DUN AND BRADSTREET/GALE

INDUSTRY

REFERENCE

HANDBOOKS

DUN AND BRADSTREET/GALE

INDUSTRY

REFERENCE

HANDBOOKS

health and medical services

Stacy A. McConnell, Editor

Linda D. Hall, Associate Editor

GALE

DETROIT • LONDON

Stacy A. McConnell, *Editor*
Linda D. Hall, *Associate Editor*
Deborah M. Burek, *Managing Editor*
Kelly Hill, *Contributing Editor*
Karin E. Koek, *Contributing Editor*
AnnaMarie L. Sheldon, *Contributing Editor*
Gerald Brennan, *Contributing Editor*

Mary Beth Trimper, *Production Director*
Evi Seoud, *Assistant Production Manager*
Cindy Range, *Production Assistant*
Deborah L. Milliken, *Production Assistant*

Theresa A. Rocklin, *Manager, Systems and Programming*
Gwen Turecki-Luczycka, *Technical Training Specialist*
Nataliya Mikheyeva, *Programmer/Analyst*
Miroslawa Bossowska, *Programmer/Analyst*

Cynthia Baldwin, *Product Design Manager*
Pamela A.E. Galbreath, *Senior Art Director*
Michelle DiMercurio, *Art Director*

While every effort has been made to ensure the reliability of the information presented in this publication, Gale Research does not guarantee the accuracy of the data contained herein. Gale accepts no payment for listing; and inclusion in the publication of any organization, agency, institution, publication, service, or individual does not imply endorsement of the editors or the publisher. Errors brought to the attention of the publisher and verified to the satisfaction of the publisher will be corrected in future editions.

This publication is a creative work fully protected by all applicable copyright laws, as well as by misappropriation, trade secret, unfair competition, and other applicable laws. The authors of this work have added value to the underlying factual material therein through one or more of the following: unique and original selection, coordination, expression, arrangement, and classification of the information.

This product includes proprietary data of Dun & Bradstreet Inc.

Extracts from *Service Industries USA* were made by special arrangement with Editorial Code and Data, Inc.

All rights to this publication will be vigorously defended.

Copyright © 1999 by The Gale Group
27500 Drake Rd.
Farmington Hills, MI 48331-3535

All rights reserved including the right of reproduction in whole or in part in any form.

ISBN 0-7876-3040-3 (set), ISBN 0-7876-3003-9

Printed in the United States of America

No part of this book may be reproduced in any form without permission in writing from the publisher, except by a reviewer who wishes to quote brief passages or entries in connection with a review written for inclusion in a magazine or newspaper.

CONTENTS

INTRODUCTION

This section presents a general introduction to the contents of *D&B/Gale Industry Reference Handbooks: Health and Medical Services*. In addition to presenting information on the book's contents, sources, organization, indices, and appendix, special explanations are provided for (1) the statistical tables and the projections used for some years of data and (2) of the industry norms and ratios used in the Dun & Bradstreet, Inc. data. Information for contacting the editors completes the introduction.

D&B/Gale Industry Reference Handbooks: Health and Medical Services is a timely compilation of information on companies, associations, consultants, trade contacts, and trade shows participating in or supporting the health and medical services industry. Recent statistics from corporate and government sources highlight financial, employment, and other trends. Descriptive materials are included on major industry issues (Foreword), industry history and trends (Industry Overview) and on recent mergers and acquisitions (Mergers & Acquisitions). Overall, *Health and Medical Services* provides an up-to-date and comprehensive guide to this industry for all—the analyst, investor, planner, marketeer, benchmarker, student, or interested member of the public.

CONTENTS AND SOURCES

Health and Medical Services covers 18 industries as defined in the Standard Industrial Classification (SIC) system. The SIC system is presently undergoing a major revision, with SIC codes in process of being replaced by North American Industry Classification System (NAICS) codes. This book is still organized by SIC code because most data providers still use the "old" system. However, an SIC to NAICS and a NAICS to SIC conversion table is provided in the appendix. Data provided in *Health and Medical Services*, shown here in chapter order, include the following categories—

Description and Context. The Foreword presents an expert view of the industry. Chapter 1 features an overview of the industry, including its history, important participants, current trends, and future directions.

Statistics. Chapter 2 presents federal government statistics and projections from 1987 to 1998. These data include establishments, employment, compensation, revenues, and ratios. Data in this chapter are drawn from the most recent edition of *Service Industries USA*.

Company Information. Chapter 3 shows financial norms and ratios for 1995, 1996 and 1997. A full discussion of norms and ratios is presented, below, under the heading **Industry Norms and Ratios**. Chapter 4 presents company capsules for leading partici-

pants in the industry in directory format, including company name, parent, address, telephone, sales, employment, company type, SIC classification, description, and name and title of the leading company officer. Chapter 5 shows companies in rank order, first by sales volume and then by employment. The data in Chapters 3-5 were prepared by and are shown by special arrangement with Dun & Bradstreet, Inc. Chapter 6 presents a summary of recent merger and acquisition activity in this industry.

Association Data. Chapter 7 presents a listing of domestic and international associations directly involved in the industry or in support of its activities. Information provided includes name of the organization, electronic access (url and/or e-mail), address, contact person, telephone and fax number, and a full description of the organization's activities, including such categories as founding date, membership, staff, local and regional groups, languages supported, publications, and other categories. Data shown are adapted from Gale's *Encyclopedia of Associations*.

Consultants. Information on industry consultants is shown in Chapter 8, adapted from Gale's *Consultants and Consulting Organizations Directory*. Categories shown include the name of the organization, e-mail and/or url for electronic access, address, leading officer, telephone and fax numbers, and a full description, including founding date, staff, special services offered, geographical areas served, and other information (e.g., seminars, workshops, conferences, etc.).

Trade Information Sources. Chapter 9 features organizations offering trade information for the health and medicine industry. The entries are adapted from Gale's *Encyclopedia of Business Information Sources* and include name of the organization, electronic contact (e-mail, url), complete address, telephone and fax numbers, and a description of the organization or special publications offered (when available).

Trade Show Information. Chapter 10 presents information needed by all those planning to visit or to participate in trade shows for the health and medicine sector. Data are drawn from Gale's *Trade Shows Worldwide* (*TSW*) or, where appropriate, from Gale's *Encyclopedia of Associations* (industry conferences). *TSW* entries include U.S. and international shows and exhibitions as well as companies, organizations, and information sources relating to the trade industry. Events, such as conferences and conventions, are included only if they feature exhibitions. Entries include the name of the show or organization, electronic access (e-mail, url), address, telephone and fax numbers, and a description including such categories as frequency of the event, audience, principal exhibits, and dates and locations.

ORGANIZATION

Health and Medical Services is organized by chapter. The 10 chapters, shown below, are followed by a Master Index. The Appendix presents an SIC to NAICS and a NAICS to SIC lookup guide. Each chapter begins with a brief description of contents and formats (if required). Additional explanatory materials are provided in this Introduction to *Chapter 2, Industry Statistics & Performance Indicators* (see **Statistics and Projections**, below) and *Chapter 3, Financial Norms and Ratios* (see **Industry Norms and Ratios**, below).

INDEX AND APPENDIX

Health and Medical Services features a single index, the **Master Index**. It shows company, organization, and personal names in alphabetical order, with page references. Also included, in alphabetical order, are industry names followed by SIC codes in parentheses.

The Appendix, **SIC/NAICS Conversion Guide**, is a two part look-up facility featuring SIC to NAICS conversions in the first part and NAICS to SIC conversions in the second part. The first part is organized by SIC codes in ascending order; the second part is sorted by NAICS codes in ascending order.

STATISTICS AND PROJECTIONS

The tables presented in Chapter 2 are drawn from federal government sources. Federal surveys are comprehensive and accurate, but they are published at some significant delay from the time of data collection. For this reason, projections were used to show data for more recent or future years in the tables in Chapter 2. In this section, terminology used in government data sources is briefly explained and the methods used in making the projections are outlined.

Terminology. Federal data make use of two terms subject to some misunderstanding. These are *establishments* and *value of shipments*.

- **Establishments** are physical locations where economic activity takes place. The establishment count for an industry is rarely the same as a census of the number of *companies* participating. There are typically more establishments than companies in an industry: many companies have multiple locations.

- **Value of Shipments** includes all products shipped from a plant, including primary and secondary products, transfers of goods to another plant, miscellaneous receipts (including contact work and work not related to the SIC at all), sales of scrap, and sales of purchased and resold products. Value of shipments, therefore, includes more than is normally associated with the concept of industry *sales*. The government makes a distinction between value of shipments and value of *product* shipments. In some SICs, the two values are very close (with value of shipments typically slightly higher). In others, there is a significant spread between the two.

Projections. The projections shown in the tables of Chapter 2 are footnoted to indicate that values are estimates. Projections are based on a curve-fitting algorithm using the least-squares method. In essence, the algorithm calculates a trend line for the data using existing data points (survey data). The trend line is the best "straight" line that can be laid over the existing points. Once the trend line has been established, it can be extended into the future. Estimated values, therefore, are points on the extended trend line indicated by past information.

INDUSTRY NORMS AND RATIOS

For each industry, two tables are presented in Chapter 3. The first, entitled **D&B Industry Norms**, presents financial norms for that industry. The second, entitled **D&B Key Business Ratios**, presents ratios. In what follows, each type of table is explained in some detail.

INDUSTRY NORMS

Each table is entitled *D&B Industry Norms* followed by the SIC code and industry name of the industry featured. Next to each year, in parenthesis, is shown the number of companies in the sample used. The "typical" balance-sheet figures are in the first column and the "common-size" balance-sheet figures (in percent) are in the second.

The Common-Size Financial Statement. The common-size balance-sheet and income statement present each item of the financial statement (e.g., *Cash*) as a percentage of its respective aggregate total (e.g., *Total Assets*). Common-size percentages are computed for all statement items for each company in the industry sample. An average for each item is then calculated and presented as the industry norm. This enables the analyst to examine the current composition of assets, liabilities and sales of a particular industry.

The Typical Financial Statement. The typical balance-sheet figures are the result of translating the common-size percentages into dollar figures. They permit, for example, a quick check of the relative size of assets and liabilities between one's own company and that company's own line of business.

Typical values are computed as follows: after the common-size percentages have been calculated for the sample, the actual financial statements are sorted by both total assets and total sales, with the median, or mid-point figure in both of these groups serving as the "typical" amount. Next, the typical balance-sheet and income statement dollar figures are computed by multiplying the item totals by the common-size percentages.

For example, if the median *Total Assets* for an SIC category is $669,599 and the common-size figure for *Cash* is 9.2 percent, then multiplying the two produces a cash figure of $61,603 for the typical balance sheet (669,559 x 0.092).

KEY BUSINESS RATIOS

This table shows data for the years 1995-1997. For each year, data are provided for the upper quartile, median, and lower quartile of the sample, providing the analyst with an even more refined set of figures. These ratios cover critical areas of business performance with indicators of solvency, efficiency and profitability.

The data serve as the basis for a profound and well-documented insight into all aspects of performance for anyone interested in the financial workings of business—executives and managers, credit executives, bankers, lenders, investors, academicians and students. An explanation of the ratios follows.

In the ratio tables shown, the figures are broken down into the median, upper, and lower quartiles. The *median* is the midpoint of all companies in the sample. The *upper* quartile shows the midpoint of the upper half, the *lower* quartile the midpoint of the lower half of the total sample.

Upper quartile figures are not always the highest numerical value, nor are lower quartile figures always the lowest numerical value. The quartile listings reflect *judgmental ranking*, thus the upper quartile represents the best condition for any given ratio and is not necessarily the highest numerical value. For example, a low numerical value is *better* for such ratios as Total Liabilities-to-Net Worth or Collection Period, indicating low liabilities and rapid collection of receivables.

Each of the 14 ratios is calculated individually for every company in the sample. These individual figures are then sorted for each ratio according to condition (best to worst). The value that falls in the middle of this series becomes the median (or mid-point) for that ratio in that line of business. The figure halfway between the median and the best condition of the series becomes the upper quartile; and the number halfway between the median and the least favorable condition of the series is the lower quartile.

In a statistical sense, each median is considered the *typical* ratio figure for a concern in a given category.

SOLVENCY RATIOS

Quick Ratio

Cash + Accounts Receivable

Current Liabilities

The Quick Ratio is computed by dividing cash plus accounts receivable by total current liabilities. Current liabilities are all the liabilities that fall due within one year. This ratio reveals the protection afforded short-term creditors in cash or near-cash assets. It shows the number of dollars of liquid assets available to cover each dollar of current debt. Any time this ratio is as much as 1 to 1 (1.0) the business is said to be in a liquid condition. The larger the ratio the greater the liquidity.

Current Ratio

Current Assets

Current Liabilities

Total current assets are divided by total current liabilities. Current assets include cash, accounts and notes receivable (less reserves for bad debts), advances on inventories, merchandise inventories and marketable securities. This ratio measures the degree to which current assets cover current liabilities. The higher the ratio the more assurance exists that the retirement of current liabilities can be made. The current ratio measures the margin of safety available to cover any possible shrinkage in the value of current assets. Normally a ratio of 2 to 1 (2.0) or better is considered good.

Current Liabilities to Net Worth

Current Liabilities

Net Worth

Current Liabilities to Net Worth is derived by dividing current liabilities by net worth. This contrasts the funds that creditors are risking temporarily with the funds permanently invested by the owners. The smaller the net worth and the larger the liabilities, the less security is afforded the creditors. Care should be exercised when selling any firm with current liabilities exceeding two-thirds (66.6 percent) of net worth.

Current Liabilities to Inventory

Current Liabilities

Inventory

Dividing current liabilities by inventory yields another indication of the extent to which the business relies on funds from disposal of unsold inventories to meet its debts. This ratio combines with Net Sales to Inventory to indicate how management controls inventory. It is possible to have decreasing liquidity while maintaining consistent sales-to-inventory ratios. Large increases in sales with corresponding increases in inventory levels can cause an inappropriate rise in current liabilities if growth isn't managed wisely.

Total Liabilities to Net Worth

$$\frac{Total\ Liabilities}{Net\ Worth}$$

This ratio is obtained by dividing total current plus long-term and deferred liabilities by net worth. The effect of long-term (funded) debt on a business can be determined by comparing this ratio with Current Liabilities to Net Worth. The difference will pinpoint the relative size of long-term debt, which, if sizable, can burden a firm with substantial interest charges. In general, total liabilities should not exceed net worth (100 percent) since in such cases creditors have more at stake than owners.

Fixed Assets to Net Worth

$$\frac{Fixed\ Assets}{Net\ Worth}$$

Fixed assets are divided by net worth. The proportion of net worth that consists of fixed assets will vary greatly from industry to industry, but generally a smaller proportion is desirable. A high ratio is unfavorable because heavy investment in fixed assets indicates that either the concern has a low net working capital and is overtrading or has utilized large funded debt to supplement working capital. Also, the larger the fixed assets, the bigger the annual depreciation charge that must be deducted from the income statement. Normally, fixed assets above 75 percent of net worth indicate possible over-investment and should be examined with care.

EFFICIENCY RATIOS

Collection Period

$$\frac{Accounts\ Receivable}{Sales\ x\ 365}$$

Accounts receivable are divided by sales and then multiplied by 365 days to obtain this figure. The quality of the receivables of a company can be determined by this relationship when compared with selling terms and industry norms. In some industries where credit sales are not the normal way of doing business, the percentage of cash sales should be taken into consideration. Generally, where most sales are for credit, any collection period more than one-third over normal selling terms (40.0 for 30-day terms) is indicative of some slow-turning receivables. When comparing the collection period of one concern with that of another, allowances should be made for possible variations in selling terms.

Sales to Inventory

$$\frac{Sales}{Inventory}$$

Obtained by dividing annual net sales by inventory. Inventory control is a prime management objective since poor controls allow inventories to become costly to store, obsolete, or insufficient to meet demands. The sales-to-inventory relationship is a guide to the rapidity at which merchandise is being moved and the effect on the flow of funds into the business. This ratio varies widely between lines of business, and a company's figure is only meaningful when compared with industry norms. Individual figures that are outside either the upper or lower quartiles for a given industry should be examined with care. Although low figures are usually the biggest problem, as they indicate excessively high inventories, extremely high turnovers might reflect insufficient merchandise to meet customer demand and result in lost sales.

Asset to Sales

Total Assets
_____
Net Sales

Assets to sales are calculated by dividing total assets by annual net sales. This ratio ties in sales and the total investment that is used to generate those sales. While figures vary greatly from industry to industry, by comparing a company's ratio with industry norms it can be determined whether a firm is overtrading (handling an excessive volume of sales in relation to investment) or undertrading (not generating sufficient sales to warrant the assets invested). Abnormally low percentages (above the upper quartile) can indicate overtrading which may lead to financial difficulties if not corrected. Extremely high percentages (below the lower quartile) can be the result of overly conservative or poor sales management, indicating a more aggressive sales policy may need to be followed.

Sales to Net Working Capital

Sales
_____
Net Working Capital

Net sales are divided by net working capital (net working capital is current assets minus current liabilities). This relationship indicates whether a company is overtrading or conversely carrying more liquid assets than needed for its volume. Each industry can vary substantially and it is necessary to compare a company with its peers to see if it is either overtrading on its available funds or being overly conservative. Companies with substantial sales gains often reach a level where their working capital becomes strained. Even if they maintain an adequate total investment for the volume being generated (Assets to Sales), that investment may be so centered in fixed assets or other noncurrent items that it will be difficult to continue meeting all current obligations without additional investment or reducing sales.

Accounts Payable to Sales

Accounts Payable
_____
Annual Net Sales

Computed by dividing accounts payable by annual net sales. This ratio measures how the company is paying its suppliers in relation to the volume being transacted. An increasing percentage, or one larger than the industry norm, indicates the firm may be using suppliers to help finance operations. This ratio is especially important to short-term creditors since a high percentage could indicate potential problems in paying vendors.

PROFITABILITY RATIOS

Return on Sales (Profit Margin)

Net Profit After Taxes
_____
Annual Net Sales

Obtained by dividing net profit after taxes by annual net sales. This reveals the profits earned per dollar of sales and therefore measures the efficiency of the operation. Return must be adequate for the firm to be able to achieve satisfactory profits for its owners. This ratio is an indicator of the firm's ability to withstand adverse conditions such as falling prices, rising costs and declining sales.

Return on Assets

Net Profit After Taxes
_____
Total Assets

Net profit after taxes divided by total assets. This ratio is the key indicator of profitability for a firm. It matches operating profits with the assets available to earn a return. Companies efficiently using their assets will have a relatively high return while less well-run businesses will be relatively low.

Return on Net Worth (Return on Equity)

Net Profit After Taxes

Net Worth

Obtained by dividing net profit after tax by net worth. This ratio is used to analyze the ability of the firm's management to realize an adequate return on the capital invested by the owners of the firm. Tendency is to look increasingly to this ratio as a final criterion of profitability. Generally, a relationship of at least 10 percent is regarded as a desirable objective for providing dividends plus funds for future growth.

USING INDUSTRY NORMS FOR FINANCIAL ANALYSIS

The principal purpose of financial analysis is to identify irregularities that require explanations to completely understand an industry's or company's current status and future potential. Comparing the industry norms with the figures of specific companies (comparative analysis) can identify these irregularities. D&B's Industry Norms are specifically formatted to accommodate this analysis.

Relative Position

Common-size and typical balance sheets provide an excellent picture of the makeup of the industry's assets and liabilities. Are assets concentrated in inventories or accounts receivable? Are payables to the trade or bank loans more important as a method for financing operations? The answers to these and other important questions are clearly shown by the Industry Norms, its common-size balance sheet approach and is then further crystallized by the typical balance sheets.

Financial Ratio Trends

Key Business Ratio changes indicate trends in the important relationships between key financial items, such as the relationship between Net Profits and Net Sales (a common indicator of profitability). Ratios that reflect short and long-term liquidity, efficiency in managing assets and controlling debt, and differ-

ent measures of profitability are all included in the Key Business Ratios sections of the Industry Norms.

Comparative Analysis

Comparing a company with its peers is a reliable method for evaluating financial status. The key to this technique is the composition of the peer group and the timeliness of the data. The D&B Industry Norms are unique in scope for sample size and in level of detail.

Sample Size

The number of firms in the sample must be representative or they will be unduly influenced by irregular figures from relatively few companies. The more than one million companies used as a basis for the Industry Norms allow for more than adequate sample sizes in most cases.

Key Business Ratios Analysis

Valuable insights into an industry's performance can be obtained by equating two related statement items in the form of a financial ratio. For really effective ratio analysis, the items compared must be meaningful and the comparison should reflect the combined effort of two potentially diverse trends. While dozens of different ratios can be computed from financial statements, the fourteen included in the Industry Norms and Key Business Ratio books are those most commonly used and were rated as the most significant as shown in a survey of financial analysts. Many of the other ratios in existence are variations on these fourteen.

The 14 Key Business Ratios are categorized into three major groups:

Solvency, or liquidity, measurements are significant in evaluating a company's ability to meet short and long-term obligations. These figures are of prime interest to credit managers of commercial companies and financial institutions.

Efficiency ratios indicate how effectively a company uses and controls its assets. This is critical information for evaluating how a company is managed.

Studying these ratios is useful for credit, marketing and investment purposes.

Profitability ratios show how successfully a business is earning a return to its owners. Those interested in mergers and acquisitions consider this key data for selecting candidates.

Recent research efforts have revealed that the use of financial analysis (via Industry Norms) is very useful in several functional areas. To follow are only a few of the more widely used applications of this unique data.

Credit

Industry Norm data has proven to be an invaluable tool in determining minimum acceptable standards for risk. The credit worthiness of an existing or potential account is immediately visible by ranking its solvency status and comparing its solvency trends to that of the industry. Short term solvency gauges, such as the quick and current ratios, are ideal indicators when evaluating an account. Balance sheet comparisons supplement this qualification by allowing a comparison of the make-up of current assets and liability items. Moreover, leverage ratios such as current liability to net worth and total liability to net worth provide valuable benchmarks to spot potential problem accounts while profitability and collection period figures provide cash flow comparisons for an overall evaluation of accounts.

In addition to evaluating individual accounts against industry standards, internal credit policies also benefit from Industry Norm data. Are receivables growing at an excessive rate as compared to the industry? If so, how does your firm's collections stack up to the industry?

Finance

Here exists a unique opportunity for financial executives to rank their firm, or their firm's subsidiaries and divisions, against its peers. Determine the efficiency of management via ratio quartile breakdowns which provides you the opportunity to pinpoint your firm's profitability position versus the industry. For example, are returns on sales and gross profit margins comparatively low thereby indicating that pric-

ing per unit may be too low or that the cost of goods is unnecessarily high?

In much the same way, matching the firm's growth and efficiency trends to that of the industry reveals conditions which prove to be vital in projecting budgets. If asset expansion exceeds the industry standard while asset utilization (as indicated by the asset to sales ratio) is sub par, should growth be slowed?

Investment executives have also utilized this diverse information when identifying optimal investment opportunities. By uncovering which industries exhibit the strongest sales growth while maintaining adequate returns, risk is minimized.

Corporate Planning

Corporate plans, competitive strategies and merger & acquisition decisions dictate a comprehensive analysis of the industry in question. Industry Norm data provides invaluable information in scrutinizing the performance of today's highly competitive, and sometimes unstable, markets. Does the liquidity of an industry provide a sufficient cushion to endure the recent record-high interest levels or is it too volatile to risk an entry? Are the profitability and equity conditions of an acquisition candidate among the best in the industry thereby qualifying it as an ideal acquisition target?

Industry Norm data provide these all-important benchmarks for setting strategic goals and measuring overall corporate performance.

Marketing and Sales

Attaining an in-depth knowledge of a potential or existing customer base is a key factor when developing successful marketing strategies and sales projections. Industry Norm data provide a competitive edge when determining market potential and market candidates. Identify those industries that meet or exceed your qualifications and take it one step further by focusing in on the specific region or size category that exhibits the greatest potential. For example, isolate the industries which have experienced the strongest growth trends in sales and inventory turnover and then fine tune marketing and sales strategies by identifying the particular segment which is the most attractive (such as firms with assets of $1 million or more).

This information can also be used in a different context by examining the industries of existing accounts. If an account's industry shows signs of faltering profitability and stagnating sales, should precautionary measures be taken? Will the next sale be profitable for your company or will it be written-off? Industry Norm data assist in answering these and many other important questions.

COMMENTS AND SUGGESTIONS

Comments on or suggestions for improvement of the usefulness, format, and coverage of *D&B/Gale Industry Reference Handbooks* are always welcome. Although every effort is made to maintain accuracy, errors may occasionally occur; the editors will be grateful if these are called to their attention. Please contact—

Editors
D&B/Gale Industry Reference Handbooks
27500 Drake Rd.
Farmington Hills, MI 48331-3535
248-699-GALE

THE BUSINESS OF HEALTH CARE:
PRESENT TRENDS AND FUTURE FORECASTS

Angela Picard

STAKEHOLDERS IN THE HEALTH CARE INDUSTRY

If one were to ask the average American citizen to describe the health care system in the United States, no doubt a variety of answers would emerge including terms like, expensive, perplexing, out of control, complex, sophisticated, full of opportunity, etc. Just like the blind men who attempt to describe the elephant, an individual's perception of the health care industry will depend in large part on what aspect of the system one is experiencing at any given time.

There are many stakeholders in the health care arena. The major players involved in the American health care system include:

    Patients (Consumers)
    Providers (Hospitals, Ambulatory Centers, Home
        Health, Physician offices, etc.)
    Payers (Insurance companies, Medicare,
        Medicaid, Managed Care)
    Professionals (Physicians, Nurses, Allied health
        practitioners)
    Professional Organizations/Associations
    Policy Makers
    Politicians
    Pharmaceutical companies
    Educators
    Researchers
    Vendors and Suppliers

One role that everyone is most likely to experience is that of being a patient. From the prenatal care received prior to delivery, to the moment of birth, to terminal care received at the point of death, everyone is personally touched by the health care system.

As a typical consumer (patient) in the American health care market, one generally expects the highest quality of service from experienced, qualified professionals. If one is fortunate enough to have insurance paid for by an employer, there is often very minimal concern given to the overall costs, but great interest in any out-of-pocket expenses.

On the other hand, as an employer or self-employed individual, the total cost of the premiums and the level of health care coverage afforded are evaluated carefully to select the best product for the price.

Whereas, the primary goal of insurance companies and other payers is to collect sufficient premiums needed to cover all the costs of claims and operational expenses. As with most purchases, those who pay for the products and services, tend to scrutinize them the most.

THE BOTTOM LINE

The New York firm of William M. Mercer, Inc. conducted a survey of nearly 4,000 employers to investigate trends in health care premiums. They found that total health benefit costs in 1997 stayed basically flat, at 0.2 percent. This outcome continues a four-year trend of premium increases of no more than 2.5 percent per year. The average health benefit cost for active and retired employees in 1997 was $3,924 per person.

In addition, growth in health care spending fell to a record low of 4.4 percent in 1996 as compared to the high of 12.9 percent in 1980. Increased managed care (HMO) enrollments and the ability of health plans to negotiate discounts are credited for this decrease in national health expenditures. However, HMO enrollments started to slow in 1997 to approximately 10 percent, following 14 percent increases annually from 1994 through 1996. Enrollments for 1998 are projected to be at 8 percent or 78.3 million members.

There is virtually no area of the United States where managed care does not exert an influence on practice patterns. Studies in *Business & Health* reveal that in areas with high HMO competition, health care utilization is lower for the entire population.

IMPACT OF AGE AND THE BABY-BOOMER GENERATION

The "graying of America" due to the large population of the baby-boomer generation is projected to have a tremendous impact on the utilization of health care resources and ultimately on Medicare funds. With increased longevity, more people are experiencing chronic illnesses such as cardiovascular disease and hypertension. Lifestyle patterns such as smoking, obesity, and exposure to prolonged stress greatly effect the need for health care services over time.

Statistics compiled by the MEDSTAT Group for 1995 indicate that the greatest percentage of inpatient and outpatient expenditures (42 percent) is incurred by persons from 35 to 54 years of age, followed closely at 31 percent by the senior population in the age group of 55 to 64. The two age groups combined utilize a total of 73 percent of the health care expenditures. These percentages are only expected to increase as more baby-boomers enter the phase of life when health care usage is at its highest.

LEADING CAUSES OF DEATH

According to the October 1998 issue of *Business and Health*, the leading causes of death for men and women in America include:

	MEN	WOMEN
Cardiovascular diseases	455,152	505,440
Cancer	281,611	256,844
Accidents	61,401	48,961
Chronic obstructive Pulmonary diseases (COPD)	53,938	45,136
Pneumonia/Influenza	37,787	33,130

As of 1998 working women between the ages of 45 and 54 comprise more than 12 million members (46 percent) of the workforce in the United States. Interestingly enough, cardiovascular diseases in women far outnumber all other causes of death, yet many women tend to fear breast cancer more. Thus, women's health issues, such as heart attacks, menopause and hormone replacement therapy, are emerging as areas of great need and concern.

HEALTH CARE AND THE INTERNET

The impact of the Internet and the World Wide Web (WWW) are so pervasive in our culture, that there is hardly an area of our lives untouched by this technology revolution. As in other segments of our global community, it serves as a valuable communication tool to link people with information, resources, special interest groups, and other individuals.

Patients have the opportunity to research diseases/conditions and look for alternative modes of treatment in order to make a more informed choice about their health care options. Specialty groups and individuals with similar conditions can offer advice and console each other through online support groups.

Providers and payers may use the Internet to monitor government legislation and proposed changes to Federal regulations affecting health care. Other health care professionals can access resources and practice standards from professional association web sites.

Physicians use e-mail and online resources to confer with colleagues, receive continuing education, or investigate the latest research breakthroughs. Researchers can collaborate with pharmaceutical companies and professionals in other countries to tackle killer diseases such as AIDS and the Ebola virus.

Health care educators are embracing the Internet as a medium for delivering distance education courses. Vendors and suppliers are able to communicate more effectively with customers and provide assess to company resources through public networks known as extranets.

With the ongoing development of web-based technologies, the Internet is becoming a focal point for business communication. However, with this technology comes the increasing need to insure privacy to all parties involved, especially for patients.

FUTURE HEALTH CARE TRENDS

In the July/August 1998 issue of the *Journal of the American Health Information Management Association* (AHIMA), industry analyst, Daniel P. Lorence, PhD, outlines the following health care trends.

1—Health care delivery relies heavily on the accurate and timely dissemination of information across long distances. Thus, the use of multimedia technology and telemedicine are anticipated to increase.

2—Providers are looking toward international markets as purchasers of American services. Managed care companies are pursuing more opportunities in the global marketplace.

3—There will be an increased demand for confidentiality of patient information. With the development of genetic testing and profiles, potentially damaging and sensitive information may be included as part of the patient record. Thus, the use of encryption technology and network firewalls to protect confidential communication will be essential.

4—Health care consumerism will drive demands for patient access to health record documentation and more stringent privacy protection measures.

5—There is a growing requirement for the use of outcomes-based decision support data in day-to-day health care delivery. Development of performance standards and comparative outcomes databases such as the ORYX initiative by the Joint Commission will continue to evolve.

6—Legislation related to limiting managed care treatment denials is proliferating. More requests for patient records and supporting documentation to substantiate the quality of care provided is anticipated.

7—Alternative care providers are becoming an integral part of the American medical practice community. Patients are exploring combinations of traditional western medicine and other complementary techniques such as acupuncture, herbalism, massage, nutritional and naturopathic remedies.

8—External audits from agencies such as the IRS, the FBI, the Inspector General, and state legislative authorities will continue to monitor health care providers to identify fraud and abuse practices.

9—A migration from older legacy database computer systems to newer integrated networks is underway driven by year 2000 compliance demands.

10—Prospective payment systems will be expanded to incorporate ambulatory services, long term and home care, and rehabilitation.

11—The Health Insurance Portability Accountability Act (HIPAA) will have a substantial impact on many aspects of health care delivery and services.

PROJECTIONS OF INCREASED HEALTH CARE COSTS

Predictions also abound that health care costs will definitely see an inevitable increase. Industry financial analysts forecast a 7 to 8 percent increase in average premiums nationwide for 1998, with annual increases in the 5 to 10 percent range over the next five years.

Elaine Zablocki reports in the *Business & Health* 1998 report titled "The State of Health Care in America" that the factors attributing to increased health care costs include:

—Desire for more health care services by aging baby boomers

—High costs of sophisticated technologies such as heart and liver transplants

—Increased bargaining power of providers

—Pressures on for-profit plans to maintain and increase earnings

—Growth of point-of-service (POS) plans, which are less tightly controlled than traditional HMOs

—Pressure for mandating additional services from managed care

—Increased use and rising costs of prescription drugs

—Rising costs of hospitalization

—The major first-time savings from decreased utilization have been achieved and are likely not repeatable

CAREERS AND EMPLOYMENT IN THE HEALTH CARE MARKET

Information from the *1998-99 Occupational Outlook Handbook* emphasizes the continued growth of career opportunities in the health care professions. The following trends are based on projections from the U.S. Bureau of Labor Statistics.

The overall labor force will grow more slowly from 1996 to 2006 as compared to the faster growth experienced during 1976 to 1986 when baby boomers were entering the work force. The number of self-employed workers is projected to increase to 11.6 million in the year 2006.

Due primarily to immigration, the diversity of ethnic groups in the work force will increase, particularly for Hispanic and Asian populations. The percentage of working women will continue to grow slowly from 46 percent to a projected 47 percent. Workers over age 45 will account for a larger share of the labor force as the baby-boomer generation ages.

There will also be a shift in demand for workers from the goods-producing sector to the service-producing sector. Business, health, and education services will account for 70 percent of the growth within the service industry.

Service and professional specialty occupations (such as health care careers) will account for approximately 2 out of every 5 job openings. This trend is due primarily to additional openings resulting from the need to replace workers who leave the occupation. Many workers may elect to leave occupations due to promotion, career or lifestyle changes such as retirement or returning to school. Others may choose to start a home-based business or stay home to care for children or elderly family members.

Employers will continue to seek higher skilled employees. Of the 25 occupations with the largest and fastest employment growth, high pay, and low unemployment, 18 require at least a bachelor's degree. Engineering and health occupations dominate this list.

Many of the fastest growing occupations are in the various health professions. Jobs in the health care services sector are expected to increase more than twice as fast as the economy as a whole and add over 3 million jobs by 2006. Correspondingly, educators specializing in the various health care professions will be needed to educate, train, and retrain the health care work force.

The following list consists of specific health care careers identified as the fastest growing occupations covered in the *1998-99 Occupational Outlook Handbook*:

- Personal and home care aides
- Physical and corrective therapy assistants and aides
- Home health aides
- Medical assistants
- Physical therapists
- Occupational therapy assistants and aides
- Occupational therapists
- Medical records technicians
- Speech-language pathologists and audiologists
- Dental hygienists
- Physician assistants
- Respiratory therapists
- Emergency medical technicians

As hospitals and insurance companies require shorter stays for recovery to reduce costs and due to trends among the elderly who desire home care services, personal and home health/care aides and related social services will be in great demand. With an aging population experiencing life-threatening and disabling conditions, the care of speech-language therapists as well as physical therapy and occupational therapy professionals, assistants, and aides will continue to be needed even more in the years ahead.

In order to manage the increased number of patient records in both paper-based and electronic formats, the demand for medical record (health information) professionals is also projected to increase. Review of medical records by third-party payers, courts, and consumers will continue to heighten as the quality of provider services are compared to industry practice standards and documentation is scrutinized for possible fraud and abuse.

Due to cost containment measures, health care support personnel such as medical assistants, physician assistants, nurse practitioners, respiratory therapists, emergency medical technicians, dental hygienists, and other multi-skilled health care providers will be needed to serve the increasing number of patients seeking care. There appears to be a sufficient number of physicians and nurses to meet health care demands for the near future.

JOB SEARCHING RESOURCES

In addition to the traditional methods of reading classified ads in newspapers and filling out paper-based applications, job seekers can now take advantage of the wealth of electronic resources found on the Internet. Most recruiter web sites allow the job seeker to post electronic resumes and search job databases at no charge. Employers generally pay a fee to gain access to job candidate information.

There are numerous web sites devoted to posting health care positions. Three examples include:

MedSearch   http://www.medsearch.com
Health Care Jobs
   Online   http://www.hcjobsonline.com
Romac International   http://www.romac.com

Many professional associations are offering online continuing education materials, bulletin boards and electronic mailing lists, which are invaluable for networking with colleagues, staying abreast of industry news, and researching career opportunities.

NEEDS OF A DIVERSE WORK FORCE

Many health care occupations have continuing education (CE) requirements that must be completed in order to maintain the professional credential. Often health care facilities provide CE training to employees or sponsor their attendance at workshops and professional meetings.

Support for continuing education and professional membership are just one of the many benefits that employees evaluate when considering a job opening. Other employer benefits that are appealing to employees, may include:

Child care services
Flexible work hours
Telecommuting opportunities
Choice of health care insurance plans
Discounts for health care services
Tuition reimbursement for college courses
Cost of living wage increases
Life insurance
Retirement plans

In markets where demand is high and supply is limited, many health care professionals may have the luxury of shopping for the best jobs that provide the benefit package they prefer.

COMPLEMENTARY AND ALTERNATIVE MEDICINE

Driven by consumer demand, alternative medicine is slowly gaining mainstream acceptance. A landmark study conducted by David M. Eisenburg, MD of the Center for Alternative Medicine Research at Deaconess Medical Center in Boston in 1990 revealed that patients spend over $10 billion a year out of their own pockets for alternative therapies. In response to these findings, the National Institutes of Health (NIH) initially established the Office of Alternative Medicine (OAM) to further research this growing phenomenon.

With the passage of the 1999 Omnibus appropriations bill in October 1998, the OAM has been updated to establish the National Center for Complementary and Alternative Medicine (NCCAM). The Center will focus on the support of basic and applied research and training and will disseminate information on complementary and alternative medicine (CAM) to practitioners and the public.

Using the $50 million appropriated by the Congress to fund the NCCAM, it will set up and carry out programs which will further the investigation and application of CAM treatments that are shown to be effective. Additional information about NCCAM, its mission, and the programs it supports are available on their web site located at http://altmed.od.nih. gov/nccam.

CONSUMER ISSUES AND CONCERNS

The growing consumer interest in using a combination of traditional medicine and alternative medicine modalities has prompted some insurers to provide coverage for complementary medical practices. Therapies such as nutritional counseling, biofeedback, acupuncture, chiropractic care, massage, and osteopathy may receive partial or full coverage depending on the type of health care plan available.

However, there is often much confusion among consumers about insurance coverage options and the types of services they provide. Despite the heralded savings of managed care during the 1990's, this health care option is not without its disadvantages. In the last five years, Americans have been literally herded into managed care plans. The health care plans provided by employers are selected based on the cost to the employer and may not offer the options needed or desired by individual employees.

In managed care (HMOs) and preferred provider networks, patients often discover that their physicians of choice are not part of the network. Frequently a patient selects a physician, within the plan, from a directory without having any knowledge of the quality of care they provide. The majority of care decisions require prior approval from the plan and all services are managed by the primary care physician referred to as the gatekeeper.

In addition, as physicians experience increasing pressure to conform to the demands of the managed care plans, many physicians elect not to participate in managed care contracts. If patients want to see a physician outside of the network, they generally incur additional out-of-pocket fees to do so.

There have also been numerous allegations that patients are denied coverage for needed health care services by managed care plans. Perhaps the newest and most aggressive state action against managed care is a 1997 Texas law allowing consumers to sue managed care entities and hold them accountable for their participation in treatment decisions.

According to the Center for Patient Advocacy, the top five complaints about HMOs include:

- Access to specialists
- Arbitrary managed care policies
- Access to and coverage for Emergency Room care
- Health plans often do not provide vital information patients need to know
- Red tape and bureaucratic requirements

The Center for Patient Advocacy (http://www.patientadvocacy.org) was established in 1995 as a national organization to articulate patient concerns to members of Congress, the executive branch, and state officials. Their mission includes "educating patients on the delivery of health care, the restrictions government and the private sector impose on patient care, and the role that they can play to affect change in the nation's health care system."

The Center sponsors a toll-free hotline (800-846-7444) where patients can seek advice from patient advocates. In addition, the Center publishes several educational brochures to help patients navigate through the maze of managed care and provides questions to ask before choosing health insurance.

Dissatisfaction with access restrictions and concerns for the quality of care received have lead to a backlash from consumers who wish to exert more control over their health care. State and federal legislators have begun to sponsor legislation and patient's rights bills in response to demands from their constituents.

For instance, the Health Insurance Portability Accountability Act (HIPAA) of 1996 was enacted as a mechanism to protect health insurance coverage for workers and their families when they change or lose their jobs. This act contains provisions to prevent insurance companies from excluding coverage to patients based on pre-existing conditions.

Additional components of HIPAA legislation are being developed to address patient confidentiality concerns. The U.S. Department of Health and Human Services Secretary, Donna E. Shalala, warned that "under the Administration's confidentiality proposals, violating medical confidentiality laws could result in criminal penalties."

MEASURING PERFORMANCE AND QUALITY

Concerns for the quality of health care date back as early as 1909 when Abraham Flexner first studied the status of medical education in the United States. Efforts at standardization were initiated by the American College of Surgeons in 1913 which was eventually replaced by the Joint Commission in 1952.

Since that time, the Joint Commission on Accreditation of Healthcare Organizations (JCAHO — http://www.jcaho.org) has become a predominant player in the health care arena. In order to receive federal funds, such as Medicare payments, organizations typically have to be Joint Commission surveyed and accredited.

Quality concepts have evolved over time as well. Even the terminology associated with quality review activities has changed from "quality assurance" to "quality assessment" to "quality improvement." Total quality management (TQM) ideas from other industries were later revamped to become known in health care circles as "continuous quality improvement (CQI)."

Regardless of the terminology used to describe the processes, the underlying premise is the same. Basically, since health care services are delivered by human beings and technology that are not perfect and prone to potential error, there is an ongoing need to evaluate performance in all areas of the organization.

Various tools (commonly referred to as QI tools) are used to assess, document, and report the results of the evaluation processes. Physician and administrative leaders of each health care organization are held accountable for monitoring quality performance activities within their given facility and taking appropriate action to correct problems found and to identify areas with opportunities for improvement.

Currently, the growing demand for objective, comparative information about the performance of health care organizations has created a need for a data-driven evaluation process that includes outcomes data. Business coalitions, purchasers (employers), and payers (insurers) choosing among plans are demanding objective evidence that they are buying good quality care for a fair price.

One of the most recent initiatives by the Joint Commission is referred to as ORYX and is designed to assist health care organizations in documenting objective, quantifiable information about their facility's performance which can be used internally and externally to demonstrate accountability to patients, payers, providers, and politicians.

Monitoring health care quality is also a primary concern of federal and state government agencies who pay for services rendered to Medicare and Medicaid patients. With the implementation of the Prospective Payment System (PPS) in 1983, the Health Care Financing Administration (HCFA —http://www.hcfa.gov) contracted with Professional Review Organizations (PROs) in every state to review patient records for the quality of care provided and the accuracy of billing practices. Other insurers/payers followed suit by implementing procedures such as pre-admission approvals, continued stay utilization review processes, and record audits.

Other organizations providing leadership in this area include the National Committee for Quality Assurance (NCQA —http://www.ncqa.org) and the National Association for Healthcare Quality (NAHQ —http://www.nahq.org). In 1992 NCQA assumed responsibility for management of the evolution of the Health Plan Employer Data and Information Set (HEDIS) with the goal of devising a standardized set of performance measures that could be used by various constituencies to compare health plans. NCQA is an independent organization that evaluates the quality of care provided by HMOs who wish to seek NCQA accreditation. The results of the HEDIS compliance audit program, referred to as "provider report cards," are also available to consumers.

FINANCIAL AND REIMBURSEMENT ISSUES

According to the American Hospital Association (AHA —http://www.aha.org), "one in five hospitals in America is losing money overall. About 29 percent of hospitals in America report a total margin of 2 percent or less—a position that many, including the business community that underwrites hospitals' capital bonds, consider unsound. That 29 percent represents 1,500 hospitals that are in trouble in communities throughout the country, large and small, urban and rural."

The last decade in the health care industry can be described as the era of down-sizing and "doing more with less." The influence of total quality management in the early 1990's resulted in the evaluation of organizational processes with an eye toward streamlining and cutting costs. With the proliferation of managed care in the second half of the 1990's, health care facilities were challenged to maintain quality while continuing to tighten their belts even further as they negotiated contracts with HMOs.

In the age of prospective payment (PPS) for inpatient services, more and more services were moved into the outpatient setting resulting in overall cost shifting. Now after fifteen years (1983-1998) of inpatient PPS, a prospective payment system for outpatient services known as Ambulatory Patient Groupings (APGs) has been proposed by HCFA.

In addition, the Balanced Budget Act of 1997 included a proposal to create a prospective payment system for home health services. This program is slated for implementation by October 1, 1999. These new payment systems will create the need for educational updates and training of health care professionals to comply with the new reimbursement requirements.

Another major change anticipated in the American health care market is the introduction of the revised 10th edition of the coding and classification system known as the International Classification of Diseases (ICD-10). The current system used in the United States is called the International Classification of Diseases, Ninth Revision, Clinical Modification (ICD-9-CM). ICD-10 is already being used in other countries such as Australia; however, the modified version for use in the United States has been slow in coming.

In America ICD-9-CM code books are used to convert medical conditions and procedures into standardized codes that are maintained in electronic databases and recorded on uniform billing claim forms (UB-92) which are submitted to payers for reimbursement. Codes for medical conditions such as con-

gestive heart failure (428.0) and procedures like chemotherapy (99.25) are also a component of calculating Diagnosis-Related Groups (DRGs) which ultimately determine the amount of reimbursement a facility receives from the government for treating Medicare patients.

GOVERNMENT EFFORTS TO FIGHT FRAUD, ABUSE, AND WASTE

In May 1995, the Clinton administration launched a comprehensive anti-fraud initiative in five states known as Operation Restore Trust (ORT) to fight fraud and abuse in the Medicare and Medicaid programs. In May 1997, Secretary Shalala announced a nationwide expansion of ORT to broaden the government's efforts to recover additional funds (10). Some of the specific strategies employed in this initiative include:

- Establishing a Fraud and Abuse Hotline (1-800-HHS-TIPS)

- Partnering with the Administration on Aging and other aging services to recognize and report fraud and abuse in nursing homes and long term care settings

- Creating $1.5 million in "Health Care Fraud and Abuse Control Grants" to be administered by HCFA, the Office of Inspector General (OIG), and the Department of Justice (DOJ)

- Expanding field offices of the Inspector General to increase coverage from 26 to 31 states to facilitate enforcement actions

- Developing a fraud and abuse database to identify health care providers who engage in fraud and/or abuse activities

- Increasing investigation efforts by the Department of Justice to enforce criminal and civil statutes applicable to health care fraud and abuse

- Implementing an incentive program to reward Medicare beneficiaries who report fraudulent activity that leads to recovery of overpayments

- Tightening standards for home health care providers

- Enforcing new requirements for durable medical equipment suppliers

- Investigating suspicious Medicare claims prior to payment through a program called the Medical Integrity Program (MIP)

- Improving health care industry compliance through educational efforts

These fraud and abuse initiatives are just some of the many components of the Health Insurance Portability and Accountability Act (HIPAA) of 1996. Due to the far reaching effects of HIPAA, many health care organizations are creating compliance programs and earmarking substantial funding to deal with this new level of government scrutiny.

RISK MANAGEMENT AND MALPRACTICE

A correlate to the efforts of quality improvement and compliance monitoring is the area of healthcare risk management. The American Society for Healthcare Risk Management (ASHRM —http://www.ashrm.org) serves as the professional association for health care professionals specializing in the field of risk assessment and control.

Their duties typically encompass the scope of services delivered throughout the entire health care organization. They work closely with insurance companies who provide liability coverage for the facility as well as administration, physicians, and employees from all areas of the facility. An effective risk management program incorporates the identification, analysis, evaluation, and elimination or reduction of possible risks to patients, visitors, and employees.

Medical malpractice is a much larger problem than most health care providers would like to admit. Interestingly enough, not all physicians are required to be insured. According to the U.S. Congressional Budget Office, medical malpractice premiums amount to less than 1% of health costs.

The 1990 Harvard Medical Practice Study reported that 80,000 people die in the United States each year due partly to medical malpractice. Their research also found that only one in eight patients that suffer due to medical negligence ever files a lawsuit and only one in sixteen recovers any damages. With such a high probability of adverse patient outcomes, health care risk managers, compliance officers, and quality improvement professionals no doubt stay very busy.

MERGERS AND ACQUISITIONS

The 1990's for the health care industry could also be dubbed the decade of "merger mania." In the early and mid-1990's, Columbia/HCA Healthcare Corporation (http://www.columbia-hca.com) marched across the United States buying up hospitals. In 1997 Columbia Healthcare faced legal charges stemming from allegations of financial misconduct and fraudulent billing practices.

Other independent healthcare organizations, located primarily in metropolitan areas, began to form alliances with other facilities. For example, the religious affiliated (Catholic) hospitals of St. Joseph's Hospital in Tampa, Florida merged with their sister-facility, St. Anthony's in St. Petersburg, Florida.

Many of these mergers were driven by the demands for cost containment (financial survival) and the desire to develop integrated health care delivery systems to better serve their communities. Many acquisitions came under close scrutiny due to anti-trust violation concerns.

Mergers among managed care organizations and other vendors of healthcare products and services have also proliferated in the late 1990's. With the demand for more sophisticated healthcare computer systems, many vendors have elected to purchase specialty companies to broaden the scope of products and services they can provide.

TRENDS IN HEALTHCARE COMPUTING

Each year the Healthcare Information and Management Systems Society (HIMSS —http://www.

himss.org) sponsors a information technology (IT) leadership survey which represents the opinions of senior executives and managers of health care providers throughout the world. In 1998 the survey was completed by 1,380 health care IT professionals. The majority of respondents (95 percent) in 1998 were from hospitals within North America. A summary of the results is provided below.

Highlights from the Ninth Annual HIMSS Leadership Survey, 1998:

- Recruiting and retaining high quality IT staff is considered the number one priority

- Increased IT utilization is driven by the need to extend diagnostic services to caregivers in remote locations and to provide remote access to patient records

- Increased reliance on IT appears to be driven by two main factors—1) the push to derive more value from existing data and 2) mergers or partnerships

- Lack of financial support is seen as the biggest barrier to successful IT implementation, although 73 percent of the respondents indicate that their IT operating budget is expected to increase in the next 12 months

- Vendors who do not fully understand the clinical needs of the provider are sited as an another barrier to successful IT implementation goals

- The biggest telecommunications challenges include the need to: 1) integrate multimedia capabilities (voice, data, and images) and 2) develop a comprehensive strategic telecommunications plan

- Case management and member services are rated as the top managed care applications supported by IT staff

- IT budgets are not dependent on the ability to identify quantifiable benefits, but rather on overall organizational spending

- One-third of health care organizations do not outsource their IT functions

- U. S. health care organizations are making slow progress toward implementing computer-based patient records (CPRs)

- The top roadblocks to fully implementing a CPR system include: 1) a lack of a standardized vocabulary, 2) inadequate IT infrastructure, 3) resistance of administrative staff, and 4) lack of adequate funding

- Internal security breaches of patient information continue to be the biggest concern

- Use of the Internet has grown from 87 percent in 1997 to 95 percent in 1998 making functions like e-mail, discussion groups, and FTP a common functionality in most health care organizations

- Use of the Internet for employee recruitment and organizational marketing are considered key business benefits of using web-based technologies

- The top clinical Internet applications used by health care providers include medical literature database searches and online patient health assessment tools

- The pace of intranet development and implementation has increased with 29 percent of the organizations having an intranet that is available to all employees

- The use of telehealth/telemedicine applications is still somewhat limited with steady growth anticipated over the next 12 months

- The top three applications used by organizations with telehealth resources include: 1) medical image transmission, 2) professional continuing education, and 3) community outreach or public health education

- Voice recognition is considered the most promising emerging technology followed by wireless information appliances, web-enabled applications, and handheld personal digital assistants for workgroups

YEAR 2000 COMPLIANCE PREPARATION

Several industry surveys report that healthcare providers are lagging behind in the race to prepare for year 2000 (Y2K) problems in the new millennium. With a finite time frame remaining, the following steps are recommended:

1—Establish an organization-wide team to research mission critical systems

2—Document and inform senior management and information technology (IT) personnel of the potential impact of Y2K problems for each department

3—Initiate contacts with vendors and suppliers for collaboration on compliance assessment

4—Identify sources for information and assistance such as Y2K training and reviewing online resources such as the web site for Rx2000 Solutions Institute (http://www.rx2000.org)

CONSULTANTS AND OUTSOURCING

Most often health care organizations utilize consultants or outsourcing companies for economic reasons. Though some outsourcing is done because skilled resources or manpower are lacking in the community, most partial or complete outsourcing of skilled services is a strategic decision.

Many executives believe that resources are better utilized when they outsource activities that are not core business functions. This allows managers to concentrate their efforts on the core operations of the organization. Furthermore, contracting for skilled services enables the organization to pay for performance rather than time, while holding a third party accountable for the quality of performance.

For functions in which workload fluctuates, total or partial outsourcing allows the organization to make the function into a variable rather than a fixed cost, thereby reducing overhead. Often quality and service

is enhanced by an outsourcing company. Thus, the organization potentially gains maximum cost-benefit.

When considering a consultant or outsourcing company, the following steps are suggested:

- Choose a consultant who understands how your business works. Get referrals from trade association members or other colleagues. Post queries on industry-specific Internet newsgroups. Select eight to ten potential consultants/firms.

- Check references relevant to the specific business. Ask questions such as, "Did they respond when called? Solve the problem? Go over budget? Would they consider working with the firm again?"

- Get resumes of everyone who will work on site and demand a detailed outline of all services to be performed.

- Develop a budget and a list of expected outcomes.

- If buying equipment and/or software, negotiate all aspects of the purchase agreement and reserve final payment until the desired performance is achieved. Fixed-price contracts are generally better than time-and-materials contracts. Beware of adding unnecessary bells and whistles.

- Be willing to pay more for a knowledgeable, unbiased consultant with a reliable service record.

LEAD, FOLLOW, OR GET OUT OF THE WAY

What is needed in health care leadership today and in the new millennium? Dwight McNeill offers these insights in his commentary titled "Time for a New Vision of Employer Leadership":

- Deal directly with the real cost drivers of consumer demand, innovation, and third-party reimbursement

- Assure the basic rights of coverage, financial security, choice and access

- Balance the market on quality and cost

- Plan for the future with funding for training, re-search and development

- Respect consumers and health care providers

- Support systems for continual improvement

Visionary health care leaders who are wise enough to know when to lead, when to follow, and when to get out of the way will best serve the needs of the myriad of stakeholders operating in the complex world of the health care industry.

—Angela Picard, MEd, RRA

Angela Picard is a health information management professional with over 18 years of experience in the healthcare industry. She has contributed to various in-dustry publications, including Professional Review Guide for the RRA and ART Examinations *(1995, 1996, and 1997 editions),* HIM Journeys: A Career Guide for Health Information Management Profes-sionals *(1997 edition),* 1998 RRA and ART Exam SUCCESS! Newsletter. *She is also the Editor and Publisher of the 1998* Certified Coding Specialist Ex-am SUCCESS Review Book.

Picard was the winner of the 1997 Literary Award from the Florida Health Information Management As-sociation (FHIMA). In addition, she served as the 1997-98 Chair of the Electronic Communication Committee which designed the web site for FHIMA.

CHAPTER 1

INDUSTRY OVERVIEW

This chapter presents a comprehensive overview of the Health and Medical Services industry. Major topics covered include an Industry Snapshot, Organization and Structure, Background and Development, Pioneers and Newsmakers in the Industry, Current Conditions, Industry Leaders, Work Force, North America and the World, and Research and Technology. A suggested list for further reading, including web sites to visit, completes the chapter. Additional company information is presented in Chapter 6 - Mergers and Acquisitions.

Industry Snapshot

Health care is one of the most dynamic sectors of the American economy. The skyrocketing cost of medical services in the 1970s and 1980s led to systemic changes that are still going on as the country enters the new millennium. High costs led insurers to move from traditional plans that paid for medical care on a fee-for-service basis to managed care plans. Combined with corporate cost-containment measures, Americans are becoming more informed health care consumers who look for the most quality for their health care dollar.

National expenditures on health care were estimated by the *U.S. Industry & Trade Outlook 1998* at $1 trillion in 1996 or about $3,760 for every American. That was an increase of about 5.6 percent over 1995, moderate when compared with the average 13.6 percent increases between 1975 and 1980 or the 10.9 percent average increases between 1980 and 1990. Health care expenditures are expected to climb to $1.161 trillion in 1998. Health care costs as a percentage of the gross domestic product should remain stable, however, at approximately 13.6 percent. That percentage is the highest in the industrialized world. Although the structural changes being wrought by managed care make it difficult to predict growth rates, the *U.S. Industry & Trade Outlook 1998* forecasts average growth of 6 to 7 percent between 1999 and 2003. Exports of American health care services rose by 6.4 percent in 1996. In 1997 they expected to reach $1 billion. As markets in Latin America are exploited more efficiently between 1998 and 2002, growth rates are expected to remain strong at around 6-7 percent.

About $350.1 billion was spent on hospital care in 1995, according to the U.S. Health Care Financing Administration. That was 36 percent of all health care expenditures. The percentage is expected to drop due pressure from managed care administrators to review hospital admissions more rigorously and to shorten hospital stays. Home health care is the fastest growing health care segment. The *U.S. Industry & Trade Outlook 1998* predicted expenditures for home health care to increase by 8.8 percent between 1997 and 1998, to $37 billion. Alternative medical treatments are a relatively invisible, but significant, segment of the American health care econ-

omy. A 1993 survey in the *New England Journal of Medicine* found that visits to providers of nontraditional therapies, including acupuncture, nutrition therapies, herbal medicine, mind/body control and the like, exceeded visits to all U.S. primary-care physicians. Many of these revenues go unaccounted for in official statistics and *U.S. Industry & Trade Outlook 1998* believes that if all alternative methods were recognized, the statistics for U.S. health care expenditures in 1995 would have been $30-$50 billion higher.

Health care is an important source of employment. In major cities, according to the *U.S. Industry & Trade Outlook 1998*, health care services are the major employer. Between 1990 and 1995 employment in the industry increased from 7.8 million to 9.3 million. That was an average rise of 3.8 percent annually, more than twice the rate for the economy as a whole. Hospitals employed 5.1 million, the most workers in the health care sector. In 1995, however, most new jobs—55,000 of 268,000 new private health care industry jobs—were created in the home health care field.

Organization and Structure

The American health and medical care industry is a vast, decentralized network of establishments, public, private and governmental. They include doctors' practices and clinics, hospitals, dentists' practices, laboratories, nursing homes, blood and organ banks, and the like. The private health care system is part of a much larger system that includes a cabinet level government agency, the Department of Health and Human Services (HHS), other federal and state government agencies, e.g. Veterans Administration, voluntary health agencies such as the American Cancer Society, and enterprises with health functions, for example, manufacturers of diagnostic equipment.

By and large though, the market for medical and dental care is dominated by the private sector. Sometimes payment is borne by government, for instance the Medicare or Medicaid programs, but services are provided almost exclusively by private physicians and dentists. As a result, services are only selectively available, based on the individual's ability to afford them or their access to medical insurance.

Doctors' Offices and Clinics

Doctors and their practices make up the heart of the American health care system. They are the first and often only contact many patients have with the health care system. The **SIC 8011: Offices and Clinics of Doctors of Medicine** includes all physicians with an M.D. degree who work out of a practice by themselves, with a couple other doctors, or in a medical clinic in which several physicians work cooperatively. **SIC 8011** includes both general and specialized medicine. General practitioners, also called family doctors, are usually the first type of doctor a patient visits regarding a health problem. If a problem persists or is serious, the primary care provider refers the patient to a specialist, the secondary care provider. Specializations in **SIC 8011** include dermatologists, gynecologists, neurologists, obstetricians, oculists, ophthalmologists, orthopedic physicians, pathologists, pediatricians, plastic surgeons, psychiatrists, psychoanalysts, surgeons, and urologists. Some practitioners who provide specialized assistance or diagnostic services, such as anesthesiologists and radiologists fall under this SIC as well. Clinics that fall in the SIC include general and specialized medical clinics, such as primary care medical clinics, ambulatory surgical centers, and emergency medical centers not part of a hospital. Throughout the 1980s and 1990s, physicians have increasingly joined together in group practices or clinics. According to Milton I. Roemer in the *International Handbook of Health Care Systems,* more than half of all American physicians now practice in groups of three or more. Individual private practice is gradually disappearing.

Dentist practices and clinics are classified separately under **SIC 8021: Offices and Clinics of Dentists.** It includes all licensed practitioners with a dental degree, D.M.D., D.D.S., and D.D.Sc. Some practice general dentistry; others practice specialized dentistry such as oral pathology, and dental surgery. Orthodontists treat teeth that have grown in irregularly, often by means of braces. Periodontists treat diseases of the gums and bones around the teeth. Endodontists treat diseases of the tooth pulp. Prosthodontists design and fit patients with prosthetic devices such as artificial teeth, dentures, bridges, and caps. Patients are almost always referred to specialists by their general dentist.

Osteopathic physicians—licensed doctors who hold a D.O. degree—and osteopathic clinics are classified under **SIC 8031: Offices and Clinics of Doctors of Osteopathy.** The basis of osteopathic medicine is the treatment of disease by the manipulation of bones. Most osteopathic physicians prescribe drugs as well.

In addition to medical doctors, dentists and osteopathic physicians, there are a variety of other specialties which fall under the general **SIC 804.** Chiropractors, under **SIC 8041: Chiropractic Offices and Clinics** treat disease primarily through manipulation of patients' vertebrae, where pressure on nerves accumulates. According to the theory of chiropractics, most disease has its origin in nerve problems. Optometrists are concerned with the correction of abnormalities in vision, such as nearsightedness, through the prescription of glasses, medication, or other means. Two other groupings are **SIC 8042: Offices and Clinics of Optometrists** and **SIC 8043: Offices and Clinics of Podiatrists.** Podiatrists treat diseases and deformities of the feet.

SIC 8049: Offices and Clinics of Health Practitioners, Not Elsewhere Classified is made up of a broad variety of miscellaneous practitioners. M.D.s are not included in this SIC even if their primary practice involves one of the following fields. For example, the office of a psychotherapist or acupuncturist who is an M.D. would not be included under **SIC 8049.** Health fields covered by this SIC include all registered and practical nurses (except nurses involved in home health care); paramedics; audiologists, speech clinicians, and speech pathologists; dental hygienists; dieticians and nutritionists; occupational therapists and physical therapists; psychotherapists, clinical psychologists and psychiatric social workers; and, physician assistants. Also included are health fields that some states do not license or certify, such as acupuncturists, practitioners of Christian Science, hypnotists, registered inhalation therapists, midwives, and naturopaths.

Hospitals

Hospitals represent another important sector of the health care system. One category is **SIC 8062: General Medical and Surgical Hospitals.** In addition, there are specialty hospitals that provide limited type of care or care for a specific type of patient. Institutions that provide diagnostic services and inpatient psychiatric and medical treatment for the mentally ill fall under **SIC 8063: Psychiatric Hospitals**. **SIC 8069: Specialty Hospitals, Except Psychiatric** covers all other specialized hospitals, including those for alcohol and drug rehabilitation, cancer, children, chronic disease, eye, ear, nose, and throat, maternity, orthopedic, and respiratory illness.

In addition to classifying hospitals by the type of services they provide, or patients they treat, hospitals can be divided by other criteria as well. So-called "community hospitals" are open to the public. Veterans hospitals are operated by the government, as are federal long-term hospitals. Similar hospitals are maintained by the Bureau of Indian Affairs for Indian reservations. Institutions like prisons frequently operate their own hospitals as well.

In general, the internal structure of most hospitals is split into an administrative staff responsible for the nursing staff and hospital administration, and a separately administered medical and ancillary staff, such as the pharmacy and various therapists.

In contrast to doctors' practices and clinics, hospitals usually have facilities where patients can sleep and remain under constant observation and supervision. Most large, general hospitals have departments for most medical specialties, laboratories and diagnostic facilities. Typical services provided by general medical and surgical hospitals include emergency care in especially equipped emergency rooms, therapy services such as respiratory therapy and physical therapy, blood banks, ultrasound and X-ray, and kitchens for patients with special nutritional needs. Many surgical procedures, and virtually all major surgical procedures, are performed in a hospital setting. Because of their size and proportionally higher revenues, hospitals are able to buy and maintain expensive diagnostic and treatment equipment that clinics and doctors' offices could never afford.

Many hospitals also offer birthing rooms, occupational therapy, and special inpatient care for patients suffering from AIDS. Some hospitals offer alcohol and chemical dependency care, psychiatric services, or geriatric services.

While hospitals traditionally delivered services to patients who remained in the hospital for two or more days during treatment, most now have outpatient departments. According to Roemer, more than half of all surgeries in community hospitals are now outpatient procedures. Other outpatient services include pain clinics and home health care services. While outpatient services are not as profitable for hospitals as inpatient services, they do bring additional, continuous revenues. Furthermore, they enable hospitals to expand their involvement in community health efforts to areas such as weight reduction and prenatal care.

A good deal of outpatient care is still performed by specialized institutions with no institutional affiliation to hospitals. These facilities employ medical and other trained staff to diagnose and treat patients with conditions of a specialized nature. Sometimes they also utilize specialized equipment. Institutions in **SIC 8092: Kidney Dialysis Centers** remove toxins from the blood of patients whose own diseased kidneys are no longer able to do so. Other specialized outpatient facilities, classified under **SIC 8093**, include alcohol treatment clinics, biofeedback centers, birth control and family planning clinics, drug treatment clinics, alcohol and drug detoxification centers, mental health clinics, treatment clinics for alcoholism and drug addiction, medical rehabilitation centers, and respiratory therapy clinics. Other facilities under **SIC 8099: Health and Allied Services, Not Elsewhere Classified** which provide specialized medical care, services or products, include blood banks and blood donor stations, plasmapheresis centers, childbirth preparation classes, sperm banks, hearing testing services, osteoporosis centers, oxygen tent service, health screening services, physical examination services not performed by physicians, and medical photography and art.

Nursing Homes

Nursing homes provide varying levels of care ranging from long-term, twenty-four-hour-a-day care for the aged and severely infirm, to low-level, minimal care patients. Patients usually reside in the nursing home. Staff members are on duty around the clock and provide help by administering medication, bathing and dressing patients, etc. Nursing homes provide meals and often social activities for their patients.

Health care is on the prescription of a physician. A registered nurse is always on duty during day shifts if not more often.

Establishments under **SIC 8051: Skilled Nursing Care Facilities** provide long-term inpatient nursing and rehabilitative services to patients with chronic and multiple disabilities who require continuous health care, but not hospital services. Care is provided around the clock and must be under the direction of a physician. The staff must include licensed nurses on duty continuously with a minimum of one full-time registered nurse on duty during each day shift. Types of establishments include convalescent homes, extended care facilities, mental retardation hospitals, and skilled nursing homes.

A number of factors distinguish one skilled nursing home from another. Some offer specialized therapeutic regimes such as physical or respiratory therapy; others serve particular target groups. Rehabilitation skilled nursing homes specialize in patients requiring shorter stays with intensive rehabilitation because of head injuries, strokes, spinal cord injuries, neurologic impairment, and the like. Others specialize in young children who have suffered traumatic accidents or birth defects. AIDS patients are a fast-growing segment of the nursing home population. Organizations such as the Association of Health Facility Survey Agencies, the American College of Health Care Administrators, and the National Association of Boards of Examiners for Nursing Home Administrators establish professional licensing and certification standards for nursing homes and their staff.

SIC 8052: Intermediate Care Facilities are similar to skilled nursing homes insofar as they provide inpatient services, often specialized. Intermediate care facilities, however, do not provide care on a continuous basis. Homes are required to be staffed 24 hours each day with as registered nurse on duty during each day shift.

SIC 8059: Nursing And Personal Care Facilities, Not Elsewhere Classified includes homes for patients who do not require the level of intensive care provided by skilled nursing homes or intermediate care facilities. Patients usually require some form of nursing care or help administering medications.

These low-level care facilities, which often provide health care, include convalescent homes, domiciliary care, homes for the mentally retarded (except skilled and intermediate care facilities), nursing homes that do not provide skilled and intermediate care, personal care facilities, personal care homes, psychiatric patients' convalescent homes, and rest homes.

Some nursing homes which are designated as skilled care nursing facilities, in fact, have a mixed population of patients some requiring skilled care and others unskilled care. Such homes are required to maintain separate beds, staff and other facilities for skilled nursing care patients.

Personal care facilities without health care under the supervision of a physician form another category of residential home care under **SIC 8361**. They are establishments for individuals who are limited in their ability to care for themselves. Medical care, however, is not a major element in the care provided in these homes. They include children's homes, rehabilitation facilities, group homes for people with a variety of limitations, halfway houses, rest homes for the aged, residential drug and alcohol treatment centers, and orphanages.

Retirement centers, also called assisted living communities, are designed for persons who are unable to function on their own, but do not require daily nursing care. Assisted living communities generally assist with bathing, dressing, housekeeping, and meals. Continuing-care retirement communities (CCRCs) are apartment complexes designed with the special needs of the elderly in mind. They provide meals, social services, health care access, and sometimes housekeeping, and in general provide a slightly higher level of care than retirement centers.

Youth crime has led to an increasing demand for juvenile treatment services and providers who are qualified and experienced in serving troubled youth. The youth sector of residential care also includes shelters, training schools, camp, ranches, and group homes.

Medical and dental laboratories provide valuable diagnostic assistance to physicians and dentists. Labs may be independent facilities or part of a clinic or hospital. Large commercial laboratories operate around the clock, including weekends and holidays. Some specialize in particular tests for which special equipment is required; equipment which would not be economical for a single hospital. Samples may be sent to labs by mail or special delivery services.

Various clinical lab tests and X-ray and imaging techniques available in medical labs enable physicians to diagnose the type and extent of an injury or illness, often without having to hospitalize the patient. Medical labs are classified under **SIC 8071: Medical Laboratories**; they include bacteriological and biological labs, blood analysis labs, X-ray and imaging labs, including dental X-rays, clinical medical labs, pathology labs, medical testing labs, and urinalysis labs. The most important X-ray and imaging techniques include mammography, computed tomography, ultrasound, magnetic resonance imaging, nuclear medicine, and interventional radiology in which images guide the physician performing treatment. These tests are performed by or under the supervision of a radiologist.

SIC 8072: Dental Laboratories produce dental prosthetics (artificial teeth and dentures), and orthodontic devices (such as braces), for the dental profession. All dental labs in this SIC manufacture their products to order.

Types of Ownership

There are, in general, three types of ownership in the health care industry: non-profit, for-profit, and government-owned. For-profit establishments are privately-owned and are subject to taxation. They may be public, shareholder-owned corporations or privately held.. Establishments may be run as single facilities, chains of one kind of facility, or groups of facilities which offer a variety of services. Clinics may be jointly owned by a group of doctors. Some medical labs are owned by doctors themselves as well. Some nursing homes are financed or owned outright by real estate investment trusts (REIT), some of which invest exclusively in health care.

There are two broad types of non-profit establishments. One is non-secular and is owned by a church or group of churches; the other is secular, and may be owned by a fraternal or charitable organization. Non-profits support themselves through their tax-ex-

empt earnings or through tax-exempt debt. Government establishments may be owned by city, state or the federal government.

Delivery of Health Care

Health care delivery in the United States is divided into three stages, primary, secondary and tertiary. Primary care is the most common and is generally the first type of medical care that is sought for a problem. It includes preventative care, such as immunizations and prenatal care, regular health checkups, and the monitoring of chronic illness, for example heart conditions. Primary care is almost always provided by private physicians in private practices or clinics. Public health clinics account for only a small percentage of primary care in America. It is frequently available outside normal medical facilities. For example, children may be immunized or tested at school and adults may be tested for cholesterol of blood pressure problems at work or the shopping mall. But when problems are detected, people are almost always referred to their private physicians.

Primary care physicians' services are generally provided on a fee basis. They are more likely to be covered in full or part by health maintenance (HMO) or preferred provider (PPO) plans. Low-income individuals without insurance must, of course, pay out-of-pocket costs, which are frequently higher than the fees charged for insured patients. Such patients often seek medical care at the outpatient departments or emergency rooms of public hospitals.

Secondary health care is provided by physicians who specialize in a particular field of medicine, such as urology. Patients may be referred to specialists by their primary physicians or they may go to them directly. However, many HMOs require that their members be referred to specialists by their primary care physicians. Tertiary health services are those provided by hospitals. In addition to their private practices, many specialists are also affiliated with one hospital or another.

Sources of Revenue

Medical services, including the diagnostic services provided by laboratories and dental care, are paid for from a number of sources. Patients without medical insurance of one kind or another must pay for their care out of their own pocket. The federal government and states administer two programs that provide medical benefits for special classes of patients. Medicaid provides coverage to low-income individuals; Medicare provides coverage for the elderly over 65 and the disabled. These two plans account for the major health expenditures of state and federal money.

Blue Cross and Blue Shield plans also provide group and individual medical and dental coverage. Traditionally not-for-profit plans intended to provide insurance to anyone who could not afford private insurance. Recently, Blues in many states have begun converting to for-profit status and operating with the stricter admission requirements used by traditional private companies.

Other insurance is provided by a variety of private plans, usually through an employer. Under a traditional indemnity insurance plan, which may or may not have included dental or pharmacy coverage, policy holders were free to visit the doctor of their choice. They were required to pay a predetermined amount every year, a deductible, after which the insurer assumed all costs.

Traditional Health Maintenance Organization (HMO) plans maintain a network of physicians, both primary and secondary care providers, who are paid a set annual rate for each member, regardless how often they visit the doctor. Members, in turn, can visit the doctor as often as they wish for their monthly premium. HMOs were conceived as a means of containing spiraling health costs in the late 1970s and early 1980s. To qualify for coverage, members must consult a member physician.

Preferred Provider Organizations (PPO) negotiate special rates with physicians, hospitals, and labs for their members. Members pay a monthly premium, and a predetermined fee for regular office visits or a percentage of specialist fees. Members are free to visit physicians who are not preferred providers. However they must reckon first with considerably higher fees, and second with the possibility that visits to specialists or hospitals are not covered by the terms of their plan.

Vendors

The medical and health care industry is dependent on a number of specialized vendors and suppliers. Drugs, and diagnostic tests and substances are purchased from pharmaceutical companies. Equipment, such as cardiac monitors, X-ray and ultrasound machinery, and treadmills, may be bought from manufacturers or rented from other companies. Plastics manufacturers produce a broad range of materials for the medical industry including catheters, disposable hypodermic syringes, gloves and hair nets. There is an entire industry involved with the by-products of the medical industry. Hospital and other waste is disposed of in special incinerators. Other companies specialize in the sterilization of reusable medical equipment or the sterilization, for example by gamma irradiation, of disposable devices such as needles and gloves once they have been used. Companies that build or operate cryogenic equipment offer hospitals and blood banks a way to preserve blood and human tissue. There is a variety of companies that offer specialized management and administrative services to doctors and hospitals. Outside companies will manage a physician's practice, an institutional pharmacy, a rehabilitation clinic, or the administration of an entire hospital. Some firms specialize in medical billing services for different segments of the medical industry; others specialize in medical cost containment. Software companies design and market systems designed to digitize and store physicians' files, X-rays, and the like. The transportation industry provides a broad variety of services extending from ambulance service, helicopter transport of the critically ill or injured, to courier services for the transport of tissue or blood specimens and important test results.

Legislation

The medical industry is regulated by a broad variety of legislation. States license or certify various medical personnel, including physicians, dentists, anesthesiologists, nurses, medical technicians, and paramedics. Hospitals and medical labs produce high amounts of dangerous waste, the disposal of which is regulated by the Environmental Protection Agency (EPA) Standards for specimen control and oversight in labs doing "high complexity" procedures are set by federal law. Federal antitrust laws regulate hospital mergers. Like other employers, medical establishments must conform to Occupational Safety and Health Administration (OSHA) regulations.

A large number of professional and specialist organizations are active in the medical and health care field. Among the most important are the American Medical Association (AMA), which represents the professional interests of American physicians; the American Hospital Association; the American Health Care Association, which represents the nursing home industry; and the American Nursing Association.

Background and Development

The history of the American health care system has, by and large, been its growth in the private sector. The rise of a recognizable class of trained, licensed, professional health providers began in the latter half of the 19th century. At first, that class was comprised primarily of physicians and pharmacists. Other practitioners, such as midwives, osteopaths and chiropractors were marginally important, and by the turn of the century, doctors began to replace midwives in aiding childbirth. Dentists formed a distinct professional class as well. However, because of older attitudes toward dental care—formed partly by the lack of anesthetics and antiseptics—people made visits to the dentist a rare occasion.

In the 1890s there were about as many physicians per capita as in the 1990s. Until the turn of the century, most training was conducted through apprenticeship to other practicing doctors. Eventually the larger universities set up schools of medicine replacing the unaffiliated, uncertified, unregulated schools that had previously offered medical training. Most doctors in the second half of the 19th century and the first few decades of the 20th worked out of their own private practice. They provided their services for a fee to their patients, although physicians perhaps felt an implicit obligation to treat patients who did not possess the means to pay. Patients paid the full fee themselves until the 1930s with the advent of the first medical insurance plans, laying the foundations of private practice and service for a fee that characterize the modern American private health care system.

Hospitals were also rare in 19th century America. Illness, among the middle and upper classes at least, was treated at home or in a physician's office. In 1875 there were only about 100 general hospitals in the U.S. "Charity hospitals" founded first in Europe and later on the east coast of the United States, were used almost exclusively by the indigent. Those hospitals, which were founded before the advent of antisepsis, were dark, dirty hotbeds of infection, to be avoided by any who had the means for alternate treatment. Because of the danger of infection, about whose cause nothing was known, surgery was practiced only on simple cases, such as the setting of simple fractures, or as a last resort, such as the amputation of gangrenous limbs.

Joseph Lister's discovery of the effectiveness of antiseptics in preventing infection during surgery, and in hospitals in general, was the impetus to begin building hospitals for the "well-to-do" classes. The discovery of anesthesia, coupled with antiseptics, eventually made surgery a more viable alternative for many patients. Once that was so, the affluent began looking for surgeons, who in turn, needed hospitals to work in. By 1900, there were 4000 general hospitals in the U.S.

The growth of hospitals in the U.S. was spurred mainly by voluntary community boards and churches. Most were private or nonprofit; municipalities built very few public hospitals. Although the nonprofit charters of early hospitals called for care of the poor, the lower classes comprised a small percentage of their patients. Paying patients—that is the middle and upper classes—paid for the hospital's day-to-day expenses; the money to build came from community fund raising or the philanthropic trusts established in the flush of the industrial revolution. The growth of surgery and the advance of medical technology, for example, with the growth of radiology after the turn of the century, encouraged the growth of hospitals; home care and private practice were increasingly unequal to the new demands.

Other specialties underwent dramatic change in the late 19th century. Dental practice paralleled medical practice: it was private and provided for a fee. Dental education was taken over by universities. Anesthetics were first used by dentists, and made dental work more attractive. Nursing took shape as a distinct profession for women following the Civil War. Education took place largely in hospitals where student nurses provided free labor. Eventually nurses training began to be organized along lines developed by Florence Nightingale. As nurses became active in helping immigrants and the urban poor, their training proved valuable since they were often the sole providers of medical help. Public health offices were first founded in response to contamination of local drinking water by sewage and waste that gave rise to periodic cholera outbreaks. Their responsibilities were later expanded to organize and administer vaccinations in schools. Unlike other hospitals, when mental hospitals were built, they were usually funded with public money, probably because the prevailing fee-for-service system could not effectively be applied.

By the early 1930s the private health care delivery system that we now know had been formed by physicians, hospitals and philanthropists. Government, usually state governments, intervened only to set standards and issue licenses. Hospitals, as well as gifts to hospitals, were given tax-exempt status, a kind of indirect government subsidy. A new element was introduced during the Great Depression: third party payment. The first health insurance plans were prepayment plans organized by hospitals which quickly evolved into Blue Cross plans throughout the country. Insurance was natural for potential patients as hospital costs increased; it helped hospitals by providing a steady flow of income. Those plans were followed later in the decade by physician's prepayment. Blue Shield, as the plan became known, provided coverage for doctors' services in hospitals, primarily surgeons whose fees were costly by then. Blue Cross and Blue Shield were very successful, exceeding even their own expectations in enrolling employer groups.

Both Blue Cross and Blue Shield were administered by tax-exempt, not-for-profit organizations. The first government health insurance was created during World War II with the implementation of the Emergency Maternal and Infant Care Program. Aimed at wives and dependents of servicemen, the program was the first national health care program directed towards a specific segment of the population. The first private insurance plans were set up during the War as well. Eventually, joining company health care

programs was made a precondition of employment. That was acceptable where government compulsion was the subject of controversy. National health insurance was first proposed around the time the Social Security Act was passed in 1935. The legislation was postponed until 1952. The opposition of President Dwight Eisenhower to the plan effectively ended Congressional debate on the subject. Nonetheless by 1952 over one-half of all Americans were covered by some form of health insurance.

Accompanying the growth of the economy from 1930 to 1960 was growth in the health care sector. During that period, according to Odin W. Anderson's *Health Services in the United States*, hospital admissions rose from 90 per 1000 in the population per year, to 145 per 1000. The number of people who visited a doctor annually grew from 30 per 1000, to 65 per 1000. Hospital beds and the number of physicians increased as well, but not enough to keep pace with demand. As a result, hospital occupancy rates jumped and hospitals prospered. To help hospitals meet demand, especially in rural areas, Congress passed the Hospital Survey & Construction Act in 1946. The law provided marching federal funds to hospitals where older sources of money, such as philanthropy, had dried up. The law introduced explicit government support of private health care where formerly it had largely existed only as tax-exemptions.

New insurance forms were introduced in the 1950s and 1960s. Group practice prepayment, in which a group of specialists provided a wide range of medical services and were each paid a salary from the premiums collected. The first were Kaiser Permanente in California and Health Insurance Plan of Greater New York, but, soon after, similar plans followed elsewhere. In 1965, federal and state government entered the health insurance field with the passage of the Medicare Act for the aged and the Medicaid Act for the poor. By that year, private and nonprofit insurance paid 40 percent of day-to-day hospital costs and 30 percent of physicians' costs. Government, in particular the federal government, was paying 50 percent and 20 percent respectively. According to figures cited by Odin Anderson, health care expenditures in the United States rose moderately between 1950 and 1965, from $78 per year to $198 per year per capita, not accounting for inflation, and from 4.6 percent to 5.9 percent of the Gross National Product. Those numbers were certainly influenced by the rise in Americans who were 65 and older, an age when disability and chronic illness increases dramatically. The growing elderly population coupled with the passage of the Medicare and Medicaid Acts helped the nursing home industry grow from 1950 onward.

Until the latter half of the 1960s, customers of the health care industry, including both patients and insurers, had not questioned the fee charged by physicians and hospitals. Hospital costs by then were rising at a rate of about 15 percent a year, according to Odin W. Anderson, and the cost of physicians was not far behind. Between 1965 and 1980 costs rocketed: health care expenditures increased from $198 per capita per year to $865, and from 5.9 percent of the GNP to 9 percent, according to Odin Anderson. The rapidly rising costs engendered concern about ways to contain costs. For the first time the practice of paying what physicians and hospitals charged was seriously questioned. Mechanisms that were developed in response included monitoring the decisions hospital physicians made, controlling access to hospital beds, and more closely controlling the hospital reimbursement rates. They were developed primarily by insurers, but Medicare and Medicaid implemented requirements for the review of the decisions made by hospital doctors, a radical step, from the point of view of the medical profession. Private insurers responded to high costs with new plans, most importantly Health Maintenance Organizations (HMOs) which paid hospitals and physicians a flat rate every year for each member. HMOs limited patients to physicians who were part of the plan and were successful in containing costs. In the 1990s, however, HMOs were increasingly criticized for taking cost containment too far and denying members necessary health care simply on the basis of expense.

The 1970s and 1980s witnessed a number of other important trends in health care. The success of high-tech medical technologies gave rise to a new class of ethical and legal issues for physicians and hospitals. Machines were able to keep the seriously infirm and handicapped patients, and even brain-dead bodies alive indefinitely, and patients and their loved ones were confronted with the question "when is it appropriate to end life support?" Advances in fertility science, in particular, the rise of surrogate mothers,

clouded the rights of parenthood. Medicine became an arena of litigation in the 1970s and 1980s as well. Hospitals and physicians became more and more frequently the targets of malpractice lawsuits. They were forced to take out expensive insurance to protect themselves, a significant factor in the rise in health care costs.

In 1986 Congress revoked the tax-exempt status of Blue Cross and Blue Shield, after the General Accounting Office criticized it as giving the Blues an unfair competitive advantage over private insurers. Not long afterwards, many Blues plans began to convert to for-profit status, putting an end to a significant middle ground between government and private insurance. That same year Congress passed a law that private hospital emergency rooms could not turn away the poor until they had been stabilized. Emergency rooms became the primary source of medical care for the indigent and uninsured. In 1990 another attempt at formulating a national health care plan was introduced by the U.S. Bipartisan Commission on Comprehensive Health Care. The Commission proposed a plan that would require all employers to provide insurance for all employees and their dependents, or to pay a tax that would go towards public coverage. The plan died when it was criticized for failing to contain health care costs. A similar fate was suffered by a national health care plan proposed by the administration of Bill Clinton.

Pioneers and Newsmakers in the Industry

Elizabeth Kenny

Elizabeth Kenny developed the world's first system of physical therapy. She was a stubborn advocate of the new techniques, despite long-standing opposition from professional medicine, particularly in her native Australia. Eventually the benefits of the "Kenny treatment" were too obvious to ignore and today physical therapists practice this treatment in hospitals and clinics the world over.

Kenny was born in Warialda, New South Wales Australia on September 20, 1886. She attended elementary school, but records indicate that she had no further education, nursing or otherwise. Around the turn of the century she began working as a volunteer nurse in the Australian outback, providing her services free to whomever needed them. Around 1911 she started treating victims of poliomyelitis. Unlike traditional treatment, Kenny applied hot packs and manipulated the affected muscles until patients were able to move and exercise autonomously. The treatment was successful with patients who were still in the early stages of the disease, recovering some use of the muscles. Encouraged, Kenny opened a small hospital of her own in the town of Clifton.

World War I interrupted her work. While serving in the Australian army, Kenny was promoted to Sister and she conceived and later patented the "Sylvia" ambulance, a stretcher on wheels intended to move the seriously injured safely over rough terrain. After the war, she returned to nursing in Australia. In 1932 Sister Kenny opened a clinic for polio and cerebral palsy patients. By that time her work had awakened considerable controversy in Australian medical circles. In direct contradiction of standard medical practice, she encouraged her patients to discard their braces and move about, to reeducate their crippled muscles. Doctors called her practices criminal and belittled her theoretical explanations of polio; Kenny was outspokenly critical of the medical profession's close-mindedness.

While some in the Australian medical community voiced their disapproval of her method, the Australian government supported her efforts. In 1934 the Queensland government provided money for polio clinics which used the Kenny treatment. Before long, Kenny clinics were opening in other cities. She traveled to Great Britain to treat polio victims and shocked the medical establishment there with her unconventional ideas. She returned to Australia to find a report by leading Queensland doctors roundly condemning her work. At the same time, however, a hospital superintendent reported that Kenny's patients recovered faster and that their muscles had greater suppleness than those of patients given conventional treatment.

In 1949, Kenny traveled to the United States where she visited the Mayo Clinic in Rochester Minnesota and was given a ward at Minneapolis General Hospital to demonstrate her treatment. Its success won over doctors in Minnesota; before long, she was offering courses in Kenny treatment at the hospital. In 1942 she opened the Sister Kenny Institute, a training center for nurses and physiotherapists from all over the world, in Minneapolis. American doctors accepted Sister Kenny's methods in a relatively short period and she became a popular figure in the U.S.; there was even a film, *Sister Kenny,* made about her life. When she returned to Australia in 1950 she encountered the same hostility from physicians that she had met years before. She died in Toowoomba in 1951. After her death, The Kenny Foundation in Minnesota continued her work.

Lavinia Dock

For nearly seventy years Lavinia Dock was a prominent figure in the women's movement in the United States and Europe. Early in her career she played a leading role in the professionalization of nursing. She trained nurses, wrote the first drug manual for nurses as well as the tremendously influential *History of Nursing,* and was in the forefront organizing the first professional association for nurses.

Lavinia Dock was born to a well-to-do family in Harrisburg, Pennsylvania on February 26, 1858. While in her early twenties she learned of a school for nurses that had opened at New York's Bellevue Hospital, the first nursing school in the United States based on principles developed by Florence Nightingale. Dock graduated from the program in 1886 and for the next couple years worked as a nurse with victims of various natural disasters. In 1888 her career began in earnest when she compiled *Materia Medica for Nurses,* a drug manual. The first book of its kind specifically for nurses, Dock's manual quickly became a standard text.

In 1890 she began working at Johns Hopkins Hospital in Baltimore with another pioneer, Isabel Robb, who was an advocate of modern nursing education. Robb and Dock became involved in the movement to raise nursing to the level of a profession, a topic she spoke on at the World's Columbian Exposition in Chicago in 1893. Dock called for a strict division of physicians' and nurses' spheres of authority. She continued to press for the organization of nurses while she was working at the Henry Street Settlement House in New York (founded by Lillian Ward.) The nurses provided the only medical care the immigrants and urban poor at Settlement House ever received; they were doing the work of independent physicians, as well as giving preventative care, providing health education and experimenting with school nursing.

In 1896 the organizational work of Dock and Robb resulted in the formation of the Nurses Associated Alumnae, the first professional organization for nurses in the United States. It was later renamed the American Nurses Association. The structure of the new group was the result of Dock's research into other women's groups and the American Medical Association. In 1899 she traveled to Great Britain and made contacts with English nursing groups and feminists. While in London in 1900, she co-founded the International Council of Nurses (ICN). She later gave help and encouragement to black nurses who were trying to organize.

Between 1900 and 1923 Dock was a contributing editor for the *American Journal of Nursing*, in whose pages she proselytized for solidarity among nurses and the independence of the profession. Her articles in the *Journal* became a meeting point for European and American nurses; she encouraged Europeans to stand up for their rights and reported news from the continent for her American readers.

In 1907 the *History of Nursing* was published. The book, which eventually ran to four volumes, was co-authored with Adelaide Nutting but most of it was Dock's work. The book was as important for the feminist movement of the day as it was for nurses. It revealed that nurses—virtually all women—had a long history of autonomous, valuable achievement stretching over centuries and continents. The book remained in print for years in successive volumes and helped support Dock during the Great Depression.

Dock's broad interests eventually led her to give up practical nursing just after the turn-of-the-century. She slowly moved from nursing activities to suffragist activities. She enjoyed a long retirement, periodically revising her *History* and maintaining occasional contacts with the ICN. She died at the age of 98 in April 1956.

Wilhelm Roentgen

Wilhelm Roentgen's accidental discovery of X-rays gave birth to the science of radiology and introduced a new age of medical diagnostics. It was also, arguably, the first piece of high-tech equipment to be used by doctors.

Roentgen was born on March 27, 1845 in the Ruhr village of Lennep. His academic career advanced haltingly. He was expelled from secondary school before he could take the exams that would have enabled him to attend university. He took courses without credit at the University of Utrecht and was allowed to enter Switzerland's Zurich Polytechnic, where in 1868 he was awarded a degree in mechanical engineering and later a Ph.D. in physics. He taught at a string of schools and published prolifically, which eventually led to an offer of a professorship in physics at the University of Wurzburg in Germany.

It was at Wurzburg, on November 8, 1895, that the 50-year-old Roentgen made his momentous discovery. While conducting and experiment with an induction coil, a device used to generate bursts of high voltage, one of Roentgen's assistants noticed that a screen coated with a barium preparation had fluoresced, even though it was on the other side of the lab and had been covered with a cloth that was impervious to light. Roentgen immediately understood the implications of the event. He repeated the experiment and christened the newly-discovered radiation X-rays, after the mathematical symbol for the unknown. The same day he made an X-ray photograph of his wife's hand.

Remarkably, Roentgen's discovery was made using common, inexpensive equipment available in virtually every chemistry or physics lab. As a result, Roentgen kept his observations secret at first, fearing that another scientist could easily repeat the experiment and publish the result before he was able to—and claim credit for the discovery. Paradoxically, however, he refused to patent his invention, and when the postwar inflation in Germany wiped out his savings, he was left penniless.

In 1901 Roentgen was awarded the first Nobel Prize in Physics. Over the next decade other researchers refined the device. The tungsten filament, the high vacuum tube, and high contrast agents such as barium sulfate that made photography of soft tissues possible, were among the discoveries that ushered in the golden age of radiology. By the time World War I broke out, most hospitals were equipped with an X-ray machine. Perhaps because he began his work with X-rays relatively late in life Roentgen did not suffer from the effects of his work. Only later were the dangers of constant exposure to X-rays discovered and many early pioneers, such as Marie Curie and Walter Bradford Cannon, died painful deaths from radiation inflicted illnesses. Wilhelm Roentgen died in 1923.

Joseph Lister

Joseph Lister was the first physician to recognize the importance of germs to human infections. That recognition led to his efforts to introduce antiseptic conditions to hospitals, and in particular, to surgery. The high rates of survival among hospital patients— previously unknown—led to the rise of surgery and of the hospital as a place of healing rather than death.

Joseph Lister was born in England on April 5, 1827. He decided early in life to become a surgeon, and after finishing his studies in 1853, he began teaching medicine at the University of Edinburgh. Lister was a physician to whom innovation apparently came easy. He invented a number of new surgical instruments: a needle for silver suture wire, a hook for retrieving objects from the ear, forceps for the sinuses, a screw tourniquet for the aorta, and blunt-ended scissors for bandages (scissors that are still used today). His work led to a professorship in surgery at Glasgow University in 1860. The following year he was put in charge of the surgical wards at the Glasgow Royal Infirmary (GRI).

Surgery was an extremely dangerous procedure at the time, one which few patients survived. Lister came to believe that cleanliness was directly related to infection in surgery. Despite great resistance from the surgeons at GRI, he insisted that they wash thoroughly with soap and water before operating. Around that time he learned of the work of Louis Pasteur that linked germs to putrefaction. Lister realized that Pasteur's theory offered a solution to the mystery of infection, and linked germs to the pus that formed in infected wounds.

Germ theory cleared up a number of anomalies, for instance why infection caused many more deaths among patients in the hospital than at home: germs were being spread back and forth among patients in hospitals. In 1865 Lister looked for an antiseptic agent to prevent infection and settled on carbolic acid. He used it for the first time on patients with compound fractures, a condition that was invariably fatal at the time. Of the first eleven fracture patients Lister treated using carbolic acid, nine survived, a stunning success.

Lister went on to apply antiseptics to all areas of surgical practice in his hospital: surgeons' hands, surgical tools, suture thread. Towels soaked in carbolic acid were hung around surgery patients. British physicians resisted adopting Lister's techniques, but his ideas caught on almost immediately in France, Germany, and the U.S. Today, although the basic materials may have changed, Lister's principles are followed in every hospital, clinic and doctor's office in the world. Lister is also famous for having licensed his name to Listerine mouthwash, for which his heirs are still paid royalties.

The Mayo Family

William Worrall Mayo, and his sons William James Mayo and Charles Horace Mayo, were among the very first successful—medically and financially—surgeons in the United States. They were important in the development of techniques for surgery of the abdomen, eye, thyroid, and ovaries. The clinic they founded became a model for group cooperative practice and through their philanthropic institute, the Mayo Foundation, became an international center for research and medical training.

William Worrell Mayo immigrated to the United States from England in 1854 and settled in Rochester Minnesota in the 1860s. He established his reputation performing operations on ovarian tumors, and soon other surgeons began traveling to Rochester to observe his technique. His sons followed in his footsteps. William James Mayo specialized in eye surgery early in his career and developed a successful procedure for removing cataracts, and later became proficient at abdominal surgery. His work led to the development of surgical treatment for appendicitis. Charles Horace Mayo pioneered the use of thyroid surgery. The Mayo Brothers developed successful methods for operating on gallstones, pyloric ulcers, and goiter.

The Mayos are most renowned for the clinic that bears their name. The Mayo Clinic grew out of the family's management of the medical operations at St. Mary's Hospital in Rochester. The clinic was revolutionary: It was a group practice at a time when American medicine was dominated by single-physician practices. It employed physicians with a broad range of expertise in diagnostics and treatment—although at first most of the medical staff were employed sorting out potential surgical patients. Also, physicians who joined the clinic were brought in as full partners to the Mayos—which was unheard of at the time. Each patient had access to the services of different specialists, the Mayo Clinic's size made it possible to obtain equipment that was beyond the means of a single-physician practice, and doctors at the Mayo Clinic had opportunities to travel, do research, and study.

The Mayo Brothers and the Mayo Clinic made surgery acceptable if not attractive to the affluent classes. Building on the discoveries of Joseph Lister, they performed operations that were both successful and, more importantly, safe compared to those of a few decades earlier. According to figures quoted by Stephen M. Ayres, between 1889 and 1892 the Mayo Brothers performed 54 abdominal operations; five years later they performed 2,157 operations of different sorts.

Targeting their practice at the middle and upper classes made the Mayo Brothers wealthy by 1915. In that year they established the Mayo Foundation for Medical Education and Research with a gift of $2.5 million. In association with the medical school of the University of Minnesota, the foundation provided promising medical students with an opportunity to do graduate work in a cutting-edge practical setting. By the time of their deaths in the early 1930s, the Mayo Clinic was one of the most respected medical institutions in the United States, a position it continued to hold in the late 1990s.

Nathan Smith Davis

Nathan Smith Davis was the main force behind the founding of the American Medical Association (AMA), the country's first national association of physicians. The organization Davis founded was responsible for the introduction of uniform standards of medical education in the United States and developed the first code of medical ethics for American physicians. Davis served the AMA his entire life and was the first editor of the *Journal of the American Medical Association.*

Nathan Smith Davis was born in 1817 and was educated as a doctor in New York state. He was elected to the New York Medical Society where he attempted to develop norms of medical education and licensure. His work in New York led him to the realization that uniform standards of education of physicians were needed for the country as a whole. In 1845, at the age of 29, Davis made a formal proposal that an national body be founded for that purpose. Though scorned, according to the AMA web site, as "impractical if not utopian" by some members of the medical establishment, a convention was called.

Delegates from 16 states and various medical societies and colleges met at New York University on May 5, 1846. Davis was named chairman. The next day a committee he chaired presented its proposals for the new organization, which included national standards of for a medical degree, uniform for all medical schools; suitable prerequisite study for medical students; and, a code of ethics for the American medical profession. One year later, on May 7, 1847, 250 delegates met at the Academy of Natural Sciences in Philadelphia and passed the resolution forming the AMA.

The AMA was founded as an organization of state, county and local medical societies, and medical colleges. Committees on medical sciences, practical medicine, surgery, obstetrics, education, medical literature, and publication were established at the same time. In addition to addressing the issue of medical education, it quickly became an outspoken critic of medical quackery and questionable patent medicines. One of its very first actions was to draw up the first nationwide code of medical ethics, based largely on the writings of Thomas Percival, a British ethicist.

In 1883 Davis was named the first editor of the AMA's new publication, the *Journal of the American Medical Association*. The weekly journal was based on the *British Medical Journal* and eventually became one of the most prestigious, respected medical publications in the world. Davis resigned as the chairman of the AMA's newly established Board of Trustees to accept the editorship and served until 1888.

Current Conditions

In 1995 Americans spent $878.8 billion dollars on personal health, over 55 percent more than in 1985 and 75 percent more than in 1980, according to the Health Care Financing Administration (HCFA). 60 percent of that was for hospital care and physicians' services, $350.1 billion and $201.6 billion respectively. $45.8 billion went to dentists, $77.9 for nursing home care, and $52.6 billion was spent for other professional services, which included everything from private nurses, podiatrists, optometrists, physical therapists and clinical psychologists, to chiropractors, naturopaths, and practitioners of Christian Science. $15.24 billion went for medical research. $4.47 billion was spent on the construction of new medical facilities.

Medical Doctors

According to the American Medical Association (AMA), there were 737,764 individuals with M.D. degrees in the United States in 1997. 598,924 or about 80 percent, were practicing physicians who dealt with patients on a regular basis; the others were representatives of pharmaceutical companies, researchers, government and company officials, and the like. A good deal of the physicians, for example, surgeons, cardiologists, and obstetricians, although office-based nonetheless worked regularly with patients in hospitals.

In general, the number of physicians, in absolute terms and in proportion to the population, has risen over the past decades, according to the AMA. The most dramatic increase was among practitioners of internal medicine. Between 1970 and 1980 their numbers rose by over 70 percent, and between 1980 and 1996 by another 70 percent. There are now 72,600 internists practicing, the largest of any medical specialty. The next largest is general practice/family practice with just under 60,000. The number of pediatricians nearly tripled between 1970 and 1996 when the number of practitioners reached 53,369. In 1996, the number of psychiatrists reached 38,407, about twice as many as in 1970. The percentage of diagnostic radiologists increased significantly as well during that period. In 1970 they made up only .06 percent of all physicians; in 1996, with 20,043 practitioners, they made up 2.7 percent. The number of surgeons, on the other hand, remained relatively stable. In 1996 there were 37,943, "a very slight rise" since 1970 according to the AMA.

The number of physicians has risen significantly in relation to the population, according to the AMA. In 1960 there was an average of one physician for every 703 people in the United States. By 1996, the ratio had improved to one for every 360. Between 1965 and 1996 the number of M.D.s not employed by the federal government increased by 169.1 percent. In 1996 California had 87,593 physicians, the most physicians in the country. However it was only 12th among the states in favorable physician/patient ratio. The District of Columbia topped the list with 136 people per physician, followed by Massachusetts with 235, New York with 253, and Maryland with 259 people per physician. According to the AMA, there is concern among some in American medicine that the number of physicians after the year 2000 will be inadequate to meet increasing demands for health care.

According to the Bureau of the Census, there were 198,500 offices and clinics of medical doctors (SIC 801) in the U.S., which employed just over 1.6 million individuals. Single physician practices and two-physician practices declined from 1990 to 1996, while group practices, of three or more physicians increased by 166.3 percent between 1980 and 1996. Approximately 89 percent of all physicians engaged in patient care practiced in metropolitan areas in 1996.

Dentists

In 1995, according to the American Dental Association figures quoted in the *Dental Practice Management Industry Report* by C.B. Dickson, there were 141,000 dentists in private practice. The year before, according to the Census Bureau, there were 110,600 dental offices and clinics (SIC 802) in the U.S., which employed 594,000 individuals, including dentists, dental technicians, hygienists, and receptionists. Those dental practices had total revenues of $45.6 billion in 1996, according to the Census Bureau's *Service Annual Survey*. The number of dentists has been growing through the 1990s at a rate of about 0. 6 percent. Most dentists and orthodontists, 90 and 95 percent respectively according to Dickson, work in practices of one or two persons. Like medical doctors, the trend in dentistry is toward group practice, but it is proceeding at a much slower pace.

Dickson reported that approximately 60 percent of the population sees a dentist regularly, and the annual cost of dentistry for that 60 percent works out to about $290 per actual patient. The likelihood that Americans will visit a dentist is directly linked to their income, the more they make, the higher the probability they will visit the dentist. One reason may be that dental insurance is not widespread and about 50 percent of dental charges are paid out-of-pocket. Of the $45.8 billion spent by Americans on dental care in 1995, according to Dickson, about 83 percent was for general dentistry procedures, such as cleanings, fillings, oral exams, crowns bridges and dentures. The other 17 percent was for work provided by specialists, primarily orthodontists, periodontists, endodontists, and oral surgeons.

Other Practitioners

In addition to medical doctors and dentists, there are a variety of other medical specialists practicing in the U.S. Doctors of Osteopathy (D.O.), like medical doctors, receive full four-year medical training. However the practice sees structural derangement, primarily in the spinal column, as the chief cause of disease. According to the American Osteopathic Association, there were approximately 40,000 D.O.s in the U.S. in 1996. The field has experienced rapid growth since 1970 when there were only 14,300 practicing D.O.s. Some D.O.s practice general medicine,

other specialties like surgery, gynecology or pediatrics. In 1992, the latest year reported, there were 14,221 offices and clinics of Osteopathy (SIC 8031) according to the Census Bureau's *1992 Census of Service Industries*. In 1995 they had revenues of $4.49 billion, according to the Census Bureau. Most D.O.s are in primary care, in fact they provide 9 percent of all primary care in the U.S. according to *Gale Business Resources,* and 15 percent in rural areas.

Optometrists (O.D.s) are qualified to diagnose diseases of the eye and prescribe glasses and drugs. Unlike opthamologists who are M.D.s, optometrists may not perform surgery. In 1995 there were approximately 29,500 practicing optometrists in the U.S. according to *Gale Business Resources*. Approximately two-thirds are in private practice according to the *Occupational Outlook Handbook (OOH)*, however, many optometrists work two or more jobs and consequently there were in 1996 about 41,000 optometrist jobs in the country. $6.3 billion was spent in optometrist clinics and offices (SIC 8042) in 1996 according to the *Service Annual Survey,* up slightly from 1995.

Podiatrists, or doctors of podiatric medicine (D.P. M.s), treat diseases and disorders of the foot. According to the *OOH,* in 1996 there were approximately 13,000 D.P.M.s in the United States. The majority of podiatrists are in solo practice and, according to *Gale Business Resources*, are concentrated in the American northeast and around the seven podiatric colleges. The Census Bureau reported total revenues of $2.49 billion for American offices and clinics of podiatrists (SIC 8043) in 1995.

There were approximately 28,800 offices and clinics of Chiropractors (SIC 8041) in 1994 according to the Census Bureau, employing about 89,000 persons. 70 percent of all chiropractors work in solo practice; most of the remainder are in group practice or employed by other chiropractors. The *OOH* reported that chiropractic practices earned some $7.3 billion revenues in 1995.

In addition to these areas of health and medicine, there is a large body of practitioners (SIC 8049 Offices and Clinics of Health Practitioners, Not Elsewhere Classified) who work in individual practices or in hospitals. Many, like physical and occupational, and respiratory therapists, psychologists, and paramedics, have won mainstream acceptance from the public and the medical establishment and their services are frequently covered by medical insurance plans. Others, like acupuncturists, naturopathists, and midwives, are accepted by wide sections of the population as alternative therapies. Practitioners face tight legal restrictions in some states and it is much rarer for treatments to be covered by insurance. Still others, like Christian Scientist practitioners, while used by a narrow circle of believers, are considered highly questionable, if not outright dangerous, by doctors and the public. There were, according to the *1992 Census of Service Industries,* 164,407 various alternative and otherwise unclassified practices in the U.S. in 1992. They enjoyed revenues of more than $10 billion in 1995.

The number of registered nurses has been rising very gradually through the 1990s, both in absolute terms and in relation to the population at large. The Department of Health and Human Services (HHS) reported that in 1996 there were 2.1 million active registered nurses in the U.S.

Hospitals

There were 6291 hospitals in the U.S. in 1995, according to the *U.S. Statistical Abstract.* That is a decrease of 674, nearly 11 percent, from 1980 levels reflecting commercialization and efforts at cost-containment that began in earnest in the 1980s. The federal government owned 299 hospitals in 1995; community hospitals totaled 5194, nonprofit hospitals 3092, state and local government hospitals 1350. All for-profit hospitals in the U.S. enjoyed revenues of about $44.6 billion in 1996, according to the Census Bureau's *Services Annual Survey.* General and surgical hospitals (SIC 8062) operating for-profit saw revenues rise from $24.16 billion in 1992 to $36.49 billion in 1996, an increase of nearly 35 percent. Nonprofits had revenues of $337.82 billion, of which $309.68 billion was earned by general and surgical hospitals, a more modest increase of 18 percent from 1992. The Bureau of Labor Statistics (BLS) reported that all hospitals employed 3.85 million persons in 1996, an increase of 1.1 million from 1980. General and surgical hospitals employed 3.51 million in 1996.

Between 1980 and 1994, according to the National Center for Health Statistics (NCHS), the number of patients discharged from non-Federal hospitals dropped from 37.83 million to 30.84. These numbers reflect the trend from inpatient to outpatient care set in motion by concern over skyrocketing health care costs in the 1980s. Per capita expenditures for hospitals between 1980 and 1995 nearly tripled, rising from $437 to $1283. By 1995, according to the HCFA, state, local and federal governments were expending $526.6 annually on hospital care. 34.1 percent patients who stayed at least one night in 1994 were covered by private health insurance, 37.6 percent by Medicare, 14.9 percent by Medicaid, while 4.7 percent paid out-of-pocket.

Indicative of the trend toward outpatient treatment, outpatient surgery increased from 3.19 million procedures in 1980 to 13.8 million in 1995, an increase of 77 percent. 16.4 percent of all surgery in 1980 were outpatient procedures while in 1995 the number had risen to 57.6 percent. In all, American hospitals treated more than 67.2 million outpatient cases in 1995, according to the NCHS, and another 96.5 million were treated in emergency rooms.

In addition to general and surgical hospitals, there were 699 specialized hospitals in the U.S. in 1992 according to the *1992 Census of Service Industries.* These included children's hospitals, tuberculosis, chronic care, and psychiatric hospitals. The American Hospital Association reported 657 psychiatric hospitals (SIC 8063) in the U.S. in 1995. They had $12.7 billion in revenues, according to the *Services Annual Survey,* with nonprofit institutions earning approximately $92.9 billion. Of the 737 psychiatric hospitals counted by the NCHS in 1993, 358 were run for profit and 266 were government institutions. There were 107,000 patients in psychiatric hospitals, a number down about 25 percent from 1985. 471 of all psychiatric hospitals in 1993 has 75 beds or more.

Other non-psychiatric specialty hospitals (SIC 8069), for profit and non profit, had revenues totaling $ 23. 51 billion in 1996, according to the *Services Annual Survey.* The number of chronic care hospitals dropped significantly between 1985 and 1993—from 44 to 26. By 1993, according to the NCHS, all but five were run by state, local or federal government;

only one was run for profit. In 1993 most were larger institutions, 22 had 75 beds or more.

$10.9 billion was contracted for hospital construction, expansion, and renovation in 1995, up about 10 percent from 1990, and 50 percent from 1980, according to the *U.S. Statistical Abstract.* Hospitals were not exempt from the trend toward networking that was at work in other parts of the medical field. According to the American Hospital Association, in the early 1990s some 11 percent of the nation's community hospitals became involved with networks—groups of hospitals, doctors, insurers and community agencies working together to provide a broad spectrum of services, to eliminate duplication of services and to better integrate care among community providers. Hospitals began forming other new group forms, such as hospital-physician organizations (PHOs), independent practice associations (IPAs), and management services organizations.

Nursing Homes and Other Personal Care Facilities

In 1992 there were 51,831 nursing and personal care facilities (SIC 805) in the United States. Of the institutions operated for profit, 10,242 were skilled nursing care facilities (SIC 8051); 3,375 were intermediate care facilities (SIC 8052); and 1337 were other types of personal care facilities (SIC 8059), according to the 1992 Census of Service Industries. Revenues for for-profit institutions totaled $44.2 billion in 1996, up from $34.7 billion in 1992, the 1996 Service Annual Survey reported. Non-profit facilities had revenues of $18.51 billion in 1996, up $3.29 billion from 1992.

Of the 16,700 nursing homes (defined as facilities that routinely provide nursing and personal care) counted by the NCHS in 1995, about 11,000 were for-profit, 4,300 nonprofit, the rest were operated by government. 9,100 were run as part of chains, the rest were independent facilities. They were concentrated overwhelmingly in the Midwest and the South, with about 5,500 in each region; the rest were divided equally between the West and Northeast. 12,600 of these homes had 50 beds or more. With 1.54 million residents, these nursing homes had an occupancy rate of about 87.4 percent.

Skilled nursing facilities, which provide nursing, personal and rehabilitative care to patients who require continuous care, experienced tremendous growth in the 1980s and 1990s. Facilities certified by Medicare increased from 5,052 in 1980 to 13,122 in 1995 according to the HCFA. Patients eligible for Medicare rose from 28.5 million to 37.5 million between 1980 and 1995, about 25 percent; expenditures, however, skyrocketed from $395 million to $9.14 billion, an increase of 2300 percent. Employment in skilled nursing facilities increased by over 45 percent, from 638,000 to 1.18 million between 1990 and 1995. Skilled nursing facilities are tending gradually to consolidate into chains, as larger companies acquire smaller independent homes. The largest, however, was the federal government in the mid-1990s, with about 125 facilities, according to *Gale Business Resources.* Smaller providers are also banding together in an increasingly competitive market to reduce duplication of administrative services, to increase their efficiency. Managed care plans are also switching patients from extended hospital stays, to take advantage of the major cost savings skilled nursing facilities offer.

Intermediate care facilities SIC 8052 provide care to individuals with incapacitating infirmities who require continuous care, but not continuous medical or nursing services. It primarily includes homes for the mentally handicapped and patients suffering from disorders of the central nervous system, such as epilepsy and cerebral palsy. Of the residential facilities for the mentally retarded in 1993, 1,765 were government-operated, up 78 percent from 1980 according to Center for Residential Services and Community Living. Private facilities increased from 14,605 to 58,790, a 76 percent change. In 1994 Medicaid spent $8.3 billion on intermediate care for the mentally handicapped, nearly 8 percent of the Medicaid budget.

Other miscellaneous residential care facilities (SIC 8059) provided minimal care for relatively healthy patients, primarily assisted living for the elderly, and to a lesser extent for psychiatric and mentally retarded patients. The $11.1 billion in 1996 revenues for this segment jumped 75 percent from $2.8 billion in 1990. More than 1.5 million people spent between $10 and $15 billion annually in the mid-1990s to live in assisted living communities, according to *Gale*

Business Resources; that amount is expected to increase to $25 billion by the year 2000. It is estimated that from a quarter to half of nursing home residents could live in assisted living for a substantially lower cost, except Medicare/Medicaid does not cover assisted living. In early 1994 there were more than 25 assisted living center worth $400 million had been financed by Real Estate Investment Trusts (REITS).

In addition to minimal care residential homes for the elderly, a broad variety of care is available for other groups, including drug and alcohol abusers, orphans, and problem juveniles. Because of a lack of foster homes, orphanages are booming. In 1990 there were about 1000 group homes for children. Homes for children born with AIDS or drug dependency, according to *Gale Business Resources*, are a particular segment that is growing rapidly. According to the National Drug and Alcohol Treatment Unit Survey in 1989, 32,000 individuals with alcohol problems and 41,000 with drug abuse problems were receiving non-hospital residential care.

Home Health Care Services

In the 1980s and 1990s, home health care services (SIC 8081) enjoyed the most dramatic growth of any health care category. National expenditures, only $2.4 billion in 1980, had increased by 1100 percent to $28.8 billion by 1995, according to HCFA statistics. The boom reflected the move away from expensive, cost-intensive hospital and nursing home stays. In 1994, according to the NCHS, 72.4 percent of home health care recipients were 65 or older, and 67.5 percent of them were women. In 1995, $6 billion, about 21 percent, of home health care costs were paid from out-of-pocket; only 12 percent of these costs were covered by private insurance. Government paid $15.79 billion in home health care costs, about 55 percent. The lion's share of that, over $15 billion, came from Medicare, up from $774 million in 1980.

According to Census Bureau figures, there were about 12,900 home health care establishments in 1994. About 43 percent were owned by for profit companies, 36.8 percent were nonprofit, the rest owned by government or other bodies. The NCHS reported, however, that 59 percent of home health care patients utilized the services of nonprofit organizations, only 30.3 were served by for profits. 41.7

percent of these institutions were concentrated in southern states in 1994, only 18.1 percent in the northeast; however, these regions had 34 and 33.7 percent of home health care patients, respectively. In 1995, for-profit institutions had revenues totaling $17.52, a rise of 32 percent from 1992 revenues. Non-profits earned $8.8, up 56 percent from 1992. The industry employed approximately 658,000 employees in 1996, according to the BLS.

Laboratories

In 1994 there were 8,800 medical labs according to the Census Bureau, and 7,500 dental labs. All laboratories employed 658,000 people in 1996, according to the BLS, up nearly 600 percent from 119,000 in 1985. The pressure in the 1980s to contain skyrocketing medical costs led insurers and health management organizations to require more testing to demonstrate the necessity of medical treatments being prescribed. The requirement brought new revenues to labs and at the same time led to higher lab costs. In 1996, medical labs had revenues of $13.26 billion, dental labs $2.77 billion, according to the *1996 Services Annual Survey*.

Specialty Facilities

Kidney dialysis centers (SIC 8092) are regulated by the federal government which grants exclusive licenses to providers to provide long-term dialysis within a designated territory. The number of dialysis patients in the U.S. increased one hundredfold in the 24 years after 1972; in 1996 there were an estimated 240,000 receiving the treatment. There were 1,119 dialysis centers in the U.S. in 1992, according to the Census Bureau. Dialysis centers are subsidized by the Health Care Financing Administration. For-profit centers had revenues of $3.38 billion in 1996, according to the *1996 Services Annual Survey*, non-profit centers earned $676 million. Dialysis centers experienced rapid growth between 1991 and 1996: 15.5 percent growth in 1992-93, 13.9 percent in 1993-94, 17.9 percent in 1995—95.

Other specialty outpatient facilities (SIC 8093) have enjoyed growth during the 1990s as insurers discourage high-cost inpatient treatment. These include drug and alcohol treatment, psychiatric care, and family planning clinics. This industry segment had revenues in 1996 of $9.58 billion, according to the 1996 Services Annual Survey. $5.95 billion was earned by nonprofit facilities.

Miscellaneous Health and Allied Services

This segment (SIC 8099) includes an extremely broad and heterogeneous combination of service types: blood and sperm banks, hearing testing, osteoporosis centers, childbirth preparation, medical illustration, oxygen tent services, and plasmapheresis centers, where red blood cells are separated from plasma and returned to the donors body. In 1992 there were 3,709 establishments working in this classification. The for-profit segment earned revenues of $20.42 billion in 1996, the non-profits earned $10.38, according to the *1996 Services Annual Survey*. Blood, now a multi-billion dollar industry, is the most important area.

Industry Leaders

Columbia/HCA Healthcare Corporation

With companies like Tenet Healthcare Corporation and Vencor Inc., Columbia/HCA Healthcare Corporation is a leader in the trend toward the corporatization of hospital care in the United States. At the end of 1997 Columbia/HCA owned and operated over 300 health care facilities, including general and surgical hospitals, psychiatric and specialty hospitals, and rehabilitation centers in 36 states in the U.S., as well as in England and Switzerland. Those facilities contained approximately 60,000 licensed beds. Its network of health care operations brought Columbia/HCA revenues totaling $18.82 billion in 1997, up about $30 million from 1996. The company was the seventh largest employer in the U.S. in 1997 with around 285,000 employees.

Columbia/HCA utilizes its size to control health care costs in its constituent hospitals. It is able to purchase medical and other supplies in huge volumes at significantly lower cost than individual hospitals could. At the same time, basic hospital administration is centralized, eliminating duplication and waste. However, facilities are managed at the local level. Many hospitals owned by Columbia/HCA

have retained their own local names and do not bear the company's name.

In early 1997, Columbia/HCA was targeted in the first of a series of federal investigations into physician relationships with the company, the company's home health operations and laboratory billings. Pamela Sherrid described the most serious in *U.S. News & World Report,* a whistle-blower suit brought by former and current employees, alleged that Columbia/HCA had systematically overbilled Medicare over a 14 year period. If found guilty of this and other suits, the company could be subject to over $1 billion in fines.

After the first series of investigations was announced, the company underwent a significant shake-up. The CEO was ousted, a new management team put in place, and a period of downsizing begun that was still underway in mid-1998. Among other things, the company was expected to rid itself of hospitals with total annual revenues of approximately $4 billion. At the same time, the company created a new senior level management position, the Senior Vice President of Ethics, Compliance and Corporate Responsibility, and gave the job to an authority in corporate ethics. His responsibility was to develop a comprehensive code of conduct and ethics, accompanied by a company-wide compliance program, the first steps of which were put in place in early 1998.

Phycor, Inc.

Phycor Inc. is one of the most successful physician practice management companies (PPMs) in the United States. PPMs manage medical clinics which provide a broad variety of specialized medical services. Founded in 1988, Phycor experienced rapid growth in the mid-1990s. Revenues nearly doubled every year between 1993 and 1997: $167,38 million in 1993, $242.48 million in 1994, $441,59 million in 1995, $766,32 million in 1996 to $1,11 billion in 1997. In 1998 it had 57 clinics which employed about 3,890 physicians and 550 physician extenders, such as physician assistants, nurse practitioners and other providers. The company had a total of 515 service sites in 28 states in the U.S. Phycor owns both urban and rural clinics. The company focuses on multi-specialty clinics with between 25 and 200 physicians. 52 percent of Phycor clinics are primary care providers. In

1997, Phycor acquired 11 new clinics, merged 103 practices into existing clinics, and helped its member clinics recruit some 400 new physicians. Phycor has also built affiliations with a number of independent physician associations (IPAs) throughout the country, some of which may eventually become Phycor members. Approximately 22,000 IPA physicians have affiliations with Phycor.

Phycor does not purchase medical clinics. Once it reaches an agreement with a clinic that matches its profile, a long-term service agreement—normally 40 years—is signed with the clinic's physicians. Phycor then provides a range of services to the clinic: It purchases all equipment and facilities. It takes over the administration of clinic's business operations. It hires and employs most non-physician personnel. Medical control of the clinic remains in the hands of its physician staff. Each clinic's operations are overseen by a Joint Policy Board comprised of representatives from Phycor, the clinic's local management and the physician staff. Phycor brings clinics a number of strengths they would not possess independently, most notably expertise in managed care contracting, access to capital, efficiencies of scale, access to medical management information systems and other resources. In addition, Phycor organizes training programs for physicians and staff on a variety of medical, managed care and administrative issues.

LabCorp

Laboratory Corporation of America Holdings, also known as LabCorp, is one of the three largest independent clinical laboratory companies in the United States. The company, founded in 1971, has approximately 17,800 full-time employees. LabCorp, based in Burlington, North Carolina, has built up a network of 25 regional laboratories plus 1,200 service sites made up of branches, patient service centers and STAT laboratories, with which it serves clients throughout the U.S. LabCorp has also set up a company courier system to pick up specimens and deliver them to lab facilities. It had nearly $1.52 billion in sales in 1997, down from $1.6 billion in 1996. In 1994 the company acquired Allied Clinical Labs, then the sixth largest independent clinical lab company in the USA. In April 1995 the company, then known as National Health Laboratories, merged with Roche Biomedical Laboratories, and took the name Laborato-

ry Corporation of America Holdings. In addition, since 1993, it has acquired 57 small laboratories worth about $182.4 million in total sales.

In 1997, LabCorp had approximately 130,000 clients and processed an average 237,000 patient specimens a day. Its laboratories are able to perform over 1700 different tests. The routine tests, such as blood tests, can be performed in any of the company's 25 major laboratories. Individual laboratories are equipped to perform a range of specialized tests, including, allergy tests, computer assisted analysis of electrocardiograms and blood pressure measurements, clinical tests for pharmaceutical companies, diagnostic genetics testing, kidney stone analysis, and cancer tests. The company also performs so-called identity tests—tests to establish disputed parentage or forensic identity in criminal cases. LabCorp says it is the largest provider of such testing in the United States. It provides drug and alcohol detection testing for private and government employers, as well as maintaining a special industrial hygiene facility in Virginia for the analysis of toxic substances.

Fresenius Medical Care

Fresenius Medical Care (FMC) is the world's largest provider of kidney dialysis care and products. FMC was created in September 1996 by the merger of the Dialysis Systems Division of Fresenius AG, in Germany, and National Medical Care Inc. The company conducts business in the U.S. and 16 other nations in the world. Two-thirds of FMC's $3.3 billion in 1997 revenues were earned by its dialysis care divisions. These services are provided primarily for patients suffering from End Stage Renal Disease. The company's 961 dialysis centers treat approximately 71,000 patients annually; in addition, the company provides inpatient dialysis for 550 U.S. hospitals.

Fresenius is the world's second largest source of dialysis equipment and supplies. It has production and distribution facilities in Germany, the U.S. and in 29 other countries. These products comprise about one-third of FMC's annual revenues and include equipment for hemodialysis and peritoneal dialysis. A full 86 percent of its worldwide product revenues in 1997 came from the sale of disposable products, primarily dialysis machine filters.

Beverly Enterprises

Beverly Enterprises is the United States' leading provider of long-term and post-acute care. At the beginning of 1998, it operated 569 skilled nursing homes and rehabilitation centers, 12 specialty hospitals, 71 outpatient therapy clinics, 34 assisted living facilities, and 5 home health agencies. Beverly's 1997 revenues of $2.74 billion were down from $3.26 billion in 1996, following a complicated divestiture of its pharmacy subsidiary. However, average occupancy of its nursing facilities was 89.1 percent in 1997 up from 87.7 percent the previous year. Skilled nursing comprised 55.9 percent of Beverly Enterprise's 1997 revenues, with pharmacy at 18 percent, rehabilitation therapy at 12.6 percent, and specialty hospitals and other services at 13.5 percent.

Beverly Enterprises has three main subsidiaries, Beverly Healthcare, the Beverly Care Alliance and Beverly Specialty Hospitals. Beverly Healthcare concentrates in the skilled nursing area. It had 63,376 licensed skilled nursing beds in 1997. The subsidiary was experiencing rapid growth. It completed 15 new buildings in 1997 and had another 21 under construction. It added 336 skilled nursing beds in high demand areas, and the daily per-patient revenues of its skilled nursing centers climbed from $109.6 in 1995 to $119.8 in 1997. The Beverly Care Alliance operated home health and hospice facilities, outpatient therapy clinics and respiratory care facilities. It added 43 outpatient clinics in 1997 and planned at least 80 more in 1998. Beverly Specialty Hospitals operated 12 acute, long-term care hospitals in 7 states in 1997. Specialty hospital revenues for the subsidiary increased from $53.5 million in 1995 to $101.5 million in 1997.

National Dentex Corporation

National Dentex Corporation (NDX) of Wayland, Massachusetts is the largest dental laboratory operator in the U.S. It runs 27 full-service laboratories and five branch laboratories in 21 states. NDX's laboratories produce a full range of dental prosthetics, including dentures, bridges, and crowns. Founded 1982, DNX's net sales have grown from $33.62 million in 1993 to $59.19 million in 1997. At the beginning of 1998, DNX had 1,212 employees. 27 of them

worked in corporate administration, the rest in the various laboratories.

Each DNX laboratory operates as a stand alone facility with its own business name under a local manager. The corporate staff is responsible for marketing, negotiating purchasing agreements for the company and its laboratories, setting quality standards sets, and providing administrative support. Each laboratory maintains its own sales force which markets and sells company services to dentists.

Work Force

Physicians

There were approximately 560,000 physician jobs held by M.D.s and D.O.s in 1996 according to the *Occupational Outlook Handbook* (OOH). About 70 percent of American physicians in 1996 were active in office-based practices, including clinics and health management organizations. There were nearly three times as many female physicians in 1996 as in 1970, their percentage of all physicians climbing from 7.6 percent to 21.3 percent. The percentage of International Medical Graduates (IMGs) among American physicians increased from 17.1 percent in 1970 to 23 percent in 1996. Nearly 47 percent of American physicians were younger than 45 in 1996, and women physicians tended to be younger than their male colleagues. According to the AMA, 17 percent of all doctors were 65 or older.

All 50 states, plus the District of Columbia and U.S. territories, license physicians. All require that an applicant graduate from an accredited medical school and pass a licensing exam. Usually a physician licensed in one state can obtain a license in another without taking the second state's licensing exam. Foreign physicians must pass an exam and complete a residency in the U.S.

According to the *OOH,* physicians earn more than most occupations. In 1995 a physician's median annual income after expenses was $160,000, according to the AMA. Physicians who owned or partly-owned their practice had higher median incomes than salaried physicians, although earnings varied by experience, geographic area, personal skills, professional reputation as well as other factors. Among specialists, surgeons had the highest median incomes with $275,200 in 1996. Radiologists were not far behind with $275,100. Psychiatrists and family practitioners were among the least well paid, with $133,700 and $139,000 of median income respectively according to the AMA.

The *OOH* predicted that, because of continuing expansion of health care and the aging of the population, employment for physicians through the year 2006 will increase more rapidly than in other occupations. The best outlook is for primary care physicians: general and family doctors, pediatricians and general internists. While the number of specialists is increasing, cost-containment measures that limit the use of specialty services are expected to reduce demand for them after the year 2000.

Dentistry

There were approximately 162,000 jobs in dentistry in 1996, according to the *OOH,* and about 90 percent of all dentists worked in private practices. Dentists are licensed by all 50 states and the District of Columbia, usually after obtaining a bachelor's degree, successfully completing two to four years of dentistry school, and, in some cases, passing a state exam. Specialists, orthodontists for example, were required to have a specialty license in 17 states in 1996. The American Dental Association reported that median income for all dentists in 1995 was $120,000, specialists earned $175,000 a year, general practitioners about $109,000. Closer attention to dental hygiene among young people and a resulting decline in tooth decay is expected to lead to slower growth in the field than in previous years.

Dental assistants prepare instruments and materials for dentists. In 1996, according to the *OOH,* there were about 202,000 dental assistant jobs. More than a third were part-time positions; sometimes dental assistants were employed by more than one dental practice. Dental assistants frequently complete special training programs after high school; they may be one year or less in duration, or two years if taken through a college. The median weekly earnings for dental assistants in 1996 were $361, though some earned as much as $516 or as little as $212. Dental hygienists, who perform clinical procedures such as

cleaning teeth and developing X-rays, earned an average $41,184 per year if working full-time in 1994. However, about half worked less than full-time, according to *Gale Business Resources*.

Other Practitioners

There were approximately 11,000 podiatrist jobs in the United States in 1996, according to the *OOH,* most in solo practice, some holding more than one job. Their median income in 1996 was about $91,400, although, according to the American Podiatric Association, those practicing less than two years earned an average $44,662 in 1995, while those who had practiced 16 to 30 years earned an average $141,135 that year. There were 7 podiatric colleges in the United States in the mid-1990s, according to the *OOH.* All fifty states require that podiatrists be licensed. There were about 41,000 jobs in 1996. The American Optometric Association reported that about 66 percent of U.S. optometrists worked in private practice. The median income for optometrists was $80,000 in 1996. The U.S. had 17 colleges of optometry in the mid-1990s; all states required that optometrists be licensed. Chiropractors held about 44,000 jobs in 1996 and some 70 percent were in private practice. Their median income in 1995, according to the American Chiropractic Association, was $80,000. There were 16 training programs for chiropractic in the U.S. in the mid-1990s. All states required that chiropractors be licensed.

Nursing

According to the *OOH,* there were nearly 2 million registered nursing (RN) jobs in 1996. Approximately two-thirds of registered nurses were employed in hospitals; three in ten worked part-time and one in ten worked more than one job. To be licensed, student nurses must successfully complete one of the 1500 programs in registered nursing, then pass a national licensing exam. Licenses must be renewed periodically. Registered nursing was projected to be one of five occupations with the most new jobs in the year 2000 and after. The most growth was predicted in hospital outpatient facilities and in home health care. Full-time registered nurses earned between $415 and $1039 weekly, depending on factors like experience, geographical location and employer.

Licensed practical nurses (LPNs) are not as highly trained as RNs. They usually receive a year of specialized training in one of about 1100 state-approved programs. In 1996 there were approximately 699,000 LPN jobs in the U.S., 32 percent in hospitals, 27 percent in nursing homes, and 13 percent in doctors' offices. LPNs earned between $318 and $673 weekly in 1996, according to the *OOH*. Job growth is expected to be highest in nursing homes.

Homemaker-Home Health Aides

Homemaker-home health aides provide daily services to the elderly living in their own homes. The approximately 697,000 jobs were held in home health agencies, visiting nurse associations, residential care facilities with home health departments, hospitals, public health and welfare departments, community volunteer agencies, and temporary help firms. Some are self-employed. Home health aides were not particularly well-paid, according to the *OOH*. Their starting wage was between $5.96 and $8.29 per hour, with pay tending to be higher in the Northeast and West than in the Midwest and South. Educational requirements for home health aides are low. With the trend toward increased home care, demand is expected to increase, abetted by the high turnover in the occupation.

Medical and Clinical Laboratory Technologists

According to the *OOH,* there were some 285,000 clinical laboratory technician and technologist jobs in 1996, more than half of which were in hospitals. Licensing requirements vary among the states. Most laboratory technicians have an associate's degree from a college or a certificate from a training program offered by a hospital, a vocational school, or the armed forces. The *OOH* reported that the average annual salary for full-time laboratory technologists in 1996 was $35,100; full-time laboratory technicians earned $26,500.

Dental Laboratory Technicians

There were approximately 47,000 dental laboratory technician jobs in 1996, according to the *OOH*. Most were employed in small privately-owned labs. One in seven were self-employed, a higher proportion than most occupations, according to the *OOH*. Most

training takes place on the job, however some colleges and vocational schools offer training. In all there were 35 accredited programs in 1995 in the United States. Dental laboratory trainees earn little more than minimum wage, but once fully-trained—after 4 or more years—they can earn upwards of $50,000 a year.

Radiologic Technologists

There were some 174,000 jobs held by radiologic technicians in 1996, according to the *OOH,* including sonographers, radiation therapists, and radiographers. More than half worked in hospitals, the rest were employed by physicians' offices, clinics, and diagnostic imaging centers. Radiologic technicians receive specialized training that lasts from 1 to 4 years, often through a junior or full college. The Joint Review on Education in Radiologic Technology, which accredits training programs, recognized 629 radiography programs and 97 radiation therapy programs in 1997. In the same year, the Joint Review on Education in Diagnostic Medical Sonography recognized 74 ultrasound programs. Licensing is not required by any state, however professional organizations like the American Registry of Diagnostic Medical Sonographers (ARDMS) certify its members competence. The median base salary for full-time radiologic technicians employed in hospitals was $28,000 a year.

Health Services Managers

In 1996 there were about 329,000 health service manager positions in the United States. Over 50 percent were employed in hospitals, another 25 percent in nursing homes and personal care facilities, and doctors' offices and clinics, while the rest worked for home health agencies and other health and allied services. Salaries varied based on the type of facility and the level of responsibility. According to the Medical Group Management Association, in 1996 administrators in small practices of 7 doctors or less earned a median salary of about $56,000 a year, while those in larger practices earned $77,000. *Modern Healthcare* reported in 1997 that half of all hospital CEOs earned $190,500 or more annually. There were 67 colleges that offered master's programs in health services administration, each generally lasting from two to three years.

North America and the World

In health care like in other industries, there is a constant give and take of human talent, products, expertise and facilities between the U.S. and the rest of the world. The most common way of "exporting" American health care services takes place in the United States—when foreigners are treated in American hospitals, clinics and other facilities. Some providers advertise their facilities in foreign countries— so-called health tourism. In early 1998, according to Piia Aarma in *Business America,* the Department of Commerce awarded a $400,000 grant to a consortium in Hawaii, to promote Hawaiian health care in China, Korea, Hong Kong, and Taiwan. Cuba has begun actively promoting its cheap health care, according to Linda Robinson in *U.S. News & World Reports,* although less than 100 Americans used it in 1997.

American hospitals and clinics have been establishing a presence abroad since the 1970s, according to Paola Trimarco and Howard Rothman in *Gale Business Resources*, at first in Canada and Western Europe, with expansion into Eastern Europe, the former Soviet Union, Asia and the Middle East in the 1990s. Nonetheless, according to Ernest Plock writing in *Business America,* Europe accounted for over half of all American health care sales abroad and the United Kingdom accounted for half of that. The affluent population in Latin America is also seen as a potential source of significant income. American companies abroad are active in other areas as well, according to Plock including managed care, emergency evacuation, home health care, dental care and health insurance.

U.S. companies also earn foreign revenues from licensing fees and royalties. American telemedicine companies, which reduce costs by utilizing the combined forces of computers and telecommunication technology, are also becoming more established in foreign markets, according to Everette James writing in *Business America.* When the medical staffing firm Olsten Corporation purchased Sogica, France's fifth largest staffing company, it established a presence in 13 countries. A growing sector is comprised of firms that provide medical care or information about available medical care in remote areas of the world. Clients of companies such as SOS Global Health-

care, are primarily companies with employees stationed in areas where medical care is not easy to obtain.

While expansion is often driven by profit motive, it can also be fueled by skyrocketing costs in the U.S. For example, Health Care International (HCI), a primary care hospital built in Scotland by two Harvard-trained doctors, can perform triple or quadruple bypass surgery for 25 percent less than it would cost in the U.S. because Scottish cost of living is significantly lower. U.S. experience with innovative means of cost-containment and financing effective health care delivery contributes in large measure to American leadership in global health care markets, according to Everette James.

Foreign graduates of medical schools, also known as International Medical Graduates (IMGs), made up 20.9 percent of all American physicians in 1980, a percentage that increased to 23 percent by 1996, according to the American Medical Association. The number of IMGs in full-time staff positions declined significantly during the same period, from 16.1 percent to 10.8 percent, a result in part of federal legislation in 1976 which limited physician immigration. The AMA predicts that those restrictions will be loosened in the next century as the per capita number of American physicians declines. In 1996, 22.2 percent of IMGs were active in Internal Medicine, another 9.8 percent in General and Family Medicine.

Dentistry does not tend to be particularly international, according to the American Dental Association. Foreign dentists frequently come to the U.S. to learn the latest procedural and technological advances. However, American dentists tend to remain in the U.S. to practice and conduct research. Osteopaths tend to remain in the U.S. as well, where salaries are higher. One reason for that, according to Nancy Hatch Woodward in *Gale Business Resources,* is that the U.S. is the only nation in the world in which osteopaths receive a medical degree. Nurses, too, earn better salaries in the U.S. than other countries, even in Europe. Nursing training is more comprehensive in the United States, and according to Trimarco and Woodward, American nursing professionals find work easily abroad because of the international nursing shortage. Practitioners of so-called alternative medicines have historically tended to have higher levels of acceptance in foreign countries. Some European countries routinely provide health insurance coverage for acupuncture, homeopathy, and the like.

Some foreign companies have successfully penetrated the American market. A notable example is the area of dialysis where two companies, Fresenius Medical Care, based in Germany, and the Gambro Group, lead the world market. Fresenius is the world's largest provider of kidney dialysis products and care. The company provided inpatient dialysis care at 550 hospitals in the U.S. in 1998. The Swedish Gambro Group is another leading producer of renal care equipment and provider of renal care, with 90 subsidiaries in 26 countries. They include COBE Laboratories and Gambro Healthcare in the United States.

Research and Technology

Research is an essential element of the health care industry. It is carried out intensively by a variety of institutions, in a variety of areas. Universities, pharmaceutical companies, small high-tech start-ups, and government labs all perform research. They look for cures for diseases like AIDS, cancer, heart disease, and diabetes; they search for the genetic bases of human biology and pathology; they develop ways of improving the chances of having a child for couples with fertility.

Perhaps one of the most revolutionary developments for the industry is telemedicine. Telemedicine enables physicians and other medical personnel to exchange medical data, video images and audio utilizing the latest communications and computer technologies, especially the Internet. Once telemedicine becomes more widespread it is expected to bring with it a number of benefits. Patients, especially those in rural and other remote areas will have access to specialized services and physicians not now available. Physicians and other health care workers who live in remote locations will be able to maintain their professional knowledge and work with professional colleagues more easily. It is expected to take over part of home health care. Above all, it is expec-

ted to increase revenues and reduce costs for patients and providers.

Certain issues remain to be resolved. The World Wide Web transcends state and national lines, but medical licenses do not; a physician with a New York medical license could not automatically practice telemedicine in Oklahoma. Insurers must agree to reimburse physicians offering telemedicine. The technology must be refined; for example the quality of medical image transmission and resolution must be higher. The technology has to be more widely distributed and it has to be accepted by doctors. The last two go hand in hand. According to investment bank Robertson Stephens, in the February 28, 1998 issue of the *Economist,* only 5 percent of American physicians used electronic medical records.

Even in the U.S. telemedicine is still in the prototype stage. Teleconferencing companies have begun to invest in the technology. Market research firm Feedback Research Services estimates the American telemedicine market is less than $100 million. According to the American Telemedicine Association (ATA), predicted growth in the field over the next few years ranges from 28 to 35 percent. Frost & Sullivan project that the American market could be worth $1.6 billion by 2004.

Another area of technological change that will affect the health care market is diagnostics. According to the *Occupational Outlook Handbook,* powerful, new tests will not only make it possible for fewer laboratory workers to perform more tests, routine tests will be greatly simplified so that personnel untrained in lab techniques—for example, physicians and patients—can perform tests that labs now perform. Powerful new sensor technology will also greatly improve diagnostic procedures. According to Charles Petit writing in *U.S. News & World Report,* one scientist is working on a breathalyzer device that will be able to detect infections by analyzing a persons breath. Other scientists are developing biosensors that will be able to diagnose DNA defects, antibody activities and other signs. These tests will not only be less expensive than current procedures, their developers say they will be as much as 100 times more precise.

In addition to sensors, micromachine technology promises to have a number of medical applications. Scientists are working on devices that can be implanted in a human body where they will continuously monitor vital signs. They will be particularly valuable for patients with serious chronic problems such as heart disease or diabetes. It is expected that they will be linked to other microdevices that will constantly administer microdoses of medication, for example insulin for a diabetic. Miniature robot surgeons are already performing some surgery, on hips for example, more accurately than human surgeons can. It is expected that, in the future, miniature robot surgeons will be performing more surgeries, such as complicated brain surgery, too delicate for any human surgeon. Some scientists even predict that in time microscopic robots will course through human blood streams, destroying cancer cells and opening blocked blood vessels.

Scientists are also expected to make great strides in the artificial generation of human tissue and the development of biomaterials which combine synthetic substances with living cells. These technologies, once developed, will make possible the production of replacement organs for humans. According to Max Busch writing in *Die Welt,* researchers are attempting to grow a human heart in a laboratory and believe the first will be implanted by the year 2008. Artificially produced organs would have a tremendous impact. In 1998. there was a severe shortage of donor organs. Doctors are working on designing new artificial organs as well.

Further Reading

1997 Beverly Enterprises Annual Report. Fort Smith, AR: Beverly Enterprises, Inc., 1998.

Aarma, Piia M. "Hawaii/Pacific District Export Council: Starting to Reap Rewards." *Business America.* September 1, 1998

Anderson, J.A. *Health Care Industry Review 1997.* Janney Montgomery Scott, 1997.

Anderson, Odin W. *Health Services in the United States: A Growth Enterprise Since 1875.* Ann Arbor: Health Administration Press, 1985.

Ayres, Stephen M.*Health Care in the United States: The Facts and the Choices.* Chicago: American Library Association, 1996.

Betts, Mitch. "Health Reform Raises Privacy Issues." *Computerworld,* April 11, 1994.

Beverly Enterprises, Inc. *Form 10-K.* Washington, DC: Securities and Exchange Commission, 1998.

Bisby, Adam. "Health Care Market Goes the Distance." *Computer Dealer News.* August 10, 1998.

Blecher, Michele Bitoun. "A Multiplier Outlier: Watchdogs Ask Why Not-for-profits Paid So Much for 22 Columbia Hospitals." *Hospitals & Health Networks.* June 20, 1998.

Brubaker Ropes, Linda. *Health Care Crisis in America.* Santa Barbara, CA: ABC-CLIO, Inc., 1991.

Burton, Virgil III, Eva Davis, and Karin Koek, eds. *Gale Business Resources.* Version 2.3. Detroit: Gale Research, 1998.

Busch, Max. "Ersatzorgane ous dem Reagenzglas.'" *Die Welt.* October 16, 1998.

"The Charm of Old Money." *Economist.* March 15, 1997.

Clapesattle, Helen. *The Brothers Mayo.* Boston: Houghton Mifflin, 1962.

COBE: A Medical Specialties Company. Lakewood, CO: COBE Laboratories, Inc., 1994.

"Corporate Background." Lexington, MA: Fresenius Medical Care, 1998.

Dickson, C.B. *Dental Practice Management Industry Report—Industry Report, et al.* Everen Securities, Inc. July 9, 1997.

Fitzpatrick, Michael. "Connected: Need a New Body Part?" *The Daily Telegraph.* September 3, 1998.

"Future Dental Care Will Be Very Different for Patients and Dentists." American Dental Association.

Available from http://www.ada.org/newsrel/9810/nr—08.html

Gambro AB Annual Report 1996. Lund, Sweden, 1997.

Girishankar, Saroja. "News & Analysis: IT Rx: Trim Costs, Move Medicine to Internet." *InternetWeek.* March 2, 1998.

Hammonds, Keith H. "Services: Health care." *Business Week.* January 12, 1998

Heterington, Laurel Traynowicz. "High Tech Meets High Touch: Telemedicine's Contribution to Patient Wellness." *Nursing Administration Quarterly.* March 22, 1998.

"How Wired is the Health Care Industry?" *Telephone IP News.* October 1, 1998.

"IT and Health Care: Bugs and Viruses." *The Economist,* February 28, 1998.

James, Everette. "Services—U.S. Firms are Leaders in the Global Economy." *Business America.* April 1, 1998

Kaufman, Martin, et al. *Dictionary of American Medical Biography.* Westport, CT: Greenwood Press, 1984.

"Laboratory Network Offers Managers the Best of Both Worlds." *LMT.* October 1994.

Lehrer, Steven. *Explorers of the Body.* New York: Doubleday & Company, 1979.

Leong, Kathy Chin. "Medical IT Managers Seek Cures." *Communications Week.* March 3, 1997.

Mason, Charles. "The Telemedicine Breakthrough," *America's Network.* January 15, 1998.

Nairn, Bede, and Geofrey Serle, eds. *Australian Dictionary of Biography.* Melbourne, Australia: Melbourne University Press, 1983.

"Nathan Smith Davis, M.D." American Medical Association: 1998. Available from http://www.ama-assn.org/about.

National Dentex Corporation, 1997 Annual Report. Wayland, MA: National Dentex Corporation, 1998.

"Nursing Home or Home Nursing?" *Forbes.* March 24, 1997.

Occupational Outlook Handbook 1998-99. Washington, DC: Bureau of Labor Statistics, 1998

Petit, Charles. "Brave New Medicine." *U.S. News & World Report.* December 1, 1997.

Physician Characteristics and Distribution in the U.S. Chicago: American Medical Association, 1997.

Plock, Ernest. "The Global Healthcare Services Market is Growing Fast as Foreign Consumers Look for Better Medical Care." *Business America.* July 1996.

Robinson, Linda. "Health Tourism." *U.S. News & World Report.* May 5, 1998.

Roemer, Milton I. "United States of America." *The International System of Health.* Westport, CT: Greenwood Press, 1988.

Sabbagh, Leslie. "Prepare to Change Your Paradigm: Telemedicine is Here to Stay." *Dermatology Times.* December 1, 1997.

Scerra, Chet. "Telemedicine Improves Access to Diabetic Eye Care." *Ophthalmology Times.* June 15, 1998.

Sherrid, Pamela. "How to Really Make a Killing in Health Care." *U.S. News & World Report.* November 2, 1998.

Sicherman, Barbara, and Carol Hurd Green, eds. *Notable American Women: The Modern Period.* Cambridge, MA: The Belknap Press of Harvard University Press, 1980.

Socioeconomic Characteristics of Medical Practice 1997/98. Chicago: American Medical Association, 1997.

Statistical Abstract of the United States. Washington, DC: GPO, 1997.

Troy, Timothy. "Does Managed Care Work?" *Opthamology Times.* November 1, 1998.

U.S. Department of Commerce, Bureau of the Census. *1996 Services Annual Survey.* Washington, DC: 1996.

U.S. Department of Commerce, Bureau of the Census. *1992 Census of Service Industries.* Washington, DC: 1995.

"U.S. Industry & Trade Outlook 1998: Health & Medical Services." *Biomedical Market Newsletter.* February 28, 1998.

—Evelyn Hauser & Gerald E. Brennan

CHAPTER 2

INDUSTRY STATISTICS & PERFORMANCE INDICATORS

This chapter presents statistical information on the Health and Medical Services industry. This view of the industry is through the lens of federal statistics. All the data shown are drawn from government sources, including the 100 percent surveys of the Economic Census and the partial surveys of services and other industries conducted annually by the U.S. Department of Commerce. Tables include general statistics, indices of change, and selected ratios.

SIC 8011 - OFFICES OF PHYSICIANS: GENERAL STATISTICS

Year	Estab-lish-ments	Employ-ment (000)	Payroll ($ mil.)	Revenues ($ mil.)		Ownership	
				SAS	Census	Sole Prop.	Partner-ships
1987	195,502	1,131.6	43,856.4	96,698.0	90,461.5	62,493	9,578
1988	191,971	1,241.8	51,118.9	108,835.0			
1989	192,224	1,304.4	55,689.3	117,213.0			
1990	193,620	1,387.2	62,970.7	128,871.0			
1991	195,610	1,454.0	68,190.5	138,576.0			
1992	197,701	1,356.7	68,731.9	151,824.0	141,429.1	63,416	8,891
1993	200,590	1,577.1	76,291.9	154,242.0			
1994	198,538[1]	1,621.4[1]	80,101.2[1]	159,616.0[1]			
1995	194,288[1]	1,663.9[1]	85,594.9[1]	167,969.0[1]			
1996	198,532[1]	1,730.5[1]	90,910.7[1]	173,483.0[1]			
1997	199,126[1]	1,793.6[1]	95,925.1[1]	186,612.0[1]			
1998	199,721[1]	1,856.6[1]	100,939.6[1]	195,135.5[1]			

Source: Data for 1987 and 1992 are from *Census of Service Industries*, Bureau of the Census, U.S. Department of Commerce. Data labeled SAS are from the *Service Annual Survey* for 1996, which also presented revisions for earlier years. Data for 1988-1991 and 1993-1995, when shown, are derived from *County Business Patterns* for those years from the Bureau of the Census. Extracted from *Service Industries USA*, 4th edition, Gale, 1998. Note: 1. Projections made by the editor.

SIC 8011 - OFFICES OF PHYSICIANS: INDICES OF CHANGE

Year	Estab-lish-ments	Employ-ment (000)	Payroll ($ mil.)	Revenues ($ mil.)		Ownership	
				SAS	Census	Sole Prop.	Partner-ships
1987	99	83	64	64	64	99	108
1988	97	92	74	72			
1989	97	96	81	77			
1990	98	102	92	85			
1991	99	107	99	91			
1992	100	100	100	100	100	100	100
1993	101	116	111	102			
1994	100[1]	120[1]	117[1]	105[1]			
1995	98[1]	123[1]	125[1]	111[1]			
1996	100[1]	128[1]	132[1]	114[1]			
1997	101[1]	132[1]	140[1]	123[1]			
1998	101[1]	137[1]	147[1]	129[1]			

Source: Same as General Statistics. The values shown reflect change from the base year, 1992, which is always 100. Data points earlier or later than 1992 are less than 1992 if less than 100 and greater than 1992 if greater than 100. Note: 1. Index based on a projected value.

SIC 8011 - OFFICES OF PHYSICIANS: SELECTED RATIOS

For 1992	Average of All Services	Analyzed Industry	Index
Employees per establishment	13	7	51
Revenues per establishment	810,117	715,369	88
Payroll per establishment	314,133	347,656	111
Payroll per employee	23,335	50,662	217
Revenue per employee	60,179	104,246	173
Sole proprietors as % of establishments	30.1	32.1	106
Partnerships as % of establishments	5.7	4.5	79

Source: Same as General Statistics. The 'Average of all Services' column represents the average of all service industries of which this SIC is a part. The Index shows the relationship between the Average and the Analyzed Industry. For example, 100 means that they are equal; 500 that the Analyzed Industry is five times the average; 50 means that the Analyzed Industry is half the national average.

SIC 8021 - OFFICES OF DENTISTS: GENERAL STATISTICS

Year	Estab-lish-ments	Employ-ment (000)	Payroll ($ mil.)	Revenues ($ mil.)		Ownership	
				SAS	Census	Sole Prop.	Partner-ships
1987	104,151	491.5	8,760.0	25,258.0	24,017.4	59,518	3,571
1988	102,241	499.4	9,957.8	27,325.0			
1989	103,279	512.9	10,588.1	29,297.0			
1990	104,654	533.2	11,618.2	31,502.0			
1991	106,362	544.5	12,321.0	33,279.0			
1992	108,804	554.6	13,039.0	36,939.0	35,523.0	63,383	3,530
1993	109,818	581.4	14,171.5	38,946.0			
1994	110,559[1]	594.3[1]	14,997.3[1]	41,663.0[1]			
1995	111,204[1]	615.3[1]	16,139.1[1]	44,909.0[1]			
1996	112,652[1]	625.6[1]	16,834.3[1]	47,417.0[1]			
1997	113,825[1]	641.2[1]	17,721.4[1]	49,331.5[1]			
1998	114,998[1]	656.9[1]	18,608.4[1]	51,818.4[1]			

Source: Data for 1987 and 1992 are from Census of Service Industries, Bureau of the Census, U.S. Department of Commerce. Data labeled SAS are from the *Service Annual Survey* for 1996, which also presented revisions for ealier years. Data for 1988-1991 and 1993-1995, when shown, are derived from *County Business Patterns* for those years from the Bureau of the Census. Extracted from *Service Industries USA*, 4th edition, Gale, 1998. Note: 1. Projections made by the editor.

SIC 8021 - OFFICES OF DENTISTS: INDICES OF CHANGE

Year	Estab-lish-ments	Employ-ment (000)	Payroll ($ mil.)	Revenues ($ mil.)		Ownership	
				SAS	Census	Sole Prop.	Partner-ships
1987	96	89	67	68	68	94	101
1988	94	90	76	74			
1989	95	92	81	79			
1990	96	96	89	85			
1991	98	98	94	90			
1992	100	100	100	100	100	100	100
1993	101	105	109	105			
1994	102[1]	107[1]	115[1]	113[1]			
1995	102[1]	111[1]	124[1]	122[1]			
1996	104[1]	113[1]	129[1]	128[1]			
1997	105[1]	116[1]	136[1]	134[1]			
1998	106[1]	118[1]	143[1]	140[1]			

Source: Same as General Statistics. The values shown reflect change from the base year, 1992, which is always 100. Data points earlier or later than 1992 are less than 1992 if less than 100 and greater than 1992 if greater than 100. Note: 1. Index based on a projected value.

SIC 8021 - OFFICES OF DENTISTS: SELECTED RATIOS

For 1992	Average of All Services	Analyzed Industry	Index
Employees per establishment	13	5	38
Revenues per establishment	810,117	326,486	40
Payroll per establishment	314,133	119,839	38
Payroll per employee	23,335	23,511	101
Revenue per employee	60,179	64,053	106
Sole proprietors as % of establishments	30.1	58.3	193
Partnerships as % of establishments	5.7	3.2	57

Source: Same as General Statistics. The 'Average of all Services' column represents the average of all service industries of which this SIC is a part. The Index shows the relationship between the Average and the Analyzed Industry. For example, 100 means that they are equal; 500 that the Analyzed Industry is five times the average; 50 means that the Analyzed Industry is half the national average.

SIC 8031 - OFFICES OF OSTEOPATHIC PHYSICIANS: GENERAL STATISTICS

| Year | Estab-lish-ments | Employ-ment (000) | Payroll ($ mil.) | Revenues ($ mil.) | | Ownership | |
				SAS	Census	Sole Prop.	Partner-ships
1987	7,314	35.6	967.0	2,280.0	2,119.2	2,840	252
1988	7,164	36.5	1,094.8	2,661.0			
1989	6,978	36.3	1,127.5	2,833.0			
1990	7,087	37.9	1,243.0	3,254.0			
1991	7,161	39.8	1,348.2	3,584.0			
1992	8,708	47.0	1,650.3	4,008.0	3,638.1	3,482	259
1993	8,554	48.9	1,715.2	4,159.0	3,689.6		
1994	8,385[1]	48.9[1]	1,763.9[1]	4,354.0[1]	3,916.3[1]		
1995	8,022[1]	49.0[1]	1,867.8[1]	4,698.0[1]	4,143.0[1]		
1996	8,374[1]	50.8[1]	1,931.7[1]	4,760.0[1]	4,369.7[1]		
1997	8,496[1]	52.5[1]	2,031.2[1]	4,995.7[1]	4,596.4[1]		
1998	8,617[1]	54.2[1]	2,130.7[1]	5,222.9[1]	4,823.1[1]		

Source: Data for 1987 and 1992 are from Census of Service Industries, Bureau of the Census, U.S. Department of Commerce. Data labeled SAS are from the *Service Annual Survey* for 1996, which also presented revisions for ealier years. Data for 1988-1991 and 1993-1995, when shown, are derived from *County Business Patterns* for those years from the Bureau of the Census. Extracted from *Service Industries USA*, 4th edition, Gale, 1998. Note: 1. Projections made by the editor.

SIC 8031 - OFFICES OF OSTEOPATHIC PHYSICIANS: INDICES OF CHANGE

| Year | Estab-lish-ments | Employ-ment (000) | Payroll ($ mil.) | Revenues ($ mil.) | | Ownership | |
				SAS	Census	Sole Prop.	Partner-ships
1987	84	76	59	57	58	82	97
1988	82	78	66	66			
1989	80	77	68	71			
1990	81	81	75	81			
1991	82	85	82	89			
1992	100	100	100	100	100	100	100
1993	98	104	104	104	101		
1994	96[1]	104[1]	107[1]	109[1]	108[1]		
1995	92[1]	104[1]	113[1]	117[1]	114[1]		
1996	96[1]	108[1]	117[1]	119[1]	120[1]		
1997	98[1]	112[1]	123[1]	125[1]	126[1]		
1998	99[1]	115[1]	129[1]	130[1]	133[1]		

Source: Same as General Statistics. The values shown reflect change from the base year, 1992, which is always 100. Data points earlier or later than 1992 are less than 1992 if less than 100 and greater than 1992 if greater than 100. Note: 1. Index based on a projected value.

SIC 8031 - OFFICES OF OSTEOPATHIC PHYSICIANS: SELECTED RATIOS

For 1992	Average of All Services	Analyzed Industry	Index
Employees per establishment	13	5	40
Revenues per establishment	810,117	417,793	52
Payroll per establishment	314,133	189,513	60
Payroll per employee	23,335	35,091	150
Revenue per employee	60,179	77,360	129
Sole proprietors as % of establishments	30.1	40.0	133
Partnerships as % of establishments	5.7	3.0	52

Source: Same as General Statistics. The 'Average of all Services' column represents the average of all service industries of which this SIC is a part. The Index shows the relationship between the Average and the Analyzed Industry. For example, 100 means that they are equal; 500 that the Analyzed Industry is five times the average; 50 means that the Analyzed Industry is half the national average.

SIC 8041 - OFFICES & CLINICS OF CHIROPRACTORS: GENERAL STATISTICS

Year	Estab-lish-ments	Employ-ment (000)	Payroll ($ mil.)	Revenues ($ mil.)		Ownership	
				SAS	Census	Sole Prop.	Partner-ships
1987	20,065	58.0	899.9	3,707.0	3,275.3	13,319	647
1988	20,056	61.0	1,049.5	4,510.0			
1989	21,701	66.7	1,179.9	5,005.0			
1990	22,899	73.0	1,317.9	5,467.0			
1991	24,572	77.2	1,460.1	5,647.0			
1992	27,329	84.7	1,652.2	6,555.0	5,917.9	17,628	790
1993	28,288	89.2	1,743.6	6,936.0	6,191.0		
1994	28,768[1]	89.1[1]	1,737.2[1]	6,757.0[1]	6,641.5[1]		
1995	29,022[1]	89.1[1]	1,766.2[1]	6,742.0[1]	7,091.9[1]		
1996	31,282[1]	99.8[1]	2,011.3[1]	6,958.0[1]	7,542.4[1]		
1997	32,580[1]	104.6[1]	2,129.8[1]	7,987.4[1]	7,992.8[1]		
1998	33,879[1]	109.3[1]	2,248.2[1]	8,392.9[1]	8,443.3[1]		

Source: Data for 1987 and 1992 are from Census of Service Industries, Bureau of the Census, U.S. Department of Commerce. Data labeled SAS are from the *Service Annual Survey* for 1996, which also presented revisions for ealier years. Data for 1988-1991 and 1993-1995, when shown, are derived from *County Business Patterns* for those years from the Bureau of the Census. Extracted from *Service Industries USA*, 4th edition, Gale, 1998. Note: 1. Projections made by the editor.

SIC 8041 - OFFICES & CLINICS OF CHIROPRACTORS: INDICES OF CHANGE

Year	Estab-lish-ments	Employ-ment (000)	Payroll ($ mil.)	Revenues ($ mil.)		Ownership	
				SAS	Census	Sole Prop.	Partner-ships
1987	73	69	54	57	55	76	82
1988	73	72	64	69			
1989	79	79	71	76			
1990	84	86	80	83			
1991	90	91	88	86			
1992	100	100	100	100	100	100	100
1993	104	105	106	106	105		
1994	105[1]	105[1]	105[1]	103[1]	112[1]		
1995	106[1]	105[1]	107[1]	103[1]	120[1]		
1996	114[1]	118[1]	122[1]	106[1]	127[1]		
1997	119[1]	123[1]	129[1]	122[1]	135[1]		
1998	124[1]	129[1]	136[1]	128[1]	143[1]		

Source: Same as General Statistics. The values shown reflect change from the base year, 1992, which is always 100. Data points earlier or later than 1992 are less than 1992 if less than 100 and greater than 1992 if greater than 100. Note: 1. Index based on a projected value.

SIC 8041 - OFFICES & CLINICS OF CHIROPRACTORS: SELECTED RATIOS

For 1992	Average of All Services	Analyzed Industry	Index
Employees per establishment	13	3	23
Revenues per establishment	810,117	216,543	27
Payroll per establishment	314,133	60,455	19
Payroll per employee	23,335	19,499	84
Revenue per employee	60,179	69,844	116
Sole proprietors as % of establishments	30.1	64.5	214
Partnerships as % of establishments	5.7	2.9	51

Source: Same as General Statistics. The 'Average of all Services' column represents the average of all service industries of which this SIC is a part. The Index shows the relationship between the Average and the Analyzed Industry. For example, 100 means that they are equal; 500 that the Analyzed Industry is five times the average; 50 means that the Analyzed Industry is half the national average.

SIC 8042 - OFFICES & CLINICS OF OPTOMETRISTS: GENERAL STATISTICS

Year	Estab- lish- ments	Employ- ment (000)	Payroll ($ mil.)	Revenues ($ mil.)		Ownership	
				SAS	Census	Sole Prop.	Partner- ships
1987	15,972	57.9	893.4	3,755.0	3,450.3	9,095	1,254
1988	15,291	58.3	964.1	4,133.0			
1989	15,049	58.9	1,007.8	4,296.0			
1990	15,320	62.6	1,116.0	4,799.0			
1991	15,425	64.1	1,181.2	5,028.0			
1992	17,135	68.6	1,301.0	5,333.0	4,939.5	9,160	1,188
1993	17,054	71.7	1,382.9	5,715.0	5,194.8		
1994	17,080[1]	72.0[1]	1,442.0[1]	6,021.0[1]	5,479.6[1]		
1995	17,028[1]	74.7[1]	1,538.5[1]	6,113.0[1]	5,764.4[1]		
1996	17,012[1]	77.3[1]	1,597.8[1]	6,313.0[1]	6,049.2[1]		
1997	17,163[1]	79.6[1]	1,676.0[1]	6,769.3[1]	6,334.1[1]		
1998	17,313[1]	82.0[1]	1,754.2[1]	7,063.6[1]	6,618.9[1]		

Source: Data for 1987 and 1992 are from Census of Service Industries, Bureau of the Census, U.S. Department of Commerce. Data labeled SAS are from the *Service Annual Survey* for 1996, which also presented revisions for ealier years. Data for 1988-1991 and 1993-1995, when shown, are derived from *County Business Patterns* for those years from the Bureau of the Census. Extracted from *Service Industries USA*, 4th edition, Gale, 1998. Note: 1. Projections made by the editor.

SIC 8042 - OFFICES & CLINICS OF OPTOMETRISTS: INDICES OF CHANGE

Year	Estab- lish- ments	Employ- ment (000)	Payroll ($ mil.)	Revenues ($ mil.)		Ownership	
				SAS	Census	Sole Prop.	Partner- ships
1987	93	84	69	70	70	99	106
1988	89	85	74	77			
1989	88	86	77	81			
1990	89	91	86	90			
1991	90	93	91	94			
1992	100	100	100	100	100	100	100
1993	100	104	106	107	105		
1994	100[1]	105[1]	111[1]	113[1]	111[1]		
1995	99[1]	109[1]	118[1]	115[1]	117[1]		
1996	99[1]	113[1]	123[1]	118[1]	122[1]		
1997	100[1]	116[1]	129[1]	127[1]	128[1]		
1998	101[1]	120[1]	135[1]	132[1]	134[1]		

Source: Same as General Statistics. The values shown reflect change from the base year, 1992, which is always 100. Data points earlier or later than 1992 are less than 1992 if less than 100 and greater than 1992 if greater than 100. Note: 1. Index based on a projected value.

SIC 8042 - OFFICES & CLINICS OF OPTOMETRISTS: SELECTED RATIOS

For 1992	Average of All Services	Analyzed Industry	Index
Employees per establishment	13	4	30
Revenues per establishment	810,117	288,271	36
Payroll per establishment	314,133	75,925	24
Payroll per employee	23,335	18,966	81
Revenue per employee	60,179	72,009	120
Sole proprietors as % of establishments	30.1	53.5	177
Partnerships as % of establishments	5.7	6.9	121

Source: Same as General Statistics. The 'Average of all Services' column represents the average of all service industries of which this SIC is a part. The Index shows the relationship between the Average and the Analyzed Industry. For example, 100 means that they are equal; 500 that the Analyzed Industry is five times the average; 50 means that the Analyzed Industry is half the national average.

SIC 8043 - OFFICES & CLINICS OF PODIATRISTS: GENERAL STATISTICS

Year	Estab-lish-ments	Employ-ment (000)	Payroll ($ mil.)	Revenues ($ mil.)		Ownership	
				SAS	Census	Sole Prop.	Partner-ships
1987	7,474	22.0	404.3		1,277.8	4,118	398
1988	7,487	24.0	501.9				
1989	6,993	23.7	515.2				
1990	7,132	24.9	576.3	1,811.0			
1991	7,246	26.6	619.8	1,957.0			
1992	7,948	26.4	624.2	2,102.0	1,920.1	4,379	350
1993	7,937	27.0	643.6	2,156.0			
1994	7,981[1]	26.8[1]	652.8[1]	2,190.0[1]			
1995	7,954[1]	27.4[1]	714.9[1]	2,388.0[1]			
1996	8,081[1]	28.6[1]	750.3[1]	2,440.0[1]			
1997	8,183[1]	29.3[1]	783.6[1]	2,554.4[1]			
1998	8,285[1]	29.9[1]	816.9[1]	2,655.8[1]			

Source: Data for 1987 and 1992 are from Census of Service Industries, Bureau of the Census, U.S. Department of Commerce. Data labeled SAS are from the *Service Annual Survey* for 1996, which also presented revisions for earlier years. Data for 1988-1991 and 1993-1995, when shown, are derived from *County Business Patterns* for those years from the Bureau of the Census. Extracted from *Service Industries USA*, 4th edition, Gale, 1998. Note: 1. Projections made by the editor.

SIC 8043 - OFFICES & CLINICS OF PODIATRISTS: INDICES OF CHANGE

Year	Estab-lish-ments	Employ-ment (000)	Payroll ($ mil.)	Revenues ($ mil.)		Ownership	
				SAS	Census	Sole Prop.	Partner-ships
1987	94	83	65		67	94	114
1988	94	91	80				
1989	88	90	83				
1990	90	94	92	86			
1991	91	101	99	93			
1992	100	100	100	100	100	100	100
1993	100	102	103	103			
1994	100[1]	101[1]	105[1]	104[1]			
1995	100[1]	104[1]	115[1]	114[1]			
1996	102[1]	108[1]	120[1]	116[1]			
1997	103[1]	111[1]	126[1]	122[1]			
1998	104[1]	113[1]	131[1]	126[1]			

Source: Same as General Statistics. The values shown reflect change from the base year, 1992, which is always 100. Data points earlier or later than 1992 are less than 1992 if less than 100 and greater than 1992 if greater than 100. Note: 1. Index based on a projected value.

SIC 8043 - OFFICES & CLINICS OF PODIATRISTS: SELECTED RATIOS

For 1992	Average of All Services	Analyzed Industry	Index
Employees per establishment	13	3	25
Revenues per establishment	810,117	241,580	30
Payroll per establishment	314,133	78,537	25
Payroll per employee	23,335	23,618	101
Revenue per employee	60,179	72,650	121
Sole proprietors as % of establishments	30.1	55.1	183
Partnerships as % of establishments	5.7	4.4	77

Source: Same as General Statistics. The 'Average of all Services' column represents the average of all service industries of which this SIC is a part. The Index shows the relationship between the Average and the Analyzed Industry. For example, 100 means that they are equal; 500 that the Analyzed Industry is five times the average; 50 means that the Analyzed Industry is half the national average.

SIC 8049 - OFFICES OF HEALTH PRACTITIONERS, NEC: GENERAL STATISTICS

Year	Estab-lish-ments	Employ-ment (000)	Payroll ($ mil.)	Revenues ($ mil.)		Ownership	
				SAS	Census	Sole Prop.	Partner-ships
1987	12,044	50.9	995.8		2,337.2	4,365	680
1988	11,740	55.6	1,240.5				
1989	12,644	67.0	1,481.6				
1990	14,968	82.0	1,835.7				
1991	16,957	91.6	2,186.0				
1992	22,260	103.5	2,572.6		6,148.1	7,906	1,151
1993	23,992	123.9	3,086.4				
1994	24,817[1]	126.3[1]	3,259.9[1]				
1995	25,445[1]	142.1[1]	3,867.9[1]				
1996	28,554[1]	153.0[1]	4,071.8[1]				
1997	30,601[1]	164.9[1]	4,430.1[1]				
1998	32,648[1]	176.8[1]	4,788.3[1]				

Source: Data for 1987 and 1992 are from Census of Service Industries, Bureau of the Census, U.S. Department of Commerce. Data labeled SAS are from the *Service Annual Survey* for 1996, which also presented revisions for ealier years. Data for 1988-1991 and 1993-1995, when shown, are derived from *County Business Patterns* for those years from the Bureau of the Census. Extracted from *Service Industries USA*, 4th edition, Gale, 1998. Note: 1. Projections made by the editor.

SIC 8049 - OFFICES OF HEALTH PRACTITIONERS, NEC: INDICES OF CHANGE

Year	Estab-lish-ments	Employ-ment (000)	Payroll ($ mil.)	Revenues ($ mil.)		Ownership	
				SAS	Census	Sole Prop.	Partner-ships
1987	54	49	39		38	55	59
1988	53	54	48				
1989	57	65	58				
1990	67	79	71				
1991	76	89	85				
1992	100	100	100		100	100	100
1993	108	120	120				
1994	111[1]	122[1]	127[1]				
1995	114[1]	137[1]	150[1]				
1996	128[1]	148[1]	158[1]				
1997	137[1]	159[1]	172[1]				
1998	147[1]	171[1]	186[1]				

Source: Same as General Statistics. The values shown reflect change from the base year, 1992, which is always 100. Data points earlier or later than 1992 are less than 1992 if less than 100 and greater than 1992 if greater than 100. Note: 1. Index based on a projected value.

SIC 8049 - OFFICES OF HEALTH PRACTITIONERS, NEC: SELECTED RATIOS

For 1992	Average of All Services	Analyzed Industry	Index
Employees per establishment	13	5	35
Revenues per establishment	810,117	276,193	34
Payroll per establishment	314,133	115,569	37
Payroll per employee	23,335	24,845	106
Revenue per employee	60,179	59,375	99
Sole proprietors as % of establishments	30.1	35.5	118
Partnerships as % of establishments	5.7	5.2	90

Source: Same as General Statistics. The 'Average of all Services' column represents the average of all service industries of which this SIC is a part. The Index shows the relationship between the Average and the Analyzed Industry. For example, 100 means that they are equal; 500 that the Analyzed Industry is five times the average; 50 means that the Analyzed Industry is half the national average.

SIC 8051 - SKILLED NURSING CARE FACILITIES: GENERAL STATISTICS

| Year | Estab-
lish-
ments | Employ-
ment
(000) | Payroll
($ mil.) | Revenues ($ mil.) | | Ownership | |
				SAS	Census	Sole Prop.	Partner- ships
1987	11,813	1,091.8	11,432.8		16,938.1	514	876
1988							
1989							
1990							
1991							
1992	12,965	1,305.1	19,342.8		28,797.8	465	1,060
1993							
1994							
1995							
1996							
1997							
1998							

Source: Data for 1987 and 1992 are from Census of Service Industries, Bureau of the Census, U.S. Department of Commerce. Data labeled SAS are from the *Service Annual Survey* for 1996, which also presented revisions for ealier years. Data for 1988-1991 and 1993-1995, when shown, are derived from *County Business Patterns* for those years from the Bureau of the Census. Extracted from *Service Industries USA*, 4th edition, Gale, 1998. Note: 1. Projections made by the editor.

SIC 8051 - SKILLED NURSING CARE FACILITIES: INDICES OF CHANGE

| Year | Estab-
lish-
ments | Employ-
ment
(000) | Payroll
($ mil.) | Revenues ($ mil.) | | Ownership | |
				SAS	Census	Sole Prop.	Partner- ships
1987	91	84	59		59	111	83
1988							
1989							
1990							
1991							
1992	100	100	100		100	100	100
1993							
1994							
1995							
1996							
1997							
1998							

Source: Same as General Statistics. The values shown reflect change from the base year, 1992, which is always 100. Data points earlier or later than 1992 are less than 1992 if less than 100 and greater than 1992 if greater than 100. Note: 1. Index based on a projected value.

SIC 8051 - SKILLED NURSING CARE FACILITIES: SELECTED RATIOS

For 1992	Average of All Services	Analyzed Industry	Index
Employees per establishment	13	101	748
Revenues per establishment	810,117	3,122,322	385
Payroll per establishment	314,133	1,491,924	475
Payroll per employee	23,335	14,821	64
Revenue per employee	60,179	31,018	52
Sole proprietors as % of establishments	30.1	3.6	12
Partnerships as % of establishments	5.7	8.2	143

Source: Same as General Statistics. The 'Average of all Services' column represents the average of all service industries of which this SIC is a part. The Index shows the relationship between the Average and the Analyzed Industry. For example, 100 means that they are equal; 500 that the Analyzed Industry is five times the average; 50 means that the Analyzed Industry is half the national average.

SIC 8052 - INTERMEDIATE CARE FACILITIES: GENERAL STATISTICS

Year	Estab-lish-ments	Employ-ment (000)	Payroll ($ mil.)	Revenues ($ mil.)		Ownership	
				SAS	Census	Sole Prop.	Partner-ships
1987	3,760	182.2	1,699.8		2,190.5	288	192
1988							
1989							
1990							
1991							
1992	6,166	278.2	3,523.1		4,207.1	203	210
1993							
1994							
1995							
1996							
1997							
1998							

Source: Data for 1987 and 1992 are from Census of Service Industries, Bureau of the Census, U.S. Department of Commerce. Data labeled SAS are from the *Service Annual Survey* for 1996, which also presented revisions for ealier years. Data for 1988-1991 and 1993-1995, when shown, are derived from *County Business Patterns* for those years from the Bureau of the Census. Extracted from *Service Industries USA*, 4th edition, Gale, 1998. Note: 1. Projections made by the editor.

SIC 8052 - INTERMEDIATE CARE FACILITIES: INDICES OF CHANGE

Year	Estab-lish-ments	Employ-ment (000)	Payroll ($ mil.)	Revenues ($ mil.)		Ownership	
				SAS	Census	Sole Prop.	Partner-ships
1987	61	65	48		52	142	91
1988							
1989							
1990							
1991							
1992	100	100	100		100	100	100
1993							
1994							
1995							
1996							
1997							
1998							

Source: Same as General Statistics. The values shown reflect change from the base year, 1992, which is always 100. Data points earlier or later than 1992 are less than 1992 if less than 100 and greater than 1992 if greater than 100. Note: 1. Index based on a projected value.

SIC 8052 - INTERMEDIATE CARE FACILITIES: SELECTED RATIOS

For 1992	Average of All Services	Analyzed Industry	Index
Employees per establishment	13	45	335
Revenues per establishment	810,117	1,160,667	143
Payroll per establishment	314,133	571,380	182
Payroll per employee	23,335	12,663	54
Revenue per employee	60,179	25,722	43
Sole proprietors as % of establishments	30.1	3.3	11
Partnerships as % of establishments	5.7	3.4	60

Source: Same as General Statistics. The 'Average of all Services' column represents the average of all service industries of which this SIC is a part. The Index shows the relationship between the Average and the Analyzed Industry. For example, 100 means that they are equal; 500 that the Analyzed Industry is five times the average; 50 means that the Analyzed Industry is half the national average.

SIC 8059 - NURSING & PERSONAL CARE, NEC: GENERAL STATISTICS

Year	Estab-lish-ments	Employ-ment (000)	Payroll ($ mil.)	Revenues ($ mil.)		Ownership	
				SAS	Census	Sole Prop.	Partner-ships
1987	1,952	59.1	596.6		934.1	334	160
1988							
1989							
1990							
1991							
1992	1,748	49.5	678.6		984.7		
1993							
1994							
1995							
1996							
1997							
1998							

Source: Data for 1987 and 1992 are from Census of Service Industries, Bureau of the Census, U.S. Department of Commerce. Data labeled SAS are from the *Service Annual Survey* for 1996, which also presented revisions for ealier years. Data for 1988-1991 and 1993-1995, when shown, are derived from *County Business Patterns* for those years from the Bureau of the Census. Extracted from *Service Industries USA*, 4th edition, Gale, 1998. Note: 1. Projections made by the editor.

SIC 8059 - NURSING & PERSONAL CARE, NEC: INDICES OF CHANGE

Year	Estab-lish-ments	Employ-ment (000)	Payroll ($ mil.)	Revenues ($ mil.)	
				SAS	Census
1987	112	119	88		95
1988					
1989					
1990					
1991					
1992	100	100	100		100
1993					
1994					
1995					
1996					
1997					
1998					

Source: Same as General Statistics. The values shown reflect change from the base year, 1992, which is always 100. Data points earlier or later than 1992 are less than 1992 if less than 100 and greater than 1992 if greater than 100. Note: 1. Index based on a projected value.

SIC 8059 - NURSING & PERSONAL CARE, NEC: SELECTED RATIOS

For 1992	Average of All Services	Analyzed Industry	Index
Employees per establishment	13	28	210
Revenues per establishment	810,117	899,610	111
Payroll per establishment	314,133	388,205	124
Payroll per employee	23,335	13,702	59
Revenue per employee	60,179	31,751	53
Sole proprietors as % of establishments	30.1	na	na
Partnerships as % of establishments	5.7	na	na

Source: Same as General Statistics. The 'Average of all Services' column represents the average of all service industries of which this SIC is a part. The Index shows the relationship between the Average and the Analyzed Industry. For example, 100 means that they are equal; 500 that the Analyzed Industry is five times the average; 50 means that the Analyzed Industry is half the national average.

SIC 8062 - GENERAL MEDICAL & SURGICAL HOSPITALS: GENERAL STATISTICS

Year	Estab-lish-ments	Employ-ment (000)	Payroll ($ mil.)	Revenues ($ mil.)		Ownership	
				SAS	Census	Sole Prop.	Partner-ships
1987	6,006	3,816.7	77,687.1		15,891.4	2	23
1988							
1989							
1990				20,442.0			
1991				22,220.0			
1992	5,624	4,411.0	120,149.7	24,162.0	24,162.3		
1993				26,683.0			
1994				27,993.0[1]			
1995				30,704.0[1]			
1996				36,496.0[1]			
1997				36,808.7[1]			
1998				39,271.6[1]			

Source: Data for 1987 and 1992 are from Census of Service Industries, Bureau of the Census, U.S. Department of Commerce. Data labeled SAS are from the *Service Annual Survey* for 1996, which also presented revisions for ealier years. Data for 1988-1991 and 1993-1995, when shown, are derived from *County Business Patterns* for those years from the Bureau of the Census. Extracted from *Service Industries USA*, 4th edition, Gale, 1998. Note: 1. Projections made by the editor.

SIC 8062 - GENERAL MEDICAL & SURGICAL HOSPITALS: INDICES OF CHANGE

Year	Estab-lish-ments	Employ-ment (000)	Payroll ($ mil.)	Revenues ($ mil.)	
				SAS	Census
1987	107	87	65		66
1988					
1989					
1990				85	
1991				92	
1992	100	100	100	100	100
1993				110	
1994				116[1]	
1995				127[1]	
1996				151[1]	
1997				152[1]	
1998				163[1]	

Source: Same as General Statistics. The values shown reflect change from the base year, 1992, which is always 100. Data points earlier or later than 1992 are less than 1992 if less than 100 and greater than 1992 if greater than 100. Note: 1. Index based on a projected value.

SIC 8062 - GENERAL MEDICAL & SURGICAL HOSPITALS: SELECTED RATIOS

For 1992	Average of All Services	Analyzed Industry	Index
Employees per establishment	13	784	5,826
Revenues per establishment	810,117	49,529,428	6,114
Payroll per establishment	314,133	21,363,746	6,801
Payroll per employee	23,335	27,238	117
Revenue per employee	60,179	63,149	105
Sole proprietors as % of establishments	30.1	na	na
Partnerships as % of establishments	5.7	na	na

Source: Same as General Statistics. The 'Average of all Services' column represents the average of all service industries of which this SIC is a part. The Index shows the relationship between the Average and the Analyzed Industry. For example, 100 means that they are equal; 500 that the Analyzed Industry is five times the average; 50 means that the Analyzed Industry is half the national average.

SIC 8063 - PSYCHIATRIC HOSPITALS: GENERAL STATISTICS

Year	Estab-lish-ments	Employ-ment (000)	Payroll ($ mil.)	Revenues ($ mil.)		Ownership	
				SAS	Census	Sole Prop.	Partner-ships
1987	787	301.9	6,654.9		2,929.7	2	6
1988							
1989							
1990				4,129.0			
1991				4,402.0			
1992	919	317.4	8,906.2	4,396.0	4,396.2		
1993				3,730.0			
1994				3,764.0[1]			
1995				3,847.0[1]			
1996				3,508.0[1]			
1997				3,453.0[1]			
1998				3,324.3[1]			

Source: Data for 1987 and 1992 are from Census of Service Industries, Bureau of the Census, U.S. Department of Commerce. Data labeled SAS are from the *Service Annual Survey* for 1996, which also presented revisions for earlier years. Data for 1988-1991 and 1993-1995, when shown, are derived from *County Business Patterns* for those years from the Bureau of the Census. Extracted from *Service Industries USA*, 4th edition, Gale, 1998. Note: 1. Projections made by the editor.

SIC 8063 - PSYCHIATRIC HOSPITALS: INDICES OF CHANGE

Year	Estab-lish-ments	Employ-ment (000)	Payroll ($ mil.)	Revenues ($ mil.)	
				SAS	Census
1987	86	95	75		67
1988					
1989					
1990				94	
1991				100	
1992	100	100	100	100	100
1993				85	
1994				86[1]	
1995				88[1]	
1996				80[1]	
1997				79[1]	
1998				76[1]	

Source: Same as General Statistics. The values shown reflect change from the base year, 1992, which is always 100. Data points earlier or later than 1992 are less than 1992 if less than 100 and greater than 1992 if greater than 100. Note: 1. Index based on a projected value.

SIC 8063 - PSYCHIATRIC HOSPITALS: SELECTED RATIOS

For 1992	Average of All Services	Analyzed Industry	Index
Employees per establishment	13	345	2,566
Revenues per establishment	810,117	16,679,455	2,059
Payroll per establishment	314,133	9,691,208	3,085
Payroll per employee	23,335	28,059	120
Revenue per employee	60,179	48,293	80
Sole proprietors as % of establishments	30.1	na	na
Partnerships as % of establishments	5.7	na	na

Source: Same as General Statistics. The 'Average of all Services' column represents the average of all service industries of which this SIC is a part. The Index shows the relationship between the Average and the Analyzed Industry. For example, 100 means that they are equal; 500 that the Analyzed Industry is five times the average; 50 means that the Analyzed Industry is half the national average.

SIC 8069 - SPECIALTY HOSPITALS, EX PSYCHIATRIC: GENERAL STATISTICS

| Year | Estab-lish-ments | Employ-ment (000) | Payroll ($ mil.) | Revenues ($ mil.) | | Ownership | |
				SAS	Census	Sole Prop.	Partner-ships
1987	505	212.0	4,581.6		898.7		6
1988							
1989							
1990				1,916.0			
1991				2,185.0			
1992	577	266.0	7,702.5	2,525.0	2,524.5		
1993				2,918.0			
1994				3,386.0[1]			
1995				3,866.0[1]			
1996				4,665.0[1]			
1997				3,249.9[1]			
1998				3,244.5[1]			

Source: Data for 1987 and 1992 are from Census of Service Industries, Bureau of the Census, U.S. Department of Commerce. Data labeled SAS are from the *Service Annual Survey* for 1996, which also presented revisions for ealier years. Data for 1988-1991 and 1993-1995, when shown, are derived from *County Business Patterns* for those years from the Bureau of the Census. Extracted from *Service Industries USA*, 4th edition, Gale, 1998. Note: 1. Projections made by the editor.

SIC 8069 - SPECIALTY HOSPITALS, EX PSYCHIATRIC: INDICES OF CHANGE

| Year | Estab-lish-ments | Employ-ment (000) | Payroll ($ mil.) | Revenues ($ mil.) | |
				SAS	Census
1987	88	80	59		36
1988					
1989					
1990				76	
1991				87	
1992	100	100	100	100	100
1993				116	
1994				134[1]	
1995				153[1]	
1996				185[1]	
1997				129[1]	
1998				128[1]	

Source: Same as General Statistics. The values shown reflect change from the base year, 1992, which is always 100. Data points earlier or later than 1992 are less than 1992 if less than 100 and greater than 1992 if greater than 100. Note: 1. Index based on a projected value.

SIC 8069 - SPECIALTY HOSPITALS, EX PSYCHIATRIC: SELECTED RATIOS

For 1992	Average of All Services	Analyzed Industry	Index
Employees per establishment	13	461	3,425
Revenues per establishment	810,117	29,352,319	3,623
Payroll per establishment	314,133	13,349,248	4,250
Payroll per employee	23,335	28,953	124
Revenue per employee	60,179	63,662	106
Sole proprietors as % of establishments	30.1	na	na
Partnerships as % of establishments	5.7	na	na

Source: Same as General Statistics. The 'Average of all Services' column represents the average of all service industries of which this SIC is a part. The Index shows the relationship between the Average and the Analyzed Industry. For example, 100 means that they are equal; 500 that the Analyzed Industry is five times the average; 50 means that the Analyzed Industry is half the national average.

SIC 8071 - MEDICAL LABORATORIES: GENERAL STATISTICS

Year	Estab-lish-ments	Employ-ment (000)	Payroll ($ mil.)	Revenues ($ mil.)		Ownership	
				SAS	Census	Sole Prop.	Partner-ships
1987	6,871	91.1	1,883.7	5,680.0	5,517.9	513	1,017
1988	6,837	99.2	2,309.9	7,171.0			
1989	7,110	110.1	2,660.5	8,470.0			
1990	7,134	118.4	3,037.2	9,996.0			
1991	7,269	130.1	3,467.1	11,458.0			
1992	8,434	138.8	3,979.9	12,882.0	12,511.3	577	956
1993	8,442	147.2	4,220.5	12,735.0	12,504.3		
1994	8,772[1]	150.9[1]	4,401.3[1]	13,007.0[1]	13,473.5[1]		
1995	8,568[1]	155.7[1]	4,577.4[1]	12,909.0[1]	14,442.7[1]		
1996	9,076[1]	165.3[1]	4,912.1[1]	13,266.0[1]	15,411.9[1]		
1997	9,345[1]	172.8[1]	5,209.8[1]	16,570.2[1]	16,381.0[1]		
1998	9,614[1]	180.4[1]	5,507.6[1]	17,699.9[1]	17,350.2[1]		

Source: Data for 1987 and 1992 are from Census of Service Industries, Bureau of the Census, U.S. Department of Commerce. Data labeled SAS are from the *Service Annual Survey* for 1996, which also presented revisions for ealier years. Data for 1988-1991 and 1993-1995, when shown, are derived from *County Business Patterns* for those years from the Bureau of the Census. Extracted from *Service Industries USA*, 4th edition, Gale, 1998. Note: 1. Projections made by the editor.

SIC 8071 - MEDICAL LABORATORIES: INDICES OF CHANGE

Year	Estab-lish-ments	Employ-ment (000)	Payroll ($ mil.)	Revenues ($ mil.)		Ownership	
				SAS	Census	Sole Prop.	Partner-ships
1987	81	66	47	44	44	89	106
1988	81	72	58	56			
1989	84	79	67	66			
1990	85	85	76	78			
1991	86	94	87	89			
1992	100	100	100	100	100	100	100
1993	100	106	106	99	100		
1994	104[1]	109[1]	111[1]	101[1]	108[1]		
1995	102[1]	112[1]	115[1]	100[1]	115[1]		
1996	108[1]	119[1]	123[1]	103[1]	123[1]		
1997	111[1]	125[1]	131[1]	129[1]	131[1]		
1998	114[1]	130[1]	138[1]	137[1]	139[1]		

Source: Same as General Statistics. The values shown reflect change from the base year, 1992, which is always 100. Data points earlier or later than 1992 are less than 1992 if less than 100 and greater than 1992 if greater than 100. Note: 1. Index based on a projected value.

SIC 8071 - MEDICAL LABORATORIES: SELECTED RATIOS

For 1992	Average of All Services	Analyzed Industry	Index
Employees per establishment	13	16	122
Revenues per establishment	810,117	1,483,440	183
Payroll per establishment	314,133	471,893	150
Payroll per employee	23,335	28,682	123
Revenue per employee	60,179	90,165	150
Sole proprietors as % of establishments	30.1	6.8	23
Partnerships as % of establishments	5.7	11.3	198

Source: Same as General Statistics. The 'Average of all Services' column represents the average of all service industries of which this SIC is a part. The Index shows the relationship between the Average and the Analyzed Industry. For example, 100 means that they are equal; 500 that the Analyzed Industry is five times the average; 50 means that the Analyzed Industry is half the national average.

SIC 8072 - DENTAL LABORATORIES: GENERAL STATISTICS

Year	Estab-lish-ments	Employ-ment (000)	Payroll ($ mil.)	Revenues ($ mil.)		Ownership	
				SAS	Census	Sole Prop.	Partner-ships
1987	7,970	40.7	683.4	1,810.0	1,596.2	3,353	585
1988	7,469	40.1	725.3	1,750.0			
1989	7,484	39.0	731.0	1,866.0			
1990	7,234	39.3	763.8	2,037.0			
1991	7,334	39.0	788.9	2,109.0			
1992	7,527	39.1	824.3	2,290.0	1,948.5	2,981	366
1993	7,505	39.7	850.1	2,331.0	2,012.7		
1994	7,417[1]	39.3[1]	877.6[1]	2,420.0[1]	2,081.2[1]		
1995	7,340[1]	40.2[1]	920.0[1]	2,615.0[1]	2,149.8[1]		
1996	7,280[1]	39.5[1]	934.1[1]	2,776.0[1]	2,218.3[1]		
1997	7,237[1]	39.5[1]	961.6[1]	2,819.8[1]	2,286.9[1]		
1998	7,194[1]	39.4[1]	989.1[1]	2,932.4[1]	2,355.4[1]		

Source: Data for 1987 and 1992 are from Census of Service Industries, Bureau of the Census, U.S. Department of Commerce. Data labeled SAS are from the *Service Annual Survey* for 1996, which also presented revisions for earlier years. Data for 1988-1991 and 1993-1995, when shown, are derived from *County Business Patterns* for those years from the Bureau of the Census. Extracted from *Service Industries USA*, 4th edition, Gale, 1998. Note: 1. Projections made by the editor.

SIC 8072 - DENTAL LABORATORIES: INDICES OF CHANGE

Year	Estab-lish-ments	Employ-ment (000)	Payroll ($ mil.)	Revenues ($ mil.)		Ownership	
				SAS	Census	Sole Prop.	Partner-ships
1987	106	104	83	79	82	112	160
1988	99	102	88	76			
1989	99	100	89	81			
1990	96	101	93	89			
1991	97	100	96	92			
1992	100	100	100	100	100	100	100
1993	100	102	103	102	103		
1994	99[1]	101[1]	106[1]	106[1]	107[1]		
1995	98[1]	103[1]	112[1]	114[1]	110[1]		
1996	97[1]	101[1]	113[1]	121[1]	114[1]		
1997	96[1]	101[1]	117[1]	123[1]	117[1]		
1998	96[1]	101[1]	120[1]	128[1]	121[1]		

Source: Same as General Statistics. The values shown reflect change from the base year, 1992, which is always 100. Data points earlier or later than 1992 are less than 1992 if less than 100 and greater than 1992 if greater than 100. Note: 1. Index based on a projected value.

SIC 8072 - DENTAL LABORATORIES: SELECTED RATIOS

For 1992	Average of All Services	Analyzed Industry	Index
Employees per establishment	13	5	39
Revenues per establishment	810,117	258,863	32
Payroll per establishment	314,133	109,514	35
Payroll per employee	23,335	21,079	90
Revenue per employee	60,179	49,825	83
Sole proprietors as % of establishments	30.1	39.6	131
Partnerships as % of establishments	5.7	4.9	85

Source: Same as General Statistics. The 'Average of all Services' column represents the average of all service industries of which this SIC is a part. The Index shows the relationship between the Average and the Analyzed Industry. For example, 100 means that they are equal; 500 that the Analyzed Industry is five times the average; 50 means that the Analyzed Industry is half the national average.

SIC 8082 - HOME HEALTH CARE SERVICES: GENERAL STATISTICS

Year	Estab- lish- ments	Employ- ment (000)	Payroll ($ mil.)	Revenues ($ mil.)		Ownership	
				SAS	Census	Sole Prop.	Partner- ships
1987	6,849	303.5	2,819.9	3,549.0	3,023.9	419	339
1988				4,589.0			
1989				5,595.0			
1990				7,556.0			
1991				9,129.0			
1992	8,045	341.9	4,853.1	11,208.0	10,413.8	606	228
1993				13,178.0			
1994				15,394.0[1]			
1995				17,987.0[1]			
1996				19,542.0[1]			
1997				20,961.5[1]			
1998				22,814.0[1]			

Source: Data for 1987 and 1992 are from Census of Service Industries, Bureau of the Census, U.S. Department of Commerce. Data labeled SAS are from the *Service Annual Survey* for 1996, which also presented revisions for ealier years. Data for 1988-1991 and 1993-1995, when shown, are derived from *County Business Patterns* for those years from the Bureau of the Census. Extracted from *Service Industries USA*, 4th edition, Gale, 1998. Note: 1. Projections made by the editor.

SIC 8082 - HOME HEALTH CARE SERVICES: INDICES OF CHANGE

Year	Estab- lish- ments	Employ- ment (000)	Payroll ($ mil.)	Revenues ($ mil.)		Ownership	
				SAS	Census	Sole Prop.	Partner- ships
1987	85	89	58	32	29	69	149
1988				41			
1989				50			
1990				67			
1991				81			
1992	100	100	100	100	100	100	100
1993				118			
1994				137[1]			
1995				160[1]			
1996				174[1]			
1997				187[1]			
1998				204[1]			

Source: Same as General Statistics. The values shown reflect change from the base year, 1992, which is always 100. Data points earlier or later than 1992 are less than 1992 if less than 100 and greater than 1992 if greater than 100. Note: 1. Index based on a projected value.

SIC 8082 - HOME HEALTH CARE SERVICES: SELECTED RATIOS

For 1992	Average of All Services	Analyzed Industry	Index
Employees per establishment	13	42	316
Revenues per establishment	810,117	1,294,449	160
Payroll per establishment	314,133	603,243	192
Payroll per employee	23,335	14,195	61
Revenue per employee	60,179	30,460	51
Sole proprietors as % of establishments	30.1	7.5	25
Partnerships as % of establishments	5.7	2.8	50

Source: Same as General Statistics. The 'Average of all Services' column represents the average of all service industries of which this SIC is a part. The Index shows the relationship between the Average and the Analyzed Industry. For example, 100 means that they are equal; 500 that the Analyzed Industry is five times the average; 50 means that the Analyzed Industry is half the national average.

SIC 8092 - KIDNEY DIALYSIS CENTERS: GENERAL STATISTICS

Year	Estab-lish-ments	Employ-ment (000)	Payroll ($ mil.)	Revenues ($ mil.)		Ownership	
				SAS	Census	Sole Prop.	Partner-ships
1987	839	16.8	316.5		824.7	18	26
1988							
1989							
1990				1,451.0			
1991				1,717.0			
1992	1,315	26.5	691.5	2,140.0	2,060.3	17	58
1993				2,468.0			
1994				2,898.0[1]			
1995				3,259.0[1]			
1996				3,385.0[1]			
1997				3,851.7[1]			
1998				4,196.1[1]			

Source: Data for 1987 and 1992 are from Census of Service Industries, Bureau of the Census, U.S. Department of Commerce. Data labeled SAS are from the *Service Annual Survey* for 1996, which also presented revisions for ealier years. Data for 1988-1991 and 1993-1995, when shown, are derived from *County Business Patterns* for those years from the Bureau of the Census. Extracted from *Service Industries USA*, 4th edition, Gale, 1998. Note: 1. Projections made by the editor.

SIC 8092 - KIDNEY DIALYSIS CENTERS: INDICES OF CHANGE

Year	Estab-lish-ments	Employ-ment (000)	Payroll ($ mil.)	Revenues ($ mil.)		Ownership	
				SAS	Census	Sole Prop.	Partner-ships
1987	64	63	46		40	106	45
1988							
1989							
1990				68			
1991				80			
1992	100	100	100	100	100	100	100
1993				115			
1994				135[1]			
1995				152[1]			
1996				158[1]			
1997				180[1]			
1998				196[1]			

Source: Same as General Statistics. The values shown reflect change from the base year, 1992, which is always 100. Data points earlier or later than 1992 are less than 1992 if less than 100 and greater than 1992 if greater than 100. Note: 1. Index based on a projected value.

SIC 8092 - KIDNEY DIALYSIS CENTERS: SELECTED RATIOS

For 1992	Average of All Services	Analyzed Industry	Index
Employees per establishment	13	20	150
Revenues per establishment	810,117	1,871,068	231
Payroll per establishment	314,133	525,868	167
Payroll per employee	23,335	26,091	112
Revenue per employee	60,179	92,833	154
Sole proprietors as % of establishments	30.1	1.3	4
Partnerships as % of establishments	5.7	4.4	77

Source: Same as General Statistics. The 'Average of all Services' column represents the average of all service industries of which this SIC is a part. The Index shows the relationship between the Average and the Analyzed Industry. For example, 100 means that they are equal; 500 that the Analyzed Industry is five times the average; 50 means that the Analyzed Industry is half the national average.

SIC 8093 - SPECIALTY OUTPATIENT FACILITIES, NEC: GENERAL STATISTICS

Year	Estab-lish-ments	Employ-ment (000)	Payroll ($ mil.)	Revenues ($ mil.)		Ownership	
				SAS	Census	Sole Prop.	Partner-ships
1987	9,044	127.4	2,307.1		2,949.0	756	544
1988							
1989							
1990				5,326.0			
1991				6,508.0			
1992	11,623	178.9	4,103.6	6,476.0	4,807.4	862	661
1993				6,999.0			
1994				7,965.0[1]			
1995				8,616.0[1]			
1996				9,586.0[1]			
1997				9,994.4[1]			
1998				10,654.6[1]			

Source: Data for 1987 and 1992 are from Census of Service Industries, Bureau of the Census, U.S. Department of Commerce. Data labeled SAS are from the *Service Annual Survey* for 1996, which also presented revisions for ealier years. Data for 1988-1991 and 1993-1995, when shown, are derived from *County Business Patterns* for those years from the Bureau of the Census. Extracted from *Service Industries USA*, 4th edition, Gale, 1998. Note: 1. Projections made by the editor.

SIC 8093 - SPECIALTY OUTPATIENT FACILITIES, NEC: INDICES OF CHANGE

Year	Estab-lish-ments	Employ-ment (000)	Payroll ($ mil.)	Revenues ($ mil.)		Ownership	
				SAS	Census	Sole Prop.	Partner-ships
1987	78	71	56		61	88	82
1988							
1989							
1990				82			
1991				100			
1992	100	100	100	100	100	100	100
1993				108			
1994				123[1]			
1995				133[1]			
1996				148[1]			
1997				154[1]			
1998				165[1]			

Source: Same as General Statistics. The values shown reflect change from the base year, 1992, which is always 100. Data points earlier or later than 1992 are less than 1992 if less than 100 and greater than 1992 if greater than 100. Note: 1. Index based on a projected value.

SIC 8093 - SPECIALTY OUTPATIENT FACILITIES, NEC: SELECTED RATIOS

For 1992	Average of All Services	Analyzed Industry	Index
Employees per establishment	13	15	114
Revenues per establishment	810,117	795,307	98
Payroll per establishment	314,133	353,056	112
Payroll per employee	23,335	22,938	98
Revenue per employee	60,179	51,672	86
Sole proprietors as % of establishments	30.1	7.4	25
Partnerships as % of establishments	5.7	5.7	100

Source: Same as General Statistics. The 'Average of all Services' column represents the average of all service industries of which this SIC is a part. The Index shows the relationship between the Average and the Analyzed Industry. For example, 100 means that they are equal; 500 that the Analyzed Industry is five times the average; 50 means that the Analyzed Industry is half the national average.

SIC 8099 - HEALTH & ALLIED SERVICES, NEC: GENERAL STATISTICS

| Year | Estab-lish-ments | Employ-ment (000) | Payroll ($ mil.) | Revenues ($ mil.) | | Ownership | |
				SAS	Census	Sole Prop.	Partner-ships
1987	4,584	64.4	1,031.3		1,656.0	327	345
1988							
1989							
1990							
1991							
1992	5,011	71.9	1,734.3		2,737.0	420	231
1993							
1994							
1995							
1996							
1997							
1998							

Source: Data for 1987 and 1992 are from Census of Service Industries, Bureau of the Census, U.S. Department of Commerce. Data labeled SAS are from the *Service Annual Survey* for 1996, which also presented revisions for ealier years. Data for 1988-1991 and 1993-1995, when shown, are derived from *County Business Patterns* for those years from the Bureau of the Census. Extracted from *Service Industries USA*, 4th edition, Gale, 1998. Note: 1. Projections made by the editor.

SIC 8099 - HEALTH & ALLIED SERVICES, NEC: INDICES OF CHANGE

| Year | Estab-lish-ments | Employ-ment (000) | Payroll ($ mil.) | Revenues ($ mil.) | | Ownership | |
				SAS	Census	Sole Prop.	Partner-ships
1987	91	90	59		61	78	149
1988							
1989							
1990							
1991							
1992	100	100	100		100	100	100
1993							
1994							
1995							
1996							
1997							
1998							

Source: Same as General Statistics. The values shown reflect change from the base year, 1992, which is always 100. Data points earlier or later than 1992 are less than 1992 if less than 100 and greater than 1992 if greater than 100. Note: 1. Index based on a projected value.

SIC 8099 - HEALTH & ALLIED SERVICES, NEC: SELECTED RATIOS

For 1992	Average of All Services	Analyzed Industry	Index
Employees per establishment	13	14	107
Revenues per establishment	810,117	1,002,318	124
Payroll per establishment	314,133	346,089	110
Payroll per employee	23,335	24,116	103
Revenue per employee	60,179	69,844	116
Sole proprietors as % of establishments	30.1	8.4	28
Partnerships as % of establishments	5.7	4.6	81

Source: Same as General Statistics. The 'Average of all Services' column represents the average of all service industries of which this SIC is a part. The Index shows the relationship between the Average and the Analyzed Industry. For example, 100 means that they are equal; 500 that the Analyzed Industry is five times the average; 50 means that the Analyzed Industry is half the national average.

SIC 8361 - RESIDENTIAL CARE: GENERAL STATISTICS

Year	Estab-lish-ments	Employ-ment (000)	Payroll ($ mil.)	Revenues ($ mil.)		Ownership	
				SAS	Census	Sole Prop.	Partner-ships
1987	18,990	338.9	3,649.4	2,837.0	2,489.8	3,694	1,004
1988	19,276	358.0	4,233.7	3,469.0			
1989	19,709	387.6	4,774.1	4,057.0			
1990	20,967	416.8	5,402.4	4,626.0			
1991	22,267	449.7	6,109.7	4,934.0			
1992	27,143	457.3	6,399.7	4,853.0	4,358.1		
1993	27,912	491.1	6,938.1	5,421.0			
1994	28,937[1]	518.2[1]	7,563.0[1]	5,905.0[1]			
1995	29,937[1]	549.9[1]	8,239.6[1]	6,437.0[1]			
1996	31,850[1]	571.8[1]	8,729.5[1]	7,244.0[1]			
1997	33,440[1]	598.0[1]	9,290.7[1]	7,377.7[1]			
1998	35,029[1]	624.2[1]	9,851.9[1]	7,814.0[1]			

Source: Data for 1987 and 1992 are from Census of Service Industries, Bureau of the Census, U.S. Department of Commerce. Data labeled SAS are from the *Service Annual Survey* for 1996, which also presented revisions for ealier years. Data for 1988-1991 and 1993-1995, when shown, are derived from *County Business Patterns* for those years from the Bureau of the Census. Extracted from *Service Industries USA*, 4th edition, Gale, 1998. Note: 1. Projections made by the editor.

SIC 8361 - RESIDENTIAL CARE: INDICES OF CHANGE

Year	Estab-lish-ments	Employ-ment (000)	Payroll ($ mil.)	Revenues ($ mil.)	
				SAS	Census
1987	70	74	57	58	57
1988	71	78	66	71	
1989	73	85	75	84	
1990	77	91	84	95	
1991	82	98	95	102	
1992	100	100	100	100	100
1993	103	107	108	112	
1994	107[1]	113[1]	118[1]	122[1]	
1995	110[1]	120[1]	129[1]	133[1]	
1996	117[1]	125[1]	136[1]	149[1]	
1997	123[1]	131[1]	145[1]	152[1]	
1998	129[1]	137[1]	154[1]	161[1]	

Source: Same as General Statistics. The values shown reflect change from the base year, 1992, which is always 100. Data points earlier or later than 1992 are less than 1992 if less than 100 and greater than 1992 if greater than 100. Note: 1. Index based on a projected value.

SIC 8361 - RESIDENTIAL CARE: SELECTED RATIOS

For 1992	Average of All Services	Analyzed Industry	Index
Employees per establishment	13	17	125
Revenues per establishment	810,117	551,634	68
Payroll per establishment	314,133	235,777	75
Payroll per employee	23,335	13,995	60
Revenue per employee	60,179	32,743	54
Sole proprietors as % of establishments	30.1	na	na
Partnerships as % of establishments	5.7	na	na

Source: Same as General Statistics. The 'Average of all Services' column represents the average of all service industries of which this SIC is a part. The Index shows the relationship between the Average and the Analyzed Industry. For example, 100 means that they are equal; 500 that the Analyzed Industry is five times the average; 50 means that the Analyzed Industry is half the national average.

CHAPTER 3

FINANCIAL NORMS AND RATIOS

Industry-specific financial norms and ratios are shown in this chapter for four industries in the Health and Medical Services sector. For each industry in the sector, balance sheets are presented for the years 1995 through 1997, with the most recent year shown first. As part of each balance sheet, additional financial averages for net sales, gross profits, net profits after tax, and working capital are shown. The number of establishments used to calculate the averages are shown for each year.

The second table in each display shows D&B Key Business Ratios for the SIC-denominated industry. These data, again, are for the years 1995 through 1997. Ratios measuring solvency (e.g., Quick ratio), efficiency (e.g., Collection period, in days), and profitability (e.g. % return on sales) are shown. A total of 14 ratios are featured. Ratios are shown for the upper quartile, median, and lowest quartile of the D&B sample.

This product includes proprietary data of Dun & Bradstreet Inc.

D&B INDUSTRY NORMS: SIC 8011 - OFFICES & CLINICS OF MEDICAL DOCTORS

	1997 (875) Estab.		1996 (1629) Estab.		1995 (1486) Estab.	
	$	%	$	%	$	%
Cash	310,405	21.7	188,407	22.0	114,146	24.3
Accounts Receivable	290,379	20.3	167,854	19.6	80,795	17.2
Notes Receivable	10,013	.7	5,138	.6	3,288	.7
Inventory	12,874	.9	7,708	.9	3,758	.8
Other Current Assets	140,183	9.8	83,927	9.8	42,746	9.1
Total Current Assets	763,854	53.4	453,034	52.9	244,733	52.1
Fixed Assets	487,779	34.1	303,164	35.4	163,939	34.9
Other Non-current Assets	178,805	12.5	100,198	11.7	61,066	13.0
Total Assets	1,430,438	100.0	856,396	100.0	469,738	100.0
Accounts Payable	91,548	6.4	58,235	6.8	27,245	5.8
Bank Loans	1,430	.1	856	.1	-	-
Notes Payable	50,065	3.5	38,538	4.5	21,138	4.5
Other Current Liabilities	367,622	25.7	219,237	25.6	119,783	25.5
Total Current Liabilities	510,665	35.7	316,866	37.0	168,166	35.8
Other Long Term	243,174	17.0	137,880	16.1	73,749	15.7
Deferred Credits	21,457	1.5	8,564	1.0	5,637	1.2
Net Worth	655,140	45.8	393,086	45.9	222,186	47.3
Total Liabilities & Net Worth	1,430,436	100.0	856,396	100.0	469,738	100.0
Net Sales	4,838,458	100.0	4,406,000	100.0	3,550,245	100.0
Gross Profits	2,559,544	52.9	2,405,676	54.6	2,009,439	56.6
Net Profit After Tax	232,246	4.8	176,240	4.0	195,263	5.5
Working Capital	253,187	-	136,166	-	76,567	-

Source: Dun & Bradstreet. Data in this table are copyright (c) 1999 of Dun & Bradstreet. Reprinted by special arrangement with D&B. *Notes:* Values in parentheses above columns indicate the number of establishments in the sample. Data shown are for all companies.

D&B KEY BUSINESS RATIOS: SIC 8011

	1997			1996			1995		
	UQ	MED	LQ	UQ	MED	LQ	UQ	MED	LQ
Solvency									
Quick ratio	2.7	1.2	.6	2.4	1.1	.5	2.6	1.1	.6
Current ratio	3.5	1.6	1.0	3.2	1.5	.9	3.3	1.5	.8
Current liabilities/Net worth (%)	17.7	58.2	154.7	19.1	60.2	146.6	18.0	52.1	130.6
Current liabilities/Investment (%)	182.8	403.1	649.3	209.7	418.5	692.4	182.8	357.6	572.5
Total liabilities/Net worth (%)	34.5	95.8	236.7	32.2	88.4	205.8	27.5	77.5	190.8
Fixed assets/Net worth (%)	30.8	68.9	140.6	28.4	66.3	139.6	27.1	64.5	127.6
Efficiency									
Collection period (days)	21.9	48.6	76.3	21.5	47.8	71.5	21.1	45.6	71.6
Sales to Inventory	214.5	110.4	50.0	183.5	103.3	53.8	210.8	114.2	49.3
Assets/Sales (%)	16.5	34.0	65.7	18.1	35.5	62.9	20.0	36.6	63.9
Sales/Net Working Capital	25.1	8.8	4.6	20.8	9.3	4.6	19.4	8.4	4.1
Accounts payable/Sales (%)	1.2	2.5	5.5	1.3	2.9	5.5	1.1	2.9	6.0
Profitability									
Return - Sales (%)	11.2	2.2	-.5	7.9	2.2	-.2	11.2	2.8	.1
Return - Assets (%)	15.7	3.3	-2.7	15.8	5.4	-1.0	16.7	5.6	-.4
Return - Net Worth (%)	33.6	7.1	-8.0	37.5	13.1	-.7	41.8	12.7	.3

Source: Dun & Bradstreet. Data in this table are copyright (c) 1999 of Dun & Bradstreet. Reprinted by special arrangement with D&B. *Note:* UQ stands for "Upper Quartile" and represents the top 25 percent of sample; MED stands for "Median"; and LQ stands for "Lower Quartile" and represents the lowest 25 percent.

D&B INDUSTRY NORMS: SIC 8021 - OFFICES AND CLINICS OF DENTISTS

	1997 (115) Estab.		1996 (269) Estab.		1995 (329) Estab.	
	$	%	$	%	$	%
Cash	45,859	21.2	39,287	28.4	27,886	23.4
Accounts Receivable	37,855	17.5	18,675	13.5	15,254	12.8
Notes Receivable	2,596	1.2	553	.4	953	.8
Inventory	1,082	.5	968	.7	477	.4
Other Current Assets	19,685	9.1	8,853	6.4	6,674	5.6
Total Current Assets	107,077	49.5	68,336	49.4	51,244	43.0
Fixed Assets	71,168	32.9	49,108	35.5	49,695	41.7
Other Non-current Assets	38,072	17.6	20,888	15.1	18,233	15.3
Total Assets	216,317	100.0	138,332	100.0	119,172	100.0
Accounts Payable	10,600	4.9	4,565	3.3	4,052	3.4
Bank Loans	-	-	138	.1	238	.2
Notes Payable	10,167	4.7	5,118	3.7	8,104	6.8
Other Current Liabilities	38,937	18.0	31,402	22.7	23,715	19.9
Total Current Liabilities	59,704	27.6	41,223	29.8	36,109	30.3
Other Long Term	44,561	20.6	29,327	21.2	27,529	23.1
Deferred Credits	2,812	1.3	1,522	1.1	1,907	1.6
Net Worth	109,240	50.5	66,262	47.9	53,628	45.0
Total Liabilities & Net Worth	216,317	100.0	138,334	100.0	119,173	100.0
Net Sales	697,172	100.0	680,641	100.0	504,936	100.0
Gross Profits	395,994	56.8	317,179	46.6	312,555	61.9
Net Profit After Tax	72,506	10.4	63,980	9.4	71,701	14.2
Working Capital	47,374	-	27,114	-	15,135	-

Source: Dun & Bradstreet. Data in this table are copyright (c) 1999 of Dun & Bradstreet. Reprinted by special arrangement with D&B. *Notes:* Values in parentheses above columns indicate the number of establishments in the sample. Data shown are for all companies.

D&B KEY BUSINESS RATIOS: SIC 8021

	1997			1996			1995		
	UQ	MED	LQ	UQ	MED	LQ	UQ	MED	LQ
Solvency									
Quick ratio	6.6	1.3	.7	3.8	1.4	.6	3.8	1.3	.5
Current ratio	8.6	1.9	.9	5.3	1.7	.8	5.3	1.5	.7
Current liabilities/Net worth (%)	8.7	32.6	92.7	12.0	34.5	86.7	10.0	39.2	132.1
Current liabilities/Investment (%)	202.7	584.6	724.3	117.6	265.9	622.6	139.5	218.2	458.6
Total liabilities/Net worth (%)	22.6	65.1	152.2	22.2	73.2	169.0	22.9	84.8	241.2
Fixed assets/Net worth (%)	25.0	72.2	109.1	19.0	52.9	110.4	30.0	76.5	159.6
Efficiency									
Collection period (days)	32.1	47.5	75.4	17.6	32.1	86.4	26.4	56.6	79.5
Sales to Inventory	122.7	92.8	72.2	82.5	26.8	17.7	171.5	58.9	34.0
Assets/Sales (%)	18.1	32.1	63.5	10.6	19.1	47.8	11.8	26.8	42.7
Sales/Net Working Capital	39.8	11.3	3.7	38.5	19.6	9.1	29.1	13.2	6.1
Accounts payable/Sales (%)	.8	3.1	6.4	1.0	2.9	4.8	1.2	1.9	3.3
Profitability									
Return - Sales (%)	28.1	12.2	2.8	36.0	5.8	.8	33.5	17.5	4.3
Return - Assets (%)	76.6	17.8	1.4	32.1	8.6	1.2	128.2	32.4	7.7
Return - Net Worth (%)	83.9	26.8	2.9	84.9	18.7	6.9	242.6	65.6	20.0

Source: Dun & Bradstreet. Data in this table are copyright (c) 1999 of Dun & Bradstreet. Reprinted by special arrangement with D&B. *Note:* UQ stands for "Upper Quartile" and represents the top 25 percent of sample; MED stands for "Median"; and LQ stands for "Lower Quartile" and represents the lowest 25 percent.

D&B INDUSTRY NORMS: SIC 8041 - OFFICES AND CLINICS OF CHIROPRACTORS

	1997 (44) Estab.		1996 (82) Estab.		1995 (86) Estab.	
	$	%	$	%	$	%
Cash	26,843	22.7	11,414	20.0	13,504	19.5
Accounts Receivable	28,972	24.5	9,987	17.5	13,781	19.9
Notes Receivable	2,365	2.0	114	.2	277	.4
Inventory	591	.5	171	.3	277	.4
Other Current Assets	7,213	6.1	3,367	5.9	4,155	6.0
Total Current Assets	65,984	55.8	25,053	43.9	31,994	46.2
Fixed Assets	46,473	39.3	22,942	40.2	30,055	43.4
Other Non-current Assets	5,794	4.9	9,074	15.9	7,202	10.4
Total Assets	118,251	100.0	57,069	100.0	69,251	100.0
Accounts Payable	2,602	2.2	3,710	6.5	1,385	2.0
Bank Loans	-	-	-	-	485	.7
Notes Payable	2,956	2.5	2,796	4.9	1,801	2.6
Other Current Liabilities	20,103	17.0	11,756	20.6	11,080	16.0
Total Current Liabilities	25,661	21.7	18,262	32.0	14,751	21.3
Other Long Term	19,866	16.8	9,359	16.4	10,665	15.4
Deferred Credits	-	-	-	-	693	1.0
Net Worth	72,725	61.5	29,448	51.6	43,144	62.3
Total Liabilities & Net Worth	118,252	100.0	57,069	100.0	69,253	100.0
Net Sales	455,340	100.0	410,542	100.0	254,699	100.0
Gross Profits	227,670	50.0	256,589	62.5	179,053	70.3
Net Profit After Tax	72,399	15.9	58,708	14.3	33,620	13.2
Working Capital	40,324	-	6,792	-	17,243	-

Source: Dun & Bradstreet. Data in this table are copyright (c) 1999 of Dun & Bradstreet. Reprinted by special arrangement with D&B. *Notes:* Values in parentheses above columns indicate the number of establishments in the sample. Data shown are for all companies.

D&B KEY BUSINESS RATIOS: SIC 8041

	1997			1996			1995		
	UQ	MED	LQ	UQ	MED	LQ	UQ	MED	LQ
Solvency									
Quick ratio	3.5	1.2	.6	3.8	.9	.4	6.5	2.6	.7
Current ratio	4.3	1.6	1.0	4.4	1.3	.5	9.9	3.9	1.0
Current liabilities/Net worth (%)	8.6	13.0	33.7	10.7	41.1	108.7	4.1	16.2	65.9
Current liabilities/Investment (%)	488.8	656.0	698.6	58.5	181.0	326.2	40.2	99.2	315.4
Total liabilities/Net worth (%)	9.6	19.3	54.7	20.7	52.6	170.1	7.4	39.4	123.2
Fixed assets/Net worth (%)	20.3	31.8	76.7	38.0	102.3	147.3	30.0	63.5	116.2
Efficiency									
Collection period (days)	33.4	66.1	112.3	79.8	139.1	190.4	102.2	124.5	222.3
Sales to Inventory	82.4	72.0	61.5	181.6	86.2	47.3	80.8	62.1	41.4
Assets/Sales (%)	8.9	18.3	23.1	9.6	31.0	101.3	15.6	31.0	69.0
Sales/Net Working Capital	14.6	6.1	1.1	36.6	12.1	1.6	17.8	7.2	2.3
Accounts payable/Sales (%)	.4	.4	.6	1.4	5.2	9.8	1.6	2.6	4.2
Profitability									
Return - Sales (%)	17.1	9.4	.6	35.4	9.2	1.8	39.2	20.0	7.8
Return - Assets (%)	4.7	-2.9	-19.1	72.3	4.5	-5.2	103.1	25.1	4.6
Return - Net Worth (%)	10.6	3.8	-4.2	149.9	7.9	-11.8	139.3	25.6	4.9

Source: Dun & Bradstreet. Data in this table are copyright (c) 1999 of Dun & Bradstreet. Reprinted by special arrangement with D&B. *Note:* UQ stands for "Upper Quartile" and represents the top 25 percent of sample; MED stands for "Median"; and LQ stands for "Lower Quartile" and represents the lowest 25 percent.

D&B INDUSTRY NORMS: SIC 8042 - OFFICES AND CLINICS OF OPTOMETRISTS

	1997 (25) Estab.		1996 (72) Estab.		1995 (86) Estab.	
	$	%	$	%	$	%
Cash	31,860	17.6	33,223	19.1	18,491	14.7
Accounts Receivable	21,361	11.8	28,005	16.1	13,963	11.1
Notes Receivable	1,448	.8	522	.3	1,384	1.1
Inventory	21,361	11.8	18,612	10.7	21,888	17.4
Other Current Assets	10,318	5.7	5,740	3.3	2,767	2.2
Total Current Assets	86,348	47.7	86,102	49.5	58,493	46.5
Fixed Assets	68,245	37.7	56,010	32.2	44,782	35.6
Other Non-current Assets	26,429	14.6	31,832	18.3	22,517	17.9
Total Assets	181,022	100.0	173,944	100.0	125,792	100.0
Accounts Payable	15,025	8.3	16,699	9.6	12,831	10.2
Bank Loans	-	-	-	-	-	-
Notes Payable	9,956	5.5	8,523	4.9	8,176	6.5
Other Current Liabilities	25,343	14.0	29,571	17.0	21,133	16.8
Total Current Liabilities	50,324	27.8	54,793	31.5	42,140	33.5
Other Long Term	53,039	29.3	43,486	25.0	21,133	16.8
Deferred Credits	181	.1	348	.2	881	.7
Net Worth	77,477	42.8	75,318	43.3	61,638	49.0
Total Liabilities & Net Worth	181,021	100.0	173,945	100.0	125,792	100.0
Net Sales	733,114	100.0	554,900	100.0	480,230	100.0
Gross Profits	338,699	46.2	365,124	65.8	252,121	52.5
Net Profit After Tax	53,517	7.3	38,843	7.0	50,424	10.5
Working Capital	36,023	-	31,310	-	16,353	-

Source: Dun & Bradstreet. Data in this table are copyright (c) 1999 of Dun & Bradstreet. Reprinted by special arrangement with D&B. *Notes:* Values in parentheses above columns indicate the number of establishments in the sample. Data shown are for all companies.

D&B KEY BUSINESS RATIOS: SIC 8042

	1997			1996			1995		
	UQ	MED	LQ	UQ	MED	LQ	UQ	MED	LQ
Solvency									
Quick ratio	1.7	1.0	.7	2.2	1.2	.7	2.3	.9	.3
Current ratio	2.8	1.5	1.3	3.2	1.8	1.0	3.7	1.9	.9
Current liabilities/Net worth (%)	32.6	54.9	71.4	17.2	53.5	123.6	10.9	39.3	140.6
Current liabilities/Investment (%)	111.9	192.1	276.8	86.9	171.2	339.3	74.5	130.7	272.6
Total liabilities/Net worth (%)	51.4	93.9	159.0	36.7	84.9	189.1	24.3	82.2	195.3
Fixed assets/Net worth (%)	37.7	62.0	123.6	35.3	55.4	100.5	32.0	54.3	134.6
Efficiency									
Collection period (days)	25.6	35.4	44.3	23.8	37.1	63.9	10.1	19.8	26.1
Sales to Inventory	34.5	26.3	20.7	59.2	14.9	9.8	37.0	21.9	11.4
Assets/Sales (%)	19.4	25.0	31.0	25.1	34.0	51.6	11.6	23.8	36.6
Sales/Net Working Capital	37.5	27.5	18.3	21.5	8.6	6.9	35.8	13.2	7.4
Accounts payable/Sales (%)	2.7	5.2	5.3	2.5	4.0	8.1	1.4	2.4	5.0
Profitability									
Return - Sales (%)	14.8	6.6	4.2	12.2	2.6	.7	22.8	15.2	3.1
Return - Assets (%)	68.7	21.2	16.7	22.4	6.9	2.7	107.1	19.8	11.2
Return - Net Worth (%)	120.5	58.3	26.5	43.5	13.1	8.1	257.1	45.9	22.4

Source: Dun & Bradstreet. Data in this table are copyright (c) 1999 of Dun & Bradstreet. Reprinted by special arrangement with D&B. *Note:* UQ stands for "Upper Quartile" and represents the top 25 percent of sample; MED stands for "Median"; and LQ stands for "Lower Quartile" and represents the lowest 25 percent.

D&B INDUSTRY NORMS: SIC 8049 - OFFICES OF HEALTH PRACTITIONERS NEC

	1997 (114) Estab.		1996 (192) Estab.		1995 (205) Estab.	
	$	%	$	%	$	%
Cash	90,565	16.4	59,256	20.4	45,644	24.7
Accounts Receivable	218,129	39.5	109,217	37.6	56,731	30.7
Notes Receivable	2,761	.5	3,776	1.3	3,141	1.7
Inventory	4,418	.8	1,743	.6	1,848	1.0
Other Current Assets	43,626	7.9	18,009	6.2	11,642	6.3
Total Current Assets	359,499	65.1	192,001	66.1	119,006	64.4
Fixed Assets	144,131	26.1	74,070	25.5	48,601	26.3
Other Non-current Assets	48,596	8.8	24,400	8.4	17,186	9.3
Total Assets	552,226	100.0	290,471	100.0	184,793	100.0
Accounts Payable	30,372	5.5	18,881	6.5	12,381	6.7
Bank Loans	-	-	-	-	-	-
Notes Payable	22,641	4.1	15,976	5.5	7,577	4.1
Other Current Liabilities	136,952	24.8	58,094	20.0	35,850	19.4
Total Current Liabilities	189,965	34.4	92,951	32.0	55,808	30.2
Other Long Term	88,908	16.1	39,504	13.6	22,360	12.1
Deferred Credits	2,209	.4	2,324	.8	1,663	.9
Net Worth	271,142	49.1	155,693	53.6	104,962	56.8
Total Liabilities & Net Worth	552,224	100.0	290,472	100.0	184,793	100.0
Net Sales	1,881,631	100.0	1,186,949	100.0	600,258	100.0
Gross Profits	724,428	38.5	491,397	41.4	379,963	63.3
Net Profit After Tax	105,371	5.6	78,339	6.6	44,419	7.4
Working Capital	169,533	-	99,051	-	63,200	-

Source: Dun & Bradstreet. Data in this table are copyright (c) 1999 of Dun & Bradstreet. Reprinted by special arrangement with D&B. *Notes:* Values in parentheses above columns indicate the number of establishments in the sample. Data shown are for all companies.

D&B KEY BUSINESS RATIOS: SIC 8049

	1997			1996			1995		
	UQ	MED	LQ	UQ	MED	LQ	UQ	MED	LQ
Solvency									
Quick ratio	4.0	2.1	.8	5.3	2.1	1.0	4.8	2.2	1.1
Current ratio	4.5	2.1	1.2	5.4	2.4	1.2	5.4	2.8	1.3
Current liabilities/Net worth (%)	19.5	48.9	134.9	12.7	37.4	88.3	9.2	32.5	105.9
Current liabilities/Investment (%)	315.3	684.3	815.4	199.2	510.5	777.5	42.6	63.2	212.8
Total liabilities/Net worth (%)	33.2	78.8	179.7	15.4	63.0	173.4	16.9	57.5	175.5
Fixed assets/Net worth (%)	18.4	43.3	87.1	15.0	36.6	93.6	14.2	39.1	84.4
Efficiency									
Collection period (days)	53.9	73.4	97.7	50.0	72.3	93.8	41.6	68.8	91.1
Sales to Inventory	57.8	31.5	21.9	216.4	72.5	53.2	112.0	80.2	44.2
Assets/Sales (%)	23.8	32.5	65.1	18.2	31.3	54.9	16.8	33.7	56.1
Sales/Net Working Capital	10.5	5.9	4.2	12.4	7.1	3.6	19.7	8.2	4.7
Accounts payable/Sales (%)	.5	1.8	4.9	1.0	2.8	6.2	1.2	3.1	7.1
Profitability									
Return - Sales (%)	8.3	3.3	.4	14.0	4.7	1.3	12.3	4.0	-.3
Return - Assets (%)	25.9	8.8	1.4	29.6	8.7	2.0	23.3	7.3	-.9
Return - Net Worth (%)	37.6	18.2	2.4	57.1	18.9	4.5	62.2	12.7	-1.1

Source: Dun & Bradstreet. Data in this table are copyright (c) 1999 of Dun & Bradstreet. Reprinted by special arrangement with D&B. *Note:* UQ stands for "Upper Quartile" and represents the top 25 percent of sample; MED stands for "Median"; and LQ stands for "Lower Quartile" and represents the lowest 25 percent.

D&B INDUSTRY NORMS: SIC 8051 - SKILLED NURSING CARE FACILITIES

	1997 (1091) Estab.		1996 (1895) Estab.		1995 (1200) Estab.	
	$	%	$	%	$	%
Cash	384,948	9.7	340,939	10.0	350,036	8.8
Accounts Receivable	861,173	21.7	763,704	22.4	771,670	19.4
Notes Receivable	7,937	.2	17,047	.5	15,911	.4
Inventory	19,843	.5	17,047	.5	23,866	.6
Other Current Assets	297,640	7.5	252,295	7.4	290,371	7.3
Total Current Assets	1,571,541	39.6	1,391,032	40.8	1,451,854	36.5
Fixed Assets	1,849,338	46.6	1,609,233	47.2	1,972,929	49.6
Other Non-current Assets	547,658	13.8	409,127	12.0	552,898	13.9
Total Assets	3,968,537	100.0	3,409,392	100.0	3,977,681	100.0
Accounts Payable	404,791	10.2	334,121	9.8	306,281	7.7
Bank Loans	3,969	.1	3,409	.1	-	-
Notes Payable	107,150	2.7	105,691	3.1	91,487	2.3
Other Current Liabilities	599,249	15.1	521,637	15.3	568,808	14.3
Total Current Liabilities	1,115,159	28.1	964,858	28.3	966,576	24.3
Other Long Term	1,460,422	36.8	1,268,294	37.2	1,599,027	40.2
Deferred Credits	51,591	1.3	30,685	.9	27,844	.7
Net Worth	1,341,366	33.8	1,145,556	33.6	1,384,233	34.8
Total Liabilities & Net Worth	3,968,538	100.0	3,409,393	100.0	3,977,680	100.0
Net Sales	6,217,006	100.0	5,282,542	100.0	5,206,048	100.0
Gross Profits	3,239,060	52.1	3,343,849	63.3	3,066,362	58.9
Net Profit After Tax	261,114	4.2	206,019	3.9	203,036	3.9
Working Capital	456,382	-	426,174	-	485,277	-

Source: Dun & Bradstreet. Data in this table are copyright (c) 1999 of Dun & Bradstreet. Reprinted by special arrangement with D&B. *Notes:* Values in parentheses above columns indicate the number of establishments in the sample. Data shown are for all companies.

D&B KEY BUSINESS RATIOS: SIC 8051

	1997			1996			1995		
	UQ	MED	LQ	UQ	MED	LQ	UQ	MED	LQ
Solvency									
Quick ratio	1.7	1.2	.8	1.8	1.2	.8	1.8	1.2	.8
Current ratio	2.4	1.5	1.0	2.4	1.5	1.0	2.5	1.6	1.1
Current liabilities/Net worth (%)	21.7	57.8	144.3	23.4	59.6	143.4	19.8	46.4	122.6
Current liabilities/Investment (%)	573.6	690.8	862.6	505.6	684.4	824.5	410.9	584.6	805.1
Total liabilities/Net worth (%)	59.3	139.9	299.8	53.0	134.4	295.4	48.5	136.3	285.7
Fixed assets/Net worth (%)	48.1	107.5	212.0	49.2	102.3	227.1	57.3	112.3	225.0
Efficiency									
Collection period (days)	26.1	38.3	52.9	26.3	38.0	55.1	25.2	36.5	54.0
Sales to Inventory	381.6	231.9	132.6	374.5	231.9	132.1	334.0	197.6	119.3
Assets/Sales (%)	37.5	76.2	126.4	36.9	76.8	127.1	45.5	86.1	136.3
Sales/Net Working Capital	20.0	9.8	5.5	19.9	9.8	5.2	20.6	9.6	5.8
Accounts payable/Sales (%)	2.5	3.9	7.1	2.2	3.8	6.9	2.1	3.3	5.8
Profitability									
Return - Sales (%)	8.3	3.9	.6	7.7	3.5	.4	6.9	3.4	.7
Return - Assets (%)	12.4	4.7	.9	11.5	4.1	.4	9.3	3.4	.5
Return - Net Worth (%)	44.4	13.7	3.3	41.2	13.4	2.4	32.6	11.5	2.3

Source: Dun & Bradstreet. Data in this table are copyright (c) 1999 of Dun & Bradstreet. Reprinted by special arrangement with D&B. *Note:* UQ stands for "Upper Quartile" and represents the top 25 percent of sample; MED stands for "Median"; and LQ stands for "Lower Quartile" and represents the lowest 25 percent.

D&B INDUSTRY NORMS: SIC 8052 - INTERMEDIATE CARE FACILITIES

	1997 (144) Estab.		1996 (341) Estab.		1995 (247) Estab.	
	$	%	$	%	$	%
Cash	269,569	10.8	196,129	11.1	209,014	10.9
Accounts Receivable	376,897	15.1	349,851	19.8	347,079	18.1
Notes Receivable	17,472	.7	5,301	.3	5,753	.3
Inventory	19,968	.8	8,835	.5	9,588	.5
Other Current Assets	194,689	7.8	139,587	7.9	147,652	7.7
Total Current Assets	878,595	35.2	699,703	39.6	719,086	37.5
Fixed Assets	1,320,388	52.9	849,890	48.1	1,012,472	52.8
Other Non-current Assets	297,025	11.9	217,332	12.3	186,003	9.7
Total Assets	2,496,008	100.0	1,766,925	100.0	1,917,561	100.0
Accounts Payable	157,248	6.3	141,354	8.0	126,559	6.6
Bank Loans	-	-	-	-	-	-
Notes Payable	49,920	2.0	47,707	2.7	40,269	2.1
Other Current Liabilities	381,889	15.3	273,873	15.5	295,304	15.4
Total Current Liabilities	589,057	23.6	462,934	26.2	462,132	24.1
Other Long Term	878,594	35.2	604,288	34.2	722,920	37.7
Deferred Credits	17,472	.7	7,068	.4	11,505	.6
Net Worth	1,010,883	40.5	692,634	39.2	721,003	37.6
Total Liabilities & Net Worth	2,496,006	100.0	1,766,924	100.0	1,917,560	100.0
Net Sales	3,794,996	100.0	3,288,168	100.0	3,330,794	100.0
Gross Profits	2,683,062	70.7	2,222,802	67.6	2,025,123	60.8
Net Profit After Tax	148,005	3.9	115,086	3.5	99,924	3.0
Working Capital	289,536	-	236,768	-	256,953	-

Source: Dun & Bradstreet. Data in this table are copyright (c) 1999 of Dun & Bradstreet. Reprinted by special arrangement with D&B. *Notes:* Values in parentheses above columns indicate the number of establishments in the sample. Data shown are for all companies.

D&B KEY BUSINESS RATIOS: SIC 8052

	1997			1996			1995		
	UQ	MED	LQ	UQ	MED	LQ	UQ	MED	LQ
Solvency									
Quick ratio	1.7	1.1	.6	2.0	1.2	.7	2.1	1.2	.7
Current ratio	2.3	1.5	.9	2.8	1.5	1.0	2.7	1.5	1.0
Current liabilities/Net worth (%)	19.1	37.5	104.2	15.6	40.3	112.0	19.3	42.9	112.0
Current liabilities/Investment (%)	284.9	526.9	655.0	432.5	580.9	711.2	317.9	561.1	752.5
Total liabilities/Net worth (%)	33.2	85.8	258.2	32.9	95.7	225.3	36.9	114.8	273.7
Fixed assets/Net worth (%)	51.1	101.6	226.7	50.2	89.1	196.1	55.1	100.7	226.3
Efficiency									
Collection period (days)	19.6	29.4	44.4	22.2	32.5	50.5	25.4	35.4	53.1
Sales to Inventory	373.2	265.4	119.7	376.0	235.2	122.4	340.3	226.3	119.1
Assets/Sales (%)	45.6	89.3	135.7	35.8	72.4	122.0	39.7	76.4	131.2
Sales/Net Working Capital	19.3	9.9	4.9	19.2	9.9	5.4	19.5	8.4	4.7
Accounts payable/Sales (%)	1.9	2.7	5.3	1.8	2.7	5.0	2.0	3.2	5.6
Profitability									
Return - Sales (%)	6.9	4.2	.9	6.7	2.1	.2	6.6	2.6	.1
Return - Assets (%)	9.6	5.1	.6	8.1	3.1	.4	7.8	3.1	.5
Return - Net Worth (%)	29.4	14.8	3.0	34.6	9.6	1.6	30.6	10.9	3.5

Source: Dun & Bradstreet. Data in this table are copyright (c) 1999 of Dun & Bradstreet. Reprinted by special arrangement with D&B. *Note:* UQ stands for "Upper Quartile" and represents the top 25 percent of sample; MED stands for "Median"; and LQ stands for "Lower Quartile" and represents the lowest 25 percent.

D&B INDUSTRY NORMS: SIC 8059 - NURSING AND PERSONAL CARE NEC

	1997 (277) Estab.		1996 (496) Estab.		1995 (320) Estab.	
	$	%	$	%	$	%
Cash	261,434	10.6	314,605	11.8	243,249	11.1
Accounts Receivable	574,661	23.3	554,558	20.8	416,372	19.0
Notes Receivable	9,865	.4	37,326	1.4	19,723	.9
Inventory	9,865	.4	10,665	.4	8,766	.4
Other Current Assets	167,712	6.8	205,293	7.7	188,463	8.6
Total Current Assets	1,023,537	41.5	1,122,447	42.1	876,573	40.0
Fixed Assets	1,104,928	44.8	1,191,766	44.7	981,762	44.8
Other Non-current Assets	337,891	13.7	351,931	13.2	333,098	15.2
Total Assets	2,466,356	100.0	2,666,144	100.0	2,191,433	100.0
Accounts Payable	241,703	9.8	255,950	9.6	168,740	7.7
Bank Loans	-	-	-	-	4,383	.2
Notes Payable	56,726	2.3	74,652	2.8	39,446	1.8
Other Current Liabilities	369,954	15.0	381,259	14.3	341,863	15.6
Total Current Liabilities	668,383	27.1	711,861	26.7	554,432	25.3
Other Long Term	813,898	33.0	850,500	31.9	642,090	29.3
Deferred Credits	76,457	3.1	58,655	2.2	56,977	2.6
Net Worth	907,620	36.8	1,045,128	39.2	937,933	42.8
Total Liabilities & Net Worth	2,466,358	100.0	2,666,144	100.0	2,191,432	100.0
Net Sales	4,443,105	100.0	3,884,985	100.0	3,961,551	100.0
Gross Profits	1,950,523	43.9	2,983,668	76.8	2,618,585	66.1
Net Profit After Tax	195,497	4.4	139,859	3.6	166,385	4.2
Working Capital	355,156	-	410,587	-	322,141	-

Source: Dun & Bradstreet. Data in this table are copyright (c) 1999 of Dun & Bradstreet. Reprinted by special arrangement with D&B. *Notes:* Values in parentheses above columns indicate the number of establishments in the sample. Data shown are for all companies.

D&B KEY BUSINESS RATIOS: SIC 8059

	1997			1996			1995		
	UQ	MED	LQ	UQ	MED	LQ	UQ	MED	LQ
Solvency									
Quick ratio	2.2	1.3	.7	2.0	1.2	.8	2.1	1.3	.7
Current ratio	3.2	1.7	1.0	2.8	1.6	1.0	3.1	1.7	1.0
Current liabilities/Net worth (%)	14.8	45.0	149.6	17.5	42.3	128.8	15.5	38.2	109.9
Current liabilities/Investment (%)	452.9	580.7	826.8	397.4	609.8	698.6	459.2	737.6	914.8
Total liabilities/Net worth (%)	33.9	107.2	294.8	40.4	110.2	275.6	37.5	105.9	254.4
Fixed assets/Net worth (%)	42.0	85.3	174.3	41.5	83.9	185.7	38.2	89.8	177.4
Efficiency									
Collection period (days)	22.3	34.3	50.0	20.8	32.5	48.8	20.0	29.0	48.7
Sales to Inventory	353.0	249.8	180.6	370.6	202.1	132.4	320.6	202.1	117.6
Assets/Sales (%)	28.1	69.2	161.5	29.6	74.3	160.3	34.2	80.3	192.1
Sales/Net Working Capital	18.6	9.0	4.2	19.4	9.0	4.7	16.4	7.2	3.5
Accounts payable/Sales (%)	2.1	3.3	6.7	2.2	3.5	6.6	1.8	2.9	5.4
Profitability									
Return - Sales (%)	8.3	4.0	.5	8.4	3.7	.1	9.3	4.1	.8
Return - Assets (%)	12.1	3.9	.5	11.9	4.0	.3	10.0	4.3	1.1
Return - Net Worth (%)	43.0	11.9	2.5	39.8	12.1	2.2	36.3	9.9	3.3

Source: Dun & Bradstreet. Data in this table are copyright (c) 1999 of Dun & Bradstreet. Reprinted by special arrangement with D&B. *Note:* UQ stands for "Upper Quartile" and represents the top 25 percent of sample; MED stands for "Median"; and LQ stands for "Lower Quartile" and represents the lowest 25 percent.

D&B INDUSTRY NORMS: SIC 8062 - GENERAL MEDICAL & SURGICAL HOSPITALS

	1997 (1485) Estab.		1996 (1353) Estab.		1995 (2400) Estab.	
	$	%	$	%	$	%
Cash	2,872,252	7.3	2,450,549	7.1	2,408,799	6.8
Accounts Receivable	7,003,573	17.8	6,178,144	17.9	6,517,926	18.4
Notes Receivable	39,346	.1	34,515	.1	35,424	.1
Inventory	747,572	1.9	690,295	2.0	708,470	2.0
Other Current Assets	2,754,214	7.0	2,208,945	6.4	2,196,258	6.2
Total Current Assets	13,416,957	34.1	11,562,448	33.5	11,866,877	33.5
Fixed Assets	16,918,744	43.0	15,221,013	44.1	15,515,497	43.8
Other Non-current Assets	9,010,215	22.9	7,731,308	22.4	8,041,137	22.7
Total Assets	39,345,916	100.0	34,514,769	100.0	35,423,511	100.0
Accounts Payable	2,282,063	5.8	1,932,827	5.6	1,912,869	5.4
Bank Loans	-	-	-	-	-	-
Notes Payable	196,730	.5	138,059	.4	141,694	.4
Other Current Liabilities	4,367,397	11.1	3,727,595	10.8	3,932,009	11.1
Total Current Liabilities	6,846,190	17.4	5,798,481	16.8	5,986,572	16.9
Other Long Term	10,702,089	27.2	9,629,621	27.9	10,485,359	29.6
Deferred Credits	118,038	.3	103,544	.3	70,847	.2
Net Worth	21,679,600	55.1	18,983,123	55.0	18,880,730	53.3
Total Liabilities & Net Worth	39,345,917	100.0	34,514,769	100.0	35,423,508	100.0
Net Sales	37,397,446	100.0	33,927,821	100.0	34,463,865	100.0
Gross Profits	26,589,584	71.1	24,394,103	71.9	23,021,862	66.8
Net Profit After Tax	2,094,257	5.6	1,662,463	4.9	1,550,874	4.5
Working Capital	6,570,768	-	5,763,967	-	5,880,303	-

Source: Dun & Bradstreet. Data in this table are copyright (c) 1999 of Dun & Bradstreet. Reprinted by special arrangement with D&B. *Notes:* Values in parentheses above columns indicate the number of establishments in the sample. Data shown are for all companies.

D&B KEY BUSINESS RATIOS: SIC 8062

	1997			1996			1995		
	UQ	MED	LQ	UQ	MED	LQ	UQ	MED	LQ
Solvency									
Quick ratio	2.1	1.5	1.1	2.1	1.5	1.1	2.2	1.5	1.1
Current ratio	2.9	2.1	1.5	2.9	2.1	1.5	2.9	2.1	1.5
Current liabilities/Net worth (%)	16.1	25.0	42.6	16.0	24.9	40.9	16.3	25.1	42.5
Current liabilities/Investment (%)	401.7	562.3	756.0	394.1	563.9	758.8	392.8	577.1	750.0
Total liabilities/Net worth (%)	41.1	73.7	124.7	39.2	77.6	129.0	41.8	83.6	142.6
Fixed assets/Net worth (%)	56.7	77.0	108.2	58.6	81.3	111.6	61.6	84.0	118.5
Efficiency									
Collection period (days)	51.5	61.3	72.3	49.6	60.6	70.5	52.2	62.4	73.7
Sales to Inventory	89.1	57.5	40.2	90.4	56.0	39.2	89.5	55.2	38.5
Assets/Sales (%)	80.4	105.9	135.3	80.7	103.8	129.5	81.7	103.4	128.0
Sales/Net Working Capital	9.8	6.1	4.1	10.6	6.4	4.2	10.5	6.4	4.3
Accounts payable/Sales (%)	3.0	4.2	6.6	2.8	4.0	6.4	2.8	4.0	6.0
Profitability									
Return - Sales (%)	9.5	5.1	2.0	8.3	4.8	1.7	7.8	4.4	1.8
Return - Assets (%)	8.2	4.8	2.0	7.9	4.6	1.6	7.2	4.2	1.8
Return - Net Worth (%)	14.2	9.0	4.4	13.9	8.5	3.4	13.5	8.2	3.7

Source: Dun & Bradstreet. Data in this table are copyright (c) 1999 of Dun & Bradstreet. Reprinted by special arrangement with D&B. *Note:* UQ stands for "Upper Quartile" and represents the top 25 percent of sample; MED stands for "Median"; and LQ stands for "Lower Quartile" and represents the lowest 25 percent.

D&B INDUSTRY NORMS: SIC 8063 - PSYCHIATRIC HOSPITALS

	1997 (70) Estab.		1996 (152) Estab.		1995 (131) Estab.	
	$	%	$	%	$	%
Cash	795,947	10.5	634,577	9.3	778,261	11.8
Accounts Receivable	2,251,392	29.7	1,610,325	23.6	1,497,163	22.7
Notes Receivable	68,224	.9	27,294	.4	26,382	.4
Inventory	22,741	.3	27,294	.4	32,977	.5
Other Current Assets	500,309	6.6	852,926	12.5	732,093	11.1
Total Current Assets	3,638,613	48.0	3,152,416	46.2	3,066,876	46.5
Fixed Assets	3,001,855	39.6	2,743,011	40.2	2,789,867	42.3
Other Non-current Assets	939,975	12.4	927,984	13.6	738,688	11.2
Total Assets	7,580,443	100.0	6,823,411	100.0	6,595,431	100.0
Accounts Payable	576,114	7.6	443,522	6.5	494,657	7.5
Bank Loans	-	-	-	-	-	-
Notes Payable	75,804	1.0	102,351	1.5	171,481	2.6
Other Current Liabilities	1,478,186	19.5	1,125,863	16.5	1,022,292	15.5
Total Current Liabilities	2,130,104	28.1	1,671,736	24.5	1,688,430	25.6
Other Long Term	1,728,341	22.8	1,480,680	21.7	1,391,636	21.1
Deferred Credits	45,483	.6	34,117	.5	52,763	.8
Net Worth	3,676,515	48.5	3,636,878	53.3	3,462,601	52.5
Total Liabilities & Net Worth	7,580,443	100.0	6,823,411	100.0	6,595,430	100.0
Net Sales	9,483,000	100.0	9,418,016	100.0	8,207,466	100.0
Gross Profits	4,969,092	52.4	4,878,532	51.8	2,733,086	33.3
Net Profit After Tax	180,177	1.9	160,106	1.7	205,187	2.5
Working Capital	1,508,509	-	1,480,680	-	1,378,445	-

Source: Dun & Bradstreet. Data in this table are copyright (c) 1999 of Dun & Bradstreet. Reprinted by special arrangement with D&B. *Notes:* Values in parentheses above columns indicate the number of establishments in the sample. Data shown are for all companies.

D&B KEY BUSINESS RATIOS: SIC 8063

	1997			1996			1995		
	UQ	MED	LQ	UQ	MED	LQ	UQ	MED	LQ
Solvency									
Quick ratio	2.5	1.6	.9	2.5	1.5	1.0	2.4	1.6	.9
Current ratio	2.9	2.0	1.3	3.5	2.2	1.4	3.1	1.9	1.2
Current liabilities/Net worth (%)	19.7	36.9	70.4	14.2	27.7	55.3	17.1	32.1	65.5
Current liabilities/Investment (%)	606.2	639.0	696.4	497.6	780.8	848.5	192.2	511.7	578.0
Total liabilities/Net worth (%)	28.1	64.9	129.0	27.4	60.0	125.5	28.7	64.9	145.5
Fixed assets/Net worth (%)	34.6	64.0	121.9	42.8	67.3	114.9	45.6	67.1	118.5
Efficiency									
Collection period (days)	41.6	61.4	91.8	37.5	57.5	80.0	42.3	61.7	77.0
Sales to Inventory	325.5	188.4	159.5	347.6	223.5	154.0	358.8	162.2	113.8
Assets/Sales (%)	51.1	76.0	101.9	48.2	80.6	110.4	56.1	84.2	107.9
Sales/Net Working Capital	9.4	5.8	4.0	9.7	6.0	3.7	9.8	5.5	3.5
Accounts payable/Sales (%)	2.0	3.8	5.9	1.7	3.2	5.5	1.8	3.4	5.8
Profitability									
Return - Sales (%)	5.8	2.6	-.7	7.1	2.5	-2.0	6.1	2.4	-.7
Return - Assets (%)	6.0	3.1	-1.8	10.6	3.0	-1.6	9.6	2.7	-1.1
Return - Net Worth (%)	18.1	5.1	-2.1	22.6	5.3	-2.5	16.3	4.5	-2.0

Source: Dun & Bradstreet. Data in this table are copyright (c) 1999 of Dun & Bradstreet. Reprinted by special arrangement with D&B. *Note:* UQ stands for "Upper Quartile" and represents the top 25 percent of sample; MED stands for "Median"; and LQ stands for "Lower Quartile" and represents the lowest 25 percent.

D&B INDUSTRY NORMS: SIC 8069 - SPECIALTY HOSPITALS EXC. PSYCHIATRIC

	1997 (109) Estab.		1996 (242) Estab.		1995 (174) Estab.	
	$	%	$	%	$	%
Cash	2,241,907	13.3	1,103,610	13.2	1,340,807	11.4
Accounts Receivable	2,798,170	16.6	1,471,481	17.6	2,034,733	17.3
Notes Receivable	16,856	.1	16,721	.2	-	-
Inventory	202,277	1.2	58,525	.7	82,330	.7
Other Current Assets	1,331,659	7.9	953,118	11.4	1,140,862	9.7
Total Current Assets	6,590,869	39.1	3,603,455	43.1	4,598,732	39.1
Fixed Assets	7,062,850	41.9	3,536,570	42.3	5,151,520	43.8
Other Non-current Assets	3,202,724	19.0	1,220,660	14.6	2,011,210	17.1
Total Assets	16,856,443	100.0	8,360,685	100.0	11,761,462	100.0
Accounts Payable	1,196,807	7.1	551,805	6.6	799,779	6.8
Bank Loans	16,856	.1	-	-	-	-
Notes Payable	101,139	.6	83,607	1.0	58,807	.5
Other Current Liabilities	2,208,194	13.1	1,095,250	13.1	1,752,458	14.9
Total Current Liabilities	3,522,996	20.9	1,730,662	20.7	2,611,044	22.2
Other Long Term	4,416,388	26.2	1,822,629	21.8	2,752,182	23.4
Deferred Credits	16,856	.1	33,443	.4	70,569	.6
Net Worth	8,900,202	52.8	4,773,951	57.1	6,327,666	53.8
Total Liabilities & Net Worth	16,856,442	100.0	8,360,685	100.0	11,761,461	100.0
Net Sales	14,531,783	100.0	10,436,471	100.0	13,984,335	100.0
Gross Profits	8,108,735	55.8	5,896,606	56.5	8,278,726	59.2
Net Profit After Tax	537,676	3.7	427,895	4.1	279,687	2.0
Working Capital	3,067,872	-	1,872,793	-	1,987,687	-

Source: Dun & Bradstreet. Data in this table are copyright (c) 1999 of Dun & Bradstreet. Reprinted by special arrangement with D&B. *Notes:* Values in parentheses above columns indicate the number of establishments in the sample. Data shown are for all companies.

D&B KEY BUSINESS RATIOS: SIC 8069

	1997			1996			1995		
	UQ	MED	LQ	UQ	MED	LQ	UQ	MED	LQ
Solvency									
Quick ratio	2.6	1.3	.8	2.6	1.4	1.0	2.4	1.4	.9
Current ratio	4.5	2.0	1.1	4.0	2.0	1.3	3.1	1.9	1.4
Current liabilities/Net worth (%)	12.8	25.2	57.7	13.3	25.7	49.4	14.5	30.4	55.2
Current liabilities/Investment (%)	287.4	638.1	829.3	327.7	572.2	752.1	549.5	629.0	806.6
Total liabilities/Net worth (%)	30.0	66.9	150.1	24.5	57.6	129.4	29.3	68.9	160.5
Fixed assets/Net worth (%)	37.8	68.4	125.1	41.3	74.6	122.1	48.3	79.4	139.3
Efficiency									
Collection period (days)	44.0	59.7	77.3	36.1	52.6	70.4	40.8	56.6	74.9
Sales to Inventory	208.7	99.4	43.4	227.0	122.5	67.0	226.5	130.6	74.9
Assets/Sales (%)	73.2	105.1	141.5	63.0	95.8	132.1	60.6	95.2	133.5
Sales/Net Working Capital	11.1	5.3	3.9	11.0	6.8	3.6	9.6	6.6	4.2
Accounts payable/Sales (%)	2.8	4.9	7.9	2.3	4.0	6.6	2.0	4.0	7.1
Profitability									
Return - Sales (%)	8.9	4.2	.7	8.2	3.8	.3	6.8	2.7	-.6
Return - Assets (%)	8.9	4.7	.6	7.6	3.7	-.5	6.8	2.9	-.5
Return - Net Worth (%)	17.7	8.3	2.6	13.8	6.9	-	11.3	6.1	.1

Source: Dun & Bradstreet. Data in this table are copyright (c) 1999 of Dun & Bradstreet. Reprinted by special arrangement with D&B. *Note:* UQ stands for "Upper Quartile" and represents the top 25 percent of sample; MED stands for "Median"; and LQ stands for "Lower Quartile" and represents the lowest 25 percent.

D&B INDUSTRY NORMS: SIC 8071 - MEDICAL LABORATORIES

	1997 (200) Estab.		1996 (273) Estab.		1995 (245) Estab.	
	$	%	$	%	$	%
Cash	180,776	14.6	164,018	14.2	153,110	16.7
Accounts Receivable	373,933	30.2	345,362	29.9	245,709	26.8
Notes Receivable	7,429	.6	6,930	.6	3,667	.4
Inventory	33,431	2.7	30,032	2.6	25,671	2.8
Other Current Assets	94,102	7.6	84,319	7.3	50,425	5.5
Total Current Assets	689,671	55.7	630,661	54.6	478,582	52.2
Fixed Assets	376,409	30.4	368,464	31.9	330,057	36.0
Other Non-current Assets	172,108	13.9	155,933	13.5	108,185	11.8
Total Assets	1,238,188	100.0	1,155,058	100.0	916,824	100.0
Accounts Payable	128,772	10.4	120,126	10.4	79,764	8.7
Bank Loans	1,238	.1	1,155	.1	-	-
Notes Payable	38,384	3.1	42,737	3.7	31,172	3.4
Other Current Liabilities	212,969	17.2	194,050	16.8	161,361	17.6
Total Current Liabilities	381,363	30.8	358,068	31.0	272,297	29.7
Other Long Term	260,020	21.0	202,135	17.5	189,783	20.7
Deferred Credits	2,476	.2	6,930	.6	3,667	.4
Net Worth	594,331	48.0	587,925	50.9	451,078	49.2
Total Liabilities & Net Worth	1,238,190	100.0	1,155,058	100.0	916,825	100.0
Net Sales	2,865,835	100.0	2,637,030	100.0	2,418,744	100.0
Gross Profits	1,447,247	50.5	1,521,566	57.7	1,298,866	53.7
Net Profit After Tax	140,426	4.9	147,674	5.6	137,868	5.7
Working Capital	308,309	-	272,594	-	206,286	-

Source: Dun & Bradstreet. Data in this table are copyright (c) 1999 of Dun & Bradstreet. Reprinted by special arrangement with D&B. *Notes:* Values in parentheses above columns indicate the number of establishments in the sample. Data shown are for all companies.

D&B KEY BUSINESS RATIOS: SIC 8071

	1997			1996			1995		
	UQ	MED	LQ	UQ	MED	LQ	UQ	MED	LQ
Solvency									
Quick ratio	2.9	1.4	.8	2.7	1.3	.8	3.0	1.6	.9
Current ratio	4.1	1.9	1.1	3.8	1.7	1.1	3.9	1.9	1.1
Current liabilities/Net worth (%)	19.8	49.7	122.7	17.5	49.0	128.2	15.7	46.0	100.1
Current liabilities/Investment (%)	252.1	475.5	635.9	246.5	506.6	718.6	216.8	367.5	680.5
Total liabilities/Net worth (%)	31.5	90.6	217.0	26.2	74.2	188.8	33.2	75.7	211.4
Fixed assets/Net worth (%)	26.4	53.6	109.0	27.4	56.9	100.9	30.1	67.5	116.5
Efficiency									
Collection period (days)	39.4	58.8	92.4	36.7	61.9	84.0	38.8	61.3	84.5
Sales to Inventory	86.8	54.7	25.7	82.1	54.7	27.5	86.5	50.5	32.5
Assets/Sales (%)	30.9	49.8	93.1	29.9	45.7	82.6	36.9	50.3	77.6
Sales/Net Working Capital	13.5	6.5	3.5	16.4	6.8	4.0	11.8	6.6	4.0
Accounts payable/Sales (%)	2.5	4.6	8.6	2.6	5.6	9.4	2.0	4.3	8.1
Profitability									
Return - Sales (%)	11.0	3.9	.3	10.8	4.8	.9	10.0	4.6	1.1
Return - Assets (%)	17.5	7.3	-.2	19.2	7.9	1.4	18.7	7.0	1.3
Return - Net Worth (%)	43.8	14.1	-.5	45.4	18.7	5.2	42.4	15.9	4.4

Source: Dun & Bradstreet. Data in this table are copyright (c) 1999 of Dun & Bradstreet. Reprinted by special arrangement with D&B. *Note:* UQ stands for "Upper Quartile" and represents the top 25 percent of sample; MED stands for "Median"; and LQ stands for "Lower Quartile" and represents the lowest 25 percent.

D&B INDUSTRY NORMS: SIC 8072 - DENTAL LABORATORIES

	1997 (55) Estab.		1996 (147) Estab.		1995 (160) Estab.	
	$	%	$	%	$	%
Cash	37,807	14.2	20,667	13.1	22,344	16.6
Accounts Receivable	84,666	31.8	52,063	33.0	40,516	30.1
Notes Receivable	799	.3	316	.2	1,077	.8
Inventory	13,312	5.0	7,573	4.8	8,615	6.4
Other Current Assets	19,170	7.2	8,993	5.7	7,807	5.8
Total Current Assets	155,754	58.5	89,612	56.8	80,359	59.7
Fixed Assets	82,802	31.1	48,276	30.6	37,150	27.6
Other Non-current Assets	27,689	10.4	19,879	12.6	17,095	12.7
Total Assets	266,245	100.0	157,767	100.0	134,604	100.0
Accounts Payable	24,494	9.2	16,408	10.4	13,191	9.8
Bank Loans	-	-	-	-	-	-
Notes Payable	5,591	2.1	6,468	4.1	5,115	3.8
Other Current Liabilities	37,274	14.0	26,189	16.6	23,421	17.4
Total Current Liabilities	67,359	25.3	49,065	31.1	41,727	31.0
Other Long Term	42,067	15.8	20,667	13.1	14,672	10.9
Deferred Credits	-	-	-	-	269	.2
Net Worth	156,818	58.9	88,033	55.8	77,935	57.9
Total Liabilities & Net Worth	266,244	100.0	157,765	100.0	134,603	100.0
Net Sales	1,146,465	100.0	958,065	100.0	759,701	100.0
Gross Profits	436,803	38.1	456,039	47.6	359,339	47.3
Net Profit After Tax	61,909	5.4	39,281	4.1	38,745	5.1
Working Capital	88,393	-	40,546	-	38,631	-

Source: Dun & Bradstreet. Data in this table are copyright (c) 1999 of Dun & Bradstreet. Reprinted by special arrangement with D&B. *Notes:* Values in parentheses above columns indicate the number of establishments in the sample. Data shown are for all companies.

D&B KEY BUSINESS RATIOS: SIC 8072

	1997			1996			1995		
	UQ	MED	LQ	UQ	MED	LQ	UQ	MED	LQ
Solvency									
Quick ratio	5.0	2.0	1.0	3.1	1.4	.9	4.5	1.7	.9
Current ratio	6.5	2.7	1.4	4.1	2.1	1.1	6.2	2.1	1.2
Current liabilities/Net worth (%)	11.3	32.2	84.3	13.8	41.0	98.8	13.6	34.8	96.8
Current liabilities/Investment (%)	216.5	347.8	565.1	134.4	305.5	499.9	137.3	268.9	528.2
Total liabilities/Net worth (%)	17.6	54.0	138.4	22.3	64.6	152.2	18.0	59.8	140.6
Fixed assets/Net worth (%)	24.5	45.8	92.8	22.8	47.1	89.8	17.6	42.9	84.3
Efficiency									
Collection period (days)	29.9	39.1	48.6	31.4	41.6	49.3	35.8	40.2	47.1
Sales to Inventory	113.9	45.4	30.5	139.1	73.0	32.9	124.7	53.0	27.6
Assets/Sales (%)	18.9	31.1	46.7	17.7	28.6	36.5	19.6	27.5	34.4
Sales/Net Working Capital	13.8	9.8	6.3	18.8	10.2	7.3	16.9	10.3	5.8
Accounts payable/Sales (%)	1.3	2.6	4.5	1.5	2.9	5.0	2.1	3.4	4.9
Profitability									
Return - Sales (%)	8.4	3.2	1.5	6.0	2.4	.6	8.3	2.5	.8
Return - Assets (%)	14.0	6.3	3.5	13.9	7.2	2.8	16.4	7.2	2.0
Return - Net Worth (%)	33.0	12.4	5.4	35.2	14.0	6.6	27.8	13.3	2.3

Source: Dun & Bradstreet. Data in this table are copyright (c) 1999 of Dun & Bradstreet. Reprinted by special arrangement with D&B. *Note:* UQ stands for "Upper Quartile" and represents the top 25 percent of sample; MED stands for "Median"; and LQ stands for "Lower Quartile" and represents the lowest 25 percent.

D&B INDUSTRY NORMS: SIC 8082 - HOME HEALTH CARE SERVICES

	1997 (419) Estab.		1996 (667) Estab.		1995 (518) Estab.	
	$	%	$	%	$	%
Cash	240,875	15.4	229,523	15.8	238,044	18.4
Accounts Receivable	681,957	43.6	642,085	44.2	575,704	44.5
Notes Receivable	7,821	.5	10,169	.7	9,056	.7
Inventory	37,539	2.4	26,148	1.8	21,993	1.7
Other Current Assets	136,079	8.7	138,005	9.5	100,910	7.8
Total Current Assets	1,104,271	70.6	1,045,930	72.0	945,707	73.1
Fixed Assets	281,542	18.0	261,482	18.0	226,400	17.5
Other Non-current Assets	178,310	11.4	145,268	10.0	121,609	9.4
Total Assets	1,564,123	100.0	1,452,680	100.0	1,293,716	100.0
Accounts Payable	165,797	10.6	168,511	11.6	146,190	11.3
Bank Loans	4,692	.3	-	-	-	-
Notes Payable	56,308	3.6	53,749	3.7	53,042	4.1
Other Current Liabilities	414,492	26.5	400,940	27.6	357,066	27.6
Total Current Liabilities	641,289	41.0	623,200	42.9	556,298	43.0
Other Long Term	187,695	12.0	167,058	11.5	141,015	10.9
Deferred Credits	3,128	.2	1,453	.1	1,294	.1
Net Worth	732,009	46.8	660,969	45.5	595,110	46.0
Total Liabilities & Net Worth	1,564,121	100.0	1,452,680	100.0	1,293,717	100.0
Net Sales	6,403,458	100.0	4,642,309	100.0	4,914,950	100.0
Gross Profits	3,041,643	47.5	2,219,024	47.8	2,270,707	46.2
Net Profit After Tax	192,104	3.0	148,554	3.2	142,534	2.9
Working Capital	462,980	-	422,730	-	389,409	-

Source: Dun & Bradstreet. Data in this table are copyright (c) 1999 of Dun & Bradstreet. Reprinted by special arrangement with D&B. *Notes:* Values in parentheses above columns indicate the number of establishments in the sample. Data shown are for all companies.

D&B KEY BUSINESS RATIOS: SIC 8082

	1997			1996			1995		
	UQ	MED	LQ	UQ	MED	LQ	UQ	MED	LQ
Solvency									
Quick ratio	2.5	1.5	1.0	2.4	1.4	1.0	2.6	1.6	1.0
Current ratio	3.1	1.9	1.2	2.8	1.7	1.2	3.0	1.8	1.2
Current liabilities/Net worth (%)	27.1	66.4	161.2	30.8	70.4	174.4	30.7	70.1	183.4
Current liabilities/Investment (%)	135.6	316.9	509.3	184.5	376.1	705.5	184.8	359.4	635.1
Total liabilities/Net worth (%)	35.3	87.9	210.8	41.8	91.9	218.8	40.4	89.2	210.5
Fixed assets/Net worth (%)	11.6	32.0	72.0	11.6	30.9	72.0	11.9	32.5	73.2
Efficiency									
Collection period (days)	37.0	54.0	79.5	36.1	50.6	75.0	36.9	51.8	75.2
Sales to Inventory	213.4	66.8	28.2	302.4	118.6	32.7	277.0	85.6	31.3
Assets/Sales (%)	22.6	34.0	53.8	22.1	32.4	53.7	21.9	31.0	51.8
Sales/Net Working Capital	18.7	8.9	4.7	20.2	9.3	5.2	18.4	9.2	4.6
Accounts payable/Sales (%)	1.6	3.0	5.5	1.4	3.0	5.5	1.3	3.1	5.8
Profitability									
Return - Sales (%)	5.8	1.4	.1	5.7	1.5	-.3	5.6	1.6	.1
Return - Assets (%)	13.0	3.8	.1	11.8	4.2	-1.0	12.7	4.7	.3
Return - Net Worth (%)	25.8	10.0	.4	25.8	10.2	-.3	24.4	10.3	.8

Source: Dun & Bradstreet. Data in this table are copyright (c) 1999 of Dun & Bradstreet. Reprinted by special arrangement with D&B. *Note:* UQ stands for "Upper Quartile" and represents the top 25 percent of sample; MED stands for "Median"; and LQ stands for "Lower Quartile" and represents the lowest 25 percent.

D&B INDUSTRY NORMS: SIC 8092 - KIDNEY DIALYSIS CENTERS

	1997 (33) Estab.		1996 (59) Estab.		1995 (29) Estab.	
	$	%	$	%	$	%
Cash	805,498	12.8	418,910	16.1	639,591	12.1
Accounts Receivable	1,975,988	31.4	798,791	30.7	1,559,333	29.5
Notes Receivable	207,667	3.3	13,010	.5	31,715	.6
Inventory	157,324	2.5	62,446	2.4	153,290	2.9
Other Current Assets	264,304	4.2	169,125	6.5	422,870	8.0
Total Current Assets	3,410,781	54.2	1,462,282	56.2	2,806,799	53.1
Fixed Assets	2,026,331	32.2	785,782	30.2	1,538,189	29.1
Other Non-current Assets	855,842	13.6	353,862	13.6	940,886	17.8
Total Assets	6,292,954	100.0	2,601,926	100.0	5,285,874	100.0
Accounts Payable	490,850	7.8	353,862	13.6	385,869	7.3
Bank Loans	-	-	-	-	-	-
Notes Payable	144,738	2.3	62,446	2.4	68,716	1.3
Other Current Liabilities	711,104	11.3	273,202	10.5	592,018	11.2
Total Current Liabilities	1,346,692	21.4	689,510	26.5	1,046,603	19.8
Other Long Term	1,340,399	21.3	476,152	18.3	729,451	13.8
Deferred Credits	6,293	.1	2,602	.1	5,286	.1
Net Worth	3,599,570	57.2	1,433,661	55.1	3,504,534	66.3
Total Liabilities & Net Worth	6,292,954	100.0	2,601,925	100.0	5,285,874	100.0
Net Sales	4,136,515	100.0	2,653,325	100.0	5,603,300	100.0
Gross Profits	1,997,937	48.3	1,541,582	58.1	2,168,477	38.7
Net Profit After Tax	384,696	9.3	305,132	11.5	571,537	10.2
Working Capital	2,064,089	-	772,772	-	1,760,196	-

Source: Dun & Bradstreet. Data in this table are copyright (c) 1999 of Dun & Bradstreet. Reprinted by special arrangement with D&B. *Notes:* Values in parentheses above columns indicate the number of establishments in the sample. Data shown are for all companies.

D&B KEY BUSINESS RATIOS: SIC 8092

	1997			1996			1995		
	UQ	MED	LQ	UQ	MED	LQ	UQ	MED	LQ
Solvency									
Quick ratio	3.9	2.5	1.3	3.9	2.4	1.4	4.1	2.5	1.5
Current ratio	4.9	3.6	2.0	4.7	2.8	1.8	4.9	3.0	1.9
Current liabilities/Net worth (%)	15.6	25.9	48.2	12.7	26.2	70.4	13.2	18.2	48.8
Current liabilities/Investment (%)	408.6	529.4	584.0	314.0	402.6	801.1	277.4	438.7	674.1
Total liabilities/Net worth (%)	28.9	48.1	160.1	18.2	57.7	103.8	17.0	43.8	90.1
Fixed assets/Net worth (%)	29.1	39.9	71.7	23.0	41.8	87.1	23.7	45.3	81.9
Efficiency									
Collection period (days)	61.3	80.3	89.1	59.8	72.5	86.3	57.3	65.7	86.9
Sales to Inventory	66.3	52.3	38.2	98.9	57.9	42.6	57.2	39.0	27.8
Assets/Sales (%)	52.0	76.0	110.4	41.2	58.3	87.8	53.7	72.1	124.5
Sales/Net Working Capital	4.4	3.6	2.5	6.1	4.3	3.5	7.0	4.9	3.5
Accounts payable/Sales (%)	2.2	3.3	4.8	2.6	4.5	7.0	2.5	4.6	6.4
Profitability									
Return - Sales (%)	16.9	8.6	5.4	19.2	10.7	3.4	14.5	8.3	5.8
Return - Assets (%)	21.5	13.6	9.2	26.2	13.6	5.8	15.7	9.9	6.2
Return - Net Worth (%)	48.0	21.3	13.3	45.1	16.5	9.7	25.2	12.9	7.8

Source: Dun & Bradstreet. Data in this table are copyright (c) 1999 of Dun & Bradstreet. Reprinted by special arrangement with D&B. *Note:* UQ stands for "Upper Quartile" and represents the top 25 percent of sample; MED stands for "Median"; and LQ stands for "Lower Quartile" and represents the lowest 25 percent.

D&B INDUSTRY NORMS: SIC 8093 - SPECIALTY OUTPATIENT CLINICS NEC

	1997 (275) Estab.		1996 (720) Estab.		1995 (696) Estab.	
	$	%	$	%	$	%
Cash	470,232	16.8	445,820	17.6	379,006	18.7
Accounts Receivable	643,770	23.0	554,741	21.9	443,863	21.9
Notes Receivable	19,593	.7	10,132	.4	4,054	.2
Inventory	30,789	1.1	22,798	.9	16,214	.8
Other Current Assets	279,900	10.0	281,170	11.1	226,998	11.2
Total Current Assets	1,444,284	51.6	1,314,661	51.9	1,070,135	52.8
Fixed Assets	999,243	35.7	990,429	39.1	788,414	38.9
Other Non-current Assets	355,473	12.7	227,976	9.0	168,222	8.3
Total Assets	2,799,000	100.0	2,533,066	100.0	2,026,771	100.0
Accounts Payable	190,332	6.8	179,848	7.1	162,142	8.0
Bank Loans	2,799	.1	-	-	-	-
Notes Payable	58,779	2.1	63,327	2.5	56,750	2.8
Other Current Liabilities	487,026	17.4	435,687	17.2	342,524	16.9
Total Current Liabilities	738,936	26.4	678,862	26.8	561,416	27.7
Other Long Term	459,036	16.4	420,489	16.6	308,069	15.2
Deferred Credits	-	-	20,265	.8	12,161	.6
Net Worth	1,601,028	57.2	1,413,451	55.8	1,145,125	56.5
Total Liabilities & Net Worth	2,799,000	100.0	2,533,067	100.0	2,026,771	100.0
Net Sales	5,012,799	100.0	5,273,504	100.0	4,141,652	100.0
Gross Profits	2,571,566	51.3	3,021,718	57.3	1,971,426	47.6
Net Profit After Tax	280,717	5.6	205,667	3.9	120,108	2.9
Working Capital	705,348	-	635,799	-	508,720	-

Source: Dun & Bradstreet. Data in this table are copyright (c) 1999 of Dun & Bradstreet. Reprinted by special arrangement with D&B. *Notes:* Values in parentheses above columns indicate the number of establishments in the sample. Data shown are for all companies.

D&B KEY BUSINESS RATIOS: SIC 8093

	1997			1996			1995		
	UQ	MED	LQ	UQ	MED	LQ	UQ	MED	LQ
Solvency									
Quick ratio	3.3	1.5	1.0	2.9	1.6	.9	2.9	1.6	.9
Current ratio	4.7	2.0	1.2	3.6	2.0	1.2	3.7	2.0	1.3
Current liabilities/Net worth (%)	11.8	30.4	77.2	16.7	37.3	80.8	16.4	40.0	83.8
Current liabilities/Investment (%)	131.1	328.4	530.4	227.6	386.4	657.7	174.2	394.1	667.9
Total liabilities/Net worth (%)	20.6	52.4	125.8	28.5	64.4	136.1	27.2	67.7	143.7
Fixed assets/Net worth (%)	27.8	61.6	100.1	37.1	69.4	112.4	37.2	69.7	114.3
Efficiency									
Collection period (days)	26.3	45.6	67.9	23.0	42.0	63.2	24.7	40.4	62.2
Sales to Inventory	177.7	69.6	40.9	226.6	96.2	42.4	182.4	68.3	40.0
Assets/Sales (%)	39.8	63.2	96.8	38.1	56.5	86.3	36.6	55.8	85.7
Sales/Net Working Capital	15.8	8.1	3.9	14.3	7.6	3.8	13.8	7.7	4.1
Accounts payable/Sales (%)	1.6	2.7	5.2	1.6	2.7	5.0	1.6	2.9	5.2
Profitability									
Return - Sales (%)	10.0	3.8	.3	6.9	2.5	.2	6.1	2.2	-.1
Return - Assets (%)	10.0	4.6	.4	10.0	4.3	-.1	10.4	3.8	-.2
Return - Net Worth (%)	22.1	7.7	.7	20.4	8.3	.1	19.7	7.6	-.3

Source: Dun & Bradstreet. Data in this table are copyright (c) 1999 of Dun & Bradstreet. Reprinted by special arrangement with D&B. *Note:* UQ stands for "Upper Quartile" and represents the top 25 percent of sample; MED stands for "Median"; and LQ stands for "Lower Quartile" and represents the lowest 25 percent.

D&B/Gale Industry Reference Handbooks

D&B INDUSTRY NORMS: SIC 8099 - HEALTH AND ALLIED SERVICES NEC

	1997 (225) Estab.		1996 (329) Estab.		1995 (271) Estab.	
	$	%	$	%	$	%
Cash	517,238	19.3	397,005	22.2	429,041	25.1
Accounts Receivable	565,478	21.1	409,523	22.9	362,377	21.2
Notes Receivable	18,760	.7	8,942	.5	10,256	.6
Inventory	77,720	2.9	44,708	2.5	54,698	3.2
Other Current Assets	391,279	14.6	236,057	13.2	198,282	11.6
Total Current Assets	1,570,475	58.6	1,096,235	61.3	1,054,654	61.7
Fixed Assets	790,597	29.5	482,844	27.0	452,971	26.5
Other Non-current Assets	318,919	11.9	209,233	11.7	201,700	11.8
Total Assets	2,679,991	100.0	1,788,312	100.0	1,709,325	100.0
Accounts Payable	214,399	8.0	180,620	10.1	167,514	9.8
Bank Loans	-	-	5,365	.3	1,709	.1
Notes Payable	29,480	1.1	37,555	2.1	27,349	1.6
Other Current Liabilities	460,958	17.2	277,188	15.5	273,492	16.0
Total Current Liabilities	704,837	26.3	500,728	28.0	470,064	27.5
Other Long Term	345,719	12.9	180,620	10.1	170,933	10.0
Deferred Credits	10,720	.4	8,942	.5	10,256	.6
Net Worth	1,618,714	60.4	1,098,024	61.4	1,058,073	61.9
Total Liabilities & Net Worth	2,679,990	100.0	1,788,314	100.0	1,709,326	100.0
Net Sales	3,499,650	100.0	3,572,971	100.0	3,398,201	100.0
Gross Profits	1,571,343	44.9	1,618,556	45.3	1,491,810	43.9
Net Profit After Tax	174,983	5.0	167,930	4.7	108,742	3.2
Working Capital	865,637	-	595,508	-	584,589	-

Source: Dun & Bradstreet. Data in this table are copyright (c) 1999 of Dun & Bradstreet. Reprinted by special arrangement with D&B. *Notes:* Values in parentheses above columns indicate the number of establishments in the sample. Data shown are for all companies.

D&B KEY BUSINESS RATIOS: SIC 8099

	1997			1996			1995		
	UQ	MED	LQ	UQ	MED	LQ	UQ	MED	LQ
Solvency									
Quick ratio	3.5	1.7	.8	3.2	1.8	1.0	3.8	1.8	1.0
Current ratio	4.3	2.6	1.4	4.8	2.6	1.5	5.4	2.8	1.4
Current liabilities/Net worth (%)	12.9	29.4	73.4	12.3	31.2	85.0	11.4	30.4	80.0
Current liabilities/Investment (%)	153.9	262.4	401.6	138.0	279.2	495.0	145.4	233.3	468.8
Total liabilities/Net worth (%)	18.7	41.0	100.1	14.8	45.3	120.4	14.0	42.2	131.7
Fixed assets/Net worth (%)	12.5	44.2	77.1	12.2	42.9	77.4	12.9	39.3	78.5
Efficiency									
Collection period (days)	30.7	44.9	70.1	35.0	47.1	67.2	33.0	44.6	61.7
Sales to Inventory	71.6	40.0	22.3	90.6	39.3	22.1	73.7	32.2	18.7
Assets/Sales (%)	38.4	57.7	91.6	34.7	54.3	84.1	35.0	59.8	100.9
Sales/Net Working Capital	8.5	4.8	3.0	9.4	5.3	3.3	9.9	5.2	2.5
Accounts payable/Sales (%)	1.4	3.9	7.6	2.0	4.2	7.8	2.1	4.3	8.8
Profitability									
Return - Sales (%)	11.9	5.2	.9	9.9	3.9	1.1	8.0	2.8	-1.3
Return - Assets (%)	16.0	7.4	1.2	16.1	6.3	1.7	11.4	5.2	-1.5
Return - Net Worth (%)	29.2	11.6	2.9	25.3	9.9	2.8	19.5	8.2	-2.6

Source: Dun & Bradstreet. Data in this table are copyright (c) 1999 of Dun & Bradstreet. Reprinted by special arrangement with D&B. *Note:* UQ stands for "Upper Quartile" and represents the top 25 percent of sample; MED stands for "Median"; and LQ stands for "Lower Quartile" and represents the lowest 25 percent.

D&B INDUSTRY NORMS: SIC 8361 - RESIDENTIAL CARE

	1997 (490) Estab.		1996 (1154) Estab.		1995 (1046) Estab.	
	$	%	$	%	$	%
Cash	519,714	12.5	379,642	13.1	329,637	13.3
Accounts Receivable	515,556	12.4	423,112	14.6	361,857	14.6
Notes Receivable	8,315	.2	8,694	.3	7,435	.3
Inventory	16,631	.4	8,694	.3	9,914	.4
Other Current Assets	424,086	10.2	344,866	11.9	267,675	10.8
Total Current Assets	1,484,302	35.7	1,165,008	40.2	976,518	39.4
Fixed Assets	1,954,123	47.0	1,350,482	46.6	1,150,013	46.4
Other Non-current Assets	719,283	17.3	382,540	13.2	351,944	14.2
Total Assets	4,157,708	100.0	2,898,030	100.0	2,478,475	100.0
Accounts Payable	195,412	4.7	162,290	5.6	151,187	6.1
Bank Loans	4,158	.1	-	-	-	-
Notes Payable	62,366	1.5	69,553	2.4	76,833	3.1
Other Current Liabilities	544,660	13.1	408,622	14.1	317,245	12.8
Total Current Liabilities	806,596	19.4	640,465	22.1	545,265	22.0
Other Long Term	956,273	23.0	643,363	22.2	545,265	22.0
Deferred Credits	83,154	2.0	31,878	1.1	37,177	1.5
Net Worth	2,311,686	55.6	1,582,324	54.6	1,350,769	54.5
Total Liabilities & Net Worth	4,157,709	100.0	2,898,030	100.0	2,478,476	100.0
Net Sales	4,914,162	100.0	4,131,327	100.0	3,398,160	100.0
Gross Profits	1,611,845	32.8	1,677,319	40.6	1,818,016	53.5
Net Profit After Tax	260,451	5.3	185,910	4.5	149,519	4.4
Working Capital	677,707	-	524,543	-	431,255	-

Source: Dun & Bradstreet. Data in this table are copyright (c) 1999 of Dun & Bradstreet. Reprinted by special arrangement with D&B. *Notes:* Values in parentheses above columns indicate the number of establishments in the sample. Data shown are for all companies.

D&B KEY BUSINESS RATIOS: SIC 8361

	1997			1996			1995		
	UQ	MED	LQ	UQ	MED	LQ	UQ	MED	LQ
Solvency									
Quick ratio	2.7	1.4	.7	2.5	1.3	.7	2.5	1.3	.7
Current ratio	4.1	2.1	1.1	4.3	2.0	1.1	3.9	1.9	1.1
Current liabilities/Net worth (%)	7.5	22.3	64.0	9.4	25.2	72.7	9.9	27.0	74.7
Current liabilities/Investment (%)	261.6	466.0	731.0	187.8	406.3	700.5	235.8	376.9	644.0
Total liabilities/Net worth (%)	13.0	49.3	178.1	17.4	59.9	164.8	17.1	57.6	156.7
Fixed assets/Net worth (%)	41.3	81.3	163.1	40.7	82.9	149.8	41.7	79.1	140.8
Efficiency									
Collection period (days)	19.4	30.1	45.1	17.9	34.0	48.2	17.9	31.8	46.7
Sales to Inventory	282.3	137.0	76.8	347.5	160.0	84.6	300.0	162.0	82.9
Assets/Sales (%)	52.4	111.2	219.6	41.9	76.7	153.0	43.7	80.6	157.4
Sales/Net Working Capital	13.4	6.1	3.0	16.3	7.1	3.3	15.2	7.1	3.4
Accounts payable/Sales (%)	1.5	2.7	4.7	1.6	2.9	5.4	1.7	3.0	5.6
Profitability									
Return - Sales (%)	10.3	4.5	1.0	8.2	3.1	.2	8.0	2.7	.2
Return - Assets (%)	8.9	3.9	.6	9.4	4.1	.3	9.1	3.2	.2
Return - Net Worth (%)	18.6	8.2	1.4	21.4	8.0	.6	19.5	7.3	.5

Source: Dun & Bradstreet. Data in this table are copyright (c) 1999 of Dun & Bradstreet. Reprinted by special arrangement with D&B. *Note:* UQ stands for "Upper Quartile" and represents the top 25 percent of sample; MED stands for "Median"; and LQ stands for "Lower Quartile" and represents the lowest 25 percent.

CHAPTER 4

COMPANY DIRECTORY

This chapter presents brief profiles of 4,926 companies in the Health and Medical Services sector. Companies are public, private, and elements of public companies ("public family members").

Each entry features the *D-U-N-S* access number for the company, the company name, its parent (if applicable), address, telephone, sales, employees, the company's primary SIC classification, a brief description of the company's business activity, and the name and title of its chairman, president, or other high-ranking officer. If the company is an exporter, importer, or both, the fact is indicated by the abbreviations EXP, IMP, and IMP EXP shown facing the *D-U-N-S* number.

Rankings of these companies are shown in Chapter 5. Additional financial data—on an aggregated, industry level—are shown in Chapter 3.

This product includes proprietary data of Dun & Bradstreet, Inc.

D-U-N-S 14-478-3610
A I H CORPORATION
1616 23rd St, Zion, IL 60099
Phone: (847) 872-4561
Sales: $25,900,000   *Employees:* 572
Company Type: Private   *Employees here:* 5
SIC: 8062
   Hospital clinic & real estate holding company
Richard J Stephenson, Chairman of the Board

D-U-N-S 03-965-8554
A INFU-TECH DELAWARE CORP
   (Parent: Kuala Healthcare Inc)
910 Sylvan Ave, Englewood Cliffs, NJ 7632
Phone: (201) 567-4600
Sales: $26,003,000   *Employees:* 213
Company Type: Public   *Employees here:* 40
SIC: 8082
   Home health care services
Jack Rosen, President

D-U-N-S 06-989-5340
ABINGTON MEMORIAL HOSPITAL
1200 Old York Rd, Abington, PA 19001
Phone: (215) 576-2000
Sales: $249,389,000   *Employees:* 2,800
Company Type: Private   *Employees here:* 2,700
SIC: 8062
   General hospital
Felix M Pilla, President

D-U-N-S 07-992-0435
ABRAHAM BETH HEALTH SERVICES
612 Allerton Ave, Bronx, NY 10467
Phone: (718) 881-3000
Sales: $90,507,000   *Employees:* 973
Company Type: Private   *Employees here:* 970
SIC: 8059
   Nursing home daycare home health care long term program
William H Frohlich, President

D-U-N-S 61-528-7000
ACCESS HEALTH INC
310 Interlocken Pkwy, Broomfield, CO 80021
Phone: (303) 466-9500
Sales: $62,073,000   *Employees:* 1,026
Company Type: Public   *Employees here:* 342
SIC: 8082
   Personal health management services
Joseph P Tallman, Chief Executive Officer

D-U-N-S 07-849-4465
ACCORD MEDICAL MANAGEMENT
414 Navarro St Ste 600, San Antonio, TX 78205
Phone: (210) 271-1800
Sales: $38,325,000   *Employees:* 425
Company Type: Private   *Employees here:* 425
SIC: 8062
   Full service medical hospital
John F Strieby, President

D-U-N-S 09-977-8649
ADAIR COUNTY PUB HOSPITAL DST CORP
Westlake Dr, Columbia, KY 42728
Phone: (502) 384-4753
Sales: $24,970,000   *Employees:* 500
Company Type: Private   *Employees here:* 379
SIC: 8062
   General hospital & medical doctor's office
Rex A Tungate, Administrator

D-U-N-S 10-235-6821
ADAMS COUNTY MEMORIAL HOSPITAL
805 High St, Decatur, IN 46733
Phone: (219) 724-2145
Sales: $27,563,000   *Employees:* 400
Company Type: Private   *Employees here:* 396
SIC: 8062
   General medical and surgical hospital
Marvin L Baird, Executive Director

D-U-N-S 07-809-3002
ADDUS HEALTHCARE, INC.
10 W Kinzie St, Chicago, IL 60610
Phone: (312) 321-6240
Sales: $95,742,000   *Employees:* 7,000
Company Type: Private   *Employees here:* 60
SIC: 8082
   Home health care
W A Wright, President

D-U-N-S 04-964-9395
ADENA HEALTH SYSTEM INC
272 Hospital Rd, Chillicothe, OH 45601
Phone: (740) 772-7500
Sales: $82,630,000   *Employees:* 882
Company Type: Private   *Employees here:* 700
SIC: 8062
   Hospital
Allen Rupiper, President

D-U-N-S 06-054-4657
ADIRONDACK MEDICAL CENTER
Lake Colby Dr, Saranac Lake, NY 12983
Phone: (518) 891-4141
Sales: $30,000,000   *Employees:* 530
Company Type: Private   *Employees here:* 425
SIC: 8062
   Acute care general hospital
Chandler Ralph, President

D-U-N-S 13-202-7194
ADMIN OF THE TUL EDUC FUND
1430 Tulane Ave, New Orleans, LA 70112
Phone: (504) 588-5104
Sales: $113,600,000   *Employees:* NA
Company Type: Private   *Employees here:* 2,000
SIC: 8011
   Medical school
John Sintich, Manager

D-U-N-S 87-851-5311
ADVANCED RADIOLOGY LLC
7253 Ambassador Rd Ste A, Baltimore, MD 21244
Phone: (410) 281-9100
Sales: $21,700,000   *Employees:* 317
Company Type: Private   *Employees here:* 60
SIC: 8011
   Radiologist
Dorothy Hunt, Executive Director

D-U-N-S 87-261-4722
ADVANTAGE CARE INC
   (Parent: New Lexington Clinic Psc)
120 Prosper Pl, Lexington, KY 40509
Phone: (606) 264-4600
Sales: $43,132,000   *Employees:* 105
Company Type: Private   *Employees here:* 105
SIC: 8011
   Health maintenance organization
Thomas Donahue, President

D-U-N-S 07-228-8525
ADVENTIST HEALTH SYSTEM/WEST
2975 Sycamore Dr, Simi Valley, CA 93065
Phone: (805) 527-2462
Sales: $39,600,000   *Employees:* NA
Company Type: Private   *Employees here:* 880
SIC: 8069
   Acute care hospital
Alan J Rice, N/A

D-U-N-S 04-122-2019
ADVENTIST HEALTH SYSTEMS GA
1035 Red Bud Rd NE, Calhoun, GA 30701
Phone: (706) 629-2895
Sales: $43,830,000   *Employees:* 371
Company Type: Private   *Employees here:* 371
SIC: 8062
   Hospital
Dennis Kiley, President

D-U-N-S 08-776-4833
ADVENTIST HEALTHCARE INC
1801 Research Blvd, Rockville, MD 20850
Phone: (301) 315-3030
Sales: $961,200,000   *Employees:* NA
Company Type: Private   *Employees here:* NA
SIC: 8062
   Operator and management of hospitals nursing homes and
      retirement centers
Cory Chamber, President

D-U-N-S 03-849-6881
ADVENTIST HEALTH SYS/SNBLT CORP
4200 Sun N Lakes Blvd, Sebring, FL 33872
Phone: (941) 453-7511
Sales: $24,200,000   *Employees:* NA
Company Type: Private   *Employees here:* 600
SIC: 8062
   General hospital
Samuel Leonor, N/A

D-U-N-S 09-891-7404
ADVENTIST HEALTH SYS/SNBLT CORP
809 E Marion Ave, Punta Gorda, FL 33950
Phone: (941) 639-3131
Sales: $28,300,000   *Employees:* NA
Company Type: Private   *Employees here:* 700
SIC: 8062
   Hospital
David Jimez, N/A

D-U-N-S 60-997-0587
ADVENTIST HEALTH SYS/SNBLT CORP
7727 Lake Underhill Rd, Orlando, FL 32822
Phone: (407) 277-8110
Sales: $26,100,000   *Employees:* NA
Company Type: Private   *Employees here:* 600
SIC: 8062
   Hospital
Rich Reiner, President

D-U-N-S 06-786-3647
ADVENTIST HEALTH SYS/SNBLT CORP
601 E Altamonte Dr, Altamonte Springs, FL 32701
Phone: (407) 830-4321
Sales: $47,100,000   *Employees:* NA
Company Type: Private   *Employees here:* 1,070
SIC: 8062
   General hospital
Rich Reiner, Branch Manager

D-U-N-S 01-028-8194
ADVENTIST HEALTH SYS/SNBLT CORP
120 N Oak St, Hinsdale, IL 60521
Phone: (630) 856-9000
Sales: $138,300,000   *Employees:* NA
Company Type: Private   *Employees here:* 2,470
SIC: 8011
   Medical doctor's office
Rob Jepson, Controller

D-U-N-S 09-566-7556
ADVENTIST HEALTH SYS/SNBLT CORP
500 Hospital Dr, Madison, TN 37115
Phone: (615) 865-2373
Sales: $37,800,000   *Employees:* NA
Company Type: Private   *Employees here:* 900
SIC: 8062
   Hospital
Milton Siepman, N/A

D-U-N-S 08-513-8790
ADVENTIST HEALTH SYS/SNBLT CORP
2201 Clear Creek Rd, Killeen, TX 76542
Phone: (254) 526-7523
Sales: $30,700,000   *Employees:* NA
Company Type: Private   *Employees here:* 750
SIC: 8062
   Hospital
Ernie W Sadau, N/A

D-U-N-S 02-974-1717
ADVENTIST HEALTH SYS/SNBLT CORP
11801 S Fwy, Fort Worth, TX 76115
Phone: (817) 293-9110
Sales: $41,500,000   *Employees:* NA
Company Type: Private   *Employees here:* 1,008
SIC: 8062
   General hospital
A D Jimenez, President

D-U-N-S 19-426-7548
ADVENTIST HEALTH SYSTEM/SUNBELT
111 N Orlando Ave, Winter Park, FL 32789
Phone: (407) 647-4400
Sales: $828,000,000   *Employees:* 17,542
Company Type: Private   *Employees here:* 100
SIC: 8062
   Operates hospitals
Mardian J Blair, President

D-U-N-S 84-801-8941
ADVENTIST HEALTH SYSTEM/SUNBELT
6801 US Highway 27 N, Sebring, FL 33870
Phone: (941) 471-1515
Sales: $113,700,000   *Employees:* NA
Company Type: Private   *Employees here:* 2,309
SIC: 8011
   Cardiologist and cardio-vascular medical office
Diana Devries, Manager

D-U-N-S 82-484-3312
ADVENTIST HEALTH SYSTEM/SUNBELT
601 E Rollins St, Orlando, FL 32803
Phone: (407) 896-6611
Sales: $221,100,000   *Employees:* NA
Company Type: Private   *Employees here:* 5,000
SIC: 8062
   Hospital
Thomas L Werner, President

D-U-N-S 93-233-3651
ADVENTIST HEALTH SYSTEM/SUNBELT
608 E Altamonte Dr, Altamonte Springs, FL 32701

Phone: (407) 834-0729
Sales: $58,900,000   *Employees:* NA
Company Type: Private   *Employees here:* 3,900
SIC: 8082
  Home health care services
Kathy Riesen, Director

D-U-N-S 80-227-1494
ADVENTIST HEALTH SYSTEM/SUNBELT
105 Redbud Dr, Portland, TN 37148
Phone: (615) 325-7301
Sales: $23,100,000   *Employees:* NA
Company Type: Private   *Employees here:* 600
SIC: 8062
  Hospital
Marcus Elliot, N/A

D-U-N-S 06-745-4694
ADVOCATE HEALTH CARE NETWORK
4440 W 95th St, Oak Lawn, IL 60453
Phone: (708) 346-3144
Sales: $178,700,000   *Employees:* NA
Company Type: Private   *Employees here:* 4,000
SIC: 8069
  Hospital
Coletta M Neuens, Chief Executive Officer

D-U-N-S 07-233-3339
ADVOCATE HEALTH CARE NETWORK
3815 Highland Ave, Downers Grove, IL 60515
Phone: (630) 963-5900
Sales: $84,800,000   *Employees:* NA
Company Type: Private   *Employees here:* 2,000
SIC: 8062
  Ret gifts/novelties
David M Mcconkey, N/A

D-U-N-S 14-408-1296
ADVOCATE HEALTH CARE NETWORK
3435 W Van Buren St, Chicago, IL 60624
Phone: (773) 265-7700
Sales: $26,400,000   *Employees:* NA
Company Type: Private   *Employees here:* 633
SIC: 8062
  Hospital
Johnny C Brown, President

D-U-N-S 09-897-4827
ADVOCATE HEALTH CARE NETWORK
450 W Highway 22, Barrington, IL 60010
Phone: (847) 381-9600
Sales: $84,800,000   *Employees:* NA
Company Type: Private   *Employees here:* 2,000
SIC: 8062
  General hospital
Russell E Feurer, Manager

D-U-N-S 60-331-2331
ADVOCATE MEDICAL GROUP, SC
1775 Dempster St 4S, Park Ridge, IL 60068
Phone: (847) 696-8655
Sales: $100,000,000   *Employees:* 1,200
Company Type: Private   *Employees here:* 75
SIC: 8093
  Medical group
Gerald Eisenberg, President

D-U-N-S 80-443-2003
AETNA HEALTH MANAGEMENT, INC
  (Parent: Ahp Holdings Inc)
151 Farmington Ave, Hartford, CT 6156
Phone: (860) 273-0123

Sales: $19,800,000   *Employees:* 290
Company Type: Public Family Member   *Employees here:* 1
SIC: 8011
  Holding company for health maintenance organizations
James W Mc Lane, President

D-U-N-S 14-746-0562
AETNA HEALTH PLANS OF CAL
  (Parent: Aetna Health Management Inc)
201 N Civic Dr Ste 300, Walnut Creek, CA 94596
Phone: (925) 941-3000
Sales: $940,000,000   *Employees:* 265
Company Type: Public Family Member *Employees here:* 265
SIC: 8011
  Health maintenance organization
Doug Werner, President

D-U-N-S 80-443-3241
AETNA HEALTH PLANS ILL INC
  (Parent: Ahp Holdings Inc)
100 N Riverside Plz Fl 20, Chicago, IL 60606
Phone: (312) 441-3000
Sales: $46,240,000   *Employees:* 265
Company Type: Public Family Member *Employees here:* 265
SIC: 8011
  Health maintenance organization
Kevin F Hickey, President

D-U-N-S 80-443-3217
AETNA HEALTH PLANS SOUTHERN NE
  (Parent: Phpsne Parent Corporation)
151 Farmington Ave, Hartford, CT 6156
Phone: (860) 273-0123
Sales: $116,738,000   *Employees:* 4
Company Type: Public Family Member   *Employees here:* 4
SIC: 8011
  Medical doctor's office
Joseph T Sebastianelli, President

D-U-N-S 10-711-1585
AETNA US HEALTHCARE AN OHIO CORP
  (Parent: Aetna Health Management Inc)
4059 Kinross Lakes Pkwy, Richfield, OH 44286
Phone: (216) 659-8000
Sales: $183,507,000   *Employees:* 5
Company Type: Public Family Member   *Employees here:* 5
SIC: 8011
  Health maintenance organization
Timothy E Nolan, Chief Executive Officer

D-U-N-S 01-034-5189
AFFILIATED COMMUNITY MED CTRS PA
101 Willmar Ave SW, Willmar, MN 56201
Phone: (320) 231-5000
Sales: $47,566,000   *Employees:* 650
Company Type: Private   *Employees here:* 500
SIC: 8011
  Medical clinic
Lynn Freeman, Chief Executive Officer

D-U-N-S 15-358-9353
AGE INC
401 Arnold St NE, Cullman, AL 35055
Phone: (256) 739-1239
Sales: $24,028,000   *Employees:* 750
Company Type: Private   *Employees here:* 4
SIC: 8059
  Owns nursing homes
Frank Brown, President

D-U-N-S 06-668-2907
AHM GEMCH, INC
  (Parent: Tenet Healthcare Corporation)
1701 Santa Anita Ave, El Monte, CA 91733
Phone: (626) 579-7777
Sales: $32,000,000   *Employees:* 340
Company Type: Public Family Member   *Employees here:* 340
SIC: 8062
  General hospital
Elizabeth Primeaux, Chief Executive Officer

D-U-N-S 07-798-7790
AHM-SMC INC
  (Parent: Tenet Healthcare Corporation)
16453 Colorado Ave, Paramount, CA 90723
Phone: (562) 531-3110
Sales: $22,500,000   *Employees:* 500
Company Type: Public Family Member   *Employees here:* 500
SIC: 8062
  General hospital
Gustavo Valdespino, Administrator

D-U-N-S 87-977-6904
AHOM HOLDINGS, INC (DE)
  (Parent: Counsel Corporation)
5200 Maryland Way Ste 400, Brentwood, TN 37027
Phone: (615) 221-8884
Sales: $30,300,000   *Employees:* 1,891
Company Type: Private   *Employees here:* 1,891
SIC: 8082
  Home health care services
Edward K Wissing, President

D-U-N-S 80-956-7001
AHS HOSPITAL CORPORATION
193 Morris Ave, Summit, NJ 7901
Phone: (908) 522-2973
Sales: $149,300,000   *Employees:* NA
Company Type: Private   *Employees here:* 3,000
SIC: 8062
  General hospital
Tom Helfrich, Manager

D-U-N-S 01-473-7857
AHS HOSPITAL CORPORATION
350 Boulevard, Passaic, NJ 7055
Phone: (973) 365-4303
Sales: $49,400,000   *Employees:* NA
Company Type: Private   *Employees here:* 1,000
SIC: 8062
  General hospitals
Irchard Oths, President

D-U-N-S 03-684-9479
AHS HOSPITAL CORPORATION
Bay & Highland Ave, Montclair, NJ 7042
Phone: (973) 429-6000
Sales: $89,500,000   *Employees:* NA
Company Type: Private   *Employees here:* 1,800
SIC: 8062
  Hospital

D-U-N-S 96-246-4756
AHS HOSPITAL CORPORATION
325 Columbia Tpke Fl 2, Florham Park, NJ 7932
Phone: (973) 660-3100
Sales: $499,900,000   *Employees:* 10,600
Company Type: Private   *Employees here:* 100
SIC: 8062
  Hospital
Richard Oths, President

D-U-N-S 60-796-3980
AIDS HEALTHCARE FOUNDATION
6255 W Sunset Blvd Fl 16, Los Angeles, CA 90028
Phone: (323) 462-2273
Sales: $31,599,000   *Employees:* 270
Company Type: Private   *Employees here:* 55
SIC: 8361
  Residential care service outpatient care & operates thrift
  stores
Michael Weinstein, President

D-U-N-S 03-011-2551
AIKEN REGIONAL MEDICAL CTRS
  (Parent: Universal Health Services)
202 University Pkwy, Aiken, SC 29801
Phone: (803) 641-5000
Sales: $47,900,000   *Employees:* 1,038
Company Type: Public Family Member   *Employees here:* 1,038
SIC: 8062
  General medical & surgical hospitals
Richard H Satcher, Chief Executive Officer

D-U-N-S 04-163-5665
AKRON GENERAL MEDICAL CENTER
400 Wabash Ave, Akron, OH 44307
Phone: (330) 384-6000
Sales: $220,534,000   *Employees:* 2,836
Company Type: Private   *Employees here:* 2,700
SIC: 8062
  General hospital
Michael A West, Chief Executive Officer

D-U-N-S 12-091-0104
ALABAMA DEPARTMENT MENTAL HEALTH
200 University Blvd, Tuscaloosa, AL 35401
Phone: (205) 759-0799
Sales: $60,000,000   *Employees:* NA
Company Type: Private   *Employees here:* 1,780
SIC: 8063
  Psychiatric hospital
James Reddoch, Branch Manager

D-U-N-S 19-732-4676
ALABAMA DEPARTMENT MENTAL HEALTH
Hwy 43 N, Mount Vernon, AL 36560
Phone: (334) 829-9411
Sales: $27,200,000   *Employees:* NA
Company Type: Private   *Employees here:* 793
SIC: 8063
  Psychiatric hospital
John T Barlette, Principal

D-U-N-S 07-546-8223
ALACARE HOME HEALTH SERVICES,
4752 Hwy 280 E, Birmingham, AL 35242
Phone: (205) 981-8000
Sales: $43,390,000   *Employees:* 700
Company Type: Private   *Employees here:* 150
SIC: 8082
  Home health care services
Charles D Beard Jr, President

D-U-N-S 15-324-8091
ALAMANCE REGIONAL MED CTR INC
1240 Huffman Mill Rd, Burlington, NC 27215
Phone: (336) 538-7000
Sales: $90,925,000   *Employees:* 1,350
Company Type: Private   *Employees here:* 1,050
SIC: 8062
  General hospital
Thomas E Ryan, President

D-U-N-S 07-394-5479
ALAMEDA HOSPITAL
2070 Clinton Ave, Alameda, CA 94501
Phone: (510) 522-3700
Sales: $35,752,000 *Employees:* 530
Company Type: Private *Employees here:* 530
SIC: 8062
General hospital
William J Cielo, President

D-U-N-S 06-062-3790
ALBANY COUNTY HOSPITAL DST
255 N 30th St, Laramie, WY 82072
Phone: (307) 742-2141
Sales: $27,338,000 *Employees:* 425
Company Type: Private *Employees here:* 425
SIC: 8062
Hospital
J M Boyd, President

D-U-N-S 05-707-0617
ALBANY GENERAL HOSPITAL, INC
1046 6th Ave SW, Albany, OR 97321
Phone: (541) 812-4000
Sales: $33,246,000 *Employees:* 550
Company Type: Private *Employees here:* 550
SIC: 8062
General hospital
Richard Delano, President

D-U-N-S 07-312-8365
ALBANY MEDICAL CENTER HOSP
43 New Scotland Ave, Albany, NY 12208
Phone: (518) 262-3125
Sales: $172,803,000 *Employees:* 6,000
Company Type: Private *Employees here:* 6,000
SIC: 8062
General medical and surgical hospital
Gary J Kochem, Vice-President

D-U-N-S 19-059-2162
ALBANY MEDICAL COLLEGE
47 New Scotland Ave, Albany, NY 12208
Phone: (518) 262-3125
Sales: $172,803,000 *Employees:* 1,568
Company Type: Private *Employees here:* 1,568
SIC: 8011
Physicians group & medical college
Dr James Mandell Md, Executive Vice-President

D-U-N-S 78-219-1183
ALBANY MEDICAL COLLEGE
47 New Scotland Ave, Albany, NY 12208
Phone: (518) 445-4378
Sales: $21,300,000 *Employees:* NA
Company Type: Private *Employees here:* 300
SIC: 8011
Medical doctor's office
Robert Baker, Branch Manager

D-U-N-S 07-473-8824
ALBEMARLE HOSPITAL
1144 N Road St, Elizabeth City, NC 27909
Phone: (252) 335-0531
Sales: $64,259,000 *Employees:* 810
Company Type: Private *Employees here:* 810
SIC: 8062
Hospital
Philip Bagby, Chief Executive Officer

D-U-N-S 06-901-9032
ALBERT EINSTEIN MEDICAL CTR
5501 Old York Rd Ste 1, Philadelphia, PA 19141

Phone: (215) 456-7890
Sales: $267,956,000 *Employees:* 4,450
Company Type: Private *Employees here:* 3,200
SIC: 8062
General hospital
Martin Goldsmith, President

D-U-N-S 10-381-7136
ALBERT EINSTEIN MEDICAL CTR
5501 Old York & Tabor Rds, Philadelphia, PA 19141
Phone: (215) 456-6200
Sales: $27,900,000 *Employees:* NA
Company Type: Private *Employees here:* 400
SIC: 8011
Medical doctor's office
Henretta Rosenburg, Manager

D-U-N-S 79-544-6699
ALBERT EINSTEIN MEDICAL CTR
1200 W Tabor Rd, Philadelphia, PA 19141
Phone: (215) 329-5715
Sales: $31,600,000 *Employees:* NA
Company Type: Private *Employees here:* 600
SIC: 8069
Specialty hospital specialty outpatient clinic
Ray Uhlhorn, President

D-U-N-S 01-602-3657
ALBERT GALLATIN HOME CARE
(Parent: Staff Builders Inc)
1983 Marcus Ave, New Hyde Park, NY 11042
Phone: (516) 358-1000
Sales: $25,000,000 *Employees:* 540
Company Type: Public Family Member *Employees here:* 85
SIC: 8082
Home health care
Gerald L Shuttlesworth, Executive Director

D-U-N-S 19-535-6928
ALBRIGHT CARE SERVICES
1 Maplewood Dr, Lewisburg, PA 17837
Phone: (717) 524-9930
Sales: $22,278,000 *Employees:* 600
Company Type: Private *Employees here:* 20
SIC: 8051
Skilled intermediate & residential care for the aged
Jerry Westling, President

D-U-N-S 07-800-5147
ALEGENT HEALTH-BERGEN MERCY
7500 Mercy Rd, Omaha, NE 68124
Phone: (402) 398-6060
Sales: $151,241,000 *Employees:* 2,500
Company Type: Private *Employees here:* 2,500
SIC: 8062
Hospital & extended care facility
Richard A Hachten Ii, President

D-U-N-S 14-714-8662
ALEGENT HEALTH-MERCY HOSPITAL
800 Mercy Dr, Council Bluffs, IA 51503
Phone: (712) 328-5000
Sales: $45,595,000 *Employees:* 690
Company Type: Private *Employees here:* 676
SIC: 8062
General medical & surgical hospital
Marie Knedler, Administrator

D-U-N-S 07-698-3956
ALEGENT HEALTH-IMMANUEL MED CTR
6901 N 72nd St, Omaha, NE 68122
Phone: (402) 572-2121

Sales: $176,237,000
Company Type: Private
SIC: 8062
  Hospital
Charles J Marr, President

Employees: 2,313
Employees here: 2,000

D-U-N-S 05-794-6774
ALEXANDRIA INOVA HOSPITAL
4320 Seminary Rd, Alexandria, VA 22304
Phone: (703) 504-3000
Sales: $122,006,000
Company Type: Private
SIC: 8062
  Hospital
H P Walters, Vice-President

Employees: 1,750
Employees here: 1,750

D-U-N-S 07-632-2411
ALEXIAN BROTHERS OF SAN JOSE,
225 N Jackson Ave, San Jose, CA 95116
Phone: (408) 259-5000
Sales: $90,000,000
Company Type: Private
SIC: 8062
  Hospital
Steven Barron, Chief Executive Officer

Employees: 1,200
Employees here: 1,200

D-U-N-S 06-620-5352
ALEXIAN BROTHERS MEDICAL CTR
800 Biesterfield Rd, Elk Grove Village, IL 60007
Phone: (847) 437-5500
Sales: $156,872,000
Company Type: Private
SIC: 8062
  Hospital
Michael Schwartz, President

Employees: 2,000
Employees here: 1,800

D-U-N-S 08-046-6774
ALICE HYDE HOSPITAL ASSN
115 Park St, Malone, NY 12953
Phone: (518) 483-3000
Sales: $23,874,000
Company Type: Private
SIC: 8062
  General hospital & skilled nursing facility
John Johnson, President

Employees: 480
Employees here: 480

D-U-N-S 08-157-2992
ALL CARE VISITING NURSE
16 City Hall Sq, Lynn, MA 1901
Phone: (781) 598-2454
Sales: $19,931,000
Company Type: Private
SIC: 8082
  Visiting nurse service
Christophe M Attaya, Chief Financial Officer

Employees: 600
Employees here: 560

D-U-N-S 06-966-5925
ALL CHILDREN'S HOSPITAL INC
801 6th St S, Saint Petersburg, FL 33701
Phone: (727) 898-7451
Sales: $129,064,000
Company Type: Private
SIC: 8069
  Children's hospital
J D Sexton, President

Employees: 1,688
Employees here: 1,683

D-U-N-S 80-019-9325
ALL SAINTS HEALTH CARE SYSTEM
3801 Spring St, Racine, WI 53405
Phone: (414) 636-4011

Sales: $250,000,000
Company Type: Private
SIC: 8062
  Hospital
Edward De Meulenaere, President

Employees: 2,700
Employees here: 2,661

D-U-N-S 15-470-7954
ALL SAINTS HEALTH SYSTEM
1400 8th Ave, Fort Worth, TX 76104
Phone: (817) 926-2544
Sales: $141,197,000
Company Type: Private
SIC: 8062
  Short-term acute care hospitals
James Schuessler, Chief Executive Officer

Employees: 1,300
Employees here: 1,200

D-U-N-S 10-350-4338
ALL SEASONS LIVING CENTERS
10900 NE 8th St Ste 900, Bellevue, WA 98004
Phone: (425) 646-5117
Sales: $21,000,000
Company Type: Private
SIC: 8059
  Operates nursing facilities
Kris Dyrud, President

Employees: 750
Employees here: 20

D-U-N-S 10-965-0481
ALLEGANY GENERAL HOSPITAL INC
25 Highland Park Dr, Uniontown, PA 15401
Phone: (724) 438-6311
Sales: $465,724,000
Company Type: Private
SIC: 8011
  Medical doctor's office
Riad Saradar, President

Employees: 5
Employees here: 5

D-U-N-S 11-342-2398
ALLEGHENY COUNTY
110 McIntyre Rd, Pittsburgh, PA 15237
Phone: (412) 369-2000
Sales: $21,700,000
Company Type: Private
SIC: 8062
  Long term nursing care facility for the elderly
Dennis Biondo, Executive Director

Employees: NA
Employees here: 450

D-U-N-S 09-421-4947
ALLEGHENY GENERAL HOSPITAL
320 E North Ave 22, Pittsburgh, PA 15212
Phone: (412) 359-3131
Sales: $477,831,000
Company Type: Private
SIC: 8062
  General hospital skilled nursing care facility and psychiatric
  hospital
Connie M Cibrone, President

Employees: 5,064
Employees here: 4,864

D-U-N-S 11-913-3924
ALLEGHENY HEALTH, EDUC & RES
120 5th Ave Ste 120, Pittsburgh, PA 15222
Phone: (412) 442-2194
Sales: $127,261,000
Company Type: Private
SIC: 8062
  General hospitals
Anthony M Sanzo, President

Employees: 1,200
Employees here: 1,200

D-U-N-S 04-870-3151
ALLEGHENY HOSPITAL CENTENIAL
1331 E Wyoming Ave, Philadelphia, PA 19124
Phone: (215) 537-7400

Sales: $34,300,000   *Employees:* NA
Company Type: Private   *Employees here:* 700
SIC: 8062
   General hospital
Ernest Emperellie, Vice-President

D-U-N-S 60-512-7364
ALLEGHENY HOSPITAL CENTENIAL
1800 Lombard St, Philadelphia, PA 19146
Phone: (215) 893-2000
Sales: $109,500,000   *Employees:* NA
Company Type: Private   *Employees here:* 2,200
SIC: 8062
   General hospital
Aronld Berman, Director

D-U-N-S 07-706-7338
ALLEGHENY HOSPITALS NJ
218a Sunset Rd, Willingboro, NJ 8046
Phone: (609) 835-2900
Sales: $88,870,000   *Employees:* 875
Company Type: Private   *Employees here:* 875
SIC: 8062
   Hospitals
Robert Mathews, President

D-U-N-S 79-096-3268
ALLEGHENY INTGRATED HEALTH GROUP
3477 Saint Vincent St, Philadelphia, PA 19149
Phone: (215) 624-3441
Sales: $117,589,000   *Employees:* 10
Company Type: Private   *Employees here:* 10
SIC: 8011
   Medical doctor's office
Dr Myron Rodas, President

D-U-N-S 87-810-7226
ALLEGHENY UNIV OF HEALTH SCENCES
320 E North Ave, Pittsburgh, PA 15212
Phone: (412) 359-6709
Sales: $199,000,000   *Employees:* NA
Company Type: Private   *Employees here:* 4,000
SIC: 8062
   3rd & 4th year medical school
Dr James E Wilberger Md, Principal

D-U-N-S 11-434-5663
ALLEGHENY UNIV OF HEALTH SCENCES
3300 Henry Ave, Philadelphia, PA 19129
Phone: (215) 842-4000
Sales: $20,000,000   *Employees:* NA
Company Type: Private   *Employees here:* 500
SIC: 8063
   Psychiatric hospital
Dr Trevor Price Md, Principal

D-U-N-S 02-105-2840
ALLEGHENY UNIV HOSPITAL GRADUATE
1 Graduate Plz, Philadelphia, PA 19146
Phone: (215) 893-2000
Sales: $40,603,000   *Employees:* 1,500
Company Type: Private   *Employees here:* 1,300
SIC: 8062
   General hospital
Arnold T Berman, President

D-U-N-S 80-727-7116
ALLEGHENY UNIVERSITY HOSPITAL
3300 Henry Ave, Philadelphia, PA 19129
Phone: (215) 842-7000

Sales: $112,644,000   *Employees:* NA
Company Type: Private   *Employees here:* NA
SIC: 8062
   Hospitals
Margaret M Mcgoldrick, Chief Operating Officer

D-U-N-S 87-651-9158
ALLEGHENY UNIVERSITY HOSPITAL
60 Township Line Rd, Elkins Park, PA 19027
Phone: (215) 663-6000
Sales: $34,300,000   *Employees:* NA
Company Type: Private   *Employees here:* 700
SIC: 8062
   General hospital
Meg Mc Goldrick, Principal

D-U-N-S 07-214-9826
ALLEGHENY VALLEY HOSPITAL
1301 Carlisle St, Natrona Heights, PA 15065
Phone: (724) 224-5100
Sales: $115,924,000   *Employees:* 1,350
Company Type: Private   *Employees here:* 1,350
SIC: 8062
   General hospital
John R England, President

D-U-N-S 07-496-1020
ALLEGHENY VALLEY SCHOOL
1996 Ewings Mill Rd, Coraopolis, PA 15108
Phone: (412) 262-3500
Sales: $51,574,000   *Employees:* 1,500
Company Type: Private   *Employees here:* 355
SIC: 8361
   Residential care facility for mentally handicapped children
Regis G Champ, Executive Director

D-U-N-S 18-646-4855
ALLEGIANT PHYSICIAN SERVICES
500 Northridge Rd Ste 500, Atlanta, GA 30350
Phone: (770) 643-5555
Sales: $57,607,000   *Employees:* 48
Company Type: Public   *Employees here:* 20
SIC: 8099
   Provider of contract medical services
Richard L Jackson, Chairman of the Board

D-U-N-S 07-276-0465
ALLEN MEMORIAL HOSPITAL CORP
1825 Logan Ave, Waterloo, IA 50703
Phone: (319) 235-3941
Sales: $72,204,000   *Employees:* 1,185
Company Type: Private   *Employees here:* 1,175
SIC: 8062
   Hospital
Richard A Seidler, President

D-U-N-S 84-952-8864
ALLIANCE HEALTH CARE, INC.
2204 E 117th St, Burnsville, MN 55337
Phone: (612) 882-1030
Sales: $24,100,000   *Employees:* 1,500
Company Type: Private   *Employees here:* 700
SIC: 8082
   Home health care services
Alana Fiala, President

D-U-N-S 10-922-0046
ALLIANCE IMAGING INC
1065 PCF Center Dr Ste 200, Anaheim, CA 92806
Phone: (714) 688-7100

Sales: $86,474,000   *Employees:* 613
Company Type: Public   *Employees here:* 70
SIC: 8099
   Medical services specializing in comprehensive magnetic
     resonance imaging services
Richard N Zehner, Chairman of the Board

D-U-N-S 07-407-9948
ALLIANT HOSPITALS, INC
200 E Chestnut St, Louisville, KY 40202
Phone: (502) 629-8000
Sales: $295,847,000   *Employees:* 3,800
Company Type: Private   *Employees here:* 3,800
SIC: 8062
   Hospital
Steven A Williams, President

D-U-N-S 18-514-5414
ALLIED SERVICES FOUNDATION
475 Morgan Hwy, Scranton, PA 18508
Phone: (717) 348-1300
Sales: $93,871,000   *Employees:* 1,954
Company Type: Private   *Employees here:* 1,042
SIC: 8093
   Outpatient & residential rehabilitation center
James L Brady, President

D-U-N-S 07-177-2503
ALLINA HEALTH SYSTEM
4050 Coon Rapids Blvd Nw, Minneapolis, MN 55433
Phone: (612) 421-8888
Sales: $49,800,000   *Employees:* NA
Company Type: Private   *Employees here:* 1,200
SIC: 8062
   General hospital
Marv Dnhe, Administrator

D-U-N-S 13-494-1343
ALLINA HEALTH SYSTEM
550 Osborne Rd NE, Minneapolis, MN 55432
Phone: (612) 421-2222
Sales: $54,000,000   *Employees:* NA
Company Type: Private   *Employees here:* 1,300
SIC: 8062
   General hospital
Marvin Dehne, Director

D-U-N-S 80-794-8708
ALLINA HEALTH SYSTEM
800 E 28th St, Minneapolis, MN 55407
Phone: (612) 863-4000
Sales: $215,100,000   *Employees:* NA
Company Type: Private   *Employees here:* 5,167
SIC: 8062
   General hospital
Gordon M Sprenger, Principal

D-U-N-S 87-682-9391
ALLINA HEALTH SYSTEM
4050 Coon Rapids Blvd Nw, Minneapolis, MN 55433
Phone: (612) 422-4522
Sales: $58,200,000   *Employees:* NA
Company Type: Private   *Employees here:* 1,400
SIC: 8062
   General hospital

D-U-N-S 11-621-3349
ALLINA HEALTH SYSTEM
5601 Smetana Dr Ste Ll, Hopkins, MN 55343
Phone: (612) 992-2000

Sales: $2,526,711,000   *Employees:* 21,000
Company Type: Private   *Employees here:* 800
SIC: 8011
   General hospitals
Gordon M Sprenger, Chief Executive Officer

D-U-N-S 14-465-2476
ALLINA SELF-INSURED
5601 Smetana Dr, Hopkins, MN 55343
Phone: (612) 992-2500
Sales: $37,775,000   *Employees:* 87
Company Type: Private   *Employees here:* 87
SIC: 8011
   Medical doctor's office
David Strand, Chief Executive Officer

D-U-N-S 03-167-2942
ALPENA GENERAL HOSPITAL
1501 W Chisholm St, Alpena, MI 49707
Phone: (517) 356-7390
Sales: $36,600,000   *Employees:* 799
Company Type: Private   *Employees here:* 793
SIC: 8062
   Hospital
John A Mcveety, Chief Executive Officer

D-U-N-S 07-395-7789
ALTA BATES MEDICAL CENTER
2450 Ashby Ave, Berkeley, CA 94705
Phone: (510) 204-4444
Sales: $287,531,000   *Employees:* 1,550
Company Type: Private   *Employees here:* 1,500
SIC: 8062
   General hospital
Albert Greene, President

D-U-N-S 08-390-6024
ALTA MED
500 Citadel Dr Ste 490, Los Angeles, CA 90040
Phone: (323) 725-8751
Sales: $24,000,000   *Employees:* 400
Company Type: Private   *Employees here:* 30
SIC: 8099
   Medical clinic
Castulo D La Rocha, President

D-U-N-S 14-474-5486
ALTERNATIVE LIVING SERVICES
450 N Sunny Slope Rd, Brookfield, WI 53005
Phone: (414) 789-9565
Sales: $130,744,000   *Employees:* 5,935
Company Type: Public   *Employees here:* 30
SIC: 8059
   Residential assisted living facilities
Timothy Buchanan, President

D-U-N-S 62-647-8747
ALTON MEMORIAL HOSPITAL
1 Memorial Dr, Alton, IL 62002
Phone: (618) 463-7311
Sales: $53,332,000   *Employees:* 1,000
Company Type: Private   *Employees here:* 1,000
SIC: 8062
   General medical hospital
Ronald Mc Mullen, President

D-U-N-S 07-652-1392
ALTRU HEALTH SYSTEM
1200 S Columbia Rd, Grand Forks, ND 58201
Phone: (701) 780-5000

Sales: $135,817,000   *Employees:* 3,200
Company Type: Private   *Employees here:* 200
SIC: 8062
   Hospital
David Molmen, Chief Operating Officer

D-U-N-S 07-941-1518
ALVIN COMMUNITY HOSPITAL, INC.
   (Parent: Clear Lk Regional Med Ctr Inc)
301 Medic Ln, Alvin, TX 77511
Phone: (281) 331-6141
Sales: $36,700,000   *Employees:* 800
Company Type: Public Family Member   *Employees here:* 800
SIC: 8062
   Hospital
Hudson Connery, President

D-U-N-S 94-436-2318
ALWAYS CARING HOME CARE SVCS
1302 Montana Ave, El Paso, TX 79902
Phone: (915) 545-4663
Sales: $21,000,000   *Employees:* 400
Company Type: Private   *Employees here:* 400
SIC: 8082
   Home health care services
Magdalene Ullrich-Allen, President

D-U-N-S 80-850-6331
AMEDISYS INC
3029 S Sherwood Frst, Baton Rouge, LA 70816
Phone: (225) 293-2662
Sales: $54,496,000   *Employees:* 700
Company Type: Public   *Employees here:* 150
SIC: 8082
   Nurse registry home health care services ambulatory surgery
   centers infusion therapy services & dme
William F Borne, Chairman of the Board

D-U-N-S 62-487-7056
AMERICA SERVICE GROUP INC
105 Westpark Dr Ste 300, Brentwood, TN 37027
Phone: (615) 373-3100
Sales: $129,890,000   *Employees:* 1,858
Company Type: Public   *Employees here:* 45
SIC: 8011
   Managed healthcare & related services
Michael Catalano, President

D-U-N-S 06-817-5637
AMERICAN BAPTIST HOMES
11985 Technology Dr, Eden Prairie, MN 55344
Phone: (612) 941-3175
Sales: $49,315,000   *Employees:* 1,340
Company Type: Private   *Employees here:* 15
SIC: 8051
   Skilled & intermediate nursing care services independent
   living and manage hud centers
Robert B Inhoff, President

D-U-N-S 06-773-8088
AMERICAN CLINICAL LABORATORIES
   (Parent: Quest Diagnostics A Cal Corp)
7470 Mission Valley Rd, San Diego, CA 92108
Phone: (619) 686-3000
Sales: $30,000,000   *Employees:* 300
Company Type: Private   *Employees here:* 280
SIC: 8071
   Medical laboratory
Nina Green, President

D-U-N-S 94-269-1734
AMERICAN HABILITATION SERVICES
15915 Katy Fwy Ste 340, Houston, TX 77094

Phone: (281) 398-7900
Sales: $66,900,000   *Employees:* 3,000
Company Type: Private   *Employees here:* 7
SIC: 8059
   Management for intermediate care facilities for the mentally
   retarded & developmentally disabled
Bill Wooten, President

D-U-N-S 09-794-7717
AMERICAN HEALTH CARE CENTERS
200 Smokerise Dr, Wadsworth, OH 44281
Phone: (330) 336-6684
Sales: $34,200,000   *Employees:* 1,500
Company Type: Private   *Employees here:* 50
SIC: 8051
   Skilled nursing homes & homes for retarded with health care
Robert Leatherman Sr, Chairman of the Board

D-U-N-S 11-870-6662
AMERICAN HEALTH CENTERS INC
52 W 8th St, Parsons, TN 38363
Phone: (901) 847-6343
Sales: $95,000,000   *Employees:* 3,000
Company Type: Private   *Employees here:* 50
SIC: 8051
   Manages & operates nursing homes
Jerry Ivey, President

D-U-N-S 05-995-1988
AMERICAN HEALTHCORP INC
1 Burton Hills Blvd, Nashville, TN 37215
Phone: (615) 665-1122
Sales: $30,537,000   *Employees:* 650
Company Type: Public   *Employees here:* 70
SIC: 8092
   Diabetes treatment centers
Thomas G Cigarran, Chairman of the Board

D-U-N-S 10-823-7371
AMERICAN HOME PRODUCTS CORP
865 Ridge Rd, Monmouth Junction, NJ 8852
Phone: (732) 329-2300
Sales: $24,600,000   *Employees:* NA
Company Type: Public Family Member   *Employees here:* 475
SIC: 8071
   Medical laboratory
Dr Alan Lewis, Research

D-U-N-S 55-628-0899
AMERICAN HOMEPATIENT INC
5200 Maryland Way Ste 400, Brentwood, TN 37027
Phone: (615) 221-8884
Sales: $387,277,000   *Employees:* 3,700
Company Type: Public   *Employees here:* 125
SIC: 8082
   Home health care services and rental and sale of home health
   care equipment and supplies
Edward K Wissing, President

D-U-N-S 04-308-9937
AMERICAN HOSPITAL MGT CORP
3800 Janes Rd, Arcata, CA 95521
Phone: (707) 822-3621
Sales: $41,344,000   *Employees:* 540
Company Type: Public   *Employees here:* 500
SIC: 8062
   General hospital
Allen E Shaw, President

D-U-N-S 06-953-5698
AMERICAN LEGION HOSPITAL
1305 Crowley Rayne Hwy, Crowley, LA 70526
Phone: (318) 783-3222

Sales: $24,965,000   *Employees:* 389
Company Type: Private   *Employees here:* 386
SIC: 8062
    General medical hospital
Leonard J Spears, Administrator

D-U-N-S 60-620-2711
AMERICAN MEDICAL HOLDINGS INC
    (Parent: Tenet Healthcare Corporation)
14001 Dallas Pkwy Ste 200, Dallas, TX 75240
Phone: (972) 789-2200
Sales: $1,426,400,000   *Employees:* NA
Company Type: Public   *Employees here:* NA
SIC: 8062
    General medical surgical & psychiatric hospitals
Robert W O Leary, Chairman of the Board

D-U-N-S 04-476-4280
AMERICAN MEDICAL LABORATORIES
14225 Newbrook Dr, Chantilly, VA 20151
Phone: (703) 802-6900
Sales: $47,700,000   *Employees:* 1,000
Company Type: Private   *Employees here:* 800
SIC: 8071
    Clinical & anatomical pathology laboratory
Timothy J Brodnik, President

D-U-N-S 07-706-2727
AMERICAN ONCOLOGIC HOSPITAL
7701 Burholme Ave Ste 1, Philadelphia, PA 19111
Phone: (215) 728-6900
Sales: $62,293,000   *Employees:* 725
Company Type: Private   *Employees here:* 725
SIC: 8069
    Specialty hospital
Dr Robert Young Md, President

D-U-N-S 06-656-5466
AMERICAN PHRM SVCS DEL
    (Parent: Mariner Post-Acute Network)
1771 W Diehl Rd Ste 210, Naperville, IL 60563
Phone: (630) 305-8000
Sales: $221,117,000   *Employees:* 1,500
Company Type: Public Family Member   *Employees here:* 165
SIC: 8051
    Pharmaceutical and infusion therapy
William R Korslin, President

D-U-N-S 14-763-1394
AMERICAN REHABILITY SERVICES
    (Parent: Mariner Post-Acute Network)
111 Westwood Pl Ste 210, Brentwood, TN 37027
Phone: (615) 377-2937
Sales: $246,292,000   *Employees:* 3,800
Company Type: Public Family Member   *Employees here:* 150
SIC: 8051
    Rehabilitation services
Kelly Gill, President

D-U-N-S 08-954-9737
AMERICAN RETIREMENT CORP
111 Westwood Pl Ste 402, Brentwood, TN 37027
Phone: (615) 221-2250
Sales: $94,212,000   *Employees:* 2,500
Company Type: Public   *Employees here:* 60
SIC: 8059
    Independent assisted living and /or nursing facilities
W E Sheriff, Chief Executive Officer

D-U-N-S 05-866-9235
AMERICAN SHARED HOSPITAL SVCS
4 Embarcadero Ctr 3260, San Francisco, CA 94111
Phone: (415) 788-5300

Sales: $37,172,000   *Employees:* 189
Company Type: Public   *Employees here:* 15
SIC: 8099
    Diagnostic imaging radiotherapy & insurance services
Dr Ernest A Bates Md, Chairman of the Board

D-U-N-S 19-620-6817
AMERICAN TRANSITIONAL HOSPITALS
    (Parent: Beverly Enterprises Inc)
112 2nd Ave N, Franklin, TN 37064
Phone: (615) 791-7099
Sales: $900,000,000   *Employees:* 1,200
Company Type: Public Family Member   *Employees here:* 13
SIC: 8011
    Acute care facility
T J Moore, President

D-U-N-S 05-566-8693
AMERICAN TRANSITIONAL HOSPITALS
1917 Ashland St, Houston, TX 77008
Phone: (713) 861-6161
Sales: $23,000,000   *Employees:* NA
Company Type: Public Family Member   *Employees here:* 566
SIC: 8062
    General hospital
Pattrick Candy, Owner

D-U-N-S 96-911-8504
AMERICARE CERTIF SPECIAL SVCS
171 Kings Hwy, Brooklyn, NY 11223
Phone: (718) 259-9300
Sales: $20,000,000   *Employees:* 300
Company Type: Private   *Employees here:* 200
SIC: 8082
    Home health care services
Martin Kleinman, President

D-U-N-S 07-594-0312
AMERICUS SUMTER COUNTY HOSPITAL AUTH
100 Wheatley Dr, Americus, GA 31709
Phone: (912) 924-6011
Sales: $39,821,000   *Employees:* 650
Company Type: Private   *Employees here:* 550
SIC: 8062
    Hospital authority
John N Cook, Chairman of the Board

D-U-N-S 14-774-7455
AMICARE HOME HEALTH SERVICES
39500 Orchard Hill Pl, Novi, MI 48375
Phone: (248) 305-7600
Sales: $80,184,000   *Employees:* 927
Company Type: Private   *Employees here:* 125
SIC: 8082
    Health services
Gary Baum, Chief Executive Officer

D-U-N-S 11-839-2133
AMISUB (IRVINE MEDICAL CENTER)
16200 Sand Canyon Ave, Irvine, CA 92618
Phone: (949) 753-2000
Sales: $27,200,000   *Employees:* 600
Company Type: Private   *Employees here:* 590
SIC: 8062
    General hospital
Richard Robinson, Chief Executive Officer

D-U-N-S 07-602-2441
AMISUB (NORTH RIDGE HOSPITAL)
    (Parent: Tenet Health System Medical)
5757 N Dixie Hwy, Fort Lauderdale, FL 33334
Phone: (954) 776-6000

Sales: $103,543,000 — Employees: 700
Company Type: Public Family Member — Employees here: 600
SIC: 8062
   Hospital
Emil Miller, Administrator

D-U-N-S 05-922-6795
AMISUB OF CALIFORNIA, INC
   (Parent: Tenet Health System Medical)
18321 Clark St, Tarzana, CA 91356
Phone: (818) 881-0800
Sales: $102,446,000 — *Employees:* 800
Company Type: Public Family Member — *Employees here:* 400
SIC: 8062
   Hospital
Robert W O Leary, Chairman of the Board

D-U-N-S 79-557-2247
AMISUB OF NORTH CAROLINA INC
   (Parent: Tenet Healthcare Corporation)
1135 Carthage St, Sanford, NC 27330
Phone: (919) 774-2100
Sales: $96,000,000 — *Employees:* 700
Company Type: Public Family Member — *Employees here:* 700
SIC: 8062
   General hospital
Elaine Hylwa, Chief Executive Officer

D-U-N-S 15-450-2637
AMISUB CULVER UNION HOSPITAL
   (Parent: Tenet Health System Medical)
1710 Lafayette Rd, Crawfordsville, IN 47933
Phone: (765) 362-2800
Sales: $29,358,000 — *Employees:* 350
Company Type: Public Family Member — *Employees here:* 350
SIC: 8062
   General hospital
Greg Starnes, Chief Executive Officer

D-U-N-S 10-903-1369
AMMONS-SPRINGMOOR ASSOCIATES
1500 Sawmill Rd, Raleigh, NC 27615
Phone: (919) 848-7000
Sales: $24,000,000 — *Employees:* 425
Company Type: Private — *Employees here:* 425
SIC: 8059
   Senior citizen residential complex
David Ammons, President

D-U-N-S 08-045-7476
AMSTERDAM MEMORIAL HOSPITAL
4988 State Highway 30, Amsterdam, NY 12010
Phone: (518) 842-3100
Sales: $30,021,000 — *Employees:* 480
Company Type: Private — *Employees here:* 480
SIC: 8062
   General hospital & skilled nursing facility
Cornelio Catena, President

D-U-N-S 07-010-1761
AMSTERDAM NURSING HOME CORP
1060 Amsterdam Ave, New York, NY 10025
Phone: (212) 678-2600
Sales: $20,897,000 — *Employees:* 340
Company Type: Private — *Employees here:* 340
SIC: 8051
   Skilled nursing home
James Davis, President

D-U-N-S 78-605-6820
AMSURG, CORP
1 Burton Hills Blvd, Nashville, TN 37215
Phone: (615) 665-1283

Sales: $57,414,000 — Employees: 64
Company Type: Public — Employees here: 50
SIC: 8062
   Owns develops & manages ambulatory surgery facilities
Thomas G Cigarran, Chairman of the Board

D-U-N-S 06-617-0804
ANAHEIM MEMORIAL HOSPITAL ASSN
1111 W La Palma Ave, Anaheim, CA 92801
Phone: (714) 774-1450
Sales: $58,528,000 — *Employees:* 775
Company Type: Private — *Employees here:* 775
SIC: 8062
   Hospital
Michael C Carter, President

D-U-N-S 93-338-9686
ANCILLA HEALTH CARE INC
1000 S Lake Park Ave, Hobart, IN 46342
Phone: (219) 947-8500
Sales: $67,459,000 — *Employees:* 800
Company Type: Private — *Employees here:* 2
SIC: 8062
   General medical & surgical hospital
Stephen L Crain, Chief Executive Officer

D-U-N-S 92-862-9484
ANCILLA HEALTH SERVICES, INC
   (Parent: Ancilla Systems Incorporated)
800 Broadway Ste 314, Fort Wayne, IN 46802
Phone: (219) 425-3635
Sales: $23,003,000 — *Employees:* 80
Company Type: Private — *Employees here:* 80
SIC: 8011
   Medical doctor's office
William Harkins, President

D-U-N-S 07-370-0643
ANDERSON AREA MEDICAL CENTER
800 N Fant St, Anderson, SC 29621
Phone: (864) 261-1000
Sales: $162,178,000 — *Employees:* 2,500
Company Type: Private — *Employees here:* 2,420
SIC: 8062
   Hospital and general family practice
John A Miller Jr, President

D-U-N-S 07-210-5505
ANDERSON INFIRMARY BENEVOLENT
2124 14th St, Meridian, MS 39301
Phone: (601) 483-8811
Sales: $135,000,000 — *Employees:* 900
Company Type: Private — *Employees here:* 881
SIC: 8062
   General medical and surgical hospital
Mark D Mc Phail, Chief Executive Officer

D-U-N-S 06-991-0263
ANDROSCOGGIN VALLEY HOSPITAL
59 Page Hill Rd, Berlin, NH 3570
Phone: (603) 752-2200
Sales: $22,380,000 — *Employees:* 345
Company Type: Private — *Employees here:* 345
SIC: 8062
   General hospital
Donald F Saunders, President

D-U-N-S 04-801-1308
ANESTHESIA ASSOCIATION OF KANSAS CITY
6400 Prospect Ave Ste 216, Kansas City, MO 64132
Phone: (816) 444-1139

Sales: $46,000,000
Company Type: Private
SIC: 8011
  Anesthesiologist physician
Mark Meisel, Chief Operating Officer

Employees: 109
Employees here: 109

D-U-N-S 06-071-6800
ANGLETON-DANBURY HOSPITAL DST
132 E Hospital Dr, Angleton, TX 77515
Phone: (409) 849-7721
Sales: $25,364,000
Company Type: Private
SIC: 8062
  General medical and surgical hospital
David A Bleakney, Administrator

Employees: 210
Employees here: 210

D-U-N-S 17-737-8619
ANNE ARUNDEL HEALTH CARE SVCS
  (Parent: Arundel Health Anne System)
Franklin & Cathedral Sts, Annapolis, MD 21401
Phone: (410) 224-2618
Sales: $138,830,000
Company Type: Private
SIC: 8093
  Diagnostic treatment & mri services
Martin L Doordan, President

Employees: 45
Employees here: 1

D-U-N-S 06-938-3289
ANNE ARUNDEL MEDICAL CENTER
64 Franklin St, Annapolis, MD 21401
Phone: (410) 267-1000
Sales: $130,365,000
Company Type: Private
SIC: 8062
  General medical & surgical hospital
Martin L Doordan, President

Employees: 1,800
Employees here: 1,800

D-U-N-S 78-898-0183
ANNE ARUNDEL MEDICAL CENTER
140 Jennifer Rd, Annapolis, MD 21401
Phone: (410) 897-6700
Sales: $134,661,000
Company Type: Private
SIC: 8062
  General hospital
Carl Brunetto, President

Employees: 50
Employees here: 50

D-U-N-S 07-157-2960
ANNIE PENN MEMORIAL HOSPITAL
618 S Main St, Reidsville, NC 27320
Phone: (336) 634-1010
Sales: $32,365,000
Company Type: Private
SIC: 8062
  General hospital
Susan Fitzgibbon, President

Employees: 500
Employees here: 498

D-U-N-S 04-034-9482
ANTELOPE VALLEY HEALTH CARE SYSTMS
1600 W Avenue J, Lancaster, CA 93534
Phone: (805) 949-5000
Sales: $129,908,000
Company Type: Private
SIC: 8062
  General hospital
Robert J Harenski, President

Employees: 1,550
Employees here: 1,510

D-U-N-S 01-271-2522
ANTHEM ALLIANCE FOR HEALTH
514 Butler Farm Rd, Hampton, VA 23666
Phone: (757) 766-7221

Sales: $22,200,000
Company Type: Private
SIC: 8011
  Health care services
Denise Curate, Branch Manager

Employees: NA
Employees here: 350

D-U-N-S 13-936-9540
ANTIETAM HEALTH SERVICES INC
  (Parent: Washington County Health Sys)
11110 Med Campus Rd 229, Hagerstown, MD 21742
Phone: (301) 665-4500
Sales: $31,816,000
Company Type: Private
SIC: 8071
  Medical laboratory pharmacy whol medical equipment child
  care center collection agency & provides bo-gin services
John J Mc Elwee Jr, President

Employees: 460
Employees here: 232

D-U-N-S 07-799-0513
APALACHEE CENTER FOR HUMANSVCS
625 E Tennessee St, Tallahassee, FL 32308
Phone: (850) 487-2930
Sales: $20,112,000
Company Type: Private
SIC: 8063
  Specialty outpatient clinic psychiatric hospital
Ron Kirkland, Executive Director

Employees: 443
Employees here: 75

D-U-N-S 05-868-5439
APPALCHIAN REGIONAL HEALTHCARE
1220 Harrodsburg Rd, Lexington, KY 40504
Phone: (606) 226-2440
Sales: $298,521,000
Company Type: Private
SIC: 8062
  General hospital
Dr Forrest W Calico, President

Employees: 4,000
Employees here: 200

D-U-N-S 07-478-1121
APPLETON MEDICAL CENTER
1818 N Meade St, Appleton, WI 54911
Phone: (920) 731-4101
Sales: $57,000,000
Company Type: Private
SIC: 8062
  Hospital
Patrick Hawley, Senior Vice-President

Employees: 1,230
Employees here: 1,230

D-U-N-S 78-757-2320
APRIA HEALTHCARE GROUP INC
3560 Hyland Ave, Costa Mesa, CA 92626
Phone: (714) 957-2000
Sales: $1,180,694,000
Company Type: Public
SIC: 8082
  Home healthcare services and pharmacy services and ret
  hospital equipment
Philip L Carter, Chief Executive Officer

Employees: 9,555
Employees here: 200

D-U-N-S 13-143-3807
ARBOR HEALTH CARE COMPANY
  (Parent: Extendcare Hlth Fclty Holdings)
105 W Michigan St, Milwaukee, WI 53203
Phone: (414) 271-9696
Sales: $96,400,000
Company Type: Private
SIC: 8051
  Operates nursing facilities and subacute care units and
  institutional pharmacies
J W Carter, President

Employees: 4,200
Employees here: 140

D-U-N-S 55-696-1936
ARCVENTURES DEVELOPMENT CORP
(Parent: Rush Prudential Health Plan)
820 W Jackson Blvd Fl 8, Chicago, IL 60607
Phone: (312) 258-5100
Sales: $22,200,000
Company Type: Private
SIC: 8011
  Leasing private medical practices & other health related
    activities
Marie Sinioris, President

Employees: 325
Employees here: 200

D-U-N-S 07-436-8234
ARCVENTURES INC
(Parent: Arcventures Development Corp)
820 W Jackson Blvd Fl 8, Chicago, IL 60607
Phone: (312) 258-5100
Sales: $32,045,000
Company Type: Private
SIC: 8082
  Home infusion therapy medical educational svc acct
    receivable & collection mgmt prenatal svcs and retail
    pharmacy
Marie E Sinioris, President

Employees: 550
Employees here: 2

D-U-N-S 07-668-0404
ARDEN HILL HOSPITAL
4 Harriman Dr, Goshen, NY 10924
Phone: (914) 294-5441
Sales: $46,392,000
Company Type: Private
SIC: 8062
  General hospital
Wayne Becker, Chief Executive Officer

Employees: 785
Employees here: 785

D-U-N-S 07-447-2382
ARIZONA BOYS RANCH INC
20061 E Rittenhouse Rd, Queen Creek, AZ 85242
Phone: (602) 987-9700
Sales: $21,753,000
Company Type: Private
SIC: 8361
  Boys residential care
Robert Thomas, President

Employees: 209
Employees here: 209

D-U-N-S 15-994-3513
ARIZONA HEART HOSPITAL INC
(Parent: Medcath Incorporated)
1930 E Thomas Rd, Phoenix, AZ 85016
Phone: (602) 532-1000
Sales: $123,000,000
Company Type: Private
SIC: 8062
  Hospital
Karen Dewitt, President

Employees: 350
Employees here: 350

D-U-N-S 01-464-1567
ARIZONA MEDICAL CLINIC LTD,
13640 N Plaza Del Rio Blv, Peoria, AZ 85381
Phone: (602) 876-3800
Sales: $27,031,000
Company Type: Private
SIC: 8011
  Medical doctor's office
Larry Schwartz, Executive Director

Employees: 216
Employees here: 200

D-U-N-S 07-566-9416
ARKANSAS CHILDRENS HOSPITAL
800 Marshall St, Little Rock, AR 72202
Phone: (501) 320-1100

Sales: $139,923,000
Company Type: Private
SIC: 8069
  Pediatric hospital
Jonathan R Bates, Chief Executive Officer

Employees: 2,200
Employees here: 2,100

D-U-N-S 11-984-1336
ARKANSAS DEPARTMENT OF HEALTH
4313 W Markham St, Little Rock, AR 72205
Phone: (501) 686-9000
Sales: $26,700,000
Company Type: Private
SIC: 8062
  General hospital
Laurance Miller, Principal

Employees: NA
Employees here: 655

D-U-N-S 07-352-4563
ARKANSAS METHODIST HOSPITAL
900 W Kingshighway, Paragould, AR 72450
Phone: (870) 239-7000
Sales: $25,742,000
Company Type: Private
SIC: 8062
  Hospital
Ronald K Rooney, President

Employees: 419
Employees here: 418

D-U-N-S 07-644-4124
ARKANSAS VALLEY REGIONAL MED CTR
1100 Carson Ave, La Junta, CO 81050
Phone: (719) 384-5412
Sales: $23,389,000
Company Type: Private
SIC: 8062
  Hospital & skilled nursing home facility
Dale D Stoll, Chief Executive Officer

Employees: 425
Employees here: 345

D-U-N-S 60-577-1161
ARL/LABSOUTH INC
3221 3rd Ave S, Birmingham, AL 35222
Phone: (205) 251-4191
Sales: $30,200,000
Company Type: Private
SIC: 8071
  Medical laboratory
Ronald Elliott, President

Employees: 630
Employees here: 140

D-U-N-S 07-215-4289
ARMSTRONG COUNTY MEM HOSP
1 Nolte Dr, Kittanning, PA 16201
Phone: (724) 543-8404
Sales: $44,921,000
Company Type: Private
SIC: 8062
  General hospital and rural clinic
Jack D Hoard, Chief Executive Officer

Employees: 870
Employees here: 868

D-U-N-S 16-120-6560
ARNETT HMO INC
(Parent: Arnett Health Systems Inc)
3768 Rome Dr, Lafayette, IN 47905
Phone: (765) 448-8200
Sales: $53,466,000
Company Type: Public Family Member
SIC: 8011
  Health maintenance organization
Jim Brunnemer, Executive Director

Employees: 46
Employees here: 46

D-U-N-S 07-368-0043
ARNOT OGDEN MEDICAL CENTER
600 Roe Ave, Elmira, NY 14905
Phone: (607) 737-4100

Sales: $55,600,000   *Employees:* 1,200
Company Type: Private   *Employees here:* 1,200
SIC: 8062
  Hospital
Anthony Cooper, President

D-U-N-S 03-771-8277
AROOSTOOK MEDICAL CENTER INC
140 Academy St, Presque Isle, ME 4769
Phone: (207) 768-4000
Sales: $38,468,000   *Employees:* 860
Company Type: Private   *Employees here:* 500
SIC: 8062
  General medical and surgical hospital
David A Peterson, President

D-U-N-S 10-279-8303
ARROWHEAD COMMUNITY HOSPITAL & MED CTR
18701 N 67th Ave, Glendale, AZ 85308
Phone: (602) 561-1000
Sales: $38,465,000   *Employees:* 160
Company Type: Private   *Employees here:* 159
SIC: 8062
  Hospital
James Burnside, Chief Financial Officer

D-U-N-S 61-524-1510
ARUNDEL HEALTH ANNE SYSTEM
64 Franklin St, Annapolis, MD 21401
Phone: (410) 267-1000
Sales: $145,302,000   *Employees:* 46
Company Type: Private   *Employees here:* 1
SIC: 8062
  General medical & surgical hospitals
Martin L Doordan, President

D-U-N-S 07-491-1249
ASBURY CENTERS INC
903 Amerine Rd, Maryville, TN 37804
Phone: (423) 982-6109
Sales: $24,791,000   *Employees:* 850
Company Type: Private   *Employees here:* 250
SIC: 8051
  Skilled nursing faciltiy and retirement facility
Bernie Bowman, President

D-U-N-S 07-482-1208
ASBURY METHODIST VILLAGE INC
201 Russell Ave, Gaithersburg, MD 20877
Phone: (301) 330-3000
Sales: $40,061,000   *Employees:* 875
Company Type: Private   *Employees here:* 575
SIC: 8059
  Continuing care retirement community
Edwin C Thomas Iii, President

D-U-N-S 07-267-7636
ASHLAND HOSPITAL CORPORATION
2201 Lexington Ave, Ashland, KY 41101
Phone: (606) 327-4000
Sales: $145,608,000   *Employees:* 1,700
Company Type: Private   *Employees here:* 1,367
SIC: 8062
  Hospital
Fred L Jackson, President

D-U-N-S 07-774-7947
ASHTABULA COUNTY MEDICAL CTR
2420 Lake Ave, Ashtabula, OH 44004
Phone: (440) 997-2262

Sales: $74,797,000   *Employees:* 900
Company Type: Private   *Employees here:* 800
SIC: 8062
  General hospital
R D Richardson, Chief Executive Officer

D-U-N-S 07-834-8141
ASPEN VALLEY HOSPITAL DST
401 Castle Creek Rd, Aspen, CO 81611
Phone: (970) 925-1120
Sales: $21,329,000   *Employees:* 180
Company Type: Private   *Employees here:* 180
SIC: 8062
  General medical & surgical hospital
Todd Stewart, Controller

D-U-N-S 96-006-1448
ASSOCIATED THERAPISTS CORP
2150 Goodlette Rd N, Naples, FL 34102
Phone: (941) 403-1750
Sales: $37,300,000   *Employees:* NA
Company Type: Public Family Member   *Employees here:* 607
SIC: 8011
  Physical therapist
Bob Sanastar, Director

D-U-N-S 62-306-7550
ASSOCIATED THERAPISTS CORP
(Parent: Integrated Health Services)
10065 Red Run Blvd, Owings Mills, MD 21117
Phone: (410) 998-8400
Sales: $60,266,000   *Employees:* 1,300
Company Type: Public Family Member   *Employees here:* 200
SIC: 8093
  Rehabilitation agency
Eleanor Harding, Treasurer

D-U-N-S 19-476-9584
ASSOCIATION/SERVICES AGED
885 Flatbush Ave Fl 4, Brooklyn, NY 11226
Phone: (718) 941-2200
Sales: $26,187,000   *Employees:* 1,300
Company Type: Private   *Employees here:* 1,300
SIC: 8361
  Home attendant service
Marilyn Freedman, President

D-U-N-S 11-751-3135
ASSOCTED REGIONAL UNIV PATHOLOGIST
(Parent: Associated Univ Pathologists)
500 Chipeta Way, Salt Lake City, UT 84108
Phone: (801) 583-2787
Sales: $74,552,000   *Employees:* 700
Company Type: Private   *Employees here:* 400
SIC: 8071
  Medical testing laboratory
Dr Carl Kjeldsberg, President

D-U-N-S 08-228-1726
ASTOR HOME FOR CHILDREN
36 Mill St, Rhinebeck, NY 12572
Phone: (914) 876-4081
Sales: $20,337,000   *Employees:* 600
Company Type: Private   *Employees here:* 200
SIC: 8361
  Children's home
Sister R Logan, Executive Director

D-U-N-S 06-695-5907
ASTORIA GENERAL HOSPITAL INC
2510 30th Ave, Long Island City, NY 11102
Phone: (718) 932-1000

Sales: $75,949,000   *Employees:* 510
Company Type: Private   *Employees here:* 510
SIC: 8062
  General hospital
Arthur Singer, President

D-U-N-S 04-065-6027
ATHENS LIMESTONE HOSPITAL
700 W Market St, Athens, AL 35611
Phone: (256) 233-9292
Sales: $35,634,000   *Employees:* 574
Company Type: Private   *Employees here:* 460
SIC: 8062
  General hospital
Phillip Dotson, Administrator

D-U-N-S 07-593-8811
ATHENS REGIONAL MEDICAL CTR
1199 Prince Ave, Athens, GA 30606
Phone: (706) 549-9977
Sales: $148,317,000   *Employees:* 1,864
Company Type: Private   *Employees here:* 1,864
SIC: 8062
  General medical and surgical hospital
John A Drew, President

D-U-N-S 07-345-1288
ATLANTA MEDICAL CLINIC LLC
100 10th St Nw, Atlanta, GA 30309
Phone: (404) 897-6846
Sales: $28,000,000   *Employees:* 300
Company Type: Private   *Employees here:* 109
SIC: 8011
  Medical doctor's office
Walton H Reeves Jr, Chairman of the Board

D-U-N-S 18-357-2551
ATLANTIC CITY MEDICAL CENTER
Jim Leeds Rd, Pomona, NJ 8240
Phone: (609) 652-1000
Sales: $55,400,000   *Employees:* NA
Company Type: Private   *Employees here:* 1,119
SIC: 8062
  General hospital
Lori Herndon, Principal

D-U-N-S 06-905-1241
ATLANTIC CITY MEDICAL CENTER
1925 Pacific Ave, Atlantic City, NJ 8401
Phone: (609) 344-4081
Sales: $210,644,000   *Employees:* 2,460
Company Type: Private   *Employees here:* 1,341
SIC: 8062
  General hospital
David P Tilton, President

D-U-N-S 79-512-4494
ATLANTIC GENERAL HOSPITAL CORP
9733 Healthway Dr, Berlin, MD 21811
Phone: (410) 641-1100
Sales: $24,103,000   *Employees:* 322
Company Type: Private   *Employees here:* 320
SIC: 8062
  General medical & surgical hospital
Cheryl Davis, Chief Financial Officer

D-U-N-S 11-295-0423
ATLANTICARE MEDICAL CENTER
500 Lynnfield St, Lynn, MA 1904
Phone: (781) 581-9200

Sales: $67,173,000   *Employees:* 1,829
Company Type: Private   *Employees here:* 1,100
SIC: 8062
  General medical & surgical hospital
Andrew Riddell, President

D-U-N-S 15-602-2097
ATLANTICARE MEDICAL CENTER
500 Lynnfield St, Lynn, MA 1904
Phone: (781) 581-9200
Sales: $70,900,000   *Employees:* NA
Company Type: Private   *Employees here:* 1,400
SIC: 8062
  General hospital
Andrew Riddell, Principal

D-U-N-S 10-334-9924
AUBURN GENERAL HOSPITAL INC
  (Parent: Universal Health Services)
Plaza 1 202 North Div St, Auburn, WA 98001
Phone: (253) 833-7711
Sales: $24,300,000   *Employees:* 538
Company Type: Public Family Member   *Employees here:* 520
SIC: 8062
  Acute care hospital
Michael M Gherardini, Administrator

D-U-N-S 04-158-7593
AUBURN MEMORIAL HOSPITAL
17 Lansing St, Auburn, NY 13021
Phone: (315) 255-7011
Sales: $54,268,000   *Employees:* 925
Company Type: Private   *Employees here:* 850
SIC: 8062
  General hospital & skilled nursing facility
Christophe J Rogers, Administrator

D-U-N-S 07-197-9140
AUDRAIN HEALTH CARE INC
620 E Monroe St, Mexico, MO 65265
Phone: (573) 581-1760
Sales: $49,834,000   *Employees:* 756
Company Type: Private   *Employees here:* 605
SIC: 8062
  General hospital
Charles P Jansen, Administrator

D-U-N-S 36-068-2249
AUGUSTA HOSPITAL CORPORATION
96 Medical Center Dr, Fishersville, VA 22939
Phone: (540) 332-4000
Sales: $97,019,000   *Employees:* 1,300
Company Type: Private   *Employees here:* 1,300
SIC: 8062
  General hospital
Richard H Graham, President

D-U-N-S 07-434-9523
AUGUSTANA LUTHERAN HOME
5434 2nd Ave, Brooklyn, NY 11220
Phone: (718) 630-6000
Sales: $20,281,000   *Employees:* 142
Company Type: Private   *Employees here:* 132
SIC: 8051
  Skilled nursing care facility
David Rose, Executive Director

D-U-N-S 02-067-2259
AURELIA OSBORN FOX MEMORIAL
1 Norton Ave, Oneonta, NY 13820
Phone: (607) 432-2000

Sales: $48,905,000   *Employees:* 640
Company Type: Private   *Employees here:* 630
SIC: 8062
    General hospital & skilled nursing facility
Anne Cole, Accountant

D-U-N-S 07-614-1209
AURORA MED CTR OF SHEBOYGAN CNTY
2629 N 7th St, Sheboygan, WI 53083
Phone: (920) 457-5033
Sales: $47,470,000   *Employees:* 703
Company Type: Private   *Employees here:* 600
SIC: 8062
    Hospital
Patrick J Trotter, President

D-U-N-S 93-295-9265
AURORA MEDICAL GROUP, INC
2414 Kohler Memorial Dr, Sheboygan, WI 53081
Phone: (920) 457-4461
Sales: $42,600,000   *Employees:* NA
Company Type: Private   *Employees here:* 700
SIC: 8011
    Medical clinic
Jerry Kamp, President

D-U-N-S 80-955-6400
AURORA MEDICAL GROUP, INC
3000 W Montana Ave, Milwaukee, WI 53215
Phone: (414) 647-6322
Sales: $108,500,000   *Employees:* 1,575
Company Type: Private   *Employees here:* 10
SIC: 8011
    Physicians practices
Elliott Huxley, President

D-U-N-S 87-862-5490
AUSTIN NORTH MEDICAL CENTER
12221 Mopac Expy N, Austin, TX 78758
Phone: (512) 901-1111
Sales: $158,471,000   *Employees:* 950
Company Type: Private   *Employees here:* 950
SIC: 8062
    Hospital
Charles Sexton, Chief Executive Officer

D-U-N-S 12-059-3165
AUSTIN STATE HOSPITAL
4110 Guadalupe St, Austin, TX 78751
Phone: (512) 452-0381
Sales: $50,000,000   *Employees:* 962
Company Type: Private   *Employees here:* 962
SIC: 8063
    Psychiatric hospital
Diane Faucher, Chief Executive Officer

D-U-N-S 09-511-6455
AUTUMN CORP
451 Winstead Ave, Rocky Mount, NC 27804
Phone: (252) 443-6265
Sales: $65,000,000   *Employees:* 1,800
Company Type: Private   *Employees here:* 40
SIC: 8059
    Nursing homes
Gerald P Cox, President

D-U-N-S 07-390-5002
AUTUMN HILLS CONVALESCENT CTRS
1080 W Sam Houston Pkwy N, Houston, TX 77043
Phone: (713) 467-2213

Sales: $45,000,000   *Employees:* 1,500
Company Type: Private   *Employees here:* 16
SIC: 8051
    Skilled and intermediate care facility
Michael Hunter, President

D-U-N-S 80-977-3211
AVIV HEALTH CARE, INC.
4509 Minnetonka Blvd, Minneapolis, MN 55416
Phone: (612) 920-4111
Sales: $21,446,000   *Employees:* 700
Company Type: Private   *Employees here:* 9
SIC: 8051
    Nursing homes
Mark Mandel, Treasurer

D-U-N-S 01-011-2167
AZALEALAND NURSING HOME INC
2040 Colonial Dr, Savannah, GA 31406
Phone: (912) 354-2752
Sales: $29,000,000   *Employees:* 87
Company Type: Private   *Employees here:* 87
SIC: 8051
    Nursing home
Charles Von Waldner, Vice-President

D-U-N-S 55-689-7692
AHP HOLDINGS, INC
    (Parent: Aetna Life Insurance Company)
151 Farmington Ave, Hartford, CT 6156
Phone: (860) 273-0123
Sales: $34,300,000   *Employees:* 500
Company Type: Public Family Member   *Employees here:* 11
SIC: 8011
    Health maintenance organization
James W Mc Lane, Chairman of the Board

D-U-N-S 80-173-8345
AMI/HTI TARZANA-ENCINO, JV
18321 Clark St, Tarzana, CA 91356
Phone: (818) 881-0800
Sales: $60,300,000   *Employees:* NA
Company Type: Private   *Employees here:* NA
SIC: 8062
    General hospital
American M Intl, Mng Ptn

D-U-N-S 88-426-3815
AMI/HTI TARZANA-ENCINO, JV
18226 Ventura Blvd, Tarzana, CA 91356
Phone: (818) 995-5462
Sales: $59,500,000   *Employees:* NA
Company Type: Private   *Employees here:* 1,200
SIC: 8062
    Hospital
Sonny Urquirco, Principal

D-U-N-S 05-921-6655
APL HEALTHCARE GROUP INC
4230 Burnham Ave, Las Vegas, NV 89119
Phone: (702) 733-7866
Sales: $50,100,000   *Employees:* 1,050
Company Type: Private   *Employees here:* 800
SIC: 8071
    Medical diagnostic laboratory
John P Schwartz, President

D-U-N-S 96-260-4781
B V M C INC
    (Parent: Galen Health Care Inc)
1604 Rock Prairie Rd, College Station, TX 77845
Phone: (409) 764-5100

Sales: $22,500,000
Company Type: Public Family Member
SIC: 8062
   Hospital
Tom Jackson, Chief Executive Officer

Employees: 500
Employees here: 438

D-U-N-S 07-799-8409
BABCOCK CENTER INC
1502 W Main St, Lexington, SC 29072
Phone: (803) 359-9717
Sales: $25,053,000
Company Type: Private
SIC: 8361
   Residential care for mentally handicapped
Risley E Linder Sr, President

Employees: 1,000
Employees here: 36

D-U-N-S 07-373-5664
BACHARACH INST FOR REHABILITATION
Jim Leeds Rd, Pomona, NJ 8240
Phone: (609) 652-7000
Sales: $25,246,000
Company Type: Private
SIC: 8069
   Comprehensive rehabilitation hospital
Richard Katherins, Administrator

Employees: 500
Employees here: 490

D-U-N-S 17-293-4556
BAKER VICTORY SERVICES
125 Martin Rd, Lackawanna, NY 14218
Phone: (716) 828-9777
Sales: $24,731,000
Company Type: Private
SIC: 8361
   Operates a home for emotionally disturbed children & a high
   school
James J Casion, Director

Employees: 340
Employees here: 35

D-U-N-S 01-070-8006
BAKERSFIELD MEMORIAL HOSPITAL
420 34th St, Bakersfield, CA 93301
Phone: (805) 327-1792
Sales: $85,702,000
Company Type: Private
SIC: 8062
   General hospital
C L Carr, President

Employees: 840
Employees here: 735

D-U-N-S 07-262-2459
BALDWIN C E SHR HSP BD
750 Morphy Ave, Fairhope, AL 36532
Phone: (334) 928-2375
Sales: $36,598,000
Company Type: Private
SIC: 8062
   General hospital
Owen Bailey, Administrator

Employees: 600
Employees here: 600

D-U-N-S 06-647-0436
BALDWIN COUNTY HOSPITAL AUTH
821 N Cobb St, Milledgeville, GA 31061
Phone: (912) 454-3500
Sales: $24,500,000
Company Type: Private
SIC: 8062
   General hospital
Brian Riddle, Chief Executive Officer

Employees: 543
Employees here: 543

D-U-N-S 07-597-4899
BALL MEMORIAL HOSPITAL INC
2401 W University Ave, Muncie, IN 47303
Phone: (765) 747-3111

Sales: $171,438,000
Company Type: Private
SIC: 8062
   General hospital
Mitch Carson, President

Employees: 2,108
Employees here: 2,100

D-U-N-S 15-069-7969
BALTIMORE MEDICAL SYSTEM INC
3501 Sinclair Ln, Baltimore, MD 21213
Phone: (410) 732-8800
Sales: $37,761,000
Company Type: Private
SIC: 8099
   Operator of community health centers
Jay Wolvovsky, Executive Director

Employees: 270
Employees here: 45

D-U-N-S 07-374-9517
BANCROFT INC
Hopkins Ln, Haddonfield, NJ 8033
Phone: (609) 429-5637
Sales: $42,084,000
Company Type: Private
SIC: 8361
   Residential treatment facility
George W Niemann Phd, President

Employees: 1,000
Employees here: 485

D-U-N-S 07-297-5253
BANNOCK REGIONAL MEDICAL CTR
651 Memorial Dr, Pocatello, ID 83201
Phone: (208) 239-1000
Sales: $55,440,000
Company Type: Private
SIC: 8062
   General hospital skilled nursing facility
Fred R Eaton, Administrator

Employees: 725
Employees here: 586

D-U-N-S 14-764-4348
BAPTIST HEALTH CARE AFFILIATES
2000 Church St, Nashville, TN 37236
Phone: (615) 329-5555
Sales: $20,091,000
Company Type: Private
SIC: 8062
   Health & wellness center & ret drugs & sundries
C D Stringfield, President

Employees: 142
Employees here: 75

D-U-N-S 60-438-2101
BAPTIST HEALTH CENTERS, INC
(Parent: Baptist Health System Inc)
3500 Blue Lake Dr, Birmingham, AL 35243
Phone: (205) 715-5900
Sales: $42,275,000
Company Type: Private
SIC: 8011
   Physician office
Allan Kennedy, President

Employees: 800
Employees here: 50

D-U-N-S 18-727-7389
BAPTIST HEALTH ENTERPRISES,
8950 N Kendall Dr, Miami, FL 33176
Phone: (305) 271-8950
Sales: $39,598,000
Company Type: Private
SIC: 8011
   Health maintenance organization
Brian Keely, President

Employees: 124
Employees here: 105

D-U-N-S 10-691-4872
BAPTIST HEALTH SERVICES CORP
2105 E South Blvd, Montgomery, AL 36116
Phone: (334) 288-2100

Sales: $86,300,000   *Employees:* 1,850
Company Type: Private   *Employees here:* 6
SIC: 8062
    Holding company for medical center home health service
       addictive disease treatment psychiatric unit & private duty
       registry
John A Holleman, Chairman of the Board

D-U-N-S 93-232-6721
BAPTIST HEALTH SYSTEM INC
315 W Hickory St, Sylacauga, AL 35150
Phone: (256) 249-5600
Sales: $23,100,000   *Employees:* NA
Company Type: Private   *Employees here:* 600
SIC: 8062
    Hospital with nursing home
Steve Johnson, President

D-U-N-S 12-629-3448
BAPTIST HEALTH SYSTEM INC
701 Princeton Ave SW, Birmingham, AL 35211
Phone: (205) 783-7226
Sales: $37,800,000   *Employees:* NA
Company Type: Private   *Employees here:* 900
SIC: 8062
    General hospital
Dana Hensley, Administrator

D-U-N-S 61-365-6909
BAPTIST HEALTH SYSTEM INC
800 Montclair Rd, Birmingham, AL 35213
Phone: (205) 592-1000
Sales: $84,800,000   *Employees:* NA
Company Type: Private   *Employees here:* 2,000
SIC: 8062
    Hospital
Dana Hensley, Principal

D-U-N-S 03-559-3854
BAPTIST HEALTH
1 Pershing Cir, North Little Rock, AR 72114
Phone: (501) 771-3000
Sales: $45,400,000   *Employees:* NA
Company Type: Private   *Employees here:* 1,100
SIC: 8062
    General hospital
Harrison Dean, Manager

D-U-N-S 86-761-4984
BAPTIST HEALTHCARE GROUP
2109 Elliston Pl, Nashville, TN 37203
Phone: (615) 340-8700
Sales: $20,100,000   *Employees:* 280
Company Type: Private   *Employees here:* 280
SIC: 8011
    Occupational medical clinic
Rich Panek, Executive Director

D-U-N-S 07-966-1963
BAPTIST HEALTHCARE SYSTEM,
2501 Kentucky Ave, Paducah, KY 42003
Phone: (502) 575-2100
Sales: $50,100,000   *Employees:* NA
Company Type: Private   *Employees here:* 1,279
SIC: 8062
    Hospital
Larry Barton, Principal

D-U-N-S 05-583-5003
BAPTIST HEALTHCARE SYSTEM,
4007 Kresge Way, Louisville, KY 40207
Phone: (502) 896-5000

Sales: $562,842,000   *Employees:* 6,850
Company Type: Private   *Employees here:* 150
SIC: 8062
    Hospitals and medical clinics
Tommy J Smith, President

D-U-N-S 60-618-2681
BAPTIST HEALTHCARE SYSTEM,
4000 Kresge Way, Louisville, KY 40207
Phone: (502) 897-8100
Sales: $84,800,000   *Employees:* NA
Company Type: Private   *Employees here:* 2,000
SIC: 8062
    Hospital
Sue S Tamme, President

D-U-N-S 07-787-5292
BAPTIST HEALTHCARE SYSTEM,
1740 Nicholasville Rd, Lexington, KY 40503
Phone: (606) 275-6100
Sales: $72,000,000   *Employees:* NA
Company Type: Private   *Employees here:* 1,700
SIC: 8062
    General hospital
William G Sisson, Principal

D-U-N-S 80-472-4367
BAPTIST HEALTHCARE SYSTEM,
1 Trillium Way, Corbin, KY 40701
Phone: (606) 528-1212
Sales: $35,700,000   *Employees:* NA
Company Type: Private   *Employees here:* 916
SIC: 8062
    Hospital
John Henson, President

D-U-N-S 15-057-0232
BAPTIST HEALTHCARE AFFLIATES INC
4007 Kresge Way, Louisville, KY 40207
Phone: (502) 896-5000
Sales: $20,312,000   *Employees:* 413
Company Type: Private   *Employees here:* 170
SIC: 8062
    General hospital
Tommy J Smith, President

D-U-N-S 01-078-7653
BAPTIST HOSPITAL OF STHEAST TEXAS
3576 College St, Beaumont, TX 77701
Phone: (409) 835-3781
Sales: $61,595,000   *Employees:* 800
Company Type: Private   *Employees here:* 800
SIC: 8062
    General hospital
David Parmer, Chief Executive Officer

D-U-N-S 07-489-2233
BAPTIST HOSPITAL OF EAST TENN
137 E Blount Ave, Knoxville, TN 37920
Phone: (423) 632-5081
Sales: $148,044,000   *Employees:* 1,800
Company Type: Private   *Employees here:* 1,800
SIC: 8062
    General hospital
Michael D Williams, President

D-U-N-S 07-601-6948
BAPTIST HOSPITAL OF MIAMI INC
8900 SW 88th St, Miami, FL 33176
Phone: (305) 596-1960

Sales: $259,711,000
Company Type: Private
SIC: 8062
   General hospital
Fred Messing, Chief Executive Officer

Employees: 3,500
Employees here: 3,050

D-U-N-S 01-039-5739
BAPTIST HOSPITAL INC
1000 W Moreno St, Pensacola, FL 32501
Phone: (850) 434-4011
Sales: $143,264,000
Company Type: Private
SIC: 8062
   General medical hospital
Alfred G Stubblefield, President

Employees: 1,641
Employees here: 1,641

D-U-N-S 01-079-1515
BAPTIST HOSPITAL ORANGE
608 Strickland Dr, Orange, TX 77630
Phone: (409) 883-9361
Sales: $33,866,000
Company Type: Private
SIC: 8062
   General hospital
David Parmer, President

Employees: 358
Employees here: 358

D-U-N-S 78-736-1476
BAPTIST HOSPITAL, INC
2000 Church St, Nashville, TN 37236
Phone: (615) 329-5555
Sales: $259,626,000
Company Type: Private
SIC: 8062
   General hospital
C D Stringfield, President

Employees: 3,500
Employees here: 2,900

D-U-N-S 10-413-7872
BAPTIST HOSPITALS HEALTH SYSTEMS
200 W Bethany Home Rd, Phoenix, AZ 85013
Phone: (602) 249-0212
Sales: $20,100,000
Company Type: Private
SIC: 8021
   Hospital
Richard Alley, President

Employees: NA
Employees here: 1,200

D-U-N-S 06-591-6447
BAPTIST MED CTR OF THE BEACHES
1350 13th Ave S, Jacksonville, FL 32250
Phone: (904) 247-2900
Sales: $37,430,000
Company Type: Private
SIC: 8062
   General hospital
Joseph Mitrick, Administrator

Employees: 501
Employees here: 501

D-U-N-S 07-210-3104
BAPTIST MEDICAL CENTER
2105 E South Blvd, Montgomery, AL 36116
Phone: (334) 288-2100
Sales: $136,779,000
Company Type: Private
SIC: 8062
   General hospital
Michael D Deboer, President

Employees: 1,700
Employees here: 1,700

D-U-N-S 07-304-5080
BAPTIST MEDICAL CENTER
6601 Rockhill Rd, Kansas City, MO 64131
Phone: (816) 361-3500

Sales: $126,078,000
Company Type: Private
SIC: 8062
   Hospital
Mike Mccoy, Chief Operating Officer

Employees: 1,500
Employees here: 1,500

D-U-N-S 06-945-2373
BAPTIST MEM HEALTHCARE SYS
660 N Main Ave, San Antonio, TX 78205
Phone: (210) 302-3000
Sales: $235,200,000
Company Type: Private
SIC: 8062
   Medical & surgical hospital
Fred R Mills, President

Employees: 5,000
Employees here: 2,300

D-U-N-S 78-998-4614
BAPTIST MEM HEALTHCARE SYS
4214 E Southcross Blvd, San Antonio, TX 78222
Phone: (210) 337-6900
Sales: $28,900,000
Company Type: Private
SIC: 8062
   Hospital
Kevin Walters, Administrator

Employees: NA
Employees here: 707

D-U-N-S 88-429-5163
BAPTIST MEM HEALTHCARE SYS
7930 Floyd Curl Dr, San Antonio, TX 78229
Phone: (210) 617-7700
Sales: $40,700,000
Company Type: Private
SIC: 8062
   General hospital
Peggy Brown, Administrator

Employees: NA
Employees here: 989

D-U-N-S 62-037-9503
BAPTIST MEM HEALTH CARE CORP
2301 S Lamar Blvd, Oxford, MS 38655
Phone: (601) 232-8100
Sales: $20,600,000
Company Type: Private
SIC: 8062
   Hospital
James Hahn, Principal

Employees: NA
Employees here: 545

D-U-N-S 14-824-4890
BAPTIST MEM HEALTH CARE CORP
899 Madison Ave, Memphis, TN 38103
Phone: (901) 227-2727
Sales: $949,199,000
Company Type: Private
SIC: 8062
   Hospitals clinics hospital management & whol hospital
     supplies
Stephen C Reynolds, President

Employees: 7,907
Employees here: 185

D-U-N-S 19-217-8671
BAPTIST MEM HOSPITAL-DESOTO
7601 Southcrest Pkwy, Southaven, MS 38671
Phone: (601) 349-4000
Sales: $33,163,000
Company Type: Private
SIC: 8062
   Hospital
Stephen Reynolds, President

Employees: 550
Employees here: 550

D-U-N-S 07-351-5678
BAPTIST MEM HOSPITAL-UNION CY
1201 Bishop St, Union City, TN 38261
Phone: (901) 885-2410

Sales: $28,066,000
Company Type: Private
SIC: 8062
  General hospital
Mike Perryman, Administrator
Employees: 475
Employees here: 475

D-U-N-S 07-351-3970
BAPTIST MEM HSPITAL-NORTH MISS
Hwy 7south, Oxford, MS 38655
Phone: (601) 232-8100
Sales: $80,373,000
Company Type: Private
SIC: 8062
  Hospital
James Hahn, Administrator
Employees: 650
Employees here: 650

D-U-N-S 82-561-5784
BAPTIST MEM HSPITAL-UNION CNTY
200 Highway 30 W, New Albany, MS 38652
Phone: (601) 538-7631
Sales: $26,788,000
Company Type: Private
SIC: 8062
  Hospital
John Tompkins, Administrator
Employees: 420
Employees here: 420

D-U-N-S 07-547-3892
BAPTIST MEM HSPTL-GLDEN TRNGLE
2520 5th St N, Columbus, MS 39701
Phone: (601) 244-1000
Sales: $72,841,000
Company Type: Private
SIC: 8062
  Hospital
Joseph H Powell, President
Employees: 780
Employees here: 769

D-U-N-S 94-758-6327
BAPTIST MEMORIAL HEALTH SVCS
899 Madison Ave, Memphis, TN 38103
Phone: (901) 227-2727
Sales: $30,613,000
Company Type: Private
SIC: 8082
  Home health care services
Stephen C Reynolds, Chief Executive Officer
Employees: NA
Employees here: NA

D-U-N-S 07-353-3812
BAPTIST MEMORIAL HOSPITAL
Division & Highland St, Blytheville, AR 72315
Phone: (870) 762-3300
Sales: $20,900,000
Company Type: Private
SIC: 8062
  Hospital
Randy King, Administrator
Employees: 467
Employees here: 325

D-U-N-S 00-704-9125
BAPTIST MEMORIAL HOSPITAL
899 Madison Ave, Memphis, TN 38103
Phone: (901) 227-2727
Sales: $428,482,000
Company Type: Private
SIC: 8062
  Hospital
Stephen C Reynolds, President
Employees: 5,680
Employees here: 4,400

D-U-N-S 06-638-5733
BAPTIST/ST ANTHONY'S HOSPITAL
1600 Wallace Blvd, Amarillo, TX 79106
Phone: (806) 376-4411

Sales: $36,700,000
Company Type: Private
SIC: 8062
  Hospital
John D Hicks, President
Employees: 800
Employees here: 800

D-U-N-S 02-062-8384
BARBERTON CITIZENS HOSPITAL INC
  (Parent: Quorum Health Group Inc)
155 5th St NE, Barberton, OH 44203
Phone: (330) 745-1611
Sales: $93,000,000
Company Type: Public Family Member
SIC: 8062
  Acute general & surgical hospital
M A Bernatovicz, President
Employees: 1,200
Employees here: 1,098

D-U-N-S 07-932-7466
BARNERT HOSPITAL
680 Broadway, Paterson, NJ 7514
Phone: (973) 977-6600
Sales: $72,349,000
Company Type: Private
SIC: 8062
  General hospital
Fred Lang, President
Employees: 850
Employees here: 840

D-U-N-S 07-195-4382
BARNES WEST COUNTY HOSPITAL
12634 Olive Blvd, Saint Louis, MO 63141
Phone: (314) 434-0600
Sales: $30,574,000
Company Type: Private
SIC: 8062
  General medical hospital
Greg Wozniak, Administrator
Employees: 200
Employees here: 200

D-U-N-S 16-109-6805
BARNES-JEWISH HOSPITAL
216 S Kingshighway Blvd, Saint Louis, MO 63110
Phone: (314) 454-7770
Sales: $59,500,000
Company Type: Private
SIC: 8011
  Medical doctor's office
Dr Peter Slavin, President
Employees: NA
Employees here: 1,000

D-U-N-S 94-949-2417
BARNES-JEWISH HOSPITAL
216 S Kingshighway Blvd, Saint Louis, MO 63110
Phone: (314) 454-7000
Sales: $235,200,000
Company Type: Private
SIC: 8062
  Hospital
Dr Peter Slavin, President
Employees: 5,000
Employees here: 3,100

D-U-N-S 94-978-7956
BARNES-JEWISH HOSPITAL
1 Barnes Hospital Plz, Saint Louis, MO 63110
Phone: (314) 362-5000
Sales: $123,000,000
Company Type: Private
SIC: 8062
  Hospital
Fred Brown, Director
Employees: NA
Employees here: 2,900

D-U-N-S 07-377-9019
BARTON MEMORIAL HOSPITAL
2170 South Ave, South Lake Tahoe, CA 96150
Phone: (530) 541-3420

Sales: $42,980,000   *Employees:* 658
Company Type: Private   *Employees here:* 574
SIC: 8062
  General hospital
William G Gordon, Chief Executive Officer

D-U-N-S 04-501-9163
BASIC AMERICAN MEDICAL, INC.
  (Parent: Columbia/Hca Healthcare Corp)
1 Park Mdws, Nashville, TN 37215
Phone: (615) 327-9551
Sales: $202,100,000   *Employees:* 4,300
Company Type: Public Family Member   *Employees here:* 15
SIC: 8062
  Owns & operates hospitals ret drugs mfr hospital furniture
    and operates rehabilitation centers
Richard A Schweinhart, Senior Vice-President

D-U-N-S 07-946-2404
BATON ROUGE CLINIC A MED CORP
8415 Goodwood Blvd, Baton Rouge, LA 70806
Phone: (225) 923-1515
Sales: $20,500,000   *Employees:* 300
Company Type: Private   *Employees here:* 255
SIC: 8011
  Medical doctors' office
Dr Steven Cavalier Md, President

D-U-N-S 15-580-5971
BATON ROUGE GENERAL MED CTR
3600 Florida Blvd, Baton Rouge, LA 70806
Phone: (225) 387-7000
Sales: $144,565,000   *Employees:* 1,790
Company Type: Private   *Employees here:* 60
SIC: 8062
  General hospital
Dr Milton Sietman, Chief Executive Officer

D-U-N-S 07-506-8247
BATON ROUGE HEALTH CARE CORP
134 McGehee Dr, Baton Rouge, LA 70815
Phone: (225) 273-4120
Sales: $39,251,000   *Employees:* 950
Company Type: Private   *Employees here:* 116
SIC: 8082
  Home health care agency
Jo A Chiasson, President

D-U-N-S 19-653-2832
BATTLE CREEK HEALTH SYSTEM
300 North Ave, Battle Creek, MI 49017
Phone: (616) 963-5521
Sales: $139,646,000   *Employees:* 1,882
Company Type: Private   *Employees here:* 150
SIC: 8062
  Healthcare organization
Stephen L Abbott, President

D-U-N-S 61-972-5419
BATTLE CREEK HEALTH SYSTEM
183 West St, Battle Creek, MI 49017
Phone: (616) 963-5521
Sales: $71,900,000   *Employees:* NA
Company Type: Private   *Employees here:* 1,600
SIC: 8069
  Acute care hospital
Steven Abbott, Principal

D-U-N-S 12-020-0423
BAXTER COUNTY REGIONAL HOSP
624 Hospital Dr, Mountain Home, AR 72653
Phone: (870) 424-1000

Sales: $68,180,000   *Employees:* 1,000
Company Type: Private   *Employees here:* 980
SIC: 8062
  Hospital
H W Anderson, Administrator

D-U-N-S 06-060-0533
BAY AREA HEALTH DISTRICT
1775 Thompson Rd, Coos Bay, OR 97420
Phone: (541) 269-8111
Sales: $57,273,000   *Employees:* 770
Company Type: Private   *Employees here:* 655
SIC: 8062
  General medical and surgical hospital and home health care
    services
Dale Jessup, Chief Executive Officer

D-U-N-S 07-479-0981
BAY AREA MEDICAL CENTER
3100 Shore Dr, Marinette, WI 54143
Phone: (715) 735-6621
Sales: $42,962,000   *Employees:* 570
Company Type: Private   *Employees here:* 510
SIC: 8062
  Hospital & outpatient services
Rick Ament, President

D-U-N-S 04-944-4565
BAY COVE HUMAN SERVICES INC
66 Canal St, Boston, MA 2114
Phone: (617) 371-3000
Sales: $23,250,000   *Employees:* 700
Company Type: Private   *Employees here:* 150
SIC: 8052
  Residential & out-patient for the mentally ill & retarded and
    substance abuse center
Daniel Boynton, President

D-U-N-S 07-293-6255
BAY HARBOR HOSPITAL INC
1437 Lomita Blvd, Harbor City, CA 90710
Phone: (310) 325-1221
Sales: $63,770,000   *Employees:* 800
Company Type: Private   *Employees here:* 540
SIC: 8062
  General hospital
Jack Weiblen, Administrator

D-U-N-S 07-706-5928
BAY HEALTH MEDICAL CENTER INC
640 S State St, Dover, DE 19901
Phone: (302) 734-4701
Sales: $122,866,000   *Employees:* NA
Company Type: Private   *Employees here:* NA
SIC: 8062
  General hospital
Dennis Clima, Chief Executive Officer

D-U-N-S 01-050-3175
BAY HOSPITAL INC
  (Parent: Columbia/Hca Healthcare Corp)
449 W 23rd St, Panama City, FL 32405
Phone: (850) 769-8341
Sales: $29,600,000   *Employees:* 650
Company Type: Public Family Member   *Employees here:* 650
SIC: 8062
  General hospital
Donald Butts, Administrator

D-U-N-S 18-005-6350
BAY MEDICAL CENTER
615 N Bonita Ave, Panama City, FL 32401
Phone: (850) 769-1511

Sales: $125,515,000   *Employees:* 1,906
Company Type: Private   *Employees here:* 1,756
SIC: 8062
    General hospital
Ronald Wolff, President

D-U-N-S 07-277-1140
BAY MEDICAL CENTER
1900 Columbus Ave, Bay City, MI 48708
Phone: (517) 894-3000
Sales: $123,599,000   *Employees:* 2,000
Company Type: Private   *Employees here:* 1,700
SIC: 8062
    Acute care general hospital
Hans Jeppesen, Chief Executive Officer

D-U-N-S 07-554-4478
BAYADA NURSES INC
290 Chester Ave, Moorestown, NJ 8057
Phone: (609) 231-1000
Sales: $47,800,000   *Employees:* 3,000
Company Type: Private   *Employees here:* 100
SIC: 8082
    Home health services
J M Baiada, President

D-U-N-S 87-663-8065
BAYER CORPORATION
400 Morgan Ln, West Haven, CT 6516
Phone: (203) 937-2000
Sales: $103,300,000   *Employees:* NA
Company Type: Private   *Employees here:* 2,000
SIC: 8071
    Medical laboratories
David Ebsworth, President

D-U-N-S 07-322-4370
BAYFRONT MEDICAL CENTER INC
701 6th St S, Saint Petersburg, FL 33701
Phone: (727) 893-6111
Sales: $161,440,000   *Employees:* 1,723
Company Type: Private   *Employees here:* 1,700
SIC: 8062
    General hospital
Sue Brody, Chief Executive Officer

D-U-N-S 10-260-9997
BAYLOR HEALTH CARE SYSTEM
3600 Gaston Ave Ste 150, Dallas, TX 75246
Phone: (214) 820-4901
Sales: $938,002,000   *Employees:* 1,409
Company Type: Private   *Employees here:* 50
SIC: 8062
    General medical & surgical hospitals
Boone Powell Jr, President

D-U-N-S 07-508-9482
BAYLOR INST FOR RHABILITATION
3505 Gaston Ave, Dallas, TX 75246
Phone: (214) 826-7030
Sales: $25,476,000   *Employees:* 450
Company Type: Private   *Employees here:* 450
SIC: 8361
    Rehabilitation center
Judith C Waterston, Executive Director

D-U-N-S 07-837-4402
BAYLOR MED CENTER-ELLIS CNTY
1405 W Jefferson St, Waxahachie, TX 75165
Phone: (972) 937-5910

Sales: $42,221,000   *Employees:* 460
Company Type: Private   *Employees here:* 305
SIC: 8062
    General hospital
Mike Lee, Executive Director

D-U-N-S 07-315-4338
BAYLOR MED CTR AT GRAPEVINE
1650 W College St, Grapevine, TX 76051
Phone: (817) 481-1588
Sales: $41,053,000   *Employees:* 450
Company Type: Private   *Employees here:* 450
SIC: 8062
    General hospital
Mark Hood, Executive Director

D-U-N-S 07-508-9052
BAYLOR MEDICAL CTR AT GARLAND
2300 Marie Curie Dr, Garland, TX 75042
Phone: (972) 487-5000
Sales: $80,021,000   *Employees:* 1,100
Company Type: Private   *Employees here:* 875
SIC: 8062
    General hospital home health care services outpatient clinic
        senior health care and psychological consulting
John Mc Whoter, Executive Director

D-U-N-S 00-528-1246
BAYLOR MEDICAL CTR AT IRVING
1901 N Macarthur Blvd, Irving, TX 75061
Phone: (972) 579-8100
Sales: $121,082,000   *Employees:* 1,600
Company Type: Private   *Employees here:* 1,500
SIC: 8062
    General hospital
Jay Macfarland, Executive Director

D-U-N-S 13-103-9331
BAYLOR UNIVERSITY MEDICAL CTR
3500 Gaston Ave, Dallas, TX 75246
Phone: (214) 820-0111
Sales: $480,807,000   *Employees:* 5,401
Company Type: Private   *Employees here:* 4,425
SIC: 8062
    General hospital
Boone Powell Jr, President

D-U-N-S 03-026-0467
BAYONNE HOSPITAL
29th St Ave E, Bayonne, NJ 7002
Phone: (201) 858-5000
Sales: $80,550,000   *Employees:* 1,200
Company Type: Private   *Employees here:* 1,164
SIC: 8062
    General hospital
Michael D Agnes, President

D-U-N-S 06-870-3636
BAYSHORE COMMUNITY HOSPITAL
727 N Beers St, Holmdel, NJ 7733
Phone: (732) 739-5900
Sales: $63,733,000   *Employees:* 1,000
Company Type: Private   *Employees here:* 1,000
SIC: 8062
    General hospital
Thomas Goldman, President

D-U-N-S 07-923-7988
BAYSTATE MEDICAL CENTER INC
759 Chestnut St, Springfield, MA 1199
Phone: (413) 784-0000

Sales: $368,733,000 | *Employees:* 5,000
Company Type: Private | *Employees here:* 4,400
SIC: 8062
  General hospital
Mark R Tolosky, Chief Executive Officer

D-U-N-S 08-430-4724
BCN-HEALTH CENTRAL
  (Parent: Blue Cross Blue Shield Of Mi)
1403 S Creyts Rd, Lansing, MI 48917
Phone: (517) 322-8000
Sales: $33,600,000 | *Employees:* 490
Company Type: Private | *Employees here:* 66
SIC: 8011
  Health maintenance organization
James C Epolito, Chief Executive Officer

D-U-N-S 07-200-6265
BEAUFORT COUNTY HOSPITAL ASSN INC
628 E 12th St, Washington, NC 27889
Phone: (252) 975-4100
Sales: $29,476,000 | *Employees:* 500
Company Type: Private | *Employees here:* 500
SIC: 8062
  Hospital
Bill Bedsole, Chief Financial Officer

D-U-N-S 07-370-7432
BEAUFORT COUNTY MEMORIAL HOSP
955 Ribaut Rd, Beaufort, SC 29902
Phone: (843) 522-5200
Sales: $58,549,000 | *Employees:* 800
Company Type: Private | *Employees here:* 780
SIC: 8062
  General hospital
David Brown, President

D-U-N-S 07-842-7325
BEAUMONT HOSPITAL INC
  (Parent: Columbia/Hca Healthcare Corp)
3080 College St, Beaumont, TX 77701
Phone: (409) 833-1411
Sales: $31,900,000 | *Employees:* 700
Company Type: Public Family Member | *Employees here:* 620
SIC: 8062
  General medical & surgical hospital
Louis Silva, Chief Executive Officer

D-U-N-S 62-179-2670
BEAUMONT REHABILITATION ASSOC L P
  (Parent: Horizon/Cms Healthcare Corp)
3340 Plaza 10 Dr, Beaumont, TX 77707
Phone: (409) 835-0835
Sales: $25,806,000 | *Employees:* 230
Company Type: Public Family Member | *Employees here:* 230
SIC: 8069
  Rehabilitation hospital
David Holly, Chairman of the Board

D-U-N-S 07-614-2215
BEAVER DAM COMMUNITY HOSPITALS
707 S University Ave, Beaver Dam, WI 53916
Phone: (920) 887-7181
Sales: $31,369,000 | *Employees:* 745
Company Type: Private | *Employees here:* 525
SIC: 8062
  General hospital and nursing home
John R Landdeck, President

D-U-N-S 14-850-5324
BECKLUND HOME HEALTH CARE,
8421 Wayzata Blvd Ste 100, Minneapolis, MN 55426
Phone: (612) 544-0315

Sales: $27,000,000 | *Employees:* 1,400
Company Type: Private | *Employees here:* 950
SIC: 8082
  Home health care
Rhoda Becklund, President

D-U-N-S 07-538-8371
BEDFORD COUNTY GENERAL HOSP
845 Union St, Shelbyville, TN 37160
Phone: (931) 685-5433
Sales: $22,909,000 | *Employees:* 349
Company Type: Private | *Employees here:* 349
SIC: 8062
  Hospital
Ronnie Riddle, Controller

D-U-N-S 07-206-2003
BEDFORD REGIONAL MEDICAL CTR
2900 16th St, Bedford, IN 47421
Phone: (812) 279-3581
Sales: $24,486,000 | *Employees:* 390
Company Type: Private | *Employees here:* 383
SIC: 8062
  General hospital
John Birdzell, Chief Executive Officer

D-U-N-S 92-757-0713
BEDFORD-NORTHEAST COMMUNITY HOSP
1301 Airport Fwy, Bedford, TX 76021
Phone: (817) 868-5740
Sales: $20,200,000 | *Employees:* NA
Company Type: Public Family Member | *Employees here:* 500
SIC: 8062
  Acute care hopsital
Randy Moresi, Chief Executive Officer

D-U-N-S 06-988-5374
BEEBE MEDICAL CENTER INC
424 Savannah Rd, Lewes, DE 19958
Phone: (302) 645-3300
Sales: $65,259,000 | *Employees:* 808
Company Type: Private | *Employees here:* 656
SIC: 8062
  General hospital
Jeffrey M Fried, President

D-U-N-S 14-828-1991
BEHAVIORAL HEALTH, INC.
3849 North Blvd Ste 200, Baton Rouge, LA 70806
Phone: (504) 381-6910
Sales: $27,981,000 | *Employees:* 209
Company Type: Private | *Employees here:* 12
SIC: 8093
  Clinic
Dr Jack Lord, President

D-U-N-S 80-684-1532
BEHAVIORAL HEALTHCARE CORP
102 Woodmont Blvd Ste 800, Nashville, TN 37205
Phone: (615) 269-3492
Sales: $223,811,000 | *Employees:* 3,846
Company Type: Private | *Employees here:* 50
SIC: 8063
  Hospital & residential treatment centers
Edward A Stack, President

D-U-N-S 11-742-9506
BEHRMAN CHIROPRACTIC CLINICS
1817 E Division St, Arlington, TX 76011
Phone: (817) 860-1005

Sales: $20,000,000
Company Type: Private
SIC: 8041
    Chiropractic clinics
Dr Michael Plambeck, President
Employees: 180
Employees here: 17

D-U-N-S 07-644-3803
BELLE BONFILS MEM BLOOD CTR
717 Yosemite Cir, Denver, CO 80220
Phone: (303) 341-4000
Sales: $24,200,000
Company Type: Private
SIC: 8099
    Blood related health services
Dr William C Dickey Md, President
Employees: 272
Employees here: 100

D-U-N-S 06-891-4605
BELLEVUE HOSPITAL INC
811 Northwest St, Bellevue, OH 44811
Phone: (419) 483-4040
Sales: $19,745,000
Company Type: Private
SIC: 8062
    General hospital
Michael K Winthrop, President
Employees: 350
Employees here: 344

D-U-N-S 00-294-5603
BELLFLOWER MEDICAL CENTER
    (Parent: Pacific Health Corporation)
9542 Artesia Blvd, Bellflower, CA 90706
Phone: (562) 925-8355
Sales: $58,918,000
Company Type: Private
SIC: 8011
    Medical center
Stan Otake, President
Employees: 400
Employees here: 400

D-U-N-S 60-382-6132
BELLIN HEALTH SYSTEMS, INC
744 S Webster Ave, Green Bay, WI 54301
Phone: (920) 433-3500
Sales: $74,500,000
Company Type: Private
SIC: 8062
    General hospital & nursing college psychiatric center and
        durable medical equipment rental
George Kerwin, President
Employees: 1,600
Employees here: 2

D-U-N-S 07-477-9430
BELLIN MEMORIAL HOSPITAL
744 S Webster Ave, Green Bay, WI 54301
Phone: (920) 433-3500
Sales: $119,761,000
Company Type: Private
SIC: 8062
    General medical hospital
George Kerwin, President
Employees: 1,650
Employees here: 1,425

D-U-N-S 07-548-3370
BELMONT CENTER COMP TREATMENT
4200 Monument Rd, Philadelphia, PA 19131
Phone: (215) 877-2000
Sales: $22,994,000
Company Type: Private
SIC: 8063
    Psychiatric hospital
Martin Goldsmith, President
Employees: 400
Employees here: 340

D-U-N-S 08-984-5531
BELOIT CLINIC SC
1905 Huebbe Pkwy, Beloit, WI 53511
Phone: (608) 364-2200

Sales: $24,000,000
Company Type: Private
SIC: 8011
    Clinic operated by physicians
James F Ruethling, Administrator
Employees: 350
Employees here: 325

D-U-N-S 07-613-9690
BELOIT MEMORIAL HOSPITAL INC
1969 W Hart Rd, Beloit, WI 53511
Phone: (608) 364-5011
Sales: $51,550,000
Company Type: Private
SIC: 8062
    Hospital
Gregory K Britton, Chief Executive Officer
Employees: 950
Employees here: 786

D-U-N-S 62-679-8177
BENEDICTINE HEALTH SYSTEM
503 E 3rd St 400, Duluth, MN 55805
Phone: (218) 720-2370
Sales: $133,591,000
Company Type: Private
SIC: 8062
    Hospitals nursing homes
Jerry Agnew, Chairman of the Board
Employees: 190
Employees here: 20

D-U-N-S 01-115-1433
BENEDICTINE LIVING COMMUNITIES
503 E 3rd St Ste 400, Duluth, MN 55805
Phone: (218) 720-2370
Sales: $21,417,000
Company Type: Private
SIC: 8051
    Non-profit owner and operator of skilled nursing care
        facilities
Chester Willer, Chairman of the Board
Employees: 565
Employees here: 3

D-U-N-S 06-892-2160
BENEFIS HEALTH CARE
1101 26th St S, Great Falls, MT 59405
Phone: (406) 761-1200
Sales: $126,593,000
Company Type: Private
SIC: 8062
    General hospital
Lloyd Smith, Chief Executive Officer
Employees: 2,000
Employees here: 1,130

D-U-N-S 07-616-4243
BENEVLENT CORP CEDAR CAMPUSES
5595 Highway Z, West Bend, WI 53095
Phone: (414) 334-9487
Sales: $25,608,000
Company Type: Private
SIC: 8051
    Skilled nursing care facility
Steven J Jaberg, Executive Director
Employees: 750
Employees here: 672

D-U-N-S 92-887-0856
BENJAMIN FRANKLIN CLINIC
800 Spruce St, Philadelphia, PA 19107
Phone: (215) 829-3450
Sales: $21,400,000
Company Type: Private
SIC: 8011
    Health care services
Deborah L Staples, Executive Director
Employees: 313
Employees here: 313

D-U-N-S 06-744-6526
BENSENVILLE HOME SOCIETY
331 S York Rd, Bensenville, IL 60106
Phone: (630) 766-5800

Sales: $35,491,000   Employees: 640
Company Type: Private   Employees here: 225
SIC: 8051
   Skilled nursing care individual & family social svc & child
   care ctr foster care adoption & apartment building operator
Dean Spencer, President

D-U-N-S 87-929-0989
BERGAN MERCY HEALTH CLINICS
7500 Mercy Rd, Omaha, NE 68124
Phone: (402) 398-6060
Sales: $172,400,000   Employees: 2,500
Company Type: Private   Employees here: 2,500
SIC: 8011
   Physicians group
Richard A Hachten Ii, President

D-U-N-S 01-094-9188
BERGEN REGIONAL MEDICAL CTR
230 E Ridgewood Ave, Paramus, NJ 7652
Phone: (201) 967-4000
Sales: $79,200,000   Employees: 1,700
Company Type: Private   Employees here: 1,700
SIC: 8062
   General medical & surgical hospital
V R Salazar, Chief Executive Officer

D-U-N-S 06-052-9989
BERKSHIRE FARM CENTER & SERVIC
13640 Rte 22, Canaan, NY 12029
Phone: (518) 781-4567
Sales: $32,890,000   Employees: 521
Company Type: Private   Employees here: 350
SIC: 8361
   Juvenile correctional home
Rose W Washington, Executive Director

D-U-N-S 02-067-3778
BERKSHIRE MEDICAL CENTER INC
725 North St, Pittsfield, MA 1201
Phone: (413) 447-2000
Sales: $135,577,000   Employees: 1,375
Company Type: Private   Employees here: 1,375
SIC: 8062
   General medical hospital
David Phelps, Chief Executive Officer

D-U-N-S 11-068-0220
BERKSHIRE PHYSICIANS SURGEONS PC
777 North St, Pittsfield, MA 1201
Phone: (413) 445-0100
Sales: $41,726,000   Employees: 240
Company Type: Private   Employees here: 200
SIC: 8011
   Medical doctor's office
Dr Peter Zwerner Md, President

D-U-N-S 10-799-8049
BERT FISH MEDICAL CENTER INC
401 Palmetto St, New Smyrna Beach, FL 32168
Phone: (904) 427-3401
Sales: $41,257,000   Employees: NA
Company Type: Private   Employees here: NA
SIC: 8062
   General medical acute care hospital
Kathy Leonard, Administrator

D-U-N-S 06-958-8515
BERWICK HOSPITAL CENTER, INC
701 E 16th St, Berwick, PA 18603
Phone: (717) 759-5000

Sales: $29,919,000   Employees: 650
Company Type: Private   Employees here: 15
SIC: 8062
   Medical & surgical hospital
Thomas Sphatt, President

D-U-N-S 07-765-1511
BESSEMER CARRAWAY MEDICAL CTR
Highway 11 S, Bessemer, AL 35021
Phone: (205) 481-7000
Sales: $47,065,000   Employees: 729
Company Type: Private   Employees here: 656
SIC: 8062
   General hospital
Dan Eagar, Treasurer

D-U-N-S 06-191-6094
BESTCARE INC
3000 Hempstead Tpke, Levittown, NY 11756
Phone: (516) 731-3770
Sales: $32,000,000   Employees: 2,000
Company Type: Private   Employees here: 40
SIC: 8082
   Provides home medical care
Lawrence Wiener, President

D-U-N-S 07-172-3621
BETH ISRAEL DEACONESS MED CTR
330 Brookline Ave, Boston, MA 2215
Phone: (617) 667-8000
Sales: $675,000,000   Employees: 7,600
Company Type: Private   Employees here: 5,000
SIC: 8062
   Hospital
Herbert Y Kressel, President

D-U-N-S 06-751-9827
BETH ISRAEL HOSPITAL ASSN
70 Parker Ave, Passaic, NJ 7055
Phone: (973) 365-5000
Sales: $53,006,000   Employees: 650
Company Type: Private   Employees here: 650
SIC: 8062
   General hospital
Jeffrey S Moll, President

D-U-N-S 07-525-5364
BETH ISRAEL MEDICAL CENTER
First Avenue At 16th St, New York, NY 10003
Phone: (212) 420-2000
Sales: $834,050,000   Employees: 8,100
Company Type: Private   Employees here: 4,000
SIC: 8062
   General hospital
Dr Robert G Newman Md, President

D-U-N-S 15-264-1213
BETH ISRAEL MEDICAL CENTER
E 16th 1st Ave, New York, NY 10003
Phone: (212) 420-2000
Sales: $113,800,000   Employees: NA
Company Type: Private   Employees here: 3,505
SIC: 8093
   Specialty outpatient clinic
Dr Robert G Newman, President

D-U-N-S 06-838-7380
BETHANIA REGIONAL HEALTH CARE CTR
1600 11th St, Wichita Falls, TX 76301
Phone: (940) 723-4111

Sales: $67,183,000   Employees: 1,800
Company Type: Private   Employees here: 1,770
SIC: 8062
    Hospital
Jeff Hausler, Chief Executive Officer

D-U-N-S 07-405-8918
BETHANY CIRCLE OF KINGS DAUGHTERS
1 Kings Daughters Dr, Madison, IN 47250
Phone: (812) 265-5211
Sales: $41,599,000   Employees: 800
Company Type: Private   Employees here: 545
SIC: 8062
    General hospital skilled nursing medical clinics and home
    health care
Roger J Allman, President

D-U-N-S 05-541-6689
BETHANY HO HOSPITAL METH CH
5025 N Paulina St, Chicago, IL 60640
Phone: (773) 271-9040
Sales: $43,394,000   Employees: 800
Company Type: Private   Employees here: 600
SIC: 8062
    General hospital skilled nursing home and retirement center
Steven Freidman, Administrator

D-U-N-S 01-064-7501
BETHANY MEDICAL CENTER
51 N 12th St, Kansas City, KS 66102
Phone: (913) 281-8400
Sales: $74,762,000   Employees: 1,200
Company Type: Private   Employees here: 1,150
SIC: 8062
    General medical and surgical hospital and outpatient medical
    clinic
Paul Herzog, President

D-U-N-S 60-919-5607
BETHESDA HEALTHCARE INC
    (Parent: Bethesda Inc)
8044 Montgomery Rd, Cincinnati, OH 45236
Phone: (513) 569-6111
Sales: $28,900,000   Employees: 421
Company Type: Private   Employees here: 3
SIC: 8011
    Primary medical care occupational physician substance abuse
    counseling fitness center mgt & physical exam & health
    screening
L T Wilburn Jr, President

D-U-N-S 06-463-8190
BETHESDA HEALTH GROUP OF ST LOUIS
3655 Vista Ave, Saint Louis, MO 63110
Phone: (314) 772-9200
Sales: $48,431,000   Employees: 1,200
Company Type: Private   Employees here: 350
SIC: 8051
    Hospital & skilled nursing facilities
John F Norwood, President

D-U-N-S 07-288-2756
BETHESDA HOSPITAL INC
619 Oak St, Cincinnati, OH 45206
Phone: (513) 569-6111
Sales: $207,594,000   Employees: 3,000
Company Type: Private   Employees here: 1,390
SIC: 8062
    General hospital
L T Wilburn Jr, President

D-U-N-S 09-986-6212
BETHESDA HOSPITAL INC
10500 Montgomery Rd, Cincinnati, OH 45242
Phone: (513) 745-1111
Sales: $63,500,000   Employees: NA
Company Type: Private   Employees here: 1,500
SIC: 8062
    General hospital
James Connelly, Principal

D-U-N-S 07-384-3419
BETHESDA LUTHERAN HOMES & SVCS
700 Hoffman Dr, Watertown, WI 53094
Phone: (920) 261-3050
Sales: $24,558,000   Employees: 1,200
Company Type: Private   Employees here: 700
SIC: 8059
    Homes with health care for retarded and thrift stores
Alexander L Napolitano, Executive Director

D-U-N-S 18-360-5492
BETHESDA LUTHERAN HOSPITAL
559 Capitol Blvd, Saint Paul, MN 55103
Phone: (651) 232-2000
Sales: $35,999,000   Employees: 490
Company Type: Private   Employees here: 490
SIC: 8062
    General hospital
Timothy H Hanson, President

D-U-N-S 07-135-8519
BETHESDA LUTHERAN MEDICAL CTR
559 Capitol Blvd, Saint Paul, MN 55103
Phone: (651) 232-2000
Sales: $27,200,000   Employees: 600
Company Type: Private   Employees here: 600
SIC: 8062
    Hospital nursing home
Timothy Hanson, President

D-U-N-S 13-210-4829
BETHESDA MEMORIAL HOSPITAL
2815 S Seacrest Blvd, Boynton Beach, FL 33435
Phone: (561) 737-7733
Sales: $119,593,000   Employees: 1,545
Company Type: Private   Employees here: 1,515
SIC: 8062
    General hospital
Robert B Hill, President

D-U-N-S 16-950-1491
BETHESDA NAVAL HOSPITAL
Rockville Pike, Bethesda, MD 20814
Phone: (301) 295-4611
Sales: $199,100,000   Employees: 4,237
Company Type: Private   Employees here: 4,237
SIC: 8062
    General hospital
Admiral B Potter, Administrator

D-U-N-S 07-415-0459
BEVERLY COMMUNITY HOSPITAL ASSN
309 W Beverly Blvd, Montebello, CA 90640
Phone: (323) 726-1222
Sales: $68,434,000   Employees: 1,100
Company Type: Private   Employees here: NA
SIC: 8062
    Hospital
Matthew Gerlack, Administrator

D-U-N-S 78-324-5137
BEVERLY ENTERPRISES - ARKANSAS
  (Parent: Beverly Hlth Rhbilitation Svcs)
5111 Rogers Ave Ste 40A, Fort Smith, AR 72919
Phone: (501) 452-6712
Sales: $112,500,000   *Employees:* 4,896
Company Type: Public Family Member   *Employees here:* 200
SIC: 8051
  Skilled care facility
William A Mathaes, President

D-U-N-S 06-540-5151
BEVERLY ENTERPRISES - MISSOURI
  (Parent: Beverly Hlth Rhbilitation Svcs)
1200 S Waldron Rd Ste 155, Fort Smith, AR 72919
Phone: (501) 452-6712
Sales: $91,400,000   *Employees:* NA
Company Type: Public Family Member   *Employees here:* NA
SIC: 8059
  Convalescent homes
David R Banks, President

D-U-N-S 04-933-4683
BEVERLY ENTERPRISES INC
1200 S Waldron Rd Ste 155, Fort Smith, AR 72919
Phone: (501) 452-6712
Sales: $3,217,099,000   *Employees:* 74,000
Company Type: Public   *Employees here:* 167
SIC: 8051
  Owns leases & manages nursing care facilities & operates
  retirement projects pharmacies and health care centers
David R Banks, Chief Executive Officer

D-U-N-S 14-417-0214
BEVERLY ENTERPRISES-FLORIDA,
  (Parent: Beverly Hlth Rhbilitation Svcs)
1200 S Waldron Rd Ste 155, Fort Smith, AR 72919
Phone: (501) 452-6712
Sales: $116,435,000   *Employees:* 5,260
Company Type: Public Family Member   *Employees here:* 8
SIC: 8059
  Operator of convalescent homes
David R Banks, President

D-U-N-S 17-443-9216
BEVERLY ENTERPRISES-MICHIGAN,
  (Parent: Beverly Hlth Rhbilitation Svcs)
5111 Rogers Ave Ste 40A, Fort Smith, AR 72919
Phone: (501) 452-6712
Sales: $103,700,000   *Employees:* 4,643
Company Type: Public Family Member   *Employees here:* 185
SIC: 8059
  Convalescent homes
David R Banks, Chairman of the Board

D-U-N-S 15-211-7024
BEVERLY ENTERPRISES-WASHINGTON
  (Parent: Beverly Hlth Rhbilitation Svcs)
1200 S Waldron Rd Ste 155, Fort Smith, AR 72919
Phone: (501) 452-6712
Sales: $96,400,000   *Employees:* 4,200
Company Type: Public Family Member   *Employees here:* 16
SIC: 8051
  Skilled nursing facilities
David R Banks, President

D-U-N-S 06-959-7581
BEVERLY ENTRPRSS-CALIFORNIA INC
  (Parent: Beverly Hlth Rhbilitation Svcs)
5111 Rogers Ave Ste 40A, Fort Smith, AR 72919
Phone: (501) 452-6712

Sales: $3,230,300,000   *Employees:* 110
Company Type: Public Family Member   *Employees here:* 5
SIC: 8051
  Skilled nursing care facility
David Banks, Chief Executive Officer

D-U-N-S 78-324-1565
BEVERLY ENTRPRSS-CONNECTICUT INC
  (Parent: Beverly Hlth Rhbilitation Svcs)
1200 S Waldron Rd Ste 155, Fort Smith, AR 72919
Phone: (501) 452-6712
Sales: $27,300,000   *Employees:* 1,200
Company Type: Public Family Member   *Employees here:* 1,200
SIC: 8051
  Skilled nursing care facility
David R Banks, Chief Executive Officer

D-U-N-S 62-309-8738
BEVERLY HOSPITAL CORP
75 Lindall St, Danvers, MA 1923
Phone: (978) 774-4400
Sales: $28,100,000   *Employees:* NA
Company Type: Private   *Employees here:* 450
SIC: 8011
  Medical doctor's office
Sheldon Aronson, Administrator

D-U-N-S 06-944-6656
BEXAR COUNTY HOSPITAL DST
4502 Medical Dr, San Antonio, TX 78229
Phone: (210) 616-4000
Sales: $321,426,000   *Employees:* 3,424
Company Type: Private   *Employees here:* 2,252
SIC: 8062
  General hospital
John Guest, President

D-U-N-S 55-710-8149
BEXAR COUNTY HOSPITAL DST
4502 Medical Dr, San Antonio, TX 78229
Phone: (210) 616-2677
Sales: $50,900,000   *Employees:* NA
Company Type: Private   *Employees here:* 1,000
SIC: 8092
  Kidney dialysis centers
Diane Carney, Manager

D-U-N-S 01-052-8560
BEXAR COUNTY MENTAL HEALTH
3031 I H 10 W, San Antonio, TX 78201
Phone: (210) 731-1300
Sales: $35,174,000   *Employees:* 600
Company Type: Private   *Employees here:* 142
SIC: 8051
  Mental health & retardation services
Ronaldo Morales, Executive Director

D-U-N-S 07-315-4940
BIG SPRING HOSPITAL CORP
  (Parent: Community Health Systems Inc)
1601 W 11th Pl, Big Spring, TX 79720
Phone: (915) 263-1211
Sales: $24,727,000   *Employees:* 325
Company Type: Public Family Member   *Employees here:* 302
SIC: 8062
  General hospital
Kenneth Randall, Executive Director

D-U-N-S 07-381-7595
BIO-MEDICAL APPLICATIONS OF TEXAS
  (Parent: Bio-Medical Applications Mgt)
95 Hayden Ave, Lexington, MA 2421
Phone: (781) 402-9000

Sales: $28,600,000   *Employees:* 500
Company Type: Public Family Member   *Employees here:* 3
SIC: 8092
    Kidney dialysis centers
A M Nogelo, Treasurer

D-U-N-S 07-087-7808
BIO-MEDICAL APPLICATIONS OF FLA
    (Parent: Fresenius Nat Med Care Hldings)
3550 Buschwood Park Dr, Tampa, FL 33618
Phone: (813) 932-9063
Sales: $57,100,000   *Employees:* 1,000
Company Type: Public Family Member   *Employees here:* 35
SIC: 8092
    Renal dialysis center
Robert Lopez, Regional Manager

D-U-N-S 07-951-6589
BIO-MEDICAL APPLICATIONS MGT
    (Parent: Fresenius Nat Med Care Hldings)
95 Hayden Ave, Lexington, MA 2421
Phone: (000) 000-0000
Sales: $685,700,000   *Employees:* 12,000
Company Type: Public Family Member   *Employees here:* 125
SIC: 8092
    Kidney dialysis center
Constantin L Hampers, President

D-U-N-S 12-157-1798
BIO-REFERENCE LABORATORIES INC
481 Edward H Ross Dr, Elmwood Park, NJ 7407
Phone: (201) 791-2600
Sales: $38,660,000   *Employees:* 420
Company Type: Public   *Employees here:* 226
SIC: 8071
    Commercial medical laboratory
Dr Marc Grodman, Chairman of the Board

D-U-N-S 07-712-0608
BIOMEDICAL SYSTEMS CORPORATION
2464 W Port Plaza Dr, Saint Louis, MO 63146
Phone: (314) 576-6800
Sales: $20,000,000   *Employees:* 95
Company Type: Private   *Employees here:* 65
SIC: 8099
    Physical examination and medical testing services
Timothy R Barrett, President

D-U-N-S 08-100-5878
BIZER ENTERPRISES
516 E Highway 131, Clarksville, IN 47129
Phone: (812) 282-2020
Sales: $25,000,000   *Employees:* 500
Company Type: Private   *Employees here:* 80
SIC: 8042
    Optometrist & opticians
Dr Jerry L Bizer, Partner

D-U-N-S 19-629-2627
BLANCHARD VALLEY REGIONAL HEALTH CTR
145 W Wallace St, Findlay, OH 45840
Phone: (419) 423-4500
Sales: $66,299,000   *Employees:* 797
Company Type: Private   *Employees here:* 655
SIC: 8062
    General hospital
Clifford Lehman, President

D-U-N-S 07-992-9733
BLESSING HOSPITAL
Broadway At 11th St, Quincy, IL 62301
Phone: (217) 223-5811

Sales: $94,783,000   *Employees:* 1,600
Company Type: Private   *Employees here:* 1,100
SIC: 8062
    General hospital
Bradford Billings, Chief Operating Officer

D-U-N-S 07-488-5492
BLOOD CARE
9000 Harry Hines Blvd, Dallas, TX 75235
Phone: (214) 351-8111
Sales: $22,932,000   *Employees:* 340
Company Type: Private   *Employees here:* 310
SIC: 8099
    Blood bank
Dr Merlyn Sayers, Chief Executive Officer

D-U-N-S 07-187-5777
BLOOD CENTERS OF PACIFIC
270 Masonic Ave, San Francisco, CA 94118
Phone: (415) 567-6400
Sales: $29,742,000   *Employees:* 400
Company Type: Private   *Employees here:* 120
SIC: 8099
    Blood bank
Dr William A Heaton, President

D-U-N-S 05-716-3172
BLOOD CTR OF SOUTHEASTERN WI INC
638 N 18th St, Milwaukee, WI 53233
Phone: (414) 933-5000
Sales: $45,231,000   *Employees:* 400
Company Type: Private   *Employees here:* 350
SIC: 8099
    Blood related health services
G E Howe, Treasurer

D-U-N-S 79-818-9502
BLOOD SERVICES CENTL OHIO REG
995 E Broad St, Columbus, OH 43205
Phone: (614) 253-7981
Sales: $21,656,000   *Employees:* 254
Company Type: Private   *Employees here:* 200
SIC: 8099
    Blood services
Dr Ambrose Ng, Principal

D-U-N-S 00-690-2498
BLOOD SYSTEMS, INC.
6210 E Oak St, Scottsdale, AZ 85257
Phone: (602) 946-4201
Sales: $118,681,000   *Employees:* 1,868
Company Type: Private   *Employees here:* 150
SIC: 8099
    Blood centers
J D Connor, President

D-U-N-S 07-205-2137
BLOOMINGTON HOSPITAL INC
601 W 2nd St, Bloomington, IN 47403
Phone: (812) 336-6821
Sales: $126,816,000   *Employees:* 2,000
Company Type: Private   *Employees here:* 1,800
SIC: 8062
    Hospital
Nancy S Carlstedt, President

D-U-N-S 06-959-5031
BLOOMSBURG HOSPITAL INC
549 Fair St, Bloomsburg, PA 17815
Phone: (717) 387-2100

Sales: $26,121,000
Company Type: Private
SIC: 8062
   General hospital with a psychiatric unit
Robert Spinelli, President

Employees: 500
Employees here: 500

D-U-N-S 07-491-1181
BLOUNT MEMORIAL HOSPITAL
907 E Lamar Alexander Pkw, Maryville, TN 37804
Phone: (423) 983-7211
Sales: $77,712,000
Company Type: Private
SIC: 8062
   General hospital
Joseph M Dawson, Administrator

Employees: 1,300
Employees here: 1,140

D-U-N-S 03-033-5392
BLUE RIDGE ORTHOPEDIC ASSOC PC
550 Hospital Dr, Warrenton, VA 20186
Phone: (540) 347-9220
Sales: $19,900,000
Company Type: Private
SIC: 8011
   Physicians
Dr David Couk Md, President

Employees: 291
Employees here: 22

D-U-N-S 08-890-7514
BLUEFIELD REGIONAL MEDICAL CTR
500 Cherry St, Bluefield, WV 24701
Phone: (304) 327-2511
Sales: $72,636,000
Company Type: Private
SIC: 8062
   General hospital
Eugene Pawlowski, President

Employees: 900
Employees here: 900

D-U-N-S 07-542-2964
BLYTHEDALE CHILDREN'S HOSPITAL
Bradhurst Ave, Valhalla, NY 10595
Phone: (914) 592-7555
Sales: $21,575,000
Company Type: Private
SIC: 8069
   Childrens' hospital
Robert Stone, President

Employees: 330
Employees here: 330

D-U-N-S 03-034-1622
BOARD OF CHILD CARE OF BALT-WA
3300 Gaither Rd, Baltimore, MD 21244
Phone: (410) 922-2100
Sales: $26,549,000
Company Type: Private
SIC: 8361
   Residential care foster homes group homes adoption agency
     & counseling for unwed mothers
Tom Curcio, Executive Director

Employees: 140
Employees here: 90

D-U-N-S 05-500-4105
BOARD OF TRUSTEES OF WELBORN
421 Chestnut St, Evansville, IN 47713
Phone: (812) 426-9411
Sales: $45,431,000
Company Type: Private
SIC: 8011
   Medical clinic
Dr John C Huus Md, Chairman of the Board

Employees: 900
Employees here: 650

D-U-N-S 07-987-1968
BOCA RATON COMMUNITY HOSPITAL INC
800 Meadows Rd, Boca Raton, FL 33486
Phone: (561) 395-7100

Sales: $152,326,000
Company Type: Private
SIC: 8062
   General hospital
Randy Pierce, President

Employees: 1,900
Employees here: 1,800

D-U-N-S 04-004-8720
BOICE-WILLIS CLINIC PA
901 N Winstead Ave, Rocky Mount, NC 27804
Phone: (252) 937-0200
Sales: $29,373,000
Company Type: Private
SIC: 8011
   Medical clinic
Dr Shalendra Varma Md, President

Employees: 350
Employees here: 290

D-U-N-S 07-792-7077
BON SCURS MEM REGIONAL MED CTR
1300 Westwood Ave, Richmond, VA 23227
Phone: (804) 254-9100
Sales: $98,100,000
Company Type: Private
SIC: 8062
   General medical & surgical hospital
Michael Robinson, Executive Vice-President

Employees: 2,100
Employees here: 1,700

D-U-N-S 18-657-6617
BON SECOURS HEALTH SYSTEM INC
2000 W Baltimore St, Baltimore, MD 21223
Phone: (410) 362-3392
Sales: $39,500,000
Company Type: Private
SIC: 8062
   General hospital
Jane Durney, Manager

Employees: NA
Employees here: 900

D-U-N-S 04-628-2893
BON SECOURS HOSPITAL BALTIMORE
2000 W Baltimore St, Baltimore, MD 21223
Phone: (410) 362-3020
Sales: $71,001,000
Company Type: Private
SIC: 8062
   General & surgical hospital
Jane Durney-Crowley, Chief Executive Officer

Employees: 1,120
Employees here: 900

D-U-N-S 07-999-4273
BON SECOURS VENICE HEALTHCARE
540 The Rialto, Venice, FL 34285
Phone: (941) 485-7711
Sales: $91,989,000
Company Type: Private
SIC: 8062
   General hospital
Roy Hess, Chief Executive Officer

Employees: 1,265
Employees here: 935

D-U-N-S 07-474-4905
BON SECOURS-DEPAUL MEDICAL CTR
150 Kingsley Ln, Norfolk, VA 23505
Phone: (757) 889-5000
Sales: $59,764,000
Company Type: Private
SIC: 8062
   General medical and surgical hospital
Mike Markwood, Secretary

Employees: 1,400
Employees here: 1,400

D-U-N-S 62-111-9940
BON SECOURS-RICHMOND HEALTH CORP
5801 Bremo Rd, Richmond, VA 23226
Phone: (804) 285-2011

Sales: $107,600,000   *Employees:* 2,300
Company Type: Private   *Employees here:* 15
SIC: 8062
    General hospital management consulting services business
    services
Chris Carney, Chief Executive Officer

D-U-N-S 82-568-5878
BON SECOURS-STUART CIRCLE HOSP
413 Stuart Cir, Richmond, VA 23220
Phone: (804) 358-7051
Sales: $36,020,000   *Employees:* 400
Company Type: Private   *Employees here:* 400
SIC: 8062
    General medical and surgical hospital
Ann E Honeycutt, Administrator

D-U-N-S 78-798-3014
BON SECOURS, INC
1525 Marriottsville Rd, Marriottsville, MD 21104
Phone: (410) 442-1333
Sales: $51,100,000   *Employees:* 1,105
Company Type: Private   *Employees here:* 5
SIC: 8062
    Provides health care & long term health care & operates
    hospitals
Sister M Flatley, President

D-U-N-S 07-804-7727
BON-SECOURS ST FRANCIS XAVIER HSP
2095 Henry Tecklenburg Dr, Charleston, SC 29414
Phone: (843) 577-1000
Sales: $47,692,000   *Employees:* 1,052
Company Type: Private   *Employees here:* 900
SIC: 8062
    Hospital
Allen P Carroll, Chief Executive Officer

D-U-N-S 07-257-6556
BORGESS MEDICAL CENTER INC
1521 Gull Rd, Kalamazoo, MI 49001
Phone: (616) 226-7000
Sales: $98,100,000   *Employees:* 2,100
Company Type: Private   *Employees here:* 2,070
SIC: 8062
    General hospital and medical clinics
R T Stack, President

D-U-N-S 06-975-0347
BOSSIER GENERAL HOSPITAL
2105 Airline Dr, Bossier City, LA 71111
Phone: (318) 741-6000
Sales: $50,594,000   *Employees:* 700
Company Type: Private   *Employees here:* 700
SIC: 8062
    General hospital
Jack Houghton, Administrator

D-U-N-S 00-549-2160
BOSTON MEDICAL CENTER CORP
1 Bostonia Ave, Boston, MA 2135
Phone: (617) 638-8000
Sales: $386,265,000   *Employees:* 4,200
Company Type: Private   *Employees here:* 2,600
SIC: 8062
    General hospital
Elaine Ullian, Chief Executive Officer

D-U-N-S 09-149-2108
BOSTON MEDICAL CENTER CORP
725 Massachusetts Ave, Boston, MA 2118
Phone: (617) 534-5000

Sales: $203,100,000   *Employees:* NA
Company Type: Private   *Employees here:* 4,000
SIC: 8062
    General hospital
Thomas Traylor, N/A

D-U-N-S 07-382-7511
BOSTON REGIONAL MEDICAL CENTER
5 Woodland Rd, Stoneham, MA 2180
Phone: (781) 979-7000
Sales: $57,441,000   *Employees:* 1,400
Company Type: Private   *Employees here:* 900
SIC: 8062
    Hospital
Charles S Ricks, President

D-U-N-S 06-794-6731
BOTHWELL REGIONAL HEALTH CTR
601 E 14th St, Sedalia, MO 65301
Phone: (660) 826-8833
Sales: $45,666,000   *Employees:* 616
Company Type: Private   *Employees here:* 606
SIC: 8062
    General medical & surgical hospital
James T Rank, Administrator

D-U-N-S 07-423-9344
BOTSFORD GENERAL HOSPITAL
28050 Grand River Ave, Farmington Hills, MI 48336
Phone: (248) 471-8000
Sales: $255,899,000   *Employees:* 1,937
Company Type: Private   *Employees here:* 1,900
SIC: 8062
    General medical & surgical osteopathic hospital
Cooper Gerson I, President

D-U-N-S 09-977-6148
BOWLING GREEN COMM HOSPITAL
250 Park St, Bowling Green, KY 42101
Phone: (502) 781-2150
Sales: $108,002,000   *Employees:* 1,250
Company Type: Private   *Employees here:* 1,250
SIC: 8062
    Hospital
Floyd H Ellis, Chairman of the Board

D-U-N-S 07-633-5041
BOYSVILLE OF MICHIGAN INC
8759 Clinton Macon Rd, Clinton, MI 49236
Phone: (517) 423-7451
Sales: $34,944,000   *Employees:* 834
Company Type: Private   *Employees here:* 200
SIC: 8361
    Residential care services
Br Francis Boylan, Executive Director

D-U-N-S 15-530-5220
BRADFORD GROUP, THE, INC
2101 Magnolia Ave S, Birmingham, AL 35205
Phone: (205) 251-7753
Sales: $22,600,000   *Employees:* 462
Company Type: Private   *Employees here:* 13
SIC: 8069
    Specialty hospital
Jerry W Crowder, President

D-U-N-S 07-402-6378
BRADFORD HOSPITAL INC
116 Interstate Pkwy, Bradford, PA 16701
Phone: (814) 368-4143

Sales: $41,721,000   *Employees:* 650
Company Type: Private   *Employees here:* 580
SIC: 8062
   General hospital
George Leonhardt, President

D-U-N-S 86-131-3625
BRADLEY COUNTY MEMORIAL HOSP
2305 Chambliss Ave Nw, Cleveland, TN 37311
Phone: (423) 559-6000
Sales: $70,531,000   *Employees:* 883
Company Type: Private   *Employees here:* 883
SIC: 8062
   Hospital
Jim Whitlock, Administrator

D-U-N-S 07-570-6176
BRADLEY EMMA PENDLETON HOSP
1011 Veterans Memorial Pk, Riverside, RI 2915
Phone: (401) 434-3400
Sales: $24,050,000   *Employees:* 403
Company Type: Private   *Employees here:* 378
SIC: 8063
   Psychiatric hospital
Daniel J Wall, President

D-U-N-S 79-777-2993
BRADLEY MEM HOSPITAL & HEALTH CTR
   (Parent: Central Conn Hlth Aliance)
81 Meriden Ave, Southington, CT 6489
Phone: (860) 276-5000
Sales: $25,124,000   *Employees:* 425
Company Type: Private   *Employees here:* 425
SIC: 8062
   General hospital
Clarence Silvia, President

D-U-N-S 14-731-9263
BRANDYWINE HEALTH SERVICES
255 Reeceville Rd, Coatesville, PA 19320
Phone: (610) 383-8581
Sales: $77,416,000   *Employees:* 75
Company Type: Private   *Employees here:* 10
SIC: 8062
   Health system
James Thornton, President

D-U-N-S 07-375-2156
BRANDYWINE HOSPITAL
201 Reeceville Rd, Coatesville, PA 19320
Phone: (610) 383-8000
Sales: $64,757,000   *Employees:* 1,300
Company Type: Private   *Employees here:* 1,245
SIC: 8062
   General hospital
James Thornton, Administrator

D-U-N-S 07-397-4065
BRATTLEBORO RETREAT
75 Linden St, Brattleboro, VT 5301
Phone: (802) 257-7785
Sales: $22,539,000   *Employees:* 550
Company Type: Private   *Employees here:* 500
SIC: 8063
   Psychiatric hospital & skilled nursing care facility
Rick Palmisano, Chief Executive Officer

D-U-N-S 03-060-1769
BREA DEVELOPMENT COMPANY LTD
380 W Central Ave, Brea, CA 92821
Phone: (714) 529-0211

Sales: $28,863,000   *Employees:* 450
Company Type: Private   *Employees here:* 450
SIC: 8062
   General hospital
Dave Yeager, Chief Executive Officer

D-U-N-S 02-145-1570
BRETHREN HOME COMMUNITY
2990 Carlisle Pike, New Oxford, PA 17350
Phone: (717) 624-2161
Sales: $20,700,000   *Employees:* 590
Company Type: Private   *Employees here:* 590
SIC: 8051
   Skilled & intermediate nursing facilities & personal care &
     independent living units
Judith C Wallace, President

D-U-N-S 14-853-6071
BRIDGEPORT HEALTH CARE CENTER
600 Bond St, Bridgeport, CT 6610
Phone: (203) 384-6400
Sales: $31,261,000   *Employees:* 550
Company Type: Private   *Employees here:* 550
SIC: 8051
   Convalescent nursing care
Christophe Massaro, Administrator

D-U-N-S 05-674-6464
BRIDGEPORT HOSPITAL INC
267 Grant St, Bridgeport, CT 6610
Phone: (203) 384-3000
Sales: $190,248,000   *Employees:* 2,050
Company Type: Private   *Employees here:* 2,029
SIC: 8062
   General hospital & medical school
Robert J Trefry, President

D-U-N-S 07-662-4261
BRIGHAM AND WOMENS HOSPITAL INC
75 Francis St, Boston, MA 2115
Phone: (617) 732-5500
Sales: $507,150,000   *Employees:* 8,000
Company Type: Private   *Employees here:* 7,500
SIC: 8062
   General hospital
Jeffrey Otten, President

D-U-N-S 07-658-6122
BRIGHAM MED GROUP FOUNDATION
20 Kent St, Brookline, MA 2445
Phone: (617) 732-7073
Sales: $27,598,000   *Employees:* 400
Company Type: Private   *Employees here:* 60
SIC: 8093
   Provides outpatient & inpatient care services
Victor J Dzau, President

D-U-N-S 61-161-1922
BRIGHAM MEDICAL CENTER INC
75 Francis St, Boston, MA 2115
Phone: (617) 732-5500
Sales: $455,966,000   *Employees:* 7,000
Company Type: Private   *Employees here:* 7,000
SIC: 8062
   Operates as a general surgical hospital and a research
     foundation
Dr H R Nesson Md, President

D-U-N-S 05-315-1817
BRIGHAM SURGICAL GROUP FOUNDATION
110 Cypress St, Brookline, MA 2445
Phone: (617) 732-7010

Sales: $37,669,000
Company Type: Private
SIC: 8011
  Medical doctor's office
Dr Michael Zinner Md, President
Employees: 350
Employees here: 300

D-U-N-S 01-200-3513
BRIGHTON MARINE HEALTH CENTER
77 Warren St, Boston, MA 2135
Phone: (617) 562-5200
Sales: $45,857,000
Company Type: Private
SIC: 8093
  Out-patient health center
Col R Hawes, President
Employees: 31
Employees here: 31

D-U-N-S 06-924-2436
BRISTOL HOSPITAL INCORPORATED
Brewster Rd, Bristol, CT 6010
Phone: (860) 585-3000
Sales: $80,000,000
Company Type: Private
SIC: 8062
  General medical and surgical hospital
Thomas D Kennedy Iii, President
Employees: 1,200
Employees here: 1,185

D-U-N-S 10-902-7870
BRITTHAVEN INC
  (Parent: Hillco Ltd)
1435 Highway 258 N, Kinston, NC 28504
Phone: (252) 523-9094
Sales: $181,013,000
Company Type: Private
SIC: 8051
  Skilled nursing facility and rest homes
Robert Hill Sr, President
Employees: 5,200
Employees here: 100

D-U-N-S 80-273-3949
BRITWILL INVESTMENTS I INC
  (Parent: Britwill Healthcare Company)
8800 N Gainey Center Dr, Scottsdale, AZ 85258
Phone: (602) 423-1954
Sales: $114,900,000
Company Type: Public Family Member
SIC: 8051
  Skilled nursing homes
Bruce Whitehead, Chairman of the Board
Employees: 5,000
Employees here: 75

D-U-N-S 82-501-4350
BRITWILL INVESTMENTS II INC
  (Parent: Unison Healthcare Corporation)
8800 N Gainey Center Dr, Scottsdale, AZ 85258
Phone: (602) 423-1954
Sales: $34,200,000
Company Type: Public Family Member
SIC: 8051
  Skilled nursing homes
Bruce Whitehead, Chairman of the Board
Employees: 1,500
Employees here: 32

D-U-N-S 07-348-2739
BROADLAWNS MEDICAL CENTER
1801 Hickman Rd, Des Moines, IA 50314
Phone: (515) 282-2200
Sales: $74,086,000
Company Type: Private
SIC: 8062
  Hospital
Willis Fry, Executive Director
Employees: 900
Employees here: 900

D-U-N-S 15-216-0461
BROCKTON HOSPITAL INC
680 Centre St, Brockton, MA 2302
Phone: (508) 941-7000

Sales: $95,819,000
Company Type: Private
SIC: 8062
  General hospital
Norman Goodman, President
Employees: 1,300
Employees here: 1,300

D-U-N-S 07-241-7892
BROKEN ARROW MEDICAL CENTER
3000 S Elm Pl, Broken Arrow, OK 74012
Phone: (918) 455-3535
Sales: $21,474,000
Company Type: Private
SIC: 8062
  General hospital
Bruce Switzer, Administrator
Employees: 450
Employees here: 403

D-U-N-S 06-740-7619
BROMENN HEALTHCARE
Virginia & Franklin Ave, Normal, IL 61761
Phone: (309) 454-1400
Sales: $86,300,000
Company Type: Private
SIC: 8062
  Hospitals
Dale S Strassheim, Chief Executive Officer
Employees: 1,850
Employees here: 1,700

D-U-N-S 07-258-1812
BRONSON METHODIST HOSPITAL
252 E Lovell St, Kalamazoo, MI 49007
Phone: (616) 341-7654
Sales: $206,505,000
Company Type: Private
SIC: 8062
  General hospital
Frank Sardone, President
Employees: 2,045
Employees here: 1,845

D-U-N-S 05-780-1953
BRONX HARBOR HEALTH CARE COMPLEX
2000 E Gun Hill Rd, Bronx, NY 10469
Phone: (718) 320-0400
Sales: $48,023,000
Company Type: Private
SIC: 8051
  Skilled nursing facility
Morris Tenenbaum, President
Employees: 750
Employees here: 750

D-U-N-S 07-325-8493
BRONX LEBANON HOSPITAL CENTER
1276 Fulton Ave, Bronx, NY 10456
Phone: (718) 590-1800
Sales: $187,900,000
Company Type: Private
SIC: 8062
  General hospital
Miguel Fuentes, President
Employees: 4,000
Employees here: 2,000

D-U-N-S 12-047-5272
BRONX LEBANON HOSPITAL CENTER
1276 Fulton Ave, Bronx, NY 10456
Phone: (718) 901-8800
Sales: $29,300,000
Company Type: Private
SIC: 8062
  General hospital
Miguel S Fuentes Jr, Manager
Employees: NA
Employees here: 600

D-U-N-S 06-386-4656
BROOKDALE UNIV HOSPITAL MED CTR
Linden Blvd At Brookdale Plz, Brooklyn, NY 11212
Phone: (718) 240-5000

Sales: $297,526,000   *Employees:* 3,725
Company Type: Private   *Employees here:* 3,700
SIC: 8062
   General medical hospital
Frank Maddalena, President

D-U-N-S 06-196-4896
BROOKHAVEN MEM HOSPITAL MED CTR
101 Hospital Rd, East Patchogue, NY 11772
Phone: (516) 654-7100
Sales: $125,608,000   *Employees:* 1,900
Company Type: Private   *Employees here:* 1,700
SIC: 8062
   Hospital
Thomas Ockers, President

D-U-N-S 04-155-5665
BROOKLYN HOSPITAL CENTER (INC)
121 De Kalb Ave, Brooklyn, NY 11201
Phone: (718) 250-8000
Sales: $303,926,000   *Employees:* 3,500
Company Type: Private   *Employees here:* 2,700
SIC: 8062
   General medical & surgical hospital
Frederick Alley, President

D-U-N-S 60-407-3221
BROOKLYN HOSPITAL CENTER (INC)
100 Parkside Ave, Brooklyn, NY 11226
Phone: (718) 940-5230
Sales: $29,300,000   *Employees:* NA
Company Type: Private   *Employees here:* 600
SIC: 8062
   General hospital
Richard Moed, Manager

D-U-N-S 07-402-9380
BROOKS MEMORIAL HOSPITAL
529 Central Ave, Dunkirk, NY 14048
Phone: (716) 366-1111
Sales: $25,119,000   *Employees:* 475
Company Type: Private   *Employees here:* 425
SIC: 8062
   General medical hospital
Richard H Ketcham, President

D-U-N-S 06-380-6194
BROTMAN PARTNERS LP
3828 Delmas Ter, Culver City, CA 90232
Phone: (310) 836-7000
Sales: $91,305,000   *Employees:* 1,200
Company Type: Private   *Employees here:* 1,200
SIC: 8062
   General hospital
John Fenton, President

D-U-N-S 07-288-5304
BROWN COUNTY GENERAL HOSPITAL
425 Home St, Georgetown, OH 45121
Phone: (937) 378-6121
Sales: $20,130,000   *Employees:* 292
Company Type: Private   *Employees here:* 268
SIC: 8062
   General surgical & medical hospital
David Wallace, Chief Executive Officer

D-U-N-S 82-558-3750
BROWN SCHOOLS INC.
   (Parent: Mccown De Leeuw & Co)
1407 W Stassney Ln, Austin, TX 78745
Phone: (512) 464-0200

Sales: $138,000,000   *Employees:* 2,200
Company Type: Private   *Employees here:* 48
SIC: 8062
   Acute psychiatric and rehabilitation hospitals
John P Harcourt, President

D-U-N-S 04-973-2910
BROWNE-MCHARDY CLINIC
4315 Houma Blvd, Metairie, LA 70006
Phone: (504) 887-5500
Sales: $22,429,000   *Employees:* 250
Company Type: Private   *Employees here:* 230
SIC: 8011
   Medical clinic
Robert L Goldstein, Cao

D-U-N-S 07-848-4102
BROWNSVILLE-VALLEY REGIONAL MED CTR
   (Parent: Columbia/Hca Healthcare Corp)
100a E Alton Gloor Blvd, Brownsville, TX 78526
Phone: (956) 831-9611
Sales: $175,000,000   *Employees:* 630
Company Type: Public Family Member   *Employees here:* 600
SIC: 8062
   Hospital health/allied services
Dr Thomas L Frist Md, President

D-U-N-S 18-777-8295
BROWNWOOD REGIONAL HOSPITAL
   (Parent: Columbia/Hca Healthcare Corp)
1501 Burnett St, Brownwood, TX 76801
Phone: (915) 646-8541
Sales: $27,000,000   *Employees:* 596
Company Type: Public Family Member   *Employees here:* 596
SIC: 8062
   Hospital
Art Layne, Administrator

D-U-N-S 06-802-7994
BRUNSWICK HOSPITAL CENTER INC
366 Broadway, Amityville, NY 11701
Phone: (516) 789-7000
Sales: $75,936,000   *Employees:* 1,300
Company Type: Private   *Employees here:* 1,300
SIC: 8062
   General medical & surgical hospital
Dr Benjamin Stein, President

D-U-N-S 07-291-9954
BRYAN MEMORIAL HOSPITAL
1600 S 48th St, Lincoln, NE 68506
Phone: (402) 489-0200
Sales: $69,850,000   *Employees:* 2,015
Company Type: Private   *Employees here:* 2,000
SIC: 8062
   General medical & surgical hospital
R L Wilson, Chief Executive Officer

D-U-N-S 03-128-2379
BRYN MAWR REHABILITATION HOSP
414 Paoli Pike, Malvern, PA 19355
Phone: (610) 251-5400
Sales: $32,009,000   *Employees:* 550
Company Type: Private   *Employees here:* 550
SIC: 8069
   Rehabilitation hospital
Barry S Rabner, President

D-U-N-S 09-354-9236
BUCHANAN GENERAL HOSPITAL
Rr 5 Box 20, Grundy, VA 24614
Phone: (540) 935-8831

Sales: $27,177,000
Company Type: Private
SIC: 8062
  General hospital
Dr J P Sutherland Md, Chairman of the Board
Employees: 400
Employees here: 400

D-U-N-S 07-487-5238
BUCKNER BAPTIST BENEVOLENCES
600 N Pearl St Ste 1900, Dallas, TX 75201
Phone: (214) 758-8000
Sales: $37,567,000
Company Type: Private
SIC: 8361
  Residential & social care centers
Dr Kenneth L Hall, President
Employees: 800
Employees here: 40

D-U-N-S 08-593-6615
BUENA VENTURA MEDICAL GROUP
2705 Loma Vista Rd, Ventura, CA 93003
Phone: (805) 656-7530
Sales: $24,000,000
Company Type: Private
SIC: 8011
  Medical clinic
Tom Becker, Administrator
Employees: 350
Employees here: 170

D-U-N-S 07-404-2292
BUFFALO GENERAL HOSPITAL
100 High St, Buffalo, NY 14203
Phone: (716) 845-5600
Sales: $279,438,000
Company Type: Private
SIC: 8062
  General medical & surgical hospital & skilled nursing facility
Carrie Frank, Chief Executive Officer
Employees: 4,249
Employees here: 3,832

D-U-N-S 07-403-9728
BUFFALO MEDICAL GROUP P C
6255 Sheridan Dr, Williamsville, NY 14221
Phone: (716) 631-5835
Sales: $53,000,000
Company Type: Private
SIC: 8011
  Medical clinic
Daniel J Scully, Chief Executive Officer
Employees: 525
Employees here: 70

D-U-N-S 78-146-8178
BUFFALO MEDICAL GROUP P C
295 Essjay Rd, Williamsville, NY 14221
Phone: (716) 631-0001
Sales: $26,400,000
Company Type: Private
SIC: 8011
  Medical doctor's office
Jean Vasiloff, Manager
Employees: NA
Employees here: 150

D-U-N-S 13-523-5778
BURDETTE TOMLIN MEMORIAL HOSP
2 Stone Harbor Blvd, Cape May Court House, NJ 8210
Phone: (609) 463-2000
Sales: $71,075,000
Company Type: Private
SIC: 8062
  Hospital
Thomas L Scott, President
Employees: 950
Employees here: 950

D-U-N-S 04-565-7301
BURKE, WINIFRD MSTRSN REHAB
785 Mamaroneck Ave, White Plains, NY 10605
Phone: (914) 948-0050

Sales: $36,234,000
Company Type: Private
SIC: 8361
  Rehabilitation center
Marybeth Walsh, Executive Director
Employees: 600
Employees here: 600

D-U-N-S 05-804-2961
BURLINGTON MEDICAL CENTER INC
602 N 3rd St, Burlington, IA 52601
Phone: (319) 753-3011
Sales: $62,193,000
Company Type: Private
SIC: 8062
  General hospital
Mark Richardson, President
Employees: 1,050
Employees here: 980

D-U-N-S 06-984-7804
BUTLER HOSPITAL
345 Blackstone Blvd, Providence, RI 2906
Phone: (401) 455-6200
Sales: $37,169,000
Company Type: Private
SIC: 8063
  Psychiatric hospital
Frank A Delmonico, President
Employees: 735
Employees here: 650

D-U-N-S 06-871-8253
BUTLER MEMORIAL HOSPITAL
911 E Brady St, Butler, PA 16001
Phone: (724) 283-6666
Sales: $70,825,000
Company Type: Private
SIC: 8062
  General hospital
Joseph Stewart, President
Employees: 1,200
Employees here: 1,185

D-U-N-S 93-292-5399
BUTTERWRTH CNTNUING CARE GROUP
4500 Breton Rd SE, Grand Rapids, MI 49508
Phone: (616) 455-7300
Sales: $25,780,000
Company Type: Private
SIC: 8051
  Skilled nursing home
Roy Eickman, Administrator
Employees: 420
Employees here: 1

D-U-N-S 07-933-6236
C A C/H DEVELOPMENT INC
  (Parent: Columbia/Hca Healthcare Corp)
2929 S Hampton Rd, Dallas, TX 75224
Phone: (214) 330-4611
Sales: $20,403,000
Company Type: Public Family Member
SIC: 8062
  General hospital
James Warren, Chief Executive Officer
Employees: 250
Employees here: 250

D-U-N-S 06-601-7138
C A COLUMBIA/H RETREAT HOSP
  (Parent: Columbia/Hca Healthcare Corp)
2621 Grove Ave, Richmond, VA 23220
Phone: (804) 254-5100
Sales: $31,784,000
Company Type: Public Family Member
SIC: 8062
  General medical & surgical hospital
Paul Baldwin, Chief Executive Officer
Employees: 320
Employees here: 320

D-U-N-S 06-323-7440
C G H MEDICAL CENTER
100 E Lefevre Rd, Sterling, IL 61081
Phone: (815) 625-0400

Sales: $47,741,000
Company Type: Private
SIC: 8062
  Hospital
Ed Andersen, Chief Executive Officer

Employees: 687
Employees here: 600

D-U-N-S 60-452-2086
C M HEALTHCARE RESOURCES INC
  (Parent: Childrens Memorial Medical Ctr)
1181 Lake Cook Rd, Deerfield, IL 60015
Phone: (847) 945-2647
Sales: $20,416,000
Company Type: Private
SIC: 8082
  Home health agency
Judith E Hicks, President

Employees: 400
Employees here: 40

D-U-N-S 07-279-6618
CABRINI MEDICAL CENTER
227 E 19th St, New York, NY 10003
Phone: (212) 995-6000
Sales: $171,077,000
Company Type: Private
SIC: 8062
  General hospital clinic services psychiatric inpatient &
    outpatient services home care services & hospice
Jeffrey Frerichs, President

Employees: 2,040
Employees here: 1,900

D-U-N-S 16-242-3545
CABS HOME ATTENDANTS SERVICE
545 Broadway Ste 1, Brooklyn, NY 11206
Phone: (718) 388-0220
Sales: $31,000,000
Company Type: Private
SIC: 8082
  Home care organization
Louis Rivera, Director

Employees: 1,400
Employees here: 1,400

D-U-N-S 06-992-5345
CAL SOUTHERN PRESBYTERIAN HOMES
1111 N Brand Blvd Ste 300, Glendale, CA 91202
Phone: (818) 247-0420
Sales: $42,881,000
Company Type: Private
SIC: 8051
  Continuing care retirement community & assisted living
    facilities
Gerald W Dingivan, Chief Executive Officer

Employees: 1,300
Employees here: 40

D-U-N-S 07-105-6238
CALDWELL MEMORIAL HOSPITAL
321 Mulberry St SW, Lenoir, NC 28645
Phone: (828) 757-5100
Sales: $37,479,000
Company Type: Private
SIC: 8062
  General hospital
Fred Soule, President

Employees: 540
Employees here: 525

D-U-N-S 07-359-4145
CALIFORNIA DEPT CORRECTIONS
5th & Western, Norco, CA 91760
Phone: (909) 689-4552
Sales: $31,200,000
Company Type: Private
SIC: 8361
  Correctional institute
Joan Gordon, Warden

Employees: NA
Employees here: 1,188

D-U-N-S 06-012-5242
CALIFORNIA DEPT HEALTH SVCS
15000 Arnold Dr, Eldridge, CA 95431
Phone: (707) 938-6000

Sales: $61,300,000
Company Type: Private
SIC: 8051
  Skilled nursing care facility
Timothy Meeker, President

Employees: NA
Employees here: 2,500

D-U-N-S 07-876-7878
CALIFORNIA DEPT MENTAL HEALTH
26501 Avenue 140, Porterville, CA 93257
Phone: (209) 782-2222
Sales: $29,900,000
Company Type: Private
SIC: 8059
  Residental facility for mentally retarded
Ruth Maples, Director

Employees: NA
Employees here: 1,250

D-U-N-S 08-358-9838
CALIFORNIA DEPT MENTAL HEALTH
3102 E Highland Ave, Patton, CA 92369
Phone: (909) 425-7000
Sales: $51,600,000
Company Type: Private
SIC: 8063
  State hospital
William Summer, Director

Employees: NA
Employees here: 1,500

D-U-N-S 07-655-9806
CALIFORNIA DEPT MENTAL HEALTH
2100 Napa Vallejo Hwy, Napa, CA 94558
Phone: (707) 253-5000
Sales: $98,600,000
Company Type: Private
SIC: 8063
  Mental hospital
Sidney Herndon, Branch Manager

Employees: NA
Employees here: 2,500

D-U-N-S 07-961-9284
CALIFORNIA DEPT MENTAL HEALTH
11400 Norwalk Blvd, Norwalk, CA 90650
Phone: (562) 863-7011
Sales: $59,400,000
Company Type: Private
SIC: 8063
  Psychiatric hospital
Bill Silva, Director

Employees: NA
Employees here: 1,300

D-U-N-S 07-251-3146
CALIFORNIA DEPT MENTAL HEALTH
2501 Harbor Blvd, Costa Mesa, CA 92626
Phone: (714) 957-5000
Sales: $67,300,000
Company Type: Private
SIC: 8063
  State hospital
Hugh Kohler, Director

Employees: NA
Employees here: 1,700

D-U-N-S 07-723-0126
CALIFORNIA DEPT MENTAL HEALTH
1878 S Lewis Rd, Camarillo, CA 93012
Phone: (805) 484-3661
Sales: $79,000,000
Company Type: Private
SIC: 8063
  Psychiatric hospital
David Freehauf, Executive Director

Employees: NA
Employees here: 1,500

D-U-N-S 07-412-1492
CALIFORNIA FAMILY HEALTH COUNCIL
3600 Wilshire Blvd, Los Angeles, CA 90010
Phone: (213) 386-5614

Sales: $25,311,000   *Employees:* 77
Company Type: Private   *Employees here:* 77
SIC: 8093
  Family planning
Margie Fites-Sigel, Chief Executive Officer

D-U-N-S 05-387-9235
CALIFORNIA HOSPITAL MEDICAL
1401 S Grand Ave, Los Angeles, CA 90015
Phone: (213) 748-2411
Sales: $109,710,000   *Employees:* 1,400
Company Type: Private   *Employees here:* 1,400
SIC: 8062
  Hospital
Melinda Beswick, President

D-U-N-S 04-874-7844
CALIFORNIA PACIFIC MED CTR
3801 Sacramento St, San Francisco, CA 94118
Phone: (415) 668-8211
Sales: $105,300,000   *Employees:* NA
Company Type: Private   *Employees here:* 2,000
SIC: 8069
  Hospital
Aubrey Serfling, Principal

D-U-N-S 07-188-2724
CALIFORNIA PACIFIC MED CTR
3700 California St, San Francisco, CA 94118
Phone: (415) 387-8700
Sales: $337,232,000   *Employees:* 3,597
Company Type: Private   *Employees here:* 2,578
SIC: 8062
  General hospital
Dr Martin Brotman Md, Chief Executive Officer

D-U-N-S 13-314-8692
CALIFORNIA PACIFIC MED CTR
2333 Buchanan St, San Francisco, CA 94115
Phone: (415) 563-4321
Sales: $57,600,000   *Employees:* NA
Company Type: Private   *Employees here:* 966
SIC: 8011
  Hospital
Dr Martin Brotman, Manager

D-U-N-S 05-874-1919
CALIFORNIA DEPT DEVELOPMENTAL SVCS
3500 Zanker Rd, San Jose, CA 95134
Phone: (408) 432-8500
Sales: $71,200,000   *Employees:* NA
Company Type: Private   *Employees here:* 1,800
SIC: 8063
  Mental health institution
Ruth Maples, N/A

D-U-N-S 07-992-0427
CALVARY HOSPITAL INC
1740 Eastchester Rd, Bronx, NY 10461
Phone: (718) 863-6900
Sales: $54,678,000   *Employees:* 690
Company Type: Private   *Employees here:* 685
SIC: 8069
  Specialty hospital
Frank A Calamari, President

D-U-N-S 06-487-1122
CALVERT MEMORIAL HOSPITAL
100 Hospital Rd, Prince Frederick, MD 20678
Phone: (410) 535-4000

Sales: $37,838,000   *Employees:* 400
Company Type: Private   *Employees here:* 398
SIC: 8062
  General hospital
James J Xinis, President

D-U-N-S 86-913-2555
CAMBRIDGE HOSPITAL PROF SVCS CORP
65 Beacon St, Somerville, MA 2143
Phone: (617) 498-2143
Sales: $27,432,000   *Employees:* 100
Company Type: Private   *Employees here:* 6
SIC: 8011
  Primary care services
John O Brien, President

D-U-N-S 01-035-7325
CAMBRIDGE MEMORIAL HOSPITAL
701 Dellwood St S, Cambridge, MN 55008
Phone: (612) 689-7700
Sales: $30,627,000   *Employees:* 770
Company Type: Private   *Employees here:* 770
SIC: 8062
  Hospital
Lenny Libuf, President

D-U-N-S 02-225-0422
CAMBRIDGE PUBLIC HEALTH COMM
65 Beacon St, Somerville, MA 2143
Phone: (617) 666-4400
Sales: $33,100,000   *Employees:* NA
Company Type: Private   *Employees here:* 663
SIC: 8062
  General hospital
Carl Zack, President

D-U-N-S 11-912-0129
CAMCARE INC
Washington St & Brooks St, Charleston, WV 25301
Phone: (304) 348-5432
Sales: $525,236,000   *Employees:* 5,500
Company Type: Private   *Employees here:* 80
SIC: 8062
  Hospital
Robert L Savage, Chief Operating Officer

D-U-N-S 07-498-0095
CAMDEN-CLARK MEMORIAL HOSP
800 Garfield Ave, Parkersburg, WV 26101
Phone: (304) 424-2111
Sales: $86,705,000   *Employees:* 1,212
Company Type: Private   *Employees here:* 1,000
SIC: 8062
  General hospital
Thomas Corder, President

D-U-N-S 03-088-7301
CAMELOT CARE CENTER INC
9160 Oakhurst Rd Ste 1, Seminole, FL 33776
Phone: (727) 596-9960
Sales: $21,397,000   *Employees:* 614
Company Type: Private   *Employees here:* 50
SIC: 8361
  Residential care & psychiatric hospital
James Bazata, Controller

D-U-N-S 93-771-5530
CAMELOT HEALTHCARE LLC
717 Curtis Dr, Rayne, LA 70578
Phone: (318) 334-8211

Sales: $54,000,000   *Employees:* 520
Company Type: Private   *Employees here:* 10
SIC: 8051
   Skilled nursing care facilities hospital management &
    consulting
Clifton L Watson, President

D-U-N-S 07-303-0801
CAMERON COMMUNITY HOSPITAL
1015 W 4th St, Cameron, MO 64429
Phone: (816) 632-2101
Sales: $23,882,000   *Employees:* 275
Company Type: Private   *Employees here:* 272
SIC: 8062
   General hospital
Joseph Abrutz Jr, Administrator

D-U-N-S 06-912-4600
CAMINO MEDICAL GROUP INC
   (Parent: El Camino Hospital)
301 Old San Francisco Rd, Sunnyvale, CA 94086
Phone: (408) 739-0551
Sales: $48,100,000   *Employees:* 700
Company Type: Private   *Employees here:* 325
SIC: 8011
   Medical clinic
Elizabeth Vilardo, President

D-U-N-S 07-351-3178
CAMPBELL CLINIC INC
1400 S Germantown Rd, Germantown, TN 38138
Phone: (901) 759-3100
Sales: $24,350,000   *Employees:* 230
Company Type: Private   *Employees here:* 130
SIC: 8011
   Orthopedic clinic
John M Vines, Chief Executive Officer

D-U-N-S 08-669-9790
CAMPBELL COUNTY HOSPITAL DST
501 S Burma Ave, Gillette, WY 82716
Phone: (307) 682-8811
Sales: $32,945,000   *Employees:* 463
Company Type: Private   *Employees here:* 450
SIC: 8062
   General medical hospital
Charles D Crow, Chief Executive Officer

D-U-N-S 01-055-0366
CANCER THERAPY
8122 Datapoint Dr Ste 250, San Antonio, TX 78229
Phone: (210) 616-5500
Sales: $70,633,000   *Employees:* 309
Company Type: Private   *Employees here:* 109
SIC: 8011
   Outpatient clinic
Dr Charles Coltman Md, Executive

D-U-N-S 19-603-1553
CANCER TREATMENT CTRS OF AMERICA
3455 W Salt Creek Ln, Arlington Heights, IL 60005
Phone: (847) 342-7300
Sales: $21,956,000   *Employees:* 600
Company Type: Private   *Employees here:* 600
SIC: 8069
   Manages inpatient cancer care programs and provides
    management services to related parties
Robert W Mayo, President

D-U-N-S 18-755-7236
CANDLER HEALTH SYSTEM INC
5353 Reynolds St, Savannah, GA 31405
Phone: (912) 692-6000

Sales: $241,710,000   *Employees:* 1,900
Company Type: Private   *Employees here:* 13
SIC: 8062
   Health services and holding company
Paul Hinchey, President

D-U-N-S 04-295-7233
CANDLER HOSPITAL INC
5353 Reynolds St, Savannah, GA 31405
Phone: (912) 356-6291
Sales: $200,320,000   *Employees:* 1,661
Company Type: Private   *Employees here:* 1,599
SIC: 8062
   General medical hospital and rehabilitation center
Paul Hinchey, President

D-U-N-S 06-875-6543
CANONSBURG GENERAL HOSPITAL
100 Medical Blvd, Canonsburg, PA 15317
Phone: (724) 745-6100
Sales: $27,616,000   *Employees:* 423
Company Type: Private   *Employees here:* 410
SIC: 8062
   General hospital
Barbara Bensaia, Acting President

D-U-N-S 09-293-7309
CANTEX HEALTH CARE CENTERS
2801 Woodside St, Dallas, TX 75204
Phone: (214) 954-4114
Sales: $27,300,000   *Employees:* 1,200
Company Type: Private   *Employees here:* 17
SIC: 8051
   Skilled long term care facilities
Albert Longo, Director

D-U-N-S 07-582-1405
CANTON-POTSDAM HOSPITAL
50 Leroy St, Potsdam, NY 13676
Phone: (315) 265-3300
Sales: $29,613,000   *Employees:* 480
Company Type: Private   *Employees here:* 472
SIC: 8062
   General hospital
Bruce C Potter, President

D-U-N-S 07-322-6227
CAPE CANAVERAL HOSPITAL
701 W Cocoa Beach Cswy, Cocoa Beach, FL 32931
Phone: (407) 799-7111
Sales: $58,689,000   *Employees:* 800
Company Type: Private   *Employees here:* 800
SIC: 8062
   Hospital
Christophe Kennedy, President

D-U-N-S 07-172-0601
CAPE COD HOSPITAL
27 Park St, Hyannis, MA 2601
Phone: (508) 771-1800
Sales: $140,000,000   *Employees:* 1,200
Company Type: Private   *Employees here:* 1,100
SIC: 8062
   General hospital primary care clinic and psychiatric care
Roy Hitching, President

D-U-N-S 84-983-7976
CAPE MEDICAL INC
17421 Telegraph Rd, Detroit, MI 48219
Phone: (313) 537-0220

Sales: $21,586,000
Company Type: Private
SIC: 8011
    Medicaid clinic plan
Susan Sarin, President

Employees: 15
Employees here: 15

D-U-N-S 11-923-8806
CAPITAL DST PHYSICIANS HEALTH PLAN
17 Columbia Cir, Albany, NY 12203
Phone: (518) 862-3700
Sales: $304,546,000
Company Type: Private
SIC: 8011
    Health maintenance organization
Diane Bergman, President

Employees: 340
Employees here: 340

D-U-N-S 62-648-8548
CAPITAL HEALTH SERVICES INC
4375 Fair Lakes Ct, Fairfax, VA 22033
Phone: (703) 818-1071
Sales: $28,000,000
Company Type: Private
SIC: 8099
    Health/allied services
Ray B Lanier, President

Employees: 700
Employees here: 9

D-U-N-S 02-313-2546
CAPITAL HEALTH SYSTEMS INC
446 Bellevue Ave, Trenton, NJ 8618
Phone: (609) 394-4000
Sales: $24,300,000
Company Type: Private
SIC: 8062
    Hospital
Al Magzie, Chief Executive Officer

Employees: NA
Employees here: 500

D-U-N-S 06-436-6065
CAPITAL HEALTH SYSTEMS INC
750 Brunswick Ave, Trenton, NJ 8638
Phone: (609) 394-6000
Sales: $152,500,000
Company Type: Private
SIC: 8062
    General medical & surgical hospital
Ronald Guy, Chief Financial Officer

Employees: 3,250
Employees here: 1,320

D-U-N-S 07-196-4001
CAPITAL REGION MEDICAL CENTER
1125 Madison St, Jefferson City, MO 65101
Phone: (573) 635-7100
Sales: $80,516,000
Company Type: Private
SIC: 8062
    General medical hospital
Ed Farnsworth, President

Employees: 1,200
Employees here: 652

D-U-N-S 80-287-2028
CAPITAL SENIOR LIVING INC
14160 Dallas Pkwy Ste 300, Dallas, TX 75240
Phone: (972) 770-5600
Sales: $30,710,000
Company Type: Public
SIC: 8059
    Senior living services
Jeffrey L Beck, Chief Executive Officer

Employees: 1,558
Employees here: 1,558

D-U-N-S 78-712-6192
CARBON SCHUYLKILL COMM HTLH
360 W Ruddle St, Coaldale, PA 18218
Phone: (717) 645-2131

Sales: $23,058,000
Company Type: Private
SIC: 8062
    General hospital
William Fegley, Chairman of the Board

Employees: 386
Employees here: 356

D-U-N-S 06-854-4899
CARBONDALE CLINIC S C
2601 W Main St, Carbondale, IL 62901
Phone: (618) 549-5361
Sales: $23,584,000
Company Type: Private
SIC: 8011
    Medical clinic operated by physicians
William Hamilton, Administrator

Employees: 264
Employees here: 260

D-U-N-S 83-477-0497
CARDIAC SOLUTIONS, INC
    (Parent: Ralin Medical Inc)
575 Virginia Dr, Fort Washington, PA 19034
Phone: (215) 540-9440
Sales: $24,000,000
Company Type: Private
SIC: 8082
    Health care services
Peter Smith, Chief Executive Officer

Employees: 135
Employees here: 25

D-U-N-S 08-605-8716
CARDIOVASCULAR CONSULTANTS INC
4330 Wornall Rd Ste 2000, Kansas City, MO 64111
Phone: (816) 931-1883
Sales: $26,779,000
Company Type: Private
SIC: 8011
    Physicians' office
Lee V Giorgi, President

Employees: 150
Employees here: 70

D-U-N-S 07-356-4361
CARE ENTERPRISES INC
    (Parent: Regency Health Services Inc)
2742 Dow Ave, Tustin, CA 92780
Phone: (714) 544-4443
Sales: $131,000,000
Company Type: Public Family Member
SIC: 8051
    Operates skilled and intermediate nursing care facilities and
        home health care agencies
Cecil R Mays, Chairman of the Board

Employees: 5,700
Employees here: 130

D-U-N-S 18-645-7628
CARE ENTERPRISES WEST
    (Parent: Care Enterprises Inc)
101 Sun Ave NE, Albuquerque, NM 87109
Phone: (505) 821-3355
Sales: $80,300,000
Company Type: Public Family Member
SIC: 8051
    Skilled nursing care facilities & rehabilitation centers
Andrew Turner, Chief Executive Officer

Employees: 3,500
Employees here: NA

D-U-N-S 05-289-0217
CARE GROUP INC
8333 Naab Rd Ste 200, Indianapolis, IN 46260
Phone: (317) 338-5050
Sales: $20,500,000
Company Type: Private
SIC: 8011
    Cardiologists
Dr Donald A Rothbaum Md, President

Employees: 300
Employees here: 265

D-U-N-S 11-823-6272
CARE GROUP INC
257 Park Ave S Fl 12A, New York, NY 10010

Phone: (212) 614-9220
Sales: $35,274,000   *Employees:* 850
Company Type: Public   *Employees here:* 30
SIC: 8082
  Home health care agency
Joe Baldi, Exec Committee

D-U-N-S 60-304-2433
CARE INITIATIVES
6915 Vista Dr, West Des Moines, IA 50266
Phone: (515) 224-4442
Sales: $85,569,000   *Employees:* 3,000
Company Type: Private   *Employees here:* 35
SIC: 8051
  Skilled and intermediate nursing facilities
Hulon Walker, President

D-U-N-S 10-147-7891
CAREFIRST OF MARYLAND, INC
10455 Mill Run Cir, Owings Mills, MD 21117
Phone: (410) 581-3000
Sales: $2,183,932,000   *Employees:* 3,700
Company Type: Private   *Employees here:* 1,300
SIC: 8011
  Managed health care insurance company
William L Jews, President

D-U-N-S 83-006-2642
CAREGIVERS INC
6323 7th Ave, Brooklyn, NY 11220
Phone: (718) 921-7999
Sales: $20,543,000   *Employees:* 1,400
Company Type: Private   *Employees here:* 1,400
SIC: 8082
  Home health care service
Elizabeth Griffith, Administrator

D-U-N-S 83-587-5402
CAREMARK INC
4801 Church St, Skokie, IL 60077
Phone: (847) 674-9800
Sales: $21,000,000   *Employees:* NA
Company Type: Public Family Member   *Employees here:* 400
SIC: 8092
  Kidney dialysis center
Nancy Whittenburg, Branch Manager

D-U-N-S 88-346-3226
CAREMARK INTERNATIONAL INC
1551 W Bay Dr, Largo, FL 33770
Phone: (727) 581-8767
Sales: $25,200,000   *Employees:* NA
Company Type: Public Family Member   *Employees here:* 400
SIC: 8011
  Clinic
Robert Dippong, Manager

D-U-N-S 87-758-0753
CARESELECT GROUP INC
5950 Berkshire Ln, Dallas, TX 75225
Phone: (214) 365-6000
Sales: $20,756,000   *Employees:* 375
Company Type: Private   *Employees here:* 20
SIC: 8099
  Physician practice management
Tom Erickson, Chief Executive Officer

D-U-N-S 15-360-0796   EXP
CARETENDERS HEALTH CORP
100 Mallard Cr Rd Ste 400, Louisville, KY 40207
Phone: (502) 899-5355

Sales: $95,183,000   *Employees:* 3,400
Company Type: Public   *Employees here:* 40
SIC: 8059
  Adult day care centers rents medical equipment and direct
  mail marketing to the elderly
William B Yarmuth, Chairman of the Board

D-U-N-S 15-338-7865
CARILION MEDICAL CENTERS INC
Bellview, Roanoke, VA 24033
Phone: (540) 981-7000
Sales: $326,931,000   *Employees:* 4,130
Company Type: Private   *Employees here:* 2,340
SIC: 8062
  General medical and surgical hospital
Thomas L Robertson, President

D-U-N-S 94-225-5191
CARILION MEDICAL CENTERS INC
101 Elm Ave SE, Roanoke, VA 24013
Phone: (540) 985-8000
Sales: $70,700,000   *Employees:* NA
Company Type: Private   *Employees here:* 1,600
SIC: 8062
  General hospital
Thomas L Robertson, Principal

D-U-N-S 15-448-1253
CARILION SERVICES INC
1212 3rd St SW, Roanoke, VA 24016
Phone: (540) 981-7900
Sales: $553,574,000   *Employees:* 935
Company Type: Private   *Employees here:* 60
SIC: 8082
  Provide health care support services
Thomas Robertson, President

D-U-N-S 06-593-3640
CARILLON HOUSE NURSING FCILTY
830 Park Ave, Huntington, NY 11743
Phone: (516) 271-5800
Sales: $21,781,000   *Employees:* 349
Company Type: Private   *Employees here:* 349
SIC: 8051
  Skilled nursing care facility
Joseph F Carillo Jr, Partner

D-U-N-S 07-171-7250
CARITAS NORWOOD HOSPITAL INC
  (Parent: Caritas Christi Inc)
800 Washington St, Norwood, MA 2062
Phone: (781) 769-4000
Sales: $35,100,000   *Employees:* 766
Company Type: Private   *Employees here:* 710
SIC: 8062
  General hospital
Delia O Connor, President

D-U-N-S 06-009-2764
CARITAS SOUTHWOOD HOSPITAL
111 Dedham St, Norfolk, MA 2056
Phone: (508) 668-0385
Sales: $31,900,000   *Employees:* 700
Company Type: Private   *Employees here:* 550
SIC: 8062
  Acute hospital
Delia O Connor, President

D-U-N-S 07-560-6517
CARLE CLINIC ASSOCIATION PC
602 W University Ave, Urbana, IL 61801
Phone: (217) 383-3311

Sales: $336,930,000
Company Type: Private
SIC: 8011
    Multi-specialty medical clinics and health insurance & health
    maintenance organization
Dr Robert C Parker Md, Chief Executive Officer

Employees: 2,615
Employees here: 1,520

D-U-N-S 07-121-7004
CARLISLE HOSPITAL
246 Parker St, Carlisle, PA 17013
Phone: (717) 249-1212
Sales: $54,506,000
Company Type: Private
SIC: 8062
    General medical hospital
Michael J Healstead, Chief Executive Officer

Employees: 675
Employees here: 625

D-U-N-S 07-816-3185
CARMEL RICHMOND NURSING HOME
88 Old Town Rd, Staten Island, NY 10304
Phone: (718) 979-5000
Sales: $24,519,000
Company Type: Private
SIC: 8051
    Nursing home
Sister M Mcbride, Treasurer

Employees: 575
Employees here: 575

D-U-N-S 07-327-2361
CARNEGIE PARTNERS INC
1760 3rd Ave, New York, NY 10029
Phone: (212) 410-8700
Sales: $35,686,000
Company Type: Private
SIC: 8051
    Skilled nursing care facility
Cornelius Sigety, Partner

Employees: 500
Employees here: 500

D-U-N-S 07-951-2778
CARNEY HOSPITAL INC
2100 Dorchester Ave, Boston, MA 2124
Phone: (617) 296-4000
Sales: $96,665,000
Company Type: Private
SIC: 8062
    General medical & surgical hospital
Joyce Murphy, President

Employees: 1,258
Employees here: 1,099

D-U-N-S 86-133-0033
CAROLINA MLT-SPECIALTY ASSOC P A
501 E McBee Ave Ste 108, Greenville, SC 29601
Phone: (864) 271-8000
Sales: $36,837,000
Company Type: Private
SIC: 8011
    Physician services
John Pettett Jr, Chief Executive Officer

Employees: 450
Employees here: 30

D-U-N-S 82-643-2890
CAROLINAS PHYSICIANS NETWORK
    (Parent: Charlotte Mecklenburg Hos)
1000 Blythe Blvd, Charlotte, NC 28203
Phone: (704) 355-7600
Sales: $34,300,000
Company Type: Private
SIC: 8011
    Managed care network
Peter Anderson, President

Employees: 500
Employees here: 165

D-U-N-S 10-281-7624
CARONDELET HEALTH NETWORK INC
1601 W Saint Marys Rd, Tucson, AZ 85745
Phone: (520) 622-5833

Sales: $246,942,000
Company Type: Private
SIC: 8062
    General hospitals
Sister S Willert, President

Employees: 5,000
Employees here: 1,500

D-U-N-S 12-375-0788
CARONDELET HEALTH NETWORK INC
350 N Wilmot Rd, Tucson, AZ 85711
Phone: (520) 296-3211
Sales: $43,100,000
Company Type: Private
SIC: 8062
    General hospital
Thomas Gagen, Principal

Employees: NA
Employees here: 1,000

D-U-N-S 07-547-3819
CARRAWAY METHDST HEALTH SYSTEMS
1600 Carraway Blvd, Birmingham, AL 35234
Phone: (205) 226-6000
Sales: $142,303,000
Company Type: Private
SIC: 8062
    General hospital
Dr Robert P Carraway, Chairman of the Board

Employees: 2,000
Employees here: 1,875

D-U-N-S 07-826-7770
CARRIER FOUNDATION INC
601 County Rd, Belle Mead, NJ 8502
Phone: (908) 281-1000
Sales: $33,583,000
Company Type: Private
SIC: 8063
    Psychiatric hospital day school and youth facility
C R Sarle, President

Employees: 600
Employees here: 510

D-U-N-S 07-494-1857
CARROLL COUNTY GENERAL HOSP
200 Memorial Ave, Westminster, MD 21157
Phone: (410) 848-3000
Sales: $65,126,000
Company Type: Private
SIC: 8062
    General hospital
William Gavin, Chairman of the Board

Employees: 1,100
Employees here: 1,100

D-U-N-S 62-140-3757
CARROLL COUNTY HEALTH SVCS CORP
200 Memorial Ave, Westminster, MD 21157
Phone: (410) 848-3000
Sales: $65,126,000
Company Type: Private
SIC: 8062
    General hospital
William Gavin, Chairman of the Board

Employees: 1,100
Employees here: 2

D-U-N-S 06-017-9843
CARSON CITY HOSPITAL
406 E Elm St, Carson City, MI 48811
Phone: (517) 584-3131
Sales: $26,985,000
Company Type: Private
SIC: 8062
    General hospital
Bruce Traverse, President

Employees: 460
Employees here: 454

D-U-N-S 07-611-3240
CARSON-TAHOE HOSPITAL
775 Fleischmann Way, Carson City, NV 89703
Phone: (702) 882-1361

Sales: $79,487,000   Employees: 1,000
Company Type: Private   Employees here: 750
SIC: 8062
  General hospital
Steve H Smith, Administrator

D-U-N-S 07-316-9765
CARTER BLOOD CENTER INC
1263 W Rosedale St, Fort Worth, TX 76104
Phone: (817) 335-4935
Sales: $34,738,000   Employees: 150
Company Type: Private   Employees here: 135
SIC: 8099
  Blood bank
Bobby Grigsby, Chief Executive Officer

D-U-N-S 79-641-7855
CARTER-WALLACE, INC
12 Acre Rd, Cranbury, NJ 8512
Phone: (609) 655-6000
Sales: $46,100,000   Employees: NA
Company Type: Public Family Member   Employees here: 900
SIC: 8071
  Medical laboratory

D-U-N-S 04-002-9613
CARTERET GENERAL HOSPITAL
3500 Arendell St, Morehead City, NC 28557
Phone: (252) 247-1616
Sales: $48,457,000   Employees: 800
Company Type: Private   Employees here: 635
SIC: 8062
  Hospital
Charles Acker, Vice-President

D-U-N-S 07-746-1275
CARY MEDICAL CENTER
37 Van Buren Rd, Caribou, ME 4736
Phone: (207) 498-3111
Sales: $20,100,000   Employees: 450
Company Type: Private   Employees here: 410
SIC: 8062
  General medical & surgical hospital
Kris Doody-Chabre, Chief Executive Officer

D-U-N-S 18-629-4641
CASA DE LAS CAMPANAS, INC
18655 W Bernardo Dr, San Diego, CA 92127
Phone: (619) 451-9152
Sales: $22,880,000   Employees: 303
Company Type: Private   Employees here: 303
SIC: 8361
  Geriatric residential care
J R Holt, Chairman of the Board

D-U-N-S 07-752-7489
CASA GRANDE COMMUNITY HOSP
1800 E Florence Blvd, Casa Grande, AZ 85222
Phone: (520) 426-6300
Sales: $62,931,000   Employees: 750
Company Type: Private   Employees here: 600
SIC: 8062
  General hospital and skilled nursing facility
Claudia Griffin, President

D-U-N-S 05-855-8636
CASTLE DENTAL CENTERS INC
1360 Post Oak Blvd, Houston, TX 77056
Phone: (713) 513-1400

Sales: $31,412,000   Employees: 800
Company Type: Public   Employees here: 95
SIC: 8021
  Dental office
Jack H Castle Jr, Chief Executive Officer

D-U-N-S 07-251-9762
CASTLE MEDICAL CENTER
640 Ulukahiki St, Kailua, HI 96734
Phone: (808) 263-5500
Sales: $62,830,000   Employees: 1,012
Company Type: Private   Employees here: 800
SIC: 8062
  General hospital
Kenneth A Finch, President

D-U-N-S 18-778-0804
CASTLEVIEW HOSPITAL INC
(Parent: Columbia/Hca Healthcare Corp)
300 Hospital Dr, Price, UT 84501
Phone: (435) 637-4800
Sales: $29,754,000   Employees: 280
Company Type: Public Family Member   Employees here: 280
SIC: 8062
  General hospital
Tommy Frist, Chairman of the Board

D-U-N-S 07-450-8557
CATAWBA MEMORIAL HOSPITAL
810 Fairgrove Church Rd, Hickory, NC 28602
Phone: (828) 326-3000
Sales: $82,631,000   Employees: 875
Company Type: Private   Employees here: 805
SIC: 8062
  Hospital
Tony Rose, President

D-U-N-S 87-435-4681
CATHEDRAL HEALTH SERVICES INC
(Parent: Cathedral Healthcare System)
219 Chestnut St, Newark, NJ 7105
Phone: (973) 690-3508
Sales: $184,550,000   Employees: 2,000
Company Type: Private   Employees here: 2,000
SIC: 8062
  General hospital intermediate care facility and home health
  care
Frank Fumai, President

D-U-N-S 62-756-7910
CATHEDRAL HEALTHCARE SYSTEM
306 Dr Martin Luther King Blvd., Newark, NJ 7102
Phone: (973) 877-5000
Sales: $74,500,000   Employees: NA
Company Type: Private   Employees here: 1,500
SIC: 8062
  Hospital
Anna Santana, Manager

D-U-N-S 62-756-7977
CATHEDRAL HEALTHCARE SYSTEM
155 Jefferson St, Newark, NJ 7105
Phone: (973) 589-1300
Sales: $26,800,000   Employees: NA
Company Type: Private   Employees here: 550
SIC: 8062
  General hospital
Dominic Calgi-V-Pres, Principal

D-U-N-S 09-473-6758
CATHOLIC BISHOP OF CHICAGO
1150 N River Rd, Des Plaines, IL 60016
Phone: (847) 824-6126

Sales: $22,400,000
Company Type: Private
SIC: 8361
   Residential care
Father J Smyth, Director

Employees: NA
Employees here: 1,000

D-U-N-S 94-818-5459
CATHOLIC HEALTH INITIATIVE
1999 Broadway Ste 2605, Denver, CO 80202
Phone: (303) 298-9100
Sales: $4,001,623,000
Company Type: Private
SIC: 8062
   Hospitals & skilled nursing homes
Patricia A Cahill, President

Employees: 45,000
Employees here: 33

D-U-N-S 00-227-1732
CATHOLIC HEALTH PARTNERS SVCS
2875 W 19th St, Chicago, IL 60623
Phone: (773) 521-1710
Sales: $23,100,000
Company Type: Private
SIC: 8062
   General medical & surgical hospital & skilled nursing home
     health agency
Mark Hennessey, Vp Finance

Employees: NA
Employees here: 556

D-U-N-S 06-858-0174
CATHOLIC HEALTH PARTNERS SVCS
2520 N Lakeview Ave, Chicago, IL 60614
Phone: (773) 388-7300
Sales: $291,630,000
Company Type: Private
SIC: 8062
   General hospital
Sister T Peck, Chief Executive Officer

Employees: 3,500
Employees here: 1,200

D-U-N-S 07-439-5450
CATHOLIC HEALTH PARTNERS SVCS
811 S Lytle St, Chicago, IL 60607
Phone: (773) 883-4343
Sales: $21,700,000
Company Type: Private
SIC: 8062
   General hospital
F S Winslow, N/A

Employees: NA
Employees here: 525

D-U-N-S 94-979-3483
CATHOLIC HEALTH PARTNERS SVCS
2900 N Lake Shore Dr, Chicago, IL 60657
Phone: (773) 975-3000
Sales: $59,200,000
Company Type: Private
SIC: 8062
   Hospital

Employees: NA
Employees here: 1,400

D-U-N-S 16-010-0897
CATHOLIC HEALTHCARE PARTNERS
3700 Kolbe Rd, Lorain, OH 44053
Phone: (440) 960-4000
Sales: $40,000,000
Company Type: Private
SIC: 8062
   General hospitals
Brian Lockwood, President

Employees: NA
Employees here: 950

D-U-N-S 17-926-4544
CATHOLIC HEALTHCARE W STHERN CAL
790 Calderwood Ln Ste 600, Pasadena, CA 91107
Phone: (626) 744-2300

Sales: $93,400,000
Company Type: Private
SIC: 8062
   General hospital
Beth O Brien, President

Employees: 2,000
Employees here: NA

D-U-N-S 12-022-9166
CATHOLIC HEALTHCARE W STHERN CAL
1050 Linden Ave, Long Beach, CA 90813
Phone: (562) 491-9000
Sales: $84,500,000
Company Type: Private
SIC: 8062
   General hospital
Tammie Brailsford, Administrator

Employees: NA
Employees here: 1,700

D-U-N-S 06-697-1599
CATHOLIC MEDICAL CENTER
8825 153rd St, Jamaica, NY 11432
Phone: (718) 558-6900
Sales: $630,234,000
Company Type: Private
SIC: 8062
   General hospital
William Mcguire, President

Employees: 3,900
Employees here: 500

D-U-N-S 06-975-4919
CAYLOR-NICKEL MEDICAL CENTER
1 Caylor Nickel Sq, Bluffton, IN 46714
Phone: (219) 824-3500
Sales: $30,383,000
Company Type: Private
SIC: 8062
   General hospital continuing care facility home health facility
Charles Caylor, Chairman of the Board

Employees: 575
Employees here: 500

D-U-N-S 10-774-1191
CAYUGA MEDICAL CTR AT ITHACA
101 Dates Dr, Ithaca, NY 14850
Phone: (607) 274-4011
Sales: $48,634,000
Company Type: Private
SIC: 8062
   Hospital
Bonnie Howell, President

Employees: 704
Employees here: 10

D-U-N-S 55-673-8169
CEDARS MEDICAL CENTER
1400 NW 12th Ave, Miami, FL 33136
Phone: (305) 325-5511
Sales: $183,614,000
Company Type: Private
SIC: 8062
   General hospital
Steven Sonenreich, Chief Executive Officer

Employees: 1,800
Employees here: 1,800

D-U-N-S 07-530-7785
CEDARS-SINAI MEDICAL CENTER
8700 Beverly Blvd, Los Angeles, CA 90048
Phone: (310) 855-4241
Sales: $681,456,000
Company Type: Private
SIC: 8062
   General hospital
Thomas M Priselac, President

Employees: 6,000
Employees here: 5

D-U-N-S 60-338-7283
CEDARS-SINAI MEDICAL CENTER
444 S Vicente Blvd, Los Angeles, CA 90048
Phone: (310) 855-5000

Sales: $273,300,000   *Employees:* NA
Company Type: Private   *Employees here:* 5,500
SIC: 8062
   General hospital
Sheldon King, President

D-U-N-S 92-923-5315
CENTEGRA HEALTH SYSTEM
4201 W Medical Center Dr, Mchenry, IL 60050
Phone: (815) 344-5555
Sales: $42,100,000   *Employees:* NA
Company Type: Private   *Employees here:* 1,000
SIC: 8062
   Hospital
Barry Finn, Branch Manager

D-U-N-S 09-157-7973
CENTER FOR NURSING REHABILITATION
1815 Cornaga Ave, Far Rockaway, NY 11691
Phone: (718) 868-8360
Sales: $42,233,000   *Employees:* 550
Company Type: Private   *Employees here:* 530
SIC: 8051
   Nursing & personal care facility
Michael Fassler, Chief Executive Officer

D-U-N-S 07-474-1034
CENTRA HEALTH INC
1920 Atherholt Rd, Lynchburg, VA 24501
Phone: (804) 947-4701
Sales: $235,200,000   *Employees:* 5,000
Company Type: Private   *Employees here:* 2,453
SIC: 8062
   General hospital
George W Dawson, President

D-U-N-S 60-281-1275
CENTRA HEALTH INC
3300 Rivermont Ave, Lynchburg, VA 24503
Phone: (804) 947-4002
Sales: $57,300,000   *Employees:* NA
Company Type: Private   *Employees here:* 1,400
SIC: 8062
   General hospital
Tom Jividen, N/A

D-U-N-S 79-574-4812
CENTRA HEALTH INC
1901 Tate Springs Rd, Lynchburg, VA 24501
Phone: (804) 947-3000
Sales: $40,800,000   *Employees:* NA
Company Type: Private   *Employees here:* 1,000
SIC: 8062
   General medical and surgical hospitals
Darell Powers, Principal

D-U-N-S 17-937-2222
CENTRACARE CLINIC
1200 6th Ave N, Saint Cloud, MN 56303
Phone: (320) 252-5131
Sales: $28,713,000   *Employees:* 500
Company Type: Private   *Employees here:* 350
SIC: 8011
   Health practitioner's office
Dr Terrance R Pladson Md, President

D-U-N-S 17-135-7288
CENTRAL ALABAMA HOME HEALTH SVCS
2641 Eastern Byp, Montgomery, AL 36117
Phone: (334) 272-3538

Sales: $29,535,000   *Employees:* 300
Company Type: Private   *Employees here:* 55
SIC: 8082
   Home medical service
George Hutchinson, President

D-U-N-S 06-800-3219
CENTRAL BAPTIST CHILDRENS HM
215 N Milwaukee Ave Ste A, Lake Villa, IL 60046
Phone: (847) 356-2391
Sales: $25,978,000   *Employees:* 500
Company Type: Private   *Employees here:* 75
SIC: 8361
   Residential care services
Donald Mertic, President

D-U-N-S 07-496-7845
CENTRAL BLOOD BANK
   (Parent: Institute For Transfusion Med)
812 5th Ave, Pittsburgh, PA 15219
Phone: (412) 456-1900
Sales: $25,511,000   *Employees:* 280
Company Type: Private   *Employees here:* 280
SIC: 8099
   Blood bank
William H Portman, President

D-U-N-S 07-435-4408
CENTRAL BROOKLYN MED GROUP PC
2 Metrotech Ctr Rm 4200, Brooklyn, NY 11201
Phone: (718) 250-4060
Sales: $25,700,000   *Employees:* 375
Company Type: Private   *Employees here:* 12
SIC: 8011
   Medical center
Dr Alexander Ellman Md, President

D-U-N-S 06-667-1595
CENTRAL CALIFORNIA FOUNDATION FOR HEALTH
1401 Garces Hwy, Delano, CA 93215
Phone: (805) 725-4800
Sales: $30,233,000   *Employees:* 450
Company Type: Private   *Employees here:* 430
SIC: 8062
   Hospital
Bahram Gaffari, Chief Financial Officer

D-U-N-S 05-665-3975
CENTRAL DU PAGE HOSPITAL ASSN
25 N Winfield Rd, Winfield, IL 60190
Phone: (630) 682-1600
Sales: $180,742,000   *Employees:* 2,300
Company Type: Private   *Employees here:* 2,250
SIC: 8062
   General acute hospital
David S Fox, President

D-U-N-S 84-219-4326
CENTRAL DU PAGE HOSPITAL ASSN
454 Pennsylvania Ave, Glen Ellyn, IL 60137
Phone: (630) 469-9200
Sales: $31,100,000   *Employees:* NA
Company Type: Private   *Employees here:* 500
SIC: 8011
   Medical doctor's office
Maureen Briney, Vice-President

D-U-N-S 01-050-7929
CENTRAL FLORIDA BLOODBANK INC
32 W Gore St, Orlando, FL 32806
Phone: (407) 849-6100

Sales: $27,000,000
Company Type: Private
SIC: 8099
   Community blood bank
Edward O Carr, President

Employees: 430
Employees here: 110

D-U-N-S 07-206-1773
CENTRAL IND REGIONAL BLOOD CTR
3450 N Meridian St, Indianapolis, IN 46208
Phone: (317) 926-2381
Sales: $24,878,000
Company Type: Private
SIC: 8099
   Blood bank
Byron B Buhner, President

Employees: 370
Employees here: 289

D-U-N-S 07-584-4548
CENTRAL IOWA HOSPITAL CORP
1200 Pleasant St, Des Moines, IA 50309
Phone: (515) 241-6201
Sales: $337,405,000
Company Type: Private
SIC: 8062
   Hospital
James Skogsbergh, President

Employees: 4,000
Employees here: 3,300

D-U-N-S 07-332-5169
CENTRAL KANSAS MEDICAL CENTER
3515 Broadway Ave, Great Bend, KS 67530
Phone: (316) 792-2511
Sales: $26,700,000
Company Type: Private
SIC: 8062
   Hospital
Gary Barnett, President

Employees: 588
Employees here: 500

D-U-N-S 07-263-0254
CENTRAL LOUISIANA HEALTHCARE
360 Jackson St Ste 123, Alexandria, LA 71301
Phone: (318) 561-9545
Sales: $77,400,000
Company Type: Private
SIC: 8062
   Hospital
Earl Denning, Chief Executive Officer

Employees: 1,661
Employees here: 1,642

D-U-N-S 07-174-5319
CENTRAL MAINE MEDICAL CENTER
300 Main St, Lewiston, ME 4240
Phone: (207) 795-2700
Sales: $86,023,000
Company Type: Private
SIC: 8062
   Acute care hospital
William W Young Jr, President

Employees: 1,200
Employees here: 1,190

D-U-N-S 05-810-4357
CENTRAL MINN GROUP HEALTH PLAN
   (Parent: Group Health Plan Inc)
1245 15th St N, Saint Cloud, MN 56303
Phone: (320) 259-7328
Sales: $31,662,000
Company Type: Private
SIC: 8011
   Community integrated service network
John J Hoefs, Executive Director

Employees: 305
Employees here: 305

D-U-N-S 07-503-5063
CENTRAL OHIO MEDICAL CLINIC
497 E Town St, Columbus, OH 43215
Phone: (614) 222-3300

Sales: $21,000,000
Company Type: Private
SIC: 8011
   Doctors of medicine
Burk Dehority, Executive Vice-President

Employees: 175
Employees here: 150

D-U-N-S 02-018-5252
CENTRAL PLAINS CLINIC
1100 E 21st St, Sioux Falls, SD 57105
Phone: (605) 335-2727
Sales: $48,537,000
Company Type: Private
SIC: 8011
   Medical clinic
D G Belton, Executive Director

Employees: 600
Employees here: 500

D-U-N-S 06-807-7197
CENTRAL SUFFOLK HOSPITAL
   (Parent: Peconic Health Corporation)
1300 Roanoke Ave, Riverhead, NY 11901
Phone: (516) 548-6000
Sales: $53,254,000
Company Type: Private
SIC: 8062
   General medical & surgical hospital
Joseph F Turner, President

Employees: 610
Employees here: 560

D-U-N-S 07-821-9730
CENTRAL TENNESSEE HOSPITAL CORP
   (Parent: Columbia/Hca Healthcare Corp)
111 Highway 70 E, Dickson, TN 37055
Phone: (615) 446-0446
Sales: $46,106,000
Company Type: Public Family Member
SIC: 8062
   General hospital
Rick Wallace, Administrator

Employees: 650
Employees here: 525

D-U-N-S 06-991-2442
CENTRAL VERMONT HOSPITAL, INC
Fisher Rd, Barre, VT 5641
Phone: (802) 229-9121
Sales: $31,100,000
Company Type: Private
SIC: 8062
   General medical & surgical hospital
Ernest Bancroft, Chairman of the Board

Employees: 683
Employees here: 683

D-U-N-S 02-023-1296
CENTRAL WASH HEALTH SVCS ASSN
1300 Fuller St, Wenatchee, WA 98801
Phone: (509) 662-1511
Sales: $67,560,000
Company Type: Private
SIC: 8062
   Hospital
Jack T Evans Jr, President

Employees: 527
Employees here: 515

D-U-N-S 06-870-8544
CENTRASTATE MEDICAL CENTER
901 W Main St, Freehold, NJ 7728
Phone: (732) 431-2000
Sales: $92,007,000
Company Type: Private
SIC: 8062
   Community hospital
Thomas Litz, President

Employees: 1,500
Employees here: 1,475

D-U-N-S 06-979-6241
CENTRE COMMUNITY HOSPITAL
1800 E Park Ave, State College, PA 16803
Phone: (814) 231-7000

Sales: $65,379,000   *Employees:* 930
Company Type: Private   *Employees here:* 882
SIC: 8062
   General medical & surgical hospital
Lance H Rose, President

D-U-N-S 78-045-0771
CENTURA HEALTH CORPORATION
825 E Pikes Peak Ave, Colorado Springs, CO 80903
Phone: (719) 636-8879
Sales: $26,400,000   *Employees:* NA
Company Type: Private   *Employees here:* 620
SIC: 8062
   General hospital
Leanord Farr, Branch Manager

D-U-N-S 06-501-1843
CENTURY HEALTHCARE CORPORATION
5555 E 71st St Ste 9220, Tulsa, OK 74136
Phone: (918) 491-0781
Sales: $44,400,000   *Employees:* 1,200
Company Type: Private   *Employees here:* 50
SIC: 8063
   Psychiatric hospital home health care services
Jerry D Dillon, Chairman of the Board

D-U-N-S 12-260-3327
CH ALLIED SERVICES INC
11133 Dunn Rd Ste, Saint Louis, MO 63136
Phone: (314) 355-2300
Sales: $147,800,000   *Employees:* 3,150
Company Type: Private   *Employees here:* 3
SIC: 8062
   Hospitals
Fred Brown, President

D-U-N-S 19-819-1371
CH ALLIED SERVICES INC
1600 E Broadway, Columbia, MO 65201
Phone: (573) 815-8000
Sales: $54,900,000   *Employees:* NA
Company Type: Private   *Employees here:* 1,300
SIC: 8062
   General hospital
Mike Shirk, N/A

D-U-N-S 07-119-7503
CHAMBERSBURG HOSPITAL (INC)
112 N 7th St, Chambersburg, PA 17201
Phone: (717) 264-5171
Sales: $87,448,000   *Employees:* 1,249
Company Type: Private   *Employees here:* 1,249
SIC: 8062
   General hospital
Norman B Epstein, President

D-U-N-S 06-054-4954
CHAMPLAIN VALLEY HOSPITAL
75 Beekman St, Plattsburgh, NY 12901
Phone: (518) 561-2000
Sales: $89,255,000   *Employees:* 1,215
Company Type: Private   *Employees here:* 1,215
SIC: 8062
   General medical and surgical hospital
Kevin J Carroll, President

D-U-N-S 07-994-1084
CHARLES COLE MEMORIAL HOSP
Us 6 E Coudersport Boro, Coudersport, PA 16915
Phone: (814) 274-9300

Sales: $29,901,000   *Employees:* 583
Company Type: Private   *Employees here:* 468
SIC: 8062
   Hospital & skilled nursing facility
David Acker, Chief Executive Officer

D-U-N-S 86-948-5623
CHARLESTON AREA HEALTH PLAN
141 Summers St, Charleston, WV 25301
Phone: (304) 348-2900
Sales: $78,369,000   *Employees:* 80
Company Type: Private   *Employees here:* 80
SIC: 8011
   Health maintenance organization
Alan Mytty, President

D-U-N-S 07-266-8940
CHARLESTON AREA MEDICAL CENTER
501 Morris St, Charleston, WV 25301
Phone: (304) 348-5432
Sales: $424,813,000   *Employees:* 6,000
Company Type: Private   *Employees here:* 2,500
SIC: 8062
   Hospital
Phillip A Goodwin, President

D-U-N-S 06-813-1960
CHARLESTON HOSPITAL, INC.
   (Parent: Columbia/Hca Healthcare Corp)
333 Laidley St, Charleston, WV 25301
Phone: (304) 347-6500
Sales: $58,762,000   *Employees:* 645
Company Type: Public Family Member   *Employees here:* 645
SIC: 8062
   General hospital
David Sirk, President

D-U-N-S 07-371-8843
CHARLESTON MEMORIAL HOSPITAL
326 Calhoun St, Charleston, SC 29401
Phone: (843) 577-0600
Sales: $32,470,000   *Employees:* 541
Company Type: Private   *Employees here:* 541
SIC: 8062
   Hospital
Thomas F Moore, Administrator

D-U-N-S 07-452-4513
CHARLOTTE MECKLENBURG HOS
1000 Blythe Blvd, Charlotte, NC 28203
Phone: (704) 355-2000
Sales: $930,337,000   *Employees:* 7,000
Company Type: Private   *Employees here:* 4,900
SIC: 8062
   General hospital specialty care hospital psychiatric hospital
   doctors' clinics and skilled nursing care facilities
Dr Harry A Nurkin, President

D-U-N-S 08-299-2397
CHARTER BEHAVIORAL HEALTH
19 Prospect St, Summit, NJ 7901
Phone: (908) 522-7000
Sales: $31,000,000   *Employees:* 180
Company Type: Private   *Employees here:* 180
SIC: 8063
   Psychiatric hospital
James Gallagher, Chief Executive Officer

D-U-N-S 88-398-9386
CHARTER BEHAVIORAL HEALTH SYSTEMS LP
3414 Peachtree Rd NE, Atlanta, GA 30326
Phone: (404) 841-9200

Sales: $66,700,000   *Employees:* 1,800
Company Type: Private   *Employees here:* 200
SIC: 8063
    Psychiatric care facility
John Gulf, Chairman of the Board

D-U-N-S 88-392-9507
CHARTER LOUISVLLE BEHAVIORAL HEALTH SYS
1405 Browns Ln, Louisville, KY 40207
Phone: (502) 896-0495
Sales: $24,000,000   *Employees:* 150
Company Type: Private   *Employees here:* 150
SIC: 8063
    Psychiatric hospital
Chuck Webb, Administrator

D-U-N-S 11-069-8065
CHARTER PROFESSIONAL SERVICES
79 Highland Ave, Salem, MA 1970
Phone: (978) 740-0406
Sales: $32,125,000   *Employees:* 5
Company Type: Private   *Employees here:* 5
SIC: 8011
    Medical doctor's office
Bonnie Boyce, Secretary

D-U-N-S 13-761-5704
CHARTER REAL BEHAVIORAL HEALTH SYS
    (Parent: Magellan Health Services Inc)
8550 Huebner Rd, San Antonio, TX 78240
Phone: (210) 699-8585
Sales: $32,648,000   *Employees:* 150
Company Type: Public Family Member   *Employees here:* 150
SIC: 8063
    Psychiatric hospital & drug addiction hospital
Irving B Sawyers Jr, Chief Executive Officer

D-U-N-S 84-846-0945
CHARTWELL HEALTHCARE, INC
16910 Dallas Pkwy Ste 200, Dallas, TX 75248
Phone: (972) 733-0009
Sales: $77,992,000   *Employees:* 6,000
Company Type: Private   *Employees here:* 65
SIC: 8051
    Owns operates and manages nursing and personal care
    facilities
Irving D Boyes, Chairman of the Board

D-U-N-S 09-416-8135
CHAUTAUQUA COUNTY CHAPTER NYS
    (Parent: Nysarc Inc)
880 E 2nd St, Jamestown, NY 14701
Phone: (716) 483-2344
Sales: $33,032,000   *Employees:* 950
Company Type: Private   *Employees here:* 100
SIC: 8093
    Rehabilitation center
Paul Cesana, Executive Director

D-U-N-S 06-984-2318
CHELSEA COMMUNITY HOSPITAL
775 S Main St, Chelsea, MI 48118
Phone: (734) 475-1311
Sales: $43,123,000   *Employees:* 900
Company Type: Private   *Employees here:* 805
SIC: 8062
    General hospital
James Miltner, Finance

D-U-N-S 07-729-4395
CHENANGO MEMORIAL HOSPITAL
179 N Broad St, Norwich, NY 13815
Phone: (607) 335-4111

Sales: $29,830,000   *Employees:* 526
Company Type: Private   *Employees here:* 466
SIC: 8062
    General hospital and skilled nursing facility
Frank Mirabito, President

D-U-N-S 07-792-3761
CHESAPEAKE HOSPITAL AUTH
736 Battlefield Blvd N, Chesapeake, VA 23320
Phone: (757) 547-8121
Sales: $121,940,000   *Employees:* 1,700
Company Type: Private   *Employees here:* 1,700
SIC: 8062
    General hospital
Donald S Buckley, President

D-U-N-S 08-106-1152
CHESAPEAKE HOSPITAL CORP
Harris Dr, Kilmarnock, VA 22482
Phone: (804) 435-8000
Sales: $24,175,000   *Employees:* 420
Company Type: Private   *Employees here:* 420
SIC: 8062
    General medical and surgical hospital
James Holmes Jr, President

D-U-N-S 07-397-0238
CHESHIRE MEDICAL CENTER
580 Court St, Keene, NH 3431
Phone: (603) 352-4111
Sales: $45,010,000   *Employees:* 822
Company Type: Private   *Employees here:* 822
SIC: 8062
    General hospital
Robert Langlais, President

D-U-N-S 07-452-4968
CHESTER CNTY HOSPITAL NURSING CTR
1 Medical Park Dr, Chester, SC 29706
Phone: (803) 581-3151
Sales: $26,376,000   *Employees:* 485
Company Type: Private   *Employees here:* 450
SIC: 8062
    Hospital
Bill Bundy, Administrator

D-U-N-S 19-850-2205
CHESTNUT HILL HOSPITAL
8835 Germantown Ave, Philadelphia, PA 19118
Phone: (215) 248-8200
Sales: $58,076,000   *Employees:* 1,000
Company Type: Private   *Employees here:* 1,000
SIC: 8062
    General hospital
Cary F Leptuck, President

D-U-N-S 04-253-1285
CHICAGO GRANT HOSPITAL, INC.
    (Parent: Columbia/Hca Healthcare Corp)
550 W Webster Ave, Chicago, IL 60614
Phone: (773) 883-2000
Sales: $53,188,000   *Employees:* 600
Company Type: Public Family Member   *Employees here:* 600
SIC: 8062
    General hospital
Nancy Hellyer, Chief Executive Officer

D-U-N-S 87-887-8644
CHICO COMMUNITY HOSPITAL INC
    (Parent: Paracelsus Healthcare Corp)
560 Cohasset Rd, Chico, CA 95926
Phone: (530) 896-5000

Sales: $20,100,000
Company Type: Public Family Member
SIC: 8062
  Hospital
Fred Hodges, Chief Financial Officer

Employees: 450
Employees here: 305

D-U-N-S 07-868-9619
CHILDREN'S HEALTH CARE
2525 Chicago Ave, Minneapolis, MN 55404
Phone: (612) 813-6100
Sales: $210,642,000
Company Type: Private
SIC: 8069
  Hospital
Brock Nelson, President

Employees: 1,994
Employees here: 1,300

D-U-N-S 15-731-4618
CHILDREN'S HEALTH SYSTEMS
9000 W Wisconsin Ave, Milwaukee, WI 53226
Phone: (414) 266-2000
Sales: $128,700,000
Company Type: Private
SIC: 8069
  Hospital educational services fundraising organization
    collection agency
Jon Vice, President

Employees: 2,600
Employees here: 2,600

D-U-N-S 07-653-6184
CHILDREN'S HOSPITAL MEDICAL CENTER N CA
747 52nd St, Oakland, CA 94609
Phone: (510) 428-3000
Sales: $112,249,000
Company Type: Private
SIC: 8062
  General hospital
Antonie H Paap, President

Employees: 2,000
Employees here: 1,900

D-U-N-S 07-484-5504
CHILDREN'S HOSPITAL
111 Michigan Ave NW, Washington, DC 20010
Phone: (202) 745-5000
Sales: $193,683,000
Company Type: Private
SIC: 8062
  Hospital
Edwin K Zeckman Jr, President

Employees: 1,810
Employees here: 1,353

D-U-N-S 07-475-8350
CHILDREN'S HOSPITAL OF KINGS
601 Childrens Ln, Norfolk, VA 23507
Phone: (757) 668-7000
Sales: $98,278,000
Company Type: Private
SIC: 8069
  Children's hospital
Robert Bonar Jr, President

Employees: 1,239
Employees here: 1,178

D-U-N-S 07-375-7627
CHILDREN'S HOSPITAL OF PHILADELPHIA
  (Parent: The Childrens Hosp Foundation)
34th St Civic Center Blvd, Philadelphia, PA 19104
Phone: (215) 590-1000
Sales: $277,560,000
Company Type: Private
SIC: 8069
  Children's hospital
Edmond F Notebaert, President

Employees: 4,000
Employees here: 3,880

D-U-N-S 06-952-3405
CHILDREN'S HOSPITAL
200 Henry Clay Ave, New Orleans, LA 70118
Phone: (504) 899-9511

Sales: $54,200,000
Company Type: Private
SIC: 8069
  Specialty hospital
Steve Worley, Executive Director

Employees: 1,100
Employees here: 1,100

D-U-N-S 07-778-5525
CHILDREN'S HOSPITAL MEDICAL CENTER
1 Perkins Sq, Akron, OH 44308
Phone: (330) 379-8200
Sales: $127,768,000
Company Type: Private
SIC: 8069
  Children's hospital
William Considine, President

Employees: 1,700
Employees here: 1,700

D-U-N-S 07-128-9326
CHILDREN'S MEDICAL CENTER
1 Childrens Plz, Dayton, OH 45404
Phone: (937) 226-8300
Sales: $90,657,000
Company Type: Private
SIC: 8069
  Children's hospital/skilled nursing home care/medical
    equipment rental
Laurence Harkness, President

Employees: 1,300
Employees here: 1,250

D-U-N-S 07-443-8755
CHILDREN'S MEMORIAL HOSPITAL
2300 N Childrens Plz, Chicago, IL 60614
Phone: (773) 880-4000
Sales: $192,686,000
Company Type: Private
SIC: 8069
  Children's hospital and pediatric outpatient clinics
Patrick Magoon, Cso

Employees: 2,000
Employees here: 2,000

D-U-N-S 06-615-8494
CHILDRENS HOSPITAL OF ORANGE CNTY
455 S Main St, Orange, CA 92868
Phone: (714) 997-3000
Sales: $92,412,000
Company Type: Private
SIC: 8069
  Pediatric hospital
Kimberly Cripe, Chief Executive Officer

Employees: 1,000
Employees here: 1,000

D-U-N-S 04-430-4145
CHILDRENS HOSPITAL OF PITTSBURGH
3705 5th Ave, Pittsburgh, PA 15213
Phone: (412) 692-5325
Sales: $150,992,000
Company Type: Private
SIC: 8069
  Specialty hospital
Ronald Violi, Chairman of the Board

Employees: 1,900
Employees here: 1,800

D-U-N-S 07-384-7261
CHILDRENS HOSPITAL OF WISCONSIN
9000 W Wisconsin Ave, Milwaukee, WI 53226
Phone: (414) 266-2000
Sales: $173,911,000
Company Type: Private
SIC: 8069
  Hospital
Jon E Vice, President

Employees: 2,000
Employees here: 2,000

D-U-N-S 05-227-7936
CHILDRENS HOSPITAL LOS ANGELES INC
4650 W Sunset Blvd, Los Angeles, CA 90027
Phone: (323) 660-2450

Sales: $167,677,000
Company Type: Private
SIC: 8069
  Hospital for children
Walter Noce, President

Employees: 2,000
Employees here: 1,950

D-U-N-S 04-868-2157
CHILDRENS HOSPITAL REGIONAL MED CTR
4800 Sand Point Way NE, Seattle, WA 98105
Phone: (206) 526-2000
Sales: $147,691,000
Company Type: Private
SIC: 8069
  Children's hospital
Treuman Katz, President

Employees: 2,150
Employees here: 2,081

D-U-N-S 93-077-5580
CHILDRENS HOSPITAL & HEALTH CTR
3020 Childrens Way, San Diego, CA 92123
Phone: (619) 576-1700
Sales: $79,200,000
Company Type: Private
SIC: 8062
  Hospital
Blair Sadler, President

Employees: 1,700
Employees here: 1,700

D-U-N-S 07-637-7316
CHILDRENS HOSPITAL OF MICH
3901 Beaubien St, Detroit, MI 48201
Phone: (313) 745-5437
Sales: $183,770,000
Company Type: Private
SIC: 8069
  Children's hospital
David Cambpell, President

Employees: 2,310
Employees here: 2,210

D-U-N-S 07-659-3722
CHILDRENS HOSPITAL CORPORATION
300 Longwood Ave Ste 300, Boston, MA 2115
Phone: (617) 355-6000
Sales: $219,844,000
Company Type: Private
SIC: 8069
  Children's hospital
David S Weiner, Chief Executive Officer

Employees: 3,907
Employees here: 3,832

D-U-N-S 07-128-4913
CHILDRENS HOSPITAL MED CTR
3333 Burnet Ave, Cincinnati, OH 45229
Phone: (513) 559-4200
Sales: $212,551,000
Company Type: Private
SIC: 8069
  Children's hospital outpatient clinics medical research
James M Anderson, President

Employees: 3,800
Employees here: 3,650

D-U-N-S 07-935-8529
CHILDRENS MED CTR OF DALLAS
1935 Motor St, Dallas, TX 75235
Phone: (214) 920-2000
Sales: $183,925,000
Company Type: Private
SIC: 8069
  Specialty hospital
George D Farr, President

Employees: 2,014
Employees here: 1,924

D-U-N-S 06-867-5719
CHILDRENS MEMORIAL HOSPITAL
8301 Dodge St, Omaha, NE 68114
Phone: (402) 390-5400

Sales: $61,711,000
Company Type: Private
SIC: 8069
  Children's hospital
Gary A Perkins, President

Employees: 849
Employees here: 587

D-U-N-S 07-058-4503
CHILDRENS SEASHORE HOUSE INC
3405 Civic Center Blvd, Philadelphia, PA 19104
Phone: (215) 895-3600
Sales: $40,807,000
Company Type: Private
SIC: 8361
  Pediatric rehabilitation hospital
Richard W Shepherd, President

Employees: 450
Employees here: 435

D-U-N-S 07-863-7576
CHILDRENS SPECIALIZED HOSPITAL
150 New Providence Rd, Mountainside, NJ 7092
Phone: (908) 233-3720
Sales: $29,400,000
Company Type: Private
SIC: 8069
  Comprehensive pediatric rehabilitation and long term care
  hospital
Richard B Ahlfeld, President

Employees: 600
Employees here: 450

D-U-N-S 05-196-8808
CHILDRENS' HOSPITAL-SAN DIEGO
3020 Childrens Way, San Diego, CA 92123
Phone: (619) 576-1700
Sales: $138,111,000
Company Type: Private
SIC: 8069
  Children's hospital
Blair L Sadler, President

Employees: 2,200
Employees here: 1,750

D-U-N-S 07-877-2852
CHINESE HOSPITAL ASSOCIATION
845 Jackson St, San Francisco, CA 94133
Phone: (415) 982-2400
Sales: $36,894,000
Company Type: Private
SIC: 8062
  Hospital
Thomas Harlan, Administrator

Employees: 275
Employees here: 275

D-U-N-S 07-478-7144
CHIPPEWA COUNTY WAR MEM HOSP
500 Osborn Blvd, Sault Sainte Marie, MI 49783
Phone: (906) 635-4460
Sales: $25,183,000
Company Type: Private
SIC: 8062
  Hospital
Dan Wakeman, Executive Director

Employees: 400
Employees here: 400

D-U-N-S 17-416-6876
CHOCTAW NATION HEALTH SERVICES
Hwy 63 A, Talihina, OK 74571
Phone: (918) 567-2211
Sales: $26,000,000
Company Type: Private
SIC: 8062
  General hospital
Rosemary Hooser, Administrator

Employees: 360
Employees here: 250

D-U-N-S 01-680-8222
CHOICECARE/HUMANA CORPORATION
(Parent: Humana Inc)
655 Eden Park Dr Ste 400, Cincinnati, OH 45202
Phone: (513) 784-5200

Sales: $36,900,000   *Employees:* 538
Company Type: Public Family Member   *Employees here:* 538
SIC: 8011
    Health maintenance organization
Jane E Rollinson, President

D-U-N-S 07-476-2295
CHOWAN HOSPITAL INC
Virginia Rd, Edenton, NC 27932
Phone: (252) 482-6258
Sales: $25,200,000   *Employees:* 495
Company Type: Private   *Employees here:* 495
SIC: 8062
    General hospital
Barbara Cale, Administrator

D-U-N-S 06-498-0105
CHRIST HOSPITAL
    (Parent: Christ Hospital Hlth Svcs Corp)
176 Palisade Ave, Jersey City, NJ 7306
Phone: (201) 795-8200
Sales: $125,634,000   *Employees:* 1,100
Company Type: Private   *Employees here:* 1,080
SIC: 8062
    General hospital
Daniel R Connell, President

D-U-N-S 14-445-7983
CHRIST HOSPITAL HEALTH SVCS CORP
176 Palisade Ave, Jersey City, NJ 7306
Phone: (201) 795-8200
Sales: $119,539,000   *Employees:* 1,200
Company Type: Private   *Employees here:* 2
SIC: 8062
    General hospital & nonprofit trust management
Paul Hoyt, President

D-U-N-S 07-486-7862
CHRISTIAN CARE CENTERS INC
1000 Wiggins Pkwy, Mesquite, TX 75150
Phone: (972) 686-3100
Sales: $21,162,000   *Employees:* 500
Company Type: Private   *Employees here:* 275
SIC: 8051
    Operates nursing homes & apartments
Dr John Losher, President

D-U-N-S 08-239-4412
CHRISTIAN CHURCH CAMPUS
12700 Shelbyville Rd, Louisville, KY 40243
Phone: (502) 254-4200
Sales: $36,196,000   *Employees:* 275
Company Type: Private   *Employees here:* 30
SIC: 8059
    Nursing facility
Dan Gilbert, President

D-U-N-S 07-542-2766
CHRISTIAN HEALTH CARE CENTER
301 Sicomac Ave, Wyckoff, NJ 7481
Phone: (201) 848-5200
Sales: $23,292,000   *Employees:* 650
Company Type: Private   *Employees here:* 650
SIC: 8063
    Psychiatric hospital & skilled long term nursing care facility
Douglas A Struyk, President

D-U-N-S 07-561-2697
CHRISTIAN HOMES INC
200 N Postville Dr, Lincoln, IL 62656
Phone: (217) 732-9651

Sales: $27,958,000   *Employees:* 1,600
Company Type: Private   *Employees here:* 25
SIC: 8051
    Skilled & intermediate nursing care facilities
George Gahr, President

D-U-N-S 03-736-3520
CHRISTIAN HOSPITAL NORTHEAST-NORTHWEST
11133 Dunn Rd, Saint Louis, MO 63136
Phone: (314) 839-3800
Sales: $42,100,000   *Employees:* NA
Company Type: Private   *Employees here:* 1,000
SIC: 8062
    General hospital
Fred Brown, President

D-U-N-S 06-855-3163
CHRISTIAN HOSPITAL NORTHEAST-NORTHWEST
11133 Dunn Rd, Saint Louis, MO 63136
Phone: (314) 355-2300
Sales: $214,995,000   *Employees:* 2,800
Company Type: Private   *Employees here:* 1,900
SIC: 8062
    General hospital
John O Shaughnessy, President

D-U-N-S 07-706-9243
CHRISTIANA CARE HEALTH SVCS
501 W 14th St, Wilmington, DE 19801
Phone: (302) 733-1000
Sales: $463,251,000   *Employees:* 5,700
Company Type: Private   *Employees here:* 1,000
SIC: 8062
    General hospital
Charles M Smith, President

D-U-N-S 02-500-8558
CHRISTIE BUILDING INC
101 W University Ave, Champaign, IL 61820
Phone: (217) 366-1321
Sales: $37,800,000   *Employees:* 550
Company Type: Private   *Employees here:* 420
SIC: 8011
    Operator of medical clinic and pharmacies and commercial
      property owner
Jack Schnitzer, President

D-U-N-S 07-560-0486
CHRISTIE CLINIC ASSOCIATION
    (Parent: Promedco Management Company)
101 W University Ave, Champaign, IL 61820
Phone: (217) 366-1200
Sales: $29,500,000   *Employees:* 430
Company Type: Public Family Member   *Employees here:* 420
SIC: 8011
    Medical clinic
Kenneth R Goodchild, Executive Director

D-U-N-S 07-732-1198
CHURCH HMES INC CONGREGATIONAL
705 New Britain Ave, Hartford, CT 6106
Phone: (860) 527-9126
Sales: $29,908,000   *Employees:* 600
Company Type: Private   *Employees here:* 450
SIC: 8051
    Skilled nursing care facility nursing/personal care individual/
      family services
Norman Harper, President

D-U-N-S 06-938-6027
CHURCH HOSPITAL CORPORATION
100 N Broadway, Baltimore, MD 21231
Phone: (410) 522-8000

Sales: $54,892,000
Company Type: Private
SIC: 8062
  General hospital
T G Whedbee, President

Employees: 1,200
Employees here: 962

D-U-N-S 01-526-6851
CHW CENTRAL COAST
1400 E Church St, Santa Maria, CA 93454
Phone: (805) 739-3000
Sales: $44,400,000
Company Type: Private
SIC: 8062
  Hospital

Employees: NA
Employees here: 900

D-U-N-S 00-511-0619
CHW CENTRAL COAST
601 E Micheltorena St, Santa Barbara, CA 93103
Phone: (805) 962-7661
Sales: $20,000,000
Company Type: Private
SIC: 8062
  General medical & surgical hospital
Daniel Herlinger, President

Employees: NA
Employees here: 415

D-U-N-S 03-087-4119
CHW CENTRAL COAST
511 Bath St, Santa Barbara, CA 93101
Phone: (805) 568-5887
Sales: $218,355,000
Company Type: Private
SIC: 8062
  General hospitals
Daniel Herlinger, President

Employees: 3,500
Employees here: 1,850

D-U-N-S 80-364-1513
CHW CENTRAL COAST
2309 Antonio Ave, Camarillo, CA 93010
Phone: (805) 484-2831
Sales: $24,300,000
Company Type: Private
SIC: 8062
  General hospital
Daniel Herlinger, Branch Manager

Employees: NA
Employees here: 500

D-U-N-S 79-783-8505
CHW MEDICAL FOUNDATION
7919 Folsom Blvd, Sacramento, CA 95826
Phone: (916) 733-3333
Sales: $115,717,000
Company Type: Private
SIC: 8099
  Medical services
Michael Wilson, President

Employees: 800
Employees here: 700

D-U-N-S 14-828-6818
CIGNA HEALTHCARE OF LOUISIANA
  (Parent: Cigna Health Corporation)
4354 S Sherwood Forest Blvd, Baton Rouge, LA 70816
Phone: (225) 295-2800
Sales: $30,576,000
Company Type: Public Family Member
SIC: 8011
  Health & allied services
Nancy Horstmann, Executive Director

Employees: 40
Employees here: 25

D-U-N-S 55-695-7140
CIGNA HEALTHCARE OF OHIO INC
  (Parent: Cigna Hcalth Corporation)
3700 Corporate Dr, Columbus, OH 43231
Phone: (614) 823-7500

Sales: $157,433,000
Company Type: Public Family Member
SIC: 8011
  Health & allied services
James D Massie, Vice-President

Employees: 500
Employees here: 200

D-U-N-S 55-695-7892
CIGNA HEALTHCARE OF TENNESSEE
  (Parent: Cigna Health Corporation)
900 Cottage Grove Rd, Bloomfield, CT 6002
Phone: (615) 595-3000
Sales: $161,089,000
Company Type: Public Family Member
SIC: 8011
  Health & allied services
David Mathis, Executive Director

Employees: 30
Employees here: 30

D-U-N-S 11-044-9063
CIGNA HEALTHCARE ARIZONA, INC.
535 N Wilmot Rd, Tucson, AZ 85711
Phone: (520) 571-6500
Sales: $28,100,000
Company Type: Public Family Member
SIC: 8011
  Medical doctor's office
Chris Kriskreutz, Manager

Employees: NA
Employees here: 450

D-U-N-S 08-545-9964
CIGNA HEALTHCARE ARIZONA, INC.
  (Parent: Cigna Health Corporation)
11001 N Black Canyon Hwy, Phoenix, AZ 85029
Phone: (602) 371-2500
Sales: $584,764,000
Company Type: Public Family Member
SIC: 8011
  Health maintenance organization
Dr Clyde A Wright Md, President

Employees: 3,000
Employees here: 900

D-U-N-S 12-031-5684
CIGNA HEALTHCARE ARIZONA, INC.
755 E McDowell Rd, Buckeye, AZ 85326
Phone: (602) 271-5111
Sales: $25,200,000
Company Type: Public Family Member
SIC: 8011
  Medical doctor's office
Jeffrey Nelson, Branch Manager

Employees: NA
Employees here: 400

D-U-N-S 02-098-0017
CIRCLES OF CARE INC
400 E Sheridan Rd, Melbourne, FL 32901
Phone: (407) 722-5200
Sales: $19,833,000
Company Type: Private
SIC: 8063
  Psychiatric hospital
James B Whitaker, President

Employees: 400
Employees here: 280

D-U-N-S 07-210-1074
CITIZENS BMC
604 Stone Ave, Talladega, AL 35160
Phone: (205) 362-8111
Sales: $20,000,000
Company Type: Private
SIC: 8062
  General hospital
Steve Johnson, President

Employees: 380
Employees here: 380

D-U-N-S 03-006-3903
CITIZENS GENERAL HOSPITAL
651 4th Ave, New Kensington, PA 15068
Phone: (724) 337-3541

Sales: $38,757,000

Employees: 800

Company Type: Private

Employees here: 800

SIC: 8062

General hospital

R E Marino, Executive Director

D-U-N-S 06-945-8024

CITIZENS MEDICAL CENTER

2701 Hospital Dr, Victoria, TX 77901

Phone: (512) 573-9181

Sales: $120,506,000

Employees: 645

Company Type: Private

Employees here: 645

SIC: 8062

General hospital

David P Brown, Administrator

D-U-N-S 05-391-9650

CITIZENS MEMRL HSP DST PLK CNT

1500 N Oakland Ave, Bolivar, MO 65613

Phone: (417) 326-6000

Sales: $29,795,000

Employees: 600

Company Type: Private

Employees here: 600

SIC: 8062

General hospital medical clinics and home health services

Donald Babb, Chief Executive Officer

D-U-N-S 07-508-6421

CITRUS MEM HEALTH FOUNDATION

502 W Highland Blvd, Inverness, FL 34452

Phone: (352) 726-1551

Sales: $71,518,000

Employees: 912

Company Type: Private

Employees here: 855

SIC: 8062

General hospital

Charles Blasband, Administrator

D-U-N-S 04-647-1330

CITRUS VALLEY MEDICAL CENTER,

1115 S Sunset Ave, West Covina, CA 91790

Phone: (626) 962-4011

Sales: $101,400,000

Employees: 1,723

Company Type: Private

Employees here: 1,720

SIC: 8062

General hospital

Peter E Makowski, President

D-U-N-S 10-733-8444

CITY OF AMES

1111 Duff Ave, Ames, IA 50010

Phone: (515) 239-2011

Sales: $47,700,000

Employees: NA

Company Type: Private

Employees here: 1,240

SIC: 8062

General hospital

Kim Russel, Principal

D-U-N-S 19-754-6609

CITY OF BOSTON

818 Harrison Ave, Boston, MA 2118

Phone: (617) 534-5365

Sales: $121,900,000

Employees: NA

Company Type: Private

Employees here: 2,400

SIC: 8062

General hospital

Lawrence Dwyer, Branch Manager

D-U-N-S 80-763-5982

CITY OF HOPE NATIONAL MED CTR

1500 Duarte Rd, Duarte, CA 91010

Phone: (626) 359-8111

Sales: $183,290,000

Employees: 2,600

Company Type: Private

Employees here: 2,600

SIC: 8062

General hospital

Dr Charles M Balch Md, President

D-U-N-S 16-193-3379

CITY OF LINCOLN

2300 S 16th St, Lincoln, NE 68502

Phone: (402) 475-1011

Sales: $45,600,000

Employees: NA

Company Type: Private

Employees here: 1,100

SIC: 8062

General hospital

Arlan Stromberg, Principal

D-U-N-S 07-374-4203

CITY OF PHILADELPHIA, TRUST

900 Walnut St, Philadelphia, PA 19107

Phone: (215) 928-3000

Sales: $63,346,000

Employees: 600

Company Type: Private

Employees here: 600

SIC: 8069

Eye & hand disorders & geriatric hospital

D M Kessler, Executive Director

D-U-N-S 06-775-5074

CITY OF QUINCY

114 Whitwell St, Quincy, MA 2169

Phone: (617) 773-6100

Sales: $60,700,000

Employees: NA

Company Type: Private

Employees here: 1,200

SIC: 8062

Hospital

Ralph Di Pisa, Director

D-U-N-S 02-101-1705

CITY OF SALEM

Dove Ave, Salem, MA 1970

Phone: (978) 745-9000

Sales: $21,500,000

Employees: NA

Company Type: Private

Employees here: 400

SIC: 8069

Hospital specialty, except psychiatric

Anthony Chiola, Manager

D-U-N-S 78-515-0244

CITY OF VIRGINIA

901 9th St N, Virginia, MN 55792

Phone: (218) 741-3340

Sales: $31,100,000

Employees: NA

Company Type: Private

Employees here: 500

SIC: 8011

Medical doctor's office

Kyle Hopstad, Manager

D-U-N-S 61-347-2190

CITY OF WOOSTER

1761 Beall Ave, Wooster, OH 44691

Phone: (330) 263-8100

Sales: $27,100,000

Employees: NA

Company Type: Private

Employees here: 650

SIC: 8062

General hospital

Richard Bajus, Administrator

D-U-N-S 07-745-6606

CITY HOSPITAL INC

Dry Run Rd, Martinsburg, WV 25401

Phone: (304) 264-1000

Sales: $54,356,000
Company Type: Private
SIC: 8062
   General hospital
Peter L Mulford, Administrator
Employees: 742
Employees here: 742

D-U-N-S 06-936-6300
CIVISTA HEALTH INC
701 E Charles St, La Plata, MD 20646
Phone: (301) 934-4633
Sales: $42,332,000
Company Type: Private
SIC: 8062
   Hospital
Susan L Hunsaker, President
Employees: 668
Employees here: 643

D-U-N-S 07-666-3889
CLALLAM CNTY PUB HOSPITAL DST 2
939 Caroline St, Port Angeles, WA 98362
Phone: (360) 457-8513
Sales: $46,720,000
Company Type: Private
SIC: 8062
   General medical & surgical hospital
Tom Stegbauer, Administrator
Employees: 670
Employees here: 665

D-U-N-S 07-515-3882
CLARA MAASS MEDICAL CENTER
1 Clara Maass Dr, Belleville, NJ 7109
Phone: (973) 450-2000
Sales: $109,275,000
Company Type: Private
SIC: 8062
   General hospital
John Calandriello, Chief Financial Officer
Employees: 1,500
Employees here: 1,500

D-U-N-S 07-805-1968
CLARENDON MEMORIAL HOSPITAL
10 Hospital St, Manning, SC 29102
Phone: (803) 435-8463
Sales: $19,869,000
Company Type: Private
SIC: 8062
   General medical and surgical hospital
Edward R Frye Jr, Administrator
Employees: 724
Employees here: 350

D-U-N-S 07-215-3828
CLARION HOSPITAL
1 Hospital Dr, Clarion, PA 16214
Phone: (814) 226-9500
Sales: $26,456,000
Company Type: Private
SIC: 8062
   General hospital
Donald Evans, Chief Executive Officer
Employees: 385
Employees here: 385

D-U-N-S 16-010-4873
CLARITY VISION INC
   (Parent: Highmark Inc)
100 Senate Ave, Camp Hill, PA 17011
Phone: (717) 760-9680
Sales: $75,700,000
Company Type: Private
SIC: 8011
   Managed vision care retail optical goods
Walter F Froh, President
Employees: 1,100
Employees here: 100

D-U-N-S 05-869-4142
CLARK MEMORIAL HOSPITAL
1220 Missouri Ave, Jeffersonville, IN 47130
Phone: (812) 282-6631

Sales: $82,023,000
Company Type: Private
SIC: 8062
   Hospital
Merle E Stepp, President
Employees: 1,338
Employees here: 1,338

D-U-N-S 07-385-6189
CLARK THEDA MEMORIAL HOSPITAL
130 2nd St, Neenah, WI 54956
Phone: (920) 729-3100
Sales: $55,600,000
Company Type: Private
SIC: 8062
   General medical and surgical hospital
Pat Hawley, Chief Financial Officer
Employees: 1,200
Employees here: 1,200

D-U-N-S 07-546-1004
CLARKSVILLE REGIONAL HEALTH SYS
1771 Madison St, Clarksville, TN 37043
Phone: (931) 552-6622
Sales: $65,990,000
Company Type: Private
SIC: 8062
   General hospital
James L Decker, President
Employees: 1,000
Employees here: 1,000

D-U-N-S 83-832-2360
CLAY PARACELSUS COUNTY HOSP
   (Parent: Paracelsus Healthcare Corp)
100 Old Jefferson St, Celina, TN 38551
Phone: (931) 243-3581
Sales: $28,878,000
Company Type: Public Family Member
SIC: 8062
   General medical and surgical hospital
Patrick Gray, Administrator
Employees: 269
Employees here: 124

D-U-N-S 92-658-1018
CLEAR LK REGIONAL MED CTR INC
   (Parent: Columbia/Hca Healthcare Corp)
500 Medical Center Blvd, Webster, TX 77598
Phone: (281) 332-2511
Sales: $55,600,000
Company Type: Public Family Member
SIC: 8062
   Acute care hospital
Donald A Shaffett, President
Employees: 1,200
Employees here: 400

D-U-N-S 15-652-1155
CLEARFIELD AREA HEALTH SVCS CORP
809 Turnpike Ave, Clearfield, PA 16830
Phone: (814) 765-5341
Sales: $75,000,000
Company Type: Private
SIC: 8062
   Holding company
Stephen A Wolfe, President
Employees: 777
Employees here: 728

D-U-N-S 07-497-9683
CLEARFIELD HOSPITAL
809 Turnpike Ave, Clearfield, PA 16830
Phone: (814) 765-5341
Sales: $46,317,000
Company Type: Private
SIC: 8062
   Hospital
Stephen A Wolfe, Chief Executive Officer
Employees: 700
Employees here: 670

D-U-N-S 95-668-9376
CLEARWATER COMMUNITY HOSPITAL LP
1521 Druid Rd E, Clearwater, FL 33756
Phone: (727) 444-4900

Sales: $27,804,000
Company Type: Private
SIC: 8062
    General hospital
Columbia H Corp, Parent

Employees: 270
Employees here: 270

D-U-N-S 07-834-2227
CLEO WALLACE CENTER INC
4400 E Iliff Ave, Denver, CO 80222
Phone: (303) 466-7391
Sales: $24,367,000
Company Type: Private
SIC: 8063
    Psychiatric facility
James M Cole, President

Employees: 500
Employees here: 120

D-U-N-S 18-791-6804
CLEVELAND CLINIC FLORIDA HOSP
2835 N Ocean Blvd, Fort Lauderdale, FL 33308
Phone: (954) 568-1000
Sales: $51,000,000
Company Type: Private
SIC: 8062
    Hospital
Harry K Moon, Chief Executive Officer

Employees: 850
Employees here: 450

D-U-N-S 01-773-0458
CLEVELAND CLINIC FOUNDATION
9500 Euclid Ave, Cleveland, OH 44195
Phone: (216) 444-2200
Sales: $1,146,856,000
Company Type: Private
SIC: 8062
    General hospital outpatient clinic and healthcare
    management services
Dr Floyd D Loop Md, Chairman of the Board

Employees: 11,500
Employees here: 8,800

D-U-N-S 07-106-3994
CLEVELAND MEMORIAL HOSPITAL
201 E Grover St, Shelby, NC 28150
Phone: (704) 487-3000
Sales: $82,303,000
Company Type: Private
SIC: 8062
    Hospital & long term care
John Young, President

Employees: 1,073
Employees here: 775

D-U-N-S 07-452-8043
CLEVELAND NEIGHBORHOOD HEALTH
12800 Shaker Blvd, Cleveland, OH 44120
Phone: (216) 991-3000
Sales: $26,143,000
Company Type: Private
SIC: 8099
    Medical service organization
James G Turner, Executive Director

Employees: 400
Employees here: 10

D-U-N-S 07-367-4814
CLIFTON SPRINGS SANITARIUM CO
2 Coulter Rd, Clifton Springs, NY 14432
Phone: (315) 462-9561
Sales: $36,909,000
Company Type: Private
SIC: 8062
    General hospital
John P Galati, President

Employees: 640
Employees here: 600

D-U-N-S 07-830-0787
CLINICAL ASSOCIATES, PA
515 S Fremont Ave, Baltimore, MD 21230
Phone: (410) 296-5300

Sales: $20,500,000
Company Type: Private
SIC: 8011
    Physicians' office including specialists
Dr Richard D Maffezzoli Md, President

Employees: 300
Employees here: 150

D-U-N-S 05-947-7513
CLINICAL LABORATORIES OF HAWAII
33 Lanihuli St, Hilo, HI 96720
Phone: (808) 935-4814
Sales: $51,344,000
Company Type: Private
SIC: 8071
    Pathological laboratories
Dr Moon S Park Md, President

Employees: 400
Employees here: 50

D-U-N-S 01-583-9376
CLINICAL LABS OF COLORADO LLC
2590 W 2nd Ave Ste 1, Denver, CO 80219
Phone: (303) 922-2210
Sales: $29,000,000
Company Type: Private
SIC: 8071
    Medical laboratory
Moon Park, Chief Executive Officer

Employees: 370
Employees here: 80

D-U-N-S 78-874-4209
CLINICAL PATHOLOGY LABS
8613 Cross Park Dr, Austin, TX 78754
Phone: (512) 339-1275
Sales: $45,000,000
Company Type: Private
SIC: 8071
    Medical laboratory
Dr Robert Connor Md, Chairman of the Board

Employees: 675
Employees here: 275

D-U-N-S 09-826-8311
CLINICAL REFERENCE LAB INC
8433 Quivira Rd, Shawnee Mission, KS 66215
Phone: (913) 492-3652
Sales: $28,155,000
Company Type: Private
SIC: 8071
    Medical lab
Timothy Sotos, Chairman of the Board

Employees: 250
Employees here: 250

D-U-N-S 11-272-6112
CLINISHARE INC
20600 Nordhoff St, Chatsworth, CA 91311
Phone: (818) 709-4221
Sales: $24,100,000
Company Type: Private
SIC: 8082
    Home health care services
Bruce Blomstrom, President

Employees: 1,500
Employees here: 150

D-U-N-S 07-288-5312
CLINTON MEMORIAL HOSPITAL
610 W Main St, Wilmington, OH 45177
Phone: (937) 382-6611
Sales: $47,075,000
Company Type: Private
SIC: 8062
    General hospital and physicians' offices
Thomas F Kurtz, President

Employees: 750
Employees here: 630

D-U-N-S 61-750-3784
CLINTRIALS RESEARCH INC
20 Burton Hills Blvd, Nashville, TN 37215
Phone: (615) 665-9665

Sales: $102,990,000
Company Type: Public
SIC: 8071
   Pharmaceutical studies
Jerry R Mitchell, Chairman of the Board

Employees: 1,500
Employees here: 140

D-U-N-S 88-464-3487
COASTAL PHYSICIAN GROUP, INC
2828 Croasdaile Dr, Durham, NC 27705
Phone: (919) 383-0355
Sales: $424,841,000
Company Type: Public
SIC: 8093
   Provides physician management services
Steven M Scott, Chairman of the Board

Employees: 1,645
Employees here: 132

D-U-N-S 06-646-6673
COBB HOSPITAL INC
3950 Austell Rd, Austell, GA 30106
Phone: (770) 732-4000
Sales: $70,900,000
Company Type: Private
SIC: 8062
   Hospital
Thomas E Hill, Chief Executive Officer

Employees: 1,525
Employees here: 1,512

D-U-N-S 06-827-5536
COBBLE HILL NURSING HOME INC
380 Henry St, Brooklyn, NY 11201
Phone: (718) 855-6789
Sales: $35,752,000
Company Type: Private
SIC: 8051
   Skilled nursing home
Dimetra Palimeros, President

Employees: 550
Employees here: 550

D-U-N-S 19-148-8576
COCOA BEACH AREA HEALTH SVC
105 South Banana River Blvd, Cocoa Beach, FL 32931
Phone: (407) 784-4211
Sales: $57,866,000
Company Type: Private
SIC: 8011
   Clinic service
Marvin Jones, Chairman of the Board

Employees: 800
Employees here: 800

D-U-N-S 07-585-9371
COFFEE REGIONAL MEDICAL CENTER
W Ward St, Douglas, GA 31533
Phone: (912) 384-1900
Sales: $44,119,000
Company Type: Private
SIC: 8062
   Hospital
George L Heck, Administrator

Employees: 530
Employees here: 530

D-U-N-S 07-306-8736
COFFEYVILLE REGL MED CTR FNDTN
1400 W 4th St, Coffeyville, KS 67337
Phone: (316) 251-1200
Sales: $20,412,000
Company Type: Private
SIC: 8062
   General hospital
Jerry Marquette, Administrator

Employees: 380
Employees here: 380

D-U-N-S 07-546-4800
COLBERT COUNTY/NORTHWEST ALABA
1300 S Montgomery Ave, Sheffield, AL 35660
Phone: (256) 386-4196

Sales: $55,464,000
Company Type: Private
SIC: 8062
   General hospital
Ralph Clark, Chief Executive Officer

Employees: 700
Employees here: 600

D-U-N-S 09-738-9779
COLISEUM PARK HOSPITAL INC
   (Parent: Columbia/Hca Healthcare Corp)
350 Hospital Dr, Macon, GA 31217
Phone: (912) 765-7000
Sales: $170,000,000
Company Type: Public Family Member
SIC: 8062
   General medical & surgical hospital
Mike Boggs, President

Employees: 1,000
Employees here: 1,000

D-U-N-S 07-316-3990
COLLOM & CARNEY CLINIC ASSN
4800 Texas Blvd, Texarkana, TX 75503
Phone: (903) 792-7151
Sales: $30,138,000
Company Type: Private
SIC: 8011
   Medical & surgical clinic
Thomas Simmons, Administrator

Employees: 400
Employees here: 355

D-U-N-S 94-879-1058
COLORADO ACCESS
501 S Cherry St Ste 700, Denver, CO 80246
Phone: (303) 355-6707
Sales: $75,000,000
Company Type: Private
SIC: 8011
   Hmo provider
David West, Executive Director

Employees: 130
Employees here: 130

D-U-N-S 18-612-0655
COLORADO PRMNT MED GROUP PC
10350 E Dakota Ave, Denver, CO 80231
Phone: (303) 344-7295
Sales: $41,200,000
Company Type: Private
SIC: 8011
   General medical service
Dr Toby Cole, President

Employees: 600
Employees here: 600

D-U-N-S 07-835-2986
COLORADO SPRNG HEALTH PRTNERS PC
209 S Nevada Ave, Colorado Springs, CO 80903
Phone: (719) 475-7700
Sales: $29,000,000
Company Type: Private
SIC: 8011
   General medical clinic
John Bell, Chairman of the Board

Employees: 468
Employees here: 296

D-U-N-S 15-459-3420
COLUMBIA-ARLINGTON HEALTHCARE LLC
1850 Town Center Pkwy, Reston, VA 20190
Phone: (703) 689-9000
Sales: $32,000,000
Company Type: Private
SIC: 8062
   General hospital
Tim Brown, President

Employees: NA
Employees here: 732

D-U-N-S 01-992-6658
COLUMBIA-ARLINGTON HEALTHCARE LLC
1701 N George Mason Dr, Arlington, VA 22205
Phone: (703) 558-5000

Sales: $500,000,000   *Employees:* 3,000
Company Type: Private   *Employees here:* 1,800
SIC: 8062
    Hospital
James Cole, President

    D-U-N-S 06-601-2626
COLUMBIA/HCA JOHN RANDOLPH MED CTR
    (Parent: Columbia/Hca Healthcare Corp)
411 W Randolph Rd, Hopewell, VA 23860
Phone: (804) 541-7492
Sales: $43,800,000   *Employees:* 950
Company Type: Public Family Member   *Employees here:* 665
SIC: 8062
    Hospital
Dan Wetta Jr, Chief Executive Officer

    D-U-N-S 07-791-9959
COLUMBIA/ALLEGHANY REGIONAL HOSPITAL INC
    (Parent: Columbia/Hca Healthcare Corp)
1 Arh Ln, Lowmoor, VA 24457
Phone: (540) 862-6230
Sales: $23,000,000   *Employees:* 510
Company Type: Public Family Member   *Employees here:* 495
SIC: 8062
    Hospital
Ward Stevens, Principal

    D-U-N-S 07-322-5906
COLUMBIA BARTOW MEMORIAL HOSP
1239 E Main St, Bartow, FL 33830
Phone: (941) 533-8111
Sales: $30,000,000   *Employees:* 245
Company Type: Private   *Employees here:* 245
SIC: 8062
    Hospital
Tom Matthews, Administrator

    D-U-N-S 36-407-5911
COLUMBIA BAY AREA HEALTHCARE
675 E Santa Clara St, San Jose, CA 95112
Phone: (408) 977-4545
Sales: $21,700,000   *Employees:* NA
Company Type: Public Family Member   *Employees here:* 450
SIC: 8062
    Hospital
William Gilbert, Principal

    D-U-N-S 80-303-8249
COLUMBIA CHICAGO OSTPTHC HOSPT
    (Parent: Columbia/Hca Healthcare Corp)
20201 Crawford Ave, Olympia Fields, IL 60461
Phone: (708) 747-4000
Sales: $170,000,000   *Employees:* 770
Company Type: Public Family Member   *Employees here:* 720
SIC: 8062
    Acute care hospital
Thomas Frist, President

    D-U-N-S 02-919-2833
COLUMBIA CHPPNHM MDCL CTR
7101 Jahnke Rd, Richmond, VA 23225
Phone: (804) 327-3313
Sales: $35,000,000   *Employees:* NA
Company Type: Public Family Member   *Employees here:* 800
SIC: 8062
    General hospital
Marylyn Tavenner, President

    D-U-N-S 96-003-8917
COLUMBIA CHPPNHM MDCL CTR
    (Parent: Columbia/Hca Healthcare Corp)
1401 Johnston Willis Dr, Richmond, VA 23235

Phone: (804) 330-2000
Sales: $112,300,000   *Employees:* 2,400
Company Type: Public Family Member   *Employees here:* 1,400
SIC: 8062
    General hospital
Marilyn Tavenner, President

    D-U-N-S 07-674-1966
COLUMBIA CSA/HS GREATER CLVLND
2351 E 22nd St, Cleveland, OH 44115
Phone: (216) 861-6200
Sales: $74,500,000   *Employees:* 1,600
Company Type: Private   *Employees here:* 1,100
SIC: 8062
    General hospital
Samuel H Turner, Chief Executive Officer

    D-U-N-S 92-984-7713
COLUMBIA CSA/HS GREATER CLVLND
29000 Center Ridge Rd, Cleveland, OH 44145
Phone: (440) 835-8000
Sales: $25,000,000   *Employees:* NA
Company Type: Private   *Employees here:* 600
SIC: 8062
    General hospital
Fred Degradis, Chief Executive Officer

    D-U-N-S 80-979-2104
COLUMBIA DUNWOODY MEDICAL CTR
    (Parent: Columbia/Hca Healthcare Corp)
4575 N Shallowford Rd, Atlanta, GA 30338
Phone: (770) 454-2000
Sales: $21,400,000   *Employees:* 477
Company Type: Public Family Member   *Employees here:* 477
SIC: 8062
    General hospital
Thomas Gilbert, Chief Executive Officer

    D-U-N-S 18-970-5197
COLUMBIA EAST HOUSTON MED CTR
    (Parent: Columbia/Hca Healthcare Corp)
13111 East Fwy, Houston, TX 77015
Phone: (713) 393-2000
Sales: $21,500,000   *Employees:* 480
Company Type: Public Family Member   *Employees here:* 280
SIC: 8062
    General hospital
Merrily Waters, Administrator

    D-U-N-S 01-843-7558
COLUMBIA EL DRADO HOSPITAL MED CTR
    (Parent: Columbia/Hca Healthcare Corp)
1400 N Wilmot Rd, Tucson, AZ 85712
Phone: (520) 886-6361
Sales: $35,325,000   *Employees:* 532
Company Type: Public Family Member   *Employees here:* 522
SIC: 8062
    Acute care hospital
Rick Smith, Chief Operating Officer

    D-U-N-S 96-260-2702
COLUMBIA FOUR RIVERS MED CTR
    (Parent: Columbia/Hca Healthcare Corp)
1015 Medical Center Pkwy, Selma, AL 36701
Phone: (334) 872-8461
Sales: $45,921,000   *Employees:* 625
Company Type: Public Family Member   *Employees here:* 600
SIC: 8062
    Hospital & clinic
John Anderson, Chief Executive Officer

    D-U-N-S 15-000-8787
COLUMBIA HEALTHCARE OF CENTL VA
10500 Quivira Rd, Shawnee Mission, KS 66215

Phone: (913) 541-5000
Sales: $49,800,000   *Employees:* NA
Company Type: Public Family Member   *Employees here:* 1,200
SIC: 8062
   General hospital
Kevin Hicks, Principal

D-U-N-S 78-267-6985
COLUMBIA HEALTHCARE OF CENTL VA
501 Medical Center Dr, Alexandria, LA 71301
Phone: (318) 449-7000
Sales: $70,300,000   *Employees:* NA
Company Type: Public Family Member   *Employees here:* 1,600
SIC: 8069
   Hospital
Lynn Truelove, Branch Manager

D-U-N-S 82-899-4285
COLUMBIA HEALTHCARE OF CENTL VA
1509 W Truman Rd, Independence, MO 64050
Phone: (816) 836-8100
Sales: $61,000,000   *Employees:* NA
Company Type: Public Family Member   *Employees here:* 1,443
SIC: 8062
   General hospital

D-U-N-S 92-830-9434
COLUMBIA HEALTHCARE OF CENTL VA
   (Parent: Columbia/Hca Healthcare Corp)
1 Park Mdws, Nashville, TN 37215
Phone: (615) 327-9551
Sales: $137,900,000   *Employees:* 2,000
Company Type: Public Family Member   *Employees here:* 1,800
SIC: 8011
   Operates physician practices and clinics
Thomas Frist, President

D-U-N-S 06-761-8009
COLUMBIA HUNTINGTON BEACH MED CTR
   (Parent: Columbia/Hca Healthcare Corp)
17772 Beach Blvd, Huntington Beach, CA 92647
Phone: (714) 842-1473
Sales: $38,632,000   *Employees:* 510
Company Type: Public Family Member   *Employees here:* 510
SIC: 8062
   General hospital
Carol Freeman, Chief Executive Officer

D-U-N-S 92-647-5948
COLUMBIA HOSPITAL CORP OF S BROWARD
   (Parent: Columbia/Hca Healthcare Corp)
8201 W Broward Blvd, Fort Lauderdale, FL 33324
Phone: (954) 473-6600
Sales: $40,200,000   *Employees:* 875
Company Type: Public Family Member   *Employees here:* 875
SIC: 8062
   General hospital
Michael Joseph, Chief Executive Officer

D-U-N-S 96-299-8688
COLUMBIA HOSPITAL CORP BAY AREA
   (Parent: Columbia/Hca Healthcare Corp)
7101 S Padre Island Dr, Corpus Christi, TX 78412
Phone: (512) 985-1200
Sales: $27,200,000   *Employees:* 600
Company Type: Public Family Member   *Employees here:* 600
SIC: 8062
   General hospital
Kirk Wilson, Administrator

D-U-N-S 05-628-7956
COLUMBIA HOSPITAL FOR WOMEN MED CTR
2425 L St Nw, Washington, DC 20037
Phone: (202) 293-6500

Sales: $97,000,000   *Employees:* 700
Company Type: Private   *Employees here:* 700
SIC: 8062
   General hospital
Gerry Beaulieu, Chief Executive Officer

D-U-N-S 07-678-1442
COLUMBIA HOSPITAL CORP KY
   (Parent: Columbia/Hca Healthcare Corp)
1 Park Mdws, Nashville, TN 37215
Phone: (615) 327-9551
Sales: $31,900,000   *Employees:* 700
Company Type: Public Family Member   *Employees here:* 240
SIC: 8062
   General hospital
Tim Brown, Chief Executive Officer

D-U-N-S 00-674-4247
COLUMBIA HOSPITAL FRANKFORT
Kings Daughters Dr, Frankfort, KY 40601
Phone: (502) 875-5240
Sales: $22,500,000   *Employees:* 500
Company Type: Private   *Employees here:* 500
SIC: 8062
   Hospital
Columbia Healthcare, Principal

D-U-N-S 07-604-0328
COLUMBIA HOSPITAL L P
2201 45th St, West Palm Beach, FL 33407
Phone: (561) 842-6141
Sales: $28,600,000   *Employees:* 630
Company Type: Private   *Employees here:* 625
SIC: 8062
   General medical hospital
Sharon Roush, Chief Executive Officer

D-U-N-S 05-410-5374
COLUMBIA HOSPITAL, INC.
2025 E Newport Ave, Milwaukee, WI 53211
Phone: (414) 961-3300
Sales: $127,982,000   *Employees:* 1,470
Company Type: Private   *Employees here:* 1,412
SIC: 8062
   General hospital
John F Schuler, President

D-U-N-S 04-423-9606
COLUMBIA LA GRANGE MEM HOSP
   (Parent: Columbia/Hca Healthcare Corp)
5101 Willow Springs Rd, La Grange, IL 60525
Phone: (708) 352-1200
Sales: $80,100,000   *Employees:* 1,719
Company Type: Public Family Member   *Employees here:* 1,719
SIC: 8062
   General medical and surgical hospital
Kathy Bigo, President

D-U-N-S 08-579-3776
COLUMBIA MED CTR OF SAN ANGELO
   (Parent: Columbia/Hca Healthcare Corp)
3501 Knickerbocker Rd, San Angelo, TX 76904
Phone: (915) 949-9511
Sales: $28,565,000   *Employees:* 650
Company Type: Public Family Member   *Employees here:* 650
SIC: 8062
   General medical hospital
Greg Angle, Chief Executive Officer

D-U-N-S 10-146-6738
COLUMBIA MEDICAL PLAN INC
   (Parent: Carefirst Of Maryland Inc)
2 Knoll North Dr, Columbia, MD 21045

Phone: (410) 997-8500
Sales: $142,181,000   *Employees:* 1,050
Company Type: Private   *Employees here:* 720
SIC: 8011
    Health maintenance organization
Dr Robert N Sheff Md, President

D-U-N-S 08-048-1708
COLUMBIA MEMORIAL HOSPITAL
71 Prospect Ave, Hudson, NY 12534
Phone: (518) 828-7601
Sales: $49,696,000   *Employees:* 1,000
Company Type: Private   *Employees here:* 750
SIC: 8062
    General medical and surgical hospital and extended care
        nursing home
Jane Ehrlich, Chief Executive Officer

D-U-N-S 07-172-3969
COLUMBIA METROWEST MEDICAL CTR
    (Parent: Columbia/Hca Healthcare Corp)
67 Union St, Natick, MA 1760
Phone: (508) 383-1000
Sales: $117,000,000   *Employees:* 2,500
Company Type: Public Family Member   *Employees here:* 1,100
SIC: 8062
    General hospital
Tom Henessey, President

D-U-N-S 96-259-2457
COLUMBIA NORTH BAY HOSPITAL
    (Parent: Columbia/Hca Healthcare Corp)
1711 W Wheeler Ave, Aransas Pass, TX 78336
Phone: (512) 758-8585
Sales: $40,000,000   *Employees:* 250
Company Type: Public Family Member   *Employees here:* 250
SIC: 8062
    General hospital
Steve Sutherlin, Chief Executive Officer

D-U-N-S 36-258-5358
COLUMBIA OUTPATIENT SURGICAL SVCS
301 NW 82nd Ave, Fort Lauderdale, FL 33324
Phone: (954) 424-1766
Sales: $25,000,000   *Employees:* 50
Company Type: Private   *Employees here:* 50
SIC: 8011
    Ambulatory surgical center
Debbie Haga-Cofer, Controller

D-U-N-S 06-536-7906
COLUMBIA PALMYRA PARK HOSPITAL
    (Parent: Columbia/Hca Healthcare Corp)
2000 Palmyra Rd, Albany, GA 31701
Phone: (912) 434-2000
Sales: $26,300,000   *Employees:* 580
Company Type: Public Family Member   *Employees here:* 580
SIC: 8062
    General medical & surgical hospital
Alan Golson, Administrator

D-U-N-S 15-039-1241
COLUMBIA PINE LK REGIONAL HOSP
1029 Med Ctr Dr Ste 200, Mayfield, KY 42066
Phone: (502) 251-4100
Sales: $25,568,000   *Employees:* NA
Company Type: Private   *Employees here:* NA
SIC: 8062
    General hospital

D-U-N-S 92-647-6821
COLUMBIA PK HEALTHCARE SYSTEMS
1 Park Mdws, Nashville, TN 37215
Phone: (615) 344-9551

Sales: $88,800,000   *Employees:* 1,903
Company Type: Private   *Employees here:* 3
SIC: 8062
    Hospitals
Jay Grinney, President

D-U-N-S 07-832-4498
COLUMBIA PUTNAM HOSPITAL INC
    (Parent: Columbia/Hca Healthcare Corp)
Highway 20 W, Palatka, FL 32177
Phone: (904) 328-5711
Sales: $27,200,000   *Employees:* 525
Company Type: Public Family Member   *Employees here:* 525
SIC: 8062
    General hospital
Rodney Smith, Chief Executive Officer

D-U-N-S 83-869-7787
COLUMBIA REGIONAL MEDICAL CTR
    (Parent: Columbia/Hca Healthcare Corp)
301 S Ripley St, Montgomery, AL 36104
Phone: (334) 269-8000
Sales: $62,489,000   *Employees:* 691
Company Type: Public Family Member   *Employees here:* 691
SIC: 8062
    General hospital
Wayne Heatherly, N/A

D-U-N-S 01-695-7078
COLUMBIA TOPS SURGICAL HOSP
17080 Red Oak Dr, Houston, TX 77090
Phone: (281) 539-2900
Sales: $28,000,000   *Employees:* 150
Company Type: Private   *Employees here:* 150
SIC: 8062
    General hospital
Rebecca Lee, Administrator

D-U-N-S 11-550-1397
COLUMBIA-HEALTHONE L L C
601 E 19th Ave, Denver, CO 80203
Phone: (303) 839-6636
Sales: $36,500,000   *Employees:* NA
Company Type: Private   *Employees here:* 850
SIC: 8062
    Medical and surgical hospital
Beverly Plena, President

D-U-N-S 11-550-1637
COLUMBIA-HEALTHONE L L C
1719 E 19th Ave, Denver, CO 80218
Phone: (303) 839-6000
Sales: $56,200,000   *Employees:* NA
Company Type: Private   *Employees here:* 1,300
SIC: 8062
    Medical and surgical hospital
Bill Adkinson, Administrator

D-U-N-S 95-997-0971
COLUMBIA-HEALTHONE L L C
4643 S Ulster St Ste 1200, Denver, CO 80237
Phone: (303) 788-2500
Sales: $471,500,000   *Employees:* 10,000
Company Type: Private   *Employees here:* 15
SIC: 8062
    Hospital nursing home ambulatory care center
Healthone I Member, N/A

D-U-N-S 01-569-2536
COLUMBIA-HEALTHONE L L C
1501 S Potomac St, Aurora, CO 80012
Phone: (303) 695-2744

Sales: $21,100,000
Company Type: Private
SIC: 8062
   Hospital
Richard Scott, President

Employees: NA
Employees here: 500

D-U-N-S 10-569-5993
COLUMBIA-HEALTHONE L L C
700 Potomac St, Aurora, CO 80011
Phone: (303) 363-7200
Sales: $25,500,000
Company Type: Private
SIC: 8062
   General hospital
Louis Garcia, N/A

Employees: NA
Employees here: 600

D-U-N-S 07-201-9193
COLUMBIA/CAPE FEAR HEALTHCARE
   (Parent: Columbia/Hca Healthcare Corp)
5301 Wrightsville Ave, Wilmington, NC 28403
Phone: (910) 452-8100
Sales: $24,592,000
Company Type: Public Family Member
SIC: 8062
   Hospital & health service
Mark Gregson, Chief Executive Officer

Employees: 501
Employees here: 480

D-U-N-S 96-299-4125
COLUMBIA/HCA HEALTHCARE CORP
400 Taylor Rd, Montgomery, AL 36117
Phone: (334) 277-8330
Sales: $20,700,000
Company Type: Public Family Member
SIC: 8062
   Hospital
John Melton, Administrator

Employees: NA
Employees here: 500

D-U-N-S 55-677-2671
COLUMBIA/HCA HEALTHCARE CORP
7300 Medical Center Dr, Canoga Park, CA 91307
Phone: (818) 712-4133
Sales: $34,300,000
Company Type: Public Family Member
SIC: 8062
   Hospital
Mark Myers, Manager

Employees: NA
Employees here: 700

D-U-N-S 80-376-5239
COLUMBIA/HCA HEALTHCARE CORP
6000 49th St N, Saint Petersburg, FL 33709
Phone: (727) 521-4411
Sales: $23,100,000
Company Type: Public Family Member
SIC: 8062
   General hospital
Steve Sutherlin, Executive Director

Employees: NA
Employees here: 534

D-U-N-S 14-993-7948
COLUMBIA/HCA HEALTHCARE CORP
11750 Bird Rd, Miami, FL 33175
Phone: (305) 223-3000
Sales: $30,600,000
Company Type: Public Family Member
SIC: 8062
   General hospital
Victor Maya, Branch Manager

Employees: NA
Employees here: 700

D-U-N-S 13-765-9629
COLUMBIA/HCA HEALTHCARE CORP
200 Industrial Blvd, Dublin, GA 31021
Phone: (912) 275-2000

Sales: $20,000,000
Company Type: Public Family Member
SIC: 8062
   Medical & surgical hospital
Richard P Cook, Administration

Employees: NA
Employees here: 500

D-U-N-S 96-257-7706
COLUMBIA/HCA HEALTHCARE CORP
5602 SW Lee Blvd, Lawton, OK 73505
Phone: (580) 531-4700
Sales: $20,200,000
Company Type: Public Family Member
SIC: 8062
   Hospital
Thomas Rine, Administrator

Employees: NA
Employees here: 500

D-U-N-S 13-104-7029
COLUMBIA/HCA HEALTHCARE CORP
2300 Patterson St, Nashville, TN 37203
Phone: (615) 342-1000
Sales: $83,400,000
Company Type: Public Family Member
SIC: 8062
   Medical center
Ron Elder, President

Employees: NA
Employees here: 1,968

D-U-N-S 19-430-3616
COLUMBIA/HCA HEALTHCARE CORP
1 Park Plz, Nashville, TN 37203
Phone: (615) 327-9551
Sales: $18,819,000,000
Company Type: Public
SIC: 8062
   Operates acute care psychiatric & specialty hospitals
   outpatient surgery centers diagnostic centers & home health
   care
Thomas F Frist Jr, Chairman of the Board

Employees: 295,000
Employees here: 80

D-U-N-S 78-606-6126
COLUMBIA/HCA HEALTHCARE CORP
1 Park Mdws, Nashville, TN 37215
Phone: (615) 344-9551
Sales: $50,700,000
Company Type: Public Family Member
SIC: 8062
   Hospital
Thomas Frist, Principal

Employees: NA
Employees here: 1,200

D-U-N-S 86-845-2772
COLUMBIA/HCA HEALTHCARE CORP
2221 Murphy Ave, Nashville, TN 37203
Phone: (615) 342-6522
Sales: $42,100,000
Company Type: Public Family Member
SIC: 8062
   Hospital
Ron Elders, President

Employees: NA
Employees here: 1,000

D-U-N-S 92-692-9290
COLUMBIA/HCA HEALTHCARE CORP
6801 E F Lowry Expy, Texas City, TX 77591
Phone: (409) 938-5000
Sales: $20,200,000
Company Type: Public Family Member
SIC: 8062
   Hospital
Alice Adams, Manager

Employees: NA
Employees here: 500

D-U-N-S 07-670-6969
COLUMBIA/HCA HEALTHCARE CORP
3901 W 15th St, Plano, TX 75075
Phone: (972) 596-6800

Sales: $51,600,000
Company Type: Public Family Member
SIC: 8062
  General hospital
Harvey Fishero, President

Employees: NA
Employees here: 1,250

D-U-N-S 79-985-3379
COLUMBIA/HCA HEALTHCARE CORP
101 E Ridge Rd, Mcallen, TX 78503
Phone: (956) 632-6000
Sales: $30,100,000
Company Type: Public Family Member
SIC: 8062
  Hospital facility
Randy Everts, Branch Manager

Employees: NA
Employees here: 735

D-U-N-S 86-713-5642
COLUMBIA/HCA HEALTHCARE CORP
500 E Mann Rd, Laredo, TX 78041
Phone: (956) 723-1131
Sales: $31,100,000
Company Type: Public Family Member
SIC: 8011
  Offices and clinics of medical doctors, nsk
Benjamin Everett, Chief Executive Officer

Employees: NA
Employees here: 500

D-U-N-S 11-848-7321
COLUMBIA/HCA HEALTHCARE CORP
12141 Richmond Ave, Houston, TX 77082
Phone: (281) 558-3444
Sales: $24,400,000
Company Type: Public Family Member
SIC: 8062
  Medical and surgical hospital
Jeffrey S Holland, President

Employees: NA
Employees here: 600

D-U-N-S 62-690-0583
COLUMBIA/HCA HEALTHCARE CORP
1615 Hillendahl Blvd, Houston, TX 77055
Phone: (713) 932-5500
Sales: $24,800,000
Company Type: Public Family Member
SIC: 8062
  General hospital
Steve Royal, N/A

Employees: NA
Employees here: 610

D-U-N-S 78-846-3271
COLUMBIA/HCA HEALTHCARE CORP
5314 Dashwood Dr, Houston, TX 77081
Phone: (713) 512-1200
Sales: $19,700,000
Company Type: Public Family Member
SIC: 8062
  General hospital
Walter Lelux, N/A

Employees: NA
Employees here: 489

D-U-N-S 07-804-0730
COLUMBUS COMMUNITY HOSPITAL
3020 18th St, Columbus, NE 68601
Phone: (402) 564-7118
Sales: $21,414,000
Company Type: Private
SIC: 8062
  General hospital
Joseph Barbaglia, Director

Employees: 315
Employees here: 295

D-U-N-S 07-593-0602
COLUMBUS DOCTORS HOSPITAL INC
616 19th St, Columbus, GA 31901
Phone: (706) 571-4262

Sales: $23,700,000
Company Type: Private
SIC: 8062
  Acute care medical facility
Hugh Wilson, Chief Executive Officer

Employees: 525
Employees here: 525

D-U-N-S 04-074-5820
COLUMBUS HOSPITAL INC
495 N 13th St, Newark, NJ 7107
Phone: (973) 268-1400
Sales: $86,883,000
Company Type: Private
SIC: 8062
  General hospital
John Magliaro, Chief Executive Officer

Employees: 900
Employees here: 843

D-U-N-S 17-813-3880
COLUMBUS REG HEALTHCR SYS INC
710 Center St, Columbus, GA 31901
Phone: (706) 571-1200
Sales: $189,987,000
Company Type: Private
SIC: 8062
  Fund development administrative functions hospital and
    nursing home and home health care
Larry S Sanders, President

Employees: 2,700
Employees here: 1,400

D-U-N-S 08-425-8789
COLUMBUS REGIONAL HOSPITAL
2400 17th St, Columbus, IN 47201
Phone: (812) 379-4441
Sales: $108,461,000
Company Type: Private
SIC: 8062
  Hospital
Doug Leonard, President

Employees: 1,300
Employees here: 1,300

D-U-N-S 07-429-4075
COMANCHE COUNTY HOSPITAL AUTH TR
3401 W Gore Blvd, Lawton, OK 73505
Phone: (580) 355-8620
Sales: $121,229,000
Company Type: Private
SIC: 8062
  General hospital
Randy Segler, Chief Executive Officer

Employees: 1,400
Employees here: 1,300

D-U-N-S 12-178-1595
COMMONWEALTH HEALTH CORP
800 Park St, Bowling Green, KY 42101
Phone: (502) 745-1500
Sales: $125,487,000
Company Type: Private
SIC: 8062
  General hospital apartment building operator
Floyd H Ellis, Chairman of the Board

Employees: 351
Employees here: 113

D-U-N-S 05-410-3577
COMMUN MEM HOSPITAL OF MENOMONEE FALLS
W180th N 8085 Town Hl, Menomonee Falls, WI 53051
Phone: (414) 251-1000
Sales: $62,334,000
Company Type: Private
SIC: 8062
  General hospital specialty outpatient facility
Robert E Drisner, President

Employees: 1,100
Employees here: 1,050

D-U-N-S 83-555-4361
COMMUNITY BEHAVIORAL HEALTH SYS
(Parent: Transitional Hospitals Corp)
3636 S I 10 Svc Rd W 30, Metairie, LA 70001
Phone: (504) 834-8340

Sales: $41,800,000
Company Type: Public Family Member
SIC: 8069
   Long term acute care
Wayne Dodge, Director

Employees: 850
Employees here: 850

D-U-N-S 16-790-6627
COMMUNITY BIO RESOURCES
   (Parent: Immuno - U S Inc)
2197 Parkway Lke Dr, Birmingham, AL 35244
Phone: (205) 403-9600
Sales: $80,000,000
Company Type: Private
SIC: 8099
   Collection of blood plasma/plasmaphersis
Paul O Ashba, Secretary

Employees: 500
Employees here: 55

D-U-N-S 80-959-7693
COMMUNITY CARE OF AMERICA INC
   (Parent: Integrated Health Services)
10065 Red Run Blvd, Owings Mills, MD 21117
Phone: (410) 998-8400
Sales: $96,100,000
Company Type: Public Family Member
SIC: 8051
   Owns leases and manages skilled nursing homes rural
     hospitals primary care clinics & home health care agencies
Robert N Elkins, Chief Executive Officer

Employees: 4,186
Employees here: 55

D-U-N-S 10-928-3879
COMMUNITY CARE SYSTEMS INC
320 N 5th St, Springfield, IL 62701
Phone: (217) 528-0122
Sales: $24,000,000
Company Type: Private
SIC: 8082
   Home care systems
Frank J Vala, President

Employees: 2,800
Employees here: 7

D-U-N-S 07-782-4209
COMMUNITY GEN HOSPITAL OF THOMASVILLE
207 Old Lexington Rd, Thomasville, NC 27360
Phone: (336) 472-2000
Sales: $26,002,000
Company Type: Private
SIC: 8062
   Hospital
Lynn I Boggs, President

Employees: 460
Employees here: 460

D-U-N-S 07-121-4142
COMMUNITY GEN OSTEOPATHIC HOSP
4300 Londonderry Rd, Harrisburg, PA 17109
Phone: (717) 652-3000
Sales: $51,398,000
Company Type: Private
SIC: 8062
   General hospital
George R Strohl Jr, President

Employees: 650
Employees here: 580

D-U-N-S 02-066-1898
COMMUNITY GENERAL HOSPITAL
Bushville Rd, Harris, NY 12742
Phone: (914) 794-3300
Sales: $63,000,000
Company Type: Private
SIC: 8062
   General hospital
Tom O Keefe, Purchasing Director

Employees: 800
Employees here: 750

D-U-N-S 06-813-3578
COMMUNITY HEALTH ASSOCIATION
Pinnell St, Ripley, WV 25271
Phone: (304) 372-2731

Sales: $22,074,000
Company Type: Private
SIC: 8062
   General hospital
Rick Rohaley, President

Employees: 320
Employees here: 320

D-U-N-S 55-649-1587
COMMUNITY HEALTH GROUP
740 Bay Blvd, Chula Vista, CA 91910
Phone: (619) 422-0422
Sales: $53,619,000
Company Type: Private
SIC: 8011
   Health maintenance organization
Gabriel Arce, Chief Executive Officer

Employees: 130
Employees here: 130

D-U-N-S 61-354-7157
COMMUNITY HEALTH INV CORP
   (Parent: Community Health Systems Inc)
155 Franklin Rd Ste 400, Brentwood, TN 37027
Phone: (615) 373-9600
Sales: $117,000,000
Company Type: Public Family Member
SIC: 8062
   General medical & surgical hospitals
E T Chaney, President

Employees: 2,500
Employees here: 8

D-U-N-S 06-689-6937
COMMUNITY HEALTH NETWORK, INC
225 Memorial Dr, Berlin, WI 54923
Phone: (920) 361-1313
Sales: $37,771,000
Company Type: Private
SIC: 8062
   Hospital & skilled nursing home
Craig W Schmidt, President

Employees: 450
Employees here: 300

D-U-N-S 94-685-4999
COMMUNITY HEALTH PLAN OF OHIO
1915 Tamarack Rd, Newark, OH 43055
Phone: (740) 348-1438
Sales: $21,040,000
Company Type: Private
SIC: 8011
   Health maintenance organization
Robert Kamp, President

Employees: 67
Employees here: 60

D-U-N-S 09-693-6109
COMMUNITY HEALTH PLAN INC
   (Parent: Kaiser Foundation Health Plan)
1 CHP Plz, Latham, NY 12110
Phone: (518) 783-3110
Sales: $575,061,000
Company Type: Private
SIC: 8011
   Health maintenance organization
John Baackes, President

Employees: 3,300
Employees here: 600

D-U-N-S 13-757-2269
COMMUNITY HEALTH SYSTEMS INC
   (Parent: Forstmann Little & Co)
155 Franklin Rd Ste 400, Brentwood, TN 37027
Phone: (615) 373-9600
Sales: $755,000,000
Company Type: Public
SIC: 8062
   Owns operates & manages 39 acute care hospitals
Wayne T Smith, President

Employees: 11,000
Employees here: 65

D-U-N-S 11-524-2349
COMMUNITY HEALTHLINK INC
72 Jaques Ave, Worcester, MA 1610
Phone: (508) 860-1154

Sales: $27,763,000   *Employees:* 261
Company Type: Private   *Employees here:* 11
SIC: 8093
   Mental health clinic
Dr Kenneth Hetzler Md, Executive Director

D-U-N-S 17-325-2115
COMMUNITY HEALTH CARE SYS OF SAN BERNARDINO
1805 Medical Center Dr, San Bernardino, CA 92411
Phone: (909) 887-6333
Sales: $74,500,000   *Employees:* 1,600
Company Type: Private   *Employees here:* 1,500
SIC: 8062
   Hospital and convalescent home
Charles Kraus, President

D-U-N-S 10-362-3765
COMMUNITY HEALTH CTR OF BRANCH CNTY
274 E Chicago St, Coldwater, MI 49036
Phone: (517) 279-5400
Sales: $36,382,000   *Employees:* 390
Company Type: Private   *Employees here:* 390
SIC: 8062
   General hospital
Randy Degroot, Chief Financial Officer

D-U-N-S 07-173-4776
COMMUNITY HEALTH COUNSELING SVCS
42 Cedar St, Bangor, ME 4401
Phone: (207) 947-0366
Sales: $42,006,000   *Employees:* 1,069
Company Type: Private   *Employees here:* 150
SIC: 8093
   Mental health center home health services and children's
   social/nursery school services
Carroll Lee, President

D-U-N-S 80-098-6242
COMMUNITY HOSPITAL OF ANDALUSIA
   (Parent: Healthtrust Inc - Hospital Co)
849 S Three Notch St, Andalusia, AL 36420
Phone: (334) 222-8466
Sales: $50,000,000   *Employees:* 323
Company Type: Public Family Member   *Employees here:* 323
SIC: 8062
   General medical & surgical hospital
Jane Sample, Chief Executive Officer

D-U-N-S 07-941-2334
COMMUNITY HOSPITAL OF BRZSPORT INC
100 Medical Dr, Lake Jackson, TX 77566
Phone: (409) 297-4411
Sales: $60,861,000   *Employees:* 523
Company Type: Private   *Employees here:* 523
SIC: 8062
   General medical & surgical hospital with 165 beds
Wesley Oswald, Chief Executive Officer

D-U-N-S 07-285-3559
COMMUNITY HOSPITAL OF LANCASTER
1100 E Orange St, Lancaster, PA 17602
Phone: (717) 397-3711
Sales: $39,694,000   *Employees:* 836
Company Type: Private   *Employees here:* 820
SIC: 8062
   General osteopathic hospital
Elam Herr, Chairman of the Board

D-U-N-S 07-360-8713
COMMUNITY HOSPITAL OF SAN BERNARDINO
1805 Medical Center Dr, San Bernardino, CA 92411
Phone: (909) 887-6333

Sales: $162,473,000   *Employees:* 1,504
Company Type: Private   *Employees here:* 1,500
SIC: 8062
   General hospital
Bruce G Satzger, Chief Executive Officer

D-U-N-S 06-370-1296
COMMUNITY HOSPITAL WILLIAMS COUNTY
433 W High St, Bryan, OH 43506
Phone: (419) 636-1131
Sales: $22,500,000   *Employees:* 500
Company Type: Private   *Employees here:* 396
SIC: 8062
   General hospital
Rusty O Brunicardi, President

D-U-N-S 05-520-5298
COMMUNITY HOSPITAL OF ANDERSON
1515 N Madison Ave, Anderson, IN 46011
Phone: (765) 642-8011
Sales: $56,420,000   *Employees:* 1,000
Company Type: Private   *Employees here:* 979
SIC: 8062
   General hospital
John Harris, Chief Financial Officer

D-U-N-S 07-629-8371
COMMUNITY HOSPITAL OF MONTEREY
23625 W R Holman Hwy, Monterey, CA 93940
Phone: (831) 624-5311
Sales: $150,251,000   *Employees:* 1,450
Company Type: Private   *Employees here:* 1,450
SIC: 8062
   Hospital
Jay M Hudson, President

D-U-N-S 07-561-2937
COMMUNITY HOSPITAL OF OTTAWA
1100 E Norris Dr, Ottawa, IL 61350
Phone: (815) 433-3100
Sales: $34,916,000   *Employees:* 550
Company Type: Private   *Employees here:* 460
SIC: 8062
   General hospital
Robert Schmelter, Chief Executive Officer

D-U-N-S 04-797-6576
COMMUNITY HOSPITAL OF SPRINGFIELD
2615 E High St, Springfield, OH 45505
Phone: (937) 325-0531
Sales: $26,884,000   *Employees:* 1,200
Company Type: Private   *Employees here:* 1,200
SIC: 8062
   Hospital
Neal Kresheck, President

D-U-N-S 05-749-4676
COMMUNITY HOSPITAL ASSN INC
1100 Balsam Ave, Boulder, CO 80304
Phone: (303) 440-2273
Sales: $109,718,000   *Employees:* 1,400
Company Type: Private   *Employees here:* 1,116
SIC: 8063
   General hospital
David Gehant, Chief Executive Officer

D-U-N-S 07-445-3556
COMMUNITY HOSPITAL CHANL INC
475 S Dobson Rd, Chandler, AZ 85224
Phone: (602) 963-4561

Sales: $76,822,000   *Employees:* 1,021
Company Type: Private   *Employees here:* 881
SIC: 8062
   General medical & surgical hospital
Kaylor E Shemberger, President

D-U-N-S 06-867-8721
COMMUNITY HOSPITAL GROUP INC
80 James St Fl 4, Edison, NJ 8820
Phone: (732) 321-7000
Sales: $200,266,000   *Employees:* 3,000
Company Type: Private   *Employees here:* 2,400
SIC: 8062
   General hospital and rehabilitation center
John P Mcgee, President

D-U-N-S 08-427-5221
COMMUNITY HOSPITAL INC
   (Parent: Columbia/Hca Healthcare Corp)
1099 Medical Center Dr, Mayfield, KY 42066
Phone: (502) 251-4100
Sales: $28,358,000   *Employees:* 500
Company Type: Public Family Member   *Employees here:* 500
SIC: 8062
   General hospital
Bill G Int, Chief Executive Officer

D-U-N-S 78-740-0381
COMMUNITY HOSPITALS OF GALEN
   (Parent: Galen Health Care Inc)
600 SW 3rd St, Pompano Beach, FL 33060
Phone: (954) 782-2000
Sales: $23,700,000   *Employees:* 525
Company Type: Public Family Member   *Employees here:* 525
SIC: 8062
   General hospital
Heather Rowan, Chief Executive Officer

D-U-N-S 07-206-8141
COMMUNITY HOSPITALS OF INDIANA
1500 N Ritter Ave, Indianapolis, IN 46219
Phone: (317) 355-1411
Sales: $444,655,000   *Employees:* 5,000
Company Type: Private   *Employees here:* 2,900
SIC: 8062
   General hospital
William E Corley, President

D-U-N-S 18-316-7055
COMMUNITY HOSPITALS OF INDIANA
7150 Clearvista Dr, Indianapolis, IN 46256
Phone: (317) 849-6262
Sales: $36,000,000   *Employees:* NA
Company Type: Private   *Employees here:* 800
SIC: 8069
   Specialty hospital
Mark Moore, Manager

D-U-N-S 60-544-8414
COMMUNITY HOSPITALS OF INDIANA
1402 E County Line Rd, Indianapolis, IN 46227
Phone: (317) 887-7000
Sales: $19,800,000   *Employees:* NA
Company Type: Private   *Employees here:* 480
SIC: 8062
   General hospital
Glen B D, Manager

D-U-N-S 01-616-4261
COMMUNITY LIVING OPTIONS INC
239 S Cherry St, Galesburg, IL 61401
Phone: (309) 343-7777

Sales: $21,250,000   *Employees:* 498
Company Type: Private   *Employees here:* 12
SIC: 8361
   Home for mentally retarded & handicapped
Jack Croc, President

D-U-N-S 07-175-4477
COMMUNITY MEDICAL CENTER INC
2827 Fort Missoula Rd, Missoula, MT 59804
Phone: (406) 728-4100
Sales: $51,753,000   *Employees:* 900
Company Type: Private   *Employees here:* 850
SIC: 8062
   General hospital
Grant M Winn, Administrator

D-U-N-S 07-755-4921
COMMUNITY MEDICAL CENTER INC
99 Highway 37, Toms River, NJ 8755
Phone: (732) 240-8000
Sales: $210,704,000   *Employees:* 2,500
Company Type: Private   *Employees here:* 2,450
SIC: 8062
   General hospital
Kevin Burchill, Executive Director

D-U-N-S 07-915-8812
COMMUNITY MEDICAL CENTER INC
1822 Mulberry St, Scranton, PA 18510
Phone: (717) 969-8000
Sales: $101,069,000   *Employees:* 1,178
Company Type: Private   *Employees here:* 1,178
SIC: 8062
   General hospital
Dr C R Hartman Md, President

D-U-N-S 07-927-5004
COMMUNITY MEMORIAL HOSPITAL
748 S Main St, Cheboygan, MI 49721
Phone: (616) 627-5601
Sales: $23,379,000   *Employees:* 400
Company Type: Private   *Employees here:* 400
SIC: 8062
   General hospital
Howard Purcell, President

D-U-N-S 07-474-1406
COMMUNITY MEMORIAL HOSPITAL
125 Buena Vista Cir, South Hill, VA 23970
Phone: (804) 447-3151
Sales: $39,266,000   *Employees:* 726
Company Type: Private   *Employees here:* 726
SIC: 8062
   Gen medical & surgical hospital
Steven Kelly, President

D-U-N-S 07-532-8450
COMMUNITY MEMORIAL HOSPITAL/SA
147 N Brent St, Ventura, CA 93003
Phone: (805) 652-5001
Sales: $85,624,000   *Employees:* 1,200
Company Type: Private   *Employees here:* 1,200
SIC: 8062
   General hospital
Dr Michael Bakst, Executive Director

D-U-N-S 01-529-4259
COMMUNITY PARTNR SOUTHERN ARIZ
4575 E Broadway Blvd, Tucson, AZ 85711
Phone: (520) 325-4268

Sales: $65,000,000
Company Type: Private
SIC: 8093
    Specialty outpatient clinic
Michael Zent, President

Employees: 82
Employees here: 82

    D-U-N-S 05-500-1382
COMMUNITY UNITED METHDST HOSP
1305 N Elm St, Henderson, KY 42420
Phone: (502) 827-7700
Sales: $64,311,000
Company Type: Private
SIC: 8062
    General hospital
Bruce Begely, Executive Director

Employees: 1,060
Employees here: 744

    D-U-N-S 17-916-3761
COMPREHENSIVE CANCER CENTERS
8201 Beverly Blvd, Los Angeles, CA 90048
Phone: (323) 966-3400
Sales: $48,800,000
Company Type: Private
SIC: 8093
    Cancer center
Michael O Brien, Chief Executive Officer

Employees: 1,600
Employees here: 160

    D-U-N-S 05-074-9829
COMPREHENSIVE CARE CORPORATION
4200 W Cypress St Ste 300, Tampa, FL 33607
Phone: (813) 876-5036
Sales: $46,063,000
Company Type: Public
SIC: 8011
    Behavioral health managed care
Chriss W Street, Chairman of the Board

Employees: 347
Employees here: 16

    D-U-N-S 78-476-8889
COMPREHENSIVE CARE MGT CORP
2401 White Plains Rd, Bronx, NY 10467
Phone: (718) 515-8600
Sales: $29,339,000
Company Type: Private
SIC: 8051
    A not-for-profit comprehensive health care management
      organization
Geraldine Taylor, Executive Vice-President

Employees: 250
Employees here: 160

    D-U-N-S 10-661-5537
COMPREHENSIVE HEALTH RESOURCES
160 Allen St, Rutland, VT 5701
Phone: (802) 775-7111
Sales: $76,379,000
Company Type: Private
SIC: 8062
    Holding company for general hospital & medical equipment
      leaser
Tom Huebner, President

Employees: 2
Employees here: 2

    D-U-N-S 06-883-6741
COMPREHENSIVE HEALTH SERVICES
2875 W Grand Blvd, Detroit, MI 48202
Phone: (313) 875-4200
Sales: $281,143,000
Company Type: Private
SIC: 8011
    Health maintenance organization
James Patton, President

Employees: 900
Employees here: 250

    D-U-N-S 07-971-8458
COMPREHENSIVE MED CARE LTD
    (Parent: Allina Health System)
9055 Springbrook Dr Nw, Minneapolis, MN 55433
Phone: (612) 780-9155

Sales: $34,300,000
Company Type: Private
SIC: 8011
    Medical clinics
Dr John C Bordwell, President

Employees: 500
Employees here: 350

    D-U-N-S 02-160-0965
COMPREHENSIVE MEDICAL IMAGING
    (Parent: Syncor International Corp)
3396 Willow Lk Ln Ste 201, Westlake Village, CA 91361
Phone: (805) 778-0882
Sales: $45,000,000
Company Type: Public Family Member
SIC: 8071
    Medical imaging
Robert Funari, Chief Executive Officer

Employees: 400
Employees here: 50

    D-U-N-S 12-254-4356
COMPUNET CLINICAL LABORATORIES
2308 Sandridge Dr, Dayton, OH 45439
Phone: (937) 296-0844
Sales: $30,104,000
Company Type: Private
SIC: 8071
    Medical laboratory (clinical)
John Charles, General Manager

Employees: 405
Employees here: 230

    D-U-N-S 60-992-9096
CONCORD HEALTH GROUP, INC
    (Parent: Multicare Companies Inc)
101 W 3rd St Fl 4, Williamsport, PA 17701
Phone: (201) 488-8818
Sales: $65,000,000
Company Type: Public Family Member
SIC: 8051
    Operates nursing homes
Moshael J Straus, Chairman of the Board

Employees: 965
Employees here: 30

    D-U-N-S 07-397-7399
CONCORD HOSPITAL INC
250 Pleasant St, Concord, NH 3301
Phone: (603) 225-2711
Sales: $54,700,000
Company Type: Private
SIC: 8062
    General medical & surgical hospital
Michael Green, President

Employees: 1,182
Employees here: 1,182

    D-U-N-S 06-871-7966
CONEMAUGH VALLEY MEM HOSP
1086 Franklin St, Johnstown, PA 15905
Phone: (814) 534-9130
Sales: $161,367,000
Company Type: Private
SIC: 8062
    General hospital
Steven E Tucker, President

Employees: 1,823
Employees here: 1,786

    D-U-N-S 13-759-7019
CONGREGATION OF THE SISTERS
519 W Houston St, San Antonio, TX 78207
Phone: (210) 228-2011
Sales: $124,400,000
Company Type: Private
SIC: 8062
    General medical hospital
Robert Nolan, Administrator

Employees: NA
Employees here: 3,000

    D-U-N-S 07-731-4268
CONNECTICUT CHILDRENS MED CTR
    (Parent: Ccmc Corp)
282 Washington St, Hartford, CT 6106
Phone: (860) 545-9000

Sales: $46,775,000   *Employees:* 1,100
Company Type: Private   *Employees here:* 850
SIC: 8069
    Hospital
Larry Gold, President

D-U-N-S 87-713-8495
CONSOLIDATED CARE CREW HOME HE
12002 Huebner Rd Ste 200, San Antonio, TX 78230
Phone: (210) 558-8228
Sales: $35,000,000   *Employees:* 535
Company Type: Private   *Employees here:* 100
SIC: 8082
    Home health care services
Daniel Orhiunu, President

D-U-N-S 93-834-0478
CONTINUE CARE HOME HEALTH
    (Parent: Continue Care Holding Corp)
401 Bailey Dr, Hollandale, MS 38748
Phone: (601) 843-6039
Sales: $35,688,000   *Employees:* 190
Company Type: Private   *Employees here:* 175
SIC: 8082
    In home health services
Carter Lack, Controller

D-U-N-S 87-724-4632
CONTINUUM CARE CORPORATION
2401 PGA Blvd Ste 146, Palm Beach Gardens, FL 33410
Phone: (561) 627-9060
Sales: $34,200,000   *Employees:* 1,500
Company Type: Private   *Employees here:* 415
SIC: 8051
    Skilled nursing facilities & assisted living facilities
Susan Dier, Chief Executive Officer

D-U-N-S 07-373-1242
CONWAY HOSPITAL INC
300 Singleton Ridge Rd, Conway, SC 29526
Phone: (843) 347-7111
Sales: $64,537,000   *Employees:* 800
Company Type: Private   *Employees here:* 700
SIC: 8062
    General hospital
Philip Clayton, President

D-U-N-S 07-566-5695
CONWAY REGIONAL MEDICAL CENTER
2302 College Ave, Conway, AR 72032
Phone: (501) 329-3831
Sales: $64,830,000   *Employees:* 788
Company Type: Private   *Employees here:* 698
SIC: 8062
    General hospital
James Summersett Iii, Chief Executive Officer

D-U-N-S 07-854-4194
COOK CHILDRENS MEDICAL CENTER
801 7th Ave, Fort Worth, TX 76104
Phone: (817) 885-4000
Sales: $59,200,000   *Employees:* 1,200
Company Type: Private   *Employees here:* 1,169
SIC: 8069
    Specialty hospital
Russell Tolman, President

D-U-N-S 83-650-3888
COOK CHILDRENS PHYSICIAN NETWRK
801 7th Ave, Fort Worth, TX 76104
Phone: (817) 885-4000

Sales: $44,610,000   *Employees:* 198
Company Type: Private   *Employees here:* 198
SIC: 8011
    Physician network
Dr Allan K Lassiter, Chief Executive Officer

D-U-N-S 06-909-8267
COOKEVILLE REGIONAL MED CTR
142 W 5th St, Cookeville, TN 38501
Phone: (931) 528-2541
Sales: $63,213,000   *Employees:* 850
Company Type: Private   *Employees here:* 850
SIC: 8062
    General hospital
William Jennings, Chief Executive Officer

D-U-N-S 06-699-1605
COOLEY DICKINSON HOSPITAL
30 Locust St, Northampton, MA 1060
Phone: (413) 582-2000
Sales: $57,583,000   *Employees:* 1,100
Company Type: Private   *Employees here:* 1,075
SIC: 8062
    General medical surgical psychiatric and substance abuse
        hospital
Craig Melin, Chief Executive Officer

D-U-N-S 01-032-0612
COOPER CLINIC PA
6801 Rogers Ave, Fort Smith, AR 72903
Phone: (501) 452-2077
Sales: $54,154,000   *Employees:* 470
Company Type: Private   *Employees here:* 200
SIC: 8011
    Physicians
John Hoffman, President

D-U-N-S 06-989-6165
COOPER HSPTL/UNIVERSITY MED CTR
3 Cooper Plz Rm 504, Camden, NJ 8103
Phone: (609) 342-2000
Sales: $352,768,000   *Employees:* 3,524
Company Type: Private   *Employees here:* 2,250
SIC: 8062
    General hospital
Kevin G Halpern, President

D-U-N-S 07-458-4749
COPLEY MEMORIAL HOSPITAL INC
2000 Ogden Ave, Aurora, IL 60504
Phone: (630) 978-6200
Sales: $72,500,000   *Employees:* 920
Company Type: Private   *Employees here:* 920
SIC: 8062
    General hospital
Marty Losof, President

D-U-N-S 84-986-5167
CORAM HEALTHCARE CORPORATION
1125 17th St Ste 2100, Denver, CO 80202
Phone: (303) 292-4973
Sales: $464,385,000   *Employees:* 2,800
Company Type: Public   *Employees here:* 20
SIC: 8093
    Infusion therapy physician practice management services and
        obstetrical and gynecological support services
Donald J Amaral, Chief Executive Officer

D-U-N-S 55-659-6336
CORNERSTONE HEALTH MANAGEMENT
    (Parent: Grancare Inc)
5080 Spectrum Dr Ste 920w, Dallas, TX 75248
Phone: (972) 715-1200

Sales: $65,000,000
Company Type: Public Family Member
SIC: 8051
Employees: 654
Employees here: 40
   Operates skilled nursing homes psychiatric facilities acute
   care hospitals and primary care networks
Dennis Johnston, Chief Executive Officer

D-U-N-S 07-368-3799
CORNING HOSPITAL
176 Denison Pkwy E, Corning, NY 14830
Phone: (607) 937-7200
Sales: $41,454,000
Company Type: Private
SIC: 8062
Employees: 740
Employees here: 570
   General hospital & nursing home
John E Pignatore, Chief Executive Officer

D-U-N-S 88-447-5534
CORNING SCICOR LTD PARTNERSHIP
8211 Scicor Dr, Indianapolis, IN 46214
Phone: (317) 271-1200
Sales: $28,700,000
Company Type: Private
SIC: 8071
Employees: 600
Employees here: 600
   Operates a medical laboratory and provides data
   management
Ed Schwenk, Controller

D-U-N-S 04-566-4596
CORNWALL HOSPITAL INC
Laurel Ave, Cornwall, NY 12518
Phone: (914) 534-7711
Sales: $30,194,000
Company Type: Private
SIC: 8062
Employees: 600
Employees here: 600
   General medical & surgical hospital
Val S Gray, Chief Executive Officer

D-U-N-S 60-608-4705
CORRECTIONAL MEDICAL SERVICES
   (Parent: Spectrum Halthcare Svcs Of Del)
12647 Olive Blvd, Saint Louis, MO 63141
Phone: (314) 878-1810
Sales: $132,000,000
Company Type: Private
SIC: 8099
Employees: 3,300
Employees here: 125
   Health/allied services
Michael Pfeiffer, Chief Operating Officer

D-U-N-S 78-533-3667
CORRECTIONAL PHYSICIANS SVCS
1787 Century Pky W B 16, Blue Bell, PA 19422
Phone: (215) 654-7450
Sales: $20,000,000
Company Type: Private
SIC: 8099
Employees: 315
Employees here: 300
   Provides health services to prisoners
Dr Kenan Umar, President

D-U-N-S 19-653-8805
CORRECTNAL HEALTHCARE SOLUTIONS
200 Highpoint Dr Ste 215, Chalfont, PA 18914
Phone: (215) 822-1050
Sales: $36,709,000
Company Type: Private
SIC: 8093
Employees: 600
Employees here: 30
   Medical service
Walter Lomax Phd, Chairman of the Board

D-U-N-S 07-160-6065
CORTLAND MEMORIAL HOSPITAL
134 Homer Ave, Cortland, NY 13045
Phone: (607) 756-3500

Sales: $44,521,000
Company Type: Private
SIC: 8062
Employees: 709
Employees here: 704
   General hospital
Thomas Carman, Chief Executive Officer

D-U-N-S 07-500-7468
COSHOCTON COUNTY MEM HOSPITAL ASSN
1460 Orange St, Coshocton, OH 43812
Phone: (740) 622-6411
Sales: $46,238,000
Company Type: Private
SIC: 8062
Employees: 480
Employees here: 463
   General hospital and skilled nursing facility
Gregory Nowak, Administrator

D-U-N-S 15-592-1315
COUNTY OF ALAMEDA
15400 Foothill Blvd, San Leandro, CA 94578
Phone: (510) 667-7800
Sales: $44,400,000
Company Type: Private
SIC: 8062
Employees: NA
Employees here: 900
   General hospital
Michael Smart, N/A

D-U-N-S 15-567-8238
COUNTY OF ALAMEDA
1411 E 31st St, Oakland, CA 94602
Phone: (510) 534-8055
Sales: $74,500,000
Company Type: Private
SIC: 8062
Employees: NA
Employees here: 1,500
   General hospital
Mike Smart, N/A

D-U-N-S 10-495-5356
COUNTY OF ALBANY
Albany Shaker Rd, Albany, NY 12211
Phone: (518) 452-7463
Sales: $24,500,000
Company Type: Private
SIC: 8051
Employees: NA
Employees here: 1,000
   Nursing home
Robert Lynch, Executive Director

D-U-N-S 80-879-2709
COUNTY OF BRADLEY
2305 Chambliss Ave Nw, Cleveland, TN 37311
Phone: (423) 559-6000
Sales: $39,000,000
Company Type: Private
SIC: 8062
Employees: NA
Employees here: 1,000
   General hospital
Jim Whitlock, Administrator

D-U-N-S 06-745-2771
COUNTY OF COOK, ILLINOIS
15900 Cicero Ave, Oak Forest, IL 60452
Phone: (708) 687-7200
Sales: $94,300,000
Company Type: Private
SIC: 8062
Employees: NA
Employees here: 2,225
   General hospital
Cynthia Henderson, Director

D-U-N-S 01-352-0861
COUNTY OF COOK, ILLINOIS
621 S Winchester Ave, Chicago, IL 60612
Phone: (312) 633-7292

Sales: $83,100,000
Company Type: Private
SIC: 8093
  Specialty outpatient clinic
John M Raba, Director

Employees: NA
Employees here: 3,000

D-U-N-S 14-617-1855
COUNTY OF COOK, ILLINOIS
1835 W Harrison St, Chicago, IL 60612
Phone: (312) 633-6000
Sales: $20,700,000
Company Type: Private
SIC: 8062
  General hospital
Dr Ruth Rothstein, Director

Employees: NA
Employees here: 500

D-U-N-S 10-758-3551
COUNTY OF ESSEX
125 Fairview Ave, Cedar Grove, NJ 7009
Phone: (973) 228-8000
Sales: $40,400,000
Company Type: Private
SIC: 8063
  Psychiatric hospital
Teresa Bielawski, Medical Doctor

Employees: NA
Employees here: 1,016

D-U-N-S 61-297-4790
COUNTY OF HILLSBOROUGH
Davis Is, Tampa, FL 33606
Phone: (813) 251-7481
Sales: $141,700,000
Company Type: Private
SIC: 8062
  General hospital
Bruce Siegel, President

Employees: NA
Employees here: 3,200

D-U-N-S 16-912-9517
COUNTY OF JEFFERSON
1515 6th Ave S, Birmingham, AL 35233
Phone: (205) 934-7900
Sales: $29,300,000
Company Type: Private
SIC: 8062
  General hospital
Dr Max Michael, Branch Manager

Employees: NA
Employees here: 700

D-U-N-S 10-888-7787
COUNTY OF KERN
1830 Flower St, Bakersfield, CA 93305
Phone: (805) 326-2000
Sales: $124,400,000
Company Type: Private
SIC: 8062
  Hospital
Gerald Starr, N/A

Employees: NA
Employees here: 2,500

D-U-N-S 09-676-7967
COUNTY OF KING
325 9th Ave, Seattle, WA 98104
Phone: (206) 223-3036
Sales: $139,300,000
Company Type: Private
SIC: 8062
  Hospital & out patient care service
David W Gitch, N/A

Employees: NA
Employees here: 2,800

D U N S 09-873-0849
COUNTY OF LEHIGH
350 S Cedarbrook Rd, Allentown, PA 18104
Phone: (610) 395-3727

Sales: $20,600,000
Company Type: Private
SIC: 8361
  Residential care services
Gloria Zimmerman, Manager

Employees: NA
Employees here: 780

D-U-N-S 07-624-4557
COUNTY OF LOS ANGELES
14445 Olive View Dr, Sylmar, CA 91342
Phone: (818) 901-3000
Sales: $124,400,000
Company Type: Private
SIC: 8062
  General hospital
Doug Bagley, Branch Manager

Employees: NA
Employees here: 2,500

D-U-N-S 04-685-2984
COUNTY OF LOS ANGELES
2829 S Grand Ave, Los Angeles, CA 90007
Phone: (213) 744-3677
Sales: $22,200,000
Company Type: Private
SIC: 8011
  Health center
Carolyn Clark, Branch Manager

Employees: NA
Employees here: 350

D-U-N-S 10-440-9842
COUNTY OF LOS ANGELES
1240 N Mission Rd, Los Angeles, CA 90033
Phone: (323) 226-3501
Sales: $52,800,000
Company Type: Private
SIC: 8069
  Women's hospital
Maria E Sanchez, Manager

Employees: NA
Employees here: 1,000

D-U-N-S 15-602-4044
COUNTY OF LOS ANGELES
441 Bauchet St, Los Angeles, CA 90012
Phone: (213) 974-5045
Sales: $31,600,000
Company Type: Private
SIC: 8069
  Specialty hospital
Rita Dineros, N/A

Employees: NA
Employees here: 600

D-U-N-S 16-161-3906
COUNTY OF LOS ANGELES
1237 N Mission Rd, Los Angeles, CA 90033
Phone: (323) 226-4855
Sales: $79,100,000
Company Type: Private
SIC: 8069
  Executive & legislative offices courts sherrifs district
    attorney's office correctional institutions and hospital
Campbell Lynette, Branch Manager

Employees: NA
Employees here: 1,500

D-U-N-S 07-413-0014
COUNTY OF LOS ANGELES
44900 60th St W, Lancaster, CA 93536
Phone: (805) 948-8580
Sales: $21,700,000
Company Type: Private
SIC: 8062
  Hospital
Jaron Gammonn, Administration

Employees: NA
Employees here: 450

D-U-N-S 61-816-6664
COUNTY OF LOS ANGELES
45010 60th St W, Lancaster, CA 93536
Phone: (805) 949-3818

Sales: $113,600,000
Company Type: Private
SIC: 8011
  Health group
Elizabeth Meany, Manager

Employees: NA
Employees here: 2,000

D-U-N-S 18-650-7216
COUNTY OF MARICOPA
2601 E Roosevelt St, Phoenix, AZ 85008
Phone: (602) 267-5011
Sales: $156,200,000
Company Type: Private
SIC: 8062
  General hospital
Frank Alaerz, Director

Employees: NA
Employees here: 3,600

D-U-N-S 09-853-7541
COUNTY OF MONTEREY
1330 Natividad Rd, Salinas, CA 93906
Phone: (831) 755-4186
Sales: $22,400,000
Company Type: Private
SIC: 8063
  Psychiatric hospital
Howard Classen, Manager

Employees: NA
Employees here: 560

D-U-N-S 07-365-7611
COUNTY OF NORTHAMPTON
Gracedale Ave, Nazareth, PA 18064
Phone: (610) 746-1900
Sales: $22,400,000
Company Type: Private
SIC: 8361
  Residential care services
Harold W Russell, Manager

Employees: NA
Employees here: 850

D-U-N-S 14-606-7459
COUNTY OF PIERCE
3629 S D St, Tacoma, WA 98408
Phone: (253) 591-6416
Sales: $22,200,000
Company Type: Private
SIC: 8011
  Health clinic specialty outpatient clinic
Jesse James, Branch Manager

Employees: NA
Employees here: 350

D-U-N-S 14-745-1975
COUNTY OF RIVERSIDE
26520 Cactus Ave, Riverside, CA 92507
Phone: (909) 486-4000
Sales: $86,800,000
Company Type: Private
SIC: 8011
  Medical doctor's office general hospital
Kenneth B Cohen, Administrator

Employees: NA
Employees here: 1,500

D-U-N-S 18-473-5199
COUNTY OF ROCKLAND
Santorum Rd Bldg 13, Pomona, NY 10970
Phone: (914) 354-0200
Sales: $71,200,000
Company Type: Private
SIC: 8093
  Health complex
George Giacobbe, N/A

Employees: NA
Employees here: 2,185

D-U-N-S 09-689-5719
COUNTY OF SAN BERNARDINO
780 E Gilbert St, San Bernardino, CA 92415
Phone: (909) 387-8111

Sales: $82,000,000
Company Type: Private
SIC: 8062
  General hospital
Charles Jervis, Director

Employees: NA
Employees here: 1,650

D-U-N-S 12-736-1731
COUNTY OF SHELBY
1075 Mullins Station Rd, Memphis, TN 38134
Phone: (901) 385-6700
Sales: $20,700,000
Company Type: Private
SIC: 8062
  Intermediate care facility
Larry Lucas, Principal

Employees: NA
Employees here: 500

D-U-N-S 08-156-0153
COUNTY OF SONOMA
3325 Chanate Rd, Santa Rosa, CA 95404
Phone: (707) 576-4000
Sales: $39,400,000
Company Type: Private
SIC: 8062
  General hospital
Cliff Coates, President

Employees: NA
Employees here: 800

D-U-N-S 13-310-5429
COUNTY OF TULARE
1062 S K St, Tulare, CA 93274
Phone: (209) 685-2500
Sales: $20,400,000
Company Type: Private
SIC: 8011
  Medical doctor's office
Ronald Probasco, Director

Employees: NA
Employees here: 320

D-U-N-S 62-062-2647
COUNTY OF UNION
40 Watchung Way, Berkeley Heights, NJ 7922
Phone: (908) 771-5700
Sales: $26,300,000
Company Type: Private
SIC: 8069
  Specialty hospital psychiatric hospital
Joseph W Sharp, Manager

Employees: NA
Employees here: 500

D-U-N-S 01-096-6935
COUNTY OF WESTCHESTER
Grasslands Reservation, Valhalla, NY 10595
Phone: (914) 285-7017
Sales: $174,200,000
Company Type: Private
SIC: 8062
  General hospital
Edward Stolzenberg, Manager

Employees: NA
Employees here: 3,500

D-U-N-S 12-415-4949
COUNTY MILWAUKEE, WISCONSIN
9455 W Watertown Plank Rd, Milwaukee, WI 53226
Phone: (414) 257-6995
Sales: $55,700,000
Company Type: Private
SIC: 8063
  Psychiatric hospital
Kathleen Eilers, Manager

Employees: NA
Employees here: 1,650

D-U-N-S 15-342-2787   EXP
COVANCE CENTRAL LABORATORY SER
  (Parent: Covance Inc)
8211 Scicor Dr, Indianapolis, IN 46214
Phone: (317) 271-1200

Sales: $33,500,000
Company Type: Public Family Member
SIC: 8071
    Clinical laboratory & data management service
Richard J Andrews, Engineering-R&D

Employees: 700
Employees here: 700

D-U-N-S 83-791-2302
COVENANT CARE CALIFORNIA INC
    (Parent: Covenant Care Inc)
30320 Rancho Viejo Rd, San Juan Capistrano, CA 92675
Phone: (949) 496-9200
Sales: $34,200,000
Company Type: Private
SIC: 8051
    Nursing homes
Jeff Mckain, President

Employees: 1,500
Employees here: 40

D-U-N-S 87-623-1200
COVENANT CARE INC
30320 Rancho Viejo Rd, San Juan Capistrano, CA 92675
Phone: (949) 496-9200
Sales: $160,000,000
Company Type: Private
SIC: 8051
    Nursing homes
Jeff Mckain, President

Employees: 3,000
Employees here: 3

D-U-N-S 18-835-0367
COVENANT HEALTH CARE SYSTEM
1126 S 70th St Rm 306, Milwaukee, WI 53214
Phone: (414) 456-2300
Sales: $73,900,000
Company Type: Private
SIC: 8062
    Hospital
E T Sheahan, Chairman of the Board

Employees: 1,587
Employees here: 190

D-U-N-S 10-232-8812
COVENANT HEALTH SYSTEM INC
3421 W 9th St, Waterloo, IA 50702
Phone: (319) 236-4111
Sales: $140,536,000
Company Type: Private
SIC: 8062
    Hospitals
Raymond F Burfeind, President

Employees: 2,050
Employees here: 1,645

D-U-N-S 07-520-9411
COVENANT HOUSE INC (NEW YORK)
346 W 17th St Fl 11, New York, NY 10011
Phone: (212) 727-4000
Sales: $58,115,000
Company Type: Private
SIC: 8361
    Residential home & emergency shelter for children
Sister M Mcgeady, President

Employees: 200
Employees here: 200

D-U-N-S 13-979-0257
COVENANT MEDICAL CENTER INC
3421 W 9th St, Waterloo, IA 50702
Phone: (319) 236-4111
Sales: $141,230,000
Company Type: Private
SIC: 8062
    Hospital
Raymond F Burfeind, President

Employees: 2,000
Employees here: 1,800

D-U-N-S 02-302-1319
COVENANT MEDICAL CENTER INC
1447 N Harrison St, Saginaw, MI 48602
Phone: (517) 771-4000

Sales: $173,800,000
Company Type: Private
SIC: 8062
    Hospital
Spencer T Maidlow, President

Employees: 3,700
Employees here: NA

D-U-N-S 19-695-1057
COVENANT NURSING & REHAB CTR
    (Parent: Covenant Care California Inc)
9289 Branstetter Pl, Stockton, CA 95209
Phone: (209) 477-5252
Sales: $55,800,000
Company Type: Private
SIC: 8059
    Convalescent homes
Jeff Garrison, Administrator

Employees: 2,500
Employees here: 130

D-U-N-S 93-192-0714
COVENANT RETIREMENT COMMUNITIES W
5115 N Francisco Ave, Chicago, IL 60625
Phone: (773) 878-2294
Sales: $91,091,000
Company Type: Private
SIC: 8059
    Retirement communities
Paul V Peterson, President

Employees: 488
Employees here: 24

D-U-N-S 07-645-3174
CRAIG HOSPITAL
3425 S Clarkson St, Englewood, CO 80110
Phone: (303) 789-8000
Sales: $35,988,000
Company Type: Private
SIC: 8069
    Specialty hospital for central nervous & spinal cord system
    trauma
Lee Larson, Chairman of the Board

Employees: 525
Employees here: 512

D-U-N-S 07-202-7931
CRAVEN REGIONAL MEDICAL CTR
2000 Neuse Blvd, New Bern, NC 28560
Phone: (252) 633-8111
Sales: $125,080,000
Company Type: Private
SIC: 8062
    General hospital
J C Barker Jr, Chairman of the Board

Employees: 1,305
Employees here: 1,203

D-U-N-S 00-541-7290
CRESTVIEW OF OHIO INC
5330 Harroun Rd, Sylvania, OH 43560
Phone: (419) 885-1444
Sales: $20,774,000
Company Type: Private
SIC: 8051
    Retirement & assisted living care
Alan Brass, President

Employees: 150
Employees here: 50

D-U-N-S 18-778-3337
CRESTWOOD HOSPITAL & NURSING HM
    (Parent: Healthtrust Inc - Hospital Co)
1 Hospital Dr SE, Huntsville, AL 35801
Phone: (256) 882-3100
Sales: $56,700,000
Company Type: Public Family Member
SIC: 8062
    Acute care medical facility
Thomas M Weiss, Chief Executive Officer

Employees: 275
Employees here: 275

D-U-N-S 06-886-2382
CRESTWOOD HOSPITALS INC
6653 Embarcadero Dr Ste Q, Stockton, CA 95219
Phone: (209) 951-4894

Sales: $122,553,000
Company Type: Private
SIC: 8069
   Sub acute psychiatric hospitals
James Dobbins Jr, Chairman of the Board

Employees: 1,400
Employees here: 5

D-U-N-S 07-794-1490
CRIPPLED CHILDREN'S HOSPITAL
2924 Brook Rd, Richmond, VA 23220
Phone: (804) 321-7474
Sales: $24,658,000
Company Type: Private
SIC: 8069
   Children's hospital
Leslie G Wyatt, Administrator

Employees: 200
Employees here: 150

D-U-N-S 07-811-9476
CRISP REGIONAL HOSPITAL
902 N 7th St, Cordele, GA 31015
Phone: (912) 276-3100
Sales: $31,659,000
Company Type: Private
SIC: 8062
   General hospital
Wayne Martin, Administrator

Employees: 730
Employees here: 553

D-U-N-S 04-406-5100
CRITTENDEN HOSPITAL ASSN
200 W Tyler Ave, West Memphis, AR 72301
Phone: (870) 735-1500
Sales: $39,307,000
Company Type: Private
SIC: 8062
   General hospital
Betsy R Hooper, Chief Executive Officer

Employees: 436
Employees here: 430

D-U-N-S 01-086-9790
CRITTENTON HOSPITAL
1101 W University Dr, Rochester, MI 48307
Phone: (248) 652-5000
Sales: $110,644,000
Company Type: Private
SIC: 8062
   General hospital
Dennis Markiewicz, Vice-President

Employees: 1,184
Employees here: 1,152

D-U-N-S 05-276-7829
CROUSE HOSPITAL INC
736 Irving Ave, Syracuse, NY 13210
Phone: (315) 470-7111
Sales: $171,278,000
Company Type: Private
SIC: 8062
   General hospital
Edward Wenzke, President

Employees: 2,400
Employees here: 2,300

D-U-N-S 17-811-5762
CROWNE INVESTMENTS INC
710 Whetstone St, Monroeville, AL 36460
Phone: (334) 743-3609
Sales: $31,400,000
Company Type: Private
SIC: 8051
   Skilled nursing care
Joseph W Jones Jr, President

Employees: 1,378
Employees here: 5

D-U-N-S 07-375-6389
CROZER-CHESTER MEDICAL CENTER
1 Medical Center Blvd, Chester, PA 19013
Phone: (610) 447-2000

Sales: $91,797,000
Company Type: Private
SIC: 8062
   Hospitals and medical clinics
Joan Richards, President

Employees: 3,300
Employees here: 2,785

D-U-N-S 96-955-7552
CROZER-KEYSTONE HEALTH SYSTEM
175 E Chester Pike, Ridley Park, PA 19078
Phone: (610) 595-6000
Sales: $49,400,000
Company Type: Private
SIC: 8062
   General hospital

Employees: NA
Employees here: 1,000

D-U-N-S 11-925-3177
CRYOLIFE INC
1655 Roberts Blvd Nw, Kennesaw, GA 30144
Phone: (770) 952-1660
Sales: $50,869,000
Company Type: Public
SIC: 8099
   Health & allied services nec
Steven G Anderson, President

Employees: 315
Employees here: 215

D-U-N-S 95-889-9361
CULLMAN MEDICAL CENTER
1912 Al Highway 157 N, Cullman, AL 35058
Phone: (256) 737-2000
Sales: $51,085,000
Company Type: Private
SIC: 8062
   General hospital
Jesse O Weatherly, President

Employees: 710
Employees here: 710

D-U-N-S 07-828-9865
CULPEPER MEMORIAL HOSPITAL INC
501 Sunset Ln, Culpeper, VA 22701
Phone: (540) 829-4100
Sales: $27,298,000
Company Type: Private
SIC: 8062
   Hospital
Lee Kirk, President

Employees: 520
Employees here: 520

D-U-N-S 80-031-5889
CULWELL HEALTH INC
400 Broad St Ste 203, Sewickley, PA 15143
Phone: (412) 741-6900
Sales: $22,700,000
Company Type: Private
SIC: 8051
   Operates skilled nursing homes
Thomas Konig, Chief Executive Officer

Employees: 1,000
Employees here: 4

D-U-N-S 07-200-5705
CUMBERLAND COUNTY HOSPITAL SYS
1638 Owen Dr, Fayetteville, NC 28304
Phone: (910) 609-4000
Sales: $242,858,000
Company Type: Private
SIC: 8062
   General hospital
John T Carlisle, Administrator

Employees: 3,100
Employees here: 3,100

D-U-N-S 96-258-2326
CUMBERLAND MEDICAL CENTER INC
   (Parent: Columbia/Hca Healthcare Corp)
150 Robeson St, Fayetteville, NC 28301
Phone: (910) 609-1000

Sales: $69,000,000   *Employees:* 475
Company Type: Public Family Member   *Employees here:* 475
SIC: 8062
   General hospital
Joel F Engles, Chief Executive Officer

D-U-N-S 07-490-2479
CUMBERLAND MEDICAL CENTER INC
421 S Main St, Crossville, TN 38555
Phone: (931) 484-9511
Sales: $49,471,000   *Employees:* 778
Company Type: Private   *Employees here:* 763
SIC: 8062
   General hospital
Edwin S Anderson, President

D-U-N-S 01-084-9131
CUYAHOGA FALLS GENERAL HOSP
1900 23rd St, Cuyahoga Falls, OH 44223
Phone: (330) 971-7000
Sales: $49,851,000   *Employees:* 825
Company Type: Private   *Employees here:* 825
SIC: 8062
   General medical and surgical hospital
Fred Anthony, President

D-U-N-S 05-227-7092
CVHS HOSPITAL CORPORATION
   (Parent: Tenet Healthcare Corporation)
555 E Hardy St, Inglewood, CA 90301
Phone: (310) 673-4660
Sales: $98,765,000   *Employees:* 1,300
Company Type: Public Family Member   *Employees here:* 1,200
SIC: 8062
   General medical and surgical hospital
John Smithhisler, Chief Executive Officer

D-U-N-S 03-884-0492
CYPRESS FAIRBANKS MEDICAL CTR
   (Parent: Tenet Healthcare Corporation)
10655 Steepletop Dr, Houston, TX 77065
Phone: (281) 890-4285
Sales: $133,000,000   *Employees:* 650
Company Type: Public Family Member   *Employees here:* 650
SIC: 8062
   Hospital
Bill Klier, President

D-U-N-S 78-783-0082
D & R PHARMACEUTICAL INC
   (Parent: Omnicare Holding Company)
4400 Ole Brickyard Cir, Louisville, KY 40218
Phone: (502) 454-0803
Sales: $35,000,000   *Employees:* 230
Company Type: Public Family Member   *Employees here:* 144
SIC: 8082
   Home health care services
Dave Wren, President

D-U-N-S 07-149-9628
DAKOTA CLINIC LTD
1702 S University Dr, Fargo, ND 58103
Phone: (701) 280-3300
Sales: $103,400,000   *Employees:* 1,500
Company Type: Private   *Employees here:* 500
SIC: 8011
   Medical clinic
Larry Solberg, Administrator

D-U-N-S 80-573-4290
DAKOTA CLINIC LTD
1702 S University Dr, Fargo, ND 58103
Phone: (701) 280-3212

Sales: $20,800,000   *Employees:* NA
Company Type: Private   *Employees here:* 375
SIC: 8011
   Physician
Bruce A Nelson, Principal

D-U-N-S 83-877-6821
DAKOTA HEARTLAND HEALTH SYSTEM
   (Parent: Paracelsus Healthcare Corp)
1711 S University Dr, Fargo, ND 58103
Phone: (701) 280-4100
Sales: $50,900,000   *Employees:* 1,100
Company Type: Public Family Member   *Employees here:* 1,085
SIC: 8062
   Hospital
Lewis Kauffman, Chief Executive Officer

D-U-N-S 06-713-1409
DALE COUNTY HOSPITAL ASSN
100 Hospital Ave, Ozark, AL 36360
Phone: (334) 774-2601
Sales: $43,909,000   *Employees:* 350
Company Type: Private   *Employees here:* 350
SIC: 8062
   Hospital
Robert Bigley, Administrator

D-U-N-S 80-513-7205
DALLAS CARDIOLOGY ASSOC PA
5420 LBJ Fwy Ste 1900, Dallas, TX 75240
Phone: (972) 391-1900
Sales: $33,000,000   *Employees:* 105
Company Type: Private   *Employees here:* 35
SIC: 8011
   Cardiologists
Keven Wheelan, President

D-U-N-S 07-670-8494
DALLAS CNTY MNTL HEALTH/RTRDTN
1380 River Bend Dr, Dallas, TX 75247
Phone: (214) 743-1200
Sales: $74,164,000   *Employees:* 1,400
Company Type: Private   *Employees here:* 100
SIC: 8361
   Social service
Jim Blagg, Director

D-U-N-S 04-904-6527
DALLAS COUNTY HOSPITAL DST
5201 Harry Hines Blvd, Dallas, TX 75235
Phone: (214) 590-8000
Sales: $561,326,000   *Employees:* 6,200
Company Type: Private   *Employees here:* 5,700
SIC: 8062
   General hospital
Dr Ron J Anderson Md, President

D-U-N-S 07-138-1008
DALLAS/FORT WORTH MED CENTER
2709 Hospital Blvd, Grand Prairie, TX 75051
Phone: (972) 641-5000
Sales: $54,042,000   *Employees:* 670
Company Type: Private   *Employees here:* 590
SIC: 8062
   General hospital alcohol & substance abuse rehabilitation
      and home health care
Robert Ficken, Chief Executive Officer

D-U-N-S 07-466-5001
DAMERON HOSPITAL ASSOCIATION
525 W Acacia St, Stockton, CA 95203
Phone: (209) 944-5550

Sales: $80,343,000   *Employees:* 1,003
Company Type: Private   *Employees here:* 916
SIC: 8062
    General hospital gift shop and pharmacy
Dr Luis Arismendi Md, President

D-U-N-S 19-904-1245
DANBURY OFFICE PHYSCN SVCS PC
95 Locust Ave, Danbury, CT 6810
Phone: (203) 797-7742
Sales: $40,000,000   *Employees:* 280
Company Type: Private   *Employees here:* 215
SIC: 8011
    Medical doctors' office
Dr George Terranova Md, President

D-U-N-S 79-084-7636
DANFORTH HOSPITAL, INC
    (Parent: Columbia/Hca Healthcare Corp)
6801 Emmett F Lowry Expy, Texas City, TX 77591
Phone: (409) 938-5000
Sales: $31,900,000   *Employees:* 698
Company Type: Public Family Member   *Employees here:* 698
SIC: 8062
    General hospital
Don Shaffett, Chief Executive Officer

D-U-N-S 03-818-1541
DANIEL FREEMAN HOSPITALS INC
4650 Lincoln Blvd, Venice, CA 90292
Phone: (310) 823-8911
Sales: $24,300,000   *Employees:* NA
Company Type: Private   *Employees here:* 500
SIC: 8062
    Hospital
Irma Odabashian Sr, N/A

D-U-N-S 02-832-2832
DANIEL FREEMAN HOSPITALS INC
333 N Prairie Ave, Inglewood, CA 90301
Phone: (310) 674-7050
Sales: $186,185,000   *Employees:* 2,500
Company Type: Private   *Employees here:* 1,420
SIC: 8062
    General hospital
Joseph Dunn Phd, Chief Executive Officer

D-U-N-S 06-601-1255
DANVILLE REGIONAL MEDICAL CTR
142 S Main St, Danville, VA 24541
Phone: (804) 799-2100
Sales: $102,338,000   *Employees:* 1,200
Company Type: Private   *Employees here:* 1,200
SIC: 8062
    Hospital
Bill M Cox, Chairman of the Board

D-U-N-S 07-849-5868
DAUGHTERS OF CHARITY H/S
1201 W 38th St, Austin, TX 78705
Phone: (512) 324-1000
Sales: $187,900,000   *Employees:* 4,000
Company Type: Private   *Employees here:* 1,875
SIC: 8062
    General hospital
Charles Barnett, President

D-U-N-S 18-341-4127
DAUGHTERS OF CHARITY H/S
601 E 15th St, Austin, TX 78701
Phone: (512) 480-1362

Sales: $70,400,000   *Employees:* NA
Company Type: Private   *Employees here:* 1,700
SIC: 8062
    General medical and surgical hospital
Rus Kyler, Chief Financial Officer

D-U-N-S 07-761-7843
DAUGHTERS OF CHARITY HEALTH
6901 Medical Pkwy, Waco, TX 76712
Phone: (254) 751-4000
Sales: $85,970,000   *Employees:* 1,500
Company Type: Private   *Employees here:* 1,187
SIC: 8062
    Acute hospital
Kent A Keahey, President

D-U-N-S 06-427-9250
DAUGHTERS OF MIRIAM CENTER
155 Hazel St, Clifton, NJ 7011
Phone: (973) 772-3700
Sales: $22,792,000   *Employees:* 500
Company Type: Private   *Employees here:* 500
SIC: 8051
    Skilled nursing care facility
Lawrence S Boss, Chairman of the Board

D-U-N-S 07-991-9833
DAUGHTERS JACOB NURSING HOME
1160 Teller Ave, Bronx, NY 10456
Phone: (718) 293-1500
Sales: $38,000,000   *Employees:* 525
Company Type: Private   *Employees here:* 525
SIC: 8051
    Skilled nursing care facility
Howard Modlin, Chairman of the Board

D-U-N-S 07-877-3694
DAVIES MEDICAL CENTER, INC
Castro & Duboce Sts, San Francisco, CA 94114
Phone: (415) 565-6600
Sales: $55,247,000   *Employees:* 900
Company Type: Private   *Employees here:* 900
SIC: 8062
    General hospital
Greg Monardo, President

D-U-N-S 07-407-1903
DAVIESS COUNTY HOSPITAL
1314 Grand Ave, Washington, IN 47501
Phone: (812) 254-2760
Sales: $22,291,000   *Employees:* 340
Company Type: Private   *Employees here:* 340
SIC: 8062
    Gen hospital
Marc A Chircop, Chief Executive Officer

D-U-N-S 01-044-2515
DAVIS MEMORIAL HOSPITAL
Gorman Ave & Reed St, Elkins, WV 26241
Phone: (304) 636-3300
Sales: $51,070,000   *Employees:* 620
Company Type: Private   *Employees here:* 575
SIC: 8062
    Hospital
Robert L Hammer Ii, Administrator

D-U-N-S 62-774-5276
DAVIS VISION INC
    (Parent: Clarity Vision Inc)
159 Express St, Plainview, NY 11803
Phone: (516) 932-9500

Sales: $150,000,000   *Employees:* 1,000
Company Type: Private   *Employees here:* 200
SIC: 8011
　　Marketer of optical medical plans
Richard David, President

D-U-N-S 07-468-2931
DAYTON OSTEOPATHIC HOSPITAL
405 W Grand Ave, Dayton, OH 45405
Phone: (937) 226-3200
Sales: $142,751,000   *Employees:* 1,800
Company Type: Private   *Employees here:* 1,400
SIC: 8062
　　General hospital
Richard J Minor, President

D-U-N-S 07-329-4654
DAYTOP VILLAGE INC
54 W 40th St, New York, NY 10018
Phone: (212) 354-6000
Sales: $32,280,000   *Employees:* 700
Company Type: Private   *Employees here:* 70
SIC: 8093
　　Non-profit drug rehabilitation center
William B O Brien, President

D-U-N-S 07-431-1838
DE KALB MEMORIAL HOSPITAL INC
1316 E 7th St, Auburn, IN 46706
Phone: (219) 925-4600
Sales: $23,520,000   *Employees:* 425
Company Type: Private   *Employees here:* 420
SIC: 8062
　　General hospital
Jack Corey, President

D-U-N-S 07-196-8200
DE PAUL HEALTH CENTER INC
12303 De Paul Dr, Bridgeton, MO 63044
Phone: (314) 344-6000
Sales: $72,100,000   *Employees:* 1,550
Company Type: Private   *Employees here:* 1,200
SIC: 8062
　　Hospital & extended care facility
Robert G Porter, President

D-U-N-S 07-327-2247
DE WITT NURSING HOME
211 E 79th St, New York, NY 10021
Phone: (212) 879-1600
Sales: $32,759,000   *Employees:* 621
Company Type: Private   *Employees here:* 621
SIC: 8051
　　Skilled nursing facility
Marilyn Lichtman, Owner

D-U-N-S 60-920-2114
DEACONESS HEALTH CARE CORP
5300 N Grand Blvd, Oklahoma City, OK 73112
Phone: (405) 949-4267
Sales: $85,699,000   *Employees:* 55
Company Type: Private   *Employees here:* 2
SIC: 8361
　　Corporate offices for health care related services
John Ellis, Administrator

D-U-N-S 07-199-8090
DEACONESS HEALTH SYS W CAMPUS
2345 Dougherty Ferry Rd, Saint Louis, MO 63122
Phone: (314) 821-5850

Sales: $28,450,000   *Employees:* 650
Company Type: Private   *Employees here:* 650
SIC: 8062
　　General medical hospitals
Joan D Ambrose, Chief Executive Officer

D-U-N-S 05-694-3277
DEACONESS HOSPITAL AN OKLA CORP
5501 N Portland Ave, Oklahoma City, OK 73112
Phone: (405) 946-5581
Sales: $77,421,000   *Employees:* 1,200
Company Type: Private   *Employees here:* 1,180
SIC: 8062
　　General hospital fitness center nursing home radiology
　　　services and home for unwed mothers
Paul Dougherty, Administrator

D-U-N-S 07-468-3814
DEACONESS HOSPITAL
311 Straight St, Cincinnati, OH 45219
Phone: (513) 559-2100
Sales: $86,200,000   *Employees:* 1,848
Company Type: Private   *Employees here:* 950
SIC: 8062
　　General medical & surgical hospital
E A Woods, President

D-U-N-S 05-682-6456
DEACONESS HOSPITAL INC
600 Mary St, Evansville, IN 47710
Phone: (812) 426-3000
Sales: $158,991,000   *Employees:* 2,300
Company Type: Private   *Employees here:* 2,050
SIC: 8062
　　General hospital
Thomas H Kramer, President

D-U-N-S 83-943-7753
DEACONESS LONG TERM CARE OF MO
8540 Blue Ridge Blvd, Kansas City, MO 64138
Phone: (816) 380-3319
Sales: $45,450,000   *Employees:* 1,850
Company Type: Private   *Employees here:* 1,500
SIC: 8059
　　Health care facility
Dennis Sever, Chief Executive Officer

D-U-N-S 07-171-8522
DEACONESS WALTHAM HOSPITAL
Hope Ave, Waltham, MA 2254
Phone: (781) 647-6000
Sales: $64,781,000   *Employees:* 1,480
Company Type: Private   *Employees here:* 727
SIC: 8062
　　Hospital
Jeanette G Clough, President

D-U-N-S 78-167-6465
DEACONESS WALTHAM HOSPITAL
20 Hope Ave, Milton, MA 2186
Phone: (781) 647-6240
Sales: $44,900,000   *Employees:* NA
Company Type: Private   *Employees here:* 740
SIC: 8011
　　Medical clinic
Jeanette Clough, President

D-U-N-S 06-892-0065
DEACONESS-BILLINGS CLINIC INC
2800 10th Ave N, Billings, MT 59101
Phone: (406) 657-4000

Sales: $162,956,000
Company Type: Private
SIC: 8062
  General hospital
Patrick Garrett, Chief Operating Officer

Employees: 1,100
Employees here: 1,095

D-U-N-S 07-384-7998
DEAN HEALTH SYSTEMS SC
1808 W Beltline Hwy, Madison, WI 53713
Phone: (608) 250-1500
Sales: $450,000,000
Company Type: Private
SIC: 8011
  Medical clinic
Michael Wilson, President

Employees: 3,000
Employees here: 100

D-U-N-S 82-508-8420
DEAN HEALTH SYSTEMS SC
580 N Washington St, Janesville, WI 53545
Phone: (608) 755-3500
Sales: $23,700,000
Company Type: Private
SIC: 8011
  Medical doctor's office
Mary Laird, Principal

Employees: NA
Employees here: 375

D-U-N-S 07-288-8035
DEARBORN COUNTY HOSPITAL
600 Wilson Creek Rd, Lawrenceburg, IN 47025
Phone: (812) 537-1010
Sales: $34,153,000
Company Type: Private
SIC: 8062
  General medical & surgical hospital
Philip Meyer, Finance

Employees: 500
Employees here: 500

D-U-N-S 05-650-3402
DEATON SPECIALTY HOSPITAL & HM
611 S Charles St, Baltimore, MD 21230
Phone: (410) 547-8500
Sales: $31,228,000
Company Type: Private
SIC: 8051
  Ventilator chronic care hospital and skilled nursing home
Errol Newport, President

Employees: 475
Employees here: 475

D-U-N-S 07-145-7964
DEBORAH HEART & LUNG CENTER
200 Trenton Rd, Browns Mills, NJ 8015
Phone: (609) 893-6611
Sales: $107,809,000
Company Type: Private
SIC: 8069
  Specialty hospital
John Ernst, Executive Director

Employees: 1,425
Employees here: 1,425

D-U-N-S 04-658-4991
DECATUR MEMORIAL HOSPITAL
2300 N Edward St, Decatur, IL 62526
Phone: (217) 877-8121
Sales: $98,851,000
Company Type: Private
SIC: 8062
  General hospital
Kenneth Smithmier, President

Employees: 1,165
Employees here: 1,143

D-U-N-S 07-953-2008
DEDHAM MEDICAL ASSOCIATES INC
1 Lyons St, Dedham, MA 2026
Phone: (781) 329-1400

Sales: $27,400,000
Company Type: Private
SIC: 8011
  Medical group of physicians & dentists
Neal Birnbaum, Chairman of the Board

Employees: 400
Employees here: 200

D-U-N-S 07-757-5298
DEFIANCE HOSPITAL INC
1206 E 2nd St, Defiance, OH 43512
Phone: (419) 782-6955
Sales: $30,986,000
Company Type: Private
SIC: 8062
  General hospital
Richard Sommer, Administrator

Employees: 350
Employees here: 346

D-U-N-S 07-993-4816
DEGRAFF MEMORIAL HOSPITAL INC
445 Tremont St, North Tonawanda, NY 14120
Phone: (716) 694-4500
Sales: $35,461,000
Company Type: Private
SIC: 8062
  General hospital & skilled nursing facility
Thomas Schifferli, President

Employees: 695
Employees here: 686

D-U-N-S 07-586-5766
DEKALB MEDICAL CENTER INC
  (Parent: Dekalb Regional Healthcare Sys)
2701 N Decatur Rd, Decatur, GA 30033
Phone: (404) 501-1000
Sales: $180,833,000
Company Type: Private
SIC: 8062
  Hospital
Pat Mathis, Chairman of the Board

Employees: 2,200
Employees here: 1,976

D-U-N-S 06-885-0890
DELANCEY STREET FOUNDATION
600 The Embarcadero, San Francisco, CA 94107
Phone: (415) 957-9800
Sales: $21,822,000
Company Type: Private
SIC: 8361
  Residential rehabilitation center
Mimi Silbert, President

Employees: 1,200
Employees here: 500

D-U-N-S 06-987-7926
DELAWARE COUNTY MEMORIAL HOSP
501 N Lansdowne Ave, Drexel Hill, PA 19026
Phone: (610) 284-8100
Sales: $96,895,000
Company Type: Private
SIC: 8062
  General hospital
Joan Richards, President

Employees: 885
Employees here: 885

D-U-N-S 05-723-1185
DELAWARE DEPT HEALTH SOCIAL SVCS
100 Sunnyside Rd, Smyrna, DE 19977
Phone: (302) 653-8556
Sales: $35,200,000
Company Type: Private
SIC: 8069
  Hospital
Arnold Morris, Principal

Employees: NA
Employees here: 750

D-U-N-S 18-288-8545
DELAWARE DEPT HEALTH SOCIAL SVCS
1901 N Dupont Hwy, New Castle, DE 19720
Phone: (302) 577-4000

Sales: $21,300,000
Company Type: Private
SIC: 8063
  State hospital
Jiro Shinono, Manager

Employees: NA
Employees here: 600

D-U-N-S 07-550-3847
DELAWARE VALLEY MEDICAL CTR
200 Oxford Valley Rd, Langhorne, PA 19047
Phone: (215) 949-5000
Sales: $47,510,000
Company Type: Private
SIC: 8062
  Hospital
Carl Brown, President

Employees: 679
Employees here: 674

D-U-N-S 16-952-8205
DELMARVA HEALTH PLAN INC
  (Parent: C F S Health Group Inc)
301 Bay St Ste 401, Easton, MD 21601
Phone: (410) 822-7223
Sales: $66,460,000
Company Type: Private
SIC: 8011
  Medical doctor's office
Dr Robert Sheff, President

Employees: 75
Employees here: 75

D-U-N-S 07-458-8567
DELNOR-COMMUNITY HOSPITAL
300 Randall Rd, Geneva, IL 60134
Phone: (630) 208-3000
Sales: $63,663,000
Company Type: Private
SIC: 8062
  General hospital
Craig Livermore, President

Employees: 985
Employees here: 985

D-U-N-S 09-568-1748
DELTA DENTAL PLAN OF TENN
240 Venture Cir, Nashville, TN 37228
Phone: (615) 356-3175
Sales: $39,602,000
Company Type: Private
SIC: 8021
  Dental plan
Dr William Manning Dds, President

Employees: 21
Employees here: 19

D-U-N-S 06-771-8981
DELTA REGIONAL MEDICAL CENTER
1400 E Union St, Greenville, MS 38703
Phone: (601) 378-3783
Sales: $50,164,000
Company Type: Private
SIC: 8062
  General hospital
Barbara Madison, Administrator

Employees: 723
Employees here: 633

D-U-N-S 79-886-5283
DEMAC CORPORATION
  (Parent: Detroit-Macomb Hospital Corp)
27472 Schoenherr Rd, Warren, MI 48093
Phone: (810) 779-9551
Sales: $31,968,000
Company Type: Private
SIC: 8011
  Health care organization
Phil Hunsberger, Executive Director

Employees: 205
Employees here: 61

D-U-N-S 60-383-4482
DENTAL-NET INC
4720 N Oracle Rd Ste 100, Tucson, AZ 85705
Phone: (520) 696-4300

Sales: $21,242,000
Company Type: Private
SIC: 8021
  Dental office and dental health maintenance organization
Dr Kenneth A Vinall Dds, Chairman of the Board

Employees: 200
Employees here: 60

D-U-N-S 00-761-2658
DENTON HOSPITAL, INC.
  (Parent: Netcare Health Systems Llc)
207 N Bonnie Brae St, Denton, TX 76201
Phone: (940) 898-7000
Sales: $89,628,000
Company Type: Private
SIC: 8062
  Hospital
Timothy Charles, Chief Executive Officer

Employees: 500
Employees here: 500

D-U-N-S 13-312-6011
DENVER, CITY & COUNTY OF
777 Bannock St Ste 278, Denver, CO 80204
Phone: (303) 436-6000
Sales: $117,100,000
Company Type: Private
SIC: 8062
  General hospital
Patrcia Gabow, N/A

Employees: NA
Employees here: 2,700

D-U-N-S 02-607-9640
DEPARTMENT OF AIR FORCE
Maxwell Airforce Base, Montgomery, AL 36112
Phone: (334) 953-7803
Sales: $22,800,000
Company Type: Private
SIC: 8062
  Hospital
Carlisle Harrison, Principal

Employees: NA
Employees here: 550

D-U-N-S 11-242-7570
DEPARTMENT OF AIR FORCE
310 W Losey St, Scott Afb, IL 62225
Phone: (618) 256-7364
Sales: $86,800,000
Company Type: Private
SIC: 8011
  Medical group
Col Robacher, Branch Manager

Employees: NA
Employees here: 1,500

D-U-N-S 96-392-3990
DEPARTMENT OF AIR FORCE
2501 Capehart Rd Ste 1105, Bellevue, NE 68123
Phone: (402) 294-0701
Sales: $38,400,000
Company Type: Private
SIC: 8062
  General hospital
Col Fronefield, Principal

Employees: NA
Employees here: 1,000

D-U-N-S 09-519-4643
DEPARTMENT OF AIR FORCE
4881 Sugar Maple Dr, Dayton, OH 45433
Phone: (937) 257-0837
Sales: $743,900,000
Company Type: Private
SIC: 8011
  Us air force medical center
Lt C Triche, Commander

Employees: NA
Employees here: 15,000

D-U-N-S 78-318-7685
DEPARTMENT OF AIR FORCE
654th Medical Group Sgm, Oklahoma City, OK 73145
Phone: (405) 734-8211

Sales: $20,600,000   *Employees:* NA
Company Type: Private   *Employees here:* 510
SIC: 8062
  Hospital
Col T Vivian, N/A

    D-U-N-S 94-173-4857
DEPARTMENT OF AIR FORCE
7321 11th St Bldg 570, Hill Air Force Base, UT 84056
Phone: (801) 777-4530
Sales: $21,100,000   *Employees:* NA
Company Type: Private   *Employees here:* 500
SIC: 8062
  Military hospital
Capt Welch, Chief

    D-U-N-S 96-588-1386
DEPARTMENT OF AIR FORCE
701 Hospital Loop, Fafb, WA 99011
Phone: (509) 247-5217
Sales: $28,100,000
Company Type: Private   *Employees here:* 450
SIC: 8011
  Medical doctor's office
Col C Hinman, Principal

    D-U-N-S 08-376-6931
DEPARTMENT OF ARMY
302 Harmon Ave, Hinesville, GA 31314
Phone: (912) 767-6857
Sales: $32,500,000   *Employees:* NA
Company Type: Private   *Employees here:* 800
SIC: 8062
  General hospital
Phillip Keating, Branch Manager

    D-U-N-S 11-190-4306
DEPARTMENT OF ARMY
Bldg 300, Indianapolis, IN 46216
Phone: (317) 546-9211
Sales: $25,000,000   *Employees:* NA
Company Type: Private   *Employees here:* 600
SIC: 8062
  Military hospital

    D-U-N-S 60-561-8248
DEPARTMENT OF ARMY
600 Caiffon Hill Rd, Fort Riley, KS 66442
Phone: (785) 239-7720
Sales: $27,500,000   *Employees:* NA
Company Type: Private   *Employees here:* 720
SIC: 8062
  General hospital
J T Hardy, Director

    D-U-N-S 15-637-7947
DEPARTMENT OF ARMY
650 Joel Dr, Fort Campbell, KY 42223
Phone: (502) 798-8041
Sales: $106,100,000   *Employees:* NA
Company Type: Private   *Employees here:* 2,700
SIC: 8062
  General hospital national security
P E Wehrle, Branch Manager

    D-U-N-S 11-190-2821
DEPARTMENT OF ARMY
Anme Bldg 2480 Llewllyn, Fort George G Meade, MD 20755
Phone: (301) 677-8392

Sales: $35,000,000   *Employees:* NA
Company Type: Private   *Employees here:* 800
SIC: 8062
  Military hospital
Col Patterson, Commander

    D-U-N-S 11-190-3241
DEPARTMENT OF ARMY
126 Mossuri Ave Atzt Cg, Fort Leonard Wood, MO 65473
Phone: (573) 596-0496
Sales: $31,100,000   *Employees:* NA
Company Type: Private   *Employees here:* 800
SIC: 8062
  Military hospital
Col R Smerz, Commander

    D-U-N-S 09-132-7304
DEPARTMENT OF ARMY
Stewart St Bldg 4500, Columbia, SC 29207
Phone: (803) 751-2183
Sales: $41,900,000   *Employees:* NA
Company Type: Private   *Employees here:* 953
SIC: 8062
  Community hospital
Col D Carol, Director

    D-U-N-S 17-021-7061
DEPARTMENT OF ARMY
3815 Roger Brooke Dr, San Antonio, TX 78234
Phone: (210) 916-6141
Sales: $54,300,000   *Employees:* NA
Company Type: Private   *Employees here:* 1,314
SIC: 8062
  General hospital
General Timboe, Director

    D-U-N-S 10-891-0068
DEPARTMENT OF ARMY
Bldg 36000, Fort Hood, TX 76544
Phone: (254) 288-8000
Sales: $24,400,000   *Employees:* NA
Company Type: Private   *Employees here:* 600
SIC: 8062
  General hospital national security
Darnell Hughes, Branch Manager

    D-U-N-S 15-609-6364
DEPARTMENT OF ARMY
Jefferson Bldg 576, Fort Eustis, VA 23604
Phone: (757) 878-7500
Sales: $21,600,000   *Employees:* NA
Company Type: Private   *Employees here:* 500
SIC: 8062
  General hospital
Col Weightman, Branch Manager

    D-U-N-S 17-237-5578
DEPARTMENT OF ARMY
9501 Farrell Rd Ste Tc11, Fort Belvoir, VA 22060
Phone: (703) 805-0510
Sales: $44,000,000   *Employees:* NA
Company Type: Private   *Employees here:* 1,000
SIC: 8062
  General hospital
Colonel S Jones, Principal

    D-U-N-S 11-549-9840
DEPARTMENT OF MENTAL HEALTH
111 Howard Ave, Cranston, RI 2920
Phone: (401) 464-3666

Sales: $40,600,000
Company Type: Private
SIC: 8063
   Psychiatric hospital intermediate care facility
James P Benedict, Principal

Employees: NA
Employees here: 1,000

D-U-N-S 00-229-0609
DEPARTMENT OF NAVY
34800 Bob Wilson Dr, San Diego, CA 92134
Phone: (619) 532-6400
Sales: $211,400,000
Company Type: Private
SIC: 8062
   General hospital
Cmdr R Nelson, Principal

Employees: NA
Employees here: 4,250

D-U-N-S 00-426-6797
DEPARTMENT OF NAVY
Camp Pendleton, Oceanside, CA 92055
Phone: (760) 725-1288
Sales: $34,300,000
Company Type: Private
SIC: 8069
   Specialty hospital
Cmdr C Burkhard, Principal

Employees: NA
Employees here: 650

D-U-N-S 61-369-2391
DEPARTMENT OF NAVY
1750 Central St, Pearl Harbor, HI 96860
Phone: (808) 471-3026
Sales: $31,100,000
Company Type: Private
SIC: 8011
   Medical clinic
Captain Murphy, Principal

Employees: NA
Employees here: 500

D-U-N-S 11-191-9171
DEPARTMENT OF NAVY
7800 3rd St, Memphis, TN 38106
Phone: (901) 874-5804
Sales: $50,500,000
Company Type: Private
SIC: 8021
   Naval hospital
Cpt Kilpatrick, Branch Manager

Employees: NA
Employees here: 2,300

D-U-N-S 06-522-1004
DES MOINES GENERAL HOSPITAL CO
603 E 12th St, Des Moines, IA 50309
Phone: (515) 263-4200
Sales: $45,440,000
Company Type: Private
SIC: 8062
   General hospital
Roy Wright, Chief Executive Officer

Employees: 540
Employees here: 510

D-U-N-S 82-523-1913
DESERT VALLEY HOSPITAL
16938 Bear Valley Rd, Victorville, CA 92392
Phone: (760) 241-8000
Sales: $36,185,000
Company Type: Private
SIC: 8062
   General hospital
John Rossfeld, Chief Executive Officer

Employees: 250
Employees here: 250

D-U-N-S 13-123-8990
DESERT VALLEY MEDICAL GROUP
16850 Bear Valley Rd, Victorville, CA 92392
Phone: (760) 242-8000

Sales: $40,000,000
Company Type: Private
SIC: 8011
   Physicians' office
Dr Prem Reddy Md, President

Employees: 460
Employees here: 300

D-U-N-S 08-221-3968
DETROIT OSTEOPATHIC HOSPITAL CORP
13355 E 10 Mile Rd, Warren, MI 48089
Phone: (810) 759-7300
Sales: $42,100,000
Company Type: Private
SIC: 8062
   General hospital ret gifts/novelties
Gary Popiel, Principal

Employees: NA
Employees here: 1,000

D-U-N-S 07-635-8100
DETROIT OSTEOPATHIC HOSPITAL CORP
150 Truax St, Trenton, MI 48183
Phone: (734) 676-4200
Sales: $29,300,000
Company Type: Private
SIC: 8062
   General hospital
Dennis Christen, Vice-President

Employees: NA
Employees here: 700

D-U-N-S 07-422-1300
DETROIT OSTEOPATHIC HOSPITAL CORP
26100 American Dr, Southfield, MI 48034
Phone: (248) 746-4300
Sales: $99,500,000
Company Type: Private
SIC: 8062
   General osteopathic hospitals
Thomas W Caulfield, President

Employees: 2,130
Employees here: 180

D-U-N-S 03-774-8076
DETROIT RECEIVING HOSPITAL AND
4201 Saint Antoine St, Detroit, MI 48201
Phone: (313) 745-3104
Sales: $225,118,000
Company Type: Private
SIC: 8069
   Trauma care hospital
Paul Broughton, Senior Vice-President

Employees: 1,740
Employees here: 1,740

D-U-N-S 06-982-9729
DETROIT-MACOMB HOSPITAL CORP
12000 E 12 Mile Rd, Warren, MI 48093
Phone: (313) 499-3000
Sales: $198,969,000
Company Type: Private
SIC: 8062
   General medical & surgical hospitals
Timothy Ryan, President

Employees: 4,030
Employees here: 175

D-U-N-S 07-276-9276
DETROIT-MACOMB HOSPITAL CORP
11800 E 12 Mile Rd, Warren, MI 48093
Phone: (810) 573-5000
Sales: $63,500,000
Company Type: Private
SIC: 8062
   General hospital
Richard Young, Principal

Employees: NA
Employees here: 1,500

D-U-N-S 78-717-6783
DIABETES TREATMENT CTRS OF AMERICA
   (Parent: American Healthcorp Inc)
1 Brtn Hls B Ste 300, Nashville, TN 37215
Phone: (615) 665-1133

Sales: $27,400,000   *Employees:* 400
Company Type: Public Family Member   *Employees here:* 60
SIC: 8011
   Diabetes treatment programs
Thomas G Cigarran, Chairman of the Board

D-U-N-S 04-746-5240
DIAGNOSTIC CLINIC HOUSTON, PA
6448 Fannin St, Houston, TX 77030
Phone: (713) 797-9191
Sales: $36,000,000   *Employees:* 346
Company Type: Private   *Employees here:* 346
SIC: 8011
   Medical clinic
Joann R Mc Clung, Administrator

D-U-N-S 07-844-4700
DIAGNOSTIC CTR HOSPITAL CORP TEXAS
   (Parent: The Methodist Hospital)
6447 Main St, Houston, TX 77030
Phone: (713) 790-0790
Sales: $42,368,000   *Employees:* 500
Company Type: Private   *Employees here:* 500
SIC: 8062
   Hospital
William A Gregory, Administrator

D-U-N-S 10-262-6660
DIAGNOSTIC HEALTH SERVICES INC
2777 N Stemmons Fwy, Dallas, TX 75207
Phone: (214) 634-0403
Sales: $52,921,000   *Employees:* 500
Company Type: Public   *Employees here:* 50
SIC: 8099
   Healthcare services & temporary help provider
Max Batzer, Chairman of the Board

D-U-N-S 14-453-5598
DIAGNOSTIC LABORATORY SERVICES
770 Kapiolani Blvd, Honolulu, HI 96813
Phone: (808) 589-5100
Sales: $38,890,000   *Employees:* 470
Company Type: Private   *Employees here:* 120
SIC: 8071
   Medical testing laboratory
Ivan Lui-Kwan, Chairman of the Board

D-U-N-S 03-810-7744
DIALYSIS CLINIC INC
1600 Hayes St Ste 300, Nashville, TN 37203
Phone: (615) 327-3061
Sales: $268,794,000   *Employees:* 3,600
Company Type: Private   *Employees here:* 60
SIC: 8092
   Operates hemodialysis clinic & wholesales medical supplies
Keith Johnson, Chairman of the Board

D-U-N-S 61-065-8775
DIALYSIS HOLDINGS, INC
   (Parent: Gambro Healthcare Patient Svcs)
1850 Gateway Dr 500, San Mateo, CA 94404
Phone: (650) 577-5700
Sales: $320,000,000   *Employees:* NA
Company Type: Public   *Employees here:* NA
SIC: 8092
   Dialysis services
Kent J Thiry, President

D-U-N-S 10-133-7863
DIANON SYSTEMS INC
200 Watson Blvd, Stratford, CT 6615
Phone: (203) 381-4000

Sales: $60,887,000   *Employees:* 500
Company Type: Public   *Employees here:* 325
SIC: 8071
   Anatomic pathology services & genetic and clinical chemistry
     testing services
Kevin Johnson, President

D-U-N-S 07-479-2540
DICKINSON CNTY HEALTH CARE SYS
1721 S Stephenson Ave, Iron Mountain, MI 49801
Phone: (906) 774-1313
Sales: $42,077,000   *Employees:* 630
Company Type: Private   *Employees here:* 610
SIC: 8062
   General medical & surgical hospital
John Schon, Chief Executive Officer

D-U-N-S 08-235-0422
DIMENSIONS HEALTH CORPORATION
9200 Basil Ct Ste 500, Upper Marlboro, MD 20774
Phone: (301) 925-9500
Sales: $233,561,000   *Employees:* 2,800
Company Type: Private   *Employees here:* 38
SIC: 8062
   Hospitals & nursing home
Winfield M Kelly Jr, President

D-U-N-S 08-768-7984
DIMENSIONS HEALTH CORPORATION
7300 Van Dusen Rd, Laurel, MD 20707
Phone: (301) 725-4300
Sales: $30,600,000   *Employees:* NA
Company Type: Private   *Employees here:* 700
SIC: 8062
   General hospital
Patrick Mutch, Principal

D-U-N-S 01-599-8511
DIMENSIONS HEALTH CORPORATION
3001 Hospital Dr, Hyattsville, MD 20785
Phone: (301) 618-2530
Sales: $38,100,000   *Employees:* NA
Company Type: Private   *Employees here:* 2,500
SIC: 8082
   Home health care services
Kris Nelson, President

D-U-N-S 78-389-9446
DIMENSIONS HEALTH CORPORATION
3001 Hospital Dr, Hyattsville, MD 20785
Phone: (301) 618-2000
Sales: $79,600,000   *Employees:* NA
Company Type: Private   *Employees here:* 1,800
SIC: 8062
   General hospital
Allan Atzrott, Branch Manager

D-U-N-S 92-931-2106
DISABLITY SVCS OF THE SOUTHWEST
1200 Circle Dr Ste 400, Fort Worth, TX 76119
Phone: (817) 531-7474
Sales: $30,500,000   *Employees:* 1,000
Company Type: Private   *Employees here:* 300
SIC: 8093
   Specialty outpatient clinic
Brenda Seawell, President

D-U-N-S 03-776-0154
DISTRICT COLUMBIA GOVERNMENT
2700 Martin Lthr Kng 10, Washington, DC 20032
Phone: (202) 373-7166

Sales: $70,300,000
Company Type: Private
SIC: 8063
   Psychiatric hospital
Guido R Zenni, Principal

Employees: NA
Employees here: 2,000

D-U-N-S 07-761-2794
DISTRICT COLUMBIA GOVERNMENT
8300 Riverton Ct, Laurel, MD 20724
Phone: (301) 497-8100
Sales: $25,800,000
Company Type: Private
SIC: 8361
   Residential care services
Wayne D Casey, Manager

Employees: NA
Employees here: 1,100

D-U-N-S 06-960-2571
DIVINE PROVIDENCE HOSPITAL
1100 Grampian Blvd, Williamsport, PA 17701
Phone: (717) 326-8101
Sales: $46,347,000
Company Type: Private
SIC: 8062
   Medical & surgical hospital
Sister J Mohl, President

Employees: 800
Employees here: 800

D-U-N-S 07-115-2086
DIVINE SAVIOR HOSPITAL NURSING HM
1015 W Pleasant St, Portage, WI 53901
Phone: (608) 742-4131
Sales: $20,585,000
Company Type: Private
SIC: 8062
   General hospital
Mike Decker, Chief Executive Officer

Employees: 350
Employees here: 225

D-U-N-S 18-056-7232
DMH HEALTH SYSTEMS
2300 N Edward St, Decatur, IL 62526
Phone: (217) 877-8121
Sales: $106,404,000
Company Type: Private
SIC: 8062
   Holding company-operating hospital
Kenneth Smithmier, President

Employees: 16
Employees here: 1

D-U-N-S 03-667-3218
DOC'S PHYSICIANS AFFILIATED
465 Columbus Ave Ste 100, Valhalla, NY 10595
Phone: (914) 747-7000
Sales: $27,400,000
Company Type: Private
SIC: 8011
   Medical center
Bob Naldi, Vp Finance

Employees: 600
Employees here: 100

D-U-N-S 80-772-6179
DOCTORS HOSPITAL SHREVEPORT INC
   (Parent: Universal Health Services)
1130 Louisiana Ave, Shreveport, LA 71101
Phone: (318) 227-1211
Sales: $20,000,000
Company Type: Public Family Member
SIC: 8069
   Acute care hospital
Charles Boyd, Chief Executive Officer

Employees: 411
Employees here: 400

D-U-N-S 02-271-5882
DOCTORS HOSPITAL
5100 W Broad St, Columbus, OH 43228
Phone: (614) 297-4000

Sales: $20,700,000
Company Type: Private
SIC: 8062
   General hospital
Richard Vincent, President

Employees: NA
Employees here: 500

D-U-N-S 07-165-4172
DOCTORS HOSPITAL
1087 Dennison Ave, Columbus, OH 43201
Phone: (614) 297-4000
Sales: $171,849,000
Company Type: Private
SIC: 8062
   General hospital & physicians office
Richard A Vincent, Chief Executive Officer

Employees: 2,000
Employees here: 1,200

D-U-N-S 06-760-4405
DOCTORS HOSPITAL OF AUGUSTA
   (Parent: Columbia/Hca Healthcare Corp)
3651 Wheeler Rd, Augusta, GA 30909
Phone: (706) 651-3232
Sales: $108,362,000
Company Type: Public Family Member
SIC: 8062
   General hospital
Michael T Kerner, President

Employees: 1,050
Employees here: 950

D-U-N-S 07-635-0883
DOCTORS HOSPITAL OF JACKSON
110 N Elm Ave, Jackson, MI 49202
Phone: (517) 787-1440
Sales: $19,926,000
Company Type: Private
SIC: 8062
   General hospital
Mike Falatko, Administrator

Employees: 234
Employees here: 231

D-U-N-S 07-913-2130
DOCTORS HOSPITAL A LTD PARTNR
5230 S 6th Street Rd, Springfield, IL 62703
Phone: (217) 529-7151
Sales: $32,794,000
Company Type: Private
SIC: 8062
   Hospital
Jim Bohl, President

Employees: 475
Employees here: 455

D-U-N-S 02-057-0412
DOCTORS HOSPITAL OF STATEN ISLAND
1050 Targee St, Staten Island, NY 10304
Phone: (718) 390-1400
Sales: $25,244,000
Company Type: Private
SIC: 8062
   General hospital
Stephen N Anderson, Executive Director

Employees: 348
Employees here: 348

D-U-N-S 04-869-8773
DOCTORS LABORATORY INC
2906 Julia Dr, Valdosta, GA 31602
Phone: (912) 244-4468
Sales: $20,588,000
Company Type: Private
SIC: 8071
   Medical laboratory
Dr Byron S Davis, President

Employees: 300
Employees here: 175

D-U-N-S 07-464-3735
DOCTORS MED CENTER-SAN PABLO
   (Parent: Tenet Healthcare Corporation)
2000 Vale Rd, San Pablo, CA 94806
Phone: (510) 235-7000

Sales: $39,000,000   *Employees:* 850
Company Type: Public Family Member   *Employees here:* 850
SIC: 8062
   General hospital
Gary Sloan, President

D-U-N-S 61-643-7240
DOCTORS OSTEOPATHIC MED CTR
(Parent: Columbia/Hca Healthcare Corp)
13681 Doctors Way, Fort Myers, FL 33912
Phone: (941) 768-5000
Sales: $32,760,000   *Employees:* 510
Company Type: Public Family Member   *Employees here:* 510
SIC: 8062
   General hospital
Valerie Jackson, President

D-U-N-S 14-420-6315
DOCTORS' HOSPITAL INC
8118 Good Luck Rd, Lanham, MD 20706
Phone: (301) 552-8118
Sales: $82,674,000   *Employees:* 850
Company Type: Private   *Employees here:* 830
SIC: 8062
   General hospital
Philip B Down, President

D-U-N-S 07-631-1620
DOMINICAN SANTA CRUZ HOSPITAL
1555 Soquel Dr, Santa Cruz, CA 95065
Phone: (831) 462-7700
Sales: $118,909,000   *Employees:* 1,300
Company Type: Private   *Employees here:* 1,275
SIC: 8062
   General hospital
Sister J Hyer, President

D-U-N-S 05-497-6824
DOMINICAN SISTERS OF ONTARIO
351 SW 9th St, Ontario, OR 97914
Phone: (541) 889-5331
Sales: $31,321,000   *Employees:* 456
Company Type: Private   *Employees here:* 455
SIC: 8062
   Hospital
Bruce C Jensen, President

D-U-N-S 07-477-5578
DOOR COUNTY MEMORIAL HOSPITAL
330 S 16th Pl, Sturgeon Bay, WI 54235
Phone: (920) 743-5566
Sales: $23,216,000   *Employees:* 440
Company Type: Private   *Employees here:* 357
SIC: 8062
   General hospital home health care skilled nursing and
     medical clinics
Gerald Worrick, President

D-U-N-S 06-936-5609
DORCHESTER GENERAL HOSPITAL
300 Byrn St, Cambridge, MD 21613
Phone: (410) 228-5511
Sales: $26,237,000   *Employees:* 420
Company Type: Private   *Employees here:* 400
SIC: 8062
   General hospital
Joseph Ross, President

D-U-N-S 82-490-1482
DOROTHY & DAVID SCHACHNE INSTITUTE
650 Amboy St, Brooklyn, NY 11212
Phone: (718) 240-6932

Sales: $35,000,000   *Employees:* 500
Company Type: Private   *Employees here:* 500
SIC: 8059
   Nursing home
Emalyn Bravo, Administrator

D-U-N-S 13-078-3541
DOUGLAS HOSPITAL INC
8954 Hospital Dr, Douglasville, GA 30134
Phone: (770) 949-1500
Sales: $27,000,000   *Employees:* 300
Company Type: Private   *Employees here:* 300
SIC: 8062
   General hospital
Diane Davis, Administration

D-U-N-S 04-743-7306
DOWNEY COMMUNITY HOSPITAL FOUNDATION
11500 Brookshire Ave, Downey, CA 90241
Phone: (562) 904-5000
Sales: $89,726,000   *Employees:* 1,100
Company Type: Private   *Employees here:* 1,000
SIC: 8062
   General hospital
Allen R Korneff, President

D-U-N-S 04-983-4302
DOWNEY COMMUNITY HEALTH CENTER
8425 Iowa St, Downey, CA 90241
Phone: (562) 862-6506
Sales: $83,705,000   *Employees:* 175
Company Type: Private   *Employees here:* 175
SIC: 8051
   Skilled nursing care facility
Harold Wilkins, Partner

D-U-N-S 07-374-9640
DOYLESTOWN HOSPITAL
595 W State St, Doylestown, PA 18901
Phone: (215) 345-2200
Sales: $88,197,000   *Employees:* 1,321
Company Type: Private   *Employees here:* 985
SIC: 8062
   General medical & surgical hospital skilled nursing &
     independent living facility
Richard A Reif, President

D-U-N-S 60-275-8674
DRAKE CENTER
151 W Galbraith Rd, Cincinnati, OH 45216
Phone: (513) 948-2500
Sales: $46,508,000   *Employees:* 700
Company Type: Private   *Employees here:* 700
SIC: 8093
   Specialty long-term care & rehabilitation hospital
Roberta J Bradford, President

D-U-N-S 06-800-3771
DREYER CLINIC INC.
1870 W Galena Blvd, Aurora, IL 60506
Phone: (630) 859-6700
Sales: $92,714,000   *Employees:* 1,000
Company Type: Private   *Employees here:* 300
SIC: 8011
   Out-patient clinic
Dr Thomas J Stemper Md, Chairman of the Board

D-U-N-S 79-986-2156
DREYER CLINIC INC.
1877 W Downer Pl, Aurora, IL 60506
Phone: (630) 859-6700

Sales: $42,600,000   *Employees:* NA
Company Type: Private   *Employees here:* 700
SIC: 8011
   Out-patient clinic
John Potter, Branch Manager

   D-U-N-S 05-512-8250
DRISCOLL CHILDRENS HOSPITAL
3533 S Alameda St, Corpus Christi, TX 78411
Phone: (512) 694-5000
Sales: $52,800,000   *Employees:* 1,070
Company Type: Private   *Employees here:* 1,030
SIC: 8069
   Children's hospital
Ted Stibbards Phd, President

   D-U-N-S 07-275-6778
DRY HARBOR, SNF INC
6135 Dry Harbor Rd, Middle Village, NY 11379
Phone: (718) 565-4200
Sales: $26,454,000   *Employees:* 225
Company Type: Private   *Employees here:* 225
SIC: 8051
   Skilled nursing facility
Jonathan Strausser, President

   D-U-N-S 12-265-2233
DU BOIS REGIONAL MEDICAL CTR
100 Hospital Ave, Du Bois, PA 15801
Phone: (814) 375-4321
Sales: $70,173,000   *Employees:* 1,040
Company Type: Private   *Employees here:* 475
SIC: 8062
   General hospital
Raymond A Graeca, President

   D-U-N-S 79-668-1179
DU BOIS REGIONAL MEDICAL CTR
Maple Ave, Du Bois, PA 15801
Phone: (814) 375-6130
Sales: $43,900,000   *Employees:* NA
Company Type: Private   *Employees here:* 750
SIC: 8011
   Medical doctor's office
Ray Greaea, Branch Manager

   D-U-N-S 05-345-6919
DU PAGE DIALYSIS, LTD.
   (Parent: Everest Healthcare Svcs Corp)
101 N Scoville Ave, Oak Park, IL 60302
Phone: (708) 386-9053
Sales: $22,900,000   *Employees:* 400
Company Type: Private   *Employees here:* 90
SIC: 8092
   Outpatient dialysis center
Dr Paul Balter Md, President

   D-U-N-S 07-810-8206
DUBLIN COMMUNITY HOSPITAL INC
   (Parent: Columbia/Hca Healthcare Corp)
200 Industrial Blvd, Dublin, GA 31021
Phone: (912) 275-2000
Sales: $105,000,000   *Employees:* 585
Company Type: Public Family Member   *Employees here:* 585
SIC: 8062
   General medical & surgical hospital
James Wood, Administrator

   D-U-N-S 62-644-9060
DUKE UNIVERSITY
Duke Hospital S Rm 1232, Durham, NC 27710
Phone: (919) 684-3411

Sales: $65,000,000   *Employees:* NA
Company Type: Private   *Employees here:* 1,100
SIC: 8011
   Surgical clinic
Paul Newman, Director

   D-U-N-S 07-432-8824
DUKES MEMORIAL HOSPITAL
Grant & Blvd, Peru, IN 46970
Phone: (765) 473-6621
Sales: $20,278,000   *Employees:* 350
Company Type: Private   *Employees here:* 350
SIC: 8062
   General medical and surgical hospital and extended nursing
      care facility
R J Johnston, President

   D-U-N-S 08-247-0576
DUNCAN REGIONAL HOSPITAL INC
1407 N Whisenant Dr, Duncan, OK 73533
Phone: (580) 252-5300
Sales: $31,764,000   *Employees:* 550
Company Type: Private   *Employees here:* 550
SIC: 8062
   Hospital
David Robertson, Administrator

   D-U-N-S 07-204-4910
DUNN MEMORIAL HOSPITAL
1600 23rd St, Bedford, IN 47421
Phone: (812) 275-3331
Sales: $27,263,000   *Employees:* 485
Company Type: Private   *Employees here:* 340
SIC: 8062
   General hospital
Bob Abel, Materials Manager

   D-U-N-S 06-529-9851
DURHAM COUNTY HOSPITAL CORP
3643 N Roxboro Rd, Durham, NC 27704
Phone: (919) 470-4000
Sales: $121,684,000   *Employees:* 2,048
Company Type: Private   *Employees here:* 1,918
SIC: 8062
   General hospital
Richard L Myers, President

   D-U-N-S 14-425-1758
DYNACARE LAB PATHOLOGY LLC
   (Parent: Dynacare Inc)
1229 Madison St Ste 604, Seattle, WA 98104
Phone: (206) 386-2672
Sales: $30,000,000   *Employees:* 352
Company Type: Private   *Employees here:* 350
SIC: 8071
   Medical laboratory
Osama Sherif, President

   D-U-N-S 07-209-4311
DCH HEALTHCARE AUTHORITY (INC)
809 University Blvd E, Tuscaloosa, AL 35401
Phone: (205) 759-7111
Sales: $221,737,000   *Employees:* 3,900
Company Type: Private   *Employees here:* 3,000
SIC: 8062
   General medical hospital
Bryan Kindred, President

   D-U-N-S 15-529-8003
DMC HEALTH CARE CENTERS INC
   (Parent: The Detroit Medical Center)
41935 W 12 Mile Rd, Novi, MI 48377
Phone: (248) 347-8000

Sales: $29,909,000
Company Type: Private
SIC: 8011
Employees: 600
Employees here: 4

Medical centers offering occupational & industrial medical care
David J Campbell, President

D-U-N-S 18-088-4413
DMS IMAGING INC
(Parent: Diagnostic Medical Systems)
2101 N University Dr, Fargo, ND 58102
Phone: (701) 237-9094
Sales: $36,100,000
Company Type: Public Family Member
SIC: 8071
Employees: 158
Employees here: 158

Operates mobile ct scanners
Kevin Moug, Treasurer

D-U-N-S 07-785-4479
E P I CORPORATION
9707 Shelbyville Rd, Louisville, KY 40223
Phone: (502) 426-2242
Sales: $41,000,000
Company Type: Public
SIC: 8052
Employees: 2,200
Employees here: 20

Nursing care facility
John P Snyder, President

D-U-N-S 06-645-9843
EAST ALABAMA HEALTH CARE AUTH
2000 Pepperell Pkwy, Opelika, AL 36801
Phone: (334) 749-3411
Sales: $107,564,000
Company Type: Private
SIC: 8062
Employees: 1,650
Employees here: 1,530

County hospital
Terry Andrus, Administrator

D-U-N-S 19-060-4744
EAST BOSTON NEIGHBORHOOD
10 Gove St, Boston, MA 2128
Phone: (617) 569-5800
Sales: $52,906,000
Company Type: Private
SIC: 8011
Employees: 450
Employees here: 400

Community health care provider
John Cradock, Chief Executive Officer

D-U-N-S 14-793-7213
EAST COOPER COMMUNITY HOSPITAL
(Parent: Tenet Health System Medical)
1200 Johnnie Dodds Blvd, Mount Pleasant, SC 29464
Phone: (843) 881-0100
Sales: $22,500,000
Company Type: Public Family Member
SIC: 8062
Employees: 500
Employees here: 500

General medical hospital & offices & clinics of doctors of medicine
Jack Dusenberry, Administrator

D-U-N-S 06-752-1070
EAST ORANGE GENERAL HOSPITAL
(Parent: Essex Valley Healthcare Inc)
300 Central Ave, East Orange, NJ 7018
Phone: (973) 672-8400
Sales: $65,482,000
Company Type: Private
SIC: 8062
Employees: 950
Employees here: 425

General acute care hospital
Mark J Chastang, President

D-U-N-S 07-499-8238
EAST OH REG HOSPITAL MART FER
90 N 4th St, Martins Ferry, OH 43935
Phone: (740) 633-1100
Sales: $39,482,000
Company Type: Private
SIC: 8062
Employees: 606
Employees here: 606

General hospital
Brian Felici, Administrator

D-U-N-S 13-195-4869
EAST PASCO MEDICAL CENTER INC
7050 Gall Blvd, Zephyrhills, FL 33541
Phone: (813) 788-0411
Sales: $105,776,000
Company Type: Private
SIC: 8062
Employees: 1,010
Employees here: 708

Acute care hospital
Paul Norman, President

D-U-N-S 07-490-9540
EAST TENNESSEE CHLD HOSPITAL ASSN
2018 W Clinch Ave, Knoxville, TN 37916
Phone: (423) 541-8000
Sales: $56,374,000
Company Type: Private
SIC: 8069
Employees: 1,000
Employees here: 900

Children's hospital
Robert Koppel, President

D-U-N-S 62-387-8154
EAST TEXAS MED CENTER-ATHENS
2000 S Palestine St, Athens, TX 75751
Phone: (903) 675-2216
Sales: $42,066,000
Company Type: Private
SIC: 8062
Employees: 353
Employees here: 353

General hospital
Patrick Wallace, Administrator

D-U-N-S 18-313-2794
EAST TEXAS MED CENTER-TYLER
1000 S Beckham Ave, Tyler, TX 75701
Phone: (903) 597-0351
Sales: $226,942,000
Company Type: Private
SIC: 8062
Employees: 1,250
Employees here: 1,225

General medical and surgical hospital and primary care clinics
Elmer Ellis, President

D-U-N-S 13-039-7573
EAST TEXAS MEDICAL CENTER
(Parent: East Tx Med Cntr Regnl Hc Syst)
1000 S Beckham Ave, Tyler, TX 75701
Phone: (903) 531-8979
Sales: $52,899,000
Company Type: Private
SIC: 8071
Employees: 300
Employees here: 3

Diagnostic reference and outpatient lab and physician consulting services
Elmer Ellis, President

D-U-N-S 07-670-7611
EAST TEXAS MED CNTR-JCKSONVILLE
501 S Ragsdale St, Jacksonville, TX 75766
Phone: (903) 586-3000
Sales: $20,489,000
Company Type: Private
SIC: 8062
Employees: 350
Employees here: 345

General medical & surgical hospital
Steve Bowen, President

D-U-N-S 08-949-1146
EASTERN IDAHO REGIONAL MED CTR
(Parent: Columbia/Hca Healthcare Corp)
3100 Channing Way, Idaho Falls, ID 83404
Phone: (208) 529-6111
Sales: $132,314,000   *Employees:* 1,300
Company Type: Public Family Member   *Employees here:* 1,300
SIC: 8062
    General hospital
Ronald G Butler, Chief Executive Officer

D-U-N-S 07-577-6468
EASTERN LONG ISLAND HOSPITAL
201 Manor Pl, Greenport, NY 11944
Phone: (516) 477-1000
Sales: $20,580,000   *Employees:* 252
Company Type: Private   *Employees here:* 250
SIC: 8062
    General psychiatric & alcohol rehabiliation hospital
John M Gwiazda, President

D-U-N-S 10-818-0597
EASTERN MAINE HEALTHCARE
489 State St, Bangor, ME 4401
Phone: (207) 945-7000
Sales: $255,142,000   *Employees:* 153
Company Type: Private   *Employees here:* 115
SIC: 8062
    General medical & surgical hospital & whol medical dental &
       hospital equipment & supplies
Norman Ledwin, President

D-U-N-S 07-173-5682
EASTERN MAINE MEDICAL CENTER
489 State St, Bangor, ME 4401
Phone: (207) 973-7000
Sales: $209,255,000   *Employees:* 2,460
Company Type: Private   *Employees here:* 2,400
SIC: 8062
    General hospital
Norman A Ledwin, President

D-U-N-S 62-085-6435
EASTERN NEW MEXICO MED CTR
405 W Country Club Rd, Roswell, NM 88201
Phone: (505) 622-8170
Sales: $25,700,000   *Employees:* NA
Company Type: Private   *Employees here:* 650
SIC: 8062
    General medical & surgical care hospital
Ron Chafer, Manager

D-U-N-S 07-365-4121
EASTON HOSPITAL
250 S 21st St, Easton, PA 18042
Phone: (610) 250-4000
Sales: $106,545,000   *Employees:* 1,425
Company Type: Private   *Employees here:* 1,412
SIC: 8062
    General hosptial
Donna A Mulholland, President

D-U-N-S 06-047-9433
EBENEZER SOCIAL MINISTRIES
3490 Lexington Ave N, Saint Paul, MN 55126
Phone: (651) 766-4300
Sales: $63,650,000   *Employees:* 4,000
Company Type: Private   *Employees here:* 60
SIC: 8051
    Operates nursing homes & retirement centers
Robert D Armitage, Executive Director

D-U-N-S 08-068-1158
ECKERD YOUTH ALTERNATIVES INC
100 Starcrest Dr Ste 201, Clearwater, FL 33765
Phone: (727) 461-2990
Sales: $48,167,000   *Employees:* 1,200
Company Type: Private   *Employees here:* 60
SIC: 8361
    Residential care for emotionally disturbed & troubled youths
Jack Eckerd, Chairman of the Board

D-U-N-S 07-854-6348
ECTOR COUNTY HOSPITAL DST
500 W 4th St, Odessa, TX 79761
Phone: (915) 640-4000
Sales: $46,433,000   *Employees:* 1,625
Company Type: Private   *Employees here:* 1,500
SIC: 8062
    Emergency surgical hospital
J M Stephans, Administrator

D-U-N-S 78-414-5096
EDEN PARK HEALTH SERVICES,
22 Holland Ave, Albany, NY 12209
Phone: (518) 436-4731
Sales: $48,000,000   *Employees:* 1,500
Company Type: Private   *Employees here:* 1,500
SIC: 8051
    Skilled nursing care facility
Bob Glock, President

D-U-N-S 06-683-0423
EDEN PARK MANAGEMENT INC
22 Holland Ave, Albany, NY 12209
Phone: (518) 436-4731
Sales: $57,300,000   *Employees:* 2,500
Company Type: Private   *Employees here:* 25
SIC: 8051
    Nursing homes
Alton P Mendleson, President

D-U-N-S 07-653-8214
EDEN TOWNSHIP HOSPITAL DST
20103 Lake Chabot Rd, Castro Valley, CA 94546
Phone: (510) 537-1234
Sales: $87,711,000   *Employees:* 968
Company Type: Private   *Employees here:* 968
SIC: 8062
    General hospitals
George Bischalaney, President

D-U-N-S 06-946-3438
EDINBURG REGIONAL MEDICAL CTR
1102 W Trenton Rd, Edinburg, TX 78539
Phone: (956) 388-6607
Sales: $92,000,000   *Employees:* 513
Company Type: Private   *Employees here:* 513
SIC: 8062
    General medical & surgical hospital
Leon Belila, Managing Director

D-U-N-S 06-847-8155
EDWARD HOSPITAL
801 S Washington St, Naperville, IL 60540
Phone: (708) 355-0450
Sales: $119,181,000   *Employees:* 1,300
Company Type: Private   *Employees here:* 1,290
SIC: 8062
    General hospital
Pamela Meyer-Davis, President

D-U-N-S 04-180-7777
EDWARD W SPARROW HOSPITAL ASSN
1215 E Michigan Ave, Lansing, MI 48912

Phone: (517) 483-2700
Sales: $258,316,000   *Employees:* 3,000
Company Type: Private   *Employees here:* 3,000
SIC: 8062
    General medical hospital
Joseph F Damore, President

D-U-N-S 12-450-2873
EDWARDS & HENSON, DDS
4990 Hwy 70 W, Kinston, NC 28504
Phone: (252) 527-6121
Sales: $21,000,000   *Employees:* 500
Company Type: Private   *Employees here:* 12
SIC: 8021
    Dental clinic
Dr George L Edwards, President

D-U-N-S 07-674-6890
EDWIN SHAW HOSPITAL
1621 Flickinger Rd, Akron, OH 44312
Phone: (330) 784-1271
Sales: $24,100,000   *Employees:* 492
Company Type: Private   *Employees here:* 492
SIC: 8069
    Physical medicine & rehab hospital and extended care
    services for addictive diseases
Daniel K Church, President

D-U-N-S 06-608-0615
EGER HEALTH CARE CENTER
140 Meisner Ave, Staten Island, NY 10306
Phone: (718) 979-1800
Sales: $30,740,000   *Employees:* 655
Company Type: Private   *Employees here:* 655
SIC: 8051
    Skilled nursing care facility
Adeline M Conroy, President

D-U-N-S 06-344-7312
EGH, INC.
(Parent: New American Healthcare Corp)
2900 SE Steele St, Portland, OR 97202
Phone: (503) 234-0411
Sales: $30,000,000   *Employees:* 283
Company Type: Public Family Member   *Employees here:* 283
SIC: 8062
    Hospital
Kay Vetaly, Acting Admin

D-U-N-S 07-347-2136
EGLESTON CHILDREN'S HOSPITAL
1405 Clifton Rd NE, Atlanta, GA 30322
Phone: (404) 325-6000
Sales: $220,000,000   *Employees:* 2,000
Company Type: Private   *Employees here:* 1,650
SIC: 8069
    Children's hospital
Alan J Gayer, President

D-U-N-S 07-814-0845
EISENHOWER MEDICAL CENTER
39000 Bob Hope Dr, Rancho Mirage, CA 92270
Phone: (760) 340-3911
Sales: $140,896,000   *Employees:* 1,800
Company Type: Private   *Employees here:* 1,700
SIC: 8062
    Hospital
Andrew W Deems, President

D-U-N-S 60-895-7254
EL CENTRO COMMUNITY HOSPITAL
1415 Ross Ave, El Centro, CA 92243
Phone: (760) 339-7157

Sales: $49,400,000   *Employees:* 630
Company Type: Private   *Employees here:* 500
SIC: 8062
    General hospital
Theodore Fox, Chief Executive Officer

D-U-N-S 19-491-8876
EL PASO HEALTHCARE SYSTEMS,
4045 N Mesa St, El Paso, TX 79902
Phone: (915) 545-6200
Sales: $140,700,000   *Employees:* 3,000
Company Type: Private   *Employees here:* 40
SIC: 8062
    General medical & surgical hospitals
Doug Matney, Chief Executive Officer

D-U-N-S 60-963-0884
EL PASO HEALTHCARE SYSTEMS,
1801 N Oregon St, El Paso, TX 79902
Phone: (915) 532-6281
Sales: $53,700,000   *Employees:* NA
Company Type: Private   *Employees here:* 1,300
SIC: 8062
    Hospital
Hank Hernandez, Branch Manager

D-U-N-S 62-267-1329
EL PASO HEALTHCARE SYSTEMS,
10301 Gateway Blvd W, El Paso, TX 79925
Phone: (915) 595-9000
Sales: $49,500,000   *Employees:* NA
Company Type: Private   *Employees here:* 1,200
SIC: 8062
    General hospital
Chris Siebenaler, Controller

D-U-N-S 01-461-5707
ELDER HEALTHCARE DEVELOPERS LLC
1770 Indial Trl Ste 400, Norcross, GA 30093
Phone: (770) 935-5841
Sales: $20,000,000   *Employees:* 1
Company Type: Private   *Employees here:* 1
SIC: 8052
    Assisted care facilities
George Schoepf, Member

D-U-N-S 08-269-4845
ELIAS F GHANEM LTD
2061 E Sahara Ave, Las Vegas, NV 89104
Phone: (702) 731-6060
Sales: $20,500,000   *Employees:* 300
Company Type: Private   *Employees here:* 150
SIC: 8011
    Medical center operations
Elias F Ghanem, President

D-U-N-S 80-513-4608
ELIM CARE, INC
7540 Market Place Dr, Eden Prairie, MN 55344
Phone: (612) 944-1164
Sales: $26,607,000   *Employees:* 15
Company Type: Private   *Employees here:* 1
SIC: 8051
    Holding company
Robert Dahl, President

D-U-N-S 05-671-4348
ELIZABETH GENERAL MEDICAL CTR
925 E Jersey St, Elizabeth, NJ 7201
Phone: (908) 289-8600

Sales: $108,635,000   *Employees:* 2,000
Company Type: Private   *Employees here:* 1,400
SIC: 8062
  General hospital
David A Fletcher, President

D-U-N-S 06-975-5411
ELKHART CLINIC LLC
303 S Nappanee St, Elkhart, IN 46514
Phone: (219) 296-3200
Sales: $20,000,000   *Employees:* 170
Company Type: Private   *Employees here:* 170
SIC: 8011
  Medical clinic
Gary Larson, Administrator

D-U-N-S 06-470-5015
ELKHART GENERAL HOSPITAL
600 East Blvd, Elkhart, IN 46514
Phone: (219) 294-2621
Sales: $109,372,000   *Employees:* 1,395
Company Type: Private   *Employees here:* 1,300
SIC: 8062
  General medical hospital
Gregory W Lintjer, President

D-U-N-S 07-399-1085
ELLIOT HOSPITAL
1 Elliot Way, Manchester, NH 3103
Phone: (603) 669-5300
Sales: $116,397,000   *Employees:* 1,517
Company Type: Private   *Employees here:* 1,514
SIC: 8062
  General medical & surgical hospital
Peter Davis, Chief Executive Officer

D-U-N-S 06-682-2784
ELLIS HOSPITAL
1101 Nott St, Schenectady, NY 12308
Phone: (518) 382-4124
Sales: $72,600,000   *Employees:* 1,560
Company Type: Private   *Employees here:* 1,535
SIC: 8062
  General hospital
G B Serrill, President

D-U-N-S 02-014-5637
ELLIS, BANDT, BIRKIN, KOLLINS
2020 Palomino Ln 100, Las Vegas, NV 89106
Phone: (702) 384-5210
Sales: $25,020,000   *Employees:* 200
Company Type: Private   *Employees here:* 116
SIC: 8011
  Radiologist
Dr Paul D Bandt Md, President

D-U-N-S 06-874-3772
ELLWOOD CITY HOSPITAL
724 Pershing St, Ellwood City, PA 16117
Phone: (724) 752-0081
Sales: $22,204,000   *Employees:* 368
Company Type: Private   *Employees here:* 340
SIC: 8062
  General hospital
Herbert Skuba, President

D-U-N-S 07-615-3501
ELMBROOK MEMORIAL HOSPITAL INC
19333 W North Ave, Brookfield, WI 53045
Phone: (414) 785-2000

Sales: $54,739,000   *Employees:* 800
Company Type: Private   *Employees here:* 800
SIC: 8062
  General hospital
Kimry Johnsrud, President

D-U-N-S 05-192-1161
ELMHURST MEMORIAL HOSPITAL
200 Berteau Ave, Elmhurst, IL 60126
Phone: (630) 833-1400
Sales: $168,896,000   *Employees:* 2,579
Company Type: Private   *Employees here:* 2,429
SIC: 8062
  General hospital
Leo F Fronza Jr, Chief Executive Officer

D-U-N-S 07-465-3270
EMANUEL MEDICAL CENTER INC
825 Delbon Ave, Turlock, CA 95382
Phone: (209) 667-4200
Sales: $57,933,000   *Employees:* 985
Company Type: Private   *Employees here:* 795
SIC: 8062
  General hospital
Robert Moen, President

D-U-N-S 06-935-6467
EMERSON HOSPITAL INC
133 Ornac, Concord, MA 1742
Phone: (978) 369-1400
Sales: $68,946,000   *Employees:* 1,300
Company Type: Private   *Employees here:* 1,200
SIC: 8062
  General hospital
Geoffrey F Cole, President

D-U-N-S 05-416-2839
EMMA L BIXBY MEDICAL CENTER
818 Riverside Ave, Adrian, MI 49221
Phone: (517) 263-0711
Sales: $40,902,000   *Employees:* 750
Company Type: Private   *Employees here:* 710
SIC: 8062
  General hospital
John Robertstad, President

D-U-N-S 03-948-4670
EMORY UNIVERSITY
550 Peachtree St NE, Atlanta, GA 30308
Phone: (404) 686-4411
Sales: $58,400,000   *Employees:* NA
Company Type: Private   *Employees here:* 1,324
SIC: 8062
  General hospital
John D Henry, N/A

D-U-N-S 79-820-5191
EMORY UNIVERSITY
1364 Clifton Rd NE, Atlanta, GA 30322
Phone: (404) 727-4881
Sales: $88,500,000   *Employees:* NA
Company Type: Private   *Employees here:* 2,000
SIC: 8062
  Hospital
Donald E Wells, Executive Director

D-U-N-S 87-477-4771
EMORY UNIVERSITY
1365 Clifton Rd NE 6400, Atlanta, GA 30322
Phone: (404) 321-0111

Sales: $68,400,000
Company Type: Private
SIC: 8011
  Medical doctor's office
Dr Rean Farrell, Director

Employees: NA
Employees here: 1,161

D-U-N-S 61-706-4910
EMPLOYEES RETIREMENT SYS ST LOUIS
1300 Convention Plz, Saint Louis, MO 63103
Phone: (314) 622-3560
Sales: $49,015,000
Company Type: Private
SIC: 8051
  Government retirement system
William C Duffe, President

Employees: 15
Employees here: 15

D-U-N-S 00-949-6758
EMSI HOLDING COMPANY
1111 W Mockingbird Ln, Dallas, TX 75247
Phone: (214) 689-3600
Sales: $104,607,000
Company Type: Private
SIC: 8099
  Holding company
John M Utley, President

Employees: 4,001
Employees here: 1

D-U-N-S 14-705-5750
ENGLEWOOD COMMUNITY HOSPITAL
  (Parent: Basic American Medical Inc)
700 Medical Blvd, Englewood, FL 34223
Phone: (941) 475-6571
Sales: $35,093,000
Company Type: Public Family Member
SIC: 8062
  General medical & surgical hospital
Terry Moore, President

Employees: 550
Employees here: 350

D-U-N-S 05-628-9481
ENGLEWOOD HOSPITAL & MED CTR
350 Engle St, Englewood, NJ 7631
Phone: (201) 894-3000
Sales: $154,994,000
Company Type: Private
SIC: 8062
  General hospital and medical clinic
Daniel A Kane, President

Employees: 2,200
Employees here: 2,170

D-U-N-S 06-594-5420
ENZO CLINICAL LABS INC
  (Parent: Enzo Biochem Inc)
60 Executive Blvd, Farmingdale, NY 11735
Phone: (516) 755-5500
Sales: $21,749,000
Company Type: Public Family Member
SIC: 8071
  Clinical medical laboratory
Elazar Rabbani Phd, Chairman

Employees: 200
Employees here: 165

D-U-N-S 07-786-0526
EPHRAIM MCDOWELL RGNAL MED CTR
217 S 3rd St, Danville, KY 40422
Phone: (606) 236-4121
Sales: $57,217,000
Company Type: Private
SIC: 8062
  General medical and surgical hospital
Thomas W Smith, President

Employees: 800
Employees here: 700

D-U-N-S 07-285-6651
EPHRATA COMMUNITY HOSPITAL
169 Martin Ave, Ephrata, PA 17522
Phone: (717) 733-0311

Sales: $47,774,000
Company Type: Private
SIC: 8062
  General hospital
John Porter, President

Employees: 755
Employees here: 755

D-U-N-S 07-815-9456
EPISCOPAL HEALTH SERVICES INC
333 Earle Ovington Blvd, Uniondale, NY 11553
Phone: (516) 228-6100
Sales: $164,300,000
Company Type: Private
SIC: 8062
  General hospitals
Jack N Farrington Phd, Chief Executive Officer

Employees: 3,500
Employees here: 300

D-U-N-S 07-578-7036
EPISCOPAL HEALTH SERVICES INC
50 Route 25a, Smithtown, NY 11787
Phone: (516) 862-3000
Sales: $59,500,000
Company Type: Private
SIC: 8062
  General hospital eating place
Lora Righter, Principal

Employees: NA
Employees here: 1,200

D-U-N-S 07-622-3015
EPISCOPAL HEALTH SERVICES INC
327 Beach 19th St, Far Rockaway, NY 11691
Phone: (718) 868-7000
Sales: $67,200,000
Company Type: Private
SIC: 8062
  General hospital
Paul Connor, N/A

Employees: NA
Employees here: 1,354

D-U-N-S 09-648-4514
EPISCOPAL HEALTH SERVICES INC
1711 Brookhaven Ave, Far Rockaway, NY 11691
Phone: (718) 869-8000
Sales: $20,800,000
Company Type: Private
SIC: 8051
  Skilled nursing care facility
Roberta D Diego, Principal

Employees: NA
Employees here: 850

D-U-N-S 07-374-1282
EPISCOPAL HOSPITAL
100 E Lehigh Ave, Philadelphia, PA 19125
Phone: (215) 427-7000
Sales: $160,527,000
Company Type: Private
SIC: 8062
  General hospital
Mark Bateman, President

Employees: 1,400
Employees here: 1,200

D-U-N-S 07-286-6585
EPISCOPAL RETIREMENT HOMES
3870 Virginia Ave, Cincinnati, OH 45227
Phone: (513) 271-9610
Sales: $34,244,000
Company Type: Private
SIC: 8361
  Homes for the aged with health care & home health care
R D Spitler, President

Employees: 1,100
Employees here: 30

D-U-N-S 80-386-4164
EQUIMED, INC.
2171 Sandy Dr, State College, PA 16803
Phone: (814) 238-0375

Sales: $99,115,000   *Employees:* 500
Company Type: Public   *Employees here:* 40
SIC: 8099
  Ophthalmology management service
Douglas R Colkitt, Chairman of the Board

D-U-N-S 87-919-6178
ERIE COUNTY MEDICAL CENTER
462 Grider St, Buffalo, NY 14215
Phone: (716) 898-3000
Sales: $172,400,000   *Employees:* 2,500
Company Type: Private   *Employees here:* 2,500
SIC: 8011
  Medical doctor's office
Paul Candino, Chief Executive Officer

D-U-N-S 11-550-1330
ERIE, NEW YORK, COUNTY OF
462 Grider St, Buffalo, NY 14215
Phone: (716) 898-3000
Sales: $109,500,000   *Employees:* NA
Company Type: Private   *Employees here:* 2,200
SIC: 8062
  General hospital
Paul Candino, President

D-U-N-S 07-490-9094
ERLANGER HEALTH SYSTEM
975 E 3rd St, Chattanooga, TN 37403
Phone: (423) 778-7000
Sales: $304,203,000   *Employees:* 2,700
Company Type: Private   *Employees here:* 2,300
SIC: 8062
  Hospital
Sylvester Reeder Iii, Chief Executive Officer

D-U-N-S 19-999-1043
ERLANGER HEALTH SYSTEM
910 Blackford St, Chattanooga, TN 37403
Phone: (423) 778-2141
Sales: $27,000,000   *Employees:* NA
Company Type: Private   *Employees here:* 600
SIC: 8069
  Specialty hospital
Susan Burkhart, Owner

D-U-N-S 62-150-6310 .
ESKATON PROPERTIES INC
5105 Manzanita Ave, Carmichael, CA 95608
Phone: (916) 334-0810
Sales: $43,441,000   *Employees:* 900
Company Type: Private   *Employees here:* 218
SIC: 8051
  Nursing home operator & home health agency
John H Breaux, President

D-U-N-S 94-528-3406
ESPLANADE GARDENS INC
5333 Everhart Rd Ste 200a, Corpus Christi, TX 78411
Phone: (512) 991-9600
Sales: $25,000,000   *Employees:* 10
Company Type: Private   *Employees here:* 10
SIC: 8361
  Residential care developer
G P Mccreless, President

D-U-N-S 07-508-2131
EUNICE REGIONAL MEDICAL CENTER
400 Moosa Blvd, Eunice, LA 70535
Phone: (318) 457-5244

Sales: $20,851,000   *Employees:* 250
Company Type: Private   *Employees here:* 200
SIC: 8062
  General medical & surgical hospital
Craig Ortego, Administrator

D-U-N-S 07-144-5985
EVANGELICAL COMMUNITY HOSP
1 Hospital Dr, Lewisburg, PA 17837
Phone: (717) 522-2000
Sales: $42,337,000   *Employees:* 760
Company Type: Private   *Employees here:* 750
SIC: 8062
  General hospital
Michael Daniloff, President

D-U-N-S 06-983-8530
EVANGELICAL HOMES OF MICHIGAN
18000 Coyle St, Detroit, MI 48235
Phone: (313) 836-5306
Sales: $27,991,000   *Employees:* 670
Company Type: Private   *Employees here:* 110
SIC: 8051
  Skilled nursing homes & homes for the aged
Rev Lowell R Schrupp, Executive

D-U-N-S 06-866-7906
EVANGELICAL LUTHERAN GOOD SAMARITAN
4800 W 57th St, Sioux Falls, SD 57106
Phone: (605) 362-3100
Sales: $649,656,000   *Employees:* 24,000
Company Type: Private   *Employees here:* 225
SIC: 8051
  Rest home with health care
Judith Ryan, President

D-U-N-S 08-294-3721
EVANSTON NORTHWESTERN
2100 Pfingsten Rd, Glenview, IL 60025
Phone: (847) 657-5800
Sales: $84,800,000   *Employees:* NA
Company Type: Private   *Employees here:* 2,000
SIC: 8062
  General hospital
Mark A Neaman, Director

D-U-N-S 06-949-0621
EVANSTON NORTHWESTERN
1301 Central St, Evanston, IL 60201
Phone: (847) 570-2000
Sales: $387,828,000   *Employees:* 4,500
Company Type: Private   *Employees here:* 100
SIC: 8062
  General hospital
Mark A Neaman, President

D-U-N-S 87-439-9603
EVANSTON NORTHWESTERN
2650 Ridge Ave, Evanston, IL 60201
Phone: (847) 570-2000
Sales: $84,800,000   *Employees:* NA
Company Type: Private   *Employees here:* 2,000
SIC: 8062
  General hospital
Mark A Neaman, Manager

D-U-N-S 94-977-1943
EVEREST HEALTHCARE SVCS CORP
101 N Scoville Ave, Oak Park, IL 60302
Phone: (708) 848-2602

Sales: $140,000,000
Company Type: Private
SIC: 8092
  Dialysis center
Dr Arthur Morris Md, President

Employees: 1,500
Employees here: 300

D-U-N-S 80-735-0053
EVERETT HOUSE
68 Fargo St, Boston, MA 2210
Phone: (617) 783-7070
Sales: $21,065,000
Company Type: Private
SIC: 8361
  Residential care services
James Traglia, Executive Director

Employees: NA
Employees here: NA

D-U-N-S 00-989-0922
EVERGREEN HEALTHCARE MGT LLC
4601 NE 77th Ave Ste 120, Vancouver, WA 98662
Phone: (360) 892-6628
Sales: $42,496,000
Company Type: Private
SIC: 8051
  Skilled nursing care management company
Andrew Martini, Chief Executive Officer

Employees: 56
Employees here: 56

D-U-N-S 15-111-1598
EVERGREEN HEALTHCARE, INC
  (Parent: Grancare Inc)
1 Ravinia Dr Ste 1500, Atlanta, GA 30346
Phone: (770) 393-0199
Sales: $101,000,000
Company Type: Public Family Member
SIC: 8052
  Operates manages & provides accounting services to nursing
    care facilities & operates an institutional pharmacy
M S Athans, President

Employees: 5,412
Employees here: 175

D-U-N-S 07-933-5493
EXAMINATION MANAGEMENT SVCS
  (Parent: Examination Mgt Svcs Inc Amer)
1111 W Mockingbird Ln, Dallas, TX 75247
Phone: (214) 689-3600
Sales: $101,971,000
Company Type: Private
SIC: 8099
  Physical examination service for insurance industry
John M Utley, President

Employees: 4,000
Employees here: 400

D-U-N-S 18-275-9829
EXAMINATION MGT SVCS INC AMER
  (Parent: Emsi Holding Company)
1111 W Mockingbird Ln, Dallas, TX 75247
Phone: (214) 638-3629
Sales: $374,000,000
Company Type: Private
SIC: 8099
  Physical examinations & inspection service for insurance
    industry
John M Utley, President

Employees: 9,350
Employees here: 410

D-U-N-S 87-768-5578
EXCELCARE SYSTEM INC
40 Palmer Ave Ste 2, Bronxville, NY 10708
Phone: (914) 337-6700
Sales: $40,000,000
Company Type: Private
SIC: 8099
  Health/allied services non-profit organization
Donald S Broas, President

Employees: 4
Employees here: 4

D-U-N-S 06-497-6525
EXECUTIVE HEALTH GROUP, MD PC
10 Rockefeller Plz Fl 4, New York, NY 10020
Phone: (212) 332-3700
Sales: $27,400,000
Company Type: Private
SIC: 8011
  Medical services
William F Flatley, President

Employees: 400
Employees here: 200

D-U-N-S 10-408-8364
EXECUTIVE OFFICE OF THE GOVERNMENT
4007 Diamond Ruby, Christiansted, VI 820
Phone: (809) 778-6311
Sales: $31,100,000
Company Type: Private
SIC: 8062
  General hospital
George Mccoy, Executive Director

Employees: NA
Employees here: 800

D-U-N-S 07-397-8389
EXETER HOSPITAL INC
10 Buzell Ave, Exeter, NH 3833
Phone: (603) 778-7311
Sales: $58,908,000
Company Type: Private
SIC: 8062
  General hospital
Kevin Callahan, President

Employees: 700
Employees here: 700

D-U-N-S 07-616-4227
EXTENDICARE FACILITIES INC
  (Parent: Extendcare Hlth Fclty Holdings)
105 W Michigan St, Milwaukee, WI 53203
Phone: (414) 271-9696
Sales: $230,651,000
Company Type: Private
SIC: 8051
  Skilled care nursing facilities
J W Carter, President

Employees: 4,591
Employees here: 10

D-U-N-S 11-753-1814
EXTENDICARE HEALTH SERVICES
  (Parent: Extendicare (canada) Inc)
105 W Michigan St Fl 8, Milwaukee, WI 53203
Phone: (414) 271-9696
Sales: $916,161,000
Company Type: Private
SIC: 8051
  Skilled care nursing facilities
Guy W Smith, President

Employees: 17,388
Employees here: 416

D-U-N-S 10-221-4558
EXTENDICARE HOMES, INC
  (Parent: Extendcare Hlth Fclty Holdings)
105 W Michigan St, Milwaukee, WI 53203
Phone: (414) 271-9696
Sales: $430,619,000
Company Type: Private
SIC: 8051
  Skilled care nursing facilities
J W Carter, President

Employees: 11,283
Employees here: 11

D-U-N-S 17-834-0790
EYEXAM 2000 OF CALIFORNIA, INC
  (Parent: United States Shoe Corporation)
1440 Chapin Ave Ste 330, Burlingame, CA 94010
Phone: (513) 583-6011
Sales: $22,500,000
Company Type: Private
SIC: 8042
  Optometrists offices
Michael Glisson, President

Employees: 450
Employees here: 14

D-U-N-S 80-728-5796
F O H P INC
3501 Rte 66, Neptune, NJ 7753
Phone: (732) 918-6700
Sales: $377,406,000   *Employees:* 350
Company Type: Private   *Employees here:* 5
SIC: 8011
   Hmo & managed health care organization
Thomas W Wilfong, President

D-U-N-S 96-153-6752
F W OF SARATOGA, INC
30 Crescent Ave, Saratoga Springs, NY 12866
Phone: (518) 584-3600
Sales: $20,085,000   *Employees:* 300
Company Type: Private   *Employees here:* 300
SIC: 8063
   Psychiatric hospital
Dr Samuel C Klagsbrun Md, Chief Executive Officer

D-U-N-S 07-880-2840
FACEY MEDICAL FOUNDATION INC
11165 Sepulveda Blvd, Mission Hills, CA 91345
Phone: (818) 365-9531
Sales: $59,133,000   *Employees:* 500
Company Type: Private   *Employees here:* 250
SIC: 8099
   Medical services organization
Dr H S Aharonian Md, President

D-U-N-S 17-202-1800
FACEY MEDICAL GROUP, PC
11165 Sepulveda Blvd, Mission Hills, CA 91345
Phone: (818) 365-9531
Sales: $36,000,000   *Employees:* 525
Company Type: Private   *Employees here:* 120
SIC: 8011
   Medical doctor's organization
Dr Frederick Russo Md, President

D-U-N-S 07-552-2888
FAIR ACRES CENTER
340 N Middletown Rd, Media, PA 19063
Phone: (610) 891-5600
Sales: $45,541,000   *Employees:* 1,100
Company Type: Private   *Employees here:* 1,100
SIC: 8361
   Nursing home with health care
Rusty Lipschutz, Acting Admin

D-U-N-S 12-364-7182
FAIR ACRES GERIATRIC CENTER
340 N Middletown Rd, Media, PA 19063
Phone: (610) 891-5700
Sales: $47,684,000   *Employees:* 1,000
Company Type: Private   *Employees here:* 998
SIC: 8059
   Nursing/personal care
Joseph T Dougherty, Administrator

D-U-N-S 07-942-8397
FAIRFIELD MEDICAL CENTER
401 N Ewing St, Lancaster, OH 43130
Phone: (740) 687-8000
Sales: $95,732,000   *Employees:* 1,300
Company Type: Private   *Employees here:* 1,287
SIC: 8062
   General hospital
Creighton E Likes Jr, Chief Executive Officer

D-U-N-S 07-216-3272
FAIRMONT GENERAL HOSPITAL INC
1325 Locust Ave, Fairmont, WV 26554

Phone: (304) 367-7100
Sales: $54,050,000   *Employees:* 850
Company Type: Private   *Employees here:* 820
SIC: 8062
   Acute care hospital
Richard W Graham, President

D-U-N-S 87-724-4210
FAIRVIEW CLINICS
2450 Riverside Ave, Minneapolis, MN 55454
Phone: (612) 672-2217
Sales: $26,000,000   *Employees:* 380
Company Type: Private   *Employees here:* 1
SIC: 8011
   Medical clinics
Gordon L Alexander Jr, Chairman of the Board

D-U-N-S 61-763-2567
FAIRVIEW EXTENDED CARE SVCS
725 North St, Pittsfield, MA 1201
Phone: (413) 447-2996
Sales: $45,237,000   *Employees:* 900
Company Type: Private   *Employees here:* 30
SIC: 8051
   Skilled nursing care facilities
David E Phelps, President

D-U-N-S 11-287-6016
FAIRVIEW HM CARE & HOSPICE INC
2450 26th Ave S, Minneapolis, MN 55406
Phone: (612) 721-2491
Sales: $26,168,000   *Employees:* 700
Company Type: Private   *Employees here:* 700
SIC: 8082
   Home health care agency
Kathy Lucas, Executive Director

D-U-N-S 00-832-4456
FAIRVIEW HOSPITAL HEALTHCARE SVCS
5200 Fairview Blvd, Wyoming, MN 55092
Phone: (651) 982-7000
Sales: $25,900,000   *Employees:* NA
Company Type: Private   *Employees here:* 680
SIC: 8062
   Hospital clinic skilled nursing
Dan Anderson, Chief Operating Officer

D-U-N-S 06-819-9611
FAIRVIEW HOSPITAL HEALTHCARE SVCS
2450 Riverside Ave, Minneapolis, MN 55454
Phone: (612) 672-6300
Sales: $96,970,000   *Employees:* 13,611
Company Type: Private   *Employees here:* 6,200
SIC: 8062
   Integrated health system
William K Maxwell, Chief Executive Officer

D-U-N-S 62-308-6824
FAIRVIEW HOSPITAL HEALTHCARE SVCS
201 E Nicollet Blvd, Burnsville, MN 55337
Phone: (612) 892-2000
Sales: $33,000,000   *Employees:* NA
Company Type: Private   *Employees here:* 800
SIC: 8062
   General hospital
Mark Enger, Administrator

D-U-N-S 07-676-2988
FAIRVIEW HOSPITAL
18101 Lorain Ave, Cleveland, OH 44111
Phone: (216) 476-7000

Sales: $151,744,000   *Employees:* 2,364
Company Type: Private   *Employees here:* 2,300
SIC: 8062
    General hospital
Thomas La Motte, President

D-U-N-S 07-149-5303
FAIRVIEW REDWING HEALTH SVCS
1407 W 4th St, Red Wing, MN 55066
Phone: (651) 388-6721
Sales: $22,846,000   *Employees:* 400
Company Type: Private   *Employees here:* 392
SIC: 8062
    General medical/surgical hospital
Scott Wordelman, Chief Executive Officer

D-U-N-S 07-697-4369
FAITH REGIONAL HEALTH SERVICES
1500 Koenigstein Ave, Norfolk, NE 68701
Phone: (402) 371-3402
Sales: $45,699,000   *Employees:* 1,050
Company Type: Private   *Employees here:* 350
SIC: 8062
    Hospital
Bob Driewer, Chief Executive Officer

D-U-N-S 03-081-5492
FALLON CLINIC INC
630 Plantation St, Worcester, MA 1605
Phone: (508) 852-0600
Sales: $113,300,000   *Employees:* NA
Company Type: Private   *Employees here:* NA
SIC: 8011
    Medical clinic
Dr Joseph Podbielski Md, President

D-U-N-S 07-827-8769
FALLSTON GENERAL HOSPITAL INC
200 Milton Ave, Fallston, MD 21047
Phone: (410) 877-3700
Sales: $48,442,000   *Employees:* 775
Company Type: Private   *Employees here:* 775
SIC: 8062
    General hospital
Lyle E Sheldon, President

D-U-N-S 07-380-0302
FALMOUTH HOSPITAL ASSOCIATION
100 Ter Heun Dr, Falmouth, MA 2540
Phone: (508) 548-5300
Sales: $48,600,000   *Employees:* 710
Company Type: Private   *Employees here:* 700
SIC: 8062
    General hospital
Gail M Frieswick, President

D-U-N-S 19-230-2503
FAMILIESFIRST INC
2100 5th St, Davis, CA 95616
Phone: (530) 753-0220
Sales: $27,192,000   *Employees:* 450
Company Type: Private   *Employees here:* 154
SIC: 8361
    Non-profit counseling center for emotionally disturbed
    children
Evelyn Praul, President

D-U-N-S 06-801-2954
FAMILY AIDES INC
120 W John St, Hicksville, NY 11801
Phone: (516) 681-2300

Sales: $47,800,000   *Employees:* 3,000
Company Type: Private   *Employees here:* 600
SIC: 8082
    Licensed home health care agency
William C Schnell, President

D-U-N-S 11-928-8934
FAMILY DENTAL
30100 Chagrin Blvd Ste 1, Cleveland, OH 44124
Phone: (216) 464-4042
Sales: $36,244,000   *Employees:* 600
Company Type: Private   *Employees here:* 30
SIC: 8021
    Dental centers
Dr Ed H Meckler Dds, President

D-U-N-S 07-855-2593
FAMILY HEALTHCARE ASSOCIATES
1300 S Fielder Rd, Arlington, TX 76013
Phone: (817) 277-2221
Sales: $30,900,000   *Employees:* 450
Company Type: Private   *Employees here:* 106
SIC: 8011
    Medical doctor's office
Dr Jim Anagnostis Md, President

D-U-N-S 06-891-0140
FAMILY PLANNING ASSOC MED GROUP
3050 E Airport Way, Long Beach, CA 90806
Phone: (562) 426-9661
Sales: $27,400,000   *Employees:* 400
Company Type: Private   *Employees here:* 52
SIC: 8011
    Medical clinics
Dr Edward C Allred Md, President

D-U-N-S 07-427-2196
FARMERS UNION HOSPITAL ASSN
1705 W 2nd St, Elk City, OK 73644
Phone: (580) 225-2511
Sales: $22,318,000   *Employees:* 295
Company Type: Private   *Employees here:* 290
SIC: 8062
    Hospital
Tim Frances, Administrator

D-U-N-S 07-313-6806
FATHER FLANAGAN'S BOY'S HOME
14100 Crawford St, Boys Town, NE 68010
Phone: (402) 498-1111
Sales: $98,725,000   *Employees:* 1,729
Company Type: Private   *Employees here:* 1,000
SIC: 8361
    Boys town
Fr V Peter, Treasurer

D-U-N-S 07-656-9144
FAULKNER HOSPITAL INC
1153 Centre St, Boston, MA 2130
Phone: (617) 522-5800
Sales: $66,191,000   *Employees:* 1,100
Company Type: Private   *Employees here:* 1,040
SIC: 8062
    Acute hospital
David J Trull, President

D-U-N-S 06-940-0745
FAUQUIER HOSPITAL INC
500 Hospital Dr, Warrenton, VA 20186
Phone: (540) 347-2550

Sales: $39,707,000   *Employees:* 700
Company Type: Private   *Employees here:* 700
SIC: 8062
   General hospital
Rodger H Baker, President

D-U-N-S 01-052-0385
FAWCETT MEMORIAL HOSPITAL INC
   (Parent: Columbia/Hca Healthcare Corp)
21298 Olean Blvd, Port Charlotte, FL 33952
Phone: (941) 629-1181
Sales: $74,834,000   *Employees:* 1,200
Company Type: Public Family Member   *Employees here:* 900
SIC: 8062
   Hospital
Dawn Rinehart, Chief Operating Officer

D-U-N-S 05-586-3963
FAXTON HOSPITAL
1676 Sunset Ave, Utica, NY 13502
Phone: (315) 738-6200
Sales: $45,734,000   *Employees:* 950
Company Type: Private   *Employees here:* 950
SIC: 8062
   General hospital
Andrew Peterson, President

D-U-N-S 36-441-5018
FAY-WEST HEALTH SYSTEM
508 S Church St, Mount Pleasant, PA 15666
Phone: (724) 547-1500
Sales: $43,380,000   *Employees:* 2
Company Type: Private   *Employees here:* 2
SIC: 8062
   Hospital management & medical services
Rodney Gunderson, Executive Director

D-U-N-S 04-066-2405
FAYETTE CNTY HOSPITAL NURSING HM
1653 Temple Ave N, Fayette, AL 35555
Phone: (205) 932-5966
Sales: $20,251,000   *Employees:* 420
Company Type: Private   *Employees here:* 418
SIC: 8062
   Hospital & skilled nursing home
Harold Reed, Chief Executive Officer

D-U-N-S 07-205-0826
FAYETTE MEMORIAL HOSPITAL
1941 Virginia Ave, Connersville, IN 47331
Phone: (765) 825-5131
Sales: $35,241,000   *Employees:* 664
Company Type: Private   *Employees here:* 564
SIC: 8062
   General hospital
David Brandon, Executive Director

D-U-N-S 02-888-3486
FEATHER RIVER HOSPITAL
5974 Pentz Rd, Paradise, CA 95969
Phone: (530) 877-9361
Sales: $34,876,000   *Employees:* 683
Company Type: Private   *Employees here:* 620
SIC: 8062
   Hospital
George Pifer, President

D-U-N-S 07-101-7115
FEDCAP REHABILITATION SERVICES
211 W 14th St, New York, NY 10011
Phone: (212) 727-4200

Sales: $42,415,000   *Employees:* 1,400
Company Type: Private   *Employees here:* 60
SIC: 8093
   Rehabilitation center
Susan Fonfa, Executive Director

D-U-N-S 10-575-2901
FHC HEALTH SYSTEMS, INC.
240 Corporate Blvd, Norfolk, VA 23502
Phone: (757) 459-5100
Sales: $129,600,000   *Employees:* 3,500
Company Type: Private   *Employees here:* 55
SIC: 8063
   Mental health services
Dozoretz Ronald I, Chairman of the Board

D-U-N-S 14-746-0232
FHP INTERNATIONAL CORPORATION
   (Parent: Pacificare Health Systems Inc)
3120 W Lake Center Dr, Santa Ana, CA 92704
Phone: (714) 825-6600
Sales: $690,200,000   *Employees:* 10,000
Company Type: Public   *Employees here:* 500
SIC: 8011
   Health maintenance organization
Westcott W Price Iii, President

D-U-N-S 96-552-3624
FINGER LAKES REGIONAL HEALTH SYS
196 North St, Geneva, NY 14456
Phone: (315) 789-4222
Sales: $54,477,000   *Employees:* 1,100
Company Type: Private   *Employees here:* 1,100
SIC: 8051
   Holding company
James J Dooley, President

D-U-N-S 12-240-0088
FIRELANDS COMMUNITY HOSPITAL CORP
1101 Decatur St, Sandusky, OH 44870
Phone: (419) 626-7400
Sales: $32,100,000   *Employees:* 703
Company Type: Private   *Employees here:* 603
SIC: 8062
   General hospital
Nelson Alward, President

D-U-N-S 18-573-0926
FIRST COMMONWEALTH, INC.
444 N Wells St Ste 600, Chicago, IL 60610
Phone: (312) 644-1800
Sales: $44,099,000   *Employees:* 55
Company Type: Public   *Employees here:* 45
SIC: 8021
   Dental benefit plan
Christophe Multhauf, Chairman of the Board

D-U-N-S 15-339-6510
FIRST HOSPITAL CORP OF PORTSMOUTH
   (Parent: Fhc Health Systems Inc)
301 Fort Ln, Portsmouth, VA 23704
Phone: (757) 393-0061
Sales: $24,934,000   *Employees:* 1,300
Company Type: Private   *Employees here:* 500
SIC: 8051
   Residential treatment center for troubled children
Dozoretz Ronald I, Chairman of the Board

D-U-N-S 87-651-8267
FIRST OPTION HEALTH PLAN OF NJ
   (Parent: F O H P Inc)
2 Bridge Ave Bldg 6, Red Bank, NJ 7701
Phone: (732) 842-5000

Sales: $377,406,000
Company Type: Private
Employees: 350
Employees here: NA
SIC: 8011
  Hmo & managed health care organization
Roger W Birnbaum, President

D-U-N-S 79-478-7119
FIRST PHYSCN CARE OF TAMPA BAY
  (Parent: First Physician Care Inc)
2701 N Rocky Point Dr, Tampa, FL 33607
Phone: (813) 289-6637
Sales: $30,900,000
Company Type: Private
Employees: 450
Employees here: 10
SIC: 8011
  Medical centers
Dr Steven A George, Chief Executive Officer

D-U-N-S 07-175-5920
FIRST PLAN OF MINNESOTA
1010 4th St, Two Harbors, MN 55616
Phone: (218) 834-7207
Sales: $32,529,000
Company Type: Private
Employees: 175
Employees here: 90
SIC: 8011
  Hmo & medical clinic
Anthony H Solem, President

D-U-N-S 93-192-3072
FIRSTHEALTH OF THE CAROLINAS
35 Memorial Dr, Pinehurst, NC 28374
Phone: (910) 215-1000
Sales: $104,500,000
Company Type: Private
Employees: 2,235
Employees here: 1,800
SIC: 8062
  Hospital management services and medical equip rental
Charles T Frock, Chief Executive Officer

D-U-N-S 19-602-2065
FISHER-TITUS MEDICAL CENTER,
272 Benedict Ave, Norwalk, OH 44857
Phone: (419) 668-8101
Sales: $39,728,000
Company Type: Private
Employees: 500
Employees here: 500
SIC: 8062
  General hospital/skilled and intermediate nursing facility
Patrick Martin, President

D-U-N-S 07-323-0567
FLAGLER HOSPITAL INC
400 Health Park Blvd, Saint Augustine, FL 32086
Phone: (904) 829-5155
Sales: $81,184,000
Company Type: Private
Employees: 780
Employees here: 450
SIC: 8062
  Hospital
James D Conzemius, President

D-U-N-S 06-842-1817
FLAGSTAFF MEDICAL CENTER INC
1200 N Beaver St, Flagstaff, AZ 86001
Phone: (520) 779-3366
Sales: $89,463,000
Company Type: Private
Employees: 1,200
Employees here: 985
SIC: 8062
  General medical & surgical hospital specialty rehabilitation
    hospital & skilled nursing care facilities
Steven Carlson, Chief Operating Officer

D-U-N-S 88-345-5354
FLETCHER HOSPITAL INC
Naples Rd, Fletcher, NC 28732
Phone: (828) 684-8501

Sales: $28,300,000
Company Type: Private
Employees: 622
Employees here: 622
SIC: 8062
  Hospital
Michael Gentry, President

D-U-N-S 07-920-8542
FLORIDA BLOOD SERVICES INC
3602 Spectrum Blvd, Tampa, FL 33612
Phone: (813) 977-5433
Sales: $30,526,000
Company Type: Private
Employees: 450
Employees here: 120
SIC: 8099
  Blood bank
Dr German F Leparc, President

D-U-N-S 80-473-7500
FLORIDA BLOOD SERVICES INC
402 Jeffords St, Clearwater, FL 33756
Phone: (727) 322-5433
Sales: $31,727,000
Company Type: Private
Employees: 500
Employees here: 150
SIC: 8099
  Blood bank services
Dr German F Leparc, President

D-U-N-S 10-186-7273
FLORIDA CONVALESCENT CENTERS
2033 Main St Ste 300, Sarasota, FL 34237
Phone: (941) 952-9411
Sales: $55,000,000
Company Type: Private
Employees: 2,400
Employees here: 3
SIC: 8051
  Skilled nursing homes
Jim Mc Carver, President

D-U-N-S 61-666-5709
FLORIDA DEPARTMENT OF HEALTH
401 NW 2nd Ave Ste N1007, Miami, FL 33128
Phone: (305) 377-7262
Sales: $29,200,000
Company Type: Private
Employees: NA
Employees here: 1,000
SIC: 8093
  Health & rehabilitative services
Anita Bock, Principal

D-U-N-S 07-981-0446
FLORIDA DEPT CHILDREN FAMILIES
20000 NW 47th Ave, Opa Locka, FL 33055
Phone: (305) 624-9671
Sales: $23,100,000
Company Type: Private
Employees: NA
Employees here: 791
SIC: 8093
  Rehabilation center
Julie Waldman, Administration

D-U-N-S 08-194-7145
FLORIDA DEPT CHILDREN FAMILIES
RR 1 Box 519, Macclenny, FL 32063
Phone: (904) 259-6211
Sales: $37,700,000
Company Type: Private
Employees: NA
Employees here: 1,150
SIC: 8063
  Hospital
C V Stotler, N/A

D-U-N-S 07-603-8090
FLORIDA DEPT CHILDREN FAMILIES
1000 SW 84th Ave, Hollywood, FL 33025
Phone: (954) 967-7000

Sales: $26,400,000
Company Type: Private
SIC: 8063
    Psychiatric hospital
Thomas Gramley, Principal
Employees: NA
Employees here: 743

D-U-N-S 02-099-3739
FLORIDA DEPT CHILDREN FAMILIES
5847 SE Highway 31, Arcadia, FL 34266
Phone: (941) 494-8200
Sales: $36,000,000
Company Type: Private
SIC: 8063
    Psychiatric state mental hospital
Dick Bradley, Branch Manager
Employees: NA
Employees here: 1,100

D-U-N-S 62-690-5186
FLORIDA DEPT ENVIRONMENTAL PROTECTION
501 S Clyde Morris Blvd, Daytona Beach, FL 32114
Phone: (904) 947-3400
Sales: $19,800,000
Company Type: Private
SIC: 8011
    General and family pratice physician surgeon
Dr June Atkinson, Branch Manager
Employees: NA
Employees here: 310

D-U-N-S 01-081-4408
FLORIDA HEALTH CARE PLAN INC
    (Parent: Halifax Hospital Medical Ctr)
350 N Clyde Morris Blvd, Daytona Beach, FL 32114
Phone: (904) 238-3200
Sales: $114,707,000
Company Type: Private
SIC: 8099
    Group health maintenance service
Edward F Simpson Jr, President
Employees: 670
Employees here: 300

D-U-N-S 15-131-3756
FLORIDA HEALTH CHOICE INC
5300 W Atl Ave Ste 302, Delray Beach, FL 33484
Phone: (561) 496-0505
Sales: $22,805,000
Company Type: Private
SIC: 8011
    Managed health care systems
Brent Casey, President
Employees: 120
Employees here: 110

D-U-N-S 00-140-9994
FLORIDA HEALTH SCIENCES CENTER
2 Columbia Dr, Tampa, FL 33606
Phone: (813) 251-7000
Sales: $274,149,000
Company Type: Private
SIC: 8062
    General hospital
Bruce Siegel, President
Employees: 3,750
Employees here: 3,500

D-U-N-S 00-274-0066
FLORIDA HOSPITAL HEARTLAND
4023 Sun N Lakes Blvd, Sebring, FL 33872
Phone: (941) 386-6462
Sales: $55,600,000
Company Type: Private
SIC: 8062
    General hospital
John Harding, President
Employees: 1,200
Employees here: 1,200

D-U-N-S 80-174-7965
FLORIDA HOSPITAL/FISH MEMORIAL
1055 Saxon Blvd, Orange City, FL 32763
Phone: (904) 851-5000

Sales: $40,029,000
Company Type: Private
SIC: 8062
    General hospital
Randy Haffner, Chief Executive Officer
Employees: 420
Employees here: 420

D-U-N-S 79-544-5683
FLORIDA HOSPITAL/WATERMAN INC
201 N Eustis St, Eustis, FL 32726
Phone: (352) 589-3333
Sales: $68,505,000
Company Type: Private
SIC: 8062
    Hospital
Ken Mattison, Chief Operating Officer
Employees: 1,200
Employees here: 1,000

D-U-N-S 61-831-0585
FLORIDA MEDICAL CENTER INC
    (Parent: Tenet Healthcare Corporation)
5000 W Oakland Park Blvd, Fort Lauderdale, FL 33313
Phone: (954) 735-6000
Sales: $117,670,000
Company Type: Public Family Member
SIC: 8062
    General short term hospital
Pat Wolfram, Chief Operating Officer
Employees: 1,350
Employees here: 1,350

D-U-N-S 80-814-8902
FLORIDA MEDICAL CLINIC, P.A.
38135 Market Sq, Zephyrhills, FL 33540
Phone: (813) 780-8440
Sales: $22,700,000
Company Type: Private
SIC: 8011
    Medical clinic
Dr Paul E Hughes Md, President
Employees: 177
Employees here: 165

D-U-N-S 82-568-6504
FLORIDA PHYSICIANS MED GROUP
2699 Lee Rd Ste 600, Winter Park, FL 32789
Phone: (407) 303-3700
Sales: $24,000,000
Company Type: Private
SIC: 8011
    Medical doctor's office
Thomas Werner, President
Employees: 350
Employees here: 30

D-U-N-S 07-322-4859
FLORIDA SHERIFFS YOUTH RANCHES
Boys Ranch, Live Oak, FL 32060
Phone: (904) 842-5501
Sales: $21,705,000
Company Type: Private
SIC: 8361
    Children's home
C T O Donnell Ii, President
Employees: 250
Employees here: 115

D-U-N-S 05-416-3209
FLOWER HOSPITAL
5200 Harroun Rd, Sylvania, OH 43560
Phone: (419) 824-1444
Sales: $46,100,000
Company Type: Private
SIC: 8062
    General hospital
William W Glover, Executive Vice-President
Employees: 1,000
Employees here: 889

D-U-N-S 96-796-7712
FLOWERS HOSPITAL, INC
    (Parent: Q H G Of Alabama Inc)
3228 W Main St, Dothan, AL 36305
Phone: (334) 793-5000

Sales: $137,731,000   *Employees:* NA
Company Type: Public Family Member   *Employees here:* NA
SIC: 8062
  General medical and surgical hospitals, nsk
Keith Granger, Chief Executive Officer

D-U-N-S 07-586-9594
FLOYD HEALTHCARE MANAGEMENT
304 Turner McCall Blvd, Rome, GA 30165
Phone: (706) 802-2000
Sales: $131,633,000   *Employees:* 1,600
Company Type: Private   *Employees here:* 1,525
SIC: 8062
  General hospital
Kurt Stuenkel, President

D-U-N-S 05-682-2091
FLOYD MEMORIAL HOSPITAL
1850 State St, New Albany, IN 47150
Phone: (812) 944-7701
Sales: $77,818,000   *Employees:* 1,200
Company Type: Private   *Employees here:* 1,000
SIC: 8062
  Hospital
Bryant R Hanson, President

D-U-N-S 07-620-3421
FOOTHILL MEMORIAL HOSPITAL
250 S Grand Ave, Glendora, CA 91741
Phone: (626) 963-8411
Sales: $25,489,000   *Employees:* 400
Company Type: Private   *Employees here:* 400
SIC: 8062
  General hospital
Bryan R Rogers, President

D-U-N-S 07-789-3386
FORREST COUNTY GENERAL HOSP
6051 Hwy 49 S, Hattiesburg, MS 39401
Phone: (601) 288-7000
Sales: $197,924,000   *Employees:* 2,800
Company Type: Private   *Employees here:* 2,500
SIC: 8062
  General hospital
William C Oliver, President

D-U-N-S 06-582-1191
FORREST S CHILTON III MEM HOSP
97 W Parkway, Pompton Plains, NJ 7444
Phone: (973) 831-5000
Sales: $83,474,000   *Employees:* 1,200
Company Type: Private   *Employees here:* 1,160
SIC: 8062
  General hospital
James J Doyle, President

D-U-N-S 07-782-9653
FORSYTH MEMORIAL HOSPITAL INC
3333 Silas Creek Pkwy, Winston Salem, NC 27103
Phone: (336) 718-5000
Sales: $260,662,000   *Employees:* 3,334
Company Type: Private   *Employees here:* 3,220
SIC: 8062
  Hospital
Paul M Wiles, President

D-U-N-S 07-383-9573
FORT ATKINSON MEM HEALTH SVCS
611 Sherman Ave E, Fort Atkinson, WI 53538
Phone: (920) 568-5401

Sales: $44,971,000   *Employees:* 625
Company Type: Private   *Employees here:* 597
SIC: 8062
  Hospital
John C Albaugh, President

D-U-N-S 01-055-2321
FORT DUNCAN MEDICAL CENTER
350 S Adams St, Eagle Pass, TX 78852
Phone: (830) 773-5321
Sales: $23,332,000   *Employees:* 350
Company Type: Private   *Employees here:* 350
SIC: 8062
  Hospital
Don Spalding, Chief Executive Officer

D-U-N-S 07-286-5629
FORT HMLTN-HGHES MEM HOSPITAL CTR
630 Eaton Ave, Hamilton, OH 45013
Phone: (513) 867-2000
Sales: $70,236,000   *Employees:* 1,286
Company Type: Private   *Employees here:* 1,196
SIC: 8062
  General medical and surgical hospital
James A Kingsbury, President

D-U-N-S 07-490-9482
FORT SANDERS REGIONAL MED CTR
1901 W Clinch Ave, Knoxville, TN 37916
Phone: (423) 541-1111
Sales: $153,526,000   *Employees:* 2,080
Company Type: Private   *Employees here:* 1,500
SIC: 8062
  General hospital and outpatient center
James R Burkhart, President

D-U-N-S 86-109-8499
FORT SANDERS-PARKWEST MED CTR
9352 Parkwest Blvd, Knoxville, TN 37923
Phone: (423) 693-5151
Sales: $227,000,000   *Employees:* 1,200
Company Type: Private   *Employees here:* 1,200
SIC: 8062
  General hospital
James Burkhart, Administrator

D-U-N-S 07-490-0317
FORT SANDERS-SEVIER MED CTR
709 Middle Creek Rd, Sevierville, TN 37862
Phone: (423) 453-7111
Sales: $19,737,000   *Employees:* 310
Company Type: Private   *Employees here:* 310
SIC: 8062
  Hospital and skilled nursing care facility
Ralph T Williams, Administrator

D-U-N-S 80-450-6285
FORT WALTON BEACH MEDICAL CTR
(Parent: Galen Health Care Inc)
1000 Mar Walt Dr, Fort Walton Beach, FL 32547
Phone: (850) 863-7501
Sales: $150,000,000   *Employees:* 750
Company Type: Public Family Member   *Employees here:* 750
SIC: 8011
  Hospital
Stephen T Braun, Administrator

D-U-N-S 02-033-5907
FORT WORTH MEDICAL PLAZA INC
(Parent: Columbia/Hca Healthcare Corp)
900 8th Ave, Fort Worth, TX 76104
Phone: (817) 336-2100

Sales: $113,774,000
Company Type: Public Family Member
SIC: 8062
    General medical & surgical hospital
Stephen Bernstein, Administrator

Employees: 1,600
Employees here: 800

D-U-N-S 87-929-1656
FORT WORTH MEDICAL PLAZA INC
900 8th Ave, Fort Worth, TX 76104
Phone: (817) 347-4700
Sales: $41,200,000
Company Type: Public Family Member
SIC: 8062
    General medical hospital
Daniel Wallus, Branch Manager

Employees: NA
Employees here: 1,000

D-U-N-S 07-316-6415
FORT WORTH OSTEOPATHIC HOSP
1000 Montgomery St, Fort Worth, TX 76107
Phone: (817) 731-4311
Sales: $32,900,000
Company Type: Private
SIC: 8062
    General hospital
David Beyer, President

Employees: 720
Employees here: 700

D-U-N-S 04-696-1926
FORUM GROUP INC
    (Parent: Host Marriott Corporation)
11320 Randon Hills Rd, Fairfax, VA 22030
Phone: (703) 277-7000
Sales: $97,900,000
Company Type: Public
SIC: 8361
    Operates retirement facilities and nursing home
Paul E Johnson Jr, President

Employees: NA
Employees here: NA

D-U-N-S 13-150-6693
FOUNDATION HEALTH A SOUTH
    (Parent: Foundtion Hlth A Fla Hlth Plan)
1340 NW 146 Ave, Fort Lauderdale, FL 33323
Phone: (954) 858-3000
Sales: $182,061,000
Company Type: Private
SIC: 8011
    Health maintenance organization
Daniel D Crowley, Chief Executive Officer

Employees: 351
Employees here: 266

D-U-N-S 84-800-3661
FOUNDATION HEALTH FEDERAL SVCS
    (Parent: Health Net)
22025 Aerojet Rd, Rancho Cordova, CA 95741
Phone: (916) 631-5000
Sales: $103,400,000
Company Type: Public Family Member
SIC: 8011
    Medical doctor's office
Gary Velasquez, President

Employees: 1,500
Employees here: 1,500

D-U-N-S 11-598-8370
FOUNDATION HEALTH SYSTEMS
    (Parent: Novant Health Inc)
1999 S Hawthorne Rd, Winston Salem, NC 27103
Phone: (336) 718-6800
Sales: $24,983,000
Company Type: Private
SIC: 8011
    Outpatient ambulatory surgery and a nursing home
William Johnson, Chief Executive Officer

Employees: 40
Employees here: 34

D-U-N-S 79-833-0908
FOUNDATION HEALTH SYSTEMS INC
21600 Oxnard St Fl 17, Woodland Hills, CA 91367

Phone: (818) 719-6775
Sales: $7,235,019,000
Company Type: Private
SIC: 8011
    Health maintenance organization
Robert Bruce, President

Employees: 2,600
Employees here: 1,200

D-U-N-S 55-692-0205
FOUNDATION MA EYE & EAR INFRMY
243 Charles St, Boston, MA 2114
Phone: (617) 523-7900
Sales: $100,708,000
Company Type: Private
SIC: 8069
    Investment holding company
Alexander Bernhard, Chairman of the Board

Employees: 1,174
Employees here: 1,174

D-U-N-S 62-525-1913
FOUNDTION HEALTH A FLA HEALTH PLAN
    (Parent: Foundation Health Systems Inc)
1340 Concord Ter, Fort Lauderdale, FL 33323
Phone: (954) 858-3000
Sales: $23,100,000
Company Type: Private
SIC: 8011
    Health maintenance organization
Steve Griffin, President

Employees: 337
Employees here: 5

D-U-N-S 07-360-9703
FOUNTAIN VALLEY REGNL HOSP
    (Parent: Ornda Healthcorp)
17100 Euclid St, Fountain Valley, CA 92708
Phone: (714) 979-1211
Sales: $60,300,000
Company Type: Public Family Member
SIC: 8062
    General and surgical hospital
Tim Smith, Chief Executive Officer

Employees: 1,300
Employees here: 1,300

D-U-N-S 02-071-6619
FOUR SEASONS NURSING CENTERS
    (Parent: Manorcare Health Services Inc)
11555 Darnestown Rd, Gaithersburg, MD 20878
Phone: (301) 979-4000
Sales: $57,300,000
Company Type: Public Family Member
SIC: 8051
    Nursing home
Stewart Bainum Jr, Chairman of the Board

Employees: 2,500
Employees here: 4

D-U-N-S 04-567-1328
FOUR WINDS INC
800 Cross River Rd, Katonah, NY 10536
Phone: (914) 763-8151
Sales: $33,144,000
Company Type: Private
SIC: 8063
    Psychiatric hospital
Dr Samuel C Klagsbrun Md, Chairman of the Board

Employees: 700
Employees here: 700

D-U-N-S 07-382-4187
FRANC CHILDR HOSP
30 Warren St, Boston, MA 2135
Phone: (617) 254-3800
Sales: $22,715,000
Company Type: Private
SIC: 8069
    Pediatric hospital with pediatric rehabilitation
Paul D Rocco, President

Employees: 400
Employees here: 400

D-U-N-S 07-884-1723
FRANCES SCHERVIER HOME & HOSP
2975 Independence Ave, Bronx, NY 10463
Phone: (718) 548-1700

Sales: $33,233,000
Company Type: Private
SIC: 8051
    Skilled nursing facility and long term home health care
Jeanne Lee, President
Employees: 500
Employees here: 470

D-U-N-S 07-800-6442
FRANCIS SAINT MEDICAL CENTER
2620 W Faidley Ave, Grand Island, NE 68803
Phone: (308) 384-4600
Sales: $104,000,000
Company Type: Private
SIC: 8062
    General hospital
Michael R Gloor, President
Employees: 950
Employees here: 665

D-U-N-S 62-082-2833
FRANCISCAN HEALTH SYSTEM WEST
11315 Bridgeport Way SW, Tacoma, WA 98499
Phone: (253) 588-1711
Sales: $285,402,000
Company Type: Private
SIC: 8062
    Hospital
Syd Bersante, Administrator
Employees: 551
Employees here: 551

D-U-N-S 14-833-4659
FRANCISCAN HEALTH SYSTEM WEST
34515 9th Ave S, Federal Way, WA 98003
Phone: (253) 927-9700
Sales: $25,900,000
Company Type: Private
SIC: 8062
    General hospital
Joe Wilcheck, Chief Operating Officer
Employees: 573
Employees here: 573

D-U-N-S 79-404-2382
FRANCISCAN HEALTH SYSTEMS OF
15 Maple Ave, Warwick, NY 10990
Phone: (914) 986-2276
Sales: $20,100,000
Company Type: Private
SIC: 8062
    Hospital
Andrew Brothers, President
Employees: 450
Employees here: 450

D-U-N-S 06-894-0329
FRANCISCAN HOSPITAL MT AIRY CAMPUS
2446 Kipling Ave, Cincinnati, OH 45239
Phone: (513) 853-5000
Sales: $78,675,000
Company Type: Private
SIC: 8062
    General hospital
Donald Stinnett, Vice-President
Employees: 1,154
Employees here: 1,154

D-U-N-S 19-333-2459
FRANCISCAN SHARED LABORATORY
    (Parent: Covenant Health Care System)
11020 W Plank Ct Ste 100, Milwaukee, WI 53226
Phone: (414) 476-3400
Sales: $25,000,000
Company Type: Private
SIC: 8071
    Medical laboratory
James E Fantus, Chief Executive Officer
Employees: 680
Employees here: 275

D-U-N-S 06-746-2101
FRANCISCAN SISTERS OF CHICAGO
1201 S Main St, Crown Point, IN 46307
Phone: (219) 738-2100

Sales: $59,200,000
Company Type: Private
SIC: 8062
    Nursing home
Steven O Leurck, Director
Employees: NA
Employees here: 1,400

D-U-N-S 11-427-6769
FRANCISCAN SKEMP HEALTHCARE
700 West Ave S, La Crosse, WI 54601
Phone: (608) 791-9700
Sales: $116,100,000
Company Type: Private
SIC: 8062
    Hospital & skilled nursing care facilities
Dr Glen Forbes Md, Chief Executive Officer
Employees: 2,481
Employees here: 2,000

D-U-N-S 07-971-3459
FRANCISCAN SKEMP MEDICAL CTR
700 West Ave S, La Crosse, WI 54601
Phone: (608) 785-0940
Sales: $47,444,000
Company Type: Private
SIC: 8062
    General hospital
Glen Forbes, President
Employees: 2,200
Employees here: 1,096

D-U-N-S 07-470-2911
FRANCSCAN MED CTR DYTON CAMPUS
1 Franciscan Way, Dayton, OH 45408
Phone: (937) 229-6000
Sales: $154,240,000
Company Type: Private
SIC: 8062
    General hospital
Duane Erwin, Chief Executive Officer
Employees: 2,054
Employees here: 2,044

D-U-N-S 07-550-1312
FRANKFORD HOSPITAL PHILA
Knights & Red Lion Rds, Philadelphia, PA 19114
Phone: (215) 612-4000
Sales: $170,800,000
Company Type: Private
SIC: 8062
    General hospital
John B Neff, President
Employees: 1,931
Employees here: 1,250

D-U-N-S 09-527-4262
FRANKFORD HOSPITAL PHILA
4900 Frankford Ave, Philadelphia, PA 19124
Phone: (215) 831-2000
Sales: $49,400,000
Company Type: Private
SIC: 8062
    General hospital
Eugene Johnson, Vice-President
Employees: NA
Employees here: 1,000

D-U-N-S 06-593-1719
FRANKLIN HOSPITAL MEDICAL CTR
900 Franklin Ave, Valley Stream, NY 11580
Phone: (516) 256-6000
Sales: $60,300,000
Company Type: Private
SIC: 8062
    General medical & surgical hospital
Albert Dicker, President
Employees: 1,300
Employees here: 1,058

D-U-N-S 06-697-7570
FRANKLIN MEDICAL CENTER
164 High St, Greenfield, MA 1301
Phone: (413) 773-0211

Sales: $58,569,000   *Employees:* 1,163
Company Type: Private   *Employees here:* 1,163
SIC: 8062
  General hospital
Harlan Smith, President

D-U-N-S 06-323-4892
FRANKLIN SQUARE HOSPITAL CTR
9000 Franklin Square Dr, Baltimore, MD 21237
Phone: (410) 682-7000
Sales: $171,248,000   *Employees:* 2,200
Company Type: Private   *Employees here:* 2,100
SIC: 8062
  General hospital
Charles D Mross, President

D-U-N-S 07-942-2382
FREDERICK C SMITH CLINIC INC
1040 Delaware Ave, Marion, OH 43302
Phone: (740) 383-7000
Sales: $30,900,000   *Employees:* 450
Company Type: Private   *Employees here:* 400
SIC: 8011
  Medical clinic
Dalsukh Madia, President

D-U-N-S 06-938-2398
FREDERICK MEMORIAL HOSPITAL
400 W 7th St, Frederick, MD 21701
Phone: (301) 698-3300
Sales: $101,661,000   *Employees:* 1,700
Company Type: Private   *Employees here:* 1,460
SIC: 8062
  General hospital
James K Kluttz, President

D-U-N-S 07-456-9526
FREEPORT MEMORIAL HOSPITAL
1045 W Stephenson St, Freeport, IL 61032
Phone: (815) 235-4131
Sales: $34,300,000   *Employees:* 750
Company Type: Private   *Employees here:* 750
SIC: 8062
  Hospital
Dennis Hamilton, President

D-U-N-S 04-091-7106
FREMONT AREA MEDICAL CENTER
450 E 23rd St, Fremont, NE 68025
Phone: (402) 721-1610
Sales: $43,230,000   *Employees:* 776
Company Type: Private   *Employees here:* 776
SIC: 8062
  Hospital & nursing care
Michael Leibert, Executive Vice-President

D-U-N-S 01-070-7941
FRENCH HOSPITAL MED CTR A CAL CORP
1911 Johnson Ave, San Luis Obispo, CA 93401
Phone: (805) 543-5353
Sales: $23,900,000   *Employees:* 530
Company Type: Private   *Employees here:* 480
SIC: 8062
  Acute care hospital
Gale Gascho, Chief Executive Officer

D-U-N-S 62-781-7356
FRESNO COMMUNITY HOSPITAL & MED CTR
  (Parent: Community Hsptals Of Cntl Cal)
Fresno & R Sts, Fresno, CA 93721
Phone: (209) 442-6000

Sales: $164,300,000   *Employees:* 3,500
Company Type: Private   *Employees here:* 2,500
SIC: 8062
  General hospital
Dr Phillip Hinton, President

D-U-N-S 07-216-5236
FRICK HOSPITAL & COMMUNITY HEALTH CTR
508 S Church St, Mount Pleasant, PA 15666
Phone: (724) 547-1500
Sales: $42,058,000   *Employees:* 750
Company Type: Private   *Employees here:* 750
SIC: 8062
  General hospital
Rodney Gunderson, Chief Executive Officer

D-U-N-S 14-791-0061
FRIENDLY HLLS HEALTH CARE NETWRK
  (Parent: Medpartners Inc)
501 S Idaho St Fl 3, La Habra, CA 90631
Phone: (714) 992-2100
Sales: $197,400,000   *Employees:* 4,200
Company Type: Public Family Member   *Employees here:* 200
SIC: 8062
  Hospital medical clinics owns/operates non-residential
    buildings and real estate holding company
Gina Glass, Assistant Controller

D-U-N-S 60-486-6954
FRIENDLY HLLS HEALTH CARE NETWRK
951 S Beach Blvd, La Habra, CA 90631
Phone: (562) 694-4711
Sales: $42,600,000   *Employees:* NA
Company Type: Public Family Member   *Employees here:* 700
SIC: 8011
  Medical clinic
Ann Minard, Branch Manager

D-U-N-S 07-553-7050
FRIENDS HOSPITAL
4641 Roosevelt Blvd, Philadelphia, PA 19124
Phone: (215) 831-4600
Sales: $31,870,000   *Employees:* 570
Company Type: Private   *Employees here:* 570
SIC: 8063
  Psychiatric hospital
Wayne A Mugrauer, Chief Executive Officer

D-U-N-S 07-399-2737
FRISBIE MEMORIAL HOSPITAL
11 Whitehall Rd, Rochester, NH 3867
Phone: (603) 332-3100
Sales: $42,667,000   *Employees:* 507
Company Type: Private   *Employees here:* 500
SIC: 8062
  General hospital
Alvin D Felgar, President

D-U-N-S 04-078-9588
FROEDTERT MEM LUTHERAN HOSP
9200 W Wisconsin Ave, Milwaukee, WI 53226
Phone: (414) 259-3000
Sales: $334,186,000   *Employees:* 2,500
Company Type: Private   *Employees here:* 2,500
SIC: 8062
  General hospital
Tom L Smallwood, Chairman of the Board

D-U-N-S 87-948-6322
FRONTIER GROUP
1 Boston Pl Ste 2000, Boston, MA 2108
Phone: (617) 720-7150

Sales: $133,817,000 Employees: 4,000
Company Type: Private Employees here: 80
SIC: 8093
   Nursing home management
Jonathan S Sherwin, Chairman of the Board

D-U-N-S 08-119-8830
FRONTIER HEALTH INC
109 W Watauga Ave, Johnson City, TN 37604
Phone: (423) 928-6545
Sales: $42,852,000 Employees: 1,100
Company Type: Private Employees here: 100
SIC: 8063
   Mental health clinics & psychiatric hospital
Doug Varney, Chief Executive Officer

D-U-N-S 04-977-2098
FRYE REGIONAL MEDICAL CENTER,
   (Parent: Tenet Health System Medical)
420 N Center St, Hickory, NC 28601
Phone: (828) 322-6070
Sales: $74,500,000 Employees: 1,600
Company Type: Public Family Member Employees here: 1,290
SIC: 8062
   General hospital specialty hospital psqchiatric facility &
      skilled nursing care facility
Dennis J Phillips, Chief Executive Officer

D-U-N-S 05-689-5998
FULTON COUNTY HEALTH CENTER
725 S Shoop Ave, Wauseon, OH 43567
Phone: (419) 335-2015
Sales: $26,543,000 Employees: 600
Company Type: Private Employees here: 420
SIC: 8062
   General hospital
E D Beck, Chief Executive Officer

D-U-N-S 07-247-5312
FULTON DEKALB HOSPITAL AUTH
80 Butler St SE, Atlanta, GA 30303
Phone: (404) 616-4307
Sales: $369,452,000 Employees: 6,700
Company Type: Private Employees here: 4,800
SIC: 8062
   General hospital
Robert Brown, Chairman of the Board

D-U-N-S 16-729-8249
FHP INTERNATIONAL CORPORATION
9930 Talbert Ave, Fountain Valley, CA 92708
Phone: (714) 964-6229
Sales: $20,400,000 Employees: NA
Company Type: Public Family Member Employees here: 320
SIC: 8011
   Medical doctor's office
Ray Chicoin, Branch Manager

D-U-N-S 96-183-4512
G B HEALTH SYSTEMS INC
   (Parent: Tenet Healthcare Corporation)
303 Parkway Dr NE, Atlanta, GA 30312
Phone: (404) 265-4000
Sales: $98,100,000 Employees: 2,100
Company Type: Public Family Member Employees here: 2,100
SIC: 8062
   Hospital
James E Lathren, Chief Executive Officer

D-U-N-S 06-627-8706
G N WILCOX MEMORIAL HOSPITAL
3420 Kuhio Hwy, Lihue, HI 96766
Phone: (808) 245-1100

Sales: $29,700,000 Employees: 653
Company Type: Private Employees here: 653
SIC: 8062
   General hospital
David W Pratt, Chairman of the Board

D-U-N-S 80-990-7694
GALEN OF ARIZONA, INC.
   (Parent: Columbia/Hca Healthcare Corp)
3929 E Bell Rd, Phoenix, AZ 85032
Phone: (602) 867-1881
Sales: $45,128,000 Employees: 450
Company Type: Public Family Member Employees here: 450
SIC: 8011
   Hospital
Rebecca Kuhn, President

D-U-N-S 13-763-6247
GALEN OF FLORIDA, INC
1000 Mar Walt Dr, Fort Walton Beach, FL 32547
Phone: (850) 862-1111
Sales: $32,800,000 Employees: NA
Company Type: Public Family Member Employees here: 750
SIC: 8062
   General hospital
David Mc Clellan, Manager

D-U-N-S 02-474-2681
GALEN OF FLORIDA, INC
13100 Fort King Rd, Dade City, FL 33525
Phone: (352) 521-1100
Sales: $21,600,000 Employees: NA
Company Type: Public Family Member Employees here: 500
SIC: 8062
   Hospital
Lisa Kelley, Chief Operating Officer

D-U-N-S 01-038-3909
GALEN OF FLORIDA, INC
   (Parent: Galen Health Care Inc)
1 Park Mdws, Nashville, TN 37215
Phone: (615) 327-9551
Sales: $107,600,000 Employees: 2,300
Company Type: Public Family Member Employees here: 1
SIC: 8062
   Hospital
Thomas Frist, Chairman of the Board

D-U-N-S 02-044-3909
GALEN OF KENTUCKY INC
305 Langdon St, Somerset, KY 42503
Phone: (606) 679-7441
Sales: $31,100,000 Employees: NA
Company Type: Public Family Member Employees here: 800
SIC: 8062
   General hospital
Kenneth Lukhard, Principal

D-U-N-S 07-406-7372
GALEN OF KENTUCKY INC
4001 Dutchmans Ln, Louisville, KY 40207
Phone: (502) 893-1000
Sales: $57,100,000 Employees: NA
Company Type: Public Family Member Employees here: 1,350
SIC: 8062
   Hospital
John Harryman, Executive Director

D-U-N-S 80-095-0230
GALEN HEALTH CARE INC
   (Parent: Columbia/Hca Healthcare Corp)
1 Park Mdws, Nashville, TN 37215
Phone: (615) 327-9551

Sales: $2,641,100,000   *Employees:* 55,900
Company Type: Public Family Member   *Employees here:* 800
SIC: 8062
   General medical and surgical hospitals
Carl F Pollard, Chairman of the Board

D-U-N-S 07-663-0060
GALEN HOSPITAL ALASKA INC
   (Parent: Galen Health Care Inc)
2801 Debarr Rd, Anchorage, AK 99508
Phone: (907) 276-1131
Sales: $86,527,000   *Employees:* 600
Company Type: Public Family Member   *Employees here:* 600
SIC: 8062
   Hospital
Ernie Meier, President

D-U-N-S 94-738-2370
GALEN HOSPITAL CORPORATION INC
8111 Township Line Rd, Indianapolis, IN 46260
Phone: (317) 875-5994
Sales: $19,800,000   *Employees:* NA
Company Type: Public Family Member   *Employees here:* 480
SIC: 8062
   Women's hospital
Steve Reed, Administrator

D-U-N-S 07-874-8373
GALEN HOSPITAL CORPORATION INC
3315 S Alameda St, Corpus Christi, TX 78411
Phone: (512) 857-1400
Sales: $39,100,000   *Employees:* NA
Company Type: Public Family Member   *Employees here:* 950
SIC: 8062
   General hospital
Steve Woeroer, N/A

D-U-N-S 00-197-2165
GALEN HOSPITAL ILLINOIS INC
   (Parent: Columbia/Hca Healthcare Corp)
2929 S Ellis Ave, Chicago, IL 60616
Phone: (312) 791-2000
Sales: $171,421,000   *Employees:* 1,700
Company Type: Public Family Member   *Employees here:* 1,600
SIC: 8062
   General hospital
Scott Winslow, Chief Executive Officer

D-U-N-S 09-592-9592
GALEN-MED, INC
   (Parent: Columbia/Hca Healthcare Corp)
2949 W Front St, Richlands, VA 24641
Phone: (540) 596-6000
Sales: $100,000,000   *Employees:* 1,975
Company Type: Public Family Member   *Employees here:* 600
SIC: 8062
   Hospital
Thomas G Frist, President

D-U-N-S 09-934-8088
GALENCARE INC
   (Parent: Columbia/Hca Healthcare Corp)
119 Oakfield Dr, Brandon, FL 33511
Phone: (813) 681-5551
Sales: $55,600,000   *Employees:* 1,200
Company Type: Public Family Member   *Employees here:* 1,200
SIC: 8062
   General medical hospital
Michael Sencel, Administration

D-U-N-S 04-913-0859
GALESBURG COTTAGE HOSPITAL
695 N Kellogg St, Galesburg, IL 61401

Phone: (309) 343-8131
Sales: $42,145,000   *Employees:* 750
Company Type: Private   *Employees here:* 750
SIC: 8062
   Hospital
Steven West, President

D-U-N-S 15-201-2134
GAMBRO HEALTHCARE PATIENT SVCS
   (Parent: Cobe Laboratories Inc)
115 Columbia, Aliso Viejo, CA 92656
Phone: (949) 831-0900
Sales: $131,815,000   *Employees:* 4,000
Company Type: Private   *Employees here:* 100
SIC: 8092
   Dialysis centers
David Barry, President

D-U-N-S 16-094-0839
GAMBRO HEALTHCARE PTENT SVCS SUP
   (Parent: Gambro Healthcare Patient Svcs)
1919 Charlotte Ave, Nashville, TN 37203
Phone: (615) 320-4200
Sales: $25,000,000   *Employees:* NA
Company Type: Private   *Employees here:* NA
SIC: 8092
   Whol kidney dialysis supplies
Larry Centella, President

D-U-N-S 07-278-4002
GARDEN CITY HOSPITAL OSTEOPATHIC
6245 Inkster Rd, Garden City, MI 48135
Phone: (734) 431-3300
Sales: $98,965,000   *Employees:* 1,200
Company Type: Private   *Employees here:* 1,200
SIC: 8062
   Osteopathic hospital
Gary R Ley, President

D-U-N-S 03-957-3720
GARDEN PARK COMMUNITY HOSPITAL L P
   (Parent: Columbia/Hca Healthcare Corp)
1520 Broad Ave, Gulfport, MS 39501
Phone: (228) 864-4210
Sales: $29,289,000   *Employees:* 300
Company Type: Public Family Member   *Employees here:* 250
SIC: 8062
   Hospital
Dr Tommy Frist Md, President

D-U-N-S 06-940-3905
GARRETT COUNTY MEMORIAL HOSP
251 N 4th St, Oakland, MD 21550
Phone: (301) 334-2155
Sales: $23,930,000   *Employees:* 356
Company Type: Private   *Employees here:* 356
SIC: 8062
   General hospital
Walter Donaldson, Administrator

D-U-N-S 07-107-1682
GASTON MEMORIAL HOSPITAL INC
2525 Court Dr, Gastonia, NC 28054
Phone: (704) 834-2000
Sales: $157,602,000   *Employees:* 1,935
Company Type: Private   *Employees here:* 1,900
SIC: 8062
   Hospital
Terry L Jones, Chief Operating Officer

D-U-N-S 04-088-3779
GATEWAY FOUNDATION INC
819 S Wabash Ave Ste 300, Chicago, IL 60605
Phone: (312) 663-1130

Sales: $38,495,000
Company Type: Private
SIC: 8093
   Drug and alcohol rehabilitation
Michael Darcy, President

Employees: 800
Employees here: 60

D-U-N-S 96-183-1419
GATEWAY HOMECARE, INC
1235 Westlakes Dr Ste 310, Berwyn, PA 19312
Phone: (610) 640-4900
Sales: $28,746,000
Company Type: Private
SIC: 8082
   Home health care provider
Michael Di Piano, President

Employees: 1,000
Employees here: NA

D-U-N-S 07-287-8424
GATEWAY REGIONAL HEALTH SYSTEM
50 Sterling Ave, Mount Sterling, KY 40353
Phone: (606) 498-1220
Sales: $23,916,000
Company Type: Private
SIC: 8062
   General hospital
Jeffrey L Buckley, Chief Executive Officer

Employees: 313
Employees here: 278

D-U-N-S 07-539-2134
GAYLORD FARM ASSOCIATION
Gaylord Farm Rd, Wallingford, CT 6492
Phone: (203) 284-2800
Sales: $34,698,000
Company Type: Private
SIC: 8361
   Rehabilitative hospital
Paul Johnson, President

Employees: 566
Employees here: 566

D-U-N-S 06-890-4689
GEAUGA COMMUNITY HOSPITAL ASSN
13207 Ravenna Rd, Chardon, OH 44024
Phone: (440) 286-6131
Sales: $24,900,000
Company Type: Private
SIC: 8062
   General hospital
Richard J Frenchie, President

Employees: 550
Employees here: 550

D-U-N-S 06-959-1238
GEISINGER MEDICAL CENTER
100 N Academy Ave, Danville, PA 17821
Phone: (717) 271-6211
Sales: $249,908,000
Company Type: Private
SIC: 8062
   General medical & surgical hospital
Frank Trembulak, Treasurer

Employees: 3,459
Employees here: 3,459

D-U-N-S 07-277-2866
GEN OAKLAND HOSPITAL OSTEOPATHIC
27351 Dequindre Rd, Madison Heights, MI 48071
Phone: (248) 967-7000
Sales: $74,583,000
Company Type: Private
SIC: 8062
   General medical & surgical osteopathic hospital
Robert A Deputat, President

Employees: 779
Employees here: 779

D-U-N-S 79-454-6903
GENERAL ELECTRIC COMPANY
3001 W Radio Dr, Florence, SC 29501
Phone: (843) 667-9799

Sales: $27,000,000
Company Type: Public Family Member
SIC: 8011
   Medical center
Steve Glover, Branch Manager

Employees: NA
Employees here: 430

D-U-N-S 92-659-1090
GENERAL HEALTH SERVICES, INC.
305 S 5th St, Enid, OK 73701
Phone: (580) 233-6100
Sales: $24,600,000
Company Type: Public Family Member
SIC: 8062
   General hospital
Frank Lopez, Chief Executive Officer

Employees: NA
Employees here: 650

D-U-N-S 07-429-4364
GENERAL HEALTH SERVICES, INC.
   (Parent: Healthtrust Inc - Hospital Co)
1 Park Plz, Nashville, TN 37202
Phone: (615) 344-9551
Sales: $59,100,000
Company Type: Public Family Member
SIC: 8062
   Health/allied services
Jack Bovender, Chief Executive Officer

Employees: 1,274
Employees here: 1

D-U-N-S 60-920-2742
GENERAL HEALTH SYSTEM
   (Parent: General Health System)
5757 Corp Blvd Ste 200, Baton Rouge, LA 70808
Phone: (225) 237-1500
Sales: $25,413,000
Company Type: Private
SIC: 8071
   Medical labs & physical fitness center
Thomas H Sawyer, President

Employees: 4,000
Employees here: 5

D-U-N-S 07-517-0662
GENERAL HOSPITAL CTR AT PASSAIC
350 Boulevard, Passaic, NJ 7055
Phone: (973) 365-4300
Sales: $109,042,000
Company Type: Private
SIC: 8062
   General medical and surgical hospital
Marie Cassese, President

Employees: 1,465
Employees here: 1,450

D-U-N-S 07-313-0411
GENERAL HOSPITAL CORPORATION
55 Fruit St, Boston, MA 2114
Phone: (617) 726-2000
Sales: $635,736,000
Company Type: Private
SIC: 8062
   General hospital
Dr James Mongan Md, President

Employees: 10,156
Employees here: 3,647

D-U-N-S 84-473-9540
GENERAL HOSPITAL CORPORATION
32 Fruit St 219, Boston, MA 2114
Phone: (617) 726-6297
Sales: $42,600,000
Company Type: Private
SIC: 8011
   Pathologist
Dr Robert Colvin, Director

Employees: NA
Employees here: 700

D-U-N-S 60-286-7673
GENERAL MEDICAL SERVICES CORP
   (Parent: Wyoming Valley Health Care Sys)
703 Rutter Ave, Kingston, PA 18704
Phone: (717) 552-7876

Sales: $45,223,000   *Employees:* 450
Company Type: Private   *Employees here:* 7
SIC: 8011
   Physicians service
Dr Joseph Weader Md, President

D-U-N-S 05-964-4484
GENESEE HOSPITAL INC
224 Alexander St, Rochester, NY 14607
Phone: (716) 263-6000
Sales: $151,004,000   *Employees:* 2,400
Company Type: Private   *Employees here:* 2,200
SIC: 8062
   General hospital
Joseph J De Silva, President

D-U-N-S 07-402-7152
GENESEE MEMORIAL HOSPITAL ASSN
127 North St, Batavia, NY 14020
Phone: (716) 343-6030
Sales: $25,719,000   *Employees:* 456
Company Type: Private   *Employees here:* 450
SIC: 8062
   General hospital
Douglas T Jones, President

D-U-N-S 07-969-7991
GENESEE REGION HOME CARE ASSN
49 Stone St, Rochester, NY 14604
Phone: (716) 325-1880
Sales: $50,036,000   *Employees:* 925
Company Type: Private   *Employees here:* 550
SIC: 8082
   Home care medical service
Anthony J Amado, Executive Director

D-U-N-S 07-367-1000
GENESEE VALLEY GROUP HEALTH ASSN
800 Carter St, Rochester, NY 14621
Phone: (716) 338-1400
Sales: $74,619,000   *Employees:* 300
Company Type: Private   *Employees here:* 160
SIC: 8011
   Health maintenance organization
Patricia L Bonino, Vice-President

D-U-N-S 61-031-1557
GENESIS ELDER CARE REHAB SERVI
   (*Parent:* Genesis Health Services Inc)
148 E State St, Kennett Square, PA 19348
Phone: (610) 444-1601
Sales: $32,400,000   *Employees:* 2,100
Company Type: Public Family Member   *Employees here:* 2,100
SIC: 8049
   Physical therapy & rehabilitation
Michael R Walker, Chairman of the Board

D-U-N-S 10-187-0251
GENESIS HEALTH INC
3627 University Blvd S, Jacksonville, FL 32216
Phone: (904) 391-1200
Sales: $40,085,000   *Employees:* 500
Company Type: Private   *Employees here:* 10
SIC: 8069
   Rehabilitation hospital outpatient surgery centers family
      physician offices & physician management services
Dr J B Brown Md, Chairman of the Board

D-U-N-S 94-001-5647
GENESIS HEALTH VENTURES INC
5601 Chestnut St, Philadelphia, PA 19139
Phone: (215) 476-2250

Sales: $28,100,000   *Employees:* NA
Company Type: Public Family Member   *Employees here:* 1,146
SIC: 8051
   Healthcare support services
Donna Wixted, Vice-President

D-U-N-S 13-108-8833
GENESIS HEALTH VENTURES INC
148 W State St, Kennett Square, PA 19348
Phone: (610) 444-6350
Sales: $1,099,823,000   *Employees:* 35,000
Company Type: Public   *Employees here:* 150
SIC: 8059
   Owns & manages long-term geriatric health care facilities
      operates pharmacies whol medical supplies & home health
      care
Michael R Walker, Chairman of the Board

D-U-N-S 78-762-6993
GENESIS LIFESTYLES INC
4901 Harrison Rd, Macon, GA 31206
Phone: (912) 474-5620
Sales: $864,000,000   *Employees:* 25
Company Type: Private   *Employees here:* 25
SIC: 8059
   Nursing/personal care
James Leverett, President

D-U-N-S 05-580-4389
GENESIS MEDICAL CENTER
1227 E Rusholme St, Davenport, IA 52803
Phone: (319) 421-6000
Sales: $189,377,000   *Employees:* 2,702
Company Type: Private   *Employees here:* 1,395
SIC: 8062
   General hospital
Leo A Bressanelli, President

D-U-N-S 84-744-0682
GENESIS MEDICAL CENTER
1401 W Central Park Ave, Davenport, IA 52804
Phone: (319) 383-1000
Sales: $54,300,000   *Employees:* NA
Company Type: Private   *Employees here:* 1,307
SIC: 8062
   General hospital
Leo Bressanelli, Manager

D-U-N-S 04-421-5663
GENESIS REHABILITATION HOSP
3599 University Blvd S, Jacksonville, FL 32216
Phone: (904) 858-7600
Sales: $31,315,000   *Employees:* 422
Company Type: Private   *Employees here:* 350
SIC: 8063
   Rehabilitation hospital
Stephen K Wilson, Executive Director

D-U-N-S 06-982-8507
GENESYS REGIONAL MEDICAL CTR
1 Genesys Pkwy, Grand Blanc, MI 48439
Phone: (810) 606-5000
Sales: $255,452,000   *Employees:* 2,800
Company Type: Private   *Employees here:* 1,500
SIC: 8062
   General medical and surgical hospitals
Gary Reetz, Vice-President

D-U-N-S 80-763-8986
GENESYS REGIONAL MEDICAL CTR
3921 Beecher Rd, Flint, MI 48532
Phone: (810) 762-4000

Sales: $42,100,000
Company Type: Private
SIC: 8062
  General hospital
Elliott Joseph, Manager

Employees: NA
Employees here: 1,000

D-U-N-S 05-596-0710
GENEVA GENERAL HOSPITAL INC
196 North St, Geneva, NY 14456
Phone: (315) 789-4222
Sales: $37,680,000
Company Type: Private
SIC: 8062
  General hospital
James Dooley, President

Employees: 845
Employees here: 845

D-U-N-S 87-446-8473
GENTLE DENTAL SERVICE CORP
900 Washington St Ste 1100, Vancouver, WA 98660
Phone: (360) 750-7975
Sales: $43,403,000
Company Type: Public
SIC: 8021
  Dentist office
Michael T Fiore, Chairman of the Board

Employees: 21
Employees here: 3

D-U-N-S 07-585-9595
GEORGE H LANIER MEMORIAL HOSP
4800 48th St, Valley, AL 36854
Phone: (334) 756-3111
Sales: $28,799,000
Company Type: Private
SIC: 8062
  General hospital
Robert J Humphrey, Chief Executive Officer

Employees: 480
Employees here: 480

D-U-N-S 06-932-9647
GEORGETOWN COUNTY MEM HOSP
606 Black River Rd, Georgetown, SC 29440
Phone: (843) 527-7000
Sales: $68,504,000
Company Type: Private
SIC: 8062
  General medical and surgical hospital
Paul Gatens Sr, Administrator

Employees: 509
Employees here: 500

D-U-N-S 06-989-4343
GERIATRIC & MEDICAL COMPANIES
  (Parent: Genesis Health Ventures Inc)
101 E State St, Kennett Square, PA 19348
Phone: (610) 444-6350
Sales: $114,900,000
Company Type: Public Family Member
SIC: 8051
  Health care srvs including rehab therapies ambulance srvs
    contract mgt financial diagnostic services & home health
    care srvs
Michael R Walker, Chairman of the Board

Employees: 5,000
Employees here: 150

D-U-N-S 09-908-3297
GERIATRIC AND MEDICAL SERVICES
  (Parent: Genesis Health Ventures Inc)
5601 Chestnut St, Philadelphia, PA 19139
Phone: (215) 476-2250
Sales: $86,100,000
Company Type: Public Family Member
SIC: 8051
  Operates skilled nursing facilities residential and
    independent care facilities
Rick Howard, President

Employees: 3,750
Employees here: 400

D-U-N-S 07-386-9844
GERIATRICS SVC CMPLEX FNDATION
630 Alton Rd, Miami, FL 33139
Phone: (305) 672-2100
Sales: $35,446,000
Company Type: Private
SIC: 8062
  Hospital
William Zubkoff Phd, Executive Director

Employees: 700
Employees here: 640

D-U-N-S 07-118-6118
GETTYSBURG HOSPITAL INC
147 Gettys St, Gettysburg, PA 17325
Phone: (717) 334-2121
Sales: $38,205,000
Company Type: Private
SIC: 8062
  General hospital
Steven Renner Cpa, President

Employees: 590
Employees here: 570

D-U-N-S 19-464-3193
GHS OSTEOPATHIC INC
4150 City Line Ave 90, Philadelphia, PA 19131
Phone: (215) 871-1000
Sales: $66,315,000
Company Type: Private
SIC: 8062
  General hospital
Harold Kramer, Chairman of the Board

Employees: 1,500
Employees here: 680

D-U-N-S 61-484-2458
GHS OSTEOPATHIC INC
1331 E Wyoming Ave, Philadelphia, PA 19124
Phone: (215) 871-1000
Sales: $36,900,000
Company Type: Private
SIC: 8062
  General hospital
Ernest Perilli, N/A

Employees: NA
Employees here: 750

D-U-N-S 07-509-0910
GILA REGIONAL MEDICAL CENTER
1313 E 32nd St, Silver City, NM 88061
Phone: (505) 388-1591
Sales: $23,700,000
Company Type: Private
SIC: 8062
  General hospital
Alfredo Ontiveros Jr, Administrator

Employees: 525
Employees here: 480

D-U-N-S 07-785-6698
GILBERT, BARBEE, MOORE, MCILVOY
201 Park St, Bowling Green, KY 42101
Phone: (502) 781-5111
Sales: $23,831,000
Company Type: Private
SIC: 8011
  Medical clinic
Thomas Babik, Administration

Employees: 300
Employees here: 245

D-U-N-S 03-733-5882
GILLETTE CHLD SPCLTY HEALTHCARE
200 University Ave E, Saint Paul, MN 55101
Phone: (651) 291-2848
Sales: $30,580,000
Company Type: Private
SIC: 8069
  Children's hospital
Margaret Perryman, President

Employees: 403
Employees here: 390

D-U-N-S 03-043-2009
GILMORE MEMORIAL HOSPITAL
1105 Earl Frye Blvd, Amory, MS 38821

Phone: (601) 256-7111
Sales: $21,271,000
Company Type: Private
SIC: 8062
   Hospital
Robert Letson, President

Employees: 420
Employees here: 420

D-U-N-S 02-155-8143
GIRLING HEALTH CARE INC
4902 Grover Ave, Austin, TX 78756
Phone: (512) 452-5781
Sales: $90,576,000
Company Type: Private
SIC: 8082
   Home health care services
Robert G Girling Iii, President

Employees: 10,000
Employees here: 310

D-U-N-S 05-320-2271
GLEN ELLYN CLINIC, S.C.
454 Pennsylvania Ave, Glen Ellyn, IL 60137
Phone: (630) 469-9200
Sales: $68,000,000
Company Type: Private
SIC: 8011
   Medical clinic
James Mini, President

Employees: 110
Employees here: 60

D-U-N-S 07-550-5289
GLEN MILLS SCHOOLS
Glen Mills Rd, Concordville, PA 19331
Phone: (610) 459-8100
Sales: $38,014,000
Company Type: Private
SIC: 8361
   Training school for delinquent adjudicated males
C D Ferrainola, Executive Director

Employees: 448
Employees here: 440

D-U-N-S 07-623-2735
GLENDALE ADVENTIST MED CTR
1509 Wilson Ter, Glendale, CA 91206
Phone: (818) 409-8000
Sales: $131,078,000
Company Type: Private
SIC: 8062
   Hospital
Robert Carmen, President

Employees: 1,400
Employees here: 1,350

D-U-N-S 06-380-2136
GLENDALE MEM HOSPITAL & HEALTH CTR
1420 S Central Ave, Glendale, CA 91204
Phone: (818) 502-1900
Sales: $101,945,000
Company Type: Private
SIC: 8062
   General hospital
Arnold R Schaeffer, President

Employees: 1,065
Employees here: 1,065

D-U-N-S 06-801-4521
GLENGARIFF CORP
Dosoris Ln, Glen Cove, NY 11542
Phone: (516) 676-1100
Sales: $20,471,000
Company Type: Private
SIC: 8051
   Skilled nursing care facility
Michael D Miness, President

Employees: 500
Employees here: 280

D-U-N-S 11-911-7406
GLENMARK ASSOCIATES INC
(Parent: Multicare Companies Inc)
1369 Stewartstown Rd, Morgantown, WV 26505
Phone: (304) 599-0395

Sales: $33,500,000
Company Type: Public Family Member
SIC: 8052
   Long term nursing & rehabilitative facilities & real estate
   holding company
Mark R Nesselroad, Chief Executive Officer

Employees: 1,800
Employees here: 40

D-U-N-S 11-450-8070
GLENOAKS MEDICAL CENTER
701 Winthrop Ave, Glendale Heights, IL 60139
Phone: (630) 545-8000
Sales: $34,798,000
Company Type: Private
SIC: 8062
   General hospital
Jorge Heyde, Executive Administrator

Employees: 625
Employees here: 613

D-U-N-S 06-054-0382
GLENS FALLS HOSPITAL
100 Park St, Glens Falls, NY 12801
Phone: (518) 792-3151
Sales: $113,867,000
Company Type: Private
SIC: 8062
   General medical and surgical hospital
David G Kruczlnicki, President

Employees: 2,100
Employees here: 1,925

D-U-N-S 07-137-3625
GLENWOOD REGIONAL MEDICAL CTR
503 McMillan Rd, West Monroe, LA 71291
Phone: (318) 329-4200
Sales: $73,578,000
Company Type: Private
SIC: 8062
   General medical & surgical hospital
Raymond L Ford, Chief Executive Officer

Employees: 1,276
Employees here: 1,183

D-U-N-S 03-115-8397
GLYNN-BRUNSWICK HOSPITAL AUTH
3100 Kemble Ave, Brunswick, GA 31520
Phone: (912) 264-7000
Sales: $116,801,000
Company Type: Private
SIC: 8062
   General hospital
Berton Whitaker, President

Employees: 1,487
Employees here: 1,272

D-U-N-S 07-361-3705
GNADEN HUETTEN MEMORIAL HOSP
211 N 12th St, Lehighton, PA 18235
Phone: (610) 377-1300
Sales: $31,704,000
Company Type: Private
SIC: 8062
   Hospital & skilled nursing home
Robert Clark, President

Employees: 690
Employees here: 600

D-U-N-S 07-952-3403
GODDARD MEDICAL ASSOCIATES PC
1 Pearl St, Brockton, MA 2301
Phone: (508) 586-3600
Sales: $41,200,000
Company Type: Private
SIC: 8011
   Group medical center
Dr Steven A Paris Md, President

Employees: 600
Employees here: 520

D-U-N-S 04-933-4311
GOLDEN STATE HEALTH CENTERS
13347 Ventura Blvd, Van Nuys, CA 91423
Phone: (818) 986-1550

Sales: $90,348,000
Company Type: Private
SIC: 8059
　　Convalescent & nursing homes
David B Weiss, Chairman of the Board

Employees: 2,000
Employees here: 16

D-U-N-S 79-997-2930
GOLDEN VALLEY MEMORIAL HOSP
1600 N 2nd St, Clinton, MO 64735
Phone: (660) 885-5511
Sales: $21,300,000
Company Type: Private
SIC: 8062
　　Hospital
Randy Wertz, Administrator

Employees: 475
Employees here: 475

D-U-N-S 80-234-9480
GOOD HEALTH HMO, INC
　　(Parent: Blue Cross/Blue Shield-Ks City)
2301 Main St, Kansas City, MO 64108
Phone: (816) 395-2222
Sales: $25,000,000
Company Type: Private
SIC: 8011
　　Health maintenance organization
John P Mescotte, President

Employees: 4
Employees here: 4

D-U-N-S 07-494-5320
GOOD SAMARITAN HOSPITAL OF MD INC
5601 Loch Raven Blvd, Baltimore, MD 21239
Phone: (410) 532-8000
Sales: $115,541,000
Company Type: Private
SIC: 8062
　　Hospital
Larry Beck, President

Employees: 1,427
Employees here: 1,427

D-U-N-S 05-361-5548
GOOD SAMARITAN HOSPITAL CORVALLIS
3600 NW Samaritan Dr, Corvallis, OR 97330
Phone: (541) 757-5111
Sales: $68,597,000
Company Type: Private
SIC: 8062
　　General hospital
Larry Mullins, President

Employees: 900
Employees here: 896

D-U-N-S 06-398-5261
GOOD SAMARITAN HOSPITAL HEALTH CTR
2222 Philadelphia Dr, Dayton, OH 45406
Phone: (937) 278-2612
Sales: $168,790,000
Company Type: Private
SIC: 8062
　　Hospital
K D Deck, President

Employees: 2,200
Employees here: 2,100

D-U-N-S 06-801-8175
GOOD SAMARITAN HOSPITAL MED CTR
1000 Montauk Hwy, West Islip, NY 11795
Phone: (516) 376-3000
Sales: $194,859,000
Company Type: Private
SIC: 8062
　　General medical and surgical hospital
Daniel P Walsh, President

Employees: 2,900
Employees here: 2,400

D-U-N-S 07-132-0501
GOOD SAMARITAN HOSPITAL
520 S 7th St, Vincennes, IN 47591
Phone: (812) 882-5220

Sales: $91,256,000
Company Type: Private
SIC: 8062
　　General hospital
A J Hidde, President

Employees: 1,600
Employees here: 1,600

D-U-N-S 06-978-1896
GOOD SAMARITAN HOSPITAL
4th & Walnut Sts, Lebanon, PA 17042
Phone: (717) 270-7500
Sales: $75,800,000
Company Type: Private
SIC: 8062
　　Hospital & ret respiratory equipment
Robert J Longo, Chief Executive Officer

Employees: 1,050
Employees here: 950

D-U-N-S 08-250-5900
GOOD SAMARITAN HOSPITAL
407 14th Ave SE, Puyallup, WA 98372
Phone: (253) 848-6661
Sales: $95,764,000
Company Type: Private
SIC: 8062
　　Acute & rehabilitation hospital
David Hamry, President

Employees: 1,481
Employees here: 1,451

D-U-N-S 07-602-3704
GOOD SAMARITAN HOSPITAL INC
N Flagler Dr, West Palm Beach, FL 33402
Phone: (561) 655-5511
Sales: $114,440,000
Company Type: Private
SIC: 8062
　　General medical and surgical hospital
C M French, President

Employees: 1,200
Employees here: 1,200

D-U-N-S 07-800-5824
GOOD SAMARITAN HOSPITAL INC
31st & Central Ave, Kearney, NE 68848
Phone: (308) 236-8511
Sales: $86,408,000
Company Type: Private
SIC: 8062
　　General hospital
William Hendrickson, President

Employees: 1,400
Employees here: 1,400

D-U-N-S 05-238-9657
GOOD SAMARITAN HOSPITAL
1225 Wilshire Blvd, Los Angeles, CA 90017
Phone: (213) 977-2121
Sales: $83,900,000
Company Type: Private
SIC: 8062
　　General hospital
Charles Munger, Chairman of the Board

Employees: 1,800
Employees here: 1,800

D-U-N-S 87-802-3050
GOOD SAMARITAN MEDICAL CENTER
235 N Pearl St, Brockton, MA 2301
Phone: (508) 427-3000
Sales: $138,929,000
Company Type: Private
SIC: 8062
　　General hospital
Gautam Parikh, Chairman of the Board

Employees: 960
Employees here: 930

D-U-N-S 07-498-7975
GOOD SAMARITAN MEDICAL CENTER
1020 Franklin St, Johnstown, PA 15905
Phone: (814) 533-1000

Sales: $34,300,000   *Employees:* 553
Company Type: Private   *Employees here:* 550
SIC: 8062
   General hospital
Timothy Carnes, Chief Executive Officer

D-U-N-S 03-017-2613
GOOD SHEPHERD HOSPITAL, INC
700 E Marshall Ave, Longview, TX 75601
Phone: (903) 236-2000
Sales: $156,737,000   *Employees:* 1,800
Company Type: Private   *Employees here:* 1,457
SIC: 8062
   General hospital
Jerry D Adair, Chief Executive Officer

D-U-N-S 07-736-8967
GOOD SHEPHERD LUTHERAN HOME
682 W Henderson Ave, Porterville, CA 93257
Phone: (209) 791-2000
Sales: $23,972,000   *Employees:* 1,000
Company Type: Private   *Employees here:* 22
SIC: 8361
   Residential care for the handicapped
David Geske Phd, President

D-U-N-S 07-327-4292
GOOD SHEPHERD SERVICES
305 7th Ave Fl 9, New York, NY 10001
Phone: (212) 243-7070
Sales: $20,280,000   *Employees:* 400
Company Type: Private   *Employees here:* 85
SIC: 8361
   Children & family services
Paulette L Monaco Sr, Executive Director

D-U-N-S 06-979-2547
GOOD SMRITAN REGIONAL MED CTR
700 E Norwegian St, Pottsville, PA 17901
Phone: (717) 621-4000
Sales: $90,685,000   *Employees:* 800
Company Type: Private   *Employees here:* 800
SIC: 8062
   General hospital
Gino Pazzaglini, Chief Executive Officer

D-U-N-S 17-492-1338
GOOD SMRTAN HOSPITAL OF CINCINNATI
   (Parent: Catholic Health Initiative)
375 Dixmyth Ave, Cincinnati, OH 45220
Phone: (513) 872-1400
Sales: $184,459,000   *Employees:* 3,042
Company Type: Private   *Employees here:* 3,000
SIC: 8062
   General medical and surgical hospital
John S Prout, Chief Executive Officer

D-U-N-S 07-870-5985
GOOD SAMARITAN HOSPITAL OF SUFFERN NY
255 Lafayette Ave, Suffern, NY 10901
Phone: (914) 368-5000
Sales: $110,728,000   *Employees:* 1,500
Company Type: Private   *Employees here:* 1,500
SIC: 8062
   General medical & surgical hospital
James Martin, President

D-U-N-S 79-867-5690
GOOD SMRTAN REGIONAL HEALTH CTR
605 N 12th St, Mount Vernon, IL 62864
Phone: (618) 242-4600

Sales: $63,413,000   *Employees:* 805
Company Type: Private   *Employees here:* 700
SIC: 8062
   General hospital
Michael Warren, Vice-President

D-U-N-S 07-779-8627
GOODWIN HOUSE INCORPORATED
4800 Fillmore Ave, Alexandria, VA 22311
Phone: (703) 578-1000
Sales: $23,237,000   *Employees:* 568
Company Type: Private   *Employees here:* 275
SIC: 8051
   Skilled nursing care facility & geriatric residential apartments
Marvin Ogburn, President

D-U-N-S 07-433-2453
GOSHEN HOSPITAL ASSOCIATION
200 High Park Ave, Goshen, IN 46526
Phone: (219) 533-2141
Sales: $50,212,000   *Employees:* 736
Company Type: Private   *Employees here:* 736
SIC: 8062
   General medical hospital
Charles Colbourn, Special Projects Coord

D-U-N-S 07-233-4287
GOTTLIEB MEMORIAL HOSPITAL
701 W North Ave, Melrose Park, IL 60160
Phone: (708) 681-3200
Sales: $97,398,000   *Employees:* 1,200
Company Type: Private   *Employees here:* 1,100
SIC: 8062
   General hospital
John Morgan, President

D-U-N-S 07-737-1433
GOULD MEDICAL FOUNDATION
600 Coffee Rd, Modesto, CA 95355
Phone: (209) 521-6097
Sales: $68,374,000   *Employees:* 680
Company Type: Private   *Employees here:* 400
SIC: 8011
   Medical clinic
Chuck Wirth, Chief Executive Officer

D-U-N-S 07-106-8589
GRACE HOSPITAL
2201 S Sterling St, Morganton, NC 28655
Phone: (828) 438-2000
Sales: $61,191,000   *Employees:* 1,000
Company Type: Private   *Employees here:* 1,000
SIC: 8062
   General hospital
V O Wilson Jr, President

D-U-N-S 08-247-1525
GRACE LIVING CENTERS
4415 Highline Blvd, Oklahoma City, OK 73108
Phone: (405) 943-1144
Sales: $43,400,000   *Employees:* 1,900
Company Type: Private   *Employees here:* 40
SIC: 8051
   Operates nursing facilities
Kenneth D Greiner, President

D-U-N-S 07-733-6659
GRADY MEMORIAL HOSPITAL
2220 W Iowa Ave, Chickasha, OK 73018
Phone: (405) 224-2300

Sales: $27,922,000   Employees: 500
Company Type: Private   Employees here: 500
SIC: 8062
    General hospital
Roger R Boid, Administrator

D-U-N-S 07-142-9567
GRAHAM HOSPITAL ASSOCIATION
210 W Walnut St, Canton, IL 61520
Phone: (309) 647-5240
Sales: $28,385,000   Employees: 500
Company Type: Private   Employees here: 495
SIC: 8062
    General hospital
D R Slaubaugh, President

D-U-N-S 62-164-0630
GRANCARE INC
    (Parent: Mariner Post-Acute Network)
1 Ravinia Dr Ste 1240, Atlanta, GA 30346
Phone: (770) 393-0199
Sales: $317,600,000   Employees: 13,800
Company Type: Public Family Member Employees here: 250
SIC: 8051
    Operates skilled nursing facilities provides home health care
      and provides contract management services
Keith B Pitts, Chairman of the Board

D-U-N-S 06-213-0166
GRAND VALLEY HEALTH PLAN INC
829 Forest Hill Ave SE, Grand Rapids, MI 49546
Phone: (616) 949-2410
Sales: $36,261,000   Employees: 49
Company Type: Private   Employees here: 35
SIC: 8011
    Health maintenance organization
Roland E Palmer, President

D-U-N-S 06-831-9094
GRAND VIEW HOSPITAL INC
N10561 Grandview Ln, Ironwood, MI 49938
Phone: (906) 932-2525
Sales: $20,371,000   Employees: 300
Company Type: Private   Employees here: 300
SIC: 8062
    General hospital
Frederick K Geissler, Administrator

D-U-N-S 86-125-0868
GRAND VIEW HOSPITAL
700 Lawn Ave, Sellersville, PA 18960
Phone: (215) 453-4000
Sales: $71,936,000   Employees: 1,572
Company Type: Private   Employees here: 1,489
SIC: 8062
    General medical & surgical hospital
Stuart Fine, Chief Executive Officer

D-U-N-S 05-497-2211
GRANDE RONDE HOSPITAL INC
900 Sunset Dr, La Grande, OR 97850
Phone: (541) 963-8421
Sales: $22,567,000   Employees: 380
Company Type: Private   Employees here: 380
SIC: 8062
    Hospital
James Mattes, Administrator

D-U-N-S 07-573-2461
GRANT COUNTY PUB HOSPITAL DST NO 1
801 E Wheeler Rd, Moses Lake, WA 98837
Phone: (509) 765-5606

Sales: $27,685,000   Employees: 470
Company Type: Private   Employees here: 470
SIC: 8062
    General medical & surgical hospital
Keith Baldwin, Administrator

D-U-N-S 07-164-3589
GRANT/RVRSIDE MTHDST HSPITALS
3535 Olentangy River Rd, Columbus, OH 43214
Phone: (614) 566-5000
Sales: $556,011,000   Employees: 8,000
Company Type: Private   Employees here: 6,000
SIC: 8062
    General hospital
Joseph G Felkner, Chief Financial Officer

D-U-N-S 93-299-8115
GRANT/RVRSIDE MTHDST HSPITALS
111 S Grant Ave, Columbus, OH 43215
Phone: (614) 461-3232
Sales: $80,500,000   Employees: NA
Company Type: Private   Employees here: 1,900
SIC: 8062
    General hospital
William W Wilkins, Chief Executive Officer

D-U-N-S 07-259-4997
GRATIOT HEALTH SYSTEM
300 E Warwick Dr, Alma, MI 48801
Phone: (517) 463-1101
Sales: $54,710,000   Employees: 818
Company Type: Private   Employees here: 810
SIC: 8062
    General hospital
Bob Baker, President

D-U-N-S 07-926-5476
GRAYS HARBOR COMMUNITY HOSP
915 Anderson Dr, Aberdeen, WA 98520
Phone: (360) 532-8330
Sales: $43,392,000   Employees: 550
Company Type: Private   Employees here: 300
SIC: 8062
    General hospital
Michael J Madden, Administrator

D-U-N-S 08-504-9112
GRAYSON COUNTY HOSPITAL FOUNDATION
910 Wallace Ave, Leitchfield, KY 42754
Phone: (502) 259-9400
Sales: $20,160,000   Employees: 360
Company Type: Private   Employees here: 280
SIC: 8062
    Hospital
Stephen L Meredith, Chief Executive Officer

D-U-N-S 06-372-2342
GREAT FALLS CLINIC LLP
1400 29th St S, Great Falls, MT 59405
Phone: (406) 454-2171
Sales: $36,794,000   Employees: 390
Company Type: Private   Employees here: 255
SIC: 8011
    Medical clinic
Gregory D Hagforf, Administrator

D-U-N-S 92-600-5901
GREAT LAKES HEALTH PLAN INC
    (Parent: Healthcor Inc)
17117 W 9 Mile Rd, Southfield, MI 48075
Phone: (248) 559-5656

Sales: $38,000,000
Company Type: Private
SIC: 8011
   Health maintenance organization
Donald Zinner, President

Employees: 150
Employees here: 150

D-U-N-S 10-233-2301
GREAT RIVER HEALTH SYSTEMS
602 N 3rd St, Burlington, IA 52601
Phone: (319) 753-3260
Sales: $23,508,000
Company Type: Private
SIC: 8062
   Holding company for general hospital
Glen L Heagle, President

Employees: 1,140
Employees here: 3

D-U-N-S 10-963-1929
GREAT VALLEY HEALTH
11 Industrial Blvd, Paoli, PA 19301
Phone: (610) 648-1644
Sales: $64,000,000
Company Type: Private
SIC: 8011
   Medical doctor's office
White Leland I, President

Employees: 882
Employees here: 35

D-U-N-S 06-487-4050
GREATER BALTIMORE MEDICAL CTR
6701 N Charles St, Baltimore, MD 21204
Phone: (410) 828-2000
Sales: $200,489,000
Company Type: Private
SIC: 8062
   General hospital
Robert P Kowal, President

Employees: 2,800
Employees here: 2,000

D-U-N-S 60-735-1392
GREATER BRISTOL HEALTH SVCS CORP
Brewster Rd, Bristol, CT 6010
Phone: (860) 585-3000
Sales: $60,300,000
Company Type: Private
SIC: 8062
   General hospital holding company
Thomas Kennedy, President

Employees: 1,300
Employees here: 5

D-U-N-S 87-849-0481
GREATER DETROIT HOSPITAL INC
3120 Carpenter St, Detroit, MI 48212
Phone: (313) 369-3000
Sales: $23,000,000
Company Type: Private
SIC: 8062
   General hospital
Sandra Peppers, Chief Executive Officer

Employees: 306
Employees here: 306

D-U-N-S 12-186-3468
GREATER LYN MNTL HTH/RTDTN ASS
37 Friend St, Lynn, MA 1902
Phone: (781) 593-1088
Sales: $20,850,000
Company Type: Private
SIC: 8361
   Operates homes for the mentally retarded and day/
    outpatient program centers
Albert W Bleau Jr, Executive Director

Employees: 800
Employees here: 70

D-U-N-S 04-080-0260
GREATER STATEN ISLAND MED GRP
1050 Clove Rd, Staten Island, NY 10301
Phone: (718) 816-6440

Sales: $26,000,000
Company Type: Private
SIC: 8011
   Prepaid medical group
David Jenkins, Administrator

Employees: 380
Employees here: 200

D-U-N-S 87-918-5320
GREATER SOUTHEAST COMMUNITY HOSPITAL CORP
1310 Southern Ave SE, Washington, DC 20032
Phone: (202) 574-6000
Sales: $130,621,000
Company Type: Private
SIC: 8062
   General hospital
Robert Winfrey, Chief Operating Officer

Employees: 1,200
Employees here: 1,200

D-U-N-S 05-860-0685
GREATER SE COMM HOSPITAL FOUNDATION
1310 Southern Ave SE, Washington, DC 20032
Phone: (202) 574-6000
Sales: $133,776,000
Company Type: Private
SIC: 8062
   Hospitals and skilled nursing homes
Dr George Gilbert, Chief Executive Officer

Employees: 2,800
Employees here: 75

D-U-N-S 07-966-8257
GREEN RIVER REG MNT HEALTH-MNT
416 W 3rd St, Owensboro, KY 42301
Phone: (502) 684-0696
Sales: $25,081,000
Company Type: Private
SIC: 8051
   Mental health and mental retardation service
Gayle J Di Cesare, President

Employees: 675
Employees here: 25

D-U-N-S 36-110-8715
GREEN SPRING HEALTH SERVICES,
   (Parent: Magellan Health Services Inc)
5565 Sterrett Pl Ste 500, Columbia, MD 21044
Phone: (410) 992-0720
Sales: $226,277,000
Company Type: Public Family Member
SIC: 8093
   Provides managed care specializing in mental health &
    substance abuse
Henry T Harbin, President

Employees: 1,500
Employees here: 600

D-U-N-S 06-685-5966
GREENE COUNTY MEMORIAL HOSP
350 Bonar Ave, Waynesburg, PA 15370
Phone: (724) 627-3101
Sales: $23,200,000
Company Type: Private
SIC: 8062
   General hospital
Raoul M Walsh, President

Employees: 270
Employees here: 265

D-U-N-S 07-287-8358
GREENE MEMORIAL HOSPITAL INC
1141 N Monroe Dr, Xenia, OH 45385
Phone: (937) 372-8011
Sales: $53,039,000
Company Type: Private
SIC: 8062
   General hospital
Michael R Stephens, President

Employees: 800
Employees here: 600

D-U-N-S 07-793-3976
GREENSVILLE MEMORIAL HOSPITAL
214 Weaver Ave, Emporia, VA 23847
Phone: (804) 348-2000

Sales: $22,984,000
Company Type: Private
SIC: 8062
   General hospital
Rosemary Check, Chief Executive Officer

Employees: 430
Employees here: 430

D-U-N-S 80-755-3508
GREENVILLE HEALTH CORPORATION
701 Grove Rd, Greenville, SC 29605
Phone: (864) 455-4069
Sales: $39,945,000
Company Type: Private
SIC: 8011
   Medical doctor's office nursing/personal care local passenger
     transportation retail drug store
Frank Pinckney, President

Employees: 407
Employees here: 400

D-U-N-S 01-491-9625
GREENVILLE HOSPITAL CORP
   (Parent: Community Health Systems Inc)
Hwy 10 W, Greenville, AL 36037
Phone: (334) 382-2671
Sales: $25,000,000
Company Type: Public Family Member
SIC: 8062
   Hospital
Tom Mcdougal Jr, Administrator

Employees: 155
Employees here: 155

D-U-N-S 07-799-0745
GREENVILLE HOSPITAL SYSTEM
701 Grove Rd, Greenville, SC 29605
Phone: (864) 455-7000
Sales: $468,782,000
Company Type: Private
SIC: 8062
   General hospitals
Frank D Pinckney, President

Employees: 5,200
Employees here: 4,000

D-U-N-S 01-013-8097
GREENWICH HOSPITAL ASSN INC
5 Perryridge Rd, Greenwich, CT 6830
Phone: (203) 863-3000
Sales: $109,381,000
Company Type: Private
SIC: 8062
   General hospital
Frank A Corvino, President

Employees: 1,300
Employees here: 1,263

D-U-N-S 07-355-3661
GREENWOOD LEFLORE HOSPITAL
1401 River Rd, Greenwood, MS 38930
Phone: (601) 459-9751
Sales: $52,535,000
Company Type: Private
SIC: 8062
   Hospital
Terrell M Cobb, Administrator

Employees: 800
Employees here: 684

D-U-N-S 03-043-2033
GRENADA LAKE MEDICAL CENTER
960 Avent Dr, Grenada, MS 38901
Phone: (601) 227-7000
Sales: $26,723,000
Company Type: Private
SIC: 8062
   General hospital and home health agency
Linda Gholston, Officer

Employees: 630
Employees here: 630

D-U-N-S 19-720-0173
GRIFFIN HEALTH SERVICES CORP
130 Division St, Derby, CT 6418
Phone: (203) 732-7528

Sales: $44,266,000
Company Type: Private
SIC: 8062
   Health services management
John Bustelos Jr, President

Employees: 1,100
Employees here: 6

D-U-N-S 07-212-8424
GRIFFIN HOSPITAL INC
130 Division St, Derby, CT 6418
Phone: (203) 735-7421
Sales: $63,860,000
Company Type: Private
SIC: 8062
   General medical & surgical hospital
John Bustelos Jr, President

Employees: 1,100
Employees here: 1,100

D-U-N-S 07-196-1007
GRIM SMITH HOSPITAL & CLINIC
315 S Osteopathy St, Kirksville, MO 63501
Phone: (660) 785-1000
Sales: $45,788,000
Company Type: Private
SIC: 8062
   General medical hospital
Charles M Boughton, Administrator

Employees: 850
Employees here: 750

D-U-N-S 01-024-5835
GRINNELL REGIONAL MEDICAL CTR
210 4th Ave, Grinnell, IA 50112
Phone: (515) 236-7511
Sales: $20,986,000
Company Type: Private
SIC: 8062
   Hospital
Todd Linden, President

Employees: 375
Employees here: 314

D-U-N-S 01-021-3700
GRITMAN MEDICAL CENTER
700 S Main St, Moscow, ID 83843
Phone: (208) 882-4511
Sales: $19,959,000
Company Type: Private
SIC: 8062
   Hospital
Dan Smigelski, Administrator

Employees: 320
Employees here: 320

D-U-N-S 07-334-1562
GROSSMONT HOSPITAL CORPORATION
5555 Grossmont Center Dr, La Mesa, CA 91942
Phone: (619) 465-0711
Sales: $159,991,000
Company Type: Private
SIC: 8062
   General hospital
Michele Tarbett, Administrator

Employees: 1,911
Employees here: 1,740

D-U-N-S 02-013-3732
GROUP HEALTH MEDICAL ASSOC PC
6565 E Carondelet Dr, Tucson, AZ 85710
Phone: (520) 721-5480
Sales: $39,269,000
Company Type: Private
SIC: 8011
   Group practice of medicine
James R Welter, Executive Director

Employees: 500
Employees here: 175

D-U-N-S 11-301-4161
GROUP HEALTH NORTHWEST
5615 W Sunset Hwy, Spokane, WA 99224
Phone: (509) 838-9100

Sales: $274,277,000   *Employees:* 1,000
Company Type: Private   *Employees here:* 400
SIC: 8011
    Health maintenance organization
Sharon Fairchild, President

D-U-N-S 55-680-5307
GROUP HEALTH PLAN, INC
2220 Riverside Ave, Minneapolis, MN 55454
Phone: (612) 371-1610
Sales: $22,200,000   *Employees:* NA
Company Type: Private   *Employees here:* 350
SIC: 8011
    Medical doctor's office
Pat Helgle, Manager

D-U-N-S 13-503-4635
GROUP HEALTH COOP OF PUGET SOUND
201 16th Ave E, Seattle, WA 98112
Phone: (206) 326-3000
Sales: $29,300,000   *Employees:* NA
Company Type: Private   *Employees here:* 600
SIC: 8062
    General hospital
Lisa Strom, Principal

D-U-N-S 15-257-7441
GROUP HEALTH COOP OF PUGET SOUND
201 16th Ave E, Seattle, WA 98112
Phone: (206) 326-3435
Sales: $48,300,000   *Employees:* NA
Company Type: Private   *Employees here:* 800
SIC: 8011
    Medical doctor's office
Pat Kennedy-Scott, Principal

D-U-N-S 07-597-3248
GROUP HEALTH COOP OF PUGET SOUND
2700 152nd Ave NE, Redmond, WA 98052
Phone: (425) 883-5151
Sales: $111,900,000   *Employees:* NA
Company Type: Private   *Employees here:* 2,250
SIC: 8062
    General hospital
Pat Kennedy-Scott, President

D-U-N-S 03-927-8577
GROVE HILL MEDICAL CENTER PC
300 Kensington Ave, New Britain, CT 6051
Phone: (860) 224-6200
Sales: $45,792,000   *Employees:* 425
Company Type: Private   *Employees here:* 275
SIC: 8093
    Outpatient specialty clinic
Robert Ferrini, Chief Executive Officer

D-U-N-S 96-257-7987
GUADALUPE MEDICAL CENTER INC
    (Parent: Columbia/Hca Healthcare Corp)
2430 W Pierce St, Carlsbad, NM 88220
Phone: (505) 887-4100
Sales: $21,300,000   *Employees:* 475
Company Type: Public Family Member *Employees here:* 450
SIC: 8062
    General hospital
Tom Mcclintock, Chief Executive Officer

D-U-N-S 07-462-0170
GUADALUPE VALLEY HOSPITAL
1215 E Court St, Seguin, TX 78155
Phone: (830) 379-2411

Sales: $35,639,000   *Employees:* 690
Company Type: Private   *Employees here:* 690
SIC: 8062
    Hospital
Don L Richey, Administrator

D-U-N-S 06-656-2703
GUARDIAN CARE, INC
5725 Paradise Dr Ste 550, Corte Madera, CA 94925
Phone: (415) 945-2200
Sales: $80,000,000   *Employees:* 1,100
Company Type: Private   *Employees here:* 32
SIC: 8051
    Subacute and skilled nursing facilities
Robert G Peirce, President

D-U-N-S 01-080-2080
GULF COAST REGIONAL BLOOD CTR
1400 La Concha Ln, Houston, TX 77054
Phone: (713) 790-1200
Sales: $41,141,000   *Employees:* 550
Company Type: Private   *Employees here:* 400
SIC: 8099
    Blood bank
Bill Teague, President

D-U-N-S 07-762-9830
GUNDERSEN CLINIC LTD
1836 South Ave, La Crosse, WI 54601
Phone: (608) 782-7300
Sales: $200,000,000   *Employees:* 2,200
Company Type: Private   *Employees here:* 1,200
SIC: 8011
    Multi-specialty medical clinic
John Katrana Phd, Officer

D-U-N-S 07-179-3673
GUNDERSEN LTHRAN HSPTL-LCROSSE
1910 South Ave, La Crosse, WI 54601
Phone: (608) 785-0530
Sales: $140,533,000   *Employees:* 1,760
Company Type: Private   *Employees here:* 1,600
SIC: 8062
    General hospital & clinic
John Katrana, Chief Executive Officer

D-U-N-S 15-771-5418
GURWIN, ROSALIND AND JOSEPH JE
68 Hauppauge Rd, Commack, NY 11725
Phone: (516) 499-6500
Sales: $30,597,000   *Employees:* 402
Company Type: Private   *Employees here:* 402
SIC: 8059
    Skilled nursing facility
Joseph Gurwin, President

D-U-N-S 06-959-8274
GUTHRIE CLINIC LTD
    (Parent: Guthrie Healthcare Systems)
Guthrie Sq, Sayre, PA 18840
Phone: (717) 888-5858
Sales: $51,600,000   *Employees:* 1,000
Company Type: Private   *Employees here:* 150
SIC: 8011
    Group health association
Dr Lynn A Smaha Md, President

D-U-N-S 07-528-7599
GUTHRIE HEALTHCARE SYSTEMS
Guthrie Sq, Sayre, PA 18840
Phone: (717) 888-6666

Sales: $132,400,000 *Employees:* 2,825
Company Type: Private *Employees here:* 1
SIC: 8062
 Hospital nursing school convalescent home group health
 association whol & rent supplies mgmt & ambulance svcs
Robert Landy, Chairman of the Board

D-U-N-S 78-740-0712
GWINNETT COMMUNITY HOSPITAL
 (Parent: Columbia/Hca Healthcare Corp)
1700 Medical Way, Snellville, GA 30078
Phone: (770) 979-0200
Sales: $22,500,000 *Employees:* 500
Company Type: Public Family Member *Employees here:* 500
SIC: 8062
 Acute care and surgical hospital
David L Harris, Administrator

D-U-N-S 07-587-7290
GWINNETT HOSPITAL SYSTEM INC
1000 Medical Center Blvd, Lawrenceville, GA 30045
Phone: (770) 995-4321
Sales: $185,654,000 *Employees:* 2,050
Company Type: Private *Employees here:* 1,300
SIC: 8062
 General hospitals and outpatient clinics
Franklin M Rinker, President

D-U-N-S 05-227-9023
GYNCOR, INC.
750 N Orleans St, Chicago, IL 60610
Phone: (312) 397-8200
Sales: $22,900,000 *Employees:* 335
Company Type: Private *Employees here:* 90
SIC: 8011
 Physician's office
Dr Norbert Gleicher Md, President

D-U-N-S 79-692-2268
GCI PROPERTIES, INC
 (Parent: Grancare Inc)
1 Ravinia Dr Ste 1500, Atlanta, GA 30346
Phone: (770) 393-0199
Sales: $53,200,000 *Employees:* 2,325
Company Type: Public Family Member *Employees here:* 1
SIC: 8051
 Skilled and intermediate nursing facility
Keith Pitts, President

D-U-N-S 96-239-7436
H C A ARLINGTON INC
 (Parent: Columbia/Hca Healthcare Corp)
3301 Matlock Rd, Arlington, TX 76015
Phone: (817) 472-4800
Sales: $36,700,000 *Employees:* 800
Company Type: Public Family Member *Employees here:* 800
SIC: 8062
 Hospital
John Fromhold, Chief Executive Officer

D-U-N-S 05-202-9311
H C A HEALTH SERVICES OF FLA
14000 Fivay Rd, Port Richey, FL 34667
Phone: (727) 863-2411
Sales: $52,900,000 *Employees:* NA
Company Type: Public Family Member *Employees here:* 1,200
SIC: 8062
 General medical and surgical services
Don Griffin, Principal

D-U-N-S 11-538-6013
H C A HEALTH SERVICES OF FLA
11375 Cortez Blvd, Brooksville, FL 34613

Phone: (352) 596-6632
Sales: $44,900,000 *Employees:* NA
Company Type: Public Family Member *Employees here:* 1,100
SIC: 8062
 General medical & surgical hospital
Dennis A Taylor, N/A

D-U-N-S 78-241-5988
H C A HEALTH SERVICES OF FLA
2020 59th St W, Bradenton, FL 34209
Phone: (941) 798-6110
Sales: $52,900,000 *Employees:* NA
Company Type: Public Family Member *Employees here:* 1,200
SIC: 8062
 Medical center
Lindell Orr, Branch Manager

D-U-N-S 07-321-6582
H C A HEALTH SERVICES OF FLA
 (Parent: Columbia/Hca Healthcare Corp)
1 Park Mdws, Nashville, TN 37215
Phone: (615) 327-9551
Sales: $239,900,000 *Employees:* 5,100
Company Type: Public Family Member *Employees here:* 4
SIC: 8062
 General hospital
Thomas F Frist Jr, Chairman of the Board

D-U-N-S 05-810-4613
H C A HEALTH SERVICES OF KANS
 (Parent: Columbia/Hca Healthcare Corp)
550 N Hillside St, Wichita, KS 67214
Phone: (316) 688-2468
Sales: $262,115,000 *Employees:* 3,080
Company Type: Public Family Member *Employees here:* 3,080
SIC: 8062
 General medical & surgical hospital
Carl W Fitch Sr, Chief Executive Officer

D-U-N-S 10-259-9743
H C A HEALTH SERVICES OF LA
 (Parent: Columbia/Hca Healthcare Corp)
3421 Medical Park Dr, Monroe, LA 71203
Phone: (318) 388-1946
Sales: $23,100,000 *Employees:* 512
Company Type: Public Family Member *Employees here:* 477
SIC: 8062
 General medical & surgical hospital
Thomas F Frist Jr, Chairman of the Board

D-U-N-S 07-398-1417
H C A HEALTH SERVICES OF NH
 (Parent: Columbia/Hca Healthcare Corp)
333 Borthwick Ave, Portsmouth, NH 3801
Phone: (603) 436-5110
Sales: $114,000,000 *Employees:* 969
Company Type: Public Family Member *Employees here:* 769
SIC: 8062
 General medical & surgical hospital & psychiatric hospital
William J Schuler, President

D-U-N-S 10-140-7138
H C A HEALTH SERVICES OF NH
1 Parkland Dr, Derry, NH 3038
Phone: (603) 432-1500
Sales: $24,800,000 *Employees:* NA
Company Type: Public Family Member *Employees here:* 500
SIC: 8062
 Medical & surgical hospital
Steven R Gordon, Manager

D-U-N-S 13-106-4644
H C A HEALTH SERVICES OF OKLA
700 NE 13th St, Oklahoma City, OK 73104

Phone: (405) 271-5194
Sales: $49,500,000
Employees: NA
Company Type: Public Family Member
Employees here: 1,200
SIC: 8062
  Medical and surgical hospital
James F O Loughlin, President

D-U-N-S 19-629-8244
H C A HEALTH SERVICES GA INC
1455 Montreal Rd, Tucker, GA 30084
Phone: (770) 270-3000
Sales: $21,400,000
Employees: NA
Company Type: Public Family Member
Employees here: 495
SIC: 8062
  Hospital
Thomas Blackburn, President

D-U-N-S 10-177-0519
H C A HEALTH SERVICES TENN INC
  (Parent: Health Services Acquisition)
1 Park Mdws, Nashville, TN 37215
Phone: (615) 327-9551
Sales: $72,100,000
Employees: 1,550
Company Type: Public Family Member
Employees here: 9
SIC: 8062
  General hospitals
Jack Bouender, President

D-U-N-S 11-869-7945
H C A HEALTH SERVICES TENN INC
391 Wallace Rd, Nashville, TN 37211
Phone: (615) 781-4000
Sales: $33,500,000
Employees: NA
Company Type: Public Family Member
Employees here: 800
SIC: 8062
  General hospital
Jeff Whitehorn, Administrator

D-U-N-S 13-766-2235
H C A HEALTH SERVICES TENN INC
5655 Frist Blvd, Hermitage, TN 37076
Phone: (615) 316-3540
Sales: $20,700,000
Employees: NA
Company Type: Public Family Member
Employees here: 500
SIC: 8062
  Hospital
Bryan Dearing, Chief Executive Officer

D-U-N-S 07-792-2409
H C A HEALTH SVCS OF VIRGINIA
  (Parent: Columbia/Hca Healthcare Corp)
1602 Skipwith Rd, Richmond, VA 23229
Phone: (804) 289-4500
Sales: $83,900,000
Employees: 1,800
Company Type: Public Family Member
Employees here: 1,800
SIC: 8062
  General hospital
Jack O Bovender, President

D-U-N-S 11-270-9142
H C A HEALTH SVCS TEXAS INC
101 E Ridge Rd, Mcallen, TX 78503
Phone: (956) 632-6000
Sales: $20,200,000
Employees: NA
Company Type: Public Family Member
Employees here: 500
SIC: 8062
  General hospital
Randall M Everts, Chief Executive Officer

D-U-N-S 78-644-4075
H C A HEALTH SVCS TEXAS INC
7600 Fannin St, Houston, TX 77054
Phone: (713) 791-7101

Sales: $24,400,000
Employees: NA
Company Type: Public Family Member
Employees here: 600
SIC: 8062
  Hospital
Judy Novak, Branch Manager

D-U-N-S 10-677-3617
H C A HIGHLAND HOSPITAL INC
  (Parent: Columbia/Hca Healthcare Corp)
1453 E Bert Kouns Industr, Shreveport, LA 71105
Phone: (318) 798-4300
Sales: $78,000,000
Employees: 650
Company Type: Public Family Member
Employees here: 642
SIC: 8062
  General medical hospital
Anthony Sala, Administrator

D-U-N-S 06-435-6538
H C A PSYCHIATRIC COMPANY
  (Parent: Columbia/Hca Healthcare Corp)
1 Park Mdws, Nashville, TN 37215
Phone: (615) 344-9551
Sales: $203,700,000
Employees: 5,500
Company Type: Public Family Member
Employees here: 55
SIC: 8063
  Hospital holding company
Thomas Frish Jr, Chairman of the Board

D-U-N-S 61-573-0652
H C A, INC.
  (Parent: Columbia/Hca Healthcare Corp)
1 Park Mdws, Nashville, TN 37215
Phone: (615) 327-9551
Sales: $826,100,000
Employees: 17,500
Company Type: Public Family Member
Employees here: 6
SIC: 8062
  General medical and psychiatric hospitals
Thomas F Frist Jr, Chief Executive Officer

D-U-N-S 07-756-1538
H C F INC
2615 Fort Amanda Rd, Lima, OH 45804
Phone: (419) 999-2010
Sales: $104,000,000
Employees: 3,000
Company Type: Private
Employees here: 40
SIC: 8051
  Skilled nursing and assisted living facilities
Richard A Unverferth, Chairman of the Board

D-U-N-S 12-237-5595
H M A DURANT INC
  (Parent: Health Management Associates)
1800 W University Blvd, Durant, OK 74701
Phone: (580) 924-3080
Sales: $30,000,000
Employees: 350
Company Type: Public Family Member
Employees here: 350
SIC: 8062
  Hospital
Joshua Putter, Chief Executive Officer

D-U-N-S 14-436-1201
H M A LOUISBURG INC
  (Parent: Health Management Associates)
100 Hospital Dr, Louisburg, NC 27549
Phone: (919) 496-5131
Sales: $40,000,000
Employees: 180
Company Type: Public Family Member
Employees here: 180
SIC: 8062
  General hospital
Thomas Hanenburg, Administrator

D-U-N-S 07-675-3169
H M HEALTH SERVICES
667 Eastland Ave SE, Warren, OH 44484
Phone: (330) 841-4000
Sales: $50,900,000   *Employees:* 1,100
Company Type: Private   *Employees here:* 1,090
SIC: 8062
  General hospital
Josephine Lawrence, Chief Executive Officer

D-U-N-S 04-918-7461
H M O COLORADO, INC
  (Parent: General Health Corporation)
700 Broadway Fl 7, Denver, CO 80203
Phone: (303) 831-3366
Sales: $224,880,000   *Employees:* 100
Company Type: Private   *Employees here:* 91
SIC: 8011
  Health maintenance organization
Steve O Dell, President

D-U-N-S 10-268-2150
H N M C INC
  (Parent: Houston Northwest Medical Ctr)
710 Fm 1960 Rd W, Houston, TX 77090
Phone: (281) 440-1000
Sales: $74,500,000   *Employees:* 1,600
Company Type: Public Family Member   *Employees here:* 1,600
SIC: 8062
  General hospital
J B Shevchuk, Chief Executive Officer

D-U-N-S 01-861-9994
H S C MEDICAL CENTER
1001 Schneider Dr, Malvern, AR 72104
Phone: (501) 337-4911
Sales: $24,000,000   *Employees:* 250
Company Type: Private   *Employees here:* 250
SIC: 8062
  General medical and surgical hospitals, nsk
Jeff Curtis, Administrator

D-U-N-S 06-713-4502
H T I MEMORIAL HOSPITAL CORP
  (Parent: Healthtrust Inc - Hospital Co)
612 W Due West Ave, Madison, TN 37115
Phone: (615) 865-3511
Sales: $50,900,000   *Employees:* 950
Company Type: Public Family Member   *Employees here:* 950
SIC: 8062
  General hospital
Allyn Harris, Chief Executive Officer

D-U-N-S 04-279-7571
HACKENSACK UNIVERSITY MED CTR
30 Prospect Ave, Hackensack, NJ 7601
Phone: (201) 996-2000
Sales: $421,265,000   *Employees:* 4,818
Company Type: Private   *Employees here:* 4,300
SIC: 8062
  Hospital with medical school affiliation
John P Ferguson, President

D-U-N-S 07-361-6930
HACKETTSTOWN COMMUNITY HOSP
651 Willow Grove St, Hackettstown, NJ 7840
Phone: (908) 852-5100
Sales: $31,007,000   *Employees:* 520
Company Type: Private   *Employees here:* 520
SIC: 8062
  General hospital
Gene C Milton, President

D-U-N-S 05-585-7643
HACKLEY HOSPITAL
1700 Clinton St, Muskegon, MI 49442
Phone: (616) 726-3511
Sales: $80,343,000   *Employees:* 1,300
Company Type: Private   *Employees here:* 1,268
SIC: 8062
  General medical & surgical hospital
Gordon A Mudler, President

D-U-N-S 06-539-9677
HALIFAX REGIONAL HOSPITAL INC
2204 Wilborn Ave, South Boston, VA 24592
Phone: (804) 575-3100
Sales: $45,247,000   *Employees:* 590
Company Type: Private   *Employees here:* 590
SIC: 8062
  Hospital
Chris Lumsden, Administrator

D-U-N-S 07-558-3393
HALIFAX REGIONAL MEDICAL CTR
250 Smith Church Rd, Roanoke Rapids, NC 27870
Phone: (252) 535-8011
Sales: $55,817,000   *Employees:* 694
Company Type: Private   *Employees here:* 623
SIC: 8062
  General hospital
M E Gilstrap, President

D-U-N-S 18-417-4886
HALLMARK HEALTH SERVICES INC
  (Parent: Regency Health Services Inc)
2742 Dow Ave, Tustin, CA 92780
Phone: (714) 544-4443
Sales: $20,400,000   *Employees:* 900
Company Type: Public Family Member   *Employees here:* 6
SIC: 8051
  Operation & management of skilled care nursing facilities
James Wodach, Senior Vice-President

D-U-N-S 08-337-9198
HALLMARK HEALTH SYSTEM
100 Hospital Rd, Malden, MA 2148
Phone: (781) 396-9250
Sales: $140,700,000   *Employees:* 3,000
Company Type: Private   *Employees here:* 1,000
SIC: 8062
  General hospital
David Lomanno, Accounting

D-U-N-S 04-913-2400
HALLMARK HEALTHCARE CORP
  (Parent: Community Health Systems Inc)
155 Franklin Rd Ste 400, Brentwood, TN 37027
Phone: (615) 373-9600
Sales: $157,000,000   *Employees:* 3,345
Company Type: Public Family Member   *Employees here:* 4
SIC: 8062
  Owns operates & manages general surgical hospitals
Wayne Smith, President

D-U-N-S 06-619-4721
HAMMOND CLINIC, LLC
7905 Calumet Ave, Munster, IN 46321
Phone: (219) 836-5800
Sales: $54,850,000   *Employees:* 600
Company Type: Private   *Employees here:* 557
SIC: 8011
  Medical clinic
Al Morrissey, Managing Partner

D-U-N-S 06-875-6204
HAMOT MEDICAL CENTER
201 State St, Erie, PA 16550
Phone: (814) 877-6000
Sales: $142,613,000   *Employees:* 1,300
Company Type: Private   *Employees here:* 1,030
SIC: 8062
    General hospital
John T Malone, President

D-U-N-S 07-204-2070
HANCOCK MEM HOSPITAL & HEALTH SVCS
801 N State St, Greenfield, IN 46140
Phone: (317) 462-5544
Sales: $44,043,000   *Employees:* 532
Company Type: Private   *Employees here:* 522
SIC: 8062
    General hospital
Rick Edwards, Chief Financial Officer

D-U-N-S 04-029-3219
HAND SURGERY ASSOCIATES OF IND
8501 Harcourt Rd, Indianapolis, IN 46260
Phone: (317) 875-9105
Sales: $20,500,000   *Employees:* 300
Company Type: Private   *Employees here:* 100
SIC: 8011
    Physicians office
Dr James Strickland Md, President

D-U-N-S 07-185-8435
HANFORD COMMUNITY HOSPITAL
450 Greenfield Ave, Hanford, CA 93230
Phone: (209) 582-4430
Sales: $47,835,000   *Employees:* 650
Company Type: Private   *Employees here:* 570
SIC: 8062
    Hospital
Darwin Remboldt, President

D-U-N-S 15-466-6218
HANGER ORTHOPEDIC GROUP INC
7700 Old Georgetown Rd, Bethesda, MD 20814
Phone: (301) 986-0701
Sales: $145,598,000   *Employees:* 1,000
Company Type: Public   *Employees here:* 40
SIC: 8361
    Provides patient care services & mfg orthotic & prosthetic
        equipment
Van R Sabel, President

D-U-N-S 07-588-6341
HANNIBAL REGIONAL HOSPITAL,
Hwy 36 W, Hannibal, MO 63401
Phone: (573) 221-0414
Sales: $40,228,000   *Employees:* 550
Company Type: Private   *Employees here:* 495
SIC: 8062
    General medical hospital
John Grossmeier, President

D-U-N-S 06-978-8644
HANOVER GENERAL HOSPITAL
300 Highland Ave, Hanover, PA 17331
Phone: (717) 637-3711
Sales: $51,072,000   *Employees:* 900
Company Type: Private   *Employees here:* 820
SIC: 8062
    General hospital
William Walb, President

D-U-N-S 09-659-2951
HARBOR BEHAVIORAL HEALTH
7809 Massachusettes Ave, New Port Richey, FL 34653
Phone: (727) 841-4200
Sales: $19,829,000   *Employees:* 460
Company Type: Private   *Employees here:* 40
SIC: 8093
    Mental health & substance abuse clinic
Dr Richard Gray, President

D-U-N-S 05-490-5930
HARBOR HOSPITAL CENTER INC
3001 S Hanover St, Baltimore, MD 21225
Phone: (410) 350-3200
Sales: $101,116,000   *Employees:* 1,150
Company Type: Private   *Employees here:* 1,130
SIC: 8062
    General hospital
L B Johnson, Chief Executive Officer

D-U-N-S 94-744-4386
HARBORSIDE HEALTHCARE CORP
470 Atlantic Ave, Boston, MA 2210
Phone: (617) 556-1515
Sales: $221,777,000   *Employees:* 7,331
Company Type: Public   *Employees here:* 25
SIC: 8051
    Provides long-term care subacute care & other specialty
        medical services
Stephen Guillard, President

D-U-N-S 03-985-0045
HARDIN MEMORIAL HOSPITAL
913 N Dixie Ave, Elizabethtown, KY 42701
Phone: (502) 737-1212
Sales: $98,051,000   *Employees:* 1,450
Company Type: Private   *Employees here:* 1,440
SIC: 8062
    Hospital
David Gray, Administrator

D-U-N-S 06-939-2991
HARFORD MEMORIAL HOSPITAL INC
501 S Union Ave, Havre De Grace, MD 21078
Phone: (410) 939-2400
Sales: $49,504,000   *Employees:* 625
Company Type: Private   *Employees here:* 625
SIC: 8062
    General hospital
Lyle E Sheldon, President

D-U-N-S 62-527-6605
HARPER HOSPITAL
3990 John R St, Detroit, MI 48201
Phone: (313) 745-8040
Sales: $277,042,000   *Employees:* 2,483
Company Type: Private   *Employees here:* 2,400
SIC: 8062
    General hospital
Paul L Broughton, President

D-U-N-S 08-097-6855
HARRIMAN CITY HOSPITAL
412 Devonia St, Harriman, TN 37748
Phone: (423) 882-1323
Sales: $23,823,000   *Employees:* 425
Company Type: Private   *Employees here:* 423
SIC: 8062
    General hospital
James Gann, Administrator

D-U-N-S 07-620-0401
HARRIMAN JONES MEDICAL GROUP
2600 Redondo Ave, Long Beach, CA 90806
Phone: (562) 988-7000
Sales: $52,999,000   *Employees:* 506
Company Type: Private   *Employees here:* 489
SIC: 8011
   Medical doctor's office
Diane Corrigan, Chief Operating Officer

D-U-N-S 07-534-0877
HARRINGTON MEMORIAL HOSPITAL
100 South St Ste 1, Southbridge, MA 1550
Phone: (508) 765-9771
Sales: $37,975,000   *Employees:* 800
Company Type: Private   *Employees here:* 700
SIC: 8062
   General hospital
Richard M Mangion, President

D-U-N-S 03-967-3769
HARRIS COUNTY HOSPITAL DST
1504 Taub Loop, Houston, TX 77030
Phone: (713) 793-2300
Sales: $91,200,000   *Employees:* NA
Company Type: Private   *Employees here:* 2,200
SIC: 8062
   General hospital
William Adams, Principal

D-U-N-S 08-697-6214
HARRIS COUNTY HOSPITAL DST
2525 Holly Hall St, Houston, TX 77054
Phone: (713) 746-6400
Sales: $315,376,000   *Employees:* 5,412
Company Type: Private   *Employees here:* 400
SIC: 8062
   Hospitals & clinics
Lois J Moore, President

D-U-N-S 18-069-7930
HARRIS COUNTY HOSPITAL DST
5656 Kelley St, Houston, TX 77026
Phone: (713) 636-5000
Sales: $49,500,000   *Employees:* NA
Company Type: Private   *Employees here:* 1,200
SIC: 8062
   General hospital
Lois J Moore, President

D-U-N-S 78-391-4153
HARRIS METHODIST ERATH COUNTY
411 N Belknap St, Stephenville, TX 76401
Phone: (254) 965-3115
Sales: $21,088,000   *Employees:* 205
Company Type: Private   *Employees here:* 205
SIC: 8062
   Hospital & clinic
Stephen R Mason, President

D-U-N-S 06-423-4636
HARRIS METHODIST FORT WORTH
1301 Pennsylvania Ave, Fort Worth, TX 76104
Phone: (817) 882-2000
Sales: $119,900,000   *Employees:* 2,560
Company Type: Private   *Employees here:* 2,560
SIC: 8062
   General hospital
Stephen Mason, President

D-U-N-S 62-606-1907
HARRIS METHODIST FORT WORTH
6100 Harris Pkwy Ste 265, Fort Worth, TX 76132

Phone: (817) 346-5050
Sales: $23,800,000   *Employees:* NA
Company Type: Private   *Employees here:* 585
SIC: 8062
   General hospital
Stansel Harvey, Manager

D-U-N-S 07-314-4958
HARRIS METHODIST H-E-B
1600 Hospital Pkwy, Bedford, TX 76022
Phone: (817) 685-4000
Sales: $93,244,000   *Employees:* 992
Company Type: Private   *Employees here:* 812
SIC: 8062
   General hospital psychiatric hospital drug and alcohol
      addiction treatment center
Stephen R Mason, President

D-U-N-S 07-452-1675
HARRIS REGIONAL HOSPITAL
68 Hospital Rd, Sylva, NC 28779
Phone: (828) 586-7000
Sales: $42,915,000   *Employees:* 700
Company Type: Private   *Employees here:* 490
SIC: 8062
   Hospital skilled nursing home and home health care
Isaac Coe, President

D-U-N-S 07-184-4583
HARRISON MEMORIAL HOSPITAL
2520 Cherry Ave, Bremerton, WA 98310
Phone: (360) 377-3911
Sales: $92,236,000   *Employees:* 1,025
Company Type: Private   *Employees here:* 995
SIC: 8062
   Hospital
Peter C Schlicher, Vice-President

D-U-N-S 06-553-3796
HARTFORD HOSPITAL
80 Seymour St, Hartford, CT 6106
Phone: (860) 545-5555
Sales: $419,242,000   *Employees:* 5,000
Company Type: Private   *Employees here:* 4,870
SIC: 8062
   General hospital
John Meehan, President

D-U-N-S 07-617-1966
HARTFORD MEMORIAL HOSPITAL
1032 E Sumner St, Hartford, WI 53027
Phone: (414) 673-2300
Sales: $23,067,000   *Employees:* 350
Company Type: Private   *Employees here:* 350
SIC: 8062
   General hospital
Mark Schwartz, President

D-U-N-S 18-328-3035
HARTWYCK AT OAK TREE INC
80 James St, Edison, NJ 8820
Phone: (732) 632-1571
Sales: $29,017,000   *Employees:* 595
Company Type: Private   *Employees here:* 10
SIC: 8051
   Skilled nursing care & personal care facility
John P Mc Gee, President

D-U-N-S 11-422-1633
HARVARD PILGRIM HEALTH CARE
26 City Hall Mall, Medford, MA 2155
Phone: (617) 381-5100

Sales: $24,900,000
Company Type: Private
SIC: 8011
  Health maintenance organization
Bruce Walton, Principal

Employees: NA
Employees here: 395

D-U-N-S 61-413-1092
HARVARD PILGRIM HEALTH CARE
3 Allied Dr, Dedham, MA 2026
Phone: (781) 431-1070
Sales: $28,700,000
Company Type: Private
SIC: 8011
  Medical doctor's office
William Schlag, Manager

Employees: NA
Employees here: 460

D-U-N-S 87-992-2037
HARVARD PILGRIM HEALTH CARE
3 Allied Dr, Dedham, MA 2026
Phone: (781) 431-1070
Sales: $31,100,000
Company Type: Private
SIC: 8011
  Health maintenance organization
William Schlag, Branch Manager

Employees: NA
Employees here: 500

D-U-N-S 15-254-8509
HARVARD PILGRIM HEALTH CARE
111 Grossman Dr, Braintree, MA 2184
Phone: (781) 849-1000
Sales: $19,800,000
Company Type: Private
SIC: 8011
  Medical doctor's office
Harvey Katz, Branch Manager

Employees: NA
Employees here: 310

D-U-N-S 07-790-1908
HATTIESBURG CLINIC PROF ASSN
415 S 28th Ave, Hattiesburg, MS 39401
Phone: (601) 264-6000
Sales: $53,245,000
Company Type: Private
SIC: 8011
  Clinic & ret drug store
Richard H Clark Jr, President

Employees: 801
Employees here: 510

D-U-N-S 08-388-6622
HAWAII DEPARTMENT OF HEALTH
221 Mahalani St, Wailuku, HI 96793
Phone: (808) 244-9056
Sales: $21,500,000
Company Type: Private
SIC: 8062
  Hospital
Dave Patton, Administrator

Employees: NA
Employees here: 480

D-U-N-S 08-454-6175
HAWAII DEPARTMENT OF HEALTH
1190 Waianuenue Ave, Hilo, HI 96720
Phone: (808) 969-4151
Sales: $31,800,000
Company Type: Private
SIC: 8062
  Hospital & gift shop
Robert Morris, Acting Ceo

Employees: NA
Employees here: 800

D-U-N-S 07-330-4214
HAYS MEDICAL CENTER INC
2220 Canterbury Dr, Hays, KS 67601
Phone: (785) 625-7301

Sales: $67,142,000
Company Type: Private
SIC: 8062
  General hospital
Steve Ronstrom, President

Employees: 900
Employees here: 450

D-U-N-S 07-450-6759
HAYWOOD REGIONAL MEDICAL CTR
262 Leroy George Dr, Clyde, NC 28721
Phone: (828) 456-7311
Sales: $51,557,000
Company Type: Private
SIC: 8062
  Acute care hospital
Grady Stokes, Chief Operating Officer

Employees: 680
Employees here: 675

D-U-N-S 60-690-4266
HEALIX INFUSION THERAPY INC
6001 Savoy Dr Ste 400, Houston, TX 77036
Phone: (713) 954-0000
Sales: $20,824,000
Company Type: Private
SIC: 8082
  Home health care services
Mort Baharloo, Chairman of the Board

Employees: 200
Employees here: 75

D-U-N-S 07-578-7333
HEALTH ACQUISITION CORP
  (Parent: National Home Health Care Corp)
17520 Hillside Ave, Jamaica, NY 11432
Phone: (718) 657-2966
Sales: $20,562,000
Company Type: Public Family Member
SIC: 8082
  Provides home health care personnel services
Richard Garofalo, President

Employees: 1,000
Employees here: 1,000

D-U-N-S 09-382-3185
HEALTH ALLIANCE PLAN OF MICH
2850 W Grand Blvd, Detroit, MI 48202
Phone: (313) 872-8100
Sales: $913,217,000
Company Type: Private
SIC: 8011
  Health maintenance organization
Cleve L Killingsworth Jr, President

Employees: 1,400
Employees here: 500

D-U-N-S 93-274-4246
HEALTH ASSOC OF KY, INC
800 Rose St A301 Ky Clnic, Lexington, KY 40506
Phone: (606) 323-5126
Sales: $34,300,000
Company Type: Private
SIC: 8011
  Manages physicians practices
James W Holsinger, Chairman of the Board

Employees: 500
Employees here: 500

D-U-N-S 07-545-7283
HEALTH CAOLC AND TCOFA
205 S Marengo St, Florence, AL 35630
Phone: (256) 767-9191
Sales: $102,341,000
Company Type: Private
SIC: 8062
  Hospital
Richard H Peck, Administrator

Employees: 1,600
Employees here: 1,600

D-U-N-S 03-093-3667
HEALTH CARE ADMINISTRATION
9311 San Pedro, San Antonio, TX 78216
Phone: (210) 340-7155

Sales: $19,900,000
Company Type: Private
SIC: 8059
  Nursing home and mental retardation centers
Robert L Bowers, Chairman of the Board

Employees: 900
Employees here: 18

D-U-N-S 07-912-4053
HEALTH CARE AUTH OF CIT OF HUN
101 Sivley Rd SW, Huntsville, AL 35801
Phone: (256) 533-8020
Sales: $349,999,000
Company Type: Private
SIC: 8062
  General hospital
Edwin D Boston, Chief Executive Officer

Employees: 4,200
Employees here: 3,500

D-U-N-S 07-211-1362
HEALTH CARE AUTH CULLMAN CNTY
1912 Al Highway 157 N, Cullman, AL 35058
Phone: (256) 734-1210
Sales: $50,857,000
Company Type: Private
SIC: 8062
  General hospital
Jessie Weatherly, President

Employees: 699
Employees here: 699

D-U-N-S 07-898-3939
HEALTH CARE AUTHORITY OF MORGA
1201 7th St SE, Decatur, AL 35601
Phone: (256) 552-0055
Sales: $82,154,000
Company Type: Private
SIC: 8062
  General hospital
Robert L Smith, Administrator

Employees: 1,000
Employees here: 1,000

D-U-N-S 04-432-5272
HEALTH CARE INDUSTRIES CORP
77 E Elmwood Dr Ste 213, Dayton, OH 45459
Phone: (937) 291-2990
Sales: $46,000,000
Company Type: Private
SIC: 8051
  Operates nursing & personal care facilities
Hugh Wall Iii, President

Employees: 1,000
Employees here: 1

D-U-N-S 15-116-5297
HEALTH CARE MID-CLMBA
1700 E 19th St, The Dalles, OR 97058
Phone: (541) 296-1111
Sales: $32,817,000
Company Type: Private
SIC: 8062
  Hospital billing service & ret & rents durable medical
    equipment own/operate medical buildings senior facility
Mark Scott, President

Employees: 500
Employees here: 15

D-U-N-S 00-790-3347
HEALTH CARE RTREMENT CORP AMER
  (Parent: Hcrc Inc)
1 Seagate, Toledo, OH 43604
Phone: (419) 252-5500
Sales: $708,110,000
Company Type: Public Family Member
SIC: 8051
  Operator long term care centers
Paul A Ormond, Chairman of the Board

Employees: 16,500
Employees here: 243

D-U-N-S 78-398-3414
HEALTH CARE RETIREMENT MANOR CARE
1 Seagate, Toledo, OH 43604
Phone: (419) 252-5500

Sales: $891,963,000
Company Type: Public
SIC: 8051
  Operator of long term nursing centers outpatient clinics &
    home health care services
Paul A Ormond, Chairman of the Board

Employees: 22,000
Employees here: 40

D-U-N-S 85-880-7852
HEALTH CARE SOLUTIONS, INC
3741 Plaza Dr, Ann Arbor, MI 48108
Phone: (734) 996-4770
Sales: $40,120,000
Company Type: Private
SIC: 8082
  Home health care services & ret pharmacy
Timothy Patton, President

Employees: 300
Employees here: 16

D-U-N-S 15-657-9385
HEALTH ENTERPRISES OF MICHIGAN
401 N Elm St, Denton, TX 76201
Phone: (940) 387-4388
Sales: $22,700,000
Company Type: Private
SIC: 8051
  Skilled nursing homes
Peter C Kern, President

Employees: 1,000
Employees here: 5

D-U-N-S 80-704-9655
HEALTH FIRST INC
8249 Devereux Dr, Melbourne, FL 32940
Phone: (407) 727-7111
Sales: $331,200,000
Company Type: Private
SIC: 8011
  Medical doctor's office
Larry Garrison, Chief Operating Officer

Employees: 4,800
Employees here: NA

D-U-N-S 07-073-3811
HEALTH FIRST MEDICAL GROUP
10535 NE Glisan St, Portland, OR 97220
Phone: (503) 254-7351
Sales: $55,000,000
Company Type: Private
SIC: 8011
  Medical clinic
Dr Matthew Shelley Md, President

Employees: 800
Employees here: 80

D-U-N-S 10-630-1567
HEALTH FIRST MEDICAL GROUP PC
2620 Thousand Oaks Blvd, Memphis, TN 38118
Phone: (901) 541-9410
Sales: $23,537,000
Company Type: Private
SIC: 8011
  Group health association
Milton Schachter, Executive Director

Employees: 350
Employees here: 65

D-U-N-S 15-279-2404
HEALTH HOSPITAL CORP OF MARION CNTY
1001 W 10th St, Indianapolis, IN 46202
Phone: (317) 630-6026
Sales: $22,800,000
Company Type: Private
SIC: 8062
  General hospital
Dr John Williams, Manager

Employees: NA
Employees here: 550

D-U-N-S 15-580-6250
HEALTH HOSPITAL CORP OF MARION CNTY
1001 W 10th St, Indianapolis, IN 46202
Phone: (317) 639-6671

Sales: $127,200,000
Company Type: Private   *Employees:* NA
SIC: 8062   *Employees here:* 3,000
  General hospital
John F Williams Jr, Manager

D-U-N-S 62-316-8457
HEALTH INVESTMENT CORPORATION
249 E Ocean Blvd Ste 1020, Long Beach, CA 90802
Phone: (562) 437-2117
Sales: $46,100,000   *Employees:* 1,000
Company Type: Private   *Employees here:* 10
SIC: 8062
  General hospital
Jens Mueller, Chairman of the Board

D-U-N-S 08-619-0493
HEALTH MANAGEMENT ASSOCIATES
5811 Pelican Bay Blvd, Naples, FL 34108
Phone: (941) 598-3051
Sales: $895,482,000   *Employees:* 10,000
Company Type: Public   *Employees here:* 52
SIC: 8062
  Operates acute care and psychiatric hospitals
Joseph V Vumbacco, President

D-U-N-S 83-100-7331
HEALTH MANAGEMENT ASSOCIATES
1970 Hospital Dr, Clarksdale, MS 38614
Phone: (601) 627-3211
Sales: $23,400,000   *Employees:* NA
Company Type: Public Family Member   *Employees here:* 616
SIC: 8062
  General hospital
David Mc Cormack, Manager

D-U-N-S 78-848-8484
HEALTH MGT ASSOC OF W VA
  (Parent: Health Management Associates)
859 Alderson St, Williamson, WV 25661
Phone: (304) 235-2500
Sales: $26,409,000   *Employees:* 230
Company Type: Public Family Member   *Employees here:* 230
SIC: 8062
  Hospital
Roger Ledux, Administrator

D-U-N-S 12-131-2458
HEALTH MIDWEST VENTURES GROUP,
  (Parent: Health Midwest)
2304 E Meyer Blvd Ste A10, Kansas City, MO 64132
Phone: (816) 751-3000
Sales: $27,400,000   *Employees:* 400
Company Type: Private   *Employees here:* 25
SIC: 8011
  Physicians clinics collection agency & commercial building
  operator
Jack L Sutherland, Chairman of the Board

D-U-N-S 11-920-2174
HEALTH NET INC
  (Parent: Baptist Hospital Inc)
44 Vantage Way Ste 300, Nashville, TN 37228
Phone: (615) 291-7000
Sales: $98,772,000   *Employees:* 6
Company Type: Private   *Employees here:* 6
SIC: 8011
  Preferred provider organization
John Hackworth, Chief Executive Officer

D-U-N-S 11-520-5437
HEALTH NET
  (Parent: Foundation Health Systems Inc)
21600 Oxnard St Fl 17, Woodland Hills, CA 91367
Phone: (818) 719-6775
Sales: $724,700,000   *Employees:* 10,500
Company Type: Public   *Employees here:* 167
SIC: 8011
  Operates hmos ppos hospitals sells life accidental death
  disability & workers' comp insurance and retails mail order
  durgs
Arthur Southam, President

D-U-N-S 10-572-2623
HEALTH PLAN OF NEVADA INC
  (Parent: Sierra Health Services Inc)
2720 N Tenaya Way, Las Vegas, NV 89128
Phone: (702) 242-7200
Sales: $358,498,000   *Employees:* 250
Company Type: Public Family Member   *Employees here:* 249
SIC: 8011
  Health maintenance organization
Jon Bunker, President

D-U-N-S 09-420-8816
HEALTH PLAN OF UPPER OHIO
52160 National Rd E, Saint Clairsville, OH 43950
Phone: (740) 695-3585
Sales: $115,168,000   *Employees:* 105
Company Type: Private   *Employees here:* 97
SIC: 8082
  Health maintenance
James Haranzo, Chairman of the Board

D-U-N-S 00-885-9667
HEALTH PLUS OF LOUISIANA INC
  (Parent: Willis-Knighton Medical Ctr)
2751 Virginia Ave Ste 2b, Shreveport, LA 71103
Phone: (318) 632-8800
Sales: $22,000,000   *Employees:* 37
Company Type: Private   *Employees here:* 37
SIC: 8011
  Hmo
James K Elrod, President

D-U-N-S 18-696-0332
HEALTH PARTNERS OF PHILADELPHIA
4700 Wissahickon Ave, Philadelphia, PA 19144
Phone: (215) 849-9606
Sales: $203,397,000   *Employees:* 300
Company Type: Private   *Employees here:* 250
SIC: 8011
  Health maintenance organization
Sonia A Madison, President

D-U-N-S 10-312-1034
HEALTH RESOURCES CORP
  (Parent: Ornda Healthcorp)
2701 S Bristol St, Santa Ana, CA 92704
Phone: (714) 754-5454
Sales: $32,106,000   *Employees:* 400
Company Type: Public Family Member   *Employees here:* 400
SIC: 8062
  General hospital
Bryan P Marsal, Chairman of the Board

D-U-N-S 15-176-5971
HEALTH RESOURCES CORPORATION
  (Parent: Community Health Care Inc)
350 7th St N, Naples, FL 34102
Phone: (941) 262-4777

Sales: $36,245,000   *Employees:* 300
Company Type: Private   *Employees here:* 5
SIC: 8071
   Medical laboratory home health care service outpatient
     surgery centers & commercial laundry service
William G Crone, President

D-U-N-S 01-937-6441
HEALTH SERVICES MEDICAL CORP
8278 Willett Pkwy, Baldwinsville, NY 13027
Phone: (315) 638-2133
Sales: $148,483,000   *Employees:* 1,100
Company Type: Private   *Employees here:* 500
SIC: 8011
   Medical doctor's office
Fred F Yanni Jr, President

D-U-N-S 94-288-6581
HEALTH SPAN HM CARE & HOSPICE
2750 Arthur St, Saint Paul, MN 55113
Phone: (651) 628-4200
Sales: $28,000,000   *Employees:* 800
Company Type: Private   *Employees here:* 800
SIC: 8082
   Home health care
Dana Brandt, President

D-U-N-S 07-159-6175
HEALTH SVCS ASSN OF CENTL NY
8278 Willett Pkwy, Baldwinsville, NY 13027
Phone: (315) 638-2133
Sales: $60,111,000   *Employees:* 724
Company Type: Private   *Employees here:* 250
SIC: 8011
   Multispecialty group medical practice and service network
Frederick F Yanni Jr, President

D-U-N-S 17-432-2818
HEALTH TECH AFFILIATES INC
   (Parent: Baptist Mem Hlth Care Corp)
1750 Madison Ave, Memphis, TN 38104
Phone: (901) 725-2900
Sales: $29,377,000   *Employees:* 400
Company Type: Private   *Employees here:* 7
SIC: 8011
   Operates medical clinics pathology labs nursing services
     retails & leases & rents medical equipment billing services
Steven Reynolds, President

D-U-N-S 94-851-1548
HEALTHACCESS INC
   (Parent: County Of Pitt)
2100 Statonburg Rd, Greenville, NC 27834
Phone: (252) 816-7730
Sales: $30,753,000   *Employees:* 80
Company Type: Private   *Employees here:* 80
SIC: 8093
   Provides respiratory services
Diane Poole, President

D-U-N-S 06-992-0916
HEALTHALLIANCE HOSPITALS INC
60 Hospital Rd, Leominster, MA 1453
Phone: (978) 343-5000
Sales: $47,444,000   *Employees:* 1,350
Company Type: Private   *Employees here:* 550
SIC: 8062
   General hospital
Thomas Sullivan, Chief Financial Officer

D-U-N-S 88-386-4324
HEALTHALLIANCE HOSPITALS INC
275 Nichols Rd, Fitchburg, MA 1420

Phone: (978) 343-5000
Sales: $40,200,000   *Employees:* NA
Company Type: Private   *Employees here:* 800
SIC: 8062
   General hospital
Douglas Fairfax, President

D-U-N-S 36-171-4207
HEALTHCARE MGT ALTERNATIVES
   (Parent: Americhoice Corporation)
100 E Penn Sq 900, Philadelphia, PA 19107
Phone: (215) 832-4500
Sales: $192,214,000   *Employees:* 196
Company Type: Private   *Employees here:* 196
SIC: 8099
   Health maintenance organization
Dr Denise Ross Md, Chief Executive Officer

D-U-N-S 09-600-0682
HEALTHCARE PARTNERS MED GROUP
1025 W Olympic Blvd, Los Angeles, CA 90015
Phone: (213) 623-2225
Sales: $110,300,000   *Employees:* 1,600
Company Type: Private   *Employees here:* 400
SIC: 8011
   Out patient facility
Dr Robert Margolis Md, President

D-U-N-S 10-206-5034
HEALTHCARE PROPERTIES INC
102 Woodmont Blvd Ste 350, Nashville, TN 37205
Phone: (615) 297-1020
Sales: $22,000,000   *Employees:* 500
Company Type: Private   *Employees here:* 11
SIC: 8059
   Operates nursing homes
Dan Mclaren, President

D-U-N-S 18-059-7627
HEALTHCARE SAN ANTONIO INC
   (Parent: Brown Schools Inc)
17720 Corporate Woods Dr, San Antonio, TX 78259
Phone: (210) 491-9400
Sales: $20,500,000   *Employees:* 300
Company Type: Private   *Employees here:* 40
SIC: 8011
   Psychiatric hospital
Allen Cross, N/A

D-U-N-S 84-935-3800
HEALTHCOR HOLDINGS INC
8150 N Central Expy, Dallas, TX 75206
Phone: (972) 233-7744
Sales: $143,205,000   *Employees:* 3,200
Company Type: Public   *Employees here:* 100
SIC: 8082
   Provider of home health services whol & rents medical
     equipment & ret drugs and sundries
S W Bazzle, Chairman of the Board

D-U-N-S 00-795-8283
HEALTHCOR, INC
17117 W 9 Mile Rd, Southfield, MI 48075
Phone: (248) 559-5656
Sales: $80,000,000   *Employees:* 236
Company Type: Private   *Employees here:* 150
SIC: 8011
   Health maintenance organization
Donald Zinner, President

D-U-N-S 15-120-0839
HEALTHCOR, INC
   (Parent: Healthcor Holdings Inc)
8150 N Central Expy, Dallas, TX 75206

Phone: (972) 233-7744
Sales: $112,188,000   *Employees:* 1,200
Company Type: Public Family Member   *Employees here:* 50
SIC: 8082
    Home health care services
S W Bazzle, Chairman of the Board

D-U-N-S 04-355-0037
HEALTHEAST COMPANIES, INC
1700 University Ave W, Saint Paul, MN 55104
Phone: (651) 232-2300
Sales: $39,900,000   *Employees:* 2,500
Company Type: Private   *Employees here:* 5
SIC: 8082
    Home health care skilled nursing home building operator
      medical doctors
Timothy H Hanson, President

D-U-N-S 15-758-0002
HEALTHEAST ST JOHN'S HOSPITAL
1575 Beam Ave, Saint Paul, MN 55109
Phone: (651) 232-7000
Sales: $98,503,000   *Employees:* 713
Company Type: Private   *Employees here:* 713
SIC: 8062
    General hospital
Timothy H Hanson, President

D-U-N-S 78-451-2527
HEALTHEAST ST JOSEPHS HOSP
69 Exchange St W, Saint Paul, MN 55102
Phone: (651) 232-1000
Sales: $111,125,000   *Employees:* 1,072
Company Type: Private   *Employees here:* 1,072
SIC: 8062
    General hospital
Timothy Hanson, President

D-U-N-S 80-948-8588
HEALTHFIRST INC
25 Broadway Fl 9, New York, NY 10004
Phone: (212) 801-6000
Sales: $88,408,000   *Employees:* 311
Company Type: Private   *Employees here:* 311
SIC: 8011
    Health maintenance organization
Paul Dickstein, Chief Executive Officer

D-U-N-S 13-943-1308
HEALTHLINK INC
12443 Olive Blvd, Saint Louis, MO 63141
Phone: (314) 989-6300
Sales: $23,200,000   *Employees:* 339
Company Type: Private   *Employees here:* 339
SIC: 8011
    Preferred provider organization
David Ott, Acting President

D-U-N-S 19-199-5430
HEALTHMARK OF WALTON INC
    (Parent: Healthmark Corporation Usa)
336 College Ave, Defuniak Springs, FL 32433
Phone: (850) 892-5171
Sales: $20,000,000   *Employees:* 150
Company Type: Private   *Employees here:* 150
SIC: 8062
    General hospital
Jon Hufstedler, Administrator

D-U-N-S 03-752-8320
HEALTHOHIO, INC
278 Barks Rd W, Marion, OH 43302
Phone: (740) 387-6355

Sales: $57,804,000   *Employees:* 90
Company Type: Private   *Employees here:* 90
SIC: 8011
    Health maintenance organization
Charles Wright, Chairman of the Board

D-U-N-S 79-705-3212
HEALTHPARTNERS, INC
8100 34th Ave S, Minneapolis, MN 55425
Phone: (612) 883-6000
Sales: $1,178,455,000   *Employees:* 7,000
Company Type: Private   *Employees here:* 1,000
SIC: 8011
    Health maintenance organization
George C Halvorson, President

D-U-N-S 13-089-6392
HEALTHPLEX INC
60 Charles Lindbergh Blvd, Uniondale, NY 11553
Phone: (516) 794-3000
Sales: $20,310,000   *Employees:* 54
Company Type: Public   *Employees here:* 54
SIC: 8021
    Provides management services licensed dental insurance
      company & develops & markets document imaging systems
Dr Stephen J Cuchel, Chairman of the Board

D-U-N-S 00-812-6893
HEALTHPLUS CORPORATION
2200 Southwest Fwy, Houston, TX 77098
Phone: (713) 522-0481
Sales: $50,000,000   *Employees:* 400
Company Type: Private   *Employees here:* 4
SIC: 8082
    Hospital acquistition company
John H Styles Sr, President

D-U-N-S 83-832-3376
HEALTHRIGHT INC
134 State St, Meriden, CT 6450
Phone: (203) 630-3356
Sales: $53,078,000   *Employees:* 60
Company Type: Private   *Employees here:* 60
SIC: 8011
    Health maintenance organization
Mark Masselli, Chairman

D-U-N-S 17-422-3495
HEALTHSOURCE HEALTH PLANS INC
701 Corporate Center Dr, Raleigh, NC 27607
Phone: (919) 854-7000
Sales: $341,000,000   *Employees:* 425
Company Type: Private   *Employees here:* 154
SIC: 8011
    Health maintenance organization
Robert J Greczyn Jr, President

D-U-N-S 36-132-3868
HEALTHSOURCE MAINE INC
    (Parent: Healthsource Inc)
2 Stonewood Dr, Freeport, ME 4032
Phone: (207) 865-5000
Sales: $124,628,000   *Employees:* 215
Company Type: Public Family Member   *Employees here:* 212
SIC: 8011
    Health maintenance organization
Richard White, Vice-President

D-U-N-S 60-939-1198
HEALTHSOURCE SOUTH CAROLINA
    (Parent: Physicians Health Systems)
146 Fairchild St, Charleston, SC 29492
Phone: (843) 884-4063

Sales: $191,115,000
Company Type: Public Family Member
SIC: 8011
   Health maintenance organization
Frank Middleton, President

Employees: 275
Employees here: 275

D-U-N-S 61-195-2193
HEALTHSOUTH OF AUSTIN, INC
   (Parent: Healthsouth Corporation)
1215 Red River St, Austin, TX 78701
Phone: (512) 474-5700
Sales: $27,500,000
Company Type: Public Family Member
SIC: 8069
   Specialty hospital
William Mitchell, Administrator

Employees: 350
Employees here: 336

D-U-N-S 13-178-7707
HEALTHSOUTH OF FT LAUDERDALE
   (Parent: Healthsouth Corporation)
4399 N Nob Hill Rd, Fort Lauderdale, FL 33351
Phone: (954) 749-0300
Sales: $28,000,000
Company Type: Public Family Member
SIC: 8069
   Specialty hospital
Kevin Conn, Administrator

Employees: 400
Employees here: 400

D-U-N-S 87-716-3980
HEALTHSOUTH OF MIDLAND, INC
   (Parent: Healthsouth Corporation)
1800 Heritage Blvd, Midland, TX 79707
Phone: (915) 520-1600
Sales: $21,000,000
Company Type: Public Family Member
SIC: 8093
   Outpatient & inpatient rehabilitation facility
Mike Munnerlyn, Administrator

Employees: 150
Employees here: 150

D-U-N-S 16-138-0696
HEALTHSOUTH OF MONTGOMERY
   (Parent: Healthsouth Corporation)
4465 Narrow Lane Rd, Montgomery, AL 36116
Phone: (334) 284-7700
Sales: $20,448,000
Company Type: Public Family Member
SIC: 8069
   Physical rehabilitation hospital
Linda Wade, Chief Executive Officer

Employees: 270
Employees here: 270

D-U-N-S 87-715-3619
HEALTHSOUTH OF NEW MEXICO
   (Parent: Healthsouth Corporation)
7000 Jefferson St NE, Albuquerque, NM 87109
Phone: (505) 344-9478
Sales: $20,000,000
Company Type: Public Family Member
SIC: 8069
   Specialty hospital
Dayle Olsen, Administrator

Employees: 274
Employees here: 200

D-U-N-S 18-403-5897
HEALTHSOUTH OF PITTSBURGH,
   (Parent: Healthsouth Corporation)
2380 McGinley Rd, Monroeville, PA 15146
Phone: (412) 856-2400
Sales: $39,000,000
Company Type: Public Family Member
SIC: 8093
   Rehabilitation hospital
Faith Deigan, Chief Executive Officer

Employees: 500
Employees here: 350

D-U-N-S 18-904-8242
HEALTHSOUTH OF SAN ANTONIO,
   (Parent: Healthsouth Corporation)
9119 Cinnamon Hl, San Antonio, TX 78240
Phone: (210) 691-0737
Sales: $25,000,000
Company Type: Public Family Member
SIC: 8069
   Rehabilitation hospital
Diane Lampe, Administrator

Employees: 370
Employees here: 220

D-U-N-S 87-715-6471
HEALTHSOUTH OF SOUTH CAROLINA,
   (Parent: Healthsouth Corporation)
2935 Colonial Dr, Columbia, SC 29203
Phone: (803) 254-7777
Sales: $35,025,000
Company Type: Public Family Member
SIC: 8069
   Rehabilitation hospital
Debbie Johnson, Administrator

Employees: 274
Employees here: 274

D-U-N-S 78-494-5040
HEALTHSOUTH OF TEXARKANA INC
   (Parent: Healthsouth Corporation)
515 W 12th St, Texarkana, TX 75501
Phone: (903) 793-0088
Sales: $25,000,000
Company Type: Public Family Member
SIC: 8069
   Rehabilitation hospital
Jeff Livingston, Chief Executive Officer

Employees: 175
Employees here: 175

D-U-N-S 15-260-8584
HEALTHSOUTH OF TREASURE COAST
   (Parent: Healthsouth Corporation)
1600 37th St, Vero Beach, FL 32960
Phone: (561) 778-2100
Sales: $40,000,000
Company Type: Public Family Member
SIC: 8069
   Rehabilitation hospital
Denise Mc Grath, Administrator

Employees: 245
Employees here: 225

D-U-N-S 06-599-7298
HEALTHSOUTH OF VIRGINIA, INC
   (Parent: Healthsouth Corporation)
7700 E Parham Rd, Richmond, VA 23294
Phone: (804) 747-5615
Sales: $43,837,000
Company Type: Public Family Member
SIC: 8062
   Hospital
Charles Stark, Chief Executive Officer

Employees: 550
Employees here: 550

D-U-N-S 78-808-2022
HEALTHSOUTH OF YORK, INC
   (Parent: Healthsouth Corporation)
1850 Normandie Dr, York, PA 17404
Phone: (717) 767-6941
Sales: $39,000,000
Company Type: Public Family Member
SIC: 8069
   Physical rehabilitation hospital
Cheryl D Fleming, Chief Executive Officer

Employees: 325
Employees here: 325

D-U-N-S 11-430-2219
HEALTHSOUTH CORPORATION
1 Healthsouth Pkwy S, Birmingham, AL 35243
Phone: (205) 967-7116

Sales: $3,017,269,000   *Employees:* 56,281
Company Type: Public   *Employees here:* 1,070
SIC: 8093
  Outpatient and inpatient rehabilitation facilities surgery &
    diagnostic centers
Richard M Scrushy, Chairman of the Board

D-U-N-S 18-930-6566
HEALTHSOUTH DOCTORS' HOSPITAL
  (Parent: Healthsouth Corporation)
5000 University Dr, Coral Gables, FL 33146
Phone: (305) 669-2484
Sales: $77,589,000   *Employees:* 717
Company Type: Public Family Member   *Employees here:* 644
SIC: 8062
  General hospital
Lincoln Mendez, Chief Financial Officer

D-U-N-S 07-545-3639
HEALTHSOUTH MEDICAL CENTER INC
  (Parent: Healthsouth Corporation)
1201 11th Ave S, Birmingham, AL 35205
Phone: (205) 930-7000
Sales: $76,917,000   *Employees:* 650
Company Type: Public Family Member   *Employees here:* 650
SIC: 8062
  General hospital
Richard M Scrushy, Chairman of the Board

D-U-N-S 94-344-4521
HEALTHSOUTH ORTHOPEDIC SVCS
  (Parent: Healthsouth Corporation)
1 Healthsouth Pkwy S, Birmingham, AL 35243
Phone: (205) 967-7116
Sales: $77,100,000   *Employees:* 1,120
Company Type: Public Family Member   *Employees here:* 85
SIC: 8011
  Orthopedic clinic
P D Brown, President

D-U-N-S 07-825-5619
HEALTHSOUTH REHABILTIATION
  (Parent: Healthsouth Corporation)
14 Hospital Dr, Toms River, NJ 8755
Phone: (732) 244-3100
Sales: $23,000,000   *Employees:* 471
Company Type: Public Family Member   *Employees here:* 451
SIC: 8069
  Rehabilitation hospital
Patricia Ostaszewski, Chief Operating Officer

D-U-N-S 87-716-0275
HEALTHSOUTH SUB-ACUTE CTR
  (Parent: Healthsouth Corporation)
175 Lancaster Blvd, Mechanicsburg, PA 17055
Phone: (717) 691-3831
Sales: $19,800,000   *Employees:* 650
Company Type: Public Family Member   *Employees here:* 650
SIC: 8093
  Rehabilitation service & instruction in the use of orthotics
Richard M Scrushy, President

D-U-N-S 62-199-1041
HEALTHSPHERE OF AMERICA INC
5135 Covington Way Ste 4, Memphis, TN 38134
Phone: (901) 386-5082
Sales: $21,782,000   *Employees:* 600
Company Type: Private   *Employees here:* 40
SIC: 8082
  Holding company and management consulting firm
Kyle E Altman, Chairman of the Board

D-U-N-S 87-715-1233
HEALTHSOUTH REHABILITATION HOSP
  (Parent: Healthsouth Corporation)
901 Clearwater Largo Rd N, Largo, FL 33770
Phone: (727) 586-2999
Sales: $22,000,000   *Employees:* 250
Company Type: Public Family Member   *Employees here:* 250
SIC: 8099
  Rehabilitation hospital & outpatient clinic
Elane Ebaugh, Administrator

D-U-N-S 83-695-4099
HEALTHTEXAS PROVIDER NETWORK
2625 Elm St, Dallas, TX 75226
Phone: (214) 820-7717
Sales: $67,264,000   *Employees:* 300
Company Type: Private   *Employees here:* 300
SIC: 8011
  Provides medical services by operating physician practices
Gary Brock, President

D-U-N-S 80-720-1413
HEALTHTRUST INC - HOSPITAL CO
401 NW 42nd Ave, Fort Lauderdale, FL 33317
Phone: (954) 587-5010
Sales: $39,500,000   *Employees:* NA
Company Type: Public Family Member   *Employees here:* 900
SIC: 8062
  Hospital
Tony Degine, Principal

D-U-N-S 16-093-6407
HEALTHTRUST INC - HOSPITAL CO
  (Parent: Columbia/Hca Healthcare Corp)
1 Park Mdws, Nashville, TN 37215
Phone: (615) 327-9551
Sales: $2,598,600,000   *Employees:* NA
Company Type: Public Family Member   *Employees here:* NA
SIC: 8062
  Operates hospitals and medical office building
James Franck, Secretary

D-U-N-S 16-074-1658
HEALTHTRUST INC - HOSPITAL CO
4000 Spencer St, Houston, TX 77007
Phone: (713) 944-6666
Sales: $53,700,000   *Employees:* NA
Company Type: Public Family Member   *Employees here:* 1,300
SIC: 8062
  General hospital
Chris Black, Purchasing Agent

D-U-N-S 78-807-0902
HEALTHTRUST INC - HOSPITAL CO
3460 S 4155 W, Salt Lake City, UT 84120
Phone: (801) 964-3100
Sales: $27,700,000   *Employees:* NA
Company Type: Public Family Member   *Employees here:* 650
SIC: 8062
  General hospital
Brian Mottishaw, Director

D-U-N-S 78-015-4456
HEALTHTRUST INC - HOSPITAL CO
3700 S Main St, Blacksburg, VA 24060
Phone: (540) 951-1111
Sales: $21,700,000   *Employees:* NA
Company Type: Public Family Member   *Employees here:* 540
SIC: 8062
  Hospital
David Williams, Manager

D-U-N-S 80-956-8413
HEALTHWISE OF AMERICA INC
   (Parent: United Healthcare Corporation)
102 Woodmont Blvd Ste 110, Nashville, TN 37205
Phone: (615) 385-4666
Sales: $208,658,000
Company Type: Public Family Member   *Employees:* 400
                                          Employees here: 4
SIC: 8011
   Health maintenance organization
Dr William W Mc Guire Md, Chairman of the Board

D-U-N-S 17-663-2974
HEART CARE CENTERS OF ILL S C
5320 159th St, Oak Forest, IL 60452
Phone: (708) 535-6000
Sales: $45,000,000   *Employees:* 22
Company Type: Private   *Employees here:* 22
SIC: 8011
   Cardio-vascular specialist
Dr Roy C Bliley Md, President

D-U-N-S 06-404-3193
HEART GROUP INC
1810 Oregon Pike, Lancaster, PA 17601
Phone: (717) 390-4650
Sales: $32,000,000   *Employees:* 132
Company Type: Private   *Employees here:* 30
SIC: 8011
   Cardiologists
Dr Richard D Gentzler Md, President

D-U-N-S 18-120-1773
HEARTLAND HEALTH SYSTEM INC
5325 Faraon St, Saint Joseph, MO 64506
Phone: (816) 271-6003
Sales: $99,900,000   *Employees:* 2,138
Company Type: Private   *Employees here:* 8
SIC: 8062
   Hospital adjustment & collection service billing &
   bookkeeping service non-profit fund raising and hmo
   insurance
Lowell Kruse, President

D-U-N-S 15-086-9683
HEARTLAND HOME HEALTH CARE SVCS
   (Parent: Health Care & Retirement Corp)
401 Center Ave Ste 116, Bay City, MI 48708
Phone: (517) 893-4504
Sales: $24,000,000   *Employees:* 2,100
Company Type: Public Family Member   *Employees here:* 300
SIC: 8082
   Home health care service
Rodney A Hildebrant, President

D-U-N-S 01-064-5919
HEARTLAND REGIONAL MEDICAL CTR
5325 Faraon St, Saint Joseph, MO 64506
Phone: (816) 271-7211
Sales: $164,763,000   *Employees:* 1,900
Company Type: Private   *Employees here:* 293
SIC: 8062
   Hospital
Lowell Kruse, President

D-U-N-S 07-776-9396
HEATHER HILL, INC
12340 Bass Lake Rd, Chardon, OH 44024
Phone: (440) 285-9151
Sales: $22,163,000   *Employees:* 550
Company Type: Private   *Employees here:* 550
SIC: 8069
   Rehabilitation hospital
Robert Harr, President

D-U-N-S 02-000-4693
HEBREW HOME FOR THE AGED DISABLED
302 Silver Ave, San Francisco, CA 94112
Phone: (415) 334-2500
Sales: $23,264,000   *Employees:* 574
Company Type: Private   *Employees here:* 574
SIC: 8051
   Skilled nursing facility
Jerry A Levine, Executive Director

D-U-N-S 06-925-0710
HEBREW HOME & HOSPITAL INC
1 Abrahms Blvd, W Hartford, CT 6117
Phone: (860) 523-3800
Sales: $25,836,000   *Employees:* 600
Company Type: Private   *Employees here:* 600
SIC: 8069
   Chronic disease hospital and long term care facility
Irving Kronenberg, President

D-U-N-S 07-091-4155
HEBREW HOME OF GREATER WASH
6121 Montrose Rd, Rockville, MD 20852
Phone: (301) 881-0300
Sales: $36,287,000   *Employees:* 700
Company Type: Private   *Employees here:* 700
SIC: 8051
   Skilled nursing care facility
Warren R Slavin, Chief Executive Officer

D-U-N-S 07-325-7008
HEBREW HOME AGED
5901 Palisade Ave, Bronx, NY 10471
Phone: (718) 549-8700
Sales: $50,316,000   *Employees:* 1,200
Company Type: Private   *Employees here:* 915
SIC: 8059
   Rest home with health care
Milton A Gilbert, President

D-U-N-S 03-083-2075
HEBREW REHABILITATION CTR FOR AGED
1200 Centre St, Boston, MA 2131
Phone: (617) 325-8000
Sales: $46,410,000   *Employees:* 830
Company Type: Private   *Employees here:* 830
SIC: 8069
   Chronic disease hospital
Maurice May, President

D-U-N-S 07-351-4887
HELENA HOSPITAL ASSOCIATION
1801 Martin Luther King Dr, Helena, AR 72342
Phone: (870) 338-5800
Sales: $20,127,000   *Employees:* 310
Company Type: Private   *Employees here:* 310
SIC: 8062
   Hospital
Steve Reeder, Administrator

D-U-N-S 17-709-7136
HELIAN HEALTH GROUP INC
   (Parent: Vencor Inc)
1105 Sanctuary Pkwy, Alpharetta, GA 30004
Phone: (770) 569-1840
Sales: $34,300,000   *Employees:* 500
Company Type: Private   *Employees here:* 21
SIC: 8011
   Medical center
Bill Winton, Chief Operating Officer

D-U-N-S 79-904-9184
HEMATLOGY ONCLOGY PHYSCIANS PC
2625 N Craycroft Rd, Tucson, AZ 85712
Phone: (520) 324-2409
Sales: $50,000,000   *Employees:* 100
Company Type: Private   *Employees here:* 40
SIC: 8011
  Internal practitioner's office
Dr Robert Brooks Md, President

D-U-N-S 08-117-9640
HEMATOLOGY CLINIC P.C
5050 NE Hoyt St Ste 256, Portland, OR 97213
Phone: (503) 239-7767
Sales: $27,000,000   *Employees:* 44
Company Type: Private   *Employees here:* 33
SIC: 8011
  Hematology clinic
Dr David Regan Md, President

D-U-N-S 06-594-0934
HEMPSTEAD GEN HOSPITAL & MED CTR
800 Front St, Hempstead, NY 11550
Phone: (516) 560-1200
Sales: $50,700,000   *Employees:* 565
Company Type: Private   *Employees here:* 565
SIC: 8062
  General hospital
Dr Milton Stapen Md, Partner

D-U-N-S 07-138-5157
HENDERSON MEMORIAL HOSPITAL
300 Wilson St, Henderson, TX 75652
Phone: (903) 657-7541
Sales: $24,568,000   *Employees:* 350
Company Type: Private   *Employees here:* 350
SIC: 8062
  General hospital
George Roberts, Administrator

D-U-N-S 06-838-2050
HENDRICK MEDICAL CENTER
1242 N 19th St, Abilene, TX 79601
Phone: (915) 670-2000
Sales: $135,109,000   *Employees:* 2,400
Company Type: Private   *Employees here:* 2,200
SIC: 8062
  General hospital
Michael C Waters, President

D-U-N-S 15-060-8644
HENDRICKS COUNTY HOSPITAL
1000 E Main St, Danville, IN 46122
Phone: (317) 745-4451
Sales: $56,326,000   *Employees:* 785
Company Type: Private   *Employees here:* 740
SIC: 8062
  General hospital and immediate care medical clinic
Dennis W Dawes, President

D-U-N-S 12-001-9070
HENNEPIN COUNTY, MINNESOTA
701 Park Ave, Minneapolis, MN 55415
Phone: (612) 347-2121
Sales: $128,200,000   *Employees:* NA
Company Type: Private   *Employees here:* 3,075
SIC: 8062
  Hospital & pharmacy
John Bluford, Administrator

D-U-N-S 07-174-1995
HENRIETTA D GOODALL HOSPITAL
25 June St, Sanford, ME 4073

Phone: (207) 324-4310
Sales: $29,615,000   *Employees:* 500
Company Type: Private   *Employees here:* 425
SIC: 8062
  General hospital
Peter G Booth, President

D-U-N-S 06-771-7165
HENRY COUNTY MEDICAL CENTER
301 Tyson Ave, Paris, TN 38242
Phone: (901) 642-1220
Sales: $26,073,000   *Employees:* 650
Company Type: Private   *Employees here:* 500
SIC: 8062
  General hospital and skilled nursing care facility
Thomas Gee, Administrator

D-U-N-S 07-313-4603
HENRY FORD HEALTH SYSTEM
1 Ford Pl, Detroit, MI 48202
Phone: (313) 876-2600
Sales: $1,937,332,000   *Employees:* 16,300
Company Type: Private   *Employees here:* 300
SIC: 8062
  Hospital
Gail L Warden, President

D-U-N-S 08-161-1246
HENRY FORD HEALTH SYSTEM
19401 Hubbard Dr, Dearborn, MI 48126
Phone: (313) 593-8100
Sales: $36,900,000   *Employees:* NA
Company Type: Private   *Employees here:* 600
SIC: 8011
  Medical center
Tom Groth, Manager

D-U-N-S 82-483-1119
HENRY FORD HEALTH SYSTEM
6777 W Maple Rd, West Bloomfield, MI 48322
Phone: (248) 661-4100
Sales: $20,200,000   *Employees:* NA
Company Type: Private   *Employees here:* 450
SIC: 8069
  Spec hospital
Linda Messina, President

D-U-N-S 17-663-8195
HENRY FORD HEALTH SYSTEM
159 Kercheval Ave, Grosse Pointe, MI 48236
Phone: (313) 640-1000
Sales: $33,500,000   *Employees:* NA
Company Type: Private   *Employees here:* 800
SIC: 8062
  Hospital
Gregory Vasse, Director

D-U-N-S 11-825-1537
HENRY FORD HEALTH SYSTEM
7800 W Outer Dr, Detroit, MI 48235
Phone: (313) 653-2000
Sales: $31,100,000   *Employees:* NA
Company Type: Private   *Employees here:* 500
SIC: 8011
  Health maintenance organization
Pat Posa, N/A

D-U-N-S 09-579-4707
HENRY MEDICAL CENTER
1133 Eagles Landing Pkwy, Stockbridge, GA 30281
Phone: (770) 389-2200

Sales: $35,500,000   *Employees:* 775
Company Type: Private   *Employees here:* 768
SIC: 8062
  General medical hospital
Joseph G Brum, President

D-U-N-S 07-159-4261
HEPBURN MEDICAL CENTER INC
214 King St, Ogdensburg, NY 13669
Phone: (315) 393-3600
Sales: $34,747,000   *Employees:* 550
Company Type: Private   *Employees here:* 550
SIC: 8062
  General medical hospital
Lorraine Kabot, President

D-U-N-S 05-994-6756
HERITAGE ENTERPRISES INC
115 W Jefferson St, Bloomington, IL 61701
Phone: (309) 828-4361
Sales: $28,725,000   *Employees:* 2,000
Company Type: Private   *Employees here:* 40
SIC: 8051
  Skilled nursing home
Joseph F Warner, President

D-U-N-S 82-573-4817
HERITAGE HOSPITAL INC
  (*Parent:* Columbia/Hca Healthcare Corp)
111 Hospital Dr, Tarboro, NC 27886
Phone: (252) 641-7700
Sales: $48,618,000   *Employees:* 300
Company Type: Public Family Member   *Employees here:* 294
SIC: 8062
  General hospital
Janet Mullaney, Chief Executive Officer

D-U-N-S 60-781-2591
HERITAGE MEDICAL MGT INC
4700 E Jackson St, Muncie, IN 47303
Phone: (765) 282-9904
Sales: $23,300,000   *Employees:* 1,050
Company Type: Private   *Employees here:* 355
SIC: 8059
  Nursing/personal care
Larry New, President

D-U-N-S 02-562-4321
HERNANDO HEALTHCARE INC
55 Ponce De Leon Blvd, Brooksville, FL 34601
Phone: (352) 796-5111
Sales: $52,574,000   *Employees:* 364
Company Type: Private   *Employees here:* 329
SIC: 8062
  General hospital
Thomas Barb, Chief Executive Officer

D-U-N-S 80-305-6571
HERRICK MEMORIAL HOSPITAL
500 E Pottawatamie St, Tecumseh, MI 49286
Phone: (517) 423-3834
Sales: $23,932,000   *Employees:* 450
Company Type: Private   *Employees here:* 440
SIC: 8062
  General hospital
John Robertstad, President

D-U-N-S 07-534-2279
HEYWOOD HENRY MEM HOSPITAL INC
242 Green St, Gardner, MA 1440
Phone: (978) 632-3420

Sales: $41,371,000   *Employees:* 714
Company Type: Private   *Employees here:* 700
SIC: 8062
  General hospital
Daniel P Moen, President

D-U-N-S 80-577-5640
HHCA TEXAS HEALTH SERVICES, LP
7502 Greenville Ave, Dallas, TX 75231
Phone: (817) 338-4855
Sales: $24,000,000   *Employees:* 250
Company Type: Private   *Employees here:* 200
SIC: 8082
  Home health care services
Mora Coriston, Chief Financial Officer

D-U-N-S 07-252-2295
HI-DESERT MEMORIAL HOSPITAL DST
6601 White Feather Rd, Joshua Tree, CA 92252
Phone: (760) 366-3711
Sales: $32,085,000   *Employees:* 550
Company Type: Private   *Employees here:* 550
SIC: 8062
  General hospital
James R Larson, President

D-U-N-S 07-131-0106
HIALEAH HOSPITAL INC
  (*Parent:* Tenet Healthcare Corporation)
651 E 25th St, Hialeah, FL 33013
Phone: (305) 693-6100
Sales: $58,400,000   *Employees:* 1,260
Company Type: Public Family Member   *Employees here:* 1,200
SIC: 8062
  General medical & surgical hospital
Cliff Bauer, Chief Executive Officer

D-U-N-S 07-784-7952
HIGH POINT REGIONAL HEALTH SYS
601 N Elm St, High Point, NC 27262
Phone: (336) 884-8400
Sales: $121,428,000   *Employees:* 1,800
Company Type: Private   *Employees here:* 1,790
SIC: 8062
  Hospital
Jeffrey S Miller, President

D-U-N-S 14-414-1967
HIGHLAND CARE CENTER, INC
9131 175th St, Jamaica, NY 11432
Phone: (718) 657-6363
Sales: $21,000,000   *Employees:* 245
Company Type: Private   *Employees here:* 245
SIC: 8051
  Skilled nursing care facility
Chaim Kaminetzky, President

D-U-N-S 06-703-0841
HIGHLAND CLNIC A PROF MED CORP
1455 E Bert Kouns, Shreveport, LA 71105
Phone: (318) 798-4500
Sales: $26,219,000   *Employees:* 250
Company Type: Private   *Employees here:* 250
SIC: 8011
  Physicians office & medical clinic
Dr James F Batte Md, President

D-U-N-S 88-401-4770
HIGHLAND HEALTH SYSTEMS INC
  (*Parent:* Community Health Systems Inc)
2412 50th St, Lubbock, TX 79412
Phone: (806) 795-8251

Sales: $39,000,000
Company Type: Public Family Member — Employees: 250 / Employees here: 250
SIC: 8062
General hospital
David Conejo, President

HIGHLAND HOSPITAL OF ROCHESTER
D-U-N-S 05-364-9430
1000 South Ave, Rochester, NY 14620
Phone: (716) 473-2200
Sales: $98,653,000 — Employees: 1,275 / Employees here: 1,275
Company Type: Private
SIC: 8062
Hospital
William Remizowski, Chief Financial Officer

HIGHLAND PARK HOSPITAL
D-U-N-S 05-665-2605
718 Glenview Ave, Highland Park, IL 60035
Phone: (847) 432-8000
Sales: $104,928,000 — Employees: 870 / Employees here: 870
Company Type: Private
SIC: 8062
General hospital
Ronald Spaeth, President

HIGHLANDS HOSPITAL CORPORATION
D-U-N-S 06-813-5516
(Parent: Consolidated Hlth Systems Inc)
Rr 23 Box North, Prestonsburg, KY 41653
Phone: (606) 886-8511
Sales: $22,500,000 — Employees: 500 / Employees here: 500
Company Type: Private
SIC: 8062
Hospital
Clarence C Traum, President

HIGHLINE COMMUNITY HOSPITAL
D-U-N-S 07-927-2761
16251 Sylvester Rd SW, Seattle, WA 98166
Phone: (206) 244-9970
Sales: $77,250,000 — Employees: 1,150 / Employees here: 770
Company Type: Private
SIC: 8062
General medical & surgical hospital
Paul Tucker, Treasurer

HILL COUNTRY MEMORIAL HOSP
D-U-N-S 07-693-2250
1020 Kerrville Hwy, Fredericksburg, TX 78624
Phone: (830) 997-4353
Sales: $25,645,000 — Employees: 400 / Employees here: 385
Company Type: Private
SIC: 8062
Hospital & medical clinic
Jerry L Durr, Chief Executive Officer

HILL PHYSICIANS MED GROUP INC
D-U-N-S 60-563-8378
2401 Crow Canyon Rd, San Ramon, CA 94583
Phone: (925) 820-8300
Sales: $189,970,000 — Employees: 4 / Employees here: 4
Company Type: Private
SIC: 8011
Independent practice association
Steve Mcdermott, Executive Director

HILLCO, LTD
D-U-N-S 07-201-8278
1435 Hwy 258 N, Kinston, NC 28501
Phone: (252) 523-9094

Sales: $233,466,000 — Employees: 6,000 / Employees here: 125
Company Type: Private
SIC: 8051
Nursing homes and rest homes
Robert Hill Sr, President

HILLCREST BAPTIST MEDICAL CTR
D-U-N-S 07-511-9024
3000 Herring Ave, Waco, TX 76708
Phone: (254) 202-2000
Sales: $133,446,000 — Employees: 2,200 / Employees here: 1,900
Company Type: Private
SIC: 8062
General acute care hospital
Richard E Scott, President

HILLCREST HEALTH CENTER INC
D-U-N-S 07-735-1757
2129 SW 59th St, Oklahoma City, OK 73119
Phone: (405) 685-6671
Sales: $46,457,000 — Employees: 875 / Employees here: 775
Company Type: Private
SIC: 8062
General hospital
Ray Brazier, Chief Executive Officer

HILLCREST HEALTHCARE SYSTEMS
D-U-N-S 61-222-5656
1120 S Utica Ave, Tulsa, OK 74104
Phone: (918) 584-1351
Sales: $263,299,000 — Employees: 564 / Employees here: 25
Company Type: Private
SIC: 8062
Medical & surgical hospital & building operator & fundraiser & rental & ret medical equipment & supplies
Donald A Lorack Jr, President

HILLCREST HOSPITAL
D-U-N-S 06-052-3693
165 Tor Ct, Pittsfield, MA 1201
Phone: (413) 443-4761
Sales: $22,500,000 — Employees: 500 / Employees here: 500
Company Type: Private
SIC: 8062
General hospital
Eugene A Dellea, President

HILLCREST MEDICAL CENTER INC
D-U-N-S 04-907-3091
1120 S Utica Ave, Tulsa, OK 74104
Phone: (918) 584-1351
Sales: $174,575,000 — Employees: 2,126 / Employees here: 1,745
Company Type: Private
SIC: 8062
General hospital
Donald A Lorack, President

HILLCREST MEDICAL NURSING INST
D-U-N-S 07-152-6487
5321 Tazewell Pike, Knoxville, TN 37918
Phone: (423) 687-6881
Sales: $27,104,000 — Employees: 765 / Employees here: 500
Company Type: Private
SIC: 8052
Intermediate care facility
Richard B Flanagan, President

HILLSDALE COMMUNITY HEALTH CTR
D-U-N-S 04-524-5479
168 S Howell St, Hillsdale, MI 49242
Phone: (517) 437-4451

Sales: $22,565,000   *Employees:* 280
Company Type: Private   *Employees here:* 280
SIC: 8062
  General hospital & skilled nursing facility
Charles A Bianchi, President

D-U-N-S 08-244-3813
HILLSDALE GROUP (INC)
1199 Howard Ave Ste 200, Burlingame, CA 94010
Phone: (650) 348-6783
Sales: $22,219,000   *Employees:* 1,600
Company Type: Private   *Employees here:* 15
SIC: 8059
  Retirement & convalescent homes
Richard Stein, Chairman of the Board

D-U-N-S 07-970-0878
HILLSIDE BEHAVIORAL HEALTH
1183 Monroe Ave, Rochester, NY 14620
Phone: (716) 256-7500
Sales: $42,851,000   *Employees:* 1,200
Company Type: Private   *Employees here:* 400
SIC: 8361
  Providing comprehensive service for child welfare & mental
  health programs
Dennis Richardson, President

D-U-N-S 62-052-9867
HILLSIDE CHILDREN'S CENTER
1337 Main St E, Rochester, NY 14609
Phone: (716) 654-4455
Sales: $29,000,000   *Employees:* NA
Company Type: Private   *Employees here:* 1,100
SIC: 8361
  Residential care services
Tess Mahnken-Weather, Branch Manager

D-U-N-S 07-853-1084
HILLSIDE MANOR REHAB & EXTEND
18215 Hillside Ave, Jamaica, NY 11432
Phone: (718) 291-8200
Sales: $37,806,000   *Employees:* 320
Company Type: Private   *Employees here:* 320
SIC: 8051
  Skilled nursing care facility
Dr Stanley Dicker, Partner

D-U-N-S 07-675-3151
HILLSIDE REHABILITATION HOSP
8747 Squires Ln NE, Warren, OH 44484
Phone: (330) 841-3700
Sales: $20,702,000   *Employees:* 345
Company Type: Private   *Employees here:* 345
SIC: 8069
  Rehabilitation & general medical hospital
William O Connor, Chief Executive Officer

D-U-N-S 06-932-4689
HILTON HEAD HEALTH SYSTEM, LP
25 Hospital Center Blvd, Hilton Head Island, SC 29926
Phone: (843) 681-6122
Sales: $83,000,000   *Employees:* 375
Company Type: Private   *Employees here:* 375
SIC: 8062
  General medical and surgical hospital
Dennis Bruns, Chief Executive Officer

D-U-N-S 15-412-7054
HIP OF NEW JERSEY, INC
1 Hip Plz, North Brunswick, NJ 8902
Phone: (732) 937-7600

Sales: $384,711,000   *Employees:* 250
Company Type: Private   *Employees here:* 235
SIC: 8011
  Health maintenance organization
Amy B Mansue, President

D-U-N-S 15-130-4714
HIP HEALTH PLAN OF FLORIDA
300 S Park Rd 400, Hollywood, FL 33021
Phone: (954) 962-3008
Sales: $295,675,000   *Employees:* 545
Company Type: Private   *Employees here:* 499
SIC: 8011
  Health maintenance organization
Steven M Cohen, President

D-U-N-S 04-023-0302
HITCHCOCK CLINIC-KEENE INC
590 Court St, Keene, NH 3431
Phone: (603) 357-3411
Sales: $24,000,000   *Employees:* 350
Company Type: Private   *Employees here:* 325
SIC: 8011
  Medical clinic
Dr William B Tomm Md, Md

D-U-N-S 61-128-2047
HMU INC
5100 Eden Ave Ste 201, Minneapolis, MN 55436
Phone: (612) 922-3418
Sales: $20,400,000   *Employees:* NA
Company Type: Private   *Employees here:* NA
SIC: 8051
  Skilled nursing care facility
Glen Urquhart, President

D-U-N-S 00-690-9717
HOAG MEMORIAL HOSPITAL PRESBT
1 Hoag Dr, Newport Beach, CA 92658
Phone: (949) 645-8600
Sales: $180,430,000   *Employees:* 2,400
Company Type: Private   *Employees here:* 2,058
SIC: 8062
  General medical hospital
Michael D Stephens, President

D-U-N-S 07-257-7877
HOLLAND COMMUNITY HOSPITAL
602 Michigan Ave, Holland, MI 49423
Phone: (616) 392-5141
Sales: $69,259,000   *Employees:* 1,120
Company Type: Private   *Employees here:* 993
SIC: 8062
  General hospital
Judeth Javorek, President

D-U-N-S 06-020-1696
HOLLAND HOME
2105 Raybrook St SE, Grand Rapids, MI 49546
Phone: (616) 235-5026
Sales: $23,440,000   *Employees:* 450
Company Type: Private   *Employees here:* 24
SIC: 8361
  Home for aged
H D Claus, President

D-U-N-S 07-744-7589
HOLLISWOOD CARE CENTER INC
19544 Woodhull Ave, Hollis, NY 11423
Phone: (718) 740-3500

Sales: $21,187,000   *Employees:* 250
Company Type: Private   *Employees here:* 250
SIC: 8051
   Skilled nursing care facility
Veena Ahuja, President

D-U-N-S 06-072-2915
HOLMES HOOPER INC
170 Mount Airy Rd Ste B1, Basking Ridge, NJ 7920
Phone: (908) 766-5000
Sales: $165,353,000   *Employees:* 1,735
Company Type: Public   *Employees here:* 110
SIC: 8099
   Physical examinations and insurance information reports
Paul W Kolacki, Chief Operating Officer

D-U-N-S 09-892-8898
HOLMES REGIONAL MEDICAL CENTER
1350 S Hickory St, Melbourne, FL 32901
Phone: (407) 727-7000
Sales: $209,570,000   *Employees:* 2,600
Company Type: Private   *Employees here:* 2,520
SIC: 8062
   General medical & surgical hospital
Stephen Bunker, President

D-U-N-S 09-457-1403
HOLY CROSS HEALTH SYSTEM CORP
3606 E Jefferson Blvd, South Bend, IN 46615
Phone: (219) 233-8558
Sales: $22,855,000   *Employees:* 17,000
Company Type: Private   *Employees here:* 16,700
SIC: 8062
   Holding company for general medical hospitals and
      management company for its members
Patricia V Csc Sr, President

D-U-N-S 14-736-0309
HOLY CROSS HOSPITAL DETROIT INC
4777 E Outer Dr, Detroit, MI 48234
Phone: (313) 369-9100
Sales: $45,453,000   *Employees:* 765
Company Type: Private   *Employees here:* 765
SIC: 8062
   General medical surgical & psychiatric hospital
Mike Breen, President

D-U-N-S 07-429-6930
HOLY CROSS HOSPITAL SILVER SPRING
1500 Forest Glen Rd, Silver Spring, MD 20910
Phone: (301) 905-0100
Sales: $181,835,000   *Employees:* 2,241
Company Type: Private   *Employees here:* 2,200
SIC: 8062
   General medical hospital
James Hamill, President

D-U-N-S 01-059-1055
HOLY CROSS HOSPITAL
2701 W 68th St, Chicago, IL 60629
Phone: (773) 471-8000
Sales: $78,880,000   *Employees:* 1,600
Company Type: Private   *Employees here:* 1,380
SIC: 8062
   General medical and surgical hospital
Mark Clement, President

D-U-N-S 07-222-8851
HOLY CROSS HOSPITAL INC
4725 N Federal Hwy, Fort Lauderdale, FL 33308
Phone: (954) 771-8000

Sales: $163,818,000   *Employees:* 2,000
Company Type: Private   *Employees here:* 1,850
SIC: 8062
   General hospital
Robert P Granger, Chief Executive Officer

D-U-N-S 19-601-5648
HOLY FAMILY HOSPITAL INC
70 East St, Methuen, MA 1844
Phone: (978) 687-0151
Sales: $70,260,000   *Employees:* 1,200
Company Type: Private   *Employees here:* 1,190
SIC: 8062
   General hospital
William L Lane, President

D-U-N-S 07-443-2808
HOLY FAMILY MEDICAL CENTER
100 N River Rd, Des Plaines, IL 60016
Phone: (847) 297-1800
Sales: $66,261,000   *Employees:* 716
Company Type: Private   *Employees here:* 716
SIC: 8062
   General medical & surgical hospital
Sister P Ann, President

D-U-N-S 06-831-9755
HOLY FAMILY MEM MED CTR INC
2300 Western Ave, Manitowoc, WI 54220
Phone: (920) 684-2011
Sales: $69,270,000   *Employees:* 1,250
Company Type: Private   *Employees here:* 830
SIC: 8062
   Hospital
Daniel Mc Ginty, Administrator

D-U-N-S 07-544-0149
HOLY NAME HOSPITAL
718 Teaneck Rd, Teaneck, NJ 7666
Phone: (201) 833-3000
Sales: $127,963,000   *Employees:* 1,800
Company Type: Private   *Employees here:* 1,780
SIC: 8062
   General medical & surgical hospital & professional nursing
      school
Michael Maron, President

D-U-N-S 07-119-5630
HOLY SPIRIT HOSPITAL SIS
503 N 21st St, Camp Hill, PA 17011
Phone: (717) 763-2100
Sales: $75,500,000   *Employees:* 1,621
Company Type: Private   *Employees here:* 1,459
SIC: 8062
   General medical hospital
Sister R Niemeyer, President

D-U-N-S 06-697-5657
HOLYOKE HOSPITAL INC
575 Beech St, Holyoke, MA 1040
Phone: (413) 534-2500
Sales: $51,250,000   *Employees:* 772
Company Type: Private   *Employees here:* 772
SIC: 8062
   General hospital
Hank J Porten, President

D-U-N-S 09-972-8776
HOLZER CLINIC INC
90 Jackson Pike, Gallipolis, OH 45631
Phone: (740) 446-5411

Sales: $40,000,000
Company Type: Private
SIC: 8011

Employees: 400
Employees here: 345

Physician's office
Robert E Daniel, Administrator

D-U-N-S 04-964-5104
HOLZER HOSPITAL FOUNDATION
100 Jackson Pike, Gallipolis, OH 45631
Phone: (740) 446-5000
Sales: $50,141,000
Company Type: Private
SIC: 8062

Employees: 700
Employees here: 694

Hospital
Adkins Charles I, President

D-U-N-S 62-111-9650
HOME ATTENDANT VENDOR AGENCY INC
3036b Nostrand Ave, Brooklyn, NY 11229
Phone: (718) 253-3888
Sales: $30,000,000
Company Type: Private
SIC: 8082

Employees: 1,200
Employees here: 1,200

Non profit home care for elderly & disabled
Kenneth A Rankin, President

D-U-N-S 10-173-3053
HOME HEALTH AND HOSPICE CARE
2402 Wayne Memorial Dr, Goldsboro, NC 27534
Phone: (919) 735-1387
Sales: $35,697,000
Company Type: Private
SIC: 8059

Employees: 1,333
Employees here: 77

Visiting nurse service
Beverly Withrow, President

D-U-N-S 10-721-7093
HOME HEALTH CORP OF AMERICA
2200 Renaissance Blvd, King Of Prussia, PA 19406
Phone: (610) 272-1717
Sales: $150,232,000
Company Type: Public
SIC: 8082

Employees: 3,068
Employees here: 113

Comprehensive home health care services
Bruce J Feldman, Chairman of the Board

D-U-N-S 62-599-4629
HOME HEALTH FOUNDATION INC
1 Water St, Haverhill, MA 1830
Phone: (978) 373-1141
Sales: $29,183,000
Company Type: Private
SIC: 8082

Employees: 1,000
Employees here: 250

Holding company provides health care homemaker extended
care and hospice services
Pheobe Goldman, Executive Director

D-U-N-S 55-594-4974
HOME HEALTH MANAGEMENT SVCS
853 Broadway Frnt 2, New York, NY 10003
Phone: (212) 420-5959
Sales: $20,100,000
Company Type: Private
SIC: 8082

Employees: 1,247
Employees here: 1,247

Home health care attendents
James Lapolla, Director

D-U-N-S 03-767-9883
HOME HEALTH VNA INC
1 Water St, Haverhill, MA 1830
Phone: (978) 373-1141

Sales: $21,891,000
Company Type: Private
SIC: 8082

Employees: 300
Employees here: 150

Healthcare and supportive services provided in the home &
community
Joan S Hull, President

D-U-N-S 93-272-4172
HOMECALL PHARMACEUTICAL SVCS
(Parent: Mid Atlantic Medical Services)
10200 Old Columbia Rd, Columbia, MD 21046
Phone: (410) 381-8530
Sales: $40,000,000
Company Type: Public Family Member
SIC: 8082

Employees: 90
Employees here: 90

Home infusion therapy service
Gretchen Murtza, President

D-U-N-S 08-963-3150
HOMECARE, INC.
(Parent: Masonic Chrty Fndtn Ct)
9 S Cherry St, Wallingford, CT 6492
Phone: (203) 269-1489
Sales: $27,000,000
Company Type: Private
SIC: 8082

Employees: 2,000
Employees here: 50

Visiting nurse service
Jon Estes, Chief Financial Officer

D-U-N-S 61-388-1606
HOMESTEAD HOSPITAL INC
160 NW 13th St, Homestead, FL 33030
Phone: (305) 248-3232
Sales: $97,000,000
Company Type: Private
SIC: 8062

Employees: 500
Employees here: 500

General hospital
Albert Boulenger, Chief Executive Officer

D-U-N-S 06-490-3974
HOMEWOOD RETIREMENT CENTER
16107 Elliott Pkwy, Williamsport, MD 21795
Phone: (301) 582-1626
Sales: $34,166,000
Company Type: Private
SIC: 8051

Employees: 980
Employees here: 50

Skilled nursing care facility
Rev Roderick J Wagner, President

D-U-N-S 05-295-3783
HOOD GENERAL HOSPITAL
(Parent: Community Health Systems Inc)
1310 Paluxy Rd, Granbury, TX 76048
Phone: (817) 573-2683
Sales: $20,000,000
Company Type: Public Family Member
SIC: 8062

Employees: 175
Employees here: 165

Hospital
John Villaneuva, Administrator

D-U-N-S 06-898-8856
HOPKINS COUNTY HOSPITAL DST
115 Airport Rd, Sulphur Springs, TX 75482
Phone: (903) 885-7671
Sales: $23,934,000
Company Type: Private
SIC: 8062

Employees: 400
Employees here: 390

General medical & surgical hospital
Richard Goddard, Administrator

D-U-N-S 00-310-4478
HOPKINS JOHNS HOSPITAL INC
600 N Wolfe St, Baltimore, MD 21287

Phone: (410) 955-5000
Sales: $601,512,000   *Employees:* 6,000
Company Type: Private   *Employees here:* 5,900
SIC: 8062
  Hospital
Ronald R Peterson, President

D-U-N-S 60-859-0105
HORIZON HEALTH CORPORATION
1500 Waters Ridge Dr, Lewisville, TX 75057
Phone: (972) 420-8200
Sales: $62,445,000   *Employees:* 1,200
Company Type: Public   *Employees here:* 90
SIC: 8063
  Psychiatric and behavioral medical services company
James K Newman, Chief Executive Officer

D-U-N-S 85-849-1533
HORIZON HOSPITAL SYSTEM, INC
110 N Main St, Greenville, PA 16125
Phone: (724) 588-2100
Sales: $70,576,000   *Employees:* 1,227
Company Type: Private   *Employees here:* 800
SIC: 8062
  General hospital
J L Heinike, President

D-U-N-S 07-146-1362
HORIZON HOUSE INC
120 S 30th St, Philadelphia, PA 19104
Phone: (215) 386-3838
Sales: $22,288,000   *Employees:* 750
Company Type: Private   *Employees here:* 200
SIC: 8361
  Rehabilitation center
Wayne Chiodo, Chief Executive Officer

D-U-N-S 94-535-3464
HORIZON PHYSICIAN NETWORK LLC
1310 13th Ave Ste 203, Columbus, GA 31901
Phone: (706) 321-0476
Sales: $21,000,000   *Employees:* 225
Company Type: Private   *Employees here:* 225
SIC: 8011
  Medical doctor's office
Edward Goffinett, Chief Executive Officer

D-U-N-S 07-609-0232
HORIZON WEST HEADQUARTERS INC
  (Parent: Horizon West Inc)
4020 Sierra College Blvd, Rocklin, CA 95677
Phone: (916) 624-6230
Sales: $80,600,000   *Employees:* 3,511
Company Type: Private   *Employees here:* 5
SIC: 8051
  Convalescent hospitals
Ellen Keykendall, President

D-U-N-S 60-515-1737
HORIZON WEST INC
4020 Sierra College Blvd, Rocklin, CA 95677
Phone: (916) 624-6230
Sales: $120,600,000   *Employees:* 5,400
Company Type: Private   *Employees here:* 41
SIC: 8059
  Through its subsidiaries of convalescent homes wholesales
    hospital supplies & pharmacy
Ellen L Kuykendall, President

D-U-N-S 15-763-8800
HORIZON/CMS HEALTHCARE CORP
  (Parent: Healthsouth Corporation)
8801 Horizon Blvd NE, Albuquerque, NM 87113
Phone: (505) 881-4961

Sales: $817,400,000   *Employees:* NA
Company Type: Public Family Member   *Employees here:* NA
SIC: 8051
  Operates rehabilitation hospitals and outpatient
    rehabilitation facilities
Richard M Scrushy, Chairman of the Board

D-U-N-S 07-146-5215
HORSHAM CLINIC (INC)
  (Parent: Universal Health Services)
722 E Butler Pike, Ambler, PA 19002
Phone: (215) 643-7800
Sales: $20,000,000   *Employees:* 250
Company Type: Public Family Member   *Employees here:* 200
SIC: 8063
  Private psychiatric hospital
Mark A Benz, Chief Executive Officer

D-U-N-S 04-412-6977
HORTON MEMORIAL HOSPITAL
60 Prospect Ave, Middletown, NY 10940
Phone: (914) 343-2424
Sales: $85,329,000   *Employees:* 1,300
Company Type: Private   *Employees here:* 1,295
SIC: 8062
  General hospital
Jeffrey Hirsch, Operations-Production-Mfg

D-U-N-S 03-877-7041
HOSPICE OF MICHIGAN INC
16250 Northland Dr, Southfield, MI 48075
Phone: (248) 559-9209
Sales: $48,896,000   *Employees:* 800
Company Type: Private   *Employees here:* 200
SIC: 8082
  Hospice
Lee R Miskowski, Chief Executive Officer

D-U-N-S 82-463-5809
HOSPICE FAMILY CARE, INC.
1125 E Southern Ave 201, Mesa, AZ 85204
Phone: (602) 926-6089
Sales: $25,726,000   *Employees:* 450
Company Type: Private   *Employees here:* 30
SIC: 8082
  Home health care services
Nancy Smith, President

D-U-N-S 12-263-1955
HOSPICE HILLSBOROUGH INC
3010 W Azeele St, Tampa, FL 33609
Phone: (813) 877-2200
Sales: $20,073,000   *Employees:* 400
Company Type: Private   *Employees here:* 390
SIC: 8093
  Out-patient hospice
Anne E Thal, President

D-U-N-S 10-771-5146
HOSPITAL OF BARSTOW, INC
  (Parent: Community Health Systems Inc)
555 S 7th Ave, Barstow, CA 92311
Phone: (760) 256-1761
Sales: $21,768,000   *Employees:* 215
Company Type: Public Family Member   *Employees here:* 215
SIC: 8062
  General hospital
Russell Judd, Chief Executive Officer

D-U-N-S 07-160-2023
HOSPITAL OF COMMUNITY-GENERAL
Broad Rd, Syracuse, NY 13215
Phone: (315) 492-5011

Sales: $82,887,000   *Employees:* 1,500
Company Type: Private   *Employees here:* 1,490
SIC: 8062
   General medical & surgical hospital
Mary Smith, Secretary

D-U-N-S 07-162-6576
HOSPITAL OF GERMANTOWN
1 Penns Ct, Philadelphia, PA 19144
Phone: (215) 951-8000
Sales: $57,893,000   *Employees:* 550
Company Type: Private   *Employees here:* 550
SIC: 8062
   Hospital
David A Ricci, President

D-U-N-S 07-271-4249
HOSPITAL OF MERCY COMMUNITY
   (Parent: Tri State Health System Inc)
160 E Main St, Port Jervis, NY 12771
Phone: (914) 856-5351
Sales: $31,900,000   *Employees:* 700
Company Type: Private   *Employees here:* 650
SIC: 8062
   General medical & surgical hospital
R A Brothers, Administrator

D-U-N-S 07-540-6579
HOSPITAL OF ST RAPHAEL
1450 Chapel St, New Haven, CT 6511
Phone: (203) 789-3000
Sales: $246,503,000   *Employees:* 3,426
Company Type: Private   *Employees here:* 3,400
SIC: 8062
   General hospital
James J Cullen, President

D-U-N-S 07-501-2203
HOSPITAL AFFLIATES OF ALHAMBRA
100 S Raymond Ave, Alhambra, CA 91801
Phone: (626) 570-1606
Sales: $29,340,000   *Employees:* 400
Company Type: Private   *Employees here:* 400
SIC: 8062
   General medical & surgical hospital
Tim Mcglew, Chief Executive Officer

D-U-N-S 07-247-3812
HOSPITAL AUTH OF COLQUITT CNTY
3131 S Main St, Moultrie, GA 31768
Phone: (912) 985-3420
Sales: $40,768,000   *Employees:* 750
Company Type: Private   *Employees here:* 725
SIC: 8062
   General hospital
James R Lowry, Administrator

D-U-N-S 06-921-1449
HOSPITAL AUTH OF HABERSHAM CNTY
Hwy 441n, Demorest, GA 30535
Phone: (706) 754-2161
Sales: $26,873,000   *Employees:* 453
Company Type: Private   *Employees here:* 453
SIC: 8062
   Hospital skilled nursing home and skilled personal care
Charles R Dwozan, Administrator

D-U-N-S 07-475-3526
HOSPITAL AUTHORITY PETERSBURG
801 S Adams St, Petersburg, VA 23803
Phone: (804) 862-5000

Sales: $99,273,000   *Employees:* 1,400
Company Type: Private   *Employees here:* 1,350
SIC: 8062
   Hospital
David H Dunham, President

D-U-N-S 01-052-0674
HOSPITAL BOARD OF DIRECTORS
2776 Cleveland Ave, Fort Myers, FL 33901
Phone: (941) 332-1111
Sales: $294,640,000   *Employees:* 4,000
Company Type: Private   *Employees here:* 2,275
SIC: 8062
   General hospital
William D Johnson, Chief Executive Officer

D-U-N-S 62-779-3425
HOSPITAL CORP OF DOUGLAS
   (Parent: Columbia/Hca Healthcare Corp)
738 W Harvard Ave, Roseburg, OR 97470
Phone: (541) 673-6641
Sales: $21,500,000   *Employees:* 480
Company Type: Public Family Member   *Employees here:* 480
SIC: 8062
   General hospital
Gwen T Selle, Chief Operating Officer

D-U-N-S 18-791-3298
HOSPITAL CORP OF UTAH INC
   (Parent: Columbia/Hca Healthcare Corp)
4525 Harding Pike, Nashville, TN 37205
Phone: (615) 327-9551
Sales: $21,300,000   *Employees:* 474
Company Type: Public Family Member   *Employees here:* 474
SIC: 8062
   General hospital
W H Connery Jr, President

D-U-N-S 07-450-3657
HOSPITAL CORP NORTH CAROLINA
   (Parent: Healthtrust Inc - Hospital Co)
218 Old Mocksville Rd, Statesville, NC 28625
Phone: (704) 873-0281
Sales: $34,500,000   *Employees:* 755
Company Type: Public Family Member   *Employees here:* 530
SIC: 8062
   General hospital skilled nursing care facility and psychiatric
   hospital
G P Lotti, Chief Executive Officer

D-U-N-S 18-791-9907
HOSPITAL CORP NORTHWEST INC
   (Parent: Columbia/Hca Healthcare Corp)
6200 N La Cholla Blvd, Tucson, AZ 85741
Phone: (520) 742-9000
Sales: $43,300,000   *Employees:* 940
Company Type: Public Family Member   *Employees here:* 940
SIC: 8062
   Hospital health/allied services
Richard L Scott, President

D-U-N-S 92-641-9516
HOSPITAL CORPORATION TENNESSEE
   (Parent: Columbia/Hca Healthcare Corp)
161 Mount Pelia Rd, Martin, TN 38237
Phone: (901) 587-4261
Sales: $26,332,000   *Employees:* 397
Company Type: Public Family Member   *Employees here:* 397
SIC: 8062
   General hospital
Coleman Foss, Chief Executive Officer

D-U-N-S 07-386-8853
HOSPITAL DEVELOPMENT & SERVICE
  (*Parent:* Columbia/Hca Healthcare Corp)
401 NW 42nd Ave, Fort Lauderdale, FL 33317
Phone: (954) 587-5010
Sales: $36,400,000   *Employees:* 795
Company Type: Public Family Member   *Employees here:* 795
SIC: 8062
  Hospital health/allied services
Anthony Degina Jr, Chief Executive Officer

D-U-N-S 07-103-6685
HOSPITAL FOR JOINT DISEASES
301 E 17th St, New York, NY 10003
Phone: (212) 598-6000
Sales: $123,008,000   *Employees:* 1,150
Company Type: Private   *Employees here:* 1,050
SIC: 8069
  Orthopedic hospital
John N Kastanis, Chief Executive Officer

D-U-N-S 07-780-3641
HOSPITAL FOR SICK CHILDREN
1731 Bunker Hill Rd NE, Washington, DC 20017
Phone: (202) 832-4400
Sales: $38,655,000   *Employees:* 450
Company Type: Private   *Employees here:* 450
SIC: 8069
  Hospital
Thomas W Chapman, President

D-U-N-S 06-924-4259
HOSPITAL FOR SPECIAL CARE
2150 Corbin Ave, New Britain, CT 6053
Phone: (860) 223-2761
Sales: $57,363,000   *Employees:* 800
Company Type: Private   *Employees here:* 800
SIC: 8069
  Hospital
David Crandall, President

D-U-N-S 79-820-4566
HOSPITAL GROUP OF AMERICA
  (*Parent:* Cooper Companies Inc)
1265 Drummers Ln Ste 107, Wayne, PA 19087
Phone: (610) 687-5151
Sales: $43,013,000   *Employees:* 761
Company Type: Public Family Member   *Employees here:* 9
SIC: 8063
  Psychiatric & drug abuse hospital
Mark Russell, President

D-U-N-S 06-847-5490
HOSPITAL GROUP OF ILLINOIS
  (*Parent:* Hospital Group Of America)
520 N Ridgeway Ave, Chicago, IL 60624
Phone: (773) 722-3113
Sales: $21,000,000   *Employees:* 300
Company Type: Public Family Member   *Employees here:* 300
SIC: 8063
  Psychiatric hospital
Mark Russell, President

D-U-N-S 11-742-3277
HOSPITAL SERVICE DIST
8166 Main St, Houma, LA 70360
Phone: (504) 873-4141
Sales: $121,885,000   *Employees:* 1,215
Company Type: Private   *Employees here:* 1,215
SIC: 8062
  Hospital
Alex Smith, Administrator

D-U-N-S 06-953-6381
HOSPITAL SERVICE DISTRICT
602 N Acadia Rd, Thibodaux, LA 70301
Phone: (504) 447-5500
Sales: $62,396,000   *Employees:* 706
Company Type: Private   *Employees here:* 704
SIC: 8062
  General hospital
David Snyder, Chief Executive Officer

D-U-N-S 07-789-1851
HOSPITAL SERVICE DISTRICT NO 1
6300 Main St, Zachary, LA 70791
Phone: (225) 658-4000
Sales: $32,462,000   *Employees:* 600
Company Type: Private   *Employees here:* 568
SIC: 8062
  Hospital
David Fuller, Chief Executive Officer

D-U-N-S 07-945-4005
HOSPITAL SERVICE DISTRICT NO 2
1125 Marguerite St, Morgan City, LA 70380
Phone: (504) 384-2200
Sales: $24,945,000   *Employees:* 400
Company Type: Private   *Employees here:* 400
SIC: 8062
  Hospital
Jim Barbuat, Chief Financial Officer

D-U-N-S 00-981-5499
HOSPITAL SERVICE DISTRICT 1
1101 Medical Center Blvd, Marrero, LA 70072
Phone: (504) 347-5511
Sales: $133,745,000   *Employees:* 1,676
Company Type: Private   *Employees here:* 1,548
SIC: 8062
  General hospital
A G Muller, Chief Executive Officer

D-U-N-S 06-641-0457
HOSPITALS OF NATIONAL MEDICAL
  (*Parent:* Tenet Healthcare Corporation)
1801 N Jackson St, Tullahoma, TN 37388
Phone: (931) 455-0601
Sales: $27,200,000   *Employees:* 600
Company Type: Public Family Member   *Employees here:* 500
SIC: 8062
  General hospital
David Wilson, Chief Executive Officer

D-U-N-S 19-373-0561
HOUSECALL MEDICAL SERVICES
  (*Parent:* Housecall Medical Resources)
305 N Hurstbourne Pkwy, Louisville, KY 40222
Phone: (502) 394-3325
Sales: $125,000,000   *Employees:* 2,000
Company Type: Public Family Member   *Employees here:* 15
SIC: 8082
  Provides home health care services & products
Daniel Kohl, President

D-U-N-S 07-911-1423
HOUSTON CNTY HEALTHCARE AUTH
1108 Ross Clark Cir, Dothan, AL 36301
Phone: (334) 793-8111
Sales: $151,940,000   *Employees:* 1,825
Company Type: Private   *Employees here:* 1,700
SIC: 8062
  General hospital
Ron Owen, Chief Executive Officer

D-U-N-S 07-248-2375
HOUSTON COUNTY HOSPITAL AUTH
1601 Watson Blvd, Warner Robins, GA 31093
Phone: (912) 922-4281
Sales: $93,449,000   *Employees:* 1,200
Company Type: Private   *Employees here:* 850
SIC: 8062
  General medical hospital
Arthur Christie, Administrator

D-U-N-S 61-275-5801
HOUSTON NORTHWEST MEDICAL CTR
   (*Parent:* Tenet Healthcare Corporation)
710 Fm 1960 Rd W, Houston, TX 77090
Phone: (281) 440-1000
Sales: $250,000,000   *Employees:* 2,100
Company Type: Public Family Member   *Employees here:* 1,600
SIC: 8062
  Holding company general medical hospital skilled nursing
   care medical services
James Kelly, Chief Executive Officer

D-U-N-S 88-479-0460
HOUSTON REHABILITATION INST
   (*Parent:* Horizon/Cms Healthcare Corp)
17506 Red Oak Dr, Houston, TX 77090
Phone: (281) 580-1212
Sales: $28,700,000   *Employees:* 250
Company Type: Public Family Member   *Employees here:* 250
SIC: 8093
  Rehabilitation services
Anne Leon, Chief Executive Officer

D-U-N-S 07-206-5816
HOWARD COMMUNITY HOSPITAL
3500 S Lafountain St, Kokomo, IN 46902
Phone: (765) 453-0702
Sales: $54,182,000   *Employees:* 900
Company Type: Private   *Employees here:* 880
SIC: 8062
  General hospital psychiatric hospital
James C Bigogno, President

D-U-N-S 03-033-4544
HOWARD COUNTY GENERAL HOSPITAL
5755 Cedar Ln, Columbia, MD 21044
Phone: (410) 740-7890
Sales: $80,437,000   *Employees:* 1,225
Company Type: Private   *Employees here:* 1,090
SIC: 8062
  General hospital
Victor A Broccolino, President

D-U-N-S 18-500-8125
HOWARD UNIVERSITY
2041 Georgia Ave Nw, Washington, DC 20060
Phone: (202) 865-6100
Sales: $120,300,000   *Employees:* NA
Company Type: Private   *Employees here:* 2,716
SIC: 8062
  Hospital
Sherman P Mccoy, President

D-U-N-S 07-479-4710
HOWARD YOUNG MEDICAL CENTER
240 Maple St, Woodruff, WI 54568
Phone: (715) 356-8000
Sales: $39,341,000   *Employees:* 550
Company Type: Private   *Employees here:* 550
SIC: 8062
  General hospital
Douglas Rosenberg, President

D-U-N-S 07-784-3308
HOWELL CHILD CARE CENTER INC
3738 Howell Day Care Rd, La Grange, NC 28551
Phone: (252) 566-9011
Sales: $39,885,000   *Employees:* 1,400
Company Type: Private   *Employees here:* 300
SIC: 8361
  Children's home
Jerald T Howell, Chairman of the Board

D-U-N-S 83-553-8125
HPI-RAMSEY, INC
   (*Parent:* Healthpartners Inc)
640 Jackson St, Saint Paul, MN 55101
Phone: (320) 634-4131
Sales: $167,800,000   *Employees:* 3,575
Company Type: Private   *Employees here:* NA
SIC: 8062
  Holding company
Terry Finzen, President

D-U-N-S 07-373-6902
HSE A INGLIS WHEELCHAIR COMMUNITY
2600 Belmont Ave, Philadelphia, PA 19131
Phone: (215) 878-5600
Sales: $31,152,000   *Employees:* 600
Company Type: Private   *Employees here:* 600
SIC: 8361
  Home for physically disabled persons
Kevin W Jones, Chief Executive Officer

D-U-N-S 07-667-4787
HUDSON VALLEY HOSPITAL CENTER
1980 Crompond Rd, Cortlandt Manor, NY 10567
Phone: (914) 737-9000
Sales: $49,989,000   *Employees:* 527
Company Type: Private   *Employees here:* 527
SIC: 8062
  General hospital
John C Federspiel, President

D-U-N-S 06-744-1436
HUGH CHATHAM MEMORIAL HOSPITAL
Parkwood Dr, Elkin, NC 28621
Phone: (336) 835-3722
Sales: $32,392,000   *Employees:* 600
Company Type: Private   *Employees here:* 325
SIC: 8062
  General hospital skilled nursing center and retirement center
Richard Osmus, Administrator

D-U-N-S 07-812-5457
HUGHSTON ORTHOPEDIC CLINIC PC
6262 Hamilton Rd, Columbus, GA 31909
Phone: (706) 324-6661
Sales: $24,000,000   *Employees:* 350
Company Type: Private   *Employees here:* 175
SIC: 8011
  Orthopedic physicians and clinic
Dr Jack C Hughston, Chairman of the Board

D-U-N-S 10-507-6228
HUMAN DEVELOPMENT ASSOCIATION,
12 Heyward St, Brooklyn, NY 11211
Phone: (718) 855-5200
Sales: $33,616,000   *Employees:* 1,450
Company Type: Private   *Employees here:* 1,450
SIC: 8082
  Provides home health care service
Rabbi Y Gruenwald, Director

D-U-N-S 04-994-4143
HUMANA INC
500 W Main St Ste 300, Louisville, KY 40202
Phone: (502) 580-1000
Sales: $7,880,000,000   *Employees:* 19,500
Company Type: Public   *Employees here:* 1,100
SIC: 8011
  Provides hmos & ppos supplemental health insurance &
  provides insurance claim processing
David A Jones, Chairman of the Board

D-U-N-S 80-534-9198
HUMANA MLITARY HEALTHCARE SVCS
  (Parent: Humana Inc)
500 W Main St Ste 300, Louisville, KY 40202
Phone: (502) 580-1000
Sales: $43,200,000   *Employees:* 628
Company Type: Public Family Member   *Employees here:* 190
SIC: 8011
  Health care services
R G Shields, President

D-U-N-S 93-887-6661
HUMILITY MARY HEALTH SYSTEM
1044 Belmont Ave, Youngstown, OH 44504
Phone: (330) 759-7484
Sales: $41,400,000   *Employees:* 900
Company Type: Private   *Employees here:* 650
SIC: 8062
  General hospital
Kevin Nolan, Chief Executive Officer

D-U-N-S 11-304-9845
HUNT ASSOC ASSSTED LIVING CORP
101 Charwood Dr, Abingdon, VA 24210
Phone: (540) 676-3300
Sales: $20,000,000   *Employees:* 35
Company Type: Private   *Employees here:* 26
SIC: 8051
  Owner/operator contractor and developer of assisted living
  communities
W H Hunt, President

D-U-N-S 07-487-8968
HUNT MEMORIAL HOSPITAL DST
4215 Joe Ramsey Blvd E, Greenville, TX 75401
Phone: (903) 408-5000
Sales: $52,157,000   *Employees:* 640
Company Type: Private   *Employees here:* 570
SIC: 8062
  General hospital an imaging center home health facility and
  employer's contract service
Richard Carter, Chief Executive Officer

D-U-N-S 78-447-1906
HUNTER CARE CENTERS INC
  (Parent: Huntco Farms Inc)
14323 S Outer 40 Ste N600, Chesterfield, MO 63017
Phone: (314) 469-3494
Sales: $41,494,000   *Employees:* 1,400
Company Type: Public Family Member   *Employees here:* 25
SIC: 8051
  Nursing homes
Raymond Tyler, President

D-U-N-S 06-988-6216
HUNTERDON MEDICAL CENTER
2100 Wescott Dr, Flemington, NJ 8822
Phone: (908) 788-6100

Sales: $82,495,000   *Employees:* 1,300
Company Type: Private   *Employees here:* 1,280
SIC: 8062
  General hospital
Lawrence N Grand, Chief Operating Officer

D-U-N-S 07-268-4152
HUNTINGTON CABELL HOSPITAL
1340 Hal Greer Blvd, Huntington, WV 25701
Phone: (304) 526-2000
Sales: $116,413,000   *Employees:* 1,600
Company Type: Private   *Employees here:* 1,600
SIC: 8062
  Hospital
W D Smith Ii, President

D-U-N-S 14-445-2273
HUNTINGTON FOUNDATION INC
Park Ave & Randolph Rd, Plainfield, NJ 7061
Phone: (908) 668-2000
Sales: $116,200,000   *Employees:* 1,686
Company Type: Private   *Employees here:* 6
SIC: 8011
  Ambulatory surg center exec physician immediate care
  medical center environmental health center and
  pathological laboratory
John Kopicki, President

D-U-N-S 06-802-0726
HUNTINGTON HOSPITAL ASSN
270 Park Ave, Huntington, NY 11743
Phone: (516) 351-2000
Sales: $105,793,000   *Employees:* 1,270
Company Type: Private   *Employees here:* 1,200
SIC: 8062
  General hospital
J R Gaudreault, President

D-U-N-S 06-474-9732
HUNTINGTON MEDICAL GROUP PC
180 E Pulaski Rd, Huntington Station, NY 11746
Phone: (516) 425-2121
Sales: $23,234,000   *Employees:* 480
Company Type: Private   *Employees here:* 290
SIC: 8011
  Offices & clinics of doctors of medicine
Thomas Mc Donagh, President

D-U-N-S 07-417-9300
HUNTSVILLE MEMORIAL HOSPITAL
485 I 45 S, Huntsville, TX 77340
Phone: (409) 291-3411
Sales: $31,429,000   *Employees:* 500
Company Type: Private   *Employees here:* 500
SIC: 8062
  General hospital
Robert Hardy, Chairman of the Board

D-U-N-S 07-423-2273
HURLEY MEDICAL CENTER, INC
1 Hurley Plz, Flint, MI 48503
Phone: (810) 257-9000
Sales: $255,304,000   *Employees:* 2,884
Company Type: Private   *Employees here:* 2,650
SIC: 8062
  General hospital
Glenn Fosdick, President

D-U-N-S 07-276-6835
HURON MEMORIAL HOSPITAL INC
1100 S Van Dyke Rd, Bad Axe, MI 48413
Phone: (517) 269-9521

Sales: $22,084,000   *Employees:* 274
Company Type: Private   *Employees here:* 274
SIC: 8062
    General medical & surgical hospital
James B Gardner, President

D-U-N-S 07-869-2712
HURON REGIONAL MEDICAL CENTER
172 4th St SE, Huron, SD 57350
Phone: (605) 353-6200
Sales: $30,000,000   *Employees:* 400
Company Type: Private   *Employees here:* 355
SIC: 8062
    Hospital
John Single, Administrator

D-U-N-S 12-199-4842
HURON VALLEY SINAI HOSPITAL
1 William Carls Dr, Commerce Township, MI 48382
Phone: (248) 360-3300
Sales: $60,783,000   *Employees:* 620
Company Type: Private   *Employees here:* 600
SIC: 8062
    General medical and surgical hospital
Elliot Joseph, Executive Vice-President

D-U-N-S 06-377-3378
HUTCHESON MEDICAL CENTER
100 Gross Crescent Cir, Fort Oglethorpe, GA 30742
Phone: (706) 858-2000
Sales: $79,067,000   *Employees:* 1,100
Company Type: Private   *Employees here:* 900
SIC: 8062
    General hospital
Dr Robert Jones, Chief Executive Officer

D-U-N-S 07-332-5425
HUTCHINSON CLINIC P A,
2101 N Waldron St, Hutchinson, KS 67502
Phone: (316) 669-2500
Sales: $35,067,000   *Employees:* 405
Company Type: Private   *Employees here:* 370
SIC: 8011
    Medical and surgical clinic lab service pharmacy and
      radiology center
Leslie Zimmerman, Administrator

D-U-N-S 07-626-2955
HUTCHINSON HOSPITAL CORP
1701 E 23rd Ave, Hutchinson, KS 67502
Phone: (316) 665-2000
Sales: $50,522,000   *Employees:* 800
Company Type: Private   *Employees here:* 800
SIC: 8062
    General hospital & skilled nursing facility
Gene Schmidt, President

D-U-N-S 07-639-2331
HUTZEL HOSPITAL
4707 Saint Antoine St, Detroit, MI 48201
Phone: (313) 745-7555
Sales: $169,691,000   *Employees:* 1,800
Company Type: Private   *Employees here:* 1,800
SIC: 8062
    General hospital
Thomas Rozek, Manager

D-U-N-S 92-647-4768
HCA HEALTH SERVICES OF FLORIDA
    (*Parent:* Columbia/Hca Healthcare Corp)
1400 Fivay Rd, Port Richey, FL 34667
Phone: (727) 863-2411

Sales: $104,381,000   *Employees:* 1,000
Company Type: Public Family Member   *Employees here:* 1,000
SIC: 8062
    General medical & surgical hospital
Don Griffin, Chief Executive Officer

D-U-N-S 07-299-8032
HCA HEALTH SERVICES OF UTAH,
    (*Parent:* Columbia/Hca Healthcare Corp)
1200 E 3900 S, Salt Lake City, UT 84124
Phone: (801) 268-7000
Sales: $67,700,000   *Employees:* 1,457
Company Type: Public Family Member   *Employees here:* 1,200
SIC: 8062
    General medical & surgical hospital
John Hanshaw, Chief Executive Officer

D-U-N-S 92-670-5104
HCA RALEIGH COMMUNITY HOSPITAL INC
    (*Parent:* Columbia/Hca Healthcare Corp)
3400 Wake Forest Rd, Raleigh, NC 27609
Phone: (919) 954-3000
Sales: $46,100,000   *Employees:* 1,000
Company Type: Public Family Member   *Employees here:* 845
SIC: 8062
    General hospital
G M Girone, Chief Executive Officer

D-U-N-S 06-975-2475
I O M HEALTH SYSTEM LP
    (*Parent:* Qhg Of Indiana)
7950 W Jefferson Blvd, Fort Wayne, IN 46804
Phone: (219) 435-7001
Sales: $157,546,000   *Employees:* 2,000
Company Type: Private   *Employees here:* 2,000
SIC: 8062
    General hospital
Marvin Kurtz, Treasurer

D-U-N-S 18-368-7664
IATROS HEALTH NETWORK INC
10 Piedmont Ctr NE, Atlanta, GA 30305
Phone: (404) 266-3643
Sales: $25,513,000   *Employees:* 600
Company Type: Public   *Employees here:* 75
SIC: 8051
    Alternative care for post-acute ventilator dependent &
      medically complex patients
Reginald D Strickland, President

D-U-N-S 07-193-0952
IBERIA GENERAL HOSPITAL & MED CTR
2315 E Main St, New Iberia, LA 70560
Phone: (318) 364-0441
Sales: $35,313,000   *Employees:* 450
Company Type: Private   *Employees here:* 450
SIC: 8062
    General medical hospital
Robert Stanley, Chief Executive Officer

D-U-N-S 00-681-8561
IDEXX VETERINARY SERVICES INC
    (*Parent:* Idexx Laboratories Inc)
2825 Kovr Dr, West Sacramento, CA 95605
Phone: (916) 372-4200
Sales: $20,700,000   *Employees:* 430
Company Type: Public Family Member   *Employees here:* 175
SIC: 8071
    Testing laboratory
David Shaw, President

D-U-N-S 10-706-3372
IHS HOME CARE
(Parent: Integrated Health Services)
1 Vantage Way Ste B300, Nashville, TN 37228
Phone: (615) 256-8755
Sales: $24,100,000 *Employees:* 1,500
Company Type: Public Family Member *Employees here:* 50
SIC: 8082
Home health care services
Chris Winkle, President

D-U-N-S 60-886-6364
ILLINI MANORS INC
115 E South St, Galesburg, IL 61401
Phone: (309) 343-1550
Sales: $31,941,000 *Employees:* 600
Company Type: Private *Employees here:* 2
SIC: 8051
Nursing homes
Donald Fike, President

D-U-N-S 07-438-9388
ILLINOIS DEPT HUMAN RESOURCES
7400 183rd St, Tinley Park, IL 60477
Phone: (708) 614-4000
Sales: $25,000,000 *Employees:* NA
Company Type: Private *Employees here:* 600
SIC: 8062
Healthcare
Abdul Basit, Director

D-U-N-S 06-085-0245
ILLINOIS DEPT HUMAN RESOURCES
100 E Jeffery St, Kankakee, IL 60901
Phone: (815) 939-8011
Sales: $42,300,000 *Employees:* NA
Company Type: Private *Employees here:* 1,350
SIC: 8063
Mental hospital
Margery Milone, Branch Manager

D-U-N-S 08-205-0543
ILLINOIS DEPT HUMAN RESOURCES
750 S State St, Elgin, IL 60123
Phone: (847) 742-1040
Sales: $42,300,000 *Employees:* NA
Company Type: Private *Employees here:* 1,250
SIC: 8063
State mental hospital & rehabilitation service
Roalda J Alderman, N/A

D-U-N-S 07-442-1934
ILLINOIS DEPT HUMAN RESOURCES
4200 N Oak Park Ave, Chicago, IL 60634
Phone: (773) 794-4000
Sales: $26,500,000 *Employees:* NA
Company Type: Private *Employees here:* 780
SIC: 8063
Mental health hospital
John Steinmetz, Branch Manager

D-U-N-S 92-748-6100
ILLINOIS DEPT HUMAN RESOURCES
1000 N Main St, Anna, IL 62906
Phone: (618) 833-5161
Sales: $20,800,000 *Employees:* NA
Company Type: Private *Employees here:* 660
SIC: 8063
Mental health institute
Shawn Jeffers, Superintendent

D-U-N-S 05-786-4449
ILLINOIS MASONIC MEDICAL CTR
836 W Wellington Ave, Chicago, IL 60657
Phone: (773) 975-1600
Sales: $224,096,000 *Employees:* 3,000
Company Type: Private *Employees here:* 2,700
SIC: 8062
General medical & surgical hospital
Bruce C Campbell, President

D-U-N-S 92-633-5803
ILLINOIS PSYCHIATRIC HOSPITAL INC
(Parent: H C A Psychiatric Company)
1 Park Mdws, Nashville, TN 37215
Phone: (615) 327-9551
Sales: $25,900,000 *Employees:* 700
Company Type: Public Family Member *Employees here:* 2
SIC: 8063
Psychiatric hospitals
David T Vandewater, President

D-U-N-S 03-055-2913
ILLINOIS VALLEY COMMUNITY HOSP
925 West St, Peru, IL 61354
Phone: (815) 223-3300
Sales: $33,502,000 *Employees:* 540
Company Type: Private *Employees here:* 540
SIC: 8062
Hospital
Ralph Berkley, Administrator

D-U-N-S 06-479-1809
IMMANUEL-ST JOSEPH OF MANKATO
1025 Marsh St, Mankato, MN 56001
Phone: (507) 625-4031
Sales: $59,747,000 *Employees:* 950
Company Type: Private *Employees here:* 950
SIC: 8062
General medical and surgical hospital
Dr Douglas Wood Md, President

D-U-N-S 12-118-3800
IN HOME HEALTH, INC
601 Carlson Pkwy Ste 500, Hopkins, MN 55305
Phone: (612) 449-7500
Sales: $110,139,000 *Employees:* 4,000
Company Type: Public *Employees here:* 119
SIC: 8082
Home health care services
Wolfgan Von Maack, President

D-U-N-S 07-836-0997
INDIAN HEALTH SERVICE
Hwy 666, Shiprock, NM 87420
Phone: (505) 368-6001
Sales: $20,600,000 *Employees:* NA
Company Type: Private *Employees here:* 525
SIC: 8062
Hospital
Dee Hutchinson, Director

D-U-N-S 96-284-8255
INDIAN PATH HOSPITAL INC
(Parent: H C A Health Services Tenn Inc)
2000 Brookside Dr, Kingsport, TN 37660
Phone: (423) 246-4311
Sales: $34,500,000 *Employees:* 755
Company Type: Public Family Member *Employees here:* 750
SIC: 8062
General hospital
Robert Bauer, Director

D-U-N-S 61-171-0427
INDIAN RIVER MEMORIAL HOSPITAL
1000 36th St, Vero Beach, FL 32960
Phone: (561) 567-4311
Sales: $100,714,000   *Employees:* 1,200
Company Type: Private   *Employees here:* 1,137
SIC: 8062
   General hospital
Michael J O Grady Jr, President

D-U-N-S 04-029-7939
INDIANA FMLY & SOCIAL SVCS ADM
498 NW 18th St, Richmond, IN 47374
Phone: (765) 966-0511
Sales: $21,700,000   *Employees:* NA
Company Type: Private   *Employees here:* 690
SIC: 8063
   Psychiatric substance abuse mr/dd care and treatment
Gene Darby, Chief Executive Officer

D-U-N-S 00-824-6485
INDIANA FMLY & SOCIAL SVCS ADM
1098 S State Road 25, Logansport, IN 46947
Phone: (219) 722-4141
Sales: $25,200,000   *Employees:* NA
Company Type: Private   *Employees here:* 800
SIC: 8063
   Mental hospital
Jeffrey Smith, Branch Manager

D-U-N-S 07-430-6879
INDIANA FMLY & SOCIAL SVCS ADM
1118 S State Road 25, Logansport, IN 46947
Phone: (219) 753-7571
Sales: $25,400,000   *Employees:* NA
Company Type: Private   *Employees here:* 807
SIC: 8063
   Mental hospital
Bob Burns, Superintendent

D-U-N-S 08-458-0919
INDIANA FMLY & SOCIAL SVCS ADM
4900 Saint Joe Rd, Fort Wayne, IN 46835
Phone: (219) 485-7554
Sales: $37,900,000   *Employees:* NA
Company Type: Private   *Employees here:* 1,120
SIC: 8063
   Training center for mentally retarded (state facility)
Ajit K Mukherjee, Superintendent

D-U-N-S 07-597-4949
INDIANA FMLY & SOCIAL SVCS ADM
P.O. Box 77, Butlerville, IN 47223
Phone: (812) 346-4401
Sales: $40,700,000   *Employees:* NA
Company Type: Private   *Employees here:* 1,300
SIC: 8063
   Phsyciatric hospital
Gregory Moore, Superintendent

D-U-N-S 07-496-1061
INDIANA HOSPITAL
Off Rt 119, Indiana, PA 15701
Phone: (724) 357-7000
Sales: $53,150,000   *Employees:* 900
Company Type: Private   *Employees here:* 897
SIC: 8062
   General hospital
Donald D Sandoval, President

D-U-N-S 07-207-3943
INDIANAPOLIS OSTEOPATHIC HOSP
3630 Guion Rd, Indianapolis, IN 46222

Phone: (317) 924-6661
Sales: $24,834,000   *Employees:* 270
Company Type: Private   *Employees here:* 222
SIC: 8062
   General hospital
David C Dyar, President

D-U-N-S 11-014-0415
INDIANPLIS NEUROSURGICAL GROUP
1801 Senate Blvd Ste 535, Indianapolis, IN 46202
Phone: (317) 926-5411
Sales: $26,400,000   *Employees:* 102
Company Type: Private   *Employees here:* 38
SIC: 8011
   Physicians office
Juluis Goodman, President

D-U-N-S 12-091-3801
INFIRMARY HEALTH SYSTEM INC
3 Mobile Infirmary Cir, Mobile, AL 36607
Phone: (334) 431-5500
Sales: $160,800,000   *Employees:* 3,425
Company Type: Private   *Employees here:* 2,100
SIC: 8062
   Integrated health care system
E C Bramlett Jr, President

D-U-N-S 07-791-1238
INFIRMARY MEDICAL CLINIC PC
   (Parent: Infirmary Health System Inc)
5 Mobile Infirmary Cir, Mobile, AL 36607
Phone: (334) 431-3033
Sales: $25,700,000   *Employees:* 375
Company Type: Private   *Employees here:* 3
SIC: 8011
   Operates physicians offices
E C Bramlett Jr, Principal

D-U-N-S 17-364-2851
INLAND VALLEY REGIONAL MED CTR
   (Parent: Universal Health Services)
36485 Inland Valley Dr, Wildomar, CA 92595
Phone: (909) 677-1111
Sales: $26,002,000   *Employees:* 350
Company Type: Public Family Member   *Employees here:* 350
SIC: 8062
   General hospital
Christopher Boyd, Chief Executive Officer

D-U-N-S 05-442-7455
INOVA HEALTH CARE SERVICES
8110 Gatehouse Rd, Springfield, VA 22150
Phone: (703) 289-2000
Sales: $682,879,000   *Employees:* 15,000
Company Type: Private   *Employees here:* 450
SIC: 8062
   General hospitals and outpatient hospital emergency centers
John K Singleton, President

D-U-N-S 10-794-1668
INOVA HEALTH CARE SERVICES
3300 Gallows Rd, Falls Church, VA 22042
Phone: (703) 698-1110
Sales: $19,800,000   *Employees:* NA
Company Type: Private   *Employees here:* 460
SIC: 8062
   General hospital
Jolene Tornabeni, Administrator

D-U-N-S 02-404-6708
INOVA HEALTH CARE SERVICES
3575 Joseph Siewick Dr, Fairfax, VA 22033
Phone: (703) 787-8687

Sales: $39,500,000   *Employees:* NA
Company Type: Private   *Employees here:* 900
SIC: 8062
  General hospital
Steven E Brown, Administrator

D-U-N-S 05-207-8508
INOVA HEALTH CARE SERVICES
2501 Parkers Ln, Alexandria, VA 22306
Phone: (703) 664-7000
Sales: $31,200,000   *Employees:* NA
Company Type: Private   *Employees here:* 715
SIC: 8062
  General hospital
Susan Herbert, Principal

D-U-N-S 15-531-7514
INSTITUTE OF PROF PRACTICE INC
Airport Rd, Montpelier, VT 5602
Phone: (802) 229-9515
Sales: $26,281,000   *Employees:* 700
Company Type: Private   *Employees here:* 6
SIC: 8361
  Residential & day care for the handicapped
Roger Strauss Phd, President

D-U-N-S 05-096-8601
INSTITUTE OF REHABILIATAION
6301 Northumberland St, Pittsburgh, PA 15217
Phone: (412) 521-9000
Sales: $32,329,000   *Employees:* 484
Company Type: Private   *Employees here:* 465
SIC: 8361
  In & out patient rehabilitation center
John A Wilson, President

D-U-N-S 06-436-7329
INSTITUTE FOR CANCER RESEARCH INC
7701 Burholme Ave, Philadelphia, PA 19111
Phone: (215) 728-6900
Sales: $23,830,000   *Employees:* 350
Company Type: Private   *Employees here:* 350
SIC: 8071
  Cancer research laboratory
Dr Robert Young Md, President

D-U-N-S 17-330-6457
INSTITUTE FOR COMMUNITY LIVING
40 Rector St Fl 8, New York, NY 10006
Phone: (212) 385-3030
Sales: $21,508,000   *Employees:* 300
Company Type: Private   *Employees here:* 33
SIC: 8052
  Operator of homes for the mentally disabled
Peter Campanelli, Chief Executive Officer

D-U-N-S 07-417-3873
INSTITUTE FOR REHABILITATION
1333 Moursund St, Houston, TX 77030
Phone: (713) 799-5000
Sales: $24,357,000   *Employees:* 466
Company Type: Private   *Employees here:* 450
SIC: 8062
  Rehabilitation hospital
Charles Beall, President

D-U-N-S 07-991-8850
INSTITUTES OF APPLIED HUMAN DEV.
3625 Bainbridge Ave, Bronx, NY 10467
Phone: (718) 231-7000

Sales: $24,000,000   *Employees:* 470
Company Type: Private   *Employees here:* 35
SIC: 8361
  Non-profit habilitation center with health care for the
   mentally retarded
Mary K St Mark, President

D-U-N-S 82-562-6245
INTEGRA HEALTH
1200 Pleasant St, Des Moines, IA 50309
Phone: (515) 241-6212
Sales: $41,420,000   *Employees:* 1,000
Company Type: Private   *Employees here:* 1,000
SIC: 8011
  Physicians group
Dr M Richards Md, President

D-U-N-S 82-469-1968
INTEGRA INC
1018 W 9th Ave, King Of Prussia, PA 19406
Phone: (610) 992-7670
Sales: $70,144,000   *Employees:* 900
Company Type: Public   *Employees here:* 30
SIC: 8093
  Multi-disciplinary provider of outpatient behavioral health
   services
John H Foster, Chairman of the Board

D-U-N-S 15-143-9767
INTEGRAMED AMERICA INC
1 Manhattanville Rd, Purchase, NY 10577
Phone: (914) 253-8000
Sales: $22,638,000   *Employees:* 175
Company Type: Public   *Employees here:* 24
SIC: 8093
  Provides consulting & technological services
Gerardo Canet, Chairman of the Board

D-U-N-S 92-866-9027
INTEGRATED HEALTH ASSOC PC
2000 Green Rd Ste 330, Ann Arbor, MI 48105
Phone: (734) 995-1442
Sales: $27,400,000   *Employees:* 400
Company Type: Private   *Employees here:* 1
SIC: 8011
  Physicians office
Dr John Mccabe Md, President

D-U-N-S 15-459-4907
INTEGRATED HEALTH SERVICES
10065 Red Run Blvd, Owings Mills, MD 21117
Phone: (410) 998-8400
Sales: $1,993,197,000   *Employees:* 86,000
Company Type: Public   *Employees here:* 1,900
SIC: 8051
  Operators & managers of skilled nursing facilities & home
   health care services
Dr Robert N Elkins Md, Chairman of the Board

D-U-N-S 94-737-8725
INTEGRATED LIVING COMMUNITIES
  (Parent: Whslc Realty Llc)
111 E Wacker Dr, Chicago, IL 60601
Phone: (773) 878-6333
Sales: $27,900,000   *Employees:* 1,500
Company Type: Private   *Employees here:* 23
SIC: 8052
  Intermediate care facility real estate agent/manager
Daniel Niedich, Chairman of the Board

D-U-N-S 08-699-5966
INTEGRIS BAPTIST MEDICAL CTR
3300 NW Expressway, Oklahoma City, OK 73112

Phone: (405) 949-3011
Sales: $215,144,000   *Employees:* 2,759
Company Type: Private   *Employees here:* 2,694
SIC: 8062
  Hospital
Stanley Hupfeld, President

    D-U-N-S 08-256-5755
INTEGRIS RUR HEALTHCARE OF OKLA
3366 NW Expressway Fl 8, Oklahoma City, OK 73112
Phone: (405) 951-2554
Sales: $117,670,000   *Employees:* 1,790
Company Type: Private   *Employees here:* 9
SIC: 8062
  General hospitals
Stan Hupfeld, Chief Executive Officer

    D-U-N-S 06-543-8822
INTEGRIS SOUTHWEST MED CTR
4401 S Western Ave, Oklahoma City, OK 73109
Phone: (405) 636-7000
Sales: $115,549,000   *Employees:* 3,000
Company Type: Private   *Employees here:* 3,000
SIC: 8062
  General hospital
Thomas R Rice, President

    D-U-N-S 07-551-0933
INTEGRTED HEALTH SVCS AT SRASOTA
    (Parent: Integrated Health Services)
2600 Courtland St, Sarasota, FL 34237
Phone: (941) 365-2926
Sales: $57,300,000   *Employees:* 2,500
Company Type: Public Family Member   *Employees here:* 1,480
SIC: 8051
  Skilled nursing facility
Robert N Elkins, Chairman of the Board

    D-U-N-S 87-819-9801
INTENSIVA HEALTHCARE CORP
7733 Forsyth Blvd Ste 800, Saint Louis, MO 63105
Phone: (314) 725-0112
Sales: $69,589,000   *Employees:* 1,500
Company Type: Public   *Employees here:* 35
SIC: 8069
  Provides long-term care hospital services
David W Cross, President

    D-U-N-S 12-087-1090
INTER VALLEY HEALTH PLAN INC
300 S Park Ave Ste 300, Pomona, CA 91766
Phone: (909) 623-6333
Sales: $131,493,000   *Employees:* 180
Company Type: Private   *Employees here:* 178
SIC: 8011
  Health maintenance organization
Mark C Covington, President

    D-U-N-S 07-616-0449
INTERFAITH MEDICAL CENTER
555 Prospect Pl, Brooklyn, NY 11238
Phone: (718) 935-7000
Sales: $199,995,000   *Employees:* 2,400
Company Type: Private   *Employees here:* 900
SIC: 8062
  General hospital
Corbett A Price, President

    D-U-N-S 06-510-6460
INTERHEALTH CORPORATION
12401 Washington Blvd, Whittier, CA 90602
Phone: (562) 698-0811

Sales: $146,573,000   *Employees:* 1,400
Company Type: Private   *Employees here:* 1,100
SIC: 8062
  General medical and surgical hospital and medical clinic
Daniel F Adams, President

    D-U-N-S 19-672-8075
INTERIM HEALTHCARE-MORRIS GROUP
2526 Ward Blvd, Wilson, NC 27893
Phone: (252) 243-7808
Sales: $47,800,000   *Employees:* 3,000
Company Type: Private   *Employees here:* 600
SIC: 8082
  Home health care services
John Morris, President

    D-U-N-S 01-842-8243
INTERIM HEALTH CARE INC
1041 E Butler Rd Ste 100, Greenville, SC 29607
Phone: (864) 627-1200
Sales: $20,924,000   *Employees:* 339
Company Type: Private   *Employees here:* 150
SIC: 8082
  Home health agency
Raymond Schroeder, President

    D-U-N-S 02-988-2669
INTERMOUNTAIN HEALTH CARE INC
777 Hospital Way, Pocatello, ID 83201
Phone: (208) 234-0777
Sales: $20,000,000   *Employees:* NA
Company Type: Private   *Employees here:* 510
SIC: 8062
  General hospital
Earl Christison, N/A

    D-U-N-S 12-055-7467
INTERMOUNTAIN HEALTH CARE INC
5770 S 3rd W, Salt Lake City, UT 84107
Phone: (801) 262-3461
Sales: $56,200,000   *Employees:* NA
Company Type: Private   *Employees here:* 1,300
SIC: 8062
  General hospital
Doug Fonnesbeck, Director

    D-U-N-S 15-592-4657
INTERMOUNTAIN HEALTH CARE INC
8 Ave And C St, Salt Lake City, UT 84143
Phone: (801) 321-1100
Sales: $121,500,000   *Employees:* NA
Company Type: Private   *Employees here:* 2,800
SIC: 8062
  General hospital
Richard M Cagen, Branch Manager

    D-U-N-S 17-452-7689
INTERMOUNTAIN HEALTH CARE INC
1034 N 500 W, Provo, UT 84604
Phone: (801) 379-7200
Sales: $99,800,000   *Employees:* NA
Company Type: Private   *Employees here:* 2,300
SIC: 8062
  Hospital
Larry R Dursteler, Principal

    D-U-N-S 08-183-0135
INTERMOUNTAIN HEALTH CARE INC
3939 Harrison Blvd, Ogden, UT 84403
Phone: (801) 625-2957

Sales: $60,600,000
Company Type: Private   *Employees:* NA
SIC: 8062   *Employees here:* 1,400
   Hospital
Thomas F Hanrahan, Branch Manager

D-U-N-S 07-308-5722
INTERMOUNTAIN HEALTH CARE INC
1400 N 500 E, Logan, UT 84341
Phone: (435) 752-2050
Sales: $24,900,000
Company Type: Private   *Employees:* NA
SIC: 8062   *Employees here:* 630
   General hospital
Richard Smith, Manager

D-U-N-S 07-190-9840
INTERNATIONAL PHILANTHROPIC HO
10445 Balboa Blvd, Granada Hills, CA 91344
Phone: (818) 360-1021
Sales: $34,459,000
Company Type: Private   *Employees:* 420
SIC: 8062   *Employees here:* 420
   General hospital
Thomas M Wallace, President

D-U-N-S 07-352-1536
INTERSTATE BLOOD BANK INC
150 Jackson Ave, Memphis, TN 38105
Phone: (901) 525-7466
Sales: $30,000,000
Company Type: Private   *Employees:* 320
SIC: 8099   *Employees here:* 50
   Blood banks and mfg blood and plasma by products
Larry Moss, President

D-U-N-S 83-620-4271
IOWA HEALTH SYSTEM
1200 Pleasant St, Des Moines, IA 50309
Phone: (515) 241-6201
Sales: $685,778,000
Company Type: Private   *Employees:* 4,110
SIC: 8062   *Employees here:* 15
   Hospital
Sam Wallace, President

D-U-N-S 19-984-3053
IOWA PHYSICIANS CLINIC FOUND
1221 Pleasant St Ste 350, Des Moines, IA 50309
Phone: (515) 241-4102
Sales: $54,469,000
Company Type: Private   *Employees:* 1,000
SIC: 8011   *Employees here:* 20
   Medical doctor's office
Dr Michael Richards, President

D-U-N-S 07-449-8064
IREDELL MEMORIAL HOSPITAL
557 Brookdale Dr, Statesville, NC 28677
Phone: (704) 873-5661
Sales: $73,585,000
Company Type: Private   *Employees:* 1,150
SIC: 8062   *Employees here:* 1,075
   General hospital
S A Nunnery, President

D-U-N-S 07-138-2592
IRVING HOSPITAL AUTHORITY
1901 N Macarthur Blvd, Irving, TX 75061
Phone: (972) 579-8100

Sales: $74,500,000
Company Type: Private   *Employees:* 1,600
SIC: 8062   *Employees here:* NA
   Leases property and hospital to others

D-U-N-S 06-750-9703
IRVINGTON GENERAL HOSPITAL
832 Chancellor Ave, Irvington, NJ 7111
Phone: (973) 399-6000
Sales: $42,159,000
Company Type: Private   *Employees:* 525
SIC: 8062   *Employees here:* 525
   General hospital
Paul Mertz, Executive Director

D-U-N-S 08-896-1180
ISABELLA GERIATRIC CENTER,
515 Audubon Ave, New York, NY 10040
Phone: (212) 781-9800
Sales: $66,614,000
Company Type: Private   *Employees:* 800
SIC: 8051   *Employees here:* 800
   Non-profit skilled nursing facilities
Edward J Mc Fadden, President

D-U-N-S 03-740-8952
ISLAND HOSPITAL
1211 24th St, Anacortes, WA 98221
Phone: (360) 293-3181
Sales: $23,936,000
Company Type: Private   *Employees:* 359
SIC: 8062   *Employees here:* 359
   Hospital
C P Sandifer, Chief Executive Officer

D-U-N-S 62-332-9372
IVONYX GROUP SERVICES, INC
17380 N Laurel Park Dr, Livonia, MI 48152
Phone: (734) 462-9290
Sales: $43,000,000
Company Type: Private   *Employees:* 160
SIC: 8082   *Employees here:* 50
   Home health care services
Richard A Breakie, Chairman of the Board

D-U-N-S 17-323-8528
IVONYX INC
   (Parent: Ivonyx Group Services Inc)
17197 N Laurel Park Dr, Livonia, MI 48152
Phone: (734) 462-9290
Sales: $26,000,000
Company Type: Private   *Employees:* 120
SIC: 8082   *Employees here:* 50
   Home health care services
Richard A Breakie, President

D-U-N-S 15-236-1283
IHC HEALTH SERVICES INC
100 N Medical Dr, Salt Lake City, UT 84113
Phone: (801) 588-2000
Sales: $98,700,000
Company Type: Private   *Employees:* NA
SIC: 8069   *Employees here:* 2,150
   Pediatrics hospital
Joseph Horton, Director

D-U-N-S 18-362-1390
IHC HEALTH SERVICES INC
36 S State St Ste 2100, Salt Lake City, UT 84111
Phone: (801) 533-8282

Sales: $1,424,812,000   *Employees:* 21,000
Company Type: Private   *Employees here:* 1,000
SIC: 8062
    General hospital
Kent Richards, President

D-U-N-S 84-853-3840
IHC HEALTH SERVICES INC
325 8th Ave, Salt Lake City, UT 84143
Phone: (801) 321-1100
Sales: $47,300,000   *Employees:* NA
Company Type: Private   *Employees here:* 3,300
SIC: 8049
    Health practitioner's office
Rick Cagen, Director

D-U-N-S 84-853-3279
IHC HEALTH SERVICES INC
1034 N 5th W St, Provo, UT 84605
Phone: (801) 373-7850
Sales: $29,000,000   *Employees:* NA
Company Type: Private   *Employees here:* 2,000
SIC: 8049
    Health practitioner's office
Mark Howard, Branch Manager

D-U-N-S 84-853-2636
IHC HEALTH SERVICES INC
3939 Harrison Blvd, Ogden, UT 84403
Phone: (801) 627-2800
Sales: $29,000,000   *Employees:* NA
Company Type: Private   *Employees here:* 2,000
SIC: 8049
    Health practitioner's office
Tom Hanrahan, Director

D-U-N-S 07-194-3559
IMG HEALTH CARE NETWORK, LLC
5640 Read Blvd, New Orleans, LA 70127
Phone: (504) 246-0800
Sales: $20,497,000   *Employees:* 210
Company Type: Private   *Employees here:* 60
SIC: 8011
    Physicians
Dr Frank Incaprera, Partner

D-U-N-S 07-284-9847
J C BLAIR MEMORIAL HOSPITAL
Warm Springs Ave, Huntingdon, PA 16652
Phone: (814) 643-2290
Sales: $25,524,000   *Employees:* 500
Company Type: Private   *Employees here:* 500
SIC: 8062
    General hospital
Richard D Alberto, Chief Executive Officer

D-U-N-S 06-200-2522
J G B HEALTH FACILITIES CORP
15 W 65th St, New York, NY 10023
Phone: (212) 769-6200
Sales: $22,444,000   *Employees:* 276
Company Type: Private   *Employees here:* 15
SIC: 8051
    Skilled nursing care facility
Dr Alan R Morse Jd, President

D-U-N-S 95-983-6107
JACK FRIEDMAN
14227 Franklin Ave, Flushing, NY 11355
Phone: (718) 670-3400

Sales: $23,803,000   *Employees:* 280
Company Type: Private   *Employees here:* 280
SIC: 8059
    Nursing/personal care
Jack Friedman, Owner

D-U-N-S 10-817-3907
JACKSON BROOK INSTITUTE
    (Parent: Community Care Systems Inc)
175 Running Hill Rd, South Portland, ME 4106
Phone: (207) 761-2200
Sales: $24,933,000   *Employees:* 400
Company Type: Private   *Employees here:* 368
SIC: 8063
    Psychiatric & alcoholism rehabilitation hospital
Steven E Katz, President

D-U-N-S 07-122-8233
JACKSON CNTY MEM HOSPITAL TR AUTH
1200 E Pecan St, Altus, OK 73521
Phone: (580) 482-4781
Sales: $36,474,000   *Employees:* 624
Company Type: Private   *Employees here:* 624
SIC: 8062
    General hospital
William G Wilson, President

D-U-N-S 07-598-0201
JACKSON CNTY SCHNECK MEM HOSP
411 W Tipton St, Seymour, IN 47274
Phone: (812) 522-2349
Sales: $37,745,000   *Employees:* 526
Company Type: Private   *Employees here:* 526
SIC: 8062
    Hospital
George James, President

D-U-N-S 07-764-6537
JACKSON COUNTY HEALTH CARE AUTH
Woods Cove Rd, Scottsboro, AL 35768
Phone: (256) 259-4444
Sales: $40,415,000   *Employees:* 458
Company Type: Private   *Employees here:* 229
SIC: 8062
    General medical & surgical hospital
Jim Armour, Chief Executive Officer

D-U-N-S 09-297-6703
JACKSON COUNTY HOSPITAL INC
4250 Hospital Dr, Marianna, FL 32446
Phone: (850) 526-2200
Sales: $28,024,000   *Employees:* 361
Company Type: Private   *Employees here:* 344
SIC: 8062
    General medical and surgical hospital and outpatient clinic
Richard L Wooten, Chief Executive Officer

D-U-N-S 03-405-4098
JACKSON HOSPITAL & CLINIC INC
1725 Pine St, Montgomery, AL 36106
Phone: (334) 293-8000
Sales: $100,437,000   *Employees:* 1,400
Company Type: Private   *Employees here:* 1,388
SIC: 8062
    General acute care hospital
Donald M Ball, President

D-U-N-S 79-609-1023
JACKSON METHODIST HEALTHCARE
1850 Chadwick Dr, Jackson, MS 39204
Phone: (601) 376-1000

Sales: $118,893,000
Company Type: Private
SIC: 8062
  Hospital
Maurice Elliott, President

Employees: 1,159
Employees here: 1,150

D-U-N-S 07-790-1924
JACKSON ST DOMINIC MEM HOSP
969 Lakeland Dr, Jackson, MS 39216
Phone: (601) 982-0121
Sales: $87,700,000
Company Type: Private
SIC: 8062
  General hospital
Sister M Dorthea, President

Employees: 1,880
Employees here: 1,880

D-U-N-S 06-874-6254
JACKSON STONEWALL MEM HOSP
Rr 33, Weston, WV 26452
Phone: (304) 269-8000
Sales: $20,153,000
Company Type: Private
SIC: 8062
  General hospital
David Shaffer, Administrator

Employees: 270
Employees here: 270

D-U-N-S 06-165-4513
JACKSON-MADISON CNTY GEN HOSP
708 W Forest Ave, Jackson, TN 38301
Phone: (901) 425-5000
Sales: $216,330,000
Company Type: Private
SIC: 8062
  General hospital
Jim Moss, President

Employees: 2,400
Employees here: 2,400

D-U-N-S 88-386-8150
JACKSONVILLE HEALTH CARE GROUP
1200 Riverplace Blvd, Jacksonville, FL 32207
Phone: (904) 346-5815
Sales: $20,500,000
Company Type: Private
SIC: 8011
  Medical center
James Clower, President

Employees: 300
Employees here: 300

D-U-N-S 07-274-0426
JAMAICA HOSPITAL INC
8900 Van Wyck Expy, Jamaica, NY 11418
Phone: (718) 206-6000
Sales: $215,599,000
Company Type: Private
SIC: 8062
  General hospital
David P Rosen, President

Employees: 3,000
Employees here: 1,550

D-U-N-S 07-498-4758
JAMESON MEMORIAL HOSPITAL
1211 Wilmington Ave, New Castle, PA 16105
Phone: (724) 658-9001
Sales: $59,219,000
Company Type: Private
SIC: 8062
  Hospital
Thomas White, President

Employees: 1,063
Employees here: 1,063

D-U-N-S 87-691-1082
JANE PHLLIPS HEALTH CARE FNDTION
3500 E Frank Phillips Blv, Bartlesville, OK 74006
Phone: (918) 333-7200

Sales: $56,215,000
Company Type: Private
SIC: 8082
  Home health care services
Mike May, Secretary

Employees: NA
Employees here: NA

D-U-N-S 03-081-9890
JAQUES ANNA HOSPITAL INC
25 Highland Ave, Newburyport, MA 1950
Phone: (978) 463-1000
Sales: $56,491,000
Company Type: Private
SIC: 8062
  General medical and surgical hospital
Allan L Desrosiers, President

Employees: 1,200
Employees here: 950

D-U-N-S 06-901-3605
JEANES HOSPITAL
7600 Central Ave, Philadelphia, PA 19111
Phone: (215) 728-2000
Sales: $81,458,000
Company Type: Private
SIC: 8062
  Hospital
G R Martin, President

Employees: 1,350
Employees here: 1,340

D-U-N-S 06-874-5512
JEANNETTE DISTRICT MEM HOSP
600 Jefferson Ave, Jeannette, PA 15644
Phone: (724) 527-3551
Sales: $37,068,000
Company Type: Private
SIC: 8062
  General hospital
Robert J Bulger, President

Employees: 725
Employees here: 700

D-U-N-S 06-872-5910
JEFFERSON HEALTH SERVICES
Coal Valley Rd, Pittsburgh, PA 15236
Phone: (412) 664-5000
Sales: $131,555,000
Company Type: Private
SIC: 8062
  General hospital
William Jennings, President

Employees: 2,600
Employees here: 2,400

D-U-N-S 07-563-9096
JEFFERSON HOSPITAL ASSOCIATION
1515 W 42nd Ave, Pine Bluff, AR 71603
Phone: (870) 541-7100
Sales: $129,545,000
Company Type: Private
SIC: 8062
  General hospital
Bob Atkinson, President

Employees: 1,788
Employees here: 1,675

D-U-N-S 03-797-0217
JEFFERSON PARISH INC
4200 Houma Blvd, Metairie, LA 70006
Phone: (504) 454-4000
Sales: $91,200,000
Company Type: Private
SIC: 8062
  General hospital
Peter J Betts, Director

Employees: NA
Employees here: 2,200

D-U-N-S 96-053-5045
JEFFERSON THMAS UNIV HOSPITALS
111 S 11th St, Philadelphia, PA 19107
Phone: (215) 955-6456

Sales: $514,900,000	*Employees:* 375
Company Type: Private	*Employees here:* NA

SIC: 8062
  Hospital
Thomas Lewis, President

D-U-N-S 07-012-8012
JENNIE EDMUNDSON MEM HOSP
933 E Pierce St, Council Bluffs, IA 51503
Phone: (712) 328-6000

Sales: $48,187,000	*Employees:* 800
Company Type: Private	*Employees here:* 750

SIC: 8062
  Hospital
Dave Holcomb, President

D-U-N-S 07-930-8110
JERSEY CITY MEDICAL CENTER
50 Baldwin Ave, Jersey City, NJ 7304
Phone: (201) 915-2000

Sales: $162,766,000	*Employees:* 1,900
Company Type: Private	*Employees here:* 1,770

SIC: 8062
  General hospital
Jonathan M Metsch Phd, President

D-U-N-S 02-035-5905
JERSEY COMMUNITY HOSPITAL
400 Maple Summit Rd, Jerseyville, IL 62052
Phone: (618) 498-6402

Sales: $20,374,000	*Employees:* 243
Company Type: Private	*Employees here:* 243

SIC: 8062
  Hospital
Lawrence Bear, Administrator

D-U-N-S 07-103-7543
JEWISH BD OF FMLY & CHLD SVCS
120 W 57th St, New York, NY 10019
Phone: (212) 582-9100

Sales: $96,068,000	*Employees:* 1,800
Company Type: Private	*Employees here:* 200

SIC: 8361
  Non-profit organization providing mental health services to
  children and adults
Fredric W Yerman, Chairman of the Board

D-U-N-S 07-684-9124
JEWISH CHILD CARE ASSN OF NY
575 Lexington Ave Fl 3, New York, NY 10022
Phone: (212) 371-1313

Sales: $44,633,000	*Employees:* 500
Company Type: Private	*Employees here:* 150

SIC: 8361
  Group foster home & family social service information
  exchange service
Stephen Sokoloff, Chairman of the Board

D-U-N-S 08-307-2660
JEWISH CHILDCARE ASSOCIATION
575 Lexington Ave Fl 3, New York, NY 10022
Phone: (212) 371-1313

Sales: $36,623,000	*Employees:* 600
Company Type: Private	*Employees here:* 400

SIC: 8361
  Children's home
Irving Goldburg, President

D-U-N-S 14-464-5033
JEWISH HOME & HOSPITAL FOR AGED
100 W Kingsbridge Rd, Bronx, NY 10468
Phone: (718) 579-0500

Sales: $24,500,000	*Employees:* NA
Company Type: Private	*Employees here:* 1,000

SIC: 8051
  Skilled nursing care facility
Harvey Finkelstein, N/A

D-U-N-S 07-772-9606
JEWISH HOME & HOSPITAL/BRONX
2545 University Ave, Bronx, NY 10468
Phone: (718) 579-0500

Sales: $74,628,000	*Employees:* 1,300
Company Type: Private	*Employees here:* 1,300

SIC: 8051
  Skilled nursing care facility
Harvey Finkelstein, President

D-U-N-S 07-368-1140
JEWISH HOME OF ROCHESTER, NY
2021 Winton Rd S, Rochester, NY 14618
Phone: (716) 427-7760

Sales: $20,890,000	*Employees:* 503
Company Type: Private	*Employees here:* 503

SIC: 8051
  Skilled nursing facility
Arnold Gissin, Administrator

D-U-N-S 00-491-7956
JEWISH HOSPITAL HEALTHCARE SVCS
150 N Eagle Creek Dr, Lexington, KY 40509
Phone: (606) 268-4800

Sales: $21,500,000	*Employees:* NA
Company Type: Private	*Employees here:* 520

SIC: 8062
  Hospital
Rebecca A Lewis, Chief Executive Officer

D-U-N-S 11-289-0132
JEWISH HOSPITAL OF CINCINNATI
3200 Burnet Ave, Cincinnati, OH 45229
Phone: (513) 569-2000

Sales: $117,000,000	*Employees:* 2,500
Company Type: Private	*Employees here:* 2,480

SIC: 8062
  General medical and surgical hospital
Warren C Falberg, President

D-U-N-S 11-289-0256
JEWISH HOSPITAL SERVICES, INC
  (Parent: Jewish Health System Inc)
3200 Burnet Ave, Cincinnati, OH 45229
Phone: (513) 569-2000

Sales: $92,000,000	*Employees:* 2,300
Company Type: Private	*Employees here:* 2,300

SIC: 8099
  Hospital medical service organization and operator of
  nonresidential buildings
Warren C Falberg, President

D-U-N-S 07-952-3353
JEWISH MEM HOSPITAL RHBLTTION CTR
59 Townsend St, Boston, MA 2119
Phone: (617) 442-8760

Sales: $50,000,000	*Employees:* 370
Company Type: Private	*Employees here:* 370

SIC: 8069
  Rehabilitation hospital
Paul D Pres-Ceo, N/A

D-U-N-S 02-122-8671
JMES R GLIDEWELL DNTL CERAMICS
4141 Macarthur Blvd, Newport Beach, CA 92660
Phone: (949) 440-2600

Sales: $46,685,000
Company Type: Private
SIC: 8072
   Dental laboratory
James R Glidewell, President

Employees: 630
Employees here: 580

D-U-N-S 04-301-8480
JOHN C LINCOLN HEALTH NETWORK
250 E Dunlap Ave, Phoenix, AZ 85020
Phone: (602) 943-2381
Sales: $133,860,000
Company Type: Private
SIC: 8062
   General medical & surgical hospital extended care and
     skilled nursing facilities
Dan C Coleman, President

Employees: 2,102
Employees here: 1,375

D-U-N-S 84-089-7110
JOHN D ARCHBOLD MEMORIAL HOSP
915 Gordon At Mimosa Gdn, Thomasville, GA 31792
Phone: (912) 246-0492
Sales: $57,300,000
Company Type: Private
SIC: 8062
   General hospital
Jason Moore, President

Employees: NA
Employees here: 1,400

D-U-N-S 60-977-6877
JOHN HEINZ INSTITUTE
150 Mundy St Ste 7, Wilkes Barre, PA 18702
Phone: (717) 826-3800
Sales: $27,260,000
Company Type: Private
SIC: 8361
   Inpatient & outpatient rehabilitation facility
James Brady, President

Employees: 345
Employees here: 345

D-U-N-S 08-019-5472
JOHN KNOX VILLAGE OF FLORIDA
651 SW 6th St, Pompano Beach, FL 33060
Phone: (954) 783-4000
Sales: $22,775,000
Company Type: Private
SIC: 8361
   Home for the aged with health care incidental
Frank H Furman, Chairman of the Board

Employees: 630
Employees here: 480

D-U-N-S 07-307-2316
JOHN KNOX VILLAGE
400 NW Murray Rd, Lees Summit, MO 64081
Phone: (816) 246-4343
Sales: $45,997,000
Company Type: Private
SIC: 8051
   Retirement community
Herman C Spahr, President

Employees: 950
Employees here: 950

D-U-N-S 11-950-1369
JOHN N DEMPSEY HOSPITAL
263 Farmington Ave, Farmington, CT 6030
Phone: (860) 679-2000
Sales: $118,954,000
Company Type: Private
SIC: 8062
   General hospital
Andrea Martin, Chief Executive Officer

Employees: 1,057
Employees here: 1,057

D-U-N-S 06-473-8859
JOHN T MATHER MEM HOSP
75 N Country Rd, Port Jefferson, NY 11777
Phone: (516) 473-1320

Sales: $94,286,000
Company Type: Private
SIC: 8062
   Hospital
Kenneth Roberts, President

Employees: 1,300
Employees here: 1,281

D-U-N-S 11-823-9458
JOHNS HOPKINS BAYVIEW MED CTR
4940 Eastern Ave, Baltimore, MD 21224
Phone: (410) 550-0100
Sales: $197,433,000
Company Type: Private
SIC: 8062
   Hospital
Judy A Reitz Rn, Chief Operating Officer

Employees: 3,300
Employees here: 3,000

D-U-N-S 15-534-8113
JOHNS HOPKINS HEALTH SYS CORP
5300 Alpha Commons Dr, Baltimore, MD 21224
Phone: (410) 955-5000
Sales: $910,535,000
Company Type: Private
SIC: 8062
   General & surgical hospitals
Ronald Peterson, President

Employees: 629
Employees here: 500

D-U-N-S 84-959-5418
JOHNS HOPKINS HOSPITAL INC
601 N Caroline St, Baltimore, MD 21287
Phone: (410) 955-6700
Sales: $53,900,000
Company Type: Private
SIC: 8011
   Medical doctor's office
Dr Rich Daves, Director

Employees: NA
Employees here: 900

D-U-N-S 06-939-0037
JOHNS HOPKINS MEDICAL SERVICES
(Parent: Johns Hopkins Health Sys Corp)
3100 Wyman Park Dr, Baltimore, MD 21211
Phone: (410) 338-3000
Sales: $114,214,000
Company Type: Private
SIC: 8011
   Health maintenance organization & healthcare management
William Kent, Chief Operating Officer

Employees: 570
Employees here: 570

D-U-N-S 62-545-5464
JOHNS HOPKINS UNIVERSITY
600 N Wolfe St Meyer 3 122, Baltimore, MD 21205
Phone: (410) 955-6647
Sales: $22,200,000
Company Type: Private
SIC: 8011
   Medical doctor's office
Judith Rohde, Director

Employees: NA
Employees here: 350

D-U-N-S 80-000-0432
JOHNS HPKINS HM CARE GROUP INC
2400 Broening Hwy, Baltimore, MD 21224
Phone: (410) 288-8000
Sales: $24,025,000
Company Type: Private
SIC: 8082
   Health care services
Marjorie Bowman, Chief Executive Officer

Employees: 350
Employees here: 300

D-U-N-S 07-202-3310
JOHNSON BETSY MEMORIAL HOSP
800 Tilghman Dr, Dunn, NC 28334
Phone: (910) 892-7161

Sales: $25,785,000   Employees: 384
Company Type: Private   Employees here: 384
SIC: 8062
  Hospital
Shannon D Brown, President

D-U-N-S 06-318-9898
JOHNSON CITY MEDICAL CTR HOSP
400 N State Of Franklin R, Johnson City, TN 37604
Phone: (423) 461-6111
Sales: $173,895,000   Employees: 2,200
Company Type: Private   Employees here: 1,738
SIC: 8062
  General hospital
Dennis Vonderfecht, President

D-U-N-S 07-488-8728
JOHNSON CY EYE & EAR HOSPITAL INC
(Parent: Columbia/Hca Healthcare Corp)
203 E Watauga Ave, Johnson City, TN 37601
Phone: (423) 926-1111
Sales: $21,034,000   Employees: 165
Company Type: Public Family Member   Employees here: 165
SIC: 8069
  Eye & ear ob-gyn podiatry & general surgery hospital health/
  allied services
Lori Fatherree, Chief Executive Officer

D-U-N-S 07-731-0985
JOHNSON MEMORIAL HOSPITAL INC
201 Chestnut Hill Rd, Stafford Springs, CT 6076
Phone: (860) 684-4251
Sales: $37,018,000   Employees: 750
Company Type: Private   Employees here: 700
SIC: 8062
  General hospital
Alfred A Lerz, President

D-U-N-S 07-597-7348
JOHNSON MEMORIAL HOSPITAL
1125 W Jefferson St, Franklin, IN 46131
Phone: (317) 736-3300
Sales: $40,725,000   Employees: 575
Company Type: Private   Employees here: 575
SIC: 8062
  General hospital
Gregg Bechtold, Chief Executive Officer

D-U-N-S 07-201-0713
JOHNSTON MEMORIAL HOSPITAL
509 N Bright Leaf Blvd, Smithfield, NC 27577
Phone: (919) 934-8171
Sales: $43,548,000   Employees: 582
Company Type: Private   Employees here: 542
SIC: 8062
  Hospital
Leland E Farnell, President

D-U-N-S 07-902-0087
JOHNSTON MEMORIAL HOSPITAL
351 Court St NE, Abingdon, VA 24210
Phone: (540) 676-7000
Sales: $43,385,000   Employees: 525
Company Type: Private   Employees here: 510
SIC: 8062
  General hospital
Clark Beil, Chief Executive Officer

D-U-N-S 06-371-5007
JOINT TOWNSHIP DST MEM HOSP
200 Saint Clair Ave, Saint Marys, OH 45885
Phone: (419) 394-3335

Sales: $31,915,000   Employees: 460
Company Type: Private   Employees here: 400
SIC: 8062
  General hospital
James Chick, President

D-U-N-S 07-355-4909
JONESBORO HEALTH SERVICES INC
(Parent: Tenet Healthcare Corporation)
3024 Stadium Dr, Jonesboro, AR 72401
Phone: (870) 972-7000
Sales: $65,000,000   Employees: 400
Company Type: Public Family Member   Employees here: 400
SIC: 8062
  Hospital
Philip H Walkley Jr, Administrator

D-U-N-S 11-330-7201
JORDAN HEALTH SERVICES INC
412 Highway 37 S, Mount Vernon, TX 75457
Phone: (903) 537-2376
Sales: $22,437,000   Employees: 4,000
Company Type: Private   Employees here: 22
SIC: 8082
  Home health care services
Mike Jordan, President

D-U-N-S 07-952-3668
JORDAN HOSPITAL (INC)
275 Sandwich St, Plymouth, MA 2360
Phone: (508) 746-2000
Sales: $66,000,000   Employees: 900
Company Type: Private   Employees here: 900
SIC: 8062
  General hospital
Alan Knight, President

D-U-N-S 07-498-6423
JOSEPH COLUMBIA/ST HEALTH SYS
19th St & Murdoch Ave, Parkersburg, WV 26101
Phone: (304) 424-4111
Sales: $92,209,000   Employees: 900
Company Type: Private   Employees here: 900
SIC: 8062
  Hospital
Stevens Mundy, Chief Executive Officer

D-U-N-S 07-599-3352
JOSEPH HAZLETON-SAINT MED CTR
687 N Church St, Hazleton, PA 18201
Phone: (717) 459-4444
Sales: $36,135,000   Employees: 600
Company Type: Private   Employees here: 500
SIC: 8062
  General hospital
Bernard C Rudegeair, President

D-U-N-S 07-303-4811
JOSEPH SAINT HEALTH CENTER
1000 Carondelet Dr, Kansas City, MO 64114
Phone: (816) 942-4400
Sales: $115,173,000   Employees: 1,550
Company Type: Private   Employees here: 1,500
SIC: 8062
  General hospital
Kevin Kast, Chief Executive Officer

D-U-N-S 06-427-9623
JOSEPHS SAINT HOSPITAL & MED CTR
703 Main St, Paterson, NJ 7503
Phone: (973) 977-2000

Sales: $286,956,000
Company Type: Private
SIC: 8062
  General hospital
Sister J Brady, President
Employees: 3,300
Employees here: 3,155

D-U-N-S 07-172-3084
JOSLIN DIABETES CENTER INC
1 Joslin Pl, Boston, MA 2215
Phone: (617) 732-2400
Sales: $43,698,000
Company Type: Private
SIC: 8011
  Specialty hospital
Dr Kenneth Quickel, President
Employees: 400
Employees here: 320

D-U-N-S 13-736-3966
JSA HEALTHCARE CORPORATION
111 2nd Ave NE Ste 1500, Saint Petersburg, FL 33701
Phone: (727) 824-0780
Sales: $41,000,000
Company Type: Private
SIC: 8011
  Medical centers
Gary L Damkoehler, President
Employees: 350
Employees here: 25

D-U-N-S 07-675-7327
JUDSON RETIREMENT COMMUNITY
2181 Ambleside Dr, Cleveland, OH 44106
Phone: (216) 721-1234
Sales: $21,748,000
Company Type: Private
SIC: 8059
  Rest home for elderly
Cynthia H Dunn, President
Employees: 331
Employees here: 255

D-U-N-S 07-561-8892
JULIA RACKLEY PERRY MEM HOSP
530 Park Ave E, Princeton, IL 61356
Phone: (815) 875-2811
Sales: $22,942,000
Company Type: Private
SIC: 8062
  General hospital
William H Spitler Iii, President
Employees: 425
Employees here: 400

D-U-N-S 13-150-6958
JUPITER MEDICAL CENTER, INC
1210 S Old Dixie Hwy, Jupiter, FL 33458
Phone: (561) 747-2234
Sales: $78,087,000
Company Type: Private
SIC: 8062
  General hospital
William Prout, Chairman of the Board
Employees: 800
Employees here: 744

D-U-N-S 07-657-5646
JUSTICE RESOURCE INSTITUTE
545 Boylston St Fl 7, Boston, MA 2116
Phone: (617) 450-0500
Sales: $32,613,000
Company Type: Private
SIC: 8361
  Residential schools & treatment centers for disabled &
  behaviorally challenging adolescents
Susan Wayne, President
Employees: 1,075
Employees here: 15

D-U-N-S 07-666-0513
KADLEC MEDICAL CENTER
888 Swift Blvd, Richland, WA 99352
Phone: (509) 946-4611

Sales: $70,267,000
Company Type: Private
SIC: 8062
  Hospital
Marcel Loh, President
Employees: 700
Employees here: 679

D-U-N-S 83-640-4475
KAISER FND HEALTH PLN OF CO INC
7701 Sheridan Blvd, Arvada, CO 80003
Phone: (303) 428-1499
Sales: $165,800,000
Company Type: Private
SIC: 8011
  Health maintenance organization
Vicki Leger, Administrator
Employees: NA
Employees here: 3,000

D-U-N-S 07-924-4208
KAISER FND HEALTH PLN/MA INC
150 Lower Westfield Rd, Holyoke, MA 1040
Phone: (413) 493-8100
Sales: $20,500,000
Company Type: Private
SIC: 8011
  Health maintenance organization medical clinic & pharmacy
J R Newsome, President
Employees: 300
Employees here: 50

D-U-N-S 03-990-3067
KAISER FOUNDATION HEALTH PLAN
2025 Morse Ave, Sacramento, CA 95825
Phone: (916) 973-5000
Sales: $124,400,000
Company Type: Private
SIC: 8062
  General hospital
Jerry Newman, N/A
Employees: NA
Employees here: 2,500

D-U-N-S 15-240-7128
KAISER FOUNDATION HEALTH PLAN
1950 Franklin St, Oakland, CA 94612
Phone: (510) 987-1000
Sales: $107,200,000
Company Type: Private
SIC: 8011
  Health maintenance organization
David G Pockell, Manager
Employees: NA
Employees here: 1,880

D-U-N-S 84-732-2922
KAISER FOUNDATION HEALTH PLAN
4867 W Sunset Blvd, Los Angeles, CA 90027
Phone: (323) 783-4011
Sales: $267,100,000
Company Type: Private
SIC: 8011
  Health maintenance
Joseph Hummel, Manager
Employees: NA
Employees here: 5,000

D-U-N-S 87-999-1719
KAISER FOUNDATION HEALTH PLAN
1011 Baldwin Park Blvd, Baldwin Park, CA 91706
Phone: (626) 851-1011
Sales: $59,500,000
Company Type: Private
SIC: 8062
  Hospital
Gary Lulejian, Director
Employees: NA
Employees here: 1,200

D-U-N-S 07-414-2431
KAISER FOUNDATION HOSPITALS
13652 Cantara St, Van Nuys, CA 91402
Phone: (818) 375-2000

Sales: $149,300,000
Company Type: Private
SIC: 8062
    General hospital medical doctor's office
Dev Mahadevan, Principal

Employees: NA
Employees here: 3,000

D-U-N-S 15-240-6708
KAISER FOUNDATION HOSPITALS
975 Sereno Dr, Vallejo, CA 94589
Phone: (707) 651-1000
Sales: $50,400,000
Company Type: Private
SIC: 8062
    General hospital
Katie Rickleff, Principal

Employees: NA
Employees here: 1,020

D-U-N-S 08-533-8291
KAISER FOUNDATION HOSPITALS
1200 El Camino Real, South San Francisco, CA 94080
Phone: (650) 742-2000
Sales: $54,400,000
Company Type: Private
SIC: 8062
    General hospital
Dianne Preston, Finance

Employees: NA
Employees here: 1,100

D-U-N-S 01-502-8657
KAISER FOUNDATION HOSPITALS
401 Bicentennial Way, Santa Rosa, CA 95403
Phone: (707) 571-4000
Sales: $59,500,000
Company Type: Private
SIC: 8011
    Medical doctor's office
Kay Stodd, Branch Manager

Employees: NA
Employees here: 1,000

D-U-N-S 07-631-4483
KAISER FOUNDATION HOSPITALS
900 Kiely Blvd, Santa Clara, CA 95051
Phone: (408) 236-6400
Sales: $124,400,000
Company Type: Private
SIC: 8062
    General hospital
Helen Wilmot, Principal

Employees: NA
Employees here: 2,500

D-U-N-S 08-289-9188
KAISER FOUNDATION HOSPITALS
275 Hospital Pkwy, San Jose, CA 95119
Phone: (408) 972-7000
Sales: $99,500,000
Company Type: Private
SIC: 8062
    General hospital
Nancy Madsen, Principal

Employees: NA
Employees here: 2,000

D-U-N-S 06-887-5947
KAISER FOUNDATION HOSPITALS
4141 Geary Blvd Rm 411, San Francisco, CA 94118
Phone: (415) 202-3510
Sales: $79,500,000
Company Type: Private
SIC: 8062
    General hospital
Janice Head, N/A

Employees: NA
Employees here: 1,600

D-U-N-S 07-337-7087
KAISER FOUNDATION HOSPITALS
4647 Zion Ave, San Diego, CA 92120
Phone: (619) 528-5000

Sales: $89,500,000
Company Type: Private
SIC: 8062
    General hospital
Kenneth F Colling, President

Employees: NA
Employees here: 1,800

D-U-N-S 15-215-0983
KAISER FOUNDATION HOSPITALS
6600 Bruceville Rd, Sacramento, CA 95823
Phone: (916) 688-2000
Sales: $49,400,000
Company Type: Private
SIC: 8062
    General hospital
Sarah Krevans, N/A

Employees: NA
Employees here: 1,000

D-U-N-S 60-438-4255
KAISER FOUNDATION HOSPITALS
10800 Magnolia Ave, Riverside, CA 92505
Phone: (909) 353-2000
Sales: $74,500,000
Company Type: Private
SIC: 8062
    General hospital
Patricia Siegal, Administrator

Employees: NA
Employees here: 1,500

D-U-N-S 08-988-2252
KAISER FOUNDATION HOSPITALS
1150 Veterans Blvd, Redwood City, CA 94063
Phone: (650) 299-2000
Sales: $74,500,000
Company Type: Private
SIC: 8062
    General hospital
John Rawls, Administrator

Employees: NA
Employees here: 1,500

D-U-N-S 13-354-2233
KAISER FOUNDATION HOSPITALS
7601 Stoneridge Dr, Pleasanton, CA 94588
Phone: (925) 847-5100
Sales: $22,200,000
Company Type: Private
SIC: 8011
    Medical doctor's office
Michele Thompson, Administration

Employees: NA
Employees here: 350

D-U-N-S 03-884-7638
KAISER FOUNDATION HOSPITALS
280 W Macarthur Blvd, Oakland, CA 94611
Phone: (510) 596-1000
Sales: $109,400,000
Company Type: Private
SIC: 8062
    General hospital
David J Artenburn, Manager

Employees: NA
Employees here: 2,200

D-U-N-S 05-305-2619
KAISER FOUNDATION HOSPITALS
1 Kaiser Plz, Oakland, CA 94612
Phone: (510) 271-5910
Sales: $3,159,000,000
Company Type: Private
SIC: 8062
    General medical & surgical hospitals
Richard A Barnaby, President

Employees: 25,000
Employees here: 250

D-U-N-S 03-856-7277
KAISER FOUNDATION HOSPITALS
200 Muir Rd, Martinez, CA 94553
Phone: (925) 372-1000

Sales: $49,400,000   *Employees:* NA
Company Type: Private   *Employees here:* 1,000
SIC: 8062
    General hospital
Michael Melewicz, Branch Manager

D-U-N-S 06-427-5795
KAISER FOUNDATION HOSPITALS
4867 W Sunset Blvd, Los Angeles, CA 90027
Phone: (323) 667-4011
Sales: $218,600,000   *Employees:* NA
Company Type: Private   *Employees here:* 4,396
SIC: 8062
    General medical and surgical hospitals, nsk
Joseph Hummel, Manager

D-U-N-S 07-412-9107
KAISER FOUNDATION HOSPITALS
6041 Cadillac Ave, Los Angeles, CA 90034
Phone: (323) 857-2000
Sales: $99,500,000   *Employees:* NA
Company Type: Private   *Employees here:* 2,000
SIC: 8062
    General hospital medical doctor's office
Kenneth Washington, Branch Manager

D-U-N-S 10-381-3358
KAISER FOUNDATION HOSPITALS
27400 Hesperian Blvd, Hayward, CA 94545
Phone: (510) 784-4000
Sales: $89,500,000   *Employees:* NA
Company Type: Private   *Employees here:* 1,800
SIC: 8062
    General hospital
Anabelle Embert, Administration

D-U-N-S 07-252-6676
KAISER FOUNDATION HOSPITALS
3288 Moanalua Rd, Honolulu, HI 96819
Phone: (808) 834-5333
Sales: $54,400,000   *Employees:* NA
Company Type: Private   *Employees here:* 1,100
SIC: 8062
    Hospital & medical research center
D J Mailer, Branch Manager

D-U-N-S 07-455-2340
KAISER FOUNDATION HOSPITALS
12301 Snow Rd, Cleveland, OH 44130
Phone: (216) 362-2000
Sales: $30,300,000   *Employees:* NA
Company Type: Private   *Employees here:* 725
SIC: 8062
    General hospital
Geoffrey D Moebius, Branch Manager

D-U-N-S 13-420-8974
KAISER FOUNDATION HOSPITALS
10200 SE Sunnyside Rd, Clackamas, OR 97015
Phone: (503) 652-2880
Sales: $49,400,000   *Employees:* NA
Company Type: Private   *Employees here:* 1,000
SIC: 8062
    General hospital
Elita Chase, N/A

D-U-N-S 18-803-2973
KAISER FOUNDATION IIOSPITALS
10180 SE Sunnyside Rd, Clackamas, OR 97015
Phone: (503) 652-2880

Sales: $99,500,000   *Employees:* NA
Company Type: Private   *Employees here:* 2,000
SIC: 8062
    General hospital
Alide Chase, Director

D-U-N-S 13-293-1809
KAISER FOUNDATION HOSPITALS
1515 N Vermont Ave, Los Angeles, CA 90027
Phone: (323) 667-4011
Sales: $233,700,000   *Employees:* NA
Company Type: Private   *Employees here:* 4,700
SIC: 8062
    Hospital
Joseph Hummel, N/A

D-U-N-S 87-866-5306
KAISER FOUNDATION HOSPITALS
27400 Hesperian Blvd, Hayward, CA 94545
Phone: (510) 784-4000
Sales: $139,900,000   *Employees:* NA
Company Type: Private   *Employees here:* 2,500
SIC: 8011
    Clinic
Dr Michael Getzell, President

D-U-N-S 87-944-4222
KAISER FOUNDATION HOSPITALS
7300 N Fresno St, Fresno, CA 93720
Phone: (209) 448-2900
Sales: $39,400,000   *Employees:* NA
Company Type: Private   *Employees here:* 800
SIC: 8062
    Plant operations
Ed Glavis, Principal

D-U-N-S 13-553-1648
KAISER FOUNDATION HOSPITALS
10180 SE Sunnyside Rd, Clackamas, OR 97015
Phone: (503) 652-2880
Sales: $99,500,000   *Employees:* NA
Company Type: Private   *Employees here:* 2,000
SIC: 8062
    General hospital
Alida Chase, Branch Manager

D-U-N-S 12-622-9707
KANSAS NEUROLOGICAL INSTITUTE
3107 SW 21st St, Topeka, KS 66604
Phone: (785) 296-5336
Sales: $23,000,000   *Employees:* 750
Company Type: Private   *Employees here:* 750
SIC: 8361
    Institution for developmentally disabled
Tim Edwards, Business Administrator

D-U-N-S 06-628-1080
KAPIOLANI MED CTR
1319 Punahou St, Honolulu, HI 96826
Phone: (808) 535-7401
Sales: $50,600,000   *Employees:* 1,027
Company Type: Private   *Employees here:* 1,027
SIC: 8069
    Specialty hospital
Fran Hallonquist, Chief Executive Officer

D-U-N-S 60-413-6119
KAPIOLANI MED CTR AT PALI MMI
98-1079 Moanalua Rd, Aiea, HI 96701
Phone: (808) 486-6000

Sales: $30,900,000   *Employees:* 450
Company Type: Private   *Employees here:* 450
SIC: 8011
    Acute care hospital
Fran Hallonquist, Chief Executive Officer

D-U-N-S 05-463-3839
KATERI RESIDENCE
150 Riverside Dr, New York, NY 10024
Phone: (212) 769-0744
Sales: $38,055,000   *Employees:* 612
Company Type: Private   *Employees here:* 612
SIC: 8051
    Skilled nursing home
Lascelles L Bond, Administrator

D-U-N-S 09-769-2644
KAUAI MEDICAL CLINIC INC
    (Parent: Wilcox Health System)
3-3420 Kuhio Hwy, Lihue, HI 96766
Phone: (808) 245-1500
Sales: $21,200,000   *Employees:* 310
Company Type: Private   *Employees here:* 280
SIC: 8011
    Outpatient medical clinic
Dr Lee A Evslin Md, President

D-U-N-S 07-463-4593
KAWEAH DELTA HEALTH CARE DST
400 W Mineral King Ave, Visalia, CA 93291
Phone: (209) 625-2211
Sales: $124,590,000   *Employees:* 2,100
Company Type: Private   *Employees here:* 1,570
SIC: 8062
    Hospital
Thomas Johnson, Chief Executive Officer

D-U-N-S 62-468-0559
KELSEY-SEYBOLD MED GROUP PA
1709 Dryden Rd Ste 1800, Houston, TX 77030
Phone: (713) 797-1551
Sales: $48,100,000   *Employees:* 700
Company Type: Private   *Employees here:* 200
SIC: 8011
    Medical clinic
Mike Fitzgerald, Managing Director

D-U-N-S 14-410-0757
KEMPER NATIONAL SERVICES INC
    (Parent: Lumbermens Mutual Casualty Co)
1601 SW 80th Ter, Fort Lauderdale, FL 33324
Phone: (954) 452-4000
Sales: $40,000,000   *Employees:* 1,000
Company Type: Private   *Employees here:* 700
SIC: 8099
    Medical cost containment services
David K Patterson, President

D-U-N-S 78-446-4489
KEN-CREST SERVICES INC
1 Plymouth Meeting Mall, Plymouth Meeting, PA 19462
Phone: (610) 825-9360
Sales: $35,005,000   *Employees:* 1,100
Company Type: Private   *Employees here:* 80
SIC: 8082
    Health services
William Nolan, Executive Director

D-U-N-S 02-195-6602
KENDAL-CROSSLANDS COMMUNITIES INC
RR 1, Kennett Square, PA 19348
Phone: (610) 388-7001

Sales: $23,115,000   *Employees:* 520
Company Type: Private   *Employees here:* 322
SIC: 8051
    Skilled nursing facility independent living apartments
John G Huber Jr, Executive Director

D-U-N-S 62-683-9211
KENDALL HEALTH CARE GROUP LTD
11750 Bird Rd, Miami, FL 33175
Phone: (305) 227-5550
Sales: $32,000,000   *Employees:* 702
Company Type: Private   *Employees here:* 702
SIC: 8062
    General hospital
Victor Maya, Chief Executive Officer

D-U-N-S 07-204-1130
KENDRICK MEMORIAL HOSPITAL
1201 Hadley Rd, Mooresville, IN 46158
Phone: (317) 831-1160
Sales: $25,175,000   *Employees:* 320
Company Type: Private   *Employees here:* 320
SIC: 8062
    General hospital
Richard V Newcomer, Chairman of the Board

D-U-N-S 03-022-8522
KENMORE MERCY HOSPITAL
2950 Elmwood Ave, Kenmore, NY 14217
Phone: (716) 879-6100
Sales: $67,267,000   *Employees:* 1,300
Company Type: Private   *Employees here:* 827
SIC: 8062
    General medical hospital & nursing home
Mary J Schimschiener Sr, Chief Executive Officer

D-U-N-S 15-103-1846
KENNEDY HEALTH SERVICES CORP
4477 W 118th St Ste 405, Hawthorne, CA 90250
Phone: (310) 973-1711
Sales: $26,000,000   *Employees:* 575
Company Type: Private   *Employees here:* 575
SIC: 8062
    Hospital
Samuel Douglas, Chairman of the Board

D-U-N-S 18-948-0064
KENNEDY HEALTH SYSTEMS
18 Laurel Rd E, Stratford, NJ 8084
Phone: (609) 346-6000
Sales: $34,300,000   *Employees:* NA
Company Type: Private   *Employees here:* 700
SIC: 8062
    General hospital
C B Dykes, Manager

D-U-N-S 07-696-1481
KENNEDY HEALTH SYSTEMS
500 Marlboro Ave, Cherry Hill, NJ 8002
Phone: (609) 488-6500
Sales: $140,700,000   *Employees:* 3,000
Company Type: Private   *Employees here:* 150
SIC: 8062
    Hospital
Richard E Murray, President

D-U-N-S 09-998-0237
KENNEDY HEALTH SYSTEMS
2201 Chapel Ave W, Cherry Hill, NJ 8002
Phone: (609) 488-6500

Sales: $29,300,000
Company Type: Private   *Employees:* NA
SIC: 8062   *Employees here:* 600
  General hospital
Mike Dennis, Administrator

D-U-N-S 04-316-0241
KENNEDY HEALTH SYSTEMS
435 Hurffville Cross Keys, Blackwood, NJ 8012
Phone: (609) 582-2802
Sales: $24,000,000   *Employees:* NA
Company Type: Private   *Employees here:* 495
SIC: 8062
  General hospital
Ann Witkowski, N/A

D-U-N-S 11-433-6910
KENNEDY HEALTH CARE FOUNDATION
19 Laurel Rd E Ste B, Stratford, NJ 8084
Phone: (609) 661-5100
Sales: $131,200,000   *Employees:* 2,800
Company Type: Private   *Employees here:* 2,800
SIC: 8062
  General hospital ambulance service real estate management
  nurses registry billing service
A R Pirolli, President

D-U-N-S 06-487-2518
KENNEDY KRIEGER CHILDRENS HOSP
707 N Broadway, Baltimore, MD 21205
Phone: (410) 502-9472
Sales: $42,736,000   *Employees:* 1,200
Company Type: Private   *Employees here:* 1,200
SIC: 8069
  Pediatric hospital & rehabilitation center
James M Anders Jr, Chief Operating Officer

D-U-N-S 03-721-7064
KENNESTONE HOSPITAL INC
677 Church St Nw, Marietta, GA 30060
Phone: (770) 793-5000
Sales: $138,300,000   *Employees:* 2,950
Company Type: Private   *Employees here:* 2,900
SIC: 8062
  General hospitals
Thomas Hill, Chief Executive Officer

D-U-N-S 07-183-9781
KENNEWICK PUBLIC HOSPITAL DST
900 S Auburn St, Kennewick, WA 99336
Phone: (509) 586-6111
Sales: $45,803,000   *Employees:* 500
Company Type: Private   *Employees here:* 480
SIC: 8062
  General hospital
Michael Tuohy, Administrator

D-U-N-S 02-046-3303
KENOSHA HOSPITAL & MEDICAL CTR
6308 8th Ave, Kenosha, WI 53143
Phone: (414) 656-2011
Sales: $74,091,000   *Employees:* 950
Company Type: Private   *Employees here:* 900
SIC: 8062
  Hospital
Richard O Schmidt Jr, President

D-U-N-S 14-796-8085
KENT COMMUNITY HOSPITAL COMPLEX
750 Fuller Ave NE, Grand Rapids, MI 49503
Phone: (616) 336-3300

Sales: $21,488,000   *Employees:* 441
Company Type: Private   *Employees here:* 441
SIC: 8069
  Long term care hospital
Lori Portfleet, Chief Executive Officer

D-U-N-S 06-985-5195
KENT COUNTY MEMORIAL HOSPITAL
455 Toll Gate Rd, Warwick, RI 2886
Phone: (401) 737-7000
Sales: $134,142,000   *Employees:* 2,000
Company Type: Private   *Employees here:* 2,000
SIC: 8062
  General hospital
Dr Robert Bauty Md, President

D-U-N-S 07-408-9095
KENTUCKY EASTER SEAL SOCIETY
2050 Versailles Rd, Lexington, KY 40504
Phone: (606) 254-5701
Sales: $22,400,000   *Employees:* NA
Company Type: Private   *Employees here:* 500
SIC: 8069
  Specialty hospital specialty outpatient clinic
Kerry G Gillihan, President

D-U-N-S 07-809-1212
KEOKUK AREA HOSPITAL
1600 Morgan St, Keokuk, IA 52632
Phone: (319) 524-7150
Sales: $24,283,000   *Employees:* 425
Company Type: Private   *Employees here:* 425
SIC: 8062
  General hospital
Allan W Zastrow, Executive Director

D-U-N-S 07-294-1925
KERLAN-JOBE ORTHOPAEDIC
6801 Park Ter Ste 500, Los Angeles, CA 90045
Phone: (310) 665-7235
Sales: $27,000,000   *Employees:* 130
Company Type: Private   *Employees here:* 110
SIC: 8011
  Orthopedic surgeons
Frank W Jobe, President

D-U-N-S 07-158-1854
KERNODLE CLINIC INC
1234 Huffman Mill Rd, Burlington, NC 27215
Phone: (336) 538-1234
Sales: $20,530,000   *Employees:* 220
Company Type: Private   *Employees here:* 180
SIC: 8011
  Medical clinic
G W Kernodle Jr, President

D-U-N-S 03-009-8404
KERSHAW COUNTY MEDICAL CENTER
Haile & Roberts St, Camden, SC 29020
Phone: (803) 432-4311
Sales: $41,589,000   *Employees:* 550
Company Type: Private   *Employees here:* 515
SIC: 8062
  Hospital
Danny J Weeks, President

D-U-N-S 07-932-9579
KESSLER INST FOR RHABILITATION
1199 Pleasant Valley Way, West Orange, NJ 7052
Phone: (973) 731-3600

Sales: $67,843,000
Company Type: Private
Employees: 1,000
Employees here: 350
SIC: 8069
  Rehabilitation hospital for the physically handicapped
Kenneth W Aitchison, President

D-U-N-S 12-254-4455
KETTERING AFFILIATED HEALTH SVCS
  (Parent: Kettering Medical Center)
3535 Southern Blvd, Dayton, OH 45429
Phone: (937) 296-7215
Sales: $248,949,000
Employees: 115
Company Type: Private
Employees here: 1
SIC: 8099
  Medical service organization
Nemi Velasco, Acct

D-U-N-S 07-128-8450
KETTERING MEDICAL CENTER
3535 Southern Blvd, Dayton, OH 45429
Phone: (937) 298-4331
Sales: $201,232,000
Employees: 2,415
Company Type: Private
Employees here: 2,100
SIC: 8062
  General hospital
Frank J Perez, President

D-U-N-S 05-423-5593
KEWANEE HOSPITAL ASSOCIATION
719 Elliott St, Kewanee, IL 61443
Phone: (309) 853-3361
Sales: $25,588,000
Employees: 300
Company Type: Private
Employees here: 290
SIC: 8062
  Hospital pharmacy & ret gifts
Roger Holloway, Chief Executive Officer

D-U-N-S 16-166-6771
KEYSTONE HEALTH PLAN EAST INC
1901 Market St, Philadelphia, PA 19103
Phone: (215) 241-2001
Sales: $1,613,046,000
Employees: 571
Company Type: Private
Employees here: 571
SIC: 8011
  Health maintenance organization
G F Dibona Jr, President

D-U-N-S 05-608-2233
KEYSTONE SERVICE SYSTEMS, INC
310 N 2nd St, Harrisburg, PA 17101
Phone: (717) 232-7509
Sales: $21,885,000
Employees: 500
Company Type: Private
Employees here: 30
SIC: 8361
  Residential care for mentally handicapped
Dennis Felty, President

D-U-N-S 06-924-4937
KIMBALL DAY HOSPITAL
320 Pomfret St, Putnam, CT 6260
Phone: (860) 928-6541
Sales: $28,200,000
Employees: 620
Company Type: Private
Employees here: 600
SIC: 8062
  General hospital and pediatric health center
Charles Schneider, President

D-U-N-S 07-827-2713
KIMBALL MEDICAL CENTER INC
600 River Ave, Lakewood, NJ 8701
Phone: (732) 886-4419

Sales: $105,750,000
Employees: 1,550
Company Type: Private
Employees here: 1,520
SIC: 8062
  General hospital
Joanne Carrocino, Executive Director

D-U-N-S 07-184-0789
KING COUNTY PUB HOSPITAL DST 2
12040 NE 128th St, Kirkland, WA 98034
Phone: (425) 899-1000
Sales: $122,459,000
Employees: 1,200
Company Type: Private
Employees here: 1,000
SIC: 8062
  General medical & surgical hospital
Anne M Mcbride, Chief Financial Officer

D-U-N-S 07-663-4252
KING COUNTY PUBLIC HOSPITAL DST 1
400 S 43rd St, Renton, WA 98055
Phone: (425) 228-3450
Sales: $133,322,000
Employees: 1,650
Company Type: Private
Employees here: 1,628
SIC: 8062
  General medical & surgical hospital
Richard D Roodman, Administrator

D-U-N-S 07-508-9391
KING'S DAUGHTERS HOSPITAL ASSN
1901 SW H K Dodgen Loop, Temple, TX 76502
Phone: (254) 771-8600
Sales: $23,441,000
Employees: 425
Company Type: Private
Employees here: 425
SIC: 8062
  General medical & surgical hospital
Tucker Bonner, Chief Executive Officer

D-U-N-S 07-260-9407
KING'S DAUGHTERS HOSPITAL
823 Grand Ave, Yazoo City, MS 39194
Phone: (601) 746-2261
Sales: $28,591,000
Employees: 190
Company Type: Private
Employees here: 190
SIC: 8062
  General hospital
Noel Hart, Administrator

D-U-N-S 07-506-8189
KING'S DAUGHTERS HOSPITAL
Hwy 51 N, Brookhaven, MS 39601
Phone: (601) 833-6011
Sales: $29,832,000
Employees: 460
Company Type: Private
Employees here: 454
SIC: 8062
  General hospital
Phillip Grady, Administrator

D-U-N-S 11-511-4654
KINGMAN HOSPITAL INC
3269 Stockton Hill Rd, Kingman, AZ 86401
Phone: (520) 757-2101
Sales: $47,408,000
Employees: 500
Company Type: Private
Employees here: 500
SIC: 8062
  General hospital skilled nursing facility
Brian Turney, Chief Operating Officer

D-U-N-S 06-887-2167
KINGS VIEW
42675 Road 44, Reedley, CA 93654
Phone: (209) 638-2505

Sales: $22,767,000
Company Type: Private
SIC: 8093
    Contract mental health services & home for emotionally
      disturbed children
Mike Waters, Chief Executive Officer

Employees: 400
Employees here: 170

D-U-N-S 13-501-2110
KINGSBORO MEDICAL GROUP P C
3245 Nostrand Ave, Brooklyn, NY 11229
Phone: (718) 615-3777
Sales: $27,400,000
Company Type: Private
SIC: 8011
    Medical group
Dr Gordon M Koota Md, Director

Employees: 400
Employees here: 120

D-U-N-S 84-467-0216
KINGSBRIDGE HEIGHTS REHABILITATION
3400 Cannon Pl 3426, Bronx, NY 10463
Phone: (718) 549-9025
Sales: $31,782,000
Company Type: Private
SIC: 8059
    Nursing home
Helen Sieger, President

Employees: 350
Employees here: 350

D-U-N-S 06-829-8306
KINGSBROOK JEWISH MEDICAL CTR
585 Schenectady Ave, Brooklyn, NY 11203
Phone: (718) 604-5000
Sales: $128,430,000
Company Type: Private
SIC: 8062
    General medical & surgical hospital
Milton Gutman, Chief Executive Officer

Employees: 2,100
Employees here: 2,100

D-U-N-S 06-054-8005
KINGSTON HOSPITAL (INC)
396 Broadway, Kingston, NY 12401
Phone: (914) 331-3131
Sales: $50,156,000
Company Type: Private
SIC: 8062
    General hospital
Anthony R Triulzi, Chief Executive Officer

Employees: 550
Employees here: 550

D-U-N-S 07-458-5795
KISHWAUKEE COMMUNITY HOSPITAL
626 Bethany Rd, Dekalb, IL 60115
Phone: (815) 756-1521
Sales: $46,635,000
Company Type: Private
SIC: 8062
    Short term acute care hospital
Robert Thebeau, President

Employees: 650
Employees here: 650

D-U-N-S 05-511-5059
KNAPP MEDICAL CENTER
1401 E 8th St, Weslaco, TX 78596
Phone: (956) 968-8567
Sales: $62,099,000
Company Type: Private
SIC: 8062
    General hospital
Robert W Vanderveer, Administrator

Employees: 1,000
Employees here: 950

D-U-N-S 05-884-1073
KNOX COMMUNITY HOSPITAL
1330 Coshocton Ave, Mount Vernon, OH 43050
Phone: (740) 393-9000

Sales: $39,286,000
Company Type: Private
SIC: 8062
    General hospital
Robert Polahar, Administrator

Employees: 453
Employees here: 453

D-U-N-S 07-183-6936
KOOTENAI HOSPITAL DISTRICT
2003 Lincoln Way, Coeur D Alene, ID 83814
Phone: (208) 666-2000
Sales: $70,674,000
Company Type: Private
SIC: 8062
    Hospital
Joseph Morris, Chief Executive Officer

Employees: 1,100
Employees here: 1,100

D-U-N-S 04-028-1073
KOSCIUSKO COMMUNITY HOSPITAL
2101 Dubois Dr, Warsaw, IN 46580
Phone: (219) 267-3200
Sales: $48,304,000
Company Type: Private
SIC: 8062
    General hospital
Wayne Hendrix, President

Employees: 600
Employees here: 480

D-U-N-S 78-167-5012
KPH-CONSOLIDATION INC
(Parent: Columbia/Hca Healthcare Corp)
22999 Highway 59 N, Kingwood, TX 77339
Phone: (281) 359-1313
Sales: $26,900,000
Company Type: Public Family Member
SIC: 8069
    Hospital and skilled nursing facility
Chuck Schuetz, Chief Executive Officer

Employees: 550
Employees here: 550

D-U-N-S 11-323-0569
KUAKINI HEALTH SYSTEM
347 N Kuakini St, Honolulu, HI 96817
Phone: (808) 536-2236
Sales: $112,324,000
Company Type: Private
SIC: 8062
    Holding company
Gary K Kajiwara, President

Employees: 1,500
Employees here: 1,455

D-U-N-S 07-770-1613
KUAKINI MEDICAL CENTER
347 N Kuakini St, Honolulu, HI 96817
Phone: (808) 536-2236
Sales: $97,696,000
Company Type: Private
SIC: 8062
    General medical and surgical hospital
Gary Kajiwara, President

Employees: 1,200
Employees here: 1,200

D-U-N-S 10-137-9774
KUALA HEALTHCARE INC
910 Sylvan Ave, Englewood Cliffs, NJ 7632
Phone: (201) 567-4600
Sales: $70,694,000
Company Type: Public
SIC: 8051
    Operates and manages skilled nursing homes and provides at
      home infusion therapy service
Jack Rosen, Chairman of the Board

Employees: 900
Employees here: 20

D-U-N-S 10-809-9169
L C RENALWEST LLC
1750 S Mesa Dr 110, Mesa, AZ 85210
Phone: (602) 926-0790

Sales: $32,013,000   *Employees:* 350
Company Type: Private   *Employees here:* 50
SIC: 8092
   Kidney dialysis treatment facility
Jeff E Weintraub, Chief Executive Officer

D-U-N-S 17-266-0524
L I C H CORPORATION
339 Hicks St, Brooklyn, NY 11201
Phone: (718) 780-1000
Sales: $150,100,000   *Employees:* 3,200
Company Type: Private   *Employees here:* 3,000
SIC: 8062
   General teaching hospital kidney dialysis center & pharmacy
Donald Snell, President

D-U-N-S 61-828-2297
L I C H CORPORATION
70 Atlantic Ave, Brooklyn, NY 11201
Phone: (718) 780-1388
Sales: $29,300,000   *Employees:* NA
Company Type: Private   *Employees here:* 600
SIC: 8062
   General hospital kidney dialysis centers ret drugs/sundries
Michael Ceyko, Manager

D-U-N-S 07-490-1141
LA FOLLETTE MEDICAL CENTER
945 East Ave, La Follette, TN 37766
Phone: (423) 562-2211
Sales: $24,000,000   *Employees:* 600
Company Type: Private   *Employees here:* 600
SIC: 8062
   Hospital
David Southerland, Administrator

D-U-N-S 07-251-6164
LA PALMA HOSPITAL MEDICAL CTR
7901 Walker St, La Palma, CA 90623
Phone: (714) 670-7400
Sales: $38,922,000   *Employees:* 360
Company Type: Private   *Employees here:* 360
SIC: 8062
   General hospital
Stephen Dixon, President

D-U-N-S 07-891-8976
LA PORTE HOSPITAL INC
1007 Lincolnway, La Porte, IN 46350
Phone: (219) 326-1234
Sales: $70,762,000   *Employees:* 1,250
Company Type: Private   *Employees here:* 925
SIC: 8062
   General medical hospital
Leigh Morris, President

D-U-N-S 06-999-2477
LA-RABIDA CHLD HOSPITAL & RES CTR
E 65th St At Lake Mich, Chicago, IL 60649
Phone: (773) 363-6700
Sales: $26,046,000   *Employees:* 339
Company Type: Private   *Employees here:* 328
SIC: 8069
   Children's hospital
Dr Paula Jaudes Md, President

D-U-N-S 07-629-0675
LABETTE COUNTY MEDICAL CENTER
South Hwy 59, Parsons, KS 67357
Phone: (316) 421-4880

Sales: $30,417,000   *Employees:* 402
Company Type: Private   *Employees here:* 343
SIC: 8062
   Hospital
Lisa Jimenez, Chief Financial Officer

D-U-N-S 07-306-7548
LABONE, INC.
   (Parent: Lab Holdings Inc)
10310 W 84th Ter, Shawnee Mission, KS 66214
Phone: (913) 888-1770
Sales: $78,926,000   *Employees:* 677
Company Type: Public   *Employees here:* 630
SIC: 8071
   Analytical testing laboratory
W T Grant Ii, Chairman of the Board

D-U-N-S 07-209-9146
LABORATORY CORP AMER HOLDINGS
1801 1st Ave S, Birmingham, AL 35233
Phone: (205) 581-3780
Sales: $21,200,000   *Employees:* NA
Company Type: Private   *Employees here:* 480
SIC: 8071
   Med test lab
Danny Cooner, Systems/Data Processing

D-U-N-S 78-911-1754
LABORATORY CORP AMER HOLDINGS
1904 Alexander Dr, Research Triangle Pa, NC 27709
Phone: (919) 549-8263
Sales: $23,000,000   *Employees:* NA
Company Type: Private   *Employees here:* 500
SIC: 8071
   Drug testing lab
Gerard C Verkerk, Branch Manager

D-U-N-S 86-142-2434
LABORATORY CORP AMER HOLDINGS
358 S Main St, Burlington, NC 27215
Phone: (336) 229-1127
Sales: $1,519,000,000   *Employees:* 18,600
Company Type: Private   *Employees here:* 300
SIC: 8071
   Clinical testing laboratory
Thomas P Mac Mahon, Chairman of the Board

D-U-N-S 05-626-7297
LABORATORY CORP AMER HOLDINGS
69 1st Ave, Raritan, NJ 8869
Phone: (908) 526-2400
Sales: $41,000,000   *Employees:* NA
Company Type: Private   *Employees here:* 800
SIC: 8071
   Medical laboratory
Ralph Monterosa, Principal

D-U-N-S 08-101-9374
LABORATORY CORP AMER HOLDINGS
6370 Wilcox Rd, Dublin, OH 43016
Phone: (614) 889-1061
Sales: $26,700,000   *Employees:* NA
Company Type: Private   *Employees here:* 608
SIC: 8071
   Med test lababoratory
Steven D Jones, Administration

D-U-N-S 01-282-2243
LABORATORY CORPORATION AMERICA
   (Parent: Laboratory Corp Amer Holdings)
358 S Main St, Burlington, NC 27215
Phone: (336) 584-5171

Sales: $464,600,000
Company Type: Public
SIC: 8071
   Clinical testing laboratory
James B Powell, President

Employees: 9,800
Employees here: 500

D-U-N-S 87-926-9405
LABORATORY CORPORATION AMERICA
750 Walnut Ave, Cranford, NJ 7016
Phone: (908) 272-2511
Sales: $30,100,000
Company Type: Public Family Member
SIC: 8099
   Blood drawing center
Donna Weeks, President

Employees: NA
Employees here: 700

D-U-N-S 06-033-2475
LABORATORY CORPORATION AMERICA
51 Charles Lindbergh Blvd, Uniondale, NY 11553
Phone: (516) 794-4646
Sales: $41,000,000
Company Type: Public Family Member
SIC: 8071
   Medical laboratory
Elias Khabboza, N/A

Employees: NA
Employees here: 800

D-U-N-S 09-240-8012
LABORATORY CORPORATION AMERICA
7777 Forest Ln Ste C350, Dallas, TX 75230
Phone: (972) 661-7500
Sales: $63,500,000
Company Type: Public Family Member
SIC: 8071
   Clinical testing laboratory
Dr Gary Smith, N/A

Employees: NA
Employees here: 1,500

D-U-N-S 08-648-5455
LABORATORY SCIENCES ARIZ LLC
   (Parent: Samaritan Health System)
1255 W Washington St, Tempe, AZ 85281
Phone: (602) 685-5000
Sales: $20,000,000
Company Type: Private
SIC: 8071
   Medical laboratory & outpatient center
Earl Buck, Chief Executive Officer

Employees: 350
Employees here: 50

D-U-N-S 04-342-7426
LAFAYETTE GENERAL HOSPITAL
1214 Coolidge Blvd, Lafayette, LA 70503
Phone: (318) 289-7991
Sales: $150,000,000
Company Type: Private
SIC: 8062
   General surgical & medical hospital
John J Burdin Jr, Executive Director

Employees: 1,400
Employees here: 1,092

D-U-N-S 07-598-4344
LAFAYETTE HOME HOSPITAL INC
2400 South St, Lafayette, IN 47904
Phone: (765) 447-6811
Sales: $94,416,000
Company Type: Private
SIC: 8062
   General hospital
John R Walling, President

Employees: 1,200
Employees here: 1,200

D-U-N-S 07-305-8257
LAFAYETTE REGIONAL HEALTH CTR
1500 State St, Lexington, MO 64067
Phone: (660) 259-2203

Sales: $28,000,000
Company Type: Private
SIC: 8062
   General hospital
Jeffrey Tarrant, Administrator

Employees: 190
Employees here: 190

D-U-N-S 07-199-1020
LAFAYETTE-GRAND HOSPITAL
   (Parent: Tenet Healthcare Corporation)
3545 Lafayette Ave, Saint Louis, MO 63104
Phone: (314) 865-6500
Sales: $55,600,000
Company Type: Public Family Member
SIC: 8062
   General medical hospital
Doug Doris, President

Employees: 1,200
Employees here: 1,100

D-U-N-S 88-385-0364
LAHEY HITCHCOCK CLINIC
41 Mall Rd, Burlington, MA 1803
Phone: (781) 273-5100
Sales: $187,900,000
Company Type: Private
SIC: 8062
   General hospital medical clinic and foundation
John A Libertino, Chief Executive Officer

Employees: 4,000
Employees here: 3,500

D-U-N-S 10-938-8330
LAHEY HITCHCOCK CLINIC
21 E Hollis St, Nashua, NH 3060
Phone: (603) 883-0323
Sales: $20,100,000
Company Type: Private
SIC: 8011
   Medical clinic
Jean Abramson, Branch Manager

Employees: NA
Employees here: 315

D-U-N-S 88-373-4683
LAHEY HITCHCOCK CLINIC
1 Medical Center Dr, Lebanon, NH 3756
Phone: (603) 650-5330
Sales: $52,000,000
Company Type: Private
SIC: 8011
   Medical clinic
Steven Plume, N/A

Employees: NA
Employees here: 1,000

D-U-N-S 08-500-8217
LAKE OF THE OZARKS GEN HOSP
54 Hospital Dr, Osage Beach, MO 65065
Phone: (573) 348-3181
Sales: $40,835,000
Company Type: Private
SIC: 8062
   General hospital
Mike Henze, Chief Executive Officer

Employees: 563
Employees here: 427

D-U-N-S 94-436-0908
LAKE CUMBERLAND HEALTHCARE
   (Parent: Columbia/Hca Healthcare Corp)
305 Langdon St, Somerset, KY 42503
Phone: (606) 679-7441
Sales: $65,000,000
Company Type: Public Family Member
SIC: 8062
   General hospital
Ken W Lukhard, President

Employees: 1,400
Employees here: 805

D-U-N-S 61-672-1148
LAKE FOREST HOSPITAL FOUNDATION
660 N Westmoreland Rd, Lake Forest, IL 60045
Phone: (847) 234-5600

Sales: $88,963,000   *Employees:* 1,500
Company Type: Private   *Employees here:* 1,200
SIC: 8062
     Hospital operator of commercial property & administrator of
     health care education
William G Ries, Chief Executive Officer

D-U-N-S 07-458-8492
LAKE FOREST HOSPITAL
660 N Westmoreland Rd, Lake Forest, IL 60045
Phone: (847) 234-5600
Sales: $94,487,000   *Employees:* NA
Company Type: Private   *Employees here:* NA
SIC: 8062
     Hospital & skilled nursing facility
William Ries, President

D-U-N-S 03-451-7193
LAKE HOSPITAL SYSTEM INC
36000 Euclid Ave, Willoughby, OH 44094
Phone: (440) 953-6050
Sales: $42,100,000   *Employees:* NA
Company Type: Private   *Employees here:* 1,000
SIC: 8062
     Hospital
Cynthia M Hardy, Chief Executive Officer

D-U-N-S 07-775-7292
LAKE HOSPITAL SYSTEM INC
10 E Washington St, Painesville, OH 44077
Phone: (440) 354-2400
Sales: $135,754,000   *Employees:* 2,200
Company Type: Private   *Employees here:* 816
SIC: 8062
     Hospital
Cynthia M Hardy, President

D-U-N-S 07-176-4062
LAKE REGION HEALTHCARE CORP
712 S Cascade St, Fergus Falls, MN 56537
Phone: (218) 736-8000
Sales: $30,343,000   *Employees:* 610
Company Type: Private   *Employees here:* 610
SIC: 8062
     General hospital
Edward J Mehl, Chief Executive Officer

D-U-N-S 07-402-5073
LAKE SHORE HOSPITAL
845 Routes 5 & 20, Irving, NY 14081
Phone: (716) 934-2654
Sales: $29,524,000   *Employees:* 600
Company Type: Private   *Employees here:* 599
SIC: 8062
     General hospital
James B Foster, Administrator

D-U-N-S 08-033-9716
LAKE SHORE NURSING HOME INC
845 Route 5 And 20, Irving, NY 14081
Phone: (716) 934-4531
Sales: $23,409,000   *Employees:* 85
Company Type: Private   *Employees here:* 85
SIC: 8059
     Nursing home
James B Foster, Chief Executive Officer

D-U-N-S 06-025-3150
LAKELAND REGIONAL MEDICAL CTR
1324 Lakeland Hills Blvd, Lakeland, FL 33805
Phone: (941) 687-1100

Sales: $241,357,000   *Employees:* 2,550
Company Type: Private   *Employees here:* 2,537
SIC: 8062
     General hospital
Jack T Stephens Jr, President

D-U-N-S 07-396-8455
LAKES REGION HOSPITAL ASSN
80 Highland St, Laconia, NH 3246
Phone: (603) 524-3211
Sales: $53,704,000   *Employees:* 900
Company Type: Private   *Employees here:* 730
SIC: 8062
     General hospital
Tom Clairmont, President

D-U-N-S 09-892-9524
LAKEVIEW CENTER INC
1221 W Lakeview Ave, Pensacola, FL 32501
Phone: (850) 432-1222
Sales: $42,453,000   *Employees:* 600
Company Type: Private   *Employees here:* 400
SIC: 8093
     Mental health substance abuse treatment & vocational
     services
Dr Morris Eaddy Phd, Chief Executive Officer

D-U-N-S 05-293-1672
LAKEVIEW COMMUNITY HOSPITAL AUTH
408 Hazen St, Paw Paw, MI 49079
Phone: (616) 657-3141
Sales: $26,177,000   *Employees:* 357
Company Type: Private   *Employees here:* 227
SIC: 8062
     Hospital & nursing home authority
Sue E Johnson-Phillip, President

D-U-N-S 07-763-7569
LAKEVIEW MED CTR INC RICE LK
1100 N Main St, Rice Lake, WI 54868
Phone: (715) 234-1515
Sales: $22,322,000   *Employees:* 270
Company Type: Private   *Employees here:* 270
SIC: 8062
     Hospital
Scott Moebius, Controller

D-U-N-S 07-763-4079
LAKEVIEW MEMORIAL HOSPITAL ASSN
927 Churchill St W, Stillwater, MN 55082
Phone: (651) 439-5330
Sales: $29,859,000   *Employees:* 450
Company Type: Private   *Employees here:* 450
SIC: 8062
     General hospital
Jeffrey Robertson, Chief Executive Officer

D-U-N-S 07-778-2241
LAKEWOOD HOSPITAL ASSOCIATION
14519 Detroit Ave, Cleveland, OH 44107
Phone: (216) 521-4200
Sales: $94,211,000   *Employees:* 1,200
Company Type: Private   *Employees here:* 1,100
SIC: 8062
     General hospital
William Baiocchi, Chief Operating Officer

D-U-N-S 13-596-8311
LANCASTER COUNTY
900 E King St, Lancaster, PA 17602
Phone: (717) 299-7850

Sales: $24,300,000
Company Type: Private
SIC: 8062
General hospital
Carol Knisely, Principal

Employees: NA
Employees here: 500

D-U-N-S 06-978-4924
LANCASTER GENERAL HOSPITAL
555 N Duke St, Lancaster, PA 17602
Phone: (717) 299-5511
Sales: $217,245,000
Company Type: Private
SIC: 8062
Hospital
Mark A Brazitis, President

Employees: 2,759
Employees here: 2,500

D-U-N-S 07-533-7485
LANCASTER HOSPITAL CORPORATION
(Parent: Paracelsus Healthcare Corp)
43830 10th St W, Lancaster, CA 93534
Phone: (805) 948-4781
Sales: $22,500,000
Company Type: Public Family Member
SIC: 8062
Hospitals
R J Messinger, President

Employees: NA
Employees here: NA

D-U-N-S 88-377-9902
LANCASTER HOSPITAL CORPORATION
(Parent: Community Health Systems Inc)
800 W Meeting St, Lancaster, SC 29720
Phone: (803) 286-1214
Sales: $30,100,000
Company Type: Public Family Member
SIC: 8062
General hospital
Robert Luther, Executive Director

Employees: 660
Employees here: 660

D-U-N-S 07-119-6364
LANCASTER MENNONITE HOSPITAL
283 Butler Rd, Lebanon, PA 17042
Phone: (717) 273-8871
Sales: $24,446,000
Company Type: Private
SIC: 8063
Psychiatric hospital
Lavern Yutzy, Chief Executive Officer

Employees: 550
Employees here: 425

D-U-N-S 07-572-6141
LANDMARK MEDICAL CENTER
115 Cass Ave, Woonsocket, RI 2895
Phone: (401) 769-4100
Sales: $50,900,000
Company Type: Private
SIC: 8062
Acute care hospital
Robert D Walker, Chairman of the Board

Employees: 1,100
Employees here: 840

D-U-N-S 78-583-7527
LANGTON LAKE PLACE, INC.
(Parent: Presbyterian Homes Of Minn Inc)
1910 County Road D W, Saint Paul, MN 55112
Phone: (651) 631-6000
Sales: $34,858,000
Company Type: Private
SIC: 8051
Nursing home
Daniel Bolhouse, President

Employees: 210
Employees here: 210

D-U-N-S 88-454-3075
LANIER PROFESSIONAL SERVICES
(Parent: Lanier Worldwide Inc)
4200 Perimeter Park S, Atlanta, GA 30341

Phone: (770) 455-7800
Sales: $20,000,000
Company Type: Public Family Member
SIC: 8099
Medical transcriptions
Dave Woodrow, Vice-President

Employees: 500
Employees here: 2

D-U-N-S 10-910-2376
LANTIS ENTERPRISES INC
4755 E Colorado Blvd, Spearfish, SD 57783
Phone: (605) 642-7736
Sales: $57,300,000
Company Type: Private
SIC: 8051
Operates skilled & intermediate nursing care facilities
Les Mahon, Chief Executive Officer

Employees: 2,500
Employees here: 45

D-U-N-S 07-422-5806
LAPEER REGIONAL HOSPITAL
(Parent: Mclaren Health Care Corp)
1375 N Main St, Lapeer, MI 48446
Phone: (810) 667-5500
Sales: $43,800,000
Company Type: Private
SIC: 8062
Hospital
Donald Kooy, President

Employees: 950
Employees here: 950

D-U-N-S 60-991-6762
LARGO MEDICAL CENTER INC
(Parent: Columbia/Hca Healthcare Corp)
201 14th St SW, Largo, FL 33770
Phone: (727) 586-1411
Sales: $60,300,000
Company Type: Public Family Member
SIC: 8062
General medical & surgical hospital
Thomas L Herron, Chief Executive Officer

Employees: 1,300
Employees here: 750

D-U-N-S 07-608-9622
LARKIN COMMUNITY HOSPITAL INC
7031 SW 62nd Ave, Miami, FL 33143
Phone: (305) 284-7700
Sales: $50,000,000
Company Type: Private
SIC: 8062
General hospital
Jack Michel, Chief Executive Officer

Employees: 400
Employees here: 400

D-U-N-S 07-495-6582
LATROBE AREA HOSPITAL INC
121 W 2nd Ave, Latrobe, PA 15650
Phone: (724) 537-1000
Sales: $102,918,000
Company Type: Private
SIC: 8062
General hospital
Douglas Clark, Administrator

Employees: 1,500
Employees here: 1,470

D-U-N-S 06-650-5975
LAUGHLIN MEMORIAL HOSPITAL
1420 Tusculum Blvd, Greeneville, TN 37745
Phone: (423) 787-5000
Sales: $35,283,000
Company Type: Private
SIC: 8062
General hospital and skilled nursing home
Charles H Whitfield Jr, Chief Executive Officer

Employees: 540
Employees here: 457

D-U-N-S 05-026-9919
LAUREATE GROUP INC
1805 Kensington Dr, Waukesha, WI 53188
Phone: (414) 548-5965

Sales: $45,000,000
Company Type: Private
SIC: 8051
   Nursing home management
Larry Weiss, Chairman of the Board

Employees: 1,500
Employees here: 18

D-U-N-S 07-805-0903
LAURENS COUNTY HEALTH CARE SYS
Us Hwy 76, Clinton, SC 29325
Phone: (864) 833-9100
Sales: $29,297,000
Company Type: Private
SIC: 8062
   General hospital
Michael Kozar, Administrator

Employees: 380
Employees here: 380

D-U-N-S 19-408-4547
LAWNWOOD MEDICAL CENTER INC
(Parent: Columbia/Hca Healthcare Corp)
1700 S 23rd St, Fort Pierce, FL 34950
Phone: (561) 461-4000
Sales: $117,066,000
Company Type: Public Family Member
SIC: 8062
   General medical & surgical hospital psychiatric hospital
Gary Cantrell, Chief Executive Officer

Employees: 1,191
Employees here: 1,066

D-U-N-S 06-925-3946
LAWRENCE AND MEMORIAL HOSP
365 Montauk Ave, New London, CT 6320
Phone: (860) 442-0711
Sales: $137,338,000
Company Type: Private
SIC: 8062
   General hospital
William Christopher, President

Employees: 1,600
Employees here: 1,153

D-U-N-S 16-372-2069
LAWRENCE CNTY GEN HOSPITAL FNDTION
2228 S 9th St, Ironton, OH 45638
Phone: (740) 532-3234
Sales: $30,392,000
Company Type: Private
SIC: 8062
   General hospital
Terry Vanderhoof, President

Employees: 543
Employees here: 495

D-U-N-S 07-951-7611
LAWRENCE GENERAL HOSPITAL
1 General St, Lawrence, MA 1841
Phone: (978) 683-4000
Sales: $84,495,000
Company Type: Private
SIC: 8062
   General medical and surgical hospital
Joseph S Mc Manus, President

Employees: 1,200
Employees here: 1,200

D-U-N-S 07-270-1832
LAWRENCE HOSPITAL INC
55 Palmer Ave, Bronxville, NY 10708
Phone: (914) 787-1000
Sales: $72,027,000
Company Type: Private
SIC: 8062
   General hospital
Roger G Dvorak, President

Employees: 860
Employees here: 760

D-U-N-S 07-305-3282
LAWRENCE MEMORIAL HOSPITAL
325 Maine St, Lawrence, KS 66044
Phone: (785) 749-6100

Sales: $50,723,000
Company Type: Private
SIC: 8062
   General hospital
Eugene W Meyer, Chief Executive Officer

Employees: 1,000
Employees here: 999

D-U-N-S 14-814-8869
LEARNING SERVICES CORPORATION
3710 University Dr, Durham, NC 27707
Phone: (919) 419-9955
Sales: $24,000,000
Company Type: Private
SIC: 8093
   Rehabilitation center
Randall Evans, President

Employees: 600
Employees here: 20

D-U-N-S 06-030-0050
LEBAUER, WEINTRAUB, BRODIE
520 N Elam Ave, Greensboro, NC 27403
Phone: (336) 547-1700
Sales: $24,000,000
Company Type: Private
SIC: 8011
   Physicians office
Dr Jeffrey Katz, President

Employees: 350
Employees here: 200

D-U-N-S 07-152-0316
LEE COUNTY COMMUNITY HOSPITAL
Rr 58, Pennington Gap, VA 24277
Phone: (540) 546-1440
Sales: $30,767,000
Company Type: Private
SIC: 8062
   General hospital
James Davis, Administrator

Employees: 420
Employees here: 413

D-U-N-S 01-145-3792
LEE REGIONAL HEALTH SYSTEM
320 Main St, Johnstown, PA 15901
Phone: (814) 533-0720
Sales: $65,000,000
Company Type: Private
SIC: 8062
   Hospital
John W Augustine, Chairman of the Board

Employees: 1,400
Employees here: 1,300

D-U-N-S 07-216-4254
LEE UPMC REGIONAL
320 Main St, Johnstown, PA 15901
Phone: (814) 533-0123
Sales: $71,792,000
Company Type: Private
SIC: 8062
   General hospital
John W Ungar, President

Employees: 1,250
Employees here: 1,050

D-U-N-S 01-082-1858
LEESBURG REGIONAL MEDICAL CTR
600 E Dixie Ave, Leesburg, FL 34748
Phone: (352) 323-5762
Sales: $106,867,000
Company Type: Private
SIC: 8062
   General hospital
Joe Depew, President

Employees: 1,275
Employees here: 1,110

D-U-N-S 07-430-4171
LEGACY HEALTH CARE INC
2101 W Enterprise Ave, Muncie, IN 47304
Phone: (765) 286-6035

Sales: $24,400,000
Company Type: Private
SIC: 8361
  Nursing home
Douglas A Bradburn, President

Employees: 1,000
Employees here: 30

D-U-N-S 15-401-9673
LEGACY MERIDIAN PARK HOSPITAL
19300 SW 65th Ave, Tualatin, OR 97062
Phone: (503) 692-1212
Sales: $55,695,000
Company Type: Private
SIC: 8062
  General hospital
Jane Cummins, President

Employees: 458
Employees here: 458

D-U-N-S 14-769-4160
LEGACY MOUNT HOOD MEDICAL CTR
24800 SE Stark St, Gresham, OR 97030
Phone: (503) 667-1122
Sales: $29,475,000
Company Type: Private
SIC: 8062
  Medical center & pharmacy
Jane Cummins, President

Employees: 306
Employees here: 306

D-U-N-S 05-097-3098
LEGACY-EMANUAL HOSPITAL HEALTH CTR
2801 N Gantenbein Ave, Portland, OR 97227
Phone: (503) 280-3200
Sales: $218,937,000
Company Type: Private
SIC: 8062
  General hospital
Jane Cummins, Vice-President

Employees: 1,978
Employees here: 1,953

D-U-N-S 06-857-2015
LEHIGH VALLEY HOSPITAL INC
  (Parent: Lehigh Valley Health Network)
Cedar Crest Blvd & I 78, Allentown, PA 18102
Phone: (610) 402-8000
Sales: $350,996,000
Company Type: Private
SIC: 8062
  General hospital
Kathern Taylor, Chairman of the Board

Employees: 3,600
Employees here: 3,600

D-U-N-S 07-201-0093
LENOIR MEMORIAL HOSPITAL INC
100 Airport Rd, Kinston, NC 28501
Phone: (252) 522-7171
Sales: $68,335,000
Company Type: Private
SIC: 8062
  General hospital
Gary Black, President

Employees: 870
Employees here: 15

D-U-N-S 07-104-5397
LENOX HILL HOSPITAL
100 E 77th St, New York, NY 10021
Phone: (212) 434-2000
Sales: $343,335,000
Company Type: Private
SIC: 8062
  General hospital
Gladys George, President

Employees: 2,955
Employees here: 2,850

D-U-N-S 03-248-9809
LESLIE PETER & CO
510 Vonderburg Dr Fl 3, Brandon, FL 33511
Phone: (813) 685-0891

Sales: $22,700,000
Company Type: Private
SIC: 8051
  Nursing home
Leslie Peter, President

Employees: NA
Employees here: NA

D-U-N-S 07-303-7343
LESTER E COX MEDICAL CENTER
1423 N Jefferson Ave, Springfield, MO 65802
Phone: (417) 269-3000
Sales: $322,556,000
Company Type: Private
SIC: 8062
  General hospital
Larry D Wallis, Chief Executive Officer

Employees: 4,200
Employees here: 1,300

D-U-N-S 15-559-7859
LESTER E COX MEDICAL CENTER
3801 S National Ave, Springfield, MO 65807
Phone: (417) 885-6000
Sales: $101,700,000
Company Type: Private
SIC: 8062
  Hospital
Robert H Bezanson, Branch Manager

Employees: NA
Employees here: 2,400

D-U-N-S 07-829-6043
LEVINDALE HEBREW GERIATRIC CTR
2434 W Belvedere Ave, Baltimore, MD 21215
Phone: (410) 466-8700
Sales: $27,995,000
Company Type: Private
SIC: 8069
  Specialty hospital & nursing home
Ronald Rothstein, Chief Executive Officer

Employees: 461
Employees here: 419

D-U-N-S 06-305-9364
LEWIS COUNTY GENERAL HOSPITAL
7785 N State St, Lowville, NY 13367
Phone: (315) 376-5200
Sales: $21,853,000
Company Type: Private
SIC: 8062
  General hospital skilled nursing home & outpatient clinic
Ernest R Mc Nelly, Chief Executive Officer

Employees: 400
Employees here: 394

D-U-N-S 01-058-3649
LEWISTOWN HOSPITAL
400 Highland Ave, Lewistown, PA 17044
Phone: (717) 242-7101
Sales: $48,828,000
Company Type: Private
SIC: 8062
  General hospital
A G Mcaleer, President

Employees: 760
Employees here: 725

D-U-N-S 14-484-6250
LEXINGTON COUNTY HEALTH SVC DST
2720 Sunset Blvd, West Columbia, SC 29169
Phone: (803) 791-2000
Sales: $138,813,000
Company Type: Private
SIC: 8062
  Hospital outpatient clinic health-oriented classes and nursing
    home
Michael Biediger, President

Employees: 2,180
Employees here: 1,200

D-U-N-S 92-608-0557
LEXINGTON HEALTH CARE GROUP
1577 New Britain Ave, Farmington, CT 6032
Phone: (860) 674-2700

Sales: $35,900,000 *Employees:* 1,000
Company Type: Public *Employees here:* 200
SIC: 8051
  Owns & manages skilled nursing care facilities
Jack Friedler, Principal

D-U-N-S 06-933-3797
LEXINGTON MEDICAL CENTER
2720 Sunset Blvd, West Columbia, SC 29169
Phone: (803) 791-2000
Sales: $122,828,000 *Employees:* 1,600
Company Type: Private *Employees here:* 1,500
SIC: 8062
  General hospital
Michael J Biediger, President

D-U-N-S 06-744-0453
LEXINGTON MEMORIAL HOSPITAL
  (Parent: Davidson Health Care Inc)
250 Hospital Dr, Lexington, NC 27295
Phone: (336) 248-5161
Sales: $30,378,000 *Employees:* 440
Company Type: Private *Employees here:* 440
SIC: 8062
  General hospital
John Cashion, President

D-U-N-S 15-515-9940
LEXINGTON SQUARE INC
1300 S Main St, Lombard, IL 60148
Phone: (630) 620-1448
Sales: $22,200,000 *Employees:* 1,000
Company Type: Private *Employees here:* 25
SIC: 8059
  Management nursing care facility
John Samatas, President

D-U-N-S 15-534-3882
LIBERTY HEALTH SYSTEM INC
  (Parent: Bon Secours Inc)
2600 Liberty Heights Ave, Baltimore, MD 21215
Phone: (410) 383-4000
Sales: $50,900,000 *Employees:* 1,100
Company Type: Private *Employees here:* 1,100
SIC: 8062
  General & psychiatric hospital
Everard O Rutledge, President

D-U-N-S 78-733-6817
LIBERTY HEALTHCARE SYSTEM INC
50 Baldwin Ave, Jersey City, NJ 7304
Phone: (201) 915-2000
Sales: $140,700,000 *Employees:* 3,000
Company Type: Private *Employees here:* 1
SIC: 8062
  General hospitals
Jonathon M Metsch, President

D-U-N-S 04-642-4750
LICKING MEMORIAL HOSPITAL
1320 W Main St, Newark, OH 43055
Phone: (740) 348-4000
Sales: $41,800,000 *Employees:* 908
Company Type: Private *Employees here:* 855
SIC: 8062
  General hospital
William Andrews, President

D-U-N-S 03-067-1002
LIFE CARE CENTERS OF AMERICA,
3570 Keith St Nw, Cleveland, TN 37312
Phone: (423) 472-9585

Sales: $443,785,000 *Employees:* 25,000
Company Type: Private *Employees here:* 275
SIC: 8051
  Skilled and intermediate care facilities
Forrest L Preston, Chairman of the Board

D-U-N-S 08-713-2502
LIFE CARE RTREMENT COMMUNITIES
200 E Grand Ave Ste 390, Des Moines, IA 50309
Phone: (515) 288-5805
Sales: $114,597,000 *Employees:* 2,000
Company Type: Private *Employees here:* 4
SIC: 8059
  Nursing/personal care
Thomas A Haeussler, Chairman of the Board

D-U-N-S 07-838-8295
LIFE MGT CTR FOR MH/MR SVCS
8929 Viscount Blvd, El Paso, TX 79925
Phone: (915) 629-2665
Sales: $20,333,000 *Employees:* 500
Company Type: Private *Employees here:* 50
SIC: 8093
  Mental rehabilitation center
Alvarado Rodriquez, Executive

D-U-N-S 83-547-7779
LIFECARE HOSPITAL NEW ORLEANS LLC
801 W Virtue St, Chalmette, LA 70043
Phone: (504) 277-5433
Sales: $23,994,000 *Employees:* 130
Company Type: Private *Employees here:* 65
SIC: 8069
  Specialty hospital
Mark Rice, Chief Executive Officer

D-U-N-S 18-341-3046
LIFELINK CORP
331 S York Rd Ste 206, Bensenville, IL 60106
Phone: (630) 766-3570
Sales: $39,778,000 *Employees:* 725
Company Type: Private *Employees here:* 45
SIC: 8051
  Holding company/management company
Robert Logston, Vice-President

D-U-N-S 15-080-2932
LIFELINK FOUNDATION INC
2111 W Swann Ave, Tampa, FL 33606
Phone: (813) 886-8111
Sales: $33,138,000 *Employees:* 281
Company Type: Private *Employees here:* 55
SIC: 8099
  Procurement foundation for kidneys livers hearts & tissue
Dr Dana L Shires Jr, Chief Executive Officer

D-U-N-S 07-199-1244
LIFEMARK HOSPITALS OF MISSOURI
  (Parent: Lifemark Hospitals Inc)
404 Keene St, Columbia, MO 65201
Phone: (573) 875-9000
Sales: $38,600,000 *Employees:* 840
Company Type: Public Family Member *Employees here:* 837
SIC: 8062
  General hospital
Thomas G Neff, Chief Executive Officer

D-U-N-S 08-079-6428
LIFEPATH INC
2014 City Line Rd, Bethlehem, PA 18017
Phone: (610) 264-5724

Sales: $22,151,000   *Employees:* 625
Company Type: Private   *Employees here:* 40
SIC: 8059
  Residential facility for challenged children & adults
David Austin Phd, Executive Director

D-U-N-S 78-280-0577
LIFEQUEST
1021 Park Ave, Quakertown, PA 18951
Phone: (215) 538-4500
Sales: $26,500,000   *Employees:* NA
Company Type: Private   *Employees here:* 545
SIC: 8062
  General hospital
Michael Hammond, Branch Manager

D-U-N-S 17-310-1668
LIFESOURCE BLOOD SERVICES
1205 Milwaukee Ave, Glenview, IL 60025
Phone: (847) 298-9660
Sales: $33,000,000   *Employees:* 450
Company Type: Private   *Employees here:* 374
SIC: 8099
  Blood bank
Patrick G Mourned, President

D-U-N-S 01-292-1818
LIMA MEMORIAL HOSPITAL
1001 Bellefontaine Ave, Lima, OH 45804
Phone: (419) 228-3335
Sales: $81,815,000   *Employees:* NA
Company Type: Private   *Employees here:* NA
SIC: 8062
  General medical & surgical hospital
John White, Chief Executive Officer

D-U-N-S 62-220-4774
LINCARE HOLDINGS INC
19337 US Highway 19 N, Clearwater, FL 33764
Phone: (727) 530-7700
Sales: $443,181,000   *Employees:* 1,200
Company Type: Public   *Employees here:* 65
SIC: 8082
  Home health respiratory therapy & ret home health equip &
    supplies
James T Kelly, Chairman of the Board

D-U-N-S 08-642-1534
LINCARE INC
  (Parent: Lincare Holdings Inc)
19337 US Highway 19 N, Clearwater, FL 33764
Phone: (727) 530-7700
Sales: $400,000,000   *Employees:* 3,500
Company Type: Public Family Member   *Employees here:* 125
SIC: 8082
  Home health respiratory therapy & ret home health
    equipment & supplies
John P Byrnes, President

D-U-N-S 05-660-0190
LINCOLN COMMUNITY MEDICAL CORP
  (Parent: Paracelsus Healthcare Corp)
515 W Greens Rd Ste 800, Houston, TX 77067
Phone: (281) 873-6623
Sales: $20,100,000   *Employees:* 450
Company Type: Public Family Member   *Employees here:* 225
SIC: 8062
  Hospital
Robert Efurd, Administrator

D-U-N-S 07-316-7827
LINCOLN HEALTH SYSTEM INC
401 E Vaughn Ave, Ruston, LA 71270

Phone: (318) 254-2100
Sales: $28,090,000   *Employees:* 510
Company Type: Private   *Employees here:* 510
SIC: 8062
  General medical & surgical hospital
Allen Tuten, President

D-U-N-S 17-603-3025
LINCOLN MEDICAL CENTER
200 Gamble Dr, Lincolnton, NC 28092
Phone: (704) 735-3071
Sales: $36,670,000   *Employees:* 504
Company Type: Private   *Employees here:* 500
SIC: 8062
  General hospital
Peter Acker, Administrator

D-U-N-S 03-044-1398
LINCOLN PK OSTEOPATHIC HOSPITAL ASSN
2021 N 12th St, Grand Junction, CO 81501
Phone: (970) 242-0920
Sales: $22,117,000   *Employees:* 300
Company Type: Private   *Employees here:* 268
SIC: 8062
  General hospital
Joe Boyle, Chief Executive Officer

D-U-N-S 83-754-7017
LINDA LOMA UNIV HEALTH CARE
11215 Mountain View Ave, Loma Linda, CA 92354
Phone: (909) 799-5298
Sales: $102,300,000   *Employees:* 1,100
Company Type: Private   *Employees here:* 850
SIC: 8011
  Provides personnel and admin services to physicians
Dr Roger Hadley Md, President

D-U-N-S 15-731-2620
LINDENGROVE INC
13700 W National Ave, New Berlin, WI 53151
Phone: (414) 797-4600
Sales: $22,061,000   *Employees:* 476
Company Type: Private   *Employees here:* 12
SIC: 8051
  Nursing home
Robert Schaefer, Chief Executive Officer

D-U-N-S 07-188-1684
LINDSAY DISTRICT HOSPITAL
740 Sequoia Ave, Lindsay, CA 93247
Phone: (209) 562-4955
Sales: $105,000,000   *Employees:* 248
Company Type: Private   *Employees here:* 248
SIC: 8062
  General hospital
Edwin Ermshar, Chief Executive Officer

D-U-N-S 17-788-7155
LITTLE CO OF MARY AFFL SVCS
  (Parent: Little Company Of Mary Hospit)
4901 W 79th St, Oak Lawn, IL 60459
Phone: (708) 424-2273
Sales: $147,067,000   *Employees:* 175
Company Type: Private   *Employees here:* 25
SIC: 8099
  Out-patient medical services & physician's office building
Sister C Mc Intyre, President

D-U-N-S 07-785-6029
LITTLE COMPANY OF MARY OF INDIANA
800 W 9th St, Jasper, IN 47546
Phone: (812) 482-2345

Sales: $46,266,000　　　　　　　　*Employees:* 780
Company Type: Private　　　　　　　*Employees here:* 780
SIC: 8062
　General hospital
Sister M Davis, President

D-U-N-S 04-094-0348
LITTLE COMPANY OF MARY HOSP
4101 Torrance Blvd, Torrance, CA 90503
Phone: (310) 540-7676
Sales: $121,842,000　　　　　　　*Employees:* 1,200
Company Type: Private　　　　　　*Employees here:* 1,000
SIC: 8062
　General hospital
Mark Costa, President

D-U-N-S 04-702-2827
LITTLE COMPANY OF MARY HOSP
2800 W 95th St, Chicago, IL 60805
Phone: (708) 422-6200
Sales: $144,536,000　　　　　　*Employees:* 2,300
Company Type: Private　　　　　*Employees here:* 2,000
SIC: 8062
　General hospital
Kathleen Mcintyre Sr, President

D-U-N-S 06-596-3506
LITTLE FLOWER CHLD SVCS OF NY
N Wading River Rd, Wading River, NY 11792
Phone: (516) 929-6200
Sales: $50,524,000　　　　　　　*Employees:* 632
Company Type: Private　　　　　*Employees here:* 371
SIC: 8361
　Non-profit organization providing child & adult care services
Mary Ryder, Executive Director

D-U-N-S 05-378-4138
LITTLE ROCK HEALTH MGT ASSOC
11401 Interstate 30, Little Rock, AR 72209
Phone: (501) 455-7100
Sales: $21,571,000　　　　　　　*Employees:* 306
Company Type: Private　　　　　*Employees here:* 306
SIC: 8062
　General hospital
Tim Hill, President

D-U-N-S 07-599-7346
LOCK HAVEN HOSPITAL
24 Cree Dr, Lock Haven, PA 17745
Phone: (717) 893-5000
Sales: $24,276,000　　　　　　　*Employees:* 410
Company Type: Private　　　　　*Employees here:* 410
SIC: 8062
　General hospital and skilled nursing care
Gary Rhodes, Chief Executive Officer

D-U-N-S 03-863-6874
LOCKPORT MEMORIAL HOSPITAL
521 East Ave, Lockport, NY 14094
Phone: (716) 434-9111
Sales: $35,252,000　　　　　　　*Employees:* 463
Company Type: Private　　　　　*Employees here:* 463
SIC: 8062
　Hospital
Michael J Vlosky, Chief Executive Officer

D-U-N-S 07-467-3807
LODI MEMORIAL HOSPITAL ASSN
975 S Fairmont Ave, Lodi, CA 95240
Phone: (209) 334-3411

Sales: $66,493,000　　　　　　　*Employees:* 950
Company Type: Private　　　　　*Employees here:* 900
SIC: 8062
　General hospital
Joseph P Harrington, Chief Executive Officer

D-U-N-S 07-267-9038
LOGAN MEDICAL FOUNDATION
20 Hospital Dr, Logan, WV 25601
Phone: (304) 792-1101
Sales: $72,925,000　　　　　　　*Employees:* 806
Company Type: Private　　　　　*Employees here:* 803
SIC: 8062
　General hospital and medical clinics
C D Morrison, President

D-U-N-S 07-688-6571
LOMA LINDA UNIVERSITY MED CTR
11234 Anderson St, Loma Linda, CA 92354
Phone: (909) 796-7311
Sales: $487,681,000　　　　　　*Employees:* 4,676
Company Type: Private　　　　*Employees here:* 4,600
SIC: 8062
　Hospital
Dr David Moorehead Md, President

D-U-N-S 07-189-9942
LONG BEACH COMMUNITY HOSPITAL ASSN
1720 Termino Ave, Long Beach, CA 90804
Phone: (562) 498-1000
Sales: $69,108,000　　　　　　　*Employees:* 1,050
Company Type: Private　　　　　*Employees here:* 1,050
SIC: 8062
　General hospital
Janet Parodi, President

D-U-N-S 06-196-1207
LONG BEACH MEDICAL CENTER
455 E Bay Dr, Long Beach, NY 11561
Phone: (516) 897-1000
Sales: $62,241,000　　　　　　　*Employees:* 830
Company Type: Private　　　　　*Employees here:* 776
SIC: 8062
　General medical & surgical hospital
Martin F Nester Jr, Chief Executive Officer

D-U-N-S 13-346-2556
LONG BEACH MEMORIAL MED CTR
2801 Atlantic Ave, Long Beach, CA 90806
Phone: (562) 933-2000
Sales: $520,972,000　　　　　　*Employees:* 4,000
Company Type: Private　　　　*Employees here:* 3,800
SIC: 8062
　General hospital
Tom Collins, President

D-U-N-S 05-935-2799
LONG ISLAND COLLEGE HOSPITAL
339 Hicks St, Brooklyn, NY 11201
Phone: (718) 780-1000
Sales: $125,500,000　　　　　　*Employees:* 2,679
Company Type: Private　　　　*Employees here:* 2,679
SIC: 8062
　General teaching hospital & kidney dialysis center
Harold L Light, President

D-U-N-S 06-474-4014
LONG ISLAND HOME LTD (INC)
400 Sunrise Hwy, Amityville, NY 11701
Phone: (516) 264-4000

Sales: $57,384,000   *Employees:* 925
Company Type: Private   *Employees here:* 925
SIC: 8063
  Psychiatric hospital & nursing home
Jean P Smith, Chief Executive Officer

D-U-N-S 06-472-7027
LONG ISLAND JEWISH MED CTR
27005 76th Ave, New Hyde Park, NY 11040
Phone: (718) 470-7000
Sales: $476,737,000   *Employees:* 6,700
Company Type: Private   *Employees here:* 5,433
SIC: 8062
  General hospitals psychiatric hospital and children's hospital
David Dantzker, President

D-U-N-S 07-851-0575
LONG ISLAND JEWISH MED CTR
7559 263rd St, Floral Park, NY 11004
Phone: (718) 470-8000
Sales: $39,800,000   *Employees:* NA
Company Type: Private   *Employees here:* 1,000
SIC: 8063
  Psychiatric hospital
Henry Hoffman, Branch Manager

D-U-N-S 19-616-1392
LONG LIFE HOME CARE SERVICES
2581 Atlantic Ave, Brooklyn, NY 11207
Phone: (718) 385-2400
Sales: $24,800,000   *Employees:* 1,545
Company Type: Private   *Employees here:* 1,545
SIC: 8082
  Home health care service
Rosie Baker, President

D-U-N-S 05-683-3833
LONGMONT UNITED HOSPITAL
1950 W Mountain View Ave, Longmont, CO 80501
Phone: (303) 651-5111
Sales: $54,562,000   *Employees:* 800
Company Type: Private   *Employees here:* 783
SIC: 8062
  General hospital
Kenneth R Huey, Chief Executive Officer

D-U-N-S 18-791-5277
LONGVIEW REGIONAL HOSPITAL
  (Parent: Columbia/Hca Healthcare Corp)
2901 N 4th St, Longview, TX 75605
Phone: (903) 758-1818
Sales: $27,200,000   *Employees:* 600
Company Type: Public Family Member   *Employees here:* 598
SIC: 8062
  General hospital
Velinda Stevens, Chief Executive Officer

D-U-N-S 08-008-0831
LONGWOOD MANAGEMENT CORP
4032 Wilshire Blvd Fl 6, Los Angeles, CA 90010
Phone: (213) 389-6900
Sales: $44,600,000   *Employees:* 2,000
Company Type: Private   *Employees here:* 25
SIC: 8059
  Convalescent & retirement homes
Jacob Friedman, President

D-U-N-S 02-520-9461
LORETTO HOSPITAL
645 S Central Ave, Chicago, IL 60644
Phone: (773) 626-4300

Sales: $24,900,000   *Employees:* 550
Company Type: Private   *Employees here:* 550
SIC: 8062
  General psychiatric and addiction hospital
Steven Drucker, President

D-U-N-S 18-517-6203
LORETTO REST NURSING HOME CO
750 E Brighton Ave, Syracuse, NY 13205
Phone: (315) 469-5561
Sales: $22,400,000   *Employees:* NA
Company Type: Private   *Employees here:* 850
SIC: 8361
  Residential care services
James Introne, President

D-U-N-S 08-614-1090
LORIEN NRSING RHBILITATION CTR
1205 York Rd, Lutherville Timonium, MD 21093
Phone: (410) 825-8400
Sales: $20,000,000   *Employees:* 300
Company Type: Private   *Employees here:* 5
SIC: 8051
  Convalescent home with health care
Louis Grimmel, President

D-U-N-S 07-370-6277
LORIS COMMUNITY HOSPITAL
3655 Mitchell St, Loris, SC 29569
Phone: (843) 756-4011
Sales: $28,714,000   *Employees:* 570
Company Type: Private   *Employees here:* 570
SIC: 8062
  General hospital with skilled nursing facilities
Alton Ewing, Administrator

D-U-N-S 11-312-1024
LOS ANGELE DEV SERV
3440 Wilshire Blvd, Los Angeles, CA 90010
Phone: (213) 383-1300
Sales: $33,923,000   *Employees:* 100
Company Type: Private   *Employees here:* 100
SIC: 8099
  Human service center
Dianne Anand, Executive Director

D-U-N-S 09-862-5437
LOS ANGELES DOCTORS HOSPITAL
  (Parent: Pacific Health Corporation)
2231 S Western Ave, Los Angeles, CA 90018
Phone: (323) 737-7372
Sales: $30,094,000   *Employees:* 450
Company Type: Private   *Employees here:* 450
SIC: 8062
  General hospital
Marc Furstman, Chief Executive Officer

D-U-N-S 78-157-9347
LOS ANGELES, COUNTY OF
1200 N State St Rm 1201, Los Angeles, CA 90033
Phone: (323) 226-5566
Sales: $59,400,000   *Employees:* NA
Company Type: Private   *Employees here:* 1,500
SIC: 8063
  Psychiatric hospital
Raul Caro, Manager

D-U-N-S 05-803-4992
LOS ROBLES REGIONAL MED CTR
  (Parent: Columbia/Hca Healthcare Corp)
215 W Janss Rd, Thousand Oaks, CA 91360
Phone: (805) 497-2727

Sales: $97,205,000   *Employees:* 800
Company Type: Public Family Member   *Employees here:* 800
SIC: 8062
  General medical & surgical hospital
Jerry Spencer, Vice-Chairman of the Board

D-U-N-S 18-051-0281
LOUDOUN HEALTHCARE INC
44045 Riverside Pkwy, Leesburg, VA 20176
Phone: (703) 777-3300
Sales: $75,805,000   *Employees:* NA
Company Type: Private   *Employees here:* NA
SIC: 8062
  Through subsidiary operates hospital
G T Ecker, President

D-U-N-S 06-936-5807
LOUDOUN HOSPITAL CENTER
224 Cornwall St Nw, Leesburg, VA 20176
Phone: (703) 777-3300
Sales: $53,615,000   *Employees:* 800
Company Type: Private   *Employees here:* 770
SIC: 8062
  General hospital
G T Ecker, President

D-U-N-S 06-949-0662
LOUIS A WEISS MEMORIAL HOSP
4646 N Marine Dr, Chicago, IL 60640
Phone: (773) 878-8700
Sales: $96,233,000   *Employees:* 1,100
Company Type: Private   *Employees here:* 1,100
SIC: 8062
  General medical & surgical hospital
Gregory A Cierlik, President

D-U-N-S 07-793-4461
LOUISE OBICI MEMORIAL HOSP
1900 N Main St, Suffolk, VA 23434
Phone: (757) 934-4000
Sales: $56,756,000   *Employees:* 1,130
Company Type: Private   *Employees here:* 1,120
SIC: 8062
  General hospital
William C Giermak, President

D-U-N-S 05-112-3271
LOUISIANA DEPT HEALTH HOSPITALS
Hwy 10, Jackson, LA 70748
Phone: (225) 634-2651
Sales: $23,800,000   *Employees:* NA
Company Type: Private   *Employees here:* 630
SIC: 8062
  General hospital
Fred Calcote, Branch Manager

D-U-N-S 08-891-8156
LOUISIANA DEPT HEALTH HOSPITALS
1978 Industrial Blvd, Houma, LA 70363
Phone: (504) 868-8140
Sales: $30,400,000   *Employees:* NA
Company Type: Private   *Employees here:* 742
SIC: 8062
  General hospital ret gifts/novelties
Danny Trahan, Principal

D-U-N-S 15-075-9678
LOUISIANA EXTENDED CARE CTRS
763 N Avery Blvd, Ridgeland, MS 39157
Phone: (601) 956-8884

Sales: $36,671,000   *Employees:* 487
Company Type: Private   *Employees here:* 4
SIC: 8051
  Skilled & intermediate care nursing homes
Glynn Beebe, President

D-U-N-S 06-974-5073
LOUISIANA STATE UNIV SYS
1501 Kings Hwy 1541, Shreveport, LA 71103
Phone: (318) 674-5240
Sales: $145,100,000   *Employees:* NA
Company Type: Private   *Employees here:* 3,500
SIC: 8062
  Hospital
Gene Hammett, Administrator

D-U-N-S 07-409-7791
LOURDES
1530 Lone Oak Rd, Paducah, KY 42003
Phone: (502) 444-2444
Sales: $99,498,000   *Employees:* 1,300
Company Type: Private   *Employees here:* 1,096
SIC: 8062
  General hospital
Bob Goodwin, Chief Executive Officer

D-U-N-S 60-279-1881
LOVELACE HEALTH SYSTEMS INC
  (Parent: Cigna Health Corporation)
5400 Gibson Blvd SE, Albuquerque, NM 87108
Phone: (505) 262-7000
Sales: $334,282,000   *Employees:* 3,183
Company Type: Public Family Member   *Employees here:* 1,967
SIC: 8011
  Health maintenance organization acute care hospital &
    outpatient medical clinic
Dr Martin Hickey, Chief Executive Officer

D-U-N-S 01-944-1377
LOWELL GENERAL HOSPITAL
295 Varnum Ave, Lowell, MA 1854
Phone: (978) 937-6000
Sales: $80,133,000   *Employees:* 1,200
Company Type: Private   *Employees here:* 1,200
SIC: 8062
  General hospital
Clementine Alexis, Chairman of the Board

D-U-N-S 78-647-4049
LOWER FLA KEYS HEALTH SYSTEMS
5900 College Rd, Key West, FL 33040
Phone: (305) 294-4692
Sales: $21,900,000   *Employees:* 487
Company Type: Private   *Employees here:* 427
SIC: 8062
  Hospital
Roberto Sanchez, Administrator

D-U-N-S 11-020-9681
LRIMG, INC
15215 National Ave, Los Gatos, CA 95032
Phone: (408) 358-1841
Sales: $109,630,000   *Employees:* 16
Company Type: Private   *Employees here:* 16
SIC: 8011
  Physician's office
Dr Dennis Penner Md, President

D-U-N-S 07-166-0492
LUBBOCK COUNTY HOSPITAL DST
602 Indiana Ave, Lubbock, TX 79415
Phone: (806) 743-3111

Sales: $96,004,000
Employees: 1,750
Company Type: Private
Employees here: 1,625
SIC: 8062
  Hospital
Jim Courtney, President

D-U-N-S 83-609-6990
LUBBOCK METHDST HOSPITAL SVCS INC
3615 19th St, Lubbock, TX 79410
Phone: (806) 784-1260
Sales: $66,198,000
Employees: 120
Company Type: Private
Employees here: 2
SIC: 8071
  Clinical laboratories magnetic resonance imaging service
Jim Houser, President

D-U-N-S 04-092-2585
LUBBOCK METHODIST HOSPITAL PRA
2107 Oxford Ave Ste 300, Lubbock, TX 79410
Phone: (806) 784-1260
Sales: $41,502,000
Employees: 157
Company Type: Private
Employees here: 100
SIC: 8011
  Medical clinics
Jim Wurts, Chief Operating Officer

D-U-N-S 09-878-6460
LUBBOCK REGIONAL
1602 10th St, Lubbock, TX 79401
Phone: (806) 766-0310
Sales: $21,963,000
Employees: 325
Company Type: Private
Employees here: 90
SIC: 8093
  Outpatient care facility
Danette Castle, Chief Executive Officer

D-U-N-S 92-642-3310
LUCERNE MEDICAL CENTER
  (*Parent:* Columbia Pk Healthcare Systems)
818 Main Ln, Orlando, FL 32801
Phone: (407) 649-6111
Sales: $79,534,000
Employees: 800
Company Type: Private
Employees here: 790
SIC: 8062
  General hospital
Rick O Connell, President

D-U-N-S 07-590-9465
LUCY LEE HOSPITAL INC
  (*Parent:* Tenet Health System Medical)
2620 N Westwood Blvd, Poplar Bluff, MO 63901
Phone: (573) 785-7721
Sales: $54,033,000
Employees: 1,000
Company Type: Public Family Member
Employees here: 750
SIC: 8062
  General hospital
William L Bradley, Director

D-U-N-S 07-482-8344
LUCY W HAYES TRNG SCH DCNS MSN
5255 Loughboro Rd Nw, Washington, DC 20016
Phone: (202) 537-4000
Sales: $65,000,000
Employees: 1,400
Company Type: Private
Employees here: 1,300
SIC: 8062
  General hospital
Robert L Sloan, Administrator

D-U-N-S 06-815-7601
LUTHER HOSPITAL
1221 Whipple St, Eau Claire, WI 54703
Phone: (715) 839-3311

Sales: $58,400,000
Employees: 1,260
Company Type: Private
Employees here: 1,200
SIC: 8062
  Hospital & ret drugs & medical equipment
Dr William Rupp, President

D-U-N-S 09-415-3541
LUTHERAN
2000 Boise Ave, Loveland, CO 80538
Phone: (970) 669-4640
Sales: $25,500,000
Employees: NA
Company Type: Private
Employees here: 800
SIC: 8062
  General hospital
Charles F Harms, N/A

D-U-N-S 09-146-0006
LUTHERAN CENTER FOR THE AGING
Rr 25 Box A, Smithtown, NY 11787
Phone: (516) 724-2200
Sales: $25,455,000
Employees: 400
Company Type: Private
Employees here: 400
SIC: 8051
  Skilled nursing facility
Gary Kleinberg, Administrator

D-U-N-S 05-539-9786
LUTHERAN GENERAL HOSPITAL
1775 Dempster St, Park Ridge, IL 60068
Phone: (847) 696-2210
Sales: $335,000,000
Employees: 4,110
Company Type: Private
Employees here: 4,000
SIC: 8062
  General hospital
Keneth J Rojek, President

D-U-N-S 07-988-9887
LUTHERAN HEALTH CARE ASSN
709 S Laclede Station Rd, Saint Louis, MO 63119
Phone: (314) 968-9313
Sales: $19,759,000
Employees: 500
Company Type: Private
Employees here: 300
SIC: 8059
  Assisted and retirement living facility and operates skilled
    nursing home
Carl A Rausch, President

D-U-N-S 02-013-7824
LUTHERAN HEALTH SYSTEM
6644 E Baywood Ave, Mesa, AZ 85206
Phone: (602) 981-2000
Sales: $35,800,000
Employees: NA
Company Type: Private
Employees here: 833
SIC: 8062
  General hospital
Robert Rundio, N/A

D-U-N-S 61-306-0722
LUTHERAN HEALTH SYSTEM
525 W Brown Rd, Mesa, AZ 85201
Phone: (602) 461-2301
Sales: $75,100,000
Employees: NA
Company Type: Private
Employees here: 3,300
SIC: 8361
  Residential care services
Bob Rundio, Director

D-U-N-S 13-457-9374
LUTHERAN HEALTH SYSTEM
2000 Boise Ave, Loveland, CO 80538
Phone: (970) 669-4640

Sales: $25,500,000

Employees: NA

Company Type: Private

Employees here: 600

SIC: 8062
   Hospital
Charles Harms, Administrator

D-U-N-S 07-175-3982
LUTHERAN HEALTH SYSTEM
4310 17th Ave SW, Fargo, ND 58103
Phone: (701) 277-7500
Sales: $665,313,000

Employees: 14,707

Company Type: Private

Employees here: 220

SIC: 8062
   Hospitals skilled care nursing homes & personal care
      retirement home
Steven Orr, Chairman of the Board

D-U-N-S 07-663-3387
LUTHERAN HEALTH SYSTEMS
1650 Cowles St, Fairbanks, AK 99701
Phone: (907) 458-5335
Sales: $26,800,000

Employees: NA

Company Type: Private

Employees here: 900

SIC: 8062
   General hospital
James H Gingerich, N/A

D-U-N-S 15-183-0536
LUTHERAN HEALTH SYSTEMS
525 W Brown Rd, Mesa, AZ 85201
Phone: (602) 461-8161
Sales: $69,700,000

Employees: NA

Company Type: Private

Employees here: 1,608

SIC: 8062
   Hospital
Jim Marovich, Branch Manager

D-U-N-S 18-265-3295
LUTHERAN HEALTH SYSTEMS
525 W Brown Rd, Mesa, AZ 85201
Phone: (602) 461-2745
Sales: $60,600,000

Employees: NA

Company Type: Private

Employees here: 1,400

SIC: 8062
   General hospital
Don Evans, Principal

D-U-N-S 07-144-6041
LUTHERAN HOME AT TOPTON PA INC
1 S Home Ave, Topton, PA 19562
Phone: (610) 682-2145
Sales: $29,909,000

Employees: 700

Company Type: Private

Employees here: 350

SIC: 8361
   Services the aged and provides home health care adoption
      foster care meals on wheels teenage pregnancy care &
      counseling
Rev Daun E Mckee Phd, President

D-U-N-S 07-690-3129
LUTHERAN HOSPITAL
1730 W 25th St, Cleveland, OH 44113
Phone: (216) 696-4300
Sales: $42,302,000

Employees: 880

Company Type: Private

Employees here: 800

SIC: 8062
   General hospital
Thomas La Motte, President

D-U-N-S 05-560-4896
LUTHERAN MEDICAL CENTER
8300 W 38th Ave, Wheat Ridge, CO 80033
Phone: (303) 425-4500

Sales: $150,437,000

Employees: 2,600

Company Type: Private

Employees here: 2,200

SIC: 8062
   General hospital and medical clinics
Jeffrey Belbert, President

D-U-N-S 06-829-2572
LUTHERAN MEDICAL CENTER
150 55th St, Brooklyn, NY 11220
Phone: (718) 630-7000
Sales: $121,800,000

Employees: 2,600

Company Type: Private

Employees here: 2,500

SIC: 8062
   Hospital
Joe Cerni, President

D-U-N-S 07-469-1015
LUTHERAN SOCIAL SERV-MIAMI VALLEY
6445 Far Hills Ave, Dayton, OH 45459
Phone: (937) 433-2140
Sales: $26,363,000

Employees: 850

Company Type: Private

Employees here: 550

SIC: 8051
   Nursing home
Willis O Serr Ii, Executive Director

D-U-N-S 14-751-9078
LUTHERAN SOCIAL SERVICES OF IL
(Parent: Lutheran Social Svcs Of Ill)
1001 E Touhy Ave Ste 50, Des Plaines, IL 60018
Phone: (847) 635-4600
Sales: $52,873,000

Employees: 3,000

Company Type: Private

Employees here: 3,000

SIC: 8361
   Residential care services
Rev Donald M Hallberg, President

D-U-N-S 06-945-8149
LUTHERAN SOCIAL SVCS OF S INC
408 W 45th St, Austin, TX 78751
Phone: (512) 459-1000
Sales: $36,688,000

Employees: 1,079

Company Type: Private

Employees here: 31

SIC: 8051
   Nursing homes & alternative living and children services
Dr Kurt Senske, President

D-U-N-S 06-974-9679
M C S A, L.L.C.
700 W Grove St, El Dorado, AR 71730
Phone: (870) 864-3290
Sales: $40,000,000

Employees: 700

Company Type: Private

Employees here: 653

SIC: 8062
   Hospital
Luther J Lewis, Chief Executive Officer

D-U-N-S 62-341-8308
M H HEALTH CARE INC
6640 Parkdale Pl Ste J, Indianapolis, IN 46254
Phone: (317) 328-7100
Sales: $99,068,000

Employees: 560

Company Type: Private

Employees here: 90

SIC: 8011
   Medical center group practice
Steve Pollom, President

D-U-N-S 06-828-9867
M J G NURSING HOME CO INC
6323 7th Ave, Brooklyn, NY 11220
Phone: (718) 921-8067

Sales: $52,821,000   *Employees:* 730
Company Type: Private   *Employees here:* 7
SIC: 8051
 Skilled nursing home
Mark Goldstein, President

D-U-N-S 10-868-9787
M V P HEALTH PLAN INC
111 Liberty St, Schenectady, NY 12305
Phone: (518) 370-4793
Sales: $356,964,000   *Employees:* 570
Company Type: Private   *Employees here:* 287
SIC: 8011
 Health maintenance organization
David Oliker, President

D-U-N-S 18-486-3074
M-CARE INC
2301 Commonwealth Blvd, Ann Arbor, MI 48105
Phone: (734) 747-8700
Sales: $155,357,000   *Employees:* 300
Company Type: Private   *Employees here:* 100
SIC: 8011
 Health maintenance organization
Ray Haggerty, President

D-U-N-S 12-801-1459
MACGREGOR MEDICAL ASSN P A
2550 Holly Hall St, Houston, TX 77054
Phone: (713) 741-2273
Sales: $103,400,000   *Employees:* 1,500
Company Type: Private   *Employees here:* 250
SIC: 8011
 Out-patient clinic
Dr James Birge, President

D-U-N-S 07-018-0245
MADERA COMMUNITY HOSPITAL INC
1250 E Almond Ave, Madera, CA 93637
Phone: (209) 673-5101
Sales: $34,305,000   *Employees:* 500
Company Type: Private   *Employees here:* 485
SIC: 8062
 General hospital
Robert C Kelley, Chief Executive Officer

D-U-N-S 04-091-2479
MADONNA REHABILITATION HOSP
5401 South St, Lincoln, NE 68506
Phone: (402) 489-7102
Sales: $32,043,000   *Employees:* 820
Company Type: Private   *Employees here:* 820
SIC: 8069
 Speciality hospital
Marsha Halpern, President

D-U-N-S 06-904-2406
MAGEE REHABILITATION HOSPITAL
6 Franklin Blvd, Philadelphia, PA 19154
Phone: (215) 587-3000
Sales: $26,777,000   *Employees:* 455
Company Type: Private   *Employees here:* 430
SIC: 8069
 Rehabilitation hospital
William Staas, Chief Executive Officer

D-U-N-S 07-215-9460
MAGEE-WOMENS HOSPITAL
300 Halket St, Pittsburgh, PA 15213
Phone: (412) 641-1000

Sales: $129,930,000   *Employees:* 1,953
Company Type: Private   *Employees here:* 1,800
SIC: 8062
 General hospital
Irma E Goertzen, President

D-U-N-S 02-249-2370
MAGELLA HEALTHCARE CORPORATION
2595 Dallas Pkwy Ste 400, Frisco, TX 75034
Phone: (972) 731-1440
Sales: $45,000,000   *Employees:* 150
Company Type: Private   *Employees here:* 12
SIC: 8011
 Physicians' office
John K Carlyle, President

D-U-N-S 04-969-3732
MAGELLAN HEALTH SERVICES INC
3414 Peachtree Rd NE, Atlanta, GA 30326
Phone: (404) 841-9200
Sales: $1,210,696,000   *Employees:* 5,000
Company Type: Public   *Employees here:* 75
SIC: 8093
 Behavioral managed care services
Henry T Harbin, President

D-U-N-S 07-297-7911
MAGIC VALLEY REGIONAL MED CTR
650 Addison Ave W, Twin Falls, ID 83301
Phone: (208) 737-2000
Sales: $52,551,000   *Employees:* 775
Company Type: Private   *Employees here:* 775
SIC: 8062
 General medical hospital-pschiatric hospital
John Bingham, Administrator

D-U-N-S 07-859-2417
MAGNOLIA REGIONAL HEALTH CTR
611 Alcorn Dr, Corinth, MS 38834
Phone: (601) 293-1000
Sales: $64,292,000   *Employees:* 800
Company Type: Private   *Employees here:* 800
SIC: 8062
 General hospital
Doug Garner, Chief Executive Officer

D-U-N-S 05-738-1535
MAIMONIDES MEDICAL CENTER
4802 10th Ave, Brooklyn, NY 11219
Phone: (718) 283-6000
Sales: $429,537,000   *Employees:* 3,950
Company Type: Private   *Employees here:* 3,950
SIC: 8062
 General hospital
Stanley Brezenoff, President

D-U-N-S 00-289-0676
MAIN LINE HOSPITALS
100 E Lancaster Ave, Wynnewood, PA 19096
Phone: (610) 645-2000
Sales: $76,100,000   *Employees:* NA
Company Type: Private   *Employees here:* 1,531
SIC: 8062
 Hospital

D-U-N-S 00-289-3498
MAIN LINE HOSPITALS
255 W Lancaster Ave, Paoli, PA 19301
Phone: (610) 648-1000
Sales: $26,000,000   *Employees:* NA
Company Type: Private   *Employees here:* 535
SIC: 8062
 Hospital

D-U-N-S 07-548-4121
MAIN LINE HOSPITALS
130 S Bryn Mawr Ave, Bryn Mawr, PA 19010
Phone: (610) 526-3000
Sales: $309,285,000   *Employees:* 3,353
Company Type: Private   *Employees here:* 1,287
SIC: 8062
  General medical & surgical hospital
Kenneth Hanover, President

D-U-N-S 07-174-4486
MAINE CAST RGNAL HEALTH FCLTIES
50 Union St, Ellsworth, ME 4605
Phone: (207) 667-5311
Sales: $29,224,000   *Employees:* 245
Company Type: Private   *Employees here:* 225
SIC: 8062
  General hospital
Paul Barrette, President

D-U-N-S 07-174-6994
MAINE GENERAL REHABILITATION &
37 Graybirch Dr, Augusta, ME 4330
Phone: (207) 622-6226
Sales: $79,388,000   *Employees:* 230
Company Type: Private   *Employees here:* 100
SIC: 8052
  Intermediate & skilled nursing home
Warren C Kesseler, President

D-U-N-S 07-173-2663
MAINE MEDICAL CENTER
22 Bramhall St, Portland, ME 4102
Phone: (207) 871-0111
Sales: $343,324,000   *Employees:* 5,000
Company Type: Private   *Employees here:* 4,200
SIC: 8062
  General hospital medical laboratories and property
Vincent Conti, President

D-U-N-S 10-119-1526
MAINE VETERANS HOME
45 Memorial Dr, Augusta, ME 4330
Phone: (207) 622-2454
Sales: $20,696,000   *Employees:* 485
Company Type: Private   *Employees here:* 25
SIC: 8052
  Skilled nursing care facility
Henry Lobl, Chief Executive Officer

D-U-N-S 07-746-1754
MAINEGENERAL MEDICAL CENTER,
6 E Chestnut St, Augusta, ME 4330
Phone: (207) 626-1000
Sales: $59,086,000   *Employees:* 967
Company Type: Private   *Employees here:* 950
SIC: 8062
  General hospital
Scott Bullock, Chief Executive Officer

D-U-N-S 00-989-7372
MANAGED CARE ASSISTANCE CORP
11821 Parklawn Dr Ste Ll, Rockville, MD 20852
Phone: (301) 984-1681
Sales: $65,000,000   *Employees:* 25
Company Type: Private   *Employees here:* 25
SIC: 8099
  Health/allied services
Michael Barch, President

D-U-N-S 87-672-4444
MANAGED CARE USA, INC
4401 Barclay Downs Dr, Charlotte, NC 28209

Phone: (704) 945-2600
Sales: $46,051,000   *Employees:* 155
Company Type: Private   *Employees here:* 110
SIC: 8099
  Managed health care
Steven M Mariano, Chairman of the Board

D-U-N-S 93-831-7419
MANAGED HEALTHCARE SYSTEMS NJ
  (Parent: Americhoice Corporation)
1 Gateway Ctr, Newark, NJ 7102
Phone: (973) 645-0800
Sales: $32,483,000   *Employees:* 33
Company Type: Private   *Employees here:* 33
SIC: 8011
  Health maintenance organization
Karen L Clark, President

D-U-N-S 80-793-6125
MANAGED HEALTHCARE SYSTEMS OF NY
  (Parent: Americhoice Corporation)
7 Hanover Sq Fl 5, New York, NY 10004
Phone: (212) 509-5999
Sales: $65,528,000   *Employees:* 119
Company Type: Private   *Employees here:* 119
SIC: 8099
  Health maintenance organization
Karen L Clark, President

D-U-N-S 06-025-9314
MANATAEE MEM HOSPITAL LTD PARTNR
206 2nd St E, Bradenton, FL 34208
Phone: (941) 746-5111
Sales: $65,000,000   *Employees:* 1,400
Company Type: Private   *Employees here:* 1,260
SIC: 8062
  General hospital
Michael J Marquez, President

D-U-N-S 06-499-3389
MANHATTAN EYE EAR THROAT HOSP
210 E 64th St, New York, NY 10021
Phone: (212) 838-9200
Sales: $39,936,000   *Employees:* 480
Company Type: Private   *Employees here:* 473
SIC: 8069
  Eye ear nose & throat hospital
George A Sarkar Phd, Executive Director

D-U-N-S 61-347-5672
MANHATTAN PREPAID HEALTH SVC PLAN
555 W 57th St Fl 18, New York, NY 10019
Phone: (212) 293-9200
Sales: $23,048,000   *Employees:* 45
Company Type: Private   *Employees here:* 45
SIC: 8011
  Nonprofit prepaid health services plan
William J White, Chief Operating Officer

D-U-N-S 15-135-0378
MANHATTAN PSYCHIATRIC CENTER
Wards Is, New York, NY 10035
Phone: (212) 369-0500
Sales: $57,400,000   *Employees:* 1,550
Company Type: Private   *Employees here:* 50
SIC: 8063
  Psychiatric hospital
Dr Michael Ford Md, Executive Director

D-U-N-S 06-047-3790
MANKATO CLINIC, LTD
1230 E Main St, Mankato, MN 56001
Phone: (507) 625-1811

Sales: $34,300,000   *Employees:* 500
Company Type: Private   *Employees here:* 425
SIC: 8011
 Medical clinics
Roger Greenwald, Administrator

D-U-N-S 08-355-4717
MANN BERKLEY EYE CENTER, PA
1200 Binz St Ste 1000, Houston, TX 77004
Phone: (713) 526-1600
Sales: $25,000,000   *Employees:* 150
Company Type: Private   *Employees here:* 65
SIC: 8011
 Ophthalmologist & optometrist
Dr Ralph G Berkeley Md, President

D-U-N-S 04-831-4108
MANORCARE HEALTH SERVICES INC
 (Parent: Manor Care Inc)
11555 Darnestown Rd, Gaithersburg, MD 20878
Phone: (301) 979-3000
Sales: $1,524,173,000   *Employees:* 30,000
Company Type: Public Family Member   *Employees here:* 200
SIC: 8051
 Nursing homes
Stewart Bainum Jr, Chairman of the Board

D-U-N-S 07-727-7507
MARATHON H M A INC
 (Parent: Health Management Associates)
3301 Overseas Hwy, Marathon, FL 33050
Phone: (305) 743-5533
Sales: $21,031,000   *Employees:* 135
Company Type: Public Family Member   *Employees here:* 135
SIC: 8062
 General medical hospital
William J Schoen, Chairman of the Board

D-U-N-S 07-448-3173
MARCUS J LAWRENCE MEDICAL CTR
202 S Willard St, Cottonwood, AZ 86326
Phone: (520) 634-2251
Sales: $33,379,000   *Employees:* 460
Company Type: Private   *Employees here:* 444
SIC: 8062
 Medical & surgical hospital
Rita Poindexter, President

D-U-N-S 07-743-4587
MARGARET MARY COMMUNITY HOSP
321 Mitchell Ave, Batesville, IN 47006
Phone: (812) 934-6624
Sales: $21,736,000   *Employees:* 400
Company Type: Private   *Employees here:* 400
SIC: 8062
 General medical & surgical hospital & skilled care facility
James Amos, Administrator

D-U-N-S 07-451-2559
MARGARET R PARDEE MEM HOSP
715 Fleming St, Hendersonville, NC 28791
Phone: (828) 696-1000
Sales: $68,735,000   *Employees:* 936
Company Type: Private   *Employees here:* 936
SIC: 8062
 General hospital and skilled nursing care facility
Frank J Aaron Jr, Chief Executive Officer

D-U-N-S 07-557-2016
MARIA PARHAM HOSPITAL ASSN
566 Ruin Creek Rd, Henderson, NC 27536
Phone: (252) 438-4143

Sales: $31,379,000   *Employees:* 373
Company Type: Private   *Employees here:* 373
SIC: 8062
 General hospital
Phil Lakernick, President

D-U-N-S 07-915-8762
MARIAN COMMUNITY HOSPITAL
100 Lincoln Ave, Carbondale, PA 18407
Phone: (717) 282-2100
Sales: $26,358,000   *Employees:* 450
Company Type: Private   *Employees here:* 450
SIC: 8062
 General medical & surgical hospital
Sist Jean Coughlin, President

D-U-N-S 07-975-6789
MARIANJOY INC
26 W 171 Roosevelt Rd, Wheaton, IL 60187
Phone: (630) 462-4000
Sales: $32,554,000   *Employees:* 800
Company Type: Private   *Employees here:* 450
SIC: 8069
 Physical rehabilitation hospital
Bruce Schurman, President

D-U-N-S 15-374-9585
MARIETTA AREA HEALTH CARE INC
401 Matthew St, Marietta, OH 45750
Phone: (740) 374-4500
Sales: $60,857,000   *Employees:* 815
Company Type: Private   *Employees here:* 814
SIC: 8062
 General medical and surgical hospital
Larry Unroe, President

D-U-N-S 06-871-7859
MARIETTA MEMORIAL HOSPITAL
401 Matthew St, Marietta, OH 45750
Phone: (740) 374-1400
Sales: $56,411,000   *Employees:* 800
Company Type: Private   *Employees here:* 800
SIC: 8062
 General hospital
Larry Unroe, President

D-U-N-S 06-885-8851
MARIN GENERAL HOSPITAL
250 Bon Air Rd, Greenbrae, CA 94904
Phone: (415) 925-7000
Sales: $106,431,000   *Employees:* 1,100
Company Type: Private   *Employees here:* 1,100
SIC: 8062
 General hospital
Henry J Buhrmann, President

D-U-N-S 13-220-3217
MARINER HEALTH OF MARYLAND,
 (Parent: Mariner Health Of Maryland)
4041 Powder Mill Rd, Beltsville, MD 20705
Phone: (301) 937-3030
Sales: $33,400,000   *Employees:* 1,500
Company Type: Public Family Member   *Employees here:* 5
SIC: 8059
 Nursing home
Dr Arthur W Stratton Md, President

D-U-N-S 06-725-7501
MARINER POST-ACUTE NETWORK,
1 Ravinia Dr, Atlanta, GA 30346
Phone: (770) 393-0199

Sales: $3,000,000,000   *Employees:* 62,000
Company Type: Public   *Employees here:* 250
SIC: 8051
    Operates long term health care facilities & mentally retarded
      facilities rehabilitation therapy services
Keith B Pitts, Chairman of the Board

D-U-N-S 78-468-6479
MARINER REHABILITATION SVCS
    (Parent: Mariner Post-Acute Network)
1633 Church St Ste 160, Nashville, TN 37203
Phone: (615) 320-7302
Sales: $23,300,000
Company Type: Public Family Member   *Employees:* NA
SIC: 8049   *Employees here:* NA
    Physical speech & occupational therapy
Arthur Stratton, President

D-U-N-S 01-082-5271
MARION COMMUNITY HOSPITAL INC
    (Parent: Columbia/Hca Healthcare Corp)
1431 SW 1st Ave, Ocala, FL 34474
Phone: (352) 401-1000
Sales: $46,100,000   *Employees:* 1,000
Company Type: Public Family Member   *Employees here:* 1,000
SIC: 8062
    General medical hospital
Steve Maham, Chief Executive Officer

D-U-N-S 62-176-8977
MARION COUNTY HOSPITAL DST
2829 E Highway 76, Mullins, SC 29574
Phone: (843) 431-2000
Sales: $89,400,000   *Employees:* 646
Company Type: Private   *Employees here:* 550
SIC: 8062
    General hospital nursing home
Clem Ham, Chief Executive Officer

D-U-N-S 07-596-3397
MARION GENERAL HOSPITAL INC
441 N Wabash Ave, Marion, IN 46952
Phone: (765) 662-1441
Sales: $80,815,000   *Employees:* 1,100
Company Type: Private   *Employees here:* 1,097
SIC: 8062
    General hospital
Albert C Knauss, President

D-U-N-S 06-906-5449
MARION GENERAL HOSPITAL INC
Mc Kinley Park Dr, Marion, OH 43302
Phone: (740) 383-8400
Sales: $51,594,000   *Employees:* 1,250
Company Type: Private   *Employees here:* 858
SIC: 8062
    General hospital
Frank Swinehart, President

D-U-N-S 07-172-3472
MARLBOROUGH HOSPITAL
57 Union St, Marlborough, MA 1752
Phone: (508) 485-1121
Sales: $32,005,000   *Employees:* 533
Company Type: Private   *Employees here:* 533
SIC: 8062
    Hospital
Anne Bourgeois, Chief Executive Officer

D-U-N-S 07-477-8614
MARQUETTE GENERAL HOSPITAL
420 W Magnetic St, Marquette, MI 49855
Phone: (906) 228-9440

Sales: $145,912,000   *Employees:* 1,950
Company Type: Private   *Employees here:* 1,857
SIC: 8062
    General hospital
William R Nemacheck, Chief Executive Officer

D-U-N-S 07-896-2719
MARSHALL HEALTHCARE AUTHORITY
Hwy 431, Boaz, AL 35957
Phone: (256) 593-8310
Sales: $44,744,000   *Employees:* 608
Company Type: Private   *Employees here:* 600
SIC: 8062
    General hospital
Marlin Hanson, Chief Executive Officer

D-U-N-S 06-780-5069
MARSHALL HOSPITAL
Marshall Way, Placerville, CA 95667
Phone: (530) 622-1441
Sales: $54,180,000   *Employees:* 800
Company Type: Private   *Employees here:* 760
SIC: 8062
    General hospital home health and outpatient x-ray &
      laboratory
Frank Nachtman, Administrator

D-U-N-S 07-896-2834
MARSHALL MEDICAL CENTER NORTH
8000 Al Highway 69, Guntersville, AL 35976
Phone: (256) 571-8000
Sales: $26,137,000   *Employees:* 450
Company Type: Private   *Employees here:* 450
SIC: 8062
    General medical and surgical hospital
Gary Gore, Administrator

D-U-N-S 07-584-1296
MARSHALLTOWN MED SURGICAL CTR
3 S 4th Ave, Marshalltown, IA 50158
Phone: (515) 754-5151
Sales: $39,521,000   *Employees:* 690
Company Type: Private   *Employees here:* 670
SIC: 8062
    Hospital
Robert B Cooper, President

D-U-N-S 07-477-6030
MARSHFIELD CLINIC
1000 N Oak Ave, Marshfield, WI 54449
Phone: (715) 387-5511
Sales: $270,000,000   *Employees:* 4,443
Company Type: Private   *Employees here:* 2,400
SIC: 8011
    Medical clinic
Robert J Devita, Executive Director

D-U-N-S 04-698-9141
MARTHA JEFFERSON HOSPITAL
459 Locust Ave, Charlottesville, VA 22902
Phone: (804) 982-7000
Sales: $80,875,000   *Employees:* 1,200
Company Type: Private   *Employees here:* 1,200
SIC: 8062
    General medical & surgical hospital
James E Haden, Chief Executive Officer

D-U-N-S 07-360-9596
MARTIN LUTHER HOSPITAL
1830 W Romneya Dr, Anaheim, CA 92801
Phone: (714) 491-5200

Sales: $46,616,000   *Employees:* 683
Company Type: Private   *Employees here:* 683
SIC: 8062
   Hospital & pharmacy
Steve Dixon, President

D-U-N-S 07-846-7651
MARTIN MEMORIAL MEDICAL CENTER
200 Hospital Ave, Stuart, FL 34994
Phone: (561) 287-5200
Sales: $151,859,000   *Employees:* 1,776
Company Type: Private   *Employees here:* 1,776
SIC: 8062
   General hospital
Richmond M Harman, President

D-U-N-S 83-764-7585
MARY BLACK HEALTH SYSTEM, INC
1700 Skylyn Dr, Spartanburg, SC 29307
Phone: (864) 573-3000
Sales: $46,100,000   *Employees:* 1,000
Company Type: Private   *Employees here:* 1,000
SIC: 8062
   General hospital
William Fox, Chief Executive Officer

D-U-N-S 06-933-3375
MARY BLACK MEMORIAL HOSPITAL
1700 Skylyn Dr, Spartanburg, SC 29307
Phone: (864) 573-3000
Sales: $46,100,000   *Employees:* 1,000
Company Type: Private   *Employees here:* 950
SIC: 8062
   General hospital
William Fox, Chief Executive Officer

D-U-N-S 07-929-2645
MARY FREE BED HOSPITAL
235 Wealthy St SE, Grand Rapids, MI 49503
Phone: (616) 242-0403
Sales: $24,106,000   *Employees:* 600
Company Type: Private   *Employees here:* 500
SIC: 8069
   Rehabilitation hospital
William Blessing, President

D-U-N-S 06-991-0297
MARY HITCHCOCK MEMORIAL HOSP
1 Medical Center Dr, Lebanon, NH 3756
Phone: (603) 650-5000
Sales: $233,446,000   *Employees:* 2,711
Company Type: Private   *Employees here:* 2,390
SIC: 8062
   General medical hospital
James W Varnum, President

D-U-N-S 06-600-2734
MARY IMMACULATE HOSPITAL INC
2 Bernardine Dr, Newport News, VA 23602
Phone: (757) 886-6000
Sales: $41,920,000   *Employees:* 900
Company Type: Private   *Employees here:* 900
SIC: 8062
   Hospital
Cynthia Farrand, Chief Executive Officer

D-U-N-S 02-067-2820
MARY IMOGENE BASSETT HOSPITAL
1 Atwell Rd, Cooperstown, NY 13326
Phone: (607) 547-3456

Sales: $143,427,000   *Employees:* 2,200
Company Type: Private   *Employees here:* 2,000
SIC: 8062
   Hospital
William F Streck, President

D-U-N-S 07-697-5077
MARY LANNING MEMORIAL HOSPITAL
715 N Saint Joseph Ave, Hastings, NE 68901
Phone: (402) 463-4521
Sales: $43,593,000   *Employees:* 800
Company Type: Private   *Employees here:* 770
SIC: 8062
   General medical and surgical hospital
W M Kearney, President

D-U-N-S 07-942-3851
MARY RUTAN HOSPITAL
205 E Palmer Rd, Bellefontaine, OH 43311
Phone: (937) 592-4015
Sales: $37,664,000   *Employees:* 463
Company Type: Private   *Employees here:* 453
SIC: 8062
   General hospital
Ewing H Crawfis, President

D-U-N-S 06-541-2223
MARY WASHINGTON HOSPITAL INC
1001 Sam Perry Blvd, Fredericksburg, VA 22401
Phone: (540) 899-1100
Sales: $146,477,000   *Employees:* 1,500
Company Type: Private   *Employees here:* 1,395
SIC: 8062
   General hospital specialty hospital
Fred Rankin Iii, President

D-U-N-S 06-939-8303
MARYLAND GENERAL HOSPITAL
827 Linden Ave, Baltimore, MD 21201
Phone: (410) 225-8000
Sales: $93,022,000   *Employees:* 1,200
Company Type: Private   *Employees here:* 1,200
SIC: 8062
   General hospital
James R Wood, Chairman of the Board

D-U-N-S 07-675-8887
MARYMOUNT HOSPITAL INC
12300 McCracken Rd, Cleveland, OH 44125
Phone: (216) 581-0500
Sales: $83,611,000   *Employees:* 1,095
Company Type: Private   *Employees here:* 1,073
SIC: 8062
   General hospital psychiatric care
Thomas J Trudell, President

D-U-N-S 17-827-8677
MARYMOUNT MEDICAL CENTER, INC
(Parent: Nazareth Health Inc)
310 E 9th St, London, KY 40741
Phone: (606) 878-6520
Sales: $28,864,000   *Employees:* 500
Company Type: Private   *Employees here:* 500
SIC: 8062
   Hospital
Lowell Jones, President

D-U-N-S 80-949-1558
MARYVIEW HOSPITAL
3636 High St, Portsmouth, VA 23707
Phone: (757) 398-2200

Sales: $99,831,000   *Employees:* 1,572
Company Type: Private   *Employees here:* 1,300
SIC: 8062
  General hospital
G R Aston Jr, Chairman of the Board

D-U-N-S 09-872-6896
MASON CITY CLINIC, P C
250 S Crescent Dr, Mason City, IA 50401
Phone: (515) 422-6510
Sales: $37,000,000   *Employees:* 380
Company Type: Private   *Employees here:* 300
SIC: 8011
  Medical clinic
Tim Thomson, President

D-U-N-S 07-373-8775
MASONIC CHARITY FOUNDATION OF NJ
902 Jacksonville Rd, Burlington, NJ 8016
Phone: (609) 239-3900
Sales: $48,756,000   *Employees:* 600
Company Type: Private   *Employees here:* 600
SIC: 8051
  Skilled nursing & residential facility for the aged members of
    the masons
T F Small Iii, Administrator

D-U-N-S 80-433-3771
MASONIC HOME OF THE GRAND
1 N Broad St, Philadelphia, PA 19107
Phone: (215) 988-1900
Sales: $36,768,000   *Employees:* 938
Company Type: Private   *Employees here:* 938
SIC: 8361
  Homes for elderly & under privileged children
Joseph E Murphy, Executive Director

D-U-N-S 87-724-4533
MASONIC HOME, INC
88 Masonic Home Rd, Charlton, MA 1507
Phone: (508) 248-7344
Sales: $28,772,000   *Employees:* 210
Company Type: Private   *Employees here:* 210
SIC: 8051
  Skilled nursing facility
Arthur Johnson, President

D-U-N-S 07-186-9382
MASONIC HOMES OF CALIFORNIA
1111 California St, San Francisco, CA 94108
Phone: (415) 776-7000
Sales: $54,840,000   *Employees:* 450
Company Type: Private   *Employees here:* 10
SIC: 8361
  Homes for aged persons & children
Stanley M Cazneaux, President

D-U-N-S 07-382-5945
MASSACHUSETTS EYE EAR INFIRMARY
243 Charles St, Boston, MA 2114
Phone: (617) 523-7900
Sales: $76,574,000   *Employees:* 1,050
Company Type: Private   *Employees here:* 1,000
SIC: 8069
  Specialty hospital
F C Smith, President

D-U-N-S 87-843-7292
MASSACHUSETTS DEPARTMENT
P.O. Box A, Hathorne, MA 1937
Phone: (508) 727-9550

Sales: $38,900,000   *Employees:* NA
Company Type: Private   *Employees here:* 1,450
SIC: 8361
  Mental retardation developmental center
Dorothy Mullen, Branch Manager

D-U-N-S 09-586-1860
MASSACHUSETTS DEPT MENTAL HEALTH
Lyman St, Westborough, MA 1581
Phone: (508) 366-4401
Sales: $30,900,000   *Employees:* NA
Company Type: Private   *Employees here:* 760
SIC: 8063
  Psychiatric care facility
Felix Vazquez, Branch Manager

D-U-N-S 07-570-0385
MASSACHUSETTS DEPT MENTAL HEALTH
60 Hodges Ave, Taunton, MA 2780
Phone: (508) 823-5100
Sales: $26,500,000   *Employees:* NA
Company Type: Private   *Employees here:* 650
SIC: 8063
  Psychiatric hospital
Garry C Phillips, Administrator

D-U-N-S 02-171-7855
MASSACHUSETTS DEPT MENTAL HEALTH
45 Hospital Rd, Medfield, MA 2052
Phone: (508) 359-7312
Sales: $20,400,000   *Employees:* NA
Company Type: Private   *Employees here:* 500
SIC: 8063
  Alcohol rehabilitation center
Barbara Leadholm, Director

D-U-N-S 60-342-0563
MASSACHUSETTS EYE & EAR ASSOC
243 Charles St, Boston, MA 2114
Phone: (617) 523-7900
Sales: $29,857,000   *Employees:* 4
Company Type: Private   *Employees here:* 4
SIC: 8011
  Eyes ears nose & throat specialists
Dr Joseph B Nadol Md, President

D-U-N-S 01-085-4255
MASSILLON COMMUNITY HOSPITAL
875 8th St NE, Massillon, OH 44646
Phone: (330) 832-8761
Sales: $42,981,000   *Employees:* 875
Company Type: Private   *Employees here:* 875
SIC: 8062
  Community hospital
Mervin F Strine, President

D-U-N-S 08-014-1872
MASSILLON HEALTH SYSTEM LLC
400 Austin Ave Nw, Massillon, OH 44646
Phone: (330) 837-7200
Sales: $36,700,000   *Employees:* 800
Company Type: Private   *Employees here:* 740
SIC: 8062
  General medical and surgical hospital
Thomas E Cecconi, Chief Executive Officer

D-U-N-S 07-853-9640
MATAGORDA COUNTY HOSPITAL DST
1115 Avenue G, Bay City, TX 77414
Phone: (409) 245-6383

Sales: $24,313,000   Employees: 600
Company Type: Private   Employees here: 450
SIC: 8062
   Two general medical & surgical hospitals & a skilled nursing
     care facility & public health clinic
Wendell H Baker, Chief Executive Officer

D-U-N-S 93-377-1123
MATRIA HEALTHCARE, INC
1850 Parkway Pl SE Fl 12, Marietta, GA 30067
Phone: (770) 423-4500
Sales: $144,533,000   Employees: 844
Company Type: Public   Employees here: 200
SIC: 8082
   Provider of pregnancy management services high-risk home
     obstetrical care & fertility specialists
Donald R Millard, President

D-U-N-S 96-772-9971
MATRIX REHABILITATION INC
   (Parent: Beverly Enterprises Inc)
3409 N Central Expy, Plano, TX 75023
Phone: (972) 398-4900
Sales: $77,000,000   Employees: 1,200
Company Type: Public Family Member   Employees here: 60
SIC: 8093
   Rehabilitation clinic
Craig Rettke, President

D-U-N-S 06-909-2286
MAURY REGIONAL HOSPITAL
1224 Trotwood Ave, Columbia, TN 38401
Phone: (931) 381-1111
Sales: $104,514,000   Employees: 1,473
Company Type: Private   Employees here: 1,407
SIC: 8062
   General hospital
William Walter, Secretary

D-U-N-S 78-594-8019
MAXICARE LOUISIANA, INC
   (Parent: Maxicare Health Plans Inc)
1515 Poydras St Ste 1130, New Orleans, LA 70112
Phone: (504) 523-7080
Sales: $20,000,000   Employees: 28
Company Type: Public Family Member   Employees here: 28
SIC: 8011
   Health care organization
John Theos, Vice-President

D-U-N-S 19-473-7029
MAY INSTITUTE
37 Purchase St, Fall River, MA 2720
Phone: (508) 675-5888
Sales: $41,703,000   Employees: 64
Company Type: Private   Employees here: 5
SIC: 8093
   Psychiatric rehabilitation center outpatient treatment
Walter P Christian, President

D-U-N-S 08-158-2637
MAY INSTITUTE INC
940 Main St, South Harwich, MA 2661
Phone: (508) 432-5530
Sales: $41,954,000   Employees: 1,000
Company Type: Private   Employees here: 30
SIC: 8361
   Residential care rehabilitation center health care incidental
Robert Whittlesey, Chairman of the Board

D-U-N-S 15-322-3151
MAYO CLINIC JACKSONVILLE INC
   (Parent: Mayo Foundation)
4500 San Pablo Rd S, Jacksonville, FL 32224
Phone: (904) 223-2000
Sales: $110,300,000   Employees: 1,600
Company Type: Private   Employees here: 978
SIC: 8011
   Subspeciality medical & surgical practice
Dr Leo F Black Md, Chairman of the Board

D-U-N-S 15-366-5211
MAYO CLINIC SCOTTSDALE
   (Parent: Mayo Foundation)
13400 E Shea Blvd, Scottsdale, AZ 85259
Phone: (602) 391-8000
Sales: $150,000,000   Employees: 1,423
Company Type: Private   Employees here: 1,400
SIC: 8011
   Medical clinic
Dr R G Tancredi Md, President

D-U-N-S 00-647-1700
MAYO FOUNDATION
200 1st St SW, Rochester, MN 55905
Phone: (507) 284-2511
Sales: $2,565,600,000   Employees: 30,497
Company Type: Private   Employees here: 16,400
SIC: 8011
   Clinical medicine hospitals & medical research & education
Dr Robert R Waller Md, President

D-U-N-S 08-540-5439
MAYO HENRY NEWHALL MEM HOSP
23845 McBean Pkwy, Santa Clarita, CA 91355
Phone: (805) 253-8000
Sales: $79,956,000   Employees: 585
Company Type: Private   Employees here: 479
SIC: 8062
   General hospital
Duffy Watson, President

D-U-N-S 07-430-7380
MCCRAY MEMORIAL HOSPITAL
951 Hospital Dr, Kendallville, IN 46755
Phone: (219) 347-1100
Sales: $22,457,000   Employees: 300
Company Type: Private   Employees here: 280
SIC: 8062
   General medical and surgical hospital and home health care
     facility
Jim Norris, Chief Executive Officer

D-U-N-S 07-468-2147
MCCULLOUGH-HYDE MEM HOSPITAL INC
110 N Poplar St, Oxford, OH 45056
Phone: (513) 523-2111
Sales: $26,564,000   Employees: 349
Company Type: Private   Employees here: 349
SIC: 8062
   General hospital
Richard Daniels, President

D-U-N-S 07-197-5775
MCDONOUGH COUNTY HOSPITAL DST
525 E Grant St, Macomb, IL 61455
Phone: (309) 833-4101
Sales: $34,164,000   Employees: 600
Company Type: Private   Employees here: 600
SIC: 8062
   General hospital and blood bank
Stephen Hopper, Chief Executive Officer

D-U-N-S 07-907-0017
MCDOWELL HOSPITAL INC
100 Rankin Dr, Marion, NC 28752
Phone: (828) 652-2125
Sales: $19,718,000   *Employees:* 310
Company Type: Private   *Employees here:* 300
SIC: 8062
   General hospital
Jeffery M Judd, Administrator

D-U-N-S 06-946-7520
MCKENNA MEMORIAL HOSPITAL
600 N Union Ave, New Braunfels, TX 78130
Phone: (830) 606-9111
Sales: $37,039,000   *Employees:* 460
Company Type: Private   *Employees here:* 456
SIC: 8062
   General hospital
Arnold Becker, Chairman

D-U-N-S 04-651-4535
MCLEAN HOSPITAL CORPORATION
115 Mill St, Belmont, MA 2478
Phone: (617) 855-2000
Sales: $49,188,000   *Employees:* 1,213
Company Type: Private   *Employees here:* 1,200
SIC: 8063
   Psychiatric hospital
Dr Steven M Mirin Md, Chief Executive Officer

D-U-N-S 95-711-7120
MCWIL GROUP LTD
209 N Beaver St, York, PA 17403
Phone: (717) 854-7857
Sales: $50,000,000   *Employees:* 1,500
Company Type: Private   *Employees here:* 5
SIC: 8059
   Holding company
Webster J Mc Cormack, Chairman of the Board

D-U-N-S 09-476-9726
MCALESTER REGIONAL HEALTH CTR AUTH
1 E Clark Bass Blvd, Mcalester, OK 74501
Phone: (918) 426-1800
Sales: $38,043,000   *Employees:* 600
Company Type: Private   *Employees here:* 550
SIC: 8062
   General hospital
Joel W Tate, Chief Executive Officer

D-U-N-S 15-009-6840
MCALLEN MEDICAL CENTER INC
   (Parent: Universal Health Services)
301 W Expressway 83, Mcallen, TX 78503
Phone: (956) 632-4000
Sales: $167,376,000   *Employees:* 1,620
Company Type: Public Family Member   *Employees here:* 1,600
SIC: 8062
   General hospital
Harold Siglar, Chief Executive Officer

D-U-N-S 62-388-3600
MCC BEHAVIORAL CARE OF CAL
   (Parent: M C C Behavioral Care Inc)
801 N Brand Blvd Ste 1150, Glendale, CA 91203
Phone: (818) 551-2200
Sales: $27,110,000   *Employees:* 150
Company Type: Public Family Member   *Employees here:* 55
SIC: 8093
   Mental health & substance abuse clinics & managed care
      company
Susan Urbanski, President

D-U-N-S 07-138-9969
MCCURTAIN MEMORIAL MEDICAL MGT
1301 Lincoln Rd, Idabel, OK 74745
Phone: (580) 286-7623
Sales: $20,114,000   *Employees:* 325
Company Type: Private   *Employees here:* 325
SIC: 8062
   General hospital
Ronald L Campbell, Chief Financial Officer

D-U-N-S 06-961-5482
MCFARLAND CLINIC P C
1215 Duff Ave, Ames, IA 50010
Phone: (515) 239-4400
Sales: $68,711,000   *Employees:* 690
Company Type: Private   *Employees here:* 502
SIC: 8011
   Medical clinic operated by group of physicians
Leo Milleman, President

D-U-N-S 07-208-8602
MCKENDREE VILLAGE INC
4343 Lebanon Pike 47, Hermitage, TN 37076
Phone: (615) 889-6990
Sales: $21,526,000   *Employees:* 395
Company Type: Private   *Employees here:* 395
SIC: 8361
   Continuing care retirement center
Bob Sullins, Chairman of the Board

D-U-N-S 05-496-8326
MCKENZIE-WILLAMETTE HOSPITAL
1460 G St, Springfield, OR 97477
Phone: (541) 726-4400
Sales: $51,979,000   *Employees:* 750
Company Type: Private   *Employees here:* 700
SIC: 8062
   General hospital
Roy Orr, Chief Executive Officer

D-U-N-S 62-798-7407
MCKENZIE-WILLAMETTE MED SVCS
1460 G St, Springfield, OR 97477
Phone: (541) 726-4400
Sales: $48,552,000   *Employees:* 850
Company Type: Private   *Employees here:* 820
SIC: 8062
   General hospital
Roy Orr, President

D-U-N-S 14-803-1495
MCKERLEY HEALTH CARE CENTERS,
   (Parent: Genesis Health Ventures Inc)
1 Fisher Ave, Penacook, NH 3303
Phone: (603) 934-2541
Sales: $26,000,000   *Employees:* 1,400
Company Type: Public Family Member   *Employees here:* 20
SIC: 8052
   Personal care facility skilled nursing care facilities
      management services & home health care services
Michael R Walker, Chairman of the Board

D-U-N-S 07-544-4281
MCLAREN REGIONAL MEDICAL CTR
   (Parent: Mclaren Health Care Corp)
401 S Ballenger Hwy, Flint, MI 48532
Phone: (810) 762-2000
Sales: $105,200,000   *Employees:* 2,250
Company Type: Private   *Employees here:* 2,000
SIC: 8062
   General hospital
Philip Incarnati, President

D-U-N-S 07-370-9784
MCLEOD RGNL MDCL CTR PEE DEE
555 E Cheves St, Florence, SC 29506
Phone: (843) 667-2000
Sales: $200,867,000   *Employees:* 2,600
Company Type: Private   *Employees here:* 2,345
SIC: 8062
   General hospital
J B Barragan, President

D-U-N-S 04-109-0523
MDI LIMITED
101 S State St 103, Monticello, IL 61856
Phone: (217) 762-7844
Sales: $31,116,000   *Employees:* 1,000
Company Type: Private   *Employees here:* 15
SIC: 8051
   Owner operator management service of nursing homes
     skilled nursing extended care
Mark G Hawthorne, Chief Financial Officer

D-U-N-S 01-012-2257
MEADOW REGIONAL MEDICAL CENTER
1703 Meadows Ln, Vidalia, GA 30474
Phone: (912) 537-8921
Sales: $29,729,000   *Employees:* 420
Company Type: Private   *Employees here:* 420
SIC: 8062
   Hospital
Barry Michael, Chief Executive Officer

D-U-N-S 18-178-5296
MEADOWBROOK RHBILITATION GROUP
2000 Powell St Ste 1203, Emeryville, CA 94608
Phone: (510) 420-0900
Sales: $20,834,000   *Employees:* 613
Company Type: Public   *Employees here:* 15
SIC: 8093
   Rehabilitation services
Ali A Dahwi, President

D-U-N-S 04-074-2017
MEADOWLANDS HOSPITAL MED CTR
   (Parent: Liberty Healthcare System Inc)
Meadowland Pkwy, Secaucus, NJ 7096
Phone: (201) 392-3100
Sales: $49,104,000   *Employees:* 625
Company Type: Private   *Employees here:* 570
SIC: 8062
   Medical & surgical hospital
Dr Paul Cavalli Md, President

D-U-N-S 06-874-8409
MEADVILLE MEDICAL CENTER
751 Liberty St, Meadville, PA 16335
Phone: (814) 333-5000
Sales: $64,215,000   *Employees:* 959
Company Type: Private   *Employees here:* 661
SIC: 8062
   Hospital
Anthony J De Fail, President

D-U-N-S 06-018-7077
MECOSTA COUNTY GENERAL HOSP
405 Winter Ave, Big Rapids, MI 49307
Phone: (616) 796-8691
Sales: $22,916,000   *Employees:* 280
Company Type: Private   *Employees here:* 280
SIC: 8062
   General medical & surgical hospital
Thomas Daugherty, Administrator

D-U-N-S 04-436-8413
MED AMERICA HEALTH SYSTEMS CORP
1 Wyoming St, Dayton, OH 45409
Phone: (937) 223-6192
Sales: $346,810,000   *Employees:* 4,300
Company Type: Private   *Employees here:* 32
SIC: 8062
   General medical and surgical hospital
T G Breitenbach, President

D-U-N-S 15-067-7920
MED-HEALTH SYSTEM
1141 N Monroe Dr, Xenia, OH 45385
Phone: (937) 372-8011
Sales: $42,600,000   *Employees:* 925
Company Type: Private   *Employees here:* 650
SIC: 8062
   Hospital
Michael Stephens, Executive Director

D-U-N-S 87-842-2070
MEDALIA HEALTHCARE LLC
1 Union St 600, Seattle, WA 98101
Phone: (206) 320-2700
Sales: $113,700,000   *Employees:* 1,650
Company Type: Private   *Employees here:* 200
SIC: 8011
   Physicians network
Derick Pasternak, Chief Executive Officer

D-U-N-S 92-757-3352
MEDCATH OF MCALLEN LTD
7621 Little Ave Ste 106, Charlotte, NC 28226
Phone: (704) 541-3228
Sales: $25,000,000   *Employees:* 175
Company Type: Private   *Employees here:* 5
SIC: 8071
   Medical laboratories
David Crane, President

D-U-N-S 60-816-1295
MEDCATH INCORPORATED
   (Parent: Medcath Intermediate Holdings)
7621 Little Ave, Charlotte, NC 28226
Phone: (704) 541-3228
Sales: $200,000,000   *Employees:* 1,800
Company Type: Private   *Employees here:* 75
SIC: 8069
   Operates heart hospitals & other specialized cardiac care
     facilities & provides practice management services
Stephen R Puckett, Chairman of the Board

D-U-N-S 07-149-4348
MEDCENTER ONE INC
300 N 7th St, Bismarck, ND 58501
Phone: (701) 224-6000
Sales: $135,365,000   *Employees:* 2,200
Company Type: Private   *Employees here:* 1,145
SIC: 8062
   General hospital and specialty medical clinic
Terrance G Brosseau, President

D-U-N-S 86-817-1596
MEDCENTER ONE INC
222 N 7th St, Bismarck, ND 58501
Phone: (701) 222-5200
Sales: $22,100,000   *Employees:* NA
Company Type: Private   *Employees here:* 400
SIC: 8011
   Medical clinic
Terry Broffeau, Manager

D-U-N-S 07-690-4705
MEDCENTRAL HEALTH SYSTEM
335 Glessner Ave, Mansfield, OH 44903
Phone: (419) 526-8000
Sales: $98,407,000   *Employees:* 2,141
Company Type: Private   *Employees here:* 1,800
SIC: 8062
    Hospital
Dr Paul Kautz, Chief Operating Officer

D-U-N-S 07-601-8845
MEDERI INC
2401 S Douglas Rd, Miami, FL 33145
Phone: (305) 447-2300
Sales: $29,098,000   *Employees:* 200
Company Type: Private   *Employees here:* 100
SIC: 8082
    Home health care services
Sandra Vasquez, President

D-U-N-S 78-933-8191
MEDICA
    (Parent: Allina Health System)
5601 Smetana Dr, Minneapolis, MN 55440
Phone: (612) 992-2000
Sales: $75,700,000   *Employees:* 1,100
Company Type: Private   *Employees here:* 2
SIC: 8011
    Health maintenance organizations
Dr K J Ehlen, President

D-U-N-S 07-733-5347
MEDICAL ARTS PATHOLOGISTS INC
1111 N Lee Ave Ste 100, Oklahoma City, OK 73103
Phone: (405) 239-7111
Sales: $27,187,000   *Employees:* 18
Company Type: Private   *Employees here:* 18
SIC: 8071
    Medical diagnostic laboratory
Bob Sebastian, President

D-U-N-S 79-731-8649
MEDICAL ASSOC OF LEHIGH VALLEY PC
1255 S Cedar Crest Blvd, Allentown, PA 18103
Phone: (610) 740-9293
Sales: $20,500,000   *Employees:* 300
Company Type: Private   *Employees here:* 12
SIC: 8011
    Medical doctor's office
Robert Stover, Owner

D-U-N-S 07-385-1529
MEDICAL ASSOC/MNMNEE FLS
W180n7950 Town Hall Rd, Menomonee Falls, WI 53051
Phone: (414) 255-2500
Sales: $50,000,000   *Employees:* 700
Company Type: Private   *Employees here:* 455
SIC: 8011
    Medical clinics with specialists
Clyde M Chumbley, President

D-U-N-S 08-537-9303
MEDICAL ASSOCIATES CLINIC P C
1000 Langworthy St, Dubuque, IA 52001
Phone: (319) 584-3000
Sales: $52,300,000   *Employees:* 761
Company Type: Private   *Employees here:* 500
SIC: 8011
    Medical clinic
Dr Edward S Alt Md, President

D-U-N-S 12-153-4762
MEDICAL BEHAVIORAL CARE OF CAL
    (Parent: Merit Behavioral Care Corp)
400 Oyster Point Blvd, South San Francisco, CA 94080
Phone: (650) 742-0980
Sales: $24,400,000   *Employees:* 800
Company Type: Public Family Member   *Employees here:* 70
SIC: 8093
    Managed mental health care & substance abuse
    administration services
Shannon R Kennedy, President

D-U-N-S 07-247-9710
MEDICAL CENTER OF CENTL GA INC
777 Hemlock St, Macon, GA 31201
Phone: (912) 633-1000
Sales: $369,384,000   *Employees:* 3,300
Company Type: Private   *Employees here:* 3,300
SIC: 8062
    Hospital
Don Faulk, Chief Executive Officer

D-U-N-S 07-764-0100
MEDICAL CENTER EAST INC
50 Medical Park Dr E, Birmingham, AL 35235
Phone: (205) 838-3000
Sales: $108,989,000   *Employees:* 1,450
Company Type: Private   *Employees here:* 1,100
SIC: 8062
    Hospital gift shop and credit union
Robert C Chapman, President

D-U-N-S 08-482-5835
MEDICAL CENTER-WEST INC
    (Parent: Columbia/Hca Healthcare Corp)
1000 Thornton Rd, Lithia Springs, GA 30122
Phone: (770) 732-7777
Sales: $69,369,000   *Employees:* 520
Company Type: Public Family Member   *Employees here:* 520
SIC: 8062
    General hospital
Deborah S Guthrie, Administrator

D-U-N-S 08-969-9508
MEDICAL CENTER, INC
710 Center St, Columbus, GA 31901
Phone: (706) 571-1000
Sales: $68,000,000   *Employees:* 1,463
Company Type: Private   *Employees here:* 1,330
SIC: 8062
    Hospital
Lance Duke, President

D-U-N-S 96-482-1482
MEDICAL CITY DALLAS HOSPITAL
    (Parent: Columbia/Hca Healthcare Corp)
7777 Forest Ln, Dallas, TX 75230
Phone: (972) 661-7000
Sales: $300,000,000   *Employees:* 2,300
Company Type: Public Family Member   *Employees here:* 2,000
SIC: 8062
    General hospital
Stephen Corbeil, Chief Executive Officer

D-U-N-S 02-033-7796
MEDICAL CLINIC OF N TEXAS P A
9003 Airport Fwy Ste 300, Fort Worth, TX 76180
Phone: (817) 514-5200
Sales: $24,000,000   *Employees:* 350
Company Type: Private   *Employees here:* 55
SIC: 8011
    Medical clinic specializing in internal medicine
David Russell, President

D-U-N-S 07-610-8810
MEDICAL CLINIC OF SACRAMENTO
3160 Folsom Blvd, Sacramento, CA 95816
Phone: (916) 733-3333
Sales: $55,000,000   *Employees:* 800
Company Type: Private   *Employees here:* 450
SIC: 8011
    Medical group
Brett De Witt, Finance

D-U-N-S 55-677-4917
MEDICAL COLLEGE OF HAMPTON RADS
714 Woodis Ave, Norfolk, VA 23510
Phone: (757) 446-5219
Sales: $59,500,000   *Employees:* NA
Company Type: Private   *Employees here:* 1,000
SIC: 8011
    Medical doctor's office
John Hamilton, Branch Manager

D-U-N-S 06-534-8054
MEDICAL COLLEGE OF GEORGIA
1120 15th St, Augusta, GA 30912
Phone: (706) 721-0211
Sales: $436,921,000   *Employees:* 7,500
Company Type: Private   *Employees here:* 6,500
SIC: 8062
    Teaching hospital & medical college
Patricia Findling-Sodomk, Executive Director

D-U-N-S 12-100-3784
MEDICAL CORPORATION AMERICA
    (Parent: Medical Care International)
1 Park Mdws, Nashville, TN 37215
Phone: (615) 327-9551
Sales: $27,400,000   *Employees:* 400
Company Type: Public Family Member   *Employees here:* 3
SIC: 8011
    Opthalmologist clinics
Donald E Steen, President

D-U-N-S 17-359-8210
MEDICAL DIAGNOSTICS INC
    (Parent: Alliance Imaging Inc)
46 Jonspin Rd, Wilmington, MA 1887
Phone: (978) 658-5357
Sales: $23,000,000   *Employees:* 150
Company Type: Public Family Member   *Employees here:* 30
SIC: 8099
    Medical services organization
Joseph Paul, President

D-U-N-S 05-092-7300
MEDICAL EDUCATION ASSIST CORP
Vet Adm Med Ctr 52 Rm 113, Mountain Home, TN 37684
Phone: (423) 929-6318
Sales: $21,635,000   *Employees:* 230
Company Type: Private   *Employees here:* 12
SIC: 8071
    Medical clinics and laboratories
Gregory L Wilgocki, Executive Director

D-U-N-S 11-066-2285
MEDICAL IMAGING SERVICES
610 Carnahan Dr, North Little Rock, AR 72113
Phone: (501) 664-1996
Sales: $25,000,000   *Employees:* 50
Company Type: Private   *Employees here:* 50
SIC: 8071
    Medical laboratory
Butch Holiday, President

D-U-N-S 19-761-7582
MEDICAL INCOME PROPERTIES 2A
400 Embassy Row NE 410, Atlanta, GA 30328
Phone: (770) 668-1080
Sales: $20,824,000   *Employees:* 325
Company Type: Public   *Employees here:* 1
SIC: 8051
    Nursing home
John Stoddard, General Partner

D-U-N-S 13-759-2036
MEDICAL INNOVATIONS INC
    (Parent: Horizon/Cms Healthcare Corp)
15333 Jfk Blvd Ste 700, Houston, TX 77032
Phone: (281) 987-8769
Sales: $60,000,000   *Employees:* 3,450
Company Type: Public Family Member   *Employees here:* 42
SIC: 8082
    Home health care service
Mark H Fisher, Chairman of the Board

D-U-N-S 07-156-6327
MEDICAL PARK HOSPITAL INC
1950 S Hawthorne Rd, Winston Salem, NC 27103
Phone: (336) 718-0600
Sales: $25,949,000   *Employees:* 260
Company Type: Private   *Employees here:* 260
SIC: 8062
    General hospital
Eduard Koehler, Administrator

D-U-N-S 17-667-7920
MEDICAL PROF ASSOC ARIZ PC
3255 E Elwood St 110, Phoenix, AZ 85034
Phone: (602) 470-5000
Sales: $34,300,000   *Employees:* 500
Company Type: Private   *Employees here:* 500
SIC: 8011
    Medical doctor's office
Mary E Rimsa, President

D-U-N-S 94-276-7575
MEDICAL RESEARCH INDUSTRIES
6200 Stirling Rd, Fort Lauderdale, FL 33314
Phone: (954) 964-6774
Sales: $40,000,000   *Employees:* 75
Company Type: Private   *Employees here:* 75
SIC: 8049
    Dietary research
Bill Tishman, Chief Executive Officer

D-U-N-S 05-742-6678
MEDICAL RESOURCES INC
155 State St, Hackensack, NJ 7601
Phone: (201) 488-6230
Sales: $202,386,000   *Employees:* 623
Company Type: Public   *Employees here:* 22
SIC: 8071
    Diagnostic imaging centers network management services &
        healthcare recruiting & placement
Duane C Montopoli, President

D-U-N-S 03-008-9726
MEDICAL SERVICES OF AMERICA
171 Monroe Ln, Lexington, SC 29072
Phone: (803) 957-0500
Sales: $97,366,000   *Employees:* 1,500
Company Type: Private   *Employees here:* 112
SIC: 8082
    Health care services & rental & retail of medical equipment
        & supplies
Ronnie L Young, President

D-U-N-S 09-777-9912
MEDICAL TEAM INC
1850 Centennial Park Dr, Reston, VA 20191
Phone: (703) 391-0400
Sales: $22,500,000
Company Type: Private
SIC: 8082
  Health care
Leslie Pembrook, President

Employees: 2,700
Employees here: 400

D-U-N-S 10-860-3267
MEDICALODGES OF KANSAS INC
  (Parent: Medicalodges Inc)
201 W 8th St, Coffeyville, KS 67337
Phone: (316) 251-6700
Sales: $34,200,000
Company Type: Private
SIC: 8051
  Operator of skilled nursing facilities
Larry L Fischer, President

Employees: 1,500
Employees here: 12

D-U-N-S 05-071-4963
MEDICALODGES INC
201 W 8th St, Coffeyville, KS 67337
Phone: (316) 251-6700
Sales: $71,136,000
Company Type: Private
SIC: 8051
  Skilled nursing homes general building contractor & leases
    equipment & buildings
S A Hann, Chairman of the Board

Employees: 2,300
Employees here: 65

D-U-N-S 11-108-8910
MEDICARE RISK NETWORK LLC
9501 Roosevelt Blvd, Philadelphia, PA 19114
Phone: (215) 612-5400
Sales: $35,000,000
Company Type: Private
SIC: 8011
  Risk contractor for medical service
Roy Powell, President

Employees: 5
Employees here: 5

D-U-N-S 15-413-1924
MEDIGROUP INC
  (Parent: Horizon Healthcare Inc)
3 Penn Plz E, Newark, NJ 7105
Phone: (973) 466-4000
Sales: $39,500,000
Company Type: Private
SIC: 8011
  Health maintenance organization
William J Marino, Chief Executive Officer

Employees: 575
Employees here: 350

D-U-N-S 03-020-8995
MEDINA MEMORIAL HOSPITAL INC
200 Ohio St, Medina, NY 14103
Phone: (716) 798-2000
Sales: $22,737,000
Company Type: Private
SIC: 8062
  Hospital & skilled nursing home
Walter Becker, Administrator

Employees: 355
Employees here: 350

D-U-N-S 08-337-9552
MEDIPLEX OF CONNECTICUT INC
  (Parent: Sunrise Healthcare Corporation)
2101 Washington St, Newton, MA 2462
Phone: (617) 969-4660
Sales: $31,900,000
Company Type: Public Family Member
SIC: 8051
  Skilled nursing
Mark Wimer, Chairman of the Board

Employees: 1,400
Employees here: 3

D-U-N-S 19-966-7429
MEDIPLEX OF MASSACHUSETTS INC
  (Parent: Mediplex Group Inc)
101 Sun Ave NE, Albuquerque, NM 87109
Phone: (505) 821-3355
Sales: $22,200,000
Company Type: Public Family Member
SIC: 8059
  Nursing homes
William T Hartigan, President

Employees: 1,000
Employees here: 6

D-U-N-S 10-676-9326
MEDIPLEX GROUP INC
  (Parent: Sun Healthcare Group Inc)
101 Sun Ave NE, Albuquerque, NM 87109
Phone: (505) 821-3355
Sales: $457,748,000
Company Type: Public Family Member
SIC: 8051
  Nursing care facilities
Dell Zulauf, President

Employees: 10,000
Employees here: 200

D-U-N-S 82-561-5396
MEDLANTIC ENTERPRISES, INC
  (Parent: Medlantic Healthcare Group)
6000 NEw Hampshire Ave NE, Washington, DC 20011
Phone: (202) 291-7964
Sales: $22,700,000
Company Type: Private
SIC: 8051
  Health care facilities
Linda Maurano, President

Employees: 1,000
Employees here: 800

D-U-N-S 13-229-6039
MEDLANTIC HEALTHCARE GROUP
100 Irving St Nw, Washington, DC 20010
Phone: (202) 877-7000
Sales: $634,169,000
Company Type: Private
SIC: 8082
  Health management services
John P Mc Daniel, Chief Executive Officer

Employees: 5,500
Employees here: 40

D-U-N-S 94-681-8697
MEDLINK OF VIRGINIA
651 Delaware Ave, Buffalo, NY 14202
Phone: (716) 881-4425
Sales: $63,500,000
Company Type: Private
SIC: 8082
  Home health care & owner of homes for adults
Mark E Hamister, Chief Executive Officer

Employees: 4,000
Employees here: 3,990

D-U-N-S 87-622-2845
MEDNET HEALTH SERVICES PC
1651 Coney Island Ave, Brooklyn, NY 11230
Phone: (718) 382-2200
Sales: $26,260,000
Company Type: Private
SIC: 8011
  Medical doctor's office
Dr Paul Rosenstock Md, President

Employees: 25
Employees here: 25

D-U-N-S 79-132-6598
MEDPARTNERS INC
3660 Arlington Ave, Riverside, CA 92506
Phone: (909) 683-6370
Sales: $47,200,000
Company Type: Public Family Member
SIC: 8011
  Medical doctor's office
Judy Carpenter, Vice-President

Employees: NA
Employees here: 781

D-U-N-S 18-311-8819
MEDREHAB INC
 (*Parent:* Mariner Post-Acute Network)
 3825 W Green Tree Rd, Milwaukee, WI 53209
Phone: (414) 247-3100
Sales: $19,700,000 | *Employees:* 1,261
Company Type: Public Family Member | *Employees here:* 588
SIC: 8049
 Residential care services
Arthur Stratton, President

D-U-N-S 12-120-5355   EXP
MEDTOX LABORATORIES INC
 (*Parent:* Medtox Scientific Inc)
 402 County Road D W, Saint Paul, MN 55112
Phone: (651) 636-7466
Sales: $28,600,000 | *Employees:* 223
Company Type: Public Family Member | *Employees here:* 215
SIC: 8071
 Toxicology reference testing laboratory
James S Arrington, Chairman of the Board

D-U-N-S 11-505-8828
MEDTOX SCIENTIFIC INC
 1238 Anthony Rd, Burlington, NC 27215
Phone: (336) 226-6311
Sales: $28,600,000 | *Employees:* 350
Company Type: Public | *Employees here:* 30
SIC: 8071
 Clinical testing lab and mfg diagnostic test reagents & kits
Richard J Braun, Chief Executive Officer

D-U-N-S 04-074-1928
MEGA CARE INC
 695 Chestnut St, Union, NJ 7083
Phone: (908) 687-7829
Sales: $26,808,000 | *Employees:* 849
Company Type: Private | *Employees here:* 6
SIC: 8051
 Nursing home
Ronald Delmauro, President

D-U-N-S 07-833-0206
MELBOURNE INTL MED ASSC INC
 200 E Sheridan Rd, Melbourne, FL 32901
Phone: (407) 725-4500
Sales: $20,500,000 | *Employees:* 300
Company Type: Private | *Employees here:* 300
SIC: 8011
 Medical doctor's office
Philip Piasecki, Administrator

D-U-N-S 08-872-9637
MEMORIAL CLINIC LTD P.S.
 500 Lilly Rd NE, Olympia, WA 98506
Phone: (360) 456-1122
Sales: $44,000,000 | *Employees:* 400
Company Type: Private. | *Employees here:* 330
SIC: 8011
 Medical clinic
Craig Wehrli, President

D-U-N-S 07-619-4356
MEMORIAL HEALTH SERVICES
 2801 Atlantic Ave, Long Beach, CA 90806
Phone: (562) 933-2000
Sales: $619,794,000 | *Employees:* 7,500
Company Type: Private | *Employees here:* 50
SIC: 8062
 Management services
Thomas J Collins, President

D-U-N-S 02-171-6881
MEMORIAL HEALTH SYSTEMS INC
 875 Sterthaus Ave, Ormond Beach, FL 32174
Phone: (904) 676-6001
Sales: $146,298,000 | *Employees:* 910
Company Type: Private | *Employees here:* 732
SIC: 8062
 General medical & surgical hospital
Richard A Lind, President

D-U-N-S 10-767-3725
MEMORIAL HEALTH VENTURES INC
 (*Parent:* Memorial Hrmann Halthcare Sys)
 9494 Southwest Fwy, Houston, TX 77074
Phone: (713) 776-4179
Sales: $20,590,000 | *Employees:* 120
Company Type: Private | *Employees here:* 112
SIC: 8082
 Home health care services
Dan Wilford, President

D-U-N-S 06-983-3523
MEMORIAL HEALTHCARE CENTER
 826 W King St, Owosso, MI 48867
Phone: (517) 723-5211
Sales: $57,046,000 | *Employees:* 1,000
Company Type: Private | *Employees here:* 820
SIC: 8062
 General hospital
Margaret Gulick, President

D-U-N-S 06-588-8422
MEMORIAL HEALTHCARE GROUP,
 (*Parent:* Columbia/Hca Healthcare Corp)
 3625 University Blvd S, Jacksonville, FL 32216
Phone: (904) 399-6111
Sales: $61,900,000 | *Employees:* 1,334
Company Type: Public Family Member | *Employees here:* 1,334
SIC: 8062
 General hospital
Winston Rushing, President

D-U-N-S 07-418-7949
MEMORIAL HERMANN HOSPITAL SYS
 7737 Southwest Fwy, Houston, TX 77074
Phone: (713) 776-5000
Sales: $615,904,000 | *Employees:* 6,500
Company Type: Private | *Employees here:* 2,300
SIC: 8062
 General medical & surgical hospital
David R Page, Chief Executive Officer

D-U-N-S 12-697-7552
MEMORIAL HERMANN HOSPITAL SYS
 11800 Astoria Blvd, Houston, TX 77089
Phone: (281) 929-6100
Sales: $26,500,000 | *Employees:* NA
Company Type: Private | *Employees here:* 650
SIC: 8062
 General hospital
Dan Martin, Manager

D-U-N-S 61-065-1135
MEMORIAL HERMANN HOSPITAL SYS
 7600 Beechnut St, Houston, TX 77074
Phone: (713) 776-5000
Sales: $68,300,000 | *Employees:* NA
Company Type: Private | *Employees here:* 1,650
SIC: 8062
 General hospital
James E Eastham, Manager

D-U-N-S 78-492-4102
MEMORIAL HERMANN HOSPITAL SYS
920 Frostwood Dr Ste 207, Houston, TX 77024
Phone: (713) 932-3000
Sales: $53,900,000
Company Type: Private
SIC: 8011
  Medical doctor's office
Leslie Gertson, Branch Manager

Employees: NA
Employees here: 900

D-U-N-S 95-790-0293
MEMORIAL HERMANN HOSPITAL SYS
7737 Southwest Fwy, Houston, TX 77074
Phone: (713) 776-5000
Sales: $207,100,000
Company Type: Private
SIC: 8062
  General medical and surgical hospitals, nsk

Employees: NA
Employees here: 5,000

D-U-N-S 05-109-8184
MEMORIAL HEALTH SYSTEMS E TEXAS
1201 W Frank Ave, Lufkin, TX 75904
Phone: (409) 634-8111
Sales: $69,179,000
Company Type: Private
SIC: 8062
  General hospital
Gary Whatley, Administrator

Employees: 880
Employees here: 770

D-U-N-S 07-550-9794
MEMORIAL HOSP
175 Madison Ave, Mount Holly, NJ 8060
Phone: (609) 267-0700
Sales: $130,360,000
Company Type: Private
SIC: 8062
  General hospital
Chester B Kaletkowski, President

Employees: 1,450
Employees here: 1,200

D-U-N-S 06-052-2653
MEMORIAL HOSPITAL OF ALBANY NY
600 Northern Blvd, Albany, NY 12204
Phone: (518) 471-3221
Sales: $51,300,000
Company Type: Private
SIC: 8062
  General hospital
Bernard Shapiro, Chief Executive Officer

Employees: 1,110
Employees here: 1,105

D-U-N-S 04-072-6275
MEMORIAL HOSPITAL OF LARAMIE CNTY
214 E 23rd St, Cheyenne, WY 82001
Phone: (307) 634-3341
Sales: $71,134,000
Company Type: Private
SIC: 8062
  Hospital
Jon M Gates, Chief Executive Officer

Employees: 900
Employees here: 450

D-U-N-S 06-599-7157
MEMORIAL HOSPITAL OF MARTINSVL
320 Hospital Dr, Martinsville, VA 24112
Phone: (540) 666-7200
Sales: $59,434,000
Company Type: Private
SIC: 8062
  General hospital and health care facility
Joseph Roach, Executive Director

Employees: 800
Employees here: 790

D-U-N-S 07-383-0994
MEMORIAL HOSPITAL AT OCONOMOWOC
791 Summit Ave, Oconomowoc, WI 53066
Phone: (414) 569-9400

Sales: $34,758,000
Company Type: Private
SIC: 8062
  Hospital
Douglas Guy, President

Employees: 604
Employees here: 604

D-U-N-S 01-037-5376
MEMORIAL HOSPITAL SHERIDAN CNTY
1401 W 5th St, Sheridan, WY 82801
Phone: (307) 672-1000
Sales: $23,831,000
Company Type: Private
SIC: 8062
  General hospital
T M Goldman, Administrator

Employees: 410
Employees here: 410

D-U-N-S 07-121-4472
MEMORIAL HOSPITAL
325 S Belmont St, York, PA 17403
Phone: (717) 843-8623
Sales: $46,285,000
Company Type: Private
SIC: 8062
  Hospital & home health care services
Sally J Dixon, President

Employees: 704
Employees here: 608

D-U-N-S 06-938-3651
MEMORIAL HOSPITAL & MEDICAL
600 Memorial Ave, Cumberland, MD 21502
Phone: (301) 777-4000
Sales: $73,598,000
Company Type: Private
SIC: 8062
  General hospital
Thomas C Dowdell, Executive Director

Employees: 1,100
Employees here: 1,000

D-U-N-S 06-921-6992
MEMORIAL HOSPITAL AND MANOR
1500 E Shotwell St, Bainbridge, GA 31717
Phone: (912) 246-3500
Sales: $22,445,000
Company Type: Private
SIC: 8062
  Hospital & nursing home
Cynthia Bickers, Asst Admin-Nursing

Employees: 400
Employees here: 400

D-U-N-S 07-491-9259
MEMORIAL HOSPITAL OF EASTON MD
219 S Washington St, Easton, MD 21601
Phone: (410) 822-1000
Sales: $75,261,000
Company Type: Private
SIC: 8062
  General hospital
Joe Ross, President

Employees: 1,241
Employees here: 1,216

D-U-N-S 06-664-6183
MEMORIAL HOSPITAL OF GARDENA,
  (Parent: Health Net)
1145 W Redondo Beach Blvd, Gardena, CA 90247
Phone: (310) 532-4200
Sales: $28,075,000
Company Type: Public Family Member
SIC: 8062
  General hospital
Frank Katsuda, Administrator

Employees: 430
Employees here: 430

D-U-N-S 06-470-1261
MEMORIAL HOSPITAL OF S BEND
615 N Michigan St, South Bend, IN 46601
Phone: (219) 234-9041

Sales: $187,162,000
Company Type: Private
SIC: 8062
  General medical hospital
Philip A Newbold, President
      Employees: 2,010
      Employees here: 2,000

D-U-N-S 07-503-8703
MEMORIAL HOSPITAL OF UN CNTY
500 London Ave, Marysville, OH 43040
Phone: (937) 644-6115
Sales: $44,089,000
Company Type: Private
SIC: 8062
  General hospital
Danny L Boggs, Chief Executive Officer
   Employees: 500
   Employees here: 465

D-U-N-S 07-947-5109
MEMORIAL HOSPITAL AT GULFPORT
4500 13th St, Gulfport, MS 39501
Phone: (228) 863-1441
Sales: $153,896,000
Company Type: Private
SIC: 8062
  General hospital
W R Burton, Administrator
   Employees: 1,900
   Employees here: 1,850

D-U-N-S 07-576-1783
MEMORIAL HOSPITAL CORPORATION
1400 E Boulder St, Colorado Springs, CO 80909
Phone: (719) 365-5000
Sales: $202,623,000
Company Type: Private
SIC: 8062
  General & surgical hospital
J R Peters, Executive Director
   Employees: 2,438
   Employees here: 2,408

D-U-N-S 12-032-2375
MEMORIAL HOSPITAL INC
401 Memorial Dr, Manchester, KY 40962
Phone: (606) 598-5104
Sales: $22,516,000
Company Type: Private
SIC: 8062
  Hospital
Jimm Bunch, President
   Employees: 315
   Employees here: 255

D-U-N-S 03-023-1377
MEMORIAL HOSPITAL INC
191 N Main St, Wellsville, NY 14895
Phone: (716) 593-1100
Sales: $20,733,000
Company Type: Private
SIC: 8062
  General hospital
William M Di Berardino, Administrator
   Employees: 380
   Employees here: 368

D-U-N-S 04-684-2829
MEMORIAL HOSPITAL PASADENA
906 E Southmore Ave, Pasadena, TX 77502
Phone: (713) 477-0411
Sales: $24,900,000
Company Type: Private
SIC: 8062
  General hospital
Dennis Knox, Chief Executive Officer
   Employees: 550
   Employees here: 550

D-U-N-S 84-847-7378
MEMORIAL HOSPITAL SELAM COUNTY
310 Salem Woodstown Rd, Salem, NJ 8079
Phone: (609) 935-1000

Sales: $23,600,000
Company Type: Private
SIC: 8093
  Provides physical therapy and through subsidiary is a general medical and surgical hospital
Joseph M Galvin Jr, President
   Employees: 775
   Employees here: 775

D-U-N-S 86-859-9317
MEMORIAL HOSPITAL WEST VOLUSIA
701 W Plymouth Ave, Deland, FL 32720
Phone: (904) 734-3320
Sales: $107,000,000
Company Type: Private
SIC: 8062
  General hospital
Richard Lind, Chief Executive Officer
   Employees: 563
   Employees here: 563

D-U-N-S 15-450-6505
MEMORIAL HOSPITAL
1101 Michigan Ave, Logansport, IN 46947
Phone: (219) 753-7541
Sales: $26,963,000
Company Type: Private
SIC: 8062
  General hospital
George W Poor, Chief Executive Officer
   Employees: 505
   Employees here: 500

D-U-N-S 07-534-1255
MEMORIAL HOSPITAL, INC
119 Belmont St, Worcester, MA 1605
Phone: (508) 793-6611
Sales: $171,781,000
Company Type: Private
SIC: 8062
  Operates hospitals family health centers & provides home health care services
Dr Peter H Levine Md, President
   Employees: 3,510
   Employees here: 2,200

D-U-N-S 06-887-7372
MEMORIAL HOSPITALS ASSN
1700 Coffee Rd, Modesto, CA 95355
Phone: (209) 526-4500
Sales: $99,982,000
Company Type: Private
SIC: 8062
  General hospital
David Benn, Chief Executive Officer
   Employees: 2,250
   Employees here: 2,000

D-U-N-S 07-682-8409
MEMORIAL HOSPITL-CANCER/ALLIED
1275 York Ave, New York, NY 10021
Phone: (212) 639-2000
Sales: $603,973,000
Company Type: Private
SIC: 8069
  Specialty hospital
Dr Paul A Marks Md, Chief Executive Officer
   Employees: 3,000
   Employees here: 2,300

D-U-N-S 04-987-6154
MEMORIAL MED CTR AT S AMBOY
540 Bordentown Ave, South Amboy, NJ 8879
Phone: (732) 721-1000
Sales: $29,435,000
Company Type: Private
SIC: 8062
  General hospital
Irv J Diamond, Chief Executive Officer
   Employees: 745
   Employees here: 700

D-U-N-S 11-017-4034
MEMORIAL MED GROUP A PROF CORP
19191 S Vermont Ave Fl 3, Torrance, CA 90502
Phone: (310) 354-4351

Sales: $21,552,000
Employees: 160
Company Type: Private
Employees here: 2
SIC: 8011
Medical doctor's office
Dr Robert Margolis Md, President

D-U-N-S 07-562-0179
MEMORIAL MEDICAL CENTER
800 N Rutledge St, Springfield, IL 62702
Phone: (217) 788-3000
Sales: $236,803,000
Employees: 2,575
Company Type: Private
Employees here: 2,535
SIC: 8062
General hospital
Robert T Clarke, President

D-U-N-S 11-075-2359
MEMORIAL MEDICAL CENTER INC
4700 Waters Ave, Savannah, GA 31404
Phone: (912) 350-8000
Sales: $327,237,000
Employees: 5,000
Company Type: Private
Employees here: 3,500
SIC: 8062
General hospital
Robert Colvin, President

D-U-N-S 03-001-8725
MEMORIAL MEDICAL CENTER INC
1615 Maple Ln, Ashland, WI 54806
Phone: (715) 682-4563
Sales: $26,794,000
Employees: 650
Company Type: Private
Employees here: 430
SIC: 8062
General hospital
Dan Hymans, President

D-U-N-S 07-456-4469
MEMORIAL MEDICAL CENTER
& Doty Rd Rr 14, Woodstock, IL 60098
Phone: (815) 338-2500
Sales: $53,211,000
Employees: 750
Company Type: Private
Employees here: NA
SIC: 8062
General hospital
Jim D Redding, Chief Executive Officer

D-U-N-S 07-508-6520
MEMORIAL MEDICAL CENTER
2450 S Telshor Blvd, Las Cruces, NM 88011
Phone: (505) 522-8641
Sales: $125,498,000
Employees: 1,450
Company Type: Private
Employees here: 1,400
SIC: 8062
General hospital
Steven Smith, President

D-U-N-S 07-258-2190
MEMORIAL MEDICAL CTR OF W MICH
1 N Atkinson Dr, Ludington, MI 49431
Phone: (616) 843-2591
Sales: $30,666,000
Employees: 450
Company Type: Private
Employees here: 450
SIC: 8062
General hospital
Robert Marquardt, President

D-U-N-S 07-452-6690
MEMORIAL MISSION HOSPITAL INC
509 Biltmore Ave, Asheville, NC 28801
Phone: (828) 255-4000

Sales: $247,494,000
Employees: 3,000
Company Type: Private
Employees here: 2,900
SIC: 8062
General hospital
Robert F Burgin, President

D-U-N-S 13-932-5237
MEMORIAL SISTERS OF CHARITY
2600 North Loop W Ste 620, Houston, TX 77092
Phone: (713) 683-2900
Sales: $30,900,000
Employees: 450
Company Type: Private
Employees here: 130
SIC: 8011
Hmo health insurance medical care & services
Richard W Todd, President

D-U-N-S 03-885-6241
MENDOCINO COAST DISTRICT HOSP
700 River Dr, Fort Bragg, CA 95437
Phone: (707) 961-1234
Sales: $20,731,000
Employees: 300
Company Type: Private
Employees here: 224
SIC: 8062
Hospital
Elizabeth J Macgard, Chief Executive Officer

D-U-N-S 18-240-6694
MENNINGER CLINIC, INCORPORATED
5800 SW 6th Ave, Topeka, KS 66606
Phone: (785) 350-5000
Sales: $57,321,000
Employees: NA
Company Type: Private
Employees here: NA
SIC: 8093
Psychiatric clinic
Efrain Bleibert, President

D-U-N-S 07-988-1579
MENNINGER FOUNDATION INC
5800 SW 6th Ave, Topeka, KS 66606
Phone: (785) 350-5000
Sales: $48,371,000
Employees: 1,100
Company Type: Private
Employees here: 975
SIC: 8063
Psychiatry hospital
Dr W W Menninger Md, Chief Executive Officer

D-U-N-S 07-691-5800
MENORAH PK CNTR FOR THE AGNG
27100 Cedar Rd, Cleveland, OH 44122
Phone: (216) 831-6500
Sales: $25,720,000
Employees: 827
Company Type: Private
Employees here: 777
SIC: 8051
Nursing home
Steven Raichilson, Executive Director

D-U-N-S 04-020-3564
MENTAL HEALTH CARE INC
5707 N 22nd St, Tampa, FL 33610
Phone: (813) 237-3914
Sales: $21,061,000
Employees: 299
Company Type: Private
Employees here: 120
SIC: 8093
Psychiatric outpatient clinic
Jay Hafferty, Director of Finance

D-U-N-S 18-222-9567
MENTAL HEALTH CORP OF DENVER
4141 E Dickenson Pl, Denver, CO 80222
Phone: (303) 757-7227

Sales: $30,000,000   *Employees:* 485
Company Type: Private   *Employees here:* 50
SIC: 8093
  Mental health out-patient clinic
Roberto Quiroz, Executive Director

D-U-N-S 08-000-8998
MENTAL HEALTH, DEPARTMENT OF
5400 Arsenal St, Saint Louis, MO 63139
Phone: (314) 644-8000
Sales: $42,100,000   *Employees:* NA
Company Type: Private   *Employees here:* 1,000
SIC: 8062
  State mental health hospital
Dr John Swiehaus, Branch Manager

D-U-N-S 07-199-5450
MENTAL HEALTH, DEPARTMENT OF
600 E 5th St, Fulton, MO 65251
Phone: (573) 592-4100
Sales: $40,700,000   *Employees:* NA
Company Type: Private   *Employees here:* 1,298
SIC: 8063
  State psychiatric hospital
Stephen Reeves, N/A

D-U-N-S 07-590-2882
MENTAL HEALTH, DEPARTMENT OF
1010 W Columbia St, Farmington, MO 63640
Phone: (573) 756-6792
Sales: $21,100,000   *Employees:* NA
Company Type: Private   *Employees here:* 670
SIC: 8063
  Psychiatric hospital
Don Barton, N/A

D-U-N-S 06-370-0231
MERCER CNTY JNT TWNSHP
800 W Main St, Coldwater, OH 45828
Phone: (419) 678-2341
Sales: $21,909,000   *Employees:* 412
Company Type: Private   *Employees here:* 392
SIC: 8062
  General medical & surgical hospital
James Isaacs, Chief Executive Officer

D-U-N-S 07-553-5187
MERCER MEDICAL CENTER
446 Bellevue Ave, Trenton, NJ 8618
Phone: (609) 394-4000
Sales: $78,210,000   *Employees:* 1,500
Company Type: Private   *Employees here:* 1,280
SIC: 8062
  Hospital
Charles E Baer, President

D-U-N-S 07-306-7480
MERCY CHILDREN'S HOSPITAL
2401 Gillham Rd, Kansas City, MO 64108
Phone: (816) 234-3000
Sales: $146,504,000   *Employees:* 2,000
Company Type: Private   *Employees here:* 1,850
SIC: 8069
  Children's hospital
Randall O'donnell Phd, President

D-U-N-S 04-867-7298
MERCY FITZGERALD HOSPITAL INC
501 S 54th St, Philadelphia, PA 19143
Phone: (215) 748-9000

Sales: $54,500,000   *Employees:* NA
Company Type: Private   *Employees here:* 1,100
SIC: 8062
  General hospital
Bernadett Mangan, President

D-U-N-S 80-466-9539
MERCY FITZGERALD HOSPITAL INC
Lansdowne Ave & Bailey Rd, Darby, PA 19023
Phone: (610) 237-4000
Sales: $194,683,000   *Employees:* NA
Company Type: Private   *Employees here:* NA
SIC: 8062
  General hospital
Plato A Marinakos, President

D-U-N-S 07-706-2511
MERCY HAVERFORD HOSPITAL
2000 Old West Chester Pik, Havertown, PA 19083
Phone: (610) 645-3600
Sales: $26,466,000   *Employees:* 500
Company Type: Private   *Employees here:* 500
SIC: 8062
  General hospital
Andrew E Harris, Chief Executive Officer

D-U-N-S 06-543-0712
MERCY HEALTH CENTER
4300 W Memorial Rd, Oklahoma City, OK 73120
Phone: (405) 755-1515
Sales: $133,661,000   *Employees:* 1,780
Company Type: Private   *Employees here:* 1,630
SIC: 8062
  General hospital
Bruce F Buchanan, President

D-U-N-S 06-795-2259
MERCY HEALTH CTR OF MANHATTAN
1823 College Ave, Manhattan, KS 66502
Phone: (785) 776-3300
Sales: $34,300,000   *Employees:* 750
Company Type: Private   *Employees here:* 750
SIC: 8062
  Hospital
Mike Nunamaker, Administrator

D-U-N-S 06-867-2617
MERCY HEALTH SERVICES
2101 Court St, Sioux City, IA 51104
Phone: (712) 279-2445
Sales: $69,500,000   *Employees:* NA
Company Type: Private   *Employees here:* 1,800
SIC: 8062
  Hospital
Verna Welte, Vice-President

D-U-N-S 08-273-1043
MERCY HEALTH SERVICES
801 5th St, Sioux City, IA 51101
Phone: (712) 279-2110
Sales: $59,300,000   *Employees:* NA
Company Type: Private   *Employees here:* 1,536
SIC: 8062
  Hospital
Deb Vanderbrooke, N/A

D-U-N-S 08-875-3090
MERCY HEALTH SERVICES
5301 E Huron River Dr, Ypsilanti, MI 48197
Phone: (734) 572-3456

Sales: $169,500,000
Company Type: Private
SIC: 8062
   Health center
Robert Laverty, President
Employees: NA
Employees here: 4,000

D-U-N-S 02-010-7678
MERCY HEALTH SERVICES
2601 Electric Ave, Port Huron, MI 48060
Phone: (810) 985-1500
Sales: $33,500,000
Company Type: Private
SIC: 8062
   General hospital
Mary Trimmer, Principal
Employees: NA
Employees here: 800

D-U-N-S 07-277-4631
MERCY HEALTH SERVICES
900 Woodward Ave, Pontiac, MI 48341
Phone: (248) 858-3000
Sales: $110,200,000
Company Type: Private
SIC: 8062
   General hospital
Thomas Feuirg, N/A
Employees: NA
Employees here: 2,600

D-U-N-S 08-160-4555
MERCY HEALTH SERVICES
1210 W Saginaw St, Lansing, MI 48915
Phone: (517) 372-3610
Sales: $42,100,000
Company Type: Private
SIC: 8062
   General hospital
Joe Damore, President
Employees: NA
Employees here: 1,000

D-U-N-S 79-664-0951
MERCY HEALTH SERVICES
1210 W Saginaw St, Lansing, MI 48915
Phone: (517) 372-3610
Sales: $72,000,000
Company Type: Private
SIC: 8062
   General hospital
Renee Rivard, Manager
Employees: NA
Employees here: 1,700

D-U-N-S 79-880-6105
MERCY HEALTH SERVICES
620 Byron Rd, Howell, MI 48843
Phone: (517) 545-6000
Sales: $31,400,000
Company Type: Private
SIC: 8062
   General hospital
C W Laudarbach Jr, Principal
Employees: NA
Employees here: 750

D-U-N-S 02-971-3625
MERCY HEALTH SERVICES
5555 Conner St, Detroit, MI 48213
Phone: (313) 579-4000
Sales: $46,400,000
Company Type: Private
SIC: 8062
   General hospital
David Spivey, Chief Executive Officer
Employees: NA
Employees here: 1,100

D-U-N-S 02-089-2584
MERCY HEALTH SERVICES
400 Hobart St, Cadillac, MI 49601
Phone: (616) 779-7200

Sales: $26,100,000
Company Type: Private
SIC: 8062
   General hospital
Dennis Renander, Principal
Employees: NA
Employees here: 675

D-U-N-S 07-421-2150
MERCY HEALTH SERVICES
5301 E Huron River Dr, Ann Arbor, MI 48106
Phone: (734) 572-3456
Sales: $148,400,000
Company Type: Private
SIC: 8062
   General hospital
Gary Saja, N/A
Employees: NA
Employees here: 3,500

D-U-N-S 03-065-4669
MERCY HEALTH SYSTEM OF KANSAS
821 Burke St, Fort Scott, KS 66701
Phone: (316) 223-2200
Sales: $31,900,000
Company Type: Private
SIC: 8062
   General hospital
Susan Barret, Chief Executive Officer
Employees: 700
Employees here: 448

D-U-N-S 04-301-8472
MERCY HEALTHCARE ARIZONA INC
350 W Thomas Rd, Phoenix, AZ 85013
Phone: (602) 285-3000
Sales: $287,795,000
Company Type: Private
SIC: 8062
   Medical & surgical hospital
Mary Yarbrough, President
Employees: 3,100
Employees here: 3,000

D-U-N-S 78-662-4866
MERCY HEALTHCARE INC
2700 NW Stewart Pkwy, Roseburg, OR 97470
Phone: (541) 673-0611
Sales: $64,202,000
Company Type: Private
SIC: 8062
   Hospital & hospital administration
Jacquetta Taylor, President
Employees: 700
Employees here: 600

D-U-N-S 07-610-1906
MERCY HEALTHCARE NORTH
2175 Rosaline Ave, Redding, CA 96001
Phone: (530) 225-6000
Sales: $184,526,000
Company Type: Private
SIC: 8062
   General hospital
George A Govier, Chief Executive Officer
Employees: 1,350
Employees here: 1,340

D-U-N-S 17-450-2682
MERCY HEALTHCARE SACRAMENTO
10540 White Rock Rd, Rancho Cordova, CA 95670
Phone: (916) 851-2000
Sales: $563,247,000
Company Type: Private
SIC: 8062
   Hospitals
Michael Erne, President
Employees: 6,131
Employees here: 450

D-U-N-S 82-519-7007
MERCY HEALTHCARE SACRAMENTO
7500 Hospital Dr, Sacramento, CA 95823
Phone: (916) 423-3000

Sales: $48,900,000   *Employees:* NA
Company Type: Private   *Employees here:* 990
SIC: 8062
    General hospital medical doctor's office
Michael Earn, Principal

D-U-N-S 06-133-1682
MERCY HOSPITAL OF WILKES BARRE PA
25 Church St, Wilkes Barre, PA 18765
Phone: (717) 826-3100
Sales: $146,767,000   *Employees:* 683
Company Type: Private   *Employees here:* 649
SIC: 8062
    General & short-term care hospital
John Nespoli, Chief Executive Officer

D-U-N-S 07-173-2499
MERCY HOSPITAL
144 State St, Portland, ME 4101
Phone: (207) 879-3000
Sales: $69,988,000   *Employees:* 917
Company Type: Private   *Employees here:* 915
SIC: 8062
    General hospital affiliated with ama residency
Howard R Buckley, President

D-U-N-S 06-699-1902
MERCY HOSPITAL (INC)
233 Carew St 271, Springfield, MA 1104
Phone: (413) 748-9000
Sales: $71,400,000   *Employees:* 1,535
Company Type: Private   *Employees here:* 1,300
SIC: 8062
    General hospital
Vincent Mc Corkle, President

D-U-N-S 02-004-7254
MERCY HOSPITAL & MEDICAL CTR
2525 S Michigan Ave, Chicago, IL 60616
Phone: (312) 567-2000
Sales: $182,038,000   *Employees:* 2,100
Company Type: Private   *Employees here:* 1,900
SIC: 8062
    General hospital
Charles Vonvorse, President

D-U-N-S 03-022-0727
MERCY HOSPITAL OF BUFFALO
565 Abbott Rd, Buffalo, NY 14220
Phone: (716) 826-7000
Sales: $107,200,000   *Employees:* 2,100
Company Type: Private   *Employees here:* 1,900
SIC: 8062
    General medical & surgical hospital
James Connolly, President

D-U-N-S 05-511-6214
MERCY HOSPITAL OF LAREDO
1515 Logan Ave, Laredo, TX 78040
Phone: (956) 718-6222
Sales: $98,623,000   *Employees:* 1,400
Company Type: Private   *Employees here:* 1,360
SIC: 8062
    Hospital
Mark Stauder, President

D-U-N-S 07-918-6011
MERCY HOSPITAL OF SCRANTON PA
746 Jefferson Ave, Scranton, PA 18510
Phone: (717) 348-7100

Sales: $106,895,000   *Employees:* 1,476
Company Type: Private   *Employees here:* 1,472
SIC: 8062
    General hospital
John Nespoli, President

D-U-N-S 08-015-6599
MERCY HOSPITAL OF TIFFIN OHIO
485 W Market St, Tiffin, OH 44883
Phone: (419) 447-3130
Sales: $25,446,000   *Employees:* 360
Company Type: Private   *Employees here:* 360
SIC: 8062
    General hospital
Mark Shugarman, Chief Executive Officer

D-U-N-S 07-581-7015
MERCY HOSPITAL OF WATERTOWN,
218 Stone St, Watertown, NY 13601
Phone: (315) 782-7400
Sales: $24,848,000   *Employees:* 610
Company Type: Private   *Employees here:* 610
SIC: 8059
    General hospital
Betty Forshaw, Executive Director

D-U-N-S 07-677-7275
MERCY HOSPITAL ANDERSON
7500 State Rd, Cincinnati, OH 45255
Phone: (513) 624-4500
Sales: $79,258,000   *Employees:* 901
Company Type: Private   *Employees here:* 901
SIC: 8062
    Hospital
Karen Ehrat, President

D-U-N-S 07-387-2178
MERCY HOSPITAL INC
3663 S Miami Ave, Miami, FL 33133
Phone: (305) 285-2714
Sales: $150,801,000   *Employees:* 2,000
Company Type: Private   *Employees here:* 1,938
SIC: 8062
    General medical & surgical hospital
Edward J Rosasco Jr, President

D-U-N-S 07-105-9190
MERCY HOSPITAL INC
2001 Vail Ave, Charlotte, NC 28207
Phone: (704) 379-5000
Sales: $110,303,000   *Employees:* 1,250
Company Type: Private   *Employees here:* 1,000
SIC: 8062
    General hospital
Harry A Nurkin Phd, President

D-U-N-S 07-347-8166
MERCY HOSPITAL MEDICAL CENTER
400 University Ave, Des Moines, IA 50314
Phone: (515) 247-8318
Sales: $275,229,000   *Employees:* 4,500
Company Type: Private   *Employees here:* 4,200
SIC: 8062
    General hospital
Thomas Reitinger, President

D-U-N-S 07-763-0069
MERCY MED CTR OF WILLISTON
1301 15th Ave W, Williston, ND 58801
Phone: (701) 774-7400

Sales: $28,206,000   *Employees:* 450
Company Type: Private   *Employees here:* 450
SIC: 8062
General hospital
Duane D Jerde, President

D-U-N-S 06-962-0524
MERCY MED CTR CEDAR RAPIDS IOWA
701 10th St SE, Cedar Rapids, IA 52403
Phone: (319) 398-6011
Sales: $100,703,000   *Employees:* 1,600
Company Type: Private   *Employees here:* 1,600
SIC: 8062
General medical and surgical hospital
A J Tinker, President

D-U-N-S 08-577-4107
MERCY MEDICAL A CORPORATION
101 Villa Dr, Daphne, AL 36526
Phone: (334) 626-2694
Sales: $30,413,000   *Employees:* 750
Company Type: Private   *Employees here:* 255
SIC: 8051
Skilled nursing care facility specialty hospital
Sister M Wilhelm, President

D-U-N-S 07-834-0460
MERCY MEDICAL CENTER
375 E Park Ave, Durango, CO 81301
Phone: (970) 247-4311
Sales: $55,143,000   *Employees:* 900
Company Type: Private   *Employees here:* 800
SIC: 8062
General hospital
Val Baciarelli, Administrator

D-U-N-S 07-298-4867
MERCY MEDICAL CENTER
1512 12th Ave Rd, Nampa, ID 83686
Phone: (208) 467-1171
Sales: $60,659,000   *Employees:* 650
Company Type: Private   *Employees here:* 542
SIC: 8062
General hospital
Joseph Messmer, Chief Executive Officer

D-U-N-S 03-078-5042
MERCY MEDICAL CENTER INC
2700 NW Stewart Pkwy, Roseburg, OR 97470
Phone: (541) 673-0611
Sales: $51,036,000   *Employees:* 652
Company Type: Private   *Employees here:* 652
SIC: 8062
Hospital
Victor J Fresolane, President

D-U-N-S 07-494-3556
MERCY MEDICAL CENTER
301 Saint Paul Pl, Baltimore, MD 21202
Phone: (410) 332-9000
Sales: $125,777,000   *Employees:* 1,300
Company Type: Private   *Employees here:* 1,250
SIC: 8062
General hospital & provides other related healthcare services
Sister H Amos, President

D-U-N-S 06-592-6099
MERCY MEDICAL CENTER
1000 N Village Ave, Rockville Centre, NY 11570
Phone: (516) 255-0111

Sales: $133,343,000   *Employees:* 1,610
Company Type: Private   *Employees here:* 1,420
SIC: 8062
General medical & surgical hospital
Vincent Dirubbio, President

D-U-N-S 04-803-0985
MERCY MEDICAL CTR OF OSHKOSH
631 Hazel St, Oshkosh, WI 54901
Phone: (920) 236-2000
Sales: $50,900,000   *Employees:* 1,100
Company Type: Private   *Employees here:* 1,060
SIC: 8062
General hospital
Joseph P Ross, President

D-U-N-S 79-886-0946
MERCY MEDICAL DEVELOPMENT,
3659 S Miami Ave Ste 4004, Miami, FL 33133
Phone: (305) 285-2922
Sales: $150,801,000   *Employees:* 365
Company Type: Private   *Employees here:* 345
SIC: 8093
Outpatient clinic performing diagnostics and rehabilitation
Maureen Mann, Administrator

D-U-N-S 07-123-4637
MERCY MEMORIAL HEALTH CENTER
1011 14th Ave Nw, Ardmore, OK 73401
Phone: (580) 223-5400
Sales: $110,000,000   *Employees:* 700
Company Type: Private   *Employees here:* 700
SIC: 8062
General hospital
Bobby G Thompson, President

D-U-N-S 87-422-7820
MERCY MOUNT CLEMENS CORP
215 North Ave, Mount Clemens, MI 48043
Phone: (810) 466-9300
Sales: $25,000,000   *Employees:* NA
Company Type: Private   *Employees here:* 600
SIC: 8062
General hospital
Jack Weiner, President

D-U-N-S 07-839-6058
MERCY MOUNT CLEMENS CORP
15855 19 Mile Rd, Clinton Township, MI 48038
Phone: (810) 263-2300
Sales: $128,721,000   *Employees:* 2,543
Company Type: Private   *Employees here:* 1,700
SIC: 8062
General medical & surgical hospital
Jack Weiner, President

D-U-N-S 06-876-0081
MERCY PROVIDENCE HOSPITAL
1004 Arch St, Pittsburgh, PA 15212
Phone: (412) 323-5600
Sales: $27,947,000   *Employees:* 783
Company Type: Private   *Employees here:* 500
SIC: 8062
General hospital
Sister J Andiorio, Chief Executive Officer

D-U-N-S 16-106-7186
MERCY SERVICES FOR AGING
34605 W 12 Mile Rd, Farmington Hills, MI 48331
Phone: (248) 305-7995

Sales: $64,420,000   *Employees:* 1,800
Company Type: Private   *Employees here:* 20
SIC: 8361
    Long term care
Karen Struve, President

D-U-N-S 06-371-6542
MERCY-MEMORIAL HOSPITAL CORP
740 N Macomb St, Monroe, MI 48162
Phone: (734) 241-1700
Sales: $68,883,000   *Employees:* 817
Company Type: Private   *Employees here:* 811
SIC: 8062
    General hospital
Richard S Hiltz, President

D-U-N-S 08-678-0400
MERCY-MEMORIAL MEDICAL CENTER
1234 Napier Ave, Saint Joseph, MI 49085
Phone: (616) 983-8300
Sales: $136,501,000   *Employees:* 2,800
Company Type: Private   *Employees here:* 2,250
SIC: 8062
    General medical hospital
Joseph Wasserman, President

D-U-N-S 15-527-7825
MERIDIA HEALTH SYSTEM
6700 Beta Dr, Cleveland, OH 44143
Phone: (440) 449-7710
Sales: $370,248,000   *Employees:* 3,200
Company Type: Private   *Employees here:* 101
SIC: 8062
    General medical & surgical hospital
Charles Miner, President

D-U-N-S 62-528-4021
MERIDIA HEALTH SYSTEM
6780 Mayfield Rd, Cleveland, OH 44124
Phone: (440) 449-4500
Sales: $67,700,000   *Employees:* NA
Company Type: Private   *Employees here:* 1,600
SIC: 8062
    General hospital
Cathy Larry, Principal

D-U-N-S 09-783-0582
MERIDIAN BEHAVIORAL HEALTH CARE
950 Michigan St, Lake City, FL 32025
Phone: (904) 758-0555
Sales: $21,300,000   *Employees:* 700
Company Type: Private   *Employees here:* 80
SIC: 8093
    Mental health clinic outpatient
Charles E Debolt, Chairman of the Board

D-U-N-S 96-540-8230
MERIDIAN HOSPITALS CORPORATION
1 Riverview Plz, Red Bank, NJ 7701
Phone: (732) 741-2700
Sales: $507,078,000   *Employees:* 7,357
Company Type: Private   *Employees here:* 2,000
SIC: 8062
    General hospital
John K Lloyd, President

D-U-N-S 18-692-9691
MERIDIAN HOSPITALS CORPORATION
425 Jack Martin Blvd, Brick, NJ 8724
Phone: (732) 840-2200

Sales: $29,300,000   *Employees:* NA
Company Type: Private   *Employees here:* 600
SIC: 8062
    General hospital
John Gribbin, N/A

D-U-N-S 02-653-6979
MERIDIAN MEDICAL GROUP INC
2839 Paces Ferry Rd SE, Atlanta, GA 30339
Phone: (770) 933-2700
Sales: $41,200,000   *Employees:* 600
Company Type: Private   *Employees here:* 70
SIC: 8011
    Medical doctor's office
Michael S Robinowitz, President

D-U-N-S 12-137-0647
MERIS LABORATORIES, INC
1075 E Brokaw Rd, San Jose, CA 95131
Phone: (408) 452-3100
Sales: $30,000,000   *Employees:* 500
Company Type: Public   *Employees here:* 200
SIC: 8071
    Clinical laboratory
Phil Tremonti, President

D-U-N-S 82-463-6104
MERIT BEHAVIORAL CARE CORP
    (Parent: Magellan Health Services Inc)
1 Maynard Dr, Park Ridge, NJ 7656
Phone: (201) 391-8700
Sales: $555,717,000   *Employees:* 2,800
Company Type: Public Family Member   *Employees here:* 90
SIC: 8093
    Behavioral health managed care
Albert S Waxman Phd, Chief Executive Officer

D-U-N-S 80-573-3490
MERITCARE HEALTH ENTERPRISES
    (Parent: Meritcare Health System)
737 Broadway, Fargo, ND 58102
Phone: (701) 234-2000
Sales: $121,421,000   *Employees:* 1,500
Company Type: Private   *Employees here:* 669
SIC: 8011
    Medical doctor's office ret drugs/sundries
Roger L Gilbertson, President

D-U-N-S 06-815-7668
MERITCARE HOSPITAL
720 4th St N, Fargo, ND 58122
Phone: (701) 234-6000
Sales: $177,544,000   *Employees:* 1,806
Company Type: Private   *Employees here:* 1,646
SIC: 8062
    Hospital
Dr Robert Gilbertson, President

D-U-N-S 15-731-3115
MERITER HEALTH SERVICES INC
309 W Washington Ave, Madison, WI 53703
Phone: (608) 258-3230
Sales: $188,983,000   *Employees:* 4,500
Company Type: Private   *Employees here:* 3
SIC: 8062
    General hospital & management services
Terri L Potter, President

D-U-N-S 05-529-6529
MERITER HOSPITAL INC
202 S Park St, Madison, WI 53715
Phone: (608) 267-6000

Sales: $158,665,000   *Employees:* 2,335
Company Type: Private   *Employees here:* 1,980
SIC: 8062
  General hospitals
Terri Potter, President

D-U-N-S 11-402-9416
MERITER MANAGEMENT SERVICES
  (Parent: Meriter Health Services Inc)
309 W Washington Ave, Madison, WI 53703
Phone: (608) 258-3209
Sales: $29,350,000   *Employees:* 351
Company Type: Private   *Employees here:* 60
SIC: 8071
  Medical testing laboratory & hospital management services
Terri L Potter, Chief Executive Officer

D-U-N-S 05-096-3727
MERLE WEST MEDICAL CENTER
2865 Daggett Ave, Klamath Falls, OR 97601
Phone: (541) 882-6311
Sales: $66,202,000   *Employees:* 1,100
Company Type: Private   *Employees here:* 930
SIC: 8062
  Hospital
Paul Stewart, President

D-U-N-S 07-244-5083
MESA GENERAL HOSPITAL MED CTR
  (Parent: Tenet Healthcare Corporation)
515 N Mesa Dr, Mesa, AZ 85201
Phone: (602) 969-9111
Sales: $100,000,000   *Employees:* 450
Company Type: Public Family Member   *Employees here:* 450
SIC: 8062
  General medical & surgical hospital
J O Lewis, Chief Executive Officer

D-U-N-S 09-136-9264
MESQUITE COMMUNITY HOSPITAL LP
3500 Interstate 30, Mesquite, TX 75150
Phone: (972) 270-3300
Sales: $37,638,000   *Employees:* 583
Company Type: Private   *Employees here:* 580
SIC: 8062
  General hospital
Raymond P Deblasi, Chief Executive Officer

D-U-N-S 82-931-8781
METHODIST CHILDREN'S HOSPITAL
3606 21st St, Lubbock, TX 79410
Phone: (806) 784-5040
Sales: $27,347,000   *Employees:* 200
Company Type: Private   *Employees here:* 200
SIC: 8069
  Specialty hospital
George Mccleskey, President

D-U-N-S 04-313-3859
METHODIST HEALTH CARE MEMPHIS
1265 Union Ave, Memphis, TN 38104
Phone: (901) 726-7000
Sales: $564,870,000   *Employees:* 8,100
Company Type: Private   *Employees here:* 5,575
SIC: 8062
  General hospitals
Gary A Shorb, President

D-U-N-S 01-986-8892
METHODIST HEALTHCARE MINISTRIE
4507 Medical Dr, San Antonio, TX 78229
Phone: (210) 692-0234

Sales: $29,824,000   *Employees:* 25
Company Type: Private   *Employees here:* 25
SIC: 8011
  Healthcare
Kevin Moriarty, Chief Executive Officer

D-U-N-S 06-306-7326
METHODIST HEALTHCARE SYSTEM OF
7550 Ih 10 W Ste 1000, San Antonio, TX 78229
Phone: (210) 377-4858
Sales: $256,800,000   *Employees:* 5,456
Company Type: Private   *Employees here:* 40
SIC: 8062
  General acute care hospital
John E Hornbeak, Chief Executive Officer

D-U-N-S 11-431-0048
METHODIST HEALTHCARE SYSTEM OF
8109 Fredericksburg Rd, San Antonio, TX 78229
Phone: (210) 692-5000
Sales: $23,800,000   *Employees:* NA
Company Type: Private   *Employees here:* 585
SIC: 8062
  Hospital
Jim Scoggin, Administrator

D-U-N-S 87-928-7845
METHODIST HEALTHCARE SYSTEM OF
1310 McCullough Ave, San Antonio, TX 78212
Phone: (210) 208-2200
Sales: $37,000,000   *Employees:* NA
Company Type: Private   *Employees here:* 900
SIC: 8062
  Hospital
Mark Bernard, Principal

D-U-N-S 07-351-3798
METHODIST HEALTHCARE-DYERSBURG HSP
400 E Tickle St, Dyersburg, TN 38024
Phone: (901) 285-2410
Sales: $31,482,000   *Employees:* 525
Company Type: Private   *Employees here:* 525
SIC: 8062
  General hospital
Richard Mc Cormick, Administrator

D-U-N-S 06-669-4803
METHODIST HOSPITAL OF SOUTHERN CAL
300 W Huntington Dr, Arcadia, CA 91007
Phone: (626) 445-4441
Sales: $115,389,000   *Employees:* 1,018
Company Type: Private   *Employees here:* 933
SIC: 8062
  Hospital diagnostic services and skilled nursing
Dennis M Lee, President

D-U-N-S 06-639-0881
METHODIST HOSPITAL LUBBOCK TEXAS
3615 19th St, Lubbock, TX 79410
Phone: (806) 792-1011
Sales: $264,703,000   *Employees:* 2,700
Company Type: Private   *Employees here:* 2,640
SIC: 8062
  General hospital
Jim Houser, Chief Executive Officer

D-U-N-S 04-178-7482
METHODIST HOSPITAL
6500 Excelsior Blvd, Minneapolis, MN 55426
Phone: (612) 993-5000

Sales: $195,035,000
Company Type: Private
SIC: 8062
  General hospital
Dr James L Reinertsen Md, President

Employees: 2,500
Employees here: 2,500

D-U-N-S 06-591-6017
METHODIST HOSPITAL INC
580 W 8th St, Jacksonville, FL 32209
Phone: (904) 798-8000
Sales: $72,166,000
Company Type: Private
SIC: 8062
  Private hospital
Ray Flores, Accounting

Employees: 900
Employees here: 900

D-U-N-S 07-485-3979
METHODIST HOSPITALS OF DALLAS
1441 N Beckley Ave, Dallas, TX 75203
Phone: (214) 947-8181
Sales: $196,277,000
Company Type: Private
SIC: 8062
  General hospital
Howard Chase, President

Employees: 3,060
Employees here: 1,825

D-U-N-S 83-704-2761
METHODIST HSPITALS OF MEMPHIS
50 N Dunlap St, Memphis, TN 38103
Phone: (901) 572-3000
Sales: $62,200,000
Company Type: Private
SIC: 8069
  Hospital
Jim Smirling, Branch Manager

Employees: NA
Employees here: 1,384

D-U-N-S 07-902-6738
METHODIST MED CTR OF OAK RIDGE
990 Oak Ridge Tpke, Oak Ridge, TN 37830
Phone: (423) 481-1101
Sales: $115,148,000
Company Type: Private
SIC: 8062
  General hospital
Dan Bonk, President

Employees: 1,500
Employees here: 1,442

D-U-N-S 07-560-7689
METHODIST MEDICAL CTR OF ILL
221 NE Glen Oak Ave, Peoria, IL 61636
Phone: (309) 672-5522
Sales: $164,550,000
Company Type: Private
SIC: 8062
  General hospital
James K Knoble, Chief Executive Officer

Employees: 2,500
Employees here: 2,100

D-U-N-S 11-008-3342
METHODIST MEDICAL GROUP INC
3615 19th St Fl 7, Lubbock, TX 79410
Phone: (806) 795-9878
Sales: $30,900,000
Company Type: Private
SIC: 8011
  Medical doctor's office
Robert J Salem, President

Employees: 450
Employees here: 450

D-U-N-S 07-085-3387
METHODST HM AGNG WYMG CNF NYS
1605 Davis Ave, Endicott, NY 13760
Phone: (607) 785-7770

Sales: $34,245,000
Company Type: Private
SIC: 8051
  Skilled nursing & assisted living facility
Keith D Chadwick, President

Employees: 1,150
Employees here: 17

D-U-N-S 88-461-9156
METRO WEST REHAB CORP
25 Railroad Sq, Haverhill, MA 1832
Phone: (978) 372-5106
Sales: $24,000,000
Company Type: Private
SIC: 8051
  Nursing home
Alfred L Arcidi, President

Employees: NA
Employees here: NA

D-U-N-S 83-442-4228
METRO WEST-MARLBOROUGH HEALTH
57 Union St, Marlborough, MA 1752
Phone: (508) 485-1121
Sales: $32,000,000
Company Type: Private
SIC: 8062
  Hospital wellness & preventive services and internal medical
    practices
Anne Bourgeois, Interim President

Employees: 4
Employees here: 4

D-U-N-S 07-112-4291
METROHEALTH SYSTEM INC
2500 Metrohealth Dr, Cleveland, OH 44109
Phone: (216) 398-6000
Sales: $271,834,000
Company Type: Private
SIC: 8062
  General hospital
Terry R White, President

Employees: 5,244
Employees here: 4,000

D-U-N-S 19-131-2321
METROPLEX ADVENTIST HOSPITAL
2201 S Clear Creek Rd, Killeen, TX 76542
Phone: (254) 526-7523
Sales: $45,000,000
Company Type: Private
SIC: 8062
  General medical and surgical hospital
Kenneth A Finch, President

Employees: 700
Employees here: 625

D-U-N-S 06-440-8933
METROPLEX HEMATOLOGY ONCOLOGY
906 W Randol Mill Rd, Arlington, TX 76012
Phone: (817) 261-4906
Sales: $24,718,000
Company Type: Private
SIC: 8011
  Cancer clinic
Dr Alfred Di Stefano Md, Partner

Employees: 125
Employees here: 117

D-U-N-S 13-420-3397
METROPOLITAN DADE COUNTY
1611 NW 12th Ave, Miami, FL 33136
Phone: (305) 585-1111
Sales: $309,100,000
Company Type: Private
SIC: 8062
  Hospital
Ira Clark, N/A

Employees: NA
Employees here: 7,000

D-U-N-S 12-407-5045
METROPOLITAN GVT NSIIVL (INC)
72 Hermitage Ave, Nashville, TN 37210
Phone: (615) 341-4000

Sales: $32,200,000   *Employees:* NA
Company Type: Private   *Employees here:* 769
SIC: 8062
  General hospital
John Stone, Director

D-U-N-S 18-613-2486
METROPOLITAN GVT NSHVL INC
72 Hermitage Ave, Nashville, TN 37210
Phone: (615) 862-4000
Sales: $28,900,000   *Employees:* NA
Company Type: Private   *Employees here:* 692
SIC: 8062
  General hospital
John M Stone, Director

D-U-N-S 07-928-8601
METROPOLITAN HOSPITAL
1919 Boston St SE, Grand Rapids, MI 49506
Phone: (616) 247-7200
Sales: $86,351,000   *Employees:* 940
Company Type: Private   *Employees here:* 875
SIC: 8062
  Hospital
Michael D Faas, President

D-U-N-S 19-679-8011
METROPOLITAN LIFE INSUR CO
2600 Lake Lucien Dr, Maitland, FL 32751
Phone: (407) 875-5545
Sales: $21,300,000   *Employees:* NA
Company Type: Private   *Employees here:* 275
SIC: 8011
  Medical doctor's office
Donna Blexrud, Branch Manager

D-U-N-S 06-951-2101
MEYER MEDICAL GROUP II, S C
11600 S Kedzie Ave, Chicago, IL 60803
Phone: (708) 239-0680
Sales: $24,000,000   *Employees:* 350
Company Type: Private   *Employees here:* 44
SIC: 8011
  Medical center
Dr Michael De Stefano Md, President

D-U-N-S 09-534-7357
MHM SERVICES, INC
8000 Towers Crescent Dr, Vienna, VA 22182
Phone: (703) 749-4600
Sales: $20,851,000   *Employees:* 330
Company Type: Public   *Employees here:* 20
SIC: 8063
  Psychiatric & chemical dependency hospital & medical
    service coordinator
Frank Baumann, Chief Executive Officer

D-U-N-S 04-241-8681
MIAMI BEACH HEALTHCARE GROUP
20900 Biscayne Blvd, Miami, FL 33180
Phone: (305) 682-7000
Sales: $30,600,000   *Employees:* NA
Company Type: Private   *Employees here:* 700
SIC: 8062
  Hospital
David M Carbone, Chief Executive Officer

D-U-N-S 07-386-9471
MIAMI BEACH HEALTHCARE GROUP
4701 N Meridian Ave, Miami, FL 33140
Phone: (305) 672-1111

Sales: $114,239,000   *Employees:* 1,700
Company Type: Private   *Employees here:* 215
SIC: 8062
  General hospital home health and medical clinics
Ralph Aleman, President

D-U-N-S 07-845-6712
MIAMI JEWISH HOME/HOSPTL AGED
5200 NE 2nd Ave, Miami, FL 33137
Phone: (305) 751-8626
Sales: $52,194,000   *Employees:* 1,200
Company Type: Private   *Employees here:* 1,051
SIC: 8051
  Skilled nursing care facilities
Seth B Goldsmith, Chief Executive Officer

D-U-N-S 07-127-1951
MIAMI VALLEY HOSPITAL
1 Wyoming St, Dayton, OH 45409
Phone: (937) 223-6192
Sales: $339,848,000   *Employees:* 3,700
Company Type: Private   *Employees here:* 3,300
SIC: 8062
  General hospital
Thomas G Breitenbach, Chief Executive Officer

D-U-N-S 80-123-5508
MICHIGAN AFFL HEALTHCARE SYS
401 W Greenlawn Ave, Lansing, MI 48910
Phone: (517) 334-2121
Sales: $195,808,000   *Employees:* 6,082
Company Type: Private   *Employees here:* 2,500
SIC: 8062
  General hospital
Dennis Litos, President

D-U-N-S 82-536-0696
MICHIGAN AFFL HEALTHCARE SYS
2727 S Pennsylvania Ave, Lansing, MI 48910
Phone: (517) 377-8310
Sales: $148,400,000   *Employees:* NA
Company Type: Private   *Employees here:* 3,500
SIC: 8062
  General hospital
Dennis Litos, Owner

D-U-N-S 19-911-8555
MICHIGAN DEPT CORRECTIONS
3855 Cooper St, Jackson, MI 49201
Phone: (517) 782-5900
Sales: $25,000,000   *Employees:* NA
Company Type: Private   *Employees here:* 600
SIC: 8062
  Prison hospital
Henry Grayson, Warden

D-U-N-S 60-259-0457
MICHIGAN MEDICAL P.C.
1300 Michigan St NE, Grand Rapids, MI 49503
Phone: (616) 456-4889
Sales: $34,300,000   *Employees:* 500
Company Type: Private   *Employees here:* 50
SIC: 8011
  Specialized medical practitioners
David Quimby, President

D-U-N-S 15-209-5840
MID AMERICA CARE FOUNDATION
7611 State Line Rd, Kansas City, MO 64114
Phone: (816) 444-0900

Sales: $57,300,000   *Employees:* 2,500
Company Type: Private   *Employees here:* 1
SIC: 8051
  Skilled & intermediate nursing care facilities
Russ Ramser, President

D-U-N-S 79-976-8361
MID AMERICA CLINICAL LABS LLC
1500 N Ritter Ave, Indianapolis, IN 46219
Phone: (317) 355-5263
Sales: $30,000,000   *Employees:* 350
Company Type: Private   *Employees here:* 350
SIC: 8071
  Clinical laboratory services
Ronald Frick, Chief Financial Officer

D-U-N-S 10-169-4685
MID ATLANTIC HEALTH GROUP INC
300 2nd Ave, Long Branch, NJ 7740
Phone: (732) 222-5200
Sales: $140,700,000   *Employees:* 3,000
Company Type: Private   *Employees here:* 2
SIC: 8062
  Holding company operates through its subsidiary as an acute care teaching hospital and chemical dependency treatment center
Christophe Dadlez, President

D-U-N-S 07-173-2523
MID COAST HOSPITAL
58 Baribeau Dr, Brunswick, ME 4011
Phone: (207) 729-0181
Sales: $35,488,000   *Employees:* 370
Company Type: Private   *Employees here:* 370
SIC: 8062
  General medical & surgical hospital
Herbert Paris, Chief Executive Officer

D-U-N-S 05-097-2314
MID COLUMBIA MEDICAL CENTER
1700 E 19th St, The Dalles, OR 97058
Phone: (541) 296-1111
Sales: $26,261,000   *Employees:* 447
Company Type: Private   *Employees here:* 422
SIC: 8062
  General medical & surgical hosptial
Mark D Scott, President

D-U-N-S 10-687-3698
MID MICHIGAN REGIONAL MED CTR
4005 Orchard Dr, Midland, MI 48640
Phone: (517) 839-3000
Sales: $63,900,000   *Employees:* 1,375
Company Type: Private   *Employees here:* 1,375
SIC: 8062
  Hospital
David A Reece, President

D-U-N-S 05-814-8305
MID VALLEY HEALTH CARE INC
525 N Santiam Hwy, Lebanon, OR 97355
Phone: (541) 258-2101
Sales: $30,000,000   *Employees:* 550
Company Type: Private   *Employees here:* 550
SIC: 8062
  General hospital
Alan Yordy, Administrator

D-U-N-S 06-802-3860
MID-ISLAND HOSPITAL, INC
4295 Hempstead Tpke, Bethpage, NY 11714
Phone: (516) 579-6000

Sales: $19,700,000   *Employees:* 440
Company Type: Private   *Employees here:* 440
SIC: 8062
  General hospital
Robert J Reed, President

D-U-N-S 07-427-9688
MIDAMERICA HEALTHCARE, INC
1102 W Macarthur St, Shawnee, OK 74804
Phone: (405) 273-2270
Sales: $28,000,000   *Employees:* 430
Company Type: Private   *Employees here:* 430
SIC: 8062
  General hospital
Robert F Maynard, President

D-U-N-S 07-765-5975
MIDDLE TENNESSEE MEDICAL CTR
400 N Highland Ave, Murfreesboro, TN 37130
Phone: (615) 849-4100
Sales: $66,218,000   *Employees:* 1,050
Company Type: Private   *Employees here:* 1,039
SIC: 8062
  General hospital
Arthur W Hastings, President

D-U-N-S 06-925-7152
MIDDLESEX HOSPITAL
28 Crescent St, Middletown, CT 6457
Phone: (860) 347-9471
Sales: $132,929,000   *Employees:* 1,257
Company Type: Private   *Employees here:* 1,174
SIC: 8062
  Hospital
Donald Wilbur, Chairman of the Board

D-U-N-S 07-134-0608
MIDELFORT CLINIC-MAYO HEALTH
733 W Clairemont Ave, Eau Claire, WI 54701
Phone: (715) 838-5222
Sales: $103,400,000   *Employees:* 1,500
Company Type: Private   *Employees here:* 800
SIC: 8011
  Medical clinics and health maintenance organization
Dr William Rupp Md, Chief Executive Officer

D-U-N-S 07-314-9411
MIDLAND COUNTY HOSPITAL DST
2200 W Illinois Ave, Midland, TX 79701
Phone: (915) 685-1111
Sales: $130,744,000   *Employees:* 1,100
Company Type: Private   *Employees here:* 1,045
SIC: 8062
  General medical & surgical hospital
Dr Harold Rubin, President

D-U-N-S 05-224-7442
MIDWAY HOSPITAL MEDICAL CTR
  (*Parent:* Tenet Healthcare Corporation)
5925 San Vicente Blvd, Los Angeles, CA 90019
Phone: (213) 938-3161
Sales: $70,000,000   *Employees:* 700
Company Type: Public Family Member   *Employees here:* 700
SIC: 8062
  General hospital
John V Fenton, Chief Executive Officer

D-U-N-S 14-826-7313
MIDWEST CITY MEM HOSPITAL AUTH
2825 Parklawn Dr, Oklahoma City, OK 73110
Phone: (405) 737-4411

Sales: $64,521,000   *Employees:* 1,000
Company Type: Private   *Employees here:* 996
SIC: 8062
  General hospital and freestanding occupational clinic
Gary Newsome, President

D-U-N-S 07-459-0969
MIDWESTERN REGIONAL MED CTR
  (Parent: A I H Corporation)
2501 Emmaus Ave, Zion, IL 60099
Phone: (847) 872-4561
Sales: $57,264,000   *Employees:* 568
Company Type: Private   *Employees here:* 478
SIC: 8069
  Hospital
Roger Carey, President

D-U-N-S 07-211-9241
MILFORD HOSPITAL INC
300 Seaside Ave, Milford, CT 6460
Phone: (203) 876-4000
Sales: $45,347,000   *Employees:* 500
Company Type: Private   *Employees here:* 500
SIC: 8062
  General hospital
Paul E Moss, President

D-U-N-S 07-534-6940
MILFORD-WHTNSVLLE RGIONAL HOSP
14 Prospect St, Milford, MA 1757
Phone: (508) 473-1190
Sales: $49,825,000   *Employees:* 1,218
Company Type: Private   *Employees here:* 1,133
SIC: 8062
  General hospital
Frances Saba, President

D-U-N-S 07-403-6476
MILLARD FILLMORE HOSPITAL
3 Gates Cir, Buffalo, NY 14209
Phone: (716) 843-7308
Sales: $236,329,000   *Employees:* 3,500
Company Type: Private   *Employees here:* 1,605
SIC: 8062
  General hospital
Carol Cassell, Chief Executive Officer

D-U-N-S 07-498-8312
MILLCREEK COMMUNITY HOSPITAL
5515 Peach St, Erie, PA 16509
Phone: (814) 864-4031
Sales: $25,705,000   *Employees:* 300
Company Type: Private   *Employees here:* 290
SIC: 8062
  Hospital
Mary L Eckert, Chief Executive Officer

D-U-N-S 06-818-7871
MILLER-DWAN MEDICAL CENTER
502 E 2nd St, Duluth, MN 55805
Phone: (218) 727-8762
Sales: $47,243,000   *Employees:* 834
Company Type: Private   *Employees here:* 811
SIC: 8062
  Hospital
William H Palmer, President

D-U-N-S 60-684-7523
MILLER'S HEALTH SYSTEMS, INC
1690 S County Farm Rd, Warsaw, IN 46580
Phone: (219) 267-7211

Sales: $55,900,000   *Employees:* 3,000
Company Type: Private   *Employees here:* 75
SIC: 8052
  Operator of skilled & intermediate nursing care facilities &
    assisted living facilities
Robert Decker, Chief Executive Officer

D-U-N-S 07-876-9643
MILLS-PENINSULA HEALTH SVCS
1783 El Camino Real, Burlingame, CA 94010
Phone: (650) 696-5400
Sales: $193,730,000   *Employees:* 2,500
Company Type: Private   *Employees here:* 1,400
SIC: 8062
  General hospital
Robert W Merwin, President

D-U-N-S 07-381-7074
MILTON HOSPITAL INC
92 Highland St, Milton, MA 2186
Phone: (617) 696-4600
Sales: $36,169,000   *Employees:* 435
Company Type: Private   *Employees here:* 435
SIC: 8062
  General medical & surgical hospital
George A Geary, President

D-U-N-S 07-116-0162
MILWAUKEE PROTESTANT HOME
2449 N Downer Ave, Milwaukee, WI 53211
Phone: (414) 332-8610
Sales: $20,191,000   *Employees:* 240
Company Type: Private   *Employees here:* 240
SIC: 8059
  Convalescent home
Mtt Furno, President

D-U-N-S 07-589-1135
MINERAL AREA OSTEOPATHIC HOSP
1212 Weber Rd, Farmington, MO 63640
Phone: (573) 756-4581
Sales: $27,706,000   *Employees:* 480
Company Type: Private   *Employees here:* 480
SIC: 8062
  Osteopathic hospital
Kenneth West, Administrator

D-U-N-S 17-045-5570
MINNESOTA DEPARTMENT HUMANSVCS
1550 Highway 71 NE, Willmar, MN 56201
Phone: (320) 231-5100
Sales: $21,800,000   *Employees:* NA
Company Type: Private   *Employees here:* 575
SIC: 8062
  Treatment center
Gregory Spartz, Principal

D-U-N-S 93-751-9890
MINNESOTA VETERANS HOMES BOARD
  (Parent: State Of Minnesota)
Veterans Service Building, Saint Paul, MN 55155
Phone: (651) 296-2076
Sales: $21,600,000   *Employees:* 950
Company Type: Private   *Employees here:* 15
SIC: 8051
  Skilled nursing care facility
Richard Zierdt, Executive Director

D-U-N-S 07-185-3980
MINOR & JAMES MEDICAL, PLLC
515 Minor Ave Ste 200, Seattle, WA 98104
Phone: (206) 623-6600

Sales: $28,490,000   *Employees:* 301
Company Type: Private   *Employees here:* 179
SIC: 8011
　Primary care medical clinic
Martin Green, Director

D-U-N-S 06-390-2704
MIRIAM HOSPITAL INC
164 Summit Ave, Providence, RI 2906
Phone: (401) 793-2500
Sales: $138,925,000   *Employees:* 1,263
Company Type: Private   *Employees here:* 1,263
SIC: 8062
　General hospital
Steven Baron, President

D-U-N-S 19-390-4265
MISERICORDIA HOME
6300 N Ridge Ave, Chicago, IL 60660
Phone: (773) 973-6300
Sales: $25,610,000   *Employees:* 720
Company Type: Private   *Employees here:* 480
SIC: 8052
　Home for children and adults with developmental disabilities
Sister R Connelly, Executive Director

D-U-N-S 13-401-6534
MISSION BAY MEMORIAL HOSPITAL
　(Parent: Notami Hospitals Of California)
3030 Bunker Hill St, San Diego, CA 92109
Phone: (619) 274-7721
Sales: $58,885,000   *Employees:* 447
Company Type: Public Family Member   *Employees here:* 380
SIC: 8062
　Health care
Debra Brehe, Chief Executive Officer

D-U-N-S 06-445-7005
MISSION HOSPITAL REGIONAL MED CTR
27700 Medical Center Rd, Mission Viejo, CA 92691
Phone: (949) 364-1400
Sales: $115,474,000   *Employees:* 1,350
Company Type: Private   *Employees here:* 1,350
SIC: 8062
　General medical & surgical hospital
Peter F Bastone, Chief Executive Officer

D-U-N-S 01-272-2138
MISSION HOSPITAL INC
900 S Bryan Rd, Mission, TX 78572
Phone: (956) 580-9000
Sales: $73,800,000   *Employees:* 531
Company Type: Private   *Employees here:* 531
SIC: 8062
　General medical hospital
Paul Ballard, Administrator

D-U-N-S 09-775-0988
MISSISSIPPI DEPT MENTAL HEALTH
4555 Hiland Dr, Meridian, MS 39301
Phone: (601) 482-6186
Sales: $30,900,000   *Employees:* NA
Company Type: Private   *Employees here:* 1,000
SIC: 8063
　Psychiatric hospital
Ramiro J Martinez, Branch Manager

D-U-N-S 08-285-4548
MISSISSIPPI M H RE CTR
1350 E Woodrow Wilson Ave, Jackson, MS 39216
Phone: (601) 981-2611

Sales: $45,488,000   *Employees:* 700
Company Type: Private   *Employees here:* 550
SIC: 8062
　General medical & surgical hospital
Mark Adams, President

D-U-N-S 07-588-6358
MISSOURI BAPTIST MEDICAL CTR
3015 N Ballas Rd, Saint Louis, MO 63131
Phone: (314) 432-1212
Sales: $98,100,000   *Employees:* 2,100
Company Type: Private   *Employees here:* 1,520
SIC: 8062
　General medical & surgical hospital
Frederick R Mills, President

D-U-N-S 07-195-6247
MISSOURI DELTA MEDICAL CENTER
1008 N Main St, Sikeston, MO 63801
Phone: (573) 471-1600
Sales: $40,318,000   *Employees:* 700
Company Type: Private   *Employees here:* 696
SIC: 8062
　General hospital
Charles D Ancell, President

D-U-N-S 92-954-5689
MISSOURI HEALTH CARE SYSTEMS LP
1000 E Walnut Lawn St, Springfield, MO 65807
Phone: (417) 882-4700
Sales: $27,200,000   *Employees:* 600
Company Type: Private   *Employees here:* 400
SIC: 8062
　General hospitals
Michelle Fischer, Chief Executive Officer

D-U-N-S 60-458-6537
MISSOURI SYSTEM, UNIVERSITY
Po Box 41, Columbia, MO 65205
Phone: (573) 882-3979
Sales: $25,200,000   *Employees:* NA
Company Type: Private   *Employees here:* 400
SIC: 8011
　Administrative offices
Don Johnson, Administrator

D-U-N-S 07-260-8367
MOBILE INFIRMARY ASSOCIATION
5 Mobile Infirmary Cir, Mobile, AL 36607
Phone: (334) 431-2400
Sales: $178,273,000   *Employees:* 3,000
Company Type: Private   *Employees here:* 3,000
SIC: 8062
　General hospital
Chandler Bramlett, President

D-U-N-S 02-086-2751
MOBILE MENTAL HEALTH CENTER
2400 Gordon Smith Dr, Mobile, AL 36617
Phone: (334) 473-4423
Sales: $20,000,000   *Employees:* 350
Company Type: Private   *Employees here:* 85
SIC: 8093
　Mental health clinic
Tom Pennington, Assoc Dir

D-U-N-S 10-909-2940
MOBILE TECHNOLOGY INC
　(Parent: Alliance Imaging Inc)
9841 Airport Blvd Fl 12, Los Angeles, CA 90045
Phone: (310) 641-8614

Sales: $69,000,000   *Employees:* 450
Company Type: Public Family Member   *Employees here:* 45
SIC: 8099
   Health screening service providing mobile medical imaging
    services
Joseph W Cilurzo, President

D-U-N-S 80-269-4455
MOHAWK VALLEY NETWORK, INC
1676 Sunset Ave, Utica, NY 13502
Phone: (315) 738-6200
Sales: $60,000,000   *Employees:* 2,350
Company Type: Private   *Employees here:* 1
SIC: 8069
   Holding company
Keith Fenstemacher, President

D-U-N-S 11-017-5023
MOLINA MEDICAL CENTER, INC
1 Golden Shore St, Long Beach, CA 90802
Phone: (562) 435-3666
Sales: $116,182,000   *Employees:* 410
Company Type: Private   *Employees here:* 295
SIC: 8011
   Medical clinics & hmo
Joseph M Molina, President

D-U-N-S 07-396-9438
MONADNOCK COMMUNITY HOSPITAL INC
452 Old Street Rd, Peterborough, NH 3458
Phone: (603) 924-7191
Sales: $21,595,000   *Employees:* 350
Company Type: Private   *Employees here:* 350
SIC: 8062
   General medical & surgical hospital
Thomas P Sheehan, Chief Executive Officer

D-U-N-S 94-570-4823
MONARCH DENTAL CORPORATION
4201 Sring Vly 320, Dallas, TX 75244
Phone: (972) 458-0923
Sales: $68,619,000   *Employees:* 260
Company Type: Public   *Employees here:* 260
SIC: 8021
   Dentist's office
Dr Warren F Melamed Dds, Chairman of the Board

D-U-N-S 04-987-5636
MONMOUTH MEDICAL CENTER
300 2nd Ave, Long Branch, NJ 7740
Phone: (732) 222-5200
Sales: $163,511,000   *Employees:* 2,400
Company Type: Private   *Employees here:* 2,200
SIC: 8062
   General hospital
Christophe M Dadlez, President

D-U-N-S 06-872-8773
MONONGAHELA VALLEY HOSPITAL INC
Country Club Rd Rr 88, Monongahela, PA 15063
Phone: (724) 258-2000
Sales: $73,245,000   *Employees:* 1,020
Company Type: Private   *Employees here:* 1,020
SIC: 8062
   General hospital
Anthony Lombardi, President

D-U-N-S 07-748-3154
MONONGALIA COUNTY GEN HOSPITAL CO
1200 J D Anderson Dr, Morgantown, WV 26505
Phone: (304) 598-1200

Sales: $82,941,000   *Employees:* 1,100
Company Type: Private   *Employees here:* 1,098
SIC: 8062
   General medical and surgical hospital
Nicholas Grubbs, Chief Financial Officer

D-U-N-S 06-791-0356
MONROE COMMUNITY HOSPITAL
435 E Henrietta Rd, Rochester, NY 14620
Phone: (716) 760-6500
Sales: $70,797,000   *Employees:* 750
Company Type: Private   *Employees here:* 750
SIC: 8051
   Skilled nursing care facility
Frank Tripodi, Executive Director

D-U-N-S 07-965-5601
MONROE MEDICAL FOUNDATION INC
529 Capp Harlan Rd, Tompkinsville, KY 42167
Phone: (502) 487-9231
Sales: $20,372,000   *Employees:* 266
Company Type: Private   *Employees here:* 266
SIC: 8062
   Hospital
Carolyn Riley, Chief Executive Officer

D-U-N-S 07-748-9672
MONSOUR MEDICAL CENTER
70 Lincoln Hwy E, Jeannette, PA 15644
Phone: (724) 527-1511
Sales: $20,216,000   *Employees:* 358
Company Type: Private   *Employees here:* 324
SIC: 8062
   Hospital
Michael N Flinn, Chief Executive Officer

D-U-N-S 04-158-1026
MONTEFIORE MEDICAL CENTER
111 E 210th St, Bronx, NY 10467
Phone: (718) 920-4321
Sales: $1,188,234,000   *Employees:* 10,794
Company Type: Private   *Employees here:* 5,500
SIC: 8062
   Non-profit general medical & surgical hospital
Dr Spencer Foreman Md, President

D-U-N-S 92-875-0736
MONTEFIORE MEDICAL CENTER
3444 Kossuth Ave, Bronx, NY 10467
Phone: (718) 920-5271
Sales: $47,100,000   *Employees:* NA
Company Type: Private   *Employees here:* 700
SIC: 8011
   Medical doctor's office
Katheline Salard, Branch Manager

D-U-N-S 07-780-6669
MONTGOMERY GENERAL HOSPITAL INC
18101 Prince Philip Dr, Olney, MD 20832
Phone: (301) 774-8882
Sales: $62,625,000   *Employees:* 1,200
Company Type: Private   *Employees here:* 1,200
SIC: 8062
   Hospital
Peter W Monge, President

D-U-N-S 05-556-9701
MONTGOMERY GENERAL HOSPITAL
401 6th Ave, Montgomery, WV 25136
Phone: (304) 442-5151

Sales: $22,517,000   *Employees:* 260
Company Type: Private   *Employees here:* 260
SIC: 8062
  General hospital skilled nursing care facility
William R Laird Iv, President

D-U-N-S 07-365-8981
MONTGOMERY HOSPITAL
1301 Powell St, Norristown, PA 19401
Phone: (610) 270-2000
Sales: $100,154,000   *Employees:* 1,330
Company Type: Private   *Employees here:* 1,300
SIC: 8062
  General medical & surgical hospital
Tim Casey, President

D-U-N-S 09-355-8864
MONTGOMERY REGIONAL HOSPITAL
  (*Parent:* Columbia/Hca Healthcare Corp)
3700 S Main St, Blacksburg, VA 24060
Phone: (540) 951-1111
Sales: $48,939,000   *Employees:* 500
Company Type: Public Family Member   *Employees here:* 500
SIC: 8062
  Acute care hospital
David Williams, Chief Executive Officer

D-U-N-S 01-063-3667
MONTROSE MEMORIAL HOSPITAL
800 S 3rd St, Montrose, CO 81401
Phone: (970) 249-2211
Sales: $26,594,000   *Employees:* 430
Company Type: Private   *Employees here:* 394
SIC: 8062
  General hospital
Tyler A Erickson, Chief Executive Officer

D-U-N-S 02-141-7399
MOORINGS, INCORPORATED
120 Moorings Park Dr, Naples, FL 34105
Phone: (941) 261-1616
Sales: $19,905,000   *Employees:* 376
Company Type: Private   *Employees here:* 376
SIC: 8361
  Continuing care retirement community with housing &
    healthcare services
Glenn Stites, Controller

D-U-N-S 07-783-2418
MOREHEAD MEMORIAL HOSPITAL
117 E Kings Hwy, Eden, NC 27288
Phone: (336) 623-9711
Sales: $43,052,000   *Employees:* 620
Company Type: Private   *Employees here:* 620
SIC: 8062
  General hospital
Robert A Enders, President

D-U-N-S 06-973-3574
MOREHOUSE GENERAL HOSPITAL
323 W Walnut Ave, Bastrop, LA 71220
Phone: (318) 281-2431
Sales: $29,082,000   *Employees:* 450
Company Type: Private   *Employees here:* 450
SIC: 8062
  Hospital
William W Bing, Administrator

D-U-N-S 07-206-2060
MORGAN COUNTY MEMORIAL HOSP
2209 John R Wooden Dr, Martinsville, IN 46151
Phone: (765) 342-8441

Sales: $25,662,000   *Employees:* 390
Company Type: Private   *Employees here:* 375
SIC: 8062
  General hospital
S D Melton, President

D-U-N-S 10-328-6316
MORNINGSIDE HSE NURSING HM CO
1000 Pelham Pkwy S, Bronx, NY 10461
Phone: (718) 409-8200
Sales: $35,889,000   *Employees:* 500
Company Type: Private   *Employees here:* 485
SIC: 8051
  Skilled nursing facility
William T Dsw, President

D-U-N-S 05-756-4148
MORNINGSIDE MINISTRIES
700 Babcock Rd, San Antonio, TX 78201
Phone: (210) 734-1000
Sales: $22,007,000   *Employees:* 650
Company Type: Private   *Employees here:* 400
SIC: 8361
  Rest home with health care & home health care services
Alvin A Loewenberg Jr, President

D-U-N-S 07-559-9308
MORRIS HOSPITAL
150 W High St, Morris, IL 60450
Phone: (815) 942-2932
Sales: $21,086,000   *Employees:* 525
Company Type: Private   *Employees here:* 525
SIC: 8062
  Hospital
Clifford Corbett, Chief Executive Officer

D-U-N-S 07-152-3823
MORRISTOWN HAMBLEN HOSPITAL
908 W 4th North St, Morristown, TN 37814
Phone: (423) 586-4231
Sales: $38,820,000   *Employees:* 490
Company Type: Private   *Employees here:* 360
SIC: 8062
  General hospital
Richard Clark, President

D-U-N-S 16-134-7315
MORTON HEALTH FOUNDATION INC
88 Washington St, Taunton, MA 2780
Phone: (508) 828-7000
Sales: $46,100,000   *Employees:* 1,000
Company Type: Private   *Employees here:* 1,000
SIC: 8062
  General hospital
Thomas C Porter, President

D-U-N-S 06-985-4495
MORTON HOSPITAL
88 Washington St, Taunton, MA 2780
Phone: (508) 828-7000
Sales: $67,498,000   *Employees:* 900
Company Type: Private   *Employees here:* 850
SIC: 8062
  General hospital and physicians' offices
Thomas C Porter, President

D-U-N-S 11-550-0191
MORTON PLANT HOSPITAL ASSN
323 Jeffords St, Clearwater, FL 33756
Phone: (727) 462-7000

Sales: $245,346,000   *Employees:* 3,000
Company Type: Private   *Employees here:* 2,100
SIC: 8062
  General hospital
Frank V Murphy Iii, President

D-U-N-S 62-267-8761
MORTON PLANT MEASE HEALTH SVCS
1240 S Fort Harrison Ave, Clearwater, FL 33756
Phone: (727) 462-7559
Sales: $37,600,000   *Employees:* 100
Company Type: Private   *Employees here:* 32
SIC: 8011
  Outpatient radiology center & ambulatory surgery center
Glen G Watkins, President

D-U-N-S 00-526-9167
MOSES CONE HEALTH SYSTEM INC
501 N Elam Ave, Greensboro, NC 27403
Phone: (336) 854-6100
Sales: $41,800,000   *Employees:* NA
Company Type: Private   *Employees here:* 952
SIC: 8062
  General hospital
Lynn Bell, Controller

D-U-N-S 78-499-9393
MOSES CONE HEALTH SYSTEM INC
801 Green Valley Rd, Greensboro, NC 27408
Phone: (336) 574-6523
Sales: $35,200,000   *Employees:* NA
Company Type: Private   *Employees here:* 750
SIC: 8069
  Specialty hospital
James Whiting, N/A

D-U-N-S 05-703-6071
MOSES H CONE MEMORIAL
1200 N Elm St, Greensboro, NC 27401
Phone: (336) 574-7881
Sales: $277,284,000   *Employees:* 4,200
Company Type: Private   *Employees here:* 3,500
SIC: 8062
  General hospitals
Dennis R Barry, President

D-U-N-S 06-959-2293
MOSES TAYLOR HOSPITAL
700 Quincy Ave, Scranton, PA 18510
Phone: (717) 340-2100
Sales: $62,322,000   *Employees:* 791
Company Type: Private   *Employees here:* 787
SIC: 8062
  General hospital with a psychiactric unit and skilled nursing
  unit
Harold A Anderson, Chief Executive Officer

D-U-N-S 17-840-1931
MOSS BEACH HOMES, INC
333 Gellert Blvd Ste 203, Daly City, CA 94015
Phone: (650) 758-0111
Sales: $29,154,000   *Employees:* 420
Company Type: Private   *Employees here:* 22
SIC: 8361
  Residential care placement for minors
Anson Hartson, Administration

D-U-N-S 04-074-6430
MOTHER FRNCS HOSP, TYLER, TX
800 E Dawson St, Tyler, TX 75701
Phone: (903) 593-8441

Sales: $164,187,000   *Employees:* 1,655
Company Type: Private   *Employees here:* 1,340
SIC: 8062
  General hospital
J L Bradley Jr, President

D-U-N-S 07-412-8380
MOTION PICTURE & TV FUND
23388 Mulholland Dr, Woodland Hills, CA 91364
Phone: (818) 876-1888
Sales: $77,402,000   *Employees:* 700
Company Type: Private   *Employees here:* 630
SIC: 8062
  Hospital & convalescent home
William Haug, President

D-U-N-S 07-381-2125
MOUNT AUBURN HOSPITAL
330 Mount Auburn St, Cambridge, MA 2138
Phone: (617) 492-3500
Sales: $132,777,000   *Employees:* 1,900
Company Type: Private   *Employees here:* 1,874
SIC: 8062
  General hospital
Francis P Lynch, President

D-U-N-S 95-884-2643
MOUNT CARMEL HOSPITAL (EAST)
6001 E Broad St, Columbus, OH 43213
Phone: (614) 868-6000
Sales: $50,900,000   *Employees:* 1,100
Company Type: Private   *Employees here:* 1,100
SIC: 8062
  General hospital
Dale St Arnold, Chief Executive Officer

D-U-N-S 07-504-0121
MOUNT CARMEL HOSPITAL WEST
5955 E Broad St, Columbus, OH 43213
Phone: (614) 225-5000
Sales: $135,900,000   *Employees:* 2,900
Company Type: Private   *Employees here:* 2,750
SIC: 8062
  General hospital
Dale St Arnold, President

D-U-N-S 07-635-7946
MOUNT CLEMENS GENERAL HOSPITAL
1000 Harrington St, Mount Clemens, MI 48043
Phone: (810) 741-4170
Sales: $165,224,000   *Employees:* 1,300
Company Type: Private   *Employees here:* 1,300
SIC: 8062
  Osteopathic hospital
Robert Milewski, Chief Executive Officer

D-U-N-S 05-522-1865
MOUNT MARTY HOSPITAL ASSN
501 Summit St, Yankton, SD 57078
Phone: (605) 665-9371
Sales: $41,400,000   *Employees:* 900
Company Type: Private   *Employees here:* 750
SIC: 8062
  General hospital
Pamela Rezac, President

D-U-N-S 07-443-3046
MOUNT SINAI HOSPITAL MED CEN
2750 W 15th St, Chicago, IL 60608
Phone: (773) 542-2000

Sales: $170,947,000   *Employees:* 1,700
Company Type: Private   *Employees here:* 1,696
SIC: 8062
   General hospital
Benn Greenspan, President

D-U-N-S 05-830-2266
MOUNT SINAI HOSPITAL (INC)
1 Gustave L Levy Pl, New York, NY 10029
Phone: (212) 241-6500
Sales: $872,112,000   *Employees:* 12,000
Company Type: Private   *Employees here:* 7,869
SIC: 8062
   General hospital
Barry Freedman, Director

D-U-N-S 08-972-7168
MOUNT SINAI HOSPITAL (INC)
8268 164th St, Jamaica, NY 11432
Phone: (718) 883-3000
Sales: $194,000,000   *Employees:* NA
Company Type: Private   *Employees here:* 3,900
SIC: 8062
   General hospital
Arnoline Jones, N/A

D-U-N-S 04-602-5144
MOUNT SINAI MED CTR
4300 Alton Rd, Miami, FL 33140
Phone: (305) 674-2032
Sales: $151,300,000   *Employees:* 3,225
Company Type: Private   *Employees here:* 3,125
SIC: 8062
   General hospital
Bob Henkel, Executive Vice-President

D-U-N-S 61-421-6927
MOUNT SINAI SCHOOL
7901 Broadway, Elmhurst, NY 11373
Phone: (718) 565-4870
Sales: $56,400,000   *Employees:* NA
Company Type: Private   *Employees here:* 850
SIC: 8011
   Hospital
Stephen Harvey, Finance

D-U-N-S 07-869-6242
MOUNT VERNON HOSPITAL INC
12 N 7th Ave, Mount Vernon, NY 10550
Phone: (914) 664-8000
Sales: $57,396,000   *Employees:* 725
Company Type: Private   *Employees here:* 700
SIC: 8062
   General medical & surgical hospital
George Haskins, Vice-President

D-U-N-S 08-680-8110
MOUNTAIN VIEW HOSPITAL, INC
   (Parent: Columbia/Hca Healthcare Corp)
1000 E Highway 6, Payson, UT 84651
Phone: (801) 465-9201
Sales: $20,100,000   *Employees:* 450
Company Type: Public Family Member   *Employees here:* 450
SIC: 8062
   General hospital
Kevin Johnson, Chief Executive Officer

D-U-N-S 83-817-7129
MOUNTAINVIEW HOSPITAL INC
   (Parent: Columbia/Hca Healthcare Corp)
3100 N Tenaya Way, Las Vegas, NV 89128
Phone: (702) 255-5000

Sales: $26,000,000   *Employees:* 575
Company Type: Public Family Member   *Employees here:* 569
SIC: 8062
   General hospital
Mark Howard, Chief Executive Officer

D-U-N-S 01-064-7840
MT CARMEL MEDICAL CENTER INC
1102 E Centennial Dr, Pittsburg, KS 66762
Phone: (316) 231-6100
Sales: $35,900,000   *Employees:* 650
Company Type: Private   *Employees here:* 620
SIC: 8062
   General hospital
Dan Lingor, President

D-U-N-S 07-445-9603
MT GRAHAM COMMUNITY HOSPITAL
1600 S 20th Ave, Safford, AZ 85546
Phone: (520) 428-1171
Sales: $21,507,000   *Employees:* 260
Company Type: Private   *Employees here:* 254
SIC: 8062
   General hospital
Karl E Johnson, Administrator

D-U-N-S 07-668-6435
MT KISCO MEDICAL GROUP, P.C.
90 S Bedford Rd, Mount Kisco, NY 10549
Phone: (914) 241-1050
Sales: $25,000,000   *Employees:* 300
Company Type: Private   *Employees here:* 275
SIC: 8011
   Medical office
John Mutschelknaus, Bus Adm

D-U-N-S 07-147-4316
MT SAINT MARY'S HOSPITAL
5300 Military Rd, Lewiston, NY 14092
Phone: (716) 297-4800
Sales: $43,341,000   *Employees:* 760
Company Type: Private   *Employees here:* 722
SIC: 8062
   General hospital
John V Winter, Vice-President

D-U-N-S 07-408-7099
MUHLENBERG COMMUNITY HOSPITAL
440 Hopkinsville St, Greenville, KY 42345
Phone: (502) 338-8000
Sales: $21,056,000   *Employees:* 450
Company Type: Private   *Employees here:* 450
SIC: 8062
   General hospital
Charles Lovell, Administrator

D-U-N-S 07-753-9708
MUHLENBERG REGIONAL MED CTR
   (Parent: Huntington Foundation Inc)
Park Ave & Randolph Rd, Plainfield, NJ 7060
Phone: (908) 668-2000
Sales: $110,897,000   *Employees:* 1,650
Company Type: Private   *Employees here:* 1,590
SIC: 8062
   General hospital
John B Rutzel, Vice-President

D-U-N-S 13-191-9672
MULTICARE COMPANIES INC
433 Hackensack Ave, Hackensack, NJ 7601
Phone: (201) 488-8818

Sales: $185,778,000   *Employees:* 15,000
Company Type: Public   *Employees here:* 120
SIC: 8051
    Nursing homes
Moshael J Straus, Chairman of the Board

D-U-N-S 19-512-8640
MULTICARE HEALTH SYSTEM
737 S Fawcett Ave, Tacoma, WA 98402
Phone: (253) 552-1400
Sales: $337,010,000   *Employees:* 4,500
Company Type: Private   *Employees here:* 1,200
SIC: 8062
    General and children's hospitals
Barry Connoley, President

D-U-N-S 15-147-4301
MULTICARE HEALTH SYSTEM
315 Martin Luther King Jr, Tacoma, WA 98405
Phone: (253) 552-1000
Sales: $99,500,000   *Employees:* NA
Company Type: Private   *Employees here:* 2,000
SIC: 8062
    Hospital
William Connoley, Manager

D-U-N-S 92-684-9415
MULTICARE HEALTH SYSTEM
317 Martin Luther King Jr, Tacoma, WA 98405
Phone: (253) 552-1400
Sales: $52,800,000   *Employees:* NA
Company Type: Private   *Employees here:* 1,000
SIC: 8069
    Children's hospital
Barry Conely, Branch Manager

D-U-N-S 07-998-9869
MUNROE RGNAL HEALTHCARE SYSTEMS
131 SW 15th St, Ocala, FL 34474
Phone: (352) 351-7327
Sales: $156,823,000   *Employees:* 1,650
Company Type: Private   *Employees here:* 1,300
SIC: 8062
    Hospital general medical & surgical acute care
Dyer T Michell, President

D-U-N-S 06-017-9595
MUNSON MEDICAL CENTER
1105 6th St, Traverse City, MI 49684
Phone: (616) 935-6000
Sales: $173,316,000   *Employees:* 2,822
Company Type: Private   *Employees here:* 2,664
SIC: 8062
    General hospital
John Rockwood, President

D-U-N-S 06-949-0167
MUNSTER MEDICAL RES FOUNDATION
901 Macarthur Blvd, Munster, IN 46321
Phone: (219) 836-1600
Sales: $148,933,000   *Employees:* 1,200
Company Type: Private   *Employees here:* 1,200
SIC: 8062
    General hospital
Donald S Powers, President

D-U-N-S 08-914-7524
MURPHY MEDICAL CENTER
2002 US Highway 64 E, Murphy, NC 28906
Phone: (828) 837-8161

Sales: $21,042,000   *Employees:* 425
Company Type: Private   *Employees here:* 425
SIC: 8062
    General & surgical hospital
Mike Stevenson, Administrator

D-U-N-S 07-965-1162
MURRAY-CALLOWAY CTY PUB HOSP
803 Poplar St, Murray, KY 42071
Phone: (502) 762-1100
Sales: $51,132,000   *Employees:* 1,000
Company Type: Private   *Employees here:* 800
SIC: 8062
    General hospital and nursing home
Stuart Poston, President

D-U-N-S 05-580-3449
MUSCATINE GENERAL HOSPITAL
1518 Mulberry Ave, Muscatine, IA 52761
Phone: (319) 264-9100
Sales: $21,744,000   *Employees:* 360
Company Type: Private   *Employees here:* 335
SIC: 8062
    Hospital
Karmon Bjella, Chief Executive Officer

D-U-N-S 07-928-4725
MUSKEGON GENERAL HOSPITAL
1700 Oak Ave, Muskegon, MI 49442
Phone: (616) 773-3311
Sales: $22,500,000   *Employees:* 500
Company Type: Private   *Employees here:* 500
SIC: 8062
    General hospital
Roger Spoelman, President

D-U-N-S 07-241-0111
MUSKOGEE MEDICAL CENTER AUTH
300 Rockefeller Dr, Muskogee, OK 74401
Phone: (918) 682-5501
Sales: $69,379,000   *Employees:* 1,000
Company Type: Private   *Employees here:* 1,000
SIC: 8062
    General medical hospital
Bill Kennedy, President

D-U-N-S 03-009-2407
MYRTLE BEACH HOSPITAL INC
(Parent: Columbia/Hca Healthcare Corp)
809 82nd Pkwy, Myrtle Beach, SC 29572
Phone: (843) 449-4411
Sales: $179,903,000   *Employees:* 811
Company Type: Public Family Member   *Employees here:* 811
SIC: 8062
    General medical & surgical hospital
Doug White, Administrator

D-U-N-S 17-817-1211
MD HEALTH PLAN INC
(Parent: Foundation Health Systems Inc)
6 Devine St Ste 3, North Haven, CT 6473
Phone: (203) 230-1000
Sales: $24,000,000   *Employees:* 351
Company Type: Private   *Employees here:* 350
SIC: 8011
    Health maintenance organization
Barbara G Bradow, President

D-U-N-S 07-611-8900
N T ENLOE MEMORIAL HOSPITAL
1531 Esplanade, Chico, CA 95926
Phone: (530) 891-7300

Sales: $117,297,000
Company Type: Private
SIC: 8062
   General hospital
Phillip R Wolfe, President
Employees: 1,700
Employees here: 1,500

D-U-N-S 07-420-4470
NACOGDOCHES COUNTY HOSPITAL DST
1204 N Mound St, Nacogdoches, TX 75961
Phone: (409) 564-4611
Sales: $57,994,000
Company Type: Private
SIC: 8062
   General hospital physical therapy and occupational health
   clinic
G W Jones, Administrator
Employees: 675
Employees here: 650

D-U-N-S 07-178-2825
NAEVE HOSPITAL
404 W Fountain St, Albert Lea, MN 56007
Phone: (507) 373-2384
Sales: $24,856,000
Company Type: Private
SIC: 8062
   General hospital
Dr Ronald Harmon Md, Chief Executive Officer
Employees: 650
Employees here: 600

D-U-N-S 06-841-5058
NAI COMMUNITY HOSPITAL OF PHOENIX
   (Parent: Tenet Healthcare Corporation)
6501 N 19th Ave, Phoenix, AZ 85015
Phone: (602) 249-3434
Sales: $40,000,000
Company Type: Public Family Member
SIC: 8062
   General hospital
Pat Walz, Chief Executive Officer
Employees: 200
Employees here: 200

D-U-N-S 07-905-2262
NALLE CLINIC COMPANY
1918 Randolph Rd, Charlotte, NC 28207
Phone: (704) 342-8000
Sales: $41,200,000
Company Type: Private
SIC: 8011
   Medical clinic
Dr C R Fernandez Md, Director
Employees: 600
Employees here: 350

D-U-N-S 07-847-2818
NAPLES COMMUNITY HOSPITAL INC
350 7th St N, Naples, FL 34102
Phone: (941) 436-5000
Sales: $174,345,000
Company Type: Private
SIC: 8062
   General medical & surgical hospital
William Crone, President
Employees: 1,800
Employees here: 1,780

D-U-N-S 07-554-9139
NASH HOSPITALS INC
2460 Curtis Ellis Dr, Rocky Mount, NC 27804
Phone: (252) 443-8012
Sales: $100,283,000
Company Type: Private
SIC: 8062
   General hospital and psychiatric & susbstance abuce center
Bryant Aldridge, President
Employees: 1,400
Employees here: 1,300

D-U-N-S 07-661-6598
NASHOBA COMMUNITY HOSPITAL CORP
200 Groton Rd, Ayer, MA 1432
Phone: (978) 784-9000

Sales: $22,496,000
Company Type: Private
SIC: 8062
   General hospital
Jeffery Kelly, President
Employees: 450
Employees here: 450

D-U-N-S 04-701-2174
NASSER SMITH PINKERTON CARDIOLOGY
8333 Naab Rd Ste 400, Indianapolis, IN 46260
Phone: (317) 338-6666
Sales: $26,000,000
Company Type: Private
SIC: 8011
   Cardioligist
Dr William K Nasser Md, President
Employees: 380
Employees here: 150

D-U-N-S 04-775-7687
NATCHEZ REGIONAL MEDICAL CTR
54 Sergeant S Prentiss Dr, Natchez, MS 39120
Phone: (601) 442-2871
Sales: $34,423,000
Company Type: Private
SIC: 8062
   General hospital
David Snyder, Administrator
Employees: 500
Employees here: 500

D-U-N-S 88-360-0546
NATCHTCHES PARISH HOSPITAL SVC DST
501 Keyser Ave, Natchitoches, LA 71457
Phone: (318) 352-1250
Sales: $21,839,000
Company Type: Private
SIC: 8062
   General hospital
Eugene Spillman, Administrator
Employees: 150
Employees here: 150

D-U-N-S 06-854-8593
NATIONAL BENEVOLENT
11780 Borman Dr Ste 200, Saint Louis, MO 63146
Phone: (314) 993-9000
Sales: $127,698,000
Company Type: Private
SIC: 8361
   Social & health services
Richard R Lance, President
Employees: 3,500
Employees here: 74

D-U-N-S 05-531-2342
NATIONAL DENTEX CORPORATION
526 Boston Post Rd, Wayland, MA 1778
Phone: (508) 358-4422
Sales: $59,196,000
Company Type: Public
SIC: 8072
   Dental laboratories
William M Mullahy, President
Employees: 1,200
Employees here: 40

D-U-N-S 96-272-4035
NATIONAL DIAGNOSTIC LABORATORY
12981 Perris Blvd Ste 101, Moreno Valley, CA 92553
Phone: (909) 485-8515
Sales: $20,000,000
Company Type: Private
SIC: 8071
   Clinical laboratory
Paricio Quines Jr, President
Employees: 15
Employees here: 15

D-U-N-S 07-545-6897
NATIONAL HEALTHCARE OF DECATUR
   (Parent: Community Health Systems Inc)
1874 Beltline Rd SW, Decatur, AL 35601
Phone: (256) 350-2211

Sales: $35,000,000   Employees: 250
Company Type: Public Family Member   Employees here: 250
SIC: 8062
  General hospital
Phillip Mazzuca, Administrator

D-U-N-S 06-910-0097
NATIONAL HEALTHCARE CORP
100 E Vine St, Murfreesboro, TN 37130
Phone: (615) 890-2020
Sales: $463,477,000   Employees: 16,000
Company Type: Public   Employees here: 150
SIC: 8051
  Owns operates & manages long-term care facilities
    retirement apartments & assisted living units & provides
    home health care
W A Adams, Chairman of the Board

D-U-N-S 36-123-6698
NATIONAL HEALTHCARE LESVILLE INC
   (Parent: Community Health Systems Inc)
1020 W Fertitta Blvd, Leesville, LA 71446
Phone: (318) 239-9041
Sales: $38,000,000   Employees: 225
Company Type: Public Family Member   Employees here: 225
SIC: 8062
  General hospital
Don Henderson, Administrator

D-U-N-S 61-159-9275
NATIONAL HOME CARE INC
   (Parent: Patient Care Inc)
100 Executive Dr Ste 130, West Orange, NJ 7052
Phone: (973) 243-5900
Sales: $32,800,000   Employees: 2,053
Company Type: Public Family Member   Employees here: 357
SIC: 8082
  Home health care service
Timothy O Toole, Chairman of the Board

D-U-N-S 11-543-5935
NATIONAL HOME HEALTH CARE CORP
700 White Plains Rd, Scarsdale, NY 10583
Phone: (914) 722-9000
Sales: $35,070,000   Employees: 2,000
Company Type: Public   Employees here: 5
SIC: 8082
  Home health care services
Frederick H Fialkow, Chief Executive Officer

D-U-N-S 07-644-3019
NATIONAL JEWISH MED & RES CTR
1400 Jackson St, Denver, CO 80206
Phone: (303) 388-4461
Sales: $28,684,000   Employees: 980
Company Type: Private   Employees here: 980
SIC: 8069
  National specialty hospital
Christine Forkner, Chief Financial Officer

D-U-N-S 04-940-5541   EXP
NATIONAL MEDICAL CARE INC
   (Parent: Fresenius Nat Med Care Hldings)
2 Leighton Ave, Lexington, MA 2420
Phone: (781) 402-9000
Sales: $1,028,600,000   Employees: 18,000
Company Type: Public Family Member   Employees here: 350
SIC: 8092
  Kidney dialysis centers
Ben J Lipps Phd, President

D-U-N-S 09-566-8091
NATIONAL MEDICAL HOSPITAL
   (Parent: Tenet Healthcare Corporation)
1411 W Baddour Pkwy, Lebanon, TN 37087
Phone: (615) 444-8262
Sales: $34,300,000   Employees: 750
Company Type: Public Family Member   Employees here: 625
SIC: 8062
  Hospital
Larry Keller, Chief Executive Officer

D-U-N-S 80-565-0447
NATIONAL MENTOR HEALTHCARE,
313 Congress St, Quincy, MA 2169
Phone: (617) 790-4800
Sales: $29,016,000   Employees: NA
Company Type: Private   Employees here: NA
SIC: 8361
  Residential care facilities
Gregory Torres, President

D-U-N-S 15-779-2052
NATIONAL MENTOR INC
   (Parent: Magellan Public Solutions Inc)
313 Congress St, Boston, MA 2210
Phone: (617) 790-4800
Sales: $88,331,000   Employees: 1,655
Company Type: Public Family Member   Employees here: 92
SIC: 8361
  Managed health care services
Gregory Torres, President

D-U-N-S 87-724-5639
NATIONAL PARK MEDICAL CENTER,
   (Parent: Tenet Healthcare Corporation)
1910 Malvern Ave, Hot Springs, AR 71901
Phone: (501) 321-1000
Sales: $36,700,000   Employees: 800
Company Type: Public Family Member   Employees here: 700
SIC: 8062
  General hospital
Jerry Mabry, Administrator

D-U-N-S 07-736-6664
NATIONAL REHABILITATION HOSP
102 Irving St Nw, Washington, DC 20010
Phone: (202) 877-1000
Sales: $60,924,000   Employees: 760
Company Type: Private   Employees here: 730
SIC: 8069
  Specialty hospital
Edward Eckenhoff, President

D-U-N-S 60-487-1038
NATIONAL SURGERY CENTERS, INC.
30 S Wacker Dr Ste 2302, Chicago, IL 60606
Phone: (312) 655-1400
Sales: $102,632,000   Employees: 519
Company Type: Public   Employees here: 24
SIC: 8093
  Outpatient surgical centers
E T Geary, Chairman of the Board

D-U-N-S 55-727-5468
NATIONS HEALTHCARE INC
1000 Mansell Exchange W, Alpharetta, GA 30022
Phone: (770) 518-3960
Sales: $81,533,000   Employees: 1,800
Company Type: Private   Employees here: 40
SIC: 8082
  Home health care service
Bob Wood, President

D-U-N-S 92-765-7031
NATIONWIDE CARE, INC
(*Parent:* Vencor Inc)
400 W Market St Ste 3300, Louisville, KY 40202
Phone: (502) 569-7300
Sales: $103,300,000   *Employees:* 4,500
Company Type: Private   *Employees here:* 50
SIC: 8051
    Intermediate & skilled nursing facilities
W B Lunsford, President

D-U-N-S 12-038-8764
NAVAJO NTION TRIBAL GOVERNMENT
516 Nizhoni Blvd, Gallup, NM 87301
Phone: (505) 722-1000
Sales: $42,200,000   *Employees:* NA
Company Type: Private   *Employees here:* 800
SIC: 8011
    Medical center
Dr Timothy Fleming, Branch Manager

D-U-N-S 08-446-2118
NAVAPACHE HEALTH CARE ASSN
2200 E Show Low Lake Rd, Show Low, AZ 85901
Phone: (520) 537-4375
Sales: $30,288,000   *Employees:* 430
Company Type: Private   *Employees here:* 430
SIC: 8062
    General hospital
Leigh Cox, Chief Executive Officer

D-U-N-S 11-192-0690
NAVY, UNITED STATES DEPT OF
6000 W Highway 98, Pensacola, FL 32512
Phone: (850) 452-6601
Sales: $86,100,000   *Employees:* NA
Company Type: Private   *Employees here:* 3,420
SIC: 8021
    Hospital
Cpt Lockhart, Branch Manager

D-U-N-S 16-967-2821
NAVY, UNITED STATES DEPT OF
H Bldg 200, Great Lakes, IL 60088
Phone: (847) 688-4668
Sales: $50,700,000   *Employees:* NA
Company Type: Private   *Employees here:* 1,200
SIC: 8062
    Naval hospital
Capt R Holden, Owner

D-U-N-S 01-918-7447
NAZARETH HEALTH INC
2051 Hamill Rd, Hixson, TN 37343
Phone: (423) 870-6101
Sales: $24,100,000   *Employees:* NA
Company Type: Private   *Employees here:* 580
SIC: 8062
    General hospital
Sean Mcmurray, Administrator

D-U-N-S 08-119-3344
NAZARETH HEALTH INC
2525 Desales Ave, Chattanooga, TN 37404
Phone: (423) 495-5656
Sales: $63,500,000   *Employees:* NA
Company Type: Private   *Employees here:* 1,500
SIC: 8062
    General hospital
L C Taylor Jr, President

D-U-N-S 06-987-3958
NAZARETH HOSPITAL (INC)
2601 Holme Ave, Philadelphia, PA 19152
Phone: (215) 335-6000
Sales: $70,608,000   *Employees:* 1,280
Company Type: Private   *Employees here:* 1,250
SIC: 8062
    General hospital
Daniel J Sinnont, President

D-U-N-S 78-478-6444
NCS, INC.
3601 Hobson Rd, Fort Wayne, IN 46815
Phone: (219) 482-6466
Sales: $20,903,000   *Employees:* 600
Company Type: Private   *Employees here:* 9
SIC: 8051
    Operator of skilled and intermediate care nursing homes
Christine Rupp, Chief Financial Officer

D-U-N-S 04-353-1607
NEBRASKA HEALTH SYSTEM
987450 Nebraska Med Ctr, Omaha, NE 68198
Phone: (402) 552-2000
Sales: $131,551,000   *Employees:* 3,800
Company Type: Private   *Employees here:* 1,400
SIC: 8062
    Hospital
Bruce R Lauritzen, Chairman of the Board

D-U-N-S 06-152-9418
NEBRASKA METHODIST HOSPITAL
8303 Dodge St, Omaha, NE 68114
Phone: (402) 390-4000
Sales: $110,000,000   *Employees:* 1,850
Company Type: Private   *Employees here:* 1,250
SIC: 8062
    Hospital
Stephen D Long, President

D-U-N-S 18-117-4434
NEIGHBORHOOD HEALTH PLAN INC
253 Summer St Fl 5, Boston, MA 2210
Phone: (617) 772-5500
Sales: $86,836,000   *Employees:* 200
Company Type: Private   *Employees here:* 163
SIC: 8011
    Health maintenance organization
James Hooley, President

D-U-N-S 03-800-4941
NEMOURS FOUNDATION (INC)
1600 Rockland Rd, Wilmington, DE 19803
Phone: (302) 651-4000
Sales: $37,600,000   *Employees:* NA
Company Type: Private   *Employees here:* 800
SIC: 8069
    Children's hospital
Thomas Ferry Phd, Administrator

D-U-N-S 80-438-3016
NEMOURS FOUNDATION (INC)
1600 Rockland Rd, Wilmington, DE 19803
Phone: (302) 651-4620
Sales: $39,700,000   *Employees:* NA
Company Type: Private   *Employees here:* 650
SIC: 8011
    Hospital
Dr Robert Doughty Md, Chief Executive Officer

D-U-N-S 03-168-2750
NEMOURS FOUNDATION (INC)
807 Nira St, Jacksonville, FL 32207

Phone: (904) 390-3600
Sales: $22,200,000　　　　　　　　　*Employees:* NA
Company Type: Private　　　　　　　*Employees here:* 350
SIC: 8011
　　Children's clinic
Dr Robert Kettrick Md, Chief Executive Officer

D-U-N-S 03-729-3792
NEMOURS FOUNDATION (INC)
1650 Prudential Dr, Jacksonville, FL 32207
Phone: (904) 858-3100
Sales: $76,389,000　　　　　　　　　*Employees:* 2,369
Company Type: Private　　　　　　　*Employees here:* 10
SIC: 8069
　　Children's hospital
W J Wadsworth, General Manager

D-U-N-S 11-417-2851
NEOMEDICA INC.
　　(Parent: National Medical Care Inc)
450 E Ohio St Fl 8, Chicago, IL 60611
Phone: (312) 951-4900
Sales: $48,915,000　　　　　　　　　*Employees:* 450
Company Type: Public Family Member　*Employees here:* 60
SIC: 8092
　　Kidney dialysis center and acute medical care service
Dr Gordon R Lang Md, Chief Executive Officer

D-U-N-S 01-178-6456
NEPONSET VALLEY HEALTH SYSTEM,
111 Dedham St, Norfolk, MA 2056
Phone: (508) 668-0385
Sales: $121,026,000　　　　　　　　*Employees:* 2,100
Company Type: Private　　　　　　　*Employees here:* 500
SIC: 8062
　　General & specialty hospitals
Yolanda Landrau, President

D-U-N-S 08-281-7073
NETWORK HEALTH SYSTEM, INC
1165 Appleton Rd, Menasha, WI 54952
Phone: (920) 727-7607
Sales: $115,000,000　　　　　　　　*Employees:* 1,291
Company Type: Private　　　　　　　*Employees here:* 150
SIC: 8011
　　Medical clinic
Dr Scott Niegard Md, Chief Executive Officer

D-U-N-S 08-188-1617
NETWORK HEALTH PLAN OF WISCONSIN
　　(Parent: Network Health System Inc)
1165 Appleton Rd, Menasha, WI 54952
Phone: (920) 727-0100
Sales: $93,250,000　　　　　　　　　*Employees:* 125
Company Type: Private　　　　　　　*Employees here:* 125
SIC: 8011
　　Health maintenance organization
Mike Wolff, President

D-U-N-S 78-808-1073
NEURO-REHAB ASSOCIATES INC
70 Butler St, Salem, NH 3079
Phone: (603) 893-2900
Sales: $50,000,000　　　　　　　　　*Employees:* 450
Company Type: Private　　　　　　　*Employees here:* 300
SIC: 8049
　　Health practitioner's office
John F Prochilo, Administrator

D-U-N-S 06-925-5172
NEW BRITAIN GENERAL HOSPITAL
100 Grand St, New Britain, CT 6052
Phone: (860) 224-5011

Sales: $144,420,000　　　　　　　　*Employees:* 3,000
Company Type: Private　　　　　　　*Employees here:* 2,450
SIC: 8062
　　General hospital
Laurence Tanner, President

D-U-N-S 07-661-8883
NEW ENGLAND BAPTIST HOSPITAL
125 Parker Hill Ave, Boston, MA 2120
Phone: (617) 754-5800
Sales: $98,187,000　　　　　　　　　*Employees:* 1,100
Company Type: Private　　　　　　　*Employees here:* 1,100
SIC: 8062
　　General hospital
Dr Alan H Robbins Md, Chief Executive Officer

D-U-N-S 01-687-7768
NEW ENGLAND HEALTH CARE
75 Kneeland St 501, Boston, MA 2111
Phone: (617) 636-5424
Sales: $90,000,000　　　　　　　　　*Employees:* 270
Company Type: Private　　　　　　　*Employees here:* 270
SIC: 8011
　　Specialized medical practitioners
Dr Douglas Payne Md, Chief Executive Officer

D-U-N-S 15-264-7749
NEW ENGLAND LONG-TERM CARE,
　　(Parent: New England Medical Center)
750 Washington St, Boston, MA 2111
Phone: (617) 636-5000
Sales: $45,800,000　　　　　　　　　*Employees:* 2,000
Company Type: Private　　　　　　　*Employees here:* 167
SIC: 8051
　　Skilled nursing care facility
Larry Smith, President

D-U-N-S 07-953-2263
NEW ENGLAND MED CTR HOSPITALS
750 Washington St, Boston, MA 2111
Phone: (617) 636-5000
Sales: $228,400,000　　　　　　　　*Employees:* 4,856
Company Type: Private　　　　　　　*Employees here:* 3,620
SIC: 8062
　　General hospital
Dr Thomas O Donnell Md, President

D-U-N-S 79-027-3114
NEW ENGLAND REHABILITATION SER
189 May St, Worcester, MA 1602
Phone: (508) 791-6351
Sales: $22,564,000　　　　　　　　　*Employees:* NA
Company Type: Private　　　　　　　*Employees here:* NA
SIC: 8062
　　Acute rehabilitation hospital
Peter Mantegazza, President

D-U-N-S 07-657-8228
NEW ENGLAND RHABILITATION HOSP
　　(Parent: Healthsouth Corporation)
2 Rehabilitation Way, Woburn, MA 1801
Phone: (781) 935-5050
Sales: $39,944,000　　　　　　　　　*Employees:* 805
Company Type: Public Family Member　*Employees here:* 805
SIC: 8093
　　Rehabilitation hospital
Mary Moscato, Chief Executive Officer

D-U-N-S 07-661-3983
NEW ENGLAND SINAI HOSPITAL
150 York St, Stoughton, MA 2072
Phone: (781) 344-0600

Sales: $38,228,000   *Employees:* 520
Company Type: Private   *Employees here:* 519
SIC: 8069
   Chronic disease/rehab hospital
Norman Spector, Chairman of the Board

D-U-N-S 07-202-9143
NEW HANOVER REGIONAL MED CTR
2131 S 17th St, Wilmington, NC 28401
Phone: (910) 343-7000
Sales: $267,848,000   *Employees:* 3,100
Company Type: Private   *Employees here:* 2,975
SIC: 8062
   General hospital
William K Atkinson, Chief Executive Officer

D-U-N-S 86-823-1978
NEW JERSEY DEPT HUMANSVCS
De Hirsch Ave, Woodbine, NJ 8270
Phone: (609) 861-6041
Sales: $31,700,000   *Employees:* NA
Company Type: Private   *Employees here:* 1,300
SIC: 8361
   Residential care services
Denise Micheletti, Chief Executive Officer

D-U-N-S 14-439-6116
NEW JERSEY DEPT HUMANSVCS
Sullivan Way, Trenton, NJ 8628
Phone: (609) 633-1500
Sales: $31,900,000   *Employees:* NA
Company Type: Private   *Employees here:* 800
SIC: 8063
   Psychiatric hospital
Joseph Jupin, President

D-U-N-S 07-514-3008
NEW JERSEY DEPT HUMANSVCS
169 Minnisink Rd, Totowa, NJ 7512
Phone: (973) 256-1700
Sales: $23,300,000   *Employees:* NA
Company Type: Private   *Employees here:* 953
SIC: 8051
   Home for mentally retarded & disabled
Richard Cesta, Manager

D-U-N-S 07-548-7009
NEW JERSEY DEPT HUMANSVCS
202 Spring Garden Rd, Hammonton, NJ 8037
Phone: (609) 567-8306
Sales: $47,600,000   *Employees:* NA
Company Type: Private   *Employees here:* 1,200
SIC: 8063
   Psychiatric hospital
William J Camarota, Branch Manager

D-U-N-S 93-250-3394
NEW LEXINGTON CLINIC, P.S.C.
1221 S Broadway, Lexington, KY 40504
Phone: (606) 255-6841
Sales: $68,800,000   *Employees:* 1,000
Company Type: Private   *Employees here:* 340
SIC: 8011
   Medical clinic
Tom Donahue, President

D-U-N-S 07-302-2683
NEW LIBERTY HOSPITAL DISTRICT
2525 Glenn Hendren Dr, Liberty, MO 64068
Phone: (816) 781-7200

Sales: $66,531,000   *Employees:* 1,050
Company Type: Private   *Employees here:* 1,050
SIC: 8062
   Hospital
Joseph W Crossett, Administrator

D-U-N-S 02-298-9727
NEW MEXICO DEPARTMENT HEALTH
Hot Springs Blvd, Las Vegas, NM 87701
Phone: (505) 454-2100
Sales: $38,500,000   *Employees:* NA
Company Type: Private   *Employees here:* 1,200
SIC: 8063
   Psychiatric hospital
Gary Buff, Manager

D-U-N-S 06-000-7481
NEW MILFORD HOSPITAL INC
21 Elm St, New Milford, CT 6776
Phone: (860) 355-2611
Sales: $38,612,000   *Employees:* 415
Company Type: Private   *Employees here:* 408
SIC: 8062
   General hospital
Richard E Pugh, President

D-U-N-S 96-260-4104
NEW PORT RICHEY HOSPITAL INC
   (Parent: Columbia/Hca Healthcare Corp)
5637 Marine Pkwy, New Port Richey, FL 34652
Phone: (727) 848-1733
Sales: $46,100,000   *Employees:* 1,000
Company Type: Public Family Member   *Employees here:* 1,000
SIC: 8062
   General hospital
Andrew Oravec Jr, Administrator

D-U-N-S 96-375-1623
NEW ULM MEDICAL CENTER
1324 5th St N, New Ulm, MN 56073
Phone: (507) 354-2111
Sales: $26,956,000   *Employees:* NA
Company Type: Private   *Employees here:* NA
SIC: 8062
   General hospital

D-U-N-S 02-152-6132
NEW VANDERBILT NURSING HOME
135 Vanderbilt Ave, Staten Island, NY 10304
Phone: (718) 447-0701
Sales: $22,034,000   *Employees:* 270
Company Type: Private   *Employees here:* 270
SIC: 8051
   Skilled nursing facility
Henry Shoen, President

D-U-N-S 13-813-2857
NEW YORK AND PRESBYTERIAN HOSP
3959 Broadway, New York, NY 10032
Phone: (212) 305-2500
Sales: $105,300,000   *Employees:* NA
Company Type: Private   *Employees here:* 2,000
SIC: 8069
   Specialty hospital
Caryn A Schwab, Senior Vice-President

D-U-N-S 62-335-6763
NEW YORK AND PRESBYTERIAN HOSP
627 W 165th St Fl 2, New York, NY 10032
Phone: (212) 305-6038

Sales: $43,200,000   *Employees:* NA
Company Type: Private   *Employees here:* 875
SIC: 8062
  General hospital
Michael Bruno, Principal

D-U-N-S 78-318-9582
NEW YORK AND PRESBYTERIAN HOSP
635 W 165th St, New York, NY 10032
Phone: (212) 305-2725
Sales: $21,000,000   *Employees:* NA
Company Type: Private   *Employees here:* 400
SIC: 8069
  Specialty hospital
Dr William Speck, President

D-U-N-S 07-327-1827
NEW YORK BLOOD CENTER, INC.
310 E 67th St, New York, NY 10021
Phone: (212) 570-3000
Sales: $210,529,000   *Employees:* 1,915
Company Type: Private   *Employees here:* 365
SIC: 8099
  Blood bank and blood research
Howard Sloan, Chairman of the Board

D-U-N-S 18-359-6527
NEW YORK BLOOD CENTER, INC.
310 E 67th St, New York, NY 10021
Phone: (212) 570-3000
Sales: $20,800,000   *Employees:* NA
Company Type: Private   *Employees here:* 400
SIC: 8071
  Medical laboratory
Jenni L Robins, Manager

D-U-N-S 05-935-0421
NEW YORK COMMUNITY HOSPITAL
2525 Kings Hwy, Brooklyn, NY 11229
Phone: (718) 692-5300
Sales: $36,021,000   *Employees:* 375
Company Type: Private   *Employees here:* 375
SIC: 8062
  General hospital
Lin H Mo, President

D-U-N-S 02-963-1173
NEW YORK CY HEALTH HSPITALS CORP
460 Brielle Ave, Staten Island, NY 10314
Phone: (718) 317-3000
Sales: $30,300,000   *Employees:* NA
Company Type: Private   *Employees here:* 620
SIC: 8062
  General hospital skilled nursing care facility
Tom Mateo, Director

D-U-N-S 06-496-1261
NEW YORK CY HEALTH HSPITALS CORP
125 Worth St, New York, NY 10013
Phone: (212) 788-3321
Sales: $3,775,931,000   *Employees:* 38,000
Company Type: Private   *Employees here:* 450
SIC: 8062
  General medical and surgical hospitals
Dr Bruce Seigel Md, President

D-U-N-S 10-505-8390
NEW YORK CY HEALTH HSPITALS CORP
Roosevelt Is, New York, NY 10044
Phone: (212) 318-8000

Sales: $49,400,000   *Employees:* NA
Company Type: Private   *Employees here:* 1,000
SIC: 8062
  General hospital
Samuel Lehrfeld, N/A

D-U-N-S 12-598-6810
NEW YORK CY HEALTH HSPITALS CORP
227 Madison St, New York, NY 10002
Phone: (212) 238-7000
Sales: $59,500,000   *Employees:* NA
Company Type: Private   *Employees here:* 1,200
SIC: 8062
  General hospital
Kenneth Geld, Principal

D-U-N-S 15-502-6818
NEW YORK CY HEALTH HSPITALS CORP
506 Lenox Ave, New York, NY 10037
Phone: (212) 939-1000
Sales: $174,200,000   *Employees:* NA
Company Type: Private   *Employees here:* 3,500
SIC: 8062
  General hospital
Bruce Goldman, N/A

D-U-N-S 17-262-8976
NEW YORK CY HEALTH HSPITALS CORP
900 Main St Rsvelt Is, New York, NY 10044
Phone: (212) 848-6000
Sales: $49,400,000   *Employees:* NA
Company Type: Private   *Employees here:* 1,000
SIC: 8062
  General hospital
Samuel Lehfseld, Director

D-U-N-S 61-849-5535
NEW YORK CY HEALTH HSPITALS CORP
462 1st Ave, New York, NY 10016
Phone: (212) 561-5251
Sales: $273,300,000   *Employees:* NA
Company Type: Private   *Employees here:* 5,500
SIC: 8062
  General hospital
Howard Cohen, N/A

D-U-N-S 80-373-4169
NEW YORK CY HEALTH HSPITALS CORP
1901 1st Ave, New York, NY 10029
Phone: (212) 423-6262
Sales: $99,500,000   *Employees:* NA
Company Type: Private   *Employees here:* 2,000
SIC: 8062
  General hospital
Stanford A Roman Jr, Senior Vice-President

D-U-N-S 08-606-0423
NEW YORK CY HEALTH HSPITALS CORP
7901 Broadway, Elmhurst, NY 11373
Phone: (718) 565-4822
Sales: $174,200,000   *Employees:* NA
Company Type: Private   *Employees here:* 3,500
SIC: 8062
  Hospital
Peter Velez, N/A

D-U-N-S 02-058-6731
NEW YORK CY HSPITALS CORP
100 N Portland Ave, Brooklyn, NY 11205
Phone: (718) 260-7500

Sales: $26,200,000 *Employees:* NA
Company Type: Private *Employees here:* 374
SIC: 8011
 Medical doctor's office
Linda Curtis, Director

D-U-N-S 04-625-4389
NEW YORK CY HEALTH HSPITALS CORP
760 Broadway, Brooklyn, NY 11206
Phone: (718) 963-8000
Sales: $124,400,000 *Employees:* NA
Company Type: Private *Employees here:* 2,500
SIC: 8062
 Hospital
Norma Noriega, N/A

D-U-N-S 07-434-5927
NEW YORK CY HEALTH HSPITALS CORP
451 Clarkson Ave, Brooklyn, NY 11203
Phone: (718) 245-3131
Sales: $298,100,000 *Employees:* NA
Company Type: Private *Employees here:* 6,000
SIC: 8062
 General hospital
Benjamin Chu, Director

D-U-N-S 10-510-2917
NEW YORK CY HEALTH HSPITALS CORP
3424 Kossuth Ave, Bronx, NY 10467
Phone: (718) 918-3426
Sales: $99,500,000 *Employees:* NA
Company Type: Private *Employees here:* 2,000
SIC: 8062
 Hospital
Emilio J Morante, N/A

D-U-N-S 07-886-9807
NEW YORK DOWNTOWN HOSPITAL
170 William St, New York, NY 10038
Phone: (212) 312-5000
Sales: $94,204,000 *Employees:* 1,100
Company Type: Private *Employees here:* 1,020
SIC: 8062
 General medical & surgical hospital
Alan H Channing, President

D-U-N-S 07-102-4277
NEW YORK EYE EAR INFIRMARY INC
310 E 14th St, New York, NY 10003
Phone: (212) 979-4000
Sales: $61,902,000 *Employees:* 600
Company Type: Private *Employees here:* 600
SIC: 8069
 Eye ear nose & throat hospital
Joseph Corcoran, President

D-U-N-S 07-275-1001
NEW YORK FLSHING HOSPITAL MED CTR
45th Ave At Parsons Blvd, Flushing, NY 11355
Phone: (718) 670-5000
Sales: $150,988,000 *Employees:* 1,450
Company Type: Private *Employees here:* 1,400
SIC: 8062
 General medical hospital
Stephen S Mills, President

D-U-N-S 07-274-4592
NEW YORK HOSPITAL MEDICAL CENT
5645 Main St, Flushing, NY 11355
Phone: (718) 670-1231

Sales: $257,810,000 *Employees:* 2,300
Company Type: Private *Employees here:* 2,200
SIC: 8062
 General hospital
Stephen S Mills, President

D-U-N-S 60-531-2412
NEW YORK HOTEL TRADES COUNCIL
305 W 44th St, New York, NY 10036
Phone: (212) 586-6400
Sales: $43,736,000 *Employees:* 143
Company Type: Private *Employees here:* 43
SIC: 8011
 Nonprofit medical centers
Gerry Parnell, Director

D-U-N-S 02-786-1251
NEW YORK MEDICAL GROUP, PC
110 E 59th St Ste Flr22, New York, NY 10022
Phone: (212) 705-5414
Sales: $75,700,000 *Employees:* 1,100
Company Type: Private *Employees here:* 80
SIC: 8011
 Physician's office
Dr Moshe Labi Md, Director

D-U-N-S 05-281-0801
NEW YORK METHODIST HOSPITAL
506 6th St, Brooklyn, NY 11215
Phone: (718) 780-3000
Sales: $272,039,000 *Employees:* 2,900
Company Type: Private *Employees here:* 2,881
SIC: 8062
 General hospital
Mark J Mundy, President

D-U-N-S 00-393-7364
NEW YORK SOCIETY FOR RELIEF
535 E 70th St, New York, NY 10021
Phone: (212) 606-1000
Sales: $154,730,000 *Employees:* 1,238
Company Type: Private *Employees here:* 1,200
SIC: 8069
 Hospital
John R Ahearn, President

D-U-N-S 12-191-1077
NEW YORK UNIVERSITY
560 1st Ave, New York, NY 10016
Phone: (212) 263-7300
Sales: $396,800,000 *Employees:* NA
Company Type: Private *Employees here:* 8,000
SIC: 8062
 Medical center
Theresa Bischoff, Principal

D-U-N-S 79-617-6675
NEW YORK, STATE OF
Nicholls Rd, Stony Brook, NY 11794
Phone: (516) 689-8333
Sales: $74,500,000 *Employees:* NA
Company Type: Private *Employees here:* 1,500
SIC: 8062
 General hospital
Lenora J Mcclean, Officer

D-U-N-S 02-152-0622
NEW YORK, STATE OF
777 Seaview Ave, Staten Island, NY 10305
Phone: (718) 667-2300

Sales: $39,800,000   *Employees:* NA
Company Type: Private   *Employees here:* 1,000
SIC: 8063
  Psychiatric hospital
Lucy Sarkis, Executive Director

D-U-N-S 78-044-5656
NEW YORK, STATE OF
8045 Winchester Blvd, Queens Village, NY 11427
Phone: (718) 217-6769
Sales: $26,300,000   *Employees:* NA
Company Type: Private   *Employees here:* 800
SIC: 8093
  Mental retarded child out patient facility
Edith Hudson, Manager

D-U-N-S 84-160-3855
NEW YORK, STATE OF
140 Old Orangeburg Rd, Orangeburg, NY 10962
Phone: (914) 359-1000
Sales: $35,800,000   *Employees:* NA
Company Type: Private   *Employees here:* 900
SIC: 8063
  Psychiatric hospital
James Bopp, Branch Manager

D-U-N-S 18-955-5873
NEW YORK, STATE OF
450 Clarkson Ave, Brooklyn, NY 11203
Phone: (718) 270-1000
Sales: $149,300,000   *Employees:* NA
Company Type: Private   *Employees here:* 3,000
SIC: 8062
  General hospital
Percy Allen, Branch Manager

D-U-N-S 62-756-9866
NEW YORK, STATE OF
998 Crooked Hill Rd, Brentwood, NY 11717
Phone: (516) 434-5267
Sales: $183,300,000   *Employees:* NA
Company Type: Private   *Employees here:* 3,000
SIC: 8011
  Medical doctor's office
Debrea Strube, Manager

D-U-N-S 62-422-6478
NEW YORK, STATE OF
75 New Scotland Ave, Albany, NY 12208
Phone: (518) 447-9611
Sales: $24,000,000   *Employees:* NA
Company Type: Private   *Employees here:* 600
SIC: 8063
  Psychiatric hospital
Jesse Nixon, N/A

D-U-N-S 07-118-3214
NEWARK BETH ISRAEL MED CTR
201 Lyons Ave, Newark, NJ 7112
Phone: (973) 926-7000
Sales: $221,592,000   *Employees:* 3,000
Company Type: Private   *Employees here:* 2,700
SIC: 8062
  General hospital
Paul A Mertz, Executive Director

D-U-N-S 07-257-5848
NEWAYGO COUNTY GEN HOSPITAL ASSN
212 S Sullivan Ave, Fremont, MI 49412
Phone: (616) 924-3300

Sales: $27,382,000   *Employees:* 500
Company Type: Private   *Employees here:* 300
SIC: 8062
  General hospital
Ned B Hughes Jr, President

D-U-N-S 96-943-8639
NEWCARE HEALTH CORPORATION
6000 Lake Forrest Dr Nw, Atlanta, GA 30328
Phone: (404) 252-2923
Sales: $32,000,000   *Employees:* 272
Company Type: Private   *Employees here:* 200
SIC: 8059
  Nursing/personal care
Chris Brogdon, Chairman of the Board

D-U-N-S 07-709-0819
NEWCOMB MEDICAL CENTER
65 S State St, Vineland, NJ 8360
Phone: (609) 691-9000
Sales: $61,737,000   *Employees:* 730
Company Type: Private   *Employees here:* 700
SIC: 8062
  General hospital
Joseph Ierardi, President

D-U-N-S 07-302-3939
NEWMAN MEMORIAL COUNTY HOSP
1201 W 12th Ave, Emporia, KS 66801
Phone: (316) 343-6800
Sales: $30,221,000   *Employees:* 490
Company Type: Private   *Employees here:* 480
SIC: 8062
  Hospital & substance abuse
Terry Lambert, Administrator

D-U-N-S 07-812-2066
NEWNAN HOSPITAL
80 Jackson St, Newnan, GA 30263
Phone: (770) 253-2330
Sales: $47,425,000   *Employees:* 549
Company Type: Private   *Employees here:* 549
SIC: 8062
  General hospital
Glenn M Flake, Administrator

D-U-N-S 79-180-3158
NEWPORT HEALTH CARE CORP
11 Friendship St, Newport, RI 2840
Phone: (401) 846-6400
Sales: $31,900,000   *Employees:* 700
Company Type: Private   *Employees here:* 700
SIC: 8062
  Health management services
Arthur Sampson, President

D-U-N-S 07-567-8177
NEWPORT HOSPITAL
11 Friendship St, Newport, RI 2840
Phone: (401) 846-6400
Sales: $54,305,000   *Employees:* 700
Company Type: Private   *Employees here:* 700
SIC: 8062
  General hospital
Arthur Sampson, President

D-U-N-S 07-342-8302
NEWTON HEALTH SYSTEMS INC
5126 Hospital Dr NE, Covington, GA 30014
Phone: (770) 786-7053

Sales: $32,633,000   *Employees:* 510
Company Type: Private   *Employees here:* 441
SIC: 8062
   General hospital
James F Weadick, Administrator

D-U-N-S 18-388-1994
NEWTON HEALTHCARE CORPORATION
600 Medical Center Dr, Newton, KS 67114
Phone: (316) 283-2700
Sales: $20,627,000   *Employees:* 380
Company Type: Private   *Employees here:* 380
SIC: 8062
   Hospital
W C Waters, President

D-U-N-S 06-857-2544
NEWTON MEMORIAL HOSPITAL
175 High St, Newton, NJ 7860
Phone: (973) 383-2121
Sales: $62,039,000   *Employees:* 677
Company Type: Private   *Employees here:* 677
SIC: 8062
   Hospital
Dennis Collette, President

D-U-N-S 13-115-6234
NEXTHEALTH INC
16600 N Lago Del Oro Pkwy, Tucson, AZ 85739
Phone: (520) 792-5800
Sales: $20,652,000   *Employees:* 370
Company Type: Public   *Employees here:* 15
SIC: 8069
   Residential care centers health & leisure resort
William O Donnell, President

D-U-N-S 06-499-1821
NHS NATIONAL HEALTH SERVICES,
777 3rd Ave Rm 18, New York, NY 10017
Phone: (212) 583-1797
Sales: $34,300,000   *Employees:* 500
Company Type: Private   *Employees here:* 30
SIC: 8011
   Medical services
Dr Richard E Winter Md, Chairman of the Board

D-U-N-S 07-993-4667
NIAGARA FALLS MEMORIAL MED CTR
621 10th St, Niagara Falls, NY 14301
Phone: (716) 278-4000
Sales: $53,000,000   *Employees:* 1,146
Company Type: Private   *Employees here:* 1,121
SIC: 8062
   Hospital
Christophe Brown, Chairman of the Board

D-U-N-S 07-816-4696
NICHOLAS DEMISAY
25 Fanning St, Staten Island, NY 10314
Phone: (718) 761-2100
Sales: $43,016,000   *Employees:* 650
Company Type: Private   *Employees here:* 650
SIC: 8051
   Skilled nursing home
Nicholas Demisay, Owner

D-U-N-S 19-758-1853
NICHOLS INST REFERENCE LABS
   (*Parent:* Quest Diagnostics A Cal Corp)
33608 Ortega Hwy, San Juan Capistrano, CA 92675
Phone: (949) 661-8000

Sales: $43,000,000   *Employees:* 900
Company Type: Private   *Employees here:* 525
SIC: 8071
   Medical diagnostic testing laboratory
Douglas Harrington, President

D-U-N-S 04-310-5071
NLVH, INC
   (*Parent:* Tenet Healthcare Corporation)
1409 E Lake Mead Blvd, North Las Vegas, NV 89030
Phone: (702) 649-7711
Sales: $75,000,000   *Employees:* 625
Company Type: Public Family Member   *Employees here:* 625
SIC: 8062
   General hospital
Ernest Libman, Chief Executive Officer

D-U-N-S 78-808-2634
NME PROPERTIES CORP.
   (*Parent:* Tenet Healthcare Corporation)
3820 State St, Santa Barbara, CA 93105
Phone: (805) 563-7000
Sales: $307,000,000   *Employees:* 7,676
Company Type: Public Family Member   *Employees here:* 1
SIC: 8099
   Medical services
Micheal Folk, Owner

D-U-N-S 18-004-5486
NOLACHUCKEY-HLST MNTL CTR INC
401 Holston Dr, Greeneville, TN 37743
Phone: (423) 639-1104
Sales: $33,500,000   *Employees:* 1,100
Company Type: Private   *Employees here:* 60
SIC: 8093
   Outpatient mental health clinic
Tom Parker, Executive Director

D-U-N-S 07-211-0869
NOLAND LLOYD HOSPITAL INC
   (*Parent:* Tenet Health System Hospitals)
701 Lloyd Noland Pkwy, Fairfield, AL 35064
Phone: (205) 783-5121
Sales: $22,332,000   *Employees:* 800
Company Type: Public Family Member   *Employees here:* 750
SIC: 8062
   General hospital and clinic
Gary Glause, Administrator

D-U-N-S 01-119-5109
NORDX
100 US Route 1 Unit 118, Scarborough, ME 4074
Phone: (207) 885-7800
Sales: $30,000,000   *Employees:* 350
Company Type: Private   *Employees here:* 350
SIC: 8071
   Medical laboratory
Stan Schosield, President

D-U-N-S 07-427-8896
NORMAN REGIONAL HOSPITAL AUTH
901 N Porter Ave, Norman, OK 73071
Phone: (405) 321-1700
Sales: $113,302,000   *Employees:* 1,370
Company Type: Private   *Employees here:* 1,181
SIC: 8062
   Hospital and medical outpatient clinics
Max Lauderdale, President

D-U-N-S 07-719-8232
NORTH ADAMS REGIONAL HOSPITAL
Hospital Ave, North Adams, MA 1247
Phone: (413) 663-3701

Sales: $35,704,000   *Employees:* 560
Company Type: Private   *Employees here:* 510
SIC: 8062
   General medical and surgical hospital
John Cronin, President

D-U-N-S 14-473-5198
NORTH ARKANSAS MEDICAL CENTER
620 N Willow St, Harrison, AR 72601
Phone: (870) 365-2000
Sales: $39,473,000   *Employees:* 713
Company Type: Private   *Employees here:* 634
SIC: 8062
   General hospital
Tim Hill, Administrator

D-U-N-S 06-137-7644
NORTH ARUNDEL HOSPITAL ASSN
301 Hospital Dr, Glen Burnie, MD 21061
Phone: (410) 787-4000
Sales: $115,435,000   *Employees:* 2,079
Company Type: Private   *Employees here:* 2,079
SIC: 8062
   General hospital
James R Walker, President

D-U-N-S 07-324-1028
NORTH BREVARD COUNTY HOSPITAL DST
951 N Washington Ave, Titusville, FL 32796
Phone: (407) 268-6111
Sales: $58,899,000   *Employees:* 980
Company Type: Private   *Employees here:* 910
SIC: 8062
   General hospital
Rod Baker, Administrator

D-U-N-S 07-224-6655
NORTH BROWARD HOSPITAL DST
201 E Sample Rd, Pompano Beach, FL 33064
Phone: (954) 941-8300
Sales: $43,200,000   *Employees:* NA
Company Type: Private   *Employees here:* 983
SIC: 8062
   General hospital ret gifts/novelties
James Chromik, Vice-President

D-U-N-S 15-465-4123
NORTH BROWARD HOSPITAL DST
3000 Coral Hills Dr, Pompano Beach, FL 33065
Phone: (954) 344-3000
Sales: $32,800,000   *Employees:* NA
Company Type: Private   *Employees here:* 750
SIC: 8062
   General hospital
Gary Muller, Administrator

D-U-N-S 07-225-2703
NORTH BROWARD HOSPITAL DST
303 SE 17th St, Fort Lauderdale, FL 33316
Phone: (954) 355-4400
Sales: $463,013,000   *Employees:* 5,400
Company Type: Private   *Employees here:* 400
SIC: 8062
   General hospital
Wil Trower, President

D-U-N-S 60-406-3917
NORTH BROWARD HOSPITAL DST
6401 N Federal Hwy, Fort Lauderdale, FL 33308
Phone: (954) 776-8501

Sales: $26,100,000   *Employees:* NA
Company Type: Private   *Employees here:* 600
SIC: 8062
   General hospital
Dorthy Mancini, Manager

D-U-N-S 60-440-7825
NORTH BROWARD HOSPITAL DST
1600 S Andrews Ave, Fort Lauderdale, FL 33316
Phone: (954) 355-5595
Sales: $39,600,000   *Employees:* NA
Company Type: Private   *Employees here:* 647
SIC: 8011
   Medical center
J R Stull Ii, President

D-U-N-S 86-834-6230
NORTH BROWARD HOSPITAL DST
4902 Eisenhower Blvd, Fort Lauderdale, FL 33308
Phone: (954) 776-8669
Sales: $41,700,000   *Employees:* NA
Company Type: Private   *Employees here:* 950
SIC: 8062
   General hospital
J R Stull Ii, President

D-U-N-S 00-352-3636
NORTH CAROLINA BAPTIST HOSP
Medical Center Blvd, Winston Salem, NC 27157
Phone: (336) 716-2011
Sales: $423,073,000   *Employees:* 5,475
Company Type: Private   *Employees here:* 5,435
SIC: 8062
   General hospital
Len B Preslar Jr, President

D-U-N-S 07-450-3525
NORTH CAROLINA DEPT OF HEALTH
1000 S Sterling St, Morganton, NC 28655
Phone: (828) 433-2111
Sales: $45,100,000   *Employees:* NA
Company Type: Private   *Employees here:* 1,380
SIC: 8063
   State mental institution
Seth Hunt, Director

D-U-N-S 84-823-0660
NORTH CAROLINA DEPT OF HEALTH
2535 Court Dr, Gastonia, NC 28054
Phone: (704) 867-4411
Sales: $29,200,000   *Employees:* NA
Company Type: Private   *Employees here:* 1,000
SIC: 8093
   Speciality outpatient clinic
Tom Waite, President

D-U-N-S 14-707-3738
NORTH CENTRAL HEALTH SERVICES
2400 South St, Lafayette, IN 47904
Phone: (765) 447-6811
Sales: $113,070,000   *Employees:* 1,700
Company Type: Private   *Employees here:* 1,700
SIC: 8062
   Hospital nursing homes and fund raising services
John R Walling, President

D-U-N-S 03-018-1754
NORTH CNTL HEALTH CARE FCILITIES
1100 Lake View Dr, Wausau, WI 54403
Phone: (715) 848-4600

Sales: $42,226,000   *Employees:* 900
Company Type: Private   *Employees here:* 362
SIC: 8051
  Nursing care facility & hospital
Tim Steller, Chief Executive Officer

D-U-N-S 07-746-7330
NORTH CNTRY HEALTH CARE ASSOC I
179 Lisbon St, Lewiston, ME 4240
Phone: (207) 786-3554
Sales: $30,000,000   *Employees:* 1,200
Company Type: Private   *Employees here:* 25
SIC: 8051
  Skilled and intermediate care facility
John F Lunt, Partner

D-U-N-S 07-341-0839
NORTH COLORADO MEDICAL CENTER,
1801 16th St, Greeley, CO 80631
Phone: (970) 352-4121
Sales: $131,476,000   *Employees:* 1,500
Company Type: Private   *Employees here:* 1,470
SIC: 8062
  Hospital
Karl Gills, President

D-U-N-S 07-648-8873
NORTH COUNTRY HEALTH SERVICES
1100 38th St Nw, Bemidji, MN 56601
Phone: (218) 751-5430
Sales: $46,212,000   *Employees:* 800
Company Type: Private   *Employees here:* 650
SIC: 8062
  Hospital
John Skjerven, President

D-U-N-S 06-991-2731
NORTH COUNTRY HOSPITAL HEALTH CTR
Prouty Dr, Newport, VT 5855
Phone: (802) 334-7331
Sales: $23,155,000   *Employees:* 350
Company Type: Private   *Employees here:* 350
SIC: 8062
  General medical & surgical hospital
Sidney A Toll, President

D-U-N-S 13-023-9924
NORTH CAROLINA DEPT HUMAN RESOURCES
820 S Boylan Ave, Raleigh, NC 27603
Phone: (919) 733-5540
Sales: $45,900,000   *Employees:* NA
Company Type: Private   *Employees here:* 1,300
SIC: 8063
  Psychiatric hospital
Michael Pedneau, Director

D-U-N-S 07-202-4631
NORTH CAROLINA DEPT HUMAN RESOURCES
2415 W Vernon Ave, Kinston, NC 28504
Phone: (252) 559-5100
Sales: $36,300,000   *Employees:* NA
Company Type: Private   *Employees here:* 1,794
SIC: 8051
  Skilled nursing care facility
Jimmie S Woodall, Director

D-U-N-S 07-202-3211
NORTH CAROLINA DEPT HUMAN RESOURCES
400 Old Smithfield Rd, Goldsboro, NC 27530
Phone: (919) 731-3545

Sales: $21,500,000   *Employees:* NA
Company Type: Private   *Employees here:* 1,066
SIC: 8051
  Mental retardation center
Jerry H Lyall, Branch Manager

D-U-N-S 09-981-6084
NORTH CAROLINA DEPT HUMAN RESOURCES
201 Stevens Mill Rd, Goldsboro, NC 27530
Phone: (919) 731-3200
Sales: $39,300,000   *Employees:* NA
Company Type: Private   *Employees here:* 1,200
SIC: 8063
  Psychiatric hospital
Dr Jerry Edwards, Principal

D-U-N-S 04-004-1691
NORTH CAROLINA DEPT HUMAN RESOURCES
1003 12th St, Butner, NC 27509
Phone: (919) 575-7211
Sales: $49,000,000   *Employees:* NA
Company Type: Private   *Employees here:* 1,500
SIC: 8063
  Psychiatric hospital job training/related services
Patsey Cristian, Principal

D-U-N-S 19-361-3346
NORTH CAROLINA DEPT HUMAN RESOURCES
C St, Butner, NC 27509
Phone: (919) 575-7734
Sales: $34,600,000   *Employees:* NA
Company Type: Private   *Employees here:* 1,600
SIC: 8361
  Residential care services
J M Hennike, Branch Manager

D-U-N-S 17-061-6536
NORTH DAKOTA DEPT HUMANSVCS
1624 23rd St SE, Jamestown, ND 58402
Phone: (701) 253-3650
Sales: $28,900,000   *Employees:* NA
Company Type: Private   *Employees here:* 758
SIC: 8062
  State hospital
Alex Schweitzer, Administration

D-U-N-S 92-857-7410
NORTH FLORIDA REGIONAL MED CTR
  (Parent: H C A Health Services Of Fla)
6500 W Newberry Rd, Gainesville, FL 32605
Phone: (352) 333-4000
Sales: $133,307,000   *Employees:* 1,800
Company Type: Public Family Member   *Employees here:* 1,650
SIC: 8062
  General hospital
Brian Robinson, President

D-U-N-S 13-231-0160
NORTH FULTON MEDICAL CENTER
  (Parent: Tenet Healthcare Corporation)
3000 Hospital Blvd, Roswell, GA 30076
Phone: (770) 751-2500
Sales: $39,000,000   *Employees:* 850
Company Type: Public Family Member   *Employees here:* 820
SIC: 8062
  General hospital
John Holland, Chief Executive Officer

D-U-N-S 17-329-5510
NORTH GENERAL HOME
  (Parent: North General Hospital)
205 E 122nd St, New York, NY 10035
Phone: (212) 427-3330

Sales: $39,100,000   *Employees:* 1,600
Company Type: Private   *Employees here:* 1,600
SIC: 8361
   Home care center for the handicapped & elderly
Eugene Mc Cabe, Chairman of the Board

D-U-N-S 09-834-3841
NORTH GENERAL HOSPITAL
1879 Madison Ave, New York, NY 10035
Phone: (212) 423-4000
Sales: $108,534,000   *Employees:* 2,565
Company Type: Private   *Employees here:* 925
SIC: 8062
   Non-profit general medical & surgical hospital
Eugene Mc Cabe, President

D-U-N-S 80-815-6913
NORTH IOWA MERCY HEALTH CENTER
1000 4th St SW, Mason City, IA 50401
Phone: (515) 424-7774
Sales: $130,822,000   *Employees:* 2,500
Company Type: Private   *Employees here:* 2,100
SIC: 8062
   General hospital & clinics
David H Vellinga, President

D-U-N-S 07-136-3634
NORTH MEMORIAL HEALTH CARE
3300 Oakdale Ave N, Minneapolis, MN 55422
Phone: (612) 520-5200
Sales: $248,197,000   *Employees:* 3,602
Company Type: Private   *Employees here:* 3,300
SIC: 8062
   General hospital
Scott R Anderson, President

D-U-N-S 07-350-6487
NORTH MISSISSIPPI MEDICAL CTR
830 S Gloster St, Tupelo, MS 38801
Phone: (601) 841-3000
Sales: $266,413,000   *Employees:* 4,148
Company Type: Private   *Employees here:* 3,655
SIC: 8062
   Hospital & skilled care nursing home
Dr Jeff Barber, President

D-U-N-S 02-090-2235
NORTH OTTAWA COMMUNITY HOSPITAL AUTH
1309 Sheldon Rd, Grand Haven, MI 49417
Phone: (616) 842-3600
Sales: $33,875,000   *Employees:* 510
Company Type: Private   *Employees here:* 484
SIC: 8062
   General hospital
Jevne Conover, President

D-U-N-S 07-058-3794
NORTH PENN HOSPITAL
100 Medical Campus Dr, Lansdale, PA 19446
Phone: (215) 368-2100
Sales: $42,799,000   *Employees:* 730
Company Type: Private   *Employees here:* 730
SIC: 8062
   General hospital
Robert Mc Kay, President

D-U-N-S 61-799-3944
NORTH PHILADELPHIA HEALTH SYS
16th & Girard Ave, Philadelphia, PA 19130
Phone: (215) 787-9000

Sales: $28,700,000   *Employees:* NA
Company Type: Private   *Employees here:* 588
SIC: 8062
   Hospital
James Gloner, Manager

D-U-N-S 62-659-7249
NORTH PHILADELPHIA HEALTH SYS
NE Cor 8th & Girard Ave, Philadelphia, PA 19122
Phone: (215) 787-2000
Sales: $76,760,000   *Employees:* 1,300
Company Type: Private   *Employees here:* 800
SIC: 8062
   General hospital
George Walsmley, President

D-U-N-S 02-017-3340
NORTH PLATTE NEB HOSPITAL CORP
601 W Leota St, North Platte, NE 69101
Phone: (308) 534-9310
Sales: $46,929,000   *Employees:* 525
Company Type: Private   *Employees here:* 522
SIC: 8062
   Hospital and home health care services
Lucinda A Bradley, President

D-U-N-S 01-033-1726
NORTH RIDGE CARE CENTER INC
5430 Boone Ave N, Minneapolis, MN 55428
Phone: (612) 536-7000
Sales: $24,675,000   *Employees:* 1,000
Company Type: Private   *Employees here:* 1,000
SIC: 8051
   Skilled nursing facility & apartments for elderly
Charles T Thompson, President

D-U-N-S 95-766-1846
NORTH SHORE HEALTH SYSTEM
972 Brush Hollow Rd, Westbury, NY 11590
Phone: (516) 876-0368
Sales: $34,300,000   *Employees:* NA
Company Type: Private   *Employees here:* 700
SIC: 8062
   Hospital and home health services
Robert Kaufman, Chairman of the Board

D-U-N-S 80-792-0368
NORTH SHORE HEALTH SYSTEM
150 Community Dr, Great Neck, NY 11021
Phone: (516) 465-8000
Sales: $329,700,000   *Employees:* 7,000
Company Type: Private   *Employees here:* 100
SIC: 8062
   Hospital and home health services
Robert Kaufman, President

D-U-N-S 62-065-5746
NORTH SHORE MEDICAL CENTER
   (Parent: Partners Healthcare Systems)
81 Highland Ave, Salem, MA 1970
Phone: (978) 741-1200
Sales: $197,515,000   *Employees:* 3,500
Company Type: Private   *Employees here:* 3,500
SIC: 8062
   Hospital
Alex Movahed, Chief Executive Officer

D-U-N-S 07-744-4198
NORTH SHORE UNIV HOSPITAL
10201 66th Rd, Forest Hills, NY 11375
Phone: (718) 830-4000

Sales: $76,383,000   *Employees:* 880
Company Type: Private   *Employees here:* 835
SIC: 8062
  General hospital
Andrew Mitchell, Vice-President

D-U-N-S 01-475-3904
NORTH SHORE UNIVERSITY HOSP
221 Jericho Tpke, Syosset, NY 11791
Phone: (516) 496-6500
Sales: $24,300,000   *Employees:* NA
Company Type: Private   *Employees here:* 500
SIC: 8062
  General hospital
John S Gallagher, President

D-U-N-S 07-236-4490
NORTH SHORE UNIVERSITY HOSP
300 Community Dr, Manhasset, NY 11030
Phone: (516) 876-6000
Sales: $425,000,000   *Employees:* 12,228
Company Type: Private   *Employees here:* 3,500
SIC: 8062
  General hospitals and specialty clinics
John S Gallagher, Co-President

D-U-N-S 96-664-6648
NORTH SHORE UNIVERSITY HOSP
10201 66th Rd, Forest Hills, NY 11375
Phone: (718) 830-4000
Sales: $39,400,000   *Employees:* NA
Company Type: Private   *Employees here:* 800
SIC: 8062
  General medical hospital

D-U-N-S 19-743-6728
NORTH SIDE HOSPITAL, INC
  (Parent: Columbia/Hca Healthcare Corp)
401 Princeton Rd, Johnson City, TN 37601
Phone: (423) 282-4111
Sales: $83,213,000   *Employees:* 350
Company Type: Public Family Member   *Employees here:* 350
SIC: 8062
  General hospital
Shaum Peroit, Chief Financial Officer

D-U-N-S 01-029-1573
NORTH SUBURBAN CLINIC LTD
  (Parent: Caremark Inc)
9977 Woods Dr, Skokie, IL 60077
Phone: (847) 674-9800
Sales: $48,100,000   *Employees:* 700
Company Type: Public Family Member   *Employees here:* 200
SIC: 8011
  Medical doctor's office
Dr Robert Rosenbloom, President

D-U-N-S 04-866-7752
NORTH SUFFOLK MENTAL HEALTH ASSN
287 Broadway 301, Chelsea, MA 2150
Phone: (617) 889-4860
Sales: $22,436,000   *Employees:* 900
Company Type: Private   *Employees here:* 80
SIC: 8093
  Substance abuse & outpatient mental health clinic
Bruce Bird, Chief Executive Officer

D-U-N-S 07-744-1517
NORTH TRIDENT REGIONAL MED CTR
  (Parent: Columbia/Hca Healthcare Corp)
9330 Medical Plaza Dr, Charleston, SC 29406
Phone: (843) 797-7000

Sales: $93,400,000   *Employees:* 2,000
Company Type: Public Family Member   *Employees here:* 1,992
SIC: 8062
  General medical & surgical hospital
Michael Layce, Chief Executive Officer

D-U-N-S 07-654-6829
NORTHBAY HEALTHCARE GROUP
1200 B Gale Wilson Blvd, Fairfield, CA 94533
Phone: (707) 429-3600
Sales: $88,731,000   *Employees:* 980
Company Type: Private   *Employees here:* 760
SIC: 8062
  General hospitals
Debra Suaiyama, President

D-U-N-S 08-351-7607
NORTHCREST MEDICAL CENTER
100 Northcrest Dr, Springfield, TN 37172
Phone: (615) 384-2411
Sales: $34,352,000   *Employees:* 410
Company Type: Private   *Employees here:* 410
SIC: 8062
  General hospital
Wiliam Kenley, Administrator

D-U-N-S 62-088-3603
NORTHEAST GEORGIA MEDICAL CTR
743 Spring St NE, Gainesville, GA 30501
Phone: (770) 535-3553
Sales: $140,943,000   *Employees:* 2,000
Company Type: Private   *Employees here:* 2,000
SIC: 8062
  Hospital
John A Ferguson Jr, President

D-U-N-S 10-818-4615
NORTHEAST HEALTH
4 White St, Rockland, ME 4841
Phone: (207) 596-8000
Sales: $58,946,000   *Employees:* 1,200
Company Type: Private   *Employees here:* 30
SIC: 8062
  General medical hospital and home health agency
Frank Mudle, Chairman of the Board

D-U-N-S 08-348-1168
NORTHEAST HOSPITAL AUTHORITY
18951 N Memorial Dr, Humble, TX 77338
Phone: (281) 540-7700
Sales: $82,921,000   *Employees:* 862
Company Type: Private   *Employees here:* 850
SIC: 8062
  Hospital
Syble Missildine, Administrator

D-U-N-S 83-827-9321
NORTHEAST HOSPITAL CORPORATION
298 Washington St, Gloucester, MA 1930
Phone: (978) 283-4000
Sales: $24,800,000   *Employees:* NA
Company Type: Private   *Employees here:* 500
SIC: 8062
  General hospital
Robert R Fanning Jr, Principal

D-U-N-S 07-380-9121
NORTHEAST HOSPITAL CORPORATION
85 Herrick St, Beverly, MA 1915
Phone: (978) 922-3000

Sales: $134,567,000   *Employees:* 2,800
Company Type: Private   *Employees here:* 1,900
SIC: 8062
    General hospital
Robert R Fanning Jr, President

D-U-N-S 79-986-2065
NORTHEAST MEDICAL CENTER, INC
9605 Holly Point Dr, Huntersville, NC 28078
Phone: (704) 895-0062
Sales: $86,800,000   *Employees:* NA
Company Type: Private   *Employees here:* 1,500
SIC: 8011
    Medical doctor's office
Angie Phillips, Principal

D-U-N-S 07-105-9489
NORTHEAST MEDICAL CENTER, INC
920 Church St N, Concord, NC 28025
Phone: (704) 783-3000
Sales: $178,432,000   *Employees:* 2,053
Company Type: Private   *Employees here:* 1,575
SIC: 8062
    General hospital
Larry Lawrence, President

D-U-N-S 07-412-0866
NORTHEAST VALLEY HEALTH CORP
1172 N Maclay Ave, San Fernando, CA 91340
Phone: (818) 898-1388
Sales: $21,207,000   *Employees:* 450
Company Type: Private   *Employees here:* 50
SIC: 8011
    Medical doctors' office
Kimberly Wyard, Executive Director

D-U-N-S 15-213-9887
NORTHEASTERN PA HEALTH CORP
700 E Broad St, Hazleton, PA 18201
Phone: (717) 450-4357
Sales: $36,499,000   *Employees:* 600
Company Type: Private   *Employees here:* 600
SIC: 8062
    General hospital
E R Moore, President

D-U-N-S 07-647-8510
NORTHEASTERN REGIONAL HOSPITAL
1235 8th St, Las Vegas, NM 87701
Phone: (505) 425-6751
Sales: $23,401,000   *Employees:* 270
Company Type: Private   *Employees here:* 243
SIC: 8062
    General hospital
Donna Beane, Chief Executive Officer

D-U-N-S 04-024-2232
NORTHEASTERN VT REGIONAL HOSP
Hospital Dr, Saint Johnsbury, VT 5819
Phone: (802) 748-8141
Sales: $20,149,000   *Employees:* 300
Company Type: Private   *Employees here:* 275
SIC: 8062
    General medical & surgical hospital
Paul Bengtson, Chief Executive Officer

D-U-N-S 07-960-6331
NORTHERN
150 Pioneer Ln, Bishop, CA 93514
Phone: (760) 873-5811

Sales: $19,899,000   *Employees:* 300
Company Type: Private   *Employees here:* 300
SIC: 8062
    Hospital
Herman J Spencer, Administrator

D-U-N-S 08-999-4438
NORTHERN ARIZONA REGIONAL BE
125 E Elm Ave Ste E, Flagstaff, AZ 86001
Phone: (520) 774-7128
Sales: $26,011,000   *Employees:* 45
Company Type: Private   *Employees here:* 17
SIC: 8093
    Administration and case management for mental health
    services
Maurice Miller, Chief Executive Officer

D-U-N-S 07-737-1961
NORTHERN CAL PRESBT HOMES
1525 Post St, San Francisco, CA 94109
Phone: (415) 922-0200
Sales: $42,849,000   *Employees:* 600
Company Type: Private   *Employees here:* 18
SIC: 8051
    Senior citizen facilities
James Aspegren, President

D-U-N-S 02-066-1757
NORTHERN DUTCHESS HOSPITAL
10 Spring Brook Ave, Rhinebeck, NY 12572
Phone: (914) 876-3001
Sales: $20,458,000   *Employees:* 400
Company Type: Private   *Employees here:* 400
SIC: 8062
    General hospital
Michael C Mazzarella, Chief Executive Officer

D-U-N-S 07-782-9216
NORTHERN HOSPITAL DST SURRY CNTY
830 Rockford St, Mount Airy, NC 27030
Phone: (336) 719-7000
Sales: $39,252,000   *Employees:* 610
Company Type: Private   *Employees here:* 470
SIC: 8062
    General hospital & home health care service
William James, Chief Executive Officer

D-U-N-S 11-386-1090
NORTHERN ILL PHYSCN GROUP PC
102 S Hennepin Ave, Dixon, IL 61021
Phone: (815) 288-7711
Sales: $22,000,000   *Employees:* 150
Company Type: Private   *Employees here:* 50
SIC: 8011
    Medical & surgical clinic
Dr David Peterson, President

D-U-N-S 07-456-1432
NORTHERN ILLINOIS MEDICAL CTR
4201 W Medical Center Dr, Mchenry, IL 60050
Phone: (815) 344-5000
Sales: $85,197,000   *Employees:* 1,000
Company Type: Private   *Employees here:* 925
SIC: 8062
    Hospital
Paul E Laudick, President

D-U-N-S 07-930-1511
NORTHERN MICHIGAN HOSPITAL
416 Connable Ave, Petoskey, MI 49770
Phone: (616) 348-4000

Sales: $82,497,000   *Employees:* 1,000
Company Type: Private   *Employees here:* 950
SIC: 8062
  General hospital
Jeffery Wendling, President

D-U-N-S 07-868-8421
NORTHERN MONTANA HOSPITAL
30 13th St, Havre, MT 59501
Phone: (406) 265-2211
Sales: $27,383,000   *Employees:* 385
Company Type: Private   *Employees here:* 140
SIC: 8062
  General hospital
David Henry, Principal

D-U-N-S 05-096-2653
NORTHERN ORE HEALTHCARE CORP
  (Parent: Columbia/Hca Healthcare Corp)
2700 SE Three Mile Ln, Mcminnville, OR 97128
Phone: (503) 472-6131
Sales: $60,000,000   *Employees:* 300
Company Type: Public Family Member   *Employees here:* 300
SIC: 8062
  General hospital
Rosemari Davis, Administrator

D-U-N-S 07-871-6123
NORTHERN WSTCHESTER HOSPITAL ASSN
400 E Main St, Mount Kisco, NY 10549
Phone: (914) 666-1200
Sales: $84,172,000   *Employees:* 1,100
Company Type: Private   *Employees here:* 1,100
SIC: 8062
  General medical and surgical hospital
Donald Davis, President

D-U-N-S 60-917-3257
NORTHMED HMO INC
109 E Front St Ste 204, Traverse City, MI 49684
Phone: (616) 935-0500
Sales: $24,596,000   *Employees:* 23
Company Type: Private   *Employees here:* 23
SIC: 8011
  Health maintenance organization
Dr Gene Tang Md, Chairman

D-U-N-S 04-972-7332
NORTHPORT HEALTH SERVICE INC
931 Fairfax Park, Tuscaloosa, AL 35406
Phone: (205) 391-3600
Sales: $52,700,000   *Employees:* 2,300
Company Type: Private   *Employees here:* 50
SIC: 8051
  Skilled nursing facilities
J N Estes, President

D-U-N-S 06-668-4887
NORTHRIDGE HOSPITAL MEDICAL
14500 Sherman Cir, Van Nuys, CA 91405
Phone: (818) 997-0101
Sales: $29,600,000   *Employees:* 650
Company Type: Private   *Employees here:* 600
SIC: 8062
  General hospital
Roger Ceaver, President

D-U-N-S 07-191-0038
NORTHRIDGE MED CENTER - ROSCOE
18300 Roscoe Blvd, Northridge, CA 91325
Phone: (818) 885-8500

Sales: $153,048,000   *Employees:* 1,600
Company Type: Private   *Employees here:* 1,550
SIC: 8062
  General hospital
Roger Seaver, Chief Executive Officer

D-U-N-S 08-969-7395
NORTHSIDE HOSPITAL INC
1000 Johnson Ferry Rd NE, Atlanta, GA 30342
Phone: (404) 851-8000
Sales: $254,687,000   *Employees:* 2,800
Company Type: Private   *Employees here:* 2,280
SIC: 8062
  General hospital and acute care facility
Sidney Kirschner, President

D-U-N-S 06-918-9801
NORTHSIDE HOSPITAL-CHEROKEE,
201 Hospital Rd, Canton, GA 30114
Phone: (770) 479-1941
Sales: $24,371,000   *Employees:* 350
Company Type: Private   *Employees here:* 335
SIC: 8062
  General hospital
Douglas M Parker, Chief Executive Officer

D-U-N-S 18-184-1362
NORTHSTAR HEALTH SERVICES INC
Po Box 1289, Indiana, PA 15701
Phone: (724) 349-7500
Sales: $32,606,000   *Employees:* 802
Company Type: Public   *Employees here:* 2
SIC: 8049
  Physical speech and occupational therapy & cardiac and
    nuclear medical services
Thomas W Zaucha, President

D-U-N-S 07-162-2146
NORTHSTERN HOSPITAL OF PHILADELPHIA
2301 E Allegheny Ave, Philadelphia, PA 19134
Phone: (215) 291-3000
Sales: $48,102,000   *Employees:* 650
Company Type: Private   *Employees here:* 650
SIC: 8062
  General hospital
Lynette Holder, Executive Director

D-U-N-S 04-232-9615
NORTHWEST COMMUNITY HOSPITAL
800 W Central Rd, Arlington Heights, IL 60005
Phone: (847) 618-1000
Sales: $183,263,000   *Employees:* 2,800
Company Type: Private   *Employees here:* 2,350
SIC: 8062
  General hospital
Bruce K Crowther, President

D-U-N-S 07-567-0463
NORTHWEST HEALTH SYSTEM INC
609 S Maple Dr, Springdale, AR 72764
Phone: (501) 751-5711
Sales: $91,606,000   *Employees:* 1,400
Company Type: Private   *Employees here:* 1,080
SIC: 8062
  General hospital
Greg Stock, Chief Executive Officer

D-U-N-S 10-657-8826
NORTHWEST HEALTHCARE CORP
325 Claremont St, Kalispell, MT 59901
Phone: (406) 756-4712

Sales: $72,425,000 — Employees: 223
Company Type: Private — Employees here: 7
SIC: 8062
Hospital nursing home health maintenance organization physician's office air ambulance service & medical equipment rental
Paul Tutvedt, Chairman of the Board

D-U-N-S 06-936-9791
NORTHWEST HOSPITAL CENTER,
5401 Old Court Rd, Randallstown, MD 21133
Phone: (410) 521-2200
Sales: $86,401,000 — Employees: 981
Company Type: Private — Employees here: 981
SIC: 8062
Hospital
Bob Fischer, President

D-U-N-S 04-302-1880
NORTHWEST KIDNEY CENTERS (INC)
700 Broadway, Seattle, WA 98122
Phone: (206) 292-2771
Sales: $40,000,000 — Employees: 330
Company Type: Private — Employees here: 240
SIC: 8092
Kidney center
Dr Christophe Blagg Md, Executive Director

D-U-N-S 79-656-7402
NORTHWEST MEDICAL CENTER
1 Spruce St, Franklin, PA 16323
Phone: (814) 437-7000
Sales: $64,198,000 — Employees: 1,200
Company Type: Private — Employees here: 800
SIC: 8062
Hospital
Henry W Gent Iii, Chairman of the Board

D-U-N-S 96-257-8266
NORTHWEST MEDICAL CENTER, INC
(Parent: Columbia/Hca Healthcare Corp)
2801 N State Road 7, Pompano Beach, FL 33063
Phone: (954) 974-0400
Sales: $29,000,000 — Employees: 485
Company Type: Public Family Member — Employees here: 485
SIC: 8062
Hospital
Gina Melby, Chief Executive Officer

D-U-N-S 15-647-5279
NORTHWEST MEDICAL TEAMS INTL
6955 SW Sandburg St, Portland, OR 97223
Phone: (503) 624-1000
Sales: $50,072,000 — Employees: 34
Company Type: Private — Employees here: 34
SIC: 8099
Medical services organization
Bas Vanderzalm, President

D-U-N-S 94-935-0441
NORTHWEST TEXAS HEALTHCARE
1501 Coulter Dr, Amarillo, TX 79106
Phone: (806) 354-1000
Sales: $76,900,000 — Employees: 2,624
Company Type: Private — Employees here: 1,520
SIC: 8062
General hospital
Michael Callahan, Chief Executive Officer

D-U-N-S 05-719-1876
NORTHWESTERN HUMAN SERVICES,
620 Germantown Pike, Lafayette Hill, PA 19444
Phone: (610) 260-4600

Sales: $176,756,000 — Employees: 4,000
Company Type: Private — Employees here: 35
SIC: 8093
Mental health center & drug & alcohol rehabilitation counseling services
Robert C Panaccio, President

D-U-N-S 06-052-5748
NORTHWESTERN MEDICAL CENTER
Fairfield St, Saint Albans, VT 5478
Phone: (802) 524-5911
Sales: $24,833,000 — Employees: 388
Company Type: Private — Employees here: 352
SIC: 8062
General hospital
Peter Hofstetter, Chief Executive Officer

D-U-N-S 05-945-7150
NORTHWESTERN MEMORIAL HOSP
250 E Superior St, Chicago, IL 60611
Phone: (312) 908-2000
Sales: $467,960,000 — Employees: 4,000
Company Type: Private — Employees here: 4,000
SIC: 8062
General hospital
Gary A Mecklenburg, President

D-U-N-S 07-152-7659
NORTON COMMUNITY HOSPITAL INC
100 15th St Nw, Norton, VA 24273
Phone: (540) 679-9600
Sales: $23,218,000 — Employees: 343
Company Type: Private — Employees here: 302
SIC: 8062
General hospital
Buford G Sturgill, Chairman of the Board

D-U-N-S 06-745-8018
NORWEGIAN AMERICAN HOSPITAL
1044 N Francisco Ave, Chicago, IL 60622
Phone: (773) 292-8200
Sales: $59,549,000 — Employees: 822
Company Type: Private — Employees here: 814
SIC: 8062
General medical and surgical hospital
Clarence Nagelvoort, President

D-U-N-S 07-547-4650
NORWOOD CLINIC INC PC
1528 Carraway Blvd, Birmingham, AL 35234
Phone: (205) 250-6000
Sales: $62,219,000 — Employees: 535
Company Type: Private — Employees here: 500
SIC: 8093
Outpatient clinic and medical association
Hank Hudson, President

D-U-N-S 07-735-6624
NOTAMI HOSPITALS OF CALIFORNIA
(Parent: Columbia/Hca Healthcare Corp)
1 Park Mdws, Nashville, TN 37215
Phone: (615) 344-9551
Sales: $31,000,000 — Employees: 680
Company Type: Public Family Member — Employees here: 1
SIC: 8062
Hospital
Richard Scott, President

D-U-N-S 96-934-9281
NOTAMI HOSPITALS OF OKLAHOMA
744 W 9th St, Tulsa, OK 74127
Phone: (918) 587-2561

Sales: $69,100,000   *Employees:* NA
Company Type: Public Family Member   *Employees here:* 1,800
SIC: 8062
   Hospital
Wayne Mc Allister, Principal

D-U-N-S 85-994-2393
NOTAMI HOSPITALS OF OKLAHOMA
   (Parent: Columbia/Hca Healthcare Corp)
1 Park Mdws, Nashville, TN 37215
Phone: (615) 327-9551
Sales: $189,700,000   *Employees:* 2,750
Company Type: Public Family Member   *Employees here:* 1
SIC: 8011
   Hospitals
Richard Scott, President

D-U-N-S 84-509-1958
NOTAMI HOSPITALS LOUISIANA INC
801 Poinciana Ave, Mamou, LA 70554
Phone: (318) 468-5261
Sales: $25,700,000   *Employees:* NA
Company Type: Public Family Member   *Employees here:* 680
SIC: 8062
   General medical/surgical hospital
J E Richardson, Chief Executive Officer

D-U-N-S 94-900-3693
NOTAMI HOSPITALS LOUISIANA INC
95 E Fairway Dr, Covington, LA 70433
Phone: (504) 867-3800
Sales: $26,500,000   *Employees:* NA
Company Type: Public Family Member   *Employees here:* 650
SIC: 8062
   General hospital
James Rogers, Administrator

D-U-N-S 13-135-6545
NOVACARE INC
1016 W 9th Ave Ste 1, King Of Prussia, PA 19406
Phone: (610) 992-7200
Sales: $1,066,451,000   *Employees:* 39,800
Company Type: Public   *Employees here:* 235
SIC: 8049
   Provides rehabilitative services and mfr orthotic & prosthetic
   devices
Timothy E Foster, Chief Executive Officer

D-U-N-S 19-735-0614
NOVACARE ORTHOTICS PROSTHETICS
   (Parent: Novacare Inc)
1016 W 9th Ave, King Of Prussia, PA 19406
Phone: (610) 992-8990
Sales: $22,800,000   *Employees:* 750
Company Type: Public Family Member   *Employees here:* 16
SIC: 8093
   Orthotic & prosthetic rehabilitation services
John H Foster, Chairman of the Board

D-U-N-S 04-840-9353
NOVACARE, INC
   (Parent: Novacare Inc)
1016 W 9th Ave Ste 1, King Of Prussia, PA 19406
Phone: (610) 992-7200
Sales: $1,066,451,000   *Employees:* 17,000
Company Type: Public Family Member   *Employees here:* 650
SIC: 8049
   Speech physical & occupational therapy
James W Mc Lane, President

D-U-N-S 11-758-4060
NOVAEON, INC
3 Station Sq Ste 105, Paoli, PA 19301

Phone: (610) 644-2700
Sales: $30,000,000   *Employees:* 450
Company Type: Private   *Employees here:* 35
SIC: 8093
   Specialty outpatient clinic
Patrick J Sullivan, President

D-U-N-S 06-886-1756
NOVATO COMMUNITY HOSPITAL
1625 Hill Rd, Novato, CA 94947
Phone: (415) 897-3111
Sales: $25,818,000   *Employees:* 330
Company Type: Private   *Employees here:* 317
SIC: 8062
   General hospital
Anne Hosfeld, Administrator

D-U-N-S 05-511-8137
NUECES COUNTY HOSPITAL DST
2606 Hospital Blvd, Corpus Christi, TX 78405
Phone: (512) 902-4000
Sales: $119,252,000   *Employees:* 1,689
Company Type: Private   *Employees here:* 1,304
SIC: 8062
   Hospital
Robert Martel, Vp Finance

D-U-N-S 04-519-7803
NURSEFINDERS INC
   (Parent: Atlantic Medical Mgt Llc)
1200 E Copeland Rd, Arlington, TX 76011
Phone: (817) 460-1181
Sales: $133,508,000   *Employees:* 450
Company Type: Private   *Employees here:* 90
SIC: 8082
   Homehealth & temporary health services
Richard L Peranton, President

D-U-N-S 12-124-9734
NURSES UNLIMITED INC
700 N Grant Ave Ste 300, Odessa, TX 79761
Phone: (915) 550-2017
Sales: $24,800,000   *Employees:* 1,600
Company Type: Private   *Employees here:* 75
SIC: 8049
   Nursing care services
Patsy Gerron, President

D-U-N-S 07-270-5783
NYACK HOSPITAL INC
160 N Midland Ave, Nyack, NY 10960
Phone: (914) 348-2000
Sales: $124,228,000   *Employees:* 1,200
Company Type: Private   *Employees here:* 1,160
SIC: 8062
   General hospital
Gregor C Anderson, President

D-U-N-S 10-731-4056
NYLCARE HEALTH PLAN OF THE SOUTH
   (Parent: Nylcare Health Plans Inc)
4500 Fuller Dr, Irving, TX 75038
Phone: (972) 791-3900
Sales: $342,210,000   *Employees:* 325
Company Type: Private   *Employees here:* 325
SIC: 8011
   Health maintenance organization
Steve Yerxa, President

D-U-N-S 92-993-0634
NYLCARE HEALTH PLANS OF MAINE
   (Parent: Nylcare Health Plans Inc)
1 Monument Sq, Portland, ME 4101
Phone: (207) 879-1995

Sales: $60,000,000   *Employees:* 100
Company Type: Private   *Employees here:* 100
SIC: 8011
  Health maintenance organization
Daniel Fishbein, President

D-U-N-S 06-595-4752
NYLCARE HEALTH PLANS, INC
  (Parent: Nylife Inc)
1 Liberty Plz, New York, NY 10006
Phone: (212) 437-1000
Sales: $2,800,000,000   *Employees:* 4,000
Company Type: Private   *Employees here:* 600
SIC: 8011
  Health maintenance organization & health services
    consultant
Joseph T Lynaugh, President

D-U-N-S 08-695-0466
NYSARC INC
  (Parent: Nysarc Inc)
471 Albany Ave, Kingston, NY 12401
Phone: (914) 331-4300
Sales: $22,404,000   *Employees:* 660
Company Type: Private   *Employees here:* 100
SIC: 8361
  Rehabilitative services & home for retarded individuals
Peter Pierri, Executive Director

D-U-N-S 08-065-5319
NYSARC, INC
2900 Vets Memorial Hwy, Bohemia, NY 11716
Phone: (516) 585-0100
Sales: $35,193,000   *Employees:* 800
Company Type: Private   *Employees here:* 200
SIC: 8361
  Non-profit rehabilitation and training center
Joseph Mammolito, Executive Director

D-U-N-S 86-780-7414
NC-SCHI
  (Parent: Quorum Health Group Inc)
6250 Hwy 83 84 Antilley, Abilene, TX 79606
Phone: (915) 695-9900
Sales: $71,545,000   *Employees:* 800
Company Type: Public Family Member   *Employees here:* 770
SIC: 8062
  General hospital
Woody Gilliland, Chief Executive Officer

D-U-N-S 07-630-0169
O'CONNOR HOSPITAL
2105 Forest Ave, San Jose, CA 95128
Phone: (408) 947-2500
Sales: $123,934,000   *Employees:* 1,000
Company Type: Private   *Employees here:* 1,000
SIC: 8062
  General hospital
Joan Bero, Chief Financial Officer

D-U-N-S 87-840-5117
OAK CREST VILLAGE, INC
8800 Walther Blvd, Baltimore, MD 21234
Phone: (410) 665-1000
Sales: $29,893,000   *Employees:* 350
Company Type: Private   *Employees here:* 350
SIC: 8059
  Personal care
Lenore Booth, President

D-U-N-S 07-466-7684
OAK VALLEY HOSPITAL DISTRICT
350 S Oak Ave, Oakdale, CA 95361

Phone: (209) 847-3011
Sales: $24,747,000   *Employees:* 425
Company Type: Private   *Employees here:* 325
SIC: 8062
  General hospital
Nancy Oliba, Administrator

D-U-N-S 07-841-0842
OAKWOOD HOSPITAL CORPORATION
18101 Oakwood Blvd, Dearborn, MI 48124
Phone: (313) 593-7000
Sales: $187,900,000   *Employees:* 4,000
Company Type: Private   *Employees here:* 3,500
SIC: 8062
  General hospital
Gerald D Fitzgerald, President

D-U-N-S 07-659-6451
OAKWOOD LIVING CENTERS OF MASS
  (Parent: Oakwood Living Centers Inc)
123 South St, Plymouth, MA 2360
Phone: (508) 746-4343
Sales: $22,100,000   *Employees:* 972
Company Type: Private   *Employees here:* 250
SIC: 8051
  Skilled nursing home & school for handicapped children
James Eden, President

D-U-N-S 14-700-2786
OAKWOOD LIVING CENTERS INC
695 Atlantic Ave Fl 11, Boston, MA 2111
Phone: (617) 790-3900
Sales: $22,100,000   *Employees:* 972
Company Type: Private   *Employees here:* 1
SIC: 8051
  Skilled nursing care facility
James Eden, President

D-U-N-S 16-706-3965
OCCUPATIONAL HEALTH SERVICES
4631 Orville Ave Ste 103, Kansas City, KS 66102
Phone: (913) 596-2774
Sales: $55,000,000   *Employees:* 800
Company Type: Private   *Employees here:* 800
SIC: 8011
  Medical doctor's office
Dr Edward Kinports, Principal

D-U-N-S 10-754-2755
OCCUPATIONAL URGENT CARE HEALTH
  (Parent: First Health Group Corp)
750 Riverpoint Dr, Broderick, CA 95605
Phone: (916) 374-4600
Sales: $23,600,000   *Employees:* 590
Company Type: Public Family Member   *Employees here:* 380
SIC: 8099
  Provides managed health care programs
James C Smith, President

D-U-N-S 07-790-0207
OCHSNER ALTON MED FOUNDATION
1516 Jefferson Hwy, Jefferson, LA 70121
Phone: (504) 842-3000
Sales: $309,917,000   *Employees:* 3,500
Company Type: Private   *Employees here:* 3,000
SIC: 8062
  General hospital
Dr Frank A Riddick Jr, Chief Executive Officer

D-U-N-S 78-834-2293
OCHSNER ALTON MED FOUNDATION
1516 Jefferson Hwy, New Orleans, LA 70121
Phone: (504) 842-3179

Sales: $82,900,000
Company Type: Private
SIC: 8062
  General hospital
Frank Riddick, Principal

Employees: NA
Employees here: 2,000

D-U-N-S 15-748-7471
OCHSNER CLINIC HEALTH SVCS CORP
1514 Jefferson Hwy, New Orleans, LA 70121
Phone: (504) 842-4000
Sales: $250,000,000
Company Type: Private
SIC: 8011
  Clinic
Dr Gary Goldstein, Chairman of the Board

Employees: 2,000
Employees here: 1,200

D-U-N-S 15-722-0732
OCHSNER HEALTH PLAN INC
1 Galleria Blvd Ste 1224, Metairie, LA 70001
Phone: (504) 836-6600
Sales: $323,738,000
Company Type: Private
SIC: 8011
  Managed health care
Lyle Luman, President

Employees: 280
Employees here: 140

D-U-N-S 06-933-3789
OCONEE MEMORIAL HOSPITAL INC
298 Memorial Dr, Seneca, SC 29672
Phone: (864) 882-3351
Sales: $56,214,000
Company Type: Private
SIC: 8062
  Hospital and skilled and intermediate care facility
W H Hudson, President

Employees: 850
Employees here: 775

D-U-N-S 82-585-6834
OCONOMWOC RESIDENTIAL PROGRAMS
36100 Genesee Lake Rd, Oconomowoc, WI 53066
Phone: (414) 569-5515
Sales: $28,000,000
Company Type: Private
SIC: 8052
  Care facility
James Balestrieri, President

Employees: 1,000
Employees here: 350

D-U-N-S 07-316-0319
ODESSA HOSPITAL LTD
520 E 6th St, Odessa, TX 79761
Phone: (915) 332-8101
Sales: $37,896,000
Company Type: Private
SIC: 8062
  Hospital
Lex Guinn, Chief Executive Officer

Employees: 350
Employees here: 346

D-U-N-S 94-571-5217
ODYSSEY HEALTHCARE INC
717 N Harwood St Ste 1500, Dallas, TX 75201
Phone: (214) 922-9711
Sales: $31,000,000
Company Type: Private
SIC: 8069
  Specialty hospital
Richard R Burnham, President

Employees: 450
Employees here: 35

D-U-N-S 18-117-0457
OGDEN MEDICAL CENTER INC
  (Parent: Healthtrust Inc - Hospital Co)
5475 S 500 E, Ogden, UT 84405
Phone: (801) 479-2111

Sales: $43,800,000
Company Type: Public Family Member
SIC: 8062
  Hospital
Steve Bateman, Chief Executive Officer

Employees: 950
Employees here: 950

D-U-N-S 00-303-1510
OHIO DEPARTMENT MENTAL HEALTH
1960 W Broad St, Columbus, OH 43223
Phone: (614) 752-0333
Sales: $25,800,000
Company Type: Private
SIC: 8063
  Psychiatric hospital
James Ignezi, Chief Executive Officer

Employees: NA
Employees here: 761

D-U-N-S 00-303-0769
OHIO DEPARTMENT MENTAL HEALTH
1708 Southpoint Dr, Cleveland, OH 44109
Phone: (216) 787-0500
Sales: $25,100,000
Company Type: Private
SIC: 8063
  Psychiatric hospital
George Gintoli, Chief Executive Officer

Employees: NA
Employees here: 738

D-U-N-S 17-264-5137
OHIO STATE UNIVERSITY
410 W 10th Ave, Columbus, OH 43210
Phone: (614) 293-8000
Sales: $169,500,000
Company Type: Private
SIC: 8062
  General hospital
R R Fraley, N/A

Employees: NA
Employees here: 4,000

D-U-N-S 07-215-2440
OHIO VALLEY GENERAL HOSPITAL
Heckel Rd, Mckees Rocks, PA 15136
Phone: (412) 777-6161
Sales: $42,398,000
Company Type: Private
SIC: 8062
  Hospital
William F Provenzano, President

Employees: 459
Employees here: 454

D-U-N-S 07-216-3892
OHIO VALLEY MEDICAL CENTER INC
2000 Eoff St, Wheeling, WV 26003
Phone: (304) 234-0123
Sales: $70,455,000
Company Type: Private
SIC: 8062
  Hospital
Thomas P Galinski, President

Employees: 975
Employees here: 950

D-U-N-S 92-647-2705
OKALOOSA HOSPITAL, INC
  (Parent: Columbia/Hca Healthcare Corp)
2190 Highway 85 N, Niceville, FL 32578
Phone: (850) 678-4131
Sales: $26,987,000
Company Type: Public Family Member
SIC: 8062
  General hospital
David Waylon, Chief Executive Officer

Employees: 450
Employees here: 446

D-U-N-S 78-447-8133
OKLAHOMA AMBULATORY CARE CORP
  (Parent: Integris Health)
3300 NW Expressway, Oklahoma City, OK 73112
Phone: (405) 949-6066

Sales: $48,615,000   Employees: NA
Company Type: Private   Employees here: NA
SIC: 8011
  Medical clinic
Stanley Hupfeld, President

D-U-N-S 08-553-2224
OKLAHOMA BLOOD INSTITUTE INC
1001 N Lincoln Blvd, Oklahoma City, OK 73104
Phone: (405) 297-5700
Sales: $27,664,000   Employees: 450
Company Type: Private   Employees here: 350
SIC: 8099
  Blood bank
Dr Ronald Gilcher Md, President

D-U-N-S 05-371-5611
OKLAHOMA CY CLINIC A PROF CORP
701 NE 10th St, Oklahoma City, OK 73104
Phone: (405) 280-5700
Sales: $37,300,000   Employees: 543
Company Type: Private   Employees here: 380
SIC: 8011
  Medical clinic
A W Coventon, Administrator

D-U-N-S 03-797-7139
OKLAHOMA DEPARTMENT HUMAN SVCS
940 NE 13th St, Oklahoma City, OK 73104
Phone: (405) 271-5911
Sales: $132,700,000   Employees: NA
Company Type: Private   Employees here: 3,200
SIC: 8062
  Hospital
Dr R T Coussons, Branch Manager

D-U-N-S 07-427-8763
OKLAHOMA ORTHPDC/ARTHRTS
1111 N Dewey Ave, Oklahoma City, OK 73103
Phone: (405) 272-9671
Sales: $23,285,000   Employees: 280
Company Type: Private   Employees here: 280
SIC: 8069
  Orthopedic hospital
James Hyde, President

D-U-N-S 07-546-1509
OKTIBBEHA COUNTY HOSPITAL
400 Hospital Rd, Starkville, MS 39759
Phone: (601) 323-4320
Sales: $28,386,000   Employees: 430
Company Type: Private   Employees here: 400
SIC: 8062
  General hospital
Arthur C Kelly, Administrator

D-U-N-S 18-273-4996
OLATHE HEALTH FOUNDATION
20333 W 151st St, Olathe, KS 66061
Phone: (913) 791-4200
Sales: $82,600,000   Employees: 1,200
Company Type: Private   Employees here: 3
SIC: 8011
  Clinic
Richard G Johnson, Principal

D-U-N-S 07-624-9945
OLATHE MEDICAL CENTER INC
20333 W 151st St, Olathe, KS 66061
Phone: (913) 791-4200

Sales: $60,283,000   Employees: 1,213
Company Type: Private   Employees here: 1,000
SIC: 8062
  Hospital
Frank Devocelle, President

D-U-N-S 03-022-3192
OLEAN GENERAL HOSPITAL INC
515 Main St, Olean, NY 14760
Phone: (716) 373-2600
Sales: $39,000,000   Employees: 850
Company Type: Private   Employees here: 350
SIC: 8062
  General hospital
Theodore W Gundlah, President

D-U-N-S 07-401-2790
OLEAN GENERAL HOSPITAL INC
2221 W State St, Olean, NY 14760
Phone: (716) 372-5300
Sales: $22,500,000   Employees: NA
Company Type: Private   Employees here: 500
SIC: 8062
  General hospital
Floyd Oathout, N/A

D-U-N-S 07-074-4388
OLMSTED MEDICAL CENTER
210 9th St SE, Rochester, MN 55904
Phone: (507) 288-3443
Sales: $44,988,000   Employees: 650
Company Type: Private   Employees here: 281
SIC: 8011
  Medical clinic & hospital
Thomas D Holets, Administrator

D-U-N-S 07-800-3837
OMAHA HOME FOR BOYS INC
4343 N 52nd St, Omaha, NE 68104
Phone: (402) 457-7000
Sales: $23,589,000   Employees: 91
Company Type: Private   Employees here: 91
SIC: 8361
  Home for boys
John C Furstenberg, Executive Director

D-U-N-S 15-415-4868
OMEGA HEALTH SYSTEMS INC
5350 Poplar Ave Ste 900, Memphis, TN 38119
Phone: (901) 683-7868
Sales: $83,314,000   Employees: 576
Company Type: Public   Employees here: 24
SIC: 8042
  Operates eye care centers
Mike Savage, Quality

D-U-N-S 94-172-1375
ONCARE
1111 Bayhill Dr Ste 125, San Bruno, CA 94066
Phone: (650) 589-5900
Sales: $71,311,000   Employees: 700
Company Type: Private   Employees here: 60
SIC: 8011
  Management services
Michael D Goldberg, Chief Executive Officer

D-U-N-S 12-558-8897
ONCOLOGY-HEMATOLGY ASSOCIATES
  (Parent: American Oncology Resources)
816 Middle St, Pittsburgh, PA 15212
Phone: (412) 231-5400

Sales: $64,000,000
Company Type: Public Family Member   *Employees:* 120
SIC: 8011   *Employees here:* 25
　　Medical doctor's office
Dr Stanley Marks Md, President

D-U-N-S 80-719-8064
ONE CALL MEDICAL, INC
20 Waterview Blvd, Parsippany, NJ 7054
Phone: (973) 257-1000
Sales: $35,000,000   *Employees:* 90
Company Type: Private   *Employees here:* 80
SIC: 8011
　　Schedules patients for diagnostic radiology services
Bruce Thomason, Chief Executive Officer

D-U-N-S 07-581-6801
ONEIDA HEALTH CARE CENTER
321 Genesee St, Oneida, NY 13421
Phone: (315) 363-6000
Sales: $35,016,000   *Employees:* 900
Company Type: Private   *Employees here:* 898
SIC: 8062
　　Hospital and skilled nursing care
Richard G Smith, Administrator

D-U-N-S 03-410-4067
ONSLOW COUNTY HOSPITAL AUTH
317 Western Blvd, Jacksonville, NC 28546
Phone: (910) 577-2345
Sales: $67,344,000   *Employees:* 1,000
Company Type: Private   *Employees here:* 1,000
SIC: 8062
　　Hospital
Doug Kramer, Chief Executive Officer

D-U-N-S 07-556-0672
ONSLOW MEMORIAL HOSPITAL INC
317 Western Blvd, Jacksonville, NC 28546
Phone: (910) 577-2345
Sales: $64,096,000   *Employees:* 786
Company Type: Private   *Employees here:* 700
SIC: 8062
　　General hospital
Douglas Kramer, Administrator

D-U-N-S 07-508-0069
OPELOUSAS GENERAL HOSPITAL
520 E Prudhomme Ln, Opelousas, LA 70570
Phone: (318) 948-3011
Sales: $41,737,000   *Employees:* 580
Company Type: Private   *Employees here:* 550
SIC: 8062
　　General medical & surgical hospital
Patrick Carrier, President

D-U-N-S 07-396-6087
OPTIMA HEALTH-CMC
100 McGregor St, Manchester, NH 3102
Phone: (603) 668-3545
Sales: $132,827,000   *Employees:* 1,432
Company Type: Private   *Employees here:* 1,422
SIC: 8062
　　General hospital
Peter Davis, Chief Executive Officer

D-U-N-S 95-866-1795
OPTIMUM REHABILITATION INC
　　(*Parent:* Frontier Group)
1 Boston Pl Ste 2300, Boston, MA 2108
Phone: (617) 720-7150

Sales: $30,000,000   *Employees:* 450
Company Type: Private   *Employees here:* 450
SIC: 8093
　　Rehabilitation center
Jonathan S Sherwin, Chairman of the Board

D-U-N-S 10-284-3331
OPTION CARE, INC (DEL)
100 Corporate N Ste 212, Deerfield, IL 60015
Phone: (847) 615-1690
Sales: $99,977,000   *Employees:* 1,156
Company Type: Public   *Employees here:* 50
SIC: 8082
　　Home infusion therapy services
Michael Rusnak, President

D-U-N-S 19-981-2579
OPTIONS HEALTH CARE (VA CORP)
　　(*Parent:* Options Healthcare Inc)
240 Corporate Blvd Fl 4, Norfolk, VA 23502
Phone: (757) 459-5200
Sales: $91,500,000   *Employees:* 3,000
Company Type: Private   *Employees here:* 275
SIC: 8093
　　Manage mental health abuse care
Ronald Dozoretz, Chairman of the Board

D-U-N-S 80-885-7361
OREGON ANESTHESIOLOGY GROUP PC
1620 SW Taylor St Ste 300, Portland, OR 97205
Phone: (503) 299-9906
Sales: $48,000,000   *Employees:* 161
Company Type: Private   *Employees here:* 161
SIC: 8011
　　Physicians' office
Reginald Bruss, President

D-U-N-S 19-651-5704
OREGON MEDICAL GROUP PC
1580 Valley River Dr, Eugene, OR 97401
Phone: (541) 687-4900
Sales: $27,400,000   *Employees:* 400
Company Type: Private   *Employees here:* 80
SIC: 8011
　　Medical group
Peter Davidson, Principal

D-U-N-S 08-240-6638
ORLANDO RGONAL HEALTHCARE SYS
1414 Kuhl Ave, Orlando, FL 32806
Phone: (407) 841-5111
Sales: $558,490,000   *Employees:* 8,000
Company Type: Private   *Employees here:* 5,250
SIC: 8062
　　General hospitals
John Hillenmeyer, President

D-U-N-S 15-251-0830
ORLANDO RGONAL HEALTHCARE SYS
9400 Turkey Lake Rd, Orlando, FL 32819
Phone: (407) 351-8500
Sales: $25,600,000   *Employees:* NA
Company Type: Private   *Employees here:* 590
SIC: 8062
　　General hospital
Cathy Canniff-Gilliam, N/A

D-U-N-S 60-651-1624
ORLANDO RGONAL HEALTHCARE SYS
92 W Miller St, Orlando, FL 32806
Phone: (407) 649-9111

Sales: $59,500,000
Company Type: Private
SIC: 8011
 Medical doctor's office
John Bozard, Executive Director

Employees: NA
Employees here: 1,000

D-U-N-S 00-805-0205
ORNDA HEALTHCORP
 (Parent: Tenet Healthcare Corporation)
3820 State St, Santa Barbara, CA 93105
Phone: (805) 563-7000
Sales: $1,227,800,000
Company Type: Public
SIC: 8062
 Owns operates & manages acute care & psychiatric hospitals
  surgery centers & hmo

Employees: 26,000
Employees here: 138

D-U-N-S 06-095-4492
ORNDA HEALTHCORP
160 NW 170th St, Miami, FL 33169
Phone: (305) 651-1100
Sales: $44,000,000
Company Type: Public Family Member
SIC: 8062
 General hospital
Louis Kauffman, Chief Operating Officer

Employees: NA
Employees here: 1,000

D-U-N-S 84-595-9766
ORNDA HEALTHCORP
160 NW 170th St, Miami, FL 33169
Phone: (305) 653-9277
Sales: $88,500,000
Company Type: Public Family Member
SIC: 8062
 General medical surgical hospitals
David Catlin, Branch Manager

Employees: NA
Employees here: 2,000

D-U-N-S 83-436-9373
ORNDA INVESTMENTS INC
 (Parent: Ahm Acquisition Co Inc)
3820 State St, Santa Barbara, CA 93105
Phone: (805) 563-7000
Sales: $1,416,900,000
Company Type: Public Family Member
SIC: 8062
 Hospitals
Jeff Barbakow, Chief Executive Officer

Employees: 30,000
Employees here: 135

D-U-N-S 07-609-9282
OROVILLE HOSPITAL
2767 Olive Hwy, Oroville, CA 95966
Phone: (530) 533-8500
Sales: $54,766,000
Company Type: Private
SIC: 8062
 General hospital
Robert Wentz, Chief Executive Officer

Employees: 800
Employees here: 800

D-U-N-S 87-796-8958
ORTHODONTIC CENTERS OF AMERICA
13000 Sawgrass Village Ci, Ponte Vedra Beach, FL 32082
Phone: (904) 273-0004
Sales: $117,326,000
Company Type: Public
SIC: 8021
 Operates orthodontic practices
Dr Gasper Lazzara Jr, Chairman of the Board

Employees: 390
Employees here: 5

D-U-N-S 07-795-4535
ORTHOPAEDIC HOSPITAL
2400 S Flower St, Los Angeles, CA 90007
Phone: (213) 742-1000

Sales: $20,227,000
Company Type: Private
SIC: 8069
 General medical and surgical hospital
James V Luck Jr, President

Employees: 376
Employees here: 376

D-U-N-S 36-301-7070
ORTHOPDIC NEUROLOGICAL REHABILITATION
200 S Santa Cruz Ave, Los Gatos, CA 95030
Phone: (408) 395-4667
Sales: $35,529,000
Company Type: Private
SIC: 8049
 Occupational physical & neurological therapists
Jill Dietrich-Capela, President

Employees: 1,200
Employees here: 25

D-U-N-S 07-867-7978
ORTHOPEDIC CONSULTANTS, PA
6465 Wayzata Blvd Ste 900, Minneapolis, MN 55426
Phone: (612) 512-5600
Sales: $37,236,000
Company Type: Private
SIC: 8011
 Clinic & surgeons
Penny M Vail, Chief Executive Officer

Employees: 200
Employees here: 30

D-U-N-S 84-900-4726
ORTHOPEDIC HOSPITAL LTD
7401 Main St, Houston, TX 77030
Phone: (713) 799-8600
Sales: $33,064,000
Company Type: Private
SIC: 8069
 Specialty hospital
John Jackson, Chief Executive Officer

Employees: 230
Employees here: 230

D-U-N-S 92-642-2973
OSCEOLA REGIONAL HOSPITAL,
 (Parent: Columbia/Hca Healthcare Corp)
700 W Oak St, Kissimmee, FL 34741
Phone: (407) 846-2266
Sales: $53,500,000
Company Type: Public Family Member
SIC: 8062
 Acute care hospital
Timothy Cook, Chief Executive Officer

Employees: 542
Employees here: 542

D-U-N-S 07-458-9433
OSF HEALTHCARE SYSTEM
5666 E State St, Rockford, IL 61108
Phone: (815) 226-2000
Sales: $63,500,000
Company Type: Private
SIC: 8062
 General hospital
David Schertz, Principal

Employees: NA
Employees here: 1,500

D-U-N-S 06-741-4946
OSF HEALTHCARE SYSTEM
800 NE Glen Oak Ave, Peoria, IL 61603
Phone: (309) 655-2850
Sales: $642,526,000
Company Type: Private
SIC: 8062
 Hospitals
Sister M Flannery, Chairman of the Board

Employees: 8,741
Employees here: 217

D-U-N-S 60-547-3255
OSF HEALTHCARE SYSTEM
530 NE Glen Oak Ave, Peoria, IL 61637
Phone: (309) 655-2000

Sales: $148,400,000
Company Type: Private
SIC: 8062
  General hospital
Sister M Canisia, N/A

Employees: NA
Employees here: 3,500

D-U-N-S 07-913-9572
OSF HEALTHCARE SYSTEM
3333 N Seminary St, Galesburg, IL 61401
Phone: (309) 344-3161
Sales: $20,400,000
Company Type: Private
SIC: 8062
  General hospital
Richard Kowalski, N/A

Employees: NA
Employees here: 530

D-U-N-S 07-142-4717
OSF HEALTHCARE SYSTEM
2200 E Washington St, Bloomington, IL 61701
Phone: (309) 662-3311
Sales: $37,800,000
Company Type: Private
SIC: 8062
  Hospital
Ken Natzke, Administration

Employees: NA
Employees here: 900

D-U-N-S 01-077-2630
OSWEGO HOSPITAL INC
110 W 6th St, Oswego, NY 13126
Phone: (315) 349-5511
Sales: $37,086,000
Company Type: Private
SIC: 8062
  General hospital
Corte J Spencer, Administrator

Employees: 650
Employees here: 550

D-U-N-S 07-761-8023
OTERO COUNTY HOSPITAL ASSN
1209 9th St, Alamogordo, NM 88310
Phone: (505) 439-2100
Sales: $29,959,000
Company Type: Private
SIC: 8062
  General hospital
Carl W Mantey, Administrator

Employees: 400
Employees here: 392

D-U-N-S 06-396-2997
OTTERBEIN HOMES
580 N State Route 741, Lebanon, OH 45036
Phone: (513) 932-2020
Sales: $37,601,000
Company Type: Private
SIC: 8361
  Home for the aged
Donald L Gilmore, President

Employees: 850
Employees here: 400

D-U-N-S 06-520-7359
OTTUMWA REGIONAL HEALTH CENTER
1001 Pennsylvania Ave, Ottumwa, IA 52501
Phone: (515) 682-7511
Sales: $46,402,000
Company Type: Private
SIC: 8062
  Hospital
Clarence Cory, President

Employees: 850
Employees here: 710

D-U-N-S 07-145-7295
OUR LADY OF LOURDES MED CTR
1600 Haddon Ave, Camden, NJ 8103
Phone: (609) 757-3500

Sales: $105,200,000
Company Type: Private
SIC: 8062
  General hospital
Alex Hatala, Chairman of the Board

Employees: 2,250
Employees here: 2,142

D-U-N-S 07-159-9021
OUR LADY OF LOURDES MEM HOSP
169 Riverside Dr, Binghamton, NY 13905
Phone: (607) 798-5111
Sales: $94,743,000
Company Type: Private
SIC: 8062
  General medical & surgical hospital
Michael Guley, President

Employees: 1,445
Employees here: 1,400

D-U-N-S 07-260-5439
OUR LADY OF LOURDES REGIONAL
611 Saint Landry St, Lafayette, LA 70506
Phone: (318) 289-2000
Sales: $106,918,000
Company Type: Private
SIC: 8062
  General hospital
Dudley Romero, President

Employees: 1,100
Employees here: 1,100

D-U-N-S 07-282-4964
OUR LADY OF MERCY MEDICAL CTR
600 E 233rd St, Bronx, NY 10466
Phone: (718) 920-9000
Sales: $212,268,000
Company Type: Private
SIC: 8062
  General hospital and medical offices
Gary S Horan, President

Employees: 2,200
Employees here: 1,500

D-U-N-S 61-208-1471
OUR LADY OF MERCY MEDICAL CTR
1870 Pelham Pkwy S, Bronx, NY 10461
Phone: (718) 430-6000
Sales: $34,300,000
Company Type: Private
SIC: 8062
  Medical center

Employees: NA
Employees here: 700

D-U-N-S 05-056-0655
OUR LADY OF THE RESURRECTION
7435 W Talcott Ave, Chicago, IL 60631
Phone: (773) 282-7000
Sales: $280,387,000
Company Type: Private
SIC: 8062
  General medical & surgical hospital
Joseph Toomey, President

Employees: 1,907
Employees here: 1,907

D-U-N-S 03-023-0817
OUR LADY OF VICTORY HOSPITAL
55 Melroy Ave, Lackawanna, NY 14218
Phone: (716) 825-8000
Sales: $44,072,000
Company Type: Private
SIC: 8062
  Hospital
John Davanzo, President

Employees: 750
Employees here: 700

D-U-N-S 09-977-0968
OUR LADY BELLEFONTE HOSPITAL INC
St Christopher Dr, Ashland, KY 41101
Phone: (606) 833-3333

Sales: $71,468,000   *Employees:* 920
Company Type: Private   *Employees here:* 902
SIC: 8062
    General hospital home health medical clinics and rents &
    retails durable medical equipment
Robert J Maher, President

D-U-N-S 06-548-0121
OUR LADY LAKE REGIONAL MED CTR
5000 Hennessy Blvd, Baton Rouge, LA 70808
Phone: (225) 765-6565
Sales: $281,224,000   *Employees:* 3,500
Company Type: Private   *Employees here:* 3,500
SIC: 8062
    General hospital
Robert C Davidge, President

D-U-N-S 78-662-1391
OUTREACH HEALTH CARE, INC
2660 S Garland Ave, Garland, TX 75041
Phone: (972) 840-3401
Sales: $183,100,000   *Employees:* 6,000
Company Type: Private   *Employees here:* 30
SIC: 8093
    Outpatient nursing service
William Ball, President

D-U-N-S 07-663-1704
OVERLAKE HOSPITAL MEDICAL CTR
1035 116th Ave NE, Bellevue, WA 98004
Phone: (425) 688-5000
Sales: $114,293,000   *Employees:* 1,600
Company Type: Private   *Employees here:* 1,600
SIC: 8062
    General hospital
Ken Graham, President

D-U-N-S 83-754-7074
OWENSBORO MERCY HEALTH SYSTEMS
811 E Parrish Ave, Owensboro, KY 42303
Phone: (502) 688-2000
Sales: $102,800,000   *Employees:* 2,200
Company Type: Private   *Employees here:* 2,134
SIC: 8062
    Hospital
Greg Carlson, President

D-U-N-S 78-951-7836
OXFORD HEALTH PLANS (PA) INC
    (Parent: Oxford Health Plans Inc)
601 Walnut St, Philadelphia, PA 19106
Phone: (215) 625-8800
Sales: $118,000,000   *Employees:* 80
Company Type: Public Family Member   *Employees here:* 80
SIC: 8011
    Health maintenance organization
Bob Azelby, Acting Ceo

D-U-N-S 07-272-9429
OZANAM HALL OF QUEENS NURSING HM
4241 201st St, Bayside, NY 11361
Phone: (718) 423-2000
Sales: $32,997,000   *Employees:* 600
Company Type: Private   *Employees here:* 600
SIC: 8051
    Skilled nursing home
James Koniarski, Finance

D-U-N-S 07-696-5391
OZARKS MEDICAL CENTER, INC
1100 Kentucky St, West Plains, MO 65775
Phone: (417) 256-9111

Sales: $51,241,000   *Employees:* 800
Company Type: Private   *Employees here:* 750
SIC: 8062
    Medical & surgical hospital
C R Brackney, Chief Executive Officer

D-U-N-S 08-236-3276
P A CARDINAL HEALTHCARE
3320 Wake Forest Rd, Raleigh, NC 27609
Phone: (919) 872-4850
Sales: $34,300,000   *Employees:* 500
Company Type: Private   *Employees here:* 178
SIC: 8011
    Multi specialty clinic
Dr Allen Hayes Md, President

D-U-N-S 18-519-3612
P C HEALTHFIRST PHYSICIAN
355 S Union Blvd, Lakewood, CO 80228
Phone: (303) 763-4900
Sales: $20,500,000   *Employees:* 300
Company Type: Private   *Employees here:* 35
SIC: 8011
    Medical doctor's office
Thomas Jeffers, Director

D-U-N-S 10-271-8459
P H C-SALT LAKE CITY INC
    (Parent: Phc/Chc Holdings Inc)
1050 E South Temple, Salt Lake City, UT 84102
Phone: (801) 350-4111
Sales: $43,800,000   *Employees:* 950
Company Type: Public Family Member   *Employees here:* 950
SIC: 8062
    Hospital
Kay Metsumura, President

D-U-N-S 36-452-5360
P M R CORPORATION
501 Washington Ave Fl 5, San Diego, CA 92103
Phone: (619) 295-2227
Sales: $67,524,000   *Employees:* 800
Company Type: Public   *Employees here:* 45
SIC: 8011
    Psychiatric management program
Allen Tepper, Chairman of the Board

D-U-N-S 11-896-5367
PACIFIC CATARACT LASER INST P S
2517 NE Kresky Ave, Chehalis, WA 98532
Phone: (360) 748-8632
Sales: $20,606,000   *Employees:* 226
Company Type: Private   *Employees here:* 100
SIC: 8011
    Ophthalmologists
Dr Robert O Ford Md, President

D-U-N-S 11-540-0368
PACIFIC HEALTH CORPORATION
    (Parent: Health Investment Corporation)
249 E Ocean Blvd Ste 440, Long Beach, CA 90802
Phone: (562) 435-1300
Sales: $46,100,000   *Employees:* 1,000
Company Type: Private   *Employees here:* 9
SIC: 8062
    General acute care hospital
James W Young, President

D-U-N-S 15-059-7060
PACIFIC HEALTH SYSTEMS INC
    (Parent: Pacificare Operations Inc)
3120 W Lake Center Dr, Santa Ana, CA 92704
Phone: (714) 825-6600

Sales: $103,400,000   *Employees:* 1,500
Company Type: Public Family Member   *Employees here:* 1,200
SIC: 8011
   Holding company
Westcott W Price Iii, Chairman of the Board

D-U-N-S 04-647-0142
PACIFIC HOMES
21021 Ventura Blvd, Woodland Hills, CA 91364
Phone: (818) 594-0200
Sales: $54,002,000   *Employees:* 1,400
Company Type: Private   *Employees here:* 35
SIC: 8361
   Residential care services skilled nursing care facility & home
   health care services
Mort Swales, President

D-U-N-S 01-920-2050
PACIFIC MEDICAL CENTER
1200 12th Ave S, Seattle, WA 98144
Phone: (206) 326-4000
Sales: $113,444,000   *Employees:* 1,100
Company Type: Private   *Employees here:* 400
SIC: 8011
   General & family health clinic
Yen Cone, Controller

D-U-N-S 19-046-1293
PACIFICA OF THE VALLEY CORP
(Parent: Doctors Corp Of America)
9449 San Fernando Rd, Sun Valley, CA 91352
Phone: (818) 767-3310
Sales: $44,000,000   *Employees:* 525
Company Type: Private   *Employees here:* 525
SIC: 8062
   General hospital
Paul Tuft, Chairman of the Board

D-U-N-S 79-868-3801
PACIFICA HOSPITAL CARE CENTER
18800 Delaware St, Huntington Beach, CA 92648
Phone: (714) 842-0611
Sales: $29,537,000   *Employees:* 300
Company Type: Private   *Employees here:* 300
SIC: 8062
   General hospital
Michael Mussman, Chief Executive Officer

D-U-N-S 17-258-1373
PACIFICARE OF CALIFORNIA
410 N 44th St, Phoenix, AZ 85008
Phone: (602) 966-6773
Sales: $21,600,000   *Employees:* NA
Company Type: Public Family Member   *Employees here:* 340
SIC: 8011
   Health maintenance organization
Cliff Klima, N/A

D-U-N-S 11-541-1076
PACIFICARE OF CALIFORNIA
1000 N Studebaker Rd, Long Beach, CA 90815
Phone: (562) 493-6411
Sales: $21,600,000   *Employees:* NA
Company Type: Public Family Member   *Employees here:* 340
SIC: 8011
   Medical doctor's office
Jane Spanier, Manager

D-U-N-S 60-967-8560
PACIFICARE OF CALIFORNIA
18000 Studebaker Rd, Cerritos, CA 90703
Phone: (562) 809-5399

Sales: $28,100,000   *Employees:* NA
Company Type: Public Family Member   *Employees here:* 450
SIC: 8011
   Medical doctor's office
Pam Polumbo, N/A

D-U-N-S 02-091-2473
PACIFICARE OF CALIFORNIA
35 W Broadway, Salt Lake City, UT 84101
Phone: (801) 355-1234
Sales: $103,000,000   *Employees:* NA
Company Type: Public Family Member   *Employees here:* 1,800
SIC: 8011
   Medical doctor's office
Steve Brewer, Director

D-U-N-S 60-661-7454
PACIFICARE OF CALIFORNIA
1525 W 2100 S, Salt Lake City, UT 84119
Phone: (801) 973-9999
Sales: $32,200,000   *Employees:* NA
Company Type: Public Family Member   *Employees here:* 520
SIC: 8011
   Medical doctor's office
Kevun Cahoon, Branch Manager

D-U-N-S 80-565-2054
PACIFICARE OF OREGON
5 Centerpointe Dr Ste 600, Lake Oswego, OR 97035
Phone: (503) 620-9324
Sales: $320,293,000   *Employees:* 210
Company Type: Private   *Employees here:* 160
SIC: 8011
   Health maintenance organization
Mary Mc Williams, President

D-U-N-S 15-036-0972
PACIFICARE OF TEXAS INC
(Parent: Pacificare Operations Inc)
8200 W Ih 10 Ste 1000, San Antonio, TX 78230
Phone: (210) 524-9800
Sales: $541,770,000   *Employees:* 180
Company Type: Public Family Member   *Employees here:* 153
SIC: 8011
   Prepaid health plan
Patrick Feyen, President

D-U-N-S 80-362-7462
PACIN HEALTHCARE-HADLEY MEM HOSP
(Parent: Doctors Community Healthcare)
4601 Martin Luther King, Washington, DC 20032
Phone: (202) 574-5700
Sales: $50,000,000   *Employees:* 350
Company Type: Private   *Employees here:* 350
SIC: 8062
   Acute care general hospital
Ana Raley, President

D-U-N-S 06-751-8811
PALISADES MEDICAL CENTER
7600 River Rd, North Bergen, NJ 7047
Phone: (201) 854-5000
Sales: $64,836,000   *Employees:* 634
Company Type: Private   *Employees here:* 629
SIC: 8062
   General hospital
Bruce J Markowitz, President

D-U-N-S 07-771-1984
PALISADES NURSING HOME CO INC
5901 Palisade Ave, Bronx, NY 10471
Phone: (718) 549-8700

Sales: $25,267,000
Company Type: Private
SIC: 8059
  Nursing home
Daniel Reingold, Owner
Employees: 500
Employees here: 500

D-U-N-S 07-698-8849
PALM BEACH GARDENS COMMUNITY HOSP
  (Parent: Tenet Healthcare Corporation)
3360 Burns Rd, Palm Beach Gardens, FL 33410
Phone: (561) 622-1411
Sales: $41,400,000
Company Type: Public Family Member
SIC: 8062
  General medical hospital
Oscar Fernandez, Chief Financial Officer
Employees: 900
Employees here: 900

D-U-N-S 07-601-1154
PALM SPRINGS GENERAL HOSPITAL
1475 W 49th St, Hialeah, FL 33012
Phone: (305) 558-2500
Sales: $53,000,000
Company Type: Private
SIC: 8062
  General hospital
Oakley G Smith, President
Employees: 600
Employees here: 600

D-U-N-S 60-264-3934
PALMETTO GENERAL HOSPITAL
  (Parent: Tenet Healthcare Corporation)
2001 W 68th St, Hialeah, FL 33016
Phone: (305) 823-5000
Sales: $57,700,000
Company Type: Public Family Member
SIC: 8062
  General hospital
Ron Stern, Chief Executive Officer
Employees: 1,245
Employees here: 1,200

D-U-N-S 80-620-1992
PALMS WEST HOSPITAL INC
  (Parent: Columbia/Hca Healthcare Corp)
13001 State Road 80, Loxahatchee, FL 33470
Phone: (561) 798-3300
Sales: $21,400,000
Company Type: Public Family Member
SIC: 8062
  General medical and surgical hospital
Alex Marceline, Chief Executive Officer
Employees: 477
Employees here: 477

D-U-N-S 07-631-3832
PALO ALTO MEDICAL FOUNDATION
300 Homer Ave, Palo Alto, CA 94301
Phone: (650) 321-4121
Sales: $110,000,000
Company Type: Private
SIC: 8011
  Medical clinic
Dr Robert W Jamplis Md, President
Employees: 1,000
Employees here: 700

D-U-N-S 07-314-4107
PALO PINTO GENERAL HOSPITAL
400 SW 25th Ave, Mineral Wells, TX 76067
Phone: (940) 325-7891
Sales: $22,814,000
Company Type: Private
SIC: 8062
  General medical & surgical hospital
Guy Hazlett, Administrator
Employees: 414
Employees here: 414

D-U-N-S 07-337-9026
PALOMAR POMERADO HEALTH SYS
15255 Innovation Dr, San Diego, CA 92128
Phone: (619) 675-5100

Sales: $188,220,000
Company Type: Private
SIC: 8062
  General acute care medical hospital
Victoria Penland, President
Employees: 2,700
Employees here: 180

D-U-N-S 10-316-2657
PALOMAR POMERADO HEALTH SYS
555 E Valley Pkwy, Escondido, CA 92025
Phone: (760) 739-3000
Sales: $59,500,000
Company Type: Private
SIC: 8062
  General hospital
Victoria M Penland, President
Employees: NA
Employees here: 1,200

D-U-N-S 07-846-2496
PAN AMERICAN HOSPITAL CORP
5959 NW 7th St, Miami, FL 33126
Phone: (305) 264-1000
Sales: $72,911,000
Company Type: Private
SIC: 8062
  General hospital
Carolina Calderin, Chief Executive Officer
Employees: 1,172
Employees here: 835

D-U-N-S 04-145-8472
PARACELSUS HEALTHCARE CORP
515 W Greens Rd Ste 800, Houston, TX 77067
Phone: (281) 774-5100
Sales: $659,219,000
Company Type: Public
SIC: 8062
  Owner/lessor/ operator of hospitals skilled nursing facilities
    & medical office buildings
Charles R Miller, President
Employees: 7,600
Employees here: 86

D-U-N-S 18-792-8312
PARACELSUS SANTA ROSA MED CTR
  (Parent: Paracelsus Healthcare Corp)
1450 Berryhill Rd, Milton, FL 32570
Phone: (850) 626-7762
Sales: $56,000,000
Company Type: Public Family Member
SIC: 8062
  General hospital
Barbara Thames, Administrator
Employees: 310
Employees here: 310

D-U-N-S 07-093-0391
PARACELSUS-DAVIS HOSPITAL,
  (Parent: Paracelsus Healthcare Corp)
1600 W Antelope Dr, Layton, UT 84041
Phone: (801) 825-9561
Sales: $43,728,000
Company Type: Public Family Member
SIC: 8062
  Hospital
Bruce Baldwin, President
Employees: 500
Employees here: 495

D-U-N-S 92-699-7321
PARADIGM HOLDINGS INC
1001 Galaxy Way Ste 300, Concord, CA 94520
Phone: (925) 676-2300
Sales: $39,080,000
Company Type: Private
SIC: 8093
  Managed care co
Michael Grisham, President
Employees: 135
Employees here: 120

D-U-N-S 06-763-1382
PARADISE VALLEY HOSPITAL INC
2400 E 4th St, National City, CA 91950
Phone: (619) 470-4321

Sales: $75,183,000
Company Type: Private
SIC: 8062
   General medical hospital
Eric Martinsen, Chief Executive Officer

Employees: 1,050
Employees here: 1,010

D-U-N-S 78-391-1217
PARAGON REHABILITATION INC
   (Parent: Centennial Healthcare Corp)
3100 W End Ave Ste 400, Nashville, TN 37203
Phone: (615) 385-1060
Sales: $78,000,000
Company Type: Public Family Member
SIC: 8049
   Contract rehabilitation physical therapy
J S Eaton, Chairman of the Board

Employees: 500
Employees here: 30

D-U-N-S 18-422-6082
PARAMOUNT CARE INC
   (Parent: Vanguard Health Ventures Inc)
1715 Indian Wood Cir, Maumee, OH 43537
Phone: (419) 891-2500
Sales: $122,646,000
Company Type: Private
SIC: 8011
   Health maintenance organization
John C Randolph, President

Employees: 127
Employees here: 127

D-U-N-S 07-176-7529
PARK COLUMBIA MEDICAL GROUP
6401 University Ave NE, Minneapolis, MN 55432
Phone: (612) 572-5710
Sales: $28,350,000
Company Type: Private
SIC: 8011
   Medical clinic
Gary A Van House, Chief Executive Officer

Employees: 275
Employees here: 20

D-U-N-S 06-848-3981
PARK JACKSON HOSPITAL FOUNDATION
7531 S Stony Island Ave, Chicago, IL 60649
Phone: (773) 947-7500
Sales: $59,907,000
Company Type: Private
SIC: 8062
   General medical hospital
Dr Peter Friedell Md, President

Employees: 750
Employees here: 750

D-U-N-S 08-489-5549
PARK LANE MED CTR KANS CY INC
5151 Raytown Rd, Kansas City, MO 64133
Phone: (816) 358-8000
Sales: $20,100,000
Company Type: Private
SIC: 8062
   Osteopathic hospital
Derell Taloney, President

Employees: 450
Employees here: 450

D-U-N-S 07-176-7966
PARK NICOLLET MEDICAL CENTER
   (Parent: Healthsystem Minnesota)
3800 Park Nicollet Blvd, Minneapolis, MN 55416
Phone: (612) 993-3123
Sales: $432,000,000
Company Type: Private
SIC: 8011
   Medical clinics
Dr James Reinertsen Md, Chief Executive Officer

Employees: 1,700
Employees here: 800

D-U-N-S 07-368-6933
PARK RIDGE NURSING HOME INC
1555 Long Pond Rd, Rochester, NY 14626
Phone: (716) 723-7000

Sales: $89,533,000
Company Type: Private
SIC: 8051
   Skilled nursing facility
Sandra Mac Williams, President

Employees: 180
Employees here: 180

D-U-N-S 07-317-1597
PARKER COUNTY HOSPITAL DST
713 E Anderson St, Weatherford, TX 76086
Phone: (817) 596-8751
Sales: $30,404,000
Company Type: Private
SIC: 8062
   General hospital
Nolan Queen, Chairman of the Board

Employees: 405
Employees here: 375

D-U-N-S 06-597-2069
PARKER JEWISH INSTITUTE
27111 76th Ave, New Hyde Park, NY 11040
Phone: (718) 289-2100
Sales: $81,178,000
Company Type: Private
SIC: 8051
   Skilled nursing home and home health care
David Glaser, President

Employees: 1,130
Employees here: 1,070

D-U-N-S 88-306-9411
PARKRIDGE HOSPITAL INC
   (Parent: Columbia/Hca Healthcare Corp)
941 Spring Creek Rd, Chattanooga, TN 37412
Phone: (423) 855-3500
Sales: $22,164,000
Company Type: Public Family Member
SIC: 8062
   Hospital
Brenda Waltz, President

Employees: 350
Employees here: 350

D-U-N-S 92-641-7809
PARKRIDGE HOSPITAL INC
   (Parent: Columbia/Hca Healthcare Corp)
2333 McCallie Ave, Chattanooga, TN 37404
Phone: (423) 698-6061
Sales: $55,600,000
Company Type: Public Family Member
SIC: 8062
   General hospital and home health facility
Solon Boggus, Chief Executive Officer

Employees: 1,200
Employees here: 785

D-U-N-S 07-359-7940
PARKVIEW COMMUNITY HOSPITAL MED CTR
3865 Jackson St, Riverside, CA 92503
Phone: (909) 688-2211
Sales: $77,248,000
Company Type: Private
SIC: 8062
   General hospital
Norm Martin, President

Employees: 1,173
Employees here: 1,173

D-U-N-S 05-683-0037
PARKVIEW HEALTH SYSTEM INC
400 W 16th St, Pueblo, CO 81003
Phone: (719) 584-4000
Sales: $62,700,000
Company Type: Private
SIC: 8062
   Holding company
C W Smith, President

Employees: 1,350
Employees here: 1,200

D-U-N-S 06-470-3861
PARKVIEW HOSPITAL INC
2200 Randallia Dr, Fort Wayne, IN 46805
Phone: (219) 484-6636

Sales: $293,129,000
Company Type: Private
SIC: 8062
  General hospital
Frank Byrne, President

Employees: 3,700
Employees here: 3,600

D-U-N-S 07-273-7620
PARKWAY HOSPITAL INC
7035 113th St, Forest Hills, NY 11375
Phone: (718) 990-4131
Sales: $79,557,000
Company Type: Private
SIC: 8062
  General medical hospital
Paul Svensson, Chief Executive Officer

Employees: 940
Employees here: 940

D-U-N-S 07-777-5278
PARMA COMMUNITY GEN HOSPITAL ASSN
7007 Powers Blvd, Cleveland, OH 44129
Phone: (440) 888-1800
Sales: $91,689,000
Company Type: Private
SIC: 8062
  General hospital
Thomas A Selden, Chief Executive Officer

Employees: 1,667
Employees here: 1,667

D-U-N-S 11-299-0452
PARTNERS IN CARE INC
  (Parent: Visiting Nurse Service Of Ny)
1250 Broadway Fl 9, New York, NY 10001
Phone: (212) 290-3151
Sales: $65,413,000
Company Type: Private
SIC: 8082
  Home health aid & rn/lpn service
Richard Flender, Chairman of the Board

Employees: 1,500
Employees here: 1,500

D-U-N-S 17-706-6792
PARTNERS NAT HEALTH PLANS OF NC
  (Parent: Carolina Medi-Plan Inc)
2085 Frontis Plaza Blvd, Winston Salem, NC 27103
Phone: (336) 760-4822
Sales: $296,389,000
Company Type: Private
SIC: 8011
  Health maintenance organization
John W Jones, President

Employees: 230
Employees here: 220

D-U-N-S 02-692-7608
PASADENA BAYSHORE HOSPITAL,
  (Parent: Columbia/Hca Healthcare Corp)
4000 Spencer Hwy, Pasadena, TX 77504
Phone: (713) 944-6666
Sales: $104,076,000
Company Type: Public Family Member
SIC: 8062
  Acute care hospital
Russell Meyers, Chief Executive Officer

Employees: 1,000
Employees here: 1,000

D-U-N-S 06-668-3962
PASADENA HOSPITAL ASSN LTD
100 W California Blvd, Pasadena, CA 91105
Phone: (626) 397-5000
Sales: $256,564,000
Company Type: Private
SIC: 8062
  General hospital and outpatient facilities
Stephen A Ralph, President

Employees: 2,800
Employees here: 2,100

D-U-N-S 07-271-3951
PASCACK VALLEY HOSPITAL ASSN
250 Old Hook Rd, Westwood, NJ 7675
Phone: (201) 358-3000

Sales: $90,700,000
Company Type: Private
SIC: 8062
  General hospital
Louis R Ycre Jr, President

Employees: 1,206
Employees here: 1,206

D-U-N-S 07-143-8667
PASSAVANT MEM AREA HOSPITAL ASSOC
1600 W Walnut St, Jacksonville, IL 62650
Phone: (217) 245-9541
Sales: $40,980,000
Company Type: Private
SIC: 8062
  Hospital
Chester Wynn, Chief Executive Officer

Employees: 670
Employees here: 664

D-U-N-S 06-990-4100
PATH LAB INC
  (Parent: Path Lab Holdings Inc)
195 Hanover St Ste 206, Portsmouth, NH 3801
Phone: (603) 431-2310
Sales: $34,000,000
Company Type: Private
SIC: 8071
  Medical diagnostic lab
P T Hirsch, President

Employees: 500
Employees here: 100

D-U-N-S 07-789-0572
PATHOLOGY LABORATORIES LTD
4200 Mamie St, Hattiesburg, MS 39402
Phone: (601) 264-3856
Sales: $21,769,000
Company Type: Private
SIC: 8071
  Pathology laboratory
Dr Thomas G Puckett, Chief Executive Officer

Employees: 300
Employees here: 200

D-U-N-S 93-221-2970
PATHWAY HEALTHCARE SERVICES
690 Canton St, Westwood, MA 2090
Phone: (781) 320-1930
Sales: $20,000,000
Company Type: Private
SIC: 8082
  Healthcare services
John Talbot, President

Employees: 700
Employees here: 50

D-U-N-S 79-607-5166
PATHWAYS, INC.
201 22nd St, Ashland, KY 41101
Phone: (606) 324-1141
Sales: $22,100,000
Company Type: Private
SIC: 8011
  Medical doctor's office specialty outpatient clinic
Richard Stai, Director

Employees: NA
Employees here: 400

D-U-N-S 07-932-9678
PATIENT CARE INC
  (Parent: Chemed Corporation)
100 Executive Dr Ste 130, West Orange, NJ 7052
Phone: (973) 243-5900
Sales: $99,565,000
Company Type: Public Family Member
SIC: 8082
  Home health care agency
Timothy S O Toole, Chairman of the Board

Employees: 5,300
Employees here: 60

D-U-N-S 05-583-9104
PATTIE A CLAY INFIRMARY
801 Eastern By Pass, Richmond, KY 40475
Phone: (606) 623-3131

Sales: $31,235,000   *Employees:* 550
Company Type: Private   *Employees here:* 550
SIC: 8062
  Hospital
Richard Thomas, Administrator

D-U-N-S 07-495-0296
PATUXENT MEDICAL GROUP, INC
  (Parent: Carefirst Of Maryland Inc)
2 Knoll North Dr, Columbia, MD 21045
Phone: (410) 997-8500
Sales: $80,787,000   *Employees:* 1,000
Company Type: Private   *Employees here:* 700
SIC: 8011
  Medical group
Dr Robert N Sheff Md, President

D-U-N-S 08-597-3683
PEACEHEALTH
1255 Hilyard St, Eugene, OR 97401
Phone: (541) 686-7171
Sales: $129,400,000   *Employees:* NA
Company Type: Private   *Employees here:* 2,600
SIC: 8062
  Hospital
Sister M Heerema, Manager

D-U-N-S 78-930-6644
PEACEHEALTH
740 E 13th Ave, Eugene, OR 97401
Phone: (541) 686-7085
Sales: $39,700,000   *Employees:* NA
Company Type: Private   *Employees here:* 2,400
SIC: 8049
  General hospital
Raymond Beaman, Director

D-U-N-S 92-652-1766
PEACEHEALTH
1162 Willamette St, Eugene, OR 97401
Phone: (541) 687-6000
Sales: $23,400,000   *Employees:* NA
Company Type: Private   *Employees here:* 370
SIC: 8011
  Medical clinic
Wes Davidson, Principal

D-U-N-S 08-858-9064
PEACEHEALTH
1614 E Kessler Blvd, Longview, WA 98632
Phone: (360) 423-1530
Sales: $52,800,000   *Employees:* NA
Company Type: Private   *Employees here:* 1,150
SIC: 8062
  General medical hospital
Mark Mc Gourty, Manager

D-U-N-S 03-926-9592
PEACEHEALTH
2901 Squalicum Pkwy, Bellingham, WA 98225
Phone: (206) 734-5400
Sales: $54,400,000   *Employees:* NA
Company Type: Private   *Employees here:* 1,100
SIC: 8062
  Hospital
John Hayward, N/A

D-U-N-S 07-663-3189
PEACEHEALTH
15325 SE 30th Pl Ste 300, Bellevue, WA 98007
Phone: (425) 747-1711

Sales: $466,797,000   *Employees:* 5,500
Company Type: Private   *Employees here:* 40
SIC: 8062
  Hospitals medical clinics and nursing homes
Keith Tromburg, Financial Analyst

D-U-N-S 01-893-9558
PEAK MEDICAL CORP
5635 Jefferson St NE, Albuquerque, NM 87109
Phone: (505) 342-0235
Sales: $65,000,000   *Employees:* 10
Company Type: Private   *Employees here:* 10
SIC: 8051
  Operates skilled nursing care facilities
Charles Gonzales, Chief Executive Officer

D-U-N-S 01-289-8990
PECONIC HEALTH CORPORATION
1116 Main Rd, Aquebogue, NY 11931
Phone: (516) 369-7100
Sales: $76,000,000   *Employees:* 1,632
Company Type: Private   *Employees here:* 3
SIC: 8062
  Holding company for hospitals
Thomas B Doolan, President

D-U-N-S 78-689-5136
PEDIATRIC SERVICES OF AMER DE
310 Technology Pkwy, Norcross, GA 30092
Phone: (770) 441-1580
Sales: $204,023,000   *Employees:* 5,000
Company Type: Public   *Employees here:* 250
SIC: 8082
  Home health care services
Joseph D Sansone, Chairman of the Board

D-U-N-S 12-094-1042
PEDIATRIC SERVICES OF AMER GA
  (Parent: Pediatric Services Of Amer De)
310 Technology Pkwy, Norcross, GA 30092
Phone: (770) 441-1580
Sales: $163,804,000   *Employees:* 5,000
Company Type: Public Family Member   *Employees here:* 250
SIC: 8082
  Home health care services rental and sales of home health
    care equipment
Joseph Sansone, President

D-U-N-S 79-149-7431
PEDIATRIX MEDICAL GROUP INC
1455 N Park Dr, Fort Lauderdale, FL 33326
Phone: (954) 384-0175
Sales: $80,833,000   *Employees:* 700
Company Type: Public   *Employees here:* 300
SIC: 8011
  Neonatal and pediatric physician management services
Dr Roger J Medel Md, President

D-U-N-S 07-914-8128
PEKIN MEMORIAL HOSPITAL
600 S 13th St, Pekin, IL 61554
Phone: (309) 347-1151
Sales: $34,523,000   *Employees:* 570
Company Type: Private   *Employees here:* 550
SIC: 8062
  General hospital
Robert J Moore, Chief Executive Officer

D-U-N-S 07-711-3033
PEMISCOT COUNTY MEMORIAL HOSP
Us Highway 61, Hayti, MO 63851
Phone: (573) 359-1372

Sales: $23,920,000   *Employees:* 750
Company Type: Private   *Employees here:* 700
SIC: 8062
  Hospital
Darrell Jean, Administrator

D-U-N-S 07-193-7171
PENDLETON MEM METHDST HOSP
5620 Read Blvd, New Orleans, LA 70127
Phone: (504) 244-5474
Sales: $106,139,000   *Employees:* 1,068
Company Type: Private   *Employees here:* 999
SIC: 8062
  General hospital
Frederick C Young Jr, President

D-U-N-S 07-744-3166
PENINSULA HOSPITAL CENTER
5115 Beach Channel Dr, Far Rockaway, NY 11691
Phone: (718) 945-7100
Sales: $64,656,000   *Employees:* 1,010
Company Type: Private   *Employees here:* 1,010
SIC: 8062
  Hospital
Robert Levine, President

D-U-N-S 07-488-8629
PENINSULA PSYCHIATRIC CENTER
  (Parent: Fort Sanders Regional Med Ctr)
Jones Bend Rd, Louisville, TN 37777
Phone: (423) 970-9800
Sales: $20,400,000   *Employees:* 550
Company Type: Private   *Employees here:* 280
SIC: 8063
  Psychiatric hospital
John Milner, Executive Vice-President

D-U-N-S 06-989-4780
PENINSULA UNITED METHDST HOMES
2 Mill Rd Ste 200, Wilmington, DE 19806
Phone: (302) 777-6800
Sales: $31,501,000   *Employees:* 1,100
Company Type: Private   *Employees here:* 34
SIC: 8361
  Continuing care retirement communities
Rev R C Stazesky, President

D-U-N-S 07-916-1360
PENN STATE GEISINGER CLINIC
100 N Academy Ave, Danville, PA 17821
Phone: (717) 271-6211
Sales: $215,656,000   *Employees:* 1,940
Company Type: Private   *Employees here:* 700
SIC: 8011
  Offices & clinics of doctors of medicine & provides non-
    commercial medical research
Frank J Trembulak, Vice-President

D-U-N-S 02-795-0542
PENN STATE GEISINGER MED CTR
100 N Academy Ave, Danville, PA 17821
Phone: (717) 271-6211
Sales: $58,967,000   *Employees:* 825
Company Type: Private   *Employees here:* 4
SIC: 8062
  General medical & surgical hospital
Frank J Trembulak, Treasurer

D-U-N-S 62-042-5363
PENN STATE GEISINGER WYOMING
1000 E Mountain Dr, Wilkes Barre, PA 18711
Phone: (717) 826-7300

Sales: $40,400,000   *Employees:* NA
Company Type: Private   *Employees here:* 821
SIC: 8062
  Hospital
Richard Somma, President

D-U-N-S 13-076-7890
PENN STATE GISINGER HEALTH PLAN
100 N Academy Ave, Danville, PA 17821
Phone: (717) 271-6211
Sales: $206,019,000   *Employees:* NA
Company Type: Private   *Employees here:* NA
SIC: 8011
  Health maintenance organization
Frank J Trembulak, Vice-President

D-U-N-S 07-927-9261
PENNOCK HOSPITAL
1009 W Green St, Hastings, MI 49058
Phone: (616) 945-3451
Sales: $32,279,000   *Employees:* 505
Company Type: Private   *Employees here:* 490
SIC: 8062
  General hospital
Daniel C Hamilton, Chief Executive Officer

D-U-N-S 07-917-9925
PENNSYLVANIA DEPT LABOR INDUST
1600 Hanover Ave, Allentown, PA 18103
Phone: (610) 740-3200
Sales: $24,000,000   *Employees:* NA
Company Type: Private   *Employees here:* 600
SIC: 8063
  State mental facility
Gregory Smith, Superintendent

D-U-N-S 08-162-1005
PENNSYLVANIA DEPT PUB WELFARE
Rr 522, Selinsgrove, PA 17870
Phone: (717) 372-5000
Sales: $26,600,000   *Employees:* NA
Company Type: Private   *Employees here:* 1,200
SIC: 8059
  Nursing and personal care, nec, nsk
Joseph J Scartelli, Principal

D-U-N-S 03-008-5716
PENNSYLVANIA DEPT PUB WELFARE
Main St, Polk, PA 16342
Phone: (814) 432-3171
Sales: $36,400,000   *Employees:* NA
Company Type: Private   *Employees here:* 1,600
SIC: 8051
  State institution for the mentally retarded
Ed Sadosky, Manager

D-U-N-S 08-079-4720
PENNSYLVANIA DEPT PUB WELFARE
1001 Sterigere St, Norristown, PA 19401
Phone: (610) 270-1015
Sales: $43,700,000   *Employees:* NA
Company Type: Private   *Employees here:* 1,100
SIC: 8063
  Psychiatric hospital
George A Kopchick Jr, Manager

D-U-N-S 07-950-0096
PENNSYLVANIA DEPT PUB WELFARE
3500 Darby Rd, Haverford, PA 19041
Phone: (610) 525-9620

Sales: $24,000,000
Company Type: Private
SIC: 8063
   Psychiatric hospital
Aiean Altenor, Principal

Employees: NA
Employees here: 600

D-U-N-S 08-063-8505
PENNSYLVANIA DEPT PUB WELFARE
Rr 22 Box West, Ebensburg, PA 15931
Phone: (814) 472-7350
Sales: $23,100,000
Company Type: Private
SIC: 8361
   Residential care for the handicapped
Alan Bellomo, Principal

Employees: NA
Employees here: 875

D-U-N-S 07-599-8401
PENNSYLVANIA DEPT PUB WELFARE
1451 Hillside Dr, Clarks Summit, PA 18411
Phone: (717) 586-2011
Sales: $20,000,000
Company Type: Private
SIC: 8063
   Mental hospital
Thomas Comerford, Principal

Employees: NA
Employees here: 500

D-U-N-S 08-073-0146
PENNSYLVANIA DEPT PUB WELFARE
1601 Mayview Rd, Bridgeville, PA 15017
Phone: (412) 257-6500
Sales: $67,300,000
Company Type: Private
SIC: 8063
   Mental health care hospital
Shirley J Dunpman, Systems/Data Processing

Employees: NA
Employees here: 1,700

D-U-N-S 07-161-3954
PENNSYLVANIA HOSPITAL
800 Spruce St, Philadelphia, PA 19107
Phone: (215) 829-3000
Sales: $222,000,000
Company Type: Private
SIC: 8062
   General hospital
Dr John Bal Md, President

Employees: 2,200
Employees here: 1,308

D-U-N-S 04-751-3981
PENNSYLVANIA STATE UNIV INC
500 University Dr, Hershey, PA 17033
Phone: (717) 531-8521
Sales: $213,900,000
Company Type: Private
SIC: 8062
   General hospital
Bruce Hamory, President

Employees: NA
Employees here: 5,100

D-U-N-S 00-235-4637
PENOBSCOT BAY MEDICAL ASSOC
331 Veranda St, Portland, ME 4103
Phone: (207) 774-5801
Sales: $47,000,000
Company Type: Private
SIC: 8093
   Outpatient health facility
Robert M Sontheimer, Chief Executive Officer

Employees: 89
Employees here: 48

D-U-N-S 07-174-4759
PENOBSCOT BAY MEDICAL CENTER
(Parent: Northeast Health)
6 Glen Cove Dr, Rockport, ME 4856
Phone: (207) 596-8000

Sales: $44,784,000
Company Type: Private
SIC: 8062
   General medical and surgical hospital & nursing home
John Bird, Chairman of the Board

Employees: 752
Employees here: 700

D-U-N-S 12-155-5130
PENTAGON CITY HOSPITAL INC
2455 Army Navy Dr, Arlington, VA 22206
Phone: (703) 553-2409
Sales: $21,500,000
Company Type: Private
SIC: 8062
   Hospital health maintenance organization & a research
   foundation
Joe Holliday, Accounting

Employees: 480
Employees here: 3

D-U-N-S 07-659-2658
PENTUCKET MEDICAL ASSOCIATES,
1 Parkway, Haverhill, MA 1830
Phone: (978) 521-3250
Sales: $30,000,000
Company Type: Private
SIC: 8011
   Primary care facility
Greg Trerotola, President

Employees: 350
Employees here: 158

D-U-N-S 03-020-5488
PEOPLE INC.
1219 N Forest Rd, Williamsville, NY 14221
Phone: (716) 634-8132
Sales: $37,975,000
Company Type: Private
SIC: 8361
   Residential care for the developmentally disabled and the
   elderly
James M Boles, Executive Director

Employees: 1,500
Employees here: 75

D-U-N-S 11-743-9547
PERMANENTE MED ASSN OF TEXAS
12720 Hillcrest Rd, Dallas, TX 75230
Phone: (972) 458-5015
Sales: $57,142,000
Company Type: Private
SIC: 8011
   Medical doctor's office
Dr William A Gillespie Md, President

Employees: 225
Employees here: 225

D-U-N-S 12-853-2041
PERMANENTE MEDICAL GROUP INC
1200 El Camino Real, South San Francisco, CA 94080
Phone: (650) 742-2000
Sales: $70,500,000
Company Type: Private
SIC: 8011
   Medical doctor's office
David Bliss, Branch Manager

Employees: NA
Employees here: 1,200

D-U-N-S 17-302-7731
PERMANENTE MEDICAL GROUP INC
2200 Ofarrell St, San Francisco, CA 94115
Phone: (415) 929-4000
Sales: $59,500,000
Company Type: Private
SIC: 8011
   Physicians
Dr Philip R Madvig Md, Branch Manager

Employees: NA
Employees here: 1,000

D-U-N-S 17-207-1219
PERMANENTE MEDICAL GROUP INC
2025 Morse Ave, Sacramento, CA 95825
Phone: (916) 973-5000

Sales: $191,500,000   *Employees:* NA
Company Type: Private   *Employees here:* 3,500
SIC: 8011
   Medical clinic
Dr Clifford Skinner, Branch Manager

D-U-N-S 07-393-2931
PERMANENTE MEDICAL GROUP INC
1950 Franklin St, Oakland, CA 94612
Phone: (510) 987-3118
Sales: $2,479,800,000   *Employees:* 19,000
Company Type: Private   *Employees here:* 500
SIC: 8011
   Manages medical offices/clinics
W H Caulfield Jr, Executive Director

D-U-N-S 18-591-6004
PERMANENTE MEDICAL GROUP INC
3801 Howe St, Oakland, CA 94611
Phone: (510) 596-1000
Sales: $145,100,000   *Employees:* NA
Company Type: Private   *Employees here:* 2,600
SIC: 8011
   Medical doctor's office
Tom Demartino, Manager

D-U-N-S 12-653-1227
PERMANENTE MEDICAL GROUP INC
2101 E Jefferson St, Rockville, MD 20852
Phone: (301) 816-2424
Sales: $29,400,000   *Employees:* NA
Company Type: Private   *Employees here:* 472
SIC: 8011
   Medical doctor's office
Martin B Bauman, N/A

D-U-N-S 96-572-3455
PERMANENTE MEDICAL GROUP, INC
4647 Zion Ave, San Diego, CA 92120
Phone: (619) 528-5497
Sales: $223,800,000   *Employees:* NA
Company Type: Private   *Employees here:* 4,500
SIC: 8062
   General hospital
Maurice Alfaro, Principal

D-U-N-S 78-541-4210
PERMANENTE MEDICAL GROUP, INC
100 S Los Robles Ave, Pasadena, CA 91101
Phone: (626) 564-3267
Sales: $21,600,000   *Employees:* NA
Company Type: Private   *Employees here:* 340
SIC: 8011
   Medical doctor's office
Tom Schipper, Manager

D-U-N-S 80-917-3180
PERMANENTE MEDICAL GROUP, INC
1800 Harrison St, Oakland, CA 94612
Phone: (510) 271-5800
Sales: $22,200,000   *Employees:* NA
Company Type: Private   *Employees here:* 350
SIC: 8011
   Medical doctor's office
Kenneth Handy, Vice-President

D-U-N-S 87-933-5164
PERMANENTE MEDICAL GROUP, INC
1071 W Shaw Ave, Fresno, CA 93711
Phone: (209) 448-4500

Sales: $48,300,000   *Employees:* NA
Company Type: Private   *Employees here:* 800
SIC: 8011
   Medical clinic
Ed Glavis, Administrator

D-U-N-S 61-867-1234
PERMANENTE MEDICAL GROUP, INC
9449 Imperial Hwy 155d, Downey, CA 90242
Phone: (562) 803-1311
Sales: $86,800,000   *Employees:* NA
Company Type: Private   *Employees here:* 1,500
SIC: 8011
   Medical doctor's office
Linda Buchanan, Branch Manager

D-U-N-S 18-165-8402
PERMANENTE MEDICAL GROUP, INC
1188 N Euclid St, Anaheim, CA 92801
Phone: (714) 778-8168
Sales: $51,200,000   *Employees:* NA
Company Type: Private   *Employees here:* 3,000
SIC: 8082
   Home health care services

D-U-N-S 13-148-9346
PERSONACARE INC
   (Parent: Theratx Incorporated)
400 W Market St, Louisville, KY 40202
Phone: (502) 569-7300
Sales: $34,200,000   *Employees:* 1,500
Company Type: Private   *Employees here:* 5
SIC: 8051
   Skilled nursing homes & retirement & rest homes
W B Lunsford, Chairman of the Board

D-U-N-S 17-492-7525
PERSONAL PHYSICIAN CARE INC
1255 Euclid Ave Ste 500, Cleveland, OH 44115
Phone: (216) 687-0015
Sales: $50,945,000   *Employees:* 125
Company Type: Private   *Employees here:* 120
SIC: 8011
   Health maintenance organization
Oscar Saffold, President

D-U-N-S 07-851-8347
PERSONAL-TOUCH HOME CARE INC
22215 Northern Blvd, Bayside, NY 11361
Phone: (718) 468-4747
Sales: $109,283,000   *Employees:* 11,500
Company Type: Private   *Employees here:* 75
SIC: 8082
   Home health care service
Dr Felix Glaubach, President

D-U-N-S 09-966-6497
PETERS BARNES-ST HOSPITAL
   (Parent: Barnes-Jewish Hospital)
10 Hospital Dr, Saint Peters, MO 63376
Phone: (314) 447-6600
Sales: $35,459,000   *Employees:* 690
Company Type: Private   *Employees here:* 690
SIC: 8062
   Hospital general medical
John J Gloss, Administrator

D-U-N-S 07-460-8977
PETERSON SID MEMORIAL HOSP
710 Water St, Kerrville, TX 78028
Phone: (830) 896-4200

Sales: $27,200,000   *Employees:* 600
Company Type: Private   *Employees here:* 500
SIC: 8062
    General hospital and skilled nursing facility
F W Hall Jr, Administrator

    D-U-N-S 11-730-1416
PHARMACO INTERNATIONAL INC
    (*Parent:* Pharmaceutical Product Dev)
4009 Banister Ln, Austin, TX 78704
Phone: (512) 447-2663
Sales: $52,700,000   *Employees:* 1,105
Company Type: Public Family Member   *Employees here:* 600
SIC: 8071
    Biological testing & clinical research & development
John D Bryer, President

    D-U-N-S 19-806-3752
PHARMCHEM LABORATORIES, INC
1505a Obrien Dr, Menlo Park, CA 94025
Phone: (650) 328-6200
Sales: $39,233,000   *Employees:* 350
Company Type: Public   *Employees here:* 260
SIC: 8071
    Drug testing services
Joseph W Halligan, President

    D-U-N-S 11-420-7053
PHELPS CNTY REGIONAL MED CTR
1000 W 10th St, Rolla, MO 65401
Phone: (573) 364-3100
Sales: $54,992,000   *Employees:* 831
Company Type: Private   *Employees here:* 800
SIC: 8062
    Hospital
David Ross, Chief Executive Officer

    D-U-N-S 07-271-0031
PHELPS MEMORIAL HOSPITAL ASSN
701 N Broadway, Tarrytown, NY 10591
Phone: (914) 366-3000
Sales: $69,932,000   *Employees:* 1,100
Company Type: Private   *Employees here:* 1,055
SIC: 8062
    General hospital
Keith F Safian, President

    D-U-N-S 06-989-5837
PHILADELPHIA GERIATRIC CENTER
5301 Old York Rd, Philadelphia, PA 19141
Phone: (215) 456-2900
Sales: $52,606,000   *Employees:* 1,000
Company Type: Private   *Employees here:* 1,000
SIC: 8051
    Extended nursing care facility & geriatric hospital
Frank Podietz, President

    D-U-N-S 07-547-8776
PHILADELPHIA PRESBYTERY HOMES
2000 Joshua Rd, Lafayette Hill, PA 19444
Phone: (610) 834-1001
Sales: $31,444,000   *Employees:* 600
Company Type: Private   *Employees here:* 22
SIC: 8361
    Residential life care intermediate & skilled care nursing
      homes
Robert Morrow, President

    D-U-N-S 07-949-5750
PHILADLPHIA AFL-CIO HOSPITAL ASSN
Cheltenham Ave Langdon St, Philadelphia, PA 19124
Phone: (215) 831-7000

Sales: $24,900,000   *Employees:* 550
Company Type: Private   *Employees here:* 460
SIC: 8062
    Hospital
Herman Matthews, President

    D-U-N-S 07-426-5794
PHILLIPS JANE MEMORIAL MED CTR
3500 E Frank Phillips Blv, Bartlesville, OK 74006
Phone: (918) 333-7200
Sales: $55,225,000   *Employees:* 815
Company Type: Private   *Employees here:* 750
SIC: 8062
    General hospital
Larry Minden, Administrator

    D-U-N-S 06-857-0985
PHOEBE HOME INC
1925 W Turner St, Allentown, PA 18104
Phone: (610) 435-9037
Sales: $21,363,000   *Employees:* 350
Company Type: Private   *Employees here:* 350
SIC: 8051
    Skilled nursing facilities
Joseph Hess, Administrator

    D-U-N-S 06-922-5209
PHOEBE PUTNEY MEMORIAL HOSP
510 W 2nd Ave, Albany, GA 31701
Phone: (912) 883-1800
Sales: $207,597,000   *Employees:* 1,950
Company Type: Private   *Employees here:* 1,940
SIC: 8062
    General hospital
Joel Wernick, President

    D-U-N-S 78-663-0384
PHOEBE-DEVITT HOMES INC
1925 W Turner St, Allentown, PA 18104
Phone: (610) 435-9037
Sales: $45,243,000   *Employees:* 8
Company Type: Private   *Employees here:* 8
SIC: 8051
    Nursing home management services
Rev Rodney Wells, President

    D-U-N-S 36-245-8218
PHOENIX AREA INDIAN HEALTH SVCS
51st & Beltline, Laveen, AZ 85339
Phone: (520) 550-3829
Sales: $21,700,000   *Employees:* NA
Company Type: Private   *Employees here:* 341
SIC: 8011
    Medical doctor's office
Henry Walden, Principal

    D-U-N-S 07-898-9977
PHOENIX BPTST HOSPITAL MED CTR INC
2224 W Northern Ave, Phoenix, AZ 85021
Phone: (602) 864-1184
Sales: $73,320,000   *Employees:* 1,023
Company Type: Private   *Employees here:* 60
SIC: 8062
    General medical & surgical hospital
Gerald L Wissink, President

    D-U-N-S 18-875-9617
PHOENIX BPTST HOSPITAL MED CTR INC
2000 W Bethany Home Rd, Phoenix, AZ 85015
Phone: (602) 249-0212

Sales: $38,700,000
Company Type: Private
SIC: 8062
   Hospital
Rich Allie, President

Employees: NA
Employees here: 900

D-U-N-S 11-044-3595
PHOENIX CHILDRENS HOSPITAL
1300 N 12th St Ste 404, Phoenix, AZ 85006
Phone: (602) 239-2400
Sales: $100,953,000
Company Type: Private
SIC: 8069
   General hospital
Burl Stamp, President

Employees: 654
Employees here: 35

D-U-N-S 80-045-8788
PHOENIX CHILDRENS HOSPITAL
1111 E McDowell Rd, Phoenix, AZ 85006
Phone: (602) 239-2400
Sales: $22,300,000
Company Type: Private
SIC: 8062
   General medical & surgical hospital
James Bands, Chief Financial Officer

Employees: NA
Employees here: 527

D-U-N-S 80-937-9092
PHOENIX HEALTHCARE OF TENN
   (Parent: Phoenix Healthcare Corporation)
3401 W End Ave Ste 470, Nashville, TN 37203
Phone: (615) 298-3666
Sales: $59,637,000
Company Type: Private
SIC: 8082
   Home health care services
Samuel Howard, Chairman

Employees: 86
Employees here: 86

D-U-N-S 02-012-8351
PHOENIX MEMORIAL HOSPITAL
1201 S 7th Ave, Phoenix, AZ 85007
Phone: (602) 258-5111
Sales: $66,283,000
Company Type: Private
SIC: 8062
   General hospital
Jeffrey Norman, Chief Executive Officer

Employees: 926
Employees here: 832

D-U-N-S 15-124-5107
PHOENIX PROGRAMS OF NEW YORK
   (Parent: Phoenix House Foundation Inc)
164 W 74th St, New York, NY 10023
Phone: (212) 595-5810
Sales: $21,822,000
Company Type: Private
SIC: 8361
   Residential nonprofit rehabilitation center for drug abuse
Mitchell S Rosenthal, President

Employees: 200
Employees here: 200

D-U-N-S 07-695-7943
PHOENIXVILLE HOSPITAL INC
140 Nutt Rd, Phoenixville, PA 19460
Phone: (610) 983-1000
Sales: $50,616,000
Company Type: Private
SIC: 8062
   General hospital
Richard E Seagrave, President

Employees: 789
Employees here: 789

D-U-N-S 07-781-6205
PHP HEALTHCARE CORPORATION
11440 Commerce Park Dr, Reston, VA 20191
Phone: (703) 758-3600

Sales: $400,130,000
Company Type: Public
SIC: 8011
   Provides integrated health care services and operates an hmo
Jack M Mazur, President

Employees: 3,300
Employees here: 123

D-U-N-S 07-125-6002
PHYCOR OF FT. SMITH, INC
   (Parent: Phycor Inc)
1500 Dodson Ave, Fort Smith, AR 72901
Phone: (501) 788-4000
Sales: $55,000,000
Company Type: Public Family Member
SIC: 8011
   Medical clinic
Jim Boswell, Executive Director

Employees: 800
Employees here: 517

D-U-N-S 88-347-2920
PHYCOR OF JACKSONVILLE, INC
2005 Riverside Ave, Jacksonville, FL 32204
Phone: (904) 387-7605
Sales: $36,900,000
Company Type: Public Family Member
SIC: 8011
   Medical doctors office (pediatrics)
Dr Stuart Z Millstone, Principal

Employees: NA
Employees here: 600

D-U-N-S 96-358-1905
PHYCOR OF KENTUCKY, INC.
   (Parent: Phycor Inc)
1221 S Broadway, Lexington, KY 40504
Phone: (606) 258-4000
Sales: $160,000,000
Company Type: Public Family Member
SIC: 8011
   Multi-specialty clinics
Tom Holets, Chief Executive Officer

Employees: 875
Employees here: 875

D-U-N-S 07-956-3599
PHYCOR OF LAFAYETTE, LLC
   (Parent: Phycor Inc)
2600 Greenbush St, Lafayette, IN 47904
Phone: (765) 448-8000
Sales: $34,300,000
Company Type: Public Family Member
SIC: 8011
   Outpatient medical clinic
Jeffrey Brown, President

Employees: 500
Employees here: 65

D-U-N-S 80-478-2092
PHYCOR OF PUEBLO INC
   (Parent: Phycor Inc)
2002 Lake Ave, Pueblo, CO 81004
Phone: (719) 560-7111
Sales: $23,000,000
Company Type: Public Family Member
SIC: 8011
   Medical clinic
Alan Taylor, Executive Director

Employees: 150
Employees here: 150

D-U-N-S 01-848-0629
PHYCOR OF ROME INC
   (Parent: Phycor Inc)
1825 Martha Berry Blvd, Rome, GA 30165
Phone: (706) 236-6307
Sales: $46,100,000
Company Type: Public Family Member
SIC: 8011
   Offices and clinics of medical doctors, nsk
Joseph Hutts, Chairman of the Board

Employees: 670
Employees here: 670

D-U-N-S 08-473-0514
PHYCOR OF VERO BEACH, INC
  (Parent: Phycor Inc)
2300 5th Ave, Vero Beach, FL 32960
Phone: (561) 567-7111
Sales: $25,000,000   *Employees:* 250
Company Type: Public Family Member   *Employees here:* 220
SIC: 8011
  Doctors' clinic & pharmacy
Michael Kissner, Executive Director

D-U-N-S 07-314-2960
PHYCOR OF WICHITA FALLS, INC
  (Parent: Phycor Inc)
501 Midwestern Pkwy E, Wichita Falls, TX 76302
Phone: (940) 766-8690
Sales: $34,300,000   *Employees:* 500
Company Type: Public Family Member   *Employees here:* 200
SIC: 8011
  Medical clinic
Ted Travis, Director

D-U-N-S 61-935-4681
PHYCOR INC
100 N Eagle Creek Dr, Lexington, KY 40509
Phone: (606) 233-1586
Sales: $36,900,000   *Employees:* NA
Company Type: Public Family Member   *Employees here:* 600
SIC: 8011
  Medical clinic
Tom Holets, Director

D-U-N-S 00-934-4326
PHYCOR INC
4235 Secor Rd, Toledo, OH 43623
Phone: (419) 473-3561
Sales: $26,400,000   *Employees:* NA
Company Type: Public Family Member   *Employees here:* 420
SIC: 8011
  Medical clinic
Barbara Yosses, Operations Manager

D-U-N-S 18-802-9607
PHYCOR INC
30 Burton Hills Blve 40, Nashville, TN 37215
Phone: (615) 665-9066
Sales: $1,119,594,000   *Employees:* 19,000
Company Type: Public   *Employees here:* 135
SIC: 8011
  Owns operates and manages multi-specialty clinics
Joseph C Hutts, Chairman of the Board

D-U-N-S 13-967-0939
PHYSICIAN ASSOCIATES FLORIDA
2301 Lucien Way Ste 230, Maitland, FL 32751
Phone: (407) 875-6600
Sales: $68,869,000   *Employees:* 710
Company Type: Private   *Employees here:* 70
SIC: 8011
  Multi specialist physicians group
Dr Edward H Lowenstein Md, President

D-U-N-S 14-746-6817
PHYSICIAN CORP OF AMERICA
  (Parent: Humana Inc)
5835 Blue Lagoon Dr, Miami, FL 33126
Phone: (305) 267-6633
Sales: $205,500,000   *Employees:* 2,980
Company Type: Public   *Employees here:* 30
SIC: 8011
  Operates hmos provides administrative services to self-
    insured & writes workers compensation insurance
Dr E S Kardatzke Md, Chairman of the Board

D-U-N-S 94-236-8507
PHYSICIAN HEALTH CORPORATION
990 Hammond Dr Ne Ste 300, Atlanta, GA 30328
Phone: (770) 673-1964
Sales: $37,408,000   *Employees:* 250
Company Type: Private   *Employees here:* 250
SIC: 8059
  Physician practice management
Sarah Garvin, President

D-U-N-S 79-964-3721
PHYSICIAN PARTNERS, INC
444 NW Elks Dr, Corvallis, OR 97330
Phone: (541) 754-1150
Sales: $30,500,000   *Employees:* NA
Company Type: Private   *Employees here:* 565
SIC: 8011
  Medical clinic
Ralph Prows, Branch Manager

D-U-N-S 06-501-4680
PHYSICIANS CLINICAL LABORATORY
3301 C St Ste 100e, Sacramento, CA 95816
Phone: (530) 444-3500
Sales: $62,831,000   *Employees:* 1,500
Company Type: Public   *Employees here:* 300
SIC: 8071
  Clinical laboratory services
Nathan L Headley, President

D-U-N-S 14-779-6809
PHYSICIANS HEALTH NETWORK,
  (Parent: United Physicians Hlth Netwrk)
7100 Eagle Crest Blvd, Evansville, IN 47715
Phone: (812) 469-7500
Sales: $39,748,000   *Employees:* 4
Company Type: Public Family Member   *Employees here:* 4
SIC: 8011
  Medical doctor's office and hospital/medical service plan
Kevin Clancy, President

D-U-N-S 17-337-6567
PHYSICIANS HEALTH PLAN, INC.
201 Executive Center Dr, Columbia, SC 29210
Phone: (803) 750-7400
Sales: $112,539,000   *Employees:* 162
Company Type: Private   *Employees here:* 124
SIC: 8011
  Health maintenance organization
William E Martin, Chief Executive Officer

D-U-N-S 78-688-9048
PHYSICIANS HEALTH SERVICES,
  (Parent: Foundation Health Systems Inc)
1 Far Mill Xing, Shelton, CT 6484
Phone: (203) 381-6400
Sales: $488,108,000   *Employees:* 1,100
Company Type: Public   *Employees here:* 5
SIC: 8011
  Holding company for a hmo an individual practice
    association & provides hmo insurance
Michael E Herbert, Chief Executive Officer

D-U-N-S 84-863-0075
PHYSICIANS HEALTHCARE PLANS,
  (Parent: Php Holdings Inc)
777 S Harbour Island Blvd, Tampa, FL 33602
Phone: (813) 273-7474
Sales: $130,393,000   *Employees:* 300
Company Type: Private   *Employees here:* 250
SIC: 8011
  Managed care plan
Michael B Fernandez, President

D-U-N-S 15-341-4586
PHYSICIANS HEALTH PLAN NTHRN IN
8101 W Jefferson Blvd, Fort Wayne, IN 46804
Phone: (219) 432-6690
Sales: $91,262,000   *Employees:* 98
Company Type: Private   *Employees here:* 98
SIC: 8011
    Health maintenance organization
Jay Gilbert, Chief Executive Officer

D-U-N-S 85-880-2630
PHYSICIANS IND MED GROUP
17190 Bernardo Center Dr, San Diego, CA 92128
Phone: (619) 675-3100
Sales: $21,000,000   *Employees:* 307
Company Type: Private   *Employees here:* 307
SIC: 8011
    Medical clinic
Karen Buck, Executive Director

D-U-N-S 09-063-0476
PHYWELL INC
10151 Deerwood Park Blvd, Jacksonville, FL 32256
Phone: (904) 996-3077
Sales: $36,000,000   *Employees:* 3
Company Type: Private   *Employees here:* 3
SIC: 8099
    Health care & mgt services
Christophe Fey, President

D-U-N-S 06-918-9124
PICKENS HEALTHCARE ASSOCIATION
1266 E Church St, Jasper, GA 30143
Phone: (706) 692-2441
Sales: $20,000,000   *Employees:* 175
Company Type: Private   *Employees here:* 175
SIC: 8062
    Hospital and nursing home
C H Wise, Administrator

D-U-N-S 06-735-3128
PIEDMONT AREA MNTL HEALTH
845 Church St N Ste 305, Concord, NC 28025
Phone: (704) 782-5505
Sales: $26,642,000   *Employees:* 429
Company Type: Private   *Employees here:* 23
SIC: 8093
    Mental health center
Dr Robert C Lorish, Director

D-U-N-S 80-624-3242
PIEDMONT HEALTHCARE SYSTEMS,
    (Parent: Tenet Healthcare Corporation)
222 S Herlong Ave, Rock Hill, SC 29732
Phone: (803) 329-1234
Sales: $62,700,000   *Employees:* 1,350
Company Type: Public Family Member   *Employees here:* 1,200
SIC: 8062
    Acute care hospital
Paul Walker, Chief Executive Officer

D-U-N-S 06-532-5466
PIEDMONT HOSPITAL INC
1968 Peachtree Rd Nw, Atlanta, GA 30309
Phone: (404) 605-5000
Sales: $239,550,000   *Employees:* 2,720
Company Type: Private   *Employees here:* 2,500
SIC: 8062
    Medical and surgical hospital
Richard B Hubbard Iii, President

D-U-N-S 05-556-9057
PIKEVILLE UNITED METHODIST HOS
911 S Bypass, Pikeville, KY 41501
Phone: (606) 437-3500
Sales: $84,282,000   *Employees:* 800
Company Type: Private   *Employees here:* 800
SIC: 8062
    Hospital
Martha O Chill, Administrator

D-U-N-S 06-775-0737
PILGRIM HEALTH CARE INC
1200 Crown Colony Dr, Quincy, MA 2169
Phone: (617) 745-1000
Sales: $803,433,000   *Employees:* 700
Company Type: Private   *Employees here:* 680
SIC: 8011
    Health maintenance organization
Greenberg Allan I, Chief Executive Officer

D-U-N-S 08-289-1326
PIMA COUNTY
2800 E Ajo Way, Tucson, AZ 85713
Phone: (520) 294-4471
Sales: $34,300,000   *Employees:* NA
Company Type: Private   *Employees here:* 800
SIC: 8062
    General hospital
Karen Shields, President

D-U-N-S 10-714-6458
PIMA COUNTY
4600 S Park Ave Ste 7, Tucson, AZ 85714
Phone: (520) 573-0228
Sales: $21,200,000   *Employees:* NA
Company Type: Private   *Employees here:* 1,400
SIC: 8082
    Home health care services
Bonnie Soukup, Administrator

D-U-N-S 05-585-7478
PINE REST CHRISTIAN HOSPITAL ASSN
300 68th St SE, Grand Rapids, MI 49548
Phone: (616) 455-5000
Sales: $29,253,000   *Employees:* 500
Company Type: Private   *Employees here:* 450
SIC: 8063
    Psychiatric hospital
Daniel Holwerda, Chief Executive Officer

D-U-N-S 07-950-6366
PINE STREET INN INC
444 Harrison Ave, Boston, MA 2118
Phone: (617) 482-4944
Sales: $26,634,000   *Employees:* 400
Company Type: Private   *Employees here:* 120
SIC: 8361
    Homeless shelter
Erik Butler, Executive Director

D-U-N-S 05-500-2216
PINEVILLE COMMUNITY HOSPITAL ASSN
850 Riverview Rd, Pineville, KY 40977
Phone: (606) 337-3051
Sales: $19,806,000   *Employees:* 355
Company Type: Private   *Employees here:* 355
SIC: 8062
    General hospital
J M Brooks, Administrator

D-U-N-S 96-725-8823
PINNACLE HEALTH HOSPITALS
2601 N 3rd St, Harrisburg, PA 17110

Phone: (717) 782-4141
Sales: $99,500,000   *Employees:* NA
Company Type: Private   *Employees here:* 2,000
SIC: 8062
   General hospital
John Kramer, President

D-U-N-S 96-725-9094
PINNACLE HEALTH HOSPITALS
205 S Front St, Harrisburg, PA 17104
Phone: (717) 782-3131
Sales: $114,500,000   *Employees:* NA
Company Type: Private   *Employees here:* 2,300
SIC: 8062
   General hospital
John Cramer, Principal

D-U-N-S 96-718-8160
PINNACLE HEALTH HOSPITALS
17 S Market Sq, Harrisburg, PA 17101
Phone: (717) 782-5678
Sales: $287,069,000   *Employees:* 4,100
Company Type: Private   *Employees here:* 5
SIC: 8062
   General hospitals
John S Cramer, President

D-U-N-S 18-792-3206
PIONEER VALLEY HOSPITAL
   (*Parent:* Paracelsus Healthcare Corp)
3460 Pioneer Pkwy, Salt Lake City, UT 84120
Phone: (801) 964-3100
Sales: $70,000,000   *Employees:* 516
Company Type: Public Family Member   *Employees here:* 500
SIC: 8062
   General hospital
Brian Mottishaw, Chief Executive Officer

D-U-N-S 07-334-2057
PIONEERS MEM HEALTHCARE DST
207 W Legion Rd, Brawley, CA 92227
Phone: (760) 344-2120
Sales: $33,308,000   *Employees:* 500
Company Type: Private   *Employees here:* 450
SIC: 8062
   General medical & surgical hospital
William Daniel, Administrator

D-U-N-S 05-640-3462
PITT COUNTY MEMORIAL HOSPITAL
2100 Stantonsburg Rd, Greenville, NC 27834
Phone: (252) 816-4100
Sales: $381,159,000   *Employees:* 3,900
Company Type: Private   *Employees here:* 3,700
SIC: 8062
   General medical and surgical hospital
Dave Mcrae, President

D-U-N-S 07-579-1871
PLAZA EMPLOYMENT AGENCY INC
50 Broadway, Lynbrook, NY 11563
Phone: (516) 887-1200
Sales: $31,721,000   *Employees:* 4,500
Company Type: Private   *Employees here:* 3,000
SIC: 8082
   Home care nursing agency
Irving Edwards, Chief Executive Officer

D-U-N-S 80-442-1931
PLEASANT CARE CORPORATION
2258 Foothill Blvd Ste 6, La Canada, CA 91011
Phone: (818) 248-9808

Sales: $45,800,000   *Employees:* 2,000
Company Type: Private   *Employees here:* 15
SIC: 8051
   Skilled nursing care facilities
Emmanuel Bernabe, President

D-U-N-S 07-269-1264
PLEASANT VALLEY HOSPITAL, INC.
2520 Valley Dr, Point Pleasant, WV 25550
Phone: (304) 675-4340
Sales: $42,764,000   *Employees:* 637
Company Type: Private   *Employees here:* 530
SIC: 8062
   General hospital
Michael Sellards, Chief Executive Officer

D-U-N-S 06-857-2460
POCONO MEDICAL CENTER
206 E Brown St, East Stroudsburg, PA 18301
Phone: (717) 421-4000
Sales: $73,596,000   *Employees:* 1,057
Company Type: Private   *Employees here:* 1,027
SIC: 8062
   General hospital
Marilyn Rettaliata, President

D-U-N-S 07-391-4723
POLLY RYON HOSPITAL AUTHORITY
1705 Jackson St, Richmond, TX 77469
Phone: (281) 342-2811
Sales: $34,768,000   *Employees:* 363
Company Type: Private   *Employees here:* 330
SIC: 8062
   General hospital
Sam L Steffee, Executive Director

D-U-N-S 04-017-6497
POLYCLINIC
1145 Broadway, Seattle, WA 98122
Phone: (206) 329-1760
Sales: $46,587,000   *Employees:* 423
Company Type: Private   *Employees here:* 423
SIC: 8011
   Primary medical clinic
Lloyd David, Executive Director

D-U-N-S 04-036-6601
POMONA UNIFIED SCHOOL DISTRICT
3530 Pomona Blvd, Pomona, CA 91768
Phone: (909) 595-1221
Sales: $49,400,000   *Employees:* NA
Company Type: Private   *Employees here:* 1,000
SIC: 8062
   Developmental center for the handicapped
Ruth Maples, President

D-U-N-S 07-724-6197
POMONA VALLEY HOSPITAL MED CTR
1798 N Garey Ave, Pomona, CA 91767
Phone: (909) 865-9500
Sales: $196,247,000   *Employees:* 2,209
Company Type: Private   *Employees here:* 2,121
SIC: 8062
   General hospital
Richard E Yochum, President

D-U-N-S 02-979-3770
PONTIAC GENERAL HOSPITAL & MED CTR
461 W Huron St, Pontiac, MI 48341
Phone: (248) 857-7700

Sales: $65,000,000
Company Type: Private
SIC: 8062
   General practice medical hospital
Robert Davis, Chief Executive Officer

Employees: 1,400
Employees here: 1,400

D-U-N-S 01-087-0863
PONTIAC OSTEOPATHIC HOSPITAL
50 N Perry St, Pontiac, MI 48342
Phone: (248) 338-5000
Sales: $97,593,000
Company Type: Private
SIC: 8062
   General osteopathic hospital
Patrick Lamerty, Chief Executive Officer

Employees: 1,300
Employees here: 970

D-U-N-S 61-353-2456
POPLAR BLUFF PHYSICIANS GROUP,
621 Pine Blvd, Poplar Bluff, MO 63901
Phone: (573) 686-4111
Sales: $41,761,000
Company Type: Private
SIC: 8062
   General hospital
Dr Ben Till Md, Chairman of the Board

Employees: 655
Employees here: 650

D-U-N-S 06-883-6915
PORT HURON HOSPITAL
1221 Pine Grove Ave, Port Huron, MI 48060
Phone: (810) 987-5000
Sales: $71,863,000
Company Type: Private
SIC: 8062
   General hospital
Donald C Fletcher, President

Employees: 950
Employees here: 934

D-U-N-S 06-832-1249
PORTAGE HEALTH SYSTEM, INC
200 Michigan St, Hancock, MI 49930
Phone: (906) 487-8000
Sales: $23,044,000
Company Type: Private
SIC: 8062
   General medical and surgical hospital rehabilitation center
     and retail pharmacy
James Bogan, Chief Executive Officer

Employees: 475
Employees here: 288

D-U-N-S 02-066-2292
PORTER HOSPITAL INC
75 South St, Middlebury, VT 5753
Phone: (802) 388-7901
Sales: $21,238,000
Company Type: Private
SIC: 8062
   General hospital
James L Daily, President

Employees: 337
Employees here: 337

D-U-N-S 18-143-5892
PORTER MEMORIAL HOSPITAL
814 La Porte Ave, Valparaiso, IN 46383
Phone: (219) 465-4600
Sales: $129,531,000
Company Type: Private
SIC: 8062
   Hospital and outpatient facilities
Wiley N Carr, President

Employees: 1,600
Employees here: 1,270

D-U-N-S 03-687-8999
PORTERCARE HOSPITAL
2525 S Downing St, Denver, CO 80210
Phone: (303) 778-1955

Sales: $135,433,000
Company Type: Private
SIC: 8062
   General hospital
Ruthita Fike, President

Employees: 2,400
Employees here: 1,670

D-U-N-S 04-980-1640
PORTLAND ADVENTIST MED CTR
10123 SE Market St, Portland, OR 97216
Phone: (503) 257-2500
Sales: $145,500,000
Company Type: Private
SIC: 8062
   General hospital
Larry Dodds, President

Employees: 3,102
Employees here: 1,450

D-U-N-S 13-482-4408
PORTLAND ADVENTIST MED CTR
10123 SE Main St, Portland, OR 97216
Phone: (503) 251-6120
Sales: $86,800,000
Company Type: Private
SIC: 8011
   Medical center
Larry Dodds, President

Employees: NA
Employees here: 1,500

D-U-N-S 07-476-2162
PORTSMOUTH GENERAL HOSPITAL
850 Crawford Pkwy, Portsmouth, VA 23704
Phone: (757) 398-4000
Sales: $36,204,000
Company Type: Private
SIC: 8062
   General hospital/home health service/visiting nurse service
Nora Paffrath, Administrator

Employees: 807
Employees here: 807

D-U-N-S 01-010-0196
POTOMAC HOSPITAL CORPORATION
2300 Opitz Blvd, Woodbridge, VA 22191
Phone: (703) 670-1313
Sales: $77,733,000
Company Type: Private
SIC: 8062
   General medical and surgical hospital
William Moss, President

Employees: 959
Employees here: 959

D-U-N-S 07-550-7442
POTTSTOWN MEMORIAL MED CTR
1600 E High St, Pottstown, PA 19464
Phone: (610) 327-7000
Sales: $75,418,000
Company Type: Private
SIC: 8062
   General hospital
John J Buckley, President

Employees: 1,100
Employees here: 962

D-U-N-S 07-119-5390
POTTSVLLE HOSPITAL WRNE CLINIC INC
420 S Jackson St, Pottsville, PA 17901
Phone: (717) 622-6120
Sales: $44,802,000
Company Type: Private
SIC: 8062
   General hospital
Donald Gintzig, President

Employees: 710
Employees here: 710

D-U-N-S 07-996-2759
POUDRE VALLEY HEALTH CARE INC
1024 S Lemay Ave, Fort Collins, CO 80524
Phone: (970) 495-7000

Sales: $150,442,000   *Employees:* 1,700
Company Type: Private   *Employees here:* 1,700
SIC: 8062
  Hospital
Steve C Ellsworth, Controller

D-U-N-S 10-932-5472
PRAIRIE CRDOVASCULAR CONS LTD
301 N 8th St, Springfield, IL 62701
Phone: (217) 788-0706
Sales: $32,508,000   *Employees:* 150
Company Type: Private   *Employees here:* 124
SIC: 8011
  Medical doctor's office
James T Dove, President

D-U-N-S 15-159-0668
PRAIRIE LAKES HEALTH CARE SYS
400 10th Ave Nw, Watertown, SD 57201
Phone: (605) 882-7000
Sales: $35,000,000   *Employees:* 500
Company Type: Private   *Employees here:* 460
SIC: 8062
  General hospital
Edmond Weiland, Chief Executive Officer

D-U-N-S 11-071-8202
PRATT MEDICAL GROUP, INC
750 Washington St 838, Boston, MA 2111
Phone: (617) 636-5000
Sales: $27,108,000   *Employees:* 33
Company Type: Private   *Employees here:* 33
SIC: 8011
  Physicians office
Dr Jeffrey Gelfand Md, President

D-U-N-S 12-499-8659
PRATT REGIONAL MED CTR CORP
200 Commodore St, Pratt, KS 67124
Phone: (316) 672-7451
Sales: $21,383,000   *Employees:* 288
Company Type: Private   *Employees here:* 282
SIC: 8062
  Hospital & skilled nursing unit
Susan Page, President

D-U-N-S 79-610-4347
PREFERRED CARE, INC
2901 Dallas Pkwy, Plano, TX 75093
Phone: (972) 398-1858
Sales: $50,300,000   *Employees:* 2,700
Company Type: Private   *Employees here:* 4
SIC: 8052
  Health care for mentally retarded & skilled nursing facility
Thomas D Scott, President

D-U-N-S 96-564-7209
PREFERRED HEALTH MANAGEMENT
20700 Ventura Blvd, Woodland Hills, CA 91364
Phone: (818) 346-3500
Sales: $32,000,000   *Employees:* 79
Company Type: Private   *Employees here:* 79
SIC: 8099
 . Health/allied services management services and billing
  services
Lou Spidelette, President

D-U-N-S 15-170-9011
PREFERRED HEALTH NETWORK OF MD
  (Parent: Health Networks Of America)
1099 Winterson Rd Ste 300, Linthicum Heights, MD 21090
Phone: (410) 850-7461

Sales: $67,333,000   *Employees:* 100
Company Type: Private   *Employees here:* 100
SIC: 8011
  Health service
Dr Dennis Batey, President

D-U-N-S 10-803-4505
PREFERRED HEALTH NETWORK INC
  (Parent: Qual-Med Inc)
153 Technology Dr Fl 2, Irvine, CA 92618
Phone: (562) 983-1616
Sales: $24,000,000   *Employees:* 600
Company Type: Private   *Employees here:* 115
SIC: 8099
  Hospital and physician marketing service
Ronald Seibel, President

D-U-N-S 79-713-2123
PREFERRED PLUS OF KANSAS INC
345 Riverview St Ste 103, Wichita, KS 67203
Phone: (316) 268-0390
Sales: $28,936,000   *Employees:* 21
Company Type: Private   *Employees here:* 21
SIC: 8011
  Health maintenance organization
Marlon Dauner, President

D-U-N-S 61-185-6667   EXP
PREMIER BIORESOURCES INC
  (Parent: Nabi)
16500 NW 15th Ave, Miami, FL 33169
Phone: (305) 625-5303
Sales: $24,000,000   *Employees:* NA
Company Type: Public Family Member   *Employees here:* NA
SIC: 8099
  Plasmapheresis center
Alfred J Fernandez, President

D-U-N-S 96-702-2237
PREMIER HEALTHCARE, INC
100 W Claredon 400, Phoenix, AZ 85013
Phone: (602) 248-0404
Sales: $53,506,000   *Employees:* 90
Company Type: Private   *Employees here:* 90
SIC: 8011
  Health maintenance organization
Dr Gerald Marshall Md, President

D-U-N-S 62-113-3628
PREMIERE ASSOC HEALTHCARE SVCS
  (Parent: Premiere Associates Inc)
6000 Meadowbrook Mall Ct, Clemmons, NC 27012
Phone: (336) 712-0444
Sales: $111,599,000   *Employees:* 100
Company Type: Public Family Member   *Employees here:* 60
SIC: 8051
  Nursing home mgmt and ret ancillary products
W S Swain, Chief Executive Officer

D-U-N-S 92-609-4905
PREMIERE ASSOCIATES INC
  (Parent: Integrated Health Services)
6000 Meadowbrook Mall Ct, Clemmons, NC 27012
Phone: (336) 712-0444
Sales: $48,100,000   *Employees:* 2,100
Company Type: Public Family Member   *Employees here:* 60
SIC: 8051
  Holding company
Stewart Swain, Chief Executive Officer

D-U-N-S 79-882-5634
PRESBYTERIAN HEALTHCARE ASSOC
(*Parent:* Novant Health Inc)
1900 Randolph Rd Ste 610, Charlotte, NC 28207
Phone: (704) 384-4920
Sales: $27,400,000 ·   *Employees:* 400
Company Type: Private   *Employees here:* 7
SIC: 8011
  Medical doctor's office
Thomas J Hardy Jr, Director

D-U-N-S 09-937-2005
PRESBYTERIAN HEALTHCARE SVCS
2100 N Dr Martin Luther K, Clovis, NM 88101
Phone: (505) 769-2141
Sales: $25,500,000   *Employees:* NA
Company Type: Private   *Employees here:* 645
SIC: 8062
  General hospital
Dennis Headlee, Manager

D-U-N-S 00-711-4655
PRESBYTERIAN HEALTHCARE SVCS
5901 Harper Dr NE, Albuquerque, NM 87109
Phone: (505) 260-6300
Sales: $580,899,000   *Employees:* 5,800
Company Type: Private   *Employees here:* 90
SIC: 8062
  Medical hospitals
James Hinton, President

D-U-N-S 15-606-4792
PRESBYTERIAN HEALTHCARE SVCS
8300 Constitution NE, Albuquerque, NM 87110
Phone: (505) 291-2000
Sales: $26,900,000   *Employees:* NA
Company Type: Private   *Employees here:* 630
SIC: 8062
  General hospital
Jim Hinton, Principal

D-U-N-S 19-455-5108
PRESBYTERIAN HEALTHCARE SVCS
1100 Central Ave SE, Albuquerque, NM 87106
Phone: (505) 841-1234
Sales: $138,800,000   *Employees:* NA
Company Type: Private   *Employees here:* 3,200
SIC: 8062
  Hospital
James Hinton, President

D-U-N-S 06-746-3950
PRESBYTERIAN HOME INC
3200 Grant St, Evanston, IL 60201
Phone: (847) 492-4800
Sales: $24,675,000   *Employees:* 505
Company Type: Private   *Employees here:* 450
SIC: 8361
  Home for the aged and retirement center
Peter Mulvey, President

D-U-N-S 06-977-9148
PRESBYTERIAN HOMES INC
1217 Slate Hill Rd, Camp Hill, PA 17011
Phone: (717) 737-9700
Sales: $59,676,000   *Employees:* 1,350
Company Type: Private   *Employees here:* 40
SIC: 8052
  Intermediate skilled & residential care for the aged home
    health care services child & elder day care facilities
Stephen Proctor, Chief Executive Officer

D-U-N-S 07-838-8055
PRESBYTERIAN HOSPITAL OF DALLAS
8200 Walnut Hill Ln, Dallas, TX 75231
Phone: (214) 345-6789
Sales: $280,178,000   *Employees:* 2,947
Company Type: Private   *Employees here:* 2,927
SIC: 8062
  Hospital
Douglas Hawthorne, President

D-U-N-S 07-451-7517
PRESBYTERIAN HOSPITAL
200 Hawthorne Ln, Charlotte, NC 28204
Phone: (704) 384-4000
Sales: $270,500,000   *Employees:* 3,100
Company Type: Private   *Employees here:* 3,075
SIC: 8062
  General hospital
Thomas Revels, President

D-U-N-S 08-396-6002
PRESBYTERIAN SENIORCARE
1215 Hulton Rd, Oakmont, PA 15139
Phone: (412) 828-5600
Sales: $45,251,000   *Employees:* 800
Company Type: Private   *Employees here:* 450
SIC: 8051
  Skilled care nursing home personal care boarding homds
    independent elderly housing and congregate independent
    elderly housing
Charles W Pruitt Jr, President

D-U-N-S 18-792-1903
PRESBYTERIAN-ORTHOPEDIC HOSP
1901 Randolph Rd, Charlotte, NC 28207
Phone: (704) 375-6790
Sales: $95,000,000   *Employees:* 475
Company Type: Private   *Employees here:* 450
SIC: 8069
  Specialty hospital
Paul Jenson, Chief Executive Officer

D-U-N-S 07-144-9748
PRESBYTRIAN HMES OF NJ FNDTON
13 Roszel Rd Ste C120, Princeton, NJ 8540
Phone: (609) 987-8900
Sales: $57,608,000   *Employees:* 1,300
Company Type: Private   *Employees here:* 23
SIC: 8059
  Retirement homes with health care
Gary Puma, President

D-U-N-S 05-922-7538
PRESBYTRIAN INTRCOMMUNITY HOSP
12401 Washington Blvd, Whittier, CA 90602
Phone: (562) 698-0811
Sales: $128,329,000   *Employees:* 1,200
Company Type: Private   *Employees here:* 1,000
SIC: 8062
  Hospital
Daniel Adams, President

D-U-N-S 06-965-9480
PRESBYTERIAN RETIREMENT COMMUNITIES
50 W Lucerne Cir, Orlando, FL 32801
Phone: (407) 839-5050
Sales: $52,215,000   *Employees:* 1,300
Company Type: Private   *Employees here:* 30
SIC: 8361
  Homes for the aged
James F Emerson, Chief Executive Officer

D-U-N-S 06-864-7668
PRESENTATION SISTERS INC
800 E 21st St, Sioux Falls, SD 57105
Phone: (605) 322-8000
Sales: $142,641,000   *Employees:* 2,200
Company Type: Private   *Employees here:* 2,100
SIC: 8062
    General medical and surgical hospital
Fredrick W Slunecka, Executive Director

D-U-N-S 14-769-4335
PRESTIGE CARE INC
501 SE Columbia Shores Bl, Vancouver, WA 98661
Phone: (503) 253-9650
Sales: $71,218,000   *Employees:* 1,950
Company Type: Private   *Employees here:* 40
SIC: 8051
    Skilled nursing center & health care facility management
Phillip G Fogg, President

D-U-N-S 07-478-9082
PREVEA CLINIC INC
1551 Dousman St, Green Bay, WI 54303
Phone: (920) 496-4700
Sales: $48,100,000   *Employees:* 700
Company Type: Private   *Employees here:* 100
SIC: 8011
    Medical clinic
John Blackburn, Administrator

D-U-N-S 17-429-1484
PRH, INC.
    (Parent: Park Ridge Health System Inc)
1555 Long Pond Rd, Rochester, NY 14626
Phone: (716) 723-7000
Sales: $27,494,000   *Employees:* 312
Company Type: Private   *Employees here:* 2
SIC: 8071
    Medical laboratory management services ret drugs/sundries
Warren Hern, President

D-U-N-S 95-900-4748
PRIMARY CARE DELIVERY CORP
4017 W Jackson St, Muncie, IN 47304
Phone: (765) 751-3150
Sales: $44,700,000   *Employees:* 650
Company Type: Private   *Employees here:* 500
SIC: 8011
    Medical doctor's office
Robert E Gildersleeve, Executive Director

D-U-N-S 17-442-0653
PRIMARY CARE RESOURCES INC
10060 Regency Cir, Omaha, NE 68114
Phone: (402) 354-1500
Sales: $46,400,000   *Employees:* 675
Company Type: Private   *Employees here:* 300
SIC: 8011
    Physicians' clinic
James Ferrando, Principal

D-U-N-S 07-674-2162
PRIMARY HEALTH SYSTEMS, PA
    (Parent: Primary Health Systems Inc)
4229 Pearl Rd, Cleveland, OH 44109
Phone: (216) 459-6300
Sales: $43,300,000   *Employees:* 940
Company Type: Private   *Employees here:* 818
SIC: 8062
    General hospital
Steven Volla, President

D-U-N-S 11-023-2766
PRIME CARE MEDICAL GROUP
16850 Bear Valley Rd, Victorville, CA 92392
Phone: (760) 241-8000
Sales: $41,200,000   *Employees:* 600
Company Type: Private   *Employees here:* 80
SIC: 8011
    Physician's office & operator of commercial buildings
Dr Prem N Reddy Md, President

D-U-N-S 60-313-4420
PRIME CARE SERVICES INC
    (Parent: Su-Pra Enterprises Inc)
30150 Telg Rd Ste 200, Franklin, MI 48025
Phone: (248) 646-5151
Sales: $20,336,000   *Employees:* 375
Company Type: Private   *Employees here:* 375
SIC: 8082
    Home health care services
Elena Szilvagyi, President

D-U-N-S 87-836-4827
PRIME MEDICAL GROUP, P.C.
1200 Brooks Ln 140, Clairton, PA 15025
Phone: (412) 469-8940
Sales: $25,000,000   *Employees:* 232
Company Type: Private   *Employees here:* 17
SIC: 8011
    Primary medical doctors
James Brooks, President

D-U-N-S 07-521-0088
PRIME MEDICAL SERVICES INC
1301 S Capital Of Texas H, Austin, TX 78746
Phone: (512) 328-2892
Sales: $95,979,000   *Employees:* 350
Company Type: Public   *Employees here:* 30
SIC: 8099
    Lithotripsy & prostatherapy equipment & services
Kennerth S Shifrin, Chairman of the Board

D-U-N-S 07-266-7132
PRINCETON COMMUNITY HOSPITAL ASSN
12th St, Princeton, WV 24740
Phone: (304) 487-7000
Sales: $60,153,000   *Employees:* 1,000
Company Type: Private   *Employees here:* 1,000
SIC: 8062
    Hospital
Dan Dunmyer, Chief Executive Officer

D-U-N-S 96-986-1939
PRINCETON HOSPITAL
1800 Mercy Dr, Orlando, FL 32808
Phone: (407) 295-5151
Sales: $32,080,000   *Employees:* 455
Company Type: Private   *Employees here:* 450
SIC: 8062
    Hospital
Russ Goldberg, Chief Executive Officer

D-U-N-S 60-250-9697
PRINCIPAL HEALTH CARE OF KANS CY
    (Parent: Coventry Health Care Inc)
1001 E 101st Ter Ste 300, Kansas City, MO 64131
Phone: (816) 941-3030
Sales: $107,465,000   *Employees:* 102
Company Type: Private   *Employees here:* 65
SIC: 8011
    Health maintenance organization
Janet Stallmeyer, Executive Director

D-U-N-S 92-645-5429
PRIORITY HEALTH INC
1231 E Beltline Ave NE, Grand Rapids, MI 49525
Phone: (616) 942-0954
Sales: $20,500,000 — *Employees:* 300
Company Type: Private — *Employees here:* 300
SIC: 8011
Medical doctor's office
Kim Horn, Chief Executive Officer

D-U-N-S 09-908-9963
PRISON HEALTH SERVICES INC
(Parent: America Service Group Inc)
105 Westpark Dr Ste 300, Brentwood, TN 37027
Phone: (800) 729-0069
Sales: $206,900,000 — *Employees:* 3,000
Company Type: Public Family Member — *Employees here:* 77
SIC: 8011
Health care service to correctional facilities
Scott L Mercy, Chief Executive Officer

D-U-N-S 07-063-2625
PRIVATE DIAGNOSTIC CLINIC PLLC
Duke University Med Ctr, Durham, NC 27710
Phone: (919) 684-6037
Sales: $150,000,000 — *Employees:* 775
Company Type: Private — *Employees here:* 775
SIC: 8011
Office of physicians
Paul Newman, Executive Director

D-U-N-S 61-471-8807
PRO-WELLNESS HEALTH MGT SVCS
(Parent: Francscan Hlth Sys Of Ohio Vly)
2360 W Dorothy Ln Ste 101, Dayton, OH 45439
Phone: (000) 000-0000
Sales: $24,000,000 — *Employees:* 350
Company Type: Private — *Employees here:* 9
SIC: 8011
Health care services
Ronald Jennings, Executive Director

D-U-N-S 06-741-4284
PROCTOR HOSPITAL
5409 N Knoxville Ave, Peoria, IL 61614
Phone: (309) 691-1000
Sales: $57,422,000 — *Employees:* 1,050
Company Type: Private — *Employees here:* 1,040
SIC: 8062
Hospital
Norman La Conte, President

D-U-N-S 15-479-1545
PROGRESSIVE HOME HEALTH SVC
132 W 31st St, New York, NY 10001
Phone: (212) 273-5500
Sales: $44,600,000 — *Employees:* 2,000
Company Type: Private — *Employees here:* 1,950
SIC: 8059
Provides health services in homes
Elliot Green, President

D-U-N-S 83-855-5647
PROMEDICA PHYSICIAN SUPPORT
5855 Monroe St, Sylvania, OH 43560
Phone: (419) 824-7200
Sales: $39,200,000 — *Employees:* 570
Company Type: Private — *Employees here:* 570
SIC: 8011
Medical doctor's office
Alan Brass, President

D-U-N-S 07-988-6479
PROTESTANT MEMORIAL MED CTR
4500 Memorial Dr, Belleville, IL 62226
Phone: (618) 233-7750
Sales: $126,925,000 — *Employees:* 2,117
Company Type: Private — *Employees here:* 1,975
SIC: 8062
General hospital
Arthur Peters, Chairman of the Board

D-U-N-S 18-566-9918
PROVENA HEALTH
2615 Washington St, Waukegan, IL 60085
Phone: (847) 249-3900
Sales: $45,500,000 — *Employees:* NA
Company Type: Private — *Employees here:* 1,080
SIC: 8062
General hospital skilled nursing care facility
Timothy Selz, President

D-U-N-S 07-914-0372
PROVENA HEALTH
600 Sager Campus, Danville, IL 61832
Phone: (217) 442-6300
Sales: $50,900,000 — *Employees:* NA
Company Type: Private — *Employees here:* 1,300
SIC: 8062
Hospital
Dennis Doran, N/A

D-U-N-S 02-249-2065
PROVENA HOSPITAL
1400 W Park St, Urbana, IL 61801
Phone: (217) 337-2000
Sales: $61,300,000 — *Employees:* NA
Company Type: Private — *Employees here:* 1,450
SIC: 8062
General hospital
Diane Friedman, President

D-U-N-S 02-249-0648
PROVENA HOSPITAL
500 W Court St, Kankakee, IL 60901
Phone: (815) 937-2490
Sales: $43,000,000 — *Employees:* NA
Company Type: Private — *Employees here:* 1,100
SIC: 8062
Hospital

D-U-N-S 07-001-4295
PROVENA HOSPITAL
333 Madison St, Joliet, IL 60435
Phone: (815) 725-7133
Sales: $97,500,000 — *Employees:* NA
Company Type: Private — *Employees here:* 2,300
SIC: 8062
General hospital specialty outpatient clinic
David Benfer, N/A

D-U-N-S 01-022-3071
PROVENA HOSPITAL
77 N Airlite St, Elgin, IL 60123
Phone: (847) 695-3200
Sales: $37,800,000 — *Employees:* NA
Company Type: Private — *Employees here:* 900
SIC: 8062
General hospital
Larry M Narum, President

D-U-N-S 19-461-1950
PROVENA HOSPITAL
812 N Logan Ave, Danville, IL 61832
Phone: (217) 443-5000

Sales: $42,200,000
Company Type: Private
SIC: 8062
   General hospital
Dennis J Doran, Personnel

Employees: NA
Employees here: 1,080

D-U-N-S 02-248-9442
PROVENA HOSPITAL
1325 N Highland Ave, Aurora, IL 60506
Phone: (630) 859-2222
Sales: $37,000,000
Company Type: Private
SIC: 8062
   General & psychiatric hospital

Employees: NA
Employees here: 880

D-U-N-S 01-764-6154
PROVENA SENIOR SERVICES
1475 Harvard Dr, Kankakee, IL 60901
Phone: (815) 937-2034
Sales: $50,000,000
Company Type: Private
SIC: 8052
   Intermediate care facility
Connie March, President

Employees: 1,300
Employees here: 20

D-U-N-S 07-780-3757
PROVIDENCE HOSPITAL
1150 Varnum St NE, Washington, DC 20017
Phone: (202) 269-7000
Sales: $133,432,000
Company Type: Private
SIC: 8062
   General hospital
Sister C Keehan, President

Employees: 1,611
Employees here: 1,611

D-U-N-S 06-883-5206
PROVIDENCE HOSPITAL
16001 W 9 Mile Rd, Southfield, MI 48075
Phone: (248) 424-3000
Sales: $322,343,000
Company Type: Private
SIC: 8062
   General medical & surgical hospital
Bryan Connolly, Chief Executive Officer

Employees: 3,100
Employees here: 2,900

D-U-N-S 07-790-0066
PROVIDENCE HOSPITAL INC
6801 Airport Blvd, Mobile, AL 36608
Phone: (334) 633-1000
Sales: $135,190,000
Company Type: Private
SIC: 8062
   General medical & surgical hospital
John R Roeder, President

Employees: 1,506
Employees here: 1,500

D-U-N-S 06-042-1294
PROVIDENCE HOSPITAL INC
1912 Hayes Ave, Sandusky, OH 44870
Phone: (419) 621-7000
Sales: $42,231,000
Company Type: Private
SIC: 8062
   General hospital
Nancy Linenkugel Sr, President

Employees: 700
Employees here: 485

D-U-N-S 05-708-0087
PROVIDENCE MILWAUKIE HOSPITAL
10150 SE 32nd Ave, Milwaukie, OR 97222
Phone: (503) 513-8300

Sales: $38,326,000
Company Type: Private
SIC: 8062
   General hospital
Russel E Danielson, Administrator

Employees: 272
Employees here: 272

D-U-N-S 13-078-5041
PROVIDENT HEALTH SERVICES INC
   (Parent: Memorial Medical Center Inc)
4700 Waters Ave, Savannah, GA 31404
Phone: (912) 350-8000
Sales: $47,800,000
Company Type: Private
SIC: 8082
   Health care delivery service
Kathy Jones, President

Employees: 3,000
Employees here: NA

D-U-N-S 07-144-8203
PSYCHIATRIC HOSPITALS OF PA
660 Thomas Rd, Lafayette Hill, PA 19444
Phone: (215) 836-7700
Sales: $20,000,000
Company Type: Private
SIC: 8063
   Psychiatric hospital
Dr Nicholas Tenaglia Md, Chairman of the Board

Employees: 350
Employees here: 338

D-U-N-S 07-819-6003
PUBLIC HOSPITAL DISTRICT 1
901 Mt View Dr Bldg 1, Shelton, WA 98584
Phone: (360) 426-1611
Sales: $19,795,000
Company Type: Private
SIC: 8062
   General hospital
George R Appel, Administrator

Employees: 300
Employees here: 300

D-U-N-S 01-019-7556
PUBLIC HOSPITAL DISTRICT 1
1415 E Kincaid St, Mount Vernon, WA 98274
Phone: (360) 424-4111
Sales: $77,325,000
Company Type: Private
SIC: 8062
   General hospital
Patrick R Mahoney, Administrator

Employees: 1,072
Employees here: 1,072

D-U-N-S 07-834-8364
PUEBLO PHYSICIANS PC
2002 Lake Ave, Pueblo, CO 81004
Phone: (719) 560-7181
Sales: $30,000,000
Company Type: Private
SIC: 8011
   Medical doctor's office
Dr Nancy Chuch Md, President

Employees: 195
Employees here: 100

D-U-N-S 09-288-1085
PUGET SOUND BLOOD CTR PROGRAM
921 Terry Ave, Seattle, WA 98104
Phone: (206) 292-6500
Sales: $46,048,000
Company Type: Private
SIC: 8071
   Biological laboratory blood bank & medical research
Peter F Acct, N/A

Employees: 630
Employees here: 350

D-U-N-S 07-474-7197
PULASKI COMMUNITY HOSPITAL
   (Parent: Columbia/Hca Healthcare Corp)
2400 Lee Hwy N, Pulaski, VA 24301
Phone: (540) 980-6822

Sales: $27,683,000
Employees: 450
Company Type: Public Family Member
Employees here: 450
SIC: 8062
  General medical & surgical hospital
Jack Nunley, Chief Executive Officer

D-U-N-S 87-804-7125
PUNTA GORDA HMA INC
  (Parent: Health Management Associates)
809 E Marion Ave, Punta Gorda, FL 33950
Phone: (941) 639-3131
Sales: $38,100,000
Employees: 830
Company Type: Public Family Member
Employees here: 680
SIC: 8062
  General and psychiatric hospital
William J Schoen, Chairman of the Board

D-U-N-S 07-669-6475
PUTNAM HOSPITAL CENTER
666 Stoneleigh Ave, Carmel, NY 10512
Phone: (914) 279-5711
Sales: $48,000,000
Employees: 1,039
Company Type: Private
Employees here: 900
SIC: 8062
  General hospital
Rodney Huebbers, Chief Executive Officer

D-U-N-S 17-519-5700
PCA FAMILY HEALTH PLAN INC
  (Parent: Physician Corp Of America)
6101 Blue Lagoon Dr, Miami, FL 33126
Phone: (305) 267-6633
Sales: $282,653,000
Employees: 1,200
Company Type: Public Family Member
Employees here: 350
SIC: 8011
  Medical doctor's office
Peter Kilissanly, President

D-U-N-S 62-648-7532
PCA HEALTH PLANS OF FLORIDA,
  (Parent: Physician Corp Of America)
6101 Blue Lagoon Dr, Miami, FL 33126
Phone: (305) 267-6633
Sales: $292,034,000
Employees: 1,200
Company Type: Public Family Member
Employees here: 700
SIC: 8011
  Health maintenance organization
Dr E S Kardatzke Md, Chairman of the Board

D-U-N-S 19-410-0582
PCA HEALTH PLANS TEXAS, INC.
  (Parent: Physician Corp Of America)
8303 Mopac Expy Ste 450, Austin, TX 78759
Phone: (512) 338-6100
Sales: $502,406,000
Employees: 580
Company Type: Public Family Member
Employees here: 200
SIC: 8011
  Health maintenance organization
Dr George Smith, Exec Dir

D-U-N-S 10-752-4639
PHC/CHC HOLDINGS INC
  (Parent: Paracelsus Healthcare Corp)
515 W Greens Rd Ste 800, Houston, TX 77067
Phone: (281) 774-5100
Sales: $83,900,000
Employees: 1,800
Company Type: Public
Employees here: 20
SIC: 8062
  Operates general accute care and psychiatric hospitals and
    manages hospitals and operates a nursing care facility
James G Vandevender, President

D-U-N-S 87-808-8269
PHC/CHC HOLDINGS INC
1050 E South Temple, Salt Lake City, UT 84102
Phone: (801) 350-4111
Sales: $31,100,000
Employees: NA
Company Type: Public Family Member
Employees here: 500
SIC: 8011
  Medical center
Kay Matsumura, Administrator

D-U-N-S 07-546-7464
Q H G OF ALABAMA INC
  (Parent: Quorum Health Group Inc)
4370 W Main St, Dothan, AL 36305
Phone: (334) 793-5000
Sales: $143,753,000
Employees: 2,220
Company Type: Public Family Member
Employees here: 1,400
SIC: 8062
  Hospital & home health care service
Keith Granger, President

D-U-N-S 78-536-9927
Q H G OF OHIO, INC
  (Parent: Quorum Health Group Inc)
1492 E Broad St, Columbus, OH 43205
Phone: (614) 251-3000
Sales: $36,700,000
Employees: 800
Company Type: Public Family Member
Employees here: 800
SIC: 8062
  General hospital
James Rieder, Chief Executive Officer

D-U-N-S 78-290-3926
Q H G OF SOUTH CAROLINA INC
  (Parent: Quorum Health Group Inc)
121 E Cedar St, Florence, SC 29506
Phone: (843) 661-3000
Sales: $74,500,000
Employees: 1,600
Company Type: Public Family Member
Employees here: 1,600
SIC: 8062
  Hospital
David Mccellam, Chief Executive Officer

D-U-N-S 36-129-4846
Q P & S CLINIC SC
1025 Maine St, Quincy, IL 62301
Phone: (217) 222-6550
Sales: $43,809,000
Employees: 440
Company Type: Private
Employees here: 400
SIC: 8011
  Medical doctor's office
Ahmad Mahmood, President

D-U-N-S 15-359-3074
QHG OF GADSDEN
  (Parent: Quorum Inc)
1007 Goodyear Ave, Gadsden, AL 35903
Phone: (256) 494-4000
Sales: $85,022,000
Employees: 1,100
Company Type: Public Family Member
Employees here: 1,000
SIC: 8062
  General hospital
William R Spray, President

D-U-N-S 07-349-4676
QUAD CITIES PATHOLOGIST GROUP
1814 E Locust St, Davenport, IA 52803
Phone: (319) 324-0471
Sales: $19,700,000
Employees: 410
Company Type: Private
Employees here: 80
SIC: 8071
  Medical laboratory
Jim King, Executive Director

D-U-N-S 07-821-3980
QUAD-C HEALTH CARE CENTERS
3901 S Fife St, Tacoma, WA 98409
Phone: (253) 474-1100
Sales: $34,456,000   *Employees:* 1,200
Company Type: Private   *Employees here:* 6
SIC: 8051
  Skilled nursing care facilities
William E Chunyk, Partner

D-U-N-S 18-217-0449
QUAL-MED INC
225 N Main St, Pueblo, CO 81003
Phone: (719) 545-3201
Sales: $36,900,000   *Employees:* NA
Company Type: Private   *Employees here:* 600
SIC: 8011
  Managed health care services
Malik Hasan, Branch Manager

D-U-N-S 80-377-7671
QUAL-MED WASHINGTON HEALTH PLAN
  (Parent: Foundation Health Systems Inc)
2331 130th Ave NE Ste 200, Bellevue, WA 98005
Phone: (425) 869-3500
Sales: $140,803,000   *Employees:* 230
Company Type: Private   *Employees here:* 130
SIC: 8011
  Health maintenance organization
Malik M Hasan, Chairman of the Board

D-U-N-S 86-698-8280
QUALITY CARE & REHAB INC
11211 Industriplex Blvd, Baton Rouge, LA 70809
Phone: (225) 295-9000
Sales: $30,000,000   *Employees:* 362
Company Type: Private   *Employees here:* 90
SIC: 8093
  Specialty outpatient clinic & speech & occupational and
    physical therapy
Sandy F Dykes, President

D-U-N-S 11-741-8244
QUALITY HM HLT G CST
1001 Howard Ave, Biloxi, MS 39530
Phone: (228) 374-2273
Sales: $30,000,000   *Employees:* 325
Company Type: Private   *Employees here:* 115
SIC: 8082
  Home health care agency
Eleanor A Rogers, Chief Executive Officer

D-U-N-S 07-412-5881
QUEEN OF ANGELE-HOLLYWOOD PRES
1300 N Vermont Ave, Los Angeles, CA 90027
Phone: (213) 413-3000
Sales: $117,936,000   *Employees:* 1,200
Company Type: Private   *Employees here:* 1,195
SIC: 8062
  General hospital
Sylverster Graff, President

D-U-N-S 80-515-8896
QUEEN OF PEACE HOSPITAL
525 N Foster St, Mitchell, SD 57301
Phone: (605) 996-6531
Sales: $35,282,000   *Employees:* 696
Company Type: Private   *Employees here:* 577
SIC: 8062
  Hospital
Ron Jacobson, Administrator

D-U-N-S 07-169-6868
QUEEN OF THE VALLEY
1000 Trancas St, Napa, CA 94558
Phone: (707) 252-4411
Sales: $84,056,000   *Employees:* 1,200
Company Type: Private   *Employees here:* 750
SIC: 8062
  Hospital
Howard Le Vont, President

D-U-N-S 18-592-1012
QUEEN'S HEALTH SYSTEMS
1099 Alakea St Ste 1100, Honolulu, HI 96813
Phone: (808) 532-6105
Sales: $499,468,000   *Employees:* 334
Company Type: Private   *Employees here:* 51
SIC: 8062
  General medical and surgical hospital
Richard L Griffith, President

D-U-N-S 83-761-6507
QUEENS BLVD EXTNDED CARE FCLTY
6111 Queens Blvd, Woodside, NY 11377
Phone: (718) 205-0287
Sales: $24,000,000   *Employees:* 360
Company Type: Private   *Employees here:* 360
SIC: 8051
  Nursing care facility
Anthony Clemenza, President

D-U-N-S 06-596-0676
QUEENS LONG ISLAND MEDICAL GR
350 S Broadway, Hicksville, NY 11801
Phone: (516) 938-0100
Sales: $50,000,000   *Employees:* 500
Company Type: Private   *Employees here:* 150
SIC: 8011
  Medical health clinic
Dr Eugene Schwalb Md, Executive

D-U-N-S 88-315-4072
QUEENS-LONG ISLAND MED GROUP
106 Eab Plz Fl 12, Uniondale, NY 11556
Phone: (516) 683-0209
Sales: $43,300,000   *Employees:* 630
Company Type: Private   *Employees here:* 630
SIC: 8011
  Medical doctor's office
Dr Eugene Schwalb, Owner

D-U-N-S 07-881-8440   EXP
QUEST DIAGNOSTICS A CAL CORP
  (Parent: Quest Diagnostics Incorporated)
33608 Ortega Hwy, San Juan Capistrano, CA 92675
Phone: (949) 728-4000
Sales: $170,000,000   *Employees:* 1,400
Company Type: Private   *Employees here:* 1,000
SIC: 8071
  Clinical & reference testing laboratory & mfg diagnostic
    testing kits
Kenneth W Freeman, Chairman of the Board

D-U-N-S 01-731-1374
QUEST DIAGNOSTICS INC MICHIGAN
  (Parent: Quest Diagnostics Incorporated)
4444 Giddings Rd, Auburn Hills, MI 48326
Phone: (248) 373-9120
Sales: $125,000,000   *Employees:* 1,350
Company Type: Private   *Employees here:* 600
SIC: 8071
  Medical laboratory
Kenneth Freeman, President

313

D-U-N-S 06-094-1960
QUEST DIAGNOSTICS INCORPORATED
1300 E Newport Center Dr, Deerfield Beach, FL 33442
Phone: (954) 481-3500
Sales: $24,100,000   *Employees:* NA
Company Type: Private   *Employees here:* 165
SIC: 8071
  Medical laboratory
Jim Tanzer, Finance

D-U-N-S 94-957-8447
QUEST DIAGNOSTICS INCORPORATED
415 Massachusetts Ave, Cambridge, MA 2139
Phone: (617) 547-8900
Sales: $41,900,000   *Employees:* NA
Company Type: Private   *Employees here:* 800
SIC: 8071
  Medical lab
Scott Cartier, Controller

D-U-N-S 13-963-2335
QUEST DIAGNOSTICS INCORPORATED
1550 E Gude Dr, Rockville, MD 20850
Phone: (301) 340-9800
Sales: $23,000,000   *Employees:* NA
Company Type: Private   *Employees here:* 500
SIC: 8071
  Medical laboratory
Vernon Wells, Vice-President

D-U-N-S 05-635-4640
QUEST DIAGNOSTICS INCORPORATED
1 Malcolm Ave, Teterboro, NJ 7608
Phone: (201) 393-5000
Sales: $1,528,695,000   *Employees:* 16,300
Company Type: Private   *Employees here:* 2,800
SIC: 8071
  Clinical laboratory testing
Kenneth W Freeman, Chairman of the Board

D-U-N-S 92-714-6845
QUEST DIAGNOSTICS INCORPORATED
1 Malcom Ave, Teterboro, NJ 7608
Phone: (800) 222-0027
Sales: $101,300,000   *Employees:* NA
Company Type: Private   *Employees here:* 2,000
SIC: 8071
  Medical laboratory
Kevin Johnson, Manager

D-U-N-S 17-079-5215
QUEST DIAGNOSTICS INCORPORATED
395 S Youngs Rd, Williamsville, NY 14221
Phone: (716) 633-1671
Sales: $25,900,000   *Employees:* NA
Company Type: Private   *Employees here:* 500
SIC: 8071
  Medical laboratory
Ted Passarelli, Manager

D-U-N-S 83-679-7563
QUEST DIAGNOSTICS INCORPORATED
875 Greentree Rd, Pittsburgh, PA 15220
Phone: (412) 920-7600
Sales: $41,000,000   *Employees:* NA
Company Type: Private   *Employees here:* 800
SIC: 8071
  Medical laboratories
Dr William Tarr, Director

D-U-N-S 08-766-0387
QUEST DIAGNOSTICS INCORPORATED
4771 Regent Blvd, Irving, TX 75063

Phone: (972) 916-3200
Sales: $30,000,000   *Employees:* NA
Company Type: Private   *Employees here:* 700
SIC: 8071
  Medical laboratory
Bill Henser, Branch Manager

D-U-N-S 61-326-0728
QUORUM HEALTH GROUP INC
103 Continental Pl, Brentwood, TN 37027
Phone: (615) 371-7979
Sales: $1,572,352,000   *Employees:* 17,000
Company Type: Public   *Employees here:* 118
SIC: 8062
  Owns operates and manages hospitals
Eugene C Fleming, Chief Operating Officer

D-U-N-S 62-099-4475
QUORUM HEALTH GROUP OF VICKSBURG
  (Parent: Quorum Health Group Inc)
100 McAuley Dr, Vicksburg, MS 39183
Phone: (601) 631-2131
Sales: $46,100,000   *Employees:* 924
Company Type: Public Family Member   *Employees here:* 900
SIC: 8062
  General hospital
Harry Alvis, Administrator

D-U-N-S 61-450-3019
QV INC
322 S Green St Ste 500, Chicago, IL 60607
Phone: (312) 697-8400
Sales: $43,616,000   *Employees:* 1,300
Company Type: Private   *Employees here:* 500
SIC: 8011
  Medical center and provider of medical services
Dean M Harrison, President

D-U-N-S 07-508-9953
R E THOMASON GENERAL HOSPITAL
4815 Alameda Ave, El Paso, TX 79905
Phone: (915) 521-7602
Sales: $164,322,000   *Employees:* 1,420
Company Type: Private   *Employees here:* 1,400
SIC: 8062
  General hospital
Pete Duarte, Chief Executive Officer

D-U-N-S 01-012-0145
R J TAYLOR MEMORIAL HOSPITAL
Macon Hwy, Hawkinsville, GA 31036
Phone: (912) 783-0200
Sales: $22,079,000   *Employees:* 550
Company Type: Private   *Employees here:* 550
SIC: 8062
  General hospital
Dan Maddock, President

D-U-N-S 61-162-4248
RADIOLOGIC SPECIALISTS OF IND
1815 N Capitol Ave, Indianapolis, IN 46202
Phone: (317) 923-3266
Sales: $20,000,000   *Employees:* 55
Company Type: Private   *Employees here:* 55
SIC: 8011
  Radiologist service
James Cairney, Director

D-U-N-S 08-210-6477
RADIOLOGICAL ASSC SACTO MD GP
1800 I St, Sacramento, CA 95814
Phone: (916) 444-0645

Sales: $24,000,000
Company Type: Private
SIC: 8071
 Radiological therapy laboratories diagnostic radiological
  imaging
Dr Michael Norton, President
Employees: 500
Employees here: 90

D-U-N-S 15-163-6586
RADIOLOGY & IMAGING INC
780 Chestnut St, Springfield, MA 1107
Phone: (413) 827-7426
Sales: $20,000,000
Company Type: Private
SIC: 8011
 Physicians' group
Dr Thomas Parker, President
Employees: 118
Employees here: 5

D-U-N-S 15-051-2911
RADIOLOGY ASSOCS TARRANT CNTY
816 W Cannon St, Fort Worth, TX 76104
Phone: (817) 336-8684
Sales: $24,639,000
Company Type: Private
SIC: 8011
 Radiology clinic
Larry Hamilton, President
Employees: 149
Employees here: 62

D-U-N-S 06-061-1282
RADIOLOGY IMAGING ASSOC PC
3333 S Bannock St Ste 600, Englewood, CO 80110
Phone: (303) 761-9190
Sales: $23,515,000
Company Type: Private
SIC: 8011
 Radiologist services
Dr James N Dreisbach Md, President
Employees: 95
Employees here: 50

D-U-N-S 07-514-6969
RAHWAY HOSPITAL
865 Stone St, Rahway, NJ 7065
Phone: (732) 381-4200
Sales: $82,571,000
Company Type: Private
SIC: 8062
 General hospital
Kirk Tice, President
Employees: 935
Employees here: 935

D-U-N-S 03-012-5934
RALEIGH GENERAL HOSPITAL
 (Parent: Columbia/Hca Healthcare Corp)
1710 Harper Rd, Beckley, WV 25801
Phone: (304) 256-4100
Sales: $140,000,000
Company Type: Public Family Member
SIC: 8062
 General hospital
Brent Marsteller, President
Employees: 1,312
Employees here: 930

D-U-N-S 10-206-8442
RAMSAY HEALTH CARE INC
1 Alhambra Plz Ste 750, Coral Gables, FL 33134
Phone: (305) 569-6993
Sales: $136,719,000
Company Type: Public
SIC: 8063
 Psychiatric hospitals
Bert Cibran, President
Employees: 2,100
Employees here: 30

D-U-N-S 07-201-3634
RANDOLPH HOSPITAL INC
364 White Oak St, Asheboro, NC 27203
Phone: (336) 625-5151

Sales: $45,537,000
Company Type: Private
SIC: 8062
 General hospital
Robert E Morrison, Chief Executive Officer
Employees: 596
Employees here: 550

D-U-N-S 06-867-7160
RAPID CITY REGIONAL HOSPITAL
353 Fairmont Blvd, Rapid City, SD 57701
Phone: (605) 341-1000
Sales: $184,151,000
Company Type: Private
SIC: 8062
 Hospital
Adil Ameer, Administrator
Employees: 2,100
Employees here: 1,935

D-U-N-S 06-869-7747
RARITAN BAY MEDICAL CTR A NJ
530 New Brunswick Ave, Perth Amboy, NJ 8861
Phone: (732) 442-3700
Sales: $141,487,000
Company Type: Private
SIC: 8062
 General hospital
Keith H Mc Laughlin, President
Employees: 1,800
Employees here: 1,700

D-U-N-S 11-238-4185
RAVENSWOOD HEALTH CARE CORP
4550 N Winchester Ave, Chicago, IL 60640
Phone: (773) 878-4300
Sales: $139,648,000
Company Type: Private
SIC: 8062
 Hospital outpatient clinic physicians' office commercial
  printing whol medical equipment & provides health care
  insurance
John Blair, President
Employees: 1,800
Employees here: 5

D-U-N-S 06-951-1418
RAVENSWOOD HOSPITAL MED CTR
4550 N Winchester Ave, Chicago, IL 60640
Phone: (773) 878-4300
Sales: $123,047,000
Company Type: Private
SIC: 8062
 General hospital
John E Blair, President
Employees: 1,250
Employees here: 1,100

D-U-N-S 02-420-0511
RAYTEL MEDICAL CORPORATION
2755 Campus Dr Ste 200, San Mateo, CA 94403
Phone: (650) 349-0800
Sales: $83,415,000
Company Type: Public
SIC: 8093
 Pacemaker monitoring & medical imaging centers
Richard Bader, Chairman of the Board
Employees: 827
Employees here: 10

D-U-N-S 01-556-9007
RCG MISSISSIPPI, INC
 (Parent: Renal Care Group Inc)
3925 W Northside Dr, Jackson, MS 39209
Phone: (601) 923-3258
Sales: $22,900,000
Company Type: Public Family Member
SIC: 8092
 Kidney dialysis center
Sam Brooks, President
Employees: 400
Employees here: 15

D-U-N-S 62-009-1892
READING HOSPITAL (INC)
6th & Spruce Sts, Reading, PA 19611
Phone: (610) 378-6000

Sales: $253,578,000   *Employees:* 55
Company Type: Private   *Employees here:* 25
SIC: 8062
  General hospital nursing school commercial operator mental
    counseling administrative laundry and sells equipment
Charles Sullivan, President

D-U-N-S 07-121-4365
READING HOSPITAL & MED CTR INC
6th & Spruce Sts, Reading, PA 19611
Phone: (610) 378-6000
Sales: $169,000,000   *Employees:* 3,600
Company Type: Private   *Employees here:* 3,500
SIC: 8062
  General medical & surgical hospital nursing school and
    operates 25 commercial buildings
Charles Sullivan, President

D-U-N-S 96-874-5281
REBSAMEN REGIONAL MEDICAL CTR
1400 Braden St, Jacksonville, AR 72076
Phone: (501) 982-9515
Sales: $22,800,000   *Employees:* 506
Company Type: Private   *Employees here:* 506
SIC: 8062
  General hospital
Thomas Siemers, Chief Executive Officer

D-U-N-S 03-815-2310
RECCO HOME CARE SERVICE INC
524 Hicksville Rd, Massapequa, NY 11758
Phone: (516) 798-6688
Sales: $24,100,000   *Employees:* 1,500
Company Type: Private   *Employees here:* 850
SIC: 8082
  Home health care service agency
Norma Recco, President

D-U-N-S 07-174-5715
REDINGTON-FAIRVIEW GEN HOSP
10 Fairview Ave, Skowhegan, ME 4976
Phone: (207) 474-5121
Sales: $24,930,000   *Employees:* 430
Company Type: Private   *Employees here:* 430
SIC: 8062
  General medical & surgical hospital
Richard Willett, Chief Executive Officer

D-U-N-S 07-815-6098
REDLANDS COMMUNITY HOSPITAL
350 Terracina Blvd, Redlands, CA 92373
Phone: (909) 335-5500
Sales: $63,418,000   *Employees:* 720
Company Type: Private   *Employees here:* 700
SIC: 8062
  Hospital
James R Holmes, Chief Executive Officer

D-U-N-S 07-810-1755
REDMOND PARK HOSPITAL INC
  (Parent: Columbia/Hca Healthcare Corp)
501 Redmond Rd Nw, Rome, GA 30165
Phone: (706) 291-0291
Sales: $101,539,000   *Employees:* 1,200
Company Type: Public Family Member   *Employees here:* 1,000
SIC: 8062
  General hospital
Charles Fowler, Chairman of the Board

D-U-N-S 18-296-2548
REGENCY HEALTH SERVICES INC
  (Parent: Sun Healthcare Group Inc)
2742 Dow Ave, Tustin, CA 92780

Phone: (714) 544-4443
Sales: $558,050,000   *Employees:* 16,170
Company Type: Public Family Member   *Employees here:* 50
SIC: 8051
  Owns operates and manages skilled nursing care facilities
    institutional pharmacy and home health care
Robert D Woltil, President

D-U-N-S 88-345-2195
REGENCY NURSING CTR OF TEXAS
5606 N Navarro St Ste 211, Victoria, TX 77904
Phone: (512) 576-0694
Sales: $22,106,000   *Employees:* 700
Company Type: Private   *Employees here:* 11
SIC: 8051
  Skilled nursing care facility
Donald Kivowitz, Chairman of the Board

D-U-N-S 07-151-0903
REGINA MEDICAL CENTER
1175 Nininger Rd, Hastings, MN 55033
Phone: (651) 480-4100
Sales: $20,491,000   *Employees:* 475
Company Type: Private   *Employees here:* 475
SIC: 8062
  General hospital skilled nursing facility & assisted living
    facility
Lynn W Olson, Chief Executive Officer

D-U-N-S 07-373-1432
REGIONAL MEDICAL CTR ORANGEBURG CLH CT
3000 Saint Matthews Rd NE, Orangeburg, SC 29118
Phone: (803) 533-2200
Sales: $90,026,000   *Employees:* 1,200
Company Type: Private   *Employees here:* 1,200
SIC: 8062
  General medical and surgical hospital
Thomas Dandridge, President

D-U-N-S 07-800-9404
REGIONAL WEST MEDICAL CENTER
4021 Avenue B, Scottsbluff, NE 69361
Phone: (308) 635-3711
Sales: $56,679,000   *Employees:* 800
Company Type: Private   *Employees here:* 800
SIC: 8062
  General hospital
David M Nitschke, President

D-U-N-S 11-038-0094
REGIONS HOSPITAL
640 Jackson St, Saint Paul, MN 55101
Phone: (651) 221-2810
Sales: $39,900,000   *Employees:* NA
Company Type: Private   *Employees here:* 1,000
SIC: 8041
  Physicians office
Lynn Solem, Manager

D-U-N-S 15-697-4321
REGIONS HOSPITAL
640 Jackson St, Saint Paul, MN 55101
Phone: (651) 221-3456
Sales: $140,700,000   *Employees:* 3,000
Company Type: Private   *Employees here:* 2,900
SIC: 8062
  Hospital
Terry Finzen, President

D-U-N-S 11-421-4281
REHABCARE GROUP
7733 Forsyth Blvd, Saint Louis, MO 63105
Phone: (314) 863-7422

Sales: $160,780,000
Company Type: Public
SIC: 8093
Employees: 1,472
Employees here: 60
Medical rehabilitation services
James M Usdan, President

D-U-N-S 62-640-0139
REHABCLINICS INC
(Parent: Novacare Inc)
1018 W 9th Ave, King Of Prussia, PA 19406
Phone: (610) 992-7600
Sales: $42,700,000
Company Type: Public Family Member
SIC: 8093
Employees: 1,400
Employees here: 18
Out-patient physical therapy services
John H Foster, Chairman of the Board

D-U-N-S 07-660-0253
REHABILITATION ASSOCIATES INC
80 Access Rd, Norwood, MA 2062
Phone: (781) 762-0703
Sales: $20,455,000
Company Type: Private
SIC: 8051
Employees: 600
Employees here: 15
Skilled nursing homes
Nicholas H Thisse, President

D-U-N-S 78-325-5672
REHABILITATION HOSPITAL OF IND
4141 Shore Dr, Indianapolis, IN 46254
Phone: (317) 329-2000
Sales: $23,966,000
Company Type: Private
SIC: 8062
Employees: 461
Employees here: 451
Physical rehabilitation hospital and outpatient services
Suzanne Smith, Chief Financial Officer

D-U-N-S 07-769-9858
REHABILITATION HSPTL PACIFIC
226 N Kuakini St, Honolulu, HI 96817
Phone: (808) 531-3511
Sales: $25,838,000
Company Type: Private
SIC: 8069
Employees: 420
Employees here: 395
Specialty hospital
William O Conner, Chief Executive Officer

D-U-N-S 07-421-7316
REHABILITATION INST OF MICH
261 Mack Ave, Detroit, MI 48201
Phone: (313) 745-1203
Sales: $37,893,000
Company Type: Private
SIC: 8069
Employees: 560
Employees here: 500
Physical medicine and rehab hospital
Dr Bruce Gans Md, President

D-U-N-S 00-600-2026
REHABILITATION SUPPORT SERVICE
2113 Western Ave, Guilderland, NY 12084
Phone: (518) 464-1511
Sales: $21,000,000
Company Type: Private
SIC: 8361
Employees: 516
Employees here: 25
Community based mental health care program
William De Vita, Executive Director

D-U-N-S 80-988-8209
REHABILITY HEALTH SERVICES
(Parent: American Rehability Services)
111 Westwood Pl Ste 210, Brentwood, TN 37027
Phone: (615) 377-2937

Sales: $83,500,000
Company Type: Public Family Member
SIC: 8093
Employees: 2,736
Employees here: 6
Specialty outpatient clinic
Kelly J Gill, President

D-U-N-S 06-847-7546
REHABILITATION INST OF CHICAGO
345 E Superior St, Chicago, IL 60611
Phone: (312) 908-6000
Sales: $41,800,000
Company Type: Private
SIC: 8069
Employees: 850
Employees here: 777
Specialty hospital
Wayne L Dph, President

D-U-N-S 06-942-5916
REHOBOTH MC KINLEY CHRISTIAN
1901 Redrock Dr, Gallup, NM 87301
Phone: (505) 863-7000
Sales: $37,980,000
Company Type: Private
SIC: 8062
Employees: 500
Employees here: 100
General hospital
David Baltezer, President

D-U-N-S 07-204-5032
REID HOSPITAL & HEALTH CARE SVC
1401 Chester Blvd, Richmond, IN 47374
Phone: (765) 983-3000
Sales: $100,261,000
Company Type: Private
SIC: 8062
Employees: 1,200
Employees here: 1,200
General hospital
Barry Macdowell, President

D-U-N-S 79-077-3667
RELIANT CARE GROUP LLC
17 W Lockwood Ave, Saint Louis, MO 63119
Phone: (314) 962-6700
Sales: $35,520,000
Company Type: Private
SIC: 8051
Employees: 1,300
Employees here: 20
Skilled nursing care facility
Joseph A Shepard, Member

D-U-N-S 60-589-8881
RENAISSANCE HEALTHCARE CORP
4720 Old Gettysburg Rd, Mechanicsburg, PA 17055
Phone: (717) 731-0300
Sales: $36,500,000
Company Type: Private
SIC: 8051
Employees: 1,600
Employees here: 24
Management of nursing & outpatient rehabilitation centers
Richard Richardson, Chairman of the Board

D-U-N-S 93-264-7886
RENAL CARE GROUP INC
2100 W End Ave Ste 800, Nashville, TN 37203
Phone: (615) 321-2333
Sales: $140,000,000
Company Type: Public
SIC: 8092
Employees: 175
Employees here: 25
Owner & operator of dialysis equipment
Sam A Brooks, Chairman of the Board

D-U-N-S 19-614-5221
RENAL TREATMENT CENTERS INC
(Parent: Total Renal Care Holdings)
1180 W Swedesford Rd, Berwyn, PA 19312
Phone: (610) 644-4796

Sales: $153,500,000
Company Type: Public Family Member
Employees: 2,687
Employees here: 180
SIC: 8092
Kidney dialysis centers
Robert L Mayer Jr, President

D-U-N-S 82-540-1110
RENEX CORP
2100 Ponce De Leon Blvd, Coral Gables, FL 33134
Phone: (305) 448-2044
Sales: $26,073,000
Company Type: Public
Employees: 250
Employees here: 25
SIC: 8082
Holding company which through subsidiaries operates as a
home health care service and kidney dialysis center
James Shea, President

D-U-N-S 16-143-3800
REPUBLIC HEALTH CORP OF ROCKWALL
(Parent: Tenet Healthcare Corporation)
6800 Scenic Dr, Rowlett, TX 75088
Phone: (972) 412-2273
Sales: $20,400,000
Company Type: Public Family Member
Employees: 455
Employees here: 384
SIC: 8062
General medical & surgical hospital with a skilled nursing
unit home health care and an outpatient clinic
Ken Teel, Administrator

D-U-N-S 15-450-2587
REPUBLIC HEALTH CORP INDANAPOLIS
3232 N Meridian St, Indianapolis, IN 46208
Phone: (317) 924-3392
Sales: $22,800,000
Company Type: Public Family Member
Employees: NA
Employees here: 550
SIC: 8062
Hospital and gift shop
Keith King, Director

D-U-N-S 15-038-3636
REPUBLIC HEALTH CORP INDANAPOLIS
(Parent: Tenet Healthcare Corporation)
3401 W End Ave Ste 700, Nashville, TN 37203
Phone: (615) 383-8599
Sales: $49,387,000
Company Type: Public Family Member
Employees: 600
Employees here: 3
SIC: 8062
General hospital
Charles Martin, Chief Executive Officer

D-U-N-S 07-022-6105
RES-CARE INC
10140 Linn Station Rd, Louisville, KY 40223
Phone: (502) 394-2100
Sales: $306,054,000
Company Type: Public
Employees: 11,900
Employees here: 155
SIC: 8052
Operates and manages intermediate care facilities and
supported living facilities and operates vocational training
centers
Ronald G Geary, Chairman of the Board

D-U-N-S 07-625-2659
RESEARCH MEDICAL CENTER
2316 E Meyer Blvd, Kansas City, MO 64132
Phone: (816) 276-4000
Sales: $112,300,000
Company Type: Private
Employees: 2,400
Employees here: 2,300
SIC: 8062
General hospital
Dan Anderson, President

D-U-N-S 13-105-2599
RESPONSE ONCOLOGY INC
1775 Moriah Woods Blvd, Memphis, TN 38117
Phone: (901) 761-7000
Sales: $101,920,000
Company Type: Public
Employees: 400
Employees here: 50
SIC: 8093
Cancer outpatient centers
Dr William H West Md, Chairman of the Board

D-U-N-S 03-089-5031
REST HAVEN CONVLSNT HM
16250 Prince Dr, South Holland, IL 60473
Phone: (708) 877-4800
Sales: $28,453,000
Company Type: Private
Employees: 900
Employees here: 20
SIC: 8051
Skilled nursing care facilities & retirement homes for the
aged
Richard C Schutt, Chief Executive Officer

D-U-N-S 06-747-6903
RESURRECTION HEALTH CARE CORP
7435 W Talcott Ave, Chicago, IL 60631
Phone: (773) 774-8000
Sales: $354,483,000
Company Type: Private
Employees: 5,200
Employees here: 2,000
SIC: 8062
General hospital
Sister V Cr, Chairman of the Board

D-U-N-S 83-662-5541
REVIVAL HOME HEALTH CARE INC
3609 13th Ave, Brooklyn, NY 11218
Phone: (718) 853-3131
Sales: $20,094,000
Company Type: Private
Employees: 400
Employees here: 50
SIC: 8082
Home health care services
Jacob Spitzer, President

D-U-N-S 05-851-8267
REX HOSPITAL
4420 Lake Boone Trl, Raleigh, NC 27607
Phone: (919) 783-3100
Sales: $197,829,000
Company Type: Private
Employees: 2,900
Employees here: 2,900
SIC: 8062
Hospital
Susan B Lewellen, Chief Operating Officer

D-U-N-S 01-044-9650
REYNOLD'S MEMORIAL HOSPITAL
800 Wheeling Ave, Glen Dale, WV 26038
Phone: (304) 845-3211
Sales: $24,692,000
Company Type: Private
Employees: 550
Employees here: 550
SIC: 8062
General hospital
John Sicurella, Chief Executive Officer

D-U-N-S 61-814-2889
RHD MEMORIAL MEDICAL CENTER
7 Medical Pkwy, Dallas, TX 75234
Phone: (972) 888-7278
Sales: $21,300,000
Company Type: Private
Employees: 475
Employees here: 475
SIC: 8062
General hospital
Thomas Casady, President

D-U-N-S 07-571-0996
RHODE ISLAND HOSPITAL
593 Eddy St, Providence, RI 2903
Phone: (401) 444-4000
Sales: $427,290,000   *Employees:* 4,133
Company Type: Private   *Employees here:* 4,133
SIC: 8062
  General hospital
Steven Baron, President

D-U-N-S 01-033-7533
RICE MEMORIAL HOSPITAL
301 Becker Ave SW, Willmar, MN 56201
Phone: (320) 235-4543
Sales: $48,578,000   *Employees:* 800
Company Type: Private   *Employees here:* 650
SIC: 8062
  Hospital
Lawrence J Massa, Chief Executive Officer

D-U-N-S 06-897-0367
RICHARDSON HOSPITAL AUTHORITY
401 W Campbell Rd, Richardson, TX 75080
Phone: (972) 231-1441
Sales: $49,199,000   *Employees:* 624
Company Type: Private   *Employees here:* 600
SIC: 8062
  General hospital
Ron Boring, President

D-U-N-S 61-464-1066
RICHMOND IMGING AFFILIATES LTD
2900 Richmond Ave, Houston, TX 77098
Phone: (713) 512-6000
Sales: $29,000,000   *Employees:* 120
Company Type: Private   *Employees here:* 120
SIC: 8011
  Imaging & diagnostic services
Dr George Allibone Md, General Partner

D-U-N-S 07-451-7954
RICHMOND MEMORIAL HOSPITAL,
925 S Long Dr, Rockingham, NC 28379
Phone: (910) 417-3000
Sales: $36,839,000   *Employees:* 516
Company Type: Private   *Employees here:* 448
SIC: 8062
  General hospital
David G Hohl, Chief Executive Officer

D-U-N-S 07-162-7178
RIDDLE MEMORIAL HOSPITAL
1068 W Baltimore Pike, Media, PA 19063
Phone: (610) 566-9400
Sales: $68,402,000   *Employees:* 1,094
Company Type: Private   *Employees here:* 1,081
SIC: 8062
  General hospital
Donald L Laughlin, President

D-U-N-S 07-611-9791
RIDEOUT MEMORIAL HOSPITAL
726 4th St, Marysville, CA 95901
Phone: (530) 742-7381
Sales: $55,719,000   *Employees:* 600
Company Type: Private   *Employees here:* 550
SIC: 8062
  General hospital
Thomas P Hayes, Chief Executive Officer

D-U-N-S 06-668-8011
RIDGECREST REGIONAL HOSPITAL
1081 N China Lake Blvd, Ridgecrest, CA 93555

Phone: (760) 446-3551
Sales: $25,013,000   *Employees:* 342
Company Type: Private   *Employees here:* 342
SIC: 8062
  General hospital
David A Mechtenberg, Chief Executive Officer

D-U-N-S 01-092-8740
RIDGEVIEW MEDICAL CENTER
500 S Maple St, Waconia, MN 55387
Phone: (612) 446-1200
Sales: $24,600,000   *Employees:* 545
Company Type: Private   *Employees here:* 540
SIC: 8062
  General hospital
John Devins, President

D-U-N-S 18-687-1018
RIO GRANDE HMO INC
  (Parent: Blue Cross Blue Sheld Of Txas)
4150 Pinnacle St Ste 203, El Paso, TX 79902
Phone: (915) 542-1547
Sales: $132,448,000   *Employees:* 37
Company Type: Private   *Employees here:* 32
SIC: 8011
  (hmo) health maintenance organization
Larry Bowermon, President

D-U-N-S 07-840-6154
RIVER DISTRICT HOSPITAL
4100 S River Rd, East China, MI 48054
Phone: (810) 329-7111
Sales: $23,641,000   *Employees:* 400
Company Type: Private   *Employees here:* 375
SIC: 8062
  General medical & surgical hospital
Frank W Poma, Administrator

D-U-N-S 18-659-0881
RIVER OAKS HOSPITAL INC
1030 River Oaks Dr, Jackson, MS 39208
Phone: (601) 932-1030
Sales: $85,254,000   *Employees:* 480
Company Type: Private   *Employees here:* 400
SIC: 8062
  Hospital
Robert Hammond, President

D-U-N-S 17-251-4655
RIVER PARK HOSPITAL ASSOC L P
  (Parent: Columbia/Hca Healthcare Corp)
1559 Sparta St, Mc Minnville, TN 37110
Phone: (931) 815-4000
Sales: $55,000,000   *Employees:* 320
Company Type: Public Family Member   *Employees here:* 320
SIC: 8062
  Hospital
Terry Gunn, Administrator

D-U-N-S 07-606-6299
RIVERSIDE COMMUNITY HEALTH
  (Parent: Columbia/Hca Healthcare Corp)
4445 Magnolia Ave, Riverside, CA 92501
Phone: (909) 788-3100
Sales: $220,000,000   *Employees:* 1,100
Company Type: Public Family Member   *Employees here:* 1,100
SIC: 8062
  General hospital
Jeff Winters, Chief Executive Officer

D-U-N-S 04-306-3478
RIVERSIDE HEALTH SYSTEMS INC
2622 W Central Ave, Wichita, KS 67203
Phone: (316) 946-5000

Sales: $27,200,000   *Employees:* 600
Company Type: Private   *Employees here:* 450
SIC: 8062
  Hospital
Robert Dixon, President

D-U-N-S 15-449-0619
RIVERSIDE HOSPITAL INC
500 J Clyde Morris Blvd, Newport News, VA 23601
Phone: (757) 594-2000
Sales: $164,300,000   *Employees:* 3,500
Company Type: Private   *Employees here:* 2,995
SIC: 8062
  General hospital
Gerald R Brink, President

D-U-N-S 07-142-9765
RIVERSIDE MEDICAL CENTER
350 N Wall St, Kankakee, IL 60901
Phone: (815) 933-1671
Sales: $91,903,000   *Employees:* 1,350
Company Type: Private   *Employees here:* 1,200
SIC: 8062
  General hospital
Dennis C Millirons, President

D-U-N-S 15-415-8760
RIVERSIDE REST HOME
276 County Farm Rd, Dover, NH 3820
Phone: (603) 742-1348
Sales: $24,208,000   *Employees:* 322
Company Type: Private   *Employees here:* 322
SIC: 8361
  Rest home
Raymond F Bower, Administrator

D-U-N-S 07-478-3291
RIVERVIEW HOSPITAL ASSN
410 Dewey St, Wisconsin Rapids, WI 54494
Phone: (715) 423-6060
Sales: $33,638,000   *Employees:* 600
Company Type: Private   *Employees here:* 475
SIC: 8062
  General hospital
Celse Berard, President

D-U-N-S 07-204-8481
RIVERVIEW HOSPITAL
395 Westfield Rd, Noblesville, IN 46060
Phone: (317) 773-0760
Sales: $51,385,000   *Employees:* 750
Company Type: Private   *Employees here:* 750
SIC: 8062
  General hospital
Seward A Horner, Administrator

D-U-N-S 07-210-5984
RIVERVIEW REGIONAL MEDICAL CTR
600 S 3rd St, Gadsden, AL 35901
Phone: (256) 543-5200
Sales: $29,600,000   *Employees:* 650
Company Type: Private   *Employees here:* 650
SIC: 8062
  General medical & surgical hospital
William J Schoen, Chairman of the Board

D-U-N-S 86-762-3944
RIVINGTON HSE HEALTH CARE FCILTY
45 Rivington St, New York, NY 10002
Phone: (212) 924-1120

Sales: $38,052,000   *Employees:* 350
Company Type: Private   *Employees here:* 350
SIC: 8059
  Nursing/personal care facility
Franklin Diaz, Administrator

D-U-N-S 07-367-5530
HURLBUT, ROBERT H
11 Goodman St S, Rochester, NY 14607
Phone: (716) 424-4770
Sales: $22,700,000   *Employees:* 1,000
Company Type: Private   *Employees here:* 175
SIC: 8051
  Skilled nursing facility
Robert H Hurlbut, Owner

D-U-N-S 06-959-8332
ROBERT PACKER HOSPITAL INC
Guthrie Sq, Sayre, PA 18840
Phone: (717) 888-6666
Sales: $99,023,000   *Employees:* 1,300
Company Type: Private   *Employees here:* 1,270
SIC: 8062
  General hospital
Russell Knight, President

D-U-N-S 07-551-6435
ROBERT WOOD JOHNSON UNIV HOSP
1 Hamilton Health Pl, Trenton, NJ 8690
Phone: (609) 586-7900
Sales: $46,244,000   *Employees:* 600
Company Type: Private   *Employees here:* 599
SIC: 8062
  General hospital
Christie Stephenson, Chief Administrator

D-U-N-S 02-078-4906
ROBERT WOOD JOHNSON UNIV HOSP
1 Robert Wood Johnson Pl, New Brunswick, NJ 8901
Phone: (732) 828-3000
Sales: $265,497,000   *Employees:* 3,100
Company Type: Private   *Employees here:* 2,830
SIC: 8062
  Hospital
Harvey Holzberg, President

D-U-N-S 07-777-9304
ROBINSON MEMORIAL HOSPITAL
6847 N Chestnut St, Ravenna, OH 44266
Phone: (330) 297-0811
Sales: $141,000,000   *Employees:* 974
Company Type: Private   *Employees here:* 959
SIC: 8062
  Hospital
Stephen Colecchi, President

D-U-N-S 08-599-1412
ROCHESTER AREA HEALTH MN ORG
  (Parent: Preferred Care Inc)
259 Monroe Ave, Rochester, NY 14607
Phone: (716) 325-3920
Sales: $282,612,000   *Employees:* 300
Company Type: Private   *Employees here:* 300
SIC: 8011
  Health maintenance organization
John Urban, President

D-U-N-S 07-367-2172
ROCHESTER GEN LONG TERM CARE
1550 Empire Blvd, Webster, NY 14580
Phone: (716) 671-4300

Sales: $19,979,000
Company Type: Private
SIC: 8051
  Skilled nursing home
Meg Bills, Administrator

Employees: 410
Employees here: 410

D-U-N-S 04-307-8385
ROCHESTER GENERAL HOSPITAL
1425 Portland Ave, Rochester, NY 14621
Phone: (716) 338-4170
Sales: $252,015,000
Company Type: Private
SIC: 8062
  General hospital
Dr Richard Constantino, President

Employees: 3,100
Employees here: 2,700

D-U-N-S 07-179-0372
ROCHESTER METHODIST HOSPITAL
200 1st St SW, Rochester, MN 55902
Phone: (507) 286-7890
Sales: $137,777,000
Company Type: Private
SIC: 8062
  Hospital
Dr Robert R Waller Md, President

Employees: 1,400
Employees here: 1,400

D-U-N-S 04-307-7668
ROCHESTER ST MARY'S HOSPITAL
89 Genesee St, Rochester, NY 14611
Phone: (716) 464-3000
Sales: $89,924,000
Company Type: Private
SIC: 8062
  General medical & surgical hospital
Stewart Putnam, President

Employees: 1,415
Employees here: 1,300

D-U-N-S 10-220-9285
ROCK COUNTY
3530 N Cnty Turnk Hwy F, Janesville, WI 53545
Phone: (608) 755-2017
Sales: $25,200,000
Company Type: Private
SIC: 8011
  Medical doctor's office
Terry A Scieszinski, N/A

Employees: NA
Employees here: 400

D-U-N-S 17-087-2626
ROCKAWAY HOME ATTENDANT SVCS
1603 Central Ave, Far Rockaway, NY 11691
Phone: (718) 471-5800
Sales: $21,000,000
Company Type: Private
SIC: 8082
  Home care service
Ade Adejunmobi, Executive Director

Employees: 1,200
Employees here: 1,200

D-U-N-S 87-929-0963
ROCKDALE HEALTH SYSTEM INC
1412 Milstead Ave NE, Conyers, GA 30012
Phone: (770) 918-3000
Sales: $30,600,000
Company Type: Private
SIC: 8062
  Health system
Nelson Toebbe, President

Employees: 671
Employees here: 671

D-U-N-S 03-005-1460
ROCKDALE HOSPITAL INC
1412 Milstead Ave NE, Conyers, GA 30012
Phone: (770) 918-3000

Sales: $57,347,000
Company Type: Private
SIC: 8062
  General medical and surgical hospital
Nelson Toebbee, President

Employees: 670
Employees here: 670

D-U-N-S 86-709-2603
ROCKFORD HEALTH SYSTEMS INC
2400 N Rockton Ave, Rockford, IL 61103
Phone: (815) 968-6861
Sales: $319,248,000
Company Type: Private
SIC: 8062
  Hospitals medical clinics managed care home health services
   and billing services
Thomas D De Fauw, President

Employees: 1,136
Employees here: 15

D-U-N-S 02-580-3297
ROCKFORD MEMORIAL HEALTH SVCS
  (Parent: Rockford Health Systems Inc)
2300 N Rockton Ave, Rockford, IL 61103
Phone: (815) 968-0051
Sales: $110,390,000
Company Type: Private
SIC: 8011
  Medical clinics/hmo's
Jack Zilavy, President

Employees: 735
Employees here: 635

D-U-N-S 07-457-8949
ROCKFORD MEMORIAL HOSPITAL
2400 N Rockton Ave, Rockford, IL 61103
Phone: (815) 968-6861
Sales: $174,884,000
Company Type: Private
SIC: 8062
  General hospital and physician offices
Tom Defauw, Chief Executive Officer

Employees: 2,800
Employees here: 2,500

D-U-N-S 06-600-1892
ROCKINGHAM MEMORIAL HOSPITAL
235 Cantrell Ave, Harrisonburg, VA 22801
Phone: (540) 433-4100
Sales: $101,039,000
Company Type: Private
SIC: 8062
  General hospital
T C Melton Jr, President

Employees: 1,465
Employees here: 1,390

D-U-N-S 06-926-3028
ROCKVILLE GENERAL HOSPITAL INC
31 Union St, Vernon Rockville, CT 6066
Phone: (860) 872-0501
Sales: $45,617,000
Company Type: Private
SIC: 8062
  General hospital
Dave Stahealski, Executive

Employees: 600
Employees here: 580

D-U-N-S 07-039-3079
ROCKWOOD CLINIC P.S.
400 E 5th Ave, Spokane, WA 99202
Phone: (509) 838-2531
Sales: $82,000,000
Company Type: Private
SIC: 8011
  Medical clinic
William Poppy, Administrator

Employees: 579
Employees here: 392

D-U-N-S 07-568-7665
ROGER WILLIAMS HOSPITAL
825 Chalkstone Ave, Providence, RI 2908
Phone: (401) 456-2000

Sales: $93,228,000
Company Type: Private
SIC: 8062
   General hospital
Thomas Slowey, Chief Financial Officer

Employees: 1,273
Employees here: 1,253

D-U-N-S 05-360-6844
ROGUE VALLEY MEDICAL CENTER
   (Parent: Asante)
2825 E Barnett Rd, Medford, OR 97504
Phone: (541) 608-4900
Sales: $128,264,000
Company Type: Private
SIC: 8062
   General hospital
Jon K Mitchell, President

Employees: 1,778
Employees here: 1,778

D-U-N-S 92-617-8229
ROME MEMORIAL HOSPITAL
1500 N James St, Rome, NY 13440
Phone: (315) 338-7020
Sales: $44,327,000
Company Type: Private
SIC: 8062
   Hospital & skilled nursing facility
Alvin White, Chief Executive Officer

Employees: 900
Employees here: 900

D-U-N-S 78-289-3754
ROPER CAREALLIANCE INC
315 Calhoun St Ste 107, Charleston, SC 29401
Phone: (843) 724-2915
Sales: $242,546,000
Company Type: Private
SIC: 8099
   Medical services organization
James Rogers, President

Employees: 40
Employees here: 40

D-U-N-S 07-799-0729
ROPER HOSPITAL INC
316 Calhoun St, Charleston, SC 29401
Phone: (843) 724-2000
Sales: $239,304,000
Company Type: Private
SIC: 8062
   Hospital
Harrison F Trammell, Chief Executive Officer

Employees: 3,500
Employees here: 3,500

D-U-N-S 07-804-6802
ROPER HOSPITAL NORTH
2750 Speissegger Dr, North Charleston, SC 29405
Phone: (843) 744-2110
Sales: $242,546,000
Company Type: Private
SIC: 8062
   Operates a general medical and surgical hospital
Ed Berdick, Chief Executive Officer

Employees: 305
Employees here: 305

D-U-N-S 05-898-9229
ROSE CARE, INC
7 Halsted Cir, Rogers, AR 72756
Phone: (501) 636-5716
Sales: $39,163,000
Company Type: Private
SIC: 8052
   Nursing home
J T Rose, Chairman of the Board

Employees: 1,500
Employees here: 20

D-U-N-S 07-645-3356
ROSE MEDICAL CENTER, INC.
   (Parent: Columbia/Hca Healthcare Corp)
4567 E 9th Ave, Denver, CO 80220
Phone: (303) 320-2121

Sales: $138,593,000
Company Type: Public Family Member
SIC: 8062
   General hospital
Phil Kalin, President

Employees: 1,325
Employees here: 1,300

D-U-N-S 06-745-6863
ROSELAND COMMUNITY HOSPITAL ASSN
45 W 111th St, Chicago, IL 60628
Phone: (773) 995-3000
Sales: $20,600,000
Company Type: Private
SIC: 8062
   General medical & surgical hospital
Oliver Krage, President

Employees: 460
Employees here: 440

D-U-N-S 62-061-5997
ROSEWOOD CARE CENTER HOLDG CO
11701 Borman Dr Ste 315, Saint Louis, MO 63146
Phone: (314) 994-9070
Sales: $22,700,000
Company Type: Private
SIC: 8051
   Skilled nursing home
Larry V Maten, President

Employees: 1,000
Employees here: 3

D-U-N-S 92-603-9637
ROSEWOOD MEDICAL CENTER INC
   (Parent: Medical Care International)
9200 Westheimer Rd, Houston, TX 77063
Phone: (713) 780-7900
Sales: $51,569,000
Company Type: Public Family Member
SIC: 8062
   General hospital
Maura Walsh, Chief Executive Officer

Employees: 425
Employees here: 425

D-U-N-S 07-105-6535
ROWAN REGIONAL MEDICAL CTR INC
612 Mocksville Ave, Salisbury, NC 28144
Phone: (704) 638-1000
Sales: $87,376,000
Company Type: Private
SIC: 8062
   General hospital
James Freeman, Chief Executive Officer

Employees: 979
Employees here: 979

D-U-N-S 06-988-8634
ROXBOROUGH MEMORIAL HOSPITAL
5800 Ridge Ave, Philadelphia, PA 19128
Phone: (215) 483-9900
Sales: $43,601,000
Company Type: Private
SIC: 8062
   Hospital
John J Donnelly Jr, President

Employees: 604
Employees here: 604

D-U-N-S 92-951-2341
ROYCO INC
831 NW 57th St, Fort Lauderdale, FL 33309
Phone: (954) 938-0999
Sales: $20,000,000
Company Type: Private
SIC: 8071
   Blood testing laboratory for kidney dialysis
Kent F Mahlke, Vice-President

Employees: 200
Employees here: 200

D-U-N-S 07-208-5236
RUSH MEDICAL FOUNDATION INC
1314 19th Ave, Meridian, MS 39301
Phone: (601) 483-0011

Sales: $48,700,000   *Employees:* 1,055
Company Type: Private   *Employees here:* 485
SIC: 8062
  General hospital
J C Mc Elroy Jr, Chief Executive Officer

D-U-N-S 07-689-1688
RUSH NORTH SHORE MEDICAL CTR
9600 Gross Point Rd, Skokie, IL 60076
Phone: (847) 677-9600
Sales: $93,073,000   *Employees:* 1,179
Company Type: Private   *Employees here:* 1,098
SIC: 8062
  General hospital
John S Frigo, President

D-U-N-S 82-658-8600
RUSH PRUDENTIAL HEALTH PLANS
233 S Wacker Dr Ste 3900, Chicago, IL 60606
Phone: (312) 234-7000
Sales: $85,000,000   *Employees:* 1,234
Company Type: Private   *Employees here:* 734
SIC: 8011
  Provides insurance through subsidiaries
Barbara Hill, President

D-U-N-S 80-835-1118
RUSH PRUDENTIAL INSURANCE CO
  (Parent: Rush Prudential Health Plans)
233 S Wacker Dr Ste 3900, Chicago, IL 60606
Phone: (312) 234-7000
Sales: $85,546,000   *Employees:* 4
Company Type: Private   *Employees here:* 4
SIC: 8011
  Point of service health insurance
Barbara Hill, President

D-U-N-S 06-861-0245
RUSH-PRESBY ST LUKES MED CTR
1653 W Congress Pkwy, Chicago, IL 60612
Phone: (312) 942-5000
Sales: $482,701,000   *Employees:* 8,500
Company Type: Private   *Employees here:* 7,000
SIC: 8062
  General hospital
Dr Leo M Henikoff Md, President

D-U-N-S 07-544-8498
RUSSELL HOSPITAL CORP
3368 Highway 280, Alexander City, AL 35010
Phone: (256) 329-7100
Sales: $31,209,000   *Employees:* 360
Company Type: Private   *Employees here:* 330
SIC: 8062
  Hospital
Frank Harris, President

D-U-N-S 07-449-5987
RUTHERFORD HOSPITAL INC
288 S Ridgecrest Ave, Rutherfordton, NC 28139
Phone: (828) 286-5000
Sales: $50,742,000   *Employees:* 850
Company Type: Private   *Employees here:* 672
SIC: 8062
  General hospital
Robert D Jones, President

D-U-N-S 06-053-1506
RUTLAND HOSPITAL INC
160 Allen St, Rutland, VT 5701
Phone: (802) 775-7111

Sales: $68,231,000   *Employees:* 1,000
Company Type: Private   *Employees here:* 1,000
SIC: 8062
  General medical and surgical hospital
Tom Huebner, Chief Executive Officer

D-U-N-S 60-538-8727
RUTLAND NURSING HOME INC
585 Schenectady Ave, Brooklyn, NY 11203
Phone: (718) 604-5000
Sales: $52,679,000   *Employees:* 725
Company Type: Private   *Employees here:* 725
SIC: 8051
  Skilled nursing care facility
Milton Gutman, Executive Director

D-U-N-S 62-066-5323
RWJ HEALTHCARE CORP
1 Robert Wood Johnson Pl, New Brunswick, NJ 8901
Phone: (732) 828-3000
Sales: $112,800,000   *Employees:* NA
Company Type: Private   *Employees here:* NA
SIC: 8062
  General hospital
Harvey A Holzberg, President

D-U-N-S 08-739-7576
RYAN WILLIAM F COMMUNITY HEALTH CTR
110 W 97th St, New York, NY 10025
Phone: (212) 316-7937
Sales: $28,079,000   *Employees:* 142
Company Type: Private   *Employees here:* 140
SIC: 8099
  Health/allied services
Barbra E Minch, Chief Executive Officer

D-U-N-S 07-384-3690
S C ADVANCED HEALTHCARE
3003 W Good Hope Rd, Milwaukee, WI 53209
Phone: (414) 352-3100
Sales: $55,000,000   *Employees:* 800
Company Type: Private   *Employees here:* 525
SIC: 8011
  Medical clinic
Dr Eugene W Monroe Md, President

D-U-N-S 18-067-0523
S C CAL
  (Parent: Tenet Health System Hospitals)
2900 S Loop 256, Palestine, TX 75801
Phone: (903) 731-1000
Sales: $32,281,000   *Employees:* 400
Company Type: Public Family Member   *Employees here:* 400
SIC: 8062
  General hospital
Larry Bozeman, Chief Executive Officer

D-U-N-S 92-669-4886
S L C O INC
  (Parent: Columbia/Hca Healthcare Corp)
13855 E 14th St, San Leandro, CA 94578
Phone: (510) 357-6500
Sales: $50,429,000   *Employees:* 600
Company Type: Public Family Member   *Employees here:* 600
SIC: 8062
  Acute care hospital
Kelly Mather, Chief Executive Officer

D-U-N-S 85-871-7085
S N F PROPERTIES, INC
  (Parent: Pleasant Care Corporation)
2258 Foothill Blvd, La Canada, CA 91011
Phone: (818) 248-9808

Sales: $20,400,000
Employees: 900
Company Type: Private
Employees here: 25
SIC: 8051
  Skilled nursing care facility
Emmanuel Bernabe, President

D-U-N-S 07-489-0476
S P ACQUISITION CORP
  (Parent: Columbia/Hca Healthcare Corp)
210 12th St, South Pittsburg, TN 37380
Phone: (423) 837-6781
Sales: $48,000,000
Employees: 170
Company Type: Public Family Member
Employees here: 143
SIC: 8062
  General medical & surgical hospital
Phil Rowland, President

D-U-N-S 16-138-7360
SAAD ENTERPRISES INC
6207 Cottage Hill Rd, Mobile, AL 36609
Phone: (334) 380-3800
Sales: $43,136,000
Employees: 1,000
Company Type: Private
Employees here: 25
SIC: 8082
  Home healthcare services
Dorothy S Saad, President

D-U-N-S 85-995-4182
SAAD ENTERPRISES INC
3725 Airport Blvd Ste 180, Mobile, AL 36608
Phone: (334) 343-9600
Sales: $20,000,000
Employees: NA
Company Type: Private
Employees here: 1,400
SIC: 8049
  Home healthcare services
Barbara Matty, Manager

D-U-N-S 13-965-3687
SAAD HEALTHCARE SERVICES, INC
  (Parent: Saad Enterprises Inc)
3725 Airport Blvd, Mobile, AL 36608
Phone: (334) 343-9600
Sales: $31,100,000
Employees: 800
Company Type: Private
Employees here: 550
SIC: 8082
  Home nursing service
Barbara Fulgham, Director

D-U-N-S 06-974-9448
SABINE VALLEY CENTER
107 Woodbine Pl, Longview, TX 75601
Phone: (903) 758-2471
Sales: $21,023,000
Employees: 550
Company Type: Private
Employees here: 80
SIC: 8093
  Mental health center
Inman White, Executive Director

D-U-N-S 07-377-4952
SACRAMENTO MEDICAL FOUNDATION
1625 Stockton Blvd, Sacramento, CA 95816
Phone: (916) 456-1500
Sales: $32,253,000
Employees: 315
Company Type: Private
Employees here: 260
SIC: 8099
  Blood bank
Dr Paul Holland Md, Chief Executive Officer

D-U-N-S 06-049-8904
SACRED HART HOSPITAL OF ALLENTOWN
421 W Chew St, Allentown, PA 18102
Phone: (610) 776-4500

Sales: $69,966,000
Employees: 1,025
Company Type: Private
Employees here: 1,000
SIC: 8062
  General hospital
Joseph Cimerola, President

D-U-N-S 07-946-4053
SACRED HEART HOSPITAL OF PENSACOLA
5151 N 9th Ave, Pensacola, FL 32504
Phone: (850) 416-7000
Sales: $175,745,000
Employees: 2,000
Company Type: Private
Employees here: 1,990
SIC: 8062
  General hospital
Patrick Madden, President

D-U-N-S 06-047-7064
SACRED HEART HOSPITAL
900 W Clairemont Ave, Eau Claire, WI 54701
Phone: (715) 839-4121
Sales: $47,300,000
Employees: 1,025
Company Type: Private
Employees here: 1,025
SIC: 8062
  General medical and surgical hospital
Stephen Ronstrom, Administrator

D-U-N-S 15-147-3808
SACRED HEART MEDICAL CENTER
101 W 8th Ave, Spokane, WA 99204
Phone: (509) 455-3131
Sales: $435,000,000
Employees: 4,074
Company Type: Private
Employees here: 3,700
SIC: 8062
  General hospital
Ryland P Davis, President

D-U-N-S 03-020-2709
SACRED HEART-ST MARYS HOSPITAL
1044 Kabel Ave, Rhinelander, WI 54501
Phone: (715) 369-6600
Sales: $38,956,000
Employees: 650
Company Type: Private
Employees here: 526
SIC: 8062
  General medical & surgical hospital
Kevin O Donnell, President

D-U-N-S 07-494-6419
SACRED HT HOSPITAL SIST CHAR
900 Seton Dr, Cumberland, MD 21502
Phone: (301) 759-4200
Sales: $64,829,000
Employees: 901
Company Type: Private
Employees here: 901
SIC: 8062
  General hospital
Edward M Dinan, President

D-U-N-S 06-762-0237
SADDLEBACK MEMORIAL MED CTR
24451 Health Center Dr, Laguna Hills, CA 92653
Phone: (949) 837-4500
Sales: $78,109,000
Employees: 1,050
Company Type: Private
Employees here: 888
SIC: 8062
  General medical & surgical hospital
Barry S Arbuckle, Chief Executive Officer

D-U-N-S 05-842-6289
SAINT AGNES MEDICAL CENTER
1303 E Herndon Ave, Fresno, CA 93720
Phone: (209) 449-3000

Sales: $93,400,000
Company Type: Private   *Employees:* 2,000
SIC: 8062   *Employees here:* 1,900
  General hospital
Ss R Nickerson, President

D-U-N-S 86-804-1906
SAINT CLARE'S HOSPITAL INC
20 Walnut St, Sussex, NJ 7461
Phone: (973) 702-2200
Sales: $99,500,000   *Employees:* NA
Company Type: Private   *Employees here:* 300
SIC: 8062
  General hospital
Joseph Trunsio, Principal

D-U-N-S 92-772-6968
SAINT CLARE'S HOSPITAL INC
24 Jardine St, Dover, NJ 7801
Phone: (973) 989-3000
Sales: $69,500,000   *Employees:* NA
Company Type: Private   *Employees here:* 1,400
SIC: 8062
  Hospital
Joseph Turnfio, President

D-U-N-S 01-089-8880
SAINT CLARE'S HOSPITAL INC
25 Pocono Rd, Denville, NJ 7834
Phone: (973) 625-6000
Sales: $225,036,000   *Employees:* 4,100
Company Type: Private   *Employees here:* 2,800
SIC: 8062
  General hospital
Katherine Mc Donagh, President

D-U-N-S 06-478-1396
SAINT CLOUD HOSPITAL INC
1406 6th Ave N, Saint Cloud, MN 56303
Phone: (320) 251-2700
Sales: $160,452,000   *Employees:* 2,000
Company Type: Private   *Employees here:* 1,750
SIC: 8062
  General hospital
John Froebenius, President

D-U-N-S 07-290-4782
SAINT ELIZABETH COMMUNITY HEALTH CTR
555 S 70th St, Lincoln, NE 68510
Phone: (402) 489-7181
Sales: $77,144,000   *Employees:* 1,150
Company Type: Private   *Employees here:* 1,040
SIC: 8062
  General hospital home health care services
Robert J Lanik, President

D-U-N-S 07-609-5801
SAINT ELIZABETH COMMUNITY HOSP
2550 Sister Mary Columba, Red Bluff, CA 96080
Phone: (530) 527-2112
Sales: $34,927,000   *Employees:* 406
Company Type: Private   *Employees here:* 388
SIC: 8062
  General hospital
George Govier, Chief Executive Officer

D-U-N-S 07-677-9651
SAINT ELIZABETH MEDICAL CTR
401 E 20th St, Covington, KY 41014
Phone: (606) 292-4000

Sales: $203,465,000   *Employees:* 2,964
Company Type: Private   *Employees here:* 815
SIC: 8062
  General medical and surgical hospital
Joseph W Gross, President

D-U-N-S 15-593-9200
SAINT ELIZABETH MEDICAL CTR
1 Medical Village Dr, Covington, KY 41017
Phone: (606) 344-2000
Sales: $73,500,000   *Employees:* NA
Company Type: Private   *Employees here:* 1,700
SIC: 8071
  Clinical testing
Joseph W Gross, Principal

D-U-N-S 07-373-1440
SAINT EUGENE COMMUNITY HOSP
301 E Jackson St, Dillon, SC 29536
Phone: (843) 774-4111
Sales: $29,326,000   *Employees:* 300
Company Type: Private   *Employees here:* 300
SIC: 8062
  Hospital
Andrew F Wood Jr, Chief Financial Officer

D-U-N-S 03-949-6344
SAINT FRANCIS HOSPITAL INC
2122 Manchester Expy, Columbus, GA 31904
Phone: (706) 596-4000
Sales: $94,691,000   *Employees:* 1,260
Company Type: Private   *Employees here:* 935
SIC: 8062
  General hospital
Michael E Garrigan, President

D-U-N-S 07-352-0447
SAINT FRANCIS HOSPITAL
  (Parent: Tenet Healthcare Corporation)
5959 Park Ave, Memphis, TN 38119
Phone: (901) 765-1000
Sales: $137,363,000   *Employees:* 1,700
Company Type: Public Family Member   *Employees here:* 1,700
SIC: 8062
  General hospital & skilled nursing care facility
Charlie Soaton, President

D-U-N-S 06-454-8175
SAINT FRANCIS HOSPITAL, INC
6161 S Yale Ave, Tulsa, OK 74136
Phone: (918) 494-2200
Sales: $342,672,000   *Employees:* 4,400
Company Type: Private   *Employees here:* 3,095
SIC: 8062
  General hospital/ret medical equipment
Mark Hutson, Vice-President

D-U-N-S 07-464-7959
SAINT FRANCIS MEMORIAL HOSP
900 Hyde St, San Francisco, CA 94109
Phone: (415) 775-4321
Sales: $86,665,000   *Employees:* 900
Company Type: Private   *Employees here:* 800
SIC: 8062
  General hospital
John G Williams, President

D-U-N-S 10-399-7755
SAINT FRNCIS HOSPITAL OF EVANSTON
355 Ridge Ave, Evanston, IL 60202
Phone: (847) 316-4000

Sales: $142,425,000   *Employees:* 1,962
Company Type: Private   *Employees here:* 1,850
SIC: 8062
   General medical surgical and teaching hospital and extended care facility
James C Gizzi, President

D-U-N-S 07-197-0222
SAINT JOHN'S MERCY HOSPITAL
200 Madison Ave, Washington, MO 63090
Phone: (314) 239-8000
Sales: $33,100,000   *Employees:* 725
Company Type: Private   *Employees here:* 713
SIC: 8062
   General hospital
Patrick Bira, Administrator

D-U-N-S 06-281-9339
SAINT JOSEPH HOSPITAL & HEALTH CTR
1907 W Sycamore St, Kokomo, IN 46901
Phone: (765) 452-5611
Sales: $56,507,000   *Employees:* 944
Company Type: Private   *Employees here:* 327
SIC: 8062
   General medical and surgical hospital
Conrad Uitts, Chairman of the Board

D-U-N-S 05-579-2063
SAINT JOSEPH HOSPITAL INC
1835 Franklin St, Denver, CO 80218
Phone: (303) 837-7111
Sales: $98,000,000   *Employees:* 2,098
Company Type: Private   *Employees here:* 2,000
SIC: 8062
   General hospital
Jeffrey Selberg, President

D-U-N-S 79-557-2205
SAINT JOSEPH HOSPITAL INC
   (Parent: Tenet Healthcare Corporation)
601 N 30th St, Omaha, NE 68131
Phone: (402) 449-4451
Sales: $60,300,000   *Employees:* 1,300
Company Type: Public Family Member   *Employees here:* 1,100
SIC: 8062
   General hospital
Matt Kurs, President

D-U-N-S 07-284-6017
SAINT JOSEPH MEDICAL CENTER
12th & Walnut Sts, Reading, PA 19604
Phone: (610) 378-2000
Sales: $76,893,000   *Employees:* 1,400
Company Type: Private   *Employees here:* 850
SIC: 8062
   General hospital
Philip Dionne, President

D-U-N-S 07-212-6816
SAINT JOSEPH'S MEDICAL CENTER
128 Strawberry Hill Ave, Stamford, CT 6902
Phone: (203) 353-2000
Sales: $55,085,000   *Employees:* 625
Company Type: Private   *Employees here:* 623
SIC: 8062
   General medical & surgical hospital & gift shops
William S Riordian, President

D-U-N-S 07-628-3175
SAINT LUKES NORTHLAND HOSP
601 S US Highway 169, Smithville, MO 64089
Phone: (816) 532-3700

Sales: $38,233,000   *Employees:* 700
Company Type: Private   *Employees here:* 150
SIC: 8062
   General hospital
James Brophy, Chief Executive Officer

D-U-N-S 07-443-9035
SAINT MARY OF NAZARETH HOSPITAL CTR
2233 W Division St, Chicago, IL 60622
Phone: (312) 770-2000
Sales: $118,826,000   *Employees:* 1,400
Company Type: Private   *Employees here:* 1,390
SIC: 8062
   General hospital
Sister M Lucille, Chairman of the Board

D-U-N-S 07-575-3301
SAINT MARY HOSPITAL & MED CTR
700 Patterson Rd, Grand Junction, CO 81506
Phone: (970) 244-6100
Sales: $74,500,000   *Employees:* 1,600
Company Type: Private   *Employees here:* 1,565
SIC: 8062
   General acute care hospital
Sister L Casey, President

D-U-N-S 80-777-9640
SAINT MARY'S HEALTHFIRST
   (Parent: St Marys Health Care Corp)
5290 Neil Rd, Reno, NV 89502
Phone: (702) 829-6000
Sales: $28,006,000   *Employees:* 100
Company Type: Private   *Employees here:* 100
SIC: 8011
   Medical doctor's office
Ronald Long, Chief Financial Officer

D-U-N-S 05-556-9545
SAINT MARYS HOSPITAL OF HUNTINGTON
2900 1st Ave, Huntington, WV 25702
Phone: (304) 526-1234
Sales: $148,833,000   *Employees:* 1,500
Company Type: Private   *Employees here:* 1,500
SIC: 8062
   General hospital
J T Jones, Executive Director

D-U-N-S 07-325-7834
SAINT PATRICK'S HOME
66 Van Cortlandt Park S, Bronx, NY 10463
Phone: (718) 519-2800
Sales: $21,893,000   *Employees:* 350
Company Type: Private   *Employees here:* 350
SIC: 8051
   Skilled nursing facility
Monsignor J Murray, President

D-U-N-S 04-593-4510
SAINT VINCENT HOSPITAL & HEALTH CTR
1233 N 30th St, Billings, MT 59101
Phone: (406) 657-7000
Sales: $55,800,000   *Employees:* 1,204
Company Type: Private   *Employees here:* 1,200
SIC: 8062
   General hospital
Pat Hermanson, Officer

D-U-N-S 11-071-2668
SAINT VINCENT HOSPITAL, LLC
   (Parent: Tenet Healthcare Corporation)
25 Winthrop St, Worcester, MA 1604
Phone: (508) 798-1234

Sales: $102,800,000   *Employees:* 2,200
Company Type: Public Family Member   *Employees here:* 2,200
SIC: 8062
   General medical & surgical hospital
Robert E Maher Jr, President

D-U-N-S 07-382-8444
SAINTS MEMORIAL MEDICAL CENTER
1 Hospital Dr, Lowell, MA 1852
Phone: (978) 458-1411
Sales: $77,362,000   *Employees:* 1,200
Company Type: Private   *Employees here:* 1,000
SIC: 8062
   General hospital & nursing home
Thom Clark, President

D-U-N-S 07-453-6996
SALEM COMMUNITY HOSPITAL
1995 E State St, Salem, OH 44460
Phone: (330) 332-1551
Sales: $54,143,000   *Employees:* 655
Company Type: Private   *Employees here:* 641
SIC: 8062
   Hospital
Eugene Zentko, Administrator

D-U-N-S 03-803-2546
SALEM HOSPITAL
665 Winter St SE, Salem, OR 97301
Phone: (503) 370-5220
Sales: $49,400,000   *Employees:* NA
Company Type: Private   *Employees here:* 1,000
SIC: 8062
   Hospital
Evan Lewis, President

D-U-N-S 04-980-2135
SALEM HOSPITAL
665 Winter St SE, Salem, OR 97301
Phone: (503) 370-5200
Sales: $164,084,000   *Employees:* 2,500
Company Type: Private   *Employees here:* 1,500
SIC: 8062
   General hospital
Dennis A Noonan, President

D-U-N-S 11-503-5115
SALICK HEALTH CARE INC
8201 Beverly Blvd, Los Angeles, CA 90048
Phone: (323) 966-3400
Sales: $48,800,000   *Employees:* 1,600
Company Type: Private   *Employees here:* 100
SIC: 8093
   Operates cancer & kidney dialysis centers home health care services & whol medical and pharmaceutical products & supplies
Michael O Brien, Chairman of the Board

D-U-N-S 07-332-7892
SALINA REGIONAL HEALTH CENTER
400 S Santa Fe Ave, Salina, KS 67401
Phone: (785) 452-7000
Sales: $59,500,000   *Employees:* 1,283
Company Type: Private   *Employees here:* 800
SIC: 8062
   General hospital
Randy Peterson, Acting Ceo

D-U-N-S 07-718-1071
SALINAS VALLEY MEMORIAL HEALTH
450 E Romie Ln, Salinas, CA 93901
Phone: (831) 757-4333

Sales: $168,007,000   *Employees:* 1,500
Company Type: Private   *Employees here:* 1,480
SIC: 8062
   General hospital
Sam Downing, Chief Executive Officer

D-U-N-S 10-668-8484
SALO INC
960 Checkrein Ave, Columbus, OH 43229
Phone: (614) 888-3130
Sales: $41,452,000   *Employees:* 3,400
Company Type: Private   *Employees here:* 3
SIC: 8082
   Home health care service
Harold A Salo, Chairman of the Board

D-U-N-S 12-254-7979
SAMARITAN HEALTH PARTNERS SHP
2222 Philadelphia Dr, Dayton, OH 45406
Phone: (937) 278-2612
Sales: $210,558,000   *Employees:* 2,200
Company Type: Private   *Employees here:* 2,165
SIC: 8062
   General hospital
K D Deck, President

D-U-N-S 10-738-8605
SAMARITAN HEALTH SYSTEM INC
1410 N 4th St, Clinton, IA 52732
Phone: (319) 244-5555
Sales: $47,675,000   *Employees:* 950
Company Type: Private   *Employees here:* 400
SIC: 8062
   General hospital
Thomas Hesselmann, Chief Executive Officer

D-U-N-S 07-244-0290
SAMARITAN HEALTH SYSTEM
1441 N 12th St, Phoenix, AZ 85006
Phone: (602) 495-4000
Sales: $1,345,613,000   *Employees:* 11,954
Company Type: Private   *Employees here:* 450
SIC: 8062
   General hospitals nursing homes personal care facilities
James C Crews, Chief Executive Officer

D-U-N-S 11-044-3561
SAMARITAN HEALTH SYSTEM
1111 E McDowell Rd, Phoenix, AZ 85006
Phone: (602) 239-2000
Sales: $153,500,000   *Employees:* NA
Company Type: Private   *Employees here:* 3,500
SIC: 8071
   Medical laboratory
Steven Seiler, Chief Executive Officer

D-U-N-S 07-246-0025
SAMARITAN HEALTH SYSTEM
1400 S Dobson Rd, Mesa, AZ 85202
Phone: (602) 835-3000
Sales: $64,900,000   *Employees:* NA
Company Type: Private   *Employees here:* 1,500
SIC: 8062
   General hospital
Bruce Pearson, N/A

D-U-N-S 09-123-9426
SAMARITAN HEALTH SYSTEM
101 Civic Center Ln, Lake Havasu City, AZ 86403
Phone: (520) 855-8185

Sales: $20,800,000   *Employees:* NA
Company Type: Private   *Employees here:* 530
SIC: 8062
  General hospital
Kevin P Poorten, Administrator

D-U-N-S 10-280-8730
SAMARITAN HEALTH SYSTEM
5555 W Thunderbird Rd, Glendale, AZ 85306
Phone: (602) 588-5555
Sales: $82,400,000   *Employees:* NA
Company Type: Private   *Employees here:* 1,900
SIC: 8062
  General hospital
Robert Curry, N/A

D-U-N-S 02-067-5211
SAMARITAN HOSPITAL
2215 Burdett Ave, Troy, NY 12180
Phone: (518) 271-3300
Sales: $63,976,000   *Employees:* 1,403
Company Type: Private   *Employees here:* 1,353
SIC: 8062
  General medical and surgical hospital
Paul A Milton, Chief Operating Officer

D-U-N-S 07-728-6243
SAMARITAN MEDICAL CENTER
830 Washington St, Watertown, NY 13601
Phone: (315) 785-4000
Sales: $129,150,000   *Employees:* 1,300
Company Type: Private   *Employees here:* 1,250
SIC: 8062
  General hospital & whol durable medical equipment
David Tinker, Chief Executive Officer

D-U-N-S 07-557-1455
SAMPSON REGIONAL MEDICAL CTR
607 Beamon St, Clinton, NC 28328
Phone: (910) 592-8511
Sales: $35,345,000   *Employees:* 600
Company Type: Private   *Employees here:* 580
SIC: 8062
  Hospital & nursing home
Lee Pridgen, Administrator

D-U-N-S 07-251-4060
SAN ANTONIO COMMUNITY HOSP
999 San Bernardino Rd, Upland, CA 91786
Phone: (909) 985-2811
Sales: $126,010,000   *Employees:* 1,800
Company Type: Private   *Employees here:* 1,750
SIC: 8062
  General hospital & pharmacy
George A Kuykendall, President

D-U-N-S 08-291-7626
SAN BENITO HEALTH CARE DST
911 Sunset Dr, Hollister, CA 95023
Phone: (831) 637-5711
Sales: $24,505,000   *Employees:* 430
Company Type: Private   *Employees here:* 270
SIC: 8062
  General hospital skilled nursing care facility
Keith Mesmer, Chief Executive Officer

D-U-N-S 13-242-6081
SAN DIEGO HOSPITAL ASSN
7901 Frost St, San Diego, CA 92123
Phone: (619) 541-3400

Sales: $149,300,000   *Employees:* NA
Company Type: Private   *Employees here:* 3,000
SIC: 8062
  General hospital
Dan Groff, Director

D-U-N-S 05-748-9239
SAN FRANCISCO CITY & COUNTY
1001 Potrero Ave, San Francisco, CA 94110
Phone: (415) 206-8000
Sales: $149,300,000   *Employees:* NA
Company Type: Private   *Employees here:* 3,000
SIC: 8062
  General hospital
Richard Cordova, Principal

D-U-N-S 16-086-8790
SAN FRANCISCO CITY & COUNTY
375 Laguna Honda Blvd, San Francisco, CA 94116
Phone: (415) 664-1580
Sales: $89,500,000   *Employees:* NA
Company Type: Private   *Employees here:* 1,800
SIC: 8062
  Skilled nursing-hosp long term care
Anthony Wagner, Exec Admin

D-U-N-S 07-527-8515
SAN GABRIEL VALLEY MED CTR
218 S Santa Anita Ave, San Gabriel, CA 91776
Phone: (626) 289-5454
Sales: $62,802,000   *Employees:* 850
Company Type: Private   *Employees here:* 850
SIC: 8062
  General hospital
Makoto Nakayama, Chief Executive Officer

D-U-N-S 07-415-5771
SAN JACINTO METHODIST HOSP
4401 Garth Rd, Baytown, TX 77521
Phone: (281) 420-8600
Sales: $74,781,000   *Employees:* 1,100
Company Type: Private   *Employees here:* 1,097
SIC: 8062
  General hospital
William Simmons, Chief Executive Officer

D-U-N-S 07-432-8048
SAN JOAQUIN COMMUNITY HOSP
2615 Eye St, Bakersfield, CA 93301
Phone: (805) 395-3000
Sales: $77,220,000   *Employees:* 900
Company Type: Private   *Employees here:* 850
SIC: 8062
  General hospital
Fred Manchur, President

D-U-N-S 88-433-3345
SAN JOAQUIN, COUNTY OF
500 W Hospital Rd, French Camp, CA 95231
Phone: (209) 468-6000
Sales: $68,500,000   *Employees:* NA
Company Type: Private   *Employees here:* NA
SIC: 8062
  General hospital
Michael N Smith, Administrator

D-U-N-S 03-043-4567
SAN JUAN REGIONAL MEDICAL CTR
801 W Maple St, Farmington, NM 87401
Phone: (505) 325-5011

Sales: $78,995,000   *Employees:* 900
Company Type: Private   *Employees here:* 787
SIC: 8062
  General hospital
Don Carlson, President

D-U-N-S 86-861-2607
SAN LEANDRO HOSPITAL
13690 E 14th St Fl 2, San Leandro, CA 94578
Phone: (510) 483-4233
Sales: $52,019,000   *Employees:* 70
Company Type: Private   *Employees here:* 70
SIC: 8361
  Residential care services
Richard Scott, Principal

D-U-N-S 86-102-2655
SAN LUIS OBISPO, COUNTY OF
2191 Johnson Ave, San Luis Obispo, CA 93401
Phone: (805) 781-5500
Sales: $24,500,000   *Employees:* NA
Company Type: Private   *Employees here:* 388
SIC: 8011
  Medical doctor's office
Susan Zepeda, Principal

D-U-N-S 18-050-1918
SAN MATEO HEALTH COMMISSION
1500 Fashion Island Blvd, San Mateo, CA 94404
Phone: (650) 573-9710
Sales: $84,170,000   *Employees:* 96
Company Type: Private   *Employees here:* 96
SIC: 8099
  Health care service
Michael W Murray, Principal

D-U-N-S 93-392-2254
SAN MATEO INDIVIDUAL PRACTICE
1150 Bayhill Dr Ste 100, San Bruno, CA 94066
Phone: (650) 588-5900
Sales: $33,951,000   *Employees:* 30
Company Type: Private   *Employees here:* 30
SIC: 8011
  Medical doctor's office
Armando Bautista, Owner

D-U-N-S 06-456-4354
SAN PEDRO PENINSULA HOSPITAL
1300 W 7th St, San Pedro, CA 90732
Phone: (310) 832-3311
Sales: $72,854,000   *Employees:* 880
Company Type: Private   *Employees here:* 556
SIC: 8062
  General hospital & skilled nursing facility
John Wilson, President

D-U-N-S 07-883-9081
SANSUM MEDICAL CLINIC INC
317 W Pueblo St, Santa Barbara, CA 93105
Phone: (805) 682-2621
Sales: $36,641,000   *Employees:* 450
Company Type: Private   *Employees here:* 420
SIC: 8011
  Medical clinic
Charles H Cox, Executive Director

D-U-N-S 18-852-2981
SANTA ANA TUSTIN RADIOLOGY
1450 N Tustin Ave Ste 132, Santa Ana, CA 92705
Phone: (714) 835-3709

Sales: $79,677,000   *Employees:* 13
Company Type: Private   *Employees here:* 1
SIC: 8011
  Diagnostic and therapeutic radiology
Dr Joseph Burgeon Md, Partner

D-U-N-S 07-882-9900
SANTA BARBARA COTTAGE HOSP
Bath & Pueblo St, Santa Barbara, CA 93102
Phone: (805) 682-7111
Sales: $83,300,000   *Employees:* 1,786
Company Type: Private   *Employees here:* 1,655
SIC: 8062
  General hospital
James L Ash, President

D-U-N-S 07-882-2939
SANTA BARBARA MDCL FNDN CLC
470 S Patterson Ave, Santa Barbara, CA 93111
Phone: (805) 681-7500
Sales: $52,747,000   *Employees:* 580
Company Type: Private   *Employees here:* 60
SIC: 8011
  Medical clinic
Dr Arthur S Greditzer Md, President

D-U-N-S 07-715-8871
SANTA CRUZ MEDICAL CLINIC
2025 Soquel Ave, Santa Cruz, CA 95062
Phone: (831) 423-4111
Sales: $30,459,000   *Employees:* 15
Company Type: Private   *Employees here:* 15
SIC: 8011
  Medical clinic
Wayne Boss, Chief Executive Officer

D-U-N-S 07-723-6933
SANTA MARTA HOSPITAL INC
319 N Humphreys Ave, Los Angeles, CA 90022
Phone: (323) 266-6500
Sales: $29,516,000   *Employees:* 430
Company Type: Private   *Employees here:* 430
SIC: 8062
  General hospital
Harry Whitney, President

D-U-N-S 06-459-8113
SANTA PAULA MEMORIAL HOSPITAL
825 N 10th St, Santa Paula, CA 93060
Phone: (805) 525-7171
Sales: $21,738,000   *Employees:* 202
Company Type: Private   *Employees here:* 202
SIC: 8062
  General hospital
William Greene, Administrator

D-U-N-S 17-021-1312
SANTA ROSA HEALTH CARE CORP
519 W Houston St, San Antonio, TX 78207
Phone: (210) 228-2011
Sales: $85,400,000   *Employees:* NA
Company Type: Private   *Employees here:* 2,061
SIC: 8062
  Medical hospital
Richard Wayne, Chief Executive Officer

D-U-N-S 06-885-6053
SANTA ROSA MEMORIAL HOSPITAL
1165 Montgomery Dr, Santa Rosa, CA 95405
Phone: (707) 546-3210

Sales: $106,863,000 *Employees:* 1,007
Company Type: Private *Employees here:* 1,000
SIC: 8062
  General hospital
James P Houser, President

D-U-N-S 07-619-7334
SANTA TERESITA HOSPITAL
819 Buena Vista St, Duarte, CA 91010
Phone: (626) 359-3243
Sales: $22,362,000 *Employees:* 425
Company Type: Private *Employees here:* 425
SIC: 8062
  General hospital and skilled nursing facility
Michael J Costello Jr, Chief Executive Officer

D-U-N-S 07-142-9054
SARAH BUSH LINCOLN HEALTH CTR
1000 Health Center Dr, Mattoon, IL 61938
Phone: (217) 258-2525
Sales: $75,041,000 *Employees:* 1,315
Company Type: Private *Employees here:* 1,216
SIC: 8062
  Hospital
Eugene A Leblond, President

D-U-N-S 07-920-8849
SARASOTA COUNTY PUB HOSPITAL BD
1700 S Tamiami Trl, Sarasota, FL 34239
Phone: (941) 917-1711
Sales: $252,935,000 *Employees:* 2,800
Company Type: Private *Employees here:* 2,700
SIC: 8062
  General hospital
Michael Covert, President

D-U-N-S 60-991-6721
SARASOTA DOCTOR'S HOSPITAL
  (Parent: Columbia/Hca Healthcare Corp)
5731 Bee Ridge Rd, Sarasota, FL 34233
Phone: (941) 342-1100
Sales: $73,071,000 *Employees:* 750
Company Type: Public Family Member *Employees here:* 600
SIC: 8062
  General hospital
William Leviense, President

D-U-N-S 14-734-8650
SARATOGA COMMUNITY HOSPITAL
15000 Gratiot Ave, Detroit, MI 48205
Phone: (313) 245-1200
Sales: $45,776,000 *Employees:* 913
Company Type: Private *Employees here:* 891
SIC: 8062
  General hospital
Michael Breen, President

D-U-N-S 06-052-3602
SARATOGA HOSPITAL (INC)
211 Church St, Saratoga Springs, NY 12866
Phone: (518) 587-3222
Sales: $54,121,000 *Employees:* 1,000
Company Type: Private *Employees here:* 1,000
SIC: 8062
  General medical and surgical hospital
David Andersen, Chief Executive Officer

D-U-N-S 16-170-6437
SARTORI MEMORIAL HOSPITAL
515 College St, Cedar Falls, IA 50613
Phone: (319) 266-3584

Sales: $21,000,000 *Employees:* 350
Company Type: Private *Employees here:* 350
SIC: 8062
  Hospital
Michael Schneiders, Chief Financial Officer

D-U-N-S 07-717-7947
SATELLITE DIALYSIS CENTERS
345 Convention Way Ste B, Redwood City, CA 94063
Phone: (650) 367-9504
Sales: $42,695,000 *Employees:* 400
Company Type: Private *Employees here:* 75
SIC: 8092
  Kidney outpatient care facility
Marke Burke, Chief Executive Officer

D-U-N-S 09-858-1689
SATILLA HEALTH SERVICES INC
410 Darling Ave, Waycross, GA 31501
Phone: (912) 283-3030
Sales: $74,928,000 *Employees:* 1,000
Company Type: Private *Employees here:* 700
SIC: 8062
  Hospital nursing home leases and retails home health care
    laundry repairs biomedical equipment and ret pharmacy
Eugene Johnson, President

D-U-N-S 06-832-1264
SAUK PRAIRIE MEMORIAL HOSPITAL
80 1st St, Prairie Du Sac, WI 53578
Phone: (608) 643-3311
Sales: $24,884,000 *Employees:* 451
Company Type: Private *Employees here:* 450
SIC: 8062
  Hospital
Bobbe L Teigen, Administrator

D-U-N-S 13-051-9531
SCAN HEALTH PLAN
3780 Klroy Arprt Way 60, Long Beach, CA 90806
Phone: (562) 989-5272
Sales: $102,954,000 *Employees:* 275
Company Type: Private *Employees here:* 180
SIC: 8011
  Health maintenance organization
Sam L Ervin, President

D-U-N-S 06-975-1287
SCH HEALTH CARE SYSTEM
2600 Saint Michael Dr, Texarkana, TX 75503
Phone: (903) 614-1000
Sales: $57,500,000 *Employees:* NA
Company Type: Private *Employees here:* 1,500
SIC: 8062
  Hospital
Don Beeler, Director

D-U-N-S 07-391-9839
SCH HEALTH CARE SYSTEM
3600 Gates Blvd, Port Arthur, TX 77642
Phone: (409) 985-7431
Sales: $26,900,000 *Employees:* NA
Company Type: Private *Employees here:* 660
SIC: 8062
  General hospital
Jack Bartow, Manager

D-U-N-S 03-776-5542
SCH HEALTH CARE SYSTEM
1919 La Branch St, Houston, TX 77002
Phone: (713) 757-1000

Sales: $94,200,000   *Employees:* NA
Company Type: Private   *Employees here:* 2,271
SIC: 8062
  General hospital
Cathy Jeffcoat, Director

D-U-N-S 05-056-3865
SCH HEALTH CARE SYSTEM
18300 Saint John Dr, Houston, TX 77058
Phone: (281) 333-5503
Sales: $20,200,000   *Employees:* NA
Company Type: Private   *Employees here:* 500
SIC: 8062
  Hospital
Thomas Pernetti, Director

D-U-N-S 06-999-7112
SCHWAB REHABILITATION HOSPITAL
1401 S California Ave, Chicago, IL 60608
Phone: (773) 522-2010
Sales: $25,916,000   *Employees:* 300
Company Type: Private   *Employees here:* 300
SIC: 8069
  Rehabilitation specialty hospital
Kathleen C Yosko, President

D-U-N-S 83-569-7350
SCOTLAND HEALTH CARE SYSTEM
500 E Lauchwood Dr, Laurinburg, NC 28352
Phone: (910) 291-7000
Sales: $75,000,000   *Employees:* 600
Company Type: Private   *Employees here:* 600
SIC: 8062
  Hospital holding company
Gregory C Wood, Chief Executive Officer

D-U-N-S 07-558-4235
SCOTLAND MEMORIAL HOSPITAL
500 E Lauchwood Dr, Laurinburg, NC 28352
Phone: (910) 291-7000
Sales: $46,482,000   *Employees:* 517
Company Type: Private   *Employees here:* 517
SIC: 8062
  General hospital
Gregory C Wood, Administrator

D-U-N-S 15-051-1517
SCOTT & WHITE CLINIC AN ASSN
2401 S 31st St, Temple, TX 76508
Phone: (254) 724-2111
Sales: $480,000,000   *Employees:* 575
Company Type: Private   *Employees here:* 438
SIC: 8011
  Medical clinic
Mike Bukosky, Executive Director

D-U-N-S 07-669-7960
SCOTT & WHITE MEMRL HOSPITAL
2401 S 31st St, Temple, TX 76508
Phone: (254) 724-2111
Sales: $335,333,000   *Employees:* 6,000
Company Type: Private   *Employees here:* 5,600
SIC: 8062
  General hospital
Dr Robert E Myers Md, President

D-U-N-S 15-111-2596
SCOTT AND WHITE HEALTH PLAN
2401 S 31st St, Temple, TX 76508
Phone: (254) 298-3000

Sales: $219,512,000   *Employees:* 245
Company Type: Private   *Employees here:* 132
SIC: 8011
  Medical doctor's office
Deny Radefeld, Chief Executive Officer

D-U-N-S 07-587-5831
SCOTTISH RITE HOSP
1001 Johnson Ferry Rd NE, Atlanta, GA 30342
Phone: (404) 256-5252
Sales: $77,100,000   *Employees:* 1,560
Company Type: Private   *Employees here:* 1,500
SIC: 8069
  Children's hospital
James E Tally Phd, President

D-U-N-S 11-553-3069
SCOTTSDALE MEMORIAL HOSPITALS
7400 E Osborn Rd, Scottsdale, AZ 85251
Phone: (602) 860-3000
Sales: $307,901,000   *Employees:* 2,500
Company Type: Private   *Employees here:* 1,105
SIC: 8062
  Acute care hospitals
Max Poll, President

D-U-N-S 15-647-2144
SCOTTSDALE MEMORIAL HOSPITALS
9003 E Shade Blvd, Scottsdale, AZ 85255
Phone: (602) 860-3009
Sales: $27,100,000   *Employees:* NA
Company Type: Private   *Employees here:* 636
SIC: 8062
  Hospital
Tom Sadvary, Vice-President

D-U-N-S 84-477-7979
SCOTTSDALE MEMORIAL HOSPITALS
9003 E Shea Blvd, Scottsdale, AZ 85260
Phone: (602) 860-3000
Sales: $43,100,000   *Employees:* NA
Company Type: Private   *Employees here:* 1,000
SIC: 8062
  Acute care hospital
Tom Sadvary, Principal

D-U-N-S 02-051-7421
SCRIPPS CLINIC MEDICAL GROUP
10170 Sorrento Valley Rd, San Diego, CA 92121
Phone: (619) 455-9100
Sales: $195,342,000   *Employees:* 325
Company Type: Private   *Employees here:* 1
SIC: 8011
  Multi specialty medical group practice
Dr Thomas Waltz Md, President

D-U-N-S 13-118-5241
SCRIPPS HEALTH
4275 Campus Point Ct, San Diego, CA 92121
Phone: (619) 678-7000
Sales: $702,334,000   *Employees:* 8,000
Company Type: Private   *Employees here:* 258
SIC: 8051
  Hospitals skilled nursing facilities home health services
Ames S Early, President

D-U-N-S 08-600-7093
SCRIPPS HEALTH
354 Santa Fe Dr, Encinitas, CA 92024
Phone: (760) 753-6501

Sales: $30,600,000
Company Type: Private
SIC: 8062
  General hospital ret drugs/sundries
Rebecca Ropchan, Principal

Employees: NA
Employees here: 625

D-U-N-S 86-705-8638
SCRIPPS HEALTH
435 H St, Chula Vista, CA 91910
Phone: (619) 691-7000
Sales: $34,700,000
Company Type: Private
SIC: 8062
  Hospital
Jeff Bills, Branch Manager

Employees: NA
Employees here: 707

D-U-N-S 80-451-0162
SCRIPPS INSTITUTIONS OF MEDICI
4275 Campus Point Ct, San Diego, CA 92121
Phone: (619) 678-7000
Sales: $702,334,000
Company Type: Private
SIC: 8062
  Hospitals outpatient medical clinics & biomedical research
Ames Early, President

Employees: 7,800
Employees here: 7,800

D-U-N-S 07-817-3754
SEA CREST HEALTH CARE CENTER
3035 W 24th St, Brooklyn, NY 11224
Phone: (718) 372-4500
Sales: $22,649,000
Company Type: Private
SIC: 8051
  Skilled nursing care facility
Ernest Dicker, Owner

Employees: 250
Employees here: 250

D-U-N-S 80-017-0532
SECURITY HEALTH PLAN OF WISCONSIN
1000 N Oak Ave, Marshfield, WI 54449
Phone: (715) 387-5043
Sales: $142,441,000
Company Type: Private
SIC: 8011
  Medical doctor's office
Robert J Devita, Executive Director

Employees: 1,006
Employees here: 1,006

D-U-N-S 00-748-2334
SELECT MEDICAL CORPORATION
4718 Old Gettysburg Rd, Mechanicsburg, PA 17055
Phone: (717) 972-1100
Sales: $60,000,000
Company Type: Private
SIC: 8093
  Operator of rehab clinics & acute care hospitals
Rocco A Ortenzio, Chairman of the Board

Employees: 1,000
Employees here: 15

D-U-N-S 02-084-7166
SELECTCARE HMO INC
  (Parent: Selectcare Inc)
2401 W Big Beaver Rd, Troy, MI 48084
Phone: (248) 637-5300
Sales: $20,300,000
Company Type: Private
SIC: 8011
  Health maintenance organization
Mark T Bertolini, Chief Executive Officer

Employees: 297
Employees here: 297

D-U-N-S 07-371-3885
SELF MEMORIAL HOSPITAL
1325 Spring St, Greenwood, SC 29646
Phone: (864) 227-4111

Sales: $102,946,000
Company Type: Private
SIC: 8062
  General hospital
John Heydel, President

Employees: 1,500
Employees here: 1,480

D-U-N-S 07-352-6097
SEMMES-MURPHEY CLINIC PC
930 Madison Ave Ste 600, Memphis, TN 38103
Phone: (901) 522-7700
Sales: $27,232,000
Company Type: Private
SIC: 8011
  Medical clinic
Dr Morris W Ray Md, Chairman of the Board

Employees: 254
Employees here: 133

D-U-N-S 11-596-0320
SENIORCARE INC
2950 Breckinridge Ln, Louisville, KY 40220
Phone: (502) 456-2172
Sales: $21,000,000
Company Type: Private
SIC: 8052
  Intermediate nursing homes
David Wren, President

Employees: 600
Employees here: 12

D-U-N-S 19-400-1277
SENSITIVE CARE INC
1000 Park Manor Dr, Fort Worth, TX 76104
Phone: (818) 810-0024
Sales: $63,011,000
Company Type: Private
SIC: 8051
  Skilled nursing care facilities
Don King, President

Employees: 1,387
Employees here: 15

D-U-N-S 15-105-8336
SENTAGE CORPORATION
5775 Wayzata Blvd 670, Minneapolis, MN 55416
Phone: (612) 541-9622
Sales: $45,000,000
Company Type: Private
SIC: 8072
  Operates dental laboratories
George E Obst, Chairman of the Board

Employees: 950
Employees here: 8

D-U-N-S 10-171-8195
SENTARA ENTERPRISES
  (Parent: Sentara Health System)
5555 Greenwich Rd Ste 600, Virginia Beach, VA 23462
Phone: (757) 687-1236
Sales: $91,689,000
Company Type: Private
SIC: 8093
  Specialty outpatient health services
Kenneth R Perry, Chairman of the Board

Employees: 331
Employees here: 107

D-U-N-S 86-704-8811
SENTARA HEALTH PLANS INC
  (Parent: Sentara Health Management)
4417 Corporation Ln, Virginia Beach, VA 23462
Phone: (757) 552-7400
Sales: $67,777,000
Company Type: Private
SIC: 8011
  Owns and manages health maintenance organization
Ted Wille Jr, President

Employees: 120
Employees here: 120

D-U-N-S 10-171-8138
SENTARA HEALTH SYSTEM
6015 Poplar Hall Dr, Norfolk, VA 23502
Phone: (757) 455-7000

Sales: $36,646,000   *Employees:* 1,700
Company Type: Private   *Employees here:* 500
SIC: 8062
  Health care system
David L Bernd, President

D-U-N-S 19-722-5642
SENTARA HEALTH SYSTEM
830 Kempsville Rd, Norfolk, VA 23502
Phone: (757) 466-6000
Sales: $43,600,000   *Employees:* NA
Company Type: Private   *Employees here:* 991
SIC: 8062
  General hospital
Mark Gavens, Branch Manager

D-U-N-S 36-421-2209
SENTARA HOSPITALS-NORFOLK
800 Independence Blvd, Virginia Beach, VA 23455
Phone: (757) 363-6100
Sales: $28,300,000   *Employees:* NA
Company Type: Private   *Employees here:* 650
SIC: 8062
  Hospital
Mark Gavens, Administrator

D-U-N-S 02-656-0623
SENTARA HOSPITALS-NORFOLK
830 Kempsville Rd, Norfolk, VA 23502
Phone: (757) 857-8100
Sales: $39,500,000   *Employees:* NA
Company Type: Private   *Employees here:* 900
SIC: 8062
  General hospital
Sentara L Anderson, N/A

D-U-N-S 05-862-4115
SENTARA HOSPITALS-NORFOLK
6015 Poplar Hall Dr, Norfolk, VA 23502
Phone: (757) 455-7020
Sales: $398,315,000   *Employees:* 5,200
Company Type: Private   *Employees here:* 200
SIC: 8062
  General & medical hospital
Richard D Hill, Chief Financial Officer

D-U-N-S 15-260-1480
SENTARA HOSPITALS-NORFOLK
600 Gresham Dr, Norfolk, VA 23507
Phone: (757) 628-3361
Sales: $132,800,000   *Employees:* NA
Company Type: Private   *Employees here:* 3,000
SIC: 8062
  General hospital
Howard P Kern, N/A

D-U-N-S 07-466-5258
SEQUOIA HOSPITAL DISTRICT
170 Alameda De Las Pulgas, Redwood City, CA 94062
Phone: (650) 369-5811
Sales: $77,377,000   *Employees:* 1,167
Company Type: Private   *Employees here:* 1,036
SIC: 8062
  General medical & surgical hospital
Glenna Vaskellas, Administrator

D-U-N-S 07-262-6120
SEROLOGICALS CORPORATION
780 Park North Blvd, Clarkston, GA 30021
Phone: (404) 296-5595

Sales: $97,534,000   *Employees:* 1,000
Company Type: Public   *Employees here:* 85
SIC: 8099
  Specialty human antiboby based products
Harold J Tenoso, President

D-U-N-S 87-478-5066
SERVICE MSTR REHABILITATION LP
3839 Forest Hill Irene Rd, Memphis, TN 38125
Phone: (901) 624-1600
Sales: $30,000,000   *Employees:* 270
Company Type: Private   *Employees here:* 50
SIC: 8093
  Rehabilitation services
Anthony B Way, President

D-U-N-S 07-121-0355
SERVICES OF LUTHERAN SOCIAL
1050 Pennsylvania Ave, York, PA 17404
Phone: (717) 848-6238
Sales: $25,056,000   *Employees:* 759
Company Type: Private   *Employees here:* 29
SIC: 8059
  Residential nursing homes & family social services
John Brndjar, President

D-U-N-S 15-378-5472
SERVICES OF NORTHWESTERN HUMAN
27 E Mount Airy Ave, Philadelphia, PA 19119
Phone: (215) 248-6700
Sales: $24,895,000   *Employees:* 2,000
Company Type: Private   *Employees here:* 300
SIC: 8093
  Mental health clinic
Hon A Porta, Chairman of the Board

D-U-N-S 87-808-2213
SETON HEALTH SYSTEM
1300 Massachusetts Ave, Troy, NY 12180
Phone: (518) 268-5000
Sales: $76,894,000   *Employees:* 1,600
Company Type: Private   *Employees here:* 880
SIC: 8062
  Hospital
Sister D Larow, N/A

D-U-N-S 07-188-0116
SETON MEDICAL CENTER
1900 Sullivan Ave, Daly City, CA 94015
Phone: (650) 992-4000
Sales: $127,491,000   *Employees:* 1,231
Company Type: Private   *Employees here:* 1,099
SIC: 8062
  Acute care hospital & skilled nursing facility
Bernadette Smith, Chief Operating Officer

D-U-N-S 09-636-2751
SHADY GROVE ADVENTIST HOSPITAL INC
9901 Medical Center Dr, Rockville, MD 20850
Phone: (301) 279-6000
Sales: $151,203,000   *Employees:* 1,300
Company Type: Private   *Employees here:* 1,300
SIC: 8062
  General medical-surgical hospital
Kiltie Leach, Chief Operating Officer

D-U-N-S 03-918-3736
SHANDS TEACHING HOSPITAL & CLINIC
1600 SW Archer Rd, Gainesville, FL 32608
Phone: (352) 395-0111

333

Sales: $505,801,000   *Employees:* 10,000
Company Type: Private   *Employees here:* 4,000
SIC: 8062
    General hospital
Paul E Metts, Chief Executive Officer

D-U-N-S 82-604-5304
SHANDS TEACHING HOSPITAL & CLINIC
428 SW A St, Gainesville, FL 32601
Phone: (352) 336-1849
Sales: $52,900,000   *Employees:* NA
Company Type: Private   *Employees here:* 1,200
SIC: 8062
    Acute hospital
Bob Williams, Administrator

D-U-N-S 07-854-4400
SHANNON CLINIC
    (*Parent:* Shannon Health System)
120 E Beauregard Ave, San Angelo, TX 76903
Phone: (915) 658-1511
Sales: $27,400,000   *Employees:* 400
Company Type: Private   *Employees here:* 340
SIC: 8011
    Medical clinic
James T Fajkus, President

D-U-N-S 92-932-7195
SHANNON HEALTH SYSTEM
120 E Harris Ave, San Angelo, TX 76903
Phone: (915) 653-6741
Sales: $137,900,000   *Employees:* 2,000
Company Type: Private   *Employees here:* 30
SIC: 8011
    Medical clinic

D-U-N-S 07-315-0963
SHANNON MEDICAL CENTER INC
120 E Harris Ave, San Angelo, TX 76903
Phone: (915) 653-6741
Sales: $60,300,000   *Employees:* 1,300
Company Type: Private   *Employees here:* 1,100
SIC: 8062
    General hospital
John Jeans, President

D-U-N-S 07-731-4938
SHARON HOSPITAL INCORPORATED
50 Hospital Hill Rd, Sharon, CT 6069
Phone: (860) 364-4141
Sales: $30,745,000   *Employees:* 500
Company Type: Private   *Employees here:* 500
SIC: 8062
    General hospital
James E Sok, President

D-U-N-S 06-874-2121
SHARON REGIONAL HEALTH SYSTEM
740 E State St, Sharon, PA 16146
Phone: (724) 983-3816
Sales: $76,379,000   *Employees:* 1,200
Company Type: Private   *Employees here:* 1,100
SIC: 8062
    General hospital
Wayne W Johnston, President

D-U-N-S 07-334-6462
SHARP CABRILLO HOSPITAL
3475 Kenyon St, San Diego, CA 92110
Phone: (619) 221-3400

Sales: $27,200,000   *Employees:* 600
Company Type: Private   *Employees here:* 597
SIC: 8062
    General medical hospital
Dan Gross, Chief Executive Officer

D-U-N-S 07-333-4666
SHARP CHULA VISTA MEDICAL CTR
751 Medical Center Ct, Chula Vista, CA 91911
Phone: (619) 421-6110
Sales: $81,102,000   *Employees:* 734
Company Type: Private   *Employees here:* 729
SIC: 8062
    General hospital
Britt Berrett, Chief Executive Officer

D-U-N-S 06-761-6557
SHARP CORONADO HOSPITAL HEALTHCARE CTR
250 Prospect Pl, Coronado, CA 92118
Phone: (619) 435-6251
Sales: $23,000,000   *Employees:* 510
Company Type: Private   *Employees here:* 500
SIC: 8062
    General hospital with a skilled nursing unit
Marcia Hall, President

D-U-N-S 01-052-2758
SHARP MEMORIAL HOSPITAL
7901 Frost St, San Diego, CA 92123
Phone: (619) 541-3400
Sales: $270,159,000   *Employees:* 3,500
Company Type: Private   *Employees here:* 3,000
SIC: 8062
    General hospital
Dan Gross, President

D-U-N-S 82-675-6306
SHARP MISSION PARK CORP
2201 Mission Ave, Oceanside, CA 92054
Phone: (760) 967-4900
Sales: $57,349,000   *Employees:* 450
Company Type: Private   *Employees here:* 70
SIC: 8011
    Primary care medical clinic
Stanley Aronovitch, President

D-U-N-S 80-132-8626
SHARP TEMECULA VALLEY
25500 Medical Center Dr, Murrieta, CA 92562
Phone: (909) 677-8606
Sales: $34,452,000   *Employees:* 481
Company Type: Private   *Employees here:* 481
SIC: 8062
    General hospital
Juanice Lovett, Chief Executive Officer

D-U-N-S 07-269-5703
SHAWNEE HILLS INC
603 Morris St, Charleston, WV 25301
Phone: (304) 345-4800
Sales: $39,370,000   *Employees:* 900
Company Type: Private   *Employees here:* 40
SIC: 8361
    Residential care
John Barnette, Executive Director

D-U-N-S 06-796-2134
SHAWNEE MISSION MEDICAL CENTER
9100 W 74th St, Shawnee Mission, KS 66204
Phone: (913) 676-2000

Sales: $157,332,000
Company Type: Private
SIC: 8062
  Acute hospital
William Robertson, Officer
Employees: 1,850
Employees here: 1,783

D-U-N-S 03-022-8597
SHEEHAN MEMORIAL HOSPITAL
425 Michigan Ave, Buffalo, NY 14203
Phone: (716) 848-2000
Sales: $37,000,000
Company Type: Private
SIC: 8062
  General hospital
Olivia S Blackwell, Administrator
Employees: 450
Employees here: 450

D-U-N-S 07-210-6305
SHELBY BAPTIST MEDICAL CENTER
1000 1st St N, Alabaster, AL 35007
Phone: (205) 620-8100
Sales: $52,155,000
Company Type: Private
SIC: 8062
  General hospital
Charles C Colvert, President
Employees: 900
Employees here: 850

D-U-N-S 07-288-6591
SHELBY COUNTY MEM HOSPITAL ASSN
915 Michigan St, Sidney, OH 45365
Phone: (937) 498-2311
Sales: $38,235,000
Company Type: Private
SIC: 8062
  Hospital
Michael Moore, President
Employees: 600
Employees here: 600

D-U-N-S 07-286-7971
SHELTERING ARM HOSPITAL FND INC
55 Hospital Dr, Athens, OH 45701
Phone: (740) 593-5551
Sales: $28,405,000
Company Type: Private
SIC: 8062
  General hospital
Richard F Castrop, President
Employees: 368
Employees here: 368

D-U-N-S 04-346-3157
SHELTERING ARMS HOSPITAL (INC)
1311 Palmyra Ave, Richmond, VA 23227
Phone: (804) 353-7039
Sales: $20,350,000
Company Type: Private
SIC: 8069
  Adult comprehensive rehabilitation hospital
Richard C Craven, President
Employees: 480
Employees here: 405

D-U-N-S 07-493-2013
SHENANDOAH MEMORIAL HOSPITAL
755 S Main St, Woodstock, VA 22664
Phone: (540) 459-4021
Sales: $21,462,000
Company Type: Private
SIC: 8062
  General hospital
Floyd Heater, Chief Executive Officer
Employees: 430
Employees here: 430

D-U-N-S 04-067-9664
SHEPHERD CENTER INC
2020 Peachtree Rd Nw, Atlanta, GA 30309
Phone: (404) 352-2020

Sales: $41,072,000
Company Type: Private
SIC: 8069
  Specialty hospital
Gary R Ulicny, Chief Executive Officer
Employees: 525
Employees here: 519

D-U-N-S 07-361-8142
SHEPHERD GOOD HOME INC
543 Saint John St, Allentown, PA 18103
Phone: (610) 776-3111
Sales: $47,736,000
Company Type: Private
SIC: 8361
  Rehab hospital skilled care life residency facility for the handicapped workshop & vocational train & wholesales film & equip
Sara T Gammon, President
Employees: 870
Employees here: 720

D-U-N-S 79-339-7332
SHEPPARD ENOCH PRATT FUNDATION
6501 N Charles St, Baltimore, MD 21204
Phone: (410) 938-3000
Sales: $69,494,000
Company Type: Private
SIC: 8063
  Psychiatric hospital
Dr Steven Sharfstein Md, Chief Executive Officer
Employees: 1,399
Employees here: 1,399

D-U-N-S 04-195-1526
SHEPPARD PRATT HEALTH SYSTEM
6501 N Charles St, Baltimore, MD 21204
Phone: (410) 938-3000
Sales: $69,494,000
Company Type: Private
SIC: 8063
  Psychiatric hospital
Dr Steven S Sharfstein Md, President
Employees: 1,254
Employees here: 1,150

D-U-N-S 93-224-4494
SHERIDAN HEALTHCARE INC
4651 Sheridan St Ste 400, Hollywood, FL 33021
Phone: (954) 964-2611
Sales: $64,665,000
Company Type: Public
SIC: 8082
  Healthcare service
Mitchell Eisenberg, President
Employees: 700
Employees here: 110

D-U-N-S 88-405-8223
SHERIDAN HEALTHCORP, INC
4651 Sheridan St Ste 400, Hollywood, FL 33021
Phone: (954) 964-2611
Sales: $98,616,000
Company Type: Private
SIC: 8082
  Healthcare services
Mitchell Eisenberg, President
Employees: 750
Employees here: 170

D-U-N-S 06-800-6824
SHERMAN HOSPITAL
934 Center St, Elgin, IL 60120
Phone: (847) 742-9800
Sales: $132,037,000
Company Type: Private
SIC: 8062
  General hospital
James Ryan, Chief Operating Officer
Employees: 1,712
Employees here: 1,300

D-U-N-S 62-392-3448
SHERMAN OAKS HEALTH SYSTEM
4911 Van Nuys Blvd, Sherman Oaks, CA 91403
Phone: (818) 784-1690

Sales: $44,430,000
Company Type: Private
SIC: 8062
  Acute hospitals
David Levinson, President

Employees: 450
Employees here: 30

D-U-N-S 78-664-2488
SHERWOOD HEALTHCARE CORP.
1302 Sherwood Dr, Greenfield, IN 46140
Phone: (317) 462-6493
Sales: $20,000,000
Company Type: Private
SIC: 8051
  Skilled nursing care facility intermediate care facility
William R Lee, President

Employees: 880
Employees here: 880

D-U-N-S 13-042-9368
SHORE HEALTH SYSTEMS
219 S Washington St, Easton, MD 21601
Phone: (410) 822-1000
Sales: $46,900,000
Company Type: Private
SIC: 8062
  Hospital data processing & collections service & diagnostic
    heart lab
Joseph P Ross, President

Employees: 1,016
Employees here: 1,016

D-U-N-S 62-077-2350
SHORE MEMORIAL HEALTH FOUNDATION
1 E New York Ave, Somers Point, NJ 8244
Phone: (609) 653-3500
Sales: $118,253,000
Company Type: Private
SIC: 8062
  Health system
Richard A Pitman, President

Employees: 1,400
Employees here: 1,400

D-U-N-S 07-162-8549
SHORE MEMORIAL HOSPITAL
1 E New York Ave, Somers Point, NJ 8244
Phone: (609) 653-3500
Sales: $109,408,000
Company Type: Private
SIC: 8062
  Hospital
Richard A Pitman, President

Employees: 1,600
Employees here: 1,450

D-U-N-S 07-492-4424
SHORE MEMORIAL HOSPITAL
9507 Hospital Ave, Nassawadox, VA 23413
Phone: (757) 442-8000
Sales: $33,561,000
Company Type: Private
SIC: 8062
  General hospital skilled nursing care facility psychiatric
    hospital
Richard Brvenik, President

Employees: 600
Employees here: 537

D-U-N-S 02-058-3787
SHORE VIEW NURSING HOME
2865 Brighton 3rd St, Brooklyn, NY 11235
Phone: (718) 891-4400
Sales: $25,035,000
Company Type: Private
SIC: 8051
  Skilled nursing care facility
Mark Dicker, Partner

Employees: 270
Employees here: 270

D-U-N-S 03-082-3074
SHRINERS HOSPITAL FOR CHILDREN
51 Blossom St, Boston, MA 2114
Phone: (617) 722-3000

Sales: $23,200,000
Company Type: Private
SIC: 8069
  Children's specialty burn hospital
Robert Bories Jr, Administrator

Employees: 250
Employees here: 220

D-U-N-S 96-666-8733
SHRINERS HSPTALS FOR CHILDREN
2425 Stockton Blvd, Sacramento, CA 95817
Phone: (916) 451-7025
Sales: $21,000,000
Company Type: Private
SIC: 8069
  Children's orthopedic hospital & burn treatment center
Margaret B Williams, Branch Manager

Employees: NA
Employees here: 400

D-U-N-S 07-442-5083
SHRINERS HSPTALS FOR CHILDREN
2900 N Rocky Point Dr, Tampa, FL 33607
Phone: (813) 281-0300
Sales: $223,100,000
Company Type: Private
SIC: 8069
  Children's orthopedic hospitals & burn treatment centers
Lewis K Molnar, Executive Vice-President

Employees: 4,500
Employees here: 130

D-U-N-S 02-165-0346
SIERRA HEALTH SERVICES INC
1225 Hancock Rd, Bullhead City, AZ 86442
Phone: (520) 758-3931
Sales: $721,724,000
Company Type: Private
SIC: 8011
  Outpatient clinic
Dr Gordon Ritter Do, President

Employees: 90
Employees here: 90

D-U-N-S 12-086-8807
SIERRA HEALTH SERVICES INC
2724 N Tenaya Way, Las Vegas, NV 89128
Phone: (702) 242-7000
Sales: $721,724,000
Company Type: Public
SIC: 8011
  Health maintenance organization & group medical providers
Dr Anthony M Marlon Md, Chairman of the Board

Employees: 2,800
Employees here: 584

D-U-N-S 01-098-2643
SIERRA NEV MMRL-MNERS HSPITALS
155 Glasson Way, Grass Valley, CA 95945
Phone: (530) 274-6000
Sales: $55,753,000
Company Type: Private
SIC: 8062
  General hospital
Tom Collier, President

Employees: 775
Employees here: 650

D-U-N-S 01-123-0315
SIERRA VIEW LOCAL HOSPITAL DST
465 W Putnam Ave, Porterville, CA 93257
Phone: (209) 784-1110
Sales: $50,404,000
Company Type: Private
SIC: 8062
  Hospital
Edwin Ermshar, Administrator

Employees: 600
Employees here: 600

D-U-N-S 06-842-3995
SIERRA VISTA COMMUNITY HOSP
300 El Camino Real, Sierra Vista, AZ 85635
Phone: (520) 458-4641

Sales: $30,745,000   *Employees:* 500
Company Type: Private   *Employees here:* 500
SIC: 8062
   Hospital
Dale Decker, Chief Executive Officer

D-U-N-S 07-295-2880
SIERRA VISTA HOSPITAL INC
   (Parent: Tenet Healthcare Corporation)
1010 Murray St, San Luis Obispo, CA 93405
Phone: (805) 546-7600
Sales: $31,000,000   *Employees:* 680
Company Type: Public Family Member   *Employees here:* 575
SIC: 8062
   General hospital
Howard Chilton, Chairman of the Board

D-U-N-S 60-563-2587
SIGNATURE HEALTH CARE CORP
   (Parent: Unison Healthcare Corporation)
15300 N 90th Pl Bldg A100, Scottsdale, AZ 85260
Phone: (602) 423-1954
Sales: $25,000,000   *Employees:* 1,100
Company Type: Public Family Member   *Employees here:* 10
SIC: 8051
   Skilled nursing care facilities
Michael A Jeffries, President

D-U-N-S 62-018-4291   EXP
SILLIKER LABORATORIES GROUP
900 Maple Rd, Homewood, IL 60430
Phone: (708) 957-7878
Sales: $21,000,000   *Employees:* 500
Company Type: Private   *Employees here:* 40
SIC: 8071
   Microbiology laboratory
Dr Russell Flowers, President

D-U-N-S 07-443-5843
SILVER CROSS HOSPITAL
1200 Maple Rd, Joliet, IL 60432
Phone: (815) 740-1100
Sales: $94,633,000   *Employees:* 1,400
Company Type: Private   *Employees here:* 1,400
SIC: 8062
   General hospital
Paul Pawlak, President

D-U-N-S 07-818-3449
SILVER LAKE NURSING HOME INC
275 Castleton Ave, Staten Island, NY 10301
Phone: (718) 447-7800
Sales: $21,002,000   *Employees:* 250
Company Type: Private   *Employees here:* 250
SIC: 8051
   Skilled nursing home
Otto Weingarten, President

D-U-N-S 62-139-4469
SILVERCREST EXTNDED CARE FCLTY
14445 87th Ave, Jamaica, NY 11435
Phone: (718) 480-4000
Sales: $31,155,000   *Employees:* 345
Company Type: Private   *Employees here:* 345
SIC: 8051
   Skilled nursing care facility
Kenneth A Carter, Administrator

D-U-N-S 07-492-0364
SINAI HOSPITAL OF BALTIMORE
2401 W Belvedere Ave, Baltimore, MD 21215
Phone: (410) 601-5678

Sales: $248,584,000   *Employees:* 2,700
Company Type: Private   *Employees here:* 2,690
SIC: 8062
   General hospital
Arthur S Wieland, Chief Financial Officer

D-U-N-S 05-204-6836
SINAI HOSPITAL
6767 W Outer Dr, Detroit, MI 48235
Phone: (313) 493-5713
Sales: $142,800,000   *Employees:* 3,045
Company Type: Private   *Employees here:* 2,900
SIC: 8062
   General hospital medical clinics & health related services and
      property & health care related management services
Eugene Miller, Chairman of the Board

D-U-N-S 18-297-0434
SINAI SAMARITAN MEDICAL CENTER
950 N 12th St, Milwaukee, WI 53233
Phone: (414) 647-3418
Sales: $87,300,000   *Employees:* 1,871
Company Type: Private   *Employees here:* 950
SIC: 8062
   Hospital
Leonard Wilk, Administrator

D-U-N-S 07-505-1706
SINGING RIVER HOSPITAL SYSTEM
2809 Denny Ave, Pascagoula, MS 39581
Phone: (228) 938-5000
Sales: $181,838,000   *Employees:* 1,700
Company Type: Private   *Employees here:* 1,325
SIC: 8062
   General medical & surgical hospitals
Robert L Lingle, Chief Executive Officer

D-U-N-S 07-291-8303
SIOUX VALLEY HSPTALS HEALTH SYSTMS
1100 S Euclid Ave, Sioux Falls, SD 57105
Phone: (605) 333-1000
Sales: $224,485,000   *Employees:* 3,500
Company Type: Private   *Employees here:* 2,900
SIC: 8062
   Hospital
Kelby K Krabbenhoft, President

D-U-N-S 87-901-7366
SIOUX VALLEY PHYSICIANS ALIANCE
   (Parent: Sioux Vly Hsptals Hlth Systms)
1201 S Euclid Ave, Sioux Falls, SD 57105
Phone: (605) 333-1000
Sales: $25,403,000   *Employees:* 240
Company Type: Private   *Employees here:* 240
SIC: 8011
   Medical centers
Fred Titze, Executive Director

D-U-N-S 60-820-4806
SISKIN HOSPITAL FOR PHYSICAL
1 Siskin Plz, Chattanooga, TN 37403
Phone: (423) 634-1200
Sales: $22,933,000   *Employees:* 323
Company Type: Private   *Employees here:* 317
SIC: 8069
   Hospital
Robert Main, President

D-U-N-S 06-894-8983
SISTER OF MERCY OF CLERM COUNT
3000 Hospital Dr, Batavia, OH 45103
Phone: (513) 732-8200

Sales: $48,081,000
Company Type: Private
SIC: 8062
 General hospital
Karen Ehrat, President

Employees: 764
Employees here: 764

D-U-N-S 07-654-1515
SISTER HAYWARD HOSPITAL
27200 Calaroga Ave, Hayward, CA 94545
Phone: (510) 264-4000
Sales: $53,561,000
Company Type: Private
SIC: 8062
 General hospital
Alan Mcbride, Chief Financial Officer

Employees: 760
Employees here: 755

D-U-N-S 07-638-0278
SISTERS OF BON SECOURS HOSP
468 Cadieux Rd, Detroit, MI 48230
Phone: (313) 343-1000
Sales: $101,905,000
Company Type: Private
SIC: 8062
 General medical and surgical hospital
Michael Serilla, Vice-President

Employees: NA
Employees here: NA

D-U-N-S 02-847-7706
SISTERS OF CHARITY HEALTH CARE
355 Bard Ave, Staten Island, NY 10310
Phone: (718) 876-1234
Sales: $94,200,000
Company Type: Private
SIC: 8062
 General medical hospital
John J Depierro, President

Employees: NA
Employees here: 1,895

D-U-N-S 80-937-9720
SISTERS OF CHARITY HEALTH CARE
91 Tompkins Ave, Staten Island, NY 10304
Phone: (718) 876-2016
Sales: $33,747,000
Company Type: Private
SIC: 8051
 Nursing home
Paul Rosenfeld, President

Employees: 400
Employees here: 400

D-U-N-S 07-287-1866
SISTERS OF MERCY OF HAMILTON
100 Riverfront Plz, Hamilton, OH 45011
Phone: (513) 867-6400
Sales: $57,500,000
Company Type: Private
SIC: 8062
 General medical hospitals
David Ferrell, President

Employees: 1,241
Employees here: 633

D-U-N-S 09-792-0672
SISTERS OF MERCY OF HAMILTON
3000 Mack Rd, Hamilton, OH 45014
Phone: (513) 870-7080
Sales: $31,400,000
Company Type: Private
SIC: 8062
 General hospital
Dave Farrell, President

Employees: NA
Employees here: 750

D-U-N-S 05-723-2456
SISTERS OF MERCY OF MERION PA
Lansdowne Ave & Bailey Rd, Darby, PA 19023
Phone: (610) 237-4000

Sales: $49,400,000
Company Type: Private
SIC: 8062
 General hospital
J D Macbride, Manager

Employees: NA
Employees here: 1,000

D-U-N-S 96-019-7044
SISTERS OF PROVIDENCE IN CAL
15031 Rinaldi St, Mission Hills, CA 91345
Phone: (818) 898-4600
Sales: $45,700,000
Company Type: Private
SIC: 8062
 General hospital
Carl W Fitch Sr, Chief Operating Officer

Employees: NA
Employees here: 925

D-U-N-S 10-794-8341
SISTERS OF PROVIDENCE IN CAL
501 S Buena Vista St, Burbank, CA 91505
Phone: (818) 843-5111
Sales: $84,500,000
Company Type: Private
SIC: 8062
 General hospital
Georgianne Johnson, Chief Operating Officer

Employees: NA
Employees here: 1,700

D-U-N-S 07-190-6283
SISTERS OF PROVIDENCE IN CAL
520 Pike St, Seattle, WA 98101
Phone: (206) 464-3355
Sales: $282,867,000
Company Type: Private
SIC: 8062
 Medical & surgical hospitals
Henry G Walker, President

Employees: 2,779
Employees here: 150

D-U-N-S 03-803-5002
SISTERS OF PROVIDENCE IN ORE
9205 SW Barnes Rd, Portland, OR 97225
Phone: (503) 297-4411
Sales: $149,300,000
Company Type: Private
SIC: 8062
 General hospital ret gifts/novelties
Don Elsom, Principal

Employees: NA
Employees here: 3,000

D-U-N-S 09-914-2093
SISTERS OF PROVIDENCE IN ORE
4805 NE Glisan St, Portland, OR 97213
Phone: (503) 230-1111
Sales: $126,400,000
Company Type: Private
SIC: 8062
 Medical center
Marvin O Uinn, N/A

Employees: NA
Employees here: 2,541

D-U-N-S 78-618-0844
SISTERS OF PROVIDENCE IN ORE
10150 SE 32nd Ave, Portland, OR 97222
Phone: (503) 652-8300
Sales: $19,900,000
Company Type: Private
SIC: 8062
 Medical center
Janice Burger, Principal

Employees: NA
Employees here: 414

D-U-N-S 06-320-7732
SISTERS OF PROVIDENCE IN ORE
1111 Crater Lake Ave, Medford, OR 97504
Phone: (541) 773-6611

Sales: $42,400,000   *Employees:* NA
Company Type: Private   *Employees here:* 860
SIC: 8062
   General hospital
Charles Wright, Manager

D-U-N-S 06-148-2048
SISTERS OF PROVIDENCE IN ORE
520 Pike St, Seattle, WA 98101
Phone: (206) 464-3355
Sales: $465,449,000   *Employees:* 6,700
Company Type: Private   *Employees here:* 120
SIC: 8062
   General medical & surgical hospitals
Henry G Walker, President

D-U-N-S 08-335-0751
SISTERS OF PROVIDENCE IN WASH
3200 Providence Dr, Anchorage, AK 99508
Phone: (907) 562-2211
Sales: $74,500,000   *Employees:* NA
Company Type: Private   *Employees here:* 1,500
SIC: 8062
   General hospital
Douglas Bruce, Principal

D-U-N-S 61-833-0963
SISTERS OF PROVIDENCE IN WASH
3200 Providence Dr, Anchorage, AK 99508
Phone: (907) 261-3173
Sales: $119,100,000   *Employees:* NA
Company Type: Private   *Employees here:* 2,393
SIC: 8062
   Home health care
Beth Van, Director

D-U-N-S 07-925-2698
SISTERS OF PROVIDENCE IN WASH
9 S 10th Ave, Yakima, WA 98902
Phone: (509) 575-5000
Sales: $49,400,000   *Employees:* NA
Company Type: Private   *Employees here:* 1,000
SIC: 8062
   Hospital
Barbara Hood, Administrator

D-U-N-S 05-730-6524
SISTERS OF PROVIDENCE IN WASH
500 17th Ave, Seattle, WA 98122
Phone: (206) 320-2000
Sales: $149,300,000   *Employees:* NA
Company Type: Private   *Employees here:* 3,000
SIC: 8062
   General hospital
Ray Crerand, Manager

D-U-N-S 05-730-6581
SISTERS OF PROVIDENCE IN WASH
520 Pike St, Seattle, WA 98101
Phone: (206) 464-3355
Sales: $1,148,867,000   *Employees:* 10,900
Company Type: Private   *Employees here:* 80
SIC: 8062
   General medical & surgical hospitals
Henry G Walker, President

D-U-N-S 82-465-4446
SISTERS OF PROVIDENCE IN WASH
12828 Gateway Dr, Seattle, WA 98168
Phone: (206) 320-2319

Sales: $119,100,000   *Employees:* NA
Company Type: Private   *Employees here:* 2,393
SIC: 8062
   General hospital
Mike Norwood, Manager

D-U-N-S 07-665-1744
SISTERS OF PROVIDENCE IN WASH
413 Lilly Rd NE, Olympia, WA 98506
Phone: (360) 491-9480
Sales: $94,500,000   *Employees:* NA
Company Type: Private   *Employees here:* 1,900
SIC: 8062
   Hospital
D L Djornson, Manager

D-U-N-S 02-314-1091
SISTERS OF PROVIDENCE IN WASH
14th & Colby St, Everett, WA 98201
Phone: (425) 261-2000
Sales: $124,200,000   *Employees:* NA
Company Type: Private   *Employees here:* 2,200
SIC: 8011
   Medical clinic
Ray Crerand, Principal

D-U-N-S 10-334-4297
SISTERS OF PROVIDENCE IN WASH
1820 Cooks Hill Rd, Centralia, WA 98531
Phone: (360) 736-2803
Sales: $36,500,000   *Employees:* NA
Company Type: Private   *Employees here:* 800
SIC: 8062
   General hospital
Maureen Comer, Principal

D-U-N-S 10-338-8039
SISTERS OF PROVIDENCE IN WASH
914 S Scheuber Rd, Centralia, WA 98531
Phone: (360) 748-4444
Sales: $36,500,000   *Employees:* NA
Company Type: Private   *Employees here:* 800
SIC: 8062
   General hospital skilled nursing care facility
Sister M Comer, Principal

D-U-N-S 06-745-0486
SISTERS OF ST FRANCIS HEALTH SVCS
1423 Chicago Rd, Chicago Heights, IL 60411
Phone: (708) 756-1000
Sales: $50,700,000   *Employees:* NA
Company Type: Private   *Employees here:* 1,200
SIC: 8062
   General hospital
Peter J Murphy, President

D-U-N-S 07-430-3694
SISTERS OF ST FRANCIS HEALTH SVCS
1515 W Dragoon Trl, Mishawaka, IN 46544
Phone: (219) 256-3935
Sales: $856,452,000   *Employees:* 9,000
Company Type: Private   *Employees here:* 25
SIC: 8062
   General medical & surgical hospital
Sister M Klein, Chairman of the Board

D-U-N-S 07-430-9642
SISTERS OF ST FRANCIS HEALTH SVCS
301 W Homer St, Michigan City, IN 46360
Phone: (219) 879-8511

Sales: $33,500,000   *Employees:* NA
Company Type: Private   *Employees here:* 800
SIC: 8062
  General hospital
Bruce Rampage, President

     D-U-N-S 07-207-0907
SISTERS OF ST FRANCIS HEALTH SVCS
1501 Hartford St, Lafayette, IN 47904
Phone: (765) 423-6011
Sales: $46,400,000   *Employees:* NA
Company Type: Private   *Employees here:* 1,100
SIC: 8062
  General hospital
Doug Eberle-Pres, Manager

     D-U-N-S 60-338-2110
SISTERS OF ST FRANCIS HEALTH SVCS
220 Overton Ave, Memphis, TN 38105
Phone: (901) 577-2700
Sales: $37,800,000   *Employees:* NA
Company Type: Private   *Employees here:* 900
SIC: 8062
  Hospital
Sister M Crone, Manager

     D-U-N-S 07-316-7496
SISTERS OF ST JOSEPH OF TEXAS
4000 24th St, Lubbock, TX 79410
Phone: (806) 796-6150
Sales: $206,242,000   *Employees:* 2,000
Company Type: Private   *Employees here:* 2,000
SIC: 8062
  Hospital
Charley Trimble, President

     D-U-N-S 09-380-7147
SISTERS CHARITY LEAVENWORTH HTH INC
4200 S 4th St, Leavenworth, KS 66048
Phone: (913) 682-1338
Sales: $57,600,000   *Employees:* 1,242
Company Type: Private   *Employees here:* 33
SIC: 8062
  Health management services
Sister M Glatt, President

     D-U-N-S 07-402-3144
SISTERS HOSPITAL
2157 Main St, Buffalo, NY 14214
Phone: (716) 862-2000
Sales: $108,790,000   *Employees:* 2,213
Company Type: Private   *Employees here:* 2,186
SIC: 8062
  General medical & surgical hospital
James M Corrigan, Chief Executive Officer

     D-U-N-S 07-566-1504
SISTERS MCY ST EDW MCY HSPT
7301 Rogers Ave, Fort Smith, AR 72903
Phone: (501) 484-6000
Sales: $132,015,000   *Employees:* 2,000
Company Type: Private   *Employees here:* 1,500
SIC: 8062
  Hospital
Michael Morgan, Chief Executive Officer

     D-U-N-S 07-625-2857
SKAGGS COMMUNITY HOSPITAL ASSOIACTION
Hwy 65 And Skaggs Rd, Branson, MO 65616
Phone: (417) 335-7000

Sales: $47,899,000   *Employees:* 530
Company Type: Private   *Employees here:* 430
SIC: 8062
  General hospital
Robert Phillips, Chief Executive Officer

     D-U-N-S 06-717-2148
SKAGIT COUNTY MEDICAL BUREAU
1100 S 2nd St, Mount Vernon, WA 98273
Phone: (360) 336-9660
Sales: $53,890,000   *Employees:* 95
Company Type: Private   *Employees here:* 95
SIC: 8011
  Medical insurance association
Roger B Mercer, President

     D-U-N-S 07-728-6706
SLOCUM-DICKSON MED GROUP PC
1729 Burrstone Rd, New Hartford, NY 13413
Phone: (315) 798-1500
Sales: $25,780,000   *Employees:* 350
Company Type: Private   *Employees here:* 340
SIC: 8011
  Medical clinic
Dr Sidney J Blatt Md, President

     D-U-N-S 13-011-4150
SMITHKLINE BEECHAM CLINICAL LABS
7600 Tyrone Ave, Van Nuys, CA 91405
Phone: (818) 989-2520
Sales: $61,100,000   *Employees:* NA
Company Type: Private   *Employees here:* 1,200
SIC: 8071
  Medical laboratory
Vijay Agganwal, Phd

     D-U-N-S 87-889-2892
SMITHKLINE BEECHAM CLINICAL LABS
3300 E Birch St, Brea, CA 92821
Phone: (714) 961-3300
Sales: $51,100,000   *Employees:* NA
Company Type: Private   *Employees here:* 1,000
SIC: 8071
  Medical lab

     D-U-N-S 06-457-4270
SMITHKLINE BEECHAM CLINICAL LABS
506 E State Pkwy, Schaumburg, IL 60173
Phone: (847) 885-2010
Sales: $19,900,000   *Employees:* NA
Company Type: Private   *Employees here:* 450
SIC: 8071
  Clinical laboratory sales department
Dr Haritio Yeung, Director

     D-U-N-S 05-616-8214   EXP
SMITHKLINE BEECHAM CLINICAL LABS
  (Parent: Smithkline Beecham Corporation)
1201 S Collegeville Rd, Collegeville, PA 19426
Phone: (610) 454-6000
Sales: $497,800,000   *Employees:* 10,500
Company Type: Private   *Employees here:* 500
SIC: 8071
  Clinical laboratory
John Okkerse, President

     D-U-N-S 05-073-7493
SMITHKLINE BEECHAM CORPORATION
343 Winter St, Waltham, MA 2451
Phone: (781) 890-6161

Sales: $25,100,000
Company Type: Private
SIC: 8071
  Medical laboratory
Norman Mckendry, Manager
Employees: NA
Employees here: 475

D-U-N-S 94-995-2279
SMITHKLINE BEECHAM CORPORATION
325 Hospital Dr, Glen Burnie, MD 21061
Phone: (410) 787-9610
Sales: $107,900,000
Company Type: Private
SIC: 8071
  Medical laboratory
Regina Adinbaum, Branch Manager
Employees: NA
Employees here: 2,400

D-U-N-S 10-122-1596
SMITHKLINE BEECHAM CORPORATION
575 Underhill Blvd, Syosset, NY 11791
Phone: (516) 677-3800
Sales: $28,400,000
Company Type: Private
SIC: 8071
  Medical laboratory
Robert Leventhal, Systems/Data Processing
Employees: NA
Employees here: 550

D-U-N-S 10-144-7928
SMITHKLINE BEECHAM CORPORATION
400 Egypt Rd, Norristown, PA 19403
Phone: (610) 631-4200
Sales: $76,200,000
Company Type: Private
SIC: 8071
  Clinical laboratory
Dorthy Miller, Manager
Employees: NA
Employees here: 1,500

D-U-N-S 18-778-3907
SMITHVLLE HEALTHCARE VENTURES LP
520 W Main St, Smithville, TN 37166
Phone: (615) 597-7171
Sales: $28,405,000
Company Type: Private
SIC: 8062
  General hospital
Alan Markowitz Phd, Chief Executive Officer
Employees: 120
Employees here: 120

D-U-N-S 19-495-9037
SMT HEALTH SERVICES, INC.
10521 Perry Hwy, Wexford, PA 15090
Phone: (724) 933-3300
Sales: $40,000,000
Company Type: Public
SIC: 8071
  Mobile diagnostic services
Jeff Bergman, President
Employees: 210
Employees here: 210

D-U-N-S 07-793-1202
SMYTH COUNTY COMMUNITY HOSP
700 Park Blvd, Marion, VA 24354
Phone: (540) 782-1234
Sales: $33,576,000
Company Type: Private
SIC: 8062
  General hospital & nursing home
Roger W Cooper, President
Employees: 530
Employees here: 435

D-U-N-S 01-019-0817
SNOHOMISH CNTY PUB HOSP
330 S Stillaguamish Ave, Arlington, WA 98223
Phone: (360) 435-2133

Sales: $26,372,000
Company Type: Private
SIC: 8062
  General hospital
Robert D Campbell, Administrator
Employees: 348
Employees here: 330

D-U-N-S 09-893-5430
SOCIAL CNCN CMMITTEE
22618 Merrick Blvd, Springfield Gardens, NY 11413
Phone: (718) 978-3700
Sales: $32,000,000
Company Type: Private
SIC: 8082
  Home patient care service
Cynthia Jenkins, Treasurer
Employees: 2,000
Employees here: 2,000

D-U-N-S 80-778-8344
SOLANO COUNTY COMM ON MED CARE
421 Executive Ct N Ste A, Suisun City, CA 94585
Phone: (707) 863-4100
Sales: $102,453,000
Company Type: Private
SIC: 8011
  Health insurance organization
Jack Horn, Executive Director
Employees: 70
Employees here: 70

D-U-N-S 02-690-2705
SOLARIS HEALTH SYSTEM
80 James St, Edison, NJ 8820
Phone: (732) 632-1500
Sales: $361,552,000
Company Type: Private
SIC: 8062
  Hospital
John Mc Gee, President
Employees: 500
Employees here: 50

D-U-N-S 07-367-5035
SOLDIERS & SAILORS HOSPITAL
418 N Main St Ste 1, Penn Yan, NY 14527
Phone: (315) 536-4431
Sales: $21,523,000
Company Type: Private
SIC: 8062
  General hospital long term care and psychiatric unit unit
Jaconna V Site, Administrator
Employees: 535
Employees here: 495

D-U-N-S 07-598-5739
SOLDIERS & SAILORS MEM HOSP
32-36 Central Ave, Wellsboro, PA 16901
Phone: (717) 724-1631
Sales: $22,132,000
Company Type: Private
SIC: 8062
  Medical & surgical hospital
Jan Fisher, Executive Director
Employees: 375
Employees here: 375

D-U-N-S 06-874-7815
SOMERSET HOSPITAL CTR FOR HEALTH
225 S Center Ave, Somerset, PA 15501
Phone: (814) 443-5000
Sales: $35,838,000
Company Type: Private
SIC: 8062
  General hospital
Michael J Farrell, Administrator
Employees: 562
Employees here: 553

D-U-N-S 06-314-1972
SOMERSET MEDICAL CENTER
110 Rehill Ave, Somerville, NJ 8876
Phone: (908) 685-2200

Sales: $115,543,000
Company Type: Private
SIC: 8062
  General hospital
Michael A Turner, President

Employees: 1,700
Employees here: 1,700

Sales: $23,425,000
Company Type: Private
SIC: 8062
  General hospital
Jerry Happel, Chief Executive Officer

Employees: 231
Employees here: 231

D-U-N-S 07-463-2621
SONOMA VALLEY HEALTHCARE DST
347 Andrieux St, Sonoma, CA 95476
Phone: (707) 935-5000
Sales: $27,622,000
Company Type: Private
SIC: 8062
  General hospital
Dennis R Burns, Administrator

Employees: 500
Employees here: 495

D-U-N-S 06-470-2889
SOUTH BEND MEDICAL FOUNDATION
530 N Lafayette Blvd, South Bend, IN 46601
Phone: (219) 234-4176
Sales: $43,653,000
Company Type: Private
SIC: 8071
  Laboratory pathology service
Dr Luis N Galup Md, President

Employees: 500
Employees here: 1

D-U-N-S 07-187-7575
SONORA COMMUNITY HOSPITAL
1 S Forest Rd, Sonora, CA 95370
Phone: (209) 532-3161
Sales: $46,234,000
Company Type: Private
SIC: 8062
  Hospital and skilled nursing facility
Larry Davis, President

Employees: 680
Employees here: 680

D-U-N-S 14-857-7166
SOUTH BROWARD HOSPITAL DST
3501 Johnson St, Hollywood, FL 33021
Phone: (954) 987-2000
Sales: $377,560,000
Company Type: Private
SIC: 8062
  General medical hospital
Frank V Sacco, Chief Executive Officer

Employees: 4,000
Employees here: 1,200

D-U-N-S 01-443-8001
SONORA QUEST LABORATORIES LLC.
1255 W Washington St, Tempe, AZ 85281
Phone: (602) 685-5000
Sales: $60,000,000
Company Type: Private
SIC: 8071
  Medical laboratory
Earl Buck, Chief Executive Officer

Employees: 850
Employees here: 700

D-U-N-S 60-907-4554
SOUTH BROWARD HOSPITAL DST
2301 N University Dr, Hollywood, FL 33024
Phone: (954) 962-9650
Sales: $28,900,000
Company Type: Private
SIC: 8062
  Hospital
J E Piriz, Principal

Employees: NA
Employees here: 664

D-U-N-S 07-543-1502
SOUND SHORE MEDICAL CENTER,
16 Guion Pl, New Rochelle, NY 10801
Phone: (914) 632-5000
Sales: $112,766,000
Company Type: Private
SIC: 8062
  General hospital
John R Spicer, President

Employees: 1,400
Employees here: 1,400

D-U-N-S 07-193-1919
SOUTH CENTL REGIONAL MED CTR
1220 Jefferson St, Laurel, MS 39440
Phone: (601) 649-4000
Sales: $68,596,000
Company Type: Private
SIC: 8062
  General hospital
G D Higginbotham, Administrator

Employees: 1,159
Employees here: 1,082

D-U-N-S 05-751-8342
SOUTH AUSTIN MEDICAL CENTER
  (*Parent:* Columbia/Hca Healthcare Corp)
901 W Ben White Blvd, Austin, TX 78704
Phone: (512) 447-2211
Sales: $28,400,000
Company Type: Public Family Member
SIC: 8062
  General hospital
Richard Klusmann, Chief Executive Officer

Employees: 625
Employees here: 625

D-U-N-S 07-567-8706
SOUTH COUNTY HOSPITAL INC
100 Kenyon Ave, Wakefield, RI 2879
Phone: (401) 782-8000
Sales: $46,664,000
Company Type: Private
SIC: 8062
  General medical & surgical hospital
Patrick Muldoon, President

Employees: 500
Employees here: 500

D-U-N-S 07-897-2262
SOUTH BALDWIN COUNTY HEALTHCAR
1613 N McKenzie St, Foley, AL 36535
Phone: (334) 943-5051
Sales: $24,354,000
Company Type: Private
SIC: 8062
  General hospital
Robert Jernigan, Administrator

Employees: 425
Employees here: 425

D-U-N-S 15-602-6098
SOUTH CROLINA DEPT MENTAL HEALTH
1801 Colonial Dr, Columbia, SC 29203
Phone: (803) 734-7038
Sales: $34,000,000
Company Type: Private
SIC: 8011
  Medical doctor's office
Dr Scully, Director

Employees: NA
Employees here: 551

D-U-N-S 07-415-2539
SOUTH BAY COMMUNITY HOSPITAL
514 N Prospect Ave, Redondo Beach, CA 90277
Phone: (310) 376-9474

D-U-N-S 14-794-3880
SOUTH CROLINA DEPT MENTAL HEALTH
Hwy 76 E, Clinton, SC 29325
Phone: (864) 833-2733

Sales: $27,100,000   *Employees:* NA
Company Type: Private   *Employees here:* 1,372
SIC: 8059
  Nursing/personal care
Bill Killion, Manager

D-U-N-S 12-218-2389
SOUTH DADE HEALTHCARE GROUP
  (Parent: Columbia/Hca Healthcare Corp)
9333 SW 152nd St, Miami, FL 33157
Phone: (305) 251-2500
Sales: $27,600,000   *Employees:* 607
Company Type: Public Family Member   *Employees here:* 500
SIC: 8062
  General medical & surgical hospital
Jude Torchia, Chief Executive Officer

D-U-N-S 08-020-2120
SOUTH DAKOTA DEPT HUMANSVCS
1000 W 31st St, Yankton, SD 57078
Phone: (605) 668-3100
Sales: $19,900,000   *Employees:* NA
Company Type: Private   *Employees here:* 641
SIC: 8063
  Mental hospital
Steven Linquist, Administrator

D-U-N-S 07-919-6093
SOUTH FLORIDA BAPTIST HOSPITAL
301 N Alexander St, Plant City, FL 33566
Phone: (813) 757-1200
Sales: $40,534,000   *Employees:* 613
Company Type: Private   *Employees here:* 600
SIC: 8062
  General hospital
Jill Moon, Chief Operating Officer

D-U-N-S 06-917-7038
SOUTH FULTON MEDICAL CENTER
1170 Cleveland Ave, Atlanta, GA 30344
Phone: (404) 305-3500
Sales: $87,398,000   *Employees:* 1,350
Company Type: Private   *Employees here:* 1,342
SIC: 8062
  Hospital
Neil Copelan, Chief Executive Officer

D-U-N-S 12-482-2495
SOUTH HILLS HEALTH SYSTEM
Coal Valley Rd, Pittsburgh, PA 15236
Phone: (412) 469-5855
Sales: $94,500,000   *Employees:* NA
Company Type: Private   *Employees here:* 1,900
SIC: 8062
  Hospital
William Jennings, President

D-U-N-S 15-374-3836
SOUTH HILLS HEALTH SYSTEM
1800 West St, Homestead, PA 15120
Phone: (412) 664-5000
Sales: $150,111,000   *Employees:* 2,700
Company Type: Private   *Employees here:* 25
SIC: 8062
  General hospital
William R Jennings, President

D-U-N-S 07-221-4018
SOUTH MIAMI HOSPITAL INC
6200 SW 73rd St, Miami, FL 33143
Phone: (305) 661-4611

Sales: $148,891,000   *Employees:* 2,200
Company Type: Private   *Employees here:* 2,200
SIC: 8062
  General hospital
Wayne Brackin, President

D-U-N-S 07-193-2578
SOUTH MISSISSIPPI HOME HEALTH
  (Parent: Deaconess Hospital)
108 Lundy Ln, Hattiesburg, MS 39401
Phone: (601) 268-1842
Sales: $28,015,000   *Employees:* 750
Company Type: Private   *Employees here:* 40
SIC: 8082
  In-home nursing service
Mary E Stainton, President

D-U-N-S 05-059-5933
SOUTH NASSAU COMMUNITIES HOSP
2445 Oceanside Rd, Oceanside, NY 11572
Phone: (516) 763-2030
Sales: $50,100,000   *Employees:* 1,085
Company Type: Private   *Employees here:* 1,035
SIC: 8062
  General medical & surgical hospital
William C Kirkwood, President

D-U-N-S 08-293-8788
SOUTH SHORE HOSPITAL CORP
8012 S Crandon Ave, Chicago, IL 60617
Phone: (773) 768-0810
Sales: $30,211,000   *Employees:* 520
Company Type: Private   *Employees here:* 500
SIC: 8062
  Medical & surgical hospital
John D Harper, President

D-U-N-S 07-659-1353
SOUTH SHORE HOSPITAL INC
55 Fogg Rd, South Weymouth, MA 2190
Phone: (781) 340-8000
Sales: $170,046,000   *Employees:* 2,375
Company Type: Private   *Employees here:* 1,775
SIC: 8062
  General hospital home care agency & visiting nurse
    association
David T Hannan, President

D-U-N-S 09-218-1775
SOUTH SHORE MNTAL HEALTH CTR INC
6 Fort St, Quincy, MA 2169
Phone: (617) 847-1950
Sales: $21,519,000   *Employees:* 195
Company Type: Private   *Employees here:* 125
SIC: 8093
  Outpatient mental health center
Harry Shulman, President

D-U-N-S 06-594-0579
SOUTHAMPTON HOSPITAL ASSN
240 Meeting House Ln, Southampton, NY 11968
Phone: (516) 726-8400
Sales: $61,088,000   *Employees:* 770
Company Type: Private   *Employees here:* 746
SIC: 8062
  Hospital
Elliot E Vose, Chairman of the Board

D-U-N-S 06-599-7694
SOUTHAMPTON MEMORIAL HOSPITAL
100 Fairview Dr, Franklin, VA 23851
Phone: (757) 569-6100

Sales: $31,525,000
Company Type: Private
SIC: 8062
  General hospital
E J Patnesky, President

Employees: 440
Employees here: 400

D-U-N-S 08-713-8129
SOUTHBORO MEDICAL GROUP INC
24 Newton St, Southborough, MA 1772
Phone: (508) 481-5500
Sales: $28,137,000
Company Type: Private
SIC: 8011
  Medical service & group practice
Dr Marvin Ostrovsky Md, President

Employees: 430
Employees here: 240

D-U-N-S 01-910-5357
SOUTHCOAST HOSPITAL GROUP INC
101 Page St, New Bedford, MA 2740
Phone: (508) 997-1515
Sales: $95,000,000
Company Type: Private
SIC: 8062
  General hospital
John B Day, Branch Manager

Employees: NA
Employees here: 1,872

D-U-N-S 94-757-8753
SOUTHCOAST HOSPITAL GROUP INC
101 Page St, New Bedford, MA 2740
Phone: (508) 961-5002
Sales: $305,386,000
Company Type: Private
SIC: 8062
  Hospital
Ronald Goodspeed, President

Employees: 3,950
Employees here: 2,000

D-U-N-S 94-758-8547
SOUTHCOAST HOSPITAL GROUP INC
363 Highland Ave, Fall River, MA 2720
Phone: (508) 679-3131
Sales: $91,000,000
Company Type: Private
SIC: 8062
  General hospital
Ronald Goodspeed, Principal

Employees: NA
Employees here: 1,794

D-U-N-S 08-372-7826
SOUTHEAST ALASKA REG HEALTH
3245 Hospital Dr, Juneau, AK 99801
Phone: (907) 463-4000
Sales: $54,653,000
Company Type: Private
SIC: 8011
  Medical doctor's office general hospital
Ethel Lund, President

Employees: 580
Employees here: 100

D-U-N-S 07-696-9583
SOUTHEAST MISSOURI HOSPITAL ASSN
1701 Lacey St, Cape Girardeau, MO 63701
Phone: (573) 334-4822
Sales: $107,030,000
Company Type: Private
SIC: 8062
  General hospital
James W Wente, Chief Executive Officer

Employees: 1,400
Employees here: 1,300

D-U-N-S 07-201-0028
SOUTHEASTERN REGIONAL MED CTR
300 W 27th St, Lumberton, NC 28358
Phone: (910) 671-5000

Sales: $112,230,000
Company Type: Private
SIC: 8062
  Hospital
J L Welsh Jr, President

Employees: 1,600
Employees here: 1,100

D-U-N-S 07-758-2369
SOUTHERN BAPTIST HOSPITAL OF FLA
800 Prudential Dr, Jacksonville, FL 32207
Phone: (904) 393-2000
Sales: $228,460,000
Company Type: Private
SIC: 8062
  General hospital
John Wilbanks, Executive Vice-President

Employees: 2,600
Employees here: 2,300

D-U-N-S 17-447-6481
SOUTHERN CAL PERMANENTE MED GROUP
5601 De Soto Ave, Woodland Hills, CA 91367
Phone: (818) 719-2000
Sales: $165,800,000
Company Type: Private
SIC: 8011
  Medical doctor's office
Joesph Ruderman, Branch Manager

Employees: NA
Employees here: 3,000

D-U-N-S 02-020-3717
SOUTHERN CAL PERMANENTE MED GROUP
4647 Zion Ave, San Diego, CA 92120
Phone: (619) 528-5000
Sales: $124,200,000
Company Type: Private
SIC: 8011
  Medical clinic
Dr Maurice J Alfaro Md, N/A

Employees: NA
Employees here: 2,200

D-U-N-S 07-144-6777
SOUTHERN CHESTER CNTY MED CTR
1015 W Baltimore Pike, West Grove, PA 19390
Phone: (610) 869-1000
Sales: $26,172,000
Company Type: Private
SIC: 8062
  General hospital
Scott K Phillips, President

Employees: 400
Employees here: 400

D-U-N-S 62-521-5389
SOUTHERN HEALTH CARE OF ALA
  (Parent: Southern Health Care Inc)
735 Broad St Ste 900, Chattanooga, TN 37402
Phone: (423) 267-8406
Sales: $23,228,000
Company Type: Private
SIC: 8062
  General hospital
Alan Tucker, President

Employees: 350
Employees here: 20

D-U-N-S 86-939-6713
SOUTHERN HEALTH MANAGEMENT
2705 Artie St SW Bldg 400, Huntsville, AL 35805
Phone: (256) 539-1776
Sales: $68,800,000
Company Type: Private
SIC: 8011
  Health maintenance organization
Bryson F Hill Jr, President

Employees: 1,000
Employees here: 185

D-U-N-S 12-182-0393
SOUTHERN HEALTH SERVICES, INC
  (Parent: Southern Health Mgt Corp)
9881 Mayland Dr, Richmond, VA 23233
Phone: (804) 747-3700

Sales: $84,621,000
Company Type: Private
SIC: 8011
   Health maintenance organization
James L Gore, President
Employees: 4
Employees here: 1

D-U-N-S 61-527-5872
SOUTHERN HEALTHCARE SYSTEMS
17617 S Harrells Ferry Rd, Baton Rouge, LA 70816
Phone: (225) 753-0864
Sales: $31,549,000
Company Type: Private
SIC: 8051
   Skilled nursing care facility
Richard Daspit, President
Employees: 634
Employees here: 6

D-U-N-S 09-439-0358
SOUTHERN ILLINOIS HOSPITAL SVCS
404 W Main St, Carbondale, IL 62901
Phone: (618) 549-0721
Sales: $35,100,000
Company Type: Private
SIC: 8062
   General hospital
George Maroney, Principal
Employees: NA
Employees here: 900

D-U-N-S 09-555-5579
SOUTHERN MANAGEMENT SERVICES
455 Indian Rocks Rd N, Largo, FL 33770
Phone: (727) 585-6333
Sales: $51,500,000
Company Type: Private
SIC: 8051
   Operates nursing homes an apartment building & ret
   building materials
William G Buckles, President
Employees: 400
Employees here: 20

D-U-N-S 08-105-5154
SOUTHERN MARYLAND HOSPITAL
7503 Surratts Rd, Clinton, MD 20735
Phone: (301) 868-8000
Sales: $97,996,000
Company Type: Private
SIC: 8062
   General hospital
Dr Francis P Chiaramonte Md, President
Employees: 1,300
Employees here: 1,270

D-U-N-S 03-957-5394
SOUTHERN MEDICAL GROUP, INC
3500 Blue Lake Dr Ste 480, Birmingham, AL 35243
Phone: (205) 715-5177
Sales: $24,970,000
Company Type: Private
SIC: 8011
   Physicians
Allan Kennedy, President
Employees: 50
Employees here: 50

D-U-N-S 07-397-1772
SOUTHERN NH REGIONAL MED CTR
8 Prospect St, Nashua, NH 3060
Phone: (603) 577-2000
Sales: $69,822,000
Company Type: Private
SIC: 8062
   General hospital
Thomas E Wilhelmsen, President
Employees: 1,014
Employees here: 1,000

D-U-N-S 17-377-7533
SOUTHERN OCEAN COUNTY HOSP
1140 Route 72 W, Manahawkin, NJ 8050
Phone: (609) 978-8900

Sales: $46,501,000
Company Type: Private
SIC: 8062
   General hospital
Joseph P Coyle, President
Employees: 600
Employees here: 550

D-U-N-S 07-501-9810
SOUTHERN OHIO MEDICAL CENTER
1248 Kinneys Ln, Portsmouth, OH 45662
Phone: (740) 354-5000
Sales: $117,860,000
Company Type: Private
SIC: 8062
   General hospital
Randal M Arnett, President
Employees: 2,000
Employees here: 6

D-U-N-S 62-800-2214
SOUTHERN OHIO MEDICAL CENTER
1805 27th St, Portsmouth, OH 45662
Phone: (740) 354-5000
Sales: $62,000,000
Company Type: Private
SIC: 8062
   General hospital
Randal M Arnett, Principal
Employees: NA
Employees here: 1,580

D-U-N-S 78-248-3911
SOUTHERN REGIONAL MEDICAL CTR
11 Upper Riverdale Rd SW, Riverdale, GA 30274
Phone: (770) 991-8000
Sales: $72,100,000
Company Type: Private
SIC: 8062
   General hospital
J R Hudson, Chief Executive Officer
Employees: 1,550
Employees here: 1,550

D-U-N-S 07-792-5782
SOUTHSIDE COMMUNITY HOSPITAL ASSN
800 Oak St, Farmville, VA 23901
Phone: (804) 392-8811
Sales: $27,900,000
Company Type: Private
SIC: 8062
   Hospital
John Greer, Administrator
Employees: 465
Employees here: 465

D-U-N-S 06-800-9935
SOUTHSIDE HOSPITAL INC
301 E Main St, Bay Shore, NY 11706
Phone: (516) 968-3000
Sales: $88,700,000
Company Type: Private
SIC: 8062
   General medical & surgical hospital
Theodore A Jospe, President
Employees: 1,900
Employees here: 1,900

D-U-N-S 36-353-5857
SOUTHSIDE VIRGINIA TRAINING CTR
W Washington St, Petersburg, VA 23803
Phone: (804) 524-7333
Sales: $52,000,000
Company Type: Private
SIC: 8361
   Residential care and training facility
Thomas J Yencha, Administrative Director
Employees: 1,600
Employees here: 1,600

D-U-N-S 07-502-6468
SOUTHSTERN OHIO REGIONAL MED CTR
1341 Clark St, Cambridge, OH 43725
Phone: (740) 439-3561

Sales: $39,131,000   *Employees:* 653
Company Type: Private   *Employees here:* 653
SIC: 8062
  General hospital
Philip Hearing, President

D-U-N-S 16-153-0308
SOUTHWEST CATHOLIC HEALTH NETWORK
2800 N Central Ave, Phoenix, AZ 85004
Phone: (602) 263-3066
Sales: $132,090,000   *Employees:* 180
Company Type: Private   *Employees here:* 165
SIC: 8011
  Health maintenance organization for the medically indigent
Kathy Byrne, President

D-U-N-S 78-663-7405
SOUTHWEST COMMUNITY HEALTH SYSTEMS
18697 Bagley Rd, Cleveland, OH 44130
Phone: (440) 816-8000
Sales: $103,643,000   *Employees:* 1,982
Company Type: Private   *Employees here:* 1,982
SIC: 8062
  Hospital
L J Schurmeier, President

D-U-N-S 06-967-1782
SOUTHWEST FLA REGIONAL MED CTR
  (Parent: Basic American Medical Inc)
2727 Winkler Ave, Fort Myers, FL 33901
Phone: (941) 939-1147
Sales: $175,000,000   *Employees:* 1,600
Company Type: Public Family Member   *Employees here:* 1,400
SIC: 8062
  General hospital
Larry Pieretti, President

D-U-N-S 07-692-0859
SOUTHWEST GENERAL HEALTH CTR
18697 Bagley Rd, Cleveland, OH 44130
Phone: (440) 816-8000
Sales: $119,344,000   *Employees:* 2,000
Company Type: Private   *Employees here:* 1,398
SIC: 8062
  General hospital
L J Schurmeier, President

D-U-N-S 08-238-7101
SOUTHWEST JEFFERSON COMMUNITY HOSP
  (Parent: Columbia/Hca Healthcare Corp)
9820 3rd Street Rd, Louisville, KY 40272
Phone: (502) 933-8100
Sales: $34,308,000   *Employees:* 350
Company Type: Public Family Member   *Employees here:* 350
SIC: 8062
  General hospital
Richard Scott, President

D-U-N-S 92-985-7472
SOUTHWEST LA HEALTH CARE SYS
1701 Oak Park Blvd, Lake Charles, LA 70601
Phone: (318) 494-3204
Sales: $99,900,000   *Employees:* 1,450
Company Type: Private   *Employees here:* 1,450
SIC: 8011
  Medical clinics
Elton L Williams, President

D-U-N-S 07-416-9962
SOUTHWEST LOUISIANA HOSPITAL ASSN
1701 Oak Park Blvd, Lake Charles, LA 70601
Phone: (318) 494-3000

Sales: $102,148,000   *Employees:* 1,500
Company Type: Private   *Employees here:* 1,470
SIC: 8062
  General hospital
Elton L Williams Jr, President

D-U-N-S 06-038-3361
SOUTHWEST MEDICAL ASSOCIATES
  (Parent: Sierra Health Services Inc)
2350 W Charleston Blvd, Las Vegas, NV 89102
Phone: (702) 877-8600
Sales: $95,678,000   *Employees:* 520
Company Type: Public Family Member   *Employees here:* 400
SIC: 8011
  Medical practice
Dr Jerry D Reeves Md, Chairman of the Board

D-U-N-S 07-331-6242
SOUTHWEST MEDICAL CENTER
315 W 15th St, Liberal, KS 67901
Phone: (316) 624-1651
Sales: $33,324,000   *Employees:* 500
Company Type: Private   *Employees here:* 478
SIC: 8062
  Hospital with skilled nursing
David Kindel, Chief Executive Officer

D-U-N-S 07-262-7599
SOUTHWEST MISS REGIONAL MED CTR
215 Marion Ave, Mc Comb, MS 39648
Phone: (601) 249-5500
Sales: $61,938,000   *Employees:* 1,000
Company Type: Private   *Employees here:* 1,000
SIC: 8062
  General hospital
Norman Price, Administrator

D-U-N-S 05-096-7926
SOUTHWEST WASHINGTON MED CTR
400 NE Mother Joseph Pl, Vancouver, WA 98664
Phone: (360) 256-2000
Sales: $164,945,000   *Employees:* 2,500
Company Type: Private   *Employees here:* 1,800
SIC: 8062
  Hospitals
Eugene Johnson, Acting Ceo

D-U-N-S 06-894-9346
SOUTHWESTERN OHIO SENIORS SVCS
11100 Springfield Pike, Cincinnati, OH 45246
Phone: (513) 782-2400
Sales: $23,143,000   *Employees:* 355
Company Type: Private   *Employees here:* 350
SIC: 8052
  Intermediate & skilled care facility for senior citizens
Jerry D Smart, President

D-U-N-S 06-052-7645
SOUTHWESTERN VT MEDICAL CENTER
100 Hospital Dr, Bennington, VT 5201
Phone: (802) 442-6361
Sales: $42,381,000   *Employees:* 650
Company Type: Private   *Employees here:* 650
SIC: 8062
  General hospital
Harvey M Yorke, President

D-U-N-S 08-226-1314
SOUTHWSTERN ILL HEALTH FCILITIES
Hwy 162 Old Edwrdsvlle Rd, Maryville, IL 62062
Phone: (618) 288-5711

Sales: $47,839,000
Company Type: Private
SIC: 8062
   General hospital
Cort Shepard, President

Employees: 600
Employees here: 470

D-U-N-S 07-567-5447
SPARKS REGIONAL MEDICAL CTR
1311 S I St, Fort Smith, AR 72901
Phone: (501) 441-4000
Sales: $121,339,000
Company Type: Private
SIC: 8062
   General hospital
Charles Shuffield, President

Employees: 1,800
Employees here: 1,800

D-U-N-S 05-207-2048
SPARTANBURG CNTY HEALTH SVCS DST
101 E Wood St, Spartanburg, SC 29303
Phone: (864) 560-6000
Sales: $279,224,000
Company Type: Private
SIC: 8062
   General hospital
Joseph Oddis, President

Employees: 2,931
Employees here: 2,533

D-U-N-S 07-952-0862
SPAULDING RHBLTATION HOSPITAL CORP
125 Nashua St, Boston, MA 2114
Phone: (617) 720-6400
Sales: $78,069,000
Company Type: Private
SIC: 8069
   Rehabilitation hospital and medical clinics
David Storto, Acting Ceo

Employees: 1,127
Employees here: 950

D-U-N-S 12-134-1200
SPECTERA INC
2811 Lord Baltimore Dr, Baltimore, MD 21244
Phone: (410) 265-6033
Sales: $56,193,000
Company Type: Private
SIC: 8011
   Provides ancillary employee benefit plans optical dental &
   prescription drug utilization review & ret optical stores
Dr Oscar Camp, Chairman of the Board

Employees: 370
Employees here: 100

D-U-N-S 07-257-5780
SPECTRUM HEALTH - DWNTWN CAMPUS
100 Michigan St NE, Grand Rapids, MI 49503
Phone: (616) 391-1774
Sales: $317,663,000
Company Type: Private
SIC: 8062
   General hospital provides emergency helicopter transport
   services and medical clinics
Phil Mccorkle, Chief Executive Officer

Employees: 3,610
Employees here: 3,400

D-U-N-S 02-019-8388
SPENCER MUNICIPAL HOSPITAL
1200 1st Ave E, Spencer, IA 51301
Phone: (712) 264-6111
Sales: $23,322,000
Company Type: Private
SIC: 8062
   General hospital
Jerry Poehling, Administrator

Employees: 439
Employees here: 439

D-U-N-S 78-695-0998
SPOHN HEALTH SYSTEMS
600 Elizabeth St, Corpus Christi, TX 78404
Phone: (512) 881-3000

Sales: $174,708,000
Company Type: Private
SIC: 8062
   General hospitals and health system management
Helen Vance, Chief Financial Officer

Employees: 2,500
Employees here: 2,200

D-U-N-S 06-944-7449
SPOHN KLEBERG MEMORIAL HOSP
600 Elizabeth St, Corpus Christi, TX 78404
Phone: (512) 595-1661
Sales: $37,327,000
Company Type: Private
SIC: 8062
   General hospital
Buddy Flores, Administrator

Employees: 350
Employees here: 350

D-U-N-S 92-652-5049
SPRING BRANCH MEDICAL CTR INC
(Parent: H C A Health Svcs Texas Inc)
8850 Long Point Rd, Houston, TX 77055
Phone: (713) 467-6555
Sales: $57,400,000
Company Type: Public Family Member
SIC: 8062
   Medical & surgical hospital
Sally Jeffcoat, Chief Executive Officer

Employees: 1,238
Employees here: 1,238

D-U-N-S 80-095-8050
SPRING HILL REGIONAL HOSPITAL
10461 Quality Dr, Spring Hill, FL 34609
Phone: (352) 688-8200
Sales: $24,290,000
Company Type: Private
SIC: 8062
   General hospital
Sonia Gonzalez, Administrator

Employees: 350
Employees here: 350

D-U-N-S 08-059-1654
SPRINGER CLINIC, INC
6160 S Yale Ave, Tulsa, OK 74136
Phone: (918) 492-7200
Sales: $59,978,000
Company Type: Private
SIC: 8011
   Medical clinic
Rick A Callis, Administrator

Employees: 425
Employees here: 300

D-U-N-S 04-703-2875
SPRINGFIELD CLINIC
1025 S 7th St, Springfield, IL 62703
Phone: (217) 528-7541
Sales: $33,100,000
Company Type: Private
SIC: 8011
   Clinic
Dr Michael A Pick Md, Managing Partner

Employees: 482
Employees here: 463

D-U-N-S 07-396-4330
SPRINGFIELD HOSPITAL
25 Ridgewood Rd, Springfield, VT 5156
Phone: (802) 885-2999
Sales: $22,634,000
Company Type: Private
SIC: 8062
   General medical & surgical hospital
Glen Cordner, Chief Executive Officer

Employees: 330
Employees here: 330

D-U-N-S 07-791-6674
SPRINGHILL HOSPITALS INC
(Parent: Southern Medical Hlth Systems)
3719 Dauphin St, Mobile, AL 36608
Phone: (334) 344-9630

Sales: $71,086,000   *Employees:* 900
Company Type: Private   *Employees here:* 900
SIC: 8062
    Hospital
William Mason, President

D-U-N-S 10-173-7229
SPRINGMOOR INC
1500 Sawmill Rd, Raleigh, NC 27615
Phone: (919) 848-7000
Sales: $22,514,000   *Employees:* 400
Company Type: Private   *Employees here:* 400
SIC: 8059
    Retirement community with health nursing facilities
Kyle W Dilday, Executive Director

D-U-N-S 19-597-3839
SPRINGWOOD ASSOC LTD PARTNR
300 Gleed Ave, East Aurora, NY 14052
Phone: (716) 652-2820
Sales: $42,300,000   *Employees:* 1,900
Company Type: Private   *Employees here:* 40
SIC: 8059
    Nursing homes
Neil M Chur, General Manager

D-U-N-S 79-005-1205
SSM HEALTH CARE OF OKLAHOMA
1000 N Lee Ave, Oklahoma City, OK 73102
Phone: (405) 272-6835
Sales: $77,100,000   *Employees:* 1,655
Company Type: Private   *Employees here:* 1,655
SIC: 8062
    Hospital management
Steve L Hunter, President

D-U-N-S 07-069-1662
SSM HEALTH CARE
12935 Gregory St, Blue Island, IL 60406
Phone: (708) 597-2000
Sales: $49,600,000   *Employees:* NA
Company Type: Private   *Employees here:* 1,175
SIC: 8062
    General hospital
Jay Crusier, Systems/Data Processing

D-U-N-S 07-711-0021
SSM HEALTH CARE
477 N Lindbergh Blvd, Saint Louis, MO 63141
Phone: (314) 994-7800
Sales: $532,283,000   *Employees:* 20,400
Company Type: Private   *Employees here:* 100
SIC: 8062
    General medical hospital skilled nursing home
Mary J Ryan Sr, President

D-U-N-S 18-203-7325
SSM HEALTH CARE
6420 Clayton Rd, Saint Louis, MO 63117
Phone: (314) 768-8000
Sales: $101,700,000   *Employees:* NA
Company Type: Private   *Employees here:* 2,400
SIC: 8062
    General hospital
Micheal Zilm, President

D-U-N-S 18-654-2874
SSM HEALTH CARE
100 Saint Marys Medical P, Jefferson City, MO 65101
Phone: (573) 635-7642

Sales: $39,000,000   *Employees:* NA
Company Type: Private   *Employees here:* 1,000
SIC: 8062
    General hospital
John Dubis, Manager

D-U-N-S 83-676-8135
SSM HEALTH CARE
707 S Mills St, Madison, WI 53715
Phone: (608) 258-6712
Sales: $59,200,000   *Employees:* NA
Company Type: Private   *Employees here:* 1,400
SIC: 8062
    Hospital
Gerald Lefert, Branch Manager

D-U-N-S 79-546-3439
SSM REHABILITATION
6420 Clayton Rd Ste 600, Saint Louis, MO 63117
Phone: (314) 768-5300
Sales: $31,895,000   *Employees:* 230
Company Type: Private   *Employees here:* 30
SIC: 8093
    Rehabilitation institute
Carla S Baum, President

D-U-N-S 06-938-0160
ST AGNES HEALTHCARE
900 S Caton Ave, Baltimore, MD 21229
Phone: (410) 368-6000
Sales: $117,300,000   *Employees:* 2,506
Company Type: Private   *Employees here:* 2,469
SIC: 8062
    General hospital
Robert E Pezzoli, President

D-U-N-S 07-870-9268
ST AGNES HOSPITAL
305 North St, White Plains, NY 10605
Phone: (914) 681-4500
Sales: $38,700,000   *Employees:* 842
Company Type: Private   *Employees here:* 697
SIC: 8062
    General hospital
Gary Horan, President

D-U-N-S 07-895-1555
ST AGNES HOSPITAL OF FOND DU LAC
430 E Division St, Fond Du Lac, WI 54935
Phone: (920) 929-2300
Sales: $93,381,000   *Employees:* 1,100
Company Type: Private   *Employees here:* 950
SIC: 8062
    Hospital
James J Sexton, Chief Executive Officer

D-U-N-S 06-905-3148
ST AGNES MEDICAL CENTER
1900 S Broad St, Philadelphia, PA 19145
Phone: (215) 339-4100
Sales: $58,513,000   *Employees:* 840
Company Type: Private   *Employees here:* 840
SIC: 8062
    General hospital
Daniel Sinnott, President

D-U-N-S 06-654-2846
ST ALEXIUS MEDICAL CENTER
900 E Broadway Ave, Bismarck, ND 58501
Phone: (701) 224-7000

Sales: $109,088,000 *Employees:* 1,875
Company Type: Private *Employees here:* 1,500
SIC: 8062
  Hospital
Richard A Tschider, Chief Executive Officer

D-U-N-S 18-549-9910
ST ALPHONSUS REGIONAL MED CTR
1055 N Curtis Rd, Boise, ID 83706
Phone: (208) 378-2121
Sales: $144,231,000 *Employees:* 1,927
Company Type: Private *Employees here:* 1,927
SIC: 8062
  Hospital
Sandra Bruce, President

D-U-N-S 04-307-6256
ST ANN'S HOME FOR AGED
1500 Portland Ave, Rochester, NY 14621
Phone: (716) 342-1700
Sales: $19,894,000 *Employees:* 750
Company Type: Private *Employees here:* 750
SIC: 8361
  Residential care services
Marie M Peartree Sr, President

D-U-N-S 04-965-3066
ST ANN'S HOSPITAL OF COLUMBUS
5955 E Broad St, Columbus, OH 43213
Phone: (614) 898-4000
Sales: $55,600,000 *Employees:* 825
Company Type: Private *Employees here:* 1
SIC: 8062
  Hospital
Joe Calvaruso, President

D-U-N-S 07-572-8170
ST ANNE'S HOSPITAL CORP
795 Middle St, Fall River, MA 2721
Phone: (508) 674-5741
Sales: $61,952,000 *Employees:* 906
Company Type: Private *Employees here:* 876
SIC: 8062
  General medical & surgical hospital
Michael W Metzler, President

D-U-N-S 07-123-6103
ST ANTHONY HOSPITAL
1000 N Lee Ave, Oklahoma City, OK 73102
Phone: (405) 272-7000
Sales: $145,742,000 *Employees:* 2,000
Company Type: Private *Employees here:* 1,950
SIC: 8062
  General medical & surgical hospital
Karen L Amen, Vice-President

D-U-N-S 06-997-4376
ST ANTHONY MEDICAL CENTER INC
1201 S Main St, Crown Point, IN 46307
Phone: (219) 738-2100
Sales: $87,579,000 *Employees:* 1,200
Company Type: Private *Employees here:* 1,000
SIC: 8062
  Medical & surgical hospital
Stephen O Leurck, President

D-U-N-S 07-588-8081
ST ANTHONY MEMORIAL HOSPITAL
503 N Maple St, Effingham, IL 62401
Phone: (217) 342-2121

Sales: $47,129,000 *Employees:* 566
Company Type: Private *Employees here:* 566
SIC: 8062
  General hospital
Anthony Pfitzer, Executive Vice-President

D-U-N-S 07-584-7038
ST ANTHONY REGIONAL HOSPITAL
311 S Clark St, Carroll, IA 51401
Phone: (712) 792-3581
Sales: $21,318,000 *Employees:* 425
Company Type: Private *Employees here:* 425
SIC: 8062
  Hospital
Gary Riedmann, Administrator

D-U-N-S 11-481-3850
ST ANTHONY'S HOSPITAL
St Anthonys Way, Alton, IL 62002
Phone: (618) 465-2571
Sales: $46,100,000 *Employees:* 1,000
Company Type: Private *Employees here:* 700
SIC: 8062
  General hospital
Sister M Plass, Chairman of the Board

D-U-N-S 05-497-2492
ST ANTHONY'S HOSPITAL
1601 SE Court Ave, Pendleton, OR 97801
Phone: (541) 276-5121
Sales: $20,829,000 *Employees:* 282
Company Type: Private *Employees here:* 282
SIC: 8062
  Hospital
Jeffrey Drop, President

D-U-N-S 06-279-3955
ST ANTHONY'S HOSPITAL INC
1200 7th Ave N, Saint Petersburg, FL 33705
Phone: (727) 825-1100
Sales: $91,517,000 *Employees:* 1,500
Company Type: Private *Employees here:* 1,312
SIC: 8062
  General hospital
Frank Murphy, Chief Executive Officer

D-U-N-S 07-711-8610
ST ANTHONY'S MEDICAL CENTER
10010 Kennerly Rd, Saint Louis, MO 63128
Phone: (314) 525-1000
Sales: $121,200,000 *Employees:* 2,589
Company Type: Private *Employees here:* 55
SIC: 8062
  General hospital psychiatric services outpatient care facilities
    adolescent rehabilitation and skilled nursing home
David P Seifert, President

D-U-N-S 19-426-7407
ST BARNABAS COMMUNITY ENTPS
4422 3rd Ave, Bronx, NY 10457
Phone: (718) 960-6100
Sales: $93,400,000 *Employees:* 2,000
Company Type: Private *Employees here:* 1
SIC: 8062
  General hospital
Dr Ronald Gade, Chairman of the Board

D-U-N-S 06-811-7787
ST BARNABAS HOSPITAL
4422 3rd Ave, Bronx, NY 10457
Phone: (718) 960-9000

Sales: $81,600,000   *Employees:* 1,750
Company Type: Private   *Employees here:* 1,500
SIC: 8062
  General hospital
Dr Ronald Gade, President

D-U-N-S 06-752-0759
ST BARNABAS MEDICAL CENTER
Old Short Hills Rd, Livingston, NJ 7039
Phone: (973) 533-5000
Sales: $121,800,000   *Employees:* 2,600
Company Type: Private   *Employees here:* 2,500
SIC: 8062
  General hospital
Ronald J Del Mauro, Chairman of the Board

D-U-N-S 05-057-3195
ST BERNARD HOSPITAL HEALTHCARE CTR
326 W 64th St, Chicago, IL 60621
Phone: (773) 962-3900
Sales: $53,238,000   *Employees:* 632
Company Type: Private   *Employees here:* 632
SIC: 8062
  General medical & surgical hospital
Sister E Van Stranton, President

D-U-N-S 07-355-5146
ST BERNARD'S HOSPITAL INC
224 E Matthews Ave, Jonesboro, AR 72401
Phone: (870) 972-4100
Sales: $137,617,000   *Employees:* 1,500
Company Type: Private   *Employees here:* 1,500
SIC: 8062
  General hospital
Ben E Owens, President

D-U-N-S 60-543-2954
ST CABRINI NURSING HOME INC
115 Broadway, Dobbs Ferry, NY 10522
Phone: (914) 693-6800
Sales: $26,193,000   *Employees:* 464
Company Type: Private   *Employees here:* 464
SIC: 8051
  Skilled nursing home
Robert G Patrick, Administrator

D-U-N-S 07-331-3744
ST CATHERINE HOSPITAL
410 E Walnut St, Garden City, KS 67846
Phone: (316) 272-2222
Sales: $23,302,000   *Employees:* 500
Company Type: Private   *Employees here:* 465
SIC: 8062
  General medical and surgical hospital
Gary Rowe, President

D-U-N-S 07-383-0705
ST CATHERINE'S HOSPITAL INC
3556 7th Ave, Kenosha, WI 53140
Phone: (414) 656-3011
Sales: $41,400,000   *Employees:* 900
Company Type: Private   *Employees here:* 800
SIC: 8062
  General hospital
Scott Abrams, Chief Financial Officer

D-U-N-S 06-149-2740
ST CHARLES MEDICAL CENTER
2500 NE Neff Rd, Bend, OR 97701
Phone: (541) 382-4321

Sales: $90,962,000   *Employees:* 1,200
Company Type: Private   *Employees here:* 1,200
SIC: 8062
  General hospital
James T Lussier, President

D-U-N-S 07-757-4580
ST CHARLES MERCY HOSPITAL
2600 Navarre Ave, Oregon, OH 43616
Phone: (419) 698-7200
Sales: $116,725,000   *Employees:* 1,903
Company Type: Private   *Employees here:* 1,651
SIC: 8062
  General hospital
Cathleen Nelson, Chief Executive Officer

D-U-N-S 14-652-2750
ST CHRIS HOSPITAL CHILDREN INC
Front St At Erie Ave, Philadelphia, PA 19134
Phone: (215) 427-5000
Sales: $132,824,000   *Employees:* 1,500
Company Type: Private   *Employees here:* 33
SIC: 8069
  Children's hospital
Calvin Bland, President

D-U-N-S 06-801-7110
ST CHARLES HOSPITAL PORT JEFFERSON NY
200 Belle Terre Rd, Port Jefferson, NY 11777
Phone: (516) 474-6000
Sales: $99,681,000   *Employees:* 1,010
Company Type: Private   *Employees here:* 985
SIC: 8062
  General hospital and medical clinics
Barry T Zeman, President

D-U-N-S 07-748-4665
ST CLAIR MEMORIAL HOSPITAL
1000 Bower Hill Rd, Pittsburgh, PA 15243
Phone: (412) 561-4900
Sales: $90,139,000   *Employees:* 1,192
Company Type: Private   *Employees here:* 1,192
SIC: 8062
  Hospital
Benjamin E Snead, President

D-U-N-S 06-813-5029
ST CLAIRE MEDICAL CENTER, INC
222 Medical Cir, Morehead, KY 40351
Phone: (606) 783-6500
Sales: $54,421,000   *Employees:* 900
Company Type: Private   *Employees here:* 600
SIC: 8062
  General hospital
Mark J Neff, President

D-U-N-S 07-115-3951
ST CLARE HOSPITAL MONROE WISCONSIN
515 22nd Ave, Monroe, WI 53566
Phone: (608) 324-2000
Sales: $51,202,000   *Employees:* 917
Company Type: Private   *Employees here:* 887
SIC: 8062
  Hospital & multi-specialty physician practice
Kenneth E Blount, President

D-U-N-S 06-820-6440
ST CLARES HOSPITAL & HEALTH CTR
415 W 51st St, New York, NY 10019
Phone: (212) 586-1500

Sales: $70,628,000   *Employees:* 855
Company Type: Private   *Employees here:* 750
SIC: 8062
  General medical & surgical hospital
James Rutherford, President

D-U-N-S 02-067-4941
ST CLARES HOSPITAL OF SCHNCTADY NY
600 McClellan St, Schenectady, NY 12304
Phone: (518) 382-2000
Sales: $61,749,000   *Employees:* 1,150
Company Type: Private   *Employees here:* 1,150
SIC: 8062
  General hospital
Jerome G Stewart, President

D-U-N-S 07-095-6867
ST DOMINIC'S HOME
500 Western Hwy, Blauvelt, NY 10913
Phone: (914) 359-3400
Sales: $23,833,000   *Employees:* 440
Company Type: Private   *Employees here:* 200
SIC: 8361
  Residential care
Sister M Flood, President

D-U-N-S 07-844-8313
ST ELIZABETH HOSPITAL
2830 Calder St, Beaumont, TX 77702
Phone: (409) 892-7171
Sales: $197,911,000   *Employees:* 3,600
Company Type: Private   *Employees here:* 2,355
SIC: 8062
  General medical and surgical hospital
Sister M Mc Carthy, Chief Executive Officer

D-U-N-S 06-579-3267
ST ELIZABETH HOSPITAL INC
225 Williamson St, Elizabeth, NJ 7202
Phone: (908) 527-5122
Sales: $103,158,000   *Employees:* 1,285
Company Type: Private   *Employees here:* 1,100
SIC: 8062
  Hospital
Elizabeth A Maloney Sr, President

D-U-N-S 07-477-8754
ST ELIZABETH HOSPITAL INC
1506 S Oneida St, Appleton, WI 54915
Phone: (920) 738-2000
Sales: $64,900,000   *Employees:* 1,398
Company Type: Private   *Employees here:* 1,368
SIC: 8062
  General hospital
Otto Cox, President

D-U-N-S 07-691-5479
ST ELIZABETH HOSPITAL MED CTR
1044 Belmont Ave, Youngstown, OH 44504
Phone: (330) 746-7211
Sales: $210,287,000   *Employees:* 2,500
Company Type: Private   *Employees here:* 2,480
SIC: 8062
  Hospital
Kevin Nolan, President

D-U-N-S 07-197-6096
ST ELIZABETH MEDICAL CENTER
2100 Madison Ave, Granite City, IL 62040
Phone: (618) 798-3000

Sales: $144,356,000   *Employees:* 930
Company Type: Private   *Employees here:* 905
SIC: 8062
  General medical hospital & medical laboratory
Theodore Eilerman, President

D-U-N-S 07-159-5474
ST ELIZABETH MEDICAL CENTER
2209 Genesee St, Utica, NY 13501
Phone: (315) 798-8100
Sales: $62,433,000   *Employees:* 1,220
Company Type: Private   *Employees here:* 1,000
SIC: 8062
  General hospital
Sister R Gleason, Chief Executive Officer

D-U-N-S 07-588-8370
ST ELIZABETH'S HOSPITAL
211 S 3rd St, Belleville, IL 62220
Phone: (618) 234-2120
Sales: $102,737,000   *Employees:* 1,600
Company Type: Private   *Employees here:* 1,600
SIC: 8062
  General hospital
Gerald M Harman, Executive Vice-President

D-U-N-S 06-439-1378
ST ELIZABETHS HOSPITAL OF CHICAGO
1431 N Claremont Ave, Chicago, IL 60622
Phone: (773) 278-2000
Sales: $82,239,000   *Employees:* 900
Company Type: Private   *Employees here:* 850
SIC: 8062
  General medical & surgical hospital
Jo A Birdzell, Chief Executive Officer

D-U-N-S 07-379-7292
ST ELZABETHS MED CTR OF BOSTON
736 Cambridge St, Boston, MA 2135
Phone: (617) 789-3000
Sales: $205,016,000   *Employees:* 2,365
Company Type: Private   *Employees here:* 2,327
SIC: 8062
  General hospital
Michael Collins, President

D-U-N-S 04-342-9182
ST FRANCES CABRINI HOSPITAL
3330 Masonic Dr, Alexandria, LA 71301
Phone: (318) 487-1122
Sales: $140,446,000   *Employees:* 1,200
Company Type: Private   *Employees here:* 1,189
SIC: 8062
  Hospital
Sister O Bordelon, President

D-U-N-S 18-974-9252
ST FRANCIS CENTRAL HOSPITAL
1200 Centre Ave, Pittsburgh, PA 15219
Phone: (412) 562-3000
Sales: $36,542,000   *Employees:* 500
Company Type: Private   *Employees here:* 500
SIC: 8062
  General hospital
John Horty, Chairman of the Board

D-U-N-S 07-499-1290
ST FRANCIS CENTRAL HOSPITAL
1200 Centre Ave, Pittsburgh, PA 15219
Phone: (412) 562-3000

Sales: $38,857,000   *Employees:* 600
Company Type: Private   *Employees here:* 560
SIC: 8062
  General hospital
Robin Z Mohr, President

D-U-N-S 80-390-3657
ST FRANCIS HEALTH SYSTEM
400 45th St, Pittsburgh, PA 15201
Phone: (412) 622-4343
Sales: $131,500,000   *Employees:* NA
Company Type: Private   *Employees here:* 2,500
SIC: 8069
  Specialty hospital
St R Wellinger, Branch Manager

D-U-N-S 06-875-1924
ST FRANCIS HOSPITAL OF NEW CASTLE
1000 S Mercer St, New Castle, PA 16101
Phone: (724) 658-3511
Sales: $32,316,000   *Employees:* 620
Company Type: Private   *Employees here:* 620
SIC: 8062
  General hospital
Robert Carlson, Chairman of the Board

D-U-N-S 11-490-0939
ST FRANCIS HOSPITAL THRD ORD (INC)
1215 Franciscan Dr, Litchfield, IL 62056
Phone: (217) 324-2191
Sales: $20,725,000   *Employees:* 370
Company Type: Private   *Employees here:* 370
SIC: 8062
  General hospital
Bob Davenport, Chief Financial Officer

D-U-N-S 06-597-4990
ST FRANCIS HOSPITAL
100 Port Washington Blvd, Roslyn, NY 11576
Phone: (516) 562-6000
Sales: $182,711,000   *Employees:* 1,759
Company Type: Private   *Employees here:* 1,759
SIC: 8069
  General hospital
Patrick J Scollard, President

D-U-N-S 07-731-4656
ST FRANCIS HOSPITAL & MED CTR
114 Woodland St, Hartford, CT 6105
Phone: (860) 714-4000
Sales: $328,669,000   *Employees:* 3,300
Company Type: Private   *Employees here:* 2,200
SIC: 8062
  General hospital
David D Eramo, President

D-U-N-S 92-899-5760
ST FRANCIS HOSPITAL & MED CTR
500 Blue Ave, Hartford, CT 6112
Phone: (860) 242-4431
Sales: $58,600,000   *Employees:* NA
Company Type: Private   *Employees here:* 1,160
SIC: 8062
  General hospital

D-U-N-S 02-120-5448
ST FRANCIS HOSPITAL & MED CTR
1700 SW 7th St, Topeka, KS 66606
Phone: (785) 295-8000

Sales: $113,535,000   *Employees:* 1,724
Company Type: Private   *Employees here:* NA
SIC: 8062
  Hospital
Sister L Colwell, President

D-U-N-S 07-947-6503
ST FRANCIS HOSPITAL INC
7th & Clayton Sts, Wilmington, DE 19805
Phone: (302) 421-4100
Sales: $116,437,000   *Employees:* 1,400
Company Type: Private   *Employees here:* 1,350
SIC: 8062
  Hospital
Steven Bjelich, President

D-U-N-S 06-582-4930
ST FRANCIS HOSPITAL INC
25 McWilliams Pl, Jersey City, NJ 7302
Phone: (201) 714-8900
Sales: $48,503,000   *Employees:* 600
Company Type: Private   *Employees here:* 600
SIC: 8062
  General & surgical hospital
Robert Chaloner, President

D-U-N-S 07-805-8344
ST FRANCIS HOSPITAL INC
St Francis Dr, Greenville, SC 29601
Phone: (864) 255-1000
Sales: $162,236,000   *Employees:* 1,500
Company Type: Private   *Employees here:* 1,081
SIC: 8062
  Hospital
Richard C Neugent, President

D-U-N-S 07-384-2056
ST FRANCIS HOSPITAL INC
3237 S 16th St, Milwaukee, WI 53215
Phone: (414) 647-5000
Sales: $119,738,000   *Employees:* 1,600
Company Type: Private   *Employees here:* 1,500
SIC: 8062
  General hospital
Gregory Banaszynski, President

D-U-N-S 61-030-0071
ST FRANCIS MED CENTER-WEST
91-2141 Fort Weaver Rd, Ewa Beach, HI 96706
Phone: (808) 678-7000
Sales: $44,933,000   *Employees:* 581
Company Type: Private   *Employees here:* 581
SIC: 8062
  General hospital
Sister G Gilroy, President

D-U-N-S 06-873-6487
ST FRANCIS MEDICAL CENTER
400 45th St, Pittsburgh, PA 15201
Phone: (412) 622-4343
Sales: $196,399,000   *Employees:* 2,800
Company Type: Private   *Employees here:* 2,591
SIC: 8062
  General hospital
Sister F Brandt, Chief Executive Officer

D-U-N-S 06-627-5660
ST FRANCIS MEDICAL CENTER
2230 Liliha St, Honolulu, HI 96817
Phone: (808) 547-6011

Sales: $128,612,000
Company Type: Private
SIC: 8062
    General medical and surgical hospital
Sister G Gilroy, Chief Executive Officer

Employees: 1,400
Employees here: 1,350

D-U-N-S 02-032-6641
ST FRANCIS MEDICAL CENTER
309 Jackson St, Monroe, LA 71201
Phone: (318) 327-4196
Sales: $149,007,000
Company Type: Private
SIC: 8062
    General medical & surgical hospital
Gerald Smith, Chief Executive Officer

Employees: 1,700
Employees here: 1,584

D-U-N-S 04-084-1306
ST FRANCIS MEDICAL CENTER
601 Hamilton Ave, Trenton, NJ 8629
Phone: (609) 599-5000
Sales: $81,877,000
Company Type: Private
SIC: 8062
    General hospital medical school & nursing school
Judith Persichilli, President

Employees: 1,150
Employees here: 1,050

D-U-N-S 07-762-6083
ST FRANCIS REGIONAL MED CTR
1455 Saint Francis Ave, Shakopee, MN 55379
Phone: (612) 403-3000
Sales: $27,901,000
Company Type: Private
SIC: 8062
    General hospital
Venetia Kuderle, President

Employees: 375
Employees here: 375

D-U-N-S 02-927-2606
ST HELENA HOSPITAL
650 Sanitarium Rd, Deer Park, CA 94576
Phone: (707) 963-3611
Sales: $59,127,000
Company Type: Private
SIC: 8062
    Hospital
Lenard Heffner, President

Employees: 875
Employees here: 750

D-U-N-S 05-005-9674
ST JAMES COMMUNITY HOSPITAL
400 S Clark St, Butte, MT 59701
Phone: (406) 723-2500
Sales: $20,600,000
Company Type: Private
SIC: 8062
    General medical & surgical hospital
Robert Rodgers, Officer

Employees: 460
Employees here: 460

D-U-N-S 07-368-3591
ST JAMES MERCY HOSPITAL
411 Canisteo St, Hornell, NY 14843
Phone: (607) 324-8000
Sales: $39,855,000
Company Type: Private
SIC: 8062
    Hospital
Paul E Shephard, Administrator

Employees: 975
Employees here: 650

D-U-N-S 07-402-5396
ST JEROME HOSPITAL
16 Bank St, Batavia, NY 14020
Phone: (716) 343-3131

Sales: $22,909,000
Company Type: Private
SIC: 8062
    General hospital
Charles W Smith Jr, Administrator

Employees: 500
Employees here: 492

D-U-N-S 06-721-1045
ST JO HOSPITAL OF PORT CHARLES
2500 Harbor Blvd, Port Charlotte, FL 33952
Phone: (941) 625-4122
Sales: $55,678,000
Company Type: Private
SIC: 8062
    Hospital
Michael L Harrington, Chief Executive Officer

Employees: 767
Employees here: 767

D-U-N-S 10-918-4176
ST JOHN AMBULATORY CARE CORP
22101 Moross Rd, Detroit, MI 48236
Phone: (313) 343-3303
Sales: $57,636,000
Company Type: Private
SIC: 8011
    Outpatient medical clinic
Patrick C Wrenn, President

Employees: 328
Employees here: 200

D-U-N-S 07-420-9875
ST JOHN HOSPITAL AND MED CTR
22101 Moross Rd, Detroit, MI 48236
Phone: (313) 343-4000
Sales: $356,845,000
Company Type: Private
SIC: 8062
    Tertiary hospital
Timothy J Grajewski, President

Employees: 3,646
Employees here: 3,500

D-U-N-S 07-242-0581
ST JOHN MEDICAL CENTER INC
1923 S Utica Ave, Tulsa, OK 74104
Phone: (918) 744-2345
Sales: $222,875,000
Company Type: Private
SIC: 8062
    General hospital
Therese Gottschalk Sr, President

Employees: 3,500
Employees here: 3,127

D-U-N-S 84-187-5040
ST JOHN'S HEALTH SYSTEM INC
1235 E Cherokee St, Springfield, MO 65804
Phone: (417) 885-2000
Sales: $296,600,000
Company Type: Private
SIC: 8062
    Osteopathic physician's office
Thomas Holes, Chief Executive Officer

Employees: 6,300
Employees here: 2

D-U-N-S 05-410-4112
ST JOHN'S HOME OF MILWAUKEE
1840 N Prospect Ave, Milwaukee, WI 53202
Phone: (414) 272-2022
Sales: $19,782,000
Company Type: Private
SIC: 8051
    Skilled nursing care facility apartment building operator
Dennis M Gralinski, President

Employees: 560
Employees here: 200

D-U-N-S 07-912-9623
ST JOHN'S HOSPITAL OF HOSPITAL SISTERS
800 E Carpenter St, Springfield, IL 62702
Phone: (217) 544-6464

Sales: $247,944,000
Company Type: Private
SIC: 8062
  General hospital
Allison Laabs, Executive Vice-President

Employees: 3,000
Employees here: 2,900

D-U-N-S 06-930-2925
ST JOHN'S RIVERSIDE HOSPITAL
967 N Broadway, Yonkers, NY 10701
Phone: (914) 964-4444
Sales: $84,738,000
Company Type: Private
SIC: 8062
  General medical & surgical hospital
James Foy, President

Employees: 1,100
Employees here: 1,100

D-U-N-S 07-195-8003
ST JOHNS MERCY MEDICAL CENTER
615 S New Ballas Rd, Saint Louis, MO 63141
Phone: (314) 569-6000
Sales: $300,169,000
Company Type: Private
SIC: 8062
  General hospital
Mark F Weber, President

Employees: 4,700
Employees here: 4,541

D-U-N-S 07-625-6809
ST JOHNS REGIONAL HEALTH CTR
1235 E Cherokee St, Springfield, MO 65804
Phone: (417) 885-2000
Sales: $280,331,000
Company Type: Private
SIC: 8062
  General hospital
Allen L Shockley, President

Employees: 4,400
Employees here: 4,000

D-U-N-S 07-626-2500
ST JOHNS REGIONAL MEDICAL CTR
2727 Mc Clelland Blvd, Joplin, MO 64804
Phone: (417) 781-2727
Sales: $170,891,000
Company Type: Private
SIC: 8062
  Hospital
Robert Bruckner, President

Employees: 2,000
Employees here: 1,310

D-U-N-S 07-157-0634
ST JOSEPH OF THE PINES INC
590 Central Dr, Southern Pines, NC 28387
Phone: (910) 692-2212
Sales: $42,815,000
Company Type: Private
SIC: 8082
  Nursing home retirement villas & home health care agency
George Kecatos, President

Employees: 1,500
Employees here: 420

D-U-N-S 60-652-5178
ST JOSEPH HEALTH CARE SYSTEM
  (Parent: Catholic Health Initiative)
7850 Jefferson St NE, Albuquerque, NM 87109
Phone: (505) 727-4700
Sales: $98,100,000
Company Type: Private
SIC: 8062
  General medical & surgical hospital
Ray H Barton Iii, President

Employees: 2,100
Employees here: 110

D-U-N-S 13-753-6702
ST JOSEPH HEALTH CENTER
300 1st Capitol Dr, Saint Charles, MO 63301
Phone: (314) 947-5000

Sales: $57,900,000
Company Type: Private
SIC: 8062
  General medical hospital
Kurt Weinmeister, President

Employees: 1,250
Employees here: 1,250

D-U-N-S 07-568-1429
ST JOSEPH HEALTH SVCS OF RI
200 High Service Ave, Providence, RI 2904
Phone: (401) 456-3000
Sales: $118,812,000
Company Type: Private
SIC: 8062
  General hospital
H J Keimig, President

Employees: 1,865
Employees here: 1,000

D-U-N-S 94-922-5973
ST JOSEPH HEALTH SVCS OF RI
21 Peace St, Providence, RI 2907
Phone: (401) 456-3000
Sales: $43,100,000
Company Type: Private
SIC: 8069
  Hospital specialty, except psychiatric
H J Keimig, President

Employees: NA
Employees here: 800

D-U-N-S 10-310-3370
ST JOSEPH HEALTH SYSTEM
440 S Batavia St, Orange, CA 92868
Phone: (714) 997-7690
Sales: $35,551,000
Company Type: Private
SIC: 8082
  Health system
Richard Statuto, Chief Executive Officer

Employees: 7,650
Employees here: 150

D-U-N-S 02-088-4524
ST JOSEPH HEALTH SYSTEM
200 M 55, Tawas City, MI 48763
Phone: (517) 362-3411
Sales: $23,495,000
Company Type: Private
SIC: 8062
  General medical & surgical hospital
Paul Schmidt, President

Employees: 500
Employees here: 375

D-U-N-S 07-587-8967
ST JOSEPH HOSPITAL OF AUGUSTA GA
2260 Wrightsboro Rd, Augusta, GA 30904
Phone: (706) 737-7400
Sales: $78,451,000
Company Type: Private
SIC: 8062
  General hospital and home health service
J W Paugh, President

Employees: 1,200
Employees here: 1,200

D-U-N-S 04-011-4852
ST JOSEPH HOSPITAL OF KIRKWOOD
525 Couch Ave, Saint Louis, MO 63122
Phone: (314) 966-1500
Sales: $54,500,000
Company Type: Private
SIC: 8062
  General hospital
Carla Baum, President

Employees: 1,178
Employees here: 1,178

D-U-N-S 07-396-2995
ST JOSEPH HOSPITAL OF NASHUA NH
172 Kinsley St, Nashua, NH 3060
Phone: (603) 882-3000

Sales: $43,350,000   *Employees:* 1,200
Company Type: Private   *Employees here:* 1,000
SIC: 8062
    General hospital
    Kenneth Ferron, Chief Operating Officer

    D-U-N-S 05-606-4314
ST JOSEPH HOSPITAL FRAN SSTRS
5000 W Chambers St, Milwaukee, WI 53210
Phone: (414) 447-2000
Sales: $168,261,000   *Employees:* 2,597
Company Type: Private   *Employees here:* 2,583
SIC: 8062
    Hospital
    Jon Wachs, President

    D-U-N-S 07-173-5286
ST JOSEPH HOSPITAL
360 Broadway, Bangor, ME 4401
Phone: (207) 262-1000
Sales: $38,561,000   *Employees:* 840
Company Type: Private   *Employees here:* 840
SIC: 8062
    General hospital
    Sister M Norberta, President

    D-U-N-S 06-760-7572
ST JOSEPH HOSPITAL OF ORANGE
1100 W Stewart Dr, Orange, CA 92868
Phone: (714) 633-9111
Sales: $221,749,000   *Employees:* 2,200
Company Type: Private   *Employees here:* 2,000
SIC: 8062
    General hospital
    Larry Ainsworth, President

    D-U-N-S 07-401-2287
ST JOSEPH HOSPITAL
2605 Harlem Rd, Buffalo, NY 14225
Phone: (716) 891-2400
Sales: $47,849,000   *Employees:* 856
Company Type: Private   *Employees here:* 849
SIC: 8062
    General hospital
    Patrick J Wiles, President

    D-U-N-S 07-466-5530
ST JOSEPH HOSPITAL, EUREKA
2700 Dolbeer St, Eureka, CA 95501
Phone: (707) 445-8121
Sales: $47,226,000   *Employees:* 617
Company Type: Private   *Employees here:* 592
SIC: 8062
    General acute care hospital
    Neil Martin, President

    D-U-N-S 06-977-6110
ST JOSEPH HOSPITAL, INC
250 College Ave, Lancaster, PA 17603
Phone: (717) 291-8211
Sales: $102,353,000   *Employees:* 1,429
Company Type: Private   *Employees here:* 1,300
SIC: 8062
    General hospital
    John Tolmie, Chief Executive Officer

    D-U-N-S 07-493-5198
ST JOSEPH MEDICAL CENTER
    (Parent: Catholic Health Initiative)
7620 York Rd, Baltimore, MD 21204
Phone: (410) 337-1000

Sales: $170,817,000   *Employees:* 2,200
Company Type: Private   *Employees here:* 2,185
SIC: 8062
    General hospital
    John Prout, Principal

    D-U-N-S 07-183-4287
ST JOSEPH MEDICAL CENTER
1717 S J St, Tacoma, WA 98405
Phone: (253) 627-4101
Sales: $179,180,000   *Employees:* 1,680
Company Type: Private   *Employees here:* 1,642
SIC: 8062
    Hospital
    Philip G Dionne, President

    D-U-N-S 07-248-1476
ST JOSEPH'S HOSPITAL
11705 Mercy Blvd, Savannah, GA 31419
Phone: (912) 925-4100
Sales: $133,561,000   *Employees:* 1,194
Company Type: Private   *Employees here:* 1,194
SIC: 8062
    General hospital
    Paul P Hinchey, President

    D-U-N-S 07-451-7533
ST JOSEPH'S HOSPITAL
428 Biltmore Ave, Asheville, NC 28801
Phone: (828) 255-3100
Sales: $88,842,000   *Employees:* 1,400
Company Type: Private   *Employees here:* 1,400
SIC: 8062
    General hospital and skilled nursing care facility
    J L Daniels, President

    D-U-N-S 07-176-5358
ST JOSEPH'S HOSPITAL
Se 3rd Burdick Expy E, Minot, ND 58701
Phone: (701) 857-2000
Sales: $55,815,000   *Employees:* 749
Company Type: Private   *Employees here:* 690
SIC: 8062
    Hospital
    Michael Mullins, Chief Executive Officer

    D-U-N-S 05-793-6155
ST JOSEPH'S HOSPITAL
555 E Market St, Elmira, NY 14901
Phone: (607) 733-6541
Sales: $47,616,000   *Employees:* 1,050
Company Type: Private   *Employees here:* 1,000
SIC: 8062
    General hospital
    Sister M Castagnaro, President

    D-U-N-S 08-877-5408
ST JOSEPH'S HOSPITAL INC
3030 W Martin Luther King, Tampa, FL 33607
Phone: (813) 879-4730
Sales: $31,700,000   *Employees:* NA
Company Type: Private   *Employees here:* 675
SIC: 8069
    Specialty hospital
    Michael Aubin, Manager

    D-U-N-S 07-668-2723
ST JOSEPH'S HOSPITAL YONKERS
127 S Broadway, Yonkers, NY 10701
Phone: (914) 378-7000

Sales: $81,406,000   *Employees:* 950
Company Type: Private   *Employees here:* 935
SIC: 8062
  General medical and surgical hospital and medical clinics
Sister M Linehan, President

D-U-N-S 06-470-7425
ST JOSEPH'S MEDICAL CENTER
801 E La Salle Ave, South Bend, IN 46617
Phone: (219) 237-7111
Sales: $137,979,000   *Employees:* 1,523
Company Type: Private   *Employees here:* 1,505
SIC: 8062
  General hospital
Robert L Beyer, President

D-U-N-S 79-736-3520
ST JOSEPH'S MEDICAL CENTER
523 N 3rd St, Brainerd, MN 56401
Phone: (218) 828-7394
Sales: $51,178,000   *Employees:* 4
Company Type: Private   *Employees here:* 4
SIC: 8011
  Medical center
Thomas K Prusak, President

D-U-N-S 07-733-0710
ST JOSEPH'S RGNL MDCL CTR N OK
1900 N 14th St, Ponca City, OK 74601
Phone: (580) 765-3321
Sales: $22,064,000   *Employees:* 446
Company Type: Private   *Employees here:* 441
SIC: 8062
  General hospital
Garry England, Chief Executive Officer

D-U-N-S 07-867-4504
ST JOSEPHS HOSPITAL & HEALTH CTR
30 7th St W, Dickinson, ND 58601
Phone: (701) 225-7200
Sales: $22,678,000   *Employees:* 450
Company Type: Private   *Employees here:* 442
SIC: 8062
  General hospital
John Studsrud, Administrator

D-U-N-S 80-011-6840
ST JOSEPHS HOSPITAL & HEALTH CTR
820 Clarksville St, Paris, TX 75460
Phone: (903) 785-4521
Sales: $89,391,000   *Employees:* 1,000
Company Type: Private   *Employees here:* 790
SIC: 8062
  General hospital
Monty Mclaurin, Administrator

D-U-N-S 07-477-8846
ST JOSEPHS HOSPITAL OF MARSHFIELD
611 Saint Joseph Ave, Marshfield, WI 54449
Phone: (715) 387-1713
Sales: $156,894,000   *Employees:* 1,715
Company Type: Private   *Employees here:* 1,715
SIC: 8062
  General hospital
Michael A Schmidt, President

D-U-N-S 07-649-1034
ST JOSEPHS HOSPITAL
2661 County Road I, Chippewa Falls, WI 54729
Phone: (715) 723-1811

Sales: $30,110,000   *Employees:* 650
Company Type: Private   *Employees here:* 600
SIC: 8062
  Hospital with a chemical dependency unit & adolescent
    treatment center
David B Fish, Chief Executive Officer

D-U-N-S 07-938-0481
ST JOSEPHS HOSPITAL OF ATLANTA
5665 Peachtree Dunwoody R, Atlanta, GA 30342
Phone: (404) 851-7001
Sales: $237,000,000   *Employees:* 2,300
Company Type: Private   *Employees here:* 2,250
SIC: 8062
  General hospital
Ronald Hogan, Chief Executive Officer

D-U-N-S 07-159-7637
ST JOSEPHS HOSPITAL HEALTH CTR
301 Prospect Ave, Syracuse, NY 13203
Phone: (315) 448-5111
Sales: $196,504,000   *Employees:* 3,200
Company Type: Private   *Employees here:* 2,800
SIC: 8062
  General hospital
Theodore M Pasinski, President

D-U-N-S 01-095-3933
ST JOSEPHS HOSPITAL NURSING
127 S Broadway, Yonkers, NY 10701
Phone: (914) 378-7000
Sales: $27,551,000   *Employees:* 320
Company Type: Private   *Employees here:* 320
SIC: 8051
  Skilled nursing home
Sister M Linehan, President

D-U-N-S 07-125-6218
ST JOSEPHS REGIONAL HEALTH CTR
300 Werner St, Hot Springs, AR 71913
Phone: (501) 622-1000
Sales: $104,178,000   *Employees:* 1,400
Company Type: Private   *Employees here:* 1,320
SIC: 8062
  Hospital
Randall J Fale, President

D-U-N-S 16-821-6281
ST JOSPEHS REGIONAL MED CTR
415 6th St, Lewiston, ID 83501
Phone: (208) 743-2511
Sales: $33,100,000   *Employees:* 725
Company Type: Private   *Employees here:* 725
SIC: 8062
  Hospital
Debra Kloster, Administration

D-U-N-S 07-615-8179
ST JOSPHS COMMUNITY HOSPITAL OF W BEND
551 S Silverbrook Dr, West Bend, WI 53095
Phone: (414) 334-5533
Sales: $31,144,000   *Employees:* 540
Company Type: Private   *Employees here:* 540
SIC: 8062
  Hospital
Gregory T Burns, Secretary

D-U-N-S 07-879-6406
ST JOSPHS MED CTR OF STOCKTON
1800 N California St, Stockton, CA 95204
Phone: (209) 943-2000

Sales: $166,025,000
Company Type: Private
SIC: 8062
   General hospital
Edward G Schroeder, President

Employees: 2,200
Employees here: 2,000

D-U-N-S 07-250-3634
ST JUDE HOSPITAL
101 E Valencia Mesa Dr, Fullerton, CA 92835
Phone: (714) 871-3280
Sales: $210,080,000
Company Type: Private
SIC: 8062
   General medical hospital
Robert Fraschetti, President

Employees: 1,454
Employees here: 1,436

D-U-N-S 07-199-5203
ST LOUIS CHILDREN'S HOSPITAL
1 Childrens Pl, Saint Louis, MO 63110
Phone: (314) 454-6000
Sales: $161,612,000
Company Type: Private
SIC: 8069
   Children's hospital
Ted Frey, President

Employees: 2,078
Employees here: 2,078

D-U-N-S 05-022-0722
ST LOUIS UNIVERSITY
221 N Grand Blvd, Saint Louis, MO 63103
Phone: (314) 977-2401
Sales: $529,919,000
Company Type: Private
SIC: 8062
   Hospital and university
Rev Very Biondi, President

Employees: 7,500
Employees here: 1,974

D-U-N-S 60-679-8718
ST LUCIE MEDICAL CENTER
   (Parent: H C A Health Services Of Fla)
1800 SE Tiffany Ave, Port Saint Lucie, FL 34952
Phone: (561) 335-4000
Sales: $71,749,000
Company Type: Public Family Member
SIC: 8062
   General medical & surgical hospital
Gary Contrell, Administrator

Employees: 850
Employees here: 600

D-U-N-S 19-220-1556
ST LUKE HEALTH SYSTEM, INC
2720 Stone Park Blvd, Sioux City, IA 51104
Phone: (712) 279-3500
Sales: $105,230,000
Company Type: Private
SIC: 8062
   Hospital real estate management & physicians practice fund
    raising & rehabilitation & recovery centers
Michael Gunsch, Chairman of the Board

Employees: 2,100
Employees here: 2,090

D-U-N-S 07-287-9455
ST LUKE HOSPITAL INC
85 N Grand Ave, Fort Thomas, KY 41075
Phone: (606) 572-3100
Sales: $64,300,000
Company Type: Private
SIC: 8062
   General medical & surgical hospital
John D Hoyle, President

Employees: 1,385
Employees here: 831

D-U-N-S 07-622-9707
ST LUKE MED CTR OF PASADENA
   (Parent: Tenet Healthcare Corporation)
2632 E Washington Blvd, Pasadena, CA 91107
Phone: (626) 797-1141

Sales: $24,900,000
Company Type: Public Family Member
SIC: 8062
   General hospital
Mark Uffer, Chief Executive Officer

Employees: 550
Employees here: 550

D-U-N-S 07-196-0660
ST LUKE'S EPISCOPAL
232 S Woods Mill Rd, Chesterfield, MO 63017
Phone: (314) 434-1500
Sales: $93,500,000
Company Type: Private
SIC: 8062
   General hospital
Dr George Tucker Md, President

Employees: 2,003
Employees here: 1,803

D-U-N-S 07-417-9060
ST LUKE'S EPISCOPAL HOSPITAL
6720 Bertner St, Houston, TX 77030
Phone: (713) 791-2011
Sales: $360,954,000
Company Type: Private
SIC: 8062
   Tertiary care hospital
Michael Jhin, President

Employees: 3,511
Employees here: 3,465

D-U-N-S 07-245-8912
ST LUKE'S HEALTH SYSTEM
   (Parent: Tenet Healthcare Corporation)
1800 E Van Buren St, Phoenix, AZ 85006
Phone: (602) 251-8100
Sales: $53,100,000
Company Type: Public Family Member
SIC: 8062
   General hospital specialty hospital nursing home
Michael Focht, President

Employees: 1,148
Employees here: 920

D-U-N-S 05-416-5675
ST LUKE'S HOSPITAL
5901 Monclova Rd, Maumee, OH 43537
Phone: (419) 893-5911
Sales: $81,053,000
Company Type: Private
SIC: 8062
   General hospital
Frank J Bartell Iii, President

Employees: 1,325
Employees here: 1,325

D-U-N-S 06-817-8268
ST LUKE'S HOSPITAL OF DULUTH
915 E 1st St, Duluth, MN 55805
Phone: (218) 726-5555
Sales: $84,370,000
Company Type: Private
SIC: 8062
   General hospital
John Strange, President

Employees: 1,500
Employees here: 1,240

D-U-N-S 05-410-3742
ST LUKE'S MEDICAL CENTER INC
2900 W Oklahoma Ave, Milwaukee, WI 53215
Phone: (414) 649-6000
Sales: $187,900,000
Company Type: Private
SIC: 8062
   General hospital
Mark Wiener, Administrator

Employees: 4,000
Employees here: 3,148

D-U-N-S 92-887-3918
ST LUKE'S MEDICAL CENTER INC
5900 S Lake Dr, Cudahy, WI 53110
Phone: (414) 769-9000

Sales: $29,300,000   *Employees:* NA
Company Type: Private   *Employees here:* 700
SIC: 8062
   General hospital
Terrence Wilson, Manager

D-U-N-S 07-383-0796
ST LUKE'S MEMORIAL HOSPITAL
3801 Spring St, Racine, WI 53405
Phone: (414) 636-2011
Sales: $50,600,000   *Employees:* 1,095
Company Type: Private   *Employees here:* 850
SIC: 8062
   General hospital
Ray L Di Iulio, President

D-U-N-S 06-522-3166
ST LUKE'S METHODIST HOSPITAL
1026 A Ave NE, Cedar Rapids, IA 52402
Phone: (319) 369-7211
Sales: $133,524,000   *Employees:* 2,000
Company Type: Private   *Employees here:* 1,275
SIC: 8062
   General hospital
Stephen Vanourny, President

D-U-N-S 07-550-6337
ST LUKE'S QUAKERTOWN HOSPITAL
1021 Park Ave, Quakertown, PA 18951
Phone: (215) 536-2400
Sales: $19,967,000   *Employees:* 277
Company Type: Private   *Employees here:* 277
SIC: 8062
   General hospital
Fred Sprissler, Chief Executive Officer

D-U-N-S 07-698-3055
ST LUKE'S REGIONAL MED CTR
2720 Stone Park Blvd, Sioux City, IA 51104
Phone: (712) 279-3500
Sales: $85,683,000   *Employees:* 1,500
Company Type: Private   *Employees here:* 1,450
SIC: 8062
   General hospital and skilled nursing center
John Daniels, Senior Vice-President

D-U-N-S 13-738-7247
ST LUKES CATARACT & LASER INST
43309 US Highway 19 N, Tarpon Springs, FL 34689
Phone: (727) 938-2020
Sales: $24,000,000   *Employees:* 350
Company Type: Private   *Employees here:* 350
SIC: 8011
   Ophthalmologist
Dr James P Gills, President

D-U-N-S 15-088-0383
ST LUKES HEALTH CARE ASSN
700 Cooper Ave, Saginaw, MI 48602
Phone: (517) 771-6000
Sales: $91,000,000   *Employees:* 1,950
Company Type: Private   *Employees here:* 1
SIC: 8062
   Hospital & ambulance service
Spencer Maidlow, President

D-U-N-S 07-366-4039
ST LUKES HOSPITAL OF BETHLEHEM PA
801 Ostrum St, Bethlehem, PA 18015
Phone: (610) 954-4000

Sales: $206,332,000   *Employees:* 3,500
Company Type: Private   *Employees here:* 2,150
SIC: 8062
   Hospital
Richard A Anderson, President

D-U-N-S 08-811-8443
ST LUKES HOSPITAL OF BETHLEHEM PA
1736 W Hamilton St, Allentown, PA 18104
Phone: (610) 770-8300
Sales: $28,300,000   *Employees:* NA
Company Type: Private   *Employees here:* 580
SIC: 8062
   Hospital

D-U-N-S 07-869-9790
ST LUKES HOSPITAL OF NEWBURGH NY
70 Du Bois St, Newburgh, NY 12550
Phone: (914) 561-4400
Sales: $33,600,000   *Employees:* 736
Company Type: Private   *Employees here:* 716
SIC: 8062
   General hospital
Arthur E Santilli, President

D-U-N-S 07-758-4365
ST LUKES HOSPITAL ASSOCIATION
4201 Belfort Rd, Jacksonville, FL 32216
Phone: (904) 296-3700
Sales: $111,844,000   *Employees:* 1,300
Company Type: Private   *Employees here:* 1,280
SIC: 8062
   General medical & surgical hospital
Dr Leo F Black, Chairman of the Board

D-U-N-S 06-816-2304
ST LUKES MDLAND RGONAL MED CTR
305 S State St, Aberdeen, SD 57401
Phone: (605) 622-5000
Sales: $65,246,000   *Employees:* 1,059
Company Type: Private   *Employees here:* 700
SIC: 8062
   General hospital
Dale Stein, President

D-U-N-S 07-835-0154
ST LUKES REGIONAL MEDICAL CTR
190 E Bannock St, Boise, ID 83712
Phone: (208) 381-2222
Sales: $192,688,000   *Employees:* 2,300
Company Type: Private   *Employees here:* 2,200
SIC: 8062
   General hospital
Edwin Dahlberg, President

D-U-N-S 05-372-4027
ST LUKES-MEMORIAL HOSPITAL CTR
1656 Champlin Ave, New Hartford, NY 13413
Phone: (315) 798-6000
Sales: $76,900,000   *Employees:* 1,650
Company Type: Private   *Employees here:* 1,500
SIC: 8062
   Hospital
Andrew Peterson, Chief Executive Officer

D-U-N-S 10-511-8939
ST LUKES-ROOSEVELT HOSPITAL CTR
1111 Amsterdam Ave, New York, NY 10025
Phone: (212) 523-5800

Sales: $598,396,000
Company Type: Private
SIC: 8062
   General hospital
Garry Gambuti, President

Employees: 8,000
Employees here: 3,000

D-U-N-S 11-165-8605
ST LUKES-ROOSEVELT HOSPITAL CTR
428 5th Ave, New York, NY 10018
Phone: (212) 523-4000
Sales: $24,300,000
Company Type: Private
SIC: 8062
   General hospital
Dr Ronald Ablow, Director

Employees: NA
Employees here: 500

D-U-N-S 62-155-0110
ST LUKES-ROOSEVELT HOSPITAL CTR
1000 10th Ave Fl 5, New York, NY 10019
Phone: (212) 523-6491
Sales: $131,700,000
Company Type: Private
SIC: 8069
   Specialty hospital
Ann Geller, Director

Employees: NA
Employees here: 2,504

D-U-N-S 07-560-5279
ST MARGARET'S HOSPITAL
600 E 1st St, Spring Valley, IL 61362
Phone: (815) 664-5311
Sales: $32,568,000
Company Type: Private
SIC: 8062
   General hospital
Tim Muntz, President

Employees: 430
Employees here: 327

D-U-N-S 79-783-5444
ST MARGRET MRCY HEALTHCARE CTRS
5454 Hohman Ave, Hammond, IN 46320
Phone: (219) 932-2300
Sales: $138,104,000
Company Type: Private
SIC: 8062
   Hospital also operates a gift shop within the hospital
James Lipinski, Chief Financial Officer

Employees: 2,859
Employees here: 1,633

D-U-N-S 78-053-7999
ST MARGRET MRCY HEALTHCARE CTRS
24 Joliet St, Dyer, IN 46311
Phone: (219) 865-2141
Sales: $31,400,000
Company Type: Private
SIC: 8062
   Medical center
Gene Diamond, Branch Manager

Employees: NA
Employees here: 750

D-U-N-S 06-883-5057
ST MARY HOSPITAL OF LIVONIA
36475 Five Mile Rd, Livonia, MI 48154
Phone: (734) 464-4800
Sales: $92,184,000
Company Type: Private
SIC: 8062
   Hospital & skilled nursing home
Mike De Rubeis, Chief Financial Officer

Employees: 1,304
Employees here: 1,304

D-U-N-S 06-580-7059
ST MARY HOSPITAL INC
308 Willow Ave, Hoboken, NJ 7030
Phone: (201) 714-8900

Sales: $70,522,000
Company Type: Private
SIC: 8062
   General hospital
Ulrich Rosa, President

Employees: 1,200
Employees here: 1,138

D-U-N-S 15-147-3840
ST MARY MEDICAL CENTER
401 W Poplar St, Walla Walla, WA 99362
Phone: (509) 525-3320
Sales: $47,536,000
Company Type: Private
SIC: 8062
   Hospital
John A Isely, President

Employees: 546
Employees here: 546

D-U-N-S 07-710-7043
ST MARY MEDICAL CENTER
Langhorne Newtown Rd, Langhorne, PA 19047
Phone: (215) 750-2000
Sales: $100,532,000
Company Type: Private
SIC: 8062
   General hospital
Thomas Mc Inerney, Chairman of the Board

Employees: 1,600
Employees here: 1,575

D-U-N-S 18-107-0442
ST MARY REGIONAL MEDICAL CTR
18300 US Highway 18, Apple Valley, CA 92307
Phone: (760) 242-2311
Sales: $61,631,000
Company Type: Private
SIC: 8062
   General hospital
Catherine Pelley, President

Employees: 700
Employees here: 700

D-U-N-S 07-566-8418
ST MARY-ROGERS MEMORIAL HOSP
1200 W Walnut St, Rogers, AR 72756
Phone: (501) 636-0200
Sales: $43,795,000
Company Type: Private
SIC: 8062
   General hospital
Michael Packnett, President

Employees: 726
Employees here: 710

D-U-N-S 07-344-5413
ST MARY'S HEALTH CARE SYSTEM
1230 Baxter St, Athens, GA 30606
Phone: (706) 548-7581
Sales: $62,700,000
Company Type: Private
SIC: 8062
   General hospital
Dennis Crum, Vice-President

Employees: 1,350
Employees here: 1,247

D-U-N-S 04-245-1914
ST MARY'S HEALTH SYSTEM INC
900 Oak Hill Ave, Knoxville, TN 37918
Phone: (423) 545-8000
Sales: $135,172,000
Company Type: Private
SIC: 8062
   Non profit hospital
Richard Williams, Chief Executive Officer

Employees: 1,732
Employees here: 1,675

D-U-N-S 07-136-3725
ST MARY'S HEALTHCARE CENTER
800 E Dakota Ave, Pierre, SD 57501
Phone: (605) 224-3100

Sales: $20,961,000   *Employees:* 450
Company Type: Private   *Employees here:* 275
SIC: 8062
   Hospital and nursing home
James D Russell, Chief Executive Officer

   D-U-N-S 07-196-9877
ST MARY'S HOSPITAL
400 N Pleasant Ave, Centralia, IL 62801
Phone: (618) 532-6731
Sales: $68,537,000   *Employees:* 950
Company Type: Private   *Employees here:* 950
SIC: 8062
   General medical hospital
James W Mcdowell, President

   D-U-N-S 06-831-9375
ST MARY'S HOSPITAL
1726 Shawano Ave, Green Bay, WI 54303
Phone: (920) 498-4200
Sales: $44,929,000   *Employees:* 571
Company Type: Private   *Employees here:* 571
SIC: 8062
   Hospital
James Coller, Administrator

   D-U-N-S 02-151-8089
ST MARY'S HOSPITAL OF BROOKLYN
170 Buffalo Ave, Brooklyn, NY 11213
Phone: (718) 221-3000
Sales: $69,800,000   *Employees:* 1,500
Company Type: Private   *Employees here:* 1,400
SIC: 8062
   Hospital
Monsignor Bennett, Chairman of the Board

   D-U-N-S 01-014-5811
ST MARY'S HOSPITAL CORPORATION
56 Franklin St, Waterbury, CT 6706
Phone: (203) 574-6000
Sales: $134,516,000   *Employees:* 1,520
Company Type: Private   *Employees here:* 1,500
SIC: 8062
   General medical & surgical hospital
Sister M Waite, President

   D-U-N-S 07-223-1954
ST MARY'S HOSPITAL INC
901 45th St, West Palm Beach, FL 33407
Phone: (561) 844-6300
Sales: $158,446,000   *Employees:* 2,000
Company Type: Private   *Employees here:* 2,000
SIC: 8062
   General hospital
Phillip Dutcher, Chief Executive Officer

   D-U-N-S 07-152-7725
ST MARY'S HOSPITAL INC
Third St NE, Norton, VA 24273
Phone: (540) 679-9100
Sales: $19,898,000   *Employees:* 370
Company Type: Private   *Employees here:* 368
SIC: 8062
   Hospital
Gary Delforge, Administrator

   D-U-N-S 07-615-0473
ST MARY'S HOSPITAL OZAUKEE
13111 N Port Washington R, Thiensville, WI 53097
Phone: (414) 243-7300

Sales: $46,238,000   *Employees:* 656
Company Type: Private   *Employees here:* 650
SIC: 8062
   General hospital
Edwin Montgomery, President

   D-U-N-S 60-413-2043
ST MARY'S MEDICAL CENTER
407 E 3rd St, Duluth, MN 55805
Phone: (218) 726-4000
Sales: $168,278,000   *Employees:* 1,631
Company Type: Private   *Employees here:* 1,611
SIC: 8062
   General medical & surgical hospital day care center and
      home care services
Peter E Person, President

   D-U-N-S 07-383-1075
ST MARY'S MEDICAL CENTER INC
3801 Spring St, Racine, WI 53405
Phone: (414) 636-4011
Sales: $51,800,000   *Employees:* 1,120
Company Type: Private   *Employees here:* 1,051
SIC: 8062
   General hospital
David Perkins, Chairman of the Board

   D-U-N-S 07-116-1129
ST MARYS HOSPITAL OF MILWAUKEE
2323 N Lake Dr, Milwaukee, WI 53211
Phone: (414) 291-1000
Sales: $120,762,000   *Employees:* 2,100
Company Type: Private   *Employees here:* 1,800
SIC: 8062
   Hospital
John Schuler, President

   D-U-N-S 06-486-9860
ST MARYS HOSPITAL OF ST MRYS CNTY
25500 Point Lookout Rd, Leonardtown, MD 20650
Phone: (301) 475-8981
Sales: $38,864,000   *Employees:* 620
Company Type: Private   *Employees here:* 620
SIC: 8062
   General hospital
Christine Wray, Administrator

   D-U-N-S 07-721-3619
ST MARYS HOSPITAL AT AMSTERDAM
427 Guy Park Ave, Amsterdam, NY 12010
Phone: (518) 842-1900
Sales: $45,453,000   *Employees:* 825
Company Type: Private   *Employees here:* 775
SIC: 8062
   General hospital
Peter Capobianco, President

   D-U-N-S 06-580-4452
ST MARYS HOSPITAL
211 Pennington Ave, Passaic, NJ 7055
Phone: (973) 470-3000
Sales: $46,715,000   *Employees:* 900
Company Type: Private   *Employees here:* 900
SIC: 8062
   General hospital
Patricia Peterson, President

   D-U-N-S 07-877-2738
ST MARYS HOSPITAL & MED CTR
450 Stanyan St, San Francisco, CA 94117
Phone: (415) 668-1000

Sales: $126,909,000
Company Type: Private
SIC: 8062
   General medical & surgical hospital
John Williams, President

Employees: 1,050
Employees here: 1,043

D-U-N-S 06-971-5746
ST MARYS HOSPITAL & MED CTR
2635 N 7th St, Grand Junction, CO 81501
Phone: (970) 244-2273
Sales: $93,400,000
Company Type: Private
SIC: 8062
   General medical & surgical hospital
Sister L Casey, Chief Executive Officer

Employees: 2,000
Employees here: 1,950

D-U-N-S 04-014-3737
ST MARYS HOSPITAL OF RICHMOND
5801 Bremo Rd, Richmond, VA 23226
Phone: (804) 285-2011
Sales: $344,658,000
Company Type: Private
SIC: 8062
   General hospital
Sister P Eck, President

Employees: 2,000
Employees here: 1,650

D-U-N-S 07-275-6984
ST MARYS HOSPITAL FOR CHILDREN
2901 216th St, Bayside, NY 11360
Phone: (718) 281-8800
Sales: $22,000,000
Company Type: Private
SIC: 8069
   Children's hospital
Dr Burton Grebin Md, President

Employees: 450
Employees here: 395

D-U-N-S 05-681-9501
ST MARYS MED CTR OF EVANSVILLE
3700 Washington Ave, Evansville, IN 47714
Phone: (812) 485-4000
Sales: $140,266,000
Company Type: Private
SIC: 8062
   General hospital
Rick Breon, President

Employees: 2,600
Employees here: 2,400

D-U-N-S 06-983-8654
ST MARYS MED CTR OF SAGINAW
830 S Jefferson Ave, Saginaw, MI 48601
Phone: (517) 776-8000
Sales: $141,141,000
Company Type: Private
SIC: 8062
   General medical & surgical hospital
Frederick Fraizer, President

Employees: 1,794
Employees here: 1,794

D-U-N-S 85-925-2777
ST MARYS REGIONAL HEALTH SYS
763 Johnsonburg Rd, Saint Marys, PA 15857
Phone: (814) 781-7500
Sales: $31,522,000
Company Type: Private
SIC: 8062
   Health management services
John Christenson, Chief Operating Officer

Employees: 500
Employees here: 500

D-U-N-S 08-111-4415
ST MARYS REGIONAL MEDICAL CTR
(Parent: Tenet Health System Medical)
1808 W Main St, Russellville, AR 72801
Phone: (501) 968-2841

Sales: $34,300,000
Company Type: Public Family Member
SIC: 8062
   General hospital
Mike Mccoy, Chief Executive Officer

Employees: 750
Employees here: 550

D-U-N-S 14-754-0926
ST MARYS REGIONAL MEDICAL CTR
235 W 6th St, Reno, NV 89520
Phone: (702) 323-2041
Sales: $133,374,000
Company Type: Private
SIC: 8062
   General medical & surgical hospital
Linda Herman, Finance

Employees: 1,400
Employees here: 1,370

D-U-N-S 07-174-3694
ST MARYS REGIONAL MEDICAL CTR
45 Golder St, Lewiston, ME 4240
Phone: (207) 777-8100
Sales: $61,788,000
Company Type: Private
SIC: 8062
   General medical & surgical hospital
James E Cassidy, President

Employees: 850
Employees here: 850

D-U-N-S 07-400-8640
ST MARYS REGIONAL MEDICAL CTR
763 Johnsonburg Rd, Saint Marys, PA 15857
Phone: (814) 781-7500
Sales: $31,259,000
Company Type: Private
SIC: 8062
   Hospital/skilled nursing facility
John Christenson, President

Employees: 660
Employees here: 660

D-U-N-S 02-046-3196
ST MICHAEL HOSPITAL
2400 W Villard Ave, Milwaukee, WI 53209
Phone: (414) 527-8000
Sales: $84,725,000
Company Type: Private
SIC: 8062
   General hospital
Jeffrey K Jenkins, Administrator

Employees: 1,027
Employees here: 999

D-U-N-S 07-477-3334
ST MICHAELS HOSPITAL
900 Illinois Ave, Stevens Point, WI 54481
Phone: (715) 346-5000
Sales: $44,761,000
Company Type: Private
SIC: 8062
   General hospital
Jeffrey Martin, President

Employees: 513
Employees here: 480

D-U-N-S 07-383-0432
ST NICHOLAS HOSPITAL
1601 N Taylor Dr, Sheboygan, WI 53081
Phone: (920) 459-8300
Sales: $47,000,000
Company Type: Private
SIC: 8062
   General hospital
Michael Stenger, Executive Vice-President

Employees: 600
Employees here: 490

D-U-N-S 07-652-0667
ST OLAF HOSPITAL ASSOCIATION
1000 1st Dr Nw, Austin, MN 55912
Phone: (507) 437-4551

Sales: $39,202,000   *Employees:* 700
Company Type: Private   *Employees here:* 650
SIC: 8062
  Hospital
Donald Brezicka, Administrator

D-U-N-S 79-404-4248
ST PATRICK HOSPITAL CORP
500 W Broadway St, Missoula, MT 59802
Phone: (406) 543-7271
Sales: $99,580,000   *Employees:* 1,170
Company Type: Private   *Employees here:* 1,170
SIC: 8069
  Acute care hospital
Larry White, President

D-U-N-S 07-711-5897
ST PATRICK HOSPITAL INC
524 S Ryan St, Lake Charles, LA 70601
Phone: (318) 491-7730
Sales: $67,500,000   *Employees:* 1,452
Company Type: Private   *Employees here:* 1,450
SIC: 8062
  Hospital
J W Hankins, President

D-U-N-S 06-053-3031
ST PETER'S HOSPITAL
315 S Manning Blvd, Albany, NY 12208
Phone: (518) 454-1550
Sales: $181,101,000   *Employees:* 2,476
Company Type: Private   *Employees here:* 2,309
SIC: 8062
  General hospital
Steven P Boyle, President

D-U-N-S 04-579-0045
ST PETER'S MEDICAL CENTER
254 Easton Ave, New Brunswick, NJ 8901
Phone: (732) 745-8600
Sales: $186,547,000   *Employees:* 2,600
Company Type: Private   *Employees here:* 2,572
SIC: 8062
  General hospital
John Matuska, President

D-U-N-S 03-272-2274
ST PETRSBURG SNCOAST MED GROUP
601 7th St S, Saint Petersburg, FL 33701
Phone: (727) 894-1818
Sales: $34,300,000   *Employees:* 500
Company Type: Private   *Employees here:* 250
SIC: 8011
  Medical clinic
Michael Reed, Administrator

D-U-N-S 05-416-3464
ST RITA'S MEDICAL CENTER
730 W Market St, Lima, OH 45801
Phone: (419) 227-3361
Sales: $135,780,000   *Employees:* 2,000
Company Type: Private   *Employees here:* 1,930
SIC: 8062
  General medical hospital
Jim Reber, President

D-U-N-S 07-262-9777
ST TAMMANY PARISH HOSPITAL DST 2
1001 Gause Blvd, Slidell, LA 70458
Phone: (504) 643-2200

Sales: $46,100,000   *Employees:* 1,000
Company Type: Private   *Employees here:* 880
SIC: 8062
  Hospital
Monica Gates, Chief Executive Officer

D-U-N-S 06-953-3768
ST TAMMANY PARISH HOSPITAL
1202 S Tyler St, Covington, LA 70433
Phone: (504) 898-4000
Sales: $127,662,000   *Employees:* 880
Company Type: Private   *Employees here:* 780
SIC: 8062
  General hospital
Thomas Stone, Administrator

D-U-N-S 07-203-5603
ST VINCENT HOSPITAL HEALTH CARE CTR
2001 W 86th St, Indianapolis, IN 46260
Phone: (317) 338-2345
Sales: $431,271,000   *Employees:* 5,075
Company Type: Private   *Employees here:* 2,943
SIC: 8062
  General hospital
Douglas D French, President

D-U-N-S 07-477-6592
ST VINCENT HOSPITAL
835 S Van Buren St, Green Bay, WI 54301
Phone: (920) 433-0111
Sales: $132,325,000   *Employees:* 2,190
Company Type: Private   *Employees here:* 2,140
SIC: 8062
  Hospital
Joseph J Neidenbach, Administrator

D-U-N-S 06-942-1618
ST VINCENT HOSPITAL INC
455 Saint Michaels Dr, Santa Fe, NM 87505
Phone: (505) 983-3361
Sales: $108,488,000   *Employees:* 1,050
Company Type: Private   *Employees here:* 1,048
SIC: 8062
  General hospital
Ronald C Winger, President

D-U-N-S 06-767-8417
ST VINCENT INFIRMARY MED CTR
No2 Saint Vincent Cir, Little Rock, AR 72205
Phone: (501) 660-3000
Sales: $215,318,000   *Employees:* 2,830
Company Type: Private   *Employees here:* 2,450
SIC: 8062
  General hospital
Diana Hueter, Chief Executive Officer

D-U-N-S 05-416-1948
ST VINCENT MERCY MEDICAL CTR
2213 Cherry St, Toledo, OH 43608
Phone: (419) 251-3232
Sales: $353,294,000   *Employees:* 4,600
Company Type: Private   *Employees here:* 4,100
SIC: 8062
  General hospital
Steven Mickus, President

D-U-N-S 12-223-4578
ST VINCENT'S AMBULATORY CARE
2565 Park St, Jacksonville, FL 32204
Phone: (904) 389-1400

Sales: $20,000,000   *Employees:* 39
Company Type: Private   *Employees here:* 10
SIC: 8011
  Family medical care center
Carol Thompson, Executive Vice-President

D-U-N-S 07-211-2618
ST VINCENT'S HOSPITAL
810 Saint Vincents Dr, Birmingham, AL 35205
Phone: (205) 939-7000
Sales: $120,600,000   *Employees:* 1,449
Company Type: Private   *Employees here:* 1,400
SIC: 8062
  Hospital
Vincent C Caponi, President

D-U-N-S 07-832-0207
ST VINCENT'S MEDICAL CENTER
  (*Parent:* Vincent Baptist/St Health Sys)
1800 Barrs St, Jacksonville, FL 32204
Phone: (904) 387-7300
Sales: $221,810,000   *Employees:* 2,447
Company Type: Private   *Employees here:* 2,342
SIC: 8062
  General hospital
John Logue, President

D-U-N-S 07-105-0132
ST VINCNTS HOSPITAL MED CTR OF NY
153 W 11th St, New York, NY 10011
Phone: (212) 604-7000
Sales: $362,829,000   *Employees:* 3,852
Company Type: Private   *Employees here:* 3,492
SIC: 8062
  General hospital
Karl P Adler, President

D-U-N-S 62-067-9688
ST. JOSEPH HEALTH SYSTEM, LLC
700 Broadway, Fort Wayne, IN 46802
Phone: (219) 425-3000
Sales: $76,059,000   *Employees:* 1,200
Company Type: Private   *Employees here:* 1,200
SIC: 8062
  General medical hospital
John T Farrell, President

D-U-N-S 07-878-1358
ST. LUKE'S HOSPITAL
3555 Cesar Chavez, San Francisco, CA 94110
Phone: (415) 647-8600
Sales: $85,839,000   *Employees:* 810
Company Type: Private   *Employees here:* 740
SIC: 8062
  General hospital
Jack Fries, President

D-U-N-S 01-439-1747
ST. MARY MEDICAL CENTER, INC
1500 S Lake Park Ave, Hobart, IN 46342
Phone: (219) 942-0551
Sales: $31,900,000   *Employees:* 700
Company Type: Private   *Employees here:* 700
SIC: 8062
  General medical hospital
Milton Triana, President

D-U-N-S 04-103-8746
ST. MARY'S HOSPITAL
1800 E Lake Shore Dr, Decatur, IL 62521
Phone: (217) 464-2966

Sales: $59,352,000   *Employees:* 1,200
Company Type: Private   *Employees here:* 1,200
SIC: 8062
  Hospital
Sister J Trstensky, President

D-U-N-S 95-813-7283
ST. MARYS DEAN VENTURES INC
1808 W Beltline Hwy, Madison, WI 53713
Phone: (608) 250-1201
Sales: $40,000,000   *Employees:* 400
Company Type: Private   *Employees here:* 12
SIC: 8011
  Medical offices
Stephen M Olson, Chief Executive Officer

D-U-N-S 93-142-2380
ST. MARYS HOSPITAL OF BLUE SPRNG
201 NW R D Mize Rd, Blue Springs, MO 64014
Phone: (816) 228-5900
Sales: $47,668,000   *Employees:* 550
Company Type: Private   *Employees here:* 550
SIC: 8062
  General hospital
N G Wages, President

D-U-N-S 06-892-1535
ST. PETERS COMMUNITY HOSPITAL
2475 E Broadway St, Helena, MT 59601
Phone: (406) 444-2100
Sales: $54,077,000   *Employees:* 700
Company Type: Private   *Employees here:* 686
SIC: 8062
  General hospital
Robert Ladenburger, President

D-U-N-S 07-529-0411
ST. ROSE DOMINICAN HOSPITAL
102 E Lake Mead Dr, Henderson, NV 89015
Phone: (702) 564-2622
Sales: $60,545,000   *Employees:* 754
Company Type: Private   *Employees here:* 738
SIC: 8062
  General hospital
Rod A Davis, President

D-U-N-S 02-839-3981
STANISLAUS COUNTY
830 Scenic Dr, Modesto, CA 95350
Phone: (209) 525-7000
Sales: $29,300,000   *Employees:* NA
Company Type: Private   *Employees here:* 600
SIC: 8062
  General medical hospital
Beverly M Finley, N/A

D-U-N-S 07-449-6142
STANLY MEMORIAL HOSPITAL INC
301 Yadkin St, Albemarle, NC 28001
Phone: (704) 983-5111
Sales: $24,200,000   *Employees:* 537
Company Type: Private   *Employees here:* 469
SIC: 8062
  General hospital
Roy Hinson, President

D-U-N-S 07-930-0828
STARR COMMONWEALTH
13725 Starr Commonwealth, Albion, MI 49224
Phone: (517) 629-5593

Sales: $30,621,000   *Employees:* 550
Company Type: Private   *Employees here:* 280
SIC: 8361
    Residential care facility
Arlin E Ness, President

D-U-N-S 03-061-5405
STATE OF KANSAS
3 Miles West Of Larned, Larned, KS 67550
Phone: (316) 285-2131
Sales: $28,900,000   *Employees:* NA
Company Type: Private   *Employees here:* 936
SIC: 8063
    Psychiatric hospital
Mani Lee, Manager

D-U-N-S 80-103-3101
STATE OF LOUISIANA
2021 Perdido St, New Orleans, LA 70112
Phone: (504) 588-3000
Sales: $41,200,000   *Employees:* NA
Company Type: Private   *Employees here:* 1,000
SIC: 8062
    General hospital
Dr Michael Butler, Administrator

D-U-N-S 01-803-7283
STATE OF LOUISIANA
4864 Jackson St, Monroe, LA 71202
Phone: (318) 330-7000
Sales: $30,700,000   *Employees:* NA
Company Type: Private   *Employees here:* 870
SIC: 8062
    General hospital
Roy Bostick, Administrator

D-U-N-S 02-766-0021
STATE OF LOUISIANA
52579 Highway 51 S, Independence, LA 70443
Phone: (504) 878-1273
Sales: $22,600,000   *Employecs:* NA
Company Type: Private   *Employees here:* 600
SIC: 8062

Leverne Meades, Principal

D-U-N-S 09-655-8267
STATE OF MARYLAND
6655 Sykesville Rd, Sykesville, MD 21784
Phone: (410) 795-2100
Sales: $42,400,000   *Employees:* NA
Company Type: Private   *Employees here:* 1,200
SIC: 8063
    Psychiatric hospital
Paula Langmead, N/A

D-U-N-S 11-822-1761
STATE OF MARYLAND
22 S Greene St, Baltimore, MD 21201
Phone: (410) 328-8976
Sales: $44,000,000   *Employees:* NA
Company Type: Private   *Employees here:* 1,000
SIC: 8062
    General hospital
John W Ashworth, Branch Manager

D-U-N-S 15-613-1963
STATE OF MARYLAND
55 Wade Ave, Baltimore, MD 21228
Phone: (410) 455-6000

Sales: $45,900,000   *Employees:* NA
Company Type: Private   *Employees here:* 1,300
SIC: 8063
    Psychiatric hospital nursing/personal care
Paul Kotula, Principal

D-U-N-S 61-709-9189
STATE OF MARYLAND
90 State Cir Ste G15, Annapolis, MD 21401
Phone: (410) 841-3900
Sales: $59,500,000   *Employees:* NA
Company Type: Private   *Employees here:* 1,000
SIC: 8011
    Medical doctor's office
Robert Edwards, Branch Manager

D-U-N-S 01-078-1052
STATE OF NEW YORK
1400 Noyes At York, Utica, NY 13502
Phone: (315) 797-6800
Sales: $47,600,000   *Employees:* NA
Company Type: Private   *Employees here:* 1,200
SIC: 8063
    Psychiatric hospital
Sarah Rudes, Principal

D-U-N-S 08-189-9205
STATE OF NEW YORK
2 Ridge Rd, Thiells, NY 10984
Phone: (914) 947-1000
Sales: $110,400,000   *Employees:* NA
Company Type: Private   *Employees here:* 2,800
SIC: 8063
    Psychiatric hospital
Fredrick Zazycki, N/A

D-U-N-S 07-159-0103
STATE OF NEW YORK
620 Madison St, Syracuse, NY 13210
Phone: (315) 473-4980
Sales: $31,900,000   *Employees:* NA
Company Type: Private   *Employees here:* 800
SIC: 8063
    Psychiatric hospital
Brian Rhodes, Administration

D-U-N-S 01-886-9735
STATE OF NEW YORK
Balltown & Consaul Rd, Schenectady, NY 12304
Phone: (518) 370-7370
Sales: $29,000,000   *Employees:* NA
Company Type: Private   *Employees here:* 1,100
SIC: 8361
    Residential care services
Michael Dillon, Administration

D-U-N-S 09-167-0018
STATE OF NEW YORK
1111 Elmwood Ave, Rochester, NY 14620
Phone: (716) 473-3230
Sales: $42,100,000   *Employees:* NA
Company Type: Private   *Employees here:* 1,059
SIC: 8063
    Psychiatric hospital
Martin H Von Holden, Executive Director

D-U-N-S 03-349-1028
STATE OF NEW YORK
8045 Winchester Blvd, Queens Village, NY 11427
Phone: (718) 464-7500

Sales: $79,100,000
Company Type: Private
SIC: 8063
  Psychiatric hospital
Charlotte Seltzer, N/A

Employees: NA
Employees here: 2,000

Sales: $23,800,000
Company Type: Private
SIC: 8063
  Psychiatric hospital
James Igmelzi, N/A

Employees: NA
Employees here: 700

D-U-N-S 07-401-2352
STATE OF NEW YORK
10310 County Rd 58, Perrysburg, NY 14129
Phone: (716) 532-5522
Sales: $25,000,000
Company Type: Private
SIC: 8051
  Skilled nursing care facility
Ivan Canuteson, N/A

Employees: NA
Employees here: 1,100

D-U-N-S 08-185-6767
STATE OF OHIO
1101 Summit Rd, Cincinnati, OH 45237
Phone: (513) 948-3600
Sales: $20,300,000
Company Type: Private
SIC: 8063
  Psychiatric hospital
Sandy Vanpelt, President

Employees: NA
Employees here: 598

D-U-N-S 07-160-0068
STATE OF NEW YORK
1 Chimney Point Dr, Ogdensburg, NY 13669
Phone: (315) 393-3000
Sales: $33,900,000
Company Type: Private
SIC: 8063
  Psychiatric hospital
John Scott, Manager

Employees: NA
Employees here: 850

D-U-N-S 13-008-5574
STATE OF SOUTH CAROLINA
2100 Bull St, Columbia, SC 29201
Phone: (803) 734-6520
Sales: $22,200,000
Company Type: Private
SIC: 8063
  Psychiatric hospital
Dr Jaime Condom, Director

Employees: NA
Employees here: 625

D-U-N-S 07-751-3497
STATE OF NEW YORK
Off Rr 25 Box A, Kings Park, NY 11754
Phone: (516) 761-3500
Sales: $118,200,000
Company Type: Private
SIC: 8063
  Psychiatric hospital
Alan Weinstock, Director

Employees: NA
Employees here: 3,000

D-U-N-S 15-695-3150
STATE LABORATORY OF HYGIENE
465 Henry Mall, Madison, WI 53706
Phone: (608) 262-1293
Sales: $23,124,000
Company Type: Private
SIC: 8071
  State public health laboratory
Ronald Laessig Phd, Director

Employees: 350
Employees here: 250

D-U-N-S 11-878-3927
STATE OF NEW YORK
400 Forest Ave, Buffalo, NY 14213
Phone: (716) 885-2261
Sales: $46,900,000
Company Type: Private
SIC: 8063
  Psychiatric hospital
George Molnar, N/A

Employees: NA
Employees here: 1,180

D-U-N-S 06-305-3656
STATE UNIVERSITY OF NY
750 E Adams St, Syracuse, NY 13210
Phone: (315) 464-8300
Sales: $340,000,000
Company Type: Private
SIC: 8062
  Hospital & medical school
Dr Gregory Eastwood Md, President

Employees: 4,800
Employees here: 4,200

D-U-N-S 01-078-1854
STATE OF NEW YORK
425 Robinson St, Binghamton, NY 13901
Phone: (607) 724-1391
Sales: $27,900,000
Company Type: Private
SIC: 8063
  Psychiatric hospital
Margret Ducan, Branch Manager

Employees: NA
Employees here: 700

D-U-N-S 86-844-8622
STATE UNIVERSITY OF NY
Health Scences Ctr L4 170, Stony Brook, NY 11794
Phone: (516) 444-2080
Sales: $99,500,000
Company Type: Private
SIC: 8062
  Hospital & medical school
Dr Norman Edelman, Vice-President

Employees: NA
Employees here: 2,000

D-U-N-S 07-581-3535
STATE OF NEW YORK
249 Glenwood Rd, Binghamton, NY 13905
Phone: (607) 770-0211
Sales: $32,200,000
Company Type: Private
SIC: 8361
  Residential care services
Richard Thamasett, Branch Manager

Employees: NA
Employees here: 1,223

D-U-N-S 62-580-0263
STATE UNIVERSITY OF NY
425 Robinson St, Binghamton, NY 13901
Phone: (607) 770-8514
Sales: $28,400,000
Company Type: Private
SIC: 8071
  Medical laboratory
Dr Rajesh Dave, Principal

Employees: NA
Employees here: 550

D-U-N-S 12-522-0152
STATE OF OHIO
1960 W Broad St, Columbus, OH 43223
Phone: (614) 274-7231

D-U-N-S 17-513-8700
STATEN ISLAND UNIVERSITY HOSP
475 Seaview Ave, Staten Island, NY 10305
Phone: (718) 226-9000

Sales: $446,916,000 *Employees:* 4,000
Company Type: Private *Employees here:* 3,400
SIC: 8062
General hospital
Rick Varone, President

D-U-N-S 19-567-7828
STATEN ISLAND UNIVERSITY HOSP
375 Seguine Ave, Staten Island, NY 10309
Phone: (718) 226-9000
Sales: $149,300,000 *Employees:* NA
Company Type: Private *Employees here:* 990
SIC: 8062
Hospital
Rick J Varone, President

D-U-N-S 07-249-0584
STATESBORO HMA INC
(Parent: Health Management Associates)
500 E Grady St, Statesboro, GA 30458
Phone: (912) 764-6671
Sales: $29,600,000 *Employees:* 650
Company Type: Public Family Member *Employees here:* 650
SIC: 8062
General hospital
Scott Campbell, Administrator

D-U-N-S 01-062-2710
STEAMBOAT SPRNGS HEALTH CARE ASN
80 Park Ave, Steamboat Springs, CO 80487
Phone: (970) 879-1322
Sales: $22,703,000 *Employees:* 260
Company Type: Private *Employees here:* 220
SIC: 8062
General medical & surgical hospital skilled nursing care
facility & child day care services
Margaret Sabin, Administrator

D-U-N-S 09-536-1564
STEP-BY-STEP INC
69 Public Sq Ste 1400, Wilkes Barre, PA 18701
Phone: (717) 829-3477
Sales: $22,359,000 *Employees:* 675
Company Type: Private *Employees here:* 50
SIC: 8361
Rehabilitation service
James Bobeck, Executive Director

D-U-N-S 06-919-4058
STEPHENS COUNTY HOSPITAL AUTH
2003 Falls Rd, Toccoa, GA 30577
Phone: (706) 886-6841
Sales: $29,206,000 *Employees:* 414
Company Type: Private *Employees here:* 414
SIC: 8062
Hospital
Edward Gambrell Jr, Administrator

D-U-N-S 04-068-5000
STERLING HEALTH CARE CORP
1500 114th Ave SE Ste 100, Bellevue, WA 98004
Phone: (425) 453-5445
Sales: $60,300,000 *Employees:* 1,300
Company Type: Private *Employees here:* 44
SIC: 8062
Owns private hospitals & outpatient facilities
Michael Cancelosi, President

D-U-N-S 09-579-2503
STERLING ROCK FLS CLINIC LTD
101 E Miller Rd, Sterling, IL 61081
Phone: (815) 625-4790

Sales: $20,943,000 *Employees:* 250
Company Type: Private *Employees here:* 200
SIC: 8011
Multi-specialty clinic
Dr Michael P Gerberi Md, President

D-U-N-S 07-122-6989
STILLWATER MEDICAL CTR AUTH
1323 W 6th Ave, Stillwater, OK 74074
Phone: (405) 372-1480
Sales: $42,546,000 *Employees:* 600
Company Type: Private *Employees here:* 523
SIC: 8062
General hospital
Jerry Moeller, President

D-U-N-S 79-244-2865
STL MANAGEMENT, INC
101 Compass Point Dr, Saint Charles, MO 63301
Phone: (314) 949-2669
Sales: $21,200,000 *Employees:* 300
Company Type: Private *Employees here:* 1
SIC: 8049
Rehabilitation services
Catherine Dulle, President

D-U-N-S 06-795-7423
STORMNT-VAIL RGIONAL HEALTH CTR
1500 SW 10th Ave, Topeka, KS 66604
Phone: (785) 354-6000
Sales: $168,783,000 *Employees:* 2,500
Company Type: Private *Employees here:* 1,742
SIC: 8062
General medical & surgical hospital
Maynard F Oliverius, President

D-U-N-S 01-745-3411
STORMONT-VAIL HEALTHCARE INC
1500 SW 10th Ave, Topeka, KS 66604
Phone: (785) 354-6000
Sales: $93,400,000 *Employees:* 2,000
Company Type: Private *Employees here:* 2,000
SIC: 8062
Acute care physician clinic
Mayard Oliverius, President

D-U-N-S 62-143-7565
STOUDER MEMORIAL HOSPITAL ASSN
920 Summit Ave, Troy, OH 45373
Phone: (937) 332-8500
Sales: $50,320,000 *Employees:* 456
Company Type: Private *Employees here:* 300
SIC: 8062
Hospital
David Meckstroth, President

D-U-N-S 11-830-3932
STRATEGIC HEALTH SERVICES,
(Parent: Camcare Inc)
501 Morris St, Charleston, WV 25301
Phone: (304) 348-3677
Sales: $37,812,000 *Employees:* 485
Company Type: Private *Employees here:* 150
SIC: 8071
Medical laboratory testing outpatient surgury collection
agency management services and linen service
Robert Savage, President

D-U-N-S 07-133-3157
STUART JENNIE MEDICAL CENTER
320 W 18th St, Hopkinsville, KY 42240
Phone: (502) 887-0100

Sales: $53,421,000   *Employees:* 575
Company Type: Private   *Employees here:* 575
SIC: 8062
  General hospital
Terry Peeples, Administrator

D-U-N-S 07-570-5475
STURDY MEMORIAL HOSPITAL INC
211 Park St, Attleboro, MA 2703
Phone: (508) 222-5200
Sales: $62,536,000   *Employees:* 1,000
Company Type: Private   *Employees here:* 1,000
SIC: 8062
  General hospital
Linda Shyavitz, President

D-U-N-S 78-717-7609
SU-PRA ENTERPRISES INC
30150 Telg Rd Ste 205, Franklin, MI 48025
Phone: (248) 646-5151
Sales: $20,560,000   *Employees:* 380
Company Type: Private   *Employees here:* 7
SIC: 8082
  Home health care services
Soledad U Dee, Secretary

D-U-N-S 06-875-9778
SUBURBAN GENERAL HOSPITAL
100 S Jackson Ave, Pittsburgh, PA 15202
Phone: (412) 734-6000
Sales: $28,140,000   *Employees:* 607
Company Type: Private   *Employees here:* 604
SIC: 8062
  General hospital
Thomas H Prickett, President

D-U-N-S 06-904-4386
SUBURBAN GENERAL HOSPITAL
2701 De Kalb Pike, Norristown, PA 19401
Phone: (610) 278-2000
Sales: $50,853,000   *Employees:* 792
Company Type: Private   *Employees here:* 707
SIC: 8062
  General hospital
Edward R Solvibile, President

D-U-N-S 06-748-2562
SUBURBAN HEIGHTS MED CTR SC
333 Dixie Hwy, Chicago Heights, IL 60411
Phone: (708) 756-0100
Sales: $27,400,000   *Employees:* 400
Company Type: Private   *Employees here:* 400
SIC: 8011
  Medical clinic
Dr Richard D Aaronson Md, President

D-U-N-S 07-479-9867
SUBURBAN HOSPITAL
8600 Old Georgetown Rd, Bethesda, MD 20814
Phone: (301) 896-3100
Sales: $124,324,000   *Employees:* 1,550
Company Type: Private   *Employees here:* 1,550
SIC: 8062
  Hospital
Brian Grissler, President

D-U-N-S 09-475-2706
SUBURBAN MED CTR HFFMN ESTATES
  (Parent: Galen Health Care Inc)
1555 Barrington Rd, Hoffman Estates, IL 60194
Phone: (847) 843-2000

Sales: $85,682,000   *Employees:* 1,070
Company Type: Public Family Member   *Employees here:* 1,070
SIC: 8062
  Medical & surgical hospital
Edward Goldberg, President

D-U-N-S 09-325-3011
SULLIVAN DIAGNSTC TRTMNT CTR
Benmosche Rd, Harris, NY 12742
Phone: (914) 794-1400
Sales: $20,744,000   *Employees:* 400
Company Type: Private   *Employees here:* 370
SIC: 8361
  Rehabilitation center
Patrick H Dollard, Chief Executive Officer

D-U-N-S 07-690-2923
SUMMA HEALTH SYSTEM
525 E Market St, Akron, OH 44304
Phone: (330) 375-3000
Sales: $348,205,000   *Employees:* 4,000
Company Type: Private   *Employees here:* 3,000
SIC: 8062
  General hospital
Elbert F Gilbert Phd, President

D-U-N-S 06-347-2302
SUMMERSVILLE MEMORIAL HOSP
400 Fairview Heights Rd, Summersville, WV 26651
Phone: (304) 872-2891
Sales: $20,274,000   *Employees:* 400
Company Type: Private   *Employees here:* 400
SIC: 8062
  General hospital
Dave Lakey, Administrator

D-U-N-S 06-280-3184
SUMMIT CARE CORPORATION
2600 W Magnolia Blvd, Burbank, CA 91505
Phone: (818) 841-8750
Sales: $197,927,000   *Employees:* 4,200
Company Type: Public   *Employees here:* 100
SIC: 8059
  Skilled nursing facilities
William C Scott, Chairman of the Board

D-U-N-S 14-781-2838
SUMMIT LANDMARK ORTHOPEDIC ASC
293 7th St W 100, Saint Paul, MN 55102
Phone: (651) 297-6909
Sales: $20,000,000   *Employees:* 140
Company Type: Private   *Employees here:* 140
SIC: 8011
  Orthopedic clinic
Jack Drogt, President

D-U-N-S 78-074-5493
SUMMIT POINTE
140 Michigan Ave W, Battle Creek, MI 49017
Phone: (616) 966-1460
Sales: $20,301,000   *Employees:* 125
Company Type: Private   *Employees here:* 125
SIC: 8093
  Specialty outpatient clinic
Ervin R Brinker, Chief Executive Officer

D-U-N-S 01-096-4083
SUMMITT COSMETIC GROUP
436 N Bedford Dr, Beverly Hills, CA 90210
Phone: (310) 276-9337

Sales: $22,000,000   *Employees:* 73
Company Type: Private   *Employees here:* 73
SIC: 8011
    Plastic surgeons
Mark Anderson, President

D-U-N-S 07-822-6792
SUMNER REGIONAL HEALTH SYSTEMS
555 Hartsville Pike, Gallatin, TN 37066
Phone: (615) 452-4210
Sales: $50,555,000   *Employees:* 700
Company Type: Private   *Employees here:* 609
SIC: 8062
    General hospital & home health care
William T Sugg, Administrator

D-U-N-S 80-680-3433
SUN CITY HOSPITAL INC
    (Parent: Healthtrust Inc - Hospital Co)
4016 State Road 674, Ruskin, FL 33573
Phone: (813) 634-3301
Sales: $19,700,000   *Employees:* 440
Company Type: Public Family Member   *Employees here:* 440
SIC: 8062
    General hospital home health and skilled nursing
Rex Etheredge, Chief Executive Officer

D-U-N-S 04-022-1665
SUN COAST HOSPITAL INC
2025 Indian Rocks Rd S, Largo, FL 33774
Phone: (727) 581-9474
Sales: $57,016,000   *Employees:* 740
Company Type: Private   *Employees here:* 740
SIC: 8069
    Osteopathic hospital
Jeffrey A Collins, Chief Executive Officer

D-U-N-S 92-876-3317
SUN COAST HOSPITAL INC
2025 Indian Rocks Rd S, Largo, FL 33774
Phone: (727) 587-7641
Sales: $42,600,000   *Employees:* NA
Company Type: Private   *Employees here:* 700
SIC: 8011
    Medical doctor's office
Margaret Coupe, Director

D-U-N-S 04-373-3369
SUN HEALTH CORPORATION
13180 N 103rd Dr, Sun City, AZ 85351
Phone: (602) 876-5301
Sales: $187,722,000   *Employees:* 2,390
Company Type: Private   *Employees here:* 1,000
SIC: 8062
    Hospital home health care & skilled nursing facility
Leland W Peterson, President

D-U-N-S 17-036-1992
SUN HEALTH CORPORATION
10401 W Thunderbird Blvd, Sun City, AZ 85351
Phone: (602) 977-7211
Sales: $51,800,000   *Employees:* NA
Company Type: Private   *Employees here:* 1,200
SIC: 8062
    General hospital
George Perez, N/A

D-U-N-S 83-547-2754
SUN HEALTH CORPORATION
13180 N 103rd SE, Sun City, AZ 85351
Phone: (602) 977-7211

Sales: $29,900,000   *Employees:* NA
Company Type: Private   *Employees here:* 700
SIC: 8062
    Hospital
Leland W Peterson, President

D-U-N-S 80-743-2380   EXP
SUN HEALTHCARE GROUP INC
101 Sun Ave NE, Albuquerque, NM 87109
Phone: (505) 821-3355
Sales: $2,010,820,000   *Employees:* 68,900
Company Type: Public   *Employees here:* 15
SIC: 8051
    Operates long term care & subacute care facilities
      institutional pharmacies rehabilitation therapy & temporary
      therapy staff
Andrew L Turner, Chairman of the Board

D-U-N-S 06-959-5304
SUNBURY COMMUNITY HOSPITAL
350 N 11th St, Sunbury, PA 17801
Phone: (717) 286-3333
Sales: $21,714,000   *Employees:* 455
Company Type: Private   *Employees here:* 455
SIC: 8062
    General medical & surgical hospital
Nicholas Prisco, Chief Executive Officer

D-U-N-S 62-288-2850
SUNCARE RESPIRATORY SERVICES
    (Parent: Sun Healthcare Group Inc)
2431 Directors Row Ste G, Indianapolis, IN 46241
Phone: (317) 244-5037
Sales: $64,000,000   *Employees:* 80
Company Type: Public Family Member   *Employees here:* 73
SIC: 8093
    Respiratory therapy whol med equip oxygen service rent
      medical equip
Tom Futch, President

D-U-N-S 55-603-1367
SUNDANCE REHABILITATION CORP
    (Parent: Sun Healthcare Group Inc)
5131 Masthead St NE, Albuquerque, NM 87109
Phone: (505) 821-3355
Sales: $326,169,000   *Employees:* 3,800
Company Type: Public Family Member   *Employees here:* 11
SIC: 8049
    Rehabilitation services
Robert A Levin, President

D-U-N-S 13-940-1103
SUNNYSIDE COMMUNITY HOSPITAL ASSN
10th St And Tacoma Ave, Sunnyside, WA 98944
Phone: (509) 837-1500
Sales: $19,806,000   *Employees:* 235
Company Type: Private   *Employees here:* 230
SIC: 8062
    General hospital
Jon Smiley, Administrator

D-U-N-S 17-516-6313
SUNNYSIDE HOME CARE PROJECT
4331 39th St Ste 5, Sunnyside, NY 11104
Phone: (718) 784-6173
Sales: $29,300,000   *Employees:* 1,200
Company Type: Private   *Employees here:* 1,200
SIC: 8361
    Home care to elderly & disabled
Judy Zangwill, Executive Director

D-U-N-S 61-596-8310
SUNPLUS HM HEALTH NURSING FCILTY
(Parent: Sun Healthcare Group Inc)
1317 W Foothill Blvd, Upland, CA 91786
Phone: (909) 949-3770
Sales: $121,800,000   *Employees:* NA
Company Type: Public Family Member   *Employees here:* NA
SIC: 8051
  Skilled nursing care facility
Sharon Guller, Director

D-U-N-S 92-616-2173
SUNRISE ASSISTED LIVING, INC
9401 Lee Hwy Ste 300, Fairfax, VA 22031
Phone: (703) 273-7500
Sales: $89,884,000   *Employees:* 3,500
Company Type: Public   *Employees here:* 100
SIC: 8361
  Manages independent & assisted living retirement
  communities
Paul J Klaassen, Chairman of the Board

D-U-N-S 06-383-3230
SUNRISE COMMUNITY, INC
9040 Sunset Dr, Miami, FL 33173
Phone: (305) 245-6150
Sales: $35,334,000   *Employees:* 1,100
Company Type: Private   *Employees here:* 350
SIC: 8052
  Home for the developmentally disabled
Leslie W Leech Jr, President

D-U-N-S 02-015-6535
SUNRISE HOSPITAL
(Parent: Columbia/Hca Healthcare Corp)
3186 S Maryland Pkwy, Las Vegas, NV 89109
Phone: (702) 731-8000
Sales: $140,700,000   *Employees:* 3,000
Company Type: Public Family Member   *Employees here:* 3,000
SIC: 8062
  General hospital
Gerald Mitchell, President

D-U-N-S 80-170-0501
SUTTER AMADOR HOSPITAL
810 Court St, Jackson, CA 95642
Phone: (209) 223-7500
Sales: $25,898,000   *Employees:* 360
Company Type: Private   *Employees here:* 360
SIC: 8062
  Hospital
Scott Stenberg, Administrator

D-U-N-S 80-288-1524
SUTTER COAST HOSPITAL
800 E Washington Blvd, Crescent City, CA 95531
Phone: (707) 464-8511
Sales: $32,125,000   *Employees:* 400
Company Type: Private   *Employees here:* 370
SIC: 8062
  General hospital
John Menaugh, Administrator

D-U-N-S 07-654-7462
SUTTER DELTA MEDICAL
3901 Lone Tree Way, Antioch, CA 94509
Phone: (925) 779-7200
Sales: $45,574,000   *Employees:* 500
Company Type: Private   *Employees here:* 475
SIC: 8062
  General medical and surgical hospital and home health care
  services
Linda Horn, Administrator

D-U-N-S 96-801-5073
SUTTER HEALTH
301 E 13th St, Merced, CA 95340
Phone: (209) 385-7000
Sales: $31,800,000   *Employees:* NA
Company Type: Private   *Employees here:* 650
SIC: 8062
  General hospital
Brian Bentley, Administrator

D-U-N-S 07-154-3870
SUTTER HEALTH CENTRAL
2800 L St, Sacramento, CA 95816
Phone: (916) 733-8800
Sales: $574,129,000   *Employees:* 4,083
Company Type: Private   *Employees here:* 435
SIC: 8062
  Hospitals
Pat Frye, Administrator

D-U-N-S 11-446-8317
SUTTER HEALTH CENTRAL
5151 F St, Sacramento, CA 95819
Phone: (916) 454-3333
Sales: $79,500,000   *Employees:* NA
Company Type: Private   *Employees here:* 1,600
SIC: 8062
  General hospital
Patrick Fry, Principal

D-U-N-S 12-615-8559
SUTTER HEALTH CENTRAL
2801 L St, Sacramento, CA 95816
Phone: (916) 454-2222
Sales: $62,200,000   *Employees:* NA
Company Type: Private   *Employees here:* 1,255
SIC: 8062
  General hospital
Lou Lazatin, Chief Operating Officer

D-U-N-S 07-154-5180
SUTTER LAKESIDE HOSPITAL
5176 Hill Rd E, Lakeport, CA 95453
Phone: (707) 263-5651
Sales: $32,476,000   *Employees:* 350
Company Type: Private   *Employees here:* 310
SIC: 8062
  General hospital
Paul Hensler, Administrator

D-U-N-S 07-612-0286
SUTTER NORTH MED FOUNDATION
826 4th St, Marysville, CA 95901
Phone: (530) 741-1300
Sales: $62,438,000   *Employees:* 400
Company Type: Private   *Employees here:* 160
SIC: 8011
  Medical clinic & urgent care clinic
Ross Gassaway, Chief Executive Officer

D-U-N-S 07-168-7859
SUTTER SOLANO MEDICAL CENTER
300 Hospital Dr, Vallejo, CA 94589
Phone: (707) 554-4444
Sales: $45,697,000   *Employees:* 542
Company Type: Private   *Employees here:* 490
SIC: 8062
  General hospital
Patrick R Brady, Chief Executive Officer

D-U-N-S 07-457-3932
SWEDISH AMERICAN HOSPITAL ASSN
1400 Charles St, Rockford, IL 61104

Phone: (815) 968-4400
Sales: $142,872,000   *Employees:* 2,494
Company Type: Private   *Employees here:* 1,670
SIC: 8062
    General hospital
Don Haring, Chief Financial Officer

D-U-N-S 07-926-4420
SWEDISH HEALTH SERVICES
747 Broadway, Seattle, WA 98122
Phone: (206) 386-6000
Sales: $297,466,000   *Employees:* 5,300
Company Type: Private   *Employees here:* 4,400
SIC: 8062
    Hospital
Richard Peterson, President

D-U-N-S 18-794-3345
SYCAMORE SHOALS HOSPITAL INC
    (Parent: Columbia/Hca Healthcare Corp)
1501 W Elk Ave, Elizabethton, TN 37643
Phone: (423) 542-1300
Sales: $21,646,000   *Employees:* 350
Company Type: Public Family Member   *Employees here:* 350
SIC: 8062
    Hospital and nursing facility
Larry R Jeter, Chief Executive Officer

D-U-N-S 07-657-8251
SYMMES HOSPITAL & MEDICAL CTR
39 Hospital Rd, Arlington, MA 2474
Phone: (781) 646-1500
Sales: $37,575,000   *Employees:* 450
Company Type: Private   *Employees here:* 450
SIC: 8062
    General hospital & skilled nursing facility
Dr Peter Goldbach Md, Chief Executive Officer

D-U-N-S 05-682-7454
T J SAMSON COMMUNITY HOSP
1301 N Race St, Glasgow, KY 42141
Phone: (502) 651-4444
Sales: $46,136,000   *Employees:* 821
Company Type: Private   *Employees here:* 821
SIC: 8062
    General medical hospital
H G Joiner, Administrator

D-U-N-S 06-512-1915
TABITHA, INC
4720 Randolph St, Lincoln, NE 68510
Phone: (402) 483-7671
Sales: $19,972,000   *Employees:* 900
Company Type: Private   *Employees here:* 900
SIC: 8361
    Home for the aged home health care hospice and housing
      services
Alfred Sward, President

D-U-N-S 07-240-5442
TAHLEQUAH HOSPITAL AUTHORITY
1400 E Downing St, Tahlequah, OK 74464
Phone: (918) 456-0641
Sales: $20,048,000   *Employees:* 295
Company Type: Private   *Employees here:* 267
SIC: 8062
    General hospital
Gary Jepson, Administrator

D-U-N-S 04-599-6246
TAHOE FOREST HOSPITAL DST
10121 Pine Ave, Truckee, CA 96161
Phone: (530) 587-6011

Sales: $35,165,000   *Employees:* 328
Company Type: Private   *Employees here:* 302
SIC: 8062
    General medical hospital and skilled nursing facility
Lawrence Long, Administrator

D-U-N-S 96-825-2536
TALBERT MEDICAL MGT CORP
    (Parent: Medpartners Inc)
3540 Howard Way, Costa Mesa, CA 92626
Phone: (714) 436-4800
Sales: $1,181,000,000   *Employees:* 29,526
Company Type: Public Family Member   *Employees here:* 40
SIC: 8099
    Health/allied services
Edwin Crawford, President

D-U-N-S 61-385-5956
TALLAHASSEE MEDICAL CENTER
    (Parent: Columbia/Hca Healthcare Corp)
2626 Capital Medical Blvd, Tallahassee, FL 32308
Phone: (850) 656-5000
Sales: $55,193,000   *Employees:* 572
Company Type: Public Family Member   *Employees here:* 35
SIC: 8062
    General medical & surgical hospital
John Freeman, Chief Financial Officer

D-U-N-S 07-919-8594
TALLAHSSEE MEM RGIONAL MED CTR
1300 Miccosukee Rd, Tallahassee, FL 32308
Phone: (850) 681-5238
Sales: $164,291,000   *Employees:* 3,300
Company Type: Private   *Employees here:* 3,000
SIC: 8062
    General hospital
Duncan Moore, President

D-U-N-S 07-820-7610
TANANA VALLEY MED SURGICAL GROUP
1001 Noble St, Fairbanks, AK 99701
Phone: (907) 459-3500
Sales: $22,000,000   *Employees:* 150
Company Type: Private   *Employees here:* 150
SIC: 8011
    Medical doctor's office
Rebecca Dean, Administrator

D-U-N-S 01-515-9549
TANDEM HEALTH CARE INC
1553 NE Arch Ave, Jensen Beach, FL 34957
Phone: (561) 225-7050
Sales: $30,000,000   *Employees:* 9
Company Type: Private   *Employees here:* 9
SIC: 8051
    Skilled nursing care facility
Jospeh Conte, President

D-U-N-S 07-321-6871
TARPON SPRINGS HOSPITAL FOUNDATION
1395 S Pinellas Ave, Tarpon Springs, FL 34689
Phone: (727) 942-5094
Sales: $59,263,000   *Employees:* 750
Company Type: Private   *Employees here:* 740
SIC: 8062
    General hospital
Joseph N Kiefer, Administrator

D-U-N-S 02-033-3597
TARRANT COUNTY
3840 S Hulen St, Fort Worth, TX 76109
Phone: (817) 735-3800

Sales: $61,660,000   *Employees:* 1,227
Company Type: Private   *Employees here:* 100
SIC: 8093
    Mental health center
James F Mc Dermott, Chief Executive Officer

D-U-N-S 08-100-9854
TAYLOR COUNTY HOSPITAL
1700 Old Lebanon Rd, Campbellsville, KY 42718
Phone: (502) 465-3561
Sales: $27,837,000   *Employees:* 459
Company Type: Private   *Employees here:* 459
SIC: 8062
    General hospital
David R Hayes, Chief Executive Officer

D-U-N-S 09-496-2362
TEAM CARE INC
    (Parent: Mariner Post-Acute Network)
1 Ravinia Dr Ste 1240, Atlanta, GA 30346
Phone: (770) 393-0199
Sales: $34,300,000   *Employees:* 500
Company Type: Public Family Member   *Employees here:* 12
SIC: 8011
    Institutional pharmacy providing pharmaceutical services
Arlene B Reynolds, President

D-U-N-S 10-159-3309
TEAYS VALLEY HEALTH SERVICES
    (Parent: Columbia/Hca Healthcare Corp)
1400 Hospital Dr, Hurricane, WV 25526
Phone: (304) 757-9800
Sales: $26,410,000   *Employees:* 330
Company Type: Public Family Member   *Employees here:* 330
SIC: 8062
    General medical & surgical hospital
Patsy Hardy, Chief Executive Officer

D-U-N-S 07-654-7363
TELECARE CORPORATION
1100 Marina Village Parkw, Alameda, CA 94501
Phone: (510) 337-7950
Sales: $61,375,000   *Employees:* 1,600
Company Type: Private   *Employees here:* 80
SIC: 8063
    Mental hospitals
Anne L Bakar, President

D-U-N-S 07-879-9095
TEMPLE HOSPITAL INC
235 N Hoover St, Los Angeles, CA 90004
Phone: (213) 382-7252
Sales: $33,920,000   *Employees:* 330
Company Type: Private   *Employees here:* 330
SIC: 8062
    Hospital
Saul Burakoff, President

D-U-N-S 07-145-4888
TEMPLE LOWER BUCKS HOSPITAL
501 Bath Rd, Bristol, PA 19007
Phone: (215) 785-9200
Sales: $69,247,000   *Employees:* 770
Company Type: Private   *Employees here:* 770
SIC: 8062
    General hospital
Nathan Bosk, Chief Executive Officer

D-U-N-S 09-523-2500
TEMPLE SURGICAL CENTER INC
60 Temple St Ste 2, New Haven, CT 6510
Phone: (203) 624-6008

Sales: $20,000,000   *Employees:* 46
Company Type: Private   *Employees here:* 46
SIC: 8011
    Ambulatory surgical center
Bart Price, President

D-U-N-S 18-457-1586
TEMPLE UNIV COMMONWEALTH SYSTM
3400 N Broad St, Philadelphia, PA 19140
Phone: (215) 707-7000
Sales: $114,300,000   *Employees:* NA
Company Type: Private   *Employees here:* 2,296
SIC: 8062
    General hospital
Paul Boehringer, Executive Director

D-U-N-S 60-712-4583
TENDERCARE MICHIGAN INC
209 E Portage Ave, Sault Sainte Marie, MI 49783
Phone: (906) 635-0020
Sales: $71,100,000   *Employees:* 3,100
Company Type: Private   *Employees here:* 25
SIC: 8051
    Skilled nursing home care & retirement home for the aged
Dr Louis B Lukenda, President

D-U-N-S 04-572-6650
TENET HEALTH SYSTEM DI, INC
    (Parent: Tenet Healthcare Corporation)
3820 State St, Santa Barbara, CA 93105
Phone: (805) 563-7000
Sales: $211,600,000   *Employees:* 4,500
Company Type: Public Family Member   *Employees here:* 5
SIC: 8062
    General medical & surgical hospital
Jeffrey Barbakow, Chairman of the Board

D-U-N-S 80-955-8216
TENET HEALTH SYSTEM DI, INC
3555 Sunset Office Dr, Saint Louis, MO 63127
Phone: (314) 822-9915
Sales: $25,200,000   *Employees:* NA
Company Type: Public Family Member   *Employees here:* 400
SIC: 8011
    Medical clinic
Nesa Joseph, Manager

D-U-N-S 61-850-8154
TENET HEALTH SYSTEM HOSPITALS
2151 Appian Way, Pinole, CA 94564
Phone: (510) 724-5000
Sales: $24,300,000   *Employees:* NA
Company Type: Public Family Member   *Employees here:* 500
SIC: 8062
    Hospital
Gary Sloan, Chief Executive Officer

D-U-N-S 03-874-6046
TENET HEALTH SYSTEM HOSPITALS
47111 Monroe St, Indio, CA 92201
Phone: (760) 347-6191
Sales: $21,700,000   *Employees:* NA
Company Type: Public Family Member   *Employees here:* 627
SIC: 8062
    General hospital
Mike Remnis, N/A

D-U-N-S 12-217-0897
TENET HEALTH SYSTEM HOSPITALS
3100 S Douglas Rd, Miami, FL 33134
Phone: (305) 445-8461

Sales: $23,900,000   *Employees:* NA
Company Type: Public Family Member   *Employees here:* 552
SIC: 8062
  General hospital
Martha Garcia, Administrator

D-U-N-S 93-226-9301
TENET HEALTH SYSTEM HOSPITALS
3600 Washington St, Hollywood, FL 33021
Phone: (954) 966-4500
Sales: $26,100,000   *Employees:* NA
Company Type: Public Family Member   *Employees here:* 600
SIC: 8062
  Acute hospital
Holly Lerner, Chief Executive Officer

D-U-N-S 06-549-7059
TENET HEALTH SYSTEM HOSPITALS
  (Parent: Tenet Healthcare Corporation)
14001 Dallas Pkwy, Dallas, TX 75240
Phone: (972) 789-2200
Sales: $2,990,884,000   *Employees:* 22,000
Company Type: Public Family Member   *Employees here:* 50
SIC: 8062
  General medical and surgical hospitals
Jeffrey C Barbakow, Chairman of the Board

D-U-N-S 61-850-8238
TENET HEALTH SYSTEM HOSPITALS
7th Medical Pkwy, Dallas, TX 75234
Phone: (972) 247-1000
Sales: $29,100,000   *Employees:* NA
Company Type: Public Family Member   *Employees here:* 712
SIC: 8062
  General hospital
Craig Sims, President

D-U-N-S 11-865-3369
TENET HEALTH SYSTEM HOSPITALS
4343 N Josey Ln, Carrollton, TX 75010
Phone: (972) 492-1010
Sales: $21,900,000   *Employees:* NA
Company Type: Public Family Member   *Employees here:* 540
SIC: 8062
  Hospital
Craig E Sims, N/A

D-U-N-S 10-209-5924
TENET HEALTH SYSTEM MEDICAL,
2010 Brookwood Medical Ct, Birmingham, AL 35209
Phone: (205) 877-1000
Sales: $84,800,000   *Employees:* NA
Company Type: Public Family Member   *Employees here:* 2,000
SIC: 8062
  General hospital
Gregory H Burfitt, Chief Executive Officer

D-U-N-S 00-968-6395
TENET HEALTH SYSTEM MEDICAL,
  (Parent: Tenet Healthcare Corporation)
3820 State St, Santa Barbara, CA 93105
Phone: (805) 563-7000
Sales: $1,426,400,000   *Employees:* 30,200
Company Type: Public Family Member   *Employees here:* 250
SIC: 8062
  Operates general medical & surgical hospitals & psychiatric
    hospitals & operates medical buildings
Michael H Focht Sr, President

D-U-N-S 07-813-8583
TENET HEALTH SYSTEM MEDICAL,
12601 Garden Grove Blvd, Garden Grove, CA 92843
Phone: (714) 537-5160

Sales: $28,300,000   *Employees:* NA
Company Type: Public Family Member   *Employees here:* 580
SIC: 8062
  General hospital
Mark A Meyers, N/A

D-U-N-S 79-667-6450
TENET HEALTH SYSTEM MEDICAL,
3360 Burns Rd, West Palm Beach, FL 33410
Phone: (561) 622-1411
Sales: $44,000,000   *Employees:* NA
Company Type: Public Family Member   *Employees here:* 1,000
SIC: 8062
  Hospital
Arlon Reynolds, Branch Manager

D-U-N-S 19-622-4299
TENET HEALTH SYSTEM MEDICAL,
5757 N Dixie Hwy, Fort Lauderdale, FL 33334
Phone: (954) 776-6000
Sales: $41,700,000   *Employees:* NA
Company Type: Public Family Member   *Employees here:* 950
SIC: 8062
  Medical & surgical hospital
Dean Danielson, Branch Manager

D-U-N-S 62-155-0581
TENET HEALTH SYSTEM MEDICAL,
2620 N Westwood Blvd, Poplar Bluff, MO 63901
Phone: (573) 785-7721
Sales: $24,100,000   *Employees:* NA
Company Type: Public Family Member   *Employees here:* 625
SIC: 8062
  General hospital
Brian Flynn, Principal

D-U-N-S 05-826-0217
TENET HEALTH SYSTEM MEDICAL,
3050 39th St, Port Arthur, TX 77642
Phone: (409) 983-4951
Sales: $24,400,000   *Employees:* NA
Company Type: Public Family Member   *Employees here:* 600
SIC: 8062
  General & surgical hospital
Luis G Silva, Branch Manager

D-U-N-S 61-814-8035
TENET HEALTH SYSTEM MEDICAL,
1313 Ewing St Lowr Level, Houston, TX 77004
Phone: (713) 527-5024
Sales: $82,900,000   *Employees:* NA
Company Type: Public Family Member   *Employees here:* 2,000
SIC: 8062
  Hospital
Susie Russell, N/A

D-U-N-S 07-846-2611
TENET HEALTH SYSTEM N SHORE
  (Parent: Tenet Healthcare Corporation)
1100 NW 95th St, Miami, FL 33150
Phone: (305) 835-6000
Sales: $50,900,000   *Employees:* 1,100
Company Type: Public Family Member   *Employees here:* 1,100
SIC: 8062
  General hospital
Steven M Klein, President

D-U-N-S 02-811-8065
TENET HEALTH SYSTEM SPALDING,
  (Parent: Tenet Healthcare Corporation)
601 S 8th St, Griffin, GA 30224
Phone: (770) 228-2721

Sales: $35,400,000   *Employees:* 772
Company Type: Public Family Member   *Employees here:* 740
SIC: 8062
  Hospital
Phil Shaw, Executive Director

D-U-N-S 13-170-8687
TENET HEALTH SYSTEM-DALLAS
  (Parent: Tenet Health System Hospitals)
7th Medical Pkwy, Dallas, TX 75234
Phone: (972) 247-1000
Sales: $46,100,000   *Employees:* 1,000
Company Type: Public Family Member   *Employees here:* 450
SIC: 8062
  General hospital
Craig Sims, President

D-U-N-S 18-840-7670
TENET HEALTH SYSTEM-DALLAS
9440 Poppy Dr, Dallas, TX 75218
Phone: (214) 324-6100
Sales: $22,300,000   *Employees:* NA
Company Type: Public Family Member   *Employees here:* 550
SIC: 8062
  General hospital
Robert Freymuller, Principal

D-U-N-S 18-866-4825
TENET HEALTH SYSTEM-DALLAS
7 Medical Pkwy, Dallas, TX 75234
Phone: (972) 247-1000
Sales: $24,400,000   *Employees:* NA
Company Type: Public Family Member   *Employees here:* 600
SIC: 8062
  General hospital
Craig Sims, Branch Manager

D-U-N-S 09-565-2848
TENET HEALTH SYSTEMS HOSPITALS
  (Parent: Tenet Healthcare Corporation)
1205 E North St, Manteca, CA 95336
Phone: (209) 823-3111
Sales: $23,483,000   *Employees:* 300
Company Type: Public Family Member   *Employees here:* 300
SIC: 8062
  General hospital
Patrick Rafferty, Administrtor

D-U-N-S 08-269-5594
TENET HEALTHCARE CORPORATION
1100 Las Tablas Rd, Templeton, CA 93465
Phone: (805) 434-2813
Sales: $26,300,000   *Employees:* NA
Company Type: Public Family Member   *Employees here:* 500
SIC: 8069
  Acute care hospital
Harold Chilton, Chief Executive Officer

D-U-N-S 05-386-6661
TENET HEALTHCARE CORPORATION
3820 State St, Santa Barbara, CA 93105
Phone: (805) 563-7000
Sales: $9,895,000,000   *Employees:* 116,800
Company Type: Public   *Employees here:* 130
SIC: 8062
  General hospitals & other healthcare operations
Jeffrey C Barbakow, Chairman of the Board

D-U-N-S 02-051-7819
TENET HEALTHCARE CORPORATION
6655 Alvarado Rd, San Diego, CA 92120
Phone: (619) 287-3270

Sales: $59,500,000   *Employees:* NA
Company Type: Public Family Member   *Employees here:* 1,200
SIC: 8062
  Hospital
Barry Veinbaun, Principal

D-U-N-S 00-677-6256
TENET HEALTHCARE CORPORATION
1100 Butte St, Redding, CA 96001
Phone: (530) 244-5400
Sales: $44,500,000   *Employees:* NA
Company Type: Public Family Member   *Employees here:* 902
SIC: 8062
  General hospital
Don Griffin, Chief Executive Officer

D-U-N-S 15-045-5632
TENET HEALTHCARE CORPORATION
1301 N Rose Dr, Placentia, CA 92870
Phone: (714) 993-2000
Sales: $26,300,000   *Employees:* NA
Company Type: Public Family Member   *Employees here:* 500
SIC: 8069
  Specialty hospital
Kenneth Rivers, Engineering-R&D

D-U-N-S 02-014-5967
TENET HEALTHCARE CORPORATION
525 N Garfield Ave, Monterey Park, CA 91754
Phone: (626) 573-2222
Sales: $52,800,000   *Employees:* NA
Company Type: Public Family Member   *Employees here:* 1,000
SIC: 8069
  Specialty hospital
Phillip Cohens, Owner

D-U-N-S 08-876-0897
TENET HEALTHCARE CORPORATION
1441 Florida Ave, Modesto, CA 95350
Phone: (209) 578-1211
Sales: $89,500,000   *Employees:* NA
Company Type: Public Family Member   *Employees here:* 1,800
SIC: 8062
  Hopsital
Steve Mitchell, Administrator

D-U-N-S 61-737-1810
TENET HEALTHCARE CORPORATION
815 Pollard Rd, Los Gatos, CA 95032
Phone: (408) 378-6131
Sales: $36,900,000   *Employees:* NA
Company Type: Public Family Member   *Employees here:* 750
SIC: 8062
  Hospital
Truman Gates, Branch Manager

D-U-N-S 17-800-3745
TENET HEALTHCARE CORPORATION
2070 Century Park E, Los Angeles, CA 90067
Phone: (310) 553-6211
Sales: $31,800,000   *Employees:* NA
Company Type: Public Family Member   *Employees here:* 650
SIC: 8062
  Hospital
John Nickens Iii, Principal

D-U-N-S 61-366-8383
TENET HEALTHCARE CORPORATION
1500 San Pablo St, Los Angeles, CA 90033
Phone: (323) 342-8500

Sales: $43,100,000   *Employees:* NA
Company Type: Public Family Member   *Employees here:* 875
SIC: 8062
  Hospital
Lee Domanico, Chief Executive Officer

D-U-N-S 14-977-7203
TENET HEALTHCARE CORPORATION
3751 Katella Ave, Los Alamitos, CA 90720
Phone: (562) 598-1311
Sales: $38,300,000   *Employees:* NA
Company Type: Public Family Member   *Employees here:* 625
SIC: 8011
  Office & clinic of doctors of medicine
Guss Valdespino, Chief Executive Officer

D-U-N-S 07-618-4290
TENET HEALTHCARE CORPORATION
3700 South St, Lakewood, CA 90712
Phone: (562) 531-2250
Sales: $28,800,000   *Employees:* NA
Company Type: Public Family Member   *Employees here:* 590
SIC: 8062
  Acute care facility
Michael Kerr, Chief Executive Officer

D-U-N-S 13-195-6690
TENET HEALTHCARE CORPORATION
6001 Webb Rd, Tampa, FL 33615
Phone: (813) 885-6666
Sales: $21,600,000   *Employees:* NA
Company Type: Public Family Member   *Employees here:* 500
SIC: 8062
  General hospital
Larry Hanan, N/A

D-U-N-S 09-556-3847
TENET HEALTHCARE CORPORATION
1501 Pasadena Ave S, Saint Petersburg, FL 33707
Phone: (727) 381-1000
Sales: $35,200,000   *Employees:* NA
Company Type: Public Family Member   *Employees here:* 750
SIC: 8069
  Acute care hospital
John Bartlett, Director

D-U-N-S 18-498-9689
TENET HEALTHCARE CORPORATION
4399 N Nob Hill Rd, Fort Lauderdale, FL 33351
Phone: (954) 749-0300
Sales: $23,400,000   *Employees:* NA
Company Type: Public Family Member   *Employees here:* 500
SIC: 8069
  Rehabilitation hospital
Rex Macklin, Manager

D-U-N-S 03-272-8842
TENET HEALTHCARE CORPORATION
5352 Linton Blvd, Delray Beach, FL 33484
Phone: (561) 498-4440
Sales: $37,300,000   *Employees:* NA
Company Type: Public Family Member   *Employees here:* 850
SIC: 8062
  Hospital
Mitchell S Feidman, N/A

D-U-N-S 14-481-9372
TENET HEALTHCARE CORPORATION
21644 State Road 7, Boca Raton, FL 33428
Phone: (561) 488-8000

Sales: $30,600,000   *Employees:* NA
Company Type: Public Family Member   *Employees here:* 700
SIC: 8062
  General hospital
Michael Jensen, N/A

D-U-N-S 12-268-8732
TENET HEALTHCARE CORPORATION
100 Medical Center Dr, Slidell, LA 70461
Phone: (504) 649-7070
Sales: $24,400,000   *Employees:* NA
Company Type: Public Family Member   *Employees here:* 600
SIC: 8062
  General medical & surgical hospital
Nick Marzocco, Executive Director

D-U-N-S 17-016-5120
TENET HEALTHCARE CORPORATION
4444 General Meyer Ave, New Orleans, LA 70131
Phone: (504) 363-7011
Sales: $34,000,000   *Employees:* NA
Company Type: Public Family Member   *Employees here:* 550
SIC: 8011
  Medical center
Rene Goux, Administrator

D-U-N-S 88-428-7467
TENET HEALTHCARE CORPORATION
180 W Esplanade Ave, Kenner, LA 70065
Phone: (504) 468-8600
Sales: $20,200,000   *Employees:* NA
Company Type: Public Family Member   *Employees here:* 500
SIC: 8062
  Hospital & acute care facility
Debra Keel, President

D-U-N-S 03-465-7387
TENET HEALTHCARE CORPORATION
2500 Belle Chasse Hwy, Gretna, LA 70056
Phone: (504) 392-3131
Sales: $24,500,000   *Employees:* NA
Company Type: Public Family Member   *Employees here:* 602
SIC: 8062
  Hospital
Jaime Weslowski, N/A

D-U-N-S 11-542-5555
TENET HEALTHCARE CORPORATION
2639 Miami St, Saint Louis, MO 63118
Phone: (314) 772-1456
Sales: $32,500,000   *Employees:* NA
Company Type: Public Family Member   *Employees here:* 775
SIC: 8062
  General medical hospital pharmacy & rehabilitation center
Cliff Ayger, Director

D-U-N-S 96-718-1751
TENET HEALTHCARE CORPORATION
180 Debuys Rd, Biloxi, MS 39531
Phone: (228) 388-0600
Sales: $45,400,000   *Employees:* NA
Company Type: Public Family Member   *Employees here:* 750
SIC: 8011
  Pediatricians
Hugh Simcoe, Owner

D-U-N-S 19-192-3432
TENET HEALTHCARE CORPORATION
175 Lancaster Blvd, Mechanicsburg, PA 17055
Phone: (717) 691-3700

Sales: $29,000,000   *Employees:* NA
Company Type: Public Family Member   *Employees here:* 550
SIC: 8069
   Rehabilitation hospital
William Wilkin, Chief Executive Officer

D-U-N-S 92-675-6883
TENET HEALTHCARE CORPORATION
3050 39th St, Port Arthur, TX 77642
Phone: (409) 985-0474
Sales: $24,400,000   *Employees:* NA
Company Type: Public Family Member   *Employees here:* 600
SIC: 8062
   Hospital
Luis G Silva, Branch Manager

D-U-N-S 96-786-5965
TENET HEALTHCARE CORPORATION
4920 NE Stalligs Dr, Nacogdoches, TX 75961
Phone: (409) 569-9481
Sales: $22,100,000   *Employees:* NA
Company Type: Public Family Member   *Employees here:* NA
SIC: 8011
   Hospital
Glen Robinson, President

D-U-N-S 12-699-2866
TENET HEALTHCARE CORPORATION
1313 Hermann Dr, Houston, TX 77004
Phone: (713) 527-5000
Sales: $62,100,000   *Employees:* NA
Company Type: Public Family Member   *Employees here:* 1,500
SIC: 8062
   General hospital
Judy Novack, N/A

D-U-N-S 87-870-4402
TENET HEALTHCARE, LTD
4200 Portsmouth St, Houston, TX 77027
Phone: (713) 964-8581
Sales: $24,400,000   *Employees:* NA
Company Type: Private   *Employees here:* 600
SIC: 8062
   General medical & surgical hospital
Eileen Briggs, Executive

D-U-N-S 93-186-3120
TENET HEALTHCARE, LTD
1625 Medical Center St, El Paso, TX 79902
Phone: (915) 747-4000
Sales: $57,900,000   *Employees:* NA
Company Type: Private   *Employees here:* 1,400
SIC: 8062
   Hospital
L M Fry, Chief Executive Officer

D-U-N-S 07-357-9336
TENET HEALTHSYSTEM DESERT INC
   (Parent: Tenet Healthcare Corporation)
1150 N Indian Canyon Dr, Palm Springs, CA 92262
Phone: (760) 323-6511
Sales: $145,000,000   *Employees:* 1,100
Company Type: Public Family Member   *Employees here:* 960
SIC: 8062
   Hospital
Robert Minkin, President

D-U-N-S 09-271-3965
TENET HEALTHSYSTEM HOSPITALS,
   (Parent: Tenet Healthcare Corporation)
6201 N Suncoast Blvd, Crystal River, FL 34428
Phone: (352) 795-6560

Sales: $41,078,000   *Employees:* 450
Company Type: Public Family Member   *Employees here:* 446
SIC: 8062
   General medical & psychiatric hospital
Michael Collins, Chief Executive Officer

D-U-N-S 05-886-9215
TENET HOSPITAL LTD
2001 N Oregon St, El Paso, TX 79902
Phone: (915) 577-6011
Sales: $90,400,000   *Employees:* 1,936
Company Type: Private   *Employees here:* 1,900
SIC: 8062
   General hospital
L M Fry, Chief Executive Officer

D-U-N-S 15-200-9973
TENNEESSE DEPT-MENTAL HEALTH
275 Stewarts Ferry Pike, Nashville, TN 37214
Phone: (615) 889-9247
Sales: $23,800,000   *Employees:* NA
Company Type: Private   *Employees here:* 1,044
SIC: 8361
   Mental health & retardation center
Julia Bratcher, Branch Manager

D-U-N-S 13-950-5515
TENNEESSE DEPT-MENTAL HEALTH
5908 Lyons View Pike, Knoxville, TN 37919
Phone: (423) 584-1561
Sales: $20,400,000   *Employees:* NA
Company Type: Private   *Employees here:* 600
SIC: 8063
   Psychiatric hospital
Richard L Thomas, Principal

D-U-N-S 08-882-3075
TENNEESSE DEPT-MENTAL HEALTH
4850 E Andrew Johnson Hwy, Greeneville, TN 37745
Phone: (423) 639-2131
Sales: $21,800,000   *Employees:* NA
Company Type: Private   *Employees here:* 1,124
SIC: 8051
   Skilled nursing care facility
Robert Erb, N/A

D-U-N-S 07-856-7484
TENNEESSE DEPT-MENTAL HEALTH
11000 Highway 64 W, Bolivar, TN 38074
Phone: (901) 658-5141
Sales: $24,200,000   *Employees:* NA
Company Type: Private   *Employees here:* 770
SIC: 8063
   Mental hospital
Mike Flynn, Administration

D-U-N-S 12-074-8033
TENNEESSE DEPT-MENTAL HEALTH
11293 Mmphis Arlington Rd, Arlington, TN 38002
Phone: (901) 867-2921
Sales: $28,600,000   *Employees:* NA
Company Type: Private   *Employees here:* 843
SIC: 8063
   Mental hospital
Mona Winfrey, Superintendent

D-U-N-S 14-761-6031
TENNESSEE HEALTHSOURCE INC
   (Parent: Healthsource Inc)
5409 Maryland Way Ste 200, Brentwood, TN 37027
Phone: (615) 373-6995

Sales: $110,781,000
Company Type: Public Family Member
SIC: 8011
  Health maintenance organization
Steve White, Chief Executive Officer
Employees: 113
Employees here: 100

D-U-N-S 01-272-5821
TENNESSEE WEST HEALTHCARE INC
708 W Forest Ave, Jackson, TN 38301
Phone: (901) 425-5000
Sales: $187,900,000
Company Type: Private
SIC: 8062
  Hospitals
Jim Moss, President
Employees: 4,000
Employees here: 2,300

D-U-N-S 04-303-7837
TERENCE COOKE HEAL CARE CTR
1249 5th Ave, New York, NY 10029
Phone: (212) 360-3600
Sales: $87,360,000
Company Type: Private
SIC: 8051
  Nursing home/long term health care facility
Daniel Leahey, President
Employees: 1,200
Employees here: 1,200

D-U-N-S 92-670-6227
TERRE HAUTE REGIONAL HOSPITAL INC
(Parent: Columbia/Hca Healthcare Corp)
3901 S 7th St, Terre Haute, IN 47802
Phone: (812) 232-0021
Sales: $68,479,000
Company Type: Public Family Member
SIC: 8062
  Acute care medical facility
Tom Ramsey, Data Processing
Employees: 800
Employees here: 800

D-U-N-S 07-295-6642
TETON COUNTY HOSPITAL DST
625 E Broadway, Jackson, WY 83001
Phone: (307) 733-3636
Sales: $29,908,000
Company Type: Private
SIC: 8062
  Hospital retail lease & service durable medical goods &
  home healthcare
John D Valiante, Administrator
Employees: 450
Employees here: 390

D-U-N-S 06-974-7012
TEXARKANA MEMORIAL HOSPITAL INC
1000 Pine St, Texarkana, TX 75501
Phone: (903) 798-8000
Sales: $100,356,000
Company Type: Private
SIC: 8062
  General hospital
Hugh R Hallgren, President
Employees: 1,285
Employees here: 1,250

D-U-N-S 07-461-5394
TEXAS CHILDREN'S HOSPITAL
6621 Fannin St, Houston, TX 77030
Phone: (713) 770-1000
Sales: $247,894,000
Company Type: Private
SIC: 8069
  General hospital
Mark Wallace, Chief Executive Officer
Employees: 3,074
Employees here: 2,600

D-U-N-S 96-807-8915
TEXAS CHILDREN'S HOSPITAL
1919 S Braeswood Blvd, Houston, TX 77030
Phone: (713) 770-7700

Sales: $25,200,000
Company Type: Private
SIC: 8011
  Medical doctor's office
Employees: NA
Employees here: 400

D-U-N-S 08-175-0325
TEXAS DEPT CRIMINAL JUSTICE
Hwy 69 N, Rusk, TX 75785
Phone: (903) 683-5781
Sales: $33,800,000
Company Type: Private
SIC: 8063
  State mental hospital
Sharron Dishongh, Principal
Employees: NA
Employees here: 1,100

D-U-N-S 07-315-3405
TEXAS HEALTH & HUMAN SVCS COMM
Hwy 70 Nw, Vernon, TX 76384
Phone: (940) 552-9901
Sales: $35,600,000
Company Type: Private
SIC: 8063
  Mental health
James E Smith, Branch Manager
Employees: NA
Employees here: 1,161

D-U-N-S 08-154-5923
TEXAS HEALTH & HUMAN SVCS COMM
1200 E Brin St, Terrell, TX 75160
Phone: (972) 563-6452
Sales: $36,800,000
Company Type: Private
SIC: 8063
  Mental hospital
Beatrice Butler, Principal
Employees: NA
Employees here: 1,200

D-U-N-S 87-804-6713
TEXAS HEALTH & HUMAN SVCS COMM
6711 S New Braunfels Ave, San Antonio, TX 78223
Phone: (210) 532-8811
Sales: $49,500,000
Company Type: Private
SIC: 8063
  Psychiatric hospital
Robert Arizpe, Principal
Employees: NA
Employees here: 1,500

D-U-N-S 02-033-6608
TEXAS HEALTH & HUMAN SVCS COMM
Hwy 87 N, Carlsbad, TX 76934
Phone: (915) 465-4391
Sales: $24,600,000
Company Type: Private
SIC: 8063
  Mental institution
R A Williams, N/A
Employees: NA
Employees here: 800

D-U-N-S 08-748-9993
TEXAS HEALTH & HUMAN SVCS COMM
1901n Lamesa Hwy, Big Spring, TX 79720
Phone: (915) 267-8216
Sales: $25,800,000
Company Type: Private
SIC: 8063
  Mental hospital
Ed Moughon, Principal
Employees: NA
Employees here: 840

D-U-N-S 61-497-4582
TEXAS HEALTH & HUMAN SVCS COMM
2501 Maple St, Abilene, TX 79602
Phone: (915) 692-4053

Sales: $39,300,000   *Employees:* NA
Company Type: Private   *Employees here:* 1,800
SIC: 8361
    State school for the mentally retarded
Bill Waddill, Superintendent

D-U-N-S 10-832-4062
TEXAS HEALTH ENTERPRISES INC
401 N Elm St, Denton, TX 76201
Phone: (940) 387-4388
Sales: $149,400,000   *Employees:* 6,500
Company Type: Private   *Employees here:* 150
SIC: 8051
    Skilled nursing home facilities
Peter C Kern, President

D-U-N-S 02-428-2746
TEXAS HEALTH SYSTEM INC
865 De Shong Dr, Paris, TX 75462
Phone: (903) 737-1111
Sales: $20,700,000   *Employees:* NA
Company Type: Private   *Employees here:* 550
SIC: 8062
    General hospital
Anthony Daigle, Administrator

D-U-N-S 09-972-2506
TEXAS HEALTH SYSTEM INC
8200 Walnut Hill Ln, Dallas, TX 75231
Phone: (214) 345-6789
Sales: $197,400,000   *Employees:* 4,200
Company Type: Private   *Employees here:* 250
SIC: 8062
    Health system
Douglas Hawthorne, President

D-U-N-S 88-428-2476
TEXAS HEALTHCARE PA
1400 S Main St Ste 414, Fort Worth, TX 76104
Phone: (817) 338-0405
Sales: $22,241,000   *Employees:* 280
Company Type: Private   *Employees here:* 60
SIC: 8011
    Medical doctor's office
Dale Schwicker, Chief Operating Officer

D-U-N-S 12-780-7857
TEXAS ONCOLOGY PA
5420 LBJ Fwy Ste 900, Dallas, TX 75240
Phone: (972) 392-8700
Sales: $64,000,000   *Employees:* 600
Company Type: Private   *Employees here:* 60
SIC: 8011
    Operates as physicians specializing in oncology and radiology
Dr Merrick H Reese Md, President

D-U-N-S 06-896-8734
TEXAS SCOTTISH RITE HOSP
2222 Welborn St, Dallas, TX 75219
Phone: (214) 521-3168
Sales: $24,500,000   *Employees:* 500
Company Type: Private   *Employees here:* 500
SIC: 8069
    Specialty hospital
Sam E Hilburn, Chairman of the Board

D-U-N-S 05-891-8483
TEXAS VISITING NURSE SERVICE
814 E Tyler Ave, Harlingen, TX 78550
Phone: (956) 412-1401

Sales: $24,399,000   *Employees:* 145
Company Type: Private   *Employees here:* 25
SIC: 8082
    Home health care services
Pamela Bryant, President

D-U-N-S 61-736-3973
TEXOMA MEDICAL CENTER INC
1000 Memorial Dr, Denison, TX 75020
Phone: (903) 416-4000
Sales: $82,369,000   *Employees:* 1,300
Company Type: Private   *Employees here:* 1,200
SIC: 8062
    General hospital
Mike Mayes, President

D-U-N-S 07-216-6259
ALTOONA HOSPITAL, THE
620 Howard Ave, Altoona, PA 16601
Phone: (814) 946-2011
Sales: $129,345,000   *Employees:* 1,518
Company Type: Private   *Employees here:* 1,518
SIC: 8062
    General hospital
James W Barner, President

D-U-N-S 07-590-7188
AMERICAN RED CROSS, THE
4050 Lindell Blvd, Saint Louis, MO 63108
Phone: (314) 658-2000
Sales: $20,200,000   *Employees:* NA
Company Type: Private   *Employees here:* 550
SIC: 8099
    Community service organization
John Forbes, Principal

D-U-N-S 03-050-7958
AMERICAN RED CROSS, THE
2425 Park Rd, Charlotte, NC 28203
Phone: (704) 376-1661
Sales: $26,800,000   *Employees:* NA
Company Type: Private   *Employees here:* 700
SIC: 8099
    Health/allied services
Frank Byrne, N/A

D-U-N-S 07-111-3054
ASHLAND HOSPITAL ASSN, THE
1025 Center St, Ashland, OH 44805
Phone: (419) 289-0491
Sales: $25,413,000   *Employees:* 650
Company Type: Private   *Employees here:* 349
SIC: 8062
    General hospital
William C Kelley Jr, President

D-U-N-S 06-041-2509
AULTMAN HOSPITAL, THE
2600 6th St SW, Canton, OH 44710
Phone: (330) 452-9911
Sales: $160,000,000   *Employees:* 3,000
Company Type: Private   *Employees here:* 2,900
SIC: 8062
    General hospital
Richard J Pryce, Chief Executive Officer

D-U-N-S 07-850-0972
AUSTIN DIAGNOSTIC CLINIC ASSN, THE
12221 Mopac Expy N, Austin, TX 78758
Phone: (512) 459-1111

Sales: $44,700,000   *Employees:* 650
Company Type: Private   *Employees here:* 450
SIC: 8011
    Diagnostic clinic
Dr James Lindley Md, Chairman

D-U-N-S 05-286-1614
BETHESDA HOSPITAL ASSN, THE
2951 Maple Ave, Zanesville, OH 43701
Phone: (740) 454-4000
Sales: $81,926,000   *Employees:* 1,200
Company Type: Private   *Employees here:* 1,100
SIC: 8062
    Operates as a hospital
Thomas Sieber, President

D-U-N-S 07-915-1171
CARLE FOUNDATION, THE
611 W Park St, Urbana, IL 61801
Phone: (217) 383-3311
Sales: $183,620,000   *Employees:* 2,043
Company Type: Private   *Employees here:* 1,900
SIC: 8062
    General hospital
Michael H Fritz, President

D-U-N-S 07-663-1951
CASEY FAMILY PROGRAM, THE
1300 Dexter Ave N Ste 400, Seattle, WA 98109
Phone: (206) 282-7300
Sales: $254,996,000   *Employees:* 375
Company Type: Private   *Employees here:* 90
SIC: 8361
    Foster care agency
Ruth Massinga, Chief Executive Officer

D-U-N-S 01-017-3482
CHARLOTTE HUNGERFORD HOSP, THE
540 Litchfield St, Torrington, CT 6790
Phone: (860) 496-6666
Sales: $64,242,000   *Employees:* 712
Company Type: Private   *Employees here:* 648
SIC: 8062
    General hospital
Roseann Griswold, President

D-U-N-S 07-553-7464
CHESTER COUNTY HOSPITAL, THE
701 E Marshall St, West Chester, PA 19380
Phone: (610) 431-5000
Sales: $75,998,000   *Employees:* 1,000
Company Type: Private   *Employees here:* 925
SIC: 8062
    General hospital
H L Pepper, President

D-U-N-S 04-643-0013
CHILDREN'S HOSPITAL, THE
700 Childrens Dr, Columbus, OH 43205
Phone: (614) 722-5950
Sales: $315,078,000   *Employees:* 2,946
Company Type: Private   *Employees here:* 2,879
SIC: 8069
    Pediatric hospital
Thomas N Hansen, Chief Executive Officer

D-U-N-S 07-870-5449
CHILDREN'S VILLAGE INC, THE
Echo Hls, Dobbs Ferry, NY 10522
Phone: (914) 693-0600

Sales: $24,168,000   *Employees:* 585
Company Type: Private   *Employees here:* 585
SIC: 8361
    Residential treatment center for disturbed children
Nan Dale, Executive Director

D-U-N-S 07-210-6867
CHILDRENS HOSPITAL OF ALA, THE
1600 7th Ave S, Birmingham, AL 35233
Phone: (205) 939-9100
Sales: $154,518,000   *Employees:* 1,947
Company Type: Private   *Employees here:* 1,944
SIC: 8069
    Children's hospital
Dr James C Dearth Md, Chief Executive Officer

D-U-N-S 07-644-3316
CHILDRENS HOSPITAL ASSN, THE
1056 E 19th Ave, Denver, CO 80218
Phone: (303) 861-8888
Sales: $161,698,000   *Employees:* 2,200
Company Type: Private   *Employees here:* 1,900
SIC: 8069
    Children's hospital
Lua Blankenship Jr, President

D-U-N-S 07-778-8040
CITY HOSPITAL ASSOCIATION, THE
425 W 5th St, East Liverpool, OH 43920
Phone: (330) 385-7200
Sales: $44,813,000   *Employees:* 650
Company Type: Private   *Employees here:* 650
SIC: 8062
    General hospital
Mel Creeley, President

D-U-N-S 07-539-4080
DANBURY HOSPITAL, THE
24 Hospital Ave, Danbury, CT 6810
Phone: (203) 797-7000
Sales: $188,761,000   *Employees:* 1,620
Company Type: Private   *Employees here:* 1,540
SIC: 8062
    General hospital
Frank J Kelly, President

D-U-N-S 94-341-2577
DETROIT MEDICAL CENTER, THE
261 Mack Ave, Detroit, MI 48201
Phone: (313) 745-1203
Sales: $28,000,000   *Employees:* NA
Company Type: Private   *Employees here:* 670
SIC: 8062
    General medical & specialty hospitals
Dr Bruce Gans, Principal

D-U-N-S 05-023-4988
DEVEREUX FOUNDATION, THE
El Colegio Rd, Goleta, CA 93117
Phone: (805) 968-2525
Sales: $24,000,000   *Employees:* NA
Company Type: Private   *Employees here:* 380
SIC: 8011
    Medical doctor's office residential care services
Thomas Mccool, N/A

D-U-N-S 18-472-3500
DEVEREUX FOUNDATION, THE
8000 Devereux Dr, Melbourne, FL 32940
Phone: (407) 242-9100

Sales: $23,400,000   *Employees:* NA
Company Type: Private   *Employees here:* 500
SIC: 8069
   Children's hospital
James Colvin, N/A

D-U-N-S 00-251-4420
DEVEREUX FOUNDATION, THE
950 E Haverford Rd 200, Bryn Mawr, PA 19010
Phone: (610) 520-3000
Sales: $199,430,000   *Employees:* 4,200
Company Type: Private   *Employees here:* 70
SIC: 8361
   Provider of human services to individuals with special needs
Ronald P Burd, President

D-U-N-S 07-177-7718
DULUTH CLINIC LTD, THE
400 E 3rd St, Duluth, MN 55805
Phone: (218) 722-8364
Sales: $202,217,000   *Employees:* 1,300
Company Type: Private   *Employees here:* 900
SIC: 8011
   Medical clinics
William Bennett, Accounting Manager

D-U-N-S 07-666-4176
EVERETT CLINIC, THE
3901 Hoyt Ave, Everett, WA 98201
Phone: (425) 259-0966
Sales: $74,567,000   *Employees:* 1,025
Company Type: Private   *Employees here:* 435
SIC: 8011
   Medical clinic
Richard Cooper, Chief Executive Officer

D-U-N-S 61-771-3888
EVERETT CLINIC, THE
Harbour Pnt 4410 106th Pl, Everett, WA 98204
Phone: (425) 259-0966
Sales: $59,500,000   *Employees:* NA
Company Type: Private   *Employees here:* 1,000
SIC: 8011
   Medical clinic
Rick C Admin, Branch Manager

D-U-N-S 06-325-4676
FINLEY HOSPITAL, THE
350 N Grandview Ave, Dubuque, IA 52001
Phone: (319) 582-1881
Sales: $48,750,000   *Employees:* 900
Company Type: Private   *Employees here:* 900
SIC: 8062
   General hospital
Kevin L Rogols, President

D-U-N-S 17-270-0247
GEORGE WASHINGTON UNIVERSITY
901 23rd St NW Ste 2500, Washington, DC 20037
Phone: (202) 994-1000
Sales: $227,500,000   *Employees:* NA
Company Type: Private   *Employees here:* 5,145
SIC: 8062
   General hospital
Peter Synowiez, Manager

D-U-N-S 17-755-0266
GEORGE WASHINGTON UNIVERSITY
2150 Pennsylvania Ave Nw, Washington, DC 20052
Phone: (202) 994-1000

Sales: $165,800,000   *Employees:* NA
Company Type: Private   *Employees here:* 3,000
SIC: 8011
   Medical doctor's office
Allan Weingold, Manager

D-U-N-S 80-241-5109
GEORGE WASHINGTON UNIVERSITY
2150 Pennsylvania Ave Nw, Washington, DC 20037
Phone: (202) 994-4513
Sales: $124,200,000   *Employees:* NA
Company Type: Private   *Employees here:* 2,200
SIC: 8011
   Medical hospital
David Alyono, Medical Doctor

D-U-N-S 06-984-0288
GRACE HOSPITAL
6071 W Outer Dr, Detroit, MI 48235
Phone: (313) 966-3300
Sales: $203,093,000   *Employees:* 2,170
Company Type: Private   *Employees here:* 2,113
SIC: 8062
   General hospital
Mark Eustis, Senior Vice-President

D-U-N-S 10-863-3884
HEALTH GROUP, THE
5425 High Mill Ave Nw, Massillon, OH 44646
Phone: (330) 832-8761
Sales: $80,581,000   *Employees:* 1,260
Company Type: Private   *Employees here:* 3
SIC: 8082
   Home health care service
Mervin F Strine, President

D-U-N-S 01-088-6422
HOSPITAL CENTER AT ORANGE, THE
188 S Essex Ave, Orange, NJ 7050
Phone: (973) 266-2200
Sales: $64,277,000   *Employees:* 900
Company Type: Private   *Employees here:* 1
SIC: 8062
   Hospital
James Romer, President

D-U-N-S 61-941-5920
HOSPITAL CENTER AT ORANGE, THE
289 Central Ave, Orange, NJ 7050
Phone: (973) 266-2500
Sales: $34,300,000   *Employees:* NA
Company Type: Private   *Employees here:* 700
SIC: 8062
   Orthopedic hospital
James Romer, Branch Manager

D-U-N-S 06-744-4927
INGALLS MEMORIAL HOSPITAL, THE
1 Ingalls Dr, Harvey, IL 60426
Phone: (708) 333-2300
Sales: $161,380,000   *Employees:* 1,845
Company Type: Private   *Employees here:* 1,845
SIC: 8062
   General medical and surgical hospital
Robert L Harris, President

D-U-N-S 03-466-4938
JACKSON CLINIC PROF ASSN, THE
616 W Forest Ave, Jackson, TN 38301
Phone: (901) 422-0200

Sales: $57,525,000   *Employees:* 630
Company Type: Private   *Employees here:* 400
SIC: 8011
   Medical clinic
Carl E Rudd, Administrator

D-U-N-S 04-214-0483
JACKSON LABORATORY, THE
600 Main St, Bar Harbor, ME 4609
Phone: (207) 288-6000
Sales: $54,769,000   *Employees:* 900
Company Type: Private   *Employees here:* 900
SIC: 8071
   Biological laboratory
Dr Kenneth Paigen, President

D-U-N-S 07-588-9337
JEFFERSON MEM HOSPITAL ASSN, THE
Hwy 61 S, Crystal City, MO 63019
Phone: (314) 933-1000
Sales: $76,523,000   *Employees:* 1,600
Company Type: Private   *Employees here:* 1,400
SIC: 8062
   General medical and surgical hospital
Mark Brodeur, Chief Executive Officer

D-U-N-S 07-511-6756
WILSON N. JONES MEM HOSP, THE
500 N Highland Ave, Sherman, TX 75092
Phone: (903) 870-4611
Sales: $64,506,000   *Employees:* 900
Company Type: Private   *Employees here:* 725
SIC: 8062
   General hospital
Merlan Knapp, Chief Financial Officer

D-U-N-S 04-253-1533
MACNEAL MEM HOSPITAL ASSN
3249 Oak Park Ave, Berwyn, IL 60402
Phone: (708) 795-9100
Sales: $162,658,000   *Employees:* 1,700
Company Type: Private   *Employees here:* 1,000
SIC: 8062
   General hospital
J L Mc Guinness, President

D-U-N-S 07-732-5645
MANCHESTER MEMORIAL HOSP
71 Haynes St, Manchester, CT 6040
Phone: (860) 646-1222
Sales: $88,762,000   *Employees:* 1,038
Company Type: Private   *Employees here:* 1,000
SIC: 8062
   General hospital
David Stahelski, Vice-President

D-U-N-S 04-294-2839
MASONIC HOMES OF KENTUCKY
240 Masonic Home Dr, Louisville, KY 40207
Phone: (502) 897-4910
Sales: $22,643,000   *Employees:* 250
Company Type: Private   *Employees here:* 250
SIC: 8361
   Residence home
Sally Bowers, Administrator

D-U-N-S 06-999-3871
MATHER FOUNDATION, THE
1615 Hinman Ave, Evanston, IL 60201
Phone: (847) 492-7400

Sales: $56,391,000   *Employees:* 381
Company Type: Private   *Employees here:* 86
SIC: 8059
   Nursing/personal care
Edward F Otto, President

D-U-N-S 07-375-8773
MEDICAL CTR AT PRINCETON, THE
253 Witherspoon St, Princeton, NJ 8540
Phone: (609) 497-4000
Sales: $117,405,000   *Employees:* 1,800
Company Type: Private   *Employees here:* 1,440
SIC: 8062
   General hospital
Dennis W Doody, President

D-U-N-S 07-548-2133
MEMORIAL HOSPITAL OF SALEM, THE
310 Salem Woodstown Rd, Salem, NJ 8079
Phone: (609) 935-1000
Sales: $49,499,000   *Employees:* 780
Company Type: Private   *Employees here:* 775
SIC: 8062
   General medical and surgical hospital
Arnold Kimmel, Chief Executive Officer

D-U-N-S 06-985-2580
MEMORIAL HOSPITAL
111 Brewster St, Pawtucket, RI 2860
Phone: (401) 729-2000
Sales: $110,956,000   *Employees:* 1,737
Company Type: Private   *Employees here:* 1,659
SIC: 8062
   General medical & surgical hospital
Francis R Dietz, President

D-U-N-S 06-875-9463
MERCY HOSPITAL OF PITTSBURGH
1400 Locust St, Pittsburgh, PA 15219
Phone: (412) 232-8111
Sales: $117,000,000   *Employees:* 2,500
Company Type: Private   *Employees here:* 2,450
SIC: 8062
   General hospital
Dr Howard Zaren, Vice-President

D-U-N-S 07-417-2719
METHODIST HOSPITAL
6565 Fannin St Stb 2 28, Houston, TX 77030
Phone: (713) 790-3311
Sales: $485,011,000   *Employees:* 4,500
Company Type: Private   *Employees here:* 3,780
SIC: 8062
   General hospital
Larry Mathis, President

D-U-N-S 13-097-9354
METHODIST HOSPITALS INC
8701 Broadway, Merrillville, IN 46410
Phone: (219) 738-5500
Sales: $57,200,000   *Employees:* NA
Company Type: Private   *Employees here:* 1,354
SIC: 8062
   General hospital
John Betjemann, Manager

D-U-N-S 06-949-0670
METHODIST HOSPITALS INC
600 Grant St, Gary, IN 46402
Phone: (219) 886-4000

Sales: $199,438,000   Employees: 3,060
Company Type: Private   Employees here: 1,671
SIC: 8062
   General hospital
John H Betjemann, President

D-U-N-S 07-775-7425
MT SINAI MEDICAL CENTER
   (Parent: Primary Health Systems Inc)
1 Mount Sinai Dr, Cleveland, OH 44106
Phone: (216) 421-4000
Sales: $250,000,000   Employees: 2,400
Company Type: Private   Employees here: 2,100
SIC: 8062
   General hospital
Robert A Schapper, Chief Executive Officer

D-U-N-S 93-756-4466
NEW YORK, THE CITY OF
8268 164th St, Jamaica, NY 11432
Phone: (718) 883-2400
Sales: $99,500,000   Employees: NA
Company Type: Private   Employees here: 2,000
SIC: 8062
   Hospital
Gladiola Sampson, Director

D-U-N-S 94-387-4917
NEW YORK, THE CITY OF
1225 Gerard Ave, Brooklyn, NY 11211
Phone: (718) 960-2740
Sales: $21,300,000   Employees: NA
Company Type: Private   Employees here: 300
SIC: 8011
   Medical clinic
Angel Laporte, Director

D-U-N-S 07-100-8221
NEW YORK FOUNDLING HOSP, THE
590 Avenue of the Americas, New York, NY 10011
Phone: (212) 633-9300
Sales: $57,777,000   Employees: 1,500
Company Type: Private   Employees here: 600
SIC: 8361
   Foster care and preventive programs for children
Michael Garber, Executive Director

D-U-N-S 07-539-7190
NORWALK HOSPITAL ASSN
Maple St, Norwalk, CT 6856
Phone: (203) 852-2000
Sales: $168,667,000   Employees: 1,660
Company Type: Private   Employees here: 1,660
SIC: 8062
   General hospital
Paul K Maloney, Chief of the Medical Staff

D-U-N-S 07-215-4917
PRESSLEY RIDGE SCHOOLS
530 Marshall Ave, Pittsburgh, PA 15214
Phone: (412) 321-6995
Sales: $33,286,000   Employees: 590
Company Type: Private   Employees here: 175
SIC: 8361
   Programs for disturbed children
William C Luster, Executive Director

D-U-N-S 96-082-3961
RESURRECTION MEDICAL CTR, THE
5645 W Addison St, Chicago, IL 60634
Phone: (773) 282-7000

Sales: $365,529,000   Employees: 985
Company Type: Private   Employees here: 985
SIC: 8062
   Hospital
Ronald E Struxness, Chief Executive Officer

D-U-N-S 11-352-1405
RICE CLINIC S C, THE
824 Illinois Ave, Stevens Point, WI 54481
Phone: (715) 342-7500
Sales: $27,400,000   Employees: 400
Company Type: Private   Employees here: 200
SIC: 8011
   Physician's clinic
Dr James H De Weerd, President

D-U-N-S 07-208-7372
RILEY HOSPITAL BENEVOLENT ASSN
1100 21st Ave, Meridian, MS 39301
Phone: (601) 693-2511
Sales: $48,189,000   Employees: 820
Company Type: Private   Employees here: 750
SIC: 8062
   Short term acute care hospital
Dr Richard Riley Md, President

D-U-N-S 05-416-9297
RIVERSIDE MERCY HOSPITAL
1600 N Superior St, Toledo, OH 43604
Phone: (419) 729-6000
Sales: $69,543,000   Employees: 912
Company Type: Private   Employees here: 857
SIC: 8062
   General hospital
Scott Shook, President

D-U-N-S 07-657-4730
SALEM HOSPITAL INC
81 Highland Ave, Salem, MA 1970
Phone: (978) 741-1200
Sales: $86,200,000   Employees: 1,848
Company Type: Private   Employees here: 1,748
SIC: 8062
   General hospital
Michael J Geancy Jr, President

D-U-N-S 07-271-6376
SOCIETY OF THE VALLEY HOSP
223 N Van Dien Ave, Ridgewood, NJ 7450
Phone: (201) 447-8000
Sales: $204,002,000   Employees: 2,150
Company Type: Private   Employees here: 2,000
SIC: 8062
   General medical & surgical hospital
Richard D Keenan, Vice-President

D-U-N-S 06-858-6106
ST GEORGE CORPORATION, THE
12251 S 80th Ave, Palos Heights, IL 60463
Phone: (708) 361-4500
Sales: $199,386,000   Employees: 2,300
Company Type: Private   Employees here: 2,185
SIC: 8062
   General hospital
Sister M Wright, President

D-U-N-S 06-986-2159
STAMFORD HOSPITAL
190 W Broad St, Stamford, CT 6902
Phone: (203) 325-7000

Sales: $124,947,000
Company Type: Private
SIC: 8062
    General hospital
Philip D Cusano, President

Employees: 1,200
Employees here: 1,200

D-U-N-S 11-284-6779
THRESHOLDS, THE
4101 N Ravenswood Ave, Chicago, IL 60613
Phone: (773) 880-6260
Sales: $25,934,000
Company Type: Private
SIC: 8093
    Psychiatric rehabilitation center
Jerry Dincin, Executive Director

Employees: 800
Employees here: 100

D-U-N-S 05-416-9354
TOLEDO HOSPITAL
2142 N Cove Blvd, Toledo, OH 43606
Phone: (419) 471-4218
Sales: $321,107,000
Company Type: Private
SIC: 8062
    General hospital
Alan Brass, Chief Executive Officer

Employees: 5,484
Employees here: 4,900

D-U-N-S 06-873-4466
UNIONTOWN HOSPITAL
500 W Berkeley St, Uniontown, PA 15401
Phone: (724) 430-5000
Sales: $73,154,000
Company Type: Private
SIC: 8062
    Hospital
Paul Bacharach, President

Employees: 900
Employees here: 900

D-U-N-S 01-070-0268
VISITING NURSES ASSOCIATION, THE
520 S La Fayette Park Pl, Los Angeles, CA 90057
Phone: (818) 525-3600
Sales: $41,056,000
Company Type: Private
SIC: 8082
    Provides home healthcare services fund raising organization
        & retailer of pharmaceutical products
June Simmons, President

Employees: 600
Employees here: 60

D-U-N-S 07-216-6887
WASHINGTON HOSPITAL
155 Wilson Ave, Washington, PA 15301
Phone: (724) 225-7000
Sales: $124,339,000
Company Type: Private
SIC: 8062
    General hospital
Telford Thomas, President

Employees: 1,470
Employees here: 1,435

D-U-N-S 01-014-2065
WATERBURY HOSPITAL
64 Robbins St, Waterbury, CT 6708
Phone: (203) 573-6000
Sales: $139,913,000
Company Type: Private
SIC: 8062
    General medical & surgical hospital
John H Tobin, President

Employees: 1,450
Employees here: 1,327

D-U-N-S 06-984-9479
WESTERLY HOSPITAL
25 Wells St, Westerly, RI 2891
Phone: (401) 596-6000

Sales: $46,124,000
Company Type: Private
SIC: 8062
    General hospital
Michael K Lally, President

Employees: 495
Employees here: 495

D-U-N-S 06-873-5141
WESTERN PENNSYLVANIA HOSP
4800 Friendship Ave, Pittsburgh, PA 15224
Phone: (412) 578-5000
Sales: $218,837,000
Company Type: Private
SIC: 8062
    General hospital
Charles M O Brien, President

Employees: 2,800
Employees here: 2,800

D-U-N-S 06-924-6494
WINDHAM COMMUNITY MEMORIAL HOSP
112 Mansfield Ave, Willimantic, CT 6226
Phone: (860) 456-9116
Sales: $49,940,000
Company Type: Private
SIC: 8062
    General medical & surgical hospital
Duane A Carlberg, President

Employees: 632
Employees here: 632

D-U-N-S 08-904-9092
THERAPEUTIC ASSOCIATES INC
15060 Ventura Blvd, Sherman Oaks, CA 91403
Phone: (818) 377-2588
Sales: $30,000,000
Company Type: Private
SIC: 8049
    Physical therapists
Warner B Owens, President

Employees: 550
Employees here: 12

D-U-N-S 07-268-1208
HERBERT J. THOMAS MEM HOSPITAL ASSN
4605 Maccorkle Ave SW, Charleston, WV 25309
Phone: (304) 766-3600
Sales: $74,667,000
Company Type: Private
SIC: 8062
    Hospital
Stephen Dexter, President

Employees: 1,000
Employees here: 975

D-U-N-S 60-279-8225
THOMAS JEFFERSON UNIVERSITY
111 Suth 11th St Ste 2210, Philadelphia, PA 19107
Phone: (215) 955-6616
Sales: $199,000,000
Company Type: Private
SIC: 8062
    General hospital
Thomas J Lewis, President

Employees: NA
Employees here: 4,000

D-U-N-S 78-214-4364
THOMAS JEFFERSON UNIVERSITY
111 S 11th St Ste 1945, Philadelphia, PA 19107
Phone: (215) 955-6735
Sales: $24,500,000
Company Type: Private
SIC: 8051
    Skilled nursing care facility
John Smalarz, Director

Employees: NA
Employees here: 1,000

D-U-N-S 07-447-6250
THOMAS-DAVIS MEDICAL CTRS PC
    (Parent: F P A Medical Management Inc)
630 N Alvernon Way, Tucson, AZ 85711
Phone: (520) 881-7100

Sales: $128,000,000   *Employees:* 1,015
Company Type: Public Family Member   *Employees here:* 485
SIC: 8011
    Primary care medical center
Glen T Randolph, Chief Operating Officer

D-U-N-S 11-045-6001
THOMAS-DAVIS MEDICAL CTRS PC
707 N Alvernon Way, Tucson, AZ 85711
Phone: (520) 322-0486
Sales: $23,700,000   *Employees:* NA
Company Type: Public Family Member   *Employees here:* 375
SIC: 8011
    Medical doctor's office
Liz Clark, Principal

D-U-N-S 07-367-4533
THOMPSON FRDERICK FERRIS HOSP
350 Parrish St, Canandaigua, NY 14424
Phone: (716) 396-6510
Sales: $35,313,000   *Employees:* 909
Company Type: Private   *Employees here:* 900
SIC: 8062
    General medical and surgical hospital and outpatient medical
    centers
Linda Janczack, President

D-U-N-S 06-847-9963
THOREK HOSPITAL & MEDICAL CTR
850 W Irving Park Rd, Chicago, IL 60613
Phone: (773) 525-6780
Sales: $51,502,000   *Employees:* 600
Company Type: Private   *Employees here:* 592
SIC: 8062
    Medical and surgical hospital
Frank A Solare, President

D-U-N-S 07-180-7895
THREE RIVERS COMMUNITY HOSPITAL
715 NW Dimmick St, Grants Pass, OR 97526
Phone: (541) 476-6831
Sales: $30,485,000   *Employees:* 613
Company Type: Private   *Employees here:* 300
SIC: 8062
    Community hospital
Jon K Mitchell, President

D-U-N-S 92-716-2974
THREE RIVERS HEALTH PLANS INC
300 Oxford Dr, Monroeville, PA 15146
Phone: (412) 858-4000
Sales: $50,000,000   *Employees:* 195
Company Type: Private   *Employees here:* 195
SIC: 8011
    Health maintenance organization
Warren Carmichael, Chairman of the Board

D-U-N-S 80-988-5106
TIDEWATER PHYS MULTI GROUP PC
    (*Parent:* Phycor Inc)
12388 Warwick Blvd, Newport News, VA 23606
Phone: (757) 596-5971
Sales: $37,800,000   *Employees:* 550
Company Type: Public Family Member   *Employees here:* 30
SIC: 8011
    Physicians office
Steve Priest, N/A

D-U-N-S 07-307-2670
TITUS COUNTY HOSPITAL DISTRICT
2001 N Jefferson Ave, Mount Pleasant, TX 75455
Phone: (903) 577-6000

Sales: $50,583,000   *Employees:* 700
Company Type: Private   *Employees here:* 693
SIC: 8062
    Hospital
Steve Jacobson, Administrator

D-U-N-S 07-497-2340
TITUSVILLE AREA HOSPITAL
406 W Oak St, Titusville, PA 16354
Phone: (814) 827-1851
Sales: $20,789,000   *Employees:* 300
Company Type: Private   *Employees here:* 285
SIC: 8062
    General hospital
Anthony Nasralla, President

D-U-N-S 08-034-8931
TOLFREE MEMORIAL HOSPITAL
335 E Houghton Ave, West Branch, MI 48661
Phone: (517) 345-3660
Sales: $20,976,000   *Employees:* 350
Company Type: Private   *Employees here:* 350
SIC: 8062
    General hospital
Douglas Pattullo, Chief Executive Officer

D-U-N-S 07-013-4325
TOMBALL HOSPITAL AUTHORITY
605 Holderrieth Blvd, Tomball, TX 77375
Phone: (281) 351-1623
Sales: $60,462,000   *Employees:* 1,100
Company Type: Private   *Employees here:* 1,060
SIC: 8062
    General hospital
Robert F Schaper, Administrator

D-U-N-S 07-227-4426
TORRANCE MEMORIAL MEDICAL CTR
3330 Lomita Blvd, Torrance, CA 90505
Phone: (310) 325-9110
Sales: $155,192,000   *Employees:* 2,000
Company Type: Private   *Employees here:* 2,000
SIC: 8062
    General hospital
George Graham, President

D-U-N-S 03-032-0196
TOTAL HEALTH CARE INC
2305 N Charles St, Baltimore, MD 21218
Phone: (410) 383-8300
Sales: $56,712,000   *Employees:* 171
Company Type: Private   *Employees here:* 90
SIC: 8011
    Health maintenance organization
Edwin R Golden, President

D-U-N-S 88-307-3371
TOTAL RENAL CARE HOLDINGS,
21250 Hawthorne Blvd, Torrance, CA 90503
Phone: (310) 792-2600
Sales: $438,205,000   *Employees:* 5,000
Company Type: Public   *Employees here:* 100
SIC: 8092
    Kidney dialysis centers
Victor Chaltiel, Chairman of the Board

D-U-N-S 03-971-1569
TOTAL RENAL CARE, INC
    (*Parent:* Total Renal Care Holdings)
21250 Hawthorne Blvd, Torrance, CA 90503
Phone: (310) 792-2600

Sales: $400,000,000
Company Type: Public Family Member
SIC: 8092
   Kidney dialysis centers
Victor Chaltiel, Chairman of the Board

Employees: 5,000
Employees here: 75

D-U-N-S 07-989-5793
TOUCHETTE REGIONAL HOSPITALINC
5900 Bond Ave, East Saint Louis, IL 62207
Phone: (618) 332-3060
Sales: $22,535,000
Company Type: Private
SIC: 8062
   General hospital
Robert Klutz, Chief Executive Officer

Employees: 300
Employees here: 300

D-U-N-S 17-013-0975
TOUCHMARK LIVING CENTERS INC
5150 SW Griffith Dr, Beaverton, OR 97005
Phone: (503) 646-5186
Sales: $35,177,000
Company Type: Private
SIC: 8051
   Skilled nursing facilities
Werner G Nistler Jr, President

Employees: 1,250
Employees here: 20

D-U-N-S 07-507-4971
TOURO INFIRMARY
1401 Foucher St, New Orleans, LA 70115
Phone: (504) 897-7011
Sales: $62,400,000
Company Type: Private
SIC: 8062
   Hospital & practical nursing school
Gary Stein, President

Employees: 1,344
Employees here: 1,323

D-U-N-S 07-879-0920
TRACY SUTTER COMMUNITY MEM HOSP
1420 N Tracy Blvd, Tracy, CA 95376
Phone: (209) 835-1500
Sales: $21,134,000
Company Type: Private
SIC: 8062
   Hospital with skilled nursing care
Gary Rapaport, Administrator

Employees: 400
Employees here: 400

D-U-N-S 80-912-9778
TRANSITIONAL HEALTH PARTNERS
400 Perimeter Center Ter, Atlanta, GA 30346
Phone: (770) 698-9040
Sales: $91,800,000
Company Type: Private
SIC: 8051
   Operator of nursing homes
J S Eaton, Chief Executive Officer

Employees: 4,000
Employees here: 50

D-U-N-S 05-167-2319
TRANSITIONAL HOSPITALS CORP
(Parent: Vencor Inc)
400 W Market St Ste 3300, Louisville, KY 40202
Phone: (502) 569-7300
Sales: $211,600,000
Company Type: Public
SIC: 8062
   Operates long term acute care hospitals
W B Lunsford, President

Employees: 4,500
Employees here: 150

D-U-N-S 10-113-1217
TRANSWORLD HEALTHCARE INC
555 Madison Ave Fl 30, New York, NY 10022
Phone: (212) 750-0064

Sales: $160,000,000
Company Type: Public
SIC: 8082
   Home infusion therapy & nursing services mail order
     pharmacy & outpatient pulmonary rehabilitation services
Timothy M Aitken, Chief Executive Officer

Employees: 430
Employees here: 13

D-U-N-S 80-937-5207
TRANSYLVANIA COMMUNITY HOSPITALASSN
90 Hospital Dr, Brevard, NC 28712
Phone: (828) 884-9111
Sales: $22,277,000
Company Type: Private
SIC: 8062
   Hospital holding company
Bob Cress, Chief Financial Officer

Employees: 350
Employees here: 350

D-U-N-S 07-450-0877
TRANSYLVANIA COMMUNITY HOSP
Hwy 64, Brevard, NC 28712
Phone: (828) 884-9111
Sales: $22,608,000
Company Type: Private
SIC: 8062
   General hospital
Robert J Bednarek, President

Employees: 500
Employees here: 500

D-U-N-S 07-144-5951
TRESSLER LUTHERAN SERVICES
960 Century Dr, Mechanicsburg, PA 17055
Phone: (717) 795-0370
Sales: $70,755,000
Company Type: Private
SIC: 8051
   Skilled nursing care independent living & assisted living
     facilities & campuses
Rev Dr T Hurlocker, President

Employees: 1,950
Employees here: 60

D-U-N-S 01-562-4091
TRI STATE HEALTH SYSTEM INC
(Parent: Franciscan Health Partnership)
255 Lafayette Ave, Suffern, NY 10901
Phone: (914) 368-5000
Sales: $184,000,000
Company Type: Private
SIC: 8062
   Hospital
James H Flynn, President

Employees: 2,500
Employees here: 1,600

D-U-N-S 07-935-3033
TRI-CITY HEALTH CENTRE, INC
7525 Scyene Rd, Dallas, TX 75227
Phone: (214) 381-7171
Sales: $30,052,000
Company Type: Private
SIC: 8062
   General hospital
Gerald Neal, Chief Executive Officer

Employees: 436
Employees here: 410

D-U-N-S 07-872-8862
TRI-CITY HOSPITAL DISTRICT
4002 Vista Way, Oceanside, CA 92056
Phone: (760) 724-8411
Sales: $139,778,000
Company Type: Private
SIC: 8062
   General hospital
John Lauri, President

Employees: NA
Employees here: NA

D-U-N-S 08-543-9313
TRIAD GROUP INC
Main, Yadkinville, NC 27055
Phone: (336) 679-8852

Sales: $41,100,000   *Employees:* 1,800
Company Type: Private   *Employees here:* 17
SIC: 8051
    Skilled nursing homes whol medical supplies and provide
    data processing services
Nolan G Brown, President

D-U-N-S 01-938-5819
TRIAD LABORATORY ALLIANCE, LLC
4380 Federal Dr Ste 100, Greensboro, NC 27410
Phone: (336) 664-6100
Sales: $20,200,000   *Employees:* 420
Company Type: Private   *Employees here:* 420
SIC: 8071
    Medical laboratory
Joseph G Williams, Chief Executive Officer

D-U-N-S 02-168-6969
TRIMARK PHYSICIANS GROUP
    (Parent: Trinity Health Systems Inc)
802 Kenyon Rd, Fort Dodge, IA 50501
Phone: (515) 574-6997
Sales: $24,000,000   *Employees:* 350
Company Type: Private   *Employees here:* 140
SIC: 8011
    Medical clinic
Dr Michael Whitters, President

D-U-N-S 07-416-4989
TRINITY COMMUNITY MEDICAL
700 Medical Pkwy, Brenham, TX 77833
Phone: (409) 836-6173
Sales: $19,854,000   *Employees:* 270
Company Type: Private   *Employees here:* 258
SIC: 8062
    General hospital with home health care
John Simms, President

D-U-N-S 11-171-2279
TRINITY HEALTH SYSTEM
4000 Johnson Rd, Steubenville, OH 43952
Phone: (740) 264-8000
Sales: $24,100,000   *Employees:* NA
Company Type: Private   *Employees here:* 625
SIC: 8062
    General hospital
Fred Brower, President

D-U-N-S 07-626-6022
TRINITY LUTHERAN HOSPITAL
3030 Baltimore Ave, Kansas City, MO 64108
Phone: (816) 751-4600
Sales: $82,435,000   *Employees:* 1,200
Company Type: Private   *Employees here:* 893
SIC: 8062
    Hospital
Ronald A Ommen, President

D-U-N-S 07-176-2694
TRINITY MEDICAL CENTER
1 Burdick Expy W, Minot, ND 58701
Phone: (701) 857-5000
Sales: $99,139,000   *Employees:* 905
Company Type: Private   *Employees here:* 850
SIC: 8062
    Medical center & rural health clinic
Terry Hoff, President

D-U-N-S 06-875-9307
TRINITY MEDICAL CENTER WEST
    (Parent: Trinity Hospital Holding Co)
4000 Johnson Rd, Steubenville, OH 43952
Phone: (740) 264-8000

Sales: $74,500,000   *Employees:* 1,600
Company Type: Private   *Employees here:* 800
SIC: 8062
    General hospital
Fred B Brower, President

D-U-N-S 94-890-9932
TRINITY MEDICAL CENTER WEST
University Blvd, Steubenville, OH 43952
Phone: (000) 000-0000
Sales: $31,100,000   *Employees:* NA
Company Type: Private   *Employees here:* 800
SIC: 8062
    Physical therapy

D-U-N-S 07-561-2895
TRINITY MEDICAL CENTER
2701 17th St, Rock Island, IL 61201
Phone: (309) 793-2121
Sales: $137,906,000   *Employees:* 2,000
Company Type: Private   *Employees here:* 1,572
SIC: 8062
    General hospitals
Eric Crowell, President

D-U-N-S 15-212-0127
TRINITY MEDICAL CNTR
    (Parent: Trinity Regional Health Sys)
2701 17th St, Rock Island, IL 61201
Phone: (309) 757-2611
Sales: $127,756,000   *Employees:* 1,800
Company Type: Private   *Employees here:* 1,800
SIC: 8062
    General hospital
Eric Crowell, President

D-U-N-S 08-726-1103
TRINITY REGNL HSPTL
802 Kenyon Rd, Fort Dodge, IA 50501
Phone: (515) 573-3100
Sales: $49,697,000   *Employees:* 825
Company Type: Private   *Employees here:* 825
SIC: 8062
    General medical and surgical hospital and rehabilitation
    center
Tom Tibbitts, Chief Executive Officer

D-U-N-S 07-462-0667
TROPICAL TEXAS CENTER FOR MENT
1901 S 24th Ave, Edinburg, TX 78539
Phone: (956) 383-0121
Sales: $26,186,000   *Employees:* 539
Company Type: Private   *Employees here:* 200
SIC: 8093
    Outpatient mental health clinic
Leory Torres, Chief Executive Officer

D-U-N-S 07-132-7894
TROVER CLINIC FOUNDATION INC
900 Hospital Dr, Madisonville, KY 42431
Phone: (502) 825-5100
Sales: $143,391,000   *Employees:* 1,158
Company Type: Private   *Employees here:* 1,100
SIC: 8062
    General medical hospital
Bobby Dampier, Chief Executive Officer

D-U-N-S 19-949-4618
TROVER CLINIC FOUNDATION INC
200 Clinic Dr, Madisonville, KY 42431
Phone: (502) 825-7230

Sales: $23,100,000
Company Type: Private
SIC: 8062
  Medical clinic
James Steinmark, Administrator

Employees: NA
Employees here: 600

D-U-N-S 07-306-7407
TRUMAN MEDICAL CENTER INC
2301 Holmes St, Kansas City, MO 64108
Phone: (816) 556-3000
Sales: $116,202,000
Company Type: Private
SIC: 8062
  Hospital
Dr E R Anderson Md, Chief Executive Officer

Employees: 2,700
Employees here: 1,800

D-U-N-S 07-626-5057
TRUMAN MEDICAL CENTER INC
7900 Lees Summit Rd, Kansas City, MO 64139
Phone: (816) 373-4415
Sales: $33,500,000
Company Type: Private
SIC: 8062
  General hospital
Ross P Marine, Principal

Employees: NA
Employees here: 800

D-U-N-S 07-674-6148
TRUMBULL MEMORIAL HOSPITAL
1350 E Market St, Warren, OH 44483
Phone: (330) 841-9011
Sales: $117,836,000
Company Type: Private
SIC: 8062
  General medical and surgical hospital and physical therapy
  services
Charles A Johns, President

Employees: 2,000
Employees here: 2,000

D-U-N-S 12-352-9489
TRUSTEES OF DARTMOUTH COLLEGE
7020 Remsen Building, Hanover, NH 3755
Phone: (603) 650-1505
Sales: $27,700,000
Company Type: Private
SIC: 8062
  Med sch
Andrew G Wallace, Manager

Employees: NA
Employees here: 600

D-U-N-S 07-758-3813
TRUSTEES OF MEASE HOSPITAL
601 Main St, Dunedin, FL 34698
Phone: (727) 733-1111
Sales: $132,668,000
Company Type: Private
SIC: 8062
  General hospital
Philip K Beauchamp, President

Employees: 1,320
Employees here: 652

D-U-N-S 06-698-5474
TRUSTEES OF NOBLE HOSPITAL INC
115 W Silver St, Westfield, MA 1085
Phone: (413) 568-2811
Sales: $29,138,000
Company Type: Private
SIC: 8062
  General medical and surgical hospital
George Koller, President

Employees: 429
Employees here: 420

D-U-N-S 18-854-7129
TSI CORP
  (Parent: Genzyme Transgenics Corp)
25 Birch St, Milford, MA 1757
Phone: (508) 478-0877

Sales: $32,421,000
Company Type: Public Family Member
SIC: 8071
  Clinical testing services
James Geraghty, President

Employees: 450
Employees here: 12

D-U-N-S 05-707-3538
TUALITY COMMUNITY HOSPITAL
334 SE 8th Ave, Hillsboro, OR 97123
Phone: (503) 681-1111
Sales: $49,337,000
Company Type: Private
SIC: 8062
  General hospital
Richard V Stenson, Administrator

Employees: 600
Employees here: 600

D-U-N-S 10-796-9818
TUALITY HEALTH CARE
335 SE 8th Ave, Hillsboro, OR 97123
Phone: (503) 681-1111
Sales: $46,100,000
Company Type: Private
SIC: 8062
  Hospital health care services data processing real estate
  operator ret medical supplies & rents medical supplies
Richard V Stenson, President

Employees: 1,000
Employees here: 85

D-U-N-S 78-792-9777
TUCSON GENERAL HOSPITAL
  (Parent: Tenet Healthcare Corporation)
3838 N Campbell Ave, Tucson, AZ 85719
Phone: (520) 327-5431
Sales: $47,600,000
Company Type: Public Family Member
SIC: 8062
  General hospital
Allen Harrington, Chief Executive Officer

Employees: 602
Employees here: 570

D-U-N-S 17-055-8746
TUFTS ASSOCIATED HEALTH PLANS
333 Wyman St, Waltham, MA 2451
Phone: (781) 466-9400
Sales: $864,994,000
Company Type: Private
SIC: 8011
  Health care services
Dr Harris A Berman Md, Chief Executive Officer

Employees: 1,000
Employees here: 990

D-U-N-S 92-669-5453
TULANE MEDICAL CENTER, LTD
1415 Tulane Ave, New Orleans, LA 70112
Phone: (504) 588-5263
Sales: $132,720,000
Company Type: Private
SIC: 8062
  Acute care hospital
Stephen A Pickett, Chief Executive Officer

Employees: 1,500
Employees here: 1,500

D-U-N-S 07-878-0699
TULARE LOCAL HOSPITAL DISTRICT
869 N Cherry St, Tulare, CA 93274
Phone: (209) 688-0821
Sales: $31,495,000
Company Type: Private
SIC: 8062
  Hospital
Robert Montion, Administrator

Employees: 500
Employees here: 500

D-U-N-S 79-782-8316
TUOLUMNE GENERAL HOSPITAL
101 Hospital Rd, Sonora, CA 95370
Phone: (209) 533-7100

Sales: $20,598,000   *Employees:* 290
Company Type: Private   *Employees here:* 270
SIC: 8062
   General hospital
Joseph Mitchell, Administrator

D-U-N-S 07-799-0505
TUOMEY
129 N Washington St, Sumter, SC 29150
Phone: (803) 778-9000
Sales: $92,631,000   *Employees:* 1,300
Company Type: Private   *Employees here:* 1,279
SIC: 8062
   Hospital
Jay Cox, President

D-U-N-S 07-794-0666
TWIN CNTY REGIONAL HEALTHCARE
200 Hospital Dr, Galax, VA 24333
Phone: (540) 236-8181
Sales: $34,010,000   *Employees:* 625
Company Type: Private   *Employees here:* 550
SIC: 8062
   Hospital
Marcus G Kuhn, President

D-U-N-S 94-836-1290
TWIN CNTY RGIONAL HEALTH CLINICS
   (Parent: Twin Cnty Regional Healthcare)
200 Hospital Dr, Galax, VA 24333
Phone: (540) 236-8181
Sales: $37,141,000   *Employees:* 500
Company Type: Private   *Employees here:* 500
SIC: 8011
   Health clinics
Marcus Kuhn, President

D-U-N-S 07-298-3463
TWIN FALLS CLINIC AND HOSP
660 Shoshone St E, Twin Falls, ID 83301
Phone: (208) 733-3700
Sales: $24,077,000   *Employees:* 275
Company Type: Private   *Employees here:* 275
SIC: 8062
   Hospital and clinic
Marley Jacksman, Administrator

D-U-N-S 00-690-2712
TMC HEALTHCARE
5301 E Grant Rd, Tucson, AZ 85712
Phone: (520) 327-5461
Sales: $246,000,000   *Employees:* 2,650
Company Type: Private   *Employees here:* 1,655
SIC: 8062
   General hospital
Henry G Walker, President

D-U-N-S 80-772-6005
U H S OF DE LA RONDE, INC.
   (Parent: Universal Health Services)
9001 Patricia St, Chalmette, LA 70043
Phone: (504) 277-8011
Sales: $1,190,210,000   *Employees:* 250
Company Type: Public Family Member   *Employees here:* 250
SIC: 8062
   General hospital
Larry A Graham, Chief Executive Officer

D-U-N-S 11-851-5873
U S H OF PENNSYLVANIA, INC
   (Parent: Universal Health Services)
Earlystown Rd, Centre Hall, PA 16828
Phone: (814) 364-2161

Sales: $22,000,000   *Employees:* 284
Company Type: Public Family Member   *Employees here:* 278
SIC: 8011
   Psychiatric hospital
Joe Barszezewski, President

D-U-N-S 04-554-6546
U S HOMECARE CORPORATION
146 Wyllys St Ste 300, Hartford, CT 6106
Phone: (860) 278-7242
Sales: $52,635,000   *Employees:* 3,700
Company Type: Public   *Employees here:* 14
SIC: 8082
   Home health care services
Jay C Huffard, Chairman of the Board

D-U-N-S 62-568-9880
U S PHYSICAL THERAPY
3040 Post Oak Blvd, Houston, TX 77056
Phone: (713) 297-9050
Sales: $38,807,000   *Employees:* 45
Company Type: Public   *Employees here:* 40
SIC: 8049
   Office of health practitioners specializing in physical therapy
J L Kosberg, Chairman of the Board

D-U-N-S 11-527-8368
U T MEDICAL GROUP INC
66 N Pauline St Ste 101, Memphis, TN 38105
Phone: (901) 448-6653
Sales: $103,400,000   *Employees:* 1,500
Company Type: Private   *Employees here:* 300
SIC: 8011
   Medical doctor's office
Brenda Jeter, Vice-President

D-U-N-S 62-143-7599
U V M C NURSING CARE INC
3130 N Dixie Hwy, Troy, OH 45373
Phone: (937) 778-6500
Sales: $20,699,000   *Employees:* 5
Company Type: Private   *Employees here:* 5
SIC: 8051
   Skilled nursing homes
David Meckstroth, President

D-U-N-S 92-995-6035
U.S. HEALTHWORKS, INC.
3655 N Point Pkwy Ste 150, Alpharetta, GA 30005
Phone: (770) 772-6282
Sales: $100,000,000   *Employees:* 2,000
Company Type: Private   *Employees here:* 40
SIC: 8011
   Physician practice management & occupational health
John Nord, President

D-U-N-S 80-646-2511
UCSF-STANFORD HEALTH CARE
725 Welch Rd, Palo Alto, CA 94304
Phone: (650) 497-8000
Sales: $52,200,000   *Employees:* NA
Company Type: Private   *Employees here:* 990
SIC: 8069
   Pediatric hospital
Chris Dawes, President

D-U-N-S 17-930-8267   EXP
UCT INTERNATIONAL INC
   (Parent: Uniholding Corp)
260 Smith St, Farmingdale, NY 11735
Phone: (516) 777-8833

Sales: $24,100,000   Employees: 76
Company Type: Public Family Member   Employees here: 76
SIC: 8071
    Medical laboratory
Paul Hokfelt, Chief Executive Officer

D-U-N-S 07-467-6867
UKIAH ADVENTIST HOSPITAL
275 Hospital Dr, Ukiah, CA 95482
Phone: (707) 462-3111
Sales: $39,272,000   Employees: 650
Company Type: Private   Employees here: 500
SIC: 8062
    General hospital
Valgene Devitt, President

D-U-N-S 08-225-4004
ULTIMATE HEALTH SERVICES INC
1115 20th St, Huntington, WV 25703
Phone: (304) 528-4600
Sales: $24,634,000   Employees: 300
Company Type: Private   Employees here: 150
SIC: 8011
    Doctors clinic
Michael Luton, Chief Executive Officer

D-U-N-S 07-145-0027
UM HOLDINGS LTD
56 Haddon Ave, Haddonfield, NJ 8033
Phone: (609) 354-2200
Sales: $39,261,000   Employees: 800
Company Type: Private   Employees here: 100
SIC: 8099
    Cardiac diagnostic testing pacemaker testing & mfg
       treadmills
John Aglialoro, Chairman of the Board

D-U-N-S 11-749-1019
UNDER 21 INC
460 W 41st St, New York, NY 10036
Phone: (212) 613-0300
Sales: $19,895,000   Employees: 422
Company Type: Private   Employees here: 422
SIC: 8361
    Emergency shelter for children
Bruce Henry, Executive Director

D-U-N-S 07-705-9152
UNDERWOOD MEMORIAL HOSPITAL
509 N Broad St, Woodbury, NJ 8096
Phone: (609) 845-0100
Sales: $88,642,000   Employees: 1,500
Company Type: Private   Employees here: 1,454
SIC: 8062
    General hospital
Steven M Jackmuff, President

D-U-N-S 10-256-0083
UNILAB CORPORATION
18448 Oxnard St, Tarzana, CA 91356
Phone: (818) 996-7300
Sales: $214,001,000   Employees: 2,100
Company Type: Public   Employees here: 400
SIC: 8071
    Clinical testing laboratories
David C Weavil, Chairman of the Board

D-U-N-S 06-070-4640
UNIMED MGT SERVICES-SAN JOSE
    (Parent: Unimed Management Services 5)
655 Lincoln Ave, San Jose, CA 95126
Phone: (408) 998-5551

Sales: $46,400,000   Employees: 675
Company Type: Private   Employees here: 288
SIC: 8011
    Medical clinic management service
John Pietrzak, Chief Executive Officer

D-U-N-S 79-141-6142
UNIMED MGT SERVICES-SAN JOSE
18550 Saint Louise Dr, Morgan Hill, CA 95037
Phone: (408) 776-8160
Sales: $34,600,000   Employees: NA
Company Type: Private   Employees here: 560
SIC: 8011
    Medical doctor's office
Diane Stunkel, Branch Manager

D-U-N-S 04-285-1733
UNION HEALTH SERVICE INC
1634 W Polk St, Chicago, IL 60612
Phone: (312) 829-4224
Sales: $21,960,000   Employees: 302
Company Type: Private   Employees here: 147
SIC: 8011
    Health maintenance organization
Helen Hrynkiw, Executive Director

D-U-N-S 00-160-5385
UNION HOSPITALASSN OF THE BRONX
260 E 188th St, Bronx, NY 10458
Phone: (718) 220-2020
Sales: $42,784,000   Employees: 550
Company Type: Private   Employees here: 550
SIC: 8062
    General hospital
Dr Ronald Gade Md, Chief Executive Officer

D-U-N-S 04-073-8627
UNION HOSPITAL
1000 Galloping Hill Rd, Union, NJ 7083
Phone: (908) 687-1900
Sales: $67,594,000   Employees: 1,284
Company Type: Private   Employees here: 1,163
SIC: 8062
    Hospital
Katherin Koyne, Vp Operations

D-U-N-S 06-937-6838
UNION HOSPITAL OF CECIL CNTY
106 Bow St, Elkton, MD 21921
Phone: (410) 398-4000
Sales: $48,003,000   Employees: 650
Company Type: Private   Employees here: 640
SIC: 8062
    Hospital
Steven Owen, President

D-U-N-S 07-452-9819
UNION HOSPITAL ASSOCIATION
659 Boulevard St, Dover, OH 44622
Phone: (330) 343-3311
Sales: $41,157,000   Employees: 634
Company Type: Private   Employees here: 634
SIC: 8062
    General hospital
William W Harding, President

D-U-N-S 07-207-5252
UNION HOSPITAL INC
1606 N 7th St, Terre Haute, IN 47804
Phone: (812) 238-7601

Sales: $220,093,000
Company Type: Private
SIC: 8062
    General hospital
Frank Shelton, President

Employees: 2,322
Employees here: 1,818

D-U-N-S 07-827-9007
UNION MEMORIAL HOSPITAL INC
201 E University Pkwy, Baltimore, MD 21218
Phone: (410) 554-2000
Sales: $171,021,000
Company Type: Private
SIC: 8062
    General hospital
Edward J Kelly Iii, President

Employees: 2,025
Employees here: 2,025

D-U-N-S 07-105-7871
UNION REGIONAL MEDICAL CENTER
600 Hospital Dr, Monroe, NC 28112
Phone: (704) 283-3100
Sales: $48,138,000
Company Type: Private
SIC: 8062
    Hospital
John Roberts, President

Employees: 750
Employees here: 750

D-U-N-S 11-952-7091
UNISON HEALTHCARE CORPORATION
8800 N Gainey Center Dr, Scottsdale, AZ 85258
Phone: (602) 423-1954
Sales: $148,674,000
Company Type: Public
SIC: 8051
    Nursing homes
Michael A Jeffries, President

Employees: 5,600
Employees here: 80

D-U-N-S 08-547-4492
UNITED CARE INC
135 S Prospect St, Ypsilanti, MI 48198
Phone: (734) 484-2200
Sales: $25,000,000
Company Type: Private
SIC: 8062
    General hospital
Rick Hillbom, N/A

Employees: NA
Employees here: 600

D-U-N-S 08-276-4093
UNITED CARE INC
10000 Telegraph Rd, Taylor, MI 48180
Phone: (313) 295-5000
Sales: $40,000,000
Company Type: Private
SIC: 8062
    General hospital
Thom Johnson, Principal

Employees: NA
Employees here: 950

D-U-N-S 60-792-0386
UNITED CARE INC
9301 Middlebelt Rd, Romulus, MI 48174
Phone: (734) 946-4370
Sales: $25,200,000
Company Type: Private
SIC: 8011
    Industrial clinic
Fred Barton, President

Employees: NA
Employees here: 400

D-U-N-S 60-896-6222
UNITED CARE INC
18101 Oakwood Blvd, Dearborn, MI 48124
Phone: (313) 593-7000

Sales: $187,900,000
Company Type: Private
SIC: 8062
    General medical & surgical hospital
Gerald Fitzgerald, President

Employees: 4,000
Employees here: 3

D-U-N-S 62-104-3231
UNITED CARE INC
845 Monroe St, Dearborn, MI 48124
Phone: (313) 561-5000
Sales: $25,200,000
Company Type: Private
SIC: 8011
    Medical doctor's office
Sandra Ziaja, Branch Manager

Employees: NA
Employees here: 400

D-U-N-S 07-237-8086
UNITED CEREBAL PALSY ASC
380 Washington Ave, Roosevelt, NY 11575
Phone: (516) 378-2000
Sales: $20,425,000
Company Type: Private
SIC: 8099
    Health organization/elementary secondary school
Sidney Schwartz, President

Employees: 600
Employees here: 450

D-U-N-S 61-320-5392
UNITED CEREBRAL PALSY ASSOCIAT
250 Marcus Blvd, Hauppauge, NY 11788
Phone: (516) 232-0011
Sales: $20,099,000
Company Type: Private
SIC: 8099
    Non-profit health care facility
Kathleen Maul, Executive Director

Employees: 550
Employees here: 100

D-U-N-S 07-282-7298
UNITED CHURCH OF CHRIST HOMES
8501 Paxton St, Hummelstown, PA 17036
Phone: (717) 566-1720
Sales: $20,115,000
Company Type: Private
SIC: 8051
    Retirement community
Catherine B Price, Executive Director

Employees: 528
Employees here: 10

D-U-N-S 07-455-6440
UNITED CHURCH HOMES INC
170 E Center St, Marion, OH 43302
Phone: (740) 382-4885
Sales: $39,735,000
Company Type: Private
SIC: 8051
    Skilled nursing home & associated retirement communities
Brian S Allen, President

Employees: 1,100
Employees here: 60

D-U-N-S 08-967-0251
UNITED COMMUNITY HOSPITAL
631 N Broad Street Ext, Grove City, PA 16127
Phone: (724) 458-5442
Sales: $25,233,000
Company Type: Private
SIC: 8062
    General hospital
Robert Turner, Chief Executive Officer

Employees: 340
Employees here: 340

D-U-N-S 09-524-2731
UNITED CRBRL PLSY/ULSTR CNTY
250 Tuytenbridge Rd, Kingston, NY 12401
Phone: (914) 336-7235

Sales: $56,863,000   *Employees:* 287
Company Type: Private   *Employees here:* 260
SIC: 8093
   Outpatient rehabilitation center pre-school education
   program adult education program and residential programs
Pam Carroad, Executive Director

D-U-N-S 04-469-5062
UNITED HEALTH SERVICES INC
409 E Doyle St, Toccoa, GA 30577
Phone: (706) 886-8493
Sales: $20,400,000   *Employees:* NA
Company Type: Private   *Employees here:* NA
SIC: 8051
   Nursing home
Neil L Pruitt, President

D-U-N-S 06-679-8372
UNITED HEALTH SVCS HOSPITALS
33-57 Harrison St, Johnson City, NY 13790
Phone: (607) 763-6000
Sales: $206,272,000   *Employees:* 2,400
Company Type: Private   *Employees here:* 900
SIC: 8062
   General medical and surgical hospitals
Matthew J Salanger, President

D-U-N-S 19-309-6484
UNITED HEALTH SVCS HOSPITALS
33-57 Harrison St, Johnson City, NY 13790
Phone: (607) 763-6000
Sales: $79,500,000   *Employees:* NA
Company Type: Private   *Employees here:* 1,600
SIC: 8062
   General hospital
Matt Salanger, Principal

D-U-N-S 15-100-0569
UNITED HEALTHCARE OF KENTUCKY
2409 Harrodsburg Rd, Lexington, KY 40504
Phone: (606) 296-6000
Sales: $111,345,000   *Employees:* 100
Company Type: Private   *Employees here:* 91
SIC: 8011
   Health maintenance organization
Budd Fisher, Chief Executive Officer

D-U-N-S 17-496-7893
UNITED HEALTHCARE OF UTAH
   (Parent: United Healthcare Services Inc)
7910 S 3500 E, Salt Lake City, UT 84121
Phone: (801) 942-6200
Sales: $145,640,000   *Employees:* 120
Company Type: Public Family Member   *Employees here:* 120
SIC: 8011
   Health maintenance organization
Thomas A Davis, President

D-U-N-S 61-347-6456
UNITED HEALTHCARE SOUTH INC
   (Parent: United Healthcare Corporation)
3700 Colonnade Pkwy, Birmingham, AL 35243
Phone: (205) 977-6300
Sales: $20,300,000   *Employees:* 508
Company Type: Public Family Member   *Employees here:* 457
SIC: 8099
   Medical services
Blair R Suelentrop, President

D-U-N-S 01-088-7560
UNITED HEALTHCARE SYSTEM, INC.
15 S 9th St, Newark, NJ 7107
Phone: (973) 268-8000

Sales: $69,800,000   *Employees:* 1,500
Company Type: Private   *Employees here:* 750
SIC: 8062
   General hospital
John Dandridge Jr, Chief Executive Officer

D-U-N-S 07-496-1426
UNITED HOSPITAL CENTER INC
Rr 19 Box South, Clarksburg, WV 26301
Phone: (304) 624-2121
Sales: $115,337,000   *Employees:* 1,400
Company Type: Private   *Employees here:* 1,393
SIC: 8062
   General hospital
Bruce C Carter, President

D-U-N-S 05-406-8200
UNITED HOSPITAL MEDICAL CTR
406 Boston Post Rd, Port Chester, NY 10573
Phone: (914) 934-3000
Sales: $71,584,000   *Employees:* 850
Company Type: Private   *Employees here:* 845
SIC: 8062
   General hospital
Kevin Dahill, President

D-U-N-S 05-606-2870
UNITED LUTHERAN PROGRAM FOR TH
4545 N 92nd St, Milwaukee, WI 53225
Phone: (414) 464-3880
Sales: $23,518,000   *Employees:* 585
Company Type: Private   *Employees here:* 585
SIC: 8051
   Continuing care retirement community
David J Keller, Executive Director

D-U-N-S 02-865-4754
UNITED MEDICAL ASSOCIATES, PC
601 Riverside Dr, Johnson City, NY 13790
Phone: (607) 729-2500
Sales: $40,285,000   *Employees:* 240
Company Type: Private   *Employees here:* 95
SIC: 8011
   Physicians
Floyd Metzger, Executive Director

D-U-N-S 96-028-5849
UNITED MEDICAL GROUP
   (Parent: St Johns Health System Inc)
615 S New Ballas Rd, Saint Louis, MO 63141
Phone: (314) 995-4437
Sales: $20,500,000   *Employees:* 300
Company Type: Private   *Employees here:* 300
SIC: 8011
   Physicians clinic
Thomas Hales, Chief Executive Officer

D-U-N-S 06-018-2888
UNITED MEMORIAL HOSPITAL ASSN
615 S Bower St, Greenville, MI 48838
Phone: (616) 754-4691
Sales: $24,514,000   *Employees:* 375
Company Type: Private   *Employees here:* 300
SIC: 8062
   General hospital
John Welch, Administrator

D-U-N-S 02-078-1076
UNITED METHODIST HOMES OF NJ
3311 Highway 33, Neptune, NJ 7753
Phone: (732) 922-9800

Sales: $27,804,000
Employees: 600
Company Type: Private
Employees here: 24
SIC: 8361
   Health care and residential care services for the elderly
James Batten, President

D-U-N-S 14-780-0734
UNITED PHYSICIANS HEALTH NETWRK
   (Parent: Health Care Ventures Inc)
7100 Eagle Crest Blvd, Evansville, IN 47715
Phone: (812) 469-7500
Sales: $43,591,000
Employees: 90
Company Type: Public Family Member
Employees here: 90
SIC: 8011
   Health maintenance organization
Kevin Clancy, President

D-U-N-S 06-802-0387
UNITED PRESBT HM AT SYOSSET
378 Syosset Woodbury Rd, Woodbury, NY 11797
Phone: (516) 921-3900
Sales: $52,000,000
Employees: 730
Company Type: Private
Employees here: 730
SIC: 8051
   Skilled nursing facility
Dr William Smith, President

D-U-N-S 06-838-7372
UNITED REGIONAL HEALTH CARE SYS
1600 8th St, Wichita Falls, TX 76301
Phone: (940) 723-1461
Sales: $138,989,000
Employees: 900
Company Type: Private
Employees here: 900
SIC: 8062
   General hospital
Jeff Hausler, Chief Executive Officer

D-U-N-S 11-971-1588
UNITED STATES HEALTH
   (Parent: Aetna-U S Healthcare Inc)
980 Jolly Rd, Blue Bell, PA 19422
Phone: (215) 628-4800
Sales: $1,717,555,000
Employees: 209
Company Type: Public Family Member
Employees here: 209
SIC: 8011
   Comprehensive managed healthcare servies
Timothy Nolan, Chief Executive Officer

D-U-N-S 00-926-5096
UNITED/DYNACARE LLC
9200 W Wisconsin Ave, Milwaukee, WI 53226
Phone: (414) 454-7500
Sales: $20,900,000
Employees: 250
Company Type: Private
Employees here: 250
SIC: 8071
   Medical laboratory
Robert Albert, General Manager

D-U-N-S 07-764-9713
UNITY HEALTH MANAGEMENT SVCS
2160 Highland Ave S, Birmingham, AL 35205
Phone: (205) 939-8600
Sales: $35,805,000
Employees: 815
Company Type: Private
Employees here: 50
SIC: 8082
   Home health care agency
Deeni Taylor, President

D-U-N-S 07-969-7819
UNITY HEALTH SYSTEM
1555 Long Pond Rd, Rochester, NY 14626
Phone: (716) 723-7000

Sales: $89,533,000
Employees: 1,150
Company Type: Private
Employees here: 955
SIC: 8062
   General hospital
Timothy R Mc Cormick, President

D-U-N-S 15-218-5872
UNITY HEALTH, INC
3933 S Broadway, Saint Louis, MO 63118
Phone: (314) 865-3333
Sales: $32,300,000
Employees: NA
Company Type: Private
Employees here: 770
SIC: 8062
   Hospital
Glenn Applebome, Branch Manager

D-U-N-S 94-231-4857
UNITY PHYSICIAN GROUP INC
1155 W 3rd St, Bloomington, IN 47404
Phone: (812) 333-2731
Sales: $39,500,000
Employees: 575
Company Type: Private
Employees here: 100
SIC: 8011
   Medical doctors office
Lawrence Rink, President

D-U-N-S 12-076-0376
UNIV OF KENTUCKY HOSPITAL
Albert B Chandler Center, Lexington, KY 40506
Phone: (606) 323-5000
Sales: $323,081,000
Employees: 2,700
Company Type: Private
Employees here: 2,650
SIC: 8062
   General hospital
Frank Butler, Chief Executive Officer

D-U-N-S 11-856-1315
UNIVERSAL CARE INC
1600 E Hill St, Long Beach, CA 90806
Phone: (562) 424-6200
Sales: $159,460,000
Employees: 1,000
Company Type: Private
Employees here: 250
SIC: 8093
   Prepaid health plan service
Howard Davis, President

D-U-N-S 09-372-5133
UNIVERSAL HEALTH SERVICES
367 S Gulph Rd Ste 2, King Of Prussia, PA 19406
Phone: (610) 768-3300
Sales: $1,442,677,000
Employees: 17,800
Company Type: Public
Employees here: 75
SIC: 8062
   General & psychiatric hospitals and ambulatory surgical
      centers
Alan B Miller, Chairman of the Board

D-U-N-S 96-284-4312
UNIVERSAL HEALTH SERVICES,
202 N Division St, Auburn, WA 98001
Phone: (253) 833-7711
Sales: $29,300,000
Employees: NA
Company Type: Public Family Member
Employees here: 600
SIC: 8062
   General medical & surgical hospitals
Micheal Gherardini, Principal

D-U-N-S 08-138-8753
UNIVERSITY OF ALABAMA HEALTH S
300 Liberty National Buil, Birmingham, AL 35233
Phone: (205) 731-9625

Sales: $376,000,000　　　　　　　　Employees: 1,800
Company Type: Private　　　　　　　Employees here: 750
SIC: 8093
　　Group practice in patient and out patient healthcare services
Dr John N Whitaker Md, President

D-U-N-S 18-927-3816
UNIVERSITY OF ALABAMA HEALTH S
301 20th St S Ste 301, Birmingham, AL 35233
Phone: (205) 731-9600
Sales: $59,500,000　　　　　　　　Employees: NA
Company Type: Private　　　　　　　Employees here: 1,000
SIC: 8011
　　Medical doctor's office health/allied services
Steven Schultz, Manager

D-U-N-S 15-385-1423
UNIVERSITY OF ARIZONA
1501 N Campbell Ave, Tucson, AZ 85724
Phone: (520) 621-2211
Sales: $108,500,000　　　　　　　Employees: NA
Company Type: Private　　　　　　Employees here: 2,500
SIC: 8062
　　Teaching hospital
Gregory A Pieverotto, President

D-U-N-S 93-983-8090
UNIVERSITY OF CALIFORNIA
1250 16th St, Santa Monica, CA 90404
Phone: (310) 319-4000
Sales: $55,000,000　　　　　　　　Employees: NA
Company Type: Private　　　　　　Employees here: 1,111
SIC: 8062
　　General hospital

D-U-N-S 06-014-2346
UNIVERSITY OF CALIFORNIA
401 Parnassus Ave, San Francisco, CA 94143
Phone: (415) 476-7000
Sales: $22,000,000　　　　　　　　Employees: NA
Company Type: Private　　　　　　Employees here: 550
SIC: 8063
　　Mental hospital
Dr Craig Van Dyke, Manager

D-U-N-S 02-021-0407
UNIVERSITY OF CALIFORNIA
200 W Arbor Dr Rm 1-121, San Diego, CA 92103
Phone: (619) 543-6654
Sales: $140,400,000　　　　　　　Employees: NA
Company Type: Private　　　　　　Employees here: 4,000
SIC: 8062
　　General hospital
Sumiyo E Kastelic, Director

D-U-N-S 07-612-4981
UNIVERSITY OF CALIFORNIA
2315 Stockton Blvd, Sacramento, CA 95817
Phone: (916) 734-2011
Sales: $211,800,000　　　　　　　Employees: NA
Company Type: Private　　　　　　Employees here: 4,218
SIC: 8071
　　Acute care hospital/trauma center
Frank J Loge, Branch Manager

D-U-N-S 06-996-1548
UNIVERSITY OF CALIFORNIA
101 The City Dr S, Orange, CA 92868
Phone: (714) 456-6011

Sales: $149,300,000　　　　　　　Employees: NA
Company Type: Private　　　　　　Employees here: 3,000
SIC: 8062
　　General hospital
Mary Piccione, Executive Director

D-U-N-S 15-572-2606
UNIVERSITY OF CALIFORNIA
101 The City Dr S, Orange, CA 92868
Phone: (714) 634-6011
Sales: $99,500,000　　　　　　　　Employees: NA
Company Type: Private　　　　　　Employees here: 2,000
SIC: 8062
　　General hospital
Mary A Piccione, Branch Manager

D-U-N-S 61-763-8705
UNIVERSITY OF CALIFORNIA
10833 Le Conte Ave, Los Angeles, CA 90095
Phone: (310) 825-9111
Sales: $206,400,000　　　　　　　Employees: NA
Company Type: Private　　　　　　Employees here: 4,150
SIC: 8062
　　General hospital
Albert Carnesale, Principal

D-U-N-S 80-113-5476
UNIVERSITY OF CALIFORNIA
9300 Campus Point Dr, La Jolla, CA 92037
Phone: (619) 657-7000
Sales: $24,300,000　　　　　　　　Employees: NA
Company Type: Private　　　　　　Employees here: 500
SIC: 8062
　　General hospital
Paul Hensler, Manager

D-U-N-S 19-848-0170
UNIVERSITY OF CHICAGO
5841 S Maryland Ave, Chicago, IL 60637
Phone: (773) 702-1000
Sales: $483,312,000　　　　　　　Employees: 4,300
Company Type: Private　　　　　　Employees here: 4,150
SIC: 8062
　　General hospital
Ralph Muller, President

D-U-N-S 62-522-7541
UNIVERSITY OF FLORIDA
Health Center Annex 13, Gainesville, FL 32610
Phone: (352) 395-0085
Sales: $25,200,000　　　　　　　　Employees: NA
Company Type: Private　　　　　　Employees here: 400
SIC: 8011
　　Medical doctor's office college/university
Ban Miripo, Branch Manager

D-U-N-S 11-954-3429
UNIVERSITY OF ILLINOIS
1740 W Taylor St, Chicago, IL 60612
Phone: (312) 996-7000
Sales: $67,700,000　　　　　　　　Employees: NA
Company Type: Private　　　　　　Employees here: 1,600
SIC: 8062
　　General hospital
James Stukel, President

D-U-N-S 10-332-5874
UNIVERSITY OF ILLINOIS
1855 W Taylor St, Chicago, IL 60612
Phone: (312) 996-6544

Sales: $25,200,000   *Employees:* NA
Company Type: Private   *Employees here:* 400
SIC: 8011
  Medical doctor's office
Toby C Dir, Director

D-U-N-S 79-220-1691
UNIVERSITY OF IA HOSPITAL & CLINIC
200 Hawkins Dr, Iowa City, IA 52242
Phone: (319) 356-1616
Sales: $571,000,000   *Employees:* 7,083
Company Type: Private   *Employees here:* 6,500
SIC: 8062
  General hospital
R E Howell, Chief Executive Officer

D-U-N-S 87-890-9357
UNIVERSITY OF KENTUCKY
800 Rose St, Lexington, KY 40536
Phone: (606) 323-5000
Sales: $134,700,000   *Employees:* NA
Company Type: Private   *Employees here:* 2,400
SIC: 8011
  Medical doctor's office
Dr James Holsinger, Principal

D-U-N-S 78-561-5451
UNIVERSITY OF MASSACHUSETTS
55 Lake Ave N, Worcester, MA 1655
Phone: (508) 856-3240
Sales: $139,900,000   *Employees:* NA
Company Type: Private   *Employees here:* 2,500
SIC: 8011
  Medical clinic school & research
Dr Aaron Lazare, Branch Manager

D-U-N-S 61-802-9383
UNIVERSITY OF MEDICINE
65 Bergen St, Newark, NJ 7107
Phone: (973) 982-6211
Sales: $47,100,000   *Employees:* NA
Company Type: Private   *Employees here:* 700
SIC: 8011
  Health clinic
Charles Carella, Chairman of the Board

D-U-N-S 15-100-9107
UNIVERSITY OF MIAMI
900 NW 17th St, Miami, FL 33136
Phone: (305) 326-6111
Sales: $23,400,000   *Employees:* NA
Company Type: Private   *Employees here:* 500
SIC: 8069
  Eye hospital
John Rossfeld, Director

D-U-N-S 62-654-6477
UNIVERSITY OF MICHIGAN
1500 E Med Ctr Dr Rm 3101, Ann Arbor, MI 48109
Phone: (734) 936-4770
Sales: $113,600,000   *Employees:* NA
Company Type: Private   *Employees here:* 2,000
SIC: 8011
  Medical doctor's office
H D Humes, Principal

D-U-N-S 62-654-6873
UNIVERSITY OF MICHIGAN
1500 E Medicl Cr Dr Univ, Ann Arbor, MI 48109
Phone: (734) 936-6376

Sales: $42,600,000   *Employees:* NA
Company Type: Private   *Employees here:* 700
SIC: 8011
  Medical doctor's office
Lazar Greenfield, Manager

D-U-N-S 78-219-4203
UNIVERSITY OF MICHIGAN
1500 E Med Ctr Dr, Ann Arbor, MI 48109
Phone: (734) 936-6776
Sales: $26,300,000   *Employees:* NA
Company Type: Private   *Employees here:* 600
SIC: 8071
  Medical laboratory
Joseph Fantone, Director

D-U-N-S 19-211-4858
UNIVERSITY OF MINNESOTA
500 Harvard St SE, Minneapolis, MN 55455
Phone: (612) 626-3000
Sales: $199,300,000   *Employees:* NA
Company Type: Private   *Employees here:* 4,784
SIC: 8062
  General hospital
Peter Rapp, Chief

D-U-N-S 61-806-4034
UNIVERSITY OF MINNESOTA
517 Umhc Hrvrd St E Riv, Minneapolis, MN 55455
Phone: (612) 626-3636
Sales: $41,400,000   *Employees:* NA
Company Type: Private   *Employees here:* 1,000
SIC: 8062
  General medical and surgical hospitals, nsk
Lou Sietti, Director

D-U-N-S 61-826-5284
UNIVERSITY OF MINNESOTA
425 E River Rd Rm 147, Minneapolis, MN 55455
Phone: (612) 376-4460
Sales: $21,500,000   *Employees:* NA
Company Type: Private   *Employees here:* 527
SIC: 8062
  General hospital

D-U-N-S 15-585-8400
UNIVERSITY OF MISSISSIPPI
2500 N State St, Jackson, MS 39216
Phone: (601) 984-1000
Sales: $316,600,000   *Employees:* NA
Company Type: Private   *Employees here:* 6,000
SIC: 8011
  Hospital
A W Conerly, Branch Manager

D-U-N-S 07-292-1000
UNIVERSITY OF NEBRASKA
600 S 42nd St, Omaha, NE 68198
Phone: (402) 559-4000
Sales: $208,200,000   *Employees:* NA
Company Type: Private   *Employees here:* 5,000
SIC: 8062
  General hospital
Joe Graham, Chief Executive Officer

D-U-N-S 95-915-7330
UNIVERSITY OF NEBRASKA
600 S 42nd St, Omaha, NE 68198
Phone: (402) 559-8658

Sales: $29,900,000
Company Type: Private
SIC: 8011
Employees: NA
Employees here: 480
   Teaches research & patient care for internal medicine
   specialties
Mike Mcglade, Administrative Director

D-U-N-S 10-349-7871
UNIVERSITY OF NEW MEXICO
2211 Lomas Blvd NE, Albuquerque, NM 87106
Phone: (505) 843-2464
Sales: $103,000,000
Company Type: Private
SIC: 8062
   Hospital
Stephen Mckernan, Chief Executive Officer
Employees: NA
Employees here: 2,375

D-U-N-S 82-635-5760
UNIVERSITY OF NEW MEXICO
2221 Lomas Blvd NE, Albuquerque, NM 87106
Phone: (505) 272-2111
Sales: $108,500,000
Company Type: Private
SIC: 8062
   Hospital
Steve Mccimerin, Director
Employees: NA
Employees here: 2,500

D-U-N-S 14-818-9517
UNIVERSITY OF NC HOSPITALS
101 Manning Dr, Chapel Hill, NC 27514
Phone: (919) 966-5111
Sales: $393,066,000
Company Type: Private
SIC: 8062
   General hospital
Eric B Munson, Executive Director
Employees: 4,746
Employees here: 4,453

D-U-N-S 10-381-9124
UNIVERSITY OF PENNSYLVANIA
3400 Spruce St, Philadelphia, PA 19104
Phone: (215) 662-4000
Sales: $223,800,000
Company Type: Private
SIC: 8062
   General hospital
William Kelly, Principal
Employees: NA
Employees here: 4,500

D-U-N-S 62-309-0982
UNIVERSITY OF PENNSYLVANIA
3400 Spruce St Fl 1, Philadelphia, PA 19104
Phone: (215) 662-3005
Sales: $21,300,000
Company Type: Private
SIC: 8011
   Medical doctor's office
Stanley Baum, Manager
Employees: NA
Employees here: 300

D-U-N-S 16-256-7846
UNIVERSITY OF ROCHESTER
300 Crittenden Way, Rochester, NY 14623
Phone: (716) 275-3575
Sales: $31,800,000
Company Type: Private
SIC: 8062
   Psychiatric hospital and school
Paul Mcathur, N/A
Employees: NA
Employees here: 650

D-U-N-S 07-947-4037
UNIVERSITY OF S ALA MED CTR
2451 Fillingim St, Mobile, AL 36617
Phone: (334) 471-7000

Sales: $145,332,000
Company Type: Private
SIC: 8062
Employees: 3,000
Employees here: 1,600
   Acute care hospital
Stephen Simmons, Administrator

D-U-N-S 19-707-3026
UNIVERSITY OF SOUTH ALABAMA
1700 Center St, Mobile, AL 36604
Phone: (256) 415-1000
Sales: $30,300,000
Company Type: Private
SIC: 8062
   General hospital
Robert Jernigan, Administrator
Employees: NA
Employees here: 725

D-U-N-S 83-804-0483
UNIVERSITY OF TEXAS AT AUSTIN
1100 Holcombe Blvd, Houston, TX 77030
Phone: (713) 792-3900
Sales: $22,200,000
Company Type: Private
SIC: 8011
   Medical doctor's office
Bernard Levin, Vice-President
Employees: NA
Employees here: 350

D-U-N-S 17-757-8994
UNIVERSITY OF TEXAS HEALTH
2800 S Macgregor Way, Houston, TX 77021
Phone: (713) 741-7803
Sales: $34,000,000
Company Type: Private
SIC: 8011
   Medical doctor's office
David R Small, Principal
Employees: NA
Employees here: 550

D-U-N-S 93-346-8860
UNIVERSITY OF TEXAS SYSTEM
5323 Harry Hines Blvd, Dallas, TX 75235
Phone: (214) 648-1802
Sales: $267,100,000
Company Type: Private
SIC: 8011
   Medical doctor's office
Scott Brady, Manager
Employees: NA
Employees here: 5,000

D-U-N-S 96-324-1518
UNIVERSITY OF TEXAS SYSTEM
5323 Harry Hines Blvd, Dallas, TX 75235
Phone: (214) 648-3787
Sales: $31,100,000
Company Type: Private
SIC: 8011
   Outpatient clinic
Dr Willis C Maddrey, Principal
Employees: NA
Employees here: 500

D-U-N-S 15-127-8744
UNIVERSITY OF UTAH
50 N Medical Dr, Salt Lake City, UT 84132
Phone: (801) 581-7606
Sales: $173,500,000
Company Type: Private
SIC: 8062
   Hospital
Dr Merle Sande, Director
Employees: NA
Employees here: 4,000

D-U-N-S 36-132-2886
UNIVERSITY OF UTAH HOSPITAL
50 N Medical Dr, Salt Lake City, UT 84132
Phone: (801) 581-2121

Sales: $272,540,000
Company Type: Private
SIC: 8062
　General hospital
Christine St Andre, Administrator

Employees: 3,600
Employees here: 3,060

D-U-N-S 10-602-6628
UNIVERSITY OF VIRGINIA
Lee St Jefferson Park Ave, Charlottesville, VA 22908
Phone: (804) 924-0211
Sales: $192,700,000
Company Type: Private
SIC: 8062
　General hospital
Michael Halseth, Manager

Employees: NA
Employees here: 4,700

D-U-N-S 12-396-8489
UNIVERSITY OF VIRGINIA
Lee St, Charlottesville, VA 22908
Phone: (804) 924-5269
Sales: $172,300,000
Company Type: Private
SIC: 8062
　General hospital
John Bright, Principal

Employees: NA
Employees here: 4,200

D-U-N-S 62-488-8194
UNIVERSITY OF VIRGINIA
Dept Of Medicine, Charlottesville, VA 22908
Phone: (804) 924-2093
Sales: $29,700,000
Company Type: Private
SIC: 8011
　Medical doctor's office
Dr Jack Gwaltney, N/A

Employees: NA
Employees here: 550

D-U-N-S 79-668-2151
UNIVERSITY OF VIRGINIA
1924 Rlington Blv Stu 211, Charlottesville, VA 22903
Phone: (804) 977-6010
Sales: $21,700,000
Company Type: Private
SIC: 8069
　Specialty hospital psychiatric hospital general hospital
Margret King, Director

Employees: NA
Employees here: 500

D-U-N-S 93-390-6547
UNIVERSITY OF VIRGINIA
412 Brandon Ave, Charlottesville, VA 22903
Phone: (804) 924-2371
Sales: $22,100,000
Company Type: Private
SIC: 8011
　Internal medicine department
Dr Frederick Hayden, Principal

Employees: NA
Employees here: 400

D-U-N-S 10-944-2707
UNIVERSITY OF WASHINGTON
1959 NE Pacific St, Seattle, WA 98195
Phone: (206) 548-3300
Sales: $113,600,000
Company Type: Private
SIC: 8011
　Medical doctor's office
Robert Mailenberg, Manager

Employees: NA
Employees here: 2,000

D-U-N-S 78-634-6643
UNIVERSITY OF WASHINGTON
1959 NE Pacific St, Seattle, WA 98195
Phone: (206) 548-4333

Sales: $74,500,000
Company Type: Private
SIC: 8062
　General hospital
R Mccormick, President

Employees: NA
Employees here: 1,500

D-U-N-S 17-419-2609
UNIVERSITY ANESTHESIOLOGY & CR
A-1305 Scaife Hall, Pittsburgh, PA 15261
Phone: (412) 648-9623
Sales: $33,017,000
Company Type: Private
SIC: 8011
　Anesthesiologists
Dr Leonard Firestone Md, President

Employees: 130
Employees here: 110

D-U-N-S 88-475-8467
UNIVERSITY COLORADO HOSPITAL AUTH
4200 E 9th Ave, Denver, CO 80220
Phone: (303) 399-1211
Sales: $234,244,000
Company Type: Private
SIC: 8062
　General medical & surgical hospital
Dennis C Brimhall, President

Employees: 2,600
Employees here: 2,595

D-U-N-S 06-966-8291
UNIVERSITY COMMUNITY HOSPITAL
3100 E Fletcher Ave, Tampa, FL 33613
Phone: (813) 971-6000
Sales: $190,700,000
Company Type: Private
SIC: 8062
　General hospital
Norm Stein, Administrator

Employees: 2,557
Employees here: 2,139

D-U-N-S 13-079-5446
UNIVERSITY HEALTH SERVICES
1350 Walton Way, Augusta, GA 30901
Phone: (706) 722-9011
Sales: $262,865,000
Company Type: Private
SIC: 8062
　General medical and surgical hospital
Donald C Bray, President

Employees: 3,800
Employees here: 3,600

D-U-N-S 10-982-6214
UNIVERSITY HEALTHCARE SYS L C
1415 Tulane Ave, New Orleans, LA 70112
Phone: (504) 588-5263
Sales: $140,700,000
Company Type: Private
SIC: 8062
　Hospital
David Fine, V Chancellor

Employees: 3,000
Employees here: 2,985

D-U-N-S 07-131-0437
UNIVERSITY HOSPITAL LTD
7201 N University Dr, Fort Lauderdale, FL 33321
Phone: (954) 721-2200
Sales: $196,200,000
Company Type: Private
SIC: 8062
　General medical and surgical hospital
James Cruickshank, Administrator

Employees: 700
Employees here: 700

D-U-N-S 60-937-3691
UNIVERSITY HSPTALS OF CLVLAND
11100 Euclid Ave, Cleveland, OH 44106
Phone: (216) 844-1000

Sales: $340,409,000
Company Type: Private
SIC: 8062
  General hospital
Farah M Walters, President
Employees: 4,700
Employees here: 4,600

D-U-N-S 06-667-7535
UNIVERSITY MED CTR SUTHERN NEV
1800 W Charleston Blvd, Las Vegas, NV 89102
Phone: (702) 383-2000
Sales: $264,843,000
Company Type: Private
SIC: 8062
  General hospital
William Hale, Chief Executive Officer
Employees: 2,487
Employees here: 2,200

D-U-N-S 82-508-1375
UNIVERSITY MEDICAL ASSOCIATES
96 Jonathan Lucas St, Charleston, SC 29401
Phone: (843) 792-2075
Sales: $25,200,000
Company Type: Private
SIC: 8011
  Ambuatory care services
David Neff, Director
Employees: NA
Employees here: 400

D-U-N-S 08-212-5345
UNIVERSITY MEDICAL CENTER
445 S Cedar Ave, Fresno, CA 93702
Phone: (209) 453-4000
Sales: $65,000,000
Company Type: Private
SIC: 8062
  General hospital
J P Hinton Phd, Chief Executive Officer
Employees: 1,400
Employees here: 1,400

D-U-N-S 11-805-9419
UNIVERSITY MEDICAL CENTER CORP
1501 N Campbell Ave, Tucson, AZ 85724
Phone: (520) 694-0111
Sales: $210,198,000
Company Type: Private
SIC: 8062
  General medical & surgical hospital
Gregory Pivirotto, President
Employees: 2,700
Employees here: 2,200

D-U-N-S 06-024-1940
UNIVERSITY MEDICAL CENTER INC
655 W 8th St, Jacksonville, FL 32209
Phone: (904) 549-5000
Sales: $228,174,000
Company Type: Private
SIC: 8062
  General hospital
W A Mcgriff Iii, President
Employees: 2,497
Employees here: 2,290

D-U-N-S 78-740-2841
UNIVERSITY MEDICAL CENTER INC
530 S Jackson St, Louisville, KY 40202
Phone: (502) 562-3000
Sales: $170,171,000
Company Type: Private
SIC: 8062
  General medical & surgical hospital
James Taylor, Chief Executive Officer
Employees: 2,000
Employees here: 2,000

D-U-N-S 02-064-5503
UNIVERSITY MEDNET
18599 Lake Shore Blvd, Cleveland, OH 44119
Phone: (216) 383-8500

Sales: $36,900,000
Company Type: Private
SIC: 8069
  Outpatient & multi-specialty clinic home health care & ret
    medical equipment & supplies
Malcolm S Henoeh, President
Employees: 750
Employees here: 300

D-U-N-S 15-070-2553
UNIVERSITY MD MED SYS CORP
22 S Greene St, Baltimore, MD 21201
Phone: (410) 328-8667
Sales: $242,700,000
Company Type: Private
SIC: 8062
  General hospital
Roger C Lipitz, Chairman of the Board
Employees: 5,158
Employees here: 4,800

D-U-N-S 61-843-8170
UNIVERSITY PHYSCN ASSOC OF NJ
30 Bergen St, Newark, NJ 7107
Phone: (973) 972-5004
Sales: $20,500,000
Company Type: Private
SIC: 8011
  Physician practice
Mike Saulich, Executive Director
Employees: 300
Employees here: 43

D-U-N-S 08-072-3943
UNIVERSITY PHYSICIANS SURGEONS
1801 6th Ave, Huntington, WV 25703
Phone: (304) 696-7210
Sales: $28,626,000
Company Type: Private
SIC: 8011
  Outpatient care
James Schneider, Treasurer
Employees: 400
Employees here: 250

D-U-N-S 14-836-8194
UNIVERSITY PHYSICIANS, INC
575 E River Rd, Tucson, AZ 85704
Phone: (520) 795-3500
Sales: $95,917,000
Company Type: Private
SIC: 8011
  Multi specialty medical group
John B Sullivan Jr, President
Employees: 800
Employees here: 150

D-U-N-S 07-214-9909
UNIVERSITY PITTSBURGH MED CTR
400 Holland Ave, Braddock, PA 15104
Phone: (412) 636-5000
Sales: $38,257,000
Company Type: Private
SIC: 8062
  General hospital
Richard Benfer, President
Employees: 600
Employees here: 600

D-U-N-S 78-451-4440
UNIVERSITY REHABILITATION HOSP
3125 Canal St, New Orleans, LA 70119
Phone: (504) 822-8222
Sales: $22,864,000
Company Type: Private
SIC: 8069
  Long-term hospital
Rob Leonhard, Chief Executive Officer
Employees: 290
Employees here: 290

D-U-N-S 61-831-4520
UNIVERSITY VIRGINIA MED CTR
1105 W Main St, Charlottesville, VA 22903
Phone: (804) 924-0211

Sales: $444,320,000   *Employees:* 4,720
Company Type: Private   *Employees here:* 4,248
SIC: 8062
    Medical center including operation of general hospitals
Mike Halseth, Executive Director

D-U-N-S 60-440-7395
UNIVERSITY WISCONSIN SYSTEM
1300 University Ave, Madison, WI 53706
Phone: (608) 262-1189
Sales: $21,400,000   *Employees:* NA
Company Type: Private   *Employees here:* 485
SIC: 8071
    Medical laboratory college/university
Arnold Brown, N/A

D-U-N-S 78-961-3726
UNIVERSITY WISCONSIN SYSTEM
1300 University Ave, Madison, WI 53706
Phone: (608) 263-4559
Sales: $38,300,000   *Employees:* NA
Company Type: Private   *Employees here:* 625
SIC: 8011
    Medical doctor's office
Phillip Farrow, Branch Manager

D-U-N-S 85-921-7432
UNIVERSITY WSCNSIN HOSPITAL CLNICS
600 Highland Ave, Madison, WI 53792
Phone: (608) 263-9635
Sales: $306,074,000   *Employees:* 5,100
Company Type: Private   *Employees here:* 5,000
SIC: 8062
    General medical hospital and medical clinics
Gordon Durzon, Administrator

D-U-N-S 01-095-7140
UNLIMITED CARE INC
245 Main St Ste 601, White Plains, NY 10601
Phone: (914) 428-8940
Sales: $117,200,000   *Employees:* 1,700
Company Type: Private   *Employees here:* 25
SIC: 8011
    Help supply services specializing in health care
Marcia Birnbaum, President

D-U-N-S 06-685-4795
UPMC MCKEESPORT
1500 5th Ave, Mc Keesport, PA 15132
Phone: (412) 664-2000
Sales: $66,400,000   *Employees:* 1,429
Company Type: Private   *Employees here:* 1,400
SIC: 8062
    General hospital
Ronald H Ott, President

D-U-N-S 07-216-4395
UPMC PASSAVANT
9100 Babcock Blvd, Pittsburgh, PA 15237
Phone: (412) 367-6700
Sales: $78,766,000   *Employees:* 4
Company Type: Private   *Employees here:* NA
SIC: 8062
    General hospital
Ralph T De Stefano, President

D-U-N-S 07-497-6044
UPMC PRESBYTERIAN
200 Lothrop St, Pittsburgh, PA 15213
Phone: (412) 647-2345

Sales: $661,871,000   *Employees:* 6,411
Company Type: Private   *Employees here:* 3,207
SIC: 8062
    General hospital
Jeffrey Romoff, President

D-U-N-S 07-217-2661
UPMC SHADYSIDE
5230 Centre Ave, Pittsburgh, PA 15232
Phone: (412) 623-2121
Sales: $206,261,000   *Employees:* 2,131
Company Type: Private   *Employees here:* 1,987
SIC: 8062
    General hospital
Henry A Mordoh, President

D-U-N-S 06-872-4186
UPMC-BEAVER VALLEY
2500 Hospital Dr, Aliquippa, PA 15001
Phone: (724) 857-1212
Sales: $35,105,000   *Employees:* 700
Company Type: Private   *Employees here:* 545
SIC: 8062
    General hospital psychiatric hospital and skilled nursing
George J Korbabes, Chief Executive Officer

D-U-N-S 13-964-4553
UPPER VALLEY MEDICAL CENTER
3130 N Dixie Hwy, Troy, OH 45373
Phone: (937) 778-6500
Sales: $115,285,000   *Employees:* 336
Company Type: Private   *Employees here:* 130
SIC: 8062
    Health system
David Meckstroth, President

D-U-N-S 07-342-2255
UPSON REGIONAL MEDICAL CENTER
801 W Gordon St, Thomaston, GA 30286
Phone: (706) 647-8111
Sales: $21,600,000   *Employees:* 482
Company Type: Private   *Employees here:* 476
SIC: 8062
    General hospital
Sam Gregory, Administrator

D-U-N-S 19-639-3888   EXP
UROCOR INC
800 Research Pkwy Ste 200, Oklahoma City, OK 73104
Phone: (405) 290-4000
Sales: $32,952,000   *Employees:* 340
Company Type: Public   *Employees here:* 340
SIC: 8071
    Diagnostic & clinical testing service company
William A Hagstrom, Chairman of the Board

D-U-N-S 01-565-6770
UROLOGY HEALTHCARE GROUP INC
3 Maryland Farms Ste 350, Brentwood, TN 37027
Phone: (615) 345-6700
Sales: $63,000,000   *Employees:* 450
Company Type: Private   *Employees here:* 450
SIC: 8011
    Manages urology practices
Robert Barnett, Chairman

D-U-N-S 03-476-5024
USDSM UNIVERSITY PHYSICIANS
2701 S Minnesota Ave, Sioux Falls, SD 57105
Phone: (605) 367-5290

Sales: $25,044,000   *Employees:* 290
Company Type: Private   *Employees here:* 40
SIC: 8011
  Medical clinic
Joseph J Cudzilo, Executive Director

D-U-N-S 12-500-5611
UTAH DEPARTMENT HUMAN SERVICES
1300 W Center St, Provo, UT 84601
Phone: (801) 344-4400
Sales: $28,100,000   *Employees:* NA
Company Type: Private   *Employees here:* 810
SIC: 8063
  State psychiatric hospital
Mark Payne, N/A

D-U-N-S 61-850-9038
UTAH SENIOR SERVICES, INC
P.O. Box 30, Cornish, UT 84308
Phone: (801) 225-8844
Sales: $20,062,000   *Employees:* 650
Company Type: Private   *Employees here:* 7
SIC: 8051
  Owner & operator of skilled care nursing facilities and
    provides home health care
Dan Heiner, President

D-U-N-S 07-692-6542
UVALDE COUNTY HOSPITAL AUTH
1025 Garner Field Rd, Uvalde, TX 78801
Phone: (830) 278-6251
Sales: $29,284,000   *Employees:* 246
Company Type: Private   *Employees here:* 246
SIC: 8062
  General hospital
Ben Durr, Administrator

D-U-N-S 00-864-1474
UW MEDICAL FOUNDATION
329 W Washington Ave, Madison, WI 53703
Phone: (608) 252-8400
Sales: $76,000,000   *Employees:* NA
Company Type: Private   *Employees here:* 1,300
SIC: 8011
  Multi specialty medical group
Tom Blinn, Branch Manager

D-U-N-S 80-790-4362
US DIAGNOSTIC INC
777 S Flagler Dr, West Palm Beach, FL 33401
Phone: (561) 832-0006
Sales: $216,222,000   *Employees:* 1,700
Company Type: Public   *Employees here:* 75
SIC: 8071
  Medical services
Joseph A Paul, President

D-U-N-S 12-994-9418
US HEALTH MANAGEMENT CORP
  (Parent: Fonar Corporation)
110 Marcus Dr, Melville, NY 11747
Phone: (516) 694-2929
Sales: $30,000,000   *Employees:* 90
Company Type: Public Family Member   *Employees here:* 35
SIC: 8071
  Health management services
Timothy R Damadian, President

D-U-N-S 08-039-2483
VAIL CLINIC, INC
181 W Meadow Dr, Vail, CO 81657
Phone: (970) 476-2451

Sales: $43,006,000   *Employees:* 500
Company Type: Private   *Employees here:* 500
SIC: 8062
  Orthopedic hospital
Clifford Eldredge, Administrator

D-U-N-S 01-055-0085
VAL VERDE COUNTY HOSPITAL DST
801 N Bedell Ave, Del Rio, TX 78840
Phone: (830) 775-8566
Sales: $27,294,000   *Employees:* 341
Company Type: Private   *Employees here:* 341
SIC: 8062
  Hospital
Waylon Cowan, Chairman of the Board

D-U-N-S 07-905-4763
VALDESE GENERAL HOSPITAL INC
Hwy 1001, Valdese, NC 28690
Phone: (828) 874-2251
Sales: $27,673,000   *Employees:* 475
Company Type: Private   *Employees here:* 475
SIC: 8062
  Hospital
Lloyd Wallace, President

D-U-N-S 07-587-7076
VALDOST-LWNDES CNTY HOSPITAL AUTH
2501 N Patterson St, Valdosta, GA 31602
Phone: (912) 259-4160
Sales: $118,487,000   *Employees:* 1,800
Company Type: Private   *Employees here:* 1,800
SIC: 8062
  General hospital
John S Bowling, Chief Executive Officer

D-U-N-S 07-850-4446
VALLEY BAPTIST MEDICAL CENTER
2101 Pease St, Harlingen, TX 78550
Phone: (956) 389-1100
Sales: $173,996,000   *Employees:* 2,100
Company Type: Private   *Employees here:* 2,088
SIC: 8062
  General medical & surgical hospital
Ben Mckibbens, President

D-U-N-S 07-188-2450
VALLEY CHILDREN'S HOSPITAL
9300 Valley Childrens Pl, Madera, CA 93638
Phone: (209) 225-3000
Sales: $138,414,000   *Employees:* 1,800
Company Type: Private   *Employees here:* 1,500
SIC: 8069
  Children's hospital
J D Northway, President

D-U-N-S 06-668-5942
VALLEY COMMUNITY HOSPITAL
  (Parent: Tenet Healthcare Corporation)
505 Plaza Dr, Santa Maria, CA 93454
Phone: (805) 925-0935
Sales: $23,000,000   *Employees:* 300
Company Type: Public Family Member   *Employees here:* 280
SIC: 8062
  General hospital
William Rassmusen, Administrator

D-U-N-S 07-249-6912
VALLEY HEALTH SYSTEM
1117 E Devonshire Ave, Hemet, CA 92543
Phone: (909) 652-2811

Sales: $162,036,000	*Employees:* 2,000
Company Type: Private	*Employees here:* 1,200

SIC: 8062
 General hospitals
John L Dist, Chief Executive Officer

D-U-N-S 19-380-4747
VALLEY HEALTH SYSTEMS INC
20 Hospital Dr, Holyoke, MA 1040
Phone: (413) 534-2500

Sales: $63,000,000	*Employees:* 1,357
Company Type: Private	*Employees here:* 900

SIC: 8062
 Operates hospital extended care facilities home health
 services mental health clinic fundraising & manages
 endowments
Hank J Porten, President

D-U-N-S 78-127-4717
VALLEY HEALTH SYSTEMS LLC
 (Parent: Quorum Health Group Inc)
2075 E Flamingo Rd, Las Vegas, NV 89119
Phone: (702) 733-8800

Sales: $39,000,000	*Employees:* 850
Company Type: Public Family Member	*Employees here:* 850

SIC: 8062
 Hospital
John L Hummer, Chief Executive Officer

D-U-N-S 01-020-3628
VALLEY HOSPITAL ASSOCIATION
515 E Dahlia Ave, Palmer, AK 99645
Phone: (907) 352-2800

Sales: $20,600,000	*Employees:* 460
Company Type: Private	*Employees here:* 425

SIC: 8062
 General hospital & pharmacy
Clifton Orme, Chief Executive Officer

D-U-N-S 07-415-0830
VALLEY HOSPITAL MED CTR INC
 (Parent: Universal Health Services)
620 Shadow Ln, Las Vegas, NV 89106
Phone: (702) 388-4000

Sales: $62,700,000	*Employees:* 1,350
Company Type: Public Family Member	*Employees here:* 1,220

SIC: 8062
 General hospital
Roger Collins, Chief Executive Officer

D-U-N-S 17-730-4805
VALLEY MENTAL HEALTH
5965 S 900 E, Salt Lake City, UT 84121
Phone: (801) 263-7100

Sales: $55,114,000	*Employees:* 820
Company Type: Private	*Employees here:* 150

SIC: 8093
 Mental health service
Dr David E Dangerfield Md, Executive Director

D-U-N-S 07-294-0307
VALLEY PRESBYTERIAN HOSPITAL
15107 Vanowen St, Van Nuys, CA 91405
Phone: (818) 782-6600

Sales: $87,617,000	*Employees:* 1,100
Company Type: Private	*Employees here:* 1,100

SIC: 8062
 General hospital
Robert Bills, President

D-U-N-S 04-023-6002
VALLEY REGIONAL HOSPITAL INC
243 Elm St, Claremont, NH 3743

Phone: (603) 542-7771

Sales: $23,998,000	*Employees:* 480
Company Type: Private	*Employees here:* 472

SIC: 8062
 General medical & surgical hospital and outpatient
 laboratory and x-ray service
Donald R Holl, President

D-U-N-S 07-426-2536
VALLEY VIEW HOSPITAL AUTH
430 N Monte Vista St, Ada, OK 74820
Phone: (580) 332-2323

Sales: $46,757,000	*Employees:* 700
Company Type: Private	*Employees here:* 700

SIC: 8062
 General hospital
Philip Fisher, President

D-U-N-S 06-151-5904
VAN WERT COUNTY HOSPITAL ASSN
1250 S Washington St, Van Wert, OH 45891
Phone: (419) 238-2390

Sales: $21,945,000	*Employees:* 354
Company Type: Private	*Employees here:* 351

SIC: 8062
 General medical & surgical hospital
Mark Minick, President

D-U-N-S 05-360-3049
VANCOUVER CLINIC INC
700 NE 87th Ave, Vancouver, WA 98664
Phone: (360) 254-1240

Sales: $41,200,000	*Employees:* 600
Company Type: Private	*Employees here:* 500

SIC: 8011
 Medical clinic
Dr Thomas Kovaric Md, Chairman of the Board

D-U-N-S 87-805-5318
VANDERBILT STALLWORTH REHABILI
2201 Capers Ave, Nashville, TN 37212
Phone: (615) 963-4004

Sales: $28,000,000	*Employees:* 200
Company Type: Private	*Employees here:* 200

SIC: 8361
 Rehabilitation hospital
Mark Tarr, Administrator

D-U-N-S 78-968-2127
VANGUARD HEALTH SYSTEMS INC
5102 W Campbell Ave, Phoenix, AZ 85031
Phone: (602) 848-5557

Sales: $29,900,000	*Employees:* NA
Company Type: Private	*Employees here:* 700

SIC: 8062
 General hospital
Melvin Cunningham, Branch Manager

D-U-N-S 17-677-9056
VANGUARD HEALTH SYSTEMS INC
20 Burton Hills Blvd, Nashville, TN 37215
Phone: (615) 665-6021

Sales: $49,200,000	*Employees:* 715
Company Type: Private	*Employees here:* 15

SIC: 8011
 Healthcare management
Charles Martin Jr, President

D-U-N-S 10-689-7630
VANTAGE HEALTHCARE CORPORATION
 (Parent: Beverly Entrprises-Indiana Inc)
5111 Rogers Ave Ste 40a, Fort Smith, AR 72919
Phone: (501) 452-6712

Sales: $41,100,000   *Employees:* NA
Company Type: Public Family Member   *Employees here:* NA
SIC: 8051
   Skilled and intermediate nursing facilities
David R Banks, President

D-U-N-S 04-746-9051
VARIETY CHILDREN'S HOSPITAL
3100 SW 62nd Ave, Miami, FL 33155
Phone: (305) 666-6511
Sales: $183,209,000   *Employees:* 2,200
Company Type: Private   *Employees here:* 2,183
SIC: 8069
   Children's hospital
William A Mcdonald, President

D-U-N-S 08-046-7954
VASSAR BROS HOSPITAL
45 Reade Pl, Poughkeepsie, NY 12601
Phone: (914) 454-8500
Sales: $97,299,000   *Employees:* 1,200
Company Type: Private   *Employees here:* 1,200
SIC: 8062
   General hospital
Ronald T Mullahey, President

D-U-N-S 07-209-4030
VAUGHAN REGIONAL MEDICAL CTR
1050 W Dallas Ave, Selma, AL 36701
Phone: (334) 872-0411
Sales: $28,838,000   *Employees:* 529
Company Type: Private   *Employees here:* 504
SIC: 8062
   General hospital
Robert E Morrow, Chief Executive Officer

D-U-N-S 18-324-1678
VAUGHAN REGIONAL MEDICAL CTR
1050 W Dallas Ave, Selma, AL 36701
Phone: (334) 872-2000
Sales: $28,838,000   *Employees:* 600
Company Type: Private   *Employees here:* 600
SIC: 8099
   Health/allied services
Jerry Horne, President

D-U-N-S 87-425-2992
VENCARE KENTUCKY, INC
   (Parent: Vencor Inc)
400 W Market St Ste 3300, Louisville, KY 40202
Phone: (502) 569-7300
Sales: $44,300,000   *Employees:* 900
Company Type: Private   *Employees here:* 82
SIC: 8069
   Specialty hospital
W B Lunsford, Chief Executive Officer

D-U-N-S 92-643-6775
VENCARE KENTUCKY, INC
601 S Carlin Springs Rd, Arlington, VA 22204
Phone: (703) 671-1200
Sales: $27,300,000   *Employees:* NA
Company Type: Private   *Employees here:* 582
SIC: 8069
   Hospital
Robert Davis, President

D-U-N-S 88-494-1253
VENCOR HOSPITAL EAST, INC
   (Parent: Vencor Inc)
3300 Aegon Ctr, Louisville, KY 40202
Phone: (502) 569-7300

Sales: $29,400,000   *Employees:* 600
Company Type: Private   *Employees here:* 180
SIC: 8069
   Specialty hospital
W B Lumsford, Chief Executive Officer

D-U-N-S 94-408-4664
VENCOR HOSPITAL EAST, INC
601 S Carlin Springs Rd, Arlington, VA 22204
Phone: (703) 671-1200
Sales: $32,800,000   *Employees:* NA
Company Type: Private   *Employees here:* 750
SIC: 8062
   Acute care hospital
Patricia Knoble, Chief Operating Officer

D-U-N-S 79-447-5707
VENCOR, INC
2800 Benedict Dr, San Leandro, CA 94577
Phone: (510) 357-8300
Sales: $31,800,000   *Employees:* NA
Company Type: Private   *Employees here:* 650
SIC: 8062
   General hospital

D-U-N-S 55-660-5095
VENCOR, INC
223 Fargo Way, Folsom, CA 95630
Phone: (916) 351-9151
Sales: $36,900,000   *Employees:* NA
Company Type: Private   *Employees here:* 750
SIC: 8062
   General hospital
Meridith Taylor, N/A

D-U-N-S 00-347-1492
VENCOR, INC
619 Northside Dr, Griffin, GA 30223
Phone: (770) 233-9228
Sales: $30,400,000   *Employees:* NA
Company Type: Private   *Employees here:* 750
SIC: 8062
   General hospital
Indu Dey, Branch Manager

D-U-N-S 87-645-7409
VENCOR, INC
1700 W 10th St, Indianapolis, IN 46222
Phone: (317) 636-4400
Sales: $29,200,000   *Employees:* NA
Company Type: Private   *Employees here:* 650
SIC: 8069
   Hospital
George Burkley, Branch Manager

D-U-N-S 13-153-0511
VENCOR, INC
400 W Market St Ste 3300, Louisville, KY 40202
Phone: (502) 569-7300
Sales: $3,116,004,000   *Employees:* 76,800
Company Type: Private   *Employees here:* 50
SIC: 8062
   Operates long-term acute care hospitals nursing centers &
     provides respiratory & rehabilitation therapies & medical
     management
Edward L Kuntz, President

D-U-N-S 12-994-2645
VENCOR, INC
2700 Martin Luther King, Detroit, MI 48208
Phone: (313) 361-8000

Sales: $22,800,000   *Employees:* NA
Company Type: Private   *Employees here:* 549
SIC: 8062
  Hospital
Dan Epley, Branch Manager

D-U-N-S 82-677-5637
VENCOR, INC
2401 S Side Blvd, Greensboro, NC 27406
Phone: (336) 271-2800
Sales: $32,800,000   *Employees:* NA
Company Type: Private   *Employees here:* 750
SIC: 8062
  General hospital
James Vroom, N/A

D-U-N-S 80-196-2226
VENCOR, INC
709 Walnut St, Chattanooga, TN 37402
Phone: (423) 266-7721
Sales: $31,400,000   *Employees:* NA
Company Type: Private   *Employees here:* 750
SIC: 8062
  General hospital
Marvin Stern, Administrator

D-U-N-S 96-354-2774
VENCOR, INC
1004 Seymour St, Pasadena, TX 77506
Phone: (713) 473-9700
Sales: $41,800,000   *Employees:* NA
Company Type: Private   *Employees here:* 950
SIC: 8069
  Hospital/long term acute care
Susan Legg, Branch Manager

D-U-N-S 07-531-3031
VERDUGO HILLS HOSPITAL
1812 Verdugo Blvd, Glendale, CA 91208
Phone: (818) 790-7100
Sales: $45,011,000   *Employees:* 450
Company Type: Private   *Employees here:* 446
SIC: 8062
  General hospital
Bernard Glossy, President

D-U-N-S 61-065-4477
VERNON HOME HEALTH CARE AGENCY
  (Parent: Outreach Health Care Inc)
2660 S Garland Ave, Garland, TX 75041
Phone: (972) 840-3401
Sales: $30,500,000   *Employees:* 1,000
Company Type: Private   *Employees here:* 20
SIC: 8093
  Outpatient health care physical therapy & home health care
William E Ball, President

D-U-N-S 08-138-9603
VETERANS ADM MED CTR
3701 Loop Rd, Tuscaloosa, AL 35404
Phone: (205) 554-2000
Sales: $62,000,000   *Employees:* 950
Company Type: Private   *Employees here:* 945
SIC: 8062
  Government hospital and nursing home
W K Ruyle, Director

D-U-N-S 04-313-1564
VETERANS AFFAIRS US DEPT
Fort Roots, North Little Rock, AR 72114
Phone: (501) 661-1202

Sales: $124,400,000   *Employees:* NA
Company Type: Private   *Employees here:* 3,000
SIC: 8062
  General hospital
George H Gray Jr, Branch Manager

D-U-N-S 19-688-3938
VETERANS AFFAIRS US DEPT
555 Willard Ave, Newington, CT 6111
Phone: (860) 666-6951
Sales: $24,200,000   *Employees:* NA
Company Type: Private   *Employees here:* 489
SIC: 8062
  General hospital
Vincent Ng, Director

D-U-N-S 82-483-5805
VETERANS AFFAIRS US DEPT
1670 Clairmont Rd, Decatur, GA 30033
Phone: (404) 728-4826
Sales: $88,500,000   *Employees:* NA
Company Type: Private   *Employees here:* 2,000
SIC: 8062
  General hospital administrative veterans' affairs
Perrault, President

D-U-N-S 87-644-2062
VETERANS AFFAIRS US DEPT
510 E Stoner Ave Rm 1w50, Shreveport, LA 71101
Phone: (318) 424-6084
Sales: $37,000,000   *Employees:* NA
Company Type: Private   *Employees here:* 900
SIC: 8062
  General hospital
Michael Hamilton, Partner

D-U-N-S 09-808-6937
VETERANS AFFAIRS US DEPT
1000 Locust St, Reno, NV 89520
Phone: (702) 786-7200
Sales: $27,000,000   *Employees:* NA
Company Type: Private   *Employees here:* 633
SIC: 8062
  General hospital administrative veterans' affairs
Gary Whitfield, Branch Manager

D-U-N-S 08-668-3091
VETERANS AFFAIRS US DEPT
2500 Overlook Ter, Madison, WI 53705
Phone: (608) 256-1901
Sales: $50,700,000   *Employees:* NA
Company Type: Private   *Employees here:* 1,200
SIC: 8062
  General hospital
Nathan L Geraths, Branch Manager

D-U-N-S 80-624-8381
VETERANS AFFAIRS US DEPT
2500 Overlook Ter, Madison, WI 53705
Phone: (608) 262-7062
Sales: $33,500,000   *Employees:* NA
Company Type: Private   *Employees here:* 800
SIC: 8062
  General hospital
Nathan Geraths, Branch Manager

D-U-N-S 62-806-7456
VETERANS HEALTH ADMINISTRATION
650 E Indian School Rd, Phoenix, AZ 85012
Phone: (602) 222-6408

Sales: $64,900,000
Company Type: Private
SIC: 8062
  General hospital
John R Fears, Manager
Employees: NA
Employees here: 1,500

Sales: $199,000,000
Company Type: Private
SIC: 8062
  Veterans hospital
Kenneth J Clark, Branch Manager
Employees: NA
Employees here: 4,000

D-U-N-S 10-600-3254
VETERANS HEALTH ADMINISTRATION
16111 Plummer St, Sepulveda, CA 91343
Phone: (818) 891-7711
Sales: $44,400,000
Company Type: Private
SIC: 8062
  Veterans medical center
Dolly G Whitehead, Manager
Employees: NA
Employees here: 900

D-U-N-S 61-816-7670
VETERANS HEALTH ADMINISTRATION
Willshire Sawtelle Blvds, Los Angeles, CA 90073
Phone: (310) 478-3711
Sales: $99,500,000
Company Type: Private
SIC: 8062
  General hospital
William K Anderson, N/A
Employees: NA
Employees here: 2,000

D-U-N-S 07-876-3885
VETERANS HEALTH ADMINISTRATION
4150 Clement St, San Francisco, CA 94121
Phone: (415) 221-4810
Sales: $99,500,000
Company Type: Private
SIC: 8062
  General hospital
Lawrence Stewart, N/A
Employees: NA
Employees here: 2,000

D-U-N-S 09-444-7042
VETERANS HEALTH ADMINISTRATION
5901 E 7th St, Long Beach, CA 90822
Phone: (562) 494-5441
Sales: $174,100,000
Company Type: Private
SIC: 8062
  General hospital administrative public health programs
Jerry Boyb, N/A
Employees: NA
Employees here: 3,500

D-U-N-S 07-335-8855
VETERANS HEALTH ADMINISTRATION
3350 La Jolla Village Dr, San Diego, CA 92161
Phone: (619) 552-8585
Sales: $24,300,000
Company Type: Private
SIC: 8062
  General hospital
Thomas A Trujillo, N/A
Employees: NA
Employees here: 500

D-U-N-S 61-272-9343
VETERANS HEALTH ADMINISTRATION
4951 Arroyo Rd, Livermore, CA 94550
Phone: (925) 447-2560
Sales: $21,700,000
Company Type: Private
SIC: 8062
  Veterans medical center
C H Nixon, Director
Employees: NA
Employees here: 450

D-U-N-S 04-601-7455
VETERANS HEALTH ADMINISTRATION
3801 Miranda Ave, Palo Alto, CA 94304
Phone: (650) 493-5000
Sales: $174,100,000
Company Type: Private
SIC: 8062
  Veterans medical center
James Goff, N/A
Employees: NA
Employees here: 3,500

D-U-N-S 03-311-9686
VETERANS HEALTH ADMINISTRATION
2615 E Clinton Ave, Fresno, CA 93703
Phone: (209) 225-6100
Sales: $42,200,000
Company Type: Private
SIC: 8069
  Medical hospital
Wayne C Tippets, N/A
Employees: NA
Employees here: 800

D-U-N-S 93-365-8478
VETERANS HEALTH ADMINISTRATION
16111 Plummer St Bldg 2, North Hills, CA 91343
Phone: (818) 895-9385
Sales: $34,300,000
Company Type: Private
SIC: 8062
  General hospital
Dr Jule D Moravec Md, Branch Manager
Employees: NA
Employees here: 700

D-U-N-S 08-515-0811
VETERANS HEALTH ADMINISTRATION
Edge Of Town, Fort Lyon, CO 81038
Phone: (719) 384-3100
Sales: $23,700,000
Company Type: Private
SIC: 8062
  General hospital
W D Smith, President
Employees: NA
Employees here: 600

D-U-N-S 08-723-1122
VETERANS HEALTH ADMINISTRATION
150 Muir Rd, Martinez, CA 94553
Phone: (925) 372-2179
Sales: $67,000,000
Company Type: Private
SIC: 8011
  Medical clinic
Hildiko Sanderford, N/A
Employees: NA
Employees here: 1,137

D-U-N-S 03-962-4291
VETERANS HEALTH ADMINISTRATION
950 Campbell Ave, West Haven, CT 6516
Phone: (203) 932-5711
Sales: $76,000,000
Company Type: Private
SIC: 8062
  General hospital
Norman E Browne, N/A
Employees: NA
Employees here: 1,500

D-U-N-S 06-668-9118
VETERANS HEALTH ADMINISTRATION
Wilshire & Sawtelle Blvd, Los Angeles, CA 90073
Phone: (310) 478-3711

D-U-N-S 19-743-0788
VETERANS HEALTH ADMINISTRATION
W Spring St, West Haven, CT 6516
Phone: (203) 932-5711

Sales: $101,500,000   *Employees:* NA
Company Type: Private   *Employees here:* 2,000
SIC: 8062
  Medical center
Vincent Ng, Branch Manager

D-U-N-S 02-181-5089
VETERANS HEALTH ADMINISTRATION
555 Willard Ave, Newington, CT 6111
Phone: (860) 666-6951
Sales: $35,000,000   *Employees:* NA
Company Type: Private   *Employees here:* 700
SIC: 8062
  Veterans medical center
Charlene R Szabl, N/A

D-U-N-S 09-685-4286
VETERANS HEALTH ADMINISTRATION
1601 Kirkwood Hwy, Wilmington, DE 19805
Phone: (302) 994-2511
Sales: $21,600,000   *Employees:* NA
Company Type: Private   *Employees here:* 500
SIC: 8062
  Veterans medical center
Dexter Dix, Director

D-U-N-S 78-324-7851
VETERANS HEALTH ADMINISTRATION
13000 Bruce D Downs Blvd, Tampa, FL 33612
Phone: (813) 972-6011
Sales: $110,700,000   *Employees:* NA
Company Type: Private   *Employees here:* 2,500
SIC: 8062
  General hospital
Richard A Silver, Branch Manager

D-U-N-S 80-793-1472
VETERANS HEALTH ADMINISTRATION
7305 N Military Trl, Palm Beach Gardens, FL 33410
Phone: (561) 882-8262
Sales: $61,800,000   *Employees:* NA
Company Type: Private   *Employees here:* 1,400
SIC: 8062
  Veterans medical center
Richard Issacs, Branch Manager

D-U-N-S 07-603-8751
VETERANS HEALTH ADMINISTRATION
1201 NW 16th St, Miami, FL 33125
Phone: (305) 324-4455
Sales: $124,000,000   *Employees:* NA
Company Type: Private   *Employees here:* 2,800
SIC: 8062
  General hospital
Thomas Doherty, Branch Manager

D-U-N-S 07-086-6512
VETERANS HEALTH ADMINISTRATION
801 S Marion St, Lake City, FL 32025
Phone: (904) 755-3016
Sales: $32,700,000   *Employees:* NA
Company Type: Private   *Employees here:* 806
SIC: 8062
  Veterans hospital
Genie Norman, Director

D-U-N-S 09-737-8632
VETERANS HEALTH ADMINISTRATION
1601 SW Archer Rd, Gainesville, FL 32608
Phone: (352) 376-1611

Sales: $68,800,000   *Employees:* NA
Company Type: Private   *Employees here:* 1,557
SIC: 8062
  Veterans hospital
Malcolm Randall, Director

D-U-N-S 78-169-2777
VETERANS HEALTH ADMINISTRATION
10000 Bay Pines Blvd, Bay Pines, FL 33744
Phone: (727) 398-6661
Sales: $97,400,000   *Employees:* NA
Company Type: Private   *Employees here:* 2,200
SIC: 8062
  In-patient and out-patient veterans hospital
Tom Weaver, Director

D-U-N-S 02-808-4333
VETERANS HEALTH ADMINISTRATION
Hwy 6 W, Iowa City, IA 52246
Phone: (319) 338-0581
Sales: $50,300,000   *Employees:* NA
Company Type: Private   *Employees here:* 1,306
SIC: 8062
  General hospital administrative veterans' affairs
Gary L Wilkinson, N/A

D-U-N-S 88-317-5820
VETERANS HEALTH ADMINISTRATION
500 W Fort St, Boise, ID 83702
Phone: (208) 336-5100
Sales: $22,500,000   *Employees:* NA
Company Type: Private   *Employees here:* 530
SIC: 8062
  Veterans medical center
Wayne Tippett, Branch Manager

D-U-N-S 07-385-9456
VETERANS HEALTH ADMINISTRATION
1707 N 12th St, Quincy, IL 62301
Phone: (217) 222-8641
Sales: $24,000,000   *Employees:* NA
Company Type: Private   *Employees here:* 438
SIC: 8011
  Clinic
Donald Lynn, Principal

D-U-N-S 02-143-9963
VETERANS HEALTH ADMINISTRATION
3001 Greenbay Rd, North Chicago, IL 60064
Phone: (847) 688-1900
Sales: $84,800,000   *Employees:* NA
Company Type: Private   *Employees here:* 2,000
SIC: 8062
  Veterans medical center
Alfred Pate, Director

D-U-N-S 06-744-5429
VETERANS HEALTH ADMINISTRATION
5th Ave & Roosevelt Rd, Hines, IL 60141
Phone: (708) 343-7200
Sales: $127,200,000   *Employees:* NA
Company Type: Private   *Employees here:* 3,000
SIC: 8062
  Veterans hospital
John Denardo, Director

D-U-N-S 06-085-5640
VETERANS HEALTH ADMINISTRATION
1900 E Main St, Danville, IL 61832
Phone: (217) 442-8000

Sales: $54,900,000
Company Type: Private
SIC: 8062
    Veterans medical center
James S Jones, Director
Employees: NA
Employees here: 1,400

D-U-N-S 01-029-9204
VETERANS HEALTH ADMINISTRATION
820 S Damen Ave, Chicago, IL 60612
Phone: (312) 666-6500
Sales: $84,800,000
Company Type: Private
SIC: 8062
    Medical center
John Denardo, N/A
Employees: NA
Employees here: 2,000

D-U-N-S 09-646-9283
VETERANS HEALTH ADMINISTRATION
333 E Huron St, Chicago, IL 60611
Phone: (312) 943-6600
Sales: $50,700,000
Company Type: Private
SIC: 8062
    Medical center
Joseph Moore, Director
Employees: NA
Employees here: 1,200

D-U-N-S 17-215-3306
VETERANS HEALTH ADMINISTRATION
1700 E 38th St, Marion, IN 46953
Phone: (765) 674-3321
Sales: $39,000,000
Company Type: Private
SIC: 8062
    Veterans medical center
Micheal Murphy, Director
Employees: NA
Employees here: 1,000

D-U-N-S 04-543-3737
VETERANS HEALTH ADMINISTRATION
5500 E Kellogg Dr, Wichita, KS 67218
Phone: (316) 685-2221
Sales: $28,500,000
Company Type: Private
SIC: 8062
    Veterans medical center
Gary Campbell, Director
Employees: NA
Employees here: 694

D-U-N-S 01-066-1569
VETERANS HEALTH ADMINISTRATION
4101 S 4th St, Leavenworth, KS 66048
Phone: (913) 682-2000
Sales: $38,400,000
Company Type: Private
SIC: 8062
    Veterans medical center
Carole Smith, Director
Employees: NA
Employees here: 1,000

D-U-N-S 08-676-5245
VETERANS HEALTH ADMINISTRATION
800 Zorn Ave, Louisville, KY 40206
Phone: (502) 895-3401
Sales: $42,100,000
Company Type: Private
SIC: 8062
    Veterans medical hospital
Robert B Wimmer, Branch Manager
Employees: NA
Employees here: 1,000

D-U-N-S 03-845-8964
VETERANS HEALTH ADMINISTRATION
510 E Stoner Ave, Shreveport, LA 71101
Phone: (318) 221-8411

Sales: $37,000,000
Company Type: Private
SIC: 8062
    Veterans medical center
Michael Hamilton, N/A
Employees: NA
Employees here: 900

D-U-N-S 07-921-9093
VETERANS HEALTH ADMINISTRATION
421 Main Rd, Easthampton, MA 1027
Phone: (413) 584-4040
Sales: $35,000,000
Company Type: Private
SIC: 8062
    Veterans medical center
Bruce Gordon, Director
Employees: NA
Employees here: 700

D-U-N-S 09-587-2032
VETERANS HEALTH ADMINISTRATION
940 Belmont St, Brockton, MA 2301
Phone: (508) 583-4500
Sales: $70,900,000
Company Type: Private
SIC: 8062
    Veterans medical center
Michael Lawson, N/A
Employees: NA
Employees here: 1,400

D-U-N-S 08-561-1036
VETERANS HEALTH ADMINISTRATION
1400 V F W Pkwy, Boston, MA 2132
Phone: (617) 323-7700
Sales: $53,000,000
Company Type: Private
SIC: 8062
    Veterans medical center
William H Kelleher, Branch Manager
Employees: NA
Employees here: 1,050

D-U-N-S 08-004-2336
VETERANS HEALTH ADMINISTRATION
200 Springs Rd, Bedford, MA 1730
Phone: (781) 275-7500
Sales: $70,900,000
Company Type: Private
SIC: 8062
    Veterans medical center
William Conte, N/A
Employees: NA
Employees here: 1,400

D-U-N-S 08-054-5684
VETERANS HEALTH ADMINISTRATION
Off U S Rt 40, Perry Point, MD 21902
Phone: (410) 642-2411
Sales: $20,000,000
Company Type: Private
SIC: 8062
    Veterans medical center
Ruford Kingsley, Branch Manager
Employees: NA
Employees here: 500

D-U-N-S 07-313-0106
VETERANS HEALTH ADMINISTRATION
10 N Green St, Baltimore, MD 21201
Phone: (410) 605-7000
Sales: $52,900,000
Company Type: Private
SIC: 8062
    Veterans medical center
Dennis H Smith, N/A
Employees: NA
Employees here: 1,200

D-U-N-S 61-485-5054
VETERANS HEALTH ADMINISTRATION
9600 North Pt, Baltimore, MD 21202
Phone: (410) 477-1800

Sales: $20,200,000
Company Type: Private
SIC: 8062
   Veterans medical center
Charles Clark, Director
Employees: NA
Employees here: 470

D-U-N-S 03-771-9846
VETERANS HEALTH ADMINISTRATION
1 Va Ctr, Augusta, ME 4330
Phone: (207) 633-8411
Sales: $50,400,000
Company Type: Private
SIC: 8062
   Veterans medical center
John H Sims, Director
Employees: NA
Employees here: 1,000

D-U-N-S 10-675-5440
VETERANS HEALTH ADMINISTRATION
5500 Armstrong Rd, Battle Creek, MI 49015
Phone: (616) 966-5600
Sales: $63,500,000
Company Type: Private
SIC: 8062
   Veterans medical center
Employees: NA
Employees here: 1,500

D-U-N-S 09-631-8480
VETERANS HEALTH ADMINISTRATION
2215 Fuller Rd, Ann Arbor, MI 48105
Phone: (734) 769-7100
Sales: $74,100,000
Company Type: Private
SIC: 8062
   Veterans medical center
Edward L Gamache, N/A
Employees: NA
Employees here: 1,750

D-U-N-S 12-001-9948
VETERANS HEALTH ADMINISTRATION
4801 8th St N, Saint Cloud, MN 56303
Phone: (320) 252-1670
Sales: $20,300,000
Company Type: Private
SIC: 8062
   Veterans center
Barry Ball, Director
Employees: NA
Employees here: 500

D-U-N-S 07-177-4624
VETERANS HEALTH ADMINISTRATION
1 Veterans Dr, Minneapolis, MN 55417
Phone: (612) 725-2000
Sales: $104,200,000
Company Type: Private
SIC: 8062
   Medical center
Charles Milbrandt, Branch Manager
Employees: NA
Employees here: 2,500

D-U-N-S 07-991-0964
VETERANS HEALTH ADMINISTRATION
Jefferson Barracks Dv, Saint Louis, MO 63125
Phone: (314) 487-0400
Sales: $93,300,000
Company Type: Private
SIC: 8062
   Veterans hospital
Donald Ziegenhorn, Branch Manager
Employees: NA
Employees here: 2,200

D-U-N-S 07-303-4399
VETERANS HEALTH ADMINISTRATION
4801 E Linwood Blvd, Kansas City, MO 64128
Phone: (816) 861-4700

Sales: $63,500,000
Company Type: Private
SIC: 8062
   Medical center
Hugh Doran, N/A
Employees: NA
Employees here: 1,500

D-U-N-S 08-226-3013
VETERANS HEALTH ADMINISTRATION
800 Hospital Dr, Columbia, MO 65201
Phone: (573) 443-2511
Sales: $42,100,000
Company Type: Private
SIC: 8062
   Veterans hospital
John Brinkers, Administration
Employees: NA
Employees here: 1,000

D-U-N-S 06-940-0638
VETERANS HEALTH ADMINISTRATION
400 Veterans Ave, Biloxi, MS 39531
Phone: (228) 388-5541
Sales: $58,200,000
Company Type: Private
SIC: 8062
   Medical center
J H Caldwell, Branch Manager
Employees: NA
Employees here: 1,400

D-U-N-S 09-546-5217
VETERANS HEALTH ADMINISTRATION
1601 Brenner Ave, Salisbury, NC 28144
Phone: (704) 638-9000
Sales: $59,600,000
Company Type: Private
SIC: 8062
   Medical center
R E Konik, N/A
Employees: NA
Employees here: 1,350

D-U-N-S 08-632-1551
VETERANS HEALTH ADMINISTRATION
2300 Ramsey St, Fayetteville, NC 28301
Phone: (910) 822-7059
Sales: $32,800,000
Company Type: Private
SIC: 8062
   Medical center
Richard Baltz, Administration
Employees: NA
Employees here: 750

D-U-N-S 04-324-1082
VETERANS HEALTH ADMINISTRATION
508 Fulton St, Durham, NC 27705
Phone: (919) 286-0411
Sales: $61,800,000
Company Type: Private
SIC: 8062
   Medical center
Barbara Small, N/A
Employees: NA
Employees here: 1,400

D-U-N-S 07-906-1172
VETERANS HEALTH ADMINISTRATION
1100 Tunnel Rd, Asheville, NC 28805
Phone: (828) 298-7911
Sales: $47,000,000
Company Type: Private
SIC: 8062
   Veterans medical center
James Christian, N/A
Employees: NA
Employees here: 1,068

D-U-N-S 05-095-2118
VETERANS HEALTH ADMINISTRATION
2101 Elm St, Fargo, ND 58102
Phone: (701) 232-3241

Sales: $26,700,000
Company Type: Private
SIC: 8062
   Medical center
Dr Ned B Nichols, Administration
             Employees: NA
Employees here: 700

    D-U-N-S 79-513-9237
VETERANS HEALTH ADMINISTRATION
718 Smyth Rd, Manchester, NH 3104
Phone: (603) 624-4366
Sales: $30,400,000   *Employees:* NA
Company Type: Private   *Employees here:* 610
SIC: 8062
   Medical center
Eugene Ochocki, Executive Director

    D-U-N-S 07-041-7068
VETERANS HEALTH ADMINISTRATION
Knollcraft & Valley Rd, Lyons, NJ 7939
Phone: (908) 647-0180
Sales: $24,300,000   *Employees:* NA
Company Type: Private   *Employees here:* 500
SIC: 8062
   General hospital
Paul Kidd, Branch Manager

    D-U-N-S 08-728-6308
VETERANS HEALTH ADMINISTRATION
385 Tremont Ave, East Orange, NJ 7018
Phone: (973) 676-1000
Sales: $99,500,000   *Employees:* NA
Company Type: Private   *Employees here:* 2,000
SIC: 8062
   Veterans hospital
Kenneth H Mizrach, Director

    D-U-N-S 09-413-7247
VETERANS HEALTH ADMINISTRATION
2100 Ridgecrest Dr SE, Albuquerque, NM 87108
Phone: (505) 265-1711
Sales: $60,600,000   *Employees:* NA
Company Type: Private   *Employees here:* 1,400
SIC: 8062
   Medical center
R M Harwell, Director

    D-U-N-S 03-835-9592
VETERANS HEALTH ADMINISTRATION
800 Irving Ave, Syracuse, NY 13210
Phone: (315) 476-7461
Sales: $64,500,000   *Employees:* NA
Company Type: Private   *Employees here:* 1,300
SIC: 8062
   Medical center
Philip P Thomas, Branch Manager

    D-U-N-S 00-820-9124
VETERANS HEALTH ADMINISTRATION
79 Middleville Rd, Northport, NY 11768
Phone: (516) 261-4400
Sales: $89,500,000   *Employees:* NA
Company Type: Private   *Employees here:* 1,800
SIC: 8062
   Medical center
Alice Wood, N/A

    D-U-N-S 07-050-1002
VETERANS HEALTH ADMINISTRATION
423 E 23rd St, New York, NY 10010
Phone: (212) 686-7500

Sales: $94,500,000   *Employees:* NA
Company Type: Private   *Employees here:* 1,900
SIC: 8062
   General hospital
John J Donnellan Jr, N/A

    D-U-N-S 13-549-5604
VETERANS HEALTH ADMINISTRATION
Rr Box 9a, Montrose, NY 10548
Phone: (914) 737-4400
Sales: $72,000,000   *Employees:* NA
Company Type: Private   *Employees here:* 1,450
SIC: 8062
   Veterans hospital
L J Kauper, Administrator

    D-U-N-S 07-368-9341
VETERANS HEALTH ADMINISTRATION
400 Fort Hill Ave, Canandaigua, NY 14424
Phone: (716) 394-2000
Sales: $55,100,000   *Employees:* NA
Company Type: Private   *Employees here:* 1,200
SIC: 8062
   Medical & surgical hospital
Stewart Collier, N/A

    D-U-N-S 07-400-4540
VETERANS HEALTH ADMINISTRATION
3495 Bailey Ave, Buffalo, NY 14215
Phone: (716) 834-9200
Sales: $89,500,000   *Employees:* NA
Company Type: Private   *Employees here:* 1,800
SIC: 8062
   Veterans medical center
Richard S Droske, N/A

    D-U-N-S 04-007-7133
VETERANS HEALTH ADMINISTRATION
130 W Kingsbridge Rd, Bronx, NY 10468
Phone: (718) 584-9000
Sales: $99,500,000   *Employees:* NA
Company Type: Private   *Employees here:* 2,000
SIC: 8062
   Medical center
Donald Colston, Branch Manager

    D-U-N-S 09-968-5570
VETERANS HEALTH ADMINISTRATION
113 Holland Ave, Albany, NY 12208
Phone: (518) 462-3311
Sales: $74,500,000   *Employees:* NA
Company Type: Private   *Employees here:* 1,500
SIC: 8062
   Medical center
Fredrick Malphurs, N/A

    D-U-N-S 07-469-5115
VETERANS HEALTH ADMINISTRATION
4100 W 3rd St, Dayton, OH 45417
Phone: (937) 268-6511
Sales: $89,000,000   *Employees:* NA
Company Type: Private   *Employees here:* 2,100
SIC: 8062
   Va hospital
Edgar Thorsland, N/A

    D-U-N-S 02-064-2948
VETERANS HEALTH ADMINISTRATION
10000 Brecksville Rd, Cleveland, OH 44141
Phone: (440) 526-3030

Sales: $57,100,000
Company Type: Private
SIC: 8062
   Medical center
Krista Ludenia, N/A

    Employees: NA
    Employees here: 1,350

Sales: $27,800,000
Company Type: Private
SIC: 8062
   General hospital administrative veterans' affairs
Allan Perry, Director

    Employees: NA
    Employees here: 613

D-U-N-S 09-162-3280
VETERANS HEALTH ADMINISTRATION
10701 East Blvd, Cleveland, OH 44106
Phone: (216) 791-3800
Sales: $57,100,000
Company Type: Private
SIC: 8062
   Veterans medical center
Christa Loudinia, N/A

    Employees: NA
    Employees here: 1,350

D-U-N-S 08-946-1255
VETERANS HEALTH ADMINISTRATION
3710 SW US Veterans Hospital, Portland, OR 97201
Phone: (503) 220-8262
Sales: $124,400,000
Company Type: Private
SIC: 8062
   Medical center
Ted Gailey, Branch Manager

    Employees: NA
    Employees here: 2,500

D-U-N-S 08-475-8143
VETERANS HEALTH ADMINISTRATION
3200 Vine St, Cincinnati, OH 45220
Phone: (513) 861-3100
Sales: $29,300,000
Company Type: Private
SIC: 8062
   Medical center
John T Carson, Branch Manager

    Employees: NA
    Employees here: 700

D-U-N-S 13-075-5341
VETERANS HEALTH ADMINISTRATION
1111 E End Blvd, Wilkes Barre, PA 18711
Phone: (717) 824-3521
Sales: $74,500,000
Company Type: Private
SIC: 8062
   Veterans hospital
Reedes Hurt, Principal

    Employees: NA
    Employees here: 1,500

D-U-N-S 08-130-7191
VETERANS HEALTH ADMINISTRATION
17273 State Route 104, Chillicothe, OH 45601
Phone: (740) 773-1141
Sales: $50,900,000
Company Type: Private
SIC: 8062
   Medical center
Troy E Page, N/A

    Employees: NA
    Employees here: 1,300

D-U-N-S 07-160-9291
VETERANS HEALTH ADMINISTRATION
Woodland & University Ave, Philadelphia, PA 19104
Phone: (215) 383-2400
Sales: $124,400,000
Company Type: Private
SIC: 8062
   Veterans medical center
William Stott, N/A

    Employees: NA
    Employees here: 2,500

D-U-N-S 80-164-3891
VETERANS HEALTH ADMINISTRATION
17273 State Route 104, Chillicothe, OH 45601
Phone: (740) 772-7015
Sales: $47,000,000
Company Type: Private
SIC: 8062
   General medical and surgical hospitals
Michael Walton, Director

    Employees: NA
    Employees here: 1,200

D-U-N-S 07-283-0664
VETERANS HEALTH ADMINISTRATION
1700 S Lincoln Ave, Lebanon, PA 17042
Phone: (717) 272-6621
Sales: $60,600,000
Company Type: Private
SIC: 8062
   Veterans hospital
Leonard Washington Jr, Administration

    Employees: NA
    Employees here: 1,222

D-U-N-S 02-071-9316
VETERANS HEALTH ADMINISTRATION
921 NE 13th St, Oklahoma City, OK 73104
Phone: (405) 270-0501
Sales: $57,900,000
Company Type: Private
SIC: 8062
   Veterans medical center
Steven J Gentling, Branch Manager

    Employees: NA
    Employees here: 1,400

D-U-N-S 07-709-3565
VETERANS HEALTH ADMINISTRATION
1400 Blackhorse Hill Rd, Coatesville, PA 19320
Phone: (610) 384-7711
Sales: $69,500,000
Company Type: Private
SIC: 8062
   Medical center
Gary W Devansky, N/A

    Employees: NA
    Employees here: 1,400

D-U-N-S 15-613-8083
VETERANS HEALTH ADMINISTRATION
1011 Honor Heights Dr, Muskogee, OK 74401
Phone: (918) 683-3261
Sales: $26,500,000
Company Type: Private
SIC: 8062
   Medical center
Dale Valentine, Branch Manager

    Employees: NA
    Employees here: 700

D-U-N-S 03-960-6165
VETERANS HEALTH ADMINISTRATION
325 New Castle Rd, Butler, PA 16001
Phone: (724) 287-4781
Sales: $31,800,000
Company Type: Private
SIC: 8062
   Veterans medical center
Michael Moreland, Director

    Employees: NA
    Employees here: 650

D-U-N-S 09-830-2391
VETERANS HEALTH ADMINISTRATION
913 NW Garden Valley Blvd, Roseburg, OR 97470
Phone: (541) 440-1000

D-U-N-S 11-952-7802
VETERANS HEALTH ADMINISTRATION
2907 Pleasant Valley Blvd, Altoona, PA 16602
Phone: (814) 943-8164

Sales: $24,300,000   *Employees:* NA
Company Type: Private   *Employees here:* 500
SIC: 8062
  Medical center
Linda Crookshank, Branch Manager

D-U-N-S 04-010-0786
VETERANS HEALTH ADMINISTRATION
830 Chalkstone Ave, Providence, RI 2908
Phone: (401) 273-7100
Sales: $50,400,000   *Employees:* NA
Company Type: Private   *Employees here:* 1,000
SIC: 8062
  General hospital
Edward H Seiler, N/A

D-U-N-S 03-980-7318
VETERANS HEALTH ADMINISTRATION
109 Bee St, Charleston, SC 29401
Phone: (843) 577-5011
Sales: $44,000,000   *Employees:* NA
Company Type: Private   *Employees here:* 1,000
SIC: 8062
  Substance abuse alcohol & detoxification outpatient clinic
Bryon Adinoff, M D

D-U-N-S 92-910-7647
VETERANS HEALTH ADMINISTRATION
2501 W 22nd St, Sioux Falls, SD 57105
Phone: (605) 336-3230
Sales: $26,200,000   *Employees:* NA
Company Type: Private   *Employees here:* 640
SIC: 8062
  Hospital
Vincent Crawford, Director

D-U-N-S 10-706-5088
VETERANS HEALTH ADMINISTRATION
1310 24th Ave S, Nashville, TN 37212
Phone: (615) 327-4751
Sales: $50,700,000   *Employees:* NA
Company Type: Private   *Employees here:* 1,200
SIC: 8062
  General hospital
Larry E Deters, N/A

D-U-N-S 15-638-5783
VETERANS HEALTH ADMINISTRATION
3400 Lebanon Rd, Murfreesboro, TN 37129
Phone: (615) 893-1360
Sales: $63,500,000   *Employees:* NA
Company Type: Private   *Employees here:* 1,500
SIC: 8062
  General hospital
Brian Heckert, N/A

D-U-N-S 09-807-4776
VETERANS HEALTH ADMINISTRATION
Sidney & Lamont St, Mountain Home, TN 37684
Phone: (615) 926-1171
Sales: $54,900,000   *Employees:* NA
Company Type: Private   *Employees here:* 1,400
SIC: 8062
  General hospital
Dr Carl Gerber, N/A

D-U-N-S 07-857-7285
VETERANS HEALTH ADMINISTRATION
1030 Jefferson Ave, Memphis, TN 38104
Phone: (901) 523-8990

Sales: $84,800,000   *Employees:* NA
Company Type: Private   *Employees here:* 2,000
SIC: 8062
  General hospital
Ken Mulholland, Branch Manager

D-U-N-S 07-838-6687
VETERANS HEALTH ADMINISTRATION
4800 Memorial Dr, Waco, TX 76711
Phone: (254) 752-6581
Sales: $58,900,000   *Employees:* NA
Company Type: Private   *Employees here:* 1,425
SIC: 8062
  General hospital
Wallace Hopkins, N/A

D-U-N-S 09-294-1541
VETERANS HEALTH ADMINISTRATION
1901 S 1st St, Temple, TX 76504
Phone: (254) 778-4811
Sales: $67,000,000   *Employees:* NA
Company Type: Private   *Employees here:* 1,619
SIC: 8062
  General hospital
Michael Hardware, N/A

D-U-N-S 07-849-3228
VETERANS HEALTH ADMINISTRATION
7400 Merton Minter St, San Antonio, TX 78284
Phone: (210) 617-5300
Sales: $124,400,000   *Employees:* NA
Company Type: Private   *Employees here:* 3,000
SIC: 8062
  General hospital
Jose R Coronado, N/A

D-U-N-S 11-255-4902
VETERANS HEALTH ADMINISTRATION
3600 Memorial Blvd, Kerrville, TX 78028
Phone: (830) 896-2020
Sales: $22,600,000   *Employees:* NA
Company Type: Private   *Employees here:* 600
SIC: 8062
  General hospital
Arnold Mouish, N/A

D-U-N-S 07-844-6044
VETERANS HEALTH ADMINISTRATION
2002 Holcombe Blvd, Houston, TX 77030
Phone: (713) 791-1414
Sales: $145,100,000   *Employees:* NA
Company Type: Private   *Employees here:* 3,500
SIC: 8062
  General hospital administrative public health programs
Robert S Stott, N/A

D-U-N-S 18-456-4268
VETERANS HEALTH ADMINISTRATION
4500 S Lancaster Rd, Dallas, TX 75216
Phone: (214) 372-7092
Sales: $91,200,000   *Employees:* NA
Company Type: Private   *Employees here:* 2,200
SIC: 8062
  Veterans medical center
Allen G Harper, Director

D-U-N-S 08-748-9811
VETERANS HEALTH ADMINISTRATION
6010 W Amarillo Blvd, Amarillo, TX 79106
Phone: (806) 355-9703

Sales: $26,500,000   *Employees:* NA
Company Type: Private   *Employees here:* 650
SIC: 8062
    Medical center
Robert Anselmi, Engineering Manager

D-U-N-S 06-322-1451
VETERANS HEALTH ADMINISTRATION
4th Plain And O St, Vancouver, WA 98661
Phone: (360) 696-4061
Sales: $25,300,000   *Employees:* NA
Company Type: Private   *Employees here:* 520
SIC: 8062
    General hospital
Ted Gailey, Chief Executive Officer

D-U-N-S 92-910-8926
VETERANS HEALTH ADMINISTRATION
9900 Veterans Dr SW, Tacoma, WA 98493
Phone: (253) 582-8440
Sales: $38,900,000   *Employees:* NA
Company Type: Private   *Employees here:* 790
SIC: 8062
    Veterans hospital
Tim Williams, Branch Manager

D-U-N-S 02-023-2971
VETERANS HEALTH ADMINISTRATION
1660 S Columbian Way, Seattle, WA 98108
Phone: (206) 762-1010
Sales: $79,500,000   *Employees:* NA
Company Type: Private   *Employees here:* 1,600
SIC: 8062
    General hospital administrative public health programs
Timothy B Williams, Manager

D-U-N-S 07-895-2454
VETERANS HEALTH ADMINISTRATION
5000 W National Ave, Milwaukee, WI 53295
Phone: (414) 384-2000
Sales: $87,000,000   *Employees:* NA
Company Type: Private   *Employees here:* 2,052
SIC: 8062
    General hospital
Russell Strubel, Branch Manager

D-U-N-S 61-414-0069
VETERANS HEALTH ADMINISTRATION
5000 W National Ave, Milwaukee, WI 53295
Phone: (414) 384-2000
Sales: $106,000,000   *Employees:* NA
Company Type: Private   *Employees here:* 2,500
SIC: 8062
    Veterans medical center
Russell Struble, Director

D-U-N-S 92-864-5308
VETERANS HOME & HOSPITAL
287 West St, Rocky Hill, CT 6067
Phone: (860) 529-2571
Sales: $23,700,000   *Employees:* 525
Company Type: Private   *Employees here:* 525
SIC: 8062
    Veterans hospital
Eugene Migliaro, Commisioner

D-U-N-S 06-925-6618
VETERANS MEMORIAL MEDICAL CTR
1 King Pl, Meriden, CT 6451
Phone: (203) 238-8200

Sales: $102,101,000   *Employees:* 1,740
Company Type: Private   *Employees here:* 1,200
SIC: 8062
    General hospital
Theodore H Horwitz, President

D-U-N-S 80-590-6799
VETERANS MEMORIAL MEDICAL CTR
883 Paddock Ave, Meriden, CT 6450
Phone: (203) 630-5241
Sales: $24,800,000   *Employees:* NA
Company Type: Private   *Employees here:* 500
SIC: 8062
    General hospital
Theodore H Horwitz, Manager

D-U-N-S 80-010-1297
VIA CHRISTI HEALTH PARTNERS,
959 N Emporia St Ste 302, Wichita, KS 67214
Phone: (316) 268-6944
Sales: $41,636,000   *Employees:* 275
Company Type: Private   *Employees here:* 5
SIC: 8011
    Provides health care services
Leroy Rheault, President

D-U-N-S 05-657-7646
VIA CHRISTI REGIONAL MED CTR
929 N Saint Francis St, Wichita, KS 67214
Phone: (316) 268-5000
Sales: $466,646,000   *Employees:* 4,100
Company Type: Private   *Employees here:* 4,000
SIC: 8062
    Hospital
Leroy Rheault, President

D-U-N-S 07-607-0184
VICTOR VALLEY COMMUNITY HOSP
15248 11th St, Victorville, CA 92392
Phone: (760) 245-8691
Sales: $60,720,000   *Employees:* 670
Company Type: Private   *Employees here:* 620
SIC: 8062
    Hospital
Ralph Parks, Chief Executive Officer

D-U-N-S 05-632-7695
VICTORIA HOSPITAL CORPORATION
(Parent: Columbia/Hca Healthcare Corp)
506 E San Antonio St, Victoria, TX 77901
Phone: (512) 575-7441
Sales: $116,000,000   *Employees:* 740
Company Type: Public Family Member   *Employees here:* 720
SIC: 8062
    General hospital
William R Blanchard, Chief Executive Officer

D-U-N-S 07-457-1365
VICTORY MEMORIAL HOSPITAL ASSN
1324 N Sheridan Rd, Waukegan, IL 60085
Phone: (847) 360-3000
Sales: $64,500,000   *Employees:* 950
Company Type: Private   *Employees here:* 950
SIC: 8062
    General hospital
Jim Mc Nichols, Chief Financial Officer

D-U-N-S 07-433-2800
VICTORY MEMORIAL HOSPITAL INC
699 92nd St, Brooklyn, NY 11228
Phone: (718) 567-1234

Sales: $50,900,000
Company Type: Private
SIC: 8062
   General hospital & skilled nursing facility
Krishin Bhatia, Administrator
Employees: 1,100
Employees here: 1,100

D-U-N-S 07-888-5886
VILLAGE CENTER FOR CARE, INC
607 Hudson St, New York, NY 10014
Phone: (212) 255-3003
Sales: $28,897,000
Company Type: Private
SIC: 8051
   Nursing home
Arthur A Webb, Chief Executive Officer
Employees: 1,050
Employees here: 200

D-U-N-S 07-216-9378
VINCENT SAINT HEALTH CENTER
232 W 25th St, Erie, PA 16544
Phone: (814) 452-5000
Sales: $146,424,000
Company Type: Private
SIC: 8062
   General hospital
Catherine Manning Sr, President
Employees: 2,300
Employees here: 2,228

D-U-N-S 00-617-5723
VINFEN CORPORATION
950 Cambridge St, Cambridge, MA 2141
Phone: (617) 441-1800
Sales: $52,345,000
Company Type: Private
SIC: 8361
   Residential care with mental health & social services
Gary Lamson, President
Employees: 1,300
Employees here: 300

D-U-N-S 83-220-2857
VINTAGE ESTATES OF SACRAMENTO
501 Jessie Ave, Sacramento, CA 95838
Phone: (916) 922-8855
Sales: $350,000,000
Company Type: Private
SIC: 8051
   Skilled nursing care facility
Sally Rapp, President
Employees: 70
Employees here: 70

D-U-N-S 07-793-3299
VIRGINIA BEACH GENERAL HOSP
1080 First Colonial Rd, Virginia Beach, VA 23454
Phone: (757) 481-8000
Sales: $107,178,000
Company Type: Private
SIC: 8062
   General hospital
Robert Graves, Chief Operating Officer
Employees: 1,717
Employees here: 1,356

D-U-N-S 07-476-1875
VIRGINIA DPT MNTL HEALTH, MR SA
4601 Ironbound Rd, Williamsburg, VA 23188
Phone: (757) 253-5161
Sales: $45,800,000
Company Type: Private
SIC: 8063
   Psychiatric hospital
John M Favret, Principal
Employees: NA
Employees here: 1,400

D-U-N-S 01-003-3819
VIRGINIA DPT MNTL HEALTH, MR SA
1301 Ridgemond Ave, Staunton, VA 24401
Phone: (540) 332-8000

Sales: $27,900,000
Company Type: Private
SIC: 8063
   Psychiatric hospital
Lynwood F Harding, Director
Employees: NA
Employees here: 850

D-U-N-S 62-738-2732
VIRGINIA DPT MNTL HEALTH, MR SA
Bldg 39, Petersburg, VA 23803
Phone: (804) 524-7400
Sales: $34,800,000
Company Type: Private
SIC: 8069
   Specialty hospital
Anponi Sulikowski, Director
Employees: NA
Employees here: 800

D-U-N-S 09-959-2701
VIRGINIA DPT MNTL HEALTH, MR SA
E End 210 Colony Rd, Madison Heights, VA 24572
Phone: (804) 947-6000
Sales: $40,400,000
Company Type: Private
SIC: 8051
   Mental retardation training center
Judy Dudley, N/A
Employees: NA
Employees here: 2,000

D-U-N-S 09-984-8467
VIRGINIA DPT MNTL HEALTH, MR SA
9901 Braddock Rd, Fairfax, VA 22032
Phone: (703) 323-4000
Sales: $20,600,000
Company Type: Private
SIC: 8069
   Specialty hospital
David Lawson, President
Employees: NA
Employees here: 440

D-U-N-S 19-488-3393
VIRGINIA MASON MEDICAL CENTER
1100 9th Ave, Seattle, WA 98101
Phone: (206) 223-6600
Sales: $377,376,000
Company Type: Private
SIC: 8011
   Medical clinics general hospital skilled nursing facility hotel
Dr Roger C Lindeman Md, Chief Executive Officer
Employees: 5,000
Employees here: 2,800

D-U-N-S 11-619-4861
VIRGINIA MEDICAL ASSOCIATES
5514 Alma Ln, Springfield, VA 22151
Phone: (703) 642-5990
Sales: $20,100,000
Company Type: Private
SIC: 8011
   Physicians office
Dr John Mamana, General Partner
Employees: 294
Employees here: 244

D-U-N-S 80-359-0827
VIRGINIA PHYSICIANS, INC
7702 E Parham Rd Ste 205, Richmond, VA 23294
Phone: (804) 346-1515
Sales: $40,000,000
Company Type: Private
SIC: 8011
   Medical doctor
Dr Hilton R Almond Md, President
Employees: 60
Employees here: 60

D-U-N-S 61-812-4945
VIRGINIA STATE DEPARTMENT HEALTH
1500 E Main St, Richmond, VA 23219
Phone: (804) 786-3561

Sales: $25,200,000   *Employees:* NA
Company Type: Private   *Employees here:* 400
SIC: 8011
  Dept of health
Randolph Gordan, Principal

  D-U-N-S 04-625-3258
VIRGINIA UNITED METHDST HOMES
7113 Three Chopt Rd, Richmond, VA 23226
Phone: (804) 673-1031
Sales: $26,781,000   *Employees:* 750
Company Type: Private   *Employees here:* 25
SIC: 8361
  Residential retirement community
Dr William J Fink, President

  D-U-N-S 06-303-5190
VISALIA MEDICAL CLINIC INC
5400 W Hillsdale Ave, Visalia, CA 93291
Phone: (209) 733-5222
Sales: $20,400,000   *Employees:* 299
Company Type: Private   *Employees here:* 299
SIC: 8011
  Medical clinic x-ray & medical lab
Gerald Moore, Administrator

  D-U-N-S 92-987-7314
VISIONQUEST NONPROFIT CORP
600 N Swan Rd, Tucson, AZ 85711
Phone: (520) 881-3950
Sales: $46,305,000   *Employees:* 900
Company Type: Private   *Employees here:* 50
SIC: 8361
  Rehabilitation service for deliquent children & including
    elementary/secondary school
Donald Barnes, President

  D-U-N-S 03-728-4452
VISITING NRS ASSOC OF CLEV
2500 E 22nd St, Cleveland, OH 44115
Phone: (216) 931-1300
Sales: $30,182,000   *Employees:* 842
Company Type: Private   *Employees here:* 30
SIC: 8082
  Home nursing care & rehabilitation
Mary L Stricklin, Chief Executive Officer

  D-U-N-S 07-779-1275
VISITING NRS ASSOCIA
5151 Wisconsin Ave Nw, Washington, DC 20016
Phone: (202) 686-2862
Sales: $180,643,000   *Employees:* 350
Company Type: Private   *Employees here:* 68
SIC: 8082
  Home nursing care & rehabilitation therapy
Linda Maurano, President

  D-U-N-S 08-075-1357
VISITING NRSE SRVC OF RCHSTR
2180 Empire Blvd, Webster, NY 14580
Phone: (716) 787-2233
Sales: $42,430,000   *Employees:* 1,073
Company Type: Private   *Employees here:* 800
SIC: 8082
  Home health care services
Sally Leiter, President

  D-U-N-S 02-444-9928
VISITING NURSE AND HOME CARE
146 New Britain Ave, Plainville, CT 6062
Phone: (860) 747-2761

Sales: $33,478,000   *Employees:* 950
Company Type: Private   *Employees here:* 5
SIC: 8082
  Home health care services
Ellen Rothberg, President

  D-U-N-S 07-380-6945
VISITING NURSE ASSN OF BOSTON
75 Arlington St, Boston, MA 2116
Phone: (617) 426-5555
Sales: $72,955,000   *Employees:* 1,250
Company Type: Private   *Employees here:* 100
SIC: 8082
  Home health care & visiting nurse services
Eileen Frietag, Chief Executive Officer

  D-U-N-S 08-643-8165
VISITING NURSE ASSN OF DEL
1 Reads Way, New Castle, DE 19720
Phone: (302) 323-8200
Sales: $33,492,000   *Employees:* 1,070
Company Type: Private   *Employees here:* 700
SIC: 8082
  Visiting nurses service
Namita Khasat, Chief Financial Officer

  D-U-N-S 07-511-9057
VISITING NURSE ASSN OF TEXAS
1440 W Mockingbird Ln, Dallas, TX 75247
Phone: (214) 689-0000
Sales: $51,415,000   *Employees:* 1,400
Company Type: Private   *Employees here:* 980
SIC: 8082
  Provider of home health care services home delivered meals
    & long term home care services
Mary Suther, President

  D-U-N-S 08-920-3947
VISITING NURSE ASSOCIATION OF
33 Evergreen Pl, East Orange, NJ 7018
Phone: (973) 673-0158
Sales: $22,413,000   *Employees:* 600
Company Type: Private   *Employees here:* 600
SIC: 8049
  Community nursing service
Mary Hanna, President

  D-U-N-S 09-157-9425
VISITING NURSE ASSOCIATION HEA
400 Lake Ave, Staten Island, NY 10303
Phone: (718) 720-2245
Sales: $23,968,000   *Employees:* 160
Company Type: Private   *Employees here:* 35
SIC: 8082
  Visiting nurse association/home care
David Lahr, Chairman

  D-U-N-S 06-922-3139
VISITING NURSE HEALTH SYSTEM
  (Parent: Visiting Nurse Health System)
133 Luckie St Nw, Atlanta, GA 30303
Phone: (404) 527-0660
Sales: $53,853,000   *Employees:* 800
Company Type: Private   *Employees here:* 190
SIC: 8082
  Home health care services
Kathy Ziegler, President

  D-U-N-S 18-610-9583
VISITING NURSE HEALTH SYSTEM
133 Luckie St Nw, Atlanta, GA 30303
Phone: (404) 527-0660

Sales: $56,016,000   *Employees:* 850
Company Type: Private   *Employees here:* 275
SIC: 8082
   Home health care services
Kathy Ziegler, President

D-U-N-S 15-770-9452
VISITING NURSE SERVICE OF NEW
   (Parent: Visiting Nurse Service Of Ny)
107 E 70th St, New York, NY 10021
Phone: (212) 794-9200
Sales: $547,205,000   *Employees:* 2,000
Company Type: Private   *Employees here:* 25
SIC: 8082
   Certified home health care agency
Carol Raphael, Chief Executive Officer

D-U-N-S 07-888-1778
VISITING NURSE SERVICE OF NY
107 E 70th St, New York, NY 10021
Phone: (212) 794-9200
Sales: $550,426,000   *Employees:* 2,500
Company Type: Private   *Employees here:* 30
SIC: 8082
   Non-profit visiting nurse service
Carol Raphael, Chief Executive Officer

D-U-N-S 15-574-9542
VISITING NURSE SERVICE OF NY
350 5th Ave Ste 530, New York, NY 10118
Phone: (212) 560-5900
Sales: $34,400,000   *Employees:* NA
Company Type: Private   *Employees here:* 2,000
SIC: 8082
   Home health care services
Georgette Nelson, Branch Manager

D-U-N-S 78-272-8703
VISITING NURSE SERVICE OF NY
350 5th Ave, New York, NY 10118
Phone: (212) 560-5900
Sales: $34,400,000   *Employees:* NA
Company Type: Private   *Employees here:* 2,000
SIC: 8082
   Home health care services
Carol Raphael, N/A

D-U-N-S 08-476-8522
VISITING NURSE SERVICE SYSTEM
150 E 9th Ave, Runnemede, NJ 8078
Phone: (609) 939-9000
Sales: $47,000,000   *Employees:* 1,300
Company Type: Private   *Employees here:* 1,100
SIC: 8082
   Home health care service
Marianne Czoch, President

D-U-N-S 07-999-6344
VISITING NURSES ASSOCIATION
600 Courtland St Ste 500, Orlando, FL 32804
Phone: (407) 628-0085
Sales: $40,856,000   *Employees:* 500
Company Type: Private   *Employees here:* 150
SIC: 8082
   Visiting nurse association
Thomas W Skemp, President

D-U-N-S 17-345-2863
VISITING NURSES ASSOCIATION OF
1 Winding Dr, Philadelphia, PA 19131
Phone: (215) 473-0772

Sales: $43,600,000   *Employees:* 400
Company Type: Private   *Employees here:* 400
SIC: 8082
   Home health services
Stephen W Holt, President

D-U-N-S 07-334-4681
VISTA HILL FOUNDATION
2355 Northside Dr, San Diego, CA 92108
Phone: (619) 563-1770
Sales: $23,560,000   *Employees:* 1,000
Company Type: Private   *Employees here:* 65
SIC: 8063
   Psychiatric hospital and management service
Gregory Zinser, President

D-U-N-S 92-810-8919
VISTA HOSPITAL SYSTEMS INC
730 Magnolia Ave, Corona, CA 91719
Phone: (909) 736-7200
Sales: $25,300,000   *Employees:* NA
Company Type: Private   *Employees here:* 771
SIC: 8093
   Specialty outpatient clinic/general hospital
Pat Sanders, Manager

D-U-N-S 11-413-6195
VITAS HEALTHCARE CORP
100 S Biscayne Blvd, Miami, FL 33131
Phone: (305) 374-4143
Sales: $213,856,000   *Employees:* 3,000
Company Type: Private   *Employees here:* 200
SIC: 8082
   Health care service
Hugh A Westbrook, Chairman of the Board

D-U-N-S 96-230-3590
VIVRA ASTHMA ALLRGY CREAMERICA
   (Parent: Vivra Specialty Partners Inc)
1850 Gateway Dr Ste 500, San Mateo, CA 94404
Phone: (650) 577-5700
Sales: $20,100,000   *Employees:* 294
Company Type: Private   *Employees here:* 6
SIC: 8011
   Asthma & allergy clinic
Joseph C Mello, President

D-U-N-S 96-230-3053
VIVRA SPECIALTY PARTNERS, INC
   (Parent: Dialysis Holdings Inc)
1850 Gateway Dr, San Mateo, CA 94404
Phone: (650) 577-5700
Sales: $250,000,000   *Employees:* 900
Company Type: Public Family Member   *Employees here:* 30
SIC: 8011
   Specialty care provider of healthcare services
Thomas Usilton, Executive Vice-President

D-U-N-S 78-244-4970
VNA OF RHODE ISLAND INC
157 Waterman St, Providence, RI 2906
Phone: (401) 444-9770
Sales: $26,171,000   *Employees:* 401
Company Type: Private   *Employees here:* 401
SIC: 8082
   Regulated medicare visiting nursing service
Susan G Belles, President

D-U-N-S 15-778-1774
VNA CARE NETWORK, INC
245 Winter St Ste 100, Waltham, MA 2451
Phone: (781) 890-2931

Sales: $37,184,000   *Employees:* 250
Company Type: Private   *Employees here:* 250
SIC: 8082
  Visiting nurse service
Susan Comporone, President

D-U-N-S 12-117-8552
VOLUNTEERS OF AMER HEALTH SVCS
7530 Market Place Dr, Eden Prairie, MN 55344
Phone: (612) 941-0305
Sales: $59,422,000   *Employees:* 1,300
Company Type: Private   *Employees here:* 3
SIC: 8051
  Holding company health care facilities
Ronald Patterson, President

D-U-N-S 08-657-5255
VOLUNTERS OF AMER CARE FCLTES
7530 Market Place Dr, Eden Prairie, MN 55344
Phone: (612) 941-0305
Sales: $54,596,000   *Employees:* 1,300
Company Type: Private   *Employees here:* 13
SIC: 8051
  Skilled health care facilities
Ronald Patterson, Chairman of the Board

D-U-N-S 15-988-0228
VA NJ HEALTHCARE SYSTEM
385 Tremont Ave, Orange, NJ 7050
Phone: (973) 676-0180
Sales: $94,500,000   *Employees:* NA
Company Type: Private   *Employees here:* 1,900
SIC: 8062
  General medical and surgical hospitals, nsk

D-U-N-S 62-728-8137
VA NJ HEALTHCARE SYSTEM
151 Knollcroft Rd, Lyons, NJ 7939
Phone: (908) 647-0180
Sales: $150,100,000   *Employees:* 3,200
Company Type: Private   *Employees here:* 1,300
SIC: 8062
  General hospital
Kenneth Mizrah, Director

D-U-N-S 07-421-3646
W A FOOTE MEMORIAL HOSPITAL
205 N East Ave, Jackson, MI 49201
Phone: (517) 788-4800
Sales: $130,726,000   *Employees:* 2,200
Company Type: Private   *Employees here:* 2,100
SIC: 8062
  Medical hospital
Georgia Fojtasek, President

D-U-N-S 04-027-7949
WABASH COUNTY HOSPITAL
710 N East St, Wabash, IN 46992
Phone: (219) 563-3131
Sales: $23,180,000   *Employees:* 375
Company Type: Private   *Employees here:* 375
SIC: 8062
  General hospital skilled care facility
David Hunter, Executive Director

D-U-N-S 07-776-3522
WADSWORTH-RTMN AREA HSPTL
195 Wadsworth Rd, Wadsworth, OH 44281
Phone: (330) 334-1504

Sales: $19,774,000   *Employees:* 290
Company Type: Private   *Employees here:* 290
SIC: 8062
  General hospital
James W Brumlow Jr, President

D-U-N-S 06-627-7021
WAHIAWA HOSPITAL ASSOCIATION
128 Lehua St, Wahiawa, HI 96786
Phone: (808) 621-8411
Sales: $20,100,000   *Employees:* 450
Company Type: Private   *Employees here:* 450
SIC: 8062
  General hospital
David Hill, President

D-U-N-S 07-202-1512
WAKEMED
3000 New Bern Ave, Raleigh, NC 27610
Phone: (919) 250-8000
Sales: $285,301,000   *Employees:* 3,500
Company Type: Private   *Employees here:* 3,200
SIC: 8062
  General hospitals
Raymond Champ, President

D-U-N-S 07-746-1762
WALDO COUNTY GENERAL HOSPITAL
118 Northport Ave, Belfast, ME 4915
Phone: (207) 338-2500
Sales: $21,228,000   *Employees:* 320
Company Type: Private   *Employees here:* 320
SIC: 8062
  General hospital
Mark Biscone, Administrator

D-U-N-S 07-895-9939
WALKER BAPTIST MEDICAL CENTER
3400 Highway 78 E, Jasper, AL 35501
Phone: (205) 387-4000
Sales: $50,190,000   *Employees:* 620
Company Type: Private   *Employees here:* 620
SIC: 8062
  General hospital
Jeff Brewer, President

D-U-N-S 15-177-3173
WALKER METHODIST HEALTH CENTER
3737 Bryant Ave S, Minneapolis, MN 55409
Phone: (612) 827-5931
Sales: $25,351,000   *Employees:* 591
Company Type: Private   *Employees here:* 591
SIC: 8051
  Skilled nursing care facility
Janet Linddo, President

D-U-N-S 06-933-1908
WALLACE THOMSON HOSPITAL
322 W South St, Union, SC 29379
Phone: (864) 427-0351
Sales: $23,823,000   *Employees:* 400
Company Type: Private   *Employees here:* 400
SIC: 8062
  General hospital
Harrell Connelly, Chief Executive Officer

D-U-N-S 14-816-8479
WALLS REGIONAL HOSPITAL
201 Walls Dr, Cleburne, TX 76031
Phone: (817) 641-2551

Sales: $31,904,000
Company Type: Private
SIC: 8062
   General medical & surgical hospital
Stephen R Mason, President

   Employees: 355
   Employees here: 355

D-U-N-S 06-647-4008
WALTON COUNTY HOSPITAL AUTH
330 Alcovy St, Monroe, GA 30655
Phone: (770) 267-8461
Sales: $24,209,000
Company Type: Private
SIC: 8062
   General hospital
Edgar C Belcher, Administrator

   Employees: 297
   Employees here: 297

D-U-N-S 82-501-2693
WARM SPRNG RHBLTTION FUNDATION
909 NE Loop 410 Ste 500, San Antonio, TX 78209
Phone: (210) 829-0009
Sales: $42,962,000
Company Type: Private
SIC: 8069
   Rehabilitation hospital
Kay Peck, President

   Employees: 600
   Employees here: 35

D-U-N-S 19-461-3949
WARREN CLINIC INC
6600 S Yale Ave Ste 1200, Tulsa, OK 74136
Phone: (918) 488-6000
Sales: $29,061,000
Company Type: Private
SIC: 8011
   Medical clinic operator
John Kabfleische, Chairman of the Board

   Employees: 390
   Employees here: 6

D-U-N-S 07-402-5883
WARREN GENERAL HOSPITAL
2 W Crescent Park, Warren, PA 16365
Phone: (814) 723-3300
Sales: $29,302,000
Company Type: Private
SIC: 8062
   General hospital
Alton M Shadt, Executive Director

   Employees: 609
   Employees here: 568

D-U-N-S 07-366-4914
WARREN HOSPITAL
185 Roseberry St, Phillipsburg, NJ 8865
Phone: (908) 859-6700
Sales: $58,227,000
Company Type: Private
SIC: 8062
   General hospital
Jeffrey Goodwin, Chief Executive Officer

   Employees: 806
   Employees here: 724

D-U-N-S 15-197-4052
WARRENSVILLE DEVELOPMENT CTR
4325 Green Rd, Cleveland, OH 44128
Phone: (216) 464-7400
Sales: $32,000,000
Company Type: Private
SIC: 8059
   Nursing/personal care
Alaric Sawyer, Superintendent

   Employees: 503
   Employees here: 503

D-U-N-S 07-056-6849
WARTBURG
Wartburg Pl, Mount Vernon, NY 10552
Phone: (914) 699-0800

Sales: $23,238,000
Company Type: Private
SIC: 8051
   Nursing home
Henriette Kole, Administrator

   Employees: 450
   Employees here: 450

D-U-N-S 07-829-7314
WASHINGTON CNTY HOSPITAL ASSN INC
251 E Antietam St, Hagerstown, MD 21740
Phone: (301) 797-2000
Sales: $130,737,000
Company Type: Private
SIC: 8062
   General hospital
Horace Murphy, President

   Employees: 1,829
   Employees here: 1,737

D-U-N-S 06-919-0452
WASHINGTON CNTY RGNAL MED CTR
610 Sparta Rd, Sandersville, GA 31082
Phone: (912) 552-3901
Sales: $20,145,000
Company Type: Private
SIC: 8062
   General hospital and skilled nursing care facility
Shirley Roberts, Chief Executive Officer

   Employees: 343
   Employees here: 343

D-U-N-S 04-017-9715
WASHINGTON DPT SCL & HEALTH SVCS
9601 Steilacoom Blvd SW, Tacoma, WA 98498
Phone: (253) 582-8900
Sales: $73,200,000
Company Type: Private
SIC: 8063
   State hospital
Dr Jerry Dennis, Chief Executive Officer

   Employees: NA
   Employees here: 1,850

D-U-N-S 06-004-0276
WASHINGTON DPT SCL & HEALTH SVCS
Maple St, Cheney, WA 99004
Phone: (509) 299-4380
Sales: $25,900,000
Company Type: Private
SIC: 8063
   Psychiatric hospital
C J Gregg, Branch Manager

   Employees: NA
   Employees here: 650

D-U-N-S 14-472-9373
WASHINGTON REGIONAL MED CTR
1125 N College Ave, Fayetteville, AR 72703
Phone: (501) 442-1000
Sales: $88,647,000
Company Type: Private
SIC: 8062
   Hospital
Patrick D Flynn, President

   Employees: 1,350
   Employees here: 1,100

D-U-N-S 79-730-3443
WASHINGTON REGIONAL MED SYS
1125 N College Ave, Fayetteville, AR 72703
Phone: (501) 442-1000
Sales: $61,900,000
Company Type: Private
SIC: 8062
   Hospital
Patrick D Flynn, President

   Employees: 1,334
   Employees here: 20

D-U-N-S 07-395-6054
WASHINGTON TOWNSHIP HEALTHCARE
2000 Mowry Ave, Fremont, CA 94538
Phone: (510) 797-1111

Sales: $127,000,000   *Employees:* 1,225
Company Type: Private   *Employees here:* 1,225
SIC: 8062
    Healthcare management company
Nancy Farber, Chief Executive Officer

D-U-N-S 06-855-2207
WASHINGTON UNIVERSITY
1 Brookings Dr, Saint Louis, MO 63130
Phone: (314) 935-5000
Sales: $941,759,000   *Employees:* 6,600
Company Type: Private   *Employees here:* 2,461
SIC: 8062
    Hospital and university
Richard A Roloff, Exec Vice Chancellor

D-U-N-S 07-904-4772
WATAUGA MEDICAL CENTER INC
336 Deerfield Rd, Boone, NC 28607
Phone: (828) 262-4100
Sales: $42,072,000   *Employees:* 520
Company Type: Private   *Employees here:* 520
SIC: 8062
    Hospital
Richard G Sparks, President

D-U-N-S 02-046-4517
WATERTOWN MEMORIAL HOSPITAL ASSN
125 Hospital Dr, Watertown, WI 53098
Phone: (920) 261-4210
Sales: $26,470,000   *Employees:* 430
Company Type: Private   *Employees here:* 350
SIC: 8062
    General hopsital
John Kosanovich, President

D-U-N-S 03-242-4293
WATSON CLINIC
1600 Lakeland Hills Blvd, Lakeland, FL 33805
Phone: (941) 680-7000
Sales: $104,260,000   *Employees:* 1,060
Company Type: Private   *Employees here:* 800
SIC: 8011
    Medical doctor's office
Dale Anderson, Administrator

D-U-N-S 01-092-4496
WATSONVILLE COMMUNITY HOSP
298 Green Valley Rd, Watsonville, CA 95076
Phone: (831) 724-4741
Sales: $50,394,000   *Employees:* 800
Company Type: Private   *Employees here:* 750
SIC: 8062
    Hospital
John Friel, Chief Executive Officer

D-U-N-S 79-144-7394
WATTS HEALTH FOUNDATION INC
10300 Compton Ave, Los Angeles, CA 90002
Phone: (323) 564-4331
Sales: $47,500,000   *Employees:* NA
Company Type: Private   *Employees here:* 900
SIC: 8069
    Alcohol rehabilitation center
Clyde W Oden, Manager

D-U-N-S 07-230-4769
WATTS HEALTH FOUNDATION INC
3405 W Imperial Hwy, Inglewood, CA 90303
Phone: (310) 671-3465

Sales: $197,509,000   *Employees:* 942
Company Type: Private   *Employees here:* 400
SIC: 8011
    Health maintenance organization
Dr Clyde W Oden, President

D-U-N-S 10-803-9603
WATTS HEALTH FOUNDATION INC
3405 W Imperial Hwy, Inglewood, CA 90303
Phone: (310) 671-3465
Sales: $20,700,000   *Employees:* NA
Company Type: Private   *Employees here:* 325
SIC: 8011
    Medical doctor's office
Dr Clyde W Oden-Pres, N/A

D-U-N-S 07-386-1106
WAUKESHA MEMORIAL HOSPITAL
725 American Ave, Waukesha, WI 53188
Phone: (414) 544-2011
Sales: $158,506,000   *Employees:* 1,275
Company Type: Private   *Employees here:* 1,260
SIC: 8062
    Hospital
Rexford W Titus Iii, President

D-U-N-S 07-476-9324
WAUSAU HOSPITALS INC
333 Pine Ridge Blvd, Wausau, WI 54401
Phone: (715) 847-2121
Sales: $109,960,000   *Employees:* 1,209
Company Type: Private   *Employees here:* 1,190
SIC: 8062
    General hospital
Paul A Spaude, President

D-U-N-S 05-096-4600
WAVERLEY GROUP INC
460 Briarwood Dr, Jackson, MS 39206
Phone: (601) 956-1013
Sales: $58,016,000   *Employees:* 1,900
Company Type: Private   *Employees here:* 20
SIC: 8051
    Skilled care nursing homes
Bobby Arnold, President

D-U-N-S 06-578-9240
WAYNE GENERAL HOSPITAL CORP
224 Hamburg Tpke, Wayne, NJ 7470
Phone: (973) 942-6900
Sales: $66,537,000   *Employees:* 941
Company Type: Private   *Employees here:* 821
SIC: 8062
    General hospital
Kenneth Kozloff, Executive Director

D-U-N-S 06-895-1417
WAYNE HOSPITAL CO INC
835 Sweitzer St, Greenville, OH 45331
Phone: (937) 548-1141
Sales: $28,221,000   *Employees:* 346
Company Type: Private   *Employees here:* 315
SIC: 8062
    General hospital
Raymond E Laughlin, President

D-U-N-S 07-585-7979
WAYNE MEMORIAL HOSPITAL
865 S 1st St, Jesup, GA 31545
Phone: (912) 427-6811

Sales: $24,936,000   Employees: 380
Company Type: Private   Employees here: 380
SIC: 8062
    General hospital
Charles Morgan Ii, Administrator

D-U-N-S 06-959-7250
WAYNE MEMORIAL HOSPITAL ASSN
601 Park St, Honesdale, PA 18431
Phone: (717) 253-1300
Sales: $32,416,000   Employees: 600
Company Type: Private   Employees here: 600
SIC: 8062
    General hospital
G R Garman, Chief Executive Officer

D-U-N-S 07-557-4855
WAYNE MEMORIAL HOSPITAL INC
2700 Wayne Memorial Dr, Goldsboro, NC 27534
Phone: (919) 736-1110
Sales: $91,425,000   Employees: 1,037
Company Type: Private   Employees here: 1,037
SIC: 8062
    Hospital
James W Hubbell, President

D-U-N-S 07-367-0689
WAYNE NEWARK COMMUNITY HOSP
111 Driving Park Ave, Newark, NY 14513
Phone: (315) 332-2022
Sales: $27,200,000   Employees: 600
Company Type: Private   Employees here: 600
SIC: 8062
    General hospital
L J Danehy, President

D-U-N-S 96-149-6049
WAYNE NEWARK COMMUNITY HOSP
Driving Park Ave, Newark, NY 14513
Phone: (315) 332-2700
Sales: $31,901,000   Employees: 700
Company Type: Private   Employees here: 700
SIC: 8062
    General care nursing home & psychiatric hospital
William Holman, Chief Executive Officer

D-U-N-S 07-119-5119
WAYNESBORO HOSPITAL
501 E Main St, Waynesboro, PA 17268
Phone: (717) 765-4000
Sales: $26,007,000   Employees: 450
Company Type: Private   Employees here: 450
SIC: 8062
    General hospital
Norman Epstein, President

D-U-N-S 07-746-8270
WEBBER HOSPITAL ASSOCIATION
1 Medical Center Dr, Biddeford, ME 4005
Phone: (207) 283-7000
Sales: $53,583,000   Employees: 765
Company Type: Private   Employees here: 765
SIC: 8062
    General hospital
Barbara Grillo, Chief Operating Officer

D-U-N-S 02-050-2530
WEIGHT WATCHERS NORTH AMERICA,
    (Parent: Weight Watchers International)
175 Crossways Park Dr W, Woodbury, NY 11797
Phone: (516) 390-1400

Sales: $183,100,000   Employees: 6,000
Company Type: Public Family Member   Employees here: 100
SIC: 8093
    Weight reduction class
Robert Mallow, Vice-President

D-U-N-S 07-216-6051
WEIRTON MEDICAL CENTER INC
601 Colliers Way, Weirton, WV 26062
Phone: (304) 797-6000
Sales: $51,805,000   Employees: 800
Company Type: Private   Employees here: 800
SIC: 8062
    Hospital
Donald R Donell, Chairman of the Board

D-U-N-S 07-404-7093
WELBORN MEMORIAL BAPTIST HOSP
401 SE 6th St, Evansville, IN 47713
Phone: (812) 426-8000
Sales: $88,020,000   Employees: 1,615
Company Type: Private   Employees here: 1,600
SIC: 8062
    General hospital
Marjorie Soyugenc, President

D-U-N-S 11-424-3124
WELLCARE MANAGEMENT GROUP INC
Hurley Avenue Ext, Kingston, NY 12401
Phone: (914) 338-4110
Sales: $143,870,000   Employees: 225
Company Type: Public   Employees here: 90
SIC: 8011
    National health management company
Joseph R Papa, Chief Executive Officer

D-U-N-S 07-658-1768
WELLESLEY NEWTON HOSPITAL
2014 Washington St, Newton, MA 2462
Phone: (617) 243-6000
Sales: $121,752,000   Employees: 1,800
Company Type: Private   Employees here: 1,800
SIC: 8062
    General hospital
John P Bihldorff, President

D-U-N-S 15-130-3468
WELLINGTON REGIONAL MED CTR
    (Parent: Universal Health Services)
10101 Forest Hill Blvd, West Palm Beach, FL 33414
Phone: (561) 798-8500
Sales: $20,100,000   Employees: 450
Company Type: Public Family Member   Employees here: 450
SIC: 8062
    General hospital
Gregory Boyer, Executive Director

D-U-N-S 95-934-5448
WELLMONT HEALTH SYSTEM INC
999 Executive Park Blvd, Kingsport, TN 37660
Phone: (423) 844-4480
Sales: $326,824,000   Employees: 3,957
Company Type: Private   Employees here: 50
SIC: 8062
    General and psychiatric hospital
Eddie George, President

D-U-N-S 95-938-6657
WELLMONT HEALTH SYSTEM INC
130 W Ravine Rd, Kingsport, TN 37660
Phone: (423) 224-4000

Sales: $93,300,000   *Employees:* NA
Company Type: Private   *Employees here:* 2,200
SIC: 8062
    General hospital
Louis Bremer, Branch Manager

D-U-N-S 96-804-7902
WELLMONT HEALTH SYSTEM INC
1 Medical Park Blvd, Bristol, TN 37620
Phone: (423) 844-1121
Sales: $80,500,000   *Employees:* NA
Company Type: Private   *Employees here:* 1,900
SIC: 8062
    Hospital
Eddie George, President

D-U-N-S 07-573-0648
WENATCHEE VALLEY CLINIC
820 N Chelan Ave, Wenatchee, WA 98801
Phone: (509) 663-8711
Sales: $100,460,000   *Employees:* 950
Company Type: Private   *Employees here:* 410
SIC: 8011
    Multi specialty medical clinic
Dr James Brown Md, Chairman of the Board

D-U-N-S 06-990-9281
WENTWORTH-DOUGLASS HOSPITAL
789 Central Ave, Dover, NH 3820
Phone: (603) 742-5252
Sales: $56,537,000   *Employees:* 645
Company Type: Private   *Employees here:* 631
SIC: 8062
    General hospital
Gregory Walker, President

D-U-N-S 06-681-9962
WESLEY HEALTH CARE CENTER INC
131 Lawrence St, Saratoga Springs, NY 12866
Phone: (518) 587-3600
Sales: $20,500,000   *Employees:* 515
Company Type: Private   *Employees here:* 515
SIC: 8051
    Skilled nursing home
G N Roberts, Executive Director

D-U-N-S 07-194-2197
WESLEY HEALTH SYSTEMS LLC
    (Parent: Quorum Health Group Inc)
5001 Hardy St, Hattiesburg, MS 39402
Phone: (601) 268-8000
Sales: $32,700,000   *Employees:* 716
Company Type: Public Family Member   *Employees here:* 716
SIC: 8062
    Hospital & skilled nursing facility
William K Ray, Administrator

D-U-N-S 80-986-1685
WESLEY WOODS GERIATRIC HOSP
1817 Clifton Rd NE, Atlanta, GA 30329
Phone: (404) 728-6200
Sales: $27,242,000   *Employees:* 301
Company Type: Private   *Employees here:* 301
SIC: 8062
    Hospital
Dr William L Minnix Jr, President

D-U-N-S 07-384-1967
WEST ALLIS MEMORIAL HOSPITAL
8901 W Lincoln Ave, Milwaukee, WI 53227
Phone: (414) 328-6000

Sales: $75,831,000   *Employees:* 1,400
Company Type: Private   *Employees here:* 1,400
SIC: 8062
    General hospital
Peter Fine, President

D-U-N-S 01-067-5726
WEST ANAHEIM COMMUNITY HOSP
    (Parent: Columbia/Hca Healthcare Corp)
3033 W Orange Ave, Anaheim, CA 92804
Phone: (714) 827-3000
Sales: $51,610,000   *Employees:* 650
Company Type: Public Family Member   *Employees here:* 650
SIC: 8062
    Hospital
David Culberson, Chief Executive Officer

D-U-N-S 01-039-8865
WEST FLA MED CTR CLINIC PA
8333 N Davis Hwy, Pensacola, FL 32514
Phone: (850) 474-8000
Sales: $91,010,000   *Employees:* 1,100
Company Type: Private   *Employees here:* 1,055
SIC: 8011
    Physicians clinic
James G Stolhanske, Administrator

D-U-N-S 13-966-6986
WEST FLORIDA REGIONAL MED CTR
    (Parent: Columbia/Hca Healthcare Corp)
8383 N Davis Hwy, Pensacola, FL 32514
Phone: (850) 494-4000
Sales: $74,500,000   *Employees:* 1,600
Company Type: Public Family Member   *Employees here:* 1,520
SIC: 8062
    Hospital rehab institute psychiatric hospital & skilled nursing
    facility
Steven C Brandt, Administrator

D-U-N-S 07-812-6554
WEST GEORGIA MEDICAL CENTER
1514 Vernon St, Lagrange, GA 30240
Phone: (706) 882-1411
Sales: $75,703,000   *Employees:* 1,400
Company Type: Private   *Employees here:* 1,270
SIC: 8062
    Hospital and skilled nursing facility
Charles L Foster Jr, Administrator

D-U-N-S 05-147-7073
WEST HILLS HOSPITAL
    (Parent: Columbia/Hca Healthcare Corp)
7300 Medical Center Dr, Canoga Park, CA 91307
Phone: (818) 884-7060
Sales: $75,825,000   *Employees:* 1,000
Company Type: Public Family Member   *Employees here:* 1,000
SIC: 8062
    General hospital skilled nursing care and convalescent home
Howard Levine, President

D-U-N-S 06-497-8562
WEST HUDSON HOSPITAL ASSN
206 Bergen Ave, Kearny, NJ 7032
Phone: (201) 955-7000
Sales: $27,200,000   *Employees:* 600
Company Type: Private   *Employees here:* 572
SIC: 8062
    Hospital
Carmen B Alecci, President

D-U-N-S 18-976-6116
WEST JERSEY HEALTH SYSTEM
Brick Rd Rr 73, Marlton, NJ 8053

Phone: (609) 596-3500
Sales: $33,900,000   *Employees:* NA
Company Type: Private   *Employees here:* 850
SIC: 8063
    General hospital
Barry D Brown, President

D-U-N-S 06-905-7115
WEST JERSEY HEALTH SYSTEM
1000 Atlantic Ave, Camden, NJ 8104
Phone: (609) 342-4000
Sales: $266,416,000   *Employees:* 4,100
Company Type: Private   *Employees here:* 1,394
SIC: 8062
    General hospital
Richard P Miller, President

D-U-N-S 07-255-9628
WEST ORANGE HEALTH CARE DST
10000 W Colonial Dr, Ocoee, FL 34761
Phone: (407) 296-1000
Sales: $49,480,000   *Employees:* 725
Company Type: Private   *Employees here:* 468
SIC: 8062
    General hospital & skilled nursing home
Richard Irwin, Chief Executive Officer

D-U-N-S 93-888-3865
WEST ORANGE HEALTHCARE INC
    (Parent: West Orange Health Care Dst)
10000 W Colonial Dr, Ocoee, FL 34761
Phone: (407) 296-1000
Sales: $104,946,000   *Employees:* 700
Company Type: Private   *Employees here:* 700
SIC: 8062
    Hospital
Alan Crowell, Chief Financial Officer

D-U-N-S 07-585-7698
WEST PACES FERRY HOSPITAL INC
    (Parent: Columbia/Hca Healthcare Corp)
3200 Howell Mill Rd Nw, Atlanta, GA 30327
Phone: (404) 351-0351
Sales: $31,900,000   *Employees:* 700
Company Type: Public Family Member   *Employees here:* 680
SIC: 8062
    General medical & surgical hospital
Thomas Anderson, Chief Executive Officer

D-U-N-S 07-140-6888
WEST PARK HOSPITAL DISTRICT
707 Sheridan Ave, Cody, WY 82414
Phone: (307) 527-7501
Sales: $23,622,000   *Employees:* 375
Company Type: Private   *Employees here:* 300
SIC: 8062
    General hospital
Doug Mcmillan, Administrator

D-U-N-S 11-820-4908
WEST SUBURBAN HEALTH CARE CORP
Erie At Austin Blvd, Oak Park, IL 60302
Phone: (708) 383-6200
Sales: $79,200,000   *Employees:* 1,700
Company Type: Private   *Employees here:* 16
SIC: 8062
    Hospital nursing school and outpatient care facility
Douglas F Dean Jr, President

D-U-N-S 06-948-2792
WEST SUBURBAN HOSPITAL MED CTR
Erie At Austin Blvd, Oak Park, IL 60302
Phone: (708) 383-6200

Sales: $147,822,000   *Employees:* 1,568
Company Type: Private   *Employees here:* 1,500
SIC: 8062
    General medical & surgical hospital
David M Cecero, President

D-U-N-S 08-579-3834
WEST TEXAS MEDICAL ASSOCIATES
3555 Knickerbocker Rd, San Angelo, TX 76904
Phone: (915) 949-9555
Sales: $30,013,000   *Employees:* 350
Company Type: Private   *Employees here:* 140
SIC: 8011
    Medical doctor's office
Dr Joe Wilkerson Md, President

D-U-N-S 18-799-6400
WEST VALLEY MEDICAL CENTER INC
    (Parent: Columbia/Hca Healthcare Corp)
1717 Arlington Ave, Caldwell, ID 83605
Phone: (208) 459-4641
Sales: $38,153,000   *Employees:* 455
Company Type: Public Family Member   *Employees here:* 455
SIC: 8062
    Hospital
Mark B Adams, Chief Executive Officer

D-U-N-S 11-343-3734
WEST VIRGINIA UNIV HOSPITALS
Medical Center Dr, Morgantown, WV 26506
Phone: (304) 598-4000
Sales: $212,663,000   *Employees:* 2,250
Company Type: Private   *Employees here:* 2,250
SIC: 8062
    General hospital
Bruce Mcclymonds, President

D-U-N-S 10-890-0671
WEST VIRGINIA UNIV MED CORP
Medical Center Dr Rm 2244, Morgantown, WV 26506
Phone: (304) 293-7413
Sales: $92,261,000   *Employees:* 1,300
Company Type: Private   *Employees here:* 15
SIC: 8011
    Academic medical group practice
W R Wright, Chief Executive Officer

D-U-N-S 62-786-5264
WEST VRGNIA RHBLTTION HOSPITAL INC
    (Parent: Healthsouth Corporation)
1160 Van Voorhis Rd, Morgantown, WV 26505
Phone: (304) 598-1100
Sales: $21,894,000   *Employees:* 357
Company Type: Public Family Member   *Employees here:* 357
SIC: 8361
    Rehabiliation hospital
Sharon Noro, Manager

D-U-N-S 16-006-9399
WESTCHESTER COUNTY HEALTH CARE
95 Grasslands Rd, Valhalla, NY 10595
Phone: (914) 493-7000
Sales: $385,000,000   *Employees:* 4,000
Company Type: Private   *Employees here:* NA
SIC: 8062
    General hospital
Edward Stolzenberg, President

D-U-N-S 07-845-6407
WESTCHESTER GENERAL HOSPITAL,
2500 SW 75th Ave, Miami, FL 33155
Phone: (305) 264-5252

Sales: $32,000,000
Employees: 500
Company Type: Private
Employees here: 220
SIC: 8062
  General surgical hospital and psychiatric hospital
Silvia Urlich, President

D-U-N-S 07-326-3436
WESTCHESTER SQUARE MEDICAL CTR
2475 Saint Raymonds Ave, Bronx, NY 10461
Phone: (718) 430-7300
Sales: $56,037,000
Employees: 700
Company Type: Private
Employees here: 700
SIC: 8062
  General hospital
Alan Kopman, President

D-U-N-S 07-606-1464
WESTERN MEDICAL CENTER
  (Parent: Tenet Healthcare Corporation)
1001 N Tustin Ave, Santa Ana, CA 92705
Phone: (714) 835-3555
Sales: $359,000,000
Employees: 1,300
Company Type: Public Family Member
Employees here: 1,300
SIC: 8062
  General hospital
Dick Butler, Chief Executive Officer

D-U-N-S 07-305-2151
WESTERN MISSOURI MEDICAL CTR
403 Burkarth Rd, Warrensburg, MO 64093
Phone: (660) 747-2500
Sales: $22,433,000
Employees: 320
Company Type: Private
Employees here: 320
SIC: 8062
  County hospital
Gregory B Vinardi, President

D-U-N-S 07-141-2241
WESTERN MONTANA CLINIC, PC
515 W Front St, Missoula, MT 59802
Phone: (406) 721-5600
Sales: $27,147,000
Employees: 350
Company Type: Private
Employees here: 274
SIC: 8011
  Medical clinic
Daniel Ramsey, Administrator

D-U-N-S 92-902-4545
WESTERN PLAINS REGIONAL HOSP
  (Parent: Columbia/Hca Healthcare Corp)
3001 Avenue A, Dodge City, KS 67801
Phone: (316) 225-8400
Sales: $50,000,000
Employees: 350
Company Type: Public Family Member
Employees here: 340
SIC: 8062
  General hospital
Ken Hutchenrider, President

D-U-N-S 07-453-2482
WESTERN RESERVE CARE SYSTEM
345 Oak Hill Ave, Youngstown, OH 44502
Phone: (330) 747-0777
Sales: $195,536,000
Employees: 2,532
Company Type: Private
Employees here: 75
SIC: 8062
  General hospital
Gary Kaatz, Chief Executive Officer

D-U-N-S 08-035-7940
WESTERN RESERVE CARE SYSTEM
500 Gypsy Ln, Youngstown, OH 44504
Phone: (330) 747-1444

Sales: $33,500,000
Employees: NA
Company Type: Private
Employees here: 798
SIC: 8062
  General hospital
Gary Kaatz, Director

D-U-N-S 86-890-5654
WESTERN WASH MED GROUP INC PS
3207 Wetmore Ave, Everett, WA 98201
Phone: (425) 259-4041
Sales: $21,000,000
Employees: 150
Company Type: Private
Employees here: 115
SIC: 8011
  Medical clinic
Henry Veldman, President

D-U-N-S 05-191-7268
WESTLAKE COMMUNITY HOSPITAL
1225 W Lake St, Melrose Park, IL 60160
Phone: (708) 681-3000
Sales: $74,640,000
Employees: 900
Company Type: Private
Employees here: 850
SIC: 8062
  General hospital
Leonard J Muller, President

D-U-N-S 07-792-9859
WESTMINSTER-CANTERBURY CORP
1600 Westbrook Ave, Richmond, VA 23227
Phone: (804) 264-6000
Sales: $21,010,000
Employees: 550
Company Type: Private
Employees here: 550
SIC: 8361
  Continuing care retirement community
W T Cunningham Jr, President

D-U-N-S 10-733-0342
WESTMORELAND HEALTH SYSTEM
532 W Pittsburgh St, Greensburg, PA 15601
Phone: (724) 832-4000
Sales: $79,200,000
Employees: 1,700
Company Type: Private
Employees here: 1,600
SIC: 8062
  Hospital rehab center ret medical equipment housecleaning
    service & commercial collection svc
Joseph J Peluso, Chief Executive Officer

D-U-N-S 00-191-9604
WESTMORELAND REGIONAL HOSP
532 W Pittsburgh St, Greensburg, PA 15601
Phone: (724) 832-4000
Sales: $107,009,000
Employees: 1,700
Company Type: Private
Employees here: 1,516
SIC: 8062
  General hospital
Joseph J Peluso, President

D-U-N-S 80-097-3042
WFSI-ILLINOIS
26w171 Roosevelt Rd, Wheaton, IL 60187
Phone: (630) 462-9271
Sales: $47,300,000
Employees: 1,024
Company Type: Private
Employees here: 1,024
SIC: 8062
  General hospital
John D Oliverio, President

D-U-N-S 09-602-5432
WHARTON HOSPITAL CORPORATION
  (Parent: Columbia/Hca Healthcare Corp)
1400 Hwy 59 Byp, Wharton, TX 77488
Phone: (409) 532-2500

Sales: $75,000,000
Company Type: Public Family Member
SIC: 8062
    General medical & surgical hospital
Michael Murphy, Chief Executive Officer

Employees: 500
Employees here: 400

D-U-N-S 06-874-2725
WHEELING HOSPITAL INC
Medical Park, Wheeling, WV 26003
Phone: (304) 243-3000
Sales: $104,741,000
Company Type: Private
SIC: 8062
    Hospital
Dr Donald H Hofoeute Md, Administrator

Employees: 1,388
Employees here: 1,120

D-U-N-S 07-185-2503
WHIDBEY GENERAL HOSPITAL PUB
101 Main St S, Coupeville, WA 98239
Phone: (360) 678-5151
Sales: $26,925,000
Company Type: Private
SIC: 8062
    General hospital
Scott Rhine, Administrator

Employees: 475
Employees here: 456

D-U-N-S 11-888-9237
WHITE COUNTY MEDICAL CENTER
3214 E Race Ave, Searcy, AR 72143
Phone: (501) 268-6121
Sales: $39,189,000
Company Type: Private
SIC: 8062
    General hospital
Ray Montgomery, Administrator

Employees: 620
Employees here: 570

D-U-N-S 05-386-6851
WHITE MEMORIAL MEDICAL CENTER
1720 E Cesar E Chavez Ave, Los Angeles, CA 90033
Phone: (323) 268-5000
Sales: $148,586,000
Company Type: Private
SIC: 8062
    General medical & surgical hospital
Robert Carman, Chief Executive Officer

Employees: 1,250
Employees here: 1,200

D-U-N-S 07-799-3665
WHITE OAK MANOR INC
2407 S Pine St, Spartanburg, SC 29302
Phone: (864) 582-7503
Sales: $72,189,000
Company Type: Private
SIC: 8051
    Skilled nursing care and independent living facilities
Bettye Cecil, President

Employees: 2,300
Employees here: 60

D-U-N-S 04-566-3903
WHITE PLAINS HOSPITAL CENTER
Davis Avenue At E Post Rd, White Plains, NY 10601
Phone: (914) 681-0600
Sales: $111,292,000
Company Type: Private
SIC: 8062
    General medical & surgical hospital
Jon B Schandler, President

Employees: 1,100
Employees here: 1,095

D-U-N-S 78-645-5121
WHITE PLINS HOSPITAL CTR FUNDATION
Davis Avenue At E Post Rd, White Plains, NY 10601
Phone: (914) 681-0600

Sales: $60,300,000
Company Type: Private
SIC: 8062
    General medical and surgical hospital
Jon B Schandler, President

Employees: 1,300
Employees here: 1,300

D-U-N-S 07-738-8999
WHITE RIVER MEDICAL CENTER
1710 Harrison St, Batesville, AR 72501
Phone: (870) 793-1200
Sales: $52,872,000
Company Type: Private
SIC: 8062
    General hospital
Gary Bebow, Chief Executive Officer

Employees: 760
Employees here: 650

D-U-N-S 07-193-9581
WHITE-WILSON MEDICAL CTR P A
1005 Mar Walt Dr, Fort Walton Beach, FL 32547
Phone: (850) 863-8100
Sales: $20,800,000
Company Type: Private
SIC: 8011
    Multi-specialty medical doctor's office
Dr Roger D Riggenbach, President

Employees: 304
Employees here: 286

D-U-N-S 07-430-3835
WHITLEY MEMORIAL HOSPITAL,
353 N Oak St, Columbia City, IN 46725
Phone: (219) 244-6191
Sales: $21,762,000
Company Type: Private
SIC: 8062
    General hospital
John Hatcher, President

Employees: 340
Employees here: 260

D-U-N-S 10-297-1330
WHITTIER HOSPITAL MED CTR INC
(Parent: Tenet Healthcare Corporation)
9080 Colima Rd, Whittier, CA 90605
Phone: (562) 945-3561
Sales: $21,600,000
Company Type: Public Family Member
SIC: 8062
    General hospital
Jeffrey Barbakow, Chief Executive Officer

Employees: 481
Employees here: 481

D-U-N-S 17-998-9165
WHSLC REALTY LLC
111 E Wacker Dr Ste 2400, Chicago, IL 60601
Phone: (773) 878-6333
Sales: $27,900,000
Company Type: Private
SIC: 8052
    Holding company for assisted living facilities
William B Kaplan, President

Employees: 1,500
Employees here: 60

D-U-N-S 07-330-7498
WICHITA CLINIC, PA
3311 E Murdock St, Wichita, KS 67208
Phone: (316) 689-9153
Sales: $80,000,000
Company Type: Private
SIC: 8011
    Medical clinic & pharmacy
Steven J Perkins, Chief Executive Officer

Employees: 750
Employees here: 500

D-U-N-S 07-156-3720
WILKES REGIONAL MEDICAL CENTER
1370 W D St, North Wilkesboro, NC 28659
Phone: (336) 651-8100

Sales: $42,396,000
Company Type: Private
SIC: 8062
   General hospital
David Henson, Administrator

Employees: 700
Employees here: 700

D-U-N-S 05-707-2407
WILLAMETTE FALLS HOSPITAL INC
1500 Division St, Oregon City, OR 97045
Phone: (503) 656-1631
Sales: $48,203,000
Company Type: Private
SIC: 8062
   General hospital home health care services
Robert Steed, Administrator

Employees: 715
Employees here: 675

D-U-N-S 07-549-2306
WILLIAM B KESSLER MEM HOSP
600 S White Horse Pike, Hammonton, NJ 8037
Phone: (609) 561-6700
Sales: $40,460,000
Company Type: Private
SIC: 8062
   General hospital
John Buertman, Chairman of the Board

Employees: 650
Employees here: 650

D-U-N-S 06-925-9398
WILLIAM BACKUS HOSPITAL
326 Washington St, Norwich, CT 6360
Phone: (860) 889-8331
Sales: $88,299,000
Company Type: Private
SIC: 8062
   General hospital
Thomas P Pipicelli, President

Employees: 1,050
Employees here: 1,045

D-U-N-S 09-912-1469
WILLIAM BEAUMONT HOSPITAL
44201 Dequindre Rd, Troy, MI 48098
Phone: (248) 828-5180
Sales: $50,700,000
Company Type: Private
SIC: 8062
   General hospital
John D Labriola, Manager

Employees: NA
Employees here: 1,200

D-U-N-S 07-636-2110
WILLIAM BEAUMONT HOSPITAL
3601 W 13 Mile Rd, Royal Oak, MI 48073
Phone: (248) 551-5000
Sales: $837,644,000
Company Type: Private
SIC: 8062
   General medical & surgical hospitals
Ted Wasson, President

Employees: 9,400
Employees here: 7,500

D-U-N-S 15-021-5747
WILLIAM N HARWIN MD PA
3840 Broadway, Fort Myers, FL 33901
Phone: (941) 275-6400
Sales: $30,000,000
Company Type: Private
SIC: 8011
   Medical office specializing in hematology & oncology
Dr William N Harwin, President

Employees: 108
Employees here: 30

D-U-N-S 07-827-8702
WILLIAM PRINCE HOSPITAL CORP
8700 Sudley Rd, Manassas, VA 20110
Phone: (703) 369-8000

Sales: $72,329,000
Company Type: Private
SIC: 8062
   Hospital
Kenneth B Swenson, Administrator

Employees: 600
Employees here: 600

D-U-N-S 07-476-0331
WILLIAMSBURG COMMUNITY HOSP
301 Monticello Ave, Williamsburg, VA 23185
Phone: (757) 259-6000
Sales: $61,001,000
Company Type: Private
SIC: 8062
   Hospital
Leslie A Donahue, President

Employees: 1,150
Employees here: 916

D-U-N-S 94-885-4369
WILLIAMSBURG COMMUNITY HOSP
301 Monticello Ave, Williamsburg, VA 23185
Phone: (757) 259-6000
Sales: $32,500,000
Company Type: Private
SIC: 8062
   Hospital
Les Donahue, Director

Employees: NA
Employees here: 800

D-U-N-S 07-822-5182
WILLIAMSON COUNTY HOSPITAL,
2021 N Carothers Rd, Franklin, TN 37067
Phone: (615) 791-0500
Sales: $51,237,000
Company Type: Private
SIC: 8062
   General hospital
Ronald G Joyner, Administrator

Employees: 610
Employees here: 600

D-U-N-S 07-917-7739
WILLIAMSPORT HOSPITAL MED CTR INC
777 Rural Ave, Williamsport, PA 17701
Phone: (717) 321-1000
Sales: $84,901,000
Company Type: Private
SIC: 8062
   General medical & surgical hospital
Donald Creamer, President

Employees: 2,633
Employees here: 1,000

D-U-N-S 83-636-8266
WILLIAMSPORT HOSPITAL MED CTR INC
1100 Grampian Blvd, Williamsport, PA 17701
Phone: (717) 326-8110
Sales: $44,400,000
Company Type: Private
SIC: 8062
   General medical and surgical hospital
Donald Creamer, Principal

Employees: NA
Employees here: 900

D-U-N-S 06-703-8877
WILLIS-KNIGHTON MEDICAL CTR
2600 Greenwood Rd, Shreveport, LA 71103
Phone: (318) 632-4600
Sales: $126,500,000
Company Type: Private
SIC: 8062
   Hospitals
James Elrod, President

Employees: 2,700
Employees here: 1,800

D-U-N-S 11-257-6319
WILLOW VALLEY MANOR
211 Willow Valley Sq, Lancaster, PA 17602
Phone: (717) 464-2741

Sales: $44,039,000

Company Type: Private

SIC: 8361
  Provides residential care
Torrey M Johnson, President

Employees: 950

Employees here: 200

D-U-N-S 07-120-6015

WILMAC CORPORATION
(*Parent:* Mc Wil Group Ltd)
209 N Beaver St, York, PA 17403
Phone: (717) 854-7857
Sales: $33,100,000
Company Type: Private
SIC: 8059
  Convalescent & skilled care facilities addictive treatment
    center apartments management consultants & real estate
    developers
Webster J Mc Cormack, Chairman of the Board

Employees: 1,490

Employees here: 37

D-U-N-S 06-266-9478

WILSON MEMORIAL HOSPITAL INC
1705 Tarboro St SW, Wilson, NC 27893
Phone: (252) 399-8040
Sales: $65,334,000
Company Type: Private
SIC: 8062
  General medical and surgical hospital
Christophe Durrer, President

Employees: 840

Employees here: 840

D-U-N-S 07-213-6468

WINCHESTER HOSPITAL
41 Highland Ave, Winchester, MA 1890
Phone: (781) 729-9000
Sales: $93,241,000
Company Type: Private
SIC: 8062
  General hospital
Stephen R Laverty, President

Employees: 2,000

Employees here: 500

D-U-N-S 07-494-4927

WINCHESTER MEDICAL CENTER INC
1840 Amherst St, Winchester, VA 22601
Phone: (540) 722-8000
Sales: $169,923,000
Company Type: Private
SIC: 8062
  General hospital
George B Caley, President

Employees: 2,006

Employees here: 1,936

D-U-N-S 06-697-4973

WING MEMORIAL HOSPITAL CORP
40 Wright St, Palmer, MA 1069
Phone: (413) 283-7651
Sales: $21,500,000
Company Type: Private
SIC: 8062
  General hospital
Richard H Scheffer, President

Employees: 480

Employees here: 340

D-U-N-S 86-119-3530

WINONA COMMUNITY MEMORIAL HOSP
855 Mankato Ave, Winona, MN 55987
Phone: (507) 454-3650
Sales: $28,693,000
Company Type: Private
SIC: 8062
  Hospital and skilled care nursing facility
Patrick Booth, Administrator

Employees: 620

Employees here: 620

D-U-N-S 07-652-1533

WINONA HEALTH SERVICES INC
855 Mankato Ave, Winona, MN 55987
Phone: (507) 454-3650

Sales: $40,000,000

Company Type: Private

SIC: 8062
  Health system
Patrick Booth, President

Employees: 675

Employees here: 625

D-U-N-S 07-921-2254

WINTER HAVEN HOSPITAL INC
200 Avenue F NE, Winter Haven, FL 33881
Phone: (941) 293-1121
Sales: $148,354,000
Company Type: Private
SIC: 8062
  General hospital
Lance W Anastasio, President

Employees: 2,420

Employees here: 2,000

D-U-N-S 07-256-2630

WINTER PARK HEALTH CARE GROUP
200 N Lakemont Ave, Winter Park, FL 32792
Phone: (407) 646-7000
Sales: $74,500,000
Company Type: Private
SIC: 8062
  Hospital
J L Builder, Partner

Employees: 1,600

Employees here: 1,579

D-U-N-S 83-614-8007

WINTER PARK MEMORIAL HOSPITAL
200 N Lakemont Ave, Winter Park, FL 32792
Phone: (407) 657-4060
Sales: $74,500,000
Company Type: Private
SIC: 8062
  Acure care & general medical & surgical hospital
Doug Degraaf, Chief Executive Officer

Employees: 1,600

Employees here: 1,600

D-U-N-S 06-593-7856

WINTHROP-UNIVERSITY HOSPITAL
259 1st St, Mineola, NY 11501
Phone: (516) 663-0333
Sales: $328,809,000
Company Type: Private
SIC: 8062
  General hospital
Martin J Delaney, President

Employees: 3,601

Employees here: 2,500

D-U-N-S 01-826-1263

WISCONSIN DEPT HEALTH FMLY SVCS
Butler Ave, Winnebago, WI 54985
Phone: (920) 235-4910
Sales: $20,400,000
Company Type: Private
SIC: 8063
  Psychatric hospital
Stanley York, N/A

Employees: NA

Employees here: 600

D-U-N-S 07-614-4526

WISCONSIN DEPT HEALTH FMLY SVCS
21425 Spring St, Union Grove, WI 53182
Phone: (414) 878-2411
Sales: $23,500,000
Company Type: Private
SIC: 8361
  Institution for developmentally disabled children & adults
James Hutchison, Director

Employees: NA

Employees here: 1,047

D-U-N-S 02-047-2866

WISCONSIN DEPT HEALTH FMLY SVCS
317 Knutson Dr, Madison, WI 53704
Phone: (608) 243-2292

Sales: $33,600,000   *Employees:* NA
Company Type: Private   *Employees here:* 1,500
SIC: 8361
    Care & training of retarded residents
Theodore Bunck, Branch Manager

D-U-N-S 07-147-4712
WOMAN'S CHRISTIAN ASSOC O JAM
207 Foote Ave, Jamestown, NY 14701
Phone: (716) 487-0141
Sales: $74,558,000   *Employees:* 1,340
Company Type: Private   *Employees here:* 1,200
SIC: 8062
    General medical & surgical hospital and psychiatric care &
    alcohol medical & cancer rehabilitation services
Mark Celmer, President

D-U-N-S 01-040-1966
WOMAN'S HOSPITAL FOUNDATION
9050 Airline Hwy, Baton Rouge, LA 70815
Phone: (225) 927-1300
Sales: $87,228,000   *Employees:* 1,250
Company Type: Private   *Employees here:* 1,200
SIC: 8062
    Women's hospital
Teri Fontenot, Administrator

D-U-N-S 07-844-7315
WOMANS HOSPITAL TEXAS INC
    (Parent: H C A Health Svcs Texas Inc)
7600 Fannin St, Houston, TX 77054
Phone: (713) 790-1234
Sales: $79,603,000   *Employees:* 900
Company Type: Public Family Member   *Employees here:* 500
SIC: 8062
    General medical & surgical hospital
Linda Russell, Chief Executive Officer

D-U-N-S 06-985-1913
WOMEN & INFANTS HOSPITAL RI
101 Dudley St, Providence, RI 2905
Phone: (401) 274-1100
Sales: $141,960,000   *Employees:* 2,000
Company Type: Private   *Employees here:* 1,800
SIC: 8069
    Ob-gyn neonatal isu specialty hospital
Mark E Crevier, Chief Financial Officer

D-U-N-S 92-661-4132
WOMENS AND CHILDRENS HOSPITAL INC
    (Parent: Columbia/Hca Healthcare Corp)
4600 Ambassador Caffery P, Lafayette, LA 70508
Phone: (318) 981-9100
Sales: $23,041,000   *Employees:* 370
Company Type: Public Family Member   *Employees here:* 370
SIC: 8069
    Specialty care hospital
Mimi Roberson, Chief Executive Officer

D-U-N-S 07-757-5421
WOOD COUNTY HOSPITAL ASSN
950 W Wooster St, Bowling Green, OH 43402
Phone: (419) 354-8900
Sales: $22,500,000   *Employees:* 500
Company Type: Private   *Employees here:* 500
SIC: 8062
    General medical and surgical hospital
Michael Miesle, Administrator

D-U-N-S 80-650-8461
WOODLAND HEALTHCARE
1207 Fairchild Ct, Woodland, CA 95695
Phone: (530) 668-2618

Sales: $22,200,000   *Employees:* NA
Company Type: Private   *Employees here:* 350
SIC: 8011
    Medical doctor's office
Bill Hunt, Principal

D-U-N-S 05-096-2604
WOODLAND PARK HOSPITAL, INC
    (Parent: New American Healthcare Corp)
10300 NE Hancock St, Portland, OR 97220
Phone: (503) 257-5500
Sales: $30,000,000   *Employees:* 325
Company Type: Public Family Member   *Employees here:* 270
SIC: 8062
    General hospital
Kay Vetaly, Administration

D-U-N-S 07-432-5234
WOODLAWN HOSPITAL
1400 E 9th St, Rochester, IN 46975
Phone: (219) 223-3141
Sales: $21,214,000   *Employees:* 458
Company Type: Private   *Employees here:* 450
SIC: 8062
    General hospital
Michael Gordon, Chief Executive Officer

D-U-N-S 07-491-0845
WOODS MEMORIAL HOSPITAL DST
Hwy 411 N, Etowah, TN 37331
Phone: (423) 263-3600
Sales: $19,939,000   *Employees:* 400
Company Type: Private   *Employees here:* 315
SIC: 8062
    General hospital and nursing facility
Alvin Hoover, Administrator

D-U-N-S 08-139-8703
WOODWARD HOSPITAL & HEALTH CTR
900 17th St, Woodward, OK 73801
Phone: (580) 256-5511
Sales: $27,007,000   *Employees:* 255
Company Type: Private   *Employees here:* 252
SIC: 8062
    General hospital
Warren K Spellman, Administrator

D-U-N-S 13-056-6375
WUESTHOFF HEALTH SYSTEMS INC
110 Longwood Ave Stop 19, Rockledge, FL 32955
Phone: (407) 636-2211
Sales: $113,872,000   *Employees:* 2,012
Company Type: Private   *Employees here:* 1,346
SIC: 8062
    Hospital
Robert Carman, President

D-U-N-S 07-921-5497
WUESTHOFF MEMORIAL HOSPITAL
110 Longwood Ave 93, Rockledge, FL 32955
Phone: (407) 636-2211
Sales: $113,872,000   *Employees:* 1,356
Company Type: Private   *Employees here:* 1,148
SIC: 8062
    General medical and surgical hospital
Robert Carman, President

D-U-N-S 06-959-4026
WVHCS-HOSPITAL
575 N River St, Wilkes Barre, PA 18764
Phone: (717) 829-8111

Sales: $197,957,000   *Employees:* 2,555
Company Type: Private   *Employees here:* 1,550
SIC: 8062
  Hospital
Pat Finan, Acting President

D-U-N-S 87-460-8490
WVHCS-HOSPITAL
562 Wyoming Ave, Kingston, PA 18704
Phone: (717) 283-7000
Sales: $69,500,000   *Employees:* NA
Company Type: Private   *Employees here:* 1,400
SIC: 8062
  Hospital
Ron Stern, Principal

D-U-N-S 06-098-3871
WYANDOTTE HOSPITAL & MED CTR
2333 Biddle St, Wyandotte, MI 48192
Phone: (734) 284-2400
Sales: $280,000,000   *Employees:* 1,700
Company Type: Private   *Employees here:* 1,700
SIC: 8062
  General hospital
William R Alvin, Administrator

D-U-N-S 06-608-6307
WYCKOFF HEIGHTS MEDICAL CTR
  (Parent: New York And Presbyterian Hosp)
374 Stockholm St, Brooklyn, NY 11237
Phone: (718) 963-7272
Sales: $69,800,000   *Employees:* 1,500
Company Type: Private   *Employees here:* 1,300
SIC: 8062
  General hospital
Dominick Gio, President

D-U-N-S 10-654-0107
WYETH LABORATORIES INC
865 Ridge Rd, Monmouth Junction, NJ 8852
Phone: (732) 329-2300
Sales: $29,600,000   *Employees:* NA
Company Type: Public Family Member   *Employees here:* 573
SIC: 8071
  Medical laboratory
Steve Clark, Principal

D-U-N-S 03-021-3862
WYOMING COUNTY COMMUNITY HOSP
400 N Main St, Warsaw, NY 14569
Phone: (716) 786-2233
Sales: $31,112,000   *Employees:* 530
Company Type: Private   *Employees here:* 526
SIC: 8062
  Hospital & extended care nursing facility
Lucy Sheedy, Chief Executive Officer

D-U-N-S 07-038-1272
WYOMING HEALTH SERVICES INC
  (Parent: Healthtrust Inc - Hospital Co)
2100 W Sunset Dr, Riverton, WY 82501
Phone: (307) 856-4161
Sales: $33,000,000   *Employees:* 235
Company Type: Public Family Member   *Employees here:* 235
SIC: 8062
  General hospital
Doug Crabtree, Chief Executive Officer

D-U-N-S 07-340-0582
WYOMING MEDICAL CENTER INC
1233 E 2nd St, Casper, WY 82601
Phone: (307) 577-7201

Sales: $95,851,000   *Employees:* 1,033
Company Type: Private   *Employees here:* 1,018
SIC: 8062
  General hospital
Chris Muirhead, Chairman of the Board

D-U-N-S 09-461-6935
YAKIMA VALLEY FRM WKRS CLINIC
518 W 1st Ave, Toppenish, WA 98948
Phone: (509) 865-5898
Sales: $46,453,000   *Employees:* 650
Company Type: Private   *Employees here:* 200
SIC: 8011
  Medical & dental clinic
Carlos Olivares, Executive Director

D-U-N-S 02-023-3946
YAKIMA VALLEY MEM HOSPITAL ASSN
2811 Tieton Dr, Yakima, WA 98902
Phone: (509) 575-8000
Sales: $90,953,000   *Employees:* 1,114
Company Type: Private   *Employees here:* 1,074
SIC: 8062
  General hospital
Richard W Linneweh, President

D-U-N-S 92-919-0296
YALE UNIVERSITY
333 Cedar St Ste 4101, New Haven, CT 6510
Phone: (203) 785-4642
Sales: $28,100,000   *Employees:* NA
Company Type: Private   *Employees here:* 450
SIC: 8011
  Pediatrics
Joseph Warshaw, Manager

D-U-N-S 07-540-6561
YALE-NEW HAVEN HOSPITAL INC
20 York St, New Haven, CT 6510
Phone: (203) 785-4242
Sales: $450,857,000   *Employees:* 5,959
Company Type: Private   *Employees here:* 5,800
SIC: 8062
  General hospital
Joseph A Zaccagnino, President

D-U-N-S 06-842-2237
YAVAPAI COMMUNITY HOSPITAL ASSN
1003 Willow Creek Rd, Prescott, AZ 86301
Phone: (520) 445-2700
Sales: $57,453,000   *Employees:* 730
Company Type: Private   *Employees here:* 660
SIC: 8062
  General medical & surgical hospital
Timothy Barnett, Chief Executive Officer

D-U-N-S 13-179-6807
YONKERS GENERAL HOSPITAL INC
2 Park Ave, Yonkers, NY 10703
Phone: (914) 964-7300
Sales: $42,803,000   *Employees:* 600
Company Type: Private   *Employees here:* 550
SIC: 8062
  General medical & surgical hospital
James Foy, Chief Executive Officer

D-U-N-S 02-018-5104
YORK GENERAL HOSPITAL, INC.
2222 Lincoln Ave, York, NE 68467
Phone: (402) 362-6671

Sales: $96,779,000   *Employees:* 190
Company Type: Private   *Employees here:* 190
SIC: 8062
   Hospital
Chuck Schulz, Chief Executive Officer

D-U-N-S 62-180-1406
YORK HANNOVER NURSING CENTERS
   (Parent: Stockbridge Inv Partners)
75 S Church St Ste 650, Pittsfield, MA 1201
Phone: (413) 448-2111
Sales: $22,700,000   *Employees:* 1,000
Company Type: Private   *Employees here:* 8
SIC: 8051
   Skilled nursing home facilities
Thomas Clarke, President

D-U-N-S 88-461-2326
YORK HEALTH SYSTEM MED GROUP
25 Monument Rd Ste 190, York, PA 17403
Phone: (717) 741-8206
Sales: $22,923,000   *Employees:* 95
Company Type: Private   *Employees here:* 30
SIC: 8011
   Group medical practice
Tom Mcgann, President

D-U-N-S 07-746-1549
YORK HOSPITAL
15 Hospital Dr, York, ME 3909
Phone: (207) 363-4321
Sales: $33,420,000   *Employees:* 509
Company Type: Private   *Employees here:* 480
SIC: 8062
   Hospital/nursing facility
Jud Knox, President

D-U-N-S 07-121-2153
YORK HOSPITAL
1001 S George St, York, PA 17403
Phone: (717) 771-2345
Sales: $228,822,000   *Employees:* 3,604
Company Type: Private   *Employees here:* 3,500
SIC: 8062
   General hospital
Bruce M Bartels, President

D-U-N-S 07-691-2468
YOUNGSTOWN OSTPTHIC HOSPITAL ASSN
100 Debartolo Pl Ste 100, Youngstown, OH 44512
Phone: (330) 726-8424
Sales: $26,953,000   *Employees:* 409
Company Type: Private   *Employees here:* 9
SIC: 8062
   General acute care hospital
John Weir, Chief Executive Officer

D-U-N-S 11-171-8029
YOUTH & FAMILY CENTERED
1705 S Capital Of Texas H, Austin, TX 78746
Phone: (512) 327-1119
Sales: $36,700,000   *Employees:* 1,500
Company Type: Private   *Employees here:* 10
SIC: 8361
   Own & operate residential care facilities
Kevin P Sheehan, Chief Executive Officer

D-U-N-S 03-024-0782
YOUTH CONSULTATION SERVICE
284 Broadway, Newark, NJ 7104
Phone: (973) 482-8411

Sales: $21,630,000   *Employees:* 750
Company Type: Private   *Employees here:* 70
SIC: 8093
   Specialty outpatient clinic residential care services
      elementary/secondary school
Harold Williams, President

D-U-N-S 78-772-6124
YOUTH SERVICES INTERNATIONAL,
2 Park Center Ct Ste 200, Owings Mills, MD 21117
Phone: (410) 356-8600
Sales: $100,353,000   *Employees:* 1,500
Company Type: Public   *Employees here:* 34
SIC: 8361
   Residential treatment facility
Timothy P Cole, Chairman of the Board

D-U-N-S 17-350-6452
YOUTH VILLAGES INC
5515 Shelby Oaks Dr, Memphis, TN 38134
Phone: (901) 252-7600
Sales: $23,709,000   *Employees:* 275
Company Type: Private   *Employees here:* 90
SIC: 8361
   Children's residential treatment center
Patrick Lawler, Administrator

D-U-N-S 07-535-4795
YOUVILLE LIFE CARE INC
1575 Cambridge St, Cambridge, MA 2138
Phone: (617) 876-4344
Sales: $43,886,000   *Employees:* 750
Company Type: Private   *Employees here:* 750
SIC: 8069
   Chronic disease hospital
T R Quigley, President

D-U-N-S 08-250-8961
YUKON-KUSKOKWIM HEALTH CORP
101 Main St, Bethel, AK 99559
Phone: (907) 543-6300
Sales: $66,511,000   *Employees:* 844
Company Type: Private   *Employees here:* 500
SIC: 8062
   Health services organization hospital alcohol rehab center
      mental health clinic & optometrist clinic
Gene Peltola, President

D-U-N-S 07-448-5996
YUMA REGIONAL MEDICAL CENTER
2400 S Avenue A, Yuma, AZ 85364
Phone: (520) 344-2000
Sales: $103,390,000   *Employees:* 1,200
Company Type: Private   *Employees here:* 1,200
SIC: 8062
   General medical/surgical hospital
Robert Olsen, Chief Executive Officer

D-U-N-S 19-609-8636
ZALE LIPSHY UNIVERSITY HOSP
5151 Harry Hines Blvd, Dallas, TX 75235
Phone: (214) 590-3000
Sales: $93,898,000   *Employees:* 650
Company Type: Private   *Employees here:* 650
SIC: 8062
   General hospital
Robert B Smith, President

D-U-N-S 07-055-9562
ZANDEX INC
1122 Taylor St, Zanesville, OH 43701
Phone: (740) 454-1400

Sales: $29,131,000   *Employees:* 1,000
Company Type: Private   *Employees here:* 15
SIC: 8052
   Intermediate care facilities
Douglas L Ramsay, Principal

   D-U-N-S 07-362-5253
22 TEXAS SERVICES, LP
120 Gibraltar Rd Ste 310, Horsham, PA 19044
Phone: (215) 441-7700
Sales: $180,000,000   *Employees:* 4,500
Company Type: Private   *Employees here:* 75
SIC: 8051
   Owns & operates skilled nursing care facilities
John H Durham, Limited Partner

CHAPTER 5

RANKINGS AND COMPANIES

The companies presented in Chapter 4 - Company Directory are arranged in this chapter in rank order based first on sales and next on employment. Each company's name, rank, location, type, sales, employment, and primary SIC are shown. Only companies with reported sales data are included in the "rankings by sales" table; similarly, only companies that report employment are ranked in the "rankings by employment" table.

Company type is either Public, Private, or Public Family Member. The last category is used to label corporate entities that belong to a group of companies, the relationship being that of a subsidiary or element of a parent. The parents of Public Family Member companies can be reviewed in the directory presented in Chapter 4.

This product includes proprietary data of Dun & Bradstreet, Inc.

D&B COMPANY RANKINGS BY SALES

Company	Rank	Location	Type	Sales ($ mil.)	Employ-ment	Primary SIC
Columbia/Hca Healthcare Corp	1	Nashville, TN	Public	18,819.0	295,000	8062
Tenet Healthcare Corporation	2	Santa Barbara, CA	Public	9,895.0	116,800	8062
Humana Inc	3	Louisville, KY	Public	7,880.0	19,500	8011
Foundation Health Systems Inc	4	Woodland Hills, CA	Private	7,235.0	2,600	8011
Catholic Health Initiative	5	Denver, CO	Private	4,001.6	45,000	8062
New York Cy Health Hspitals Corp	6	New York, NY	Private	3,775.9	38,000	8062
Beverly Entrprss-California Inc	7	Fort Smith, AR	Public Family Member	3,230.3	110	8051
Beverly Enterprises Inc	8	Fort Smith, AR	Public	3,217.1	74,000	8051
Kaiser Foundation Hospitals	9	Oakland, CA	Private	3,159.0	25,000	8062
Vencor, Inc	10	Louisville, KY	Private	3,116.0	76,800	8062
Healthsouth Corporation	11	Birmingham, AL	Public	3,017.3	56,281	8093
Mariner Post-Acute Network	12	Atlanta, GA	Public	3,000.0	62,000	8051
Tenet Health System Hospitals	13	Dallas, TX	Public Family Member	2,990.9	22,000	8062
Nylcare Health Plans, Inc	14	New York, NY	Private	2,800.0	4,000	8011
Galen Health Care Inc	15	Nashville, TN	Public Family Member	2,641.1	55,900	8062
Healthtrust Inc - Hospital Co	16	Nashville, TN	Public Family Member	2,598.6	NA	8062
Mayo Foundation	17	Rochester, MN	Private	2,565.6	30,497	8011
Allina Health System	18	Hopkins, MN	Private	2,526.7	21,000	8011
Permanente Medical Group Inc	19	Oakland, CA	Private	2,479.8	19,000	8011
Carefirst Of Maryland, Inc	20	Owings Mills, MD	Private	2,183.9	3,700	8011
Sun Healthcare Group Inc	21	Albuquerque, NM	Public	2,010.8	68,900	8051
Integrated Health Services	22	Owings Mills, MD	Public	1,993.2	86,000	8051
Henry Ford Health System	23	Detroit, MI	Private	1,937.3	16,300	8062
United States Health	24	Blue Bell, PA	Public Family Member	1,717.6	209	8011
Keystone Health Plan East Inc	25	Philadelphia, PA	Private	1,613.0	571	8011
Quorum Health Group Inc	26	Brentwood, TN	Public	1,572.4	17,000	8062
Quest Diagnostics Incorporated	27	Teterboro, NJ	Private	1,528.7	16,300	8071
Manorcare Health Services Inc	28	Gaithersburg, MD	Public Family Member	1,524.2	30,000	8051
Laboratory Corp Amer Holdings	29	Burlington, NC	Private	1,519.0	18,600	8071
Universal Health Services	30	King Of Prussia, PA	Public	1,442.7	17,800	8062
American Medical Holdings Inc	31	Dallas, TX	Public	1,426.4	NA	8062
Tenet Health System Medical	32	Santa Barbara, CA	Public Family Member	1,426.4	30,200	8062
Ihc Health Services Inc	33	Salt Lake City, UT	Private	1,424.8	21,000	8062
Ornda Investments Inc	34	Santa Barbara, CA	Public Family Member	1,416.9	30,000	8062
Samaritan Health System	35	Phoenix, AZ	Private	1,345.6	11,954	8062
Ornda Healthcorp	36	Santa Barbara, CA	Public	1,227.8	26,000	8062
Magellan Health Services Inc	37	Atlanta, GA	Public	1,210.7	5,000	8093
U H S Of De La Ronde, Inc.	38	Chalmette, LA	Public Family Member	1,190.2	250	8062
Montefiore Medical Center	39	Bronx, NY	Private	1,188.2	10,794	8062
Talbert Medical Mgt Corp	40	Costa Mesa, CA	Public Family Member	1,181.0	29,526	8099
Apria Healthcare Group Inc	41	Costa Mesa, CA	Public	1,180.7	9,555	8082
Healthpartners, Inc	42	Minneapolis, MN	Private	1,178.5	7,000	8011
Sisters Of Providence In Wash	43	Seattle, WA	Private	1,148.9	10,900	8062
Cleveland Clinic Foundation	44	Cleveland, OH	Private	1,146.9	11,500	8062
Phycor Inc	45	Nashville, TN	Public	1,119.6	19,000	8011
Genesis Health Ventures Inc	46	Kennett Square, PA	Public	1,099.8	35,000	8059
Novacare Inc	47	King Of Prussia, PA	Public	1,066.5	39,800	8049
Novacare, Inc	48	King Of Prussia, PA	Public Family Member	1,066.5	17,000	8049
National Medical Care Inc	49	Lexington, MA	Public Family Member	1,028.6	18,000	8092
Adventist Healthcare Inc	50	Rockville, MD	Private	961.2	NA	8062
Baptist Mem Health Care Corp	51	Memphis, TN	Private	949.2	7,907	8062
Washington University	52	Saint Louis, MO	Private	941.8	6,600	8062
Aetna Health Plans Of Cal	53	Walnut Creek, CA	Public Family Member	940.0	265	8011
Baylor Health Care System	54	Dallas, TX	Private	938.0	1,409	8062
Charlotte Mecklenburg Hos	55	Charlotte, NC	Private	930.3	7,000	8062
Extendicare Health Services	56	Milwaukee, WI	Private	916.2	17,388	8051
Health Alliance Plan Of Mich	57	Detroit, MI	Private	913.2	1,400	8011
Johns Hopkins Health Sys Corp	58	Baltimore, MD	Private	910.5	629	8062
American Transitional Hospitals	59	Franklin, TN	Public Family Member	900.0	1,200	8011
Health Management Associates	60	Naples, FL	Public	895.5	10,000	8062
Health Care Retirement Manor Care	61	Toledo, OH	Public	892.0	22,000	8051
Mount Sinai Hospital (Inc)	62	New York, NY	Private	872.1	12,000	8062
Tufts Associated Health Plans	63	Waltham, MA	Private	865.0	1,000	8011
Genesis Lifestyles Inc	64	Macon, GA	Private	864.0	25	8059
Sisters Of St Francis Health Svcs	65	Mishawaka, IN	Private	856.5	9,000	8062
William Beaumont Hospital	66	Royal Oak, MI	Private	837.6	9,400	8062
Beth Israel Medical Center	67	New York, NY	Private	834.0	8,100	8062
Adventist Health System/Sunbelt	68	Winter Park, FL	Private	828.0	17,542	8062
H C A, Inc.	69	Nashville, TN	Public Family Member	826.1	17,500	8062
Horizon/Cms Healthcare Corp	70	Albuquerque, NM	Public Family Member	817.4	NA	8051

D&B COMPANY RANKINGS BY SALES

Company	Rank	Location	Type	Sales ($ mil.)	Employ- ment	Primary SIC
Pilgrim Health Care Inc	71	Quincy, MA	Private	803.4	700	8011
Community Health Systems Inc	72	Brentwood, TN	Public	755.0	11,000	8062
Department Of Air Force	73	Dayton, OH	Private	743.9	NA	8011
Health Net	74	Woodland Hills, CA	Public	724.7	10,500	8011
Sierra Health Services Inc	75	Las Vegas, NV	Public	721.7	2,800	8011
Sierra Health Services Inc	76	Bullhead City, AZ	Private	721.7	90	8011
Health Care Rtrement Corp Amer	77	Toledo, OH	Public Family Member	708.1	16,500	8051
Scripps Health	78	San Diego, CA	Private	702.3	8,000	8051
Scripps Institutions Of Medici	79	San Diego, CA	Private	702.3	7,800	8062
Fhp International Corporation	80	Santa Ana, CA	Public	690.2	10,000	8011
Iowa Health System	81	Des Moines, IA	Private	685.8	4,110	8062
Bio-Medical Applications Mgt	82	Lexington, MA	Public Family Member	685.7	12,000	8092
Inova Health Care Services	83	Springfield, VA	Private	682.9	15,000	8062
Cedars-Sinai Medical Center	84	Los Angeles, CA	Private	681.5	6,000	8062
Beth Israel Deaconess Med Ctr	85	Boston, MA	Private	675.0	7,600	8062
Lutheran Health System	86	Fargo, ND	Private	665.3	14,707	8062
Upmc Presbyterian	87	Pittsburgh, PA	Private	661.9	6,411	8062
Paracelsus Healthcare Corp	88	Houston, TX	Public	659.2	7,600	8062
Evangelical Lutheran	89	Sioux Falls, SD	Private	649.7	24,000	8051
Osf Healthcare System	90	Peoria, IL	Private	642.5	8,741	8062
General Hospital Corporation	91	Boston, MA	Private	635.7	10,156	8062
Medlantic Healthcare Group	92	Washington, DC	Private	634.2	5,500	8082
Catholic Medical Center	93	Jamaica, NY	Private	630.2	3,900	8062
Memorial Health Services	94	Long Beach, CA	Private	619.8	7,500	8062
Memorial Hermann Hospital Sys	95	Houston, TX	Private	615.9	6,500	8062
Memorial Hospitl-Cancer/Allied	96	New York, NY	Private	604.0	3,000	8069
Hopkins Johns Hospital Inc	97	Baltimore, MD	Private	601.5	6,000	8062
St Lukes-Roosevelt Hospital Ctr	98	New York, NY	Private	598.4	8,000	8062
Cigna Healthcare Arizona, Inc.	99	Phoenix, AZ	Public Family Member	584.8	3,000	8011
Presbyterian Healthcare Svcs	100	Albuquerque, NM	Private	580.9	5,800	8062
Community Health Plan Inc	101	Latham, NY	Private	575.1	3,300	8011
Sutter Health Central	102	Sacramento, CA	Private	574.1	4,083	8062
University Of Ia Hospital & Clinic	103	Iowa City, IA	Private	571.0	7,083	8062
Methodist Health Care Memphis	104	Memphis, TN	Private	564.9	8,100	8062
Mercy Healthcare Sacramento	105	Rancho Cordova, CA	Private	563.2	6,131	8062
Baptist Healthcare System	106	Louisville, KY	Private	562.8	6,850	8062
Dallas County Hospital Dst	107	Dallas, TX	Private	561.3	6,200	8062
Orlando Rgonal Healthcare Sys	108	Orlando, FL	Private	558.5	8,000	8062
Regency Health Services Inc	109	Tustin, CA	Public Family Member	558.0	16,170	8051
Grant/Rvrside Mthdst Hspitals	110	Columbus, OH	Private	556.0	8,000	8062
Merit Behavioral Care Corp	111	Park Ridge, NJ	Public Family Member	555.7	2,800	8093
Carilion Services Inc	112	Roanoke, VA	Private	553.6	935	8082
Visiting Nurse Service Of Ny	113	New York, NY	Private	550.4	2,500	8082
Visiting Nurse Service Of New	114	New York, NY	Private	547.2	2,000	8082
Pacificare Of Texas Inc	115	San Antonio, TX	Public Family Member	541.8	180	8011
Ssm Health Care	116	Saint Louis, MO	Private	532.3	20,400	8062
St Louis University	117	Saint Louis, MO	Private	529.9	7,500	8062
Camcare Inc	118	Charleston, WV	Private	525.2	5,500	8062
Long Beach Memorial Med Ctr	119	Long Beach, CA	Private	521.0	4,000	8062
Jefferson Thmas Univ Hospitals	120	Philadelphia, PA	Private	514.9	375	8062
Brigham And Womens Hospital Inc	121	Boston, MA	Private	507.1	8,000	8062
Meridian Hospitals Corporation	122	Red Bank, NJ	Private	507.1	7,357	8062
Shands Teaching Hospital & Clinic	123	Gainesville, FL	Private	505.8	10,000	8062
Pca Health Plans Texas, Inc.	124	Austin, TX	Public Family Member	502.4	580	8011
Columbia-Arlington Healthcare Llc	125	Arlington, VA	Private	500.0	3,000	8062
Ahs Hospital Corporation	126	Florham Park, NJ	Private	499.9	10,600	8062
Queen's Health Systems	127	Honolulu, HI	Private	499.5	334	8062
Smithkline Beecham Clinical Labs	128	Collegeville, PA	Private	497.8	10,500	8071
Physicians Health Services	129	Shelton, CT	Public	488.1	1,100	8011
Loma Linda University Med Ctr	130	Loma Linda, CA	Private	487.7	4,676	8062
Methodist Hospital	131	Houston, TX	Private	485.0	4,500	8062
University Of Chicago	132	Chicago, IL	Private	483.3	4,300	8062
Rush-Presby St Lukes Med Ctr	133	Chicago, IL	Private	482.7	8,500	8062
Baylor University Medical Ctr	134	Dallas, TX	Private	480.8	5,401	8062
Scott & White Clinic An Assn	135	Temple, TX	Private	480.0	575	8011
Allegheny General Hospital	136	Pittsburgh, PA	Private	477.8	5,064	8062
Long Island Jewish Med Ctr	137	New Hyde Park, NY	Private	476.7	6,700	8062
Columbia-Healthone L L C	138	Denver, CO	Private	471.5	10,000	8062
Greenville Hospital System	139	Greenville, SC	Private	468.8	5,200	8062
Northwestern Memorial Hosp	140	Chicago, IL	Private	468.0	4,000	8062

D&B COMPANY RANKINGS BY SALES

Company	Rank	Location	Type	Sales ($ mil.)	Employ-ment	Primary SIC
Peacehealth	141	Bellevue, WA	Private	466.8	5,500	8062
Via Christi Regional Med Ctr	142	Wichita, KS	Private	466.6	4,100	8062
Allegany General Hospital Inc	143	Uniontown, PA	Private	465.7	5	8011
Sisters Of Providence In Ore	144	Seattle, WA	Private	465.4	6,700	8062
Laboratory Corporation America	145	Burlington, NC	Public	464.6	9,800	8071
Coram Healthcare Corporation	146	Denver, CO	Public	464.4	2,800	8093
National Healthcare Corp	147	Murfreesboro, TN	Public	463.5	16,000	8051
Christiana Care Health Svcs	148	Wilmington, DE	Private	463.3	5,700	8062
North Broward Hospital Dst	149	Fort Lauderdale, FL	Private	463.0	5,400	8062
Mediplex Group Inc	150	Albuquerque, NM	Public Family Member	457.7	10,000	8051
Brigham Medical Center Inc	151	Boston, MA	Private	456.0	7,000	8062
Yale-New Haven Hospital Inc	152	New Haven, CT	Private	450.9	5,959	8062
Dean Health Systems Sc	153	Madison, WI	Private	450.0	3,000	8011
Staten Island University Hosp	154	Staten Island, NY	Private	446.9	4,000	8062
Community Hospitals Of Indiana	155	Indianapolis, IN	Private	444.7	5,000	8062
University Virginia Med Ctr	156	Charlottesville, VA	Private	444.3	4,720	8062
Life Care Centers Of America	157	Cleveland, TN	Private	443.8	25,000	8051
Lincare Holdings Inc	158	Clearwater, FL	Public	443.2	1,200	8082
Total Renal Care Holdings	159	Torrance, CA	Public	438.2	5,000	8092
Medical College Of Georgia	160	Augusta, GA	Private	436.9	7,500	8062
Sacred Heart Medical Center	161	Spokane, WA	Private	435.0	4,074	8062
Park Nicollet Medical Center	162	Minneapolis, MN	Private	432.0	1,700	8011
St Vincent Hospital Health Care Ctr	163	Indianapolis, IN	Private	431.3	5,075	8062
Extendicare Homes, Inc	164	Milwaukee, WI	Private	430.6	11,283	8051
Maimonides Medical Center	165	Brooklyn, NY	Private	429.5	3,950	8062
Baptist Memorial Hospital	166	Memphis, TN	Private	428.5	5,680	8062
Rhode Island Hospital	167	Providence, RI	Private	427.3	4,133	8062
North Shore University Hosp	168	Manhasset, NY	Private	425.0	12,228	8062
Coastal Physician Group, Inc	169	Durham, NC	Public	424.8	1,645	8093
Charleston Area Medical Center	170	Charleston, WV	Private	424.8	6,000	8062
North Carolina Baptist Hosp	171	Winston Salem, NC	Private	423.1	5,475	8062
Hackensack University Med Ctr	172	Hackensack, NJ	Private	421.3	4,818	8062
Hartford Hospital	173	Hartford, CT	Private	419.2	5,000	8062
Php Healthcare Corporation	174	Reston, VA	Public	400.1	3,300	8011
Lincare Inc	175	Clearwater, FL	Public Family Member	400.0	3,500	8082
Total Renal Care, Inc	176	Torrance, CA	Public Family Member	400.0	5,000	8092
Sentara Hospitals-Norfolk	177	Norfolk, VA	Private	398.3	5,200	8062
New York University	178	New York, NY	Private	396.8	NA	8062
University Of Nc Hospitals	179	Chapel Hill, NC	Private	393.1	4,746	8062
Evanston Northwestern	180	Evanston, IL	Private	387.8	4,500	8062
American Homepatient Inc	181	Brentwood, TN	Public	387.3	3,700	8082
Boston Medical Center Corp	182	Boston, MA	Private	386.3	4,200	8062
Westchester County Health Care	183	Valhalla, NY	Private	385.0	4,000	8062
Hip Of New Jersey, Inc	184	North Brunswick, NJ	Private	384.7	250	8011
Pitt County Memorial Hospital	185	Greenville, NC	Private	381.2	3,900	8062
South Broward Hospital Dst	186	Hollywood, FL	Private	377.6	4,000	8062
F O H P Inc	187	Neptune, NJ	Private	377.4	350	8011
First Option Health Plan Of Nj	188	Red Bank, NJ	Private	377.4	350	8011
Virginia Mason Medical Center	189	Seattle, WA	Private	377.4	5,000	8011
University Of Alabama Health S	190	Birmingham, AL	Private	376.0	1,800	8093
Examination Mgt Svcs Inc Amer	191	Dallas, TX	Private	374.0	9,350	8099
Meridia Health System	192	Cleveland, OH	Private	370.2	3,200	8062
Fulton Dekalb Hospital Auth	193	Atlanta, GA	Private	369.5	6,700	8062
Medical Center Of Centl Ga Inc	194	Macon, GA	Private	369.4	3,300	8062
Baystate Medical Center Inc	195	Springfield, MA	Private	368.7	5,000	8062
Resurrection Medical Ctr, The	196	Chicago, IL	Private	365.5	985	8062
St Vincnts Hospital Med Ctr Of Ny	197	New York, NY	Private	362.8	3,852	8062
Solaris Health System	198	Edison, NJ	Private	361.6	500	8062
St Luke's Episcopal Hospital	199	Houston, TX	Private	361.0	3,511	8062
Western Medical Center	200	Santa Ana, CA	Public Family Member	359.0	1,300	8062
Health Plan Of Nevada Inc	201	Las Vegas, NV	Public Family Member	358.5	250	8011
M V P Health Plan Inc	202	Schenectady, NY	Private	357.0	570	8011
St John Hospital And Med Ctr	203	Detroit, MI	Private	356.8	3,646	8062
Resurrection Health Care Corp	204	Chicago, IL	Private	354.5	5,200	8062
St Vincent Mercy Medical Ctr	205	Toledo, OH	Private	353.3	4,600	8062
Cooper Hsptl/University Med Ctr	206	Camden, NJ	Private	352.8	3,524	8062
Lehigh Valley Hospital Inc	207	Allentown, PA	Private	351.0	3,600	8062
Vintage Estates Of Sacramento	208	Sacramento, CA	Private	350.0	70	8051
Health Care Auth Of Cit Of Hun	209	Huntsville, AL	Private	350.0	4,200	8062
Summa Health System	210	Akron, OH	Private	348.2	4,000	8062

D&B COMPANY RANKINGS BY SALES

Company	Rank	Location	Type	Sales ($ mil.)	Employ- ment	Primary SIC
Med America Health Systems Corp	211	Dayton, OH	Private	346.8	4,300	8062
St Marys Hospital Of Richmond	212	Richmond, VA	Private	344.7	2,000	8062
Lenox Hill Hospital	213	New York, NY	Private	343.3	2,955	8062
Maine Medical Center	214	Portland, ME	Private	343.3	5,000	8062
Saint Francis Hospital, Inc	215	Tulsa, OK	Private	342.7	4,400	8062
Nylcare Health Plan Of The South	216	Irving, TX	Private	342.2	325	8011
Healthsource Health Plans Inc	217	Raleigh, NC	Private	341.0	425	8011
University Hsptals Of Clvland	218	Cleveland, OH	Private	340.4	4,700	8062
State University Of Ny	219	Syracuse, NY	Private	340.0	4,800	8062
Miami Valley Hospital	220	Dayton, OH	Private	339.8	3,700	8062
Central Iowa Hospital Corp	221	Des Moines, IA	Private	337.4	4,000	8062
California Pacific Med Ctr	222	San Francisco, CA	Private	337.2	3,597	8062
Multicare Health System	223	Tacoma, WA	Private	337.0	4,500	8062
Carle Clinic Association Pc	224	Urbana, IL	Private	336.9	2,615	8011
Scott & White Memrl Hospital	225	Temple, TX	Private	335.3	6,000	8062
Lutheran General Hospital	226	Park Ridge, IL	Private	335.0	4,110	8062
Lovelace Health Systems Inc	227	Albuquerque, NM	Public Family Member	334.3	3,183	8011
Froedtert Mem Lutheran Hosp	228	Milwaukee, WI	Private	334.2	2,500	8062
Health First Inc	229	Melbourne, FL	Private	331.2	4,800	8011
North Shore Health System	230	Great Neck, NY	Private	329.7	7,000	8062
Winthrop-University Hospital	231	Mineola, NY	Private	328.8	3,601	8062
St Francis Hospital & Med Ctr	232	Hartford, CT	Private	328.7	3,300	8062
Memorial Medical Center Inc	233	Savannah, GA	Private	327.2	5,000	8062
Carilion Medical Centers Inc	234	Roanoke, VA	Private	326.9	4,130	8062
Wellmont Health System Inc	235	Kingsport, TN	Private	326.8	3,957	8062
Sundance Rehabilitation Corp	236	Albuquerque, NM	Public Family Member	326.2	3,800	8049
Ochsner Health Plan Inc	237	Metairie, LA	Private	323.7	280	8011
Univ Of Kentucky Hospital	238	Lexington, KY	Private	323.1	2,700	8062
Lester E Cox Medical Center	239	Springfield, MO	Private	322.6	4,200	8062
Providence Hospital	240	Southfield, MI	Private	322.3	3,100	8062
Bexar County Hospital Dst	241	San Antonio, TX	Private	321.4	3,424	8062
Toledo Hospital	242	Toledo, OH	Private	321.1	5,484	8062
Pacificare Of Oregon	243	Lake Oswego, OR	Private	320.3	210	8011
Dialysis Holdings, Inc	244	San Mateo, CA	Public	320.0	NA	8092
Rockford Health Systems Inc	245	Rockford, IL	Private	319.2	1,136	8062
Spectrum Health - Dwntwn Campus	246	Grand Rapids, MI	Private	317.7	3,610	8062
Grancare Inc	247	Atlanta, GA	Public Family Member	317.6	13,800	8051
University Of Mississippi	248	Jackson, MS	Private	316.6	NA	8011
Harris County Hospital Dst	249	Houston, TX	Private	315.4	5,412	8062
Children's Hospital, The	250	Columbus, OH	Private	315.1	2,946	8069
Ochsner Alton Med Foundation	251	Jefferson, LA	Private	309.9	3,500	8062
Main Line Hospitals	252	Bryn Mawr, PA	Private	309.3	3,353	8062
Metropolitan Dade County	253	Miami, FL	Private	309.1	NA	8062
Scottsdale Memorial Hospitals	254	Scottsdale, AZ	Private	307.9	2,500	8062
Nme Properties Corp.	255	Santa Barbara, CA	Public Family Member	307.0	7,676	8099
University Wscnsin Hospital Clnics	256	Madison, WI	Private	306.1	5,100	8062
Res-Care Inc	257	Louisville, KY	Public	306.1	11,900	8052
Southcoast Hospital Group Inc	258	New Bedford, MA	Private	305.4	3,950	8062
Capital Dst Physicians Health Plan	259	Albany, NY	Private	304.5	340	8011
Erlanger Health System	260	Chattanooga, TN	Private	304.2	2,700	8062
Brooklyn Hospital Center (Inc)	261	Brooklyn, NY	Private	303.9	3,500	8062
St Johns Mercy Medical Center	262	Saint Louis, MO	Private	300.2	4,700	8062
Medical City Dallas Hospital	263	Dallas, TX	Public Family Member	300.0	2,300	8062
Appalchian Regional Healthcare	264	Lexington, KY	Private	298.5	4,000	8062
New York Cy Health Hspitals Corp	265	Brooklyn, NY	Private	298.1	NA	8062
Brookdale Univ Hospital Med Ctr	266	Brooklyn, NY	Private	297.5	3,725	8062
Swedish Health Services	267	Seattle, WA	Private	297.5	5,300	8062
St John's Health System Inc	268	Springfield, MO	Private	296.6	6,300	8062
Partners Nat Health Plans Of Nc	269	Winston Salem, NC	Private	296.4	230	8011
Alliant Hospitals, Inc	270	Louisville, KY	Private	295.8	3,800	8062
Hip Health Plan Of Florida	271	Hollywood, FL	Private	295.7	545	8011
Hospital Board Of Directors	272	Fort Myers, FL	Private	294.6	4,000	8062
Parkview Hospital Inc	273	Fort Wayne, IN	Private	293.1	3,700	8062
Pca Health Plans Of Florida	274	Miami, FL	Public Family Member	292.0	1,200	8011
Catholic Health Partners Svcs	275	Chicago, IL	Private	291.6	3,500	8062
Mercy Healthcare Arizona Inc	276	Phoenix, AZ	Private	287.8	3,100	8062
Alta Bates Medical Center	277	Berkeley, CA	Private	287.5	1,550	8062
Pinnacle Health Hospitals	278	Harrisburg, PA	Private	287.1	4,100	8062
Josephs Saint Hospital & Med Ctr	279	Paterson, NJ	Private	287.0	3,300	8062
Franciscan Health System West	280	Tacoma, WA	Private	285.4	551	8062

D&B COMPANY RANKINGS BY SALES

Company	Rank	Location	Type	Sales ($ mil.)	Employment	Primary SIC
Wakemed	281	Raleigh, NC	Private	285.3	3,500	8062
Sisters Of Providence In Cal	282	Seattle, WA	Private	282.9	2,779	8062
Pca Family Health Plan Inc	283	Miami, FL	Public Family Member	282.7	1,200	8011
Rochester Area Health Mn Org	284	Rochester, NY	Private	282.6	300	8011
Our Lady Lake Regional Med Ctr	285	Baton Rouge, LA	Private	281.2	3,500	8062
Comprehensive Health Services	286	Detroit, MI	Private	281.1	900	8011
Our Lady Of The Resurrection	287	Chicago, IL	Private	280.4	1,907	8062
St Johns Regional Health Ctr	288	Springfield, MO	Private	280.3	4,400	8062
Presbyterian Hospital Of Dallas	289	Dallas, TX	Private	280.2	2,947	8062
Wyandotte Hospital & Med Ctr	290	Wyandotte, MI	Private	280.0	1,700	8062
Buffalo General Hospital	291	Buffalo, NY	Private	279.4	4,249	8062
Spartanburg Cnty Health Svcs Dst	292	Spartanburg, SC	Private	279.2	2,931	8062
Children's Hospital Of Philadelphia	293	Philadelphia, PA	Private	277.6	4,000	8069
Moses H Cone Memorial	294	Greensboro, NC	Private	277.3	4,200	8062
Harper Hospital	295	Detroit, MI	Private	277.0	2,483	8062
Mercy Hospital Medical Center	296	Des Moines, IA	Private	275.2	4,500	8062
Group Health Northwest	297	Spokane, WA	Private	274.3	1,000	8011
Florida Health Sciences Center	298	Tampa, FL	Private	274.1	3,750	8062
Cedars-Sinai Medical Center	299	Los Angeles, CA	Private	273.3	NA	8062
New York Cy Health Hspitals Corp	300	New York, NY	Private	273.3	NA	8062
University Of Utah Hospital	301	Salt Lake City, UT	Private	272.5	3,600	8062
New York Methodist Hospital	302	Brooklyn, NY	Private	272.0	2,900	8062
Metrohealth System Inc	303	Cleveland, OH	Private	271.8	5,244	8062
Presbyterian Hospital	304	Charlotte, NC	Private	270.5	3,100	8062
Sharp Memorial Hospital	305	San Diego, CA	Private	270.2	3,500	8062
Marshfield Clinic	306	Marshfield, WI	Private	270.0	4,443	8011
Dialysis Clinic Inc	307	Nashville, TN	Private	268.8	3,600	8092
Albert Einstein Medical Ctr	308	Philadelphia, PA	Private	268.0	4,450	8062
New Hanover Regional Med Ctr	309	Wilmington, NC	Private	267.8	3,100	8062
Kaiser Foundation Health Plan	310	Los Angeles, CA	Private	267.1	NA	8011
University Of Texas System	311	Dallas, TX	Private	267.1	NA	8011
West Jersey Health System	312	Camden, NJ	Private	266.4	4,100	8062
North Mississippi Medical Ctr	313	Tupelo, MS	Private	266.4	4,148	8062
Robert Wood Johnson Univ Hosp	314	New Brunswick, NJ	Private	265.5	3,100	8062
University Med Ctr Suthern Nev	315	Las Vegas, NV	Private	264.8	2,487	8062
Methodist Hospital Lubbock Texas	316	Lubbock, TX	Private	264.7	2,700	8062
Hillcrest Healthcare Systems	317	Tulsa, OK	Private	263.3	564	8062
University Health Services	318	Augusta, GA	Private	262.9	3,800	8062
H C A Health Services Of Kans	319	Wichita, KS	Public Family Member	262.1	3,080	8062
Forsyth Memorial Hospital Inc	320	Winston Salem, NC	Private	260.7	3,334	8062
Baptist Hospital Of Miami Inc	321	Miami, FL	Private	259.7	3,500	8062
Baptist Hospital, Inc	322	Nashville, TN	Private	259.6	3,500	8062
Edward W Sparrow Hospital Assn	323	Lansing, MI	Private	258.3	3,000	8062
New York Hospital Medical Cent	324	Flushing, NY	Private	257.8	2,300	8062
Methodist Healthcare System	325	San Antonio, TX	Private	256.8	5,456	8062
Pasadena Hospital Assn Ltd	326	Pasadena, CA	Private	256.6	2,800	8062
Botsford General Hospital	327	Farmington Hills, MI	Private	255.9	1,937	8062
Genesys Regional Medical Ctr	328	Grand Blanc, MI	Private	255.5	2,800	8062
Hurley Medical Center, Inc	329	Flint, MI	Private	255.3	2,884	8062
Eastern Maine Healthcare	330	Bangor, ME	Private	255.1	153	8062
Casey Family Program, The	331	Seattle, WA	Private	255.0	375	8361
Northside Hospital Inc	332	Atlanta, GA	Private	254.7	2,800	8062
Reading Hospital (Inc)	333	Reading, PA	Private	253.6	55	8062
Sarasota County Pub Hospital Bd	334	Sarasota, FL	Private	252.9	2,800	8062
Rochester General Hospital	335	Rochester, NY	Private	252.0	3,100	8062
All Saints Health Care System	336	Racine, WI	Private	250.0	2,700	8062
Houston Northwest Medical Ctr	337	Houston, TX	Public Family Member	250.0	2,100	8062
Mt Sinai Medical Center	338	Cleveland, OH	Private	250.0	2,400	8062
Ochsner Clinic Health Svcs Corp	339	New Orleans, LA	Private	250.0	2,000	8011
Vivra Specialty Partners, Inc	340	San Mateo, CA	Public Family Member	250.0	900	8011
Geisinger Medical Center	341	Danville, PA	Private	249.9	3,459	8062
Abington Memorial Hospital	342	Abington, PA	Private	249.4	2,800	8062
Kettering Affiliated Health Svcs	343	Dayton, OH	Private	248.9	115	8099
Sinai Hospital Of Baltimore	344	Baltimore, MD	Private	248.6	2,700	8062
North Memorial Health Care	345	Minneapolis, MN	Private	248.2	3,602	8062
St John's Hospital Of Hospital	346	Springfield, IL	Private	247.9	3,000	8062
Texas Children's Hospital	347	Houston, TX	Private	247.9	3,074	8069
Memorial Mission Hospital Inc	348	Asheville, NC	Private	247.5	3,000	8062
Carondelet Health Network Inc	349	Tucson, AZ	Private	246.9	5,000	8062
Hospital Of St Raphael	350	New Haven, CT	Private	246.5	3,426	8062

D&B COMPANY RANKINGS BY SALES

Company	Rank	Location	Type	Sales ($ mil.)	Employ-ment	Primary SIC
American Rehability Services	351	Brentwood, TN	Public Family Member	246.3	3,800	8051
Tmc Healthcare	352	Tucson, AZ	Private	246.0	2,650	8062
Morton Plant Hospital Assn	353	Clearwater, FL	Private	245.3	3,000	8062
Cumberland County Hospital Sys	354	Fayetteville, NC	Private	242.9	3,100	8062
University Md Med Sys Corp	355	Baltimore, MD	Private	242.7	5,158	8062
Roper Carealliance Inc	356	Charleston, SC	Private	242.5	40	8099
Roper Hospital North	357	North Charleston, SC	Private	242.5	305	8062
Candler Health System Inc	358	Savannah, GA	Private	241.7	1,900	8062
Lakeland Regional Medical Ctr	359	Lakeland, FL	Private	241.4	2,550	8062
H C A Health Services Of Fla	360	Nashville, TN	Public Family Member	239.9	5,100	8062
Piedmont Hospital Inc	361	Atlanta, GA	Private	239.5	2,720	8062
Roper Hospital Inc	362	Charleston, SC	Private	239.3	3,500	8062
St Josephs Hospital Of Atlanta	363	Atlanta, GA	Private	237.0	2,300	8062
Memorial Medical Center	364	Springfield, IL	Private	236.8	2,575	8062
Millard Fillmore Hospital	365	Buffalo, NY	Private	236.3	3,500	8062
Baptist Mem Healthcare Sys	366	San Antonio, TX	Private	235.2	5,000	8062
Barnes-Jewish Hospital	367	Saint Louis, MO	Private	235.2	5,000	8062
Centra Health Inc	368	Lynchburg, VA	Private	235.2	5,000	8062
University Colorado Hospital Auth	369	Denver, CO	Private	234.2	2,600	8062
Kaiser Foundation Hospitals	370	Los Angeles, CA	Private	233.7	NA	8062
Dimensions Health Corporation	371	Upper Marlboro, MD	Private	233.6	2,800	8062
Hillco, Ltd	372	Kinston, NC	Private	233.5	6,000	8051
Mary Hitchcock Memorial Hosp	373	Lebanon, NH	Private	233.4	2,711	8062
Extendicare Facilities Inc	374	Milwaukee, WI	Private	230.7	4,591	8051
York Hospital	375	York, PA	Private	228.8	3,604	8062
Southern Baptist Hospital Of Fla	376	Jacksonville, FL	Private	228.5	2,600	8062
New England Med Ctr Hospitals	377	Boston, MA	Private	228.4	4,856	8062
University Medical Center Inc	378	Jacksonville, FL	Private	228.2	2,497	8062
George Washington University	379	Washington, DC	Private	227.5	NA	8062
Fort Sanders-Parkwest Med Ctr	380	Knoxville, TN	Private	227.0	1,200	8062
East Texas Med Center-Tyler	381	Tyler, TX	Private	226.9	1,250	8062
Green Spring Health Services	382	Columbia, MD	Public Family Member	226.3	1,500	8093
Detroit Receiving Hospital And	383	Detroit, MI	Private	225.1	1,740	8069
Saint Clare's Hospital Inc	384	Denville, NJ	Private	225.0	4,100	8062
H M O Colorado, Inc	385	Denver, CO	Private	224.9	100	8011
Sioux Valley Hsptals Health Systms	386	Sioux Falls, SD	Private	224.5	3,500	8062
Illinois Masonic Medical Ctr	387	Chicago, IL	Private	224.1	3,000	8062
Behavioral Healthcare Corp	388	Nashville, TN	Private	223.8	3,846	8063
Permanente Medical Group, Inc	389	San Diego, CA	Private	223.8	NA	8062
University Of Pennsylvania	390	Philadelphia, PA	Private	223.8	NA	8062
Shriners Hsptals For Children	391	Tampa, FL	Private	223.1	4,500	8069
St John Medical Center Inc	392	Tulsa, OK	Private	222.9	3,500	8062
Pennsylvania Hospital	393	Philadelphia, PA	Private	222.0	2,200	8062
St Vincent's Medical Center	394	Jacksonville, FL	Private	221.8	2,447	8062
Harborside Healthcare Corp	395	Boston, MA	Public	221.8	7,331	8051
St Joseph Hospital Of Orange	396	Orange, CA	Private	221.7	2,200	8062
Dch Healthcare Authority (Inc)	397	Tuscaloosa, AL	Private	221.7	3,900	8062
Newark Beth Israel Med Ctr	398	Newark, NJ	Private	221.6	3,000	8062
American Phrm Svcs Del	399	Naperville, IL	Public Family Member	221.1	1,500	8051
Adventist Health System/Sunbelt	400	Orlando, FL	Private	221.1	NA	8062
Akron General Medical Center	401	Akron, OH	Private	220.5	2,836	8062
Union Hospital Inc	402	Terre Haute, IN	Private	220.1	2,322	8062
Egleston Children's Hospital	403	Atlanta, GA	Private	220.0	2,000	8069
Riverside Community Health	404	Riverside, CA	Public Family Member	220.0	1,100	8062
Childrens Hospital Corporation	405	Boston, MA	Private	219.8	3,907	8069
Scott And White Health Plan	406	Temple, TX	Private	219.5	245	8011
Legacy-Emanual Hospital Health Ctr	407	Portland, OR	Private	218.9	1,978	8062
Western Pennsylvania Hosp	408	Pittsburgh, PA	Private	218.8	2,800	8062
Kaiser Foundation Hospitals	409	Los Angeles, CA	Private	218.6	NA	8062
Chw Central Coast	410	Santa Barbara, CA	Private	218.4	3,500	8062
Lancaster General Hospital	411	Lancaster, PA	Private	217.2	2,759	8062
Jackson-Madison Cnty Gen Hosp	412	Jackson, TN	Private	216.3	2,400	8062
Us Diagnostic Inc	413	West Palm Beach, FL	Public	216.2	1,700	8071
Penn State Geisinger Clinic	414	Danville, PA	Private	215.7	1,940	8011
Jamaica Hospital Inc	415	Jamaica, NY	Private	215.6	3,000	8062
St Vincent Infirmary Med Ctr	416	Little Rock, AR	Private	215.3	2,830	8062
Integris Baptist Medical Ctr	417	Oklahoma City, OK	Private	215.1	2,759	8062
Allina Health System	418	Minneapolis, MN	Private	215.1	NA	8062
Christian Hospital NE-NW	419	Saint Louis, MO	Private	215.0	2,800	8062
Unilab Corporation	420	Tarzana, CA	Public	214.0	2,100	8071

D&B COMPANY RANKINGS BY SALES

Company	Rank	Location	Type	Sales ($ mil.)	Employment	Primary SIC
Pennsylvania State Univ Inc	421	Hershey, PA	Private	213.9	NA	8062
Vitas Healthcare Corp	422	Miami, FL	Private	213.9	3,000	8082
West Virginia Univ Hospitals	423	Morgantown, WV	Private	212.7	2,250	8062
Childrens Hospital Med Ctr	424	Cincinnati, OH	Private	212.6	3,800	8069
Our Lady Of Mercy Medical Ctr	425	Bronx, NY	Private	212.3	2,200	8062
University Of California	426	Sacramento, CA	Private	211.8	NA	8071
Tenet Health System Di, Inc	427	Santa Barbara, CA	Public Family Member	211.6	4,500	8062
Transitional Hospitals Corp	428	Louisville, KY	Public	211.6	4,500	8062
Department Of Navy	429	San Diego, CA	Private	211.4	NA	8062
Community Medical Center Inc	430	Toms River, NJ	Private	210.7	2,500	8062
Atlantic City Medical Center	431	Atlantic City, NJ	Private	210.6	2,460	8062
Children's Health Care	432	Minneapolis, MN	Private	210.6	1,994	8069
Samaritan Health Partners Shp	433	Dayton, OH	Private	210.6	2,200	8062
New York Blood Center, Inc.	434	New York, NY	Private	210.5	1,915	8099
St Elizabeth Hospital Med Ctr	435	Youngstown, OH	Private	210.3	2,500	8062
University Medical Center Corp	436	Tucson, AZ	Private	210.2	2,700	8062
St Jude Hospital	437	Fullerton, CA	Private	210.1	1,454	8062
Holmes Regional Medical Center	438	Melbourne, FL	Private	209.6	2,600	8062
Eastern Maine Medical Center	439	Bangor, ME	Private	209.3	2,460	8062
Healthwise Of America Inc	440	Nashville, TN	Public Family Member	208.7	400	8011
University Of Nebraska	441	Omaha, NE	Private	208.2	NA	8062
Phoebe Putney Memorial Hosp	442	Albany, GA	Private	207.6	1,950	8062
Bethesda Hospital Inc	443	Cincinnati, OH	Private	207.6	3,000	8062
Memorial Hermann Hospital Sys	444	Houston, TX	Private	207.1	NA	8062
Prison Health Services Inc	445	Brentwood, TN	Public Family Member	206.9	3,000	8011
Bronson Methodist Hospital	446	Kalamazoo, MI	Private	206.5	2,045	8062
University Of California	447	Los Angeles, CA	Private	206.4	NA	8062
St Lukes Hospital Of Bethlehem Pa	448	Bethlehem, PA	Private	206.3	3,500	8062
United Health Svcs Hospitals	449	Johnson City, NY	Private	206.3	2,400	8062
Upmc Shadyside	450	Pittsburgh, PA	Private	206.3	2,131	8062
Sisters Of St Joseph Of Texas	451	Lubbock, TX	Private	206.2	2,000	8062
Penn State Gisinger Health Plan	452	Danville, PA	Private	206.0	NA	8011
Physician Corp Of America	453	Miami, FL	Public	205.5	2,980	8011
St Elzabeths Med Ctr Of Boston	454	Boston, MA	Private	205.0	2,365	8062
Pediatric Services Of Amer De	455	Norcross, GA	Public	204.0	5,000	8082
Society Of The Valley Hosp	456	Ridgewood, NJ	Private	204.0	2,150	8062
H C A Psychiatric Company	457	Nashville, TN	Public Family Member	203.7	5,500	8063
Saint Elizabeth Medical Ctr	458	Covington, KY	Private	203.5	2,964	8062
Health Partners Of Philadelphia	459	Philadelphia, PA	Private	203.4	300	8011
Boston Medical Center Corp	460	Boston, MA	Private	203.1	NA	8062
Grace Hospital	461	Detroit, MI	Private	203.1	2,170	8062
Memorial Hospital Corporation	462	Colorado Springs, CO	Private	202.6	2,438	8062
Medical Resources Inc	463	Hackensack, NJ	Public	202.4	623	8071
Duluth Clinic Ltd, The	464	Duluth, MN	Private	202.2	1,300	8011
Basic American Medical, Inc.	465	Nashville, TN	Public Family Member	202.1	4,300	8062
Kettering Medical Center	466	Dayton, OH	Private	201.2	2,415	8062
Mcleod Rgnl Mdcl Ctr Pee Dee	467	Florence, SC	Private	200.9	2,600	8062
Greater Baltimore Medical Ctr	468	Baltimore, MD	Private	200.5	2,800	8062
Candler Hospital Inc	469	Savannah, GA	Private	200.3	1,661	8062
Community Hospital Group Inc	470	Edison, NJ	Private	200.3	3,000	8062
Gundersen Clinic Ltd	471	La Crosse, WI	Private	200.0	2,200	8011
Medcath Incorporated	472	Charlotte, NC	Private	200.0	1,800	8069
Interfaith Medical Center	473	Brooklyn, NY	Private	200.0	2,400	8062
Methodist Hospitals Inc	474	Gary, IN	Private	199.4	3,060	8062
Devereux Foundation, The	475	Bryn Mawr, PA	Private	199.4	4,200	8361
St George Corporation, The	476	Palos Heights, IL	Private	199.4	2,300	8062
University Of Minnesota	477	Minneapolis, MN	Private	199.3	NA	8062
Bethesda Naval Hospital	478	Bethesda, MD	Private	199.1	4,237	8062
Allegheny Univ Of Health Scences	479	Pittsburgh, PA	Private	199.0	NA	8062
Thomas Jefferson University	480	Philadelphia, PA	Private	199.0	NA	8062
Veterans Health Administration	481	Los Angeles, CA	Private	199.0	NA	8062
Detroit-Macomb Hospital Corp	482	Warren, MI	Private	199.0	4,030	8062
Wvhcs-Hospital	483	Wilkes Barre, PA	Private	198.0	2,555	8062
Summit Care Corporation	484	Burbank, CA	Public	197.9	4,200	8059
Forrest County General Hosp	485	Hattiesburg, MS	Private	197.9	2,800	8062
St Elizabeth Hospital	486	Beaumont, TX	Private	197.9	3,600	8062
Rex Hospital	487	Raleigh, NC	Private	197.8	2,900	8062
North Shore Medical Center	488	Salem, MA	Private	197.5	3,500	8062
Watts Health Foundation Inc	489	Inglewood, CA	Private	197.5	942	8011
Johns Hopkins Bayview Med Ctr	490	Baltimore, MD	Private	197.4	3,300	8062

D&B COMPANY RANKINGS BY SALES

Company	Rank	Location	Type	Sales ($ mil.)	Employ-ment	Primary SIC
Friendly Hlls Health Care Netwrk	491	La Habra, CA	Public Family Member	197.4	4,200	8062
Texas Health System Inc	492	Dallas, TX	Private	197.4	4,200	8062
St Josephs Hospital Health Ctr	493	Syracuse, NY	Private	196.5	3,200	8062
St Francis Medical Center	494	Pittsburgh, PA	Private	196.4	2,800	8062
Methodist Hospitals Of Dallas	495	Dallas, TX	Private	196.3	3,060	8062
Pomona Valley Hospital Med Ctr	496	Pomona, CA	Private	196.2	2,209	8062
University Hospital Ltd	497	Fort Lauderdale, FL	Private	196.2	700	8062
Michigan Affl Healthcare Sys	498	Lansing, MI	Private	195.8	6,082	8062
Western Reserve Care System	499	Youngstown, OH	Private	195.5	2,532	8062
Scripps Clinic Medical Group	500	San Diego, CA	Private	195.3	325	8011
Methodist Hospital	501	Minneapolis, MN	Private	195.0	2,500	8062
Good Samaritan Hospital Med Ctr	502	West Islip, NY	Private	194.9	2,900	8062
Mercy Fitzgerald Hospital Inc	503	Darby, PA	Private	194.7	NA	8062
Mount Sinai Hospital (Inc)	504	Jamaica, NY	Private	194.0	NA	8062
Mills-Peninsula Health Svcs	505	Burlingame, CA	Private	193.7	2,500	8062
Children's Hospital	506	Washington, DC	Private	193.7	1,810	8062
University Of Virginia	507	Charlottesville, VA	Private	192.7	NA	8062
St Lukes Regional Medical Ctr	508	Boise, ID	Private	192.7	2,300	8062
Children's Memorial Hospital	509	Chicago, IL	Private	192.7	2,000	8069
Healthcare Mgt Alternatives	510	Philadelphia, PA	Private	192.2	196	8099
Permanente Medical Group Inc	511	Sacramento, CA	Private	191.5	NA	8011
Healthsource South Carolina	512	Charleston, SC	Public Family Member	191.1	275	8011
University Community Hospital	513	Tampa, FL	Private	190.7	2,557	8062
Bridgeport Hospital Inc	514	Bridgeport, CT	Private	190.2	2,050	8062
Columbus Reg Healthcr Sys Inc	515	Columbus, GA	Private	190.0	2,700	8062
Hill Physicians Med Group Inc	516	San Ramon, CA	Private	190.0	4	8011
Notami Hospitals Of Oklahoma	517	Nashville, TN	Public Family Member	189.7	2,750	8011
Genesis Medical Center	518	Davenport, IA	Private	189.4	2,702	8062
Meriter Health Services Inc	519	Madison, WI	Private	189.0	4,500	8062
Danbury Hospital, The	520	Danbury, CT	Private	188.8	1,620	8062
Palomar Pomerado Health Sys	521	San Diego, CA	Private	188.2	2,700	8062
Bronx Lebanon Hospital Center	522	Bronx, NY	Private	187.9	4,000	8062
Daughters Of Charity H/S	523	Austin, TX	Private	187.9	4,000	8062
Lahey Hitchcock Clinic	524	Burlington, MA	Private	187.9	4,000	8062
Oakwood Hospital Corporation	525	Dearborn, MI	Private	187.9	4,000	8062
St Luke's Medical Center Inc	526	Milwaukee, WI	Private	187.9	4,000	8062
Tennessee West Healthcare Inc	527	Jackson, TN	Private	187.9	4,000	8062
United Care Inc	528	Dearborn, MI	Private	187.9	4,000	8062
Sun Health Corporation	529	Sun City, AZ	Private	187.7	2,390	8062
Memorial Hospital Of S Bend	530	South Bend, IN	Private	187.2	2,010	8062
St Peter's Medical Center	531	New Brunswick, NJ	Private	186.5	2,600	8062
Daniel Freeman Hospitals Inc	532	Inglewood, CA	Private	186.2	2,500	8062
Multicare Companies Inc	533	Hackensack, NJ	Public	185.8	15,000	8051
Gwinnett Hospital System Inc	534	Lawrenceville, GA	Private	185.7	2,050	8062
Cathedral Health Services Inc	535	Newark, NJ	Private	184.6	2,000	8062
Mercy Healthcare North	536	Redding, CA	Private	184.5	1,350	8062
Good Smrtan Hospital Of Cincinnati	537	Cincinnati, OH	Private	184.5	3,042	8062
Rapid City Regional Hospital	538	Rapid City, SD	Private	184.2	2,100	8062
Tri State Health System Inc	539	Suffern, NY	Private	184.0	2,500	8062
Childrens Med Ctr Of Dallas	540	Dallas, TX	Private	183.9	2,014	8069
Childrens Hospital Of Mich	541	Detroit, MI	Private	183.8	2,310	8069
Carle Foundation, The	542	Urbana, IL	Private	183.6	2,043	8062
Cedars Medical Center	543	Miami, FL	Private	183.6	1,800	8062
Aetna Us Healthcare An Ohio Corp	544	Richfield, OH	Public Family Member	183.5	5	8011
New York, State	545	Brentwood, NY	Private	183.3	NA	8011
City Of Hope National Med Ctr	546	Duarte, CA	Private	183.3	2,600	8062
Northwest Community Hospital	547	Arlington Heights, IL	Private	183.3	2,800	8062
Variety Children's Hospital	548	Miami, FL	Private	183.2	2,200	8069
Outreach Health Care, Inc	549	Garland, TX	Private	183.1	6,000	8093
Weight Watchers North America	550	Woodbury, NY	Public Family Member	183.1	6,000	8093
St Francis Hospital	551	Roslyn, NY	Private	182.7	1,759	8069
Foundation Health A South	552	Fort Lauderdale, FL	Private	182.1	351	8011
Mercy Hospital & Medical Ctr	553	Chicago, IL	Private	182.0	2,100	8062
Singing River Hospital System	554	Pascagoula, MS	Private	181.8	1,700	8062
Holy Cross Hospital Silver Spring	555	Silver Spring, MD	Private	181.8	2,241	8062
St Peter's Hospital	556	Albany, NY	Private	181.1	2,476	8062
Britthaven Inc	557	Kinston, NC	Private	181.0	5,200	8051
Dekalb Medical Center Inc	558	Decatur, GA	Private	180.8	2,200	8062
Central Du Page Hospital Assn	559	Winfield, IL	Private	180.7	2,300	8062
Visiting Nrs Associa	560	Washington, DC	Private	180.6	350	8082

D&B COMPANY RANKINGS BY SALES

Company	Rank	Location	Type	Sales ($ mil.)	Employ- ment	Primary SIC
Hoag Memorial Hospital Presbt	561	Newport Beach, CA	Private	180.4	2,400	8062
22 Texas Services, Lp	562	Horsham, PA	Private	180.0	4,500	8051
Myrtle Beach Hospital Inc	563	Myrtle Beach, SC	Public Family Member	179.9	811	8062
St Joseph Medical Center	564	Tacoma, WA	Private	179.2	1,680	8062
Advocate Health Care Network	565	Oak Lawn, IL	Private	178.7	NA	8069
Northeast Medical Center, Inc	566	Concord, NC	Private	178.4	2,053	8062
Mobile Infirmary Association	567	Mobile, AL	Private	178.3	3,000	8062
Meritcare Hospital	568	Fargo, ND	Private	177.5	1,806	8062
Northwestern Human Services	569	Lafayette Hill, PA	Private	176.8	4,000	8093
Alegent Health-Immanuel Med Ctr	570	Omaha, NE	Private	176.2	2,313	8062
Sacred Heart Hospital Of Pensacola	571	Pensacola, FL	Private	175.7	2,000	8062
Brownsville-Valley Regional Med	572	Brownsville, TX	Public Family Member	175.0	630	8062
Southwest Fla Regional Med Ctr	573	Fort Myers, FL	Public Family Member	175.0	1,600	8062
Rockford Memorial Hospital	574	Rockford, IL	Private	174.9	2,800	8062
Spohn Health Systems	575	Corpus Christi, TX	Private	174.7	2,500	8062
Hillcrest Medical Center Inc	576	Tulsa, OK	Private	174.6	2,126	8062
Naples Community Hospital Inc	577	Naples, FL	Private	174.3	1,800	8062
County Of Westchester	578	Valhalla, NY	Private	174.2	NA	8062
New York Cy Health Hspitals Corp	579	Elmhurst, NY	Private	174.2	NA	8062
New York Cy Health Hspitals Corp	580	New York, NY	Private	174.2	NA	8062
Veterans Health Administration	581	Long Beach, CA	Private	174.1	NA	8062
Veterans Health Administration	582	Palo Alto, CA	Private	174.1	NA	8062
Valley Baptist Medical Center	583	Harlingen, TX	Private	174.0	2,100	8062
Childrens Hospital Of Wisconsin	584	Milwaukee, WI	Private	173.9	2,000	8069
Johnson City Medical Ctr Hosp	585	Johnson City, TN	Private	173.9	2,200	8062
Covenant Medical Center Inc	586	Saginaw, MI	Private	173.8	3,700	8062
University Of Utah	587	Salt Lake City, UT	Private	173.5	NA	8062
Munson Medical Center	588	Traverse City, MI	Private	173.3	2,822	8062
Albany Medical Center Hosp	589	Albany, NY	Private	172.8	6,000	8062
Albany Medical College	590	Albany, NY	Private	172.8	1,568	8011
Bergan Mercy Health Clinics	591	Omaha, NE	Private	172.4	2,500	8011
Erie County Medical Center	592	Buffalo, NY	Private	172.4	2,500	8011
University Of Virginia	593	Charlottesville, VA	Private	172.3	NA	8062
Doctors Hospital	594	Columbus, OH	Private	171.8	2,000	8062
Memorial Hospital, Inc	595	Worcester, MA	Private	171.8	3,510	8062
Ball Memorial Hospital Inc	596	Muncie, IN	Private	171.4	2,108	8062
Galen Hospital Illinois Inc	597	Chicago, IL	Public Family Member	171.4	1,700	8062
Crouse Hospital Inc	598	Syracuse, NY	Private	171.3	2,400	8062
Franklin Square Hospital Ctr	599	Baltimore, MD	Private	171.2	2,200	8062
Cabrini Medical Center	600	New York, NY	Private	171.1	2,040	8062
Union Memorial Hospital Inc	601	Baltimore, MD	Private	171.0	2,025	8062
Mount Sinai Hospital Med Cen	602	Chicago, IL	Private	170.9	1,700	8062
St Johns Regional Medical Ctr	603	Joplin, MO	Private	170.9	2,000	8062
St Joseph Medical Center	604	Baltimore, MD	Private	170.8	2,200	8062
Frankford Hospital Phila	605	Philadelphia, PA	Private	170.8	1,931	8062
University Medical Center Inc	606	Louisville, KY	Private	170.2	2,000	8062
South Shore Hospital Inc	607	South Weymouth, MA	Private	170.0	2,375	8062
Coliseum Park Hospital Inc	608	Macon, GA	Public Family Member	170.0	1,000	8062
Columbia Chicago Ostpthc Hospt	609	Olympia Fields, IL	Public Family Member	170.0	770	8062
Quest Diagnostics A Cal Corp	610	SJ Capistrano, CA	Private	170.0	1,400	8071
Winchester Medical Center Inc	611	Winchester, VA	Private	169.9	2,006	8062
Hutzel Hospital	612	Detroit, MI	Private	169.7	1,800	8062
Mercy Health Services	613	Ypsilanti, MI	Private	169.5	NA	8062
Ohio State University	614	Columbus, OH	Private	169.5	NA	8062
Reading Hospital & Med Ctr Inc	615	Reading, PA	Private	169.0	3,600	8062
Elmhurst Memorial Hospital	616	Elmhurst, IL	Private	168.9	2,579	8062
Good Samaritan Hospital Health Ctr	617	Dayton, OH	Private	168.8	2,200	8062
Stormnt-Vail Rgional Health Ctr	618	Topeka, KS	Private	168.8	2,500	8062
Norwalk Hospital Assn	619	Norwalk, CT	Private	168.7	1,660	8062
St Mary's Medical Center	620	Duluth, MN	Private	168.3	1,631	8062
St Joseph Hospital Fran Sstrs	621	Milwaukee, WI	Private	168.3	2,597	8062
Salinas Valley Memorial Health	622	Salinas, CA	Private	168.0	1,500	8062
Hpi-Ramsey, Inc	623	Saint Paul, MN	Private	167.8	3,575	8062
Childrens Hospital Los Angeles Inc	624	Los Angeles, CA	Private	167.7	2,000	8069
McAllen Medical Center Inc	625	Mcallen, TX	Public Family Member	167.4	1,620	8062
St Josphs Med Ctr Of Stockton	626	Stockton, CA	Private	166.0	2,200	8062
George Washington University	627	Washington, DC	Private	165.8	NA	8011
Kaiser Fnd Health Pln Of Co Inc	628	Arvada, CO	Private	165.8	NA	8011
Southern Cal Permanente Med	629	Woodland Hills, CA	Private	165.8	NA	8011
Holmes Hooper Inc	630	Basking Ridge, NJ	Public	165.4	1,735	8099

D&B COMPANY RANKINGS BY SALES

Company	Rank	Location	Type	Sales ($ mil.)	Employ-ment	Primary SIC
Mount Clemens General Hospital	631	Mount Clemens, MI	Private	165.2	1,300	8062
Southwest Washington Med Ctr	632	Vancouver, WA	Private	164.9	2,500	8062
Heartland Regional Medical Ctr	633	Saint Joseph, MO	Private	164.8	1,900	8062
Methodist Medical Ctr Of Ill	634	Peoria, IL	Private	164.6	2,500	8062
R E Thomason General Hospital	635	El Paso, TX	Private	164.3	1,420	8062
Episcopal Health Services Inc	636	Uniondale, NY	Private	164.3	3,500	8062
Fresno Community Hospital	637	Fresno, CA	Private	164.3	3,500	8062
Riverside Hospital Inc	638	Newport News, VA	Private	164.3	3,500	8062
Tallahssee Mem Rgional Med Ctr	639	Tallahassee, FL	Private	164.3	3,300	8062
Mother Frncs Hosp, Tyler, Tx	640	Tyler, TX	Private	164.2	1,655	8062
Salem Hospital	641	Salem, OR	Private	164.1	2,500	8062
Holy Cross Hospital Inc	642	Fort Lauderdale, FL	Private	163.8	2,000	8062
Pediatric Services Of Amer Ga	643	Norcross, GA	Public Family Member	163.8	5,000	8082
Monmouth Medical Center	644	Long Branch, NJ	Private	163.5	2,400	8062
Deaconess-Billings Clinic Inc	645	Billings, MT	Private	163.0	1,100	8062
Jersey City Medical Center	646	Jersey City, NJ	Private	162.8	1,900	8062
MacNeal Mem Hospital Assn	647	Berwyn, IL	Private	162.7	1,700	8062
Community Hospital - SB	648	San Bernardino, CA	Private	162.5	1,504	8062
St Francis Hospital Inc	649	Greenville, SC	Private	162.2	1,500	8062
Anderson Area Medical Center	650	Anderson, SC	Private	162.2	2,500	8062
Valley Health System	651	Hemet, CA	Private	162.0	2,000	8062
Childrens Hospital Assn, The	652	Denver, CO	Private	161.7	2,200	8069
St Louis Children's Hospital	653	Saint Louis, MO	Private	161.6	2,078	8069
Bayfront Medical Center Inc	654	Saint Petersburg, FL	Private	161.4	1,723	8062
Ingalls Memorial Hospital, The	655	Harvey, IL	Private	161.4	1,845	8062
Conemaugh Valley Mem Hosp	656	Johnstown, PA	Private	161.4	1,823	8062
Cigna Healthcare Of Tennessee	657	Bloomfield, CT	Public Family Member	161.1	30	8011
Infirmary Health System Inc	658	Mobile, AL	Private	160.8	3,425	8062
Rehabcare Group	659	Saint Louis, MO	Public	160.8	1,472	8093
Episcopal Hospital	660	Philadelphia, PA	Private	160.5	1,400	8062
Saint Cloud Hospital Inc	661	Saint Cloud, MN	Private	160.5	2,000	8062
Aultman Hospital, The	662	Canton, OH	Private	160.0	3,000	8062
Covenant Care Inc	663	SJ Capistrano, CA	Private	160.0	3,000	8051
Phycor Of Kentucky, Inc.	664	Lexington, KY	Public Family Member	160.0	875	8011
Transworld Healthcare Inc	665	New York, NY	Public	160.0	430	8082
Grossmont Hospital Corporation	666	La Mesa, CA	Private	160.0	1,911	8062
Universal Care Inc	667	Long Beach, CA	Private	159.5	1,000	8093
Deaconess Hospital Inc	668	Evansville, IN	Private	159.0	2,300	8062
Meriter Hospital Inc	669	Madison, WI	Private	158.7	2,335	8062
Waukesha Memorial Hospital	670	Waukesha, WI	Private	158.5	1,275	8062
Austin North Medical Center	671	Austin, TX	Private	158.5	950	8062
St Mary's Hospital Inc	672	West Palm Beach, FL	Private	158.4	2,000	8062
Gaston Memorial Hospital Inc	673	Gastonia, NC	Private	157.6	1,935	8062
I O M Health System Lp	674	Fort Wayne, IN	Private	157.5	2,000	8062
Cigna Healthcare Of Ohio Inc	675	Columbus, OH	Public Family Member	157.4	500	8011
Shawnee Mission Medical Center	676	Shawnee Mission, KS	Private	157.3	1,850	8062
Hallmark Healthcare Corp	677	Brentwood, TN	Public Family Member	157.0	3,345	8062
St Josephs Hospital Of Marshfield	678	Marshfield, WI	Private	156.9	1,715	8062
Alexian Brothers Medical Ctr	679	Elk Grove Village, IL	Private	156.9	2,000	8062
Munroe Rgnal Healthcare Systems	680	Ocala, FL	Private	156.8	1,650	8062
Good Shepherd Hospital, Inc	681	Longview, TX	Private	156.7	1,800	8062
County Of Maricopa	682	Phoenix, AZ	Private	156.2	NA	8062
M-Care Inc	683	Ann Arbor, MI	Private	155.4	300	8011
Torrance Memorial Medical Ctr	684	Torrance, CA	Private	155.2	2,000	8062
Englewood Hospital & Med Ctr	685	Englewood, NJ	Private	155.0	2,200	8062
New York Society For Relief	686	New York, NY	Private	154.7	1,238	8069
Childrens Hospital Of Ala, The	687	Birmingham, AL	Private	154.5	1,947	8069
Francscan Med Ctr Dyton Campus	688	Dayton, OH	Private	154.2	2,054	8062
Memorial Hospital At Gulfport	689	Gulfport, MS	Private	153.9	1,900	8062
Fort Sanders Regional Med Ctr	690	Knoxville, TN	Private	153.5	2,080	8062
Renal Treatment Centers Inc	691	Berwyn, PA	Public Family Member	153.5	2,687	8092
Samaritan Health System	692	Phoenix, AZ	Private	153.5	NA	8071
Northridge Med Center - Roscoe	693	Northridge, CA	Private	153.0	1,600	8062
Capital Health Systems Inc	694	Trenton, NJ	Private	152.5	3,250	8062
Boca Raton Community Hospital Inc	695	Boca Raton, FL	Private	152.3	1,900	8062
Houston Cnty Healthcare Auth	696	Dothan, AL	Private	151.9	1,825	8062
Martin Memorial Medical Center	697	Stuart, FL	Private	151.9	1,776	8062
Fairview Hospital	698	Cleveland, OH	Private	151.7	2,364	8062
Mount Sinai Med Ctr	699	Miami, FL	Private	151.3	3,225	8062
Alegent Health-Bergen Mercy	700	Omaha, NE	Private	151.2	2,500	8062

D&B COMPANY RANKINGS BY SALES

Company	Rank	Location	Type	Sales ($ mil.)	Employ-ment	Primary SIC
Shady Grove Adventist Hospital Inc	701	Rockville, MD	Private	151.2	1,300	8062
Genesee Hospital Inc	702	Rochester, NY	Private	151.0	2,400	8062
Childrens Hospital Of Pittsburgh	703	Pittsburgh, PA	Private	151.0	1,900	8069
New York Flshing Hospital Med Ctr	704	Flushing, NY	Private	151.0	1,450	8062
Mercy Hospital Inc	705	Miami, FL	Private	150.8	2,000	8062
Mercy Medical Development	706	Miami, FL	Private	150.8	365	8093
Poudre Valley Health Care Inc	707	Fort Collins, CO	Private	150.4	1,700	8062
Lutheran Medical Center	708	Wheat Ridge, CO	Private	150.4	2,600	8062
Community Hospital Of Monterey	709	Monterey, CA	Private	150.3	1,450	8062
Home Health Corp Of America	710	King Of Prussia, PA	Public	150.2	3,068	8082
South Hills Health System	711	Homestead, PA	Private	150.1	2,700	8062
L I C H Corporation	712	Brooklyn, NY	Private	150.1	3,200	8062
Va Nj Healthcare System	713	Lyons, NJ	Private	150.1	3,200	8062
Davis Vision Inc	714	Plainview, NY	Private	150.0	1,000	8011
Fort Walton Beach Medical Ctr	715	Fort Walton Beach, FL	Public Family Member	150.0	750	8011
Lafayette General Hospital	716	Lafayette, LA	Private	150.0	1,400	8062
Mayo Clinic Scottsdale	717	Scottsdale, AZ	Private	150.0	1,423	8011
Private Diagnostic Clinic Pllc	718	Durham, NC	Private	150.0	775	8011
Texas Health Enterprises Inc	719	Denton, TX	Private	149.4	6,500	8051
Ahs Hospital Corporation	720	Summit, NJ	Private	149.3	NA	8062
Kaiser Foundation Hospitals	721	Van Nuys, CA	Private	149.3	NA	8062
New York, State	722	Brooklyn, NY	Private	149.3	NA	8062
San Diego Hospital Assn	723	San Diego, CA	Private	149.3	NA	8062
San Francisco City & County	724	San Francisco, CA	Private	149.3	NA	8062
Sisters Of Providence In Ore	725	Portland, OR	Private	149.3	NA	8062
Sisters Of Providence In Wash	726	Seattle, WA	Private	149.3	NA	8062
Staten Island University Hosp	727	Staten Island, NY	Private	149.3	NA	8062
University Of California	728	Orange, CA	Private	149.3	NA	8062
St Francis Medical Center	729	Monroe, LA	Private	149.0	1,700	8062
Munster Medical Res Foundation	730	Munster, IN	Private	148.9	1,200	8062
South Miami Hospital Inc	731	Miami, FL	Private	148.9	2,200	8062
Saint Marys Hospital Of Huntington	732	Huntington, WV	Private	148.8	1,500	8062
Unison Healthcare Corporation	733	Scottsdale, AZ	Public	148.7	5,600	8051
White Memorial Medical Center	734	Los Angeles, CA	Private	148.6	1,250	8062
Health Services Medical Corp	735	Baldwinsville, NY	Private	148.5	1,100	8011
Mercy Health Services	736	Ann Arbor, MI	Private	148.4	NA	8062
Michigan Affl Healthcare Sys	737	Lansing, MI	Private	148.4	NA	8062
Osf Healthcare System	738	Peoria, IL	Private	148.4	NA	8062
Winter Haven Hospital Inc	739	Winter Haven, FL	Private	148.4	2,420	8062
Athens Regional Medical Ctr	740	Athens, GA	Private	148.3	1,864	8062
Baptist Hospital Of East Tenn	741	Knoxville, TN	Private	148.0	1,800	8062
West Suburban Hospital Med Ctr	742	Oak Park, IL	Private	147.8	1,568	8062
Ch Allied Services Inc	743	Saint Louis, MO	Private	147.8	3,150	8062
Childrens Hospital Regional Med	744	Seattle, WA	Private	147.7	2,150	8069
Little Co Of Mary Affl Svcs	745	Oak Lawn, IL	Private	147.1	175	8099
Mercy Hospital Of Wilkes Barre Pa	746	Wilkes Barre, PA	Private	146.8	683	8062
Interhealth Corporation	747	Whittier, CA	Private	146.6	1,400	8062
Mercy Children's Hospital	748	Kansas City, MO	Private	146.5	2,000	8069
Mary Washington Hospital Inc	749	Fredericksburg, VA	Private	146.5	1,500	8062
Vincent Saint Health Center	750	Erie, PA	Private	146.4	2,300	8062
Memorial Health Systems Inc	751	Ormond Beach, FL	Private	146.3	910	8062
Marquette General Hospital	752	Marquette, MI	Private	145.9	1,950	8062
St Anthony Hospital	753	Oklahoma City, OK	Private	145.7	2,000	8062
United Healthcare Of Utah	754	Salt Lake City, UT	Public Family Member	145.6	120	8011
Ashland Hospital Corporation	755	Ashland, KY	Private	145.6	1,700	8062
Hanger Orthopedic Group Inc	756	Bethesda, MD	Public	145.6	1,000	8361
Portland Adventist Med Ctr	757	Portland, OR	Private	145.5	3,102	8062
University Of S Ala Med Ctr	758	Mobile, AL	Private	145.3	3,000	8062
Arundel Health Anne System	759	Annapolis, MD	Private	145.3	46	8062
Louisiana State Univ Sys	760	Shreveport, LA	Private	145.1	NA	8062
Permanente Medical Group Inc	761	Oakland, CA	Private	145.1	NA	8011
Veterans Health Administration	762	Houston, TX	Private	145.1	NA	8062
Tenet Healthsystem Desert Inc	763	Palm Springs, CA	Public Family Member	145.0	1,100	8062
Baton Rouge General Med Ctr	764	Baton Rouge, LA	Private	144.6	1,790	8062
Little Company Of Mary Hosp	765	Chicago, IL	Private	144.5	2,300	8062
Matria Healthcare, Inc	766	Marietta, GA	Public	144.5	844	8082
New Britain General Hospital	767	New Britain, CT	Private	144.4	3,000	8062
St Elizabeth Medical Center	768	Granite City, IL	Private	144.4	930	8062
St Alphonsus Regional Med Ctr	769	Boise, ID	Private	144.2	1,927	8062
Wellcare Management Group Inc	770	Kingston, NY	Public	143.9	225	8011

D&B COMPANY RANKINGS BY SALES

Company	Rank	Location	Type	Sales ($ mil.)	Employ-ment	Primary SIC
Q H G Of Alabama Inc	771	Dothan, AL	Public Family Member	143.8	2,220	8062
Mary Imogene Bassett Hospital	772	Cooperstown, NY	Private	143.4	2,200	8062
Trover Clinic Foundation Inc	773	Madisonville, KY	Private	143.4	1,158	8062
Baptist Hospital Inc	774	Pensacola, FL	Private	143.3	1,641	8062
Healthcor Holdings Inc	775	Dallas, TX	Public	143.2	3,200	8082
Swedish American Hospital Assn	776	Rockford, IL	Private	142.9	2,494	8062
Sinai Hospital	777	Detroit, MI	Private	142.8	3,045	8062
Dayton Osteopathic Hospital	778	Dayton, OH	Private	142.8	1,800	8062
Presentation Sisters Inc	779	Sioux Falls, SD	Private	142.6	2,200	8062
Hamot Medical Center	780	Erie, PA	Private	142.6	1,300	8062
Security Health Plan Of Wisconsin	781	Marshfield, WI	Private	142.4	1,006	8011
Saint Frncis Hospital Of Evanston	782	Evanston, IL	Private	142.4	1,962	8062
Carraway Methdst Health Systems	783	Birmingham, AL	Private	142.3	2,000	8062
Columbia Medical Plan Inc	784	Columbia, MD	Private	142.2	1,050	8011
Women & Infants Hospital Ri	785	Providence, RI	Private	142.0	2,000	8069
County Of Hillsborough	786	Tampa, FL	Private	141.7	NA	8062
Raritan Bay Medical Ctr A Nj	787	Perth Amboy, NJ	Private	141.5	1,800	8062
Covenant Medical Center Inc	788	Waterloo, IA	Private	141.2	2,000	8062
All Saints Health System	789	Fort Worth, TX	Private	141.2	1,300	8062
St Marys Med Ctr Of Saginaw	790	Saginaw, MI	Private	141.1	1,794	8062
Robinson Memorial Hospital	791	Ravenna, OH	Private	141.0	974	8062
Northeast Georgia Medical Ctr	792	Gainesville, GA	Private	140.9	2,000	8062
Eisenhower Medical Center	793	Rancho Mirage, CA	Private	140.9	1,800	8062
Qual-Med Washington Health Plan	794	Bellevue, WA	Private	140.8	230	8011
El Paso Healthcare Systems	795	El Paso, TX	Private	140.7	3,000	8062
Hallmark Health System	796	Malden, MA	Private	140.7	3,000	8062
Kennedy Health Systems	797	Cherry Hill, NJ	Private	140.7	3,000	8062
Liberty Healthcare System Inc	798	Jersey City, NJ	Private	140.7	3,000	8062
Mid Atlantic Health Group Inc	799	Long Branch, NJ	Private	140.7	3,000	8062
Regions Hospital	800	Saint Paul, MN	Private	140.7	3,000	8062
Sunrise Hospital	801	Las Vegas, NV	Public Family Member	140.7	3,000	8062
University Healthcare Sys L C	802	New Orleans, LA	Private	140.7	3,000	8062
Covenant Health System Inc	803	Waterloo, IA	Private	140.5	2,050	8062
Gundersen Lthran Hsptl-Lcrosse	804	La Crosse, WI	Private	140.5	1,760	8062
St Frances Cabrini Hospital	805	Alexandria, LA	Private	140.4	1,200	8062
University Of California	806	San Diego, CA	Private	140.4	NA	8062
St Marys Med Ctr Of Evansville	807	Evansville, IN	Private	140.3	2,600	8062
Cape Cod Hospital	808	Hyannis, MA	Private	140.0	1,200	8062
Everest Healthcare Svcs Corp	809	Oak Park, IL	Private	140.0	1,500	8092
Raleigh General Hospital	810	Beckley, WV	Public Family Member	140.0	1,312	8062
Renal Care Group Inc	811	Nashville, TN	Public	140.0	175	8092
Arkansas Childrens Hospital	812	Little Rock, AR	Private	139.9	2,200	8069
Waterbury Hospital	813	Waterbury, CT	Private	139.9	1,450	8062
Kaiser Foundation Hospitals	814	Hayward, CA	Private	139.9	NA	8011
University Of Massachusetts	815	Worcester, MA	Private	139.9	NA	8011
Tri-City Hospital District	816	Oceanside, CA	Private	139.8	NA	8062
Ravenswood Health Care Corp	817	Chicago, IL	Private	139.6	1,800	8062
Battle Creek Health System	818	Battle Creek, MI	Private	139.6	1,882	8062
County Of King	819	Seattle, WA	Private	139.3	NA	8062
United Regional Health Care Sys	820	Wichita Falls, TX	Private	139.0	900	8062
Good Samaritan Medical Center	821	Brockton, MA	Private	138.9	960	8062
Miriam Hospital Inc	822	Providence, RI	Private	138.9	1,263	8062
Anne Arundel Health Care Svcs	823	Annapolis, MD	Private	138.8	45	8093
Lexington County Health Svc Dst	824	West Columbia, SC	Private	138.8	2,180	8062
Presbyterian Healthcare Svcs	825	Albuquerque, NM	Private	138.8	NA	8062
Rose Medical Center, Inc.	826	Denver, CO	Public Family Member	138.6	1,325	8062
Valley Children's Hospital	827	Madera, CA	Private	138.4	1,800	8069
Adventist Health Sys/Snblt Corp	828	Hinsdale, IL	Private	138.3	NA	8011
Kennestone Hospital Inc	829	Marietta, GA	Private	138.3	2,950	8062
Childrens' Hospital-San Diego	830	San Diego, CA	Private	138.1	2,200	8069
St Margret Mrcy Healthcare Ctrs	831	Hammond, IN	Private	138.1	2,859	8062
Brown Schools Inc.	832	Austin, TX	Private	138.0	2,200	8062
St Joseph's Medical Center	833	South Bend, IN	Private	138.0	1,523	8062
Trinity Medical Center	834	Rock Island, IL	Private	137.9	2,000	8062
Columbia Healthcare Of Centl Va	835	Nashville, TN	Public Family Member	137.9	2,000	8011
Shannon Health System	836	San Angelo, TX	Private	137.9	2,000	8011
Rochester Methodist Hospital	837	Rochester, MN	Private	137.8	1,400	8062
Flowers Hospital, Inc	838	Dothan, AL	Public Family Member	137.7	NA	8062
St Bernard's Hospital Inc	839	Jonesboro, AR	Private	137.6	1,500	8062
Saint Francis Hospital	840	Memphis, TN	Public Family Member	137.4	1,700	8062

D&B COMPANY RANKINGS BY SALES

Company	Rank	Location	Type	Sales ($ mil.)	Employment	Primary SIC
Lawrence And Memorial Hosp	841	New London, CT	Private	137.3	1,600	8062
Baptist Medical Center	842	Montgomery, AL	Private	136.8	1,700	8062
Ramsay Health Care Inc	843	Coral Gables, FL	Public	136.7	2,100	8063
Mercy-Memorial Medical Center	844	Saint Joseph, MI	Private	136.5	2,800	8062
Mount Carmel Hospital West	845	Columbus, OH	Private	135.9	2,900	8062
Altru Health System	846	Grand Forks, ND	Private	135.8	3,200	8062
St Rita's Medical Center	847	Lima, OH	Private	135.8	2,000	8062
Lake Hospital System Inc	848	Painesville, OH	Private	135.8	2,200	8062
Berkshire Medical Center Inc	849	Pittsfield, MA	Private	135.6	1,375	8062
Portercare Hospital	850	Denver, CO	Private	135.4	2,400	8062
Medcenter One Inc	851	Bismarck, ND	Private	135.4	2,200	8062
Providence Hospital Inc	852	Mobile, AL	Private	135.2	1,506	8062
St Mary's Health System Inc	853	Knoxville, TN	Private	135.2	1,732	8062
Hendrick Medical Center	854	Abilene, TX	Private	135.1	2,400	8062
Anderson Infirmary Benevolent	855	Meridian, MS	Private	135.0	900	8062
University Of Kentucky	856	Lexington, KY	Private	134.7	NA	8011
Anne Arundel Medical Center	857	Annapolis, MD	Private	134.7	50	8062
Northeast Hospital Corporation	858	Beverly, MA	Private	134.6	2,800	8062
St Mary's Hospital Corporation	859	Waterbury, CT	Private	134.5	1,520	8062
Kent County Memorial Hospital	860	Warwick, RI	Private	134.1	2,000	8062
John C Lincoln Health Network	861	Phoenix, AZ	Private	133.9	2,102	8062
Frontier Group	862	Boston, MA	Private	133.8	4,000	8093
Greater Se Comm Hospital	863	Washington, DC	Private	133.8	2,800	8062
Hospital Service District 1	864	Marrero, LA	Private	133.7	1,676	8062
Mercy Health Center	865	Oklahoma City, OK	Private	133.7	1,780	8062
Benedictine Health System	866	Duluth, MN	Private	133.6	190	8062
St Joseph's Hospital	867	Savannah, GA	Private	133.6	1,194	8062
St Luke's Methodist Hospital	868	Cedar Rapids, IA	Private	133.5	2,000	8062
Nursefinders Inc	869	Arlington, TX	Private	133.5	450	8082
Hillcrest Baptist Medical Ctr	870	Waco, TX	Private	133.4	2,200	8062
Providence Hospital	871	Washington, DC	Private	133.4	1,611	8062
St Marys Regional Medical Ctr	872	Reno, NV	Private	133.4	1,400	8062
Mercy Medical Center	873	Rockville Centre, NY	Private	133.3	1,610	8062
King County Public Hospital Dst 1	874	Renton, WA	Private	133.3	1,650	8062
North Florida Regional Med Ctr	875	Gainesville, FL	Public Family Member	133.3	1,800	8062
Cypress Fairbanks Medical Ctr	876	Houston, TX	Public Family Member	133.0	650	8062
Middlesex Hospital	877	Middletown, CT	Private	132.9	1,257	8062
Optima Health-Cmc	878	Manchester, NH	Private	132.8	1,432	8062
St Chris Hospital Children Inc	879	Philadelphia, PA	Private	132.8	1,500	8069
Sentara Hospitals-Norfolk	880	Norfolk, VA	Private	132.8	NA	8062
Mount Auburn Hospital	881	Cambridge, MA	Private	132.8	1,900	8062
Tulane Medical Center, Ltd	882	New Orleans, LA	Private	132.7	1,500	8062
Oklahoma Department Human Svcs	883	Oklahoma City, OK	Private	132.7	NA	8062
Trustees Of Mease Hospital	884	Dunedin, FL	Private	132.7	1,320	8062
Rio Grande Hmo Inc	885	El Paso, TX	Private	132.4	37	8011
Guthrie Healthcare Systems	886	Sayre, PA	Private	132.4	2,825	8062
St Vincent Hospital	887	Green Bay, WI	Private	132.3	2,190	8062
Eastern Idaho Regional Med Ctr	888	Idaho Falls, ID	Public Family Member	132.3	1,300	8062
Southwest Catholic Health Network	889	Phoenix, AZ	Private	132.1	180	8011
Sherman Hospital	890	Elgin, IL	Private	132.0	1,712	8062
Sisters Mcy St Edw Mcy Hspt	891	Fort Smith, AR	Private	132.0	2,000	8062
Correctional Medical Services	892	Saint Louis, MO	Private	132.0	3,300	8099
Gambro Healthcare Patient Svcs	893	Aliso Viejo, CA	Private	131.8	4,000	8092
St Lukes-Roosevelt Hospital Ctr	894	New York, NY	Private	131.7	NA	8069
Floyd Healthcare Management	895	Rome, GA	Private	131.6	1,600	8062
Jefferson Health Services	896	Pittsburgh, PA	Private	131.6	2,600	8062
Nebraska Health System	897	Omaha, NE	Private	131.6	3,800	8062
St Francis Health System	898	Pittsburgh, PA	Private	131.5	NA	8069
Inter Valley Health Plan Inc	899	Pomona, CA	Private	131.5	180	8011
North Colorado Medical Center	900	Greeley, CO	Private	131.5	1,500	8062
Kennedy Health Care Foundation	901	Stratford, NJ	Private	131.2	2,800	8062
Glendale Adventist Med Ctr	902	Glendale, CA	Private	131.1	1,400	8062
Care Enterprises Inc	903	Tustin, CA	Public Family Member	131.0	5,700	8051
North Iowa Mercy Health Center	904	Mason City, IA	Private	130.8	2,500	8062
Alternative Living Services	905	Brookfield, WI	Public	130.7	5,935	8059
Midland County Hospital Dst	906	Midland, TX	Private	130.7	1,100	8062
Washington Cnty Hospital Assn Inc	907	Hagerstown, MD	Private	130.7	1,829	8062
W A Foote Memorial Hospital	908	Jackson, MI	Private	130.7	2,200	8062
Greater SE Community Hospital	909	Washington, DC	Private	130.6	1,200	8062
Physicians Healthcare Plans	910	Tampa, FL	Private	130.4	300	8011

D&B COMPANY RANKINGS BY SALES

Company	Rank	Location	Type	Sales ($ mil.)	Employment	Primary SIC
Anne Arundel Medical Center	911	Annapolis, MD	Private	130.4	1,800	8062
Memorial Hosp	912	Mount Holly, NJ	Private	130.4	1,450	8062
Magee-Womens Hospital	913	Pittsburgh, PA	Private	129.9	1,953	8062
Antelope Valley Health Care Systms	914	Lancaster, CA	Private	129.9	1,550	8062
America Service Group Inc	915	Brentwood, TN	Public	129.9	1,858	8011
Fhc Health Systems, Inc.	916	Norfolk, VA	Private	129.6	3,500	8063
Jefferson Hospital Association	917	Pine Bluff, AR	Private	129.5	1,788	8062
Porter Memorial Hospital	918	Valparaiso, IN	Private	129.5	1,600	8062
Peacehealth	919	Eugene, OR	Private	129.4	NA	8062
Altoona Hospital, The	920	Altoona, PA	Private	129.3	1,518	8062
Samaritan Medical Center	921	Watertown, NY	Private	129.1	1,300	8062
All Children's Hospital Inc	922	Saint Petersburg, FL	Private	129.1	1,688	8069
Mercy Mount Clemens Corp	923	Clinton Township, MI	Private	128.7	2,543	8062
Children's Health Systems	924	Milwaukee, WI	Private	128.7	2,600	8069
St Francis Medical Center	925	Honolulu, HI	Private	128.6	1,400	8062
Kingsbrook Jewish Medical Ctr	926	Brooklyn, NY	Private	128.4	2,100	8062
Presbytrian Intrcommunity Hosp	927	Whittier, CA	Private	128.3	1,200	8062
Rogue Valley Medical Center	928	Medford, OR	Private	128.3	1,778	8062
Hennepin County, Minnesota	929	Minneapolis, MN	Private	128.2	NA	8062
Thomas-Davis Medical Ctrs Pc	930	Tucson, AZ	Public Family Member	128.0	1,015	8011
Columbia Hospital, Inc.	931	Milwaukee, WI	Private	128.0	1,470	8062
Holy Name Hospital	932	Teaneck, NJ	Private	128.0	1,800	8062
Children's Hospital Medical Center	933	Akron, OH	Private	127.8	1,700	8069
Trinity Medical Cntr	934	Rock Island, IL	Private	127.8	1,800	8062
National Benevolent	935	Saint Louis, MO	Private	127.7	3,500	8361
St Tammany Parish Hospital	936	Covington, LA	Private	127.7	880	8062
Seton Medical Center	937	Daly City, CA	Private	127.5	1,231	8062
Allegheny Health, Educ & Res	938	Pittsburgh, PA	Private	127.3	1,200	8062
Health Hospital Corp Of Marion	939	Indianapolis, IN	Private	127.2	NA	8062
Veterans Health Administration	940	Hines, IL	Private	127.2	NA	8062
Washington Township Healthcare	941	Fremont, CA	Private	127.0	1,225	8062
Protestant Memorial Med Ctr	942	Belleville, IL	Private	126.9	2,117	8062
St Marys Hospital & Med Ctr	943	San Francisco, CA	Private	126.9	1,050	8062
Bloomington Hospital Inc	944	Bloomington, IN	Private	126.8	2,000	8062
Benefis Health Care	945	Great Falls, MT	Private	126.6	2,000	8062
Willis-Knighton Medical Ctr	946	Shreveport, LA	Private	126.5	2,700	8062
Sisters Of Providence In Ore	947	Portland, OR	Private	126.4	NA	8062
Baptist Medical Center	948	Kansas City, MO	Private	126.1	1,500	8062
San Antonio Community Hosp	949	Upland, CA	Private	126.0	1,800	8062
Mercy Medical Center	950	Baltimore, MD	Private	125.8	1,300	8062
Christ Hospital	951	Jersey City, NJ	Private	125.6	1,100	8062
Brookhaven Mem Hospital Med Ctr	952	East Patchogue, NY	Private	125.6	1,900	8062
Bay Medical Center	953	Panama City, FL	Private	125.5	1,906	8062
Long Island College Hospital	954	Brooklyn, NY	Private	125.5	2,679	8062
Memorial Medical Center	955	Las Cruces, NM	Private	125.5	1,450	8062
Commonwealth Health Corp	956	Bowling Green, KY	Private	125.5	351	8062
Craven Regional Medical Ctr	957	New Bern, NC	Private	125.1	1,305	8062
Housecall Medical Services	958	Louisville, KY	Public Family Member	125.0	2,000	8082
Quest Diagnostics Inc Michigan	959	Auburn Hills, MI	Private	125.0	1,350	8071
Stamford Hospital	960	Stamford, CT	Private	124.9	1,200	8062
Healthsource Maine Inc	961	Freeport, ME	Public Family Member	124.6	215	8011
Kaweah Delta Health Care Dst	962	Visalia, CA	Private	124.6	2,100	8062
Congregation Of The Sisters	963	San Antonio, TX	Private	124.4	NA	8062
County Of Kern	964	Bakersfield, CA	Private	124.4	NA	8062
County Of Los Angeles	965	Sylmar, CA	Private	124.4	NA	8062
Kaiser Foundation Health Plan	966	Sacramento, CA	Private	124.4	NA	8062
Kaiser Foundation Hospitals	967	Santa Clara, CA	Private	124.4	NA	8062
New York Cy Health Hspitals Corp	968	Brooklyn, NY	Private	124.4	NA	8062
Veterans Affairs Us Dept	969	North Little Rock, AR	Private	124.4	NA	8062
Veterans Health Administration	970	Philadelphia, PA	Private	124.4	NA	8062
Veterans Health Administration	971	Portland, OR	Private	124.4	NA	8062
Veterans Health Administration	972	San Antonio, TX	Private	124.4	NA	8062
Washington Hospital	973	Washington, PA	Private	124.3	1,470	8062
Suburban Hospital	974	Bethesda, MD	Private	124.3	1,550	8062
Nyack Hospital Inc	975	Nyack, NY	Private	124.2	1,200	8062
George Washington University	976	Washington, DC	Private	124.2	NA	8011
Sisters Of Providence In Wash	977	Everett, WA	Private	124.2	NA	8011
Southern Cal Permanente Med	978	San Diego, CA	Private	124.2	NA	8011
Veterans Health Administration	979	Miami, FL	Private	124.0	NA	8062
O'connor Hospital	980	San Jose, CA	Private	123.9	1,000	8062

D&B COMPANY RANKINGS BY SALES

Company	Rank	Location	Type	Sales ($ mil.)	Employ-ment	Primary SIC
Bay Medical Center	981	Bay City, MI	Private	123.6	2,000	8062
Ravenswood Hospital Med Ctr	982	Chicago, IL	Private	123.0	1,250	8062
Hospital For Joint Diseases	983	New York, NY	Private	123.0	1,150	8069
Arizona Heart Hospital Inc	984	Phoenix, AZ	Private	123.0	350	8062
Barnes-Jewish Hospital	985	Saint Louis, MO	Private	123.0	NA	8062
Bay Health Medical Center Inc	986	Dover, DE	Private	122.9	NA	8062
Lexington Medical Center	987	West Columbia, SC	Private	122.8	1,600	8062
Paramount Care Inc	988	Maumee, OH	Private	122.6	127	8011
Crestwood Hospitals Inc	989	Stockton, CA	Private	122.6	1,400	8069
King County Pub Hospital Dst 2	990	Kirkland, WA	Private	122.5	1,200	8062
Alexandria Inova Hospital	991	Alexandria, VA	Private	122.0	1,750	8062
Chesapeake Hospital Auth	992	Chesapeake, VA	Private	121.9	1,700	8062
City Of Boston	993	Boston, MA	Private	121.9	NA	8062
Hospital Service Dist	994	Houma, LA	Private	121.9	1,215	8062
Little Company Of Mary Hosp	995	Torrance, CA	Private	121.8	1,200	8062
Lutheran Medical Center	996	Brooklyn, NY	Private	121.8	2,600	8062
St Barnabas Medical Center	997	Livingston, NJ	Private	121.8	2,600	8062
Sunplus Hm Health Nursing Fcilty	998	Upland, CA	Public Family Member	121.8	NA	8051
Wellesley Newton Hospital	999	Newton, MA	Private	121.8	1,800	8062
Durham County Hospital Corp	1000	Durham, NC	Private	121.7	2,048	8062
Intermountain Health Care Inc	1001	Salt Lake City, UT	Private	121.5	NA	8062
High Point Regional Health Sys	1002	High Point, NC	Private	121.4	1,800	8062
Meritcare Health Enterprises	1003	Fargo, ND	Private	121.4	1,500	8011
Sparks Regional Medical Ctr	1004	Fort Smith, AR	Private	121.3	1,800	8062
Comanche County Hospital Auth Tr	1005	Lawton, OK	Private	121.2	1,400	8062
St Anthony's Medical Center	1006	Saint Louis, MO	Private	121.2	2,589	8062
Baylor Medical Ctr At Irving	1007	Irving, TX	Private	121.1	1,600	8062
Neponset Valley Health System	1008	Norfolk, MA	Private	121.0	2,100	8062
St Marys Hospital Of Milwaukee	1009	Milwaukee, WI	Private	120.8	2,100	8062
Horizon West Inc	1010	Rocklin, CA	Private	120.6	5,400	8059
St Vincent's Hospital	1011	Birmingham, AL	Private	120.6	1,449	8062
Citizens Medical Center	1012	Victoria, TX	Private	120.5	645	8062
Howard University	1013	Washington, DC	Private	120.3	NA	8062
Harris Methodist Fort Worth	1014	Fort Worth, TX	Private	119.9	2,560	8062
Bellin Memorial Hospital	1015	Green Bay, WI	Private	119.8	1,650	8062
St Francis Hospital Inc	1016	Milwaukee, WI	Private	119.7	1,600	8062
Bethesda Memorial Hospital	1017	Boynton Beach, FL	Private	119.6	1,545	8062
Christ Hospital Health Svcs Corp	1018	Jersey City, NJ	Private	119.5	1,200	8062
Southwest General Health Ctr	1019	Cleveland, OH	Private	119.3	2,000	8062
Nueces County Hospital Dst	1020	Corpus Christi, TX	Private	119.3	1,689	8062
Edward Hospital	1021	Naperville, IL	Private	119.2	1,300	8062
Sisters Of Providence In Wash	1022	Anchorage, AK	Private	119.1	NA	8062
Sisters Of Providence In Wash	1023	Seattle, WA	Private	119.1	NA	8062
John N Dempsey Hospital	1024	Farmington, CT	Private	119.0	1,057	8062
Dominican Santa Cruz Hospital	1025	Santa Cruz, CA	Private	118.9	1,300	8062
Jackson Methodist Healthcare	1026	Jackson, MS	Private	118.9	1,159	8062
Saint Mary Of Nazareth Hospital Ctr	1027	Chicago, IL	Private	118.8	1,400	8062
St Joseph Health Svcs Of Ri	1028	Providence, RI	Private	118.8	1,865	8062
Blood Systems, Inc.	1029	Scottsdale, AZ	Private	118.7	1,868	8099
Valdost-Lwndes Cnty Hospital Auth	1030	Valdosta, GA	Private	118.5	1,800	8062
Shore Memorial Health Foundation	1031	Somers Point, NJ	Private	118.3	1,400	8062
State Of New York	1032	Kings Park, NY	Private	118.2	NA	8063
Oxford Health Plans (Pa) Inc	1033	Philadelphia, PA	Public Family Member	118.0	80	8011
Queen Of Angele-Hollywood Pres	1034	Los Angeles, CA	Private	117.9	1,200	8062
Southern Ohio Medical Center	1035	Portsmouth, OH	Private	117.9	2,000	8062
Trumbull Memorial Hospital	1036	Warren, OH	Private	117.8	2,000	8062
Florida Medical Center Inc	1037	Fort Lauderdale, FL	Public Family Member	117.7	1,350	8062
Integris Rur Healthcare Of Okla	1038	Oklahoma City, OK	Private	117.7	1,790	8062
Allegheny Intgrated Health Group	1039	Philadelphia, PA	Private	117.6	10	8011
Medical Ctr At Princeton, The	1040	Princeton, NJ	Private	117.4	1,800	8062
Orthodontic Centers Of America	1041	Ponte Vedra Beach, FL	Public	117.3	390	8021
St Agnes Healthcare	1042	Baltimore, MD	Private	117.3	2,506	8062
N T Enloe Memorial Hospital	1043	Chico, CA	Private	117.3	1,700	8062
Unlimited Care Inc	1044	White Plains, NY	Private	117.2	1,700	8011
Denver, City & County	1045	Denver, CO	Private	117.1	NA	8062
Lawnwood Medical Center Inc	1046	Fort Pierce, FL	Public Family Member	117.1	1,191	8062
Columbia Metrowest Medical Ctr	1047	Natick, MA	Public Family Member	117.0	2,500	8062
Community Health Inv Corp	1048	Brentwood, TN	Public Family Member	117.0	2,500	8062
Jewish Hospital Of Cincinnati	1049	Cincinnati, OH	Private	117.0	2,500	8062
Mercy Hospital Of Pittsburgh	1050	Pittsburgh, PA	Private	117.0	2,500	8062

D&B COMPANY RANKINGS BY SALES

Company	Rank	Location	Type	Sales ($ mil.)	Employ- ment	Primary SIC
Glynn-Brunswick Hospital Auth	1051	Brunswick, GA	Private	116.8	1,487	8062
Aetna Health Plans Southern Ne	1052	Hartford, CT	Public Family Member	116.7	4	8011
St Charles Mercy Hospital	1053	Oregon, OH	Private	116.7	1,903	8062
St Francis Hospital Inc	1054	Wilmington, DE	Private	116.4	1,400	8062
Beverly Enterprises-Florida	1055	Fort Smith, AR	Public Family Member	116.4	5,260	8059
Huntington Cabell Hospital	1056	Huntington, WV	Private	116.4	1,600	8062
Elliot Hospital	1057	Manchester, NH	Private	116.4	1,517	8062
Truman Medical Center Inc	1058	Kansas City, MO	Private	116.2	2,700	8062
Huntington Foundation Inc	1059	Plainfield, NJ	Private	116.2	1,686	8011
Molina Medical Center, Inc	1060	Long Beach, CA	Private	116.2	410	8011
Franciscan Skemp Healthcare	1061	La Crosse, WI	Private	116.1	2,481	8062
Victoria Hospital Corporation	1062	Victoria, TX	Public Family Member	116.0	740	8062
Allegheny Valley Hospital	1063	Natrona Heights, PA	Private	115.9	1,350	8062
Chw Medical Foundation	1064	Sacramento, CA	Private	115.7	800	8099
Integris Southwest Med Ctr	1065	Oklahoma City, OK	Private	115.5	3,000	8062
Somerset Medical Center	1066	Somerville, NJ	Private	115.5	1,700	8062
Good Samaritan Hospital Of Md Inc	1067	Baltimore, MD	Private	115.5	1,427	8062
Mission Hospital Regional Med Ctr	1068	Mission Viejo, CA	Private	115.5	1,350	8062
North Arundel Hospital Assn	1069	Glen Burnie, MD	Private	115.4	2,079	8062
Methodist Hospital Of Southern Cal	1070	Arcadia, CA	Private	115.4	1,018	8062
United Hospital Center Inc	1071	Clarksburg, WV	Private	115.3	1,400	8062
Upper Valley Medical Center	1072	Troy, OH	Private	115.3	336	8062
Joseph Saint Health Center	1073	Kansas City, MO	Private	115.2	1,550	8062
Health Plan Of Upper Ohio	1074	Saint Clairsville, OH	Private	115.2	105	8082
Methodist Med Ctr Of Oak Ridge	1075	Oak Ridge, TN	Private	115.1	1,500	8062
Network Health System, Inc	1076	Menasha, WI	Private	115.0	1,291	8011
Britwill Investments I Inc	1077	Scottsdale, AZ	Public Family Member	114.9	5,000	8051
Geriatric & Medical Companies	1078	Kennett Square, PA	Public Family Member	114.9	5,000	8051
Florida Health Care Plan Inc	1079	Daytona Beach, FL	Private	114.7	670	8099
Life Care Rtrement Communities	1080	Des Moines, IA	Private	114.6	2,000	8059
Pinnacle Health Hospitals	1081	Harrisburg, PA	Private	114.5	NA	8062
Good Samaritan Hospital Inc	1082	West Palm Beach, FL	Private	114.4	1,200	8062
Temple Univ Commonwealth Systm	1083	Philadelphia, PA	Private	114.3	NA	8062
Overlake Hospital Medical Ctr	1084	Bellevue, WA	Private	114.3	1,600	8062
Miami Beach Healthcare Group	1085	Miami, FL	Private	114.2	1,700	8062
Johns Hopkins Medical Services	1086	Baltimore, MD	Private	114.2	570	8011
H C A Health Services Of Nh	1087	Portsmouth, NH	Public Family Member	114.0	969	8062
Wuesthoff Health Systems Inc	1088	Rockledge, FL	Private	113.9	2,012	8062
Wuesthoff Memorial Hospital	1089	Rockledge, FL	Private	113.9	1,356	8062
Glens Falls Hospital	1090	Glens Falls, NY	Private	113.9	2,100	8062
Beth Israel Medical Center	1091	New York, NY	Private	113.8	NA	8093
Fort Worth Medical Plaza Inc	1092	Fort Worth, TX	Public Family Member	113.8	1,600	8062
Adventist Health System/Sunbelt	1093	Sebring, FL	Private	113.7	NA	8011
Medalia Healthcare Llc	1094	Seattle, WA	Private	113.7	1,650	8011
Admin Of The Tul Educ Fund	1095	New Orleans, LA	Private	113.6	NA	8011
County Of Los Angeles	1096	Lancaster, CA	Private	113.6	NA	8011
University Of Michigan	1097	Ann Arbor, MI	Private	113.6	NA	8011
University Of Washington	1098	Seattle, WA	Private	113.6	NA	8011
St Francis Hospital & Med Ctr	1099	Topeka, KS	Private	113.5	1,724	8062
Pacific Medical Center	1100	Seattle, WA	Private	113.4	1,100	8011
Norman Regional Hospital Auth	1101	Norman, OK	Private	113.3	1,370	8062
Fallon Clinic Inc	1102	Worcester, MA	Private	113.3	NA	8011
North Central Health Services	1103	Lafayette, IN	Private	113.1	1,700	8062
Rwj Healthcare Corp	1104	New Brunswick, NJ	Private	112.8	NA	8062
Sound Shore Medical Center	1105	New Rochelle, NY	Private	112.8	1,400	8062
Allegheny University Hospital	1106	Philadelphia, PA	Private	112.6	NA	8062
Physicians Health Plan, Inc.	1107	Columbia, SC	Private	112.5	162	8011
Beverly Enterprises - Arkansas	1108	Fort Smith, AR	Public Family Member	112.5	4,896	8051
Kuakini Health System	1109	Honolulu, HI	Private	112.3	1,500	8062
Columbia Chppnhm Mdcl Ctr	1110	Richmond, VA	Public Family Member	112.3	2,400	8062
Research Medical Center	1111	Kansas City, MO	Private	112.3	2,400	8062
Children's Hospital Medical Center	1112	Oakland, CA	Private	112.2	2,000	8062
Southeastern Regional Med Ctr	1113	Lumberton, NC	Private	112.2	1,600	8062
Healthcor, Inc	1114	Dallas, TX	Public Family Member	112.2	1,200	8082
Group Health Coop Of Puget Sound	1115	Redmond, WA	Private	111.9	NA	8062
St Lukes Hospital Association	1116	Jacksonville, FL	Private	111.8	1,300	8062
Premiere Assoc Healthcare Svcs	1117	Clemmons, NC	Public Family Member	111.6	100	8051
United Healthcare Of Kentucky	1118	Lexington, KY	Private	111.3	100	8011
White Plains Hospital Center	1119	White Plains, NY	Private	111.3	1,100	8062
Healtheast St Josephs Hosp	1120	Saint Paul, MN	Private	111.1	1,072	8062

D&B COMPANY RANKINGS BY SALES

Company	Rank	Location	Type	Sales ($ mil.)	Employ-ment	Primary SIC
Memorial Hospital	1121	Pawtucket, RI	Private	111.0	1,737	8062
Muhlenberg Regional Med Ctr	1122	Plainfield, NJ	Private	110.9	1,650	8062
Tennessee Healthsource Inc	1123	Brentwood, TN	Public Family Member	110.8	113	8011
Good Samaritan Hospital Of Suffern	1124	Suffern, NY	Private	110.7	1,500	8062
Veterans Health Administration	1125	Tampa, FL	Private	110.7	NA	8062
Crittenton Hospital	1126	Rochester, MI	Private	110.6	1,184	8062
State Of New York	1127	Thiells, NY	Private	110.4	NA	8063
Rockford Memorial Health Svcs	1128	Rockford, IL	Private	110.4	735	8011
Mercy Hospital Inc	1129	Charlotte, NC	Private	110.3	1,250	8062
Healthcare Partners Med Group	1130	Los Angeles, CA	Private	110.3	1,600	8011
Mayo Clinic Jacksonville Inc	1131	Jacksonville, FL	Private	110.3	1,600	8011
Mercy Health Services	1132	Pontiac, MI	Private	110.2	NA	8062
In Home Health, Inc	1133	Hopkins, MN	Public	110.1	4,000	8082
Mercy Memorial Health Center	1134	Ardmore, OK	Private	110.0	700	8062
Nebraska Methodist Hospital	1135	Omaha, NE	Private	110.0	1,850	8062
Palo Alto Medical Foundation	1136	Palo Alto, CA	Private	110.0	1,000	8011
Wausau Hospitals Inc	1137	Wausau, WI	Private	110.0	1,209	8062
Community Hospital Assn Inc	1138	Boulder, CO	Private	109.7	1,400	8063
California Hospital Medical	1139	Los Angeles, CA	Private	109.7	1,400	8062
Lrimg, Inc	1140	Los Gatos, CA	Private	109.6	16	8011
Allegheny Hospital Centenial	1141	Philadelphia, PA	Private	109.5	NA	8062
Erie, New York, County	1142	Buffalo, NY	Private	109.5	NA	8062
Shore Memorial Hospital	1143	Somers Point, NJ	Private	109.4	1,600	8062
Kaiser Foundation Hospitals	1144	Oakland, CA	Private	109.4	NA	8062
Greenwich Hospital Assn Inc	1145	Greenwich, CT	Private	109.4	1,300	8062
Elkhart General Hospital	1146	Elkhart, IN	Private	109.4	1,395	8062
Personal-Touch Home Care Inc	1147	Bayside, NY	Private	109.3	11,500	8082
Clara Maass Medical Center	1148	Belleville, NJ	Private	109.3	1,500	8062
St Alexius Medical Center	1149	Bismarck, ND	Private	109.1	1,875	8062
General Hospital Ctr At Passaic	1150	Passaic, NJ	Private	109.0	1,465	8062
Medical Center East Inc	1151	Birmingham, AL	Private	109.0	1,450	8062
Sisters Hospital	1152	Buffalo, NY	Private	108.8	2,213	8062
Elizabeth General Medical Ctr	1153	Elizabeth, NJ	Private	108.6	2,000	8062
North General Hospital	1154	New York, NY	Private	108.5	2,565	8062
Aurora Medical Group, Inc	1155	Milwaukee, WI	Private	108.5	1,575	8011
University Of Arizona	1156	Tucson, AZ	Private	108.5	NA	8062
University Of New Mexico	1157	Albuquerque, NM	Private	108.5	NA	8062
St Vincent Hospital Inc	1158	Santa Fe, NM	Private	108.5	1,050	8062
Columbus Regional Hospital	1159	Columbus, IN	Private	108.5	1,300	8062
Doctors Hospital Of Augusta	1160	Augusta, GA	Public Family Member	108.4	1,050	8062
Bowling Green Comm Hospital	1161	Bowling Green, KY	Private	108.0	1,250	8062
Smithkline Beecham Corporation	1162	Glen Burnie, MD	Private	107.9	NA	8071
Deborah Heart & Lung Center	1163	Browns Mills, NJ	Private	107.8	1,425	8069
Bon Secours-Richmond Health Corp	1164	Richmond, VA	Private	107.6	2,300	8062
Galen Of Florida, Inc	1165	Nashville, TN	Public Family Member	107.6	2,300	8062
East Alabama Health Care Auth	1166	Opelika, AL	Private	107.6	1,650	8062
Principal Health Care Of Kans Cy	1167	Kansas City, MO	Private	107.5	102	8011
Kaiser Foundation Health Plan	1168	Oakland, CA	Private	107.2	NA	8011
Mercy Hospital Of Buffalo	1169	Buffalo, NY	Private	107.2	2,100	8062
Virginia Beach General Hosp	1170	Virginia Beach, VA	Private	107.2	1,717	8062
Southeast Missouri Hospital Assn	1171	Cape Girardeau, MO	Private	107.0	1,400	8062
Westmoreland Regional Hosp	1172	Greensburg, PA	Private	107.0	1,700	8062
Memorial Hospital West Volusia	1173	Deland, FL	Private	107.0	563	8062
Our Lady Of Lourdes Regional	1174	Lafayette, LA	Private	106.9	1,100	8062
Mercy Hospital Of Scranton Pa	1175	Scranton, PA	Private	106.9	1,476	8062
Leesburg Regional Medical Ctr	1176	Leesburg, FL	Private	106.9	1,275	8062
Santa Rosa Memorial Hospital	1177	Santa Rosa, CA	Private	106.9	1,007	8062
Easton Hospital	1178	Easton, PA	Private	106.5	1,425	8062
Marin General Hospital	1179	Greenbrae, CA	Private	106.4	1,100	8062
Dmh Health Systems	1180	Decatur, IL	Private	106.4	16	8062
Pendleton Mem Methdst Hosp	1181	New Orleans, LA	Private	106.1	1,068	8062
Department Of Army	1182	Fort Campbell, KY	Private	106.1	NA	8062
Veterans Health Administration	1183	Milwaukee, WI	Private	106.0	NA	8062
Huntington Hospital Assn	1184	Huntington, NY	Private	105.8	1,270	8062
East Pasco Medical Center Inc	1185	Zephyrhills, FL	Private	105.8	1,010	8062
Kimball Medical Center Inc	1186	Lakewood, NJ	Private	105.8	1,550	8062
California Pacific Med Ctr	1187	San Francisco, CA	Private	105.3	NA	8069
New York And Presbyterian Hosp	1188	New York, NY	Private	105.3	NA	8069
St Luke Health System, Inc	1189	Sioux City, IA	Private	105.2	2,100	8062
Mclaren Regional Medical Ctr	1190	Flint, MI	Private	105.2	2,250	8062

D&B COMPANY RANKINGS BY SALES

Company	Rank	Location	Type	Sales ($ mil.)	Employ- ment	Primary SIC
Our Lady Of Lourdes Med Ctr	1191	Camden, NJ	Private	105.2	2,250	8062
Dublin Community Hospital Inc	1192	Dublin, GA	Public Family Member	105.0	585	8062
Lindsay District Hospital	1193	Lindsay, CA	Private	105.0	248	8062
West Orange Healthcare Inc	1194	Ocoee, FL	Private	104.9	700	8062
Highland Park Hospital	1195	Highland Park, IL	Private	104.9	870	8062
Wheeling Hospital Inc	1196	Wheeling, WV	Private	104.7	1,388	8062
Emsi Holding Company	1197	Dallas, TX	Private	104.6	4,001	8099
Maury Regional Hospital	1198	Columbia, TN	Private	104.5	1,473	8062
Firsthealth Of The Carolinas	1199	Pinehurst, NC	Private	104.5	2,235	8062
Hca Health Services Of Florida	1200	Port Richey, FL	Public Family Member	104.4	1,000	8062
Watson Clinic	1201	Lakeland, FL	Private	104.3	1,060	8011
Veterans Health Administration	1202	Minneapolis, MN	Private	104.2	NA	8062
St Josephs Regional Health Ctr	1203	Hot Springs, AR	Private	104.2	1,400	8062
Pasadena Bayshore Hospital	1204	Pasadena, TX	Public Family Member	104.1	1,000	8062
Francis Saint Medical Center	1205	Grand Island, NE	Private	104.0	950	8062
H C F Inc	1206	Lima, OH	Private	104.0	3,000	8051
Beverly Enterprises-Michigan	1207	Fort Smith, AR	Public Family Member	103.7	4,643	8059
Southwest Community Health	1208	Cleveland, OH	Private	103.6	1,982	8062
Amisub (North Ridge Hospital)	1209	Fort Lauderdale, FL	Public Family Member	103.5	700	8062
Dakota Clinic Ltd	1210	Fargo, ND	Private	103.4	1,500	8011
Foundation Health Federal Svcs	1211	Rancho Cordova, CA	Public Family Member	103.4	1,500	8011
Macgregor Medical Assn P A	1212	Houston, TX	Private	103.4	1,500	8011
Midelfort Clinic-Mayo Health	1213	Eau Claire, WI	Private	103.4	1,500	8011
Pacific Health Systems Inc	1214	Santa Ana, CA	Public Family Member	103.4	1,500	8011
U T Medical Group Inc	1215	Memphis, TN	Private	103.4	1,500	8011
Yuma Regional Medical Center	1216	Yuma, AZ	Private	103.4	1,200	8062
Bayer Corporation	1217	West Haven, CT	Private	103.3	NA	8071
Nationwide Care, Inc	1218	Louisville, KY	Private	103.3	4,500	8051
St Elizabeth Hospital Inc	1219	Elizabeth, NJ	Private	103.2	1,285	8062
Pacificare Of California	1220	Salt Lake City, UT	Public Family Member	103.0	NA	8011
University Of New Mexico	1221	Albuquerque, NM	Private	103.0	NA	8062
Clintrials Research Inc	1222	Nashville, TN	Public	103.0	1,500	8071
Scan Health Plan	1223	Long Beach, CA	Private	103.0	275	8011
Self Memorial Hospital	1224	Greenwood, SC	Private	102.9	1,500	8062
Latrobe Area Hospital Inc	1225	Latrobe, PA	Private	102.9	1,500	8062
Owensboro Mercy Health Systems	1226	Owensboro, KY	Private	102.8	2,200	8062
Saint Vincent Hospital, Llc	1227	Worcester, MA	Public Family Member	102.8	2,200	8062
St Elizabeth's Hospital	1228	Belleville, IL	Private	102.7	1,600	8062
National Surgery Centers, Inc.	1229	Chicago, IL	Public	102.6	519	8093
Solano County Comm On Med Care	1230	Suisun City, CA	Private	102.5	70	8011
Amisub Of California, Inc	1231	Tarzana, CA	Public Family Member	102.4	800	8062
St Joseph Hospital, Inc	1232	Lancaster, PA	Private	102.4	1,429	8062
Health Caolc And Tcofa	1233	Florence, AL	Private	102.3	1,600	8062
Danville Regional Medical Ctr	1234	Danville, VA	Private	102.3	1,200	8062
Linda Loma Univ Health Care	1235	Loma Linda, CA	Private	102.3	1,100	8011
Southwest Louisiana Hospital Assn	1236	Lake Charles, LA	Private	102.1	1,500	8062
Veterans Memorial Medical Ctr	1237	Meriden, CT	Private	102.1	1,740	8062
Examination Management Svcs	1238	Dallas, TX	Private	102.0	4,000	8099
Glendale Mem Hospital & Health	1239	Glendale, CA	Private	101.9	1,065	8062
Response Oncology Inc	1240	Memphis, TN	Public	101.9	400	8093
Sisters Of Bon Secours Hosp	1241	Detroit, MI	Private	101.9	NA	8062
Lester E Cox Medical Center	1242	Springfield, MO	Private	101.7	NA	8062
Ssm Health Care	1243	Saint Louis, MO	Private	101.7	NA	8062
Frederick Memorial Hospital	1244	Frederick, MD	Private	101.7	1,700	8062
Redmond Park Hospital Inc	1245	Rome, GA	Public Family Member	101.5	1,200	8062
Veterans Health Administration	1246	West Haven, CT	Private	101.5	NA	8062
Citrus Valley Medical Center	1247	West Covina, CA	Private	101.4	1,723	8062
Quest Diagnostics Incorporated	1248	Teterboro, NJ	Private	101.3	NA	8071
Harbor Hospital Center Inc	1249	Baltimore, MD	Private	101.1	1,150	8062
Community Medical Center Inc	1250	Scranton, PA	Private	101.1	1,178	8062
Rockingham Memorial Hospital	1251	Harrisonburg, VA	Private	101.0	1,465	8062
Evergreen Healthcare, Inc	1252	Atlanta, GA	Public Family Member	101.0	5,412	8052
Phoenix Childrens Hospital	1253	Phoenix, AZ	Private	101.0	654	8069
Indian River Memorial Hospital	1254	Vero Beach, FL	Private	100.7	1,200	8062
Foundation Ma Eye & Ear Infrmy	1255	Boston, MA	Private	100.7	1,174	8069
Mercy Med Ctr Cedar Rapids Iowa	1256	Cedar Rapids, IA	Private	100.7	1,600	8062
St Mary Medical Center	1257	Langhorne, PA	Private	100.5	1,600	8062
Wenatchee Valley Clinic	1258	Wenatchee, WA	Private	100.5	950	8011
Jackson Hospital & Clinic Inc	1259	Montgomery, AL	Private	100.4	1,400	8062
Texarkana Memorial Hospital Inc	1260	Texarkana, TX	Private	100.4	1,285	8062

D&B/Gale Industry Reference Handbooks

D&B COMPANY RANKINGS BY SALES

Company	Rank	Location	Type	Sales ($ mil.)	Employ-ment	Primary SIC
Youth Services International	1261	Owings Mills, MD	Public	100.4	1,500	8361
Nash Hospitals Inc	1262	Rocky Mount, NC	Private	100.3	1,400	8062
Reid Hospital & Health Care Svc	1263	Richmond, IN	Private	100.3	1,200	8062
Montgomery Hospital	1264	Norristown, PA	Private	100.2	1,330	8062
Advocate Medical Group, Sc	1265	Park Ridge, IL	Private	100.0	1,200	8093
Galen-Med, Inc	1266	Richlands, VA	Public Family Member	100.0	1,975	8062
Mesa General Hospital Med Ctr	1267	Mesa, AZ	Public Family Member	100.0	450	8062
U.S. Healthworks, Inc.	1268	Alpharetta, GA	Private	100.0	2,000	8011
Memorial Hospitals Assn	1269	Modesto, CA	Private	100.0	2,250	8062
Option Care, Inc (Del)	1270	Deerfield, IL	Public	100.0	1,156	8082
Heartland Health System Inc	1271	Saint Joseph, MO	Private	99.9	2,138	8062
Southwest La Health Care Sys	1272	Lake Charles, LA	Private	99.9	1,450	8011
Maryview Hospital	1273	Portsmouth, VA	Private	99.8	1,572	8062
Intermountain Health Care Inc	1274	Provo, UT	Private	99.8	NA	8062
St Charles Hospital Port Jefferson	1275	Port Jefferson, NY	Private	99.7	1,010	8062
St Patrick Hospital Corp	1276	Missoula, MT	Private	99.6	1,170	8069
Patient Care Inc	1277	West Orange, NJ	Public Family Member	99.6	5,300	8082
Detroit Osteopathic Hospital Corp	1278	Southfield, MI	Private	99.5	2,130	8062
Kaiser Foundation Hospitals	1279	San Jose, CA	Private	99.5	NA	8062
Kaiser Foundation Hospitals	1280	Clackamas, OR	Private	99.5	NA	8062
Kaiser Foundation Hospitals	1281	Los Angeles, CA	Private	99.5	NA	8062
Kaiser Foundation Hospitals	1282	Clackamas, OR	Private	99.5	NA	8062
Multicare Health System	1283	Tacoma, WA	Private	99.5	NA	8062
New York Cy Health Hspitals Corp	1284	New York, NY	Private	99.5	NA	8062
New York Cy Health Hspitals Corp	1285	Bronx, NY	Private	99.5	NA	8062
New York, The City	1286	Jamaica, NY	Private	99.5	NA	8062
Pinnacle Health Hospitals	1287	Harrisburg, PA	Private	99.5	NA	8062
Saint Clare's Hospital Inc	1288	Sussex, NJ	Private	99.5	NA	8062
State University Of Ny	1289	Stony Brook, NY	Private	99.5	NA	8062
University Of California	1290	Orange, CA	Private	99.5	NA	8062
Veterans Health Administration	1291	East Orange, NJ	Private	99.5	NA	8062
Veterans Health Administration	1292	Bronx, NY	Private	99.5	NA	8062
Veterans Health Administration	1293	San Francisco, CA	Private	99.5	NA	8062
Veterans Health Administration	1294	Los Angeles, CA	Private	99.5	NA	8062
Lourdes	1295	Paducah, KY	Private	99.5	1,300	8062
Hospital Authority Petersburg	1296	Petersburg, VA	Private	99.3	1,400	8062
Trinity Medical Center	1297	Minot, ND	Private	99.1	905	8062
Equimed, Inc.	1298	State College, PA	Public	99.1	500	8099
M H Health Care Inc	1299	Indianapolis, IN	Private	99.1	560	8011
Robert Packer Hospital Inc	1300	Sayre, PA	Private	99.0	1,300	8062
Garden City Hospital Osteopathic	1301	Garden City, MI	Private	99.0	1,200	8062
Decatur Memorial Hospital	1302	Decatur, IL	Private	98.9	1,165	8062
Health Net Inc	1303	Nashville, TN	Private	98.8	6	8011
Cvhs Hospital Corporation	1304	Inglewood, CA	Public Family Member	98.8	1,300	8062
Father Flanagan's Boy's Home	1305	Boys Town, NE	Private	98.7	1,729	8361
Ihc Health Services Inc	1306	Salt Lake City, UT	Private	98.7	NA	8069
Highland Hospital Of Rochester	1307	Rochester, NY	Private	98.7	1,275	8062
Mercy Hospital Of Laredo	1308	Laredo, TX	Private	98.6	1,400	8062
Sheridan Healthcorp, Inc	1309	Hollywood, FL	Private	98.6	750	8082
California Dept Mental Health	1310	Napa, CA	Private	98.6	NA	8063
Healtheast St John's Hospital	1311	Saint Paul, MN	Private	98.5	713	8062
Medcentral Health System	1312	Mansfield, OH	Private	98.4	2,141	8062
Children's Hospital Of Kings	1313	Norfolk, VA	Private	98.3	1,239	8069
New England Baptist Hospital	1314	Boston, MA	Private	98.2	1,100	8062
Bon Scurs Mem Regional Med Ctr	1315	Richmond, VA	Private	98.1	2,100	8062
Borgess Medical Center Inc	1316	Kalamazoo, MI	Private	98.1	2,100	8062
G B Health Systems Inc	1317	Atlanta, GA	Public Family Member	98.1	2,100	8062
Missouri Baptist Medical Ctr	1318	Saint Louis, MO	Private	98.1	2,100	8062
St Joseph Health Care System	1319	Albuquerque, NM	Private	98.1	2,100	8062
Hardin Memorial Hospital	1320	Elizabethtown, KY	Private	98.1	1,450	8062
Saint Joseph Hospital Inc	1321	Denver, CO	Private	98.0	2,098	8062
Southern Maryland Hospital	1322	Clinton, MD	Private	98.0	1,300	8062
Forum Group Inc	1323	Fairfax, VA	Public	97.9	NA	8361
Kuakini Medical Center	1324	Honolulu, HI	Private	97.7	1,200	8062
Pontiac Osteopathic Hospital	1325	Pontiac, MI	Private	97.6	1,300	8062
Serologicals Corporation	1326	Clarkston, GA	Public	97.5	1,000	8099
Provena Hospital	1327	Joliet, IL	Private	97.5	NA	8062
Veterans Health Administration	1328	Bay Pines, FL	Private	97.4	NA	8062
Gottlieb Memorial Hospital	1329	Melrose Park, IL	Private	97.4	1,200	8062
Medical Services Of America	1330	Lexington, SC	Private	97.4	1,500	8082

D&B COMPANY RANKINGS BY SALES

Company	Rank	Location	Type	Sales ($ mil.)	Employ-ment	Primary SIC
Vassar Bros Hospital	1331	Poughkeepsie, NY	Private	97 3	1,200	8062
Los Robles Regional Med Ctr	1332	Thousand Oaks, CA	Public Family Member	97.2	800	8062
Augusta Hospital Corporation	1333	Fishersville, VA	Private	97.0	1,300	8062
Columbia Hospital For Women Med	1334	Washington, DC	Private	97.0	700	8062
Homestead Hospital Inc	1335	Homestead, FL	Private	97.0	500	8062
Fairview Hospital Healthcare Svcs	1336	Minneapolis, MN	Private	97.0	13,611	8062
Delaware County Memorial Hosp	1337	Drexel Hill, PA	Private	96.9	885	8062
York General Hospital, Inc.	1338	York, NE	Private	96.8	190	8062
Carney Hospital Inc	1339	Boston, MA	Private	96.7	1,258	8062
Arbor Health Care Company	1340	Milwaukee, WI	Private	96.4	4,200	8051
Beverly Enterprises-Washington	1341	Fort Smith, AR	Public Family Member	96.4	4,200	8051
Louis A Weiss Memorial Hosp	1342	Chicago, IL	Private	96.2	1,100	8062
Community Care Of America Inc	1343	Owings Mills, MD	Public Family Member	96.1	4,186	8051
Jewish Bd Of Fmly & Chld Svcs	1344	New York, NY	Private	96.1	1,800	8361
Lubbock County Hospital Dst	1345	Lubbock, TX	Private	96.0	1,750	8062
Amisub Of North Carolina Inc	1346	Sanford, NC	Public Family Member	96.0	700	8062
Prime Medical Services Inc	1347	Austin, TX	Public	96.0	350	8099
University Physicians, Inc	1348	Tucson, AZ	Private	95.9	800	8011
Wyoming Medical Center Inc	1349	Casper, WY	Private	95.9	1,033	8062
Brockton Hospital Inc	1350	Brockton, MA	Private	95.8	1,300	8062
Good Samaritan Hospital	1351	Puyallup, WA	Private	95.8	1,481	8062
Addus Healthcare, Inc.	1352	Chicago, IL	Private	95.7	7,000	8082
Fairfield Medical Center	1353	Lancaster, OH	Private	95.7	1,300	8062
Southwest Medical Associates	1354	Las Vegas, NV	Public Family Member	95.7	520	8011
Caretenders Health Corp	1355	Louisville, KY	Public	95.2	3,400	8059
American Health Centers Inc	1356	Parsons, TN	Private	95.0	3,000	8051
Presbyterian-Orthopedic Hosp	1357	Charlotte, NC	Private	95.0	475	8069
Southcoast Hospital Group Inc	1358	New Bedford, MA	Private	95.0	NA	8062
Blessing Hospital	1359	Quincy, IL	Private	94.8	1,600	8062
Our Lady Of Lourdes Mem Hosp	1360	Binghamton, NY	Private	94.7	1,445	8062
Saint Francis Hospital Inc	1361	Columbus, GA	Private	94.7	1,260	8062
Silver Cross Hospital	1362	Joliet, IL	Private	94.6	1,400	8062
Sisters Of Providence In Wash	1363	Olympia, WA	Private	94.5	NA	8062
South Hills Health System	1364	Pittsburgh, PA	Private	94.5	NA	8062
Va Nj Healthcare System	1365	Orange, NJ	Private	94.5	NA	8062
Veterans Health Administration	1366	New York, NY	Private	94.5	NA	8062
Lake Forest Hospital	1367	Lake Forest, IL	Private	94.5	NA	8062
Lafayette Home Hospital Inc	1368	Lafayette, IN	Private	94.4	1,200	8062
County Of Cook, Illinois	1369	Oak Forest, IL	Private	94.3	NA	8062
John T Mather Mem Hosp	1370	Port Jefferson, NY	Private	94.3	1,300	8062
American Retirement Corp	1371	Brentwood, TN	Public	94.2	2,500	8059
Lakewood Hospital Association	1372	Cleveland, OH	Private	94.2	1,200	8062
New York Downtown Hospital	1373	New York, NY	Private	94.2	1,100	8062
Sch Health Care System	1374	Houston, TX	Private	94.2	NA	8062
Sisters Of Charity Health Care	1375	Staten Island, NY	Private	94.2	NA	8062
Zale Lipshy University Hosp	1376	Dallas, TX	Private	93.9	650	8062
Allied Services Foundation	1377	Scranton, PA	Private	93.9	1,954	8093
St Luke's Episcopal	1378	Chesterfield, MO	Private	93.5	2,003	8062
Houston County Hospital Auth	1379	Warner Robins, GA	Private	93.4	1,200	8062
Catholic Healthcare W Sthern Cal	1380	Pasadena, CA	Private	93.4	2,000	8062
North Trident Regional Med Ctr	1381	Charleston, SC	Public Family Member	93.4	2,000	8062
Saint Agnes Medical Center	1382	Fresno, CA	Private	93.4	2,000	8062
St Barnabas Community Entps	1383	Bronx, NY	Private	93.4	2,000	8062
St Marys Hospital & Med Ctr	1384	Grand Junction, CO	Private	93.4	2,000	8062
Stormont-Vail Healthcare Inc	1385	Topeka, KS	Private	93.4	2,000	8062
St Agnes Hospital Of Fond Du Lac	1386	Fond Du Lac, WI	Private	93.4	1,100	8062
Veterans Health Administration	1387	Saint Louis, MO	Private	93.3	NA	8062
Wellmont Health System Inc	1388	Kingsport, TN	Private	93.3	NA	8062
Network Health Plan Of Wisconsin	1389	Menasha, WI	Private	93.2	125	8011
Harris Methodist H-E-B	1390	Bedford, TX	Private	93.2	992	8062
Winchester Hospital	1391	Winchester, MA	Private	93.2	2,000	8062
Roger Williams Hospital	1392	Providence, RI	Private	93.2	1,273	8062
Rush North Shore Medical Ctr	1393	Skokie, IL	Private	93.1	1,179	8062
Maryland General Hospital	1394	Baltimore, MD	Private	93.0	1,200	8062
Barberton Citizens Hospital Inc	1395	Barberton, OH	Public Family Member	93.0	1,200	8062
Dreyer Clinic Inc.	1396	Aurora, IL	Private	92.7	1,000	8011
Tuomey	1397	Sumter, SC	Private	92.6	1,300	8062
Childrens Hospital Of Orange City	1398	Orange, CA	Private	92.4	1,000	8069
West Virginia Univ Med Corp	1399	Morgantown, WV	Private	92.3	1,300	8011
Harrison Memorial Hospital	1400	Bremerton, WA	Private	92.2	1,025	8062

D&B COMPANY RANKINGS BY SALES

Company	Rank	Location	Type	Sales ($ mil.)	Employ-ment	Primary SIC
Joseph Columbia/St Health Sys	1401	Parkersburg, WV	Private	92.2	900	8062
St Mary Hospital Of Livonia	1402	Livonia, MI	Private	92.2	1,304	8062
Centrastate Medical Center	1403	Freehold, NJ	Private	92.0	1,500	8062
Edinburg Regional Medical Ctr	1404	Edinburg, TX	Private	92.0	513	8062
Jewish Hospital Services, Inc	1405	Cincinnati, OH	Private	92.0	2,300	8099
Bon Secours Venice Healthcare	1406	Venice, FL	Private	92.0	1,265	8062
Riverside Medical Center	1407	Kankakee, IL	Private	91.9	1,350	8062
Transitional Health Partners	1408	Atlanta, GA	Private	91.8	4,000	8051
Crozer-Chester Medical Center	1409	Chester, PA	Private	91.8	3,300	8062
Parma Community Gen Hospital	1410	Cleveland, OH	Private	91.7	1,667	8062
Sentara Enterprises	1411	Virginia Beach, VA	Private	91.7	331	8093
Northwest Health System Inc	1412	Springdale, AR	Private	91.6	1,400	8062
St Anthony's Hospital Inc	1413	Saint Petersburg, FL	Private	91.5	1,500	8062
Options Health Care (Va Corp)	1414	Norfolk, VA	Private	91.5	3,000	8093
Wayne Memorial Hospital Inc	1415	Goldsboro, NC	Private	91.4	1,037	8062
Beverly Enterprises - Missouri	1416	Fort Smith, AR	Public Family Member	91.4	NA	8059
Brotman Partners Lp	1417	Culver City, CA	Private	91.3	1,200	8062
Physicians Health Plan Nthrn In	1418	Fort Wayne, IN	Private	91.3	98	8011
Good Samaritan Hospital	1419	Vincennes, IN	Private	91.3	1,600	8062
Harris County Hospital Dst	1420	Houston, TX	Private	91.2	NA	8062
Jefferson Parish Inc	1421	Metairie, LA	Private	91.2	NA	8062
Veterans Health Administration	1422	Dallas, TX	Private	91.2	NA	8062
Covenant Retirement Communities	1423	Chicago, IL	Private	91.1	488	8059
West Fla Med Ctr Clinic Pa	1424	Pensacola, FL	Private	91.0	1,100	8011
Southcoast Hospital Group Inc	1425	Fall River, MA	Private	91.0	NA	8062
St Lukes Health Care Assn	1426	Saginaw, MI	Private	91.0	1,950	8062
St Charles Medical Center	1427	Bend, OR	Private	91.0	1,200	8062
Yakima Valley Mem Hospital Assn	1428	Yakima, WA	Private	91.0	1,114	8062
Alamance Regional Med Ctr Inc	1429	Burlington, NC	Private	90.9	1,350	8062
Pascack Valley Hospital Assn	1430	Westwood, NJ	Private	90.7	1,206	8062
Good Smritan Regional Med Ctr	1431	Pottsville, PA	Private	90.7	800	8062
Children's Medical Center	1432	Dayton, OH	Private	90.7	1,300	8069
Girling Health Care Inc	1433	Austin, TX	Private	90.6	10,000	8082
Abraham Beth Health Services	1434	Bronx, NY	Private	90.5	973	8059
Tenet Hospital Ltd	1435	El Paso, TX	Private	90.4	1,936	8062
Golden State Health Centers	1436	Van Nuys, CA	Private	90.3	2,000	8059
St Clair Memorial Hospital	1437	Pittsburgh, PA	Private	90.1	1,192	8062
Regional Medical Ctr Orangeburg	1438	Orangeburg, SC	Private	90.0	1,200	8062
Alexian Brothers Of San Jose	1439	San Jose, CA	Private	90.0	1,200	8062
New England Health Care	1440	Boston, MA	Private	90.0	270	8011
Rochester St Mary's Hospital	1441	Rochester, NY	Private	89.9	1,415	8062
Sunrise Assisted Living, Inc	1442	Fairfax, VA	Public	89.9	3,500	8361
Downey Community Hospital	1443	Downey, CA	Private	89.7	1,100	8062
Denton Hospital, Inc.	1444	Denton, TX	Private	89.6	500	8062
Park Ridge Nursing Home Inc	1445	Rochester, NY	Private	89.5	180	8051
Unity Health System	1446	Rochester, NY	Private	89.5	1,150	8062
Ahs Hospital Corporation	1447	Montclair, NJ	Private	89.5	NA	8062
Kaiser Foundation Hospitals	1448	Hayward, CA	Private	89.5	NA	8062
Kaiser Foundation Hospitals	1449	San Diego, CA	Private	89.5	NA	8062
San Francisco City & County	1450	San Francisco, CA	Private	89.5	NA	8062
Tenet Healthcare Corporation	1451	Modesto, CA	Public Family Member	89.5	NA	8062
Veterans Health Administration	1452	Buffalo, NY	Private	89.5	NA	8062
Veterans Health Administration	1453	Northport, NY	Private	89.5	NA	8062
Flagstaff Medical Center Inc	1454	Flagstaff, AZ	Private	89.5	1,200	8062
Marion County Hospital Dst	1455	Mullins, SC	Private	89.4	646	8062
St Josephs Hospital & Health Ctr	1456	Paris, TX	Private	89.4	1,000	8062
Champlain Valley Hospital	1457	Plattsburgh, NY	Private	89.3	1,215	8062
Veterans Health Administration	1458	Dayton, OH	Private	89.0	NA	8062
Lake Forest Hospital Foundation	1459	Lake Forest, IL	Private	89.0	1,500	8062
Allegheny Hospitals Nj	1460	Willingboro, NJ	Private	88.9	875	8062
St Joseph's Hospital	1461	Asheville, NC	Private	88.8	1,400	8062
Columbia Pk Healthcare Systems	1462	Nashville, TN	Private	88.8	1,903	8062
Manchester Memorial Hosp	1463	Manchester, CT	Private	88.8	1,038	8062
Northbay Healthcare Group	1464	Fairfield, CA	Private	88.7	980	8062
Southside Hospital Inc	1465	Bay Shore, NY	Private	88.7	1,900	8062
Washington Regional Med Ctr	1466	Fayetteville, AR	Private	88.6	1,350	8062
Underwood Memorial Hospital	1467	Woodbury, NJ	Private	88.6	1,500	8062
Emory University	1468	Atlanta, GA	Private	88.5	NA	8062
Ornda Healthcorp	1469	Miami, FL	Public Family Member	88.5	NA	8062
Veterans Affairs Us Dept	1470	Decatur, GA	Private	88.5	NA	8062

D&B COMPANY RANKINGS BY SALES

Company	Rank	Location	Type	Sales ($ mil.)	Employ-ment	Primary SIC
Healthfirst Inc	1471	New York, NY	Private	88.4	311	8011
National Mentor Inc	1472	Boston, MA	Public Family Member	88.3	1,655	8361
William Backus Hospital	1473	Norwich, CT	Private	88.3	1,050	8062
Doylestown Hospital	1474	Doylestown, PA	Private	88.2	1,321	8062
Welborn Memorial Baptist Hosp	1475	Evansville, IN	Private	88.0	1,615	8062
Eden Township Hospital Dst	1476	Castro Valley, CA	Private	87.7	968	8062
Jackson St Dominic Mem Hosp	1477	Jackson, MS	Private	87.7	1,880	8062
Valley Presbyterian Hospital	1478	Van Nuys, CA	Private	87.6	1,100	8062
St Anthony Medical Center Inc	1479	Crown Point, IN	Private	87.6	1,200	8062
Chambersburg Hospital (Inc)	1480	Chambersburg, PA	Private	87.4	1,249	8062
South Fulton Medical Center	1481	Atlanta, GA	Private	87.4	1,350	8062
Rowan Regional Medical Ctr Inc	1482	Salisbury, NC	Private	87.4	979	8062
Terence Cooke Heal Care Ctr	1483	New York, NY	Private	87.4	1,200	8051
Sinai Samaritan Medical Center	1484	Milwaukee, WI	Private	87.3	1,871	8062
Woman's Hospital Foundation	1485	Baton Rouge, LA	Private	87.2	1,250	8062
Veterans Health Administration	1486	Milwaukee, WI	Private	87.0	NA	8062
Columbus Hospital Inc	1487	Newark, NJ	Private	86.9	900	8062
Neighborhood Health Plan Inc	1488	Boston, MA	Private	86.8	200	8011
County Of Riverside	1489	Riverside, CA	Private	86.8	NA	8011
Department Of Air Force	1490	Scott Afb, IL	Private	86.8	NA	8011
Northeast Medical Center, Inc	1491	Huntersville, NC	Private	86.8	NA	8011
Permanente Medical Group, Inc	1492	Downey, CA	Private	86.8	NA	8011
Portland Adventist Med Ctr	1493	Portland, OR	Private	86.8	NA	8011
Camden-Clark Memorial Hosp	1494	Parkersburg, WV	Private	86.7	1,212	8062
Saint Francis Memorial Hosp	1495	San Francisco, CA	Private	86.7	900	8062
Galen Hospital Alaska Inc	1496	Anchorage, AK	Public Family Member	86.5	600	8062
Alliance Imaging Inc	1497	Anaheim, CA	Public	86.5	613	8099
Good Samaritan Hospital Inc	1498	Kearney, NE	Private	86.4	1,400	8062
Northwest Hospital Center	1499	Randallstown, MD	Private	86.4	981	8062
Metropolitan Hospital	1500	Grand Rapids, MI	Private	86.4	940	8062
Baptist Health Services Corp	1501	Montgomery, AL	Private	86.3	1,850	8062
Bromenn Healthcare	1502	Normal, IL	Private	86.3	1,850	8062
Deaconess Hospital	1503	Cincinnati, OH	Private	86.2	1,848	8062
Salem Hospital Inc	1504	Salem, MA	Private	86.2	1,848	8062
Geriatric And Medical Services	1505	Philadelphia, PA	Public Family Member	86.1	3,750	8051
Navy, United States Dept	1506	Pensacola, FL	Private	86.1	NA	8021
Central Maine Medical Center	1507	Lewiston, ME	Private	86.0	1,200	8062
Daughters Of Charity Health	1508	Waco, TX	Private	86.0	1,500	8062
St. Luke's Hospital	1509	San Francisco, CA	Private	85.8	810	8062
Bakersfield Memorial Hospital	1510	Bakersfield, CA	Private	85.7	840	8062
Deaconess Health Care Corp	1511	Oklahoma City, OK	Private	85.7	55	8361
St Luke's Regional Med Ctr	1512	Sioux City, IA	Private	85.7	1,500	8062
Suburban Med Ctr Hffmn Estates	1513	Hoffman Estates, IL	Public Family Member	85.7	1,070	8062
Community Memorial Hospital/Sa	1514	Ventura, CA	Private	85.6	1,200	8062
Care Initiatives	1515	West Des Moines, IA	Private	85.6	3,000	8051
Rush Prudential Insurance Co	1516	Chicago, IL	Private	85.5	4	8011
Santa Rosa Health Care Corp	1517	San Antonio, TX	Private	85.4	NA	8062
Horton Memorial Hospital	1518	Middletown, NY	Private	85.3	1,300	8062
River Oaks Hospital Inc	1519	Jackson, MS	Private	85.3	480	8062
Northern Illinois Medical Ctr	1520	Mchenry, IL	Private	85.2	1,000	8062
Qhg Of Gadsden	1521	Gadsden, AL	Public Family Member	85.0	1,100	8062
Rush Prudential Health Plans	1522	Chicago, IL	Private	85.0	1,234	8011
Williamsport Hospital Med Ctr Inc	1523	Williamsport, PA	Private	84.9	2,633	8062
Advocate Health Care Network	1524	Downers Grove, IL	Private	84.8	NA	8062
Advocate Health Care Network	1525	Barrington, IL	Private	84.8	NA	8062
Baptist Health System Inc	1526	Birmingham, AL	Private	84.8	NA	8062
Baptist Healthcare System	1527	Louisville, KY	Private	84.8	NA	8062
Evanston Northwestern	1528	Evanston, IL	Private	84.8	NA	8062
Evanston Northwestern	1529	Glenview, IL	Private	84.8	NA	8062
Tenet Health System Medical	1530	Birmingham, AL	Public Family Member	84.8	NA	8062
Veterans Health Administration	1531	Chicago, IL	Private	84.8	NA	8062
Veterans Health Administration	1532	Memphis, TN	Private	84.8	NA	8062
Veterans Health Administration	1533	North Chicago, IL	Private	84.8	NA	8062
St John's Riverside Hospital	1534	Yonkers, NY	Private	84.7	1,100	8062
St Michael Hospital	1535	Milwaukee, WI	Private	84.7	1,027	8062
Southern Health Services, Inc	1536	Richmond, VA	Private	84.6	4	8011
Catholic Healthcare W Sthern Cal	1537	Long Beach, CA	Private	84.5	NA	8062
Sisters Of Providence In Cal	1538	Burbank, CA	Private	84.5	NA	8062
Lawrence General Hospital	1539	Lawrence, MA	Private	84.5	1,200	8062
St Luke's Hospital Of Duluth	1540	Duluth, MN	Private	84.4	1,500	8062

D&B COMPANY RANKINGS BY SALES

Company	Rank	Location	Type	Sales ($ mil.)	Employ- ment	Primary SIC
Pikeville United Methodist Hos	1541	Pikeville, KY	Private	84.3	800	8062
Northern Wstchester Hospital Assn	1542	Mount Kisco, NY	Private	84.2	1,100	8062
San Mateo Health Commission	1543	San Mateo, CA	Private	84.2	96	8099
Queen Of The Valley	1544	Napa, CA	Private	84.1	1,200	8062
Good Samaritan Hospital	1545	Los Angeles, CA	Private	83.9	1,800	8062
H C A Health Svcs Of Virginia	1546	Richmond, VA	Public Family Member	83.9	1,800	8062
Phc/Chc Holdings Inc	1547	Houston, TX	Public	83.9	1,800	8062
Downey Community Health Center	1548	Downey, CA	Private	83.7	175	8051
Marymount Hospital Inc	1549	Cleveland, OH	Private	83.6	1,095	8062
Rehability Health Services	1550	Brentwood, TN	Public Family Member	83.5	2,736	8093
Forrest S Chilton III Mem Hosp	1551	Pompton Plains, NJ	Private	83.5	1,200	8062
Raytel Medical Corporation	1552	San Mateo, CA	Public	83.4	827	8093
Columbia/Hca Healthcare Corp	1553	Nashville, TN	Public Family Member	83.4	NA	8062
Omega Health Systems Inc	1554	Memphis, TN	Public	83.3	576	8042
Santa Barbara Cottage Hosp	1555	Santa Barbara, CA	Private	83.3	1,786	8062
North Side Hospital, Inc	1556	Johnson City, TN	Public Family Member	83.2	350	8062
County Of Cook, Illinois	1557	Chicago, IL	Private	83.1	NA	8093
Hilton Head Health System, Lp	1558	Hilton Head Island, SC	Private	83.0	375	8062
Monongalia County Gen Hospital	1559	Morgantown, WV	Private	82.9	1,100	8062
Northeast Hospital Authority	1560	Humble, TX	Private	82.9	862	8062
Ochsner Alton Med Foundation	1561	New Orleans, LA	Private	82.9	NA	8062
Tenet Health System Medical	1562	Houston, TX	Public Family Member	82.9	NA	8062
Hospital Of Community-General	1563	Syracuse, NY	Private	82.9	1,500	8062
Doctors' Hospital Inc	1564	Lanham, MD	Private	82.7	850	8062
Catawba Memorial Hospital	1565	Hickory, NC	Private	82.6	875	8062
Adena Health System Inc	1566	Chillicothe, OH	Private	82.6	882	8062
Olathe Health Foundation	1567	Olathe, KS	Private	82.6	1,200	8011
Rahway Hospital	1568	Rahway, NJ	Private	82.6	935	8062
Northern Michigan Hospital	1569	Petoskey, MI	Private	82.5	1,000	8062
Hunterdon Medical Center	1570	Flemington, NJ	Private	82.5	1,300	8062
Trinity Lutheran Hospital	1571	Kansas City, MO	Private	82.4	1,200	8062
Samaritan Health System	1572	Glendale, AZ	Private	82.4	NA	8062
Texoma Medical Center Inc	1573	Denison, TX	Private	82.4	1,300	8062
Cleveland Memorial Hospital	1574	Shelby, NC	Private	82.3	1,073	8062
St Elizabeths Hospital Of Chicago	1575	Chicago, IL	Private	82.2	900	8062
Health Care Authority Of Morga	1576	Decatur, AL	Private	82.2	1,000	8062
Clark Memorial Hospital	1577	Jeffersonville, IN	Private	82.0	1,338	8062
County Of San Bernardino	1578	San Bernardino, CA	Private	82.0	NA	8062
Rockwood Clinic P.S.	1579	Spokane, WA	Private	82.0	579	8011
Bethesda Hospital Assn, The	1580	Zanesville, OH	Private	81.9	1,200	8062
St Francis Medical Center	1581	Trenton, NJ	Private	81.9	1,150	8062
Lima Memorial Hospital	1582	Lima, OH	Private	81.8	NA	8062
St Barnabas Hospital	1583	Bronx, NY	Private	81.6	1,750	8062
Nations Healthcare Inc	1584	Alpharetta, GA	Private	81.5	1,800	8082
Jeanes Hospital	1585	Philadelphia, PA	Private	81.5	1,350	8062
St Joseph's Hospital Yonkers	1586	Yonkers, NY	Private	81.4	950	8062
Flagler Hospital Inc	1587	Saint Augustine, FL	Private	81.2	780	8062
Parker Jewish Institute	1588	New Hyde Park, NY	Private	81.2	1,130	8051
Sharp Chula Vista Medical Ctr	1589	Chula Vista, CA	Private	81.1	734	8062
St Luke's Hospital	1590	Maumee, OH	Private	81.1	1,325	8062
Martha Jefferson Hospital	1591	Charlottesville, VA	Private	80.9	1,200	8062
Pediatrix Medical Group Inc	1592	Fort Lauderdale, FL	Public	80.8	700	8011
Marion General Hospital Inc	1593	Marion, IN	Private	80.8	1,100	8062
Patuxent Medical Group, Inc	1594	Columbia, MD	Private	80.8	1,000	8011
Horizon West Headquarters Inc	1595	Rocklin, CA	Private	80.6	3,511	8051
Health Group, The	1596	Massillon, OH	Private	80.6	1,260	8082
Bayonne Hospital	1597	Bayonne, NJ	Private	80.6	1,200	8062
Capital Region Medical Center	1598	Jefferson City, MO	Private	80.5	1,200	8062
Grant/Rvrside Mthdst Hspitals	1599	Columbus, OH	Private	80.5	NA	8062
Wellmont Health System Inc	1600	Bristol, TN	Private	80.5	NA	8062
Howard County General Hospital	1601	Columbia, MD	Private	80.4	1,225	8062
Baptist Mem Hspital-North Miss	1602	Oxford, MS	Private	80.4	650	8062
Dameron Hospital Association	1603	Stockton, CA	Private	80.3	1,003	8062
Hackley Hospital	1604	Muskegon, MI	Private	80.3	1,300	8062
Care Enterprises West	1605	Albuquerque, NM	Public Family Member	80.3	3,500	8051
Amicare Home Health Services	1606	Novi, MI	Private	80.2	927	8082
Lowell General Hospital	1607	Lowell, MA	Private	80.1	1,200	8062
Columbia La Grange Mem Hosp	1608	La Grange, IL	Public Family Member	80.1	1,719	8062
Baylor Medical Ctr At Garland	1609	Garland, TX	Private	80.0	1,100	8062
Bristol Hospital Incorporated	1610	Bristol, CT	Private	80.0	1,200	8062

D&B COMPANY RANKINGS BY SALES

Company	Rank	Location	Type	Sales ($ mil.)	Employ-ment	Primary SIC
Community Bio Resources	1611	Birmingham, AL	Private	80.0	500	8099
Guardian Care, Inc	1612	Corte Madera, CA	Private	80.0	1,100	8051
Healthcor, Inc	1613	Southfield, MI	Private	80.0	236	8011
Wichita Clinic, Pa	1614	Wichita, KS	Private	80.0	750	8011
Mayo Henry Newhall Mem Hosp	1615	Santa Clarita, CA	Private	80.0	585	8062
Santa Ana Tustin Radiology	1616	Santa Ana, CA	Private	79.7	13	8011
Womans Hospital Texas Inc	1617	Houston, TX	Public Family Member	79.6	900	8062
Dimensions Health Corporation	1618	Hyattsville, MD	Private	79.6	NA	8062
Parkway Hospital Inc	1619	Forest Hills, NY	Private	79.6	940	8062
Lucerne Medical Center	1620	Orlando, FL	Private	79.5	800	8062
Kaiser Foundation Hospitals	1621	San Francisco, CA	Private	79.5	NA	8062
Sutter Health Central	1622	Sacramento, CA	Private	79.5	NA	8062
United Health Svcs Hospitals	1623	Johnson City, NY	Private	79.5	NA	8062
Veterans Health Administration	1624	Seattle, WA	Private	79.5	NA	8062
Carson-Tahoe Hospital	1625	Carson City, NV	Private	79.5	1,000	8062
Maine General Rehabilitation &	1626	Augusta, ME	Private	79.4	230	8052
Mercy Hospital Anderson	1627	Cincinnati, OH	Private	79.3	901	8062
Bergen Regional Medical Ctr	1628	Paramus, NJ	Private	79.2	1,700	8062
Childrens Hospital & Health Ctr	1629	San Diego, CA	Private	79.2	1,700	8062
West Suburban Health Care Corp	1630	Oak Park, IL	Private	79.2	1,700	8062
Westmoreland Health System	1631	Greensburg, PA	Private	79.2	1,700	8062
County Of Los Angeles	1632	Los Angeles, CA	Private	79.1	NA	8069
State Of New York	1633	Queens Village, NY	Private	79.1	NA	8063
Hutcheson Medical Center	1634	Fort Oglethorpe, GA	Private	79.1	1,100	8062
California Dept Mental Health	1635	Camarillo, CA	Private	79.0	NA	8063
San Juan Regional Medical Ctr	1636	Farmington, NM	Private	79.0	900	8062
Labone, Inc.	1637	Shawnee Mission, KS	Public	78.9	677	8071
Holy Cross Hospital	1638	Chicago, IL	Private	78.9	1,600	8062
Upmc Passavant	1639	Pittsburgh, PA	Private	78.8	4	8062
Franciscan Hospital Mt Airy Campus	1640	Cincinnati, OH	Private	78.7	1,154	8062
St Joseph Hospital Of Augusta Ga	1641	Augusta, GA	Private	78.5	1,200	8062
Charleston Area Health Plan	1642	Charleston, WV	Private	78.4	80	8011
Mercer Medical Center	1643	Trenton, NJ	Private	78.2	1,500	8062
Saddleback Memorial Med Ctr	1644	Laguna Hills, CA	Private	78.1	1,050	8062
Jupiter Medical Center, Inc	1645	Jupiter, FL	Private	78.1	800	8062
Spaulding Rhbltation Hospital Corp	1646	Boston, MA	Private	78.1	1,127	8069
H C A Highland Hospital Inc	1647	Shreveport, LA	Public Family Member	78.0	650	8062
Paragon Rehabilitation Inc	1648	Nashville, TN	Public Family Member	78.0	500	8049
Chartwell Healthcare, Inc	1649	Dallas, TX	Private	78.0	6,000	8051
Floyd Memorial Hospital	1650	New Albany, IN	Private	77.8	1,200	8062
Potomac Hospital Corporation	1651	Woodbridge, VA	Private	77.7	959	8062
Blount Memorial Hospital	1652	Maryville, TN	Private	77.7	1,300	8062
Healthsouth Doctors' Hospital	1653	Coral Gables, FL	Public Family Member	77.6	717	8062
Deaconess Hospital An Okla Corp	1654	Oklahoma City, OK	Private	77.4	1,200	8062
Brandywine Health Services	1655	Coatesville, PA	Private	77.4	75	8062
Motion Picture & Tv Fund	1656	Woodland Hills, CA	Private	77.4	700	8062
Central Louisiana Healthcare	1657	Alexandria, LA	Private	77.4	1,661	8062
Sequoia Hospital District	1658	Redwood City, CA	Private	77.4	1,167	8062
Saints Memorial Medical Center	1659	Lowell, MA	Private	77.4	1,200	8062
Public Hospital District 1	1660	Mount Vernon, WA	Private	77.3	1,072	8062
Highline Community Hospital	1661	Seattle, WA	Private	77.2	1,150	8062
Parkview Community Hospital Med	1662	Riverside, CA	Private	77.2	1,173	8062
San Joaquin Community Hosp	1663	Bakersfield, CA	Private	77.2	900	8062
Saint Elizabeth Community Health	1664	Lincoln, NE	Private	77.1	1,150	8062
Healthsouth Orthopedic Svcs	1665	Birmingham, AL	Public Family Member	77.1	1,120	8011
Scottish Rite Hosp	1666	Atlanta, GA	Private	77.1	1,560	8069
Ssm Health Care Of Oklahoma	1667	Oklahoma City, OK	Private	77.1	1,655	8062
Matrix Rehabilitation Inc	1668	Plano, TX	Public Family Member	77.0	1,200	8093
Healthsouth Medical Center Inc	1669	Birmingham, AL	Public Family Member	76.9	650	8062
Northwest Texas Healthcare	1670	Amarillo, TX	Private	76.9	2,624	8062
St Lukes-Memorial Hospital Ctr	1671	New Hartford, NY	Private	76.9	1,650	8062
Seton Health System	1672	Troy, NY	Private	76.9	1,600	8062
Saint Joseph Medical Center	1673	Reading, PA	Private	76.9	1,400	8062
Community Hospital Chanl Inc	1674	Chandler, AZ	Private	76.8	1,021	8062
North Philadelphia Health Sys	1675	Philadelphia, PA	Private	76.8	1,300	8062
Massachusetts Eye Ear Infirmary	1676	Boston, MA	Private	76.6	1,050	8069
Jefferson Mem Hospital Assn, The	1677	Crystal City, MO	Private	76.5	1,600	8062
Nemours Foundation (Inc)	1678	Jacksonville, FL	Private	76.4	2,369	8069
North Shore Univ Hospital	1679	Forest Hills, NY	Private	76.4	880	8062
Comprehensive Health Resources	1680	Rutland, VT	Private	76.4	2	8062

D&B COMPANY RANKINGS BY SALES

Company	Rank	Location	Type	Sales ($ mil.)	Employ- ment	Primary SIC
Sharon Regional Health System	1681	Sharon, PA	Private	76.4	1,200	8062
Smithkline Beecham Corporation	1682	Norristown, PA	Private	76.2	NA	8071
Main Line Hospitals	1683	Wynnewood, PA	Private	76.1	NA	8062
St. Joseph Health System, Llc	1684	Fort Wayne, IN	Private	76.1	1,200	8062
Peconic Health Corporation	1685	Aquebogue, NY	Private	76.0	1,632	8062
Uw Medical Foundation	1686	Madison, WI	Private	76.0	NA	8011
Veterans Health Administration	1687	West Haven, CT	Private	76.0	NA	8062
Chester County Hospital, The	1688	West Chester, PA	Private	76.0	1,000	8062
Astoria General Hospital Inc	1689	Long Island City, NY	Private	75.9	510	8062
Brunswick Hospital Center Inc	1690	Amityville, NY	Private	75.9	1,300	8062
West Allis Memorial Hospital	1691	Milwaukee, WI	Private	75.8	1,400	8062
West Hills Hospital	1692	Canoga Park, CA	Public Family Member	75.8	1,000	8062
Loudoun Healthcare Inc	1693	Leesburg, VA	Private	75.8	NA	8062
Good Samaritan Hospital	1694	Lebanon, PA	Private	75.8	1,050	8062
West Georgia Medical Center	1695	Lagrange, GA	Private	75.7	1,400	8062
Clarity Vision Inc	1696	Camp Hill, PA	Private	75.7	1,100	8011
Medica	1697	Minneapolis, MN	Private	75.7	1,100	8011
New York Medical Group, Pc	1698	New York, NY	Private	75.7	1,100	8011
Holy Spirit Hospital Sis	1699	Camp Hill, PA	Private	75.5	1,621	8062
Pottstown Memorial Med Ctr	1700	Pottstown, PA	Private	75.4	1,100	8062
Memorial Hospital Of Easton Md	1701	Easton, MD	Private	75.3	1,241	8062
Paradise Valley Hospital Inc	1702	National City, CA	Private	75.2	1,050	8062
Lutheran Health System	1703	Mesa, AZ	Private	75.1	NA	8361
Sarah Bush Lincoln Health Ctr	1704	Mattoon, IL	Private	75.0	1,315	8062
Clearfield Area Health Svcs Corp	1705	Clearfield, PA	Private	75.0	777	8062
Colorado Access	1706	Denver, CO	Private	75.0	130	8011
Nlvh, Inc	1707	North Las Vegas, NV	Public Family Member	75.0	625	8062
Scotland Health Care System	1708	Laurinburg, NC	Private	75.0	600	8062
Wharton Hospital Corporation	1709	Wharton, TX	Public Family Member	75.0	500	8062
Satilla Health Services Inc	1710	Waycross, GA	Private	74.9	1,000	8062
Fawcett Memorial Hospital Inc	1711	Port Charlotte, FL	Public Family Member	74.8	1,200	8062
Ashtabula County Medical Ctr	1712	Ashtabula, OH	Private	74.8	900	8062
San Jacinto Methodist Hosp	1713	Baytown, TX	Private	74.8	1,100	8062
Bethany Medical Center	1714	Kansas City, KS	Private	74.8	1,200	8062
Herbert J. Thomas Mem Hospital	1715	Charleston, WV	Private	74.7	1,000	8062
Westlake Community Hospital	1716	Melrose Park, IL	Private	74.6	900	8062
Jewish Home & Hospital/Bronx	1717	Bronx, NY	Private	74.6	1,300	8051
Genesee Valley Group Health Assn	1718	Rochester, NY	Private	74.6	300	8011
Gen Oakland Hospital Osteopathic	1719	Madison Heights, MI	Private	74.6	779	8062
Everett Clinic, The	1720	Everett, WA	Private	74.6	1,025	8011
Woman's Christian Assoc O Jam	1721	Jamestown, NY	Private	74.6	1,340	8062
Assocted Regional Univ Pathologist	1722	Salt Lake City, UT	Private	74.6	700	8071
Bellin Health Systems, Inc	1723	Green Bay, WI	Private	74.5	1,600	8062
Cathedral Healthcare System	1724	Newark, NJ	Private	74.5	NA	8062
Columbia Csa/Hs Greater Clvlnd	1725	Cleveland, OH	Private	74.5	1,600	8062
Community Health Care Sys	1726	San Bernardino, CA	Private	74.5	1,600	8062
County Of Alameda	1727	Oakland, CA	Private	74.5	NA	8062
Frye Regional Medical Center	1728	Hickory, NC	Public Family Member	74.5	1,600	8062
H N M C Inc	1729	Houston, TX	Public Family Member	74.5	1,600	8062
Irving Hospital Authority	1730	Irving, TX	Private	74.5	1,600	8062
Kaiser Foundation Hospitals	1731	Redwood City, CA	Private	74.5	NA	8062
Kaiser Foundation Hospitals	1732	Riverside, CA	Private	74.5	NA	8062
New York, State	1733	Stony Brook, NY	Private	74.5	NA	8062
Q H G Of South Carolina Inc	1734	Florence, SC	Public Family Member	74.5	1,600	8062
Saint Mary Hospital & Med Ctr	1735	Grand Junction, CO	Private	74.5	1,600	8062
Sisters Of Providence In Wash	1736	Anchorage, AK	Private	74.5	NA	8062
Trinity Medical Center West	1737	Steubenville, OH	Private	74.5	1,600	8062
University Of Washington	1738	Seattle, WA	Private	74.5	NA	8062
Veterans Health Administration	1739	Albany, NY	Private	74.5	NA	8062
Veterans Health Administration	1740	Wilkes Barre, PA	Private	74.5	NA	8062
West Florida Regional Med Ctr	1741	Pensacola, FL	Public Family Member	74.5	1,600	8062
Winter Park Health Care Group	1742	Winter Park, FL	Private	74.5	1,600	8062
Winter Park Memorial Hospital	1743	Winter Park, FL	Private	74.5	1,600	8062
Dallas Cnty Mntl Health/Rtrdtn	1744	Dallas, TX	Private	74.2	1,400	8361
Veterans Health Administration	1745	Ann Arbor, MI	Private	74.1	NA	8062
Kenosha Hospital & Medical Ctr	1746	Kenosha, WI	Private	74.1	950	8062
Broadlawns Medical Center	1747	Des Moines, IA	Private	74.1	900	8062
Covenant Health Care System	1748	Milwaukee, WI	Private	73.9	1,587	8062
Mission Hospital Inc	1749	Mission, TX	Private	73.8	531	8062
Memorial Hospital & Medical	1750	Cumberland, MD	Private	73.6	1,100	8062

D&B COMPANY RANKINGS BY SALES

Company	Rank	Location	Type	Sales ($ mil.)	Employ-ment	Primary SIC
Pocono Medical Center	1751	East Stroudsburg, PA	Private	73.6	1,057	8062
Iredell Memorial Hospital	1752	Statesville, NC	Private	73.6	1,150	8062
Glenwood Regional Medical Ctr	1753	West Monroe, LA	Private	73.6	1,276	8062
Saint Elizabeth Medical Ctr	1754	Covington, KY	Private	73.5	NA	8071
Phoenix Bptst Hospital Med Ctr Inc	1755	Phoenix, AZ	Private	73.3	1,023	8062
Monongahela Valley Hospital Inc	1756	Monongahela, PA	Private	73.2	1,020	8062
Washington Dpt Scl & Health Svcs	1757	Tacoma, WA	Private	73.2	NA	8063
Uniontown Hospital	1758	Uniontown, PA	Private	73.2	900	8062
Sarasota Doctor's Hospital	1759	Sarasota, FL	Public Family Member	73.1	750	8062
Visiting Nurse Assn Of Boston	1760	Boston, MA	Private	73.0	1,250	8082
Logan Medical Foundation	1761	Logan, WV	Private	72.9	806	8062
Pan American Hospital Corp	1762	Miami, FL	Private	72.9	1,172	8062
San Pedro Peninsula Hospital	1763	San Pedro, CA	Private	72.9	880	8062
Baptist Mem Hsptl-Glden Trngle	1764	Columbus, MS	Private	72.8	780	8062
Bluefield Regional Medical Ctr	1765	Bluefield, WV	Private	72.6	900	8062
Ellis Hospital	1766	Schenectady, NY	Private	72.6	1,560	8062
Copley Memorial Hospital Inc	1767	Aurora, IL	Private	72.5	920	8062
Northwest Healthcare Corp	1768	Kalispell, MT	Private	72.4	223	8062
Barnert Hospital	1769	Paterson, NJ	Private	72.3	850	8062
William Prince Hospital Corp	1770	Manassas, VA	Private	72.3	600	8062
Allen Memorial Hospital Corp	1771	Waterloo, IA	Private	72.2	1,185	8062
White Oak Manor Inc	1772	Spartanburg, SC	Private	72.2	2,300	8051
Methodist Hospital Inc	1773	Jacksonville, FL	Private	72.2	900	8062
De Paul Health Center Inc	1774	Bridgeton, MO	Private	72.1	1,550	8062
H C A Health Services Tenn Inc	1775	Nashville, TN	Public Family Member	72.1	1,550	8062
Southern Regional Medical Ctr	1776	Riverdale, GA	Private	72.1	1,550	8062
Lawrence Hospital Inc	1777	Bronxville, NY	Private	72.0	860	8062
Baptist Healthcare System	1778	Lexington, KY	Private	72.0	NA	8062
Mercy Health Services	1779	Lansing, MI	Private	72.0	NA	8062
Veterans Health Administration	1780	Montrose, NY	Private	72.0	NA	8062
Grand View Hospital	1781	Sellersville, PA	Private	71.9	1,572	8062
Battle Creek Health System	1782	Battle Creek, MI	Private	71.9	NA	8069
Port Huron Hospital	1783	Port Huron, MI	Private	71.9	950	8062
Lee Upmc Regional	1784	Johnstown, PA	Private	71.8	1,250	8062
St Lucie Medical Center	1785	Port Saint Lucie, FL	Public Family Member	71.7	850	8062
United Hospital Medical Ctr	1786	Port Chester, NY	Private	71.6	850	8062
Nc-Schi	1787	Abilene, TX	Public Family Member	71.5	800	8062
Citrus Mem Health Foundation	1788	Inverness, FL	Private	71.5	912	8062
Our Lady Bellefonte Hospital Inc	1789	Ashland, KY	Private	71.5	920	8062
Mercy Hospital (Inc)	1790	Springfield, MA	Private	71.4	1,535	8062
Oncare	1791	San Bruno, CA	Private	71.3	700	8011
Prestige Care Inc	1792	Vancouver, WA	Private	71.2	1,950	8051
California Dept Developmental Svcs	1793	San Jose, CA	Private	71.2	NA	8063
County Of Rockland	1794	Pomona, NY	Private	71.2	NA	8093
Medicalodges Inc	1795	Coffeyville, KS	Private	71.1	2,300	8051
Memorial Hospital Of Laramie Cnty	1796	Cheyenne, WY	Private	71.1	900	8062
Tendercare Michigan Inc	1797	Sault Sainte Marie, MI	Private	71.1	3,100	8051
Springhill Hospitals Inc	1798	Mobile, AL	Private	71.1	900	8062
Burdette Tomlin Memorial Hosp	1799	Cape May CH, NJ	Private	71.1	950	8062
Bon Secours Hospital Baltimore	1800	Baltimore, MD	Private	71.0	1,120	8062
Atlanticare Medical Center	1801	Lynn, MA	Private	70.9	NA	8062
Cobb Hospital Inc	1802	Austell, GA	Private	70.9	1,525	8062
Veterans Health Administration	1803	Brockton, MA	Private	70.9	NA	8062
Veterans Health Administration	1804	Bedford, MA	Private	70.9	NA	8062
Butler Memorial Hospital	1805	Butler, PA	Private	70.8	1,200	8062
Monroe Community Hospital	1806	Rochester, NY	Private	70.8	750	8051
La Porte Hospital Inc	1807	La Porte, IN	Private	70.8	1,250	8062
Tressler Lutheran Services	1808	Mechanicsburg, PA	Private	70.8	1,950	8051
Carilion Medical Centers Inc	1809	Roanoke, VA	Private	70.7	NA	8062
Kuala Healthcare Inc	1810	Englewood Cliffs, NJ	Public	70.7	900	8051
Kootenai Hospital District	1811	Coeur D Alene, ID	Private	70.7	1,100	8062
Cancer Therapy	1812	San Antonio, TX	Private	70.6	309	8011
St Clares Hospital & Health Ctr	1813	New York, NY	Private	70.6	855	8062
Nazareth Hospital (Inc)	1814	Philadelphia, PA	Private	70.6	1,280	8062
Horizon Hospital System, Inc	1815	Greenville, PA	Private	70.6	1,227	8062
Bradley County Memorial Hosp	1816	Cleveland, TN	Private	70.5	883	8062
St Mary Hospital Inc	1817	Hoboken, NJ	Private	70.5	1,200	8062
Permanente Medical Group Inc	1818	S San Francisco, CA	Private	70.5	NA	8011
Ohio Valley Medical Center Inc	1819	Wheeling, WV	Private	70.5	975	8062
Daughters Of Charity H/S	1820	Austin, TX	Private	70.4	NA	8062

D&B COMPANY RANKINGS BY SALES

Company	Rank	Location	Type	Sales ($ mil.)	Employ- ment	Primary SIC
Columbia Healthcare Of Centl Va	1821	Alexandria, LA	Public Family Member	70.3	NA	8069
District Columbia Government	1822	Washington, DC	Private	70.3	NA	8063
Kadlec Medical Center	1823	Richland, WA	Private	70.3	700	8062
Holy Family Hospital Inc	1824	Methuen, MA	Private	70.3	1,200	8062
Fort Hmltn-Hghes Mem Hospital	1825	Hamilton, OH	Private	70.2	1,286	8062
Du Bois Regional Medical Ctr	1826	Du Bois, PA	Private	70.2	1,040	8062
Integra Inc	1827	King Of Prussia, PA	Public	70.1	900	8093
Midway Hospital Medical Ctr	1828	Los Angeles, CA	Public Family Member	70.0	700	8062
Pioneer Valley Hospital	1829	Salt Lake City, UT	Public Family Member	70.0	516	8062
Mercy Hospital	1830	Portland, ME	Private	70.0	917	8062
Sacred Hart Hospital Of Allentown	1831	Allentown, PA	Private	70.0	1,025	8062
Phelps Memorial Hospital Assn	1832	Tarrytown, NY	Private	69.9	1,100	8062
Bryan Memorial Hospital	1833	Lincoln, NE	Private	69.8	2,015	8062
Southern Nh Regional Med Ctr	1834	Nashua, NH	Private	69.8	1,014	8062
St Mary's Hospital Of Brooklyn	1835	Brooklyn, NY	Private	69.8	1,500	8062
United Healthcare System, Inc.	1836	Newark, NJ	Private	69.8	1,500	8062
Wyckoff Heights Medical Ctr	1837	Brooklyn, NY	Private	69.8	1,500	8062
Lutheran Health Systems	1838	Mesa, AZ	Private	69.7	NA	8062
Intensiva Healthcare Corp	1839	Saint Louis, MO	Public	69.6	1,500	8069
Riverside Mercy Hospital	1840	Toledo, OH	Private	69.5	912	8062
Mercy Health Services	1841	Sioux City, IA	Private	69.5	NA	8062
Saint Clare's Hospital Inc	1842	Dover, NJ	Private	69.5	NA	8062
Veterans Health Administration	1843	Coatesville, PA	Private	69.5	NA	8062
Wvhcs-Hospital	1844	Kingston, PA	Private	69.5	NA	8062
Sheppard Enoch Pratt Fundation	1845	Baltimore, MD	Private	69.5	1,399	8063
Sheppard Pratt Health System	1846	Baltimore, MD	Private	69.5	1,254	8063
Muskogee Medical Center Auth	1847	Muskogee, OK	Private	69.4	1,000	8062
Medical Center-West Inc	1848	Lithia Springs, GA	Public Family Member	69.4	520	8062
Holy Family Mem Med Ctr Inc	1849	Manitowoc, WI	Private	69.3	1,250	8062
Holland Community Hospital	1850	Holland, MI	Private	69.3	1,120	8062
Temple Lower Bucks Hospital	1851	Bristol, PA	Private	69.2	770	8062
Memorial Health Systems E Texas	1852	Lufkin, TX	Private	69.2	880	8062
Long Beach Community Hospital	1853	Long Beach, CA	Private	69.1	1,050	8062
Notami Hospitals Of Oklahoma	1854	Tulsa, OK	Public Family Member	69.1	NA	8062
Cumberland Medical Center Inc	1855	Fayetteville, NC	Public Family Member	69.0	475	8062
Mobile Technology Inc	1856	Los Angeles, CA	Public Family Member	69.0	450	8099
Emerson Hospital Inc	1857	Concord, MA	Private	68.9	1,300	8062
Mercy-Memorial Hospital Corp	1858	Monroe, MI	Private	68.9	817	8062
Physician Associates Florida	1859	Maitland, FL	Private	68.9	710	8011
New Lexington Clinic, P.S.C.	1860	Lexington, KY	Private	68.8	1,000	8011
Southern Health Management	1861	Huntsville, AL	Private	68.8	1,000	8011
Veterans Health Administration	1862	Gainesville, FL	Private	68.8	NA	8062
Margaret R Pardee Mem Hosp	1863	Hendersonville, NC	Private	68.7	936	8062
Mcfarland Clinic P C	1864	Ames, IA	Private	68.7	690	8011
Monarch Dental Corporation	1865	Dallas, TX	Public	68.6	260	8021
Good Samaritan Hospital Corvallis	1866	Corvallis, OR	Private	68.6	900	8062
South Centl Regional Med Ctr	1867	Laurel, MS	Private	68.6	1,159	8062
St Mary's Hospital	1868	Centralia, IL	Private	68.5	950	8062
Florida Hospital/Waterman Inc	1869	Eustis, FL	Private	68.5	1,200	8062
Georgetown County Mem Hosp	1870	Georgetown, SC	Private	68.5	509	8062
San Joaquin, County	1871	French Camp, CA	Private	68.5	NA	8062
Terre Haute Regional Hospital Inc	1872	Terre Haute, IN	Public Family Member	68.5	800	8062
Beverly Community Hospital Assn	1873	Montebello, CA	Private	68.4	1,100	8062
Riddle Memorial Hospital	1874	Media, PA	Private	68.4	1,094	8062
Emory University	1875	Atlanta, GA	Private	68.4	NA	8011
Gould Medical Foundation	1876	Modesto, CA	Private	68.4	680	8011
Lenoir Memorial Hospital Inc	1877	Kinston, NC	Private	68.3	870	8062
Memorial Hermann Hospital Sys	1878	Houston, TX	Private	68.3	NA	8062
Rutland Hospital Inc	1879	Rutland, VT	Private	68.2	1,000	8062
Baxter County Regional Hosp	1880	Mountain Home, AR	Private	68.2	1,000	8062
Glen Ellyn Clinic, S.C.	1881	Glen Ellyn, IL	Private	68.0	110	8011
Medical Center, Inc	1882	Columbus, GA	Private	68.0	1,463	8062
Kessler Inst For Rhabilitation	1883	West Orange, NJ	Private	67.8	1,000	8069
Sentara Health Plans Inc	1884	Virginia Beach, VA	Private	67.8	120	8011
Hca Health Services Of Utah	1885	Salt Lake City, UT	Public Family Member	67.7	1,457	8062
Meridia Health System	1886	Cleveland, OH	Private	67.7	NA	8062
University Of Illinois	1887	Chicago, IL	Private	67.7	NA	8062
Union Hospital	1888	Union, NJ	Private	67.6	1,284	8062
Central Wash Health Svcs Assn	1889	Wenatchee, WA	Private	67.6	527	8062
P M R Corporation	1890	San Diego, CA	Public	67.5	800	8011

D&B COMPANY RANKINGS BY SALES

Company	Rank	Location	Type	Sales ($ mil.)	Employment	Primary SIC
St Patrick Hospital Inc	1891	Lake Charles, LA	Private	67.5	1,452	8062
Morton Hospital	1892	Taunton, MA	Private	67.5	900	8062
Ancilla Health Care Inc	1893	Hobart, IN	Private	67.5	800	8062
Onslow County Hospital Auth	1894	Jacksonville, NC	Private	67.3	1,000	8062
Preferred Health Network Of Md	1895	Linthicum Heights, MD	Private	67.3	100	8011
California Dept Mental Health	1896	Costa Mesa, CA	Private	67.3	NA	8063
Pennsylvania Dept Pub Welfare	1897	Bridgeville, PA	Private	67.3	NA	8063
Kenmore Mercy Hospital	1898	Kenmore, NY	Private	67.3	1,300	8062
Healthtexas Provider Network	1899	Dallas, TX	Private	67.3	300	8011
Episcopal Health Services Inc	1900	Far Rockaway, NY	Private	67.2	NA	8062
Bethania Regional Health Care Ctr	1901	Wichita Falls, TX	Private	67.2	1,800	8062
Atlanticare Medical Center	1902	Lynn, MA	Private	67.2	1,829	8062
Hays Medical Center Inc	1903	Hays, KS	Private	67.1	900	8062
Veterans Health Administration	1904	Temple, TX	Private	67.0	NA	8062
Veterans Health Administration	1905	Martinez, CA	Private	67.0	NA	8011
American Habilitation Services	1906	Houston, TX	Private	66.9	3,000	8059
Charter Behavioral Health Systems	1907	Atlanta, GA	Private	66.7	1,800	8063
Isabella Geriatric Center	1908	New York, NY	Private	66.6	800	8051
Wayne General Hospital Corp	1909	Wayne, NJ	Private	66.5	941	8062
New Liberty Hospital District	1910	Liberty, MO	Private	66.5	1,050	8062
Yukon-Kuskokwim Health Corp	1911	Bethel, AK	Private	66.5	844	8062
Lodi Memorial Hospital Assn	1912	Lodi, CA	Private	66.5	950	8062
Delmarva Health Plan Inc	1913	Easton, MD	Private	66.5	75	8011
Upmc Mckeesport	1914	Mc Keesport, PA	Private	66.4	1,429	8062
Ghs Osteopathic Inc	1915	Philadelphia, PA	Private	66.3	1,500	8062
Blanchard Valley Regional Health	1916	Findlay, OH	Private	66.3	797	8062
Phoenix Memorial Hospital	1917	Phoenix, AZ	Private	66.3	926	8062
Holy Family Medical Center	1918	Des Plaines, IL	Private	66.3	716	8062
Middle Tennessee Medical Ctr	1919	Murfreesboro, TN	Private	66.2	1,050	8062
Merle West Medical Center	1920	Klamath Falls, OR	Private	66.2	1,100	8062
Lubbock Methdst Hospital Svcs Inc	1921	Lubbock, TX	Private	66.2	120	8071
Faulkner Hospital Inc	1922	Boston, MA	Private	66.2	1,100	8062
Jordan Hospital (Inc)	1923	Plymouth, MA	Private	66.0	900	8062
Clarksville Regional Health Sys	1924	Clarksville, TN	Private	66.0	1,000	8062
Managed Healthcare Systems Of Ny	1925	New York, NY	Private	65.5	119	8099
East Orange General Hospital	1926	East Orange, NJ	Private	65.5	950	8062
Partners In Care Inc	1927	New York, NY	Private	65.4	1,500	8082
Centre Community Hospital	1928	State College, PA	Private	65.4	930	8062
Wilson Memorial Hospital Inc	1929	Wilson, NC	Private	65.3	840	8062
Beebe Medical Center Inc	1930	Lewes, DE	Private	65.3	808	8062
St Lukes Mdland Rgonal Med Ctr	1931	Aberdeen, SD	Private	65.2	1,059	8062
Carroll County General Hosp	1932	Westminster, MD	Private	65.1	1,100	8062
Carroll County Health Svcs Corp	1933	Westminster, MD	Private	65.1	1,100	8062
Autumn Corp	1934	Rocky Mount, NC	Private	65.0	1,800	8059
Community Partnr Southern Ariz	1935	Tucson, AZ	Private	65.0	82	8093
Concord Health Group, Inc	1936	Williamsport, PA	Public Family Member	65.0	965	8051
Cornerstone Health Management	1937	Dallas, TX	Public Family Member	65.0	654	8051
Duke University	1938	Durham, NC	Private	65.0	NA	8011
Jonesboro Health Services Inc	1939	Jonesboro, AR	Public Family Member	65.0	400	8062
Lake Cumberland Healthcare	1940	Somerset, KY	Public Family Member	65.0	1,400	8062
Lee Regional Health System	1941	Johnstown, PA	Private	65.0	1,400	8062
Lucy W Hayes Trng Sch Dcns Msn	1942	Washington, DC	Private	65.0	1,400	8062
Managed Care Assistance Corp	1943	Rockville, MD	Private	65.0	25	8099
Manataee Mem Hospital Ltd Partnr	1944	Bradenton, FL	Private	65.0	1,400	8062
Peak Medical Corp	1945	Albuquerque, NM	Private	65.0	10	8051
Pontiac General Hospital & Med Ctr	1946	Pontiac, MI	Private	65.0	1,400	8062
University Medical Center	1947	Fresno, CA	Private	65.0	1,400	8062
Samaritan Health System	1948	Mesa, AZ	Private	64.9	NA	8062
St Elizabeth Hospital Inc	1949	Appleton, WI	Private	64.9	1,398	8062
Veterans Health Administration	1950	Phoenix, AZ	Private	64.9	NA	8062
Palisades Medical Center	1951	North Bergen, NJ	Private	64.8	634	8062
Conway Regional Medical Center	1952	Conway, AR	Private	64.8	788	8062
Sacred Ht Hospital Sist Char	1953	Cumberland, MD	Private	64.8	901	8062
Deaconess Waltham Hospital	1954	Waltham, MA	Private	64.8	1,480	8062
Brandywine Hospital	1955	Coatesville, PA	Private	64.8	1,300	8062
Sheridan Healthcare Inc	1956	Hollywood, FL	Public	64.7	700	8082
Peninsula Hospital Center	1957	Far Rockaway, NY	Private	64.7	1,010	8062
Conway Hospital Inc	1958	Conway, SC	Private	64.5	800	8062
Midwest City Mem Hospital Auth	1959	Oklahoma City, OK	Private	64.5	1,000	8062
Wilson N. Jones Mem Hosp, The	1960	Sherman, TX	Private	64.5	900	8062

D&B COMPANY RANKINGS BY SALES

Company	Rank	Location	Type	Sales ($ mil.)	Employ-ment	Primary SIC
Veterans Health Administration	1961	Syracuse, NY	Private	64.5	NA	8062
Victory Memorial Hospital Assn	1962	Waukegan, IL	Private	64.5	950	8062
Mercy Services For Aging	1963	Farmington Hills, MI	Private	64.4	1,800	8361
Community United Methdst Hosp	1964	Henderson, KY	Private	64.3	1,060	8062
St Luke Hospital Inc	1965	Fort Thomas, KY	Private	64.3	1,385	8062
Magnolia Regional Health Ctr	1966	Corinth, MS	Private	64.3	800	8062
Hospital Center At Orange, The	1967	Orange, NJ	Private	64.3	900	8062
Albemarle Hospital	1968	Elizabeth City, NC	Private	64.3	810	8062
Charlotte Hungerford Hosp, The	1969	Torrington, CT	Private	64.2	712	8062
Meadville Medical Center	1970	Meadville, PA	Private	64.2	959	8062
Mercy Healthcare Inc	1971	Roseburg, OR	Private	64.2	700	8062
Northwest Medical Center	1972	Franklin, PA	Private	64.2	1,200	8062
Onslow Memorial Hospital Inc	1973	Jacksonville, NC	Private	64.1	786	8062
Great Valley Health	1974	Paoli, PA	Private	64.0	882	8011
Oncology-Hematolgy Associates	1975	Pittsburgh, PA	Public Family Member	64.0	120	8011
Suncare Respiratory Services	1976	Indianapolis, IN	Public Family Member	64.0	80	8093
Texas Oncology Pa	1977	Dallas, TX	Private	64.0	600	8011
Samaritan Hospital	1978	Troy, NY	Private	64.0	1,403	8062
Mid Michigan Regional Med Ctr	1979	Midland, MI	Private	63.9	1,375	8062
Griffin Hospital Inc	1980	Derby, CT	Private	63.9	1,100	8062
Bay Harbor Hospital Inc	1981	Harbor City, CA	Private	63.8	800	8062
Bayshore Community Hospital	1982	Holmdel, NJ	Private	63.7	1,000	8062
Delnor-Community Hospital	1983	Geneva, IL	Private	63.7	985	8062
Ebenezer Social Ministries	1984	Saint Paul, MN	Private	63.7	4,000	8051
Bethesda Hospital Inc	1985	Cincinnati, OH	Private	63.5	NA	8062
Detroit-Macomb Hospital Corp	1986	Warren, MI	Private	63.5	NA	8062
Laboratory Corporation America	1987	Dallas, TX	Public Family Member	63.5	NA	8071
Medlink Of Virginia	1988	Buffalo, NY	Private	63.5	4,000	8082
Nazareth Health Inc	1989	Chattanooga, TN	Private	63.5	NA	8062
Osf Healthcare System	1990	Rockford, IL	Private	63.5	NA	8062
Veterans Health Administration	1991	Kansas City, MO	Private	63.5	NA	8062
Veterans Health Administration	1992	Battle Creek, MI	Private	63.5	NA	8062
Veterans Health Administration	1993	Murfreesboro, TN	Private	63.5	NA	8062
Redlands Community Hospital	1994	Redlands, CA	Private	63.4	720	8062
Good Smrtan Regional Health Ctr	1995	Mount Vernon, IL	Private	63.4	805	8062
City Of Philadelphia, Trust	1996	Philadelphia, PA	Private	63.3	600	8069
Cookeville Regional Med Ctr	1997	Cookeville, TN	Private	63.2	850	8062
Sensitive Care Inc	1998	Fort Worth, TX	Private	63.0	1,387	8051
Community General Hospital	1999	Harris, NY	Private	63.0	800	8062
Urology Healthcare Group Inc	2000	Brentwood, TN	Private	63.0	450	8011
Valley Health Systems Inc	2001	Holyoke, MA	Private	63.0	1,357	8062
Casa Grande Community Hosp	2002	Casa Grande, AZ	Private	62.9	750	8062
Physicians Clinical Laboratory	2003	Sacramento, CA	Public	62.8	1,500	8071
Castle Medical Center	2004	Kailua, HI	Private	62.8	1,012	8062
San Gabriel Valley Med Ctr	2005	San Gabriel, CA	Private	62.8	850	8062
Parkview Health System Inc	2006	Pueblo, CO	Private	62.7	1,350	8062
Piedmont Healthcare Systems	2007	Rock Hill, SC	Public Family Member	62.7	1,350	8062
St Mary's Health Care System	2008	Athens, GA	Private	62.7	1,350	8062
Valley Hospital Med Ctr Inc	2009	Las Vegas, NV	Public Family Member	62.7	1,350	8062
Montgomery General Hospital Inc	2010	Olney, MD	Private	62.6	1,200	8062
Sturdy Memorial Hospital Inc	2011	Attleboro, MA	Private	62.5	1,000	8062
Columbia Regional Medical Ctr	2012	Montgomery, AL	Public Family Member	62.5	691	8062
Horizon Health Corporation	2013	Lewisville, TX	Public	62.4	1,200	8063
Sutter North Med Foundation	2014	Marysville, CA	Private	62.4	400	8011
St Elizabeth Medical Center	2015	Utica, NY	Private	62.4	1,220	8062
Touro Infirmary	2016	New Orleans, LA	Private	62.4	1,344	8062
Hospital Service District	2017	Thibodaux, LA	Private	62.4	706	8062
Commun Mem Hospital	2018	Menomonee Falls, WI	Private	62.3	1,100	8062
Moses Taylor Hospital	2019	Scranton, PA	Private	62.3	791	8062
American Oncologic Hospital	2020	Philadelphia, PA	Private	62.3	725	8069
Long Beach Medical Center	2021	Long Beach, NY	Private	62.2	830	8062
Norwood Clinic Inc Pc	2022	Birmingham, AL	Private	62.2	535	8093
Methodist Hspitals Of Memphis	2023	Memphis, TN	Private	62.2	NA	8069
Sutter Health Central	2024	Sacramento, CA	Private	62.2	NA	8062
Burlington Medical Center Inc	2025	Burlington, IA	Private	62.2	1,050	8062
Tenet Healthcare Corporation	2026	Houston, TX	Public Family Member	62.1	NA	8062
Knapp Medical Center	2027	Weslaco, TX	Private	62.1	1,000	8062
Access Health Inc	2028	Broomfield, CO	Public	62.1	1,026	8082
Newton Memorial Hospital	2029	Newton, NJ	Private	62.0	677	8062
Southern Ohio Medical Center	2030	Portsmouth, OH	Private	62.0	NA	8062

D&B COMPANY RANKINGS BY SALES

Company	Rank	Location	Type	Sales ($ mil.)	Employ-ment	Primary SIC
Veterans Adm Med Ctr	2031	Tuscaloosa, AL	Private	62.0	950	8062
St Anne's Hospital Corp	2032	Fall River, MA	Private	62.0	906	8062
Southwest Miss Regional Med Ctr	2033	Mc Comb, MS	Private	61.9	1,000	8062
New York Eye Ear Infirmary Inc	2034	New York, NY	Private	61.9	600	8069
Memorial Healthcare Group	2035	Jacksonville, FL	Public Family Member	61.9	1,334	8062
Washington Regional Med Sys	2036	Fayetteville, AR	Private	61.9	1,334	8062
Veterans Health Administration	2037	Durham, NC	Private	61.8	NA	8062
Veterans Health Administration	2038	Palm Beach Gds, FL	Private	61.8	NA	8062
St Marys Regional Medical Ctr	2039	Lewiston, ME	Private	61.8	850	8062
St Clares Hospital Of Schnctady Ny	2040	Schenectady, NY	Private	61.7	1,150	8062
Newcomb Medical Center	2041	Vineland, NJ	Private	61.7	730	8062
Childrens Memorial Hospital	2042	Omaha, NE	Private	61.7	849	8069
Tarrant County	2043	Fort Worth, TX	Private	61.7	1,227	8093
St Mary Regional Medical Ctr	2044	Apple Valley, CA	Private	61.6	700	8062
Baptist Hospital Of Stheast Texas	2045	Beaumont, TX	Private	61.6	800	8062
Telecare Corporation	2046	Alameda, CA	Private	61.4	1,600	8063
California Dept Health Svcs	2047	Eldridge, CA	Private	61.3	NA	8051
Provena Hospital	2048	Urbana, IL	Private	61.3	NA	8062
Grace Hospital	2049	Morganton, NC	Private	61.2	1,000	8062
Smithkline Beecham Clinical Labs	2050	Van Nuys, CA	Private	61.1	NA	8071
Southampton Hospital Assn	2051	Southampton, NY	Private	61.1	770	8062
Williamsburg Community Hosp	2052	Williamsburg, VA	Private	61.0	1,150	8062
Columbia Healthcare Of Centl Va	2053	Independence, MO	Public Family Member	61.0	NA	8062
National Rehabilitation Hosp	2054	Washington, DC	Private	60.9	760	8069
Dianon Systems Inc	2055	Stratford, CT	Public	60.9	500	8071
Community Hospital Of Brzsport Inc	2056	Lake Jackson, TX	Private	60.9	523	8062
Marietta Area Health Care Inc	2057	Marietta, OH	Private	60.9	815	8062
Huron Valley Sinai Hospital	2058	Commerce Twnsh, MI	Private	60.8	620	8062
Victor Valley Community Hosp	2059	Victorville, CA	Private	60.7	670	8062
City Of Quincy	2060	Quincy, MA	Private	60.7	NA	8062
Mercy Medical Center	2061	Nampa, ID	Private	60.7	650	8062
Intermountain Health Care Inc	2062	Ogden, UT	Private	60.6	NA	8062
Lutheran Health Systems	2063	Mesa, AZ	Private	60.6	NA	8062
Veterans Health Administration	2064	Albuquerque, NM	Private	60.6	NA	8062
Veterans Health Administration	2065	Lebanon, PA	Private	60.6	NA	8062
St. Rose Dominican Hospital	2066	Henderson, NV	Private	60.5	754	8062
Tomball Hospital Authority	2067	Tomball, TX	Private	60.5	1,100	8062
Ami/Hti Tarzana-Encino, Jv	2068	Tarzana, CA	Private	60.3	NA	8062
Fountain Valley Regnl Hosp	2069	Fountain Valley, CA	Public Family Member	60.3	1,300	8062
Franklin Hospital Medical Ctr	2070	Valley Stream, NY	Private	60.3	1,300	8062
Greater Bristol Health Svcs Corp	2071	Bristol, CT	Private	60.3	1,300	8062
Largo Medical Center Inc	2072	Largo, FL	Public Family Member	60.3	1,300	8062
Saint Joseph Hospital Inc	2073	Omaha, NE	Public Family Member	60.3	1,300	8062
Shannon Medical Center Inc	2074	San Angelo, TX	Private	60.3	1,300	8062
Sterling Health Care Corp	2075	Bellevue, WA	Private	60.3	1,300	8062
White Plins Hospital Ctr Fundation	2076	White Plains, NY	Private	60.3	1,300	8062
Olathe Medical Center Inc	2077	Olathe, KS	Private	60.3	1,213	8062
Associated Therapists Corp	2078	Owings Mills, MD	Public Family Member	60.3	1,300	8093
Princeton Community Hospital Assn	2079	Princeton, WV	Private	60.2	1,000	8062
Health Svcs Assn Of Centl Ny	2080	Baldwinsville, NY	Private	60.1	724	8011
Alabama Department Mental Health	2081	Tuscaloosa, AL	Private	60.0	NA	8063
Medical Innovations Inc	2082	Houston, TX	Public Family Member	60.0	3,450	8082
Mohawk Valley Network, Inc	2083	Utica, NY	Private	60.0	2,350	8069
Northern Ore Healthcare Corp	2084	Mcminnville, OR	Public Family Member	60.0	300	8062
Nylcare Health Plans Of Maine	2085	Portland, ME	Private	60.0	100	8011
Select Medical Corporation	2086	Mechanicsburg, PA	Private	60.0	1,000	8093
Sonora Quest Laboratories Llc.	2087	Tempe, AZ	Private	60.0	850	8071
Springer Clinic, Inc	2088	Tulsa, OK	Private	60.0	425	8011
Park Jackson Hospital Foundation	2089	Chicago, IL	Private	59.9	750	8062
Bon Secours-Depaul Medical Ctr	2090	Norfolk, VA	Private	59.8	1,400	8062
Immanuel-St Joseph Of Mankato	2091	Mankato, MN	Private	59.7	950	8062
Presbyterian Homes Inc	2092	Camp Hill, PA	Private	59.7	1,350	8052
Phoenix Healthcare Of Tenn	2093	Nashville, TN	Private	59.6	86	8082
Veterans Health Administration	2094	Salisbury, NC	Private	59.6	NA	8062
Norwegian American Hospital	2095	Chicago, IL	Private	59.5	822	8062
Ami/Hti Tarzana-Encino, Jv	2096	Tarzana, CA	Private	59.5	NA	8062
Barnes-Jewish Hospital	2097	Saint Louis, MO	Private	59.5	NA	8011
Episcopal Health Services Inc	2098	Smithtown, NY	Private	59.5	NA	8062
Everett Clinic, The	2099	Everett, WA	Private	59.5	NA	8011
Kaiser Foundation Health Plan	2100	Baldwin Park, CA	Private	59.5	NA	8062

D&B COMPANY RANKINGS BY SALES

Company	Rank	Location	Type	Sales ($ mil.)	Employment	Primary SIC
Kaiser Foundation Hospitals	2101	Santa Rosa, CA	Private	59.5	NA	8011
Medical College Of Hampton Rads	2102	Norfolk, VA	Private	59.5	NA	8011
New York Cy Health Hspitals Corp	2103	New York, NY	Private	59.5	NA	8062
Orlando Rgonal Healthcare Sys	2104	Orlando, FL	Private	59.5	NA	8011
Palomar Pomerado Health Sys	2105	Escondido, CA	Private	59.5	NA	8062
Permanente Medical Group Inc	2106	San Francisco, CA	Private	59.5	NA	8011
Salina Regional Health Center	2107	Salina, KS	Private	59.5	1,283	8062
State Of Maryland	2108	Annapolis, MD	Private	59.5	NA	8011
Tenet Healthcare Corporation	2109	San Diego, CA	Public Family Member	59.5	NA	8062
University Of Alabama Health S	2110	Birmingham, AL	Private	59.5	NA	8011
Memorial Hospital Of Martinsvl	2111	Martinsville, VA	Private	59.4	800	8062
Volunteers Of Amer Health Svcs	2112	Eden Prairie, MN	Private	59.4	1,300	8051
California Dept Mental Health	2113	Norwalk, CA	Private	59.4	NA	8063
Los Angeles, County	2114	Los Angeles, CA	Private	59.4	NA	8063
St. Mary's Hospital	2115	Decatur, IL	Private	59.4	1,200	8062
Mercy Health Services	2116	Sioux City, IA	Private	59.3	NA	8062
Tarpon Springs Hospital Foundation	2117	Tarpon Springs, FL	Private	59.3	750	8062
Jameson Memorial Hospital	2118	New Castle, PA	Private	59.2	1,063	8062
Catholic Health Partners Svcs	2119	Chicago, IL	Private	59.2	NA	8062
Cook Childrens Medical Center	2120	Fort Worth, TX	Private	59.2	1,200	8069
Franciscan Sisters Of Chicago	2121	Crown Point, IN	Private	59.2	NA	8062
Ssm Health Care	2122	Madison, WI	Private	59.2	NA	8062
National Dentex Corporation	2123	Wayland, MA	Public	59.2	1,200	8072
Facey Medical Foundation Inc	2124	Mission Hills, CA	Private	59.1	500	8099
St Helena Hospital	2125	Deer Park, CA	Private	59.1	875	8062
General Health Services, Inc.	2126	Nashville, TN	Public Family Member	59.1	1,274	8062
Mainegeneral Medical Center	2127	Augusta, ME	Private	59.1	967	8062
Penn State Geisinger Med Ctr	2128	Danville, PA	Private	59.0	825	8062
Northeast Health	2129	Rockland, ME	Private	58.9	1,200	8062
Bellflower Medical Center	2130	Bellflower, CA	Private	58.9	400	8011
Exeter Hospital Inc	2131	Exeter, NH	Private	58.9	700	8062
Adventist Health System/Sunbelt	2132	Altamonte Springs, FL	Private	58.9	NA	8082
Veterans Health Administration	2133	Waco, TX	Private	58.9	NA	8062
North Brevard County Hospital Dst	2134	Titusville, FL	Private	58.9	980	8062
Mission Bay Memorial Hospital	2135	San Diego, CA	Public Family Member	58.9	447	8062
Charleston Hospital, Inc.	2136	Charleston, WV	Public Family Member	58.8	645	8062
Cape Canaveral Hospital	2137	Cocoa Beach, FL	Private	58.7	800	8062
St Francis Hospital & Med Ctr	2138	Hartford, CT	Private	58.6	NA	8062
Franklin Medical Center	2139	Greenfield, MA	Private	58.6	1,163	8062
Beaufort County Memorial Hosp	2140	Beaufort, SC	Private	58.5	800	8062
Anaheim Memorial Hospital Assn	2141	Anaheim, CA	Private	58.5	775	8062
St Agnes Medical Center	2142	Philadelphia, PA	Private	58.5	840	8062
Emory University	2143	Atlanta, GA	Private	58.4	NA	8062
Hialeah Hospital Inc	2144	Hialeah, FL	Public Family Member	58.4	1,260	8062
Luther Hospital	2145	Eau Claire, WI	Private	58.4	1,260	8062
Warren Hospital	2146	Phillipsburg, NJ	Private	58.2	806	8062
Allina Health System	2147	Minneapolis, MN	Private	58.2	NA	8062
Veterans Health Administration	2148	Biloxi, MS	Private	58.2	NA	8062
Covenant House Inc (New York)	2149	New York, NY	Private	58.1	200	8361
Chestnut Hill Hospital	2150	Philadelphia, PA	Private	58.1	1,000	8062
Waverley Group Inc	2151	Jackson, MS	Private	58.0	1,900	8051
Nacogdoches County Hospital Dst	2152	Nacogdoches, TX	Private	58.0	675	8062
Emanuel Medical Center Inc	2153	Turlock, CA	Private	57.9	985	8062
St Joseph Health Center	2154	Saint Charles, MO	Private	57.9	1,250	8062
Tenet Healthcare, Ltd	2155	El Paso, TX	Private	57.9	NA	8062
Veterans Health Administration	2156	Oklahoma City, OK	Private	57.9	NA	8062
Hospital Of Germantown	2157	Philadelphia, PA	Private	57.9	550	8062
Cocoa Beach Area Health Svc	2158	Cocoa Beach, FL	Private	57.9	800	8011
Healthohio, Inc	2159	Marion, OH	Private	57.8	90	8011
New York Foundling Hosp, The	2160	New York, NY	Private	57.8	1,500	8361
Palmetto General Hospital	2161	Hialeah, FL	Public Family Member	57.7	1,245	8062
St John Ambulatory Care Corp	2162	Detroit, MI	Private	57.6	328	8011
Presbytrian Hmes Of Nj Fndton	2163	Princeton, NJ	Private	57.6	1,300	8059
Allegiant Physician Services	2164	Atlanta, GA	Public	57.6	48	8099
California Pacific Med Ctr	2165	San Francisco, CA	Private	57.6	NA	8011
Sisters Charity Leavenworth Hth Inc	2166	Leavenworth, KS	Private	57.6	1,242	8062
Cooley Dickinson Hospital	2167	Northampton, MA	Private	57.6	1,100	8062
Jackson Clinic Prof Assn, The	2168	Jackson, TN	Private	57.5	630	8011
Sch Health Care System	2169	Texarkana, TX	Private	57.5	NA	8062
Sisters Of Mercy Of Hamilton	2170	Hamilton, OH	Private	57.5	1,241	8062

D&B COMPANY RANKINGS BY SALES

Company	Rank	Location	Type	Sales ($ mil.)	Employ-ment	Primary SIC
Yavapai Community Hospital Assn	2171	Prescott, AZ	Private	57.5	730	8062
Boston Regional Medical Center	2172	Stoneham, MA	Private	57.4	1,400	8062
Proctor Hospital	2173	Peoria, IL	Private	57.4	1,050	8062
Amsurg, Corp	2174	Nashville, TN	Public	57.4	64	8062
Manhattan Psychiatric Center	2175	New York, NY	Private	57.4	1,550	8063
Spring Branch Medical Ctr Inc	2176	Houston, TX	Public Family Member	57.4	1,238	8062
Mount Vernon Hospital Inc	2177	Mount Vernon, NY	Private	57.4	725	8062
Long Island Home Ltd (Inc)	2178	Amityville, NY	Private	57.4	925	8063
Hospital For Special Care	2179	New Britain, CT	Private	57.4	800	8069
Sharp Mission Park Corp	2180	Oceanside, CA	Private	57.3	450	8011
Rockdale Hospital Inc	2181	Conyers, GA	Private	57.3	670	8062
Menninger Clinic, Incorporated	2182	Topeka, KS	Private	57.3	NA	8093
Centra Health Inc	2183	Lynchburg, VA	Private	57.3	NA	8062
Eden Park Management Inc	2184	Albany, NY	Private	57.3	2,500	8051
Four Seasons Nursing Centers	2185	Gaithersburg, MD	Public Family Member	57.3	2,500	8051
Integrted Health Svcs At Srasota	2186	Sarasota, FL	Public Family Member	57.3	2,500	8051
John D Archbold Memorial Hosp	2187	Thomasville, GA	Private	57.3	NA	8062
Lantis Enterprises Inc	2188	Spearfish, SD	Private	57.3	2,500	8051
Mid America Care Foundation	2189	Kansas City, MO	Private	57.3	2,500	8051
Bay Area Health District	2190	Coos Bay, OR	Private	57.3	770	8062
Midwestern Regional Med Ctr	2191	Zion, IL	Private	57.3	568	8069
Ephraim McDowell Rgnal Med Ctr	2192	Danville, KY	Private	57.2	800	8062
Methodist Hospitals Inc	2193	Merrillville, IN	Private	57.2	NA	8062
Permanente Med Assn Of Texas	2194	Dallas, TX	Private	57.1	225	8011
Bio-Medical Applications Of Fla	2195	Tampa, FL	Public Family Member	57.1	1,000	8092
Galen Of Kentucky Inc	2196	Louisville, KY	Public Family Member	57.1	NA	8062
Veterans Health Administration	2197	Cleveland, OH	Private	57.1	NA	8062
Veterans Health Administration	2198	Cleveland, OH	Private	57.1	NA	8062
Memorial Healthcare Center	2199	Owosso, MI	Private	57.0	1,000	8062
Sun Coast Hospital Inc	2200	Largo, FL	Private	57.0	740	8069
Appleton Medical Center	2201	Appleton, WI	Private	57.0	1,230	8062
United Crbrl Plsy/Ulstr Cnty	2202	Kingston, NY	Private	56.9	287	8093
Louise Obici Memorial Hosp	2203	Suffolk, VA	Private	56.8	1,130	8062
Total Health Care Inc	2204	Baltimore, MD	Private	56.7	171	8011
Crestwood Hospital & Nursing Hm	2205	Huntsville, AL	Public Family Member	56.7	275	8062
Regional West Medical Center	2206	Scottsbluff, NE	Private	56.7	800	8062
Wentworth-Douglass Hospital	2207	Dover, NH	Private	56.5	645	8062
Saint Joseph Hospital & Health Ctr	2208	Kokomo, IN	Private	56.5	944	8062
Jaques Anna Hospital Inc	2209	Newburyport, MA	Private	56.5	1,200	8062
Community Hospital Of Anderson	2210	Anderson, IN	Private	56.4	1,000	8062
Marietta Memorial Hospital	2211	Marietta, OH	Private	56.4	800	8062
Mount Sinai School	2212	Elmhurst, NY	Private	56.4	NA	8011
Mather Foundation, The	2213	Evanston, IL	Private	56.4	381	8059
East Tennessee Chld Hospital Assn	2214	Knoxville, TN	Private	56.4	1,000	8069
Hendricks County Hospital	2215	Danville, IN	Private	56.3	785	8062
Jane Phllips Health Care Fndtion	2216	Bartlesville, OK	Private	56.2	NA	8082
Oconee Memorial Hospital Inc	2217	Seneca, SC	Private	56.2	850	8062
Columbia-Healthone L L C	2218	Denver, CO	Private	56.2	NA	8062
Intermountain Health Care Inc	2219	Salt Lake City, UT	Private	56.2	NA	8062
Spectera Inc	2220	Baltimore, MD	Private	56.2	370	8011
Westchester Square Medical Ctr	2221	Bronx, NY	Private	56.0	700	8062
Visiting Nurse Health System	2222	Atlanta, GA	Private	56.0	850	8082
Paracelsus Santa Rosa Med Ctr	2223	Milton, FL	Public Family Member	56.0	310	8062
Miller's Health Systems, Inc	2224	Warsaw, IN	Private	55.9	3,000	8052
Halifax Regional Medical Ctr	2225	Roanoke Rapids, NC	Private	55.8	694	8062
St Joseph's Hospital	2226	Minot, ND	Private	55.8	749	8062
Covenant Nursing & Rehab Ctr	2227	Stockton, CA	Private	55.8	2,500	8059
Saint Vincent Hospital & Health Ctr	2228	Billings, MT	Private	55.8	1,204	8062
Sierra Nev Mmrl-Mners Hspitals	2229	Grass Valley, CA	Private	55.8	775	8062
Rideout Memorial Hospital	2230	Marysville, CA	Private	55.7	600	8062
County Milwaukee, Wisconsin	2231	Milwaukee, WI	Private	55.7	NA	8063
Legacy Meridian Park Hospital	2232	Tualatin, OR	Private	55.7	458	8062
St Jo Hospital Of Port Charles	2233	Port Charlotte, FL	Private	55.7	767	8062
Arnot Ogden Medical Center	2234	Elmira, NY	Private	55.6	1,200	8062
Clark Theda Memorial Hospital	2235	Neenah, WI	Private	55.6	1,200	8062
Clear Lk Regional Med Ctr Inc	2236	Webster, TX	Public Family Member	55.6	1,200	8062
Florida Hospital Heartland	2237	Sebring, FL	Private	55.6	1,200	8062
Galencare Inc	2238	Brandon, FL	Public Family Member	55.6	1,200	8062
Lafayette-Grand Hospital	2239	Saint Louis, MO	Public Family Member	55.6	1,200	8062
Parkridge Hospital Inc	2240	Chattanooga, TN	Public Family Member	55.6	1,200	8062

D&B COMPANY RANKINGS BY SALES

Company	Rank	Location	Type	Sales ($ mil.)	Employ-ment	Primary SIC
St Ann's Hospital Of Columbus	2241	Columbus, OH	Private	55.6	825	8062
Colbert County/Northwest Alaba	2242	Sheffield, AL	Private	55.5	700	8062
Bannock Regional Medical Ctr	2243	Pocatello, ID	Private	55.4	725	8062
Atlantic City Medical Center	2244	Pomona, NJ	Private	55.4	NA	8062
Davies Medical Center, Inc	2245	San Francisco, CA	Private	55.2	900	8062
Phillips Jane Memorial Med Ctr	2246	Bartlesville, OK	Private	55.2	815	8062
Tallahassee Medical Center	2247	Tallahassee, FL	Public Family Member	55.2	572	8062
Mercy Medical Center	2248	Durango, CO	Private	55.1	900	8062
Valley Mental Health	2249	Salt Lake City, UT	Private	55.1	820	8093
Veterans Health Administration	2250	Canandaigua, NY	Private	55.1	NA	8062
Saint Joseph's Medical Center	2251	Stamford, CT	Private	55.1	625	8062
Florida Convalescent Centers	2252	Sarasota, FL	Private	55.0	2,400	8051
Health First Medical Group	2253	Portland, OR	Private	55.0	800	8011
Medical Clinic Of Sacramento	2254	Sacramento, CA	Private	55.0	800	8011
Occupational Health Services	2255	Kansas City, KS	Private	55.0	800	8011
Phycor Of Ft. Smith, Inc	2256	Fort Smith, AR	Public Family Member	55.0	800	8011
River Park Hospital Assoc L P	2257	Mc Minnville, TN	Public Family Member	55.0	320	8062
S C Advanced Healthcare	2258	Milwaukee, WI	Private	55.0	800	8011
University Of California	2259	Santa Monica, CA	Private	55.0	NA	8062
Phelps Cnty Regional Med Ctr	2260	Rolla, MO	Private	55.0	831	8062
Ch Allied Services Inc	2261	Columbia, MO	Private	54.9	NA	8062
Veterans Health Administration	2262	Mountain Home, TN	Private	54.9	NA	8062
Veterans Health Administration	2263	Danville, IL	Private	54.9	NA	8062
Church Hospital Corporation	2264	Baltimore, MD	Private	54.9	1,200	8062
Hammond Clinic, Llc	2265	Munster, IN	Private	54.9	600	8011
Masonic Homes Of California	2266	San Francisco, CA	Private	54.8	450	8361
Jackson Laboratory, The	2267	Bar Harbor, ME	Private	54.8	900	8071
Oroville Hospital	2268	Oroville, CA	Private	54.8	800	8062
Elmbrook Memorial Hospital Inc	2269	Brookfield, WI	Private	54.7	800	8062
Gratiot Health System	2270	Alma, MI	Private	54.7	818	8062
Concord Hospital Inc	2271	Concord, NH	Private	54.7	1,182	8062
Calvary Hospital Inc	2272	Bronx, NY	Private	54.7	690	8069
Southeast Alaska Reg Health	2273	Juneau, AK	Private	54.7	580	8011
Volunters Of Amer Care Fcltes	2274	Eden Prairie, MN	Private	54.6	1,300	8051
Longmont United Hospital	2275	Longmont, CO	Private	54.6	800	8062
Carlisle Hospital	2276	Carlisle, PA	Private	54.5	675	8062
Mercy Fitzgerald Hospital Inc	2277	Philadelphia, PA	Private	54.5	NA	8062
St Joseph Hospital Of Kirkwood	2278	Saint Louis, MO	Private	54.5	1,178	8062
Amedisys Inc	2279	Baton Rouge, LA	Public	54.5	700	8082
Finger Lakes Regional Health Sys	2280	Geneva, NY	Private	54.5	1,100	8051
Iowa Physicians Clinic Found	2281	Des Moines, IA	Private	54.5	1,000	8011
St Claire Medical Center, Inc	2282	Morehead, KY	Private	54.4	900	8062
Kaiser Foundation Hospitals	2283	S San Francisco, CA	Private	54.4	NA	8062
Kaiser Foundation Hospitals	2284	Honolulu, HI	Private	54.4	NA	8062
Peacehealth	2285	Bellingham, WA	Private	54.4	NA	8062
City Hospital Inc	2286	Martinsburg, WV	Private	54.4	742	8062
Newport Hospital	2287	Newport, RI	Private	54.3	700	8062
Department Of Army	2288	San Antonio, TX	Private	54.3	NA	8062
Genesis Medical Center	2289	Davenport, IA	Private	54.3	NA	8062
Auburn Memorial Hospital	2290	Auburn, NY	Private	54.3	925	8062
Children's Hospital	2291	New Orleans, LA	Private	54.2	1,100	8069
Howard Community Hospital	2292	Kokomo, IN	Private	54.2	900	8062
Marshall Hospital	2293	Placerville, CA	Private	54.2	800	8062
Cooper Clinic Pa	2294	Fort Smith, AR	Private	54.2	470	8011
Salem Community Hospital	2295	Salem, OH	Private	54.1	655	8062
Saratoga Hospital (Inc)	2296	Saratoga Springs, NY	Private	54.1	1,000	8062
St. Peters Community Hospital	2297	Helena, MT	Private	54.1	700	8062
Fairmont General Hospital Inc	2298	Fairmont, WV	Private	54.0	850	8062
Dallas/Fort Worth Med Center	2299	Grand Prairie, TX	Private	54.0	670	8062
Lucy Lee Hospital Inc	2300	Poplar Bluff, MO	Public Family Member	54.0	1,000	8062
Pacific Homes	2301	Woodland Hills, CA	Private	54.0	1,400	8361
Allina Health System	2302	Minneapolis, MN	Private	54.0	NA	8062
Camelot Healthcare Llc	2303	Rayne, LA	Private	54.0	520	8051
Johns Hopkins Hospital Inc	2304	Baltimore, MD	Private	53.9	NA	8011
Memorial Hermann Hospital Sys	2305	Houston, TX	Private	53.9	NA	8011
Skagit County Medical Bureau	2306	Mount Vernon, WA	Private	53.9	95	8011
Visiting Nurse Health System	2307	Atlanta, GA	Private	53.9	800	8082
Lakes Region Hospital Assn	2308	Laconia, NH	Private	53.7	900	8062
El Paso Healthcare Systems	2309	El Paso, TX	Private	53.7	NA	8062
Healthtrust Inc - Hospital Co	2310	Houston, TX	Public Family Member	53.7	NA	8062

D&B COMPANY RANKINGS BY SALES

Company	Rank	Location	Type	Sales ($ mil.)	Employ-ment	Primary SIC
Community Health Group	2311	Chula Vista, CA	Private	53.6	130	8011
Loudoun Hospital Center	2312	Leesburg, VA	Private	53.6	800	8062
Webber Hospital Association	2313	Biddeford, ME	Private	53.6	765	8062
Sister Hayward Hospital	2314	Hayward, CA	Private	53.6	760	8062
Premier Healthcare, Inc	2315	Phoenix, AZ	Private	53.5	90	8011
Osceola Regional Hospital	2316	Kissimmee, FL	Public Family Member	53.5	542	8062
Arnett Hmo Inc	2317	Lafayette, IN	Public Family Member	53.5	46	8011
Stuart Jennie Medical Center	2318	Hopkinsville, KY	Private	53.4	575	8062
Alton Memorial Hospital	2319	Alton, IL	Private	53.3	1,000	8062
Central Suffolk Hospital	2320	Riverhead, NY	Private	53.3	610	8062
Hattiesburg Clinic Prof Assn	2321	Hattiesburg, MS	Private	53.2	801	8011
St Bernard Hospital Healthcare Ctr	2322	Chicago, IL	Private	53.2	632	8062
Memorial Medical Center	2323	Woodstock, IL	Private	53.2	750	8062
Gci Properties, Inc	2324	Atlanta, GA	Public Family Member	53.2	2,325	8051
Chicago Grant Hospital, Inc.	2325	Chicago, IL	Public Family Member	53.2	600	8062
Indiana Hospital	2326	Indiana, PA	Private	53.2	900	8062
St Luke's Health System	2327	Phoenix, AZ	Public Family Member	53.1	1,148	8062
Healthright Inc	2328	Meriden, CT	Private	53.1	60	8011
Greene Memorial Hospital Inc	2329	Xenia, OH	Private	53.0	800	8062
Beth Israel Hospital Assn	2330	Passaic, NJ	Private	53.0	650	8062
Buffalo Medical Group P C	2331	Williamsville, NY	Private	53.0	525	8011
Niagara Falls Memorial Med Ctr	2332	Niagara Falls, NY	Private	53.0	1,146	8062
Palm Springs General Hospital	2333	Hialeah, FL	Private	53.0	600	8062
Veterans Health Administration	2334	Boston, MA	Private	53.0	NA	8062
Harriman Jones Medical Group	2335	Long Beach, CA	Private	53.0	506	8011
Diagnostic Health Services Inc	2336	Dallas, TX	Public	52.9	500	8099
East Boston Neighborhood	2337	Boston, MA	Private	52.9	450	8011
H C A Health Services Of Fla	2338	Port Richey, FL	Public Family Member	52.9	NA	8062
H C A Health Services Of Fla	2339	Bradenton, FL	Public Family Member	52.9	NA	8062
Shands Teaching Hospital & Clinic	2340	Gainesville, FL	Private	52.9	NA	8062
Veterans Health Administration	2341	Baltimore, MD	Private	52.9	NA	8062
East Texas Medical Center	2342	Tyler, TX	Private	52.9	300	8071
Lutheran Social Services Of Il	2343	Des Plaines, IL	Private	52.9	3,000	8361
White River Medical Center	2344	Batesville, AR	Private	52.9	760	8062
M J G Nursing Home Co Inc	2345	Brooklyn, NY	Private	52.8	730	8051
County Of Los Angeles	2346	Los Angeles, CA	Private	52.8	NA	8069
Driscoll Childrens Hospital	2347	Corpus Christi, TX	Private	52.8	1,070	8069
Multicare Health System	2348	Tacoma, WA	Private	52.8	NA	8069
Peacehealth	2349	Longview, WA	Private	52.8	NA	8062
Tenet Healthcare Corporation	2350	Monterey Park, CA	Public Family Member	52.8	NA	8069
Santa Barbara Mdcl Fndn Clc	2351	Santa Barbara, CA	Private	52.7	580	8011
Northport Health Service Inc	2352	Tuscaloosa, AL	Private	52.7	2,300	8051
Pharmaco International Inc	2353	Austin, TX	Public Family Member	52.7	1,105	8071
Rutland Nursing Home Inc	2354	Brooklyn, NY	Private	52.7	725	8051
U S Homecare Corporation	2355	Hartford, CT	Public	52.6	3,700	8082
Philadelphia Geriatric Center	2356	Philadelphia, PA	Private	52.6	1,000	8051
Hernando Healthcare Inc	2357	Brooksville, FL	Private	52.6	364	8062
Magic Valley Regional Med Ctr	2358	Twin Falls, ID	Private	52.6	775	8062
Greenwood Leflore Hospital	2359	Greenwood, MS	Private	52.5	800	8062
Vinfen Corporation	2360	Cambridge, MA	Private	52.3	1,300	8361
Medical Associates Clinic P C	2361	Dubuque, IA	Private	52.3	761	8011
Presbyterian Retirement	2362	Orlando, FL	Private	52.2	1,300	8361
Ucsf-Stanford Health Care	2363	Palo Alto, CA	Private	52.2	NA	8069
Miami Jewish Home/Hosptl Aged	2364	Miami, FL	Private	52.2	1,200	8051
Hunt Memorial Hospital Dst	2365	Greenville, TX	Private	52.2	640	8062
Shelby Baptist Medical Center	2366	Alabaster, AL	Private	52.2	900	8062
San Leandro Hospital	2367	San Leandro, CA	Private	52.0	70	8361
Lahey Hitchcock Clinic	2368	Lebanon, NH	Private	52.0	NA	8011
Southside Virginia Training Ctr	2369	Petersburg, VA	Private	52.0	1,600	8361
United Presbt Hm At Syosset	2370	Woodbury, NY	Private	52.0	730	8051
Mckenzie-Willamette Hospital	2371	Springfield, OR	Private	52.0	750	8062
Weirton Medical Center Inc	2372	Weirton, WV	Private	51.8	800	8062
St Mary's Medical Center Inc	2373	Racine, WI	Private	51.8	1,120	8062
Sun Health Corporation	2374	Sun City, AZ	Private	51.8	NA	8062
Community Medical Center Inc	2375	Missoula, MT	Private	51.8	900	8062
West Anaheim Community Hosp	2376	Anaheim, CA	Public Family Member	51.6	650	8062
California Dept Mental Health	2377	Patton, CA	Private	51.6	NA	8063
Columbia/Hca Healthcare Corp	2378	Plano, TX	Public Family Member	51.6	NA	8062
Guthrie Clinic Ltd	2379	Sayre, PA	Private	51.6	1,000	8011
Marion General Hospital Inc	2380	Marion, OH	Private	51.6	1,250	8062

D&B COMPANY RANKINGS BY SALES

Company	Rank	Location	Type	Sales ($ mil.)	Employ-ment	Primary SIC
Allegheny Valley School	2381	Coraopolis, PA	Private	51.6	1,500	8361
Rosewood Medical Center Inc	2382	Houston, TX	Public Family Member	51.6	425	8062
Haywood Regional Medical Ctr	2383	Clyde, NC	Private	51.6	680	8062
Beloit Memorial Hospital Inc	2384	Beloit, WI	Private	51.5	950	8062
Thorek Hospital & Medical Ctr	2385	Chicago, IL	Private	51.5	600	8062
Southern Management Services	2386	Largo, FL	Private	51.5	400	8051
Visiting Nurse Assn Of Texas	2387	Dallas, TX	Private	51.4	1,400	8082
Community Gen Osteopathic Hosp	2388	Harrisburg, PA	Private	51.4	650	8062
Riverview Hospital	2389	Noblesville, IN	Private	51.4	750	8062
Clinical Laboratories Of Hawaii	2390	Hilo, HI	Private	51.3	400	8071
Memorial Hospital Of Albany Ny	2391	Albany, NY	Private	51.3	1,110	8062
Holyoke Hospital Inc	2392	Holyoke, MA	Private	51.3	772	8062
Ozarks Medical Center, Inc	2393	West Plains, MO	Private	51.2	800	8062
Williamson County Hospital	2394	Franklin, TN	Private	51.2	610	8062
St Clare Hospital Monroe Wisconsin	2395	Monroe, WI	Private	51.2	917	8062
Permanente Medical Group, Inc	2396	Anaheim, CA	Private	51.2	NA	8082
St Joseph's Medical Center	2397	Brainerd, MN	Private	51.2	4	8011
Murray-Calloway Cty Pub Hosp	2398	Murray, KY	Private	51.1	1,000	8062
Bon Secours, Inc	2399	Marriottsville, MD	Private	51.1	1,105	8062
Smithkline Beecham Clinical Labs	2400	Brea, CA	Private	51.1	NA	8071
Cullman Medical Center	2401	Cullman, AL	Private	51.1	710	8062
Hanover General Hospital	2402	Hanover, PA	Private	51.1	900	8062
Davis Memorial Hospital	2403	Elkins, WV	Private	51.1	620	8062
Mercy Medical Center Inc	2404	Roseburg, OR	Private	51.0	652	8062
Cleveland Clinic Florida Hosp	2405	Fort Lauderdale, FL	Private	51.0	850	8062
Personal Physician Care Inc	2406	Cleveland, OH	Private	50.9	125	8011
Bexar County Hospital Dst	2407	San Antonio, TX	Private	50.9	NA	8092
Dakota Heartland Health System	2408	Fargo, ND	Public Family Member	50.9	1,100	8062
H M Health Services	2409	Warren, OH	Private	50.9	1,100	8062
H T I Memorial Hospital Corp	2410	Madison, TN	Public Family Member	50.9	950	8062
Landmark Medical Center	2411	Woonsocket, RI	Private	50.9	1,100	8062
Liberty Health System Inc	2412	Baltimore, MD	Private	50.9	1,100	8062
Mercy Medical Ctr Of Oshkosh	2413	Oshkosh, WI	Private	50.9	1,100	8062
Mount Carmel Hospital (East)	2414	Columbus, OH	Private	50.9	1,100	8062
Provena Health	2415	Danville, IL	Private	50.9	NA	8062
Tenet Health System N Shore	2416	Miami, FL	Public Family Member	50.9	1,100	8062
Veterans Health Administration	2417	Chillicothe, OH	Private	50.9	NA	8062
Victory Memorial Hospital Inc	2418	Brooklyn, NY	Private	50.9	1,100	8062
Cryolife Inc	2419	Kennesaw, GA	Public	50.9	315	8099
Health Care Auth Cullman Cnty	2420	Cullman, AL	Private	50.9	699	8062
Suburban General Hospital	2421	Norristown, PA	Private	50.9	792	8062
Rutherford Hospital Inc	2422	Rutherfordton, NC	Private	50.7	850	8062
Lawrence Memorial Hospital	2423	Lawrence, KS	Private	50.7	1,000	8062
Columbia/Hca Healthcare Corp	2424	Nashville, TN	Public Family Member	50.7	NA	8062
Hempstead Gen Hospital & Med Ctr	2425	Hempstead, NY	Private	50.7	565	8062
Navy, United States Dept	2426	Great Lakes, IL	Private	50.7	NA	8062
Sisters Of St Francis Health Svcs	2427	Chicago Heights, IL	Private	50.7	NA	8062
Veterans Affairs Us Dept	2428	Madison, WI	Private	50.7	NA	8062
Veterans Health Administration	2429	Nashville, TN	Private	50.7	NA	8062
Veterans Health Administration	2430	Chicago, IL	Private	50.7	NA	8062
William Beaumont Hospital	2431	Troy, MI	Private	50.7	NA	8062
Phoenixville Hospital Inc	2432	Phoenixville, PA	Private	50.6	789	8062
Kapiolani Med Ctr	2433	Honolulu, HI	Private	50.6	1,027	8069
St Luke's Memorial Hospital	2434	Racine, WI	Private	50.6	1,095	8062
Bossier General Hospital	2435	Bossier City, LA	Private	50.6	700	8062
Titus County Hospital District	2436	Mount Pleasant, TX	Private	50.6	700	8062
Sumner Regional Health Systems	2437	Gallatin, TN	Private	50.6	700	8062
Little Flower Chld Svcs Of Ny	2438	Wading River, NY	Private	50.5	632	8361
Hutchinson Hospital Corp	2439	Hutchinson, KS	Private	50.5	800	8062
Department Of Navy	2440	Memphis, TN	Private	50.5	NA	8021
S L C O Inc	2441	San Leandro, CA	Public Family Member	50.4	600	8062
Sierra View Local Hospital Dst	2442	Porterville, CA	Private	50.4	600	8062
Kaiser Foundation Hospitals	2443	Vallejo, CA	Private	50.4	NA	8062
Veterans Health Administration	2444	Augusta, ME	Private	50.4	NA	8062
Veterans Health Administration	2445	Providence, RI	Private	50.4	NA	8062
Watsonville Community Hosp	2446	Watsonville, CA	Private	50.4	800	8062
Stouder Memorial Hospital Assn	2447	Troy, OH	Private	50.3	456	8062
Hebrew Home Aged	2448	Bronx, NY	Private	50.3	1,200	8059
Preferred Care, Inc	2449	Plano, TX	Private	50.3	2,700	8052
Veterans Health Administration	2450	Iowa City, IA	Private	50.3	NA	8062

D&B COMPANY RANKINGS BY SALES

Company	Rank	Location	Type	Sales ($ mil.)	Employ- ment	Primary SIC
Goshen Hospital Association	2451	Goshen, IN	Private	50.2	736	8062
Walker Baptist Medical Center	2452	Jasper, AL	Private	50.2	620	8062
Delta Regional Medical Center	2453	Greenville, MS	Private	50.2	723	8062
Kingston Hospital (Inc)	2454	Kingston, NY	Private	50.2	550	8062
Holzer Hospital Foundation	2455	Gallipolis, OH	Private	50.1	700	8062
Apl Healthcare Group Inc	2456	Las Vegas, NV	Private	50.1	1,050	8071
Baptist Healthcare System	2457	Paducah, KY	Private	50.1	NA	8062
South Nassau Communities Hosp	2458	Oceanside, NY	Private	50.1	1,085	8062
Northwest Medical Teams Intl	2459	Portland, OR	Private	50.1	34	8099
Genesee Region Home Care Assn	2460	Rochester, NY	Private	50.0	925	8082
Austin State Hospital	2461	Austin, TX	Private	50.0	962	8063
Community Hospital Of Andalusia	2462	Andalusia, AL	Public Family Member	50.0	323	8062
Healthplus Corporation	2463	Houston, TX	Private	50.0	400	8082
Hematlogy Onclogy Physcians Pc	2464	Tucson, AZ	Private	50.0	100	8011
Jewish Mem Hospital Rhblttion Ctr	2465	Boston, MA	Private	50.0	370	8069
Larkin Community Hospital Inc	2466	Miami, FL	Private	50.0	400	8062
McWil Group Ltd	2467	York, PA	Private	50.0	1,500	8059
Medical Assoc/Mnmnee Fls	2468	Menomonee Falls, WI	Private	50.0	700	8011
Neuro-Rehab Associates Inc	2469	Salem, NH	Private	50.0	450	8049
Pacin Healthcare-Hadley Mem Hosp	2470	Washington, DC	Private	50.0	350	8062
Provena Senior Services	2471	Kankakee, IL	Private	50.0	1,300	8052
Queens Long Island Medical Gr	2472	Hicksville, NY	Private	50.0	500	8011
Three Rivers Health Plans Inc	2473	Monroeville, PA	Private	50.0	195	8011
Western Plains Regional Hosp	2474	Dodge City, KS	Public Family Member	50.0	350	8062
Hudson Valley Hospital Center	2475	Cortlandt Manor, NY	Private	50.0	527	8062
Windham Community Memorial	2476	Willimantic, CT	Private	49.9	632	8062
Cuyahoga Falls General Hosp	2477	Cuyahoga Falls, OH	Private	49.9	825	8062
Audrain Health Care Inc	2478	Mexico, MO	Private	49.8	756	8062
Milford-Whtnsvlle Rgional Hosp	2479	Milford, MA	Private	49.8	1,218	8062
Allina Health System	2480	Minneapolis, MN	Private	49.8	NA	8062
Columbia Healthcare Of Centl Va	2481	Shawnee Mission, KS	Public Family Member	49.8	NA	8062
Trinity Regnl Hsptl	2482	Fort Dodge, IA	Private	49.7	825	8062
Columbia Memorial Hospital	2483	Hudson, NY	Private	49.7	1,000	8062
Ssm Health Care	2484	Blue Island, IL	Private	49.6	NA	8062
Harford Memorial Hospital Inc	2485	Havre De Grace, MD	Private	49.5	625	8062
El Paso Healthcare Systems	2486	El Paso, TX	Private	49.5	NA	8062
H C A Health Services Of Okla	2487	Oklahoma City, OK	Public Family Member	49.5	NA	8062
Harris County Hospital Dst	2488	Houston, TX	Private	49.5	NA	8062
Texas Health & Human Svcs Comm	2489	San Antonio, TX	Private	49.5	NA	8063
Memorial Hospital Of Salem, The	2490	Salem, NJ	Private	49.5	780	8062
West Orange Health Care Dst	2491	Ocoee, FL	Private	49.5	725	8062
Cumberland Medical Center Inc	2492	Crossville, TN	Private	49.5	778	8062
Ahs Hospital Corporation	2493	Passaic, NJ	Private	49.4	NA	8062
Crozer-Keystone Health System	2494	Ridley Park, PA	Private	49.4	NA	8062
El Centro Community Hospital	2495	El Centro, CA	Private	49.4	630	8062
Frankford Hospital Phila	2496	Philadelphia, PA	Private	49.4	NA	8062
Kaiser Foundation Hospitals	2497	Clackamas, OR	Private	49.4	NA	8062
Kaiser Foundation Hospitals	2498	Sacramento, CA	Private	49.4	NA	8062
Kaiser Foundation Hospitals	2499	Martinez, CA	Private	49.4	NA	8062
New York Cy Health Hspitals Corp	2500	New York, NY	Private	49.4	NA	8062
New York Cy Health Hspitals Corp	2501	New York, NY	Private	49.4	NA	8062
Pomona Unified School District	2502	Pomona, CA	Private	49.4	NA	8062
Salem Hospital	2503	Salem, OR	Private	49.4	NA	8062
Sisters Of Mercy Of Merion Pa	2504	Darby, PA	Private	49.4	NA	8062
Sisters Of Providence In Wash	2505	Yakima, WA	Private	49.4	NA	8062
Republic Health Corp Indanapolis	2506	Nashville, TN	Public Family Member	49.4	600	8062
Tuality Community Hospital	2507	Hillsboro, OR	Private	49.3	600	8062
American Baptist Homes	2508	Eden Prairie, MN	Private	49.3	1,340	8051
Vanguard Health Systems Inc	2509	Nashville, TN	Private	49.2	715	8011
Richardson Hospital Authority	2510	Richardson, TX	Private	49.2	624	8062
McLean Hospital Corporation	2511	Belmont, MA	Private	49.2	1,213	8063
Meadowlands Hospital Med Ctr	2512	Secaucus, NJ	Private	49.1	625	8062
Employees Retirement Sys St Louis	2513	Saint Louis, MO	Private	49.0	15	8051
North Carolina Dept Human	2514	Butner, NC	Private	49.0	NA	8063
Montgomery Regional Hospital	2515	Blacksburg, VA	Public Family Member	48.9	500	8062
Neomedica Inc.	2516	Chicago, IL	Public Family Member	48.9	450	8092
Aurelia Osborn Fox Memorial	2517	Oneonta, NY	Private	48.9	640	8062
Mercy Healthcare Sacramento	2518	Sacramento, CA	Private	48.9	NA	8062
Hospice Of Michigan Inc	2519	Southfield, MI	Private	48.9	800	8082
Lewistown Hospital	2520	Lewistown, PA	Private	48.8	760	8062

D&B COMPANY RANKINGS BY SALES

Company	Rank	Location	Type	Sales ($ mil.)	Employ-ment	Primary SIC
Comprehensive Cancer Centers	2521	Los Angeles, CA	Private	48.8	1,600	8093
Salick Health Care Inc	2522	Los Angeles, CA	Private	48.8	1,600	8093
Masonic Charity Foundation Of Nj	2523	Burlington, NJ	Private	48.8	600	8051
Finley Hospital, The	2524	Dubuque, IA	Private	48.8	900	8062
Rush Medical Foundation Inc	2525	Meridian, MS	Private	48.7	1,055	8062
Cayuga Medical Ctr At Ithaca	2526	Ithaca, NY	Private	48.6	704	8062
Heritage Hospital Inc	2527	Tarboro, NC	Public Family Member	48.6	300	8062
Oklahoma Ambulatory Care Corp	2528	Oklahoma City, OK	Private	48.6	NA	8011
Falmouth Hospital Association	2529	Falmouth, MA	Private	48.6	710	8062
Rice Memorial Hospital	2530	Willmar, MN	Private	48.6	800	8062
Mckenzie-Willamette Med Svcs	2531	Springfield, OR	Private	48.6	850	8062
Central Plains Clinic	2532	Sioux Falls, SD	Private	48.5	600	8011
St Francis Hospital Inc	2533	Jersey City, NJ	Private	48.5	600	8062
Carteret General Hospital	2534	Morehead City, NC	Private	48.5	800	8062
Fallston General Hospital Inc	2535	Fallston, MD	Private	48.4	775	8062
Bethesda Health Group Of St Louis	2536	Saint Louis, MO	Private	48.4	1,200	8051
Menninger Foundation Inc	2537	Topeka, KS	Private	48.4	1,100	8063
Kosciusko Community Hospital	2538	Warsaw, IN	Private	48.3	600	8062
Group Health Coop Of Puget Sound	2539	Seattle, WA	Private	48.3	NA	8011
Permanente Medical Group, Inc	2540	Fresno, CA	Private	48.3	NA	8011
Willamette Falls Hospital Inc	2541	Oregon City, OR	Private	48.2	715	8062
Riley Hospital Benevolent Assn	2542	Meridian, MS	Private	48.2	820	8062
Jennie Edmundson Mem Hosp	2543	Council Bluffs, IA	Private	48.2	800	8062
Eckerd Youth Alternatives Inc	2544	Clearwater, FL	Private	48.2	1,200	8361
Union Regional Medical Center	2545	Monroe, NC	Private	48.1	750	8062
Northstern Hospital Of Philadelphia	2546	Philadelphia, PA	Private	48.1	650	8062
Camino Medical Group Inc	2547	Sunnyvale, CA	Private	48.1	700	8011
Kelsey-Seybold Med Group Pa	2548	Houston, TX	Private	48.1	700	8011
North Suburban Clinic Ltd	2549	Skokie, IL	Public Family Member	48.1	700	8011
Premiere Associates Inc	2550	Clemmons, NC	Public Family Member	48.1	2,100	8051
Prevea Clinic Inc	2551	Green Bay, WI	Private	48.1	700	8011
Sister Of Mercy Of Clerm Count	2552	Batavia, OH	Private	48.1	764	8062
Bronx Harbor Health Care Complex	2553	Bronx, NY	Private	48.0	750	8051
Union Hospital Of Cecil Cnty	2554	Elkton, MD	Private	48.0	650	8062
Eden Park Health Services	2555	Albany, NY	Private	48.0	1,500	8051
Oregon Anesthesiology Group Pc	2556	Portland, OR	Private	48.0	161	8011
Putnam Hospital Center	2557	Carmel, NY	Private	48.0	1,039	8062
S P Acquisition Corp	2558	South Pittsburg, TN	Public Family Member	48.0	170	8062
Aiken Regional Medical Ctrs	2559	Aiken, SC	Public Family Member	47.9	1,038	8062
Skaggs Community Hospital	2560	Branson, MO	Private	47.9	530	8062
St Joseph Hospital	2561	Buffalo, NY	Private	47.8	856	8062
Southwstern Ill Health Fcilities	2562	Maryville, IL	Private	47.8	600	8062
Hanford Community Hospital	2563	Hanford, CA	Private	47.8	650	8062
Bayada Nurses Inc	2564	Moorestown, NJ	Private	47.8	3,000	8082
Family Aides Inc	2565	Hicksville, NY	Private	47.8	3,000	8082
Interim Healthcare-Morris Group	2566	Wilson, NC	Private	47.8	3,000	8082
Provident Health Services Inc	2567	Savannah, GA	Private	47.8	3,000	8082
Ephrata Community Hospital	2568	Ephrata, PA	Private	47.8	755	8062
C G H Medical Center	2569	Sterling, IL	Private	47.7	687	8062
Shepherd Good Home Inc	2570	Allentown, PA	Private	47.7	870	8361
American Medical Laboratories	2571	Chantilly, VA	Private	47.7	1,000	8071
City Of Ames	2572	Ames, IA	Private	47.7	NA	8062
Bon-Secours St Francis Xavier Hsp	2573	Charleston, SC	Private	47.7	1,052	8062
Fair Acres Geriatric Center	2574	Media, PA	Private	47.7	1,000	8059
Samaritan Health System Inc	2575	Clinton, IA	Private	47.7	950	8062
St. Marys Hospital Of Blue Sprng	2576	Blue Springs, MO	Private	47.7	550	8062
St Joseph's Hospital	2577	Elmira, NY	Private	47.6	1,050	8062
New Jersey Dept HumanSvcs	2578	Hammonton, NJ	Private	47.6	NA	8063
State Of New York	2579	Utica, NY	Private	47.6	NA	8063
Tucson General Hospital	2580	Tucson, AZ	Public Family Member	47.6	602	8062
Affiliated Community Med Ctrs PA	2581	Willmar, MN	Private	47.6	650	8011
St Mary Medical Center	2582	Walla Walla, WA	Private	47.5	546	8062
Delaware Valley Medical Ctr	2583	Langhorne, PA	Private	47.5	679	8062
Watts Health Foundation Inc	2584	Los Angeles, CA	Private	47.5	NA	8069
Aurora Med Ctr Of Sheboygan Cnty	2585	Sheboygan, WI	Private	47.5	703	8062
Franciscan Skemp Medical Ctr	2586	La Crosse, WI	Private	47.4	2,200	8062
Healthalliance Hospitals Inc	2587	Leominster, MA	Private	47.4	1,350	8062
Newnan Hospital	2588	Newnan, GA	Private	47.4	549	8062
Kingman Hospital Inc	2589	Kingman, AZ	Private	47.4	500	8062
Ihc Health Services Inc	2590	Salt Lake City, UT	Private	47.3	NA	8049

D&B COMPANY RANKINGS BY SALES

Company	Rank	Location	Type	Sales ($ mil.)	Employment	Primary SIC
Sacred Heart Hospital	2591	Eau Claire, WI	Private	47.3	1,025	8062
Wfsi-Illinois	2592	Wheaton, IL	Private	47.3	1,024	8062
Miller-Dwan Medical Center	2593	Duluth, MN	Private	47.2	834	8062
St Joseph Hospital, Eureka	2594	Eureka, CA	Private	47.2	617	8062
Medpartners Inc	2595	Riverside, CA	Public Family Member	47.2	NA	8011
St Anthony Memorial Hospital	2596	Effingham, IL	Private	47.1	566	8062
Adventist Health Sys/Snblt Corp	2597	Altamonte Springs, FL	Private	47.1	NA	8062
Montefiore Medical Center	2598	Bronx, NY	Private	47.1	NA	8011
University Of Medicine	2599	Newark, NJ	Private	47.1	NA	8011
Clinton Memorial Hospital	2600	Wilmington, OH	Private	47.1	750	8062
Bessemer Carraway Medical Ctr	2601	Bessemer, AL	Private	47.1	729	8062
Penobscot Bay Medical Assoc	2602	Portland, ME	Private	47.0	89	8093
St Nicholas Hospital	2603	Sheboygan, WI	Private	47.0	600	8062
Veterans Health Administration	2604	Asheville, NC	Private	47.0	NA	8062
Veterans Health Administration	2605	Chillicothe, OH	Private	47.0	NA	8062
Visiting Nurse Service System	2606	Runnemede, NJ	Private	47.0	1,300	8082
North Platte Neb Hospital Corp	2607	North Platte, NE	Private	46.9	525	8062
Shore Health Systems	2608	Easton, MD	Private	46.9	1,016	8062
State Of New York	2609	Buffalo, NY	Private	46.9	NA	8063
Connecticut Childrens Med Ctr	2610	Hartford, CT	Private	46.8	1,100	8069
Valley View Hospital Auth	2611	Ada, OK	Private	46.8	700	8062
Clallam Cnty Pub Hospital Dst 2	2612	Port Angeles, WA	Private	46.7	670	8062
St Marys Hospital	2613	Passaic, NJ	Private	46.7	900	8062
Jmes R Glidewell Dntl Ceramics	2614	Newport Beach, CA	Private	46.7	630	8072
South County Hospital Inc	2615	Wakefield, RI	Private	46.7	500	8062
Kishwaukee Community Hospital	2616	Dekalb, IL	Private	46.6	650	8062
Martin Luther Hospital	2617	Anaheim, CA	Private	46.6	683	8062
Polyclinic	2618	Seattle, WA	Private	46.6	423	8011
Drake Center	2619	Cincinnati, OH	Private	46.5	700	8093
Southern Ocean County Hosp	2620	Manahawkin, NJ	Private	46.5	600	8062
Scotland Memorial Hospital	2621	Laurinburg, NC	Private	46.5	517	8062
Hillcrest Health Center Inc	2622	Oklahoma City, OK	Private	46.5	875	8062
Yakima Valley Frm Wkrs Clinic	2623	Toppenish, WA	Private	46.5	650	8011
Ector County Hospital Dst	2624	Odessa, TX	Private	46.4	1,625	8062
Hebrew Rehabilitation Ctr For Aged	2625	Boston, MA	Private	46.4	830	8069
Ottumwa Regional Health Center	2626	Ottumwa, IA	Private	46.4	850	8062
Mercy Health Services	2627	Detroit, MI	Private	46.4	NA	8062
Primary Care Resources Inc	2628	Omaha, NE	Private	46.4	675	8011
Sisters Of St Francis Health Svcs	2629	Lafayette, IN	Private	46.4	NA	8062
Unimed Mgt Services-San Jose	2630	San Jose, CA	Private	46.4	675	8011
Arden Hill Hospital	2631	Goshen, NY	Private	46.4	785	8062
Divine Providence Hospital	2632	Williamsport, PA	Private	46.3	800	8062
Clearfield Hospital	2633	Clearfield, PA	Private	46.3	700	8062
Visionquest Nonprofit Corp	2634	Tucson, AZ	Private	46.3	900	8361
Memorial Hospital	2635	York, PA	Private	46.3	704	8062
Little Company Of Mary Of Indiana	2636	Jasper, IN	Private	46.3	780	8062
Robert Wood Johnson Univ Hosp	2637	Trenton, NJ	Private	46.2	600	8062
Aetna Health Plans Ill Inc	2638	Chicago, IL	Public Family Member	46.2	265	8011
Coshocton County Mem Hospital	2639	Coshocton, OH	Private	46.2	480	8062
St Mary's Hospital Ozaukee	2640	Thiensville, WI	Private	46.2	656	8062
Sonora Community Hospital	2641	Sonora, CA	Private	46.2	680	8062
North Country Health Services	2642	Bemidji, MN	Private	46.2	800	8062
T J Samson Community Hosp	2643	Glasgow, KY	Private	46.1	821	8062
Westerly Hospital	2644	Westerly, RI	Private	46.1	495	8062
Central Tennessee Hospital Corp	2645	Dickson, TN	Public Family Member	46.1	650	8062
Carter-Wallace, Inc	2646	Cranbury, NJ	Public Family Member	46.1	NA	8071
Flower Hospital	2647	Sylvania, OH	Private	46.1	1,000	8062
Hca Raleigh Community Hospital	2648	Raleigh, NC	Public Family Member	46.1	1,000	8062
Health Investment Corporation	2649	Long Beach, CA	Private	46.1	1,000	8062
Marion Community Hospital Inc	2650	Ocala, FL	Public Family Member	46.1	1,000	8062
Mary Black Health System, Inc	2651	Spartanburg, SC	Private	46.1	1,000	8062
Mary Black Memorial Hospital	2652	Spartanburg, SC	Private	46.1	1,000	8062
Morton Health Foundation Inc	2653	Taunton, MA	Private	46.1	1,000	8062
New Port Richey Hospital Inc	2654	New Port Richey, FL	Public Family Member	46.1	1,000	8062
Pacific Health Corporation	2655	Long Beach, CA	Private	46.1	1,000	8062
Phycor Of Rome Inc	2656	Rome, GA	Public Family Member	46.1	670	8011
Quorum Health Group Of Vicksburg	2657	Vicksburg, MS	Public Family Member	46.1	924	8062
St Anthony's Hospital	2658	Alton, IL	Private	46.1	1,000	8062
St Tammany Parish Hospital Dst 2	2659	Slidell, LA	Private	46.1	1,000	8062
Tenet Health System-Dallas	2660	Dallas, TX	Public Family Member	46.1	1,000	8062

D&B COMPANY RANKINGS BY SALES

Company	Rank	Location	Type	Sales ($ mil.)	Employ- ment	Primary SIC
Tuality Health Care	2661	Hillsboro, OR	Private	46.1	1,000	8062
Comprehensive Care Corporation	2662	Tampa, FL	Public	46.1	347	8011
Managed Care Usa, Inc	2663	Charlotte, NC	Private	46.1	155	8099
Puget Sound Blood Ctr Program	2664	Seattle, WA	Private	46.0	630	8071
Anesthesia Association Of Kansas	2665	Kansas City, MO	Private	46.0	109	8011
Health Care Industries Corp	2666	Dayton, OH	Private	46.0	1,000	8051
John Knox Village	2667	Lees Summit, MO	Private	46.0	950	8051
Columbia Four Rivers Med Ctr	2668	Selma, AL	Public Family Member	45.9	625	8062
North Carolina Dept Human	2669	Raleigh, NC	Private	45.9	NA	8063
State Of Maryland	2670	Baltimore, MD	Private	45.9	NA	8063
Brighton Marine Health Center	2671	Boston, MA	Private	45.9	31	8093
Kennewick Public Hospital Dst	2672	Kennewick, WA	Private	45.8	500	8062
New England Long-Term Care	2673	Boston, MA	Private	45.8	2,000	8051
Pleasant Care Corporation	2674	La Canada, CA	Private	45.8	2,000	8051
Virginia Dpt Mntl Health, Mr Sa	2675	Williamsburg, VA	Private	45.8	NA	8063
Grove Hill Medical Center Pc	2676	New Britain, CT	Private	45.8	425	8093
Grim Smith Hospital & Clinic	2677	Kirksville, MO	Private	45.8	850	8062
Saratoga Community Hospital	2678	Detroit, MI	Private	45.8	913	8062
Faxton Hospital	2679	Utica, NY	Private	45.7	950	8062
Sisters Of Providence In Cal	2680	Mission Hills, CA	Private	45.7	NA	8062
Faith Regional Health Services	2681	Norfolk, NE	Private	45.7	1,050	8062
Sutter Solano Medical Center	2682	Vallejo, CA	Private	45.7	542	8062
Bothwell Regional Health Ctr	2683	Sedalia, MO	Private	45.7	616	3062
Rockville General Hospital Inc	2684	Vernon Rockville, CT	Private	45.6	600	8062
City Of Lincoln	2685	Lincoln, NE	Private	45.6	NA	8062
Alegent Health-Mercy Hospital	2686	Council Bluffs, IA	Private	45.6	690	8062
Sutter Delta Medical	2687	Antioch, CA	Private	45.6	500	8062
Fair Acres Center	2688	Media, PA	Private	45.5	1,100	8361
Randolph Hospital Inc	2689	Asheboro, NC	Private	45.5	596	8062
Provena Health	2690	Waukegan, IL	Private	45.5	NA	8062
Mississippi M H Re Ctr	2691	Jackson, MS	Private	45.5	700	8062
Holy Cross Hospital Detroit Inc	2692	Detroit, MI	Private	45.5	765	8062
St Marys Hospital At Amsterdam	2693	Amsterdam, NY	Private	45.5	825	8062
Deaconess Long Term Care Of Mo	2694	Kansas City, MO	Private	45.4	1,850	8059
Des Moines General Hospital Co	2695	Des Moines, IA	Private	45.4	540	8062
Board Of Trustees Of Welborn	2696	Evansville, IN	Private	45.4	900	8011
Baptist Health	2697	North Little Rock, AR	Private	45.4	NA	8062
Tenet Healthcare Corporation	2698	Biloxi, MS	Public Family Member	45.4	NA	8011
Milford Hospital Inc	2699	Milford, CT	Private	45.3	500	8062
Presbyterian Seniorcare	2700	Oakmont, PA	Private	45.3	800	8051
Halifax Regional Hospital Inc	2701	South Boston, VA	Private	45.2	590	8062
Phoebe-Devitt Homes Inc	2702	Allentown, PA	Private	45.2	8	8051
Fairview Extended Care Svcs	2703	Pittsfield, MA	Private	45.2	900	8051
Blood Ctr Of Southeastern Wi Inc	2704	Milwaukee, WI	Private	45.2	400	8099
General Medical Services Corp	2705	Kingston, PA	Private	45.2	450	8011
Galen Of Arizona, Inc.	2706	Phoenix, AZ	Public Family Member	45.1	450	8011
North Carolina Dept Of Health	2707	Morganton, NC	Private	45.1	NA	8063
Verdugo Hills Hospital	2708	Glendale, CA	Private	45.0	450	8062
Cheshire Medical Center	2709	Keene, NH	Private	45.0	822	8062
Autumn Hills Convalescent Ctrs	2710	Houston, TX	Private	45.0	1,500	8051
Clinical Pathology Labs	2711	Austin, TX	Private	45.0	675	8071
Comprehensive Medical Imaging	2712	Westlake Village, CA	Public Family Member	45.0	400	8071
Heart Care Centers Of Ill S C	2713	Oak Forest, IL	Private	45.0	22	8011
Laureate Group Inc	2714	Waukesha, WI	Private	45.0	1,500	8051
Magella Healthcare Corporation	2715	Frisco, TX	Private	45.0	150	8011
Metroplex Adventist Hospital	2716	Killeen, TX	Private	45.0	700	8062
Sentage Corporation	2717	Minneapolis, MN	Private	45.0	950	8072
Olmsted Medical Center	2718	Rochester, MN	Private	45.0	650	8011
Fort Atkinson Mem Health Svcs	2719	Fort Atkinson, WI	Private	45.0	625	8062
St Francis Med Center-West	2720	Ewa Beach, HI	Private	44.9	581	8062
St Mary's Hospital	2721	Green Bay, WI	Private	44.9	571	8062
Armstrong County Mem Hosp	2722	Kittanning, PA	Private	44.9	870	8062
Deaconess Waltham Hospital	2723	Milton, MA	Private	44.9	NA	8011
H C A Health Services Of Fla	2724	Brooksville, FL	Public Family Member	44.9	NA	8062
City Hospital Association, The	2725	East Liverpool, OH	Private	44.8	650	8062
Pottsvlle Hospital Wrne Clinic Inc	2726	Pottsville, PA	Private	44.8	710	8062
Penobscot Bay Medical Center	2727	Rockport, ME	Private	44.8	752	8062
St Michaels Hospital	2728	Stevens Point, WI	Private	44.8	513	8062
Marshall Healthcare Authority	2729	Boaz, AL	Private	44.7	608	8062
Austin Diagnostic Clinic Assn, The	2730	Austin, TX	Private	44.7	650	8011

D&B COMPANY RANKINGS BY SALES

Company	Rank	Location	Type	Sales ($ mil.)	Employ-ment	Primary SIC
Primary Care Delivery Corp	2731	Muncie, IN	Private	44.7	650	8011
Jewish Child Care Assn Of Ny	2732	New York, NY	Private	44.6	500	8361
Cook Childrens Physician Netwrk	2733	Fort Worth, TX	Private	44.6	198	8011
Longwood Management Corp	2734	Los Angeles, CA	Private	44.6	2,000	8059
Progressive Home Health Svc	2735	New York, NY	Private	44.6	2,000	8059
Cortland Memorial Hospital	2736	Cortland, NY	Private	44.5	709	8062
Tenet Healthcare Corporation	2737	Redding, CA	Public Family Member	44.5	NA	8062
Sherman Oaks Health System	2738	Sherman Oaks, CA	Private	44.4	450	8062
Century Healthcare Corporation	2739	Tulsa, OK	Private	44.4	1,200	8063
Chw Central Coast	2740	Santa Maria, CA	Private	44.4	NA	8062
County Of Alameda	2741	San Leandro, CA	Private	44.4	NA	8062
Veterans Health Administration	2742	Sepulveda, CA	Private	44.4	NA	8062
Williamsport Hospital Med Ctr Inc	2743	Williamsport, PA	Private	44.4	NA	8062
Rome Memorial Hospital	2744	Rome, NY	Private	44.3	900	8062
Vencare Kentucky, Inc	2745	Louisville, KY	Private	44.3	900	8069
Griffin Health Services Corp	2746	Derby, CT	Private	44.3	1,100	8062
Coffee Regional Medical Center	2747	Douglas, GA	Private	44.1	530	8062
First Commonwealth, Inc.	2748	Chicago, IL	Public	44.1	55	8021
Memorial Hospital Of Un Cnty	2749	Marysville, OH	Private	44.1	500	8062
Our Lady Of Victory Hospital	2750	Lackawanna, NY	Private	44.1	750	8062
Hancock Mem Hospital & Health	2751	Greenfield, IN	Private	44.0	532	8062
Willow Valley Manor	2752	Lancaster, PA	Private	44.0	950	8361
Department Of Army	2753	Fort Belvoir, VA	Private	44.0	NA	8062
Memorial Clinic Ltd P.S.	2754	Olympia, WA	Private	44.0	400	8011
Ornda Healthcorp	2755	Miami, FL	Public Family Member	44.0	NA	8062
Pacifica Of The Valley Corp	2756	Sun Valley, CA	Private	44.0	525	8062
State Of Maryland	2757	Baltimore, MD	Private	44.0	NA	8062
Tenet Health System Medical	2758	West Palm Beach, FL	Public Family Member	44.0	NA	8062
Veterans Health Administration	2759	Charleston, SC	Private	44.0	NA	8062
Dale County Hospital Assn	2760	Ozark, AL	Private	43.9	350	8062
Du Bois Regional Medical Ctr	2761	Du Bois, PA	Private	43.9	NA	8011
Youville Life Care Inc	2762	Cambridge, MA	Private	43.9	750	8069
Healthsouth Of Virginia, Inc	2763	Richmond, VA	Public Family Member	43.8	550	8062
Adventist Health Systems Ga	2764	Calhoun, GA	Private	43.8	371	8062
Q P & S Clinic Sc	2765	Quincy, IL	Private	43.8	440	8011
Columbia/Hca John Randolph Med	2766	Hopewell, VA	Public Family Member	43.8	950	8062
Lapeer Regional Hospital	2767	Lapeer, MI	Private	43.8	950	8062
Ogden Medical Center Inc	2768	Ogden, UT	Public Family Member	43.8	950	8062
P H C-Salt Lake City Inc	2769	Salt Lake City, UT	Public Family Member	43.8	950	8062
St Mary-Rogers Memorial Hosp	2770	Rogers, AR	Private	43.8	726	8062
New York Hotel Trades Council	2771	New York, NY	Private	43.7	143	8011
Paracelsus-Davis Hospital	2772	Layton, UT	Public Family Member	43.7	500	8062
Pennsylvania Dept Pub Welfare	2773	Norristown, PA	Private	43.7	NA	8063
Joslin Diabetes Center Inc	2774	Boston, MA	Private	43.7	400	8011
South Bend Medical Foundation	2775	South Bend, IN	Private	43.7	500	8071
Qv Inc	2776	Chicago, IL	Private	43.6	1,300	8011
Roxborough Memorial Hospital	2777	Philadelphia, PA	Private	43.6	604	8062
Sentara Health System	2778	Norfolk, VA	Private	43.6	NA	8062
Visiting Nurses Association	2779	Philadelphia, PA	Private	43.6	400	8082
Mary Lanning Memorial Hospital	2780	Hastings, NE	Private	43.6	800	8062
United Physicians Health Netwrk	2781	Evansville, IN	Public Family Member	43.6	90	8011
Johnston Memorial Hospital	2782	Smithfield, NC	Private	43.5	582	8062
Eskaton Properties Inc	2783	Carmichael, CA	Private	43.4	900	8051
Gentle Dental Service Corp	2784	Vancouver, WA	Public	43.4	21	8021
Grace Living Centers	2785	Oklahoma City, OK	Private	43.4	1,900	8051
Bethany Ho Hospital Meth Ch	2786	Chicago, IL	Private	43.4	800	8062
Grays Harbor Community Hosp	2787	Aberdeen, WA	Private	43.4	550	8062
Alacare Home Health Services	2788	Birmingham, AL	Private	43.4	700	8082
Johnston Memorial Hospital	2789	Abingdon, VA	Private	43.4	525	8062
Fay-West Health System	2790	Mount Pleasant, PA	Private	43.4	2	8062
St Joseph Hospital Of Nashua Nh	2791	Nashua, NH	Private	43.3	1,200	8062
Mt Saint Mary's Hospital	2792	Lewiston, NY	Private	43.3	760	8062
Hospital Corp Northwest Inc	2793	Tucson, AZ	Public Family Member	43.3	940	8062
Primary Health Systems, Pa	2794	Cleveland, OH	Private	43.3	940	8062
Queens-Long Island Med Group	2795	Uniondale, NY	Private	43.3	630	8011
Fremont Area Medical Center	2796	Fremont, NE	Private	43.2	776	8062
Humana Mlitary Healthcare Svcs	2797	Louisville, KY	Public Family Member	43.2	628	8011
New York And Presbyterian Hosp	2798	New York, NY	Private	43.2	NA	8062
North Broward Hospital Dst	2799	Pompano Beach, FL	Private	43.2	NA	8062
Saad Enterprises Inc	2800	Mobile, AL	Private	43.1	1,000	8082

D&B COMPANY RANKINGS BY SALES

Company	Rank	Location	Type	Sales ($ mil.)	Employ-ment	Primary SIC
Advantage Care Inc	2801	Lexington, KY	Private	43.1	105	8011
Chelsea Community Hospital	2802	Chelsea, MI	Private	43.1	900	8062
Carondelet Health Network Inc	2803	Tucson, AZ	Private	43.1	NA	8062
Scottsdale Memorial Hospitals	2804	Scottsdale, AZ	Private	43.1	NA	8062
St Joseph Health Svcs Of Ri	2805	Providence, RI	Private	43.1	NA	8069
Tenet Healthcare Corporation	2806	Los Angeles, CA	Public Family Member	43.1	NA	8062
Morehead Memorial Hospital	2807	Eden, NC	Private	43.1	620	8062
Nicholas Demisay	2808	Staten Island, NY	Private	43.0	650	8051
Hospital Group Of America	2809	Wayne, PA	Public Family Member	43.0	761	8063
Vail Clinic, Inc	2810	Vail, CO	Private	43.0	500	8062
Ivonyx Group Services, Inc	2811	Livonia, MI	Private	43.0	160	8082
Nichols Inst Reference Labs	2812	SJ Capistrano, CA	Private	43.0	900	8071
Provena Hospital	2813	Kankakee, IL	Private	43.0	NA	8062
Massillon Community Hospital	2814	Massillon, OH	Private	43.0	875	8062
Barton Memorial Hospital	2815	South Lake Tahoe, CA	Private	43.0	658	8062
Bay Area Medical Center	2816	Marinette, WI	Private	43.0	570	8062
Warm Sprng Rhblttion Fundation	2817	San Antonio, TX	Private	43.0	600	8069
Harris Regional Hospital	2818	Sylva, NC	Private	42.9	700	8062
Cal Southern Presbyterian Homes	2819	Glendale, CA	Private	42.9	1,300	8051
Frontier Health Inc	2820	Johnson City, TN	Private	42.9	1,100	8063
Hillside Behavioral Health	2821	Rochester, NY	Private	42.9	1,200	8361
Northern Cal Presbt Homes	2822	San Francisco, CA	Private	42.8	600	8051
St Joseph Of The Pines Inc	2823	Southern Pines, NC	Private	42.8	1,500	8082
Yonkers General Hospital Inc	2824	Yonkers, NY	Private	42.8	600	8062
North Penn Hospital	2825	Lansdale, PA	Private	42.8	730	8062
Union HospitalAssn Of The Bronx	2826	Bronx, NY	Private	42.8	550	8062
Pleasant Valley Hospital, Inc.	2827	Point Pleasant, WV	Private	42.8	637	8062
Kennedy Krieger Childrens Hosp	2828	Baltimore, MD	Private	42.7	1,200	8069
Rehabclinics Inc	2829	King Of Prussia, PA	Public Family Member	42.7	1,400	8093
Satellite Dialysis Centers	2830	Redwood City, CA	Private	42.7	400	8092
Frisbie Memorial Hospital	2831	Rochester, NH	Private	42.7	507	8062
Aurora Medical Group, Inc	2832	Sheboygan, WI	Private	42.6	NA	8011
Dreyer Clinic Inc.	2833	Aurora, IL	Private	42.6	NA	8011
Friendly Hlls Health Care Netwrk	2834	La Habra, CA	Public Family Member	42.6	NA	8011
General Hospital Corporation	2835	Boston, MA	Private	42.6	NA	8011
Med-Health System	2836	Xenia, OH	Private	42.6	925	8062
Sun Coast Hospital Inc	2837	Largo, FL	Private	42.6	NA	8011
University Of Michigan	2838	Ann Arbor, MI	Private	42.6	NA	8011
Stillwater Medical Ctr Auth	2839	Stillwater, OK	Private	42.5	600	8062
Evergreen Healthcare Mgt Llc	2840	Vancouver, WA	Private	42.5	56	8051
Lakeview Center Inc	2841	Pensacola, FL	Private	42.5	600	8093
Visiting Nrse Srvc Of Rchstr	2842	Webster, NY	Private	42.4	1,073	8082
Fedcap Rehabilitation Services	2843	New York, NY	Private	42.4	1,400	8093
Sisters Of Providence In Ore	2844	Medford, OR	Private	42.4	NA	8062
State Of Maryland	2845	Sykesville, MD	Private	42.4	NA	8063
Ohio Valley General Hospital	2846	Mckees Rocks, PA	Private	42.4	459	8062
Wilkes Regional Medical Center	2847	North Wilkesboro, NC	Private	42.4	700	8062
Southwestern Vt Medical Center	2848	Bennington, VT	Private	42.4	650	8062
Diagnostic Ctr Hospital Corp Texas	2849	Houston, TX	Private	42.4	500	8062
Evangelical Community Hosp	2850	Lewisburg, PA	Private	42.3	760	8062
Civista Health Inc	2851	La Plata, MD	Private	42.3	668	8062
Lutheran Hospital	2852	Cleveland, OH	Private	42.3	880	8062
Illinois Dept Human Resources	2853	Kankakee, IL	Private	42.3	NA	8063
Illinois Dept Human Resources	2854	Elgin, IL	Private	42.3	NA	8063
Springwood Assoc Ltd Partnr	2855	East Aurora, NY	Private	42.3	1,900	8059
Baptist Health Centers, Inc	2856	Birmingham, AL	Private	42.3	800	8011
Center For Nursing Rehabilitation	2857	Far Rockaway, NY	Private	42.2	550	8051
Providence Hospital Inc	2858	Sandusky, OH	Private	42.2	700	8062
North Cntl Health Care Fcilities	2859	Wausau, WI	Private	42.2	900	8051
Baylor Med Center-Ellis Cnty	2860	Waxahachie, TX	Private	42.2	460	8062
Navajo Ntion Tribal Government	2861	Gallup, NM	Private	42.2	NA	8011
Provena Hospital	2862	Danville, IL	Private	42.2	NA	8062
Veterans Health Administration	2863	Fresno, CA	Private	42.2	NA	8069
Irvington General Hospital	2864	Irvington, NJ	Private	42.2	525	8062
Galesburg Cottage Hospital	2865	Galesburg, IL	Private	42.1	750	8062
Centegra Health System	2866	Mchenry, IL	Private	42.1	NA	8062
Christian Hospital NE-NW	2867	Saint Louis, MO	Private	42.1	NA	8062
Columbia/Hca Healthcare Corp	2868	Nashville, TN	Public Family Member	42.1	NA	8062
Detroit Osteopathic Hospital Corp	2869	Warren, MI	Private	42.1	NA	8062
Genesys Regional Medical Ctr	2870	Flint, MI	Private	42.1	NA	8062

D&B COMPANY RANKINGS BY SALES

Company	Rank	Location	Type	Sales ($ mil.)	Employ- ment	Primary SIC
Lake Hospital System Inc	2871	Willoughby, OH	Private	42.1	NA	8062
Mental Health, Department	2872	Saint Louis, MO	Private	42.1	NA	8062
Mercy Health Services	2873	Lansing, MI	Private	42.1	NA	8062
State Of New York	2874	Rochester, NY	Private	42.1	NA	8063
Veterans Health Administration	2875	Louisville, KY	Private	42.1	NA	8062
Veterans Health Administration	2876	Columbia, MO	Private	42.1	NA	8062
Bancroft Inc	2877	Haddonfield, NJ	Private	42.1	1,000	8361
Dickinson Cnty Health Care Sys	2878	Iron Mountain, MI	Private	42.1	630	8062
Watauga Medical Center Inc	2879	Boone, NC	Private	42.1	520	8062
East Texas Med Center-Athens	2880	Athens, TX	Private	42.1	353	8062
Frick Hospital & Community Health	2881	Mount Pleasant, PA	Private	42.1	750	8062
Community Health Counseling Svcs	2882	Bangor, ME	Private	42.0	1,069	8093
May Institute Inc	2883	South Harwich, MA	Private	42.0	1,000	8361
Mary Immaculate Hospital Inc	2884	Newport News, VA	Private	41.9	900	8062
Department Of Army	2885	Columbia, SC	Private	41.9	NA	8062
Quest Diagnostics Incorporated	2886	Cambridge, MA	Private	41.9	NA	8071
Community Behavioral Health Sys	2887	Metairie, LA	Public Family Member	41.8	850	8069
Licking Memorial Hospital	2888	Newark, OH	Private	41.8	908	8062
Moses Cone Health System Inc	2889	Greensboro, NC	Private	41.8	NA	8062
Rehablitation Inst Of Chicago	2890	Chicago, IL	Private	41.8	850	8069
Vencor, Inc	2891	Pasadena, TX	Private	41.8	NA	8069
Poplar Bluff Physicians Group	2892	Poplar Bluff, MO	Private	41.8	655	8062
Opelousas General Hospital	2893	Opelousas, LA	Private	41.7	580	8062
Berkshire Physicians Surgeons Pc	2894	Pittsfield, MA	Private	41.7	240	8011
Bradford Hospital Inc	2895	Bradford, PA	Private	41.7	650	8062
May Institute	2896	Fall River, MA	Private	41.7	64	8093
North Broward Hospital Dst	2897	Fort Lauderdale, FL	Private	41.7	NA	8062
Tenet Health System Medical	2898	Fort Lauderdale, FL	Public Family Member	41.7	NA	8062
Via Christi Health Partners	2899	Wichita, KS	Private	41.6	275	8011
Bethany Circle Of Kings Daughters	2900	Madison, IN	Private	41.6	800	8062
Kershaw County Medical Center	2901	Camden, SC	Private	41.6	550	8062
Lubbock Methodist Hospital Pra	2902	Lubbock, TX	Private	41.5	157	8011
Adventist Health Sys/Snblt Corp	2903	Fort Worth, TX	Private	41.5	NA	8062
Hunter Care Centers Inc	2904	Chesterfield, MO	Public Family Member	41.5	1,400	8051
Corning Hospital	2905	Corning, NY	Private	41.5	740	8062
Salo Inc	2906	Columbus, OH	Private	41.5	3,400	8082
Integra Health	2907	Des Moines, IA	Private	41.4	1,000	8011
Humility Mary Health System	2908	Youngstown, OH	Private	41.4	900	8062
Mount Marty Hospital Assn	2909	Yankton, SD	Private	41.4	900	8062
Palm Beach Gardens Community	2910	Palm Beach Gds, FL	Public Family Member	41.4	900	8062
St Catherine's Hospital Inc	2911	Kenosha, WI	Private	41.4	900	8062
University Of Minnesota	2912	Minneapolis, MN	Private	41.4	NA	8062
Heywood Henry Mem Hospital Inc	2913	Gardner, MA	Private	41.4	714	8062
American Hospital Mgt Corp	2914	Arcata, CA	Public	41.3	540	8062
Bert Fish Medical Center Inc	2915	New Smyrna Beach, FL	Private	41.3	NA	8062
Colorado Prmnt Med Group Pc	2916	Denver, CO	Private	41.2	600	8011
Fort Worth Medical Plaza Inc	2917	Fort Worth, TX	Public Family Member	41.2	NA	8062
Goddard Medical Associates Pc	2918	Brockton, MA	Private	41.2	600	8011
Meridian Medical Group Inc	2919	Atlanta, GA	Private	41.2	600	8011
Nalle Clinic Company	2920	Charlotte, NC	Private	41.2	600	8011
Prime Care Medical Group	2921	Victorville, CA	Private	41.2	600	8011
State Of Louisiana	2922	New Orleans, LA	Private	41.2	NA	8062
Vancouver Clinic Inc	2923	Vancouver, WA	Private	41.2	600	8011
Union Hospital Association	2924	Dover, OH	Private	41.2	634	8062
Gulf Coast Regional Blood Ctr	2925	Houston, TX	Private	41.1	550	8099
Triad Group Inc	2926	Yadkinville, NC	Private	41.1	1,800	8051
Vantage Healthcare Corporation	2927	Fort Smith, AR	Public Family Member	41.1	NA	8051
Tenet Healthsystem Hospitals	2928	Crystal River, FL	Public Family Member	41.1	450	8062
Shepherd Center Inc	2929	Atlanta, GA	Private	41.1	525	8069
Visiting Nurses Association, The	2930	Los Angeles, CA	Private	41.1	600	8082
Baylor Med Ctr At Grapevine	2931	Grapevine, TX	Private	41.1	450	8062
E P I Corporation	2932	Louisville, KY	Public	41.0	2,200	8052
Jsa Healthcare Corporation	2933	Saint Petersburg, FL	Private	41.0	350	8011
Laboratory Corp Amer Holdings	2934	Raritan, NJ	Private	41.0	NA	8071
Laboratory Corporation America	2935	Uniondale, NY	Public Family Member	41.0	NA	8071
Quest Diagnostics Incorporated	2936	Pittsburgh, PA	Private	41.0	NA	8071
Passavant Mem Area Hospital Assoc	2937	Jacksonville, IL	Private	41.0	670	8062
Emma L Bixby Medical Center	2938	Adrian, MI	Private	40.9	750	8062
Visiting Nurses Association	2939	Orlando, FL	Private	40.9	500	8082
Lake Of The Ozarks Gen Hosp	2940	Osage Beach, MO	Private	40.8	563	8062

D&B COMPANY RANKINGS BY SALES

Company	Rank	Location	Type	Sales ($ mil.)	Employ- ment	Primary SIC
Childrens Seashore House Inc	2941	Philadelphia, PA	Private	40.8	450	8361
Centra Health Inc	2942	Lynchburg, VA	Private	40.8	NA	8062
Hospital Auth Of Colquitt Cnty	2943	Moultrie, GA	Private	40.8	750	8062
Johnson Memorial Hospital	2944	Franklin, IN	Private	40.7	575	8062
Baptist Mem Healthcare Sys	2945	San Antonio, TX	Private	40.7	NA	8062
Indiana Fmly & Social Svcs Adm	2946	Butlerville, IN	Private	40.7	NA	8063
Mental Health, Department	2947	Fulton, MO	Private	40.7	NA	8063
Allegheny Univ Hospital Graduate	2948	Philadelphia, PA	Private	40.6	1,500	8062
Department Of Mental Health	2949	Cranston, RI	Private	40.6	NA	8063
South Florida Baptist Hospital	2950	Plant City, FL	Private	40.5	613	8062
William B Kessler Mem Hosp	2951	Hammonton, NJ	Private	40.5	650	8062
Jackson County Health Care Auth	2952	Scottsboro, AL	Private	40.4	458	8062
County Of Essex	2953	Cedar Grove, NJ	Private	40.4	NA	8063
Penn State Geisinger Wyoming	2954	Wilkes Barre, PA	Private	40.4	NA	8062
Virginia Dpt Mntl Health, Mr Sa	2955	Madison Heights, VA	Private	40.4	NA	8051
Missouri Delta Medical Center	2956	Sikeston, MO	Private	40.3	700	8062
United Medical Associates, Pc	2957	Johnson City, NY	Private	40.3	240	8011
Hannibal Regional Hospital	2958	Hannibal, MO	Private	40.2	550	8062
Columbia Hospital Corp Of S	2959	Fort Lauderdale, FL	Public Family Member	40.2	875	8062
Healthalliance Hospitals Inc	2960	Fitchburg, MA	Private	40.2	NA	8062
Health Care Solutions, Inc	2961	Ann Arbor, MI	Private	40.1	300	8082
Genesis Health Inc	2962	Jacksonville, FL	Private	40.1	500	8069
Asbury Methodist Village Inc	2963	Gaithersburg, MD	Private	40.1	875	8059
Florida Hospital/Fish Memorial	2964	Orange City, FL	Private	40.0	420	8062
Catholic Healthcare Partners	2965	Lorain, OH	Private	40.0	NA	8062
Columbia North Bay Hospital	2966	Aransas Pass, TX	Public Family Member	40.0	250	8062
Danbury Office Physcn Svcs Pc	2967	Danbury, CT	Private	40.0	280	8011
Desert Valley Medical Group	2968	Victorville, CA	Private	40.0	460	8011
Excelcare System Inc	2969	Bronxville, NY	Private	40.0	4	8099
H M A Louisburg Inc	2970	Louisburg, NC	Public Family Member	40.0	180	8062
Healthsouth Of Treasure Coast	2971	Vero Beach, FL	Public Family Member	40.0	245	8069
Holzer Clinic Inc	2972	Gallipolis, OH	Private	40.0	400	8011
Homecall Pharmaceutical Svcs	2973	Columbia, MD	Public Family Member	40.0	90	8082
Kemper National Services Inc	2974	Fort Lauderdale, FL	Private	40.0	1,000	8099
M C S A, L.L.C.	2975	El Dorado, AR	Private	40.0	700	8062
Medical Research Industries	2976	Fort Lauderdale, FL	Private	40.0	75	8049
Nai Community Hospital Of Phoenix	2977	Phoenix, AZ	Public Family Member	40.0	200	8062
Northwest Kidney Centers (Inc)	2978	Seattle, WA	Private	40.0	330	8092
Smt Health Services, Inc.	2979	Wexford, PA	Public	40.0	210	8071
St. Marys Dean Ventures Inc	2980	Madison, WI	Private	40.0	400	8011
United Care Inc	2981	Taylor, MI	Private	40.0	NA	8062
Virginia Physicians, Inc	2982	Richmond, VA	Private	40.0	60	8011
Winona Health Services Inc	2983	Winona, MN	Private	40.0	675	8062
Greenville Health Corporation	2984	Greenville, SC	Private	39.9	407	8011
New England Rhabilitation Hosp	2985	Woburn, MA	Public Family Member	39.9	805	8093
Manhattan Eye Ear Throat Hosp	2986	New York, NY	Private	39.9	480	8069
Healtheast Companies, Inc	2987	Saint Paul, MN	Private	39.9	2,500	8082
Regions Hospital	2988	Saint Paul, MN	Private	39.9	NA	8041
Howell Child Care Center Inc	2989	La Grange, NC	Private	39.9	1,400	8361
St James Mercy Hospital	2990	Hornell, NY	Private	39.9	975	8062
Americus Sumter County Hospital	2991	Americus, GA	Private	39.8	650	8062
Long Island Jewish Med Ctr	2992	Floral Park, NY	Private	39.8	NA	8063
New York, State	2993	Staten Island, NY	Private	39.8	NA	8063
Lifelink Corp	2994	Bensenville, IL	Private	39.8	725	8051
Physicians Health Network	2995	Evansville, IN	Public Family Member	39.7	4	8011
United Church Homes Inc	2996	Marion, OH	Private	39.7	1,100	8051
Fisher-Titus Medical Center	2997	Norwalk, OH	Private	39.7	500	8062
Fauquier Hospital Inc	2998	Warrenton, VA	Private	39.7	700	8062
Nemours Foundation (Inc)	2999	Wilmington, DE	Private	39.7	NA	8011
Peacehealth	3000	Eugene, OR	Private	39.7	NA	8049
Community Hospital Of Lancaster	3001	Lancaster, PA	Private	39.7	836	8062
Delta Dental Plan Of Tenn	3002	Nashville, TN	Private	39.6	21	8021
Adventist Health System/West	3003	Simi Valley, CA	Private	39.6	NA	8069
North Broward Hospital Dst	3004	Fort Lauderdale, FL	Private	39.6	NA	8011
Baptist Health Enterprises	3005	Miami, FL	Private	39.6	124	8011
Marshalltown Med Surgical Ctr	3006	Marshalltown, IA	Private	39.5	690	8062
Bon Secours Health System Inc	3007	Baltimore, MD	Private	39.5	NA	8062
Healthtrust Inc - Hospital Co	3008	Fort Lauderdale, FL	Public Family Member	39.5	NA	8062
Inova Health Care Services	3009	Fairfax, VA	Private	39.5	NA	8062
Medigroup Inc	3010	Newark, NJ	Private	39.5	575	8011

D&B COMPANY RANKINGS BY SALES

Company	Rank	Location	Type	Sales ($ mil.)	Employ-ment	Primary SIC
Sentara Hospitals-Norfolk	3011	Norfolk, VA	Private	39.5	NA	8062
Unity Physician Group Inc	3012	Bloomington, IN	Private	39.5	575	8011
East Oh Reg Hospital Mart Fer	3013	Martins Ferry, OH	Private	39.5	606	8062
North Arkansas Medical Center	3014	Harrison, AR	Private	39.5	713	8062
County Of Sonoma	3015	Santa Rosa, CA	Private	39.4	NA	8062
Kaiser Foundation Hospitals	3016	Fresno, CA	Private	39.4	NA	8062
North Shore University Hosp	3017	Forest Hills, NY	Private	39.4	NA	8062
Shawnee Hills Inc	3018	Charleston, WV	Private	39.4	900	8361
Howard Young Medical Center	3019	Woodruff, WI	Private	39.3	550	8062
Crittenden Hospital Assn	3020	West Memphis, AR	Private	39.3	436	8062
North Carolina Dept Human	3021	Goldsboro, NC	Private	39.3	NA	8063
Texas Health & Human Svcs Comm	3022	Abilene, TX	Private	39.3	NA	8361
Knox Community Hospital	3023	Mount Vernon, OH	Private	39.3	453	8062
Ukiah Adventist Hospital	3024	Ukiah, CA	Private	39.3	650	8062
Group Health Medical Assoc Pc	3025	Tucson, AZ	Private	39.3	500	8011
Community Memorial Hospital	3026	South Hill, VA	Private	39.3	726	8062
Um Holdings Ltd	3027	Haddonfield, NJ	Private	39.3	800	8099
Northern Hospital Dst Surry Cnty	3028	Mount Airy, NC	Private	39.3	610	8062
Baton Rouge Health Care Corp	3029	Baton Rouge, LA	Private	39.3	950	8082
Pharmchem Laboratories, Inc	3030	Menlo Park, CA	Public	39.2	350	8071
St Olaf Hospital Association	3031	Austin, MN	Private	39.2	700	8062
Promedica Physician Support	3032	Sylvania, OH	Private	39.2	570	8011
White County Medical Center	3033	Searcy, AR	Private	39.2	620	8062
Rose Care, Inc	3034	Rogers, AR	Private	39.2	1,500	8052
Southstern Ohio Regional Med Ctr	3035	Cambridge, OH	Private	39.1	653	8062
Galen Hospital Corporation Inc	3036	Corpus Christi, TX	Public Family Member	39.1	NA	8062
North General Home	3037	New York, NY	Private	39.1	1,600	8361
Paradigm Holdings Inc	3038	Concord, CA	Private	39.1	135	8093
County Of Bradley	3039	Cleveland, TN	Private	39.0	NA	8062
Doctors Med Center-San Pablo	3040	San Pablo, CA	Public Family Member	39.0	850	8062
Healthsouth Of Pittsburgh	3041	Monroeville, PA	Public Family Member	39.0	500	8093
Healthsouth Of York, Inc	3042	York, PA	Public Family Member	39.0	325	8069
Highland Health Systems Inc	3043	Lubbock, TX	Public Family Member	39.0	250	8062
North Fulton Medical Center	3044	Roswell, GA	Public Family Member	39.0	850	8062
Olean General Hospital Inc	3045	Olean, NY	Private	39.0	850	8062
Ssm Health Care	3046	Jefferson City, MO	Private	39.0	NA	8062
Valley Health Systems Llc	3047	Las Vegas, NV	Public Family Member	39.0	850	8062
Veterans Health Administration	3048	Marion, IN	Private	39.0	NA	8062
Sacred Heart-St Marys Hospital	3049	Rhinelander, WI	Private	39.0	650	8062
La Palma Hospital Medical Ctr	3050	La Palma, CA	Private	38.9	360	8062
Massachusetts Department	3051	Hathorne, MA	Private	38.9	NA	8361
Veterans Health Administration	3052	Tacoma, WA	Private	38.9	NA	8062
Diagnostic Laboratory Services	3053	Honolulu, HI	Private	38.9	470	8071
St Marys Hospital Of St Mrys Cnty	3054	Leonardtown, MD	Private	38.9	620	8062
St Francis Central Hospital	3055	Pittsburgh, PA	Private	38.9	600	8062
Morristown Hamblen Hospital	3056	Morristown, TN	Private	38.8	490	8062
U S Physical Therapy	3057	Houston, TX	Public	38.8	45	8049
Citizens General Hospital	3058	New Kensington, PA	Private	38.8	800	8062
Phoenix Bptst Hospital Med Ctr Inc	3059	Phoenix, AZ	Private	38.7	NA	8062
St Agnes Hospital	3060	White Plains, NY	Private	38.7	842	8062
Bio-Reference Laboratories Inc	3061	Elmwood Park, NJ	Public	38.7	420	8071
Hospital For Sick Children	3062	Washington, DC	Private	38.7	450	8069
Columbia Huntington Beach Med	3063	Huntington Beach, CA	Public Family Member	38.6	510	8062
New Milford Hospital Inc	3064	New Milford, CT	Private	38.6	415	8062
Lifemark Hospitals Of Missouri	3065	Columbia, MO	Public Family Member	38.6	840	8062
St Joseph Hospital	3066	Bangor, ME	Private	38.6	840	8062
New Mexico Department Health	3067	Las Vegas, NM	Private	38.5	NA	8063
Gateway Foundation Inc	3068	Chicago, IL	Private	38.5	800	8093
Aroostook Medical Center Inc	3069	Presque Isle, ME	Private	38.5	860	8062
Arrowhead Community Hospital &	3070	Glendale, AZ	Private	38.5	160	8062
Department Of Air Force	3071	Bellevue, NE	Private	38.4	NA	8062
Veterans Health Administration	3072	Leavenworth, KS	Private	38.4	NA	8062
Providence Milwaukie Hospital	3073	Milwaukie, OR	Private	38.3	272	8062
Accord Medical Management	3074	San Antonio, TX	Private	38.3	425	8062
Tenet Healthcare Corporation	3075	Los Alamitos, CA	Public Family Member	38.3	NA	8011
University Wisconsin System	3076	Madison, WI	Private	38.3	NA	8011
University Pittsburgh Med Ctr	3077	Braddock, PA	Private	38.3	600	8062
Shelby County Mem Hospital Assn	3078	Sidney, OH	Private	38.2	600	8062
Saint Lukes Northland Hosp	3079	Smithville, MO	Private	38.2	700	8062
New England Sinai Hospital	3080	Stoughton, MA	Private	38.2	520	8069

D&B COMPANY RANKINGS BY SALES

Company	Rank	Location	Type	Sales ($ mil.)	Employment	Primary SIC
Gettysburg Hospital Inc	3081	Gettysburg, PA	Private	38.2	590	8062
West Valley Medical Center Inc	3082	Caldwell, ID	Public Family Member	38.2	455	8062
Dimensions Health Corporation	3083	Hyattsville, MD	Private	38.1	NA	8082
Punta Gorda Hma Inc	3084	Punta Gorda, FL	Public Family Member	38.1	830	8062
Kateri Residence	3085	New York, NY	Private	38.1	612	8051
Rivington Hse Health Care Fcilty	3086	New York, NY	Private	38.1	350	8059
McAlester Regional Health Ctr Auth	3087	Mcalester, OK	Private	38.0	600	8062
Glen Mills Schools	3088	Concordville, PA	Private	38.0	448	8361
Daughters Jacob Nursing Home	3089	Bronx, NY	Private	38.0	525	8051
Great Lakes Health Plan Inc	3090	Southfield, MI	Private	38.0	150	8011
National Healthcare Lesville Inc	3091	Leesville, LA	Public Family Member	38.0	225	8062
Rehoboth Mc Kinley Christian	3092	Gallup, NM	Private	38.0	500	8062
Harrington Memorial Hospital	3093	Southbridge, MA	Private	38.0	800	8062
People Inc.	3094	Williamsville, NY	Private	38.0	1,500	8361
Indiana Fmly & Social Svcs Adm	3095	Fort Wayne, IN	Private	37.9	NA	8063
Odessa Hospital Ltd	3096	Odessa, TX	Private	37.9	350	8062
Rehabilitation Inst Of Mich	3097	Detroit, MI	Private	37.9	560	8069
Calvert Memorial Hospital	3098	Prince Frederick, MD	Private	37.8	400	8062
Strategic Health Services	3099	Charleston, WV	Private	37.8	485	8071
Hillside Manor Rehab & Extend	3100	Jamaica, NY	Private	37.8	320	8051
Adventist Health Sys/Snblt Corp	3101	Madison, TN	Private	37.8	NA	8062
Baptist Health System Inc	3102	Birmingham, AL	Private	37.8	NA	8062
Christie Building Inc	3103	Champaign, IL	Private	37.8	550	8011
Osf Healthcare System	3104	Bloomington, IL	Private	37.8	NA	8062
Provena Hospital	3105	Elgin, IL	Private	37.8	NA	8062
Sisters Of St Francis Health Svcs	3106	Memphis, TN	Private	37.8	NA	8062
Tidewater Phys Multi Group Pc	3107	Newport News, VA	Public Family Member	37.8	550	8011
Allina Self-Insured	3108	Hopkins, MN	Private	37.8	87	8011
Community Health Network, Inc	3109	Berlin, WI	Private	37.8	450	8062
Baltimore Medical System Inc	3110	Baltimore, MD	Private	37.8	270	8099
Jackson Cnty Schneck Mem Hosp	3111	Seymour, IN	Private	37.7	526	8062
Florida Dept Children Families	3112	Macclenny, FL	Private	37.7	NA	8063
Geneva General Hospital Inc	3113	Geneva, NY	Private	37.7	845	8062
Brigham Surgical Group Foundation	3114	Brookline, MA	Private	37.7	350	8011
Mary Rutan Hospital	3115	Bellefontaine, OH	Private	37.7	463	8062
Mesquite Community Hospital Lp	3116	Mesquite, TX	Private	37.6	583	8062
Otterbein Homes	3117	Lebanon, OH	Private	37.6	850	8361
Morton Plant Mease Health Svcs	3118	Clearwater, FL	Private	37.6	100	8011
Nemours Foundation (Inc)	3119	Wilmington, DE	Private	37.6	NA	8069
Symmes Hospital & Medical Ctr	3120	Arlington, MA	Private	37.6	450	8062
Buckner Baptist Benevolences	3121	Dallas, TX	Private	37.6	800	8361
Caldwell Memorial Hospital	3122	Lenoir, NC	Private	37.5	540	8062
Baptist Med Ctr Of The Beaches	3123	Jacksonville, FL	Private	37.4	501	8062
Physician Health Corporation	3124	Atlanta, GA	Private	37.4	250	8059
Spohn Kleberg Memorial Hosp	3125	Corpus Christi, TX	Private	37.3	350	8062
Associated Therapists Corp	3126	Naples, FL	Public Family Member	37.3	NA	8011
Oklahoma Cy Clinic A Prof Corp	3127	Oklahoma City, OK	Private	37.3	543	8011
Tenet Healthcare Corporation	3128	Delray Beach, FL	Public Family Member	37.3	NA	8062
Orthopedic Consultants, Pa	3129	Minneapolis, MN	Private	37.2	200	8011
Vna Care Network, Inc	3130	Waltham, MA	Private	37.2	250	8082
American Shared Hospital Svcs	3131	San Francisco, CA	Public	37.2	189	8099
Butler Hospital	3132	Providence, RI	Private	37.2	735	8063
Twin Cnty Rgional Health Clinics	3133	Galax, VA	Private	37.1	500	8011
Oswego Hospital Inc	3134	Oswego, NY	Private	37.1	650	8062
Jeannette District Mem Hosp	3135	Jeannette, PA	Private	37.1	725	8062
McKenna Memorial Hospital	3136	New Braunfels, TX	Private	37.0	460	8062
Johnson Memorial Hospital Inc	3137	Stafford Springs, CT	Private	37.0	750	8062
Mason City Clinic, P C	3138	Mason City, IA	Private	37.0	380	8011
Methodist Healthcare System	3139	San Antonio, TX	Private	37.0	NA	8062
Provena Hospital	3140	Aurora, IL	Private	37.0	NA	8062
Sheehan Memorial Hospital	3141	Buffalo, NY	Private	37.0	450	8062
Veterans Affairs Us Dept	3142	Shreveport, LA	Private	37.0	NA	8062
Veterans Health Administration	3143	Shreveport, LA	Private	37.0	NA	8062
Clifton Springs Sanitarium Co	3144	Clifton Springs, NY	Private	36.9	640	8062
Choicecare/Humana Corporation	3145	Cincinnati, OH	Public Family Member	36.9	538	8011
Ghs Osteopathic Inc	3146	Philadelphia, PA	Private	36.9	NA	8062
Henry Ford Health System	3147	Dearborn, MI	Private	36.9	NA	8011
Phycor Inc	3148	Lexington, KY	Public Family Member	36.9	NA	8011
Phycor Of Jacksonville, Inc	3149	Jacksonville, FL	Public Family Member	36.9	NA	8011
Qual-Med Inc	3150	Pueblo, CO	Private	36.9	NA	8011

D&B COMPANY RANKINGS BY SALES

Company	Rank	Location	Type	Sales ($ mil.)	Employ-ment	Primary SIC
Tenet Healthcare Corporation	3151	Los Gatos, CA	Public Family Member	36.9	NA	8062
University Mednet	3152	Cleveland, OH	Private	36.9	750	8069
Vencor, Inc	3153	Folsom, CA	Private	36.9	NA	8062
Chinese Hospital Association	3154	San Francisco, CA	Private	36.9	275	8062
Richmond Memorial Hospital	3155	Rockingham, NC	Private	36.8	516	8062
Carolina Mlt-Specialty Assoc P A	3156	Greenville, SC	Private	36.8	450	8011
Texas Health & Human Svcs Comm	3157	Terrell, TX	Private	36.8	NA	8063
Great Falls Clinic Llp	3158	Great Falls, MT	Private	36.8	390	8011
Masonic Home Of The Grand	3159	Philadelphia, PA	Private	36.8	938	8361
Correctnal Healthcare Solutions	3160	Chalfont, PA	Private	36.7	600	8093
Alvin Community Hospital, Inc.	3161	Alvin, TX	Public Family Member	36.7	800	8062
Baptist/St Anthony's Hospital	3162	Amarillo, TX	Private	36.7	800	8062
H C A Arlington Inc	3163	Arlington, TX	Public Family Member	36.7	800	8062
Massillon Health System Llc	3164	Massillon, OH	Private	36.7	800	8062
National Park Medical Center	3165	Hot Springs, AR	Public Family Member	36.7	800	8062
Q H G Of Ohio, Inc	3166	Columbus, OH	Public Family Member	36.7	800	8062
Youth & Family Centered	3167	Austin, TX	Private	36.7	1,500	8361
Lutheran Social Svcs Of S Inc	3168	Austin, TX	Private	36.7	1,079	8051
Louisiana Extended Care Ctrs	3169	Ridgeland, MS	Private	36.7	487	8051
Lincoln Medical Center	3170	Lincolnton, NC	Private	36.7	504	8062
Sentara Health System	3171	Norfolk, VA	Private	36.6	1,700	8062
Sansum Medical Clinic Inc	3172	Santa Barbara, CA	Private	36.6	450	8011
Jewish Childcare Association	3173	New York, NY	Private	36.6	600	8361
Alpena General Hospital	3174	Alpena, MI	Private	36.6	799	8062
Baldwin C E Shr Hsp Bd	3175	Fairhope, AL	Private	36.6	600	8062
St Francis Central Hospital	3176	Pittsburgh, PA	Private	36.5	500	8062
Columbia-Healthone L L C	3177	Denver, CO	Private	36.5	NA	8062
Renaissance Healthcare Corp	3178	Mechanicsburg, PA	Private	36.5	1,600	8051
Sisters Of Providence In Wash	3179	Centralia, WA	Private	36.5	NA	8062
Sisters Of Providence In Wash	3180	Centralia, WA	Private	36.5	NA	8062
Northeastern Pa Health Corp	3181	Hazleton, PA	Private	36.5	600	8062
Jackson Cnty Mem Hospital Tr Auth	3182	Altus, OK	Private	36.5	624	8062
Hospital Development & Service	3183	Fort Lauderdale, FL	Public Family Member	36.4	795	8062
Pennsylvania Dept Pub Welfare	3184	Polk, PA	Private	36.4	NA	8051
Community Health Ctr Of Branch	3185	Coldwater, MI	Private	36.4	390	8062
North Carolina Dept Human	3186	Kinston, NC	Private	36.3	NA	8051
Hebrew Home Of Greater Wash	3187	Rockville, MD	Private	36.3	700	8051
Grand Valley Health Plan Inc	3188	Grand Rapids, MI	Private	36.3	49	8011
Health Resources Corporation	3189	Naples, FL	Private	36.2	300	8071
Family Dental	3190	Cleveland, OH	Private	36.2	600	8021
Burke, Winifrd Mstrsn Rehab	3191	White Plains, NY	Private	36.2	600	8361
Portsmouth General Hospital	3192	Portsmouth, VA	Private	36.2	807	8062
Christian Church Campus	3193	Louisville, KY	Private	36.2	275	8059
Desert Valley Hospital	3194	Victorville, CA	Private	36.2	250	8062
Milton Hospital Inc	3195	Milton, MA	Private	36.2	435	8062
Joseph Hazleton-Saint Med Ctr	3196	Hazleton, PA	Private	36.1	600	8062
Dms Imaging Inc	3197	Fargo, ND	Public Family Member	36.1	158	8071
New York Community Hospital	3198	Brooklyn, NY	Private	36.0	375	8062
Bon Secours-Stuart Circle Hosp	3199	Richmond, VA	Private	36.0	400	8062
Community Hospitals Of Indiana	3200	Indianapolis, IN	Private	36.0	NA	8069
Diagnostic Clinic Houston, Pa	3201	Houston, TX	Private	36.0	346	8011
Facey Medical Group, Pc	3202	Mission Hills, CA	Private	36.0	525	8011
Florida Dept Children Families	3203	Arcadia, FL	Private	36.0	NA	8063
Phywell Inc	3204	Jacksonville, FL	Private	36.0	3	8099
Bethesda Lutheran Hospital	3205	Saint Paul, MN	Private	36.0	490	8062
Craig Hospital	3206	Englewood, CO	Private	36.0	525	8069
Lexington Health Care Group	3207	Farmington, CT	Public	35.9	1,000	8051
Mt Carmel Medical Center Inc	3208	Pittsburg, KS	Private	35.9	650	8062
Morningside Hse Nursing Hm Co	3209	Bronx, NY	Private	35.9	500	8051
Somerset Hospital Ctr For Health	3210	Somerset, PA	Private	35.8	562	8062
Unity Health Management Svcs	3211	Birmingham, AL	Private	35.8	815	8082
Lutheran Health System	3212	Mesa, AZ	Private	35.8	NA	8062
New York, State	3213	Orangeburg, NY	Private	35.8	NA	8063
Alameda Hospital	3214	Alameda, CA	Private	35.8	530	8062
Cobble Hill Nursing Home Inc	3215	Brooklyn, NY	Private	35.8	550	8051
North Adams Regional Hospital	3216	North Adams, MA	Private	35.7	560	8062
Baptist Healthcare System	3217	Corbin, KY	Private	35.7	NA	8062
Home Health And Hospice Carc	3218	Goldsboro, NC	Private	35.7	1,333	8059
Continue Care Home Health	3219	Hollandale, MS	Private	35.7	190	8082
Carnegie Partners Inc	3220	New York, NY	Private	35.7	500	8051

D&B COMPANY RANKINGS BY SALES

Company	Rank	Location	Type	Sales ($ mil.)	Employ-ment	Primary SIC
Guadalupe Valley Hospital	3221	Seguin, TX	Private	35.6	690	8062
Athens Limestone Hospital	3222	Athens, AL	Private	35.6	574	8062
Texas Health & Human Svcs Comm	3223	Vernon, TX	Private	35.6	NA	8063
St Joseph Health System	3224	Orange, CA	Private	35.6	7,650	8082
Orthopdic Neurological	3225	Los Gatos, CA	Private	35.5	1,200	8049
Reliant Care Group Llc	3226	Saint Louis, MO	Private	35.5	1,300	8051
Henry Medical Center	3227	Stockbridge, GA	Private	35.5	775	8062
Bensenville Home Socicty	3228	Bensenville, IL	Private	35.5	640	8051
Mid Coast Hospital	3229	Brunswick, ME	Private	35.5	370	8062
Degraff Memorial Hospital Inc	3230	North Tonawanda, NY	Private	35.5	695	8062
Peters Barnes-St Hospital	3231	Saint Peters, MO	Private	35.5	690	8062
Geriatrics Svc Cmplex Fndation	3232	Miami, FL	Private	35.4	700	8062
Tenet Health System Spalding	3233	Griffin, GA	Public Family Member	35.4	772	8062
Sampson Regional Medical Ctr	3234	Clinton, NC	Private	35.3	600	8062
Sunrise Community, Inc	3235	Miami, FL	Private	35.3	1,100	8052
Columbia El Drado Hospital Med	3236	Tucson, AZ	Public Family Member	35.3	532	8062
Iberia General Hospital & Med Ctr	3237	New Iberia, LA	Private	35.3	450	8062
Thompson Frderick Ferris Hosp	3238	Canandaigua, NY	Private	35.3	909	8062
Laughlin Memorial Hospital	3239	Greeneville, TN	Private	35.3	540	8062
Queen Of Peace Hospital	3240	Mitchell, SD	Private	35.3	696	8062
Care Group Inc	3241	New York, NY	Public	35.3	850	8082
Lockport Memorial Hospital	3242	Lockport, NY	Private	35.3	463	8062
Fayette Memorial Hospital	3243	Connersville, IN	Private	35.2	664	8062
Delaware Dept Health Social Svcs	3244	Smyrna, DE	Private	35.2	NA	8069
Moses Cone Health System Inc	3245	Greensboro, NC	Private	35.2	NA	8069
Tenet Healthcare Corporation	3246	Saint Petersburg, FL	Public Family Member	35.2	NA	8069
Nysarc, Inc	3247	Bohemia, NY	Private	35.2	800	8361
Touchmark Living Centers Inc	3248	Beaverton, OR	Private	35.2	1,250	8051
Bexar County Mental Health	3249	San Antonio, TX	Private	35.2	600	8051
Tahoe Forest Hospital Dst	3250	Truckee, CA	Private	35.2	328	8062
Upmc-Beaver Valley	3251	Aliquippa, PA	Private	35.1	700	8062
Caritas Norwood Hospital Inc	3252	Norwood, MA	Private	35.1	766	8062
Southern Illinois Hospital Svcs	3253	Carbondale, IL	Private	35.1	NA	8062
Englewood Community Hospital	3254	Englewood, FL	Public Family Member	35.1	550	8062
National Home Health Care Corp	3255	Scarsdale, NY	Public	35.1	2,000	8082
Hutchinson Clinic P A	3256	Hutchinson, KS	Private	35.1	405	8011
Healthsouth Of South Carolina	3257	Columbia, SC	Public Family Member	35.0	274	8069
Oneida Health Care Center	3258	Oneida, NY	Private	35.0	900	8062
Ken-Crest Services Inc	3259	Plymouth Meeting, PA	Private	35.0	1,100	8082
Columbia Chppnhm Mdcl Ctr	3260	Richmond, VA	Public Family Member	35.0	NA	8062
Consolidated Care Crew Home He	3261	San Antonio, TX	Private	35.0	535	8082
D & R Pharmaceutical Inc	3262	Louisville, KY	Public Family Member	35.0	230	8082
Department Of Army	3263	Ft Meade, MD	Private	35.0	NA	8062
Dorothy & David Schachne Institute	3264	Brooklyn, NY	Private	35.0	500	8059
Medicare Risk Network Llc	3265	Philadelphia, PA	Private	35.0	5	8011
National Healthcare Of Decatur	3266	Decatur, AL	Public Family Member	35.0	250	8062
One Call Medical, Inc	3267	Parsippany, NJ	Private	35.0	90	8011
Prairie Lakes Health Care Sys	3268	Watertown, SD	Private	35.0	500	8062
Veterans Health Administration	3269	Newington, CT	Private	35.0	NA	8062
Veterans Health Administration	3270	Easthampton, MA	Private	35.0	NA	8062
Boysville Of Michigan Inc	3271	Clinton, MI	Private	34.9	834	8361
Saint Elizabeth Community Hosp	3272	Red Bluff, CA	Private	34.9	406	8062
Community Hospital Of Ottawa	3273	Ottawa, IL	Private	34.9	550	8062
Feather River Hospital	3274	Paradise, CA	Private	34.9	683	8062
Langton Lake Place, Inc.	3275	Saint Paul, MN	Private	34.9	210	8051
Virginia Dpt Mntl Health, Mr Sa	3276	Petersburg, VA	Private	34.8	NA	8069
Glenoaks Medical Center	3277	Glendale Heights, IL	Private	34.8	625	8062
Polly Ryon Hospital Authority	3278	Richmond, TX	Private	34.8	363	8062
Memorial Hospital At Oconomowoc	3279	Oconomowoc, WI	Private	34.8	604	8062
Hepburn Medical Center Inc	3280	Ogdensburg, NY	Private	34.7	550	8062
Carter Blood Center Inc	3281	Fort Worth, TX	Private	34.7	150	8099
Scripps Health	3282	Chula Vista, CA	Private	34.7	NA	8062
Gaylord Farm Association	3283	Wallingford, CT	Private	34.7	566	8361
North Carolina Dept Human	3284	Butner, NC	Private	34.6	NA	8361
Unimed Mgt Services-San Jose	3285	Morgan Hill, CA	Private	34.6	NA	8011
Pekin Memorial Hospital	3286	Pekin, IL	Private	34.5	570	8062
Hospital Corp North Carolina	3287	Statesville, NC	Public Family Member	34.5	755	8062
Indian Path Hospital Inc	3288	Kingsport, TN	Public Family Member	34.5	755	8062
International Philanthropic Ho	3289	Granada Hills, CA	Private	34.5	420	8062
Quad-C Health Care Centers	3290	Tacoma, WA	Private	34.5	1,200	8051

D&B COMPANY RANKINGS BY SALES

Company	Rank	Location	Type	Sales ($ mil.)	Employment	Primary SIC
Sharp Temecula Valley	3291	Murrieta, CA	Private	34.5	481	8062
Natchez Regional Medical Ctr	3292	Natchez, MS	Private	34.4	500	8062
Visiting Nurse Service Of Ny	3293	New York, NY	Private	34.4	NA	8082
Visiting Nurse Service Of Ny	3294	New York, NY	Private	34.4	NA	8082
Northcrest Medical Center	3295	Springfield, TN	Private	34.4	410	8062
Southwest Jefferson Community	3296	Louisville, KY	Public Family Member	34.3	350	8062
Madera Community Hospital Inc	3297	Madera, CA	Private	34.3	500	8062
Ahp Holdings, Inc	3298	Hartford, CT	Public Family Member	34.3	500	8011
Allegheny Hospital Centenial	3299	Philadelphia, PA	Private	34.3	NA	8062
Allegheny University Hospital	3300	Elkins Park, PA	Private	34.3	NA	8062
Carolinas Physicians Network	3301	Charlotte, NC	Private	34.3	500	8011
Columbia/Hca Healthcare Corp	3302	Canoga Park, CA	Public Family Member	34.3	NA	8062
Comprehensive Med Care Ltd	3303	Minneapolis, MN	Private	34.3	500	8011
Department Of Navy	3304	Oceanside, CA	Private	34.3	NA	8069
Freeport Memorial Hospital	3305	Freeport, IL	Private	34.3	750	8062
Good Samaritan Medical Center	3306	Johnstown, PA	Private	34.3	553	8062
Health Assoc Of Ky, Inc	3307	Lexington, KY	Private	34.3	500	8011
Helian Health Group Inc	3308	Alpharetta, GA	Private	34.3	500	8011
Hospital Center At Orange, The	3309	Orange, NJ	Private	34.3	NA	8062
Kennedy Health Systems	3310	Stratford, NJ	Private	34.3	NA	8062
Mankato Clinic, Ltd	3311	Mankato, MN	Private	34.3	500	8011
Medical Prof Assoc Ariz Pc	3312	Phoenix, AZ	Private	34.3	500	8011
Mercy Health Ctr Of Manhattan	3313	Manhattan, KS	Private	34.3	750	8062
Michigan Medical P.C.	3314	Grand Rapids, MI	Private	34.3	500	8011
National Medical Hospital	3315	Lebanon, TN	Public Family Member	34.3	750	8062
Nhs National Health Services	3316	New York, NY	Private	34.3	500	8011
North Shore Health System	3317	Westbury, NY	Private	34.3	NA	8062
Our Lady Of Mercy Medical Ctr	3318	Bronx, NY	Private	34.3	NA	8062
P A Cardinal Healthcare	3319	Raleigh, NC	Private	34.3	500	8011
Phycor Of Lafayette, Llc	3320	Lafayette, IN	Public Family Member	34.3	500	8011
Phycor Of Wichita Falls, Inc	3321	Wichita Falls, TX	Public Family Member	34.3	500	8011
Pima County	3322	Tucson, AZ	Private	34.3	NA	8062
St Marys Regional Medical Ctr	3323	Russellville, AR	Public Family Member	34.3	750	8062
St Petrsburg Sncoast Med Group	3324	Saint Petersburg, FL	Private	34.3	500	8011
Team Care Inc	3325	Atlanta, GA	Public Family Member	34.3	500	8011
Veterans Health Administration	3326	North Hills, CA	Private	34.3	NA	8062
Methodst Hm Agng Wymg Cnf Nys	3327	Endicott, NY	Private	34.2	1,150	8051
Episcopal Retirement Homes	3328	Cincinnati, OH	Private	34.2	1,100	8361
American Health Care Centers	3329	Wadsworth, OH	Private	34.2	1,500	8051
Britwill Investments Ii Inc	3330	Scottsdale, AZ	Public Family Member	34.2	1,500	8051
Continuum Care Corporation	3331	Palm Beach Gds,FL	Private	34.2	1,500	8051
Covenant Care California Inc	3332	SJ Capistrano, CA	Private	34.2	1,500	8051
Medicalodges Of Kansas Inc	3333	Coffeyville, KS	Private	34.2	1,500	8051
Personacare Inc	3334	Louisville, KY	Private	34.2	1,500	8051
Homewood Retirement Center	3335	Williamsport, MD	Private	34.2	980	8051
McDonough County Hospital Dst	3336	Macomb, IL	Private	34.2	600	8062
Dearborn County Hospital	3337	Lawrenceburg, IN	Private	34.2	500	8062
Twin Cnty Regional Healthcare	3338	Galax, VA	Private	34.0	625	8062
Path Lab Inc	3339	Portsmouth, NH	Private	34.0	500	8071
South Crolina Dept Mental Health	3340	Columbia, SC	Private	34.0	NA	8011
Tenet Healthcare Corporation	3341	New Orleans, LA	Public Family Member	34.0	NA	8011
University Of Texas Health	3342	Houston, TX	Private	34.0	NA	8011
San Mateo Individual Practice	3343	San Bruno, CA	Private	34.0	30	8011
Los Angele Dev Serv	3344	Los Angeles, CA	Private	33.9	100	8099
Temple Hospital Inc	3345	Los Angeles, CA	Private	33.9	330	8062
State Of New York	3346	Ogdensburg, NY	Private	33.9	NA	8063
West Jersey Health System	3347	Marlton, NJ	Private	33.9	NA	8063
North Ottawa Community Hospital	3348	Grand Haven, MI	Private	33.9	510	8062
Baptist Hospital Orange	3349	Orange, TX	Private	33.9	358	8062
Texas Dept Criminal Justice	3350	Rusk, TX	Private	33.8	NA	8063
Sisters Of Charity Health Care	3351	Staten Island, NY	Private	33.7	400	8051
Riverview Hospital Assn	3352	Wisconsin Rapids, WI	Private	33.6	600	8062
Human Development Association	3353	Brooklyn, NY	Private	33.6	1,450	8082
Bcn-Health Central	3354	Lansing, MI	Private	33.6	490	8011
St Lukes Hospital Of Newburgh Ny	3355	Newburgh, NY	Private	33.6	736	8062
Wisconsin Dept Health Fmly Svcs	3356	Madison, WI	Private	33.6	NA	8361
Carrier Foundation Inc	3357	Belle Mead, NJ	Private	33.6	600	8063
Smyth County Community Hosp	3358	Marion, VA	Private	33.6	530	8062
Shore Memorial Hospital	3359	Nassawadox, VA	Private	33.6	600	8062
Illinois Valley Community Hosp	3360	Peru, IL	Private	33.5	540	8062

D&B COMPANY RANKINGS BY SALES

Company	Rank	Location	Type	Sales ($ mil.)	Employ- ment	Primary SIC
Covance Central Laboratory Ser	3361	Indianapolis, IN	Public Family Member	33.5	700	8071
Glenmark Associates Inc	3362	Morgantown, WV	Public Family Member	33.5	1,800	8052
H C A Health Services Tenn Inc	3363	Nashville, TN	Public Family Member	33.5	NA	8062
Henry Ford Health System	3364	Grosse Pointe, MI	Private	33.5	NA	8062
Mercy Health Services	3365	Port Huron, MI	Private	33.5	NA	8062
Nolachuckey-Hlst Mntl Ctr Inc	3366	Greeneville, TN	Private	33.5	1,100	8093
Sisters Of St Francis Health Svcs	3367	Michigan City, IN	Private	33.5	NA	8062
Truman Medical Center Inc	3368	Kansas City, MO	Private	33.5	NA	8062
Veterans Affairs Us Dept	3369	Madison, WI	Private	33.5	NA	8062
Western Reserve Care System	3370	Youngstown, OH	Private	33.5	NA	8062
Visiting Nurse Assn Of Del	3371	New Castle, DE	Private	33.5	1,070	8082
Visiting Nurse And Home Care	3372	Plainville, CT	Private	33.5	950	8082
York Hospital	3373	York, ME	Private	33.4	509	8062
Mariner Health Of Maryland	3374	Beltsville, MD	Public Family Member	33.4	1,500	8059
Marcus J Lawrence Medical Ctr	3375	Cottonwood, AZ	Private	33.4	460	8062
Southwest Medical Center	3376	Liberal, KS	Private	33.3	500	8062
Pioneers Mem Healthcare Dst	3377	Brawley, CA	Private	33.3	500	8062
Pressley Ridge Schools	3378	Pittsburgh, PA	Private	33.3	590	8361
Albany General Hospital, Inc	3379	Albany, OR	Private	33.2	550	8062
Frances Schervier Home & Hosp	3380	Bronx, NY	Private	33.2	500	8051
Baptist Mem Hospital-Desoto	3381	Southaven, MS	Private	33.2	550	8062
Four Winds Inc	3382	Katonah, NY	Private	33.1	700	8063
Lifelink Foundation Inc	3383	Tampa, FL	Private	33.1	281	8099
Cambridge Public Health Comm	3384	Somerville, MA	Private	33.1	NA	8062
Saint John's Mercy Hospital	3385	Washington, MO	Private	33.1	725	8062
Springfield Clinic	3386	Springfield, IL	Private	33.1	482	8011
St Jospehs Regional Med Ctr	3387	Lewiston, ID	Private	33.1	725	8062
Wilmac Corporation	3388	York, PA	Private	33.1	1,490	8059
Orthopedic Hospital Ltd	3389	Houston, TX	Private	33.1	230	8069
Chautauqua County Chapter Nys	3390	Jamestown, NY	Private	33.0	950	8093
University Anesthesiology & Cr	3391	Pittsburgh, PA	Private	33.0	130	8011
Dallas Cardiology Assoc Pa	3392	Dallas, TX	Private	33.0	105	8011
Fairview Hospital Healthcare Svcs	3393	Burnsville, MN	Private	33.0	NA	8062
Lifesource Blood Services	3394	Glenview, IL	Private	33.0	450	8099
Wyoming Health Services Inc	3395	Riverton, WY	Public Family Member	33.0	235	8062
Ozanam Hall Of Queens Nursing	3396	Bayside, NY	Private	33.0	600	8051
Urocor Inc	3397	Oklahoma City, OK	Public	33.0	340	8071
Campbell County Hospital Dst	3398	Gillette, WY	Private	32.9	463	8062
Fort Worth Osteopathic Hosp	3399	Fort Worth, TX	Private	32.9	720	8062
Berkshire Farm Center & Servic	3400	Canaan, NY	Private	32.9	521	8361
Health Care Mid-Clmba	3401	The Dalles, OR	Private	32.8	500	8062
Galen Of Florida, Inc	3402	Fort Walton Beach, FL	Public Family Member	32.8	NA	8062
National Home Care Inc	3403	West Orange, NJ	Public Family Member	32.8	2,053	8082
North Broward Hospital Dst	3404	Pompano Beach, FL	Private	32.8	NA	8062
Vencor Hospital East, Inc	3405	Arlington, VA	Private	32.8	NA	8062
Vencor, Inc	3406	Greensboro, NC	Private	32.8	NA	8062
Veterans Health Administration	3407	Fayetteville, NC	Private	32.8	NA	8062
Doctors Hospital A Ltd Partnr	3408	Springfield, IL	Private	32.8	475	8062
Doctors Osteopathic Med Ctr	3409	Fort Myers, FL	Public Family Member	32.8	510	8062
De Witt Nursing Home	3410	New York, NY	Private	32.8	621	8051
Veterans Health Administration	3411	Lake City, FL	Private	32.7	NA	8062
Wesley Health Systems Llc	3412	Hattiesburg, MS	Public Family Member	32.7	716	8062
Charter Real Behavioral Health Sys	3413	San Antonio, TX	Public Family Member	32.6	150	8063
Newton Health Systems Inc	3414	Covington, GA	Private	32.6	510	8062
Justice Resource Institute	3415	Boston, MA	Private	32.6	1,075	8361
Northstar Health Services Inc	3416	Indiana, PA	Public	32.6	802	8049
St Margaret's Hospital	3417	Spring Valley, IL	Private	32.6	430	8062
Marianjoy Inc	3418	Wheaton, IL	Private	32.6	800	8069
First Plan Of Minnesota	3419	Two Harbors, MN	Private	32.5	175	8011
Prairie Crdovascular Cons Ltd	3420	Springfield, IL	Private	32.5	150	8011
Department Of Army	3421	Hinesville, GA	Private	32.5	NA	8062
Tenet Healthcare Corporation	3422	Saint Louis, MO	Public Family Member	32.5	NA	8062
Williamsburg Community Hosp	3423	Williamsburg, VA	Private	32.5	NA	8062
Managed Healthcare Systems Nj	3424	Newark, NJ	Private	32.5	33	8011
Sutter Lakeside Hospital	3425	Lakeport, CA	Private	32.5	350	8062
Charleston Memorial Hospital	3426	Charleston, SC	Private	32.5	541	8062
Hospital Service District No 1	3427	Zachary, LA	Private	32.5	600	8062
Tsi Corp	3428	Milford, MA	Public Family Member	32.4	450	8071
Wayne Memorial Hospital Assn	3429	Honesdale, PA	Private	32.4	600	8062
Genesis Elder Care Rehab Servi	3430	Kennett Square, PA	Public Family Member	32.4	2,100	8049

D&B COMPANY RANKINGS BY SALES

Company	Rank	Location	Type	Sales ($ mil.)	Employ-ment	Primary SIC
Hugh Chatham Memorial Hospital	3431	Elkin, NC	Private	32.4	600	8062
Annie Penn Memorial Hospital	3432	Reidsville, NC	Private	32.4	500	8062
Institute Of Rehabiliataion	3433	Pittsburgh, PA	Private	32.3	484	8361
St Francis Hospital Of New Castle	3434	New Castle, PA	Private	32.3	620	8062
Unity Health, Inc	3435	Saint Louis, MO	Private	32.3	NA	8062
S C Cal	3436	Palestine, TX	Public Family Member	32.3	400	8062
Daytop Village Inc	3437	New York, NY	Private	32.3	700	8093
Pennock Hospital	3438	Hastings, MI	Private	32.3	505	8062
Sacramento Medical Foundation	3439	Sacramento, CA	Private	32.3	315	8099
Metropolitan Gvt Nshvl (Inc)	3440	Nashville, TN	Private	32.2	NA	8062
Pacificare Of California	3441	Salt Lake City, UT	Public Family Member	32.2	NA	8011
State Of New York	3442	Binghamton, NY	Private	32.2	NA	8361
Charter Professional Services	3443	Salem, MA	Private	32.1	5	8011
Sutter Coast Hospital	3444	Crescent City, CA	Private	32.1	400	8062
Health Resources Corp	3445	Santa Ana, CA	Public Family Member	32.1	400	8062
Firelands Community Hospital Corp	3446	Sandusky, OH	Private	32.1	703	8062
Hi-Desert Memorial Hospital Dst	3447	Joshua Tree, CA	Private	32.1	550	8062
Princeton Hospital	3448	Orlando, FL	Private	32.1	455	8062
Arcventures Inc	3449	Chicago, IL	Private	32.0	550	8082
Madonna Rehabilitation Hosp	3450	Lincoln, NE	Private	32.0	820	8069
L C Renalwest Llc	3451	Mesa, AZ	Private	32.0	350	8092
Bryn Mawr Rehabilitation Hosp	3452	Malvern, PA	Private	32.0	550	8069
Marlborough Hospital	3453	Marlborough, MA	Private	32.0	533	8062
Ahm Gemch, Inc	3454	El Monte, CA	Public Family Member	32.0	340	8062
Bestcare Inc	3455	Levittown, NY	Private	32.0	2,000	8082
Columbia-Arlington Healthcare Llc	3456	Reston, VA	Private	32.0	NA	8062
Heart Group Inc	3457	Lancaster, PA	Private	32.0	132	8011
Kendall Health Care Group Ltd	3458	Miami, FL	Private	32.0	702	8062
Metro West-Marlborough Health	3459	Marlborough, MA	Private	32.0	4	8062
Newcare Health Corporation	3460	Atlanta, GA	Private	32.0	272	8059
Preferred Health Management	3461	Woodland Hills, CA	Private	32.0	79	8099
Social Cncn Cmmittee	3462	Springfield Gdms, NY	Private	32.0	2,000	8082
Warrensville Development Ctr	3463	Cleveland, OH	Private	32.0	503	8059
Westchester General Hospital	3464	Miami, FL	Private	32.0	500	8062
Demac Corporation	3465	Warren, MI	Private	32.0	205	8011
Illini Manors Inc	3466	Galesburg, IL	Private	31.9	600	8051
Joint Township Dst Mem Hosp	3467	Saint Marys, OH	Private	31.9	460	8062
Walls Regional Hospital	3468	Cleburne, TX	Private	31.9	355	8062
Wayne Newark Community Hosp	3469	Newark, NY	Private	31.9	700	8062
Beaumont Hospital Inc	3470	Beaumont, TX	Public Family Member	31.9	700	8062
Caritas Southwood Hospital	3471	Norfolk, MA	Private	31.9	700	8062
Columbia Hospital Corp Ky	3472	Nashville, TN	Public Family Member	31.9	700	8062
Danforth Hospital, Inc	3473	Texas City, TX	Public Family Member	31.9	698	8062
Hospital Of Mercy Community	3474	Port Jervis, NY	Private	31.9	700	8062
Mediplex Of Connecticut Inc	3475	Newton, MA	Public Family Member	31.9	1,400	8051
Mercy Health System Of Kansas	3476	Fort Scott, KS	Private	31.9	700	8062
New Jersey Dept HumanSvcs	3477	Trenton, NJ	Private	31.9	NA	8063
Newport Health Care Corp	3478	Newport, RI	Private	31.9	700	8062
St. Mary Medical Center, Inc	3479	Hobart, IN	Private	31.9	700	8062
State Of New York	3480	Syracuse, NY	Private	31.9	NA	8063
West Paces Ferry Hospital Inc	3481	Atlanta, GA	Public Family Member	31.9	700	8062
Ssm Rehabilitation	3482	Saint Louis, MO	Private	31.9	230	8093
Friends Hospital	3483	Philadelphia, PA	Private	31.9	570	8063
Antietam Health Services Inc	3484	Hagerstown, MD	Private	31.8	460	8071
Hawaii Department Of Health	3485	Hilo, HI	Private	31.8	NA	8062
Sutter Health	3486	Merced, CA	Private	31.8	NA	8062
Tenet Healthcare Corporation	3487	Los Angeles, CA	Public Family Member	31.8	NA	8062
University Of Rochester	3488	Rochester, NY	Private	31.8	NA	8062
Vencor, Inc	3489	San Leandro, CA	Private	31.8	NA	8062
Veterans Health Administration	3490	Butler, PA	Private	31.8	NA	8062
C A Columbia/H Retreat Hosp	3491	Richmond, VA	Public Family Member	31.8	320	8062
Kingsbridge Heights Rehabilitation	3492	Bronx, NY	Private	31.8	350	8059
Duncan Regional Hospital Inc	3493	Duncan, OK	Private	31.8	550	8062
Florida Blood Services Inc	3494	Clearwater, FL	Private	31.7	500	8099
Plaza Employment Agency Inc	3495	Lynbrook, NY	Private	31.7	4,500	8082
Gnaden Huetten Memorial Hosp	3496	Lehighton, PA	Private	31.7	690	8062
New Jersey Dept HumanSvcs	3497	Woodbine, NJ	Private	31.7	NA	8361
St Joseph's Hospital Inc	3498	Tampa, FL	Private	31.7	NA	8069
Central Minn Group Health Plan	3499	Saint Cloud, MN	Private	31.7	305	8011
Crisp Regional Hospital	3500	Cordele, GA	Private	31.7	730	8062

D&B COMPANY RANKINGS BY SALES

Company	Rank	Location	Type	Sales ($ mil.)	Employ-ment	Primary SIC
Albert Einstein Medical Ctr	3501	Philadelphia, PA	Private	31.6	NA	8069
County Of Los Angeles	3502	Los Angeles, CA	Private	31.6	NA	8069
Aids Healthcare Foundation	3503	Los Angeles, CA	Private	31.6	270	8361
Southern Healthcare Systems	3504	Baton Rouge, LA	Private	31.5	634	8051
Southampton Memorial Hospital	3505	Franklin, VA	Private	31.5	440	8062
St Marys Regional Health Sys	3506	Saint Marys, PA	Private	31.5	500	8062
Peninsula United Methdst Homes	3507	Wilmington, DE	Private	31.5	1,100	8361
Tulare Local Hospital District	3508	Tulare, CA	Private	31.5	500	8062
Methodist Healthcare-Dyersburg	3509	Dyersburg, TN	Private	31.5	525	8062
Philadelphia Presbytery Homes	3510	Lafayette Hill, PA	Private	31.4	600	8361
Huntsville Memorial Hospital	3511	Huntsville, TX	Private	31.4	500	8062
Castle Dental Centers Inc	3512	Houston, TX	Public	31.4	800	8021
Crowne Investments Inc	3513	Monroeville, AL	Private	31.4	1,378	8051
Mercy Health Services	3514	Howell, MI	Private	31.4	NA	8062
Sisters Of Mercy Of Hamilton	3515	Hamilton, OH	Private	31.4	NA	8062
St Margret Mrcy Healthcare Ctrs	3516	Dyer, IN	Private	31.4	NA	8062
Vencor, Inc	3517	Chattanooga, TN	Private	31.4	NA	8062
Maria Parham Hospital Assn	3518	Henderson, NC	Private	31.4	373	8062
Beaver Dam Community Hospitals	3519	Beaver Dam, WI	Private	31.4	745	8062
Dominican Sisters Of Ontario	3520	Ontario, OR	Private	31.3	456	8062
Genesis Rehabilitation Hosp	3521	Jacksonville, FL	Private	31.3	422	8063
Bridgeport Health Care Center	3522	Bridgeport, CT	Private	31.3	550	8051
St Marys Regional Medical Ctr	3523	Saint Marys, PA	Private	31.3	660	8062
Pattie A Clay Infirmary	3524	Richmond, KY	Private	31.2	550	8062
Deaton Specialty Hospital & Hm	3525	Baltimore, MD	Private	31.2	475	8051
Russell Hospital Corp	3526	Alexander City, AL	Private	31.2	360	8062
California Dept Corrections	3527	Norco, CA	Private	31.2	NA	8361
Inova Health Care Services	3528	Alexandria, VA	Private	31.2	NA	8062
Silvercrest Extnded Care Fclty	3529	Jamaica, NY	Private	31.2	345	8051
Hse A Inglis Wheelchair Community	3530	Philadelphia, PA	Private	31.2	600	8361
St Josphs Community Hospital Of W	3531	West Bend, WI	Private	31.1	540	8062
Mdi Limited	3532	Monticello, IL	Private	31.1	1,000	8051
Wyoming County Community Hosp	3533	Warsaw, NY	Private	31.1	530	8062
Central Du Page Hospital Assn	3534	Glen Ellyn, IL	Private	31.1	NA	8011
Central Vermont Hospital, Inc	3535	Barre, VT	Private	31.1	683	8062
City Of Virginia	3536	Virginia, MN	Private	31.1	NA	8011
Columbia/Hca Healthcare Corp	3537	Laredo, TX	Public Family Member	31.1	NA	8011
Department Of Army	3538	Ft L Wood, MO	Private	31.1	NA	8062
Department Of Navy	3539	Pearl Harbor, HI	Private	31.1	NA	8011
Executive Office Of The	3540	Christiansted, VI	Private	31.1	NA	8062
Galen Of Kentucky Inc	3541	Somerset, KY	Public Family Member	31.1	NA	8062
Harvard Pilgrim Health Care	3542	Dedham, MA	Private	31.1	NA	8011
Henry Ford Health System	3543	Detroit, MI	Private	31.1	NA	8011
Phc/Chc Holdings Inc	3544	Salt Lake City, UT	Public Family Member	31.1	NA	8011
Saad Healthcare Services, Inc	3545	Mobile, AL	Private	31.1	800	8082
Trinity Medical Center West	3546	Steubenville, OH	Private	31.1	NA	8062
University Of Texas System	3547	Dallas, TX	Private	31.1	NA	8011
Hackettstown Community Hosp	3548	Hackettstown, NJ	Private	31.0	520	8062
Cabs Home Attendants Service	3549	Brooklyn, NY	Private	31.0	1,400	8082
Charter Behavioral Health	3550	Summit, NJ	Private	31.0	180	8063
Notami Hospitals Of California	3551	Nashville, TN	Public Family Member	31.0	680	8062
Odyssey Healthcare Inc	3552	Dallas, TX	Private	31.0	450	8069
Sierra Vista Hospital Inc	3553	San Luis Obispo, CA	Public Family Member	31.0	680	8062
Defiance Hospital Inc	3554	Defiance, OH	Private	31.0	350	8062
Family Healthcare Associates	3555	Arlington, TX	Private	30.9	450	8011
First Physcn Care Of Tampa Bay	3556	Tampa, FL	Private	30.9	450	8011
Frederick C Smith Clinic Inc	3557	Marion, OH	Private	30.9	450	8011
Kapiolani Med Ctr At Pali Mmi	3558	Aiea, HI	Private	30.9	450	8011
Massachusetts Dept Mental Health	3559	Westborough, MA	Private	30.9	NA	8063
Memorial Sisters Of Charity	3560	Houston, TX	Private	30.9	450	8011
Methodist Medical Group Inc	3561	Lubbock, TX	Private	30.9	450	8011
Mississippi Dept Mental Health	3562	Meridian, MS	Private	30.9	NA	8063
Lee County Community Hospital	3563	Pennington Gap, VA	Private	30.8	420	8062
Healthaccess Inc	3564	Greenville, NC	Private	30.8	80	8093
Sharon Hospital Incorporated	3565	Sharon, CT	Private	30.7	500	8062
Sierra Vista Community Hosp	3566	Sierra Vista, AZ	Private	30.7	500	8062
Eger Health Care Center	3567	Staten Island, NY	Private	30.7	655	8051
Capital Senior Living Inc	3568	Dallas, TX	Public	30.7	1,558	8059
Adventist Health Sys/Snblt Corp	3569	Killeen, TX	Private	30.7	NA	8062
State Of Louisiana	3570	Monroe, LA	Private	30.7	NA	8062

D&B COMPANY RANKINGS BY SALES

Company	Rank	Location	Type	Sales ($ mil.)	Employ-ment	Primary SIC
Memorial Medical Ctr Of W Mich	3571	Ludington, MI	Private	30.7	450	8062
Cambridge Memorial Hospital	3572	Cambridge, MN	Private	30.6	770	8062
Starr Commonwealth	3573	Albion, MI	Private	30.6	550	8361
Baptist Memorial Health Svcs	3574	Memphis, TN	Private	30.6	NA	8082
Columbia/Hca Healthcare Corp	3575	Miami, FL	Public Family Member	30.6	NA	8062
Dimensions Health Corporation	3576	Laurel, MD	Private	30.6	NA	8062
Miami Beach Healthcare Group	3577	Miami, FL	Private	30.6	NA	8062
Rockdale Health System Inc	3578	Conyers, GA	Private	30.6	671	8062
Scripps Health	3579	Encinitas, CA	Private	30.6	NA	8062
Tenet Healthcare Corporation	3580	Boca Raton, FL	Public Family Member	30.6	NA	8062
Gurwin, Rosalind And Joseph Je	3581	Commack, NY	Private	30.6	402	8059
Gillette Chld Spclty Healthcare	3582	Saint Paul, MN	Private	30.6	403	8069
Cigna Healthcare Of Louisiana	3583	Baton Rouge, LA	Public Family Member	30.6	40	8011
Barnes West County Hospital	3584	Saint Louis, MO	Private	30.6	200	8062
American Healthcorp Inc	3585	Nashville, TN	Public	30.5	650	8092
Florida Blood Services Inc	3586	Tampa, FL	Private	30.5	450	8099
Disablty Svcs Of The Southwest	3587	Fort Worth, TX	Private	30.5	1,000	8093
Physician Partners, Inc	3588	Corvallis, OR	Private	30.5	NA	8011
Vernon Home Health Care Agency	3589	Garland, TX	Private	30.5	1,000	8093
Three Rivers Community Hospital	3590	Grants Pass, OR	Private	30.5	613	8062
Santa Cruz Medical Clinic	3591	Santa Cruz, CA	Private	30.5	15	8011
Labette County Medical Center	3592	Parsons, KS	Private	30.4	402	8062
Mercy Medical A Corporation	3593	Daphne, AL	Private	30.4	750	8051
Parker County Hospital Dst	3594	Weatherford, TX	Private	30.4	405	8062
Louisiana Dept Health Hospitals	3595	Houma, LA	Private	30.4	NA	8062
Vencor, Inc	3596	Griffin, GA	Private	30.4	NA	8062
Veterans Health Administration	3597	Manchester, NH	Private	30.4	NA	8062
Lawrence Cnty Gen Hospital	3598	Ironton, OH	Private	30.4	543	8062
Caylor-Nickel Medical Center	3599	Bluffton, IN	Private	30.4	575	8062
Lexington Memorial Hospital	3600	Lexington, NC	Private	30.4	440	8062
Lake Region Healthcare Corp	3601	Fergus Falls, MN	Private	30.3	610	8062
Ahom Holdings, Inc (De)	3602	Brentwood, TN	Private	30.3	1,891	8082
Kaiser Foundation Hospitals	3603	Cleveland, OH	Private	30.3	NA	8062
New York Cy Health Hspitals Corp	3604	Staten Island, NY	Private	30.3	NA	8062
University Of South Alabama	3605	Mobile, AL	Private	30.3	NA	8062
Navapache Health Care Assn	3606	Show Low, AZ	Private	30.3	430	8062
Central California Foundation For	3607	Delano, CA	Private	30.2	450	8062
Newman Memorial County Hosp	3608	Emporia, KS	Private	30.2	490	8062
South Shore Hospital Corp	3609	Chicago, IL	Private	30.2	520	8062
Arl/Labsouth Inc	3610	Birmingham, AL	Private	30.2	630	8071
Cornwall Hospital Inc	3611	Cornwall, NY	Private	30.2	600	8062
Visiting Nrs Assoc Of Clev	3612	Cleveland, OH	Private	30.2	842	8082
Collom & Carney Clinic Assn	3613	Texarkana, TX	Private	30.1	400	8011
St Josephs Hospital	3614	Chippewa Falls, WI	Private	30.1	650	8062
Compunet Clinical Laboratories	3615	Dayton, OH	Private	30.1	405	8071
Columbia/Hca Healthcare Corp	3616	Mcallen, TX	Public Family Member	30.1	NA	8062
Laboratory Corporation America	3617	Cranford, NJ	Public Family Member	30.1	NA	8099
Lancaster Hospital Corporation	3618	Lancaster, SC	Public Family Member	30.1	660	8062
Los Angeles Doctors Hospital	3619	Los Angeles, CA	Private	30.1	450	8062
Tri-City Health Centre, Inc	3620	Dallas, TX	Private	30.1	436	8062
Amsterdam Memorial Hospital	3621	Amsterdam, NY	Private	30.0	480	8062
West Texas Medical Associates	3622	San Angelo, TX	Private	30.0	350	8011
Adirondack Medical Center	3623	Saranac Lake, NY	Private	30.0	530	8062
American Clinical Laboratories	3624	San Diego, CA	Private	30.0	300	8071
Columbia Bartow Memorial Hosp	3625	Bartow, FL	Private	30.0	245	8062
Dynacare Lab Pathology Llc	3626	Seattle, WA	Private	30.0	352	8071
Egh, Inc.	3627	Portland, OR	Public Family Member	30.0	283	8062
H M A Durant Inc	3628	Durant, OK	Public Family Member	30.0	350	8062
Home Attendant Vendor Agency Inc	3629	Brooklyn, NY	Private	30.0	1,200	8082
Huron Regional Medical Center	3630	Huron, SD	Private	30.0	400	8062
Interstate Blood Bank Inc	3631	Memphis, TN	Private	30.0	320	8099
Mental Health Corp Of Denver	3632	Denver, CO	Private	30.0	485	8093
Meris Laboratories, Inc	3633	San Jose, CA	Public	30.0	500	8071
Mid America Clinical Labs Llc	3634	Indianapolis, IN	Private	30.0	350	8071
Mid Valley Health Care Inc	3635	Lebanon, OR	Private	30.0	550	8062
Nordx	3636	Scarborough, ME	Private	30.0	350	8071
North Cntry Health Care Assoc I	3637	Lewiston, ME	Private	30.0	1,200	8051
Novaeon, Inc	3638	Paoli, PA	Private	30.0	450	8093
Optimum Rehabilitation Inc	3639	Boston, MA	Private	30.0	450	8093
Pentucket Medical Associates	3640	Haverhill, MA	Private	30.0	350	8011

D&B COMPANY RANKINGS BY SALES

Company	Rank	Location	Type	Sales ($ mil.)	Employ-ment	Primary SIC
Pueblo Physicians Pc	3641	Pueblo, CO	Private	30.0	195	8011
Quality Care & Rehab Inc	3642	Baton Rouge, LA	Private	30.0	362	8093
Quality Hm Hlt G Cst	3643	Biloxi, MS	Private	30.0	325	8082
Quest Diagnostics Incorporated	3644	Irving, TX	Private	30.0	NA	8071
Service Mstr Rehabilitation Lp	3645	Memphis, TN	Private	30.0	270	8093
Tandem Health Care Inc	3646	Jensen Beach, FL	Private	30.0	9	8051
Therapeutic Associates Inc	3647	Sherman Oaks, CA	Private	30.0	550	8049
Us Health Management Corp	3648	Melville, NY	Public Family Member	30.0	90	8071
William N Harwin Md Pa	3649	Fort Myers, FL	Private	30.0	108	8011
Woodland Park Hospital, Inc	3650	Portland, OR	Public Family Member	30.0	325	8062
Otero County Hospital Assn	3651	Alamogordo, NM	Private	30.0	400	8062
Berwick Hospital Center, Inc	3652	Berwick, PA	Private	29.9	650	8062
Dmc Health Care Centers Inc	3653	Novi, MI	Private	29.9	600	8011
Lutheran Home At Topton Pa Inc	3654	Topton, PA	Private	29.9	700	8361
Church Hmes Inc Congregational	3655	Hartford, CT	Private	29.9	600	8051
Teton County Hospital Dst	3656	Jackson, WY	Private	29.9	450	8062
Charles Cole Memorial Hosp	3657	Coudersport, PA	Private	29.9	583	8062
California Dept Mental Health	3658	Porterville, CA	Private	29.9	NA	8059
Sun Health Corporation	3659	Sun City, AZ	Private	29.9	NA	8062
University Of Nebraska	3660	Omaha, NE	Private	29.9	NA	8011
Vanguard Health Systems Inc	3661	Phoenix, AZ	Private	29.9	NA	8062
Oak Crest Village, Inc	3662	Baltimore, MD	Private	29.9	350	8059
Lakeview Memorial Hospital Assn	3663	Stillwater, MN	Private	29.9	450	8062
Massachusetts Eye & Ear Assoc	3664	Boston, MA	Private	29.9	4	8011
King's Daughters Hospital	3665	Brookhaven, MS	Private	29.8	460	8062
Chenango Memorial Hospital	3666	Norwich, NY	Private	29.8	526	8062
Methodist Healthcare Ministrie	3667	San Antonio, TX	Private	29.8	25	8011
Citizens Memrl Hsp Dst Plk Cnt	3668	Bolivar, MO	Private	29.8	600	8062
Castleview Hospital Inc	3669	Price, UT	Public Family Member	29.8	280	8062
Blood Centers Of Pacific	3670	San Francisco, CA	Private	29.7	400	8099
Meadow Regional Medical Center	3671	Vidalia, GA	Private	29.7	420	8062
G N Wilcox Memorial Hospital	3672	Lihue, HI	Private	29.7	653	8062
University Of Virginia	3673	Charlottesville, VA	Private	29.7	NA	8011
Henrietta D Goodall Hospital	3674	Sanford, ME	Private	29.6	500	8062
Canton-Potsdam Hospital	3675	Potsdam, NY	Private	29.6	480	8062
Bay Hospital Inc	3676	Panama City, FL	Public Family Member	29.6	650	8062
Northridge Hospital Medical	3677	Van Nuys, CA	Private	29.6	650	8062
Riverview Regional Medical Ctr	3678	Gadsden, AL	Private	29.6	650	8062
Statesboro Hma Inc	3679	Statesboro, GA	Public Family Member	29.6	650	8062
Wyeth Laboratories Inc	3680	Monmouth Junction, NJ	Public Family Member	29.6	NA	8071
Pacifica Hospital Care Center	3681	Huntington Beach, CA	Private	29.5	300	8062
Central Alabama Home Health Svcs	3682	Montgomery, AL	Private	29.5	300	8082
Lake Shore Hospital	3683	Irving, NY	Private	29.5	600	8062
Santa Marta Hospital Inc	3684	Los Angeles, CA	Private	29.5	430	8062
Christie Clinic Association	3685	Champaign, IL	Public Family Member	29.5	430	8011
Beaufort County Hospital Assn Inc	3686	Washington, NC	Private	29.5	500	8062
Legacy Mount Hood Medical Ctr	3687	Gresham, OR	Private	29.5	306	8062
Memorial Med Ctr At S Amboy	3688	South Amboy, NJ	Private	29.4	745	8062
Childrens Specialized Hospital	3689	Mountainside, NJ	Private	29.4	600	8069
Permanente Medical Group Inc	3690	Rockville, MD	Private	29.4	NA	8011
Vencor Hospital East, Inc	3691	Louisville, KY	Private	29.4	600	8069
Health Tech Affiliates Inc	3692	Memphis, TN	Private	29.4	400	8011
Boice-Willis Clinic Pa	3693	Rocky Mount, NC	Private	29.4	350	8011
Amisub Culver Union Hospital	3694	Crawfordsville, IN	Public Family Member	29.4	350	8062
Meriter Management Services	3695	Madison, WI	Private	29.4	351	8071
Hospital Affliates Of Alhambra	3696	Alhambra, CA	Private	29.3	400	8062
Comprehensive Care Mgt Corp	3697	Bronx, NY	Private	29.3	250	8051
Saint Eugene Community Hosp	3698	Dillon, SC	Private	29.3	300	8062
Warren General Hospital	3699	Warren, PA	Private	29.3	609	8062
Bronx Lebanon Hospital Center	3700	Bronx, NY	Private	29.3	NA	8062
Brooklyn Hospital Center (Inc)	3701	Brooklyn, NY	Private	29.3	NA	8062
County Of Jefferson	3702	Birmingham, AL	Private	29.3	NA	8062
Detroit Osteopathic Hospital Corp	3703	Trenton, MI	Private	29.3	NA	8062
Group Health Coop Of Puget Sound	3704	Seattle, WA	Private	29.3	NA	8062
Kennedy Health Systems	3705	Cherry Hill, NJ	Private	29.3	NA	8062
L I C H Corporation	3706	Brooklyn, NY	Private	29.3	NA	8062
Meridian Hospitals Corporation	3707	Brick, NJ	Private	29.3	NA	8062
St Luke's Medical Center Inc	3708	Cudahy, WI	Private	29.3	NA	8062
Stanislaus County	3709	Modesto, CA	Private	29.3	NA	8062
Sunnyside Home Care Project	3710	Sunnyside, NY	Private	29.3	1,200	8361

D&B COMPANY RANKINGS BY SALES

Company	Rank	Location	Type	Sales ($ mil.)	Employ- ment	Primary SIC
Universal Health Services	3711	Auburn, WA	Public Family Member	29.3	NA	8062
Veterans Health Administration	3712	Cincinnati, OH	Private	29.3	NA	8062
Laurens County Health Care Sys	3713	Clinton, SC	Private	29.3	380	8062
Garden Park Community Hospital L	3714	Gulfport, MS	Public Family Member	29.3	300	8062
Uvalde County Hospital Auth	3715	Uvalde, TX	Private	29.3	246	8062
Pine Rest Christian Hospital Assn	3716	Grand Rapids, MI	Private	29.3	500	8063
Maine Cast Rgnal Health Fclties	3717	Ellsworth, ME	Private	29.2	245	8062
Stephens County Hospital Auth	3718	Toccoa, GA	Private	29.2	414	8062
Florida Department Of Health	3719	Miami, FL	Private	29.2	NA	8093
North Carolina Dept Of Health	3720	Gastonia, NC	Private	29.2	NA	8093
Vencor, Inc	3721	Indianapolis, IN	Private	29.2	NA	8069
Home Health Foundation Inc	3722	Haverhill, MA	Private	29.2	1,000	8082
Moss Beach Homes, Inc	3723	Daly City, CA	Private	29.2	420	8361
Trustees Of Noble Hospital Inc	3724	Westfield, MA	Private	29.1	429	8062
Zandex Inc	3725	Zanesville, OH	Private	29.1	1,000	8052
Tenet Health System Hospitals	3726	Dallas, TX	Public Family Member	29.1	NA	8062
Mederi Inc	3727	Miami, FL	Private	29.1	200	8082
Morehouse General Hospital	3728	Bastrop, LA	Private	29.1	450	8062
Warren Clinic Inc	3729	Tulsa, OK	Private	29.1	390	8011
Hartwyck At Oak Tree Inc	3730	Edison, NJ	Private	29.0	595	8051
National Mentor Healthcare	3731	Quincy, MA	Private	29.0	NA	8361
Azalealand Nursing Home Inc	3732	Savannah, GA	Private	29.0	87	8051
Clinical Labs Of Colorado Llc	3733	Denver, CO	Private	29.0	370	8071
Colorado Sprng Health Prtners Pc	3734	Colorado Springs, CO	Private	29.0	468	8011
Hillside Children's Center	3735	Rochester, NY	Private	29.0	NA	8361
Ihc Health Services Inc	3736	Ogden, UT	Private	29.0	NA	8049
Ihc Health Services Inc	3737	Provo, UT	Private	29.0	NA	8049
Northwest Medical Center, Inc	3738	Pompano Beach, FL	Public Family Member	29.0	485	8062
Richmond Imging Affiliates Ltd	3739	Houston, TX	Private	29.0	120	8011
State Of New York	3740	Schenectady, NY	Private	29.0	NA	8361
Tenet Healthcare Corporation	3741	Mechanicsburg, PA	Public Family Member	29.0	NA	8069
Preferred Plus Of Kansas Inc	3742	Wichita, KS	Private	28.9	21	8011
Baptist Mem Healthcare Sys	3743	San Antonio, TX	Private	28.9	NA	8062
Bethesda Healthcare Inc	3744	Cincinnati, OH	Private	28.9	421	8011
Metropolitan Gvt Nshvl Inc	3745	Nashville, TN	Private	28.9	NA	8062
North Dakota Dept HumanSvcs	3746	Jamestown, ND	Private	28.9	NA	8062
South Broward Hospital Dst	3747	Hollywood, FL	Private	28.9	NA	8062
State Of Kansas	3748	Larned, KS	Private	28.9	NA	8063
Village Center For Care, Inc	3749	New York, NY	Private	28.9	1,050	8051
Clay Paracelsus County Hosp	3750	Celina, TN	Public Family Member	28.9	269	8062
Marymount Medical Center, Inc	3751	London, KY	Private	28.9	500	8062
Brea Development Company Ltd	3752	Brea, CA	Private	28.9	450	8062
Vaughan Regional Medical Ctr	3753	Selma, AL	Private	28.8	529	8062
Vaughan Regional Medical Ctr	3754	Selma, AL	Private	28.8	600	8099
Tenet Healthcare Corporation	3755	Lakewood, CA	Public Family Member	28.8	NA	8062
George H Lanier Memorial Hosp	3756	Valley, AL	Private	28.8	480	8062
Masonic Home, Inc	3757	Charlton, MA	Private	28.8	210	8051
Gateway Homecare, Inc	3758	Berwyn, PA	Private	28.7	1,000	8082
Heritage Enterprises Inc	3759	Bloomington, IL	Private	28.7	2,000	8051
Loris Community Hospital	3760	Loris, SC	Private	28.7	570	8062
Centracare Clinic	3761	Saint Cloud, MN	Private	28.7	500	8011
Corning Scicor Ltd Partnership	3762	Indianapolis, IN	Private	28.7	600	8071
Harvard Pilgrim Health Care	3763	Dedham, MA	Private	28.7	NA	8011
Houston Rehabilitation Inst	3764	Houston, TX	Public Family Member	28.7	250	8093
North Philadelphia Health Sys	3765	Philadelphia, PA	Private	28.7	NA	8062
Winona Community Memorial Hosp	3766	Winona, MN	Private	28.7	620	8062
National Jewish Med & Res Ctr	3767	Denver, CO	Private	28.7	980	8069
University Physicians Surgeons	3768	Huntington, WV	Private	28.6	400	8011
Bio-Medical Applications Of Texas	3769	Lexington, MA	Public Family Member	28.6	500	8092
Columbia Hospital L P	3770	West Palm Beach, FL	Private	28.6	630	8062
Medtox Laboratories Inc	3771	Saint Paul, MN	Public Family Member	28.6	223	8071
Medtox Scientific Inc	3772	Burlington, NC	Public	28.6	350	8071
Tenneese Dept-Mental Health	3773	Arlington, TN	Private	28.6	NA	8063
King's Daughters Hospital	3774	Yazoo City, MS	Private	28.6	190	8062
Columbia Med Ctr Of San Angelo	3775	San Angelo, TX	Public Family Member	28.6	650	8062
Veterans Health Administration	3776	Wichita, KS	Private	28.5	NA	8062
Minor & James Medical, Pllc	3777	Seattle, WA	Private	28.5	301	8011
Rest Haven Convlsnt Hm	3778	South Holland, IL	Private	28.5	900	8051
Deaconess Health Sys W Campus	3779	Saint Louis, MO	Private	28.5	650	8062
Sheltering Arm Hospital Fnd Inc	3780	Athens, OH	Private	28.4	368	8062

D&B COMPANY RANKINGS BY SALES

Company	Rank	Location	Type	Sales ($ mil.)	Employ-ment	Primary SIC
Smithvlle Healthcare Ventures Lp	3781	Smithville, TN	Private	28.4	120	8062
Smithkline Beecham Corporation	3782	Syosset, NY	Private	28.4	NA	8071
South Austin Medical Center	3783	Austin, TX	Public Family Member	28.4	625	8062
State University Of Ny	3784	Binghamton, NY	Private	28.4	NA	8071
Oktibbeha County Hospital	3785	Starkville, MS	Private	28.4	430	8062
Graham Hospital Association	3786	Canton, IL	Private	28.4	500	8062
Community Hospital Inc	3787	Mayfield, KY	Public Family Member	28.4	500	8062
Park Columbia Medical Group	3788	Minneapolis, MN	Private	28.3	275	8011
Adventist Health Sys/Snblt Corp	3789	Punta Gorda, FL	Private	28.3	NA	8062
Fletcher Hospital Inc	3790	Fletcher, NC	Private	28.3	622	8062
Sentara Hospitals-Norfolk	3791	Virginia Beach, VA	Private	28.3	NA	8062
St Lukes Hospital Of Bethlehem Pa	3792	Allentown, PA	Private	28.3	NA	8062
Tenet Health System Medical	3793	Garden Grove, CA	Public Family Member	28.3	NA	8062
Wayne Hospital Co Inc	3794	Greenville, OH	Private	28.2	346	8062
Mercy Med Ctr Of Williston	3795	Williston, ND	Private	28.2	450	8062
Kimball Day Hospital	3796	Putnam, CT	Private	28.2	620	8062
Clinical Reference Lab Inc	3797	Shawnee Mission, KS	Private	28.2	250	8071
Suburban General Hospital	3798	Pittsburgh, PA	Private	28.1	607	8062
Southboro Medical Group Inc	3799	Southborough, MA	Private	28.1	430	8011
Beverly Hospital Corp	3800	Danvers, MA	Private	28.1	NA	8011
Cigna Healthcare Arizona, Inc.	3801	Tucson, AZ	Public Family Member	28.1	NA	8011
Department Of Air Force	3802	Fafb, WA	Private	28.1	NA	8011
Genesis Health Ventures Inc	3803	Philadelphia, PA	Public Family Member	28.1	NA	8051
Pacificare Of California	3804	Cerritos, CA	Public Family Member	28.1	NA	8011
Utah Department Human Services	3805	Provo, UT	Private	28.1	NA	8063
Yale University	3806	New Haven, CT	Private	28.1	NA	8011
Lincoln Health System Inc	3807	Ruston, LA	Private	28.1	510	8062
Ryan William F Community Health	3808	New York, NY	Private	28.1	142	8099
Memorial Hospital Of Gardena	3809	Gardena, CA	Public Family Member	28.1	430	8062
Baptist Mem Hospital-Union Cy	3810	Union City, TN	Private	28.1	475	8062
Jackson County Hospital Inc	3811	Marianna, FL	Private	28.0	361	8062
South Mississippi Home Health	3812	Hattiesburg, MS	Private	28.0	750	8082
Saint Mary's Healthfirst	3813	Reno, NV	Private	28.0	100	8011
Atlanta Medical Clinic Llc	3814	Atlanta, GA	Private	28.0	300	8011
Capital Health Services Inc	3815	Fairfax, VA	Private	28.0	700	8099
Columbia Tops Surgical Hosp	3816	Houston, TX	Private	28.0	150	8062
Detroit Medical Center, The	3817	Detroit, MI	Private	28.0	NA	8062
Health Span Hm Care & Hospice	3818	Saint Paul, MN	Private	28.0	800	8082
Healthsouth Of Ft Lauderdale	3819	Fort Lauderdale, FL	Public Family Member	28.0	400	8069
Lafayette Regional Health Ctr	3820	Lexington, MO	Private	28.0	190	8062
Midamerica Healthcare, Inc	3821	Shawnee, OK	Private	28.0	430	8062
Oconomwoc Residential Programs	3822	Oconomowoc, WI	Private	28.0	1,000	8052
Vanderbilt Stallworth Rehabili	3823	Nashville, TN	Private	28.0	200	8361
Levindale Hebrew Geriatric Ctr	3824	Baltimore, MD	Private	28.0	461	8069
Evangelical Homes Of Michigan	3825	Detroit, MI	Private	28.0	670	8051
Behavioral Health, Inc.	3826	Baton Rouge, LA	Private	28.0	209	8093
Christian Homes Inc	3827	Lincoln, IL	Private	28.0	1,600	8051
Mercy Providence Hospital	3828	Pittsburgh, PA	Private	27.9	783	8062
Grady Memorial Hospital	3829	Chickasha, OK	Private	27.9	500	8062
St Francis Regional Med Ctr	3830	Shakopee, MN	Private	27.9	375	8062
Albert Einstein Medical Ctr	3831	Philadelphia, PA	Private	27.9	NA	8011
Integrated Living Communities	3832	Chicago, IL	Private	27.9	1,500	8052
Southside Community Hospital Assn	3833	Farmville, VA	Private	27.9	465	8062
State Of New York	3834	Binghamton, NY	Private	27.9	NA	8063
Virginia Dpt Mntl Health, Mr Sa	3835	Staunton, VA	Private	27.9	NA	8063
Whslc Realty Llc	3836	Chicago, IL	Private	27.9	1,500	8052
Taylor County Hospital	3837	Campbellsville, KY	Private	27.8	459	8062
Clearwater Community Hospital Lp	3838	Clearwater, FL	Private	27.8	270	8062
United Methodist Homes Of Nj	3839	Neptune, NJ	Private	27.8	600	8361
Veterans Health Administration	3840	Roseburg, OR	Private	27.8	NA	8062
Community Healthlink Inc	3841	Worcester, MA	Private	27.8	261	8093
Mineral Area Osteopathic Hosp	3842	Farmington, MO	Private	27.7	480	8062
Healthtrust Inc - Hospital Co	3843	Salt Lake City, UT	Public Family Member	27.7	NA	8062
Trustees Of Dartmouth College	3844	Hanover, NH	Private	27.7	NA	8062
Grant County Pub Hospital Dst No 1	3845	Moses Lake, WA	Private	27.7	470	8062
Pulaski Community Hospital	3846	Pulaski, VA	Public Family Member	27.7	450	8062
Valdese General Hospital Inc	3847	Valdese, NC	Private	27.7	475	8062
Oklahoma Blood Institute Inc	3848	Oklahoma City, OK	Private	27.7	450	8099
Sonoma Valley Healthcare Dst	3849	Sonoma, CA	Private	27.6	500	8062
Canonsburg General Hospital	3850	Canonsburg, PA	Private	27.6	423	8062

D&B COMPANY RANKINGS BY SALES

Company	Rank	Location	Type	Sales ($ mil.)	Employment	Primary SIC
South Dade Healthcare Group	3851	Miami, FL	Public Family Member	27.6	607	8062
Brigham Med Group Foundation	3852	Brookline, MA	Private	27.6	400	8093
Adams County Memorial Hospital	3853	Decatur, IN	Private	27.6	400	8062
St Josephs Hospital Nursing	3854	Yonkers, NY	Private	27.6	320	8051
Department Of Army	3855	Fort Riley, KS	Private	27.5	NA	8062
Healthsouth Of Austin, Inc	3856	Austin, TX	Public Family Member	27.5	350	8069
Prh, Inc.	3857	Rochester, NY	Private	27.5	312	8071
Cambridge Hospital Prof Svcs Corp	3858	Somerville, MA	Private	27.4	100	8011
Dedham Medical Associates Inc	3859	Dedham, MA	Private	27.4	400	8011
Diabetes Treatment Ctrs Of America	3860	Nashville, TN	Public Family Member	27.4	400	8011
Doc's Physicians Affiliated	3861	Valhalla, NY	Private	27.4	600	8011
Executive Health Group, Md Pc	3862	New York, NY	Private	27.4	400	8011
Family Planning Assoc Med Group	3863	Long Beach, CA	Private	27.4	400	8011
Health Midwest Ventures Group	3864	Kansas City, MO	Private	27.4	400	8011
Integrated Health Assoc Pc	3865	Ann Arbor, MI	Private	27.4	400	8011
Kingsboro Medical Group P C	3866	Brooklyn, NY	Private	27.4	400	8011
Medical Corporation America	3867	Nashville, TN	Public Family Member	27.4	400	8011
Oregon Medical Group Pc	3868	Eugene, OR	Private	27.4	400	8011
Presbyterian Healthcare Assoc	3869	Charlotte, NC	Private	27.4	400	8011
Rice Clinic S C, The	3870	Stevens Point, WI	Private	27.4	400	8011
Shannon Clinic	3871	San Angelo, TX	Private	27.4	400	8011
Suburban Heights Med Ctr Sc	3872	Chicago Heights, IL	Private	27.4	400	8011
Northern Montana Hospital	3873	Havre, MT	Private	27.4	385	8062
Newaygo County Gen Hospital Assn	3874	Fremont, MI	Private	27.4	500	8062
Methodist Children's Hospital	3875	Lubbock, TX	Private	27.3	200	8069
Albany County Hospital Dst	3876	Laramie, WY	Private	27.3	425	8062
Beverly Entrprss-Connecticut Inc	3877	Fort Smith, AR	Public Family Member	27.3	1,200	8051
Cantex Health Care Centers	3878	Dallas, TX	Private	27.3	1,200	8051
Vencare Kentucky, Inc	3879	Arlington, VA	Private	27.3	NA	8069
Culpeper Memorial Hospital Inc	3880	Culpeper, VA	Private	27.3	520	8062
Val Verde County Hospital Dst	3881	Del Rio, TX	Private	27.3	341	8062
Dunn Memorial Hospital	3882	Bedford, IN	Private	27.3	485	8062
John Heinz Institute	3883	Wilkes Barre, PA	Private	27.3	345	8361
Wesley Woods Geriatric Hosp	3884	Atlanta, GA	Private	27.2	301	8062
Semmes-Murphey Clinic Pc	3885	Memphis, TN	Private	27.2	254	8011
Alabama Department Mental Health	3886	Mount Vernon, AL	Private	27.2	NA	8063
Amisub (Irvine Medical Center)	3887	Irvine, CA	Private	27.2	600	8062
Bethesda Lutheran Medical Ctr	3888	Saint Paul, MN	Private	27.2	600	8062
Columbia Hospital Corp Bay Area	3889	Corpus Christi, TX	Public Family Member	27.2	600	8062
Columbia Putnam Hospital Inc	3890	Palatka, FL	Public Family Member	27.2	525	8062
Hospitals Of National Medical	3891	Tullahoma, TN	Public Family Member	27.2	600	8062
Longview Regional Hospital	3892	Longview, TX	Public Family Member	27.2	600	8062
Missouri Health Care Systems Lp	3893	Springfield, MO	Private	27.2	600	8062
Peterson Sid Memorial Hosp	3894	Kerrville, TX	Private	27.2	600	8062
Riverside Health Systems Inc	3895	Wichita, KS	Private	27.2	600	8062
Sharp Cabrillo Hospital	3896	San Diego, CA	Private	27.2	600	8062
Wayne Newark Community Hosp	3897	Newark, NY	Private	27.2	600	8062
West Hudson Hospital Assn	3898	Kearny, NJ	Private	27.2	600	8062
Familiesfirst Inc	3899	Davis, CA	Private	27.2	450	8361
Medical Arts Pathologists Inc	3900	Oklahoma City, OK	Private	27.2	18	8071
Buchanan General Hospital	3901	Grundy, VA	Private	27.2	400	8062
Western Montana Clinic, Pc	3902	Missoula, MT	Private	27.1	350	8011
Mcc Behavioral Care Of Cal	3903	Glendale, CA	Public Family Member	27.1	150	8093
Pratt Medical Group, Inc	3904	Boston, MA	Private	27.1	33	8011
Hillcrest Medical Nursing Inst	3905	Knoxville, TN	Private	27.1	765	8052
City Of Wooster	3906	Wooster, OH	Private	27.1	NA	8062
Scottsdale Memorial Hospitals	3907	Scottsdale, AZ	Private	27.1	NA	8062
South Crolina Dept Mental Health	3908	Clinton, SC	Private	27.1	NA	8059
Arizona Medical Clinic Ltd	3909	Peoria, AZ	Private	27.0	216	8011
Woodward Hospital & Health Ctr	3910	Woodward, OK	Private	27.0	255	8062
Becklund Home Health Care	3911	Minneapolis, MN	Private	27.0	1,400	8082
Brownwood Regional Hospital	3912	Brownwood, TX	Public Family Member	27.0	596	8062
Central Florida Bloodbank Inc	3913	Orlando, FL	Private	27.0	430	8099
Douglas Hospital Inc	3914	Douglasville, GA	Private	27.0	300	8062
Erlanger Health System	3915	Chattanooga, TN	Private	27.0	NA	8069
General Electric Company	3916	Florence, SC	Public Family Member	27.0	NA	8011
Hematology Clinic P.C	3917	Portland, OR	Private	27.0	44	8011
Homecare, Inc.	3918	Wallingford, CT	Private	27.0	2,000	8082
Kerlan-Jobe Orthopaedic	3919	Los Angeles, CA	Private	27.0	130	8011
Veterans Affairs Us Dept	3920	Reno, NV	Private	27.0	NA	8062

D&B COMPANY RANKINGS BY SALES

Company	Rank	Location	Type	Sales ($ mil.)	Employ-ment	Primary SIC
Okaloosa Hospital, Inc	3921	Niceville, FL	Public Family Member	27.0	450	8062
Carson City Hospital	3922	Carson City, MI	Private	27.0	460	8062
Memorial Hospital	3923	Logansport, IN	Private	27.0	505	8062
New Ulm Medical Center	3924	New Ulm, MN	Private	27.0	NA	8062
Youngstown Ostpthic Hospital Assn	3925	Youngstown, OH	Private	27.0	409	8062
Whidbey General Hospital Pub	3926	Coupeville, WA	Private	26.9	475	8062
Kph-Consolidation Inc	3927	Kingwood, TX	Public Family Member	26.9	550	8069
Presbyterian Healthcare Svcs	3928	Albuquerque, NM	Private	26.9	NA	8062
Sch Health Care System	3929	Port Arthur, TX	Private	26.9	NA	8062
Community Hospital Of Springfield	3930	Springfield, OH	Private	26.9	1,200	8062
Hospital Auth Of Habersham Cnty	3931	Demorest, GA	Private	26.9	453	8062
Mega Care Inc	3932	Union, NJ	Private	26.8	849	8051
American Red Cross, The	3933	Charlotte, NC	Private	26.8	NA	8099
Cathedral Healthcare System	3934	Newark, NJ	Private	26.8	NA	8062
Lutheran Health Systems	3935	Fairbanks, AK	Private	26.8	NA	8062
Memorial Medical Center Inc	3936	Ashland, WI	Private	26.8	650	8062
Baptist Mem Hspital-Union Cnty	3937	New Albany, MS	Private	26.8	420	8062
Virginia United Methdst Homes	3938	Richmond, VA	Private	26.8	750	8361
Cardiovascular Consultants Inc	3939	Kansas City, MO	Private	26.8	150	8011
Magee Rehabilitation Hospital	3940	Philadelphia, PA	Private	26.8	455	8069
Grenada Lake Medical Center	3941	Grenada, MS	Private	26.7	630	8062
Arkansas Department Of Health	3942	Little Rock, AR	Private	26.7	NA	8062
Central Kansas Medical Center	3943	Great Bend, KS	Private	26.7	588	8062
Laboratory Corp Amer Holdings	3944	Dublin, OH	Private	26.7	NA	8071
Veterans Health Administration	3945	Fargo, ND	Private	26.7	NA	8062
Piedmont Area Mntl Health	3946	Concord, NC	Private	26.6	429	8093
Pine Street Inn Inc	3947	Boston, MA	Private	26.6	400	8361
Elim Care, Inc	3948	Eden Prairie, MN	Private	26.6	15	8051
Pennsylvania Dept Pub Welfare	3949	Selinsgrove, PA	Private	26.6	NA	8059
Montrose Memorial Hospital	3950	Montrose, CO	Private	26.6	430	8062
McCullough-Hyde Mem Hospital Inc	3951	Oxford, OH	Private	26.6	349	8062
Board Of Child Care Of Balt-Wa	3952	Baltimore, MD	Private	26.5	140	8361
Fulton County Health Center	3953	Wauseon, OH	Private	26.5	600	8062
Illinois Dept Human Resources	3954	Chicago, IL	Private	26.5	NA	8063
Lifequest	3955	Quakertown, PA	Private	26.5	NA	8062
Massachusetts Dept Mental Health	3956	Taunton, MA	Private	26.5	NA	8063
Memorial Hermann Hospital Sys	3957	Houston, TX	Private	26.5	NA	8062
Notami Hospitals Louisiana Inc	3958	Covington, LA	Public Family Member	26.5	NA	8062
Veterans Health Administration	3959	Amarillo, TX	Private	26.5	NA	8062
Veterans Health Administration	3960	Muskogee, OK	Private	26.5	NA	8062
Watertown Memorial Hospital Assn	3961	Watertown, WI	Private	26.5	430	8062
Mercy Haverford Hospital	3962	Havertown, PA	Private	26.5	500	8062
Clarion Hospital	3963	Clarion, PA	Private	26.5	385	8062
Dry Harbor, Snf Inc	3964	Middle Village, NY	Private	26.5	225	8051
Teays Valley Health Services	3965	Hurricane, WV	Public Family Member	26.4	330	8062
Health Mgt Assoc Of W Va	3966	Williamson, WV	Public Family Member	26.4	230	8062
Advocate Health Care Network	3967	Chicago, IL	Private	26.4	NA	8062
Buffalo Medical Group P C	3968	Williamsville, NY	Private	26.4	NA	8011
Centura Health Corporation	3969	Colorado Springs, CO	Private	26.4	NA	8062
Florida Dept Children Families	3970	Hollywood, FL	Private	26.4	NA	8063
Indianplis Neurosurgical Group	3971	Indianapolis, IN	Private	26.4	102	8011
Phycor Inc	3972	Toledo, OH	Public Family Member	26.4	NA	8011
Chester Cnty Hospital Nursing Ctr	3973	Chester, SC	Private	26.4	485	8062
Snohomish Cnty Pub Hosp	3974	Arlington, WA	Private	26.4	348	8062
Lutheran Social Serv-Miami Valley	3975	Dayton, OH	Private	26.4	850	8051
Marian Community Hospital	3976	Carbondale, PA	Private	26.4	450	8062
Hospital Corporation Tennessee	3977	Martin, TN	Public Family Member	26.3	397	8062
Columbia Palmyra Park Hospital	3978	Albany, GA	Public Family Member	26.3	580	8062
County Of Union	3979	Berkeley Heights, NJ	Private	26.3	NA	8069
New York, State	3980	Queens Village, NY	Private	26.3	NA	8093
Tenet Healthcare Corporation	3981	Placentia, CA	Public Family Member	26.3	NA	8069
Tenet Healthcare Corporation	3982	Templeton, CA	Public Family Member	26.3	NA	8069
University Of Michigan	3983	Ann Arbor, MI	Private	26.3	NA	8071
Institute Of Prof Practice Inc	3984	Montpelier, VT	Private	26.3	700	8361
Mid Columbia Medical Center	3985	The Dalles, OR	Private	26.3	447	8062
Mednet Health Services Pc	3986	Brooklyn, NY	Private	26.3	25	8011
Dorchester General Hospital	3987	Cambridge, MD	Private	26.2	420	8062
Highland Clnic A Prof Med Corp	3988	Shreveport, LA	Private	26.2	250	8011
New York Cy Health Hspitals Corp	3989	Brooklyn, NY	Private	26.2	NA	8011
Veterans Health Administration	3990	Sioux Falls, SD	Private	26.2	NA	8062

D&B COMPANY RANKINGS BY SALES

Company	Rank	Location	Type	Sales ($ mil.)	Employ-ment	Primary SIC
St Cabrini Nursing Home Inc	3991	Dobbs Ferry, NY	Private	26.2	464	8051
Association/Services Aged	3992	Brooklyn, NY	Private	26.2	1,300	8361
Tropical Texas Center For Ment	3993	Edinburg, TX	Private	26.2	539	8093
Lakeview Community Hospital Auth	3994	Paw Paw, MI	Private	26.2	357	8062
Southern Chester Cnty Med Ctr	3995	West Grove, PA	Private	26.2	400	8062
Vna Of Rhode Island Inc	3996	Providence, RI	Private	26.2	401	8082
Fairview Hm Care & Hospice Inc	3997	Minneapolis, MN	Private	26.2	700	8082
Cleveland Neighborhood Health	3998	Cleveland, OH	Private	26.1	400	8099
Marshall Medical Center North	3999	Guntersville, AL	Private	26.1	450	8062
Bloomsburg Hospital Inc	4000	Bloomsburg, PA	Private	26.1	500	8062
Adventist Health Sys/Snblt Corp	4001	Orlando, FL	Private	26.1	NA	8062
Mercy Health Services	4002	Cadillac, MI	Private	26.1	NA	8062
North Broward Hospital Dst	4003	Fort Lauderdale, FL	Private	26.1	NA	8062
Tenet Health System Hospitals	4004	Hollywood, FL	Public Family Member	26.1	NA	8062
Henry County Medical Center	4005	Paris, TN	Private	26.1	650	8062
Renex Corp	4006	Coral Gables, FL	Public	26.1	250	8082
La-Rabida Chld Hospital & Res Ctr	4007	Chicago, IL	Private	26.0	339	8069
Northern Arizona Regional Be	4008	Flagstaff, AZ	Private	26.0	45	8093
Waynesboro Hospital	4009	Waynesboro, PA	Private	26.0	450	8062
A Infu-Tech Delaware Corp	4010	Englewood Cliffs, NJ	Public	26.0	213	8082
Community Gen Hospital	4011	Thomasville, NC	Private	26.0	460	8062
Inland Valley Regional Med Ctr	4012	Wildomar, CA	Public Family Member	26.0	350	8062
Choctaw Nation Health Services	4013	Talihina, OK	Private	26.0	360	8062
Fairview Clinics	4014	Minneapolis, MN	Private	26.0	380	8011
Greater Staten Island Med Grp	4015	Staten Island, NY	Private	26.0	380	8011
Ivonyx Inc	4016	Livonia, MI	Private	26.0	120	8082
Kennedy Health Services Corp	4017	Hawthorne, CA	Private	26.0	575	8062
Main Line Hospitals	4018	Paoli, PA	Private	26.0	NA	8062
Mckerley Health Care Centers	4019	Penacook, NH	Public Family Member	26.0	1,400	8052
Mountainview Hospital Inc	4020	Las Vegas, NV	Public Family Member	26.0	575	8062
Nasser Smith Pinkerton Cardiology	4021	Indianapolis, IN	Private	26.0	380	8011
Central Baptist Childrens Hm	4022	Lake Villa, IL	Private	26.0	500	8361
Medical Park Hospital Inc	4023	Winston Salem, NC	Private	25.9	260	8062
Thresholds, The	4024	Chicago, IL	Private	25.9	800	8093
Schwab Rehabilitation Hospital	4025	Chicago, IL	Private	25.9	300	8069
A I H Corporation	4026	Zion, IL	Private	25.9	572	8062
Fairview Hospital Healthcare Svcs	4027	Wyoming, MN	Private	25.9	NA	8062
Franciscan Health System West	4028	Federal Way, WA	Private	25.9	573	8062
Illinois Psychiatric Hospital Inc	4029	Nashville, TN	Public Family Member	25.9	700	8063
Quest Diagnostics Incorporated	4030	Williamsville, NY	Private	25.9	NA	8071
Washington Dpt Scl & Health Svcs	4031	Cheney, WA	Private	25.9	NA	8063
Sutter Amador Hospital	4032	Jackson, CA	Private	25.9	360	8062
Rehabilitation Hsptl Pacific	4033	Honolulu, HI	Private	25.8	420	8069
Hebrew Home & Hospital Inc	4034	W Hartford, CT	Private	25.8	600	8069
Novato Community Hospital	4035	Novato, CA	Private	25.8	330	8062
Beaumont Rehabilitation Assoc L P	4036	Beaumont, TX	Public Family Member	25.8	230	8069
District Columbia Government	4037	Laurel, MD	Private	25.8	NA	8361
Ohio Department Mental Health	4038	Columbus, OH	Private	25.8	NA	8063
Texas Health & Human Svcs Comm	4039	Big Spring, TX	Private	25.8	NA	8063
Johnson Betsy Memorial Hosp	4040	Dunn, NC	Private	25.8	384	8062
Butterwrth Cntnuing Care Group	4041	Grand Rapids, MI	Private	25.8	420	8051
Slocum-Dickson Med Group Pc	4042	New Hartford, NY	Private	25.8	350	8011
Arkansas Methodist Hospital	4043	Paragould, AR	Private	25.7	419	8062
Hospice Family Care, Inc.	4044	Mesa, AZ	Private	25.7	450	8082
Menorah Pk Cntr For The Agng	4045	Cleveland, OH	Private	25.7	827	8051
Genesee Memorial Hospital Assn	4046	Batavia, NY	Private	25.7	456	8062
Millcreek Community Hospital	4047	Erie, PA	Private	25.7	300	8062
Central Brooklyn Med Group Pc	4048	Brooklyn, NY	Private	25.7	375	8011
Eastern New Mexico Med Ctr	4049	Roswell, NM	Private	25.7	NA	8062
Infirmary Medical Clinic Pc	4050	Mobile, AL	Private	25.7	375	8011
Notami Hospitals Louisiana Inc	4051	Mamou, LA	Public Family Member	25.7	NA	8062
Morgan County Memorial Hosp	4052	Martinsville, IN	Private	25.7	390	8062
Hill Country Memorial Hosp	4053	Fredericksburg, TX	Private	25.6	400	8062
Misericordia Home	4054	Chicago, IL	Private	25.6	720	8052
Benevlent Corp Cedar Campuses	4055	West Bend, WI	Private	25.6	750	8051
Orlando Rgonal Healthcare Sys	4056	Orlando, FL	Private	25.6	NA	8062
Kewanee Hospital Association	4057	Kewanee, IL	Private	25.6	300	8062
Columbia Pine Lk Regional Hosp	4058	Mayfield, KY	Private	25.6	NA	8062
J C Blair Memorial Hospital	4059	Huntingdon, PA	Private	25.5	500	8062
Iatros Health Network Inc	4060	Atlanta, GA	Public	25.5	600	8051

D&B/Gale Industry Reference Handbooks

D&B COMPANY RANKINGS BY SALES

Company	Rank	Location	Type	Sales ($ mil.)	Employ-ment	Primary SIC
Central Blood Bank	4061	Pittsburgh, PA	Private	25.5	280	8099
Columbia-Healthone L L C	4062	Aurora, CO	Private	25.5	NA	8062
Lutheran	4063	Loveland, CO	Private	25.5	NA	8062
Lutheran Health System	4064	Loveland, CO	Private	25.5	NA	8062
Presbyterian Healthcare Svcs	4065	Clovis, NM	Private	25.5	NA	8062
Foothill Memorial Hospital	4066	Glendora, CA	Private	25.5	400	8062
Baylor Inst For Rhabilitation	4067	Dallas, TX	Private	25.5	450	8361
Lutheran Center For The Aging	4068	Smithtown, NY	Private	25.5	400	8051
Mercy Hospital Of Tiffin Ohio	4069	Tiffin, OH	Private	25.4	360	8062
Ashland Hospital Assn, The	4070	Ashland, OH	Private	25.4	650	8062
General Health System	4071	Baton Rouge, LA	Private	25.4	4,000	8071
Sioux Valley Physicians Aliance	4072	Sioux Falls, SD	Private	25.4	240	8011
Indiana Fmly & Social Svcs Adm	4073	Logansport, IN	Private	25.4	NA	8063
Angleton-Danbury Hospital Dst	4074	Angleton, TX	Private	25.4	210	8062
Walker Methodist Health Center	4075	Minneapolis, MN	Private	25.4	591	8051
California Family Health Council	4076	Los Angeles, CA	Private	25.3	77	8093
Veterans Health Administration	4077	Vancouver, WA	Private	25.3	NA	8062
Vista Hospital Systems Inc	4078	Corona, CA	Private	25.3	NA	8093
Palisades Nursing Home Co Inc	4079	Bronx, NY	Private	25.3	500	8059
Bacharach Inst For Rehabilitation	4080	Pomona, NJ	Private	25.2	500	8069
Doctors Hospital Of Staten Island	4081	Staten Island, NY	Private	25.2	348	8062
United Community Hospital	4082	Grove City, PA	Private	25.2	340	8062
Caremark International Inc	4083	Largo, FL	Public Family Member	25.2	NA	8011
Chowan Hospital Inc	4084	Edenton, NC	Private	25.2	495	8062
Cigna Healthcare Arizona, Inc.	4085	Buckeye, AZ	Public Family Member	25.2	NA	8011
Indiana Fmly & Social Svcs Adm	4086	Logansport, IN	Private	25.2	NA	8063
Missouri System, University	4087	Columbia, MO	Private	25.2	NA	8011
Rock County	4088	Janesville, WI	Private	25.2	NA	8011
Tenet Health System Di, Inc	4089	Saint Louis, MO	Public Family Member	25.2	NA	8011
Texas Children's Hospital	4090	Houston, TX	Private	25.2	NA	8011
United Care Inc	4091	Romulus, MI	Private	25.2	NA	8011
United Care Inc	4092	Dearborn, MI	Private	25.2	NA	8011
University Medical Associates	4093	Charleston, SC	Private	25.2	NA	8011
University Of Florida	4094	Gainesville, FL	Private	25.2	NA	8011
University Of Illinois	4095	Chicago, IL	Private	25.2	NA	8011
Virginia State Department Health	4096	Richmond, VA	Private	25.2	NA	8011
Chippewa County War Mem Hosp	4097	Sault Sainte Marie, MI	Private	25.2	400	8062
Kendrick Memorial Hospital	4098	Mooresville, IN	Private	25.2	320	8062
Bradley Mem Hospital & Health Ctr	4099	Southington, CT	Private	25.1	425	8062
Brooks Memorial Hospital	4100	Dunkirk, NY	Private	25.1	475	8062
Ohio Department Mental Health	4101	Cleveland, OH	Private	25.1	NA	8063
Smithkline Beecham Corporation	4102	Waltham, MA	Private	25.1	NA	8071
Green River Reg Mnt Health-Mnt	4103	Owensboro, KY	Private	25.1	675	8051
Services Of Lutheran Social	4104	York, PA	Private	25.1	759	8059
Babcock Center Inc	4105	Lexington, SC	Private	25.1	1,000	8361
Usdsm University Physicians	4106	Sioux Falls, SD	Private	25.0	290	8011
Shore View Nursing Home	4107	Brooklyn, NY	Private	25.0	270	8051
Ellis, Bandt, Birkin, Kollins	4108	Las Vegas, NV	Private	25.0	200	8011
Ridgecrest Regional Hospital	4109	Ridgecrest, CA	Private	25.0	342	8062
Albert Gallatin Home Care	4110	New Hyde Park, NY	Public Family Member	25.0	540	8082
Bizer Enterprises	4111	Clarksville, IN	Private	25.0	500	8042
Columbia Csa/Hs Greater Clvlnd	4112	Cleveland, OH	Private	25.0	NA	8062
Columbia Outpatient Surgical Svcs	4113	Fort Lauderdale, FL	Private	25.0	50	8011
Department Of Army	4114	Indianapolis, IN	Private	25.0	NA	8062
Esplanade Gardens Inc	4115	Corpus Christi, TX	Private	25.0	10	8361
Franciscan Shared Laboratory	4116	Milwaukee, WI	Private	25.0	680	8071
Gambro Healthcare Ptent Svcs Sup	4117	Nashville, TN	Private	25.0	NA	8092
Good Health Hmo, Inc	4118	Kansas City, MO	Private	25.0	4	8011
Greenville Hospital Corp	4119	Greenville, AL	Public Family Member	25.0	155	8062
Healthsouth Of San Antonio	4120	San Antonio, TX	Public Family Member	25.0	370	8069
Healthsouth Of Texarkana Inc	4121	Texarkana, TX	Public Family Member	25.0	175	8069
Illinois Dept Human Resources	4122	Tinley Park, IL	Private	25.0	NA	8062
Mann Berkley Eye Center, Pa	4123	Houston, TX	Private	25.0	150	8011
Medcath Of Mcallen Ltd	4124	Charlotte, NC	Private	25.0	175	8071
Medical Imaging Services	4125	North Little Rock, AR	Private	25.0	50	8071
Mercy Mount Clemens Corp	4126	Mount Clemens, MI	Private	25.0	NA	8062
Michigan Dept Corrections	4127	Jackson, MI	Private	25.0	NA	8062
Mt Kisco Medical Group, P.C.	4128	Mount Kisco, NY	Private	25.0	300	8011
Phycor Of Vero Beach, Inc	4129	Vero Beach, FL	Public Family Member	25.0	250	8011
Prime Medical Group, P.C.	4130	Clairton, PA	Private	25.0	232	8011

D&B COMPANY RANKINGS BY SALES

Company	Rank	Location	Type	Sales ($ mil.)	Employ- ment	Primary SIC
Signature Health Care Corp	4131	Scottsdale, AZ	Public Family Member	25.0	1,100	8051
State Of New York	4132	Perrysburg, NY	Private	25.0	NA	8051
United Care Inc	4133	Ypsilanti, MI	Private	25.0	NA	8062
Foundation Health Systems	4134	Winston Salem, NC	Private	25.0	40	8011
Adair County Pub Hospital Dst Corp	4135	Columbia, KY	Private	25.0	500	8062
Southern Medical Group, Inc	4136	Birmingham, AL	Private	25.0	50	8011
American Legion Hospital	4137	Crowley, LA	Private	25.0	389	8062
Hospital Service District No 2	4138	Morgan City, LA	Private	24.9	400	8062
Wayne Memorial Hospital	4139	Jesup, GA	Private	24.9	380	8062
First Hospital Corp Of Portsmouth	4140	Portsmouth, VA	Private	24.9	1,300	8051
Jackson Brook Institute	4141	South Portland, ME	Private	24.9	400	8063
Redington-Fairview Gen Hosp	4142	Skowhegan, ME	Private	24.9	430	8062
Geauga Community Hospital Assn	4143	Chardon, OH	Private	24.9	550	8062
Harvard Pilgrim Health Care	4144	Medford, MA	Private	24.9	NA	8011
Intermountain Health Care Inc	4145	Logan, UT	Private	24.9	NA	8062
Loretto Hospital	4146	Chicago, IL	Private	24.9	550	8062
Memorial Hospital Pasadena	4147	Pasadena, TX	Private	24.9	550	8062
Philadlphia Afl-Cio Hospital Assn	4148	Philadelphia, PA	Private	24.9	550	8062
St Luke Med Ctr Of Pasadena	4149	Pasadena, CA	Public Family Member	24.9	550	8062
Services Of Northwestern Human	4150	Philadelphia, PA	Private	24.9	2,000	8093
Sauk Prairie Memorial Hospital	4151	Prairie Du Sac, WI	Private	24.9	451	8062
Central Ind Regional Blood Ctr	4152	Indianapolis, IN	Private	24.9	370	8099
Naeve Hospital	4153	Albert Lea, MN	Private	24.9	650	8062
Mercy Hospital Of Watertown	4154	Watertown, NY	Private	24.8	610	8059
Indianapolis Osteopathic Hosp	4155	Indianapolis, IN	Private	24.8	270	8062
Northwestern Medical Center	4156	Saint Albans, VT	Private	24.8	388	8062
Columbia/Hca Healthcare Corp	4157	Houston, TX	Public Family Member	24.8	NA	8062
H C A Health Services Of Nh	4158	Derry, NH	Public Family Member	24.8	NA	8062
Long Life Home Care Services	4159	Brooklyn, NY	Private	24.8	1,545	8082
Northeast Hospital Corporation	4160	Gloucester, MA	Private	24.8	NA	8062
Nurses Unlimited Inc	4161	Odessa, TX	Private	24.8	1,600	8049
Veterans Memorial Medical Ctr	4162	Meriden, CT	Private	24.8	NA	8062
Asbury Centers Inc	4163	Maryville, TN	Private	24.8	850	8051
Oak Valley Hospital District	4164	Oakdale, CA	Private	24.7	425	8062
Baker Victory Services	4165	Lackawanna, NY	Private	24.7	340	8361
Big Spring Hospital Corp	4166	Big Spring, TX	Public Family Member	24.7	325	8062
Metroplex Hematology Oncology	4167	Arlington, TX	Private	24.7	125	8011
Reynold's Memorial Hospital	4168	Glen Dale, WV	Private	24.7	550	8062
North Ridge Care Center Inc	4169	Minneapolis, MN	Private	24.7	1,000	8051
Presbyterian Home Inc	4170	Evanston, IL	Private	24.7	505	8361
Crippled Children's Hospital	4171	Richmond, VA	Private	24.7	200	8069
Radiology Assocs Tarrant Cnty	4172	Fort Worth, TX	Private	24.6	149	8011
Ultimate Health Services Inc	4173	Huntington, WV	Private	24.6	300	8011
American Home Products Corp	4174	Monmouth Junction, NJ	Public Family Member	24.6	NA	8071
General Health Services, Inc.	4175	Enid, OK	Public Family Member	24.6	NA	8062
Ridgeview Medical Center	4176	Waconia, MN	Private	24.6	545	8062
Texas Health & Human Svcs Comm	4177	Carlsbad, TX	Private	24.6	NA	8063
Northmed Hmo Inc	4178	Traverse City, MI	Private	24.6	23	8011
Columbia/Cape Fear Healthcare	4179	Wilmington, NC	Public Family Member	24.6	501	8062
Henderson Memorial Hospital	4180	Henderson, TX	Private	24.6	350	8062
Bethesda Lutheran Homes & Svcs	4181	Watertown, WI	Private	24.6	1,200	8059
Carmel Richmond Nursing Home	4182	Staten Island, NY	Private	24.5	575	8051
United Memorial Hospital Assn	4183	Greenville, MI	Private	24.5	375	8062
San Benito Health Care Dst	4184	Hollister, CA	Private	24.5	430	8062
Baldwin County Hospital Auth	4185	Milledgeville, GA	Private	24.5	543	8062
County Of Albany	4186	Albany, NY	Private	24.5	NA	8051
Jewish Home & Hospital For Aged	4187	Bronx, NY	Private	24.5	NA	8051
San Luis Obispo, County	4188	San Luis Obispo, CA	Private	24.5	NA	8011
Tenet Healthcare Corporation	4189	Gretna, LA	Public Family Member	24.5	NA	8062
Texas Scottish Rite Hosp	4190	Dallas, TX	Private	24.5	500	8069
Thomas Jefferson University	4191	Philadelphia, PA	Private	24.5	NA	8051
Bedford Regional Medical Ctr	4192	Bedford, IN	Private	24.5	390	8062
Lancaster Mennonite Hospital	4193	Lebanon, PA	Private	24.4	550	8063
Columbia/Hca Healthcare Corp	4194	Houston, TX	Public Family Member	24.4	NA	8062
Department Of Army	4195	Fort Hood, TX	Private	24.4	NA	8062
H C A Health Svcs Texas Inc	4196	Houston, TX	Public Family Member	24.4	NA	8062
Legacy Health Care Inc	4197	Muncie, IN	Private	24.4	1,000	8361
Medical Behavioral Care Of Cal	4198	S San Francisco, CA	Public Family Member	24.4	800	8093
Tenet Health System Medical	4199	Port Arthur, TX	Public Family Member	24.4	NA	8062
Tenet Health System-Dallas	4200	Dallas, TX	Public Family Member	24.4	NA	8062

D&B COMPANY RANKINGS BY SALES

Company	Rank	Location	Type	Sales ($ mil.)	Employ-ment	Primary SIC
Tenet Healthcare Corporation	4201	Slidell, LA	Public Family Member	24.4	NA	8062
Tenet Healthcare Corporation	4202	Port Arthur, TX	Public Family Member	24.4	NA	8062
Tenet Healthcare, Ltd	4203	Houston, TX	Private	24.4	NA	8062
Texas Visiting Nurse Service	4204	Harlingen, TX	Private	24.4	145	8082
Northside Hospital-Cherokee	4205	Canton, GA	Private	24.4	350	8062
Cleo Wallace Center Inc	4206	Denver, CO	Private	24.4	500	8063
Institute For Rehabilitation	4207	Houston, TX	Private	24.4	466	8062
South Baldwin County Healthcar	4208	Foley, AL	Private	24.4	425	8062
Campbell Clinic Inc	4209	Germantown, TN	Private	24.4	230	8011
Matagorda County Hospital Dst	4210	Bay City, TX	Private	24.3	600	8062
Auburn General Hospital Inc	4211	Auburn, WA	Public Family Member	24.3	538	8062
Capital Health Systems Inc	4212	Trenton, NJ	Private	24.3	NA	8062
Chw Central Coast	4213	Camarillo, CA	Private	24.3	NA	8062
Daniel Freeman Hospitals Inc	4214	Venice, CA	Private	24.3	NA	8062
Lancaster County	4215	Lancaster, PA	Private	24.3	NA	8062
North Shore University Hosp	4216	Syosset, NY	Private	24.3	NA	8062
St Lukes-Roosevelt Hospital Ctr	4217	New York, NY	Private	24.3	NA	8062
Tenet Health System Hospitals	4218	Pinole, CA	Public Family Member	24.3	NA	8062
University Of California	4219	La Jolla, CA	Private	24.3	NA	8062
Veterans Health Administration	4220	Altoona, PA	Private	24.3	NA	8062
Veterans Health Administration	4221	San Diego, CA	Private	24.3	NA	8062
Veterans Health Administration	4222	Lyons, NJ	Private	24.3	NA	8062
Spring Hill Regional Hospital	4223	Spring Hill, FL	Private	24.3	350	8062
Keokuk Area Hospital	4224	Keokuk, IA	Private	24.3	425	8062
Lock Haven Hospital	4225	Lock Haven, PA	Private	24.3	410	8062
Walton County Hospital Auth	4226	Monroe, GA	Private	24.2	297	8062
Riverside Rest Home	4227	Dover, NH	Private	24.2	322	8361
Adventist Health Sys/Snblt Corp	4228	Sebring, FL	Private	24.2	NA	8062
Belle Bonfils Mem Blood Ctr	4229	Denver, CO	Private	24.2	272	8099
Stanly Memorial Hospital Inc	4230	Albemarle, NC	Private	24.2	537	8062
Tenneesse Dept-Mental Health	4231	Bolivar, TN	Private	24.2	NA	8063
Veterans Affairs Us Dept	4232	Newington, CT	Private	24.2	NA	8062
Chesapeake Hospital Corp	4233	Kilmarnock, VA	Private	24.2	420	8062
Children's Village Inc, The	4234	Dobbs Ferry, NY	Private	24.2	585	8361
Mary Free Bed Hospital	4235	Grand Rapids, MI	Private	24.1	600	8069
Atlantic General Hospital Corp	4236	Berlin, MD	Private	24.1	322	8062
Alliance Health Care, Inc.	4237	Burnsville, MN	Private	24.1	1,500	8082
Clinishare Inc	4238	Chatsworth, CA	Private	24.1	1,500	8082
Edwin Shaw Hospital	4239	Akron, OH	Private	24.1	492	8069
Ihs Home Care	4240	Nashville, TN	Public Family Member	24.1	1,500	8082
Nazareth Health Inc	4241	Hixson, TN	Private	24.1	NA	8062
Quest Diagnostics Incorporated	4242	Deerfield Beach, FL	Private	24.1	NA	8071
Recco Home Care Service Inc	4243	Massapequa, NY	Private	24.1	1,500	8082
Tenet Health System Medical	4244	Poplar Bluff, MO	Public Family Member	24.1	NA	8062
Trinity Health System	4245	Steubenville, OH	Private	24.1	NA	8062
Uct International Inc	4246	Farmingdale, NY	Public Family Member	24.1	76	8071
Twin Falls Clinic And Hosp	4247	Twin Falls, ID	Private	24.1	275	8062
Bradley Emma Pendleton Hosp	4248	Riverside, RI	Private	24.0	403	8063
Age Inc	4249	Cullman, AL	Private	24.0	750	8059
Johns Hpkins Hm Care Group Inc	4250	Baltimore, MD	Private	24.0	350	8082
Alta Med	4251	Los Angeles, CA	Private	24.0	400	8099
Ammons-Springmoor Associates	4252	Raleigh, NC	Private	24.0	425	8059
Beloit Clinic Sc	4253	Beloit, WI	Private	24.0	350	8011
Buena Ventura Medical Group	4254	Ventura, CA	Private	24.0	350	8011
Cardiac Solutions, Inc	4255	Fort Washington, PA	Private	24.0	135	8082
Charter Louisvlle Behavioral Health	4256	Louisville, KY	Private	24.0	150	8063
Community Care Systems Inc	4257	Springfield, IL	Private	24.0	2,800	8082
Devereux Foundation, The	4258	Goleta, CA	Private	24.0	NA	8011
Florida Physicians Med Group	4259	Winter Park, FL	Private	24.0	350	8011
H S C Medical Center	4260	Malvern, AR	Private	24.0	250	8062
Heartland Home Health Care Svcs	4261	Bay City, MI	Public Family Member	24.0	2,100	8082
Hhca Texas Health Services, Lp	4262	Dallas, TX	Private	24.0	250	8082
Hitchcock Clinic-Keene Inc	4263	Keene, NH	Private	24.0	350	8011
Hughston Orthopedic Clinic Pc	4264	Columbus, GA	Private	24.0	350	8011
Institutes Of Applied Human Dev.	4265	Bronx, NY	Private	24.0	470	8361
Kennedy Health Systems	4266	Blackwood, NJ	Private	24.0	NA	8062
La Follette Medical Center	4267	La Follette, TN	Private	24.0	600	8062
Learning Services Corporation	4268	Durham, NC	Private	24.0	600	8093
Lebauer, Weintraub, Brodie	4269	Greensboro, NC	Private	24.0	350	8011
Md Health Plan Inc	4270	North Haven, CT	Private	24.0	351	8011

D&B COMPANY RANKINGS BY SALES

Company	Rank	Location	Type	Sales ($ mil.)	Employ-ment	Primary SIC
Medical Clinic Of N Texas P A	4271	Fort Worth, TX	Private	24.0	350	8011
Metro West Rehab Corp	4272	Haverhill, MA	Private	24.0	NA	8051
Meyer Medical Group Ii, S C	4273	Chicago, IL	Private	24.0	350	8011
New York, State	4274	Albany, NY	Private	24.0	NA	8063
Pennsylvania Dept Labor Indust	4275	Allentown, PA	Private	24.0	NA	8063
Pennsylvania Dept Pub Welfare	4276	Haverford, PA	Private	24.0	NA	8063
Preferred Health Network Inc	4277	Irvine, CA	Private	24.0	600	8099
Premier Bioresources Inc	4278	Miami, FL	Public Family Member	24.0	NA	8099
Pro-Wellness Health Mgt Svcs	4279	Dayton, OH	Private	24.0	350	8011
Queens Blvd Extnded Care Fclty	4280	Woodside, NY	Private	24.0	360	8051
Radiological Assc Sacto Md Gp	4281	Sacramento, CA	Private	24.0	500	8071
St Lukes Cataract & Laser Inst	4282	Tarpon Springs, FL	Private	24.0	350	8011
Trimark Physicians Group	4283	Fort Dodge, IA	Private	24.0	350	8011
Veterans Health Administration	4284	Quincy, IL	Private	24.0	NA	8011
Valley Regional Hospital Inc	4285	Claremont, NH	Private	24.0	480	8062
Lifecare Hospital New Orleans Llc	4286	Chalmette, LA	Private	24.0	130	8069
Good Shepherd Lutheran Home	4287	Porterville, CA	Private	24.0	1,000	8361
Visiting Nurse Association Hea	4288	Staten Island, NY	Private	24.0	160	8082
Rehabilitation Hospital Of Ind	4289	Indianapolis, IN	Private	24.0	461	8062
Island Hospital	4290	Anacortes, WA	Private	23.9	359	8062
Hopkins County Hospital Dst	4291	Sulphur Springs, TX	Private	23.9	400	8062
Herrick Memorial Hospital	4292	Tecumseh, MI	Private	23.9	450	8062
Garrett County Memorial Hosp	4293	Oakland, MD	Private	23.9	356	8062
Pemiscot County Memorial Hosp	4294	Hayti, MO	Private	23.9	750	8062
Gateway Regional Health System	4295	Mount Sterling, KY	Private	23.9	313	8062
French Hospital Med Ctr A Cal	4296	San Luis Obispo, CA	Private	23.9	530	8062
Tenet Health System Hospitals	4297	Miami, FL	Public Family Member	23.9	NA	8062
Cameron Community Hospital	4298	Cameron, MO	Private	23.9	275	8062
Alice Hyde Hospital Assn	4299	Malone, NY	Private	23.9	480	8062
St Dominic's Home	4300	Blauvelt, NY	Private	23.8	440	8361
Gilbert, Barbee, Moore, McIlvoy	4301	Bowling Green, KY	Private	23.8	300	8011
Memorial Hospital Sheridan Cnty	4302	Sheridan, WY	Private	23.8	410	8062
Institute For Cancer Research Inc	4303	Philadelphia, PA	Private	23.8	350	8071
Harriman City Hospital	4304	Harriman, TN	Private	23.8	425	8062
Wallace Thomson Hospital	4305	Union, SC	Private	23.8	400	8062
Jack Friedman	4306	Flushing, NY	Private	23.8	280	8059
Harris Methodist Fort Worth	4307	Fort Worth, TX	Private	23.8	NA	8062
Louisiana Dept Health Hospitals	4308	Jackson, LA	Private	23.8	NA	8062
Methodist Healthcare System	4309	San Antonio, TX	Private	23.8	NA	8062
State Of Ohio	4310	Columbus, OH	Private	23.8	NA	8063
Tenneesse Dept-Mental Health	4311	Nashville, TN	Private	23.8	NA	8361
Youth Villages Inc	4312	Memphis, TN	Private	23.7	275	8361
Columbus Doctors Hospital Inc	4313	Columbus, GA	Private	23.7	525	8062
Community Hospitals Of Galen	4314	Pompano Beach, FL	Public Family Member	23.7	525	8062
Dean Health Systems Sc	4315	Janesville, WI	Private	23.7	NA	8011
Gila Regional Medical Center	4316	Silver City, NM	Private	23.7	525	8062
Thomas-Davis Medical Ctrs Pc	4317	Tucson, AZ	Public Family Member	23.7	NA	8011
Veterans Health Administration	4318	Fort Lyon, CO	Private	23.7	NA	8062
Veterans Home & Hospital	4319	Rocky Hill, CT	Private	23.7	525	8062
River District Hospital	4320	East China, MI	Private	23.6	400	8062
West Park Hospital District	4321	Cody, WY	Private	23.6	375	8062
Memorial Hospital Selam County	4322	Salem, NJ	Private	23.6	775	8093
Occupational Urgent Care Health	4323	Broderick, CA	Public Family Member	23.6	590	8099
Omaha Home For Boys Inc	4324	Omaha, NE	Private	23.6	91	8361
Carbondale Clinic S C	4325	Carbondale, IL	Private	23.6	264	8011
Vista Hill Foundation	4326	San Diego, CA	Private	23.6	1,000	8063
Health First Medical Group Pc	4327	Memphis, TN	Private	23.5	350	8011
De Kalb Memorial Hospital Inc	4328	Auburn, IN	Private	23.5	425	8062
United Lutheran Program For Th	4329	Milwaukee, WI	Private	23.5	585	8051
Radiology Imaging Assoc Pc	4330	Englewood, CO	Private	23.5	95	8011
Great River Health Systems	4331	Burlington, IA	Private	23.5	1,140	8062
Wisconsin Dept Health Fmly Svcs	4332	Union Grove, WI	Private	23.5	NA	8361
St Joseph Health System	4333	Tawas City, MI	Private	23.5	500	8062
Tenet Health Systems Hospitals	4334	Manteca, CA	Public Family Member	23.5	300	8062
King's Daughters Hospital Assn	4335	Temple, TX	Private	23.4	425	8062
Holland Home	4336	Grand Rapids, MI	Private	23.4	450	8361
South Bay Community Hospital	4337	Redondo Beach, CA	Private	23.4	231	8062
Lake Shore Nursing Home Inc	4338	Irving, NY	Private	23.4	85	8059
Northeastern Regional Hospital	4339	Las Vegas, NM	Private	23.4	270	8062
Devereux Foundation, The	4340	Melbourne, FL	Private	23.4	NA	8069

D&B COMPANY RANKINGS BY SALES

Company	Rank	Location	Type	Sales ($ mil.)	Employ- ment	Primary SIC
Health Management Associates	4341	Clarksdale, MS	Public Family Member	23.4	NA	8062
Peacehealth	4342	Eugene, OR	Private	23.4	NA	8011
Tenet Healthcare Corporation	4343	Fort Lauderdale, FL	Public Family Member	23.4	NA	8069
University Of Miami	4344	Miami, FL	Private	23.4	NA	8069
Arkansas Valley Regional Med Ctr	4345	La Junta, CO	Private	23.4	425	8062
Community Memorial Hospital	4346	Cheboygan, MI	Private	23.4	400	8062
Fort Duncan Medical Center	4347	Eagle Pass, TX	Private	23.3	350	8062
Spencer Municipal Hospital	4348	Spencer, IA	Private	23.3	439	8062
St Catherine Hospital	4349	Garden City, KS	Private	23.3	500	8062
Heritage Medical Mgt Inc	4350	Muncie, IN	Private	23.3	1,050	8059
Mariner Rehabilitation Svcs	4351	Nashville, TN	Public Family Member	23.3	NA	8049
New Jersey Dept HumanSvcs	4352	Totowa, NJ	Private	23.3	NA	8051
Christian Health Care Center	4353	Wyckoff, NJ	Private	23.3	650	8063
Oklahoma Orthpdc/Arthrts	4354	Oklahoma City, OK	Private	23.3	280	8069
Hebrew Home For The Aged	4355	San Francisco, CA	Private	23.3	574	8051
Bay Cove Human Services Inc	4356	Boston, MA	Private	23.3	700	8052
Wartburg	4357	Mount Vernon, NY	Private	23.2	450	8051
Goodwin House Incorporated	4358	Alexandria, VA	Private	23.2	568	8051
Huntington Medical Group Pc	4359	Huntington Station, NY	Private	23.2	480	8011
Southern Health Care Of Ala	4360	Chattanooga, TN	Private	23.2	350	8062
Norton Community Hospital Inc	4361	Norton, VA	Private	23.2	343	8062
Door County Memorial Hospital	4362	Sturgeon Bay, WI	Private	23.2	440	8062
Greene County Memorial Hosp	4363	Waynesburg, PA	Private	23.2	270	8062
Healthlink Inc	4364	Saint Louis, MO	Private	23.2	339	8011
Shriners Hospital For Children	4365	Boston, MA	Private	23.2	250	8069
Wabash County Hospital	4366	Wabash, IN	Private	23.2	375	8062
North Country Hospital Health Ctr	4367	Newport, VT	Private	23.2	350	8062
Southwestern Ohio Seniors Svcs	4368	Cincinnati, OH	Private	23.1	355	8052
State Laboratory Of Hygiene	4369	Madison, WI	Private	23.1	350	8071
Kendal-Crosslands Communities Inc	4370	Kennett Square, PA	Private	23.1	520	8051
Adventist Health System/Sunbelt	4371	Portland, TN	Private	23.1	NA	8062
Baptist Health System Inc	4372	Sylacauga, AL	Private	23.1	NA	8062
Catholic Health Partners Svcs	4373	Chicago, IL	Private	23.1	NA	8062
Columbia/Hca Healthcare Corp	4374	Saint Petersburg, FL	Public Family Member	23.1	NA	8062
Florida Dept Children Families	4375	Opa Locka, FL	Private	23.1	NA	8093
Foundtion Health A Fla Health Plan	4376	Fort Lauderdale, FL	Private	23.1	337	8011
H C A Health Services Of La	4377	Monroe, LA	Public Family Member	23.1	512	8062
Pennsylvania Dept Pub Welfare	4378	Ebensburg, PA	Private	23.1	NA	8361
Trover Clinic Foundation Inc	4379	Madisonville, KY	Private	23.1	NA	8062
Hartford Memorial Hospital	4380	Hartford, WI	Private	23.1	350	8062
Carbon Schuylkill Comm Htlh	4381	Coaldale, PA	Private	23.1	386	8062
Manhattan Prepaid Health Svc Plan	4382	New York, NY	Private	23.0	45	8011
Portage Health System, Inc	4383	Hancock, MI	Private	23.0	475	8062
Womens And Childrens Hospital Inc	4384	Lafayette, LA	Public Family Member	23.0	370	8069
Ancilla Health Services, Inc	4385	Fort Wayne, IN	Private	23.0	80	8011
American Transitional Hospitals	4386	Houston, TX	Public Family Member	23.0	NA	8062
Columbia/Alleghany Regional	4387	Lowmoor, VA	Public Family Member	23.0	510	8062
Greater Detroit Hospital Inc	4388	Detroit, MI	Private	23.0	306	8062
Healthsouth Rehabiltiation	4389	Toms River, NJ	Public Family Member	23.0	471	8069
Kansas Neurological Institute	4390	Topeka, KS	Private	23.0	750	8361
Laboratory Corp Amer Holdings	4391	RTP, NC	Private	23.0	NA	8071
Medical Diagnostics Inc	4392	Wilmington, MA	Public Family Member	23.0	150	8099
Phycor Of Pueblo Inc	4393	Pueblo, CO	Public Family Member	23.0	150	8011
Quest Diagnostics Incorporated	4394	Rockville, MD	Private	23.0	NA	8071
Sharp Coronado Hospital Healthcare	4395	Coronado, CA	Private	23.0	510	8062
Valley Community Hospital	4396	Santa Maria, CA	Public Family Member	23.0	300	8062
Belmont Center Comp Treatment	4397	Philadelphia, PA	Private	23.0	400	8063
Greensville Memorial Hospital	4398	Emporia, VA	Private	23.0	430	8062
Julia Rackley Perry Mem Hosp	4399	Princeton, IL	Private	22.9	425	8062
Siskin Hospital For Physical	4400	Chattanooga, TN	Private	22.9	323	8069
Blood Care	4401	Dallas, TX	Private	22.9	340	8099
York Health System Med Group	4402	York, PA	Private	22.9	95	8011
Mecosta County General Hosp	4403	Big Rapids, MI	Private	22.9	280	8062
Bedford County General Hosp	4404	Shelbyville, TN	Private	22.9	349	8062
St Jerome Hospital	4405	Batavia, NY	Private	22.9	500	8062
Du Page Dialysis, Ltd.	4406	Oak Park, IL	Private	22.9	400	8092
Gyncor, Inc.	4407	Chicago, IL	Private	22.9	335	8011
Rcg Mississippi, Inc	4408	Jackson, MS	Public Family Member	22.9	400	8092
Casa De Las Campanas, Inc	4409	San Diego, CA	Private	22.9	303	8361
University Rehabilitation Hosp	4410	New Orleans, LA	Private	22.9	290	8069

D&B COMPANY RANKINGS BY SALES

Company	Rank	Location	Type	Sales ($ mil.)	Employ- ment	Primary SIC
Holy Cross Health System Corp	4411	South Bend, IN	Private	22.9	17,000	8062
Fairview Redwing Health Svcs	4412	Red Wing, MN	Private	22.8	400	8062
Palo Pinto General Hospital	4413	Mineral Wells, TX	Private	22.8	414	8062
Florida Health Choice Inc	4414	Delray Beach, FL	Private	22.8	120	8011
Department Of Air Force	4415	Montgomery, AL	Private	22.8	NA	8062
Health Hospital Corp Of Marion	4416	Indianapolis, IN	Private	22.8	NA	8062
Novacare Orthotics Prosthetics	4417	King Of Prussia, PA	Public Family Member	22.8	750	8093
Rebsamen Regional Medical Ctr	4418	Jacksonville, AR	Private	22.8	506	8062
Republic Health Corp Indanapolis	4419	Indianapolis, IN	Public Family Member	22.8	NA	8062
Vencor, Inc	4420	Detroit, MI	Private	22.8	NA	8062
Daughters Of Miriam Center	4421	Clifton, NJ	Private	22.8	500	8051
John Knox Village Of Florida	4422	Pompano Beach, FL	Private	22.8	630	8361
Kings View	4423	Reedley, CA	Private	22.8	400	8093
Medina Memorial Hospital Inc	4424	Medina, NY	Private	22.7	355	8062
Franc Childr Hosp	4425	Boston, MA	Private	22.7	400	8069
Steamboat Sprngs Health Care Asn	4426	Steamboat Springs, CO	Private	22.7	260	8062
Culwell Health Inc	4427	Sewickley, PA	Private	22.7	1,000	8051
Florida Medical Clinic, P.A.	4428	Zephyrhills, FL	Private	22.7	177	8011
Health Enterprises Of Michigan	4429	Denton, TX	Private	22.7	1,000	8051
Hurlbut, Robert H	4430	Rochester, NY	Private	22.7	1,000	8051
Leslie Peter & Co	4431	Brandon, FL	Private	22.7	NA	8051
Medlantic Enterprises, Inc	4432	Washington, DC	Private	22.7	1,000	8051
Rosewood Care Center Holdg Co	4433	Saint Louis, MO	Private	22.7	1,000	8051
York Hannover Nursing Centers	4434	Pittsfield, MA	Private	22.7	1,000	8051
St Josephs Hospital & Health Ctr	4435	Dickinson, ND	Private	22.7	450	8062
Sea Crest Health Care Center	4436	Brooklyn, NY	Private	22.6	250	8051
Masonic Homes Of Kentucky	4437	Louisville, KY	Private	22.6	250	8361
Integramed America Inc	4438	Purchase, NY	Public	22.6	175	8093
Springfield Hospital	4439	Springfield, VT	Private	22.6	330	8062
Transylvania Community Hosp	4440	Brevard, NC	Private	22.6	500	8062
Bradford Group, The, Inc	4441	Birmingham, AL	Private	22.6	462	8069
State Of Louisiana	4442	Independence, LA	Private	22.6	NA	8062
Veterans Health Administration	4443	Kerrville, TX	Private	22.6	NA	8062
Grande Ronde Hospital Inc	4444	La Grande, OR	Private	22.6	380	8062
Hillsdale Community Health Ctr	4445	Hillsdale, MI	Private	22.6	280	8062
New England Rehabilitation Ser	4446	Worcester, MA	Private	22.6	NA	8062
Brattleboro Retreat	4447	Brattleboro, VT	Private	22.5	550	8063
Touchette Regional HospitalInc	4448	East Saint Louis, IL	Private	22.5	300	8062
Montgomery General Hospital	4449	Montgomery, WV	Private	22.5	260	8062
Memorial Hospital Inc	4450	Manchester, KY	Private	22.5	315	8062
Springmoor Inc	4451	Raleigh, NC	Private	22.5	400	8059
Ahm-Smc Inc	4452	Paramount, CA	Public Family Member	22.5	500	8062
B V M C Inc	4453	College Station, TX	Public Family Member	22.5	500	8062
Columbia Hospital Frankfort	4454	Frankfort, KY	Private	22.5	500	8062
Community Hospital Williams	4455	Bryan, OH	Private	22.5	500	8062
East Cooper Community Hospital	4456	Mount Pleasant, SC	Public Family Member	22.5	500	8062
Eyexam 2000 Of California, Inc	4457	Burlingame, CA	Private	22.5	450	8042
Gwinnett Community Hospital	4458	Snellville, GA	Public Family Member	22.5	500	8062
Highlands Hospital Corporation	4459	Prestonsburg, KY	Private	22.5	500	8062
Hillcrest Hospital	4460	Pittsfield, MA	Private	22.5	500	8062
Lancaster Hospital Corporation	4461	Lancaster, CA	Public Family Member	22.5	NA	8062
Medical Team Inc	4462	Reston, VA	Private	22.5	2,700	8082
Muskegon General Hospital	4463	Muskegon, MI	Private	22.5	500	8062
Olean General Hospital Inc	4464	Olean, NY	Private	22.5	NA	8062
Veterans Health Administration	4465	Boise, ID	Private	22.5	NA	8062
Wood County Hospital Assn	4466	Bowling Green, OH	Private	22.5	500	8062
Nashoba Community Hospital Corp	4467	Ayer, MA	Private	22.5	450	8062
McCray Memorial Hospital	4468	Kendallville, IN	Private	22.5	300	8062
Memorial Hospital And Manor	4469	Bainbridge, GA	Private	22.4	400	8062
J G B Health Facilities Corp	4470	New York, NY	Private	22.4	276	8051
Jordan Health Services Inc	4471	Mount Vernon, TX	Private	22.4	4,000	8082
North Suffolk Mental Health Assn	4472	Chelsea, MA	Private	22.4	900	8093
Western Missouri Medical Ctr	4473	Warrensburg, MO	Private	22.4	320	8062
Browne-McHardy Clinic	4474	Metairie, LA	Private	22.4	250	8011
Visiting Nurse Association	4475	East Orange, NJ	Private	22.4	600	8049
Nysarc Inc	4476	Kingston, NY	Private	22.4	660	8361
Catholic Bishop Of Chicago	4477	Des Plaines, IL	Private	22.4	NA	8361
County Of Monterey	4478	Salinas, CA	Private	22.4	NA	8063
County Of Northampton	4479	Nazareth, PA	Private	22.4	NA	8361
Kentucky Easter Seal Society	4480	Lexington, KY	Private	22.4	NA	8069

D&B COMPANY RANKINGS BY SALES

Company	Rank	Location	Type	Sales ($ mil.)	Employ-ment	Primary SIC
Loretto Rest Nursing Home Co	4481	Syracuse, NY	Private	22.4	NA	8361
Androscoggin Valley Hospital	4482	Berlin, NH	Private	22.4	345	8062
Santa Teresita Hospital	4483	Duarte, CA	Private	22.4	425	8062
Step-By-Step Inc	4484	Wilkes Barre, PA	Private	22.4	675	8361
Noland Lloyd Hospital Inc	4485	Fairfield, AL	Public Family Member	22.3	800	8062
Lakeview Med Ctr Inc Rice Lk	4486	Rice Lake, WI	Private	22.3	270	8062
Farmers Union Hospital Assn	4487	Elk City, OK	Private	22.3	295	8062
Phoenix Childrens Hospital	4488	Phoenix, AZ	Private	22.3	NA	8062
Tenet Health System-Dallas	4489	Dallas, TX	Public Family Member	22.3	NA	8062
Daviess County Hospital	4490	Washington, IN	Private	22.3	340	8062
Horizon House Inc	4491	Philadelphia, PA	Private	22.3	750	8361
Albright Care Services	4492	Lewisburg, PA	Private	22.3	600	8051
Transylvania Community	4493	Brevard, NC	Private	22.3	350	8062
Texas Healthcare Pa	4494	Fort Worth, TX	Private	22.2	280	8011
Hillsdale Group (Inc)	4495	Burlingame, CA	Private	22.2	1,600	8059
Ellwood City Hospital	4496	Ellwood City, PA	Private	22.2	368	8062
Anthem Alliance For Health	4497	Hampton, VA	Private	22.2	NA	8011
Arcventures Development Corp	4498	Chicago, IL	Private	22.2	325	8011
County Of Los Angeles	4499	Los Angeles, CA	Private	22.2	NA	8011
County Of Pierce	4500	Tacoma, WA	Private	22.2	NA	8011
Group Health Plan, Inc	4501	Minneapolis, MN	Private	22.2	NA	8011
Johns Hopkins University	4502	Baltimore, MD	Private	22.2	NA	8011
Kaiser Foundation Hospitals	4503	Pleasanton, CA	Private	22.2	NA	8011
Lexington Square Inc	4504	Lombard, IL	Private	22.2	1,000	8059
Mediplex Of Massachusetts Inc	4505	Albuquerque, NM	Public Family Member	22.2	1,000	8059
Nemours Foundation (Inc)	4506	Jacksonville, FL	Private	22.2	NA	8011
Permanente Medical Group, Inc	4507	Oakland, CA	Private	22.2	NA	8011
State Of South Carolina	4508	Columbia, SC	Private	22.2	NA	8063
University Of Texas At Austin	4509	Houston, TX	Private	22.2	NA	8011
Woodland Healthcare	4510	Woodland, CA	Private	22.2	NA	8011
Parkridge Hospital Inc	4511	Chattanooga, TN	Public Family Member	22.2	350	8062
Heather Hill, Inc	4512	Chardon, OH	Private	22.2	550	8069
Lifepath Inc	4513	Bethlehem, PA	Private	22.2	625	8059
Soldiers & Sailors Mem Hosp	4514	Wellsboro, PA	Private	22.1	375	8062
Lincoln Pk Osteopathic Hospital	4515	Grand Junction, CO	Private	22.1	300	8062
Regency Nursing Ctr Of Texas	4516	Victoria, TX	Private	22.1	700	8051
Medcenter One Inc	4517	Bismarck, ND	Private	22.1	NA	8011
Oakwood Living Centers Inc	4518	Boston, MA	Private	22.1	972	8051
Oakwood Living Centers Of Mass	4519	Plymouth, MA	Private	22.1	972	8051
Pathways, Inc.	4520	Ashland, KY	Private	22.1	NA	8011
Tenet Healthcare Corporation	4521	Nacogdoches, TX	Public Family Member	22.1	NA	8011
University Of Virginia	4522	Charlottesville, VA	Private	22.1	NA	8011
Huron Memorial Hospital Inc	4523	Bad Axe, MI	Private	22.1	274	8062
R J Taylor Memorial Hospital	4524	Hawkinsville, GA	Private	22.1	550	8062
Community Health Association	4525	Ripley, WV	Private	22.1	320	8062
St Joseph's Rgnl Mdcl Ctr N Ok	4526	Ponca City, OK	Private	22.1	446	8062
Lindengrove Inc	4527	New Berlin, WI	Private	22.1	476	8051
New Vanderbilt Nursing Home	4528	Staten Island, NY	Private	22.0	270	8051
Morningside Ministries	4529	San Antonio, TX	Private	22.0	650	8361
Health Plus Of Louisiana Inc	4530	Shreveport, LA	Private	22.0	37	8011
Healthcare Properties Inc	4531	Nashville, TN	Private	22.0	500	8059
Healthsouth Rehabilitation Hosp	4532	Largo, FL	Public Family Member	22.0	250	8099
Northern Ill Physcn Group Pc	4533	Dixon, IL	Private	22.0	150	8011
St Marys Hospital For Children	4534	Bayside, NY	Private	22.0	450	8069
Summitt Cosmetic Group	4535	Beverly Hills, CA	Private	22.0	73	8011
Tanana Valley Med Surgical Group	4536	Fairbanks, AK	Private	22.0	150	8011
U S H Of Pennsylvania, Inc	4537	Centre Hall, PA	Public Family Member	22.0	284	8011
University Of California	4538	San Francisco, CA	Private	22.0	NA	8063
Lubbock Regional	4539	Lubbock, TX	Private	22.0	325	8093
Union Health Service Inc	4540	Chicago, IL	Private	22.0	302	8011
Cancer Treatment Ctrs Of America	4541	Arlington Heights, IL	Private	22.0	600	8069
Van Wert County Hospital Assn	4542	Van Wert, OH	Private	21.9	354	8062
Mercer Cnty Jnt Twnshp	4543	Coldwater, OH	Private	21.9	412	8062
Lower Fla Keys Health Systems	4544	Key West, FL	Private	21.9	487	8062
Tenet Health System Hospitals	4545	Carrollton, TX	Public Family Member	21.9	NA	8062
West Vrgnia Rhbltion Hospital Inc	4546	Morgantown, WV	Public Family Member	21.9	357	8361
Saint Patrick's Home	4547	Bronx, NY	Private	21.9	350	8051
Home Health Vna Inc	4548	Haverhill, MA	Private	21.9	300	8082
Keystone Service Systems, Inc	4549	Harrisburg, PA	Private	21.9	500	8361
Lewis County General Hospital	4550	Lowville, NY	Private	21.9	400	8062

D&B COMPANY RANKINGS BY SALES

Company	Rank	Location	Type	Sales ($ mil.)	Employ- ment	Primary SIC
Natchtches Parish Hospital Svc Dst	4551	Natchitoches, LA	Private	21.8	150	8062
Delancey Street Foundation	4552	San Francisco, CA	Private	21.8	1,200	8361
Phoenix Programs Of New York	4553	New York, NY	Private	21.8	200	8361
Minnesota Department HumanSvcs	4554	Willmar, MN	Private	21.8	NA	8062
Tenneesse Dept-Mental Health	4555	Greeneville, TN	Private	21.8	NA	8051
Healthsphere Of America Inc	4556	Memphis, TN	Private	21.8	600	8082
Carillon House Nursing Fcilty	4557	Huntington, NY	Private	21.8	349	8051
Pathology Laboratories Ltd	4558	Hattiesburg, MS	Private	21.8	300	8071
Hospital Of Barstow, Inc	4559	Barstow, CA	Public Family Member	21.8	215	8062
Whitley Memorial Hospital	4560	Columbia City, IN	Private	21.8	340	8062
Arizona Boys Ranch Inc	4561	Queen Creek, AZ	Private	21.8	209	8361
Enzo Clinical Labs Inc	4562	Farmingdale, NY	Public Family Member	21.7	200	8071
Judson Retirement Community	4563	Cleveland, OH	Private	21.7	331	8059
Muscatine General Hospital	4564	Muscatine, IA	Private	21.7	360	8062
Santa Paula Memorial Hospital	4565	Santa Paula, CA	Private	21.7	202	8062
Margaret Mary Community Hosp	4566	Batesville, IN	Private	21.7	400	8062
Sunbury Community Hospital	4567	Sunbury, PA	Private	21.7	455	8062
Florida Sheriffs Youth Ranches	4568	Live Oak, FL	Private	21.7	250	8361
Advanced Radiology Llc	4569	Baltimore, MD	Private	21.7	317	8011
Allegheny County	4570	Pittsburgh, PA	Private	21.7	NA	8062
Catholic Health Partners Svcs	4571	Chicago, IL	Private	21.7	NA	8062
Columbia Bay Area Healthcare	4572	San Jose, CA	Public Family Member	21.7	NA	8062
County Of Los Angeles	4573	Lancaster, CA	Private	21.7	NA	8062
Healthtrust Inc - Hospital Co	4574	Blacksburg, VA	Public Family Member	21.7	NA	8062
Indiana Fmly & Social Svcs Adm	4575	Richmond, IN	Private	21.7	NA	8063
Phoenix Area Indian Health Svcs	4576	Laveen, AZ	Private	21.7	NA	8011
Tenet Health System Hospitals	4577	Indio, CA	Public Family Member	21.7	NA	8062
University Of Virginia	4578	Charlottesville, VA	Private	21.7	NA	8069
Veterans Health Administration	4579	Livermore, CA	Private	21.7	NA	8062
Blood Services Centl Ohio Reg	4580	Columbus, OH	Private	21.7	254	8099
Sycamore Shoals Hospital Inc	4581	Elizabethton, TN	Public Family Member	21.6	350	8062
Medical Education Assist Corp	4582	Mountain Home, TN	Private	21.6	230	8071
Youth Consultation Service	4583	Newark, NJ	Private	21.6	750	8093
Department Of Army	4584	Fort Eustis, VA	Private	21.6	NA	8062
Galen Of Florida, Inc	4585	Dade City, FL	Public Family Member	21.6	NA	8062
Minnesota Veterans Homes Board	4586	Saint Paul, MN	Private	21.6	950	8051
Pacificare Of California	4587	Phoenix, AZ	Public Family Member	21.6	NA	8011
Pacificare Of California	4588	Long Beach, CA	Public Family Member	21.6	NA	8011
Permanente Medical Group, Inc	4589	Pasadena, CA	Private	21.6	NA	8011
Tenet Healthcare Corporation	4590	Tampa, FL	Public Family Member	21.6	NA	8062
Upson Regional Medical Center	4591	Thomaston, GA	Private	21.6	482	8062
Veterans Health Administration	4592	Wilmington, DE	Private	21.6	NA	8062
Whittier Hospital Med Ctr Inc	4593	Whittier, CA	Public Family Member	21.6	481	8062
Monadnock Community Hospital Inc	4594	Peterborough, NH	Private	21.6	350	8062
Cape Medical Inc	4595	Detroit, MI	Private	21.6	15	8011
Blythedale Children's Hospital	4596	Valhalla, NY	Private	21.6	330	8069
Little Rock Health Mgt Assoc	4597	Little Rock, AR	Private	21.6	306	8062
Memorial Med Group A Prof Corp	4598	Torrance, CA	Private	21.6	160	8011
Mckendree Village Inc	4599	Hermitage, TN	Private	21.5	395	8361
Soldiers & Sailors Hospital	4600	Penn Yan, NY	Private	21.5	535	8062
South Shore Mntal Health Ctr Inc	4601	Quincy, MA	Private	21.5	195	8093
Institute For Community Living	4602	New York, NY	Private	21.5	300	8052
Mt Graham Community Hospital	4603	Safford, AZ	Private	21.5	260	8062
City Of Salem	4604	Salem, MA	Private	21.5	NA	8069
Columbia East Houston Med Ctr	4605	Houston, TX	Public Family Member	21.5	480	8062
Hawaii Department Of Health	4606	Wailuku, HI	Private	21.5	NA	8062
Hospital Corp Of Douglas	4607	Roseburg, OR	Public Family Member	21.5	480	8062
Jewish Hospital Healthcare Svcs	4608	Lexington, KY	Private	21.5	NA	8062
North Carolina Dept Human	4609	Goldsboro, NC	Private	21.5	NA	8051
Pentagon City Hospital Inc	4610	Arlington, VA	Private	21.5	480	8062
University Of Minnesota	4611	Minneapolis, MN	Private	21.5	NA	8062
Wing Memorial Hospital Corp	4612	Palmer, MA	Private	21.5	480	8062
Kent Community Hospital Complex	4613	Grand Rapids, MI	Private	21.5	441	8069
Broken Arrow Medical Center	4614	Broken Arrow, OK	Private	21.5	450	8062
Shenandoah Memorial Hospital	4615	Woodstock, VA	Private	21.5	430	8062
Aviv Health Care, Inc.	4616	Minneapolis, MN	Private	21.4	700	8051
Benedictine Living Communities	4617	Duluth, MN	Private	21.4	565	8051
Columbus Community Hospital	4618	Columbus, NE	Private	21.4	315	8062
Benjamin Franklin Clinic	4619	Philadelphia, PA	Private	21.4	313	8011
Columbia Dunwoody Medical Ctr	4620	Atlanta, GA	Public Family Member	21.4	477	8062

D&B COMPANY RANKINGS BY SALES

Company	Rank	Location	Type	Sales ($ mil.)	Employ-ment	Primary SIC
H C A Health Services Ga Inc	4621	Tucker, GA	Public Family Member	21.4	NA	8062
Palms West Hospital Inc	4622	Loxahatchee, FL	Public Family Member	21.4	477	8062
University Wisconsin System	4623	Madison, WI	Private	21.4	NA	8071
Camelot Care Center Inc	4624	Seminole, FL	Private	21.4	614	8361
Pratt Regional Med Ctr Corp	4625	Pratt, KS	Private	21.4	288	8062
Phoebe Home Inc	4626	Allentown, PA	Private	21.4	350	8051
Aspen Valley Hospital Dst	4627	Aspen, CO	Private	21.3	180	8062
St Anthony Regional Hospital	4628	Carroll, IA	Private	21.3	425	8062
Albany Medical College	4629	Albany, NY	Private	21.3	NA	8011
Delaware Dept Health Social Svcs	4630	New Castle, DE	Private	21.3	NA	8063
Golden Valley Memorial Hosp	4631	Clinton, MO	Private	21.3	475	8062
Guadalupe Medical Center Inc	4632	Carlsbad, NM	Public Family Member	21.3	475	8062
Hospital Corp Of Utah Inc	4633	Nashville, TN	Public Family Member	21.3	474	8062
Meridian Behavioral Health Care	4634	Lake City, FL	Private	21.3	700	8093
Metropolitan Life Insur Co	4635	Maitland, FL	Private	21.3	NA	8011
New York, The City	4636	Brooklyn, NY	Private	21.3	NA	8011
Rhd Memorial Medical Center	4637	Dallas, TX	Private	21.3	475	8062
University Of Pennsylvania	4638	Philadelphia, PA	Private	21.3	NA	8011
Gilmore Memorial Hospital	4639	Amory, MS	Private	21.3	420	8062
Community Living Options Inc	4640	Galesburg, IL	Private	21.3	498	8361
Dental-Net Inc	4641	Tucson, AZ	Private	21.2	200	8021
Porter Hospital Inc	4642	Middlebury, VT	Private	21.2	337	8062
Waldo County General Hospital	4643	Belfast, ME	Private	21.2	320	8062
Woodlawn Hospital	4644	Rochester, IN	Private	21.2	458	8062
Northeast Valley Health Corp	4645	San Fernando, CA	Private	21.2	450	8011
Kauai Medical Clinic Inc	4646	Lihue, HI	Private	21.2	310	8011
Laboratory Corp Amer Holdings	4647	Birmingham, AL	Private	21.2	NA	8071
Pima County	4648	Tucson, AZ	Private	21.2	NA	8082
Stl Management, Inc	4649	Saint Charles, MO	Private	21.2	300	8049
Holliswood Care Center Inc	4650	Hollis, NY	Private	21.2	250	8051
Christian Care Centers Inc	4651	Mesquite, TX	Private	21.2	500	8051
Tracy Sutter Community Mem Hosp	4652	Tracy, CA	Private	21.1	400	8062
Columbia-Healthone L L C	4653	Aurora, CO	Private	21.1	NA	8062
Department Of Air Force	4654	Hill Air Force Base, UT	Private	21.1	NA	8062
Mental Health, Department	4655	Farmington, MO	Private	21.1	NA	8063
Harris Methodist Erath County	4656	Stephenville, TX	Private	21.1	205	8062
Morris Hospital	4657	Morris, IL	Private	21.1	525	8062
Everett House	4658	Boston, MA	Private	21.1	NA	8361
Mental Health Care Inc	4659	Tampa, FL	Private	21.1	299	8093
Muhlenberg Community Hospital	4660	Greenville, KY	Private	21.1	450	8062
Murphy Medical Center	4661	Murphy, NC	Private	21.0	425	8062
Community Health Plan Of Ohio	4662	Newark, OH	Private	21.0	67	8011
Johnson Cy Eye & Ear Hospital Inc	4663	Johnson City, TN	Public Family Member	21.0	165	8069
Marathon H M A Inc	4664	Marathon, FL	Public Family Member	21.0	135	8062
Sabine Valley Center	4665	Longview, TX	Private	21.0	550	8093
Westminster-Canterbury Corp	4666	Richmond, VA	Private	21.0	550	8361
Silver Lake Nursing Home Inc	4667	Staten Island, NY	Private	21.0	250	8051
All Seasons Living Centers	4668	Bellevue, WA	Private	21.0	750	8059
Always Caring Home Care Svcs	4669	El Paso, TX	Private	21.0	400	8082
Caremark Inc	4670	Skokie, IL	Public Family Member	21.0	NA	8092
Central Ohio Medical Clinic	4671	Columbus, OH	Private	21.0	175	8011
Edwards & Henson, Dds	4672	Kinston, NC	Private	21.0	500	8021
Healthsouth Of Midland, Inc	4673	Midland, TX	Public Family Member	21.0	150	8093
Highland Care Center, Inc	4674	Jamaica, NY	Private	21.0	245	8051
Horizon Physician Network Llc	4675	Columbus, GA	Private	21.0	225	8011
Hospital Group Of Illinois	4676	Chicago, IL	Public Family Member	21.0	300	8063
New York And Presbyterian Hosp	4677	New York, NY	Private	21.0	NA	8069
Physicians Ind Med Group	4678	San Diego, CA	Private	21.0	307	8011
Rehabilitation Support Service	4679	Guilderland, NY	Private	21.0	516	8361
Rockaway Home Attendant Svcs	4680	Far Rockaway, NY	Private	21.0	1,200	8082
Sartori Memorial Hospital	4681	Cedar Falls, IA	Private	21.0	350	8062
Seniorcare Inc	4682	Louisville, KY	Private	21.0	600	8052
Shriners Hsptals For Children	4683	Sacramento, CA	Private	21.0	NA	8069
Silliker Laboratories Group	4684	Homewood, IL	Private	21.0	500	8071
Western Wash Med Group Inc Ps	4685	Everett, WA	Private	21.0	150	8011
Grinnell Regional Medical Ctr	4686	Grinnell, IA	Private	21.0	375	8062
Tolfree Memorial Hospital	4687	West Branch, MI	Private	21.0	350	8062
St Mary's Healthcare Center	4688	Pierre, SD	Private	21.0	450	8062
Sterling Rock Fls Clinic Ltd	4689	Sterling, IL	Private	20.9	250	8011
Interim Health Care Inc	4690	Greenville, SC	Private	20.9	339	8082

D&B COMPANY RANKINGS BY SALES

Company	Rank	Location	Type	Sales ($ mil.)	Employ-ment	Primary SIC
Ncs, Inc.	4691	Fort Wayne, IN	Private	20.9	600	8051
Baptist Memorial Hospital	4692	Blytheville, AR	Private	20.9	467	8062
United/Dynacare Llc	4693	Milwaukee, WI	Private	20.9	250	8071
Amsterdam Nursing Home Corp	4694	New York, NY	Private	20.9	340	8051
Jewish Home Of Rochester, Ny	4695	Rochester, NY	Private	20.9	503	8051
Eunice Regional Medical Center	4696	Eunice, LA	Private	20.9	250	8062
Mhm Services, Inc	4697	Vienna, VA	Public	20.9	330	8063
Greater Lyn Mntl Hth/Rtdtn Ass	4698	Lynn, MA	Private	20.8	800	8361
Meadowbrook Rhbilitation Group	4699	Emeryville, CA	Public	20.8	613	8093
St Anthony's Hospital	4700	Pendleton, OR	Private	20.8	282	8062
Healix Infusion Therapy Inc	4701	Houston, TX	Private	20.8	200	8082
Medical Income Properties 2a	4702	Atlanta, GA	Public	20.8	325	8051
Dakota Clinic Ltd	4703	Fargo, ND	Private	20.8	NA	8011
Episcopal Health Services Inc	4704	Far Rockaway, NY	Private	20.8	NA	8051
Illinois Dept Human Resources	4705	Anna, IL	Private	20.8	NA	8063
New York Blood Center, Inc.	4706	New York, NY	Private	20.8	NA	8071
Samaritan Health System	4707	Lake Havasu City, AZ	Private	20.8	NA	8062
White-Wilson Medical Ctr P A	4708	Fort Walton Beach, FL	Private	20.8	304	8011
Titusville Area Hospital	4709	Titusville, PA	Private	20.8	300	8062
Crestview Of Ohio Inc	4710	Sylvania, OH	Private	20.8	150	8051
Careselect Group Inc	4711	Dallas, TX	Private	20.8	375	8099
Sullivan Diagnstc Trtmnt Ctr	4712	Harris, NY	Private	20.7	400	8361
Memorial Hospital Inc	4713	Wellsville, NY	Private	20.7	380	8062
Mendocino Coast District Hosp	4714	Fort Bragg, CA	Private	20.7	300	8062
St Francis Hospital Thrd Ord (Inc)	4715	Litchfield, IL	Private	20.7	370	8062
Hillside Rehabilitation Hosp	4716	Warren, OH	Private	20.7	345	8069
Brethren Home Community	4717	New Oxford, PA	Private	20.7	590	8051
Columbia/Hca Healthcare Corp	4718	Montgomery, AL	Public Family Member	20.7	NA	8062
County Of Cook, Illinois	4719	Chicago, IL	Private	20.7	NA	8062
County Of Shelby	4720	Memphis, TN	Private	20.7	NA	8062
Doctors Hospital	4721	Columbus, OH	Private	20.7	NA	8062
H C A Health Services Tenn Inc	4722	Hermitage, TN	Public Family Member	20.7	NA	8062
Idexx Veterinary Services Inc	4723	West Sacramento, CA	Public Family Member	20.7	430	8071
Texas Health System Inc	4724	Paris, TX	Private	20.7	NA	8062
Watts Health Foundation Inc	4725	Inglewood, CA	Private	20.7	NA	8011
U V M C Nursing Care Inc	4726	Troy, OH	Private	20.7	5	8051
Maine Veterans Home	4727	Augusta, ME	Private	20.7	485	8052
Nexthealth Inc	4728	Tucson, AZ	Public	20.7	370	8069
Newton Healthcare Corporation	4729	Newton, KS	Private	20.6	380	8062
Pacific Cataract Laser Inst P S	4730	Chehalis, WA	Private	20.6	226	8011
Baptist Mem Health Care Corp	4731	Oxford, MS	Private	20.6	NA	8062
County Of Lehigh	4732	Allentown, PA	Private	20.6	NA	8361
Department Of Air Force	4733	Oklahoma City, OK	Private	20.6	NA	8062
Indian Health Service	4734	Shiprock, NM	Private	20.6	NA	8062
Roseland Community Hospital Assn	4735	Chicago, IL	Private	20.6	460	8062
St James Community Hospital	4736	Butte, MT	Private	20.6	460	8062
Valley Hospital Association	4737	Palmer, AK	Private	20.6	460	8062
Virginia Dpt Mntl Health, Mr Sa	4738	Fairfax, VA	Private	20.6	NA	8069
Tuolumne General Hospital	4739	Sonora, CA	Private	20.6	290	8062
Memorial Health Ventures Inc	4740	Houston, TX	Private	20.6	120	8082
Doctors Laboratory Inc	4741	Valdosta, GA	Private	20.6	300	8071
Divine Savior Hospital Nursing Hm	4742	Portage, WI	Private	20.6	350	8062
Eastern Long Island Hospital	4743	Greenport, NY	Private	20.6	252	8062
Health Acquisition Corp	4744	Jamaica, NY	Public Family Member	20.6	1,000	8082
Su-Pra Enterprises Inc	4745	Franklin, MI	Private	20.6	380	8082
Caregivers Inc	4746	Brooklyn, NY	Private	20.5	1,400	8082
Kernodle Clinic Inc	4747	Burlington, NC	Private	20.5	220	8011
Baton Rouge Clinic A Med Corp	4748	Baton Rouge, LA	Private	20.5	300	8011
Care Group Inc	4749	Indianapolis, IN	Private	20.5	300	8011
Clinical Associates, Pa	4750	Baltimore, MD	Private	20.5	300	8011
Elias F Ghanem Ltd	4751	Las Vegas, NV	Private	20.5	300	8011
Hand Surgery Associates Of Ind	4752	Indianapolis, IN	Private	20.5	300	8011
Healthcare San Antonio Inc	4753	San Antonio, TX	Private	20.5	300	8011
Jacksonville Health Care Group	4754	Jacksonville, FL	Private	20.5	300	8011
Kaiser Fnd Health Pln/Ma Inc	4755	Holyoke, MA	Private	20.5	300	8011
Medical Assoc Of Lehigh Valley Pc	4756	Allentown, PA	Private	20.5	300	8011
Melbourne Intl Med Assc Inc	4757	Melbourne, FL	Private	20.5	300	8011
P C Healthfirst Physician	4758	Lakewood, CO	Private	20.5	300	8011
Priority Health Inc	4759	Grand Rapids, MI	Private	20.5	300	8011
United Medical Group	4760	Saint Louis, MO	Private	20.5	300	8011

D&B COMPANY RANKINGS BY SALES

Company	Rank	Location	Type	Sales ($ mil.)	Employ-ment	Primary SIC
University Physcn Assoc Of Nj	4761	Newark, NJ	Private	20.5	300	8011
Wesley Health Care Center Inc	4762	Saratoga Springs, NY	Private	20.5	515	8051
Img Health Care Network, Llc	4763	New Orleans, LA	Private	20.5	210	8011
Regina Medical Center	4764	Hastings, MN	Private	20.5	475	8062
East Texas Med Cntr-Jcksonville	4765	Jacksonville, TX	Private	20.5	350	8062
Glengariff Corp	4766	Glen Cove, NY	Private	20.5	500	8051
Northern Dutchess Hospital	4767	Rhinebeck, NY	Private	20.5	400	8062
Rehabilitation Associates Inc	4768	Norwood, MA	Private	20.5	600	8051
Healthsouth Of Montgomery	4769	Montgomery, AL	Public Family Member	20.4	270	8069
United Cerebal Palsy Asc	4770	Roosevelt, NY	Private	20.4	600	8099
C M Healthcare Resources Inc	4771	Deerfield, IL	Private	20.4	400	8082
Coffeyville Regl Med Ctr Fndtn	4772	Coffeyville, KS	Private	20.4	380	8062
C A C/H Development Inc	4773	Dallas, TX	Public Family Member	20.4	250	8062
County Of Tulare	4774	Tulare, CA	Private	20.4	NA	8011
Fhp International Corporation	4775	Fountain Valley, CA	Public Family Member	20.4	NA	8011
Hallmark Health Services Inc	4776	Tustin, CA	Public Family Member	20.4	900	8051
Hmu Inc	4777	Minneapolis, MN	Private	20.4	NA	8051
Massachusetts Dept Mental Health	4778	Medfield, MA	Private	20.4	NA	8063
Osf Healthcare System	4779	Galesburg, IL	Private	20.4	NA	8062
Peninsula Psychiatric Center	4780	Louisville, TN	Private	20.4	550	8063
Republic Health Corp Of Rockwall	4781	Rowlett, TX	Public Family Member	20.4	455	8062
S N F Properties, Inc	4782	La Canada, CA	Private	20.4	900	8051
Tenneesse Dept-Mental Health	4783	Knoxville, TN	Private	20.4	NA	8063
United Health Services Inc	4784	Toccoa, GA	Private	20.4	NA	8051
Visalia Medical Clinic Inc	4785	Visalia, CA	Private	20.4	299	8011
Wisconsin Dept Health Fmly Svcs	4786	Winnebago, WI	Private	20.4	NA	8063
Jersey Community Hospital	4787	Jerseyville, IL	Private	20.4	243	8062
Monroe Medical Foundation Inc	4788	Tompkinsville, KY	Private	20.4	266	8062
Grand View Hospital Inc	4789	Ironwood, MI	Private	20.4	300	8062
Sheltering Arms Hospital (Inc)	4790	Richmond, VA	Private	20.3	480	8069
Astor Home For Children	4791	Rhinebeck, NY	Private	20.3	600	8361
Prime Care Services Inc	4792	Franklin, MI	Private	20.3	375	8082
Life Mgt Ctr For Mh/Mr Svcs	4793	El Paso, TX	Private	20.3	500	8093
Baptist Healthcare Affliates Inc	4794	Louisville, KY	Private	20.3	413	8062
Healthplex Inc	4795	Uniondale, NY	Public	20.3	54	8021
Summit Pointe	4796	Battle Creek, MI	Private	20.3	125	8093
Selectcare Hmo Inc	4797	Troy, MI	Private	20.3	297	8011
State Of Ohio	4798	Cincinnati, OH	Private	20.3	NA	8063
United Healthcare South Inc	4799	Birmingham, AL	Public Family Member	20.3	508	8099
Veterans Health Administration	4800	Saint Cloud, MN	Private	20.3	NA	8062
Augustana Lutheran Home	4801	Brooklyn, NY	Private	20.3	142	8051
Good Shepherd Services	4802	New York, NY	Private	20.3	400	8361
Dukes Memorial Hospital	4803	Peru, IN	Private	20.3	350	8062
Summersville Memorial Hosp	4804	Summersville, WV	Private	20.3	400	8062
Fayette Cnty Hospital Nursing Hm	4805	Fayette, AL	Private	20.3	420	8062
Orthopaedic Hospital	4806	Los Angeles, CA	Private	20.2	376	8069
Monsour Medical Center	4807	Jeannette, PA	Private	20.2	358	8062
American Red Cross, The	4808	Saint Louis, MO	Private	20.2	NA	8099
Bedford-Northeast Community Hosp	4809	Bedford, TX	Public Family Member	20.2	NA	8062
Columbia/Hca Healthcare Corp	4810	Lawton, OK	Public Family Member	20.2	NA	8062
Columbia/Hca Healthcare Corp	4811	Texas City, TX	Public Family Member	20.2	NA	8062
H C A Health Svcs Texas Inc	4812	Mcallen, TX	Public Family Member	20.2	NA	8062
Henry Ford Health System	4813	West Bloomfield, MI	Private	20.2	NA	8069
Sch Health Care System	4814	Houston, TX	Private	20.2	NA	8062
Tenet Healthcare Corporation	4815	Kenner, LA	Public Family Member	20.2	NA	8062
Triad Laboratory Alliance, Llc	4816	Greensboro, NC	Private	20.2	420	8071
Veterans Health Administration	4817	Baltimore, MD	Private	20.2	NA	8062
Milwaukee Protestant Home	4818	Milwaukee, WI	Private	20.2	240	8059
Grayson County Hospital	4819	Leitchfield, KY	Private	20.2	360	8062
Jackson Stonewall Mem Hosp	4820	Weston, WV	Private	20.2	270	8062
Northeastern Vt Regional Hosp	4821	Saint Johnsbury, VT	Private	20.1	300	8062
Washington Cnty Rgnal Med Ctr	4822	Sandersville, GA	Private	20.1	343	8062
Brown County General Hospital	4823	Georgetown, OH	Private	20.1	292	8062
Helena Hospital Association	4824	Helena, AR	Private	20.1	310	8062
United Church Of Christ Homes	4825	Hummelstown, PA	Private	20.1	528	8051
Mccurtain Memorial Medical Mgt	4826	Idabel, OK	Private	20.1	325	8062
Apalachee Center For HumanSvcs	4827	Tallahassee, FL	Private	20.1	443	8063
Baptist Healthcare Group	4828	Nashville, TN	Private	20.1	280	8011
Baptist Hospitals Health Systems	4829	Phoenix, AZ	Private	20.1	NA	8021
Cary Medical Center	4830	Caribou, ME	Private	20.1	450	8062

D&B COMPANY RANKINGS BY SALES

Company	Rank	Location	Type	Sales ($ mil.)	Employ-ment	Primary SIC
Chico Community Hospital Inc	4831	Chico, CA	Public Family Member	20.1	450	8062
Franciscan Health Systems	4832	Warwick, NY	Private	20.1	450	8062
Home Health Management Svcs	4833	New York, NY	Private	20.1	1,247	8082
Lahey Hitchcock Clinic	4834	Nashua, NH	Private	20.1	NA	8011
Lincoln Community Medical Corp	4835	Houston, TX	Public Family Member	20.1	450	8062
Mountain View Hospital, Inc	4836	Payson, UT	Public Family Member	20.1	450	8062
Park Lane Med Ctr Kans Cy Inc	4837	Kansas City, MO	Private	20.1	450	8062
Virginia Medical Associates	4838	Springfield, VA	Private	20.1	294	8011
Vivra Asthma Allrgy Creamerica	4839	San Mateo, CA	Private	20.1	294	8011
Wahiawa Hospital Association	4840	Wahiawa, HI	Private	20.1	450	8062
Wellington Regional Med Ctr	4841	West Palm Beach, FL	Public Family Member	20.1	450	8062
United Cerebral Palsy Associat	4842	Hauppauge, NY	Private	20.1	550	8099
Revival Home Health Care Inc	4843	Brooklyn, NY	Private	20.1	400	8082
Baptist Health Care Affiliates	4844	Nashville, TN	Private	20.1	142	8062
F W Of Saratoga, Inc	4845	Saratoga Springs, NY	Private	20.1	300	8063
Hospice Hillsborough Inc	4846	Tampa, FL	Private	20.1	400	8093
Utah Senior Services, Inc	4847	Cornish, UT	Private	20.1	650	8051
Tahlequah Hospital Authority	4848	Tahlequah, OK	Private	20.0	295	8062
Allegheny Univ Of Health Scences	4849	Philadelphia, PA	Private	20.0	NA	8063
Americare Certif Special Svcs	4850	Brooklyn, NY	Private	20.0	300	8082
Behrman Chiropractic Clinics	4851	Arlington, TX	Private	20.0	180	8041
Biomedical Systems Corporation	4852	Saint Louis, MO	Private	20.0	95	8099
Chw Central Coast	4853	Santa Barbara, CA	Private	20.0	NA	8062
Citizens Bmc	4854	Talladega, AL	Private	20.0	380	8062
Columbia/Hca Healthcare Corp	4855	Dublin, GA	Public Family Member	20.0	NA	8062
Correctional Physicians Svcs	4856	Blue Bell, PA	Private	20.0	315	8099
Doctors Hospital Shreveport Inc	4857	Shreveport, LA	Public Family Member	20.0	411	8069
Elder Healthcare Developers Llc	4858	Norcross, GA	Private	20.0	1	8052
Elkhart Clinic Llc	4859	Elkhart, IN	Private	20.0	170	8011
Healthmark Of Walton Inc	4860	Defuniak Springs, FL	Private	20.0	150	8062
Healthsouth Of New Mexico	4861	Albuquerque, NM	Public Family Member	20.0	274	8069
Hood General Hospital	4862	Granbury, TX	Public Family Member	20.0	175	8062
Horsham Clinic (Inc)	4863	Ambler, PA	Public Family Member	20.0	250	8063
Hunt Assoc Asssted Living Corp	4864	Abingdon, VA	Private	20.0	35	8051
Intermountain Health Care Inc	4865	Pocatello, ID	Private	20.0	NA	8062
Laboratory Sciences Ariz Llc	4866	Tempe, AZ	Private	20.0	350	8071
Lanier Professional Services	4867	Atlanta, GA	Public Family Member	20.0	500	8099
Lorien Nrsing Rhbilitation Ctr	4868	Lutherville Tim., MD	Private	20.0	300	8051
Maxicare Louisiana, Inc	4869	New Orleans, LA	Public Family Member	20.0	28	8011
Mobile Mental Health Center	4870	Mobile, AL	Private	20.0	350	8093
National Diagnostic Laboratory	4871	Moreno Valley, CA	Private	20.0	15	8071
Pathway Healthcare Services	4872	Westwood, MA	Private	20.0	700	8082
Pennsylvania Dept Pub Welfare	4873	Clarks Summit, PA	Private	20.0	NA	8063
Pickens Healthcare Association	4874	Jasper, GA	Private	20.0	175	8062
Psychiatric Hospitals Of Pa	4875	Lafayette Hill, PA	Private	20.0	350	8063
Radiologic Specialists Of Ind	4876	Indianapolis, IN	Private	20.0	55	8011
Radiology & Imaging Inc	4877	Springfield, MA	Private	20.0	118	8011
Royco Inc	4878	Fort Lauderdale, FL	Private	20.0	200	8071
Saad Enterprises Inc	4879	Mobile, AL	Private	20.0	NA	8049
Sherwood Healthcare Corp.	4880	Greenfield, IN	Private	20.0	880	8051
St Vincent's Ambulatory Care	4881	Jacksonville, FL	Private	20.0	39	8011
Summit Landmark Orthopedic Asc	4882	Saint Paul, MN	Private	20.0	140	8011
Temple Surgical Center Inc	4883	New Haven, CT	Private	20.0	46	8011
Veterans Health Administration	4884	Perry Point, MD	Private	20.0	NA	8062
Rochester Gen Long Term Care	4885	Webster, NY	Private	20.0	410	8051
Tabitha, Inc	4886	Lincoln, NE	Private	20.0	900	8361
St Luke's Quakertown Hospital	4887	Quakertown, PA	Private	20.0	277	8062
Gritman Medical Center	4888	Moscow, ID	Private	20.0	320	8062
Woods Memorial Hospital Dst	4889	Etowah, TN	Private	19.9	400	8062
All Care Visiting Nurse	4890	Lynn, MA	Private	19.9	600	8082
Doctors Hospital Of Jackson	4891	Jackson, MI	Private	19.9	234	8062
Moorings, Incorporated	4892	Naples, FL	Private	19.9	376	8361
Blue Ridge Orthopedic Assoc Pc	4893	Warrenton, VA	Private	19.9	291	8011
Health Care Administration	4894	San Antonio, TX	Private	19.9	900	8059
Sisters Of Providence In Ore	4895	Portland, OR	Private	19.9	NA	8062
Smithkline Beecham Clinical Labs	4896	Schaumburg, IL	Private	19.9	NA	8071
South Dakota Dept HumanSvcs	4897	Yankton, SD	Private	19.9	NA	8063
Northern	4898	Bishop, CA	Private	19.9	300	8062
St Mary's Hospital Inc	4899	Norton, VA	Private	19.9	370	8062
Under 21 Inc	4900	New York, NY	Private	19.9	422	8361

D&B COMPANY RANKINGS BY SALES

Company	Rank	Location	Type	Sales ($ mil.)	Employ- ment	Primary SIC
St Ann's Home For Aged	4901	Rochester, NY	Private	19.9	750	8361
Clarendon Memorial Hospital	4902	Manning, SC	Private	19.9	724	8062
Trinity Community Medical	4903	Brenham, TX	Private	19.9	270	8062
Circles Of Care Inc	4904	Melbourne, FL	Private	19.8	400	8063
Harbor Behavioral Health	4905	New Port Richey, FL	Private	19.8	460	8093
Pineville Community Hospital Assn	4906	Pineville, KY	Private	19.8	355	8062
Sunnyside Community Hospital Assn	4907	Sunnyside, WA	Private	19.8	235	8062
Aetna Health Management, Inc	4908	Hartford, CT	Public Family Member	19.8	290	8011
Community Hospitals Of Indiana	4909	Indianapolis, IN	Private	19.8	NA	8062
Florida Dept Environmental	4910	Daytona Beach, FL	Private	19.8	NA	8011
Galen Hospital Corporation Inc	4911	Indianapolis, IN	Public Family Member	19.8	NA	8062
Harvard Pilgrim Health Care	4912	Braintree, MA	Private	19.8	NA	8011
Healthsouth Sub-Acute Ctr	4913	Mechanicsburg, PA	Public Family Member	19.8	650	8093
Inova Health Care Services	4914	Falls Church, VA	Private	19.8	NA	8062
Public Hospital District 1	4915	Shelton, WA	Private	19.8	300	8062
St John's Home Of Milwaukee	4916	Milwaukee, WI	Private	19.8	560	8051
Wadsworth-Rtmn Area Hsptl	4917	Wadsworth, OH	Private	19.8	290	8062
Lutheran Health Care Assn	4918	Saint Louis, MO	Private	19.8	500	8059
Bellevue Hospital Inc	4919	Bellevue, OH	Private	19.7	350	8062
Fort Sanders-Sevier Med Ctr	4920	Sevierville, TN	Private	19.7	310	8062
McDowell Hospital Inc	4921	Marion, NC	Private	19.7	310	8062
Columbia/Hca Healthcare Corp	4922	Houston, TX	Public Family Member	19.7	NA	8062
Medrehab Inc	4923	Milwaukee, WI	Public Family Member	19.7	1,261	8049
Mid-Island Hospital, Inc	4924	Bethpage, NY	Private	19.7	440	8062
Quad Cities Pathologist Group	4925	Davenport, IA	Private	19.7	410	8071
Sun City Hospital Inc	4926	Ruskin, FL	Public Family Member	19.7	440	8062

D&B COMPANY RANKINGS BY EMPLOYMENT

Company	Rank	Location	Type	Sales ($ mil.)	Employ-ment	Primary SIC
Columbia/Hca Healthcare Corp	1	Nashville, TN	Public	18,819.0	295,000	8062
Tenet Healthcare Corporation	2	Santa Barbara, CA	Public	9,895.0	116,800	8062
Integrated Health Services	3	Owings Mills, MD	Public	1,993.2	86,000	8051
Vencor, Inc	4	Louisville, KY	Private	3,116.0	76,800	8062
Beverly Enterprises Inc	5	Fort Smith, AR	Public	3,217.1	74,000	8051
Sun Healthcare Group Inc	6	Albuquerque, NM	Public	2,010.8	68,900	8051
Mariner Post-Acute Network	7	Atlanta, GA	Public	3,000.0	62,000	8051
Healthsouth Corporation	8	Birmingham, AL	Public	3,017.3	56,281	8093
Galen Health Care Inc	9	Nashville, TN	Public Family Member	2,641.1	55,900	8062
Catholic Health Initiative	10	Denver, CO	Private	4,001.6	45,000	8062
Novacare Inc	11	King Of Prussia, PA	Public	1,066.5	39,800	8049
New York Cy Health Hspitals Corp	12	New York, NY	Private	3,775.9	38,000	8062
Genesis Health Ventures Inc	13	Kennett Square, PA	Public	1,099.8	35,000	8059
Mayo Foundation	14	Rochester, MN	Private	2,565.6	30,497	8011
Tenet Health System Medical	15	Santa Barbara, CA	Public Family Member	1,426.4	30,200	8062
Manorcare Health Services Inc	16	Gaithersburg, MD	Public Family Member	1,524.2	30,000	8051
Ornda Investments Inc	17	Santa Barbara, CA	Public Family Member	1,416.9	30,000	8062
Talbert Medical Mgt Corp	18	Costa Mesa, CA	Public Family Member	1,181.0	29,526	8099
Ornda Healthcorp	19	Santa Barbara, CA	Public	1,227.8	26,000	8062
Kaiser Foundation Hospitals	20	Oakland, CA	Private	3,159.0	25,000	8062
Life Care Centers Of America	21	Cleveland, TN	Private	443.8	25,000	8051
Evangelical Lutheran	22	Sioux Falls, SD	Private	649.7	24,000	8051
Health Care Retirement Manor Care	23	Toledo, OH	Public	892.0	22,000	8051
Tenet Health System Hospitals	24	Dallas, TX	Public Family Member	2,990.9	22,000	8062
Allina Health System	25	Hopkins, MN	Private	2,526.7	21,000	8011
Ihc Health Services Inc	26	Salt Lake City, UT	Private	1,424.8	21,000	8062
Ssm Health Care	27	Saint Louis, MO	Private	532.3	20,400	8062
Humana Inc	28	Louisville, KY	Public	7,880.0	19,500	8011
Permanente Medical Group Inc	29	Oakland, CA	Private	2,479.8	19,000	8011
Phycor Inc	30	Nashville, TN	Public	1,119.6	19,000	8011
Laboratory Corp Amer Holdings	31	Burlington, NC	Private	1,519.0	18,600	8071
National Medical Care Inc	32	Lexington, MA	Public Family Member	1,028.6	18,000	8092
Universal Health Services	33	King Of Prussia, PA	Public	1,442.7	17,800	8062
Adventist Health System/Sunbelt	34	Winter Park, FL	Private	828.0	17,542	8062
H C A, Inc.	35	Nashville, TN	Public Family Member	826.1	17,500	8062
Extendicare Health Services	36	Milwaukee, WI	Private	916.2	17,388	8051
Holy Cross Health System Corp	37	South Bend, IN	Private	22.9	17,000	8062
Novacare, Inc	38	King Of Prussia, PA	Public Family Member	1,066.5	17,000	8049
Quorum Health Group Inc	39	Brentwood, TN	Public	1,572.4	17,000	8062
Health Care Rtrement Corp Amer	40	Toledo, OH	Public Family Member	708.1	16,500	8051
Henry Ford Health System	41	Detroit, MI	Private	1,937.3	16,300	8062
Quest Diagnostics Incorporated	42	Teterboro, NJ	Private	1,528.7	16,300	8071
Regency Health Services Inc	43	Tustin, CA	Public Family Member	558.0	16,170	8051
National Healthcare Corp	44	Murfreesboro, TN	Public	463.5	16,000	8051
Inova Health Care Services	45	Springfield, VA	Private	682.9	15,000	8062
Multicare Companies Inc	46	Hackensack, NJ	Public	185.8	15,000	8051
Lutheran Health System	47	Fargo, ND	Private	665.3	14,707	8062
Grancare Inc	48	Atlanta, GA	Public Family Member	317.6	13,800	8051
Fairview Hospital Healthcare Svcs	49	Minneapolis, MN	Private	97.0	13,611	8062
North Shore University Hosp	50	Manhasset, NY	Private	425.0	12,228	8062
Bio-Medical Applications Mgt	51	Lexington, MA	Public Family Member	685.7	12,000	8092
Mount Sinai Hospital (Inc)	52	New York, NY	Private	872.1	12,000	8062
Samaritan Health System	53	Phoenix, AZ	Private	1,345.6	11,954	8062
Res-Care Inc	54	Louisville, KY	Public	306.1	11,900	8052
Cleveland Clinic Foundation	55	Cleveland, OH	Private	1,146.9	11,500	8062
Personal-Touch Home Care Inc	56	Bayside, NY	Private	109.3	11,500	8082
Extendicare Homes, Inc	57	Milwaukee, WI	Private	430.6	11,283	8051
Community Health Systems Inc	58	Brentwood, TN	Public	755.0	11,000	8062
Sisters Of Providence In Wash	59	Seattle, WA	Private	1,148.9	10,900	8062
Montefiore Medical Center	60	Bronx, NY	Private	1,188.2	10,794	8062
Ahs Hospital Corporation	61	Florham Park, NJ	Private	499.9	10,600	8062
Health Net	62	Woodland Hills, CA	Public	724.7	10,500	8011
Smithkline Beecham Clinical Labs	63	Collegeville, PA	Private	497.8	10,500	8071
General Hospital Corporation	64	Boston, MA	Private	635.7	10,156	8062
Columbia-Healthone L L C	65	Denver, CO	Private	471.5	10,000	8062
Fhp International Corporation	66	Santa Ana, CA	Public	690.2	10,000	8011
Girling Health Care Inc	67	Austin, TX	Private	90.6	10,000	8082
Health Management Associates	68	Naples, FL	Public	895.5	10,000	8062
Mediplex Group Inc	69	Albuquerque, NM	Public Family Member	457.7	10,000	8051
Shands Teaching Hospital & Clinic	70	Gainesville, FL	Private	505.8	10,000	8062

D&B COMPANY RANKINGS BY EMPLOYMENT

Company	Rank	Location	Type	Sales ($ mil.)	Employment	Primary SIC
Laboratory Corporation America	71	Burlington, NC	Public	464.6	9,800	8071
Apria Healthcare Group Inc	72	Costa Mesa, CA	Public	1,180.7	9,555	8082
William Beaumont Hospital	73	Royal Oak, MI	Private	837.6	9,400	8062
Examination Mgt Svcs Inc Amer	74	Dallas, TX	Private	374.0	9,350	8099
Sisters Of St Francis Health Svcs	75	Mishawaka, IN	Private	856.5	9,000	8062
Osf Healthcare System	76	Peoria, IL	Private	642.5	8,741	8062
Rush-Presby St Lukes Med Ctr	77	Chicago, IL	Private	482.7	8,500	8062
Beth Israel Medical Center	78	New York, NY	Private	834.0	8,100	8062
Methodist Health Care Memphis	79	Memphis, TN	Private	564.9	8,100	8062
Brigham And Womens Hospital Inc	80	Boston, MA	Private	507.1	8,000	8062
Grant/Rvrside Mthdst Hspitals	81	Columbus, OH	Private	556.0	8,000	8062
Orlando Rgonal Healthcare Sys	82	Orlando, FL	Private	558.5	8,000	8062
Scripps Health	83	San Diego, CA	Private	702.3	8,000	8051
St Lukes-Roosevelt Hospital Ctr	84	New York, NY	Private	598.4	8,000	8062
Baptist Mem Health Care Corp	85	Memphis, TN	Private	949.2	7,907	8062
Scripps Institutions Of Medici	86	San Diego, CA	Private	702.3	7,800	8062
Nme Properties Corp.	87	Santa Barbara, CA	Public Family Member	307.0	7,676	8099
St Joseph Health System	88	Orange, CA	Private	35.6	7,650	8082
Beth Israel Deaconess Med Ctr	89	Boston, MA	Private	675.0	7,600	8062
Paracelsus Healthcare Corp	90	Houston, TX	Public	659.2	7,600	8062
Medical College Of Georgia	91	Augusta, GA	Private	436.9	7,500	8062
Memorial Health Services	92	Long Beach, CA	Private	619.8	7,500	8062
St Louis University	93	Saint Louis, MO	Private	529.9	7,500	8062
Meridian Hospitals Corporation	94	Red Bank, NJ	Private	507.1	7,357	8062
Harborside Healthcare Corp	95	Boston, MA	Public	221.8	7,331	8051
University Of Ia Hospital & Clinic	96	Iowa City, IA	Private	571.0	7,083	8062
Addus Healthcare, Inc.	97	Chicago, IL	Private	95.7	7,000	8082
Brigham Medical Center Inc	98	Boston, MA	Private	456.0	7,000	8062
Charlotte Mecklenburg Hos	99	Charlotte, NC	Private	930.3	7,000	8062
Healthpartners, Inc	100	Minneapolis, MN	Private	1,178.5	7,000	8011
North Shore Health System	101	Great Neck, NY	Private	329.7	7,000	8062
Baptist Healthcare System	102	Louisville, KY	Private	562.8	6,850	8062
Fulton Dekalb Hospital Auth	103	Atlanta, GA	Private	369.5	6,700	8062
Long Island Jewish Med Ctr	104	New Hyde Park, NY	Private	476.7	6,700	8062
Sisters Of Providence In Ore	105	Seattle, WA	Private	465.4	6,700	8062
Washington University	106	Saint Louis, MO	Private	941.8	6,600	8062
Memorial Hermann Hospital Sys	107	Houston, TX	Private	615.9	6,500	8062
Texas Health Enterprises Inc	108	Denton, TX	Private	149.4	6,500	8051
Upmc Presbyterian	109	Pittsburgh, PA	Private	661.9	6,411	8062
St John's Health System Inc	110	Springfield, MO	Private	296.6	6,300	8062
Dallas County Hospital Dst	111	Dallas, TX	Private	561.3	6,200	8062
Mercy Healthcare Sacramento	112	Rancho Cordova, CA	Private	563.2	6,131	8062
Michigan Affl Healthcare Sys	113	Lansing, MI	Private	195.8	6,082	8062
Albany Medical Center Hosp	114	Albany, NY	Private	172.8	6,000	8062
Cedars-Sinai Medical Center	115	Los Angeles, CA	Private	681.5	6,000	8062
Charleston Area Medical Center	116	Charleston, WV	Private	424.8	6,000	8062
Chartwell Healthcare, Inc	117	Dallas, TX	Private	78.0	6,000	8051
Hillco, Ltd	118	Kinston, NC	Private	233.5	6,000	8051
Hopkins Johns Hospital Inc	119	Baltimore, MD	Private	601.5	6,000	8062
Outreach Health Care, Inc	120	Garland, TX	Private	183.1	6,000	8093
Scott & White Memrl Hospital	121	Temple, TX	Private	335.3	6,000	8062
Weight Watchers North America	122	Woodbury, NY	Public Family Member	183.1	6,000	8093
Yale-New Haven Hospital Inc	123	New Haven, CT	Private	450.9	5,959	8062
Alternative Living Services	124	Brookfield, WI	Public	130.7	5,935	8059
Presbyterian Healthcare Svcs	125	Albuquerque, NM	Private	580.9	5,800	8062
Care Enterprises Inc	126	Tustin, CA	Public Family Member	131.0	5,700	8051
Christiana Care Health Svcs	127	Wilmington, DE	Private	463.3	5,700	8062
Baptist Memorial Hospital	128	Memphis, TN	Private	428.5	5,680	8062
Unison Healthcare Corporation	129	Scottsdale, AZ	Public	148.7	5,600	8051
Camcare Inc	130	Charleston, WV	Private	525.2	5,500	8062
H C A Psychiatric Company	131	Nashville, TN	Public Family Member	203.7	5,500	8063
Medlantic Healthcare Group	132	Washington, DC	Private	634.2	5,500	8082
Peacehealth	133	Bellevue, WA	Private	466.8	5,500	8062
Toledo Hospital	134	Toledo, OH	Private	321.1	5,484	8062
North Carolina Baptist Hosp	135	Winston Salem, NC	Private	423.1	5,475	8062
Methodist Healthcare System	136	San Antonio, TX	Private	256.8	5,456	8062
Evergreen Healthcare, Inc	137	Atlanta, GA	Public Family Member	101.0	5,412	8052
Harris County Hospital Dst	138	Houston, TX	Private	315.4	5,412	8062
Baylor University Medical Ctr	139	Dallas, TX	Private	480.8	5,401	8062
Horizon West Inc	140	Rocklin, CA	Private	120.6	5,400	8059

D&B COMPANY RANKINGS BY EMPLOYMENT

Company	Rank	Location	Type	Sales ($ mil.)	Employ-ment	Primary SIC
North Broward Hospital Dst	141	Fort Lauderdale, FL	Private	463.0	5,400	8062
Patient Care Inc	142	West Orange, NJ	Public Family Member	99.6	5,300	8082
Swedish Health Services	143	Seattle, WA	Private	297.5	5,300	8062
Beverly Enterprises-Florida	144	Fort Smith, AR	Public Family Member	116.4	5,260	8059
Metrohealth System Inc	145	Cleveland, OH	Private	271.8	5,244	8062
Britthaven Inc	146	Kinston, NC	Private	181.0	5,200	8051
Greenville Hospital System	147	Greenville, SC	Private	468.8	5,200	8062
Resurrection Health Care Corp	148	Chicago, IL	Private	354.5	5,200	8062
Sentara Hospitals-Norfolk	149	Norfolk, VA	Private	398.3	5,200	8062
University Md Med Sys Corp	150	Baltimore, MD	Private	242.7	5,158	8062
H C A Health Services Of Fla	151	Nashville, TN	Public Family Member	239.9	5,100	8062
University Wscnsin Hospital Clnics	152	Madison, WI	Private	306.1	5,100	8062
St Vincent Hospital Health Care Ctr	153	Indianapolis, IN	Private	431.3	5,075	8062
Allegheny General Hospital	154	Pittsburgh, PA	Private	477.8	5,064	8062
Baptist Mem Healthcare Sys	155	San Antonio, TX	Private	235.2	5,000	8062
Barnes-Jewish Hospital	156	Saint Louis, MO	Private	235.2	5,000	8062
Baystate Medical Center Inc	157	Springfield, MA	Private	368.7	5,000	8062
Britwill Investments I Inc	158	Scottsdale, AZ	Public Family Member	114.9	5,000	8051
Carondelet Health Network Inc	159	Tucson, AZ	Private	246.9	5,000	8062
Centra Health Inc	160	Lynchburg, VA	Private	235.2	5,000	8062
Community Hospitals Of Indiana	161	Indianapolis, IN	Private	444.7	5,000	8062
Geriatric & Medical Companies	162	Kennett Square, PA	Public Family Member	114.9	5,000	8051
Hartford Hospital	163	Hartford, CT	Private	419.2	5,000	8062
Magellan Health Services Inc	164	Atlanta, GA	Public	1,210.7	5,000	8093
Maine Medical Center	165	Portland, ME	Private	343.3	5,000	8062
Memorial Medical Center Inc	166	Savannah, GA	Private	327.2	5,000	8062
Pediatric Services Of Amer De	167	Norcross, GA	Public	204.0	5,000	8082
Pediatric Services Of Amer Ga	168	Norcross, GA	Public Family Member	163.8	5,000	8082
Total Renal Care Holdings	169	Torrance, CA	Public	438.2	5,000	8092
Total Renal Care, Inc	170	Torrance, CA	Public Family Member	400.0	5,000	8092
Virginia Mason Medical Center	171	Seattle, WA	Private	377.4	5,000	8011
Beverly Enterprises - Arkansas	172	Fort Smith, AR	Public Family Member	112.5	4,896	8051
New England Med Ctr Hospitals	173	Boston, MA	Private	228.4	4,856	8062
Hackensack University Med Ctr	174	Hackensack, NJ	Private	421.3	4,818	8062
Health First Inc	175	Melbourne, FL	Private	331.2	4,800	8011
State University Of Ny	176	Syracuse, NY	Private	340.0	4,800	8062
University Of Nc Hospitals	177	Chapel Hill, NC	Private	393.1	4,746	8062
University Virginia Med Ctr	178	Charlottesville, VA	Private	444.3	4,720	8062
St Johns Mercy Medical Center	179	Saint Louis, MO	Private	300.2	4,700	8062
University Hsptals Of Clvland	180	Cleveland, OH	Private	340.4	4,700	8062
Loma Linda University Med Ctr	181	Loma Linda, CA	Private	487.7	4,676	8062
Beverly Enterprises-Michigan	182	Fort Smith, AR	Public Family Member	103.7	4,643	8059
St Vincent Mercy Medical Ctr	183	Toledo, OH	Private	353.3	4,600	8062
Extendicare Facilities Inc	184	Milwaukee, WI	Private	230.7	4,591	8051
22 Texas Services, Lp	185	Horsham, PA	Private	180.0	4,500	8051
Evanston Northwestern	186	Evanston, IL	Private	387.8	4,500	8062
Mercy Hospital Medical Center	187	Des Moines, IA	Private	275.2	4,500	8062
Meriter Health Services Inc	188	Madison, WI	Private	189.0	4,500	8062
Methodist Hospital	189	Houston, TX	Private	485.0	4,500	8062
Multicare Health System	190	Tacoma, WA	Private	337.0	4,500	8062
Nationwide Care, Inc	191	Louisville, KY	Private	103.3	4,500	8051
Plaza Employment Agency Inc	192	Lynbrook, NY	Private	31.7	4,500	8082
Shriners Hsptals For Children	193	Tampa, FL	Private	223.1	4,500	8069
Tenet Health System Di, Inc	194	Santa Barbara, CA	Public Family Member	211.6	4,500	8062
Transitional Hospitals Corp	195	Louisville, KY	Public	211.6	4,500	8062
Albert Einstein Medical Ctr	196	Philadelphia, PA	Private	268.0	4,450	8062
Marshfield Clinic	197	Marshfield, WI	Private	270.0	4,443	8011
Saint Francis Hospital, Inc	198	Tulsa, OK	Private	342.7	4,400	8062
St Johns Regional Health Ctr	199	Springfield, MO	Private	280.3	4,400	8062
Basic American Medical, Inc.	200	Nashville, TN	Public Family Member	202.1	4,300	8062
Med America Health Systems Corp	201	Dayton, OH	Private	346.8	4,300	8062
University Of Chicago	202	Chicago, IL	Private	483.3	4,300	8062
Buffalo General Hospital	203	Buffalo, NY	Private	279.4	4,249	8062
Bethesda Naval Hospital	204	Bethesda, MD	Private	199.1	4,237	8062
Arbor Health Care Company	205	Milwaukee, WI	Private	96.4	4,200	8051
Beverly Enterprises-Washington	206	Fort Smith, AR	Public Family Member	96.4	4,200	8051
Boston Medical Center Corp	207	Boston, MA	Private	386.3	4,200	8062
Devereux Foundation, The	208	Bryn Mawr, PA	Private	199.4	4,200	8361
Friendly Hlls Health Care Netwrk	209	La Habra, CA	Public Family Member	197.4	4,200	8062
Health Care Auth Of Cit Of Hun	210	Huntsville, AL	Private	350.0	4,200	8062

D&B COMPANY RANKINGS BY EMPLOYMENT

Company	Rank	Location	Type	Sales ($ mil.)	Employ-ment	Primary SIC
Lester E Cox Medical Center	211	Springfield, MO	Private	322.6	4,200	8062
Moses H Cone Memorial	212	Greensboro, NC	Private	277.3	4,200	8062
Summit Care Corporation	213	Burbank, CA	Public	197.9	4,200	8059
Texas Health System Inc	214	Dallas, TX	Private	197.4	4,200	8062
Community Care Of America Inc	215	Owings Mills, MD	Public Family Member	96.1	4,186	8051
North Mississippi Medical Ctr	216	Tupelo, MS	Private	266.4	4,148	8062
Rhode Island Hospital	217	Providence, RI	Private	427.3	4,133	8062
Carilion Medical Centers Inc	218	Roanoke, VA	Private	326.9	4,130	8062
Iowa Health System	219	Des Moines, IA	Private	685.8	4,110	8062
Lutheran General Hospital	220	Park Ridge, IL	Private	335.0	4,110	8062
Pinnacle Health Hospitals	221	Harrisburg, PA	Private	287.1	4,100	8062
Saint Clare's Hospital Inc	222	Denville, NJ	Private	225.0	4,100	8062
Via Christi Regional Med Ctr	223	Wichita, KS	Private	466.6	4,100	8062
West Jersey Health System	224	Camden, NJ	Private	266.4	4,100	8062
Sutter Health Central	225	Sacramento, CA	Private	574.1	4,083	8062
Sacred Heart Medical Center	226	Spokane, WA	Private	435.0	4,074	8062
Detroit-Macomb Hospital Corp	227	Warren, MI	Private	199.0	4,030	8062
Emsi Holding Company	228	Dallas, TX	Private	104.6	4,001	8099
Appalchian Regional Healthcare	229	Lexington, KY	Private	298.5	4,000	8062
Bronx Lebanon Hospital Center	230	Bronx, NY	Private	187.9	4,000	8062
Central Iowa Hospital Corp	231	Des Moines, IA	Private	337.4	4,000	8062
Children's Hospital Of Philadelphia	232	Philadelphia, PA	Private	277.6	4,000	8069
Daughters Of Charity H/S	233	Austin, TX	Private	187.9	4,000	8062
Ebenezer Social Ministries	234	Saint Paul, MN	Private	63.7	4,000	8051
Examination Management Svcs	235	Dallas, TX	Private	102.0	4,000	8099
Frontier Group	236	Boston, MA	Private	133.8	4,000	8093
Gambro Healthcare Patient Svcs	237	Aliso Viejo, CA	Private	131.8	4,000	8092
General Health System	238	Baton Rouge, LA	Private	25.4	4,000	8071
Hospital Board Of Directors	239	Fort Myers, FL	Private	294.6	4,000	8062
In Home Health, Inc	240	Hopkins, MN	Public	110.1	4,000	8082
Jordan Health Services Inc	241	Mount Vernon, TX	Private	22.4	4,000	8082
Lahey Hitchcock Clinic	242	Burlington, MA	Private	187.9	4,000	8062
Long Beach Memorial Med Ctr	243	Long Beach, CA	Private	521.0	4,000	8062
Medlink Of Virginia	244	Buffalo, NY	Private	63.5	4,000	8082
Northwestern Human Services	245	Lafayette Hill, PA	Private	176.8	4,000	8093
Northwestern Memorial Hosp	246	Chicago, IL	Private	468.0	4,000	8062
Nylcare Health Plans, Inc	247	New York, NY	Private	2,800.0	4,000	8011
Oakwood Hospital Corporation	248	Dearborn, MI	Private	187.9	4,000	8062
South Broward Hospital Dst	249	Hollywood, FL	Private	377.6	4,000	8062
St Luke's Medical Center Inc	250	Milwaukee, WI	Private	187.9	4,000	8062
Staten Island University Hosp	251	Staten Island, NY	Private	446.9	4,000	8062
Summa Health System	252	Akron, OH	Private	348.2	4,000	8062
Tennessee West Healthcare Inc	253	Jackson, TN	Private	187.9	4,000	8062
Transitional Health Partners	254	Atlanta, GA	Private	91.8	4,000	8051
United Care Inc	255	Dearborn, MI	Private	187.9	4,000	8062
Westchester County Health Care	256	Valhalla, NY	Private	385.0	4,000	8062
Wellmont Health System Inc	257	Kingsport, TN	Private	326.8	3,957	8062
Maimonides Medical Center	258	Brooklyn, NY	Private	429.5	3,950	8062
Southcoast Hospital Group Inc	259	New Bedford, MA	Private	305.4	3,950	8062
Childrens Hospital Corporation	260	Boston, MA	Private	219.8	3,907	8069
Catholic Medical Center	261	Jamaica, NY	Private	630.2	3,900	8062
Dch Healthcare Authority (Inc)	262	Tuscaloosa, AL	Private	221.7	3,900	8062
Pitt County Memorial Hospital	263	Greenville, NC	Private	381.2	3,900	8062
St Vincnts Hospital Med Ctr Of Ny	264	New York, NY	Private	362.8	3,852	8062
Behavioral Healthcare Corp	265	Nashville, TN	Private	223.8	3,846	8063
Alliant Hospitals, Inc	266	Louisville, KY	Private	295.8	3,800	8062
American Rehability Services	267	Brentwood, TN	Public Family Member	246.3	3,800	8051
Childrens Hospital Med Ctr	268	Cincinnati, OH	Private	212.6	3,800	8069
Nebraska Health System	269	Omaha, NE	Private	131.6	3,800	8062
Sundance Rehabilitation Corp	270	Albuquerque, NM	Public Family Member	326.2	3,800	8049
University Health Services	271	Augusta, GA	Private	262.9	3,800	8062
Florida Health Sciences Center	272	Tampa, FL	Private	274.1	3,750	8062
Geriatric And Medical Services	273	Philadelphia, PA	Public Family Member	86.1	3,750	8051
Brookdale Univ Hospital Med Ctr	274	Brooklyn, NY	Private	297.5	3,725	8062
American Homepatient Inc	275	Brentwood, TN	Public	387.3	3,700	8082
Carefirst Of Maryland, Inc	276	Owings Mills, MD	Private	2,183.9	3,700	8011
Covenant Medical Center Inc	277	Saginaw, MI	Private	173.8	3,700	8062
Miami Valley Hospital	278	Dayton, OH	Private	339.8	3,700	8062
Parkview Hospital Inc	279	Fort Wayne, IN	Private	293.1	3,700	8062
U S Homecare Corporation	280	Hartford, CT	Public	52.6	3,700	8082

D&B COMPANY RANKINGS BY EMPLOYMENT

Company	Rank	Location	Type	Sales ($ mil.)	Employ-ment	Primary SIC
St John Hospital And Med Ctr	281	Detroit, MI	Private	356.8	3,646	8062
Spectrum Health - Dwntwn Campus	282	Grand Rapids, MI	Private	317.7	3,610	8062
York Hospital	283	York, PA	Private	228.8	3,604	8062
North Memorial Health Care	284	Minneapolis, MN	Private	248.2	3,602	8062
Winthrop-University Hospital	285	Mineola, NY	Private	328.8	3,601	8062
Dialysis Clinic Inc	286	Nashville, TN	Private	268.8	3,600	8092
Lehigh Valley Hospital Inc	287	Allentown, PA	Private	351.0	3,600	8062
Reading Hospital & Med Ctr Inc	288	Reading, PA	Private	169.0	3,600	8062
St Elizabeth Hospital	289	Beaumont, TX	Private	197.9	3,600	8062
University Of Utah Hospital	290	Salt Lake City, UT	Private	272.5	3,600	8062
California Pacific Med Ctr	291	San Francisco, CA	Private	337.2	3,597	8062
Hpi-Ramsey, Inc	292	Saint Paul, MN	Private	167.8	3,575	8062
Cooper Hsptl/University Med Ctr	293	Camden, NJ	Private	352.8	3,524	8062
Horizon West Headquarters Inc	294	Rocklin, CA	Private	80.6	3,511	8051
St Luke's Episcopal Hospital	295	Houston, TX	Private	361.0	3,511	8062
Memorial Hospital, Inc	296	Worcester, MA	Private	171.8	3,510	8062
Baptist Hospital Of Miami Inc	297	Miami, FL	Private	259.7	3,500	8062
Baptist Hospital, Inc	298	Nashville, TN	Private	259.6	3,500	8062
Brooklyn Hospital Center (Inc)	299	Brooklyn, NY	Private	303.9	3,500	8062
Care Enterprises West	300	Albuquerque, NM	Public Family Member	80.3	3,500	8051
Catholic Health Partners Svcs	301	Chicago, IL	Private	291.6	3,500	8062
Chw Central Coast	302	Santa Barbara, CA	Private	218.4	3,500	8062
Episcopal Health Services Inc	303	Uniondale, NY	Private	164.3	3,500	8062
Fhc Health Systems, Inc.	304	Norfolk, VA	Private	129.6	3,500	8063
Fresno Community Hospital	305	Fresno, CA	Private	164.3	3,500	8062
Lincare Inc	306	Clearwater, FL	Public Family Member	400.0	3,500	8082
Millard Fillmore Hospital	307	Buffalo, NY	Private	236.3	3,500	8062
National Benevolent	308	Saint Louis, MO	Private	127.7	3,500	8361
North Shore Medical Center	309	Salem, MA	Private	197.5	3,500	8062
Ochsner Alton Med Foundation	310	Jefferson, LA	Private	309.9	3,500	8062
Our Lady Lake Regional Med Ctr	311	Baton Rouge, LA	Private	281.2	3,500	8062
Riverside Hospital Inc	312	Newport News, VA	Private	164.3	3,500	8062
Roper Hospital Inc	313	Charleston, SC	Private	239.3	3,500	8062
Sharp Memorial Hospital	314	San Diego, CA	Private	270.2	3,500	8062
Sioux Valley Hsptals Health Systms	315	Sioux Falls, SD	Private	224.5	3,500	8062
St John Medical Center Inc	316	Tulsa, OK	Private	222.9	3,500	8062
St Lukes Hospital Of Bethlehem Pa	317	Bethlehem, PA	Private	206.3	3,500	8062
Sunrise Assisted Living, Inc	318	Fairfax, VA	Public	89.9	3,500	8361
Wakemed	319	Raleigh, NC	Private	285.3	3,500	8062
Geisinger Medical Center	320	Danville, PA	Private	249.9	3,459	8062
Medical Innovations Inc	321	Houston, TX	Public Family Member	60.0	3,450	8082
Hospital Of St Raphael	322	New Haven, CT	Private	246.5	3,426	8062
Infirmary Health System Inc	323	Mobile, AL	Private	160.8	3,425	8062
Bexar County Hospital Dst	324	San Antonio, TX	Private	321.4	3,424	8062
Caretenders Health Corp	325	Louisville, KY	Public	95.2	3,400	8059
Salo Inc	326	Columbus, OH	Private	41.5	3,400	8082
Main Line Hospitals	327	Bryn Mawr, PA	Private	309.3	3,353	8062
Hallmark Healthcare Corp	328	Brentwood, TN	Public Family Member	157.0	3,345	8062
Forsyth Memorial Hospital Inc	329	Winston Salem, NC	Private	260.7	3,334	8062
Community Health Plan Inc	330	Latham, NY	Private	575.1	3,300	8011
Correctional Medical Services	331	Saint Louis, MO	Private	132.0	3,300	8099
Crozer-Chester Medical Center	332	Chester, PA	Private	91.8	3,300	8062
Johns Hopkins Bayview Med Ctr	333	Baltimore, MD	Private	197.4	3,300	8062
Josephs Saint Hospital & Med Ctr	334	Paterson, NJ	Private	287.0	3,300	8062
Medical Center Of Centl Ga Inc	335	Macon, GA	Private	369.4	3,300	8062
Php Healthcare Corporation	336	Reston, VA	Public	400.1	3,300	8011
St Francis Hospital & Med Ctr	337	Hartford, CT	Private	328.7	3,300	8062
Tallahssee Mem Rgional Med Ctr	338	Tallahassee, FL	Private	164.3	3,300	8062
Capital Health Systems Inc	339	Trenton, NJ	Private	152.5	3,250	8062
Mount Sinai Med Ctr	340	Miami, FL	Private	151.3	3,225	8062
Altru Health System	341	Grand Forks, ND	Private	135.8	3,200	8062
Healthcor Holdings Inc	342	Dallas, TX	Public	143.2	3,200	8082
L I C H Corporation	343	Brooklyn, NY	Private	150.1	3,200	8062
Meridia Health System	344	Cleveland, OH	Private	370.2	3,200	8062
St Josephs Hospital Health Ctr	345	Syracuse, NY	Private	196.5	3,200	8062
Va Nj Healthcare System	346	Lyons, NJ	Private	150.1	3,200	8062
Lovelace Health Systems Inc	347	Albuquerque, NM	Public Family Member	334.3	3,183	8011
Ch Allied Services Inc	348	Saint Louis, MO	Private	147.8	3,150	8062
Portland Adventist Med Ctr	349	Portland, OR	Private	145.5	3,102	8062
Cumberland County Hospital Sys	350	Fayetteville, NC	Private	242.9	3,100	8062

D&B COMPANY RANKINGS BY EMPLOYMENT

Company	Rank	Location	Type	Sales ($ mil.)	Employment	Primary SIC
Mercy Healthcare Arizona Inc	351	Phoenix, AZ	Private	287.8	3,100	8062
New Hanover Regional Med Ctr	352	Wilmington, NC	Private	267.8	3,100	8062
Presbyterian Hospital	353	Charlotte, NC	Private	270.5	3,100	8062
Providence Hospital	354	Southfield, MI	Private	322.3	3,100	8062
Robert Wood Johnson Univ Hosp	355	New Brunswick, NJ	Private	265.5	3,100	8062
Rochester General Hospital	356	Rochester, NY	Private	252.0	3,100	8062
Tendercare Michigan Inc	357	Sault Sainte Marie, MI	Private	71.1	3,100	8051
H C A Health Services Of Kans	358	Wichita, KS	Public Family Member	262.1	3,080	8062
Texas Children's Hospital	359	Houston, TX	Private	247.9	3,074	8069
Home Health Corp Of America	360	King Of Prussia, PA	Public	150.2	3,068	8082
Methodist Hospitals Inc	361	Gary, IN	Private	199.4	3,060	8062
Methodist Hospitals Of Dallas	362	Dallas, TX	Private	196.3	3,060	8062
Sinai Hospital	363	Detroit, MI	Private	142.8	3,045	8062
Good Smrtan Hospital Of Cincinnati	364	Cincinnati, OH	Private	184.5	3,042	8062
American Habilitation Services	365	Houston, TX	Private	66.9	3,000	8059
American Health Centers Inc	366	Parsons, TN	Private	95.0	3,000	8051
Aultman Hospital, The	367	Canton, OH	Private	160.0	3,000	8062
Bayada Nurses Inc	368	Moorestown, NJ	Private	47.8	3,000	8082
Bethesda Hospital Inc	369	Cincinnati, OH	Private	207.6	3,000	8062
Care Initiatives	370	West Des Moines, IA	Private	85.6	3,000	8051
Cigna Healthcare Arizona, Inc.	371	Phoenix, AZ	Public Family Member	584.8	3,000	8011
Columbia-Arlington Healthcare Llc	372	Arlington, VA	Private	500.0	3,000	8062
Community Hospital Group Inc	373	Edison, NJ	Private	200.3	3,000	8062
Covenant Care Inc	374	SJ Capistrano, CA	Private	160.0	3,000	8051
Dean Health Systems Sc	375	Madison, WI	Private	450.0	3,000	8011
Edward W Sparrow Hospital Assn	376	Lansing, MI	Private	258.3	3,000	8062
El Paso Healthcare Systems	377	El Paso, TX	Private	140.7	3,000	8062
Family Aides Inc	378	Hicksville, NY	Private	47.8	3,000	8082
H C F Inc	379	Lima, OH	Private	104.0	3,000	8051
Hallmark Health System	380	Malden, MA	Private	140.7	3,000	8062
Illinois Masonic Medical Ctr	381	Chicago, IL	Private	224.1	3,000	8062
Integris Southwest Med Ctr	382	Oklahoma City, OK	Private	115.5	3,000	8062
Interim Healthcare-Morris Group	383	Wilson, NC	Private	47.8	3,000	8082
Jamaica Hospital Inc	384	Jamaica, NY	Private	215.6	3,000	8062
Kennedy Health Systems	385	Cherry Hill, NJ	Private	140.7	3,000	8062
Liberty Healthcare System Inc	386	Jersey City, NJ	Private	140.7	3,000	8062
Lutheran Social Services Of Il	387	Des Plaines, IL	Private	52.9	3,000	8361
Memorial Hospitl-Cancer/Allied	388	New York, NY	Private	604.0	3,000	8069
Memorial Mission Hospital Inc	389	Asheville, NC	Private	247.5	3,000	8062
Mid Atlantic Health Group Inc	390	Long Branch, NJ	Private	140.7	3,000	8062
Miller's Health Systems, Inc	391	Warsaw, IN	Private	55.9	3,000	8052
Mobile Infirmary Association	392	Mobile, AL	Private	178.3	3,000	8062
Morton Plant Hospital Assn	393	Clearwater, FL	Private	245.3	3,000	8062
New Britain General Hospital	394	New Britain, CT	Private	144.4	3,000	8062
Newark Beth Israel Med Ctr	395	Newark, NJ	Private	221.6	3,000	8062
Options Health Care (Va Corp)	396	Norfolk, VA	Private	91.5	3,000	8093
Prison Health Services Inc	397	Brentwood, TN	Public Family Member	206.9	3,000	8011
Provident Health Services Inc	398	Savannah, GA	Private	47.8	3,000	8082
Regions Hospital	399	Saint Paul, MN	Private	140.7	3,000	8062
St John's Hospital Of Hospital	400	Springfield, IL	Private	247.9	3,000	8062
Sunrise Hospital	401	Las Vegas, NV	Public Family Member	140.7	3,000	8062
University Healthcare Sys L C	402	New Orleans, LA	Private	140.7	3,000	8062
University Of S Ala Med Ctr	403	Mobile, AL	Private	145.3	3,000	8062
Vitas Healthcare Corp	404	Miami, FL	Private	213.9	3,000	8082
Physician Corp Of America	405	Miami, FL	Public	205.5	2,980	8011
Saint Elizabeth Medical Ctr	406	Covington, KY	Private	203.5	2,964	8062
Lenox Hill Hospital	407	New York, NY	Private	343.3	2,955	8062
Kennestone Hospital Inc	408	Marietta, GA	Private	138.3	2,950	8062
Presbyterian Hospital Of Dallas	409	Dallas, TX	Private	280.2	2,947	8062
Children's Hospital, The	410	Columbus, OH	Private	315.1	2,946	8069
Spartanburg Cnty Health Svcs Dst	411	Spartanburg, SC	Private	279.2	2,931	8062
Good Samaritan Hospital Med Ctr	412	West Islip, NY	Private	194.9	2,900	8062
Mount Carmel Hospital West	413	Columbus, OH	Private	135.9	2,900	8062
New York Methodist Hospital	414	Brooklyn, NY	Private	272.0	2,900	8062
Rex Hospital	415	Raleigh, NC	Private	197.8	2,900	8062
Hurley Medical Center, Inc	416	Flint, MI	Private	255.3	2,884	8062
St Margret Mrcy Healthcare Ctrs	417	Hammond, IN	Private	138.1	2,859	8062
Akron General Medical Center	418	Akron, OH	Private	220.5	2,836	8062
St Vincent Infirmary Med Ctr	419	Little Rock, AR	Private	215.3	2,830	8062
Guthrie Healthcare Systems	420	Sayre, PA	Private	132.4	2,825	8062

D&B COMPANY RANKINGS BY EMPLOYMENT

Company	Rank	Location	Type	Sales ($ mil.)	Employ- ment	Primary SIC
Munson Medical Center	421	Traverse City, MI	Private	173.3	2,822	8062
Abington Memorial Hospital	422	Abington, PA	Private	249.4	2,800	8062
Christian Hospital NE-NW	423	Saint Louis, MO	Private	215.0	2,800	8062
Community Care Systems Inc	424	Springfield, IL	Private	24.0	2,800	8082
Coram Healthcare Corporation	425	Denver, CO	Public	464.4	2,800	8093
Dimensions Health Corporation	426	Upper Marlboro, MD	Private	233.6	2,800	8062
Forrest County General Hosp	427	Hattiesburg, MS	Private	197.9	2,800	8062
Genesys Regional Medical Ctr	428	Grand Blanc, MI	Private	255.5	2,800	8062
Greater Baltimore Medical Ctr	429	Baltimore, MD	Private	200.5	2,800	8062
Greater Se Comm Hospital	430	Washington, DC	Private	133.8	2,800	8062
Kennedy Health Care Foundation	431	Stratford, NJ	Private	131.2	2,800	8062
Mercy-Memorial Medical Center	432	Saint Joseph, MI	Private	136.5	2,800	8062
Merit Behavioral Care Corp	433	Park Ridge, NJ	Public Family Member	555.7	2,800	8093
Northeast Hospital Corporation	434	Beverly, MA	Private	134.6	2,800	8062
Northside Hospital Inc	435	Atlanta, GA	Private	254.7	2,800	8062
Northwest Community Hospital	436	Arlington Heights, IL	Private	183.3	2,800	8062
Pasadena Hospital Assn Ltd	437	Pasadena, CA	Private	256.6	2,800	8062
Rockford Memorial Hospital	438	Rockford, IL	Private	174.9	2,800	8062
Sarasota County Pub Hospital Bd	439	Sarasota, FL	Private	252.9	2,800	8062
Sierra Health Services Inc	440	Las Vegas, NV	Public	721.7	2,800	8011
St Francis Medical Center	441	Pittsburgh, PA	Private	196.4	2,800	8062
Western Pennsylvania Hosp	442	Pittsburgh, PA	Private	218.8	2,800	8062
Sisters Of Providence In Cal	443	Seattle, WA	Private	282.9	2,779	8062
Integris Baptist Medical Ctr	444	Oklahoma City, OK	Private	215.1	2,759	8062
Lancaster General Hospital	445	Lancaster, PA	Private	217.2	2,759	8062
Notami Hospitals Of Oklahoma	446	Nashville, TN	Public Family Member	189.7	2,750	8011
Rehability Health Services	447	Brentwood, TN	Public Family Member	83.5	2,736	8093
Piedmont Hospital Inc	448	Atlanta, GA	Private	239.5	2,720	8062
Mary Hitchcock Memorial Hosp	449	Lebanon, NH	Private	233.4	2,711	8062
Genesis Medical Center	450	Davenport, IA	Private	189.4	2,702	8062
All Saints Health Care System	451	Racine, WI	Private	250.0	2,700	8062
Columbus Reg Healthcr Sys Inc	452	Columbus, GA	Private	190.0	2,700	8062
Erlanger Health System	453	Chattanooga, TN	Private	304.2	2,700	8062
Medical Team Inc	454	Reston, VA	Private	22.5	2,700	8082
Methodist Hospital Lubbock Texas	455	Lubbock, TX	Private	264.7	2,700	8062
Palomar Pomerado Health Sys	456	San Diego, CA	Private	188.2	2,700	8062
Preferred Care, Inc	457	Plano, TX	Private	50.3	2,700	8052
Sinai Hospital Of Baltimore	458	Baltimore, MD	Private	248.6	2,700	8062
South Hills Health System	459	Homestead, PA	Private	150.1	2,700	8062
Truman Medical Center Inc	460	Kansas City, MO	Private	116.2	2,700	8062
Univ Of Kentucky Hospital	461	Lexington, KY	Private	323.1	2,700	8062
University Medical Center Corp	462	Tucson, AZ	Private	210.2	2,700	8062
Willis-Knighton Medical Ctr	463	Shreveport, LA	Private	126.5	2,700	8062
Renal Treatment Centers Inc	464	Berwyn, PA	Public Family Member	153.5	2,687	8092
Long Island College Hospital	465	Brooklyn, NY	Private	125.5	2,679	8062
Tmc Healthcare	466	Tucson, AZ	Private	246.0	2,650	8062
Williamsport Hospital Med Ctr Inc	467	Williamsport, PA	Private	84.9	2,633	8062
Northwest Texas Healthcare	468	Amarillo, TX	Private	76.9	2,624	8062
Carle Clinic Association Pc	469	Urbana, IL	Private	336.9	2,615	8011
Children's Health Systems	470	Milwaukee, WI	Private	128.7	2,600	8069
City Of Hope National Med Ctr	471	Duarte, CA	Private	183.3	2,600	8062
Foundation Health Systems Inc	472	Woodland Hills, CA	Private	7,235.0	2,600	8011
Holmes Regional Medical Center	473	Melbourne, FL	Private	209.6	2,600	8062
Jefferson Health Services	474	Pittsburgh, PA	Private	131.6	2,600	8062
Lutheran Medical Center	475	Brooklyn, NY	Private	121.8	2,600	8062
Lutheran Medical Center	476	Wheat Ridge, CO	Private	150.4	2,600	8062
Mcleod Rgnl Mdcl Ctr Pee Dee	477	Florence, SC	Private	200.9	2,600	8062
Southern Baptist Hospital Of Fla	478	Jacksonville, FL	Private	228.5	2,600	8062
St Barnabas Medical Center	479	Livingston, NJ	Private	121.8	2,600	8062
St Marys Med Ctr Of Evansville	480	Evansville, IN	Private	140.3	2,600	8062
St Peter's Medical Center	481	New Brunswick, NJ	Private	186.5	2,600	8062
University Colorado Hospital Auth	482	Denver, CO	Private	234.2	2,600	8062
St Joseph Hospital Fran Sstrs	483	Milwaukee, WI	Private	168.3	2,597	8062
St Anthony's Medical Center	484	Saint Louis, MO	Private	121.2	2,589	8062
Elmhurst Memorial Hospital	485	Elmhurst, IL	Private	168.9	2,579	8062
Memorial Medical Center	486	Springfield, IL	Private	236.8	2,575	8062
North General Hospital	487	New York, NY	Private	108.5	2,565	8062
Harris Methodist Fort Worth	488	Fort Worth, TX	Private	119.9	2,560	8062
University Community Hospital	489	Tampa, FL	Private	190.7	2,557	8062
Wvhcs-Hospital	490	Wilkes Barre, PA	Private	198.0	2,555	8062

D&B COMPANY RANKINGS BY EMPLOYMENT

Company	Rank	Location	Type	Sales ($ mil.)	Employ- ment	Primary SIC
Lakeland Regional Medical Ctr	491	Lakeland, FL	Private	241.4	2,550	8062
Mercy Mount Clemens Corp	492	Clinton Township, MI	Private	128.7	2,543	8062
Western Reserve Care System	493	Youngstown, OH	Private	195.5	2,532	8062
St Agnes Healthcare	494	Baltimore, MD	Private	117.3	2,506	8062
Alegent Health-Bergen Mercy	495	Omaha, NE	Private	151.2	2,500	8062
American Retirement Corp	496	Brentwood, TN	Public	94.2	2,500	8059
Anderson Area Medical Center	497	Anderson, SC	Private	162.2	2,500	8062
Bergan Mercy Health Clinics	498	Omaha, NE	Private	172.4	2,500	8011
Columbia Metrowest Medical Ctr	499	Natick, MA	Public Family Member	117.0	2,500	8062
Community Health Inv Corp	500	Brentwood, TN	Public Family Member	117.0	2,500	8062
Community Medical Center Inc	501	Toms River, NJ	Private	210.7	2,500	8062
Covenant Nursing & Rehab Ctr	502	Stockton, CA	Private	55.8	2,500	8059
Daniel Freeman Hospitals Inc	503	Inglewood, CA	Private	186.2	2,500	8062
Eden Park Management Inc	504	Albany, NY	Private	57.3	2,500	8051
Erie County Medical Center	505	Buffalo, NY	Private	172.4	2,500	8011
Four Seasons Nursing Centers	506	Gaithersburg, MD	Public Family Member	57.3	2,500	8051
Froedtert Mem Lutheran Hosp	507	Milwaukee, WI	Private	334.2	2,500	8062
Healtheast Companies, Inc	508	Saint Paul, MN	Private	39.9	2,500	8082
Integrted Health Svcs At Srasota	509	Sarasota, FL	Public Family Member	57.3	2,500	8051
Jewish Hospital Of Cincinnati	510	Cincinnati, OH	Private	117.0	2,500	8062
Lantis Enterprises Inc	511	Spearfish, SD	Private	57.3	2,500	8051
Mercy Hospital Of Pittsburgh	512	Pittsburgh, PA	Private	117.0	2,500	8062
Methodist Hospital	513	Minneapolis, MN	Private	195.0	2,500	8062
Methodist Medical Ctr Of Ill	514	Peoria, IL	Private	164.6	2,500	8062
Mid America Care Foundation	515	Kansas City, MO	Private	57.3	2,500	8051
Mills-Peninsula Health Svcs	516	Burlingame, CA	Private	193.7	2,500	8062
North Iowa Mercy Health Center	517	Mason City, IA	Private	130.8	2,500	8062
Salem Hospital	518	Salem, OR	Private	164.1	2,500	8062
Scottsdale Memorial Hospitals	519	Scottsdale, AZ	Private	307.9	2,500	8062
Southwest Washington Med Ctr	520	Vancouver, WA	Private	164.9	2,500	8062
Spohn Health Systems	521	Corpus Christi, TX	Private	174.7	2,500	8062
St Elizabeth Hospital Med Ctr	522	Youngstown, OH	Private	210.3	2,500	8062
Stormnt-Vail Rgional Health Ctr	523	Topeka, KS	Private	168.8	2,500	8062
Tri State Health System Inc	524	Suffern, NY	Private	184.0	2,500	8062
Visiting Nurse Service Of Ny	525	New York, NY	Private	550.4	2,500	8082
University Medical Center Inc	526	Jacksonville, FL	Private	228.2	2,497	8062
Swedish American Hospital Assn	527	Rockford, IL	Private	142.9	2,494	8062
University Med Ctr Suthern Nev	528	Las Vegas, NV	Private	264.8	2,487	8062
Harper Hospital	529	Detroit, MI	Private	277.0	2,483	8062
Franciscan Skemp Healthcare	530	La Crosse, WI	Private	116.1	2,481	8062
St Peter's Hospital	531	Albany, NY	Private	181.1	2,476	8062
Atlantic City Medical Center	532	Atlantic City, NJ	Private	210.6	2,460	8062
Eastern Maine Medical Center	533	Bangor, ME	Private	209.3	2,460	8062
St Vincent's Medical Center	534	Jacksonville, FL	Private	221.8	2,447	8062
Memorial Hospital Corporation	535	Colorado Springs, CO	Private	202.6	2,438	8062
Winter Haven Hospital Inc	536	Winter Haven, FL	Private	148.4	2,420	8062
Kettering Medical Center	537	Dayton, OH	Private	201.2	2,415	8062
Columbia Chppnhm Mdcl Ctr	538	Richmond, VA	Public Family Member	112.3	2,400	8062
Crouse Hospital Inc	539	Syracuse, NY	Private	171.3	2,400	8062
Florida Convalescent Centers	540	Sarasota, FL	Private	55.0	2,400	8051
Genesee Hospital Inc	541	Rochester, NY	Private	151.0	2,400	8062
Hendrick Medical Center	542	Abilene, TX	Private	135.1	2,400	8062
Hoag Memorial Hospital Presbt	543	Newport Beach, CA	Private	180.4	2,400	8062
Interfaith Medical Center	544	Brooklyn, NY	Private	200.0	2,400	8062
Jackson-Madison Cnty Gen Hosp	545	Jackson, TN	Private	216.3	2,400	8062
Monmouth Medical Center	546	Long Branch, NJ	Private	163.5	2,400	8062
Mt Sinai Medical Center	547	Cleveland, OH	Private	250.0	2,400	8062
Portercare Hospital	548	Denver, CO	Private	135.4	2,400	8062
Research Medical Center	549	Kansas City, MO	Private	112.3	2,400	8062
United Health Svcs Hospitals	550	Johnson City, NY	Private	206.3	2,400	8062
Sun Health Corporation	551	Sun City, AZ	Private	187.7	2,390	8062
South Shore Hospital Inc	552	South Weymouth, MA	Private	170.0	2,375	8062
Nemours Foundation (Inc)	553	Jacksonville, FL	Private	76.4	2,369	8069
St Elzabeths Med Ctr Of Boston	554	Boston, MA	Private	205.0	2,365	8062
Fairview Hospital	555	Cleveland, OH	Private	151.7	2,364	8062
Mohawk Valley Network, Inc	556	Utica, NY	Private	60.0	2,350	8069
Meriter Hospital Inc	557	Madison, WI	Private	158.7	2,335	8062
Gci Properties, Inc	558	Atlanta, GA	Public Family Member	53.2	2,325	8051
Union Hospital Inc	559	Terre Haute, IN	Private	220.1	2,322	8062
Alegent Health-Immanuel Med Ctr	560	Omaha, NE	Private	176.2	2,313	8062

D&B COMPANY RANKINGS BY EMPLOYMENT

Company	Rank	Location	Type	Sales ($ mil.)	Employ-ment	Primary SIC
Childrens Hospital Of Mich	561	Detroit, MI	Private	183.8	2,310	8069
Bon Secours-Richmond Health Corp	562	Richmond, VA	Private	107.6	2,300	8062
Central Du Page Hospital Assn	563	Winfield, IL	Private	180.7	2,300	8062
Deaconess Hospital Inc	564	Evansville, IN	Private	159.0	2,300	8062
Galen Of Florida, Inc	565	Nashville, TN	Public Family Member	107.6	2,300	8062
Jewish Hospital Services, Inc	566	Cincinnati, OH	Private	92.0	2,300	8099
Little Company Of Mary Hosp	567	Chicago, IL	Private	144.5	2,300	8062
Medical City Dallas Hospital	568	Dallas, TX	Public Family Member	300.0	2,300	8062
Medicalodges Inc	569	Coffeyville, KS	Private	71.1	2,300	8051
New York Hospital Medical Cent	570	Flushing, NY	Private	257.8	2,300	8062
Northport Health Service Inc	571	Tuscaloosa, AL	Private	52.7	2,300	8051
St George Corporation, The	572	Palos Heights, IL	Private	199.4	2,300	8062
St Josephs Hospital Of Atlanta	573	Atlanta, GA	Private	237.0	2,300	8062
St Lukes Regional Medical Ctr	574	Boise, ID	Private	192.7	2,300	8062
Vincent Saint Health Center	575	Erie, PA	Private	146.4	2,300	8062
White Oak Manor Inc	576	Spartanburg, SC	Private	72.2	2,300	8051
Mclaren Regional Medical Ctr	577	Flint, MI	Private	105.2	2,250	8062
Memorial Hospitals Assn	578	Modesto, CA	Private	100.0	2,250	8062
Our Lady Of Lourdes Med Ctr	579	Camden, NJ	Private	105.2	2,250	8062
West Virginia Univ Hospitals	580	Morgantown, WV	Private	212.7	2,250	8062
Holy Cross Hospital Silver Spring	581	Silver Spring, MD	Private	181.8	2,241	8062
Firsthealth Of The Carolinas	582	Pinehurst, NC	Private	104.5	2,235	8062
Q H G Of Alabama Inc	583	Dothan, AL	Public Family Member	143.8	2,220	8062
Sisters Hospital	584	Buffalo, NY	Private	108.8	2,213	8062
Pomona Valley Hospital Med Ctr	585	Pomona, CA	Private	196.2	2,209	8062
Arkansas Childrens Hospital	586	Little Rock, AR	Private	139.9	2,200	8069
Brown Schools Inc.	587	Austin, TX	Private	138.0	2,200	8062
Childrens Hospital Assn, The	588	Denver, CO	Private	161.7	2,200	8069
Childrens' Hospital-San Diego	589	San Diego, CA	Private	138.1	2,200	8069
Dekalb Medical Center Inc	590	Decatur, GA	Private	180.8	2,200	8062
E P I Corporation	591	Louisville, KY	Public	41.0	2,200	8052
Englewood Hospital & Med Ctr	592	Englewood, NJ	Private	155.0	2,200	8062
Franciscan Skemp Medical Ctr	593	La Crosse, WI	Private	47.4	2,200	8062
Franklin Square Hospital Ctr	594	Baltimore, MD	Private	171.2	2,200	8062
Good Samaritan Hospital Health Ctr	595	Dayton, OH	Private	168.8	2,200	8062
Gundersen Clinic Ltd	596	La Crosse, WI	Private	200.0	2,200	8011
Hillcrest Baptist Medical Ctr	597	Waco, TX	Private	133.4	2,200	8062
Johnson City Medical Ctr Hosp	598	Johnson City, TN	Private	173.9	2,200	8062
Lake Hospital System Inc	599	Painesville, OH	Private	135.8	2,200	8062
Mary Imogene Bassett Hospital	600	Cooperstown, NY	Private	143.4	2,200	8062
Medcenter One Inc	601	Bismarck, ND	Private	135.4	2,200	8062
Our Lady Of Mercy Medical Ctr	602	Bronx, NY	Private	212.3	2,200	8062
Owensboro Mercy Health Systems	603	Owensboro, KY	Private	102.8	2,200	8062
Pennsylvania Hospital	604	Philadelphia, PA	Private	222.0	2,200	8062
Presentation Sisters Inc	605	Sioux Falls, SD	Private	142.6	2,200	8062
Saint Vincent Hospital, Llc	606	Worcester, MA	Public Family Member	102.8	2,200	8062
Samaritan Health Partners Shp	607	Dayton, OH	Private	210.6	2,200	8062
South Miami Hospital Inc	608	Miami, FL	Private	148.9	2,200	8062
St Joseph Hospital Of Orange	609	Orange, CA	Private	221.7	2,200	8062
St Joseph Medical Center	610	Baltimore, MD	Private	170.8	2,200	8062
St Josphs Med Ctr Of Stockton	611	Stockton, CA	Private	166.0	2,200	8062
Variety Children's Hospital	612	Miami, FL	Private	183.2	2,200	8069
W A Foote Memorial Hospital	613	Jackson, MI	Private	130.7	2,200	8062
St Vincent Hospital	614	Green Bay, WI	Private	132.3	2,190	8062
Lexington County Health Svc Dst	615	West Columbia, SC	Private	138.8	2,180	8062
Grace Hospital	616	Detroit, MI	Private	203.1	2,170	8062
Childrens Hospital Regional Med	617	Seattle, WA	Private	147.7	2,150	8069
Society Of The Valley Hosp	618	Ridgewood, NJ	Private	204.0	2,150	8062
Medcentral Health System	619	Mansfield, OH	Private	98.4	2,141	8062
Heartland Health System Inc	620	Saint Joseph, MO	Private	99.9	2,138	8062
Upmc Shadyside	621	Pittsburgh, PA	Private	206.3	2,131	8062
Detroit Osteopathic Hospital Corp	622	Southfield, MI	Private	99.5	2,130	8062
Hillcrest Medical Center Inc	623	Tulsa, OK	Private	174.6	2,126	8062
Protestant Memorial Med Ctr	624	Belleville, IL	Private	126.9	2,117	8062
Ball Memorial Hospital Inc	625	Muncie, IN	Private	171.4	2,108	8062
John C Lincoln Health Network	626	Phoenix, AZ	Private	133.9	2,102	8062
Bon Scurs Mem Regional Med Ctr	627	Richmond, VA	Private	98.1	2,100	8062
Borgess Medical Center Inc	628	Kalamazoo, MI	Private	98.1	2,100	8062
G B Health Systems Inc	629	Atlanta, GA	Public Family Member	98.1	2,100	8062
Genesis Elder Care Rehab Servi	630	Kennett Square, PA	Public Family Member	32.4	2,100	8049

D&B COMPANY RANKINGS BY EMPLOYMENT

Company	Rank	Location	Type	Sales ($ mil.)	Employ-ment	Primary SIC
Glens Falls Hospital	631	Glens Falls, NY	Private	113.9	2,100	8062
Heartland Home Health Care Svcs	632	Bay City, MI	Public Family Member	24.0	2,100	8082
Houston Northwest Medical Ctr	633	Houston, TX	Public Family Member	250.0	2,100	8062
Kaweah Delta Health Care Dst	634	Visalia, CA	Private	124.6	2,100	8062
Kingsbrook Jewish Medical Ctr	635	Brooklyn, NY	Private	128.4	2,100	8062
Mercy Hospital & Medical Ctr	636	Chicago, IL	Private	182.0	2,100	8062
Mercy Hospital Of Buffalo	637	Buffalo, NY	Private	107.2	2,100	8062
Missouri Baptist Medical Ctr	638	Saint Louis, MO	Private	98.1	2,100	8062
Neponset Valley Health System	639	Norfolk, MA	Private	121.0	2,100	8062
Premiere Associates Inc	640	Clemmons, NC	Public Family Member	48.1	2,100	8051
Ramsay Health Care Inc	641	Coral Gables, FL	Public	136.7	2,100	8063
Rapid City Regional Hospital	642	Rapid City, SD	Private	184.2	2,100	8062
St Joseph Health Care System	643	Albuquerque, NM	Private	98.1	2,100	8062
St Luke Health System, Inc	644	Sioux City, IA	Private	105.2	2,100	8062
St Marys Hospital Of Milwaukee	645	Milwaukee, WI	Private	120.8	2,100	8062
Unilab Corporation	646	Tarzana, CA	Public	214.0	2,100	8071
Valley Baptist Medical Center	647	Harlingen, TX	Private	174.0	2,100	8062
Saint Joseph Hospital Inc	648	Denver, CO	Private	98.0	2,098	8062
Fort Sanders Regional Med Ctr	649	Knoxville, TN	Private	153.5	2,080	8062
North Arundel Hospital Assn	650	Glen Burnie, MD	Private	115.4	2,079	8062
St Louis Children's Hospital	651	Saint Louis, MO	Private	161.6	2,078	8069
Francscan Med Ctr Dyton Campus	652	Dayton, OH	Private	154.2	2,054	8062
National Home Care Inc	653	West Orange, NJ	Public Family Member	32.8	2,053	8082
Northeast Medical Center, Inc	654	Concord, NC	Private	178.4	2,053	8062
Bridgeport Hospital Inc	655	Bridgeport, CT	Private	190.2	2,050	8062
Covenant Health System Inc	656	Waterloo, IA	Private	140.5	2,050	8062
Gwinnett Hospital System Inc	657	Lawrenceville, GA	Private	185.7	2,050	8062
Durham County Hospital Corp	658	Durham, NC	Private	121.7	2,048	8062
Bronson Methodist Hospital	659	Kalamazoo, MI	Private	206.5	2,045	8062
Carle Foundation, The	660	Urbana, IL	Private	183.6	2,043	8062
Cabrini Medical Center	661	New York, NY	Private	171.1	2,040	8062
Union Memorial Hospital Inc	662	Baltimore, MD	Private	171.0	2,025	8062
Bryan Memorial Hospital	663	Lincoln, NE	Private	69.8	2,015	8062
Childrens Med Ctr Of Dallas	664	Dallas, TX	Private	183.9	2,014	8069
Wuesthoff Health Systems Inc	665	Rockledge, FL	Private	113.9	2,012	8062
Memorial Hospital Of S Bend	666	South Bend, IN	Private	187.2	2,010	8062
Winchester Medical Center Inc	667	Winchester, VA	Private	169.9	2,006	8062
St Luke's Episcopal	668	Chesterfield, MO	Private	93.5	2,003	8062
Alexian Brothers Medical Ctr	669	Elk Grove Village, IL	Private	156.9	2,003	8062
Bay Medical Center	670	Bay City, MI	Private	123.6	2,000	8062
Benefis Health Care	671	Great Falls, MT	Private	126.6	2,000	8062
Bestcare Inc	672	Levittown, NY	Private	32.0	2,000	8082
Bloomington Hospital Inc	673	Bloomington, IN	Private	126.8	2,000	8062
Carraway Methdst Health Systems	674	Birmingham, AL	Private	142.3	2,000	8062
Cathedral Health Services Inc	675	Newark, NJ	Private	184.6	2,000	8062
Catholic Healthcare W Sthern Cal	676	Pasadena, CA	Private	93.4	2,000	8062
Children's Hospital Medical Center	677	Oakland, CA	Private	112.2	2,000	8062
Children's Memorial Hospital	678	Chicago, IL	Private	192.7	2,000	8069
Childrens Hospital Los Angeles Inc	679	Los Angeles, CA	Private	167.7	2,000	8069
Childrens Hospital Of Wisconsin	680	Milwaukee, WI	Private	173.9	2,000	8069
Columbia Healthcare Of Centl Va	681	Nashville, TN	Public Family Member	137.9	2,000	8011
Covenant Medical Center Inc	682	Waterloo, IA	Private	141.2	2,000	8062
Doctors Hospital	683	Columbus, OH	Private	171.8	2,000	8062
Egleston Children's Hospital	684	Atlanta, GA	Private	220.0	2,000	8069
Elizabeth General Medical Ctr	685	Elizabeth, NJ	Private	108.6	2,000	8062
Golden State Health Centers	686	Van Nuys, CA	Private	90.3	2,000	8059
Heritage Enterprises Inc	687	Bloomington, IL	Private	28.7	2,000	8051
Holy Cross Hospital Inc	688	Fort Lauderdale, FL	Private	163.8	2,000	8062
Homecare, Inc.	689	Wallingford, CT	Private	27.0	2,000	8082
Housecall Medical Services	690	Louisville, KY	Public Family Member	125.0	2,000	8082
I O M Health System Lp	691	Fort Wayne, IN	Private	157.5	2,000	8062
Kent County Memorial Hospital	692	Warwick, RI	Private	134.1	2,000	8062
Life Care Rtrement Communities	693	Des Moines, IA	Private	114.6	2,000	8059
Longwood Management Corp	694	Los Angeles, CA	Private	44.6	2,000	8059
Mercy Children's Hospital	695	Kansas City, MO	Private	146.5	2,000	8069
Mercy Hospital Inc	696	Miami, FL	Private	150.8	2,000	8062
National Home Health Care Corp	697	Scarsdale, NY	Public	35.1	2,000	8082
New England Long-Term Care	698	Boston, MA	Private	45.8	2,000	8051
North Trident Regional Med Ctr	699	Charleston, SC	Public Family Member	93.4	2,000	8062
Northeast Georgia Medical Ctr	700	Gainesville, GA	Private	140.9	2,000	8062

D&B COMPANY RANKINGS BY EMPLOYMENT

Company	Rank	Location	Type	Sales ($ mil.)	Employ-ment	Primary SIC
Ochsner Clinic Health Svcs Corp	701	New Orleans, LA	Private	250.0	2,000	8011
Pleasant Care Corporation	702	La Canada, CA	Private	45.8	2,000	8051
Progressive Home Health Svc	703	New York, NY	Private	44.6	2,000	8059
Sacred Heart Hospital Of Pensacola	704	Pensacola, FL	Private	175.7	2,000	8062
Saint Agnes Medical Center	705	Fresno, CA	Private	93.4	2,000	8062
Saint Cloud Hospital Inc	706	Saint Cloud, MN	Private	160.5	2,000	8062
Services Of Northwestern Human	707	Philadelphia, PA	Private	24.9	2,000	8093
Shannon Health System	708	San Angelo, TX	Private	137.9	2,000	8011
Sisters Mcy St Edw Mcy Hspt	709	Fort Smith, AR	Private	132.0	2,000	8062
Sisters Of St Joseph Of Texas	710	Lubbock, TX	Private	206.2	2,000	8062
Social Cncn Cmmittee	711	Springfield Gdns, NY	Private	32.0	2,000	8082
Southern Ohio Medical Center	712	Portsmouth, OH	Private	117.9	2,000	8062
Southwest General Health Ctr	713	Cleveland, OH	Private	119.3	2,000	8062
St Anthony Hospital	714	Oklahoma City, OK	Private	145.7	2,000	8062
St Barnabas Community Entps	715	Bronx, NY	Private	93.4	2,000	8062
St Johns Regional Medical Ctr	716	Joplin, MO	Private	170.9	2,000	8062
St Luke's Methodist Hospital	717	Cedar Rapids, IA	Private	133.5	2,000	8062
St Mary's Hospital Inc	718	West Palm Beach, FL	Private	158.4	2,000	8062
St Marys Hospital & Med Ctr	719	Grand Junction, CO	Private	93.4	2,000	8062
St Marys Hospital Of Richmond	720	Richmond, VA	Private	344.7	2,000	8062
St Rita's Medical Center	721	Lima, OH	Private	135.8	2,000	8062
Stormont-Vail Healthcare Inc	722	Topeka, KS	Private	93.4	2,000	8062
Torrance Memorial Medical Ctr	723	Torrance, CA	Private	155.2	2,000	8062
Trinity Medical Center	724	Rock Island, IL	Private	137.9	2,000	8062
Trumbull Memorial Hospital	725	Warren, OH	Private	117.8	2,000	8062
U.S. Healthworks, Inc.	726	Alpharetta, GA	Private	100.0	2,000	8011
University Medical Center Inc	727	Louisville, KY	Private	170.2	2,000	8062
Valley Health System	728	Hemet, CA	Private	162.0	2,000	8062
Visiting Nurse Service Of New	729	New York, NY	Private	547.2	2,000	8082
Winchester Hospital	730	Winchester, MA	Private	93.2	2,000	8062
Women & Infants Hospital Ri	731	Providence, RI	Private	142.0	2,000	8069
Children's Health Care	732	Minneapolis, MN	Private	210.6	1,994	8069
Southwest Community Health	733	Cleveland, OH	Private	103.6	1,982	8062
Legacy-Emanual Hospital Health Ctr	734	Portland, OR	Private	218.9	1,978	8062
Galen-Med, Inc	735	Richlands, VA	Public Family Member	100.0	1,975	8062
Saint Frncis Hospital Of Evanston	736	Evanston, IL	Private	142.4	1,962	8062
Allied Services Foundation	737	Scranton, PA	Private	93.9	1,954	8093
Magee-Womens Hospital	738	Pittsburgh, PA	Private	129.9	1,953	8062
Marquette General Hospital	739	Marquette, MI	Private	145.9	1,950	8062
Phoebe Putney Memorial Hosp	740	Albany, GA	Private	207.6	1,950	8062
Prestige Care Inc	741	Vancouver, WA	Private	71.2	1,950	8051
St Lukes Health Care Assn	742	Saginaw, MI	Private	91.0	1,950	8062
Tressler Lutheran Services	743	Mechanicsburg, PA	Private	70.8	1,950	8051
Childrens Hospital Of Ala, The	744	Birmingham, AL	Private	154.5	1,947	8069
Penn State Geisinger Clinic	745	Danville, PA	Private	215.7	1,940	8011
Botsford General Hospital	746	Farmington Hills, MI	Private	255.9	1,937	8062
Tenet Hospital Ltd	747	El Paso, TX	Private	90.4	1,936	8062
Gaston Memorial Hospital Inc	748	Gastonia, NC	Private	157.6	1,935	8062
Frankford Hospital Phila	749	Philadelphia, PA	Private	170.8	1,931	8062
St Alphonsus Regional Med Ctr	750	Boise, ID	Private	144.2	1,927	8062
New York Blood Center, Inc.	751	New York, NY	Private	210.5	1,915	8099
Grossmont Hospital Corporation	752	La Mesa, CA	Private	160.0	1,911	8062
Our Lady Of The Resurrection	753	Chicago, IL	Private	280.4	1,907	8062
Bay Medical Center	754	Panama City, FL	Private	125.5	1,906	8062
Columbia Pk Healthcare Systems	755	Nashville, TN	Private	88.8	1,903	8062
St Charles Mercy Hospital	756	Oregon, OH	Private	116.7	1,903	8062
Boca Raton Community Hospital Inc	757	Boca Raton, FL	Private	152.3	1,900	8062
Brookhaven Mem Hospital Med Ctr	758	East Patchogue, NY	Private	125.6	1,900	8062
Candler Health System Inc	759	Savannah, GA	Private	241.7	1,900	8062
Childrens Hospital Of Pittsburgh	760	Pittsburgh, PA	Private	151.0	1,900	8069
Grace Living Centers	761	Oklahoma City, OK	Private	43.4	1,900	8051
Heartland Regional Medical Ctr	762	Saint Joseph, MO	Private	164.8	1,900	8062
Jersey City Medical Center	763	Jersey City, NJ	Private	162.8	1,900	8062
Memorial Hospital At Gulfport	764	Gulfport, MS	Private	153.9	1,900	8062
Mount Auburn Hospital	765	Cambridge, MA	Private	132.8	1,900	8062
Southside Hospital Inc	766	Bay Shore, NY	Private	88.7	1,900	8062
Springwood Assoc Ltd Partnr	767	East Aurora, NY	Private	42.3	1,900	8059
Waverley Group Inc	768	Jackson, MS	Private	58.0	1,900	8051
Ahom Holdings, Inc (De)	769	Brentwood, TN	Private	30.3	1,891	8082
Battle Creek Health System	770	Battle Creek, MI	Private	139.6	1,882	8062

D&B COMPANY RANKINGS BY EMPLOYMENT

Company	Rank	Location	Type	Sales ($ mil.)	Employ- ment	Primary SIC
Jackson St Dominic Mem Hosp	771	Jackson, MS	Private	87.7	1,880	8062
St Alexius Medical Center	772	Bismarck, ND	Private	109.1	1,875	8062
Sinai Samaritan Medical Center	773	Milwaukee, WI	Private	87.3	1,871	8062
Blood Systems, Inc.	774	Scottsdale, AZ	Private	118.7	1,868	8099
St Joseph Health Svcs Of Ri	775	Providence, RI	Private	118.8	1,865	8062
Athens Regional Medical Ctr	776	Athens, GA	Private	148.3	1,864	8062
America Service Group Inc	777	Brentwood, TN	Public	129.9	1,858	8011
Baptist Health Services Corp	778	Montgomery, AL	Private	86.3	1,850	8062
Bromenn Healthcare	779	Normal, IL	Private	86.3	1,850	8062
Deaconess Long Term Care Of Mo	780	Kansas City, MO	Private	45.4	1,850	8059
Nebraska Methodist Hospital	781	Omaha, NE	Private	110.0	1,850	8062
Shawnee Mission Medical Center	782	Shawnee Mission, KS	Private	157.3	1,850	8062
Deaconess Hospital	783	Cincinnati, OH	Private	86.2	1,848	8062
Salem Hospital Inc	784	Salem, MA	Private	86.2	1,848	8062
Ingalls Memorial Hospital, The	785	Harvey, IL	Private	161.4	1,845	8062
Atlanticare Medical Center	786	Lynn, MA	Private	67.2	1,829	8062
Washington Cnty Hospital Assn Inc	787	Hagerstown, MD	Private	130.7	1,829	8062
Houston Cnty Healthcare Auth	788	Dothan, AL	Private	151.9	1,825	8062
Conemaugh Valley Mem Hosp	789	Johnstown, PA	Private	161.4	1,823	8062
Children's Hospital	790	Washington, DC	Private	193.7	1,810	8062
Meritcare Hospital	791	Fargo, ND	Private	177.5	1,806	8062
Anne Arundel Medical Center	792	Annapolis, MD	Private	130.4	1,800	8062
Autumn Corp	793	Rocky Mount, NC	Private	65.0	1,800	8059
Baptist Hospital Of East Tenn	794	Knoxville, TN	Private	148.0	1,800	8062
Bethania Regional Health Care Ctr	795	Wichita Falls, TX	Private	67.2	1,800	8062
Cedars Medical Center	796	Miami, FL	Private	183.6	1,800	8062
Charter Behavioral Health Systems	797	Atlanta, GA	Private	66.7	1,800	8063
Dayton Osteopathic Hospital	798	Dayton, OH	Private	142.8	1,800	8062
Eisenhower Medical Center	799	Rancho Mirage, CA	Private	140.9	1,800	8062
Glenmark Associates Inc	800	Morgantown, WV	Public Family Member	33.5	1,800	8052
Good Samaritan Hospital	801	Los Angeles, CA	Private	83.9	1,800	8062
Good Shepherd Hospital, Inc	802	Longview, TX	Private	156.7	1,800	8062
H C A Health Svcs Of Virginia	803	Richmond, VA	Public Family Member	83.9	1,800	8062
High Point Regional Health Sys	804	High Point, NC	Private	121.4	1,800	8062
Holy Name Hospital	805	Teaneck, NJ	Private	128.0	1,800	8062
Hutzel Hospital	806	Detroit, MI	Private	169.7	1,800	8062
Jewish Bd Of Fmly & Chld Svcs	807	New York, NY	Private	96.1	1,800	8361
Medcath Incorporated	808	Charlotte, NC	Private	200.0	1,800	8069
Medical Ctr At Princeton, The	809	Princeton, NJ	Private	117.4	1,800	8062
Mercy Services For Aging	810	Farmington Hills, MI	Private	64.4	1,800	8361
Naples Community Hospital Inc	811	Naples, FL	Private	174.3	1,800	8062
Nations Healthcare Inc	812	Alpharetta, GA	Private	81.5	1,800	8082
North Florida Regional Med Ctr	813	Gainesville, FL	Public Family Member	133.3	1,800	8062
Phc/Chc Holdings Inc	814	Houston, TX	Public	83.9	1,800	8062
Raritan Bay Medical Ctr A Nj	815	Perth Amboy, NJ	Private	141.5	1,800	8062
Ravenswood Health Care Corp	816	Chicago, IL	Private	139.6	1,800	8062
San Antonio Community Hosp	817	Upland, CA	Private	126.0	1,800	8062
Sparks Regional Medical Ctr	818	Fort Smith, AR	Private	121.3	1,800	8062
Triad Group Inc	819	Yadkinville, NC	Private	41.1	1,800	8051
Trinity Medical Cntr	820	Rock Island, IL	Private	127.8	1,800	8062
University Of Alabama Health S	821	Birmingham, AL	Private	376.0	1,800	8093
Valdost-Lwndes Cnty Hospital Auth	822	Valdosta, GA	Private	118.5	1,800	8062
Valley Children's Hospital	823	Madera, CA	Private	138.4	1,800	8069
Wellesley Newton Hospital	824	Newton, MA	Private	121.8	1,800	8062
St Marys Med Ctr Of Saginaw	825	Saginaw, MI	Private	141.1	1,794	8062
Baton Rouge General Med Ctr	826	Baton Rouge, LA	Private	144.6	1,790	8062
Integris Rur Healthcare Of Okla	827	Oklahoma City, OK	Private	117.7	1,790	8062
Jefferson Hospital Association	828	Pine Bluff, AR	Private	129.5	1,788	8062
Santa Barbara Cottage Hosp	829	Santa Barbara, CA	Private	83.3	1,786	8062
Mercy Health Center	830	Oklahoma City, OK	Private	133.7	1,780	8062
Rogue Valley Medical Center	831	Medford, OR	Private	128.3	1,778	8062
Martin Memorial Medical Center	832	Stuart, FL	Private	151.9	1,776	8062
Gundersen Lthran Hsptl-Lcrosse	833	La Crosse, WI	Private	140.5	1,760	8062
St Francis Hospital	834	Roslyn, NY	Private	182.7	1,759	8069
Alexandria Inova Hospital	835	Alexandria, VA	Private	122.0	1,750	8062
Lubbock County Hospital Dst	836	Lubbock, TX	Private	96.0	1,750	8062
St Barnabas Hospital	837	Bronx, NY	Private	81.6	1,750	8062
Detroit Receiving Hospital And	838	Detroit, MI	Private	225.1	1,740	8069
Veterans Memorial Medical Ctr	839	Meriden, CT	Private	102.1	1,740	8062
Memorial Hospital	840	Pawtucket, RI	Private	111.0	1,737	8062

D&B COMPANY RANKINGS BY EMPLOYMENT

Company	Rank	Location	Type	Sales ($ mil.)	Employment	Primary SIC
Holmes Hooper Inc	841	Basking Ridge, NJ	Public	165.4	1,735	8099
St Mary's Health System Inc	842	Knoxville, TN	Private	135.2	1,732	8062
Father Flanagan's Boy's Home	843	Boys Town, NE	Private	98.7	1,729	8361
St Francis Hospital & Med Ctr	844	Topeka, KS	Private	113.5	1,724	8062
Bayfront Medical Center Inc	845	Saint Petersburg, FL	Private	161.4	1,723	8062
Citrus Valley Medical Center	846	West Covina, CA	Private	101.4	1,723	8062
Columbia La Grange Mem Hosp	847	La Grange, IL	Public Family Member	80.1	1,719	8062
Virginia Beach General Hosp	848	Virginia Beach, VA	Private	107.2	1,717	8062
St Josephs Hospital Of Marshfield	849	Marshfield, WI	Private	156.9	1,715	8062
Sherman Hospital	850	Elgin, IL	Private	132.0	1,712	8062
Ashland Hospital Corporation	851	Ashland, KY	Private	145.6	1,700	8062
Baptist Medical Center	852	Montgomery, AL	Private	136.8	1,700	8062
Bergen Regional Medical Ctr	853	Paramus, NJ	Private	79.2	1,700	8062
Chesapeake Hospital Auth	854	Chesapeake, VA	Private	121.9	1,700	8062
Children's Hospital Medical Center	855	Akron, OH	Private	127.8	1,700	8069
Childrens Hospital & Health Ctr	856	San Diego, CA	Private	79.2	1,700	8062
Frederick Memorial Hospital	857	Frederick, MD	Private	101.7	1,700	8062
Galen Hospital Illinois Inc	858	Chicago, IL	Public Family Member	171.4	1,700	8062
MacNeal Mem Hospital Assn	859	Berwyn, IL	Private	162.7	1,700	8062
Miami Beach Healthcare Group	860	Miami, FL	Private	114.2	1,700	8062
Mount Sinai Hospital Med Cen	861	Chicago, IL	Private	170.9	1,700	8062
N T Enloe Memorial Hospital	862	Chico, CA	Private	117.3	1,700	8062
North Central Health Services	863	Lafayette, IN	Private	113.1	1,700	8062
Park Nicollet Medical Center	864	Minneapolis, MN	Private	432.0	1,700	8011
Poudre Valley Health Care Inc	865	Fort Collins, CO	Private	150.4	1,700	8062
Saint Francis Hospital	866	Memphis, TN	Public Family Member	137.4	1,700	8062
Sentara Health System	867	Norfolk, VA	Private	36.6	1,700	8062
Singing River Hospital System	868	Pascagoula, MS	Private	181.8	1,700	8062
Somerset Medical Center	869	Somerville, NJ	Private	115.5	1,700	8062
St Francis Medical Center	870	Monroe, LA	Private	149.0	1,700	8062
Unlimited Care Inc	871	White Plains, NY	Private	117.2	1,700	8011
Us Diagnostic Inc	872	West Palm Beach, FL	Public	216.2	1,700	8071
West Suburban Health Care Corp	873	Oak Park, IL	Private	79.2	1,700	8062
Westmoreland Health System	874	Greensburg, PA	Private	79.2	1,700	8062
Westmoreland Regional Hosp	875	Greensburg, PA	Private	107.0	1,700	8062
Wyandotte Hospital & Med Ctr	876	Wyandotte, MI	Private	280.0	1,700	8062
Nueces County Hospital Dst	877	Corpus Christi, TX	Private	119.3	1,689	8062
All Children's Hospital Inc	878	Saint Petersburg, FL	Private	129.1	1,688	8069
Huntington Foundation Inc	879	Plainfield, NJ	Private	116.2	1,686	8011
St Joseph Medical Center	880	Tacoma, WA	Private	179.2	1,680	8062
Hospital Service District 1	881	Marrero, LA	Private	133.7	1,676	8062
Parma Community Gen Hospital	882	Cleveland, OH	Private	91.7	1,667	8062
Candler Hospital Inc	883	Savannah, GA	Private	200.3	1,661	8062
Central Louisiana Healthcare	884	Alexandria, LA	Private	77.4	1,661	8062
Norwalk Hospital Assn	885	Norwalk, CT	Private	168.7	1,660	8062
Mother Frncs Hosp, Tyler, Tx	886	Tyler, TX	Private	164.2	1,655	8062
National Mentor Inc	887	Boston, MA	Public Family Member	88.3	1,655	8361
Ssm Health Care Of Oklahoma	888	Oklahoma City, OK	Private	77.1	1,655	8062
Bellin Memorial Hospital	889	Green Bay, WI	Private	119.8	1,650	8062
East Alabama Health Care Auth	890	Opelika, AL	Private	107.6	1,650	8062
King County Public Hospital Dst 1	891	Renton, WA	Private	133.3	1,650	8062
Medalia Healthcare Llc	892	Seattle, WA	Private	113.7	1,650	8011
Muhlenberg Regional Med Ctr	893	Plainfield, NJ	Private	110.9	1,650	8062
Munroe Rgnal Healthcare Systems	894	Ocala, FL	Private	156.8	1,650	8062
St Lukes-Memorial Hospital Ctr	895	New Hartford, NY	Private	76.9	1,650	8062
Coastal Physician Group, Inc	896	Durham, NC	Public	424.8	1,645	8093
Baptist Hospital Inc	897	Pensacola, FL	Private	143.3	1,641	8062
Peconic Health Corporation	898	Aquebogue, NY	Private	76.0	1,632	8062
St Mary's Medical Center	899	Duluth, MN	Private	168.3	1,631	8062
Ector County Hospital Dst	900	Odessa, TX	Private	46.4	1,625	8062
Holy Spirit Hospital Sis	901	Camp Hill, PA	Private	75.5	1,621	8062
Danbury Hospital, The	902	Danbury, CT	Private	188.8	1,620	8062
McAllen Medical Center Inc	903	Mcallen, TX	Public Family Member	167.4	1,620	8062
Welborn Memorial Baptist Hosp	904	Evansville, IN	Private	88.0	1,615	8062
Providence Hospital	905	Washington, DC	Private	133.4	1,611	8062
Mercy Medical Center	906	Rockville Centre, NY	Private	133.3	1,610	8062
Baylor Medical Ctr At Irving	907	Irving, TX	Private	121.1	1,600	8062
Bellin Health Systems, Inc	908	Green Bay, WI	Private	74.5	1,600	8062
Blessing Hospital	909	Quincy, IL	Private	94.8	1,600	8062
Christian Homes Inc	910	Lincoln, IL	Private	28.0	1,600	8051

D&B COMPANY RANKINGS BY EMPLOYMENT

Company	Rank	Location	Type	Sales ($ mil.)	Employ-ment	Primary SIC
Columbia Csa/Hs Greater Clvlnd	911	Cleveland, OH	Private	74.5	1,600	8062
Community Health Care Sys	912	San Bernardino, CA	Private	74.5	1,600	8062
Comprehensive Cancer Centers	913	Los Angeles, CA	Private	48.8	1,600	8093
Floyd Healthcare Management	914	Rome, GA	Private	131.6	1,600	8062
Fort Worth Medical Plaza Inc	915	Fort Worth, TX	Public Family Member	113.8	1,600	8062
Frye Regional Medical Center	916	Hickory, NC	Public Family Member	74.5	1,600	8062
Good Samaritan Hospital	917	Vincennes, IN	Private	91.3	1,600	8062
H N M C Inc	918	Houston, TX	Public Family Member	74.5	1,600	8062
Health Caolc And Tcofa	919	Florence, AL	Private	102.3	1,600	8062
Healthcare Partners Med Group	920	Los Angeles, CA	Private	110.3	1,600	8011
Hillsdale Group (Inc)	921	Burlingame, CA	Private	22.2	1,600	8059
Holy Cross Hospital	922	Chicago, IL	Private	78.9	1,600	8062
Huntington Cabell Hospital	923	Huntington, WV	Private	116.4	1,600	8062
Irving Hospital Authority	924	Irving, TX	Private	74.5	1,600	8062
Jefferson Mem Hospital Assn, The	925	Crystal City, MO	Private	76.5	1,600	8062
Lawrence And Memorial Hosp	926	New London, CT	Private	137.3	1,600	8062
Lexington Medical Center	927	West Columbia, SC	Private	122.8	1,600	8062
Mayo Clinic Jacksonville Inc	928	Jacksonville, FL	Private	110.3	1,600	8011
Mercy Med Ctr Cedar Rapids Iowa	929	Cedar Rapids, IA	Private	100.7	1,600	8062
North General Home	930	New York, NY	Private	39.1	1,600	8361
Northridge Med Center - Roscoe	931	Northridge, CA	Private	153.0	1,600	8062
Nurses Unlimited Inc	932	Odessa, TX	Private	24.8	1,600	8049
Overlake Hospital Medical Ctr	933	Bellevue, WA	Private	114.3	1,600	8062
Porter Memorial Hospital	934	Valparaiso, IN	Private	129.5	1,600	8062
Q H G Of South Carolina Inc	935	Florence, SC	Public Family Member	74.5	1,600	8062
Renaissance Healthcare Corp	936	Mechanicsburg, PA	Private	36.5	1,600	8051
Saint Mary Hospital & Med Ctr	937	Grand Junction, CO	Private	74.5	1,600	8062
Salick Health Care Inc	938	Los Angeles, CA	Private	48.8	1,600	8093
Seton Health System	939	Troy, NY	Private	76.9	1,600	8062
Shore Memorial Hospital	940	Somers Point, NJ	Private	109.4	1,600	8062
Southeastern Regional Med Ctr	941	Lumberton, NC	Private	112.2	1,600	8062
Southside Virginia Training Ctr	942	Petersburg, VA	Private	52.0	1,600	8361
Southwest Fla Regional Med Ctr	943	Fort Myers, FL	Public Family Member	175.0	1,600	8062
St Elizabeth's Hospital	944	Belleville, IL	Private	102.7	1,600	8062
St Francis Hospital Inc	945	Milwaukee, WI	Private	119.7	1,600	8062
St Mary Medical Center	946	Langhorne, PA	Private	100.5	1,600	8062
Telecare Corporation	947	Alameda, CA	Private	61.4	1,600	8063
Trinity Medical Center West	948	Steubenville, OH	Private	74.5	1,600	8062
West Florida Regional Med Ctr	949	Pensacola, FL	Public Family Member	74.5	1,600	8062
Winter Park Health Care Group	950	Winter Park, FL	Private	74.5	1,600	8062
Winter Park Memorial Hospital	951	Winter Park, FL	Private	74.5	1,600	8062
Covenant Health Care System	952	Milwaukee, WI	Private	73.9	1,587	8062
Aurora Medical Group, Inc	953	Milwaukee, WI	Private	108.5	1,575	8011
Grand View Hospital	954	Sellersville, PA	Private	71.9	1,572	8062
Maryview Hospital	955	Portsmouth, VA	Private	99.8	1,572	8062
Albany Medical College	956	Albany, NY	Private	172.8	1,568	8011
West Suburban Hospital Med Ctr	957	Oak Park, IL	Private	147.8	1,568	8062
Ellis Hospital	958	Schenectady, NY	Private	72.6	1,560	8062
Scottish Rite Hosp	959	Atlanta, GA	Private	77.1	1,560	8069
Capital Senior Living Inc	960	Dallas, TX	Public	30.7	1,558	8059
Alta Bates Medical Center	961	Berkeley, CA	Private	287.5	1,550	8062
Antelope Valley Health Care Systms	962	Lancaster, CA	Private	129.9	1,550	8062
De Paul Health Center Inc	963	Bridgeton, MO	Private	72.1	1,550	8062
H C A Health Services Tenn Inc	964	Nashville, TN	Public Family Member	72.1	1,550	8062
Joseph Saint Health Center	965	Kansas City, MO	Private	115.2	1,550	8062
Kimball Medical Center Inc	966	Lakewood, NJ	Private	105.8	1,550	8062
Manhattan Psychiatric Center	967	New York, NY	Private	57.4	1,550	8063
Southern Regional Medical Ctr	968	Riverdale, GA	Private	72.1	1,550	8062
Suburban Hospital	969	Bethesda, MD	Private	124.3	1,550	8062
Bethesda Memorial Hospital	970	Boynton Beach, FL	Private	119.6	1,545	8062
Long Life Home Care Services	971	Brooklyn, NY	Private	24.8	1,545	8082
Mercy Hospital (Inc)	972	Springfield, MA	Private	71.4	1,535	8062
Cobb Hospital Inc	973	Austell, GA	Private	70.9	1,525	8062
St Joseph's Medical Center	974	South Bend, IN	Private	138.0	1,523	8062
St Mary's Hospital Corporation	975	Waterbury, CT	Private	134.5	1,520	8062
Altoona Hospital, The	976	Altoona, PA	Private	129.3	1,518	8062
Elliot Hospital	977	Manchester, NH	Private	116.4	1,517	8062
Providence Hospital Inc	978	Mobile, AL	Private	135.2	1,506	8062
Community Hospital	979	San Bernardino, CA	Private	162.5	1,504	8062
Allegheny Univ Hospital Graduate	980	Philadelphia, PA	Private	40.6	1,500	8062

D&B COMPANY RANKINGS BY EMPLOYMENT

Company	Rank	Location	Type	Sales ($ mil.)	Employ-ment	Primary SIC
Allegheny Valley School	981	Coraopolis, PA	Private	51.6	1,500	8361
Alliance Health Care, Inc.	982	Burnsville, MN	Private	24.1	1,500	8082
American Health Care Centers	983	Wadsworth, OH	Private	34.2	1,500	8051
American Phrm Svcs Del	984	Naperville, IL	Public Family Member	221.1	1,500	8051
Autumn Hills Convalescent Ctrs	985	Houston, TX	Private	45.0	1,500	8051
Baptist Medical Center	986	Kansas City, MO	Private	126.1	1,500	8062
Britwill Investments Ii Inc	987	Scottsdale, AZ	Public Family Member	34.2	1,500	8051
Centrastate Medical Center	988	Freehold, NJ	Private	92.0	1,500	8062
Clara Maass Medical Center	989	Belleville, NJ	Private	109.3	1,500	8062
Clinishare Inc	990	Chatsworth, CA	Private	24.1	1,500	8082
Clintrials Research Inc	991	Nashville, TN	Public	103.0	1,500	8071
Continuum Care Corporation	992	Palm Beach Gdns, FL	Private	34.2	1,500	8051
Covenant Care California Inc	993	SJ Capistrano, CA	Private	34.2	1,500	8051
Dakota Clinic Ltd	994	Fargo, ND	Private	103.4	1,500	8011
Daughters Of Charity Health	995	Waco, TX	Private	86.0	1,500	8062
Eden Park Health Services	996	Albany, NY	Private	48.0	1,500	8051
Everest Healthcare Svcs Corp	997	Oak Park, IL	Private	140.0	1,500	8092
Foundation Health Federal Svcs	998	Rancho Cordova, CA	Public Family Member	103.4	1,500	8011
Ghs Osteopathic Inc	999	Philadelphia, PA	Private	66.3	1,500	8062
Good Samaritan Hospital Of Suffern	1000	Suffern, NY	Private	110.7	1,500	8062
Green Spring Health Services	1001	Columbia, MD	Public Family Member	226.3	1,500	8093
Hospital Of Community-General	1002	Syracuse, NY	Private	82.9	1,500	8062
Ihs Home Care	1003	Nashville, TN	Public Family Member	24.1	1,500	8082
Integrated Living Communities	1004	Chicago, IL	Private	27.9	1,500	8052
Intensiva Healthcare Corp	1005	Saint Louis, MO	Public	69.6	1,500	8069
Kuakini Health System	1006	Honolulu, HI	Private	112.3	1,500	8062
Lake Forest Hospital Foundation	1007	Lake Forest, IL	Private	89.0	1,500	8062
Latrobe Area Hospital Inc	1008	Latrobe, PA	Private	102.9	1,500	8062
Laureate Group Inc	1009	Waukesha, WI	Private	45.0	1,500	8051
Macgregor Medical Assn P A	1010	Houston, TX	Private	103.4	1,500	8011
Mariner Health Of Maryland	1011	Beltsville, MD	Public Family Member	33.4	1,500	8059
Mary Washington Hospital Inc	1012	Fredericksburg, VA	Private	146.5	1,500	8062
McWil Group Ltd	1013	York, PA	Private	50.0	1,500	8059
Medical Services Of America	1014	Lexington, SC	Private	97.4	1,500	8082
Medicalodges Of Kansas Inc	1015	Coffeyville, KS	Private	34.2	1,500	8051
Mercer Medical Center	1016	Trenton, NJ	Private	78.2	1,500	8062
Meritcare Health Enterprises	1017	Fargo, ND	Private	121.4	1,500	8011
Methodist Med Ctr Of Oak Ridge	1018	Oak Ridge, TN	Private	115.1	1,500	8062
Midelfort Clinic-Mayo Health	1019	Eau Claire, WI	Private	103.4	1,500	8011
New York Foundling Hosp, The	1020	New York, NY	Private	57.8	1,500	8361
North Colorado Medical Center	1021	Greeley, CO	Private	131.5	1,500	8062
Pacific Health Systems Inc	1022	Santa Ana, CA	Public Family Member	103.4	1,500	8011
Partners In Care Inc	1023	New York, NY	Private	65.4	1,500	8082
People Inc.	1024	Williamsville, NY	Private	38.0	1,500	8361
Personacare Inc	1025	Louisville, KY	Private	34.2	1,500	8051
Physicians Clinical Laboratory	1026	Sacramento, CA	Public	62.8	1,500	8071
Recco Home Care Service Inc	1027	Massapequa, NY	Private	24.1	1,500	8082
Rose Care, Inc	1028	Rogers, AR	Private	39.2	1,500	8052
Saint Marys Hospital Of Huntington	1029	Huntington, WV	Private	148.8	1,500	8062
Salinas Valley Memorial Health	1030	Salinas, CA	Private	168.0	1,500	8062
Self Memorial Hospital	1031	Greenwood, SC	Private	102.9	1,500	8062
Southwest Louisiana Hospital Assn	1032	Lake Charles, LA	Private	102.1	1,500	8062
St Anthony's Hospital Inc	1033	Saint Petersburg, FL	Private	91.5	1,500	8062
St Bernard's Hospital Inc	1034	Jonesboro, AR	Private	137.6	1,500	8062
St Chris Hospital Children Inc	1035	Philadelphia, PA	Private	132.8	1,500	8069
St Francis Hospital Inc	1036	Greenville, SC	Private	162.2	1,500	8062
St Joseph Of The Pines Inc	1037	Southern Pines, NC	Private	42.8	1,500	8082
St Luke's Hospital Of Duluth	1038	Duluth, MN	Private	84.4	1,500	8062
St Luke's Regional Med Ctr	1039	Sioux City, IA	Private	85.7	1,500	8062
St Mary's Hospital Of Brooklyn	1040	Brooklyn, NY	Private	69.8	1,500	8062
Tulane Medical Center, Ltd	1041	New Orleans, LA	Private	132.7	1,500	8062
U T Medical Group Inc	1042	Memphis, TN	Private	103.4	1,500	8011
Underwood Memorial Hospital	1043	Woodbury, NJ	Private	88.6	1,500	8062
United Healthcare System, Inc.	1044	Newark, NJ	Private	69.8	1,500	8062
Whslc Realty Llc	1045	Chicago, IL	Private	27.9	1,500	8052
Wyckoff Heights Medical Ctr	1046	Brooklyn, NY	Private	69.8	1,500	8062
Youth & Family Centered	1047	Austin, TX	Private	36.7	1,500	8361
Youth Services International	1048	Owings Mills, MD	Public	100.4	1,500	8361
Wilmac Corporation	1049	York, PA	Private	33.1	1,490	8059
Glynn-Brunswick Hospital Auth	1050	Brunswick, GA	Private	116.8	1,487	8062

D&B COMPANY RANKINGS BY EMPLOYMENT

Company	Rank	Location	Type	Sales ($ mil.)	Employ-ment	Primary SIC
Good Samaritan Hospital	1051	Puyallup, WA	Private	95.8	1,481	8062
Deaconess Waltham Hospital	1052	Waltham, MA	Private	64.8	1,480	8062
Mercy Hospital Of Scranton Pa	1053	Scranton, PA	Private	106.9	1,476	8062
Maury Regional Hospital	1054	Columbia, TN	Private	104.5	1,473	8062
Rehabcare Group	1055	Saint Louis, MO	Public	160.8	1,472	8093
Columbia Hospital, Inc.	1056	Milwaukee, WI	Private	128.0	1,470	8062
Washington Hospital	1057	Washington, PA	Private	124.3	1,470	8062
General Hospital Ctr At Passaic	1058	Passaic, NJ	Private	109.0	1,465	8062
Rockingham Memorial Hospital	1059	Harrisonburg, VA	Private	101.0	1,465	8062
Medical Center, Inc	1060	Columbus, GA	Private	68.0	1,463	8062
Hca Health Services Of Utah	1061	Salt Lake City, UT	Public Family Member	67.7	1,457	8062
St Jude Hospital	1062	Fullerton, CA	Private	210.1	1,454	8062
St Patrick Hospital Inc	1063	Lake Charles, LA	Private	67.5	1,452	8062
Community Hospital Of Monterey	1064	Monterey, CA	Private	150.3	1,450	8062
Hardin Memorial Hospital	1065	Elizabethtown, KY	Private	98.1	1,450	8062
Human Development Association	1066	Brooklyn, NY	Private	33.6	1,450	8082
Medical Center East Inc	1067	Birmingham, AL	Private	109.0	1,450	8062
Memorial Hosp	1068	Mount Holly, NJ	Private	130.4	1,450	8062
Memorial Medical Center	1069	Las Cruces, NM	Private	125.5	1,450	8062
New York Flshing Hospital Med Ctr	1070	Flushing, NY	Private	151.0	1,450	8062
Southwest La Health Care Sys	1071	Lake Charles, LA	Private	99.9	1,450	8011
Waterbury Hospital	1072	Waterbury, CT	Private	139.9	1,450	8062
St Vincent's Hospital	1073	Birmingham, AL	Private	120.6	1,449	8062
Our Lady Of Lourdes Mem Hosp	1074	Binghamton, NY	Private	94.7	1,445	8062
Optima Health-Cmc	1075	Manchester, NH	Private	132.8	1,432	8062
St Joseph Hospital, Inc	1076	Lancaster, PA	Private	102.4	1,429	8062
Upmc Mckeesport	1077	Mc Keesport, PA	Private	66.4	1,429	8062
Good Samaritan Hospital Of Md Inc	1078	Baltimore, MD	Private	115.5	1,427	8062
Deborah Heart & Lung Center	1079	Browns Mills, NJ	Private	107.8	1,425	8069
Easton Hospital	1080	Easton, PA	Private	106.5	1,425	8062
Mayo Clinic Scottsdale	1081	Scottsdale, AZ	Private	150.0	1,423	8011
R E Thomason General Hospital	1082	El Paso, TX	Private	164.3	1,420	8062
Rochester St Mary's Hospital	1083	Rochester, NY	Private	89.9	1,415	8062
Baylor Health Care System	1084	Dallas, TX	Private	938.0	1,409	8062
Samaritan Hospital	1085	Troy, NY	Private	64.0	1,403	8062
Becklund Home Health Care	1086	Minneapolis, MN	Private	27.0	1,400	8082
Bon Secours-Depaul Medical Ctr	1087	Norfolk, VA	Private	59.8	1,400	8062
Boston Regional Medical Center	1088	Stoneham, MA	Private	57.4	1,400	8062
Cabs Home Attendants Service	1089	Brooklyn, NY	Private	31.0	1,400	8082
California Hospital Medical	1090	Los Angeles, CA	Private	109.7	1,400	8062
Caregivers Inc	1091	Brooklyn, NY	Private	20.5	1,400	8082
Comanche County Hospital Auth Tr	1092	Lawton, OK	Private	121.2	1,400	8062
Community Hospital Assn Inc	1093	Boulder, CO	Private	109.7	1,400	8063
Crestwood Hospitals Inc	1094	Stockton, CA	Private	122.6	1,400	8069
Dallas Cnty Mntl Health/Rtrdtn	1095	Dallas, TX	Private	74.2	1,400	8361
Episcopal Hospital	1096	Philadelphia, PA	Private	160.5	1,400	8062
Fedcap Rehabilitation Services	1097	New York, NY	Private	42.4	1,400	8093
Glendale Adventist Med Ctr	1098	Glendale, CA	Private	131.1	1,400	8062
Good Samaritan Hospital Inc	1099	Kearney, NE	Private	86.4	1,400	8062
Health Alliance Plan Of Mich	1100	Detroit, MI	Private	913.2	1,400	8011
Hospital Authority Petersburg	1101	Petersburg, VA	Private	99.3	1,400	8062
Howell Child Care Center Inc	1102	La Grange, NC	Private	39.9	1,400	8361
Hunter Care Centers Inc	1103	Chesterfield, MO	Public Family Member	41.5	1,400	8051
Interhealth Corporation	1104	Whittier, CA	Private	146.6	1,400	8062
Jackson Hospital & Clinic Inc	1105	Montgomery, AL	Private	100.4	1,400	8062
Lafayette General Hospital	1106	Lafayette, LA	Private	150.0	1,400	8062
Lake Cumberland Healthcare	1107	Somerset, KY	Public Family Member	65.0	1,400	8062
Lee Regional Health System	1108	Johnstown, PA	Private	65.0	1,400	8062
Lucy W Hayes Trng Sch Dcns Msn	1109	Washington, DC	Private	65.0	1,400	8062
Manatee Mem Hospital Ltd Partnr	1110	Bradenton, FL	Private	65.0	1,400	8062
Mckerley Health Care Centers	1111	Penacook, NH	Public Family Member	26.0	1,400	8052
Mediplex Of Connecticut Inc	1112	Newton, MA	Public Family Member	31.9	1,400	8051
Mercy Hospital Of Laredo	1113	Laredo, TX	Private	98.6	1,400	8062
Nash Hospitals Inc	1114	Rocky Mount, NC	Private	100.3	1,400	8062
Northwest Health System Inc	1115	Springdale, AR	Private	91.6	1,400	8062
Pacific Homes	1116	Woodland Hills, CA	Private	54.0	1,400	8361
Pontiac General Hospital & Med Ctr	1117	Pontiac, MI	Private	65.0	1,400	8062
Quest Diagnostics A Cal Corp	1118	SJ Capistrano, CA	Private	170.0	1,400	8071
Rehabclinics Inc	1119	King Of Prussia, PA	Public Family Member	42.7	1,400	8093
Rochester Methodist Hospital	1120	Rochester, MN	Private	137.8	1,400	8062

D&B COMPANY RANKINGS BY EMPLOYMENT

Company	Rank	Location	Type	Sales ($ mil.)	Employ- ment	Primary SIC
Saint Joseph Medical Center	1121	Reading, PA	Private	76.9	1,400	8062
Saint Mary Of Nazareth Hospital Ctr	1122	Chicago, IL	Private	118.8	1,400	8062
Shore Memorial Health Foundation	1123	Somers Point, NJ	Private	118.3	1,400	8062
Silver Cross Hospital	1124	Joliet, IL	Private	94.6	1,400	8062
Sound Shore Medical Center	1125	New Rochelle, NY	Private	112.8	1,400	8062
Southeast Missouri Hospital Assn	1126	Cape Girardeau, MO	Private	107.0	1,400	8062
St Francis Hospital Inc	1127	Wilmington, DE	Private	116.4	1,400	8062
St Francis Medical Center	1128	Honolulu, HI	Private	128.6	1,400	8062
St Joseph's Hospital	1129	Asheville, NC	Private	88.8	1,400	8062
St Josephs Regional Health Ctr	1130	Hot Springs, AR	Private	104.2	1,400	8062
St Marys Regional Medical Ctr	1131	Reno, NV	Private	133.4	1,400	8062
United Hospital Center Inc	1132	Clarksburg, WV	Private	115.3	1,400	8062
University Medical Center	1133	Fresno, CA	Private	65.0	1,400	8062
Visiting Nurse Assn Of Texas	1134	Dallas, TX	Private	51.4	1,400	8082
West Allis Memorial Hospital	1135	Milwaukee, WI	Private	75.8	1,400	8062
West Georgia Medical Center	1136	Lagrange, GA	Private	75.7	1,400	8062
Sheppard Enoch Pratt Fundation	1137	Baltimore, MD	Private	69.5	1,399	8063
St Elizabeth Hospital Inc	1138	Appleton, WI	Private	64.9	1,398	8062
Elkhart General Hospital	1139	Elkhart, IN	Private	109.4	1,395	8062
Wheeling Hospital Inc	1140	Wheeling, WV	Private	104.7	1,388	8062
Sensitive Care Inc	1141	Fort Worth, TX	Private	63.0	1,387	8051
St Luke Hospital Inc	1142	Fort Thomas, KY	Private	64.3	1,385	8062
Crowne Investments Inc	1143	Monroeville, AL	Private	31.4	1,378	8051
Berkshire Medical Center Inc	1144	Pittsfield, MA	Private	135.6	1,375	8062
Mid Michigan Regional Med Ctr	1145	Midland, MI	Private	63.9	1,375	8062
Norman Regional Hospital Auth	1146	Norman, OK	Private	113.3	1,370	8062
Valley Health Systems Inc	1147	Holyoke, MA	Private	63.0	1,357	8062
Wuesthoff Memorial Hospital	1148	Rockledge, FL	Private	113.9	1,356	8062
Alamance Regional Med Ctr Inc	1149	Burlington, NC	Private	90.9	1,350	8062
Allegheny Valley Hospital	1150	Natrona Heights, PA	Private	115.9	1,350	8062
Florida Medical Center Inc	1151	Fort Lauderdale, FL	Public Family Member	117.7	1,350	8062
Healthalliance Hospitals Inc	1152	Leominster, MA	Private	47.4	1,350	8062
Jeanes Hospital	1153	Philadelphia, PA	Private	81.5	1,350	8062
Mercy Healthcare North	1154	Redding, CA	Private	184.5	1,350	8062
Mission Hospital Regional Med Ctr	1155	Mission Viejo, CA	Private	115.5	1,350	8062
Parkview Health System Inc	1156	Pueblo, CO	Private	62.7	1,350	8062
Piedmont Healthcare Systems	1157	Rock Hill, SC	Public Family Member	62.7	1,350	8062
Presbyterian Homes Inc	1158	Camp Hill, PA	Private	59.7	1,350	8052
Quest Diagnostics Inc Michigan	1159	Auburn Hills, MI	Private	125.0	1,350	8071
Riverside Medical Center	1160	Kankakee, IL	Private	91.9	1,350	8062
South Fulton Medical Center	1161	Atlanta, GA	Private	87.4	1,350	8062
St Mary's Health Care System	1162	Athens, GA	Private	62.7	1,350	8062
Valley Hospital Med Ctr Inc	1163	Las Vegas, NV	Public Family Member	62.7	1,350	8062
Washington Regional Med Ctr	1164	Fayetteville, AR	Private	88.6	1,350	8062
Touro Infirmary	1165	New Orleans, LA	Private	62.4	1,344	8062
American Baptist Homes	1166	Eden Prairie, MN	Private	49.3	1,340	8051
Woman's Christian Assoc O Jam	1167	Jamestown, NY	Private	74.6	1,340	8062
Clark Memorial Hospital	1168	Jeffersonville, IN	Private	82.0	1,338	8062
Memorial Healthcare Group	1169	Jacksonville, FL	Public Family Member	61.9	1,334	8062
Washington Regional Med Sys	1170	Fayetteville, AR	Private	61.9	1,334	8062
Home Health And Hospice Care	1171	Goldsboro, NC	Private	35.7	1,333	8059
Montgomery Hospital	1172	Norristown, PA	Private	100.2	1,330	8062
Rose Medical Center, Inc.	1173	Denver, CO	Public Family Member	138.6	1,325	8062
St Luke's Hospital	1174	Maumee, OH	Private	81.1	1,325	8062
Doylestown Hospital	1175	Doylestown, PA	Private	88.2	1,321	8062
Trustees Of Mease Hospital	1176	Dunedin, FL	Private	132.7	1,320	8062
Sarah Bush Lincoln Health Ctr	1177	Mattoon, IL	Private	75.0	1,315	8062
Raleigh General Hospital	1178	Beckley, WV	Public Family Member	140.0	1,312	8062
Craven Regional Medical Ctr	1179	New Bern, NC	Private	125.1	1,305	8062
St Mary Hospital Of Livonia	1180	Livonia, MI	Private	92.2	1,304	8062
All Saints Health System	1181	Fort Worth, TX	Private	141.2	1,300	8062
Associated Therapists Corp	1182	Owings Mills, MD	Public Family Member	60.3	1,300	8093
Association/Services Aged	1183	Brooklyn, NY	Private	26.2	1,300	8361
Augusta Hospital Corporation	1184	Fishersville, VA	Private	97.0	1,300	8062
Blount Memorial Hospital	1185	Maryville, TN	Private	77.7	1,300	8062
Brandywine Hospital	1186	Coatesville, PA	Private	64.8	1,300	8062
Brockton Hospital Inc	1187	Brockton, MA	Private	95.8	1,300	8062
Brunswick Hospital Center Inc	1188	Amityville, NY	Private	75.9	1,300	8062
Cal Southern Presbyterian Homes	1189	Glendale, CA	Private	42.9	1,300	8051
Children's Medical Center	1190	Dayton, OH	Private	90.7	1,300	8069

D&B COMPANY RANKINGS BY EMPLOYMENT

Company	Rank	Location	Type	Sales ($ mil.)	Employ-ment	Primary SIC
Columbus Regional Hospital	1191	Columbus, IN	Private	108.5	1,300	8062
Cvhs Hospital Corporation	1192	Inglewood, CA	Public Family Member	98.8	1,300	8062
Dominican Santa Cruz Hospital	1193	Santa Cruz, CA	Private	118.9	1,300	8062
Duluth Clinic Ltd, The	1194	Duluth, MN	Private	202.2	1,300	8011
Eastern Idaho Regional Med Ctr	1195	Idaho Falls, ID	Public Family Member	132.3	1,300	8062
Edward Hospital	1196	Naperville, IL	Private	119.2	1,300	8062
Emerson Hospital Inc	1197	Concord, MA	Private	68.9	1,300	8062
Fairfield Medical Center	1198	Lancaster, OH	Private	95.7	1,300	8062
First Hospital Corp Of Portsmouth	1199	Portsmouth, VA	Private	24.9	1,300	8051
Fountain Valley Regnl Hosp	1200	Fountain Valley, CA	Public Family Member	60.3	1,300	8062
Franklin Hospital Medical Ctr	1201	Valley Stream, NY	Private	60.3	1,300	8062
Greater Bristol Health Svcs Corp	1202	Bristol, CT	Private	60.3	1,300	8062
Greenwich Hospital Assn Inc	1203	Greenwich, CT	Private	109.4	1,300	8062
Hackley Hospital	1204	Muskegon, MI	Private	80.3	1,300	8062
Hamot Medical Center	1205	Erie, PA	Private	142.6	1,300	8062
Horton Memorial Hospital	1206	Middletown, NY	Private	85.3	1,300	8062
Hunterdon Medical Center	1207	Flemington, NJ	Private	82.5	1,300	8062
Jewish Home & Hospital/Bronx	1208	Bronx, NY	Private	74.6	1,300	8051
John T Mather Mem Hosp	1209	Port Jefferson, NY	Private	94.3	1,300	8062
Kenmore Mercy Hospital	1210	Kenmore, NY	Private	67.3	1,300	8062
Largo Medical Center Inc	1211	Largo, FL	Public Family Member	60.3	1,300	8062
Lourdes	1212	Paducah, KY	Private	99.5	1,300	8062
Mercy Medical Center	1213	Baltimore, MD	Private	125.8	1,300	8062
Mount Clemens General Hospital	1214	Mount Clemens, MI	Private	165.2	1,300	8062
North Philadelphia Health Sys	1215	Philadelphia, PA	Private	76.8	1,300	8062
Pontiac Osteopathic Hospital	1216	Pontiac, MI	Private	97.6	1,300	8062
Presbyterian Retirement	1217	Orlando, FL	Private	52.2	1,300	8361
Presbytrian Hmes Of Nj Fndton	1218	Princeton, NJ	Private	57.6	1,300	8059
Provena Senior Services	1219	Kankakee, IL	Private	50.0	1,300	8052
Qv Inc	1220	Chicago, IL	Private	43.6	1,300	8011
Reliant Care Group Llc	1221	Saint Louis, MO	Private	35.5	1,300	8051
Robert Packer Hospital Inc	1222	Sayre, PA	Private	99.0	1,300	8062
Saint Joseph Hospital Inc	1223	Omaha, NE	Public Family Member	60.3	1,300	8062
Samaritan Medical Center	1224	Watertown, NY	Private	129.1	1,300	8062
Shady Grove Adventist Hospital Inc	1225	Rockville, MD	Private	151.2	1,300	8062
Shannon Medical Center Inc	1226	San Angelo, TX	Private	60.3	1,300	8062
Southern Maryland Hospital	1227	Clinton, MD	Private	98.0	1,300	8062
St Lukes Hospital Association	1228	Jacksonville, FL	Private	111.8	1,300	8062
Sterling Health Care Corp	1229	Bellevue, WA	Private	60.3	1,300	8062
Texoma Medical Center Inc	1230	Denison, TX	Private	82.4	1,300	8062
Tuomey	1231	Sumter, SC	Private	92.6	1,300	8062
Vinfen Corporation	1232	Cambridge, MA	Private	52.3	1,300	8361
Visiting Nurse Service System	1233	Runnemede, NJ	Private	47.0	1,300	8082
Volunteers Of Amer Health Svcs	1234	Eden Prairie, MN	Private	59.4	1,300	8051
Volunters Of Amer Care Fcltes	1235	Eden Prairie, MN	Private	54.6	1,300	8051
West Virginia Univ Med Corp	1236	Morgantown, WV	Private	92.3	1,300	8011
Western Medical Center	1237	Santa Ana, CA	Public Family Member	359.0	1,300	8062
White Plins Hospital Ctr Fundation	1238	White Plains, NY	Private	60.3	1,300	8062
Network Health System, Inc	1239	Menasha, WI	Private	115.0	1,291	8011
Fort Hmltn-Hghes Mem Hospital	1240	Hamilton, OH	Private	70.2	1,286	8062
St Elizabeth Hospital Inc	1241	Elizabeth, NJ	Private	103.2	1,285	8062
Texarkana Memorial Hospital Inc	1242	Texarkana, TX	Private	100.4	1,285	8062
Union Hospital	1243	Union, NJ	Private	67.6	1,284	8062
Salina Regional Health Center	1244	Salina, KS	Private	59.5	1,283	8062
Nazareth Hospital (Inc)	1245	Philadelphia, PA	Private	70.6	1,280	8062
Glenwood Regional Medical Ctr	1246	West Monroe, LA	Private	73.6	1,276	8062
Highland Hospital Of Rochester	1247	Rochester, NY	Private	98.7	1,275	8062
Leesburg Regional Medical Ctr	1248	Leesburg, FL	Private	106.9	1,275	8062
Waukesha Memorial Hospital	1249	Waukesha, WI	Private	158.5	1,275	8062
General Health Services, Inc.	1250	Nashville, TN	Public Family Member	59.1	1,274	8062
Roger Williams Hospital	1251	Providence, RI	Private	93.2	1,273	8062
Huntington Hospital Assn	1252	Huntington, NY	Private	105.8	1,270	8062
Bon Secours Venice Healthcare	1253	Venice, FL	Private	92.0	1,265	8062
Miriam Hospital Inc	1254	Providence, RI	Private	138.9	1,263	8062
Medrehab Inc	1255	Milwaukee, WI	Public Family Member	19.7	1,261	8049
Health Group, The	1256	Massillon, OH	Private	80.6	1,260	8082
Hialeah Hospital Inc	1257	Hialeah, FL	Public Family Member	58.4	1,260	8062
Luther Hospital	1258	Eau Claire, WI	Private	58.4	1,260	8062
Saint Francis Hospital Inc	1259	Columbus, GA	Private	94.7	1,260	8062
Carney Hospital Inc	1260	Boston, MA	Private	96.7	1,258	8062

D&B COMPANY RANKINGS BY EMPLOYMENT

Company	Rank	Location	Type	Sales ($ mil.)	Employ-ment	Primary SIC
Middlesex Hospital	1261	Middletown, CT	Private	132.9	1,257	8062
Sheppard Pratt Health System	1262	Baltimore, MD	Private	69.5	1,254	8063
Bowling Green Comm Hospital	1263	Bowling Green, KY	Private	108.0	1,250	8062
East Texas Med Center-Tyler	1264	Tyler, TX	Private	226.9	1,250	8062
Holy Family Mem Med Ctr Inc	1265	Manitowoc, WI	Private	69.3	1,250	8062
La Porte Hospital Inc	1266	La Porte, IN	Private	70.8	1,250	8062
Lee Upmc Regional	1267	Johnstown, PA	Private	71.8	1,250	8062
Marion General Hospital Inc	1268	Marion, OH	Private	51.6	1,250	8062
Mercy Hospital Inc	1269	Charlotte, NC	Private	110.3	1,250	8062
Ravenswood Hospital Med Ctr	1270	Chicago, IL	Private	123.0	1,250	8062
St Joseph Health Center	1271	Saint Charles, MO	Private	57.9	1,250	8062
Touchmark Living Centers Inc	1272	Beaverton, OR	Private	35.2	1,250	8051
Visiting Nurse Assn Of Boston	1273	Boston, MA	Private	73.0	1,250	8082
White Memorial Medical Center	1274	Los Angeles, CA	Private	148.6	1,250	8062
Woman's Hospital Foundation	1275	Baton Rouge, LA	Private	87.2	1,250	8062
Chambersburg Hospital (Inc)	1276	Chambersburg, PA	Private	87.4	1,249	8062
Home Health Management Svcs	1277	New York, NY	Private	20.1	1,247	8082
Palmetto General Hospital	1278	Hialeah, FL	Public Family Member	57.7	1,245	8062
Sisters Charity Leavenworth Hth Inc	1279	Leavenworth, KS	Private	57.6	1,242	8062
Memorial Hospital Of Easton Md	1280	Easton, MD	Private	75.3	1,241	8062
Sisters Of Mercy Of Hamilton	1281	Hamilton, OH	Private	57.5	1,241	8062
Children's Hospital Of Kings	1282	Norfolk, VA	Private	98.3	1,239	8069
New York Society For Relief	1283	New York, NY	Private	154.7	1,238	8069
Spring Branch Medical Ctr Inc	1284	Houston, TX	Public Family Member	57.4	1,238	8062
Rush Prudential Health Plans	1285	Chicago, IL	Private	85.0	1,234	8011
Seton Medical Center	1286	Daly City, CA	Private	127.5	1,231	8062
Appleton Medical Center	1287	Appleton, WI	Private	57.0	1,230	8062
Horizon Hospital System, Inc	1288	Greenville, PA	Private	70.6	1,227	8062
Tarrant County	1289	Fort Worth, TX	Private	61.7	1,227	8093
Howard County General Hospital	1290	Columbia, MD	Private	80.4	1,225	8062
Washington Township Healthcare	1291	Fremont, CA	Private	127.0	1,225	8062
St Elizabeth Medical Center	1292	Utica, NY	Private	62.4	1,220	8062
Milford-Whtnsvlle Rgional Hosp	1293	Milford, MA	Private	49.8	1,218	8062
Champlain Valley Hospital	1294	Plattsburgh, NY	Private	89.3	1,215	8062
Hospital Service Dist	1295	Houma, LA	Private	121.9	1,215	8062
McLean Hospital Corporation	1296	Belmont, MA	Private	49.2	1,213	8063
Olathe Medical Center Inc	1297	Olathe, KS	Private	60.3	1,213	8062
Camden-Clark Memorial Hosp	1298	Parkersburg, WV	Private	86.7	1,212	8062
Wausau Hospitals Inc	1299	Wausau, WI	Private	110.0	1,209	8062
Pascack Valley Hospital Assn	1300	Westwood, NJ	Private	90.7	1,206	8062
Saint Vincent Hospital & Health Ctr	1301	Billings, MT	Private	55.8	1,204	8062
Advocate Medical Group, Sc	1302	Park Ridge, IL	Private	100.0	1,200	8093
Alexian Brothers Of San Jose	1303	San Jose, CA	Private	90.0	1,200	8062
Allegheny Health, Educ & Res	1304	Pittsburgh, PA	Private	127.3	1,200	8062
American Transitional Hospitals	1305	Franklin, TN	Public Family Member	900.0	1,200	8011
Arnot Ogden Medical Center	1306	Elmira, NY	Private	55.6	1,200	8062
Barberton Citizens Hospital Inc	1307	Barberton, OH	Public Family Member	93.0	1,200	8062
Bayonne Hospital	1308	Bayonne, NJ	Private	80.6	1,200	8062
Bethany Medical Center	1309	Kansas City, KS	Private	74.8	1,200	8062
Bethesda Health Group Of St Louis	1310	Saint Louis, MO	Private	48.4	1,200	8051
Bethesda Hospital Assn, The	1311	Zanesville, OH	Private	81.9	1,200	8062
Bethesda Lutheran Homes & Svcs	1312	Watertown, WI	Private	24.6	1,200	8059
Beverly Entrprss-Connecticut Inc	1313	Fort Smith, AR	Public Family Member	27.3	1,200	8051
Bristol Hospital Incorporated	1314	Bristol, CT	Private	80.0	1,200	8062
Brotman Partners Lp	1315	Culver City, CA	Private	91.3	1,200	8062
Butler Memorial Hospital	1316	Butler, PA	Private	70.8	1,200	8062
Cantex Health Care Centers	1317	Dallas, TX	Private	27.3	1,200	8051
Cape Cod Hospital	1318	Hyannis, MA	Private	140.0	1,200	8062
Capital Region Medical Center	1319	Jefferson City, MO	Private	80.5	1,200	8062
Central Maine Medical Center	1320	Lewiston, ME	Private	86.0	1,200	8062
Century Healthcare Corporation	1321	Tulsa, OK	Private	44.4	1,200	8063
Christ Hospital Health Svcs Corp	1322	Jersey City, NJ	Private	119.5	1,200	8062
Church Hospital Corporation	1323	Baltimore, MD	Private	54.9	1,200	8062
Clark Theda Memorial Hospital	1324	Neenah, WI	Private	55.6	1,200	8062
Clear Lk Regional Med Ctr Inc	1325	Webster, TX	Public Family Member	55.6	1,200	8062
Community Hospital Of Springfield	1326	Springfield, OH	Private	26.9	1,200	8062
Community Memorial Hospital/Sa	1327	Ventura, CA	Private	85.6	1,200	8062
Cook Childrens Medical Center	1328	Fort Worth, TX	Private	59.2	1,200	8069
Danville Regional Medical Ctr	1329	Danville, VA	Private	102.3	1,200	8062
Deaconess Hospital An Okla Corp	1330	Oklahoma City, OK	Private	77.4	1,200	8062

D&B COMPANY RANKINGS BY EMPLOYMENT

Company	Rank	Location	Type	Sales ($ mil.)	Employ- ment	Primary SIC
Delancey Street Foundation	1331	San Francisco, CA	Private	21.8	1,200	8361
Eckerd Youth Alternatives Inc	1332	Clearwater, FL	Private	48.2	1,200	8361
Fawcett Memorial Hospital Inc	1333	Port Charlotte, FL	Public Family Member	74.8	1,200	8062
Flagstaff Medical Center Inc	1334	Flagstaff, AZ	Private	89.5	1,200	8062
Florida Hospital Heartland	1335	Sebring, FL	Private	55.6	1,200	8062
Florida Hospital/Waterman Inc	1336	Eustis, FL	Private	68.5	1,200	8062
Floyd Memorial Hospital	1337	New Albany, IN	Private	77.8	1,200	8062
Forrest S Chilton III Mem Hosp	1338	Pompton Plains, NJ	Private	83.5	1,200	8062
Fort Sanders-Parkwest Med Ctr	1339	Knoxville, TN	Private	227.0	1,200	8062
Galencare Inc	1340	Brandon, FL	Public Family Member	55.6	1,200	8062
Garden City Hospital Osteopathic	1341	Garden City, MI	Private	99.0	1,200	8062
Good Samaritan Hospital Inc	1342	West Palm Beach, FL	Private	114.4	1,200	8062
Gottlieb Memorial Hospital	1343	Melrose Park, IL	Private	97.4	1,200	8062
Greater SE Community Hospital	1344	Washington, DC	Private	130.6	1,200	8062
Healthcor, Inc	1345	Dallas, TX	Public Family Member	112.2	1,200	8082
Hebrew Home Aged	1346	Bronx, NY	Private	50.3	1,200	8059
Hillside Behavioral Health	1347	Rochester, NY	Private	42.9	1,200	8361
Holy Family Hospital Inc	1348	Methuen, MA	Private	70.3	1,200	8062
Home Attendant Vendor Agency Inc	1349	Brooklyn, NY	Private	30.0	1,200	8082
Horizon Health Corporation	1350	Lewisville, TX	Public	62.4	1,200	8063
Houston County Hospital Auth	1351	Warner Robins, GA	Private	93.4	1,200	8062
Indian River Memorial Hospital	1352	Vero Beach, FL	Private	100.7	1,200	8062
Jaques Anna Hospital Inc	1353	Newburyport, MA	Private	56.5	1,200	8062
Kennedy Krieger Childrens Hosp	1354	Baltimore, MD	Private	42.7	1,200	8069
King County Pub Hospital Dst 2	1355	Kirkland, WA	Private	122.5	1,200	8062
Kuakini Medical Center	1356	Honolulu, HI	Private	97.7	1,200	8062
Lafayette Home Hospital Inc	1357	Lafayette, IN	Private	94.4	1,200	8062
Lafayette-Grand Hospital	1358	Saint Louis, MO	Public Family Member	55.6	1,200	8062
Lakewood Hospital Association	1359	Cleveland, OH	Private	94.2	1,200	8062
Lawrence General Hospital	1360	Lawrence, MA	Private	84.5	1,200	8062
Lincare Holdings Inc	1361	Clearwater, FL	Public	443.2	1,200	8082
Little Company Of Mary Hosp	1362	Torrance, CA	Private	121.8	1,200	8062
Lowell General Hospital	1363	Lowell, MA	Private	80.1	1,200	8062
Martha Jefferson Hospital	1364	Charlottesville, VA	Private	80.9	1,200	8062
Maryland General Hospital	1365	Baltimore, MD	Private	93.0	1,200	8062
Matrix Rehabilitation Inc	1366	Plano, TX	Public Family Member	77.0	1,200	8093
Miami Jewish Home/Hosptl Aged	1367	Miami, FL	Private	52.2	1,200	8051
Montgomery General Hospital Inc	1368	Olney, MD	Private	62.6	1,200	8062
Munster Medical Res Foundation	1369	Munster, IN	Private	148.9	1,200	8062
National Dentex Corporation	1370	Wayland, MA	Public	59.2	1,200	8072
North Cntry Health Care Assoc I	1371	Lewiston, ME	Private	30.0	1,200	8051
Northeast Health	1372	Rockland, ME	Private	58.9	1,200	8062
Northwest Medical Center	1373	Franklin, PA	Private	64.2	1,200	8062
Nyack Hospital Inc	1374	Nyack, NY	Private	124.2	1,200	8062
Olathe Health Foundation	1375	Olathe, KS	Private	82.6	1,200	8011
Orthopdic Neurological	1376	Los Gatos, CA	Private	35.5	1,200	8049
Parkridge Hospital Inc	1377	Chattanooga, TN	Public Family Member	55.6	1,200	8062
Pca Family Health Plan Inc	1378	Miami, FL	Public Family Member	282.7	1,200	8011
Pca Health Plans Of Florida	1379	Miami, FL	Public Family Member	292.0	1,200	8011
Presbytrian Intrcommunity Hosp	1380	Whittier, CA	Private	128.3	1,200	8062
Quad-C Health Care Centers	1381	Tacoma, WA	Private	34.5	1,200	8051
Queen Of Angele-Hollywood Pres	1382	Los Angeles, CA	Private	117.9	1,200	8062
Queen Of The Valley	1383	Napa, CA	Private	84.1	1,200	8062
Redmond Park Hospital Inc	1384	Rome, GA	Public Family Member	101.5	1,200	8062
Regional Medical Ctr Orangeburg	1385	Orangeburg, SC	Private	90.0	1,200	8062
Reid Hospital & Health Care Svc	1386	Richmond, IN	Private	100.3	1,200	8062
Rockaway Home Attendant Svcs	1387	Far Rockaway, NY	Private	21.0	1,200	8082
Saints Memorial Medical Center	1388	Lowell, MA	Private	77.4	1,200	8062
Sharon Regional Health System	1389	Sharon, PA	Private	76.4	1,200	8062
St Anthony Medical Center Inc	1390	Crown Point, IN	Private	87.6	1,200	8062
St Charles Medical Center	1391	Bend, OR	Private	91.0	1,200	8062
St Frances Cabrini Hospital	1392	Alexandria, LA	Private	140.4	1,200	8062
St Joseph Hospital Of Augusta Ga	1393	Augusta, GA	Private	78.5	1,200	8062
St Joseph Hospital Of Nashua Nh	1394	Nashua, NH	Private	43.3	1,200	8062
St Mary Hospital Inc	1395	Hoboken, NJ	Private	70.5	1,200	8062
St. Joseph Health System, Llc	1396	Fort Wayne, IN	Private	76.1	1,200	8062
St. Mary's Hospital	1397	Decatur, IL	Private	59.4	1,200	8062
Stamford Hospital	1398	Stamford, CT	Private	124.9	1,200	8062
Sunnyside Home Care Project	1399	Sunnyside, NY	Private	29.3	1,200	8361
Terence Cooke Heal Care Ctr	1400	New York, NY	Private	87.4	1,200	8051

D&B COMPANY RANKINGS BY EMPLOYMENT

Company	Rank	Location	Type	Sales ($ mil.)	Employ-ment	Primary SIC
Trinity Lutheran Hospital	1401	Kansas City, MO	Private	82.4	1,200	8062
Vassar Bros Hospital	1402	Poughkeepsie, NY	Private	97.3	1,200	8062
Yuma Regional Medical Center	1403	Yuma, AZ	Private	103.4	1,200	8062
St Joseph's Hospital	1404	Savannah, GA	Private	133.6	1,194	8062
St Clair Memorial Hospital	1405	Pittsburgh, PA	Private	90.1	1,192	8062
Lawnwood Medical Center Inc	1406	Fort Pierce, FL	Public Family Member	117.1	1,191	8062
Allen Memorial Hospital Corp	1407	Waterloo, IA	Private	72.2	1,185	8062
Crittenton Hospital	1408	Rochester, MI	Private	110.6	1,184	8062
Concord Hospital Inc	1409	Concord, NH	Private	54.7	1,182	8062
Rush North Shore Medical Ctr	1410	Skokie, IL	Private	93.1	1,179	8062
Community Medical Center Inc	1411	Scranton, PA	Private	101.1	1,178	8062
St Joseph Hospital Of Kirkwood	1412	Saint Louis, MO	Private	54.5	1,178	8062
Foundation Ma Eye & Ear Infrmy	1413	Boston, MA	Private	100.7	1,174	8069
Parkview Community Hospital Med	1414	Riverside, CA	Private	77.2	1,173	8062
Pan American Hospital Corp	1415	Miami, FL	Private	72.9	1,172	8062
St Patrick Hospital Corp	1416	Missoula, MT	Private	99.6	1,170	8069
Sequoia Hospital District	1417	Redwood City, CA	Private	77.4	1,167	8062
Decatur Memorial Hospital	1418	Decatur, IL	Private	98.9	1,165	8062
Franklin Medical Center	1419	Greenfield, MA	Private	58.6	1,163	8062
Jackson Methodist Healthcare	1420	Jackson, MS	Private	118.9	1,159	8062
South Centl Regional Med Ctr	1421	Laurel, MS	Private	68.6	1,159	8062
Trover Clinic Foundation Inc	1422	Madisonville, KY	Private	143.4	1,158	8062
Option Care, Inc (Del)	1423	Deerfield, IL	Public	100.0	1,156	8082
Franciscan Hospital Mt Airy Campus	1424	Cincinnati, OH	Private	78.7	1,154	8062
Harbor Hospital Center Inc	1425	Baltimore, MD	Private	101.1	1,150	8062
Highline Community Hospital	1426	Seattle, WA	Private	77.2	1,150	8062
Hospital For Joint Diseases	1427	New York, NY	Private	123.0	1,150	8069
Iredell Memorial Hospital	1428	Statesville, NC	Private	73.6	1,150	8062
Methodst Hm Agng Wymg Cnf Nys	1429	Endicott, NY	Private	34.2	1,150	8051
Saint Elizabeth Community Health	1430	Lincoln, NE	Private	77.1	1,150	8062
St Clares Hospital Of Schnctady Ny	1431	Schenectady, NY	Private	61.7	1,150	8062
St Francis Medical Center	1432	Trenton, NJ	Private	81.9	1,150	8062
Unity Health System	1433	Rochester, NY	Private	89.5	1,150	8062
Williamsburg Community Hosp	1434	Williamsburg, VA	Private	61.0	1,150	8062
St Luke's Health System	1435	Phoenix, AZ	Public Family Member	53.1	1,148	8062
Niagara Falls Memorial Med Ctr	1436	Niagara Falls, NY	Private	53.0	1,146	8062
Great River Health Systems	1437	Burlington, IA	Private	23.5	1,140	8062
Rockford Health Systems Inc	1438	Rockford, IL	Private	319.2	1,136	8062
Louise Obici Memorial Hosp	1439	Suffolk, VA	Private	56.8	1,130	8062
Parker Jewish Institute	1440	New Hyde Park, NY	Private	81.2	1,130	8051
Spaulding Rhbltation Hospital Corp	1441	Boston, MA	Private	78.1	1,127	8069
Bon Secours Hospital Baltimore	1442	Baltimore, MD	Private	71.0	1,120	8062
Healthsouth Orthopedic Svcs	1443	Birmingham, AL	Public Family Member	77.1	1,120	8011
Holland Community Hospital	1444	Holland, MI	Private	69.3	1,120	8062
St Mary's Medical Center Inc	1445	Racine, WI	Private	51.8	1,120	8062
Yakima Valley Mem Hospital Assn	1446	Yakima, WA	Private	91.0	1,114	8062
Memorial Hospital Of Albany Ny	1447	Albany, NY	Private	51.3	1,110	8062
Bon Secours, Inc	1448	Marriottsville, MD	Private	51.1	1,105	8062
Pharmaco International Inc	1449	Austin, TX	Public Family Member	52.7	1,105	8071
Baylor Medical Ctr At Garland	1450	Garland, TX	Private	80.0	1,100	8062
Beverly Community Hospital Assn	1451	Montebello, CA	Private	68.4	1,100	8062
Carroll County General Hosp	1452	Westminster, MD	Private	65.1	1,100	8062
Carroll County Health Svcs Corp	1453	Westminster, MD	Private	65.1	1,100	8062
Children's Hospital	1454	New Orleans, LA	Private	54.2	1,100	8069
Christ Hospital	1455	Jersey City, NJ	Private	125.6	1,100	8062
Clarity Vision Inc	1456	Camp Hill, PA	Private	75.7	1,100	8011
Commun Mem Hospital	1457	Menomonee Falls, WI	Private	62.3	1,100	8062
Connecticut Childrens Med Ctr	1458	Hartford, CT	Private	46.8	1,100	8069
Cooley Dickinson Hospital	1459	Northampton, MA	Private	57.6	1,100	8062
Dakota Heartland Health System	1460	Fargo, ND	Public Family Member	50.9	1,100	8062
Deaconess-Billings Clinic Inc	1461	Billings, MT	Private	163.0	1,100	8062
Downey Community Hospital	1462	Downey, CA	Private	89.7	1,100	8062
Episcopal Retirement Homes	1463	Cincinnati, OH	Private	34.2	1,100	8361
Fair Acres Center	1464	Media, PA	Private	45.5	1,100	8361
Faulkner Hospital Inc	1465	Boston, MA	Private	66.2	1,100	8062
Finger Lakes Regional Health Sys	1466	Geneva, NY	Private	54.5	1,100	8051
Frontier Health Inc	1467	Johnson City, TN	Private	42.9	1,100	8063
Griffin Health Services Corp	1468	Derby, CT	Private	44.3	1,100	8062
Griffin Hospital Inc	1469	Derby, CT	Private	63.9	1,100	8062
Guardian Care, Inc	1470	Corte Madera, CA	Private	80.0	1,100	8051

D&B COMPANY RANKINGS BY EMPLOYMENT

Company	Rank	Location	Type	Sales ($ mil.)	Employ- ment	Primary SIC
H M Health Services	1471	Warren, OH	Private	50.9	1,100	8062
Health Services Medical Corp	1472	Baldwinsville, NY	Private	148.5	1,100	8011
Hutcheson Medical Center	1473	Fort Oglethorpe, GA	Private	79.1	1,100	8062
Ken-Crest Services Inc	1474	Plymouth Meeting, PA	Private	35.0	1,100	8082
Kootenai Hospital District	1475	Coeur D Alene, ID	Private	70.7	1,100	8062
Landmark Medical Center	1476	Woonsocket, RI	Private	50.9	1,100	8062
Liberty Health System Inc	1477	Baltimore, MD	Private	50.9	1,100	8062
Linda Loma Univ Health Care	1478	Loma Linda, CA	Private	102.3	1,100	8011
Louis A Weiss Memorial Hosp	1479	Chicago, IL	Private	96.2	1,100	8062
Marin General Hospital	1480	Greenbrae, CA	Private	106.4	1,100	8062
Marion General Hospital Inc	1481	Marion, IN	Private	80.8	1,100	8062
Medica	1482	Minneapolis, MN	Private	75.7	1,100	8011
Memorial Hospital & Medical	1483	Cumberland, MD	Private	73.6	1,100	8062
Menninger Foundation Inc	1484	Topeka, KS	Private	48.4	1,100	8063
Mercy Medical Ctr Of Oshkosh	1485	Oshkosh, WI	Private	50.9	1,100	8062
Merle West Medical Center	1486	Klamath Falls, OR	Private	66.2	1,100	8062
Midland County Hospital Dst	1487	Midland, TX	Private	130.7	1,100	8062
Monongalia County Gen Hospital	1488	Morgantown, WV	Private	82.9	1,100	8062
Mount Carmel Hospital (East)	1489	Columbus, OH	Private	50.9	1,100	8062
New England Baptist Hospital	1490	Boston, MA	Private	98.2	1,100	8062
New York Downtown Hospital	1491	New York, NY	Private	94.2	1,100	8062
New York Medical Group, Pc	1492	New York, NY	Private	75.7	1,100	8011
Nolachuckey-Hlst Mntl Ctr Inc	1493	Greeneville, TN	Private	33.5	1,100	8093
Northern Wstchester Hospital Assn	1494	Mount Kisco, NY	Private	84.2	1,100	8062
Our Lady Of Lourdes Regional	1495	Lafayette, LA	Private	106.9	1,100	8062
Pacific Medical Center	1496	Seattle, WA	Private	113.4	1,100	8011
Peninsula United Methdst Homes	1497	Wilmington, DE	Private	31.5	1,100	8361
Phelps Memorial Hospital Assn	1498	Tarrytown, NY	Private	69.9	1,100	8062
Physicians Health Services	1499	Shelton, CT	Public	488.1	1,100	8011
Pottstown Memorial Med Ctr	1500	Pottstown, PA	Private	75.4	1,100	8062
Qhg Of Gadsden	1501	Gadsden, AL	Public Family Member	85.0	1,100	8062
Riverside Community Health	1502	Riverside, CA	Public Family Member	220.0	1,100	8062
San Jacinto Methodist Hosp	1503	Baytown, TX	Private	74.8	1,100	8062
Signature Health Care Corp	1504	Scottsdale, AZ	Public Family Member	25.0	1,100	8051
St Agnes Hospital Of Fond Du Lac	1505	Fond Du Lac, WI	Private	93.4	1,100	8062
St John's Riverside Hospital	1506	Yonkers, NY	Private	84.7	1,100	8062
Sunrise Community, Inc	1507	Miami, FL	Private	35.3	1,100	8052
Tenet Health System N Shore	1508	Miami, FL	Public Family Member	50.9	1,100	8062
Tenet Healthsystem Desert Inc	1509	Palm Springs, CA	Public Family Member	145.0	1,100	8062
Tomball Hospital Authority	1510	Tomball, TX	Private	60.5	1,100	8062
United Church Homes Inc	1511	Marion, OH	Private	39.7	1,100	8051
Valley Presbyterian Hospital	1512	Van Nuys, CA	Private	87.6	1,100	8062
Victory Memorial Hospital Inc	1513	Brooklyn, NY	Private	50.9	1,100	8062
West Fla Med Ctr Clinic Pa	1514	Pensacola, FL	Private	91.0	1,100	8011
White Plains Hospital Center	1515	White Plains, NY	Private	111.3	1,100	8062
Marymount Hospital Inc	1516	Cleveland, OH	Private	83.6	1,095	8062
St Luke's Memorial Hospital	1517	Racine, WI	Private	50.6	1,095	8062
Riddle Memorial Hospital	1518	Media, PA	Private	68.4	1,094	8062
South Nassau Communities Hosp	1519	Oceanside, NY	Private	50.1	1,085	8062
Lutheran Social Svcs Of S Inc	1520	Austin, TX	Private	36.7	1,079	8051
Justice Resource Institute	1521	Boston, MA	Private	32.6	1,075	8361
Cleveland Memorial Hospital	1522	Shelby, NC	Private	82.3	1,073	8062
Visiting Nrse Srvc Of Rchstr	1523	Webster, NY	Private	42.4	1,073	8082
Healtheast St Josephs Hosp	1524	Saint Paul, MN	Private	111.1	1,072	8062
Public Hospital District 1	1525	Mount Vernon, WA	Private	77.3	1,072	8062
Driscoll Childrens Hospital	1526	Corpus Christi, TX	Private	52.8	1,070	8069
Suburban Med Ctr Hffmn Estates	1527	Hoffman Estates, IL	Public Family Member	85.7	1,070	8062
Visiting Nurse Assn Of Del	1528	New Castle, DE	Private	33.5	1,070	8082
Community Health Counseling Svcs	1529	Bangor, ME	Private	42.0	1,069	8093
Pendleton Mem Methdst Hosp	1530	New Orleans, LA	Private	106.1	1,068	8062
Glendale Mem Hospital & Health	1531	Glendale, CA	Private	101.9	1,065	8062
Jameson Memorial Hospital	1532	New Castle, PA	Private	59.2	1,063	8062
Community United Methdst Hosp	1533	Henderson, KY	Private	64.3	1,060	8062
Watson Clinic	1534	Lakeland, FL	Private	104.3	1,060	8011
St Lukes Mdland Rgonal Med Ctr	1535	Aberdeen, SD	Private	65.2	1,059	8062
John N Dempsey Hospital	1536	Farmington, CT	Private	119.0	1,057	8062
Pocono Medical Center	1537	East Stroudsburg, PA	Private	73.6	1,057	8062
Rush Medical Foundation Inc	1538	Meridian, MS	Private	48.7	1,055	8062
Bon-Secours St Francis Xavier Hsp	1539	Charleston, SC	Private	47.7	1,052	8062
Apl Healthcare Group Inc	1540	Las Vegas, NV	Private	50.1	1,050	8071

D&B COMPANY RANKINGS BY EMPLOYMENT

Company	Rank	Location	Type	Sales ($ mil.)	Employ- ment	Primary SIC
Burlington Medical Center Inc	1541	Burlington, IA	Private	62.2	1,050	8062
Columbia Medical Plan Inc	1542	Columbia, MD	Private	142.2	1,050	8011
Doctors Hospital Of Augusta	1543	Augusta, GA	Public Family Member	108.4	1,050	8062
Faith Regional Health Services	1544	Norfolk, NE	Private	45.7	1,050	8062
Good Samaritan Hospital	1545	Lebanon, PA	Private	75.8	1,050	8062
Heritage Medical Mgt Inc	1546	Muncie, IN	Private	23.3	1,050	8059
Long Beach Community Hospital	1547	Long Beach, CA	Private	69.1	1,050	8062
Massachusetts Eye Ear Infirmary	1548	Boston, MA	Private	76.6	1,050	8069
Middle Tennessee Medical Ctr	1549	Murfreesboro, TN	Private	66.2	1,050	8062
New Liberty Hospital District	1550	Liberty, MO	Private	66.5	1,050	8062
Paradise Valley Hospital Inc	1551	National City, CA	Private	75.2	1,050	8062
Proctor Hospital	1552	Peoria, IL	Private	57.4	1,050	8062
Saddleback Memorial Med Ctr	1553	Laguna Hills, CA	Private	78.1	1,050	8062
St Joseph's Hospital	1554	Elmira, NY	Private	47.6	1,050	8062
St Marys Hospital & Med Ctr	1555	San Francisco, CA	Private	126.9	1,050	8062
St Vincent Hospital Inc	1556	Santa Fe, NM	Private	108.5	1,050	8062
Village Center For Care, Inc	1557	New York, NY	Private	28.9	1,050	8051
William Backus Hospital	1558	Norwich, CT	Private	88.3	1,050	8062
Du Bois Regional Medical Ctr	1559	Du Bois, PA	Private	70.2	1,040	8062
Putnam Hospital Center	1560	Carmel, NY	Private	48.0	1,039	8062
Aiken Regional Medical Ctrs	1561	Aiken, SC	Public Family Member	47.9	1,038	8062
Manchester Memorial Hosp	1562	Manchester, CT	Private	88.8	1,038	8062
Wayne Memorial Hospital Inc	1563	Goldsboro, NC	Private	91.4	1,037	8062
Wyoming Medical Center Inc	1564	Casper, WY	Private	95.9	1,033	8062
Kapiolani Med Ctr	1565	Honolulu, HI	Private	50.6	1,027	8069
St Michael Hospital	1566	Milwaukee, WI	Private	84.7	1,027	8062
Access Health Inc	1567	Broomfield, CO	Public	62.1	1,026	8082
Everett Clinic, The	1568	Everett, WA	Private	74.6	1,025	8011
Harrison Memorial Hospital	1569	Bremerton, WA	Private	92.2	1,025	8062
Sacred Hart Hospital Of Allentown	1570	Allentown, PA	Private	70.0	1,025	8062
Sacred Heart Hospital	1571	Eau Claire, WI	Private	47.3	1,025	8062
Wfsi-Illinois	1572	Wheaton, IL	Private	47.3	1,024	8062
Phoenix Bptst Hospital Med Ctr Inc	1573	Phoenix, AZ	Private	73.3	1,023	8062
Community Hospital Chanl Inc	1574	Chandler, AZ	Private	76.8	1,021	8062
Monongahela Valley Hospital Inc	1575	Monongahela, PA	Private	73.2	1,020	8062
Methodist Hospital Of Southern Cal	1576	Arcadia, CA	Private	115.4	1,018	8062
Shore Health Systems	1577	Easton, MD	Private	46.9	1,016	8062
Thomas-Davis Medical Ctrs Pc	1578	Tucson, AZ	Public Family Member	128.0	1,015	8011
Southern Nh Regional Med Ctr	1579	Nashua, NH	Private	69.8	1,014	8062
Castle Medical Center	1580	Kailua, HI	Private	62.8	1,012	8062
East Pasco Medical Center Inc	1581	Zephyrhills, FL	Private	105.8	1,010	8062
Peninsula Hospital Center	1582	Far Rockaway, NY	Private	64.7	1,010	8062
St Charles Hospital Port Jefferson	1583	Port Jefferson, NY	Private	99.7	1,010	8062
Santa Rosa Memorial Hospital	1584	Santa Rosa, CA	Private	106.9	1,007	8062
Security Health Plan Of Wisconsin	1585	Marshfield, WI	Private	142.4	1,006	8011
Dameron Hospital Association	1586	Stockton, CA	Private	80.3	1,003	8062
Alton Memorial Hospital	1587	Alton, IL	Private	53.3	1,000	8062
American Medical Laboratories	1588	Chantilly, VA	Private	47.7	1,000	8071
Babcock Center Inc	1589	Lexington, SC	Private	25.1	1,000	8361
Bancroft Inc	1590	Haddonfield, NJ	Private	42.1	1,000	8361
Baxter County Regional Hosp	1591	Mountain Home, AR	Private	68.2	1,000	8062
Bayshore Community Hospital	1592	Holmdel, NJ	Private	63.7	1,000	8062
Bio-Medical Applications Of Fla	1593	Tampa, FL	Public Family Member	57.1	1,000	8092
Carson-Tahoe Hospital	1594	Carson City, NV	Private	79.5	1,000	8062
Chester County Hospital, The	1595	West Chester, PA	Private	76.0	1,000	8062
Chestnut Hill Hospital	1596	Philadelphia, PA	Private	58.1	1,000	8062
Childrens Hospital Of Orange Cnty	1597	Orange, CA	Private	92.4	1,000	8069
Clarksville Regional Health Sys	1598	Clarksville, TN	Private	66.0	1,000	8062
Coliseum Park Hospital Inc	1599	Macon, GA	Public Family Member	170.0	1,000	8062
Columbia Memorial Hospital	1600	Hudson, NY	Private	49.7	1,000	8062
Community Hospital Of Anderson	1601	Anderson, IN	Private	56.4	1,000	8062
Culwell Health Inc	1602	Sewickley, PA	Private	22.7	1,000	8051
Davis Vision Inc	1603	Plainview, NY	Private	150.0	1,000	8011
Disablity Svcs Of The Southwest	1604	Fort Worth, TX	Private	30.5	1,000	8093
Dreyer Clinic Inc.	1605	Aurora, IL	Private	92.7	1,000	8011
East Tennessee Chld Hospital Assn	1606	Knoxville, TN	Private	56.4	1,000	8069
Fair Acres Geriatric Center	1607	Media, PA	Private	47.7	1,000	8059
Flower Hospital	1608	Sylvania, OH	Private	46.1	1,000	8062
Gateway Homecare, Inc	1609	Berwyn, PA	Private	28.7	1,000	8082
Good Shepherd Lutheran Home	1610	Porterville, CA	Private	24.0	1,000	8361

D&B COMPANY RANKINGS BY EMPLOYMENT

Company	Rank	Location	Type	Sales ($ mil.)	Employ- ment	Primary SIC
Grace Hospital	1611	Morganton, NC	Private	61.2	1,000	8062
Group Health Northwest	1612	Spokane, WA	Private	274.3	1,000	8011
Guthrie Clinic Ltd	1613	Sayre, PA	Private	51.6	1,000	8011
Hanger Orthopedic Group Inc	1614	Bethesda, MD	Public	145.6	1,000	8361
Hca Health Services Of Florida	1615	Port Richey, FL	Public Family Member	104.4	1,000	8062
Hca Raleigh Community Hospital	1616	Raleigh, NC	Public Family Member	46.1	1,000	8062
Health Acquisition Corp	1617	Jamaica, NY	Public Family Member	20.6	1,000	8082
IIcalth Care Authority Of Morga	1618	Decatur, AL	Private	82.2	1,000	8062
Health Care Industries Corp	1619	Dayton, OH	Private	46.0	1,000	8051
Health Enterprises Of Michigan	1620	Denton, TX	Private	22.7	1,000	8051
Health Investment Corporation	1621	Long Beach, CA	Private	46.1	1,000	8062
Herbert J. Thomas Mem Hospital	1622	Charleston, WV	Private	74.7	1,000	8062
Home Health Foundation Inc	1623	Haverhill, MA	Private	29.2	1,000	8082
Hurlbut, Robert H	1624	Rochester, NY	Private	22.7	1,000	8051
Integra Health	1625	Des Moines, IA	Private	41.4	1,000	8011
Iowa Physicians Clinic Found	1626	Des Moines, IA	Private	54.5	1,000	8011
Kemper National Services Inc	1627	Fort Lauderdale, FL	Private	40.0	1,000	8099
Kessler Inst For Rhabilitation	1628	West Orange, NJ	Private	67.8	1,000	8069
Knapp Medical Center	1629	Weslaco, TX	Private	62.1	1,000	8062
Lawrence Memorial Hospital	1630	Lawrence, KS	Private	50.7	1,000	8062
Legacy Health Care Inc	1631	Muncie, IN	Private	24.4	1,000	8361
Lexington Health Care Group	1632	Farmington, CT	Public	35.9	1,000	8051
Lexington Square Inc	1633	Lombard, IL	Private	22.2	1,000	8059
Lucy Lee Hospital Inc	1634	Poplar Bluff, MO	Public Family Member	54.0	1,000	8062
Marion Community Hospital Inc	1635	Ocala, FL	Public Family Member	46.1	1,000	8062
Mary Black Health System, Inc	1636	Spartanburg, SC	Private	46.1	1,000	8062
Mary Black Memorial Hospital	1637	Spartanburg, SC	Private	46.1	1,000	8062
May Institute Inc	1638	South Harwich, MA	Private	42.0	1,000	8361
Mdi Limited	1639	Monticello, IL	Private	31.1	1,000	8051
Mediplex Of Massachusetts Inc	1640	Albuquerque, NM	Public Family Member	22.2	1,000	8059
Medlantic Enterprises, Inc	1641	Washington, DC	Private	22.7	1,000	8051
Memorial Healthcare Center	1642	Owosso, MI	Private	57.0	1,000	8062
Midwest City Mem Hospital Auth	1643	Oklahoma City, OK	Private	64.5	1,000	8062
Morton Health Foundation Inc	1644	Taunton, MA	Private	46.1	1,000	8062
Murray-Calloway Cty Pub Hosp	1645	Murray, KY	Private	51.1	1,000	8062
Muskogee Medical Center Auth	1646	Muskogee, OK	Private	69.4	1,000	8062
New Lexington Clinic, P.S.C.	1647	Lexington, KY	Private	68.8	1,000	8011
New Port Richey Hospital Inc	1648	New Port Richey, FL	Public Family Member	46.1	1,000	8062
North Ridge Care Center Inc	1649	Minneapolis, MN	Private	24.7	1,000	8051
Northern Illinois Medical Ctr	1650	Mchenry, IL	Private	85.2	1,000	8062
Northern Michigan Hospital	1651	Petoskey, MI	Private	82.5	1,000	8062
O'connor Hospital	1652	San Jose, CA	Private	123.9	1,000	8062
Oconomwoc Residential Programs	1653	Oconomowoc, WI	Private	28.0	1,000	8052
Onslow County Hospital Auth	1654	Jacksonville, NC	Private	67.3	1,000	8062
Pacific Health Corporation	1655	Long Beach, CA	Private	46.1	1,000	8062
Palo Alto Medical Foundation	1656	Palo Alto, CA	Private	110.0	1,000	8011
Pasadena Bayshore Hospital	1657	Pasadena, TX	Public Family Member	104.1	1,000	8062
Patuxent Medical Group, Inc	1658	Columbia, MD	Private	80.8	1,000	8011
Philadelphia Geriatric Center	1659	Philadelphia, PA	Private	52.6	1,000	8051
Princeton Community Hospital Assn	1660	Princeton, WV	Private	60.2	1,000	8062
Rosewood Care Center Holdg Co	1661	Saint Louis, MO	Private	22.7	1,000	8051
Rutland Hospital Inc	1662	Rutland, VT	Private	68.2	1,000	8062
Saad Enterprises Inc	1663	Mobile, AL	Private	43.1	1,000	8082
Saratoga Hospital (Inc)	1664	Saratoga Springs, NY	Private	54.1	1,000	8062
Satilla Health Services Inc	1665	Waycross, GA	Private	74.9	1,000	8062
Select Medical Corporation	1666	Mechanicsburg, PA	Private	60.0	1,000	8093
Serologicals Corporation	1667	Clarkston, GA	Public	97.5	1,000	8099
Southern Health Management	1668	Huntsville, AL	Private	68.8	1,000	8011
Southwest Miss Regional Med Ctr	1669	Mc Comb, MS	Private	61.9	1,000	8062
St Anthony's Hospital	1670	Alton, IL	Private	46.1	1,000	8062
St Josephs Hospital & Health Ctr	1671	Paris, TX	Private	89.4	1,000	8062
St Tammany Parish Hospital Dst 2	1672	Slidell, LA	Private	46.1	1,000	8062
Sturdy Memorial Hospital Inc	1673	Attleboro, MA	Private	62.5	1,000	8062
Tenet Health System-Dallas	1674	Dallas, TX	Public Family Member	46.1	1,000	8062
Tuality Health Care	1675	Hillsboro, OR	Private	46.1	1,000	8062
Tufts Associated Health Plans	1676	Waltham, MA	Private	865.0	1,000	8011
Universal Care Inc	1677	Long Beach, CA	Private	159.5	1,000	8093
Vernon Home Health Care Agency	1678	Garland, TX	Private	30.5	1,000	8093
Vista Hill Foundation	1679	San Diego, CA	Private	23.6	1,000	8063
West Hills Hospital	1680	Canoga Park, CA	Public Family Member	75.8	1,000	8062

D&B COMPANY RANKINGS BY EMPLOYMENT

Company	Rank	Location	Type	Sales ($ mil.)	Employ-ment	Primary SIC
York Hannover Nursing Centers	1681	Pittsfield, MA	Private	22.7	1,000	8051
Zandex Inc	1682	Zanesville, OH	Private	29.1	1,000	8052
Harris Methodist H-E-B	1683	Bedford, TX	Private	93.2	992	8062
Delnor-Community Hospital	1684	Geneva, IL	Private	63.7	985	8062
Emanuel Medical Center Inc	1685	Turlock, CA	Private	57.9	985	8062
Resurrection Medical Ctr, The	1686	Chicago, IL	Private	365.5	985	8062
Northwest Hospital Center	1687	Randallstown, MD	Private	86.4	981	8062
Homewood Retirement Center	1688	Williamsport, MD	Private	34.2	980	8051
National Jewish Med & Res Ctr	1689	Denver, CO	Private	28.7	980	8069
North Brevard County Hospital Dst	1690	Titusville, FL	Private	58.9	980	8062
Northbay Healthcare Group	1691	Fairfield, CA	Private	88.7	980	8062
Rowan Regional Medical Ctr Inc	1692	Salisbury, NC	Private	87.4	979	8062
Ohio Valley Medical Center Inc	1693	Wheeling, WV	Private	70.5	975	8062
St James Mercy Hospital	1694	Hornell, NY	Private	39.9	975	8062
Robinson Memorial Hospital	1695	Ravenna, OH	Private	141.0	974	8062
Abraham Beth Health Services	1696	Bronx, NY	Private	90.5	973	8059
Oakwood Living Centers Inc	1697	Boston, MA	Private	22.1	972	8051
Oakwood Living Centers Of Mass	1698	Plymouth, MA	Private	22.1	972	8051
H C A Health Services Of Nh	1699	Portsmouth, NH	Public Family Member	114.0	969	8062
Eden Township Hospital Dst	1700	Castro Valley, CA	Private	87.7	968	8062
Mainegeneral Medical Center	1701	Augusta, ME	Private	59.1	967	8062
Concord Health Group, Inc	1702	Williamsport, PA	Public Family Member	65.0	965	8051
Austin State Hospital	1703	Austin, TX	Private	50.0	962	8063
Good Samaritan Medical Center	1704	Brockton, MA	Private	138.9	960	8062
Meadville Medical Center	1705	Meadville, PA	Private	64.2	959	8062
Potomac Hospital Corporation	1706	Woodbridge, VA	Private	77.7	959	8062
Austin North Medical Center	1707	Austin, TX	Private	158.5	950	8062
Baton Rouge Health Care Corp	1708	Baton Rouge, LA	Private	39.3	950	8082
Beloit Memorial Hospital Inc	1709	Beloit, WI	Private	51.5	950	8062
Burdette Tomlin Memorial Hosp	1710	Cape May CH, NJ	Private	71.1	950	8062
Chautauqua County Chapter Nys	1711	Jamestown, NY	Private	33.0	950	8093
Columbia/Hca John Randolph Med	1712	Hopewell, VA	Public Family Member	43.8	950	8062
East Orange General Hospital	1713	East Orange, NJ	Private	65.5	950	8062
Faxton Hospital	1714	Utica, NY	Private	45.7	950	8062
Francis Saint Medical Center	1715	Grand Island, NE	Private	104.0	950	8062
H T I Memorial Hospital Corp	1716	Madison, TN	Public Family Member	50.9	950	8062
Immanuel-St Joseph Of Mankato	1717	Mankato, MN	Private	59.7	950	8062
John Knox Village	1718	Lees Summit, MO	Private	46.0	950	8051
Kenosha Hospital & Medical Ctr	1719	Kenosha, WI	Private	74.1	950	8062
Lapeer Regional Hospital	1720	Lapeer, MI	Private	43.8	950	8062
Lodi Memorial Hospital Assn	1721	Lodi, CA	Private	66.5	950	8062
Minnesota Veterans Homes Board	1722	Saint Paul, MN	Private	21.6	950	8051
Ogden Medical Center Inc	1723	Ogden, UT	Public Family Member	43.8	950	8062
P H C-Salt Lake City Inc	1724	Salt Lake City, UT	Public Family Member	43.8	950	8062
Port Huron Hospital	1725	Port Huron, MI	Private	71.9	950	8062
Samaritan Health System Inc	1726	Clinton, IA	Private	47.7	950	8062
Sentage Corporation	1727	Minneapolis, MN	Private	45.0	950	8072
St Joseph's Hospital Yonkers	1728	Yonkers, NY	Private	81.4	950	8062
St Mary's Hospital	1729	Centralia, IL	Private	68.5	950	8062
Veterans Adm Med Ctr	1730	Tuscaloosa, AL	Private	62.0	950	8062
Victory Memorial Hospital Assn	1731	Waukegan, IL	Private	64.5	950	8062
Visiting Nurse And Home Care	1732	Plainville, CT	Private	33.5	950	8082
Wenatchee Valley Clinic	1733	Wenatchee, WA	Private	100.5	950	8011
Willow Valley Manor	1734	Lancaster, PA	Private	44.0	950	8361
Saint Joseph Hospital & Health Ctr	1735	Kokomo, IN	Private	56.5	944	8062
Watts Health Foundation Inc	1736	Inglewood, CA	Private	197.5	942	8011
Wayne General Hospital Corp	1737	Wayne, NJ	Private	66.5	941	8062
Hospital Corp Northwest Inc	1738	Tucson, AZ	Public Family Member	43.3	940	8062
Metropolitan Hospital	1739	Grand Rapids, MI	Private	86.4	940	8062
Parkway Hospital Inc	1740	Forest Hills, NY	Private	79.6	940	8062
Primary Health Systems, Pa	1741	Cleveland, OH	Private	43.3	940	8062
Masonic Home Of The Grand	1742	Philadelphia, PA	Private	36.8	938	8361
Margaret R Pardee Mem Hosp	1743	Hendersonville, NC	Private	68.7	936	8062
Carilion Services Inc	1744	Roanoke, VA	Private	553.6	935	8082
Rahway Hospital	1745	Rahway, NJ	Private	82.6	935	8062
Centre Community Hospital	1746	State College, PA	Private	65.4	930	8062
St Elizabeth Medical Center	1747	Granite City, IL	Private	144.4	930	8062
Amicare Home Health Services	1748	Novi, MI	Private	80.2	927	8082
Phoenix Memorial Hospital	1749	Phoenix, AZ	Private	66.3	926	8062
Auburn Memorial Hospital	1750	Auburn, NY	Private	54.3	925	8062

D&B COMPANY RANKINGS BY EMPLOYMENT

Company	Rank	Location	Type	Sales ($ mil.)	Employ-ment	Primary SIC
Genesee Region Home Care Assn	1751	Rochester, NY	Private	50.0	925	8082
Long Island Home Ltd (Inc)	1752	Amityville, NY	Private	57.4	925	8063
Med-Health System	1753	Xenia, OH	Private	42.6	925	8062
Quorum Health Group Of Vicksburg	1754	Vicksburg, MS	Public Family Member	46.1	924	8062
Copley Memorial Hospital Inc	1755	Aurora, IL	Private	72.5	920	8062
Our Lady Bellefonte Hospital Inc	1756	Ashland, KY	Private	71.5	920	8062
Mercy Hospital	1757	Portland, ME	Private	70.0	917	8062
St Clare Hospital Monroe Wisconsin	1758	Monroe, WI	Private	51.2	917	8062
Saratoga Community Hospital	1759	Detroit, MI	Private	45.8	913	8062
Citrus Mem Health Foundation	1760	Inverness, FL	Private	71.5	912	8062
Riverside Mercy Hospital	1761	Toledo, OH	Private	69.5	912	8062
Memorial Health Systems Inc	1762	Ormond Beach, FL	Private	146.3	910	8062
Thompson Frderick Ferris Hosp	1763	Canandaigua, NY	Private	35.3	909	8062
Licking Memorial Hospital	1764	Newark, OH	Private	41.8	908	8062
St Anne's Hospital Corp	1765	Fall River, MA	Private	62.0	906	8062
Trinity Medical Center	1766	Minot, ND	Private	99.1	905	8062
Mercy Hospital Anderson	1767	Cincinnati, OH	Private	79.3	901	8062
Sacred Ht Hospital Sist Char	1768	Cumberland, MD	Private	64.8	901	8062
Anderson Infirmary Benevolent	1769	Meridian, MS	Private	135.0	900	8062
Ashtabula County Medical Ctr	1770	Ashtabula, OH	Private	74.8	900	8062
Bluefield Regional Medical Ctr	1771	Bluefield, WV	Private	72.6	900	8062
Board Of Trustees Of Welborn	1772	Evansville, IN	Private	45.4	900	8011
Broadlawns Medical Center	1773	Des Moines, IA	Private	74.1	900	8062
Chelsea Community Hospital	1774	Chelsea, MI	Private	43.1	900	8062
Columbus Hospital Inc	1775	Newark, NJ	Private	86.9	900	8062
Community Medical Center Inc	1776	Missoula, MT	Private	51.8	900	8062
Comprehensive Health Services	1777	Detroit, MI	Private	281.1	900	8011
Davies Medical Center, Inc	1778	San Francisco, CA	Private	55.2	900	8062
Eskaton Properties Inc	1779	Carmichael, CA	Private	43.4	900	8051
Fairview Extended Care Svcs	1780	Pittsfield, MA	Private	45.2	900	8051
Finley Hospital, The	1781	Dubuque, IA	Private	48.8	900	8062
Good Samaritan Hospital Corvallis	1782	Corvallis, OR	Private	68.6	900	8062
Hallmark Health Services Inc	1783	Tustin, CA	Public Family Member	20.4	900	8051
Hanover General Hospital	1784	Hanover, PA	Private	51.1	900	8062
Hays Medical Center Inc	1785	Hays, KS	Private	67.1	900	8062
Health Care Administration	1786	San Antonio, TX	Private	19.9	900	8059
Hospital Center At Orange, The	1787	Orange, NJ	Private	64.3	900	8062
Howard Community Hospital	1788	Kokomo, IN	Private	54.2	900	8062
Humility Mary Health System	1789	Youngstown, OH	Private	41.4	900	8062
Indiana Hospital	1790	Indiana, PA	Private	53.2	900	8062
Integra Inc	1791	King Of Prussia, PA	Public	70.1	900	8093
Jackson Laboratory, The	1792	Bar Harbor, ME	Private	54.8	900	8071
Jordan Hospital (Inc)	1793	Plymouth, MA	Private	66.0	900	8062
Joseph Columbia/St Health Sys	1794	Parkersburg, WV	Private	92.2	900	8062
Kuala Healthcare Inc	1795	Englewood Cliffs, NJ	Public	70.7	900	8051
Lakes Region Hospital Assn	1796	Laconia, NH	Private	53.7	900	8062
Mary Immaculate Hospital Inc	1797	Newport News, VA	Private	41.9	900	8062
Memorial Hospital Of Laramie Cnty	1798	Cheyenne, WY	Private	71.1	900	8062
Mercy Medical Center	1799	Durango, CO	Private	55.1	900	8062
Methodist Hospital Inc	1800	Jacksonville, FL	Private	72.2	900	8062
Morton Hospital	1801	Taunton, MA	Private	67.5	900	8062
Mount Marty Hospital Assn	1802	Yankton, SD	Private	41.4	900	8062
Nichols Inst Reference Labs	1803	SJ Capistrano, CA	Private	43.0	900	8071
North Cntl Health Care Fcilities	1804	Wausau, WI	Private	42.2	900	8051
North Suffolk Mental Health Assn	1805	Chelsea, MA	Private	22.4	900	8093
Oneida Health Care Center	1806	Oneida, NY	Private	35.0	900	8062
Palm Beach Gardens Community	1807	Palm Beach Gdns, FLA	Public Family Member	41.4	900	8062
Rest Haven Convlsnt Hm	1808	South Holland, IL	Private	28.5	900	8051
Rome Memorial Hospital	1809	Rome, NY	Private	44.3	900	8062
S N F Properties, Inc	1810	La Canada, CA	Private	20.4	900	8051
Saint Francis Memorial Hosp	1811	San Francisco, CA	Private	86.7	900	8062
San Joaquin Community Hosp	1812	Bakersfield, CA	Private	77.2	900	8062
San Juan Regional Medical Ctr	1813	Farmington, NM	Private	79.0	900	8062
Shawnee Hills Inc	1814	Charleston, WV	Private	39.4	900	8361
Shelby Baptist Medical Center	1815	Alabaster, AL	Private	52.2	900	8062
Springhill Hospitals Inc	1816	Mobile, AL	Private	71.1	900	8062
St Catherine's Hospital Inc	1817	Kenosha, WI	Private	41.4	900	8062
St Claire Medical Center, Inc	1818	Morehead, KY	Private	54.4	900	8062
St Elizabeths Hospital Of Chicago	1819	Chicago, IL	Private	82.2	900	8062
St Marys Hospital	1820	Passaic, NJ	Private	46.7	900	8062

D&B COMPANY RANKINGS BY EMPLOYMENT

Company	Rank	Location	Type	Sales ($ mil.)	Employment	Primary SIC
Tabitha, Inc	1821	Lincoln, NE	Private	20.0	900	8361
Uniontown Hospital	1822	Uniontown, PA	Private	73.2	900	8062
United Regional Health Care Sys	1823	Wichita Falls, TX	Private	139.0	900	8062
Vencare Kentucky, Inc	1824	Louisville, KY	Private	44.3	900	8069
Visionquest Nonprofit Corp	1825	Tucson, AZ	Private	46.3	900	8361
Vivra Specialty Partners, Inc	1826	San Mateo, CA	Public Family Member	250.0	900	8011
Westlake Community Hospital	1827	Melrose Park, IL	Private	74.6	900	8062
Wilson N. Jones Mem Hosp, The	1828	Sherman, TX	Private	64.5	900	8062
Womans Hospital Texas Inc	1829	Houston, TX	Public Family Member	79.6	900	8062
Delaware County Memorial Hosp	1830	Drexel Hill, PA	Private	96.9	885	8062
Bradley County Memorial Hosp	1831	Cleveland, TN	Private	70.5	883	8062
Adena Health System Inc	1832	Chillicothe, OH	Private	82.6	882	8062
Great Valley Health	1833	Paoli, PA	Private	64.0	882	8011
Lutheran Hospital	1834	Cleveland, OH	Private	42.3	880	8062
Memorial Health Systems E Texas	1835	Lufkin, TX	Private	69.2	880	8062
North Shore Univ Hospital	1836	Forest Hills, NY	Private	76.4	880	8062
San Pedro Peninsula Hospital	1837	San Pedro, CA	Private	72.9	880	8062
Sherwood Healthcare Corp.	1838	Greenfield, IN	Private	20.0	880	8051
St Tammany Parish Hospital	1839	Covington, LA	Private	127.7	880	8062
Allegheny Hospitals Nj	1840	Willingboro, NJ	Private	88.9	875	8062
Asbury Methodist Village Inc	1841	Gaithersburg, MD	Private	40.1	875	8059
Catawba Memorial Hospital	1842	Hickory, NC	Private	82.6	875	8062
Columbia Hospital Corp Of S	1843	Fort Lauderdale, FL	Public Family Member	40.2	875	8062
Hillcrest Health Center Inc	1844	Oklahoma City, OK	Private	46.5	875	8062
Massillon Community Hospital	1845	Massillon, OH	Private	43.0	875	8062
Phycor Of Kentucky, Inc.	1846	Lexington, KY	Public Family Member	160.0	875	8011
St Helena Hospital	1847	Deer Park, CA	Private	59.1	875	8062
Armstrong County Mem Hosp	1848	Kittanning, PA	Private	44.9	870	8062
Highland Park Hospital	1849	Highland Park, IL	Private	104.9	870	8062
Lenoir Memorial Hospital Inc	1850	Kinston, NC	Private	68.3	870	8062
Shepherd Good Home Inc	1851	Allentown, PA	Private	47.7	870	8361
Northeast Hospital Authority	1852	Humble, TX	Private	82.9	862	8062
Aroostook Medical Center Inc	1853	Presque Isle, ME	Private	38.5	860	8062
Lawrence Hospital Inc	1854	Bronxville, NY	Private	72.0	860	8062
St Joseph Hospital	1855	Buffalo, NY	Private	47.8	856	8062
St Clares Hospital & Health Ctr	1856	New York, NY	Private	70.6	855	8062
Asbury Centers Inc	1857	Maryville, TN	Private	24.8	850	8051
Barnert Hospital	1858	Paterson, NJ	Private	72.3	850	8062
Care Group Inc	1859	New York, NY	Public	35.3	850	8082
Cleveland Clinic Florida Hosp	1860	Fort Lauderdale, FL	Private	51.0	850	8062
Community Behavioral Health Sys	1861	Metairie, LA	Public Family Member	41.8	850	8069
Cookeville Regional Med Ctr	1862	Cookeville, TN	Private	63.2	850	8062
Doctors Med Center-San Pablo	1863	San Pablo, CA	Public Family Member	39.0	850	8062
Doctors' Hospital Inc	1864	Lanham, MD	Private	82.7	850	8062
Fairmont General Hospital Inc	1865	Fairmont, WV	Private	54.0	850	8062
Grim Smith Hospital & Clinic	1866	Kirksville, MO	Private	45.8	850	8062
Lutheran Social Serv-Miami Valley	1867	Dayton, OH	Private	26.4	850	8051
Mckenzie-Willamette Med Svcs	1868	Springfield, OR	Private	48.6	850	8062
North Fulton Medical Center	1869	Roswell, GA	Public Family Member	39.0	850	8062
Oconee Memorial Hospital Inc	1870	Seneca, SC	Private	56.2	850	8062
Olean General Hospital Inc	1871	Olean, NY	Private	39.0	850	8062
Otterbein Homes	1872	Lebanon, OH	Private	37.6	850	8361
Ottumwa Regional Health Center	1873	Ottumwa, IA	Private	46.4	850	8062
Rehablitation Inst Of Chicago	1874	Chicago, IL	Private	41.8	850	8069
Rutherford Hospital Inc	1875	Rutherfordton, NC	Private	50.7	850	8062
San Gabriel Valley Med Ctr	1876	San Gabriel, CA	Private	62.8	850	8062
Sonora Quest Laboratories Llc.	1877	Tempe, AZ	Private	60.0	850	8071
St Lucie Medical Center	1878	Port Saint Lucie, FL	Public Family Member	71.7	850	8062
St Marys Regional Medical Ctr	1879	Lewiston, ME	Private	61.8	850	8062
United Hospital Medical Ctr	1880	Port Chester, NY	Private	71.6	850	8062
Valley Health Systems Llc	1881	Las Vegas, NV	Public Family Member	39.0	850	8062
Visiting Nurse Health System	1882	Atlanta, GA	Private	56.0	850	8082
Childrens Memorial Hospital	1883	Omaha, NE	Private	61.7	849	8069
Mcga Care Inc	1884	Union, NJ	Private	26.8	849	8051
Geneva General Hospital Inc	1885	Geneva, NY	Private	37.7	845	8062
Matria Healthcare, Inc	1886	Marietta, GA	Public	144.5	844	8082
Yukon-Kuskokwim Health Corp	1887	Bethel, AK	Private	66.5	844	8062
St Agnes Hospital	1888	White Plains, NY	Private	38.7	842	8062
Visiting Nrs Assoc Of Clev	1889	Cleveland, OH	Private	30.2	842	8082
Bakersfield Memorial Hospital	1890	Bakersfield, CA	Private	85.7	840	8062

D&B COMPANY RANKINGS BY EMPLOYMENT

Company	Rank	Location	Type	Sales ($ mil.)	Employment	Primary SIC
Lifemark Hospitals Of Missouri	1891	Columbia, MO	Public Family Member	38.6	840	8062
St Agnes Medical Center	1892	Philadelphia, PA	Private	58.5	840	8062
St Joseph Hospital	1893	Bangor, ME	Private	38.6	840	8062
Wilson Memorial Hospital Inc	1894	Wilson, NC	Private	65.3	840	8062
Community Hospital Of Lancaster	1895	Lancaster, PA	Private	39.7	836	8062
Boysville Of Michigan Inc	1896	Clinton, MI	Private	34.9	834	8361
Miller-Dwan Medical Center	1897	Duluth, MN	Private	47.2	834	8062
Phelps Cnty Regional Med Ctr	1898	Rolla, MO	Private	55.0	831	8062
Hebrew Rehabilitation Ctr For Aged	1899	Boston, MA	Private	46.4	830	8069
Long Beach Medical Center	1900	Long Beach, NY	Private	62.2	830	8062
Punta Gorda Hma Inc	1901	Punta Gorda, FL	Public Family Member	38.1	830	8062
Menorah Pk Cntr For The Agng	1902	Cleveland, OH	Private	25.7	827	8051
Raytel Medical Corporation	1903	San Mateo, CA	Public	83.4	827	8093
Cuyahoga Falls General Hosp	1904	Cuyahoga Falls, OH	Private	49.9	825	8062
Penn State Geisinger Med Ctr	1905	Danville, PA	Private	59.0	825	8062
St Ann's Hospital Of Columbus	1906	Columbus, OH	Private	55.6	825	8062
St Marys Hospital At Amsterdam	1907	Amsterdam, NY	Private	45.5	825	8062
Trinity Regnl Hsptl	1908	Fort Dodge, IA	Private	49.7	825	8062
Cheshire Medical Center	1909	Keene, NH	Private	45.0	822	8062
Norwegian American Hospital	1910	Chicago, IL	Private	59.5	822	8062
T J Samson Community Hosp	1911	Glasgow, KY	Private	46.1	821	8062
Madonna Rehabilitation Hosp	1912	Lincoln, NE	Private	32.0	820	8069
Riley Hospital Benevolent Assn	1913	Meridian, MS	Private	48.2	820	8062
Valley Mental Health	1914	Salt Lake City, UT	Private	55.1	820	8093
Gratiot Health System	1915	Alma, MI	Private	54.7	818	8062
Mercy-Memorial Hospital Corp	1916	Monroe, MI	Private	68.9	817	8062
Marietta Area Health Care Inc	1917	Marietta, OH	Private	60.9	815	8062
Phillips Jane Memorial Med Ctr	1918	Bartlesville, OK	Private	55.2	815	8062
Unity Health Management Svcs	1919	Birmingham, AL	Private	35.8	815	8082
Myrtle Beach Hospital Inc	1920	Myrtle Beach, SC	Public Family Member	179.9	811	8062
Albemarle Hospital	1921	Elizabeth City, NC	Private	64.3	810	8062
St. Luke's Hospital	1922	San Francisco, CA	Private	85.8	810	8062
Beebe Medical Center Inc	1923	Lewes, DE	Private	65.3	808	8062
Portsmouth General Hospital	1924	Portsmouth, VA	Private	36.2	807	8062
Logan Medical Foundation	1925	Logan, WV	Private	72.9	806	8062
Warren Hospital	1926	Phillipsburg, NJ	Private	58.2	806	8062
Good Smrtan Regional Health Ctr	1927	Mount Vernon, IL	Private	63.4	805	8062
New England Rhabilitation Hosp	1928	Woburn, MA	Public Family Member	39.9	805	8093
Northstar Health Services Inc	1929	Indiana, PA	Public	32.6	802	8049
Hattiesburg Clinic Prof Assn	1930	Hattiesburg, MS	Private	53.2	801	8011
Alvin Community Hospital, Inc.	1931	Alvin, TX	Public Family Member	36.7	800	8062
Amisub Of California, Inc	1932	Tarzana, CA	Public Family Member	102.4	800	8062
Ancilla Health Care Inc	1933	Hobart, IN	Private	67.5	800	8062
Baptist Health Centers, Inc	1934	Birmingham, AL	Private	42.3	800	8011
Baptist Hospital Of Stheast Texas	1935	Beaumont, TX	Private	61.6	800	8062
Baptist/St Anthony's Hospital	1936	Amarillo, TX	Private	36.7	800	8062
Bay Harbor Hospital Inc	1937	Harbor City, CA	Private	63.8	800	8062
Beaufort County Memorial Hosp	1938	Beaufort, SC	Private	58.5	800	8062
Bethany Circle Of Kings Daughters	1939	Madison, IN	Private	41.6	800	8062
Bethany Ho Hospital Meth Ch	1940	Chicago, IL	Private	43.4	800	8062
Buckner Baptist Benevolences	1941	Dallas, TX	Private	37.6	800	8361
Cape Canaveral Hospital	1942	Cocoa Beach, FL	Private	58.7	800	8062
Carteret General Hospital	1943	Morehead City, NC	Private	48.5	800	8062
Castle Dental Centers Inc	1944	Houston, TX	Public	31.4	800	8021
Chw Medical Foundation	1945	Sacramento, CA	Private	115.7	800	8099
Citizens General Hospital	1946	New Kensington, PA	Private	38.8	800	8062
Cocoa Beach Area Health Svc	1947	Cocoa Beach, FL	Private	57.9	800	8011
Community General Hospital	1948	Harris, NY	Private	63.0	800	8062
Conway Hospital Inc	1949	Conway, SC	Private	64.5	800	8062
Divine Providence Hospital	1950	Williamsport, PA	Private	46.3	800	8062
Elmbrook Memorial Hospital Inc	1951	Brookfield, WI	Private	54.7	800	8062
Ephraim McDowell Rgnal Med Ctr	1952	Danville, KY	Private	57.2	800	8062
Gateway Foundation Inc	1953	Chicago, IL	Private	38.5	800	8093
Good Smritan Regional Med Ctr	1954	Pottsville, PA	Private	90.7	800	8062
Greater Lyn Mntl Hth/Rtdtn Ass	1955	Lynn, MA	Private	20.8	800	8361
Greene Memorial Hospital Inc	1956	Xenia, OH	Private	53.0	800	8062
Greenwood Leflore Hospital	1957	Greenwood, MS	Private	52.5	800	8062
H C A Arlington Inc	1958	Arlington, TX	Public Family Member	36.7	800	8062
Harrington Memorial Hospital	1959	Southbridge, MA	Private	38.0	800	8062
Health First Medical Group	1960	Portland, OR	Private	55.0	800	8011

D&B COMPANY RANKINGS BY EMPLOYMENT

Company	Rank	Location	Type	Sales ($ mil.)	Employ-ment	Primary SIC
Health Span Hm Care & Hospice	1961	Saint Paul, MN	Private	28.0	800	8082
Hospice Of Michigan Inc	1962	Southfield, MI	Private	48.9	800	8082
Hospital For Special Care	1963	New Britain, CT	Private	57.4	800	8069
Hutchinson Hospital Corp	1964	Hutchinson, KS	Private	50.5	800	8062
Isabella Geriatric Center	1965	New York, NY	Private	66.6	800	8051
Jennie Edmundson Mem Hosp	1966	Council Bluffs, IA	Private	48.2	800	8062
Jupiter Medical Center, Inc	1967	Jupiter, FL	Private	78.1	800	8062
Longmont United Hospital	1968	Longmont, CO	Private	54.6	800	8062
Los Robles Regional Med Ctr	1969	Thousand Oaks, CA	Public Family Member	97.2	800	8062
Loudoun Hospital Center	1970	Leesburg, VA	Private	53.6	800	8062
Lucerne Medical Center	1971	Orlando, FL	Private	79.5	800	8062
Magnolia Regional Health Ctr	1972	Corinth, MS	Private	64.3	800	8062
Marianjoy Inc	1973	Wheaton, IL	Private	32.6	800	8069
Marietta Memorial Hospital	1974	Marietta, OH	Private	56.4	800	8062
Marshall Hospital	1975	Placerville, CA	Private	54.2	800	8062
Mary Lanning Memorial Hospital	1976	Hastings, NE	Private	43.6	800	8062
Massillon Health System Llc	1977	Massillon, OH	Private	36.7	800	8062
Medical Behavioral Care Of Cal	1978	S San Francisco, CA	Public Family Member	24.4	800	8093
Medical Clinic Of Sacramento	1979	Sacramento, CA	Private	55.0	800	8011
Memorial Hospital Of Martinsvl	1980	Martinsville, VA	Private	59.4	800	8062
National Park Medical Center	1981	Hot Springs, AR	Public Family Member	36.7	800	8062
Nc-Schi	1982	Abilene, TX	Public Family Member	71.5	800	8062
Noland Lloyd Hospital Inc	1983	Fairfield, AL	Public Family Member	22.3	800	8062
North Country Health Services	1984	Bemidji, MN	Private	46.2	800	8062
Nysarc, Inc	1985	Bohemia, NY	Private	35.2	800	8361
Occupational Health Services	1986	Kansas City, KS	Private	55.0	800	8011
Oroville Hospital	1987	Oroville, CA	Private	54.8	800	8062
Ozarks Medical Center, Inc	1988	West Plains, MO	Private	51.2	800	8062
P M R Corporation	1989	San Diego, CA	Public	67.5	800	8011
Phycor Of Ft. Smith, Inc	1990	Fort Smith, AR	Public Family Member	55.0	800	8011
Pikeville United Methodist Hos	1991	Pikeville, KY	Private	84.3	800	8062
Presbyterian Seniorcare	1992	Oakmont, PA	Private	45.3	800	8051
Q H G Of Ohio, Inc	1993	Columbus, OH	Public Family Member	36.7	800	8062
Regional West Medical Center	1994	Scottsbluff, NE	Private	56.7	800	8062
Rice Memorial Hospital	1995	Willmar, MN	Private	48.6	800	8062
S C Advanced Healthcare	1996	Milwaukee, WI	Private	55.0	800	8011
Saad Healthcare Services, Inc	1997	Mobile, AL	Private	31.1	800	8082
Terre Haute Regional Hospital Inc	1998	Terre Haute, IN	Public Family Member	68.5	800	8062
Thresholds, The	1999	Chicago, IL	Private	25.9	800	8093
Um Holdings Ltd	2000	Haddonfield, NJ	Private	39.3	800	8099
University Physicians, Inc	2001	Tucson, AZ	Private	95.9	800	8011
Visiting Nurse Health System	2002	Atlanta, GA	Private	53.9	800	8082
Watsonville Community Hosp	2003	Watsonville, CA	Private	50.4	800	8062
Weirton Medical Center Inc	2004	Weirton, WV	Private	51.8	800	8062
Alpena General Hospital	2005	Alpena, MI	Private	36.6	799	8062
Blanchard Valley Regional Health	2006	Findlay, OH	Private	66.3	797	8062
Hospital Development & Service	2007	Fort Lauderdale, FL	Public Family Member	36.4	795	8062
Suburban General Hospital	2008	Norristown, PA	Private	50.9	792	8062
Moses Taylor Hospital	2009	Scranton, PA	Private	62.3	791	8062
Phoenixville Hospital Inc	2010	Phoenixville, PA	Private	50.6	789	8062
Conway Regional Medical Center	2011	Conway, AR	Private	64.8	788	8062
Onslow Memorial Hospital Inc	2012	Jacksonville, NC	Private	64.1	786	8062
Arden Hill Hospital	2013	Goshen, NY	Private	46.4	785	8062
Hendricks County Hospital	2014	Danville, IN	Private	56.3	785	8062
Mercy Providence Hospital	2015	Pittsburgh, PA	Private	27.9	783	8062
Baptist Mem Hsptl-Glden Trngle	2016	Columbus, MS	Private	72.8	780	8062
Flagler Hospital Inc	2017	Saint Augustine, FL	Private	81.2	780	8062
Little Company Of Mary Of Indiana	2018	Jasper, IN	Private	46.3	780	8062
Memorial Hospital Of Salem, The	2019	Salem, NJ	Private	49.5	780	8062
Gen Oakland Hospital Osteopathic	2020	Madison Heights, MI	Private	74.6	779	8062
Cumberland Medical Center Inc	2021	Crossville, TN	Private	49.5	778	8062
Clearfield Area Health Svcs Corp	2022	Clearfield, PA	Private	75.0	777	8062
Fremont Area Medical Center	2023	Fremont, NE	Private	43.2	776	8062
Anaheim Memorial Hospital Assn	2024	Anaheim, CA	Private	58.5	775	8062
Fallston General Hospital Inc	2025	Fallston, MD	Private	48.4	775	8062
Henry Medical Center	2026	Stockbridge, GA	Private	35.5	775	8062
Magic Valley Regional Med Ctr	2027	Twin Falls, ID	Private	52.6	775	8062
Memorial Hospital Selam County	2028	Salem, NJ	Private	23.6	775	8093
Private Diagnostic Clinic Pllc	2029	Durham, NC	Private	150.0	775	8011
Sierra Nev Mmrl-Mners Hspitals	2030	Grass Valley, CA	Private	55.8	775	8062

D&B COMPANY RANKINGS BY EMPLOYMENT

Company	Rank	Location	Type	Sales ($ mil.)	Employ-ment	Primary SIC
Holyoke Hospital Inc	2031	Holyoke, MA	Private	51.3	772	8062
Tenet Health System Spalding	2032	Griffin, GA	Public Family Member	35.4	772	8062
Bay Area Health District	2033	Coos Bay, OR	Private	57.3	770	8062
Cambridge Memorial Hospital	2034	Cambridge, MN	Private	30.6	770	8062
Columbia Chicago Ostpthc Hospt	2035	Olympia Fields, IL	Public Family Member	170.0	770	8062
Southampton Hospital Assn	2036	Southampton, NY	Private	61.1	770	8062
Temple Lower Bucks Hospital	2037	Bristol, PA	Private	69.2	770	8062
St Jo Hospital Of Port Charles	2038	Port Charlotte, FL	Private	55.7	767	8062
Caritas Norwood Hospital Inc	2039	Norwood, MA	Private	35.1	766	8062
Hillcrest Medical Nursing Inst	2040	Knoxville, TN	Private	27.1	765	8052
Holy Cross Hospital Detroit Inc	2041	Detroit, MI	Private	45.5	765	8062
Webber Hospital Association	2042	Biddeford, ME	Private	53.6	765	8062
Sister Of Mercy Of Clerm Count	2043	Batavia, OH	Private	48.1	764	8062
Hospital Group Of America	2044	Wayne, PA	Public Family Member	43.0	761	8063
Medical Associates Clinic P C	2045	Dubuque, IA	Private	52.3	761	8011
Evangelical Community Hosp	2046	Lewisburg, PA	Private	42.3	760	8062
Lewistown Hospital	2047	Lewistown, PA	Private	48.8	760	8062
Mt Saint Mary's Hospital	2048	Lewiston, NY	Private	43.3	760	8062
National Rehabilitation Hosp	2049	Washington, DC	Private	60.9	760	8069
Sister Hayward Hospital	2050	Hayward, CA	Private	53.6	760	8062
White River Medical Center	2051	Batesville, AR	Private	52.9	760	8062
Services Of Lutheran Social	2052	York, PA	Private	25.1	759	8059
Audrain Health Care Inc	2053	Mexico, MO	Private	49.8	756	8062
Ephrata Community Hospital	2054	Ephrata, PA	Private	47.8	755	8062
Hospital Corp North Carolina	2055	Statesville, NC	Public Family Member	34.5	755	8062
Indian Path Hospital Inc	2056	Kingsport, TN	Public Family Member	34.5	755	8062
St. Rose Dominican Hospital	2057	Henderson, NV	Private	60.5	754	8062
Penobscot Bay Medical Center	2058	Rockport, ME	Private	44.8	752	8062
Age Inc	2059	Cullman, AL	Private	24.0	750	8059
All Seasons Living Centers	2060	Bellevue, WA	Private	21.0	750	8059
Benevlent Corp Cedar Campuses	2061	West Bend, WI	Private	25.6	750	8051
Bronx Harbor Health Care Complex	2062	Bronx, NY	Private	48.0	750	8051
Casa Grande Community Hosp	2063	Casa Grande, AZ	Private	62.9	750	8062
Clinton Memorial Hospital	2064	Wilmington, OH	Private	47.1	750	8062
Emma L Bixby Medical Center	2065	Adrian, MI	Private	40.9	750	8062
Fort Walton Beach Medical Ctr	2066	Fort Walton Beach, FL	Public Family Member	150.0	750	8011
Freeport Memorial Hospital	2067	Freeport, IL	Private	34.3	750	8062
Frick Hospital & Community Health	2068	Mount Pleasant, PA	Private	42.1	750	8062
Galesburg Cottage Hospital	2069	Galesburg, IL	Private	42.1	750	8062
Horizon House Inc	2070	Philadelphia, PA	Private	22.3	750	8361
Hospital Auth Of Colquitt Cnty	2071	Moultrie, GA	Private	40.8	750	8062
Johnson Memorial Hospital Inc	2072	Stafford Springs, CT	Private	37.0	750	8062
Kansas Neurological Institute	2073	Topeka, KS	Private	23.0	750	8361
Mckenzie-Willamette Hospital	2074	Springfield, OR	Private	52.0	750	8062
Memorial Medical Center	2075	Woodstock, IL	Private	53.2	750	8062
Mercy Health Ctr Of Manhattan	2076	Manhattan, KS	Private	34.3	750	8062
Mercy Medical A Corporation	2077	Daphne, AL	Private	30.4	750	8051
Monroe Community Hospital	2078	Rochester, NY	Private	70.8	750	8051
National Medical Hospital	2079	Lebanon, TN	Public Family Member	34.3	750	8062
Novacare Orthotics Prosthetics	2080	King Of Prussia, PA	Public Family Member	22.8	750	8093
Our Lady Of Victory Hospital	2081	Lackawanna, NY	Private	44.1	750	8062
Park Jackson Hospital Foundation	2082	Chicago, IL	Private	59.9	750	8062
Pemiscot County Memorial Hosp	2083	Hayti, MO	Private	23.9	750	8062
Riverview Hospital	2084	Noblesville, IN	Private	51.4	750	8062
Sarasota Doctor's Hospital	2085	Sarasota, FL	Public Family Member	73.1	750	8062
Sheridan Healthcorp, Inc	2086	Hollywood, FL	Private	98.6	750	8082
South Mississippi Home Health	2087	Hattiesburg, MS	Private	28.0	750	8082
St Ann's Home For Aged	2088	Rochester, NY	Private	19.9	750	8361
St Marys Regional Medical Ctr	2089	Russellville, AR	Public Family Member	34.3	750	8062
Tarpon Springs Hospital Foundation	2090	Tarpon Springs, FL	Private	59.3	750	8062
Union Regional Medical Center	2091	Monroe, NC	Private	48.1	750	8062
University Mednet	2092	Cleveland, OH	Private	36.9	750	8069
Virginia United Methdst Homes	2093	Richmond, VA	Private	26.8	750	8361
Wichita Clinic, Pa	2094	Wichita, KS	Private	80.0	750	8011
Youth Consultation Service	2095	Newark, NJ	Private	21.6	750	8093
Youville Life Care Inc	2096	Cambridge, MA	Private	43.9	750	8069
St Joseph's Hospital	2097	Minot, ND	Private	55.8	749	8062
Beaver Dam Community Hospitals	2098	Beaver Dam, WI	Private	31.4	745	8062
Memorial Med Ctr At S Amboy	2099	South Amboy, NJ	Private	29.4	745	8062
City Hospital Inc	2100	Martinsburg, WV	Private	54.4	742	8062

D&B COMPANY RANKINGS BY EMPLOYMENT

Company	Rank	Location	Type	Sales ($ mil.)	Employ-ment	Primary SIC
Corning Hospital	2101	Corning, NY	Private	41.5	740	8062
Sun Coast Hospital Inc	2102	Largo, FL	Private	57.0	740	8069
Victoria Hospital Corporation	2103	Victoria, TX	Public Family Member	116.0	740	8062
Goshen Hospital Association	2104	Goshen, IN	Private	50.2	736	8062
St Lukes Hospital Of Newburgh Ny	2105	Newburgh, NY	Private	33.6	736	8062
Butler Hospital	2106	Providence, RI	Private	37.2	735	8063
Rockford Memorial Health Svcs	2107	Rockford, IL	Private	110.4	735	8011
Sharp Chula Vista Medical Ctr	2108	Chula Vista, CA	Private	81.1	734	8062
Crisp Regional Hospital	2109	Cordele, GA	Private	31.7	730	8062
M J G Nursing Home Co Inc	2110	Brooklyn, NY	Private	52.8	730	8051
Newcomb Medical Center	2111	Vineland, NJ	Private	61.7	730	8062
North Penn Hospital	2112	Lansdale, PA	Private	42.8	730	8062
United Presbt Hm At Syosset	2113	Woodbury, NY	Private	52.0	730	8051
Yavapai Community Hospital Assn	2114	Prescott, AZ	Private	57.5	730	8062
Bessemer Carraway Medical Ctr	2115	Bessemer, AL	Private	47.1	729	8062
Community Memorial Hospital	2116	South Hill, VA	Private	39.3	726	8062
St Mary-Rogers Memorial Hosp	2117	Rogers, AR	Private	43.8	726	8062
American Oncologic Hospital	2118	Philadelphia, PA	Private	62.3	725	8069
Bannock Regional Medical Ctr	2119	Pocatello, ID	Private	55.4	725	8062
Jeannette District Mem Hosp	2120	Jeannette, PA	Private	37.1	725	8062
Lifelink Corp	2121	Bensenville, IL	Private	39.8	725	8051
Mount Vernon Hospital Inc	2122	Mount Vernon, NY	Private	57.4	725	8062
Rutland Nursing Home Inc	2123	Brooklyn, NY	Private	52.7	725	8051
Saint John's Mercy Hospital	2124	Washington, MO	Private	33.1	725	8062
St Jospehs Regional Med Ctr	2125	Lewiston, ID	Private	33.1	725	8062
West Orange Health Care Dst	2126	Ocoee, FL	Private	49.5	725	8062
Clarendon Memorial Hospital	2127	Manning, SC	Private	19.9	724	8062
Health Svcs Assn Of Centl Ny	2128	Baldwinsville, NY	Private	60.1	724	8011
Delta Regional Medical Center	2129	Greenville, MS	Private	50.2	723	8062
Fort Worth Osteopathic Hosp	2130	Fort Worth, TX	Private	32.9	720	8062
Misericordia Home	2131	Chicago, IL	Private	25.6	720	8052
Redlands Community Hospital	2132	Redlands, CA	Private	63.4	720	8062
Healthsouth Doctors' Hospital	2133	Coral Gables, FL	Public Family Member	77.6	717	8062
Holy Family Medical Center	2134	Des Plaines, IL	Private	66.3	716	8062
Wesley Health Systems Llc	2135	Hattiesburg, MS	Public Family Member	32.7	716	8062
Vanguard Health Systems Inc	2136	Nashville, TN	Private	49.2	715	8011
Willamette Falls Hospital Inc	2137	Oregon City, OR	Private	48.2	715	8062
Heywood Henry Mem Hospital Inc	2138	Gardner, MA	Private	41.4	714	8062
Healtheast St John's Hospital	2139	Saint Paul, MN	Private	98.5	713	8062
North Arkansas Medical Center	2140	Harrison, AR	Private	39.5	713	8062
Charlotte Hungerford Hosp, The	2141	Torrington, CT	Private	64.2	712	8062
Cullman Medical Center	2142	Cullman, AL	Private	51.1	710	8062
Falmouth Hospital Association	2143	Falmouth, MA	Private	48.6	710	8062
Physician Associates Florida	2144	Maitland, FL	Private	68.9	710	8011
Pottsvlle Hospital Wrne Clinic Inc	2145	Pottsville, PA	Private	44.8	710	8062
Cortland Memorial Hospital	2146	Cortland, NY	Private	44.5	709	8062
Hospital Service District	2147	Thibodaux, LA	Private	62.4	706	8062
Cayuga Medical Ctr At Ithaca	2148	Ithaca, NY	Private	48.6	704	8062
Memorial Hospital	2149	York, PA	Private	46.3	704	8062
Aurora Med Ctr Of Sheboygan Cnty	2150	Sheboygan, WI	Private	47.5	703	8062
Firelands Community Hospital Corp	2151	Sandusky, OH	Private	32.1	703	8062
Kendall Health Care Group Ltd	2152	Miami, FL	Private	32.0	702	8062
Alacare Home Health Services	2153	Birmingham, AL	Private	43.4	700	8082
Amedisys Inc	2154	Baton Rouge, LA	Public	54.5	700	8082
Amisub (North Ridge Hospital)	2155	Fort Lauderdale, FL	Public Family Member	103.5	700	8062
Amisub Of North Carolina Inc	2156	Sanford, NC	Public Family Member	96.0	700	8062
Assocted Regional Univ Pathologist	2157	Salt Lake City, UT	Private	74.6	700	8071
Aviv Health Care, Inc.	2158	Minneapolis, MN	Private	21.4	700	8051
Bay Cove Human Services Inc	2159	Boston, MA	Private	23.3	700	8052
Beaumont Hospital Inc	2160	Beaumont, TX	Public Family Member	31.9	700	8062
Bossier General Hospital	2161	Bossier City, LA	Private	50.6	700	8062
Camino Medical Group Inc	2162	Sunnyvale, CA	Private	48.1	700	8011
Capital Health Services Inc	2163	Fairfax, VA	Private	28.0	700	8099
Caritas Southwood Hospital	2164	Norfolk, MA	Private	31.9	700	8062
Clearfield Hospital	2165	Clearfield, PA	Private	46.3	700	8062
Colbert County/Northwest Alaba	2166	Sheffield, AL	Private	55.5	700	8062
Columbia Hospital Corp Ky	2167	Nashville, TN	Public Family Member	31.9	700	8062
Columbia Hospital For Women Med	2168	Washington, DC	Private	97.0	700	8062
Covance Central Laboratory Ser	2169	Indianapolis, IN	Public Family Member	33.5	700	8071
Daytop Village Inc	2170	New York, NY	Private	32.3	700	8093

D&B COMPANY RANKINGS BY EMPLOYMENT

Company	Rank	Location	Type	Sales ($ mil.)	Employ- ment	Primary SIC
Drake Center	2171	Cincinnati, OH	Private	46.5	700	8093
Exeter Hospital Inc	2172	Exeter, NH	Private	58.9	700	8062
Fairview Hm Care & Hospice Inc	2173	Minneapolis, MN	Private	26.2	700	8082
Fauquier Hospital Inc	2174	Warrenton, VA	Private	39.7	700	8062
Four Winds Inc	2175	Katonah, NY	Private	33.1	700	8063
Geriatrics Svc Cmplex Fndation	2176	Miami, FL	Private	35.4	700	8062
Harris Regional Hospital	2177	Sylva, NC	Private	42.9	700	8062
Hebrew Home Of Greater Wash	2178	Rockville, MD	Private	36.3	700	8051
Holzer Hospital Foundation	2179	Gallipolis, OH	Private	50.1	700	8062
Hospital Of Mercy Community	2180	Port Jervis, NY	Private	31.9	700	8062
Illinois Psychiatric Hospital Inc	2181	Nashville, TN	Public Family Member	25.9	700	8063
Institute Of Prof Practice Inc	2182	Montpelier, VT	Private	26.3	700	8361
Kadlec Medical Center	2183	Richland, WA	Private	70.3	700	8062
Kelsey-Seybold Med Group Pa	2184	Houston, TX	Private	48.1	700	8011
Lutheran Home At Topton Pa Inc	2185	Topton, PA	Private	29.9	700	8361
M C S A, L.L.C.	2186	El Dorado, AR	Private	40.0	700	8062
Medical Assoc/Mnmnee Fls	2187	Menomonee Falls, WI	Private	50.0	700	8011
Mercy Health System Of Kansas	2188	Fort Scott, KS	Private	31.9	700	8062
Mercy Healthcare Inc	2189	Roseburg, OR	Private	64.2	700	8062
Mercy Memorial Health Center	2190	Ardmore, OK	Private	110.0	700	8062
Meridian Behavioral Health Care	2191	Lake City, FL	Private	21.3	700	8093
Metroplex Adventist Hospital	2192	Killeen, TX	Private	45.0	700	8062
Midway Hospital Medical Ctr	2193	Los Angeles, CA	Public Family Member	70.0	700	8062
Mississippi M H Re Ctr	2194	Jackson, MS	Private	45.5	700	8062
Missouri Delta Medical Center	2195	Sikeston, MO	Private	40.3	700	8062
Motion Picture & Tv Fund	2196	Woodland Hills, CA	Private	77.4	700	8062
Newport Health Care Corp	2197	Newport, RI	Private	31.9	700	8062
Newport Hospital	2198	Newport, RI	Private	54.3	700	8062
North Suburban Clinic Ltd	2199	Skokie, IL	Public Family Member	48.1	700	8011
Oncare	2200	San Bruno, CA	Private	71.3	700	8011
Pathway Healthcare Services	2201	Westwood, MA	Private	20.0	700	8082
Pediatrix Medical Group Inc	2202	Fort Lauderdale, FL	Public	80.8	700	8011
Pilgrim Health Care Inc	2203	Quincy, MA	Private	803.4	700	8011
Prevea Clinic Inc	2204	Green Bay, WI	Private	48.1	700	8011
Providence Hospital Inc	2205	Sandusky, OH	Private	42.2	700	8062
Regency Nursing Ctr Of Texas	2206	Victoria, TX	Private	22.1	700	8051
Saint Lukes Northland Hosp	2207	Smithville, MO	Private	38.2	700	8062
Sheridan Healthcare Inc	2208	Hollywood, FL	Public	64.7	700	8082
St Mary Regional Medical Ctr	2209	Apple Valley, CA	Private	61.6	700	8062
St Olaf Hospital Association	2210	Austin, MN	Private	39.2	700	8062
St. Mary Medical Center, Inc	2211	Hobart, IN	Private	31.9	700	8062
St. Peters Community Hospital	2212	Helena, MT	Private	54.1	700	8062
Sumner Regional Health Systems	2213	Gallatin, TN	Private	50.6	700	8062
Titus County Hospital District	2214	Mount Pleasant, TX	Private	50.6	700	8062
University Hospital Ltd	2215	Fort Lauderdale, FL	Private	196.2	700	8062
Upmc-Beaver Valley	2216	Aliquippa, PA	Private	35.1	700	8062
Valley View Hospital Auth	2217	Ada, OK	Private	46.8	700	8062
Wayne Newark Community Hosp	2218	Newark, NY	Private	31.9	700	8062
West Orange Healthcare Inc	2219	Ocoee, FL	Private	104.9	700	8062
West Paces Ferry Hospital Inc	2220	Atlanta, GA	Public Family Member	31.9	700	8062
Westchester Square Medical Ctr	2221	Bronx, NY	Private	56.0	700	8062
Wilkes Regional Medical Center	2222	North Wilkesboro, NC	Private	42.4	700	8062
Health Care Auth Cullman Cnty	2223	Cullman, AL	Private	50.9	699	8062
Danforth Hospital, Inc	2224	Texas City, TX	Public Family Member	31.9	698	8062
Queen Of Peace Hospital	2225	Mitchell, SD	Private	35.3	696	8062
Degraff Memorial Hospital Inc	2226	North Tonawanda, NY	Private	35.5	695	8062
Halifax Regional Medical Ctr	2227	Roanoke Rapids, NC	Private	55.8	694	8062
Columbia Regional Medical Ctr	2228	Montgomery, AL	Public Family Member	62.5	691	8062
Alegent Health-Mercy Hospital	2229	Council Bluffs, IA	Private	45.6	690	8062
Calvary Hospital Inc	2230	Bronx, NY	Private	54.7	690	8069
Gnaden Huetten Memorial Hosp	2231	Lehighton, PA	Private	31.7	690	8062
Guadalupe Valley Hospital	2232	Seguin, TX	Private	35.6	690	8062
Marshalltown Med Surgical Ctr	2233	Marshalltown, IA	Private	39.5	690	8062
Mcfarland Clinic P C	2234	Ames, IA	Private	68.7	690	8011
Peters Barnes-St Hospital	2235	Saint Peters, MO	Private	35.5	690	8062
C G H Medical Center	2236	Sterling, IL	Private	47.7	687	8062
Central Vermont Hospital, Inc	2237	Barre, VT	Private	31.1	683	8062
Feather River Hospital	2238	Paradise, CA	Private	34.9	683	8062
Martin Luther Hospital	2239	Anaheim, CA	Private	46.6	683	8062
Mercy Hospital Of Wilkes Barre Pa	2240	Wilkes Barre, PA	Private	146.8	683	8062

D&B COMPANY RANKINGS BY EMPLOYMENT

Company	Rank	Location	Type	Sales ($ mil.)	Employ-ment	Primary SIC
Franciscan Shared Laboratory	2241	Milwaukee, WI	Private	25.0	680	8071
Gould Medical Foundation	2242	Modesto, CA	Private	68.4	680	8011
Haywood Regional Medical Ctr	2243	Clyde, NC	Private	51.6	680	8062
Notami Hospitals Of California	2244	Nashville, TN	Public Family Member	31.0	680	8062
Sierra Vista Hospital Inc	2245	San Luis Obispo, CA	Public Family Member	31.0	680	8062
Sonora Community Hospital	2246	Sonora, CA	Private	46.2	680	8062
Delaware Valley Medical Ctr	2247	Langhorne, PA	Private	47.5	679	8062
Labone, Inc.	2248	Shawnee Mission, KS	Public	78.9	677	8071
Newton Memorial Hospital	2249	Newton, NJ	Private	62.0	677	8062
Carlisle Hospital	2250	Carlisle, PA	Private	54.5	675	8062
Clinical Pathology Labs	2251	Austin, TX	Private	45.0	675	8071
Green River Reg Mnt Health-Mnt	2252	Owensboro, KY	Private	25.1	675	8051
Nacogdoches County Hospital Dst	2253	Nacogdoches, TX	Private	58.0	675	8062
Primary Care Resources Inc	2254	Omaha, NE	Private	46.4	675	8011
Step-By-Step Inc	2255	Wilkes Barre, PA	Private	22.4	675	8361
Unimed Mgt Services-San Jose	2256	San Jose, CA	Private	46.4	675	8011
Winona Health Services Inc	2257	Winona, MN	Private	40.0	675	8062
Rockdale Health System Inc	2258	Conyers, GA	Private	30.6	671	8062
Clallam Cnty Pub Hospital Dst 2	2259	Port Angeles, WA	Private	46.7	670	8062
Dallas/Fort Worth Med Center	2260	Grand Prairie, TX	Private	54.0	670	8062
Evangelical Homes Of Michigan	2261	Detroit, MI	Private	28.0	670	8051
Florida Health Care Plan Inc	2262	Daytona Beach, FL	Private	114.7	670	8099
Passavant Mem Area Hospital Assoc	2263	Jacksonville, IL	Private	41.0	670	8062
Phycor Of Rome Inc	2264	Rome, GA	Public Family Member	46.1	670	8011
Rockdale Hospital Inc	2265	Conyers, GA	Private	57.3	670	8062
Victor Valley Community Hosp	2266	Victorville, CA	Private	60.7	670	8062
Civista Health Inc	2267	La Plata, MD	Private	42.3	668	8062
Fayette Memorial Hospital	2268	Connersville, IN	Private	35.2	664	8062
Lancaster Hospital Corporation	2269	Lancaster, SC	Public Family Member	30.1	660	8062
Nysarc Inc	2270	Kingston, NY	Private	22.4	660	8361
St Marys Regional Medical Ctr	2271	Saint Marys, PA	Private	31.3	660	8062
Barton Memorial Hospital	2272	South Lake Tahoe, CA	Private	43.0	658	8062
St Mary's Hospital Ozaukee	2273	Thiensville, WI	Private	46.2	656	8062
Eger Health Care Center	2274	Staten Island, NY	Private	30.7	655	8051
Poplar Bluff Physicians Group	2275	Poplar Bluff, MO	Private	41.8	655	8062
Salem Community Hospital	2276	Salem, OH	Private	54.1	655	8062
Cornerstone Health Management	2277	Dallas, TX	Public Family Member	65.0	654	8051
Phoenix Childrens Hospital	2278	Phoenix, AZ	Private	101.0	654	8069
G N Wilcox Memorial Hospital	2279	Lihue, HI	Private	29.7	653	8062
Southstern Ohio Regional Med Ctr	2280	Cambridge, OH	Private	39.1	653	8062
Mercy Medical Center Inc	2281	Roseburg, OR	Private	51.0	652	8062
Affiliated Community Med Ctrs PA	2282	Willmar, MN	Private	47.6	650	8011
American Healthcorp Inc	2283	Nashville, TN	Public	30.5	650	8092
Americus Sumter County Hospital	2284	Americus, GA	Private	39.8	650	8062
Ashland Hospital Assn, The	2285	Ashland, OH	Private	25.4	650	8062
Austin Diagnostic Clinic Assn, The	2286	Austin, TX	Private	44.7	650	8011
Baptist Mem Hspital-North Miss	2287	Oxford, MS	Private	80.4	650	8062
Bay Hospital Inc	2288	Panama City, FL	Public Family Member	29.6	650	8062
Berwick Hospital Center, Inc	2289	Berwick, PA	Private	29.9	650	8062
Beth Israel Hospital Assn	2290	Passaic, NJ	Private	53.0	650	8062
Bradford Hospital Inc	2291	Bradford, PA	Private	41.7	650	8062
Central Tennessee Hospital Corp	2292	Dickson, TN	Public Family Member	46.1	650	8062
Christian Health Care Center	2293	Wyckoff, NJ	Private	23.3	650	8063
City Hospital Association, The	2294	East Liverpool, OH	Private	44.8	650	8062
Columbia Med Ctr Of San Angelo	2295	San Angelo, TX	Public Family Member	28.6	650	8062
Community Gen Osteopathic Hosp	2296	Harrisburg, PA	Private	51.4	650	8062
Cypress Fairbanks Medical Ctr	2297	Houston, TX	Public Family Member	133.0	650	8062
Deaconess Health Sys W Campus	2298	Saint Louis, MO	Private	28.5	650	8062
H C A Highland Hospital Inc	2299	Shreveport, LA	Public Family Member	78.0	650	8062
Hanford Community Hospital	2300	Hanford, CA	Private	47.8	650	8062
Healthsouth Medical Center Inc	2301	Birmingham, AL	Public Family Member	76.9	650	8062
Healthsouth Sub-Acute Ctr	2302	Mechanicsburg, PA	Public Family Member	19.8	650	8093
Henry County Medical Center	2303	Paris, TN	Private	26.1	650	8062
Kishwaukee Community Hospital	2304	Dekalb, IL	Private	46.6	650	8062
Memorial Medical Center Inc	2305	Ashland, WI	Private	26.8	650	8062
Mercy Medical Center	2306	Nampa, ID	Private	60.7	650	8062
Morningside Ministries	2307	San Antonio, TX	Private	22.0	650	8361
Mt Carmel Medical Center Inc	2308	Pittsburg, KS	Private	35.9	650	8062
Naeve Hospital	2309	Albert Lea, MN	Private	24.9	650	8062
Nicholas Demisay	2310	Staten Island, NY	Private	43.0	650	8051

D&B COMPANY RANKINGS BY EMPLOYMENT

Company	Rank	Location	Type	Sales ($ mil.)	Employ- ment	Primary SIC
Northridge Hospital Medical	2311	Van Nuys, CA	Private	29.6	650	8062
Northstern Hospital Of Philadelphia	2312	Philadelphia, PA	Private	48.1	650	8062
Olmsted Medical Center	2313	Rochester, MN	Private	45.0	650	8011
Oswego Hospital Inc	2314	Oswego, NY	Private	37.1	650	8062
Primary Care Delivery Corp	2315	Muncie, IN	Private	44.7	650	8011
Riverview Regional Medical Ctr	2316	Gadsden, AL	Private	29.6	650	8062
Sacred Heart-St Marys Hospital	2317	Rhinelander, WI	Private	39.0	650	8062
Southwestern Vt Medical Center	2318	Bennington, VT	Private	42.4	650	8062
St Josephs Hospital	2319	Chippewa Falls, WI	Private	30.1	650	8062
Statesboro Hma Inc	2320	Statesboro, GA	Public Family Member	29.6	650	8062
Ukiah Adventist Hospital	2321	Ukiah, CA	Private	39.3	650	8062
Union Hospital Of Cecil Cnty	2322	Elkton, MD	Private	48.0	650	8062
Utah Senior Services, Inc	2323	Cornish, UT	Private	20.1	650	8051
West Anaheim Community Hosp	2324	Anaheim, CA	Public Family Member	51.6	650	8062
William B Kessler Mem Hosp	2325	Hammonton, NJ	Private	40.5	650	8062
Yakima Valley Frm Wkrs Clinic	2326	Toppenish, WA	Private	46.5	650	8011
Zale Lipshy University Hosp	2327	Dallas, TX	Private	93.9	650	8062
Marion County Hospital Dst	2328	Mullins, SC	Private	89.4	646	8062
Charleston Hospital, Inc.	2329	Charleston, WV	Public Family Member	58.8	645	8062
Citizens Medical Center	2330	Victoria, TX	Private	120.5	645	8062
Wentworth-Douglass Hospital	2331	Dover, NH	Private	56.5	645	8062
Aurelia Osborn Fox Memorial	2332	Oneonta, NY	Private	48.9	640	8062
Bensenville Home Society	2333	Bensenville, IL	Private	35.5	640	8051
Clifton Springs Sanitarium Co	2334	Clifton Springs, NY	Private	36.9	640	8062
Hunt Memorial Hospital Dst	2335	Greenville, TX	Private	52.2	640	8062
Pleasant Valley Hospital, Inc.	2336	Point Pleasant, WV	Private	42.8	637	8062
Palisades Medical Center	2337	North Bergen, NJ	Private	64.8	634	8062
Southern Healthcare Systems	2338	Baton Rouge, LA	Private	31.5	634	8051
Union Hospital Association	2339	Dover, OH	Private	41.2	634	8062
Little Flower Chld Svcs Of Ny	2340	Wading River, NY	Private	50.5	632	8361
St Bernard Hospital Healthcare Ctr	2341	Chicago, IL	Private	53.2	632	8062
Windham Community Memorial	2342	Willimantic, CT	Private	49.9	632	8062
Jackson Clinic Prof Assn, The	2343	Jackson, TN	Private	57.5	630	8011
Arl/Labsouth Inc	2344	Birmingham, AL	Private	30.2	630	8071
Brownsville-Valley Regional Med	2345	Brownsville, TX	Public Family Member	175.0	630	8062
Columbia Hospital L P	2346	West Palm Beach, FL	Private	28.6	630	8062
Dickinson Cnty Health Care Sys	2347	Iron Mountain, MI	Private	42.1	630	8062
El Centro Community Hospital	2348	El Centro, CA	Private	49.4	630	8062
Grenada Lake Medical Center	2349	Grenada, MS	Private	26.7	630	8062
Jmes R Glidewell Dntl Ceramics	2350	Newport Beach, CA	Private	46.7	630	8072
John Knox Village Of Florida	2351	Pompano Beach, FL	Private	22.8	630	8361
Puget Sound Blood Ctr Program	2352	Seattle, WA	Private	46.0	630	8071
Queens-Long Island Med Group	2353	Uniondale, NY	Private	43.3	630	8011
Johns Hopkins Health Sys Corp	2354	Baltimore, MD	Private	910.5	629	8062
Humana Mlitary Healthcare Svcs	2355	Louisville, KY	Public Family Member	43.2	628	8011
Columbia Four Rivers Med Ctr	2356	Selma, AL	Public Family Member	45.9	625	8062
Fort Atkinson Mem Health Svcs	2357	Fort Atkinson, WI	Private	45.0	625	8062
Glenoaks Medical Center	2358	Glendale Heights, IL	Private	34.8	625	8062
Harford Memorial Hospital Inc	2359	Havre De Grace, MD	Private	49.5	625	8062
Lifepath Inc	2360	Bethlehem, PA	Private	22.2	625	8059
Meadowlands Hospital Med Ctr	2361	Secaucus, NJ	Private	49.1	625	8062
Nlvh, Inc	2362	North Las Vegas, NV	Public Family Member	75.0	625	8062
Saint Joseph's Medical Center	2363	Stamford, CT	Private	55.1	625	8062
South Austin Medical Center	2364	Austin, TX	Public Family Member	28.4	625	8062
Twin Cnty Regional Healthcare	2365	Galax, VA	Private	34.0	625	8062
Jackson Cnty Mem Hospital Tr Auth	2366	Altus, OK	Private	36.5	624	8062
Richardson Hospital Authority	2367	Richardson, TX	Private	49.2	624	8062
Medical Resources Inc	2368	Hackensack, NJ	Public	202.4	623	8071
Fletcher Hospital Inc	2369	Fletcher, NC	Private	28.3	622	8062
De Witt Nursing Home	2370	New York, NY	Private	32.8	621	8051
Davis Memorial Hospital	2371	Elkins, WV	Private	51.1	620	8062
Huron Valley Sinai Hospital	2372	Commerce Twnshp, MI	Private	60.8	620	8062
Kimball Day Hospital	2373	Putnam, CT	Private	28.2	620	8062
Morehead Memorial Hospital	2374	Eden, NC	Private	43.1	620	8062
St Francis Hospital Of New Castle	2375	New Castle, PA	Private	32.3	620	8062
St Marys Hospital Of St Mrys Cnty	2376	Leonardtown, MD	Private	38.9	620	8062
Walker Baptist Medical Center	2377	Jasper, AL	Private	50.2	620	8062
White County Medical Center	2378	Searcy, AR	Private	39.2	620	8062
Winona Community Memorial Hosp	2379	Winona, MN	Private	28.7	620	8062
St Joseph Hospital, Eureka	2380	Eureka, CA	Private	47.2	617	8062

D&B COMPANY RANKINGS BY EMPLOYMENT

Company	Rank	Location	Type	Sales ($ mil.)	Employ-ment	Primary SIC
Bothwell Regional Health Ctr	2381	Sedalia, MO	Private	45.7	616	8062
Camelot Care Center Inc	2382	Seminole, FL	Private	21.4	614	8361
Alliance Imaging Inc	2383	Anaheim, CA	Public	86.5	613	8099
Meadowbrook Rhbilitation Group	2384	Emeryville, CA	Public	20.8	613	8093
South Florida Baptist Hospital	2385	Plant City, FL	Private	40.5	613	8062
Three Rivers Community Hospital	2386	Grants Pass, OR	Private	30.5	613	8062
Kateri Residence	2387	New York, NY	Private	38.1	612	8051
Central Suffolk Hospital	2388	Riverhead, NY	Private	53.3	610	8062
Lake Region Healthcare Corp	2389	Fergus Falls, MN	Private	30.3	610	8062
Mercy Hospital Of Watertown	2390	Watertown, NY	Private	24.8	610	8059
Northern Hospital Dst Surry Cnty	2391	Mount Airy, NC	Private	39.3	610	8062
Williamson County Hospital	2392	Franklin, TN	Private	51.2	610	8062
Warren General Hospital	2393	Warren, PA	Private	29.3	609	8062
Marshall Healthcare Authority	2394	Boaz, AL	Private	44.7	608	8062
South Dade Healthcare Group	2395	Miami, FL	Public Family Member	27.6	607	8062
Suburban General Hospital	2396	Pittsburgh, PA	Private	28.1	607	8062
East Oh Reg Hospital Mart Fer	2397	Martins Ferry, OH	Private	39.5	606	8062
Memorial Hospital At Oconomowoc	2398	Oconomowoc, WI	Private	34.8	604	8062
Roxborough Memorial Hospital	2399	Philadelphia, PA	Private	43.6	604	8062
Tucson General Hospital	2400	Tucson, AZ	Public Family Member	47.6	602	8062
Albright Care Services	2401	Lewisburg, PA	Private	22.3	600	8051
All Care Visiting Nurse	2402	Lynn, MA	Private	19.9	600	8082
Amisub (Irvine Medical Center)	2403	Irvine, CA	Private	27.2	600	8062
Astor Home For Children	2404	Rhinebeck, NY	Private	20.3	600	8361
Baldwin C E Shr Hsp Bd	2405	Fairhope, AL	Private	36.6	600	8062
Bethesda Lutheran Medical Ctr	2406	Saint Paul, MN	Private	27.2	600	8062
Bexar County Mental Health	2407	San Antonio, TX	Private	35.2	600	8051
Burke, Winifrd Mstrsn Rehab	2408	White Plains, NY	Private	36.2	600	8361
Cancer Treatment Ctrs Of America	2409	Arlington Heights, IL	Private	22.0	600	8069
Carrier Foundation Inc	2410	Belle Mead, NJ	Private	33.6	600	8063
Central Plains Clinic	2411	Sioux Falls, SD	Private	48.5	600	8011
Chicago Grant Hospital, Inc.	2412	Chicago, IL	Public Family Member	53.2	600	8062
Childrens Specialized Hospital	2413	Mountainside, NJ	Private	29.4	600	8069
Church Hmes Inc Congregational	2414	Hartford, CT	Private	29.9	600	8051
Citizens Memrl Hsp Dst Plk Cnt	2415	Bolivar, MO	Private	29.8	600	8062
City Of Philadelphia, Trust	2416	Philadelphia, PA	Private	63.3	600	8069
Colorado Prmnt Med Group Pc	2417	Denver, CO	Private	41.2	600	8011
Columbia Hospital Corp Bay Area	2418	Corpus Christi, TX	Public Family Member	27.2	600	8062
Corning Scicor Ltd Partnership	2419	Indianapolis, IN	Private	28.7	600	8071
Cornwall Hospital Inc	2420	Cornwall, NY	Private	30.2	600	8062
Correctnal Healthcare Solutions	2421	Chalfont, PA	Private	36.7	600	8093
Dmc Health Care Centers Inc	2422	Novi, MI	Private	29.9	600	8011
Doc's Physicians Affiliated	2423	Valhalla, NY	Private	27.4	600	8011
Family Dental	2424	Cleveland, OH	Private	36.2	600	8021
Fulton County Health Center	2425	Wauseon, OH	Private	26.5	600	8062
Galen Hospital Alaska Inc	2426	Anchorage, AK	Public Family Member	86.5	600	8062
Goddard Medical Associates Pc	2427	Brockton, MA	Private	41.2	600	8011
Hammond Clinic, Llc	2428	Munster, IN	Private	54.9	600	8011
Healthsphere Of America Inc	2429	Memphis, TN	Private	21.8	600	8082
Hebrew Home & Hospital Inc	2430	W Hartford, CT	Private	25.8	600	8069
Hospital Service District No 1	2431	Zachary, LA	Private	32.5	600	8062
Hospitals Of National Medical	2432	Tullahoma, TN	Public Family Member	27.2	600	8062
Hse A Inglis Wheelchair Community	2433	Philadelphia, PA	Private	31.2	600	8361
Hugh Chatham Memorial Hospital	2434	Elkin, NC	Private	32.4	600	8062
Iatros Health Network Inc	2435	Atlanta, GA	Public	25.5	600	8051
Illini Manors Inc	2436	Galesburg, IL	Private	31.9	600	8051
Jewish Childcare Association	2437	New York, NY	Private	36.6	600	8361
Joseph Hazleton-Saint Med Ctr	2438	Hazleton, PA	Private	36.1	600	8062
Kosciusko Community Hospital	2439	Warsaw, IN	Private	48.3	600	8062
La Follette Medical Center	2440	La Follette, TN	Private	24.0	600	8062
Lake Shore Hospital	2441	Irving, NY	Private	29.5	600	8062
Lakeview Center Inc	2442	Pensacola, FL	Private	42.5	600	8093
Learning Services Corporation	2443	Durham, NC	Private	24.0	600	8093
Longview Regional Hospital	2444	Longview, TX	Public Family Member	27.2	600	8062
Mary Free Bed Hospital	2445	Grand Rapids, MI	Private	24.1	600	8069
Masonic Charity Foundation Of Nj	2446	Burlington, NJ	Private	48.8	600	8051
Matagorda County Hospital Dst	2447	Bay City, TX	Private	24.3	600	8062
McAlester Regional Health Ctr Auth	2448	Mcalester, OK	Private	38.0	600	8062
McDonough County Hospital Dst	2449	Macomb, IL	Private	34.2	600	8062
Meridian Medical Group Inc	2450	Atlanta, GA	Private	41.2	600	8011

D&B COMPANY RANKINGS BY EMPLOYMENT

Company	Rank	Location	Type	Sales ($ mil.)	Employ-ment	Primary SIC
Missouri Health Care Systems Lp	2451	Springfield, MO	Private	27.2	600	8062
Nalle Clinic Company	2452	Charlotte, NC	Private	41.2	600	8011
Ncs, Inc.	2453	Fort Wayne, IN	Private	20.9	600	8051
New York Eye Ear Infirmary Inc	2454	New York, NY	Private	61.9	600	8069
Northeastern Pa Health Corp	2455	Hazleton, PA	Private	36.5	600	8062
Northern Cal Presbt Homes	2456	San Francisco, CA	Private	42.8	600	8051
Ozanam Hall Of Queens Nursing	2457	Bayside, NY	Private	33.0	600	8051
Palm Springs General Hospital	2458	Hialeah, FL	Private	53.0	600	8062
Peterson Sid Memorial Hosp	2459	Kerrville, TX	Private	27.2	600	8062
Philadelphia Presbytery Homes	2460	Lafayette Hill, PA	Private	31.4	600	8361
Preferred Health Network Inc	2461	Irvine, CA	Private	24.0	600	8099
Prime Care Medical Group	2462	Victorville, CA	Private	41.2	600	8011
Rehabilitation Associates Inc	2463	Norwood, MA	Private	20.5	600	8051
Republic Health Corp Indanapolis	2464	Nashville, TN	Public Family Member	49.4	600	8062
Rideout Memorial Hospital	2465	Marysville, CA	Private	55.7	600	8062
Riverside Health Systems Inc	2466	Wichita, KS	Private	27.2	600	8062
Riverview Hospital Assn	2467	Wisconsin Rapids, WI	Private	33.6	600	8062
Robert Wood Johnson Univ Hosp	2468	Trenton, NJ	Private	46.2	600	8062
Rockville General Hospital Inc	2469	Vernon Rockville, CT	Private	45.6	600	8062
S L C O Inc	2470	San Leandro, CA	Public Family Member	50.4	600	8062
Sampson Regional Medical Ctr	2471	Clinton, NC	Private	35.3	600	8062
Scotland Health Care System	2472	Laurinburg, NC	Private	75.0	600	8062
Seniorcare Inc	2473	Louisville, KY	Private	21.0	600	8052
Sharp Cabrillo Hospital	2474	San Diego, CA	Private	27.2	600	8062
Shelby County Mem Hospital Assn	2475	Sidney, OH	Private	38.2	600	8062
Shore Memorial Hospital	2476	Nassawadox, VA	Private	33.6	600	8062
Sierra View Local Hospital Dst	2477	Porterville, CA	Private	50.4	600	8062
Southern Ocean County Hosp	2478	Manahawkin, NJ	Private	46.5	600	8062
Southwstern Ill Health Fcilities	2479	Maryville, IL	Private	47.8	600	8062
St Francis Central Hospital	2480	Pittsburgh, PA	Private	38.9	600	8062
St Francis Hospital Inc	2481	Jersey City, NJ	Private	48.5	600	8062
St Nicholas Hospital	2482	Sheboygan, WI	Private	47.0	600	8062
Stillwater Medical Ctr Auth	2483	Stillwater, OK	Private	42.5	600	8062
Texas Oncology Pa	2484	Dallas, TX	Private	64.0	600	8011
Thorek Hospital & Medical Ctr	2485	Chicago, IL	Private	51.5	600	8062
Tuality Community Hospital	2486	Hillsboro, OR	Private	49.3	600	8062
United Cerebal Palsy Asc	2487	Roosevelt, NY	Private	20.4	600	8099
United Methodist Homes Of Nj	2488	Neptune, NJ	Private	27.8	600	8361
University Pittsburgh Med Ctr	2489	Braddock, PA	Private	38.3	600	8062
Vancouver Clinic Inc	2490	Vancouver, WA	Private	41.2	600	8011
Vaughan Regional Medical Ctr	2491	Selma, AL	Private	28.8	600	8099
Vencor Hospital East, Inc	2492	Louisville, KY	Private	29.4	600	8069
Visiting Nurse Association	2493	East Orange, NJ	Private	22.4	600	8049
Visiting Nurses Association, The	2494	Los Angeles, CA	Private	41.1	600	8082
Warm Sprng Rhblttion Fundation	2495	San Antonio, TX	Private	43.0	600	8069
Wayne Memorial Hospital Assn	2496	Honesdale, PA	Private	32.4	600	8062
Wayne Newark Community Hosp	2497	Newark, NY	Private	27.2	600	8062
West Hudson Hospital Assn	2498	Kearny, NJ	Private	27.2	600	8062
William Prince Hospital Corp	2499	Manassas, VA	Private	72.3	600	8062
Yonkers General Hospital Inc	2500	Yonkers, NY	Private	42.8	600	8062
Brownwood Regional Hospital	2501	Brownwood, TX	Public Family Member	27.0	596	8062
Randolph Hospital Inc	2502	Asheboro, NC	Private	45.5	596	8062
Hartwyck At Oak Tree Inc	2503	Edison, NJ	Private	29.0	595	8051
Walker Methodist Health Center	2504	Minneapolis, MN	Private	25.4	591	8051
Brethren Home Community	2505	New Oxford, PA	Private	20.7	590	8051
Gettysburg Hospital Inc	2506	Gettysburg, PA	Private	38.2	590	8062
Halifax Regional Hospital Inc	2507	South Boston, VA	Private	45.2	590	8062
Occupational Urgent Care Health	2508	Broderick, CA	Public Family Member	23.6	590	8099
Pressley Ridge Schools	2509	Pittsburgh, PA	Private	33.3	590	8361
Central Kansas Medical Center	2510	Great Bend, KS	Private	26.7	588	8062
Children's Village Inc, The	2511	Dobbs Ferry, NY	Private	24.2	585	8361
Dublin Community Hospital Inc	2512	Dublin, GA	Public Family Member	105.0	585	8062
Mayo Henry Newhall Mem Hosp	2513	Santa Clarita, CA	Private	80.0	585	8062
United Lutheran Program For Th	2514	Milwaukee, WI	Private	23.5	585	8051
Charles Cole Memorial Hosp	2515	Coudersport, PA	Private	29.9	583	8062
Mesquite Community Hospital Lp	2516	Mesquite, TX	Private	37.6	583	8062
Johnston Memorial Hospital	2517	Smithfield, NC	Private	43.5	582	8062
St Francis Med Center-West	2518	Ewa Beach, HI	Private	44.9	581	8062
Columbia Palmyra Park Hospital	2519	Albany, GA	Public Family Member	26.3	580	8062
Opelousas General Hospital	2520	Opelousas, LA	Private	41.7	580	8062

D&B COMPANY RANKINGS BY EMPLOYMENT

Company	Rank	Location	Type	Sales ($ mil.)	Employ- ment	Primary SIC
Pca Health Plans Texas, Inc.	2521	Austin, TX	Public Family Member	502.4	580	8011
Santa Barbara Mdcl Fndn Clc	2522	Santa Barbara, CA	Private	52.7	580	8011
Southeast Alaska Reg Health	2523	Juneau, AK	Private	54.7	580	8011
Rockwood Clinic P.S.	2524	Spokane, WA	Private	82.0	579	8011
Omega Health Systems Inc	2525	Memphis, TN	Public	83.3	576	8042
Carmel Richmond Nursing Home	2526	Staten Island, NY	Private	24.5	575	8051
Caylor-Nickel Medical Center	2527	Bluffton, IN	Private	30.4	575	8062
Johnson Memorial Hospital	2528	Franklin, IN	Private	40.7	575	8062
Kennedy Health Services Corp	2529	Hawthorne, CA	Private	26.0	575	8062
Medigroup Inc	2530	Newark, NJ	Private	39.5	575	8011
Mountainview Hospital Inc	2531	Las Vegas, NV	Public Family Member	26.0	575	8062
Scott & White Clinic An Assn	2532	Temple, TX	Private	480.0	575	8011
Stuart Jennie Medical Center	2533	Hopkinsville, KY	Private	53.4	575	8062
Unity Physician Group Inc	2534	Bloomington, IN	Private	39.5	575	8011
Athens Limestone Hospital	2535	Athens, AL	Private	35.6	574	8062
Hebrew Home For The Aged	2536	San Francisco, CA	Private	23.3	574	8051
Franciscan Health System West	2537	Federal Way, WA	Private	25.9	573	8062
A I H Corporation	2538	Zion, IL	Private	25.9	572	8062
Tallahassee Medical Center	2539	Tallahassee, FL	Public Family Member	55.2	572	8062
Keystone Health Plan East Inc	2540	Philadelphia, PA	Private	1,613.0	571	8011
St Mary's Hospital	2541	Green Bay, WI	Private	44.9	571	8062
Bay Area Medical Center	2542	Marinette, WI	Private	43.0	570	8062
Friends Hospital	2543	Philadelphia, PA	Private	31.9	570	8063
Johns Hopkins Medical Services	2544	Baltimore, MD	Private	114.2	570	8011
Loris Community Hospital	2545	Loris, SC	Private	28.7	570	8062
M V P Health Plan Inc	2546	Schenectady, NY	Private	357.0	570	8011
Pekin Memorial Hospital	2547	Pekin, IL	Private	34.5	570	8062
Promedica Physician Support	2548	Sylvania, OH	Private	39.2	570	8011
Goodwin House Incorporated	2549	Alexandria, VA	Private	23.2	568	8051
Midwestern Regional Med Ctr	2550	Zion, IL	Private	57.3	568	8069
Gaylord Farm Association	2551	Wallingford, CT	Private	34.7	566	8361
St Anthony Memorial Hospital	2552	Effingham, IL	Private	47.1	566	8062
Benedictine Living Communities	2553	Duluth, MN	Private	21.4	565	8051
Hempstead Gen Hospital & Med Ctr	2554	Hempstead, NY	Private	50.7	565	8062
Hillcrest Healthcare Systems	2555	Tulsa, OK	Private	263.3	564	8062
Lake Of The Ozarks Gen Hosp	2556	Osage Beach, MO	Private	40.8	563	8062
Memorial Hospital West Volusia	2557	Deland, FL	Private	107.0	563	8062
Somerset Hospital Ctr For Health	2558	Somerset, PA	Private	35.8	562	8062
M H Health Care Inc	2559	Indianapolis, IN	Private	99.1	560	8011
North Adams Regional Hospital	2560	North Adams, MA	Private	35.7	560	8062
Rehabilitation Inst Of Mich	2561	Detroit, MI	Private	37.9	560	8069
St John's Home Of Milwaukee	2562	Milwaukee, WI	Private	19.8	560	8051
Good Samaritan Medical Center	2563	Johnstown, PA	Private	34.3	553	8062
Franciscan Health System West	2564	Tacoma, WA	Private	285.4	551	8062
Albany General Hospital, Inc	2565	Albany, OR	Private	33.2	550	8062
Arcventures Inc	2566	Chicago, IL	Private	32.0	550	8082
Baptist Mem Hospital-Desoto	2567	Southaven, MS	Private	33.2	550	8062
Brattleboro Retreat	2568	Brattleboro, VT	Private	22.5	550	8063
Bridgeport Health Care Center	2569	Bridgeport, CT	Private	31.3	550	8051
Bryn Mawr Rehabilitation Hosp	2570	Malvern, PA	Private	32.0	550	8069
Center For Nursing Rehabilitation	2571	Far Rockaway, NY	Private	42.2	550	8051
Christie Building Inc	2572	Champaign, IL	Private	37.8	550	8011
Cobble Hill Nursing Home Inc	2573	Brooklyn, NY	Private	35.8	550	8051
Community Hospital Of Ottawa	2574	Ottawa, IL	Private	34.9	550	8062
Duncan Regional Hospital Inc	2575	Duncan, OK	Private	31.8	550	8062
Englewood Community Hospital	2576	Englewood, FL	Public Family Member	35.1	550	8062
Geauga Community Hospital Assn	2577	Chardon, OH	Private	24.9	550	8062
Grays Harbor Community Hosp	2578	Aberdeen, WA	Private	43.4	550	8062
Gulf Coast Regional Blood Ctr	2579	Houston, TX	Private	41.1	550	8099
Hannibal Regional Hospital	2580	Hannibal, MO	Private	40.2	550	8062
Healthsouth Of Virginia, Inc	2581	Richmond, VA	Public Family Member	43.8	550	8062
Heather Hill, Inc	2582	Chardon, OH	Private	22.2	550	8069
Hepburn Medical Center Inc	2583	Ogdensburg, NY	Private	34.7	550	8062
Hi-Desert Memorial Hospital Dst	2584	Joshua Tree, CA	Private	32.1	550	8062
Hospital Of Germantown	2585	Philadelphia, PA	Private	57.9	550	8062
Howard Young Medical Center	2586	Woodruff, WI	Private	39.3	550	8062
Kershaw County Medical Center	2587	Camden, SC	Private	41.6	550	8062
Kingston Hospital (Inc)	2588	Kingston, NY	Private	50.2	550	8062
Kph-Consolidation Inc	2589	Kingwood, TX	Public Family Member	26.9	550	8069
Lancaster Mennonite Hospital	2590	Lebanon, PA	Private	24.4	550	8063

D&B COMPANY RANKINGS BY EMPLOYMENT

Company	Rank	Location	Type	Sales ($ mil.)	Employ-ment	Primary SIC
Loretto Hospital	2591	Chicago, IL	Private	24.9	550	8062
Memorial Hospital Pasadena	2592	Pasadena, TX	Private	24.9	550	8062
Mid Valley Health Care Inc	2593	Lebanon, OR	Private	30.0	550	8062
Pattie A Clay Infirmary	2594	Richmond, KY	Private	31.2	550	8062
Peninsula Psychiatric Center	2595	Louisville, TN	Private	20.4	550	8063
Philadlphia Afl-Cio Hospital Assn	2596	Philadelphia, PA	Private	24.9	550	8062
R J Taylor Memorial Hospital	2597	Hawkinsville, GA	Private	22.1	550	8062
Reynold's Memorial Hospital	2598	Glen Dale, WV	Private	24.7	550	8062
Sabine Valley Center	2599	Longview, TX	Private	21.0	550	8093
St Luke Med Ctr Of Pasadena	2600	Pasadena, CA	Public Family Member	24.9	550	8062
St. Marys Hospital Of Blue Sprng	2601	Blue Springs, MO	Private	47.7	550	8062
Starr Commonwealth	2602	Albion, MI	Private	30.6	550	8361
Therapeutic Associates Inc	2603	Sherman Oaks, CA	Private	30.0	550	8049
Tidewater Phys Multi Group Pc	2604	Newport News, VA	Public Family Member	37.8	550	8011
Union HospitalAssn Of The Bronx	2605	Bronx, NY	Private	42.8	550	8062
United Cerebral Palsy Associat	2606	Hauppauge, NY	Private	20.1	550	8099
Westminster-Canterbury Corp	2607	Richmond, VA	Private	21.0	550	8361
Newnan Hospital	2608	Newnan, GA	Private	47.4	549	8062
St Mary Medical Center	2609	Walla Walla, WA	Private	47.5	546	8062
Hip Health Plan Of Florida	2610	Hollywood, FL	Private	295.7	545	8011
Ridgeview Medical Center	2611	Waconia, MN	Private	24.6	545	8062
Baldwin County Hospital Auth	2612	Milledgeville, GA	Private	24.5	543	8062
Lawrence Cnty Gen Hospital	2613	Ironton, OH	Private	30.4	543	8062
Oklahoma Cy Clinic A Prof Corp	2614	Oklahoma City, OK	Private	37.3	543	8011
Osceola Regional Hospital	2615	Kissimmee, FL	Public Family Member	53.5	542	8062
Sutter Solano Medical Center	2616	Vallejo, CA	Private	45.7	542	8062
Charleston Memorial Hospital	2617	Charleston, SC	Private	32.5	541	8062
Albert Gallatin Home Care	2618	New Hyde Park, NY	Public Family Member	25.0	540	8082
American Hospital Mgt Corp	2619	Arcata, CA	Public	41.3	540	8062
Caldwell Memorial Hospital	2620	Lenoir, NC	Private	37.5	540	8062
Des Moines General Hospital Co	2621	Des Moines, IA	Private	45.4	540	8062
Illinois Valley Community Hosp	2622	Peru, IL	Private	33.5	540	8062
Laughlin Memorial Hospital	2623	Greeneville, TN	Private	35.3	540	8062
St Josphs Community Hospital Of W	2624	West Bend, WI	Private	31.1	540	8062
Tropical Texas Center For Ment	2625	Edinburg, TX	Private	26.2	539	8093
Auburn General Hospital Inc	2626	Auburn, WA	Public Family Member	24.3	538	8062
Choicecare/Humana Corporation	2627	Cincinnati, OH	Public Family Member	36.9	538	8011
Stanly Memorial Hospital Inc	2628	Albemarle, NC	Private	24.2	537	8062
Consolidated Care Crew Home He	2629	San Antonio, TX	Private	35.0	535	8082
Norwood Clinic Inc Pc	2630	Birmingham, AL	Private	62.2	535	8093
Soldiers & Sailors Hospital	2631	Penn Yan, NY	Private	21.5	535	8062
Marlborough Hospital	2632	Marlborough, MA	Private	32.0	533	8062
Columbia El Drado Hospital Med	2633	Tucson, AZ	Public Family Member	35.3	532	8062
Hancock Mem Hospital & Health	2634	Greenfield, IN	Private	44.0	532	8062
Mission Hospital Inc	2635	Mission, TX	Private	73.8	531	8062
Adirondack Medical Center	2636	Saranac Lake, NY	Private	30.0	530	8062
Alameda Hospital	2637	Alameda, CA	Private	35.8	530	8062
Coffee Regional Medical Center	2638	Douglas, GA	Private	44.1	530	8062
French Hospital Med Ctr A Cal	2639	San Luis Obispo, CA	Private	23.9	530	8062
Skaggs Community Hospital	2640	Branson, MO	Private	47.9	530	8062
Smyth County Community Hosp	2641	Marion, VA	Private	33.6	530	8062
Wyoming County Community Hosp	2642	Warsaw, NY	Private	31.1	530	8062
Vaughan Regional Medical Ctr	2643	Selma, AL	Private	28.8	529	8062
United Church Of Christ Homes	2644	Hummelstown, PA	Private	20.1	528	8051
Central Wash Health Svcs Assn	2645	Wenatchee, WA	Private	67.6	527	8062
Hudson Valley Hospital Center	2646	Cortlandt Manor, NY	Private	50.0	527	8062
Chenango Memorial Hospital	2647	Norwich, NY	Private	29.8	526	8062
Jackson Cnty Schneck Mem Hosp	2648	Seymour, IN	Private	37.7	526	8062
Buffalo Medical Group P C	2649	Williamsville, NY	Private	53.0	525	8011
Columbia Putnam Hospital Inc	2650	Palatka, FL	Public Family Member	27.2	525	8062
Columbus Doctors Hospital Inc	2651	Columbus, GA	Private	23.7	525	8062
Community Hospitals Of Galen	2652	Pompano Beach, FL	Public Family Member	23.7	525	8062
Craig Hospital	2653	Englewood, CO	Private	36.0	525	8069
Daughters Jacob Nursing Home	2654	Bronx, NY	Private	38.0	525	8051
Facey Medical Group, Pc	2655	Mission Hills, CA	Private	36.0	525	8011
Gila Regional Medical Center	2656	Silver City, NM	Private	23.7	525	8062
Irvington General Hospital	2657	Irvington, NJ	Private	42.2	525	8062
Johnston Memorial Hospital	2658	Abingdon, VA	Private	43.4	525	8062
Methodist Healthcare-Dyersburg	2659	Dyersburg, TN	Private	31.5	525	8062
Morris Hospital	2660	Morris, IL	Private	21.1	525	8062

D&B COMPANY RANKINGS BY EMPLOYMENT

Company	Rank	Location	Type	Sales ($ mil.)	Employ-ment	Primary SIC
North Platte Neb Hospital Corp	2661	North Platte, NE	Private	46.9	525	8062
Pacifica Of The Valley Corp	2662	Sun Valley, CA	Private	44.0	525	8062
Shepherd Center Inc	2663	Atlanta, GA	Private	41.1	525	8069
Veterans Home & Hospital	2664	Rocky Hill, CT	Private	23.7	525	8062
Community Hospital Of Brzsport Inc	2665	Lake Jackson, TX	Private	60.9	523	8062
Berkshire Farm Center & Servic	2666	Canaan, NY	Private	32.9	521	8361
Camelot Healthcare Llc	2667	Rayne, LA	Private	54.0	520	8051
Culpeper Memorial Hospital Inc	2668	Culpeper, VA	Private	27.3	520	8062
Hackettstown Community Hosp	2669	Hackettstown, NJ	Private	31.0	520	8062
Kendal-Crosslands Communities Inc	2670	Kennett Square, PA	Private	23.1	520	8051
Medical Center-West Inc	2671	Lithia Springs, GA	Public Family Member	69.4	520	8062
New England Sinai Hospital	2672	Stoughton, MA	Private	38.2	520	8069
South Shore Hospital Corp	2673	Chicago, IL	Private	30.2	520	8062
Southwest Medical Associates	2674	Las Vegas, NV	Public Family Member	95.7	520	8011
Watauga Medical Center Inc	2675	Boone, NC	Private	42.1	520	8062
National Surgery Centers, Inc.	2676	Chicago, IL	Public	102.6	519	8093
Scotland Memorial Hospital	2677	Laurinburg, NC	Private	46.5	517	8062
Pioneer Valley Hospital	2678	Salt Lake City, UT	Public Family Member	70.0	516	8062
Rehabilitation Support Service	2679	Guilderland, NY	Private	21.0	516	8361
Richmond Memorial Hospital	2680	Rockingham, NC	Private	36.8	516	8062
Wesley Health Care Center Inc	2681	Saratoga Springs, NY	Private	20.5	515	8051
Edinburg Regional Medical Ctr	2682	Edinburg, TX	Private	92.0	513	8062
St Michaels Hospital	2683	Stevens Point, WI	Private	44.8	513	8062
H C A Health Services Of La	2684	Monroe, LA	Public Family Member	23.1	512	8062
Astoria General Hospital Inc	2685	Long Island City, NY	Private	75.9	510	8062
Columbia Huntington Beach Med	2686	Huntington Beach, CA	Public Family Member	38.6	510	8062
Columbia/Alleghany Regional	2687	Lowmoor, VA	Public Family Member	23.0	510	8062
Doctors Osteopathic Med Ctr	2688	Fort Myers, FL	Public Family Member	32.8	510	8062
Lincoln Health System Inc	2689	Ruston, LA	Private	28.1	510	8062
Newton Health Systems Inc	2690	Covington, GA	Private	32.6	510	8062
North Ottawa Community Hospital	2691	Grand Haven, MI	Private	33.9	510	8062
Sharp Coronado Hospital Healthcare	2692	Coronado, CA	Private	23.0	510	8062
Georgetown County Mem Hosp	2693	Georgetown, SC	Private	68.5	509	8062
York Hospital	2694	York, ME	Private	33.4	509	8062
United Healthcare South Inc	2695	Birmingham, AL	Public Family Member	20.3	508	8099
Frisbie Memorial Hospital	2696	Rochester, NH	Private	42.7	507	8062
Harriman Jones Medical Group	2697	Long Beach, CA	Private	53.0	506	8011
Rebsamen Regional Medical Ctr	2698	Jacksonville, AR	Private	22.8	506	8062
Memorial Hospital	2699	Logansport, IN	Private	27.0	505	8062
Pennock Hospital	2700	Hastings, MI	Private	32.3	505	8062
Presbyterian Home Inc	2701	Evanston, IL	Private	24.7	505	8361
Lincoln Medical Center	2702	Lincolnton, NC	Private	36.7	504	8062
Jewish Home Of Rochester, Ny	2703	Rochester, NY	Private	20.9	503	8051
Warrensville Development Ctr	2704	Cleveland, OH	Private	32.0	503	8059
Baptist Med Ctr Of The Beaches	2705	Jacksonville, FL	Private	37.4	501	8062
Columbia/Cape Fear Healthcare	2706	Wilmington, NC	Public Family Member	24.6	501	8062
Adair County Pub Hospital Dst Corp	2707	Columbia, KY	Private	25.0	500	8062
Ahm-Smc Inc	2708	Paramount, CA	Public Family Member	22.5	500	8062
Ahp Holdings, Inc	2709	Hartford, CT	Public Family Member	34.3	500	8011
Annie Penn Memorial Hospital	2710	Reidsville, NC	Private	32.4	500	8062
B V M C Inc	2711	College Station, TX	Public Family Member	22.5	500	8062
Bacharach Inst For Rehabilitation	2712	Pomona, NJ	Private	25.2	500	8069
Beaufort County Hospital Assn Inc	2713	Washington, NC	Private	29.5	500	8062
Bio-Medical Applications Of Texas	2714	Lexington, MA	Public Family Member	28.6	500	8092
Bizer Enterprises	2715	Clarksville, IN	Private	25.0	500	8042
Bloomsburg Hospital Inc	2716	Bloomsburg, PA	Private	26.1	500	8062
Carnegie Partners Inc	2717	New York, NY	Private	35.7	500	8051
Carolinas Physicians Network	2718	Charlotte, NC	Private	34.3	500	8011
Centracare Clinic	2719	Saint Cloud, MN	Private	28.7	500	8011
Central Baptist Childrens Hm	2720	Lake Villa, IL	Private	26.0	500	8361
Christian Care Centers Inc	2721	Mesquite, TX	Private	21.2	500	8051
Cigna Healthcare Of Ohio Inc	2722	Columbus, OH	Public Family Member	157.4	500	8011
Cleo Wallace Center Inc	2723	Denver, CO	Private	24.4	500	8063
Columbia Hospital Frankfort	2724	Frankfort, KY	Private	22.5	500	8062
Community Bio Resources	2725	Birmingham, AL	Private	80.0	500	8099
Community Hospital Inc	2726	Mayfield, KY	Public Family Member	28.4	500	8062
Community Hospital Williams	2727	Bryan, OH	Private	22.5	500	8062
Comprehensive Med Care Ltd	2728	Minneapolis, MN	Private	34.3	500	8011
Daughters Of Miriam Center	2729	Clifton, NJ	Private	22.8	500	8051
Dearborn County Hospital	2730	Lawrenceburg, IN	Private	34.2	500	8062

D&B COMPANY RANKINGS BY EMPLOYMENT

Company	Rank	Location	Type	Sales ($ mil.)	Employ-ment	Primary SIC
Denton Hospital, Inc.	2731	Denton, TX	Private	89.6	500	8062
Diagnostic Ctr Hospital Corp Texas	2732	Houston, TX	Private	42.4	500	8062
Diagnostic Health Services Inc	2733	Dallas, TX	Public	52.9	500	8099
Dianon Systems Inc	2734	Stratford, CT	Public	60.9	500	8071
Dorothy & David Schachne Institute	2735	Brooklyn, NY	Private	35.0	500	8059
East Cooper Community Hospital	2736	Mount Pleasant, SC	Public Family Member	22.5	500	8062
Edwards & Henson, Dds	2737	Kinston, NC	Private	21.0	500	8021
Equimed, Inc.	2738	State College, PA	Public	99.1	500	8099
Facey Medical Foundation Inc	2739	Mission Hills, CA	Private	59.1	500	8099
Fisher-Titus Medical Center	2740	Norwalk, OH	Private	39.7	500	8062
Florida Blood Services Inc	2741	Clearwater, FL	Private	31.7	500	8099
Frances Schervier Home & Hosp	2742	Bronx, NY	Private	33.2	500	8051
Genesis Health Inc	2743	Jacksonville, FL	Private	40.1	500	8069
Glengariff Corp	2744	Glen Cove, NY	Private	20.5	500	8051
Grady Memorial Hospital	2745	Chickasha, OK	Private	27.9	500	8062
Graham Hospital Association	2746	Canton, IL	Private	28.4	500	8062
Group Health Medical Assoc Pc	2747	Tucson, AZ	Private	39.3	500	8011
Gwinnett Community Hospital	2748	Snellville, GA	Public Family Member	22.5	500	8062
Health Assoc Of Ky, Inc	2749	Lexington, KY	Private	34.3	500	8011
Health Care Mid-Clmba	2750	The Dalles, OR	Private	32.8	500	8062
Healthcare Properties Inc	2751	Nashville, TN	Private	22.0	500	8059
Healthsouth Of Pittsburgh	2752	Monroeville, PA	Public Family Member	39.0	500	8093
Helian Health Group Inc	2753	Alpharetta, GA	Private	34.3	500	8011
Henrietta D Goodall Hospital	2754	Sanford, ME	Private	29.6	500	8062
Highlands Hospital Corporation	2755	Prestonsburg, KY	Private	22.5	500	8062
Hillcrest Hospital	2756	Pittsfield, MA	Private	22.5	500	8062
Homestead Hospital Inc	2757	Homestead, FL	Private	97.0	500	8062
Huntsville Memorial Hospital	2758	Huntsville, TX	Private	31.4	500	8062
J C Blair Memorial Hospital	2759	Huntingdon, PA	Private	25.5	500	8062
Jewish Child Care Assn Of Ny	2760	New York, NY	Private	44.6	500	8361
Kennewick Public Hospital Dst	2761	Kennewick, WA	Private	45.8	500	8062
Keystone Service Systems, Inc	2762	Harrisburg, PA	Private	21.9	500	8361
Kingman Hospital Inc	2763	Kingman, AZ	Private	47.4	500	8062
Lanier Professional Services	2764	Atlanta, GA	Public Family Member	20.0	500	8099
Life Mgt Ctr For Mh/Mr Svcs	2765	El Paso, TX	Private	20.3	500	8093
Lutheran Health Care Assn	2766	Saint Louis, MO	Private	19.8	500	8059
Madera Community Hospital Inc	2767	Madera, CA	Private	34.3	500	8062
Mankato Clinic, Ltd	2768	Mankato, MN	Private	34.3	500	8011
Marymount Medical Center, Inc	2769	London, KY	Private	28.9	500	8062
Medical Prof Assoc Ariz Pc	2770	Phoenix, AZ	Private	34.3	500	8011
Memorial Hospital Of Un Cnty	2771	Marysville, OH	Private	44.1	500	8062
Mercy Haverford Hospital	2772	Havertown, PA	Private	26.5	500	8062
Meris Laboratories, Inc	2773	San Jose, CA	Public	30.0	500	8071
Michigan Medical P.C.	2774	Grand Rapids, MI	Private	34.3	500	8011
Milford Hospital Inc	2775	Milford, CT	Private	45.3	500	8062
Montgomery Regional Hospital	2776	Blacksburg, VA	Public Family Member	48.9	500	8062
Morningside Hse Nursing Hm Co	2777	Bronx, NY	Private	35.9	500	8051
Muskegon General Hospital	2778	Muskegon, MI	Private	22.5	500	8062
Natchez Regional Medical Ctr	2779	Natchez, MS	Private	34.4	500	8062
Newaygo County Gen Hospital Assn	2780	Fremont, MI	Private	27.4	500	8062
Nhs National Health Services	2781	New York, NY	Private	34.3	500	8011
P A Cardinal Healthcare	2782	Raleigh, NC	Private	34.3	500	8011
Palisades Nursing Home Co Inc	2783	Bronx, NY	Private	25.3	500	8059
Paracelsus-Davis Hospital	2784	Layton, UT	Public Family Member	43.7	500	8062
Paragon Rehabilitation Inc	2785	Nashville, TN	Public Family Member	78.0	500	8049
Path Lab Inc	2786	Portsmouth, NH	Private	34.0	500	8071
Phycor Of Lafayette, Llc	2787	Lafayette, IN	Public Family Member	34.3	500	8011
Phycor Of Wichita Falls, Inc	2788	Wichita Falls, TX	Public Family Member	34.3	500	8011
Pine Rest Christian Hospital Assn	2789	Grand Rapids, MI	Private	29.3	500	8063
Pioneers Mem Healthcare Dst	2790	Brawley, CA	Private	33.3	500	8062
Prairie Lakes Health Care Sys	2791	Watertown, SD	Private	35.0	500	8062
Queens Long Island Medical Gr	2792	Hicksville, NY	Private	50.0	500	8011
Radiological Assc Sacto Md Gp	2793	Sacramento, CA	Private	24.0	500	8071
Rehoboth Mc Kinley Christian	2794	Gallup, NM	Private	38.0	500	8062
Sharon Hospital Incorporated	2795	Sharon, CT	Private	30.7	500	8062
Sierra Vista Community Hosp	2796	Sierra Vista, AZ	Private	30.7	500	8062
Silliker Laboratories Group	2797	Homewood, IL	Private	21.0	500	8071
Solaris Health System	2798	Edison, NJ	Private	361.6	500	8062
Sonoma Valley Healthcare Dst	2799	Sonoma, CA	Private	27.6	500	8062
South Bend Medical Foundation	2800	South Bend, IN	Private	43.7	500	8071

D&B COMPANY RANKINGS BY EMPLOYMENT

Company	Rank	Location	Type	Sales ($ mil.)	Employ-ment	Primary SIC
South County Hospital Inc	2801	Wakefield, RI	Private	46.7	500	8062
Southwest Medical Center	2802	Liberal, KS	Private	33.3	500	8062
St Catherine Hospital	2803	Garden City, KS	Private	23.3	500	8062
St Francis Central Hospital	2804	Pittsburgh, PA	Private	36.5	500	8062
St Jerome Hospital	2805	Batavia, NY	Private	22.9	500	8062
St Joseph Health System	2806	Tawas City, MI	Private	23.5	500	8062
St Marys Regional Health Sys	2807	Saint Marys, PA	Private	31.5	500	8062
St Petrsburg Sncoast Med Group	2808	Saint Petersburg, FL	Private	34.3	500	8011
Sutter Delta Medical	2809	Antioch, CA	Private	45.6	500	8062
Team Care Inc	2810	Atlanta, GA	Public Family Member	34.3	500	8011
Texas Scottish Rite Hosp	2811	Dallas, TX	Private	24.5	500	8069
Transylvania Community Hosp	2812	Brevard, NC	Private	22.6	500	8062
Tulare Local Hospital District	2813	Tulare, CA	Private	31.5	500	8062
Twin Cnty Rgional Health Clinics	2814	Galax, VA	Private	37.1	500	8011
Vail Clinic, Inc	2815	Vail, CO	Private	43.0	500	8062
Visiting Nurses Association	2816	Orlando, FL	Private	40.9	500	8082
Westchester General Hospital	2817	Miami, FL	Private	32.0	500	8062
Wharton Hospital Corporation	2818	Wharton, TX	Public Family Member	75.0	500	8062
Wood County Hospital Assn	2819	Bowling Green, OH	Private	22.5	500	8062
Community Living Options Inc	2820	Galesburg, IL	Private	21.3	498	8361
Chowan Hospital Inc	2821	Edenton, NC	Private	25.2	495	8062
Westerly Hospital	2822	Westerly, RI	Private	46.1	495	8062
Edwin Shaw Hospital	2823	Akron, OH	Private	24.1	492	8069
Bcn-Health Central	2824	Lansing, MI	Private	33.6	490	8011
Bethesda Lutheran Hospital	2825	Saint Paul, MN	Private	36.0	490	8062
Morristown Hamblen Hospital	2826	Morristown, TN	Private	38.8	490	8062
Newman Memorial County Hosp	2827	Emporia, KS	Private	30.2	490	8062
Covenant Retirement Communities	2828	Chicago, IL	Private	91.1	488	8059
Louisiana Extended Care Ctrs	2829	Ridgeland, MS	Private	36.7	487	8051
Lower Fla Keys Health Systems	2830	Key West, FL	Private	21.9	487	8062
Chester Cnty Hospital Nursing Ctr	2831	Chester, SC	Private	26.4	485	8062
Dunn Memorial Hospital	2832	Bedford, IN	Private	27.3	485	8062
Maine Veterans Home	2833	Augusta, ME	Private	20.7	485	8052
Mental Health Corp Of Denver	2834	Denver, CO	Private	30.0	485	8093
Northwest Medical Center, Inc	2835	Pompano Beach, FL	Public Family Member	29.0	485	8062
Strategic Health Services	2836	Charleston, WV	Private	37.8	485	8071
Institute Of Rehabiliataion	2837	Pittsburgh, PA	Private	32.3	484	8361
Springfield Clinic	2838	Springfield, IL	Private	33.1	482	8011
Upson Regional Medical Center	2839	Thomaston, GA	Private	21.6	482	8062
Sharp Temecula Valley	2840	Murrieta, CA	Private	34.5	481	8062
Whittier Hospital Med Ctr Inc	2841	Whittier, CA	Public Family Member	21.6	481	8062
Alice Hyde Hospital Assn	2842	Malone, NY	Private	23.9	480	8062
Amsterdam Memorial Hospital	2843	Amsterdam, NY	Private	30.0	480	8062
Canton-Potsdam Hospital	2844	Potsdam, NY	Private	29.6	480	8062
Columbia East Houston Med Ctr	2845	Houston, TX	Public Family Member	21.5	480	8062
Coshocton County Mem Hospital	2846	Coshocton, OH	Private	46.2	480	8062
George H Lanier Memorial Hosp	2847	Valley, AL	Private	28.8	480	8062
Hospital Corp Of Douglas	2848	Roseburg, OR	Public Family Member	21.5	480	8062
Huntington Medical Group Pc	2849	Huntington Station, NY	Private	23.2	480	8011
Manhattan Eye Ear Throat Hosp	2850	New York, NY	Private	39.9	480	8069
Mineral Area Osteopathic Hosp	2851	Farmington, MO	Private	27.7	480	8062
Pentagon City Hospital Inc	2852	Arlington, VA	Private	21.5	480	8062
River Oaks Hospital Inc	2853	Jackson, MS	Private	85.3	480	8062
Sheltering Arms Hospital (Inc)	2854	Richmond, VA	Private	20.3	480	8069
Valley Regional Hospital Inc	2855	Claremont, NH	Private	24.0	480	8062
Wing Memorial Hospital Corp	2856	Palmer, MA	Private	21.5	480	8062
Columbia Dunwoody Medical Ctr	2857	Atlanta, GA	Public Family Member	21.4	477	8062
Palms West Hospital Inc	2858	Loxahatchee, FL	Public Family Member	21.4	477	8062
Lindengrove Inc	2859	New Berlin, WI	Private	22.1	476	8051
Baptist Mem Hospital-Union Cy	2860	Union City, TN	Private	28.1	475	8062
Brooks Memorial Hospital	2861	Dunkirk, NY	Private	25.1	475	8062
Cumberland Medical Center Inc	2862	Fayetteville, NC	Public Family Member	69.0	475	8062
Deaton Specialty Hospital & Hm	2863	Baltimore, MD	Private	31.2	475	8051
Doctors Hospital A Ltd Partnr	2864	Springfield, IL	Private	32.8	475	8062
Golden Valley Memorial Hosp	2865	Clinton, MO	Private	21.3	475	8062
Guadalupe Medical Center Inc	2866	Carlsbad, NM	Public Family Member	21.3	475	8062
Portage Health System, Inc	2867	Hancock, MI	Private	23.0	475	8062
Presbyterian-Orthopedic Hosp	2868	Charlotte, NC	Private	95.0	475	8069
Regina Medical Center	2869	Hastings, MN	Private	20.5	475	8062
Rhd Memorial Medical Center	2870	Dallas, TX	Private	21.3	475	8062

D&B COMPANY RANKINGS BY EMPLOYMENT

Company	Rank	Location	Type	Sales ($ mil.)	Employ-ment	Primary SIC
Valdese General Hospital Inc	2871	Valdese, NC	Private	27.7	475	8062
Whidbey General Hospital Pub	2872	Coupeville, WA	Private	26.9	475	8062
Hospital Corp Of Utah Inc	2873	Nashville, TN	Public Family Member	21.3	474	8062
Healthsouth Rehabiltiation	2874	Toms River, NJ	Public Family Member	23.0	471	8069
Cooper Clinic Pa	2875	Fort Smith, AR	Private	54.2	470	8011
Diagnostic Laboratory Services	2876	Honolulu, HI	Private	38.9	470	8071
Grant County Pub Hospital Dst No 1	2877	Moses Lake, WA	Private	27.7	470	8062
Institutes Of Applied Human Dev.	2878	Bronx, NY	Private	24.0	470	8361
Colorado Sprng Health Prtners Pc	2879	Colorado Springs, CO	Private	29.0	468	8011
Baptist Memorial Hospital	2880	Blytheville, AR	Private	20.9	467	8062
Institute For Rehabilitation	2881	Houston, TX	Private	24.4	466	8062
Southside Community Hospital Assn	2882	Farmville, VA	Private	27.9	465	8062
St Cabrini Nursing Home Inc	2883	Dobbs Ferry, NY	Private	26.2	464	8051
Campbell County Hospital Dst	2884	Gillette, WY	Private	32.9	463	8062
Lockport Memorial Hospital	2885	Lockport, NY	Private	35.3	463	8062
Mary Rutan Hospital	2886	Bellefontaine, OH	Private	37.7	463	8062
Bradford Group, The, Inc	2887	Birmingham, AL	Private	22.6	462	8069
Levindale Hebrew Geriatric Ctr	2888	Baltimore, MD	Private	28.0	461	8069
Rehabilitation Hospital Of Ind	2889	Indianapolis, IN	Private	24.0	461	8062
Antietam Health Services Inc	2890	Hagerstown, MD	Private	31.8	460	8071
Baylor Med Center-Ellis Cnty	2891	Waxahachie, TX	Private	42.2	460	8062
Carson City Hospital	2892	Carson City, MI	Private	27.0	460	8062
Community Gen Hospital	2893	Thomasville, NC	Private	26.0	460	8062
Desert Valley Medical Group	2894	Victorville, CA	Private	40.0	460	8011
Harbor Behavioral Health	2895	New Port Richey, FL	Private	19.8	460	8093
Joint Township Dst Mem Hosp	2896	Saint Marys, OH	Private	31.9	460	8062
King's Daughters Hospital	2897	Brookhaven, MS	Private	29.8	460	8062
Marcus J Lawrence Medical Ctr	2898	Cottonwood, AZ	Private	33.4	460	8062
McKenna Memorial Hospital	2899	New Braunfels, TX	Private	37.0	460	8062
Roseland Community Hospital Assn	2900	Chicago, IL	Private	20.6	460	8062
St James Community Hospital	2901	Butte, MT	Private	20.6	460	8062
Valley Hospital Association	2902	Palmer, AK	Private	20.6	460	8062
Ohio Valley General Hospital	2903	Mckees Rocks, PA	Private	42.4	459	8062
Taylor County Hospital	2904	Campbellsville, KY	Private	27.8	459	8062
Jackson County Health Care Auth	2905	Scottsboro, AL	Private	40.4	458	8062
Legacy Meridian Park Hospital	2906	Tualatin, OR	Private	55.7	458	8062
Woodlawn Hospital	2907	Rochester, IN	Private	21.2	458	8062
Dominican Sisters Of Ontario	2908	Ontario, OR	Private	31.3	456	8062
Genesee Memorial Hospital Assn	2909	Batavia, NY	Private	25.7	456	8062
Stouder Memorial Hospital Assn	2910	Troy, OH	Private	50.3	456	8062
Magee Rehabilitation Hospital	2911	Philadelphia, PA	Private	26.8	455	8069
Princeton Hospital	2912	Orlando, FL	Private	32.1	455	8062
Republic Health Corp Of Rockwall	2913	Rowlett, TX	Public Family Member	20.4	455	8062
Sunbury Community Hospital	2914	Sunbury, PA	Private	21.7	455	8062
West Valley Medical Center Inc	2915	Caldwell, ID	Public Family Member	38.2	455	8062
Hospital Auth Of Habersham Cnty	2916	Demorest, GA	Private	26.9	453	8062
Knox Community Hospital	2917	Mount Vernon, OH	Private	39.3	453	8062
Sauk Prairie Memorial Hospital	2918	Prairie Du Sac, WI	Private	24.9	451	8062
Baylor Inst For Rhabilitation	2919	Dallas, TX	Private	25.5	450	8361
Baylor Med Ctr At Grapevine	2920	Grapevine, TX	Private	41.1	450	8062
Brea Development Company Ltd	2921	Brea, CA	Private	28.9	450	8062
Broken Arrow Medical Center	2922	Broken Arrow, OK	Private	21.5	450	8062
Carolina Mlt-Specialty Assoc P A	2923	Greenville, SC	Private	36.8	450	8011
Cary Medical Center	2924	Caribou, ME	Private	20.1	450	8062
Central California Foundation For	2925	Delano, CA	Private	30.2	450	8062
Chico Community Hospital Inc	2926	Chico, CA	Public Family Member	20.1	450	8062
Childrens Seashore House Inc	2927	Philadelphia, PA	Private	40.8	450	8361
Community Health Network, Inc	2928	Berlin, WI	Private	37.8	450	8062
East Boston Neighborhood	2929	Boston, MA	Private	52.9	450	8011
Eyexam 2000 Of California, Inc	2930	Burlingame, CA	Private	22.5	450	8042
Familiesfirst Inc	2931	Davis, CA	Private	27.2	450	8361
Family Healthcare Associates	2932	Arlington, TX	Private	30.9	450	8011
First Physcn Care Of Tampa Bay	2933	Tampa, FL	Private	30.9	450	8011
Florida Blood Services Inc	2934	Tampa, FL	Private	30.5	450	8099
Franciscan Health Systems	2935	Warwick, NY	Private	20.1	450	8062
Frederick C Smith Clinic Inc	2936	Marion, OH	Private	30.9	450	8011
Galen Of Arizona, Inc.	2937	Phoenix, AZ	Public Family Member	45.1	450	8011
General Medical Services Corp	2938	Kingston, PA	Private	45.2	450	8011
Herrick Memorial Hospital	2939	Tecumseh, MI	Private	23.9	450	8062
Holland Home	2940	Grand Rapids, MI	Private	23.4	450	8361

D&B COMPANY RANKINGS BY EMPLOYMENT

Company	Rank	Location	Type	Sales ($ mil.)	Employment	Primary SIC
Hospice Family Care, Inc.	2941	Mesa, AZ	Private	25.7	450	8082
Hospital For Sick Children	2942	Washington, DC	Private	38.7	450	8069
Iberia General Hospital & Med Ctr	2943	New Iberia, LA	Private	35.3	450	8062
Kapiolani Med Ctr At Pali Mmi	2944	Aiea, HI	Private	30.9	450	8011
Lakeview Memorial Hospital Assn	2945	Stillwater, MN	Private	29.9	450	8062
Lifesource Blood Services	2946	Glenview, IL	Private	33.0	450	8099
Lincoln Community Medical Corp	2947	Houston, TX	Public Family Member	20.1	450	8062
Los Angeles Doctors Hospital	2948	Los Angeles, CA	Private	30.1	450	8062
Marian Community Hospital	2949	Carbondale, PA	Private	26.4	450	8062
Marshall Medical Center North	2950	Guntersville, AL	Private	26.1	450	8062
Masonic Homes Of California	2951	San Francisco, CA	Private	54.8	450	8361
Memorial Medical Ctr Of W Mich	2952	Ludington, MI	Private	30.7	450	8062
Memorial Sisters Of Charity	2953	Houston, TX	Private	30.9	450	8011
Mercy Med Ctr Of Williston	2954	Williston, ND	Private	28.2	450	8062
Mesa General Hospital Med Ctr	2955	Mesa, AZ	Public Family Member	100.0	450	8062
Methodist Medical Group Inc	2956	Lubbock, TX	Private	30.9	450	8011
Mobile Technology Inc	2957	Los Angeles, CA	Public Family Member	69.0	450	8099
Morehouse General Hospital	2958	Bastrop, LA	Private	29.1	450	8062
Mountain View Hospital, Inc	2959	Payson, UT	Public Family Member	20.1	450	8062
Muhlenberg Community Hospital	2960	Greenville, KY	Private	21.1	450	8062
Nashoba Community Hospital Corp	2961	Ayer, MA	Private	22.5	450	8062
Neomedica Inc.	2962	Chicago, IL	Public Family Member	48.9	450	8092
Neuro-Rehab Associates Inc	2963	Salem, NH	Private	50.0	450	8049
Northeast Valley Health Corp	2964	San Fernando, CA	Private	21.2	450	8011
Novaeon, Inc	2965	Paoli, PA	Private	30.0	450	8093
Nursefinders Inc	2966	Arlington, TX	Private	133.5	450	8082
Odyssey Healthcare Inc	2967	Dallas, TX	Private	31.0	450	8069
Okaloosa Hospital, Inc	2968	Niceville, FL	Public Family Member	27.0	450	8062
Oklahoma Blood Institute Inc	2969	Oklahoma City, OK	Private	27.7	450	8099
Optimum Rehabilitation Inc	2970	Boston, MA	Private	30.0	450	8093
Park Lane Med Ctr Kans Cy Inc	2971	Kansas City, MO	Private	20.1	450	8062
Pulaski Community Hospital	2972	Pulaski, VA	Public Family Member	27.7	450	8062
Sansum Medical Clinic Inc	2973	Santa Barbara, CA	Private	36.6	450	8011
Sharp Mission Park Corp	2974	Oceanside, CA	Private	57.3	450	8011
Sheehan Memorial Hospital	2975	Buffalo, NY	Private	37.0	450	8062
Sherman Oaks Health System	2976	Sherman Oaks, CA	Private	44.4	450	8062
St Josephs Hospital & Health Ctr	2977	Dickinson, ND	Private	22.7	450	8062
St Mary's Healthcare Center	2978	Pierre, SD	Private	21.0	450	8062
St Marys Hospital For Children	2979	Bayside, NY	Private	22.0	450	8069
Symmes Hospital & Medical Ctr	2980	Arlington, MA	Private	37.6	450	8062
Tenet Healthsystem Hospitals	2981	Crystal River, FL	Public Family Member	41.1	450	8062
Teton County Hospital Dst	2982	Jackson, WY	Private	29.9	450	8062
Tsi Corp	2983	Milford, MA	Public Family Member	32.4	450	8071
Urology Healthcare Group Inc	2984	Brentwood, TN	Private	63.0	450	8011
Verdugo Hills Hospital	2985	Glendale, CA	Private	45.0	450	8062
Wahiawa Hospital Association	2986	Wahiawa, HI	Private	20.1	450	8062
Wartburg	2987	Mount Vernon, NY	Private	23.2	450	8051
Waynesboro Hospital	2988	Waynesboro, PA	Private	26.0	450	8062
Wellington Regional Med Ctr	2989	West Palm Beach, FL	Public Family Member	20.1	450	8062
Glen Mills Schools	2990	Concordville, PA	Private	38.0	448	8361
Mid Columbia Medical Center	2991	The Dalles, OR	Private	26.3	447	8062
Mission Bay Memorial Hospital	2992	San Diego, CA	Public Family Member	58.9	447	8062
St Joseph's Rgnl Mdcl Ctr N Ok	2993	Ponca City, OK	Private	22.1	446	8062
Apalachee Center For HumanSvcs	2994	Tallahassee, FL	Private	20.1	443	8063
Kent Community Hospital Complex	2995	Grand Rapids, MI	Private	21.5	441	8069
Door County Memorial Hospital	2996	Sturgeon Bay, WI	Private	23.2	440	8062
Lexington Memorial Hospital	2997	Lexington, NC	Private	30.4	440	8062
Mid-Island Hospital, Inc	2998	Bethpage, NY	Private	19.7	440	8062
Q P & S Clinic Sc	2999	Quincy, IL	Private	43.8	440	8011
Southampton Memorial Hospital	3000	Franklin, VA	Private	31.5	440	8062
St Dominic's Home	3001	Blauvelt, NY	Private	23.8	440	8361
Sun City Hospital Inc	3002	Ruskin, FL	Public Family Member	19.7	440	8062
Spencer Municipal Hospital	3003	Spencer, IA	Private	23.3	439	8062
Crittenden Hospital Assn	3004	West Memphis, AR	Private	39.3	436	8062
Tri-City Health Centre, Inc	3005	Dallas, TX	Private	30.1	436	8062
Milton Hospital Inc	3006	Milton, MA	Private	36.2	435	8062
Central Florida Bloodbank Inc	3007	Orlando, FL	Private	27.0	430	8099
Christie Clinic Association	3008	Champaign, IL	Public Family Member	29.5	430	8011
Greensville Memorial Hospital	3009	Emporia, VA	Private	23.0	430	8062
Idexx Veterinary Services Inc	3010	West Sacramento, CA	Public Family Member	20.7	430	8071

D&B COMPANY RANKINGS BY EMPLOYMENT

Company	Rank	Location	Type	Sales ($ mil.)	Employ-ment	Primary SIC
Memorial Hospital Of Gardena	3011	Gardena, CA	Public Family Member	28.1	430	8062
Midamerica Healthcare, Inc	3012	Shawnee, OK	Private	28.0	430	8062
Montrose Memorial Hospital	3013	Montrose, CO	Private	26.6	430	8062
Navapache Health Care Assn	3014	Show Low, AZ	Private	30.3	430	8062
Oktibbeha County Hospital	3015	Starkville, MS	Private	28.4	430	8062
Redington-Fairview Gen Hosp	3016	Skowhegan, ME	Private	24.9	430	8062
San Benito Health Care Dst	3017	Hollister, CA	Private	24.5	430	8062
Santa Marta Hospital Inc	3018	Los Angeles, CA	Private	29.5	430	8062
Shenandoah Memorial Hospital	3019	Woodstock, VA	Private	21.5	430	8062
Southboro Medical Group Inc	3020	Southborough, MA	Private	28.1	430	8011
St Margaret's Hospital	3021	Spring Valley, IL	Private	32.6	430	8062
Transworld Healthcare Inc	3022	New York, NY	Public	160.0	430	8082
Watertown Memorial Hospital Assn	3023	Watertown, WI	Private	26.5	430	8062
Piedmont Area Mntl Health	3024	Concord, NC	Private	26.6	429	8093
Trustees Of Noble Hospital Inc	3025	Westfield, MA	Private	29.1	429	8062
Accord Medical Management	3026	San Antonio, TX	Private	38.3	425	8062
Albany County Hospital Dst	3027	Laramie, WY	Private	27.3	425	8062
Ammons-Springmoor Associates	3028	Raleigh, NC	Private	24.0	425	8059
Arkansas Valley Regional Med Ctr	3029	La Junta, CO	Private	23.4	425	8062
Bradley Mem Hospital & Health Ctr	3030	Southington, CT	Private	25.1	425	8062
De Kalb Memorial Hospital Inc	3031	Auburn, IN	Private	23.5	425	8062
Grove Hill Medical Center Pc	3032	New Britain, CT	Private	45.8	425	8093
Harriman City Hospital	3033	Harriman, TN	Private	23.8	425	8062
Healthsource Health Plans Inc	3034	Raleigh, NC	Private	341.0	425	8011
Julia Rackley Perry Mem Hosp	3035	Princeton, IL	Private	22.9	425	8062
Keokuk Area Hospital	3036	Keokuk, IA	Private	24.3	425	8062
King's Daughters Hospital Assn	3037	Temple, TX	Private	23.4	425	8062
Murphy Medical Center	3038	Murphy, NC	Private	21.0	425	8062
Oak Valley Hospital District	3039	Oakdale, CA	Private	24.7	425	8062
Rosewood Medical Center Inc	3040	Houston, TX	Public Family Member	51.6	425	8062
Santa Teresita Hospital	3041	Duarte, CA	Private	22.4	425	8062
South Baldwin County Healthcar	3042	Foley, AL	Private	24.4	425	8062
Springer Clinic, Inc	3043	Tulsa, OK	Private	60.0	425	8011
St Anthony Regional Hospital	3044	Carroll, IA	Private	21.3	425	8062
Canonsburg General Hospital	3045	Canonsburg, PA	Private	27.6	423	8062
Polyclinic	3046	Seattle, WA	Private	46.6	423	8011
Genesis Rehabilitation Hosp	3047	Jacksonville, FL	Private	31.3	422	8063
Under 21 Inc	3048	New York, NY	Private	19.9	422	8361
Bethesda Healthcare Inc	3049	Cincinnati, OH	Private	28.9	421	8011
Baptist Mem Hspital-Union Cnty	3050	New Albany, MS	Private	26.8	420	8062
Bio-Reference Laboratories Inc	3051	Elmwood Park, NJ	Public	38.7	420	8071
Butterwrth Cntnuing Care Group	3052	Grand Rapids, MI	Private	25.8	420	8051
Chesapeake Hospital Corp	3053	Kilmarnock, VA	Private	24.2	420	8062
Dorchester General Hospital	3054	Cambridge, MD	Private	26.2	420	8062
Fayette Cnty Hospital Nursing Hm	3055	Fayette, AL	Private	20.3	420	8062
Florida Hospital/Fish Memorial	3056	Orange City, FL	Private	40.0	420	8062
Gilmore Memorial Hospital	3057	Amory, MS	Private	21.3	420	8062
International Philanthropic Ho	3058	Granada Hills, CA	Private	34.5	420	8062
Lee County Community Hospital	3059	Pennington Gap, VA	Private	30.8	420	8062
Meadow Regional Medical Center	3060	Vidalia, GA	Private	29.7	420	8062
Moss Beach Homes, Inc	3061	Daly City, CA	Private	29.2	420	8361
Rehabilitation Hsptl Pacific	3062	Honolulu, HI	Private	25.8	420	8069
Triad Laboratory Alliance, Llc	3063	Greensboro, NC	Private	20.2	420	8071
Arkansas Methodist Hospital	3064	Paragould, AR	Private	25.7	419	8062
New Milford Hospital Inc	3065	New Milford, CT	Private	38.6	415	8062
Palo Pinto General Hospital	3066	Mineral Wells, TX	Private	22.8	414	8062
Stephens County Hospital Auth	3067	Toccoa, GA	Private	29.2	414	8062
Baptist Healthcare Affliates Inc	3068	Louisville, KY	Private	20.3	413	8062
Mercer Cnty Jnt Twnshp	3069	Coldwater, OH	Private	21.9	412	8062
Doctors Hospital Shreveport Inc	3070	Shreveport, LA	Public Family Member	20.0	411	8069
Lock Haven Hospital	3071	Lock Haven, PA	Private	24.3	410	8062
Memorial Hospital Sheridan Cnty	3072	Sheridan, WY	Private	23.8	410	8062
Molina Medical Center, Inc	3073	Long Beach, CA	Private	116.2	410	8011
Northcrest Medical Center	3074	Springfield, TN	Private	34.4	410	8062
Quad Cities Pathologist Group	3075	Davenport, IA	Private	19.7	410	8071
Rochester Gen Long Term Care	3076	Webster, NY	Private	20.0	410	8051
Youngstown Ostpthic Hospital Assn	3077	Youngstown, OH	Private	27.0	409	8062
Greenville Health Corporation	3078	Greenville, SC	Private	39.9	407	8011
Saint Elizabeth Community Hosp	3079	Red Bluff, CA	Private	34.9	406	8062
Compunet Clinical Laboratories	3080	Dayton, OH	Private	30.1	405	8071

D&B COMPANY RANKINGS BY EMPLOYMENT

Company	Rank	Location	Type	Sales ($ mil.)	Employ-ment	Primary SIC
Hutchinson Clinic P A	3081	Hutchinson, KS	Private	35.1	405	8011
Parker County Hospital Dst	3082	Weatherford, TX	Private	30.4	405	8062
Bradley Emma Pendleton Hosp	3083	Riverside, RI	Private	24.0	403	8063
Gillette Chld Spclty Healthcare	3084	Saint Paul, MN	Private	30.6	403	8069
Gurwin, Rosalind And Joseph Je	3085	Commack, NY	Private	30.6	402	8059
Labette County Medical Center	3086	Parsons, KS	Private	30.4	402	8062
Vna Of Rhode Island Inc	3087	Providence, RI	Private	26.2	401	8082
Adams County Memorial Hospital	3088	Decatur, IN	Private	27.6	400	8062
Alta Med	3089	Los Angeles, CA	Private	24.0	400	8099
Always Caring Home Care Svcs	3090	El Paso, TX	Private	21.0	400	8082
Bellflower Medical Center	3091	Bellflower, CA	Private	58.9	400	8011
Belmont Center Comp Treatment	3092	Philadelphia, PA	Private	23.0	400	8063
Blood Centers Of Pacific	3093	San Francisco, CA	Private	29.7	400	8099
Blood Ctr Of Southeastern Wi Inc	3094	Milwaukee, WI	Private	45.2	400	8099
Bon Secours-Stuart Circle Hosp	3095	Richmond, VA	Private	36.0	400	8062
Brigham Med Group Foundation	3096	Brookline, MA	Private	27.6	400	8093
Buchanan General Hospital	3097	Grundy, VA	Private	27.2	400	8062
C M Healthcare Resources Inc	3098	Deerfield, IL	Private	20.4	400	8082
Calvert Memorial Hospital	3099	Prince Frederick, MD	Private	37.8	400	8062
Chippewa County War Mem Hosp	3100	Sault Sainte Marie, MI	Private	25.2	400	8062
Circles Of Care Inc	3101	Melbourne, FL	Private	19.8	400	8063
Cleveland Neighborhood Health	3102	Cleveland, OH	Private	26.1	400	8099
Clinical Laboratories Of Hawaii	3103	Hilo, HI	Private	51.3	400	8071
Collom & Carney Clinic Assn	3104	Texarkana, TX	Private	30.1	400	8011
Community Memorial Hospital	3105	Cheboygan, MI	Private	23.4	400	8062
Comprehensive Medical Imaging	3106	Westlake Village, CA	Public Family Member	45.0	400	8071
Dedham Medical Associates Inc	3107	Dedham, MA	Private	27.4	400	8011
Diabetes Treatment Ctrs Of America	3108	Nashville, TN	Public Family Member	27.4	400	8011
Du Page Dialysis, Ltd.	3109	Oak Park, IL	Private	22.9	400	8092
Executive Health Group, Md Pc	3110	New York, NY	Private	27.4	400	8011
Fairview Redwing Health Svcs	3111	Red Wing, MN	Private	22.8	400	8062
Family Planning Assoc Med Group	3112	Long Beach, CA	Private	27.4	400	8011
Foothill Memorial Hospital	3113	Glendora, CA	Private	25.5	400	8062
Franc Childr Hosp	3114	Boston, MA	Private	22.7	400	8069
Good Shepherd Services	3115	New York, NY	Private	20.3	400	8361
Health Midwest Ventures Group	3116	Kansas City, MO	Private	27.4	400	8011
Health Resources Corp	3117	Santa Ana, CA	Public Family Member	32.1	400	8062
Health Tech Affiliates Inc	3118	Memphis, TN	Private	29.4	400	8011
Healthplus Corporation	3119	Houston, TX	Private	50.0	400	8082
Healthsouth Of Ft Lauderdale	3120	Fort Lauderdale, FL	Public Family Member	28.0	400	8069
Healthwise Of America Inc	3121	Nashville, TN	Public Family Member	208.7	400	8011
Hill Country Memorial Hosp	3122	Fredericksburg, TX	Private	25.6	400	8062
Holzer Clinic Inc	3123	Gallipolis, OH	Private	40.0	400	8011
Hopkins County Hospital Dst	3124	Sulphur Springs, TX	Private	23.9	400	8062
Hospice Hillsborough Inc	3125	Tampa, FL	Private	20.1	400	8093
Hospital Affliates Of Alhambra	3126	Alhambra, CA	Private	29.3	400	8062
Hospital Service District No 2	3127	Morgan City, LA	Private	24.9	400	8062
Huron Regional Medical Center	3128	Huron, SD	Private	30.0	400	8062
Integrated Health Assoc Pc	3129	Ann Arbor, MI	Private	27.4	400	8011
Jackson Brook Institute	3130	South Portland, ME	Private	24.9	400	8063
Jonesboro Health Services Inc	3131	Jonesboro, AR	Public Family Member	65.0	400	8062
Joslin Diabetes Center Inc	3132	Boston, MA	Private	43.7	400	8011
Kings View	3133	Reedley, CA	Private	22.8	400	8093
Kingsboro Medical Group P C	3134	Brooklyn, NY	Private	27.4	400	8011
Larkin Community Hospital Inc	3135	Miami, FL	Private	50.0	400	8062
Lewis County General Hospital	3136	Lowville, NY	Private	21.9	400	8062
Lutheran Center For The Aging	3137	Smithtown, NY	Private	25.5	400	8051
Margaret Mary Community Hosp	3138	Batesville, IN	Private	21.7	400	8062
Medical Corporation America	3139	Nashville, TN	Public Family Member	27.4	400	8011
Memorial Clinic Ltd P.S.	3140	Olympia, WA	Private	44.0	400	8011
Memorial Hospital And Manor	3141	Bainbridge, GA	Private	22.4	400	8062
Northern Dutchess Hospital	3142	Rhinebeck, NY	Private	20.5	400	8062
Oregon Medical Group Pc	3143	Eugene, OR	Private	27.4	400	8011
Otero County Hospital Assn	3144	Alamogordo, NM	Private	30.0	400	8062
Pine Street Inn Inc	3145	Boston, MA	Private	26.6	400	8361
Presbyterian Healthcare Assoc	3146	Charlotte, NC	Private	27.4	400	8011
Rcg Mississippi, Inc	3147	Jackson, MS	Public Family Member	22.9	400	8092
Response Oncology Inc	3148	Memphis, TN	Public	101.9	400	8093
Revival Home Health Care Inc	3149	Brooklyn, NY	Private	20.1	400	8082
Rice Clinic S C, The	3150	Stevens Point, WI	Private	27.4	400	8011

D&B COMPANY RANKINGS BY EMPLOYMENT

Company	Rank	Location	Type	Sales ($ mil.)	Employment	Primary SIC
River District Hospital	3151	East China, MI	Private	23.6	400	8062
S C Cal	3152	Palestine, TX	Public Family Member	32.3	400	8062
Satellite Dialysis Centers	3153	Redwood City, CA	Private	42.7	400	8092
Shannon Clinic	3154	San Angelo, TX	Private	27.4	400	8011
Sisters Of Charity Health Care	3155	Staten Island, NY	Private	33.7	400	8051
Southern Chester Cnty Med Ctr	3156	West Grove, PA	Private	26.2	400	8062
Southern Management Services	3157	Largo, FL	Private	51.5	400	8051
Springmoor Inc	3158	Raleigh, NC	Private	22.5	400	8059
St. Marys Dean Ventures Inc	3159	Madison, WI	Private	40.0	400	8011
Suburban Heights Med Ctr Sc	3160	Chicago Heights, IL	Private	27.4	400	8011
Sullivan Diagnstc Trtmnt Ctr	3161	Harris, NY	Private	20.7	400	8361
Summersville Memorial Hosp	3162	Summersville, WV	Private	20.3	400	8062
Sutter Coast Hospital	3163	Crescent City, CA	Private	32.1	400	8062
Sutter North Med Foundation	3164	Marysville, CA	Private	62.4	400	8011
Tracy Sutter Community Mem Hosp	3165	Tracy, CA	Private	21.1	400	8062
University Physicians Surgeons	3166	Huntington, WV	Private	28.6	400	8011
Visiting Nurses Association	3167	Philadelphia, PA	Private	43.6	400	8082
Wallace Thomson Hospital	3168	Union, SC	Private	23.8	400	8062
Woods Memorial Hospital Dst	3169	Etowah, TN	Private	19.9	400	8062
Hospital Corporation Tennessee	3170	Martin, TN	Public Family Member	26.3	397	8062
Mckendree Village Inc	3171	Hermitage, TN	Private	21.5	395	8361
Bedford Regional Medical Ctr	3172	Bedford, IN	Private	24.5	390	8062
Community Health Ctr Of Branch	3173	Coldwater, MI	Private	36.4	390	8062
Great Falls Clinic Llp	3174	Great Falls, MT	Private	36.8	390	8011
Morgan County Memorial Hosp	3175	Martinsville, IN	Private	25.7	390	8062
Orthodontic Centers Of America	3176	Ponte Vedra Beach, FL	Public	117.3	390	8021
Warren Clinic Inc	3177	Tulsa, OK	Private	29.1	390	8011
American Legion Hospital	3178	Crowley, LA	Private	25.0	389	8062
Northwestern Medical Center	3179	Saint Albans, VT	Private	24.8	388	8062
Carbon Schuylkill Comm Htlh	3180	Coaldale, PA	Private	23.1	386	8062
Clarion Hospital	3181	Clarion, PA	Private	26.5	385	8062
Northern Montana Hospital	3182	Havre, MT	Private	27.4	385	8062
Johnson Betsy Memorial Hosp	3183	Dunn, NC	Private	25.8	384	8062
Mather Foundation, The	3184	Evanston, IL	Private	56.4	381	8059
Citizens Bmc	3185	Talladega, AL	Private	20.0	380	8062
Coffeyville Regl Med Ctr Fndtn	3186	Coffeyville, KS	Private	20.4	380	8062
Fairview Clinics	3187	Minneapolis, MN	Private	26.0	380	8011
Grande Ronde Hospital Inc	3188	La Grande, OR	Private	22.6	380	8062
Greater Staten Island Med Grp	3189	Staten Island, NY	Private	26.0	380	8011
Laurens County Health Care Sys	3190	Clinton, SC	Private	29.3	380	8062
Mason City Clinic, P C	3191	Mason City, IA	Private	37.0	380	8011
Memorial Hospital Inc	3192	Wellsville, NY	Private	20.7	380	8062
Nasser Smith Pinkerton Cardiology	3193	Indianapolis, IN	Private	26.0	380	8011
Newton Healthcare Corporation	3194	Newton, KS	Private	20.6	380	8062
Su-Pra Enterprises Inc	3195	Franklin, MI	Private	20.6	380	8082
Wayne Memorial Hospital	3196	Jesup, GA	Private	24.9	380	8062
Moorings, Incorporated	3197	Naples, FL	Private	19.9	376	8361
Orthopaedic Hospital	3198	Los Angeles, CA	Private	20.2	376	8069
Careselect Group Inc	3199	Dallas, TX	Private	20.8	375	8099
Casey Family Program, The	3200	Seattle, WA	Private	255.0	375	8361
Central Brooklyn Med Group Pc	3201	Brooklyn, NY	Private	25.7	375	8011
Grinnell Regional Medical Ctr	3202	Grinnell, IA	Private	21.0	375	8062
Hilton Head Health System, Lp	3203	Hilton Head Island, SC	Private	83.0	375	8062
Infirmary Medical Clinic Pc	3204	Mobile, AL	Private	25.7	375	8011
Jefferson Thmas Univ Hospitals	3205	Philadelphia, PA	Private	514.9	375	8062
New York Community Hospital	3206	Brooklyn, NY	Private	36.0	375	8062
Prime Care Services Inc	3207	Franklin, MI	Private	20.3	375	8082
Soldiers & Sailors Mem Hosp	3208	Wellsboro, PA	Private	22.1	375	8062
St Francis Regional Med Ctr	3209	Shakopee, MN	Private	27.9	375	8062
United Memorial Hospital Assn	3210	Greenville, MI	Private	24.5	375	8062
Wabash County Hospital	3211	Wabash, IN	Private	23.2	375	8062
West Park Hospital District	3212	Cody, WY	Private	23.6	375	8062
Maria Parham Hospital Assn	3213	Henderson, NC	Private	31.4	373	8062
Adventist Health Systems Ga	3214	Calhoun, GA	Private	43.8	371	8062
Central Ind Regional Blood Ctr	3215	Indianapolis, IN	Private	24.9	370	8099
Clinical Labs Of Colorado Llc	3216	Denver, CO	Private	29.0	370	8071
Healthsouth Of San Antonio	3217	San Antonio, TX	Public Family Member	25.0	370	8069
Jewish Mem Hospital Rhblttion Ctr	3218	Boston, MA	Private	50.0	370	8069
Mid Coast Hospital	3219	Brunswick, ME	Private	35.5	370	8062
Nexthealth Inc	3220	Tucson, AZ	Public	20.7	370	8069

D&B COMPANY RANKINGS BY EMPLOYMENT

Company	Rank	Location	Type	Sales ($ mil.)	Employ-ment	Primary SIC
Spectera Inc	3221	Baltimore, MD	Private	56.2	370	8011
St Francis Hospital Thrd Ord (Inc)	3222	Litchfield, IL	Private	20.7	370	8062
St Mary's Hospital Inc	3223	Norton, VA	Private	19.9	370	8062
Womens And Childrens Hospital Inc	3224	Lafayette, LA	Public Family Member	23.0	370	8069
Ellwood City Hospital	3225	Ellwood City, PA	Private	22.2	368	8062
Sheltering Arm Hospital Fnd Inc	3226	Athens, OH	Private	28.4	368	8062
Mercy Medical Development	3227	Miami, FL	Private	150.8	365	8093
Hernando Healthcare Inc	3228	Brooksville, FL	Private	52.6	364	8062
Polly Ryon Hospital Authority	3229	Richmond, TX	Private	34.8	363	8062
Quality Care & Rehab Inc	3230	Baton Rouge, LA	Private	30.0	362	8093
Jackson County Hospital Inc	3231	Marianna, FL	Private	28.0	361	8062
Choctaw Nation Health Services	3232	Talihina, OK	Private	26.0	360	8062
Grayson County Hospital	3233	Leitchfield, KY	Private	20.2	360	8062
La Palma Hospital Medical Ctr	3234	La Palma, CA	Private	38.9	360	8062
Mercy Hospital Of Tiffin Ohio	3235	Tiffin, OH	Private	25.4	360	8062
Muscatine General Hospital	3236	Muscatine, IA	Private	21.7	360	8062
Queens Blvd Extnded Care Fclty	3237	Woodside, NY	Private	24.0	360	8051
Russell Hospital Corp	3238	Alexander City, AL	Private	31.2	360	8062
Sutter Amador Hospital	3239	Jackson, CA	Private	25.9	360	8062
Island Hospital	3240	Anacortes, WA	Private	23.9	359	8062
Baptist Hospital Orange	3241	Orange, TX	Private	33.9	358	8062
Monsour Medical Center	3242	Jeannette, PA	Private	20.2	358	8062
Lakeview Community Hospital Auth	3243	Paw Paw, MI	Private	26.2	357	8062
West Vrgnia Rhblttion Hospital Inc	3244	Morgantown, WV	Public Family Member	21.9	357	8361
Garrett County Memorial Hosp	3245	Oakland, MD	Private	23.9	356	8062
Medina Memorial Hospital Inc	3246	Medina, NY	Private	22.7	355	8062
Pineville Community Hospital Assn	3247	Pineville, KY	Private	19.8	355	8062
Southwestern Ohio Seniors Svcs	3248	Cincinnati, OH	Private	23.1	355	8052
Walls Regional Hospital	3249	Cleburne, TX	Private	31.9	355	8062
Van Wert County Hospital Assn	3250	Van Wert, OH	Private	21.9	354	8062
East Texas Med Center-Athens	3251	Athens, TX	Private	42.1	353	8062
Dynacare Lab Pathology Llc	3252	Seattle, WA	Private	30.0	352	8071
Commonwealth Health Corp	3253	Bowling Green, KY	Private	125.5	351	8062
Foundation Health A South	3254	Fort Lauderdale, FL	Private	182.1	351	8011
Md Health Plan Inc	3255	North Haven, CT	Private	24.0	351	8011
Meriter Management Services	3256	Madison, WI	Private	29.4	351	8071
Amisub Culver Union Hospital	3257	Crawfordsville, IN	Public Family Member	29.4	350	8062
Arizona Heart Hospital Inc	3258	Phoenix, AZ	Private	123.0	350	8062
Bellevue Hospital Inc	3259	Bellevue, OH	Private	19.7	350	8062
Beloit Clinic Sc	3260	Beloit, WI	Private	24.0	350	8011
Boice-Willis Clinic Pa	3261	Rocky Mount, NC	Private	29.4	350	8011
Brigham Surgical Group Foundation	3262	Brookline, MA	Private	37.7	350	8011
Buena Ventura Medical Group	3263	Ventura, CA	Private	24.0	350	8011
Dale County Hospital Assn	3264	Ozark, AL	Private	43.9	350	8062
Defiance Hospital Inc	3265	Defiance, OH	Private	31.0	350	8062
Divine Savior Hospital Nursing Hm	3266	Portage, WI	Private	20.6	350	8062
Dukes Memorial Hospital	3267	Peru, IN	Private	20.3	350	8062
East Texas Med Cntr-Jcksonville	3268	Jacksonville, TX	Private	20.5	350	8062
F O H P Inc	3269	Neptune, NJ	Private	377.4	350	8011
First Option Health Plan Of Nj	3270	Red Bank, NJ	Private	377.4	350	8011
Florida Physicians Med Group	3271	Winter Park, FL	Private	24.0	350	8011
Fort Duncan Medical Center	3272	Eagle Pass, TX	Private	23.3	350	8062
H M A Durant Inc	3273	Durant, OK	Public Family Member	30.0	350	8062
Hartford Memorial Hospital	3274	Hartford, WI	Private	23.1	350	8062
Health First Medical Group Pc	3275	Memphis, TN	Private	23.5	350	8011
Healthsouth Of Austin, Inc	3276	Austin, TX	Public Family Member	27.5	350	8069
Henderson Memorial Hospital	3277	Henderson, TX	Private	24.6	350	8062
Hitchcock Clinic-Keene Inc	3278	Keene, NH	Private	24.0	350	8011
Hughston Orthopedic Clinic Pc	3279	Columbus, GA	Private	24.0	350	8011
Inland Valley Regional Med Ctr	3280	Wildomar, CA	Public Family Member	26.0	350	8062
Institute For Cancer Research Inc	3281	Philadelphia, PA	Private	23.8	350	8071
Johns Hpkins Hm Care Group Inc	3282	Baltimore, MD	Private	24.0	350	8082
Jsa Healthcare Corporation	3283	Saint Petersburg, FL	Private	41.0	350	8011
Kingsbridge Heights Rehabilitation	3284	Bronx, NY	Private	31.8	350	8059
L C Renalwest Llc	3285	Mesa, AZ	Private	32.0	350	8092
Laboratory Sciences Ariz Llc	3286	Tempe, AZ	Private	20.0	350	8071
Lebauer, Weintraub, Brodie	3287	Greensboro, NC	Private	24.0	350	8011
Medical Clinic Of N Texas P A	3288	Fort Worth, TX	Private	24.0	350	8011
Medtox Scientific Inc	3289	Burlington, NC	Public	28.6	350	8071
Meyer Medical Group Ii, S C	3290	Chicago, IL	Private	24.0	350	8011

D&B COMPANY RANKINGS BY EMPLOYMENT

Company	Rank	Location	Type	Sales ($ mil.)	Employment	Primary SIC
Mid America Clinical Labs Llc	3291	Indianapolis, IN	Private	30.0	350	8071
Mobile Mental Health Center	3292	Mobile, AL	Private	20.0	350	8093
Monadnock Community Hospital Inc	3293	Peterborough, NH	Private	21.6	350	8062
Nordx	3294	Scarborough, ME	Private	30.0	350	8071
North Country Hospital Health Ctr	3295	Newport, VT	Private	23.2	350	8062
North Side Hospital, Inc	3296	Johnson City, TN	Public Family Member	83.2	350	8062
Northside Hospital-Cherokee	3297	Canton, GA	Private	24.4	350	8062
Oak Crest Village, Inc	3298	Baltimore, MD	Private	29.9	350	8059
Odessa Hospital Ltd	3299	Odessa, TX	Private	37.9	350	8062
Pacin Healthcare-Hadley Mem Hosp	3300	Washington, DC	Private	50.0	350	8062
Parkridge Hospital Inc	3301	Chattanooga, TN	Public Family Member	22.2	350	8062
Pentucket Medical Associates	3302	Haverhill, MA	Private	30.0	350	8011
Pharmchem Laboratories, Inc	3303	Menlo Park, CA	Public	39.2	350	8071
Phoebe Home Inc	3304	Allentown, PA	Private	21.4	350	8051
Prime Medical Services Inc	3305	Austin, TX	Public	96.0	350	8099
Pro-Wellness Health Mgt Svcs	3306	Dayton, OH	Private	24.0	350	8011
Psychiatric Hospitals Of Pa	3307	Lafayette Hill, PA	Private	20.0	350	8063
Rivington Hse Health Care Fcilty	3308	New York, NY	Private	38.1	350	8059
Saint Patrick's Home	3309	Bronx, NY	Private	21.9	350	8051
Sartori Memorial Hospital	3310	Cedar Falls, IA	Private	21.0	350	8062
Slocum-Dickson Med Group Pc	3311	New Hartford, NY	Private	25.8	350	8011
Southern Health Care Of Ala	3312	Chattanooga, TN	Private	23.2	350	8062
Southwest Jefferson Community	3313	Louisville, KY	Public Family Member	34.3	350	8062
Spohn Kleberg Memorial Hosp	3314	Corpus Christi, TX	Private	37.3	350	8062
Spring Hill Regional Hospital	3315	Spring Hill, FL	Private	24.3	350	8062
St Lukes Cataract & Laser Inst	3316	Tarpon Springs, FL	Private	24.0	350	8011
State Laboratory Of Hygiene	3317	Madison, WI	Private	23.1	350	8071
Sutter Lakeside Hospital	3318	Lakeport, CA	Private	32.5	350	8062
Sycamore Shoals Hospital Inc	3319	Elizabethton, TN	Public Family Member	21.6	350	8062
Tolfree Memorial Hospital	3320	West Branch, MI	Private	21.0	350	8062
Transylvania Community	3321	Brevard, NC	Private	22.3	350	8062
Trimark Physicians Group	3322	Fort Dodge, IA	Private	24.0	350	8011
Visiting Nrs Associa	3323	Washington, DC	Private	180.6	350	8082
West Texas Medical Associates	3324	San Angelo, TX	Private	30.0	350	8011
Western Montana Clinic, Pc	3325	Missoula, MT	Private	27.1	350	8011
Western Plains Regional Hosp	3326	Dodge City, KS	Public Family Member	50.0	350	8062
Bedford County General Hosp	3327	Shelbyville, TN	Private	22.9	349	8062
Carillon House Nursing Fcilty	3328	Huntington, NY	Private	21.8	349	8051
McCullough-Hyde Mem Hospital Inc	3329	Oxford, OH	Private	26.6	349	8062
Doctors Hospital Of Staten Island	3330	Staten Island, NY	Private	25.2	348	8062
Snohomish Cnty Pub Hosp	3331	Arlington, WA	Private	26.4	348	8062
Comprehensive Care Corporation	3332	Tampa, FL	Public	46.1	347	8011
Diagnostic Clinic Houston, Pa	3333	Houston, TX	Private	36.0	346	8011
Wayne Hospital Co Inc	3334	Greenville, OH	Private	28.2	346	8062
Androscoggin Valley Hospital	3335	Berlin, NH	Private	22.4	345	8062
Hillside Rehabilitation Hosp	3336	Warren, OH	Private	20.7	345	8069
John Heinz Institute	3337	Wilkes Barre, PA	Private	27.3	345	8361
Silvercrest Extnded Care Fclty	3338	Jamaica, NY	Private	31.2	345	8051
Norton Community Hospital Inc	3339	Norton, VA	Private	23.2	343	8062
Washington Cnty Rgnal Med Ctr	3340	Sandersville, GA	Private	20.1	343	8062
Ridgecrest Regional Hospital	3341	Ridgecrest, CA	Private	25.0	342	8062
Val Verde County Hospital Dst	3342	Del Rio, TX	Private	27.3	341	8062
Ahm Gemch, Inc	3343	El Monte, CA	Public Family Member	32.0	340	8062
Amsterdam Nursing Home Corp	3344	New York, NY	Private	20.9	340	8051
Baker Victory Services	3345	Lackawanna, NY	Private	24.7	340	8361
Blood Care	3346	Dallas, TX	Private	22.9	340	8099
Capital Dst Physicians Health Plan	3347	Albany, NY	Private	304.5	340	8011
Daviess County Hospital	3348	Washington, IN	Private	22.3	340	8062
United Community Hospital	3349	Grove City, PA	Private	25.2	340	8062
Urocor Inc	3350	Oklahoma City, OK	Public	33.0	340	8071
Whitley Memorial Hospital	3351	Columbia City, IN	Private	21.8	340	8062
Healthlink Inc	3352	Saint Louis, MO	Private	23.2	339	8011
Interim Health Care Inc	3353	Greenville, SC	Private	20.9	339	8082
La-Rabida Chld Hospital & Res Ctr	3354	Chicago, IL	Private	26.0	339	8069
Foundtion Health A Fla Health Plan	3355	Fort Lauderdale, FL	Private	23.1	337	8011
Porter Hospital Inc	3356	Middlebury, VT	Private	21.2	337	8062
Upper Valley Medical Center	3357	Troy, OH	Private	115.3	336	8062
Gyncor, Inc.	3358	Chicago, IL	Private	22.9	335	8011
Queen's Health Systems	3359	Honolulu, HI	Private	499.5	334	8062
Judson Retirement Community	3360	Cleveland, OH	Private	21.7	331	8059

D&B COMPANY RANKINGS BY EMPLOYMENT

Company	Rank	Location	Type	Sales ($ mil.)	Employ-ment	Primary SIC
Sentara Enterprises	3361	Virginia Beach, VA	Private	91.7	331	8093
Blythedale Children's Hospital	3362	Valhalla, NY	Private	21.6	330	8069
Mhm Services, Inc	3363	Vienna, VA	Public	20.9	330	8063
Northwest Kidney Centers (Inc)	3364	Seattle, WA	Private	40.0	330	8092
Novato Community Hospital	3365	Novato, CA	Private	25.8	330	8062
Springfield Hospital	3366	Springfield, VT	Private	22.6	330	8062
Teays Valley Health Services	3367	Hurricane, WV	Public Family Member	26.4	330	8062
Temple Hospital Inc	3368	Los Angeles, CA	Private	33.9	330	8062
St John Ambulatory Care Corp	3369	Detroit, MI	Private	57.6	328	8011
Tahoe Forest Hospital Dst	3370	Truckee, CA	Private	35.2	328	8062
Arcventures Development Corp	3371	Chicago, IL	Private	22.2	325	8011
Big Spring Hospital Corp	3372	Big Spring, TX	Public Family Member	24.7	325	8062
Healthsouth Of York, Inc	3373	York, PA	Public Family Member	39.0	325	8069
Lubbock Regional	3374	Lubbock, TX	Private	22.0	325	8093
Mccurtain Memorial Medical Mgt	3375	Idabel, OK	Private	20.1	325	8062
Medical Income Properties 2a	3376	Atlanta, GA	Public	20.8	325	8051
Nylcare Health Plan Of The South	3377	Irving, TX	Private	342.2	325	8011
Quality Hm Hlt G Cst	3378	Biloxi, MS	Private	30.0	325	8082
Scripps Clinic Medical Group	3379	San Diego, CA	Private	195.3	325	8011
Woodland Park Hospital, Inc	3380	Portland, OR	Public Family Member	30.0	325	8062
Community Hospital Of Andalusia	3381	Andalusia, AL	Public Family Member	50.0	323	8062
Siskin Hospital For Physical	3382	Chattanooga, TN	Private	22.9	323	8069
Atlantic General Hospital Corp	3383	Berlin, MD	Private	24.1	322	8062
Riverside Rest Home	3384	Dover, NH	Private	24.2	322	8361
C A Columbia/H Retreat Hosp	3385	Richmond, VA	Public Family Member	31.8	320	8062
Community Health Association	3386	Ripley, WV	Private	22.1	320	8062
Gritman Medical Center	3387	Moscow, ID	Private	20.0	320	8062
Hillside Manor Rehab & Extend	3388	Jamaica, NY	Private	37.8	320	8051
Interstate Blood Bank Inc	3389	Memphis, TN	Private	30.0	320	8099
Kendrick Memorial Hospital	3390	Mooresville, IN	Private	25.2	320	8062
River Park Hospital Assoc L P	3391	Mc Minnville, TN	Public Family Member	55.0	320	8062
St Josephs Hospital Nursing	3392	Yonkers, NY	Private	27.6	320	8051
Waldo County General Hospital	3393	Belfast, ME	Private	21.2	320	8062
Western Missouri Medical Ctr	3394	Warrensburg, MO	Private	22.4	320	8062
Advanced Radiology Llc	3395	Baltimore, MD	Private	21.7	317	8011
Columbus Community Hospital	3396	Columbus, NE	Private	21.4	315	8062
Correctional Physicians Svcs	3397	Blue Bell, PA	Private	20.0	315	8099
Cryolife Inc	3398	Kennesaw, GA	Public	50.9	315	8099
Memorial Hospital Inc	3399	Manchester, KY	Private	22.5	315	8062
Sacramento Medical Foundation	3400	Sacramento, CA	Private	32.3	315	8099
Benjamin Franklin Clinic	3401	Philadelphia, PA	Private	21.4	313	8011
Gateway Regional Health System	3402	Mount Sterling, KY	Private	23.9	313	8062
Prh, Inc.	3403	Rochester, NY	Private	27.5	312	8071
Healthfirst Inc	3404	New York, NY	Private	88.4	311	8011
Fort Sanders-Sevier Med Ctr	3405	Sevierville, TN	Private	19.7	310	8062
Helena Hospital Association	3406	Helena, AR	Private	20.1	310	8062
Kauai Medical Clinic Inc	3407	Lihue, HI	Private	21.2	310	8011
McDowell Hospital Inc	3408	Marion, NC	Private	19.7	310	8062
Paracelsus Santa Rosa Med Ctr	3409	Milton, FL	Public Family Member	56.0	310	8062
Cancer Therapy	3410	San Antonio, TX	Private	70.6	309	8011
Physicians Ind Med Group	3411	San Diego, CA	Private	21.0	307	8011
Greater Detroit Hospital Inc	3412	Detroit, MI	Private	23.0	306	8062
Legacy Mount Hood Medical Ctr	3413	Gresham, OR	Private	29.5	306	8062
Little Rock Health Mgt Assoc	3414	Little Rock, AR	Private	21.6	306	8062
Central Minn Group Health Plan	3415	Saint Cloud, MN	Private	31.7	305	8011
Roper Hospital North	3416	North Charleston, SC	Private	242.5	305	8062
White-Wilson Medical Ctr P A	3417	Fort Walton Beach, FL	Private	20.8	304	8011
Casa De Las Campanas, Inc	3418	San Diego, CA	Private	22.9	303	8361
Union Health Service Inc	3419	Chicago, IL	Private	22.0	302	8011
Minor & James Medical, Pllc	3420	Seattle, WA	Private	28.5	301	8011
Wesley Woods Geriatric Hosp	3421	Atlanta, GA	Private	27.2	301	8062
American Clinical Laboratories	3422	San Diego, CA	Private	30.0	300	8071
Americare Certif Special Svcs	3423	Brooklyn, NY	Private	20.0	300	8082
Atlanta Medical Clinic Llc	3424	Atlanta, GA	Private	28.0	300	8011
Baton Rouge Clinic A Med Corp	3425	Baton Rouge, LA	Private	20.5	300	8011
Care Group Inc	3426	Indianapolis, IN	Private	20.5	300	8011
Central Alabama Home Health Svcs	3427	Montgomery, AL	Private	29.5	300	8082
Clinical Associates, Pa	3428	Baltimore, MD	Private	20.5	300	8011
Doctors Laboratory Inc	3429	Valdosta, GA	Private	20.6	300	8071
Douglas Hospital Inc	3430	Douglasville, GA	Private	27.0	300	8062

D&B COMPANY RANKINGS BY EMPLOYMENT

Company	Rank	Location	Type	Sales ($ mil.)	Employ-ment	Primary SIC
East Texas Medical Center	3431	Tyler, TX	Private	52.9	300	8071
Elias F Ghanem Ltd	3432	Las Vegas, NV	Private	20.5	300	8011
F W Of Saratoga, Inc	3433	Saratoga Springs, NY	Private	20.1	300	8063
Garden Park Community Hospital L	3434	Gulfport, MS	Public Family Member	29.3	300	8062
Genesee Valley Group Health Assn	3435	Rochester, NY	Private	74.6	300	8011
Gilbert, Barbee, Moore, McIlvoy	3436	Bowling Green, KY	Private	23.8	300	8011
Grand View Hospital Inc	3437	Ironwood, MI	Private	20.4	300	8062
Hand Surgery Associates Of Ind	3438	Indianapolis, IN	Private	20.5	300	8011
Health Care Solutions, Inc	3439	Ann Arbor, MI	Private	40.1	300	8082
Health Partners Of Philadelphia	3440	Philadelphia, PA	Private	203.4	300	8011
Health Resources Corporation	3441	Naples, FL	Private	36.2	300	8071
Healthcare San Antonio Inc	3442	San Antonio, TX	Private	20.5	300	8011
Healthtexas Provider Network	3443	Dallas, TX	Private	67.3	300	8011
Heritage Hospital Inc	3444	Tarboro, NC	Public Family Member	48.6	300	8062
Home Health Vna Inc	3445	Haverhill, MA	Private	21.9	300	8082
Hospital Group Of Illinois	3446	Chicago, IL	Public Family Member	21.0	300	8063
Institute For Community Living	3447	New York, NY	Private	21.5	300	8052
Jacksonville Health Care Group	3448	Jacksonville, FL	Private	20.5	300	8011
Kaiser Fnd Health Pln/Ma Inc	3449	Holyoke, MA	Private	20.5	300	8011
Kewanee Hospital Association	3450	Kewanee, IL	Private	25.6	300	8062
Lincoln Pk Osteopathic Hospital	3451	Grand Junction, CO	Private	22.1	300	8062
Lorien Nrsing Rhbilitation Ctr	3452	Lutherville Tim., MD	Private	20.0	300	8051
M-Care Inc	3453	Ann Arbor, MI	Private	155.4	300	8011
McCray Memorial Hospital	3454	Kendallville, IN	Private	22.5	300	8062
Medical Assoc Of Lehigh Valley Pc	3455	Allentown, PA	Private	20.5	300	8011
Melbourne Intl Med Assc Inc	3456	Melbourne, FL	Private	20.5	300	8011
Mendocino Coast District Hosp	3457	Fort Bragg, CA	Private	20.7	300	8062
Millcreek Community Hospital	3458	Erie, PA	Private	25.7	300	8062
Mt Kisco Medical Group, P.C.	3459	Mount Kisco, NY	Private	25.0	300	8011
Northeastern Vt Regional Hosp	3460	Saint Johnsbury, VT	Private	20.1	300	8062
Northern	3461	Bishop, CA	Private	19.9	300	8062
Northern Ore Healthcare Corp	3462	Mcminnville, OR	Public Family Member	60.0	300	8062
P C Healthfirst Physician	3463	Lakewood, CO	Private	20.5	300	8011
Pacifica Hospital Care Center	3464	Huntington Beach, CA	Private	29.5	300	8062
Pathology Laboratories Ltd	3465	Hattiesburg, MS	Private	21.8	300	8071
Physicians Healthcare Plans	3466	Tampa, FL	Private	130.4	300	8011
Priority Health Inc	3467	Grand Rapids, MI	Private	20.5	300	8011
Public Hospital District 1	3468	Shelton, WA	Private	19.8	300	8062
Rochester Area Health Mn Org	3469	Rochester, NY	Private	282.6	300	8011
Saint Eugene Community Hosp	3470	Dillon, SC	Private	29.3	300	8062
Schwab Rehabilitation Hospital	3471	Chicago, IL	Private	25.9	300	8069
Stl Management, Inc	3472	Saint Charles, MO	Private	21.2	300	8049
Tenet Health Systems Hospitals	3473	Manteca, CA	Public Family Member	23.5	300	8062
Titusville Area Hospital	3474	Titusville, PA	Private	20.8	300	8062
Touchette Regional HospitalInc	3475	East Saint Louis, IL	Private	22.5	300	8062
Ultimate Health Services Inc	3476	Huntington, WV	Private	24.6	300	8011
United Medical Group	3477	Saint Louis, MO	Private	20.5	300	8011
University Physcn Assoc Of Nj	3478	Newark, NJ	Private	20.5	300	8011
Valley Community Hospital	3479	Santa Maria, CA	Public Family Member	23.0	300	8062
Mental Health Care Inc	3480	Tampa, FL	Private	21.1	299	8093
Visalia Medical Clinic Inc	3481	Visalia, CA	Private	20.4	299	8011
Selectcare Hmo Inc	3482	Troy, MI	Private	20.3	297	8011
Walton County Hospital Auth	3483	Monroe, GA	Private	24.2	297	8062
Farmers Union Hospital Assn	3484	Elk City, OK	Private	22.3	295	8062
Tahlequah Hospital Authority	3485	Tahlequah, OK	Private	20.0	295	8062
Virginia Medical Associates	3486	Springfield, VA	Private	20.1	294	8011
Vivra Asthma Allrgy Creamerica	3487	San Mateo, CA	Private	20.1	294	8011
Brown County General Hospital	3488	Georgetown, OH	Private	20.1	292	8062
Blue Ridge Orthopedic Assoc Pc	3489	Warrenton, VA	Private	19.9	291	8011
Aetna Health Management, Inc	3490	Hartford, CT	Public Family Member	19.8	290	8011
Tuolumne General Hospital	3491	Sonora, CA	Private	20.6	290	8062
University Rehabilitation Hosp	3492	New Orleans, LA	Private	22.9	290	8069
Usdsm University Physicians	3493	Sioux Falls, SD	Private	25.0	290	8011
Wadsworth-Rtmn Area Hsptl	3494	Wadsworth, OH	Private	19.8	290	8062
Pratt Regional Med Ctr Corp	3495	Pratt, KS	Private	21.4	288	8062
United Crbrl Plsy/Ulstr Cnty	3496	Kingston, NY	Private	56.9	287	8093
U S H Of Pennsylvania, Inc	3497	Centre Hall, PA	Public Family Member	22.0	284	8011
Egh, Inc.	3498	Portland, OR	Public Family Member	30.0	283	8062
St Anthony's Hospital	3499	Pendleton, OR	Private	20.8	282	8062
Lifelink Foundation Inc	3500	Tampa, FL	Private	33.1	281	8099

D&B COMPANY RANKINGS BY EMPLOYMENT

Company	Rank	Location	Type	Sales ($ mil.)	Employ-ment	Primary SIC
Baptist Healthcare Group	3501	Nashville, TN	Private	20.1	280	8011
Castleview Hospital Inc	3502	Price, UT	Public Family Member	29.8	280	8062
Central Blood Bank	3503	Pittsburgh, PA	Private	25.5	280	8099
Danbury Office Physcn Svcs Pc	3504	Danbury, CT	Private	40.0	280	8011
Hillsdale Community Health Ctr	3505	Hillsdale, MI	Private	22.6	280	8062
Jack Friedman	3506	Flushing, NY	Private	23.8	280	8059
Mecosta County General Hosp	3507	Big Rapids, MI	Private	22.9	280	8062
Ochsner Health Plan Inc	3508	Metairie, LA	Private	323.7	280	8011
Oklahoma Orthpdc/Arthrts	3509	Oklahoma City, OK	Private	23.3	280	8069
Texas Healthcare Pa	3510	Fort Worth, TX	Private	22.2	280	8011
St Luke's Quakertown Hospital	3511	Quakertown, PA	Private	20.0	277	8062
J G B Health Facilities Corp	3512	New York, NY	Private	22.4	276	8051
Cameron Community Hospital	3513	Cameron, MO	Private	23.9	275	8062
Chinese Hospital Association	3514	San Francisco, CA	Private	36.9	275	8062
Christian Church Campus	3515	Louisville, KY	Private	36.2	275	8059
Crestwood Hospital & Nursing Hm	3516	Huntsville, AL	Public Family Member	56.7	275	8062
Healthsource South Carolina	3517	Charleston, SC	Public Family Member	191.1	275	8011
Park Columbia Medical Group	3518	Minneapolis, MN	Private	28.3	275	8011
Scan Health Plan	3519	Long Beach, CA	Private	103.0	275	8011
Twin Falls Clinic And Hosp	3520	Twin Falls, ID	Private	24.1	275	8062
Via Christi Health Partners	3521	Wichita, KS	Private	41.6	275	8011
Youth Villages Inc	3522	Memphis, TN	Private	23.7	275	8361
Healthsouth Of New Mexico	3523	Albuquerque, NM	Public Family Member	20.0	274	8069
Healthsouth Of South Carolina	3524	Columbia, SC	Public Family Member	35.0	274	8069
Huron Memorial Hospital Inc	3525	Bad Axe, MI	Private	22.1	274	8062
Belle Bonfils Mem Blood Ctr	3526	Denver, CO	Private	24.2	272	8099
Newcare Health Corporation	3527	Atlanta, GA	Private	32.0	272	8059
Providence Milwaukie Hospital	3528	Milwaukie, OR	Private	38.3	272	8062
Aids Healthcare Foundation	3529	Los Angeles, CA	Private	31.6	270	8361
Baltimore Medical System Inc	3530	Baltimore, MD	Private	37.8	270	8099
Clearwater Community Hospital Lp	3531	Clearwater, FL	Private	27.8	270	8062
Greene County Memorial Hosp	3532	Waynesburg, PA	Private	23.2	270	8062
Healthsouth Of Montgomery	3533	Montgomery, AL	Public Family Member	20.4	270	8069
Indianapolis Osteopathic Hosp	3534	Indianapolis, IN	Private	24.8	270	8062
Jackson Stonewall Mem Hosp	3535	Weston, WV	Private	20.2	270	8062
Lakeview Med Ctr Inc Rice Lk	3536	Rice Lake, WI	Private	22.3	270	8062
New England Health Care	3537	Boston, MA	Private	90.0	270	8011
New Vanderbilt Nursing Home	3538	Staten Island, NY	Private	22.0	270	8051
Northeastern Regional Hospital	3539	Las Vegas, NM	Private	23.4	270	8062
Service Mstr Rehabilitation Lp	3540	Memphis, TN	Private	30.0	270	8093
Shore View Nursing Home	3541	Brooklyn, NY	Private	25.0	270	8051
Trinity Community Medical	3542	Brenham, TX	Private	19.9	270	8062
Clay Paracelsus County Hosp	3543	Celina, TN	Public Family Member	28.9	269	8062
Monroe Medical Foundation Inc	3544	Tompkinsville, KY	Private	20.4	266	8062
Aetna Health Plans Ill Inc	3545	Chicago, IL	Public Family Member	46.2	265	8011
Aetna Health Plans Of Cal	3546	Walnut Creek, CA	Public Family Member	940.0	265	8011
Carbondale Clinic S C	3547	Carbondale, IL	Private	23.6	264	8011
Community Healthlink Inc	3548	Worcester, MA	Private	27.8	261	8093
Medical Park Hospital Inc	3549	Winston Salem, NC	Private	25.9	260	8062
Monarch Dental Corporation	3550	Dallas, TX	Public	68.6	260	8021
Montgomery General Hospital	3551	Montgomery, WV	Private	22.5	260	8062
Mt Graham Community Hospital	3552	Safford, AZ	Private	21.5	260	8062
Steamboat Sprngs Health Care Asn	3553	Steamboat Springs, CO	Private	22.7	260	8062
Woodward Hospital & Health Ctr	3554	Woodward, OK	Private	27.0	255	8062
Blood Services Centl Ohio Reg	3555	Columbus, OH	Private	21.7	254	8099
Semmes-Murphey Clinic Pc	3556	Memphis, TN	Private	27.2	254	8011
Eastern Long Island Hospital	3557	Greenport, NY	Private	20.6	252	8062
Browne-McHardy Clinic	3558	Metairie, LA	Private	22.4	250	8011
C A C/H Development Inc	3559	Dallas, TX	Public Family Member	20.4	250	8062
Clinical Reference Lab Inc	3560	Shawnee Mission, KS	Private	28.2	250	8071
Columbia North Bay Hospital	3561	Aransas Pass, TX	Public Family Member	40.0	250	8062
Comprehensive Care Mgt Corp	3562	Bronx, NY	Private	29.3	250	8051
Desert Valley Hospital	3563	Victorville, CA	Private	36.2	250	8062
Eunice Regional Medical Center	3564	Eunice, LA	Private	20.9	250	8062
Florida Sheriffs Youth Ranches	3565	Live Oak, FL	Private	21.7	250	8361
H S C Medical Center	3566	Malvern, AR	Private	24.0	250	8062
Health Plan Of Nevada Inc	3567	Las Vegas, NV	Public Family Member	358.5	250	8011
Healthsouth Rehabilitation Hosp	3568	Largo, FL	Public Family Member	22.0	250	8099
Hhca Texas Health Services, Lp	3569	Dallas, TX	Private	24.0	250	8082
Highland Clnic A Prof Med Corp	3570	Shreveport, LA	Private	26.2	250	8011

D&B COMPANY RANKINGS BY EMPLOYMENT

Company	Rank	Location	Type	Sales ($ mil.)	Employ-ment	Primary SIC
Highland Health Systems Inc	3571	Lubbock, TX	Public Family Member	39.0	250	8062
Hip Of New Jersey, Inc	3572	North Brunswick, NJ	Private	384.7	250	8011
Holliswood Care Center Inc	3573	Hollis, NY	Private	21.2	250	8051
Horsham Clinic (Inc)	3574	Ambler, PA	Public Family Member	20.0	250	8063
Houston Rehabilitation Inst	3575	Houston, TX	Public Family Member	28.7	250	8093
Masonic Homes Of Kentucky	3576	Louisville, KY	Private	22.6	250	8361
National Healthcare Of Decatur	3577	Decatur, AL	Public Family Member	35.0	250	8062
Phycor Of Vero Beach, Inc	3578	Vero Beach, FL	Public Family Member	25.0	250	8011
Physician Health Corporation	3579	Atlanta, GA	Private	37.4	250	8059
Renex Corp	3580	Coral Gables, FL	Public	26.1	250	8082
Sea Crest Health Care Center	3581	Brooklyn, NY	Private	22.6	250	8051
Shriners Hospital For Children	3582	Boston, MA	Private	23.2	250	8069
Silver Lake Nursing Home Inc	3583	Staten Island, NY	Private	21.0	250	8051
Sterling Rock Fls Clinic Ltd	3584	Sterling, IL	Private	20.9	250	8011
U H S Of De La Ronde, Inc.	3585	Chalmette, LA	Public Family Member	1,190.2	250	8062
United/Dynacare Llc	3586	Milwaukee, WI	Private	20.9	250	8071
Vna Care Network, Inc	3587	Waltham, MA	Private	37.2	250	8082
Lindsay District Hospital	3588	Lindsay, CA	Private	105.0	248	8062
Uvalde County Hospital Auth	3589	Uvalde, TX	Private	29.3	246	8062
Columbia Bartow Memorial Hosp	3590	Bartow, FL	Private	30.0	245	8062
Healthsouth Of Treasure Coast	3591	Vero Beach, FL	Public Family Member	40.0	245	8069
Highland Care Center, Inc	3592	Jamaica, NY	Private	21.0	245	8051
Maine Cast Rgnal Health Fclties	3593	Ellsworth, ME	Private	29.2	245	8062
Scott And White Health Plan	3594	Temple, TX	Private	219.5	245	8011
Jersey Community Hospital	3595	Jerseyville, IL	Private	20.4	243	8062
Berkshire Physicians Surgeons Pc	3596	Pittsfield, MA	Private	41.7	240	8011
Milwaukee Protestant Home	3597	Milwaukee, WI	Private	20.2	240	8059
Sioux Valley Physicians Aliance	3598	Sioux Falls, SD	Private	25.4	240	8011
United Medical Associates, Pc	3599	Johnson City, NY	Private	40.3	240	8011
Healthcor, Inc	3600	Southfield, MI	Private	80.0	236	8011
Sunnyside Community Hospital Assn	3601	Sunnyside, WA	Private	19.8	235	8062
Wyoming Health Services Inc	3602	Riverton, WY	Public Family Member	33.0	235	8062
Doctors Hospital Of Jackson	3603	Jackson, MI	Private	19.9	234	8062
Prime Medical Group, P.C.	3604	Clairton, PA	Private	25.0	232	8011
South Bay Community Hospital	3605	Redondo Beach, CA	Private	23.4	231	8062
Beaumont Rehabilitation Assoc L P	3606	Beaumont, TX	Public Family Member	25.8	230	8069
Campbell Clinic Inc	3607	Germantown, TN	Private	24.4	230	8011
D & R Pharmaceutical Inc	3608	Louisville, KY	Public Family Member	35.0	230	8082
Health Mgt Assoc Of W Va	3609	Williamson, WV	Public Family Member	26.4	230	8062
Maine General Rehabilitation &	3610	Augusta, ME	Private	79.4	230	8052
Medical Education Assist Corp	3611	Mountain Home, TN	Private	21.6	230	8071
Orthopedic Hospital Ltd	3612	Houston, TX	Private	33.1	230	8069
Partners Nat Health Plans Of Nc	3613	Winston Salem, NC	Private	296.4	230	8011
Qual-Med Washington Health Plan	3614	Bellevue, WA	Private	140.8	230	8011
Ssm Rehabilitation	3615	Saint Louis, MO	Private	31.9	230	8093
Pacific Cataract Laser Inst P S	3616	Chehalis, WA	Private	20.6	226	8011
Dry Harbor, Snf Inc	3617	Middle Village, NY	Private	26.5	225	8051
Horizon Physician Network Llc	3618	Columbus, GA	Private	21.0	225	8011
National Healthcare Lesville Inc	3619	Leesville, LA	Public Family Member	38.0	225	8062
Permanente Med Assn Of Texas	3620	Dallas, TX	Private	57.1	225	8011
Wellcare Management Group Inc	3621	Kingston, NY	Public	143.9	225	8011
Medtox Laboratories Inc	3622	Saint Paul, MN	Public Family Member	28.6	223	8071
Northwest Healthcare Corp	3623	Kalispell, MT	Private	72.4	223	8062
Kernodle Clinic Inc	3624	Burlington, NC	Private	20.5	220	8011
Arizona Medical Clinic Ltd	3625	Peoria, AZ	Private	27.0	216	8011
Healthsource Maine Inc	3626	Freeport, ME	Public Family Member	124.6	215	8011
Hospital Of Barstow, Inc	3627	Barstow, CA	Public Family Member	21.8	215	8062
A Infu-Tech Delaware Corp	3628	Englewood Cliffs, NJ	Public	26.0	213	8082
Angleton-Danbury Hospital Dst	3629	Angleton, TX	Private	25.4	210	8062
Img Health Care Network, Llc	3630	New Orleans, LA	Private	20.5	210	8011
Langton Lake Place, Inc.	3631	Saint Paul, MN	Private	34.9	210	8051
Masonic Home, Inc	3632	Charlton, MA	Private	28.8	210	8051
Pacificare Of Oregon	3633	Lake Oswego, OR	Private	320.3	210	8011
Smt Health Services, Inc.	3634	Wexford, PA	Public	40.0	210	8071
Arizona Boys Ranch Inc	3635	Queen Creek, AZ	Private	21.8	209	8361
Behavioral Health, Inc.	3636	Baton Rouge, LA	Private	28.0	209	8093
United States Health	3637	Blue Bell, PA	Public Family Member	1,717.6	209	8011
Demac Corporation	3638	Warren, MI	Private	32.0	205	8011
Harris Methodist Erath County	3639	Stephenville, TX	Private	21.1	205	8062
Santa Paula Memorial Hospital	3640	Santa Paula, CA	Private	21.7	202	8062

D&B COMPANY RANKINGS BY EMPLOYMENT

Company	Rank	Location	Type	Sales ($ mil.)	Employ- ment	Primary SIC
Barnes West County Hospital	3641	Saint Louis, MO	Private	30.6	200	8062
Covenant House Inc (New York)	3642	New York, NY	Private	58.1	200	8361
Crippled Children's Hospital	3643	Richmond, VA	Private	24.7	200	8069
Dental-Net Inc	3644	Tucson, AZ	Private	21.2	200	8021
Ellis, Bandt, Birkin, Kollins	3645	Las Vegas, NV	Private	25.0	200	8011
Enzo Clinical Labs Inc	3646	Farmingdale, NY	Public Family Member	21.7	200	8071
Healix Infusion Therapy Inc	3647	Houston, TX	Private	20.8	200	8082
Mederi Inc	3648	Miami, FL	Private	29.1	200	8082
Methodist Children's Hospital	3649	Lubbock, TX	Private	27.3	200	8069
Nai Community Hospital Of Phoenix	3650	Phoenix, AZ	Public Family Member	40.0	200	8062
Neighborhood Health Plan Inc	3651	Boston, MA	Private	86.8	200	8011
Orthopedic Consultants, Pa	3652	Minneapolis, MN	Private	37.2	200	8011
Phoenix Programs Of New York	3653	New York, NY	Private	21.8	200	8361
Royco Inc	3654	Fort Lauderdale, FL	Private	20.0	200	8071
Vanderbilt Stallworth Rehabili	3655	Nashville, TN	Private	28.0	200	8361
Cook Childrens Physician Netwrk	3656	Fort Worth, TX	Private	44.6	198	8011
Healthcare Mgt Alternatives	3657	Philadelphia, PA	Private	192.2	196	8099
Pueblo Physicians Pc	3658	Pueblo, CO	Private	30.0	195	8011
South Shore Mntal Health Ctr Inc	3659	Quincy, MA	Private	21.5	195	8093
Three Rivers Health Plans Inc	3660	Monroeville, PA	Private	50.0	195	8011
Benedictine Health System	3661	Duluth, MN	Private	133.6	190	8062
Continue Care Home Health	3662	Hollandale, MS	Private	35.7	190	8082
King's Daughters Hospital	3663	Yazoo City, MS	Private	28.6	190	8062
Lafayette Regional Health Ctr	3664	Lexington, MO	Private	28.0	190	8062
York General Hospital, Inc.	3665	York, NE	Private	96.8	190	8062
American Shared Hospital Svcs	3666	San Francisco, CA	Public	37.2	189	8099
Aspen Valley Hospital Dst	3667	Aspen, CO	Private	21.3	180	8062
Behrman Chiropractic Clinics	3668	Arlington, TX	Private	20.0	180	8041
Charter Behavioral Health	3669	Summit, NJ	Private	31.0	180	8063
H M A Louisburg Inc	3670	Louisburg, NC	Public Family Member	40.0	180	8062
Inter Valley Health Plan Inc	3671	Pomona, CA	Private	131.5	180	8011
Pacificare Of Texas Inc	3672	San Antonio, TX	Public Family Member	541.8	180	8011
Park Ridge Nursing Home Inc	3673	Rochester, NY	Private	89.5	180	8051
Southwest Catholic Health Network	3674	Phoenix, AZ	Private	132.1	180	8011
Florida Medical Clinic, P.A.	3675	Zephyrhills, FL	Private	22.7	177	8011
Central Ohio Medical Clinic	3676	Columbus, OH	Private	21.0	175	8011
Downey Community Health Center	3677	Downey, CA	Private	83.7	175	8051
First Plan Of Minnesota	3678	Two Harbors, MN	Private	32.5	175	8011
Healthsouth Of Texarkana Inc	3679	Texarkana, TX	Public Family Member	25.0	175	8069
Hood General Hospital	3680	Granbury, TX	Public Family Member	20.0	175	8062
Integramed America Inc	3681	Purchase, NY	Public	22.6	175	8093
Little Co Of Mary Affl Svcs	3682	Oak Lawn, IL	Private	147.1	175	8099
Medcath Of Mcallen Ltd	3683	Charlotte, NC	Private	25.0	175	8071
Pickens Healthcare Association	3684	Jasper, GA	Private	20.0	175	8062
Renal Care Group Inc	3685	Nashville, TN	Public	140.0	175	8092
Total Health Care Inc	3686	Baltimore, MD	Private	56.7	171	8011
Elkhart Clinic Llc	3687	Elkhart, IN	Private	20.0	170	8011
S P Acquisition Corp	3688	South Pittsburg, TN	Public Family Member	48.0	170	8062
Johnson Cy Eye & Ear Hospital Inc	3689	Johnson City, TN	Public Family Member	21.0	165	8069
Physicians Health Plan, Inc.	3690	Columbia, SC	Private	112.5	162	8011
Oregon Anesthesiology Group Pc	3691	Portland, OR	Private	48.0	161	8011
Arrowhead Community Hospital &	3692	Glendale, AZ	Private	38.5	160	8062
Ivonyx Group Services, Inc	3693	Livonia, MI	Private	43.0	160	8082
Memorial Med Group A Prof Corp	3694	Torrance, CA	Private	21.6	160	8011
Visiting Nurse Association Hea	3695	Staten Island, NY	Private	24.0	160	8082
Dms Imaging Inc	3696	Fargo, ND	Public Family Member	36.1	158	8071
Lubbock Methodist Hospital Pra	3697	Lubbock, TX	Private	41.5	157	8011
Greenville Hospital Corp	3698	Greenville, AL	Public Family Member	25.0	155	8062
Managed Care Usa, Inc	3699	Charlotte, NC	Private	46.1	155	8099
Eastern Maine Healthcare	3700	Bangor, ME	Private	255.1	153	8062
Cardiovascular Consultants Inc	3701	Kansas City, MO	Private	26.8	150	8011
Carter Blood Center Inc	3702	Fort Worth, TX	Private	34.7	150	8099
Charter Louisvlle Behavioral Health	3703	Louisville, KY	Private	24.0	150	8063
Charter Real Behavioral Health Sys	3704	San Antonio, TX	Public Family Member	32.6	150	8063
Columbia Tops Surgical Hosp	3705	Houston, TX	Private	28.0	150	8062
Crestview Of Ohio Inc	3706	Sylvania, OH	Private	20.8	150	8051
Great Lakes Health Plan Inc	3707	Southfield, MI	Private	38.0	150	8011
Healthmark Of Walton Inc	3708	Defuniak Springs, FL	Private	20.0	150	8062
Healthsouth Of Midland, Inc	3709	Midland, TX	Public Family Member	21.0	150	8093
Magella Healthcare Corporation	3710	Frisco, TX	Private	45.0	150	8011

D&B COMPANY RANKINGS BY EMPLOYMENT

Company	Rank	Location	Type	Sales ($ mil.)	Employ-ment	Primary SIC
Mann Berkley Eye Center, Pa	3711	Houston, TX	Private	25.0	150	8011
Mcc Behavioral Care Of Cal	3712	Glendale, CA	Public Family Member	27.1	150	8093
Medical Diagnostics Inc	3713	Wilmington, MA	Public Family Member	23.0	150	8099
Natchtches Parish Hospital Svc Dst	3714	Natchitoches, LA	Private	21.8	150	8062
Northern Ill Physcn Group Pc	3715	Dixon, IL	Private	22.0	150	8011
Phycor Of Pueblo Inc	3716	Pueblo, CO	Public Family Member	23.0	150	8011
Prairie Crdovascular Cons Ltd	3717	Springfield, IL	Private	32.5	150	8011
Tanana Valley Med Surgical Group	3718	Fairbanks, AK	Private	22.0	150	8011
Western Wash Med Group Inc Ps	3719	Everett, WA	Private	21.0	150	8011
Radiology Assocs Tarrant Cnty	3720	Fort Worth, TX	Private	24.6	149	8011
Texas Visiting Nurse Service	3721	Harlingen, TX	Private	24.4	145	8082
New York Hotel Trades Council	3722	New York, NY	Private	43.7	143	8011
Augustana Lutheran Home	3723	Brooklyn, NY	Private	20.3	142	8051
Baptist Health Care Affiliates	3724	Nashville, TN	Private	20.1	142	8062
Ryan William F Community Health	3725	New York, NY	Private	28.1	142	8099
Board Of Child Care Of Balt-Wa	3726	Baltimore, MD	Private	26.5	140	8361
Summit Landmark Orthopedic Asc	3727	Saint Paul, MN	Private	20.0	140	8011
Cardiac Solutions, Inc	3728	Fort Washington, PA	Private	24.0	135	8082
Marathon H M A Inc	3729	Marathon, FL	Public Family Member	21.0	135	8062
Paradigm Holdings Inc	3730	Concord, CA	Private	39.1	135	8093
Heart Group Inc	3731	Lancaster, PA	Private	32.0	132	8011
Colorado Access	3732	Denver, CO	Private	75.0	130	8011
Community Health Group	3733	Chula Vista, CA	Private	53.6	130	8011
Kerlan-Jobe Orthopaedic	3734	Los Angeles, CA	Private	27.0	130	8011
Lifecare Hospital New Orleans Llc	3735	Chalmette, LA	Private	24.0	130	8069
University Anesthesiology & Cr	3736	Pittsburgh, PA	Private	33.0	130	8011
Paramount Care Inc	3737	Maumee, OH	Private	122.6	127	8011
Metroplex Hematology Oncology	3738	Arlington, TX	Private	24.7	125	8011
Network Health Plan Of Wisconsin	3739	Menasha, WI	Private	93.2	125	8011
Personal Physician Care Inc	3740	Cleveland, OH	Private	50.9	125	8011
Summit Pointe	3741	Battle Creek, MI	Private	20.3	125	8093
Baptist Health Enterprises	3742	Miami, FL	Private	39.6	124	8011
Florida Health Choice Inc	3743	Delray Beach, FL	Private	22.8	120	8011
Ivonyx Inc	3744	Livonia, MI	Private	26.0	120	8082
Lubbock Methdst Hospital Svcs Inc	3745	Lubbock, TX	Private	66.2	120	8071
Memorial Health Ventures Inc	3746	Houston, TX	Private	20.6	120	8082
Oncology-Hematolgy Associates	3747	Pittsburgh, PA	Public Family Member	64.0	120	8011
Richmond Imaging Affiliates Ltd	3748	Houston, TX	Private	29.0	120	8011
Sentara Health Plans Inc	3749	Virginia Beach, VA	Private	67.8	120	8011
Smithvlle Healthcare Ventures Lp	3750	Smithville, TN	Private	28.4	120	8062
United Healthcare Of Utah	3751	Salt Lake City, UT	Public Family Member	145.6	120	8011
Managed Healthcare Systems Of Ny	3752	New York, NY	Private	65.5	119	8099
Radiology & Imaging Inc	3753	Springfield, MA	Private	20.0	118	8011
Kettering Affiliated Health Svcs	3754	Dayton, OH	Private	248.9	115	8099
Tennessee Healthsource Inc	3755	Brentwood, TN	Public Family Member	110.8	113	8011
Beverly Entrprss-California Inc	3756	Fort Smith, AR	Public Family Member	3,230.3	110	8051
Glen Ellyn Clinic, S.C.	3757	Glen Ellyn, IL	Private	68.0	110	8011
Anesthesia Association Of Kansas	3758	Kansas City, MO	Private	46.0	109	8011
William N Harwin Md Pa	3759	Fort Myers, FL	Private	30.0	108	8011
Advantage Care Inc	3760	Lexington, KY	Private	43.1	105	8011
Dallas Cardiology Assoc Pa	3761	Dallas, TX	Private	33.0	105	8011
Health Plan Of Upper Ohio	3762	Saint Clairsville, OH	Private	115.2	105	8082
Indianplis Neurosurgical Group	3763	Indianapolis, IN	Private	26.4	102	8011
Principal Health Care Of Kans Cy	3764	Kansas City, MO	Private	107.5	102	8011
Cambridge Hospital Prof Svcs Corp	3765	Somerville, MA	Private	27.4	100	8011
H M O Colorado, Inc	3766	Denver, CO	Private	224.9	100	8011
Hematlogy Onclogy Physcians Pc	3767	Tucson, AZ	Private	50.0	100	8011
Los Angele Dev Serv	3768	Los Angeles, CA	Private	33.9	100	8099
Morton Plant Mease Health Svcs	3769	Clearwater, FL	Private	37.6	100	8011
Nylcare Health Plans Of Maine	3770	Portland, ME	Private	60.0	100	8011
Preferred Health Network Of Md	3771	Linthicum Heights, MD	Private	67.3	100	8011
Premiere Assoc Healthcare Svcs	3772	Clemmons, NC	Public Family Member	111.6	100	8051
Saint Mary's Healthfirst	3773	Reno, NV	Private	28.0	100	8011
United Healthcare Of Kentucky	3774	Lexington, KY	Private	111.3	100	8011
Physicians Health Plan Nthrn In	3775	Fort Wayne, IN	Private	91.3	98	8011
San Mateo Health Commission	3776	San Mateo, CA	Private	84.2	96	8099
Biomedical Systems Corporation	3777	Saint Louis, MO	Private	20.0	95	8099
Radiology Imaging Assoc Pc	3778	Englewood, CO	Private	23.5	95	8011
Skagit County Medical Bureau	3779	Mount Vernon, WA	Private	53.9	95	8011
York Health System Med Group	3780	York, PA	Private	22.9	95	8011

D&B COMPANY RANKINGS BY EMPLOYMENT

Company	Rank	Location	Type	Sales ($ mil.)	Employ-ment	Primary SIC
Omaha Home For Boys Inc	3781	Omaha, NE	Private	23.6	91	8361
Healthohio, Inc	3782	Marion, OH	Private	57.8	90	8011
Homecall Pharmaceutical Svcs	3783	Columbia, MD	Public Family Member	40.0	90	8082
One Call Medical, Inc	3784	Parsippany, NJ	Private	35.0	90	8011
Premier Healthcare, Inc	3785	Phoenix, AZ	Private	53.5	90	8011
Sierra Health Services Inc	3786	Bullhead City, AZ	Private	721.7	90	8011
United Physicians Health Netwrk	3787	Evansville, IN	Public Family Member	43.6	90	8011
Us Health Management Corp	3788	Melville, NY	Public Family Member	30.0	90	8071
Penobscot Bay Medical Assoc	3789	Portland, ME	Private	47.0	89	8093
Allina Self-Insured	3790	Hopkins, MN	Private	37.8	87	8011
Azalealand Nursing Home Inc	3791	Savannah, GA	Private	29.0	87	8051
Phoenix Healthcare Of Tenn	3792	Nashville, TN	Private	59.6	86	8082
Lake Shore Nursing Home Inc	3793	Irving, NY	Private	23.4	85	8059
Community Partnr Southern Ariz	3794	Tucson, AZ	Private	65.0	82	8093
Ancilla Health Services, Inc	3795	Fort Wayne, IN	Private	23.0	80	8011
Charleston Area Health Plan	3796	Charleston, WV	Private	78.4	80	8011
Healthaccess Inc	3797	Greenville, NC	Private	30.8	80	8093
Oxford Health Plans (Pa) Inc	3798	Philadelphia, PA	Public Family Member	118.0	80	8011
Suncare Respiratory Services	3799	Indianapolis, IN	Public Family Member	64.0	80	8093
Preferred Health Management	3800	Woodland Hills, CA	Private	32.0	79	8099
California Family Health Council	3801	Los Angeles, CA	Private	25.3	77	8093
Uct International Inc	3802	Farmingdale, NY	Public Family Member	24.1	76	8071
Brandywine Health Services	3803	Coatesville, PA	Private	77.4	75	8062
Delmarva Health Plan Inc	3804	Easton, MD	Private	66.5	75	8011
Medical Research Industries	3805	Fort Lauderdale, FL	Private	40.0	75	8049
Summit Cosmetic Group	3806	Beverly Hills, CA	Private	22.0	73	8011
San Leandro Hospital	3807	San Leandro, CA	Private	52.0	70	8361
Solano County Comm On Med Care	3808	Suisun City, CA	Private	102.5	70	8011
Vintage Estates Of Sacramento	3809	Sacramento, CA	Private	350.0	70	8051
Community Health Plan Of Ohio	3810	Newark, OH	Private	21.0	67	8011
Amsurg, Corp	3811	Nashville, TN	Public	57.4	64	8062
May Institute	3812	Fall River, MA	Private	41.7	64	8093
Healthright Inc	3813	Meriden, CT	Private	53.1	60	8011
Virginia Physicians, Inc	3814	Richmond, VA	Private	40.0	60	8011
Evergreen Healthcare Mgt Llc	3815	Vancouver, WA	Private	42.5	56	8051
Deaconess Health Care Corp	3816	Oklahoma City, OK	Private	85.7	55	8361
First Commonwealth, Inc.	3817	Chicago, IL	Public	44.1	55	8021
Radiologic Specialists Of Ind	3818	Indianapolis, IN	Private	20.0	55	8011
Reading Hospital (Inc)	3819	Reading, PA	Private	253.6	55	8062
Healthplex Inc	3820	Uniondale, NY	Public	20.3	54	8021
Anne Arundel Medical Center	3821	Annapolis, MD	Private	134.7	50	8062
Columbia Outpatient Surgical Svcs	3822	Fort Lauderdale, FL	Private	25.0	50	8011
Medical Imaging Services	3823	North Little Rock, AR	Private	25.0	50	8071
Southern Medical Group, Inc	3824	Birmingham, AL	Private	25.0	50	8011
Grand Valley Health Plan Inc	3825	Grand Rapids, MI	Private	36.3	49	8011
Allegiant Physician Services	3826	Atlanta, GA	Public	57.6	48	8099
Arnett Hmo Inc	3827	Lafayette, IN	Public Family Member	53.5	46	8011
Arundel Health Anne System	3828	Annapolis, MD	Private	145.3	46	8062
Temple Surgical Center Inc	3829	New Haven, CT	Private	20.0	46	8011
Anne Arundel Health Care Svcs	3830	Annapolis, MD	Private	138.8	45	8093
Manhattan Prepaid Health Svc Plan	3831	New York, NY	Private	23.0	45	8011
Northern Arizona Regional Be	3832	Flagstaff, AZ	Private	26.0	45	8093
U S Physical Therapy	3833	Houston, TX	Public	38.8	45	8049
Hematology Clinic P.C	3834	Portland, OR	Private	27.0	44	8011
Cigna Healthcare Of Louisiana	3835	Baton Rouge, LA	Public Family Member	30.6	40	8011
Foundation Health Systems	3836	Winston Salem, NC	Private	25.0	40	8011
Roper Carealliance Inc	3837	Charleston, SC	Private	242.5	40	8099
St Vincent's Ambulatory Care	3838	Jacksonville, FL	Private	20.0	39	8011
Health Plus Of Louisiana Inc	3839	Shreveport, LA	Private	22.0	37	8011
Rio Grande Hmo Inc	3840	El Paso, TX	Private	132.4	37	8011
Hunt Assoc Asssted Living Corp	3841	Abingdon, VA	Private	20.0	35	8051
Northwest Medical Teams Intl	3842	Portland, OR	Private	50.1	34	8099
Managed Healthcare Systems Nj	3843	Newark, NJ	Private	32.5	33	8011
Pratt Medical Group, Inc	3844	Boston, MA	Private	27.1	33	8011
Brighton Marine Health Center	3845	Boston, MA	Private	45.9	31	8093
Cigna Healthcare Of Tennessee	3846	Bloomfield, CT	Public Family Member	161.1	30	8011
San Mateo Individual Practice	3847	San Bruno, CA	Private	34.0	30	8011
Maxicare Louisiana, Inc	3848	New Orleans, LA	Public Family Member	20.0	28	8011
Genesis Lifestyles Inc	3849	Macon, GA	Private	864.0	25	8059
Managed Care Assistance Corp	3850	Rockville, MD	Private	65.0	25	8099

D&B COMPANY RANKINGS BY EMPLOYMENT

Company	Rank	Location	Type	Sales ($ mil.)	Employ- ment	Primary SIC
Methodist Healthcare Ministrie	3852	San Antonio, TX	Private	29.8	25	8011
Northmed Hmo Inc	3853	Traverse City, MI	Private	24.6	23	8011
Heart Care Centers Of Ill S C	3854	Oak Forest, IL	Private	45.0	22	8011
Delta Dental Plan Of Tenn	3855	Nashville, TN	Private	39.6	21	8021
Gentle Dental Service Corp	3856	Vancouver, WA	Public	43.4	21	8021
Preferred Plus Of Kansas Inc	3857	Wichita, KS	Private	28.9	21	8011
Medical Arts Pathologists Inc	3858	Oklahoma City, OK	Private	27.2	18	8071
Dmh Health Systems	3859	Decatur, IL	Private	106.4	16	8062
Lrimg, Inc	3860	Los Gatos, CA	Private	109.6	16	8011
Cape Medical Inc	3861	Detroit, MI	Private	21.6	15	8011
Elim Care, Inc	3862	Eden Prairie, MN	Private	26.6	15	8051
Employees Retirement Sys St Louis	3863	Saint Louis, MO	Private	49.0	15	8051
National Diagnostic Laboratory	3864	Moreno Valley, CA	Private	20.0	15	8071
Santa Cruz Medical Clinic	3865	Santa Cruz, CA	Private	30.5	15	8011
Santa Ana Tustin Radiology	3866	Santa Ana, CA	Private	79.7	13	8011
Allegheny Intgrated Health Group	3867	Philadelphia, PA	Private	117.6	10	8011
Esplanade Gardens Inc	3868	Corpus Christi, TX	Private	25.0	10	8361
Peak Medical Corp	3869	Albuquerque, NM	Private	65.0	10	8051
Tandem Health Care Inc	3870	Jensen Beach, FL	Private	30.0	9	8051
Phoebe-Devitt Homes Inc	3871	Allentown, PA	Private	45.2	8	8051
Health Net Inc	3872	Nashville, TN	Private	98.8	6	8011
Aetna Us Healthcare An Ohio Corp	3873	Richfield, OH	Public Family Member	183.5	5	8011
Allegany General Hospital Inc	3874	Uniontown, PA	Private	465.7	5	8011
Charter Professional Services	3875	Salem, MA	Private	32.1	5	8011
Medicare Risk Network Llc	3876	Philadelphia, PA	Private	35.0	5	8011
U V M C Nursing Care Inc	3877	Troy, OH	Private	20.7	5	8051
Aetna Health Plans Southern Ne	3878	Hartford, CT	Public Family Member	116.7	4	8011
Excelcare System Inc	3879	Bronxville, NY	Private	40.0	4	8099
Good Health Hmo, Inc	3880	Kansas City, MO	Private	25.0	4	8011
Hill Physicians Med Group Inc	3881	San Ramon, CA	Private	190.0	4	8011
Massachusetts Eye & Ear Assoc	3882	Boston, MA	Private	29.9	4	8011
Metro West-Marlborough Health	3883	Marlborough, MA	Private	32.0	4	8062
Physicians Health Network	3884	Evansville, IN	Public Family Member	39.7	4	8011
Rush Prudential Insurance Co	3885	Chicago, IL	Private	85.5	4	8011
Southern Health Services, Inc	3886	Richmond, VA	Private	84.6	4	8011
St Joseph's Medical Center	3887	Brainerd, MN	Private	51.2	4	8011
Upmc Passavant	3888	Pittsburgh, PA	Private	78.8	4	8062
Phywell Inc	3889	Jacksonville, FL	Private	36.0	3	8099
Comprehensive Health Resources	3890	Rutland, VT	Private	76.4	2	8062
Fay-West Health System	3891	Mount Pleasant, PA	Private	43.4	2	8062
Elder Healthcare Developers Llc	3892	Norcross, GA	Private	20.0	1	8052

CHAPTER 6

MERGERS & ACQUISITIONS

The following essay presents a look at merger and acquisition activity in the Health and Medical Services sector. A general overview of M&A activity is followed by a listing of actual merger and acquisition events. Purchasing companies are listed in alphabetical order, with a paragraph set aside for each acquisition.

This essay discusses recent merger and acquisition activity in the industry and its effect on the industry. The essay is followed by a list of significant acquisitions and mergers.

Nearly every market segment in the health and medical services industry has seen increased levels of merger and acquisition activity over the past two years. The total number of health care mergers and acquisitions in the United States reached 1,183 in 1997, a 19 percent jump from 1996. Lines between health insurance companies and health and medical service providers have blurred as companies strive to offer a broader range of services to clients, who are increasingly concerned about the rising cost of health care products and services. As a result, size has become a crucial element for success because larger health care companies are able to use their sizable customer bases to secure less expensive rates from physicians, insurance providers, hospitals, and other heath care providers.

Nowhere is this phenomenon more evident than in the managed care segment of the health and medical services industry. Because more than one quarter of the U.S. population belongs to a health maintenance organization (HMO), and more than one half has joined some sort of a managed care plan, larger HMO and managed care companies are able to shop around for cheaper doctors, medical services, etc., for inclusion in their networks. To remain competitive in an industry that appears to be increasingly driven by insurers, as well as cost, doctors, hospitals, and other health care providers have begun merging together as a means of reducing costs, streamlining operations, and gaining access to the reduced prices to which members of a network have access. For example, Phycor Inc. and MedPartners Inc., the two largest physician management companies in the United States, merged in a stock and debt transaction valued at $8 billion in November of 1997.

Over the past two years a number of mergers have taken place among managed care and HMO companies that have significantly reduced the number of players in the industry segment. For example, United Health Care Corp. bought MetraHealth Companies, Inc., based in McLean, Virginia, for $1.59 billion in January of 1996. Upon completion of the acquisition, United Health Care became the largest

managed care services firm in the United States with estimated yearly sales in excess of $8 billion. In August of 1998, a $5.5 billion merger between United Health Care and Humana Inc. was called off by Humana after United Health Care posted a whopping $900 million second quarter loss. Despite this setback, both Humana and United Health Care remain on the acquisition trail, and it seems only a matter of time before at least one of these firms is a partner in the creation of a new industry behemoth.

Other noteworthy managed care and HMO transactions include the $8.9 billion purchase of U.S. Health Care Inc. by Aetna Life and Casualty Co. in April of 1996. Upon completion of the transaction, Aetna/U.S. Health Care became one of the largest managed health care providers in the United States. In February of 1997, PacifiCare Health Systems Inc. became the fifth largest health maintenance organization in the United States when it bought FHP International Corp., a managed health company, for $2.2 billion. Also, Cigna Corp. bought Healthsource Inc., a health maintenance organization based in Hooksett, New Hampshire, for $1.7 billion in early 1997. Finally, on April 1, 1997, Foundation Health Corp. and Health Systems International, Inc. merged to form Foundation Health Systems Inc., a leading managed health care provider with annual revenues in excess of $7.5 billion. The transaction was valued at roughly $3 billion.

Because cost is shaping the health care industry more dramatically than any other factor, the home health care services segment has seen more intense growth than any other portion of the health and medical services industry—it now accounts for more than $30 billion annually. Between 1990 and 1995 the number of home health care firms in the United States grew from 11,765 to 18,874, an increase of roughly 60 percent. Because most of the industry giants, such as Columbia/HCA Health Care Corp. and Olsten Corp., have diversified into home health care services, smaller firms have had to either acquire or be acquired to remain competitive.

American Home Patient Inc., one of the leading home health care companies in the United States, is a prime example of growth via acquisitions. During 1997, the company completed twenty-seven acquisitions. In October alone, American Home Patient bought AAYS of Nevada, a Los Vegas-based provider of respiratory therapies and home medical equipment; Medical Options, an Orlando, Florida-based provider of respiratory therapies and home medical equipment; Summit Home Care, a home health care services provider located in Utica, New York; Total Mobility, a Los Vegas-based provider of respiratory therapies and home medical equipment; and United Clinical Services, a Cedar Grove, New Jersey-based provider of respiratory and infusion therapies and home medical equipment. The company's 1998 purchases included Carolina Home Oxygen Medical Supply, a North Carolina-based provider of respiratory therapies and home medical equipment, in January; National Medical Systems, a privately owned home health care company based in Little Rock, Arkansas, in February; Volunteer Medical Oxygen and Hospital Equipment, a respiratory therapies and home medical equipment provider based in Nashville, Tennessee, in March; and Greenbrier Respiratory Care Services, a home health care company based in Lewisburg, West Virginia, in July.

As an increasing number of patients are treated at home, hospitals themselves must consolidate to remain competitive. In 1997, 181 hospital deals were completed, up from 133 two years prior. One of the more noteworthy marriages was the merging of North Shore Health System and Long Island Jewish Medical Center into one of the largest hospital systems in the United States, with 13 hospitals, two nursing homes, and a $2.5 billion annual budget, in October of 1997. Also, University of California at San Francisco Medical Center and Stanford University Medical Center merged to form UCFS Stanford Health Care, on November 1, 1997.

Long-term care is another industry sector which has seen intense merger and acquisition activity over the past two years. Long-term care is currently growing at a rate of eight percent annually. According to industry analysts, the number of elderly patients requiring long-term care will grow from seven million to more than nine million over the next five or six years. Hoping to capitalize on this trend, many health care industry leaders have diversified into long-term care, the result of which is similar to the home health care industry: a frenetic pace of merger and acquisition among the smaller players seeking

either growth via acquisitions or security via a buy-out. The number of long-term care transactions in 1996 reached 121, nearly double the amount in 1995. This number jumped even higher in 1997 because the stock prices of long-term care companies tumbled a bit due to Medicare and Medicaid reform concerns in late 1996. Lower stock prices fueled purchases in the industry segment throughout 1997.

A major acquisition in the long-term care sector took place in September of 1997 when Genesis Health Ventures Inc. bought Multicare Companies Inc., an elder care services provider, for $1.4 billion. In October of 1997, Sun Health Care Group, Inc. bought Regency Health Services, Inc., a nursing center operator based in Tustin, California, for $367 million in cash and the assumption of $258 million in debt. Two major transactions also took place in November of 1997: Extendicare Inc. bought Arbor Health Care Co. for $432 million; and GranCare, Inc. and Living Centers of America Inc. merged to form Paragon Health Network, the third largest long-term care company in the United States with annual revenues of roughly $1.9 billion.

Several smaller segments of the health and medical services industry have also seen increased levels of merger and acquisition activity. For example, in the assisted living sector, Seattle, Washington-based Emeritus Corp. launched a $313 million takeover bid of Costa Mesa, California-based rival ARV Assisted Living Inc. Although the takeover attempt failed, most analysts believe that the bid was a sign of impending activity in this ancillary market sector. Consolidation has also heated up in the kidney dialysis market segment, as evidenced by the $1.3 billion stock swap between Total Renal Care Holdings Inc. and Renal Treatment Centers Inc. in February of 1998. The purchase doubled the size of Total Renal Care, solidifying its position as the second largest dialysis center in the United States, with a 15 percent market share. Even radiologists have felt pressure to merge to remain competitive: on October 1, 1997, Radiology Associates, based in Everett, Washington, and Puget Sound Radiology, also based in Washington, merged to form Radia Medical Imaging Inc., the largest radiology group in the state.

Despite the many lucrative niche markets in the health and medical services industry, most of the industry's players have sought and continue to seek a position within a comprehensive health care network, as a means of gaining access to less expensive products and services, as well as large client bases. Accordingly, many significant mergers over the past two years reflect this trend: in October of 1997, HealthSouth Corp. bought Horizon/CMS Health Care Corp., which owns 139 long term care complexes, 12 specialty hospitals, and 35 institutional pharmacies, for $1.7 billion; in January of 1998, Integrated Health Services Inc. bought Horizon/CMS Health Care Corp. for $1.15 billion in cash and $100 million in assumed debt; and in August of 1998, Columbia/HCA Health Care Corp. bought Value Health Inc., a health care insurance, pharmaceutical benefits, and disease management company based in Avon, Connecticut, for $1.3 billion.

Despite antitrust concerns regarding the creation of these large, integrated health care networks, most industry analysts believe that the potential for continued consolidation in the industry is high both within specialized industry segments, as well as across the health and medical services industry as a whole. Many analysts predict that over the next few years, the number of large heath care companies will shrink as merger and acquisition activity intensifies.

Mergers and Acquisitions

Aetna Life and Casualty Co. bought **U.S. Health Care Inc.** for $8.9 billion in April of 1996. Upon completion of the transaction, **Aetna/U.S. Health Care** became one of the largest managed health care providers in the United States. [*Business Week,* 4/15/96, p. 41.]

Alexian Brothers Health System bought **Hoffman Estates Medical Center** and **Woodland Hospital,** both located in Chicago, Illinois, from **Columbia/HCA Health Care Corp.** in August of 1998. [*Modern Health Care,* 8/24/98, p. 18.]

Alliance Imaging Inc. bought **Medical Consultants Imaging Co.,** a mobile magnetic resonance imaging, cat scan, and related health care services provider based in Cleveland, Ohio, in November of 1997. [*Business Wire,* 1/24/97.]

Altius Health Plans bought the Utah-based health plan holdings of **PacifiCare Health Systems, Inc.** in October of 1998. [*PR Newswire,* 10/2/98.]

AMEDISYS, Inc. bought **Alliance Home Health, Inc.,** a mobile infusion therapy services company located in Tulsa, Oklahoma, in a stock swap on January 7, 1998. [*PR Newswire,* 1/7/98.]

American HomePatient Inc. bought **Greenbrier Respiratory Care Services,** a home health care company based in Lewisburg, West Virginia, on July 9, 1998. [*Business Wire,* 7/9/98.]

—bought **Volunteer Medical Oxygen and Hospital Equipment,** a respiratory therapies and home medical equipment provider based in Nashville, Tennessee, on March 10, 1998. [*Business Wire,* 3/10/98.]

—bought **National Medical Systems,** a privately owned home health care company based in Little Rock, Arkansas, on February 6, 1998. [*Business Wire,* 2/6/98.]

—bought **Carolina Home Oxygen Medical Supply,** a North Carolina-based provider of respiratory therapies and home medical equipment, on January 14, 1998. [*Business Wire,* 1/14/98.]

—bought **AAYS of Nevada,** a Los Vegas-based provider of respiratory therapies and home medical equipment, in October of 1997. [*Business Wire,* 10/28/97.]

—bought **Medical Options,** an Orlando, Florida-based provider of respiratory therapies and home medical equipment, in October of 1997. [*Business Wire,* 10/28/97.]

—bought **Summit Home Care,** a home health care services provider located in Utica, New York, in October of 1997. [*Business Wire,* 10/28/97.]

—bought **Total Mobility,** a Los Vegas-based provider of respiratory therapies and home medical equipment, in October of 1997. [*Business Wire,* 10/28/97.]

—bought **United Clinical Services,** a Cedar Grove, New Jersey-based provider of respiratory and infusion therapies and home medical equipment, in October of 1997. [*Business Wire,* 10/28/97.]

—bought **C-P Medical, Inc.,** a home health care services provider based in Worthington, Ohio, in September of 1997. [*Business Wire,* 9/4/97.]

—bought the respiratory and medical equipment holdings of **Headley Home Care Medical Services,** based in Franksville, Wisconsin, in August of 1998. [*The Business Journal-Milwaukee,* 8/22/97, p. 9.]

—bought **Cross Medical Equipment,** a home health care medical products provider based in Oneida, Tennessee. [*Business Wire,* 3/26/97.]

—bought **Krieger Medical Inc.,** a home medical e-quipment firm based in Houston, Texas, in March of 1997. [*Business Wire,* 3/19/97.]

—bought **United Medical Corp.,** an owner and operator of four home health care centers in Missouri and Illinois, in March of 1997. [*Business Wire,* 3/26/97.]

—bought **Choice Health Services Inc.,** a Maryland-based home health care provider specializing in home infusion, intravenous nutrition, medical equipment, respiratory services, and rehabilitation equipment and services, in February of 1997. [*Business Wire,* 2/5/97.]

—bought **Home Medical Services Inc.,** an Alabama-based home health care provider specializing in intravenous nutrition, medical equipment, and respiratory services, in February of 1997. [*Business Wire,* 2/5/97.]

—bought **PrimaCare Health Resources of Rochester Inc.,** a home health care provider based in New York, in January of 1997. [*Business Wire,* 1/27/97.]

AmeriPath Inc. bought **Shoals Pathology Associates, P.C.,** an inpatient and outpatient anatomic pathology practice located in Muscle Shoals, Alabama, in August of 1998. [*PR Newswire,* 8/20/98.]

—bought **H. Michael Jones, M.D., P.A.,** a hospital-based anatomic pathology practice located in Hen-

derson, North Carolina, in August of 1998. [*PR Newswire,* 8/20/98.]

—bought **The Dermatopathology Laboratory,** an anatomic pathology practice located in Pittsburgh, Pennsylvania, in December of 1997. [*PR Newswire,* 12/19/98.]

—bought **Laboratory Physicians,** an anatomic pathology practice located in Jacksonville, Florida, in December of 1997. [*PR Newswire,* 12/19/98.]

ARV Assisted Living, Inc. bought 13 senior citizen housing complexes from **Hillsdale Group, L.P.,** located in Burlingame, California, for $88 million in February of 1998. [*Business Wire,* 2/12/98.]

Atria Communities, Inc. bought **Atria St. George,** an assisted living complex located in St. George, Utah, in February of 1998. [*Business Wire,* 2/24/98.]

—bought **Atria Highland Crossing,** an assisted living complex located in Fort Wright, Kentucky, in February of 1998. [*Business Wire,* 2/24/98.]

—bought **Atria Cottage Village,** an assisted living complex located in Lubbock, Texas, in March of 1998. [*Business Wire,* 2/24/98.]

Banyan Health Care Services, Inc. and **NuMed Home Health Care, Inc.** merged in February of 1998. [*Business Wire,* 2/18/98.]

—bought **National Health Enterprises Inc.,** a home health care staffing services provider based in Philadelphia, Pennsylvania, in January of 1998. [*Business Wire,* 2/18/98.]

—bought **STAT** and **ELLIS,** two staffing divisions of **International Nursing Services, Inc.,** in late 1997. [*Business Wire,* 2/18/98.]

—bought **PAXXON,** a staffing division of **International Nursing Services, Inc.,** in October of 1997. [*Business Wire,* 2/18/98.]

Benefit Partners Inc. bought **Health Insurance Plan of California,** a health insurance purchasing pool owned by **Humana, Inc.,** in February of 1998. [*PR Newswire,* 2/17/98.]

Brookdale Living Communities, Inc. bought **Harbor Village Retirement Community,** located in Chicago, Illinois, for $16.75 million in November of 1997. [*PR Newswire,* 11/24/97.]

California Pacific Medical Center bought **Davies Medical Center,** a struggling AIDS treatment facility located in San Francisco, California, in June of 1998. [*San Francisco Business Times,* 4/3/98, p. 1.]

Caretenders Health Corp. bought **Metro Home Care, Inc.,** a home health services provider based in Fort Myers, Florida, on January 8, 1998. [*PR Newswire,* 1/8/98.]

—bought **Nelson Care, Inc.,** an adult day care health services provider based in Cleveland, Ohio, on January 2, 1998. [*PR Newswire,* 1/2/98.]

Catholic Health Initiatives bought **Jewish Hospital Lexington,** a 174-bed facility, from **Jewish Hospital Health Care Services,** a hospital system located in Louisville, Kentucky, in November of 1998. [*Modern Health Care,* 10/50/98, p. 18.]

Catholic Health Care West bought the hospital division of **UniHealth,** including 8 hospitals in California, for $5 million in late 1998. [*Modern Health Care,* 10/26/98, p. 24.]

—bought **Emergency Physicians Medical Group,** a physician staffing provider serving hospital emergency rooms in California, Nevada, and Hawaii, in late 1997. [*PR Newswire,* 11/20/97.]

Children's Comprehensive Services Inc. bought **Ameris Health Systems, Inc.,** an operator of residential juvenile sex offender programs in the southeastern United States, for $12.5 million in cash on September 10, 1998. [*Business Wire,* 9/10/98.]

—bought **Ventures Management Services,** a day treatment centers management firm based in Gainesville, Florida, for $2.7 million in stock on January 22, 1998. [*Business Wire,* 1/22/98.]

Cigna Corp. bought **Healthsource Inc.,** a health maintenance organization based in Hooksett, New Hampshire, for $1.7 billion in early 1997. [*Best's Review,* 4/97, p. 20.]

Columbia/HCA Health Care Corp. bought a hospital located in San Jose, California, from **Alexian Brothers Health System** in August of 1998. [*Modern Health Care,* 8/24/98, p. 18.]

—bought **Value Health Inc.,** a health care, pharmaceutical benefits, and disease management company based in Avon, Connecticut, for $1.3 billion on August 6, 1998. [*PR Newswire,* 8/6/97.]

Dental Care Alliance, Inc. bought two dental practices, one located in Ocala, Florida, and one located in Jacksonville, Florida, for a total of roughly $1.15 million in cash and notes on September 17, 1998. [*Business Wire,* 9/17/98.]

Dental Services of America bought a dental practice located in Plantation, Florida, from Alan J. Zukor, D.D.S., in August of 1998. [*Business Wire,* 8/18/98.]

Diagnostic Health Services, Inc. bought **Medical Diagnostic Imaging Inc.,** a mobile ultrasound services provider based in Huntsville, Alabama, on December 3, 1997. [*Business Wire,* 12/3/97.]

Emeritus Corp. bought **ARV Assisted Living, Inc.** for $17.50 per share for all outstanding shares of the assisted living facility operator on December 19, 1997. [*Business Wire,* 12/19/97.]

Express Scripts Inc. bought **ValueRx,** the pharmacy benefit management subsidiary of **Columbia/HCA Health Care Corp.,** for $445 million in cash on April 1, 1998. [*PR Newswire,* 4/1/98.]

Extendicare Inc. bought **Arbor Health Care Co.,** a long-term care provider, for $432 million, in November of 1997. [*Business Wire,* 11/26/97.]

FHC Health Systems, Inc. bought **Value Behavioral Health,** a subsidiary of **Columbia/HCA Health Care Corp.,** for $206.5 million on June 18, 1998. Upon completion of the transaction, FHC Health Systems became the second largest behavioral health company in the United States. [*PR Newswire,* 6/18/98.]

Foundation Health Systems Inc. bought **Physician Health Services, Inc.,** a 440,000 member health plan located in Shelton, Connecticut, for $271 million in January of 1998. [*Business Wire,* 1/5/98.]

—bought **PACC Health Plans Inc.,** a 116,000 member health plan operating in Oregon and Washington, in the summer of 1997. [*Business Wire,* 4/9/97.]

—bought **Advantage Health Corp.,** a group of managed health care providers located in Pittsburgh, Pennsylvania, for $12.5 million in cash on April 4, 1997. [*Business Wire,* 4/4/97.]

Foundation Health Corp. and **Health Systems International, Inc.** merged to form **Foundation Health Systems Inc.,** a leading managed health care provider with annual revenues in excess of $7.5 billion, on April 1, 1997. The transaction was valued at roughly $3 billion. [*Business Wire,* 4/9/97.]

Fountain View, Inc bought **Summit Care Corp.,** a rehabilitative care, infusion therapy and related health care services provider based in Burbank California, for $274 million, on February 13, 1998. [*Business Wire,* 2/9/98.]

Franciscan Sisters of Allegheny Health System, Eastern Mercy Health System, and **Sisters of Providence Health System** merged to form **Catholic Health East,** based in Radnor, Pennsylvania, in October of 1997. [*The Bond Buyer,* 1/6/98, p. 1.]

Genesis Health Ventures Inc. bought **Vitalink Pharmacy Services Inc.** for roughly $680 million in cash, notes, and assumed debt in August of 1998. [*Business Wire,* 8/31/98.]

—bought **Multicare Companies Inc.,** an elder care services provider, for $1.4 billion in September of 1997. [*PR Newswire,* 6/16/97.]

GranCare, Inc. and **Living Centers of America Inc.** merged to form **Paragon Health Network,** the third largest long-term care company in the United States with annual revenues of roughly $1.9 billion, on November 4, 1997. [*PR Newswire,* 11/4/97.]

Grand Court Lifestyles, Inc. bought an adult living community in Carrollton, Georgia, in October of 1998. [*PR Newswire,* 10/27/98.]

Green Springs Health Services, Inc. bought an 80 percent stake in **CHC,** an employee assistance pro-

gram provider based in Canada, in December of 1997. [*PR Newswire,* 12/16/97.]

Greenbriar Corp. bought **Villa Residential Care Homes, Inc.,** including 12 assisted living communities in Texas, on December 31, 1997.[*PR Newswire,* 1/6/98.]

Guardian Health Corp. bought three rehabilitation hospitals located in California from **Tenet Health Care Corp.** on November 12, 1997. [*Business Wire,* 11/6/97.]

Hanger Orthopedic Group, Inc. bought **G&F Enterprises, Inc.,** an advanced prosthetic and orthopedic services provider based in El Paso, Texas, in October of 1998. [*PR Newswire,* 10/8/98.]

Harborside Health Care Corp. bought two long-term care communities located in Toledo, Ohio, from **JAD Enterprises, Inc.** in the second quarter of 1998. [*Business Wire,* 2/10/98.]

Health Management Associates Inc. bought **Riley Memorial Hospital,** a general acute care facility located in Meridian, Mississippi, on January 2, 1998. [*PR Newswire,* 1/27/98.]

—bought **River Oaks Health System,** a general acute care facility located in Mississippi, in January of 1998. [*PR Newswire,* 11/11/97.]

—bought **Southwest Hospital,** a general acute care facility located in Pulaski County, Arkansas, on November 1, 1997. [*PR Newswire,* 11/11/97.]

HealthMax Inc. bought **HMO California,** the California-based subsidiary of **Humana, Inc,.** in November of 1997. [*PR Newswire,* 11/3/97.]

HealthSouth Corp. bought **Horizon/CMS Health Care Corp.,** which includes 139 long term care complexes, 12 specialty hospitals, and 35 institutional pharmacies, for $1.7 billion in October of 1997. [*Modern Health Care,* 11/10/97, p. 49.]

—bought **Cedar Court Physical Rehabilitation Hospital,** located in Melbourne, Australia, on October 23, 1997. [*PR Newswire,* 12/5/97.]

Humana Inc. bought **ChoiceCare Corp.,** owner of a health maintenance organization in Cincinnati, Ohio, for $250 million in cash on October 17, 1997. [*PR Newswire,* 10/17/97.]

—bought **Physician Corporation of America,** owner of health maintenance organizations in Florida, Texas, and Puerto Rico, for $400 million in cash on September 8, 1997. [*PR Newswire,* 9/8/97.]

—bought **Health Direct, Inc.,** a managed health care services provider based in Chicago, Illinois, for $20.5 million in cash in January of 1997. [*PR Newswire,* 1/8/97.]

Idora Silver Mines Inc. bought **Nurses Station of America Inc.,** a New York-based heathcare provider serving automobile and work accident victims, in September of 1998. [*Business Wire,* 9/10/98.]

InSight Health Services Corp. bought **Redwood City MRI,** a magnetic resonance imaging center located in Redwood City, California, in November of 1997. [*Business Wire,* 11/13/97.]

Integrated Health Services Inc. bought **Horizon/CMS Health Care Corp.,** which includes 139 long term care complexes, 12 specialty hospitals, and 35 institutional pharmacies, from Birmingham, Alabama-based **HealthSouth Corp.,** for $1.15 billion in cash and $100 million in assumed debt in January of 1998. [*PR Newswire,* 1/2/98.]

Interim Health Care Inc. bought the Arizona-based homecare operations of **Columbia/HCA Heathcare Corp.** on September 25, 1998. [*PR Newswire,* 10/1/98.]

International Nursing Services, Inc. bought **Cymedix Corp.,** a privately owned Internet-based medical information and communications management operation, for seven million shares on December 22, 1997. [*Business Wire,* 12/22/97.]

Jewish Hospital Health Care Services Inc. bought **Jewish Hospital Lexington** from **Humana,** a managed care firm based in Louisville, Kentucky, in November of 1997. [*Modern Health Care,* 10/50/98, p. 18.]

Kaiser Permanente of the Mid-Atlantic States bought **Humana Group Health Plans, Inc.,** based in Washington, D.C., in February of 1997. [*PR Newswire,* 2/1/97.]

Laboratory Specialists of America Inc. bought **Accu-Path Medical Laboratory, Inc.,** a drug testing business based in Arkansas, in December of 1997. [*Business Wire,* 12/8/97.]

Magellan Health Services Inc. bought **Merit Behavioral Care Corp.,** a mental health and substance abuse employee assistance provider, for $625 million in February of 1998. [*PR Newswire,* 2/6/98.]

—bought **Allied Health Group,** a specialty care management and claims processing firm based in Florida, on December 10, 1997. [*PR Newswire,* 12/10/97.]

—bought **Human Affairs International Inc.,** the Salt Lake City, Utah-based behavioral health subsidiary of **Aetna/U.S. Health Care Inc.,** for $122.1 million in cash on December 5, 1997. [*Philadelphia Business Journal,* 12/12/97, p. 39.]

McKesson Health Systems Group bought **MedManagement L.L.C.,** a pharmacy management, purchasing, consulting, and information services firm located in Plymouth, Minnesota, on September 14, 1998. [*Business Wire,* 9/14/98.]

MedCath Inc. bought **Ultimed, Inc.,** a cardiovascular disease management services firm based in Los Angeles, California, on May 16, 1997. [*Business Wire,* 5/16/97.]

Medical Industries of America Inc. bought **Care America Integrated Health Care Services Inc.,** a privately owned home health care services provider based in Florida, for $200,000 in January of 1998. [*Business Wire,* 1/16/98.]

Medical Technology Consolidation Group, Inc. bought 10 **Health Care Agencies,** independently owned home health care delivery services in Texas, California, Illinois, and Minnesota, in December of 1997. [*PR Newswire,* 12/3/97.]

Medshares Management Group Inc. bought home health care agencies in California, Nevada, New Mexico, and Texas from **Columbia/HCA Heathcare Corp.** on October 19, 1998. [*PR Newswire,* 10/19/98.]

—bought home health care agencies in Arkansas, Illinois, Indiana, Kentucky, South Carolina, Utah, and Virginia from **Columbia/HCA Heathcare Corp.** on October 1, 1998. [*PR Newswire,* 10/1/98.]

Memorial Mission Medical Center bought **St. Joseph's Hospital** located in Asheville, North Carolina, for $90 million in October of 1998. [*Modern Health Care,* 11/2/98, p. 21.]

Merit Behavioral Care Corp. bought **CMG Health Inc.,** a behavioral health managed care company, for $51.5 million in cash and 750,000 shares on September 12, 1997. [*Business Wire,* 9/16/97.]

Multi-Plan, Inc. bought **Preferred Plan,** a preferred provider company serving the southeastern United States, from **PacifiCare Health Systems** in November of 1997. [*PR Newswire,* 11/25/97.]

New York Health Care, Inc. bought three New Jersey-based home health care units, with combined annual revenues of $3.6 million, in February of 1998. [*Business Wire,* 2/12/98.]

NewCare Health Corp. bought **Renaissance Senior Living, Inc.,** an assisted living facilities owner and operator based in Florida, for $2 million in early 1998. [*PR Newswire,* 12/17/97.]

—bought **Iatros Health Network, Inc.,** a health care facilities lease and management firm, for $17 million in stock in December of 1997. [*PR Newswire,* 12/23/97.]

North Shore Health System and **Long Island Jewish Medical Center** merged into one of the largest hospital systems in the United States, with 13 hospitals, two nursing homes, and a $2.5 billion annual budget, in October of 1997. [*LI Business News,* 1/19/98, p. 32.]

PacifiCare Health Systems Inc. bought **FHP International Corp.,** a managed health company, for $2.2

billion in February of 1997. Upon completion of the acquisition, PacifiCare Health Systems became the fifth largest health maintenance organization in the United States, with annual revenues in excess of $10 billion. [*Business Wire,* 2/20/97.]

Pediatric Services of America Inc. bought **Texas Air Supply Home Medical Equipment, Inc.,** a home health equipment services provider based in Fort Worth, Texas, on January 15, 1998. [*Business Wire,* 1/15/98.]

—bought **Kids Nurses, Inc.,** a pediatric home nursing provider based in St. Louis, Missouri, in January of 1998. [*Business Wire,* 1/15/98.]

—bought **Cyber HomeCare, Inc.,** a respiratory therapy and medical equipment services provider based in Rockville Center, New York, in December of 1997. [*Business Wire,* 12/1/97.]

—bought **IntraCare, Inc.** and **Intravenous Treatment Centers, Inc.,** two home infusion service providers based in Little Falls, New Jersey, in November of 1997. [*Business Wire,* 11/10/97.]

—bought **Pediatric Physical Therapy, Inc.,** an outpatient physical therapy services provider based in St. Louis, Missouri, in November of 1997. [*Business Wire,* 11/10/97.]

Pediatrix Medical Group Inc. bought **Border Neonatal Associates,** based in El Paso, Texas, in February of 1998. [*Business Wire,* 2/13/98.]

PhyCor Inc. and **MedPartners Inc.,** the two largest physician management companies in the United States, merged in a stock and debt transaction valued at $8 billion in November of 1997. The newly merged firm, worth an estimated $8.4 billion in annual revenues, retained the Phycor name. [*American Medical News,* 11/17/97, p. 1.]

Presbyterian Health Services bought **FHP of New Mexico,** a subsidiary of **PacifiCare Health Systems** in November of 1997. [*PR Newswire,* 11/25/97.]

Prime Health of Alabama, Inc. bought the Alabama-based operations of **Humana, Inc.** in January of 1997. [*PR Newswire,* 1/16/97.]

Principal Health Care, Inc. bought **FHP of Illinois,** a subsidiary of **PacifiCare Health Systems** in October of 1997. [*PR Newswire,* 10/2/97.]

Radiology Associates and **Puget Sound Radiology** merged to form Radia Medical Imaging Inc. on October 1, 1997. [*Puget Sound Business Journal,* 11/28/97, p. 11A.]

RehabCare Group Inc. bought **Therapeutic Systems, Ltd.,** a contract therapy services provider serving nursing homes and school districts in Chicago, Illinois, in September of 1998. [*Business Wire,* 9/9/98.]

Renex Corp. bought **Dialysis Services of Atlanta, Inc.,** an inpatient dialysis treatment provider based in Georgia, in December of 1997. [*Business Wire,* 12/12/97.]

Res-Care Inc. bought **Tangram Rehabilitation Network, Inc.,** a San Marcos, Texas-based health care provider serving acquired brain injury patients, in October of 1998. [*PR Newswire,* 10/19/98.]

—bought **Creative Networks, LLC,** a privately held supported living services provider based in Phoenix, Arizona, in January of 1998. [*PR Newswire,* 1/6/98.]

—bought Maryland-based **Other Options,** a heathcare services provider serving persons with developmental disabilities, in December of 1997. [*PR Newswire,* 12/2/97.]

Rural/Metro Corp. bought Argentina-based **Emergencias Cardio Coronarias,** the leading ambulance company of Latin America, in early 1998. [*Business Wire,* 1/22/98.]

—bought Argentina-based **United Medical Services Inc.,** a medical transport services provider based in Lynnwood, Washington, in early 1998. [*Business Wire,* 1/15/98.]

Henry Schein Inc. bought **Meer Dental Supply Co.,** a comprehensive dental supplies distributor based in Canton, Michigan, in August of 1998. [*PR Newswire,* 8/3/98.]

St. Mary's Medical Center, based in Evansville, Indiana, bought **Welborn Memorial Baptist Hospital,** also based in Evansville, in October of 1998. [*Modern Health Care,* 10/12/98, p. 20.]

Summit Care Corp. bought **Briarcliff Nursing and Rehabilitation Center,** based in McAllen, Texas, for $9.8 million on December 1, 1997. [*Business Wire,* 12/8/97.]

Sun Health Care Group, Inc. bought **Heim Plan Unternehmensgruppe,** a long-term health care facilities owner and operator based in Germany, for $15.1 million in cash in January of 1998. [*PR Newswire,* 1/7/98.]

—bought 18 skilled nursing facilities from **Health Care Capital, Inc.** for $14.6 million in cash and the assumption of $13.2 million in annual leases in December of 1997. [*PR Newswire,* 12/12/97.]

—bought **Regency Health Services, Inc.,** a nursing center operator based in Tustin, California, for $367 million in cash and the assumption of $258 million in debt on October 8, 1997. [*PR Newswire,* 10/8/97.]

Sunrise Assisted Living, Inc. bought **Karrington Health, Inc.,** a health care provider serving senior citizens, for approximately $89 million in stock in October of 1998. [*PR Newswire,* 10/19/98.]

Superior National Insurance Group Inc. bought **Business Insurance Group Inc.,** a subsidiary of Woodland Hills, California-based **Foundation Health Systems,** for $285 million in cash in May of 1998. [*Business Wire,* 5/5/98.]

Tenet Health Care Corp. bought the bankrupt **Allegheny Health, Education, and Research Foundation** for $345 million in cash on September 29, 1998. [*Pittsburgh Business Times,* 10/2/98, p. 53.]

—bought **Queen of Angels-Hollywood Presbyterian Medical Center,** based in Hollywood, California, in December of 1997. [*Business Wire,* 12/19/97.]

Total of Florida Holdings Company, Inc. bought **PacifiCare of Florida,** a subsidiary of **PacifiCare Health Systems,** in August of 1997. [*PR Newswire,* 8/15/97.]

Total Renal Care Holdings Inc. bought **Renal Treatment Centers Inc.** for 35.2 million shares on February 27, 1998. The deal, valued at roughly $1.3 billion, doubled the size of Total Renal Care and strengthened its position as the second largest dialysis service provider in the United States. [*Business Wire,* 2/27/98.]

UCI Medical Affiliates Inc. bought **MainStreet Health Care Corp. of Atlanta,** a primary care medical office operator based in Georgia, in March of 1998. [*PR Newswire,* 2/13/98.]

United Health Care Corp. bought **MetraHealth Companies, Inc.,** based in McLean, Virginia, for $1.59 billion in January of 1996. Upon completions of the acquisition, United Health Care became the largest managed care services firm in the United States with estimated yearly sales in excess of $8 billion.[*Best's Review* 1/96, p. 126.]

United Health Care Services, Inc. bought **HealthPartners of Arizona, Inc.,** a health plan serving residents of Arizona, in October of 1998. [*PR Newswire,* 10/5/98.]

—bought **Principal Health Care of Texas Inc.,** a health plan serving residents of South Texas, in August of 1998. [*PR Newswire,* 8/12/98.]

Universal Health Services, Inc. bought **Hospital San Pablo Inc.,** the largest privately owned hospital in Puerto Rico, in December of 1997. [*PR Newswire,* 12/16/97.]

University of California at San Francisco Medical Center and **Stanford University Medical Center** merged to form **UCFS Stanford Health Care** on November 1, 1997. [*PR Newswire,* 12/16/97.]

Wellpoint Health Networks Inc. bought **Cerulean Cos.,** the parent company of **Blue Cross and Blue Shield of Georgia** for $500 million in the fourth quarter of 1998. [*Modern Health Care,* 7/13/98, p. 12.]

—bought the group health and life insurance operations of **John Hancock Mutual Life Insurance Co.** for $86.7 million on March 3, 1997. [*National Under-*

writer Life & Health-Financial Services Edition, 10/21/96, p. 3.]

—bought the group health and life insurance subsidiary of **Massachusetts Mutual Life Insurance Co.** for $380 million in early 1996. [*National Underwriter Life & Health-Financial Services Edition,* 1/15/96, p. 1.]

Bibliography

Bellandi, Deanna. "The People Strike Back: Hospitals' Mergers, Closures Spawn Cadres of Local Activists." *Modern Healthcare,* 8/31/98, p. 60.

Fine, Howard. "Feds Put Brakes on Fast-Growing Home Health Care." *Los Angeles Business Journal,* 11/10/97, p. 30.

Freeman, Paul. "Radiologists Latest to Feel Urge to Merge." *Puget Sound Business Journal,* 11/28/97, p. 11A.

Gordon, Lawrence J. "Banking: Financing Trends in an Acquisitive Health Care Market." *Journal of Health Care Finance,* Summer 1998, p. 39.

"Health Care: Managed Care." *Standard & Poor's Industry Survey,* 7/30/98.

Japsen, Bruce. "Emeritus Ends Takeover: Attempt Signals Aggression in Assisted Living Industry." *Modern Healthcare,* 2/23/98, p. 49.

Josefak, Lisa. "More Hospitals Expected to Unite." *LI Business News,* 1/19/98, p. 32.

Niedzielski, Joe. "Mega Managed Care Deal Redefines Market." *National Underwriter Life & Health-Financial Services Edition,* 4/8/96, p. 1.

Novarro, Leonard. "Can Mergers Save These Markets?" *Hospitals & Health Networks,* 2/20/98, p. 72.

Rauber, Chris. "Health Care Giants Sort Through Spoils of Merger Battles." *San Francisco Business Times,* 1/2/98, p. 8A.

Sharpe, Anita. "Acquisition Hungry Humana is Back in the Hunt Again." *The Wall Street Journal,* 11/17/98, p. B4.

Shinkman, Ron. "Consolidation Trend Increases Odds for Conflicts of Interest." *Modern Healthcare,* 1/19/98, p. 30.

Snow, Charlotte. "Renal-Care Biggies Plan Merger.-" *Modern Healthcare,* 11/24/97, p. 20.

Tokarski, Cathy. "United, Humana Call Off Merger." *American Medical News,* 8/24/98, p. 10.

"United HealthCare Corp." *Best's Review-Life-Health Insurance Edition,* 1/96, p. 126.

—AnnaMarie L. Sheldon is a freelance writer and editor based in Orlando, Florida.

CHAPTER 7

ASSOCIATIONS

This chapter presents a selection of business and professional associations active in the Health and Medical Services sector. The information shown is adapted from Gale's *Encyclopedia of Associations* series and provides detailed and comprehensive information on nonprofit membership organizations.

Entries are arranged in alphabetical order. Categories included are e-mail address (when provided), description, founding date, number of memberships, staff; regional, state, and local group counts; national groups; budget, publications, and other information.

ABDUS SALAM INTERNATIONAL CENTRE FOR THEORETICAL PHYSICS (ASICTP)

e-mail: sci_info@ictp.trieste.it
url: http://www.ictp.trieste.it/
Strada Costiera 11
I-34014 Trieste, Italy
Prof. Miguel Angel Virasoro, Dir.
PH: 39 40 2240111
FX: 39 40 224163
Description: Seeks to foster advanced studies and research in physical and mathematical sciences, especially in developing countries. Provides an international forum for contacts among scientists and facilities for its visitors, associates, and fellows to conduct research. Programs consist of workshops, extended courses, and topical meetings on research subjects as well as research work throughout the year. Bestows grants for research sessions or for seminars offering training in research techniques. **Founded:** 1964. **Membership:** 600. **Staff:** 130. Multinational. **Languages:** English. **Budget:** $20,000,000. **Publication:** *News from ICTP* (in English), quarterly. Newsletter. Contains general information on ICTP activities. Price: Free. Circulation: 1,000. Advertising: not accepted. Alternate Formats: online ■ *Preprints*, 400/year ■ *Report of Scientific Activities*, annual ■ Brochures. **Formerly:** (1997) International Centre for Theoretical Physics.

THE ABUSE INSTITUTE (TAI)

14622 Ventura Blvd., No. 748
Sherman Oaks, CA 91403-3600
Sanford Holst, Exec.Dir.
Description: Works with abuse service centers to increase public awareness of abuse. Generates support for abuse centers and disseminates methods for treating abuse. **Founded:** 1996. **Staff:** 5.

ACADEMY OF DENTAL MATERIALS (ADM)

e-mail: dentmatr@airmail.net
3302 Gaston Ave.
Dallas, TX 75246
Dr. Victoria Marker, Ed.
PH: (214)828-8378
FX: (214)828-8458
Description: Active members are licensed dentists, members of academic institutions, industrial employees, and individuals active or interested in dental materials. Coordinates activities relating to the use of dental materials. **Founded:** 1940. **Membership:** 300. Multinational. **Languages:** English. **Budget:** $90,000. **Publication:** *ADM Newsletter*, 3/year ■ *Dental Materials*, bimonthly. Journal. Covers scientific research. Price: included in membership dues; $195.00 for nonmembers. ISSN: 0109-5641. Circulation: 900. Advertising: accepted. Alternate Formats: microform ■ *Transactions of the Academy of Dental Materials* ■ Directory, periodic. **Formerly:** (1983) American Academy for Plastics Research in Dentistry.

ACADEMY OF DENTISTRY INTERNATIONAL (ADI)

5125 MacArthur Blvd. NW, Ste. 50
Washington, DC 20016-3315
Henry J. Sazima, D.D.S., Exec.Dir.
PH: (202)364-8349
FX: (202)364-8349
Description: Dentists; membership by invitation only. Works to further dentistry and the study of prevention of dental diseases worldwide. Disseminates and promotes the exchange of scientific information and fosters research. **Founded:** 1974. **Membership:** 2000. **Staff:** 2. Multinational. **National Groups:** 55. **Languages:** English. **Budget:** $130,000. **Publication:** *International Communicator*, semiannual. Newsletter. Price: included in membership dues. ISSN: 1057-5237. Circulation: 2,100. Advertising: not accepted ■ *Roster of ADI*, periodic.

ACADEMY OF DENTISTRY FOR PERSONS WITH DISABILITIES

url: http://www.bgsm.edu/dentistry/foscod
211 E. Chicago Ave., Ste. 948
Chicago, IL 60611
John S. Rutkauskas, D.D.S., Exec.Dir.
PH: (312)440-2661
FX: (312)440-2824
Description: Dentists, dental hygienists, dental assistants, and allied professionals specializing in improving oral health of persons with special dental needs. Promotes dental education, research, legislation to improve oral health and sensitivity of parents, advocacy, and related professional groups. **Founded:** 1952. **Membership:** 500. **Staff:** 3. **Languages:** English. **Budget:** $150,000. **Publication:** *Interface*, quarterly. Newsletter ■ *Membership Referral Roster*, annual ■ *Special Care in Dentistry*, bimonthly. **Formerly:** Academy of Dentistry for the Handicapped.

ACADEMY OF GENERAL DENTISTRY (AGD)

url: http://www.AGD.org
211 E. Chicago Ave., Ste. 1200
Chicago, IL 60611
Harold E. Donnell, Jr., Exec.Dir.
PH: (312)440-4300
FX: (312)440-0559
Description: Dentists dedicated to promoting the continuing education and professional development of general practitioners. **Founded:** 1952. **Membership:** 34500. **Staff:** 72. Multinational. **Local Groups:** 35. **Languages:** English. **Budget:** $8,013,599. **Publication:** *AGD Impact*, 11/year. Newspaper. Covers issues, legislation, and trends that affect the practice and role of dentistry in the health care community. Price: included in membership dues; $25.00 for nonmembers. ISSN: 0194-729X. Circulation: 36,000. Advertising: accepted. Alternate Formats: microform ■ *Dentalnotes*, quarterly. Newsletter. Provides information on the latest dental issues and trends; intended for the national media and to be displayed in dentists' reception areas. Price: free to national media; $20.00/year for all others. Circulation: 540. Advertising: not accepted ■ *General Dentistry*, bimonthly. Journal. Provides research and clinical reports for the continuing education of general dentists. Contains advertisers' index, book reviews, and quizzes. Price: included in membership dues; $30.00/year for nonmembers. ISSN: 0363-6771. Circulation: 65,000. Advertising: accepted. Alternate Formats: microform ■ Membership Directory, biennial.

ACADEMY FOR IMPLANTS AND TRANSPLANTS (AIT)

PO Box 223
Springfield, VA 22150
Anthony J. Viscido, D.D.S., Sec.-Treas.
PH: (703)451-0001
FX: (703)451-0004
Description: Dentists united to: motivate and assist men and women in the general practice of dentistry in the field of implants and transplants; encourage and promote the art and science of implant and transplant dentistry; assist in research in this and allied fields. Conducts seminars; teaches implantology. **Founded:** 1972. **Membership:** 180. **Regional Groups:** 15. **Languages:** English. **Publication:** *Implant Update*, quarterly. Newsletter. Discusses developments in the field of implant and transplant dentistry. Price: included in membership dues. Circulation: 268. Advertising: not accepted ■ Journal, periodic.

ACADEMY OF LASER DENTISTRY

e-mail: acohen@laserdentistry.org
url: http://www.laserdentistry.org
10435 Vernon Ave.
Huntington Woods, MI 48070
Alison Cohen, Exec.Dir.
PH: (248)548-7171
FX: (248)548-7174
Description: Dentists, hygienists, dental academicians and researchers, and corporate laser and laser accessory dental vendors. Promotes clinical education, research, and development of

standards and guidelines for the safe and ethical use of dental laser technology. Conducts educational programs. Provides certification. **Founded:** 1993. **Membership:** 500. **Staff:** 1. Multinational. **Languages:** English. **Budget:** $250,000. **Publication:** *Wavelengths*, quarterly. Clinical case studies, industry and academy news. Price: included in membership. Advertising: accepted. **Formed by Merger of:** American Academy of Laser Dentistry.

ACADEMY OF MANAGED CARE PHARMACY (AMCP)
1650 King St., Ste. 402
Alexandria, VA 22314-2747
Judith A. Cahill, Exec.Dir.
Description: Professional society for pharmacists working for managed care health services. Promotes the "development and application of pharmaceutical care in order to ensure appropriate outcomes for all individuals." Represents the views and interests of managed care pharmacy. Conducts educational courses and continuing professional development programs for members. **Founded:** 1989. **Membership:** 4300. **Staff:** 14. **Languages:** English.

ACADEMY OF MANAGED CARE PROVIDERS (AMCP)
e-mail: academymcp@aol.com
6285 E. Spring St., No. 404
Long Beach, CA 90808-4000
Dr. John Russell, Pres.
PH: (562)596-8660
TF: 800297-2627
FX: (562)596-2486
Description: Works to promote excellence in the provision of health care services in a managed care environment. Conducts continuing education programs; offers consulting services; maintains speakers' bureau. **Founded:** 1993. **Membership:** 1500.

ACADEMY OF OPERATIVE DENTISTRY (AOD)
320 West Indian School Rd.
Phoenix, AZ 85013
Dr. William E. Hawkins, Pres.
PH: (602)248-9445
FX: (602)263-1122
Description: Dentists and persons in allied industries. Seeks to ensure quality education in operative dentistry. **Founded:** 1972. **Membership:** 1000. **Languages:** English. **Budget:** $100,000. **Publication:** *Membership Roster*, periodic. Price: $15.00. Advertising: not accepted ▪ *Operative Dentistry*, 4/year.

ACADEMY OF ORAL DYNAMICS (AOD)
8919 Sudley Rd.
Manassas, VA 22110
Dr. E. Paul Byrne, Sec.
PH: (703)368-8527
FX: (703)331-0356
Description: Professional society of dentists. Promotes the study of oral dynamics, especially as it applies to the use of natural teeth in restoring and maintaining a healthy, functioning mouth; disseminates information gained through research. Conducts educational programs. Publications: none. **Founded:** 1950. **Membership:** 75. Multinational. **Languages:** English, Japanese. **Formerly:** (1950) International Academy of Oral Dynamics.

ACADEMY OF OSSEOINTEGRATION
e-mail: academy@osseo.org
url: http://www.osseo.org
401 N. Michigan Ave.
Chicago, IL 60611-4267
Thomas Stautzenbach, Exec.Dir.
PH: (312)321-5169
TF: 800656-7736
Description: Works for the advancement of osseointegration among dentists, physicians and related professionals. Conducts research and educational programs; disseminates information to the public and medical agencies; provides a forum for interdis-

ciplinary discussions. **Founded:** 1987. **Membership:** 4500. **Staff:** 13. Multinational. **Budget:** $2,000,000.

ACADEMY OF PHARMACEUTICAL RESEARCH AND SCIENCE (APRS)
url: http://www.aphanet.org
American Pharmaceutical Association
2215 Constitution Ave. NW
Washington, DC 20037
Naomi U. Kaminsky, Scientific Affairs Program Mng.
PH: 800-237-2742
FX: (202)628-0443
Description: A part of American Pharmaceutical Association. Pharmaceutical scientists from industry and academia. Objective is to serve the profession of pharmacy by developing knowledge and integrating the process of science into the profession. Sponsors national meetings to provide a forum for presentation and discussion of original research, controversial topics, and continuing communication. Provides consultation and advice to: pharmacists on scientific matters as they relate to policy; congressional committees on bills of interest to pharmaceutical scientists; governmental agencies. **Founded:** 1965. **Membership:** 3000. **Staff:** 3. **Local Groups:** 1. **Languages:** English Formerly (1987) Academy of Pharmaceutical Sciences.

ACADEMY FOR SPORTS DENTISTRY (ASD)
e-mail: sportdds@uic.edu
c/o Mailcode 555
University of Illinois College of Dentistry
801 S. Paulina St.
Chicago, IL 60612
Susan D. Ferry, Exec.Sec.
PH: (312)413-0174
FX: (312)996-3535
Description: Dentists, dental students, physicians, athletic trainers, and others interested in the study and prevention of dental injuries incurred during sports participation. Purpose is to foster research, development, and education in all sciences related to sports dentistry and its relationship to the body as a whole. Encourages utilization of this knowledge in promoting better approaches to the prevention and treatment of athletic injuries and oral disease. Facilitates the exchange of ideas and experience among members. **Founded:** 1983. **Membership:** 750. **Staff:** 1. **National Groups:** 1. **Languages:** English.

ACCREDITATION COUNCIL FOR CONTINUING MEDICAL EDUCATION (ACCME)
url: http://www.accme.org
515 N. State St., Ste. 7340
Chicago, IL 60610
Murray Kopelow, MD, Exec.Dir. & Sec.
PH: (312)464-2500
FX: (312)464-2586
Description: Acts as an accrediting agency for sponsors of continuing medical education for physicians. Sponsoring participants are: American Board of Medical Specialties; American Hospital Association; American Medical Association; Association of American Medical Colleges; Association for Hospital Medical Education; Council of Medical Specialty Societies; Federation of State Medical Boards of the United States. Publications: none. **Convention/Meeting:** none. **Founded:** 1981. **Staff:** 11. **Languages:** English. **Formerly:** Liaison Committee on Continuing Medical Education.

ACCREDITATION REVIEW COMMITTEE ON EDUCATION FOR PHYSICIAN ASSISTANTS (ARC-PA)
e-mail: mccartys@mfldclin.edu
1000 N. Oak Ave.
Marshfield, WI 54449-5788
John E. McCarty, Exec.Dir.
PH: (715)389-3785
FX: (715)387-5163
Description: Serves as an accrediting review body for physician assistant education nationwide. Makes recommendations to

Commission on Accreditation of Allied Health Education Programs. **Founded:** 1971. **Membership:** 15. **Languages:** English. **Budget:** $80,000 Formerly (1972) Joint Review Committee on Educational Programs for Physician's Assistants; (1987) Joint Review on Educational Programs for Physician Assistants; (1989) Accreditation Committee on Education for Physicians Assistants.

ACCREDITATION REVIEW COMMITTEE ON EDUCATION IN SURGICAL TECHNOLOGY (ARC-ST)
7108-C S. Alton Way
Englewood, CO 80112-2106
Annamarie Dubies-Appel, Exec.Dir.
PH: (303)694-9262
FX: (303)694-3655
Description: Reviews accreditation applications of surgical techology programs in hospitals, community colleges, technical schools, and universities and makes recommendations to the Commission on Accreditation of Allied Health Education Programs. Collaborates with American College of Surgeons, American Hospital Association, and the Association of Surgical Technologists. **Founded:** 1974. **Staff:** 2. **Languages:** English. **Budget:** $67,000. **Publication:** *Surgical Technology: A Growing Career*. Brochure. Contains information on careers in surgical technology, educational requirements, and a list of accredited programs. Price: free (first copy); $1.00/each additional copy. **Formerly:** (1987) Joint Review Committee on Education for the Surgical Technologist; (1990) Accreditation Review Committee for Educational Programs in Surgical Technology.

ACOUSTIC NEUROMA ASSOCIATION OF CANADA (ANAC)
e-mail: anac@compusmart.ab.ca
PO Box 369
Edmonton, AB, Canada T5J 2J6
Peggy Bray, Pres.
PH: (403)428-3384
Description: For people with acoustic neuroma, Bell's Palsy, and other neuromuscular disorders, their families, health care professionals, and other interested individuals. Seeks to improve the quality of life of people with neuromuscular diseases; promotes research into the causes and treatment of acoustic neuroma. Conducts charitable programs; provides support and services to people with neuromuscular disorders; maintains speakers' bureau. **Founded:** 1983. **Membership:** 2000. **Staff:** 2. **Languages:** English, French. **Budget:** C$200,000. **Publication:** *Connection*, quarterly. Newsletter. Circulation: 2,000. Advertising: accepted.

ACTA ODONTOLOGICA SCANDINAVICA FOUNDATION (AOSF)
Faculty of Odontology
Medicinaregatan 12
Goteborg University
S-41390 Goteborg, Sweden
Gunnar E. Carlson, Contact
Description: Dental educators and schools; dentists. Seeks to advance the study, teaching, and practice of dentistry; encourages professional development of members. Serves as a forum for the exchange of information among members; sponsors continuing dental education courses. Multinational. **Languages:** English, Swedish.

ACTION CANCER
e-mail: info.actioncancer.cinni@nics.gov.uk
1 Marlborough Park
Belfast, Antrim BT9 6XS, Northern Ireland
Peter S. Quigley, MIPR, Contact
PH: 44 1232 661081
FX: 44 1232 683931
Description: Works to heighten awareness of the importance of early cancer detection. Offers breast and cervical cancer screening services for women, and testicular and prostatic screening services for men. Provides counselling for cancer patients, families, and friends. Maintains research lab. Disseminates information. **Founded:** 1973. **Staff:** 42. **Local Groups:** 40. **Budget:**

L1,100,000. **Publication:** *Action Cancer News* (in English), quarterly. Magazine. ISSN: 1355-8749. Advertising: not accepted ■ Annual Report.

ACTION HEALTH (AH)
The Gate House
25 Gwydir St.
Cambridge CB1 2LG, England
Philippa Young, Dir.
PH: 44 1223 480853
FX: 44 1223 480853
Description: Health care personnel and organizations with operations worldwide. Promotes increased availability of primary health care services in previously underserved areas. Provides training courses for health care personnel working in developing areas; supports community development, educational, public health, and population control initiatives. **Founded:** 1984. **Staff:** 5. Multinational. **Languages:** English. **Budget:** $224,000.

ACTION HEALTH INC. (AHI)
PO Box 803
Yaba Post Office
Lagos, Lagos, Nigeria
Description: Individuals interested in the health and well-being of Nigerian youth. Promotes increased availability of health and social services for youth; works to improve public understanding of reproductive health and related issues. Conducts educational programs for youth; sponsors reproductive health clinics. **Languages:** English. **Publication:** *Growing Up* (in English), periodic. Newsletter.

ACTION IN INTERNATIONAL MEDICINE (AIM)
125 High Holborn
London WC1V 6QA, England
Dr. Christopher Rose, Contact
PH: 44 0171 4053090
FX: 44 0171 4053093
Description: Health care providers and health services. Promotes increased access to quality health care among underserved populations worldwide. Works to establish health care infrastructure in developing areas; provides support and assistance to grass roots health services. Multinational. **Languages:** English.

ACUPUNCTURE FOUNDATION OF CANADA INSTITUTE (AFCI)
e-mail: info@afcinstitute.com
url: http://www.afcinstitute.com
2131 Lawrence Ave. E
Scarborough, ON, Canada M1R 5G4
Cheryll Kwok, Exec.Dir.
PH: (416)752-3988
FX: (416)752-4398
Description: Licensed professional acupuncturists. Promotes continuing professional development of members. Seeks to gain recognition for acupuncture as a legitimate medical and dental technique. Represents members' interests before professional organizations, government agencies, and the public. Conducts educational programs for members. **Founded:** 1995. **Membership:** 1000. **Staff:** 3. **Languages:** English, French. **Budget:** C$800,000. **Publication:** *Acupuncture Canada*, periodic. Newsletter. Advertising: accepted ■ Brochure, periodic ■ Directory, periodic.

ACUPUNTURE FOUNDATION OF CANADA (AFC)
e-mail: info@afciinstitute.ca
url: http://www.afcinstitute.com
2131 Lawarence Ave. E.
Scarborough, ON, Canada M1R 5G4
Cheryll Kwok, Exec.Dir.
PH: (416)752-3988
FX: (416)752-4398
Description: Promotes acupuncture's legimate place in health care by initiating and supporting research in acupuncture. **Founded:** 1974. **Membership:** 900. **Staff:** 2. **Budget:** C$150,000. **Publi-**

cation: Newsletter (in English), semiannual. Price: free, for members only. Circulation: 1,000. Advertising: accepted.

AD HOC GROUP FOR MEDICAL RESEARCH FUNDING (AHGMRF)
e-mail: adhoc@aamc.org
url: http://www.aamc.org/research/adhocqp/
2450 N St. NW
Washington, DC 20037-1126
Richard M. Knapp, Ph.D., Chmn.
PH: (202)828-0525
FX: (202)828-1125
Description: Organizations engaged in or supporting biomedical and behavioral research. Goals are to assess federal funding for biomedical and behavioral research and advocate appropriate funding for the National Institutes of Health. Founded: 1982. Membership: 200. Languages: English. Publication: Annual Report. Price: free. Advertising: not accepted ■ Brochure, annual.

ADVOCATES FOR YOUTH
url: http://www.advocatesforyouth.org
1025 Vermont Ave. NW, Ste. 200
Washington, DC 20005
James Wagoner, Exec.Dir. & Pres.
PH: (202)347-5700
FX: (202)347-2263
Description: Objectives are to: reduce the incidence of unintended teenage pregnancy and childbearing and promote adolescent health through education; to prevent the proliferation of the human immunodeficiency virus (HIV) among adolescents; motivate teens to think and act responsibly about birth control and parenting; conduct programs and advocacy campaigns to assure minors' access to family planning information and services. Provides technical assistance on program planning, implementation, and evaluation of sexuality education in the U.S. and, through International Center on Adolescent Fertility, to health, education, and social service workers worldwide. Operates Support Center for School-Based Health Care and media project. Monitors legislative activities for various organizations concerned with youth issues. Conducts research to evaluate promising prevention strategies. Compiles statistics; maintains speakers' bureau. Founded: 1980. Staff: 30. Multinational. Languages: English, French. Budget: $2,000,000. Publication: *Linkx*, quarterly. Newsletter. Details school-based health care ■ *Options*, quarterly. Newsletter ■ *Passages* (in English, French, and Spanish), quarterly ■ Reports. Formerly: Center for Population Options.

ADVOCATES FOR YOUTH'S MEDIA PROJECT
10999 Riverside Dr., Ste. 300
North Hollywood, CA 91602-2239
Description: Serves as an advisory and information resource for the entertainment industry to encourage positive and relevant messages about family planning, sexuality, and reproductive health, especially in programming directed toward adolescents. Conducts research and charitable programs. Operates speakers' bureau. Founded: 1983. Staff: 5. Languages: English. Budget: $300,000. Formerly: Center for Population Options' Media Project.

AESCULAPIAN CLUB (AC)
Harvard Medical School
25 Shaphduck St., Bldg. A, Rm. 206
Boston, MA 02115
Sandy Gollis, Adm.
PH: (617)432-1540
FX: (617)734-4382
Description: Social organization of graduates of Harvard Medical School or physicians who have held teaching appointments there for three years. Languages: English.

AFRICAN ASSOCIATION OF DERMATOLOGY (AAD)
Rabito Clinic
PO Box 7286
Accra, Ghana
Dr. Edmund N. Delle, Contact
PH: 233 21 774526
FX: 233 21 777465
Description: Dermatologists. Seeks to advance the study and practice of dermatology; encourages continuing professional development of members. Serves as a forum for the exchange of information among members; conducts educational programs. Multinational. Languages: English.

AFRICAN COMMISSION OF HEALTH AND HUMAN RIGHTS PROMOTERS (ACHHRP)
Rabito Clinic
PO Box 7286
North
Accra, Ghana
PH: 233 21 774526
FX: 233 21 777465
Description: Health and human rights organizations. Promotes respect for the rights of the individual and the rule of law; seeks to increase availability of health care services among previously underserved populations. Publicizes human rights abuses; makes available health care programs. Multinational. Languages: English.

AFRICAN LASER, ATOMIC AND MOLECULAR SCIENCES NETWORK (ALAMSN)
Scientific Faculty
Department of Physics
PO Box 321
Khartoum, Sudan
Farouk Habbani, Contact
Description: Physicists and other individuals with an interest in molecular sciences and related technologies. Seeks to advance the study, teaching, and practice of the molecular sciences. Serves as a forum for the exchange of information among members; sponsors research and educational programs. Multinational. Languages: English.

AFRICAN LEAGUE AGAINST RHEUMATISM (ALAR)
Hopital Mongi Slim
2046 La Marsa, Tunisia
Leith Zakraoui, Contact
PH: 216 1 759360
FX: 216 1 765118
Description: Health care professionals specializing in the treatment of rheumatic diseases. Seeks to improve the diagnosis and treatment of rheumatic disorders. Serves as a forum for the exchange of information among members; sponsors continuing professional development courses; makes available health care services. Multinational. Languages: Arabic, English.

AFRICAN MEDICAL AND RESEARCH FOUNDATION - CANADA (AMREF CANA)
e-mail: amref@web.net
59 Front St. E
Toronto, ON, Canada M5E 1B3
Seana Massey, Exec.Dir.
PH: (416)601-6984
FX: (416)601-6984
Description: Medical and public health professionals in Canada (3) and Africa (600). Seeks to identify and address health needs in rural areas of Africa. Develops, implements, and evaluates public health programs and services; encourages enhancement of local administrative capabilities through training, education, and community participation; facilitates increased participation by women in community development. Conducts outreach activities. Founded: 1957. Membership: 603. Staff: 3. Multinational. Languages: English, French. Publication: Newsletter (in English), periodic. Circulation: 1,700. Advertising: not accepted ■ Brochure, periodic. Circulation: 1,700.

AFRICAN MEDICAL AND RESEARCH FOUNDATION -
  DENMARK (AMRFD)
12 H.C. Andersens Blvd.
DK-1553 Copenhagen, Denmark
Thomas Federspiel, Contact
PH: 45 33157533
FX: 45 33156802
Description: Medical and public health professionals. Seeks to i-
dentify and address health needs in rural Africa. Develops, im-
plements, and evaluates public health programs; encourages
enhancement of local administrative capacities through training.
Multinational. **Languages:** Danish, English.

AFRICAN MEDICAL AND RESEARCH FOUNDATION -
  FRANCE (AMRFF)
66 bis rue St. Didier
F-75116 Paris, France
Dominique Gautheron, Contact
PH: 33 1 45538684
FX: 33 1 46422321
Description: Medical and public health professionals. Seeks to i-
dentify and address health needs in rural Africa. Develops, im-
plements, and evaluates public health programs; encourages
enhancement of local administrative capacities through training.
Multinational. **Languages:** English, French.

AFRICAN MEDICAL AND RESEARCH FOUNDATION -
  ITALY (AMREF -IT)
(Fondzione Africana per la Medicina e la Ricerca)
e-mail: amrefit@tin.it
P.za. Hartiri di Belfiore 4
I-00195 Rome, Italy
Thomas Simmons, Exec.Dir.
PH: 39 6 3202222
FX: 39 6 3202227
Description: Provides health care services to people in eastern
Africa. Identifies health needs and evaluates and implements me-
thods and programs to meet those needs. Maintains projects
which emphasize affordable health care for people in underdeveloped, rural areas. Operates mobile health service facilities, airborn support for health centers in remote areas, and radio communication services with over 100 two-way radio stations.
Conducts training programs for rural health care workers and research into the control of hydatid disease, malaria, and sleeping
sickness. Applies knowledge from the behavioral and social sciences to health care improvement initiatives. Writes articles and
information for training manuals, health education materials,
and medical journals. Disseminates information. Offers consultancy services. **Founded:** 1988. **Membership:** 6000. **Staff:** 6. Multinational. **Languages:** Italian.

AFRICAN MEDICAL AND RESEARCH FOUNDATION -
  KENYA (AMREF)
url: http://www.amref.org
PO Box 30125
Nairobi, Kenya
Dr. Michael S. Gerber, Dir.Gen.
PH: 254 2 501301
FX: 254 2 609518
Description: Purpose is to improve the health of people living in
5 east and south African countries. Focuses efforts on developing
low-cost healthcare for people in rural areas. Program includes:
training of community health workers; planning and evaluation
of health projects; consulting services; primary healthcare education; operation of a medical radio communication network within
the region; ground mobile health services for nomadic and pastoral peoples; the Flying Doctor Service (funded by the Flying
Doctors' Society of Africa), which provides airborne support for
remote medical, surgical, and public health facilities. Conducts
medical research, particularly into the control of malaria, sleeping sickness, and hydatid disease; applies behavioral and social
sciences in health improvement. Offers computerized services.
Founded: 1957. **Staff:** 600. Multinational. **National Groups:** 5.
Languages: English. **Budget:** $12,100,000. **Publication:** *Afya* (in

English), quarterly ▪ *AMREF-in-Action* (in English), annual ▪
AMREF News (in English), quarterly ▪ *Cobasheca* (in English),
quarterly ▪ *Defender* (in English), quarterly ▪ *Research Papers*,
periodic ▪ *Training Manuals*, periodic ▪ Reports. **Formerly:** Flying Doctors Service.

AFRICAN MEDICAL AND RESEARCH FOUNDATION -
  SWEDEN (AMREF -SW)
e-mail: amref@bok.bonnier.se
Box 3159
S-103 63 Stockholm, Sweden
Helena Bonnier, Chairperson
PH: 46 8 6968040
FX: 46 8 6968041
Description: Aims to improve the health of people in eastern Africa. Seeks to indentify health needs and develop, implement,
and evaluate methods and programmes to meet those needs
through service, training and research. Programmes include: primary health care; training of community health workers; training
of rural health staff through continuing education, teacher training and correspondence courses; development, printing, and distribution of training manuals, medical journals, and health education materials; application of behavioral and social sciences to
health improvement; airborne support for remote health facilities, including surgical, medical, and public health services;
grounds mobile health services for nomadic pastoralists; medical
research into the control of hydatid disease, and malaria. Multinational.

AFRICAN MEDICAL AND RESEARCH FOUNDATION -
  UGANDA (AMREF/UGAN)
e-mail: amrefug@imul.com
url: http://www.amref.org
PO Box 10663
Kampala, Uganda
D. Shuey, Director
PH: 256 41 250319
FX: 256 41 344565
Description: Purpose is to improve the health of people living in
Uganda. Focus is on public heath education, sanitation, medical
auxilaries, preventive medicine, health care teams, and clinics.
Founded: 1957. **Staff:** 62. **Budget:** $3,000,000.

AFRICAN MEDICAL AND RESEARCH FOUNDATION -
  UNITED KINGDOM (AMRFUK)
8 Bourdon St., 2nd Fl.
London W1X 9HX, England
Alexander Heroys, Dir.
PH: 44 0171 4093230
FX: 44 0171 6292006
Description: Health care personnel and organizations with oper-
ations in Africa. Seeks to increase the quality and availability of
African health care services. Provides support and assistance to
African health care providers; sponsors programs in areas inclu-
ding public health, education, and child welfare. Makes available
emergency relief services. **Founded:** 1967. **Staff:** 3. Multinational.
Languages: English. **Budget:** $571,000.

AFRICAN MEDICAL AND RESEARCH FOUNDATION, U.S.A.
  (AMREF)
19 W. 44th St., Ste. 1707-8
New York, NY 10036
Ellen S. Subin, Pres.
PH: (212)768-2440
FX: (212)768-4230
Description: U.S. branch of the African Medical and Research
Foundation. Voluntary organization providing medical services
to aid and augment health programs in developing nations and in
rural areas of East Africa. Attempts to reach isolated peoples
and outlying medical facilities through a network of 100 two-way
radios, clinic-equipped mobile units, and a "Flying Doctor Service." Undertakes research programs in the field of medicine and
general health surveys. Engages in national surveys. Designs and
implements primary health care projects. Provides health educa-

tion courses through its training center to train health educators and is implementing a program of continuing education for health workers. **Founded:** 1957. **Regional Groups:** 9. **Languages:** English. **Budget:** $15,000,000. **Publication:** *AFYA*, bimonthly. Journal ▪ *Defender: Health Journal for Africa*, bimonthly ▪ *Rural Health Series*, periodic. **Formerly:** African Research Foundation; (1973) African Medical and Research Foundation; (1981) International Medical and Research Foundation.

AFRICAN REGIONAL COUNCIL OF THE WORLD FEDERATION FOR THE WORLD FEDERATION FOR MENTAL HEALTH (ARCWFMH)
PO Box 50209
Lusaka, Zambia
Isaac Mwendapole, Contact
PH: 260 5 224689
FX: 260 5 224585
Description: Mental health professionals and organizations. Seeks to advance the diagnosis and treatment of mental illness. Facilitates exchange of information among members; provides assistance and consulting services to mental health care programs. Multinational. **Languages:** English.

AFRICAN RESEARCH AND DEVELOPMENT NETWORK FOR THE INDUSTRIAL PRODUCTION OF DRUGS AND MEDICINAL PLANTS
e-mail: oaustrc.lagos@rcl.dircon.co.uk
Port Authority Bldg., 4th Fl.
26-28 Marina
PMB 2359
Lagos, Nigeria
PH: 234 1 2633289
FX: 234 1 2636093
Description: Manufacturers of pharmaceuticals and growers of medicinal plants. Seeks to advance the African pharmaceuticals industries. Facilitates communication and cooperation among members; sponsors research and development programs; conducts promotional activities. Multinational. **Languages:** English.

AFRICAN UNION OF SPORTS MEDICINE (AUSM)
Faculte Medecine
Boite Postale V 166
Abidjan, Cote d'Ivoire
Constant Roux, Contact
PH: 225 466704
FX: 225 466727
Description: Physicians and other health care professionals with an interest in sports medicine. Promotes excellence in the practice of sports medicine; seeks to advance scholarship and expertise in the field. Facilitates exchange of information among members; sponsors research and educational programs. Multinational. **Languages:** English, French.

AID INTERNATIONAL (AIDI)
1776 Peachtree St. NW, Ste. 450
Atlanta, GA 30309
O. J. Brown, Pres.
PH: (404)875-3891
FX: (404)872-6253
Description: Health care personnel. Seeks to improve the quality and availability of health care and social services in developing regions worldwide. Provides emergency relief and medical services; conducts training programs for medical technicians and paramedics. Maintains emergency disaster management team. Multinational. **Languages:** English.

AKHA ASSOCIATION IN THAILAND (AAT)
PO Box 66
Muang Chiang Rai 57000, Thailand
Luka Chermui, Admin.
PH: 66 53 713169
FX: 66 53 713169
Description: Seeks to increase accessibility of primary health care services. Operates Akha Medical Clinic. **Founded:** 1995.

Staff: 7. **Languages:** Akan, English. **Budget:** 600,000 Bht. **Publication:** *VDO, Radio, Picture*. Advertising: accepted.

AKTION A-B-C FIR BILDUNG A GESONDHEET AM
157 Avenue Pasteur
Boite Postale 1744
L-1017 Luxembourg, Luxembourg
Description: Promotes improved public health programs. Works to increase availability of primary health care services. **Languages:** Dutch.

AL ATTA' CENTRE FOR THE AGED
PO Box 21358
Beit Hanina
Jerusalem, Israel
Nora Kurt, Contact
PH: 972 2 812032
Description: Promotes improved care for elderly people residing in nursing homes. Conducts surveys to determine the needs of nursing home residents; sponsors training programs for individuals working with elderly people. **Languages:** Arabic, English.

ALAN GUTTMACHER INSTITUTE (AGI)
e-mail: info@agi-usa.org
url: http://www.agi-usa.org
120 Wall St., 21st Fl.
New York, NY 10005
Jeannie I. Rosoff, Pres.
PH: (212)248-1111
FX: (212)248-1951
Description: Fosters sound public policies on voluntary fertility control and population issues and encourages responsive reproductive health programs through policy analysis, public education, and research in the U.S. and internationally. Compiles statistics and conducts policy-relevant research on the provision of services relating to reproductive health care. **Founded:** 1968. **Staff:** 60. **Languages:** English. **Budget:** $6,000,000. **Publication:** *Family Planning Perspectives*, bimonthly. Journal. Focuses on reproductive health issues. Price: $42.00/year for individuals; $52.00/year for institutions; $62.00 foreign subscriptions; $10.00 per back issue. ISSN: 0014-7354. Circulation: 7,000. Advertising: accepted ▪ *The Guttmacher Report*, bimonthly. Journal. Links federal and state policy policy devlopments on all aspects of reproductive health and rights. Price: $35.00/year for individuals; $45.00/year for institutions; $55.00 foreign subscriptions; $8.00/ back issue. ISSN: 1096-7699 ▪ *International Family Planning Perspectives* (in English, French, and Spanish), quarterly. Journal. Highlights population and reproductive health research and program achievements in developing countries. Price: $36.00/year for individuals; $46.00/year for institutions; $56.00 outside U.S.; $10.00/back issues. ISSN: 0162-2749. Circulation: 30,000. Advertising: accepted ▪ *Sex and America's Teenagers*. Book. Discusses teenage sexual and reproductive behavior ▪ *Testing Positive: Sexually Transmitted Disease and the Public Health Response* ▪ Annual Report ▪ *Into a New World: Young Women's Sexual and Reproductive Lives*. Book ▪ *Contraception Counts: State-by-State Information* ▪ *Cost to Employer Health Plans of Covering Contraceptives*. Reprint. **Formerly:** (1975) Center for Family Planning Program Development; (1977) Research and Development Division of Planned Parenthood Federation of America.

ALBANIAN FAMILY PLANNING ASSOCIATION
Rr. Jul variboba, No. 9
Tirana, Albania
PH: 355 42 27762
FX: 355 42 27530
Description: Works to improve reproductive health services available to women in Albania. Promotes increased awareness of family planning. **Founded:** 1993. **Languages:** Albanian.

ALL INDIA NATURE CURE FEDERATION
15 Rajghat Colony
New Delhi 110 002, Delhi, India
J.H. Chinchalkar, Pres.

PH: 91 11 3317396
Description: Promotes use of natural medical treatments including herbs and meditation, particularly in cases of acute and chronic disorders. Gathers and disseminates information on effective natural remedies; conducts educational and training programs. **Founded:** 1951. **Membership:** 51. **Staff:** 3. **Languages:** English, Hindi. **Budget:** Rs 200,000. **Publication:** *Parishad Prabha* (in English and Hindi), monthly. Magazine. Contains information on naturopathy, yoga treatments, and news of naturopathy activities. Price: Rs 4.00. Circulation: 5,000. Advertising: accepted. **Also Known As:** Akhil Bharatiya - Prakritik Chikitsa Parishad.

ALLIANCE FOR ALTERNATIVES IN HEALTHCARE (AAH)
e-mail: ahhhnins@aol.com
url: http://www.alternativeinsurance.com
PO Box 6279
Thousand Oaks, CA 91359-6279
Steve Gorman, Pres.
PH: (805)494-7818
FX: (805)494-8528
Description: Holistic physicians; employers; interested individuals. Seeks to enhance public recognition of holistic, homeopathic, naturopathic, chiropractic, and acupuncture treatments. (Holistic medicine focuses on the treatment of the entire body, rather than on any one organ or system; homeopathic medicine treats diseases by administering minute quantities of a substance that would produce the disease's symptoms in a healthy person; naturopathic medicine avoids the use of surgery and drugs, focusing instead on natural agents, such as sunshine and fresh air, or on physical means, such as manipulation or acupuncture.) Encourages health insurance systems to cover holistic, homeopathic, and naturopathic treatments in their policies. Attends exhibitions to disseminate information on holistic, homeopathic, and naturopathic medicine to health care providers and the public. Offers group medical, dental, and vision plans to members. Manages network of holistic and natural providers who offer discounts to subscribers of the Holistic Health Network. Convention/Meeting: none. **Founded:** 1983. **Membership:** 1500. **Staff:** 4. **Languages:** English. **Publication:** *Natural Marketing News*, periodic ■ *Press Releases*, periodic. **Formerly:** Alternative Health Insurance Services; (1989) Natural Marketing Association.

ALLIANCE OF THE AMERICAN DENTAL ASSOCIATION (AADA)
211 E. Chicago Ave., No. 918
Chicago, IL 60611
Margaret Gay, Exec.Dir.
PH: (312)440-2865
FX: (312)440-2587
Description: Spouses of dentists. Promotes public dental health and creates public awareness of dentistry. Conducts preventive dental health education programs and assists organized dentistry in encouraging state and national legislation that benefits the public and dentistry. Maintains legislative projects and leadership skill development. **Founded:** 1955. **Membership:** 12000. **Staff:** 2. **National Groups:** 1. **Languages:** English. **Budget:** $300,000. **Publication:** *Connection*, quarterly. Newsletter. Circulation: 500 ■ *Key*, quarterly. Newsletter. ISSN: 1075-9794. Circulation: 12,000. Advertising: not accepted. **Formerly:** Auxiliary to the American Dental Association; (1982) Women's Auxiliary to the American Dental Association.

ALLIANCE FOR CANNABIS THERAPEUTICS (ACT)
PO Box 21210
Dept. E
Washington, DC 20009
Robert Randall, Pres.
PH: (202)483-8595
FX: (703)354-5695
Description: Works to end federal prohibition of cannabis in medicine and to "construct a medically meaningful, ethically correct and compassionate system of regulation which permits the seriously ill to legally obtain cannabis." **Founded:** 1980. **Staff:** 1. **Languages:** English.

ALLIANCE OF CARDIOVASCULAR PROFESSIONALS
e-mail: SeanMcE@aol.com
url: http://www.acp-online.com
910 Charles St.
Fredericksburg, VA 22401
Peggy McElgunn, Exec.Dir.
PH: (540)370-0102
FX: (540)370-0015
Description: Dedicated to meeting educational needs, developing programs to meet those needs, and providing a structure to offer the cardiovascular and pulmonary technology professional a key to the future as a valuable member of the medical team. Seeks advancement for members through communication and education. Provides coordinated programs to orient the newer professional to his field and continuing educational opportunities for technologist personnel. Has established guidelines for educational programs in the hospital and university setting. Works with educators and physicians to provide basic, advanced, and in-service programs for technologists. Sponsors registration and certification programs which provide technology professionals with further opportunity to clarify their level of expertise. Compiles statistics. **Founded:** 1967. **Membership:** 3200. **Staff:** 8. **Multinational. Languages:** English. **Budget:** $350,000. Formed by Merger of (1993) National Society for Cardiovascular Technology; (1995) ASCP; (1995) Society for Cardiovascular Management; National Society for Pulmonary Technology.

ALLIANCE FOR LUNG CANCER ADVOCACY, SUPPORT AND EDUCATION (ALCASE)
e-mail: info@alcase.org
1601 Lincoln Ave.
Vancouver, WA 98660
Susan McCarthy, Dir.
PH: (360)696-2436
FX: (360)699-1944
Description: Lung cancer patients, their families, and other persons who have been previously treated for the disease. Provides moral and physical support to lung cancer patients and their families in order to assist them in leading normal and productive lives. Serves as a forum for discussion and information exchange among individuals who are undergoing or have undergone treatment for lung cancer. Works with professionals to develop physical and psychological rehabilitation programs. Maintains volunteer program which allows patients who are in remission to visit hospitalized lung cancer patients to offer guidance and information on nonmedical treatments and therapies. Conducts discussions; operates speakers' bureau. Presently inactive. **Founded:** 1979. **Membership:** 250. **Languages:** English. **Publication:** *Miracle of Believing* ■ *Spirit and Breath Association Bulletin*, monthly. Newsletter. For lung cancer patients. Includes calendar of events ■ *Spirit and Breath Exercise Book for People Who Had Lung Cancer* ■ *Treading the Right Path to Health and Fitness*. **Formerly:** (1998) Spirit and Breath.

ALLIANCE FOR THE MENTALLY ILL
url: http://www.nami.org
200 N. Glebe Rd., Ste. 1015
Arlington, VA 22203-3754
Laurie Flynn, Contact
PH: (703)524-7600
FX: (703)524-9094
Description: Mentally ill persons and their families. Works to inform the public about mental illness and enhance the lives of people who are mentally ill. Conducts research and educational programs. **Founded:** 1979. **Membership:** 160000. **Staff:** 80. **National Groups:** 1. **Languages:** English, Spanish. **Budget:** $22,000,000.

ALLIANCE FOR THE PRUDENT USE OF ANTIBIOTICS (APUA)
e-mail: apua@opal.tufts.edu
url: http://www.healthsci.tufts.edu/apua/apua.html
PO Box 1372
Boston, MA 02117
Stuart B. Levy, M.D., Pres.
PH: (617)636-0966
FX: (617)636-6765
Description: International membership of physicians, scientists, and medical and public health personnel; other individuals supporting prudent use of antibiotics. (Believes that extensive use of antibiotics leads to development of resistant strains of pathogenic and common, nonpathogenic bacteria with resistance traits transferable from one bacterium to others. These resistant strains are no longer susceptible to antibiotics and therefore can undermine treatment of infectious bacterial diseases.) Advocates and defines "good usage" of antibiotics; informs and educates the public about the dangers of misusing and overusing antibiotics and other antimicrobial agents; provides data to individuals and organizations interested in preventing antibiotic misuse and overuse. Informs and educates medical and paramedical personnel worldwide about the defined and specific action of antibiotics and the necessity of controlling their dispensation and prescription. Supports research projects. Maintains speakers' bureau; plans to offer computerized services. **Founded:** 1981. **Membership:** 1000. **Staff:** 3. Multinational. **National Groups:** 13. **Languages:** Chinese, English.

ALLIED BEAUTY ASSOCIATION (ABA)
3625 Dufferin St., Ste. 235
Downsview, ON, Canada M3K 1Z2
Marc Speir, Exec.Dir.
PH: (416)635-1282
FX: (416)635-1705
Description: Individuals and corporations engaged in the beauty industries. Promotes growth and development of members' businesses. Represents members' interests; conducts public relations campaigns; serves as a clearinghouse on the Canadian beauty industries. **Languages:** English, French. **Publication:** *Riben Nehrah Quarterly.* Newsletter ▪ Brochure.

ALOPECIA AREATA SUPPORT AND INFORMATION SERVICE (AASIS)
2255B Queen St. E
Toronto, ON, Canada M4E 1G3
Lindy Barrow, Contact
PH: (416)690-8063
Description: Individuals with alopecia areata (a condition of the skin causing irritation of the scalp and the bearded areas of the face); dermatologists and other health care professionals. Promotes advancement in the diagnosis and treatment of alopecia areata; seeks to improve the quality of life of people with the condition. Provides support and services to members. **Languages:** English, French. **Publication:** *Canadian Student Press Style Guide.* Book.

ALPHA EPSILON DELTA
University of Virginia
Garrett Hall of Medicine
McCormick Rd.
Charlottesville, VA 22903
Dr. Thomas Pearce, Pres.
PH: (804)924-0311
FX: (804)924-8907
Description: Honor society of men and women in the field of premedical study. **Founded:** 1926. **Membership:** 88600. **Regional Groups:** 5. **Languages:** English. **Budget:** $220,000. **Publication:** *The Scalpel,* semiannual ▪ Newsletter, bimonthly.

ALPHA OMEGA ALPHA HONOR MEDICAL SOCIETY
e-mail: eharris@alphaomegaalpha.org
url: http://www.pharos.org
525 Middlefield Rd., Ste. 130
Menlo Park, CA 94025
Edward D. Harris, Jr., Exec.Sec.
PH: (650)329-0291
FX: (650)329-1618
Description: Honor society for men and women studying medicine at graduate and postgraduate levels. Sponsors "Leaders in American Medicine" videotape series; underwrites visiting professorships. **Founded:** 1902. **Membership:** 72000. **Regional Groups:** 124. **Languages:** English. **Publication:** *The Pharos,* quarterly. Journal. Contains nontechnical articles of medical interest. Circulation: 72,000. Advertising: not accepted. **Formerly:** Alpha Omega Alpha.

ALPHA OMEGA INTERNATIONAL DENTAL FRATERNITY
1314 Bedford Ave., Ste. 206
Baltimore, MD 21208
Stephanie Block, Exec.Dir.
PH: (410)602-3300
TF: 800677-8468
FX: (410)602-3394
Description: Professional fraternity - dentistry. Encourages fraternalism and monitors discrimination in dental schools. Maintains the Alpha Omega Foundation, which sends funds to dental schools in Israel and the U.S. Holds continuing education seminars. **Founded:** 1907. **Membership:** 15000. **Staff:** 4. Multinational. **Local Groups:** 125. **Languages:** English. **Budget:** $500,000. **Publication:** *Alpha Omega International Dental Fraternity Newsletter,* quarterly. Provides information on dental education in the United States and Israel. Price: included in membership dues. Circulation: 11,500 ▪ *Alpha Omegan,* quarterly.

ALPHA TAU DELTA (ATD)
url: http://www.atdnursin.org
150 Cruickshank Dr.
Folsom, CA 95630
Kerri L. Kaye, Natl. Corresponding Sec.
Description: Professional fraternity - nursing. Seeks to further educational standards for the nursing profession. Maintains scholarship program for members only. **Founded:** 1921. **Membership:** 6000. **National Groups:** 1. **Languages:** English.

ALS SOCIETY OF CANADA
e-mail: alssoc@inforamp.net
url: http://www.als.ca
6 Adelaide St. E, Ste. 220
Toronto, ON, Canada M5C 1H6
Suzanne Lawson, Natl. Exec. Dir.
PH: (416)362-0269
TF: 800267-4ALS
FX: (416)362-0414
Description: Individuals interested in amyotropic lateral sclerosis or ALS (also known as Lou Gehrig's Disease). Works to: heighten public awareness and understanding of the disease; encourage research among medical and scientific communities. **Founded:** 1977. **Membership:** 3295. **Staff:** 5. **National Groups:** 1. **Languages:** French. **Budget:** C$3,389,000. **Publication:** *ALS Q and A.* Brochure ▪ *An Overview for People with ALS* (in English and French). Book. Price: C$3.00. Circulation: 10,000. Advertising: not accepted ▪ *Breathing Strategies* ▪ *Communication Strategies For People Living With ALS* ▪ *Coping with Grief* ▪ *Drinking and Swallowing Strategies* ▪ *Mobility Strategies* ▪ *Resources for ALS Healthcare Providers* ▪ Newsletter (in English), 3/year. Contains information on ALS treatment, research, and events. Circulation: 6,000. Advertising: not accepted.

ALS FORBES NORRIS RESEARCH CENTER (ALSNRF)
3698 California St., Rm. 545
San Francisco, CA 94118
Robert G. Miller, M.D., Contact

PH: (415)923-3604
FX: (415)673-5184
Description: Serves as clearinghouse for laboratory and clinical research into neuromuscular diseases, primarily Amyotrophic Lateral Sclerosis (Lou Gehrig's Disease). ALS is a paralytic and usually fatal disease of the motor neurons, nerves which innervate the muscles to allow movement. Although patients maintain their full intellectual capacities, they gradually lose their ability to move, talk, and breathe. Conducts monthly support group for ALS patients and families in the San Francisco Bay area. Sponsors the ALS Research Center at the California Pacific Medical Center in San Francisco, CA and maintains an extensive bank of ALS patient information. Offers educational programs and a speakers' bureau. Convention/Meeting: none. **Founded:** 1981. **Staff:** 17. **Local Groups:** 3. **Languages:** English. **Budget:** $300,000. **Publication:** *Forbes Norris Research Center – Support Group Newsletter*, monthly. Price: free. Advertising: not accepted ▪ Newsletter, semiannual. **Formerly:** (1994) ALS and Neuromuscular Research Foundation.

AMBULATORY PEDIATRIC ASSOCIATION (APA)
e-mail: ambpeds@aol.com
url: http://www.ambpeds.org
6728 Old McLean Village Dr.
Mc Lean, VA 22101
Marge Degnon, Exec.Sec.
PH: (703)556-9222
FX: (703)556-8729
Description: Health care providers interested in the care of children in ambulatory care facilities, particularly directors of outpatient departments in private, university, and other teaching hospitals and those engaged in public health work or private practice. Aims to improve methods of care of children. Studies methods of research and the teaching of outpatient care. Conducts collaborative research; compiles statistics; presents annual scientific program. **Founded:** 1960. **Membership:** 1700. **Staff:** 3. **Regional Groups:** 10. **Languages:** English. **Budget:** $300,000. Formerly (1967) Association for Ambulatory Pediatric Services.

AMERICAN ACADEMY OF ADDICTION PSYCHIATRY (AAAP)
7301 Mission Rd., Ste. 252
Prairie Village, KS 66208
Jeanne G. Trumble, Exec.Dir.
PH: (913)262-6161
FX: (913)262-4311
Description: Psychiatrists and other health care and mental health professionals treating people with addictive behaviors. Promotes excellence in the treatment of addictions; seeks to insure availability of addiction treatment programs; encourages improvement in the training of health and mental health care providers treating people with addictive behaviors. Conducts educational programs to raise public awareness of addiction and related diseases; provides consulting services to public policy makers. Serves as a clearinghouse on addictions and their treatment; provides support and assistance to addictions research. **Founded:** 1985. **Membership:** 1000. Multinational. **Regional Groups:** 9. **Languages:** English.

AMERICAN ACADEMY OF ALTERNATIVE MEDICINE (AAAM)
16126 E Warren
Detroit, MI 48224-0224
Dr. B. Alli, Contact
PH: (313)882-0641
FX: (313)882-0972
Description: Advocates of alternative medicine. Promotes increased reliance on alternative treatments by medical professionals. Conducts research; sponsors training programs for health care professionals wishing to make use of alternative therapies. **Founded:** 1994. **Membership:** 800. **Staff:** 5. **Languages:** English. **Publication:** Newsletter, periodic. Advertising: accepted.

AMERICAN ACADEMY OF AMBULATORY CARE NURSING (AAACN)
e-mail: aaacn@mail.ajj.com
url: http://www.inurse.com/~aaacn
East Holly Ave., Box 56
Pitman, NJ 08071-0056
Cynthia R. Nowicki, EdD,RN, Contact
PH: (609)256-2350
TF: 800262-6877
FX: (609)589-7463
Description: Nurses with administrative/management responsibilities in ambulatory care. To improve the quality and efficiency of ambulatory care through continuing education programs. Program goals are to enhance the leadership and supervisory skills of nurse administrators, and improve members' abilities to influence organizational decisions. Conducts skill building workshops; provides educators to members' groups for in-service educational programs. **Founded:** 1978. **Membership:** 1900. **Staff:** 5. **Local Groups:** 17. **Languages:** English. **Budget:** $150,000. Formerly American Academy of Ambulatory Nursing Administration.

AMERICAN ACADEMY OF ANESTHESIOLOGIST ASSISTANTS (AAAA)
url: http://www.shoestringnet.com/AAAA
PO Box 81362
Wellesley, MA 02181-0004
Sherri L. Oken, CAE, Assn.Mgr.
PH: 800-757-5858
FX: (781)239-3259
Description: Active anesthesiologist assistants who have graduated from an accredited training program. Establishes and maintains the standards of the profession. Fosters and encourages continuing education and research. Sponsors educational meetings to all graduates and student anesthesiologist assistants. **Founded:** 1975. **Membership:** 450. **Budget:** $24,000.

AMERICAN ACADEMY OF CHILD AND ADOLESCENT PSYCHIATRY (AACAP)
url: http://www.aacap.org
3615 Wisconsin Ave. NW
Washington, DC 20016-3007
Virginia Q. Anthony, Exec.Dir.
PH: (202)966-7300
TF: 800333-7636
FX: (202)966-2891
Description: Professional society of degreed physicians who have completed an additional five years of residency in child and adolescent psychiatry. Seeks to stimulate and advance medical contributions to the knowledge and treatment of psychiatric illnesses of children and adolescents. **Founded:** 1953. **Membership:** 6000. **Staff:** 23. Multinational. **Regional Groups:** 53. **Languages:** English. **Budget:** $3,000,000. Formerly (1986) American Academy of Child Psychiatry.

AMERICAN ACADEMY OF CLINICAL NEUROPHYSIOLOGY
4700 W. Lake Ave.
Glenview, IL 60025-1485
Anne M. Cordes, Exec.Dir.
PH: (847)375-4712
FX: (847)375-4777
Description: Clinical neurophysiologists. Fosters an understanding of the function of the nervous system among health professionals, scientists, and the public by serving as a forum for interaction and the communication of new developments. Offers educational programs. **Founded:** 1985. **Membership:** 800. **Staff:** 5. **Languages:** English.

AMERICAN ACADEMY OF CLINICAL PSYCHIATRISTS (AACP)
e-mail: info-aacp@aacp.com
url: http://www.aacp.com
PO Box 3212
San Diego, CA 92163
Alicia A. Munoz, Exec.Dir.

PH: (619)298-0538
FX: (619)298-3601
Description: Practicing board-eligible or board-certified psychiatrists. Promotes the scientific practice of psychiatric medicine. Conducts educational and teaching research. Founded: 1975. Membership: 600. Staff: 1. Languages: English. Budget: $125,000.

AMERICAN ACADEMY OF CLINICAL TOXICOLOGY (AACT)
777 E. Park Dr.
PO Box 8820
Harrisburg, PA 17105-8820
Edward P. Krenzelok, Ph.D., Pres.
PH: (717)558-7847
FX: (717)558-7841
Description: Physicians, veterinarians, pharmacists, nurses research scientists, and analytical chemists. Objectives are to: unite medical scientists and facilitate the exchange of information; encourage the development of therapeutic methods and technology; Conducts professional training in poison information and emergency service personnel. Founded: 1968. Membership: 550. Staff: 1. Multinational. Languages: English. Budget: $150,000.

AMERICAN ACADEMY OF DENTAL ELECTROSURGERY (AADE)
PO Box 374, Planetarium Sta.
New York, NY 10024
Dr. Maurice J. Oringer, D.D.S., Exec.Sec.
PH: (212)595-1925
Description: Dentists who are qualified by special training to use electrosurgery therapeutically and research scientists who investigate the behavior of the therapeutic electrosurgical high frequency currents and their effects on the oral structures. Purposes are: to improve the clinical uses of electrosurgery in dentistry; to introduce instruction in dental electrosurgery at the undergraduate basic science and clinical level; to promote postgraduate training in electrosurgery; to promote research by qualified investigators; to improve electronic circuitry and clinical techniques. Conducts 2 scientific programs annually consisting of panel symposia, essays, clinical lectures, and table clinics. Founded: 1963. Membership: 200. Staff: 1. Languages: English. Budget: $10,000. Publication: "Current" Events (in English), quarterly. Newsletter. Covers academy activities and providing information about electrosurgery techniques, circuitry, and equipment. Price: included in membership dues. Advertising: not accepted.

AMERICAN ACADEMY OF DENTAL GROUP PRACTICE (AADGP)
e-mail: aadgp@hibcc.org
url: http://www.hibcc.org/aadgp/aadgp.htm
5110 N. 40th St., Ste. 250
Phoenix, AZ 85018
Robert A. Hankin, Ph.D., Exec.Dir.
PH: (602)381-1185
FX: (602)381-1093
Description: Active dentists and dental group practices. Purpose is to improve the level of dental service provided by members through exchanging and expanding of ideas and techniques for patient treatment and practice administration. Promotes group practice and research; accumulates and disseminates information; seeks to achieve the proper recognition for the aims and goals of group practice. Helps support an accreditation program as a system of voluntary peer review. Founded: 1973. Membership: 1575. Staff: 2. Regional Groups: 3. Languages: English. Publication: AADGP Contact, quarterly. Newsletter. Price: included in membership dues. Circulation: 1,500. Advertising: accepted ■ Membership Directory, biennial.

AMERICAN ACADEMY OF DENTAL PRACTICE ADMINISTRATION (AADPA)
c/o Kathleen Uebel
1063 Whippoorwill Ln.
Palatine, IL 60067
Kathleen Uebel, Exec.Dir.
PH: (847)934-4404
Description: Professional society of dentists interested in efficient administration of dental practice. Offers educational programs. Founded: 1956. Membership: 250. Multinational. Languages: English. Publication: American Academy of Dental Practice Administration – Communicator, 3/year. Newsletter. Price: Free, for members only. Advertising: not accepted ■ American Academy of Dental Practice Administration – Roster, annual. Price: for members only ■ Essay Tapes, annual.

AMERICAN ACADEMY OF DERMATOLOGY (AAD)
url: http://www.aad.org
930 N. Meacham Rd.
Schaumburg, IL 60173
Bradford W. Claxton, Exec.Dir.
PH: (847)330-0230
FX: (847)330-0050
Description: Professional society of medical doctors specializing in skin diseases. Conducts educational programs. Provides placement service; compiles statistics. Founded: 1938. Membership: 11200. Staff: 63. Multinational. Languages: English. Budget: $11,500,000. Formerly American Academy of Dermatology and Syphilology.

AMERICAN ACADEMY OF ESTHETIC DENTISTRY (AAED)
1807 S. Washington St., Ste. 106
Naperville, IL 60565
Lanny L. Hardy, Exec.Dir.
PH: (630)355-0424
TF: 800993-2626
FX: (630)355-0474
Description: Dentists seeking to advance the art and science of esthetic dentistry (dentistry concerned with restorative procedures of natural teeth). Founded: 1975. Membership: 125. Multinational. Languages: English. Budget: $500,000. Publication: Esthetics, semiannual. Newsletter. Presents information on the restoration of natural teeth. Includes calendar of events and research updates. Price: included in membership dues. Circulation: 200 ■ Journal of Esthetic Dentistry.

AMERICAN ACADEMY OF FAMILY PHYSICIANS (AAFP)
e-mail: fp@aafp.org
url: http://www.aafp.org
8880 Ward Pky.
Kansas City, MO 64114
Robert Graham, M.D., Exec.VP
PH: (816)333-9700
TF: 800274-2237
FX: (816)822-0580
Description: Professional society of family physicians who provide continuing comprehensive care to patients. Founded: 1947. Membership: 81000. Staff: 300. Local Groups: 200. Languages: English. Budget: $54,000,000. Publication: AAFP Reporter, monthly. Newsletter. Covers socioeconomic issues and legislative news affecting medicine; includes member news. Available to selected media. Circulation: 59,000. Advertising: not accepted ■ American Academy of Family Physicians, annual. Membership Directory ■ American Family Physician, 16/year. Journal. Includes book reviews, newsletter, calendar of events, and therapeutic, product, and subject indexes. Price: free to qualified recipients; $50.00/year for nonmembers. ISSN: 0002-838X. Circulation: 150,000. Advertising: accepted. Alternate Formats: CD-ROM ■ Family Practice Management, 10/year. Covers practice management and socioeconomic issues ■ Annual Report. Formerly: (1971) American Academy of General Practice.

AMERICAN ACADEMY OF FIXED PROSTHODONTICS (AAFP)
e-mail: secaafp@worldnet.att.net
url: http://www.prosthodontics.org/aafp
PO Box 1409
Bodega Bay, CA 94923-1409
Dr. Robert S. Staffanou, Sec.
PH: (707)875-3040
TF: 800785-9188
FX: (707)875-2927
Description: Dentists. Provides 2-day professional continuing education course in the specialty of fixed prosthodontics. Founded: 1952. Membership: 535. Multinational. Languages: English. Budget: $230,000. Publication: *American Academy of Fixed Prosthodontics Newsletter*, semiannual. Price: included in membership dues. Circulation: 600. Advertising: not accepted ▪ *Journal of Prosthetic Dentistry*, monthly ▪ *Meeting Program/Directory*, annual. Formerly: (1991) American Academy of Crown and Bridge Prosthodontics.

AMERICAN ACADEMY OF GNATHOLOGIC ORTHOPEDICS (AAGO)
1585 N. Barrington Rd., Ste. 106
Hoffman Estates, IL 60194
John Rothchild, D.D.S., Exec.Dir.
PH: (847)884-1220
FX: (847)884-1638
Description: Dentists dealing with the prevention or correction of malocclusion and bony misformation of the jaw and face. Conducts activities in the fields of maxillofacial orthopedics/ orthodontics and preventative and corrective orthodontics. Founded: 1970. Membership: 700. Staff: 1. National Groups: 1. Languages: English. Budget: $100,000. Publication: *American Academy of Gnathologic Orthopedics—Journal*, quarterly. Includes scientific articles and case reports on orthodontic treatment. Price: $80.00 plus postage in U.S.; $85.00 Canada; $100.00 foreign. ISSN: 0886-1064. Circulation: 400. Advertising: accepted ▪ *American Academy of Gnathologic Orthopedics—Membership Roster*, annual. Membership Directory. Price: included in membership dues. Circulation: 400 ▪ Articles. On the Crozat Method.

AMERICAN ACADEMY OF GOLD FOIL OPERATORS (AAGFO)
17922 Tallgrass Ct.
Noblesville, IN 46060
Dr. Ronald K. Harris, Sec.-Treas.
PH: (317)867-3011
FX: (317)867-3011
Description: Dentists who perform restorative procedures utilizing gold foil, cast gold, and the rubber dam. Formulates and applies new ideas for research on gold restorations and the rubber dam; encourages members of the dental profession and research institutions in the armed forces, government, dental schools, and private enterprise to study gold restorations and rubber dam procedures. Presents chair demonstrations at dental schools. Founded: 1952. Membership: 320. Staff: 1. Multinational. Languages: English. Publication: *Journal of Operative Dentistry*, bimonthly ▪ *Roster*, biennial.

AMERICAN ACADEMY OF THE HISTORY OF DENTISTRY (AAHD)
100 S. Vail Ave.
Arlington Heights, IL 60005-1866
Aletha A. Kowitz, Sec.-Treas.
PH: (847)670-7561
Description: Seeks to stimulate interest, study, and research in the history of dentistry and promote the teaching of dental history. Founded: 1951. Membership: 500. Multinational. Languages: English. Budget: $10,000. Publication: *Journal of the History of Dentistry*, 3/year. Includes articles on the history of dentistry, book reviews, and 5yr cummulative index. Price: $45.00/year. ISSN: 0007-5132. Circulation: 750. Advertising: accepted.

AMERICAN ACADEMY OF HUSBAND-COACHED CHILDBIRTH (AAHCC)
url: http://www.bradleybirth.com
PO Box 5224
Sherman Oaks, CA 91413
Marjie Hathaway, Exec.Dir.
PH: (818)788-6662
TF: 8004-A-BIRTH
FX: (818)788-1580
Description: Trains instructors in the Bradley method of natural childbirth. Provides referals to Bradley teachers. Founded: 1970. Membership: 1200. Languages: English. For-Profit.

AMERICAN ACADEMY OF IMPLANT DENTISTRY (AAID)
e-mail: aaid@aaid-implant.org
url: http://aaid-implant.org
211 E. Chicago Ave., Ste. 750
Chicago, IL 60611
J. Vincent Shuck, Exec.Dir.
PH: (312)335-1550
FX: (312)335-9090
Description: Dedicated to furthering scientific research and development in the field of implantology. Founded: 1952. Membership: 2500. Staff: 6. Multinational. Regional Groups: 4. Languages: English. Budget: $1,200,000. Publication: *American Academy of Implant Dentistry*, annual. Directory. Arranged geographically and alphabetically. Price: free to members. Circulation: 2,500. Advertising: not accepted ▪ *Journal of Oral Implantology*, quarterly. Contains original manuscripts, clinical presentations, research annotations, and educational reports pertinent to dental studies. Price: included in membership dues; $75.00/year for nonmembers; $100.00/year for libraries, corporations, and institutes. Advertising: accepted. Formerly: American Academy of Implant Dentures.

AMERICAN ACADEMY OF IMPLANT PROSTHODONTICS (AAIP)
5555 Peachtree-Dunwoody Rd. NE, Ste. 140
Atlanta, GA 30342
M. Ford, Contact
Description: Experts in dental implantology; dental school professors. Encourages continuing education, advancement, and research in implant dentistry; believes that prosthodontics and implantology education and research should take place in academic institutions. Promotes the surgical insertion of dental transplants and the design and insertion of prosthodontic devices to replace missing teeth. Emphasizes research on the construction and maintenance of fixed and removable prostheses. Conducts continuing education courses in conjunction with dental schools. Maintains speakers' bureau and small library; bestows awards. Founded: 1980. Membership: 300. Languages: English. Budget: $100,000. Publication: *The Dental Implant - Clinical and Biological Response of Oral Tissues* ▪ *Implant Prosthodontics - Surgical and Prosthetic Techniques for Dental Implants* ▪ Membership Directory, periodic ▪ Newsletter, 3/year.

AMERICAN ACADEMY OF INSURANCE MEDICINE (AAIM)
e-mail: info@aaimedicine.org
url: http://www.aaimedicine.org
PO Box 59811
Potomac, MD 20859-9811
Dr. Bell, 2nd VP & Medical Dir.
PH: (301)365-3572
FX: (301)365-7705
Description: Professional society of medical directors of life insurance companies. Founded: 1889. Membership: 800. Languages: English. Publication: *Journal of Insurance Medicine*, quarterly. Price: included in membership dues; $45.00/year for nonmembers. Advertising: accepted. Formerly: (1992) Association of Life Insurance Medical Directors of America.

AMERICAN ACADEMY OF MEDICAL ADMINISTRATORS (AAMA)
e-mail: info@aameda.org
url: http://www.aameda.org
30555 Southfield Rd., Ste. 150
Southfield, MI 48076-7747
Thomas R. O'Donovan, Ph.D., Pres.
PH: (248)540-4310
FX: (248)645-0590
Description: Individuals involved in medical administration at the executive- or middle-management levels. Promotes educational courses for the training of persons in medical administration. Conducts research. Offers placement service. **Founded:** 1957. **Membership:** 3800. **Staff:** 9. **State Groups:** 50. **Languages:** English. **Budget:** $1,200,000. **Publication:** *American Academy of Medical Administrators – Executive* (in English), bimonthly. Newsletter. Covers membership activities. Includes triennial membership directory;also contains calendar of events, book reviews, and lists of new members. Price: included in membership dues; $60.00/year for nonmembers. Circulation: 10,000. Advertising: accepted ■ *Journal of Cardiovascular Management* ■ *Journal of Oncology Management*.

AMERICAN ACADEMY OF MEDICAL ADMINISTRATORS RESEARCH AND EDUCATIONAL FOUNDATION (AAMA)
url: http://www.aameda.org
30555 Southfield Rd., Ste. 150
Southfield, MI 48076
Thomas R. O'Donovan, Ph.D., Pres.
PH: (810)540-4310
FX: (810)645-0590
Description: Individuals with health care backgrounds. Conducts research in the health care field and seminars geared toward professional development. Maintains placement services. **Founded:** 1957. **Membership:** 3800. **Staff:** 9. **State Groups:** 50. **Languages:** English. **Publication:** *AAMA Executive*, bimonthly. Newsletter. Covers management topics, industry trends, current developments in health care administration, and association news. Includes book reviews. Price: included in membership dues; $110.00/year for nonmembers. Circulation: 4,000. Advertising: not accepted.

AMERICAN ACADEMY OF NEUROLOGICAL AND ORTHOPAEDIC SURGEONS (FAANAOS)
2300 S. Rancho Dr., Ste. 202
Las Vegas, NV 89102-4508
TF: 888432-2667
Description: Neurological and orthopaedic surgeons, neurologists, physiatrists, and professionals in allied medical or surgical specialties. Provides and encourages information about and understanding of neurological and orthopaedic medicine and surgery, a branch of medicine that deals with diseases and injuries to the human neuromusculo-skeletal system; seeks to improve patient care. Maintains American Board of Neurological and Orthopaedic Medicine and Surgery and American Board of Spinal Surgery. Sponsors charitable program. Maintains a complete collection of recordings of scientific meetings since 1977. Operates 40 colleges of experts in individual disciplines related to neurological and orthopaedic medicine and surgery. Acronym stands for Fellowship of the American Academy of Neurological and Orthopaedic Surgeons. **Founded:** 1977. **Membership:** 1100. Multinational. **Languages:** English. **Publication:** *American Academy of Neurological and Orthopaedic Surgeons – Directory*, biennial ■ *Journal of Neurological and Orthopaedic Surgery*, quarterly. Price: $125.00/year in U.S.; $135.00/year outside U.S. ISSN: 0890-6599. Circulation: 1,000. Advertising: accepted.

AMERICAN ACADEMY OF NEUROLOGICAL SURGERY
2128 Taubman
University Hospital
Ann Arbor, MI 48109
Dr. Julian Hoff, Sec.
PH: (313)936-5015
FX: (313)936-9294
Description: Leaders in the field of neurological surgery united for neurosurgical education. **Founded:** 1938. **Membership:** 168. **Languages:** English. **Budget:** $70,000.

AMERICAN ACADEMY OF NEUROLOGY (AAN)
e-mail: aan@aan.com
url: http://www.aan.com
1080 Montreal Ave.
St. Paul, MN 55116-2325
Jan W. Kolehmainen, Exec.Dir.
Description: Professional society of medical doctors specializing in brain and nervous system diseases. Maintains placement service. Sponsors research and educational programs. Compiles statistics. Publishes scientific journal. **Founded:** 1948. **Membership:** 14500. **Staff:** 65. Multinational. **Languages:** English. **Budget:** $12,000,000. **Publication:** *AAN Governmental Report*, bimonthly. Newsletter. Includes news on legislative affairs ■ *AANews*, monthly. Newsletter. General information and placement publication ■ *American Academy of Neurology Membership Directory*, annual ■ *ICD-9-CM for Neurologists*. Booklet. To aid users of ICD-9 diagnostic codes ■ *Medical Specialty of Neurology*. Brochure. Discusses neurology as a career ■ *Neurologist*. Brochure. For patients ■ *Neurology*, monthly. Journal. Includes research reports ■ *Patient Information Guide for Neurology*. Handbook for patients to find educational information about disorders.

AMERICAN ACADEMY OF NURSE PRACTITIONERS (AANP)
e-mail: admin@aanp.org
url: http://www.aanp.org
LBJ Bldg.
PO Box 12846
Austin, TX 78711
Zo DeMarchi, Dir. of Association Services
PH: (512)442-4262
FX: (512)442-6469
Description: Groups (2000) and individuals (1600) promoting high standards of health care delivered by nurse practitioners. Acts as a forum to enhance the identity and continuity of nurse practitioners. Addresses national and state legislative issues that affect members; acts as a resource center on legislative activity. Supports continuing education programs. Encourages research in the field. Compiles statistics. **Founded:** 1985. **Membership:** 8140. **Staff:** 16. **Languages:** English.

AMERICAN ACADEMY OF NURSING (AAN)
600 Maryland Ave., NW, Ste. 100
Washington, DC 20024-2571
Nancy Fugate Woods, Pres.
PH: (202)544-4444
FX: (202)554-2641
Description: Purposes are to: advance new concepts in nursing and health care; identify and explore issues in health, the professions, and society that concern nursing; examine interrelationships among the segments within nursing and the interaction among nurses as these affect the development of the nursing profession; identify and propose resolutions to issues and problems confronting nursing and health, including alternative plans for implementation. Sponsors symposia. **Founded:** 1973. **Membership:** 800. **Staff:** 3. **Languages:** English. **Budget:** $300,000.

AMERICAN ACADEMY OF OPHTHALMOLOGY (AAO)
url: http://www.eyenet.org
655 Beach St.
San Francisco, CA 94109
H. Dunbar Hoskins, M.D., Exec.VP
PH: (415)561-8500
FX: (415)561-8533
Description: Ophthalmologists concerned with high-quality eye care and the continuing education of members. Sponsors Basic and Clinical Science Course for practitioners and residents to maintain current status (includes annual self-assessment); offers information on new techniques. Operates museum of ophthalmological instruments and artifacts. Operates American Aca-

demy of Ophthalmology Government Affairs Office which serves as a liaison between the AAO and the federal government, monitors pending legislation affecting ophthalmology, and prepares statements and testimonies to be presented to congressional committees and regulatory agencies. Also operates Foundation of the American Academy of Ophthalmology, which functions as the charitable arm of the academy. Current activities of the foundation include National Eye Care Project; Oral Histories Program. **Founded:** 1896. **Membership:** 20000. **Staff:** 150. Multinational. **Languages:** English Absorbed (1981) American Association of Ophthalmology.

AMERICAN ACADEMY OF ORAL AND MAXILLOFACIAL PATHOLOGY (AAOMP)
e-mail: aaomp@b-online.com
710 E. Ogden Ave No. 600
Naperville, IL 60563-8614
Ann Spehar, CAE, Exec.Dir.
PH: (630)369-2406
TF: 888552-2667
FX: (630)369-2488
Description: Professional society of oral pathologists. **Founded:** 1946. **Membership:** 800. **Staff:** 1. **Languages:** English. **Budget:** $110,000. **Publication:** *Oral Radiology and Endodontics.* Journal ▪ *Oral Surgery, Oral Medicine, Oral Pathology,* monthly. **Formerly:** (1994) American Academy Oral Pathology.

AMERICAN ACADEMY OF ORAL AND MAXILLOFACIAL RADIOLOGY (AAOMR)
e-mail: ocarroll@fiona.umsmed.edu
url: http://www.aaomr.org
PO Box 55722
Jackson, MS 39296
Dr. M. Kevin O'Carroll, Exec.Sec.
PH: (601)984-6060
FX: (601)984-6086
Description: Dentists and other professionals who specialize in oral and maxillofacial rediology in clinical practice, teaching or research. Serves as authoritative body on radiation hygiene and hazards for the American Dental Association. **Founded:** 1949. **Membership:** 500. Multinational. **Languages:** English. **Publication:** *AAOMR Newsletter,* quarterly. Price: free. Circulation: 500. Advertising: not accepted ▪ *Oral and Maxillofacial Radiology Section of Oral Surgery, Oral Medicine, Oral Pathology, Oral Radiology, and Endodontics,* monthly. Journal. Price: included in membership dues that are active and associate; $42.00 for corporate memberships ▪ *Roster of Membership,* annual. **Formerly:** (1968) American Academy of Oral Roentgenology; (1991) American Academy of Dental Radiology.

AMERICAN ACADEMY OF ORAL MEDICINE (AAOM)
e-mail: cmiller@pop.uky.edu
url: http://www.aaom.com
Univ. Kentucky Col. of Dent.
Lexington, KY 40536-5598
Craig S. Miller, DDS, Sec.
PH: (606)272-6455
FX: (606)323-1042
Description: Dental educators, specialists, general dentists, and physicians interested in the study of diseases of the mouth. Promotes the study of the cause, prevention, and control of diseases of the teeth, their supporting structures, adnexa (accessory parts of the structures), and related subjects; fosters better scientific understanding between the fields of dentistry and medicine. Maintains speakers' bureau; offers continuing education lectures and seminars. **Founded:** 1946. **Membership:** 800. **Staff:** 1. **Regional Groups:** 4. **Languages:** English. **Budget:** $30,000. **Publication:** *American Association of Stomatologists Newsletter,* quarterly. Advertising: not accepted ▪ *The Clinician's Guide to the Treatment of the Medically-Compromised Dental Patient* ▪ *The Clinician's Guide to Treatment of Common Oral Conditions* (in English and Spanish), every 3-5 years. Monograph. Price: $11.95. Advertising: accepted ▪ *The Clinician's Guide to Treatment of HIV-infected Patients* ▪ *Oral Surgery, Oral Medicine, Oral Pathology,*

Oral Radiology and Endodontics. Journal ▪ Monograph, periodic. Price: included in membership dues; $12.00/year for nonmembers. Advertising: accepted.

AMERICAN ACADEMY OF OROFACIAL PAIN (AAOP)
19 Mantua Rd.
Mount Royal, NJ 08061
Ms. Dale Ziegler, Exec.Dir.
PH: (609)423-3629
FX: (609)423-3420
Description: Medical and dental doctors. Seeks to further knowledge of Orofacial Pain and Temporomandibular Disorders. Maintains patient referral program. **Founded:** 1975. **Membership:** 220. **Staff:** 1. **Languages:** English. **Budget:** $100,000. **Publication:** *Journal of Orofacial Pain,* quarterly. Price: $60.00/year ▪ *Orofacial Pain: Guidelines for Classification, Assessment, and Management* ▪ *Temporomandibular Disorders: Guidelines for Classificiation, Assessment, and Management.* **Formerly:** (1979) American Academy of Craniomandibular Orthopedics; (1992) American Academy of Craniomandibular Disorders.

AMERICAN ACADEMY OF ORTHODONTICS FOR THE GENERAL PRACTITIONER (AAOGP)
920 Bascom Hill Dr.
Baraboo, WI 53913-1281
Jackie Hemmrich, Sec.
Description: Licensed dentists. Provides dentists in general practice with an organization through which they can augment their basic knowledge and training in orthodontics. Offers continuing education courses for dentists and auxiliary personnel; sponsors seminars. Provides facilities and audiovisual material for its affiliated study clubs. **Founded:** 1959. **Membership:** 250. **Staff:** 1. **State Groups:** 5. **Languages:** English. **Publication:** *American Academy of Orthodontics for the General Practitioner – Continuing Education,* annual. Brochure. Lists AAOGP-sponsored continuing education courses, seminars, and meetings for the coming year. Price: free. Advertising: accepted ▪ *International Journal of Orthodontics,* semiannual.

AMERICAN ACADEMY OF PEDIATRIC DENTISTRY (AAPD)
211 E. Chicago Ave., Ste. 700
Chicago, IL 60611
Dr. John A. Bogert, Exec.Dir.
PH: (312)337-2169
FX: (312)337-6329
Description: Professional society of dentists whose practice is limited to children; teachers and researchers in pediatric dentistry. Seeks to advance the specialty of pediatric dentistry through practice, education, and research. Sponsors graduate student pediatric dentistry award program. **Founded:** 1947. **Membership:** 4200. **Staff:** 13. **Regional Groups:** 45. **Languages:** English. **Budget:** $2,500,000. **Publication:** *American Academy of Pediatric Dentistry – Membership Roster,* annual. Membership Directory. Circulation: 3,300. Advertising: accepted ▪ *American Academy of Pediatric Dentistry – Newsletter,* bimonthly. Includes employment listings, meetings calendar, research updates, and obituaries. Price: included in membership dues. Circulation: 4,300. Advertising: accepted ▪ *Pediatric Dentistry,* bimonthly. Journal. Includes employment listings and conference proceedings. Price: included in membership dues; $50.00/year for nonmembers; $65.00/year for institutions. ISSN: 0164-1263. Circulation: 4,900. Advertising: accepted ▪ Pamphlets. **Formerly:** (1984) American Academy of Pedodontics.

AMERICAN ACADEMY OF PEDIATRICS (AAP)
e-mail: kidsdocs@aap.org
url: http://www.aap.org
141 Northwest Point Blvd.
PO Box 927
Elk Grove Village, IL 60009-0927
Joe M. Sanders, Jr., Exec.Dir.
PH: (847)228-5005
FX: (847)228-5097
Description: Professional medical society of pediatricians and

pediatric subspecialists. Operates small member library of books and journals on pediatric medicine, office practice, and child health care policy. Maintains 48 committees, councils, and tasks forces including: Accident and Poison Prevention; Early Childhood, Adoption and Dependent Care; Infectious Diseases. Operates 41 sections. Sponsors Pediatrics Review and Education Program (PREP), a self-assessment, continuing education program for practicing pediatricians. **Founded:** 1930. **Membership:** 51000. **Staff:** 250. **State Groups:** 66. **Languages:** English.

AMERICAN ACADEMY OF PERIODONTOLOGY (AAP)

e-mail: dawn@perio.org
url: http://www.perio.org
737 N. Michigan Ave., Ste. 800
Chicago, IL 60611-2615
Alice DeForest, Exec.Dir.
PH: (312)787-5518
FX: (312)787-3670
Description: Professional society of dentists specializing in treatment of supporting and surrounding tissues of the teeth and their diseases. **Founded:** 1914. **Staff:** 38. **Languages:** English. **Budget:** $6,700,000. **Publication:** *AAP News*, monthly. Newsletter ■ *Directory of Members*, annual ■ *Journal of Periodontology*, monthly. **Absorbed:** (1967) American Society of Periodontists.

AMERICAN ACADEMY OF PHYSICIAN ASSISTANTS (AAPA)

e-mail: aapa@aapa.org
url: http://www.aapa.org
950 N. Washington St.
Alexandria, VA 22314-1552
Stephen C. Crane, Exec.VP
PH: (703)836-2272
FX: (703)684-1924
Description: Physician assistants who have graduated from an accredited program and/or are certified by the National Commission on Certification of Physician Assistants; individuals who are enrolled in an accredited PA educational program. Purposes are to: enhance public access to quality, cost- effective health care, educate the public about the physician assistant profession; represent physician assistants' interests before Congress, government agencies, and health-related organizations; assure the competence of physician assistants through development of educational curricula and accreditation programs; provide services for members. Organizes annual National PA Day. Develops research and education programs; compiles statistics. **Founded:** 1968. **Membership:** 25100. **Staff:** 57. **Local Groups:** 59. **Languages:** English. **Budget:** $6,659,000.

AMERICAN ACADEMY OF PHYSIOLOGIC DENTISTRY (AAPD)

567 S. Washington St.
Naperville, IL 60540
William Kopperud, D.D.S., Sec.
PH: (630)355-2625
FX: (630)355-7243
Description: Dentists and members of related professions. To advance the science and art of dentistry in any of its phases that pertain to the total person. Presently inactive. **Founded:** 1958. **Membership:** 75. **Languages:** English.

AMERICAN ACADEMY OF PODIATRIC SPORTS MEDICINE (AAPSM)

1729 Glastonberry Rd.
Potomac, MD 20854
Larry I. Shane, Exec.Dir.
PH: (301)424-7440
Description: Podiatrists, medical doctors, and athletic trainers interested in promoting professional participation and research in sports medicine. Directs 12 committees that deal with individual sports. Compiles statistics. **Founded:** 1970. **Membership:** 800. **Languages:** English.

AMERICAN ACADEMY OF PROCEDURAL CODERS (AAPC)

e-mail: aapc@worldnet.att.net
url: http://www.cdcreate.com
145 W Crystal Ave.
Salt Lake City, UT 84115-3020
Lan C. England, Exec.Dir.
PH: (801)487-5590
TF: 800626-2633
FX: (801)485-7803
Description: Medical coding specialists. Promotes high standards of outpatient coding through education and cerification. **Founded:** 1988. **Membership:** 5300. **Staff:** 30. **Local Groups:** 125. **Languages:** English.

AMERICAN ACADEMY OF PSYCHIATRY AND THE LAW (AAPL)

e-mail: execoff@aol.com
url: http://aapl.org
1 Regency Dr.
PO Box 30
Bloomfield, CT 06002-0030
Jacquelyn T. Coleman, CAE, Exec.Dir.
PH: (860)242-5450
TF: 800331-1389
FX: (860)286-0787
Description: Psychiatrists who are members in good standing of the American Psychiatric Association or the American Academy of Child and Adolescent Psychiatry. Seeks to exchange ideas and experience in those areas where psychiatry and the law overlap; develop standards of practice in the relationship of psychiatry to the law and encourage the development of training programs for psychiatrists seeking skill and knowledge in this area; stimulate and encourage research in the field; improve relationships between psychiatrists and other professionals in the field; inform the public of problems in the area of psychiatry and the law and the potential contributions from psychiatry. **Founded:** 1969. **Membership:** 1900. **Staff:** 3. Multinational. **Regional Groups:** 11. **Languages:** English. **For-Profit. Budget:** $500,000. **Publication:** *Journal of the American Academy of Psychiatry and the Law* (in English), quarterly. Scholarly articles on forensicy psychiatry. Price: $95.00 library/institutions; $5.00 individuals; $5.00 non US mailings. Circulation: 2,500. Advertising: not accepted ■ *Newsletter of the American Academy of Psychiatry and Law*, 3/year ■ Membership Directory, annual.

AMERICAN ACADEMY OF RESTORATIVE DENTISTRY (AARD)

13 Mirada Rd.
Colorado Springs, CO 80906-4306
Donald H. Downs, D.D.S., Sec.-Treas.
PH: (719)576-8840
FX: (719)633-1060
Description: Professional society of dentists practicing restorative dentistry, and educators interested in dentistry as it applies to treatment of the natural teeth to restore and maintain a healthy functioning mouth as part of a healthy body. **Founded:** 1928. **Membership:** 285. **Languages:** English. **Budget:** $45,000. **Publication:** *Journal of Prosthetic Dentistry*, periodic ■ *Roster*, annual. **Formerly:** (1928) American Society of Dental Ceramics.

AMERICAN ACADEMY OF SOMNOLOGY (AAS)

PO Box 29124
Las Vegas, NV 89126
David L. Hopper, Ph.D., Founder & Pres.
PH: (877)649-0920
FX: (702)458-5833
Description: Clinicians, researchers, and students in the field of somnology; interested individuals. Promotes advancement of somnology as a health care specialty. (Somnology is the study of sleep and sleep disorders.) Advocates standardization of university programs in somnology and a multidisciplinary approach to the study and treatment of sleep disorders; conducts continuing education program. Sponsors American Board of Somnology to evaluate qualifications of applicants, administer examinations,

and confer diplomate status on qualified individuals. Provides a forum for somnology clinicians and researchers to present findings and exchange ideas. Maintains speakers' bureau. **Founded:** 1986. **Membership:** 75. **Staff:** 6. **Languages:** English.

AMERICAN ACADEMY OF SPORTS PHYSICIANS (AASP)
17445 Oak Creek Court
Encino, CA 91316
Janie Zimmer, Coord.
PH: (818)501-4433
FX: (818)501-8855
Description: Clinical physicians engaged in the practice of sports medicine who have made contributions in research, academics, or related fields. Objectives are to educate and inform physicians whose practices comprise mainly sports medicine and to register and recognize physicians who have expertise in sports medicine. Sponsors seminars. **Founded:** 1979. **Membership:** 150. **Languages:** English.

AMERICAN APITHERAPY SOCIETY (AAS)
url: http://www.beesting.com
5370 Carmel Rd.
Hillsboro, OH 45133
Linda Kay, Contact
PH: (937)466-9214
FX: (937)466-9215
Description: Beekeepers, physicians, scientists, and others interested in apitherapy, the therapeutic use of honey bee products. Purpose is to collect and disseminate information in the field and to provide a forum for researchers to present the results of their work. Encourages investigation of hive products in order to provide a scientific foundation for their curative properties and use in human medicine. Seeks to prove the effectiveness of bee venom in treating inflammatory diseases such as arthritis and rheumatism. Gains funding for clinical laboratory studies through contributions. Supports selected research and fundraising projects for the investigation of apitherapeutic agents. Compiles statistics. **Founded:** 1989. **Membership:** 2500. **Staff:** 3. Multinational. **Regional Groups:** 9. **Languages:** English. **Budget:** $50,000. **Publication:** *BeeWell Newsletter*, quarterly. Price: free. Circulation: 1,500. Advertising: not accepted ■ Brochures. Contains information on bee venom, honey, pollen, and beeswax ■ Journal, annual ■ Proceedings, annual. Price: free. Circulation: 300. Advertising: not accepted. **Formerly:** (1989) North American Apio-Therapy Society.

AMERICAN ASSEMBLY FOR MEN IN NURSING (AAMN)
437 Twin Bay Dr.
Pensacola, FL 32534-1350
Leland B. Cohen, Pres.
PH: (518)782-9400
FX: (518)782-9530
Description: Registered nurses. Works to: help eliminate prejudice in nursing; interest men in the nursing profession; provide opportunities for the discussion of common problems; encourage education and promote further professional growth; advise and assist in areas of professional inequity; help develop sensitivities to various social needs; promote the principles and practices of positive health care. Acts as a clearinghouse for information on men in nursing. Conducts educational programs. **Founded:** 1971. **Staff:** 4. **State Groups:** 4. **Languages:** English. Formerly (1982) National Male Nurse Association.

AMERICAN ASSOCIATION FOR ACCREDITATION OF AMBULATORY SURGERY FACILITIES (AAAASF)
1202 Allanson Rd.
Mundelein, IL 60060
Daniel C. Morello, M.D., Pres.
PH: (847)949-6058
FX: (847)566-4580
Description: Board-certified surgeon-operated ambulatory surgical facilities. To maintain high standards through adherence to a voluntary program of inspection and accreditation of ambulatory surgery facilities. **Founded:** 1981. **Membership:** 400. **Languages:**

English. Formerly (1994) American Association for Accreditation of Ambulatory Plastic Surgery Facilities.

AMERICAN ASSOCIATION OF AMBULATORY SURGERY CENTERS (AAASC)
e-mail: aaasc@sba.com
401 N. Michigan Ave.
Chicago, IL 60611-4267
Thomas E. Stautzenbach, Exec.Dir.
TF: 800237-3768
FX: (312)321-6869
Description: Physicians, nurses and administrators involved in planning ambulatory surgery centers. Seeks to advance ambulatory surgery centers for all outpatient surgery. **Founded:** 1978. **Membership:** 400. **Staff:** 4. **Languages:** English. **For-Profit.** Formerly (1986) Society for Office-Based Surgery; (1996) American Society of Outpatient Surgeons.

AMERICAN ASSOCIATION OF ANATOMISTS (AAA)
c/o Dr. Duane E. Haines
University of Mississippi Medical Center
2500 N. State St.
Jackson, MS 39216
Dr. Duane E. Haines, Sec.-Treas.
PH: (601)984-1772
FX: (601)984-1655
Description: Professional society of anatomists and scientists in related fields. **Founded:** 1888. **Membership:** 2500. **Languages:** English. **Publication:** *Anatomical News*, quarterly. Newsletter. Includes list of employment opportunities. Price: included in membership dues. Circulation: 2,500 ■ *Anatomical Record*, monthly ■ *Developmental Dynamics*, monthly ■ *Directory, Departments of Anatomy, U.S. and Canada*, triennial.

AMERICAN ASSOCIATION OF BLOOD BANKS (AABB)
e-mail: aabb@aabb.org
url: http://Www.aabb.org
8101 Glenbrook Rd.
Bethesda, MD 20814
Karen Lipton, JD, CEO
PH: (301)907-6977
FX: (301)907-6895
Description: Community and hospital blood centers and transfusion and transplantation services, physicians, nurses, technologists, administrators, blood donor recruiters, scientists, and individuals involved in related activities. Encourages the voluntary donation of blood and other tissues and organs through education, public information, and research. Operates the National Blood Exchange; inspects and accredits blood banks and parentage testing laboratories; sponsors the National Blood Foundation; maintains a rare donor file and reference laboratory system. Maintains over 40 scientific, technical, and administrative committees and three councils. **Founded:** 1947. **Membership:** 11500. **Staff:** 63. Multinational. **Languages:** English. **Budget:** $6,800,000. **Publication:** *AABB News Briefs*, 11/year. Newsletter. Includes calendar of events, employment listings, and government affairs update. Price: included in membership dues. ISSN: 8756-6095. Circulation: 11,500. Advertising: accepted ■ *American Association of Blood Banks–Membership Directory*, biennial. Lists institutional and individual members in alphabetical and geographic order. Price: included in membership dues; $50.00 for nonmembers ■ *Blood Bank Week*. Newsletter. Covers scientific, legislative, and regulatory events affecting blood banking and transfusion medicine. Price: $98.00/year for members; $128.00/year for nonmembers. ISSN: 0747-2420. Circulation: 1,400 ■ *Directory of Community Blood Centers*, biennial. Price: $25.00 for participating members; $50.00 for nonmembers. Circulation: 1,000. Advertising: not accepted ■ *Standards for Blood Banks and Transfusion Services*, every 18 months. Price: $20.00 for members; $35.00 for nonmembers. Circulation: 35,000. Advertising: not accepted ■ *Technical Manual*, triennial. Price: $48.00 for members; $60.00 for nonmembers; $45.00 for students. Circulation: 35,000. Advertising: not accepted ■ *Transfusion*, monthly. Journal. Presents scientific, technical, and administrative papers relating to the field of blood

banking. Includes advertisers index and convention abstract. Price: included in membership dues; $135.00/year for nonmember individuals; $195.00/year for institutions. ISSN: 0041-1132. Circulation: 12,800. Advertising: accepted ■ Books ■ Monographs.

AMERICAN ASSOCIATION FOR CANCER EDUCATION (AACE)
e-mail: gkrawiec@cancer.org
url: http://rpci.med.buffalo.edu/clinic/educations/aace2.html
PO Box 601
Snellville, GA 30278-0601
Virginia Krawiec, MPA, Sec.
Description: Physicians, dentists, nurses, health educators, social workers, and occupational therapists; others interested in cancer education. Provides a forum for individuals concerned with the study and improvement of cancer education focusing on prevention, early detection, treatment, and rehabilitation. **Founded:** 1966. **Membership:** 550. **Languages:** English. **Publication:** *Journal of Cancer Education*, quarterly. Price: $95.00 for members; $195.00 for institutions and libraries. ISSN: 0885-8195. Circulation: 800. Advertising: accepted ■ Membership Directory, annual. **Supersedes:** Cancer Coordinators.

AMERICAN ASSOCIATION OF CARDIOVASCULAR AND PULMONARY REHABILITATION (AACVPR)
e-mail: aacvpr@tmahq.com
url: http://www.aacvpr.org
7611 Elmwood Ave., Ste. 201
Middleton, WI 53562
Robin Brown, Exec.Dir.
PH: (608)831-6989
FX: (608)831-5122
Description: Allied health professionals involved in the field of cardiovascular and pulmonary rehabilitation. Fosters the improvement of clinical practice in CVPR; promotes scientific CVPR research; seeks the advancement of CVPR education for health care professionals and the public. **Founded:** 1985. **Membership:** 3000. Multinational. **Languages:** English. **Budget:** $1,000,000.

AMERICAN ASSOCIATION OF CERTIFIED ORTHOPTISTS (AACO)
501 Hill St.
Waycross, GA 31501
Jill T. Clark, Pres.
Description: Orthoptists certified by the American Orthoptic Council, after completing a minimum of 24 months' special training, to treat defects in binocular function. Assists in postgraduate instruction courses; conducts programs and courses at international, national, and regional meetings; helps individual orthoptists with special or unusual problem cases; trains new orthoptists. Operates a placement listing. **Founded:** 1940. **Membership:** 350. **Languages:** English Formerly (1963) American Association of Orthopic Technicians.

AMERICAN ASSOCIATION OF CHAIRMEN OF DEPARTMENTS OF PSYCHIATRY (AACDP)
e-mail: a0tasm01@ulkyvm.louisville.edu
url: http://www.aacdp.org
American Association of Chairmen of Departments of Psychiatr
Department of Psychiatry and Behavioral Sciences
University of Louisville School of Medicine
Louisville, KY 40292
Allan Tasman, M.D., Pres.
PH: (502)852-1126
FX: (502)852-1115
Description: Chairmen of departments of psychiatry in colleges of medicine. Purposes are: to promote medical education, research, and patient care, particularly as these concern psychiatry; to promote the growth and continuing development of psychiatry; to provide a forum for discussion and exchange of ideas among the chairmen of departments of psychiatry in medical schools; to provide appropriate liaison between chairmen and in-

dividuals and organizations whose activities bear on the objectives of the association. **Founded:** 1967. **Membership:** 136. **Staff:** 1. **Languages:** English. **Budget:** $40,000.

AMERICAN ASSOCIATION OF COLLEGES OF NURSING (AACN)
1 Dupont Cir. NW, Ste. 530
Washington, DC 20036
Dr. Geraldine Bednash, Exec.Dir.
PH: (202)463-6930
FX: (202)785-8320
Description: Institutions offering baccalaureate and/or graduate degrees in nursing. Seeks to advance the practice of professional nursing by improving the quality of baccalaureate and graduate programs, promoting research, and developing academic leaders. Works with other professional nursing organizations and organizations in other health professions to evaluate and improve health care. Conducts educational programs on masters and doctoral nursing education and faculty practice; sponsors executive development series for new and aspiring deans of nursing. **Founded:** 1969. **Membership:** 461. **Staff:** 13. **Languages:** English. **Budget:** $1,000,000. **Publication:** *Data Base for Graduate Education in Nursing*. Price: $6.00 ■ *The Ecoomic Investment in Nursing Education*. Price: $5.00 ■ *Enrollment and Graduations in Baccalaureate and Graduate Programs in Nursing*, annual. Report ■ *Essentials of College and University Education for Professional Nursing*. Price: $2.75 for members; $3.75 for nonmembers ■ *Executive Development Series II: The Dean's Role in Organizational Assessment and Development*. Price: $26.95 for members; $36.95 for nonmembers ■ *Faculty Salaries in Baccalaureate and Graduate Programs in Nursing*, annual. Report ■ *Issue Bulletin*, 3/year. Examines issues in nursing education and research ■ *Journal of Professional Nursing*, bimonthly ■ *Meet the Press and Succeed: A Handbook for Nurse Educators*. Price: $4.75 for members; $5.75 for nonmembers ■ *Position Statement on Nursing Research*. Price: $3.00 ■ *Primary Health Care: Nurses Lead the Way – A Global Perspective*. Price: $10.00 for members; $15.00 for nonmembers ■ *Salaries of Administrative Nursing Faculty in Baccalaureate and Graduate Programs in Nursing*, biennial. Report ■ *Salaries of Deans in Baccalaureate and Graduate Programs in Nursing*, annual. Report. Price: $28.00 ■ *Special Report on Institutional Resources and Budgets in Baccalaureate and Graduate Programs in Nursing*, biennial. Price: $25.00 ■ *Syllabus*, bimonthly. Newsletter. Advertising: accepted ■ Annual Report.

AMERICAN ASSOCIATION OF COLLEGES OF PHARMACY (AACP)
e-mail: prtaacp@aol.com
url: http://www.aacp.org
1426 Prince St.
Alexandria, VA 22314
Richard P. Penna, Exec.VP
PH: (703)739-2330
FX: (703)836-8982
Description: College of pharmacy programs accredited by American Council on Pharmaceutical Education; corporations and individuals. Compiles statistics. **Founded:** 1900. **Membership:** 2500. **Staff:** 15. **Languages:** English. **Budget:** $2,900,000 Formerly (1925) American Conference of Pharmaceutical Faculties.

AMERICAN ASSOCIATION FOR COMMUNITY DENTAL PROGRAMS
3101 Burnet Ave.
Cincinnati, OH 45229-3014
Lawrence F. Hill, Contact
PH: (513)357-7380
FX: (513)357-7385
Description: Community dental programs. Conducts educational programs. **Founded:** 1983. **Membership:** 200. **Staff:** 1. **Budget:** $10,000.

AMERICAN ASSOCIATION OF COMMUNITY PSYCHIATRISTS (AACP)

PO Box 282189
Dallas, TX 75228-0218
Charles Huffine, M.D., Pres.
PH: (503)698-3544
FX: (503)698-8100
Description: Psychiatrists and psychiatry residents practicing in community mental health centers (CMHCs) or similar programs that provide care to populations of the mentally ill regardless of their ability to pay. Works to address issues faced by psychiatrists who practice within CMHCs, with the goal of ensuring quality patient care. Purposes are to: increase the number of psychiatrists who choose careers in community mental health; clarify and solve mutual problems regarding community mental health psychiatric practice; inform and educate the public about the community psychiatrist's role in treating the mentally ill; encourage research and training in psychiatry in the community mental health setting; establish liaison with similar professional associations and foster local and regional groups interested in public community psychiatry. Works to deal with issues such as professional burnout, the function of the psychiatrist within CMHCs, assuring relevant continuing medical education, and improving care in CMHCs. Proposes and promotes standards and guidelines of psychiatric practice and staffing in CMHCs; fosters a multidisciplinary approach to CMHC psychiatric care employing nurses, psychiatrists, psychologists, and social workers. Operates work groups in areas such as residency and fellowship training, standards of care, psychiatric leadership in community settings, and CMHCs and the homeless. Disseminates information on legislative activities, local and regional programs, treatment methods, and other matters relating to community psychiatry. **Founded:** 1984. **Membership:** 350. **Regional Groups:** 7. **Languages:** English.

AMERICAN ASSOCIATION OF DENTAL EXAMINERS (AADE)

211 E. Chicago Ave., Ste. 760
Chicago, IL 60611
Molly S. Nadler, Exec.Dir.
PH: (312)440-7464
FX: (312)440-3525
Description: Present and past members of state dental examining boards and board administrators. To assist member agencies with problems related to state dental board examinations and licensure, and enforcement of the state dental practice act. Conducts research; compiles statistics. **Founded:** 1883. **Membership:** 850. **Staff:** 3. **Languages:** English. **Budget:** $200,000. **Publication:** *American Association of Dental Examiners Bulletin*, quarterly, 3-4/year. Newsletter. Price: available to members and related organizations ▪ Proceedings, annual. **Formerly:** National Association of Dental Examiners.

AMERICAN ASSOCIATION FOR DENTAL RESEARCH (AADR)

e-mail: research@iadv.com
1619 Duke St.
Alexandria, VA 20005
John J. Clarkson, Ph.D., Exec.Dir.
PH: (703)548-0066
FX: (703)548-1883
Description: Dentists, researchers, dental schools, and dental products manufacturing companies. Seeks to promote better dental health and research activities. Presents current research information at annual meeting. Sponsors competitions; sponsors seminars. **Founded:** 1972. **Membership:** 5000. **Staff:** 14. **Regional Groups:** 40. **Languages:** English. **Budget:** $3,000,000. **Publication:** *Advances in Dental Research*, periodic ▪ *Dental Materials* ▪ *Dental Research Newsletter*, bimonthly. Association and professional newsletter for dental researchers. Includes calendar of events. Price: included in membership dues. Circulation: 4,500. Advertising: accepted. Also Cited As: *Around IADR & AADR* ▪ *Journal of Dental Research*, 16/year. Provides information on all sciences relevant to dentistry and to the oral cavity and associated structures in health and disease. Price: $38.00/year for members; $16.00/year for student members; $270.00/year (within U.S.) and $280/year (foreign). ISSN: 0022-0345. Circulation: 6,500. Advertising: accepted. Alternate Formats: microform ▪ *Journal of Oral Implantology*, quarterly ▪ Membership Directory, periodic.

AMERICAN ASSOCIATION OF DENTAL SCHOOLS (AADS)

e-mail: aads@aads.jhu.edu
url: http://www.aads.jhu.edu
1625 Massachusetts Ave. NW, Ste. 600
Washington, DC 20036
Richard Valachovic, Exec.Dir.
PH: (202)667-9433
FX: (202)667-0642
Description: Individuals interested in dental education; schools of dentistry, graduate dentistry, and dental auxiliary education in the U.S., Canada, and Puerto Rico; affiliated institutions of the federal government. To promote better teaching and education in dentistry and dental research and to facilitate exchange of ideas among dental educators. Sponsors meetings, conferences, and workshops; conducts surveys, studies, and special projects and publishes their results. Maintains 37 sections representing teaching and administrative areas of dentistry. **Founded:** 1923. **Membership:** 3600. **Staff:** 40. Multinational. **Languages:** English. **Budget:** $4,901,938. **Publication:** *Admission Requirements of United States and Canadian Dental Schools*, annual. Catalog. Helps students decide on a career in dentistry, and explains how to go about it. Price: $25.00. Advertising: not accepted ▪ *Bulletin of Dental Education*, monthly ▪ *Directory of Dental Educators*, periodic ▪ *Directory of Institutional Members*, annual ▪ *Journal of Dental Education*, monthly ▪ Proceedings, annual.

AMERICAN ASSOCIATION OF DIABETES EDUCATORS (AADE)

url: http://www.aadenet.org
100 W. Monroe, 4th Fl.
Chicago, IL 60603-1901
James J. Balija, Exec.Dir.
PH: (312)644-2233
TF: 800338-DMED
FX: (312)644-4411
Description: Nurses, dietitians, social workers, physicians, pharmacists, podiatrists, and others involved in teaching diabetes management to diabetics. Purposes are: to provide educational opportunities for the professional growth and development of members; to promote the development of quality diabetes education for the diabetic consumer; to foster communication and cooperation among individuals and organizations involved in diabetes patient education. Offers continuing education programs for diabetes educators. **Founded:** 1973. **Membership:** 11000. **Staff:** 11. **Local Groups:** 104. **Languages:** English. **Budget:** $2,580,000.

AMERICAN ASSOCIATION OF DIRECTORS OF PSYCHIATRIC RESIDENCY TRAINING (AADPRT)

Executive Office
University of Connecticut Health Center
Dept. of Psychiatry
Farmington, CT 06030
David Goldberg, M.D., Exec.Sec.
PH: (860)679-6729
FX: (860)679-6675

AMERICAN ASSOCIATION OF ELECTRODIAGNOSTIC MEDICINE (AAEM)

e-mail: AAEM@aol.com
url: http://www.pitt.edu/~nab4/aaem.html
421 1st Ave., SW, Ste. 300 East
Rochester, MN 55902
Shirlyn A. Adkins, J.D., Exec.Dir.
PH: (507)288-0100
FX: (507)288-1225
Description: M.D.'s and D.O.'s or foreign equivalent degrees who practice or are interested in electrodiagnostic medicine. Ob-

jective is to increase and extend knowledge of electomyography and electrodiagnostic medicine, and to improve patient care. **Founded:** 1953. **Membership:** 4226. **Staff:** 12. Multinational. **Languages:** English. **Budget:** $1,500,000. **Publication:** *AAEM Case Reports*, periodic. Monograph. Price: $8.00. Advertising: not accepted ▪ *AAEM Minimonographs*, 2-3/year. Price: $10.00. Advertising: not accepted ▪ *American Association of Electrodiagnostic Medicine – Membership Directory*, annual. Price: included in membership dues; $15.00 for nonmembers. Advertising: not accepted ▪ *Guidelines*, periodic ▪ *Muscle & Nerve*, monthly. Price: included in fellow/associate membership. ISSN: 6148-639X. **Formerly:** (1990) American Association of Electromyography and Electrodiagnosis.

AMERICAN ASSOCIATION OF ENDODONTISTS (AAE)
e-mail: webmaster@aae.org
211 E. Chicago Ave., Ste. 1100
Chicago, IL 60611
Irma S. Kudo, Exec.Dir.
PH: (312)266-7255
FX: (312)266-9867
Description: Endodontic specialists and other interested professionals. (Endodontics is a branch of dentistry that deals with the soft tissues inside the tooth.) Seeks to promote the exchange of ideas, to stimulate research, and to encourage the highest standard of quality care in the practice of endodontics. **Founded:** 1943. **Membership:** 4800. **Staff:** 19. Multinational. **Languages:** English. **Budget:** $2,600,000. **Publication:** *Communique*, quarterly. Newsletter ▪ *Endodontics*, semiannual. Newsletter ▪ *Glossary: Contemporary Terminology for Endodontics* ▪ *Journal of Endodontics*, monthly. Advertising: accepted ▪ *Membership Roster*, annual ▪ *Tooth Pain Guide*. Brochure ▪ *Your Guide to Endodontic Retreatment*. Brochure ▪ *Your Guide to Endodontic Surgery*. Brochure ▪ *Your Guide to Endodontic Treatment* (in English and Spanish). Brochure ▪ Brochure ▪ Brochure ▪ Brochure ▪ Brochure.

AMERICAN ASSOCIATION FOR FUNCTIONAL ORTHODONTICS (AAFO)
106 S. Kent St.
Winchester, VA 22601
Dr. Craig C. Stoner, Pres.
PH: (540)662-2200
TF: 800441-3850
FX: (540)662-2200
Description: Dentists involved in orthodontic malocclusions and temporomandibular joint dysfunctions by utilization of functional appliances. Purpose is to facilitate exchange of information and case reports on current developments in this type of treatment. Sponsors seminars; offers members discounts on accredited seminars sponsored by other organizations. **Founded:** 1981. **Membership:** 1800. **Languages:** English. **For-Profit. Budget:** $450,000. **Publication:** *Functional Orthodontist: A Journal of Functional Jaw Orthopedics*, bimonthly. Includes AAFO accredited course listings and new product information. Price: included in membership dues; $79.00/year for nonmembers. ISSN: 8756-3150. Circulation: 7,000. Advertising: accepted ▪ Membership Directory, annual. **Formerly:** (1984) Northern Virginia Functional Jaw Study Club; (1985) American Association of Functional Orthodontists.

AMERICAN ASSOCIATION FOR GERIATRIC PSYCHIATRY (AAGP)
e-mail: main@aagpgpa.org
url: http://www.aagpgpa.org
7910 Woodmont Ave., 7th Fl.
Bethesda, MD 20814
Janet L. Pailet, J.D., Exec.Dir.
PH: (301)654-7850
FX: (301)654-4137
Description: Psychiatrists interested in promoting better mental health care for the elderly. Maintains placement service and speakers' bureau. **Founded:** 1978. **Membership:** 1468. **Staff:** 10. **Languages:** English. **For-Profit. Budget:** $2,000,000.

AMERICAN ASSOCIATION OF GYNECOLOGICAL LAPAROSCOPISTS (AAGL)
e-mail: generalmail@aagl.com
url: http://www.pages.prodigy.com/CA/jmp/jmp.html
13021 E. Florence Ave.
Santa Fe Springs, CA 90670
Jordan M. Phillips, M.D., Bd.Chm.
TF: 800554-2245
FX: (562)946-0073
Description: Physicians who specialize in obstetrics and gynecology and who are interested in gynecological endoscopic procedures. Purposes are to: teach; demonstrate; exchange ideas; distribute literature; stimulate interest in gynecological laparoscopy; maintain and improve medical standards in medical schools and hospitals regarding gynecological laparoscopy; maintain and improve the ethics, practice, and efficiency of the medical practice pertaining to obstetrics and laparoscopy. Conducts seminars and workshops. **Founded:** 1972. **Membership:** 7200. **Staff:** 14. **Languages:** English.

AMERICAN ASSOCIATION FOR HEALTH EDUCATION
e-mail: aahe@aahperd.org
url: http://www.aahperd.org/aahe.aahe.html
1900 Association Dr.
Reston, VA 20191
Becky J. Smith, Ph.D., Exec.Dir.
PH: (703)476-3437
TF: 800213-7193
FX: (703)476-6638
Description: Professionals who have responsibility for health education in schools, colleges, communities, hospitals and clinics, and industries. Purposes are advancement of health education through program activities and federal legislation; encouragement of close working relationships between all health education and health service organizations; achievement of good health and well-being for all Americans automatically, without conscious thought and endeavor. Member of the American Alliance for Health, Physical Education, Recreation and Dance. **Founded:** 1937. **Membership:** 11000. **Staff:** 7. **Languages:** English. Formerly (1974) School Health Division of American Association for Health, Physical Education and Recreation; (1997) Association for the Advancement of Health Education.

AMERICAN ASSOCIATION OF HEALTH PLANS (AAHP)
url: http://www.aahp.org
1129 20th St. NW, Ste. 600
Washington, DC 20036
Karen Ignagni, Pres.
PH: (202)778-3200
FX: (202)331-7487
Description: Supports the managed health care industry. Lobbies; conducts research programs and workshops; compiles statistics. Maintains placement service. **Founded:** 1959. **Membership:** 1000. **Staff:** 100. **Languages:** English. **Budget:** $18,000,000. **Publication:** *healthplan*, bimonthly. Magazine. Price: $75.00/year. Advertising: accepted ▪ *Profile of Health Plans and URDS*, annual. Survey. Contains enrollment, demographics for HMOs, PPOs, and UROs. Price: $149.00. **Formed by Merger of:** (1995) Group Health Association of America; (1995) American Managed Care and Review Association.

AMERICAN ASSOCIATION OF HOSPITAL DENTISTS (AAHD)
url: http://www.bgsm.edu/dentistry/foscod
211 E. Chicago Ave., No. 948
Chicago, IL 60611
John S. Rutkauskas, D.D.S., Exec.Dir.
PH: (312)440-2661
FX: (312)440-2824
Description: Directors and staff members of dental departments in hospitals. Promotes dental education programs in hospitals. Offers examinations. **Founded:** 1927. **Membership:** 500. **Staff:** 3. **Languages:** English. **Budget:** $150,000. **Publication:** *InterFace*, quarterly. Newsletter. Reports on trends, legislation, policy chan-

ges, and issues that affect the practices of hospital dentists. Includes calendar of events. Price: included in membership dues; $25.00/year for nonmembers. ISSN: 0887-6304. Advertising: accepted ■ *Oral Facial Emergencies* ■ *Oral Medicine in Hospital Practice* ■ *Special Care in Dentistry*, bimonthly. **Formerly:** American Association of Hospital Dental Chiefs.

AMERICAN ASSOCIATION OF IMMUNOLOGISTS (AAI)
e-mail: infoaai@aai.faseb.org
url: http://www.sciencexchange.com/aai
9650 Rockville Pike
Bethesda, MD 20814-3994
M. Michele Hogan, Ph.D., Contact
PH: (301)530-7178
FX: (301)571-1816
Description: Scientists engaged in immunological research including aspects of virology, bacteriology, biochemistry, genetics, and related disciplines. Goals are to advance knowledge of immunology and related disciplines and to facilitate the interchange of information among investigators in various fields. Promotes interaction between laboratory investigators and clinicians. Conducts training courses, symposia, workshop, and lectures. Compiles statistics. **Founded:** 1913. **Membership:** 5500. **Staff:** 17. Multinational. **Languages:** English. **Budget:** $600,000.

AMERICAN ASSOCIATION OF INTEGRATED HEALTHCARE DELIVERY SYSTEMS
e-mail: sreed@aaihds.org
url: http://www.aaihds.org
4435 Waterfront Dr., Ste. 101
PO Box 4913
Glen Allen, VA 23058-4913
Douglas L. Chaet, Chm.
PH: (804)747-5823
FX: (804)747-5316
Description: Physicians, hospital executives and board members, health plan executives, and other key entities and professionals employed by all forms of IDDSs including PHOS, IPA POSOS, and MSOS. Seeks to provide advocacy for issues related to integrated healthcare through research, education, and communication. Conducts educational and research programs; maintains speakers' bureau and information clearinghouse. **Founded:** 1993. **Membership:** 900. **Staff:** 12. **Languages:** English. **Budget:** $500,000. Formerly (1998) American Association of Physician-Hospital Organizations.

AMERICAN ASSOCIATION OF MANAGED CARE NURSES (AAMCN)
e-mail: sreed@aamcn.org
url: http://www.aamcn.org
4435 Waterfront Dr., Ste. 101
PO Box 4975
Glen Allen, VA 23058-4975
Marilyn Doughman, Pres.
PH: (804)747-9698
FX: (804)747-5316
Description: Managed health care professionals, including registered nurses, licensed practical nurses, and nurse practitioners. Seeks to enhance the abilities of members to meet the future needs of the managed health care profession through education. Provides courses towards certification in managed care nursing. **Founded:** 1994. **Membership:** 400. **Staff:** 12. **State Groups:** 3. **Languages:** English. **Budget:** $150,000.

AMERICAN ASSOCIATION OF MEDICAL ASSISTANTS (AAMA)
url: http://www.aama_ntl.org
20 N. Wacker Dr., Ste. 1575
Chicago, IL 60606-2903
Donald A. Balasa, Exec.Dir.
PH: (312)899-1500
TF: 800228-2262
FX: (312)899-1259
Description: Medical assistants are allied health professionals who work primarily in anbilatory (out patient) settings and perform clinical and administrative procedures. Activities include a certification program consisting of study and an examination, passage of which entitles the individual to become credentialed as a Certified Medical Assistant. Conducts accreditation of one- and two-year programs in medical assisting in conjunction with the commission on Accreditation of Allied Health Education Programs. Provides assistance and information to institutions of higher learning desirous of initiating courses for medical assistants. Awards continuing education units for selected educational programs. **Founded:** 1956. **Membership:** 20000. **Staff:** 21. **State Groups:** 46. **Languages:** English. **Budget:** $1,500,000. **Publication:** *Accounts Receivable and Collection for the Medical Practice.* Price: $20.00 for members; $30.00 for nonmembers ■ *AIDS Concepts for Medical Assistnts – Part I.* Price: $15.00 for member; $25.00 for nonmember ■ *Human Relations for the Medical Office.* Price: $30.00 for member; $50.00 for nonmember ■ *Law for the Medical Office.* Price: $30.00 for member; $50.00 for nonmember ■ *Managing Managed Care.* Price: $15.00 for member; $25.00 for nonmember ■ *Medical Office Management – Part I.* Price: $22.00 for member; $32.00 for nonmember ■ *PMA*, bimonthly. Journal. Includes association news, index of advertisers, continuing education articles, and calendar of events. Price: included in membership dues; $30.00/year for nonmembers and students. ISSN: 0033-0140. Circulation: 14,000. Advertising: accepted ■ *Urinalysis Today.* Price: $30.00 for member; $50.00 for nonmember ■ Brochures ■ Pamphlets.

AMERICAN ASSOCIATION OF MEDICAL SOCIETY EXECUTIVES (AAMSE)
e-mail: aamse@aamse.org
url: http://www.aamse.org
515 N. State St.
Chicago, IL 60610
Robin Kriegel, CAE, Exec.Dir.
PH: (312)464-2555
FX: (312)464-2467
Description: Professional society of executives of national, state, regional, or county medical and specialty societies. Conducts continuing education seminars. Makes available management resources and operational evaluations. **Founded:** 1947. **Membership:** 1200. **Staff:** 4. **Languages:** English. **Budget:** $520,000. **Publication:** *Hotline*, monthly ■ *Who's Who in Medical Society Management*, annual. **Formerly:** Medical Society Executives Association.

AMERICAN ASSOCIATION FOR MEDICAL TRANSCRIPTION (AAMT)
e-mail: aamt@sna.com
url: http://www.aamt.org
PO Box 576187
Modesto, CA 95357-6187
Claudia Tessier, Exec.Dir.
PH: (209)551-0883
TF: 800982-2182
FX: (209)551-9317
Description: Medical transcriptionists, their supervisors, teachers and students of medical transcription, owners and managers of medical transcription services, and other interested health personnel. Purpose is to provide information about the profession of medical transcription and to provide continuing education for medical transcriptionists. (Medical transcriptionists translate patients' records of medical care and treatment from oral dictation to printed form.) Advocates professional recognition of medical transcriptionists in county, state, and national medical societies and in health care facilities nationwide. Sponsors voluntary certification/credentialing program. Offers updates on developments in medicine and curricula, and on new transcription methods and equipment; sponsors and encourages research in the field. Establishes guidelines for education of medical transcriptionists. Fosters positive relations among medical transcriptionists, the public, members of allied health services, and the legislature. **Founded:** 1978. **Membership:** 9500. **Staff:** 15. **Local Groups:** 145. **Languages:** English. **Budget:** $1,400,000. **Publication:** *The AAMT Book of Style for Medical Transcription* ■ *BIS Source*, quarterly.

Newsletter ∎ *Cert Alert*, quarterly. Newsletter ∎ *Journal of the American Association for Medical Transcription*, bimonthly. Offers guidance in quality assurance for medical transcription, medican and nonmedical educational articles, word lists, and technology updates. Price: included in membership dues; $150.00/year for nonmembers; $30.00/issue. ISSN: 0745-2624. Circulation: 10,000. Advertising: accepted ∎ *The Leading Edge*, bimonthly. Newsletter ∎ *Model Curriculum for Medical Transcription* ∎ *Model Job Description: Medical Transcriptionist*.

AMERICAN ASSOCIATION OF MENTAL HEALTH PROFESSIONALS IN CORRECTIONS (AAMHPC)
PO Box 160208
Sacramento, CA 95816-0208
John S. Zil, MD, JD, Pres.
Description: Psychiatrists, psychologists, social workers, nurses, and other mental health professionals; individuals working in correctional settings. Fosters the progress of behavioral sciences related to corrections. Goals are: to improve the treatment, rehabilitation, and care of the mentally ill, mentally retarded, and emotionally disturbed; to promote research and professional education in psychiatry and allied fields in corrections; to advance standards of correctional services and facilities; to foster cooperation between individuals concerned with the medical, psychological, social, and legal aspects of corrections; to share knowledge with other medical practitioners, scientists, and the public. Conducts scientific meetings to contribute to the advancement of the therapeutic community in all its institutional settings, including correctional institutions, hospitals, churches, schools, industry, and the family. **Founded:** 1940. **Membership:** 2000. **Staff:** 4. **Languages:** English. **Budget:** $100,000. Formerly (1978) Medical Correctional Society of the American Correctional Association.

AMERICAN ASSOCIATION OF NEUROLOGICAL SURGEONS (AANS)
e-mail: info@aans.org
url: http://www.aans.org
22 S. Washington St.
Park Ridge, IL 60068-4287
Robert E. Draba, Ph.D., Exec.Dir.
PH: (847)692-9500
FX: (847)692-2589
Description: Neurological surgeons united to promote excellence in neurological surgery and its related sciences. Provides funding to foster research in the neurosciences. Conducts specialized education. The largest publisher of neurosurgical books in the world. **Founded:** 1931. **Membership:** 5011. **Staff:** 55. **Languages:** English. **Budget:** $11,000,000. **Publication:** *American Association of Neurological Surgeons Bulletin*, quarterly. Price: included in membership dues. Circulation: 4,976. Advertising: accepted ∎ *Directory of Neurological Surgery*, annual. Price: $50.00 for members. Circulation: 5,000. Advertising: accepted ∎ *Journal of Neurosurgery*, monthly. Price: $100.00/year for members; $110.00/year for nonmembers; $60.00/year for residents. Circulation: 12,000. Advertising: accepted ∎ *Neurosurgical Operative Atlas*. Booklets ∎ *Neurosurgical Topics*, quarterly. Books. Price: $85.00 for members; $95.00 for nonmembers; $75.00 for residents. Advertising: not accepted. Alternate Formats: CD-ROM ∎ *Neurosurgical Topics Series*. Books ∎ *Self-Assessment in Neurological Surgery*, triennial. Booklet. Contains multiple choice and patient management tests. Price: $175.00/copy for members; $225.00/copy for nonmembers; $145.00 for residents. Advertising: not accepted. **Formerly:** (1966) Harvey Cushing Society.

AMERICAN ASSOCIATION OF NEUROPATHOLOGISTS (AANP)
e-mail: aanp@mail.med.umn.edu
Box 174, Univ. of Minnesota Medical School
420 Delaware St. SE
Minneapolis, MN 55455
H. Brent Clark, Ph.D., Sec.-Treas.
PH: (612)625-0956
FX: (612)625-0440

Description: Professional society of physicians specializing in neuropathology. Seeks to advance research and training in neuropathology. Offers placement service. **Founded:** 1924. **Membership:** 810. **Languages:** English. **Budget:** $50,000. **Publication:** *Journal of Neuropathology and Experimental Neurology*, monthly ∎ *Roster of Members*, annual. **Formerly:** (1932) Club of Neuropathologists.

AMERICAN ASSOCIATION OF NEUROSCIENCE NURSES (AANN)
e-mail: AssnNeuro@aol.com
url: http://www.AANN.org
224 N. Des Plaines, No. 601
Chicago, IL 60661
Shelly Johnson, Exec.Dir.
PH: (312)993-0043
FX: (312)993-0362
Description: Registered nurses engaged in or primarily interested in neurosurgical or neurological nursing. Objectives are to: foster interest, education, and high standards of practice in the field of neuroscience nursing; encourage continuing growth in the field; provide a medium for communication among neuroscience nurses in the U.S. and Canada. Has developed clinical and surgical core curriculum for neuroscience nursing practice. **Founded:** 1968. **Membership:** 4000. **Staff:** 5. **Multinational.** **Regional Groups:** 77. **Languages:** English. **Budget:** $750,000.

AMERICAN ASSOCIATION OF NURSE ANESTHETISTS (AANA)
url: http://www.aana.com
222 S. Prospect
Park Ridge, IL 60068-4001
John F. Garde, Exec.Dir.
PH: (847)692-7050
FX: (847)692-6968
Description: Active registered professional nurses who have successfully completed an accredited program in nurse anesthesia and passed a national examination for certification. Advances the art and science of anesthesiology; promotes research in anesthesia; develops educational standards and techniques for the administration of anesthesia. Sponsors continuing education; promotes biennial recertification. **Founded:** 1931. **Membership:** 27222. **Staff:** 56. **State Groups:** 52. **Languages:** English. **Budget:** $12,000,000.

AMERICAN ASSOCIATION OF OCCUPATIONAL HEALTH NURSES (AAOHN)
e-mail: aaohn@aaohn.org
url: http://www.aaohn.org
2920 Brandywine Rd., Ste. 100
Atlanta, GA 30341-4146
Ann Cox, CAE, Exec.Dir.
PH: (770)455-7757
FX: (770)455-7271
Description: Registered professional nurses employed by business and industrial firms; nurse educators, nurse editors, nurse writers, and others interested in occupational health nursing. Promotes and sets standards for the profession. Provides and approves continuing education; maintains governmental affairs program; offers placement service. **Founded:** 1942. **Membership:** 13000. **Staff:** 23. **Local Groups:** 144. **Languages:** English. **Budget:** $3,000,000. Formerly (1977) American Association of Industrial Nurses.

AMERICAN ASSOCIATION OF OFFICE NURSES (AAON)
e-mail: aaonmail@aaon.org
url: http://www.aaon.org
109 Kinderkamack Rd.
Montvale, NJ 07645
Joyce Logan, Exec.Dir.
PH: (201)391-2600
TF: 800457-7504
FX: (201)573-8543
Description: Nurses working primarily in physicians' offices. Pro-

motes improvement of the image of the office nurse. Encourages professional growth and development; facilitates exchange of information among members. Provides continuing education opportunities. Issues publications. **Founded:** 1988. **Membership:** 4000. **Staff:** 3. **Regional Groups:** 21. **Languages:** English. **Budget:** $350,000.

AMERICAN ASSOCIATION OF ORAL AND MAXILLOFACIAL SURGEONS (AAOMS)
9700 W. Bryn Mawr
Rosemont, IL 60018-5701
Barbara N. Moles, Exec.Dir.
PH: (847)678-6200
TF: 800822-6637
FX: (847)678-6286
Description: Dentists specializing in disease diagnosis and surgical, adjunctive, and esthetic treatment of diseases, injuries, and defects of the oral and maxillofacial region (jaw deformities, dental implants, infections, and oral cancer). **Founded:** 1918. **Membership:** 6100. **Staff:** 46. **State Groups:** 53. **Languages:** English. **Budget:** $9,000,000. **Publication:** *AAOMS Digest*, 6/year. Newsletter. Contains association news and events ■ *AAOMS Directory*, annual ■ *AAOMS Forum*, 4/year ■ *Journal of Oral Maxillofacial Surgery*, monthly ■ *Office Anesthesia Evaluation Manual* ■ *Report of Annual Meeting* ■ *Surgical Update*, 3/year ■ Annual Report. **Formerly:** (1944) American Society of Exodontists; (1977) American Society of Oral Surgeons.

AMERICAN ASSOCIATION OF ORTHODONTISTS (AAO)
e-mail: aao@worldnet.att.net
url: http://www.aaortho.org
401 N. Lindbergh Blvd.
St. Louis, MO 63141-7816
Ronald S. Moen, Exec.Dir.
PH: (314)993-1700
FX: (314)997-1745
Description: Professional society of orthodontists. To advance the art and science of orthodontics through continuing education, encouragement of research and cooperation with other health groups. Maintains museum. **Founded:** 1901. **Membership:** 12000. **Staff:** 31. Multinational. **State Groups:** 51. **Languages:** English. **Budget:** $10,000,000. **Publication:** *AAO Bulletin*, bimonthly. Newsletter. Includes meetings schedules. Price: included in membership dues. Advertising: accepted. Also Cited As: *Orthodontic Bulletin* ■ *American Association of Orthodontists Membership Directory*, biennial. Price: $35.00 for members; $65.00 for nonmembers. Advertising: accepted ■ *American Journal of Orthodontics and Dentofacial Orthopedics*, monthly. Price: included in membership dues. Advertising: accepted ■ Pamphlets. **Formerly:** American Society of Orthodontists.

AMERICAN ASSOCIATION OF PATHOLOGISTS' ASSISTANTS (AAPA)
url: http://meds.quennsu.ca/medicine/aapahome.htm
8030 Old Cedar Ave. S., Ste. 225
Bloomington, MN 55425-1215
Don Stacey, Pres.
PH: (612)853-2243
TF: 800532-2272
FX: (612)854-1402
Description: Pathologists' assistants and individuals qualified by academic and practical training to provide service in anatomic pathology under the direction of a qualified pathologist who is responsible for the performance of the assistant. Promotes the mutual association of trained pathologists' assistants and informs the public and the medical profession concerning the goals of this profession. Compiles statistics on salaries, geographic distribution, and duties of pathologists' assistants. Sponsors a continuing medical education program; offers placement services for members only. **Founded:** 1972. **Membership:** 337. **Languages:** English. **Publication:** *AAPA Newsletter*, quarterly. Includes employment and educational opportunity listings. Price: included in membership dues. Circulation: 350. Advertising: not accepted ■ Membership Directory, biennial.

AMERICAN ASSOCIATION FOR PEDIATRIC OPHTHALMOLOGY AND STRABISMUS
url: http://med-aapos.bu.edu
PO Box 193832
San Francisco, CA 94119
Sue A. Brown, Admin.
PH: (415)561-8505
FX: (415)561-8575
Description: Ophthalmologists who limit their practice largely to children. Encourages quality eye care for children by establishing high ethical standards of practice, supporting educational training programs for pediatric ophthalmologists, and promoting basic research in children's eye diseases. Conducts research programs. **Founded:** 1974. **Membership:** 844. Multinational. **Languages:** English. **Budget:** $140,000. Formerly (1978) American Association of Pediatric Ophthalmology.

AMERICAN ASSOCIATION OF PHARMACEUTICAL SCIENTISTS (AAPS)
e-mail: aaps@aaps.org
url: http://www.aaps.org
1650 King St.
Alexandria, VA 22314-2747
John B. Cox, CAE, Exec.Dir.
PH: (703)548-3000
FX: (703)684-7349
Description: Pharmaceutical scientists. Provides a forum for exchange of scientific information; serves as a resource in forming public policies to regulate pharmaceutical sciences and related issues of public concern. Promotes pharmaceutical sciences and provides for recognition of individual achievement; works to foster career growth and the development of members. Offers placement service. **Founded:** 1986. **Membership:** 7000. **Staff:** 20. Multinational. **Regional Groups:** 4. **Languages:** English. **Budget:** $3,600,000. **Publication:** *AAPS Newsletter*, monthly. Price: included in membership dues. Circulation: 7,000. Advertising: accepted ■ *Journal of Pharmaceutical and Biomedical Analysis*, monthly. Features original research reports and authoritative reviews on pharmaceutical and biomedical analysis. Price: $70.00/year for members; $136.00/year for nonmembers. ISSN: 0731-7085. Advertising: accepted ■ *Journal of Pharmaceutical Marketing and Management*, quarterly. Focuses on the use of pharmaceuticals in health care, with particular emphasis on drug marketing and management. Price: $26.25 in U.S.; $36.75 outside U.S. ISSN: 0883-7597. Circulation: 500. Advertising: not accepted ■ *Pharmaceutical Research*, monthly. Journal. Reports on applied and basic research in the pharmaceutical-biomedical sciences; includes research reports. Price: $50.00/year for members; $110.00/year for nonmembers. ISSN: 0724-8741. Circulation: 7,000. Advertising: accepted.

AMERICAN ASSOCIATION OF PHYSICISTS IN MEDICINE (AAPM)
e-mail: strofi@aapm.acp.org
url: http://www.aapm.org
One Physics Ellipse
College Park, MD 20740-3846
Sal Trofi, Jr., Exec.Dir.
PH: (301)209-3350
FX: (301)209-0862
Description: Persons professionally engaged in application of physics to medicine and biology in medical research and educational institutions;encourages interest and training in medical physics and related fields; promotes high professional standards; disseminates technical information. Maintains placement service. Conducts research programs. Member society of American Institute of Physics. **Founded:** 1958. **Membership:** 4500. **Staff:** 9. **Regional Groups:** 20. **Languages:** English. **Budget:** $3,000,000.

AMERICAN ASSOCIATION OF POISON CONTROL
  CENTERS (AAPCC)
e-mail: aapcc@aol.com
3201 New Mexico Ave. NW, Ste. 310
Washington, DC 20016
Rose Ann Soloway, RN, Admin.
PH: (202)362-7217
Description: Individuals and organizations engaged in operation
of poison control centers. Has established standards for poison
information, control centers and specialists in poison informa-
tion. Compiles statistics about poison exposures in the United
States. **Founded:** 1958. **Membership:** 1000. **Languages:** English.

AMERICAN ASSOCIATION OF PSYCHIATRIC SERVICES
  FOR CHILDREN (AAPSC)
220 Hibiscus Dr.
Rochester, NY 14618-4440
Dr. Sydney Koret, Exec.Dir.
TF: 800777-6910
Description: Fosters prevention and treatment of mental and e-
motional disorders of the child, adolescent, and family; furthers
the development and application of clinical knowledge; researches and supports projects dealing with child and adolescent mental health; offers a national focus for the clinical point of view;
acts as an information clearinghouse; provides accreditation services. Maintains speakers bureau and roster of available staff
positions. Sponsors educational programs; compiles statistics.
Founded: 1948. **Membership:** 165. **Staff:** 2. **Languages:** English.
Formerly (1970) American Association of Psychiatric Clinics for
Children.

AMERICAN ASSOCIATION OF PSYCHIATRIC
  TECHNICIANS (AAPT)
2059 S. 3rd St.
Niles, MI 49120
George Blake, Dir. & Pres.
PH: (616)684-3164
TF: 800391-7589
FX: (616)683-0032
Description: Psychiatric technicians, behavioral health technicians, mental health workers, counselors, social workers, psychiatric nurses, psychologists, and other individuals and companies interested in mental health. Promotes professionalism in mental
health industry. Encourages further education of mental health
workers and provides national certification of mental health
workers. Works with colleges, schools, and mental health facilities to develop education and training. Awards accreditation to
mental health worker training programs. Promotes the last
Wednesday in January as "Nationally Certified Psychiatric Technicians Day," and the first full week in September as "Mental
Health Workers Week." Conducts educational programs; offers
placement information; compiles statistics. Work with states to
help them set up their own "State Board of Psychiatric Technicians.". **Founded:** 1991. **Membership:** 8000. **Staff:** 3. **Regional
Groups:** 10. **Languages:** English. Also Known As Mental Health
Workers Association; National Certification Board.

AMERICAN ASSOCIATION OF PUBLIC HEALTH
  DENTISTRY (AAPHD)
e-mail: natoff@aol.com
url: http://www.pitt.edu/~aaphd
10619 Jousting Ln.
Richmond, VA 23235
Dr. B. Alex White, DDS, Pres.
PH: (804)272-8344
FX: (804)272-0802
Description: Professional society of dentists, dental hygienists,
health educators, and others actively engaged in dental public
health. Sponsors competitions. **Founded:** 1937. **Membership:** 800.
Staff: 1. Multinational. **Languages:** English. **Budget:** $69,000.
Publication: *American Association of Public Health Dentistry–Communique*, quarterly. Newsletter. Price: included in mem-
bership dues; $20.00/year for nonmembers. Circulation: 800. Ad-
vertising: accepted ∎ *Journal of Public Health Dentistry*, quarterly.

Covers fluoridation, sealants, demographics, and utilization of
dental services. Includes research reports and book reviews.
Price: included in membership dues; $100.00/year for nonmem-
bers in U.S.; $100.00/year for nonmembers outside U.S.;
$135.00/year airmail. ISSN: 0022-4006. Circulation: 1,500. Adver-
tising: accepted. Alternate Formats: microform. **Formerly:** (1983)
American Association of Public Health Dentists.

AMERICAN ASSOCIATION OF SPINAL CORD INJURY
  NURSES (AASCIN)
75-20 Astoria Blvd.
Jackson Heights, NY 11370
Dr. Vivian Beyda, Exec.Admin.
PH: (718)803-3782
FX: (718)803-0414
Description: Nurses who care for patients with spinal cord
impairment; nurses interested in the field of spinal cord impairment; persons who have provided extraordinary service to improve the quality of life for spinal cord impairment patients. Purposes are to: promote and improve nursing care of spinal cord
impairment patients; develop and advance related education and
research; recognize nurses whose careers are devoted to the
problems of spinal cord impairment; keep medical personnel informed of state-of-the-art techniques. Focuses on topics such as
sexuality and spinal cord impairment, care of respiratory dependent spinal cord impairment patients, alcohol and drug dependent
spinal cord impairment patients, and planning for care in the
community. Monitors and participates in legislative and regulatory activities affecting spinal cord impairment and professional
nursing practice. Conducts research and educational programs.
Founded: 1983. **Membership:** 1200. **Staff:** 5. **Languages:** English.

AMERICAN ASSOCIATION OF STOMATOLOGISTS (AAS)
32 Cobblestone Way
Freehold, NJ 07728
Dr. David A. Lederman, Pres.
PH: (732)901-7575
FX: (732)866-8830
Description: Serves as a coordinating organization representing
the American Academy of Oral Medicine and the Organization
of Teachers of Oral Diagnosis, and their members. Acts as a
voice for diagnostic and therapeutic disciplines in dentistry; seeks
to establish oral diagnosis, radiology, and medicine as recognized
specialty in dentistry; encourages excellence in the field to ensure
excellence in patient care. **Founded:** 1985. **Membership:** 1000.
Languages: English. **Publication:** *AAS News*, 3/year. Newsletter.
Formerly: (1993) Academy of Oral Diagnosis, Radiology, and
Medicine.

AMERICAN ASSOCIATION OF UTILIZATION
  MANAGEMENT NURSES (AAUMN)
1926 Waukegan Rd., Ste. 1
Glenview, IL 60025-1770
David L. Stumph, CAE, Exec.Dir.
Description: Works to promote effective, quality healthcare.
Conducts education programs; provides networking opportuni-
ties. **Founded:** 1994. **Membership:** 1200. **Staff:** 3. **Budget:**
$175,000.

AMERICAN ASSOCIATION OF WOMEN DENTISTS (AAWD)
e-mail: aawd@sba.com
401 N. Michigan Ave.
Chicago, IL 60611-4267
Deene Alongi, Exec.Dir.
PH: (312)527-6757
TF: 800920-2293
FX: (312)527-6640
Description: Female dentists and dental students. Encourages
young women to pursue an academic degree in dentistry and to
advance the status of women already in the dental profession.
Founded: 1921. **Membership:** 900. **Staff:** 2. **Regional Groups:** 17.
Languages: English. **Budget:** $135,000. **Publication:** *AAWD Mem-
bership Directory*, annual ∎ *The Chronicle*, bimonthly. Newsletter.
Includes book reviews, listings of employment opportunities,

obituaries, research updates, and statistics. Price: included in membership dues; $30.00/year for nonmembers. Circulation: 2,000. Advertising: accepted. **Formerly:** (1978) Association of American Women Dentists.

AMERICAN ASSOCIATION FOR WOMEN RADIOLOGISTS (AAWR)

e-mail: aawr@acr.org
url: http://www.aawr.org
1891 Preston White Dr.
Reston, VA 20191
Ann Rosser, Exec.Dir.
PH: (703)648-8939
FX: (703)391-1757
Description: Physicians involved in diagnostic or therapeutic radiology, nuclear medicine, or radiologic physics. Facilitates exchange of knowledge and information as it relates to women in radiology; encourages publication of materials on radiology and medicine by members; supports women who are training in the field and encourages women at all levels to participate in radiological societies. Maintains ad hoc committees on affirmative action, radiation therapists, and policy on pregnancy. **Founded:** 1981. **Membership:** 1700. **Staff:** 2. **Local Groups:** 3. **Languages:** English. Formerly (1991) American Association of Women Radiologists.

AMERICAN AUTO IMMUNE RELATED DISEASES ASSOCIATION

e-mail: aarda@aol.com
url: http://www.aarda.org
Michigan National Bank Bldg.
15475 Gratiot
Detroit, MI 48205
Virginia Ladd, Exec.Dir.
PH: (313)371-8600
TF: 800598-4668
FX: (313)371-6002
Description: Promotes national focus and collaborative efforts among state and national volunteer health groups on autoimmunity, the major cause of serious chronic diseases. Offers research and educational programs; maintains speakers' bureau. **Founded:** 1991. **Staff:** 5. **Languages:** English. **Budget:** $400,000.

AMERICAN BLOOD RESOURCES ASSOCIATION (ABRA)

PO Box 669
Annapolis, MD 21404-0669
James P. Reilly, Pres.
PH: (410)263-8296
FX: (410)263-2298
Description: Operators of blood plasma centers and U.S. plasma fractionators. Represents the interests of plasma collection centers and promotes plasma as an important part of the blood industry. Has developed code of ethics. Conducts specialized education program; compiles statistics; maintains speakers' bureau. **Founded:** 1972. **Membership:** 100. **Staff:** 10. **Languages:** English. **Publication:** *The Fax Letter*, monthly ■ *Journal of the ABRA*, quarterly. Focuses on the business, operation, regulation, and scientific needs of the commercial blood and plasma collection industry. Includes industry news. Price: included in membership dues; $75.00/year for nonmembers; $100.00/year for foreign. Circulation: 3,400. Advertising: accepted.

AMERICAN BOARD OF ABDOMINAL SURGERY (ABAS)

url: http://www.abdominalsurg.org
675 Main St.
Melrose, MA 02176
Louis F. Alfano, M.D., Exec.Sec.
PH: (617)665-6102
FX: (617)665-4127
Description: Specialists in abdominal surgery. Improves the quality of graduate education for abdominal surgery. Establishes minimum educational and training standards for the specialty. Determines whether candidates have received adequate preparation as defined by the board. Provides comprehensive examina-

tions to determine the ability and fitness of candidates. Certifies surgeons who have satisfied the requirements of the board as a protection to the public and the profession. Gives oral and written examinations in abdominal surgery. **Founded:** 1957. **Membership:** 1865. **Staff:** 2. Multinational. **Languages:** English. **Budget:** $25,000.

AMERICAN BOARD OF ALTERNATIVE MEDICINE (ABAM)

16126 E Warren
Detroit, MI 48224-0224
Dr. B. Alli, Contact
PH: (313)882-0641
Description: Practitioners of alternative medicine. Promotes increased use of alternative treatments including mind-body intervention, bioelectromagnetic therapy, and herbal medicines. Conducts research and educational programs; maintains hall of fame. **Founded:** 1994. **Membership:** 800. **Staff:** 5. **Languages:** English. **Publication:** Newsletter, periodic.

AMERICAN BOARD OF ANESTHESIOLOGY (ABA)

4101 Lake Boone Trail, Ste. 510
Raleigh, NC 27607-7506
Francis P. Hughes, Ph.D., Exec.V.P.
PH: (919)881-2570
FX: (919)881-2575
Description: Certification board which seeks to elevate and maintain the standards of the practice of anesthesiology and to establish criteria of fitness for the designation of a specialist in this field. Advises the Accreditation Council for Graduate Medical Education of the American Medical Association concerning training of individuals seeking certification. Arranges and conducts examinations to determine the competence of physicians who apply; issues certificates to those who meet the required standards. **Founded:** 1938. **Membership:** 12. **Staff:** 13. **Languages:** English.

AMERICAN BOARD OF CARDIOVASCULAR PERFUSION (ABCP)

url: http://www.abcp.org
207 N. 25th Ave.
Hattiesburg, MS 39401
Drs. Mark and Beth Richmond, Exec.Dirs.
PH: (601)582-3309
Description: Certified clinical perfusionists. Seeks to protect the public through the establishment and maintenance of standards in the field. Has established qualifications for examination and procedures for recertification. Administers annual board examinations. **Founded:** 1975. **Membership:** 3000. Multinational. **Languages:** English.

AMERICAN BOARD OF CHELATION THERAPY (ABCT)

1407-B N. Wells St.
Chicago, IL 60610-1305
Jack Hank, Exec.Dir.
TF: 800356-2228
FX: (312)266-3688
Description: Purpose is to define and establish qualifications required of licensed physicians and surgeons for certification in the field of chelation therapy. (Chelation therapy is used in cases of blood poisoning and involves the use of metal binding and bioinorganic agents intravenously infused into the bloodstream to "pick up" and remove calcium, lead, or other toxic heavy metals and restore cellular homeostasis. Because of lack of controlled studies for conditions other than calcinosis, digitalis toxicity, and excessive body storage of heavy metals, chelation therapy is not considered standard medical procedure.) Stresses that proper use of chelation therapy requires knowledge of nutrition and exercise and expertise in assisting patients in implementing lifestyle changes. Refers candidate physicians to sponsor ingorganizations for teaching workshops, audio and video learning aids, and reading and study materials. Has created series of testing procedures designed to be comprehensive and unbiased. Administers oral and written examinations and conducts reviews of candidates' background experience and patient records. Maintains standards

through process of recertification and reexamination. Sponsored by the American Holistic Medical Association, American College for Advancement in Medicine, Great Lakes Association of Clinical Medicine, and the International Oxidative Medical Association. **Founded:** 1982. **Languages:** English.

AMERICAN BOARD OF DENTAL PUBLIC HEALTH (ABDPH)
e-mail: standen@nersp.nerdc.ufl.edu
1321 NW 47th Ter.
Gainesville, FL 32605
Stanley Lotzkar, D.D.S., Exec.Sec.
PH: (352)378-6301
Description: Board whose purpose is to investigate the qualifications of, administer examinations to, and certify as diplomates, dentists specializing in dental public health. Sponsored by American Association of Public Health Dentistry. **Founded:** 1950. **Membership:** 5. **Languages:** English. **Publication:** *ABDPH Membership Directory*, triennial ∎ Newsletter, annual.

AMERICAN BOARD OF DERMATOLOGY (ABD)
1 Ford Pl.
Detroit, MI 48202-3450
Harry J. Hurley, M.D., Exec.Dir.
PH: (313)874-1088
FX: (313)872-3221
Description: Examining and certifying body. Seeks to assure provision of competent care for patients with cutaneous diseases, via capable board representation. Establishes requirements of postdoctoral training. Creates and conducts annual comprehensive examination to determine the competence of physicians who meet the requirements for examination by the board. Issues appropriate certificate to those who satisfactorily complete examination. Member of American Board of Medical Specialties. **Founded:** 1932. **Membership:** 15. **Languages:** English.

AMERICAN BOARD OF ENDODONTICS (ABE)
e-mail: abe@aae.org
211 E. Chicago Ave., Ste. 1150
Chicago, IL 60611
Dr. Harold E. Goodis
PH: (312)266-7310
FX: (312)266-9982
Description: Dentists who have successfully completed study and training in an advanced endodontics education program that is accredited by the Commission on Dental Accreditation of the American Dental Association Primary objective is to protect the public by raising the standards of endodontic practice and requiring candidates for diplomate status to show strong evidence of specialized skills and knowledge in endodontics. Administers examinations and certifies dentists who successfully complete the examinations. **Staff:** 1. **Languages:** English. **Publication:** *Membership Roster*, annual. Published in conjunction with American Association of Endodontists.

AMERICAN BOARD OF FAMILY PRACTICE (ABFP)
e-mail: general@abfp.org
url: http://www.abfp.org
2228 Young Dr.
Lexington, KY 40505
Robert F. Avant, M.D., Exec.Dir.
PH: (606)269-5626
TF: 888995-5700
FX: (606)335-7501
Description: Certifying board for physicians specializing in family practice. Conducts certification/recertification examinations. **Founded:** 1969. **Languages:** English. **Publication:** *Journal of the American Board of Family Practice*, bimonthly. Price: $60.00 institution; $35.00 physician. ISSN: 0893-8652. Circulation: 55,000. Advertising: accepted.

AMERICAN BOARD OF HEALTH PHYSICS (ABHP)
1313 Dolley Madison Blvd., Ste. 402
Mc Lean, VA 22101-3926
Richard J. Burk, Jr., Exec.Sec.
PH: (703)790-1745
FX: (703)790-9063
Description: Certifying body. Promotes the health physics profession by establishing standards and procedures for certification and conducting certification examinations. Issues written proof of certification. **Founded:** 1960. **Membership:** 8. **Languages:** English.

AMERICAN BOARD OF MEDICAL SPECIALTIES (ABMS)
url: http://www.abms.org/abms
1007 Church St., Ste. 404
Evanston, IL 60201-5913
J. Lee Dockery, M.D., Exec.VP
PH: (847)491-9091
FX: (847)328-3596
Description: Primary medical specialty boards and conjoint boards; organizations with related interests are associate members. Acts as spokesman for approved medical specialty boards as a group; is actively concerned with the establishment, maintenance, and elevation of standards for the education and qualification of physicians recognized as specialists through the certification procedures of its members; cooperates with other groups concerned in establishing standards, policies, and procedures for ensuring the maintenance of continued competence of such physicians. Compiles statistics. **Founded:** 1933. **Membership:** 30. **Staff:** 17. **Languages:** English. **Budget:** $2,500,000. **Publication:** *ABMS Directory of Board Certified Medical Specialists*, annual. Four volumes listing over 500,000 specialists certified by 24 U.S. medical specialty boards. Arranged by specialty, name, and location. Price: $425.00/copy. ISSN: 0884-1543. Advertising: not accepted ∎ *ABMS Record*, quarterly. Newsletter. Reports on legislative-judicial events related to medical education. Includes meeting reports. Price: free. Advertising: not accepted ∎ *American Board of Medical Specialties–Annual Report and Reference Handbook*. Guide to medical specialty bo ards and specialty certification. Price: $5.00. Advertising: not accepted. **Supersedes:** Advisory Board for Medical Specialties.

AMERICAN BOARD OF NEUROLOGICAL SURGERY (ABNS)
6550 Fannin St., No. 2139
Houston, TX 77030-2722
Dr. Donald Quest, Sec.-Treas.
PH: (713)790-6015
FX: (713)794-0207
Description: Certification board to investigate qualifications of, administer examinations to, and certify as diplomates medical doctors specializing in neurological surgery. Works to stimulate development of adequate training facilities and aids in evaluating residencies under consideration by the Accreditation Council on Graduate Medical Education of the American Medical Association. **Founded:** 1940. **Staff:** 2. **Languages:** English. **Publication:** *Newsletter to Diplomates*, semiannual.

AMERICAN BOARD OF NEUROSCIENCE NURSING (ABNN)
e-mail: AssnNeuro@aol.com
url: http://www.AANN.org
224 N. Des Plaines, Ste. 601
Chicago, IL 60661
Shelly Johnson, Exec.Dir.
PH: (312)993-0256
FX: (312)993-0362
Description: Certifying body for registered nurses who have passed a written examination demonstrating achievement in neuroscience nursing. Objective is to promote excellence in the field by encouraging professional growth and individual study; granting neuroscience nursing certification; measuring knowledge and level of theory required for certification; establishing certification standards. Administers certifying examination. Publications:

none. **Founded:** 1978. **Staff:** 2. **Languages:** English Formerly (1984) Neurosurgical Nurses.

AMERICAN BOARD OF OBSTETRICS AND GYNECOLOGY (ABOG)
2915 Vine St.
Dallas, TX 75204-1069
Norman F. Gant, M.D., Exec.Dir.
PH: (214)871-1619
FX: (214)871-1943
Description: Certification board to establish qualifications, conduct examinations, and certify as diplomates those doctors whom the board finds qualified to specialize in obstetrics and gynecology. **Founded:** 1927. **Membership:** 15. **Languages:** English.

AMERICAN BOARD FOR OCCUPATIONAL HEALTH NURSES (ABOHN)
201 E. Ogden Ave., Ste. 114
Hinsdale, IL 60521-3652
Sharon D. Kemerer, MSN, Exec.Dir.
PH: (630)789-5799
FX: (630)789-8901
Description: Occupational health nurses. Establishes standards and confers initial and ongoing certification in occupational health nursing. Conducts seminal certification examination. Convention/Meeting: none. **Founded:** 1972. **Membership:** 6100. **Staff:** 4. Multinational. **Languages:** English. **Budget:** $700,000.

AMERICAN BOARD OF OPHTHALMOLOGY (ABO)
111 Presidential Blvd., Ste. 241
Bala Cynwyd, PA 19004
Dennis O'Day, M.D., Exec.Dir.
PH: (610)664-1175
FX: (610)664-6503
Description: Medical specialty board to determine the adequacy of training, the professional preparation, and ophthalmic knowledge of ophthalmologists who wish to be certified. Works to improve the standards of graduate medical education and the facilities for special ophthalmic training. **Founded:** 1916. **Membership:** 17. **Staff:** 6. **Languages:** English. Formerly (1933) American Board for Ophthalmic Examinations.

AMERICAN BOARD OF ORAL AND MAXILLOFACIAL PATHOLOGY
4830 W. Kennedy Blvd., Ste. 690
PO Box 25915
Tampa, FL 33622-5915
Clarita Wendrich, Exec.Sec.
PH: (813)286-2444
FX: (813)289-5279
Description: Works to encourage the study and promote and improve the practice of oral pathology; arrange, conduct, and control examinations to determine the competence of applicants; grant and issue certificates. **Founded:** 1948. **Membership:** 260. **Languages:** English. **Budget:** $50,000. **Formerly:** American Board of Oral Pathology.

AMERICAN BOARD OF ORAL AND MAXILLOFACIAL SURGERY (ABOMS)
625 N. Michigan Ave., Ste. 1820
Chicago, IL 60611
Sheryl Mouts, Sec.
PH: (312)642-0070
FX: (312)642-8584
Description: Certification board to establish qualifications, conduct examinations, and certify surgeons whom the board finds qualified to practice oral and maxillofacial medicine, including diagnostic, surgical, and adjunctive treatment of the diseases, injuries, and defects of the oral and maxillofacial regions. **Founded:** 1946. **Membership:** 3580. **Staff:** 3. **Languages:** English. **Formerly:** (1978) American Board of Oral Surgery.

AMERICAN BOARD OF ORTHODONTICS (ABO)
e-mail: amboard@stlnet.com
url: http://www.americanboardortho.com
401 N. Lindbergh Blvd., Ste. 308
St. Louis, MO 63141
Sally Bowers, Exec.Sec.
PH: (314)432-6130
FX: (314)432-8170
Description: Certification board to investigate the qualifications of, administer examinations to, and certify as diplomates dentists specializing in orthodontics (prevention and correction of irregularities and faulty positions of the teeth). Sponsored by the American Association of Orthodontists. **Founded:** 1929. **Languages:** English. **Publication:** *American Board of Orthodontics Directory*, annual. Lists diplomates. **Formerly:** (1938) American Board of Orthodontia.

AMERICAN BOARD OF PATHOLOGY (ABP)
PO Box 25915
Tampa, FL 33622
William H. Hartmann, M.D., Exec.VP
PH: (813)286-2444
FX: (813)289-5279
Description: Seeks to: encourage study of pathology; maintain profesional standards and advance practice in the field; maintain registry of certified pathologists; participate in the evaluation and review of graduate medical education programs in pathology. Examines doctors of medicine or osteopathy who have had three to five years postgraduate training in laboratory medicine and pathology and certifies qualified and successful applicants as specialists in pathology. **Founded:** 1936. **Membership:** 12. **Staff:** 12. **Languages:** English. **Publication:** *The American Board of Pathology*, 2-3/year. Newsletter ■ *Information Booklet*, annual.

AMERICAN BOARD OF PEDIATRIC DENTISTRY (ABPD)
e-mail: jrroche@compuserve.com
1193 Woodgate Dr.
Carmel, IN 46033
James R. Roche, D.D.S., Exec.Sec.-Treas.
PH: (317)573-0877
FX: (317)846-7235
Description: Certification board whose purpose is to investigate the qualifications of, administer examinations to, and certify as diplomates, dentists specializing in the care of children. Sponsored by American Academy of Pediatric Dentistry. **Founded:** 1940. **Membership:** 1031. **Staff:** 10. Multinational. **Languages:** English. **Publication:** *Directory of Diplomates*, biennial. Lists all board certified pediatric dentists. Price: $28.00. Advertising: accepted. **Formerly:** (1986) American Board of Pedodontics.

AMERICAN BOARD OF PEDIATRICS (ABP)
e-mail: abpeds@abpeds.org
url: http://www.abp.org
111 Silver Cedar Ct.
Chapel Hill, NC 27514
James A. Stockman, M.D., Pres.
PH: (919)929-0461
FX: (919)929-9255
Description: Certification board to establish qualifications, conduct examinations, and certify as diplomates those whom the board finds qualified as specialists in pediatrics. **Founded:** 1933. **Membership:** 250. **Staff:** 50. **Languages:** English.

AMERICAN BOARD OF PERI ANESTHESIA NURSING CERTIFICATION (ABPANC)
475 Riverside Dr., 7th Fl.
New York, NY 10115-0089
Linda Ziolkowski, R.N., Pres.
TF: 800622-7262
FX: (212)367-4256
Description: Administers examination to individuals wishing to attain post-anesthesia nursing certification. Convention/Meeting: none. **Founded:** 1985. **Staff:** 2. **Languages:** English.

AMERICAN BOARD OF PERIODONTOLOGY (ABP)
e-mail: abperio@msn.com
url: http://www.perio.org
4157 Mountain Rd. No. 249
Pasadena, MD 21122
Gerald M. Bowers, Exec.Sec.-Treas.
PH: (410)437-3749
FX: (410)437-4021
Description: Conducts examinations to determine the qualifications and competence of periodontists who voluntarily apply for certification as diplomates in the field of periodontology. Maintains registry of holders of diplomate certificates. **Founded:** 1939. **Staff:** 2. **Languages:** English.

AMERICAN BOARD OF PROSTHODONTICS (ABP)
c/o Dr. William D. Culpepper
PO Box 8437
Atlanta, GA 30306
Dr. William D. Culpepper, Exec.Dir.
PH: (404)876-2625
FX: (404)872-8804
Description: Seeks to advance the science and art of prosthodontics by encouraging its study and improving its practice. Certifies dentists who specialize in the field of fixed, removable, and maxillofacial prosthodontics. Approved by the American Dental Association and the Council on Dental Education. **Languages:** English.

AMERICAN BOARD OF PSYCHIATRY AND NEUROLOGY (ABPN)
500 Lake Cook Rd., Ste. 335
Deerfield, IL 60015
Stephen C. Scheiber, M.D., Exec.VP
PH: (847)945-7900
FX: (847)945-1146
Description: Physicians with specialized training in psychiatry, neurology, child neurology, child adolescent psychiatry, clinical neurophysiology, and geriatric psychiatry. Determines eligibility requirements, administers examinations, and certifies physicians. Convention/Meeting: none. **Founded:** 1934. **Languages:** English.

AMERICAN BOARD OF RADIOLOGY (ABR)
e-mail: info@theabr.org
5255 E. Williams Cir., Ste. 3200
Tucson, AZ 85711-7401
M. Paul Capp, M.D., Exec.Dir.
PH: (520)790-2900
FX: (520)790-3200
Description: Certification board to establish qualifications, conduct examinations, and certify physicians in the specialty of radiology and physicists in radiological physics and related branches (science dealing with X-rays or rays from radioactive substances for medical use). **Founded:** 1934. **Membership:** 23. **Languages:** English. **Publication:** Booklets. On examinations in diagnostic radiology, radiological physics, radiation oncology, and special competence in nuclear radiology.

AMERICAN BOARD OF SLEEP MEDICINE
1610 14th St. NW, Ste. 302
Rochester, MN 55901-0246
Charlene Wibben, Exam.Coord.
PH: (507)285-4377
FX: (507)287-6008
Description: Works to encourage the study and elevate the standards of sleep medicine. Offers certification in sleep medicine to licensed physicians and individuals with Ph.D.s in health related fields. **Founded:** 1991. **Languages:** English.

AMERICAN BOARD OF SPINAL SURGERY (ABSS)
2300 S. Rancho Dr., Ste. 202
Las Vegas, NV 89102-4508
Kazem Fathie, M.D., Chm.
TF: 888432-2667
Description: Spinal surgeons seeking to advance knowledge and provide education in the field of spinal surgery. Conducts charitable, education, and research programs; maintains hall of fame; offers placement service; compiles statistics; maintains speakers' bureau. **Founded:** 1977. **Membership:** 450. Multinational. **Languages:** English. **Publication:** *Journal of Neurological and Orthopaedic Surgery*, quarterly. Price: $125.00/year in U.S.; $135.00/year outside U.S. Circulation: 1,000.

AMERICAN BOARD OF SURGERY (ABS)
url: http://www.absurgery.org
1617 John F. Kennedy Blvd., Ste. 860
Philadelphia, PA 19103
Dr. Wallace P. Ritchie, Jr., Exec.Dir.
PH: (215)568-4000
FX: (215)563-5718
Description: Examining and certifying board in general surgery; also certifies in Pediatric Surgery, General Vascular Surgery, Surgical Critical Care, and Hand Surgery. Membership is drawn from 23 national and regional surgical and specialty societies and organizations. Currently offers Recertification in General Surgery, Pediatric Surgery, General Vascular Surgery, and Surgical Critical Care. **Founded:** 1937. **Membership:** 29. **Languages:** English.

AMERICAN BOARD OF TOXICOLOGY (ABT)
PO Box 30054
Raleigh, NC 27622
Sue Moore, Exec.Dir.
PH: (919)782-0036
FX: (919)782-0036
Description: Certifies toxicologists. Administers annual certification and recertification exams. **Founded:** 1979. **Staff:** 1. **Languages:** English.

AMERICAN BRAIN TUMOR ASSOCIATION (ABTA)
e-mail: info@abta.org
url: http://www.abta.org
2720 River Rd., Ste. 146
Des Plaines, IL 60018
Naomi Berkowitz, Exec.Dir.
PH: (847)827-9910
TF: 800886-2282
FX: (847)827-9918
Description: Seeks to eliminate brain tumors by funding and encouraging research; providing educational materials and objective resource information to patients, their families, and the medical professionals who treat them. Promotes excellence in patient care; and advocates the investigation of innovative research and treatment approaches. **Founded:** 1973. **Staff:** 12. **Languages:** English. **Publication:** *A Brain Tumor-Sharing Hope* (in English and Spanish). Pamphlet ▪ *A Primer of Brain Tumors*. Booklet ▪ *About Ependymoma*. Pamphlet ▪ *About Glioblastoma Multiforme and Anaplastic Astrocytoma*. Pamphlet ▪ *About Medulloblastoma/PNET*. Pamphlet ▪ *About Meningioma*. Pamphlet ▪ *About Metastatic Tumors to the Brain and Spine*. Booklet ▪ *About Oligodendroglioma and Mixed Glioma*. Pamphlet ▪ *About Pituitary Tumors*. Pamphlet ▪ *Alex's Journey: The Story of a Child with a Brain Tumor*. Booklet ▪ *Chemotherapy of Brain Tumors*. Booklet ▪ *Coping with a Brain Tumor: Part 1; From Diagnosis to Treatment*. Booklet ▪ *Coping with a Brain Tumor: Part 2; During and After Treatment*. Booklet ▪ *Dictionary for Brain Tumor Patients*. Booklet ▪ *The Message Line*, 3/year. Newsletter. Price: free to patients and family members ▪ *Organizing a Support Group*. Pamphlet ▪ *Radiation Therapy of Brain Tumors: Part 1; A Basic Guide*. Pamphlet ▪ *Radiation Therapy of Brain Tumors: Part 2; Background and Research Guide*. Booklet ▪ *Using a Medical Library*. Pamphlet ▪ *When Your Child is Ready to Return to School*. Pamphlet ▪ Brochures. **Formerly:** (1992) Association for Brain Tumor Research.

AMERICAN CANCER SOCIETY (ACS)
url: http://www.cancer.org
1599 Clifton Rd. NE
Atlanta, GA 30329
John R. Seffrin, Ph.D., CEO
PH: (404)320-3333
TF: 800ACS-2345
FX: (404)329-7530
Description: Provides special services to cancer patients. Sponsors Reach to Recovery, Can. Surmount, and I Can Cope. Conducts medical and educational programs. **Founded:** 1913. **Staff:** 390. Multinational. **Local Groups:** 3,300. **Languages:** English. **Publication:** *American Cancer Society.* Annual Report. Price: free. Circulation: 100,000. Advertising: not accepted ▪ *CA-A Cancer Journal for Clinicians,* bimonthly. Covers cancer treatment, prevention, and diagnosis. Price: free for health professionals. ISSN: 0007-9235. Circulation: 400,000. Advertising: accepted. Alternate Formats: microform ▪ *Cancer,* semimonthly. Medical journal covering cancer prevention, research, diagnosis, and treatment. Includes proceedings supplements covering ACS conferences. Price: $75.00/year for individuals; $125.00/year for institutions. ISSN: 0008-543X. Circulation: 20,000. Advertising: accepted ▪ *Cancer Facts and Figures,* annual. Report providing statistical information on the major sites of cancer including incidence, mortality and survival rates, and risk factors. Price: free. Circulation: 500,000. Advertising: not accepted ▪ *Cancer News,* 3/year. Magazine for ACS volunteers and donors; includes news of society activities. Price: free. ISSN: 0008-5464. Circulation: 230,000. Advertising: not accepted. **Absorbed:** (1969) Reach to Recovery Foundation. **Formerly:** (1944) American Society for the Control Cancer.

AMERICAN CENTRAL EUROPEAN DENTAL INSTITUTE (ACEDI)
60 Federal St.
Boston, MA 02110-2510
Dr. Arnold Watkin, Chm.
PH: (617)423-6165
FX: (617)426-0006
Description: Dentists and others serving in capacities related to the dental profession. Seeks to advance standards in the profession of dentistry. Conducts educational programs; maintains speakers' bureau. **Founded:** 1991. **Membership:** 2. **Staff:** 3. Multinational. **Languages:** Czech, English. **Budget:** $100,000. **Publication:** *ACEDI,* annual. Newsletter.

AMERICAN CHIROPRACTIC REGISTRY OF RADIOLOGIC TECHNOLOGISTS (ACRRT)
2330 Gull Rd.
Kalamazoo, MI 49001
Dr. Edward Maurer, Exec.VP
PH: (616)343-6666
Description: Chiropractic assistants and radiologic technologists employed in chiropractic offices. Educates the general public concerning the importance of having highly skilled radiologic technologists (those who administer X-rays) in chiropractic offices. Serves as a national certifying agency for individuals in the field; maintains registry of certified chiropractic radiologic technologists. **Founded:** 1982. **Membership:** 2000. **Staff:** 2. **Languages:** English. **Publication:** *Wavelengths,* bimonthly. Newsletter.

AMERICAN CLINICAL AND CLIMATOLOGICAL ASSOCIATION (ACCA)
200 1st St. SW
1601 Guggenheim Bldg.
Rochester, MN 55905
Dr. Lynwood H. Smith, Sec.-Treas.
PH: (507)284-3320
FX: (507)284-2053
Description: Internists interested in the clinical study of disease. **Founded:** 1884. **Membership:** 375. **Languages:** English.

AMERICAN COLLEGE OF APOTHECARIES (ACA)
PO Box 341266
Memphis, TN 38184-1266
Dr. D. C. Huffman, Jr., Exec.VP
PH: (901)383-8119
FX: (901)383-8882
Description: Professional society of pharmacists owning and operating ethical prescription pharmacies, including hospital pharmacists, pharmacy students, and faculty of colleges of pharmacy. Primary objective is the translation, transformation, and dissemination of knowledge, research data, and recent developments in the pharmaceutical industry and public health. Sponsors Community Pharmacy Residency Program; offers continuing education courses. Conducts research programs; sponsors charitable program; compiles statistics; operates speakers' bureau. **Founded:** 1940. **Membership:** 1000. **Staff:** 7. **State Groups:** 24. **Languages:** English. **Budget:** $250,000.

AMERICAN COLLEGE OF CARDIOLOGY (ACC)
url: http://www.acc.org
9111 Old Georgetown Rd.
Bethesda, MD 20814-1699
David J. Feild, Exec.VP
PH: (301)897-5400
TF: 800253-4636
FX: (301)897-9745
Description: Professional society of physicians, surgeons, and scientists specializing in cardiology (heart) and cardiovascular (circulatory) diseases. Operates Heart House Learning Center. Maintains numerous committees. **Founded:** 1949. **Membership:** 241000. **Staff:** 140. Multinational. **State Groups:** 38. **Languages:** English. **Budget:** $30,000,000.

AMERICAN COLLEGE OF CARDIOVASCULAR ADMINISTRATORS (ACCA)
e-mail: info@aameda.org
url: http://www.aameda.org
30555 Southfield Rd., Ste, 150
Southfield, MI 48076
Roy Redman, Pres.
PH: (248)540-4598
FX: (248)645-0590
Description: A chapter of the American Academy of Medical Administrators. Upper- and middle-level managers of health care professionals in the cardiovascular health care field; associate members are junior supervisors, salespersons, and individuals. Represents members within the medical industry; provides credentialing of cardiology administrators. Serves as a forum for the exchange of information. Conducts research; offers educational programs. **Founded:** 1986. **Membership:** 1200. **Staff:** 9. **State Groups:** 50. **Languages:** English. **Publication:** *Journal of Cardiovacular Management,* bimonthly. Advertising: accepted.

AMERICAN COLLEGE OF CHEST PHYSICIANS (ACCP)
e-mail: accp@chestnet.org
url: http://www/chestnet.org
3300 Dundee Rd.
Northbrook, IL 60062
Alvin Lever, Exec.VP/CEO
PH: (847)498-1400
TF: 800343-ACCP
FX: (847)498-5460
Description: Professional society of physicians and surgeons specializing in diseases of the chest (heart and lungs). Promotes undergraduate and postgraduate medical education and research in the field. Sponsors forums. Maintains placement service; conducts educational programs. **Founded:** 1935. **Membership:** 15000. **Staff:** 52. Multinational. **Languages:** English. **Budget:** $10,000,000. **Publication:** *American College of Chest Physicians Membership Directory,* annual. Arranged geographically and by specialty. Price: included in membership dues. Circulation: 15,000. Advertising: accepted ▪ *Chest: For Pulmonologists, Cardiologists, Cardiothoracic Surgeons, and Related Specialists,* monthly. Journal. Presents clinical investigations and case reports in

cardiopulmonary medical and surgical specialties. Contains author and subject indexes. Price: included in membership dues; $120.00/year for nonmembers; $150.00/year for institutions. Circulation: 23,000. Advertising: accepted ■ Books ■ Brochures. On smoking and health ■ Films ■ Reports.

AMERICAN COLLEGE OF CLINICAL PHARMACOLOGY (ACCP)
e-mail: accp1ssu@aol.com
url: http://www.accp1.org
3 Ellinwood Court
New Hartford, NY 13413-1105
Susan Ulrich, Exec.Dir.
PH: (315)768-6117
FX: (315)768-6119
Description: Strives to be the premier professional society with the size, influence, and diversity of membership consistent with the breadth of the discipline of clinical pharmacology. Provides educational programs and forum for membership, health professionals, students, and the public. Assists in the development and dissemination of basic and clinical knowledge to improve rational drug use and patient outcomes. Serves as a forum for active public debate to influence scientific, regulatory, and public health policy issues. Provides oppurtunities to influence future directions of the College. Supports and encourages the discovery and development efforts designed to provide improved therapeutic modalities. **Founded:** 1969. **Membership:** 1000. **Staff:** 1. Multinational. **Local Groups:** 14. **Languages:** English. **Budget:** $325,000.

AMERICAN COLLEGE OF DENTISTS (ACD)
url: http://www.acdentists.org
839-J Quince Orchard Blvd.
Gaithersburg, MD 20878
Dr. Stephen Ralls, Exec.Dir.
PH: (301)977-3223
FX: (301)977-3330
Description: Dentists and others serving in capacities related to the dental profession. Seeks to advance the standards of the profession of dentistry. Conducts educational and research programs. Maintains speakers' bureau and charitable programs. **Founded:** 1920. **Membership:** 7000. **Staff:** 6. **Local Groups:** 46. **Languages:** English. **Budget:** $1,000,000. **Publication:** *American College of Dentists News and Views*, quarterly. Newsletter. Price: included in membership dues. Circulation: 6,500. Advertising: not accepted ■ *Journal of the American College of Dentists*, quarterly. Includes news and reserach reports. Price: included in membership dues; $40.00/year for nonmembers. ISSN: 0002-7979. Circulation: 5,000. Advertising: not accepted.

AMERICAN COLLEGE OF DOMICILIARY MIDWIVES (ACDM)
e-mail: goodnews@best.com
url: http://www.goodnewsnet.org/college/index.html/acdm
3889 Middlefield Rd.
Palo Alto, CA 94303-4718
Faith Gibson, Exec.Dir.
Description: Strives to preserve lawful access to home-based maternity care as provided by community midwives and family-practice physicians..

AMERICAN COLLEGE HEALTH ASSOCIATION (ACHA)
e-mail: acha@access.digex.net
url: http://www.clbalt.com/acha.org
PO Box 28937
Baltimore, MD 21240-8937
Doyle Randol, Exec.Dir.
PH: (410)859-1500
FX: (410)859-1510
Description: Institutions (930) and individuals (2500)Provides an organization in which institutions of higher education and interested individuals may work together to promote health in its broadest aspects for students and all other members of the college community. Offers continuing education programs for health professionals. Maintains placement listings for physicians and other personnel seeking positions in college health. Compiles statistics. Conducts seminars and training programs. **Founded:** 1920. **Membership:** 3438. **Staff:** 20. **Local Groups:** 11. **Languages:** English. **Budget:** $2,000,000. **Publication:** *ACHA Action*, quarterly. Newsletter. Includes calendar of events, college health resource listings, annual report, and leadership directory. Price: included in membership dues. Circulation: 3,000. Advertising: not accepted ■ *Health Information Series*. Pamphlets ■ *Journal of American College Health*, bimonthly. Advertising: accepted ■ *Membership Profile Directory*, periodic ■ Catalog. Lists publications ■ Monographs ■ Reports. **Formerly:** American Student Health Association.

AMERICAN COLLEGE OF HEALTH CARE ADMINISTRATORS (ACHCA)
e-mail: info@achca.org
url: http://www.achca.org
325 S. Patrick St.
Alexandria, VA 22314
Karen S. Tucker, CAE, Pres. & CEO
PH: (703)739-7900
TF: 88888A-CHCA
FX: (703)739-7901
Description: Persons actively engaged in the administration of long-term care facilities, such as nursing homes, retirement communities, assisted living facilities, and subacute care programs. ACHCA administers professional certification programs for assisted living, subacute and nursing home administrators. ACHCA also administers the Assisted Living Administrator Certificate Program. Works to elevate the standards in the field and to develop and promote a code of ethics and standards of education and training. Seeks to inform allied professions and the public that good administration of long-term care facilities calls for special formal academic training and experience. Encourages research in all aspects of geriatrics, the chronically ill, and administration. Maintains placement service. Conducts research and special education programs. **Founded:** 1962. **Membership:** 6400. **Staff:** 18. **State Groups:** 48. **Languages:** English. **Budget:** $2,500,000. **Formerly** American College of Nursing Home Administrators.

AMERICAN COLLEGE OF HEALTHCARE INFORMATION ADMINISTRATORS (ACHIA)
e-mail: info@aameda.org
url: http://www.aameda.org
30555 Southfield Rd., Ste. 150
Southfield, MI 48076
Lt. James A. Studebaker, Pres.
PH: (248)540-4310
FX: (248)645-0590
Description: Healthcare leaders serving in a management position in the information field. Works to promote the advancement of members' knowledge, professional standing, credentialing, and personal achievements in information technology, management, and strategic planning. Conducts an employment referral and educational programs. **Founded:** 1991. **Membership:** 200. **Languages:** English.

AMERICAN COLLEGE OF HOME HEALTH ADMINISTRATORS (ACHHA)
30555 Southfield Rd., Ste. 150
Southfield, MI 48076
Thomas R. O'Donovan, Pres.
PH: (248)540-4310
FX: (248)645-0590
Description: Home health administrators, executives, and managers at all levels. Promotes professional indentification within the home health care field and seeks to facilitate the career and professional development of members. Represents the interests of the home health care industry within the medical community and before government agencies and the public; makes available to members discounts on educational programs conducted by the ACHHA or the American Academy of Medical Administrators; offers professional referral services; holds examinations and

confers professional certification. **Founded:** 1957. **Membership:** 3500. **Staff:** 8. Multinational. **Regional Groups:** 7. **Languages:** English.

AMERICAN COLLEGE OF HOME OBSTETRICS (ACHO)
2821 Rose St.
Franklin Park, IL 60131
Gregory White, M.D., Pres.
PH: (847)455-2030
Description: Physicians interested in cooperating with families who wish to give birth in the home. Objective is to accumulate and exchange data on home birth. Maintains speakers' bureau; compiles statistics. Plans to conduct research. **Founded:** 1978. **Membership:** 30. **Languages:** English.

AMERICAN COLLEGE OF MANAGED CARE ADMINISTRATORS (ACMCA)
e-mail: aama@netquest.com
30555 Southfield Rd., Ste. 150
Southfield, MI 48076
Eugene A. Migliaccio, Pres.
PH: (810)540-4310
FX: (810)645-0590
Description: Managers of professionals who are directly or indirectly providing managed healthcare. Works to promote the advancement of members' professional standing, education, and personal achievement and develop innovative concepts in managed care administration. Conducts an employment referral and educational programs. **Founded:** 1994. **Membership:** 600. **Staff:** 8. **Languages:** English.

AMERICAN COLLEGE OF MANAGED CARE MEDICINE (ACMCM)
4435 Waterfront Dr., Ste. 101
Glen Allen, VA 23060
Dr. William Tindall, Contact
PH: (804)527-1906
FX: (804)747-5316
Description: Physicians and other health care providers working for managed care organizations. Seeks to advance the effectiveness of managed care health services. Conducts continuing professional development courses for health care providers and bestows Managed Care Certification; facilitates exchange of information among members; sponsors research; maintains speakers' bureau. **Founded:** 1995. **Membership:** 2000. **Languages:** English. **Publication:** *American Journal of Integrated Health Care*, quarterly. Circulation: 25,000. Advertising: accepted.

AMERICAN COLLEGE OF MEDICAL PHYSICS
e-mail: acmp@acr.org
url: http://www.acmp.org
1891 Preston White Dr.
Reston, VA 22091
Laura Fleming Jones, Exec.Dir.
PH: (703)648-8966
FX: (703)648-9176
Description: Covers socioeconomic aspects of practice, management issues, reimbursement, licensure, and practice standards. **Founded:** 1982. **Membership:** 400. **Regional Groups:** 9. **Languages:** English.

AMERICAN COLLEGE OF MEDICAL PRACTICE EXECUTIVES (ACMPE)
url: http://www.mgma.com
104 Inverness Ter. E.
Englewood, CO 80112-5306
Andrea M. Rossiter, Sr. VP
PH: (303)397-7869
FX: (303)643-4427
Description: Professional credentialing organization. Membership is drawn from Medical Group Management Association and beyond Works to encourage medical group practice administrators to improve and maintain their proficiency and to provide appropriate recognition; to establish a program with uniform standards of admission, advancement, certification and fellowship in order to achieve the highest possible standards in the profession of medical group practice administration; to participate in the development of educational and research programs for the advancement of the profession; to inform the medical profession and the public of the value of trained and experienced men and women in the management of the administrative affairs of all forms of group practice; to instill in its membership a constant awareness of the high ideals and traditions of the medical profession and medical group administration so that its members will conduct themselves in such a manner as to augment those ideals and traditions. Conducts educational programs such as Management Education Programs and Group Practice Governance Leadership Institute. **Founded:** 1956. **Membership:** 3000. **Staff:** 9. **Languages:** English. **Budget:** $1,000,000. **Publication:** *College Review*, semiannual. Professional manuscripts submitted to the College for advancement to fellow status; arranged by subject and author. Price: $10.00/copy to members; $16.00/copy to affiliates; $22.00/copy to nonmembers. Advertising: not accepted ∎ *Your Pathway to Excellence.* Brochure. Provides general information regarding ACMPE membership application. **Formerly:** (1976) American College of Clinic Managers; (1993) American College of Medical Group Administrators.

AMERICAN COLLEGE OF MEDICAL TOXICOLOGY (ACMT)
777 E. Park Dr.
PO Box 8820
Harrisburg, PA 17105-8820
J. Ward Donovan, M.D., Pres.
PH: (717)558-7846
FX: (717)558-7841
Description: Seeks to advance the science, study and practice of medical toxicology by fostering the development of medical toxicology in its provision of emergency, consultation, forensic, legal, community and industrial services; and by otherwise striving to advance and elevate the science, study and practice of medical toxicology. **Founded:** 1993. **Membership:** 210. **Staff:** 3. **Languages:** English. Formerly American Board of Medical Toxicology.

AMERICAN COLLEGE OF MEDICINE (ACM)
e-mail: iaos@aol.com
4711 Golf Rd., Ste. 408
Skokie, IL 60076
Randall T. Bellows, M.D., Dir.
PH: (847)568-1500
TF: 8006214002
FX: (847)568-1527
Description: Promotes and recognizes the specific needs of general practitioners and provides continuing medical education programs to physicians for maintaining competence in the practice of medicine. **Founded:** 1981. **Languages:** English. **Publication:** *Comprehensive Therapy*, monthly. **Absorbed:** American Society of Contemporary Medicine and Surgery. **Formerly:** (1984) American College of General Practice.

AMERICAN COLLEGE OF MENTAL HEALTH ADMINISTRATION (ACMHA)
e-mail: lawhel@aol.com
url: http://www.newmexico.com/acmha
7625 W. Hutchinson Ave.
Pittsburgh, PA 15218-1248
Lawrence A. Heller, Ph.D., Exec.Dir.
PH: (412)244-0670
FX: (412)244-9916
Description: Mental health clinician administrators. **Founded:** 1980. **Membership:** 200. **Staff:** 2. **Languages:** English. **Budget:** $55,000.

AMERICAN COLLEGE OF NEUROPSYCHIATRISTS (ACN)
28595 Orchard Lake Rd., Ste. 335
Farmington Hills, MI 48334
Louis E. Rentz, Exec.Dir.

PH: (810)553-9877
FX: (810)553-5957
Description: Psychiatrists, neurologists, physicians in training, and persons in interrelated professions. Promotes study and research in neurology and psychiatry in the osteopathic profession. Maintains specialized education programs. **Founded:** 1937. **Membership:** 420. **Staff:** 2. **Languages:** English.

AMERICAN COLLEGE OF NEUROPSYCHOPHARMACOLOGY (ACNP)
e-mail: acnp@acnp.org
url: http://www.acnp.org
320 Centre Bldg.
2014 Broadway
Nashville, TN 37203
Oakley Ray, Ph.D., Exec.Sec.
PH: (615)322-2075
FX: (615)343-0662
Description: Experienced investigators whose work is related to neuropsychopharmacology. Promotes and encourages the scientific study and application of neuropsychopharmacology. Conducts study groups and plenary sessions. **Founded:** 1961. **Membership:** 757. **Staff:** 8. Multinational. **Languages:** English.

AMERICAN COLLEGE OF NURSE-MIDWIVES (ACNM)
e-mail: info@acnm.org
url: http://www.midwife.org
818 Connecticut Ave., Ste. 900
Washington, DC 20006
Helen Marieskind
PH: (202)728-9860
FX: (202)289-9897
Description: Seeks to develop and support the profession of certified nurse-midwives in order to promote the health and well-being of women and infants within their families and communities. A CNM is a licensed health care practitioner educated in the two disciplines of nursing and midwifery. Provides gynecological services and care of mothers and babies throughout the maternity cycle; members have completed an ACNM accredited program of study and clinical experience in midwifery and passed a national certification exam. Cooperates with allied groups to enable nurse-midwives to concentrate their efforts in the improvement of services for mothers and newborn babies. Seeks to identify areas of nurse-midwifery practices as they relate to the total service and educational aspects of maternal and newborn care. Studies and evaluates activities of nurse-midwives in order to establish qualifications; cooperates in planning and developing educational programs. conducts research and continuing education workshops. sponsors research. Compiles statistics. Maintains speakers' bureau and archives; offers placement service. **Founded:** 1955. **Membership:** 6200. **Staff:** 38. **Local Groups:** 53. **Languages:** English. **Budget:** $2,200,000. Absorbed (1968) American Association of Nurse-Midwives. Formerly (1969) American College of Nurse-Midwifery.

AMERICAN COLLEGE OF OBSTETRICIANS AND GYNECOLOGISTS (ACOG)
e-mail: mgraves@acog.org
url: http://www.acog.org
409 12th St. SW
PO Box 96920
Washington, DC 20090-6920
Ralph Hale, M.D., Exec.Dir.
PH: (202)638-5577
FX: (202)484-8107
Description: Physicians specializing in childbirth and the diseases of women. Sponsors continuing professional development program. **Founded:** 1951. **Membership:** 38000. **Staff:** 200. **State Groups:** 50. **Languages:** English. **Budget:** $38,000,000. Formerly (1956) American Academy of Obstetrics and Gynecology.

AMERICAN COLLEGE OF ONCOLOGY ADMINISTRATORS (ACOA)
e-mail: info@aameda.org
url: http://www.aameda.org
30555 Southfield Rd., Ste. 150
Southfield, MI 48076
Janet L. Jones, RN, Pres.
PH: (248)540-4310
FX: (248)645-0590
Description: Oncology administrators, managers and consultants. Brings together all components of oncology management to develop creative strategies, quality programs, and sound evaluation mechanisms. Promotes advancement of members through continuing education and research in oncology management. Conducts educational programs. **Founded:** 1991. **Membership:** 700. **Staff:** 8. **Languages:** English.

AMERICAN COLLEGE OF ORAL AND MAXILLOFACIAL SURGEONS (ACOMS)
url: http://www.acoms.org
1100 NW Loop 410, Ste. 506
San Antonio, TX 78213-2266
Robert Green, Exec.Dir.
PH: (210)344-5674
TF: 800522-6676
FX: (210)344-9754
Description: Diplomates of the American Board of Oral and Maxillofacial Surgery who practice oral and maxillofacial surgery. To advance the integrity of the profession through continuing education, exchange of ideas, certification procedures, and cooperation with allied groups. **Founded:** 1975. **Membership:** 2500. **Staff:** 3. **Languages:** English. **Budget:** $750,000. **Publication:** *ACOMS Review*, quarterly. Circulation: 6,000. Advertising: not accepted. **Formerly:** (1975) Association of Diplomates of the American Board of Oral Surgery.

AMERICAN COLLEGE OF OSTEOPATHIC OBSTETRICIANS AND GYNECOLOGISTS (ACOOG)
e-mail: acoog@mich.com
url: http://www.acoog@mich.com
900 Auburn Rd.
Pontiac, MI 48342-3365
J. Polsinelli, D.O., Exec.Dir.
PH: (248)332-6360
TF: 800875-6360
FX: (248)332-4607
Description: Osteopathic physicians and surgeons specializing in obstetrics and gynecology. Conducts educational programs, and reviews osteopathic obstetric and gynecologic residency training programs. Holds annual postgraduate course and annual convention. **Founded:** 1934. **Membership:** 790. **Staff:** 3. **Languages:** English. **Budget:** $320,000.

AMERICAN COLLEGE OF PHYSICIAN EXECUTIVES (ACPE)
url: http://www.acpe.org
4890 W. Kennedy Blvd., Ste. 200
Tampa, FL 33609
Roger S. Schenke, Exec.VP
PH: (813)287-2000
TF: 800562-8088
FX: (813)287-8993
Description: Physicians whose primary professional responsibility is the management of health care organizations. Provides for continuing education and certification of the physician executive and the advancement and recognition of the physician executive and the profession. Offers specialized career planning, counseling, recruitment and placement services, and research and information data on physician managers. **Founded:** 1974. **Membership:** 11500. **Staff:** 32. Multinational. **Languages:** English. **Budget:** $8,000,000. **Publication:** *American College of Physician Executives – Membership Directory*, annual. Price: included in membership dues. Circulation: 11,500. Advertising: not accepted ■ *College Digest*, bimonthly. Newsletter. Includes employment oppor-

tunity. Price: included in membership dues. Circulation: 11,500. Advertising: not accepted. Also Cited As: *Academy Digest* ▪ *Fundamentals of Medical Management: A Guide for the Physician Executive*. Book. Includes discussion of organizational theory, effective communication, negotiating skills, conflict management, and organizational politics. Price: $40.00 for members; $50.00 for nonmembers ▪ *Get the Job You Want and the Money You're Worth*. Monograph. Outlines a step-by-step strategy to planning a successful job pursuit, with advice on structuring your resume and setting up personal networking. Price: $15.00 for members; $25.00 for nonmembers ▪ *Health Care Quality Management for the 21st Century*. Book. Attempts to place the current health care delivery crisis into historical perspective. Price: $65.00 for members; $75.00 for nonmembers ▪ *International Health Care: A Bibliography*. Contains material on international health care systems such as up-to-date lists of citations from the literature. Price: $20.00 for members; $40.00 for nonmembers ▪ *Managing in an Academic Health Care Environment*. Book. Provides an overview of managing in this unique environment. Price: $40.00 for members; $50.00 for nonmembers ▪ *Medical Directors: What, Why, How*. Monograph. Covers the possible responsibilities for the position of Medical Director. Price: $15.00 for members; $20.00 for nonmembers ▪ *New Leadership in Health Care Management – The Physician Executive*. Book. Outlines the knowledge base physician executives must master in order to effectively compete and succeed. Price: $35.00 for members; $49.00 for nonmembers ▪ *Physician Executive: Journal of Management*, monthly. Includes recurring columns on health economics and health law. Price: included in membership dues; $48.00/year for nonmembers. Circulation: 10,000. Advertising: accepted. Also Cited As: *Medical Director* ▪ *Roads to Medical Management: Physician Executives' Career Decisions*. Monograph. Tracks the career moves of 15 physician executives into medical management. Price: $19.95 for members; $24.95 for nonmembers ▪ *The Shifting Sources of Power and Influence*. Monograph. Details how influence can be gained and used in the struggle for organizational power. Price: $20.95 for members; $25.95 for nonmembers ▪ *Top Docs: Managing the Search for Physician Leaders*. Monograph. Covers how to recruit physician leaders, what pitfalls to avoid, and when and how to use a recruiter. Price: $27.00 for members; $32.00 for nonmembers ▪ *Using Outplacement Services Effectively*. Monograph. Covers the what, when, why, and how of outplacement. Price: $4.95 for members; $5.95 for nonmembers ▪ *Women in Medical Management*. Report. Provides information on current perceptions about women in medical management. Price: $20.00 for members; $40.00 for nonmembers. **Absorbed:** (1989) American Academy of Medical Directors.

AMERICAN COLLEGE OF PROSTHODONTISTS (ACP)
e-mail: acpros@aol.com
url: http://www.prosthodontics.org
211 E Chicago Ave., Ste. 1000
Chicago, IL 60611-2616
Steve Hines, Exec.Dir.
PH: (312)573-1260
FX: (312)573-1257
Description: Dentists specializing in prosthetics who are either board certified, board eligible, or under training in approved graduate or residency programs. Seeks to improve prosthodontic treatment for patients by encouraging educational activities designed to bring new ideas, techniques, and research into clinical practice. Sponsors annual prosthodontic research competition. **Founded:** 1970. **Membership:** 2600. **Staff:** 6. **Regional Groups:** 40. **Languages:** English. **Budget:** $1,400,000. **Publication:** *Journal of Prosthodontics*, quarterly ▪ *Journal of Prosthodontics – Clinical Journal*. Articles ▪ Newsletter, 4/year. ACP Messenger – Membership Newsletter. Price: included in membership dues. ISSN: 0736-346X. Circulation: 2,300. Advertising: accepted.

AMERICAN COLLEGE OF RADIATION ONCOLOGY (ACRO)
e-mail: info@acro.org
url: http://www.acro.org
2021 Spring Rd., Ste. 600
Oak Brook, IL 60523-1860
Del Stauffer, Contact
PH: (630)368-3733
FX: (630)571-7837
Description: Radiation oncologists, physicists, and administrators. Seeks to ensure that regulatory legislation is fair to radiation oncologists. Lobbies on behalf of radiation onocolgy physicians. Represents physicans in fee disputes with Medicare. **Founded:** 1989. **Membership:** 1500. **Staff:** 4. **Languages:** English. **Budget:** $250,000. **Publication:** *ACRO Bulletin*, quarterly. Newsletter. Price: included in membership dues. Circulation: 1,500. Advertising: not accepted.

AMERICAN COLLEGE OF RADIOLOGY (ACR)
url: http://www.acr.org
1891 Preston White Dr.
Reston, VA 20191
John J. Curry, Exec.Dir.
PH: (703)648-8900
TF: 800ACR-LINE
FX: (703)648-9176
Description: Principal organization serving radiologists with programs which focus on the practice of radiology and the delivery of comprehensive radiological health services. These programs in medical sciences, education, and in practice management, serve the public interest and the interests of the medical community in which radiologists serve in both diagnostic and therapeutic roles. Seeks to "advance the science of radiology, improve radiologic service to the patient, study the economic aspects of the practice of radiology, and encourage imrroved and continuing education for radiologists and allied professional fields". **Founded:** 1923. **Membership:** 20000. **Staff:** 150. **State Groups:** 53. **Languages:** English. **Budget:** $16,000,000. **Publication:** Booklets ▪ Books ▪ Bulletin, monthly ▪ Directory, annual ▪ Pamphlets.

AMERICAN COLLEGE OF RHEUMATOLOGY (ACR)
e-mail: acr@rheumatology.org
url: http://www.rheumatology.org
1800 Century Pl., Ste. 250
Atlanta, GA 30345
Mark Andrejeski, Exec.VP
PH: (404)633-3777
FX: (404)633-1870
Description: Rheumatologists and rheumatology health professionals. Provides unified leadership in research, education, and the care of people with rheumatic diseases. **Founded:** 1934. **Membership:** 6500. **Staff:** 23. **Languages:** English. **Budget:** $4,600,000. Formerly (1989) American Rheumatism Association.

AMERICAN COLLEGE OF SPORTS MEDICINE (ACSM)
e-mail: pipacsm@acsm.org
url: http://www.acsm.org
PO Box 1440
Indianapolis, IN 46206-1440
James R. Whitehead, Exec.VP
PH: (317)637-9200
FX: (317)634-7817
Description: Promotes and integrates scientific research, education, and practical applications of sports medicine and exercise science to maintain and enhance physical performance, fitness, health, and quality of life. Certifies fitness leaders, fitness instructors, exercise test technologists, exercise specialists, health/fitness program directors, and U.S. military fitness personnel. Grants continuing medical education (CME) and continuing education credits (CEC). Operates more than 50 committees. **Founded:** 1954. **Membership:** 15800. **Staff:** 30. Multinational. **Regional Groups:** 12. **Languages:** English. **Budget:** $4,400,000.

AMERICAN COLLEGE OF SURGEONS (ACS)
e-mail: postmaster@facs.org
url: http://www.facs.org
633 N. Saint Clair St.
Chicago, IL 60611-3211
Paul A. Ebert, M.D., Dir.
PH: (312)202-5000
FX: (312)202-5001
Description: Professional association of surgeons worldwide organized primarily to improve the quality of care for surgical patients by elevating the standards of surgical education and practice. Conducts nationwide programs to improve emergency medical services and hospital cancer programs. Sponsors continuing education and self-assessment courses for surgeons in practice. **Founded:** 1913. **Membership:** 55600. **Staff:** 200. Multinational. **Local Groups:** 67. **Languages:** English. **Budget:** $35,000,000.

AMERICAN COLLEGE OF TOXICOLOGY (ACT)
e-mail: ekagan@act.faseb.org
url: http://landaus.com/toxicology/
9650 Rockville Pike
Bethesda, MD 20814
Carol C. Lemire, Exec.Dir.
PH: (301)571-1840
FX: (301)571-1852
Description: Individuals interested in toxicology and related disciplines such as analytical chemistry, biology, pathology, teratology, and immunology. Addresses toxicological issues. Disseminates information and provides a forum for discussion of approaches to problems in the field in order to advance toxicological science and better serve society during the annual meeting. **Founded:** 1977. **Membership:** 750. **Staff:** 2. Multinational. **Languages:** English. **Budget:** $100,000.

AMERICAN CORRECTIONAL HEALTH SERVICES ASSOCIATION (ACHSA)
e-mail: achsa@achsa.meinet.com
PO Box 2307
Dayton, OH 45401-2307
Francine W. Rickenbach, CAE, Exec.Dir.
PH: (937)586-3708
FX: (937)586-3699
Description: Health care providers, individuals, or organizations interested in improving the quality of correctional health services. Aims are: to promote the provision of health services to incarcerated persons consistent in quality and quantity with acceptable health care practices; to promote and encourage continuing education and provide technical and professional guidance for correctional health care personnel; to establish a forum for the sharing and discussion of correctional health care issues. Conducts conferences on correctional health care management, nursing, mental health, juvenile corrections, dentistry, and related subjects. Maintains placement service. **Founded:** 1975. **Membership:** 1100. **Staff:** 3. **State Groups:** 8. **Languages:** English. **Budget:** $200,000. **Publication:** *CORHEALTH*, bimonthly. Newsletter. Includes book reviews, conference calendar, list of new members, and chapter news. Price: included in membership dues. Circulation: 1,600. Advertising: accepted ■ Brochures. Provides information on policy matters.

AMERICAN COUNCIL FOR HEALTH CARE REFORM (ACHCR)
712 W. Broad St., Ste. B2
Falls Church, VA 22046-3222
William Shaker, Pres.
PH: (703)908-9220
TF: 800240-6423
FX: (703)908-9467
Description: Organized to eliminate what the council terms unnecessary and costly federal and state health care regulations and laws, such as certificate of public need restrictions that limit public choice in the selection of health care providers. Supports health care reform, based on Consumer choice. Testifies before congressional and state legislative committees. Coordinates grass roots support for free market approaches to health care delivery and health, safety, and consumer-oriented projects. Works to achieve public access to medical practice information. Supports medical savings accounts. **Founded:** 1982. **Membership:** 500000. **Staff:** 6. **Languages:** English. **Budget:** $3,000,000.

AMERICAN COUNCIL ON SCIENCE AND HEALTH (ACSH)
e-mail: acsh@acsh.org
url: http://www.acsh.org
1995 Broadway, 2nd Fl.
New York, NY 10023-5860
Dr. Elizabeth M. Whelan, Pres.
PH: (212)362-7044
FX: (212)362-4919
Description: Provides consumers with scientifically balanced evaluations of food, chemicals, the environment, and human health. Council personnel participate in government regulatory proceedings, congressional hearings, radio and television programs, public debates and other forums, and write regularly for professional and scientific journals, popular magazines, and newspaper columns. Holds national press conferences; produces documentary films. Maintains speakers' bureau. **Founded:** 1978. **Membership:** 2000. **Staff:** 11. **Languages:** English. **Budget:** $1,000,000. **Publication:** *Cigarettes: What the Warning Label Doesn't Tell You* ■ *Directory of Scientific Advisors*, triennial. Advertising: not accepted ■ *Media Updates*, semiannual. Advertising: not accepted ■ *News From ACSH*, semiannual ■ *Priorities*, quarterly. Magazine. Health and environmental reports for consumers. Price: $6.25 single copy; $25.00 annual subscription. Circulation: 6,500 ■ Papers ■ Reports. On health risks and benefits associated with public health and environmental issues.

AMERICAN DEBATE ASSOCIATION
US Naval Academy
Department of History
Annapolis, MD 21402-5044
Dr. Brett O'Donnell, Pres.
PH: (410)293-6291
FX: (410)293-2256
Description: Colleges and universities. Promotes and helps to develop intercollegiate policy debate at all levels. Offers resources to assist in initiating debate programs. Sponsors rules governing debate tournaments. **Founded:** 1984. **Membership:** 100. **Languages:** English.

AMERICAN DENTAL ASSISTANTS ASSOCIATION (ADAA)
e-mail: ADAA1@aol.com
url: http://www.members.aol.com/adaa1/index.html
203 N. LaSalle St., Ste. 1320
Chicago, IL 60601-1225
Lawrence H. Sepin, Exec.Dir.
PH: (312)541-1550
TF: 800SEE-ADAA
FX: (312)541-1496
Description: Individuals employed as dental assistants in dental offices, clinics, hospitals, or institutions; instructors of dental assistants; dental students. Sponsors workshops and seminars; maintains governmental liaison. Offers group insurance; maintains scholarship trust fund. Dental Assisting National Board examines members who are candidates for title of Certified Dental Assistant. **Founded:** 1923. **Membership:** 16000. **Staff:** 10. **Local Groups:** 175. **Languages:** English. **Budget:** $1,250,000. **Publication:** *The Dental Assistant*, bimonthly. Journal. Features articles pertaining to dental assisting. Price: included in membership dues; $20.00/yr. for nonmembers. ISSN: 0011-8508. Circulation: 18,000. Advertising: accepted.

AMERICAN DENTAL ASSOCIATION (ADA)
e-mail: publicinfo@ada.org
url: http://www.ada.org
211 E. Chicago Ave.
Chicago, IL 60611
John S. Zapp, D.D.S., Exec.Dir.

PH: (312)440-2500
FX: (312)440-7494
Description: Professional society of dentists. Encourages the improvement of the health of the public and promotes the art and science of dentistry in matters of legislation and regulations. Inspects and accredits dental schools and schools for dental hygienists, assistants, and laboratory technicians. Conducts research programs at ADA Health Foundation Research Institute. Produces most of the dental health education material used in the U.S. Sponsors National Children's Dental Health Month. Compiles statistics on personnel, practice, and dental care needs and attitudes of patients with regard to dental health. Sponsors 11 councils. **Founded:** 1859. **Membership:** 141878. **Staff:** 380. **Local Groups:** 529. **Languages:** English. **Budget:** $57,000,000. **Publication:** *ADA News*, biweekly. Price: $50.00 for nonmembers. ISSN: 0895-2930. Circulation: 140,000. Advertising: accepted ▪ *American Dental Directory*, annual. Lists dentists in the United States; includes biographical information. Price: $125.00; $250.00 CD-ROM. Circulation: 1,100. Advertising: not accepted ▪ *Index to Dental Literature*, quarterly. Indexes worldwide literature on dentistry. Price: $225.00/Annual cumulation; $250.00/four quarters. ISSN: 0019-3992. Circulation: 900. Advertising: not accepted ▪ *Journal of the American Dental Association*, monthly. Price: $85.00 for nonmembers. ISSN: 0002-8177. Advertising: accepted. **Absorbed:** (1897) Southern Dental Association. **Formerly:** (1922) National Dental Association.

AMERICAN DENTAL HYGIENISTS' ASSOCIATION (ADHA)
e-mail: mail@adha.net
url: http://www.adha.org
444 N. Michigan Ave., Ste. 3400
Chicago, IL 60611
Stanley B. Peck, Exec.Dir.
PH: (312)440-8900
TF: 800243-ADHA
FX: (312)440-6780
Description: Professional organization of licensed dental hygienists possessing a degree or certificate in dental hygiene granted by an accredited school of dental hygiene. Administers Dental Hygiene Candidate Aptitude Testing Program and makes available scholarships, research grants, and continuing education programs. Maintains accrediting service through the American Dental Association's Commission on Dental Accreditation. Compiles statistics. **Founded:** 1923. **Membership:** 30000. **Staff:** 40. **Local Groups:** 360. **Languages:** English. **Budget:** $4,200,000. **Publication:** *American Dental Hygienists' Association Access*, 10/year. Magazine. Covers current dental hygiene topics, regulatory and legislative developments, and association news. Includes membership profiles. Price: included in membership dues; $30.00/year for nonmembers. Circulation: 30,000. Advertising: accepted ▪ *Dental Hygiene*, 9/year. Journal. Includes association news, book reviews, abstracts, government news, and information on research and new products. Price: included in membership dues; $40.00/year for nonmembers. ISSN: 0091-3979. Circulation: 30,000. Advertising: accepted. Alternate Formats: microform.

AMERICAN DENTAL INSTITUTE (DI)
2509 N. Campbell, No. 9
Tucson, AZ 85719
Soaring Bear, Pres.
PH: (520)626-6133
Description: Conducts educational programs and research on nonsurgical dentistry and preventive health measures, stressing dental selfhelp and herbal treatments. Provides advisory services and information on research in progress. Operates speakers' bureau; compiles statistics. **Founded:** 1980. **Staff:** 1. **Languages:** English. **Publication:** *Dental Self Help*. Book. **Formerly:** (1992) Dental Information.

AMERICAN DENTAL SOCIETY OF ANESTHESIOLOGY (ADSA)
e-mail: adsa@compuserve.com
211 E. Chicago Ave., Ste. 780
Chicago, IL 60611

PH: (312)664-8270
TF: 800722-7788
FX: (312)642-9713
Description: Dentists and physicians. Encourages study and progress in dental anesthesiology. **Founded:** 1953. **Membership:** 3200. **State Groups:** 21. **Languages:** English. **Budget:** $350,000. **Publication:** *ADSA Directory*, annual ▪ *ADSA Pulse*, bimonthly. Newsletter. Includes society news, calendar of events, and research updates. Price: included in membership dues; $5.00/year for nonmembers. ISSN: 0274-9793. Circulation: 4,000 ▪ *Anesthesia Progress*, bimonthly. Price: $30.00/year for members; $35.00/year for nonmembers; $55.00/year for institutions.

AMERICAN DENTAL SOCIETY OF EUROPE (ADSE)
e-mail: 100305.1136@compuserve.com
Flat 2, Hacourt House
19A Cavendish Sq.
London W1M 9AD, England
Lloyd Searson, Hon.Sec.
PH: 44 171 6374518
FX: 44 171 6291869
Description: Graduates of North American schools of dentistry who practice in Europe. Seeks the interchange of dental information and the advancement of the profession. Offers scholarship for European dentists to study in the United States. **Founded:** 1873. **Membership:** 250. Multinational. **Languages:** English. **Budget:** $40,000.

AMERICAN DIABETES ASSOCIATION (ADA)
url: http://www.diabetes.org
1660 Duke St.
Alexandria, VA 22314
John H. Graham, IV, CEO
PH: (703)549-1500
TF: 800ADA-DISC
FX: (703)836-7439
Description: Physicians, laypersons, and health professionals interested in diabetes mellitus. Promotes research, information and advocacy to find a prevention and cure for diabetes and to improve the lives of all people with diabetes. Promotes public awareness of diabetes as a serious disease. Conducts educational programs and provides information to people with diabetes and the health professionals who care for them. Administers research grants. **Founded:** 1940. **Membership:** 280000. **Staff:** 829. **Local Groups:** 800. **Languages:** English, Spanish. **Budget:** $88,000,000.

AMERICAN DIOPTER AND DECIBEL SOCIETY (ADDS)
3518 5th Ave.
Pittsburgh, PA 15213
Albert W. Biglan, M.D., Exec.Dir.
PH: (412)682-6300
FX: (412)682-8137
Description: Physicians who specialize in ophthalmology (the eye and its diseases), otolaryngology (the ear and throat and their diseases), rhinology (the nose and its diseases), or allied sciences. Devotes any available income in excess of cost of operation or other resources to research and educational projects. **Founded:** 1960. **Membership:** 200. **Languages:** English.

AMERICAN ENDODONTIC SOCIETY (AES)
1440 N. Harbor Blvd., Ste. 719
Fullerton, CA 92635
Dr. Ramon Werts, Exec.Dir.
PH: (714)870-5590
Description: Dentists united topromote and provide educational and scientific information on simplified root canal therapy for the general practitioner. Conducts research programs. **Founded:** 1969. **Membership:** 10000. **Staff:** 2. **Languages:** English. **Publication:** *American Endodontic Society Newsletter*, quarterly. Contains society news, member profiles, and instructional articles ▪ *Hotline*, periodic.

AMERICAN EPILEPSY SOCIETY (AES)
e-mail: info@aesnet.org
url: http://www.aesnet.org
638 Prospect Ave.
Hartford, CT 06105-4240
Suzanne C. Berry, CAE
PH: (860)586-7505
FX: (860)586-7550
Description: Clinicians, scientists investigating basic and clinical aspects of epilepsy, and related professional workers with an active interest in seizure disorders. Seeks to promote interdisciplinary communication, scientific investigation and exchange of clinical information about epilepsy. **Founded:** 1946. **Membership:** 1898. **Staff:** 500. Multinational. **Languages:** English. **Budget:** $500,000. **Publication:** *Epilepsia*, monthly. Journal. Published in conjunction with the International League Against Epilepsy. Price: included in membership fee. Advertising: accepted. **Formerly:** (1959) American League Against Epilepsy.

AMERICAN EQUILIBRATION SOCIETY (AES)
url: http://www.prosthodontics.org/aes
8726 N. Ferris Ave.
Morton Grove, IL 60053
Mr. Shel Marcus, Office Dir.
PH: (847)965-2888
FX: (847)965-4888
Description: Dentists, orthodontists, oral surgeons, and physicians interested in study and proficiency in the diagnosis and treatment of occlusal and temporomandibular joint disorders. Bestows Student Recognition Certificates annually to outstanding graduating students. **Founded:** 1955. **Membership:** 1100. **Languages:** English. **Budget:** $75,000. **Publication:** *American Equilibration Society Newsletter*, 3/year. Price: included in membership dues. Advertising: not accepted ■ *Roster*, annual ■ *TMJ Update*, bimonthly. Price: included in membership dues. Advertising: not accepted.

AMERICAN FEDERATION FOR MEDICAL RESEARCH
e-mail: afmr@dc.sba.com
url: http://www.afmr.org
1200 19th St. NW, Ste. 300
Washington, DC 20036
Pat McFadden, Contact
PH: (202)429-5161
FX: (202)223-4579
Description: Provides a forum for young clinical scientists (under 43); promotes and encourages original research in clinical and laboratory medicine. Offers specialized education program; maintains information services on membership status, files, and National Abstracting Processing. Annual scientific program presents sections on: Cardiovascular; Dermatology; Endocrinology; Gastroenterology; Genetics; Hematology; Immunology and Connective Tissue; Infectious Disease; Metabolism; Neoplastic Disease; Patient Care; Pulmonary; Renal and Electrolytes. **Founded:** 1940. **Membership:** 6000. **Staff:** 3. **Local Groups:** 19. **Languages:** English. **Budget:** $1,300,000. Formerly (1998) American Federation for Clinical Research.

AMERICAN INTERNATIONAL HEALTH ALLIANCE (AIHA)
e-mail: aiha@aiha.com
1212 New York Ave. NW, Ste. 825
Washington, DC 20005
James Smith, Exec.Dir.
PH: (202)789-1136
FX: (202)789-1277
Description: Institutional health care providers. Promotes increased availability of health care services in previously underserved areas worldwide. Creates partnerships between hospitals in the United States and their counterparts abroad to facilitate sharing of technology and expertise; sponsors educational programs; serves as a clearinghouse on international health issues and emerging medical technologies and practices. **Founded:** 1992. Multinational. **Languages:** English.

AMERICAN FORENSIC ASSOCIATION (AFA)
e-mail: James.W.Pratt@uwrf.edu
Box 256
River Falls, WI 54022
James W. Pratt, Exec.Sec.
PH: (715)425-3198
TF: 800228-5424
FX: (715)425-9533
Description: High school and college directors of forensics and debate coaches. Promotes debate and other speech activities. Sponsors annual collegiate National Individual Events Tournament and National Debate Tournament; sells debate ballots; makes studies of professional standards and debate budgets. Supports research grants. **Founded:** 1949. **Membership:** 900. Multinational. **Regional Groups:** 4. **Languages:** English.

AMERICAN FOUNDATION FOR ALTERNATIVE HEALTH CARE, RESEARCH AND DEVELOPMENT (AFAHCRD)
25 Landfield Ave.
Monticello, NY 12701
Edwin M. Field, Exec.Dir.
PH: (914)794-8181
FX: (914)794-5861
Description: Serves as an alternative health care information resource center. Compiles data. **Founded:** 1978. **Languages:** English. **Budget:** $50,000. **Formerly:** (1985) American Foundation for Alternative Health Care.

AMERICAN FOUNDATION FOR HEALTH (AFH)
2107 Dwight Way
Berkeley, CA 94704
Dr. Ken Matsumura, Exec.Dir.
PH: (510)644-3366
Description: Individuals interested in improving the delivery of health care services. Encourages recording of personal medical data. Conducts educational research projects and activities. **Founded:** 1979. **Membership:** 17000. **Staff:** 18. **Languages:** English. **Publication:** *Health Features*, periodic. Newsletter.

AMERICAN FOUNDATION FOR HEALTH CARE REFORM
712 W. Broad St., Ste. B2
Falls Church, VA 22046-3222
William Shaker, Pres.
PH: (703)908-9220
FX: (703)908-9467
Description: Provides financial support to medical research projects aimed at improving healthcare in the U.S. Has supported cancer research projects at George Washington University in Washington, DC. **Founded:** 1980. **Staff:** 2. **Languages:** English. **Publication:** *Heart to Heart*, periodic. Newsletter. **Formerly:** Heart to Heart Foundation.

AMERICAN FOUNDATION FOR MATERNAL AND CHILD HEALTH (AFMCH)
439 E. 51st St., 4th Fl.
New York, NY 10022
Doris Haire, Pres.
PH: (212)759-5510
FX: (212)935-0191
Description: Serves as a clearinghouse for interdisciplinary research on maternal and child health; focuses on the perinatal or birth period and its effect on infant development. Sponsors medical research designed to improve application of technology in maternal and child health; conducts educational programs; compiles statistics. Operates extensive reference library. **Founded:** 1972. **Staff:** 1. **Languages:** English.

AMERICAN FOUNDATION OF TRADITIONAL CHINESE MEDICINE (AFTCM)
505 Beach St.
San Francisco, CA 94133
Barbara Bernie, Pres., Chrm. and CEO
PH: (415)776-0502
FX: (415)776-9053

Description: Practitioners and individuals interested in contributing to the advancement of traditional Chinese medicine for the improvement of health care. (Traditional Chinese medicine is a holistic form of medicine that offers additional insights into how the human body functions relative to the disease process. Diagnosis is obtained by taking 6 wrist pulses, one for each major organ of the body; the abnormal pulse indicates the organ affected. Treatment is administered by treating the causes instead of the symptoms. Forms of treatment include acupuncture, herbs, exercise and diet regulation.) Seeks to: encourage the use of Eastern and Western medicine in hospitals and clinics providing more treatment options for patients; improve standards and regulations of the profession; increase communication between East and West for cooperative research. Offers masters' teaching workshops and continuing education courses for practitioners in techniques, theory, and methods; provides referral service. Maintains clinic for administering traditional Chinese medicine. Is currently working to establish an International Health Center that will bring medical experts of different backgrounds together for exchange of information and exploration of complementary forms of medical treatment. **Founded:** 1982. **Staff:** 4. **Languages:** English. **Publication:** *Gateways*, quarterly. Newsletter. Includes developments in traditional Chinese medical research. Price: included in membership dues; $3.00/copy for nonmembers. Advertising: accepted. **Formerly:** (1992) International Health Center.

AMERICAN GUILD OF PATIENT ACCOUNT MANAGEMENT (AGPAM)
1200 19th St., NW, Ste. 300
Washington, DC 20036-2401
PH: (202)857-1100
Description: Business offices, credit and collection managers, and admitting officers for hospitals, clinics, and other health care organizations. To educate members, exchange information and techniques, and keep members abreast of new regulations relating to their field. Seeks proper recognition for the financial aspect of hospital and clinic management. Offers certification program. Administers examinations in April and October for qualification as Certified Patient Account Manager (CPAM) and Certified Clinic Account Manager (CCAM). Maintains placement services; sponsors seminars and workshops on a local, regional, and national level. Operates speakers' bureau. **Founded:** 1968. **Membership:** 4000. **Languages:** English. **Budget:** $250,000. **Publication:** *Journal of Patient Account Management*, 8/year. Lists employment opportunities; includes annual membership list. Price: included in membership dues; $30.00/year for nonmembers. Circulation: 4,500. Advertising: not accepted. **Formerly:** (1981) American Guild of Patient Account Managers.

AMERICAN GYNECOLOGICAL AND OBSTETRICAL SOCIETY (AGOS)
50 North Medical Dr.
Salt Lake City, UT 84132
Paul B. Underwood, Jr., Sec.
PH: (801)581-5501
FX: (801)581-7199
Description: Works to cultivate and promote knowledge concerning obstetrics and gynecology. **Founded:** 1981. **Membership:** 243. **Staff:** 1. **Languages:** English. Formed by Merger of American Gynecological Society; American Association of Obstetricians and Gynecologists.

AMERICAN HAIR LOSS COUNCIL (AHLC)
url: http://www.ahlc.org
401 N. Michigan Ave., 22nd Fl.
Chicago, IL 60611-4212
Russell Bodnar, Exec.Dir.
PH: (312)321-5128
FX: (312)245-1080
Description: Dermatologists, plastic surgeons, cosmetologists, barbers, and interested others. Provides nonbiased information regarding treatments for hair loss in both men and women. Facilitates communication and information exchange between professionals in different areas of specialization. Conducts educational

programs; compiles statistics. **Founded:** 1985. **Membership:** 420. **Staff:** 2. **Languages:** English. **Budget:** $200,000.

AMERICAN HEALTH ASSISTANCE FOUNDATION (AHAF)
e-mail: sbarnard@ahaf.org
url: http://www.ahaf.org
15825 Shady Grove Rd., Ste. 140
Rockville, MD 20850
Eugene H. Michaels, Pres.
PH: (301)948-3244
TF: 800437-2423
FX: (301)258-9454
Description: Established to support medical research. Four programs within the foundation are Alzheimer's Family Relief Program, Coronary Heart Disease Research, National Glaucoma Research, and Alzheimer's Disease Research. **Founded:** 1973. **Staff:** 22. **Languages:** English. **Publication:** *Alzheimer's Research Review*, quarterly. Newsletter. Updates the work of Alzheimer's disease researchers. Provides tips for families with members who have the disease.

AMERICAN HEALTH CARE ADVISORY ASSOCIATION (AHCAA)
PO Box 15485
Austin, TX 78761-5485
Nick Keeling, Pres.
Description: Acts as an advisory organization promoting improved health care and reduction in medical costs. Gathers information concerning medical and insurance costs. **Founded:** 1982. **Membership:** 25000. **Languages:** English. **Publication:** *Vitality Health Gram*, quarterly.

AMERICAN HEALTH CARE ASSOCIATION (AHCA)
1201 L St. NW
Washington, DC 20005
Dr. Paul R. Willging, Exec.VP
PH: (202)842-4444
FX: (202)842-3860
Description: Federation of state associations of long-term health care facilities. Promotes standards for professionals in long-term health care delivery and quality care for patients and residents in a safe environment. Focuses on issues of availability, quality, affordability, and fair payment. Operates as liaison with governmental agencies, Congress, and professional associations. Compiles statistics. **Founded:** 1949. **Membership:** 11000. **Staff:** 67. **State Groups:** 51. **Languages:** English. **Budget:** $9,000,000. **Publication:** *AHCA Notes*, monthly. Newsletter. Covers legislation and regulations. Price: included in membership dues ■ *Provider: For Long Term Care Professionals*, monthly. Magazine. Includes buyers' guide, news reports, advertisers' index, a listing of new products and services, and calendar of events. Price: free to long-term health care professionals; $48.00/year for nonmembers and libraries. ISSN: 0360-4069. Circulation: 24,000. Advertising: accepted. Alternate Formats: microform ■ *Thinking About a Nursing Home?* ■ *Welcome to Our Nursing Home* ■ Manuals. **Absorbed:** (1984) National Council of Health Centers. **Formed by Merger of:** American Association of Nursing Homes; National Association of Registered Nursing Homes. **Formerly:** (1975) American Nursing Home Association.

AMERICAN HEALTH DECISIONS (AHD)
1445 Market St., Ste. 380
Denver, CO 80202
Judy Hutchison, M.A., Exec.Off.
PH: (303)820-5635
FX: (303)534-8774
Description: Confederation of state health programs. Assists in establishing public education programs about health care and policy; works to increase availability of quality medical care. Promotes personal autonomy on ethical issues, such as patients making the decision to refuse or accept treatment. Addresses problems arising from ethical conflicts over new medical technologies and disease prevention. Maintains research and educational pro-

grams; disseminates information. **Founded:** 1989. **Membership:** 21. **Languages:** English.

AMERICAN HEALTH FOUNDATION (AHF)
320 E. 43rd St.
New York, NY 10017
Dr. Ernst Wynder, Pres
PH: (212)953-1900
FX: (212)687-2339
Description: Devoted to promoting preventive medicine, emphasizing four major fields: research (nutrition, environmental carcinogenesis, molecular biology, experimental pathology, and epidemiology); clinical research and service for children (through screening and intervention); public health action (educating laymen and medical and government personnel in the principles of preventive medicine); health economics research (investigating direct and indirect costs of major diseases and comparing them with preventive approaches). Maintains Naylor Dana Institute for Disease Prevention and the Child Health Center in Valhalla, NY and The Mahoney Institute for Health Promotion Research in New York City. **Founded:** 1969. **Staff:** 200. **Languages:** English. **Budget:** $15,000,000. **Publication:** *Preventive Medicine,* bimonthly. Journal. Contains scientific, preventive medicine and public health information. Price: $264.00 institutional subscription; $132.00 personal subscription. ISSN: 0091-7435. Circulation: 1,450. Advertising: accepted. **Formerly:** (1968) Environmental Health Foundation.

AMERICAN HEALTH INFORMATION MANAGEMENT ASSOCIATION (AMRA)
url: http://www.ahima.org
919 N. Michigan Ave., Ste. 1400
Chicago, IL 60611
Linda Kloss, Exec.Dir.
PH: (312)787-2672
FX: (312)787-9793
Description: Registered record administrators; accredited record technicians with expertise in health information management, biostatistics, classification systems, and systems analysis. Sponsors Independent Study Programs in Medical Record Technology and coding. Conducts annual qualification examinations to credential medical record personnel as Registered Record Administrators (RRA), Accredited Record Technicians (ART) and Certified Coding Specialists (CCS). Maintains Foundation of Research and Education Library, Scholarships and loans. **Founded:** 1928. **Membership:** 35000. **Staff:** 70. **State Groups:** 52. **Languages:** English. **Budget:** $6,000,000. **Publication:** *From the Couch: Official Newsletter of the Mental Health Record Section of the American Medical Record Association,* quarterly. Price: included in membership dues. Circulation: 800. Advertising: not accepted ■ *The Gavel: AMRA State Presidents' Newsletter,* quarterly. Price: included in membership dues. Advertising: not accepted ■ *Journal of AHIMA,* 10/year. Price: $72.00. ISSN: 1060-5487. Circulation: 35,000. Advertising: accepted ■ *Journal of AMRA: America's Health Information Leaders,* monthly. Contains articles on the theory, practice, and current issues in health information management. Includes book reviews and calendar of events. Price: included in membership dues; $45.00/year for nonmembers. ISSN: 0273-9976. Circulation: 31,000. Advertising: accepted. Alternate Formats: microform ■ *Medical Record Educator,* quarterly. Newsletter. Provides association and academic news; includes reading list. Price: $15.00/year. Circulation: 200. Advertising: not accepted ■ *QA Section Connection,* bimonthly. Newsletter. Provides educational information on the management and methodology of health care quality assurance programs. Includes annual subject index. Price: included in membership dues. Circulation: 3,000. Advertising: not accepted ■ *Spectrum,* quarterly. Newsletter. Price: included in membership dues. Circulation: 1,400. Advertising: not accepted. **Formerly:** (1928) American Association of Medical Record Librarians; (1938) Association of Record Librarians of North America; (1991) American Medical Records Association.

AMERICAN HEALTH LAWYERS ASSOCIATION (AHLA)
e-mail: info@healthlawyers.org
url: http://www.healthlawyers.org
1120 Connecticut Ave. NW, Ste. 950
Washington, DC 20036-3902
Marietta Gaden, Dir.
PH: (202)833-1100
FX: (202)833-1105
Description: Attorneys who represent or are employees of hospitals or other health organizations. Works to disseminate information on health care law and legislation; keep members abreast of court decisions in the health care field; conduct legal seminars and institutes. Maintains a collection of leading decisions in health law, model agreements, and memoranda. **Founded:** 1968. **Membership:** 3300. **Staff:** 7. **Languages:** English. **Budget:** $1,500,000. **Publication:** *Journal of Health and Hospital Law,* quarterly. Covers current healthcare issues and cases and their impact on the health care arena. Price: $150.00/year. Advertising: not accepted ■ *Membership Roster,* annual ■ *Reporter,* bimonthly. Newsletter. Price: free to members. Advertising: not accepted. **Formerly:** (1971) Society of Hospital Attorneys; (1984) American Society of Hospital Attorneys; (1995) American Academy of Hospital Attorneys; (1998) American Academy of Healthcare Attorneys.

AMERICAN HEALTH PLANNING ASSOCIATION (AHPA)
e-mail: hsann@aol.com
7245 Arlington Blvd., Ste. 300
Falls Church, VA 22042
Dean Montgomery, Contact
PH: (703)573-3103
FX: (703)573-1276
Description: State and local health planning agencies and affiliated organizations and individuals. Conducts research; disseminates information; serves as clearinghouse for health planning activities and concepts; sponsors programs of technical assistance; provides continuing education. **Founded:** 1970. **Languages:** English. **Publication:** *National Directory of Health Planning, Policy, and Regulatory Agencies,* annual. Price: $125.00 ■ *TODAY in Health Planning,* quarterly. **Formerly:** (1977) American Association for Comprehensive Health Planning.

AMERICAN HEALTHCARE RADIOLOGY ADMINISTRATORS (AHRA)
e-mail: info@ahraonline.org
url: http://ahraonline.org
PO Box 334
Sudbury, MA 01776
Mary S. Reitter, Exec.Dir.
PH: (978)443-7591
TF: 800443-AHRA
FX: (978)443-8046
Description: Radiology and healthcare managers. Works to improve management of radiology departments in hospitals, physician practices, and other health care facilities; to provide a forum for publication of educational, scientific, and professional materials. Has established code of ethics for the profession. Provides liaison between related organizations such as radiology, health care and management groups, and government agencies. Compiles statistics; conducts specialized education programs. **Founded:** 1973. **Membership:** 3900. **Staff:** 7. Multinational. **Languages:** English. **Budget:** $2,400,000. **Publication:** *Link,* monthly. Newsletter. Price: for members. Circulation: 4,000. Advertising: accepted. Also Cited As: *AHRA Link* ■ *Radiology Management,* bimonthly. Advertising: accepted ■ Membership Directory, annual. **Formerly:** (1986) American Hospital Radiology Administrators.

AMERICAN HEART ASSOCIATION (AHA)
url: http://www.americanheart.org
7272 Greenville Ave.
Dallas, TX 75231-4596
M. Cass Wheeler, CEO

PH: (214)373-6300
TF: 800242-1793
FX: (214)987-4334
Description: Physicians, scientists, and laypersons. Supports research, education, and community service programs with the objective of reducing premature death and disability from cardiovascular diseases and stroke; coordinates the efforts of physicians, nurses, health professionals, and others engaged in the fight against heart and circulatory disease. Financed entirely by voluntary contributions of the public, principally during the Heart Campaign held in February. **Founded:** 1924. **Membership:** 26000. **Staff:** 392. **State Groups:** 56. **Languages:** English. **Budget:** $000,000. Absorbed (1983) Intersociety Commission for Heart Disease Resources; (1993) Courage Stroke Network.

AMERICAN INSTITUTE OF ORAL BIOLOGY (AIOB)
PO Box 7184
Loma Linda, CA 92354-7184
June J. Barrientos, Exec.Sec.
PH: (909)824-4671
FX: (909)478-4285
Description: Dental and medical health professionals united for continuing education. Conducts lectures. **Founded:** 1943. **Membership:** 150. **Staff:** 1. **Languages:** English. **Publication:** *AIOB Proceedings Manual*, annual. Price: $75.00. ISSN: 0098-6119. Advertising: not accepted.

AMERICAN-ISRAELI OPHTHALMOLOGICAL SOCIETY
130 E. 67th St., Ste. 1C
New York, NY 10021-6136
B. Rubin, Sec./Contact
PH: (212)879-6824
FX: (212)734-2682
Description: Ophthalmologists. Seeks to facilitate communication between American and Israeli ophthalmologists. Provides training for Israeli opthalmologists in the United States. Organizes conventions. **Founded:** 1974. **Membership:** 450. Multinational. **Languages:** English.

AMERICAN JUVENILE ARTHRITIS ORGANIZATION (AJAO)
1330 W. Peachtree St.
Atlanta, GA 30309
Janet Austin, PhD., Contact
PH: (404)872-7100
TF: 800283-7800
FX: (404)872-9559
Description: Parents, health care professionals, and others interested in the problems of juvenile arthritis. Serves as advocate for the needs of those affected by juvenile arthritis. A council of the Arthritis Foundation. **Founded:** 1980. **Membership:** 2500. **Staff:** 3. **Languages:** English.

AMERICAN LEBANESE MEDICAL ASSOCIATION (ALMA)
e-mail: jjabre@bu.edu
url: http://med-www.bu.edu/ALMA/lebanon
65 Arlington Rd.
Woburn, MA 01801
Joe F. Jabre, M.D., Contact
PH: (617)937-3071
FX: (617)937-3081
Description: Health care professionals with Lebanese heritage, or with and interest in providing assistance to the people of Lebanon. Promotes increased access to improved health care for all religious and cultural communities in Lebanon. Fosters development of medical education institutions and health care facilities in Lebanon. Gathers and distributes Lebanese medical and scientific publications; conducts continuing professional education programs for members. Plans to operate library in conjunction with the Lebanese Medical Association. **Founded:** 1994. **Languages:** English.

AMERICAN LICENSED PRACTICAL NURSES ASSOCIATION (ALPNA)
1090 Vermont Ave. NW, Ste. 1200
Washington, DC 20005
Paul M. Tendler, Exec.Dir.
PH: (202)682-9000
Description: Licensed practical nurses. Promotes the practical nursing profession; lobbies and maintains relations with the government on issues and legislation that may have an impact on LPNs. Conducts continuing education classes. Facilitates discussion of issues affecting the nursing and health professions. **Founded:** 1984. **Membership:** 6200. **Languages:** English. **Budget:** $150,000.

AMERICAN LYME DISEASE FOUNDATION (ALDF)
url: http://www.aldf.com
Mill Pond Offices
293 Rte. 100, Ste. 204
Somers, NY 10589
David L. Weld
PH: (914)277-6970
TF: 800876-LYME
FX: (914)277-6974
Description: Health care professionals and other individuals with an interest in Lyme Disease, a disorder transmitted to humans by the deer tick. Works to control the spread of Lyme Disease, and to improve treatments for the disorder. Maintains physician referral service; produces educational materials and conducts public and professional education programs; supports Lyme Disease research. **Founded:** 1990. **Staff:** 7. **Languages:** English. **Budget:** $850,000.

AMERICAN MANAGED BEHAVIORAL HEALTHCARE ASSOCIATION (AMBHA)
url: http://www.ambha.org
700 13th St. NW, Ste. 950
Washington, DC 20005
E. Clarke Ross, D.P.A., Exec.Dir.
PH: (202)434-4565
FX: (202)434-4564
Description: Managed behavioral healthcare organizations. Works to advance the value of managed behavioral healthcare and promotes the inclusion of mental illnesses and addiction disorders in benefit coverage. **Founded:** 1994. **Membership:** 12. **Staff:** 2. **Budget:** $400,000.

AMERICAN MEDICAL ASSOCIATION (AMA)
url: http://www.ama-assn.org/
515 N. State St.
Chicago, IL 60610
John Seward, Exec.VP
PH: (312)464-5000
FX: (312)464-5830
Description: County medical societies and physicians. Disseminates scientific information to members and the public. Informs members on significant medical and health legislation on state and national levels and represents the profession before Congress and governmental agencies. Cooperates in setting standards for medical schools, hospitals, residency programs, and continuing medical education courses. Offers physician placement service and counseling on practice management problems. Operates library which lends material and provides specific medical information to physicians. Ad-hoc committees are formed for such topics as health care planning and principles of medical ethics. **Founded:** 1847. **Membership:** 297000. **State Groups:** 54. **Languages:** English. **Publication:** *American Medical News*, weekly. Newspaper. Covers news and opinions on key issues of political, social, and economic significance concerning the practice and delivery of medical care. Price: included in membership dues; $99.00/year for nonmembers; $49.50/year for medical students, interns, and residents. Circulation: 362,200 ▪ *Archives of Dermatology*, monthly. Journal. Oriented to the dermatologic clinician. Includes book reviews, employment opportunity listings, annual index, and index of advertisers. Price: $67.50/year for

members; $135.00/year for nonmembers; $67.50/year for residents and medical students. ISSN: 0003-987X. Circulation: 14,000. Advertising: accepted. Alternate Formats: online ▪ *Archives of Family Medicine*, monthly. Oriented to physicians in family and general practice. Price: $47.50 for members; $95.00 for nonmembers. Circulation: 83,000. Advertising: accepted ▪ *Archives of General Psychiatry*, monthly. Journal. Oriented toward the psychiatric clinician. Includes employment opportunity listings, book reviews, annual index, and index of advertisers. Price: $47.50/year for members; $95.00/year for nonmembers; $47.50/year for residents and medical students. ISSN: 0003-990X. Circulation: 27,500. Advertising: accepted. Alternate Formats: microform; online ▪ *Archives of Internal Medicine*, semimonthly. Journal. Oriented toward physicians in internal medicine. Includes employment opportunity listings, annual index, and index of advertisers. Price: $57.50/year for members; $115.00/year for nonmembers; $57.50/year for residents and medical students. ISSN: 0003-9926. Circulation: 87,000. Advertising: accepted. Alternate Formats: microform; online ▪ *Archives of Neurology*, monthly. Journal. Oriented toward the neurologic clinician. Includes employment opportunity listings, annual index, and index of advertisers. Price: $72.50/year for members; $145.00/year for nonmembers; $72.50/year for residents and medical students. ISSN: 0003-9942. Circulation: 12,500. Advertising: accepted. Alternate Formats: microform; online ▪ *Archives of Ophthalmology*, monthly. Journal. Includes employment opportunity listings, case reports, book reviews, annual index, and index of advertisers. Price: $55.00/year for members; $110.00/year for nonmembers; $55.00/year for residents and medical students. ISSN: 0003-9950. Circulation: 20,000. Advertising: accepted. Alternate Formats: microform; online ▪ *Archives of Otolaryngology – Head and Neck Surgery*, monthly. Journal. Oriented toward the otolaryngolic clinician. Includes employment opportunity listings, annual index, and index of advertisers. Price: $62.50/year for members; $125.00/year for nonmembers; $62.50/year for residents and medical students. ISSN: 0886-4470. Circulation: 12,000. Advertising: accepted. Alternate Formats: microform; online ▪ *Archives of Pediatrics & Adolescent Medicine*, monthly. Journal. Oriented toward the pediatric clinician. Includes book reviews, employment opportunity listings, annual index, and index of advertisers. Price: $50.00/year for members; $100.00/year for nonmembers; $50.00/year for residents and medical students. ISSN: 1072-4710. Circulation: 35,000. Advertising: accepted. Alternate Formats: microform; online. Also Cited As: *American Journal of Diseases of Children* ▪ *Archives of Surgery*, monthly. Journal. Oriented toward general surgeons. Includes employment opportunity listings, calendar of events, book reviews, index of advertisers, and annual index. Price: $50.00/year for members; $100.00/year for nonmembers; $50.00/year for medical students and residents. ISSN: 0004-0010. Circulation: 24,500. Advertising: accepted. Alternate Formats: microform; online ▪ *Journal of the American Medical Association*, weekly. Covers topics in general medicine; includes employment opportunity listings, book reviews, calendar of events, case reports, and obituaries. Price: included in membership dues; $120.00/year for nonmembers; $60.00/year for medical students and residents. ISSN: 0098-7484. Circulation: 361,000. Advertising: accepted. Alternate Formats: online. **Absorbed:** (1994) American Association of Senior Physicians.

AMERICAN MEDICAL ASSOCIATION ALLIANCE (AMAA)
515 N. State St.
Chicago, IL 60610-0174
Hazel J. Lewis, Exec.Dir.
PH: (312)464-4470
FX: (312)464-5020
Description: Physicians' spouses. Serves as the volunteer arm of the American Medical Association. Promotes the goals of the medical profession and works to meet public health needs. Raises more than $2 million annually for the American Medical Association Education and Research Foundation, which provides assistance to medical schools and students. Sponsors the Shape Up for Life Campaign, a nationwide auxiliary program to promote good health. Maintains Project Bank, an information clearinghouse of community projects initiated by auxiliaries across the country. Implements community health projects on such concerns as child abuse prevention, adolescent health, family violence, AIDS education, seatbelt usage, pre- and postnatal care, drug abuse, suicide prevention, proper nutrition, drunk driving prevention, venereal disease awareness, and services to the aging. Works with the AMA to promote sound health legislation; conducts public education programs, letter-writing campaigns, and personal interviews with legislators involved in health matters. **Founded:** 1922. **Membership:** 70000. **Staff:** 15. **National Groups:** 100. **Languages:** English. **Budget:** $1,500,000. **Publication:** *Facets Magazine*, bimonthly. Includes information on community health projects, public health issues, socioeconomic health care issues, and physician family concerns. Price: included in membership dues; $7.00/year for nonmembers. ISSN: 0163-0512. Circulation: 80,000. Advertising: not accepted ▪ *Horizons Newsletter*, bimonthly. Covers topics of concern to the families of resident physicians and medical students. Price: free to resident physicians and medical students. Circulation: 6,000. Advertising: not accepted ▪ *Newsline*, bimonthly. Includes information on health periodicals and health projects. Price: included in membership dues. Circulation: 8,000. Advertising: not accepted. **Formerly:** (1975) Women's Auxilliary to the American Medical Association; (1993) American Medical Association Auxilliary.

AMERICAN MEDICAL ASSOCIATION EDUCATION AND RESEARCH FOUNDATION (AMA-ERF)
url: http://www.ama-assn.org/med-sci/arf.htm
515 N. State St.
Chicago, IL 60610
P. John Seward, M.D., Exec.VP
PH: (312)464-4543
FX: (312)464-5842
Description: Managed by members of the Board of Trustees of the American Medical Association. Receives and distributes funds to benefit medical education in U.S. medical schools and to support medical research and innovative pilot programs in health care. AMA-ERF funds consist of contributions from physicians, medical societies and auxiliaries, foundations, private industry, and the public. Accepts bequests and other gifts for allocation to various projects in medicine. Convention/Meeting: none. **Founded:** 1962. **Languages:** English. **Formed by Merger of:** American Medical Education Foundation; American Medical Research Foundation.

AMERICAN MEDICAL DIRECTORS ASSOCIATION (AMDA)
url: http://www.amda.com
10480 Little Patuxent Pky., Ste. 760
Columbia, MD 21044
Lorraine Tarnove, Exec.Dir.
PH: (410)740-9743
TF: 800876-AMDA
FX: (410)740-4572
Description: Physicians providing care in long-term facilities including nursing homes. Sponsors continuing medical education in geriatrics and medical administration. Promotes improved long term care. **Founded:** 1975. **Membership:** 5900. **Staff:** 12. **State Groups:** 35. **Languages:** English. **Budget:** $1,500,000.

AMERICAN MEDICAL GROUP ASSOCIATION (AMGA)
e-mail: amga@va.amga.org
url: http://www.amga.org
1422 Duke St.
Alexandria, VA 22314-3430
Dr. Donald W. Fisher, CEO
PH: (703)838-0033
FX: (703)548-1890
Description: Trade association for group practice integrate a delivery systems and IPAS representing more than 45,000 physicians. Fosters accreditation of medical clinics; compiles statistics on group practice; sponsors research, patient education, insurance programs, and capitation management assistance. Conducts symposia; makes available consulting services. **Founded:** 1949. **Membership:** 250. **Staff:** 43. **Languages:** English. **Budget:** $5,000,000. **Publication:** *American Medical Group Associa-*

tion–*Executive News Service*, 22/year. Newsletter. Covers federal health care legislation and regulations affecting physician and hospital reimbursement under Medicare. Price: included in membership dues. Circulation: 1,600. Advertising: not accepted ∎ *Executive News Service*, biweekly. Price: available to members only ∎ *Group Practice Journal*, bimonthly. Covers market trends, health care policy and legislation, and management topics affecting the medical profession. Includes advertiser index. Price: included in membership dues; $65.00/year for nonmembers. ISSN: 0199-5103. Circulation: 47,000. Advertising: accepted ∎ *Quality Source*, quarterly. Covers quality measurement and outcomes information. Price: included in membership dues ∎ Books. Topics include administration and operation of clinics ∎ Directory, annual. Price: $225.00/year. Advertising: accepted. **Formerly:** American Group Practice Association; (1974) American Association of Medical Clinics.

AMERICAN MEDICAL NETWORK
url: http://www.wncguide.com/hend_co/oma/
PO Box 604
Hendersonville, NC 28793
Description: Practicing physicians. Represents doctors' concerns for their patients; establishes a national quality database for use in negotiating managed care contracts; educates laymen and policy makers on quality of care issues; and influences health care policy. **Founded:** 1996.

AMERICAN MEDICAL STUDENT ASSOCIATION (AMSA)
url: http://www.amsa.org
1902 Association Dr.
Reston, VA 22091
Paul R. Wright, Exec.Dir.
PH: (703)620-6600
TF: 800767-2266
FX: (703)620-5873
Description: Medical students; local, state, and national organizations; premedical students, interns, and residents. Seeks to improve medical education by making it relevant to today's needs and by making the process by which physicians are trained more humanistic. Contributes to the improvement of health care of all people; involves its members in the social, moral, and ethical obligations of the profession of medicine. Serves as a mechanism through which students may actively participate in the fields of community health through various student health programs. Addresses political issues relating to the nation's health care delivery system and other medical and health issues. Offers specialized education and placement services; conducts research; operates speakers' bureau. Maintains standing committees and interest groups which publish newsletters, organize educational workshops, and initiate special projects. **Founded:** 1950. **Membership:** 30000. **Staff:** 30. **Local Groups:** 140. **Languages:** English. **Budget:** $2,500,000. **Publication:** *The New Physician*, 9/year. Magazine. Price: included in membership dues; $25.00/year. Circulation: 28,000. Advertising: accepted. **Formerly:** (1975) Student American Medical Association.

AMERICAN MEDICAL TECHNOLOGISTS (AMT)
e-mail: amtmail@aol.com
710 Higgins Rd.
Park Ridge, IL 60068
Gerard P. Boe, Ph.D., Exec.Dir.
PH: (847)823-5169
TF: 800275-1268
FX: (847)823-0458
Description: National professional registry of medical laboratory technologists, technicians, medical assistants, dental assistants, and phlebotomists. Maintains job information service. Sponsors AMT Institute for Education, which has developed continuing education programs. **Founded:** 1939. **Membership:** 25000. **Staff:** 19. **State Groups:** 38. **Languages:** English. **Publication:** *AMT Events and Continuing Education Supplement*, 6/yr. Journal. Includes book reviews and legislative updates. Price: included in membership dues; $35.00/year for nonmembers in the U.S.; $45.00/year for foreign nonmembers. ISSN: 0746-9217. Circula-

tion: 25,000. Advertising: accepted. Alternate Formats: microform ∎ *AMT Newsletter*, 3/year. Contains societal news and information.

AMERICAN MEDICAL WOMEN'S ASSOCIATION (AMWA)
url: http://amwa-doc.org
801 N. Fairfax St., Ste. 400
Alexandria, VA 22314
Eileen McGrath, Exec.Dir.
PH: (703)838-0500
FX: (703)549-3864
Description: Women holding a M.D. or D.O. degree from approved medical colleges; women interns, residents, and medical students. Promotes women's health issues in medical education and public policy. Seeks to find solutions to problems common to women studying or practicing medicine, such as career advancement and the integration of professional and family responsibilities. Provides student members with educational loans and personal counseling. Sponsors continuing medical education programs. **Founded:** 1915. **Membership:** 11000. **Staff:** 25. **Local Groups:** 160. **Languages:** English. **Budget:** $1,500,000. **Publication:** *What's Happening in AMWA*, semiannual. Newsletter. Price: included in membership dues. Circulation: 13,000 ∎ Journal, bimonthly ∎ Newsletter, quarterly.

AMERICAN MENTAL HEALTH COUNSELORS ASSOCIATION (AMHCA)
e-mail: amhca@prodigy.net
801 N. Fairfax, Ste. 304
Alexandria, VA 22314
Beth Powell, Dir., Public Policy & Legislation
PH: (703)548-6002
FX: (703)548-5233
Description: Professional counselors employed in mental health services; students. Aims to: deliver quality mental health services to children, youth, adults, families, and organizations; improve the availability and quality of counseling services through licensure and certification, training standards, and consumer advocacy. Supports specialty and special interest networks. Fosters communication among members. A division of the American Counseling Association. **Founded:** 1976. **Membership:** 9800. **Staff:** 4. **Languages:** English. **For-Profit. Budget:** $1,100,000.

AMERICAN MENTAL HEALTH FOUNDATION (AMHF)
1049 5th Ave.
New York, NY 10028-0113
Dr. Valentine W. Zetlin, Pres.
PH: (212)737-9027
Description: Dedicated to extensive and intensive research in the theories and techniques of treatment of emotional illness, and to the implementation of reforms in the mental health system. Efforts have resulted in development of better and less expensive treatment methods. Findings are disseminated in English and other major languages. Is currently engaged in a long-term research project to determine which approaches hold hope for improvements in prevention, treatment, and mental health policy. **Founded:** 1924. **Languages:** English.

AMERICAN NEUROLOGICAL ASSOCIATION (ANA)
5841 Cedar Lake Rd. S., Ste. 204
Minneapolis, MN 55416-1491
Linda J. Wilkenson, Exec.Dir.
PH: (612)545-6284
FX: (612)545-6073
Description: Physicians and scientists interested in the form, functioning, and disorders of the nervous system. Conducts research programs. **Founded:** 1875. **Membership:** 960. **Staff:** 2. **Languages:** English. **Budget:** $400,000. **Publication:** *Annals of Neurology*, monthly. Journal. Includes book reviews. Price: included in membership dues; $68.00/year for nonmembers; $84.00/year for institutions; $52.50/year for students. Advertising: accepted.

AMERICAN NEUROPSYCHIATRIC ASSOCIATION (ANA)
PO Box CN10018001
New Hope, PA 18938
Pat Arnold, Account Exec.
Description: Conducts educational and research programs.
Founded: 1987. **Membership:** 425. **Staff:** 1. Multinational. **Languages:** English. **Budget:** $40,000.

AMERICAN NURSES ASSOCIATION (ANA)
url: http://www.nursingworld.org
600 Maryland Ave. SW, Ste. 100 W.
Washington, DC 20024-2571
Beverly L. Malone, PhD,RN, Pres.
PH: (202)651-7000
TF: 800637-0323
FX: (202)651-7001
Description: Member associations representing registered nurses. Sponsors American Nurses Foundation (for research), American Academy of Nursing, Center for Ethics and Human Rights, International Nursing Center, Ethnic/Racial Minority Fellowship Programs, and American Nurses Credentialing Center. Maintains hall of fame. **Founded:** 1896. **Membership:** 210000. **Staff:** 175. **Local Groups:** 860. **Languages:** English. **Budget:** $17,000,000 Formerly (1911) Nurses Associated Alumnae of United States and Canada.

AMERICAN NURSES IN BUSINESS ASSOCIATION (ANBA)
6671 SW Fwy
Houston, TX 77074-2212
Sharon Mathis, Pres. & CEO
PH: (713)771-5016
Description: Nursing students, companies, self-employed nurses, registered nurses, and licensed vocational nurses. Serves as support group for nurses interested in seeking business opportunities. Provides business-related information. Sponsors speakers' bureau; offers placement service. **Founded:** 1992. **Membership:** 30. **Staff:** 1. **Local Groups:** 2. **Languages:** English.

AMERICAN NURSES' FOUNDATION (ANF)
e-mail: anf@ana.org
url: http://www.nursingworld.org/anf
600 Maryland Ave. SW, Ste. 100W
Washington, DC 20024-2571
Geraldine Marullo, MSN RN, Exec. Dir.
PH: (202)651-7227
FX: (202)488-8461
Description: Board of trustees elected by the board of directors of the American Nurses' Association. Provides continuing education opportunities. Sponsors demonstration projects, research, and other programs for nurses to enhance health care delivery. **Founded:** 1955. **Staff:** 7. **Languages:** English.

AMERICAN OPHTHALMOLOGICAL SOCIETY (AOS)
e-mail: ander011@mc.duke.edu
PO Box 19340
San Francisco, CA 94119-3940
W. Banks Anderson, M.D., Exec. Officer
PH: (415)561-8578
FX: (919)684-2230
Description: Professional honorary society of physicians specializing in the functions and treatment of the eye. **Founded:** 1864. **Membership:** 225. **Languages:** English.

AMERICAN ORGANIZATION OF NURSE EXECUTIVES (AONE)
One N. Franklin, 34th Fl.
Chicago, IL 60606
Marjorie Beyers, RN, Exec.Dir.
PH: (312)422-2800
FX: (312)422-4503
Description: Provides leadership, professional development, advocacy, and research to advance nursing practice and patient care, promote nursing leadership and excellence, and shape healthcare public policy. Supports and enhances the manage-

ment, leadership, educational, and professional development of nursing leaders. Offers placement service through Career Development and Referral Center. **Founded:** 1967. **Membership:** 6000. **Staff:** 11. **State Groups:** 69. **Languages:** English. **Budget:** $2,700,000. Formerly (1977) American Society for Hospital Nursing Service Administrators; (1984) American Society for Nursing Service Administrators.

AMERICAN ORTHODONTIC SOCIETY (AOS)
11884 Greenville Ave., No. 112
Dallas, TX 75243-3537
Tom Chapman, Exec.Dir.
PH: (214)234-4000
TF: 800448-1601
FX: (972)234-4290
Description: General and pediatric dentists. Objectives are: to make orthodontic information readily available to any ethical dentist; to zealously protect the right of members to pursue orthodontic knowledge; to keep a watchful eye on third party services and government programs. Offers courses in orthodontic techniques. Conducts educational programs. **Founded:** 1974. **Membership:** 1900. **Staff:** 4. **Languages:** English. **Budget:** $900,000. **Publication:** *American Orthodontic Society Newsletter*, quarterly. Provides information on the society's seminars and conventions and news of interest to members. Price: included in membership dues. Circulation: 4,000. Advertising: not accepted ▪ *American Orthodontic Society Technique Directory*, biennial. Membership Directory. Lists members by city and state; includes the type of orthodontic technique used by listee. Price: $150.00. Advertising: accepted ▪ Brochures.

AMERICAN ORTHOPAEDIC SOCIETY FOR SPORTS MEDICINE (AOSSM)
e-mail: aossm@aossm.org
url: http://www.sportsmed.org
6300 N. River Rd., Ste. 200
Rosemont, IL 60018
Duane Messner, Pres.
PH: (847)292-4900
FX: (847)292-4905
Description: Orthopedic surgeons working in sports medicine; others in related fields involved in the care of athletes. Increases the knowledge and improves care of athletic injuries. Performs educational and research functions; disseminates information. **Founded:** 1972. **Membership:** 1100. **Staff:** 5. **Languages:** English. **Budget:** $1,000,000.

AMERICAN ORTHOPSYCHIATRIC ASSOCIATION (ORTHO)
e-mail: amerortho@aol.com
330 7th Ave., 18th Fl.
New York, NY 10001-3010
Gale Siegel, MSW, Exec.Dir.
PH: (212)564-5930
FX: (212)564-6180
Description: Psychiatrists, psychologis ts, social workers, and educators; psychiatric nurses and lawyers; others in related fields, including anthropology, sociology, and economics. Seeks to unite and provide a common meeting ground for those engaged in the study and treatment of problems of human behavior. Fosters research and disseminates information concerning scientific work in the field of mental health. **Founded:** 1924. **Membership:** 5200. **Staff:** 7. **Languages:** English. **For-Profit. Budget:** $800,000.

AMERICAN ORTHOPTIC COUNCIL (AOC)
3914 Nakoma Rd.
Madison, WI 53711
Leslie France, Adm.Asst.
PH: (608)233-5383
FX: (608)263-4247
Description: Ophthalmologists and orthoptists. Directs practice of orthoptists; determines qualifications of candidates; regulates training and certification of orthoptists; supervises the practice

of orthoptists after certification. **Founded:** 1935. **Membership:** 20. **Languages:** English.

AMERICAN OSLER SOCIETY (AOS)

Loma Linda University School of Medicine
Center of Perinatal Biology
Loma Linda, CA 92350
Lawrence D. Longo, Sec.-Treas.
PH: (909)824-4325
FX: (909)824-4029
Description: Physicians, librarians, and scientistsunited to further a humanistic approach to the study and practice of medicine as exemplified in the life work of Sir William Osler (1849-1919). **Founded:** 1970. **Membership:** 135. **Languages:** English. **Publication:** *Osler Biographical Directory*, annual ■ *The Persisting Osler.* Book ■ *The Persisting Osler II.* Book.

AMERICAN OSTEOPATHIC ACADEMY OF SPORTS MEDICINE (AOASM)

e-mail: aoasm@tmahq.com
7611 Elmwood Ave., Ste. 201
Middleton, WI 53562
Sheila Endicott, Exec.Dir.
PH: (608)831-4400
FX: (608)831-5122
Description: Members of the American Osteopathic Association and students enrolled in approved colleges of osteopathic medicine. Objectives are to promote education, development of high ethical standards, communication, and research in the field of sports medicine. Conducts study programs, lectures, forums, and seminars. Encourages publication of articles and dissertations in scientific and professional journals. Sponsors student academy organizations at osteopathic education institutions. Maintains speakers' bureau. **Founded:** 1975. **Membership:** 500. Multinational. **Languages:** English.

AMERICAN OSTEOPATHIC COLLEGE OF ANESTHESIOLOGISTS (AOCA)

17201 E. US Hwy. 40, No. 204
Independence, MO 64055
Tom Pence, Pres.
PH: (816)373-4700
TF: 800842-AOCA
FX: (816)373-1529
Description: Members of American Osteopathic Association who are engaged in the practice of anesthesiology. **Founded:** 1952. **Membership:** 500. **Languages:** English. **Budget:** $100,000 Formerly (1952) American Osteopathic Society of Anesthesiologists.

AMERICAN OSTEOPATHIC COLLEGE OF DERMATOLOGY (AOCD)

e-mail: aocd@kvmo.net
PO Box 7525
Kirksville, MO 63501-7525
Rebecca A. Mansfield, Exec.Dir.
PH: (660)665-2184
FX: (660)626-2714
Description: Members of the osteopathic profession certified or involved in dermatology. Conducts specialized education programs. **Founded:** 1958. **Membership:** 250. **Staff:** 2. **Languages:** English.

AMERICAN OSTEOPATHIC COLLEGE OF RADIOLOGY (AOCR)

119 E. 2nd St.
Milan, MO 63556
Pamela A. Smith, Exec.Dir.
PH: (816)265-4011
FX: (816)265-3494
Description: Certified radiologists, residents-in-training, and others active in the field of radiology. **Founded:** 1941. **Membership:** 730. **Languages:** English. **Budget:** $400,000. **Publication:** *Viewbox*, quarterly ■ Membership Directory, annual.

AMERICAN PARKINSON'S DISEASE ASSOCIATION (APDA)

e-mail: apda@admin.con2.com
1250 Hylan Blvd., Ste. 4B
Staten Island, NY 10305
John Pillarella, res.
PH: (718)981-8001
TF: 800223-2732
FX: (718)981-4399
Description: Works to find the cure for Parkinson's disease and to alleviate the suffering of its victims by subsidizing information and referral centers and providing funds for research. Offers counseling services to patients and their families. Maintains 43 information and referral centers. Conducts symposia. **Founded:** 1961. **Membership:** 2000. **Staff:** 13. **Local Groups:** 400. **Languages:** English. **Publication:** *American Parkinson Disease Association – Newsletter* (in English), quarterly. Includes association and research news, and calendar of events. Price: free. Circulation: 250,000. Advertising: not accepted ■ *Be Active! A Suggested Exercise Program for People with Parkinson's Disease.* Booklet ■ *Be Independent! To Help the Patient with Parkinson's Disease in the Activities of Daily Living.* Booklet ■ *Coping With Parkinson's Disease.* Booklet ■ *Let's Communicate: Speech Problems and Swallowing Problems in Parkinson's Disease.* Booklet ■ *Parkinson's Disease Handbook.* Booklet ■ Annual Report.

AMERICAN PATHOLOGY FOUNDATION (APF)

1202 Allanson Rd.
Mundelein, IL 60060
Edward J. Stygar, Jr., Exec.Dir.
PH: (847)949-6055
FX: (847)566-4580
Description: Board-certified pathologists. Objectives are: to promote the practice of pathology in private laboratories; to provide for exchange of information that will improve anatomic and clinical pathology; to cooperate in the development of the art and sciences of medicine and pathology. Compiles statistics. **Founded:** 1959. **Membership:** 650. **Staff:** 3. **Languages:** English. **Publication:** Directory, annual ■ Newsletter, quarterly. **Formerly:** Private Practitioners of Pathology Foundation.

AMERICAN PEDIATRIC SOCIETY (APS)

e-mail: info@aps.spr.org
3400 Research Forest Dr., Ste. B7
Spring, TX 77381-4259
Dr. Norman I. Siegel, Sec.-Treas.
PH: (281)296-0244
FX: (281)296-0255
Description: Professional academic society of M.D. educators and researchers interested in the study of children and their diseases, prevention of illness, and promotion of health in childhood. Maintains archives. **Founded:** 1888. **Membership:** 1400. **Staff:** 9. **Languages:** English. **Budget:** $1,000,000.

AMERICAN PHARMACEUTICAL ASSOCIATION - ACADEMY OF PHARMACY PRACTICE AND MANAGEMENT (APLA-APPM)

url: http://www.aphanet.org
2215 Constitution Ave. NW
Washington, DC 20037
Janet N. Edwards, Assoc.Dir., Practice Development
PH: (202)628-4410
TF: 800237-APHA
FX: (202)783-2351
Description: Pharmacists concerned with rendering professional services directly to the public, without regard for status of employment or environment of practice. Purposes are to provide a forum and mechanism whereby pharmacists may meet to discuss and implement programs and activities relevant and helpful to the practitioner of pharmacy; to recommend programs and courses of action which should be undertaken or implemented by the profession; to coordinate academy efforts so as to be an asset to the progress of the profession. Provides and cosponsors continuing education meetings, seminars, and workshops; produces audiovisual materials. **Founded:** 1965. **Membership:** 21000. **Staff:** 2.

Languages: English. Formerly (1966) General Practice Section of APhA; (1975) Academy of General Practice of Pharmacy; (1987) Academy of Pharmacy Practice; (1995) Academy of Pharmacy Practice and Management.

AMERICAN PHYSICAL SOCIETY (APS)
e-mail: exoffice@aps.org
url: http://aps.org
1 Physics Ellipse
College Park, MD 20740-3844
Judy R. Franz, Exec. Officer
PH: (301)209-3269
FX: (301)209-0865
Description: Scientists worldwide, dedicated to the advancement and the diffusion of the knowledge of physics. Publishes some of the leading international physics journals, organizes major scientific meetings, and provides strong outreach programs in physics education and in international and public affairs. **Founded:** 1899. **Membership:** 40000. **Staff:** 165. Multinational. **Regional Groups:** 5. **Languages:** English. **Budget:** $30,000,000.

AMERICAN PHYSIOLOGICAL SOCIETY (APS)
e-mail: info@aps.faseb.org
url: http://www.faseb.org/aps/
9650 Rockville Pike
Bethesda, MD 20814-3991
Martin Frank, Exec.Dir.
PH: (301)530-7164
FX: (301)571-8305
Description: Professional society of physiologists. **Founded:** 1887. **Membership:** 8200. **Staff:** 65. **Languages:** English. **Budget:** $13,000,000.

AMERICAN POLARITY THERAPY ASSOCIATION (APTA)
e-mail: satvahq@aol.com
2888 Bluff St., Ste. 149
Boulder, CO 80301
Gary Peterson, Exec.Dir.
PH: (303)545-2080
FX: (303)545-2161
Description: Dedicated to the advancement of polarity therapy. Polarity therapy is a non-diagnostic holistic health system, supplementing and supporting medical treatment. Polarity techniques include bodywork, diet, exercise and self awareness for health maintenance. Develops and disseminates educational and support materials; registers practitioners; holds competitions. **Founded:** 1984. **Membership:** 1200. **Staff:** 3. **State Groups:** 6. **Languages:** English. **Budget:** $250,000.

AMERICAN PROFESSIONAL PRACTICE ASSOCIATION (APPA)
e-mail: ppsone@msn.com
url: http://www.appa-assn.com
292 Madison Ave., 4th Fl.
New York, NY 10017
Ms. Pat Arden, Exec.Dir./CEO
PH: (212)949-5900
TF: 800221-2168
FX: (212)949-5910
Description: Provides physicians with economic benefits and services including the following: unsecured loan plans; equipment, furniture, and automobile leasing; seminars and information programs; low-cost group insurance; group purchase discounts; investment opportunities; local, travel, and personal service programs. **Founded:** 1959. **Membership:** 70000. **Staff:** 15. **Languages:** English. **Publication:** *APPA Digest*, quarterly. Newsletter. Provides business advice on private practice; also covers APPA activities. Price: included in membership dues. Circulation: 19,000.

AMERICAN PROSTHODONTIC SOCIETY (APS)
919 N. Michigan Ave., Ste. 2406
Chicago, IL 60611
Alan C. Keyes, D.D.S., Exec.Dir.

PH: (312)944-7618
FX: (312)266-2431
Description: Dentists interested in the discipline of prosthodontics (the art and science of replacing missing teeth and supporting structures). **Founded:** 1928. **Membership:** 1300. **Staff:** 4. Multinational. **Languages:** English. **Budget:** $150,000. **Publication:** *Journal of Prosthetic Dentistry*, monthly. Published in conjunction with 21 other prosthodonic organizations. Price: included in membership dues.

AMERICAN PSEUDO-OBSTRUCTION AND HIRSCHSPRUNG'S DISEASE SOCIETY (APHS)
e-mail: aphs@mail.tiac.net
url: http://www.tiac.net/users/aphs
158 Pleasant St.
North Andover, MA 01845
Anthony P. Giglio, Chairman of the Board
PH: (978)685-4477
TF: 800394-APHS
FX: (978)685-4488
Description: Parents, health care professionals, and other interested individuals. Provides support services for families such as the Family Assistance Program; conducts educational programs. **Founded:** 1988. **Membership:** 1800. **Staff:** 5. Multinational. **Languages:** English. **Budget:** $250,000. Formed by Merger of (1993) North American Pediatric Pseudo-Obstruction Society; American Hirschsprung's Disease Association.

AMERICAN PSYCHIATRIC ASSOCIATION (APA)
url: http://www.psych.org
1400 K St. NW
Washington, DC 20005
Steven Mirin, M.D., Med.Dir.
PH: (202)682-6000
FX: (202)682-6114
Description: Psychiatrists. Seeks to further the study of the nature, treatment, and prevention of mental disorders. Assists in formulating programs to meet mental health needs; compiles and disseminates facts and figures about psychiatry; furthers psychiatric education and research. **Founded:** 1844. **Membership:** 40000. **Staff:** 190. **Regional Groups:** 77. **Languages:** English. **Budget:** $25,000,000. Formerly (1892) Association of Medical Superintendents of American Institutions for Insane; (1921) American Medico Psychological Association.

AMERICAN PSYCHIATRIC NURSES ASSOCIATION (APNA)
e-mail: info@apna.org
url: http://www.apna.org
1200 19th St. NW, Ste. 300
Washington, DC 20036
Timothy Gordon, Exec.Dir.
PH: (202)857-1133
FX: (202)223-4579
Description: Provides leadership to advance psychiatric mental health nursing practice, improve mental health care for families, individuals, groups and communities, and shape health policy for the delivery of mental health serivces. **Founded:** 1987. **Membership:** 2600. **Staff:** 7. **Local Groups:** 2. **Languages:** English. **Budget:** $490,000.

AMERICAN PUBLIC HEALTH ASSOCIATION (APHA)
e-mail: comments@apha.org
url: http://www.apha.org
1015 15th St. NW
Washington, DC 20005
Mohammad Akhter, MD, Exec.Dir.
PH: (202)789-5600
FX: (202)789-5661
Description: Professional organization of physicians, nurses, educators, academicians, environmentalists, epidemiologists, new professionals, social workers, health administrators, optometrists, podiatrists, pharmacists, dentists, nutritionists, health planners, other community and mental health specialists, and interested consumers. Seeks to protect and promote personal,

mental, and environmental health. Services include: promulgation of standards; establishment of uniform practices and procedures; development of the etiology of communicable diseases; research in public health; exploration of medical care programs and their relationships to public health. Sponsors job placement service. **Founded:** 1872. **Membership:** 32000. **Staff:** 65. **Languages:** English. **Budget:** $9,600,000.

AMERICAN RADIOLOGICAL NURSES ASSOCIATION (ARNA)
e-mail: arna@rsna.org
2021 Spring Rd., Ste. 600
Oak Brook, IL 60521
Betty Rohr, Exec.Sec.
PH: (708)571-9072
FX: (708)571-7837
Description: Radiological nurses. Seeks to provide, promote, and maintain continuity of quality patient care through education, standards of care, professional growth, and collaboration with other health care providers. **Founded:** 1981. **Membership:** 1514. **Staff:** 3. **State Groups:** 23. **Languages:** English. **Budget:** $175,000.

AMERICAN REGISTRY OF MEDICAL ASSISTANTS (ARMA)
69 Southwick Rd., Ste. A
Westfield, MA 01085-4729
Annette H. Heyman, Dir.
PH: (413)562-7336
TF: 800527-2762
Description: Medical assistants who have completed an accredited medical assistant training course or who have trained with a physician. Objectives are to: establish and maintain high training standards for medical assistants; promote greater efficiency within the profession; raise awareness of medical assistants within the medical community. **Convention/Meeting:** none. **Founded:** 1950. **Membership:** 5000. **Staff:** 4. **Languages:** English. **Publication:** *The Medical Assistant* (in English), annual. Journal. Information of interest to the medical community. Price: included in membership dues. Advertising: accepted ■ *Registry Connection*, quarterly ■ *200 Ways to Put Your Talent To Work in the Health Field*. Pamphlet. Price: free ■ Brochures. Price: included in application fee and annual fee of; members. Advertising: accepted.

AMERICAN REGISTRY OF PATHOLOGY (ARP)
c/o Armed Forces Institute of Pathology
14th St. & Alaska Ave. NW
Washington, DC 20306-6000
Donald West King, M.D., Exec.Dir.
PH: (202)782-2143
FX: (202)782-4567
Description: Engages in cooperative enterprises in medical research and education with the Armed Forces Institute of Pathology. Functions as a fiscal agent in the management of research grants and monies derived from tuition fees publications and contributions. Serves as a link between, and encourages cooperation among, the military and civilian medical, dental, and veterinary communities for the mutual benefit of military and civilian medicine. Provides personnel and other services in support of research in a variety of Offers 38 continuing medical education courses annually. Bestows annual John Hill Brinton Award in recognition of outstanding young researcher, John Shaw Billings Lifetime Achievement Awart to senior AFIP staff member, Callender-Binford fellowships. **Founded:** 1976. **Staff:** 8. **Languages:** English. **Budget:** $3,100,000.

AMERICAN REGISTRY OF RADIOLOGIC TECHNOLOGISTS (ARRT)
1255 Northland Dr.
St. Paul, MN 55120
Jerry B. Reid, Exec.Dir.
PH: (612)687-0048
Description: Radiologic certification boards that administer examinations, issues certificates of registration to radiographers, nuclear medicine technologists, and radiation therapists, and investigates the qualifications of practicing radiologic technolo-

gists. Governed by trustees appointed from American College of Radiology and American Society of Radiologic Technologists. **Convention/Meeting:** none. **Founded:** 1922. **Membership:** 220895. **Staff:** 34. **Languages:** English. **Publication:** *Directory of Registered Technologists*, biennial ■ Annual Report. Advertising: not accepted. **Formerly:** American Registry of X-Ray Technicians; (1936) American Registry of Radiological Technicians.

AMERICAN ROENTGEN RAY SOCIETY (ARRS)
url: http://www.arrs.org
c/o Paul R. Fullagar
1891 Preston White Dr.
Reston, VA 22091
Paul R. Fullagar, Exec.Dir.
PH: (703)648-8992
TF: 800438-2777
FX: (703)264-8863
Description: Trade association for board certified radiologists. Offers many educational programs. **Founded:** 1900. **Membership:** 12500. **Staff:** 21. Multinational. **Languages:** English. **Publication:** *American Journal of Roentgenology* (in English), monthly, Peer reviewed. Price: $175.00/year. ISSN: 0361-803X. Circulation: 26,000. Advertising: accepted. Alternate Formats: CD-ROM ■ *ARRS Memo*, quarterly. Newsletter ■ *Categorical Course Syllabi*. **Formerly:** (1906) Roentgen Society of the U.S.

AMERICAN SCHOOL HEALTH ASSOCIATION (ASHA)
e-mail: swooley@asha.web.org
url: http://www.ashaweb.org
7263 State Rte. 43
PO Box 708
Kent, OH 44240
Susan F. Wooley, Ph.D., Exec.Dir.
PH: (330)678-1601
TF: 800445-2742
FX: (330)678-4526
Description: School physicians, school nurses, dentist, nurses, nutritionists, health educators, dental hygentist, school-based professionals and public health workers. Promotes coordinated school health programs that include health education, health services, a healthful school environment, physical education, nutrition services, and psycho-social health services offered in schools collaboratively with families and other members of the community. Offers professional reference materials. Conducts pilot programs that inform materials developement, provides technical assistance to school professionals, advocates for school health, and complies statistics. **Founded:** 1927. **Membership:** 4000. **Staff:** 15. **State Groups:** 16. **Languages:** English. **Budget:** $900,000. **Publication:** *A Pocketguide to Health and Health Problems in School Physical Activities*. Book ■ *ASHA NetworkNews*, periodic. Newsletter ■ *Building Effective Coalitions to Prevent the Spread of HIV*. Book ■ *Guidelines for Comprehensive School Heath Programs*. Book ■ *Health Counseling*. Book ■ *Healthy Students 2000: An Agenda for Continuous Improvement in America's Schools*. Book ■ *How Physicians Work and How to Work with Physicians: A Guide for Educators to Enhance HIV Eduation Intiatives*. Book ■ *Implementation Guide for the Standards of School Nursing Practice*. Book ■ *Journal of School Health*, 10/year. Includes articles, research papers, reports, commentaries, teaching techniques, and health service application. Price: $85.00/year; $95.00/year for institutions; $110.00/year outside U.S.; $8.50/copy for members. ISSN: 0022-4391. Circulation: 7,200. Advertising: accepted ■ *The PULSE*, quarterly. Price: included in membership. Circulation: 4,000. Advertising: accepted ■ *The Role of the Nurse in the School Setting: A Historical Perspective*. Book ■ *School-Based HIV Prevention: A Multidisciplinary Approach*. Book ■ *School Health in America*. Survey ■ *Science and Health Experiments and Demonstrations in Smoking Education*. Book ■ *Sexuality Education Within Comprehensive School Health Education*. Book ■ *Standards of School Nursing Practice*. Book ■ *Teaching Human Sexuality*. Book ■ *Thinking Ahead: Preparing for Controversy*. Book ■ *Topical Index of Articles From the Journal*, annual. **Formerly:** (1936) American Association of School Physicians.

AMERICAN SHOULDER AND ELBOW SURGEONS (ASES)
e-mail: gjohnsonp@aaos.org
6300 N. River Rd., Ste. 727
Rosemont, IL 60018-4226
Karen Jared, Mgr.
PH: (847)698-1629
FX: (847)823-0536
Description: Orthopedic surgeons. Purpose is to promote the exchange and dissemination of information on shoulder and elbow surgery and treatment. Sponsors educational courses. Founded: 1982. Membership: 146. Languages: English.

AMERICAN SKIN ASSOCIATION (ASA)
150 E. 58th St., 33rd Fl.
New York, NY 10155-0002
Joyce Weidler, Mng.Dir.
PH: (212)753-8260
TF: 800499-SKIN
FX: (212)688-6547
Description: Supports research on skin diseases. Promotes public education on prevention and treatment of skin disorders. Founded: 1987. Membership: 100. Staff: 2. Languages: English. Budget: $400,000.

AMERICAN SLEEP APNEA ASSOCIATION (ASAA)
e-mail: asaa@nicom.com
url: http://www.sleepapnea.org
1424 K St. NW
Washington, DC 20005
Christin Engelhardt, Exec.Dir.
PH: (202)293-3650
FX: (202)293-3656
Description: Individuals affected by sleep apnea; health care professionals. Promotes public awareness of sleep apnea; encourages research on the causes and treatments of breathing abnormalities during sleep. Sponsors educational programs and support groups through the A.W.A.K.E. Network. Serves as an advocate for people with sleep apnea. Convention/Meeting: none. Founded: 1990. Membership: 5000. Staff: 3. Local Groups: 225. Languages: English. Budget: $250,000.

AMERICAN SLEEP DISORDERS ASSOCIATION (ASDA)
e-mail: asda@asda.org
url: http://www.asda.org
1610 14th St. NW, Ste. 300
Rochester, MN 55901
Jerry Barrett, Exec.Dir.
PH: (507)287-6006
FX: (507)287-6008
Description: Sleep disorders centers and individuals united to provide full diagnostic and treatment services and to improve the quality of care for patients with all types of sleep disorders. Fosters educational activities at medical schools and in continuing medical education programs; conducts site visits to assure minimum standards at member centers; trains and evaluates the competence of individuals who care for patients with sleep disorders. Conducts research programs, including a cooperative case study series on all patients seen by sleep disorders centers throughout the country. Founded: 1975. Membership: 2900. Staff: 19. Languages: English. For-Profit. Budget: $1,300,000. Formerly American Association of Sleep Disorders Centers; (1987) Association of Sleep Disorders Centers.

AMERICAN SOCIETY OF ABDOMINAL SURGEONS (ASAS)
e-mail: office@abdominalsurg.org
url: http://www.ardominalsurg.org
675 Main St.
Melrose, MA 02176
Louis F. Alfano, M.D., Exec.Sec.
PH: (617)665-6102
FX: (617)665-4127
Description: Medical doctors specializing in abdominal surgery. Sponsors extensive program of surgical education including study courses, postgraduate programs, lectures, and demonstrations.

Founded: 1959. Membership: 3900. Staff: 6. Multinational. Languages: English. Budget: $25,000.

AMERICAN SOCIETY FOR ADOLESCENT PSYCHIATRY (ASAP)
e-mail: addpsych@aol.com
4340 East West Hwy., Ste. 401
Bethesda, MD 20814
Ann Loew, Exec.Dir.
PH: (301)718-6502
TF: 800899-6338
FX: (301)656-0989
Description: Qualified psychiatrists concerned with the behavior of adolescents. Provides for the exchange of psychiatric knowledge; encourages the development of adequate standards and training facilities; stimulates research in the psychopathology and treatment of adolescents. Consults with national organizations interested in the welfare of youth and adolescence. Founded: 1967. Membership: 800. Multinational. Regional Groups: 20. Languages: English.

AMERICAN SOCIETY OF ANESTHESIOLOGISTS (ASA)
e-mail: mail@asahq.org
url: http://www.asahq.org
520 N. Northwest Hwy.
Park Ridge, IL 60068-2573
Glenn W. Johnson, Exec.Dir.
PH: (708)825-5586
FX: (708)825-1692
Description: Professional society of physicians specializing or interested in anesthesiology. Seeks "to develop and further the specialty of anesthesiology for the general elevation of the standards of medical practice." Encourages education, research, and scientific progress in anesthesiology. Conducts refresher courses and other postgraduate educational activities. Maintains placement service. Founded: 1905. Membership: 34000. Staff: 42. State Groups: 48. Languages: English. Budget: $15,375,000. Formerly (1911) Long Island Society of Anesthetists; (1936) New York Society of Anesthetists; (1945) American Society of Anesthetists.

AMERICAN SOCIETY FOR AUTOMATION IN PHARMACY (ASAP)
url: http://www.asapnet.com
492 Norristown Rd., Ste. 160
Blue Bell, PA 19422
William A. Lockwood, Jr., Exec.Dir.
PH: (610)825-7783
FX: (610)825-7641
Description: Pharmaceutical software developers; pharmaceutical and insurance companies; related organizatios. Addresses issues related to computer use in the pharmaceutical industry. Founded: 1989. Membership: 500. Staff: 3. Languages: English. Publication: *Byteline*, quarterly. Advertising: not accepted.

AMERICAN SOCIETY FOR BARIATRIC SURGERY (ASBS)
e-mail: mallorygn@aol.com
url: http://www.asbs.org
6717 NW 11th Pl., Ste. C
Gainesville, FL 32605
Georgeann Mallory, Exec.Dir.
PH: (352)331-4900
FX: (352)332-3583
Description: Works to advance the art and science of bariatric surgery. Supports clinical and laboratory investigations; promotes guidelines for ethical patient care; conducts educational programs for physicians, paramedicals and lay people; provides a forum for the exchange of ideas. Founded: 1983. Membership: 375. Staff: 2. Multinational.

AMERICAN SOCIETY FOR BIOCHEMISTRY AND MOLECULAR BIOLOGY (ASBMB)

e-mail: asbmb@asbmb.faseb.org
url: http://www.faseb.org/asbmb
9650 Rockville Pike
Bethesda, MD 20814
Charles C. Hancock, Exec. Officer
PH: (301)530-7145
FX: (301)571-1824
Description: Biochemists and molecular biologists who have conducted and published original investigations in biological chemistry and/or molecular biology. Operates placement service. Founded: 1906. Membership: 9300. Staff: 17. Multinational. Languages: English. Budget: $10,000,000. Formerly (1987) American Society of Biological Chemists.

AMERICAN SOCIETY OF CATARACT AND REFRACTIVE SURGERY (ASCRS)

e-mail: ascrs@ascrs.org
url: http://www.ascrs.org
4000 Legato Rd. No., 850
Fairfax, VA 22033
David A. Karcher, Exec.Dir.
PH: (703)591-2220
TF: 800451-1339
FX: (703)591-0614
Description: Ophthalmologists interested in anterior segment surgery and refractive corneal surgery. Offers continuing medical education to ophthalmologists on cataract and refractive surgery techniques, intraocular lens designs, and related research areas; assists allied health care professionals in ophthalmology on medical and surgical care of pseudophakic (lens implant) patients. Works to improve public education in the field of eye care. Conducts research in ocular pathology in cataract and refractive surgery. Compiles statistics. Founded: 1974. Membership: 7500. Staff: 21. Multinational. Languages: English. Budget: $5,000,000. Formerly (1986) American Intra-Ocular Implant Society.

AMERICAN SOCIETY OF CHILDBIRTH EDUCATORS (ASCE)

PO Box 2282
Sedona, AZ 86339
Dr. James C. Sasmor, Corporate Sec.
PH: (520)284-9897
FX: (520)284-9897
Description: Seeks to provide a medium for the exchange and dissemination of information relating to prepared childbirth as a shared family experience and disseminate information to qualified professionals regarding standards, techniques, and skills relevant to the concept of prepared birth. Presently inactive. Founded: 1972. Languages: English.

AMERICAN SOCIETY FOR CLINICAL EVOKED POTENTIALS (ASCEP)

14 Soundview Ave., No. 51
White Plains, NY 10606
Mrs. S. Moss, Exec.Sec.
PH: (914)761-4713
Description: Physicians in physical medicine and rehabilitation, neurology, neurosurgery, ophthalmology, and anesthesiology. Purpose is to study the central nervous system's transmissions and to teach electrodiagnostic reading of evoked potentials. (Evoked potential is the sum of the stimulus-evoked bioelectrical potentials from the peripheral nerve, retina, or cochlear mechanism, from the spinal cord or central conduction pathways, and from cortical and subcortical structures.) Teaches and encourages the practice of and research in the clinical application of evoked potentials for the betterment of patient care. Conducts seminars and workshops; maintains speakers' bureau. Founded: 1981. Membership: 410. Multinational. Languages: English. Publication: Membership Directory, periodic ▪ Journal.

AMERICAN SOCIETY FOR CLINICAL INVESTIGATION (ASCI)

6900 Grove Rd.
Thorofare, NJ 08086
David Ginsburg, M.D., Sec.Treas.
PH: (609)848-1000
TF: 800257-8290
FX: (609)848-5274
Description: Physician scientists with meritorious original clinical investigations. Active members are doctors under age 48; emeritus members are those over age 48. Promotes cultivation of clinical research by methods of natural sciences, correlation of science with the art of medical practice, encouragement of scientific investigation by medical practitioners, and publication of papers on the methods and results of clinical research. Founded: 1909. Membership: 2600. Staff: 2. Languages: English. Budget: $2,000,000.

AMERICAN SOCIETY FOR CLINICAL LABORATORY SCIENCE (ASCLS)

url: http://www.ascls.org
7910 Woodmont Ave., Ste. 530
Bethesda, MD 20814
Elissa Passiment, EdM, Exec.Dir.
PH: (301)657-2768
FX: (301)657-2909
Description: Primarily clinical laboratory personnel who have an associate or baccalaureate degree and clinical training and specialists who hold at least a master's degree in one of the major fields of clinical laboratory science such as bacteriology, mycology, or biochemistry; also includes technicians, specialists, and educators with limited certificates and students enrolled in approved programs of clinical laboratory studies and military medical technology schools. Promotes and maintains high standards in clinical laboratory methods and research and advances standards of education and training of personnel. Conducts educational program of seminars and workshops. Sponsors award competition to encourage the writing of scientific papers. Approves programs of continuing education and maintains records on participation in continuing education programs for members. Maintains speakers' bureau. Founded: 1932. Membership: 20000. Staff: 11. Languages: English. Budget: $1,900,000. Publication: *ASCLS Today*, monthly. Newsletter. Price: included in membership dues. ISSN: 0895-3597. Circulation: 17,000. Advertising: accepted ▪ *Clinical Laboratory Science*, bimonthly. Journal. Price: included in membership dues; $40.00 for individuals; $60.00 for corporations. ISSN: 0894-959X. Circulation: 22,000. Advertising: accepted ▪ Books ▪ Brochures ▪ Manuals ▪ Videos. Formerly: American Society of Medical Technologists; (1936) American Society of Clinical Laboratory Technicians; (1993) American Society for Medical Technology.

AMERICAN SOCIETY OF CLINICAL PATHOLOGISTS (ASCP)

2100 W. Harrison
Chicago, IL 60612
Robert C. Rock, M.D., Sr.VP
PH: (312)738-1336
TF: 800621-4142
FX: (312)738-1619
Description: Works to promote public health and safety by the appropriate application of pathology and laboratory medicine. Provides educational, scientific, and charitable services. Founded: 1922. Membership: 65000. Staff: 194. Languages: English. Publication: *American Journal of Clinical Pathology*, monthly ▪ *ASCP News*, 8/year. Newsletter ▪ *Laboratory Medicine*, monthly ▪ *Pathology Patterns*, semiannual ▪ Membership Directory, biennial.

AMERICAN SOCIETY OF CLINICAL PSYCHOPHARMACOLOGY (ASCP)

PO Box 2257
New York, NY 10116
Paul H. Wender, M.D., Pres.

PH: (212)268-4260
FX: (212)268-4434
Description: Works to encourage clinical research in psychopharmacology and provide continuing education for members. Sponsors research; facilitates exchange of information; conducts professional educational programs and; provides educational programs on the treatment of psychiatric disorders for patients and families; develops relationships with mental health advocacy groups; advocates public policies which promote research and the delivery of high quality care. **Founded:** 1992. **Membership:** 1200. **Staff:** 2. **Languages:** English.

AMERICAN SOCIETY FOR COLPOSCOPY AND CERVICAL PATHOLOGY (ASCCP)
url: http://ww.asccp.org
18-20 W Washington St.
Hagerstown, MD 21740
Kathleen Poole, Admin.Dir.
TF: 800787-7227
Description: Gynecologists, family physicians, pathologists, nurses, and other individuals interested in promoting the accurate and ethical application of colposcopy (the examination of the lower genital tract by means of a colposcope). Organizes and approves training programs and audio visual materials in the diagnosis and management of lower genital tract disease. Conducts accredited postgraduate courses. **Founded:** 1964. **Membership:** 3600. **Staff:** 3. **Languages:** English. **Budget:** $1,200,000. Formerly American Society for Colposcopy and Colpomicroscopy.

AMERICAN SOCIETY OF CONSULTANT PHARMACISTS (ASCP)
e-mail: info@ascp.com
url: http://www.ascp.com
1321 Duke St.
Alexandria, VA 22314-3563
R. Timothy Webster, Exec.Dir.
PH: (703)739-1300
FX: (703)739-1321
Description: Registered pharmacists and educators who are largely concerned with pharmaceutical procedures within nursing homes and related health facilities. Works to: improve consultant pharmacist services to nursing homes and other long-term care facilities; define professional standards and to promote the certification of the profession; exchange information; sponsor and encourage the development of educational facilities and courses for the advancement of the profession; promote wider public information efforts; represent the interests of the profession before legislative and administrative branches of government; sponsor group service programs; promote public health and welfare. Conducts surveys of long-term care pharmacy operations. Sponsors educational and research programs. Maintains information center, hall of fame, and speakers' bureau; operates placement service; compiles statistics. **Founded:** 1969. **Membership:** 6500. **Staff:** 45. Multinational. **Languages:** English. **For-Profit. Budget:** $7,000,000.

AMERICAN SOCIETY OF CONTEMPORARY OPHTHALMOLOGY (ASCO)
e-mail: iaos@aol.com
4711 Golf Rd., Ste. 408
Skokie, IL 60076
Randall T. Bellows, M.D., Dir.
PH: (847)568-1500
TF: 800621-4002
FX: (847)568-1527
Description: Ophthalmologists interested in promoting clinical investigative advances in ophthalmology. Offers continuing medical education courses approved by the American Council for Continuing Medical Education (ACCME) on new opthalmic developments in medical, therapeutic, diagnostic, and surgical procedures. **Founded:** 1966. **Membership:** 6000. Multinational. **Languages:** English. Formerly (1970) Society for Cryo-Opthamology.

AMERICAN SOCIETY FOR DENTAL AESTHETICS (ASDA)
635 Madison Ave.
New York, NY 10022
Irwin Smigel, DDS, Pres.
PH: (212)751-3263
FX: (212)308-5182
Description: Accredited dentists practicing aesthetic concepts in dentistry, including porcelain lamination (a technique where porcelain veneer is chemically fused to teeth to lengthen them, close spaces, or recontour the entire mouth). Dentists must have 5 years experience and submit 5 "before and after" photos of their work in aesthetic dentistry to qualify for membership. Promotes development, research, and teaching of aesthetic concepts in dentistry. Although centered in New York City, the group promotes expansion of aesthetic dentistry concepts in other states and abroad. Sponsors educational programs on tooth and crown repair, aesthetic fillings, orthodontics, periodontics, implantology, and other topics. **Founded:** 1978. **Membership:** 200. **Staff:** 2. **Languages:** English. **Publication:** *ASDA Today*, semiannual. Journal. Circulation: 3,000. Advertising: accepted.

AMERICAN SOCIETY OF DENTISTRY FOR CHILDREN (ASDC)
e-mail: asdckids@aol.com
url: http://www.cudental.creighton.edu/ASDC
875 N. Michigan Ave., Ste. 4040
Chicago, IL 60611-1901
Peter Fos, Exec. Dir.
PH: (312)943-1244
FX: (312)943-5341
Description: General practitioners and specialists interested in dentistry for children. Conducts specialized education and research programs. **Founded:** 1927. **Membership:** 5000. **Staff:** 5. Multinational. **State Groups:** 50. **Languages:** English. **Budget:** $650,000. **Publication:** *Dental Recap*, bimonthly. Newsletter. Contains news about children's dental health concerns. Includes scientific references and governmental activities related to children's health. Price: included in membership dues. Circulation: 8,500. Advertising: accepted ■ *Directory of the Membership of the American Society of Dentistry for Children*, annual. Membership Directory ■ *Journal of Dentistry for Children*, bimonthly.

AMERICAN SOCIETY FOR DERMATOLOGIC SURGERY (ASDS)
url: http://www.asds-net.org
PO Box 4014
Schaumburg, IL 60173
Cheryl K. Nordstedt, Exec.Dir.
PH: (847)330-9830
FX: (847)330-1090
Description: Physicians specializing in dermatologic surgery. Purpose is to maintain the highest possible standards in medical education, clinical practice, and patient care. Seeks to promote high standards in allied health professions and services as they relate to dermatology. Maintains audiovisual library. **Founded:** 1970. **Membership:** 2350. **Languages:** English. **Budget:** $900,000.

AMERICAN SOCIETY OF DERMATOPATHOLOGY (ASDP)
930 N. Meacham Rd.
Schaumburg, IL 60173-6016
Victoria Przybyszeski, Account Mgr.
PH: (847)330-9830
FX: (847)330-1135
Description: Seeks to: improve the quality of dermatopathology (the study of abnormal skin conditions, especially the structural and functional changes produced by disease); aid in the dissemination of information; encourage continuing education and research. **Founded:** 1962. **Membership:** 965. **Staff:** 1. **Languages:** English.

AMERICAN SOCIETY OF ECHOCARDIOGRAPHY (ASE)
e-mail: ase@mercury.interpath.com
url: http://www.aseho.org
4101 Lake Boone Trl., Ste. 201
Raleigh, NC 27607
Sharon Perry, Exec.Dir.
PH: (919)787-5181
FX: (919)787-4916
Description: Physicians and sonographers specializing in ultrasound heart imaging and diagnosis. Promotes excellence in the ultrasonic examination of the heart and assists in establishing standards for education of physicians and cardiac-sonographers in echocardiography. Sponsors educational activities including distribution of self-testing materials, continuing education calendar, and annual scientific sessions. Maintains liaison with governmental agencies and other professional groups. **Founded:** 1976. **Membership:** 5500. **Staff:** 4. Multinational. **Languages:** English. **Budget:** $1,500,000.

AMERICAN SOCIETY OF EXTRA-CORPOREAL
   TECHNOLOGY (AMSECT)
e-mail: webmaster@amsect.org
url: http://www.amsect.org
11480 Sunset Hills Rd., No. 210E
Reston, VA 20190-5208
George M. Cate, Exec.Dir.
PH: (703)435-8556
FX: (703)435-0056
Description: Perfusionists, technologists, doctors, nurses, and others actively employed and using the applied skills relating to the practice of extracorporeal technology (involving heart-lung machines); student members. Disseminates information necessary to the proper practice of the technology. Conducts programs in continuing education and professional-public liaison and hands-on workshops. Maintains placement service. **Founded:** 1964. **Membership:** 3000. **Staff:** 5. **Regional Groups:** 11. **Languages:** English. **Budget:** $600,000. **Publication:** *AMSECT Today*, 11/year. Magazine. Includes calendar of events, reading and employment opportunities lists, and reports of regional events. Price: included in membership dues; $55.00/year for nonmembers. ISSN: 0747-3079. Circulation: 2,800. Advertising: accepted ▪ *Journal of Extra-Corporeal Technology*, quarterly. Covers dialysis, hemodynamics, organs and tissues, oxygenation, and research. Includes book reviews, case studies and membership directory. Price: included in membership dues; $70.00/year for nonmembers. ISSN: 0022-1058. Circulation: 2,800. Advertising: not accepted. **Formerly:** (1968) American Society of Extracorporeal Circulation Technicians.

AMERICAN SOCIETY OF FORENSIC ODONTOLOGY
   (ASFO)
Northwestern University Dental School
240 E. Huron
Chicago, IL 60611
Peter Tsay, Sec.
PH: (312)503-0900
FX: (312)503-9898
Description: Individuals interested in furthering the field of forensic dentistry. Conducts research and specialized education programs. Maintains library. **Founded:** 1966. **Membership:** 450. **Regional Groups:** 1. **Languages:** English. **Publication:** *Field Workbook in Forensic Odontology* ▪ Membership Directory, annual ▪ Newsletter, quarterly.

AMERICAN SOCIETY OF GENERAL SURGEONS
e-mail: asgs-info@theasgs.org
url: http://www.theasgs.org
2122 Grove
Glenview, IL 60025
L. Jack Carow, III, Exec.Dir.
PH: (847)998-4577
FX: (847)998-4577
Description: Board certified general surgeons and subspecialists who perform general surgery. **Founded:** 1993. **Budget:** $250,000.

AMERICAN SOCIETY FOR GERIATRIC DENTISTRY
   (ASGD)
url: http://www.bgsm.edu/dentistry/foscod
211 E. Chicago Ave., Ste. 948
Chicago, IL 60611
John S. Rutkauskas, D.D.S., Exec.Dir.
PH: (312)440-2661
FX: (312)440-2824
Description: Devoted to the maintenance and improvement of the oral health of the elderly. Promotes the continuing education of the practitioner of geriatric dentistry; auxiliary and nursing home administrators and personnel; hygienists, nurses, and students. Maintains speakers' bureau. **Founded:** 1965. **Membership:** 500. **Staff:** 3. Multinational. **Regional Groups:** 3. **Languages:** English. **Budget:** $150,000. **Publication:** *ASGD - Interface*, quarterly. Newsletter. Includes book reviews and calendar of events. Price: included in membership dues; $25.00/year for nonmembers. Circulation: 600. Advertising: accepted ▪ *Special Care in Dentistry*, bimonthly. Published in cooperation with American Association of Hospital Dentists and Academy of Dentistry for persons with disabilities.

AMERICAN SOCIETY OF HEALTH SYSTEM PHARMACISTS
   (ASHP)
7272 Wisconsin Ave.
Bethesda, MD 20814
Kate Gibbons
PH: (301)657-3000
FX: (301)657-1251
Description: Professional society of pharmacists employed by hospitals, HMOs, clinics, and other health systems. Provides personnel placement service for members; sponsors professional and personal liability program. Conducts educational and exhibit programs. Has 30 practice interest areas, special sections for home care practitioners and clinical specialists, and research and education foundation. **Founded:** 1942. **Membership:** 30000. **Staff:** 170. Multinational. **State Groups:** 50. **Languages:** English. **Budget:** $26,000,000.

AMERICAN SOCIETY FOR HEALTHCARE EDUCATION
   AND TRAINING OF THE AMERICAN HOSPITAL
   ASSOCIATION (ASHET)
1 N. Franklin
Chicago, IL 60606
Linda N. Brooks, Dir.
PH: (312)422-3721
FX: (312)422-4575
Description: Educators and trainers from hospitals and other healthcare institutions involved in staff development, and patient and community education. Purposes are: to foster professional development of members; to demonstrate the value of comprehensive education as a management strategy; to promote continuing education among all healthcare personnel; to develop coordination among organizations involved in the education of healthcare personnel; to formulate information and evaluation programs; to recommend action on national issues relating to healthcare education. Conducts educational programs. Sponsors competitions. **Founded:** 1970. **Membership:** 1500. **Staff:** 3. **State Groups:** 50. **Languages:** English. **Budget:** $350,000. **Publication:** *Healthcare Education Dateline*, 3/year. Newsletter. Price: for members. Circulation: 1,600. Advertising: not accepted ▪ *Hospitals*, biweekly ▪ *Journal of Healthcare Education and Training*, periodic. **Formerly:** (1973) American Society for Hospital Education and Training; (1981) American Society for Health Manpower Education and Training.

AMERICAN SOCIETY FOR HISTOCOMPATIBILITY AND
   IMMUNOGENETICS (ASHI)
PO Box 15804
Lenexa, KS 66285
Michael P. Flanagan, Exec.Dir.
PH: (913)541-0009
FX: (913)541-0156
Description: Scientists, physicians, and technologists involved in

research and clinical activities related to histocompatibility testing (a state of mutual tolerance that allows some tissues to be grafted effectively to others). Conducts proficiency testing and educational programs. Maintains liaison with regulatory agencies; offers placement services and laboratory accreditation. Has co-sponsored development of histocompatability specialist and laboratory certification program. **Founded:** 1968. **Membership:** 1000. **Languages:** English. **Budget:** $2,000,000. Formerly American Association for Clinical Histocompatibility Testing.

AMERICAN SOCIETY FOR INVESTIGATIVE PATHOLOGY (ASIP)
e-mail: asip@pathol.faseb.org
url: http://www.asip.uthscsa.edu/
9650 Rockville Pke.
Bethesda, MD 20814-3993
Frances A. Pitlick, Ph.D., Exec. Officer
PH: (301)530-7130
FX: (301)571-1879
Description: Experimental research pathologists who have made significant contributions to the knowledge of disease. **Founded:** 1976. **Membership:** 2300. **Staff:** 6. Multinational. **Languages:** English. **Budget:** $500,000. **Publication:** *The American Journal of Pathology*, monthly. Research papers in experimental pathology. Covers cell injury and death, inflammatory reactions, disturbances in circulation, and neoplastic growth. Price: included in membership dues; $195.00/year for nonmembers; $290.00/year for institutions. ISSN: 0002-9440. Circulation: 5,500. Advertising: accepted. Alternate Formats: microform ■ *ASIP Newsletter*, bimonthly. Contains articles on public policy issues and research opportunities. Includes new members and personnel promotions and appointments. Price: included in membership dues. Circulation: 2,300. Advertising: not accepted ■ Membership Directory, annual. **Formed by Merger of:** (1992) American Association of Pathologists and Bacteriologists; American Society for Experimental Pathology. **Formerly:** (1992) American Association of Pathologists.

AMERICAN SOCIETY OF LIPO-SUCTION SURGERY (ASLSS)
401 N. Michigan Ave.
Chicago, IL 60611-4212
Jeffery Knezozich, Exec.Dir.
PH: (312)527-6713
FX: (312)344-1815
Description: Surgeons specializing in dermatology, general surgery, gynecology, otolaryngology, plastic and reconstructive surgery, and cosmetic surgery. Trains surgeons in the art and methods of lipo-suction surgery. (Lipo-suction surgery is a procedure wherein fatty tissue is removed from the body by suction. It is not meant to reduce weight but to adjust body contours. Liposuction surgery is not currently part of the ordinary medical school curriculum.) Conducts workshops and seminars. **Founded:** 1982. **Membership:** 650. **Languages:** English.

AMERICAN SOCIETY OF MASTER DENTAL TECHNOLOGISTS (ASMDT)
PO Box 640248
Oakland Gardens, NY 11364
Sue Heppenheimer, Exec.Sec.
PH: (718)428-0075
FX: (718)631-4507
Description: Dental lab technicians. Dedicated to the upgrading of dental technology. Seeks to provide educational resources such as texts, instructors, and guidance for technicians interested in becoming master dental technologists. Conducts associate and master level courses in conjunction with New York University School of Dentistry, Dept. of Continuing Education. **Founded:** 1976. **Membership:** 125. **Languages:** English.

AMERICAN SOCIETY OF MAXILLOFACIAL SURGEONS (ASMS)
444 E. Algonquin Rd.
Arlington Heights, IL 60005
Catherine A. Hay, Exec.Dir.
PH: (847)228-8375
FX: (847)228-6509
Description: Professional society of doctors of medicine and doctors of dental surgery who have at least five years of recognized graduate training and experience in maxillofacial surgery. Seeks to stimulate and advance knowledge of the science and art of maxillofacial surgery and improve and elevate the standard of practice. **Founded:** 1947. **Membership:** 385. **Staff:** 3. **Languages:** English. **Publication:** *Maxillofacial News*, quarterly. Newsletter. Circulation: 385. Advertising: accepted.

AMERICAN SOCIETY FOR MEDICINE AND SCIENCE (ASMS)
e-mail: medical@colpittswt.com
875 Providence Hwy.
Dedham, MA 02026-6868
Joel P. Krensky, Chm.
PH: (781)326-7800
TF: 800972-7777
FX: (781)326-2921
Description: Not an association. Organizes medical and scientific conventions worldwide for nonprofit organizations. **Languages:** English. **For-Profit. Status Note:** (1998) Formerly American Academy of Medicine and Science.

AMERICAN SOCIETY FOR NEURAL TRANSPLANTATION (ASNT)
e-mail: jkordowe@rush.edu
url: http://www.neuraltransplant.org
U.S. Department ofT of Neurological Sciences
Research Center for Brain Repair
Rush-Presbyterian-St. Luke's Medical Center
Chicago, IL 60612
Jeffrey H. Kordower, Ph.D., Pres.
Description: Basic and clinical neuroscientists who utilize transplantation and related technologies to better understand the way the nervous system functions. Provides an interactive forum for scientists to discuss their data and important issues in the areas of neural transplantation, nervous system regeneration, and plasticity. Also provides leadership in the area of education with the emphasis on the training and education of young investigators. **Membership:** 200.

AMERICAN SOCIETY OF NEUROIMAGING (ASN)
e-mail: 103053.222@compuserve.com
5841 Cedar Lake Rd. S, Ste. 204
Minneapolis, MN 55416
Linda J. Wilkenson, Exec.Dir.
PH: (612)545-6291
FX: (612)545-6073
Description: Neurologists, neurosurgeons, neuroradiologists, and scientists. Promotes the development of computerized tomography (CT scanning), magnetic resonance imaging (MRI), neurosonology, and other neurodiagnostic techniques for clinical service, teaching, and research. Encourages the collaboration of members to improve techniques through educational programs and scientific research. Holds annual certification exam in MRI and neurosonology. **Founded:** 1977. **Membership:** 800. **Staff:** 3. Multinational. **Languages:** English. **Budget:** $500,000. **Publication:** *Journal of Neuroimaging*, quarterly. Circulation: 1,000. Advertising: accepted ■ Newsletter, semiannual. **Formerly:** (1980) Society for Computerized Tomography and Neuroimaging.

AMERICAN SOCIETY OF NEURORADIOLOGY (ASNR)
e-mail: asnrgant@interaccess.com
url: http://www.rad.rpsdmc.edu/~ajnr/index.html
2210 Midwest Rd., Ste. 207
Oak Brook, IL 60521
James B. Gantenberg, CHE, Exec.Dir./CEO

PH: (630)574-0220
FX: (630)574-0661
Description: Neuroradiologists who spend at least half of their time practicing neuroradiology. Fosters education, basic science research, and communication in neuroradiology. **Founded:** 1962. **Membership:** 2700. **Staff:** 10. **Languages:** English. **Publication:** *American Journal of Neuroradiology*, 10/year. Price: included in membership dues; $210.00/year for nonmembers; $270.00/year for nonmembers outside the U.S.; $90.00 in training. ISSN: 0195-6108. Circulation: 6,500. Advertising: accepted ■ *Membership Roll*, annual.

AMERICAN SOCIETY OF NEUROREHABILITATION
e-mail: loriandersonl@compuserve.com
5841 Cedar Lk. Rd., Ste. 204
Minneapolis, MN 55416
Lori Anderson, Exec.Dir.
PH: (612)545-6324
FX: (612)545-6073
Description: Neurologists, neurosurgeons, psychiatrists, pediatricians, and other medical professionals interested in disorders of the nervous system. Rehabilitates and monitors patients with neurological disabilities. Acts as an advocate for patients; liases with other neurological organizations. Promotes research. **Founded:** 1990. **Membership:** 700. **Languages:** English. **Publication:** *Journal of Neurologic Rehabilitation* ■ Newsletter, quarterly.

AMERICAN SOCIETY OF NUCLEAR CARDIOLOGY (ASNC)
e-mail: admin@asnc.org
url: http://www.asnc.org
9111 Old Georgetown Rd.
Bethesda, MD 20814
William D. Nelligan, Exec.Dir.
PH: (301)493-2360
FX: (301)493-2376
Description: Physicians, scientists, technologist, biomedical engineers and health care workers. Seeks to foster optimal delivery of nuclear cardiology services and promote research. Provides continuing medical education opportunities; establishes guidelines and standards for training and practice; provides information on lisensure requirments. **Founded:** 1993. **Membership:** 2900. **Staff:** 4. Multinational. **Regional Groups:** 28. **Languages:** English. **Budget:** $1,000,000.

AMERICAN SOCIETY OF OPHTHALMIC ADMINISTRATORS (ASOA)
e-mail: ascrs@ascrs.org
url: http://www.ascrs.org
4000 Legato Rd., No. 850
Fairfax, VA 22033
Lucy Santiago, Exec.Dir.
PH: (703)591-2220
TF: 800451-1339
FX: (703)591-0614
Description: A division of the American Society of Cataract and Refractive Surgery. Persons involved with the administration of an ophthalmic office or clinic. Facilitates the exchange of ideas and information in order to improve management practices and working conditions. Offers placement services. **Founded:** 1986. **Membership:** 1900. **Staff:** 21. **Languages:** English. **Publication:** *A Manager's Survival Guide to Employee Rights* ■ *Administrative Eyecare*, quarterly. Magazine. Price: $45.00/year. ISSN: 1060-5991. Circulation: 7,000. Advertising: accepted ■ *Effective Interviews for Every Situation* ■ *Guidebook to Medical Practice Finances Reporting* ■ *Managed Care and Contracting*. Manual. Price: $150.00 for members; $225.00 for nonmembers ■ *marketing Ophthalmology* ■ *Ophthalmic Practice Management I & II*. Alternate Formats: CD-ROM ■ *Ophthalmic Reimbursement Manual*. Price: $90.00 for members; $145.00 for nonmembers ■ *Performance Appraisals: The Latest Legal Nightmare*.

AMERICAN SOCIETY OF OPHTHALMIC REGISTERED NURSES (ASORN)
PO Box 193030
San Francisco, CA 94119
Sue Brown, Exec.Admin.
PH: (415)561-8513
FX: (415)561-8575
Description: Registered nurses specializing in the field of ophthalmology. Promotes excellence in ophthalmic nursing for the best and safest care of patients with eye disorders or injuries. Facilitates continuing education through the study, discussion, and exchange of knowledge, experience, and ideas in the field. Represents members' interests before governmental agencies, hospitals, industries, research organizations, technical societies, universities, and other professional associations. Conducts educational programs. **Founded:** 1976. **Membership:** 1200. **Staff:** 4. Multinational. **Local Groups:** 27. **Languages:** English. **Budget:** $325,000.

AMERICAN SOCIETY FOR PEDIATRIC NEUROSURGERY (ASPN)
c/o M.L. Walker, Sec.
100 N. Medical Dr.
Salt Lake City, UT 84113
Mike Scott, Pres.
Description: Pediatric neurosurgeons dedicated to the advancement and development of their specialty. Represents the interests of pediatric neurosurgery as they relate to government, the public, universities, and professional societies. Supports basic and clinical research in pediatric neurosurgery. Provides leadership in undergraduate, graduate, and continuing education in the field of pediatric neurosurgery. **Founded:** 1978. **Membership:** 63. **Languages:** English.

AMERICAN SOCIETY OF PERIANESTHESIA NURSES (ASPAN)
url: http://www.aspan.org/index.htm
6900 Grove Rd.
Thorofare, NJ 08086
Terry R. McLean, RN, CP, Pres.
PH: (609)845-5557
FX: (609)848-1881
Description: Nurses practicing in all phases of ambulatory surgery, preanesthesia and post anesthesia care. Promotes quality and cost effective care for patients, their families, and the community through public and professional education, research and standards of practice. Offers continuing education programs. **Founded:** 1980. **Membership:** 10000.

AMERICAN SOCIETY OF PHARMACOGNOSY (ASP)
School of Pharmacy
Northeast Louisiana University
Monroe, LA 71209
Dr. William J. Keller, Sec.
PH: (318)342-5252
FX: (318)342-5274
Description: Professional society of pharmacognosists (persons engaged in the study of drugs from a natural origin) and others interested in the plant sciences and natural products. **Founded:** 1959. **Membership:** 1000. **Languages:** English. **Budget:** $100,000. Supersedes Plant Science Seminar.

AMERICAN SOCIETY FOR PHARMACOLOGY AND EXPERIMENTAL THERAPEUTICS (ASPET)
e-mail: aspetinfo@faseb.org
url: http://www.faseb.org/aspet
9650 Rockville Pike
Bethesda, MD 20814-3995
Christine K. Carrico, Ph.D., Exec. Officer
PH: (301)530-7060
FX: (301)530-7061
Description: Scientific society of investigators in pharmacology and toxicology interested in research and promotion of pharma-

cological knowledge and its use among scientists and the public. **Founded:** 1908. **Membership:** 4300. **Staff:** 5. **Languages:** English.

AMERICAN SOCIETY OF PLASTIC AND RECONSTRUCTIVE SURGICAL NURSES (ASPRSN)

e-mail: asprsn@mail.ajj.com
E. Holly Ave.
Box 56
Pitman, NJ 08071
Ron Brady, Exec.Dir.
PH: (609)256-2340
FX: (609)589-7463
Description: Registered nurses, licensed practical nurses, and licensed vocational nurses working with plastic surgeons or interested in plastic and reconstructive nursing. Objectives are: to enhance leadership qualities of nurses in the field of plastic surgery; to increase the skills, knowledge, and understanding of personnel in plastic surgery nursing through continuing education; to study existing practices and new developments in the field; to encourage participation and interest in professional organizations; to cooperate with others in the profession. **Founded:** 1975. **Membership:** 1700. **State Groups:** 25. **Languages:** English. **Budget:** $400,000.

AMERICAN SOCIETY OF POST ANESTHESIA NURSES (ASPAN)

11512 Allecingie Pkwy.
Richmond, VA 23235
Keven Dill, Dir.
PH: (804)379-5516
FX: (609)848-1881
Description: Postanesthesia nurses. Promotes upgrading of standards of postanesthesia patient care and the professional growth of licensed nurses involved in the care of patients in the immediate postanesthesia period. Provides forum for exchange of knowledge and ideas on patient care; facilitates cooperation among postanesthesia nurses and physicians and other medical personnel; encourages specialization and research in the field. Promotes public awareness and understanding of the care of postanesthesia patients. Conducts courses. **Founded:** 1980. **Membership:** 11500. Multinational. **State Groups:** 42. **Languages:** English. **Budget:** $1,000,000.

AMERICAN SOCIETY OF RADIOLOGIC TECHNOLOGISTS (ASRT)

url: http://www.asrt.org
15000 Central Ave. SE
Albuquerque, NM 87123
Joan Parsons, Exec.VP, Operations
PH: (505)298-4500
TF: 800444-2778
FX: (505)298-5063
Description: Professional society of diagnostic radiography, radiation therapy, ultrasound, and nuclear medicine technologists. Advances the science of radiologic technology; establishes and maintains high standards of education; evaluates the quality of patient care; improves the welfare and socioeconomics of radiologic technologists. Operates ASRT Educational Foundation, which provides educational materials to radiologic technologists. **Founded:** 1920. **Membership:** 67000. **Staff:** 64. **State Groups:** 50. **Languages:** English. **Budget:** $6,000,000. **Publication:** *ASRT Scanner*, monthly. Magazine. Includes calendar of events, member profiles, state affiliate news, educational opportunities, and research updates. Price: included in membership dues. ISSN: 0161-3863. Circulation: 67,000. Advertising: accepted ■ *Radiation Therapist*, semiannual. Journal. Price: included in membership dues; $25.00/year for nonmembership in U.S.; $50.00/year for nonmembers outside U.S. Circulation: 13,000. Advertising: accepted ■ *Radiologic Technology*, bimonthly. Journal. Includes advertisers and cumulative annual author and title indexes, book reviews, literature abstracts, and calendar of events. Price: included in membership dues; $49.00/year for nonmembers; $75.00/year for nonmembers outside the U.S.; $29.50/year for students. ISSN: 0033-8397. Circulation: 70,000. **Formerly:** (1934) American

Society of Radiographers; (1964) American Society of X-Ray Technicians.

AMERICAN SOCIETY OF REGIONAL ANESTHESIA (ASRA)

e-mail: 75112.2053@compuserve.com
1910 Byrd Ave., No. 100
PO Box 11086
Richmond, VA 23230-1086
John A. Hinckley, Exec.Sec.
PH: (804)282-0010
FX: (804)282-0090
Description: Physicians and research Ph.D.s. Conducts educational workshops. Sponsors annual refresher course. **Founded:** 1974. **Membership:** 8000. **Staff:** 4. Multinational. **Languages:** English. **Budget:** $1,000,000.

AMERICAN SOCIETY FOR STEREOTACTIC AND FUNCTIONAL NEUROSURGERY (ASSFN)

c/o Philip L. Gildenberg, M.D.
6624 Fannin, Ste. 1620
Houston, TX 77030
Philip L. Gildenberg, M.D., VP
PH: (713)790-0795
FX: (713)669-0388
Description: Neurosurgeons practicing stereotactic surgery united to promote communication in the field. (Stereotactic surgery utilizes a technique for inserting delicate instruments in precise areas of the nervous system.) Compiles statistics. Plans to establish museum. **Founded:** 1968. **Membership:** 300. **Staff:** 2. **Languages:** English. **Publication:** *Stereotactic and Functional Neurosurgery*, bimonthly. Journal. **Formerly:** (1972) International Society for Research in Stereoencephalotomy, American Branch.

AMERICAN SOCIETY FOR THE STUDY OF ORTHODONTICS (ASSO)

50-12 204th St.
Oakland Gardens, NY 11364
Daisy N. Buchalter, Exec.Sec.
PH: (718)224-8898
Description: Members of the American Dental Association or other societies, with special interest in orthodontics but not limited to those who practice in the field. Purposes are to: preserve the highest ideals in orthodontics and in dentistry; encourage and assist the diffusion of orthodontic knowledge to all dentists who include orthodontics as an integral part of their health service or limit their practice to orthodontics; institute an intensive program of fundamental and advanced studies and guidance for its members in theoretical, didactic, and applied orthodontics; encourage the orthodontic departments of university dental schools to provide both short and extended courses in orthodontics; to establish discussion and clinical study groups throughout the U.S. Conducts lectures, panel discussions, postgraduate seminars, table clinics, and consultation service. **Founded:** 1945. **Languages:** English. **Publication:** *ASSO Newsletter*, quarterly ■ *International Journal of Orthodontics*, 3/year. **Formerly:** (1962) New York Society for the Study of Orthodontics.

AMERICAN SOCIETY FOR THERAPEUTIC RADIOLOGY AND ONCOLOGY (ASTRO)

url: http://www.astro.org
1891 Preston White Dr.
Reston, VA 20191
Gregg Robinson, COO
PH: (703)716-7588
TF: 800962-7876
FX: (703)476-8167
Description: Physicians who limit their practice to radiation therapy; associate members are scientists and health care personnel who have a major interest "in furthering the aims of the society"; junior members are residents who have completed one year of training in radiation therapy. Aim is "to extend the benefits of radiation therapy to patients with cancer or other disorders, to advance its scientific basis, and to provide for the education and professional fellowship of its members.". **Founded:** 1955. **Mem-**

bership: 4200. **Staff:** 6. Multinational. **Languages:** English. **Budget:** $2,100,000. Formerly (1983) American Society of Therapeutic Radiologists.

AMERICAN SOCIETY FOR VIROLOGY (ASV)
e-mail: lguarino@bioch.tamu.edu
url: http://www.mcw.edu/asv
Department of Biochemistry
Texas A&M University
College Station, TX 77843-2128
Linda A. Guarino, Ph.D., Membership Chm.
PH: (409)845-7556
FX: (409)845-9274
Description: Individuals possessing professional degrees who have published original investigations in virology, and are actively engaged in virological research. Serves as a forum for discussion and exchange of information among members. Makes available to members discount subscriptions to scholarly journals; represents members on national and international scientific councils. **Founded:** 1981. **Languages:** English.

AMERICAN SPORTS MEDICINE ASSOCIATION BOARD OF CERTIFICATION (ASMA)
660 W. Duarte Rd.
Arcadia, CA 91007
Joe S. Borland, Bd.Chm.
PH: (626)445-1978
Description: Verifies and qualifies the educational competency of active athletic trainers and sports medicine trainers for certification. Establishes competency standards of education required for the prevention and care of athletic injuries and sports medicine. Maintains speakers' bureau. **Founded:** 1978. **Membership:** 1400. **Staff:** 4. **Languages:** German, Italian. **Budget:** $40,000.

AMERICAN STUDENT DENTAL ASSOCIATION (ASDA)
211 E. Chicago Ave., Ste. 1160
Chicago, IL 60611
Karen S. Cervenka, CAE, Exec. Dir.
PH: (312)440-2795
FX: (312)440-2820
Description: Predoctoral and postdoctoral dental students organized to improve the quality of dental education and to promote the accessibility of oral health care. Additional membership categories include predental, postdoctoral, international and associate. Represents dental students before legislative bodies, organizations, and associations that affect dental students. Disseminates information to dental students. Sponsors advocacy program and "externships" including Washington National Helath Policy, Chicago Administrative, State Governm ent Affairs, and Research. **Founded:** 1971. **Membership:** 12500. **Staff:** 8. **Local Groups:** 54. **Languages:** English. **Budget:** $1,000,000. **Publication:** *ASDA Handbook*, annual. Price: $20.00 in U.S.; $30.00 outside U.S. ■ *ASDA News*, monthly ■ *Dentistry*, quarterly. **Formerly:** (1971) Student American Dental Association.

AMERICAN SUBACUTE CARE ASSOCIATION (ASCA)
e-mail: ASCAMail@aol.com
1720 Kennedy Causeway, Ste. 109
North Bay Village, FL 33141
Mike Freedman, Pres.
PH: (305)864-0396
FX: (305)868-0905
Description: Executives of subacute care companies, vendors, and allied legal and financial professionals; physicians, nurses, physical therapists, occupational therapists, and other healthcare professionals involved in subacute care. Dedicated to advancing the field of subacute care. **Founded:** 1993. **Membership:** 375. **Staff:** 5. **Languages:** English. **Budget:** $50,000.

AMERICAN SURGICAL ASSOCIATION (ASA)
c/o Robert P. Jones, Jr., Ed.D.
13 Elm St.
Manchester, MA 01944-1314
John L. Cameron, M.D., Sec.

PH: (508)526-8330
FX: (508)526-7521
Description: Surgeons organized to promote the science and art of surgery. Bestows medallion for scientific achievement. **Founded:** 1880. **Membership:** 949. **Staff:** 1. **Languages:** English.

AMERICAN SYRINGOMYELIA ALLIANCE PROJECT (ASAP)
url: http://www.syringo.org
PO Box 1586
Longview, TX 75606-1586
Don White, Co.-Founder/Chair.
PH: (903)236-7079
TF: 800ASAP-282
FX: (903)757-7456
Description: Seeks to increase awareness of and promote research on syringomyelia, a rare spinal disorder. Conducts fundraising activities and children's services. **Founded:** 1988. **Membership:** 1500. **Staff:** 1. **National Groups:** 1. **Languages:** English. **Budget:** $45,000. **Publication:** *Syringomyelia Connections*, bimonthly. Newsletter. Price: $20.00. Circulation: 1,500. Advertising: not accepted ■ *What Is Syringomyelia*. Brochure. ASAP.

AMERICA'S BLOOD CENTERS
e-mail: abe@americasblood.org
url: http://www.americasblood.org
725 15th St. NW, Ste. 700
Washington, DC 20005
Jim MacPherson, Exec.Dir.
PH: (202)393-5725
FX: (202)393-1282
Description: Independent, nonprofit, federally licensed blood centers serving defined geographic areas that collectively provide about half of the nation's volunteer donor blood supply. Purpose is to ensure an optimal supply of blood, blood components, and blood derivatives and the development of a comprehensive range of the highest quality blood services to meet the needs of the American people. Compiles data and statistics; conducts research concerning organizational, administrative, fiscal, and operational phases of blood banking; establishes liaison and conducts cooperative activities of all kinds with national, regional, and local associations, groups, and organizations having a relationship of any kind to the drawing, processing, storing, or distribution of blood. **Founded:** 1962. **Membership:** 67. **Staff:** 7. **Languages:** English. **Budget:** $1,200,000. **Publication:** *CCBC Newsletter*, weekly. Includes calendar of events and list of employment opportunities. Price: free to members; $216.00/year for nonmembers (U.S. and Canada); $240.00/year for nonmembers (outside the U.S. and Canada). Circulation: 500. Advertising: accepted ■ Membership Directory, semiannual. **Formerly:** (1971) Community Blood Bank Council; (1998) Council of Community Blood Centers.

AMYOTROPHIC LATERAL SCLEROSIS ASSOCIATION (ALSA)
21021 Ventura Blvd., Ste. 321
Woodland Hills, CA 91364
Michael W. Havlicek, Exec.VP
PH: (818)340-7500
TF: 800782-4747
FX: (818)340-2060
Description: Patients; relatives and friends of patients; doctors, neurologists, physical therapists, nurses, and professional organizations dedicated to finding the cause, prevention, and cure for amyotrophic lateral sclerosis (ALS). Offers help and information to ALS patients and their families. Funds ALS-specific research at major medical institutions. Works with other agencies, including the government, to increase their involvement on a priority basis in ALS research. Conducts patient meetings. **Founded:** 1985. **Membership:** 250000. **Staff:** 16. **Regional Groups:** 135. **Languages:** English, Spanish. **Budget:** $3,000,000. **Publication:** *Amyotrophic Lateral Sclerosis Association – Link*, quarterly. Newspaper. Includes book reviews and research and chapter news. Price: free. Circulation: 75,000. Advertising: accepted. **Also Known As:** ALS Association. **Formed by Merger of:** National

ALS Foundation; Amyotrophic Lateral Sclerosis Society of America.

AMYOTROPHIC LATERAL SCLEROSIS SOCIETY OF CANADA (ALSSC)

(Societe Canadienne de la Sclerose Laterale Amyotrophique)
220-6 Adelaide St. E
Toronto, ON, Canada M5C 1H6
Jan Rodman, Exec.Dir.
PH: (416)362-0269
FX: (416)362-0414
Description: Health care professionals; individuals with amyotrophic lateral sclerosis (ALS) and their families. Promotes advancement in the diagnosis of ALS and seeks to find a cure for the disease; works to improve the quality of life for people with ALS and their families. Provides support and services to people with ALS and their families; sponsors research and educational programs. **Languages:** English, French.

ANAESTHETIC RESEARCH SOCIETY (ARS)

e-mail: p.m.hopkins@leeds.ac.uk
Academic Unit of Anaesthesia
St. James University Hospital
Leeds IS9 7TF, England
Dr. P.M. Hopkins, Hon.Sec.
PH: 44 113 2065274
FX: 44 113 2064140
Description: Facilitates the presentation of members' research in anesthesiology (clinical or experimental, completed or in progress). **Founded:** 1958. **Membership:** 660. **Languages:** English. **Publication:** *Proceedings* (in English), 3/year. Journal. Included in the *British Journal of Anaesthesia*. Price: L150.00/year. ISSN: 0007-0912. Circulation: 10,500. Advertising: accepted.

ANATOMICAL SOCIETY (AS)

(Anatomische Gesellschaft)
e-mail: buchard@enet.eu_czebeck.de
url: http://www.azst/iu-cuebech.de/ezatpes.html
Institut fur Anatomie
Medizinische Universitat zu Lubeck
Ratzeburger Allee 160
D-23538 Lubeck, Germany
Dr. Wolfgang Kuhnel, M.D., Sec.
PH: 49 451 5004030
FX: 49 451 5004034
Description: Anatomists, histochemists, histologists, biologists. **Founded:** 1886. **Membership:** 1056. **Staff:** 5. Multinational. **Languages:** English, French. **Publication:** *Annals of Anatomy.* Journal ■ *Verhandlungen der Anatomischen Gesellschaft* (in English, French, and German), annual. Proceedings. Price: DM 180.00. ISSN: 0066-1562. Advertising: not accepted.

ANATOMICAL SOCIETY OF GREAT BRITAIN AND IRELAND

e-mail: gillian.morris-kay@human-anatomy.ox.ac.uk
url: http://www.sm.ic.ac.uk/anatsoc/home.htm
Department of Human Anatomy
University of Oxford
South Parks Rd.
Oxford OX1 3QX, England
Prof. G.M. Morriss-Kay, Sec.
PH: 44 1865 272165
FX: 44 1865 272420
Description: Individuals involved in anatomical science. Promotes development and advancement in anatomy and related science through research and education. Offers program for graduate students. **Founded:** 1887. **Membership:** 650. **Staff:** 1. **Languages:** English. **Publication:** *Journal of Anatomy* (in English), 8/year. Contains research information in the anatomical sciences.

ANATOMICAL SOCIETY OF SOUTHERN AFRICA (ASSA)

(Anatomiese Vereniging van Suider-Afrika)
e-mail: anatom3@op1_up.ac.za
Faculty of Veterinary Science
Private Bag X04
Onderstepoort 0110, Republic of South Africa
Prof. H.B. Groenewald, Sec.
PH: 27 12 5298247
FX: 27 12 5298320
Description: Individuals from 5 countries interested in the study of anatomy. Aims to: promote the study of anatomy; encourage anatomical research; represent anatomists of Southern Africa at the international level. Organizes seminars and workshops. Bestows awards. **Founded:** 1969. **Membership:** 200. Multinational. **Languages:** Afrikaans, English. **Budget:** R 12,000. **Publication:** *Newsletter of the ASSA* (in English), semiannual. Advertising: not accepted ■ *Proceedings* (in English), annual.

ANATOMICAL SOCIETY OF WEST AFRICA (ASWA)

Department of Anatomy
University of Ibadan
Ibadan, Oyo, Nigeria
Dr. M. Shokunbi, Contact
PH: 234 22 400550
Description: Anatomists and anatomy educators and students. Seeks to advance the study and teaching of anatomy. Facilitates exchange of information among members; conducts research and educational programs. Multinational. **Languages:** English.

ANDEAN COOPERATION IN HEALTH (ACH)

525 23rd St. NW
Washington, DC 20037
PH: (202)861-3200
FX: (202)223-5971
Description: Public and private sector health organizations and agencies in Andean countries. Seeks to improve access to quality health care for people in the Andean region. Coordinates members' activities; identifies and devises means to meet areas of need in the health care delivery systems of members. Multinational. **Languages:** English, Spanish.

ANDEAN RURAL HEALTH CARE (ARHC)

e-mail: arhcsara@aol.com
518 Lakeshore Dr.
Lake Junaluska, NC 28745
David Shanklin, Contact
PH: (704)452-3544
FX: (704)452-7790
Description: Volunteers united to improve the health care available to people living in rural areas of Bolivia. Collaborates with Bolivian health organizations and government agencies to develop and expand health care services. Trains indigenous people to operate and maintain public health services. Conducts research to determine health care needs in rural Bolivia. Maintains home visitation programs; sponsors volunteer work teams from the U.S. to support Bolivian health care services. **Languages:** English, Spanish. **Budget:** $1,200,000.

ANIMAL HEALTH INSTITUTE (AHI)

url: http://www.ahi.org
501 Wythe St.
PO Box 1417-D50
Alexandria, VA 22313-1480
Alexander S. Mathews, Pres. CEO
PH: (703)684-0011
FX: (703)684-0125
Description: Represents manufacturers of animal health products (vaccines, pharmaceuticals, and feed additives used in modern food production; and medicines for household pets). Works with government agencies and legislators; prepares position papers; compiles and disseminates information. Sponsors AHI Foundation. **Founded:** 1941. **Membership:** 22. **Staff:** 17. **Languages:** English. **Budget:** $2,500,000. **Publication:** *AHI quarterly,* quarterly. Newsletter. Covers developments of significance to an-

imal health, livestock, and veterinary industries. Includes legislative and regulatory updates and research. Price: free. Circulation: 2,500. Advertising: not accepted ∎ *Net Sales Survey*, annual ∎ *Source Book*, annual. Provides information on members, governmental agencies, and allied organizations ∎ Directory, annual. Provides information on membership activities ∎ Report, annual ∎ Surveys. Provides information on research and development.

ANTHROPOSOPHICAL NURSES ASSOCIATION OF AMERICA
103 Hermitage Dr.
Elkton, MD 21921
Catherine Barnes, Sec.
PH: (410)392-3283
FX: (410)392-0862
Description: Seeks to further the practice of anthroposophical nursing in the U.S. (Anthroposophy is a 20th century religious system centering on human development.) Encourages nurses to apply their knowledge of humankind to nursing practices. Promotes members' continued education. **Founded:** 1985. **Membership:** 90. **Languages:** English.

ANTIGUA PLANNED PARENTHOOD ASSOCIATION (APPA)
Bishopgate St.
PO Box 419
St. Johns, Antigua-Barbuda
Dr. Marlene Joseph
PH: (268)462-0947
FX: (268)462-1187
Description: Promotes family planning and maternal and infant health care as a way to improve the quality of life for individuals living in Antigua Barbuda. Seeks to reduce the number of unwanted pregnancies and abortions. Provides contraceptive services for men and women. Sponsors programs on family plannng and sex education. Acts as an advocate for family planning on the national level. Conducts research. **Founded:** 1970. **Membership:** 52. **Staff:** 6. **Languages:** English. **Publication:** *Family Fare* (in English). Newsletter. Covers reproductive health issues, family planning and family life education issues. Price: EC$5.00. Advertising: not accepted.

APPROPRIATE HEALTH RESOURCES AND TECHNOLOGIES ACTION GROUP (AHRTAG)
1 London Bridge St.
London SE1 9SG, England
K. Attawell, Co-Dir.
PH: 44 171 3781403
FX: 44 171 4036003
Description: Primary health care specialists in developing countries. Addresses the problems of disease, disability, and high infant mortality. Promotes better primary health care in developing countries through the dissemination of information to health workers and the establishment of advisory services. Participates in the design and development of low-cost health equipment. Conducts courses and surveys. **Founded:** 1977. **Membership:** 70. **Staff:** 22. Multinational. **Languages:** English. **Budget:** L1,300,000. **Publication:** *AIDS Action* (in English, French, Portuguese, and Spanish), quarterly. Newsletter. ISSN: 0953-0096 ∎ *Annual Report* ∎ *CBR News* (in English), quarterly. Newsletter. ISSN: 0963-5556 ∎ *Child Health Dialogue* (in Chinese, English, French, Gujarati, Hindi, Portuguese, Spanish, Tamil, Urdu, and Vietnamese), quarterly. Newsletter. ISSN: 0950-0235 ∎ *Health Action* (in English), quarterly. Newsletter. ISSN: 0969-479X.

ARAB CENTRE FOR MEDICAL LITERATURE (ACML)
Box 5225
Safat 13053, Kuwait
Dr. Abdul Rahman Al-Awadi, Contact
PH: 965 5338610
FX: 965 5338618
Description: Physicians and medical writers. Promotes dissemination of medical knowledge. Encourages publication of medical texts; sponsors research and educational programs; facilitates communication among doctors in the Arab World. Multinational. **Languages:** Arabic, English.

ARAB FEDERATION OF SPORTS MEDICINE (AFSM)
PO Box 7559
Doha, Qatar
Description: Physicians specializing in sports medicine. Seeks to advance the practice of sports medicine; encourages continuing professional development of members. Facilitates exchange of information among members; conducts educational programs. Multinational. **Languages:** Arabic, English.

ARAB FORUM FOR PRIMARY HEALTH CARE AND COMMUNITY BASED REHABILITATION
32 avenue Tour Hassan, Apt. 7
Rabat, Morocco
PH: 212 7 726336
FX: 212 7 726340
Description: Health care organizations and institutions. Promotes increased availability of quality primary health care and rehabilitation services in the Arab World. Facilitates communication and cooperation among members; conducts public health programs; sponsors research and educational initiatives. Multinational. **Languages:** Arabic, English.

ARAB MEDICAL UNION (AMU)
Union des Medecins Arabes
Mahrajene
PO Box 290
1082 Tunis, Tunisia
Aziz El Matri, Contact
PH: 216 1 886800
FX: 216 1 889293
Description: Physicians and other health care professionals. Seeks to increase availability and quality of health care services in the Arab World; promotes professional advancement of members. Makes available health services; sponsors research; conducts continuing professional development courses. Multinational. **Languages:** Arabic, English.

ARAB ORTHODOX SOCIETY FOR THE RELIEF OF THE SICK (AOSRS)
PO Box 21358
Old City
Jerusalem, Israel
Nura Kurt, Contact
PH: 972 2 271958
Description: Works to insure availability of health care and social services; promotes preventive health care. Provides medical relief services in times of emergency. **Languages:** Arabic, English.

ARAB PHYSICS EDUCATION NETWORK (APEN)
Faculty of Science
Physics Department
University of Cairo
Giza, Egypt
R. K. Wassef, Contact
PH: 20 2 5720095
FX: 20 2 3545296
Description: Physicists and physics educators, students, and institutions. Seeks to advance the study and teaching of physics. Serves as a forum for the exchange of information among members; sponsors research and educational programs. Multinational. **Languages:** Arabic, English.

ARCHAEUS PROJECT (AP)
url: http://www.fivemtn.org
PO Box 7079
Kamuela, HI 96743
Dennis Stillings, Dir.
PH: (808)885-6773
FX: (808)885-9863
Description: Business, medical, academic, and engineering pro-

fessionals, scientists, psychologists, psi researchers, and interested others. Investigates the effects of ordinary and altered states of consciousness on conditions of health and disease; studies the relationships between the mind, body, and matter, and the implications of these relationships for medicine. Sponsors lecture series, seminars, and workshops; conducts cyberphysiology (science of self-regulation in physiology) research. **Founded:** 1981. **Staff:** 3. Multinational. **Languages:** French, German. **Budget:** $239,000. **Publication:** *Healing Island*, quarterly. Journal. Contains items on health care, health care costs, and the integration of alternative with mainstream medicine, Hawaii as a health/healing destination. Price: free on request at present. ISSN: 0895-125X. Advertising: not accepted ■ *Project 2010*. Monograph ■ *Tape Catalog*.

ARGENTINIAN ASSOCIATION OF DERMATOLOGY (AAD)
(Asociacion Argentina de Dermatologia)
Mexico 1720
1100 Buenos Aires, Argentina
Dr. Lidia Ester Valle, Pres.
PH: 54 1 3812737
FX: 54 1 3812737
Description: Dermatologists in Argentina. Bestows awards; provides educational programs. **Founded:** 1907. **Membership:** 910. **Staff:** 2. **Local Groups:** 6. **Languages:** English, Spanish. **Budget:** 10 A. **Publication:** *Indice General* (in English and Spanish), periodic. Price: 150.00 A/year. Advertising: accepted. Alternate Formats: CD-ROM ■ *Journal of Argentine Dermatology* (in English and Spanish). Price: 150.00 A/year. Advertising: accepted. Alternate Formats: CD-ROM ■ *Revista Argentina de Dermatologia* (in English and Spanish), quarterly. Includes summary in English. Price: 150.00 A/year. Advertising: accepted.

ARS MEDICA PRO HUMANITATE INTERNATIONAL (AMHI)
Avenue Abbe Huyberechts 14
B-1340 Ottignies, Belgium
Dr. Bernard De Spiegelier, Contact
Description: Physicians and public health organizations. Seeks to advance medical research and the study and practice of medicine. Serves as a clearinghouse on medical research; makes available health services; sponsors research and educational programs. Multinational. **Languages:** English, French.

ARTHRITIS CARE (AC)
18 Stephenson Way
London NW1 2HD, England
Richard Gutch, CEO
PH: 44 171 9161500
FX: 44 171 9161505
Description: Individuals with arthritis and concerned others. Seeks to: increase awareness of the problems associated with rheumatic diseases; disseminate information; establish a nationwide network of branches; improve welfare facilities; provide information, advice and practical aid. Maintains hotels, a residential home for severely disabled persons, and self catering units. Provides home-visiting service. Advises on non-medical enquiries. Assists needy members. **Founded:** 1948. **Membership:** 67000. **Staff:** 100. **Local Groups:** 650. **Languages:** English. **Budget:** L6,935,241. **Publication:** *Arthritis News* (in English), quarterly. Magazine. Price: L6.00/year. ISSN: 0144-6339. Circulation: 100,000. Advertising: accepted. Alternate Formats: magnetic tape ■ *Young Arthritis News*. Magazine. Price: included in membership dues. **Formerly:** British Rheumatism and Arthritis Association.

ARTHRITIS AND RESEARCH CAMPAIGN
e-mail: rue@arc.org.uk.
Copeman House
St. Mary's Court
St. Mary's Gate
Chesterfield, Derbyshire S41 7TD, England
F. Logan, Chief Exec.
PH: 44 1246 558033
FX: 44 1246 558007

Description: Voluntary helpers, donators and support staff. Conducts research and education to find the cause of rheumatic disease. In pursuit of these objectives mounts a wide ranging research program involving people, projects and centers - usually at university medical schools. Currently running at over 15 million pounds per year. The income raised to meet this commitment comes entirely from voluntary donations. **Founded:** 1936. **Membership:** 40000. **Staff:** 71. **Budget:** L16,200,000. **Publication:** *Arthritis Today*, 3/year. Booklets ■ Booklets. **Formerly:** Arthritis and Rheumatism Council for Research.

ARTHRITIS FOUNDATION (AF)
url: http://www.arthritis.org
1330 W. Peachtree St.
Atlanta, GA 30309
Don L. Riggin, CAE, CEO & President
PH: (404)872-7100
TF: 800283-7800
FX: (404)872-0457
Description: Seeks to: discover the cause and improve the methods for the treatment and prevention of arthritis and other rheumatic diseases; increase the number of scientists investigating rheumatic diseases; provide training in rheumatic diseases for more doctors; extend knowledge of arthritis and other rheumatic diseases to the lay public, emphasizing the socioeconomic as well as medical aspects of these diseases. **Founded:** 1948. **Membership:** 700000. **Staff:** 750. **Local Groups:** 71. Formerly Arthritis and Rheumatism Foundation.

ARTHRITIS HEALTH PROFESSIONS ASSOCIATION (AHPA)
1314 Spring St. NW
60 Executive Park S., Ste. 150
Atlanta, GA 30329
Julie Epps, Exec.Dir.
PH: (404)633-3777
FX: (404)633-1870
Description: Nurses, occupational and physical therapists, social workers, psychologists, vocational counselors, physicians, pharmacists, and other health professionals concerned with the practice, education, and research of rheumatic diseases. Seeks to establish a scientific base of knowledge to improve the quality and provision of health services to individuals with rheumatic diseases. Disseminates information regarding the study and treatment of rheumatic diseases. Develops and implements medical and scientific programs in the field of rheumatology. A section of the Arthritis Foundation. **Founded:** 1965. **Membership:** 2000. **Staff:** 3. **Local Groups:** 13. **Languages:** English. **Budget:** $230,000.

ARTHRITIS SOCIETY (AS)
e-mail: dmorrice@arthritis.ca
url: http://www.arthritis.ca
393 University Ave., Ste. 1700
Toronto, ON, Canada M5G 1E6
Denis Morrice, Pres.
PH: (416)979-7228
FX: (416)979-8366
Description: Individuals with arthritis and their families; health care professionals and institutions with an interest in arthritis and other rheumatic diseases. Promotes research in arthritis prevention, treatment, and patient care. Conducts public education programs and continuing professional training courses for health care providers; sponsors research; maintains speakers' bureau. **Founded:** 1948. **Languages:** English, French. **Publication:** *Arthritis News*, quarterly. Journal. ISSN: 0820-9006. Circulation: 20,000. Advertising: accepted.

ASEAN ASSOCIATION OF RADIOLOGY
Department of Radiological Sciences
Santa Tomas University Hospital
Espana
Manila, Philippines
PH: 63 2 7313001
Description: Radiologists and health care facilities in southeast-

ern Asia. Seeks to advance the study, teaching, and practice of radiology; promotes professional advancement of radiologists. Serves as a clearinghouse on radiology; conducts research and educational programs. Multinational. **Languages:** English, Filipino.

ASEAN CARDIOLOGISTS' FEDERATION
Indonesia Heart Association
Rumah Sakit Jantung, Harapan Kita
Jalan Jend
Jakarta, Indonesia
Description: Cardiologists and health care facilities. Seeks to advance the study, teaching, and practice of cardiology; promotes professional development of cardiologists. Functions as a clearinghouse on cardiology; conducts continuing professional education courses. Multinational. **Languages:** English, Indonesian.

ASEAN FEDERATION FOR PSYCHIATRIC AND MENTAL HEALTH
Panpreecha AFPMH
Somdet Chaopraya Hospital
Klongsan
Bangkok 10600, Thailand
Dr. Chutitaya, Contact
PH: 66 2 4371298
FX: 66 2 4375456
Description: Psychiatrists and other mental health professionals; mental health care facilities. Promotes increased access to mental health care; seeks to advance the study, teaching, and practice of psychiatry. Facilitates exchange of information among members; provides support and assistance to mental health care institutions. Multinational. **Languages:** English, Thai.

ASEAN INSTITUTE FOR HEALTH DEVELOPMENT
e-mail: directad@mahidol.ac.th
25/5 Phutthamonthon 4 Rd.
Salaya
Mahido University
Nakhon Pathom 73170, Thailand
Dr. Boongium Tragoolvonse, Contact
PH: 66 2 4419040
FX: 66 2 4419044
Description: National health agencies. Seeks to improve the availability and quality of primary health care services in Southeast Asia. Facilitates establishment of local health services and facilities; serves as a clearinghouse on public health policies and programs. Multinational. **Languages:** English, Thai.

ASEAN NEUROLOGICAL SOCIETY
Clinical Neuroscience Society
Department of Neurology
Singapore General Hospital
Singapore 169606, Singapore
Dr. Lim Shih Hui, Contact
PH: 65 2223322
FX: 65 2203321
Description: Health care professionals with an interest in neurology. Seeks to advance neurological study, teaching, and practice. Facilitates exchange of information among members; sponsors research and continuing professional development programs. Multinational. **Languages:** Chinese, English.

ASEAN PEDIATRIC FEDERATION
Academy of Medicine
Singapore Paediatric Society
Chapter of Physicians
Singapore 169854, Singapore
Monica Wong, Contact
PH: 65 2238968
FX: 65 2255155
Description: Pediatrists and other health care professionals with an interest in pediatrics. Seeks to advance pediatric study, teaching, and practice. Facilitates exchange of information among

members; sponsors continuing professional development courses. Multinational. **Languages:** Chinese, English.

ASHP FOUNDATION
7272 Wisconsin Ave.
Bethesda, MD 20814
Joseph A. Oddis, Exec.VP
PH: (301)657-3000
FX: (301)657-1251
Description: Established for pharmaceutical care and research purposes. Offers fellowships, grants, awards, and anticoagulation and renal dialysis traineeships. **Founded:** 1968. **Languages:** English. Also Known As American Society of Hospital Pharmacists Research and Education Foundation; ASHP Research and Education Foundation.

ASIA AND OCEANIA FEDERATION OF OBSTETRICS AND GYNECOLOGY (AOFOG)
National University Hospital
Department of Obstetrics and Gynaecology
Lower Kent Ridge Rd.
Singapore 119074, Singapore
S. S. Ratnam, Contact
Description: Obstetricians and gynecologists. Seeks to advance the study, teaching, and practice of obstetrics and gynecology; promotes professional development of members. Serves as a forum for the exchange of information among members; sponsors research and educational programs. Multinational. **Languages:** Chinese, English.

ASIA PACIFIC ACADEMY OF OPHTHALMOLOGY (APAO)
e-mail: wll@pacific.net.sg
Gleneagles Hospital
Annexe Block 02-38
6A Napier Rd.
Singapore 258500, Singapore
PH: 65 4666666
FX: 65 7333360

ASIA-PACIFIC ACADEMY OF OPHTHALMOLOGY (APAO)
e-mail: wll@pacific.net.sg
Eye Clinic Singapore
6A Napier Rd.
102-38 Gleneagles Ave. Blk
Singapore 309028, Singapore
Prof. Arthur S.M. Lim, Contact
PH: 65 4666666
FX: 65 7333360
Description: National ophthalmological societies, ophthalmologists, and scientists in 21 countries. Promotes research, exchange, and dissemination of scientific information on diseases of the eye including blinding diseases. Encourages closer relations among members to improve the teaching and practice of ophthalmology. Maintains liaison with International Agency for the Prevention of Blindness and the International Federation of Ophthalmological Societies. Encourages support of the World Health Organization Programme for Prevention of Blindness. Sponsors Holmes Lecture on Preventative Ophthalmology and Ocampo Lecture on Clinical Research; organizes workshops and instructional courses on advances in ophthalmology. **Founded:** 1958. Multinational. **Budget:** $3,700.**Description:** Ophthalmologists. Seeks to advance ophthalmological study, teaching, and practice. Facilitates exchange of information among members; conducts continuing professional development courses. Multinational. **Languages:** Chinese, English.

ASIA PACIFIC ASSOCIATION OF SOCIETIES OF PATHOLOGISTS (APASP)
Department of Pathology
Beijing Medical University
Beijing 100083, People's Republic of China
Dr. Jie Zheng, Contact
Description: Professional associations representing pathologists. Seeks to advance the study, teaching, and practice of pathology.

Facilitates exchange of information among members; sponsors research and continuing professional development programs. Multinational. **Languages:** Chinese, English.

ASIA PACIFIC ENDODONTIC CONFEDERATION (APEC)
e-mail: spcheung@hkuxa.hku.hk
url: http://www.hku.hk/consden/apec.htm
Prince Philip Dental Hospital
34 Hospital Rd.
Hong Kong, Hong Kong
Dr. Gary Cheung, Contact
PH: 852 28590288
FX: 852 25599013
Description: Endodontists. Seeks to advance the study, teaching, and practice of endodontia. Serves as a forum for the exchange of information among members; sponsors research and continuing professional development programs. Multinational. **Languages:** Chinese, English.

ASIA PACIFIC INTRAOCULAR IMPLANT ASSOCIATION (APIIA)
e-mail: wll@pacific.net.sg
Annexe Block 02-38
Gleneagles Hospital
6A Napier Rd.
Singapore 258500, Singapore
Arthur S. M. Lim, Contact
PH: 65 4666666
FX: 65 7333360
Description: Ophthalmologists and ocular surgeons with an interest in intraocular implants. Seeks to advance the study, teaching, and practice of intraocular implantology. Facilitates exchange of information among members; sponsors research and continuing professional development programs. Multinational. **Languages:** Chinese, English.

ASIA PACIFIC LEAGUE OF ASSOCIATIONS FOR RHEUMATISM (APLAR)
Department of Medicine
Prince of Wales Hospital
Chinese University of Hong Kong
Shatin, Hong Kong
Edmund K. Li, Contact
Description: Health care professionals with an interest in rheumatism. Seeks to advance the prevention, diagnosis, and treatment of rheumatism and related disorders. Serves as a clearinghouse on rheumatism; facilitates exchange of information among members; conducts research and continuing professional development programs. Multinational. **Languages:** Chinese, English.

ASIA PACIFIC PUBLIC HEALTH NUTRITION ASSOCIATION (APPHNA)
e-mail: zaksabry@uclink.berkeley.edu
Public Health Nutrition Program
421 Warren Hall
University of California
Berkeley, CA 94720-7360
Zak Sabry, Contact
PH: (510)642-3852
FX: (510)643-6981
Description: Public health practitioners and nutritionists. Promotes nutrition as a vital component of good health. Develops and implements national and international public health nutrition strategies; sponsors research and educational programs. Multinational. **Languages:** English.

ASIA PACIFIC SOCIETY OF PERIODONTOLOGY (APSP)
741-1 Hangnam, 2-dong
Yongsan-gu
Seoul 140-212, Republic of Korea
Son Seong-Hee, Contact
PH: 82 2 7926114
FX: 82 2 7926116
Description: Periondontists. Seeks to advance the study, teach-

ing, and practice of periodontology. Facilitates communication among members; sponsors research and continuing professional development programs. Multinational. **Languages:** English, Korean.

ASIA PACIFIC TRAVEL HEALTH ASSOCIATION (APTHA)
University of Hong Kong
7 Sassoon Rd.
Hong Kong, Hong Kong
A. J. Hedley, Contact
PH: 852 28199280
FX: 852 28559528
Description: Health care professionals and travel organizations. Promotes availability of quality health care for travelers. Recruits physicians to provide health care services for tourists; serves as a clearinghouse on health services geared to the needs of travelers. Multinational. **Languages:** Chinese, English.

ASIAN ACADEMY OF AESTHETIC DENTISTRY (AAAD)
268 Orchard Rd. 05-02
Singapore 0923, Singapore
Dr. Chee Peng Sum, Contact
PH: 65 7343162
FX: 65 7321979
Description: Dentists practicing aesthetic dentistry. Seeks to advance the study, teaching, and practice of aesthetic dentistry. Gathers and disseminates information on aesthetic dentistry; sponsors research and continuing professional development programs. Multinational. **Languages:** Chinese, English.

ASIAN ACADEMY OF PREVENTIVE DENTISTRY (AAPD)
e-mail: sakaio1@college.fdcnet.ac.jp
Fukuoka Dental College
Department of Preventive Dentistry
2-15-1 Tamura
Fukuoka 814-01, Japan
Osamu Sakai, Contact
PH: 81 92 8014011
FX: 81 92 8014909
Description: Dentists with an interest in preventive dentistry. Seeks to advance the study, teaching, and practice of preventive dentistry. Gathers and disseminates information on preventive dentistry; sponsors research and continuing professional development programs. Multinational. **Languages:** English, Japanese.

ASIAN AND PACIFIC ISLANDER AMERICAN HEALTH FORUM
e-mail: hforum@apiahf.org
url: http://www.apiahf.org/apiahf
942 Market St. Ste 200
San Francisco, CA 94102
Tessie Guillermo, Exec.Dir.
PH: (415)954-9959
FX: (415)954-9999
Description: Promotes policy, program, and research efforts for the improvement of health status of all Asian and Pacific Islander Americans. Examines and review the distribution of factors associated with health problems and issues facing Asian and Pacific Islander Americans, including infectious diseases, diabetes, hypertension, cancer, HIV/AIDS, substance abuse, and mental health disorders. Compiles statistics. Conducts research programs. **Founded:** 1986. **Membership:** 350. **Staff:** 17. **Languages:** English. **Budget:** $1,400,000.

ASIAN ASSOCIATION OF ORAL AND MAXILLO FACIAL SURGEONS (AAOMFS)
Maxillo-Facial Unit
Ripas Hospital
Bandar Seri Begawan, Brunei Darussalam
Dr. N. Ravindranathan, Contact
PH: 673 2 447583
Description: Oral and maxillofacial surgeons. Seeks to advance the practice of oral and maxillofacial surgery. Facilitates exchange of information among members; conducts research and con-

tinuing professional development programs. Multinational. **Languages:** Arabic, English.

ASIAN ASSOCIATION OF PEDIATRIC SURGEONS (AAPS)
Hyushu University
3-1-1 Maidashi
Higashi-ku
Fukuoka 812-82, Japan
Sachiyo Suita, Contact
PH: 81 92 6425573
FX: 81 92 6425580
Description: Pediatric surgeons. Seeks to advance the practice of pediatric surgery. Facilitates exchange of information among members; sponsors research, training, and continuing professional development programs. Multinational. **Languages:** English, Japanese.

ASIAN-AUSTRALASIAN SOCIETY OF NEUROLOGICAL SURGEONS (AASNS)
e-mail: leigh.atkinson@hcn.net.au
201 Wickham Terrace
Brisbane, QLD 4000, Australia
PH: 61 7 38393393
FX: 61 7 38322005

ASIAN - AUSTRALASIAN SOCIETY OF NEUROLOGICAL SURGEONS (AASNS)
201 Wickham Terr.
Brisbane, QLD 4000, Australia
Dr. Leigh Atkinson, Sec.
PH: 61 7 38393393
FX: 61 7 38322005
Description: Neurosurgeons seeking to advance neurosurgical studies and promote understanding between members from different countries. Conducts educational programs. **Founded:** 1964. **Membership:** 5000. Multinational. **National Groups:** 16. **Languages:** English. **Budget:** $A 6,000. **Publication:** Newsletter (in English), annual. **Price:** Free.**Description:** Neurological surgeons. Seeks to advance the practice of neurological surgery; promotes continuing professional development among members. Serves as a clearinghouse on neurological surgery; sponsors training courses. Multinational. **Languages:** English.

ASIAN DERMATOLOGICAL ASSOCIATION (ADA)
20 Des Vouex Rd.
Central
Hong Kong, Hong Kong
Dr. Shin-chak Chiu, Contact
Description: Dermatologists and medical students with an interest in dermatology. Seeks to advance the study, teaching, and practice of dermatology. Facilitates exchange of information among members; sponsors research and educational programs. Multinational. **Languages:** Chinese, English.

ASIAN FEDERATION OF CATHOLIC MEDICAL ASSOCIATIONS (AFCMA)
Catholic University Medical College
505 Banpo-dong
Sochu-ku
Seoul 137 701, Republic of Korea
PH: 82 2 5935141
FX: 82 2 5323112
Description: Catholic medical associations. Seeks to increase the availability of quality health care services in previously underserved areas of Asia; promotes adherence to high standards of ethics and practice among Catholic health care services and institutions. Facilitates communication and cooperation among members; makes available health services; conducts exchange and continuing professional development programs. Multinational. **Languages:** English, Korean.

ASIAN FEDERATION OF SOCIETIES FOR ULTRASOUND IN MEDICINE AND BIOLOGY (AFSUMB)
Department of Obstetrics and Gynecology
National Taiwan University Hospital
1 Chang-Fe St.
Taipei 10016, Taiwan
Dr. Hsi-Yao Chen, Contact
PH: 886 2 3816939
Description: Ultrasonographers and other medical professionals with an interest in ultrasound technology. Promotes application of ultrasonography in a variety of medical and biological specialties; seeks to advance the practice of ultrasonography. Serves as a clearinghouse on ultrasound technology and its uses; sponsors research and educational programs. Multinational. **Languages:** Chinese, English.

ASIAN FEDERATION OF SPORTS MEDICINE (AFSM)
e-mail: chan6150@cuhk.edu.hk
Orthopaedics and Traumatology
Faculty of Medicine
Chinese University of Hong Kong
Shatin, Hong Kong
Dr. Kai-Ming Chan, Contact
PH: 852 26096893
FX: 852 26035821
Description: Health care professionals specializing in sports medicine. Seeks to advance the study, teaching, and practice of sports medicine. Facilitates exchange of information among members; sponsors research and educational programs. Multinational. **Languages:** Chinese, English.

ASIAN FLUID MECHANICS COMMITTEE (AFMC)
Centre for Atmospheric Sciences
Indian Institute of Science
Bangalore 560 012, Mysore, India
R. Narasimha, Contact
Description: Engineers and physicists with an interest in fluid mechanics. Seeks to advance scholarship in the field of fluid mechanics. Gathers and disseminates information on fluid mechanics and related fields; conducts research and educational programs. Multinational. **Languages:** English, Hindi.

ASIAN HEALTH INSTITUTE (AHI)
e-mail: ahi@mx6.mesh.net.or.jp
987-30 Minamiyama
Komenogi, Nisshin-Shi
Aichi-gun
Aichi 470-01, Japan
Sato Hikaru, M.D., Gen.Sec.
PH: 81 5617 31950
FX: 81 5617 31990
Description: Promotes improved public health, particularly in Asia. Conducts public educational campaigns to create indigenous leadership for public health initiatives in the region. **Founded:** 1980. **Membership:** 7700. **Staff:** 10. Multinational. **Languages:** English, French. **Budget:** 000,000¥. **Publication:** *Ajia no Kenko* (in English and Japanese), bimonthly. Magazine. Member Newsletter. Price: free. Circulation: 11,000. Advertising: not accepted ▪ *Aju no Kodomo* (in English and Japanese), annual. Magazine. Children's magazine on the live of children in Asian countries. Price: free. Circulation: 17,000. Advertising: not accepted ▪ *Asian Health Institute* (in English), quarterly. Newsletter. Forum for training course alumni, grassroots health workers. Price: free. Circulation: 1,000. Advertising: not accepted.

ASIAN AND OCEANIA SOCIETY FOR INTRAVENOUS ANESTHESIA (AOSIA)
Murakami-cho 383
Fushimi-ku
Kyoto 612, Japan
PH: 81 75 6112008
FX: 81 75 6033816
Description: Anesthesiologists. Promotes increased use of intravenous anesthetics; seeks to advance the study, teaching,

and practice of anesthesiology. Facilitates exchange of information among members; sponsors research and continuing professional development programs. Multinational. **Languages:** English, Japanese.

ASIAN OCEANIA SOCIETY OF REGIONAL ANESTHESIA (AOSRA)
Philippine Society of Anaesthesiologists
PMA Bldg.
Quezon City, Philippines
Dr. Alfonso Doloroso, Contact
PH: 63 2 975852
FX: 63 2 975852
Description: Anesthesiologists. Promotes increased use of regional anesthetics; seeks to advance anesthesiological study and practice. Serves as a clearinghouse on regional anesthesia; sponsors research and continuing professional development programs. Multinational. **Languages:** English, Filipino.

ASIAN AND OCEANIAN SOCIETY OF NEURORADIOLOGY AND HEAD AND NECK RADIOLOGY (AOSNHNR)
Taipei Veterans General Hospital
Department of Radiology
201 Section 2
Taipei, Taiwan
PH: 886 2 8757357
FX: 886 2 8733643
Description: Radiologists, neurologists, and otorhinolaryngologists. Seeks to advance the practice of neuroradiology and head and neck radiology. Facilitates exchange of information among members; sponsors research and continuing professional development programs. Multinational. **Languages:** Chinese, English.

ASIAN-OCEANIC GLAUCOMA SOCIETY (AOGS)
Singapore National Eye Centre
11 Third Hospital Ave.
Singapore 168751, Singapore
Dr. Steve Seah, Contact
PH: 65 2277255
FX: 65 2277290
Description: Ophthalmologists specializing in the treatment of glaucoma. Promotes early diagnosis and effective treatment of glaucoma; seeks to advance the science and practice of glaucomatology. Serves as a clearinghouse on the diagnosis and treatment of glaucoma; sponsors research and continuing professional development programs. Multinational. **Languages:** Chinese, English.

ASIAN ORAL IMPLANT ACADEMY (AOIA)
268 Orchard Rd. 05-07
Singapore 0923, Singapore
Dr. Dominic Leung, Contact
PH: 65 7343162
FX: 65 7321979
Description: Dentists specializing in oral implantology. Seeks to advance the practice of oral implantology. Facilitates communication and cooperation among members; conducts continuing professional development programs. Multinational. **Languages:** Chinese, English.

ASIAN PACIFIC ASSOCIATION FOR MEDICAL INFORMATICS (APAMI)
e-mail: lunkc@nusvm.bitnet
url: http://bullseye.aims.org.sg/apami/
National University Hospital
Department of Community, Occupational and Family Medicine
Lower Kent Ridge Rd.
Singapore 0511, Singapore
Lun Kwok Chan, Contact
PH: 65 7724296
FX: 65 7791489
Description: Medical information and information management organizations. Seeks to advance the practice of medical information management; promotes development and implementation of new medical informatics technologies. Serves as a clearinghouse on medical information management; sponsors research and educational programs. Multinational. **Languages:** Chinese, English.

ASIAN PACIFIC DENTAL FEDERATION/ASIAN PACIFIC REGIONAL ORGANISATION (APDF/APRO)
e-mail: toffee@pacific.net.sg
242 Tanjong Katong Rd.
Singapore 437030, Singapore
Dr. Oliver Hennedige, Sec.Gen.
PH: 65 3453125
FX: 65 3442116
Description: National dental associations in Australia, Bangladesh, Guam, Hong Kong, India, Indonesia, Japan, Malaysia, Mongolia, Myanmar, Nepal, New Zealand, Pakistan, Philippines, Republic of Korea, Singapore, Sri Lanka, Taiwan, and Thailand. Works to improve dental and general health in the Asia Pacific region. Encourages education and research links between national dental associations. **Founded:** 1955. **Membership:** 19. Multinational. **Languages:** English. **Publication:** *APDF/APRO Technical Report*, periodic ∎ *Dentistry in the Asian Pacific Region*, periodic. **Also Known As:** Asian Pacific Regional Organisation of the International Dental Federation.

ASIAN AND PACIFIC FEDERATION OF CLINICAL BIOCHEMISTRY (APFCB)
Clinical Biochemistry Laboratories
Department of Pathology
Singapore General Hospital
Singapore 0316, Singapore
Dr. Tan It Koon, Contact
PH: 65 3214914
FX: 65 2226826
Description: Biochemists and clinical biochemistry institutions. Seeks to advance the study, teaching, and practice of clinical biochemistry. Facilitates communication and cooperation among members; sponsors research and educational programs. Multinational. **Languages:** Chinese, English.

ASIAN AND PACIFIC FEDERATION OF ORGANIZATIONS FOR CANCER RESEARCH AND CONTROL (APFOCRC)
Seoul National University Hospital
28 Yunkun-dong
Conggno-ku
Seoul 110-744, Republic of Korea
Dr. J. Kim, Contact
PH: 82 2 7602314
FX: 82 2 7448307
Description: Cancer researchers and research institutions; organizations providing care to people with cancer. Seeks to discover more effective methods for the treatment and eventual cure of cancer; works to improve the quality of life of people with cancer. Serves as a clearinghouse on cancer and cancer research; facilitates exchange of information among cancer researchers; provides support and services to people with cancer. Multinational. **Languages:** English, Korean.

ASIAN-PACIFIC RESOURCE AND RESEARCH CENTRE FOR WOMEN (ARROW)
e-mail: arrow@po.jaring.my
url: http://asiaconnect.com.my/arrow/
Block F, 2nd Fl.
Anjung Felda
Jalan Maktab
54000 Kuala Lumpur, Malaysia
Rashidah Abdullah
PH: 60 3 2929913
FX: 60 3 2929958
Description: Gathers and disseminates information on family planning, maternal and child health, and women's reproductive rights. Works to establish models for the development and implementation of family planning programs that respect women's rights. **Founded:** 1993. **Staff:** 7. **Languages:** English, Malay. **For-Profit. Publication:** *Arrows for Change* (in English), 3/year. Bul-

letin. Focuses on the gender dimension of women and health. ISSN: 1396-6666. Advertising: not accepted ■ *Gender and Women's Health: Information Package, No. 2, 1997* ■ *Reappraising Population Policies and Family Planning Programmes: An Annotated Bibliography Series 1, 1994* ■ *Towards Women-Centered Reproductive Health: Information Package No. 1, 1994* ■ *Women-Centered and Gender-Sensitive Experiences: Changing Our Perspectives, Policies, and Programmes on Womens Health in Asia and the Pacific Ref. Kit.*

ASIAN-PACIFIC SOCIETY OF CARDIOLOGY (APSC)
Seoul National University Hospital, Rm. 9603
28 Yunkun-Dong
Chongno-ku
Seoul 110 744, Republic of Korea
Dr. Jung Don Seo, Contact
PH: 82 2 7602262
FX: 82 2 7438694
Description: Cardiologists and other health care professionals and scientists with an interest in cardiology. Seeks to advance cardiological study, teaching, and practice. Serves as a forum for the exchange of information among members; sponsors research programs and continuing professional development courses. Multinational. **Languages:** English, Korean.

ASIAN-PACIFIC SOCIETY OF CARDIOVASCULAR AND INTERVENTIONAL RADIOLOGY (APSCIR)
Department of Radiology
Grattan St.
Parkville, VIC 34052, Australia
Dr. Ken Thompson, Contact
Description: Cardiovascular and interventional radiologists. Seeks to advance the study, teaching, and practice of radiology. Serves as a forum for the exchange of information among members; sponsors research and continuing professional development programs. Multinational. **Languages:** English.

ASIAN PACIFIC SOCIETY FOR NEUROCHEMISTRY (APSN)
e-mail: peterD@qimr.edu.au
Clinical Research Center
Royal Brisbane Hospital Federation
Royal Brisbane Hospital
Brisbane, QLD 4029, Australia
Peter Dodd, Contact
PH: 61 7 3620495
FX: 61 7 3620108
Description: Neurologists and chemists with an interest in neurology. Seeks to advance the study, teaching, and practice of neurochemistry. Gathers and disseminates information on neurochemistry; sponsors research and educational programs. Multinational. **Languages:** English.

ASIAN PHARMACEUTICAL PRODUCTS COUNCIL (APPC)
Bhai Mohan Singh Group of Companies
15 Aurangreb Rd.
New Delhi 110 011, Delhi, India
Dr. Bhai Mohan Singh, Contact
PH: 91 11 3016675
FX: 91 11 6466784
Description: Manufacturers of pharmaceuticals. Promotes growth and development of the Asian pharmaceuticals industries. Represents members' commercial and regulatory interests; sponsors research; conducts promotional activities. Multinational. **Languages:** English, Hindi.

ASIAN PHYSICS EDUCATION NETWORK (APEN)
UNESCO/ROTSEA
Jalan M.H. Thamrin 14
Tromolpos 1273 JKT
10012 Jakarta, Indonesia
Fumin Zhang, Contact
PH: 62 21 3141308
FX: 62 21 3150382
Description: Physics educators, students, and educational institu-

tions. Seeks to advance physics pedagogy and scholarship. Serves as a forum for the exchange of information among members; conducts research and educational programs. Multinational. **Languages:** English, Indonesian.

ASIAN SOCIETY OF CARDIOTHORACIC ANAESTHESIA (ASCA)
Singapore Society of Anaesthesiologists
114 Middle Rd., Ste. 05-01
Singapore 0718, Singapore
Maureen Groh, Contact
PH: 65 3363875
FX: 65 3397843
Description: Anesthesiologists specializing in cardiothoracic anesthesia. Seeks to advance the profession of cardiothoracic anesthesia; promotes continuing professional development among members. Serves as a forum for the exchange of information among members; sponsors research and training programs. Multinational. **Languages:** Chinese, English.

ASIAN SOCIETY FOR CARDIOVASCULAR SURGERY (ASCS)
Seoul National University Hospital
28 Yon-gon-dong
Chongo-gu
Seoul 110-744, Republic of Korea
Ahn Hyuk, Contact
PH: 82 2 7603349
FX: 82 2 7643644
Description: Cardiovascular surgeons. Seeks to advance the practice of cardiovascular surgery; promotes continuing professional development among members. Facilitates exchange of information among members; sponsors research and educational programs. Multinational. **Languages:** English, Korean.

ASIAN SOCIETY FOR HEPATO-BILIARY-PANCREATIC SURGERY (ASHBPS)
Department of Surgery
Chinese University of Hong Kong
Shatin, Hong Kong
Arthur K. C. Li, Contact
PH: 852 26322623
FX: 852 26453602
Description: Surgeons specializing in operations on the liver, biliary system, and pancreas. Seeks to advance the practice of hepatic, biliary, and pancreatic surgery; promotes continuing professional development of members. Serves as a forum for the exchange of information among members; sponsors research and educational programs. Multinational. **Languages:** Chinese, English.

ASIAN SOCIETY FOR SOLID STATE IONICS (ASSSI)
e-mail: phychowd@leonis.nus.sg
National University of Singapore
Department of Physics
Lower Kent Ridge Rd.
Singapore 0511, Singapore
Dr. B. V. R. Chowdari, Contact
PH: 65 7722956
FX: 65 7776126
Description: Physicists and other scientists with an interest in solid state ionics. Seeks to advance the study of solid state ionics and related fields. Facilitates exchange of information among members; sponsors research and educational programs. Multinational. **Languages:** Chinese, English.

ASIAN SOCIETY FOR STEREOTACTIC FUNCTIONAL AND COMPUTER ASSISTED NEUROSURGERY
Department of Neurosurgery
3-39-15 Showa-machi
Maebashi
Gunma 371, Japan
C. Ohye, Contact

PH: 81 272 207111
FX: 81 272 336300
Description: Neurosurgeons. Promotes increased use of stereotactic and computer asssisted neurosurgical techniques; seeks to advance surgical assistive technologies. Facilitates exchange of information among members; provides support to surgical technology research programs; sponsors continuing professional development courses. Multinational. **Languages:** English, Japanese.

ASIAN SURGICAL ASSOCIATION (ASA)
Department of Surgery
University of Hong Kong
Queen Mary Hospital
Hong Kong, Hong Kong
John Wong, Contact
PH: 852 28554235
FX: 852 28559950
Description: Surgeons. Seeks to advance surgical practice. Facilitates exchange of information among members; sponsors continuing professional development courses. Multinational. **Languages:** Chinese, English.

ASOCIACION ARGENTINA DE PROTECCION FAMILIAR (AAPF)
Aguero 1355/59
Capital Federal
1425 Buenos Aires, Argentina
Olga Alicia Vigliola, M.D., Exec.Dir.
PH: 54 1 8261216
FX: 54 1 8248416
Description: Works to improve the quality of family life in Argentina. Supports and promotes reproductive rights and equal parenting duties. Operates family planning centers; conducts research and educational programs on subjects including the importance of the father figure; sexual health and the transmission of STDs, and birth control methods. Offers training for health and professionals and social workers. Maintains speakers bureau. **Founded:** 1966. **Membership:** 160. **Languages:** Spanish. **Budget:** $800,000.

ASOCIACION DEMOGRAFICA SALVADORENA (ADS)
e-mail: ads_dire@sal.gbm.net
Edificio Profamilia
25 Av. Norte No. 583
Apartado Postal 1338
San Salvador, El Salvador
Llc. Jorge Hernandez Isussl, Exec.Dir.
PH: 503 2250588
FX: 503 2250879
Description: Promotes responsible parenthood and family planning. Encourages public knowledge of contraception, family planning, AIDS, and other sexually transmitted diseases. Promotes family planning as a basic human right. Sponsors educational programs on family planning for teens and adults. Conducts research provide medical services, by the openning of a private hospital. **Founded:** 1962. **Membership:** 220. **Staff:** 6. **Languages:** Spanish. **Budget:** C 5,800,000. **Publication:** *Anniversary Magazine* (in Spanish), annual. Provides summary of covering and institutional goals. Price: free. Circulation: 1,000. Also Cited As: *members, institutions private and government, local and internationals* ▪ *Informative News - Carta Informativa* (in Spanish), quarterly. Price: free. Circulation: 2,000. Advertising: accepted ▪ *Memoria de Labores* (in Spanish), annual. Annual Report. Price: free. Circulation: 1,000 ▪ *National Family Health Survey* (in English and Spanish), quinquennial. Price: free. Circulation: 1,500.

ASOCIACION HONDURENA DE PLANIFICACION DE FAMILIA (ASHONPLAFA)
Calle Principal, entre: Colonias Alameda y Ruben Dario
Apartado Postal 625
Tegucigalpa, Honduras
Alejandro Flores Aguilar, Exec.Dir.

PH: 504 323235
FX: 504 325140
Description: Works to enhance the quality of life of people living in Honduras through the promotion of responsible parenthood and family planning. Advocates family planning as a basic human right. Secks to reduce the number of unwanted pregnancies and abortions. Provides programs in family planning, sex education, and health. **Languages:** Spanish.

ASOCIACION NACIONAL CONTRA EL CANCER (ANCEC)
Apdo 7358, Zona 5
Ciudad de Panama
Panama City, Panama
PH: 507 2258404
FX: 507 2255366
Description: Works to educate Panamanian women on prevention and detect of breast cancer. Helps treat women with breast or uterine cancer. Informs women on prevention, self-testing, and importance of regular gynecological examinations. Maintains clinics offering mammograms and Pap smears. **Languages:** Spanish.

ASOCIACION PRO-BIENESTAR DE LA FAMILIA COLOMBIANA (PROFAMILIA)
e-mail: profamil@colomsat.net.co
url: http://www.profamilia.com
Calle 34, Numero 14-52
Bogota, Colombia
Maria Isabel Plata, Exec.Dir.
PH: 57 1 2872100
FX: 57 1 2875530
Description: Promotes sexual health and reproductive rights in Colombia. Seeks to: improve maternal and child health by increasing the time between pregnancies; foster awareness of the possible effects of demographics on the socio-economic development of Colombia. Operates 35 family planning clinics in Colombia offering legal, medical, and educational services. Has established the Population Management Training Centre for staff employed at the clinics. Provides continuing education programs for gynecologists, obstetricians, and other doctors. Conducts studies and surveys; sponsors lectures, seminars, and workshops. **Founded:** 1965. **Staff:** 1200. **State Groups:** 40. **Languages:** English, Spanish. **Budget:** $24,000,000. **Publication:** *Anatomia y fisiologia de la Reproduccion Femenina y Masculina.* Booklet ▪ *Annual Report* (in English and Spanish). Pamphlet. Lists accomplishments of previous year. Price: free. Circulation: 1,000. Advertising: not accepted ▪ *Cada dia Cada Instante.* Video ▪ *Disfunciones Sexuales.* Booklet ▪ *Enfermedades de Transmision Sexual.* Booklet ▪ *Erase una Vez.* Video ▪ *Fecundacion, Maternidad y Lactancia.* Booklet ▪ *Historia de los Metodos Antic..* Booklet ▪ *Novedades Anticonceptivas y Metodos en Investigacion.* Booklet ▪ *Planificacion Familiar y Metodes Anticonceptivos.* Video ▪ *Planificacion Familiar y Metodos Anticonceptivos.* Booklet ▪ *Profamilia, Planificacion, Poblacion y Desarrollo* (in Spanish), semiannual. Video. ISSN: 0122-0977. Advertising: accepted ▪ *RL 6 Temas.* Booklet ▪ *Sindrome de Inmunodeficiencia Adquirida - SIDA.* Booklet. **Also Known As:** Profamilia.

ASOCIACION PRO-BIENESTAR DE LA FAMILIA ECUATORIANA (APROFE)
e-mail: aprofe@aprofe.org.ec
Noguchi 1516 y Letamendi
Apartado Postal 5954
Guayaquil, Ecuador
Dr. Paolo Marangoni, Exec. Dir.
PH: 593 4 400888
FX: 593 4 419667
Description: Works to enhance the quality of life for people living in Ecuador through the promotion of responsible parenthood and family planning. Encourages public knowledge of family planning, contraception, AIDS, and other sexually transmitted diseases. Provides contraceptive and health care services. Sponsors educational programs. Conducts research. **Founded:** 1965. **Membership:** 20. **Staff:** 379. **Languages:** Spanish. **Budget:** S

3,600,000. **Publication:** *Family Planning in Ecuador* (in Spanish). Reports. Features the history of Aprofe and information on family planning in Eucador.

ASOCIACION PRO-BIENESTAR DE LA FAMILIA DE GUATEMALA (APROFAM)
e-mail: aprofam@guate.net
url: http://www.centoamerica.com/aprofa
9a Calle 0-57, Zona 1
Apartado Postal 1004
Guatemala City, Guatemala
Mrs. Blanca Guerra de Nicol, Contact
PH: 502 2 305488
FX: 502 2 514017
Description: Educators, doctors, social workers, and others interested in improving the quality of life through the promotion of family planning. Advocates family planning as a basic human right. Conducts family development program that stresses self-sufficiency and offers help in how to improve family income and health. Works to educate the public on family planning, contraception, AIDS, and other sexually transmitted diseases. Operates a clinic for women from which it provides contraceptive and health care services such as instruction in pre- and post-natal care; tests and treatment for infertility; tests to detect cervical and uterine cancer; coloscopies; and ultrasound. Conducts research. **Founded:** 1964. **Membership:** 90. **Staff:** 457. **National Groups:** 34. **Languages:** Spanish. **Budget:** Q 32,000,000. **Publication:** *Calendario Demagrafico* (in Spanish), annual. Journal. demographics, the environment ■ *Calendario Demografico* (in Spanish), annual.

ASOCIACION PUERTORRIQUENA PRO-BIENESTAR DE LA FAMILIA (APPBF)
e-mail: profamilia@upr1.upr.clu.edu
Calle Padre las Casas 117
Urbanizacion El Vedado
Hato Rey, Puerto Rico 00919
Idalia Colon Rondon, Exec.Dir.
PH: (787)765-7373
FX: (787)766-6920
Description: Offers educational and medical services for family planning. Emphasizes education as a means to prevent unwanted pregnancies. Sponsors peer-counseling program on sexually transmitted diseases and AIDS. Conducts periodic seminars and workshops. **Founded:** 1954. **Languages:** Spanish. **Publication:** *La Voz De Profamilia* (in Spanish), quarterly. Newsletter. Price: free. Circulation: 3,000. Advertising: not accepted. **Also Known As:** Profamilia.

ASOCIATIA HANDICAPATILOR NEUROMOTORI DIN ROMANIA (AHNR)
e-mail: ahnr@ahnr.sorostm.ro
Str. Sava Tekelija Nr. 2
R-2900 Arad, Romania
Ioana Monica Antoci, Pres.
PH: 40 57 272707
FX: 40 57 272707
Description: Works to protect the rights of citizens suffering from motor neuron diseases (MND). Faciliates exchange of information and experience regarding the care of persons with this disease. **Founded:** 1990. **Membership:** 35000. **Staff:** 6. **Regional Groups:** 14. **Languages:** English, French.

ASSIST INTERNATIONAL (AI)
e-mail: assistintl@aol.com
Scotts Valley, CA 95067-6396
Robert J. Pagett, Pres.
PH: (408)438-4582
FX: (408)439-9602
Description: Health care organizations. Procures used cardiac care monitoring systems and other medical equipment in the United States for distribution among underserved populations in the developing world. Distributes medical equipment, food,

pharmaceuticals, and other supplies in needy areas worldwide. Multinational. **Languages:** English.

ASSOCIACAO BRASILEIRA DE DISTROFIA MUSCULAR
e-mail: mayazatz@usp.br
Rua Eng Teixeira Soares, 715 Butanta
05505-030 Sao Paulo, SP, Brazil
Mayana Zatz, Ph.D., Pres.
PH: 55 11 8146582
FX: 55 11 8187419
Description: Promotes interest in muscular dystrophy research among medical and scientific communities and the public in Brazil. Disseminates information. **Founded:** 1981. **Publication:** Newsletter (in Portuguese), 3/year.

ASSOCIACAO PORTUGUESA DE MIASTENIA GRAVIS E DOENCAS NEUROMUSCULARES (APMG-DNM)
Hospital de Santa Maria
P-1699 Lisbon, Portugal
Fernando Morgado, Contact
PH: 351 1 7901217
FX: 351 1 7976882
Description: Promotes interest in neuromuscular diseases research among medical and scientific communities and the public in Portugal. Disseminates information. **Founded:** 1989. **Membership:** 720. **Staff:** 5. **Languages:** English. **Publication:** *Boletim Informative* (in Portuguese), quarterly. Journal. Contains news about neuromuscular dystrophy and information for patients. Price: free. Circulation: 800. Advertising: not accepted.

ASSOCIATED HEALTH FOUNDATION (AHF)
99 Madison Ave.
New York, NY 10016
Edward Birnbaum, Pres.
PH: (212)889-4455
TF: 800722-8668
Description: Extends life-saving services to members through incentive benefits. Contributes to hospitals and institutions that carry on research. **Founded:** 1937. **Membership:** 20000. **Staff:** 4. **Languages:** English.

ASSOCIATED MEDICAL SERVICES (AMS)
e-mail: 73252.3302@compuserve.com
14 Prince Arthur Ave., Ste. 101
Toronto, ON, Canada M5R 1A9
Boyd Upper, Pres.
PH: (416)924-3368
FX: (416)323-3338
Description: Health services. Promotes increased availability of quality health care. Facilitates communication and cooperation among members; represents members' interests before government agencies, professional medical organizations, and the public. **Languages:** English, French.

ASSOCIATED PROFESSIONAL SLEEP SOCIETIES (APSS)
e-mail: asda@asda.org
1610 14th St. NW, Ste. 300
Rochester, MN 55901
Jerry Barrett, Exec.Dir.
PH: (507)287-6006
FX: (507)287-6008
Description: Members are the Sleep Research Society and American Sleep Disorders Association. Works to facilitate sleep research and development of sleep disorder s medicine by encouraging cooperation and exchange of information among members. **Founded:** 1985. Multinational. **Languages:** English. **Budget:** $750,000 Formerly Association of Professional Sleep Societies.

ASSOCIATES OF CLINICAL PHARMACOLOGY (ACP)
16425 Maplewild Ave. SW
Seattle, WA 98166-3165
Denise F. Olson, Exec.Dir.
PH: (206)246-6994

Description: Individuals engaged in clinical pharmacology and other related research professions, including clinical monitors and research associates, nurses, pharmacists, pharmacologists, physicians, and regulatory professionals. Promotes professional growth in the field through the dissemination of information, the exchange of ideas, and the development of educational programs. Provides continuing education credits to pharmacy and nursing professionals through the American Council on Pharmaceutical Education and the American Nurses Association. **Founded:** 1977. **Membership:** 4100. **Staff:** 4. **Languages:** English. **Budget:** $1,000,000.

ASSOCIATION OF ACADEMIC HEALTH CENTERS (AHC)
e-mail: ahc@acadhlthctrs.org
url: http://www.ahcnet.org
1400 16th St. NW, Ste. 720
Washington, DC 20036
Roger J. Bulger, M.D., Pres.
PH: (202)265-9600
Description: Chief executive officers of university-based academic health centers in the U.S. and Canada. Interdisciplinary in focus, with a primary interest in total health manpower education. Sponsors task forces and forums to advance public policy dialogue on health and science issues. Develops research and education programs. Publishes, reports, books, and issues papers. **Founded:** 1969. **Membership:** 102. **Staff:** 12. **Languages:** English. **Publication:** *General Meetings*, periodic ▪ Directory, periodic ▪ Reports. On special projects. **Formerly:** Organization of University Health Center Administrators.

ASSOCIATION FOR ACADEMIC SURGERY (AAS)
e-mail: aas@prri.com
13 Elm St.
Manchester, MA 01944
Kevin Cuff, Exec.Dir.
PH: (978)526-8336
FX: (978)526-4018
Description: Active (1550) and senior (1150) surgeons with backgrounds in all surgical specialties in academic surgical centers at chief resident level or above. Encourages young surgeons to pursue careers in academic surgery; supports them in establishing themselves as investigators and educators by providing a forum in which senior surgical residents and junior faculty members may present papers on subjects of clinical or laboratory investigations; promotes interchange of ideas between senior surgical residents, junior faculty, and established academic surgeons; facilitates communication among academic surgeons in all surgical fields. Maintains placement service. **Founded:** 1966. **Membership:** 2700. **Languages:** English.

ASSOCIATION OF AFRICAN OPTOMETRIC EDUCATORS (AAOE)
Morny Optical Centre
PO Box 1814
Kumasi, Ghana
Francis Kojovi Morny, Contact
PH: 233 51 22511
FX: 233 51 25306
Description: Optometry educators. Seeks to advance optometric scholarship and practice. Sponsors training programs for optometric personnel; makes available continuing professional development courses for members. Multinational. **Languages:** English.

ASSOCIATION OF ANAESTHETISTS OF GREAT BRITAIN AND IRELAND
e-mail: aagbi@compuserve.com
url: http://www.ncl.ac.uk/~naoaes/aagbi.html
9 Bedford Sq.
London WC1B 3RA, England
Lesley Ogg, Admin. Mgr.
PH: 44 171 6311650
FX: 44 171 6314352
Description: Ordinary Members, Trainee Members and Associate Members. Aims to promote education and research in anaesthesia and to bring together as many members as is possible at the three annual meetings to disseminate relevant information both at home and abroad. **Founded:** 1932. **Membership:** 6000. **Staff:** 7. **Publication:** *Anaesthesia* (in English), monthly. Journal. Price: free to members.

ASSOCIATION OF ASIA PACIFIC PHYSICAL SOCIETIES (AAPPS)
Research Center for Advanced Science and Technology
University of Tokyo
4-6-1 Komaba
Tokyo 153, Japan
Dr. Yasuhiro Shiraki, Contact
PH: 81 3 34814428
FX: 81 3 34814572
Description: Physicists, physics educators and students, and educational institutions. Seeks to advance physics scholarship and practice. Facilitates exchange of information among members; sponsors research and educational programs. Multinational. **Languages:** English, Japanese.

ASSOCIATION OF BIOLOGICAL MANUFACTURERS OF JAPAN (ABMJ)
(Saikin Siezai Kyokai)
TH-1 Bldg. Iidabashi, 9th Fl.
3-11, Tsukudo-cho
Shinjuku-ku
Tokyo 162, Japan
Hisao Nakagawa, Exec.Dir.
PH: 81 3 32696591
FX: 81 3 32696592
Description: Manufacturers of vaccines, toxoids, and anti-sera. Monitors use and supply of vaccines in Japan. Works with government agencies to promote research and educational activities on the importance of vaccinations. Promotes international awareness and cooperation. Works in cooperation with the Expanded Programme on Immunization of the World Health Organization. **Founded:** 1946. **Membership:** 22. **Staff:** 4. **Languages:** English, Japanese. **Budget:** 80,000,000¥. **Publication:** *Minimum Requirements for Biological Products*, periodic. Includes standards and specifications for biological products.

ASSOCIATION OF BRITISH DENTAL SURGERY ASSISTANTS
DSA House
29 London St.
Fleetwood FY7 6JY, England
Lyn Ripley
Description: Represents the interests of dental surgery assistants in England. Promotes increased pay and improved status and working conditions. Supports educational programs and training and post-qualification courses. **Founded:** 1940. **Membership:** 2500. **Staff:** 2. **Publication:** *British Dental Surgery Assistant*, quarterly. Newsletter. ISSN: 0007-0629.

ASSOCIATION OF BRITISH NEUROLOGISTS
e-mail: abn@abnoffice.demon.co.uk
Ormond House, 4th Fl.
27 Boswell St.
London WC1N 3JZ, England
Dr. Michael Donaghy, Contact
PH: 44 171 4054060
FX: 44 171 4054070
Description: Trainee and consultant in the neurological sciences. To promote the advancement of the neurological sciences, including the practice of neurology in the British Isles. **Founded:** 1933. **Membership:** 800.

ASSOCIATION FOR THE ADVANCEMENT OF APPLIED SPORT PSYCHOLOGY

e-mail: vkrane@bgnet.bgsu.edu
url: http://www.spot.colorado.edu/~aaasp/
Univ. of Memphis
Dept. of Psychology
Memphis, TN 38152-1389
Maureen Weiss, Pres.
PH: (419)372-7233
FX: (419)372-0383
Description: Promotes the development of research, theory, and intervention strategies in sport psychology. Concerned with ethical and professional issues related to the development of sport psychology and to the provision of psychological services in sport and exercise settings. Sponsors research and educational programs. **Founded:** 1986. **Membership:** 1000. Multinational. **Languages:** English.

ASSOCIATION FOR THE ADVANCEMENT OF MEDICAL INSTRUMENTATION (AAMI)

3330 Washington Blvd., Ste. 400
Arlington, VA 22201
Michael J. Miller, Pres.
PH: (703)525-4890
TF: 800332-2264
FX: (703)276-0793
Description: Clinical engineers, biomedical equipment technicians, physicians, hospital administrators, consultants, engineers, manufacturers of medical devices, nurses researchers and others interested in medical instrumentation. Purpose is to improve the quality of medical care through the application, development, and management of technology. Maintains placement service. Offers certification programs for biomedical equipment technicians and clinical engineers. Produces numerous standards and recommended practices on medical devices and procedures. Offers educational programs. **Founded:** 1967. **Membership:** 7000. **Staff:** 35. Multinational. **Languages:** English. **Budget:** $4,000,000. **Publication:** *AAMI News*, monthly. Newsletter. Informs members on legislative and regulatory proposals, proposed and final AAMI standards, and association policies and programs. Price: included in membership dues; $105.00/year for nonmembers. ISSN: 0739-0270. Circulation: 7,000. Advertising: accepted ▪ *Biomedical Instrumentation & Technology*, bimonthly. Includes advertisers and annual subject indexes, book reviews, statistics, association news, information on medical instrumentation. Price: included in membership dues; $72.00 for individual nonmembers; $96.00 for institutional nonmembers. ISSN: 0883-9093. Circulation: 7,000. Advertising: accepted ▪ *Directory of Members*, annual. Membership Directory ▪ *Medical Device Research Report*, bimonthly. Newsletter. Informs members of latest medical research information. Price: included in membership dues; $60.00 for nonmembers. ISSN: 1074-9519. Circulation: 7,000. Advertising: accepted.

ASSOCIATION FOR THE ADVANCEMENT OF WOUND CARE (AAWC)

950 West Valley Rd., Ste. 2800
Wayne, PA 19087
Diane Krasner, MS, RN, Exec.Dir.
PH: 800-237-7285
TF: 800237-7285
FX: (610)688-8050
Description: Works to advance the cause of wound care through education, research, clinical practice and public policy. Provides a forum for communication and partnership among all people involved in wound care. **Founded:** 1995. **Membership:** 600. **Staff:** 1. Multinational. **Budget:** $100,000.

ASSOCIATION FOR AMBULATORY BEHAVIORAL HEALTHCARE

url: http://www.aabh.org
301 N. Fairfax St., Ste. 109
Alexandria, VA 22314
Mark A. Knight, MSW, Exec. Officer
PH: (703)836-2274
FX: (703)836-0083
Description: Individuals interested in the development and improvement of partial hospitalization within the continuum of psychiatric treatment. To support, encourage, and stimulate the expansion of partial hospitalization services. Sponsors educational discussions on partial hospitalization, including clinical research and administrative issues. Provides consultation services to stimulate and support the study, evaluation, and implementation of partial hospitalization services. Collaborates with other groups in establishing standards of operation and performance in the field. Monitors local and national legislative activity directly related to partial hospitalization. **Founded:** 1965. **Membership:** 1100. **Staff:** 9. **Regional Groups:** 26. **Languages:** English. **Budget:** $750,000. Formerly (1975) Partial Hospitalization Study Group; (1979) Federation of Partial Hospitalization Study Groups; (1996) American Association for Partial Hospitalization.

ASSOCIATION OF AMERICAN CANCER INSTITUTES (AACI)

Elm & Carlton Sts.
Buffalo, NY 14263
Dr. Edwin A. Mirand, Sec.-Treas.
PH: (716)845-3028
FX: (716)845-8178
Description: Directors of cancer centers. Informs members of important legislative and program developments in the field. Promotes discussion among cancer center leadership throughout the world; fosters collaboration between members on research, education, and service programs; works to further educational and training opportunities in related biomedical sciences; advises federal, state, and local governments, and private and civic organizations concerning cancer research and related health topics. **Founded:** 1959. **Membership:** 85. Multinational. **Languages:** English. **Budget:** $130,000. **Publication:** *AACI Newsletter*, periodic. Price: free. Advertising: not accepted. **Formerly:** (1968) Association of Cancer Institute Directors.

ASSOCIATION OF AMERICAN INDIAN PHYSICIANS (AAIP)

e-mail: aaip@ionet.net
url: http://www.aaip.com
1235 Sovereign Row, Ste. C-9
Oklahoma City, OK 73108-1833
Margaret Knight, Exec.Dir.
PH: (405)946-7072
FX: (405)946-7651
Description: Physicians (M.D. or D.O.) of American Indian descent. Encourages American Indians to enter the health professions. Provides a forum for the interchange of ideas and information of mutual interest to physicians of Indian descent. Establishes contracts with government agencies to provide consultation and other expert opinion regarding health care of American Indians and Alaskan Natives; receives contracts and grant monies and other forms of assistance from these sources. Supports and encourages all other agencies and organizations, Indian and non-Indian, working to improve health conditions of American Indians and Alaskan Natives. Locates scholarship funds for Indian professional students; provides counseling assistance; preserves American Indian culture. Conducts seminars for students interested in health careers and for counselors in government and other schools where American Indian children are taught. **Founded:** 1971. **Membership:** 220. **Staff:** 3. **Languages:** English. **Publication:** Newsletter, quarterly. Circulation: 4,500. Advertising: accepted.

ASSOCIATION OF AMERICAN MEDICAL COLLEGES (AAMC)

e-mail: webmaster@aamc.org
url: http://www.aamc.org
2450 N St. NW
Washington, DC 20037
Jordan J. Cohen, M.D., Pres.
PH: (202)828-0400
FX: (202)828-1125

Description: Medical schools, graduate affiliate medical colleges, academic societies, teaching hospitals, and individuals interested in the advancement of medical education, biomedical research, and healthcare. Provides centralized application service. Offers management education program for medical school deans, teaching hospital directors, department chairmen, and service chiefs of affiliated hospitals. Develops and administers the Medical College Admissions Test (MCAT). Operates student loan program. Maintains information management system and institutional profile system. Compiles statistics. **Founded:** 1876. **Membership:** 2200. **Staff:** 250. **Languages:** English. **Budget:** $21,000,000. **Publication:** *Academic Medicine,* monthly. Journal. Provides scholarly articles on physician education and workforce issues. Price: $70.00/year in U.S.; $120.00 Canada and foreign. ISSN: 1040-2446. Circulation: 3,500. Advertising: accepted. Also Cited As: *Journal of Medical Education* ■ *Curriculum Directory,* annual ■ *Directory of American Medical Education,* annual ■ *Medical School Admission Requirements,* annual ■ Reports, annual ■ Reports, semiannual.

ASSOCIATION OF AMERICAN PHYSICIANS (AAP)
e-mail: bhansen@vapop.ucsd.edu
Department of Medicine
9500 Gilmun Dr.
La Jolla, CA 92093-0673
Stuart Kornfeld, MD, Pres.
PH: (619)534-6651
FX: (619)534-6653
Description: Medical school faculty and clinical investigators. **Founded:** 1886. **Membership:** 1200. **Languages:** English. **Publication:** *Transactions of the Association of American Physicians,* annual. Proceedings. Proceedings of the annual meeting; includes membership list and obituaries. Price: included in membership dues; $50.00/copy for nonmembers. Circulation: 1,500.

ASSOCIATION OF AMERICAN PHYSICIANS AND SURGEONS (AAPS)
e-mail: 71161.1263@compuserve.com
url: http://www.appsonline.org
1601 N. Tucson Blvd., Ste. 9
Tucson, AZ 85716
Jane M. Orient, M.D., Exec.Dir.
PH: (520)327-4885
TF: 800635-1196
FX: (520)325-4230
Description: Physicians dedicated to preserving and promoting quality medical care. Represents physicians in the socioeconomic and legal aspects of medical practice such as medical economics, public relations, and legislation. Makes available legal consultation services. **Founded:** 1943. **Membership:** 4500. **Staff:** 3. **Languages:** English. **Publication:** *A Letter to My Colleagues: The Solution to Today's Health Economic Crisis,* monthly. Newsletter ■ *AAPS News,* monthly. Newsletter. Covers developments affecting health care and the profession. Includes legislative news, calendar of events, and health law commentary. Price: included in membership dues; $35.00/year for nonmembers. ISSN: 8750-9687. Advertising: not accepted ■ *The Canadian Model: Could it Work Here?* ■ *How to Challenge Health Insurers Who Refuse to Pay Legitimate Claims: A Guide for Patients* ■ *John Q. Privatepractice, RIP* ■ *The Political Fallacy that Medical Care is a Right* ■ *Relative Value Scales: Fundamental Economic Principles* ■ Audiotapes ■ Videos.

ASSOCIATION OF ASIAN/PACIFIC COMMUNITY HEALTH ORGANIZATIONS (AAPCHO)
1440 Broadway, Ste. 510
Oakland, CA 94612-2025
Stephen P. Jiang, Contact
PH: (510)272-9536
Description: Works to improve access to culturally and linguistically appropriate health care in order to improve the health status of Asians and Pacific Islanders with a special focus on the medically underserved. **Founded:** 1987. **Membership:** 13. **Staff:** 13. **Languages:** Chinese, Hindi. **Budget:** $950,000. **Publication:**

Behind the Mask: AIDS <el3> It Affects All of Us. Video ■ *Hepatitis B.* Brochure ■ *Parent's Guide to Common Childhood Illnesses.* Brochure ■ *Thalassemia Among Asians.* Brochure.

ASSOCIATION OF BEHAVIORAL HEALTHCARE MANAGEMENT (ABHM)
60 Revere Dr., Ste. 500
Northbrook, IL 60062
John Wakman, Exec.Dir.
PH: (847)480-9626
FX: (847)480-9282
Description: Administrators of services for the emotionally disturbed, mentally ill, mentally retarded, developmentally disabled, and those with problems of alcohol and substance abuse. Objectives are to: further the education of administrators; develop criteria for and certify the competence of administrators; promote adherence to a code of ethics. Aids in developing professional administrative skills and administration of services. Sponsors educational workshops. **Founded:** 1959. **Membership:** 900. **Languages:** English. **Budget:** $250,000. Formerly (1969) American Society of Mental Health Business Administrators; (1997) Association of Mental Heath Administrators.

ASSOCIATION OF BLACK CARDIOLOGISTS (ABC)
url: http://www.abcardio.org
225 Peachtree St., Ste. 1420
Atlanta, GA 30303
B. Waine Kong, PhD,JD, CEO
PH: (404)582-8777
TF: 800753-9222
FX: (404)582-8778
Description: Physicians and other health professionals interested in lowering mortality and morbidity resulting from cardiovascular diseases. Seeks to improve prevention and treatment of cardiovascular diseases. Conducts educational and research programs; bestows awards; maintains speakers' bureau. **Founded:** 1974. **Membership:** 500. **Staff:** 5. **Languages:** English. **Budget:** $3,000,000.

ASSOCIATION OF BLACK NURSING FACULTY (ABNF)
5823 Queens Cove
Lisle, IL 60532
Sallie Tucker-Allen, Ph.D., Exec.Dir.
PH: (630)969-3809
FX: (630)969-3895
Description: Black nursing faculty teaching in nursing programs accredited by the National League for Nursing Works to promote health-related issues and educational concerns of interest to the black community and ABNF. Serves as a forum for communication and the exchange of information among members; develops strategies for expressing concerns to other individuals, institutions, and communities. Assists members in professional development; develops and sponsors continuing education activities; fosters networking and guidance in employment and recruitment activities. Promotes health-related issues of legislation, government programs, and community activities. Supports black consumer advocacy issues. Encourages research. Maintains speakers' bureau and hall of fame. Offers charitable program and placement services. Compiles statistics. Is establishing a computer-assisted job bank; plans to develop bibliographies related to research groups. **Founded:** 1987. **Membership:** 127. **State Groups:** 25. **Languages:** English. **Budget:** $25,000. **Publication:** *ABNF Journal,* bimonthly. Includes research reports and scholarly papers. Price: $125.00/year. ISSN: 1046-7041. Circulation: 400. Advertising: accepted ■ *ABNF Newsletter,* quarterly. Includes member profiles and activities, research abstracts, conference information, job opportunities, and fellowship information. Price: included in membership dues; $25.00/year. Advertising: accepted ■ *Membership Directory of the ABNF,* annual.

ASSOCIATION OF CAMP NURSES (ACN)
8504 Thorsonvein
Bemidji, MN 56601
Linda Ebner Erceg, RN, Pres.

PH: (218)586-2633
FX: (218)586-3631
Description: Works to promote and develop the nursing practice in the camp community. Maintains resource center; provides consulting services; supports camp nursing research; conducts educational programs. **Founded:** 1990. **Membership:** 300. Multinational. **Regional Groups:** 8. **Languages:** English. **Budget:** $6,000.

ASSOCIATION OF CHILD AND ADOLESCENT PSYCHIATRIC NURSES (ACAPN)
1211 Locust St.
Philadelphia, PA 19107
Linda Finke, Pres.
PH: (215)545-2843
TF: 800826-2950
FX: (215)545-8107
Description: Nurses and others interested in child and adolescent psychiatry. Works to promote mental health of infants, children, adolescents, and their families through clinical practice, public policy, and research. **Founded:** 1971. **Membership:** 500. **Local Groups:** 25. **Languages:** English. Formerly (1992) Advocates for Child Psychiatric Nursing.

ASSOCIATION FOR CHILDBIRTH AT HOME, INTERNATIONAL (ACHI)
PO Box 430
Glendale, CA 91209
Tonya Brooks, Founder & Pres.
PH: (818)386-1082
FX: (818)386-9374
Description: Parents, midwives, doctors, childbirth educators, other professionals, and interested individuals, all of whom support childbirth at home. Purposes are to bring accurate information and competent support to parents seeking home birth and safe hospital birth; to identify and implement correct obstetrical and pediatric practice. Offers parent education classes, leader training programs, international resource and referral service, and professional education seminars and programs; instructs parents, childbirth educators, midwives, and physicians in safe home birth and noninterventive alternative techniques. Conducts research; compiles statistics. Maintains speakers' bureau. **Founded:** 1972. **Membership:** 30000. **Staff:** 8. Multinational. **Local Groups:** 120. **Languages:** English. **Budget:** $150,000. Formerly Association for Childbirth at Home.

ASSOCIATION OF CLINICAL SCIENTISTS
e-mail: 103040.2027@compuserve.com
PO Box 1287
Middlebury, VT 05753
Dr. F. William Sunderman, Jr., Sec.-Treas.
Description: Professional society of physicians and scientists working in various fields of laboratory medicine. Seeks to promote education and research in clinical science by practical methods; maintain and improve the accuracy of measurements in clinical laboratories and promote uniformity in clinical laboratory procedures; encourage cooperation between physicians and nonphysicians concerned with the application of scientific methods to medical practice. **Founded:** 1949. **Membership:** 500. **Staff:** 1. **Languages:** English. Formerly (1956) Clinical Science Club.

ASSOCIATION OF COMMUNITY CANCER CENTERS (ACCC)
url: http://www.assoc-cancer-ctrs.org
11600 Nebel St., Ste. 201
Rockville, MD 20852
Lee E. Mortenson, Exec.Dir.
PH: (301)984-9496
FX: (301)770-1949
Description: Institutions (517), individuals (300), and 14 state oncology societies involved in the provision of community cancer care. Fosters communication among providers of community cancer care; seeks to improve the quality of care available to can-

cer patients in community settings; encourages clinical research utilizing the community as a setting. **Founded:** 1974. **Membership:** 817. **Staff:** 13. **State Groups:** 14. **Languages:** English. **Publication:** *Cancer DRGs: A Comparative Report on Key Cancer DRGs*, annual. Advertising: not accepted ■ *Community Cancer Programs in the U.S.*, annual. Reference guide to freestanding and hospital-based cancer programs. Price: $50.00 non-profit organizations; $150.00 others. Advertising: accepted ■ *Compendia-Based Drug Bulletin*, quarterly ■ *Critical Pathways*, periodic ■ *Oncology Issues*, bimonthly. Journal. Provides information on community cancer programs for association members, who are physicians, nurses, social workers, and other health professionals. Price: $40.00/year. Circulation: 18,000 ■ *Standards for Cancer Programs*, periodic.

ASSOCIATION FOR CONTINUING EDUCATION (ACE)
PO Box 774168
Steamboat Springs, CO 80477
Shirlee Finney, Exec.Dir.
PH: (303)879-0911
TF: 800525-3402
FX: (303)879-2952
Description: Physicians, dentists, and allied health professionals pursuing continuing education credit in their fields. Conducts weekly educational program. Convention/Meeting: none. **Founded:** 1982. **Membership:** 2000. **Languages:** English. **For-Profit.** **Budget:** $120,000. **Publication:** Membership Directory, annual.

ASSOCIATION FOR FACULTY IN THE MEDICAL HUMANITIES (AFMH)
e-mail: shhv@aol.com
6728 Old McLean Village Dr.
Mc Lean, VA 22101
George K. Degnon, Exec.Dir.
PH: (703)556-9222
FX: (703)556-8729
Description: A section of the Society for Health and Human Values. Faculty in the humanities at medical schools. Promotes teaching and research in the humanities in the context of medical education; closer links among scholars in the humanities who work in medical education; interdisciplinary teaching and research among humanities scholars, scientists, and clinicians; alliances with colleagues who relate in a scholarly way to the humanities in contexts other than medical education. **Founded:** 1983. **Membership:** 350. **Languages:** English. **Publication:** Membership Directory, annual.

ASSOCIATION OF FAMILY PRACTICE ADMINISTRATORS (AFPA)
e-mail: fbomar@umich.edu
url: http://www.uams.edu/afpa/
Dept. of Family Medicine
PO Box 8729
Kansas City, MO 64114
Francine Bomar, Board Member
PH: (734)998-7122
FX: (734)998-7335
Description: Administrators and coordinators of family practice residency training programs. Promotes professionalism in family practice administration. Serves as a network for sharing of information and fellowship among members. Provides technical assistance to members; functions as a liaison to related professional organizations. **Languages:** English.

ASSOCIATION OF FAMILY PRACTICE RESIDENCY DIRECTORS (AFPRD)
e-mail: afprd@aafp.org
url: http://www.afprd.org
8880 Ward Pky.
Kansas City, MO 64114-2797
Julie Dostal, M.D., Pres.
PH: (816)333-9700
TF: 800274-2237
FX: (816)333-9855

Description: Promotes excellence in family practice graduate education. Provides representation for residency directors at a national level and provides a political voice for them in appropriate arenas. Promotes cooperation and communication between residency programs and different branches of the family practice specialty. Dedicated to improving of education of family physicians. Provides a network for mutual assistance among FP. residency directors. **Founded:** 1990. **Membership:** 410. **Languages:** English. **For-Profit. Publication:** *Highlights*, 3/year. Newsletter. Price: free for members. Circulation: 410. Advertising: accepted.

ASSOCIATION OF HEALTH FACILITY SURVEY AGENCIES (AHFSA)

Missouri Department of Health
Bureau of Hospital Licensing
920 Wildwood Dr.
Jefferson City, MO 65102
Michele Reznick, Admin.
PH: (573)751-6302
FX: (573)526-3621
Description: Directors of state or territorial health facility licensure and certification programs; staff members of a state or territorial health facility licensure and certification agency; employees of the federal Health Care Financing Administration; interested individuals. (The term health facilities refers to health/medical institutions including hospitals, nursing homes, rehabilitation centers, reproductive health centers, independent clinical laboratories, hospices, and ambulatory surgical centers.) Purposes are to: exchange information among members and between members and the Association of State and Territorial Health Officials; constitute a "reservoir of expertise" to aid in the guidance of ASTHO; improve the quality of health facility licensure and certification programs; provide a forum for state and territorial issues at the national level. Has a representative on an ASTHO standing committee and liaises with the federal Department of Health and Human Services and the HCFA. Has developed new training programs with the HHS and testified before the U.S. Senate Special Committee on Aging on survey and certification procedures. Bestows annual Surveyor of the Year Award. **Founded:** 1968. **Membership:** 51. **Languages:** English Formerly (1991) Association of Health Facility Licensure and Certification Directors.

ASSOCIATION OF HEALTH OCCUPATIONS TEACHER EDUCATORS (AHOTE)

School of Education Rm. 346
Louisville, KY 40292
Dr. Patricia K. Leitsch, Pres.
PH: (502)852-0608
Description: Educators of health occupations education teachers; graduate students preparing to teach health occupations. Purposes are to: plan and implement professional development of health occupations teachers; to facilitate sharing of teacher education curriculum materials; to investigate and disseminate innovative strategies for health occupations teacher education delivery systems; to attempt to impact national issues relating to health occupations teacher education personnel and programs. Identifies needed research relating to health occupations and encourages dissemination of findings that have implications for the field. Cooperates with other organizations engaged in the preparation of health personnel and programs. Operates speakers' bureau. **Founded:** 1978. **Membership:** 28. **Languages:** English. **Publication:** *Health Occupations Personnel in Teacher Education*, annual ▪ *Journal of Health Occupations Education*, semiannual ▪ *Membership List*, annual.

ASSOCIATION FOR HEALTH SERVICES RESEARCH (AHSR)

e-mail: info@ahsr.org
url: http://www.ahsr.org
1130 Connecticut Ave. NW, Ste. 700
Washington, DC 20036
PH: (202)223-2477
FX: (202)835-8972

Description: Individuals and organizations concerned with health services research. Objectives are to educate the public concerning the need for and contribution of health services research in improving health care in the U.S.; to foster productive cooperation among researchers, public and private funding agencies, health professionals, policymakers, and the public; to represent the views of members in the development and implementation of national legislative and administrative policies concerning health services research. Disseminates research findings to public and private sector officials. **Founded:** 1981. **Membership:** 2800. **Staff:** 21. Multinational. **Languages:** English. **Budget:** $4,000,000. **Publication:** *HSR Reports*, quarterly. Newsletter. Covers legislative news and association activities. Includes conference calendar, employment listings, and training opportunities. Price: free with membership. Circulation: 3,000. Advertising: accepted.

ASSOCIATION OF HEALTHCARE INTERNAL AUDITORS (AHIA)

url: http://www.ahia.org
926 Great Pond Dr., Ste. 1003
Altamonte Springs, FL 32714-7244
Thomas A. Monahan, CAE, Exec.Dir.
PH: (202)429-5134
FX: (202)223-4579
Description: Health care internal auditors and other interested individuals. Promotes cost containment and increased productivity in health care institutions through internal auditing. Serves as a forum for the exchange of experience, ideas, and information among members; provides continuing professional education courses and informs members of developments in health care internal auditing. Offers employment clearinghouse services. **Founded:** 1981. **Membership:** 1000. **Staff:** 2. **Local Groups:** 4. **Languages:** English. **Publication:** *New Perspectives on Healthcare Auditing*, quarterly. Journal. Contains book reviews, audit findings, and local and regional group news. Circulation: 1,000. Advertising: accepted. **Formerly:** (1989) Healthcare Internal Audit Group.

ASSOCIATION FOR MACULAR DISEASES (AMD)

e-mail: macula@macula.org
210 E. 64th St.
New York, NY 10021
Nikolai Stevenson, Pres.
PH: (212)605-3719
FX: (212)605-3795
Description: Individuals afflicted with macular diseases, and their families. (The macula of the eye is the posterior middle portion of the retina responsible for central vision. Disorders involving the macula include inflammations, tumors, retinal growths, and degenerative problems.) Purposes are to: disseminate information on available resources such as recorded material and low vision aids; promote public awareness of macular diseases; encourage growth of research into the causes, treatment, and possible prevention of macular diseases; inform the public of the need for postmortem donation of eyes having a history of macular disease and advise on procedures for making such a donation. Provides counseling programs and group sharing for afflicted persons and their families. **Founded:** 1977. **Membership:** 6000. **Languages:** English. Formerly Association for Mascular Degeneration.

ASSOCIATION OF MANAGED HEALTHCARE ORGANIZATIONS

url: http://www.amho.org
1 Bridge Plaza, Ste. 350
Fort Lee, NJ 07024
Bradley Kalish
PH: (703)255-5340
TF: 800642-2515
FX: (201)947-8406
Description: Seeks to advance the development, growth and success of network-based managed health care organizations(PPOs PSOs IPAs, etc.). Provides its members with a variety of educational and networking opportunities. Advocates the needs and

interests of its members before local, state and federal legislators and regulators. Promotes network-based managed health care to payors, employers and the general public through a variety of media outlets. **Founded:** 1983. **Membership:** 1300. **Staff:** 5. **Regional Groups:** 11. **Languages:** English. **Budget:** $1,000,000. **Publication:** *AAPPO Journal/PPO Perspectives*, bimonthly. Newsletter. Contains information on product innovations, systems, trends, and individuals in the managed care field. Price: included in membership dues; $50.00/year for nonmembers. Advertising: accepted ■ *Directory of Operational PPOs*, annual. Contains information on approximately 1000 PPO organizations and products. Price: free to organizational members; $225.00 for individual members; $425.00 for nonmembers ■ *Summary of PPO Legislation on a State Level*, annual. Provides information on state laws and regulations that govern the organization and operation of PPOs. Price: free to organizational members; $50.00 for individual members; $100.00 for nonmembers ■ Bibliography. Lists current reports, speeches, articles, and books on PPOs. **Formerly:** (1998) American Association of Preferred Provider Organizations.

ASSOCIATION OF MEDICAL EDUCATION AND RESEARCH IN SUBSTANCE ABUSE (AMERSA)
Brown University
Center for Alcohol and Addiction Studies
Box G-BH
Providence, RI 02912
David C. Lewis, M.D., Exec.Dir.
PH: (401)785-8263
FX: (401)444-1850
Description: Medical school faculty members and others concerned with general medical education who are involved with providing information on alcohol and drug-related topics to medical professionals and students. **Founded:** 1976. **Membership:** 400. **Languages:** English. **Publication:** *Substance Abuse*, quarterly. Journal. Price: included in membership dues; $40.00/year for nonmembers ■ Membership Directory, biennial.

ASSOCIATION OF MEDICAL SCHOOL PEDIATRIC DEPARTMENT CHAIRMEN (AMSPDC)
e-mail: jbartholomew@abpeds.org
c/o Jean Bartholomew
111 Silver Cedar Ct.
Chapel Hill, NC 27514-1651
Russell Chesney, M.D., Sec.-Treas.
PH: (919)942-1993
FX: (919)929-9255
Description: Chairmen of the department of pediatrics of each accredited medical school in the United States and Canada. Fosters education and research in the field of child health and human development. Is cooperating with other national pediatric groups to consider problems of pediatric education, research, and care. **Founded:** 1961. **Membership:** 145. **Languages:** English.

ASSOCIATION OF MINORITY HEALTH PROFESSIONS SCHOOLS (AMHPS)
507 Capitol Court, Ste. 200
Washington, DC 20002
Dale P. Dirks, Wash.Rep.
PH: (202)544-7499
FX: (202)546-7105
Description: Predominantly black health professions schools. Seeks to: increase the number of minorities in health professions; improve the health of blacks in the U.S.; increase the federal resources available to minority schools and students. Provides information to the U.S. Congress; conducts educational programs. **Founded:** 1978. **Membership:** 11. **Staff:** 2. **Languages:** English. **Publication:** *Study of the Health Status of Minorities in the U.S.*, periodic.

ASSOCIATION FOR MOLECULAR PATHOLOGY (AMP)
e-mail: amp@pathol.faseb.org
url: http://www.zapruder.path.med.umich.edu/users/amp/
9650 Rockville Pike
Bethesda, MD 20814-3993
Frances A. Pitlick, Ph.D., Contact
PH: (301)571-1880
FX: (301)571-1879
Description: Individuals interested in, or engaged in the practice of, molecular pathology. Promotes clinical practice, basic research, and education in the field. Represents members' interests within the health care industry. Develops and maintains liaison with other organizations and agencies concerned with molecular pathology; serves as a forum for the exchange of ideas and information among members. Participates in the development of regulatory and credentialing policies applied to molecular pathology; promulgates guidlines for molecular pathology training programs. Conducts educational programs to increase public awareness of molecular pathology. **Languages:** English.

ASSOCIATION OF NURSES ENDORSING TRANSPLANTATION (ANET)
PO Box 541234
Merritt Island, FL 32954-1234
Mary Gainey, RNC, Exec.Dir.
PH: (407)459-3777
FX: (407)459-3777
Description: Registered nurses, LVNs, LPNs, student nurses, chaplains, social workers, hospitals, health care facilities. Promotes organ and tissue donation for transplantation and research. **Founded:** 1983. **Membership:** 75. **Staff:** 2. **Languages:** English. Formerly (1983) Consortium of Registered Nurses for Eye Acquisition.

ASSOCIATION OF OPERATING ROOM NURSES (AORN)
url: http://www.aorn.org/
2170 S. Parker Rd.
Ste. 300
Denver, CO 80231-5711
Lola M. Fehr, R.N.,, Exec.Dir.
PH: (303)755-6300
TF: 800755-2676
FX: (303)750-3212
Description: Professional perioperative (operating room) nurses. Provides education, representation, and standards for quality patient care. **Founded:** 1949. **Membership:** 47000. **Staff:** 100. Multinational. **Local Groups:** 390. **Languages:** English. **Budget:** $10,000,000.

ASSOCIATION OF OPTOMETRIC EDUCATORS (AOE)
NSU College of Optometry
1001 N. Grand Ave.
Tahlequah, OK 74464-7017
Dr. George Foster, Dean
PH: (918)456-5511
FX: (918)458-2104
Description: Teachers in schools and colleges of optometry. Works to enhance the professional and academic status and conditions of service of optometric educators and to promote communication among members. Concerned with faculty welfare, faculty-administration relations, faculty-student relations, and faculty-professional relations. **Founded:** 1972. **Membership:** 100. **Languages:** English.

ASSOCIATION OF OTOLARYNGOLOGY ADMINISTRATORS (AOA)
2283 Wrightsboro Rd.
Augusta, GA 30904-4717
Beth Williams, Adm.
PH: (706)737-9262
FX: (706)738-3531
Description: Persons employed in a managerial capacity for private or academic group medical practices specializing in otolaryngology (the study of the ear, nose, and throat). Seeks to: pro-

mote the concept of professional management in otolaryngology; provide a forum for interaction and exchange of information between otolaryngological managers; present educational programs. Maintains data exchange service for members researching specific topics. **Founded:** 1983. **Membership:** 730. **Regional Groups:** 8. **Languages:** English. **Budget:** $100,000. **Publication:** *Oto's Scope*, 3/year.

ASSOCIATION OF PAKISTANI PHYSICIANS (APPNA)
url: http://www.appna.org
6414 S. Cast Ave., Ste. L2
Westmont, IL 60559
Durdana Gilani, M.D., Pres.
PH: (630)968-8585
FX: (630)968-8677
Description: Physicians and dentists who are native to Pakistan but now live and practice in North America. Purposes are: to support medical education and research and advance the interests of medicine and medical organizations; to foster scientific development and education in order to improve the quality of medicine and health care; to facilitate better relations among Pakistani physicians and between them and the people of North America. Assists Pakistani physicians newly arrived in North America in orientation and adjustment. Arranges for donation of medical literature and medical supplies to Pakistan, and for lecture tours, medical conferences, and seminars to be held there. Participates in medical relief and charitable activities in Pakistan and North America; cooperates with other medical organizations in North America. Offers scientific programs for which continuing medical education credits are awarded. **Founded:** 1976. **Membership:** 1200. **Staff:** 2. **Languages:** Baluchi, Panjabi. **Budget:** $150,000. **Publication:** Bulletin, monthly ■ Newsletter, quarterly.

ASSOCIATION OF PATHOLOGY CHAIRS (APC)
e-mail: apc@pathol.faseb.org
9650 Rockville Pike
Bethesda, MD 20814-3993
Frances A. Pitlick, Ph.D., Admin.
PH: (301)571-1880
FX: (301)571-1879
Description: Chairs of medical school departments of pathology. Acts as a communications center for exchange of information and for workshops on innovations for teaching and resident training, department administration, and relationships with governmental and other nonuniversity agencies. Compiles statistics. **Founded:** 1967. **Membership:** 152. **Regional Groups:** 4. **Languages:** English. **Publication:** Newsletter, quarterly. Price: available to members only. Circulation: 350. Advertising: not accepted. **Formerly:** (1970) American Association of Chairmen of Medical School Departments of Pathology; (1993) Association of Pathology Chairmen.

ASSOCIATION OF PEDIATRIC ONCOLOGY NURSES (APON)
e-mail: apon@amctec.com
url: http://www.apon.org/
4700 W. Lake Ave.
Glenview, IL 60025-1485
M. Kathleen Klaeser, CAE, Exec.Dir.
PH: (708)375-4724
FX: (708)375-4777
Description: Scientific and educational association seeking to establish lines of communication among nurses caring for children and adolescents with cancer. Encourages updating of literature and development of standards of care for children with cancer. Plans regional workshops. **Founded:** 1973. **Membership:** 2000. **Regional Groups:** 37. **Languages:** English.

ASSOCIATION OF PEDIATRIC ONCOLOGY SOCIAL WORKERS (APOSW)
All Childrens Hospital
St. Petersburg, FL 33701
Lynda Walker, Pres.
PH: (813)360-1319

Description: Social workers involved with pediatric cancer patients in medical settings nationwide. Purposes are to: advance the practice, enhance knowledge, and develop policy and programs of pediatric oncology social work; foster quality and effectiveness of the social work practice of pediatric oncology; promote solidarity among social workers; provide community and professional education; formulate and record local and federal legislation related to pediatric oncology. **Founded:** 1977. **Membership:** 200. **Languages:** English.

ASSOCIATION OF PHYSICIAN ASSISTANT PROGRAMS (APAP)
950 N. Washington St.
Alexandria, VA 22314
Don Pederson, Pres.
PH: (703)548-5538
FX: (703)684-1924
Description: Educational institutions with training programs for assistants to primary care and surgical physicians. Assists in the development and organization of educational curricula for physician assistant (PA) programs to assure the public of competent PAs; contributes to defining the roles of PAs in the field of medicine to maximize their benefit to the public; serves as a public information center on the profession; coordinates program logistics such as admissions and career placements. Sponsors Annual Survey of Physician Assistant Educational Programs in the United States. Conducts research projects; compiles statistics. **Founded:** 1972. **Staff:** 2. **Languages:** English. **Publication:** *Annual Report on Physician Assistant Education in the U.S.*, annual. Provides data on physician assistant education, employment, and trends affecting the profession. Includes statistics. Price: $25.00/copy. ISSN: 0883-0703. Advertising: not accepted ■ *APAP Update*, monthly. Newsletter. For physician assistant program faculty and others concerned with curricula and government/ legislative developments affecting the profession. Price: included in membership dues ■ *National Directory of Physician Assistant Programs*, annual. Describes curriculum, university and institutional affiliations, entrance requirements, selection factors, credentials awarded, and financial aid. Price: $25.00/copy. Advertising: accepted.

ASSOCIATION OF PHYSICIAN ASSISTANTS IN CARDIOVASCULAR SURGERY (APACVS)
url: http://www.apacvs.org
11250 Roger Bacon Dr. Ste., 8
Reston, VA 20190
Richard A. Guggok, Exec.Dir.
PH: (703)707-0476
FX: (703)435-4390
Description: Physician assistants who work with cardiovascular surgeons. Objective is to assist in defining the role of physician assistants in the field of cardiovascular surgery through educational forums. **Founded:** 1981. **Membership:** 600. **Languages:** English. **Budget:** $100,000.

ASSOCIATION OF POLYSOMNOGRAPHIC TECHNOLOGISTS (APT)
e-mail: lgordon@applmeapro.com
url: http://www.aptwed.org
PO Box 14861
Lenexa, KS 66285-4861
Linda Gordon, Exec. Dir.
PH: (913)541-1991
FX: (913)541-0156
Description: Individuals who practice polysomnography in research or clinical settings. (Polysomnographic technology deals with the measurement and recording of multiple physiological activity, such as eye movement and heart rate, during sleep.) Seeks to establish standards for polysomnographic technology and provide education and training for people entering in the field. Acts as a forum for communication among members. **Founded:** 1978. **Membership:** 1600. **Languages:** English.

**ASSOCIATION OF PROFESSIONAL BASEBALL
PHYSICIANS (APBP)**
c/o Dr. Leonard J. Michienzi
6515 Barrie Rd.
Edina, MN 55435
PH: (612)920-5663
TF: 800747-3641
FX: (612)924-1659
Description: Physicians and surgeons of the professional baseball
teams in the U.S. Aim is to provide the best possible medical
care to all players and associated personnel. Conducts drug
abuse seminars on topics such as the use of amphetamines,
steroids, and cocaine by athletes. Publications: none. **Founded:**
1970. **Membership:** 36. **Languages:** English.

ASSOCIATION OF PROFESSORS OF CARDIOLOGY (APC)
e-mail: sthayer@acc.org
9111 Old Georgetown Rd.
Bethesda, MD 20814-1699
Donald J. Jablonski, CAE, Contact
PH: (301)493-2330
FX: (301)897-9745
Description: Directors or acting directors of divisions of cardio-
logy in accredited medical schools in the U.S. and Puerto Rico.
Conducts educational and scientific programs with respect to
cardiology. Publications: none. **Founded:** 1990. **Membership:** 115.
Staff: 2. **Languages:** English. **Budget:** $30,000.

**ASSOCIATION OF PROFESSORS OF GYNECOLOGY AND
OBSTETRICS (APGO)**
409 12th St. SW
Washington, DC 20024
Donna Wachter, Exec.Dir.
PH: (202)863-2507
FX: (202)863-2514
Description: Departments of obstetrics and gynecology in approved medical schools in the U.S. and Canada, and in non-uni-
versity teaching hospitals with active educational program for undergraduate medical students in ob/gyn. Works to consider
problems relating to the departments of obstetrics and gynecology; to advance and improve the study of gynecology and obstetrics; to provide a means of exchanging information relating to
the programs of study, teaching methods, and research activities
of such departments. Compiles statistics. **Founded:** 1962. **Membership:** 1500. **Staff:** 4. **Languages:** English. **Budget:** $600,000.

ASSOCIATION OF PROFESSORS OF MEDICINE (APM)
e-mail: apm@im.org
url: http://www.im.org/apm
2501 M St. NW, Ste. 550
Washington, DC 20037-1308
Tod Ibrahim, Exec.Dir.
PH: (202)861-7700
FX: (202)861-9731
Description: Heads of departments of internal medicine in medical schools. Conducts educational programs; compiles statistics.
Founded: 1954. **Membership:** 152. **Staff:** 7. **Languages:** English.
Publication: *APM Update*, quarterly. Newsletter. Circulation:
1,500. Advertising: not accepted ■ *Federal Health Policy Update*,
quarterly. Circulation: 1,500 ■ Directory, annual. **Formerly:** Aca-
demic Medicine Club.

ASSOCIATION OF PROGRAM DIRECTORS IN SURGERY
4900B 31st St.
Arlington, VA 22206
Thomas F. Fise, Contact
PH: (703)820-7400
FX: (703)931-4520
Description: Program directors in surgery. Conducts educational
programs and scientific meetings. **Founded:** 1978. **Membership:**
507. **Staff:** 5. Multinational. **Languages:** English.

**ASSOCIATION OF PSYCHOLOGY POSTDOCTORAL AND
INTERNSHIP CENTERS (APPIC)**
e-mail: appic@aol.com
733 15th St. NW, Ste. 719
Washington, DC 20005-2112
Connie Hercey, Exec. Officer
PH: (202)347-0022
FX: (202)347-8480
Description: Veterans Administration hospitals, medical centers,
state hospitals, university counseling centers, and other facilities
that provide internship and postdoctoral programs in professional psychology. Promotes activities that assist in the development of professional psychology training programs. Serves as a
clearinghouse to provide Ph.D. candidates with internship placement assistance at member facilities. Conducts workshops and
seminars on training procedures in clinical psychology at the
Ph.D. level. **Founded:** 1968. **Membership:** 550. **Staff:** 2. Multinational. **Languages:** English. **Budget:** $500,000. **Publication:**
APPIC Newsletter, semiannual. Price: $10.00 free for members.
Advertising: not accepted ■ *Internship and Postdoctoral Programs
in Professional Psychology*, annual. Directory. **Formerly:** (1991)
Association of Psychology Internship Centers.

ASSOCIATION OF REHABILITATION NURSES (ARN)
e-mail: info@rehabnurse.org
url: http://www.rehabnurse.org
4700 W. Lake Ave.
Glenview, IL 60025-1485
Anne Cordes, R.N.,, Exec.Dir.
PH: (847)375-4710
TF: 800229-7530
FX: (847)375-4777
Description: Registered nurses concerned with or actively engaged in the practice of rehabilitation nursing; others interested
in rehabilitation. Works to advance the quality of rehabilitation
nursing practice through educational opportunities and to facilitate the exchange of ideas. Committees involve members in issues of organizational, local, and national importance and provi-
de an avenue to effect change. Has formed the Rehabilitation
Nursing Foundation to promote, develop, and engage in educational activities and scientific research in the rehabilitation field.
Founded: 1974. **Membership:** 9000. **Staff:** 9. **Local Groups:** 89.
Languages: English. **For-Profit. Budget:** $2,500,000.

**ASSOCIATION OF REPRODUCTIVE HEALTH
PROFESSIONALS (ARHP)**
e-mail: arhp@aol.com
url: http://www.arhp.org
2401 Pennsylvania Ave. NW, Ste. 350
Washington, DC 20037-1718
Wayne C. Shields, Pres.
PH: (202)466-3825
FX: (202)466-3826
Description: Professionals in reproductive health, including obstetricians, gynecologists, family practitioners, pediatricians,
nurse clinicians, researchers, educators, counselors, and administrators. Interested in contraception, sexually transmitted diseases, HIV/AIDS, menopause, urogenital disorders, sexuality, cancer prevention/detection, abortion and infertility. Maintains
speakers' bureau; sponsors clinical and public educational programs. **Founded:** 1963. **Membership:** 2000. **Staff:** 10. **Languages:**
English. **Budget:** $4,000,000. **Publication:** *Clinical Proceedings* ■
Health and Sexuality, quarterly. Newsletter. Circulation: 15,000.
Advertising: not accepted ■ Journal, bimonthly. Advertising: accepted ■ Journals ■ Videos. **Formerly:** (1973) American Association of Parenthood Physicians; (1982) Association of Planned
Parenthood Physicians; (1987) Association of Planned Parenthood Professionals.

**ASSOCIATION FOR RESEARCH OF CHILDHOOD CANCER
(AROCC)**
PO Box 251
Buffalo, NY 14225-0251
Ann O'Donnell, Exec. Officer

PH: (716)681-4433
Description: Parents who have lost children to various pediatric cancers; persons supporting cancer research. Seeks to fund the expansion and continuation of research in pediatric cancer centers and to provide seed money for pilot projects in cancer research. Offers support to parents of children with cancer. Bestows research and clinical investigation grants; offers research and medical student fellowships. **Founded:** 1971. **Membership:** 1000. **Regional Groups:** 2. **Languages:** English. **Publication:** *AROCC – Newsletter*, quarterly. Contains book reviews; donations list; memorial list. Price: included in membership dues. Circulation: 1,000 ■ *Parent/Child Handbook*.

ASSOCIATION FOR RESEARCH IN NERVOUS AND MENTAL DISEASE (ARNMD)
630 West 168th Street
Box 23
New York, NY 10032
James E. Goldman, M.D., Sec.Treas.
PH: (212)740-7608
FX: (212)305-4548
Description: Individuals engaged in the practice or research of neurology, neurosurgery, or psychiatry who are members of neurologic or psychiatric societies. **Founded:** 1920. **Membership:** 950. **Languages:** English. **Budget:** $25,000. Formerly (1922) Neuropsychiatric Research Society.

ASSOCIATION FOR RESEARCH IN VISION AND OPHTHALMOLOGY (ARVO)
e-mail: mem@arvo.arvo.org
url: http://www.faseb.org/arvo/
9650 Rockville Pike
Bethesda, MD 20814-3998
Joanne G. Angle, Exec.Dir.
PH: (301)571-1844
FX: (301)571-8311
Description: Professional society of researchers in vision and ophthalmology. To encourage ophthalmic research in the field of blinding eye disease. Administers Scientific Review Fight for Sight/Prevent Blindness America research program. Operates placement service. Maintains 13 scientific sections. **Founded:** 1928. **Membership:** 10200. **Staff:** 15. Multinational. **Languages:** English. **Budget:** $3,262,100. Formerly (1970) Association for Research in Ophthalmology.

ASSOCIATION FOR RESPONSIBLE MEDICINE (AARM)
PO Box 270986
Tampa, FL 33688
Ray McEachern, Exec.Dir.
PH: (813)933-6236
FX: (813)933-6236
Description: Individuals requiring the services of acute care hospitals; individuals the group feels are victims of medical malpractice. Seeks to "reduce the incidence of medical mistakes that cause injury to patients." Conducts background and malpractice record checks of physicians upon request; gathers and disseminates information on malpractice suits and insurance claims. **Founded:** 1994. **Membership:** 1200. **Staff:** 1.

ASSOCIATION OF SCHOOLS OF ALLIED HEALTH PROFESSIONS (ASAHP)
1730 M St. NW, Ste. 500
Washington, DC 20036
Tom Elwood, Ph.D., Exec.Dir.
PH: (202)293-4848
FX: (202)293-4852
Description: National allied health professional membership organizations, clinical service programs, academic institutions, and other institutions and organizations whose interests include the advancement of allied health education, research, and service delivery. Aims include: to provide communication among schools and colleges of allied health professions; to promote development of new programs; to encourage research and to provide liaison with other health organizations, professional groups, and

educational and governmental institutions. Sponsors short-term institutes for allied health education, administration, and practice. Conducts research programs. **Founded:** 1967. **Membership:** 750. **Staff:** 6. **Languages:** English. **Publication:** *Allied Health Trends*, monthly. Newsletter ■ *Journal of Allied Health*, quarterly ■ Directory, annual. **Formerly:** (1974) Association of Schools of Allied Health Professions; (1992) American Society of Allied Health Professions.

ASSOCIATION OF SCHOOLS OF PUBLIC HEALTH (ASPH)
url: http://www.asph.org
1660 L St. NW, Ste. 204
Washington, DC 20036
Michael K. Gemmell, Exec.Dir.
PH: (202)296-1099
FX: (202)296-1252
Description: Accredited graduate schools of public health. Provides focus for the enhancement of academic public health programs. Serves as an information center for governmental and private groups, and individuals whose concerns overlap those of higher education for public health. **Founded:** 1941. **Membership:** 28. **Staff:** 13. **Languages:** English. **Budget:** $350,000.

ASSOCIATION OF STATE AND TERRITORIAL DENTAL DIRECTORS (ASTDD)
Minnesota Dept. of Health
717 Delaware St. SE
Minneapolis, MN 55440
Dr. Robert Isman, Sec.-Treas.
PH: (612)623-5529
FX: (612)623-5442
Description: Directors of state and territorial dental programs. Provides a forum for consideration of dental health administrative problems and policies on the state and territorial level; promotes constructive plans for better administrative procedures. **Membership:** 53. **Languages:** English.

ASSOCIATION OF STATE AND TERRITORIAL DIRECTORS OF NURSING (ASTDN)
Office of Local and Border Health
1740 W. Adams, Rm. 201
Phoenix, AZ 85007
Abby Horak, RN, CS, MSN
PH: (913)296-7100
FX: (913)296-1231
Description: Directors of nursing in the states and territories. Serves as a channel for sharing methods, techniques, and information to increase the effectiveness of public health nursing services; cooperates with other professional groups in public health and related fields. **Founded:** 1935. **Membership:** 54. **Languages:** English. Formerly Association of State and Territorial Directors of Public Health Nursing.

ASSOCIATION OF STATE AND TERRITORIAL HEALTH OFFICIALS (ASTHO)
e-mail: cbeversd@astho.org
url: http://www.astho.org
1275 K St., NW, Ste. 800
Washington, DC 20005-4006
Cheryl A. Beversdorf, Exec.VP
PH: (202)371-9090
FX: (202)371-9797
Description: Represents the executive officer of the department of public health of each of the U.S. states, territories and possessions and is engaged in a wide range of legislative, educational, scientific and programmatic issues and activities on behalf of public health. Seeks to "formulate and influence sound national public health policy and to assist state health officials in the development and implementation of programs and policies to promote health and prevent disease, injury and disability." Serves as a primary information resource to state health agencies on a wide range of issues, including HIV/AIDS, immunizations, tobacco-use control, primary care, maternal and child health, school health and the environment. Its sixteen affiliate organiza-

tions represent state public health specialty associations for chronic disease programs, dental health, emergency medical services, epidemiology, health facility survey agencies, HIV/AIDS, local health liaisons, maternal and child health programs, nursing services, nutrition services, public health laboratories, public health promotion and education, public health statistics and information systems, social work and vector control services. **Founded:** 1942. **Membership:** 55. **Staff:** 27. **Languages:** English. **Budget:** $2,000,000. Formerly (1975) Association of State and Territorial Health Officers.

ASSOCIATION FOR SURGICAL EDUCATION (ASE)

SIU School of Medicine
Department of Surgery
PO Box 19230
Springfield, IL 62794-1611
Sue Kedner, Pres.
PH: (217)785-3835
Description: Surgeons and individuals involved or interested in undergraduate surgical education. Purpose is to develop and disseminate information on motivation, techniques, research, and applications for presenting curricula in undergraduate surgical education. Acts as forum for research in surgical education; serves as information clearinghouse. Compiles statistics; maintains speakers' bureau. Conducts educational programs. **Founded:** 1980. **Membership:** 700. **Staff:** 2. **Languages:** English. **Budget:** $85,000. **Publication:** *Focus on Surgical Education*, quarterly. Journal. Price: included in membership dues. Circulation: 700. Advertising: not accepted.

ASSOCIATION OF SURGICAL TECHNOLOGISTS (AST)

e-mail: ast@ast.org
url: http://www.ast.org
7108-C S. Alton Way, Ste.100
Englewood, CO 80112-2106
William J. Teutsch, Exec.Dir.
PH: (303)694-9130
Description: Individuals who have received specific education and training to deliver surgical patient care in the operating room. Membership categories are available for both certified and student surgical technologists. Emphasis is placed on encouraging members to participate actively in a continuing education program. Aims are: to study, discuss, and exchange knowledge, experience, and ideas in the field of surgical technology; to promote a high standard of surgical technology performance in the community for quality patient care; to stimulate interest in continuing education. Local groups sponsor workshops and institutes. Conducts research. **Founded:** 1969. **Membership:** 17500. **Staff:** 25. **Languages:** English. **Budget:** $980,000. **Publication:** *AST Core Curriculum for Surgical First Assisting*. Book ▪ *AST Core Curriculum for Surgical Technology*. Book ▪ *The Surgical Technologist*, monthly. Journal. Covers surgical procedures and equipment, aseptic techniques, medical law, and legislation. Also includes association news, and annual subject index. Price: included in membership dues; $36.00/year for nonmembers. ISSN: 0164-4238. Circulation: 18,000. Advertising: accepted ▪ *Surgical Technologist Certifying Exam Study Guide*. Book. **Formerly:** (1978) Association of Operating Room Technicians.

ASSOCIATION OF TECHNICAL PERSONNEL IN OPHTHALMOLOGY (ATPO)

e-mail: jcahpo@jcahpo.org
PO Box 193940
San Francisco, CA 94119-3190
Tisha Kehn, Manager
PH: (651)731-7582
TF: 800482-4858
FX: (651)731-0410
Description: Opthalmic assistants, technicians, technologists, surgical and keratorefractive techs, photographers, nurses, and orthoptists. Promotes high standards and professional ethics dedicated to quality opthalmic medical care under the direction of an opthalmologist. Recognizes the utilization of opthalmalic medical personnel to perform certain non-medical procedures or tests as

a means of enhancing the productivity of opthalmologists and thereby increasing the availability of opthalmologists to provide the highest level of medical service and comprehensive vision care to their patients. **Founded:** 1969. **Membership:** 1000. **Staff:** 2. **Languages:** English. Formerly (1989) American Association of Certified Allied Health Personnel in Ophthalmology.

ASSOCIATION OF THE BRITISH PHARMACEUTICAL INDUSTRY

e-mail: abpi@abpi.org.uk
url: http://www.abpi.org.uk
12 Whitehall
London SW1A 2DY, England
D.B.L. George, Sec.
PH: 44 171 9303477
FX: 44 171 7471411
Description: Pharmaceutical companies conducting business in the United Kingdom involved in research and development, or those companies interested in pharmaceutical matters. Represents manufacturers of medicines not advertised to the public. **Founded:** 1930. **Membership:** 101. **Staff:** 65. **Budget:** L5,500,000.

ASSOCIATION OF CANADIAN FACULTIES OF DENTISTRY (ACFD)

(Association des Facultes Dentaires du Canada)
1815 Alta Vista Dr., Ste. 105
Ottawa, ON, Canada K1G 3Y6
Jose Chiasson, Exec.Sec.-Treas.
PH: (613)738-7732
FX: (613)738-2107
Description: Dental school faculties. Promotes improvement of dental education; seeks to advance the teaching, study, and practice of dentistry. Conducts research and educational programs; facilitates exchange of information among members. **Languages:** English, French.

ASSOCIATION OF CANADIAN MEDICAL COLLEGES (ACMC)

(Association des Facultes de Medecine du Canada)
774 Echo Dr.
Ottawa, ON, Canada K1S 5P2
David Hawkins, Exec.Dir.
PH: (613)730-0687
FX: (613)730-1196
Description: Colleges of medicine. Promotes excellence in the study and teaching of medicine; seeks to advance the profession of medicine through improved medical education. Conducts research and educational programs; facilitates exchange of information among members. **Languages:** English, French.

ASSOCIATION OF CANADIAN PHARMACEUTICAL PHYSICIANS (ACPP)

(Association Canadienne des Medecins de l'Industrie Pharmaceutique)
2150 Boulevard Saint-Elzear E
Laval, PQ, Canada H7L 4A8
Geoffrey Heseltine, Contact
PH: (514)331-9220
FX: (514)856-3845
Description: Pharmaceutical physicians. Promotes excellence in the practice of pharmaceutical medicine; encourages professional advancement of members. Facilitates communication and cooperation among members; conducts research and educational programs. **Languages:** English, French.

ASSOCIATION OF CARDIOTHORACIC ANAESTHETISTS

The Royal Hospitals NHS Trust
The London Chest Hospital
Bonner Rd.
London E2 9SX, England
Dr. Robert Feneck, Chm.
PH: 44 181 9804433
FX: 44 181 9832324
Description: Consultants who are currently engaged in the prac-

tice of cardiothoracic anaesthesia. To further the development of the art and science of caring for patients undergoing heart and chest surgery. **Founded:** 1984. **Membership:** 200. **Publication:** Articles. Produced in association with the British Journal of Intensive Care.

ASSOCIATION CENTRAFRICAINE POUR LE BIEN-ETRE FAMILIAL (ACABEF)
BP 1366
Bangui, Central African Republic
Eregani Clement, Exec.Dir.
PH: 236 615435
FX: 236 616700
Description: Promotes and supports the use of family planning techniques for citizens of the Central African Republic. Fosters family welfare through educational programs and counseling. **Founded:** 1987. **Membership:** 537. **Staff:** 25. **Languages:** English, French. **Budget:** 000,000 Fr CFA.

ASSOCIATION OF CHARTERED PHYSIOTHERAPISTS IN SPORTS MEDICINE (ACPSM)
81 Heol W. Plas Coity
Budgend CF35 6BA, England
Nicola Pillips, Hon.Sec.
PH: 44 115 9627681
FX: 44 115 9606993
Description: Chartered physiotherapists specializing in sports injuries. Seeks to improve techniques and facilities for the prevention and treatment of sports injuries. Offers sports physiotherapy courses and produces and educational journal. **Founded:** 1975. **Membership:** 954. **Languages:** English. **Publication:** *Directory*, biennial ■ *Physiotherapy in Sport* (in English), 3/year. Newsletter.

ASSOCIATION FOR CHILD PSYCHOLOGY AND PSYCHIATRY (ACPP)
e-mail: admin@acpp.co.uk
St. Saviours House
39/41 Union St.
London SE1 1SD, England
Frederick Wentworth-Bowyer, Chief Exec.
PH: 44 171 4037458
FX: 44 171 4037081
Description: Professionals working in the field of child mental health. Encourages dissemination of scientific research and information. **Founded:** 1956. **Membership:** 2750. **Staff:** 6. Multinational. **National Groups:** 15. **Languages:** English. **Publication:** *Child Psychology and Psychiatry Review*, quarterly ■ *Journal of Child Psychology and Psychiatry* (in English), 8/year. Advertising: accepted.

ASSOCIATION OF CLINICAL BIOCHEMISTS
2 Carlton House Terrace
London SW1Y 5AF, England
Hilary Crosweller, Admin. Officer
PH: 44 171 9303333
FX: 44 171 9303553
Description: University graduates in science or medicine occupied in the practice of clinical biochemistry, mainly in district, general and teaching hospitals. Associate members from related disciplines, such as cytogenetics, microbiology and immunology. To promote the advancement of clinical biochemistry. It is consulted by government health departments and many other organisations. Has an education committee, primarily concerned with postgraduate education, a scientific committee and a publications committee. **Founded:** 1953. **Membership:** 2321. **Staff:** 2. **Publication:** *Annals of Clinical Biochemistry*, bimonthly ■ *Clinical Biochemistry in Medicine Series*, periodic ■ Handbook, annual ■ Newsletter, monthly.

ASSOCIATION OF CLINICAL RESEARCH FOR THE PHARMACEUTICAL INDUSTRY
e-mail: 100757.1240@compuserve.com
url: http://www.dashnet.com/acrpi
PO Box 1208
Maidenhead SL6 3GD, England
Judi Reader, Contact
PH: 44 1628 829900
FX: 44 1628 829922
Description: Any person who is engaged in the design, organization or conduct of clinical trials for the pharmaceutical industry. Aims to establish and maintain the professional identity of members; to facilitate communications between members of clinical research departments in the industry, to provide a forum for discussion and to foster good relations with other professional groups. **Founded:** 1978. **Membership:** 3000. **Staff:** 6. **Publication:** *Clinical Research Focus*, every six weeks. Advertising: accepted ■ *Handbook of Clinical Research*. Price: L33.50.

ASSOCIATION FOR COMMON EUROPEAN NURSING DIAGNOSES, INTERVENTIONS AND OUTCOMES
Royal College of Nursing
20 Cavendish Sq.
London W1M 0AB, England
Ms. D. Ralston, Contact
PH: 44 171 6473412
Description: Nurses and nursing organizations. Promotes adoption of standardized nursing accreditation and practice throughout Europe. Drafts model nursing standards of training and practice; facilitates communication and cooperation among members. Multinational. **Languages:** English.

ASSOCIATION OF COMMUNITY HEALTH COUNCILS FOR ENGLAND AND WALES
30 Drayton Park
London N5 1PB, England
Toby Harris, Dir.
PH: 44 171 6098405
FX: 44 171 7001152
Description: Community Health Councils set up to monitor the National Health Service. Provides a forum for member CHCs, provides information and advisory services to CHCs and represents the user of health services at a national level. **Founded:** 1977. **Membership:** 206. **Staff:** 10. **Publication:** *CHC News* (in English), 10/year ■ *Factsheets for the Public*, periodic ■ *Health News Briefings*, 10/year ■ *Perspectives - Brief Topic Papers*, 10/year.

ASSOCIATION CONGOLAISE POUR LE BIEN-ETRE FAMILIAL
850, ave. des 3 Martyrs
Plateau des 15 Ans
PO Box 945
Brazzaville, Congo
Florent Mboungou, Contact
PH: 242 826331
FX: 242 826631
Description: Seeks to improve the quality of family life in the Congo. Works to improve living conditions where underdevelopment impairs the family structure. Promotes awareness of the importance of family life for the well-being of society. **Founded:** 1987. **Membership:** 450. **Staff:** 14. **National Groups:** 1. **Languages:** French. **Budget:** $220,000. **Publication:** *BIEN-ETRE* (in French), periodic. Magazine. Price: 800.00 Fr CFA. Advertising: accepted.

ASSOCIATION OF COUNTY PUBLIC HEALTH OFFICERS
County Hall
Trowbridge BA14 8JW, England
N. Durnford, Hon.Sec.
PH: 44 1225 713562
FX: 44 1225 713987
Description: Co-ordinates and liaises on matters of common in-

terest regarding environmental health. **Founded:** 1947. **Membership:** 30.

ASSOCIATION OF DEMOCRATIC PHARMACISTS
(Verein Demokratischer Pharmazeutinnen und Pharmazeuten)
Grindelalle 182
D-20144 Hamburg, Germany
Thomas Hammer, Contact
PH: 49 40 458768
FX: 49 40 458768
Description: Promotes the interests of registered pharmacists in Germany. Concerned with issues focusing on environmental and public health policies. **Founded:** 1989. **Membership:** 160. **Publication:** *VDPP-Rundbriet* (in German), bimonthly. Journal. Circulation: 250. Advertising: not accepted.

ASSOCIATION DENTAIRE FRANCAISE (ADF)
e-mail: adf@adf.asso.fr
url: http://www.adf.asso.fr
6, rue G. Tell
F-75017 Paris, France
Dr. Michel Chabre, Contact
PH: 33 1 44010270
FX: 33 1 47639028
Description: Federation of dental associations in France. Promotes and defends the dental profession; works for the evaluation and standardization of dental products. **Founded:** 1970. **Membership:** 33000. **Languages:** French. **Publication:** *Les Cahiers de F A.D.F* (in French), quarterly. Price: free. Advertising: accepted.

ASSOCIATION OF DENTAL DEALERS IN EUROPE (ADDE)
e-mail: uwanner@swissonline.ch
Moosstrasse 2
Gumligen
CH-3073 Berne, Switzerland
Dr. Ulrich Wanner, Contact
PH: 41 31 9527892
FX: 41 31 9527683
Description: Manufacturers of dental equipment and supplies. Promotes growth and development of members' businesses; seeks to advance dental technologies. Represents members' interests before labor, industrial, and professional organizations, government agencies, and the public; sponsors research and development programs. Multinational. **Languages:** English, French.

ASSOCIATION FOR DENTAL EDUCATION IN EUROPE (ADEE)
e-mail: marsan@eucmax.sim.ucm.es
url: http://www/linux.odont.ku.dk/adee
Facultad de Odontologia
Universidad Computense
E-28040 Madrid, Spain
Prof. Mariano Sanz, Sec.Gen.
PH: 34 1 3941905
FX: 34 1 3941910
Description: Teachers of dentistry. Objectives are: to further dental education in Europe; to evaluate the goals and methods of dental education; to assess training programs for teachers; to promote ties among dentistry teachers. Holds lectures, seminars, and working discussion groups in conjunction with annual meeting. **Founded:** 1975. **Membership:** 85. Multinational. **Languages:** English. **Publication:** Proceedings (in English), annual.

ASSOCIATION FOR THE DEVELOPMENT OF TROPICAL ATMOSPHERIC PHYSICS
(Association pour le Developpement de la Physique de l'Atmosphere Tropicale)
Boite Postale 5271
Dakar, Senegal
Simeon Fongang, Contact
PH: 221 259364
FX: (fon)gang@ucad.sn
Description: Physicists and meteorologists. Promotes advance-

ment in the study of tropical atmospheric physics. Facilitates exchange of information among members; sponsors research and educational programs. Multinational. **Languages:** English, French.

ASSOCIATION OF EUROPEAN CANCER LEAGUES (AECL)
e-mail: ics@uicc.ch
url: http://www.uicc.ch/ecl/
5 Northumberland Rd.
Dublin 4, Ireland
Tom Hudson, Contact
PH: 353 1 6681855
FX: 353 1 6687599
Description: National cancer societies. Promotes advancement in the prevention, diagnosis, and treatment of cancer; seeks to improve the quality of life of people with cancer and their families. Facilitates communication and cooperation among members; sponsors research and educational programs; provides support and services to people with cancer. Multinational. **Languages:** English, Irish Gaelic.

ASSOCIATION OF EUROPEAN PAEDIATRIC CARDIOLOGISTS (AEPC)
St. Radboud Hospital
Department of Paediatric Cardiology
Geert Grootplein Zuid
NL-6500 HB Nijmegen, Netherlands
Dr. Otto Daniels, Contact
PH: 31 24 3614427
FX: 31 24 3619052
Description: Physicians specializing in pediatric cardiology. Seeks to advance pediatric cardiological study, teaching, and practice. Serves as a clearinghouse on pediatric cardiology; conducts research and continuing professional development programs. Multinational. **Languages:** Dutch, English.

ASSOCIATION OF EUROPEAN PSYCHIATRISTS (AEP)
e-mail: aep@chl.lu
url: http://www.santel.lu/CHL/aep/uk-aep.html
Clinique Psychiatrique
CHU
Place de l'Hopital
F-67091 Strasbourg, France
Armande Martin, Contact
PH: 33 3 88793630
FX: 33 3 88794919
Description: Psychiatrists. Seeks to advance psychiatric scholarship and practice. Facilitates communication and cooperation among members; sponsors research and continuing professional development programs. Multinational. **Languages:** English, French.

ASSOCIATION FOR EYE RESEARCH (AER)
Institut fur Experimentelle Ophthalmologie
Universitats-Augenklinik
Sigmund-Freud-Strasse 25
D-53105 Bonn, Germany
Dr. A. Wegener, Contact
Description: Ophthalmological researchers and research institutions. Seeks to advance the science and practice of ophthalmology. Facilitates exchange of information among members; sponsors joint research projects involving members; sponsors training programs. Multinational. **Languages:** English, German.

ASSOCIATION OF FACULTIES OF PHARMACY OF CANADA (AFPC)
University of British Columbia
Vancouver, BC, Canada V6T 1Z3
Kevin Moody, Exec.Dir.
PH: (604)822-4451
FX: (604)822-3035
Description: Educators engaged in postsecondary pharmacy programs. Promotes excellence in pharmacy education; encourages continuing professional development among members. Facili-

tates exchange of information among members; conducts research and educational programs. **Languages:** English, French.

ASSOCIATION OF FRENCH-SPEAKING DERMATOLOGISTS (AFSD)

(Association des Dermatologistes Francophone)
Hopital Henri Mondor
51 avenue du Marechal de Lattre de Tassigny
F-94010 Cretell, France
Jean Revuz, Contact
PH: 33 1 49812501
FX: 33 1 49812502
Description: Dermatologists and dermatology students and educators. Seeks to advance the study, teaching, and practice of dermatology. Establishes standards for dermatological certification and practice; sponsors continuing professional development courses. Multinational. **Languages:** English, French.

ASSOCIATION OF FRENCH-SPEAKING PHYSICIANS OF CANADA (AFSPC)

(Association des Medicins de Langue Francaise du Canada)
8355 Boulevard Saint-Laurent
Montreal, PQ, Canada H2P 2Z6
Andre de Seve, Adm.Dir.
PH: (514)388-2228
TF: 800387-2228
FX: (514)388-5335
Description: French-speaking physicians practicing in Canada. Seeks to increase availability and quality of health care in French-speaking areas of Canada; promotes professional advancement of members. Makes available health services in underserved areas; facilitates communication and cooperation among members. **Languages:** English, French.

ASSOCIATION OF GERMAN DENTAL MANUFACTURERS

(Verband der Deutschen Dental-Industrie)
e-mail: russegger@vddi.de
url: http://www.vddi.de
Kirchwag 12
D-50858 Cologne, Germany
Harald Russegger, Sec.Gen.
PH: 49 221 9486280
FX: 49 221 483428
Description: Companies manufacturing dental equipment and supplies. Establishes international standards and technical harmonization for dental equipment. Represents members' interests before government bodies, international agencies, and the public. Maintains liaison with organizations representing dentists, dental technicians, and dental supply dealers and distributors. Compiles statistics. **Founded:** 1917. **Membership:** 185. **Staff:** 7. **Languages:** German. **Publication:** *The German Dental Industry* (in Danish, English, French, and Spanish), biennial. Brochure. Price: free. Advertising: not accepted.

ASSOCIATION OF GERMAN RADIOLOGISTS AND NUCLEAR PHYSICIANS

(Berufsverband der Deutschen Radiologen und Nuklearmediziner eV)
Sonnenstr. 3
D-80331 Munich, Germany
RA Dipl.-Kfm. Udo H. Cramer, Contact
PH: 49 89 592690
FX: 49 89 553896
Description: Radiologists and nuclear physicians in Germany. Promotes and represents the interests of members. **Membership:** 1200. **Staff:** 25. **Languages:** English. **Publication:** *Roubgeupraxis mit Migliedes-Info* (in German), 10/year, monthly except January and July. Price: Free. Circulation: 2,000. Advertising: accepted.

ASSOCIATION FOR HEALTH-CARE INSTITUTIONS

(Verbond der Verzorgingsinstellingen)
Guimardstraat 1
B-1040 Brussels, Belgium
A. Aernoudt, Adm.Dir.
PH: 32 2 5118008
FX: 32 2 5135269
Description: Hospitals; psychiatric hospitals; nursing homes; homes for elderly people. Promotes high standards of health service. Fosters exchange and cooperation; offers consultative services; makes recommendations to government authorities. **Founded:** 1938. **Membership:** 325. **Staff:** 20. **Languages:** Dutch, English. **Publication:** *Hospitalia* (in Dutch), quarterly ■ *VVI-Information* (in Dutch), 11/year.

ASSOCIATION FOR HEALTH WITHOUT VACCINATION (AHWV)

(Association pour la Sante sans Vaccination)
6, rue Jean Perrin
F-94400 Vitry-sur-Seine, France
Isabelle Staffalo, Dir.
PH: 33 1 46816109
FX: 33 1 46816109
Description: Professionals in France who believe that illness is related to mental state and that harmony between mind and body is the key to health. Advocates the patient's freedom of choice in medical treatment and the cessation of obligatory human and animal vaccination. Works to influence public policy and obtain favorable legislation; provides individual legal and practical assistance. Offers cost reductions on a broad range of products. Disseminates information. Organizes classes, debates, and roundtables. **Founded:** 1987. **Membership:** 800. **Languages:** French. **Budget:** 180,000 Fr.

ASSOCIATION OF HONG KONG NURSING STAFF (AHKNS)

e-mail: info@nurse.org.hk
url: http://www.nurse.org.hk
Hing Wan Commercial Bldg., Rm. 25, 3/F
25-27 Parkes St.
Yaumatei
Kowloon, Hong Kong
Mr. Michael M.K Ho, Chm.
PH: 852 27306655
FX: 852 27366020
Description: Registered, enrolled, and student nurses. Seeks to advance the nursing profession; promotes professional development of members. Represents members' legal and professional interests. Conducts continuing professional education and training courses; makes available to members services including legal advice and travel and merchandise discounts. **Founded:** 1977. **Membership:** 12000. **Staff:** 13. **Languages:** Chinese, English. **Publication:** *AHKNS Newsletter* (in Chinese and English), quarterly. Price: free. Circulation: 15,000. Advertising: accepted. **Formerly:** (1990) Association of Government Nursing Staff.

ASSOCIATION OF HYGIENE - LIFE CULTIVATION, HONG KONG

Melbourne Plaza, Ste. 1011
33 Queen's Rd.
Central
Hong Kong, Hong Kong
Dr. Thomas A. Wong, Pres.
PH: 852 25227337
FX: 852 25218886
Description: Health care practitioners making use of fingertip accupuncture, herbal therapies, and other traditional Asian forms of medicine. Promotes effective practice of alternative medical techniques; seeks to insure safety of alternative medicines. Conducts continuing professional development courses for members; makes available medicinal teas and other alternative health care products. **Founded:** 1971. **Languages:** Chinese, English. **Publication:** Newsletter, annual.

ASSOCIATION OF INTERNATIONAL HEALTH RESEARCHERS (AIHR)

2665 Pleasant Valley Rd.
Mobile, AL 36606
Dr. Roy E. Kadel, Pres.
PH: (334)473-3946

Description: Individuals interested in quality health research. Works to: promote a better understanding of scientifically effective research techniques and methodologies; encourage interaction among individuals in international health research. Compiles statistics. **Founded:** 1982. **Membership:** 123. Multinational. Regional Groups: 5. **Languages:** English.

ASSOCIATION IVOIRIENNE DE BIEN-ETRE FAMILIAL (AIBEF)
Treichville
Bd. Giscard d'Estaing
BP 5315
Abidjan 01, Cote d'Ivoire
Paul Agodio, Exec.Dir.
PH: 225 251811
FX: 225 251868
Description: Promotes advances in women's health care and family planning programs. Publications: none. **Convention/ Meeting:** none. **Founded:** 1979. **Membership:** 650. **Staff:** 61. **Languages:** French. **Budget:** $796,758.

ASSOCIATION OF LOCAL OFFICIAL HEALTH AGENCIES (ALOHA)
e-mail: mail@alphaweb.org
url: http://www.alphaweb.org
415 Yonge St., Ste. 1618
Toronto, ON, Canada M5B 2E7
Gordon White, Exec.Dir.
PH: (416)595-0006
FX: (416)595-0030
Description: Local public health agencies. Promotes increased availability and effectiveness of public health programs. Lobbies for improved legislation governing public health; facilitates communication and cooperation among members; publicizes public health programs. **Languages:** English, French.

ASSOCIATION DES MEDECINS DE LANGUE FRANCAISE DU CANADA (AMLFC)
e-mail: amlfc@videotron.net
8355, blvd. St. Laurent
Montreal, PQ, Canada H2P 2Z6
Andre de Seve, Adm.Dir.
PH: (514)388-2228
FX: (514)388-5335
Description: French speaking doctors united for scientific and technical exchange. Conducts research; disseminates information. **Founded:** 1902. **Membership:** 5000. **Staff:** 6. **Languages:** French.

ASSOCIATION OF MEDICAL DOCTORS OF ASIA (AMDAI)
e-mail: nakanot@amda.or.jp
url: http://www.amda.or.jp
310-1 Nazaru
Okayama 701-12, Japan
Shigeru Sugahami, Pres.
PH: 81 86 2847730
FX: 81 86 2846758
Description: Physicians, medical students, and organizations are members; nurses and other health care personnel and organizations are associate members. Promotes and works to strengthen partnership among Asian doctors. Seeks to insure adequate medical care for people in underserved areas. Conducts emergency relief and rehabilitation operations in areas affected by natural disasters or human conflicts; implements community health development programs in rural areas; facilitates continuing professional education and training of members. **Founded:** 1984. **Membership:** 665. Multinational. **Languages:** English, French. **Publication:** *AMDA International* (in English and Japanese), quarterly. Newsletter. Price: free to members; 2,000.00¥/year to nonmembers. Circulation: 1,000 ■ *Harukanaru Yume* (in Japanese). Book ■ *International Collaboration of Medical Care* (in English and Japanese), monthly. Journal. Price: free to members; 500.00¥/ copy to nonmembers. Circulation: 1,000 ■ *International Medical Cooperation - Proceedings of the Hayabashibara Forum 1993* (in

English and Japanese) ■ *Proceedings of the 1994 Okayama NGO Summit* (in English and Japanese) ■ *Ruwandakarano Shogen* (in Japanese). Book ■ *Tobidase! AMDA* (in Japanese). Report. **Also Known As:** AMDA International.

ASSOCIATION FOR MEDICAL EDUCATION IN THE EASTERN MEDITERRANEAN (AMEEM)
Jordan University of Science and Technology
PO Box 3030
Irbid, Jordan
Sa'ad Hijazi, Contact
PH: 962 2 295111
FX: 962 2 295123
Description: Medical schools, educators, and students. Seeks to advance medical scholarship and practice. Serves as a clearinghouse on medical education; encourages communication and cooperation among members; sponsors research programs and continuing professional development courses. Multinational. **Languages:** English.

ASSOCIATION FOR MEDICAL EDUCATION IN EUROPE (AMEE)
e-mail: 1.a.cumming@dundee.ac.uk
url: http://www.dundee.ac.uk/MedEd/AMEE/
Centre for Medical Education
Tay Park House
484 Perth Rd.
Dundee DD2 1LR, Scotland
R. M. Harden, Contact
PH: 44 1382 631967
Description: Medical schools, educators, and students. Seeks to advance medical scholarship and practice. Serves as a clearinghouse on medical education; encourages communication and cooperation among members; sponsors research programs and continuing professional development courses. Multinational. **Languages:** English.

ASSOCIATION FOR MEDICAL EDUCATION IN THE WESTERN PACIFIC REGION (AMEWPR)
Fukuoka University School of Medicine
Department of Psychiatry
7-45-1 Nanakuma
Fukuoka 814-01, Japan
Masahisa Nishizono, Contact
PH: 81 92 8011011
FX: 81 92 8633150
Description: Medical schools, educators, and students. Seeks to advance medical scholarship and practice. Serves as a clearinghouse on medical education; encourages communication and cooperation among members; sponsors research programs and continuing professional development courses. Multinational. **Languages:** English, Japanese.

ASSOCIATION OF MEDICAL RESEARCH CHARITIES (AMRC)
e-mail: info@amrc.org.uk
url: http://www.amrc.org.uk
29-35 Farringdon Rd.
London EC1M 3JB, England
Diana A. Garnham, Gen.Sec.
PH: 44 171 4046454
FX: 44 171 4046448
Description: Medical research charities. Furthers the advancement of medical research in the United Kingdom. Focuses attention on the collective effectiveness of members. Provides information, advice and guidance to members and others. **Founded:** 1987. **Membership:** 100. **Staff:** 5. **Languages:** English. **Publication:** *Handbook*, annual. Booklet. Lists member charities that award funding for medical research. Price: free to individual researchers. Circulation: 6,500. Advertising: not accepted ■ Newsletter. Features member information.

ASSOCIATION OF MEDICAL SCHOOLS IN AFRICA (AMSA)
Easterna and Southern Africa Regional Office UNICEF
United Nations Office
Gigiri
Nairobi, Kenya
Description: Medical schools. Seeks to advance medical scholarship and practice. Facilitates communication and exchange among members; sponsors research and educational programs. Multinational. **Languages:** English.

ASSOCIATION OF MEDICAL SCHOOLS IN EUROPE (AMSE)
e-mail: helmut.gruber@univie.ac.at
University of Vienna
Wahringerstrabe 13
A-1090 Vienna, Austria
Helmut Gruber, Contact
PH: 43 1 4088366
FX: 43 1 40480224
Description: Deans of medical schools; representatives of medical deans in 25 countries. Provides a forum for the exchange of ideas and information. Objectives are: to address important questions concerning medical education, with special emphasis on policies affecting the future of medical education in Europe; to discuss practical issues such as admission criteria and organizational problems; to analyze the relationship between medical schools and health service organizations; to assess the impact of medical science on medical education. **Founded:** 1979. Multinational. **Languages:** English. **Budget:** $13,000. **Publication:** *AMSE Newsletter*, quarterly. **Formerly:** (1992) Association of Medical Deans in Europe.

ASSOCIATION OF MEDICAL SPECIALISTS IN THE PHARMACEUTICAL INDUSTRIES (AMSPI)
(Asociacio de Medicos Especialistas en la Industria Farmaceutica)
Canifarma av. Cuauhtemoc 1481
03310 Mexico City, DF, Mexico
Fabian Llorens, MD, Pres.
PH: 52 5 6290979
FX: 52 5 5814938
Description: Physicians employed in the pharmaceutical industry. Facilitates academic and professional advancement of members. Provides financial and technical assistance to members; conducts educational programs. **Founded:** 1967. **Membership:** 100. **Staff:** 9. **Languages:** English, Spanish. **Budget:** $5,000.

ASSOCIATION OF MEDICAL TECHNOLOGISTS
Isotopes Section
The Royal Hospital
Wolverhampton WV2 1BT, England
Ms. V. Seymour, Sec.
PH: 44 1902 644964
Description: Aims to contribute to the advancement of medical and allied technologies. **Founded:** 1952. **Membership:** 250. **Publication:** *Job Placement*, monthly. Bulletin ▪ Journal, quarterly.

ASSOCIATION OF MULTIPLE SCLEROSIS THERAPY CENTRES (SCOTLAND) (AMSTCS)
Howemoss Crescent
Kirkhill Industrial Estate
Dyce
Aberdeen AB2 0GN, Scotland
Dr. Colin Webster, Contact
PH: 44 01224 771105
Description: Multiple sclerosis therapy centers. Seeks to advance the treatment of multiple sclerosis; promotes an improved quality of life for people with multiple sclerosis and their families. Facilitates communication and cooperation among members; conducts research and educational programs; participates in charitable activities; compiles statistics. **Founded:** 1992. **Membership:** 12. **Staff:** 40. **Languages:** English. **Budget:** L400,000.

ASSOCIATION OF MUSCLE DISORDERS
Hatboyu cad. No. 12
Yesilkoy
Istanbul, Turkey
Prof. Dr. Coskun Odzemir, Contact
PH: 90 212 5730975
FX: 90 212 6630168
Description: Promotes study and research of neurological muscle diseases. Works as a support group for individuals suffering with muscle disorders. Conducts educational programs. **Founded:** 1978. **Membership:** 1000. **Staff:** 5. **Languages:** English. **Budget:** TL 16,000. **Publication:** *Hope and Life* (in English and Turkish), quarterly. Journal. Provides information about neuromuscular disorders and activities. Price: free. Circulation: 3,000. Advertising: accepted. Alternate Formats: magnetic tape ▪ Pamphlets.

ASSOCIATION OF NATURAL MEDICATION PRACTITIONERS OF CANADA (ANMPC)
(Association des Practiciens en Medication Naturelle du Canada)
5485 1ere Ave.
Charlesbourg, PQ, Canada G1H 2V6
Jules Guy Pollquin, Pres.
PH: (418)623-7244
FX: (418)624-0630
Description: Physicians and other health care professionals using natural medications to replace synthetic pharmaceuticals. Promotes increased use of natural remedies. Conducts research on the efficacy of natural medications; sponsors continuing professional development courses; serves as a clearinghouse on natural medications and other alternative medical procedures. **Languages:** English, French.

ASSOCIATION DES NEUROLOGUES LIBERAUX DE LANGUE FRANCAISE (ANLLF)
39, blvd. du Roi
F-78000 Versailles, France
Dr. Pierre Hinault, Exec. Officer
PH: 3301 39532064
FX: 3301 39519244
Description: French-speaking clinical neurologists working in the private sector. Provides for information exchange and organizes post-university teaching adapted to meet the needs of members. Makes arrangements for follow-up treatment of patients who have relocated. **Founded:** 1987. **Membership:** 560. **Staff:** 27. **Local Groups:** 3. **Languages:** French. **Budget:** 500,000 Fr. **Publication:** *Neurologie Liberale* (in French), quarterly. Price: free. Advertising: not accepted.

ASSOCIATION OF NORDIC CANCER REGISTRIES (ANCR)
Montebello
N-0310 Oslo, Norway
PH: 47 22451300
FX: 47 22451370
Description: National cancer registries. Promotes availability of data on cancer patients; seeks to advance the prevention, diagnosis, and treatment of cancer. Serves as a clearinghouse on cancer and its treatment; sponsors health screenings and other services; conducts research. Multinational. **Languages:** English, Norwegian.

ASSOCIATION OF NURSERY TRAINING COLLEGES
The Princess Christian College
26 Wilbraham Rd.
Fellowfield
Manchester M14 6JX, England
Marilyn Randle, Contact
PH: 44 161 2244560
FX: 44 161 2564142
Description: Private colleges providing nursery nurse training. Aims to foster co-operation between like minded organizations, to exchange information and promote interest in the training of a nursery nurse. **Founded:** 1931. **Membership:** 18.

ASSOCIATION OF PAEDIATRIC ANAESTHETISTS OF GREAT BRITAIN AND IRELAND (APA)
Royal Belfast Hospital for Sick Children
Belfast, Belfast BT12 6BF, Northern Ireland
Dr. P. Crean, Contact
PH: 353 1232 263056
FX: 353 1232 235340
Description: Pediatric anesthetists practicing in Great Britain and Ireland and outside the British Isles. Promotes the study of pediatric anesthesiology. Collects and disseminates information; conducts research; advises other professional bodies on matters pertaining to pediatric anesthesiology. **Founded:** 1973. **Membership:** 320. Multinational. **Languages:** English. **Publication:** *Paediatric Anaesthesia*, bimonthly ▪ *Yearbook*.

ASSOCIATION OF PEDIATRIC SOCIETIES OF THE SOUTHEAST ASIAN REGION (APSSEAR)
Medical Center Manila
PO Box EA 100
Manila, Philippines
Prof. Perla D. Santos Ocampo, Sec.Gen.
PH: 63 2 5247874
FX: 63 2 7216569
Description: Pediatrics societies in Asian countries and the Pacific region. Works to disseminate information for the benefit of children and child health in the Southeast Asian region and surrounding countries. Encourages research. Participates in the fellowship program sponsored by the Australian College of Pediatrics. **Founded:** 1974. **Membership:** 20. Multinational. **Languages:** English. **Publication:** *Association of Pediatric Societies of the Southeast Asian Region* (in English), quarterly. Bulletin ▪ *State of Asian Children*. Report.

ASSOCIATION OF THE PHARMACEUTICAL COMPANIES' REPRESENTATIVES IN POLAND (APCRP)
Kubickiego 7 m. 7
PL-02-954 Warsaw, Poland
Mr. J. Kowalczyk, Dir.
PH: 48 22 6425870
FX: 48 22 6517199
Description: Pharmaceutical manufacturing companies maintaining operations in Poland. Promotes creation of a business climate favorable to members. Represents members' interests before government agencies and trade organizations; conducts educational and charitable programs. **Founded:** 1993. **Membership:** 57. **Staff:** 4. **Languages:** English, Polish. **Publication:** *Informative Bulletin*, monthly. Newsletter.

ASSOCIATION OF PHILLIPINE MIDWIVES (APM)
100 Parkway Forest Dr.
Willowdale, ON, Canada M2J 1L6
Liz Marquez, Contact
PH: (416)491-3960
Description: Canadian midwives of Filipion descent. Promotes excellence in the practice of midwifery; encourages continuing professional development of members. Facilitates communication and cooperation among members; conducts educational programs. **Languages:** English, Filipino.

ASSOCIATION OF POLICE SURGEONS
e-mail: christine@fscisoc.demon.co.uk
Clarke House
18A Mount Parade
Harrogate HG1 1BX, England
Dr. M.A. Knight, Contact
PH: 44 1423 509727
Description: Members are medical practitioners who regularly assist or advise the police in medical or forensic cases. To promote the best interests of police surgeons; advancement of medico legal knowledge in all its aspects; liaison between appointed police surgeons and other medical practitioners; practical and theoretical study of the subject by lectures, discussions, correspondence and any other means. **Founded:** 1951. **Membership:** 1050. **Staff:** 1.

ASSOCIATION OF PORT HEALTH AUTHORITIES
Dutton House
46 Church St.
Runcorn WA7 1LL, England
Peter Rotheram, Contact
PH: 44 1928 580440
FX: 44 1928 581596
Description: Local authorities, port health authorities in the United Kingdom, Ireland and the Channel Islands. Promoting the health and safety of seafarers, discussing issues on imported food, environmental health etc with central government, EU organisations etc. **Founded:** 1899. **Membership:** 70. **Staff:** 2. **Budget:** L60,000. **Publication:** *Lookout Newsletter*, monthly. Advertising: not accepted.

ASSOCIATION POUR LA LUTTE CONTRE LE PSORIASIS (APLCP)
Contre Le Psoriasis
1 Rue des Bois
F-95520 Osny, France
Mrs. Nichele Allaire, Contact
PH: 33 1 30322917
FX: 33 1 30374581
Description: National psoriasis organizations. Acts as advisory, consulting, and coordinating body for member groups implementing medical, social, and psychological research into psoriasis. Seeks to influence related social legislation and to collect all available information on psoriasis. Promotes public awareness of psoriasis and works to remove the social stigma associated with skin conditions. **Founded:** 1973. **Membership:** 30. **Staff:** 4. Multinational. **Languages:** English. **Publication:** *IFPA Newsletter* (in English), quarterly.

ASSOCIATION FOR PROTECTION OF THE MOROCCAN FAMILY (APMF)
(Association Marocaine pour la Protection de la Famille Marocaine)
Boite Postale 5046
Souissi
Rabat, Morocco
PH: 212 7 691647
Description: Seeks to protect the civil and human rights of women; promotes family planning education. Provides instruction in basic family health care practices; makes available family planning services. **Founded:** 1963. **Languages:** Arabic, English.

ASSOCIATION FOR PUBLIC HEALTH
e-mail: donald.reid@hea.org.uk
Hamilton House
Mabledon Pl.
London WC1H 9TX, England
Donald Reid, Contact
PH: 44 171 4131896
FX: 44 171 3886079
Description: NHS, local authority and voluntary sector professionals and managers. Aims to ensure that the health needs of the UK become a permanent feature of national policy and spending decisions. **Founded:** 1992. **Membership:** 400. **Staff:** 2. **Publication:** *Newsletter* (in English), 3/year. Price: free to members. Circulation: 450. Advertising: not accepted ▪ *Policy Manifesto*.

ASSOCIATION FOR QUALITY IN HEALTHCARE
47 Southgate St.
Hants, Hants. SO23 9EH, England
Virginia Sherwood, Contact
PH: 44 1962 877700
FX: 44 1962 877701
Description: Anyone interested in promoting measurable and continuous improvement in the quality of healthcare for the benefit of the public. Dedicated solely to all aspects of the subject of measuring and improving the quality of healthcare services. **Founded:** 1986. **Membership:** 600. **Staff:** 2. Multinational. **Regional Groups:** 9. **Publication:** *Journal for the Association for*

Quality Healthcare (in English), quarterly. Price: L75.00. ISSN: 1351-5969. Circulation: 750. Advertising: accepted ▪ *Quality Times* (in English), quarterly. Newsletter. Price: L20.00. Circulation: 750. Advertising: accepted.

ASSOCIATION OF RADICAL MIDWIVES (ARM)
e-mail: arm@radmid.demon.co.uk
url: http://www.radmid.demon.co.uk
62 Greetby Hill
Ormskirk, Lancs. L39 2DT, England
Ishbel Kargar, Admin.Sec.
PH: 44 1695 572776
FX: 44 1695 572776
Description: Midwives, mothers, health professionals, and interested individuals. Supports the interests of midwives. Provides supportive services and information to women experiencing difficulty in securing adequate and sympathetic maternity care. **Founded:** 1976. **Membership:** 1700. **Staff:** 1. **Local Groups:** 50. **Languages:** English. **Budget:** L25,000. **Publication:** *Choices in Childbirth* (in English). Booklet. Price:. Advertising: not accepted ▪ *Midwifery Matters* (in English), quarterly. Magazine. Price: L2.00/copy nonmembers; free to members. ISSN: 0961-1479. Circulation: 1,750. Advertising: accepted.

ASSOCIATION POUR LA RECHERCHE SUR LA SCLEROSE LATERALE AMYOTROPHIQUE (ARS)
e-mail: a.r.s.@wanadoo.fr
url: http://www.infobisogen.fr/agora/associations/ARS
24 rue Lacharriere
F-75011 Paris, France
Claude Blanchard, Pres.
PH: 33 1 43389989
FX: 33 1 43383159
Description: Promotes interest in amyotropic lateral sclerosis or ALS (a rare progressive degenerative disease of the motor neurons, characterized by atrophy of the muscles of the hands, forearms, and legs spreading to involve most of the body; also called Lou Gehrig's Disease) research among medical and scientific communities and the public. Faciliates exchange of information with ALS patients, researchers, clinics, and discussion/ support groups. **Founded:** 1985. **Membership:** 2500. **Staff:** 5. **National Groups:** 1. **Budget:** 1,750,000 Fr. **Publication:** Booklets (in French). Price: free. Advertising: accepted ▪ Magazine (in French), annual. Price: Free. Advertising: accepted ▪ Newsletter (in French), quarterly. Price: Free. Advertising: accepted ▪ Reports.

ASSOCIATION OF SCHOOLS OF PUBLIC HEALTH IN THE EUROPEAN REGIONAL (ASPHER)
(Association des Ecoles de Sante Publique de la Regional Europeenne)
Nottingham Health Authority
Forest House
Berkeley Ave.
Nottingham NG5 1PG, England
Maurice Beaver
PH: 44 115 9691691
Description: Schools of public health and other institutions offering graduate instruction in public health. Promotes the study and development of education in public health and health services. Conducts workshops and seminars. Organizes exchange of students and staff between member schools. **Founded:** 1966. **Membership:** 65. Multinational. **Languages:** English, French.

ASSOCIATION SUISSE DE PLANNING FAMILIAL ET D'EDUCATION SEXUELLE (ASPFES)
e-mail: aspfes@bluewin.ch
7, chemin de la Gueta
CH-1073 Savigny, Switzerland
Ms. Christine Magistretti, Contact
PH: 41 27 7840246
FX: 41 27 7840246
Description: Promotes family planning and responsible parenthood as a means to improve the quality of life for individuals in Switzerland. Advocates family planning as a basic human right. Works to reduce the number of unwanted pregnancies and abortions. Offers programs in sex education, family planning, and health. Provides contraceptive and health care services. Conducts research. **Founded:** 1993. **Membership:** 250. **Staff:** 3. **Languages:** French, German. **Publication:** *ASPFES Info-Bulletin* (in French, German, and Italian), quarterly. Newsletter.

ASSOCIATION OF SUPERVISORS OF MIDWIVES
Corporate Services
Lowestoft Rd.
Gorleston
Great Yarmouth NR31 6LA, England
Elayne Guest, Contact
PH: 44 1493 452269
FX: 44 1493 452819
Description: Qualified midwives nominated as Supervisors of Midwives. Promotes a high standard of Supervision of Midwives in the practice and teaching of midwifery. Offers support to members and represents the interests of Supervisors of Midwives at national and international levels. **Founded:** 1910. **Membership:** 350. **Publication:** *Risk Management in Midwifery Practice.* Price: L1.50/each ▪ *Supervision The Why's and Wherefore's.* Booklet ▪ *Teaching Package About Midwifery Supervisor.* Price: L10.00/each ▪ Annual Report, annual.

ASSOCIATION OF SURGEONS OF GREAT BRITAIN AND IRELAND
e-mail: admin@asgbi.org.uk
35-43 Lincoln's Inn Fields
London WC2A 3PN, England
Mr. RHS Lane, Hon. Sec.
PH: 44 171 9730300
FX: 44 171 4309235
Description: General surgeons. Concerned with the advancement of the science and art of surgery and the promoting of friendship amongst surgeons. The Association is the speciality association for general surgery and is recognised as such by Government as well as by the profession. **Founded:** 1920. **Membership:** 2000. **Staff:** 4. **Publication:** *British Journal of Surgery,* monthly.

ASSOCIATION TUNISIENNE DU PLANNING FAMILIAL (ATPF)
9, rue Essoyouti
El Menzah
TN-1004 Tunis, Tunisia
Mr. Lotfi Labbane
PH: 216 1 232419
FX: 216 1 767263
Description: Advocates family planning as a basic human right. Works to reduce the number of unwanted pregnancies and abortions. Attempts to stop the spread of AIDS and other sexually transmitted diseases. Offers programs in sex education, family planning, and health. Provides contraceptive and health care services. Acts as an advocate for family planning on the national level. **Languages:** Arabic, French. **Publication:** *Bulletin de l'Association* (in Arabic and French), quarterly. Newsletter. Price: free. Advertising: not accepted.

ASSOCIATION OF UNIVERSITY ANESTHESIOLOGISTS (AUA)
2033 6th Ave., No. 804
Seattle, WA 98121
Shirley Bishop, Exec.Dir.
PH: (206)441-6020
FX: (206)441-8262
Description: Academic anesthesiologists from medical school faculties. Encourages members to pursue original investigations in the clinic and the laboratory; develops methods of teaching anesthesiology. **Founded:** 1953. **Membership:** 600. **Languages:** English. Formerly (1990) Association of University Anesthetists.

ASSOCIATION OF UNIVERSITY PROFESSORS OF OPHTHALMOLOGY (AUPO)

PO Box 420369
San Francisco, CA 94142-0369
Steve M. Podos, M.D., Exec.VP
PH: (415)561-8548
FX: (415)561-8575
Description: Heads of departments or divisions of ophthalmology in accredited medical schools throughout the U.S. and Canada; directors of ophthalmology residency programs in institutions not connected to medical schools. Promotes medical education, research, and patient care relating to ophthalmology. Operates Ophthalmology Matching Program and faculty placement service, which aids ophthalmologists interested in being associated with university ophthalmology programs to locate such programs. **Founded:** 1966. **Membership:** 246. **Staff:** 3. **Languages:** English.

ASSOCIATION OF UNIVERSITY PROGRAMS IN HEALTH ADMINISTRATION (AUPHA)

1110 Vermont Ave., NW
Ste. 220
Washington, DC 20005-3500
Henry Fernandez, CEO
PH: (703)524-5500
FX: (703)525-4791
Description: Universities offering graduate and undergraduate study in health services and hospital administration. To improve the quality of education in health services administration. Undertakes research and educational programs, such as studies of the criteria used for selection of students and curriculum patterns adopted by various universities. Conducts faculty institutes on topics relating to health administration. Compiles statistics. **Founded:** 1948. **Membership:** 1200. **Staff:** 14. **Languages:** English. **Budget:** $1,800,000. **Publication:** *AUPHA Exchange*, bimonthly. Newsletter ▪ *Health Services Administration Education*, biennial. Directory ▪ *Journal of Health Administration Education*, quarterly. **Formerly:** (1973) Association of University Programs in Hospital Administration.

ASSOCIATION OF UNIVERSITY RADIOLOGISTS (AUR)

e-mail: aurc@rsna.org
2021 Spring Rd., Ste. 600
Oak Brook, IL 60523-1860
Jennifer Boylan, Exec. Sec.
PH: (630)368-3730
FX: (630)571-7837
Description: Physician and non-physician scientists who have been appointed to a university faculty. Seeks to: encourage excellence in laboratory and clinical investigation, teaching, and clinical practice; stimulate interest in academic radiology as a medical career; advance radiology as a medical science; provide a forum for university based radiologists to present and discuss results of research, teaching, and administrative issues. **Founded:** 1953. **Membership:** 1600. **Staff:** 6. **Languages:** English.

ASSOCIATION OF VASCULAR AND INTERVENTIONAL RADIOGRAPHERS

e-mail: avir@rsna.org
2021 Spring Rd., Ste. 600
Oak Brook, IL 60523
Betty Rohr, Exec.Sec.
PH: (630)571-2266
FX: (630)571-7837
Description: Cardiovascular and interventional radiographers and allied health care professionals. **Founded:** 1988. **Membership:** 1469. **Staff:** 2.

ASSOCIATION FOR VOLUNTARY SURGICAL CONTRACEPTION (AVSC)

Box 57964
Nairobi, Kenya
Description: Promotes family planning through provision of voluntary sterilization services; seeks to raise public awareness of surgical contraception. Makes available technical assistance for local family planning agencies; trains physicians and nurses in performing surgical contraception. **Languages:** English.

ASSOCIATION OF WOMEN SURGEONS (AWS)

e-mail: aws@adminsys.com
url: http://www.womensurgeons.org
414 Plaza Dr., Ste. 209
Westmont, IL 60559
Judith Keel, Exec.Dir.
PH: (630)655-0392
FX: (630)655-0391
Description: Women surgeons, interns, and residents; retired women surgeons; women in medical school interested in a career in surgery; interested individuals. Promotes the professional and personal goals of women surgeons and women involved and interested in the medical profession. Encourages interaction between women surgeons internationally. Serves as a network for the exchange of ideas and information. **Founded:** 1981. **Membership:** 1300. Multinational. **Languages:** English.

ASSOCIATION OF WOMEN'S HEALTH, OBSTETRIC, AND NEONATAL NURSES (AWHONN)

e-mail: lisad@awhonn.org
url: http://www.awhonn.org
700 14th St. NW, Ste. 600
Washington, DC 20005-2019
Gail Kincaide, Exec.Dir.
PH: (202)662-1600
FX: (202)737-0575
Description: Members are registered nurses; associate members are allied health workers with an interest in obstetric, women's health, and neonatal (OGN) nursing. Promotes and establishes the highest standards of OGN nursing practice, education, and research; cooperates with all members of the health team; stimulates interest in OGN nursing. Sponsors educational meetings, audiovisual programs, and continuing education courses. **Founded:** 1969. **Membership:** 22000. **Staff:** 30. **State Groups:** 62. **Languages:** English. **Budget:** $2,950,000. Formerly Nurses Association of the American College of Obstetricians and Gynecologists; (1993) NAACOG: The Organization of Obstetric, Gynecologic, and Neonatal Nurses.

ASSOCIATION OF WORKERS FOR CHILDREN WITH EMOTIONAL AND BEHAVIOURAL DIFFICULTIES

e-mail: awccbd@mistral.co.uk
Charlton Ct.
East Sutton, Kent ME17 3DQ, England
Allan Rimmer, Admin. Officer
PH: 44 1622 8434104
FX: 44 1622 844220
Description: All professions involved in work with children and young people with emotional and behavioural difficulties and those who are involved in training. Promotes meeting the needs of children and young people with emotional and/or behavioural difficulties, in a variety of settings including education. **Founded:** 1953. **Membership:** 1000. **Regional Groups:** 6. **Publication:** *Emotional and Behavioral Difficulties*, 3/year. Journal. Multidisciplinary practitioners journal ▪ Newsletter, semiannuaal.

ASSOCIAZIONE ITALIANA DI ANESTESIA ODONTO-STOMATOLOGICA (AINOS)

Casella Postale 1630
I-40100 Bologna, Italy
Dr. Luigi Baldinelli, Gen.Sec.
PH: 39 51 247784
FX: 39 51 247784
Description: Physicians concerned with dental anesthesiology. Sponsors educational and research programs. **Founded:** 1972. **Membership:** 60. **Staff:** 1. **Languages:** Italian. **Budget:** 2,000,000 Lr. **Publication:** *Giornale di Anestesia Stomatologica* (in Italian), quarterly. Magazine. Price: free for members. ISSN: 0391-5670. Advertising: accepted.

ATAXIA
The Stable
Wiggins Yard
Bridge St.
Godalming, Surrey GU7 1HW, England
Sue Grice, Contact
PH: 44 1483 417111
FX: 44 1483 424006
Description: Fundraising organization supporting research into Friedreich's, Cerebellar, and other ataxias (hereditary spinal diseases which cause the loss of muscular coordination). Offers support services for ataxia sufferers and their families. **Founded:** 1965. **Membership:** 2700. **Staff:** 2. Multinational. **Languages:** English. **Publication:** *Ataxian* (in English), quarterly. Magazine ■ *Fax/Ataxian*, periodic. Videos ■ Brochures (in English), periodic ■ Newsletter (in English), quarterly. Advertising: accepted. **Also Known As:** Friedreich's Ataxia Group.

ATTENTION DEFICIT INFORMATION NETWORK (ADIN)
475 Hillside Ave.
Needham, MA 02194
Moira Munns, Pres.
PH: (617)455-9895
FX: (617)444-5466
Description: People with Attention Deficit Disorders (ADD), their families, and other individuals with an interest in ADD. Promotes improved quality of life for people with ADD. Works to expand home, school, and work-based strategies for aiding people with ADD; advocates for improved responsiveness to the needs of people with ADD by schools, businesses, and organizations. Provides support and information to families of people with ADD; conducts educational programs; maintains speakers' bureau. **Founded:** 1988. **State Groups:** 20. **Languages:** English.

AUSTRALIAN DENTAL ASSOCIATION (ADA)
e-mail: adainc@ozemail.com.au
url: http://www.ada.org.au
75 Lithgow St.
PO Box 520
St. Leonards, NSW 2065, Australia
Dr. Robert J.F. Butler, Contact
PH: 61 2 99064412
FX: 61 2 99064917
Description: Dentists, specialists, and dental students. Represents dentists' interests nationally and internationally. Seeks to improve the dental health of the community. Sponsors educational and research programs; cosponsors the Australian Dental Research Fund. **Founded:** 1928. **Membership:** 7500. **Staff:** 15. **State Groups:** 7. **Languages:** English. **Budget:** $A 1,700,000. **Publication:** *ADA News Bulletin* (in English), 11/year ■ *Australian Dental Journal* (in English), bimonthly ■ *Facts and Figures - Australian Dentistry*, annual ■ Directory (in English), biennial.

AUSTRALIAN INSTITUTE OF RADIOGRAPHY (AIR)
e-mail: ausumrad@internet.com.au
PO Box 1169
Collingwood, VIC 3069, Australia
E.M. Hughes, Gen.Sec.
PH: 61 3 94193336
FX: 61 3 94160783
Description: Diagnostic radiographers, radiation therapists, and sonographers in Australia. Fosters cooperation and exchange of information between members. Conducts educational and research projects; prepares guidelines and policies for the practice of radiography in Australia. Encourages high professional standards. Disseminates information; offers educational programs and seminars. **Founded:** 1950. **Membership:** 3800. **Staff:** 6. **Languages:** English. **Publication:** *Radiographer* (in English), 3/year, April, August, December. Journal. Price: $A 45.00. ISSN: 0033-8273. Circulation: 4,000. Advertising: accepted ■ *Spectrum* (in English), monthly. **Formerly:** Australasian Institute of Radiography.

AUSTRIAN PHYSICAL SOCIETY
e-mail: oepg@ati87.ati.ac.at
Atominstitut der Osterr. Universitaten
Schuttelstr. 115
A-1020 Vienna, Austria
Christoph Leubner, Sec.
Description: Physicists, physics teachers, and others with an interest in the physical sciences. Seeks to improve the quality of physics education, research, and knowledge. **Membership:** 1100. **Staff:** 1. **Languages:** English, German. **Publication:** *OPG Mitteilugsblatter* (in German), quarterly. Newsletter. Contains information on internal happenings and the field of physics in Austria. Price: included in membership dues. Advertising: accepted.

AUSTRIAN SOCIETY OF ACUPUNCTURE AND AURICULAR THERAPY (ASAAT)
(Osterreichische Gesellschaft fur Akupunktur)
url: http://www.akupunktur.at
Kaiserin-Elisabeth Hospital
Huglgasse 1-3
A-1150 Vienna, Austria
Manfred Richart, Sec.
PH: 43 1 981045758
FX: 43 1 981045759
Description: Promotes the acceptance of acupuncture as a recognized healing method in the western medical world. Works in conjunction with the World Health Organization to disseminate and standardize nomenclature. Offers training course. **Founded:** 1954. **Membership:** 2147. **Staff:** 3. Multinational. **Languages:** Chinese, English.

AUXILIARY TO THE AMERICAN PHARMACEUTICAL ASSOCIATION
7327 Danbury Way
Clearwater, FL 34624
Nan Tower, Pres.
PH: (813)531-1729
Description: Individuals related to members in the American Pharmaceutical Association; others interested in pharmacy. Grants low-interest loans to pharmacy students annually. **Founded:** 1936. **Membership:** 400. **Languages:** English. Formerly (1975) Women's Auxiliary of the American Pharmaceutical Association.

AUXILIARY TO THE NATIONAL DENTAL ASSOCIATION (ANDA)
5506 Connecticut Ave.
Washington, DC 20015
Hazel Harper, Pres.
PH: (202)244-7555
FX: (202)244-5992
Description: Spouses and widows of dentists. Fosters professional, educational, ethical, and social measures that are conducive to the welfare of the dental profession; promotes and participates in health programs and projects; sponsors a student aid fund; encourages and correlates activities of local units throughout the country. Presents scholarships. Sponsors competitions; maintains charitable program. **Founded:** 1936. **Membership:** 250. **Regional Groups:** 6. **Languages:** English. **Publication:** *ANDA Yearbook*. Directory ■ *President's Newsletter*, periodic. **Formerly:** (1979) Ladies Auxiliary to the National Dental Association.

AUXILIARY TO THE NATIONAL MEDICAL ASSOCIATION (ANMA)
1012 10th St. NW
Washington, DC 20001
Sherman Word Dennis, Pres.
PH: (202)371-1674
FX: (202)289-2662
Description: Spouses of active members of the National Medical Association; widows and widowers of former members. Purposes are to: create a greater interest in the NMA; assist and encourage the medical profession in its efforts to educate and serve the

public in matters of sanitation and health; develop and promote a national program on health and education with subcategories in community needs, legislation, and human relations. Conducts workshops on teenage pregnancy, breast self-examinations, high blood pressure screening, and sickle cell anemia screening. Plans and implements an annual youth forum under the auspices of the March of Dimes Birth Defects Foundation. Provides youth with professional guidance and the opportunity for peer exchange in the areas of mental and physical health; deals with the health of newborns, health services, nutrition, and teenage pregnancy. Also conducts programs for youth on parenting, socially transmitted diseases, nutrition, birth defects, and continued education after pregnancy. **Founded:** 1935. **Membership:** 1000. **Staff:** 1. **Local Groups:** 40. **Languages:** English. **Publication:** Book. Covers standard procedures ▪ Membership Directory, periodic. Price: available to members only ▪ Newsletter, quarterly. **Formerly:** (1975) Women's Auxiliary to the National Medical Association.

AVENUES, NATIONAL SUPPORT GROUP FOR ARTHROGRYPOSIS MULTIPLEX CONGENITA
e-mail: avenues@sonnet.com
url: http://www.sonnet.com/avenues/
PO Box 5192
Sonora, CA 95370
Mary Anne Schmidt, Dir.
PH: (209)928-3688
Description: Individuals with arthrogryposis multiplex congentia (AMC), their families and friends, and interested professionals. (AMC, a birth defect, is a muscle and/or nerve syndrome affecting some or all of the body's limbs.) Purpose is to share positive attitudes and selfhelp ideas for the handicapped and for all who deal with them. **Founded:** 1980. **Membership:** 1200. **Languages:** English. **Publication:** *Avenues*, semiannual. Newsletter. Lists doctors and families interested in corresponding with others about arthrogryposis. Price: included in membership dues; $10.00 annual donation requested for members in U.S.; $15.00 annual donation requested for members outside U.S. Circulation: 1,200. Advertising: not accepted ▪ Audiotapes ▪ Bibliography ▪ Pamphlet. Price: $1.00.

AVSC INTERNATIONAL (AVSC)
e-mail: info@avsc.org
url: http://www.avsc.org
79 Madison Ave., 7th Fl.
New York, NY 10016-7802
Amy E. Pollack, Pres.
PH: (212)561-8000
FX: (212)779-9439
Description: Seeks to provide women and men with access to voluntary and safe contraception. Helps countries and institutions develop, improve, and expand systems for the provision of clinic-based contraception services. Special expertise in female sterilization and vasectomy. **Founded:** 1943. **Membership:** 8000. **Staff:** 200. Multinational. **Languages:** Arabic, English. **Budget:** $25,000,000. **Publication:** *AVSC News*, quarterly. Newsletter. Price: free, for members only and family planning community ▪ Brochures. **Formerly:** (1985) Association for Voluntary Sterilization; (1994) Association for Voluntary Surgical Contraception.

BANGLADESH ASSOCIATION FOR MATERNAL AND NEONATAL HEALTH (BAMANEH)
11-KA, Shyamoli, St. No. 2
Dhaka 1207, Bangladesh
Dr. A.I. Begum
PH: 880 2 311168
FX: 880 2 866992
Description: Focuses on the health and safety of women and infants.

BANGLADESH MEDICAL ASSOCIATION OF NORTH AMERICA (BMA)
c/o S. Hasan
1575 Woodward Ave., Ste. 212
Bloomfield Hills, MI 48302
F. Hasan, M.D., Pres.
PH: (248)338-8182
FX: (248)338-9520
Description: Physicians who are from Bangladesh or have graduated from a medical college in Bangladesh. Seeks to bring together and improve communication between physicians who are of Bangladeshi origin or have trained in Bangladesh, and are currently residents of the United States or Canada, and other physicians. Assists medical students and physicians in obtaining specialized medical training and in post-training job placement in North America. Publications: none. **Founded:** 1982. **Membership:** 200. **Languages:** English.

BANGLADESH MEDICAL STUDIES AND RESEARCH INSTITUTE (BMSRI)
e-mail: bmch@bangla.net
35 H Rd., No. 14 A
Dhanmondi Residential Area
Dhaka, Bangladesh
Dr. Anis Waiz, Dir.
PH: 880 2 9120792
FX: 880 2 9125655
Description: Promotes medical studies and research with the object of raising the standard of medical education in Bangladesh. Encourages growth in Bangladesh's pharmaceutical, medical, and surgical instrument industries. Conducts research in disease prevention and treatment and on medical applications of indigenous plants and herbs. Offers refresher courses and monthly academic seminar; organizes conferences, lectures, seminars, and study groups. Operates speakers' bureau. Maintains the Bangladesh Medical College which grants degrees in medicine and surgery and the Dental College which grants degrees in dentistry. **Founded:** 1984. **Membership:** 15. **Staff:** 366. **Languages:** English. **Budget:** Tk 421,000. **Publication:** *Annual Report and Prospectus* (in English), annual. Directory. Price: free. Advertising: not accepted. Alternate Formats: online ▪ *Bangladesh Medical College* (in Bengali and English), quarterly. Journal. **Also Known As:** Bangladesh Medical College.

BANJA LA MORTSOGOLO (BLM)
e-mail: blantyre@cix.compulink.oc.uk
PO Box 3008
Blantyre, Malawi
Dorothy Ngoma, Prog.Dir.
PH: 265 652496
FX: 265 652284
Description: Promotes child spacing and increased public awareness of population control and family planning issues. Conducts educational and social programs to change traditional attitudes toward family size and the role of women in society. Makes available maternal and child health care; operates clinics and hospitals. Sponsors contraceptive education and distribution campaigns. **Founded:** 1987. **Membership:** 150. **Local Groups:** 15. **Languages:** English. **Budget:** $750,000.

BARBADOS DENTAL ASSOCIATION (BDA)
PO Box 95
Bridgetown, Barbados
Dr. Ronald Ramsay, Contact
PH: (246)228-6488
FX: (246)228-6488
Description: Promotes dentistry and the interests of dental professionals in Barbados; works to improve the dental and general health of the public. Conducts educational programs at schools. Offers competitions for school children to foster dental health awareness. **Founded:** 1965. **Membership:** 34. **Staff:** 1. **Local Groups:** 1. **Languages:** English.

BARBADOS FAMILY PLANNING ASSOCIATION (BFPA)
Bay St.
Bridgetown, Barbados
Mr. George Griffith, Contact
PH: (246)426-2027
FX: (246)427-6611
Description: Promotes family planning as a basic human right. Encourages family planning activities in Barbados. Offers educational programs in family planning, sexually transmitted diseases, and health care. Provides contraceptive services. Acts as an advocate for family planning on a national level. **Founded:** 1954. **Staff:** 33. **Languages:** English. **Budget:** BD$1,100,000. **Publication:** *Annual Report* (in English), always May ∎ *Family*, semiannual. Newsletter. Price: free. Circulation: 5,000. Advertising: accepted.

BAROMEDICAL NURSES ASSOCIATION (BNA)
url: http://www.members.aol.com/PGBATZ/bna.html
PO Box 24113
Halethorpe, MD 21227
Laura Josefsen, Pres.
PH: (410)789-5690
Description: Registered nurses practicing baromedicine (hyperbaric medicine), involved in research related to baromedical nursing, completing basic orientation in baromedicine, or contributing to literature on baromedicine or baromedical nursing. Defines, develops, and promotes the status and standards of baromedical nursing. Facilitates professional activities and continuing education programs. Provides a forum for the exchange of ideas, information, and support; maintains speakers' bureau. **Founded:** 1985. **Membership:** 160. **Staff:** 1. **Regional Groups:** 6. **Languages:** English.

BATES ASSOCIATION OF GREAT BRITAIN
e-mail: bagb@sta.clara.net
PO Box 25
Shoreham-by-Sea BN43 6ZF, England
Peter Mansfield, Sec.
PH: 44 1273 871166
FX: 44 1273 871166
Description: Teachers of Bates Method vision education. To advance the knowledge and practice of vision education. **Founded:** 1954. **Membership:** 25. **Publication:** *Seeing* (in English), quarterly. Journal. Price: L5.00. Circulation: 200. Advertising: not accepted ∎ *Vision Education News*, quarterly. Newsletter. Circulation: 500. **Formerly:** (1989) London Association of Eyesight Training.

BATH INSTITUTE FOR RHEUMATIC DISEASES
Trim Bridge
Bath, Avon BA1 1HD, England
Terry Hyde, Exec.Dir.
PH: 44 1225 448444
FX: 44 1225 336809

BATTEN DISEASE SUPPORT AND RESEARCH ASSOCIATION (BDSRA)
e-mail: BDSRA1@bdsra.org
url: http://www.bdsra.org
2600 Parsons Ave.
Columbus, OH 43207
Lance W. Johnson, Exec.Dir.
PH: (614)927-4298
TF: 800448-4570
FX: (614)445-4246
Description: Families of children afflicted with Batten Disease; health care professionals; interested others. (Batten Disease, is a degenerative neurological disease affecting children, causing seizures, dementia, loss of motor skills, and blindness.) Represents the interest of individuals with Batten; seeks to educate the public and professional community concerning the needs of Battens Disease patients. Provides information and referral services. Conducts support group activities. Maintains registry. **Founded:** 1987. **Membership:** 400. **Staff:** 1. Multinational. **State Groups:** 14. **Languages:** English. **Budget:** $250,000. **Publication:** *Family Directory*, annual. Price: free; available to member

families only. Circulation: 350. Advertising: not accepted ∎ *Illuminator*, quarterly. Newsletter. Provides information on research, education, meetings, and other topics of interest. Price: free. Circulation: 700. Advertising: not accepted.

BELARUSIAN PHYSICAL SOCIETY
e-mail: imafbel@imaph.bas-net.by
Institute of Molecular & Atomic Physics
National Academy of Sciences of Belarus
70 F. Skorina Prospekt
220072 Minsk, Belarus
Dr. E.A. Ershov-Pavlov, Sec.
PH: 375 172 685346
FX: 375 172 393064
Description: Physicists, physics teachers, and others with an interest in the physical sciences. Seeks to improve the quality of physics education, research, and knowledge. **Founded:** 1991. **Membership:** 134. **Languages:** English, Russian.

BELGIAN ASSOCIATION OF PHYSICIANS IN THE PHARMACEUTICAL INDUSTRY (BAPPI)
(Association Belge des Medecins de l'Industrie Pharmaceutique)
Vossemberg 73
B-3080 Tervuren, Belgium
Henri Pintens, Dir.
PH: 32 2 7670108
FX: 32 2 4222799
Description: Physicians working in the pharmaceutical industry. Promotes thorough testing to determine the safety and effectiveness of all pharmaceutical products. Conducts research and educational programs; maintains speakers' bureau. **Membership:** 160. **Staff:** 6. **Languages:** Dutch, English. **Budget:** 900,000 BFr. **Publication:** *ABEMIP News* (in English), bimonthly. Newsletter. Contains information on regulatory, clinical studies, health economic issues, internet news. Price: free. Circulation: 160. Advertising: accepted.

BELGIAN PHYSICAL SOCIETY
Belgian Institute for Space Aeronomy
Ringlaan 3
B-1180 Brussels, Belgium
J. Ingels, Sec.
PH: 32 2 3730378
FX: 32 2 3748423
Description: Physicists, physics teachers, and others with an interest in the physical sciences. Seeks to improve the quality of physics education, research, and knowledge. **Membership:** 480. **Publication:** *Physicalia Magazine* (in Dutch, English, and French), 3/month. Journal. Advertising: accepted.

BELGIAN ROYAL SOCIETY OF DERMATOLOGY AND VENEROLOGY (BSD)
(Societe Royale Belge de Dermatologie et Venerologie)
Dept. of Dermatology
University Hospital
B-9000 Gent, Belgium
Prof.Dr. E. Van Hecke, Sec.
PH: 32 9 2402287
FX: 32 9 2404996
Description: Dermatologists and other scientists interested in dermatology. Conducts biennial postgraduate course. **Founded:** 1901. **Membership:** 500. **Languages:** Dutch, English. **Publication:** *Dermatology* (in English), 10/year.

BELIZE FAMILY LIFE ASSOCIATION (BFLA)
e-mail: bfla@btl.net
127 Barrack Rd.
PO Box 529
Belize City, Belize
Mrs. Jewel Quallo, Exec.Dir.
PH: 501 2 31018
FX: 501 2 32667
Description: Works to enhance the quality of life in Belize

through promotion of family planning and maternal and infant health care. Encourages public awareness of methods of contraception. Offers educational programs in family planning, sex education, and health care. Conducts AIDS education and counselling. Provides contraceptive services. Also provides diagnosis and treatment of STDs, testing for cervical cancer, and counselling and support (including pre-natal education and post-natal services) for young parents. **Founded:** 1985. **Membership:** 5000. **Staff:** 17. **Languages:** English. **Publication:** *Annual Report* ▪ *Information Sheets* ▪ *Journey* (in English), quarterly. Newsletter. Price: free. Circulation: 1,000. Advertising: not accepted ▪ Brochures.

BELL'S PALSY RESEARCH FOUNDATION
e-mail: bellspalsy@aol.com
9121 E. Tanque Verde, Ste. 105-286
Tucson, AZ 85719
Colleen Pier, Founder & Pres.
PH: (520)749-4614
Description: Provides information and support to those diagnosed with facial paralysis. Offers research programs. Convention/Meeting: none. **Founded:** 1995. **Staff:** 5. Multinational. **For-Profit. Budget:** $2,000.

BENIGN ESSENTIAL BLEPHAROSPASM RESEARCH
  FOUNDATION (BEBRF)
e-mail: bebrf@ih2000.net
url: http://www.blepharospasm.org/~bebrf/
PO Box 12468
Beaumont, TX 77726-2468
Mattie Lou Koster, Contact
PH: (409)832-0788
FX: (409)832-0890
Description: Victims of benign essential blepharospasm (BEB), a rare disorder of unknown cause characterized by an involuntary forcible closure of the eyelids. Purpose is to undertake, promote, and develop research into the cause and cure of BEB and related disorders and infirmities of the facial musculature, such as Meige's Syndrome (involving muscle spasms of the eyes, lower face, mouth, tongue, throat, and respiratory system). Seeks to foster public awareness of the disorder in order to guarantee detection at the onset of symptoms. Encourages continuity and cooperation among neurologists, neuro-ophthalmologists, ophthalmologists, plastic surgeons, psychologists, psychiatrists, and other medical professionals in rendering correct diagnoses, implementing effective treatment, improving surgical procedure, and discovering a cure. Organizes seminars, clinical studies, and other programs in continuing education; sponsors fundraising activities. Endeavors to locate sufferers of the disorder and to compile data in order to determine the incidence of BEB and to advise on available treatment. Carries out research activities in areas such as brain tissue collection and experimental treatments. **Founded:** 1981. **Membership:** 6000. **Staff:** 2. **Local Groups:** 170. **Languages:** English. **Budget:** $300,000. **Publication:** *BEBRF Newsletter*, bimonthly. Includes research reports and statistics. Price: $15.00/year. Circulation: 6,000. Advertising: not accepted ▪ *Blepharospasm and Related Disorders*. Price: $16.00 ▪ *Medical Handbook*, annual. Contains articles by physicians and reprints of materials appearing in medical journals. Price: free. Circulation: 8,000. Advertising: not accepted ▪ Films ▪ Journal ▪ Pamphlets.

BENJAMIN FRANKLIN LITERARY AND MEDICAL
  SOCIETY (BFLMS)
PO Box 567
Indianapolis, IN 46206
Cory SerVaas, M.D., Pres. & CEO
PH: (317)636-8881
FX: (317)634-1791
Description: Individuals, industries, and businesses united to support research and promote sciences, literature, and the arts in order to achieve greater public understanding of science and the humanities. Major emphasis is on the dissemination of health, preventive medicine, and nutrition information to the health community and the public. Advocates a preventive approach to

health care including proper nutrition, daily exercise, and good health habits. Offers training in cardiopulmonary resuscitation and other life-saving skills; conducts health education programs. Sponsors the Children's Better Health Institute, which publishes material designed to educate children of preschool through elementary school levels on health, nutrition, safety, and exercise, and provides parents with medical information concerning infants and children. Operates Medical Education and Research Foundation, which disseminates medical information in lay terms, covering concepts and developments in preventive medicine, safety procedures and techniques, health dangers, proper dietary habits, and reports on new and developing treatments and medications for cancer patients and techniques used for early detection of cancer. Sponsors the Saturday Evening Post Society which conducts national health surveys; publicizes advances in science, medicine, nutrition, and preventive medicine; funds research projects; and encourages commercial manufacturers to produce innovative health equipment. Is named for Benjamin Franklin (1706-90), who founded the Pennsylvania Gazette in 1728, which eventually became the Saturday Evening Post. (The society purchased this magazine from the Curtis Publishing Company in 1982.) Franklin was also a strong supporter of the arts and sciences. **Founded:** 1976. **Membership:** 2300000. **Staff:** 100. **Languages:** English. **Publication:** *Child Life*, 8/year. Magazine. Promotes reading and good health habits in children between the ages of seven and nine. Includes "Ask the Doctor" column, poems, and short stories. Price: $14.95/year. ISSN: 0009-3971. Circulation: 75,000. Advertising: accepted. Alternate Formats: microform ▪ *Children's Digest*, 8/year. Magazine. Promotes reading and good health habits in children between the ages of eight and ten. Includes book reviews. Price: $14.95/year. Circulation: 115,000. Advertising: accepted. Alternate Formats: microform ▪ *Children's Playmate Magazine*, 8/year. Promotes reading and good health habits for children between the ages of five and seven. Includes book reviews. Price: $14.95/year. ISSN: 0009-4161. Circulation: 130,000. Advertising: accepted. Alternate Formats: microform ▪ *Humpty Dumpty*, 8/year. Magazine. Promotes reading and good health habits for children between the ages of four and six. Price: $14.95/year. ISSN: 0273-7590. Circulation: 260,000. Advertising: accepted. Alternate Formats: microform ▪ *Jack and Jill*, 8/year. Magazine. Promotes reading and good health habits for children between the ages of six and eight. Price: $14.95/year. ISSN: 0021-3829. Circulation: 340,000. Advertising: accepted. Alternate Formats: microform ▪ *Mecidal Update Newsletter*, monthly. Includes foundation news and research updates. Price: $12.00/year. Circulation: 25,000 ▪ *Saturday Evening Post*, bimonthly ▪ *Turtle Magazine for Preschool Kids*, 8/year. Promotes reading and good health, safety, and nutrition habits for children between the ages of two and five. Includes book reviews. Price: $14.95/year. ISSN: 0191-3654. Circulation: 500,000. Advertising: accepted. Alternate Formats: microform.

BERMUDA DENTAL ASSOCIATION (BDA)
PO Box 3059
Hamilton HM HX, Bermuda
Description: Dentists in Bermuda. Promotes dentistry; represents members' interests. Sponsors study club. **Membership:** 25. **Languages:** English.

BETTER VISION INSTITUTE (BVI)
url: http://www.visionsite.org
1655 N. Fort Meyer Dr., Ste. 200
Arlington, VA 22209
Susan Burton, Exec.VP
PH: (703)243-1508
TF: 800424-8422
FX: (703)243-1537
Description: Advisory council of the Vision Council of America. Carried out in consultation with a board of eye care professionals who inform the public of the need for more adequate vision care. **Founded:** 1929. **Membership:** 500. Multinational. **Languages:** English.

BIOCHEMICAL SOCIETY - ENGLAND (BS)
e-mail: genadmin@biochemsoc.org.uk
url: http://www.biochemsoc.org.uk
59 Portland Pl.
London W1N 3AJ, England
G.D. Jones, Exec.Sec.
PH: 44 171 5805530
FX: 44 171 6377626
Description: Biochemists in 70 countries working in industrial production, health services, and industrial and higher education research. Objectives are to promote biochemistry and to provide a forum for information exchange and discussion of teaching and research in biochemistry. Maintains 16 specialized biochemical groups. **Founded:** 1911. **Membership:** 9000. **Staff:** 35. Multinational. **Regional Groups:** 6. **Languages:** English. **Publication:** *Biochemical Journal*, semimonthly ▪ *Biochemical Society Transactions*, bimonthly ▪ *Biochemist*, bimonthly ▪ *Clinical Science*, monthly ▪ *Essays in Biochemistry*, annual ▪ *Symposium Proceedings*, annual.

BIOELECTROCHEMICAL SOCIETY (BES)
e-mail: marosa@cica.es
Department of Biochemistry
Faculty of Biology
Apartado 1095
E-41080 Seville, Spain
Prof. M.A. De La Rosa, Contact
PH: 34 5 4557088
FX: 34 5 4620154
Description: Electrochemists, biochemists, electrophysiologists, and biophysicists. Promotes research; sponsors seminars and workshops; administers schools of bioelectrochemistry. Bestows Luigi Galvani Prize. **Founded:** 1978. **Membership:** 200. Multinational. **Languages:** English. **Publication:** *Bioelectrochemistry and Bioenergetics*, 6/yr ▪ *Newsletter*, 3-4/year.

BIOMEDICAL ENGINEERING SOCIETY (BMES)
e-mail: bmes@netcom.com
url: http://mecca.mecca.org/BME/BMES/society/bmeshm.html
PO Box 2399
Culver City, CA 90231
Rita M. Schaffer, Exec.Dir.
PH: (310)618-9322
Description: Biomedical, chemical, electrical, and mechanical engineers, physicians, managers, and university professors representing all fields of biomedical engineering; students and corporations. Encourages the development, dissemination, integration, and utilization of knowledge in biomedical engineering. **Founded:** 1968. **Membership:** 2000. Multinational. **Languages:** English. **Budget:** $180,000. **Publication:** *Annals of Biomedical Engineering*, bimonthly. Journal ▪ *BMES Bulletin*, quarterly ▪ *BMES Membership Directory*, annual. Price: $50.00 ▪ *Planning a Career in Biomedical Engineering*. Brochure.

BLACK MENTAL HEALTH ALLIANCE (BMHA)
e-mail: bhealthall@aol.com
1800 N. Charles Street, 7th floor
Baltimore, MD 21201
Jan Desper Maybin, Exec.Dir.
PH: (410)837-2642
TF: 888729-BMHA
FX: (410)837-2646
Description: Seeks to increase clinicians, clergy, educators, and social service professionals awareness of African-Americans mental health needs and concerns on issues including stress, violence, racism, susbstance abuse, and parenting. Provides consultation, public information, and resource referrals. Conducts a public awareness campaign; educates the community about available resources; develops programs that benefit African-American children and families. Offers training to human service workers, teachers, police officers, and other service providers who work with culturally diverse populations. Maintains speakers' bureau. Provides the Family Outreach Support Group designed to provide mental health services to African American family members of mentally ill person. The support group provides emotional support, education and interaction for family members experiencing the stresses of caring for and/or living with a mentally ill relative. Provides a resource referral service; maintains an extensive list of African American mental health professionals who are sensitive to and appreciate cultural differences. Offers programs that invest in the needs of African American adult and adolescent females who are at risk of, or have, HIV or AIDS. Offers the "Free Yourself Stop Smoking and Prevention" program. This program includes a community coalition, vendor/merchant education, support groups, smoking cessation classes, exersice classes, and nutrition counseling. Provides mental health therapy to children and families in two schools, including after school activities and African-centered summer camp for youth 10-14 years. **Founded:** 1984. **Membership:** 250. **Staff:** 6. Local. **Local Groups:** 1. **Languages:** English.

BLACK PSYCHIATRISTS OF AMERICA (BPA)
666 Carlston Ave.
Oakland, CA 94610-1733
Dr. Isaac Slaughter, Exec.Off.
PH: (510)465-1800
FX: (510)465-1508
Description: Black psychiatrists, either in practice or training, united to promote black behavioral science and foster high quality psychiatric care for blacks and minority group members. Sponsors public information service. Maintains speakers' bureau and biographical archives; compiles statistics; conducts educational programs. Offers placement service. **Founded:** 1968. **Membership:** 1600. **Staff:** 1. **Regional Groups:** 4. **Languages:** English.

BLESSINGS INTERNATIONAL (BI)
e-mail: 75554.3572@compuserve.com
5881 S Garnett Rd.
Tulsa, OK 74146-6812
Harold Harder, Pres.
PH: (918)250-8101
FX: (918)250-1281
Description: Health care providers and other individuals. Seeks to increase the availability and quality of health care services among previously underserved communities worldwide. Procures and distributes pharmaceuticals and medical and surgical supplies; sends teams of volunteers to assist in the operation of local health services in developing and economically disadvantaged areas. Multinational. **Languages:** English.

BOTSWANA VACCINE INSTITUTE STAFF UNION
Private Bag 0031
Gaborone, Botswana
Elliot Modise, Gen.Sec.
Description: Staff of the Botswana Vaccine Institute. Seeks to obtain optimal conditions of employment for members. Represents members in contract negotiations. **Languages:** English.

BRAIN INFORMATION SERVICE (BIS)
e-mail: mchase@ucla.edu
url: http://bisleep.medsch.ucla.edu
43-367 CHS/UCLA School of Medicine
Los Angeles, CA 90095-1746
Dr. Michael H. Chase, Dir.
PH: (310)825-3417
FX: (310)206-3499
Description: A cooperative effort of the UCLA Brain Research Institute and the Biomedical Library. Purpose is to provide rapid, accurate, and complete information in the basic brain sciences to aid investigators and teachers in the field. Subject area of the service includes alcohol and sleep research; it does not cover the literature of diagnosis and treatment of neurological diseases. **Founded:** 1964. **Staff:** 6. Multinational. **Languages:** English. **Publication:** *Brain Information Service-Sleep Research*, annual. Compilation of abstracts of sleep research papers presented at the annual meeting of the Association of Professional Sleep Societies. Price: $92.00/copy. ISSN: 0093-0407. **Advertising:** not accepted.

**BRAZILIAN ASSOCIATION OF PHYSICIANS IN THE
PHARMACEUTICAL INDUSTRY**
(Asociacao Brasiliera de Medicos Assessores da Industria
Farmaceutica)
rua Pamplona 788
3 andar, sala 32
01405-001 Sao Paulo, SP, Brazil
D.C. Brandao, M.D., Pres.
PH: 55 11 2532848
FX: 55 11 2532848
Description: Physicians employed by manufacturers of pharma-
ceuticals. Promotes effective research, development, and testing
of pharmaceutical products. Conducts research and educational
programs; makes available marketing support. **Founded:** 1974.
Membership: 120. **Languages:** English, Portuguese.

**BRAZILIAN ASSOCIATION FOR THE PROMOTION OF
APPROPRIATE TECHNOLOGY IN HEALTHCARE**
(Associacao Brasileira de Tecnologia Alternativa na Promocao
da Saude)
e-mail: taps@tsp.com.br
Caixa Postal 20396
04041-990 Sao Paulo, SP, Brazil
Hildegard Bromberg Richter, Chm. of the Bd.
PH: 55 11 5720466
FX: 55 11 5720465
Description: Promotes health and domestic development in
Brazil with emphasis on improving health care through appropri-
ate technology. Functional in the following areas: health and nu-
trition; technical assistance; training and publications. **Founded:**
1981. **Membership:** 40. **Staff:** 4. **Languages:** Portuguese. **Budget:**
$50,000. **Publication:** *Onde nao ha medico* (in Portuguese). Book
■ *Voce sabe se alimentar?* (in Portuguese). Book. **Also Known As:
Temas Atuais na Promocao da Saude.**

BREAST CANCER CARE
Kiln House
210 New Kings Rd.
London SW6 4NZ, England
PH: 44 171 3842984
FX: 44 171 3843387
Description: Provides emotional and practical support to people
who have or think they may have, breast cancer. Operates advice
line, one-to-one volunteer support, and prothesis fitting. **Founded:** 1973. **Staff:** 15. **Languages:** English. **Budget:** L700,000. **Publication:** Books ■ Newsletter (in English), quarterly. Price: free
to members ■ Pamphlets. Contains information on breast awareness, breast surgery, and breast cancer treatments. **Formerly:**
(1993) Breast Care and Masectomy Association.

BREAST CANCER SUPPORT SERVICE - NEW ZEALAND
PO Box 7125
52 Riddiford St.
Wellington 5, New Zealand
Corrianne Simpson, Exec.Officer
PH: 64 4 3898421
FX: 64 4 3895994
Description: Works directly with breast cancer patients. Provides
counselling and support. Disseminates information. **Founded:**
1975. **Membership:** 200. **Staff:** 1. **Regional Groups:** 35. **Lang-
uages:** English.

**BREAST CANCER SUPPORT SERVICE - NORTHERN
IRELAND**
40 Eglantine Ave.
Belfast, Antrim BT9 6DX, Northern Ireland
Betty M.E. McCrum, Contact
PH: 44 1232 663281
FX: 44 1232 660081
Description: Promotes awareness of breast care and early detec-
tion of breast cancer. Supports the rehabilitation of women who
have breast cancer and breast surgery. **Founded:** 1974. **Regional
Groups:** 13. **Publication:** *Coping with Breast Cancer.* Booklet.
Price:. **Formerly:** Breast Care and Mastectomy Support Service.

BRITAIN - NEPAL MEDICAL TRUST (BNMT)
18 East St.
Tonbridge, Kent TN9 1HG, England
I. A. Baker, Chm.
PH: 44 1732 360284
FX: 44 1732 363876
Description: Health care professionals and health organizations.
Seeks to improve the health of the people of Nepal. Works with
Nepalese government agencies to increase delivery of health ser-
vices in underserved areas. Evaluates health programs and makes
recommendations for their improvement; distributes medical e-
quipment, medications, and other supplies. **Founded:** 1968. **Staff:**
153. Multinational. **Languages:** English. **Budget:** $689,000.

**BRITISH ACUPUNCTURE ASSOCIATION AND REGISTER
(BAAR)**
34 Alderney St.
Westminster
London SW1V 4EU, England
E. Welton Johnson, Exec. Officer
PH: 44 181 9732309
Publication: *BAAR Journal* (in English), semiannual. Adverti-
sing: not accepted ■ *Directory* (in English), periodic ■ Books, pe-
riodic ■ Papers, periodic. **Also Known As:** British Acupuncture
Association.

BRITISH ACUPUNCTURE COUNCIL
1 The Ridgeway
Stratford-upon-Avon, Warwickshire CV37 9JL, England
Yvonne Matthews, Coun.Sec.
PH: 44 1789 298798
Description: Practitioners of acupuncture belonging to the Coun-
cil of Acupuncture. Member groups include the following British
Acupuncture Association and Register, Chung San Acupuncture
Society, International Register of Oriental Medicine, Register of
Traditional Chinese Medicine, and Traditional Acupuncture So-
ciety. Promotes the use of traditional Chinese acupuncture. En-
courages exchange of ideas. Organizes seminars, study tours of
China, and educational courses. Maintains charitable program.
Founded: 1976. **Membership:** 1435. Multinational. **Languages:**
English. **Publication:** *Register of Members* (in English), semian-
nual. Membership Directory ■ *TAS Newsletter* (in English), quar-
terly ■ Journal (in English), semiannual. **Formerly:** Traditional
Acupuncture Society.

BRITISH ASSOCIATION FOR CANCER RESEARCH (BACR)
e-mail: info@iob.primex.ac.uk
url: http://www.icr.ac.uk
Institute of Biology
20 Queensberry Pl.
London SW7 2DZ, England
Mrs. B.J. Cavilla, Exec.Sec.
PH: 44 171 5818333
FX: 44 171 8239409
Description: Laboratory and clinical cancer research workers.
Conducts and promotes research into the prevention, causes,
treatment, and cure of cancer. **Founded:** 1960. **Membership:**
1300. **Staff:** 1. **Languages:** English. **Publication:** *British Journal of
Cancer* (in English), monthly. Advertising: accepted.

BRITISH ASSOCIATION OF DAY SURGERY
35-43 Lincoln's Inn Fields
London WC2A 3PN, England
David Ralphs, Sec.
PH: 44 171 9730308
FX: 44 171 9730314
Description: Nurses, managers, surgeons and anaesthetists. To
encourage the expansion of day surgery and to promote education, research and high-quality treatment in this field. Organises
seminars, meetings and holds an annual conference. Advice is
provided to Royal Colleges, NHS Executive, regional commissions and trusts including private health organisations. **Founded:**
1990. **Membership:** 1000. **Publication:** *Journal of One Day Surgery* (in English), quarterly. Price: L18.00. Advertising: accepted.

BRITISH ASSOCIATION OF DENTAL NURSES
11 Pharos St.
Fleetwood FY7 6BG, England
Pamela A. Swain, Exec.Sec.
PH: 44 1253 778631
FX: 44 1253 773266
Description: Dental nurses throughout the UK plus associate overseas members. To support, encourage and provide advice
for dental nurses; to develop and maintain nationally recognised
standards and protect the professional status of the dental nurse.
Founded: 1940. **Staff:** 4. **Publication:** *The British Dental Nurses
Journal* (in English), quarterly, always March, June, September,
and December. Price: L35.00/UK and surface overseas; L40.00/
airmail. ISSN: 1356-3807. Advertising: accepted. **Formerly:**
(1994) ABDSA.

BRITISH ASSOCIATION OF DERMATOLOGISTS (BAD)
19 Fitzroy St.
London W1B 5HQ, England
Dr. M.L. Price, Hon. Sec.
PH: 44 171 3830266
FX: 44 171 3885263
Description: Medical professionals united to further the knowledge and teaching of dermatology. Promotes the interests of
members and their patients. Conducts medical and scientific research; disseminates information. **Founded:** 1921. **Membership:**
850. **Staff:** 9. Multinational. **National Groups:** 6. **Languages:**
English. **Publication:** *British Journal of Dermatology* (in English),
monthly.

BRITISH ASSOCIATION OF DOMICILIARY CARE
OFFICERS
2 Saint Catherines Close
Sindlesham
Wokingham, Berks. RG41 5BZ, England
M. Uttley, Contact
PH: 44 1734 790888
Description: Membership is open to managers of home help,
home care, day care, domiciliary care, community meals services
and any other service encompassing care in the community. Aims
to develop good practice and service delivery, to promote nation-
al standards and to facilitate the exchange of information and
ideas with other professionals.. **Membership:** 150. **Publication:**
BADCO Matters, quarterly ■ *Practice & Policy Guidelines &
Codes of Practice*, semiannual.

BRITISH ASSOCIATION OF MEDICAL MANAGERS
e-mail: bamm@premier.co.uk
Kingsway
Cheadle SR8 2NY, England
Dr. Jenny Simpson, Contact
PH: 44 161 4914229
FX: 44 161 4914254
Description: Doctors from all specialties and at all levels of interest in management are invited to apply for membership.
Junior doctors are warmly welcomed and non medical managers
are welcome to apply for associate membership. Concerned with
the promotion of quality healthcare by improving and supporting
the contribution of doctors in management. Unites doctors with
an interest in healthcare management. Members are keen to
learn from, and work with each other to ensure a meaningful and
effective contribution to the management of organisations. **Founded:** 1991. **Membership:** 800. **Staff:** 8. **Publication:** *Clinician in
Management*, bimonthly ■ Newsletter.

BRITISH ASSOCIATION OF ORAL AND MAXILLOFACIAL
SURGEONS
35-43 Lincoln's Inn Fields
London WC2A 3PN, England
Description: Aims to promote the advancement of education and
research into the development of oral and maxillofacial surgery
in the British Isles; to encourage, and assist postgraduate education, study and research in oral and maxillofacial surgery. Arranges regular meetings at which lectures and demonstrations

will be given. **Founded:** 1962. **Membership:** 1200. **Publication:**
British Journal of Oral & Maxillofacial Surgery, bimonthly.

BRITISH ASSOCIATION OF PAEDIATRIC SURGEONS
(BAPS)
e-mail: honsec@baps.org.uk
url: http://baps.org.uk
Nicolson St.
Edinburgh EH8 9DW, Scotland
Mr. D. Burge, Hon.Sec.
PH: 44 131 6683975
FX: 44 131 6671905
Description: Pediatric surgeons, consultants, and trainees.
Works to improve the techniques of study, practice, and research
in pediatric surgery; fosters professional relations among pedia-
tric surgeons. Sponsors training program. **Founded:** 1953. **Mem-
bership:** 700. **Staff:** 1. **Languages:** English. **Publication:** *Journal
of Pediatric Surgery* (in English), periodic.

BRITISH ASSOCIATION OF PHARMACEUTICAL
PHYSICIANS
1 Wimpole St.
London W1M 8AE, England
Elizabeth Borg, Contact
PH: 44 171 4918610
FX: 44 171 4992405
Description: Fully registered medical practitioners practising
pharmaceutical medicine in, or on behalf of, the pharmaceutical
industry or in the statutory regulatory authority. Assists and ad-
vises members in all matters pertaining to the execution of their
professional duties relating to the pharmaceutical industry.
Founded: 1957. **Membership:** 700. **Staff:** 3. **Publication:** *Pharma-
ceutical Physician*, bimonthly.

BRITISH ASSOCIATION OF PHARMACEUTICAL
WHOLESALERS
19a South St.
Farnham, Surrey GU9 7QU, England
J.M. Watts, OBE, Exec.Dir.
PH: 44 1252 711412
FX: 44 1252 726561
Description: Membership open to all full-time pharmaceutical
wholesalers who are able to comply with the Association's Code
of Practice. There is also an Associate Membership category o-
pen to manufacturers and providers of services to the industry.
Representative body for all full-time pharmaceutical wholesalers
in discussion with Department of Health, manufacturers and
other pharmaceutical industry bodies. **Founded:** 1967. **Membership:** 59. **Staff:** 3. **Publication:** *Members Directory* ■ Newsletters.

BRITISH ASSOCIATION OF SPORT AND MEDICINE
e-mail: big.hill@mds.gmw.ac.uk
Medical School of St. Bartholomews Hospital
Charterhouse Sq.
London EC1M 6BQ, England
Barry Hill, Contact
PH: 44 171 2533244
FX: 44 171 2510774
Description: Medical professionals, GPs, hospital doctors,
chartered physiotherapists and sports scientists. Concerned with
the postgraduate education of medical professionals with regard
to sports medicine. **Founded:** 1953. **Membership:** 1400. **Staff:** 2.
Publication: *British Journal of Sport Medicine*, quarterly.

BRITISH DENTAL ASSOCIATION (BDA)
e-mail: enquiries@bda-dentistry.org.uk
url: http://www.bda-dentistry.org.uk
64 Wimpole St.
London W1M 8AL, England
John Hunt, CEO
PH: 44 171 9350875
FX: 44 171 4875232
Description: Professional association and trade union for dental
surgeons in the United Kingdom. Promotes dentristry and the

provision of dental services to the public. Represents members' interests individually and collectively before the government. **Founded:** 1880. **Membership:** 10000. **Staff:** 64. **Local Groups:** 130. **Languages:** English. **Publication:** *BDA News*, monthly. Newsletter. Advertising: accepted ■ *British Dental Journal*, bimonthly.

BRITISH DENTAL HYGIENISTS' ASSOCIATION
13 The Ridge
Yatton
Bristol BS19 4DQ, England
A. Craddock, Contact
PH: 44 1934 876389

BRITISH DENTAL TRADE ASSOCIATION (BDTA)
e-mail: admin@bdta.org.uk
url: http://www.bdta-dentistry.org.uk.
Merritt House
Hill Ave.
Amersham, Bucks. HP6 5BQ, England
Tony Reed, Exec.Dir.
PH: 44 1494 431010
FX: 44 1494 431360
Description: Companies manufacturing dental equipment and supplies. Establishes international standards and technical harmonization for dental equipment. Represents members' interests before government bodies, international agencies, and the public. Maintains liaison with organizations representing dentists, dental technicians, and dental supply dealers and distributors. Compiles statistics. **Founded:** 1923. **Membership:** 105. **Staff:** 5. **Languages:** English. **Publication:** *Dental Trader*, quarterly. Journal. Price: L25.00/year. Circulation: 300. Advertising: accepted.

BRITISH DIABETIC ASSOCIATION
10 Queen Anne St.
London W1M 0BD, England
Michael Cooper, Dir. General
PH: 44 171 3231531
FX: 44 171 6373644
Description: Open to everyone. Life and annual subscription rates. Provides help and advice to everyone living with diabetes and those who care for them. Represents people with diabetes on matters affecting the individual. Supports diabetes research. **Founded:** 1934. **Membership:** 143000. **Staff:** 100. **Regional Groups:** 450. **Publication:** *Balance*, bimonthly. Magazines.

BRITISH EPILEPSY ASSOCIATION
e-mail: epilepsy@bea.org.uk
url: http://www.epilepsy.org.uk
Anstey House
40 Hanover Sq.
Leeds LS3 1BE, England
Lucy Laville, Contact
PH: 44 113 2439393
TF: 0800 309030
FX: 44 113 2428804
Description: Association is owned by its members. Provides care in the community for the country's estimated 420,000 people with epilepsy. Publications on all aspects of epilepsy counselling, advice, information and support and the National Epilepsy Helpline. Around 140 regional groups and branch - regional office in Belfast. National information centre provides extensive service to public and professionals. **Founded:** 1950. **Membership:** 20000. **Staff:** 36. **Regional Groups:** 140. **Publication:** *Epilepsy Today* (in English), quarterly. Magazine. Advertising: not accepted ■ *Seizure* (in English), quarterly. Journal. Advertising: not accepted.

BRITISH FLUORIDATION SOCIETY
e-mail: bfs@liv.ac.uk
url: http://derweb.ac.uk/bfs/index.html
4th Fl., Dental School
University of Liverpool
Liverpool L69 38X, England
Sheila Jones, Info. Officer
PH: 44 151 7065216
FX: 44 151 7065845
Description: Promotes dental health by fluoridation of water supplies. **Founded:** 1969.

BRITISH HEART FOUNDATION (BHF)
14 Fitzhardinge St.
London W1H 4DH, England
Maj.Gen. L.F.H. Busk, CB, Dir.Gen.
PH: 44 171 9350185
FX: 44 171 4865820
Description: Funds research into the causes and prevention diagnosis and treatment of cardiovascular disease. Sponsors postgraduate medical education; distributes fellowships and research funds. Organizes symposia, and workshops for health care and research professionals. Provides cardiac equipment for hospitals and ambulance services. Supports heart patients through rehabilitation programmes, heart support groups and BHF nurses. Conducts fundraising events. Compiles statistics. **Founded:** 1961. **Staff:** 190. **Local Groups:** 430. **Languages:** English. **Publication:** *BHF Heart News* (in English), bimonthly. Newsletter. Magazine for heart patients. Price: L7.00/year. Circulation: 30,000. Advertising: not accepted ■ *Grant Regulations*. Booklet ■ *Medical Reports* (in English), periodic ■ *Newsbeat* (in English), quarterly. Newsletter ■ *Teenage Newsletter* (in English), annual ■ Annual Report (in English) ■ Catalog (in English), annual ■ Pamphlets, periodic ■ Videos, periodic.

BRITISH HOLISTIC MEDICAL ASSOCIATION
Royal Shrewsbury Hospital South
Rowland Thomas House
Mytton Oak Rd.
Shrewsbury SY3 8XF, England
Kathryn Crockford, Contact
PH: 44 1743 261155
FX: 44 1743 353637
Description: Professional corporate/associate membership (for the lay public) nurse/student membership and overseas membership. To educate doctors and other healthcare professionals in the principles and practice of holistic medicine, to encourage research studies and publication of work carried out in the field of holistic medicine and to bring together holistic healthcare practitioners for mutual support and further personal and professional development. **Founded:** 1983. **Membership:** 800. **Staff:** 3. **Publication:** Newsletter, quarterly.

BRITISH HOMEOPATHIC ASSOCIATION
url: http://www.nhsconfed.net/bha
27a Devonshire St.
London W1N 1RJ, England
Enid Segall, Gen.Sec.
PH: 44 171 9352163
Description: The Association is a registered charity supported by a membership of people who, being convinced of the efficacy of the homoeopathic system of medicine, give regular subscriptions or donations for its maintenance. Aims to support, extend and develop homoeopathy. Puts the general public in touch with homoeopathic doctors, veterinary surgeons and pharmacies. Also book publishers, maintaining in print a number of books on various aspects of homoeopathy as well as the magazine. **Founded:** 1902. **Membership:** 5000. **Staff:** 3. **Publication:** *Homoeopathy*, bimonthly ■ Books.

BRITISH INSTITUTE OF RADIOLOGY (BIR)
e-mail: anyone@bir.org.uk
url: http://www.bir.org.uk
36 Portland Pl.
London W1N 4AT, England
Mary-Anne Piggott, CEO
PH: 44 171 5804085
FX: 44 171 2553209
Description: Medical radiologists, scientists, and allied professionals in 55 countries. Conducts seminars; bestows awards. **Founded:** 1897. **Membership:** 2000. **Staff:** 16. Multinational. **Local Groups:** 4. **Languages:** English. **Budget:** L1,000,000. **Publication:** *British Journal of Radiology* (in English), monthly. Multidisciplinary research. Price: L210.00 in the U.K.; L230.00 outside of the U.K. ISSN: 0007-1285. Circulation: 4,000. Advertising: accepted. Also Cited As: *BJR* ▪ *Current Research in Osteoporosis and Bone Mineral Measurement.* Proceedings. Price: L32.00 ▪ *Reccomendations for Brachytherapy Dosimetry.* Report. Price: L10.00 ▪ Membership Directory (in English), periodic ▪ Reports. **Absorbed:** (1927) Rontgen Society. **Formerly:** (1924) British Association for the Advancement of Radiology and Physiotherapy.

BRITISH INSTITUTE OF SURGICAL TECHNOLOGISTS
School of Dentristry, Rm. 888
St. Chads Queensway
Birmingham, Kent B4 6NN, England
Glyn Thomas, Contact
PH: 44 121 2378611
FX: 44 121 2372931
Description: Maintains standards as a professional institute. **Founded:** 1935. **Membership:** 500. **Publication:** *Journal of the British Institute of Surgical Technologists,* annual.

BRITISH MEDICAL ACUPUNCTURE SOCIETY
e-mail: bmasadmin@aol.com
url: http://users.aol.com/acubmas/bumas.html
Newton House
Newton Ln.
Lower Whitley
Warrington WA4 4JA, England
Jean Marcus, Contact
PH: 44 1925 730727
FX: 44 1925 730492
Description: Medically qualified practitioners. Concerned with the training of medical practitioners in acupuncture. Geographic listings of medically qualified practitioners of acupuncture. **Founded:** 1980. **Membership:** 1450. **Staff:** 3. Multinational. **Regional Groups:** 4. **Publication:** *Acupuncture in Medicine* (in English), semiannual. Journal. Price: L10.00. ISSN: 0964-5284. Circulation: 1,900. Advertising: accepted. Alternate Formats: online; magnetic tape.

BRITISH MEDICAL ASSOCIATION (BMA)
url: http://www.bma.org.uk
Tavistock Sq.
London WC1H 9JP, England
Dr. E.M. Armstrong, Sec.
PH: 44 171 3874499
FX: 44 171 3836400
Description: Independent trade union for British physicians. Disseminates scientific information. **Founded:** 1832. **Membership:** 117490. **Staff:** 640. **Regional Groups:** 203. **Languages:** English. **Publication:** *BMA News Review.* Newsletter ▪ *BMJ Specialist Journals* ▪ *British Medical Journal* (in English), weekly. Price: included in membership dues. ISSN: 0959-8138. Circulation: 120,000. Advertising: accepted ▪ *Student BMJ.* Journal.

BRITISH ORTHODONTIC SOCIETY
Grays Inn Rd.
London WC1X 8LD, England
C.J.R. Kettler, Sec.
PH: 44 171 8372193
FX: 44 171 8372193
Description: Persons interested in orthodontics eligible for membership. Members (normally resident in the UK), honorary members, life members, international members, associate members, retired members, laboratory and trades members. Concerned with the promotion of the study and practice of orthodontics. Orthodontics is a speciality of dentistry and involves the treatment of abnormalities of jaw size and dental arch relationship and irregularities of tooth position. **Founded:** 1994. **Membership:** 1600. **Staff:** 1. **Publication:** *BOS Newsletter,* 3/year ▪ *British Journal of Orthodontics,* quarterly.

BRITISH ORTHOPTIC SOCIETY
Tavistock House North
Tavistock Sq.
London WC1H 9HX, England
Joanna Brown, Contact
PH: 44 171 3877992
FX: 44 171 3832584
Description: Orthoptists, including students and retired orthoptists. Members work in both NHS and private practice. **Founded:** 1937. **Membership:** 1200. **Publication:** *British Orthoptic Journal,* annual. Price: price on request. Advertising: accepted.

BRITISH RETINITIS PIGMENTOSA SOCIETY
PO Box 350
Buckingham, Bucks. MK18 5EL, England
Mrs. M.L. Cantor, Contact
PH: 44 12806 363
FX: 44 12806 515
Description: RP sufferers and their families and interested multi disciplinary members. Aims to help RP sufferers and their families cope with living with RP and to raise money for medical research. **Founded:** 1976. **Membership:** 3000. **Staff:** 1. **Publication:** Handbook, annual ▪ Newsletter, quarterly.

BRITISH SOCIETY FOR CLINICAL NEUROPHYSIOLOGY
Dundee Royal Infirmary
EEG Department
Barrau Rd.
Dundee, Scotland
Dr. Alan Forster, Contact
PH: 44 382 660111
Description: Medical practitioners, scientists and technologists. Medical and scientific study of electrical activity which can be recorded from the nervous system. **Founded:** 1942. **Membership:** 350. **Publication:** Papers. **Formerly:** (1992) EEG Society.

BRITISH SOCIETY FOR DERMATOPATHOLOGY (BSD)
e-mail: admin@bod.org.uk
British Assn. of Dermatologists
19 Fitzroy Sq.
London W1P 5HQ, England
PH: 44 171 3830266
FX: 44 171 3885263
Description: Doctors and residents specializing in dermatopathology. Conducts research; disseminates information. **Founded:** 1976. **Membership:** 200. **Languages:** English.

BRITISH SOCIETY FOR IMMUNOLOGY
e-mail: bsi@immunology.org
url: http://www.immunology.org
Triangle House
Broomhill Rd.
London SW18 4HX, England
Kevin Horlock, Contact
PH: 44 181 8752400
FX: 44 181 8752424
Description: Immunologists. To advance the science of immunology for the benefit of the public. **Founded:** 1956. **Membership:** 4200. **Staff:** 10. Multinational. **Regional Groups:** 18. **Publication:** *Clinical & Experimental Immunology,* monthly. Journal. Advertising: accepted ▪ *Immunology,* monthly. Journal ▪ *Immunology News,* bimonthly. Newsletter.

BRITISH SOCIETY OF PERIODONTOLOGY
44 Pool Rd.
Hook, Hants. RG27 8RD, England
Mrs. A. Hallowes, Contact
PH: 44 1252 843598
FX: 44 1252 844018
Description: Members are dental surgeons. To promote for the benefit of the public the art and science of dentistry and in particular the art and science of periodontology. **Founded:** 1949. **Membership:** 675. **Publication:** *Journal of Clinical Periodontology*, monthly.

BRITISH SOCIETY FOR RHEUMATOLOGY
e-mail: bsr@rheumatology.org.uk
url: http://www.oup.co.uk/guest/bsr
41 Eagle St.
London WC1R 4AR, England
Ms. Anne Mansfield, Gen.Sec.
PH: 44 171 2423313
FX: 44 171 2423277
Description: Hospital doctors, non-clinical scientists, general practitioners, other professions allied to medicine (eg nursing; physiotherapy). For the treatment and prevention of rheumatic diseases, education and research. **Founded:** 1983. **Membership:** 1400. **Staff:** 5. **Publication:** *British Journal of Rheumatology*, monthly.

BRITISH SOCIETY FOR THE STUDY OF PROSTHETIC DENTISTRY
e-mail: mchan@ulth.northy.nhs.uk
Clarendon Way
Leeds, W. Yorkshire LS2 9LU, England
Mr. Martin Chan, Contact
PH: 44 113 2336277
Description: Ordinary and Honorary Members. Ordinary membership shall be available to those dentists, doctors or scientists who profess an interest in prosthetic dentistry and shall be by election. Established to advance education in prosthetic dentistry for the benefit of the public. **Founded:** 1953. **Membership:** 390. Multinational. **Publication:** *BSSPD Proceedings*, annual.

BRITISH VACUUM COUNCIL
76 Portland Pl.
London W1N 3DH, England
Susan Lippmann, Contact
PH: 44 171 4704800
FX: 44 171 4704848
Description: Two representatives from each of the 3 bodies affiliated to the Council which are: The Institute of Physics, The Institution of Electrical Engineers and the Faraday Division of The Royal Society of Chemistry. To promote and advance the understanding and teaching of vacuum science, technology and its applications by co-ordinating and promoting conferences, seminars and courses and publications in these fields; encouraging excellence amongst postgraduate students and other young research workers in these fields. **Founded:** 1969. **Staff:** 1.

BROOKS ADVISORY CENTRES
e-mail: brookcentres@compuserve.com.uk
165 Gray's Inn Rd.
London WCIX 8UD, England
PH: 44 71 7139000
FX: 44 71 833
Description: Seeks to decrease the incidence of unwanted pregnancy among young women. Conducts educational programs in matters of sex, contraception, and reproductive and social responsibility. **Founded:** 1964. **Languages:** English.

BROTHER TO BROTHER INTERNATIONAL (BBI)
e-mail: mveitenh@worldvision.org
url: http://www.bbi.org
PO Box 27634
Tempe, AZ 85285-7634
Mike Veitenhans, Program Mgr.

PH: (602)345-9200
FX: (602)345-2747
Description: Works to procure excess inventory, such as pharmaceuticals, medical supplies, personal care products, clothing, educational material, seed and food, from corporations throughout the United States. Donated excess inventory or technical information is then provided to national and international non-profits across the United States and around the world. Provides a network for U.S. charities during domestic and international emergencies. **Founded:** 1982. **Staff:** 9. Multinational. **Languages:** English. **Publication:** *For the Children*. Annual Report. Advertising: not accepted.

BULGARIA SOCIETY OF OPHTALMOLOGY
c/o Eye Clinic, Fifth City Clinical Hospital
Stolebov 67 - A
1233 Sofia, Bulgaria
Tsvetan Markov, Pres.
PH: 359 2 312117
FX: 359 2 325171
Description: Fosters research in fundamental ophtalmic studies. **Founded:** 1927.

BULGARIAN ANATOMICAL SOCIETY
e-mail: dolapchi@medfac.acad.bg
Katedra po Anatomia
Sv.G.Sofiiski 1
BG-1431 Sofia, Bulgaria
Vasil Vasilev, Pres.
PH: 359 2 518623
FX: 359 2 594094
Description: Fosters research in histochemistry and elctronic microscopy. **Founded:** 1962. **Membership:** 100. **Budget:** 500,000 Lv.

BULGARIAN DERMATOLOGICAL SOCIETY (BDS)
(Balgarsko Dermatologichno Drujestvo)
Georgi Sofiisky St. 1
BG-1431 Sofia, Bulgaria
Dr. Nikolai Tsankov, M.D., Pres.
PH: 359 2 517342
FX: 359 2 5212754
Description: Dermatologists and individuals interested in furthering the development of dermatology in Bulgaria. Coordinates efforts in combatting the spread of skin and venereal diseases. Furthers post-graduate education. Conducts educational and research programs. **Founded:** 1923. **Membership:** 400. **Staff:** 8. **Local Groups:** 7. **Languages:** Bulgarian, English. **Publication:** *Dermatologia i Venerologia Bulgaran* (in Bulgarian), quarterly. Journal. Price: 25.00 Lv. ISSN: 0417-0792. Circulation: 1,000. Advertising: accepted ∎ Books ∎ Monographs.

BULGARIAN FAMILY PLANNING ASSOCIATION (BFPA)
e-mail: bfpa@online.bg
67 Dondukov St.
BG-1504 Sofia, Bulgaria
Prof. Todor Chernev, Pres.
PH: 359 2 9433710
FX: 359 2 9433710
Description: Health care professionals and other individuals with an interest in reproductive health and population control. Promotes availability of reproductive health and family planning services. Provides counseling and family planning services; makes available sexually transmitted disease and AIDS prevention programs. **Founded:** 1992. **Membership:** 350. **Staff:** 7. **Regional Groups:** 10. **Languages:** Bulgarian, English. **Publication:** *Family Planning* (in Bulgarian), quarterly. Newsletter. Price: free. Circulation: 1,000. Advertising: not accepted ∎ Brochures.

BULGARIAN PSYCHOLOGICAL ASSOCIATION
Liulin Planina 14
BG-1606 Sofia, Bulgaria
Dontcho Gradev, PhD, Pres.
PH: 359 2 541295

Description: Supports scientific work in the field of psychology. **Founded:** 1969. **Membership:** 720. **Languages:** English. **Budget:** 500,000 Lv. **Publication:** *Balgarsko Spisanie po Psihologia* (in Bulgarian and English), quarterly. Journal. Price: 400.00 Lv. ISSN: 0861-7831. Advertising: not accepted.

BULGARIAN SOCIETY OF HISTORY OF MEDICINE
Katedra po Sotsialna Meditsina
Bialo more 8
BG-1504 Sofia, Bulgaria
Miladin Apostolov, Pres.
PH: 359 2 4344532
FX: 359 2 442388
Description: Stimulates interest in the history of medicine and of folk medicine. **Founded:** 1957. **Membership:** 210. **National Groups:** 1. **Languages:** English, French. **Publication:** *Asklepios*, annual. Magazine. ISSN: 1310-0637. Advertising: accepted. **Formerly:** (1997) Scientific Society of History of Medicine.

BULGARIAN SOCIETY OF MEDICAL GEOGRAPHY
Tsentar po Hygiene
D.Nestorov 95
BG-1431 Sofia, Bulgaria
Prof. Iordan Naumov, M.D., Pres.
PH: 359 2 5812541
FX: 359 2 9581277
Description: Fosters teaching and research in medical geography. **Founded:** 1970. **Membership:** 100. **Staff:** 15. **Regional Groups:** 2. **Languages:** Bulgarian, English. **Publication:** Journal (in Bulgarian), bimonthly. Price: 3,000.00 Lv. ISSN: 0018-8247. Advertising: accepted.

BULGARIAN SOCIETY OF PHYSIOLOGICAL SCIENCES
e-mail: bps@iph.bio.acad.bg
Institute of Physiology
Akad. G. Bonchev Blok 23
BG-1113 Sofia, Bulgaria
Prof. Angel Vassilev, Pres.
PH: 359 2 7133770
FX: 359 2 719109
Description: Fosters research in labour physiology, chronobiology, pathophysiology, and general physiology. **Founded:** 1954. **Membership:** 110. **Regional Groups:** 6. **Languages:** English.

BULGARIAN SOCIETY OF SPORT MEDICINE AND KINESTHERAPY
Gurguliat 1
BG-1000 Sofia, Bulgaria
Slavcho Savov, Pres.
PH: 359 2 894145
Description: Fosters research in sport medicine and kinestherapy. **Founded:** 1953. **Membership:** 300. **Staff:** 200. **State Groups:** 1. **Publication:** *Vaprosi na Fizicheskata Kultura* (in Bulgarian), quarterly. Journal. Features information on sports and nauka. ISSN: 1340-3393.

BULGARIAN STOMATOLOGICAL UNION
Veliko Tarnovo 9
BG-4000 Plovdiv, Bulgaria
Krasimir Kumanov, Pres.
Description: Represents the interests of dentists. **Founded:** 1992.

BURGER KING CANCER CARING CENTER
url: http://www.trfn.clpgh.org/cancercaring
4117 Liberty Ave.
Pittsburgh, PA 15224
Rebecca Whitlinger, Exec.Dir.
PH: (412)622-1212
FX: (412)622-1216
Description: Cancer patients, professionals, and interested individuals. Helps patients cope with the psychological impact of cancer. Emphasizes the importance of the patient's attitude and emotions in the recovery process. Offers consulting services to help establish and maintain innovative programs such as selfhelp groups, and patient/professional communication systems. Increases public awareness through television and radio appearances, and newspaper and magazine articles. Conducts lecture and workshop. Offers support groups including groups for children who have a family member with cancer. **Founded:** 1981. **Membership:** 7000. **Staff:** 5. **Languages:** English. **Budget:** $250,000. **Publication:** *Live Well with Cancer*, monthly. Newsletter. Provides emotional support and resource information for cancer patients, family members, and the professional community; includes book reviews. Price: free. Circulation: 10,000. Advertising: accepted. **Absorbed:** (1993) Cancer Guidance Hotline. **Formerly:** (1982) Lifeline Institute.

C/SEC
22 Forest Rd.
Framingham, MA 01701
Norma Shulman, Dir.
PH: (508)877-8266
Description: Childbirth groups, doctors, laypersons, and nurses. Established out of concern for the lack of resources available to couples who anticipate or have had a cesarean delivery. Goals are to: improve the cesarean childbirth experience and make the cesarean delivery a good and meaningful childbirth experience for each couple; provide information and promote education on cesarean prevention and vaginal birth after cesarean; change attitudes and policies that affect the cesarean childbirth experience. Offers support for cesarean couples through informal discussion meetings, telephone contact, and personal reply to letters. Provides information on many aspects of cesarean childbirth in order to make couples aware of exactly what the procedure entails and what options are available. Works with doctors, hospitals, childbirth educators, and others in the medical community to effect policy changes and to promote family-centered maternity care for cesarean couples. Conducts in-service programs for hospital staffs and has spoken at conventions and workshops on childbirth. Acronym C/SEC stands for Cesareans/Support, Education and Concern. **Founded:** 1972. **Membership:** 2000. **Languages:** English. Formerly (1976) C/SEC (Cesarean Sections: Education and Concern).

CAJAL CLUB (CC)
University of Colorado Health Sciences Center
Department of Cellular & Structural Biology, B-111
4200 E. 9th Ave.
Denver, CO 80262
Dr. David Whitlock, Apical Dendrite
PH: (303)315-4129
FX: (303)315-4729
Description: Neuroanatomists who meet for discussion and the presentation of papers on prospective research, technique, and history of neurology. (Club is named after Sr. Don Santiago Ramon y Cajal, a founder of and Nobel laureate for the science of neuroanatomy.) **Founded:** 1947. **Membership:** 450. **Languages:** English. **Publication:** *History of Cajal Club*, quinquennial ▪ Proceedings, periodic.

CAMEROON NATIONAL ASSOCIATION FOR FAMILY WELFARE (CAMNAFAW)
BP 11994
Yaounde, Cameroon
Mrs. Grace F. Walla, Exec.Dir.
PH: 237 237984
FX: 237 237984
Description: Encourages public awareness of family planning and responsible parenthood through youth programs in Cameroon. Works to reduce the number of unwanted pregnancies and abortions. Advocates family planning as a basic human right. Sponsors programs in sex education, family planning, and health. Provides contraceptive services. **Founded:** 1987. **Membership:** 220. **Staff:** 16. **Languages:** English, French. **Budget:** $310,000. **Publication:** *CAMNAFAW - The Road so Far* (in English and French), periodic. Brochure. Containing information on youth and planning issues ▪ *Youth and Sexuality* (in English and French). Book-

let. Price: 100.00 Fr CFA ▪ *Youth Prepare for Responsible Parenthood* (in English and French). Booklet. Price: 100.00 Fr CFA.

CANADIAN ACADEMY OF CHILD PSYCHIATRY (CACP)
596 Davis Dr.
Newmarket, ON, Canada L3Y 2T9
Jennifer Steadman, Sec.-Treas.
PH: (905)859-4420
FX: (905)830-5972
Description: Child psychiatrists and other individuals with an interest in the psychiatric treatment of children. Seeks to advance the study and practice of child psychiatry. Conducts research and continuing professional development programs; facilitates exchange of information among members. Languages: English, French.

CANADIAN ACADEMY OF DENTURISM (CAD)
2 Athabascan Ave., Ste. 201
Sherwood Park, AB, Canada T8A 4E3
John G. Ashton, Registrar
PH: (403)467-5541
FX: (403)467-9263
Description: Dentists and related health professionals. Promotes advancement in the study and practice of denturism. Conducts continuing professional education programs. Sponsors research. Membership: 90. Languages: English, French. Publication: *Academy Report*, annual. Journal. Circulation: 2,000.

CANADIAN ACADEMY OF ENDODONTICS (CAE)
(Academie Canadienne d'Endodontie)
url: http://www.jimcarroll.forbin.com/images/bpig.ipg
11215 Jasper Ave., Ste. 365
Edmonton, AB, Canada T5K 0L5
Dr. Carl Hawrish, Exec.Sec.
PH: (403)482-3636
FX: (403)451-3535
Description: Member dentists of the Canadian Dental Association or other Canadian national dental associations who have been graduated for at least 3 years or have earned recognition by graduate or postgraduate training, teaching, or research. Works to maintain and improve public health through the advancement of endodontics. Sponsors competitions and bestows awards; maintains speakers' bureau; compiles statistics. Founded: 1965. Membership: 200. Languages: English, French. Budget: C$25,000. Publication: *Roster* (in English), annual ▪ Newsletter (in English), 2-3/year. Price: free to members. Circulation: 200. Advertising: accepted.

CANADIAN ACADEMY OF ORAL RADIOLOGY (CAOR)
(Academie Canadienne de Radiologie Buccale)
Faculty of Dentistry
University of Toronto
Toronto, ON, Canada M5G 1G6
Grace Petrikowski, Sec.-Treas.
PH: (416)979-4900
Description: Oral radiologists. Seeks to advance the study, teaching, and practice of oral radiology. Conducts researchs; makes available continuing professional education courses. Languages: English, French.

CANADIAN ACADEMY OF PERIODONTOLOGY (CAP)
1815 Alta Vista Dr., Unit 103
Ottawa, ON, Canada K1G 3Y6
Description: Periodontologists, educators, and students. Promotes advancement in the practice and teaching of periodontology. Conducts continuing professional education courses for members. Maintains speakers' bureau. Membership: 300. Languages: English, French. Publication: *CAPsule*, 3/year. Newsletter. Advertising: accepted ▪ Directory, annual. Advertising: accepted.

CANADIAN ACADEMY OF SPORT MEDICINE (CASM)
e-mail: jburke@casm-acms.org
url: http://www.casm-acms.org
1600 James Naismith Dr., Ste. 506
Gloucester, ON, Canada K1B 5N4
Jacqueline Burke, Contact
PH: (613)748-5851
FX: (613)748-5792
Description: Health care professionals with an interest in sports medicine. Promotes development and application of improved sports medical techniques; facilitates professional advancement of members. Serves as a clearinghouse on sports medicine; conducts educational programs; participates in charitable activities. Founded: 1970. Membership: 500. Staff: 1. Languages: English, French. Publication: *Clinical Journal of Sport Medicine*, periodic. Advertising: accepted.

CANADIAN ADULT CONGENTIAL HEART NETWORK
e-mail: bbandc@enterprise.ca
url: http://www.cachnet.org
191 The West Mall, Ste. 1105
Etobicoke, ON, Canada M9C 5K8
Dr. Gary Webb, Pres.
PH: (416)620-5391
FX: (416)620-5392
Description: Represents the interests of Canadian adults who were born with heart defects. Encourages efforts to educate the public on the problems and treatment of heart disease. Works as a support network for congenital heart patients. Founded: 1992. Membership: 86. Regional Groups: 15. Languages: English, French. Budget: C$30,000. Publication: *CACH News* (in English), quarterly. Newsletter. Circulation: 130. Advertising: not accepted. Also Known As: CACH Network.

CANADIAN ANAESTHETISTS' SOCIETY (CAS)
(Societe Canadienne des Anesthesistes)
e-mail: cas@multinet.net
url: http://www.cas.ca
1 Eglinton Ave. E., Ste. 208
Toronto, ON, Canada M4P 3A1
Ann Andrews, Exec.Dir.
PH: (416)480-0602
FX: (416)480-0320
Description: Professional anaesthetists and students. Promotes the art and science of anesthesia in Canada. Advocates measures designed to improve health care in Canada and hospital standards regarding anesthesia. Works in conjunction with the Canadian Medical Association. Conducts discussion sessions, panels, refresher courses, and workshops. Maintains C.A.S. International Education Fund for aid to developing countries. Founded: 1920. Membership: 2250. Staff: 6. Local Groups: 10. Languages: English, French. Budget: C$1,100,000. Publication: *Canadian Journal of Anaesthesia* (in English and French), monthly. Price: C$156.00/individual; C$204.00/institution. ISSN: 0832-610X. Circulation: 5,000. Advertising: accepted ▪ *CAS Members' Guide* (in English and French), annual. Directory ▪ *CAS-SCA Newsletter* (in English and French), quarterly ▪ *CJA Annual Meeting Supplement* (in English and French). Report. Formerly: (1924) Canadian Society of Anaesthetists; (1943) Anaesthesia Section of the Canadian Medical Association.

CANADIAN ASSOCIATION FOR ANATOMY, NEUROBIOLOGY AND CELL BIOLOGY (CAANCB)
url: http://www.usak.ca/anatomy
Dept. of Anatomy and Cell Biology
Univ. of Saskatchewan
Saskatoon, SK, Canada S7N 5E5
Dr. Ban Rosser, Sec.
PH: (306)966-4075
FX: (306)966-4298
Description: Represents members' interests. Founded: 1957. Membership: 125. Publication: Bulletin (in English), annual. Price: included in membership dues. Advertising: accepted.

CANADIAN ASSOCIATION OF BLUE CROSS PLANS (CABCP)
185 The West Mall, Ste. 600
Etobicoke, ON, Canada M9C 5P1
Gerald M. Devlin, Pres.
PH: (416)626-1688
FX: (416)444-2000
Description: Blue Cross health plans. Seeks to advance the health insurance industry. Facilitates communication and cooperation among members; serves as a clearinghouse on health insurance. **Languages:** English, French.

CANADIAN ASSOCIATION OF BURN NURSES (CABN)
425 Cosburn Ave.
Toronto, ON, Canada M4J 2N2
Kathy Popovske, Pres.
PH: (416)926-7021
FX: (416)926-5064
Description: Nurses specializing in the treatment of burns. Promotes professional advancement of members. Facilitates exchange of information among members; conducts continuing professional education programs. **Languages:** English, French.

CANADIAN ASSOCIATION OF CARDIO-PULMONARY TECHNOLOGISTS (CACPT)
PO Box 848, Sta. A
Toronto, ON, Canada M5W 1G3
John Fedirko, Pres.
PH: (416)243-3600
FX: (416)243-3631
Description: Medical technologists specializing in cardio-pulmonary practice. Promotes professional advancement of members. Supports cardio-pulmonary research; conducts continuing professional education programs. **Languages:** English, French.

CANADIAN ASSOCIATION FOR CHILD NEUROLOGY (CACN)
(Association Canadienne de Neurologie Pediatrique)
906 12th St. SW, Ste. 810
Calgary, AB, Canada T2R 1K7
William J. Logan, Pres.
PH: (403)219-9575
Description: Neurologists with an interest in neurological disorders in children. Seeks to advance the practice of child neurology; promotes professional development of members. Serves as a clearinghouse on child neurology; conducts continuing professional education courses; provides support and assistance to research projects. **Languages:** English, French.

CANADIAN ASSOCIATION FOR CLINICAL MICROBIOLOGISTS AND INFECTIOUS DISEASES (CACMID)
(Association Canadienne de Microbiologie Clinique et des Maladies)
RR 1
Sutton West, ON, Canada L0E 1R0
A. V. Seefried, Sec.
PH: (905)722-5648
Description: Microbiologists and other scientists and medical professionals engaged in the clinical study of infectious diseases. Seeks to advance the biological and medical sciences; promotes professional development of members. Serves as a clearinghouse on the clinical study of infectious diseases; facilitates exchange of information among members; conducts research and educational programs. **Languages:** English, French.

CANADIAN ASSOCIATION FOR COMMUNITY CARE (CACC)
(Association Canadienne de Soins et Services Communautaires)
e-mail: cacc@trytel.com
url: http://www.csc-efc.ca/cacc
701-45 Rideau St.
Ottawa, ON, Canada K1N 5W8
Dr. Taylor Alexander, Pres.
PH: (613)241-7510
FX: (613)241-5923
Description: Home health care services and long-term care facilities. Promotes development of a "range of high-quality, flexible, responsive and accessible community care services" in Canada. Serves as a clearinghouse on community care services; conducts public advocacy on behalf of members, consumers, and researchers; develops standards of practice and facilities in community care; serves as liaison between members and government, consumers, and related organizations. **Founded:** 1980. **Membership:** 300. **Staff:** 7. **Languages:** English, French. **Formerly:** HomeSupport Canada; Canadian Long Term Care Association.

CANADIAN ASSOCIATION OF CRITICAL CARE NURSES (CACCN)
e-mail: accn@execulink.com
url: http://www.execulink.com/~accn
PO Box 22006
London, ON, Canada N6C 5Y3
Gwyne McDonald, Pres.
PH: (519)649-5284
FX: (519)668-2499
Description: Critical care nurses. Promotes professional advancement of members and improvement in the practice of critical care nursing. Conducts continuing professional education programs for members. **Founded:** 1985. **Membership:** 1050. **Staff:** 1. **Languages:** English, French. **Publication:** *Official Journal of the CACCN*, quarterly. ISSN: 1201-2580. Circulation: 1,100. Advertising: accepted ▪ *Standards for Critical Care Nursing Practice (2nd Edition)* ▪ *Study Guide for Critical Care Nursing Certification Examination*.

CANADIAN ASSOCIATION FOR DENTAL RESEARCH (CADR)
(Association Canadienne de Recherches Dentaires)
e-mail: edyen@umixg.ubc.ca
Faculty of Dentistry
University of British Columbia
Vancouver, BC, Canada V6T 1Z3
Edwin Yen, Pres.
PH: (604)822-5773
FX: (604)822-4532
Description: Dentists, dental schools, and dental research facilities. Seeks to advance the practice of dentistry. Sponsors dental research projects; conducts continuing professional education courses. **Languages:** English, French.

CANADIAN ASSOCIATION OF ELECTRONEUROPHYSIOLOGY TECHNOLOGISTS
(Association Canadienne des Technologues en Electroneurophysiologie)
Eastern Ontario Children's Hospital
410 Smyth Rd.
Ottawa, ON, Canada K1H 8L1
Patricia Tremaine, Pres.
PH: (613)737-2315
FX: (613)738-3218
Description: Medical technologists specializing in electroneurophysiology. Promotes professional advancement of members; works to advance the practice of electroneurophysiology. Represents members' interests; conducts continuing professional development courses. **Languages:** English, French.

CANADIAN ASSOCIATION OF EMERGENCY PHYSICIANS
(Association Canadienne des Medecins d'Urgence)
1785 Alta Vista Dr., Ste. 104
Ottawa, ON, Canada K1G 3Y6
Julie Smith, Sec.
PH: (613)523-3343
FX: (613)523-0190
Description: Emergency physicians. Promotes professional advancement of members; seeks to improve the availability and quality of emergency medical services. Facilitates exchange of information among members; conducts continuing professional development courses. **Languages:** English, French.

CANADIAN ASSOCIATION OF GENERAL SURGEONS
(CAGS)
Health Sciences Center
300 Prince Phillip Dr.
St. John's, NF, Canada A1B 3V6
Roger Keith, Sec.
PH: (902)737-6558
Description: General surgeons. Promotes professional development of members; seeks to advance the practice of general surgery. Represents members' collective interests; conducts continuing professional education courses. **Languages:** English, French.

**CANADIAN ASSOCIATION OF HEALTH CARE
AUXILIARIES**
(Association des Auxiliares Benevoles des Establissements de
Sante du Canada)
17 York St., Ste. 100
Ottawa, ON, Canada K1N 9J6
PH: (613)238-8005
FX: (613)238-6924
Description: Organizations providing support and assistance to health care facilities. Promotes increased availability of health services. Facilitates exchange of information among members; serves as a clearinghouse on health care services. **Languages:** English, French.

CANADIAN ASSOCIATION OF INTERNS AND RESIDENTS
(CAIR)
e-mail: cair@infoshare.ca
151 Slater St., Ste. 412
Ottawa, ON, Canada K1P 5H3
Marielle Bouillon, Office Mgr.
PH: (613)234-6448
FX: (613)234-5292
Description: Medical residents, interns, and other physicians-intraining. Promotes professional advancement of members. Represents members' interests before medical organizations, government agencies, and the public in matters including medical education, licensure, certification, and entry into practice. **Founded:** 1973. **Membership:** 4700. **Staff:** 2. **Languages:** English, French. **Budget:** C$500,000. **Publication:** Newsletter, periodic.

CANADIAN ASSOCIATION OF MEDICAL BIOCHEMISTS
(CAMB)
(L'Association des Biochimistes Medical du Canada)
Department of Pathology
Royal University Hospital
Saskatoon, SK, Canada S7N 0W0
Jay Kayla, Pres.
PH: (306)655-2251
FX: (306)655-2223
Description: Medical biochemists. Promotes professional development of members; seeks to advance the science of medical biochemistry. Represents members' interests; conducts continuing professional education courses. **Languages:** English, French.

CANADIAN ASSOCIATION OF MEDICAL CLINICS (CAMC)
(Association Canadienne des Cliniques Medicales)
500 Parliament St.
Toronto, ON, Canada M4X 1P4
Deryck O. Evelyn, Exec.Dir.

PH: (416)966-3641
Description: Medical clinics. Promotes growth and development of the health care industry; seeks to improve the delivery of health care services. Represents members' interests; facilitates communication and cooperation among members. **Languages:** English, French.

**CANADIAN ASSOCIATION OF MEDICAL
MICROBIOLOGISTS (CAMM)**
(Association Canadienne des Medecins Microbiologistes)
711 Concession St.
Hamilton, ON, Canada L8V 1C3
W. David Colby, Pres.
PH: (905)527-4322
FX: (905)575-2581
Description: Medical microbiologists. Seeks to advance the science of medical microbiology; promotes professional advancement of members. Facilitates communication and cooperation among members; conducts research and educational programs. **Languages:** English, French.

**CANADIAN ASSOCIATION OF MEDICAL RADIATION
TECHNOLOGISTS (CAMRT)**
(Association Canadienne des Technologues en Radiation
Medicale)
url: http://www.camrt.com
294 Albert St., Ste. 601
Ottawa, ON, Canada K1P 6E6
Richard Lauzon, Ph.D., Exec.Dir.
PH: (613)234-0012
FX: (613)234-1097
Description: Certifies medical radiation technologists in the fields of radiography, radiation therapy, and nuclear medicine. Provides standards in the training and certification of members; promotes and maintains code of ethics. Participates in the accreditation of medical radiation technologist training programs; organizes continuing education programs. Advises private and governmental organizations involved in the fields of health and education. Provides placement assistance, professional liability insurance and numerous other member benefits. **Founded:** 1942. **Membership:** 10100. **Staff:** 15. **Languages:** English, French. **Publication:** *CAMRT News* (in English and French), 5/year. Newsletter. Contains activity information and education programmes. Price: Available to members only. Circulation: 10,000. Advertising: accepted ▪ *Canadian Journal of Medical Radiation Technology* (in English and French), quarterly. Price: included in membership dues. Circulation: 10,000. Advertising: accepted.

CANADIAN ASSOCIATION OF NEUROPATHOLOGISTS
(CAN)
(Association Canadienne de Neuropathologistes)
e-mail: davidr@ihsc.on.ca
London Health Sciences Centre
Victoria Campus
375 South St.
London, ON, Canada N5Y 2T1
David Ramsey, Sec.-Treas.
PH: (519)667-6758
FX: (519)667-6749
Description: Neuropathologists and other health care professionals with an interest in the field. Promotes professional development of members; seeks to advance the practice of neuropathology. Facilitates exchange of information among members; conducts continuing professional education programs. **Languages:** English, French.

CANADIAN ASSOCIATION OF NEUROSCIENCE NURSES
(CANN)
(Association Canadienne des Infirmieres en Sciences
Neurologiques)
83 Mountfield Crescent
Saint John, NB, Canada E2M 5R4
Janice Kenney, Pres.

PH: (506)648-6446
FX: (506)648-6060
Description: Neuroscience nurses. Seeks to advance the practice of neuroscience nursing; promotes professional development of members. Facilitates exchange of information among members; conducts continuing professional development courses. **Languages:** English, French.

CANADIAN ASSOCIATION OF NURSE ADMINISTRATORS (CANN)
PO Box 3272
Prince Albert, ON, Canada L9L 1C3
Dr. Bonnie Lynn Wright, Pres.
PH: (905)985-1918
Description: Professional nurse administrators. Promotes professional advancement of members; seeks to improve the practice of administrative nursing. Facilitates exchange of information among members; conducts continuing professional development programs. **Languages:** English, French.

CANADIAN ASSOCIATION OF NURSES IN AIDS CARE
(Association Canadienne des Infirmieres et Infirmiers en Sidologie)
1331 Nelson St., Apt. 6
Vancouver, BC, Canada V6E 1J8
Andrew Johnson, Pres.
PH: (604)669-1030
FX: (604)669-5975
Description: Nurses engaged in the care of people with AIDS and HIVSeeks to improve the quality of life of people with AIDS and HIV, and to advance the prevention and treatment of autoimmune diseases. Provides support and services to people with AIDS and HIV; makes available continuing professional development programs. **Languages:** English, French.

CANADIAN ASSOCIATION OF NURSES IN INDEPENDENT PRACTICE (CANIP)
3240 66th Ave. SW, Ste. 117
Calgary, AB, Canada T3E 6M5
Betty Gourlay, Pres.
PH: (403)246-2368
Description: Registered nurses in independent practice. Promotes improved public access to health care; seeks to increase the role of nurses in the delivery of health care services. Develops business and practice guidelines for members. Provides support and assistance to members; conducts educational programs to raise public awareness of nursing and other health care services; sponsors business and continuing professional development courses for members. Conducts lobbying activities; undertakes research projects; compiles statistics. **Founded:** 1985. **Membership:** 250. **Languages:** English, French. **Publication:** *Visions*, quarterly. Newsletter. Circulation: 500 ■ Brochure ■ Directory, periodic.

CANADIAN ASSOCIATION OF NURSES IN ONCOLOGY (CANO)
(Association Canadienne des Infirmieres en Oncologie)
370 King St. W, Ste. 304
Box 1
Toronto, ON, Canada M5V 1J9
Doris Howell, Pres.
PH: (416)596-6565
FX: (416)596-1808
Description: Nurses specializing in oncology. Seeks to advance the professional of oncological nursing. Conducts continuing professional development programs. **Languages:** English, French.

CANADIAN ASSOCIATION OF ORTHODONTISTS (CAO)
(Association Canadienne des Orthodontistes)
2175 Sheppard Ave. E, Ste. 310
Willowdale, ON, Canada M2J 1W8
Diane Gaunt, Admin.

PH: (416)491-3186
FX: (416)491-1670
Description: Orthodontists. Promotes excellence in the practice of orthodonture. Conducts continuing professional development courses for members. **Languages:** English, French.

CANADIAN ASSOCIATION OF PAEDIATRIC SURGEONS (CAPS)
(Association Canadienne de la Chirurgie Pediatrique)
e-mail: secretary@caps.ca
3175 Ste. Catherine Rd.
Montreal, PQ, Canada H3T 1C5
Salem Yazbeck, Sec.-Treas.
PH: (514)345-4688
FX: (514)345-4964
Description: Pediatric surgeons and other health care professionals with an interest in the field. Seeks to advance the practice of pediatric surgery; promotes professional development of members. Facilitates communication and cooperation among members; makes available continuing professional education courses. **Languages:** English, French.

CANADIAN ASSOCIATION OF PATHOLOGISTS (CAP)
(Association Canadienne des Pathologistes)
Royal Alexandria Hospital
10240 Kingsway
Edmonton, AB, Canada T5H 3V9
Joan Sweet, Sec.-Treas.
PH: (403)477-4366
FX: (403)477-4715
Description: Pathologists and other health care professionals with an interest in pathology. Promotes professional development of members; seeks to advance the study and practice of pathology. Facilitates communication and cooperation among members; conducts continuing professional education programs. **Languages:** English, French.

CANADIAN ASSOCIATION OF PEDIATRIC NURSES (CAPN)
College of Nursing
University of Saskatchewan
Saskatoon, SK, Canada S7N 3J7
Susan Fowler-Kerry, Pres.
PH: (306)966-9241
FX: (306)966-6703
Description: Nurses specializing in pediatrics. Promotes professional development of members; seeks to advance the practice of pediatric nursing. Encourages exchange of information among members; makes available continuing professional education courses. **Languages:** English, French.

CANADIAN ASSOCIATION OF PEDIATRIC SURGEONS (CAPS)
e-mail: SECRETARY@CAPS.CA
url: http://www.acs.ucalgary.ca/~postuma/capshome.html
Hopital Ste. Justine
3175 Cote Ste. Catherine
Montreal, PQ, Canada H3T 1C5
Dr. Salam Yazbeck, Sec.-Treas.
PH: (514)345-4688
FX: (514)345-4964
Description: Pediatric surgeons and other health care professionals with an interest in pediatric surgery. Seeks to advance the practice of pediatric surgery; works to improve diagnostic, treatment, and research techniques in the field. Facilitates exchange of information among members; conducts research and educational programs. **Founded:** 1968. **Membership:** 120. **Staff:** 30. **Languages:** English, French. **Budget:** C$37,500. **Publication:** *Capsule*, quarterly. Newsletter.

CANADIAN ASSOCIATION OF PHYSICISTS (CAP)
e-mail: cap@physics.uottawa.ca
url: http://www.cap.ca
McDonald Bldg., Ste. 112
150 Louis Pasteur Ave.
Ottawa, ON, Canada K1N 9N1
F.M. Ford, Exec.Dir.
PH: (613)562-5614
FX: (613)562-5615
Description: Physicists, educators, and students. Promotes advancement of Canadian physics; encourages study and interest in physics and the physical sciences. Serves as a forum for exchange of ideas and information among members. Conducts educational programs. Founded: 1945. Membership: 1600. Staff: 3. Languages: English, French. Publication: *Physics in Canada* (in English and French), bimonthly. Journal. Circulation: 2,000.

CANADIAN ASSOCIATION OF POISON CONTROL CENTRES
Children's Hospital
840 Sherbrooke St.
Winnipeg, MB, Canada R3A 1S1
M. Tennenbain, Pres.
PH: (204)787-2444
FX: (204)787-4807
Description: Poison control centers. Promotes increased public awareness of poisoning prevention and the steps to take in case of poisoning. Facilitates communication and cooperation among members; conducts educational and promotional programs. Languages: English, French.

CANADIAN ASSOCIATION OF PUBLIC HEALTH DENTISTRY
(L'Association Canadienne des Dentistes en Sante Communautaire)
8230 105th St.
Edmonton, AB, Canada T6E 5H9
Gordon Thompson, Pres.
PH: (403)432-1012
FX: (403)433-4864
Description: Public health dentists. Seeks to advance the practice of public health dentistry; encourages continuing professional development of members. Sponsors research and educational programs. Languages: English, French.

CANADIAN ASSOCIATION OF RADIOLOGISTS (CAR)
(Association Canadienne des Radiologistes)
5101 rue Buchan, Bureau 510
Montreal, PQ, Canada H4P 2R9
Suzanne Charette, Exec.Dir.
PH: (514)738-3111
FX: (514)738-5199
Description: Physicians specializing in radiology; other individuals with an interest in the field. Seeks to advance the practice of radiology; promotes continuing professional development of members. Represents the medical, scientific, and economic interests of radiologists; sponsors research and educational programs. Languages: English, French.

CANADIAN ASSOCIATION FOR SCHOOL HEALTH (CASH)
e-mail: dmccall@eln.etc.bc.ca
2835 Country Woods Dr.
Surrey, BC, Canada V4A 9P9
Doug McCall, Exec.Dir.
PH: (604)535-7664
FX: (604)531-6454
Description: School health services. Promotes increased availability and quality of school health programs. Serves as a clearinghouse on school health services; facilitates communication and cooperation among members. Languages: English, French.

CANADIAN ASSOCIATION OF UNIVERSITY SCHOOLS OF NURSING (CAUSN)
(Association Canadienne des Ecoles Universitaires de Nursing)
350 Albert St., Ste. 325
Ottawa, ON, Canada K1R 1B1
Wendy McBride, Exec.Dir.
PH: (613)563-1236
FX: (613)563-7739
Description: University schools of nursing. Promotes excellence in the study, teaching, and practice of nursing. Facilitates communication and cooperation among members; sponsors research and educational programs. Languages: English, French.

CANADIAN BRAIN TISSUE BANK (CBTC)
(Banque Canadienne de Tissue du Cerveau)
100 College St., Ste. 127
Toronto, ON, Canada M5G 1L5
PH: (416)977-3398
FX: (416)964-2165
Description: Neurologists, psychiatrists, and other individuals with an interest in the structure and function of the brain. Seeks to advance understanding of the brain and its function; promotes professional development of members. Maintains brain tissue bank for research and study; provides support and assistance to brain research programs; conducts educational programs. Languages: English, French.

CANADIAN CANCER SOCIETY (CCS)
e-mail: ccs@cancer.ca
url: http://www.cancer.ca
10 Alcorn Ave., Ste. 200
Toronto, ON, Canada M4V 3B1
Dorothy Lamont, CEO
PH: (416)961-7223
FX: (416)961-4189
Description: Community-based volunteers. Promotes research into the causes, detection, and cure of cancer; seeks to improve the quality of life of people with cancer. Conducts fundraising activities benefitting cancer research; sponsors volunteer training programs; makes available educational courses. Founded: 1938. Languages: English, French. Publication: *Progress Against Cancer*, 3/year. Magazine. Circulation: 10,000. Advertising: not accepted.

CANADIAN CARDIOVASCULAR SOCIETY (CCS)
(Societe Canadienne de Cardiologie)
e-mail: ccsinfo@ccs.ca
url: http://www.ccs.ca
222 Queen St., Ste. 1403
Ottawa, ON, Canada K1P 5V9
Chuck Shields, Exec.Dir.
PH: (613)569-3407
FX: (613)569-6574
Description: Physicians, surgeons, and scientists practicing or conducting research in cardiology and related fields. Promotes the growth and collection of current cardiology information and facilitates its dissemination for the improvement of public health. Founded: 1946. Membership: 1045. Staff: 3. Languages: English, French. Publication: *Abstract Program* (in English and French), annual. Formerly: (1962) Canadian Heart Association.

CANADIAN CHIROPRACTIC EXAMINING BOARD (CCEB)
1020 Centre St. N
Calgary, AB, Canada T2E 2P9
Murray C. McEwen, Chm.
PH: (403)230-9003
FX: (403)299-8162
Description: Chiropractic practitioners and educators. Promotes excellence in the practice of chiropractic. Conducts examinations and bestows certification upon chiropractic practitioners; develops standards of practice for chiropractors. Languages: English, French.

CANADIAN CLINICAL NURSE SPECIALIST GROUP
(CCNSG)
1283 Aldridge Crescent
Burlington, ON, Canada L7M 1C5
Deborah McLeod, Pres.
PH: (905)336-1367
Description: Nurses engaged in clinical practice. Promotes professional development of members; seeks to advance the practice of clinical nursing. Facilitates communication and cooperation among members; sponsors continuing professional education courses. **Languages:** English, French.

CANADIAN COLLEGE OF HEALTH SERVICE EXECUTIVES
e-mail: cchse@canlinks.com
url: http://www.canlinks.com/cchse
350 Sparks St., Ste. 402
Ottawa, ON, Canada K1R 7S8
Gaston C. Levac, CHE, Pres./CEO
PH: (613)235-7218
FX: (613)235-5451
Publication: *Healthcare Management Forum* (in English and French), quarterly, always March, June, September, and December. Journal. Contains articles on innovations in health services. Price: C$74.90 in Canada; C$90.00 in U.S.; C$100.00 International. ISSN: 0840-4704. Circulation: 4,200. Advertising: accepted.

CANADIAN COLLEGE OF PHYSICISTS IN MEDICINE
(CCPM)
e-mail: abaillie@bccancer.bc.ca
399 Royal Ave.
Kelowna, BC, Canada V1Y 5L3
Dr. A. Baillie, Contact
PH: (250)712-3914
FX: (250)712-3911
Description: Physical scientists engaged in medical research. Promotes advancement of the physical sciences as applied to the practice of medicine. Conducts research and educational programs; serves as a clearinghouse on medicine and the physical sciences. **Founded:** 1976. **Membership:** 120. **Languages:** English, French.

CANADIAN COUNCIL OF CARDIOVASCULAR NURSES
(CCCN)
(Conseil Canadien des Infirmieres en Nursing
Cardiovasculaire)
160 George St., Ste. 200
Ottawa, ON, Canada K1N 9M2
Lynne Maxwell, Pres.
PH: (613)241-4361
FX: (613)241-3278
Description: Nurses specializing in cardiovascular practice. Promotes advancement of cardiovascular nursing; facilitates continuing professional development of members. Serves as a forum for the exchange of information among members; conducts educational and training programs. **Languages:** English, French.

CANADIAN COUNCIL ON HEALTH SERVICES
ACCREDITATION (CCHSA)
e-mail: heie@cchsa.ca
url: http://www.cchsa.ca
1730 St. Laurent Blvd., Ste. 430
Ottawa, ON, Canada K1G 5L1
Elma G. Heidemann, Exec.Dir.
PH: (613)738-3800
FX: (613)738-3755
Description: Agencies and organizations accrediting health care services including mental health care, cancer treatment centers, home health care, and community health. Seeks to ensure high standards of ethics, practice, and equipment and facilities among Canadian health services. Formulates and enforces standards; conducts research and educational programs. **Founded:** 1958. **Membership:** 1350. **Staff:** 60. **Languages:** English, French. **Budget:** C$6,700,000. **Publication:** *The Accreditation Standard,* quar-

terly. Newsletter ■ *Standards.* Manual ■ Annual Report ■ Reports. **Formerly:** (1995) Canadian Council on Health Facilities Accreditation.

CANADIAN COUNCIL ON MULTICULTURAL HEALTH
(CCMH)
(Conseil Canadien de la Sante Multiculturelle)
1017 Wilson Ave., Ste. 400
Downsview, ON, Canada M3K 1Z1
Judith Lynam, Pres.
PH: (416)630-8835
FX: (416)638-6076
Description: Health care professionals and other individuals with an interest in public health. Promotes increased availability of health care services among previously underserved populations. Serves as a clearinghouse on multicultural health and related issues; makes available support and assistance to health care services. **Languages:** English, French.

CANADIAN DENTAL ASSOCIATION (CDA)
(Association Dentair Canadienne)
e-mail: cdaa@cyberus.ca
1785 Alta Vista Dr.
Ottawa, ON, Canada K1G 3Y6
A. Jardine Neilson, Exec.Dir.
PH: (613)521-5495
TF: 800345-5137
FX: (613)521-5572
Description: Dentists. Seeks to advance the profession of dentistry. Facilitates exchange of information among members; sponsors continuing professional education courses. **Languages:** English, French.

CANADIAN DENTAL HYGIENISTS' ASSOCIATION (CDHA)
96 Centerpointe Dr.
Nepean, ON, Canada K2G 1B6
Carol Matheson Worobey, Exec.Dir.
PH: (613)224-5515
FX: (613)224-7283
Description: Dental hygienists. Promotes development of standards of ethics and practice in the field of dental hygiene; facilitates professional advancement of members. Provides dental hygiene services to previously underserved populations; conducts educational programs. **Languages:** English, French.

CANADIAN DERMATOLOGY ASSOCIATION (CDA)
e-mail: cda.chadwick@rcpsc.edu
774 Echo Dr., Ste. 521
Ottawa, ON, Canada K1S 5N8
Dr. Dana W. Hanson, Contact
PH: (613)730-6262
FX: (613)730-1116
Description: Certified dermatologists and related professionals interested in the professional advancement of dermatology. Promotes continuing education programs in dermatology. Conducts research on adverse dermatological reactions. Sponsors Cutaneous Adverse Reaction Program and annual SunAwareness Week. Provides public education program on skin cancer prevention. **Founded:** 1926. **Membership:** 600. **Staff:** 2. **Languages:** English, French. **Publication:** *Canadian Dermatology Association Bulletin,* quarterly ■ *Journal of Cutaneous Medicine and Surgery* (in English and French), quarterly. Advertising: accepted ■ *Roster,* annual. Directory.

CANADIAN DIABETES ASSOCIATION (CDA)
(Association Canadienne du Diabete)
15 Toronto St., Ste. 1001
Toronto, ON, Canada M5C 2E3
Jim O'Brien, Exec.Dir.
PH: (416)363-3373
FX: (416)363-3393
Description: People with diabetes and their families; health care professionals with an interest in diabetes. Seeks to advance the prevention, diagnosis, and treatment of diabetes. Provides sup-

port and services to people with diabetes and their families; sponsors research and educational programs. **Languages:** English, French.

CANADIAN DIABETES ASSOCIATION - DIABETES EDUCATOR SECTION
url: http://www.diabetes.ca
15 Toronto St., Ste. 800
Toronto, ON, Canada M5C 2E3
Jennifer Belding, Contact
PH: (416)363-3373
TF: 800226-8464
FX: (416)363-3393
Description: Organizations and individuals with an interest in diabetes. Promotes increased public awareness of the causes, prevention, and treatment of diabetes. Conducts research and educational programs. **Languages:** English, French.

CANADIAN DRUG MANUFACTURERS ASSOCIATION (CDMA)
(Association Canadienne des Fabricants de Produits Pharmacetiques)
4120 Yonge St., Ste. 606
Toronto, ON, Canada M2P 2B8
Jack Kay, Chm.
PH: (416)223-2333
FX: (416)223-2425
Description: Manufacturers of pharmaceutical products. Promotes growth and development of the domestic pharmaceuticals industry. Represents members' collective interests before scientific, labor, and industrial organizations, government agencies, and the public. **Languages:** English, French.

CANADIAN FEDERATION OF MENTAL HEALTH NURSES (CFMHN)
e-mail: waustin@ua-nursing-ualberta-ca
Faculty of Nursing
Clinical Sciences Bldg., 3rd Fl.
University of Alberta
Edmonton, AB, Canada T6G 2G3
Wendy Austin, Pres.
PH: (403)492-5250
FX: (403)492-2551
Description: Nurses engaged in mental health practice. Promotes professional development of members; seeks to advance the practice of mental health nursing. Facilitates communication and cooperation among members; sponsors continuing professional education programs. **Languages:** English, French.

CANADIAN FOUNDATION FOR THE STUDY OF INFANT DEATHS (CFSID)
e-mail: sidscanada@inforamp.net
url: http://www.sidscanada.org/sids.html
586 Eglinton Ave. E, Ste. 308
Toronto, ON, Canada M4P 1P2
Beverley DeBruyn, Exec.Dir.
PH: (416)488-3260
TF: 800END-SIDS
FX: (416)488-3864
Description: Health care providers, families who have lost a child to sudden infant death syndrome, and other individuals with an interest in SIDSProvides emotional support to families that have experienced the loss of a child to SIDS. Operates network of support groups; serves as a clearinghouse on SIDS and grief; provides educational programs for general public; conducts fundraising activities benefitting SIDS research projects. **Founded:** 1973. **Membership:** 200. **Staff:** 3. **Languages:** English, French. **Budget:** C$260,000. **Publication:** *Baby's Breath* (in English and French), quarterly. Newsletter. Price: free. ISSN: 1192-9294. Circulation: 3,000. Advertising: not accepted.

CANADIAN FRIENDS OF THE AMERICAN-ISRAEL MEDICAL FOUNDATION (CFAIMF)
600 University Ave., Ste. 656
Toronto, ON, Canada M5G 1X5
N. Zamel, Contact
PH: (416)586-4473
Description: Supporters of the American-Israel Medical Foundation and its programs. Seeks to advance the practice of medicine. Provides support and assistance to the programs of the American-Israel Medical Foundation. **Languages:** English, French.

CANADIAN GERONTOLOGICAL NURSING ASSOCIATION (CGNA)
(Association Canadienne des Infirmiers et Infirmieres en Gerontologie)
911 Maitland St.
London, ON, Canada N5Y 2X2
Nancy Bol, Pres.
PH: (519)685-4000
Description: Nurses specializing in gerontological practice. Promotes professional development of members; seeks to advance the practice of gerontological nursing. Serves as a forum for the exchange of information among members; conducts continuing professional education programs. **Languages:** English, French.

CANADIAN HEALTH CARE GUILD (CHCG)
17410 17th Ave., Ste. 200
Edmonton, AB, Canada T5S 1E9
Gerrie Dakers, Dir.
PH: (403)483-8126
TF: 800252-7984
FX: (403)484-3341
Description: Medical technicians, ambulance drivers, and other health care personnel. Seeks to obtain optimal conditions of employment for members. Represents members in negotiations with employers. **Languages:** English, French.

CANADIAN HEALTH CARE MATERIAL MANAGEMENT ASSOCIATION (CHCMMA)
231 E 15th St.
North Vancouver, BC, Canada V7L 2L7
Tony Clayton, Pres.
PH: (604)984-5800
FX: (604)984-5838
Description: Materials management professionals employed by health care facilities. Promotes excellence in the field of health care materials management. Facilitates communication and cooperation among members; sponsors continuing professional development courses. **Languages:** English, French.

CANADIAN HEALTH COALITION (CHC)
(Coalition Canadienne de la Sante)
2841 Riverside Dr.
Ottawa, ON, Canada K1V 8X7
Kathleen Connors, Chair
PH: (613)521-3400
FX: (613)521-4655
Description: Individuals and organizations with an interest in health care. Promotes increased availability and quality of health services. Monitors the performance of health care facilities and services and makes recommendations for their improvement. **Languages:** English, French.

CANADIAN HEALTH ECONOMICS RESEARCH ASSOCIATION (CHERA)
(Association Canadienne pour la Recerche en Economie de la Sante)
e-mail: chera@post.queensv.ca
url: http://qhp.queen.ca/chera
Abramsky Hall, 3rd Fl.
Queen's University
Kingston, ON, Canada K7L 3N6
Bill Swan, Exec.Coor.

PH: (613)545-6000
FX: (613)545-6353
Description: Economists, administrators, political scientists, sociologists, social workers, policymakers, and other individuals with an interest in the economics of health care. Facilitates communication and exchange of information among members. Gathers and disseminates health economics information. Promotes quality research in health economics and related fields. Maintains registry of health economics researchers and research projects in Canada. Maintains Internet server. **Founded:** 1983. **Membership:** 330. **Staff:** 1. **Budget:** C$30,000. **Publication:** *CHERAction*, quarterly. Newsletter ■ *Membership Registry*, annual. Directory.

CANADIAN HEALTH RECORD ASSOCIATION (CHRA)
(College des Archivists Medicale du Canada)
e-mail: chragen@ibm.net
1090 Don Mills Rd., Ste. 501
Don Mills, ON, Canada M3C 3R6
Deborah Del Duca, Exec.Dir.
PH: (416)447-4900
FX: (416)447-4598
Description: Librarians, archivists, and other individuals engaged in the maintenance of medical records. Promotes excellence in the practice of medical records management. Facilitates communication and cooperation among members; sponsors continuing professional development courses for medical records managers. **Languages:** English, French.

CANADIAN HOLISTIC NURSES ASSOCIATION (CHNA)
e-mail: lpross@axionet.com
209-6051 Gilbert Rd.
Richmond, BC, Canada V7C 3V3
Lois Ross, Pres.
PH: (604)244-1096
FX: (604)241-4580
Description: Registered nurses are members; health care providers including registered psychiatric nurses, massage therapists, physiotherapists, nursing students, and chiropractors are associate members. Seeks to further the development of the field of holistic nursing. Promotes use of a conceptual framework based on nursing principles and human environmental field theory in the treatment of patients; encourages employment of noninvasive strategies for promoting health and wellness. Promulgates and enforces standards of practice in holistic nursing; provides consulting services and other support to members; interacts with health care consumer and provider organizations to influence health policy formation. **Founded:** 1988. **Membership:** 140. **Languages:** English, French. **Publication:** Newsletter, semiannual. Advertising: accepted.

CANADIAN INSTITUTE OF HEALTH CARE AND BUSINESS (CIHCB)
1851 Eglinton Ave. W
Toronto, ON, Canada M6E 2H9
M. Lapuente, Consultant
PH: (416)785-5572
Description: Business professionals working in the field of health care. Promotes effective application of business principles within the health care industries. Sponsors continuing professional education courses for members. **Languages:** English, French.

CANADIAN INSTITUTE FOR HEALTH INFORMATION (CIHI)
url: http://www.cici.ca
250 Ferrand Dr.
Don Mills, ON, Canada M3C 2T9
Rheal LeBlanc, Pres.
PH: (416)429-0464
FX: (416)429-1953
Description: Hospital medical records departments and other individuals and organizations with an interest in health information management. Promotes more effective practice of medical records management; seeks to insure free access to medical in-

formation by patients. Serves as a forum for the exchange of information among members; sponsors educational programs. **Languages:** English, French.

CANADIAN INSTITUTE OF PUBLIC HEALTH INSPECTORS (CIPHI)
(Institut Canadien des Inspecteurs en Hygiene Publique)
38 Auriga Dr., Ste. 200
Nepean, ON, Canada K2E 8A5
James Bradley, Exec.Dir.
PH: (613)224-7566
FX: (613)224-6055
Description: Public health inspectors. Seeks to advance the profession of public health inspection; promotes adherence to high standards of ethics and practice among members. Conducts advocacy campaigns to increase public appreciation of the role of public health inspectors; sponsors educational and training programs. **Languages:** English, French.

CANADIAN INTRAVENOUS NURSES ASSOCIATION (CINA)
e-mail: cinacsot@idirect.com
url: http://www.web.idirect.com/~csotcina
4433 Sheppard Ave. E, Ste. 200
Agincourt, ON, Canada M1S 1V3
Pamela Smith, Exec. Officer
PH: (416)292-0687
FX: (416)292-1038
Description: Registered nurses specializing in intravenous therapy or employed in supervisory, educational, or administrative positions related to intravenous therapy. Works to establish and promote standards of intravenous therapy. Offers educational programs designed to enhance patient care and safety. Facilitates discussion of intravenous therapy issues. **Founded:** 1975. **Membership:** 575. **Staff:** 1. **Local Groups:** 6. **Languages:** English. **Publication:** *CINA Journal*, annual. Advertising: accepted ■ *CINA Mainliner*, quarterly. Newsletter.

CANADIAN MEDIC ALERT FOUNDATION (CMAF)
(La Fondation Canadienne Medic-Alert)
e-mail: medicalert@flexnet.com
144 Front St. W, Ste. 300
Toronto, ON, Canada M5J 2L7
Sheilagh Tippet-Fayges, Pres.
PH: (416)696-0267
TF: 800668-1507
FX: (416)696-0156
Description: Promotes wearing of medic alert jewelry, inscribed with personal medical information of use to health care professionals in case the wearer is rendered unconcious. Facilitates distribution and use of medic alert jewelry. **Languages:** English, French.

CANADIAN MEDICAL ASSOCIATION
url: http://www.cma.ca
1867 Alta Vista Dr.
Ottawa, ON, Canada K1G 3Y6
Dr. Victor Dirnfield, Pres.
PH: (613)731-9331
FX: (613)731-9013
Description: Seeks to improve medical care for persons living in Canada. Works to maintain high standards of hospital care and health related services. Encourages constant improvement in the medical profession.

CANADIAN MEDICAL AND BIOLOGICAL ENGINEERING SOCIETY (CMBES)
(Societe Canadienne de Genie Biomedical)
e-mail: sally.chapman@nrc.ca
Bldg. 55, Rm. 382
Ottawa, ON, Canada K1A 0R8
Sally Chapman, Sec.
PH: (613)993-1686
FX: (613)954-2216
Description: Medical and biological engineers. Seeks to advance

the study and profession of medical and biological engineering and related fields. Sponsors research and educational programs. **Languages:** English, French.

CANADIAN MEDICAL FOUNDATION (CMF)
1867 Alta Vista Dr.
Ottawa, ON, Canada K1G 3Y6
PH: (613)731-9331
Description: Health care professionals. Seeks to advance the study and practice of medicine. Makes available health care services; sponsors educational programs. **Languages:** English, French.

CANADIAN MEDICAL MALPRACTICE PREVENTION ASSOCIATION (CMMPA)
2900 Warden Ave. No. 92093
Scarborough, ON, Canada M1W 3Y8
Sharon Roberts, Pres.
PH: (416)969-1587
FX: (416)496-2825
Description: Individuals with an interest in medical malpractice and related issues. Promotes effective medical treatment and reform of legal medical malpractice procedures. Maintains speakers' bureau. **Founded:** 1987. **Languages:** English, French.

CANADIAN MEDICAL PROTECTIVE ASSOCIATION (CMPA)
(Association Canadienne de Protection Medicale)
2100 Drummond, Ste. 120
Montreal, PQ, Canada H3G 1X1
Stuart B. Lee, Sec.-Treas.
PH: (514)285-1984
Description: Physicians and other health care professionals. Seeks to protect the commercial and professional interests of members. Provides support and assistance to medical professionals; advocates legal reform. **Languages:** English, French.

CANADIAN MENTAL HEALTH ASSOCIATION
(Association Canadienne pour la Sante Mentale)
e-mail: cmha@interlog.com
url: http://www.icomm.ca/cmhcan
2160 Yonge St.
Toronto, ON, Canada M4S 2Z3
Edward J. Pennington, Gen.Dir.
PH: (416)484-7750
FX: (416)484-4617
Description: Mental health professionals and other individuals with an interest in community mental health. Works to enable individuals, groups, and communities to increase control over and enhance their mental health. Serves as a social advocate to encourage public action to strengthen community mental health services; conducts lobbying activities. Promotes mental health research; organizes and operates grass roots programs to help people whose mental health is at risk make use of the services available to them. Sponsors educational programs. **Founded:** 1918. **Local Groups:** 135. **Languages:** English, French. **Publication:** Newsletter (in English and French), quarterly ■ Pamphlets.

CANADIAN NATURAL HEALTH ASSOCIATION (CNHA)
url: http://www.natural-health.org
439 Wellington St. W, Ste. 5
Toronto, ON, Canada M5V 1E7
Mark Ansara, Contact
PH: (416)977-2642
FX: (416)977-1536
Description: Holistic health care educators. Seeks to raise public awareness of holistic health care and the importance of a healthy lifestyle. Conducts educational programs; maintains speakers' bureau. **Founded:** 1960. **Membership:** 900. **Staff:** 2. **Languages:** English, French. **Budget:** C$170,000. **Publication:** Living Naturally, bimonthly. Newsletter ■ Directory, annual.

CANADIAN NETWORK OF TOXICOLOGY CENTRES (CNTC)
e-mail: DWARNER@TOX.UOGUELPH.CA
url: http://www.uoguelph.ca/cntc/
2nd Fl., Bovey Bldg.
Gordon St.
University of Guelph
Guelph, ON, Canada N1G 2W1
Dr. Len Ritter, Exec.Dir.
PH: (519)837-3320
FX: (519)837-3861
Description: University based toxicology research centers. Seeks to improve human and environmental health through increased understanding of toxic substances and their impact on the environment. Coordinates research efforts of research team members; advises government agencies and industrial organizations concerned with the release of toxic substances into the environment. Supports educational programs in toxicology at all levels. Serves as a clearinghouse on toxicology and environmental health issues. **Founded:** 1988. **Membership:** 300. **Languages:** English, French. **Budget:** C$2,000,000. **Publication:** Canadian Network of Toxicology Centres (in English and French). Brochure. Advertising: not accepted. Alternate Formats: online ■ CNTC News, semiannual. Newsletter. Advertising: not accepted. Alternate Formats: online ■ Toxicology Educators Resource Guide for Secondary Schhol Audiences. Alternate Formats: online ■ ToxTalk (in English and French), semiannual. Alternate Formats: online.

CANADIAN NEUROLOGICAL SOCIETY (CNS)
(Societe Canadienne de Neurologie)
906 12th Ave., Ste. 810
Calgary, AB, Canada T2R 1K7
Oksana Suchowersky, Pres.
PH: (403)229-9544
Description: Neurologists, scientists, and other individuals with an interest in neurology and related fields. Seeks to advance the study and practice of the neurological sciences; promotes professional development of members. Facilitates exchange of information among members; sponsors research and educational programs. **Languages:** English, French.

CANADIAN NEUROSURGERY SOCIETY (CNS)
(Societe Canadienne de Neurochirurgie)
906 12th Ave., Ste. 810
Calgary, AB, Canada T2R 1K7
John P. Girvin, Pres.
PH: (403)229-9544
Description: Neurosurgeons, neurologists, and other individuals with an interest in neurosurgery. Seeks to improve neurosurgical techniques; promotes professional development of members. Sponsors research and educational programs; facilitates communication and cooperation among members. **Languages:** English, French.

CANADIAN NURSES ASSOCIATION (CNA)
(Association des Infirmieres et Infirmiers du Canada)
e-mail: commdiv@cna-nurses.ca
url: http://www.cna-nurses.ca
50 Driveway
Ottawa, ON, Canada K2P 1E2
Dr. Mary Ellen Jeans, Exec.Dir.
PH: (613)237-2133
FX: (613)237-3520
Description: Works to advance the quality of nursing in the interests of the public. Promotes high standards of nursing practice, education, research, and administration in order to achieve quality nursing care in the public interest. Also promotes uniform and high quality regulatory practices in the public interest and in collaboration with nursing regulatory bodies. Acts in the public interest for Canadian nursing and nurses, providing national and international leadership in nursing and health issues. **Founded:** 1908. **Membership:** 111708. **Staff:** 80. **Local Groups:** 11. **Languages:** English, French. **Publication:** Canadian Nurse/

Infirmiere Canadienne (in English and French), 11/year. Journal. Price: C$36.00. ISSN: 0008-4581. Circulation: 114,000. Advertising: accepted. Alternate Formats: microform ∎ Monograph, periodic ∎ Pamphlets, periodic.

CANADIAN NURSES FOUNDATION (CNF)
   (Fondation des Infirmieres et Infirmiers du Canada)
   e-mail: cnf@cnursesfdn.ca
   url: http://www.magma.ca/~cnf/
   50 Driveway
   Ottawa, ON, Canada K2P 1E2
   Beverly Campbell, Exec.Dir.
   PH: (613)237-2133
   FX: (613)237-3520
   Description: Nurses and nursing students. Promotes professional advancement of members. Provides support and assistance to members; sponsors research and educational programs. **Languages:** English, French.

CANADIAN NURSES RESPIRATORY SOCIETY (CNRS)
   (Societe Canadienne des Infirmieres en Sante Respiratoire)
   10 Cowan Ave.
   St. John's, NF, Canada A1E 3N5
   Pamela Baker, Pres.
   PH: (709)737-4253
   FX: (709)737-6795
   Description: Nurses specializing in the treatment of respiratory diseases. Promotes excellence in the practice of nursing; encourages professional development of members. Serves as a forum for the exchange of information among members; sponsors research and educational programs. **Languages:** English, French.

CANADIAN NURSING RESEARCH GROUP (CNRG)
   (Groupe Canadien de Recherche Infirmiere)
   Faculty of Nursing
   PO Box 440
   University of New Brunswick
   Fredericton, NB, Canada E3B 5A3
   Judith Wuest, Pres.
   PH: (506)453-4642
   FX: (506)453-4503
   Description: Nurse researchers. Seeks to advance the study and profession of nursing. Facilitates exchange of information among members; provides support and assistance to nurse researchers; conducts educational programs. **Languages:** English, French.

CANADIAN OBSTETRIC GYNECOLOGIC AND NEONATAL
   NURSES (COGNN)
   315 Oakwood Ave.
   Winnipeg, MB, Canada R3L 1E8
   Vera Rosolowich, Pres.
   PH: (204)774-6581
   FX: (204)774-7834
   Description: Nurses specializing in obstetric, gynecologic, and neonatal practice. Seeks to advance the practice of ob/gyn and neonatal nursing. Serves as a forum for the exchange of information among members; sponsors research and educational programs. **Languages:** English, French.

CANADIAN OCCUPATIONAL HEALTH NURSES
   ASSOCIATION (COHNA)
   (Association Canadienne des Infirmieres et Infirmiers en Sante du Travail)
   3777 Kingsway, Ste. 5
   Burnaby, BC, Canada V5H 3Z7
   Sharon Blaney, Pres.
   PH: (604)432-4012
   FX: (604)432-9456
   Description: Nurses specializing in occupational health. Seeks to advance the study and practice of occupational health nursing. Facilitates communication among members; sponsors research and educational programs. **Languages:** English, French.

CANADIAN OPHTHALMOLOGICAL SOCIETY (COS)
   (Societe Canadienne d'Ophthalmologie)
   1525 Carling Ave., Ste. 610
   Ottawa, ON, Canada K1Z 8R9
   Hubert Drouin, Exec.Dir.
   PH: (613)729-6779
   TF: 800267-5763
   FX: (613)729-7209
   Description: Ophthalmologists and ophthalmology students. Seeks to advance the study and practice of ophthalmology. Facilitates exchange of information among members; sponsors research and educational programs. **Languages:** English, French.

CANADIAN ORTHOPAEDIC NURSES ASSOCIATION
   (CONA)
   (Association Canadienne des Infirmieres et Infirmiers en Orthopedie)
   43 Wellesley St. E
   Toronto, ON, Canada M4Y 1H1
   Pamela Gossmann, Pres.
   PH: (416)967-8622
   Description: Nurses specializing in orthopedic practice. Promotes advancement of the profession of orthopedic nursing. Sponsors continuing professional development courses for members. **Languages:** English, French.

CANADIAN ORTHOPTIC COUNCIL (COC)
   (Conseil Canadien d'Orthoptique)
   506 71st Ave. SW, Ste. 5
   Calgary, AB, Canada T2V 4V4
   Carolyn M. B. Skov, Sec.-Treas.
   PH: (403)253-6700
   Description: Health care professionals specializing in orthoptics and occular surgery. Seeks to advance the study and practice of orthoptics. Serves as a forum for the exchange of information among members; sponsors research and educational programs. **Languages:** English, French.

CANADIAN PAEDIATRIC SOCIETY (CPS)
   (Societe Canadienne de Pediatrie)
   e-mail: webmaster@cps.ca
   url: http://www.cps.ca
   2204 Walkley Rd., Ste. 100
   Ottawa, ON, Canada K1G 4G8
   Nicole Menzies, Contact
   PH: (613)526-9397
   FX: (613)526-3332
   Description: Professional organization of paediatricians serving on committees and sections focusing on adolescent medicine, bioethics, drug therapy, hazardous substances, fetus and newborns, Indian and Inuit health, infectious disease and immunization, injury prevention, paediatric practice, nutrition, and psychological paediatrics. Provides services to Canadian children and to its membership. Serves as an advocate on issues relating to child health and welfare. Provides continuing education for the maintenance of competence of its members. Establishes Canadian standards/guidelines for paediatric care and practice, and promotes the interest of paediatricians. **Founded:** 1922. **Membership:** 1954. **Staff:** 15. **Languages:** English, French. **Publication:** *Clinical Practice Guidelines* (in English and French), periodic. Paper ∎ *CPS News* (in English and French), bimonthly. Newsletter ∎ *Paediatrics & Child Health* (in English and French), bimonthly. Journal ∎ *Well Beings*. Book ∎ *Your Child's Best Shot: A Parent's Guide to Vaccination*. Book ∎ Reports. **Formerly:** (1951) Canadian Society for the Study of Diseases of Children.

CANADIAN PHYSIOLOGICAL SOCIETY
   e-mail: buchan@cs.ubc.ca
   url: http://www.physiology.ubc.ca
   Department of Physiology
   2146 Health Sciences Hall
   Vancouver, BC, Canada V6T 1Z3
   Dr. A.M. Buchan, Professor

PH: (604)822-2083
FX: (604)822-6048
Description: Physiologists, students, and other individuals with an interest in physiology and related fields. Seeks to advance the study and applications of physiology. Facilitates exchange of information among members; and between members and scholars and scientists working in related fields. **Languages:** English, French. **Publication:** *Physiology Canada*, semiannual. Journal. ISSN: 0822-9058. Circulation: 600.

CANADIAN PSORIASIS FOUNDATION (CPF)

e-mail: cpfdon@istar.ca
1306 Wellington St., Ste. 500A
Ottawa, ON, Canada K1Y 3B2
Don Rutherford, Exec.Dir.
PH: (613)728-4000
FX: (613)728-8913
Description: People with psoriasis and their families; health care providers with an interest in dermatology. Promotes an improved quality of life for people with psoriasis; seeks advancement in the prevention and treatment of psoriasis and related disorders. Maintains support groups; conducts research and educational programs. **Founded:** 1983. **Membership:** 1200. **Staff:** 1. **Languages:** English, French. **Budget:** C$135,000. **Publication:** *CPF Newsletter*, 3/year. Circulation: 3,000 ▪ Brochure.

CANADIAN PSYCHIATRIC ASSOCIATION (CPA)

(Association des Psychiatres du Canada)
url: http://www.cpa.medical.org
260-441 MacLaren St.
Ottawa, ON, Canada K2P 2H3
B. Alex Saunders, Exec. Officer
PH: (613)234-2815
FX: (613)234-9857
Description: Works to improve mental health and psychiatric care delivery systems in Canada. Fosters high standards among Canadian psychiatrists; promotes continuing education of members; encourages and participates in educational programs for patient care providers; promotes research into psychiatric disorders; represents members before government bodies and licensing bureaus, universities, and related organizations. **Founded:** 1951. **Membership:** 2400. **Staff:** 16. **State Groups:** 10. **Languages:** English, French. **Budget:** C$2,000,000. **Publication:** *Canadian Journal of Psychiatry* (in English and French), 10/year. Price: C$85.60/year in Canada; C$105.00/year outside Canada. Circulation: 3,300. Advertising: accepted ▪ *CPA Bulletin* (in English and French), bimonthly ▪ *Journal of Psychiatry and Neuroscience* (in English and French), 5/year. Price: C$71.00 individual; C$90.00 institutional. Circulation: 2,650. Advertising: accepted ▪ *Membership Directory* (in English and French), biennial.

CANADIAN PUBLIC HEALTH ASSOCIATION

e-mail: info@cpha.ca
url: http://www.cpha.ca
1565 Carling Ave., Ste. 400
Ottawa, ON, Canada K1Z 8R1
Gerald Dafoe, CEO
PH: (613)725-3769
FX: (613)725-9826
Description: Works to mobilize national charitable and volunteer resources to address public health concerns worldwide. Conducts immunization, maternal and child health, and nutritional programs in at-risk areas. **Languages:** English, French.

CANADIAN REFERENCE CENTRE FOR CANCER PATHOLOGY (CRCCP)

(Centre Canadien de Consultation en Pathologie Oncologique)
60 Ruskin St.
Ottawa, ON, Canada K1Y 4M9
Dr. Jane Thomas, Dir.
PH: (613)728-1723
FX: (613)728-0811
Description: Cancer pathologists and other scientists and health care professionals with an interest in cancer pathology. Seeks to

advance the practice of cancer pathology; encourages continuing professional development of members. Serves as a clearinghouse on cancer pathology; sponsors research and educational programs. **Languages:** English, French.

CANADIAN RHEUMATOLOGY ASSOCIATION (CRA)

(La Societe Canadienne de Rhumatologie)
1560 Sherbrooke St. E
Montreal, PQ, Canada H2L 4K8
Simon Carette, Pres.
PH: (514)876-7131
FX: (514)876-6630
Description: Rheumatologists, people with rheumatic diseases, and other individuals with an interest in rheumatology. Seeks to advance rheumatological study and practice. Serves as a clearinghouse on rheumatology; sponsors research and educational programs. **Languages:** English, French.

CANADIAN SCHIZOPHRENIA FOUNDATION (CSF)

e-mail: centre@orthomed.org
url: http://www.orthomed.org
16 Florence Ave.
Toronto, ON, Canada M2N 1E9
Steven Carter, Exec.Dir.
PH: (416)733-2117
FX: (416)733-2352
Description: People with schizophrenia and their families, mental health professionals, and others with an interest in schizophrenia and related conditions. Promotes an improved quality of life for people with schizophrenia; seeks to identify more effective treatments for the disorder. Facilitates communication among mental health professionals studying schizophrenia; sponsors research. **Founded:** 1969. **Languages:** English, French. **Publication:** *Health Naturally*, periodic. Magazine ▪ *Nutrition and Mental Health*, quarterly. Newsletter.

CANADIAN SLEEP SOCIETY (CSS)

url: http://www.bisleep.medsch.ucla.edu/WFSRS/CSS/css.html
3080 Yonge St., Ste. 5055
Toronto, ON, Canada M4N 3N1
Dr. Charles George, Pres.
PH: (416)483-6260
FX: (416)483-7081
Description: Scientists, health care professionals, students, and other individuals with an interest in sleep; corporations manufacturing sleep-related products. Promotes increased understanding of sleep and sleep disorders and their treatment. Sponsors research and educational programs. **Founded:** 1986. **Membership:** 220. **Staff:** 2. **Languages:** English, French. **Publication:** *Vigilance*, 3/year. Newsletter. Circulation: 300. Advertising: accepted ▪ Brochure.

CANADIAN SOCIETY OF ALLERGY AND CLINICAL IMMUNOLOGY (CSACI)

e-mail: CSACI@RCPSC.EDU
774 Echo Dr.
Ottawa, ON, Canada K1S 5N8
Dr. Zave Chad, Pres.
PH: (613)730-6272
FX: (613)730-1116
Description: Allergists, immunologists, and others with an interest in the diagnosis and treatment of allergic and immunological disorders. Seeks to advance the understanding and treatment of allergic and immunological diseases. Conducts continuing professional education courses; sponsors research; maintains speakers' bureau; compiles statistics. **Founded:** 1945. **Membership:** 225. **Staff:** 1. **Languages:** English, French. **Publication:** Newsletter, periodic ▪ Journal, periodic.

CANADIAN SOCIETY OF CARDIOLOGY TECHNOLOGISTS (CSCT)
(Societe Canadienne des Technologistes en Cardiologie)
PO Box 3121
Winnipeg, MB, Canada R3C 4E6
Patricia Lively, Exec.V.Pres.
Description: Cardiology technologists. Seeks to advance the practice of cardiology; promotes professional development of members. Facilitates exchange of information among members; sponsors research and educational programs. **Languages:** English, French.

CANADIAN SOCIETY OF CLINICAL NEUROPHYSIOLOGISTS (CSCN)
(Societe Canadienne de Neurophysiologistes Cliniques)
e-mail: brains@accns.org
906 12th Ave., Ste. 810
Calgary, AB, Canada T2R 1K7
Lucile Edwards, Exec.Dir.
PH: (403)229-9544
FX: (403)229-1661
Description: Neurophysiologists and other individuals with an interest in the field. Seeks to advance the study and practice of neurophysiology. Facilitates exchange of information among members; sponsors research and educational programs. **Languages:** English, French.

CANADIAN SOCIETY FOR CLINICAL PHARMACOLOGY (CSCP)
33 Russell St.
Toronto, ON, Canada M5S 2S1
C. Van Der Giussen, Contact
PH: (416)595-6119
FX: (416)595-6619
Description: Clinical pharmacologists and other health care professionals and scientists with and interest in pharmacy. Seeks to advance the study, teaching, and practice of clinical pharmacology. Serves as a network linking members; sponsors research and educational programs. **Languages:** English, French.

CANADIAN SOCIETY FOR EXERCISE PHYSIOLOGY (CSEP)
e-mail: info@csep.ca
url: http://www.csep.ca
185 Somerset St. W, Ste. 202
Ottawa, ON, Canada K2P 0J2
William E. Hearst, Exec.Dir.
PH: (613)234-3755
FX: (613)234-3565
Description: Exercise physiologists, educators, students, and other individuals with an interest in exercise physiology. Promotes and seeks to ensure excellence in the study, teaching, and practice of exercise physiology. Conducts research and educational programs. **Founded:** 1967. **Membership:** 320. **Staff:** 2. **Languages:** English, French. **Publication:** *Canadian Journal of Applied Physiology,* bimonthly.

CANADIAN SOCIETY OF GASTROENTEROLOGY NURSES AND ASSOCIATES (CSGNA)
e-mail: ledress@istar.ca
url: http://www.webray.com/esgna
36 Adelaide St. E
PO Box 366
Toronto, ON, Canada M5C 2J5
Terry LeDressay, Pres.
PH: (905)668-4982
Description: Gastroenterology nurses, medical technicians, and sales representatives of medical equipment and pharmaceutical manufacturers. Promotes excellence in the teaching and practice of gastroenterological nursing. Facilitates communication among members; produces patient education materials. Conducts continuing professional education programs; maintains speakers' bureau. **Founded:** 1985. **Membership:** 510. **Languages:** English, French. **Budget:** C$60,000. **Publication:** *Guiding Light,* 3/year. Newsletter. Price: free to members.

CANADIAN SOCIETY FOR IMMUNOLOGY (CSI)
(Societe Canadienne d'Immunologie)
795 McDermot Ave.
Winnipeg, MB, Canada R3E 0W3
Donna A. Chow, Sec.-Treas.
PH: (204)789-3316
Description: Immunologists and other health care professionals and scientists with an interest in immunology. Seeks to advance immunological study, research, and practice. Promotes ongoing professional development of members. Serves as a network linking members; sponsors research and educational programs. **Languages:** English, French.

CANADIAN SOCIETY FOR INTERNATIONAL HEALTH (SCIH)
(Societe Canadienne de Sante Internationale)
e-mail: csih@fox.nstn.ca
url: http://www.csih.org
170 Laurier Ave. W, Ste. 902
Ottawa, ON, Canada K1P 5V5
Charles A. Shields, Jr., Exec.Dir.
PH: (613)230-2654
FX: (613)230-8401
Description: Health care services and individuals and organizations with an interest in global public health. Promotes increased availability and quality of health services in previously underserved areas worldwide. Provides support and assistance to health services; lobbies for more effective public health policies; sponsors research. Multinational. **Languages:** English, French.

CANADIAN SOCIETY FOR MEDICAL LABORATORY SCIENCE
e-mail: khdavis@csmls.org
url: http://www.csmls.org
PO Box 2830 LCD 1
Hamilton, ON, Canada L8N 3N8
E. Valerie Booth, Exec.Dir.
PH: (905)528-8642
FX: (905)528-4968
Description: Laboratory technologists in 20 countries. Seeks to maintain high standards of medical laboratory technology to insure effective and economical laboratory services. Promotes the interests of medical laboratory technologists. Emphasizes the importance of continuing education; sponsors courses. Communicates with government authorities concerning issues affecting members. Offers insurance program to members. Organizes national medical laboratory week annually. Bestows awards. **Founded:** 1937. **Membership:** 15000. **Staff:** 17. **Languages:** English, French. **Budget:** C$2,000,000. **Publication:** *Annual Roster.* Advertising: not accepted. Alternate Formats: online ■ *Canadian Journal of Medical Laboratory Science* (in English and French), bimonthly. Advertising: accepted ■ *Catalogs of Continuing Education* ■ *Guidelines for Laboratory Safety.* Manual. Canadian Society of Laboratory Technologies; Societe Canadienne Des Technologistes De Laboratoire.

CANADIAN SOCIETY OF PLANT PHYSIOLOGISTS (CSPP)
(Societe Canadienne de Physiologie Vegetale)
Department of Biology
University of Waterloo
Waterloo, ON, Canada N2L 3G1
Carol A. Peterson, Pres.
PH: (519)885-1211
FX: (519)746-0614
Description: Botanists and other scientists with an interest in plant physiology. Seeks to advance the study of physiology as it applies to plants; promotes ongoing professional development of members. Functions as a clearinghouse on plant physiology; facilitates communication among members; sponsors research and educational programs. **Languages:** English, French.

CANADIAN SOCIETY FOR PSYCHOMOTOR LEARNING AND SPORT PSYCHOLOGY
(Societe Canadienne d'Apprentissage Psychomoteur et de Psychologie du Sport)
e-mail: tegabrie@acs.ucalgary.ca
Faculty of Kinesiology
University of Calgary
Calgary, AB, Canada T2N 1N4
Tina Gabriele, Sec.-Treas.
PH: (403)220-3428
FX: (403)289-9117
Description: Health care professionals and other individuals with an interest in psychomotor learning and sports psychology. Seeks to advance the study and practice of sports psychology. Gathers and disseminates information; sponsors research and educational programs. **Languages:** English, French.

CANADIAN THORACIC SOCIETY (CTS)
(Societe Canadienne de Thoracologie)
4223 Du Moulin E
Cap-Rouge, PQ, Canada G1Y 1L4
Yvon Cormier, Pres.
PH: (418)656-4747
FX: (418)656-4762
Description: Physicians and other health care professionals with an interest in thoracic surgery. Seeks to advance the study and practice of thoracic medicine. Serves as a clearinghouse on thoracic medicine; conducts continuing professional education programs for members. **Languages:** English, French.

CANADIAN WHOLESALE DRUG ASSOCIATION (CWDA)
(Association des Grossistes en Medicaments du Canada)
110 rue Sherbrooke W, Bureau 2206
Montreal, PQ, Canada H3A 1G8
Desmond Lartigue, Pres.
PH: (514)842-8627
FX: (514)842-3061
Description: Dealers in wholesale pharmaceuticals. Seeks to advance the pharmaceutical wholesale and distribution industries. Facilitates exchange of information among members; represents members before labor and industrial organizations, government agencies, and the public. **Languages:** English, French.

CANADIANS FOR HEALTH RESEARCH (CHR)
(Canadiens pour la Recherche Medicale)
CP 126
Westmount, PQ, Canada H3Z 2T1
Patricia Guyda, Pres.
PH: (514)398-7478
FX: (514)398-8361
Description: Health care professionals and scientists with an interest in health research. Seeks to advance medical research; promotes continuing professional development of members. Serves as a forum for the exchange of information among members; sponsors research and educational programs. **Languages:** English, French.

CANCER BIOTHERAPY RESEARCH GROUP
e-mail: 72520.3014@compuserve.com
url: http://www.CBRG.org
PO Box 680757
Franklin, TN 37068-0757
Rosalie A. Crispin, Exec.Dir.
PH: (615)791-6393
FX: (615)791-4719
Description: Practicing oncologists, cancer management professionals, hospitals, and biopharmaceutical companies interested in using biologicals alone and with other agents in the treatment of all types of cancer. Promotes and sponsors research into biotherapy and other innovative cell biology technologies such as tumor-infiltrating lymphocytes, autologous vaccines and activated lymphocytes, pulsed LAK cells, and peripheral and bone marrow stem cells. Conducts cancer trials, and studies; provides networking opportunities. **Founded:** 1987. **Membership:** 100. **Staff:** 5.

Languages: English. **Formerly:** (1997) National Biotherapy Study Group.

CANCER CARE (CC)
1180 Avenue of the Americas
New York, NY 10036
Diane Blum, Exec.Dir.
PH: (212)221-3300
FX: (212)719-0263
Description: Promotes and aids the development of social services to patients and families of patients stricken by cancer, throughout the U.S. and worldwide. Offers professional social work counseling and guidance to help patients and families cope with the emotional and psychological consequences of cancer. Sponsors programs of professional consultation and education. Conducts social research on the impact of a catastrophic illness and on the alleviation of the emotional, economic, and social effects of cancer. Provides facts and guidelines on social services and related needs of the catastrophically ill through a public relations and public affairs program. Provides financial assistance to eligible families for certain home care, child care, transportation, and medical treatment costs. Testifies before government officials on national health insurance, Medicaid, Medicare, and multi-faceted problems of the aging. Holds symposia. **Founded:** 1944. **Membership:** 20000. **Staff:** 85. **Local Groups:** 38. **Languages:** English, Spanish. **Budget:** $7,197,600. **Publication:** *Currents*, quarterly. Newsletter ■ Annual Report. Price: free. Advertising: not accepted. **Formerly:** (1986) National Cancer Foundation; (1991) National Cancer Care Foundation.

CANCER CONTROL SOCIETY (CCS)
2043 N. Berendo St.
Los Angeles, CA 90027
Norman Fritz, Pres.
PH: (213)663-7801
Description: Cancer patients, doctors, and interested individuals. Educates the public on the prevention and control of cancer and other diseases through nutrition, tests, and nontoxic alternative therapies, such as Laetrile, Gerson, Hoxsey, Koch, Enzymes, Wheat Grass, Immunology, Mega-Vitamins and Minerals, Detoxification and Nutrition, and DMSO and Chelation Therapy. Provides information through a 24-hour telephone hot line, direct mail, doctor and patient lists, speakers, films, cancer clinic tours, and Cancer Book House. **Founded:** 1973. **Membership:** 5500. **Languages:** English. **Publication:** *Cancer Book House List*, biennial ■ *Cancer Control Journal*, periodic. Reports on one specific cancer-related topic in each issue. Price: included in membership dues. Circulation: 20,000. Advertising: not accepted ■ *Doctor and Clinic Directory*, 6/year ■ *Patient Directory*, 6/year.

CANCER FEDERATION (CFI)
PO Box 1298
Banning, CA 92220-0009
John Steinbacher, Exec.Dir.
Description: Physicians, scientists, nurses, and laymen (both cancer patients and nonpatients). Promotes research and education in the field of cancer immunology. Seeks to discover appropriate cancer therapies using natural biological modifiers. Funds research at major centers throughout the U.S., including the University of California (Riverside and Santa Barbara), University of Hawaii, and University of Pittsburgh, on biological modifiers, such as lymphokines; killer cells; Interleukin I and II; diet; and psychological aspects of cancer. Compiles statistics; conducts research and education in cancer therapy, including vaccines, and in psychological programming for patients. Offers counseling program for cancer patients and their families. Sponsors public medical conferences and in-service courses for nurses on the psychology of cancer, and research projects at many universities and hospitals in the field of immunology. Sponsors charitable program. **Founded:** 1977. **Membership:** 1500. **Staff:** 4. **Languages:** English. **Budget:** $600,000. **Publication:** *Challenge of the Cancer Federation*, quarterly. Newsletter. Provides general information on cancer research and treatments. Contains information on federation activities and book reviews. Price: included in

membership dues. Circulation: 2,000. Advertising: accepted ■ Audiotapes ■ Booklets ■ Books ■ Monographs ■ Videos.

CANCER INFORMATION SERVICE (CIS)
NCI/NIH, Bldg. 31, 10A07
31 Center Dr., MSC 2580
Bethesda, MD 20892-2580
Chris Thomsen, Chief
TF: 8004-CANCER
FX: (301)402-0555
Description: Funded by the National Cancer Institute. Trained counselors provide information about cancer causes, prevention, detection, diagnosis, rehabilitation, and research. Provides technical assistance to state and regional organizations conducting cancer education activities. Offers publications on cancer. **Founded:** 1975. **Regional Groups:** 19. **Languages:** English.

CANCER INFORMATION SERVICE (CANADA) (CIS)
(Service d'Information sur le Cancer)
328 Mountain Park Ave.
Hamilton, ON, Canada L8V 4X2
Patricia Payne, Mgr.
PH: (905)387-1153
TF: 800263-6750
FX: (905)387-0376
Description: Promotes increased public awareness of cancer and its detection, treatment, and prevention. Serves as a clearinghouse on cancer; sponsors research and educational programs. **Languages:** English, French.

CANCER RESEARCH FUND OF THE DAMON RUNYON - WALTER WINCHELL FOUNDATION (CRFDR-WWF)
675 3rd Ave., 25 Fl.
New York, NY 10017
Rebecca R. Kry, Exec.Dir.
PH: (212)532-7000
TF: 800445-2494
FX: (212)686-1935
Description: Nonprofit organization dedicated to advancing cancer research through the funding of initial postdoctoral fellowships and junior faculty awards. Monies are raised through the Fund's Broadway Theatre Ticket Service and the solicitation of individuals, foundations and corporations. **Founded:** 1946. **Staff:** 11. **Languages:** English. **Publication:** Annual Report, annual ■ Brochures ■ Newsletter, 3/year. **Formerly:** Damon Runyon Foundation for Cancer Research; (1973) Damon Runyon Memorial Fund for Cancer Research; (1988) Damon Runyon - Walter Winchell Cancer Fund; (1993) Damon Runyon - Walter Winchell Cancer Research Fund.

CANCER RESEARCH SOCIETY (CRS)
(Societe de Recherche sur le Cancer)
e-mail: crs@cam.org
1 Place Ville Marie, Ste. 2332
Montreal, PQ, Canada H3B 3M5
Ivy Steinberg, Exec.Dir.
PH: (514)861-9227
FX: (514)861-9220
Description: Health care professionals and research scientists with an interest in cancer. Seeks to advance cancer research. Serves as a forum for the exchange of information among members; sponsors research and educational programs. **Languages:** English, French.

CANDLELIGHTERS CHILDHOOD CANCER FOUNDATION (CCCF)
e-mail: info@candlelighters.org
url: http://www.candlelighters.org
7910 Woodmont Ave., Ste. 460
Bethesda, MD 20814-3015
PH: (301)657-8401
TF: 800366-2223
FX: (301)718-2686
Description: Children and adolescents with cancer, their family

members, survivors of childhood cancer, and professionals who work with them. Educates, supports, serves, and advocates for families and individuals touched by childhood cancer, empowering them to meet the challenges they face. Coordinates a network of more than 400 peer support groups and contacts for parents of children/adolescents with cancer. Offers newsletters, other publications, literature and searches through the Information Clearinghouse. Makes referrals to volunteers who can assist with health insurance problems, second opinions, and employment issues. Local groups offer meetings at which parents share information and emotional support and hear speakers. Many chapters offer parent-to-parent visitation, transportation, blood or wig banks, speakers' bureaus, meetings for young people, and bereavement groups. Named for the Chinese proverb, "It is better to light one candle than to curse the darkness.". **Founded:** 1970. **Membership:** 40000. **Staff:** 3. Multinational. **Local Groups:** 400. **Languages:** English. **Budget:** $600,000. **Publication:** *Bone Marrow Transplant Guide*. Handbook. Price: $7.50. Advertising: not accepted ■ *CCCF Bibliography and Resource Guide*, annual. Annotated reviews of books, articles, pamphlets, and videos. Price: $5.00 in U.S.; $8.00 in Canada and Mexico; $12.00 all other countries. Circulation: 5,000. Advertising: not accepted ■ *CCCF Quarterly Newsletter*. Articles, poetry, and reviews pertaining to living with and

CANDLELIGHTERS CHILDHOOD CANCER FOUNDATION CANADA (CCCFC)
(Fondation des Eclaireurs pour le Cancer dans l'Enfance Canada)
e-mail: staff@candlelighters.ca
url: http://www.candlelighters.ca
55 Eglinton Ave. E, Ste. 401
Toronto, ON, Canada M4P 1G8
Eleanor Pask, Exec.Dir.
PH: (416)489-6440
FX: (416)489-9812
Description: Volunteers. Seeks to improve the quality of life of children with cancer and their families. Seeks to advance the detection, prevention, and treatment of childhood cancers. Provides assistance to children with cancer; maintains support groups; sponsors educational and recreational programs. **Languages:** English, French.

CARDIOVASCULAR CREDENTIALING INTERNATIONAL (CCI)
e-mail: ccircvt@nettek.net
4456 Corporation Ln., Ste. 120
Virginia Beach, VA 23462
Julia Dow, Exec.Dir.
PH: (804)497-3380
TF: 800326-0268
FX: (804)497-3491
Description: Cardiovascular technologists involved in the allied health professions. Conducts testing of allied health professionals throughout the U.S. and Canada. Provides study guides and reliability and validity testing. Compiles statistics. **Founded:** 1988. **Membership:** 15000. **Staff:** 5. Multinational. **Languages:** English. **Budget:** $250,000. Formed by Merger of National Board of Cardiovascular Technology; Cardiovascular Credentialing International. **Formerly** (1984) National Board for Cardiopulmonary Credentialing; (1986) National Board for Cardiovascular and Pulmonary Credentialing.

CASE MANAGEMENT SOCIETY OF AMERICA (CMSA)
e-mail: cmsa@cmsa.org
url: http://www.cmsa.org
8201 Cantrell Rd., Ste. 230
Little Rock, AR 72227-2448
Jeanne Boling, Exec.Dir.
PH: (501)225-2229
FX: (501)221-9068
Description: Case management and allied healthcare professionals. Offers members a voice in the future through opportunities for professional leadership and networking opportunities, case

management legislative impact and visibility, publications, educational workshops, seminars, conferences, recognition and fellowship opportunities. **Founded:** 1990. **Membership:** 6500. **Staff:** 14. Multinational. **Local Groups:** 100. **Languages:** English.

CATECHOLAMINE CLUB (CC)

Dept. of Pharmacology and Toxicology
School of Pharmacy
Lawrence, KS 66045
Walter R Dixon, Ph.D., Sec.-Treas.
PH: (785)864-3951
FX: (785)864-5219
Description: Neuroscience researchers throughout the world interested in catecholamines. Provides a forum for presentation and detailed discussion of studies done by outstanding researchers in the field. (Catecholamines are certain chemical compounds with a similar basic structure, three of which are found in the human body, including norepinephrine, dopamine, and epinephrine. All three compounds function in brain chemistry. Norepinephrine and dopamine act as agents that transfer nerve impulses; epinephrine mainly initiates physiological and metabolic responses in stress situations. The functions of these compounds are significant in the study of the biochemistry of the brain and nervous system and of nervous and brain disorders.) Maintains speakers' bureau. **Founded:** 1969. **Membership:** 350. **Languages:** English.

CATHOLIC HEALTH ASSOCIATION OF CANADA

e-mail: chac@web.net
url: http://www.net-globe.com/chac/
1247 Kilborn Pl.
Ottawa, ON, Canada K1H 6K9
Mr. Richard Haughian, Pres.
PH: (613)731-7148
FX: (613)731-7797
Description: Works to administer Christian principles within the Canadian healthcare system. Fosters competent and efficient health care services. Disseminates health information.

CATHOLIC MEDICAL ASSOCIATION

e-mail: cahmed@cathmed.com
url: http://www.cathmed.com
850 Elm Grove Rd.
Elm Grove, WI 53122
Michael J. Herzog, Dir.
PH: (414)784-3435
FX: (414)782-8788
Description: Catholic physicians and dentists with a priest-moderator for each local group. **Founded:** 1932. **Membership:** 3500. **Staff:** 4. **Local Groups:** 90. **Languages:** English. **Budget:** $100,000. **Publication:** *The Linacre Quarterly.* **Formerly:** (1998) National Federation of Catholic Physicians Guilds.

CATHOLIC MEDICAL MISSION BOARD (CMMB)

e-mail: cmmb@compuserve.com
10 W. 17th St.
New York, NY 10011-5765
Terry Kirch, Pres./Dir.
PH: (212)242-7757
TF: 800678-5969
FX: (212)807-9161
Description: Provides health care assistance to clinical facilities in developing and transitional countries. Financial aid granted to students matriculated in accredited health care education programs in their own mission countries. Placement program assists health providers interested in volunteering for short- and long-term tours of service at selected clinical sites around the world. Conducts charitable programs. Convention/Meeting: none. **Founded:** 1928. **Staff:** 30. Multinational. **Languages:** English. **Budget:** $3,100,000. **Publication:** *Medical Mission News,* quarterly. Magazine. Provides information on CMMB's programs. Recipients of shipments and health care placement opportunities are features. Price: free. Circulation: 30,000. Advertising: not accepted ■ Annual Report. Price: free. Advertising: not accepted.

CCHS FAMILY SUPPORT NETWORK

e-mail: vanderlaanm@hartwick.edu
71 Maple St.
Oneonta, NY 13820
Mary Vanderlaan, Founder
PH: (607)432-8872
Description: Seeks to provide support to families with a CCHS child. Supports CCHS research; shares information on ventilation methods and technologies; conducts educational programs; collects data on CCHS. **Founded:** 1990. **Membership:** 300. Multinational. **Formerly** (1998) Central Hypoventilation Syndrome Parent Support Group.

CENTER FOR ATTITUDINAL HEALING (CAH)

url: http://www.healingcenter.org
33 Buchanan Dr.
Sausalito, CA 94965
Don Goewey, Exec.Dir.
PH: (415)331-6161
FX: (415)331-4545
Description: Nonsectarian organization established to supplement traditional health care by offering free services in attitudinal healing for both children and adults with life-threatening illnesses, or other crises. (The concept of attitudinal healing is based on the belief that it is possible to choose peace rather than conflict, and love rather than fear; the center defines health as inner peace and healing as the process of letting go of fear.) Offers support groups and arranges home and hospital visits for children, youth, and adults. Offers volunteer training program. Maintains speakers' bureau; conducts educational programs and charitable activities. **Founded:** 1975. **Membership:** 12000. **Staff:** 10. Multinational. **Languages:** English. **Budget:** $500,000.

CENTER FOR HUMANE OPTIONS IN CHILDBIRTH EXPERIENCES (CHOICE)

3474 N. High St.
Columbus, OH 43214
Abby Kinne, Dir.
PH: (614)263-2229
FX: (614)449-0140
Description: Medical professionals, paraprofessionals, and interested individuals. Purpose is to teach and encourage parents, parents-to-be, groups, and interested individuals working in family-oriented childbirth in hospital birth centers and out-of-hospital situations. Trains and certifies attendants to attend or coach births. Acts as consumer advocate for hospital births. Services include medical referrals, childbirth education classes, and supplementary prenatal care. Sponsors community educational programs; operates speakers' bureau; compiles statistics. Convention/Meeting: none. **Founded:** 1977. **Membership:** 1200. **Local Groups:** 1. **Languages:** English.

CENTER FOR MEDICAL CONSUMERS (CMC)

237 Thompson St.
New York, NY 10012
Arthur A. Levin, Dir.
PH: (212)674-7105
FX: (212)674-7100
Description: Provides people with the information they need to understand medical conditions and obtain appropriate health care. **Founded:** 1976. **Staff:** 3. Local. **Languages:** English. **Budget:** $150,000. **Publication:** *HealthFacts,* monthly. Newsletter. Helps consumers determine the risks and effectiveness of common medical procedures. Presents all treatment options, including nonmedical. Price: $25.00/year. ISSN: 0738-811X. Circulation: 13,000. Advertising: not accepted ■ Reports. **Formerly:** (1998) Center for Medical Consumers and Health Care Information.

CENTER FOR PROFESSIONAL WELL-BEING (CWBHP)
e-mail: cpwb@mindspring.com
url: http://www.cpwb.org
21 W. Colony Pl., Ste. 150
Durham, NC 27705
John-Henry Pfifferling, Ph.D., Pres.
PH: (919)489-9167
FX: (919)419-0011
Description: Society serving health and other professional associations. Promotes the well-being of health professionals and their families through: preventive education on manifestations of disabilities; increased awareness about the stresses inherent in the system of providing health services; efforts to improve and maintain effectiveness. Provides information on treatment centers. Conducts research and supports efforts to study the incidence and causes of professional impairment, with prevention as a goal. Maintains speakers' bureau; provides individual consulting and counseling. Offers workshops on The Joy of Medicine, Physician Burnout, and Preventive Malpractice Strategies; sponsors retreats, seminars, and lectures. **Founded:** 1979. **Membership:** 800. **Staff:** 2. Multinational. **Languages:** English. **Budget:** $160,000. **Publication:** *Being Well: Bulletin of the Society for Professional Well-Being,* quarterly. Price: included in membership dues; $55.00 ▪ Booklets ▪ Monographs ▪ Videos. **Formerly:** (1993) Center for the Well-Being of Health Professionals.

CENTER FOR REPRODUCTIVE HEALTH AND FAMILY
    HEALTH
e-mail: rafh@bdvn.vnmail.vdn.net
C12 Bai Cat Linh
Dong Da
Hanoi, Vietnam
Prof. Nguyen Thi Hoai Duc, MD, Dir.
PH: 84 4 8234288
FX: 84 4 8234288
Description: Promotes availability of family planning and reproductive health services throughout Vietnam, and particularly in rural areas. Provides assistance to rural development programs operating in Vietnam; works to integrate population control and family planning activities into development programs. **Founded:** 1993. **Membership:** 12. **Staff:** 10. **National Groups:** 1. **Languages:** English, French. **For-Profit. Budget:** 200,000 Dg. **Publication:** *Midwife.* Booklets ▪ *Reproductive Health,* quarterly. Magazine ▪ *Women's health Rain Drops - STDs Prevention What's cannot poured out* (in Vietnamese), annual. Video.

CENTER FOR RESEARCH IN AMBULATORY HEALTH
    CARE ADMINISTRATION (CRAHCA)
e-mail: bgreen@mgma.com
url: http://www.mgma.com
104 Inverness Ter. E.
Englewood, CO 80112-5306
Barry R. Greene, Ph.D., VP
PH: (303)397-7879
FX: (303)397-1827
Description: Seeks to advance the art and science of medical group practice management to improve the health of our communties. Vision is to be the source of excellence and innovation as the leading association in providing quality and timely services and resources for medical practice management and leadership. Develops and advances research-based knowledge in the field of ambulatory health care by improving education, management technology, publications, and database services. Research is directed toward health care economics, policy development and analysis, alternative organizational models for health care delivery, evaluation methodologies, models of provider team leadership, and the social aspects of health services organizations and the communities in which they serve. Research interests include provider reimbursement and the analysis of ambulatory health care and medical practice costs. The evolution and impact of integrated and managed care systems and the role of access and quality in the production and management of ambulatory care services will be examined. The impact of these areas on health system reform will be studied. **Founded:** 1973. **Staff:** 19. **Lang-**

uages: English. **Budget:** $1,500,000. **Publication:** *An Assessment Manual for Medical Groups, 3rd Edition* ▪ *Budgeting and Cost Management for Medical Groups* ▪ *Directions: Quality Assurance Manual for Physician Office Laboratories* ▪ *Financial Management For Medical Groups* ▪ *In-House Supervisory Training Program* ▪ *Integrated Health Care: Reorganizing the Physician, Hospital and Health Plan Relationships* ▪ *Medical Group Practices Face the Uncertain Future: Challenges, Opportunities and Strategies.* Advertising: not accepted ▪ *Physician Recruitment and Retention: A Guide for Rural Medical Group Practice* ▪ *The Pysician Manager in Group Practice* ▪ *Quality Improvement: Practical Applications for Medical Group Practice* ▪ *Telephone Nursing: The Manual* ▪ *Twelve Key Strategies to Improve Cash Flow in Medical Groups.* **Also Known As:** CRAHCA.

CENTER FOR THE STUDY OF PSYCHIATRY AND
    PSYCHOLOGY
4628 Chestnut St.
Bethesda, MD 20814
Peter R. Breggin, M.D., Dir.
PH: (301)652-5580
FX: (301)652-5924
Description: Fosters prevention and treatment of mental and emotional disorders. Promotes alternatives to administering psychiatric drugs to children. Convention/Meeting: none. **Founded:** 1971. **Languages:** English Formerly (1995) Center for the Study of Psychiatry.

CENTER FOR THE WELL BEING OF HEALTH
    PROFESSIONALS
e-mail: profwellbe@aol.com
21 W. Colony Pl., Ste. 150
Durham, NC 27705-5589
PH: (919)489-9167
FX: (919)403-8605
Description: Offers presentations on all areas relevant to professional well-being. Works to find a balance between personal and professional lives.

CENTRAL AMERICAN FEDERATION OF SPORTS
    MEDICINE
(Confederacion Centroamericano de Medicina del Deporte)
e-mail: rbrenesr@irazu.una.ac.cr
Apartado Postal 172
Heredia 3000, Costa Rica
Dr. Rafeal Brenes Rojas, Pres.
PH: 506 2378956
FX: 506 2378956
Description: Promotes the advancement of sports medicine in Central America. **Founded:** 1986. **Membership:** 6. Multinational.

CENTRAL SOCIETY FOR CLINICAL RESEARCH (CSCR)
1481 W. 10th St., No. 111P
Indianapolis, IN 46202-2803
Dr. Morton Arnsdorf, Sec.-Treas.
Description: Individuals who have accomplished a meritorious original investigation in the clinical or allied sciences of medicine and who enjoy an unimpeachable moral standing in the profession. Objectives are: the advancement of medical science; the cultivation of clinical research; the correlation of science with the art of medical practice; the encouragement of scientific investigation by the medical practitioner; the diffusion of a scientific spirit among the members of the society; the sponsorship of scientific meetings; the publication of papers on the methods and results of clinical research. **Founded:** 1928. **Membership:** 1294. **Staff:** 1. **Languages:** English. **Budget:** $100,000.

CENTRE FOR AFRICAN FAMILY STUDIES (CAFS)

(Centre d'Etudes de la Famille Africaine)
e-mail: admin@cafs.org
Pamstech House
Woodvale Grove
Westlands
Nairobi, Kenya
Dr. Pape Syr Diagne, Dir.
PH: 254 2 448618
FX: 254 2 448621
Description: Works to raise public awareness about family planning and reproductive health promotes the significance of family planning in national development. Provides technical assistance to family planning associations; organizes training course for managers, supervisors, and other personnel employed in family planning programs and organizations. Conducts research; disseminates information; compiles statistics. **Founded:** 1975. **Staff:** 34. Multinational. **Languages:** English, French. **Publication:** *African Journal of Fertility, Sexuality and Reproductive Health* (in English and French), biennial. Advertising: accepted ■ *CAFS Information Brochure* (in English and French), annual. Price: free. Circulation: 2,000. Advertising: not accepted ■ *CAFS News* (in English and French), semiannual. Newsletter. Includes family planning issues. Price: free. Circulation: 1,500. Advertising: accepted ■ *Family Life Education Curriculum Guidelines* ■ *Introduction to Family Life Education in Africa* ■ *Programme of Activities* (in English and French), annual ■ *Research Reports*, periodic ■ *Women and Health* (in English), semiannual. Newsletter.

CENTRE FOR DEVELOPMENT AND HEALTH (CDH)

(Centre pour le Developpement et la Sante)
16 Rue Freres Simmonds
Cite Militaire
PO Box 1666
Port-au-Prince, Haiti
PH: 509 232740
FX: 509 232307
Description: Seeks to improve the quality of life in Haiti. Conducts health and education programs. **Founded:** 1974. **Languages:** English, French.

CENTRE FOR DEVELOPMENT AND POPULATION ACTIVITIES -EGYPT (CEDPA)

e-mail: cedpa@idsc.gov.eg
53 Manial St., Ste. 500
Manial el Rodah
PO Box 110
Cairo 11451, Egypt
PH: 20 2 3654565
FX: 20 2 3654568
Description: Seeks to enhance the managerial and technical capabilities of family planning, health, and development professionals. Conducts reproductive health programs focusing on the need of women and youth. Facilitates creation of primary health care services in rural and developing areas; makes available financial assistance to local health and development initiatives. Sponsors training programs for health and development personnel. **Founded:** 1975. **Languages:** Arabic, English.

CENTRE FOR DEVELOPMENT AND POPULATION ACTIVITIES -INDIA (CEDPA)

4/2 Shanti Niketan
New Delhi 110 021, Delhi, India
PH: 91 11 672841
FX: 91 11 6885850
Description: Health and development professionals from developing countries. Seeks to improve family planning and reproduction health programs worldwide; promotes increased availability of reproductive health services in previously underserved areas. Provides managerial training, technical assistance, and financial support to grass roots population and family planning programs. Conducts training courses for reproduction health and family planning service personnel; sponsors training of women to operate and administer health clinics. Gathers and disseminates information on reproductive health and family planning. Main forces of organization is in empowering women to become full partners in development and helping the girl child to have better options in their lives. **Founded:** 1975. **Staff:** 35. Multinational. **Languages:** English, Hindi.

CENTRE FOR DEVELOPMENT AND POPULATION ACTIVITIES -KENYA (CEDPA)

e-mail: njuki@nke.cedpa.permanet.org
Mama Nginna St.
PO Box 63051
Nairobi, Kenya
PH: 254 2 245129
FX: 254 2 252924
Description: Family planning, health, and development professionals. Promotes increased availability and effectiveness of population control, reproductive health, and development programs. Conducts continuing professional education courses for members; sponsors reproductive health training for women in areas underserved by the medical system. Maintains community-level health initiatives including AIDS awareness, contraception education, and environmental consciousness-raising. Operates Better Life Options for Girls and Young Women Program, which provides health education and awareness programs. **Founded:** 1975. **Staff:** 35. **Languages:** English. **Budget:** $3,400,000.

CENTRE FOR DEVELOPMENT AND POPULATION ACTIVITIES -NEPAL (CEDPA)

e-mail: russelln@npl.healthnet.org
GPO 8975
Bhatbotani
Kathmandu, Nepal
PH: 977 1 413156
FX: 977 1 421696
Description: Seeks to improve the technical and managerial capacities of indigenous planning, health, and development professionals. Promotes empowerment of women. Provides training and technical assistance to development, reproductive health, family planning, and environmental protection programs. Conducts educational programs to raise public awareness of population, reproductive health, and development issues. **Founded:** 1975. **Languages:** English, Nepali.

CENTRE FOR DEVELOPMENT AND POPULATION ACTIVITIES -NIGERIA (CEDPAN)

e-mail: cedpa@usaid.gov
Adeola Hopewell St., Plot 1601
Victoria Island, Lagos, Nigeria
Ifenne Enyantu, Country Dir.
PH: 234 1 2618539
FX: 234 1 2615592
Description: Seeks to improve the technical and managerial capacities of indigenous planning, health, and development professionals. Promotes empowerment of women. Provides training and technical assistance to development, reproductive health, family planning, and environmental protection programs. Conducts educational programs to raise public awareness of population, reproductive health, and development issues. **Founded:** 1996. **Staff:** 31. **Local Groups:** 34. **Languages:** English. **Publication:** *Women on the Move* (in English), periodic. Journal. Price: free. Advertising: not accepted.

CENTRE FOR DEVELOPMENT AND POPULATION ACTIVITIES -ROMANIA (CEDPA)

B-dul Primaverii 31, Etaj 1, Apt. 3
Bucharest, Romania
PH: 40 1 2113929
FX: 40 1 2120790
Description: Seeks to improve the technical and managerial capacities of indigenous planning, health, and development professionals. Promotes empowerment of women. Provides training and technical assistance to development, reproductive health, family planning, and environmental protection programs. Conducts educational programs to raise public awareness of popula-

tion, reproductive health, and development issues. **Languages:** English, Romanian.

CENTRE MURAZ
01 Boite Postale 153
Bobo-Dioulasso 01, Burkina Faso
Phillipe Vandeperre, Dir.
PH: 226 970102
FX: 226 970457
Description: Medical researchers and health care professionals. Promotes improved diagnostic techniques and treatments of common diseases. Conducts research and educational programs; makes available health services. Multinational. **Languages:** English, French.

CERTIFIED PERINATAL EDUCATORS ASSOCIATION
3941 Park Dr. No. 20-114
El Dorado Hills, CA 95762
Claudia Lowe, Dir.
PH: (415)893-0439
Description: Certified perinatal educators and practitioners. Provides educational counseling for women and families in the childbearing years. Conducts educational programs and home-study certification. **Founded:** 1983. **Languages:** English. **For-Profit.**

CFIDS ASSOCIATION OF AMERICA
e-mail: cfids@cfids.org
url: http://CFIDS.org/cfids
PO Box 220398
Charlotte, NC 28222-0398
Kim Kenney, Exec. Officer
PH: 800-442-3437
FX: (704)365-9755
Description: Individuals with chronic fatigue and immune dysfunction syndrome (chronic viral illness associated with dysfunction of the immune system; formerly called chronic Epstein-Barr virus); doctors, nurses, and government officials. Advocates continued research into the cause and cure of the syndrome. Funds pilot medical research projects. **Founded:** 1986. **Membership:** 23000. **Staff:** 12. **Languages:** English. **Budget:** $1,500,000. **Publication:** *The CFIDS Chronicle*, quarterly. Journal. Contains research and medical articles, advocacy efforts reports, practical tips on living with CFIDS and book and media reviews. Price: included in membership dues. Circulation: 25,000. Advertising: accepted. **Formerly:** (1994) CFIDS Association.

CHARCOT-MARIE-TOOTH ASSOCIATION (CMTA)
e-mail: cmtassoc@aol.com
url: http://www.charcot-marie-tooth.org
601 Upland Ave.
Upland, PA 19015
Pat Dreibelbis, Dir. of Program Services
PH: (610)499-7486
TF: 800606-CMTA
FX: (610)499-7487
Description: Charcot-Marie-Tooth patients and their families, medical professionals treating the disorder, and interested individuals. (Charcot-Marie-Tooth Disease, also known as peroneal muscular atrophy or hereditary motor sensory neuropathy, is a progressive neurological disorder beginning in childhood or adult life with weakness and muscle wasting in feet, legs, hands, and arms.) Works to inform and educate patients and their families, the medical community, and the public about medical treatment for CMT. Offers support groups for patients and their families; disseminates educational materials; encourages and funds research; sponsors lay and professional symposia. Makes available videotapes; maintains speakers' bureau. **Founded:** 1983. **Membership:** 12000. **Staff:** 3. **Regional Groups:** 20. **Languages:** English. **Publication:** *A Physician's Guide to CMT Disorder.* Handbook. Price: $20.00. Advertising: not accepted ∎ *Charcot-Marie-Tooth Disorders.* Pamphlets ∎ *CMT Facts I,* periodic. Booklets. Price: $3.00. Advertising: not accepted ∎ *CMT-Facts II,* periodic. Booklets. Price: $5.00. Advertising: not accepted ∎ *CMTA Report,* bimonthly. Newsletter. Containing articles on CMT to-

pics, research news, patient profiles, and meeting and program announcements. Price: with membership. ISSN: 1067-0181. Circulation: 10,000. Advertising: not accepted. **Formerly:** (1990) National Foundation for Peroneal Muscular Atrophy.

CHARCOT-MARIE-TOOTH INTERNATIONAL (CMTI)
e-mail: cmtint@vaxxine.com
url: http://www.cmtint.org
1 Springbank Dr.
St. Catharines, ON, Canada L2S 2K1
Linda Crabtree, Exec.Dir. & Pres.
PH: (905)687-3670
FX: (905)687-8753
Description: Individuals in Canada, the U.S., Canada, France, Great Britain, Ireland, and New Zealand who work toward the dissemination of information and research concerning Charcot-Marie-Tooth Disease also known as Peroneal Muscular Atrophy and Hereditary Motor and Sensory Neuropathy. (CMT is marked by degeneration of motor and sensory nerves in the feet and hands.) Aims to: provide information to persons with CMT, the medical community, and the public; gather data and promote research; ensure the psychological well-being of people with CMT; establish an international network for information and counseling. **Founded:** 1984. **Membership:** 5000. **Staff:** 3. Multinational. **National Groups:** 1. **For-Profit. Budget:** C$125,000. **Publication:** *CMT Newsletter,* bimonthly. Articles on coping, research and assistive devices. ISSN: 0831-6279. Circulation: 2,000. Advertising: not accepted ∎ Booklets. Provide information on specific Charcot-Marie-Tooth problems. **Also Known As:** Charcot-Marie-Tooth Disease/Peroral Muscular Antrophy International Association.

CHEMICAL INDUSTRY INSTITUTE OF TOXICOLOGY (CIIT)
e-mail: ciitinfo@ciit.org
url: http://www.ciit.org
PO Box 12137
Research Triangle Park, NC 27709
Dr. Roger O. McClellan, CEO & Pres.
PH: (919)558-1200
FX: (919)558-1300
Description: Chemical and pharmaceutical companies. Aims to develop the scientific data required for evaluation of the potential health risks of chemicals, pharmaceuticals, and consumer products. Works to: understand human health risk from occupational or environmental exposures; improve species extrapolations used in product safety evaluations; update the existing toxicological testing and investigation of commodity chemicals; develop improved testing methods; train professional toxicologists; serve health and environmental needs of the public through research in toxicology. Maintains scientific advisory panel. Provides fellowships for graduate and postdoctoral toxicological training. Conducts workshops. **Founded:** 1974. **Membership:** 37. **Staff:** 160. **Languages:** English.

CHI DELTA MU
Grand Chapter
1003 K St., NW, Ste. 400
Washington, DC 20001-4425
Tracy M. Walton, Jr., Sec.
PH: (202)842-1111
FX: (202)842-0222
Description: To improve relationships among physicians, dentists, and pharmacists so that they may better serve their respective communities. Maintains revolving loan funds. **Founded:** 1913. **Membership:** 650. **Staff:** 1. **State Groups:** 7. **Languages:** English. **Publication:** *Chi Delta Mu News,* quarterly. Newsletter ∎ *Dragon,* annual. Magazine. Advertising: accepted ∎ Proceedings, annual.

CHI ETA PHI SORORITY
3029 13th St. NW
Washington, DC 20009
Catherine W. Binns, R.N., Contact

PH: (202)232-3858
FX: (202)232-3460
Description: Professional sorority - registered and student nurses. Objectives are to: encourage continuing education; stimulate friendship among members; develop working relationships with other professional groups for the improvement and delivery of health care services. Sponsors leadership training seminars every two years and holds additional seminars at the local, regional, and national levels. Offers educational programs for entrance into nursing and allied health fields. Maintains health screening and consumer health education programs; volunteers assistance to senior citizens; sponsors recruitment and retention programs for minority students in nursing. Operates speakers' bureau on health education. **Founded:** 1932. **Membership:** 5000. **Staff:** 1. **Languages:** English.

CHILD AND FAMILY CONSULTATION CENTRE (CFCC)
Shu'Fat
Anata Rd.
PO Box 51819
Jerusalem, Israel
Dr. Elia Awwad, Contact
PH: 972 2 826697
Description: Promotes improved child and family mental health and counseling services. Conducts training courses for mental health personnel working with children and families; sponsors research. **Languages:** Arabic, English.

CHILD NEUROLOGY SOCIETY (CNS)
e-mail: cns@tc.umn.edu
3900 Northwoods Dr., Ste. 175
St. Paul, MN 55112-6966
Mary Currey, Exec.Dir.
PH: (612)486-9447
FX: (612)486-9436
Description: Neurologists certified by the American Board of Psychiatry and Neurology and specializing in child neurology; individuals eligible for the certifying examination and those who have made significant contributions to the field of child neurology; individuals enrolled in approved child neurology training programs. To advance child neurology by establishing a scientific forum for professionals in the field; to define areas of pediatric neurological practices and to make known these procedures among professionals and medical students. Promotes interest in the field of child neurology among medical students. Advertises positions available in pediatric neurology. **Founded:** 1971. **Membership:** 1000. **Staff:** 2. **Languages:** English. **Budget:** $200,000. **Publication:** *Annals of Neurology*, monthly. Journal ■ Booklets.

CHILDBIRTH EDUCATORS - NEW ZEALAND
94 Rattray St.
Christchurch 4, New Zealand
Wendy Maw, National Coord.
PH: 64 3 3488920
Description: Promotes education concerning the principles of natural childbirth; facilitates communication and cooperation among parents and medical professionals. Provides educational opportunities to parents and parents-to-be. **Founded:** 1986. **Membership:** 180. **National Groups:** 1. **Languages:** English. **Budget:** NZ$4,500. **Publication:** *News & Views* (in English), quarterly, always March, June, September, and December. Magazine. Advertising: accepted.

CHILDBIRTH WITHOUT PAIN EDUCATION ASSOCIATION (CWPEA)
20134 Snowden
Detroit, MI 48235
Flora Hommel, Exec.Dir.
PH: (313)341-3816
Description: Former and current students of the Lamaze-Pavlov (psychoprophylactic) method of painless childbirth; physicians, nurses, midwifes, and interested individuals. Sponsors classes and films for women with or without partners, nurses, midwifes and medical and lay groups about the method, which is based on

conditioning reflexes to help prevent pain, thus allowing for natural, usually drug-free childbirth. Works to provide a method-trained registered nurse (monitrice) in attendance at the birth where possible. Collects data for further development of the method; surveys maternity services. Sponsors childbirth teacher and monitrice training and certification. Provides teen pregnancy programs. Offers referral service. **Founded:** 1958. **Membership:** 2000. **Staff:** 5. **National Groups:** 8. **Languages:** English, French. **Budget:** $30,000. Also Known As Lamaze Birth Without Pain Education Association.

CHILDREN AND ADULTS WITH ATTENTION DEFICIT DISORDER (CHADD)
e-mail: national@chadd.org
url: http://www.chadd.org
499 NW 70th Ave., Ste. 101
Plantation, FL 33317
PH: (954)587-3700
TF: 800233-4050
FX: (954)587-4599
Description: Parents, adults, and professionals with an interest in attention-deficit disorders. (ADD is a neurologically-based disorder which affects an individual's behavior and learning. The disorder is characterized by deficits in attention span and impulse control, and is often accompanied by hyperactivity.) Goals are to: maintain a support group for parents of children with ADD; provide a forum for continuing education for parents and professionals about ADD; act as a resource for information about ADD; assure that the best educational opportunities are available to children with ADD so that their specific difficulties will be recognized and appropriately managed within educational settings. Operates speakers' bureau. **Founded:** 1987. **Membership:** 29000. **Staff:** 8. **Local Groups:** 625. **Languages:** English. **Publication:** *ATTENTION*, quarterly, 2/year. Magazine. Circulation: 50,000. Advertising: accepted ■ *Inside Chadd*, quarterly, 8/year. Newsletter ■ Booklets ■ Brochures. **Formerly:** (1993) Children with Attention-Deficit Disorders.

CHILDREN'S HEART ASSOCIATION FOR SUPPORT AND EDUCATION (CHASE)
Hospital for Sick Children
Cardiac Clinic
Division of Cardiology
Toronto, ON, Canada M5G 1X8
Sandra Clarke, Pres.
PH: (416)410-2427
Description: Parents of children with congential heart defects. Works to improve the quality of life of children with cardiological problems and their families. Maintains network of support groups for members; encourages exchange of information among members and between members and cardiologists; conducts social and educational activities; works to increase public awareness of pediatric cardiology. Provides support and assistance to the Hospital for Sick Children's Division of Pediatric Cardiology. **Founded:** 1983. **Membership:** 550. Multinational. **Languages:** English, French. **Publication:** *Straight from the Heart*, monthly. Newsletter.

CHILDREN'S HEARTLINK (CHL)
e-mail: chl@mtn.org
url: http://www.childrensheartlink.org
5075 Arcadia Ave.
Minneapolis, MN 55436-2306
Claudia Liebrecht, Pres.
PH: (612)928-4860
FX: (612)928-4859
Description: Medical charity and service agency. Advocates the prevention and treatment of heart disease in needy children throughout the world; helps selected developing countries expand and improve their cardiac services for children. Provides: treatment for needy children with heart disease; support for rheumatic fever prevention programs; education and training opportunities for foreign physicians, nurses, and other medical professionals; technical advice and problem-solving assistance; medi-

cal equipment and supplies. Organizes fund-raising events. **Founded:** 1969. **Staff:** 9. Multinational. **Regional Groups:** 1. **Languages:** English. **Budget:** $1,760,000. Formerly (1994) Children's Heart Fund.

CHILDREN'S LEUKEMIA RESEARCH ASSOCIATION (NLA)
585 Stewart Ave., Ste. 536
Garden City, NY 11530
Allan D. Weinberg, Exec.Dir.
PH: (516)222-1944
FX: (516)222-0457
Description: Promotes leukemia research and public awareness of the disease. Provides financial aid to leukemia patients and their families, based on need. **Founded:** 1965. **Staff:** 4. **Languages:** English. **Formerly:** (1994) National Leukemia Association.

CHINA ANTICANCER ASSOCIATION (CACA)
e-mail: caca@mail.zlnet.com.cn
url: http://www.caca.org.cn
Huan-Hu-Xi Rd.
Tiyuanbei
Tianjin 300060, People's Republic of China
Zhang Tian-ze, Pres.
PH: 86 22 3359958
FX: 86 22 23526512
Description: Physicians, researchers, and interested individuals in the People's Republic of China. Conducts research programs concentrating on the prevention of cancer. Sponsors research exchange with cancer experts in other countries. Maintains 23 academic commissions. Offers educational programs; disseminates information to the public about cancer prevention. Organizes academic conferences and symposia. **Founded:** 1985. **Membership:** 20000. **Staff:** 6. **National Groups:** 1. **Languages:** Chinese, English. **Budget:** 60,000 Yu. **Publication:** *Cancer Research on Prevention and Treatment* (in Chinese), quarterly. Journal. Price: 4.00 Yu/issue. ISSN: 1000-8578. Circulation: 5,000. Advertising: accepted. Also Cited As: *Cancer Res.Prevent. and Treat* ▪ *Chinese Journal for Cancer Research* (in English), quarterly. Price: 4.00 Yu/issue. ISSN: 1000-9604. Circulation: 4,000. Advertising: not accepted ▪ *Chinese Journal of Clinical Oncology* (in Chinese), monthly. Includes English abstracts. Price: 8.00 Yu/issue; $6.80. ISSN: 1000-8179. Circulation: 5,000. Advertising: accepted.

CHINESE AMERICAN MEDICAL SOCIETY (CAMS)
e-mail: hw5@columbia.edu
url: http://www.camsociety.org
281 Edgewood Ave.
Teaneck, NJ 07666
Dr. H. H. Wang, Exec.Dir.
PH: (201)833-1506
FX: (201)833-8252
Description: Physicians of Chinese origin residing in the U.S. and Canada. Seeks to advance medical knowledge, scientific research, and interchange of information among members and to promote the health status of Chinese Americans. Conducts educational meetings; supports research. Maintains placement service. Sponsors limited charitable program. **Founded:** 1962. **Membership:** 700. **Regional Groups:** 4. **Languages:** English. **Publication:** *Chinese American Medical Society – Newsletter*, 3-4/year. Includes membership news, announcements, and calendar of events. Price: included in membership dues. Circulation: 700. Advertising: accepted ▪ Membership Directory, biennial. **Formerly:** (1985) American Chinese Medical Society.

CHINESE NURSING ASSOCIATION
42 Dongsi Xi Da Jie
Beijing 100710, People's Republic of China
Wang Chunsheng, Sec.Gen.
PH: 86 10 65265331
FX: 86 10 65123754
Description: Nurses and nursing attendants in the People's Republic of China. Promotes research and advanced technological developments in the nursing profession; represents members' interests. Conducts educational programs. **Founded:** 1909. **Mem-

bership:** 240000. **Languages:** English, Japanese. **Publication:** *Chinese Journal of Nursing* (in Chinese), monthly. Price: 3.90 Yu. Advertising: accepted.

CHINESE SOCIETY OF BIOCHEMICAL AND MOLECULAR BIOLOGY (CSBMB)
15 Datun Rd.
Chaoyang District
Beijing 100101, People's Republic of China
Lian-fang Du, Chief of Sec. Office
PH: 86 21 4374430
FX: 86 21 4338357
Description: Biochemical professionals in the People's Republic of China. Promotes the development of science and technology in the fields of agriculture, engineering, general studies, and medicine. Unites members to facilitate academic exchanges and discussions. Organizes national academic projects. Participates in international biochemistry events. **Founded:** 1979. **Membership:** 2500. **Staff:** 6. **Local Groups:** 27. **Languages:** Chinese, English. **Budget:** 500,000 Yu. **Publication:** *Chemistry of Life* (in Chinese), bimonthly ▪ *Chinese Biochemical Journal* (in Chinese), bimonthly. **Formerly:** (1996) Chinese Biochemical Society.

CHINESE TAIPEI PEDIATRIC ASSOCIATION (CTPA)
e-mail: pediatr@pediatr.org.tw
url: http://www.pediatr.org.tw
10-1F, No. 69, Hang-Chow S. Rd
Sec. 1
Taipei 10022, Taiwan
Prof. Tso-Ren Wang, Pres.
PH: 886 2 23516446
FX: 886 2 23516448
Description: Pediatricians and others working in the field of pediatric medicine in 6 countries. Promotes the health and welfare of infants, children, and adolescents. Encourages research and teaching in the field; sponsors educational and scientific programs. Facilitates information exchange. **Founded:** 1960. **Membership:** 2600. **Staff:** 5. Multinational. **Languages:** Chinese, English. **Budget:** $300,000. **Publication:** *Acta Paediatrica Sinica* (in Chinese and English), bimonthly. Journal. Price: NTs 2,000.00/year; $80.00/year. ISSN: 0001-6578. Circulation: 3,000. Advertising: not accepted ▪ *Members' Directory* (in Chinese), triennial ▪ *Supplement* (in Chinese), semiannual. For the purpose of continuing medical education. **Formerly:** (1989) Pediatric Association of Republic of China.

CHOICE
1233 Locust St., Fl. 3
Philadelphia, PA 19107
Trina Johnston, Exec.Dir.
PH: (215)985-3355
FX: (215)985-3369
Description: Concerned with reproductive health care, child care, and HIV/AIDS. Goal of CHOICE, which began as an outgrowth of the Clergy Consultation Service, is to make available, with dignity and concern, high-quality medical and social services to all people at every economic level. Operates resource information hotlines; provides training and consulting services. Conducts training programs. **Founded:** 1971. **Membership:** 1500. **Staff:** 30. **Languages:** English. **Budget:** $1,000,000. **Publication:** *The Choice is Yours*, periodic. Directory. Directory of HIV testing services ▪ *Where to Find*, periodic. Directory. Lists family planning services. Price: free. Circulation: 8,800. Advertising: not accepted. **Also Known As:** Concern for Health Options - Information, Care and Education.

CHOSEN
e-mail: chosew4jay@aol.com
3642 W. 26th St.
Erie, PA 16506
Carl C. Eldred, Exec.Dir.
PH: (814)833-3023
FX: (814)833-4091
Description: Interdenominational organization supporting over-

seas Christian medical mission work. Procures new and used medical equipment for mission hospitals in economically deprived nations; repairs and modifies equipment; prepares equipment for shipping. Provides training in infection control (operating room and sterile departments) and in the proper use and maintenance of equipment for all mission hospital staffs. **Founded:** 1969. **Membership:** 160. **Staff:** 5. **Languages:** English. **Budget:** $1,900,000. **Publication:** *CHOSEN Mission Project Newsletter*, quarterly. Price: free. Circulation: 800. Advertising: not accepted. **Also Known As:** Christian Hospitals Overseas Secure Equipment Needs. **Formerly:** (1988) CHOSEN Mission Project.

CHRISTIAN DENTAL SOCIETY (CDS)
PO Box 177
Sumner, IA 50674
Richard Haw, D.D.S., Sec.
PH: (319)578-8843
TF: 800CDS-SENT
Description: Encourages dentists of the American Dental Association to donate their professional services to Christian schools, clinics, and hospitals. Members also supply materials and equipment to missions. Maintains speakers' bureau. **Founded:** 1962. **Membership:** 800. **Staff:** 1. Multinational. **Languages:** English. **Publication:** *CDS News Update*, monthly. Newsletter ■ *CDS Newsletter*, quarterly. Circulation: 3,000. Advertising: accepted ■ *Keys to a Joyful Practice* ■ *Portable Mission Dentistry*. **Formerly:** (1962) Presbyterian Missionary Committee.

CHRISTIAN HEALTH ASSOCIATION OF KENYA (CHAK)
PO Box 30690
Nairobi, Kenya
N. Olembo, M.D., Contact
PH: 254 2 441920
FX: 254 2 440306
Description: Fosters improved health in Kenya through programs in health education. Compiles statistics on youth and population. Disseminates information. Organizes training courses in health, AIDS/HIV prevention, essential drugs program and family planning. Provides forum for memebers to network. Acts as advocate with the government Ministry of Health and donors on behalf of members. **Founded:** 1930. **Membership:** 230. **Staff:** 45. **Languages:** English. **Budget:** 40,000,000 KSh. **Publication:** *AIDS for Health Workers* (in English). Manuals. Price: 400.00 KSh. Advertising: not accepted ■ *CHAK Quarterly News* (in English). Newsletter. Price: for members. Advertising: accepted.

CHRISTIAN HEALTH ASSOCIATION OF MALAWI (CHAM)
Presidential Way
PO Box 30378
Lilongwe 3, Malawi
Regent L. Gondwe, Exec.Sec.
PH: 265 730966
FX: 265 734987
Description: Health care facilities operated by Christian denominations. Promotes accessibility of health care services, and increased public awareness of the role of Christian churches in the provision of health care. Facilitates communication and cooperation among members; conducts public advocacy and lobbying campaigns on public health and related issues. Conducts training programs for health care personnel and social workers; sponsors AIDS awareness programs. **Founded:** 1967. **Membership:** 148. **Staff:** 30. **Languages:** English. **Budget:** $250,000. **Formerly:** Private Hospital Association of Malawi.

CHRISTIAN MEDICAL & DENTAL SOCIETY (CMDS)
e-mail: main@christian-doctors.com
url: http://www.cmds.org
PO Box 5
Bristol, TN 37621-0005
David Stevens, M.D., Exec.Dir.
PH: (423)844-1000
FX: (423)844-1005
Description: The Christian Medical & Dental Society serves as a voice and ministry for Christian doctors. Its mission is to "change

the heart of healthcare." Founded in 1931, CMDS promotes positions and addresses policies on health care issues; conducts overseas and domestic mission projects; coordinates a network of Christian doctors for fellowship and professional growth; sponsors student ministries in medical and dental schools; distributes educational and inspirational resouurces; holds marriage and family conferences; provides Third World missionary doctors with continuing education resources; and conducts academic exchange programs overseas. **Founded:** 1931. **Membership:** 12000. **Staff:** 50. Multinational. **Regional Groups:** 6. **Languages:** English. **Budget:** $3,800,000. **Publication:** *Christian Doctor's Digest*, 8/year. Magazine. Price: included in membership dues. Circulation: 12,000. Advertising: not accepted ■ *Today's Christian Doctor*, quarterly. Journal. Contains articles on medical and ethical issues. Price: included in membership dues. ISSN: 0009-546X. Circulation: 15,000. Advertising: accepted. **Formerly:** (1988) Christian Medical Society.

CHRISTIAN MEDICAL AND DENTAL SOCIETY OF CANADA (CMDS)
e-mail: cmds@oncomdis.on.ca
url: http://www.cmdsemas.ca
PO Box 160
Warkworth, ON, Canada K0K 3K0
Ellen Watson, Exec.Asst.
PH: (705)924-3246
TF: 888256-8653
FX: (705)924-3384
Description: Christian physicians, dentists, and medical and dental students. Seeks to present "a positive witness of God our Father and our Saviour, Jesus Christ, to the medical and dental professions and to the recipients of health care." Serves as a Christian voice within the medical community and before government agencies, medical and dental associations, policy makers, and patients. Facilitates communication among members; makes available to members opportunities for overseas voluntary service; sponsors social and fellowship activities. **Membership:** 1200. **Staff:** 2. **Languages:** English, French. **Budget:** C$250,000. **Publication:** *Focus*, quarterly. Magazine. Circulation: 1,800 ■ *NUCLEUS*, quarterly. Journal ■ *Spotlight*, periodic. Newsletter.

CHRONIC FATIGUE IMMUNE DISFUNCTION SYNDROME (CFIDS) ACTIVATION NETWORK (CAN)
e-mail: cfidsnet@aol.com
PO Box 345
Larchmont, NY 10538
Ms. Jane Perlmutter, Contact
PH: (212)280-4726
FX: (914)636-6515
Description: Works to prompt government into action on research issues concerning Chronic Fatigue Immune Disfunction Syndrome (CFIDS). (CFIDS is a disease that affects women more than men and causes flu-like symptoms such as aches, pains, and muscle weakness.) Promotes public awareness and knowledge of the disease. Provides information on CFIDS on local and national television and radio. Maintains political action committee to obtain government funding for further research. Compiles statistics. **Founded:** 1991. **Membership:** 1000. **Staff:** 3. **Languages:** English.

CHRONIC GRANULOMATOUS DISEASE ASSOCIATION (CGDA)
e-mail: amhurley@pacificnet.net
url: http://www.pacific.net.r
2616 Monterey Rd.
San Marino, CA 91108-1646
Mary Hurley, Pres.
PH: (626)441-4118
Description: Seeks to improve the quality of life of people with chronic granulomatous disease (CGD) and their families (CGD is chracterized by the presence of multiple granulomas, or nodular inflammatory lesions). Provides support and services to people with CGD; assists in the formation of support networks

for people with CGD; maintains international registry of CGD patients; compiles statistics. **Founded:** 1982. **Languages:** English.

CHURCHES MEDICAL COUNCIL (CMC)
PO Box 3269
Boroko, Papua New Guinea
Mark Fitzmaurice, Contact
PH: 675 2362
FX: 675 3230422
Description: Health care programs and services operated by religious organizations. Promotes effective delivery of health care to previously underserved populations. Facilitates communication and cooperation among members. Sponsors public health and educational programs; makes available health services. **Founded:** 1960. **Membership:** 24. **National Groups:** 1. **Languages:** English. **Budget:** 40,000 K.

CITIZENS FOR HEALTH
e-mail: cfh@ares.csd.net
url: http://www.citizens.org
PO Box 2260
Boulder, CO 80306
Susan Haeger, Exec.Dir.
PH: (303)417-0772
TF: 800357-2211
FX: (303)417-9378
Description: Lobbies government to assure continued access to dietary supplements and herbs, as well as truthful information on their benefits. Seeks to protect the right of individuals to make informed health care choices from a range of traditional and alternative therapies. Holds public forums; organizes rallies. **Founded:** 1991. Multinational. **Local Groups:** 150. **Languages:** English. **Publication:** *Action Alert*, periodic. Bulletin ▪ *FAX Hotline* ▪ *The Natural Activist*, bimonthly. Newsletter. Price: included in full member dues.

CITY OF HOPE (COH)
url: http://www.cityofhope.org
1500 E. Duarte Rd.
Duarte, CA 91010
Dr. Charles Balch, CEO
PH: (626)359-8111
FX: (626)301-8115
Description: Supports the National Pilot Medical Center and the Beckman Research Institute, which are engaged in treatment, research, and medical education in catastrophic diseases including cancer; leukemia; blood, heart and lung diseases; certain hereditary maladies; and metabolic disorders, such as diabetes. Patient care is available on a national and nonsectarian basis. Provides physician referrals. Offers free consulting service to doctors and hospitals. Seeks to influence medicine and science through 80 pilot research programs. From its staff and 200 laboratories, during the past decade over 3000 original findings have emerged in diseases treated as well as studies in diabetes, Alzheimer's disease, AIDS, Huntington's disease, genetics, and brain and nerve function. Receives nationwide support from nearly 500 chartered auxiliaries in over 230 cities, 32 states and Washington, DC, and from management, labor, fraternal and benevolent organizations, individuals, and special campaigns. **Founded:** 1913. **Languages:** English. **Budget:** $000,000.

CLINICAL DENTAL TECHNICIANS ASSOCIATION
e-mail: chris@cdta.org.uk
url: http://www.CDTA.org.uk
7 The Studios
The Row
New Ash Green, Kent DA3 8JL, England
Mr. C.J. Allen, Contact
PH: 44 1474 879430
FX: 44 1474 879430
Description: Dental technicians seeking legal status in the United Kingdom to train and qualify to make and fit dentures directly with the public under Act of Parliament. **Founded:** 1950. **Membership:** 115. **Staff:** 2. **Budget:** L120,000. **Publication:** *The Denturist*, monthly. Newsletter. **Formerly:** Association for Denture Prosthesis.

CLINICAL IMMUNOLOGY SOCIETY (CIS)
e-mail: info@clinimmsoc.org
url: http://www.clinimmsoc.org
611 E. Wells St.
Milwaukee, WI 53202
Susan J. Nelson, Contact
PH: (414)224-8095
FX: (414)276-3349
Description: Investigators and clinicians concerned with immunologic diseases. Promotes research on: the causes and mechanisms of immunologic diseases; improved treatment, evaluation, and prevention of diseases related to immunity. Facilitates exchange of ideas and findings; fosters excellence in research and medical practice. Works to increase public awareness and knowledge of immunologically-mediated diseases. Conducts scientific, educational programs. **Founded:** 1986. **Membership:** 1000. **Languages:** English. **Budget:** $500,000.

CLINICAL MAGNETIC RESONANCE SOCIETY (CMRS)
e-mail: cmrs@one.net
url: http://www.cmrs.com
2600 Euclid Ave.
Cincinnati, OH 45219
Stephen J. Pomeranz, M.D., Pres.
PH: (513)221-0070
TF: 800823-2677
FX: (513)221-0825
Description: Physicians whose work in magnetic resonance imaging is clinically oriented, other health care professionals, and radiological technologists. Supports and nurtures the educational interests and sophistication of the community practitioner of clinical magnetic resonance. Offers accredited educational program at the Annual Meeting. **Founded:** 1995. **Membership:** 750. **Staff:** 2. Multinational.

COLLEGE OF AMERICAN PATHOLOGISTS (CAP)
325 Waukegan Rd.
Northfield, IL 60093-2750
Lee VanBremen, Ph.D.,, Exec.VP
PH: (847)832-7000
TF: 800323-4040
FX: (847)832-8000
Description: Physicians practicing the specialty of pathology (diagnosis, treatment, observation, and understanding of the progress of disease or medical condition) obtained by morphologic, microscopic, chemical, microbiologic, serologic, or any other type of laboratory examination made on the patient. Fosters improvement of education, research, and medical laboratory service to physicians, hospitals, and the public. Provides job placement information for members. Conducts laboratory accreditation program and laboratory proficiency testing surveys. Maintains spokepersons network; provides free health information to the public; compiles statistics; sponsors educational programs. **Founded:** 1947. **Membership:** 15116. **Staff:** 356. **Languages:** English. **Budget:** $69,000,000. **Publication:** *Archives of Pathology and Laboratory Medicine*, monthly. Journal. Price: free to members; $135.00 US and Canada; $185.00 other countries. ISSN: 0003-9985. Circulation: 15,000. Advertising: accepted ▪ *CAP TODAY*, monthly. Newspaper. Includes scientific abstracts. Price: included in membership dues; $40.00 US; $60.00 US possessions and the rest of North America; $95.00 other Countries. ISSN: q891-1525. Circulation: 48,000. Advertising: accepted ▪ *College of American Pathologists–Directory*, annual. Price: included in membership dues ▪ *College of American Pathologists–Job Placement Bulletin*, bimonthly. Updating service providing job listings. Price: included in membership dues. Advertising: not accepted.

COLLEGE OF DIPLOMATES THE AMERICAN BOARD OF ORTHODONTICS (CDABO)
e-mail: 105673.1513@compuserve.com
427 Kenwood St.
Delmar, NY 12054
Elizabeth Matterson, Exec. Dir.
PH: (518)439-0981
FX: (518)439-0980
Description: Members are diplomates of the American Board of Orthodontics who qualify by passing qualifying examinations. Promotes self-evaluation and ongoing professional improvement among orthodontists. Conducts seminars. **Membership:** 1726. **Staff:** 2. **Languages:** English. **Budget:** $275,000. **Publication:** *The Diplomate*, semiannual. Newsletter. Price: for members only. Advertising: not accepted.

COLLEGE OF FAMILY PHYSICIANS OF CANADA (CFPC)
(College des Medecins de Famille du Canada)
e-mail: info@cfpc.ca
url: http://www.cfpc.ca
2630 Skymark Ave.
Mississauga, ON, Canada L4W 5A4
Dr. Calvin Gutkin, Exec.Dir.
PH: (905)629-0900
FX: (905)629-0893
Description: National medical association of family physicians and general practitioners. Members must maintain a minimum of 50 hours of continuing medical education credits annually. Works to maintain standards of family medicine training in the 16 Canadian medical schools through support of the Departments of Family Medicine and the accreditation of family practice residency programs. Administers certification examinations in emergency medicine and family medicine. Runs practice assessment program. Offers public education programs on family medicine topics. **Founded:** 1954. **Membership:** 14000. **Staff:** 50. **State Groups:** 10. **Languages:** English, French. **Budget:** C$7,000,000. **Publication:** *Canadian Family Physician* (in English and French), monthly. Journal. Price: C$8.56/issue. ISSN: 0008-350X. Circulation: 31,500. Advertising: accepted ▪ *CFPC-Liaison Newsletter*, quarterly ▪ *Self-Evaluation* (in English and French), bimonthly. Home study program ▪ *Stress Without Distress: A Guide to the Management of Stress in Family Physicians.*. Price: C$20.00. Also Cited As: *Stress sans Detresse: un Guide pour Aider les Medecins de Famille a Maitriser le Stress.*

COLLEGIUM INTERNATIONALE NEURO-PSYCHOPHARMACOLOGICUM (CINP)
e-mail: cinp@ctrvax.vanderbilt.edu
url: http://www.vanderbilt.edu/cinp
2014 Broadway, Ste. 320
Nashville, TN 37203
Oakley Ray, Ph.D., Sec., Presidents Committee
PH: (615)322-2075
FX: (615)343-0662
Description: Individuals engaged in experimental and clinical neuropsychopharmacological research and teachers in this field. Purposes are to advance the experimental and clinical aspects of the neuropsychopharmacological sciences; facilitate international relations between branches of the neuropsychopharmacological disciplines; further the international exchange of information and promote personal relations; consider the medico-social problems of psychopharmacology. **Founded:** 1957. **Membership:** 1000. Multinational. **Languages:** English.

COLOMBIAN PEDRIATRIC SOCIETY (CPS)
(Sociedad Colombiana de Pediatria)
Carrera 5, No. 67-28
Santa Fe
Bogota, Colombia
Dr. Jose Serrato, M.D., Pres.
PH: 57 1 2550047
FX: 57 1 3104215
Description: Health care professionals specializing in pediatric and adolescent medicine. Facilitates exchange of information a-mong members; establishes unified guidelines for pediatric diagnosis and treatment. Conducts national immunization programs. **Founded:** 1917. **Membership:** 1984. **Staff:** 10. **Regional Groups:** 21. **Languages:** English, Spanish. **Budget:** 20,000,000 CoP. **Publication:** *ACTA Pediatrica* (in Spanish), 3/year ▪ *Pediatria* (in Spanish), quarterly. Journal. Price: free for members. Circulation: 2,000. Advertising: accepted ▪ *Revista Colombiana de Pediatria y Puericultura* (in Spanish), quarterly. **Absorbed:** (1988) Colombian Pediatric Federation.

COLOMBIAN SOCIETY OF DERMATOLOGY (CSD)
(Sociedad Colombiana de Dermatologia)
Apartado Aereo 90123
Bogota, Colombia
Dr. Maria Duran
PH: 57 1 2575568
FX: 57 1 2182596
Description: Dermatologists interested in furthering the study and profession of dermatology in Colombia. Conducts research; disseminates information. **Founded:** 1947. **Membership:** 300. **Languages:** Spanish. **Publication:** *Revista de la Sociedad Colombiana de Dermatologia* (in Spanish), bimonthly. Journal.

COMMISSION ON ACCREDITATION OF ALLIED HEALTH EDUCATION PROGRAMS (CAAHEP)
e-mail: 75767.1444@compuserve.com
url: http://www.caahep.org
35 E. Wacker Dr., Ste. 1970
Chicago, IL 60601-2208
Mr. L.M. Detmer, MHA, Exec.Dir.
PH: (312)553-9355
FX: (312)553-9616
Description: Serves as an nationally recognized accrediting agency for allied health programs in 18 occupational areas. **Founded:** 1994. **Membership:** 70. **Staff:** 4. **Languages:** English. **For-Profit.** **Budget:** $550,000. **Formerly:** (1994) Committee on Allied Health Education and Accreditation.

COMMISSION ON GRADUATES OF FOREIGN NURSING SCHOOLS (CGFNS)
e-mail: nichols@compuserve.com
3600 Market St., Ste. 400
Philadelphia, PA 19104
Barbara Nichols, RN,MSN, Exec. Officer
PH: (215)222-8454
FX: (215)662-0425
Description: Established to help ensure safe nursing care for the American public while assisting nurses educated outside the United States in assesing their ability to become licensed, as well as to practice, in the U.S. Offers a certification program with credentials review and exam of nursing knowledge and English-language proficiency for registered nurses. Provides the CGFNS Credentials Evaluation Service which can evaluate any nurse's academic records in terms of U.S. comparability. Conducts studies and surveys; participates in policy discussions concerning international nursing education, licensure, and practice. **Founded:** 1977. **Staff:** 40. Multinational. **Languages:** English.

COMMISSIONED OFFICERS ASSOCIATION OF THE UNITED STATES PUBLIC HEALTH SERVICE (COA)
e-mail: mikecoa@aol.com
url: http://www.coausphs.org
8201 Corporate Dr., Ste. 560
Landover, MD 20785
Michael Lord, Exec.Dir.
PH: (301)731-9080
FX: (301)731-9084
Description: Commissioned officers of the U.S. Public Health Service; includes career active duty, retired, and inactive reserve officers who are physicians, dentists, scientists, engineers, pharmacists, nurses, and other types of professional personnel. Acts as a spokesman for the Commissioned Corps, as an information center for its members, and "as a sounding board where views and concerns of the Corps may be brought to the proper authori-

ties for official action.". **Founded:** 1910. **Membership:** 7300. **Staff:** 6. **Local Groups:** 45. **Languages:** English. **Budget:** $750,000. Absorbed (1976) United States Public Health Service Clinical Society.

COMMITTEE ON ACCREDITATION FOR OPTHALMIC MEDICAL PERSONNEL (COA-OMP)

e-mail: jcahpo@jcahpo.org
2025 Woodlane Dr.
St. Paul, MN 55125-2995
Mr. Edward Wilson, M.D., Pres.
PH: (612)731-2944
TF: 800284-3937
FX: (612)731-0410
Description: Individuals from collaborating health organizations including the Association of Technical Personnel in Ophthalmology and Joint Commission on Allied Health Personnel in Ophthalmology Evaluates ophthalmic educational programs applying for accreditation from the Commission on Accreditation of Allied Health Education Programs. Reviews and revises guidelines, maintains policies, and approves processes that comply with standards established for national accrediting agencies. Analyzes self-study reports; provides teams of representatives to conduct site visits of programs. Compiles statistics. **Founded:** 1987. **Membership:** 4. **Staff:** 1. **Languages:** English. **Publication:** *Educational Programs for Ophthalmic Medical Personnel*, 3/year. Brochure. Price: free. Advertising: not accepted. **Formerly:** (1988) Joint Review Committee for the Ophthalmic Medical Assistant; (1989) Joint Review Commission for the Ophthalmic Medical Personnel; (1997) Joint Review Committee for Opthalmic Medical Personnel.

COMMITTEE FOR FREEDOM OF CHOICE IN MEDICINE (CFCM)

e-mail: ambio@ix.netcom.com
url: http://www.ambio@ix.netcom.com
1180 Walnut Ave.
Chula Vista, CA 91911
Mike Culbert, Chm. Emeritus
PH: (619)429-8200
TF: 800227-4473
FX: (619)429-8004
Description: Purpose is to support freedom of choice for any therapy which shows clear evidence of efficacy and to prohibit the interference of government or any third party in the relationship between an informed patient and his or her physician. Activities include: publishing information to keep members apprised of the latest developments in research and treatment; directing people with questions concerning alternative therapy to physicians in their areas; maintaining an information service for physicians interested in expanding their knowledge of metabolic/ nutritional treatment; providing educational exhibits for programs and seminars being conducted by various medical groups. Conducts research; compiles statistics on people with degenerative diseases who have been treated with metabolic therapy. Operates speakers' bureau. **Founded:** 1972. **Membership:** 30000. **Staff:** 5. **Local Groups:** 30. **Languages:** English. **Publication:** *Choice Magazine*, quarterly. Includes science corner and heart, cancer, drug, and court watch sections. Price: included in membership dues ■ Audiotapes ■ Books ■ Brochures ■ Pamphlets ■ Reprints ■ Videos. **Formerly:** (1985) Committee for Freedom of Choice in Cancer Therapy.

COMMITTEE OF INTERNS AND RESIDENTS (CIR)

386 Park Ave. S., Rm. 1502
New York, NY 10016
John Ronches, Exec.Dir.
PH: (212)725-5500
FX: (212)779-2413
Description: Medical and dental interns, residents, chief residents, and fellows (collectively referred to as house staff officers) at 50 member hospitals located in New York, New Jersey, and Washington, DC. Purposes include representing house staff in matters pertaining to compensation, benefits, hours, working conditions, and other issues affecting their employment, education, training, and the quality of health services and patient care. **Founded:** 1957. **Membership:** 5000. **Staff:** 20. **Languages:** English. **Publication:** *News*, monthly. **Formerly:** (1974) Committee of Interns and Residents in New York City.

COMMITTEE FOR NATIONAL HEALTH INSURANCE (CNHI)

1757 N St. NW
Washington, DC 20036
Denise E. Holmes, Dir.
PH: (202)223-9685
FX: (202)293-3457
Description: Persons from health care fields; government, labor, academic, business, economic, and citizen's organizations. Conducts research and education on the health care system in the U.S., its problems and the ways in which to bring about reform through enactment of a comprehensive national health insurance program. **Founded:** 1969. **Membership:** 100. **Staff:** 3. **Languages:** English. **Publication:** *Health Security News*, bimonthly. Newsletter.

COMMITTEE FOR THE PROMOTION OF MEDICAL RESEARCH

191 Hayward St.
Yonkers, NY 10704
Ellen M. Cosgrove, Exec.Sec.
PH: (914)968-0262
Description: Is concerned with the administration of medical research grants. Convention/Meeting: none. **Founded:** 1944. **Staff:** 1. **Languages:** English.

COMMITTEE FOR TRUTH IN PSYCHIATRY (CTIP)

e-mail: andrel@pie.org
url: http://www.i1.net/~juli/shocked.html
PO Box 1214
New York, NY 10003
Linda Andre, Dir.
PH: (212)473-4786
Description: Former psychiatric patients who have had electroconvulsive therapy (ECT), working to bring about truthfully informed consent to shock treatment. Works to retain ECT's current FDA classification as a high-risk procedure. Has submitted a proposal to the Food and Drug Administration regarding a statement of information about ECT that would be given to patients before they give consent for treatment. Seeks endorsements for the CTIP statement. Also has petitioned the FDA for an animal and human CAT scan study of ECT. Convention/ Meeting: none. **Founded:** 1984. **Membership:** 500. Multinational. **Languages:** English.

COMMONWEALTH DENTAL ASSOCIATION (CDA)

e-mail: 100641.1544@compuserve.com
64 Wimpole St.
London W1M 8AL, England
Dr. S. Prince Akpabio, OBE, Exec.Sec.
PH: 44 171 9350875
FX: 44 171 4875232
Description: Local dental associations. Serves as a forum for discussion of matters of interest to members; works to coordinate members' activities. Promotes dental hygiene and oral health. Develops primary preventive dental strategies; conducts training programs for dental health workers; provides technical support to members in implementing programs. Holds educational courses. **Founded:** 1991. **Membership:** 44. **Staff:** 1. Multinational. **Languages:** English. **Publication:** *CDA News* (in English), semiannual. Newsletter. Advertising: accepted.

COMMONWEALTH MEDICAL ASSOCIATION (CMA)

e-mail: com_med_assn@compuserve.com
BMA House
Tavistock Sq.
London WC1H 9JP, England
Dr. J.D.J. Havard, Sec.

PH: 44 171 3836095
FX: 44 171 3836195
Description: National medical associations in Commonwealth countries. Provides technical assistance and cooperation to the national medical associations of Commonwealth developing countries. Offers educational programs and conducts projects in areas such as reproductive health, women's health, youth health, medical ethics and human rights. Conducts studies; acts as a clearinghouse for news and information. **Founded:** 1962. **Membership:** 38. **Staff:** 5. Multinational. **National Groups:** 38. **Languages:** English. **Budget:** L150,000. **Publication:** *Adolescent Health* ■ *CommonHealth* (in English), 3/year. Bulletin. Price: L15.00 per year. Circulation: 600. Advertising: not accepted ■ *Medical Ethics in the Protection of Human Rights.*

COMMONWEALTH NURSES FEDERATION (CNF)
Royal College of Nursing
20 Cavendish Sq.
London W1M 0AB, England
Patricia M. Larby, Exec.Sec.
PH: 44 171 4933539
FX: 44 171 6473413
Description: Organization of national nurses associations in Commonwealth countries. Strives to further the development of nursing and midwifery for the benefit of the community in Commonwealth nations; promotes the advancement of the profession. Encourages the use of facilities within the various regions of the Commonwealth for further education of nurses; promotes cooperation and coordinated activities among member associations. Seeks to create closer links among national nurses' associations within the Commonwealth as a means of providing mutual help and support. Offers assistance to governments and health agencies to facilitate the delivery of appropriate health services. Disseminates professional information, advice, and assistance. Supports regional and pan-Commonwealth educational nursing projects. **Founded:** 1973. **Membership:** 50. **Staff:** 1. Multinational. **National Groups:** 50. **Languages:** English. **Publication:** *CNF Newsletter* (in English), semiannual. ISSN: 0268-4063. Advertising: accepted ■ *Directory of Nursing Associations and Chief Nursing Officers in Countries of the Commonwealth*, periodic ■ *Reports of Workshops*, periodic.

COMMONWEALTH PHARMACEUTICAL ASSOCIATION (CPA)
e-mail: eharden@compuserve.com
url: http://www.jr2.ox.ac.uk/pharmacy/CPA/CPAhomepage.html
1 Lambeth High St.
London SE1 7JN, England
Mr. Philip Green, Sec.
PH: 44 171 7359141
FX: 44 171 5823401
Description: Pharmaceutical organizations in 39 Commonwealth countries; pharmacists. Objectives are to: maintain the honor and traditions of the profession and promote high standards of conduct, practice, and education at all levels; encourage close links among members in the profession and facilitate personal contacts between pharmacists and students; disseminate information about the professional practice of pharmacy and the pharmaceutical sciences. **Founded:** 1970. **Membership:** 300. Multinational. **Regional Groups:** 6. **Languages:** English. **Publication:** *Newsletter* (in English), quarterly. Advertising: not accepted.

COMMONWEALTH REGIONAL HEALTH SECRETARIAT (CRHS)
e-mail: crgcs@ken.healthnet.org
PO Box 1009
Arusha, United Republic of Tanzania
Prof. K. Thairu, CEO; Reg.Sec.
PH: 255 57 8362
FX: 255 57 8292
Description: Ministries of health from the Commonwealth countries of Botswana, Kenya, Lesotho, Malawi, Mauritius, Namibia, Seychelles, Swaziland, Tanzania, Uganda, Zambia, and Zimbabwe. Seeks better health for the people of eastern, central, and southern Africa; promotes cooperation among members to achieve this goal and coordinates health activities of member ministries. Conducts research and training courses. Disseminates health information. **Founded:** 1974. **Membership:** 14. **Staff:** 27. Multinational. **Languages:** English. **Budget:** $2,000,000. **Publication:** *CRHCS News* (in English), semiannual. Newsletter. Price: frec. ISSN: 0856-4043. Circulation: 2,000. Advertising: accepted ■ *Inventory of Training Institutions and Courses* (in English), periodic ■ Annual Report (in English).

COMMUNITY HEALTH NURSES ASSOCIATION OF CANADA (CHNAC)
106 Bellevista Dr.
Dartmouth, NS, Canada B2W 2X7
Donna L. Smith, Contact
Description: Community health nurses and provincial organizations. Seeks to advance the practice of community health nursing and enhance members' professional status. Represents members' interests before government agencies and medical associations; provides support, services, and assistance to members. **Founded:** 1989. **Membership:** 2500. **Languages:** English, French. **Publication:** *CHNAC*, quarterly. Newsletter.

COMPANY CHEMISTS ASSOCIATION
1 Thane Rd. West
Nottingham NG2 3AA, England
M.J. Oliver, Contact
PH: 44 115 9592831
FX: 44 115 9595097
Description: Companies engaged in running community pharmacies. Covers the interests of multiple retail chemists..

COMPREHENSIVE HEALTH EDUCATION FOUNDATION (CHEF)
22323 Pacific Hwy. S.
Seattle, WA 98198
Carl J. Nickerson, Ed.D., Pres.
PH: (206)824-2907
FX: (206)824-3072
Description: Encourages and supports improvement of health through education. Seeks to improve health education in the schools and community, enhance the public image of health educators, and stimulate community support of health education. Produces and disseminates health education information and materials. Initiates and supports innovations in health education. Supports the Health Education Fund, which sponsors pilot programs, offers scholarships for health education studies, and bestows leadership/recognition and professional enrichment awards. **Founded:** 1974. **Staff:** 40. **Languages:** English.

COMPUTERIZED MEDICAL IMAGING SOCIETY (CMIS)
c/o Natl. Biomedical Research Found.
Georgetown Univ. Med. Center
3900 Reservoir Rd. NW
Washington, DC 20007
Robert S. Ledley, Editor-in-Chief
PH: (202)687-2121
FX: (202)687-1662
Description: Physicians and other medical personnel concerned with computerized tomography (a diagnostic technique using X-ray photographs in which the shadows of structures before and behind the section under scrutiny do not show), and other radiological diagnostic procedures. Provides a forum for the exchange of information concerning the medical use of computerized tomography in radiological diagnosis. **Founded:** 1976. **Membership:** 350. **Staff:** 2. **Languages:** English. Formerly (1983) Computerized Tomography Society; (1988) Computerized Radiology Society.

CONTACT LENS ASSOCIATION OF OPHTHALMOLOGISTS (CLAO)

e-mail: 102177.15772@compuserve.com
url: http://www.clao.org
721 Papworth Ave., Ste. 205 & 206
Metairie, LA 70005
John S. Massare, Exec.Dir.
PH: (504)835-3937
FX: (504)833-5884
Description: To advance quality medical eyecare for the public by providing comprehensive ophthalmologists and other eye care professionals with education and training in contact lenses, refractive surgery, and related eyecare science. **Founded:** 1963. **Membership:** 2000. **Staff:** 4. Multinational. **Languages:** English. **Budget:** $1,000,000.

CONTINUING CARE AT HOME ASSOCIATION

54 Glasshouse Ln.
Countess Wear
Exeter EX2 7BU, England
Heather Hutchinson, Memb.Sec.
Description: Health and social service professionals. To improve the relief at home of those people suffering from chronic illness and disability, and to advance the learning and understanding of those caring for such persons. **Founded:** 1992.

COORDINATION OF JAPANESE-NICARAGUAN ACUPUNCTURISTS

(Coordinacion Japon-Nicaragua de Acupunctura)
8-28-9 Kinuta
Setagaya-ku
Tokyo 157, Japan
Takanobu Hirayama, Contact
PH: 81 3 34159292
FX: 81 3 34159292
Description: Serves as a support group for Japanese practitioners of acupuncture and moxibustion. Promotes availability of acupuncture in developing countries. Recruits and trains acupuncturists to practice in developing areas; constructs clinics. **Languages:** English, Japanese. **Budget:** $26,426.

CORONARY CLUB (CC)

url: http://www.heartline-news.org
9500 Euclid Ave.
Mailcode EE-37
Cleveland, OH 44195
Kathryn E. Ryan-Muldoon, Adm.Asst.
PH: (216)444-3690
TF: 800478-4255
FX: (216)444-9385
Description: Heart patients, doctors, nurses, therapists, educators, and other health professionals involved in cardiac care. **Founded:** 1969. **Membership:** 9000. **Staff:** 2. Multinational. **Languages:** English.

CORPORATE ANGEL NETWORK (CAN)

e-mail: info@corpangelnetwork.org
Westchester County Airport
One Loop Rd.
White Plains, NY 10604
Judith Haims, Admin.
PH: (914)328-1313
FX: 800-328-4226
Description: U.S. corporations that own aircraft and volunteer empty seats to cancer patients in need of transportation to or from recognized treatment centers. Patients must be able to board the aircraft unassisted, not require special equipment or services en route, and have proper medical authorization for the flight. CAN will transport one attendant or family member with the patient; patient must arrange his or her own ground transportation. Convention/Meeting: none. **Founded:** 1981. **Membership:** 550. **Staff:** 3. **Languages:** English. **Budget:** $170,000. **Publication:** Bulletin, quarterly.

COUNCIL FOR INTERNATIONAL ORGANIZATIONS OF MEDICAL SCIENCES (CIOMS)

(Conseil des Organisations Internationales des Sciences Medicales)
World Health Org.
Ave. Appia
CH-1211 Geneva, Switzerland
Dr. Zbigniew Bankowski, Sec. Gen.
PH: 41 22 7913406
FX: 41 22 7910746
Description: International organizations of medical sciences. Promotes and coordinates medical and scientific activities of member associations and national institutions affiliated with the council. Maintains collaborative relations with the World Health Organization and United Nations Educational, Scientific and Cultural Organization. Serves the scientific interests of the international biomedical community. **Founded:** 1949. **Membership:** 103. **Staff:** 3. Multinational. **Languages:** English, French. **Publication:** *Calendar of International and Regional Congresses of Medical Sciences*, annual ■ *International Nomenclature of Diseases* ■ *Proceedings of Round Table Conferences* ■ Directory, periodic.

COUNCIL ON ACCREDITATION OF NURSE ANESTHESIA EDUCATIONAL PROGRAMS/SCHOOLS

222 Prespect Ave.
Park Ridge, IL 60068-4010
Betty Horton, Exec. Officer
PH: (847)692-7050
FX: (847)692-7137
Description: Nurse anesthesia programs. To provide accreditation and to evaluate the education offered by educational institutions and programs. Functions within the framework of the American Association of Nurse Anesthetists. Conducts on-site reviews and educational workshops. Compiles statistics. **Founded:** 1975. **Membership:** 90. **Staff:** 3. **Languages:** English. **Budget:** $500,000. **Publication:** *Educational Standards and Guidelines* ■ *List of Accredited Nurse Anesthesia Educational Program/ Schools*, semiannual. Directory ■ *Policies and Procedures Manual.* **Supersedes:** Approval of Schools Committee.

COUNCIL ON ARTERIOSCLEROSIS, THROMBOSIS AND VASCULAR BIOLOGY OF THE AMERICAN HEART ASSOCIATION

e-mail: joannp@amhart.org
7320 Greenville Ave.
Dallas, TX 75231
Dr. Trudy Forte, Chair
PH: (214)706-1293
FX: (214)706-1341
Description: Professional society of physicians and others interested in cardiovascular diseases, especially arteriosclerosis (hardening of the arteries). **Founded:** 1946. **Membership:** 1014. **Staff:** 7. **Languages:** English. Formerly (1959) American Society for the Study of Arteriosclerosis; (1997) Council on Arteriosclerosis of the American Heart Association.

COUNCIL ON CERTIFICATION OF NURSE ANESTHETISTS (CCNA)

e-mail: 75777.1571@compuserve.com
url: http://www.aana.com
222 S. Prospect Ave.
Park Ridge, IL 60068
Susan S. Caulk, Dir., Certification
PH: (847)692-7050
FX: (847)692-7082
Description: Sets certification standards and policies; confers certification upon entry-level nurse anesthetists. Conducts research. Works within the framework of the American Association of Nurse Anesthetists. **Founded:** 1975. **Membership:** 11. **Staff:** 2. **Languages:** English Supersedes Exam Committee, American Association of Nurse Anesthetists.

COUNCIL ON DIAGNOSTIC IMAGING
e-mail: cdisec@aol.com
PO Box 25
Palatine, IL 60078-0025
Dr. Lawrence Pyzik, Sec.-Treas.
PH: (847)705-1177
FX: (847)705-1178
Description: Professional society of chiropractic roentgenologists, educators, students, and chiropractors interested in roentgenology. **Founded:** 1936. **Membership:** 2000. **Staff:** 1. **Languages:** English. **Budget:** $100,000. **Publication:** *Topics in Diagnostic Radiology and Advanced Imaging*, quarterly. Journal. Covers diagnostic radiology, advanced imaging, thermology, and case studies. Price: $50.00; $75.00 only in U.S.A.; $100.00 outside of U.S.A. Circulation: 2,000. Advertising: accepted. **Formerly:** (1963) National Council of Chiropractic Roentgenologists; (1968) American Council on Chiropractic Roentgenology; (1970) American Chiropractic Council on Roentgenology; (1983) Council on Roentgeneology to the American Chiropractic Association.

COUNCIL ON EDUCATION FOR PUBLIC HEALTH (CEPH)
1015 15th St. NW
Washington, DC 20005
Patricia P. Evans, Exec.Dir.
PH: (202)789-1050
FX: (202)789-1895
Description: Participants are professional associations representing public health practice (American Public Health Association) and public health education (Association of Schools of Public Health). Seeks to strengthen educational programs in schools of public health and graduate public health programs through accreditation, consultation, research, and other appropriate services; and to encourage the development of experimental and innovative programs which will ensure educational quality. **Founded:** 1974. **Staff:** 3. **Languages:** English. **Budget:** $250,000.

COUNCIL ON FAMILY HEALTH (CFH)
url: http://www.cfhinfo.org
225 Park Ave. S., 17th Fl.
New York, NY 10003
William I. Bergman, Pres.
PH: (212)598-3617
FX: (212)598-3665
Description: Manufacturers of prescription and over-the-counter medications. Provides the public and interested organizations with information on proper usage of medications and other family health concerns, such as safety in the home. **Founded:** 1966. **Membership:** 32. **Languages:** English. **Budget:** $300,000. **Publication:** *How to Prevent Drug Interactions* (in English and Spanish). Brochure. Price: free single copy with SASE. Advertising: not accepted ▪ *The Medicine Label...Your Roadmap to Good Health*. Price: free single copy with SASE ▪ *Medicines and You: A Guide for Older Americans* (in English and Spanish). Brochure. Price: free single copy. Advertising: not accepted ▪ *Nonprescription Medicines: A Consumer's Dictionary of Terms* (in English and Spanish). Brochure. Price: free single copy with SASE ▪ *Ten Guides to Proper Medicine Use* (in English and Spanish). Price: free single copy with SASE.

COUNCIL ON GERIATRIC CARDIOLOGY
777 W Putnam Ave.
Greenwich, CT 06830
Sarah Howell, Exec.Dir.
PH: (203)531-0916
FX: (203)531-0450
Description: Geriatric cardiologists and physicians in related fields are members; medical practitioners certified in specialties other than geriatrics or cardiologists are fellows; other individuals with an interest in geriatric cardiology are nonphysician members. Works to improve the clinical and therapeutic management of older individuals with cardiovascular disease; encourages use of preventive measures to avert the onset of cardiovascular aging and disease. Promotes more effective public policy and education regarding cardiac health. Conducts educational programs for physicians, other health care professionals, and the public. Supports research into cardiovascular aging and diseases relevant to older people. Serves as a clearinghouse on geriatric cardiology. Sponsors competitions. **Founded:** 1986. **Membership:** 500. **Staff:** 10. Multinational. **Languages:** English.

COUNCIL ON HEALTH INFORMATION AND EDUCATION (CHIE)
2272 Colorado Blvd., No. 1228
Los Angeles, CA 90041
D. Andre, Dir.
Description: Promotes health and fitness of Americans through the dissemination of information on health care, nutrition, and exercise. Warns against fads in health and nutrition; conducts research on health and exercise products; reviews books on health, fitness, nutrition, sexuality, and sports. **Founded:** 1978. **Languages:** English. **Publication:** Pamphlets.

COUNCIL FOR MEDICAL AFFAIRS (CFMA)
PO Box 10944
Chicago, IL 60610
Gail Cates, Contact
PH: (312)464-4649
FX: (312)464-5830
Description: Membership is limited to: American Board of Medical Specialties; American Hospital Association; American Medical Association; Association of American Medical Colleges; Council of Medical Specialty Societies. Each organization is represented by a chief executive officer and the two highest elected officials. Provides a forum for members of the organizations represented to consider issues related to medical education, and to initiate the necessary steps for their consideration by the five parent organizations. **Founded:** 1980. **Membership:** 15. **Staff:** 1. **Languages:** English. **Supersedes:** Coordinating Council on Medical Education.

COUNCIL ON MEDICAL EDUCATION - OF THE AMERICAN MEDICAL ASSOCIATION (CME-AMA)
515 N. State St.
Chicago, IL 60610
Dr. Marvin Dunn, Sec.
PH: (312)464-4395
FX: (312)464-5830
Description: A council of the American Medical Association. Participates in the accreditation of and provides consultation to medical school programs, graduate medical educational programs, and continuing medical educational programs. Provides information on medical education at all levels. **Founded:** 1847. **Membership:** 12. **Staff:** 50. **Languages:** English. **Publication:** *Allied Health Education Directory*, annual ▪ *Annual Report of Medical Education in the Journal of the AMA* ▪ *Continuing Education Courses for Physicians Supplement to the Journal of the AMA*, semiannual ▪ *Directory of Graduate Medical Education Programs*, annual.

COUNCIL OF MEDICAL SPECIALTY SOCIETIES (CMSS)
e-mail: mailbox@cmss.org
url: http://www.cmss.org
51 Sherwood Ter., Ste. Y
Lake Bluff, IL 60044
Rebecca R. Gschwend, MA,MBA, Exec.VP
PH: (847)295-3456
FX: (847)295-3759
Description: National medical specialty societies representing 325,000 physicians. Purpose is to improve the quality of medical care in the United States and to foster excellence in the education of physicians. Provides a forum for discussion by specialty societies of national issues affecting the practice and teaching of medicine. Promotes communication among specialty organizations involved in the principal disciplines of medicine. **Founded:** 1965. **Membership:** 17. **Staff:** 3. **Languages:** English. **For-Profit. Budget:** $350,000. **Formerly:** Tri-College Council.

COUNCIL ON RESIDENT EDUCATION IN OBSTETRICS AND GYNECOLOGY (CREOG)
e-mail: dnehra@acog.org
PO Box 96920
Washington, DC 20090-6920
DeAnne Nehra, Assoc.Dir.
PH: (202)863-2554
FX: (202)863-4994
Description: A semiautonomous nonregulatory organization founded by the American College of Obstetricians and Gynecologists and comprised of national specialty organizations. Works to promote and maintain high standards of resident training in obstetrics and gynecology. Services include: consultative site visits to residency programs; clearinghouse for residency positions; conferences; a resident data bank; national in-training examination. **Founded:** 1967. **Membership:** 450. **Staff:** 3. **Languages:** English.

COUNCIL FOR PROFESSIONS SUPPLEMENTARY TO MEDICINE
Park House
184 Kensington Park Rd.
London SE11 4BU, England
Mike Hall, Registrar
PH: 44 171 5820866
FX: 44 171 8209684
Description: Those wishing to practise as state registered arts therapists, chiropodists, dietitians, medical laboratory scientific officers, occupational therapists, orthoptists, prosthetists/orthotists, physiotherapists, or radiographers must register at CPSM. State Registration is required for the NHS. and Local Authority Social Services and is a univeral kitemark of professional excellence. To implement as effectively as possible the Professions Supplementary to Medicines Act, 1960, and EC Directives 89/48 and 92/51 with particular reference to the duty laid on the Council at Boards by Parliament, of promoting high standards of professional education and professional conduct. **Founded:** 1960. **Membership:** 98000. **Staff:** 23. **Publication:** Annual Report, annual.

CREDENTIALING COMMISSION (CC)
917 Locust St., Ste. 1100
St. Louis, MO 63101-1413
Mark S. Birenbaum, Ph.D., Admin.
PH: (314)241-1445
FX: (314)241-1449
Description: Autonomous certifying agency for general supervison, medical technologists, laboratory technicians, and physician office laboratory technicians. Maintains Continuing Education for Professional Advancement (CEPA) program to approve and record continuing education unit credits. Convention/Meeting: none. **Founded:** 1962. **Staff:** 5. **Languages:** English. **Formerly:** Accrediting Commission.

CZECH ASSOCIATION FOR FAMILY PLANNING AND SEX EDUCATION (CAFPSE)
Podolski Nabrezi 157
CZ-147 10 Prague, Czech Republic
PH: 42 2 434951
FX: 42 2 66412031
Description: Health care professionals and other individuals and organizations with an interest in reproductive health, family planning, and population control. Promotes increased availability of family planning services and improved access to sex education. Makes available reproductive health care services; conducts educational programs to raise public awareness of population issues; lobbies for improved public policies governing reproductive health, sex education, and family planning services. **Founded:** 1990. **Languages:** Czech, English.

CZECH DERMATOVENEROLOGICAL SOCIETY (CDS)
(Ceska Dermatovenerologicka Spolecnost)
Department Dermatology
University Hospital
Alej Svobody 80
CZ-306 40 Plzen, Czech Republic
Prof.Dr. Vladimir Resl, CSc, Exec. Officer
PH: 42 79 7703300
FX: 42 79 532820
Description: Dermatologists in Czech Republic. Promotes the study of dermatological diseases; encourages research and exchange of information. Operates postgraduate educational programs. **Founded:** 1922. **Membership:** 700. **State Groups:** 1. **Languages:** English. **Budget:** Kcs 5,000. **Publication:** *Ceskoslovenska Dermatologie* (in Czech, English, and Slovak), quarterly. Journal. Price: $2.00. ISSN: 0009-0514. Advertising: accepted ■ *Journal of Czechoslovak Dermatology*, quarterly. **Formerly:** Czechoslovakia Dermatovenerological Society; Ceskoslovenska Dermatovenerologicka Spolecnost.

CZECH MEDICAL ASSOCIATION (CZMA)
e-mail: iss@czechmed.aset.cz
PO Box 88
Sokolska 31
CZ-120 26 Prague, Czech Republic
A. Stoceky
PH: 420 2 24915195
FX: 420 2 24216836
Description: Physicians, pharmacists, and other medical personnel. **Founded:** 1968. **For-Profit. Publication:** *Medical Congresses and Symposia*, annual.

CZECH RADIOLOGICAL SOCIETY (CRS)
(Ceska Radiologicka Spolecnost)
Budinova 2
CZ-180 81 Prague, Czech Republic
Prof. Jaromir Kolar, M.D., Scientific Sec.
PH: 420 2 822431
FX: 420 2 822431
Description: Diagnostic radiologists in the Czech Republic. Disseminates information on developments in diagnostic imaging. Acts as a forum for discussion among professionals. **Founded:** 1929. **Membership:** 100. **Local Groups:** 2. **Languages:** Czech, Slovak. **Budget:** Kcs 35,000. **Publication:** *Ceska Radiologie* (in Czech and Slovak), bimonthly. Journal. Covers all fields of interest in diagnostic radiology, radio-therapy and nuclear medicine. Price: Kcs 288.00/year. ISSN: 0069-2344. Advertising: accepted. **Formerly:** (1993) Czechoslovak Radiological Society.

DANISH DENTAL ASSOCIATION (DDA)
(Dansk Tandlaegeforening)
e-mail: dtf-dk@inet.uni-c.dk
Amaliegade 17
Postboks 143
DK-1256 Copenhagen, Denmark
Karsten Thuen, Chief Exec.
PH: 45 33157711
FX: 45 33151637
Description: Danish dentists. Represents members' interests; promotes dental health care in Denmark. Offers postgraduate training. Maintains placement services; compiles statistics. **Founded:** 1873. **Membership:** 6150. **Staff:** 52. **Regional Groups:** 11. **Languages:** Danish, English. **For-Profit. Budget:** 43,000,000 DKr. **Publication:** *Tandlaegebladet* (in Danish), 18/year. Journal. Provides scientific information. Advertising: accepted. Also Cited As: *Journal of the Danish Dental Association*.

DANISH DENTAL MANUFACTURERS
Borsen
DK-1217 Copenhagen, Denmark
Mette Herget, Sec.
PH: 45 33950500
FX: 45 33325216
Description: Companies manufacturing dental equipment and

supplies. Establishes international standards and technical harmonization for dental equipment. Represents members' interests before government bodies, international agencies, and the public. Maintains liaison with organizations representing dentists, dental technicians, and dental supply dealers and distributors. Compiles statistics. **Languages:** Danish, English.

DANISH DERMATOLOGICAL SOCIETY (DDS)
(Dansk Dermatologisk Selskab)
Bispebjerg Hospital
Dept. of Dermatology D
Bispebjerg Bakke 23
DK-2400 Copenhagen, Denmark
Hanne Fogh, Sec.
PH: 45 3531 3107
FX: 45 3531 3113
Description: Dermatologists in Denmark, Norway, and Sweden. Promotes advances in dermatology and venereology. Offers courses for members. **Founded:** 1899. **Membership:** 295. **Languages:** English, German. **Budget:** 311,000 DKr.

DANISH PHYSICAL SOCIETY
e-mail: alstrom@nbi.dk
url: http://www.nbi.dk/dfs/
Niels Bohr Institute
Blegdamsvej 17
DK-2100 Copenhagen, Denmark
P. Alstrom, Pres.
PH: 45 35 325214
FX: 45 35 325425
Description: Physicists, physics teachers, and others with an interest in the physical sciences. Seeks to improve the quality of physics education, research, and knowledge. **Membership:** 457.

DANNEMILLER MEMORIAL EDUCATIONAL FOUNDATION (DMEF)
e-mail: dmef@txdirect.net
url: http://www.pain.com
12500 Network Blvd., Ste. 101
San Antonio, TX 78249
Larry Vervack, Exec. Dir
PH: (210)641-8311
TF: 800328-2308
FX: (210)641-8329
Description: Conducts annual Anesthesia Review Course in June for M.D. anesthesiologists and in the fall for nurse anesthesiologists, and review course of current concepts in anesthesiology. Sponsors weekend anesthesia and pain management meetings. **Founded:** 1971. **Membership:** 30. **Staff:** 9. Multinational. **Languages:** English. **For-Profit. Budget:** $1,750,000. Formerly (1984) Society of Air Force Anesthesiologists.

DEAF-REACH
e-mail: office@deaf-reach.org
url: http://www.deaf-reach.org/
3521 12th St. NE
Washington, DC 20017
Sarah Brown, Exec.Dir.
PH: (202)832-6681
FX: (202)832-8454
Description: Committed to maximizing the self-sufficiency of deaf people needing special services by providing referral, education, advocacy, counseling, and housing. Seeks to establish residential homes and provide psychological, physical, spiritual, and social aid to deaf persons with mental and emotional problems. Operates Otis House and Kearny House, group homes for mentally ill deaf persons, designed to help meet the residents' emotional and social needs and teach them independent living skills. Administers the Community Housing for the Hearing Impaired Program which also provides a group home. Offers intake, referral, housing placement assistance, and personal counseling; provides day-programs for learning disabled, deaf adults. Works in community advocacy for the mentally ill hearing impaired. Conducts workshops. Activities are conducted primarily in the Washington, DC, area. **Founded:** 1972. **Staff:** 28. Local. **Languages:** English. **Budget:** $1,000,000. Formerly (1990) National Health Care Foundation for the Deaf.

DELTA DENTAL PLANS ASSOCIATION (DDPA)
1515 W. 22nd St., No. 1200
Oak Brook, IL 60521
Carl Zimmerman, Pres.
PH: (630)574-6001
Description: Active state dental service corporations; inactive state dental service corporations; state dental societies; foreign dental service plans. Seeks to increase the availability of dental service to the public by assisting state dental societies in the formation of dental service corporations and by coordinating the activities of dental service corporations and helping them in the development of dental care programs for application to multistate and national accounts. A dental service corporation (or dental service plan) refers to a nonprofit corporation organized by the dental profession to provide prepaid dental care coverage to the public on a group basis. Maintains speakers' bureau; conducts specialized education programs; compiles statistics. Holds marketing, management, financial, and educational workshops, seminars, and conferences. **Founded:** 1965. **Membership:** 37. **Staff:** 13. **Languages:** English. **Budget:** $2,000,000. **Publication:** *The Communicator*, quarterly. Newsletter. Covers members news. Advertising: not accepted ■ *Legal Briefs*, quarterly. Newsletter. Covers legislative issues. Advertising: not accepted. **Formerly:** National Association of Dental Service Plans.

DELTA OMEGA
University of Minnesota
School of Public Health
Box 197 Mail
Minneapolis, MN 55455
Leonard Schuman, M.D., Contact
PH: (612)624-6669
FX: (612)626-6931
Description: Honorary society - men and women, public health. Promotes research and scholarly attainment; sponsors lectures. Publications: none. **Founded:** 1924. **Membership:** 4000. **Local Groups:** 18. **Languages:** English.

DELTA SIGMA DELTA
W323 S3380 Hwy. E
Dousman, WI 53118
Dr. John H. Prey, Supreme Scribe
PH: (414)968-2030
TF: 800335-8744
FX: (414)968-5850
Description: Maintains museum; offers educational programs. **Founded:** 1882. **Membership:** 26732. Multinational. **Local Groups:** 38. **Languages:** English. **Budget:** $218,000. **Publication:** *Alumni Directory*, quadrennial. ISSN: 0011-9474. Circulation: 26,000. Advertising: not accepted ■ *Desmos*, quarterly. Magazine. Includes chapter news, scientific articles, and announcements. Price: free to members. ISSN: 0011-9474. Circulation: 26,000. Advertising: not accepted.

DENIP
url: http://www.unamec.be
Leuvenstraat 29
B-1800 Vivoorde, Belgium
Ms. N. Van Lent, Sec.
PH: 32 2 2510509
FX: 32 2 2524398
Description: Companies manufacturing dental equipment and supplies. Establishes international standards and technical harmonization for dental equipment. Represents members' interests before government bodies, international agencies, and the public. Maintains liaison with organizations representing dentists, dental technicians, and dental supply dealers and distributors. Compiles statistics. **Languages:** Dutch, French.

DENTAL ASSISTING NATIONAL BOARD (DANB)
216 E. Ontario St.
Chicago, IL 60611
Cynthia Durley, Exec.Dir.
PH: (312)642-3368
TF: 800FOR-DANB
FX: (312)642-8507
Description: Certifying agency that administers examinations to dental assistants. **Founded:** 1948. **Staff:** 21. **Languages:** English. **Budget:** $1,000,000. **Formerly:** Certifying Board of the American Dental Assistants Association.

DENTAL ASSOCIATION OF THAILAND (DAT)
71 Ladprao 95
Bangkapi
Bangkok 10310, Thailand
Thanin Ratananakin, DDS,MS, Sec.Gen.
PH: 66 2 5394748
FX: 66 2 5141100
Description: Licensed dentists. Promotes dental health and the advancement of the profession. **Founded:** 1947. **Membership:** 3500. **Staff:** 4. **Languages:** English, Thai. **Budget:** 5,000,000 Bht. **Publication:** *Dental Association of Thailand* (in Thai), bimonthly. Journal. With English abstracts. Price: $100.00/year. ISSN: 0045-9917. Advertising: accepted ▪ *News Letter of the Dental Association of Thailand*, periodic. ISSN: 0857-5800.

DENTAL ASSOCIATION OF ZIMBABWE
PO Box 3303
Harare, Zimbabwe
Dr. W.D. Sithole, Pres.
PH: 263 4 861639
FX: 263 4 707300
Description: Dentists and others working in the field of dentistry. Promotes dental health and the efficient practice of dentistry. Works to enhance the professional standing of members. **Membership:** 80. **Staff:** 1. **Regional Groups:** 2. **Languages:** English. **Publication:** Newsletter (in English), periodic. Advertising: accepted.

DENTAL GROUP MANAGEMENT ASSOCIATION (DGMA)
c/o Ann Pakalski
North Point Dental Group
7040 N. Port Washington
Glendale, WI 53217
Lynn Moore, Exec. Officer
PH: (414)224-1020
FX: (414)251-6148
Description: Dental group business managers and others interested in group practice management. **Founded:** 1951. **Membership:** 200. **Regional Groups:** 2. **Languages:** English. **Publication:** *DGMA Communicator*, bimonthly. Newsletter. Includes job listings and membership profiles. Price: free. Circulation: 300. Also Cited As: *The Communicator* ▪ Newsletter, semimonthly.

DENTAL HEALTH INTERNATIONAL (DHI)
e-mail: 102024.3671@compuserve.com
847 S. Milledge Ave.
Athens, GA 30605
Barry Simmons, D.D.S., Pres.
PH: (706)546-1715
FX: (706)546-1715
Description: Dentists, dental hygienists, dental technicians, and the International Association of Dental Students. Purposes are to promote dental health programs in developing countries; to provide general dental care using portable modular dental units in areas without electricity or water. Utilizes minimal fee structure to support projects; professionals in the field of dentistry donate their services for a period of 3 months. Volunteer dentists and dental technicians collect permanent non-obsolete dental equipment in their local areas and rendevous with the equipment in the host country and assist with the installation of it. Serves "pro-United States" countries. Convention/Meeting:

none. **Founded:** 1973. **Staff:** 1. Multinational. **Languages:** English.

DENTURIST ASSOCIATION OF CANADA
e-mail: dentcba@mb.sympatico.ca
url: http://www.denturist.org
PO Box 46114, RPO Westdale
Winnipeg, MB, Canada R3R 3S3
Ms. Gerry Hansen, Chief Adm. Officer
PH: (204)897-1087
FX: (204)895-9595
Description: Professional denturists, denturist students, and educators. Seeks to advance the profession of denturism and to establish educational standards in the field. Formulates standards of ethics and practice; represents members' interests before legislative bodies and the public; facilitates exchange of information among members; monitors advancements in the field of denturism. **Founded:** 1971. **Membership:** 1800. **Staff:** 2. **Languages:** English, French. **Publication:** *Journal of Canadian Denturism*, quarterly. Circulation: 2,000. Advertising: accepted.

DEPRESSION AND RELATED AFFECTIVE DISORDERS ASSOCIATION (DRADA)
e-mail: drada@welchlink.welch.vhu.edu
url: http://www.med.vhu.edu/drada/
Johns Hopkins Hospital Meyer 3-181
600 N. Wolfe St.
Baltimore, MD 21287-7381
James R. O'Hair, Pres.
PH: (410)955-4647
FX: (410)614-3241
Description: Individuals with affective disorders, their families and friends, and mental health professionals. (Affective disorders include depressive illnesses and manic-depression.) Provides support services including referrals, educational programs, networking, and consultation. Encourages and facilitates the formation of local support groups for those with affective disorders; provides training for support group leaders. Conducts research and educational programs; maintains speakers' bureau. **Founded:** 1986. **Membership:** 1300. **Staff:** 5. **Budget:** $210,000.

DEPRESSIVES ANONYMOUS: RECOVERY FROM DEPRESSION (DARFD)
329 E. 62nd St.
New York, NY 10021
Dr. Helen DeRosis, Founder
PH: (212)689-2600
Description: Individuals suffering from depression or anxiety. A selfhelp organization which helps people deal with their anxiety or depression through weekly meeting and sharing of experiences. Conducts research; offers classes. Disseminates information. Interested people may send a SASE or ask for a collect call at the above number. **Founded:** 1977. **Membership:** 3000. **Languages:** English.

DERMATOLOGICAL SOCIETY OF MALAYSIA (DSM)
(Persatuan Dermatologi Malaysia)
url: http://www.jaring.my/enrich/pdm/
Hospital Kuala Lumpur
Jalan Pahang
50586 Kuala Lumpur, Malaysia
Dr. Suraiya H. Hussein, Pres.
PH: 60 3 2905271
FX: 60 3 2985927
Description: Dermatologists and other practitioners interested in dermatology. Promotes the research and development of dermatological medicine in Malaysia. Organizes scientific seminars and congresses. **Founded:** 1975. **Membership:** 83. **Languages:** English. **Publication:** *Malaysian Journal of Dermatology* (in English), annual. Price: free. Advertising: accepted.

DERMATOLOGICAL SOCIETY OF SINGAPORE (DSS)
e-mail: nsc@poutic.net.org
url: http://medweb.nvs.sg/nsc/nsc.html
1 Mandalay Rd.
Singapore 308205, Singapore
Dr. Joyce Lim, Pres.
PH: 65 2534455
FX: 65 2533255
Description: Dermatologists in Singapore. Holds clinico-pathological sessions for dermatologists. Maintains research fund. Founded: 1972. Membership: 90. Staff: 1. Languages: English. Publication: *Proceedings of Dermatological Society of Singapore* (in English), annual. Journal. Price: Free for members.

DERMATOLOGY FOUNDATION (DF)
1560 Sherman Ave., Ste. 870
Evanston, IL 60201-4802
Sandra Rahn Goldman, Exec.Dir.
PH: (708)328-2256
FX: (708)328-0509
Description: Members of national and regional dermatological societies; board-certified dermatologists. Raises funds for the control of skin diseases through research, improved education, and better patient care. Stimulates interest of graduate physicians in academic dermatology. Supports basic and clinical investigations. Founded: 1964. Membership: 3300. Staff: 4. Languages: English. Budget: $450,000.

DERMATOLOGY NURSES' ASSOCIATION (DNA)
e-mail: dna@mail.ajj.com
Box 56, N. Woodbury Rd.
Pitman, NJ 08071
Catherine A. Brown, R.N., Exec.Dir.
PH: (609)256-2330
Description: Addresses professional issues involving dermatology nurses; develops high standards of dermatologic nursing care; facilitates communication and interdisciplinary cooperation among members. Conducts educational meetings. Founded: 1982. Membership: 1600. Languages: English.

DES ACTION, U.S.A.
e-mail: desact@well.com
url: http://www.desaction.org
1615 Broadway, Ste. 510
Oakland, CA 94612
Nora Cody, Exec.Dir.
PH: (510)465-4011
TF: 800DES-9288
FX: (510)465-4815
Description: DES-exposed persons and others "working to try to ameliorate the problems caused by DES." DES (diethylstilbestrol) is a synthetic estrogen in use since 1938 and often prescribed for prevention of miscarriage, diabetes during pregnancy, difficulty in conceiving, staining during pregnancy, and cessation of premature labor. It has since been found that, in some cases, daughters born to women taking DES in the first five months of pregnancy have developed cervical and vaginal abnormalities, a very small percentage of which have resulted in cancer, and a greater number of DES daughters experience problems with pregnancies, including seven times the rate of tubal pregnancy and twice the rate of miscarriage. DES mothers have a higher risk of breast cancer. There have been some reports of urinary problems, genital abnormalities, and infertility among DES sons, although research has not been completed in this area. Goal is to reach DES-exposed persons and to stress to them the need for medical attention and monitoring; to educate professionals and the public. Worked for passage of the first national DES legislation in 1992. Offers support, counseling, and doctor referral service. Maintains speakers' bureau. Founded: 1977. Membership: 3000. Staff: 3. State Groups: 30. Languages: Spanish. For-Profit. Budget: $130,000. Publication: *DES Action Voice: A Focus on Diethylstilbestrol Exposure*, quarterly. Newsletter. Includes medical question and answer column; book reviews; legislation and litigation news; conference reports. Price: $35.00/year. Circulation:

3,000. Advertising: not accepted ▪ *Fertility and Pregnancy Guide for DES Daughters and Sons*. Price: $6.00. Formerly: (1986) DES Action, National.

DIABETES FOUNDATION
177a Tennison Rd.
London SE25 5NF, England
Arthur Bennett, Hon. Sec.
PH: 44 181 6565467
Description: Mostly diabetics of all age groups in addition to professionals in the medical field and diabetic specialists. Aims to raise funds for research into the cure for diabetes and education to enable diabetics to avoid the long term complications of the disease. Provides blood glucose monitor packs entirely free of charge to all diabetic children under the age of 18 who are UK residents and UK senior citizens who are diabetic and over the age of 65. Founded: 1982. Membership: 10000. Staff: 6. Publication: *Diabetic Life*, semiannual ▪ *Newsnotes*, semiannual.

DIABETES RESEARCH INSTITUTE FOUNDATION (DRIF)
e-mail: info@drif.org
url: http://drinet.med.miami.edu/
3440 Hollywood Blvd., Ste. 100
Hollywood, FL 33021
Robert A. Pearlman, Exec.VP
PH: (954)964-4040
TF: 800321-3437
FX: (954)964-7036
Description: Works to improve the quality of life for individuals with diabetes and to find a cure for diabetes. Acts as an information clearinghouse. Offers referral services. Fosters research on diabetes. Conducts educational programs; maintains speakers' bureau. Compiles statistics. Founded: 1971. Membership: 10000. Staff: 15. Multinational. Regional Groups: 2. Languages: English.

DIABETIC ASSOCIATION OF LUXEMBOURG (DAL)
(Association Luxembourgeoise du Diabete)
22, rue Goethe
BP 1316
Luxembourg, Luxembourg
Dr. Roger Wirion, Sec.
PH: 352 474545
FX: 352 220836
Description: Diabetics and health care providers. Aims to promote the medical, scientific, and social concerns of diabetics. Collaborates with doctors, related organizations, and interested individuals. Provides diabetes prevention information. Sponsors biennial diabetes education week. Participates in European programs for diabetic children. Founded: 1979. Membership: 700. Staff: 12. Languages: English, French. Budget: 700,000 LFr. Publication: *Journal du Diabetique* (in French and German), quarterly. Magazine. Price: included in membership fee. Circulation: 800. Advertising: accepted.

DINSHAH HEALTH SOCIETY (DHS)
url: http://www.wj.net/dinshah
PO Box 707
Malaga, NJ 08328-0707
Darius Dinshah, Pres.
PH: (609)692-4686
Description: Health professionals and other interested individuals who use and promote chromopathy as a therapy. (Chromopathy, or color therapy, involves the use of projected colors of light to treat specific health problems.) Seeks to stimulate interest in and knowledge of chromopathy and other lesser-known methods of health restoration and maintenance such as vegetarianism and mind-power. Founded: 1975. Membership: 3300. Multinational. Languages: English. Publication: *Es Werde Licht* (in German). Book. Advertising: not accepted ▪ *Let There Be Light* (in German). Book. Advertising: not accepted. Also Cited As: *Es Werde Licht* ▪ Brochures ▪ Manuals ▪ Newsletter, 3-5/year.

DIRECT RELIEF INTERNATIONAL (DRI)
27 S. La Patera Ln.
Santa Barbara, CA 93117
Max Goff, Exec.Dir.
PH: (805)964-4767
FX: (805)681-4838
Description: Donates contributed pharmaceuticals, medical supplies, and equipment to health facilities and locally coordinated health projects in medically underdeveloped areas of the world. Provides emergency assistance to refugees and other victims of natural disaster and civil strife. **Founded:** 1948. **Staff:** 23. Multinational. **Languages:** Spanish. **Budget:** $28,500,000. **Publication:** *Presidents' Report*, annual. Contains a Summary of year's accomplishments with financial report included. Price: available upon request ▪ *Program Reports*, periodic ▪ *Response*, 3/year. Newsletter. **Formerly:** (1982) Direct Relief Foundation.

DIVING DENTISTS SOCIETY (DDS)
e-mail: frgt12c@prodigy.com
1101 N. Calvert St.
Baltimore, MD 21202-3861
Leonore Chizever, Exec.Dir.
PH: (410)837-5852
FX: (410)752-0779
Description: North American dentists interested in scuba and other forms of diving. Researches and proposes solutions to the dental problems of scuba divers. **Founded:** 1978. **Membership:** 100. **Staff:** 1. **Languages:** English.

DKT INTERNATIONAL - VIETNAM (DKTIVN)
8 Trang Thi, No. 13
Hanoi, Vietnam
Andrew Piller, Contact
PH: 84 4 260043
FX: 84 4 260262
Description: Population and public health programs operating in Vietnam. Seeks to increase availability of primary health care and family planning services. Makes available health services; conducts educational programs to raise public awareness of population issues. **Staff:** 6. **Languages:** English, French. **Budget:** $400,000.

DOCARE INTERNATIONAL (DI)
1750 NE 168th St.
North Miami Beach, FL 33162-3021
Anslie M. Stark, Exec.Sec.
Description: Volunteer organization of medical doctors, osteopathic physicians, nurses, dentists, veterinarians, pharmacists, optometrists, podiatrists, and laypersons with special skills. Serves as a medical outreach program providing health care services to people in remote areas of Mexico, Central America, and the Caribbean. Is concerned with those deprived of medical care due to terrain, language, and cultural barriers. Conducts two to three one-week medical missions per year to areas in need until physicians or health care specialists are provided by the host country government. Has provided care to the Tarahumara Indians of northern Mexico, the Tepehuan Indians of Central Mexico, Mayan Indians in the Yucatan jungle, and an orphanage in Honduras. **Founded:** 1961. **Membership:** 150. Multinational. **Languages:** English. **Publication:** *DOCARE Flyer*, quarterly. Newsletter. Includes stories about members, meetings, planned missions, and election of officers. Price: included in membership dues. Circulation: 150. Advertising: not accepted.

DOCTORS FOR ARTISTS (DFA)
57 W. 57th St.
New York, NY 10019
Dr. Lambert Macias, Dir.
PH: (212)355-1950
FX: (212)319-0782
Description: Doctors in New York directly or indirectly involved with the arts. Established to provide performing and visual artists with specialized health care at a reduced rate, and treatment especially sympathetic to their needs. Artists receive a 20%

discount on medical services, including office visits and surgery; membership is represented in some 23 areas of specialized medicine. Although there are no plans to expand outside New York, assistance is offered to individuals wishing to establish similar groups in other parts of the country. **Founded:** 1984. **Membership:** 20. **Staff:** 1. **Languages:** English.

DOCTORS FOR DEVELOPING COUNTRIES
(Comitato Collaborazione Medica)
e-mail: cmedica@arpnet.it
c/c Postale 13404108
Corso Giovanni Lanza 100
I-10133 Turin, Italy
Dr. Roberto Masino, Sec.
PH: 39 11 6602793
FX: 39 11 6602798
Description: Operates public health projects in developing countries. **Founded:** 1968. **Membership:** 70. **Staff:** 2. **Languages:** English, French. **Budget:** 500,000 Lr. **Publication:** *A Colour Atlas of Surgical Cases in the Tropics* (in English). Book. Price: $30.00/copy ▪ *Volontari per lo sviluppo* (in Italian), bimonthly. Magazine. Price: $10.00.

DOCTORS OUGHT TO CARE (DOC)
e-mail: esolberg@bcm.tmc.edu
url: http://www.bcm.tmc.edu/doc
5615 Kirby Dr., No. 440
Houston, TX 77005
Luke Burchard, M.D., Chm.
PH: (713)528-1487
FX: (713)528-2146
Description: A physician-led organization of medical students, teachers, parents, and other concerned individuals working to counteract the promotion of unhealthy products, primarily tobacco and alcohol. Works through school programs, health professionals' offices, hospitals, media, and Super Health 2000, a health promotion effort which attempts to counter the effects of advertising unhealthy products. Seeks to launch a broad health promotion effort aimed at educating the public, particularly teenagers and children, on the "lethal" lifestyles of tobacco and alcohol use. Campaigns through television commercials, radio, sports events, posters and t-shirts, and its speakers' bureau to promote the image of good health through community-wide reinforcement of the positive role model of the health professional. Serves as a resource center on tobacco and alcohol issues. **Founded:** 1977. **Membership:** 1374. **Staff:** 3. Multinational. **Local Groups:** 76. **Languages:** English. **Budget:** $150,000. **Publication:** *The Journal of Medical Activism*, quarterly. Newsletter. Fights advertising and promotion of unhealthy products by the tobacco and alcohol industry. Includes information on the pro-health community. Price: included in membership dues. Circulation: 3,000. Advertising: not accepted.

DOCTORS TO THE WORLD (DTTW)
e-mail: dttw@aol.com
url: http://rwsa.com/VTTW/index.html
3654 S. Oneida Way
PO Box 37167
Denver, CO 80237
Othnid J. Seiden, M.D., Contact
PH: (303)758-5405
FX: (303)758-4124
Description: Physicians, nurses, and technical and support professionals. Service organization dedicated to providing medical assistance to underpriveledged and needy areas throughout the world. Provided emergency care for individuals involved in the 1988 earthquake in Armenia, the 1989 revolution in Rumania, and the 1990 earthquake in Peru. Participated in relief efforts in Homestead, Florida, in 1989, during and after hurricane Hugo. Operates support facilities in West Indies, Netherlands Antilles, and Central and South America. Operates Street Smart program for inner city youths. Offers homeless individuals medical services, food, clothing, shelter, and aid in obtaining employment. Conducts speakers' bureau and educational programs. **Founded:**

1980. **Membership:** 2800. Multinational. **Languages:** English. **Publication:** *Doctors to the World Newsletter*, semiannual. Price: free. Circulation: 5,000. Advertising: accepted.

DOCTORS WITHOUT BORDERS
url: http://www.dwb.org
6 East 39th St., 8th Floor
New York, NY 10016
Joelle Tanguy, Exec.Dir.
PH: (212)679-6800
TF: 888392-0392
FX: (212)679-7016
Description: Medical and non-medical professionals. Provides assistance to victims of war, natural and man-made disasters, and epidemics, and to others who lack access to health care. Each year more than 2,000 volunteers provide relief in more than 80 countries. **Founded:** 1971. **Staff:** 10. Multinational. **Languages:** English. **Budget:** $6,000,000. **Publication:** *Alert*, 3/year. Newsletter. Contains articles on the fields where Doctors Without Borders are active. Price: free. Advertising: not accepted ▪ *Populations in Dangers*, annual. Book. Contains a look at 5 people in crisis and the humanitarian response. Price: $19.00. ISSN: 9780-9525. Advertising: not accepted. Medecins Sans Fronteres AKA.

DOCTORS WITHOUT BORDERS - ARMENIA
 (Medicines Sans Frontiers)
e-mail: msff@msff.arminco.com
Raffi St. 8A
Yerevan, Armenia
Sonia Peyrassol, Contact
PH: 374 885 2151146
FX: 374 885 2151146
Description: Provides medical assistance to the underprivileged in Armenia. Operates children's psychological trauma program. **Founded:** 1988. **Membership:** 20. **Languages:** Armenian, English.

DOCTORS WITHOUT BORDERS - AZERBAIJAN (DWD)
 (Medicins Sans Frontieres - Azerbaijan)
ul. Sheikh Shamil 4, kv. 8
Baku, Azerbaijan
Philip Rijckaert, Contact
PH: 994 12 926618
FX: 994 12 926695
Description: Physicians and other health care personnel. Provides medical assistance to the underpriveleged in Azerbaijan; makes available emergency relief. **Languages:** Azerbaijani, English.

DOCTORS WITHOUT BORDERS - FRANCE (DWB)
 (Medecins Sans Frontieres)
e-mail: office@paris.msf.org
8, rue St. Sabin
F-75544 Paris, France
Dr. Philippe Biberson, Pres.
PH: 33 1 40212929
FX: 33 1 48066868
Description: Physicians and other members of the medical profession. Provides medical assistance to victims of war or natural disasters. Is presently rendering aid in the crisis-stricken areas of Africa. Sponsors professional training for physicians. **Founded:** 1971. **Membership:** 3500. **Staff:** 110. Multinational. **National Groups:** 5. **Languages:** English, French. **Budget:** 000,000 Fr. **Publication:** *Medecins Sans Frontieres* (in French), quarterly ▪ *Medical and Surgical Guidelines*, periodic ▪ *Medical News* (in English and French), quarterly. Journal ▪ *MSF Info*, 10/year ▪ *Populations in Danger* (in English, French, and Spanish). Book.

DOCTORS WITHOUT BORDERS - GREECE (DWB)
 (Medecins Sans Frontieres Grece)
11A, rue Paioniou
GR-104 40 Athens, Greece
Description: Medical professionals. Provides medical assistance to victims of war or natural disaster. Sponsors training programs

for physicians wishing to participate in relief activities. Multinational. **Languages:** French, Greek.

DOCTORS OF THE WORLD (DW)
e-mail: dow@interserv.com
375 W Broadway, 4th Fl.
New York, NY 10012-4324
Derick G. Wong, Exec.Dir.
PH: (212)529-1556
FX: (212)529-1571
Description: Physicians and other health care professionals. Seeks to increase the availability and quality of health services in developing regions worldwide. Recruits and trains volunteers from the United States to provide professional assistance to local health care services in developing areas. Multinational. **Languages:** English.

DOMINICA PLANNED PARENTHOOD ASSOCIATION
 (DPPA)
e-mail: dppa@tod.dm
64 King George V St.
PO Box 247
Roseau, Dominica
Willie Fevrier, Contact
PH: (809)448-4043
FX: (809)448-0991
Description: Works to improve the quality of life of individuals living in Dominica by promoting responsible parenthood and family planning. Offers educational programs on family planning and contraception to teens and adults. Encourages public awareness of AIDS and other sexually transmitted diseases. Seeks to decrease the number of unwanted pregnancies and abortions. **Staff:** 5. **Languages:** English.

DOMINICAN SOCIETY OF PEDIATRICS (SDP)
 (Sociedad Dominicana de Pediatria)
Clinica Infantil Dr. Robert Reid Cabral
Centro de Los Heroes
Santo Domingo, Dominican Republic
Dr. Rodolfo Nunez-Musa, Pres.
PH: (809)533-3222
FX: (809)535-1052
Description: Pediatric physicians in the Dominican Republic. Sponsors educational programs. **Founded:** 1947. **Membership:** 850. **Staff:** 7. **National Groups:** 1. **Publication:** *Archivo Dominicanos de Pediatria* (in Spanish), 3/year. Journal. Price: Free to members. ISSN: 0004-0606. Advertising: accepted ▪ *Committee Papers*. Reports ▪ *Bulletin*, monthly.

DOOLEY FOUNDATION/INTERMED
e-mail: dooleyfdn@aol.com
420 Lexington Ave., Rm. 2428
New York, NY 10170
Verne Chaney, M.D., Founder & Pres.
PH: (212)687-3620
FX: (212)599-6137
Description: Assists Third World countries in the development of medical care systems through self-help projects in disease prevention, health education, personnel development, and research and medical aid to refugees. Presently operates programs in Laos, Honduras, Nepal, and Nicaragua. Convention/Meeting: none. **Founded:** 1961. **Staff:** 7. Multinational. **Languages:** English. **Budget:** $500,000. **Publication:** *Intermed Journal*, semiannual. Brochure. Circulation: 10,000. Advertising: not accepted ▪ *INTERMED Journal*, semiannual. Advertising: not accepted. **Formerly:** Dooley Foundation/INTERMED; (1962) Dr. Thomas A. Dooley Foundation; (1978) Thomas A. Dooley Foundation; (1980) Thomas A. Dooley Foundation/INTERMED U.S.A.

DOULAS OF NORTH AMERICA (DONA)
e-mail: AskDONA@aol.com
url: http://www.dona.com/
1100 23rd Ave. E
Seattle, WA 98112
Sandy Szalay, Pres. of the Board
PH: (206)324-5440
FX: (206)325-0472
Description: Seeks to help doulas provide quality labor support to birthing women. Offers certification program for doulas; provides continuing education opporrnties; establishes standards of practice and code of ethics; compiles statistics. **Founded:** 1992. **Membership:** 2000. **Staff:** 3. Multinational. **Regional Groups:** 8.

DRUG, CHEMICAL AND ALLIED TRADES ASSOCIATION (DCAT)
2 Roosevelt Ave., Ste. 301
Syosset, NY 11791
Tara Powers, Membership Svc.Dir.
PH: (516)496-3317
FX: (516)496-2231
Description: Manufacturers of drugs, chemicals, and related products (packaging, cosmetics, essential oils); publications, advertising agencies, agents, brokers, and importers. **Founded:** 1890. **Membership:** 500. **Staff:** 6. **Languages:** English. **Budget:** $800,000. **Publication:** *DCAT Digest*, monthly. Newsletter. Contains information on drug and chemical manufacturing, with emphasis on federal regulation. Price: free, for members only. Circulation: 2,500. Advertising: not accepted ■ Directory, annual. Provides information on membership activities. Price: available to members only. **Formerly:** (1959) Drug, Chemical and Allied Trades Section of the New York Board of Trade.

DRUG INFORMATION ASSOCIATION (DIA)
e-mail: dia@diahome.org
url: http://www.diahome.org
321 Norristown Rd., Ste. 225
Ambler, PA 19002-2755
Joseph R. Assenzo, PhD, Exec.Dir.
PH: (215)628-2288
FX: (215)641-1229
Description: Persons who handle drug information in government, industry, the medical and pharmaceutical professions, and allied fields. Seeks to provide mutual instruction on the technology of drug information processing in all areas, including collecting, selecting, abstracting, indexing, coding, vocabulary building, terminology standardizing, computerizing data storage and retrieval, tabulating, correlating, computing, evaluating, writing, editing, reporting, and publishing. Conducts workshops, symposia, and seminars. **Founded:** 1965. **Membership:** 13000. **Languages:** English.

DUTCH ASSOCIATION FOR DERMATOLOGY AND VENEREOLOGY (DADV)
(Nederlandse Vereniging voor Dermatologie en Venereologie)
Postbus 8552
NL-3503 RN Utrecht, Netherlands
Ms. Auguste Glastra
PH: 31 30 2474695
FX: 31 30 2474439
Description: Physicians and interested individuals. Promotes the study of dermatology and venereal infection and treatment. **Founded:** 1896. **Membership:** 500. **Publication:** *Nederlands Tydschrift Voor Dermatologie en Veneredogie* (in Dutch), 8/year. Magazine. ISSN: 0925-2604. Advertising: accepted.

DUTCH SOCIETY OF CARDIOLOGY (DSC)
(Nederlandse Vereniging voor Cardiologie)
Medisch Spectrum Twente
PO Box 50000
NL-7500 KA Enschede, Netherlands
Dr. G.P. Molhock, Exec. Officer
PH: 31 53 4872103
FX: 31 53 4872107
Description: Promotes the profession of cardiology, cardiological research, and cardiac care in the Netherlands. Defends the professional interests of members. **Publication:** *Cardiologie* (in Dutch and English), monthly. Journal. Price: 163.00 f; $100.00. ISSN: 0929-7456. Advertising: not accepted.

DYSAUTONOMIA FOUNDATION (DF)
20 E. 46th St., 3rd Fl.
New York, NY 10017
Lenore F. Roseman, Exec.Dir.
PH: (212)949-6644
FX: (212)682-7625
Description: Parents, relatives, friends, and benefactors of children afflicted with Familial dysautonomia, a Jewish genetic disease of the autonomic nervous system. Purpose is to fund research to find the gene for FD & ultimately have a carrier test for the general Jewish population as well as the causes and cure of the disease. **Founded:** 1954. **Membership:** 8000. **Staff:** 2. **Languages:** English. **Budget:** $1,000,000. **Publication:** *DYS/COURSE*, semiannual. Newsletter. Includes research updates. Price: free. Circulation: 5,000. Advertising: not accepted ■ *Dysautonomia Foundation–Journal*, annual. Price: free upon aid of $250 or more. Circulation: 500. Advertising: accepted. **Formerly:** (1969) Dysautonomia Association.

DYSTONIA MEDICAL RESEARCH FOUNDATION
e-mail: dystfndt@aol.com
url: http://www.ziplink.net/users/dystonia
1 E. Wacker Dr., Ste. 2430
Chicago, IL 60601-2001
Valerie F. Levitin, PhD., Exec.Dir.
PH: (312)755-0198
TF: 800377-DYST
FX: (312)803-0138
Description: Dystonia patients and their families; medical personnel; health agencies; interested individuals. Promotes and funds research and encourages increased public awareness of dystonia, a neurologic muscular disorder causing muscles to jerk and contract into abnormal positions. Disseminates information concerning dystonia. Sponsors patient and family support groups. **Founded:** 1977. **Membership:** 25000. **Staff:** 6. Multinational. **National Groups:** 5. **Languages:** English. **For-Profit.** **Budget:** $1,600,000. **Publication:** *Dystonia Dialogue*, quarterly. Newsletter. Includes foundation and chapter news and research updates. Price: free. Circulation: 12,000. Advertising: not accepted ■ Brochures.

DYSTROPHIC EPIDERMOLYSIS BULLOSA RESEARCH ASSOCIATION OF AMERICA (DEBRA)
e-mail: debraorg@erols.com
url: http://www.debra.org
40 Rector St.
New York, NY 10006
Miram Feder, Exec.Dir.
PH: (212)513-4090
FX: (212)513-4099
Description: People with Epidermolysis Bullosa and their families; other interested individuals. (Epidermolysis Bullosa represents a group of inherited disorders of the skin characterized by formation of blisters resulting from the most minimal trauma.) To raise funds to promote and support research into the cause, nature, and treatment of EB in all its forms; to relieve the physical and mental distress of victims by providing practical advice, guidance, support, and other assistance. Distributes educational material to the public and medical professionals. Works for federal funding for biomedical research of EB and related disorders. Offers children's services; conducts educational programs. **Founded:** 1979. **Membership:** 4000. **Staff:** 5. **Languages:** English. Also Known As DEBRA of America.

ECOLOGICAL PHYSICIANS ASSOCIATION
(Okologischer Arztebund eV)
e-mail: oekologischer.aerztebuld@t-online.de
url: http://www.dremeu.de/info/oekoaertte/oeaebuld.htm
Bundesgeschaftsstelle
Braunschweiger Str. 53b
D-28205 Bremen, Germany
Erik Petersen, Contact
PH: 49 421 4984251
FX: 49 421 4984252
Description: Promotes the return to a natural life existence as well as the preservation of human health. Provides information and treatment. Seeks to contribute to building ecological awareness. German section of the International Doctors for the Environment (ISDE). **Founded:** 1987. **Membership:** 500. **Publication:** *Arzt und Umwelt-Oekologisches Aerzteblatt* (in German), quarterly. Journal. Price: DM 65.00. ISSN: 1431-3146. Circulation: 3,000. Advertising: accepted.

ECRI
e-mail: info@ecri.org
5200 Butler Pke.
Plymouth Meeting, PA 19462
Joel J. Nobel, M.D., Pres.
PH: (610)825-6000
FX: (610)834-1275
Description: Improves the safety, performance, reliability, and cost effectiveness of health care technology through research testing, and publication of results. Provides technical consulting and accident investigation and educational programs. Functions as a worldwide information clearinghouse for health care technology assessment and hazards and deficiencies in medical devices; sponsors seminars. Provides information and technical assistance for planning, procurement and management of medical equipment. Conducts research; compiles statistics and operates speakers' bureau. **Founded:** 1955. **Membership:** 5000. **Staff:** 200. Multinational. **Languages:** English. **Publication:** *Health Devices,* monthly ▪ *Health Devices Alerts,* weekly ▪ *Health Devices Sourcebook,* annual. Directory ▪ *Health Technology Trends,* monthly. Newsletter ▪ *Healthcare Environmental Management,* monthly ▪ *Healthcare Product Comparison System,* monthly ▪ *Healthcare Risk Control,* monthly ▪ *Healthcare Technology Assessment Reports: Executive Briefings,* monthly ▪ *Hospital Hazardous Materials Management,* monthly. Newsletter ▪ *Operating Room Risk Management,* bimonthly ▪ *Technology for Anesthesia,* periodic. Includes information on medical equipment and research updates. Price: $125.00/year ▪ *Technology for Cardiology,* monthly. Newsletter. Reports on ECRI comparative product evaluations; offers hazard reports on medical devices and device operation data. Includes research updates. Price: $125.00/year ▪ *Technology for Respiratory Therapy,* monthly. Newsletter. Evaluates medical devices and summarizes reported problems, hazards, and recalls. Includes research updates and health care technology abstracts. Price: $125.00/year. **Formerly:** (1968) Graduate Pain Research Foundation; (1979) Emergency Care Research Institute.

EDUCATIONAL COMMISSION FOR FOREIGN MEDICAL GRADUATES (ECFMG)
url: http://www.ecfmg.org
3624 Market St.
Philadelphia, PA 19104
Nancy E. Gary, M.D., Pres. & CEO
PH: (215)386-5900
FX: (215)386-9196
Description: Sponsoring organizations are American Board of Medical Specialties; American Medical Association; Association of American Medical Colleges; Association for Hospital Medical Education; the Federation of State Medical Boards of the U.S.; National Medical Association. Aims to provide information to graduates of foreign medical schools regarding entry into graduate medical education and the U.S. health care system; evaluate the qualifications of graduates of foreign medical schools; identify the cultural and professional needs of graduates of foreign medical schools and assist in the establishment of educational

policies and programs; provides international access to testing and evaluation programs to meet theses needs. Sponsors exchange visitor program to enable physicians from other countries to participate in graduate medical education or training. Gathers and disseminates data about graduates of foreign medical schools. Convention/Meeting: none. **Founded:** 1956. **Membership:** 20. **Staff:** 80. Multinational. **Languages:** English. **For-Profit.** **Publication:** *Educational Commission for Foreign Medical Graduates – Annual Report.* Details organizations history and programs. Price: free. Circulation: 8,000. Advertising: not accepted ▪ *Educational Commission for Foreign Medical Graduates – Information Booklet,* annual. Provides procedures for fulfilling ECFMG examination and certification requirements. Price: free. Circulation: 320,000. Advertising: not accepted. **Formerly:** (1974) Educational Council for Foreign Medical Graduates.

EGYPTIAN FAMILY PLANNING ASSOCIATION (EFPA)
e-mail: efpa@idsc.gov.eg
url: http://www.geocities.com/westhollywood/5988/index.html
3 Aba Dawoud Al Zahery St.
Off Makram Ebeid
Nasr City
Cairo, Egypt
Dr. Abdel-Salam Hassan, Exec.Dir.
PH: 20 2 2706374
FX: 20 2 2706372
Description: Non-governmental, non-profit organization providing leadership to voluntary endeavors launched in the field of population and family planning. Contributes towards the realization of the objectives of the national population policy through its efforts in improving and propagating of family planning services particularly among the socially underprivileged sectors of the population and in deprived areas. Raises women's awareness of their reproductive rights; acts as an integral part of women's human rights; solicits support for women's status; and improves youth awareness of health matters in relation to reproductive and sexual behavior in light of the prevailing cultural, social, and economic values. **Founded:** 1958. **Membership:** 25. **Staff:** 26. **Languages:** English, French. **Budget:** LE 15,000,000.

EGYPTIAN GENERAL MEDICAL DOCTORS' ASSOCIATION (EGMDA)
17 El Magdy St.
Mohandissen
Giza, Egypt
PH: 20 2 704482
FX: 20 2 704494
Description: Physicians and medical students. Promotes maintenance of high standards of professional conduct and practice among members. Provides public health care services in areas including family planning, maternal and child care, and geriatric care. **Founded:** 1984. **Languages:** Arabic, English.

EGYPTIAN POPULATION SERVICES SOCIETY (EPSS)
12 Sayem El Dahr St.
Rod El Faraq
Shoubra
Cairo, Egypt
PH: 20 2 33703
Description: Health care professionals and other individuals with an interest in family planning and related health services. Promotes increased availability primary health care in previously underserved areas. Makes available family planning, reproductive health, and pediatric health care services. Conducts surveys to determine medical needs of underserved communities. **Founded:** 1989. **Languages:** Arabic, English.

EMOTIONS ANONYMOUS (EA)
e-mail: eaisc@mtn.org
url: http://www.mtn.org/ea
PO Box 4245
St. Paul, MN 55104-0245
Karen Mead, Dir.

PH: (612)647-9712
FX: (612)647-1593
Description: "Fellowship of men and women who share their experience, strength, and hope with each other, that they may solve their common problem and help others recover from emotional illness." Uses the Twelve Steps of Alcoholics Anonymous World Services, adapted to emotional problems. Disseminates literature and information; provides telephone referrals to local chapters. **Founded:** 1971. **Staff:** 4. Multinational. **National Groups:** 1,300. **Languages:** English. **Budget:** $225,000.

ENDOMETRIOSIS ASSOCIATION (EA)
e-mail: endo@endometriosisassn.org
8585 N. 76th Pl.
Milwaukee, WI 53223
Mary Lou Ballweg, Exec.Dir.
PH: (414)355-2200
TF: 800992-3636
FX: (414)355-6065
Description: Women who have endometriosis and others interested in the condition. (Endometriosis is a disorder in which endometrial tissue, which lines the uterus, is also found in other locations in the body, usually the abdomen. Symptoms can include extremely painful menstruation, infertility, painful sexual intercourse, and heavy or irregular bleeding.) Disseminates information on the treatment, research, and attitudes concerning endometriosis. Offers selfhelp support and informational meetings for women with endometriosis and others. Conducts public education programs; maintains speakers' bureau; gathers data on individual experiences with endometriosis; conducts and promotes research. **Founded:** 1980. **Staff:** 13. Multinational. **Regional Groups:** 200. **Languages:** English.

ENGLISH NATIONAL BOARD FOR NURSING, MIDWIFERY AND HEALTH VISITING
e-mail: enb.resources@easynet.co
url: http://www.enb.org.uk/
170 Tottenham Court Rd.
London W1P 0HA, England
A.P. Smith, Chief Exec.
PH: 44 171 3883131
FX: 44 171 3834031
Description: The Board consists of 10 members who were appointed by the Secretary of State for Health - 7 non-executive members consisting of a nurse, midwife, and health visitor, and someone currently in education, and 3 executive members. Main purpose is to ensure that the institutions it approves conduct education programmes which equip nurses, midwives and health visitors to meet existing and changing health care needs. **Founded:** 1983. **Staff:** 180.

EPILEPSY ASSOCIATION OF SCOTLAND (EAS)
url: http://www.greenchannel.com/fnnpe
48 Govan Rd.
Glasgow G51 1JL, Scotland
Judy Cochrane, Contact
PH: 44 0141 4274911
FX: 44 0141 4191709
Description: Individuals and organizations with an interest in epilepsy. Seeks to improve the quality of life of people with epilepsy; promotes advancement in the diagnosis and treatment of epilepsy. Provides information, support, and counseling services to people with epilepsy; conducts educational programs to raise public awareness of epilepsy; sponsors training courses for health care personnel working with people with epilepsy; makes available advocacy services on behalf of people with epilepsy and their families; lobbies local and national government agencies on legislation affecting people with epilepsy. to members. **Founded:** 1954. **Membership:** 400. **Staff:** 31. **Languages:** English. **Publication:** *Epilepsy News*, 3/year. Newsletter ■ Proceedings (in English, French, and German), annual ■ Booklets.

EPILEPSY CANADA (EC)
e-mail: epilepsy@epilepsy.ca
url: http://www.epilepsy.ca
1470 Peel St., Ste. 745
Montreal, PQ, Canada H3A 1T1
Denise Crepin, Exec.Dir.
PH: (514)845-7855
FX: (514)845-7866
Description: People with epilepsy and their families; health care professionals with an interest in epilepsy and related disorders. Seeks to improve the quality of life of people affected by epilepsy through promotion and support of research. Offers education and awareness initiatives that build understanding and acceptance of epilepsy. **Founded:** 1966. **Languages:** English, French. **Publication:** *Lumina*, semiannual. Newsletter. ISSN: 1181-8212. Circulation: 12,000. Advertising: not accepted ■ Brochure.

EPILEPSY FOUNDATION
e-mail: postmaster@efa.org
url: http://www.efa.org
4351 Garden City Dr.
Landover, MD 20785
Cindy Brownstein, Interim CEO
PH: (301)459-3700
TF: 800EFA-1000
FX: (301)577-2684
Description: National voluntary health agency which serves as the "focal point for the fight against epilepsy in the United States." Augmented by 64 affiliates in the U.S. committed to preventing and controlling epilepsy and improving the lives of those who have it. Provides federal government liaison. The foundation supports medical, social, rehabilitational, legal, employment, and information, education, and advocacy programs. Sponsors research in causes of epilepsy, prevention, psychosocial needs, and improved methods of treatment. Provides research and training grants and fellowships to students and professionals. Assistance and counseling for epilepsy patients and their families is provided through local organizations and the National Information Center on Epilepsy. Annual projects include National Epilepsy Month (November), School Alert (a national educational program for schools), selection of the Epilepsy Poster Child, and a continuing professional and public education and information program. Maintains a resource center. Provides members with access to mail order pharmacy program. Compiles statistics; maintains placement program. **Founded:** 1967. **Membership:** 16000. **Staff:** 60. Multinational. **Languages:** Spanish. **Publication:** *Epilepsy Advances*, quarterly. Newsletter. Includes calendar of events. Price: free to selected audience. Circulation: 3,000. Advertising: not accepted. Also Cited As: *Epilepsy Advances in Clinical and Experimental Research* ■ *Epilepsy USA*, 8/year. Newspaper. Provides information on national legislation and administrative political decisions that affect the disabled, people with epilepsy, and others. Circulation: 23,000. Advertising: not accepted ■ *In Touch*, quarterly. Newsletter. For adults with epilepsy. Price: free. Circulation: 27,000. **Formed by Merger of:** Epilepsy Foundation; Epilepsy Association of America.

EPILEPSY SUPPORT FOUNDATION
No. 3 Crocket Rd.
PO Box A104
Avondale
Harare, Zimbabwe
Tendai Mundanda, Dir.
PH: 263 4 724071
Description: Seeks to improve the quality of life for persons with epilepsy. Raises public awareness about epilepsy and its effects. Disseminates information. **Founded:** 1990. **Membership:** 1205. **Staff:** 6. **Languages:** English, Shona. **Publication:** *Epilepsy Back Up* (in English and Shona), bimonthly. Newsletter. Price: Available to members only. Circulation: 1,300. Advertising: accepted ■ Pamphlets, periodic. Contains information on epilepsy for patients, service providers, medical personnel, and various professionals.

ESTONIAN CARDIAC SOCIETY
(Eesti Kardioloogide Selts)
Sutiste Tee 19
EE-0034 Tallinn, Estonia
Jaan Eha, Chm.
PH: 372 2 525384
FX: 372 2 525384
Description: Physicians and scientists interested in the field of cardiology. **Founded:** 1963.

ESTONIAN CENTRE FOR HEALTH EDUCATION AND PROMOTION
(Eesti Tervisekasvatuse Keskus)
e-mail: root@tervis.ee
Ruutli St. 24
EE-0001 Tallinn, Estonia
Anu Kasmel, Dir.
PH: 372 2 440801
FX: 372 2 440800
Description: Conducts health education activities in Estonia to prevent disease. **Founded:** 1993. **Staff:** 10. **State Groups:** 15. **Languages:** English, Finnish. **Budget:** 350,000 Rb. **Publication:** *Tervist* (in Estonian), monthly. Newsletter. Price: free. Circulation: 2,000. Advertising: not accepted.

ESTONIAN HEALTH PROTECTION ASSOCIATION
(Eesti Tervikaitse Selts)
Paldiski Mnt. 81
EE-0109 Tallinn, Estonia
Neemi Puussaar, Contact
PH: 372 2 426614
FX: 372 2 476051
Description: Promotes better health care for people living in Estonia. **Founded:** 1967. **Membership:** 248. **Local Groups:** 20. **Languages:** English, German. **Publication:** *Estonian Health Protection Association 1967-1992* (in Estonian). Brochure. Contains information on 25 years of the association. Advertising: not accepted.

ESTONIAN MEDICAL ASSOCIATION
(Eesti Arstide Liit)
e-mail: eal@gennet.ee
Pepleri 32
EE-2400 Tartu, Estonia
Katrin Rehemaa, Sec.Gen.
PH: 372 7 430029
FX: 372 7 430029
Description: Promotes the educational and professional interests of physicians. **Founded:** 1921. **Membership:** 2864. **Staff:** 3. **Regional Groups:** 20. **Publication:** *Esti Arstide Liidu Teataja* (in Estonian), monthly. Journal. Circulation: 2,600. **Formerly:** Estonian Doctor's Association.

ESTONIAN PHYSICAL SOCIETY
e-mail: teet@fi.tartu.ee
url: http://www.physic.ut.ee/efs/
Tartu University
Tahe 4
EE-2400 Tartu, Estonia
T. Ord, Sec.
PH: 372 7 465576
FX: 372 7 465570
Description: Physicists, physics teachers, and others with an interest in the physical sciences. Seeks to improve the quality of physics education, research, and knowledge. **Founded:** 1989. **Membership:** 209. **National Groups:** 1. **Languages:** English, Estonian. **Budget:** $30,000. **Publication:** *Annual of the Estonian Physical Society* (in English and Estonian). Price: $45.00. ISSN: 1406-0574. Advertising: accepted.

ESTONIAN PHYSIOLOGY ASSOCIATION
(Eesti Fusiology Selts)
e-mail: eero.vasar@ut.ee
Naituse St. 2
EE-2400 Tartu, Estonia
Eero Vasar, Pres.
PH: 372 7 465334
FX: 372 7 422044
Description: Promotes scientific contact among physiologists. **Membership:** 60. **Languages:** English, Finnish.

ESTONIAN SOCIETY OF FAMILY DOCTORS
(Eesti Perearstide Selts)
Puusepa St. 1a
EE-2400 Tartu, Estonia
Margus Lember, Chm.
PH: 372 7 449212
FX: 372 7 449213
Description: Family physicians and general practitioners in Estonia. **Founded:** 1991.

EUROPEAN ASSOCIATION OF CARDIOTHORACIC ANAESTHESIOLOGISTS (EACTA)
rue Washington, 129
B-1050 Brussels, Belgium
Mary Roe, Mgr.
PH: 32 2 3465643
FX: 32 2 3463637
Description: Physician anesthesiologists. Provides a forum for scientific discussion of issues in cardiothoracic anesthesiology. **Founded:** 1986. **Membership:** 500. Multinational. **Languages:** English.

EUROPEAN ASSOCIATION OF CENTRES OF MEDICAL ETHICS (EACME)
Kapucijnenvoer 35
B-3000 Louvain, Belgium
Prof.Dr. P. Schotsmans, Sec.Gen.
PH: 32 76 336951
FX: 32 76 336952
Description: Medical ethics centers. Promotes critical public and professional concern regarding ethical issues encountered in the practice of medicine. Gathers and disseminates information; conducts research and makes research tools available to members; coordinates collaborative research efforts among members. Encourages continuing ethical education for health care professionals. **Founded:** 1985. **Membership:** 46. Multinational. **Publication:** *EACME News* (in English), periodic. Bulletin.

EUROPEAN ASSOCIATION FOR CRANIO-MAXILLO-FACIAL SURGERY (EACMFS)
The Clock House
39 North St.
Midhurst, W. Sussex GU29 9DS, England
Mr. J. Williams, Sec.Gen.
PH: 1730 815726
Description: Surgeons involved in oral and cranio-maxillofacial surgery. Encourages discussion and conducts medical courses on subjects such as orthognathic and temporomandibular joint surgery and plastic and aesthetic surgery. Maintains speakers' bureau. **Founded:** 1970. **Membership:** 800. Multinational. **National Groups:** 2. **Languages:** English, French. **Publication:** *Journal of Cranio-maxillo-facial Surgery* (in English), bimonthly. Price: included in membership dues. Advertising: accepted.

EUROPEAN ASSOCIATION OF DENTAL GRAPHOLOGY
(Association Dentologique Europeene de Graphologues)
Avenue Vandersmissen 27
B-1040 Brussels, Belgium
Aline Verbist, Contact
PH: 32 2 7713645
Description: Dental graphologists. Promotes adherence to high standards of ethics and practice by members. Establishes standards for dental graphology certification; sponsors continuing pro-

fessional development courses. Multinational. **Languages:** English, French.

EUROPEAN ASSOCIATION OF MULTIDISCIPLINARY PRACTICE IN CHILD, ADOLESCENT AND FAMILY MENTAL HEALTH
(Association Europeene de Pratiques Multidisciplinaires en Sante Mentale de l'Enfant, l'Adolescent et de la Familie)
4 rue Ed Branly
F-77000 Melun, France
Martine Pattin, Contact
PH: 33 1 60689990
FX: 33 1 64377024
Description: Mental health practitioners. Promotes a multidisciplinary approach in the provision of child, adolescent, and family mental health services. Encourages cooperation among members and arranges joint mental health programs; conducts research and continuing professional training programs. Multinational. **Languages:** English, French.

EUROPEAN ASSOCIATION OF NEUROSURGICAL SOCIETIES (EANS)
e-mail: gjerris@rh.dk
url: http://www.eans.org
University Clinic of Neurosurgery
Rigshospitalet
Blegdamsuej 9
DK-2100 Copenhagen, Denmark
L. Calliauw, Sec.
PH: 45 3542390
Description: European neurological societies in 32 countries. Sponsors annual training course. **Founded:** 1971. **Membership:** 8000. Multinational. **Languages:** English. **Publication:** *Acta Neurochirurgica* (in English), 3-4/year. Journal ■ *EANS Bulletin* (in English), semiannual ■ Directory (in English), annual ■ Directory (in English), annual.

EUROPEAN ASSOCIATION OF NEW MEDICAL TECHNIQUES (EANMT)
(Association Europeene de Methodes Medicales Nouvelles)
Route d'Esch 7
L-1470 Luxembourg, Luxembourg
Robert van Sinay, Contact
PH: 352 250226
Description: Physicians and other health care professionals. Promotes advancement of medical practice through the introduction of new techniques and technologies. Identifies and evaluates new medical methods and equipment; sponsors research; conducts training programs for health care personnel. Multinational. **Languages:** English, French.

EUROPEAN ASSOCIATION OF POISONS CENTRES AND CLINICAL TOXICOLOGISTS (EAPCCT)
(Association Europeenne des Centres Anti-Poisons et de Toxicologie Clinique)
National Posions Information Service
(Birmingham Centre)
City Hospital
Birmingham, W. Midlands B18 7QH, England
Dr. Allister Vale, Pres.
PH: 44 121 5074123
FX: 44 121 5075580
Description: Physicians and scientists working in clinical toxicology and related fields. Association works to improve contacts between clinical toxicologists and poisons information specialists. Regularly organizes joint meetings with the World Health Organization and the European Commission. Is a member of the International Union on Toxicology (IUTOX). **Founded:** 1964. **Membership:** 300. Multinational. **Languages:** English. **Publication:** *Journal of Toxicology: Clinical Toxicology* (in English), bimonthly. Advertising: not accepted ■ *Newsletter* (in English), quarterly. **Formerly:** (1990) European Association of Poison Control Centres.

EUROPEAN ASSOCIATION FOR THE STUDY OF DIABETES (EASD)
e-mail: easd@rz.uni-duesseldorf.de
url: http://www.rz.uni-duesseldorf.de/WWW/EASD
Merowingerstr, 29
D-40223 Dusseldorf, Germany
Viktor Joergens, M.D., Exec.Dir.
PH: 49 211 316738
FX: 49 211 3190987
Description: Individuals and firms in 55 countries. Promotes research into the disease of diabetes. Sponsors postgraduate education courses. **Founded:** 1964. **Membership:** 5500. **Staff:** 2. Multinational. **Languages:** English. **Publication:** *Diabetologia* (in English), periodic. Journal. Price: Included in membership fee. Advertising: accepted ■ *Membership List*, triennial.

EUROPEAN BANK OF FROZEN BLOOD OF RARE GROUPS (EBFBRG)
(Banque Europeenne de Sange Congele de Groupes Rares)
Plesmanlaan 125
NL-1066 CX Amsterdam, Netherlands
Mrs. M.A.M. Overbeeke, Exec. Officer
PH: 31 20 5123373
FX: 31 20 5123685
Description: Individuals representing national blood banks and research centers. **Founded:** 1969. **Membership:** 54. Multinational. **Languages:** English, French.

EUROPEAN BRAIN AND BEHAVIOUR SOCIETY (EBBS)
e-mail: ebbs@snv.jussieu.fr
Institut des Neurosciences
9 quai St. Bernard
F-75005 Paris, France
Susan J. Sara, Sec.
PH: 33 1 44273252
FX: 33 1 44273460
Description: Scientists with an interest in the study of the brain and behavior. Promotes and facilitates exchange of information among members and between members and others working in related fields. Conducts research and and educational programs. **Founded:** 1966. **Membership:** 550. **Staff:** 1. Multinational. **Languages:** Dutch, English. **Publication:** Books (in English), biennial. Advertising: not accepted ■ Newsletter, periodic.

EUROPEAN CHEMORECEPTION RESEARCH ORGANIZATION (ECRO)
(Organisation Europeenne pour les Recherches Chimiosensorielles)
e-mail: jean.pierre.calame@roche.com
url: http://www.csv.warwichac.uk/~pssao/ecro.html
Givaudan-Roure
Ueberlandstr. 138
CH-8600 Dubendorf, Switzerland
Dr. Jean Pierre Calame, Exec.Sec.-Treas.
PH: 41 1 8242488
FX: 41 1 8242925
Description: Scientists in academic and industrial laboratories in 29 countries. Promotes research involving chemoreception, or the chemical senses, including taste and smell. Fosters exchange of information on chemoreception. Conducts summer schools to provide practical training in the field for young people. **Founded:** 1970. **Membership:** 440. **Staff:** 7. Multinational. **Languages:** English, French. **Budget:** 15,000 SFr. **Publication:** *Chemical Senses* (in English), quarterly ■ *Chemoreception References* (in English), quarterly ■ *ECRO News Letter* (in English), semiannual. Newsletter.

**EUROPEAN DEPARTMENT FOR THE QUALITY OF
MEDICINES (EDQM)**
(European Pharmacopoeia)
e-mail: 100536.3157@compuserve.com
Coun. of Europe
226 Avenue de Colmar
BP 907
F-67029 Strasbourg, France
Dr. A. Artiges, Dir.
PH: 33 3 88412000
FX: 33 3 88412771
Description: European countries. Works to develop a European
pharmacopoeia (an officially sanctioned book describing drugs,
chemicals, and medical preparations). Seeks to establish uniform
control methods and standards of quality for medicines in mem-
ber countries. **Founded:** 1964. **Membership:** 26. **Staff:** 80. Multi-
national. **Languages:** English, French. **Publication:** *European
Pharmacopoeia* (in English and French), quadrennial. Book.
Price: 2,100.00 Fr 850 (adder dum). Circulation: 12,000. Advertising: accepted. Alternate Formats: CD-ROM ■ *Pharmeuropa:
European Pharmacopoeia Forum* (in English and French), quarterly. Booklet. Price: 900.00 Fr. Advertising: not accepted. **Formerly:** (1996) European Pharmacopoeia Commission.

**EUROPEAN DIABETES PREGNANCY STUDY GROUP
(EDPSG)**
e-mail: easd@uni-duesseldorf.de
url: http://www.uni-duesseldorf.de/WWW/EASD
Merowingerstr. 29
D-40223 Dusseldorf, Germany
Dr. Viktor Jorgens, Exec.Dir.
PH: 49 211 316738
FX: 49 211 3190987
Description: A study group of the European Association for the
Study of Diabetes. Members are diabetologists, obstetricians, pa-
thologists, and pediatricians in 10 countries united to promote
better understanding and more effective investigation of the
problems of pregnancy and diabetes. **Founded:** 1965. **Staff:** 3.
Multinational. **Languages:** English. **Publication:** *Diabetologia* (in
English), monthly. Journal. Price: included in membership dues.
Advertising: accepted.

**EUROPEAN FEDERATION OF PHARMACEUTICAL
INDUSTRIES' ASSOCIATIONS (EFPIA)**
(Federation Europeenne des Associations de l'Industrie
Pharmaceutique)
250, ave. Louise, bte. 91
B-1050 Brussels, Belgium
Brian Ager, Dir.Gen.
PH: 32 2 6262555
FX: 32 2 6262566
Description: European national associations for pharmaceuticals.
Monitors the development of the European pharmaceuticals in-
dustry with respect to public health interests. **Founded:** 1978.
Membership: 16. Multinational. **Languages:** English, French.
Publication: *Annual Report* (in English and French). Advertising:
not accepted ■ *Conference Proceedings* (in English and French),
biennial.

EUROPEAN HEALTH POLICY FORUM (EHPF)
(Forum Europeen de Politique de Sante)
e-mail: 106053.2765@compuserve.com
School of Public Health
Leuven University
PO Box 214
B-3000 Louvain, Belgium
Prof. Mia Defever, Dir.
PH: 32 16 336978
FX: 32 50 220541
Description: Leading policymakers in a broad range of health
care fields and industries representing 25 countries. Purposes
are: to inform members of new developments in health care poli-
cy and research; to facilitate communication between policyma-
kers in different fields; to draw attention to new research and its

implications for health policy. Sponsors the development and
transfer of health information systems. **Founded:** 1981. **Staff:** 3.
Multinational. **Languages:** English. **Publication:** *Health Policy*,
monthly. Journal ■ Papers, periodic ■ Proceedings, periodic.

**EUROPEAN HEALTHCARE MANAGEMENT ASSOCIATION
(EHMA)**
e-mail: ehma@iol.ie
url: http://www.iol.ie/~EHMA/
Vergemount Hall
Clonskeagh
Dublin 6, Ireland
Philip C. Berman, Dir.
PH: 353 1 2839299
FX: 353 1 2838653
Description: Policy makers, senior managers, personnel directors, academic institutions, and research organizations in the
healthcare sector. Seeks to improve healthcare in Europe by raising standards of managerial performance in the health sector.
Fosters cooperation between health service organizations and
institutions in the field of healthcare management education and
training. Promotes the continuing education and development of
healthcare managers. Offers advice and support to national governments in Europe; evaluates members' management development programs. **Founded:** 1966. **Membership:** 200. **Staff:** 4. Multinational. **Languages:** English, French. **Publication:** *Conference
Proceedings* (in English), annual. Journal ■ *Health Services Administration Education and Research* (in English), annual. Directory ■ *Management Development for Health Care: An International Perspective* (in English) ■ *Management Education and
Training in the Health Sector: A Perspective for Italy* (in English) ■
Newsletter (in English), bimonthly. **Formerly:** (1987) European
Association of Programmes in Health Services Studies.

EUROPEAN LEAGUE AGAINST RHEUMATISM (EULAR)
(Ligue Europeenne Contre le Rhumatisme)
e-mail: eular@bluewin.ch
url: http://www.eular.org
Witikonerstrasse 15
CH-8032 Zurich, Switzerland
Fred K. Wyss, Exec.Sec.
PH: 41 1 3839690
FX: 41 1 3839810
Description: Members of social and scientific organizations and
pharmaceutical firms in 36 countries. Maintains small collection
of rheumatology journals. **Founded:** 1947. **Membership:** 12000.
Staff: 2. Multinational. **Regional Groups:** 4. **Languages:** English,
French. **Publication:** *EULAR Manual* (in English, French, and
German), quadrennial ■ *Rheumatology in Europe* (in English,
French, and German), quarterly. Bulletin.

EUROPEAN MEDICAL RESEARCH COUNCILS (EMRC)
e-mail: BSchaller@esf.org
url: http://www.esf.org
1, quai Lezay Marnesia
F-67080 Strasbourg, France
Dr. Ingrid Wuenning, Sec.
PH: 33 388 767118
FX: 33 388 370532
Description: A committee of the European Science Foundation.
National medical research councils or equivalent organizations.
Promotes public medical and biomedical research. Exchanges information on topics including scientific policies of various research organizations, and information on planned or undertaken
but unpublished research programs in specific fields of interdisciplinary and priority research. Encourages the creation of research projects through the coordination and cooperation of research groups on an international level. Identifies and defines research problems in member countries and prompts members to
influence national policies pertaining to research grants in those
areas. **Founded:** 1971. **Membership:** 25. **Staff:** 2. Multinational.
Languages: English.

EUROPEAN MIDWIVES LIAISON COMMITTEE (EEC-LCM)
(Comite de Liaison des Sages-Femmes Europeennes)
e-mail: mariannemead@compuserve.com
7 Dalestones
W. Hunsbury
Northampton NN4 9UU, England
Marianne Mead, Contact
PH: 44 1604 702121
FX: 44 1604 702121
Description: Representatives of associations of midwives in the European Union. Promotes the interests of midwives; represents midwife associations before the Commission of the European Communities and other organizations. **Founded:** 1968. **Membership:** 16. Multinational. **National Groups:** 16. **Languages:** English, French. **Formerly:** EEC Midwives Liaison Committee.

EUROPEAN ORGANIZATION FOR CARIES RESEARCH (ORCA)
(Organisme Europeen de Recherche sur la Carie)
e-mail: stoesse@zmkh_ef.uni_jena_de
University of Jenna
Preventative Dentistry
Nordhauser Str. 78
D-99089 Erfurt, Germany
Dr. Lutz Stoesser, Sec.Gen.
PH: 49 361 741 1205
FX: 49 361 741 1105
Description: Scientists and organizations in 24 countries engaged in research on dental caries. Promotes research on dental caries and evaluates research findings. Establishes contact among organizations and individuals involved in similar research. **Founded:** 1953. **Membership:** 300. Multinational. **Languages:** English. **Budget:** $30,000. **Publication:** *Caries Research* (in English), bimonthly.

EUROPEAN ORGANIZATION FOR RESEARCH AND TREATMENT OF CANCER (EORTC)
(Organisation Europeenne pour la Recherche et le Traitement du Cancer)
e-mail: eortc@eortc.be
url: http://www.eortc.be
83, ave. Mounier, bte. 11
B-1200 Brussels, Belgium
F. Meunier, M.D., Dir.Gen.
PH: 32 2 7741630
FX: 32 2 7723545
Description: Doctors, pharmacologists, clinicians, statisticians, computer analysts, and others in 25 countries involved in the development of anticancer therapies. Aims to develop cancer research in Europe through the coordination of joint research projects by hospitals and laboratories. Maintains screening program of potential anticancer agents and clinical research groups formed to carry out trials with new therapeutic agents. Maintains EORTC New Drug Development Office to coordinate the development of new anticancer medications; operates EORTC Central Office and Data Center to coordinate and conduct cancer clinical trials performed by a network of 2000 doctors in over 300 hospitals in Europe; conducts educational and research programs as well as health, economics, and quality of life studies. Compiles statistics. **Founded:** 1962. **Membership:** 2500. **Staff:** 40. Multinational. **Regional Groups:** 36. **Languages:** English. **Publication:** *EORTC Organisation, Activities and Current Research*, annual. Directory. Price: free. Circulation: 5,000. Alternate Formats: online ■ *European Journal of Cancer* (in English), monthly. **Formerly:** (1968) Groupe Europeen de Chimiotherapie Anticancereuse.

EUROPEAN ORTHODONTIC SOCIETY (EOS)
e-mail: eoslondon@compuserve.com
49 Hallam St., Flat 31
London W1N 5LL, England
Prof. J.P. Moss, Hon.Sec.
PH: 44 171 9352795
FX: 44 171 9352795
Description: Orthodontists in 64 countries promoting the science of orthodontics. **Founded:** 1907. **Membership:** 2500. **Staff:** 1. Multinational. **Languages:** English. **Publication:** *European Journal of Orthodontics* (in English), bimonthly. ISSN: 0141-5387. Circulation: 3,000. Advertising: accepted. Also Cited As: *EJO*. **Formerly:** (1935) European Orthodontia Society.

EUROPEAN PHYSICAL SOCIETY (EPS)
34 Rue Marc Seguin
F-68060 Mulhouse, France
Mr. David Lee, Sec.Gen.
PH: 33 38 9329440
FX: 33 38 9329449
Description: Individuals, laboratories, and organizations concerned with physics. Promotes the advancement of physics by providing: a forum for discussion of topics in the field; a means whereby action can be taken on matters concerning physics. Sponsors conferences; develops scholarship programs for postgraduate study; organizes visits of lecturers to different countries; examines and seeks to standardize methods of teaching physics in schools and universities. Studies problems of physicists in the less developed regions of Europe. Cooperates in establishing standards for physics publications; presents the views of physicists to publishers of physics journals. **Founded:** 1968. **Membership:** 70000. **Staff:** 6. Multinational. **National Groups:** 31. **Languages:** English. **Budget:** 4,000,000 Fr. **Publication:** *Address Booklet* (in English), 3-4/year ■ *European Journal of Physics* (in English), quarterly. Price: L144.00. ISSN: 0143-0807 ■ *Europhysics Conference Abstracts* (in English), 7-9/year. Price: 360.00 SFr ■ *Europhysics Letters*, 3/month. Price: 1,600.00 SFr. ISSN: 0295-5075 ■ *Europhysics News*, monthly. Price: 135.00 SFr. ISSN: 0531-7479. Advertising: accepted ■ *Proceedings*, triennial.

EUROPEAN PROPRIETARY MEDICINES MANUFACTURERS' ASSOCIATION
(Europaischer Fachverband der Arzneimittel-Hersteller)
e-mail: aesgp@innet.be
url: http://www.club.innet.be/~pub00568
7, ave. de Tervuren
B-1040 Brussels, Belgium
Dr. Hubertus Cranz, Dir.
PH: 32 2 7355130
FX: 32 2 7355222
Description: National European proprietary medicines associations. (Proprietary medicines are packaged, over-the-counter drugs.) Advocates self-medication, defined as the therapeutic use of drugs that are safe, effective, and available without prescription. Objectives are to: encourage the involvement of the pharmaceutical industry in European national health care systems; promote and maintain high standards of production, distribution, and advertising of proprietary drugs; ensure that the interests of the proprietary drug industry are recognized by institutions responsible for health legislation; enhance cooperation and the exchange of information among members, and with international professional, industrial, and governmental organizations; represent member associations in the World Federation of Proprietary Medicines' Manufacturers. Compiles statistics. **Founded:** 1964. **Membership:** 25. **Staff:** 6. Multinational. **Languages:** English. **Publication:** *Annual Meeting Proceedings* (in English) ■ *Developing Self-Medication in Central and Eastern Europe*. Price: 7.00 BFr/copy ■ *Self-Medication and the Pharmacist*, periodic. Price: 7.00 BFr/copy ■ *Summary of Product Characteristics for Non-Prescription Medicines in the EC*.

EUROPEAN PUBLIC HEALTH ALLIANCE
e-mail: epha@club.innet.be
33 Rue de Pascale
B-1040 Brussels, Belgium
Andrews Hayes, Sec.
PH: 32 2 2303056
FX: 32 2 2310940
Description: Strives to improve public health care in Europe through policy monitoring and development. Works to heighten public awareness on current public health reforms. Communi-

cates with other organizations with similar interests. **Founded:** 1993. **Membership:** 60. **Staff:** 4. Multinational. **Languages:** Dutch, English. **Budget:** 285,567 BFr. **Publication:** *Commercial Sponsorship and NGOs* (in English and French). Discusses the potential advantages and disadvantages of commercial sponsorship and NGOs ▪ *European Public Health Update* (in English and French), 10/year. Newsletter. Price: 130.00 BFr NGOs; 260.00 BFr industry. Circulation: 500. Advertising: not accepted ▪ *The Fifth Environmental Action Programme and its Implications for Public Health* (in English and French). Prepared for the European Public Health Alliance by the Institution of Environmental Health Officers ▪ *Future of EC Activities in the Area of Public Health* (in English and French). Discussion of how the public health chapter in the Maastricht Treaty may be best interpreted and put into effect ▪ *Guide to Directories of Health Related NGOs in Belgium* (in English and French). Book. A comprehensive guide to directories of health-related organisations in Belgium, both disease specific and general ▪ *Health in Europe* (in English and French). An EPHA response to the Commission communication on the framework for action in the field of public health ▪ *Public Health and the EU - an Overview* (in English and French). Book. Thirteen chapters introducing a range of health related EU policies ▪ *Research Priorities for Public Health in Europe* (in English and French). The final report of a major EPHA conference held in Brussels, Belgium in July 1993.

EUROPEAN REGIONAL ORGANIZATION OF THE INTERNATIONAL DENTAL FEDERATION (ERO)
Postfach 41 01 68
D-50861 Cologne, Germany
Marion Bader, Sec.
PH: 49 221 4001204
FX: 49 221 4001214
Description: National dental associations belonging to the International Dental Federation. Works to establish common professional and health policies in European nations. Provides for the exchange of information; fosters cooperation among members. **Founded:** 1955. **Membership:** 30. **Staff:** 2. Multinational. **Languages:** English, French. **Budget:** DM 90,000. **Publication:** *ERO Circular Letter* (in English, French, and German), quarterly. Newsletter. Price: free. Advertising: not accepted.

EUROPEAN SOCIETY OF BIOMECHANICS (ESB)
e-mail: l.blankevoort@orthp.azn.nl
800 Orthopedie
Postbus 9101
NL-6500 HB NIJMEGEN
D-21073 Hamburg, Germany
Dr. L. Blankevoort, Contact
PH: 49 24 3616959
FX: 49 24 3540555
Description: Engineers, surgeons, and physicians interested in the mechanics (musculoskeletal, cardiovascular, dental, and athletic) of the human body; universities and research institutions. Promotes biomechanics research; organizes courses, symposia, and seminars. **Founded:** 1976. **Membership:** 250. Multinational. **Languages:** English. **Publication:** Proceedings, biennial.

EUROPEAN SOCIETY FOR CARDIOVASCULAR SURGERY (ESCVS)
(Societe Europeenne de Chirurgie Cardiovasculaire)
Cliniques Universitaires U.C.L.
B-5530 Yvoir, Belgium
Dr. Jean-Claude Schoevaerdts, Gen.Sec.
PH: 32 81 423159
FX: 32 81 423158
Description: European Chapter of the International Society Cardiovascular Surgery. Members are cardiac and vascular surgeons. Promotes the study of cardiovascular diseases; facilitates exchange of information and ideas concerning cardiovascular diseases. **Founded:** 1952. **Membership:** 1100. **Staff:** 9. Multinational. **National Groups:** 40. **Languages:** English. **Publication:** *Cardiovascular Surgery* (in English), bimonthly. Journal. Price: $50.00. Advertising: accepted.

EUROPEAN SOCIETY OF CHILD AND ADOLESCENT PSYCHIATRY (ESCAP)
(Societe Europeene de Psychiatrie de l'Enfant et de l'Adolescent)
Academisch Ziekenhuis Utrecht
Kinder en Juegdpsychiatrie
Postbus 85500
NL-3508 GA Utrecht, Netherlands
Prof. H. Remschmidt, Pres.
PH: 31 30 2506362
FX: 31 30 2505444
Description: National societies. **Founded:** 1954. **Membership:** 28. Multinational. **Languages:** English, French. **Publication:** *European Child and Adolescent Psychiatry* (in English), quarterly. Journal. Advertising: not accepted.

EUROPEAN SOCIETY OF COMPARATIVE PHYSIOLOGY AND BIOCHEMISTRY (ESCPB)
e-mail: a.pequeux@ulg.ac.be
url: http://www.al.umi/pmm.it/escpb
Laboratory of Animal Physiology
Univ. of Liege
22, quai Van Beneden
B-4020 Liege, Belgium
Andre Pequeux, Ph.D., Gen.Sec.
PH: 32 43 665046
FX: 32 43 665020
Description: Individuals in 27 countries. Promotes the advancement of comparative and environmental physiology and biochemistry. Conducts summer courses. **Founded:** 1978. **Membership:** 500. **Staff:** 2. Multinational. **Languages:** English. **Publication:** *ESCPB News* (in English), periodic. Newsletter. Price: free to members. Advertising: accepted ▪ *Proceedings*, annual ▪ Books (in English).

EUROPEAN SOCIETY OF NEURORADIOLOGY (ESNR)
(Servizio di Neuroradiologia)
e-mail: leonardi@centauro.it
url: http://www.esnr.org
MGR Congressi
Via Servio Tullio, 4
I-20123 Milan, Italy
Prof. Marco Leonardi, M.D., Sec.Gen.
PH: 39 2 43007247
FX: 39 2 43007247
Description: Mission is accomplish the following: to promote neuroradiology in all its fields; to coordinate work and documents in neuroradiology and to ensure the circulation throughout Europe; to coordinate relations with general radiology and the clinical specialties concerning the nervous system; to contribute to the development of unified methods of teaching neuroradiology and unified standards for training and certification in neuroradiology; to promote and coordinate relations among the existing European national neuroradiological societies or national sections of the ESNR in countries where there are no existing societies; to form European research teams to deal with specific neuroradiological issues. **Founded:** 1969. **Membership:** 650. **Staff:** 1. Multinational. **Languages:** English. **Publication:** *Neuroradiology* (in English), bimonthly. Journal. Advertising: accepted ▪ Directory, periodic.

EUROPEAN SOCIETY FOR NONINVASIVE CARDIOVASCULAR DYNAMICS (ESNICVD)
e-mail: sjuznic@ibmi.mf.uni-/j.si
Institute of Physiology
Faculty of Medicine
Zaloska 4
SLO-91105 Ljubljana, Slovenia
Dr. Susara Juznic, Sec.-Treas.
PH: 386 61 317152
FX: 386 61 1324181
Description: Scientists and professionals in 17 countries active in fields such as biology, cardiology, physiology, sports science, hydraulics, and physics who seek better knowledge of the cardio-

vascular system. Promotes the exchange of ideas in noninvasive cardiovascular research. Fosters the study of cardiovascular function from a mechanical point of reference to gain knowledge applicable to medical practice and technical disciplines. Works to standardize methods used to study the mechanical activity of the cardiovascular system. **Founded:** 1960. **Membership:** 54. Multinational. **Languages:** English. **Publication:** *Bibliotheca Cardiologica* (in English), periodic. Advertising: not accepted ■ *Cardiovascular* (in English), annual. Newsletter. Includes information on conferences, working groups, and ESNICVD. Price: Included in membership dues. Advertising: accepted ■ *Journal of Cardiovascular Diagnosis and Procedures*, quarterly. Advertising: accepted ■ *Proceedings of Congress*, biennial. **Formerly:** (1970) European Society for Ballistocardiographic Research; (1978) European Society for Ballistocardiography and Cardiovascular Dynamics.

EUROPEAN SOCIETY OF OPHTHALMIC PLASTIC AND RECONSTRUCTIVE SURGERY
PO Box 100888
Doberaner Str. 40
D-18055 Postock, Germany
Prof. Rudolf F. Guthoff, Dir.
PH: 49 381 4948501
FX: 49 381 4948502
Description: Surgeons interested in plastic surgery around the eyes. Aims to promote teaching of ophthalmic plastic surgery and to exchange new ideas. **Founded:** 1981. **Membership:** 250. Multinational. **Languages:** English. **Publication:** *Orbit Journal*, quarterly.

EUROPEAN SOCIETY OF PAEDIATRIC RADIOLOGY (ESPR)
Hopital Des Enfants Malades
Service de Radiologie
149 rue de Sevres
F-75743 Paris, France
Prof. Francis Brunelle, Gen.Sec.
PH: 33 1 44495173
FX: 33 1 44495170
Description: Radiologists involved or interested in pediatric radiology. Seeks to contribute to the advancement of the clinical and scientific aspects of pediatric radiology in European countries through educational activities. Conducts Annual postgraduate courses; sponsors research programs. **Founded:** 1963. **Membership:** 471. Multinational. **Languages:** English. **Budget:** 50,000 Fr. **Publication:** *Paediatric Radiology*, annual ■ *Pediakic Radiology* (in English and Spanish), annual. Includes proceedings. Price: $98.00. Also Cited As: *Official Journal* ■ Bulletin (in English), semiannual.

EUROPEAN SOCIETY OF PATHOLOGY (ESP)
Department of Pathology, Medical Faculty
Hospital of Joao
P-4200 Porto, Portugal
Prof. G. Kloppel, Pres. ESP
PH: 351 2 590591
FX: 351 2 5503940
Description: Pathologists and other medical doctors in 49 countries with an interest in pathology. Fosters communication among pathologists; promotes publication of works on pathology and the development of a European school of pathology. **Founded:** 1964. **Membership:** 1352. Multinational. **Languages:** English, French. **Publication:** *European Pathology Newsletter*, periodic ■ *Pathology Research and Practice*, periodic. Journal ■ *Pathology Update*, periodic. Journal.

EUROPEAN SOCIETY OF REGIONAL ANAESTHESIA (ESRA)
(Societe Europeenne d'Anesthesie Loco-Regionale)
Kempenlaan 12
B-2300 Turnhout, Belgium
Andre Van Zundert, MD,PhD, Sec.Gen.
PH: 32 14 422773
FX: 32 14 439284

Description: Doctors of medicine specializing in anesthesiology in 30 countries. Seeks to reduce the risks and heighten the effectiveness of anesthesia by improving techniques of anesthesiology. Provides professional training; conducts workshops and seminars. **Founded:** 1980. **Membership:** 2200. Multinational. **Regional Groups:** 7. **Languages:** English, French. **Publication:** *International Monitor on Regional Anesthesia* (in English), quarterly ■ *Newsletter*, annual ■ *Yearbook*.

EUROPEAN UNION OF MEDICAL SPECIALISTS (UEMS)
e-mail: uems@optinet.be
20, ave. de la Couronne
B-1050 Brussels, Belgium
Dr. R. Peiffer, Gen.Sec.
PH: 32 2 6495164
FX: 32 2 6403730
Description: Medical specialists in 18 countries. Works to ensure high quality care for patients. Fosters communication among members; promotes members' interests. **Founded:** 1958. **Membership:** 24. Multinational. **National Groups:** 24. **Languages:** English, French.

EUROTOX
e-mail: einohietansn@utu.fin
url: http://www.uta.fl/eurotox/
Turku University Hospital
Department of Clinical Physiology
SF-20520 Turku, Finland
Eino Hietanen, Ph.D., Sec.Gen.
PH: 358 2 2612664
FX: 358 2 2611666
Description: Industrial, university, and government toxicology researchers in 50 countries. Purpose is to encourage and advance research in the field of drug toxicity and in other areas of toxicology. Fosters exchange of information concerning problems in toxicology. Topics of interest have included the effects of drugs on the human fetus, toxicological methods and their reliability, toxicity problems of organs such as the liver and the nervous system, carcinogenesis, and sensitization. Sponsors working groups and training courses in toxicology. **Founded:** 1962. **Membership:** 6000. Multinational. **National Groups:** 25. **Languages:** English. **Publication:** *EUROTOX* (in English), 3/year. Newsletter. Contains news and views on a variety of toxicological issues. Price: 100.00 f/year. ISSN: 1015-3780. Circulation: 4,500. Advertising: accepted. Also Cited As: *EUROTOX Newsl* ■ *EUROTOX Membership Directory* (in English), periodic. Contains names and addresses of members. Price: Available to members only. Advertising: accepted ■ *Proceedings of the Annual Meeting* (in English). **Formed by Merger of:** (1939) European Society of Toxicology; (1939) Federation of European Societies of Toxicology.

EVANS SYNDROME RESEARCH AND SUPPORT GROUP
5630 Devon St.
c/o Lou Addington
Port Orange, FL 32127
Lou Addington, Contact
PH: (904)760-3031
FX: (904)760-5583
Description: Provides mutual support and ongoing research for parents and concerned friends and caregivers of children with Evans Syndrome. (Evans Syndrome is a rare auto immune disease.) Facilitates networking and exchange of information. Distributes literature. Developing a group of interested physicians in immunology, genetics, and hematology/oncology. Works to formulate questions for caregivers/patients to ask their doctors. Publications: none. **Convention/Meeting:** none. **Founded:** 1992. **Languages:** English.

FACULTY OF DENTAL SURGERY (FDS)
e-mail: fds@rcseng.ac.uk
url: http://www.rcseng.ac.uk
35-43 Lincoln's Inn Fields
London WC2A 3PN, England
Anne O'Mara, Courses Admin.

PH: 44 171 4053474
FX: 44 171 8319438

FACULTY OF HOMEOPATHY
2 Powis Place
London WC1N 3HT, England
Mrs. Wincott, Chief Exec.
PH: 44 171 8379469
FX: 44 171 2787900
Description: Professional body responsible for regulating the education, training and practice of homeopathy by medically qualified doctors, veterinary surgeons, dentists, pharmacists and other statutorily registered health care professionals. Accredited postgraduate training courses lead to the primary health care certificate and, for doctors and vets, medical/veterinary membership of the faculty. **Founded:** 1950. **Membership:** 800. **Staff:** 12. **Publication:** *British Homoeopathic Journal*, quarterly. Price: free to member; L40.00. ISSN: 0007-0785. Circulation: 1,500. Advertising: accepted.

FACULTY OF PUBLIC HEALTH MEDICINE
e-mail: enquiries@fphm.org.uk
4 St Andrew's Pl.
London NW1 4LB, England
Miss Linda Frankland, Faculty Sec.
PH: 44 171 9350243
FX: 44 171 2246973
Description: Principally trainees and consultants in public health medicine. To promote, for the public benefit, the advancement of education in the field of public health medicine; and to develop public health medicine with a view to maintaining the highest possible standards of professional competence and practice, and act as an authoritative body for the purpose of consultation in matters of education or public interest concerning public health medicine. **Founded:** 1972. **Membership:** 2500. **Staff:** 11. **Publication:** *HFA 2000 News*, quarterly ■ *Journal of Public Health Medicine*, quarterly ■ *Public Health Physician*, quarterly ■ Reports.

FAMILIARES Y AMIGOS DE ENFERMOS DE LA NEURONA MOTORA (FYADENMAC)
e-mail: consult@mailinternet.com.mx
Maestro Rural Num. 74
Col. Un Hogar para Nostros
11330 Mexico City, DF, Mexico
Armando Nava Escobedo, Pres.
PH: 52 5 3411595
FX: 52 5 3411121
Description: Promotes interest in motor neurone disease (MND) research among medical and scientific communities and the public in Mexico. Offers support services to MND sufferers and their families. Disseminates information about the disease. **Founded:** 1982. **Membership:** 34. **Staff:** 17. **Languages:** English, German.

FAMILIES AGAINST CANCER TERROR (FACT)
521 Hillsboro Pkwy
Syracuse, NY 13214-2030
Gertrude Swerdlow, Founder
TF: 800422-6237
Description: Works for the creation of a new and more vigorous national policy on cancer based on incremental research to achieve cancer prevention, treatment and intervention. Endorses the following: an increase in national cancer research appropriations from seven to ten dollars per person; the ability of cancer patients to obtain medical treatment; a continuing health alert on the risks of tobacco and fatty foods; psychological counseling for cancer patients and their families; a federal cancer program that works with local and state programs; and a better informed public. Conducts educational programs; provides patient support services, patient advocacy, and crisis referral. Maintains speakers' bureau Convention/Meeting: none. **Founded:** 1985. **Membership:** 600. **Staff:** 2. **Languages:** English.

FAMILIES OF S.M.A. (FSMA)
e-mail: sma@interaccess.com
url: http://www.abacus96.com/fsma/
PO Box 196
Libertyville, IL 60048-0196
Marilyn Naiditch, Sec.
PH: (847)367-7620
TF: 800886-1762
FX: (847)367-7623
Description: Individuals with Spinal Muscular Atrophy; their families; medical professionals; and interested others. Major funder of SMA research. Promotes public awareness. SMA diseases include: Infantile Progressive SMA (Werdnig-Hoffman Disease), Juvenile Progressive SMA (Kugelberg-Welander Disease) and Adult Progressive SMA (Aran-Duchenne Type). **Founded:** 1985. **Membership:** 2000. **Staff:** 7. Multinational. **State Groups:** 3. **Languages:** English, German. **Publication:** *Direction*, quarterly. Newsletter. Includes research updates and information network. Price: $20.00/year for families in U.S.; $25.00/year for professionals in U.S.; $35.00/year outside U.S. Circulation: 2,000. Advertising: accepted ■ *Living with SMA*. Video ■ *Understanding Muscular Atrophy* (in English, French, and Spanish).

FAMILY HEALTH CARE ASSOCIATION OF AMERICA
e-mail: fitaa@juno.com
url: http://www.fhaa.org
PO Box 1208
Jamestown, NC 27282
PH: (910)887-3484
Description: Provides educational, charitable, and research programs. Also offers a speakers bureau.Publications: none. **Founded:** 1996. **Staff:** 6. **Budget:** $35,000.

FAMILY HEALTH INTERNATIONAL (FHI)
url: http://www.fhi.org
PO Box 13950
Durham, NC 27709
Dr. Theodore King, Contact
PH: (919)544-7040
FX: (919)544-7261
Description: Biomedical researchers and technical assistants. Promotes increased availability, safety, effectiveness, acceptability, and ease of using family planning methods. Works to improve the delivery of voluntary fertility planning and primary health care services, and reduce the spread of sexually transmitted diseases, especially HIV infection. Conducts, analyzes, and disseminates research on contraception and distribution of family planning services. Supports a program of contraceptive safety and health records. Maintains library of 8000 monographs, journals, and reports. Operates computerized services. **Founded:** 1971. **Membership:** 300. **Staff:** 300. Multinational. **Languages:** English. **Publication:** *Biennial Report*. Price: free. Advertising: not accepted ■ *Family Health International – Network* (in English, French, and Spanish), quarterly. Bulletin. Covers reproductive health and family planning for health care personnel and policymakers in developing countries. Price: free. ISSN: 0270-3637. Circulation: 70,000. Advertising: not accepted ■ *Publications Catalog*, annual. **Formerly:** (1982) International Fertility Research Program.

FAMILY AND HEALTH SECTION OF THE NATIONAL COUNCIL ON FAMILY RELATIONS (FHS)
e-mail: ncfr3989@ncfr.com
url: http://www.ncfr.com
3989 Central Ave. NE, Ste. 550
Minneapolis, MN 55421
Mary Jo Czaplewski, Ph.D., Exec.Dir.
PH: (612)781-9331
TF: 888781-9331
FX: (612)781-9348
Description: A section of the National Council on Family Relations. Health and education professionals. Serves as a forum for all professionals involved in interdisciplinary work in the family and health fields. Presents clinical research and educational pro-

grams at NCFR conferences. **Founded:** 1984. **Membership:** 345. **Languages:** English. **Publication:** *Family Health News*, periodic. Newsletter. **Formerly:** (1991) Family and Health Section.

FAMILY RESEARCH INSTITUTE (FRI)
PO Box 62640
Colorado Springs, CO 80962-2640
Dr. Paul Cameron, Exec. Officer
PH: (303)681-3113
FX: (303)681-3427
Description: Promotes information about sexual, family, and substance abuse issues. Conducts research and educational programs. Maintains speakers' bureau; compiles statistics. **Founded:** 1982. **Membership:** 1900. **Staff:** 6. Multinational. **Languages:** English. **Publication:** *Family Research Report*, bimonthly. Newsletter. Price: $25.00/year. Circulation: 2,000. Advertising: not accepted.

FAMILY OF THE FUTURE HEALTH CARE
(Banja la Misogolo)
PO Box 3008
Blantyre, Malawi
PH: 265 652496
FX: 265 652284
Description: Promotes population control, family planning, and reproductive health. Makes available reproductive health care services in urban areas; conducts campaigns encouraging male factory workers to participate in family planning and population control programs. **Founded:** 1987. **Languages:** English.

FAMILY GUIDANCE ASSOCIATION OF ETHIOPIA (FGAE)
PO Box 5716
Addis Ababa, Ethiopia
Mr. Ato Teka Feyera, Contact
PH: 251 1 518909
FX: 251 1 512192
Description: Promotes family planning and responsible parenthood as a means to enhance the quality of life for people living in Ethiopia. Works to stop the spread of AIDS and other sexually transmitted diseases. Provides contraceptive services. Sponsors programs in family planning, sex education, and health. Conducts research. **Founded:** 1966. **Membership:** 3668. **Staff:** 193. **National Groups:** 1. **Languages:** Amharic, English. **Publication:** *FGAE Print and Audio Visual Material Catalogue* ▪ Newsletter, semiannual ▪ Pamphlets ▪ Proceedings.

FAMILY LIFE PROMOTION AND SERVICES (FLPS)
Mumbi House
Temple Rd.
PO Box 19608
Nairobi, Kenya
PH: 254 2 339087
FX: 254 2 339087
Description: Promotes family planning and reproductive health education. Encourages and facilitates increased participation by women in economic and social development programs. **Founded:** 1987. **Languages:** English.

FAMILY PLANNING ASSOCIATION OF CYPRUS (FPA)
25 Bouboulina St.
Nicosia, Cyprus
Despo Hadjiloizou, Acting Exec. Dir.
PH: 357 2 442093
FX: 357 2 367495
Description: Promotes and defends the right of women and men including young people to decide freely the number and spacing of their children and the right to the highest possible level of sexual & reproductive health. **Founded:** 1971. **Membership:** 300. **Staff:** 3. **Languages:** English, Greek. **Budget:** $55,000. **Publication:** *Family Law in Cyprus* (in Greek). Booklet. Price: Free. Cyprus Family Planning Association.

FAMILY PLANNING ASSOCIATION OF ENGLAND (FPA)
2-12 Pentonville Rd.
London N1 9FP, England
Anne Weyman, CEO
PH: 44 171 8375432
FX: 44 171 8373034
Description: Promotes family plannning and sexual health in England. Conducts public education programs; conducts research. **Founded:** 1936. **Staff:** 36. **Languages:** English. **Publication:** *Contraceptive Education Bulletin* (in English), quarterly. Newsletter. Price: L12.00; L18.00 overseas. Advertising: not accepted.

FAMILY PLANNING ASSOCIATION OF ESTONIA (FPA)
e-mail: eppl@teleport.ee
Kooli 7
EE-0001 Tallinn, Estonia
Helle Karro, President
PH: 372 6 446656
FX: 372 2 6313934
Description: Works to improve reproductive health and family planning services and to increase the availability of such services. Conducts research and educational programs; organizes youth services. **Founded:** 1994. **Membership:** 167. **Staff:** 2. **Languages:** Estonian. **Budget:** 2,000,000 Rb. **Publication:** *Bulletin of FPA of Estonia* (in Estonian), biennial. Covers important areas of sexuality, health and education. Price: free. Advertising: accepted.

FAMILY PLANNING ASSOCIATION OF GREECE (FPAG)
e-mail: cop-fpag@othfoethnet.gr
121 Solonos St.
GR-106 78 Athens, Greece
Dr. Elizabeth Mestheneos, Contact
PH: 30 1 3806390
FX: 30 1 3806390
Description: Works to enhance the quality of life for individuals living in Greece by promoting family planning, sex education, and responsible parenthood. Works to stop the spread of AIDS and other sexually transmitted diseases through education and contraceptive services. Sponsors programs in family planning and health. Conducts research. **Founded:** 1977. **Membership:** 850. **Staff:** 2. **Languages:** Greek. **Budget:** $27,000. **Publication:** *Family Planning/Sexual Behaivor*. Pamphlets ▪ *FPA's Newsletter* (in Greek), quarterly. Articles about family planning. Price: included in membership dues. Advertising: accepted ▪ *Sex Education* (in Greek). Proceedings. Price: $4.00. Advertising: not accepted.

FAMILY PLANNING ASSOCIATION OF HONG KONG
e-mail: fpahk@pamplan.org.hk
Southorn Centre, 10/F
130 Hennessy Rd.
Wanchai, Hong Kong
Dr. Susan Fan, Exec.Dir.
PH: 852 25754477
FX: 852 28346767
Description: Health care providers and other interested individuals. Promotes availability of effective family planning services. Conducts educational and advocacy programs to increase public awareness of family planning techniques and services. Makes available: premarital, youth, and women's health services; sexuality education and counseling programs. Works to strengthen ties between family planning services and other public and private social welfare organizations; conducts research in family planning and youth sexuality. Sponsors competitions; compiles statistics. **Founded:** 1950. **Membership:** 150. **Staff:** 200. **Languages:** Chinese, English. **Budget:** HK$70,000,000. **Publication:** *Contraceptive Methods*. Video. Price: $26.00 ▪ *Family Life Education Handbook for Teachers*. Price: $17.00 ▪ *Marriage: Crisis and Future in the Modern World*. Book. Price: $8.00 ▪ *Puberty News*. Video. Price: $26.00.

FAMILY PLANNING ASSOCIATION OF INDIA (FPAI)
e-mail: fpai@giasbm01.vsnl.net.in
Bajaj Bhavan
Nariman Point
Bombay 400 021, Maharashtra, India
E.S. Lala, Sec.Gen.
PH: 91 22 2029000
FX: 91 22 2029038
Description: Works to improve the quality of life for people living in India by promoting family planning and responsible parenthood. Advocates family planning as a basic human right. Works to reduce the number of unwanted pregnancies and abortions. Provides contraceptive and health care services including maternal and child health services. Offers programmes in family life and sexuality education and counselling. Conducts research and training of health professionals, NGOs and other categories of personnel. **Founded:** 1949. **Membership:** 2979. **Staff:** 2491. **Languages:** English, Hindi Suriname Hindustanti. **Budget:** Rs 000,000.

FAMILY PLANNING ASSOCIATION OF KENYA (FPAK)
e-mail: fpak@ken.healthnet.org
PO Box 30581
Nairobi, Kenya
PH: 254 2 215676
FX: 254 2 213757
Description: Believes that planned parenthood is a fundamental human right and that voluntary family planning is an important health measure. Works to provide clients with affordable, accessible, quality service in a dignified and confidential atmosphere. Advocates equal rights and the empowerment of women. **Founded:** 1961. **Languages:** English. **Budget:** 864,800 KSh.

FAMILY PLANNING ASSOCIATION OF SRI LANKA (FPASL)
e-mail: dayafpas@slt.lk
PO Box 365
37/27 Bullers Ln.
Colombo 7, Sri Lanka
Mr. Daya Abeywickrema, Exec.Dir.
PH: 94 1 584153
FX: 94 1 580915
Description: Advocates family planning as a basic human right and as a means to enhance the quality of life for individuals living in Sri Lanka. Works to reduce the number of unwanted pregnancies and abortions. Offers programs in sex education, family planning, and health. Provides contraceptive and health care services. Conducts research. Promotes the empowerment of women and gender equality and reproductive and sexual health for youth. **Founded:** 1953. **Membership:** 350. **Staff:** 200. **Local Groups:** 17. **Languages:** Sinhalese, Tamil. **Budget:** CRs 65,000,000. **Publication:** *Annual Report* (in English). Magazine. Contains reports of the year's activities. Price: free. Circulation: 500. Advertising: not accepted.

FAMILY PLANNING ASSOCIATION OF TURKEY
  (Turkiye Aile Planlamasi Dernegi)
e-mail: tapd@adanet.tr
url: http://www.ada.net.tr/TAPD
Atac Sokak 73/3
TR-06420 Ankara, Turkey
Dr. Kemal Demir, Pres.
PH: 90 312 4318355
FX: 90 312 4342946
Description: Promotes enhanced awareness of family planning rights and services throughout Turkey. Advocates reproductive health including family planning as a basic human right. Disseminates information. Works for the advancement of women's studies, health, and rights. **Founded:** 1963. **Membership:** 1500. **Staff:** 70. **Languages:** English. **Budget:** TL 235,000. **Publication:** *Islam and Family Planning* (in Turkish). Booklet. Price: free. Circulation: 20,000. Advertising: not accepted ■ Books ■ Newsletters ■ Brochures.

FAMILY PLANNING AUSTRALIA (FPA)
e-mail: fpa@actonline.com.au
url: http://www.actonline.com.au/fpa
9/114 Maitland St.
Hackett, ACT 2602, Australia
Susan King, Pres.
PH: 61 2 62305255
FX: 61 2 62305344
Description: Promotes improved education and research in family planning. Seeks to heighten governmental and public awareness of the population problems of local communities and the world. Believes that the availability and use of contraceptives is a basic human right. **Membership:** 8. **Staff:** 6. **State Groups:** 8. **Budget:** $A 250,000. **Formerly:** (1992) Family Planning Federation of Australia.

FAMILY PLANNING INTERNATIONAL ASSISTANCE (FPIA)
e-mail: fpia@ppfa.org
url: http://www.ppfa.org/ppfa
810 7th Ave.
New York, NY 10019
Dr. Daniel R. Weintraub, VP
PH: (212)261-4764
FX: (212)247-6274
Description: Provides financial, technical, and commodity assistance to organizations in developing countries interested in reproductive health programs. Convention/Meeting: none. **Founded:** 1971. **Staff:** 18. Multinational. **Languages:** English. **For-Profit. Budget:** $3,200.

**FAMILY PLANNING INTERNATIONAL ASSISTANCE -
  KENYA (FPIA)**
e-mail: FPIA@form-net.com
Box 53538
Nairobi, Kenya
Joellen Lambiotte, Regional Dir.
PH: 254 2 521855
FX: 254 2 520028
Description: Family planning organization that works to improve reproductive health in developing countries. Multinational. **Languages:** English, French.

**FAMILY PLANNING INTERNATIONAL ASSISTANCE -
  THAILAND (FPIA)**
Yada Bldg., 5th Fl.
56 Silom Rd.
Bangkok 10500, Thailand
Easter Dasmariens, Contact
Description: Health care professionals, family planning and population organizations, and other interested individuals. Promotes increased availability of family planning services. Conducts educational programs to raise public awareness of population issues and family planning services; provides support and assistance to reproductive health and family planning clinics. **Languages:** English, Thai.

FAMILY PLANNING PRIVATE SECTOR (FPPS)
PO Box 46042
Nairobi, Kenya
PH: 254 2 224626
FX: 254 2 23039
Description: Promotes increased awareness of population control issues and family planning services. Facilitates increased participation by women in economic and social development; conducts reproductive health education courses for men and women. **Founded:** 1984. **Languages:** English.

**FAMILY PLANNING AND SEXUAL HEALTH ASSOCIATION
  (FPSHA)**
58 Saltoniskiu
2034 Vilnius, Lithuania
Esmeralda Kuliesyte, Exec.Dir.
PH: 370 2 790319
FX: 370 2 790319

Description: Health care professionals with an interest in reproductive medicine; individuals interested in family planning and sexual health. Seeks to avoid unwanted pregnancies and to eliminate the spread of sexually transmitted diseases. Promotes increased availability of reproductive health services; facilitates advancement of reproductive medicine. Serves as a clearinghouse on family planning and sexual health; conducts public education programs; sponsors continuing professional development courses; lobbies for improved public policies dealing with reproductive health issues. **Founded:** 1995. **Membership:** 238. **Staff:** 3. **Languages:** English, Lithuanian. **Budget:** $30,000. **Publication:** Newsletter, quarterly ▪ Brochure ▪ Bulletin.

FDI WORLD DENTAL FEDERATION
e-mail: general@fdi.org.uk
url: http://www.fdi.org.uk/worldental
7 Carlisle St.
London W1V 5RG, England
Dr. Per Ake Zillen, Exec.Dir.
PH: 44 171 9357852
FX: 44 171 4860183
Description: National Dental Associates and individual dentists worldwide. A federation of National Dental Association and individual member dentists with the aim of helping to promote oral health worldwide. **Founded:** 1900. **Membership:** 600000. **Staff:** 20. Multinational. **National Groups:** 116. **Languages:** French, German. **Publication:** *Community Dental Health* (in English), quarterly ▪ *The European Journal of Prosthodontics and Restorative Dentistry* (in English), quarterly ▪ *FDI World* (in English, French, German, and Spanish), bimonthly ▪ *Gerodontology* (in English), semiannual ▪ *International Dental Journal* (in English, French, German, and Spanish), bimonthly.

FEDERACION NACIONAL DE EMPRESAS DE INSTRUMENTACION CIENTIFICA, MEDICA, TECNICA Y DENTAL (FENIN)
e-mail: 100416.2116@compuserve.com
Juan Bravo 10-3o planta
E-28006 Madrid, Spain
Ramon Perez Bordo, Sec.
PH: 34 1 5759800
FX: 34 1 4353478
Description: Companies manufacturing medical equipment and supplies. Establishes international standards and technical harmonization for medical equipment. Represents members' interests before government bodies, international agencies, and the public. Maintains liaison with organizations representing dentists, dental technicians, and dental supply dealers and distributors. Compiles statistics. **Founded:** 1978. **Membership:** 14. **Staff:** 4. **Regional Groups:** 2. **Languages:** Spanish. **Budget:** $1,000,000. **Publication:** *Noticias Fenin* (in Spanish), monthly. Newsletter. Price: free. Circulation: 600. Advertising: not accepted.

FEDERACION DE PLANIFICACION FAMILIAR DE ESPANA (FPFE)
Almagro 28
E-28010 Madrid, Spain
Ms. Isabel Serrano, Pres.
PH: 34 1 3199276
FX: 34 1 3081589
Description: Works to improve the quality of life for individuals living in Spain by promoting responsible parenthood and family planning. Attempts to stop the spread of AIDS and other sexually transmitted diseases through education and contraceptive services. Offers programs in family planning and health care. Acts as an advocate for family planning on the national level. **Founded:** 1987. **Membership:** 450. **Staff:** 12. **Regional Groups:** 7. **Languages:** Spanish. **Budget:** 75,000,000 Ptas. **Publication:** *Boletin de la Federacion de Planificacion Familiar de Espana* (in Spanish), quarterly. Magazine. Circulation: 2,500. Advertising: accepted.

FEDERAL PHYSICIANS ASSOCIATION (FPA)
e-mail: fedphy@aol.com
PO Box 45150
Washington, DC 20026
Dennis W. Boyd, Exec.Dir.
PH: (703)455-5947
TF: 800403-3374
FX: (703)455-8282
Description: Civil service physicians employed by or retired from the federal government. Objectives are: to improve the health care of patients served by federal civil service physicians; to advance the practice of medicine within the federal government; to better the working conditions and benefits of federal civil service physicians. Conducts specialized education programs. **Founded:** 1978. **Membership:** 500. **Staff:** 1. Multinational. **National Groups:** 1. **Languages:** English. **Budget:** $30,000. **Publication:** *The Federal Physician*, bimonthly. Newsletter. Price: $37.50/year. ISSN: 1070-9029. Circulation: 500. Advertising: accepted. **Formerly:** (1982) American Academy of Federal Civil Service Physicians.

FEDERATED AMBULATORY SURGERY ASSOCIATION (FASA)
700 N. Fairfax St., No. 306
Alexandria, VA 22314
Gail D. Durant, Exec.Dir.
PH: (703)836-8808
Description: Physicians, nurses, health administrators, and other individuals representing more than 400 outpatient surgery facilities. Promotes the concept of freestanding ambulatory (outpatient) surgical care. Facilitates exchange of knowledge and ideas regarding the care of ambulatory surgical patients. Represents members' interests at national level. Provides information to members, other organizations, and the public regarding government activities, legislation, statistical studies, group purchase programs, and the availability of malpractice insurance. Sponsors seminars, educational programs, and panel discussions; conducts studies and surveys in the field. **Founded:** 1974. **Membership:** 1200. **Staff:** 2. **Languages:** English. Formerly Society for the Advancement of Freestanding Ambulatory Surgical Care; (1986) Freestanding Ambulatory Surgery Association.

FEDERATION FOR ACCESSIBLE NURSING EDUCATION AND LICENSURE (FANEL)
PO Box 1418
Lewisburg, WV 24901
Twyla Wallace, Pres.
PH: (304)645-4357
FX: (304)645-4357
Description: Registered nurses, licensed practical nurses, educators, health organizations, schools, and hospital administrators seeking to maintain licensure through current educational programs for RNs and LPNs. **Founded:** 1983. **Languages:** English.

FEDERATION OF ASSOCIATIONS OF REGULATORY BOARDS (FARB)
400 S. Union St., Ste. 295
PO Box 4389
Montgomery, AL 36103-4389
Randolph P. Reaves, Contact
PH: (334)834-2415
FX: (334)269-6379
Description: National associations of regulatory boards united to exchange information and engage in programs and joint activities relating to the education and licensing of professionals and to cooperate in solving the mutual problems of members. Conducts attorney certification course. **Founded:** 1973. **Membership:** 9. **Languages:** English. **Publication:** *FARB Facts*, periodic. **Formerly:** (1985) Federation of Associations of Health Regulatory Boards.

**FEDERATION OF EUROPEAN BIOCHEMICAL SOCIETIES
(FEBS)**
e-mail: marko.dolinar@ijs.si
url: http://ubeclu.unibe.ch/mci/febs
Dept. of Biochemistry and Mol. Biology
Jozef Stefan Inst.
Jamova 39
SLO-1000 Ljubljana, Slovenia
Prof. Vito Turk, Gen.Sec.
PH: 386 61 1257080
FX: 386 61 273594
Description: Purpose is to further research and education in the
field of biochemistry and to disseminate research findings. Holds
advanced courses; offers fellowships. **Founded:** 1964. **Member-
ship:** 39000. Multinational. **Languages:** English, French. **Budget:**
7,000,000 Din. **Publication:** *European Journal of Biochemistry*, bi-
weekly ■ *FEBS Letters* (in English), weekly.

**FEDERATION OF FAMILIES FOR CHILDREN'S MENTAL
HEALTH (FFCMH)**
e-mail: ffcmh@crosslink.net
url: http://www.ffcmh.org
1021 Prince St.
Alexandria, VA 22314
Barbara Huff
PH: (703)684-7710
FX: (703)836-1040

**FEDERATION OF NURSES AND HEALTH PROFESSIONALS
(FNHP)**
e-mail: fnhp2@aol.com
url: http://www.aft.org
555 New Jersey Ave. NW
Washington, DC 20001
Lou Nayman, Field Dir.
PH: (202)879-4491
TF: 800238-1133
FX: (202)879-4597
Description: Collective bargaining organization of registered
nurses, licensed practical nurses, and other professional and
technical employees in the health field. Works to improve members' professional standards through promoting continuing education, advancing their economic status, and securing working
conditions conducive to optimum performance and the most effective delivery of health care. Seeks to have an impact on
legislation affecting national health insurance, cost containment,
utilization of manpower resources, consumer health education,
health personnel training funds, allocation of health research
grants, and other national health issues. Maintains legal defense
fund to provide assistance to members whose legal or contractual
rights have been violated. **Founded:** 1978. **Membership:** 54000.
Staff: 3. **National Groups:** 1. **Languages:** English. **Publication:**
Healthwire, bimonthly. Newsletter. Includes book reviews. Price:
included in membership dues. Circulation: 50,000. Advertising:
not accepted ■ *Stat*, quarterly. Newsletter. Price: free. Circulation: 500. Advertising: not accepted ■ Brochures, periodic. Covers unions and health issues ■ Pamphlets.

FEDERATION OF ORTHODONTIC ASSOCIATIONS (FOA)
711 Giddings Ave.
Sheboygan Falls, WI 53085
Dr. Robert Weber, Treas.
PH: (920)467-4070
Description: Orthodontically oriented dental associations united
to increase members' knowledge of orthodontics on the postgraduate level. **Founded:** 1969. **Languages:** English. **Publication:** *International Journal of Orthodontics*, semiannual. Includes annual
index, book reviews, and news from associations represented by
the federation. Price: $20.00/year. ISSN: 0020-7500. Circulation:
1,100. Advertising: accepted. Alternate Formats: microform.

**FEDERATION OF SPECIAL CARE ORGANIZATIONS AND
DENTISTRY**
url: http://www.bgsm.edu/dentistry/foscod
211 E. Chicago Ave., Ste. 948
Chicago, IL 60611-9361
John S. Rutkauskas, DDS, Exec.Dir.
PH: (312)440-2660
FX: (312)440-7494
Description: Dentists and dental care providers. Seeks to improve the effectiveness of health care providers in providing
quality patient care, especially for patients who for reasons of
medical diagnosis, disabilities, or frailties prevalent in advanced
age require special care and/or special settings for dental care.
Conducts educational programs. **Founded:** 1987. **Membership:**
1500. Multinational. **Languages:** English. **Budget:** $400,000.

**FEDERATION OF STATE MEDICAL BOARDS OF THE
UNITED STATES (FSMB)**
url: http://www.fsmb.org
Federation Pl.
400 Fuller Wiser Rd., Ste. 300
Euless, TX 76039-3855
Dr. James Winn, M.D., Exec.VP
PH: (817)868-4000
FX: (817)868-4097
Description: State medical examining and licensing boards (in-
cluding fourteen osteopathic boards). **Founded:** 1912. **Member-
ship:** 69. **Staff:** 105. **Languages:** English. **Publication:** *Exchange*,
triennial ■ *Federation Bulletin*, quarterly. Advertising: not accep-
ted ■ *FSMB NewsLine*, monthly ■ *Handbook*, annual. Directory.
Formed by Merger of: (1912) American Confederation of
Reciprocating, Examining and Licensing Medical Boards; American Confederation of State Medical Examining Boards.

FEDERATION OF THE EUROPEAN DENTAL INDUSTRY
(Federation de l'Industrie Dentaire en Europe)
Kirchweg 2
D-50858 Cologne, Germany
Harald Russegger, Sec.Gen.
PH: 49 221 9486280
FX: 49 221 483428
Description: National associations of companies engaged in the
manufacture of dental instruments and supplies. Functions as a
platform for coordination of development and works to harmo-
nize international standards within the industry; represents mem-
bers' interests before government and European Community
agencies. Promotes environmental protection, bar coding
(HIBC), market statistics (project). **Founded:** 1957. **Membership:** 11. Multinational. **Languages:** English. **Publication:** *FIDE -
European Dental Industry* (in English), biennial. Brochure. Membership brochure. Advertising: not accepted ■ *FIDE News* (in
English), 1-2/year. Newsletter. Price: free; Available to members
only. Advertising: not accepted. **Also Known As:** Vereinigung
der Europaischen Dental-Industrie.

**FEDERATION OF FAMILY PLANNING ASSOCIATIONS OF
MALAYSIA (FFPAM)**
e-mail: ffeam@po.jaring.mg
81-B Jalan SS 15/5A
Subang Jaya
47500 Petaling Jaya, Malaysia
PH: 60 3 7337514
FX: 60 3 7346638
Description: Promotes and advocates family health including
family planning, women's development, family life education,
youth sexuality, AIDS and sexually transmitted disease prevention, through service, research training and activities. Thus,
improving the quality of life of individuals living in Malaysia..
Languages: Malay.

FEDERATION FRANCOPHONE BELGE POUR LE PLANNING FAMILIAL ET L'EDUCATION SEXUELLE
34, rue de la Tulipe
B-1050 Brussels, Belgium
Dominique Robichez, Contact
PH: 32 2 5028203
FX: 32 2 5025613
Description: Advocates family planning as a basic human right. Works to reduce the number of unwanted pregnancies and abortions. Attempts to stop the spread of AIDS and other sexually transmitted diseases through education and contraceptive services. Sponsors programs in family planning and health. Acts as an advocate for family planning on a national level. **Founded:** 1963. **Membership:** 37. **Staff:** 8. **Languages:** French. **Publication:** *En Question* (in French), semiannual. Newsletter. Price: 200.00 BFr.

FEDERATION OF FRENCH-LANGUAGE GYNECOLOGISTS AND OBSTETRICIANS
(Federation des Gynecologues et Obstetriciens de Langue Francaise)
Clinique Universitaire Baudelocque
123, blvd. de Port-Royal
F-75674 Paris, France
Prof. Jean-Rene Zorn, Contact
PH: 33 1 42341143
FX: 33 1 42341231
Description: French-speaking gynecologists and obstetricians. Purpose is to promote scientific study in the French language of all aspects of the biology of human reproduction. Conducts training sessions and travel and exchange programs. Maintains permanent committees to deal with special topics. **Founded:** 1950. **Membership:** 2000. Multinational. **Languages:** French. **Publication:** *Journal de Gynecologie Obstetrique et Biologie de la Reproduction* (in French), bimonthly. Price: 906.00 Fr. ISSN: 0368-2315. Advertising: accepted.

FEDERATION OF HUNGARIAN MEDICAL SOCIETIES (MOTESZ)
(Magyar Orvostudomanyi Tarsasagok es Egyesuletek Szovetsege)
e-mail: motesz@mail.elender.hu
Nador utca 36
H-1051 Budapest, Hungary
Dr. Bela Szalma, Exec.Dir.
PH: 36 1 3123807
FX: 36 1 1837918
Description: Medical, dental and natural scientific societies comprising 32,000 individuals. Works to enhance the medical and sciences in Hungary. Promotes the development of international relations in the field of health. Conducts educational programs; bestows awards. **Founded:** 1966. **Membership:** 83. **Staff:** 24. Multinational. **Languages:** English, German. **Budget:** 36,270,000 Ft. **Publication:** *MOTESZ Calendar* (in English and Hungarian), annual. Magazine. Price: Free. Advertising: accepted ∎ *MOTESZ Magazine* (in Hungarian), bimonthly. Scientific journal. Price: Free to members. Advertising: accepted.

FEDERATION OF MEDICAL SOCIETIES OF HONG KONG
Duke of Windsor Social Service Bldg., 4/F
15 Hennessy Rd.
Wanchai, Hong Kong
Kitty Leung, Adm.Mgr.
PH: 852 25278898
FX: 852 28650345
Description: Medical and dental associations and related professional organizations. Promotes advancement of the medical, dental, and related sciences. Represents the interests of the medical community. Coordinates activities of members; conducts educational programs. **Founded:** 1965. **Membership:** 95. **Languages:** Chinese, English. **Publication:** *Hong Kong Medical Diary*, monthly. Bulletin. Circulation: 7,500. Advertising: accepted ∎ *Medical and Dental Directory of Hong Kong*, quadrennial. Circulation: 4,000. Advertising: accepted.

FEDERATION OF SCANDINAVIAN SOCIETIES OF OBSTETRICS AND GYNECOLOGY
(Nordisk Forening for Obstetrikk og Gynekologi)
Obst Gyn. Dept.
University Hospital
N-7006 Trondheim, Norway
Mette H. Moen, M.D., Sec.Gen.
PH: 47 73 998000
FX: 47 73 997602
Description: Gynecologists and obstetricians from Nordic countries. Conducts educational programs; sponsors competitions. **Founded:** 1933. **Membership:** 3212. Multinational. **National Groups:** 5. **Languages:** Swedish. **Budget:** 550,000 NKr. **Publication:** *Acta Obstetrica Gynecologicia Scandinavica* (in English), 10/year. Journal. Includes supplements. Price: 1,770.00 DKr. Circulation: 4,600. Advertising: accepted ∎ *Bulletin* (in Danish, English, Norwegian, and Swedish), quarterly. Newsletter. **Formerly:** Scandinavian Association of Obstetrics and Gynecology; Nordisk Forening for Obstretik Och Gynekologi.

FEDERATION OF THE TRADE UNIONS IN HEALTH CARE
Maria Luiza 45
BG-1202 Sofia, Bulgaria
Ivan Kokalov, Pres.
PH: 359 2 882097
FX: 359 2 831814
Description: Defends and represents members' interests. **Founded:** 1990. **Membership:** 51739. **Staff:** 9. **Local Groups:** 539. **Languages:** English, French.

FELLOWSHIP OF ASSOCIATES OF MEDICAL EVANGELISM (FAME)
PO Box 688
Columbus, IN 47202-0688
Robert E. Reeves, Exec.Dir.
PH: (812)379-4351
FX: (812)379-1105
Description: Builds hospitals and clinics and provides mobile medical units for Christian missionaries outside the U.S.; secures and ships medicine and medical supplies. Conducts charitable programs; maintains speakers' bureau. **Founded:** 1970. **Staff:** 83. Multinational. **Languages:** English. **Publication:** *Spreading the Fame of Christ*, quarterly. Newsletter. Advertising: not accepted.

FIBROMYALGIA ALLIANCE OF AMERICA (FMAA)
e-mail: masaathoff@aol.com
PO Box 21990
Columbus, OH 43221-0990
Mary Anne Saathoff, R.N., Pres.
PH: (614)457-4222
FX: (614)457-2729
Description: Individuals with fibromyalgia, their families and friends, health care professionals. (Fibromyalgia is a chronic condition of severe muscle aching and severe fatigue, along with a sleep disorder. Pain can be sharp and stabbing and appears in muscles, tendons, and ligaments. Treatments are often ineffective; the condition can be functionally disabling.) Serves as an international informational clearinghouse on fibromyalgia. Promotes research, conducts charitable programs, operates speakers' bureau. Provides printed material and audiovisual resources to fibromyalgia patients, hospitals, and health care professionals. **Founded:** 1986. **Membership:** 8000. **Staff:** 4. Multinational. **Local Groups:** 6. **Languages:** English. **Budget:** $200,000. **Publication:** *Fibromyalgia Syndrome*. Booklet. Provides an overview of fibromyalgia. Price: $4.00. Circulation: 70,000. Advertising: not accepted ∎ *The Fibromyalgia Times*, quarterly. Newsletter. Price: $25.00 membership. Circulation: 8,000. Advertising: not accepted. **Formerly:** (1990) Central Ohio Fibrositis Association; (1995) Fibromyalgia Association of Central Ohio; (1997) Fibromyalgia Alliance.

FINNISH ASSOCIATION FOR MENTAL HEALTH (FAMH)
(Suomen Mielenterveysseura-Foreningen for Mental Halsa i Finland)
e-mail: Pirkko.Lahti@mielenterveysseura.fi
Maistraatinportti 4 A
FIN-00240 Helsinki, Finland
Ms. Pirkko Lahti, Exec.Dir.
PH: 358 9 615516
FX: 358 9 61551770
Description: Voluntary organization for professional and lay people. Promotes mental health through programs of prevention. Introduces new procedures in voluntary and statutory mental health work. Provides support and crisis services; offers vocational training programs. Maintains 21 crisis centers. **Founded:** 1897. **Membership:** 90. **Languages:** English, Finnish. **Publication:** *Mielenterveys* (in Finnish), bimonthly. Includes mental health information. Price: FM 230.00/year. Circulation: 12,000. Advertising: accepted. Also Cited As: *Mental Health* ■ *Perheterapia* (in Finnish), quarterly. Provides family therapy information. Also Cited As: *Family Therapy* ■ Books (in Finnish) ■ Journals ■ Newsletter (in English), annual. Price: free. Advertising: not accepted.

FINNISH BIOCHEMICAL SOCIETY (FBS)
(Societas Biochemica, Biophysica et Microbiologica Fenniae)
e-mail: jarmo.juuti@helsinki.fi
url: http://www.helsinki.fi/~juuti/biabio.html
Dept. of Biosciences
Division of Genetics
PO Box 56
FIN-00014 Helsinki, Finland
Jarmo Juuti, Sec.
PH: 358 9 70859104
FX: 358 9 70859098
Description: Scientists promoting biochemical, biophysical, and microbiological research in Finland. Organizes symposia. **Founded:** 1945. **Membership:** 1200. **Regional Groups:** 2. **Languages:** English, French. **Budget:** FM 150,000. **Publication:** Newsletter, periodic. Price: Available to members only. Advertising: accepted.

FINNISH CARDIAC SOCIETY (FCS)
(Suomen Kardiologinen Seura)
e-mail: fcs@fimnet.fi
url: http://www.fimnet.fi/fcs/
Kuopio University Hospital
Dept. of Medicine
PO Box 1777
FIN-70211 Kuopio, Finland
Matti Halinen, Pres.
PH: 358 208 315555
FX: 358 207 315555
Description: Physicians practicing in Finland. Encourages contact between cardiology specialists and doctors interested in the field. Organizes educational courses. **Founded:** 1969. **Membership:** 559. **Staff:** 1. **Languages:** English, Finnish. **Publication:** *Sydanaani (Cardiac Sound)* (in Finnish), periodic. Newsletter. Price: Available to members only. ISSN: 0788-0227. Advertising: not accepted.

FINNISH DERMATOLOGICAL SOCIETY (FDS)
(Suomen Ihotautilaakariyhdistys Ry)
Dept. of Dermatology
PO Box 160
FIN-00029 Hyks, Finland
Antti Lauerma, MD, Secretary
PH: 358 9 471961639
FX: 358 9 94716561
Description: Professional organization for dermatologists in Finland. Conducts educational programs. **Founded:** 1916. **Membership:** 251. **Staff:** 5. **Languages:** English, Finnish. **Budget:** FM 100,000. **Publication:** *Skinfo* (in Finnish), 4-6/year. Newsletter. Price: Available to members only. Advertising: not accepted.

FINNISH MEDICAL ASSOCIATION
(Suomen Laakariliitto)
e-mail: fma@fimnet.fi
Makelankatu 2
PO Box 49
Helsinki, Finland
Dr. Markku Aarimaa, Sec.Gen.
PH: 358 9 393091
FX: 358 9 3930794
Description: Physicians' organizations. Promotes formation and implementation of effective national health policies. Develops and administers national training programs for physicians and confers professional certification. Conducts research on health systems and services. Facilitates international cooperation in the provision of health care in underserved areas. **Founded:** 1910. **Membership:** 17500. **Staff:** 55. **Languages:** English, Finnish. **Publication:** *Finnish Medical Journal*, 36/year ■ *Information Newsletter*, 15/year ■ *Newsletter for the General Press*, 15/year ■ Books ■ Manuals.

FINNISH SOCIETY OF CLINICAL NEUROPHYSIOLOGY (FSCN)
(Suomen Kliinisen Neurofysiologian Yhdistys)
Division of Clinical Neurophysiology
University Hospital
FIN-00290 Helsinki, Finland
Tapani Salmi, M.D., Sec.
PH: 358 0 4713876
FX: 358 0 4714088
Description: Physicians who specialize in clinical neurophysiology. Promotes research in new techniques and applications in the field. Disseminates current information. Encourages training and education of residents in clinical neurophysiology. Conducts Annual course and semiannual seminar. **Founded:** 1972. **Membership:** 95. **Languages:** English, Finnish. **Budget:** FM 10,000. **Publication:** *Membership List*, periodic.

FINNISH SOCIETY FOR DERMATOPATHOLOGY (FSD)
(Suomen Dermatopatologiyhdistys)
Department of Dermatology
Meilahdentie 2
FIN-00250 Helsinki, Finland
Arja-Leena Kariniemi, M.D., Exec. Officer
PH: 358 0 4716263
FX: 358 0 4716474
Description: Medical doctors. Promotes the study of dermatopathology. **Founded:** 1984. **Membership:** 119. **Staff:** 3. **Languages:** English, Finnish. **Budget:** FM 1,000.

FLEISCHNER SOCIETY (FS)
e-mail: richard_webb@radmac.1.ucsf.edu
c/o Dept. of Radiology
University of California, San Francisco
San Francisco, CA 94143-0628
W. Richard Webb, M.D., Sec.
PH: (415)476-5926
FX: (415)476-0616
Description: Physicians interested in the radiological aspects of pulmonary disease and the basic disciplines of anatomy, physiology, pathology, and clinical medicine upon which radiological interpretation rests. To foster the continuing development of chest radiology as an art and a science; to improve methods of teaching radiological diagnosis of chest disease; to stimulate research in chest radiology; to provide meetings for the reading and discussion of papers and the dissemination of information. Conducts annual course in diseases of the chest. **Founded:** 1969. **Membership:** 65. **Languages:** English.

FLYING DENTISTS ASSOCIATION (FDA)
e-mail: efritcher@amsn.com
url: http://www.iserv.net/~fda
820 S. Mariposa
La Habra, CA 90631
Dr. Ernest Fritcher, DDS, Exec.Sec.

PH: (562)697-1454
Description: Members of the American Dental Association who have an active aircraft pilot's license. Many members make use of private air travel in conducting their dental practice. **Founded:** 1960. **Membership:** 500. **Regional Groups:** 4. **Languages:** English. **Budget:** $121,000. **Publication:** *Flight Watch*, monthly.

FLYING DOCTORS OF AMERICA (FDOA)
e-mail: FDOAmerica@aol.com
4015 Holcomb Bridge Rd., Ste. 350922
Norcross, GA 30092
Allan Gathercoal, Founder/Director
PH: (770)447-6319
Description: Volunteer physicians, dentists, pharmacists, and support members. Flies volunteer health care professionals and other individuals to Third World countries to provide medical care to impoverished people. Maintains speakers' bureau. **Founded:** 1990. **Membership:** 7500. **Staff:** 7. Multinational. **Languages:** English. **Publication:** *Touch and Go*, quarterly. Newsletter ▪ Brochure.

FOCUS
Department of Ophthalmology
Loyola University Med. Center
2160 S. 1st Ave.
Maywood, IL 60153
James E. McDonald, M.D., Pres.
PH: (708)216-3408
FX: (708)216-3557
Description: Volunteer eye surgeons. Allows American ophthalmologists the opportunity to represent their profession and country by working overseas in an area of desperate need. Doctors pay their own transportation and expenses, and contribute two working weeks of their vacation time to treating patients in Nigeria, where eye care would otherwise not be available. Medical equipment and drugs have been donated by U.S. drug and medical supply firms to the clinics operated by Focus in these countries. Group is unrelated to association of same name. **Founded:** 1961. **Membership:** 400. **Languages:** English.

FORUM FOR MEDICAL AFFAIRS (FORUM)
760 Riverside Ave.
Jacksonville, FL 32204-3335
Donald F. Foy, Sr., Exec.VP
PH: (904)356-1571
FX: (904)353-1247
Description: Presidents, presidents-elect, and past presidents of state medical associations, members of the American Medical Association and the House of Delegates, editors of state medical association journals, executive directors of state medical associations, and representatives of AMA-recognized medical specialty societies. Publications: none. **Founded:** 1944. **Membership:** 800. **Languages:** English. **Formerly:** (1972) Conference of Presidents and Officers of State Medical Associations.

FOUNDATION FOR ADVANCEMENT IN CANCER THERAPY (FACT)
Box 1242, Old Chelsea Sta.
New York, NY 10113
Ruth Sackman, Pres.
PH: (212)741-2790
FX: (212)924-3634
Description: Believes that cancer is a symptom of imbalance in body chemistry; thus, to control the disease, not only must any tumors be destroyed, but the body must also be regenerated through the "total person approach" which emphasizes nutrition, detoxification, and mind-body cohesion. Asserts the right of the public to be informed of the "nontoxic biological" adjuncts and alternatives to surgery, chemotherapy, and radiotherapy, but cautions that patients be discriminating; disseminates information concerning only those preventive schemes and nontoxic therapies that have been verified as "safe" by long-term clinical tests. Does not intend to discredit traditional therapies, but to complement them; works cooperatively with established practitioners and in-

stit utions. Seeks the elimination of carcinogens from the environment; supports cancer and nutrition research and compiles statistics; maintains speakers' bureau. **Founded:** 1971. **Membership:** 2500. **Staff:** 3. Multinational. **Regional Groups:** 1. **Languages:** English. **Budget:** $80,000. **Publication:** *Cancer Forum*, bimonthly. Magazine. Price: included in membership dues. Advertising: not accepted. **Formerly:** (1988) Foundation for Alternative Cancer Therapies.

FOUNDATION FOR ADVANCES IN MEDICINE AND SCIENCE (FAMS)
e-mail: fams@holonet.net
url: http://www.scanning-fams.org/
PO Box 832
Mahwah, NJ 07430-0832
Tony Bourgholtzer, Bd.Chm.
PH: (201)818-1010
FX: (201)818-0086
Description: Clinical cardiologists, scientists, and scanning electron microscopists. Disseminates resource information in clinical medicine and science. Funds research projects. **Founded:** 1983. **Membership:** 400. **Staff:** 3. **Languages:** English. **Budget:** $400,000. Formerly (1990) Foundation for Advances in Clincal Medicine and Science.

FOUNDATION OF AMERICAN COLLEGE OF HEALTH CARE ADMINISTRATORS (FACHCA)
e-mail: info@achea.org
url: http://www.achca.org
325 S. Patrick St.
Alexandria, VA 22314
Karen S. Tucker, CAE, Pres.CEO
PH: (703)739-7900
TF: 88888A-CHCA
FX: (703)739-7901
Description: Individuals dedicated to the improvement of the administration of long-term care facilities. Conducts professional training programs and research in administration. **Founded:** 1971. **Membership:** 2000. **Staff:** 1. **Languages:** English. **Budget:** $250,000. Formerly (1983) Foundation of American College of Nursing Home Administrators.

FOUNDATION FOR FUNDAMENTAL RESEARCH ON MATTER (FOM)
(Stichting voor Fundamenteel Onderzoek der Materie)
e-mail: press@fom.nl
url: http://www.fom.nl
Postbus 3021
NL-3502 GA Utrecht, Netherlands
Dr. K.H. Chang, Dir.
PH: 31 30 6001211
FX: 31 30 6014406
Description: Promotes and supports research and educational programs in pure and applied physics. Research interests include high-energy and nuclear physics, thermonuclear research and plasmaphysics, atomic physics, statistical and mathematical physics, solid-state physics, semiconductor physics, materials science, computational physics, hydrodynamics, quantum electronics, soft matter condensed physics, and scientific instrumentation. Operates 5 research institutes and 150 research groups, made up of university physics faculty. Conducts national massive parallel computing and materials research programs. **Founded:** 1946. **Staff:** 1000. **Languages:** Dutch, English. **Budget:** 000,000 f. **Publication:** *FOM-Jaarboek* (in Dutch), annual ▪ Proceedings, periodic.

FOUNDATION FOR HEALTH (FFH)
e-mail: gbonadio@imcnet.net
337 East Ave.
Watertown, NY 13601-3829
George Bonadio, Exec.Dir.
PH: (315)782-6664
TF: 800724-7460
FX: (315)782-6664

Description: Gathers and disseminates information regarding health; seeks to publicize "natural" laws of health in an effort to make excellent health and long, useful lives common throughout the world. Proclaims the simplicity and inexpensiveness of maintaining one's health in contrast to the complexity and expense of disease. Researches and develops nutrition and health related projects and programs Convention/Meeting: none. **Founded:** 1972. **Languages:** English. **Publication:** *Ask the Nutritionist*, weekly. Newspaper ■ *Seven Disciplines of Health.*

FOUNDATION FOR ICHTHYOSIS AND RELATED SKIN TYPES (FIRST)
e-mail: ichthyosis@aol.com
url: http://www.libertynet.org/~ichthyos/
PO Box 669
Ardmore, PA 19003
Mark S. Levitan, Exec.Dir.
PH: (610)789-3995
TF: 800545-3286
FX: (610)789-4366
Description: Persons suffering from ichthyosis (a rare hereditary disease that causes the skin to be thick, dry, taut, and scaly) and related diseases; doctors, dermatologists, and others interested in the disease. Acts as a support group for persons with ichthyosis; puts families of sufferers in touch with one another. Provides education about technical, social, and psychological aspects of the disease. Conducts research programs; maintains speakers' bureau; compiles statistics. **Founded:** 1980. **Membership:** 8000. **Staff:** 2. Multinational. **Regional Groups:** 8. **Languages:** English. **Budget:** $100,000. Formerly (1986) National Ichthyosis Foundation.

FOUNDATION FOR INFORMED MEDICAL DECISION MAKING
PO Box 5457
Hanover, NH 03755-5457
John Billings, Acting Pres.
PH: (603)650-1180
FX: (603)650-1125
Description: Gathers and contributes scientific research information for use in videotape programs on shared decision making topics. **Founded:** 1989. **Staff:** 4. Multinational. **Languages:** English. **Publication:** Video.

FOUNDATION FOR INNOVATION IN MEDICINE (FIM)
411 North Ave. E.
Cranford, NJ 07016
Stephen L. DeFelice, M.D., Chm.
PH: (908)272-2967
FX: (908)272-4583
Description: Seeks to regenerate interest in medical discovery and innovation, which the foundation believes flourished in the U.S. in the 1940s and 1950s, but has since declined despite "vastly increased public and private expenditures in research and development." Intends to monitor the state of innovation by conducting seminars and conferences. Encourages clinical research on natural substances and substances with little commercial value. **Founded:** 1976. Multinational. **Languages:** English, French. **Publication:** *From Oysters to Insulin: Nature and Medicine at Odds.* Book. Price: $15.95 ■ *Nutraceutical White Paper.* Price: $10.00. Advertising: not accepted.

FOUNDATION FOR INTERNATIONAL SELF HELP DEVELOPMENT (FISH)
19 Gordon Town Rd.
Kingston, Jamaica
PH: (809)927-6715
Description: Seeks to improve the health and nutrition of the needy in Jamaica. Maintains medical, dental, and eye care clinic. Plans to operate programs in areas including community development, reforestation, and energy conservation and alternative fuels. **Founded:** 1985. **Languages:** English.

FOUNDATION FOR PROMOTION OF RESPONSIBLE PARENTHOOD -ARUBA (FPRP)
PO Box 2256
Bernhardstraat 75
San Nicolas, Aruba
Reginald Andrews, Pres.
PH: 297 8 48833
FX: 297 8 41107
Description: Works to improve the quality of life of people living in Aruba through promotion of family planning and maternal and infant health care. Sponsors programs in family planning, sex education, and basic health care. Offers contraceptive services. Conducts research. **Founded:** 1970. **Staff:** 4. **Languages:** Dutch.

FOUNDATION FOR THE PROMOTION OF RESPONSIBLE PARENTHOOD -NETHERLANDS ANTILLES (FPRP)
(Fundashon Famia Plania)
Bitterstraat No.1A
Curacao, Netherlands Antilles
John I. Samander, M.D., Pres.
PH: 599 9 611487
FX: 599 9 611024
Description: Advocates responsible parenthood and family planning. Seeks to reduce the number of unwanted pregnancies and abortions. Encourages public knowledge of AIDS and other sexually transmitted diseases. Offers educational programs on family planning and maternal and infant health care. **Membership:** 11. **Languages:** Dutch. **Budget:** 357,300 NAf.

FOUNDATION FOR REVITALIZATION OF LOCAL HEALTH (FRLHT)
e-mail: root@frlht.ernet.in
50 MSH Layout, 2nd Stage, 3rd Main
Anandnagar
Bangalore 560 024, Karnataka, India
Darshan Shankar, Dir.
PH: 91 80 3336909
FX: 91 80 3334167
Description: Promotes traditional medicine as an integral part of public health programs in developing areas. Facilitates international cooperation in understanding the theoretical foundation and epistemology of traditional medical practices; works to preserve the biodiversity upon which traditional medicine depends. Gathers and disseminates information on medicinal plants. Constructs traditional medical centers. **Founded:** 1991. **Languages:** English, Hindi. **Budget:** $1,140,625. **Publication:** *Amruth*, bimonthly. Magazine. Advertising: accepted.

FRED HOLLOWS FOUNDATION (FHF)
2414 Gardeners Rd., Ste. 1 Level
Rosebery, NSW 2018, Australia
PH: 61 2 6695899
FX: 61 2 6695188
Description: Ophthalmological health care providers and other individuals and organizations with an interest in visual impairment. Promotes increased access to visual health care in previously underserved areas. Provides visual care including eye examinations and cataract surgeries; establishes ocular lens factories; gathers and distributes ophthalmological supplies and equipment. Multinational. **Languages:** English.

FRED HOLLOWS FOUNDATION - VIETNAM (FHFVN)
4 Nguyen Cong Tru
Hai Ba Trung District
Hanoi, Vietnam
Bich Dover, Contact
PH: 84 4 212304
FX: 84 4 212304
Description: Ophthalmological health care providers and other individuals and organizations with an interest in visual impairment. Promotes increased access to visual health care in previously underserved areas. Provides visual care including eye examinations and cataract surgeries; establishes ocular lens facto-

ries; gathers and distributes ophthalmological supplies and equipment. **Staff:** 4. **Languages:** English, French.

FRENCH DIABETES ASSOCIATION (FDA)
(Association Francaise des Diabetiques)
58, rue Alexandre Dumas
F-75544 Paris, France
Mr. Levesque, Pres.
PH: 33 1 40092425
FX: 33 1 40092030
Description: Individuals with diabetes in France. Works to inform, assist, and defend diabetics. Furthers public understanding of diabetes by disseminating information to the public and medical specialists. **Founded:** 1938. **Membership:** 30000. **Staff:** 16. **Local Groups:** 118. **Languages:** English, French. **Publication:** *Equilibre* (in French), quarterly. Magazine. Price: 150.00 Fr/year. ISSN: 1158-0879. Circulation: 30,000. Advertising: accepted. Alternate Formats: online; magnetic tape ■ *Medical and Informations sur le Diabete*, periodic.

FRENCH-LANGUAGE ASSOCIATION FOR THE STUDY OF DIABETES AND METABOLIC DISORDERS
(Association de Langue Francaise pour l'Etude du Diabete et des Maladies Metaboliques)
CHU
Boite Postale 1542
F-21034 Dijon, France
Jean-Marcel Brun, Contact
PH: 33 3 80293453
FX: 33 3 80293519
Description: Health care professionals and researchers with an interest in diabetes and other metabolic disorders. Seeks to advance the prevention, diagnosis, and treatment of metabolic disorders. Provides support and services to people with diabetes and their families; serves as a clearinghouse on research on metabolic disorders; sponsors research and continuing professional development programs. Multinational. **Languages:** English, French.

FRENCH-LANGUAGE NEURO-ANESTHETIC-RESUSCITATION ASSOCIATION
(Association de Neuro-Anesthesie-Reanimation de Langue Francaise)
12 rue de l'Ecole de Medicine
F-75100 Paris, France
Description: Neurologists and anesthesiologists. Seeks to increase awareness of resuscitation techniques among members. Conducts training programs for members; serves as a clearinghouse on neuro-anesthetic resuscitation. Multinational. **Languages:** English, French.

FRENCH SOCIETY FOR CLINICAL NEUROPHYSIOLOGY (FLSCN)
(Societe de Neurophysiologie Clinique de Langue Francaise)
Hospital Saint Vincent DePaul
82, ave. Denfert Rochereau
F-75014 Paris, France
Dr. Bernard Gueguen, Sec.Gen.
PH: 33 01 45658189
FX: 33 01 45654122
Description: Medical specialists in electroencephalography, electromyography, and other functional explorations of the nervous system; researchers concerned with human and animal neurophysiology. Promotes clinical and experimental exploration of the nervous system. **Founded:** 1948. **Membership:** 550. Multinational. **Languages:** English, French. **Budget:** $50,000. **Publication:** *Neurophysiologie Clinique* (in English and French), quarterly. Journal. Price: 700.00 Fr/year. Advertising: accepted.

FRIENDS OF THE JOSE CARRERAS INTERNATIONAL LEUKEMIA FOUNDATION
Fred Hutchinson Cancer Research Ctr., D5-100
PO Box 19024
Seattle, WA 98109-1024
Dorothy Thomas, Treas.
PH: (206)667-7108
FX: (206)667-6498
Description: Raises funds for research into the treatment and cure of leukemia and related blood disorders. Maintains research programs. **Founded:** 1989. **Staff:** 1. Multinational. **Languages:** English. **Publication:** *Friends to Friends*, 3/year. Newsletter. Current news about the Foundation. Advertising: not accepted.

FRONTIER NURSING SERVICE (FNS)
url: http://www.barefoot.com/fns
132 FNS Dr.
Wendover, KY 41775
Deanna Severance, Dir.
PH: (606)672-2317
FX: (606)672-3022
Description: Provides health care to persons in approximately 1000 square miles of eastern Kentucky using a 40-bed hospital, two primary care centers, three rural health clinics, and a home health agency. Operates Frontier School of Midwifery and Family Nursing. Provides social and ancillary services; conducts research on health services; compiles statistics; offers educational programs. Maintains a hall of fame and museum. **Founded:** 1925. **Membership:** 15. **Staff:** 350. **Languages:** English.

F.S.H. (FACIOSCAPULOHUMERAL) SOCIETY
e-mail: info@fshsociety.org
url: http://www.fishsociety.org
3 Westwood Rd.
Lexington, MA 02420
Daniel Paul Perez, Pres.
PH: (781)860-0501
FX: (781)860-0599
Description: Individuals, families, and medical and business professionals interested in Facioscapulohumeral Muscular Dystrophy. (FSHD is an inheritable disease that causes a progressive loss of skeletal muscle with weakness of facial, scapular, and upper arm muscles.) Promotes research, solicits contributions and grants, and disperses information on FSHD. Offers support groups, acts as clearinghouse for researchers, clinicians and patients to facilitate participation in FSHD studies. Funds Research on FSHD. **Founded:** 1992. **Membership:** 700. **Staff:** 1. Multinational. **Regional Groups:** 6. **Languages:** English. For-Profit. **Budget:** $60,000. **Publication:** *F.S.H. Watch*, semiannual. Newsletter. Contains updates on FSHD Internationally and cites current research articles. Circulation: 2,000. Advertising: accepted.

FUNDACION MEXICANA PARA LA PLANEACION FAMILIAR (MEXFAM)
e-mail: info@mexfam.org.mx
Calle Juarez 208
Tlalpan
14000 Mexico City, DF, Mexico
Ramona Pando de Cosio, Chm. of the Board
PH: 52 5 5737100
FX: 52 5 5732318
Description: Promotes responsible parenthood and family planning. Advocates family planning as a basic human right. Works to reduce the number of unwanted pregnancies and abortions. Encourages public awareness of family planning, contraception, and sexually transmitted diseases. Offers educational programs for teens and adults. Acts as an advocate for family planning on a national level. Conducts research. **Languages:** Spanish. **Budget:** 5,000,000 MP.

GENERAL ASSOCIATION OF MUNICIPAL HEALTH AND TECHNICAL EXPERTS (GAMHTE)

(Association Generale des Hygienistes et Techniciens
Municipaux)
83 Av. Foch
BP 3916
F-75761 Paris, France
Alain Lasalmonie, Sec.Gen.
Description: Engineers, engineering consultants, technicians, architects, scientists, administrators, and municipal and private services in 32 countries. Objectives are to: stimulate fundamental and applied research on urban and rural public hygiene; disseminate findings of such research; encourage the exchange of information and ideas among members. Areas of interest include city planning, energy management, traffic problems, and pollution prevention. Operates information service; organizes field tours. **Founded:** 1905. **Membership:** 1200. **Staff:** 5. Multinational. **Local Groups:** 5. **Languages:** French. **Publication:** *Techniques Sciences-Methodes*, monthly. **Absorbed:** (1911) Union des Services Municipaux et des Travaux Publics. **Formerly:** Association Generale des Ingenieurs, Architectes et Hygienistes Municipaux de France, Algerie, Tunisie, Belgique, Suisse et Luxembourg.

GENERAL COUNCIL AND REGISTER OF NATUROPATHS

e-mail: admin@naturopathy.org.uk
url: http://www.naturopathy.org.uk
6 Netherhall Gardens
London NW3 5RR, England
M.W.F. Szewiel, Contact
PH: 44 1458 840072
FX: 44 1458 840075
Description: Fully qualified naturopathic practitioners. Maintains educational, professional and ethical standards and the safe practice of naturopathy for the benefit and protection of the public. **Founded:** 1964. **Membership:** 250. **Publication:** Membership Directory, annual. Price: L10.00.

GENERAL DENTAL COUNCIL

37 Wimpole St.
London W1M 8DQ, England
Mrs. R.M.J. Hepplewhite
PH: 44 171 4862171
FX: 44 171 2243294
Description: President (a registered dentist elected by the Council), 6 lay members appointed by The Queen on the advice of her Privy Council, 18 elected members (registered dentists), 17 nominated members (registered dentists nominated by dental authorities), 1. elected dental auxiliary, 4 Chief Dental Officers (ex officio), 3 members appointed by the General Medical Council. A statutory body, established by the Dentists Act, whose concerns are the maintenance of a register of dentists, the promotion of high standards of dental education at all its stages and of professional conduct among dentists, and certain functions in relation to sick dentists. The Council also has responsibilities in relation to the training, enrollment and conduct of dental auxiliaries. **Founded:** 1956. **Membership:** 50. **Staff:** 32. **Publication:** *Dentists Register*, annual. Price: L15.50; L18.50 overseas. Advertising: not accepted. Alternate Formats: diskette ▪ *Minutes of Meeting of the Council and Professional Conduct Committee*, annual. Proceedings. Price: L10.00 ▪ *Roles of Dental Auxiliaries*, annual. Price: L8.00.

GENERAL DENTAL PRACTITIONERS ASSOCIATION

Victoria Rd.
Barnsley, N. Yorkshire S70 2BB, England
Marjorie Blackburne, Contact
PH: 44 1226 299020
FX: 44 1226 299629

GENERAL MEDICAL COUNCIL

178 Great Portland St.
London W1N 6JE, England
Finlay Scott, Chief Exec. & Registrar

PH: 44 171 5807642
FX: 44 171 9153641
Description: Doctors elected by UK doctors or appointed by UK universities with medical schools and by Royal Colleges. Lay members nominated by Privy Council. Protects the public by overseeing medical education, keeping a register of qualified doctors and taking action where a doctor's fitness to pratise is in doubt. **Founded:** 1858. **Membership:** 102. **Staff:** 180. **Publication:** *Duties of a Doctor - Guidance on Professional Ethics*. Price: free ▪ *GMC News Review*, semiannual. Newsletter. Price: free ▪ *Medical Register*, annual. Price: L110.00 printed; L150.00 CD-ROM. Alternate Formats: CD-ROM ▪ Annual Report, annual. Advertising: not accepted.

GENERIC PHARMACEUTICAL INDUSTRY ASSOCIATION (GPIA)

1620 Eye St. NW, Ste. 800
Washington, DC 20006-4005
Dr. Alice Till, Pres.
PH: (202)833-9070
FX: (202)833-9612
Description: Manufacturers and distributors of generic medicines and providers of technical services and goods. Members are dedicated to providing quality pharmaceuticals to consumers at affordable prices. **Founded:** 1981. **Membership:** 43. **Staff:** 6. **Languages:** English. **Budget:** $2,000,000. **Publication:** *Seven Quick Facts to Remember about Generic Drugs*.

GEORGIAN PLANNED PARENTHOOD FEDERATION (IPPF)

37 Kostava St.
380009 Tbilisi, Georgia
PH: 7 8832 996197
FX: 7 8832 998108
Description: Promotes availability of reproductive health and family planning services. Sponsors women's health care and family planning programs. **Founded:** 1993. **Languages:** English, Russian.

GERMAN ASSOCIATION OF NON-MEDICAL PRACTITIONERS

(Verband Deutscher Heilpraktiker)
url: http://www.heilpraktiker-vdh.de
Ernst-Grote-Str. 13
D-30916 Isernhagen, Germany
Ekkehard S. Scharnick, Pres.
PH: 49 511 616980
FX: 49 511 6169820
Description: Promotes and protects the interests of non-medical health practitioners. Seeks to raise public awareness of holistic medicine. **Founded:** 1963. **Membership:** 3250. **Budget:** DM 1,300,000.

GERMAN DENTAL ASSOCIATION

(BundeszahnArztekammer-BZAK)
Universitatsstr. 71-73
D-50931 Cologne, Germany
Dr. Detlef Schulze-Wilk, Contact
PH: 49 221 40010
FX: 49 221 404035
Description: Promotes the dental sciences in Germany and represents German dentistry internationally. Promotes dental education and continuing education. Represents the interests of members to authorities, associations, and the public. **Founded:** 1953. **Membership:** 76390. **Publication:** *Zahnarztlidie MiHerCu-ugen* (in German), bimonthly. Journal. Contains professional and scientific papers. Price: free for dentists. Advertising: accepted. **Formerly:** National Association of German Dentists; Bundesverband der Deutschen Zahnarzte.

GERMAN DERMATOLOGICAL SOCIETY (GRS)
(Deutsche Dermatologische Gesellschaft)
Dept. of Dermatology
Univ. of Tuebingen
Liebermeisterstr. 25
D-72076 Tuebingen, Germany
Prof. Dr. Gernot Rassner, Pres.
PH: 49 7071 2983473
FX: 49 7071 295113
Description: Individuals united to promote dermatology. Conducts educational and research programs. **Founded:** 1888. **Membership:** 1800. Multinational. **Languages:** English, German. **Publication:** *Der Hautarzt*, periodic.

GERMAN PHYSICAL SOCIETY
(Deutsche Physikalische Gesellschaft)
e-mail: dpg@dpg-physik.de
url: http://www.dpg-physik.de
Hauptstrasse 5
D-53604 Bad Honnef, Germany
Dr. Volker Haselbarth, Sec.
PH: 49 2224 92320
FX: 49 2224 923250
Description: Physicists, physics teachers, and others with an interest in the physical sciences. Seeks to improve the quality of physics education, research, and knowledge. **Membership:** 30700. **Languages:** English, German.

GERMAN SOCIETY OF ANAESTHESIOLOGY AND
INTENSIVE CARE MEDICINE (GSAIM)
(Deutsche Gesellschaft fur Anaesthesiologie und
Intensivmedizin)
e-mail: dgai@dgai-ev.de
url: http://www.dgai-nuernberg.de
Geschaeftsstelle
Roritzerstrasse 27
D-90419 Nuernberg, Germany
Prof. Klaus van Ackern, Contact
PH: 49 11 933780
FX: 49 11 3938195
Description: Promotes scientific advancement and high standards of practice in anesthesiology and intensive care medicine. **Founded:** 1953. **Membership:** 8770. **Publication:** *Anaesthesie, Intensivmedizin, Notfallmedizin, Schmerztherapie* (in German), periodic. Advertising: accepted ■ *Anaesthesiologie und Intensivmedizin* (in German), periodic ■ *Der Anaesthesist* (in German), periodic.

GERMAN WOMEN PHYSICIANS ASSOCIATION
(Deutscher Arztinnenbund)
Herbert-Lewin-Str. 1
D-50931 Cologne, Germany
Rosmarie Hennings, Contact
PH: 49 221 4004540
FX: 49 221 4004541
Description: Promotes solidarity among women doctors. Represents members' interests in the medical sphere. Cultivates international contacts. **Founded:** 1924. **Membership:** 1800. **Regional Groups:** 30. **Languages:** Dutch, English. **Publication:** *Aerztin*, bimonthly. Magazine.

GERSON INSTITUTE (GI)
e-mail: mail@gerson.org
url: http://www.GERSON.ORG
PO Box 430
Bonita, CA 91908-0430
Charlotte Gerson, Pres.
PH: (619)585-7600
FX: (619)585-7610
Description: Individuals interested in health information. Purpose is to educate the public on nutritional health and to disseminate information about the Gerson therapy for healing. (The Gerson therapy was developed by Max Gerson, M.D., and seeks to prevent disease as well as to restore the natural healing mech-

anism in patients suffering from cancer and other degenerative diseases without the use of standard toxic therapies. Therapy includes a detoxification program to help the body eliminate toxins and waste materials that interfere with metabolism and healing and an intensive nutrition program.) Acts as consultant to operating physicians at hospital near Tijuana, Mexico and Sedona, Arizona; assists and trains physicians who want to learn the Gerson therapy. Presents lectures on health; conducts medical and nutritional research. **Founded:** 1977. **Membership:** 3000. **Staff:** 10. **Languages:** English. **Budget:** $900,000. **Publication:** *A Cancer Therapy - Results of 50 Cases* (in English, German, Japanese, and Romanian). Includes historical reviews and therapy details. Price: $25.00/year inside U.S.; $30.00/year outside U.S. Circulation: 3,000. Advertising: not accepted ■ *Censored for Curing Cancer* ■ *Healing Newsletter*, bimonthly ■ Videos.

GLAUCOMA FOUNDATION
e-mail: glaucoma@mindspring.com
url: http://www.glaucoma-foundation.org/info
33 Maiden Ln.
New York, NY 10038
John W. Corwin, Exec.Dir.
PH: (212)504-1900
TF: 800GLAUCOMA
FX: (212)504-1933
Description: Individuals who have been affected by glaucoma and interested others. Works to increase public awareness and to provide research funding. Provides information about glaucoma to the medical and lay communities. Targets and funds the following areas for research: optic nerve regeneration; molecular genetics. Sponsors educational and research programs. **Founded:** 1984. **Staff:** 8. Multinational. **Languages:** English. **Budget:** $1,750,000. Formed by Merger of (1994) National Glaucoma Trust and The Glaucoma Foundation.

GLAUCOMA RESEARCH FOUNDATION (ARF)
e-mail: info@glaucoma.org
url: http://www.glaucoma.org
490 Post St., Ste. 830
San Francisco, CA 94102
Tara L. Steele, Exec.Dir.
PH: (415)986-3162
TF: 800826-6693
FX: (415)986-3763
Description: Dedicated to protecting the sight and independence of individuals with glaucoma through research and education, with the ultimate goal of finding a cure. Funds serveral research programs including Shaffer International Fellowship and Clinician-Scientist Fellowship. **Founded:** 1978. **Staff:** 10. **Languages:** English. **Budget:** $1,200,000. Formerly (1993) Foundation for Glaucoma Research.

GLAUCOMA SOCIETY OF THE INTERNATIONAL
CONGRESS OF OPHTHALMOLOGY (GSICO)
e-mail: yoshikit-gif@umin.u-tokyo.ac.jp
c/o Y. Kitazawa, M.D.
Gifu University
Tsukasa-Machi 40
Gifu 500, Japan
Y. Kitazawa, M.D., Pres.
PH: 81 582 672272
FX: 81 582 659012
Description: Ophthalmologists with a special interest in glaucoma. Provides a forum for the exchange of information obtained through research on glaucoma. **Founded:** 1978. **Membership:** 60. Multinational. **Languages:** English. **Publication:** *Glaucoma Updates I-IV*, quadrennial. Advertising: accepted ■ *Transaction*, quadrennial.

GLOBAL HUMAN RESEARCH FOUNDATION (GHR)
14-4-14 Satyakrishna Nivas
Kolagatlavari St.
Vizianagaram 535 002, Andhra Pradesh, India
Dr. Row P. Bhaskar, Social Scientist & Chm.

PH: 91 892227283
FX: 91 892227283
Description: Seeks to curtail the spread of infectious diseases, with particular emphasis on slowing the AIDS epidemic. Conducts preventive health education programs; serves as a clearinghouse for development organizations interested in public health issues. Makes available health care services. **Languages:** English, Hindi.

GLOBAL OUTREACH MISSION
e-mail: glmiss1@aol.com
PO Box 2010
Buffalo, NY 14231-2010
Dr. Vaughn V. Chapman, Dir.
Description: Seeks to share the Gospel through the medium of dentistry. Provides dental services and conducts dental education programs in undeveloped or rural areas and cities overseas coupled with "the good news of the Gospel." Trains dentists, dental assistants, laboratory technicians, and hygenists for overseas service in their Overseas Training Seminar. **Founded:** 1950. **Membership:** 4564. Multinational. **Languages:** English. **Budget:** $150,000. **Publication:** *The Missionary Dentist*, quarterly. Newsletter. Advertising: not accepted. **Also Known As:** Worldwide Dental Health Service. **Formerly:** (1998) Missionary Dentists.

GLOBAL VACCINE AWARENESS LEAGUE (GVAL)
11875 Pigeon Pass Rd., Ste. B-14-223
Moreno Valley, CA 92553
Michelle Helms, Founder
PH: (909)247-4910
FX: (909)247-4910
Description: Dedicated to disseminating information on the serious side effects of government sponsored vaccinations. Conducts educational programs; promotes parents right to choose whether or not to vaccinate their children; supports research; conducts fundraising events. **Founded:** 1995. **Membership:** 160. **Staff:** 6. **Languages:** English.

GRENADA PLANNED PARENTHOOD ASSOCIATION (GPPA)
Deponthieu St.
PO Box 127
St. George's, Grenada
Mr. Allan Bierzynski, Pres.
PH: (809)440-3341
FX: (809)440-8071
Description: Advocates responsible parenthood and family planning. Promotes family planning as a basic human right. Encourages public awareness of contraception, family planning, and sexually transmitted diseases. Provides contraceptive health care services. Sponsors educational programs. Conducts research. **Founded:** 1964. **Membership:** 26. **Staff:** 12. **Languages:** English. **Publication:** Annual Report. Advertising: accepted.

GROUP OF FRANCOPHONE DENTISTS' ASSOCIATIONS (GADEF)
(Groupement des Associations Dentaires Francophones)
22, ave. de Villiers
F-75017 Paris, France
Dr. Jacques Charon, Hon.Pres.
PH: 33 1 47660232
Description: National dental associations. Promotes use of the French language for international professional relations and works to advance dental science and public health. Maintains contacts in industrialized and developing countries. **Founded:** 1971. **Membership:** 26. Multinational. **Languages:** French. **Publication:** *Bulletin du GADEF*, semiannual ■ *Directory* (in French), quarterly.

GROUP FOR THE ADVANCEMENT OF PSYCHIATRY (GAP)
PO Box 28218
Dallas, TX 75228
Frances Roton, Contact

PH: (972)613-3044
FX: (972)613-5532
Description: Independent group of psychiatrists organized in working committees interested in applying the principles of psychiatry toward the study of human relations. Works closely with specialists in many other disciplines. Investigates such subjects as school desegregation, use of nuclear energy, religion, psychiatry in the armed forces, mental retardation, cross-cultural communication, medical uses of hypnosis, and the college experience. Maintains 25 committees. **Founded:** 1946. **Membership:** 300. **Staff:** 2. **Languages:** English. **Budget:** $750,000.

GUAM LYTICO AND BODIG ASSOCIATION
PO Box 1458
Agana, Guam 96910
Madeleine Z. Bordallo
PH: 671 4772293
FX: 671 4772294
Description: Provides supportive services and information to individuals stricken with disease.

GUARDIANS OF HYDROCEPHALUS RESEARCH FOUNDATION (GHRF)
2618 Avenue Z
Brooklyn, NY 11235-2023
Katherine Soriano, Nat. VP
PH: (718)743-4473
TF: 800458-8655
FX: (718)743-1171
Description: Hydrocephalics and their families, health care professionals, and other concerned individuals. Seeks to find the cause and cure of hydrocephalus. (Hydrocephalus is the buildup of cerebrospinal fluid in the brain cavity, which can cause brain damage or death if untreated.) Disseminates information on hydrocephalus; conducts public awareness and fundraising projects. Plans to conduct research and educational programs, and to operate computerized services. **Founded:** 1977. **Membership:** 5000. **Staff:** 2. **Local Groups:** 2. **Languages:** English. **Publication:** *An Introduction to Hydrocephalus* ■ *Journal Ad Book*, annual ■ Newsletter, quarterly. Includes news briefs and fundraising and project information. Price: included in membership dues.

GUILLAIN-BARRE SYNDROME FOUNDATION INTERNATIONAL (GBSFI)
e-mail: GBINT@ix.netcom.com
url: http://www.webmast.com/gbs/
PO Box 262
Wynnewood, PA 19096
Robert and Estelle Benson, Founders
PH: (610)667-0131
FX: (610)667-7036
Description: Individuals concerned with Guillain-Barre syndrome (Acute Idiopathic Polyneuritis), a rare, paralyzing, potentially catastrophic disorder of the peripheral nerves. Objectives are to: educate the public and medical community about the availability of support groups and maintain their awareness of the disorder; foster research on cause, prevention, and treatment; encourage financial support for research; develop nationwide support groups. Arranges for recovered or recovering patients to visit patients in acute care and rehabilitation hospitals; assists patients in dealing with disabilities should complete recovery not occur. Maintains steering committee of physicians, some of who have had the disorder. **Founded:** 1980. **Membership:** 15000. **Staff:** 2. Multinational. **Regional Groups:** 148. **Languages:** French, German. **Publication:** *Communicator*, quarterly. Newsletter ■ *Guide for Caregivers*. Handbook ■ *Guillain-Barre Syndrome, an Overview for the Layperson*. Booklet. Advertising: not accepted. **Formerly:** (1988) Guillian-Barre Syndrome Support Group; (1990) Guillian-Barre Syndrome Support Group International.

GUYANA RESPONSIBLE PARENTHOOD ASSOCIATION (GRPA)
70 Quamina St.
S. Cummingsburg
Georgetown, Guyana
Ms. Beverly Braithwaite, Chm.
PH: 592 2 53286
FX: 592 2 52144
Description: Promotes family planning as a basic human right. Works to educate the public on family planning, sex education, AIDS, and other sexually transmitted diseases. Seeks to reduce the number of unwanted pregnancies and abortions. Provides contraceptive and health care services. Provides sexual and reproductive health services, including the Pap Smear. **Founded:** 1973. **Membership:** 4000. **Staff:** 40. **Languages:** English. **Publication:** *Inside the Family* (in English), semiannual. Newsletter. Price: free. Circulation: 100. Advertising: not accepted.

GYNECOLOGIC SURGERY SOCIETY (GSS)
6900 Grove Rd.
Thorofare, NJ 08086-9431
John Marlow, Pres.
PH: (609)848-1000
FX: (609)853-5991
Description: Individuals interested in gynecologic surgery. Facilitates communication among members. Conducts educational programs and demonstrations of new surgical techniques. **Founded:** 1979. **Membership:** 700. **Languages:** English.

HAITIAN CHILDHOOD INSTITUTE (HCI)
(Institut Haitien de l'Enfance)
41, rue Borno
PO Box 15606
Petion-Ville, Haiti
PH: 509 573101
FX: 509 572269
Description: Promotes improved maternal and child health. Conducts research; develops health outreach programs. **Founded:** 1985. **Languages:** English, French.

HARVEY SOCIETY (HS)
Mt. Sinai School of Medicine
Institute of Gene Therapy
1190 5th Ave., Box 1218
New York, NY 10029
Dr. Savio Woo, Sec.
PH: (212)824-7728
FX: (212)803-6740
Description: Persons with a Ph.D. or M.D. degree active or interested in making contributions to the literature of medical and biological science. Seeks to disseminate knowledge and promote the development of the biomedical sciences. Sponsors a series of public lectures delivered by leaders in the field. Society is named after William Harvey (1578-1657), who identified the circulation of blood. **Founded:** 1905. **Membership:** 1600. **Languages:** English. **Publication:** *Harvey Lectures*, annual. Book. Contains lectures given during the year. Advertising: not accepted.

HEALTH EDUCATION FOUNDATION (HEF)
e-mail: hefmona@erols.com
2600 Virginia Ave. NW, Ste. 502
Washington, DC 20037
Morris E. Chafetz, M.D., Pres.
PH: (202)338-3501
FX: (202)965-6520
Description: Seeks to develop cost-effective health promotion programs for government, industry, and the business community; helps people make informed decisions about their physical and mental health; participates in research for analysis and development of standards and programs to meet public health needs. Convention/Meeting: none. **Founded:** 1975. **Staff:** 3. **Languages:** English.

HEALTH FIRST INTERNATIONAL (HFI)
508 N. 1st St.
Sartell, MN 56377
Elsie Harper, Exec.Dir.
PH: (320)252-5857
Description: Disseminates information on low-cost health care. Offers classes in nutrition, diet management, stress and anger control, family life, drug abuse recognition, and how to stop smoking; holds well-baby clinics. Compiles statistics. Plans to conduct cooking, physical therapy, and exercise classes. **Founded:** 1989. **Membership:** 250. **Staff:** 2. Multinational. **Local Groups:** 1. **Languages:** English.

HEALTH INFORMATION RESOURCE CENTER (HIRC)
e-mail: hlthinfo@aol.com
url: http://www.acpinc.com/healthinfo.html
621 E. Park Ave.
Libertyville, IL 60048
Patricia Henze, Exec.Dir.
PH: (847)816-8660
TF: 800828-8225
FX: (847)816-8662
Description: Provides information and referral services to many organizations that use or produce consumer health information materials. Conducts market research. Convention/Meeting: none. **Founded:** 1993. **Staff:** 2. **Languages:** English. **For-Profit.**

HEALTH MEDIA EDUCATION (HME)
1207 De Haro St.
San Francisco, CA 94107
Ruth Davidow, Dir.
PH: (415)282-9318
Description: Produces and distributes materials that provide consumers and health personnel with information needed to plan and implement community health programs. Services include: rental and sale of films; free exhibitions; discussions, and classes. **Founded:** 1974. **Membership:** 150. **Languages:** English.

HEALTH MINISTRIES (HM)
e-mail: ic_hartunbm@lcms.org
url: http://www.lcms.org
Board for Human Care Ministries
1333 S. Kirkwood Rd.
St. Louis, MO 63122
Bruce M. Hartung, Ph.D., Dir.
PH: (314)965-9917
FX: (314)965-0277
Description: Consultants to all boards and commissions of the Lutheran Church-Missouri Synod having a relationship to the "healing mission" of the church and health issues of professional church workers. **Staff:** 5. **Languages:** English. **Budget:** $165,000. **Publication:** *AIDS Alert*. Newsletter ■ *Cross and Caduceus*, 3/year. Newsletter. Focuses on health and wellness issues. Price: free. Circulation: 12,000. Advertising: not accepted ■ *Gesundheit*. Newsletter. Circulation: 35 ■ *Parish Nurse*, quarterly. Newsletter. **Formerly:** (1969) Council for Christian Medical Work; (1981) Commission on Health and Healing; (1986) Health and Healing Ministries.

HEALTH OCCUPATIONS STUDENTS OF AMERICA (HOSA)
6021 Morriss Rd., Ste. 110
Flower Mound, TX 75028-3762
Dr. Jim Koeninger, Exec.Dir.
PH: (214)506-9780
TF: 800321-HOSA
FX: (214)506-9919
Description: Secondary and postsecondary students enrolled in health occupations education programs; health professionals and others interested in assisting and supporting the activities of HOSA; alumni of health occupations education programs and individuals who have made significant contributions to the field. Primary aim is to improve the quality of healthcare for all Americans by urging members to develop self-improvement skills. Operates within health occupation education programs in public

high schools and postsecondary institutions. Encourages members to develop an understanding of current healthcare issues, environmental concerns, and survival needs worldwide. Conducts programs to help individuals improve their occupational skills and develop leadership qualities. Conducts exhibits, management workshops, and medical facility tours; provides social and recreational activities. Maintains speakers' bureau; compiles statistics. **Founded:** 1975. **Membership:** 52000. **Local Groups:** 2,100. **Languages:** English. **Budget:** $750,000. **Publication:** *HOSA Leaders Directory*, annual ■ *HOSA Leaders' Update*, quarterly ■ *HOSA News Magazine*, quarterly ■ *Story of HOSA*. Video ■ Brochure ■ Handbook. **Also Known As:** National HOSA.

HEALTH PHYSICS SOCIETY (HPS)
1313 Dolley Madison Blvd., Ste. 402
Mc Lean, VA 22101-3926
Richard J. Burk, Jr., Exec.Sec.
PH: (703)790-1745
FX: (703)790-9063
Description: Persons engaged in some form of activity in the field of health physics (the profession devoted to radiation protection). To improve public understanding of the problems and needs in radiation protection; to promote health physics as a profession. Maintains Elda E. Anderson Memorial Fund to be used for teachers, researchers, and others. Provides placement service at annual meeting. Cosponsors American Board of Health Physics for certification of health physicists. **Founded:** 1956. **Membership:** 6890. **Staff:** 10. **Local Groups:** 41. **Languages:** English.

HEALTH PROFESSIONS COUNCIL ZIMBABWE
PO Box A410 Avondale
Harare, Zimbabwe
Mr. D.G. Bessant, Registrar
PH: 263 754930
FX: 263 756731
Description: Scientists engaged in medical and related research. Promotes and coordinates members' activities; facilitates communication among members and between members and international biomedical and research organizations. **Languages:** English.

HEALTH RESEARCH COUNCIL OF NEW ZEALAND (HRC)
e-mail: info@hrc.govt.nz
url: http://www.hrc.govt.nz
PO Box 5541
Wellesley St.
Auckland, New Zealand
Dr. Bruce A. Scoggins, Dir.
PH: 64 9 3798227
FX: 64 9 3779988
Description: Initiates and supports general health-related research, including the biomedical, public health, Maori, and clinical fields in New Zealand. Coordinates health research on a national basis and administers and disburses government research funding. Bestows awards. **Founded:** 1990. **Staff:** 20. **Budget:** NZ$37,200,000. **Publication:** *HRC Annual Report*. Price: free. Advertising: not accepted ■ *HRC Newsletter* (in English), quarterly. Contains information on health research in New Zealand. Circulation: 2,000. Advertising: not accepted ■ *Maori Health Research Newsletter*, semiannual ■ *Pacific Health Research News* (in English), semiannual. Newsletter. Contains information on research being done on Pacific Island health. Circulation: 500. Advertising: not accepted. **Formerly:** (1937) Medical Research Council of New Zealand.

HEALTH SCIENCE CENTER (HSC)
10180 Committee Medical College
Hanoi, Vietnam
Dr. Le Cao Dai, Contact
PH: 84 4 63514
FX: 84 4 63514
Description: Health care providers. Seeks to increase access to quality health services among previously underserved popula-

tions. Makes available primary medical care; sponsors research and educational programs. **Languages:** English, French.

HEALTH SECURITY ACTION COUNCIL (HSAC)
1757 N St. NW
Washington, DC 20036
Denise E. Holmes, Dir.
PH: (202)223-9685
FX: (202)293-3457
Description: Individuals and organizations united to increase grass roots support for national health insurance and progressive health plans through publicity and education. Conducts surveys on the effects of federal legislative actions on state and local health programs. **Founded:** 1969. **Staff:** 3. **Languages:** English.

HEALTH SERVICES UNION OF AUSTRALIA (HSUA)
PO Box 655
Carlton South, VIC 3053, Australia
Robert Elliott, Sec.
PH: 61 3 96638224
FX: 61 3 96638225
Description: Workers in the health care industries. Seeks to advance the economic well-being and improve the conditions of employment of members. Represents members in negotiations with employers. **Membership:** 90000. **Languages:** English.

HEALTH AND SOCIAL POLICY CORPORATION
(Corporacion de Salud y Politicas Sociale)
Roman Diez 228 Of. 401
Providencia
Santiago, Chile
Giorgio Solimano, M.D., Pres.
PH: 56 2 2641261
FX: 56 2 2352312
Description: Promotes health reform and the development of related social policy for the citizens of Chile. Focuses primarily on the health concerns of young people and women. Supports applied research. **Founded:** 1990. **Staff:** 30. **Languages:** English, Spanish. **Budget:** $350,000.

HEALTH VOLUNTEERS OVERSEAS (HVO)
e-mail: hvo@aol.com
PO Box 65157, Washington Sta.
Washington, DC 20035-5157
Nancy Kelly, Exec.Dir.
PH: (202)296-0928
FX: (202)296-8018
Description: Physicians, dentists, nurses, and physical therapists. Works to improve health care in developing countries through the participation of trained health and medical volunteers. Programs include Anesthesia, Dentistry, General Surgery, Oral and Maxillofacial Surgery, Internal Medicine, Orthopaedics, and Pediatrics and physical therapy. HVO has program sites in St. Lucia, Uganda, Brazil, Guyana, India, Philippines, Malawi, Indonesia, South Africa, Guyana, Vietnam, Kenya, Bhutan, and Zimbabwe. **Founded:** 1986. **Membership:** 1800. **Staff:** 12. Multinational. **Languages:** English. **Budget:** $6,000,000. **Publication:** *A Guide for Short-Term Volunteer Medical Workers in Developing Countries* ■ *The Volunteer Connection*, quarterly. Newsletter.

HEALTH VOLUNTEERS OVERSEAS - VIETNAM (HVOVN)
9 Cao ba Quat
Ba Dinh District
Hanoi, Vietnam
Theresa Egan, Contact
PH: 84 4 234678
FX: 84 4 269678
Description: Volunteers assisting health care organizations. Promotes increased access to quality health care for people living in previously underserved areas worldwide. Provides support and assistance to health care services. **Staff:** 2. **Languages:** English, French. **Budget:** $150,000.

HEALTH WORKERS UNION OF THE RUSSIAN FEDERATION

e-mail: ckprz@online.ru
42 Leninsky Prospect
PO Box 117119
Moscow, Russia
Vladimir Panchekhin, Contact
PH: 7 95 9387762
FX: 7 95 9388134
Description: Physicians, nurses, pharmacists, paramedical personnel, and medical students and trainees. Promotes professional advancement of members; works to maintain high standards of practice and ethics in the field of medicine. Represents members' interests before government agencies; promulgates and enforces standards of practice and conduct. **Founded:** 1990. **Membership:** 3100022. **Staff:** 1000. **Local Groups:** 23,094. **Languages:** English, Russian. **Budget:** 000,000 Rb. **Publication:** *Profsoiuznaya Tema* (in Russian), quarterly. Information on protection of health workers' rights and interests. Price: available to members only. Circulation: 5,600. Advertising: not accepted.

HEALTHCARE COMPLIANCE PACKAGING COUNCIL (HCPC)

e-mail: pgmayberry@aol.com
url: http://www.unitdose.org
1101 Connecticut Ave., Ste. 1000
Washington, DC 20036
Peter G. Mayberry, Staff Dir.
PH: (202)828-2328
FX: (202)828-2400
Description: Promotes the use of "unit-dose blister packaging" as a way of insuring compliance with pharmaceutical regimens and other benefits. Conducts speakers' bureau. Compiles statistics. Sponsors research and educational programs. **Founded:** 1991. **Membership:** 65. **Staff:** 3. **Languages:** English. **Budget:** $200,000.

HEALTHCARE FINANCIAL MANAGEMENT ASSOCIATION (HFMA)

e-mail: tarya@hfma.org
url: http://www.hfma.org
2 Westbrook Corporate Financial Center, Ste. 700
Westchester, IL 60154-5700
Richard L. Clarke, Pres.
TF: 800531-HFMA
FX: (708)531-0032
Description: Financial management professionals employed by hospitals and long-term care facilities, public accounting and consulting firms, insurance companies, medical groups, managed care organizations, government agencies, and other organizations. Conducts conferences, including annual conference in late June, audio teleconferences. Publishes books on healthcare financial issues. A Fellowship in Healthcare Financial Management (FHFMA) as well as the Certified Healthcare Professional (CHFP) in Fianace and Accounting, Financial Management of Physician Practices, Managed Care, and Patient Financial Services are offered. **Founded:** 1946. **Membership:** 34000. **Staff:** 80. **State Groups:** 70. **Languages:** English. **Budget:** $12,000,000. **Publication:** *Healthcare Financial Management*, monthly. Magazine. Includes industry news, articles on financial management in all types of facilities across the healthcare continuum. Price: $82.00 /year for nonmembers. ISSN: 0735-0732. Circulation: 35,000. Advertising: accepted. Alternate Formats: microform ▪ *Notes from National*, monthly. Newsletter. Price: included in membership dues. Circulation: 1,450 ▪ *Patient Accounts*, monthly. Newsletter. Covers the financial operations of business office and patient accounting functions, including preadmission information gathering. Price: $60.00/year for members; $108.00/year for nonmembers. Circulation: 2,000 ▪ Books ▪ Videos. **Formerly:** (1968) American Association of Hospital Accountants; (1982) Hospital Financial Management Association.

HEALTHCARE FINANCING STUDY GROUP (HFSG)

1919 Pennsylvania Ave. NW, Ste. 800
Washington, DC 20006
Michael Colopy, Dir.
PH: (202)887-1400
FX: (202)466-3215
Description: Investment banking, law, consulting, and accounting firms involved in providing capital financing for health care institutions. Analyzes legislative and regulatory proposals from the standpoint of the health care financial community. Provides forum for exchange of information concerning health care financing. **Founded:** 1973. **Membership:** 40. **Languages:** English. **Publication:** Bulletin, periodic ▪ Newsletter, monthly. **Formerly:** (1981) Hospital Financing Study Group.

THE HEALTHCARE FORUM (THF)

url: http://www.thfnet.org
425 Market St., 16th Fl.
San Francisco, CA 94105
Kathryn E. Johnson, CEO & Pres.
PH: (415)356-4200
FX: (415)421-8837
Description: Individuals and organizational leaders worldwide. Provides education and applied research services. Works to create healthier communities through innovative leadership thinking, organizational learning and mastering change. **Founded:** 1927. **Membership:** 1000. **Staff:** 44. Multinational. **Languages:** English. **Budget:** $6,000,000. **Publication:** *Healthcare Forum Journal*, bimonthly. Price: $55.00/year. ISSN: 0899-9287. Circulation: 27,000. Advertising: accepted. Alternate Formats: online ▪ *VIS*. **Formerly:** Association of Western Hospitals.

HEALTHCARE FORUM

url: http://www.thfnet.org
425 Market St., 16th Fl.
San Francisco, CA 94105
Kathryn E. Johnson, CEO & Pres.
PH: (415)356-4400
FX: (415)356-9300
Description: Healthcare leaders and executives. Promotes visionary leadership and motivation in healthcare. Conducts leadership development education programs; produces computer based educational materials. Sponsors research activities. **Founded:** 1927. **Membership:** 1100. **Staff:** 40. Multinational. **Languages:** English. **Budget:** $8,000,000. **Publication:** *Healthcare Forum Journal*, bimonthly. Price: $55.00. Circulation: 27,000. Advertising: accepted. Alternate Formats: online.

HEALTHNET BOTSWANA

e-mail: sysop@bot.healthnet.org
Private Bag 0038
Gaborone, Botswana
T. Gaamangwe, Contact
PH: 267 352000
FX: 267 353100
Description: Health care workers. Promotes exchange of information among members and between members and their counterparts abroad. Maintains computer-based telecommunications system to disseminate public health, medical, and environmental information. **Languages:** English.

HEALTHNET SOUTH AFRICA (HNSA)

e-mail: roger@hst.db.healthlink.org.za
504 General Bldg.
Corner Smith and Field Sts.
Durban 4001, Republic of South Africa
Roger Day, Contact
PH: 27 31 3072954
FX: 27 31 3040775
Description: Hospitals, clinics, and other health care facilities; telecommunications and satellite communications networks. Promotes improved communication and cooperation among health care facilities. Serves as a clearinghouse on medicine and telecommunications; maintains electronic network linking members;

conducts educational and training programs for health care and telecommunications professionals. Multinational. **Languages:** Afrikaans, English.

HEALTHNET ZIMBABWE (HZ)
e-mail: borland@healthnet.zw
PO Box MP 167
University of Zimbabwe
Harare, Zimbabwe
Dr. Bob Borland, Contact
PH: 263 4 303211
FX: 263 4 333407
Description: Health care professionals. Promotes increased use of electronic communications to advance the practice of health care. Serves as a clearinghouse on medicine. **Languages:** English.

HEALTHY MOTHERS, HEALTHY BABIES (HMHB)
409 12th St. SW, Rm. 309
Washington, DC 20024
Anita Boles, Exec.Dir.
PH: (202)863-2458
FX: (202)554-4346
Description: Coalition of national and state organizations concerned with maternal and child health. Serves as a network through which members share ideas and information regarding issues such as prenatal care, nutrition for pregnant women, and infant mortality. **Founded:** 1981. **Membership:** 110. **National Groups:** 110. **Languages:** English. **Budget:** $1,000,000.

HEART DISEASE RESEARCH FOUNDATION (HDRF)
50 Court St.
Brooklyn, NY 11201
Dr. Yoshiaki Omura, M.D., Dir., Med. Research
PH: (718)649-6210
Description: Promotes research aimed at the prevention, early diagnosis, and treatment of cardiovascular disease and related medico-social problems. Supports and conducts research, both basic and clinical, in the early diagnosis, prevention, and treatment of cardiovascular diseases using a multidisciplinary approach. Studies include the effects of acupuncture and electrotherapeutics on blood chemistry and the cardiovascular system, the clinical applications of these methods, and the noninvasive early diagnostic methods of cardiovascular diseases. Sponsors postgraduate continuing medical educational courses for physicians, dentists, and medical researchers. Conducts public education programs on the heart and heart disease. Answers questions from the public and professionals; supplies available educational information on cardiovascular diseases and research. **Founded:** 1962. **Staff:** 24. **Languages:** English.

HELLENIC SOCIETY OF DERMATOLOGY AND VENEREOLOGY
University of Athens
A. Sygros Hospital
5 Ionos Dragoumi St. Kessariani
GR-161 21 Athens, Greece
Prof. J.D. Stratigos, M.D., Contact
PH: 30 1 7210839
FX: 30 1 7211122
Description: Offers awards; Conducts educational programs; compiles statistics. Maintains museum. **Membership:** 600. **Languages:** English, Greek. **Budget:** 5,000,000 Dr. **Publication:** *Hellenic Dermato-Venereological Review* (in Greek), quarterly.

HERBALIST ASSOCIATION OF MALAWI (HAM)
PO Box 280
Zomba, Malawi
PH: 265 322222
Description: Traditional healers and birth assistants. Represents members' interests before government agencies and professional organizations. Seeks to ensure availability of health care services in rural areas. Facilitates exchange of information among members; conducts research and educational programs; sponsors collaborative efforts involving traditional and Western medical

research. **Founded:** 1953. **Membership:** 25000. **Languages:** English.

HEREDITARY DISEASE FOUNDATION (HDF)
e-mail: cures@hdfoundation.org
url: http://www.hdtoundation.org
1427 7th St., Ste. 2
Santa Monica, CA 90401
Nancy S. Wexler, Ph.D., Pres.
PH: (310)458-4183
FX: (310)458-3937

HISPANIC DENTAL ASSOCIATION
188 W. Randolph St., Ste. 1811
Chicago, IL 60606
Sandy Reed, Exec.Dir.
PH: (312)577-4013
FX: (312)577-0052
Description: Promotes dentistry in the hispanic community. **Founded:** 1990. **Membership:** 700. **Staff:** 2.

HOLISTIC DENTAL ASSOCIATION (HDA)
e-mail: hda@frontier.net
url: http://www.frontier.net/~hda
PO Box 5007
Durango, CO 81301
Dr. Dick Shepard, Exec.Dir.
PH: (970)259-1091
FX: (970)259-1091
Description: Dentists, chiropractors, dental hygienists, physical therapists, and medical doctors. Goals are: to provide a holistic approach to better dental care for patients; to expand techniques, medications, and philosophies that pertain to extractions, anesthetics, fillings, crowns, and orthodontics. Encourages use of homeopathic medications, acupuncture, cranial osteopathy, nutritional techniques, and physical therapy in treating patients in addition to conventional treatments. Sponsors training and educational seminars. **Founded:** 1980. **Membership:** 200. **Staff:** 1. **Languages:** English. **Publication:** *Communicator*, quarterly. Newsletter. Includes calendar of events and research updates. Price: included in membership dues. Circulation: 200. Advertising: accepted. **Formerly:** Holistic Dental Association International.

HOME BIRTH ASSOCIATION
PO Box 7093
Wellesley St.
Auckland, New Zealand
Linda McKay, Sec.
PH: 64 9 6206214
FX: 64 9 6206214
Description: Encourages natural childbirth methods. Disseminates information. **Founded:** 1978. **Membership:** 700. **Languages:** English. **Publication:** *A Guide to Healthy Pregnancy and Childbirth.* ISBN: 0-473-02178-1. Price: NZ$18.00 ▪ *Home Birth* (in English), quarterly. Newsletter. Advertising: accepted.

HOME HEALTH SERVICES AND STAFFING ASSOCIATION (HHSSA)
e-mail: mbenner@hhssa.org
115D S. Asaph St.
Alexandria, VA 22314-3110
David Savitsky, Pres.
PH: (703)836-9863
Description: Works to lobby federal and state governments on behalf of home health agencies. **Founded:** 1978. **Membership:** 35. **Staff:** 2. **Budget:** $500,000.

HOME HEALTHCARE NURSES ASSOCIATION (HHNA)
e-mail: HHNA@aol.com
7794 Grow Dr.
Pensacola, FL 32514
Belinda E. Puetz, Ph.D.,, Admin.
TF: 800558-4462

Description: Works to develop and promote the specialty of home healthcare nursing. Provides a forum for members to exchange information; influences public policy affecting the practice; fosters excellence in practice. **Founded:** 1993. **Membership:** 1800. **Staff:** 5. Multinational. **Local Groups:** 9.

HONG KONG ASSOCIATION OF DENTAL SURGERY ASSISTANTS (HKADSA)
Tutor DSA's Office
Department of Conservative Dentistry, 6/F
Prince Philip Dental Hospital
Hong Kong, Hong Kong
Ms. Maggie A. Crosswaite, Chair
PH: 852 28590325
FX: 852 25599013
Description: Dental surgery assistants and trainees. Promotes the study and practice of dental surgery assistance; seeks to further the professional development of members. Serves as a clearinghouse on dental surgery assistance. Facilitates exchange of information among members; conducts educational and continuing professional development courses; sponsors social activities; maintains speakers' bureau. **Founded:** 1987. **Membership:** 60. **Languages:** Chinese, English. **Publication:** Newsletter (in English), monthly. Price: included in membership dues.

HONG KONG DENTAL ASSOCIATION
e-mail: hkda@hkda.org
8/F Duke of Windsor Social Services Bldg.
15 Hennesey Rd.
Wanchai, Hong Kong
Dr. Chan Sai Kwing, Hon.Sec.
PH: 852 2 5285327
FX: 852 2 5290755
Description: Dentists, orthodontists, and others with an interest in the provision of dental care in Hong Kong. Promotes the welfare of the dental profession; encourages continuing professional education of members. Represents members' interests before government agencies and the public. Conducts research to advance dental practice; disseminates information to encourage public dental health maintenance. Maintains liaison with other dental organizations worldwide. Operates speakers' bureau; sponsors competitions; compiles statistics. **Founded:** 1950. **Membership:** 1200. **Staff:** 6. **Languages:** Chinese, English. **Publication:** *Hong Kong Dental Association Newsletter*, monthly ▪ *Hong Kong Dental Association Yearbook* (in Chinese and English), annual. Circulation: 1,200. Advertising: accepted.

HONG KONG DENTAL HYGIENISTS' ASSOCIATION (HKDHA)
Prince Philip Dental Hospital, 3/F
34 Hospital Rd.
Hong Kong, Hong Kong
Ms. P. Dando, Sec.
PH: 852 28590299
FX: 852 28587874
Description: Dental hygienists and students of dental hygiene. Promotes the study and practice of dental hygiene. Represents the dental hygiene profession; serves as a clearinghouse for government agencies and public and private organizations with an interest in dental hygiene. Conducts educational programs. **Founded:** 1981. **Membership:** 60. **Languages:** Chinese, English. **Budget:** HK$3,000. **Publication:** *HKDHA Newsletter*, quarterly.

HONG KONG GYNAECOLOGICAL ENDOSCOPY SOCIETY (HKGES)
Department of Obstetrics and Gynaecology
Prince of Wales Hospital
30-32 Ngan Shing St.
New Territories, Hong Kong
Dr. P. M. Yuen, Sec.
PH: 852 26322810
FX: 852 26360008
Description: Gynecological endoscopists and other health care professionals. Promotes advancement of the practice of gynecol-

ogical endoscopy. Conducts continuing professional education programs. **Founded:** 1994. **Membership:** 134. **Languages:** Chinese, English. **Publication:** *Endovision*, quarterly. Newsletter.

HONG KONG INSTITUTE OF FAMILY MEDICINE
18 Fu Kin St.
Tai Wai
Shatin
New Territories, Hong Kong
Dr. Anthony K.Y. Lee, V.Chm.
PH: 852 26083311
FX: 852 26053334
Description: Seeks to advance the study, theory, and practice of family medicine; encourages professional advancement of individuals engaged in the provision of family medical services. Conducts research and continuing professional development programs. **Founded:** 1994. **Staff:** 5. **Languages:** Chinese, English.

HONG KONG LABORATORY TECHNICIANS' ASSOCIATION
url: http://www.hkabc.net/ycau/hklta.htm
PO Box 80401
Cheung Sha Wan Post Office
Hong Kong, Hong Kong
Yun-Woon Chui, Pres.
PH: 852 23611551
FX: 852 27252793
Description: Medical and laboratory technicians. Promotes professional competence in the practice of medical and laboratory technology. Seeks to secure optimal conditions of employment for members. Formulates and enforces standards of practice and ethics for the field. Represents members in negotiations with employers. Conducts continuing professional development and other educational and training programs for members; sponsors research projects. Provides laboratory equipment, job referral, and discount shopping services to members. **Founded:** 1972. **Membership:** 400. **Staff:** 2. **Languages:** Chinese, English. **Publication:** *Laboratory and Labtek*, monthly. Newsletter.

HONG KONG MEDICAL ASSOCIATION
e-mail: hkma@hkma.org
url: http://www.hkma.org
Duke of Windsor Social Service Bldg., 5/F
15 Hennessy Rd.
Wanchai, Hong Kong
Yvonne Leung, CEO
PH: 852 25278285
FX: 852 28650943
Description: Physicians and other health care professionals. Seeks to advance the profession and practice of medicine. Promotes professional advancement of members. Represents members' interests before government agencies and the public. Conducts continuing professional development courses; sponsors research projects; holds social and charitable activities. **Founded:** 1920. **Membership:** 4800. **Staff:** 15. **Languages:** Chinese, English. **Publication:** *HK Medical Journal*, quarterly. Circulation: 4,800. Advertising: accepted ▪ *HKMA News*, monthly. Newsletter. Circulation: 4,800. Advertising: accepted. **Formerly:** (1970) Hong Kong Chinese Medical Association.

HONG KONG PAEDIATRIC HAEMATOLOGY AND ONCOLOGY STUDY GROUP (HKPHOSG)
url: http://Medicine.org.hk/hkphosg
Prince of Wales Hospital
Lady Pao Children's Cancer Centre, Rm. G15
30-32 Ngan Shing St.
New Territories, Hong Kong
Dr. Chung Wing Luk, Sec.
Description: Physicians with an interest in pediatric hematology and oncology. Seeks to advance methods of diagnosis and treatment of pediatric hematological and oncological problems. Conducts educational and continuing professional development courses for members. Compiles statistics. **Founded:** 1993. **Member-**

ship: 43. **Languages:** Chinese, English. **Publication:** Newsletter, monthly.

HONG KONG PATHOLOGY SOCIETY
Department of Pathology
Queen Mary Hospital
Pokfulam Rd.
Hong Kong, Hong Kong
Dr. Ui-Soon Khoo, Chm.
PH: 852 28554410
FX: 852 28190760
Description: Medical doctors in the field of pathology. Seeks to advance the profession of pathology. Serves as a forum for discussion and exchange of information among members. Conducts continuing professional development programs; sponsors research; holds competitions and social functions. **Founded:** 1982. **Membership:** 45. **Languages:** Chinese, English. **Publication:** Newsletter, quarterly.

HONG KONG PHARMACEUTICALS MANUFACTURERS ASSOCIATION
12A Cheung Wah Industrial Bldg.
12 Shipyard Ln.
Quarry Bay
Hong Kong, Hong Kong
Mr. Sin Lam Kwong, Pres.
PH: 852 25621289
FX: 852 25657913
Description: Producers of pharmaceuticals and related products in Hong Kong. Represents and promotes the economic and regulatory interests of the industry. **Languages:** Chinese, English.

HONG KONG SEX EDUCATION ASSOCIATION (HKSEA)
PO Box 50419
Sai Ying Pun Post Office
Hong Kong, Hong Kong
Mr. Li Man Chiu, Contact
PH: 852 28554486
FX: 852 28551345
Description: Individuals working in the fields of sex education, family planning, social work, psychology, and medicine; students. Promotes availability of quality educational programs dealing with sexuality, which the group defines as "those aspects of the human body that relate specifically to being male or female." Conducts research and educational programs; gathers and disseminates information. **Founded:** 1985. **Membership:** 100. **Languages:** Chinese, English. **Publication:** *Sex Forum*, semiannual. Newsletter ■ Bulletin.

HONG KONG SOCIETY OF DERMATOLOGY AND VENEREOLOGY (HKSD)
url: http://www.medicine.org.hk/hksdv/
Sai Ying Pun Jockey Club Clinic, 3rd Fl.
Queen's Rd. W.
Hong Kong, Hong Kong
Dr. Y.M. Tang, Contact
PH: 852 25409804
FX: 852 25409804
Description: Dermatologists and physicians in Hong Kong. Stimulates interest in dermatology; promotes exchange and cooperation among members; encourages discussions to address problems in the field. Inspires high standards of dermatological care. Fosters international contacts; disseminates information. **Founded:** 1983. **Membership:** 150. **Languages:** English. **Budget:** HK$150,000.

HONG KONG SOCIETY OF MINIMAL ACCESS SURGERY
Duke of Windsor Social Service Bldg., 4/F
15 Hennessy Rd.
Wanchai, Hong Kong
Dr. Samuel P.Y. Kwok, Contact
PH: 852
Description: Medical practitioners, scientists and researchers, and other individuals with an interest in laparoscopy and other minimal access surgical techniques. Seeks to advance the practice of minimal access surgery. Promotes continuing professional advancement of members. Conducts public education programs and continuing professional development courses; facilitates international exchange among minimal access surgeons; sponsors research projects; makes available scholarships and other assistance to minimal access surgery students. Provides charitable medical care; assists in the development of hospitals and other health care facilities. **Founded:** 1992. **Membership:** 369. **Languages:** Chinese, English. **Publication:** *Elsa Journal*, quarterly. Advertising: accepted.

HONG KONG SOCIETY FOR NURSING EDUCATION
PO Box 98898
Tsimshatsui Post Office
Kowloon, Hong Kong
Mr. Bing-Shu Cheng, Contact
Description: Nurses and nursing educators. Promotes excellence in nursing education; seeks to advance the practice of nursing. Represents the interests of the nursing profession; facilitates communication among nurses and nursing educators; conducts continuing professional development courses; sponsors research; maintains liaison with nursing education organizations worldwide. **Founded:** 1985. **Membership:** 150. **Languages:** Chinese, English. **Publication:** Newsletter, periodic. Alternate Formats: online.

HONG KONG SOCIETY OF ORAL IMPLANTOLOGY
e-mail: hksoi@netvigator.com
Takshing House, Rm. 704
20 Des Voeux Rd.
Central
Hong Kong, Hong Kong
Dr. Caesar Wong, Contact
PH: 852 25225571
FX: 852 25243557
Description: Registered dental and medical practitioners; dental and medical students. Seeks to advance the practice of oral implantology; promotes professional development of members. Establishes standards of professional conduct and practice; conducts research, educational, and continuing professional development courses; makes available to members technical and other assistance. **Founded:** 1995. **Membership:** 100. **Staff:** 3. Multinational. **Languages:** Chinese, English. **Publication:** *Newsletter of the Hong Kong Society of Oral Implantology* (in English), quarterly. Price: free. Circulation: 150. Advertising: accepted.

HOSPICE AND PALLIATIVE NURSES ASSOCIATION (HPNA)
e-mail: hnafan@pipeline.com
url: http://www.roxane.com/HNA
211 N. Whitfield St., Ste. 375
Pittsburgh, PA 15206
Susan Mann, Pres.
PH: (412)361-2470
FX: (412)361-2425
Description: Registered nurses engaged in end of life care in all settings. Promotes excellence in the specialties of hospice and palliative nursing. Conducts education and research programs. Has the only certification boards in hospice nursing. **Founded:** 1985. **Membership:** 3000. **Staff:** 5. **Regional Groups:** 8. **Languages:** English. **Budget:** $300,000. Formerly (1998) Hospice Nurses Association.

HOSPITAL DOCTORS' ASSOCIATION
London Rd.
Ascot SL5 7EN, England
Pam Morrisroe, Chief Exec.
PH: 44 1344 26613
Description: All hospital doctors below consultant level. The organisation exclusively representing junior doctors interests. It is concerned with their pay and terms and condition of service. At present it is concerned with the changes in specialist training and

the reduction in hours of work. **Founded:** 1966. **Membership:** 600. **Staff:** 1. **Publication:** *Official Reference Directory*, annual.

HUNGARIAN DERMATOLOGICAL SOCIETY (HDS)
(Magyar Dermatologiai Tarsulat)
e-mail: huderm@sote.hu
Department of Dermatology
University Medical School
PO Box 99
H-7624 Pecs, Hungary
Sarolta Karpati, M.D., Exec. Officer
PH: 36 1 2100310
FX: 36 1 1340566
Description: Promotes dermatological practice and research. Monitors progress in the field of dermatology. Participates in international forums. **Founded:** 1928. **Membership:** 500. **Staff:** 3. Multinational. **Local Groups:** 3. **Languages:** English, Hungarian. **Budget:** $40,000. **Publication:** *Borgyogyaszati es Venerologiai Szemle* (in Hungarian), bimonthly. Journal. Accepts English and German papers. Contains English abstracts. Price: $8.00/year. Advertising: accepted ▪ *Progress of Dermatology and Venereology*. Yearbook.

HUNGARIAN SOCIETY OF CARDIOLOGY (HSC)
(Magyar Kardiologusok Tarsasaga)
Hungarian Institute of Cardiology
Hallerutca 29
Postafiok 88
H-1096 Budapest, Hungary
Prof. Istvan Preda, M.D., Gen.Sec.
PH: 36 1 2151220
FX: 36 1 2155217
Description: Cardiologists and other medical specialists. Promotes development of cardiology; facilitates scientific exchanges of information among members. Monitors standards in cardiology training programs; provides cardiologists with ethical advice. Conducts educational, research, and public service programs. **Founded:** 1955. **Membership:** 1200. **Local Groups:** 17. **Languages:** English, Hungarian. **Publication:** *Cardiologia Hungarica* (in Hungarian), quarterly. Journal. Price: included in membership fee. Advertising: accepted.

HUNTINGTON'S DISEASE SOCIETY OF AMERICA (HDSA)
e-mail: curehd@hdsa.ttisms.com
url: http://hdsa.mgh.harvard.edu
140 W. 22nd St., 6th Fl.
New York, NY 10011-2420
Barbara Boyle, Exec.Dir.
PH: (212)242-1968
TF: 800345-4372
FX: (212)243-2443
Description: Individuals and groups of volunteers concerned with Huntington's disease, an inherited and terminal neurological condition causing progressive brain and nerve deterioration. Goals are to: identify HD families; educate the public and professionals, with emphasis on increasing consumer awareness of HD; promote and support basic and clinical research into the causes and cure of HD; maintain patient services program, coordinated with various community services, to assist families in meeting the social, economic, and emotional problems resulting from HD. Is working to change the attitude of the working community toward the HD patient, enhance the HD patient's lifestyle, and promote better health care and treatment, both in the community and in facilities. Has launched nationwide campaign in support of federal and state legislation establishing clinics, genetic counseling and screening centers, and diagnostic and treatment centers for HD patients and those suffering from other chronic, debilitating diseases. Actively cooperates with researchers in ongoing studies; cosponsors and supports workshops and symposia; provides grants to individual researchers; sponsors brain donor program. Crisis intervention and other support services are available. **Founded:** 1986. **Membership:** 45000. **Staff:** 12. National Groups: **3,331.** Languages: **English.** Budget: **$2,000,000.** Publication: *Huntington's Disease Society of America – Marker*,

3/year. Newsletter. Price: free. Circulation: 45,000. Advertising: not accepted ▪ Booklets ▪ Pamphlets. **Formed by Merger of: Huntington Disease Foundation of America; National Huntington's Disease Association.**

HUNTINGTON SOCIETY OF CANADA (HSC)
e-mail: info@hsc-ca.org
url: http://www.hsc-ca.org
13 Water St. N
PO Box 1269
Cambridge, ON, Canada N1R 7G6
Rod Morrison, Exec.Dir.
PH: (519)622-1002
FX: (519)622-7370
Description: Individuals with Huntington's disease (a hereditary neurological disorder) and their families; health care professionals and others with an interest in Huntington's disease and related disorders. Seeks to identify the cause and find a cure for Huntington's disease; promotes an improved quality of life for people with Huntington's disease. Serves as a clearinghouse on Huntington's disease; conducts research and educational programs; maintains speakers' bureau. **Founded:** 1973. **Membership:** 8000. **Staff:** 20. **National Groups:** 1. **Languages:** English, French. **Budget:** C$1,500,000. **Publication:** *Horizon*, quarterly. Newsletter. ISSN: 0827-7605. Circulation: 10,000. Advertising: accepted.

HUNTINGTON'S DISEASE ASSOCIATION (HDA)
108 Battersea High St.
London SW11 3HP, England
PH: 44 171 2237000
FX: 44 171 2239489
Description: Individuals united to provide assistance, treatment, and information on the effects of Huntington's Disease, a hereditary nervous disorder causing terminal physical and mental disability. Services include: counseling program designed for families and involved professionals; network of regional advisers and local groups throughout the country; confidential telephone and correspondence service; financial assistance; aid to patients undergoing presymptomatic tests or brain tissue donations. Encourages research on the medical and social effects of Huntington's Disease; raises funds. **Founded:** 1971. **Membership:** 4000. **Staff:** 10. **Local Groups:** 40. **Languages:** English. **Budget:** L250,000. **Publication:** *Facing Huntington's Disease*, periodic. Booklet ▪ Newsletter (in English), semiannual. Advertising: accepted ▪ Pamphlets, periodic. **Formerly:** (1991) Association to Combat Huntington's Disease.

HYDROCEPHALUS ASSOCIATION (HA)
url: http://neurosurgery.mgh.harvard.edu/ha/
870 Market St., Ste. 955
San Francisco, CA 94102
Emily Fudge, Exec. Dir.
PH: (415)732-7040
FX: (415)732-7044
Description: People with hydrocephalus and their families, health care professionals with an interest in hydrocephalus, and interested businesses and foundations. Works to improve the quality of life of people with hydrocephalus through education. Conducts training for families of people with hydrocephalus; sponsors social gatherings; facilitates networking among families of people with hydrocephalus and between organizations representing people with hydrocephalus. **Founded:** 1983. **Staff:** 2. **Languages:** English.

HYDROCEPHALUS RESEARCH FOUNDATION (HRF)
e-mail: ann_liakos@atlmug.org
1670 Green Oak Circle
Lawrenceville, GA 30243
Ann Marie Liakos, Exec. Dir.
PH: (770)995-9570
FX: (770)995-8982
Description: Persons with hydrocephalus, their families, and the professionals who specialize in their education, therapy and health care. Goals are to: familiarize the public with hydroce-

phalus and eliminate stigma associated with the condition; define and help resolve specific problems that parents of children with hydrocephalus encounter; collect and disseminate information pertaining to hydrocephalus and inform parents of the educational rights of these children. Conducts symposia with physicians in the field of hydrocephalus aimed at informing parents. Compiles statistics. **Founded:** 1979. **Membership:** 500. **Languages:** English. **Publication:** *Hydrocephalus News and Notes*, quarterly. Newsletter. Price: included in membership dues ▪ *Survey on Hydrocephalus*. Statistics on hydrocephalus types and related side affects. **Formerly:** (1998) National Hydrocephalus Foundation.

HYSTERECTOMY EDUCATIONAL RESOURCES AND SERVICES FOUNDATION (HERS)
e-mail: hersfdn@aol.com
url: http://www.dca.net/hers/
422 Bryn Mawr Ave.
Bala Cynwyd, PA 19004
Nora W. Coffey, Pres.
PH: (610)667-7757
FX: (610)667-8096
Description: Helps women make informed decisions regarding hysterectomy. Provides educational materials concerning hysterectomy and alternative procedures. Functions as a referral service matching women who have had or will have a hysterectomy for one-to-one sharing of experiences and concerns. Offers referral list of doctors for second opinions. Also provides legal referrals. Maintains speakers' bureau. **Founded:** 1982. **Staff:** 5. Multinational. **Languages:** English, Spanish. **Budget:** $90,000. Also Known As HERS Foundation.

IBERO-LATIN AMERICAN COLLEGE OF DERMATOLOGY (ILACD)
(Colegio Ibero-Latino-Americano de Dermatologia)
Av. Callao 852, Piso 2
1023 Buenos Aires, Argentina
Prof.Dra. Ana Kaminsky, Pres.
FX: 54 1 8117581
Description: Iberian or Latin American doctors in 29 countries working in various fields related to dermatology including mycology (the study of fungi), venereology (the study of sexually transmitted diseases), the treatment of leprosy, dermatologic surgery, and criosurgery. Seeks to foster a working relationship between Ibero-Latin American specialists and those in other countries. **Founded:** 1948. **Membership:** 2210. Multinational. **Languages:** Portuguese, Spanish. **Budget:** $50,000. **Publication:** *Boletin del CILAD* (in Portuguese and Spanish), quarterly. Bulletin. Contains information about the activities of the college. Price: free for members. Advertising: not accepted ▪ *Ciladerma*, bimonthly. Magazine ▪ *Medicina Cutanea Ibero-Latino-Americana* (in Portuguese and Spanish), bimonthly. Advertising: accepted ▪ Directory, periodic ▪ Monographs, periodic.

ICELANDIC CARDIAC SOCIETY (ICS)
(Hjartasjukdomafelag Islenskra Laekna)
Sidumula 37
IS-105 Reykjavik, Iceland
Uggi Agnarsson, M.D.
PH: 354 1 5812560
FX: 354 1 5525703
Description: Physicians and scientists interested in the field of cardiology. **Founded:** 1968. **Membership:** 33. **National Groups:** 1. **Languages:** Danish, English.

ICELANDIC DENTAL ASSOCIATION
(Tannlaeknafelag Islands)
e-mail: tfi@tv.is
Sidumuli 35
PO Box 8596
IS-128 Reykjavik, Iceland
Sigridur Dagbjartsdottir, Exec. Officer
PH: 354 1 5534646
FX: 354 1 5533562

Description: Professional association of active and retired dentists. Conducts charitable activities; provides emergency dental assistance. Conducts educational programs. **Founded:** 1927. **Membership:** 308. **Staff:** 2. **Local Groups:** 4. **Languages:** English, Swedish. **Publication:** *Journal of Dentistry*, annual. Also Cited As: Tannlaeknabladid ▪ *Newsletter*, monthly.

ICELANDIC PHYSICAL SOCIETY
e-mail: ario@raunvis.hi.is
url: http://www.os.is/ei/
Science Institute
Dunhaga 3
IS-107 Reykjavik, Iceland
Dr. Ari Olafssonn, Pres.
PH: 354 5254800
Description: Physicists, physics teachers, and others with an interest in the physical sciences. Seeks to improve the quality of physics education, research, and knowledge. **Founded:** 1977. **Membership:** 70. **Publication:** *Edlisfraedi a Islandi* (in English and Icelandic), biennial. Journal. Advertising: not accepted.

IEEE ENGINEERING IN MEDICINE AND BIOLOGY SOCIETY (EMBS)
e-mail: soc.emb@ieee.org
url: http://www.bae.ncsu.edu/bae/courses/bae465/embs.html
Bldg. M-55, Rm. 382
Ottawa, ON, Canada K1A 0R8
Sally Chapman, Exec.Sec.
PH: (613)993-4005
FX: (613)954-2216
Description: A society of the Institute of Electrical and Electronics Engineers. Concerned with concepts and methods of the physical and engineering sciences applied in biology and medicine, including formalized mathematical theory, experimental science, technological development, and practical clinical application. Disseminates information on current methods and technologies used in biomedical and clinical engineering. **Founded:** 1950. **Membership:** 8500. Multinational. **Local Groups:** 37. **Languages:** English. **Publication:** *Engineering in Medicine and Biology Magazine*, semiannual ▪ *Transaction on Biomedical Engineering*, monthly.

IMMUNE DEFICIENCY FOUNDATION (IDF)
e-mail: idf@clark.net
url: http://www.primaryimmune.org
25 W. Chesapeake Ave.
Towson, MD 21204
Thomas L. Moran, Pres.
PH: (410)321-6647
TF: 800296-4433
FX: (410)321-9165
Description: Immune deficiency patients, their families, and medical professionals. Promotes education and research in primary immune deficiency diseases. Holds medical symposia; bestows patient scholarship and research awards. **Founded:** 1980. **Membership:** 11500. **Staff:** 6. **Local Groups:** 14. **Languages:** English.

IMMUNIZATION ACTION COALITION (IAC)
e-mail: mail@immunize.org
url: http://www.immunize.org
1573 Selby Ave., Ste. 234
St. Paul, MN 55104
Deborah L. Wexler, M.D., Exec.Dir.
PH: (612)647-9009
FX: (612)647-9131
Description: Works to boost immunization rates. Promotes awareness of and responsibility for immunization of all people against all vaccine-preventable diseases. Conducts educational and outreach programs; develops print and audiovisual educational materials. **Founded:** 1990. **Staff:** 7. Multinational. **Languages:** English. **Budget:** $400,000.

**IMPLANTED DEFIBRILATOR ASSOCIATION OF
  SCOTLAND (IDAS)**
6 Argyll St.
Brechin
Angus DD9 6JL, Scotland
Peter Slater, Sec.
Description: Individuals with implanted defibrilating devices and
their families. Promotes and improved quality of life for people
with implanted defibrilators. Sponsors support groups for members; advocates on behalf of members before medical organizations and the public; conducts educational programs; participates
in charitable activities. **Founded:** 1994. **Languages:** English.
Budget: L4,000. **Publication:** *Vital Spark*, periodic. Newsletter.

INDENT
e-mail: com@fme.nl
url: http://www.fme.nl/INDENT
Postbus 190
NL-2700 AD Zoetermeer, Netherlands
Mr. F.J.H.J. Donders, Sec.Gen.
PH: 31 79 3531100
FX: 31 79 3531365
Description: Companies manufacturing dental equipment and
supplies. Establishes international standards and technical har-
monization for dental equipment. Represents members' interests
before government bodies, international agencies, and the public.
Maintains liaison with organizations representing dentists, dental
technicians, and dental supply dealers and distributors. Compiles
statistics. **Founded:** 1978. **Membership:** 19. **Staff:** 2. **Languages:**
Dutch. **Publication:** *INDENT Export Group, the Netherlands* (in
English). Brochure. Contains information regarding products
and activities of members of the INDENT export group. Advertising: not accepted. **Formerly:** (1993) VNFTP.

INDEPENDENT ASSOCIATION OF GERMAN DENTISTS
  (Freier Verband Deutscher Zahnarzte)
Mallwitzstr. 16
D-53177 Bonn, Germany
Dr. Ralph Gutmann, Contact
PH: 49 228 85570
FX: 49 228 347967
Description: Represents and promotes the professional interests
of German dentists. **Founded:** 1955. **Membership:** 26000. **Staff:**
30. **National Groups:** 1. **Languages:** English. **Publication:** *Der
Freie Zahnarzt* (in German), monthly. Magazine. Informs mem-
bers of relevant politics, science, technologies, and service sup-
plies of the association. Price: free to dentists. Circulation:
55,000. Advertising: accepted. Also Cited As: *The Independent
Dentist*.

**INDEPENDENT CITIZENS RESEARCH FOUNDATION FOR
  THE STUDY OF DEGENERATIVE DISEASES (ICRFSDD)**
PO Box 91
Ardsley, NY 10502
Mark Bereday, Exec.Dir.
PH: (914)478-1862
Description: Individuals united to seek and publish information
of aid to those affected by degenerative diseases. Makes available in bulletin form documented information on the multiple and
contributing causes of degenerative diseases, testing procedures
for their early detection, and possible approaches to therapy and
prevention. Seeks out factors in the environment that are
detrimental to health. Supports research on calibrated transcuta-
neous electric nerve stimulation and preventive medicine techniques. Maintains 400 volume library on maintenance of health
and prevention of disease. Seeks out factors in the environment
that are detrimental to health. **Founded:** 1957. **Languages:** English. **Publication:** Newsletter, bimonthly.

INDEPENDENT LIVING CENTRE
Millbrook House
Millbrook Lane
Topsham Rd.
Exeter EX2 6ES, England
Mrs. Sue Morris, Contact
PH: 44 1392 59260
FX: 44 1392 435357
Description: Provides a permanent exhibition and demonstration
centre of equipment for people of all ages with a variety of needs
and disabilities providing information to their families, carers,
health professionals, students and the general public. **Founded:**
1986. **Staff:** 1. **Publication:** Brochure.

INDIAN DENTAL ASSOCIATION (IDA)
83 Dewan Bahadur Rd.
R S Puram
Coimbatore 641 002, Tamil Nadu, India
Dr. V.M. Veerabahu, Hon.Gen.Sec.
PH: 91 422 453684
FX: 91 442 449555
Description: Dental surgeons; dental students. Promotes the
dental profession and educates the public concerning the contri-
butions of dental professionals. Offers educational and public
service programs; conducts research programs. **Founded:** 1945.
Membership: 6000. **Staff:** 25. **Local Groups:** 103. **Languages:**
English. **Budget:** $3,000. **Publication:** *Journal of IDA* (in English),
monthly. Price: Rs 250.00. Advertising: accepted ■ Directory (in
English), annual.

INDIAN DENTAL ASSOCIATION U.S.A.
146-02 89th Ave.
Jamaica, NY 11435
Dr. Simla, Pres.
PH: (718)523-8438
FX: (718)523-4114
Description: Dentists in the U.S. who are of Asian-Indian de-
scent. Seeks to further the professional education of members.
Conducts social events. **Founded:** 1983. **Membership:** 345. **State
Groups:** 2. **Languages:** English. **Publication:** *IDA Newsletter*,
monthly.

INDIAN DRUG MANUFACTURERS ASSOCIATION
102B Poonam Chambers
Dr. A. B. Rd.
Worli
Bombay 400 018, Maharashtra, India
Dinesh B. Mody, Pres.
PH: 91 22 4926308
FX: 91 22 4950723
Description: Pharmaceutical manufacturers. Seeks to advance
the domestic pharmaceuticals industry. Represents members' in-
terests; gathers and disseminates industry information. **Founded:**
1948. **Membership:** 389. **Languages:** English, Hindi.

INDIAN MUSCULAR DYSTROPHY ASSOCIATION (IMDA)
21-136 Batchupet
Malchilipatnam 521 001, India
R. Janardana Rao
PH: 91 8 6722817
Description: Individuals in India who work toward the dissemi-
nation of information and research concerning muscular
dystrophy, a hereditary disease characterized by progressive de-
terioration of muscles. **Founded:** 1982. **Membership:** 850. **Staff:**
1. **State Groups:** 7. **Languages:** English. **Publication:** *Bridge* (in
English), quarterly. Newsletter. Advertising: not accepted ■
Varadhi.

INDIANS INTO MEDICINE (INMED)
e-mail: inmed@mail.med.und.nodak.edu
url: http://www.med.und.nodak.edu/depts/inmed/home.htm
University of North Dakota
School of Medicine and Health Services
PO Box 9037
Grand Forks, ND 58202-9037
Eugene DeLorme, J.D., Dir.
PH: (701)777-3037
FX: (701)777-3277
Description: Support program for American Indian students. Seeks to: increase the awareness of and interest in healthcare professions among young American Indians; recruit and enroll American Indians in healthcare education programs; place American health professionals in service to Indian communities. Coordinates financial and personal support for students in healthcare curricula. Provides referral and counseling services. Maintains 2000 volume library. Provides summer enrichment sessions at the junior high, high school and pre-medical levels. Founded: 1973. Staff: 9. Languages: English. Publication: Serpent, Staff and Drum, quarterly. Newsletter. Price: free. Advertising: not accepted.

INDONESIAN PLANNED PARENTHOOD ASSOCIATION (IPPA)
e-mail: pkbinet@idola.net.id
Jalan Hang Jebat III/F3
PO Box 6017
Kebayoran Baru
12060 Jakarta, Indonesia
Pandu Kusumd Hadi, Contact
PH: 62 21 7207372
FX: 62 21 7394088
Description: Works to improve the quality of life for individuals living in Indonesia through responsible parenthood and family planning. Advocates family planning as a basic human right. Offers programs in family planning, sex education, and health care. Provides contraceptive and health care services. Conducts research. Founded: 1957. Membership: 1500. Staff: 110. National Groups: 1. Languages: English, Indonesian. Publication: IPPA's News Letter (in English and Indonesian), semiannual. Newsletter. Price: free. Circulation: 2,000. Advertising: not accepted ▪ Kabar (in English and Indonesian), quarterly. Magazine. Price: free. ISSN: 0216-0269. Circulation: 2,000. Advertising: not accepted ▪ Brochures.

INDONESIAN SOCIETY FOR PERINATOLOGY (PERINASIA)
(Perkumpulan Perinatologi Indonesia)
e-mail: perinasi@centrin.net.id
Jalan Tebet Utara IA/22
12820 Jakarta, Indonesia
Dr. Hadi Pratomo, MPH, Contact
PH: 62 21 8281243
FX: 62 21 8281243
Description: Obstetricians, gynecologists, pediatricians, midwives, and interested others. Strives to reduce the perinatal mortality rate; works to improve prenatal, natal, and postnatal health care; seeks improved medical facilities. Holds workshops, congresses, seminars, and symposia on perinatal health care and related subjects. Advocates research in safe birth practices; promotes the use of preventive medicine in prenatal care. Encourages community participation in health care improvement programs. Offers technical assistance to government authorities. Cooperates with similar international organizations. Conducts surveys. Disseminates information. Founded: 1981. Membership: 200. Staff: 8. Local Groups: 19. Languages: English, Indonesian. Budget: 000,000 Rp. Publication: Perinasia Bulletin (in Indonesian), quarterly. Price: Free. ISSN: 0215-9422. Circulation: 1,000. Advertising: accepted ▪ Proceedings, periodic.

INDUSTRIAL BIOTECHNOLOGY ASSOCIATION OF CANADA (IBAC)
e-mail: info@biotech.ca
url: http://www.biotech.com
420-130 Albert St.
Ottawa, ON, Canada K1P 5G4
Joyce Groote, Pres.
PH: (613)230-5585
FX: (613)563-8850
Description: Biotechnology operating companies and providers of services to the industry. Promotes growth and development of the domestic biotechnology industry. Represents members' interests before government agencies and scientific and industrial organizations. Founded: 1987. Membership: 65. Staff: 4. Languages: English, French. Publication: IBAC Fax, monthly. Newsletter. Alternate Formats: online.

INFECTION CONTROL NURSES' ASSOCIATION
Wirral Hospital
Clatterbridge
Bebington, Cheshire L63 4JY, England
Janet Roberts, Contact
PH: 44 151 6047411
Description: Infection control nurses and allied professionals. Concerned with the education of public and health care staff in infection. Founded: 1969. Membership: 1000. Publication: Journal on Nursing.

INFLAMMATION RESEARCH ASSOCIATION (IRA)
url: http://www.mindport.net/~hauki/inflammation/
Ciba-Geigy Corp.
556 Morris Ave.
Summit, NJ 07901
Barry Weichman, Pres.
FX: (908)277-2405
Description: Brings together scientists with an interest in inflammation research. Encourages the communication and discussion of science..

INFORMATION CENTER AGAINST DRUG-INDUCED SUFFERING (ICADIS)
4-1-8, 102 Minato-cho
Hyogo-ku
Kobe 652, Japan
Koichi Izumi, Contact
PH: 81 78 5772064
FX: 81 78 5772083
Description: Works to prevent inappropriate use of medicines, and to make medical practice more considerate of patient needs and preferences. Provides financial assistance to health organizations in Malaysia, the Philippines, and Thailand. Makes available consulting services on medications and their side affects and patients' rights in Japan. Founded: 1979. Membership: 400. Staff: 2. Multinational. Languages: English, Japanese. Budget: $74,190. Publication: Yakugai Iroyohigai Joho Center News (in Japanese). Newsletter. Contains news of information center against drug-induced suffering. Price: included in membership dues. Advertising: not accepted.

THE INFORMATION EXCHANGE (TIE)
120 N. Main St.
New City, NY 10956
Bert Pepper, M.D., Exec.Dir.
PH: (914)634-0050
FX: (914)634-1690
Description: Information dissemination for young adults with serious ongoing mental/emotional disorders. (Defines young adult patients as persons 18-35 years old who have a psychiatric disorder, are socially disabled, and have needed mental health services for at least two years. The psychiatric disorder may be a major mental illness or personality disorder, or a mixture of emotional problems with substance abuse or other disabilities.) Goals are to gather information about young adults and effective program initiatives for them; to disseminate information to professionals

and the public; to create an awareness of the needs of young adults and their families. Provides consultation and teaching about the patients and on effective ways of meeting their needs. Conducts presentations for professional and community groups. **Founded:** 1983. Multinational. **Languages:** English. Formerly (1994) The Information Exchange on Young Adult Chronic Patients.

INFORMED HOMEBIRTH/INFORMED BIRTH AND PARENTING (IH/IBP)
PO Box 3675
Ann Arbor, MI 48106
Rahima Baldwin, Pres.
PH: (313)662-6857
Description: Expectant and new parents, childbirth educators, midwives, nurses, preschool and elementary school teachers, and others interested in safe childbirth alternatives. Seeks to provide information on alternatives in childbirth methods, parenting, and developmental education. Childbirth Educator Training Program leading to certification as Childbirth Educator; Childbirth Assistant Training emphasizing practical skills to help the birthing woman and the primary caregiver. **Founded:** 1977. **Staff:** 2. **Languages:** English. Formerly (1981) Informed Homebirth.

INSTITUT MARCHOUX
Boite Postale 251
Bamako, Mali
Fr. S. Keita, Dir.
PH: 223 225131
FX: 223 222845
Description: Medical researchers and health care professionals. Promotes improved diagnostic techniques and treatments of common diseases. Conducts research and educational programs; makes available health services. **Founded:** 1935. **Staff:** 72. Multinational. **Languages:** English, French. **Budget:** $30,000. **Also Known As:** Obsrvatoire de la Lepre en Afrique.

INSTITUT PIERRE RICHET
01 Boite Postale 1500
Bouake, Cote d'Ivoire
Dr. Francois Riviere, Dir.
PH: 225 633746
FX: 225 632738
Description: Medical researchers and health care professionals. Promotes improved diagnostic techniques and treatments of common diseases. Conducts research and educational programs; makes available health services. Multinational. **Languages:** English, French.

INSTITUTE OF ARTIC MEDICINE
e-mail: olli.arjamao@oulu.fi
Aapistie 1
FIN-90220 Oulu, Finland
Olli Arjamaa, M.D., Sec.Gen.
PH: 358 8 5376200
FX: 358 8 5376203
Description: Promotes research into arctic medicine; encourages cooperation among researchers. Disseminates reports and other information to persons engaged in arctic medicine. **Founded:** 1969. **Membership:** 6. **Staff:** 3. Multinational. **Languages:** English, Finnish. **Budget:** $1,000,000. **Publication:** *International Journal of Circumpolar Health* (in English), quarterly. Price: $75.00. ISSN: 0782-226X. Circulation: 1,600. Advertising: accepted ∎ Monographs ∎ Proceedings. **Formerly:** Nordic Council for Artic Medical Research; Nordiska Samarbetskommitten for Artisk Medicinsk Forskning.

INSTITUTE OF BIOMEDICAL SCIENCE
e-mail: 101771.3572@compuserve.com
12 Coldbath Sq.
London EC1R 5HL, England
PH: 44 171 6368192
FX: 44 171 4364946
Description: Biomedical scientists (medical laboratory scientists)

and related staff in the National Health Service, private sector and overseas. To promote the study and development of biomedical science and maintain high standards of professional education and practice. **Founded:** 1912. **Publication:** *Biomedical Scientist*, monthly. Advertising: accepted ∎ *British Journal of Biomedical Science*, quarterly.

INSTITUTE OF CERTIFIED PROFESSIONAL BUSINESS CONSULTANTS (ICPBC)
330 S. Wells St., Ste. 1422
Chicago, IL 60606-7101
Barbara Boden, Exec.Dir.
PH: (312)360-0384
TF: 800447-1684
FX: (312)360-0388
Description: Individuals providing business advisory services to physicians and dentists. Maintains code of ethics, rules of professional conduct, and certification program; administers examination and conducts review course. Membership by successful completion of certification examination only. **Founded:** 1975. **Membership:** 295. **Staff:** 3. **Languages:** English. **Publication:** *Institute of Certified Professional Business Consultants – Membership Directory*, annual. Advertising: not accepted ∎ *Institute of Certified Professional Business Consultants – Newsletter*, quarterly. Price: available to members only.

INSTITUTE FOR COMPLEMENTARY MEDICINE (ICM)
PO Box 194
London SE16 1QZ, England
Anthony Baird, Sec.
PH: 44 171 2375165
FX: 44 171 2375175
Description: Individuals united to promote the practice of alternative medicine. Seeks to establish educational standards for practitioners and to establish ties between therapy groups, organizations, teachers, and practitioners. Cooperates with the British government to develop natural therapy curricula. Maintains British Register of Complementary Practitions. Conducts research; disseminates information. Advises groups establishing healing practices on legal, organizational, and practical matters. **Founded:** 1982. **Membership:** 6000. **Staff:** 8. **Languages:** English. **Publication:** *Journal for Complementary Medicine* (in English), semiannual ∎ *Newsletter* (in English), quarterly. Supplement to journal. **Absorbed:** (1969) Healing Research Trust.

INSTITUTE FOR DIAGNOSTIC RADIOLOGY (IDR)
(Institut fur Diagnotische Radiologie)
e-mail: Hari@adr.ks.se
Inselspital
CH-3010 Bern, Switzerland
Dr. M. Blery, Sec.Gen.
PH: 41 31 6322435
FX: 41 31 6324874
Description: National European societies of radiology representing 20,000 radiologists. Objectives are to: promote radiology as a unified scientific and clinical discipline; further and monitor the application of radiology in biology and medicine; investigate the theoretical and technical problems connected with different applications of radiation; coordinate study and examination programs in the field of radiology in member countries; standardize training for radiologists and nonmedical assistants; encourage a constructive rapport with scientific, professional, and industrial organizations; promote international exchange of medical and paramedical personnel. **Founded:** 1962. **Membership:** 34. Multinational. **Languages:** English, French. **Publication:** *European Radiology* (in English), bimonthly. Newsletter. Price: free. Advertising: accepted. **Also Known As:** Association Europeenne de Radiologie; Europaische Gesellschaft f. Radiologie. **Formerly:** European Association of Radiology.

INSTITUTE OF FAMILY MEDICINE (IFM)
University of Arhus
HOEG-Guldbergs Gade 8
DK-8000 Arhus, Denmark
Frede Olesen, Contact
Description: Health care researchers and primary care providers. Promotes more effective research, study, and practice in the field of family medicine. Conducts research. **Languages:** Danish, English.

INSTITUTE OF HEALTH EDUCATION
e-mail: anthony.blinkhorn@man.ac.uk
url: http://www.salford.ac.uk/ti/gsc/html/auth/summary.html
University Dental Hospital
Dept. of Oral Health and Development
Higher Cambridge St.
Manchester M15 6FH, England
Prof. A.S. Blinkhorn, Gen.Sec.
PH: 44 161 2756610
FX: 44 161 2756610
Description: Members are individuals concerned with the promotion of health and the prevention of illness in all sections of the community at home, school, work and leisure. **Founded:** 1962. **Membership:** 1000. **Publication:** *International Journal of Health Education*, quarterly. Advertising: accepted.

INSTITUTE FOR HEALTH MANAGEMENT
e-mail: nzi@nzi.nl
Postbus 9697
NL-3506 GR Utrecht, Netherlands
Mrs. J.E.M. Geraerts, PR Officer
PH: 31 30 2739700
FX: 31 30 273560
Description: Seeks to develop a "sound, humane, and financially feasible health service" in the Netherlands. Conducts scientific research; offers advisory services; maintains educational programs. Disseminates information to health institutions and health care services. **Founded:** 1968. **Staff:** 130. **Local Groups:** 7. **Languages:** Dutch, English. **Budget:** 19,500,000 f. **Publication:** *NZI Notities*, bimonthly. Magazine. Price: free. Advertising: not accepted.

INSTITUTE OF HEALTH SERVICES MANAGEMENT
e-mail: mailbox@ihsm.co.uk
url: http://www.insm.co.uk
7-10 Chandos St.
London W1M 9DE, England
Karen Caines, Dir.
PH: 44 171 4607654
FX: 44 171 4607655
Description: Those involved in the management and administration of health care. To promote excellence in health services management and the development of good managers, to affect health services policy and its implementation and to create and sustain a professional community of health services managers. It is a forum, network and management development association for individuals both inside and outside the NHS. **Founded:** 1902. **Membership:** 8000. **Staff:** 22. **State Groups:** 3. **Publication:** *Health Management*. Magazine ▪ *The IHSM Health and Social Services Yearbook* (in English), annual. Also Cited As: *The Yearbook*.

INSTITUTE OF OPHTHALMOLOGY
e-mail: ams.admin@vcl.ac.uk
Bath St.
London EC1V 9EL, England
Prof. A.M. Sillito, Dir. of Research
PH: 44 171 6086800
FX: 44 171 6086877
Description: Teaching and research into eye diseases and other causes of blindness. **Founded:** 1948. **Staff:** 185.

INSTITUTE OF PHARMACY MANAGEMENT INTERNATIONAL
14 Mamignog Close
Bearsted
Kent ME14 4PR, England
Mrs. Ruth Rogers, Contact
PH: 44 1622 735708
FX: 44 1622 735108
Description: Members are pharmaceutical chemists, and managers in the pharmaceutical industry. Provides research and study of management within the pharmaceutical industry and profession of pharmacy in hospital and community practice with particular reference to the National Health Service pharmaceutical service; sales and marketing activitie in connection with OTC medicines and allied healthcare products. Hosts twice in a year conferences on management subjects. **Founded:** 1964. **Membership:** 795. **Publication:** *IPMI Institute News*, quarterly. Journal. Price: L40.00 a year; free to members. Circulation: 750. Advertising: accepted.

INSTITUTE OF PHYSICS (IOP)
e-mail: physics@iop.org
url: http://www.iop.org
76 Portland Pl.
London WIN 3DH, England
Alun Jones, Chief Exec.
PH: 44 171 4704800
FX: 44 171 4704848
Description: Professional body for physicists in Great Britain and Ireland. Chartered by a royal charter to "promote the advancement and dissemination of knowledge and education in the science of pure and applied physics." Represents the physics community to government and other legislative or policy-making bodies. Sets and supports professional standards and qualifications. **Founded:** 1960. **Membership:** 22000. **Staff:** 220. **Regional Groups:** 12. **Languages:** English. **Budget:** L18,000,000. **Publication:** *Classical and Quantum Gravity* (in English), monthly. Journal ▪ *Clinical Physics and Physiological Measurement* (in English), quarterly. Journal ▪ *Engineering Optics* (in English), quarterly. Journal ▪ *European Journal of Physics* (in English), quarterly ▪ *Europhysics Letters* (in English), semimonthly. Magazine ▪ *Inverse Problems* (in English), bimonthly. Journal ▪ *Journal of Physics A: Mathematical and General* (in English), semimonthly ▪ *Journal of Physics B: Atomic, Molecular and Optical Physics* (in English), semimonthly ▪ *Journal of Physics C: Condensed Matter* (in English), weekly ▪ *Journal of Physics D: Applied Physics* (in English), monthly ▪ *Journal of Physics E: Scientific Instruments* (in English), monthly ▪ *Journal of Physics G: Nuclear and Particle Physics* (in English), monthly ▪ *Journal of Radiological Protection* (in English), quarterly ▪ *Liquids* (in English), monthly. Journal ▪ *Nonlinearity* (in English), quarterly. Journal ▪ *Physics Education* (in English), bimonthly. Journal ▪ *Physics in Medicine and Biology* (in English), monthly. Journal ▪ *Physics World* (in English), monthly. Magazine ▪ *Plasma Physics and Controlled Fusion* (in English), monthly. Journal ▪ *Reports on Progress in Physics* (in English), monthly ▪ *Semiconductor Science and Technology* (in English), monthly. Journal ▪ *Superconductor Science and Technology* (in English), periodic. Journal. **Formed by Merger of:** Institute of Physics; Physical Society.

INSTITUTE OF PSYCHIATRY
De Crespigny Park
Denmark Hill
London SE5 8AF, England
D. Llewellyn, Sec.
PH: 44 171 7035411
Description: To promote excellence in the research, development and teaching of psychiatry and its allied subjects and to apply and disseminate this knowledge through the development of treatment for the relief of suffering. **Founded:** 1948. **Staff:** 525. **Publication:** Annual Report, annual.

INSTITUTE OF SOCIAL PSYCHIATRY
London Rd.
Stapleford Tawney
Romford RM4 1SR, England
Mrs. N. Weeks, Contact
PH: 44 1992 814661
FX: 44 1708 688583
Description: Aims to further and finance, if feasible, research into psychiatry. Runs a nursing home for elderly mentally handicapped. The Institute of Social Psychiatry is a Registered Charity. **Founded:** 1947.

INSTITUTE OF SPORTS MEDICINE
University College London Medical School
67-73 Riding House St.
London W1P 7LD, England
Description: Established to develop postgraduate medical research, teaching and treatment in sports medicine. It runs courses and seminars on different aspects of this specialist subject. **Founded:** 1959.

INSTITUTE OF STERILE SERVICES MANAGEMENT
Cliftonville
Northampton NN1 5BD, England
Mrs. P.A. Oliver, Dir. of Education
PH: 44 1604 602576
FX: 44 1604 602576
Description: Different grades of membership - Fellow, Member, Student member, Associate, Corporate, Honorary, Associate Technician. Aims to organise and initiate training programmes for members/students, with the object of achieving high professional standards; provides a forum for members through regional branches to consider and discuss matters relating to sterilization and disinfection and promotes and encourages research and development in the world of sterile service. **Publication:** *The ISSM Journal* (in English), quarterly. ISSN: 0951-2578. Advertising: accepted ■ *Official Reference Book*, annual ■ *Training Handbook for Steril Service Personnel*.

INSTITUTE FOR THE DEVELOPMENT OF EMOTIONAL AND LIFE SKILLS (IDEALS)
4400 East- West Hwy., Ste. 28
Bethesda, MD 20814
Dr. William Nordling, Exec.Dir.
PH: (301)986-1479
FX: (301)699-8835
Description: Goals include developing and researching effective programs for improving emotional and interpersonal skills and providing high-quality training and supervision for mental health professionals, managers, workers, and the public. Conducts training programs for professionals in the areas of mental health, health care, human services, education, and business; sponsors training programs for laypeople in the areas of improving interpersonal relations, problem solving, and effective functioning in family and in business settings. Offers programs for workers and managers in communication, goal planning, motivation, negotiation, stress and time management, personnel management, and supervision. Convention/Meeting: none. **Founded:** 1972. **Membership:** 12. **Staff:** 6. **Languages:** English.

INSTITUTE FOR LABOR AND MENTAL HEALTH (ILMH)
3137 Telegraph Ave.
Oakland, CA 94609
Dr. Richard Epstein, Dir.
PH: (510)653-6166
Description: Purpose is to help working people with problems related to the workplace. Seeks to identify conditions at work that cause stress; believes that education and communication about common work problems are the first steps in dealing with job stress. Assists unions in handling grievances and stress-related disabilities; provides counseling to union members and their families; offers legal and worker compensation assistance to working people. Provides consultation to government and businesses on ways to reduce stress. Develops ongoing stress pro-

grams; operates summer institute on occupational stress. **Founded:** 1977. **Membership:** 50. **Staff:** 6. **Languages:** English.

INSTITUTE FOR MENTAL HEALTH INITIATIVES (IMHI)
e-mail: instmhi@aol.com
url: http://www.imhi.org/imhi
4545 42nd St. NW, Ste. 311
Washington, DC 20016
Suzanne Stutman, Pres.
PH: (202)364-7111
FX: (202)363-3891
Description: Uses a public health approach to promote mental health and prevent emotional disorders. Seeks to transform complex mental health concepts into positive models of human interaction. Gathers knowledge derived from clinical and research findings on good mental health, which it then adapts for use by the media, educators, health and mental health professionals, community leaders, and parents. Conducts meetings and workshops; consults with media professionals; creates training videos, discussion guides, and public service announcements. Works to influence perceptions and attitudes through the power of commercial mass media. **Founded:** 1982. **Staff:** 5. **Languages:** English. **Budget:** $400,000.

INSTITUTE ON PSYCHIATRIC SERVICES/AMERICAN PSYCHIATRIC ASSOCIATION
e-mail: JGruber@psych.org
1400 K St. NW
Washington, DC 20005
Jill L. Gruber, Coord.
PH: (202)682-6314
FX: (202)682-6345
Description: Annual meeting sponsored by the American Psychiatric Association. Open to employees of all psychiatric and related health and educational facilities. Includes lectures by experts in the field and workshops and accredited courses on problems, programs, and trends. Offers on-site Job Bank, which lists opportunities for mental health professionals. Organized scientific exhibits. **Founded:** 1949. **Staff:** 13. Multinational. **Languages:** English Formerly (1995) Institute on Hospital and Community Psychiatry.

INSTITUTION OF PHYSICS AND ENGINEERING IN MEDICINE AND BIOLOGY
e-mail: r.w.neilson@ipemb.org.uk
url: http://www.ipemb.org.uk
4 Compleshon Rd.
York YO2 1PE, England
Robert W. Neilson, Gen.Sec.
PH: 44 171 2427750
FX: 44 171 8315225
Description: Scientists and engineers working in the field of medical physics and bioengineering. Promotes for public benefit the advancement of physics and engineering applied to medicine and biology and to advance public education in this field. Represents the needs and interests of engineering and physical sciences in the provision and advancement of health care. **Founded:** 1943. **Membership:** 2400. **Staff:** 6. Multinational. **Publication:** *Medical Engineering and Physics*. Journal. Price: $652.00/year in North Central and South America; L410.00 rest of world. ISSN: 1350-4533. Advertising: accepted ■ *Physics in Medicine and Biology*, monthly. Journal. Price: $1,080.00/year in U.S., Canada, and Mexico; L575.00/year for rest of world. ISSN: 0031-9155. Advertising: accepted ■ *Physiological Measurement*, quarterly. Journal. Price: $297.00/year in U.S., Canada, and Mexico; L173.00/year for rest of world. Advertising: accepted ■ *Scope*, quarterly. Magazine. Price: free. ISSN: 0964-9565. Circulation: 2,400. Advertising: accepted. **Formerly:** Industry of Physical Sciences in Medicine.

INTERAMERICAN COLLEGE OF PHYSICIANS AND SURGEONS (ICPS)
url: http://www.icps.org
915 Broadway, Ste. 1105
New York, NY 10010
Dr. Rene F. Rodriguez, Pres.
PH: (212)777-3642
FX: (212)505-7984
Description: Physicians in countries of the Americas. Encourages understanding and communication among members concerning all aspects of medical practice. Promotes health education in Hispanic communities in the Western Hemisphere. Maintains library of Spanish language medical books. **Founded:** 1979. **Membership:** 4000. **Staff:** 1. Multinational. **Languages:** English, Spanish. **Publication:** *Interamerican Medical Directory*, biennial ∎ *Medico Interamericano*, monthly.

INTERAMERICAN HEART FOUNDATION (IAHF)
e-mail: beatrizc@ix.netcom.com
url: http://www.interamericanhcart.org
7272 Greenville Ave.
Dallas, TX 75231-4596
Beatriz Champagne, Ph.D., Exec.Dir.
PH: (214)706-1218
FX: (214)373-0268
Description: The InterAmerican Heart Program was created in September, 1992 under the auspices of the International Society and Federation of Cardiology with the support of the American Heart Association, the InterAmerican Society of Cardiology and heart foundations and societies throughout the American continent. **Founded:** 1992. **Membership:** 31. Multinational. **Languages:** English, Portuguese. Formerly International Cardiology Foundation; (1998) Interamerican Heart Cardiology Foundation.

INTERAMERICAN MEDICAL AND HEALTH ASSOCIATION (IMHA)
3025 St. James Dr.
Boca Raton, FL 33434
Dr. Maurizio Luca-Moretti, Pres.
PH: (407)483-6573
FX: (407)483-3239
Description: Academicians of national academies of medicine, deans of medical facilities, and professors of medical science. Promotes the work of biomedical and health scientists and the effectiveness of science in the promotion of human welfare. Facilitates networking among members and their institutions. Conducts research programs on medical and public health issues; current research focuses on nutrition and AIDS. **Founded:** 1989. **Membership:** 4000. **Staff:** 6. **Languages:** English. **Budget:** $25,000. **Publication:** *Journal of the Interamerican Medical and Health Association*, 3/year. Price: $60.00/year for institutions in North America; $60.00/year for insititutions in Europe and Japan; $30.00/year for individuals in North America; $30.00/year for individuals in Europe and Japan. ISSN: 1060-3085. Circulation: 4,000. Advertising: accepted.

INTERCHURCH MEDICAL ASSISTANCE (IMA)
e-mail: ima@ecunet.org
url: http://www.interchurch.org
College Ave. at Blue Ridge
Box 429
New Windsor, MD 21776
Paul Derstine, Exec.Dir.
PH: (410)635-8720
FX: (410)635-8726
Description: Denominational-founded autonomous organization for the solicitation, collection, and distribution of pharmaceutical, medical, dental, and hospital supplies for use in the overseas charity medical programs of American Protestant churches, relief agencies, and other American charitable organizations. **Founded:** 1961. **Membership:** 12. **Staff:** 7. Multinational. **Languages:** English. **Budget:** $15,500,000. **Publication:** *Interchurch Medical Newsletter*, quarterly ∎ Annual Report, annual.

INTERGOVERNMENTAL HEALTH POLICY PROJECT (IHPP)
e-mail: dick.merritt@ncsl.org
444 N. Capital St. Ste 515
Washington, DC 20001
Richard E. Merritt, Dir.
PH: (202)624-8698
FX: (202)737-1069
Description: Provides information on state health legislation and programs to state executive officials, legislators, legislative staff, and others. Serves as information clearinghouse; responds to specific information requests on state programs. Compiles statistics. Offers a customized legislative tracking service to customers. **Founded:** 1979. **Staff:** 10. **Languages:** English. **Budget:** $1,500,000. **Publication:** *State Health Notes*, 24/year. Newsletter. Price: $297.00. Circulation: 2,000 ∎ Newsletter, bimonthly ∎ Newsletter, 10/year ∎ Monograph, annual. Summarizes state legislation relating to health care.

INTERNATIONAL ACADEMY FOR CHILD BRAIN DEVELOPMENT (IACBD)
e-mail: chipm@earthlink.net
url: http://www.iahp.org
8801 Stenton Ave.
Wyndmoor, PA 19038
Neil Harvey, Ph.D., Sec.
PH: (215)233-2050
FX: (215)233-3940
Description: Professionals from a variety of disciplines including physicians, psychologists, and anthropologists, who are interested in the physical and psychological processes involved in child brain development. Seeks to gain recognition for the study of child brain development as a discipline in itself and establish criteria for the certification of child brain developmentalists. Provides a forum for presentation of scholarly works in the field; offers courses in child-brain development; conducts field research and prepares reports of results. **Founded:** 1985. Multinational. **Languages:** English, French. For-Profit. **Publication:** *The In-Report*, quarterly. Journal.

INTERNATIONAL ACADEMY OF GNATHOLOGY-AMERICAN SECTION (IAG)
1428 Medical-Dental Blvd.
Seattle, WA 98101
Dr. Olin Loomis, Contact
PH: (206)624-2535
FX: (206)622-2722
Description: Dentists and educators interested in the science of gnathology. (Gnathology is the science that treats the biology of chewing and the jaws and cheeks as related to the rest of the body.) Areas of concern include morphology, anatomy, psychology, physiology, pathology, and therapy of the mouth. **Founded:** 1964. **Membership:** 3000. Multinational. **Languages:** English. **Publication:** *Journal of Gnathology*, annual.

INTERNATIONAL ACADEMY OF HEALTH CARE PROFESSIONALS (IAHCP)
70 Glen Cove Rd., Ste. 209
Roslyn Heights, NY 11577
Dr. Henry H. Reiter, Pres.
PH: (516)621-0620
Description: Nurses, psychologists, social workers, and medical and health care professionals. Provides for educational exchange among members. Offers research and educational materials to Third World health care institutions. **Founded:** 1984. **Membership:** 39. **Staff:** 3. Multinational. **Languages:** English. **Publication:** *Membership Brochure* ∎ Newsletter, periodic.

INTERNATIONAL ACADEMY OF MYODONTICS (IAM)
c/o Harry N. Cooperman, D.D.S.
800 Airport Blvd.
Doylestown, PA 18901
Harry N. Cooperman, D.D.S., Pres.

PH: (215)345-1149
FX: (215)609-2588
Description: Dentists who specialize in the treatment of head and neck syndromes that cause dental or oral malfunction. Works with physicians and dentists in the field of myodontics, especially those working on the treatment of Cooperman-Muira Syndrome, also known as uvula-tongue malposture syndrome. **Founded:** 1970. **Membership:** 1100. Multinational. **Regional Groups:** 2. **Languages:** English.

INTERNATIONAL ACADEMY OF MYODONTICS, OCEANIC CHAPTER (IAM)
57 Darlinghurst Rd.
Potts Point
Sydney, NSW 2011, Australia
Dr. Harry Rich, Pres.
PH: 61 2 3585563
Description: Practicing dental surgeons organized to study and apply theory and practical use of myodontic principles. **Founded:** 1985. **Membership:** 6. Multinational. **Languages:** English, German.

INTERNATIONAL ACADEMY OF ORAL MEDICINE AND TOXICOLOGY (IAOMT)
PO Box 608531
Orlando, FL 32860-8531
Michael F. Ziff, D.D.S., Exec.Dir.
PH: (407)298-2450
FX: (407)298-3075
Description: Dentists, physicians, and medical scientists. Encourages, sponsors, and disseminates scientific research on the biocompatibility of materials used in dentistry. Offers educational programs; maintains speakers' bureau. **Founded:** 1984. **Membership:** 310. **Staff:** 1. Multinational. **National Groups:** 6. **Languages:** English. **Publication:** *Bio-Probe Newsletter*, bimonthly. Review of scientific literature and legislative activities. Price: included in membership dues ■ *IN VIVO*, quarterly. Newsletter. Available to members only. Price: included in membership dues ■ Membership Directory. Indexed alphabetically and geographically.

INTERNATIONAL ACADEMY OF SPORTS VISION (NASV)
e-mail: nasv@mindspring.com
url: http://www.al.com/nasv/
200 S. Progress Ave.
Harrisburg, PA 17109
Dr. A. I. Garner, Exec.Dir.
PH: (717)652-8080
FX: (717)652-8878
Description: Optometrists and opthalmologists; athletic trainers, team physicians, coaches, and students; educational institutions and eyewear manufacturers. Purpose is to: provide comprehensive vision care for individuals active in sports and fitness programs; foster the promotion and advancement of research, development, and education in the field; facilitate the design, development, and fitting of both protective and corrective contact lenses and eyewear for athletes; advance and enhance the role of the sports specialist to the public through a public relations program. Acts as a forum for the discussion and exchange of information in the areas of developmental vision, vision training, and therapy. Offers referral services. Bestows the Blanton Collier Award; maintains speakers' bureau; compiles statistics. **Founded:** 1984. **Membership:** 1000. **Staff:** 5. Multinational. **Languages:** English. **Budget:** $125,000. **Publication:** *Journal of the International Academy of Sports Vision* ■ *SportsVision*, quarterly. Magazine ■ *Update*, quarterly ■ Audiotapes ■ Membership Directory, annual ■ Videos. **Formerly:** (1991) National Academy of Sports Vision.

INTERNATIONAL ACUPUNCTURE INSTITUTE
301 Nathan Rd., Rm. 1304
Kowloon, Hong Kong
Dr. Lo Chi Kwong, Dir.
PH: 852 2 7711066
FX: 852 2 3888836

Description: Acupuncturists and other health care professionals; individuals with an interest in acupuncture. Promotes effective practice of acupuncture; devises and maintains standards of practice. Conducts research and educational programs. **Founded:** 1978. **Membership:** 700. **National Groups:** 2. **Languages:** Chinese, English. **Publication:** *Clinical Acupuncture* (in English). Book. Price: $20.00.

INTERNATIONAL AGENCY FOR RESEARCH ON CANCER (IARC)
(Centre International de Recherche sur le Cancer)
e-mail: lastname@iarc.fr
url: http://www.iarc.fr
150, cours Albert Thomas
F-69372 Lyon, France
Dr. Paul Kleihues, Dir.
PH: 33 472738485
FX: 33 472738575
Description: Cancer research arm of the World Health Organization. Representatives of nations involved in international collaboration in cancer research. Generates and disseminates information on the causes and prevention of cancer; conducts research in the field of cancer epidemiology, biostatistics, and environmental carcinogenesis. Evaluates and examines populations with unusually high or low frequencies of cancer and identifies the role of environmental factors including cultural and dietary habits and chemicals. Assists governments in cancer control programs. Maintains laboratories and collaborates with scientists working in national laboratories. Organizes training courses; compiles statistics. **Founded:** 1965. **Membership:** 16. **Staff:** 180. Multinational. **Languages:** English, French. **Budget:** $17,000,000. **Publication:** *Biennial Report* (in English and French). Circulation: 4,000. Advertising: not accepted ■ *Directory of On-Going Research in Cancer Epidemiology* (in English), biennial ■ *IAR Cancer Disc CD-ROM*, annual ■ *Scientific Publications Series* (in English), periodic. ISSN: 0300-5085 ■ *Technical Report Series* (in English and French), periodic ■ Monographs (in English), 3/year. ISSN: 0250-9555.

INTERNATIONAL ALOE SCIENCE COUNCIL (IASC)
e-mail: iasc@airmail.net
url: http://www.iasc.org
415 E. Airport Fwy, No. 365
Irving, TX 75062
Gene Hale, Mgr.Dir.
PH: (972)258-8772
FX: (972)258-8777
Description: Manufacturers and marketers of foods, drugs, and cosmetics containing gel of the aloe vera plant. Goals are: to provide scientific research for support of product claims; to educate members on the plant and its products and uses; to act as a liaison for government agency regulations on aloe vera business. **Founded:** 1981. **Membership:** 175. **Staff:** 2. Multinational. **National Groups:** 1. **Languages:** English. **Budget:** $175,000. **Publication:** *Inside Aloe*, monthly. Journal. Price: included in membership dues. Circulation: 1,500. Advertising: accepted. **Formerly:** (1989) National Aloe Science Council.

INTERNATIONAL ANATOMICAL NOMENCLATURE COMMITTEE (IANC)
Department of Anatomy
UMDS
Guy's Campus
London Bridge SE1 9RT, England
Prof. Murray Brookes, Hon.Sec.
PH: 44 181 8866134
FX: 44 181 3720941
Description: Anatomists, cytologists, embryologists, zoologists, and anthropologists. Works to establish and standardize structural and developmental terminology in the science fields. **Founded:** 1950. **Membership:** 400. **Staff:** 3. Multinational. **Languages:** English. **Budget:** L5,000. **Publication:** *Nomina Anatomica* (in English and Latin), quinquennial. Book. Contains anatomical word lists. (ISBN: 0-443-04085-0). Price: L30.00 3000. Adverti-

sing: not accepted ■ *Nomina Embryologica* (in English and Latin), quinquennial. Book ■ *Nomina Histologica* (in English and Latin), quinquennial. Book.

INTERNATIONAL ANESTHESIA RESEARCH SOCIETY (IARS)

2 Summit Park Dr., Ste. 140
Cleveland, OH 44131-2553
Anne F. Maggiore, Exec.Dir.
PH: (216)642-1124
FX: (216)642-1127
Description: Anesthesiologists and other doctors of medicine and dentistry in 50 countries interested in the specialty of anesthesiology; associate members are registered nurses, physician assistants, and respiratory therapists. Fosters progress and research in all phases of anesthesiology. **Founded:** 1922. **Membership:** 15000. **Staff:** 5. Multinational. **Languages:** English. **Publication:** *Anesthesia & Analgesia*, monthly. Journal. Contains research articles and clinical reports on anesthesia and anesthesia-related subjects. Includes book reviews and employment listings. Price: $110.00/year for members; $150.00/year for nonmember institutions. ISSN: 0003-2999. Circulation: 21,000. Advertising: accepted. Alternate Formats: microform.

INTERNATIONAL ASSOCIATION OF AGRICULTURAL MEDICINE AND RURAL HEALTH (IAAMRH)

(Association Internationale de Medecine Agricole et de Sante Rurale)
e-mail: sakuchp@valley.or.jp
Saku Central Hospital
197, Usuda
Minamisaku-gun
Nagano 384-03, Japan
Shosui Matsushima, M.D., Acting Sec.Gen.
PH: 81 267 823131
FX: 81 267 829602
Description: Physicians, nurses, paramedics, and other health care professionals in 40 countries. Studies problems of agricultural medicine and rural health around the world. Seeks means of averting the detrimental effects of certain agricultural and rural work conditions. **Founded:** 1961. **Membership:** 450. Multinational. **National Groups:** 4. **Languages:** English, French. **Publication:** *Agricultural Medicine and Rural Health* (in English), semiannual. Circulation: 500. Advertising: accepted ■ *Journal*, quarterly.

INTERNATIONAL ASSOCIATION OF CANCER REGISTRIES (IACR)

(Association Internationale des Registres du Cancer)
e-mail: whelan@iacr.fr
url: http://www.dep.iarc.fr/resour/iacr/iacr.htm
150, cours Albert Thomas
F-69372 Lyon, France
Dr. D.M. Parkin, Deputy Sec.
PH: 33 472 738485
FX: 33 472 738575
Description: Population-based cancer registries in 100 countries. Encourages the development and application of cancer registration and morbidity techniques to studies of defined populations. Endeavors to increase global awareness of the importance of producing accurate and comparable morbidity and mortality data which can be used to generate etiological hypotheses for cancer and as a basis for epidemiological studies, health planning, and other aspects of cancer control. **Founded:** 1966. **Membership:** 410. Multinational. **Languages:** English. **Publication:** *Cancer Incidence in Five Continents* (in English), 5/year. Book. Price: $198.00 Vol. VII. Advertising: not accepted. Alternate Formats: diskette ■ *International Association of Cancer Registries' Newsletter*, biennial.

INTERNATIONAL ASSOCIATION OF CANCER VICTORS AND FRIENDS (IACVF)

e-mail: iacvf@inetworld.net
7740 W. Manchester, Ste. 203
Playa del Rey, CA 90293
Ann Cinquita, Exec.Sec.
PH: (310)822-5032
FX: (310)822-4193
Description: Encourages independent research on cancer therapies and disseminates information on "nontoxic" chemotherapies. Works directly with cancer patients providing one-on-one services. Offers educational programs on topics including carcinogens in air, food, and water and nutrition in relation to cancer. **Founded:** 1963. **Membership:** 4000. **Staff:** 2. Multinational. **National Groups:** 10. **Languages:** English. **Budget:** $50,000. **Publication:** *Cancer Victors Journal*, quarterly. Provides news on nontoxic cancer treatments and breakthroughs in cancer research; includes studies on carcinogenic conditions. Price: included in membership dues. ISSN: 0891-0766. Circulation: 5,000. Advertising: accepted ■ Audiotapes. Advertising: accepted ■ Books ■ Pamphlets ■ Reprints. **Formerly:** (1985) International Association of Cancer Victims and Friends.

INTERNATIONAL ASSOCIATION FOR CHILD AND ADOLESCENT PSYCHIATRY AND ALLIED PROFESSIONS (IACAPAP)

e-mail: donald.cohen@yale.edu
PO Box 207900
New Haven, CT 06520-7900
Donald J. Cohen, M.D., Pres.
PH: (203)785-5759
FX: (203)785-7402
Description: National societies; others in the field of child and adolescent psychiatry and allied professions. Promotes collaboration among related professions including pediatrics, psychology, public health, social work, education, nursing, and others involved in research and practice in the field of child and adolescent psychiatry. **Founded:** 1948. **Membership:** 50. Multinational. **National Groups:** 50. **Languages:** English, French. **Publication:** *IACAPAP Newsletter*, quarterly ■ Monograph, semiannual. **Also Known As:** Association Internationale de Psychiatrie de l'Enfant et de l'Adolescent et des Professions Associees. **Formerly:** (1978) International Association for Child Psychiatry and Allied Professions.

INTERNATIONAL ASSOCIATION OF CORONERS AND MEDICAL EXAMINERS (IACME)

PO Box 899
Mansfield, LA 71052
Jack Grindle, M.D., Contact
PH: (318)872-0516
FX: (318)872-4495
Description: Educational seminar involving all aspects of death investigation such as pathology, autopsy, crime scene investigation, mass disasters and anthropology. Offers continuing medical education credit. **Founded:** 1938. **Membership:** 335. Multinational. **Languages:** English. **Publication:** *RECAP*, quarterly. Newsletter. Price: included in membership dues. Advertising: not accepted.

INTERNATIONAL ASSOCIATION FOR DANCE MEDICINE AND SCIENCE (IADMS)

e-mail: iadms@aol.com
2555 Andrew Dr.
Superior, CO 80027
PH: (303)494-9450
FX: (393)494-9450
Description: Serves as a forum for reeducation, promotion of research and public services in the field of dance medicine and science. Committed to providing continuing education for the dance and medical communities as well as the public regarding appropriate training for dance. Offers educational programs. **Founded:** 1990. **Membership:** 390. Multinational. **Budget:** $20,000.

INTERNATIONAL ASSOCIATION FOR DENTAL RESEARCH (IADR)

e-mail: research@iadr.com
url: http://medhlp.netvsa.net/iadr/iadr.htm
1619 Duke St.
Alexandria, VA 22314
John J. Clarkson, Ph.D., Exec.Dir.
PH: (703)548-0066
FX: (703)548-1883
Description: Individuals engaged or interested in advancing research in the various aspects of dental and related sciences. Founded: 1920. Membership: 9500. Staff: 14. Multinational. Languages: English. Budget: $2,500,000. Publication: *Advances in Dental Research*, periodic. Journal. Covers developments in dental research and the chemistry, biology, and function of the oral cavity. Also includes conference proceedings. Circulation: 1,100. Advertising: accepted. Alternate Formats: microform ■ *Critical Reviews in Oral Biology and Medicine*, quarterly ■ *IADReports and Dental Research*, quarterly. Newsletter. Includes calender of events. Price: included in membership dues. Circulation: 11,000. Advertising: accepted ■ *Journal of Dental Research*, monthly. Disseminates new information and knowledge on all sciences relevant to dentistry, the oral cavity, and associated structures in health and disease ■ *Journal of Oral Implantology*, quarterly ■ *Program and Abstracts*, annual ■ *Special Care in Dentistry*, bimonthly.

INTERNATIONAL ASSOCIATION OF DENTAL STUDENTS (IADS)

e-mail: general@fdi.org.uk
url: http://www.unite.co.uk/customers/iads/
7 Carlisle St.
London W1V 5RG, England
PH: 44 171 9357852
FX: 44 171 4860183
Description: Coordinating body between National Association of Dental students. Association members in 52 countries. Promotes international contact among dental students; facilitates exchange of students between member countries; develops international programs. Organises annual concerts. Conducts competitions. Founded: 1951. Membership: 52. Multinational. National Groups: 47. Languages: English. Publication: *ADS Newsletter*, semiannual. Circulation: 1,200. Advertising: accepted ■ *IADS Exchange Guide* (in English). Manual. Advertising: not accepted. Alternate Formats: online.

INTERNATIONAL ASSOCIATION FOR MATERNAL AND NEONATAL HEALTH (IAMENEH)

e-mail: lamaneh@span.ch
url: http://www.llmatweb.hcuge.ch/lamaneh
16, chemin Grande Gorge
CH-1255 Veyrier, Switzerland
Mrs. Gerda M. Santschi, Exec.Sec.
PH: 41 22 7840658
FX: 41 22 7840658
Description: Medical professionals and individuals interested in improving maternal and neonatal care throughout the world, especially at the primary health care level. Objectives are to: promote and finance basic and applied research in the field of human reproduction and publish and distribute the findings; improve the standards of medical and paramedical care in the field of obstetrics and gynecology; foster and finance research programs on social problems related to maternal and perinatal health; purpose curriculum on improving maternal and perinatal health to higher education institutions; disseminate scientific information concerning women, mothers, fetuses, newborns, and children. Supports projects to improve maternal and neonatal care in developing countries. Founded: 1977. Membership: 4500. Staff: 2. Multinational. National Groups: 39. Languages: English, French. Budget: $300,000. Publication: *High Risk Mothers and Newborns - Detection, Management and Prevention*. Book. Circulation: 2,000. Advertising: accepted ■ *Maternal and Child Care in Developing Countries - Assessment, Promotion and Implementation*. Book ■ *Maternal and Infant Mortality*. Book ■ *Practi-cal Issues in Safe Motherhood - Proceedings of the Vth International Congress for Maternal and Neonatal Health of IAMANEH* ■ *Primary Maternal and Neonatal Health - A Global Concern*. Book ■ *Proceedings of Congress*, triennial ■ *Proceedings of Workshop*, annual ■ Annual Report. Formerly: (1994) Mother and Child International.

INTERNATIONAL ASSOCIATION OF MEDICAL LABORATORY TECHNOLOGISTS (IAMLT)

(Association Internationale des Technologistes de Laboratoire Medical)
url: http://www.iamlt.se
Adolf Fredriks Kyrkogata 11
S-111 37 Stockholm, Sweden
Margareta Haag, Exec.Dir.
PH: 46 8 103031
FX: 46 8 109061
Description: Member of the World Health Organization. National societies united to provide a means of communication among medical laboratory technologists in 39 countries. Promotes the continued education of health laboratory workers; plans curriculum for courses in health laboratory technology and management. Advises governments and governmental agencies on these matters and on validation of examinations leading to qualifications in medical laboratory subjects. Maintains travel and development fund. Founded: 1954. Membership: 39. Staff: 1. Multinational. State Groups: 39. Languages: English, French. Budget: 105,000 SFr. Publication: *Curriculum for a Course in Health Safety* (in English). Journal. Price: 13.00 SFr/pack of five. Advertising: not accepted ■ *International Directory of Medical Laboratory Science Education* (in English), periodic. Details medical lab education worldwide. Price: $40.00 includes postage. Advertising: accepted ■ *MedTec International* (in English), semiannual. Journal. Covers information for medical laboratory technologists. Price: NZ$25.00/year. Circulation: 17,000. Advertising: accepted.

INTERNATIONAL ASSOCIATION FOR MEDICAL RESEARCH AND CULTURAL EXCHANGE (AIRMEC)

(Association Internationale pour la Recherche Medicale et les Echanges Culturels)
2, blvd. Pershing
F-75017 Paris, France
PH: 33 1 55379015
FX: 33 1 55379040
Description: Medical and pharmaceutical professionals. Fosters and participates in the development of medical research. Initiates scientific exchange among members throughout the world. Organizes activities such as conferences, conventions, and workshops to facilitate medico-pharmaceutical comparison. Promotes and contributes to postgraduate medical and pharmaceutical study. Founded: 1956. Membership: 2000. Multinational. Languages: French. Publication: *Medecine d'Afrique Noire*, monthly.

INTERNATIONAL ASSOCIATION OF OCULAR SURGEONS (IAOS)

e-mail: iaos@aol.com
4711 Golf Rd., Ste. 408
Skokie, IL 60076
Randall T. Bellows, M.D., Dir.
PH: (847)568-1500
TF: 800621-4002
FX: (847)568-1527
Description: A division of the American Society of Contemporary Ophthalmology. Seeks to develop a global community of ophthalmic surgeons who examine and deliberate on all aspects of ocular surgery; encourage information exchange among members; disseminate information about contemporary diagnostic and surgical procedures. Founded: 1981. Membership: 900. Multinational. Languages: English. Publication: *Annals of Ophthalmology*. Continuing medical education for ophthalmologists. Price: $120.00. ISSN: 1079-4794. Circulation: 2,500. Advertising: accepted.

INTERNATIONAL ASSOCIATION OF ORAL AND MAXILLOFACIAL SURGEONS (IAOMS)
Medical College of Virginia
Box 410, MCV
Richmond, VA 23298
Dr. Daniel M. Laskin, Exec.Dir.
PH: (804)828-8515
FX: (804)828-1753
Description: Oral and maxillofacial surgeons in 63 countries promoting the science of oral surgery. Sponsors educational programs. **Founded:** 1962. **Membership:** 3000. **Staff:** 1. Multinational. **National Groups:** 63. **Languages:** English. **Publication:** *I.A.O.M.S.*, semiannual. Newsletter ▪ *International Journal of Oral and Maxillofacial Surgery*, bimonthly. Advertising: accepted ▪ *Registry of Fellows* ▪ *Rules and Regulations of the IAOMS.* **Foreign language name:** Association Internationale de Chirurgie Buccale et Maxillo-Faciale.

INTERNATIONAL ASSOCIATION OF PAEDIATRIC DENTISTRY (IAPD)
e-mail: m.hector@mds.qmw.ac.uk
Dept. of Child Dental Health
London Hospital Medical College Dental School
Turner St.
London E1 2AD, England
Dr. M.P. Hector, Hon.Sec./Treas.
PH: 44 171 3777000
FX: 44 171 3777058
Description: Dentists, dental and medical libraries, bookshops, and research institutions in 36 countries. Encourages research and foster progress in the field of children's dental health. Provides a forum for the exchange of information concerning children's dentistry worldwide. **Founded:** 1969. **Membership:** 700. Multinational. **Languages:** English, French. **Publication:** *International Journal of Paediatric Dentistry.*, quarterly ▪ *Newsletter*, semiannual.

INTERNATIONAL ASSOCIATION OF PARENTS AND PROFESSIONALS FOR SAFE ALTERNATIVES IN CHILDBIRTH (NAPSAC)
Rte. 1, Box 646
Marble Hill, MO 63764-9725
Lee Stewart, Pres.
PH: (573)238-2010
Description: Parents, midwives, physicians, nurses, health officials, social workers, and childbirth educators in 10 countries who are "dedicated to exploring, examining, implementing, and establishing family-centered childbirth programs which meet the needs of families as well as provide the safe aspects of medical science."Promotes education concerning the principles of natural childbirth; facilitates communication and cooperation among parents, medical professionals, and childbirth educators; assists in the establishment of maternity and childbearing centers. Provides educational opportunities to parents and parents-to-be, enabling them to assume more personal responsibility for pregnancy, childbirth, infant care, and child rearing. **Founded:** 1975. **Membership:** 1000. **Staff:** 2. Multinational. **National Groups:** 10. **Languages:** English. **Budget:** $50,000. **Publication:** *Childbirth Activitists Handbook.* Price: $12.95. Circulation: 1,500. Advertising: not accepted ▪ *Emergency Childbirth.* Price: $12.95 ▪ *Five Standards for Safe Childbearing* ▪ *NAPSAC Directory of Alternative Birth Services and Consumer Guide*, biennial. Lists midwives, birth centers, noninterventive physicians, and educators for safe alternatives in childbirth. Price: $7.95/copy. Circulation: 500. Advertising: accepted ▪ *NAPSAC News*, quarterly. Newsletter. Includes association news, book reviews, and calendar of events. Price: included in membership dues. ISSN: 0192-1223. Circulation: 2,000. Advertising: accepted ▪ *Safe Alternatives in Childbirth.* Price: $9.95 ▪ *Transitions.* Price: $10.95 ▪ *21st Century Obstetrics Now.* Price: $14.95/2 vol. **Formerly:** (1979) National Association of Parents and Professionals for Safe Alternatives in Childbirth.

INTERNATIONAL ASSOCIATION FOR THE STUDY OF LUNG CANCER (IASLC)
e-mail: hansenhh@rh.dk
The Finsen Institute/Rigshospitalet
Department of Oncology - 5074
Blegdamsvej 9
DK-2100 Copenhagen, Denmark
Heine H. Hansen, M.D.
PH: 45 35454090
FX: 45 31356906
Description: Oncologists promoting research and treatment of lung cancer. Collects and disseminates information; conducts periodic seminars and symposia. **Founded:** 1974. **Membership:** 1100. Multinational. **Languages:** English. **Publication:** *IASLC Membership Directory*, annual ▪ *Lung Cancer*, bimonthly.

INTERNATIONAL ASSOCIATION OF FORENSIC NURSING (IAFN)
e-mail: iafn@slackinc.com
url: http://www.members.aol.com/COCFCI/IAFN.html
6900 Grove Rd.
Thorofare, NJ 08086
Debi Maines, Exec.Dir.
PH: (609)848-8356
FX: (609)848-5274
Description: Sexual assault nurse examiners, forensic nurse investigators, educators, researcher consultants, nurse coroners, nurse attorneys and emergency/trauma nurses. Works to develop, promote and disseminate information about the science of forensic nursing. Sets standards of practice; promotes the exchange of ideas; participates in research projects; encourages a holistic approach to victims of violent crime; develops educational programs at the undergraduate, graduate and postgraduate levels; protects the legal, civil and human rights of victims, perpetrators and families. **Founded:** 1990. **Membership:** 1100. **Staff:** 3. Multinational. **Languages:** English. **Budget:** $100,000.

INTERNATIONAL ASSOCIATION OF FORENSIC TOXICOLOGISTS (TIAFT)
e-mail: spiehluaa@aol.com
url: http://www.cbft.auipd.it/tiaft/
422 Tustin
Newport Beach, CA 92663
Vina Spiehler, Sec.
PH: (714)642-0574
FX: (714)642-2852
Description: Police, medical examiners, coroners, pharmacists, pharmacologists, toxicologists, hospital and lab workers and individuals actively engaged in analytical toxicology or allied areas. Promotes cooperation of effort among members and encourages research in forensic toxicology. Organization applicants must be recommended by two TIAFT sponsors and approved by the Regional Representative of a TIAFT officer. **Founded:** 1965. **Membership:** 1200. Multinational. **Languages:** English.

INTERNATIONAL ASSOCIATION OF HOLISTIC MEDICINE
BernaDean University
21757 Devonshire, No. 16
Chatsworth, CA 91311
Adele Kadans, Pres.
PH: (702)880-4247
TF: 800542-3792
FX: (702)878-3837
Description: Works to: establish standards for public retreats for the study of health practices; operate health havens as pilot studies; approve and supervise retreats operated by others. **Founded:** 1954. Multinational. **Languages:** English. **Publication:** *Holistic Health Quarterly.* Journal. **Formerly:** (1998) Holistic Health Havens.

INTERNATIONAL ASSOCIATION OF MEDICAL EQUIPMENT REMARKETERS (IAMER)
5620 Highway 78
Sachse, TX 75048
Tom Norman, Pres.
PH: (214)414-3038
FX: (214)414-6348
Description: Dealers, lessors, refurbishers, and services of medical equipment. Promotes ethical business practices and delivers high quality previously owned medical equipment. Offers educational and research programs and maintains a speakers bureau. **Founded:** 1994. **Membership:** 150. **Staff:** 2. Multinational. **Budget:** $200,000.

INTERNATIONAL ASSOCIATION OF ORTHODONTICS (IAO)
e-mail: worldheadquarters@iaortho.com
url: http://www.iaortho.com/index.htm
1100 Lake St., No. 240
Oak Park, IL 60301
Joanna Carey, Exec.Dir.
PH: (708)445-0320
TF: 800447-8770
FX: (708)445-0321
Description: Dentists. Promotes the study and dissemination of information on the cause, control, treatment, and prevention of malocclusion of the teeth; facilitates exchange of ideas and experiences, based on a biomechanical approach, between the various fields of dentistry related to orthodontics. **Founded:** 1961. **Membership:** 1800. **Staff:** 3. Multinational. **Regional Groups:** 15. **Languages:** English. **Budget:** $350,000. **Publication:** *IAO Directory of Orthodontic Suppliers*, annual. Price: included in membership dues; $10.00 for nonmembers. Circulation: 1,900 ▪ *IAO Straight Talk*, monthly. Newsletter. Provides information on membership activities. Price: included in membership dues; $15.00/year for nonmembers. Circulation: 2,200. Advertising: not accepted ▪ *International Association of Orthodontics – Directory of Members*, annual. Price: included in membership dues; $15.00 for nonmembers. Circulation: 1,900 ▪ *Journal of General Orthodontics*, quarterly. Contains clinical articles on orthodontics, self-assessment, troubleshooting, and new products. Price: $40.00/year. ISSN: 1048-1990. Circulation: 3,500. Advertising: accepted. **Formerly:** International Academy of Orthodontics.

INTERNATIONAL ASSOCIATION OF PHYSICIANS IN AIDS CARE (IAPAC)
e-mail: iapac@aol.com
url: http://www.iapac.org
225 W. Washington, Ste. 2200
Chicago, IL 60606
Gordon Nary, Pres.
PH: (312)419-7295
FX: (312)419-7160
Description: Provides educational programs to caregivers, physicians and patients. Promotes public policy reform and research. **Founded:** 1995. **Membership:** 7500. **Staff:** 8. Multinational. **Languages:** English, Spanish. **Budget:** $1,500,000. Absorbed (1995) Physicians Assoc. for AIDS Care.

INTERNATIONAL ATHEROSCLEROSIS SOCIETY (IAS)
e-mail: ajackson@bcm.tmc.edu
url: http://athero.med.bcm.tmc.edu/ias
6550 Fannin, No. 1423
Houston, TX 77030
Ann Sterens Jackson, Exec.Dir.
PH: (713)797-9620
FX: (713)797-9507
Description: Scientists and other professionals involved in research in the field of atherosclerosis; corporations and firms supporting aims of the IAS. Promotes the advancement of science, research, and teaching in the field of atherosclerosis throughout the world. (Atherosclerosis is a form of arteriosclerosis characterized by the deposition of fatty substances in and fibrosis of the inner layer of the arteries.) Advocates an interdisciplinary approach to the study of atherosclerosis and related diseases. Facilitates international communication and exchange of knowledge among scientists in the field. Assists in the organization of exchange visits among scientists at various research centers. Fosters and encourages young researchers by arranging contacts, and offering travel support to world gatherings in the field. Coordinates activities in atherosclerosis research. **Founded:** 1979. **Membership:** 7835. **Staff:** 3. Multinational. **National Groups:** 36. **Languages:** English. **Publication:** *Proceedings of Symposia*, triennial ▪ *Roster of Member Societies* ▪ Newsletter, semiannual.

INTERNATIONAL BILLING ASSOCIATION
7315 Wisconsin Ave., Ste. 424-East
Bethesda, MD 20814
Sanford J. Hill, Pres.
PH: (301)961-8680
Description: Companies who provide third paty medical billing services.

INTERNATIONAL BRAIN RESEARCH ORGANIZATION (IBRO)
(Organisation Internationale de Recherche sur le Cerveau)
e-mail: ibro@pratique.fr
51, Blvd. de Montmorency
F-75016 Paris, France
Dr. David Ottoson, Sec.Gen.
PH: 33 1 46479292
FX: 33 1 45206006
Description: Scientists working in neuroanatomy, neuroendocrinology, the behavioral sciences, neurocommunications and biophysics, brain pathology, and clinical and health-related sciences. Works to promote international cooperation in research on the nervous system. Sponsors fellowships, exchange of scientific workers, and traveling teams of instructors to supplement local teachings. Organizes international neuroscience symposia and workshops. **Founded:** 1960. **Membership:** 35000. Multinational. **Publication:** *Directory of Members*, periodic ▪ *Neuroscience*, bimonthly ▪ *News*, 3/year.

INTERNATIONAL BUNDLE BRANCH BLOCK ASSOCIATION (IBBBA)
6631 W. 83rd St.
Los Angeles, CA 90045-2899
Rita Kurtz Lewis, Exec.Dir.
PH: (310)670-9132

INTERNATIONAL BUREAU FOR EPILEPSY (IBE)
(Bureau International pour l'Epilepsie)
e-mail: ibe@xs4all.nl
Postbus 21
NL-2100 AA Heemstede, Netherlands
Mr. Richard Holmes, Pres.
PH: 31 23 5291019
FX: 31 23 5470119
Description: National organizations and individuals interested in the medical, social, and scientific aspects of epilepsy. Focuses on aspects of daily life with epilepsy. Facilitates exchange of information and experience regarding the care of persons with epilepsy. Provides material on how to organize and finance nonmedical societies. Organizes training sessions. Works to build an international film library on epilepsy. **Founded:** 1961. **Membership:** 51. **Staff:** 2. Multinational. **National Groups:** 51. **Languages:** English. **Budget:** $100,000. **Publication:** *A Manual for Epilepsy Self-Help Groups* ▪ *Epilepsy Education Manual* ▪ *Epilepsy Passport*. Handbook ▪ *International Epilepsy News* (in English and Japanese), quarterly. Magazine. Contains information on epilepsy. Price: $10.00/year. ISSN: 1381-0189. Circulation: 19,000. Advertising: not accepted. Also Cited As: *I.E. News* ▪ *The Recommended Reading List on Epilepsy and Employment* ▪ *Vocational Scenarios*. Manual ▪ Annual Report.

INTERNATIONAL CENTER FOR THE HEALTH SCIENCES (ICHS)
Barracks Hill
PO Box 4744
Charlottesville, VA 22905-4744
Warren E. Grupe, MD, Medical Dir.
PH: (804)971-6921
FX: (804)971-7605
Description: Works to improve the health of all people through creative health education programs designed to meet the unique needs and capabilities of communities around the world. Sponsors collaborative research; develops and strengthens current preventative and curative care; manages and implements health science education programs in cooperation with US institutions in Central America, Africa and the former Soviet Union; advocates for the health care needs of all people. **Founded:** 1991. **Staff:** 5. Multinational. **Languages:** English.

INTERNATIONAL CESAREAN AWARENESS NETWORK (ICAN)
e-mail: icaninc@aol.com
url: http://www.childbirth.org/section/ican.html
1304 Kingsdale Ave.
Redondo Beach, CA 90278-3926
April Kubachka, Pres.
PH: (310)542-6400
FX: (310)542-5368
Description: Men and women concerned with the increasing rate of cesarean births. Objectives are: to promote vaginal births; to offer encouragement, information, and support for women wanting vaginal births after cesarean (VBAC); to assist in organizing and informing new parents and cesarean parents on preventing future cesareans by opposing unnecessary medical intervention during the birth process and by working to make hospital routines more responsive to women in labor. Provides support network to link women anticipating a VBAC and VBAC mothers, supportive physicians, midwives, and child birth educators. **Founded:** 1982. **Membership:** 2000. Multinational. **Regional Groups:** 40. **Languages:** English. Formerly (1992) Cesarean Prevention Movement.

INTERNATIONAL CHILD CARE - CANADA (ICC)
Box 2125, Sta. B
St. Catharines, ON, Canada L2M 6P5
PH: (905)688-0632
Description: Health care personnel. Promotes global availability of community-based health care, with emphasis on the prevention of tuberculosis, maternal and child health, and provision of primary health care services. Cooperates with local administrative bodies to strengthen public health programs in the Dominican Republic and Haiti. Conducts primary health care and immunization services. Sponsors health care training courses for people living in underserved areas. Multinational. **Languages:** English, French.

INTERNATIONAL CHILD CARE - HAITI (ICC)
Delmas 31, No. 38
Port-au-Prince, Haiti
PH: 509 464104
Description: Christian health care workers. Seeks to control and treat tuberculosis and increase availability of maternal and child health care services in developing areas. Conducts immunization programs; trains local leaders to promote and maintain community-based primary health care services. Multinational. **Languages:** English, French.

INTERNATIONAL CHILDBIRTH EDUCATION ASSOCIATION (ICEA)
e-mail: info@icea.org
url: http://www.icea.org/
PO Box 20048
Minneapolis, MN 55420-0048
Doris Olson, Mgr.

PH: (612)854-8660
FX: (612)854-8772
Description: Purposes are: to further the educational, physical, and emotional preparation of expectant parents for childbearing and breastfeeding; to increase public awareness on current issues related to childbearing; to cooperate with physicians, nurses, physical therapists, hospitals, health, education, and welfare agencies, and other individuals and groups interested in furthering parental participation and minimal obstetric intervention in uncomplicated labors; to promote development of safe, low-cost alternatives in childbirth that recognize the rights and responsibilities of those involved. Develops, publishes, and distributes literature pertaining to family-centered maternity care. Offers a teacher certifi cation program for childbirth educat ors. Conducts workshops. Operates mail order book store in Minneapolis, MN which makes available literature on all aspects of childbirth education and family-centered maternity care. **Founded:** 1960. **Membership:** 12000. **Staff:** 8. Multinational. **Local Groups:** 275. **Languages:** English. **Budget:** $500,000.

INTERNATIONAL COLLEGE OF DENTISTS (ICD)
url: http://www.icd.org
51 Monroe St., Ste. 1501
Rockville, MD 20850-2421
Richard G. Shaffer, D.D.S., Sec.Gen.
PH: (301)251-8861
FX: (301)738-9143
Description: Dentists who have made outstanding contributions to the profession. Acclaims meritorious service to dentistry; fosters growth and diffusion of dental information; upholds high standards in dental education. Supports the Dental Career Option Seminar for Students. Promotes continuing education through the International Clinicians Program. Operates charitable programs. **Founded:** 1928. **Membership:** 7900. **Staff:** 2. Multinational. **Languages:** English. **Budget:** $500,000. **Publication:** *Globe*, annual. Journal ▪ *Key*, annual. Magazine. Advertising: not accepted ▪ *Keynotes*, semiannual. Newsletter. Advertising: not accepted ▪ *Roster*, periodic.

INTERNATIONAL COLLEGE FOR HEALTH COOPERATION IN DEVELOPING COUNTRIES -ITALY
e-mail: cuamm@windnet.neol.it
url: http://www.geocities.com/CapitolHill
Via San Francesco 126
I-35121 Padua, Italy
Paolo Chiodini, Contact
PH: 39 49 8751649
FX: 39 49 8574738
Description: Works to improve public health and increase the availability of health care services and preventive medical programs in developing countries. Facilitates cooperation among international development agencies with health-related programs. Conducts educational and training programs in health related areas including community development and water supply and sanitation. Makes available emergency medical relief services. **Founded:** 1950. **Membership:** 280. **Staff:** 13. Multinational. **Languages:** English, Italian. **Budget:** $3,000,000. **Publication:** *CUAMM Notizie - Salute E Sviluppo* (in Italian), weekly. Journal. Price: free. Advertising: not accepted.

INTERNATIONAL COLLEGE OF SURGEONS (ICS)
e-mail: info@icsglobal.org
url: http://www.icsglobal.org
1516 N. Lake Shore Dr.
Chicago, IL 60610
Max Downham, Exec.Dir.
PH: (312)642-3555
FX: (312)787-1624
Description: General surgeons and surgical specialists in 110 countries maintaining official relations with the World Health Organization. Promotes the universal teaching and advancement of surgery and its allied sciences. Maintains International Museum of Surgical Sciences containing specialty rooms showing the growth and perfection of many surgical specialties. Maintains lib-

rary open to researchers, individuals working in the profession, and the public. Organizes postgraduate clinics around the world; conducts lecture series and periodic congresses; offers grants, scholarships, and loans for residencies, research, and advanced study in surgery. Sends surgical teaching teams to developing countries. Bestows honorary fellowship. **Founded:** 1935. **Membership:** 14000. **Staff:** 12. Multinational. **National Groups:** 70. **Languages:** English. **Budget:** $2,000,000. **Publication:** *International College of Surgeons Newsletter*, quarterly. Covers college news and business. Circulation: 10,000. Advertising: accepted ∎ *International Surgery*, quarterly. Journal. Presents papers on clinical, experimental, cultural, and historical topics pertinent to surgery and related fields. Contains book reviews. Price: $25.00/year for members; $50.00/year for nonmembers. ISSN: 0020-8868. Circulation: 10,000. Advertising: accepted.

INTERNATIONAL COMMITTEE AGAINST MENTAL
ILLNESS (ICAMI)
PO Box 1921, Grand Central Sta.
New York, NY 10163-1921
Dr. Robert Cancro, Pres.
PH: (212)263-6214
Description: Fosters psychosocial rehabilitation and mental health research, services, and information systems. Provides technical assistance to professional rehabilitation organizations in expanding or installing computer information systems in psychiatry and in planning workshops, symposia, and conferences. Organizes international consortium of voluntary agencies and rehabilitation groups. Conducts research; operates speakers' bureau. Has worked on projects in Colombia, Indonesia, Iran, Israel, Kuwait, Liberia, Nepal, Pakistan, and Yugoslavia. The committee is a direct outgrowth of a pioneering psychiatric treatment project in Haiti that is now operated by the Haitian government. **Founded:** 1958. Multinational. **Languages:** English.

INTERNATIONAL COMMITTEE OF CATHOLIC NURSES
AND MEDIO-SOCIAL ASSISTANTS (ICCN)
(Comite International Catholique des Infirmieres et Assistantes Medico Sociales)
43 Sq. Vergote
B-1030 Brussels, Belgium
An Verlinde, Gen.Sec.
PH: 32 2 7321050
FX: 32 2 7348460
Description: Professional Catholic nursing associations, Catholic nursing and medico-social work schools, and other Catholic groups representing the nursing profession in 57 countries. Works to encourage the development of members and ensure their technical ability in accordance with Christian moral principles. Promotes development of the nursing profession in general; fosters health and social welfare measures consistent with Christian principles and scientific progress while respecting individual religious convictions. Provides assistance to nursing schools and associations in developing countries; facilitates exchange of statistics between hospital establishments and medico-social organizations. **Founded:** 1928. **Membership:** 79. **Staff:** 1. Multinational. **Regional Groups:** 5. **Languages:** English, French. **Publication:** *CICIAMS News* (in English, French, and German), quarterly. Price: $45.00. Advertising: not accepted. **Formerly:** (1946) International Study Committee of Catholic Nursing Associations.

INTERNATIONAL COMMITTEE FOR LIFE ASSURANCE
MEDICINE (ICLAM)
(Comite International de Medecine d'Assurances sur la Vie)
e-mail: Hanreparislife@compuserve.com
41, ave. George V
F-75008 Paris, France
Dr. Jacques Chouty, Gen.Sec.
PH: 33 1 47208199
FX: 33 1 47233881
Description: Medical doctors working in life insurance and reinsurance companies in 41 countries. Promotes fraternal benefit life insurance; facilitates contact and cooperation among members. Establishes societies of life assurance medicine in countries

where they do not exist. **Founded:** 1899. **Membership:** 81. Multinational. **Languages:** English. **Publication:** *Annals of Life Assurance Medicine* (in English), triennial.

INTERNATIONAL CONFEDERATION OF MIDWIVES (ICM)
(Confederation Internationale des Sages-Femmes)
e-mail: 100702.2405@Compuserve.com
10 Barley Mow Passage
Chiswick
London W4 4PH, England
Miss J. Walker, Sec.Gen.
PH: 44 181 9946477
FX: 44 181 9951332
Description: National midwives' associations in 66 countries. Seeks to improve the standard of care provided to mothers, babies, and the family by promoting midwifery education and disseminating information about the art and science of midwifery. **Founded:** 1919. **Membership:** 77. **Staff:** 2. Multinational. **Regional Groups:** 4. **Languages:** English, French. **Budget:** L24,000. **Publication:** *A Birthday for Midwives - Seventy Five Years of International Collaboration*. Book ∎ *Congress Proceedings*, triennial ∎ *International Code of Ethics for Midwives, 1993*. Book ∎ *International Midwifery Matters*, 3/year. Newsletter ∎ *Introductory Brochure* ∎ *Maternity Care in the World* ∎ *Planning for Action for Midwives* ∎ *Workshop Report*.

INTERNATIONAL CONFERENCE ON MECHANICS IN
MEDICINE AND BIOLOGY (ICMMB)
e-mail: wjyang@engin.umich.edu
2150 G.G. Brown Bldg.
Ann Arbor, MI 48109-2125
Wen-Jei Yang, Coord.
PH: (734)764-9910
FX: (734)647-3170
Description: Organizes conferences and disseminates information on mechanics in medicine and biology worldwide. Conducts research; offers seminars and short courses. **Founded:** 1977. Multinational. **Languages:** English. **Publication:** *Advances in Cardiovascular Physics* ∎ *Digest*, biennial ∎ *Directory of Conference Participants*, biennial ∎ *Proceedings of the International Conference on Mechanics in Medicine and Biology*, biennial.

INTERNATIONAL CONGRESS OF ORAL
IMPLANTOLOGISTS (ICOI)
e-mail: icoi@dentalimplants.com
248 Lorraine Ave., 3rd Fl.
Upper Montclair, NJ 07043
R. Craig Johnson, Exec.Dir.
PH: (973)783-6300
FX: (973)783-1175
Description: Dentists and oral surgeons dedicated to the teaching of and research in oral implantology (branch of dentistry dealing with dental implants placed into or on top of the jaw bone). Offers fellowship and course certification programs. Compiles statistics and maintains registry of current research in the field. Sponsors classes, seminars, and workshops at universities, hospitals, and societies worldwide. Provides consultation and patient information/referral services. **Founded:** 1975. **Membership:** 3000. Multinational. **Languages:** English. **Budget:** $1,000,000. **Publication:** *ICOI News*, periodic. Newsletter. Price: included in membership dues. Circulation: 3,000 ∎ *Implant Dentistry*, quarterly. Journal. Includes scientific manuscripts, new product reports, membership updates, and calendar of seminars. Price: included in membership dues; $76.00 for nonmembers; $95.00 for nonmembers outside U.S. ISSN: 0190-2024. Circulation: 6,000. Advertising: accepted ∎ *Membership Directory*, annual. **Formerly:** (1976) International College of Oral Implantologists.

INTERNATIONAL CORRESPONDENCE SOCIETY OF
OBSTETRICIANS AND GYNECOLOGISTS (ICSOG)
url: http://www.obgynet.com
PO Box 1130
Northborough, MA 01532
Dean M. Laux, Exec.Sec.

PH: (508)842-7027
FX: (508)842-7062
Description: Physicians concerned with obstetrics and gynecology and related surgery; medical schools and libraries; civilian and military hospitals; others with research interests. **Founded:** 1960. **Membership:** 3000. Multinational. **Languages:** English. **Publication:** *The Collected Letters*, monthly. Newsletter. Price: $115.00. ISSN: 0443-9058. Circulation: 3,000. Advertising: not accepted.

INTERNATIONAL COUNCIL OF NURSES (ICN)
   (Conseil International des Infirmieres)
e-mail: ICN@uni2a.unige.ch
3, place Jean-Marteau
CH-1201 Geneva, Switzerland
Judith A. Oulton, Exec.Dir.
PH: 41 22 9080100
FX: 41 22 9080101
Description: ICN works in collaboration with its national nurses' association. Provides a medium through which members can work together to promote the health of people and the care of the sick. Objectives are to: improve the standards and status of nursing; promote the development of strong national nurses' associations; serve as the authoritative voice for nurses and the nursing profession worldwide. **Founded:** 1899. **Membership:** 112. **Staff:** 15. Multinational. **National Groups:** 112. **Languages:** English, French. **Publication:** *International Nursing Review* (in English), bimonthly. Journal. Contains information on nursing and health issues. Advertising: not accepted ▪ Brochures, periodic.

INTERNATIONAL COUNCIL OF SOCIETIES OF
   PATHOLOGY (ICSP)
1501 N. Campbell Ave.
Tucson, AZ 85724
F. K. Mostofi, M.D., Sec.-Treas.
PH: (602)626-6097
FX: (602)626-1027
Description: National pathology societies. Distributes teaching sets and professional aids to pathology societies worldwide. Offers seminars and specialized education; conducts professional training and research programs. **Founded:** 1962. **Membership:** 60. **Staff:** 1. Multinational. **Languages:** English. **Budget:** $2,000.

INTERNATIONAL DENTAL HEALTH FOUNDATION (IDHF)
e-mail: idhf@aol.com
1111-60F S. Lakes Dr., Ste. 345
Reston, VA 22091
Patricia L. Cartwright, Exec.Dir.
PH: (703)860-9244
FX: (703)860-9245
Description: Dentists, dental hygienists, and other dental professionals. Advocates a method of treating periodontal disease that de-emphasizes cleaning and surgery and instead concentrates on eliminating the disease-causing bacteria. **Founded:** 1981. **Membership:** 450. **Staff:** 2. Multinational. **Languages:** English. **Publication:** *Annotations* (in English), bimonthly. Newsletter. Price: included in membership dues. Circulation: 450 ▪ *Seminar Brochures* ▪ Brochures.

INTERNATIONAL DIABETES FEDERATION (IDF)
   (Federation Internationale du Diabete)
e-mail: idf@idf.org
url: http://www.idf.org
1, rue Defacqz
B-1000 Brussels, Belgium
H. Williams, Exec.Dir.
PH: 32 2 5385511
FX: 32 2 5385114
Description: National diabetes associations; diabetes sections of national academies; endocrinology, metabolic, and diabetes societies; diabetes supplies companies are supporting members; association represents over one million individuals through its national associations. Objectives are: to improve the quality of life in the global diabetic community; to promote the exchange of information; to improve standards of treatment; to develop educa-

tional methods designed to patients a better understanding of their disease; to educate the public in the early recognition of the disease and the importance of its medically supervised treatment; to encourage medical, scientific, and socioeconomic research. Maintains liaison with the World Health Organization. Compiles statistics. Provides professional training courses through the IDF Educational Foundation. **Founded:** 1949. **Membership:** 1100. **Staff:** 5. Multinational. **National Groups:** 147. **Languages:** English, French. **Publication:** *The Economics of Diabetes & Diabetes Care: Costing Diabetes, the cause for Prevention* ▪ *IDF Bulletin* (in English), quarterly. Journal. Advertising: accepted ▪ *IDF Diabetes Voice*, 3/year ▪ *Triennial Report*.

INTERNATIONAL DIABETIC ATHLETES ASSOCIATION
   (IDAA)
e-mail: idaa@diabetes-exercise.org
url: http://www.getnet.com/~idaa/
1647 W. Bethany Home Rd., No. B
Phoenix, AZ 85015
Paula Harper, RN, CDE, Pres.
PH: (602)433-2113
TF: 800898-IDAA
FX: (602)433-9331
Description: Individuals with diabetes and healthcare professionals. Promotes the participation of individuals with diabetes in sports activities. Provides a network and support group for athletes with diabetes. Conducts educational programs to increase self care skills for individuals with diabetes and counseling skills for healthcare professionals. Offers blood sugar screenings; sponsors volunteer services and speakers' bureau. Conducts children's services. **Founded:** 1985. **Membership:** 3500. **Staff:** 2. Multinational. **Regional Groups:** 12. **Languages:** Catalan, Danish. **Budget:** $50,000.

INTERNATIONAL ELECTROLOGY EDUCATORS (IEE)
132 Great Rd., No. 200
Stow, MA 01775
Lauren Hunte, Contact
PH: (978)461-0313
FX: (617)237-9039
Description: Electrology schools and teachers. Purposes are to instruct teachers and standardize the curriculum and teaching of electrology. Conducts educational programs and regional educational conferences for electrology educators. **Founded:** 1979. **Membership:** 55. Multinational. **Languages:** English. **Publication:** *IEE Directory of Schools*, periodic ▪ *Perspectives*, quarterly. Advertising: accepted. **Formerly:** (1982) National Electrology Educators; (1985) International Electrology Educators; (1993) Institute of Electrology Educators.

INTERNATIONAL ERGOPHTHALMOLOGICAL SOCIETY
   (Societas Ergophthalmologica Internationalis)
55 Front St.
Nanaimo, BC, Canada V9R 5H9
Dr. B.T. Philipson, Pres.
PH: (250)753-1612
FX: (250)753-2767
Description: National ergophthalmological associations in 47 countries; interested individuals. Promotes scientific research in the area of industrial ophthalmology (ergophthalmology) and the establishment and development of professional contacts. Conducts periodic symposia. **Founded:** 1966. **Membership:** 150. Multinational. **National Groups:** 15. **Languages:** English, French. **Publication:** *Problems of Industrial Medicine in Ophthalmology*, periodic ▪ Handbook, periodic.

INTERNATIONAL EYE FOUNDATION (IEF)
e-mail: info@ief.permanet.org
7801 Norfolk Ave., Ste. 200
Bethesda, MD 20814
Victoria M. Sheffield, Exec.Dir.
PH: (301)986-1830
FX: (301)986-1876
Description: Qualified ophthalmologists who are members of the

Society of Eye Surgeons. Promotes the prevention of blindness worldwide. Disseminates information to ophthalmologists on recent advances in eye surgery and trains physicians, nurses, paramedical personnel, and technicians in the care and treatment of eye patients. Aids in the establishment of eye care delivery systems and eye banks; provides eye tissues for operations. Collaborates with governments and international health agencies. **Founded:** 1961. **Staff:** 21. Multinational. **Languages:** English. **Budget:** $2,500,000. **Publication:** *International Eye Foundation – Eye to Eye*, semiannual. Newsletter. Concerned with the prevention of blindness in the developing countries; includes information on foundation programs. Price: free. Circulation: 2,000 ▪ Annual Report, annual. Circulation: 1,500.

INTERNATIONAL FEDERATION OF ASSOCIATIONS OF PHARMACEUTICAL PHYSICIANS (IFAPP)
43 Galgenstraat
B-3078 Everberg, Belgium
Dr. Herman F.J. Lahon, Contact
Description: National organizations representing 4000 physicians in 25 countries specializing in pharmaceutical medicine. Encourages contact among members. **Founded:** 1975. **Membership:** 25. **Staff:** 10. Multinational. **National Groups:** 25. **Languages:** English. **Publication:** *International Journal of Pharmaceutical Medicine: IFAPP Section* (in English), bimonthly. Newsletter. Price: free. Circulation: 4,000. Advertising: accepted.

INTERNATIONAL FEDERATION OF CATHOLIC MEDICAL ASSOCIATIONS (FIAMC)
(Federation Internationale des Associations Medicales Catholiques)
Palazzo San Calisto
V-00120 Vatican City, Vatican City
Prof. Walter Osswald, Pres.
PH: 39 6 69887372
FX: 39 6 69887372
Description: National associations and guilds of Catholic physicians. Seeks to: coordinate the efforts of Catholic medical associations worldwide; promote Christian principles throughout the medical profession; discuss and find new ethical approaches to biotechnological problems. Encourages the development of Catholic medical associations globally to assist in the moral, spiritual, and technical advancement of the Catholic physician; participates in the development of the medical profession. Maintains speakers' bureau. **Founded:** 1950. **Membership:** 52. Multinational. **National Groups:** 64. **Languages:** English, French. **Budget:** $32,000. **Publication:** *Catholic Medical Quarterly* (in English) ▪ *Decisions* (in English), quarterly ▪ *Linacre Bulletin* (in English), quarterly ▪ Journal (in English, Flemish, and French), quarterly.

INTERNATIONAL FEDERATION OF CATHOLIC PHARMACISTS
(Federation Internationale des Pharmaciens Catholiques)
12 Rue du Berceau
B-1495 Villeri la Ville, Belgium
Ann Janssens, Sec.Gen.
PH: 32 71 7799524
FX: 32 71 875043
Description: National associations of Catholic pharmacists. Seeks Christian solutions to all problems affecting the profession; promotes international understanding among members. Sponsors study commissions and regional study days. **Founded:** 1950. **Membership:** 20. Multinational. **Languages:** English, French. **Publication:** *Acta-FIPC*, biennial ▪ *Listing-FIPC*, biennial.

INTERNATIONAL FEDERATION OF CERVICAL PATHOLOGY AND COLPOSCOPY (IFCPC)
(Federacion Internacional de Patologia Cervical y Colposcopia)
Instituto Nazionale Tumori
Via Venezian, 1
I-20133 Milan, Italy
Giuseppe De Palo, M.D., Exec.Off.
PH: 39 2 2390324
FX: 39 2 2367430
Description: Federation of national societies encouraging basic and applied research and the dissemination of information concerning uterine cervical pathology and colposcopy. **Founded:** 1972. **Membership:** 30. Multinational. **Languages:** English, French.

INTERNATIONAL FEDERATION OF DENTAL ANESTHESIOLOGY SOCIETIES (IFDAS)
e-mail: jameskg@ozenail.com.au
13 Corinna Chambers
Corinna St.
Woden, ACT 2606, Australia
Dr. J. Grainger, Sec.Gen.
PH: 61 26 2822605
FX: 61 26 2815321
Description: Societies of dental and medical practitioners in 14 countries. Promotes and encourages the study and practice of improved methods for administering anesthesia, analgesia, and sedation in dentistry and its related branches. Works to bring the benefits of these methods to people throughout the world. Facilitates the international exchange of information, research, and technology in the field. **Founded:** 1982. **Membership:** 10. Multinational. **Languages:** English. **Publication:** *IFDAS Newsletter* (in English), semiannual.

INTERNATIONAL FEDERATION OF GYNECOLOGY AND OBSTETRICS (FIGO)
(Federation Internationale de Gynecologie et d'Obstetrique)
e-mail: secret@figo.win-uk.net
27 Sussex Pl.
Regent's Park
London NW1 4RG, England
Dr. Giuseppe Benagiano, Sec.Gen.
PH: 44 171 7232951
FX: 44 171 2580737
Description: Objectives are to: promote and assist in the development of scientific and research work relating to all facets of gynecology and obstetrics; improve the physical and mental health of women, mothers, and their children; provide an exchange of information and ideas; improve teaching standards; promote international cooperation among medical bodies. Acts as liaison with World Health Organization and other international organizations. **Founded:** 1954. **Membership:** 101. **Staff:** 4. Multinational. **Languages:** English, French. **Publication:** *Figo*, triennial. Book. Provides results of treatment in gynecological cancer ▪ *International Journal of Gynecology and Obstetrics*, monthly ▪ Newsletter, 3/year.

INTERNATIONAL FEDERATION FOR HEALTH
(Federation Internationale pour la Sante)
BP 312
F-45304 Lithariers, France
Yves Machelard, Dir.
PH: 33 1 46660327
FX: 33 1 46745270
Description: Associations in 7 countries concerned with health and a balanced environment. Acts to unify and broaden the scope and capabilities of member associations. Favors the development of alternative medical treatments. Advocates the patient's freedom of choice in medical treatment and the cessation of obligatory human and animal vaccination. Works to influence public policy and obtain favorable health care legislation. Provides individual legal, moral, and practical support; offers opportunities for the exchange of ideas. Makes available cost reductions on a variety of products. Conducts radio, educational, and children's programs. **Founded:** 1980. **Membership:** 3000. **Staff:** 2. Multinational. **National Groups:** 2. **Languages:** French. **Budget:** 1,300,000 Fr.

INTERNATIONAL FEDERATION OF HEALTH FUNDS (FHF)
e-mail: administrator@fnf.com
url: http://www.fhf.com
39 Friar St.
Reading, Berks. RG1 1DZ, England
Kenneth N. Groom, Sec.Gen.
PH: 44 1734 566544
FX: 44 1734 393464
Description: Nongovermental organizations involved in the execution of independent health care finance (100); associations of health funds (11) and individuals (26) in 20 countries. Promotes the study and development of independent health care services. Encourages research and the exchange of information. Operates conferences and meetings; information and research; sharing of infromation in cohesive network of member health funds. Offers study tours and educational programmes. **Founded:** 1968. **Membership:** 100. **Staff:** 5. Multinational. **Languages:** English. **For-Profit. Budget:** L425,000. **Publication:** *Conference Proceedings,* biennial ▪ *Membership Directory,* annual ▪ *National Commentaries,* biennial ▪ *Newsletter,* quarterly ▪ Booklets, periodic. **Formerly:** (1989) International Federation of Voluntary Health Service Funds.

INTERNATIONAL FEDERATION OF HEALTH RECORDS
   ORGANIZATIONS (IFHRO)
c/o Philip Roxborough
2/365 Richardson Rd.
Mount Roskill
Auckland, New Zealand
Philip Roxborough, Sec.-Treas.
PH: 64 9 6267975
FX: 64 9 6267975
Description: Organizations in 19 countries working in the health records field; persons involved in the field of health records in countries where no national organizations exist are associate members; individuals who have made significant contributions to the federation are honorary members. Objectives are to: improve health records standards in hospitals, dispensaries, and various health and medical institutions; promote efficient methods of health records in patient care, statistics, research, and teaching; provide a worldwide forum for individuals working in the health records field; encourage the international exchange of education requirements and training programs in the field of health records. Works closely with the World Health Organization and jointly sponsors workshops and research and educational projects in the health records field. **Founded:** 1968. **Membership:** 19. Multinational. **Languages:** English. **Publication:** *International Health Records,* quarterly. Newsletter. Price: $10.00/year. Circulation: 300. Advertising: not accepted. **Also Known As:** Federation Internationale de Associations du Dossier de Sante. **Formerly:** (1976) International Federation of Medical Record Organizations.

INTERNATIONAL FEDERATION OF INFANTILE AND
   JUVENILE GYNECOLOGY (IFIJG)
   (Federation Internationale de Gynecologie Infantile et
      Juvenile)
e-mail: grpagyn@hol.gr
9 Kanari St.
GR-106 71 Athens, Greece
Prof. George Creatsas, MD, Pres.
PH: 30 1 7770850
FX: 30 1 3620484
Description: Gynecologists and pediatricians in 43 countries. Promotes the diagnosis and treatment of gynecological problems during childhood and adolescence. Maintains the FIGO Joint Committee for the Study of Gynecological Problems in Childhood and Adolescence. **Founded:** 1972. **Membership:** 3850. Multinational. **National Groups:** 40. **Languages:** English, French. **Publication:** *Gynecologie* (in French), periodic. Magazine. Advertising: accepted ▪ *Pediatric and Adolescent Gynecology* (in English), periodic. Newsletter.

INTERNATIONAL FEDERATION OF MULTIPLE
   SCLEROSIS SOCIETIES (IFMSS)
e-mail: info@ifmss.org.uk
url: http://www.ifmss.org.uk
10 Heddon St.
London W1R 7LJ, England
Richard Hamilton, Sec. General
PH: 44 171 7349120
FX: 44 171 2872587
Description: Key aims are to stimulate scientific research at a global scale, disseminate information internationally, assist the development of national MS societies, and encourage full integration and participation of all people affected by MS. **Founded:** 1967. **Membership:** 36. **Staff:** 6. Multinational. **Languages:** English, French. **Publication:** *Annual Report* (in English). Magazine. Price: free. Advertising: not accepted ▪ *Federation Updates,* biennial ▪ *MS Management* ▪ *MS Research in Progress* ▪ *MS Therapeutic Claims.*

INTERNATIONAL FEDERATION OF
   OPHTHALMOLOGICAL SOCIETIES (IFOS)
e-mail: bspivey@cccare.com
url: http://www.icoph.org
Columbia-Cornell Care, L.L.C.
900 Third Ave., Ste. 500
New York, NY 10022
Bruce E. Spivey, MD, Sec.-Gen.
PH: (212)588-7301
FX: (212)588-7307
Description: The ICO represents opthalmologic organizations throughout the world. Dedicated to international exchange in ophthalmology. Encourages the study and improvement of ophthalmologic education; formulates international standards. Advocates the prevention and treatment of preventable blindness in developing nations, particularly Africa. Supports the International Agency for the Prevention of Blindness. **Founded:** 1857. Multinational.

INTERNATIONAL FEDERATION OF SPORTS MEDICINE
   (FIMS)
url: http://cac.psu.edu/~hgk2/fims/index.html
Rio Grande do Sul State University
91330-250 Porto Alegre, Rio Grande do Sul, Brazil
Prof. Eduardo H. de Rose, Contact
PH: 55 51 3348083
FX: 55 51 2272295
Description: National federations of physicians, physiologists, and individuals interested in maintaining and improving physical and mental health through sporting activities such as physical education, gymnastics, games, and other sports. Conducts scientific studies of the pathological and normal effects of sporting activities. **Founded:** 1928. Multinational. **Languages:** English, French. **Publication:** *FIMS Directory,* annual ▪ *The World of Sports Medicine,* quarterly.

INTERNATIONAL FEDERATION OF SURGICAL COLLEGES
   (IFSC)
e-mail: ifsc.us-muldoon@mail.med.upenn.edu
c/o S.W.A. Gunn, M.D., M.S., FRCSC, Hon. Sec.-Gen.
CH-1279 Bogis-Bossey, Switzerland
Prof. John Tetblanche, Pres.
PH: 41 22 7762161
FX: 41 22 7766417
Description: National colleges, academies, and associations of surgery in 50 countries; interested individuals. Works to improve standards of surgery throughout the world. Promotes cooperation and exchange of medical and surgical information among surgical institutions. Encourages high standards of education, training, and research in surgery and its allied sciences. Supports clinical and scientific congresses in the surgical community. Fosters cooperation in developing the best possible standards of surgical facilities and treatment, and in providing appropriate surgical training in countries requesting aid. Collaborates with the World Health Organization in attempts to strengthen rural surgi-

cal health services in developing countries; maintains distribution facility for journals to Third World nations. **Founded:** 1958. **Membership:** 795. **Staff:** 1. Multinational. **National Groups:** 57. **Languages:** English. **Budget:** $89,000. **Publication:** *World Journal of Surgery* ▪ Newsletter (in English), annual. Advertising: not accepted.

INTERNATIONAL FRENCH-SPEAKING ASSOCIATION FOR ODONTOLOGICAL RESEARCH
(Association Internationale Francophone de Recherche Odontologique)
Faculte d'Odontologie de Reims
2 rue du General Koenig
F-51100 Reims, France
Dr. Marie Pascale Hippolyte, Contact
PH: 33 3 26053450
FX: 33 3 26053480
Description: Odontologists and ondontology researchers. Seeks to advance odontological research, study, and practice. Serves as a clearinghouse on developments in odontology; sponsors educational and continuing professional development programs. Multinational. **Languages:** English, French.

INTERNATIONAL GLAUCOMA ASSOCIATION (IGA)
e-mail: iga@kcl.qc.uk
url: http://www.iga.org.uk/fga/
Denmark Hill
London SE5 9RS, England
Betsy M. Wright, Chief Exec.
PH: 44 171 7373265
FX: 44 171 3465929
Description: Glaucoma patients. Seeks to educate the public about glaucoma, its causes, detection, and treatment. Provides patients, doctors, opticians, optometrists, and others a forum for the exchange of ideas on glaucoma. Supports research; bestows grants. Conducts surveys; disseminates information. **Founded:** 1974. **Membership:** 14500. **Staff:** 9. Multinational. **Languages:** English, French. **Publication:** *Glaucoma 98 - A Guide for Patients* ▪ Newsletter (in English), semiannual. Price: Available to members only ▪ Pamphlets. **Formerly:** (1974) Glaucoma Association.

INTERNATIONAL GRAVIMETRIC BUREAU (IGB)
(Bureau Gravimetric International)
url: http://www.obs-mlp.fr/uggl/bgl.html
18, ave. E. Belin
F-31401 Toulouse, France
Dr. Georges Balmino, Exec. Officer
PH: 33 561 332980
FX: 33 561 253098
Description: Individuals and organizations interested in the earth's gravity field. Objectives are to collect and distribute gravity data and to provide advice, guidance, and standards for the acquisition of data. Aims to contribute to the knowledge of the earth's gravity field by conducting theoretical studies and measurements of gravity, and by maintaining a bibliography. **Founded:** 1951. **Membership:** 250. **Staff:** 7. Multinational. **Languages:** English, French. **Budget:** $4,000. **Publication:** *Bulletin d'Information* (in English and French), semiannual. Booklets. Includes maps and charts. Price: 75.00 Fr ▪ *Bulletin d'Information*, semiannual.

INTERNATIONAL GROUP FOR SCIENTIFIC RESEARCH IN STOMATOLOGY AND ODONTOLOGY (GIRSO)
(Groupement International pour la Recherche Scientifique en Stomatologie et Odontologie)
Faculte de Medecine ULB
Rte. de Lennik 808/621
B-1070 Brussels, Belgium
Dr. Roland Rodembourg, Sec.
PH: 32 2 5556361
FX: 32 2 5556361
Description: Physicians and dentists doing basic research in stomatology (the science dealing with the treatment of the mouth and its diseases). Encourages exchange of material, docu-

mentation, and visits. **Founded:** 1957. **Membership:** 100. Multinational. **Languages:** English, French. **Publication:** *Bulletin* (in English and French), quarterly.

INTERNATIONAL HEALTH EVALUATION ASSOCIATION (IHEA)
6412 Dahlonega Rd.
Bethesda, MD 20816
Dr. Marianne. Floor, M.D., Exec.VP
PH: (301)765-1179
FX: (301)365-5958
Description: Users, suppliers, and manufacturers of computer-based health evaluation systems including clinics, hospitals, physicians, medical students, and research institutions. Is dedicated to the improvement of health care through: the advancement of computer-based health testing and evaluation techniques; the refinement of associated data-processing systems and biomedical devices; the development of a low-cost, high-quality health programs. Believes the technique of computer-based health evaluation can be used in the areas of testing industrial workers and others exposed to environmental hazards, mandatory tests conducted by governmental agencies, and pre-admission hospital testing. Sponsors seminars on clinical preventive medicine for the discussion of medical results, operational techniques, new applications, and cost-effectiveness data. Conducts research; compiles statistics; maintains library; operates speakers' bureau. **Founded:** 1971. **Membership:** 300. **Staff:** 2. Multinational. **Regional Groups:** 3. **Languages:** English. **Budget:** $50,000. **Publication:** *Proceedings of Annual Symposia* (in English and Japanese), quarterly. Price: free. Advertising: accepted. Alternate Formats: CD-ROM ▪ *Regional Newsletter*, periodic ▪ Newsletter, quarterly.

INTERNATIONAL HEALTH EXCHANGE (IHE)
8-10 Dryden St.
London WC2E 9NA, England
Alice Tligui, Dir.
PH: 44 0171 8365833
FX: 44 0171 3791239
Description: Health care professionals; organizations operating health programs in developing areas worldwide. Promotes availability of effective health services in previously underserved areas. Recruits volunteers and places them with health services in developing areas that require assistance. Conducts research and educational programs; maintains speakers' bureau. **Founded:** 1980. **Membership:** 1200. **Staff:** 3. Multinational. **Languages:** English. **Budget:** L200,000. **Publication:** *Health Exchange Magazine*, monthly. ISSN: 1336-3858. Circulation: 1,600. Advertising: accepted.

INTERNATIONAL HEALTH FOUNDATION
e-mail: hansenkda@aol.com
6501 Bright Mountain Rd.
Mc Lean, VA 22101
Kenneth D. Hansen, MD, Exec.Dir.
FX: (703)356-4143
Description: Provides governmental organizations and health providers with methods for improving health services. Focuses on medical systems and medical and legal affairs. Offers assistance to developing countries. Sponsors educational programs; conducts research. Maintains speakers' bureau. Distinct from organization of same name listed in index. **Founded:** 1972. Multinational. **Languages:** English.

INTERNATIONAL HEALTH POLICY AND MANAGEMENT INSTITUTE (IHPMI)
c/o Paul Detrick
Christian Health Services Dev. Corp.
10133 Dunn Rd., Ste. 400
St. Louis, MO 63136
Paul Detrick, Treas.
PH: (314)355-0095
Description: Health policymakers, hospital presidents, physicians, business leaders, and educators. Dedicated to improving and expanding knowledge of health care economics and manage-

ment systems. Goals are to: facilitate discussion for the exchange of health care techniques, strategies, and ideas at the theoretical and applied levels to improve the financing and delivery of health care; encourage research and understanding of health policy issues; examine and compare health care systems of industrialized and developing countries; promote the need to maintain access to quality health care while limiting costs within a free market framework. Conducts research and cross-cultural comparative studies on multihospital systems, government health regulations, health systems analysis and planning, health care finance and investment, alternative health care delivery systems, economics of aging, health care cost effectiveness within free market systems, and medical ethics. Disseminates research results; monitors and reports on events affecting health care; conducts demonstration projects. **Founded:** 1983. **Membership:** 100. Multinational. **Languages:** English. **Publication:** *International Perspectives*, quarterly. Newsletter. Contains excerpts from other publications. Price: included in membership dues. Circulation: 3,500. Advertising: accepted. **Formerly:** (1991) International Health Economics and Management Institute.

INTERNATIONAL INSTITUTE FOR BIOENERGETIC ANALYSIS (IIBA)
e-mail: iibanet@aol.com
url: http://www.bioenergetic-therapy.com
144 E. 36th St., Ste. 1A
New York, NY 10016
John Bustelos, Jr., Exec.Dir.
PH: (212)532-7742
FX: (212)532-5331
Description: Works to promote research and education in the fields of mental and physical health as they relate to biological energy processes. Areas of interest include: the role of muscle tension in emotional and physical illness, relationship of body structure and body movement, energy dynamics, disturbances in motility as a factor in illness, genetic factors, principles and methods of therapy, and growth and development of the child in response to patterns of child rearing. Conducts lectures, 1-day patient workshops, professional weekend workshops, seminars, and exercise classes. **Founded:** 1956. **Membership:** 1700. **Staff:** 2. Multinational. **Regional Groups:** 50. **Languages:** English, French. **Publication:** *Bioenergetic Analysis*, periodic. Journal ■ Books ■ Brochures ■ Membership Directory, periodic ■ Papers. **Formerly:** (1979) Institute for Bioenergetic Analysis.

INTERNATIONAL INSTITUTE OF CONCERN FOR PUBLIC HEALTH (IICPH)
e-mail: iicph@compuserve.com
710-264 Queens Quay W
Toronto, ON, Canada M5J 1B5
Dr. Rosalie Bertell, Pres.
PH: (416)260-0575
FX: (416)260-3404
Description: Promotes dissemination of information on public health and related topics including environmental and occupational health and human rights. Serves as a clearinghouse on international public health and related issues; assists in the development of model health-related human rights legislation. Conducts research and educational programs; compiles statistics; maintains speakers' bureau. Provides support and assistance to communities wishing to maintain their own public health databases. **Founded:** 1984. **Membership:** 80. **Staff:** 2. Multinational. **Languages:** English, French. **Budget:** C$100,000. **Publication:** *International Perspectives in Public Health*, annual. Journal. ISSN: 8755-5328 ■ Newsletter, bimonthly. Contains articles relating to the environment, work and health.

INTERNATIONAL INSTITUTE OF DENTAL ERGONOMICS AND TECHNOLOGY (IIDET)
(Institut International d'Ergonomie et Technology Dentaire)
Loehrstrasse 1 39
D-56068 Koblenz, Germany
Dr. Karlheinz Kimmel, Exec. Officer

PH: 49 261 34818
FX: 49 261 34609
Description: Experts from 10 countries in dental equipment development, ergonomics, quality assurance, and infection control. **Founded:** 1973. **Membership:** 120. **Staff:** 3. Multinational. **Languages:** English, German. **Budget:** DM 30,000. **Publication:** Annual Report (in English and German).

INTERNATIONAL ISOTOPE SOCIETY (IIS)
144 Ramblewood Rd.
Moorestown, NJ 08057
Dr. Dale W. Blackburn, Treas.
PH: (609)235-1360
FX: (609)235-6801
Description: Individuals who conduct or have conducted research in the field of isotope synthesis or the applications of isotopes and isotopically-labelled compounds; corporations that support the IIS or its members. (Isotopic labelling involves the placement of minute quantities of radioactive material within a chemical structure, so that the structure in question can be traced in a chemical or biological system and identified by the label's radioactivity.) Seeks to advance knowledge of the sythesis, measurement, and applications of isotopically labelled compounds. Serves as a forum for discussion among scientists working with isotopes; acts as liaison between members, other scientific organizations, and governments worldwide. Assists in maintaining links between academic and industrial organizations that use isotopes. Disseminates information to the public to promote awareness of the practical applications of isotopes. Plans to conduct educational programs. **Founded:** 1986. **Membership:** 500. **Staff:** 1. Multinational. **National Groups:** 3. **Languages:** English.

INTERNATIONAL JOSEPH DISEASES FOUNDATION (IJDF)
PO Box 2550
Livermore, CA 94551-2550
Rose Marie Silva, Exec.Dir.
PH: (510)371-1287
FX: (510)371-1288
Description: Geneticists, neurologists, patients and their families, and individuals interested in Joseph disease. (Joseph disease is a neurological genetic disorder of the motor system affecting all races and many ethnic groups, which is often misdiagnosed as multiple sclerosis, or Parkinson's disease.) Offers diagnostic services and treatment at free clinics. Provides genetic counseling to individuals concerned with inheriting the disorder or passing it on to future generations. Locates families throughout the world affected by the disease. Educates the medical profession and the public on Joseph disease in an effort to promote more accurate diagnosis and better treatment. Diagnostic marker to identify carriers of the disorder is now available. Conducts research; maintains speakers' bureau. **Founded:** 1977. **Membership:** 1800. Multinational. **Languages:** Portuguese. **Budget:** $10,000. **Publication:** *IJDF Newsletter*, quarterly. Includes research developments. Advertising: not accepted.

INTERNATIONAL LEAGUE AGAINST EPILEPSY (ILAE)
e-mail: iku@mara.de
c/o Dr. Peter Wolf
Klinik Mara I
Maraweg 21
D-33617 Bielefeld, Germany
Dr. Peter Wolf, Contact
PH: 49 521 1444897
FX: 49 521 1444637
Description: Fosters development of and cooperation among associations with common interests. **Founded:** 1909. **Membership:** 62. Multinational. **National Groups:** 62. **Publication:** *Epigraph* ■ *Epilepsia*, monthly. Journal. Contains scientific papers and meeting abstracts for professional researchers in the field of epilepsy. Includes book reviews and research reports. Price: $99.00 for ILAE members. Advertising: accepted.

INTERNATIONAL LEAGUE AGAINST RHEUMATISM (ILAR)
c/o Charles M. Plotz, M.D.
SUNY Downstate Med. Center
450 Clarkson Ave.
Brooklyn, NY 11203
Charles M. Plotz, M.D., Treas.
PH: (718)270-1662
FX: (718)270-1951
Description: Physicians interested in rheumatism. Promotes research and education in rheumatic disease. Facilitates communication among members and with United Nations Educational, Scientific and Cultural Organization and World Health Organization. **Founded:** 1927. **Membership:** 12000. Multinational. **National Groups:** 63. **Languages:** English. **Publication:** *Handbook*, quadrennial.

INTERNATIONAL LEAGUE OF DERMATOLOGICAL SOCIETIES (ILDS)
e-mail: bnichols@mtgmgr.win.net
5250 Avenida Navarra
Sarasota, FL 34242-2095
Barbara Nichols, Admin. Officer
Description: Works to stimulate cooperation between dermatology societies and encourage worldwide advancement of the profession. Promotes personal and professional relations among the dermatologists of the world. Provides educational programs; represents dermatology in commissions and health organizations. **Founded:** 1957. **Membership:** 102. **Staff:** 2. Multinational. **National Groups:** 102. **Languages:** English.

INTERNATIONAL LIFELINE
e-mail: negpa@aol.com
PO Box 32714
Oklahoma City, OK 73123
Robert E. Watkins, Pres.
PH: (405)728-2828
FX: (405)946-5512
Description: Volunteer medical personnel. Members donate time and services in emerging nations in the Caribbean for short-term assignments. Conducts charitable programs; offers children's services. Publications: none. **Convention/Meeting:** none. **Founded:** 1978. **Staff:** 3. Multinational. **Local Groups:** 106. **Languages:** Creole, French.

INTERNATIONAL LIVEDO RETICULARIS NETWORK (ILRN)
e-mail: pandjpalm@aol.com
700 N Bentsen Palm Dr., No. 313
Mission, TX 78572-9450
PH: (956)584-8039
Description: Persons with Livedo Reticularis and interested others. Livedo Reticularis is a peripheral vascular condition characterized by a reddish blue mottling of the skin. It affects the extremities. Sponsors research programs. Publications: none. **Convention/Meeting:** none. **Founded:** 1995. Multinational. **Languages:** English.

INTERNATIONAL MYELOMA FOUNDATION
e-mail: TheIMF@aol.com
2120 Stanley Hills Dr.
Los Angeles, CA 90046
Susie Novis, Exec.Dir.
TF: 800452-CURE
FX: (213)656-1182
Description: Sponsors research in multiple myeloma, a blood cancer. **Founded:** 1990. Multinational. **Languages:** English. **Publication:** *Myeloma Today*, quarterly. Price: $25.00 U.S. subscribers; $35.00 international subscribers. Circulation: 10,000.

INTERNATIONAL NEURAL NETWORK SOCIETY (INNS)
e-mail: 70712.3265@compuserve.com
1250 24th St. NW, Ste. 300
Washington, DC 20037
Stephanie Dickinson, Exec.Dir.
PH: (202)466-4667
FX: (202)466-2888
Description: Individuals interested in theoretical and computational understanding of the brain. Provides a forum for neurocomputing and theoretical approaches to neuroscience. Promotes research into behavioral processes and models of the brain. Encourages development of computing applications which use neural modeling concepts. **Founded:** 1987. **Membership:** 2000. **Staff:** 3. Multinational. **Languages:** English. **Publication:** *INNS Newsletter*, quarterly. Includes calendar of events and special interest group information ▪ *INNS Series on Neural Networks*. Published in conjunction with Lawrence Erlbaum Associates ▪ *Neural Networks*, bimonthly. Journal.

INTERNATIONAL NEUROMODULATION SOCIETY
e-mail: sherrikae.calkins@mail.tju.edu
1015 Chestnut St., Ste. 1400
Philadelphia, PA 19107
Sherri Kae Calkins, Contact
PH: (215)955-2364
FX: (215)923-4939
Description: Individuals with an interest in implantable technologies that impact on the nervous system. Promotes advancement of neuromodulation technologies and techniques; encourages continuing professional development of members. Serves as a forum for the exchange of scientific information on neuromodulation; conducts research and educational programs. **Founded:** 1994. **Languages:** English.

INTERNATIONAL OCULOPLASTIC SOCIETY (IOSI)
630 Park Ave.
New York, NY 10021
Pierre Guibor, M.D., Dir.
PH: (212)734-1010
FX: (201)871-8474
Description: Surgeons specializing in ophthalmology, otolaryngology, dermatology, and plastic surgery. Sponsors professional education and clinically applied research in the prevention, diagnosis, and treatment of disorders of the eye, orbit, adnexa, face, and skin. Seeks to promote and establish successful forms of patient care and treatment through open discussions, seminars, and instructional courses on clinical research, surgery, and medical advances. Conducts educational and charitable programs. Maintains speakers' bureau and placement servic. Compiles statistics. **Founded:** 1978. **Membership:** 3000. **Staff:** 4. Multinational. **Local Groups:** 2. **Languages:** French, Spanish. **Budget:** $100,000.

INTERNATIONAL OLYMPIC ASSOCIATION FOR MEDICO-SPORT RESEARCH (IOAMSR)
(Association Olympique Internationale pour la Recherche MedicoSportive)
Chateau de Vidy
CH-1007 Lausanne, Switzerland
Juan Antonio Samaranch, Contact
PH: 41 21 6216111
FX: 41 21 6216116
Description: Medical research programs sponsored by the International Olympic Committee. Seeks to advance sports medical research and practice. Conducts research programs; serves as a clearinghouse on sports medicine. Multinational. **Languages:** English, French.

INTERNATIONAL ONTOLOGICAL AID (IOA)
(Aide Ontologique Internationale)
115 rue Lamarcq
F-75018 Paris, France
PH: 33 1 42265290
FX: 33 1 42250792
Description: Dentists and dental organizations. Seeks to increase

access to dental health care in underprivileged areas worldwide. Develops dental services at rural hospitals; makes available dental care; supports local dental health centers through provision of equipment and supplies, technical expertise, and voluntary assistance. Conducts educational and training programs for indigenous dental care providers. Multinational. **Languages:** English, French.

INTERNATIONAL ONTOLOGICAL AID - VIETNAM (IOA)

(Aide Ontologique Internationale)
19/30 Tran Binh Trong
P5 Binh Thanh
Ho Chi Minh City, Vietnam
PH: 84 8 940797
FX: 84 8 298540
Description: Dentists and dental organizations. Seeks to increase access to dental health care in underprivileged areas of Vietnam. Develops dental services at rural hospitals; makes available dental care; supports local dental health centers through provision of equipment and supplies, technical expertise, and voluntary assistance. Conducts educational and training programs for indigenous dental care providers. **Staff:** 4. **Languages:** English, French. **Budget:** $100,000.

INTERNATIONAL ORGANIZATION AGAINST TRACHOMA (IOAT)

(Organisation Internationale pour la Lutte Contre le Trachome)
e-mail: coscasgabriel@compuserve.com
Universite de Paris-Val-de-Marne
Centre Hospitalier Intercommunal
Clinique Ophtalmologique de Creteil
F-94010 Creteil, France
Gabriel Coscas, Pres.
PH: 33 1 45175220
FX: 33 1 45175227
Description: Circulates information in 20 countries on current trachoma research (trachoma is a chronic, contagious eye disease) and supplies the latest information on etiology, diagnosis, epidemiology, prevention, and treatment, thus providing a scientific basis for the fight against the disease. Promotes research on trachoma; facilitates the adoption of sanitary and other regulations aimed at implementing the fight against trachoma. Maintains close contact with the World Health Organization and other institutions engaged in the fight against trachoma. **Founded:** 1923. **Membership:** 1200. **Staff:** 5. Multinational. **Languages:** English, French. **Publication:** *Revue Internationale du Trachome* (in English and French), semiannual. Journal. Circulation: 800. Advertising: accepted.

INTERNATIONAL ORGANIZATION FOR COOPERATION IN HEALTH CARE (IOCHC)

(Medicus Mundi Internationalis)
64, rue des Deux Eglises
B-1210 Brussels, Belgium
Frederica Wyckmans, Liaison Ofcr.
PH: 32 2 2310605
FX: 32 2 2311852
Description: National branches and organizations of physicians and paramedical personnel. Promotes the fields of health care and disease prevention as a necessary part of development of all nations. Encourages primary health care through comprehensive, integrated, long-term health programs. Documents socio-medical information on developing countries to assess the medical needs and demands of those countries. Other aims include: encouraging dialogue with the Third World; strengthening relations between national branches and European governments; profiling experts serving IOCHC; providing field workers with practical conclusions, recommendations, and moral support regarding new strategies, methods, or operations. Offers training programs. **Founded:** 1963. **Membership:** 8. **Staff:** 1. Multinational. **National Groups:** 8. **Languages:** English, French. **Budget:** 2,400,000 BFr. **Publication:** Newsletter (in French), quarterly. Advertising: accepted ■ Proceedings, periodic. Contains meeting reports.

INTERNATIONAL ORGANIZATION FOR FORENSIC ODONTO-STOMATOLOGY (IOFOS)

The Forge
Burnt House Ln.
Battisford
Stowmarket, Suffolk IP14 2ND, England
Graham Ritchie, Pres.
PH: 44 1449 612247
FX: 44 1449 612247
Description: National professional societies active in the field of forensic odonto-stomatology. Promotes forensic dentistry worldwide. Fosters cooperation among members; collects and disseminates information and ideas on forensic dentistry. Compiles statistics. Supports educational and research programs. **Founded:** 1973. **Membership:** 1500. Multinational. **National Groups:** 23. **Languages:** English. **Budget:** DM 8,000. **Publication:** *Forensic Odontology, Its Scope and History* (in English). Book. Out of Print, but obtainable through co. Pres ■ *International Journal of Forensic Odonto-Homatology* ■ *IOFOS Newsletter* (in English), 3/year ■ *The Journal of Forensic Odonto-Stomatology* (in English), semiannual. Price: DM 25.00. Advertising: not accepted. **Formerly:** (1981) International Society of Forensic Odonto-Stomatology.

INTERNATIONAL ORGANIZATION FOR MEDICAL PHYSICS (IOMP)

Radiation Physics Dept.
University Hospital
90185 UMEA
Prof. Gary D. Fullerton, Contact
Description: A member of the International Union of Physical and Engineering Sciences in Medicine. National organizations of medical physics representing 10,000 individuals. Fosters international cooperation in medical physics; promotes communication between various branches of medical physics and allied subjects. Conducts training programs. Has established 43 libraries in developing countries. **Founded:** 1963. Multinational. **Budget:** $50,000. **Publication:** *Clinical Physics and Physiological Measurement*, bimonthly ■ *Medical Physics World*, semiannual ■ *Physics in Medicine and Biology*, monthly.

INTERNATIONAL ORTHOPTIC ASSOCIATION (IOA)

Moorfields Eye Hospital
City Rd.
London EC1V 2PD, England
Bronia Unwin, Sec.-Treas.
PH: 44 171 2533411
Description: Orthoptists in 22 countries certified to treat defects in binocular vision, faulty visual habits, and low visual acuity. Organizes and conducts an international congress of orthoptists; shares information through newsletters. **Founded:** 1967. **Membership:** 4000. Multinational. **Languages:** English. **Budget:** L7,000. **Publication:** *Abstracts of Congress* (in English, French, and German), quadrennial. Journal. Price: L20.00. Advertising: accepted ■ *Newsletter* (in English), annual.

INTERNATIONAL PERIMETRIC SOCIETY (IPS)

e-mail: michael_wall@uiowa.edu
url: http://www.webeye.obhth.wiswa.edu/isps/
Department of Neurology
200 Hawkins Dr., No. 2007 RCP
Iowa City, IA 52242
Michael Wall, M.D., Sec.
PH: (319)356-8758
FX: (319)356-4505
Description: Opthalmologists, scientists, and technicians in 20 countries working in the field of perimetry (visual field testing) and related areas. Promotes the study of normal and abnormal visual function and encourages worldwide cooperation and friendship among those working in the field. **Founded:** 1974. **Membership:** 225. Multinational. **Languages:** English. **Budget:** $50,000. **Publication:** *Perimetry Update*, biennial. Proceedings. Circulation: 300.

INTERNATIONAL PHARMACEUTICAL EXCIPIENTS COUNCIL (IPEC)

e-mail: ipec@iscorp.com
1361 Alps Rd., Bldg. 3
Wayne, NJ 07470
Louis Blecher, Chm.
PH: (973)628-3231
FX: (973)628-3794
Description: Pharmaceutical and excipient manufacturing companies. Promotes the use of inactive ingredients (excipients) in pharmaceuticals that do not affect the safety or effectiveness of the final product. Encourages harmonization of worldwide standards to facilitate uniformity of product. Seeks to ensure the safety and quality of excipients and represent the interests of members. Develops safety guidelines and good manufacturing practices guidelines. Provides expertise and information to the U.S. Food and Drug Administration, U.S. Pharmacopoeia and equivalents in Europe and Japan. **Founded:** 1991. **Membership:** 25. Multinational. **Languages:** English. **Budget:** $300,000. **Publication:** *IPEC Newsletter*, quarterly. Price: Free, for members only.

INTERNATIONAL PHARMACEUTICAL FEDERATION (IPF)
(Federation Internationale Pharmaceutique)

e-mail: int.phar.fed@fip.nl
url: http://www.pharmweb.net/
Andries Bickerweg 5
NL-2517 JP The Hague, Netherlands
A.W. Davidson, Gen.Sec.
PH: 31 70 3021976
FX: 31 70 3633914
Description: Pharmaceutical organizations, pharmacists, and other interested organizations in 85 countries. Objectives are to: develop pharmacy at the international level in professional and scientific fields; extend the role of the pharmacist in the health care field; foster communication among members; act as a clearinghouse; collaborate with efforts to improve pharmaceutical structures in various countries; advocate and support measures to ensure distribution, dispensation, and proper use of medicines. Exchanges opinions on professional and ethical issues; develops research and study programs; fosters cooperation among pharmacists, teachers, research workers, and the practitioners in the field of drug information; improves methods for assembling, selecting, summarizing, indexing, storing, classifying, and analyzing clinical and social surveys. Subjects studied include biopharmaceutics, pharmacokinetics and drug metabolism, administrative and social pharmacy, pharmacognosy, and the history of pharmacy. Collaborates with World Health Organization. **Founded:** 1912. **Membership:** 4000. **Staff:** 6. Multinational. **Languages:** English, French. **Budget:** 4,000,000 f. **Publication:** *International Pharmacy Journal* (in English, French, German, and Spanish), bimonthly. ISSN: 1010-0923. Circulation: 5,000. Advertising: accepted ■ *Scientific Congress Proceedings*, biennial.

INTERNATIONAL PLANNED PARENTHOOD FEDERATION -AFRICA REGIONAL OFFICE

e-mail: ippfaro@ken.healthnet.org
PO Box 30234
Nairobi, Kenya
Mr. Kodio Efu, Reg.Dir.
PH: 254 2 720280
FX: 254 2 726596
Description: Co-ordinates activities of Planned Parenthood member associations operating in sub-Saharan Africa. Advocates family planning as a basic human right. Works to heighten governmental and public awareness of the population problems of local communities in Africa. Seeks to extend and improve family and sexual and reproductive health planning services. Conducts research on human fertility and contraception. **Founded:** 1971. **Staff:** 42. Multinational. **Languages:** English, French. **Budget:** 15,075 KSh. **Publication:** *Adam & Eve and the Serpent* (in English). Book. Price: 5.00 KSh. Advertising: not accepted ■ *Africa Link* (in English and French), semiannual. Magazine. Reports on sexual and reproductive health programmes of family planning associations in the region and provides related information on

global events. Price: free. ISSN: 0250-698X. Circulation: 4,500. Advertising: not accepted ■ *Contraceptive Update: A Handbook for Health Workers* ■ *Legal and Policy Barriers Affecting Sexual and Reproductive Health Service in: Burkina Faso, Senegal, Swaziland, Zambia* ■ *Regional Conference of Women, Islam and Family Planning, Niamey, Niger.* Report.

INTERNATIONAL PLANNED PARENTHOOD FEDERATION EAST AND SOUTH EAST ASIA AND OCEANIA REGION

e-mail: anandake@ippf.org
Regents College, Inner Circle
Regent's Park
London NW1 4NS, England
Mahdi Nawi, Acting Regional Dir.
PH: 44 171 4877900
FX: 44 171 4877970
Description: Works to co-ordinate activities for Planned Parenthood offices operating in the Asia and Oceania region. Advocates family planning as a basic human right. Works to increase governmental and public awareness of population problems in local regions. Promotes effective family planning programs. Conducts research on human fertility and contraception. **Founded:** 1960. **Membership:** 25. **Staff:** 17. Multinational. **Languages:** Malay. **Budget:** $1,228,300. **Publication:** *People and Development Challenges* (in English), semiannual. Magazine. Price: free. Circulation: 3,500. Advertising: not accepted.

INTERNATIONAL PLANNED PARENTHOOD FEDERATION -TUNIS

e-mail: awro@ippf.intl.tn
Arab World Regional Office
2, Place Virgile
Notre Dame
TN-1082 Tunis, Tunisia
PH: 216 1 847344
FX: 216 1 788661
Description: Advocates family planning as a basic human right in Tunisia. Works to increase governmental and public awareness of population problems. Promotes effective family planning services. Conducts research on human fertility and contraception. **Languages:** Arabic, French.

INTERNATIONAL PLANNED PARENTHOOD FEDERATION -UNITED KINGDOM (IPPF)
(Federation Internationale pour la Planification Familiale)

e-mail: info@ippf.org
url: http://www.ippf.org
Regent's College
Inner Circle
Regent's Park
London NW1 4NS, England
Mrs. Ingar Brueggemann, Sec.Gen.
PH: 44 171 4877900
FX: 44 171 4877950
Description: National, independent, and nongovernmental family planning associations. Works to: initiate and support family planning services and sexual and reproductive health services throughout the world; heighten governmental and public awareness of the population issues. Promotes effective family planning services in order to improve the well-being of parents and their children; concerns itself with the efficacy and safety of various methods of contracepton. Seeks to: create strong volunteer participation; promote family planning and sexual and reproductive health as a basic human right; extend and improve services; meet the needs of young people; improve the status of women; increase male involvement in family planning; develop human financial and material resources; stimulate research on subjects related to human fertility and disseminate the findings of such research; encourage and coordinate training of the federation's professional workers. **Founded:** 1952. **Membership:** 150. **Staff:** 292. Multinational. **National Groups:** 154. **Languages:** Arabic, English. **Budget:** $000,000. **Publication:** *Family Planning Handbook for Doctors* (in English, French, and Spanish), periodic. Advertising: not accepted ■ *IPPF Annual Report* (in Arabic, English,

French, and Spanish) ▪ *IPPF Directory of Contraceptives*, periodic. Booklet ▪ *IPPF Medical Bulletin* (in English, French, and Spanish), bimonthly ▪ *Open File*, monthly. Newsletter ▪ *People and the Planet* (in English), quarterly. Magazine. Price: $25.00. Advertising: not accepted ▪ *Planned Parenthood Challenges* (in English), semiannual. Magazine. Price: Free to affiliates and members. Advertising: not accepted.

INTERNATIONAL PLANNED PARENTHOOD FEDERATION, WESTERN HEMISPHERE REGION (IPPF/WHR)
e-mail: info@ippfwhr.org
url: http://www.ippfwhr.org
120 Wallstreet, 9th Fl.
New York, NY 10005
Hernan Sanhueza, Regional Dir.
PH: (212)248-6400
FX: (212)248-2441
Description: Independent family planning organizations in Canada, Latin America, Caribbean Islands, and the United States. Views family planning as "the expression of the human right of couples to have only the children they want and to have them when they want them." Works to extend the practice of voluntary family planning by providing information, education, and services to couples. Seeks to persuade governments to establish national family planning programs. Conducts research programs; maintains speakers' bureau; sponsors specialized education programs. **Founded:** 1952. **Membership:** 46. **Staff:** 65. Multinational. **Languages:** English, Spanish. **Budget:** $21,779,220. **Publication:** *Forum* (in English and Spanish), quarterly. Magazine. Includes calendar of events. Distributed primarily to affiliated family planning programs ▪ Annual Report (in English and Spanish). Advertising: not accepted.

INTERNATIONAL PSYCHO-ONCOLOGY SOCIETY (IPOS)
e-mail: marchint@mskcc.org
url: http://www.ipos.org/iposmis.htm
1275 York Ave., Box. 421
New York, NY 10021
Uwe Koch, M.D.
PH: (212)639-7051
FX: (212)717-3087
Description: Addresses the two major psychological dimensions of cancer: the psychological response of patients to cancer and the behavioral and social factors that influence risk, detection and survival. .

INTERNATIONAL RESEARCH GROUP ON COLOUR VISION DEFICIENCIES (IRGCVD)
e-mail: coa09@cc.keele.ac.uk
url: http://orlab.optom.unsw.edu.au./IRGCVD/
Dept. of Communication and Neuroscience
Keele University
Stafford ST5 5BG, England
Prof. J.D. Moreland, Contact
PH: 44 1782 583060
FX: 44 1782 583055
Description: Ophthalmologists, optometrists, physicists, physiologists, psychologists, and zoologists. Seeks to collaborate on the study of congenital and acquired color vision deficiencies. **Founded:** 1971. **Membership:** 200. Multinational. **Languages:** English. **Publication:** *Daltoniana* (in English), quarterly. Newsletter ▪ *Proceedings of the IRGCVD Symposia*, biennial.

INTERNATIONAL RETT SYNDROME ASSOCIATION (IRSA)
e-mail: irsa@paltech.com
url: http://www2.paltech.com/irsa/irsa.htm
9121 Piscataway Rd., No. 2B
Clinton, MD 20735
Kathy Hunter, Pres.
PH: (301)856-3334
TF: 800818-RETT
FX: (301)856-3336
Description: Parents of children with Rett Syndrome; interested professionals and supporters. (A child afflicted with Rett Syn-

drome, which strikes only females, seems normal until 7 to 18 months of age, when autistic-like withdrawal sets in; though this symptom eases in time, higher brain functions continue to deteriorate, leading to severe retardation. The child also loses purposeful use of her hands, wringing them in a constant "handwashing" movement in front of the face or chest. The syndrome is named for Dr. Andreas Rett, of Vienna, Austria, who described it in 1966. Research has not yet revealed a cause, but since the syndrome affects only girls, it is likely that it has a genetic origin in some defect of the X chromosome.) Provides support to parents; encourages research; collects and disseminates information. Assists in identifying syndrome victims; conducts activities aimed at the prevention, treatment, and eventual eradication of Rett Syndrome. **Founded:** 1985. **Membership:** 2000. **Staff:** 3. Multinational. **State Groups:** 20. **Languages:** English. **Budget:** $350,000. **Publication:** *Educational and Therapeutic Intervention in Rett Syndrome.* Journal. Explores a variety of treatment strategies & learning approaches, decisions about placement and/or inclusion in classrooms. Price: $5.00 members; $10.00 non-members ▪ *International Rett Syndrome Association – Newsletter*, quarterly. Price: included in membership dues. Circulation: 3,500. Advertising: not accepted ▪ *Orthopedic Problems in Rett Syndrome* ▪ *The Parent Idea Book* ▪ *Rett Sydrome: A Physician's Approach.* Video ▪ *Rett Syndrome: A Closer Look.* Video ▪ *Rett Syndrome: A Conversation with Families.* Video ▪ *Rett Syndrome: A Therapeutic Approach.* Video ▪ *Understanding Rett Syndrome* ▪ *What is Rett Syndrome.* **Formerly:** (1985) International Rett's Syndrome Association.

INTERNATIONAL SKELETAL SOCIETY (ISS)
e-mail: harry.genant@oarg.ucsf.edu
University of California
Dept. of Radiology
505 Parnassus Ave., No. M392
San Francisco, CA 94143-0628
Harry K. Genant, M.D., Contact
PH: (415)476-4864
FX: (415)476-8550
Description: Physicians and scientists interested in skeletal muscle disease. Seeks to advance the science of skeletal radiology; brings together radiologists and individuals in related disciplines; provides continuing education courses. **Founded:** 1973. **Membership:** 433. Multinational. **Languages:** English. **Publication:** *Skeletal Radiology*, 8/year. Journal. Contains scientific articles and case reports. Price: included in membership dues. Circulation: 1,200. Advertising: accepted ▪ Membership Directory, annual ▪ Newsletter, semiannual.

INTERNATIONAL SOCIETY FOR ADOLESCENT PSYCHIATRY
e-mail: rlandy7257@aol.com
730 Soundview Ave.
Bronx, NY 10473
Rosalie Landy, Admin.Dir.
PH: (718)542-0394
Description: Psychiatrists, psychologists, psychoanalysts, social workers, sociologists, pediatricians, educators, and health care professionals involved in the treatment of adolescents. Seeks to advance treatment of psychiatric illnesses of adolescents. Maintains research and educational programs. **Founded:** 1985. **Membership:** 900. Multinational. **Languages:** English. **Publication:** *International Annals of Adolescent Psychiatry*, triennial. Monograph. Price: included in membership dues ▪ Newsletter, 3/year. Price: included in membership dues.

INTERNATIONAL SOCIETY OF BLOOD TRANSFUSION (ISBT)
(Societe Internationale de Transfusion Sanguine)
PO Box 111
Royal Lancaster Infirmary
Ashton Rd.
Lancaster LA1 4GT, England
Dr. H.H. Gunser, Sec.Gen.

PH: 44 1524 306272
FX: 44 1524 306273
Description: Members of national blood bank societies in 105 countries. Works toward solving the scientific, technical, social, and ethical problems related to the transfusion of blood. Encourages closer relations among individuals dealing with such problems; standardizes methods and equipment. Facilitates the exchange of information among members. **Founded:** 1937. **Membership:** 1300. Multinational. **National Groups:** 105. **Languages:** English, French. **Publication:** *Transfusion Today*, quarterly ■ *Vox Sanguinis*, quarterly.

**INTERNATIONAL SOCIETY FOR CARDIOVASCULAR
  SURGERY (ISCVS)**
13 Elm St.
Manchester, MA 01944-1314
William T. Maloney, Exec.Dir.
PH: (508)526-8330
FX: (508)526-4018
Description: Encourages exchange and cooperation between cardiovascular specialists. Promotes discussion of ideas pertinent to the cardiovascular disease field and stimulates investigation and study of cardiovascular diseases. **Founded:** 1951. **Membership:** 2500. **Staff:** 12. Multinational. **Languages:** English. **Publication:** *Cardiovascular Surgery*, bimonthly. Journal. Advertising: accepted. **Formerly:** (1983) International Cardiovascular Society.

**INTERNATIONAL SOCIETY OF CHEMICAL ECOLOGY
  (ISCE)**
e-mail: iscesec@ucraci.ucr.edu
url: http://www.isce.ucr.edu/
Dept. of Entomology
Univ. of California
Riverside, CA 92521
Dr. Jocelyn Miller, Sec.
PH: (909)787-5821
FX: (813)974-3263
Description: Chemists, ecologists, biologists, and others with an interest in chemical ecology. Purpose is to promote understanding of the origin, function, and importance of natural chemicals that mediate interactions within and among organisms. Seeks to broaden the scope of chemical ecology and to stimulate cooperation and exchange of information among members of diverse scientific fields. Conducts educational programs designed to foster knowledge in the area of chemical ecology. **Founded:** 1983. **Membership:** 750. Multinational. **Languages:** English. **Budget:** $75,000. **Publication:** *ISCE Newsletter*, 3/year. Advertising: accepted ■ *Journal of Chemical Ecology*, monthly ■ *Proceedings of the Annual Meeting*.

**INTERNATIONAL SOCIETY FOR CLINICAL LABORATORY
  TECHNOLOGY (ISCLT)**
e-mail: isclt@aol.com
917 Locust St., Ste. 1100
St. Louis, MO 63101-1413
Mark S. Birenbaum, PhD, Admin.
PH: (314)241-1445
FX: (314)241-1449
Description: Clinical laboratory supervisors, technologists and technicians; physician's office laboratory technicians. Conducts educational programs; maintains placement service; offers specialized education. **Founded:** 1962. **Membership:** 6000. Multinational. **State Groups:** 12. **Languages:** English. **Publication:** *ISCLT Alert*, periodic. Features condensed reports of important news and legislative developments ■ *ISCLT Newsletter*, bimonthly. **Formerly:** International Society of Clinical Laboratory Technologists.

**INTERNATIONAL SOCIETY FOR DERMATOLOGIC
  SURGERY (ISDS)**
e-mail: straficano@aad.org
PO Box 4014
Schaumburg, IL 60168-4014
Sherrie Traficano, Exec.Dir.

PH: (847)330-9830
FX: (847)330-0050
Description: Dermatologists, otolaryngologists, plastic surgeons, and skin surgery specialists. Goals are to: promote high standards of patient care; provide for continuing education and research in dermatologic surgery; encourage public interest in the field. Provides a forum for the exchange of ideas and methodology in dermatologic surgery and related basic sciences. **Founded:** 1976. **Membership:** 1200. Multinational. **Languages:** English. **Publication:** *Journal of Dermatologic Surgery and Oncology*, monthly ■ Directory, annual.

INTERNATIONAL SOCIETY OF DERMATOLOGY (ISD)
930 N. Meacham Rd.
Schaumburg, IL 60173
Dr. Degas Karlel, Pres.
PH: (847)330-9830
FX: (847)330-0050
Description: Dermatologists and general physicians. Promotes interest, education, and research in dermatology. **Founded:** 1957. **Membership:** 2000. Multinational. **Languages:** English. **Budget:** $75,000. **Publication:** *International Journal of Dermatology*, monthly ■ Directory, biennial. **Formerly:** (1984) International Society of Tropical Dermatology; (1997) International Society of Dermatology: Tropical, Geographic, and Ecologic.

**INTERNATIONAL SOCIETY OF DERMATOLOGY:
  TROPICAL, GEOGRAPHIC, AND ECOLOGICAL -
  COLOMBIA**
Aparatado Aereo 90123
Bogota, Colombia
Dr. Maria M. Duran, Sec.Gen.
PH: 57 1 2575936
FX: 57 1 2182596
Description: Promotes the study of dermatology. Concerned with the education and tracking of skin diseases. Multinational. **Publication:** *International Journal of Dermatology* (in English), 10/year. Practical dematology for practicioners all over the world. Advertising: accepted.

**INTERNATIONAL SOCIETY OF ELECTROCARDIOLOGY
  (ISE)**
e-mail: peter.w.macfarlane@clinmed.gla.ac.uk
University Department of Medical Cardiology
Royal Infirmary
10 Alexandra Parade
Glasgow G31 2ER, Scotland
Prof. Peter W. Macfarlane, Sec.
PH: 44 141 2114724
FX: 44 141 5526114
Description: Researchers and physicians in 25 countries in cardiovascular physiology and pathology, cardiology, biomathematics, biophysics, and computer science who are interested in electrocardiology. Sponsors International Committee on Electrocardiology to develop professional programs. **Founded:** 1994. **Membership:** 300. Multinational. **Languages:** English. **Publication:** *Proceedings* (in English), annual. Advertising: not accepted.

**INTERNATIONAL SOCIETY AND FEDERATION OF
  CARDIOLOGY (ISFC)**
(Societe et Federation Internationale de Cardiologie)
e-mail: isfc@compuserve.com
Case Postale 117
CH-1211 Geneva, Switzerland
Marianne B. de Figueiredo, Exec.Sec.
PH: 41 22 3476755
FX: 41 22 3471028
Description: Societies of cardiology and heart foundations. Promotes international study, prevention, and treatment of cardiovascular diseases; encourages, coordinates, and assists the development of educational and scientific programs focusing on cardiovascular problems. **Founded:** 1978. **Membership:** 64. **Staff:** 2. Multinational. **National Groups:** 125. **Languages:** English, French. **Publication:** *Heartbeat*, quarterly. **Formed by Merger of:**

International Cardiology Federation; International Society of Cardiology.

INTERNATIONAL SOCIETY FOR GENERAL RELATIVITY AND GRAVITATION
e-mail: M.A.H.MacCallum@qmw.ac.uk
url: http://www.maths.qmw.ac.uk/hyperspace/
School of Mathematical Sciences
Queen Mary and Westfield College
Mile End Rd.
London E1 4NS, England
M.A.H. MacCallum, Sec.
PH: 44 171 9755445
FX: 44 181 9819587
Description: Scientists from 38 countries active in the field of general relativity and gravitation. Offers information services. Founded: 1957. Membership: 400. Staff: 2. Multinational. Publication: Contains technical scientific articles on relativity and gravitation.. (in English). Journal. ISSN: 0001-7701. Advertising: not accepted ▪ General Relativity and Gravitation, monthly ▪ Directory, periodic. Also Known As: GRG Committee. Formerly: (1971) International Committee on General Relativity and Gravitation.

INTERNATIONAL SOCIETY FOR HEART RESEARCH
Dept. of Medicine
University of Louisville Health Science Center
550 S. Jackson
Louisville, KY 40292
Roberto Bolli, M.D., Sec.Gen.
PH: (502)852-1837
FX: (502)852-6474
Description: Professionals and investigators in the field of experimental cardiology united to foster multidisciplinary approaches for finding solutions to the problems of heart disease. Conducts research in cardiac metabolism. Founded: 1967. Membership: 2000. Multinational. Publication: Advances in Myocardiology. Journal ▪ Journal of Molecular and Cellular Cardiology, monthly. Formerly: International Society for Cardiovascular Research.

INTERNATIONAL SOCIETY OF INTERNAL MEDICINE (ISIM)
(Societe Internationale de Medecine Interne)
e-mail: r.streuli@rsl.ch
url: http://www.acponline.org/isim/
Regional Hospital
CH-4900 Langenthal, Switzerland
Dr. Rolf A. Streuli, Sec.Gen.
PH: 41 62 9163102
FX: 41 62 9164155
Description: Internal medicine specialists. Promotes scientific knowledge in internal medicine; furthers the education of young internists; encourages friendship among physicians in all countries. Federation of Societies of Internal Medicine from 43 countries. Founded: 1948. Membership: 2000. Multinational. National Groups: 48. Languages: English.

INTERNATIONAL SOCIETY FOR MAGNETIC RESONANCE IN MEDICINE
e-mail: info@ismrm.org
url: http://ismrm.org
2118 Milvia St., Ste. 201
Berkeley, CA 94704
Jane Tiemann, Exec.Dir.
PH: (510)841-1899
FX: (510)841-2340
Description: Devoted to furthering the development and application of MRI and its techniques in medicine and biology. Sponsors educational and research programs. Founded: 1981. Membership: 5000. Staff: 9. Multinational. Languages: English. Formerly (1995) Society for Magnetic Resonance.

INTERNATIONAL SOCIETY ON METABOLIC EYE DISEASE (ISMED)
1125 Park Ave.
New York, NY 10128
Heskel M. Haddad, M.D., Sec.-Treas.
PH: (212)427-1246
FX: (212)360-7009
Description: Ophthalmologists, pediatricians, endocrinologists, internists, and paramedical personnel in 20 countries. Promotes the study of metabolic eye problems and biochemical and genetic aspects of such problems. Founded: 1971. Membership: 600. Multinational. Languages: English. Publication: Metabolic, Pediatric, and Systemic Ophthalmology, quarterly. Journal. Price: $160.00/year. Advertising: not accepted ▪ Book.

INTERNATIONAL SOCIETY OF NEUROPATHOLOGY
(Societe Internationale de Neuropathologie)
e-mail: jra20@cam.ac.uk
url: http://www.his.path.cam.ac.uk/npsoc/welcome.html
Dept. of Histopathology
Addenbrooke's Hospital
Cambridge CB2 2QQ, England
Dr. Janice R. Anderson, Sec.Gen.
PH: 44 1 223217170
FX: 44 1 223216980
Description: Members of national societies of neuropathology in 30 countries. Works to foster the formation of national and regional societies of neuropathology and to promote cooperation among these societies. Maintains liaison with international organizations in various fields of neurological sciences. Encourages the exchange of information and persons engaged in neuropathology. Initiates research projects. Founded: 1972. Membership: 2500. Multinational. Languages: English. Publication: Brain Pathology, quarterly. Journal. Price: $70.00 individual; $120.00 insitutional. Advertising: accepted ▪ Membership Directory, periodic. Alternate Formats: online. Supersedes: International Committee of Neuropathology.

INTERNATIONAL SOCIETY FOR PHARMACOECONOMICS AND OUTCOMES RESEARCH
CN-5256, No. 319
Princeton, NJ 08543-5256
Marilyn Dix-Smith, Exec.Dir.
Description: Researchers who study the effectiveness of treatments. Founded: 1995.

INTERNATIONAL SOCIETY FOR PLASTINATION (ISP)
url: http://www.kfunigraz.ac.at/anaww/plast/index.html
University of Maryland at Baltimore, BRB
Anatomical Service Div.
School of Medicine, Rm. B-026
Baltimore, MD 21201
Ronald S. Wade, Treas.
PH: (410)706-3313
FX: (410)706-8107
Description: Anatomists, pathologists, and technologists. Seeks to share information about plastination, a means of infiltrating biological specimens with curable polymers. Founded: 1984. Membership: 200. Multinational. Languages: English. Publication: Journal of the International Society for Plastination, semiannual. Price: $10.00/issue. ISSN: 1090-2171. Circulation: 200. Advertising: accepted.

INTERNATIONAL SOCIETY OF PROFESSIONAL AROMATHERAPISTS
ISPA House,
82 Ashby Rd.
Hinckley LE10 1SN, England
Lisa Brown, Admin.
PH: 44 1455 637987
FX: 44 1455 890956
Description: Various categories of membership, the main group of which has trained with or meet the high standards required by ISPA accredited schools. Only this category of membership is

entitled to use the letter MISPATo develop and stimulate high professional standards, through qualification and practice. Accredited schools across the country. Local practitioner lists and public hot-line service. **Founded:** 1990. **Membership:** 2300. **Staff:** 3. Multinational. **National Groups:** 1. **Publication:** *Aromatherapy World* (in English), quarterly. Journal. Price: L3.75; by subscription. Circulation: 2,500. Advertising: accepted.

INTERNATIONAL SOCIETY OF PSYCHIATRIC CONSULTATION LIAISON NURSES (ISPCLN)
7794 Grow Dr.
Pensacola, FL 32514
Belinda E. Puetz, Admin.
PH: (850)474-4147
FX: (850)484-8762
Description: Nurses engaged in the practice of, or with an interest in, psychiatric consultation liaison nursing. Promotes development of psychiatric consultation nursing as a subspecialty of psychiatric and mental health nursing. Seeks to advance understanding of mind-body interaction in healing and wellness. Facilitates communication among members and serves as a clearinghouse on psychiatric consultation liaison nursing. Makes available networking opportunities and professional conference discounts to members. **Founded:** 1986. **Membership:** 250. Multinational. **Languages:** English.

INTERNATIONAL SOCIETY OF RADIOGRAPHERS AND RADIOLOGICAL TECHNOLOGISTS (ISRRT)
(Societe Internationale des Radiographes et Techniciens de Radiologie)
e-mail: isrrt@compuserve.com
url: http://users.aol.com/isrrt.isrrt.html
170 W The Donway, Ste. 404
Don Mills, ON, Canada M3C 2G3
T.J.D. West, Sec.Gen.
PH: (416)510-0805
FX: (416)445-4268
Description: National radiographic societies and other organizations having radiographers as members. Objectives are to: advance the science and practice of radiography, radiotherapy, and allied subjects by promoting improved standards of training and research in technical aspects of radiation medicine and protection; make results of research and experience available to practitioners; raise funds to further these objectives. Compiles statistics and maintains museum. Has established educational trust fund. Conducts teachers' seminars. **Founded:** 1959. **Membership:** 57. **Staff:** 1. Multinational. **National Groups:** 57. **Languages:** English. **Budget:** C$100,000. **Publication:** *Newsletter* (in English), semiannual. Contains radiation medicine articles and international news. Price: L6.50/year. ISSN: 1027-0671. Circulation: 2,500. Advertising: accepted ■ *Professional Standards for the Education of Medical Radiation Technologists* ■ *Quality Control Handbook* ■ *Role of Radiographers* ■ *Teaching Guides*, periodic ■ Proceedings, periodic. **Formerly:** International Society of Radiographers and Radiological Technicians.

INTERNATIONAL SOCIETY OF SURGERY (ISS)
(Societe Internationale de Chirurgie)
e-mail: 101762,1434@compuserve.com
url: http://www.surgery.nbs.ch
Netzibodenstr. 34
PO Box 1527
CH-4133 Pratteln, Switzerland
Dr. Thomas Ruedi, Sec.Gen.
PH: 41 61 8114770
FX: 41 61 8114775
Description: Surgeons from 80 countries wishing to contribute to the progress of science by researching and discussing surgical problems at congresses and general assemblies. **Founded:** 1902. **Membership:** 3700. **Staff:** 3. Multinational. **National Groups:** 80. **Languages:** English. **Budget:** $320,000. **Publication:** *ISS/SIC*, 2-3/year. Newsletter ■ *Membership Booklet*, biennial. Price: for members only. Circulation: 4,000. Advertising: accepted ■ *World*

Journal of Surgery (in English), monthly. Scientific publication on general surgery. Circulation: 7,000. Advertising: accepted.

INTERNATIONAL SOCIETY FOR THE STUDY OF DISSOCIATION (ISSD)
4700 W. Lake Ave.
Glenview, IL 60025
Jeffrey W. Engle, Exec.Dir.
PH: (847)375-4718
FX: (847)375-4777
Description: Mental health professionals; students. Promotes a greater understanding of the field of dissociation. Conducts research into the diagnosis and treatment of multiple personalities and dissociation. Sponsors educational programs. **Founded:** 1982. **Membership:** 1900. **Staff:** 2. Multinational. **Languages:** English. **Budget:** $300,000. Formerly International Society for the Study of Multiple Personalities and Dissociation.

INTERNATIONAL SOCIETY FOR THYMOLOGY AND IMMUNOTHERAPY
(Internationale Gesellschaft fur Thymologie und Immuntherapie)
e-mail: biofger@aol.com
Am Stadtpark 18
D-38667 Bad Harzburg, Germany
Hildegarde Rieger, Contact
PH: 49 5322 6520
FX: 49 5322 3017
Description: Promotes the study of thymology and immunotherapy treatment. Disseminates information on the different areas of thymus research and the therapeutic applications of thymus elements. **Founded:** 1975. **Membership:** 100. Multinational. **Budget:** $10,000.

INTERNATIONAL SOCIETY ON TOXICOLOGY (IST)
e-mail: mebg@em.uni-frankfurt.de
University of Frankfurt
Kennedyallee 104
D-60596 Frankfurt, Germany
Mr. Dietrich Mebs, Sec.
PH: 69 63017563
FX: 69 63015882
Description: Biochemists, pharmacologists, immunologists, herpetologists, physiologists, microbiologists, ichthyologists, physicians, and others studying animal, plant, and microbial toxins (poisons and venoms). Seeks to advance knowledge on the properties of toxins and antitoxins derived from plant and animal tissues. **Founded:** 1961. **Membership:** 600. Multinational. **Regional Groups:** 3. **Publication:** *Toxicon: An International Journal Devoted to the Exchange of Knowledge on the Poisons Derived from Animals, Plants, and Microorganisms*, monthly. Includes meeting announcements. Price: DM 110.00/year for members; DM 635.25/year for institutions. ISSN: 0041-0101. Advertising: accepted. Alternate Formats: microform ■ Membership Directory, periodic. Advertising: not accepted ■ Newsletter, quarterly.

INTERNATIONAL SOCIETY OF TROPICAL PEDIATRICS (ISTP)
Medical Center Manila, Ste. 326
1122 Gen. Luna St.
Ermita, Philippines
Prof. Perla D. Santos Ocampo, Exec.Dir.
PH: 63 2 5247874
FX: 63 2 7216569
Description: Promotes pediatrics in tropical and sub-tropical regions. Encourages pediatricians to familiarize themselves with diseases unique to these climates. **Founded:** 1986. **Membership:** 100. **Languages:** English.

INTERNATIONAL STRABISMOLOGICAL ASSOCIATION (ISA)
702 Rotary Cir.
Indianapolis, IN 46202
Eugene Helveston, Sec.

PH: (317)274-1214
FX: (317)274-1111
Description: Ophthalmologists specializing in strabismus (eye movement disorders). Encourages research and education among members. Bestows quadrennial Linksz Medal an Award to outstanding strabismologists. Bestows quadrennial Biecschowsky lectureship to an outstanding strabismologist. **Founded:** 1966. **Membership:** 400. **Staff:** 1. Multinational. **Languages:** English. **Publication:** *Proceedings Volume*, quadrennial ▪ Membership Directory, periodic. **Also Known As:** Association Internationale de Strabisme.

INTERNATIONAL TRANSACTIONAL ANALYSIS ASSOCIATION (ITAA)
e-mail: info@itaa-net.org
url: http://www.ita-net.org
Analysis Association
450 Pacific Ave., Ste. 250
San Francisco, CA 94133-4640
Susan Sevilla, Exec.Dir.
PH: (415)989-5640
FX: (415)989-9343
Description: Educational corporation of persons in medical and behavioral sciences, including psychiatrists, psychologists, social workers, nurses, educators, marriage and family counselors, clergy, and organizational consultants. Maintains standards of practice and teaching of transactional analysis, which involves group therapy, social dynamics, and personality theory based on analysis of the "transactions" or interactions between persons. (The book, *Games People Play*, covers basic transactional analysis theory; its author, Dr. Eric Berne, was ITAA founder.). **Founded:** 1958. **Membership:** 2500. **Staff:** 3. Multinational. **Languages:** English. **Budget:** $400,000. **Publication:** *International Transactional Analysis Association Membership Directory*, annual. Price: $10.00 ▪ *ITAA Membership Directory*, annual ▪ *Script*, 9/year. Newsletter ▪ *Transactional Analysis Journal*, quarterly. **Formerly:** (1961) San Francisco Social Psychiatry Seminar.

INTERNATIONAL TRANSPLANT NURSES SOCIETY (ITNS)
e-mail: jnla74a@prodigy.com
url: http://www.transweb.org/itns
651 Holiday Dr., Ste. 300
Pittsburgh, PA 15220-2740
Beth A. Kassalen, MBA, Exec.Dir.
PH: (412)928-3667
FX: (412)928-4951
Description: Nurses, LVNs, LPNs, and others involved in patient care for organ transplantation. Works to encourage cooperation among all medical disciplines involved in transplantation, disseminate information, and establish certification for this nursing specialty. **Founded:** 1992. **Membership:** 1200. **Staff:** 1. Multinational. **State Groups:** 13. **Languages:** English. **Budget:** $150,000.

INTERNATIONAL TRAUMA ANESTHESIA AND CRITICAL CARE SOCIETY (ITACCS)
url: http://www.trauma.itaccs.com
PO Box 4826
Baltimore, MD 21211
Christopher M. Grande, MD,MPH, Exec.Dir.
PH: (410)235-7697
FX: (410)235-8084
Description: Healthcare professionals involved in trauma and critical care anesthesiology. Works to gain recognition for trauma anesthesiology as a discipline within anesthesiology and critical care medicine. Promotes cooperation and information sharing among healthcare professionals. Sponsors seminars and workshops; conducts research and educational programs; provides children's services; holds competitions; maintains speakers' bureau and placement service. **Founded:** 1988. **Membership:** 1000. Multinational. **Languages:** English.

INTERNATIONAL TREMOR FOUNDATION (ITF)
e-mail: UPF_ITF@msn.com
833 W. Washington Blvd.
Chicago, IL 60607
Judy Rosner, Exec.Dir.
PH: (312)733-1893
FX: (312)733-1896
Description: Individuals suffering from tremors, their families and friends and health care professionals. (Tremor is a common symptom of neurologic disease and may be due to trauma, tumor, stroke or degenerative disease. The hands and head are most often affected. Current treatment includes drug therapy and surgical intervention.) Promotes research and development of clinical care programs. Provides patient information and referrals. **Founded:** 1988. **Membership:** 25000. **Staff:** 2. Multinational. **Regional Groups:** 9. **Languages:** English. **Publication:** Newsletter, quarterly. Includes research reports and networking information. Price: included in membership dues. Circulation: 25,000. Advertising: not accepted.

INTERNATIONAL UNION AGAINST CANCER (UICC)
(Union Internationale Contre le Cancer)
e-mail: info@uicc.org
3, rue du Conseil General
CH-1205 Geneva, Switzerland
A.J. Turnbull, Exec.Dir.
PH: 41 22 8091811
FX: 41 22 8091810
Description: Voluntary cancer leagues and societies, national organizations, private or public cancer research institutions, and ministries of health in 86 countries. Promotes a comprehensive international campaign against cancer. Directs activities in fields of prevention, research, and treatment; sponsors special projects in fields including cervical cancer, head and neck cancer, and exchange of information on unproven methods in cancer treatment. Facilitates training courses for researchers and health professionals; makes available advisory visits by cancer experts. Bestows numerous fellowships and awards. **Founded:** 1933. **Membership:** 290. **Staff:** 19. Multinational. **Languages:** English. **Budget:** $4,000,000. **Publication:** *International Calendar of Meetings on Cancer* (in English), semiannual. Price: free. Circulation: 10,000. Advertising: accepted. Alternate Formats: online ▪ *International Journal of Cancer and Predictive Oncology*, 30/year ▪ *UICC International Directory of Cancer Institutes and Organizations*, quadrennial. Alternate Formats: online ▪ *UICC News*, quarterly. Alternate Formats: online.

INTERNATIONAL UNION OF BIOCHEMISTRY AND MOLECULAR BIOLOGY (IUBMB)
e-mail: kleinkauf@chemie.tu-berlin.de
url: http://www.iubmb.unibe.ch
Technical University Berlin, Sekr. OE 2
Franklinstrasse 29
D-10587 Berlin, Germany
Dr. Horst Kleinkauf, Exec.Off. & Gen.Sec.
PH: 49 30 31424205
FX: 49 30 31424783
Description: National academies, research councils, or biochemical societies; associate members are regional bodies representing several national biochemical and molecular biology societies; special members are organizations representing individual biochemists. Promotes international cooperation in the research, discussion, and publication of matters relating to biochemistry and molecular biology. Seeks to: standardize methods, nomenclature, and symbols used in biochemistry and molecular biology; contribute to the advancement of biochemistry; promote high standards; aid biochemists and molecular biologists in developing countries. Supports interest group meetings; sponsors discussions. **Founded:** 1955. **Membership:** 65. Multinational. **Languages:** English. **Publication:** *Biochemical Education*, quarterly ▪ *Biochemical Nomenclature and Related Documents*, periodic. Standardizes and codifies the nomenclature of natural products. Advertising: not accepted ▪ *Biochemistry and Molecular Biology International*, monthly ▪ *BioFactors*, quarterly ▪ *Journal of Bio-*

technology and Applied Biochemistry, bimonthly. Covers applications of biochemical research with emphasis on biotechnology. ISSN: 0161-7354 ■ *Trends in Biochemical Sciences*, monthly. **Formerly:** (1991) National Union of Biochemistry.

INTERNATIONAL UNION OF IMMUNOLOGICAL SOCIETIES (IUIS)
Lister Research Laboratories
University Department of Surgery
Royal Infirmary, Laurston Pl.
Edinburgh EH3 9YW, Scotland
Keith James, Sec.Gen.
PH: 44 131 5363831
FX: 44 131 6676190
Description: National professional societies of basic and applied immunologists. Encourages the orderly development and utilization of the science of immunology. Promotes the application of new developments to clinical and veterinary problems and standardizes reagents and nomenclature. Conducts educational symposia and scientific meetings. **Founded:** 1969. **Membership:** 51. Multinational. **Regional Groups:** 4. **Languages:** English. **Budget:** $100,000. **Publication:** *The Immunologist*, bimonthly. Journal. Advertising: accepted.

INTERNATIONAL UNION OF PHARMACOLOGY (IUPHAR)
e-mail: w.c.bowman@strath.ac.uk
url: http://www.medfac.unimelb.edu.au/iuphar/plenary.htm
University of Strathclyde
Dept. of Physiology & Pharmacology
204 George St.
Glasgow G1 1XW, Scotland
Prof. W.C. Bowman
PH: 44 141 5524400
FX: 44 141 5522562
Description: National and international societies in pharmacology and related disciplines representing approximately 30,000 individuals. Purpose is to promote cooperation between pharmacological societies and encourage free international exchange of ideas and research. Acts as a forum for participation between related scientific bodies. Works to standardize the use of drugs worldwide and rationally define the receptors and ion channels on which they act. **Founded:** 1966. **Membership:** 52. Multinational. **National Groups:** 52. **Languages:** English. **Budget:** $60,000. **Publication:** *Congress Proceedings*, quadrennial ■ *Directory of IUPHAR*, annual ■ *IUPHAR Newsletter*, semiannual.

INTERNATIONAL UNION FOR PHYSICAL AND ENGINEERING SCIENCES IN MEDICINE (IUPESM)
e-mail: iupesm@amc.uva.nl
AMC, University of Amsterdam
Dept. of Medical Physics & Informatics
Meibergdreef 15
NL-1105 AZ Amsterdam, Netherlands
Prof.Dr.Ir. Jos. A.E. Spaan, Sec.Gen.
PH: 31 20 5665200
FX: 31 20 6917233
Description: A joint project of the International Organization for Medical Physics and the International Federation of Medical and Biological Engineering. Promotes the application of engineering and physics to medicine. Represents the professional interests and views of engineering and physical scientists in the health care community. Coordinates and seeks backing for technology transfer to developing countries. Seeks to promote the coordination of IOMP and IFMBE activities on national and international levels. Promotes cooperation among members, related organizations, and governments. Organizes scientific conferences and seminars. Sponsors regional support programs; maintains working groups. **Founded:** 1982. **Membership:** 2. Multinational. **National Groups:** 35. **Languages:** English.

INTERNATIONAL UNION OF PHYSIOLOGICAL SCIENCES (IUPS)
e-mail: suorsoni@infobiogen.fr
url: http://www.nas.edu/iups/
Batiment Cervi
Hopital de la Pitie-Salpetriere
83, blvd. de l'Hopital
F-75651 Paris, France
Susan Orsoni, Exec.Sec.
PH: 33 1 42177537
FX: 33 1 42177575
Description: Physiological societies united to exchange scientific information. Coordinates research and educational programs. **Founded:** 1953. **Membership:** 52. **Staff:** 1. Multinational. **National Groups:** 52. **Languages:** English. **Publication:** *News in Physiological Sciences* (in English), quarterly. Journal. Price: $105.00 institution. ISSN: 0886-1714 ■ *World Directory of Physiologists* (in English), periodic.

INTERNATIONAL UNION OF PURE AND APPLIED PHYSICS (IUPAP)
(Union Internationale de Physique Pure et Appliquee)
url: http://www.umanitoba.ca/IUPAP/IUPAP.html
Vittens Gata 11
S-421 65V Frolunda, Sweden
Prof. Jan S. Nilsson, Pres. Designate
PH: 46 31 282828
FX: 46 31 7734628
Description: National physics committees or groups of physicists from 47 countries. Aims to stimulate and promote international cooperation in physics and the use of international symbols, units, nomenclature, and standards; provides assistance in organizing committees and meetings; encourages research and publication of papers and tables. Fosters free circulation of scientists. **Founded:** 1922. Multinational. **Languages:** English, French. **Budget:** $300,000. **Publication:** *General Report*, triennial ■ *News-Bulletin*, periodic.

INTERNATIONAL UNION OF RETICULOENDOTHELIAL SOCIETIES (IURES)
e-mail: maps@csra.net
c/o Dr. Sherwood M. Reichard
Med. College of Georgia
1120 15th St.
Augusta, GA 30912
Dr. Sherwood M. Reichard, Exec.Dir.
PH: (706)722-7511
FX: (702)722-7515
Description: Reticuloendothelial and related research societies concerned with the body's defenses against disease and cancer. Works to advance research and understanding of the reticuloendothelial system. (RES is a diffuse system of cells arising from mesenchyme and comprising all phagocytic cells of the body excluding circulating leukocytes.) Fosters and maintains scientific cooperation and communication among individual scientists and regional and national societies worldwide. Maintains liaison with the International Council of Scientific Unions, World Health Organization, and similar organizations to facilitate the appropriate representation of RES research. Sponsors international scientific conferences, seminars, workshops, and training courses. **Founded:** 1975. **Membership:** 3000. Multinational. **Languages:** English. **Publication:** *Proceedings of International Meetings*, biennial.

INTERNATIONAL UNION OF TOXICOLOGY
e-mail: kai.savolainen@uku.fi
url: http://www.ehsc.orst.edu/iutox
National Public Health Institute
Department of Environmental Medicine
PO Box 95
FIN-70701 Kuopio, Finland
K.M. Savoleinen, Sec.Gen.
PH: 358 17 162400
FX: 358 17 162424
Description: National organizations of toxicologists and other

scientists and medical professionals with an interest in toxicology. Seeks to advance the teaching, study, and practice of toxicology. Facilitates exchange of information among toxicologists worldwide; conducts research and educational programs; sponsors continuing professional development programs for members. **Founded:** 1980. **Membership:** 22. Multinational. **Languages:** English, Finnish. **Publication:** *Broadsheet*, periodic. Newsletter ■ *Proceedings of the International Congresses of Toxicology*, biennial.

INTERSOCIETY COMMITTEE ON PATHOLOGY INFORMATION (ICPI)
4733 Bethesda Ave., Ste. 700
Bethesda, MD 20814
Eileen M. Lavine, Info. Counsel
PH: (301)656-2944
FX: (301)656-3179
Description: One representative from each sponsoring society: American Society for Investigative Pathology; American Society of Clinical Pathologists; Association of Pathology Chairs; College of American Pathologists; U.S. & Canadian Academy of Pathology Disseminates information about the medical practice and research achievements of pathology. Produces career information. Convention/Meeting: none. **Founded:** 1957. **Membership:** 5. **Staff:** 2. **Languages:** English. **Publication:** *Directory of Pathology Training Programs: Residencies and Fellowships in US and Canada*, annual. Price: $25.00; $5.00 for medical students/ residents; free to medical schools/libraries/teaching hospita. Circulation: 2,500. Advertising: not accepted ■ *Pathology as a Career in Medicine*. Brochure.

INTERSTATE POSTGRADUATE MEDICAL ASSOCIATION OF NORTH AMERICA (IPMANA)
PO Box 5474
Madison, WI 53705
H. B. Maroney, Exec.Dir.
PH: (608)231-9045
FX: (608)257-1401
Description: Presents annual four-day teaching program in various branches of medicine and medical research, aimed at the family practitioner who must keep up with new developments in a short time away from his practice. Publications: none. **Founded:** 1916. **Staff:** 2. **Languages:** English. **Budget:** $250,000.

INTERSUBJECTS MEDICAL CLUB
Oborishte 35
BG-1504 Sofia, Bulgaria
Prof. Damian Damianov, D.Sc., Pres.
PH: 359 2 441157
FX: 359 2 441590
Description: Stimulates interest in medical research. **Founded:** 1993. **Membership:** 20. **Staff:** 1. **Regional Groups:** 2. **Languages:** Bulgarian, English. **Publication:** *ARS Medicina* (in Bulgarian), quarterly. Journal. Price: $5.00. Circulation: 1,000. Advertising: accepted ■ Proceedings.

IRISH CANCER SOCIETY (ICS)
e-mail: ics@uicc.ch
url: http://www.uicc.ch/ecl/
5 Northumberland Rd.
Dublin 4, Ireland
Tom Hudson, Contact
PH: 353 1 6681855
FX: 353 1 6687599
Description: National cancer societies. Promotes advancement in the prevention, diagnosis, and treatment of cancer; seeks to improve the quality of life of people with cancer and their families. Facilitates communication and cooperation among members; sponsors research and educational programs; provides support and services to people with cancer. **Languages:** English, Irish Gaelic.

IRISH FAMILY PLANNING ASSOCIATION (IFPA)
Unity Building
16-17 Lower O'Connell St.
Dublin 1, Ireland
Tony O'Brien, Exec.Dir.
PH: 353 1 8780366
FX: 353 1 8780375
Description: Works to improve the quality of life for individuals living in Ireland by promoting family planning and responsible parenthood. Advocates family planning as a basic human right. Offers programs in sex education, family planning, and health. Provides contraceptive and health care services. Conducts research. **Languages:** English.

IRISH MOTOR NEURONE DISEASE ASSOCIATION
Carmichael House
N. Brunswick St.
Dublin 7, Ireland
Eithne Frost, Contact
PH: 353 1 8730422
FX: 353 1 8735737
Description: Promotes interest in motor neurone disease (MND) research among medical and scientific communities and the public in Ireland. Offers support services to MND sufferers and their families. Disseminates information about the disease. **Founded:** 1985. **Staff:** 4. **Publication:** *IMNDA Newsletter* (in English), quarterly.

ISLAMIC MEDICAL ASSOCIATION (IMA)
e-mail: imana@aol.com
url: http://www.imana.org
950 75th St.
Downers Grove, IL 60516
Khursheed Mallick, M.D., Exec.Dir.
PH: (630)852-2122
FX: (630)435-1429
Description: Muslim physicians and allied health professionals. Unites Muslim physicians and allied health professionals in the U.S. and Canada for the improvement of professional and social contact; provides assistance to Muslim communities worldwide. Charitable programs include: donation of books, journals, and educational and research materials to medical institutions; donation of medical supplies and equipment to charity medical institutions in Muslim countries. Maintains speakers' bureau to present Islamic viewpoints on medical topics; sponsors placement service; offers assistance in orientation. **Founded:** 1967. **Membership:** 6000. **Staff:** 1. **Languages:** Arabic, Bengali. **Budget:** $125,000. **Publication:** *Al-Itiknga*, quarterly. Newsletter ■ *The Journal of IMA*, quarterly. Price: $50.00/year. Circulation: 2,500. Advertising: accepted. Alternate Formats: online. Also Cited As: *JIMA* ■ *The Mediview*, quarterly. Newsletter.

ISRAEL CANCER ASSOCIATION (ICA)
(Haagudah Lemilchama Besartan Beyisrael)
e-mail: ica@netvision.net.il
url: http://www.cancer.org.il
7 Revivim St.
PO Box 437
IL-53104 Givatayim, Israel
Mrs. Miri Ziv, Dir.Gen.
PH: 972 3 5721616
FX: 972 3 5719578
Description: Encourages and facilitates research on cancer prevention and early diagnosis. Supports cancer medical treatment services, and finances rehabilitation and social welfare programs for cancer patients. Provides educational programs. **Founded:** 1952. **Staff:** 160. **Local Groups:** 52. **Languages:** English, Hebrew. **Budget:** 15,420,000 IS. **Publication:** *Adcan* (in Hebrew), semiannual. Advertising: not accepted ■ *Bama* (in Hebrew), periodic. Journal. Includes information on medical, psychosocial, and welfare aspects of cancer.

ISRAEL MEDICAL ASSOCIATION
788 Marlee Ave., Ste. 309
Toronto, ON, Canada M6B 3K1
Dr. Dafna Gladman, Pres.
Description: Physicians, medical residents and interns, and medical students. Promotes professional and cultural interaction between physicians in Canada and Israel. Conducts educational programs. **Founded:** 1958. **Membership:** 400. **Staff:** 1. Multinational. **Languages:** English, Hebrew. **Publication:** Newsletter, quarterly.

ISRAEL PHYSICAL SOCIETY (IPS)
e-mail: havlin@ophir.ph.biu.ac.il
url: http://org.ph.biu.ac.il/ips/
U.S. Department of of Physics
Bar-Ilan University
IL-52900 Ramat-Gan, Israel
Prof. Shlomo Havlin, Pres.
PH: 972 3 5318436
FX: 972 3 5353298
Publication: *Annals of the Israel Physical Society.* Book.

ISRAEL SOCIETY BIOCHEMISTRY AND MOLECULAR BIOLOGY
e-mail: shimons@leonardo.1s.huji.ac.il
The Weizmann Institute of Science
PO Box 26
IL-76100 Rehovot, Israel
Prof. S. Schuldiner, Sec.
PH: 972 8 343808
FX: 972 2 634625
Description: Works to further the fields of Biochemistry and Molecular Biology through sponsoring awards and conducting research programs. **Founded:** 1990. **Membership:** 750. **Staff:** 3. **Languages:** English, Hebrew. **Budget:** 40,000 IS. **Formerly:** Israel Biochemical Society; Biochemical Society of Israel.

ISRAELI ARTHRITIS FOUNDATION (IAF)
192A Arlozorov Str.
IL-64923 Tel Aviv, Israel
Dr. Michael Ehrenfeld, Exec. Officer
PH: 972 3 6962760
FX: 972 3 6962759
Description: Seeks to aid individuals suffering from arthritis in Israel. Offers physiotherapy services; provides counseling. Conducts educational programs. Offers children's services. Compiles statistics; disseminates information. Maintains speakers' bureau; coordinates social activities. **Founded:** 1986. **Membership:** 2500. **Staff:** 2. **Local Groups:** 10. **Languages:** Hebrew. **Budget:** 100,000 IS. **Publication:** *Inbar* (in Hebrew), 2-3/year. Journal. Includes articles written by physicians. Circulation: 5,000. Advertising: accepted ■ Pamphlet, monthly. **Formerly:** (1992) Israeli League Against Rheumatism.

ISRAELI DERMATOLOGICAL SOCIETY (IDS)
Dermatology Out Patient Clinic
MEIR Hospital
IL-44281 Kfar-Saba, Israel
David Abraham, M.D., Sec.
PH: 972 9 7470769
FX: 972 9 7425027
Description: Dermatologists and dermatopathologists. Organizes postgraduate educational programs; conducts research. **Founded:** 1927. **Membership:** 232. **Local Groups:** 3. **Languages:** English, Hebrew.

ITALIAN PHYSICAL SOCIETY (IPS)
(Societa Italiana di Fisica)
e-mail: sif@sif.it
url: http://www.sif.it
Via Castiglione 101
I-40136 Bologna, Italy
Renato Ricci, Pres.

PH: 39 51 331554
FX: 39 51 581340
Description: Physicists, scientists, academics, and researchers. Promotes the study and development of physics in Italy. Offers annual courses at the Enrico Fermi International School of Physics. Publishes several journals of physics. **Founded:** 1897. **Membership:** 5000. **Staff:** 11. **Languages:** English, Italian. **Publication:** *Europhysics Letters* (in English), bimonthly. Published in conjunction with European Physical Society ■ *Giornale di Fisica* (in Italian), quarterly. Journal ■ *Nuovo Cimento Section C* (in English), bimonthly ■ *Nuovo Cimento Sections A, B, and D* (in English), monthly ■ *Nuovo Saggiatore* (in English and Italian), bimonthly ■ *Rivista del Nuovo Cimento* (in English), monthly.

ITALIAN SOCIETY OF ANATOMY (ISA)
(Societa Italiana di Anatomia)
e-mail: motta@axrma.uniroma1.it
Istituto di Anatomia Umana Normale
Via A. Borelli No. 50
I-00161 Rome, Italy
Prof. Pietro Motta, Pres.
PH: 39 6 4462623
FX: 39 6 4452349
Description: Fosters the study of anatomy, histology, and embryology in Italy. **Founded:** 1929. **Membership:** 400. **Staff:** 10. **Languages:** English, Italian. **Budget:** 30,000,000 Lr. **Publication:** *Italian Journal of Anatomy and Embriology* (in English and Italian), quarterly. Price: 150.00 Lr Italy; 200.00 Lr international. ISSN: 0004-0223. Advertising: not accepted ■ Papers (in English), periodic.

IUD CLAIMS INFORMATION SOURCE (ICIS)
PO Box 84151
Seattle, WA 98104
Constance Miller, Mng.Dir.
PH: (206)329-1371
FX: (206)623-4251
Description: Provides information and referrals to women filing lawsuits because of injuries sustained through use of an intrauterine contraceptive device (IUD). Offers professional seminars in claims filing and resolution. Maintains speakers' bureau. **Founded:** 1989. **Staff:** 1. **Languages:** English.

JAMAICA CANCER SOCIETY (JCS)
e-mail: bagarcic@infochan.com
16 Lady Musgrave Rd.
Kingston 5, Jamaica
Mrs. Barbara Garcia, Adm. Off.
PH: (876)927-4933
FX: (876)978-1918
Description: Health care professionals, people with cancer and their families, and other interested individuals. Promotes and encourages research into the causes and cure of cancer, and improved treatments for people with cancer. Conducts public education programs on cancer detection and treatment; offers specialized training for cancer doctors and nurses. Operates cancer screening clinics. **Founded:** 1955. **Membership:** 1200. **Staff:** 25. **National Groups:** 1. **Budget:** J$12,000. **Publication:** *Can Survive* (in English), biennial. Newsletter. Price: Free. Advertising: accepted ■ Brochure.

JAPAN ASSOCIATION OF INTERNATIONAL COOPERATION FOR ORAL HEALTH (JAICOH)
National Leprosarium Tama
Zenshou-en
4-1-1 Aoba-cho
Tokyo 189, Japan
Masao Murai, Contact
PH: 81 423 951101
FX: 81 423 942410
Description: Facilitates international cooperation to improve oral health in Cambodia, China, and the Solomon Islands. Conducts research on eating habits and nutrition and their impact on oral health. Sends technical staff to assist local oral health pro-

grams in developing regions; sponsors oral health advocacy activities. Multinational. **Languages:** English, Japanese. **Budget:** $105,337.

JAPAN MEDICAL FOUNDATION FOR VANUATU (JMFV)
Taiho Bldg., 2F
Shinsai Bashisuji
Chuo-ku
Osaka 542, Japan
Wakako Iwasaki, Contact
PH: 81 6 2521420
FX: 81 6 2520492
Description: Works to improve public health on Vanuatu, particularly in the areas of dental and visual health. Conducts eye examinations; produces and disseminates educational materials; trains indigenous people and provides dental and visual health screenings. Collects and distributes eyeglasses. Sponsors exchange of artwork between Japanese and Vanuatan children. **Founded:** 1984. **Languages:** English, Japanese. **Budget:** $301,289.

JAPAN MEDICAL PRODUCTS INTERNATIONAL TRADE ASSOCIATION
7-1, Nihonbashi-Honcho 4-chome,
Chuo-ku
Tokyo 103, Japan
Kuniichiro Ohno, Mng.Dir.
PH: 81 3 32412106
FX: 81 3 32412109
Description: Pharmaceutical, proprietary medicine, medical and dental instrument manufacturers and distributors; general trading companies; crude drug distributors; surgical dressing manufacturers. Promotes the export of pharmaceutical, and medical and dental supplies. Advocates fair trade practices and information exchange. Issues trade-related certificates including manufacturer, country of origin, and trademark. Conducts research and overseas market surveys. Cooperate with governmental and other organizations. Works in conjunction with the World Health Organization. **Founded:** 1953. **Membership:** 155. **Staff:** 7. **Languages:** English, Japanese. **Publication:** *Japan Medical Instrument Catalog, 9th Ed.* (in English, French, and Spanish), periodic. Includes the names of the medical equipment and instruments in English, French, and Spanish. Price: 160.00¥ includes airmail and registration fee ▪ *Japan Pharmaceutical Reference (JPR), 4th Ed.*, periodic. Includes description of Japanese pharmaceutical products marketed internationally. Price: 200.00¥ includes airmail and registered fee. ISSN: 0917-7825 ▪ *Membership Directory*, biennial. Includes name of member firms, addresses, phone & fax numbers, export roducts, etc. **Formerly:** (1992) Japan Pharmaceutical, Medical, and Dental Supply Exporters Association.

JAPANESE NURSING ASSOCIATION
e-mail: webmaster@nurse.or.jp
url: http://www.nurse.or.jp
5-8-2 Jingu-mae
Shibuya-ku
Tokyo 150-8331, Japan
PH: 81 3 34008331
FX: 81 3 34008767
Description: Promotes the status of nurses in Japan.

JAPANESE ORGANIZATION FOR INTERNATIONAL COOPERATION IN FAMILY PLANNING (JOICFP)
e-mail: joicfp@i.bekkoame.or.jp
url: http://www.bekkoame.or.jp/i/joicfp
Hoken Kaikan Shinkan Building
1-10 Ichigaya Tamachi
Tokyo 162-0843, Japan
Masao Sawaki, Chairman
PH: 81 3 32685875
FX: 81 3 32357090
Description: Provides assistance to reproductive health and family planning programs in 12 countries worldwide. Works closely with Japanese government agencies and international development organizations including UNFPA and IPPF to devise

projects and train staff. Promotes the use of videotapes and films in reproductive health/family planning education programs. **Founded:** 1968. **Membership:** 39. **Staff:** 52. Multinational. **Languages:** English, Japanese. **Budget:** 829,565¥. **Publication:** *Adolescent Women - Voices Unheard, Marian's Monolog*. Film ▪ *Guatemala Family Planning on IEC for Adolescents*. Report ▪ *Integration* (in English), quarterly. Magazine. Price: 20.00¥. Advertising: not accepted ▪ *JOICFP News* (in English), monthly. Newsletter ▪ *Sekaito Jinko* (in Japanese), monthly. Magazine. Also Cited As: *Women and Population* ▪ Monographs.

JOINT CARE COUNCIL
PO Box 3016
London WC1A 2QJ, England
Sheila Scott, Contact
PH: 44 171 4361871
FX: 44 171 4361193
Description: Independent care providers. Represents the four major representatives for the independent sector - i.e. BFCHP; IHA; NCHA; RNHA. Each association's membership includes residential or nursing home owners, providers of rehabilitation, care for mentally ill or disabled and short term care and convalescence. **Founded:** 1988. **Membership:** 4.

JOINT COMMISSION ON ALLIED HEALTH PERSONNEL IN OPHTHALMOLOGY (JCAHPO)
e-mail: jcahpo@jcahpo.org
url: http://www.jcahpo.org
2025 Woodlane Dr.
St. Paul, MN 55125-2995
Alice O. Gelinas, Exec.Dir.
PH: (612)731-2944
TF: 800284-3937
FX: (612)731-0410
Description: A certifying agency for allied health personnel. Objectives are: to encourage the establishment of medically oriented programs for training allied health personnel in ophthalmology; to develop standards of education and training in the field; to examine, certify, and recertify ophthalmic medical personnel, and encourage their continued occupational development. Conducts national certifying examinations. **Founded:** 1969. **Staff:** 24. **Languages:** English. **Budget:** $1,600,000.

JOINT COMMISSION ON SPORTS MEDICINE AND SCIENCE (JCSMS)
Oklahoma State University
Student Health Center
Stillwater, OK 74078
Donald L. Cooper, M.D., Co-Chm.
PH: (405)744-7031
FX: (405)744-6556
Description: Provides a forum and acts as a catalyst for the promotion of increased communication among the various organizations interested in the health and safety of sports participants and to help them convey to the public necessary information on that subject. Seeks to stimulate various organizations for continuous research on pertinent questions and problems in the field of sports injury prevention and care and for the acquisition of valid statistics on the incidence and epidemiology of injuries in sports activities. Also plays a role in helping corporations contact those sports organizations so that they can be of mutual benefit to each other. **Founded:** 1966. **Languages:** English. Formerly (1988) Joint Commission on Competitive Safeguards and the Medical Aspects of Sports.

JOINT REVIEW COMMITTEE ON EDUCATION IN DIAGNOSTIC MEDICAL SONOGRAPHY (JRCDMS)
7108-C S. Alton Way
Englewood, CO 80112
Annamarie Dubies-Appel, Exec.Dir.
PH: (303)741-3533
FX: (303)741-3655
Description: Participants are physicians and medical ultrasonographers. In collaboration with the Commission on Accreditation

for Allied Health Education Programs, accredits post-secondary education programs in diagnostic medical sonography. (Sonography utilizes ultrasonic waves to take two-dimensional pictures of internal body structures.) Convention/Meeting: none. **Founded:** 1979. **Membership:** 8. **Staff:** 2. **Languages:** English. **Budget:** $83,000. **Publication:** *JRCDMS News*, semiannual. Newsletter. Circulation: 300. Advertising: not accepted.

JOINT REVIEW COMMITTEE ON EDUCATION IN RADIOLOGIC TECHNOLOGY (JRCERT)
e-mail: jrcert@mail.idt.net
url: http://hudson.idt.net/jrcert
20 N. Wacker Dr., Ste. 900
Chicago, IL 60606
Marilyn Fay, Exec.Dir.
PH: (312)704-5300
FX: (312)704-5304
Description: Purpose is to evaluate and accredit educational programs in the fields of radiography and radiation therapy. **Founded:** 1969. **Membership:** 9. **Staff:** 10. **Languages:** English. **Budget:** $800,000. **Publication:** *JRCERT Review*, 3/year. Newsletter. Includes interpretations of educational standards. Price: $6.00/ year. Circulation: 6,000. Advertising: not accepted.

JOINT REVIEW COMMITTEE ON EDUCATIONAL PROGRAMS FOR THE EMT-PARAMEDIC (JRCEMT-P)
7108-C S. Alton Way, Ste. 150
Englewood, CO 80112
Anna Marie Appel, Exec. Officer
PH: (303)694-6191
Description: Cooperates with the Committee on Allied Health Education and Accreditation to accredit emergency medical technician-paramedic training programs across the U.S. Establishes national education standards and programs for the EMT-paramedic. Compiles statistics. **Founded:** 1979. **Membership:** 16. **Languages:** English. **Budget:** $60,000. **Publication:** *Chairmans Newsletter*, semiannual.

JORDANIAN ASSOCIATION FOR FAMILY PLANNING AND PROTECTION (JAFPP)
e-mail: jafpp@80.com.jo
Abdali-Amman Commercial Center Bldg., 6th Fl.
PO Box 8066
Amman, Jordan
Mr. Basem Abu Raad, Exec.Dir.
PH: 962 6 678083
FX: 962 6 674534
Description: Social workers and health care professionals in Jordan. Advocates responsible parenthood and family planning in Jordan. Operates family planning clinics and mobile units for rural areas. Offers advice to paretns on issues such as child spacing, marital problems, and child rearing; encourages couples to plan children according to financial means. Provides medical assistance to couples with infertility problems and helps them to overcome the social stigma attached to infertility through counseling services. Conducts annual family planning week. Organizes family planning courses for social workers and volunteers, lectures, workshops, siminar for targeting youth and women on the fields of reproductive health, commmunication skills, sexual health, population issues. Advocacy targeting decision makers. **Founded:** 1964. **Membership:** 200. **Staff:** 89. **Local Groups:** 3. **Languages:** Arabic, English. **Budget:** 850,000 JD. **Publication:** *Selected Lectures in Family Planning* ▪ Brochures, periodic.

JOSLIN DIABETES CENTER (JDC)
url: http://www.joslin.harvard.edu
1 Joslin Pl.
Boston, MA 02136
Dr. Kenneth E. Quickel, Pres.
PH: (617)732-2400
FX: (617)732-2562
Description: Investigates new methods in the clinical treatment of diabetes; conducts research at its Elliott P. Joslin Research Laboratory. Supports two camps for diabetic children and main-

tains diabetes treatment unit to instruct diabetic patients in the proper management of their disease. Compiles statistics on grants for research on diabetes. Offers specialized education programs for health care professionals, including annual course for practicing physicians with the Harvard Medical School. **Founded:** 1898. **Staff:** 350. **Languages:** English. **Budget:** $41,000,000. Formed by Merger of Diabetes Foundation; Joslin Clinic. Formerly (1981) Joslin Diabetes Foundation.

JUVENILE DIABETES FOUNDATION IN ISRAEL (JDFI)
(Haagudah LeSukereth Neurim Beyisrael)
5 Jabotinsky St.
IL-63479 Tel Aviv, Israel
Ofra Bajrach, Contact
PH: 972 3 5462717
FX: 972 3 5463830
Description: Strives to improve the situation of children and young adults with Juvenile diabetes in Israel. Conducts fundraising activities and research programs. **Founded:** 1981. **Membership:** 2000. **Staff:** 2. **Languages:** English, Hebrew. **Budget:** 760,000 IS. **Publication:** *Ad-Kan* (in Hebrew), semiannual. Price: free. Advertising: accepted ▪ *Update* (in Hebrew), semiannual ▪ Newsletter, quarterly.

JUVENILE DIABETES FOUNDATION INTERNATIONAL (JDFI)
e-mail: jbroch@jdf.usa.com
120 Wall St.
New York, NY 10005-3904
Brian Beauchamp, Public Info.Mgr.
PH: (212)785-9500
TF: 800JDF-CURE
FX: (212)785-9595
Description: Juvenile diabetics and their families. Objectives are: to solicit funds for diabetes research; to provide counseling and support services to juvenile diabetics and their families; to educate the public. Programs include: workshops that provide a forum for scientific discussion; efforts to stimulate government research funding. Holds seminars, discussion groups, and parent counseling. Conducts specialized education programs. **Founded:** 1970. Multinational. **Local Groups:** 114. **Languages:** English, Spanish. Formerly (1983) Juvenile Diabetes Foundation.

KABIRO KAWAGWARE HEALTH CARE TRUST (KKHCT)
PO Box 55454
Nairobi, Kenya
PH: 254 2 565162
Description: Promotes increased availability of family planning and reproductive health services in previously underserved areas. Distributes contraceptives; makes available maternal and child health care services; sponsors family planning education programs. **Founded:** 1982. **Languages:** English.

KARAKALPAK CENTER OF THE HUMAN REPRODUCTION AND FAMILY PLANNING (PERZENT)
e-mail: perzent@nukus.silk.org
PO Box 27
742012 Nukus, Uzbekistan
Oral Ataniyazova, Dir.
PH: 7 136122 75517
FX: 7 131622 75517
Description: Works to improve the status of women and children. Promotes family planning and increased availability of reproductive health services in Uzbekistan. Conducts research on the affects of environmental quality on human reproductive health. Provides ecological education training for trainers and family planning services. Monitors drinking water quality. **Founded:** 1992. **Membership:** 498. **Staff:** 4. Multinational. **Languages:** English, Russian. **Budget:** $30,000. **Publication:** *Perzent* (in Russian), monthly. Bulletin. Circulation: 600. Advertising: not accepted.

KENYA CATHOLIC SECRETARIAT (KCS)
PO Box 48062
Nairobi, Kenya
PH: 254 2 443133
FX: 254 2 442910
Description: Catholic medical services. Promotes improved public education in primary health care and family planning. Gathers and disseminates information; facilitates communication and cooperation between health care and population control programs in Kenya. **Founded:** 1957. **Languages:** English.

KENYA MEDICAL WOMEN'S ASSOCIATION (KMWA)
Kabarnet Rd.
PO Box 49877
Nairobi, Kenya
PH: 254 2 560813
FX: 254 2 560813
Description: Woman physicians. Encourages and assists in the professional advancement of members. Promotes improved public health through maintenance of high professional and practice standards. Sponsors public clinics offering primary health care and screening services for women. Serves as an advocate for family planning and maternal and child health programs. **Founded:** 1983. **Languages:** English.

KERATO-REFRACTIVE SOCIETY (KRS)
PO Box 796728
Dallas, TX 75379
Ronald A. Schachar, M.D., Exec.Sec.
PH: (972)601-5750
FX: (972)713-9722
Description: Ophthalmologists and scientists interested in the latest advances in keratorefractive and laser techniques. (Keratorefraction is a surgical procedure in which the shape of the cornea and iris is changed in order to correct nearsightedness and astigmatism. The procedure is now performed with a diamond knife; use of lasers is still in the investigational stage.) Purpose is to keep professionals and others informed of the most recent advances and developments in ophthalmologic care. Conducts research and raises funds. Sponsors training programs. **Founded:** 1979. **Membership:** 2000. **Languages:** English.

KOREAN-AMERICAN MEDICAL ASSOCIATION (KAMA)
162 Deer Run
Watchung, NJ 07060
Bong H. Hyun, MD, Exec.VP
PH: (908)755-KAMA
FX: (908)755-5322
Description: Korean-American physicians. Purpose is to provide a social and scientific forum for the exchange of scholarly information among members and between Korean-Americans and Korean physicans. Plans to offer scholarship program and to form liaisons with other health care professional societies. **Founded:** 1974. **Membership:** 4300. **Languages:** English, Korean. **Publication:** Membership Directory, quinquennial ∎ Newsletter, 3/year. **Formerly:** Korean-American Medical Association of America.

LA LECHE LEAGUE (LLL)
(Ligue La Leche)
e-mail: laleche@cam.org
PO Box 37046
St.-Hubert, PQ, Canada J3Y 8N3
Lucie Baillot, Dir.
PH: (514)990-8917
FX: (514)926-8420
Description: French-speaking Canadians with an interest in breastfeeding. Promotes breastfeeding as the most healthy method of nourishing infants. Provides support and services to women wishing to breastfeed. Conducts charitable programs. **Founded:** 1960. **Membership:** 802. **Staff:** 4. **Languages:** French. **Publication:** *La Voie Lactee* (in French), bimonthly. Magazine. Price: C$15.00. Circulation: 1,200. Advertising: accepted.

LAM FOUNDATION
e-mail: lamfoundtn@Juno.com
url: http://Lam.uc.edu
10105 Beacon Hills Dr.
Cincinnati, OH 45241
Sue Byrnes, Exec.Dir.
PH: (513)777-6899
FX: (513)777-4109
Description: Works to find a cure for LAM (lymphangioleimyomatosis), a progressive, fatal lung disease that affects women. Provides information and support; conducts education programs; promotes and funds clinical research; sponsors a tissue bank; supports a national registry of LAM patients. **Founded:** 1995.

LAMAZE INTERNATIONAL
e-mail: lamaze@dc.sba.com
url: http://www/lamaze-childbirth.com
1200 19th St. NW, No. 300
Washington, DC 20036-2422
Linda Harmon, Exec.Dir.
PH: (202)857-1128
TF: 800368-4404
FX: (202)223-4579
Description: Physicians, nurses, nurse-midwives, certified teachers of psychoprophylatic (Lamaze) method of childbirth, other professionals, parents, and others interested in Lamaze childbirth preparation and family-centered maternity care. Disseminates information about the theory and practical application of psychoprophylaxis in obstetrics; administers teacher training courses and certifies qualified Lamaze teachers; provides educational lectures, public forums, films, and written materials; maintains national and local teacher and physician referral service. Also presents materials to prospective parents concerning the demands of childrearing. National office serves as information clearinghouse. **Founded:** 1960. **Membership:** 5000. **Staff:** 5. Multinational. **Local Groups:** 25. **Languages:** English, Spanish. **Budget:** $1,800,000. Formerly (1998) American Society for Psychoprophylaxis in Obstetrics.

LATIN AMERICAN ASSOCIATION OF NATIONAL ACADEMIES OF MEDICINE (ALANAM)
1200 Mariposa Ave., E-201
Coral Gables, FL 33146
Alberto Cardenas-Escovar, M.D., Sec.
PH: (305)665-7341
FX: (305)446-3340
Description: National academies of medicine in Argentina, Brazil, Bolivia, Chile, Colombia, Ecuador, Mexico, Paraguay, Peru, Uruguay, and Venezuela. Coordinates research on problems of public health, social security, medical research and education, and related topics. **Founded:** 1967. **Membership:** 11. Multinational. **Languages:** Portuguese, Spanish. **Publication:** *Memoirs* (in Spanish), biennial.

LATIN AMERICAN ASSOCIATION OF PHYSIOLOGICAL SCIENCES
(Asociacion Latinoamericana de Ciencias Fisiologicas)
e-mail: pzapata@genes.bio.puc.cl
Maria Luisa Santander 0363
Casilla 16164
Santiago, Chile
Dr. Patricio Zapata, Exec.Sec.
PH: 56 2 2093503
FX: 56 2 2225515
Description: Physiological societies in Central America, South America, Mexico, and the Caribbean. Unites Latin American societies of the physiological sciences in an effort to stimulate and coordinate research and educational programs; encourages the exchange of scientific information. Promotes the establishment of faculties and research programs; encourages the implementation of modern educational methods in the teaching of the physiological sciences. **Founded:** 1956. **Membership:** 2500. Multinational. **National Groups:** 14. **Languages:** English, Portuguese. **Budget:** $5,000. **Publication:** *Acta Physiologica et Pharmacologica*

Latinoamericana (in English, Portuguese, and Spanish), quarterly. Journal.

LATIN AMERICAN CENTRE FOR PHYSICS (CLAF)
(Centro Latino-Americano de Fisica)
e-mail: clad@cat.cbpf.br
url: http://alexandria.cat.cbpf.br/CLAF
Avenida Wenceslau Braz 71
22290-140 Rio de Janeiro, RJ, Brazil
Carlos Alberto Aragao de Carvalho, Dir.
PH: 55 21 2955096
FX: 55 21 2955145
Description: Governments of Latin American countries united for cooperation in the field of physics. Promotes the application of physics to agriculture, energy, formal education, technology, and communications. Conducts research; sponsors teaching programs. **Founded:** 1962. **Membership:** 13. **Staff:** 6. Multinational. **Languages:** English, French. **Budget:** $600,000.

LATIN AND MEDITERRANEAN GROUP FOR SPORT MEDICINE (LMGSM)
(Groupement Latin et Mediterraneen de Medecine du Sport)
23, blvd. Carabacel
F-06000 Nice, France
Dr. Francisque Commandre, Sec.Gen.
PH: 33 93 853377
FX: 33 93 130762
Description: Physicians in 27 Mediterranean countries interested in the medical study of sports and exercise. Objectives are to further sports medicine and to conduct studies on medical problems related to amateur and professional sports and physical activity in general. Offers continuing education classes to members. Operates speakers' bureau. **Founded:** 1956. **Membership:** 2000. Multinational. **Languages:** French. **Publication:** *Apunto* (in Spanish), periodic ■ *Archivos de Medicina del Deporte* (in Spanish), quarterly ■ *Cinesiologie* (in French), bimonthly ■ *Medecine du Sport* (in English, French, Italian, and Portuguese), bimonthly ■ *Medecine du Sud-Est* (in French), quarterly.

LATVIAN PHYSICAL SOCIETY
e-mail: bzzs@lanet.lv
Nuclear Research Center
Miera Str. 31
LV2169 Salaspils, Latvia
F. Berzins, Pres.
PH: 371 2 945840
FX: 371 2 7901212
Description: Physicists, physics teachers, and others with an interest in the physical sciences. Seeks to improve the quality of physics education, research, and knowledge. **Founded:** 1992. **Membership:** 75. **Languages:** English, Latvian.

LATVIA'S ASSOCIATION FOR FAMILY PLANNING AND SEXUAL HEALTH
(Association Papardes Zieds)
e-mail: lfpa@mailbox.riga.lv
url: http://www.iclub.lv/lfpa
3 Valnu Iela
LV-1050 Riga, Latvia
Ilze Melgalve, Exec.Dir.
PH: 371 7 242700
FX: 371 7 821227
Description: Promotes family planning. Gathers and disseminates family planning information; conducts family planning education courses for health care professionals, educators, and social workers. **Founded:** 1994. **Membership:** 380. **Staff:** 3. Multinational. **Languages:** English, Latvian. **Budget:** 45,000 Rb. **Publication:** *Abortion*. Brochure ■ *Contraception*. Brochure ■ *Happy Relations*. Brochure ■ *Papardes Lapa* (in Latvian), semiannual. Newsletter. Advertising: not accepted. Alternate Formats: magnetic tape ■ *STD*. Brochure. Papardes Zieds.

LEUKEMIA SOCIETY OF AMERICA (LSA)
e-mail: infocenter@leukemia.org
url: http://www.leukemia.org
600 3rd Ave.
New York, NY 10016
Dwayne Howell, Pres. & CEO
PH: (212)573-8484
TF: 800955-4LSA
FX: (212)856-9686
Description: Raises funds to combat leukemia, lymphoma, Hodgkin's Disease and myeloma through research, patient service, and public and professional education and advocacy. Sponsors medical symposia; conducts research; provides financial aid for patients and free information; sponsors support groups. Free information available through 1-800-955-4. LSA or website: www.leukemia.org. **Founded:** 1949. **Staff:** 375. **Local Groups:** 58. **Languages:** English. **Publication:** *Educational Literature* (in English and Spanish). Brochures. Price: free. Alternate Formats: online ■ *Leukemia Society of America – Newsline*, quarterly. Newsletter. Provides information on advances in the research into leukemia, lymphoma, Hodgkin's Disease and Myeloma. Includes research updates. Price: free. Circulation: 77,000. **Formerly:** (1955) Robert Roesler de Villiers Foundation.

LIAISON COMMITTEE ON MEDICAL EDUCATION (LCME)
e-mail: Harry_Jonas@ama-assn.org
515 N. State St.
Chicago, IL 60610
Harry S. Jonas, M.D., Sec.
PH: (312)464-4933
FX: (312)464-5830
Description: Sponsored by the American Medical Association and the Association of American Medical Colleges; membership is drawn from these groups and the Committee on Accreditation of Canadian Medical Schools, as well as two students, one federal participant, and two public members. Principle function is to conduct accrediting activities in undergraduate medical education. Conducts research on medical education programs; maintains data banks on medical schools in the U.S. and Canada. Compiles statistics. **Founded:** 1942. **Membership:** 18. **Staff:** 8. **Languages:** English. **Budget:** $320,000. **Publication:** *Functions and Structure of a Medical School* ■ *Report on Medical Education in U.S.*, annual ■ *Status of Accreditation of M.D. Programs in the U.S. and Canada*, quarterly.

LIFEGAIN INSTITUTE (LI)
e-mail: HRI@healthyaulureHRI@healthyculture.com
url: http://www.healthyculture.com
115 Dunder Rd.
Burlington, VT 05401
Judd Allen, Ph.D., Pres.
PH: (802)862-8855
FX: (802)862-6389
Description: People who work with health promotion programs in hospitals, corporations, colleges, and communities. Promotes healthy practices such as exercise, nutrition, safety, and the reduction or curtailment of smoking and alcohol consumption through health promotion programs that provide a supportive environment. Maintains speakers' bureau. Compiles data on improvements cutural support nationwide. **Founded:** 1977. **Membership:** 600. **Languages:** English. **Budget:** $50,000. **Publication:** *American Journal of Health Promotion*, quarterly ■ *Lifegain: A Culture-Based Approach to Positive Health*. Book ■ *Lifegain Healthy Communities System* ■ Articles. **Also Known As:** Human Resources Institute.

LIGA INTERNATIONAL (LI)
e-mail: liga@earthlink.net
url: http://www.sdaworld.com/liga//
19531 Campus Dr., Ste. 20
Santa Ana, CA 92707
Jacquelyn Hanson, Pres.
PH: (714)852-8611
FX: (714)852-8739

Description: Physicians, dentists, nurses, pilots, technicians, assistants, educators, and laypeople interested in providing medical and educational assistance to impoverished people of rural MexicoLiga (Spanish word for "league") seeks to stimulate interest and support for establishing and maintaining educational, charitable, and medical programs among underprivileged inhabitants of Mexico; exchange scientific information between medical and educational groups. Sponsors monthly trips to clinics in Ocoroni, El Fuerte, San Blas, in Sinaloa Mexico. Operates speakers' bureau. **Founded:** 1948. **Membership:** 700. **Staff:** 1. Multinational. **Local Groups:** 5. **Languages:** English, Spanish. **Publication:** *Liga High Flying Times*, quarterly. Newsletter ▪ Brochure. **Also Known As:** Flying Doctors of Mercy.

LIPID NURSE TASK FORCE (LNTF)
e-mail: lntf@tmahq.com
url: http://www.lntf.org
7611 Elmwood Ave., Ste. 202
Middleton, WI 53562-3161
Alice Holbrow, Exec.Dir.
PH: (608)831-5683
FX: (608)831-5122
Description: Works to develop and promote the role of nurses in managing of patients with lipid disorders. Defines a certification process; disseminates information to increase consumer awareness; funds a training grant; seeks to have lipid nursing designated a nursing specialty. **Founded:** 1991. **Membership:** 500. **Staff:** 3. **Budget:** $200,000.

LOK SWASTHYA PARAMPARA SAMVARDHAN (LSPSS)
e-mail: system@cimh.frlht.ernet.in
Ayurbedic Trust Complex
Trichy Rd.
PO Box 7102
Coimbatore 641 045, Tamil Nadu, India
Dr. G.G. Gangadharan, Exec.Dir.
PH: 91 422 313188
FX: 91 422 314953
Description: Village healers, midwives, folk practitioners, and other individuals interested in traditional healing methods. Seeks to revitalize folk traditions in areas including: childcare, nutrition, and home remedies for common ailments. Encourages the integration of folk medicine and organized health care systems in India. Cultivates medicinal gardens, forests, and nurseries. Fosters communication among members; gathers and disseminates information. **Founded:** 1985. **Membership:** 1214. **Staff:** 8. **Languages:** English, Hindi. **Publication:** Newsletter (in English), quarterly. Circulation: 1,200. Advertising: not accepted. **Formerly:** Lok Swasthya Parampara Samvardhan Samithi.

LONG TERM CARE CAMPAIGN (LTCC)
url: http://www.geocities.com/capitolhill/lobby/4936/
P.O. Box 27394
Washington, DC 20038
Kevin Donnellan, Chair
PH: (202)434-3744
FX: (202)434-6403
Description: Consumer, provider, business, labor, ciuk, older adult, and disability groups. Works to make long term health care accessible and affordable for all families. **Founded:** 1987. **Membership:** 143. **Staff:** 2. **National Groups:** 143. **Languages:** English. **Budget:** $300,000. **Publication:** *The Campaigner*, quarterly. Newsletter. Long Term Care issues and legislative updates. Circulation: 7,000. Advertising: not accepted ▪ *The Time Is Now*. Videos.

LYME DISEASE FOUNDATION (LDF)
e-mail: lymefnd@aol.com
url: http://www.lyme.org
1 Financial Plaza, 18th Fl.
Hartford, CT 06103
Karen Vanderhoof-Forschner, Chm. & Pres.

PH: (860)525-2000
TF: 800886-LYME
FX: (860)525-8425
Description: Seeks to educate medical professionals and the public about Lyme Borreliosis (Lyme disease), which is spread to humans by ticks with symptoms including rashes, joint swelling and pain, fever, severe headaches, and heart arrhythmia. Provides treatment protocols, diagnostic guidelines, and photographic case histories. Assists in the formation of support groups; offers referral service; maintains speakers' bureau. Sponsors medical seminars; provides videotape and slide programs; conducts research. Maintains registry of infected pregnant women and congenital cases. Works in cooperation with Congress, Centers for Disease Control, and National Institutes of Health. **Founded:** 1988. **Staff:** 4. **Local Groups:** 200. **Languages:** English. **Budget:** $400,000. **Publication:** *Journal of Spirochetal and Tick Bourne Disease*, quarterly. Price: $75.00/year. ISSN: 1060-0051. Circulation: 500. Advertising: accepted ▪ *Lymelight*, quarterly. Newsletter. Price: $30.00/year. Advertising: accepted ▪ *Monthly Update*. Price: $50.00/year. Advertising: accepted ▪ Pamphlets. **Formerly:** (1992) Lyme Borreliosis Foundation.

LYMPHOMA RESEARCH FOUNDATION OF AMERICA (LRFA)
e-mail: lrfa@aol.com
url: http://www.lymphoma.org
8800 Venice Blvd., Ste. 207
Los Angeles, CA 90034
Ellen Cohen, President
PH: (310)204-7040
FX: (310)204-7043
Description: Nationally recognized leader for funding lymphoma research and providing patien t resources, including support groups, "cell-mates" buddy system and patient he lpline; also distributes educational material and clinical trials information. **Founded:** 1991. **Languages:** English.

MADRE
e-mail: madre@igc.apc.org
url: http://www.madre.org
121 W. 27th St., Rm. 301
New York, NY 10001
Vivian Stromberg, Exec.Dir.
PH: (212)627-0444
FX: (212)675-3704
Description: Seeks to further the possibilities for peace through a women's human rights agenda in the U.S. and abroad. Conducts health campaign to raise funds for improved health care for women and children, including delivery of medical supplies and training workshops by midwives and health professionals. Addresses the effects of U.S. policies on women and children in the U.S. and abroad; conducts educational tours in the U.S. on issues related women's human rights throughout the world. ("Madre" is Spanish for "mother."). **Founded:** 1983. **Membership:** 23000. **Staff:** 6. Multinational. **Languages:** English, Spanish. **Publication:** *MADRE* (in English), quarterly. Newsletter. Circulation: 20,000. Advertising: not accepted ▪ Brochures.

MAKE TODAY COUNT (MTC)
1235 E. Cherokee St.
Springfield, MO 65804-2203
Connie Zimmerman, Exec.Dir.
PH: (417)885-3324
TF: 800432-2273
FX: (417)888-8761
Description: Cancer patients and others with life-threatening illnesses, and their immediate families. Works to bring members and their neighbors together to discuss openly the false implications and the realities of life-threatening diseases. Takes a positive approach to the problems of serious illness in order to lessen the emotional trauma for all concerned. Assists professionals in communicating with and meeting the needs of seriously ill patients. Maintains speakers' bureau and referral service; plans educational programs, films, and tapes. **Founded:** 1974. **Member-

ship: 5000. **Staff:** 3. **Local Groups:** 200. **Languages:** English. **Publication:** *Chapter Directory*, annual ▪ *Make Today Count Newsletter*, bimonthly. Offers emotional support to people with cancer or other life-threatening illnesses, and to their family members, friends, and professionals. Price: $10.00/year ▪ *Make Today Count - Until Tomorrow Comes.*

MALAYSIAN ORGANISATION OF PHARMACEUTICAL INDUSTRIES (MOPI)
5B Lorong Rahim Kajai 13
Taman Tun Dr. Ismail
60000 Kuala Lumpur, Malaysia
Mr. David Ho Sue San, Contact
PH: 60 3 7173486
FX: 60 3 7173487
Description: Manufacturers of pharmaceuticals and related products. Seeks to protect and advance the pharmaceutical industry. Represents member's's interests before government bodies, international trade and labor organizations, and the public. **Founded:** 1981. **Membership:** 32. **Staff:** 1. **Languages:** English, Malay.

MALAYSIAN SOCIETY OF RADIOGRAPHERS (MSR)
(Persatuan Juru X-Ray Malaysia)
General Hospital
Department of Radiology
50586 Jalan Pahang
Kuala Lumpur, Malaysia
M.R.B. Hashim, Pres.
PH: 60 3 2906674
FX: 60 3 2989845
Description: Radiographers working in diagnostic and radiotherapeutic specialties. Represents the interests of radiographers and allied practitioners through professional and social activities. Works to foster interest in radiography and radiotherapeutic technique and to improve the standards of practice. Operates a research program in radiation protection. Sponsors weekend lectures, technical sessions, seminars, symposia, workshops, and conferences. **Founded:** 1968. **Membership:** 400. **Languages:** English, Malay. **Publication:** *Journal*, annual ▪ *Newsletter* (in English and Malay), quarterly. Price: Free for members. Circulation: 400.

MALIGNANT HYPERTHERMIA ASSOCIATION (MHA)
Toronto General Hospital
200 Elizabeth St., OCRW-2, Rm. 834
Toronto, ON, Canada M5G 2C4
Dr. Morris Altman, Exec.Dir.
PH: (416)340-3238
FX: (416)340-4960
Description: Individuals with malignant hyperthermia (high fever and muscle rigidity, usually brought on by a reaction to certain anesthetics, to which some individuals are genetically predisposed), their families, and interested health care professionals. Seeks to advance the prevention and treatment of malignant hyperthermia. Conducts research; operates charitable programs; maintains support groups. **Founded:** 1979. **Membership:** 2200. **Languages:** English, French. **Publication:** *Hotline*, semiannual. Newsletter.

MALTESE DIABETES ASSOCIATION (MDA)
(Ghaqda Kontra d-Dijabete)
PO Box 413
Valletta CMR 01, Malta
Marie-Louise Mifsuo, Sec.
PH: 356 235158
Description: Individuals with type I or type II diabetes and their families. Furthers awareness of the health problems associated with diabetes and encourages the study of causes and treatments. Works to safeguard the social and economic interests of diabetic individuals. Conducts lectures and discussions; distributes educational materials; disseminates information. **Founded:** 1981. **Membership:** 850. **Languages:** English. **Budget:** 1,000 ML. **Publication:** *Id-Dijabete u Sahhtek* (in Maltese), quarterly. Magazine. Price: Free to members. Circulation: 900. Advertising: accepted ▪

Int u d-dijabete. Booklet. Also Cited As: *You and Diabetes* ▪ *What is Diabetes?*. Brochure.

MANAGEMENT SOCIETY FOR HEALTHCARE PROFESSIONALS
88 Lockhart Rd., 8/F
Wanchai, Hong Kong
Dr. Dickens Yeung, Contact
Description: Managerial and adminstrative staff of health care services; medical, paramedical, and nursing professionals. Promotes effective delivery of health care and patient care and management services. Seeks to facilitate the professional development of members. Represents members' interests; collaborates with government agencies in establishment of public health policies and programs; facilitates exchange of information among members. Conducts educational programs; sponsors social activities. **Founded:** 1984. **Languages:** Chinese, English.

MAP INTERNATIONAL (MAP)
e-mail: map@map.org
url: http://www.map.org
PO Box 215000
Brunswick, GA 31521-5000
Paul B. Thompson, Pres./CEO
PH: (912)265-6010
TF: 800225-8550
FX: (912)265-6170
Description: Non-profit Christian relief and development organization that promotes the health of people living in the world's poorest communities. Works with partners in the areas of community health development, disease prevention and eradication, relief and rehabilitation and global health advocacy. Promotes access to health services and essential medicines in more than 100 countries each year. **Founded:** 1954. **Staff:** 100. Multinational. **Regional Groups:** 5. **Languages:** English, French. **Budget:** $000,000. **Publication:** *MAP International Report*, bimonthly. Newsletter ▪ *Our Health*, semiannual. Magazine ▪ Annual Report. **Formerly:** (1976) Medical Assistance Programs.

MAP INTERNATIONAL - KENYA
e-mail: pokaalet@map.org
url: http://www.map.org
Studio House on Argwings Kodhek
Chaka Rd.
PO Box 21663
Nairobi, Kenya
Emily Chengo, Finance, Administration Dir.
PH: 254 2 569513
FX: 254 2 714422
Description: Provides training, consultancy, and health education services. Disseminates information about AIDS and other health issues. Provides a forum for the exchange of information. **Membership:** 10. **Staff:** 18. **Publication:** *A Pastoral Counselling Manual for AIDS*. Booklet. Advertising: accepted ▪ *AIDS in Africa, the Churches Opportunity*. Booklet ▪ *AIDS in Your Community*. Booklet ▪ *Community Balanced Development*. Booklet ▪ *Facts and Feelings About AIDS*. Booklet ▪ *Giving and Getting AIDS*. Booklet ▪ *Growing Together*. Booklet ▪ *Helpers for a Healing Community*. Booklet ▪ *Patterns for Life*. Booklet ▪ *Springs of Life*. Video. Educational AIDS video for church leaders.

MARIE CURIE CANCER CARE (MCCC)
e-mail: info@mariecurie.org.uk
28 Belgrave Sq.
London SW1X 8QG, England
PH: 44 0171 2353325
FX: 44 0171 8232380
Description: Health care professionals and other individuals working with people with cancer. Seeks to improve the quality of life of people with cancer; promotes increased availability and cf-fectiveness of cancer care. Operates network of cancer care centers; provides nursing and other care to people with cancer; makes available support and assistance to cancer research pro-

jects. Conducts educational programs. **Founded:** 1948. **Languages:** English. **Publication:** Pamphlets.

MARIE STOPES INTERNATIONAL (MSI)
url: http://www.mariestopes.org.uk
153 Cleveland St.
London W1P 5GP, England
Dr. Timothy Black, CEO
PH: 44 171 5747400
FX: 44 171 5747418
Description: Provides a wide range of maternal health and family planning services. Programs conducted include: contraceptive social marketing; male oriented services. Specializes in working with indigenous personnel to develop clinical family planning services and social marketing programs. **Founded:** 1975. Multinational.

MARIE STOPES INTERNATIONAL - VIETNAM (MSIVN)
Nghe An Clinic
21 Phan Dinh Phung St.
Vinh City, Vietnam
Hoang Nhat An, Contact
PH: 84 38 41804
Description: Maternal and child health organizations, health care providers, and other interested individuals. Seeks to increase access to health and family planning services among previously underserved populations. Conducts social marketing of contraceptives; sponsors male-oriented family planning campaigns. Develops locally administered family planning services and social marketing programs. **Staff:** 11. **Languages:** English, French. **Budget:** $100,000.

MATERNITY ALLIANCE - ENGLAND (MA)
e-mail: ma@mail-pro-net.co.uk
45 Beech St.
London EC2P 2LX, England
Christine Gowdridge, Contact
PH: 44 171 5588583
FX: 44 171 5588584
Description: Individuals and organizations concerned with rights and services for parents and babies. Campaigns for improvements in rights and services for mothers, fathers, and babies. Concerns include: improvement in health care before conception and the first year of life; financial support for low income families; protection of working mothers' rights; and availability of transportation and housing. Conducts research on child health services, homeless families, sugar content of baby foods, and parents with special needs. **Founded:** 1979. **Staff:** 7. **Languages:** English. **Budget:** L179,000. **Publication:** *Getting Fit for Pregnancy* (in English) ▪ *Maternity Action* (in English), periodic. Bulletin. Price: L3.00/issue; L12.00/year ▪ *Money for Mothers and Babies* (in Bengali, Cantonese, and English), periodic ▪ *Pregnant at Work* (in English), annual ▪ *Thinking About a Baby - A Man's Guide to Pre-Pregnancy Health* (in English), periodic.

MATERNITY CENTER ASSOCIATION (MCA)
e-mail: mcabirth@aol.com
281 Park Ave. S, 5th Fl.
New York, NY 10010
Maureen Corry, Exec.Dir.
PH: (212)777-5000
FX: (212)777-9320
Description: Laypersons, physicians, nurses, nurse-midwives, childbirth educators, and public health workers interested in improvement of maternity care, maternal and infant health, and family life. A national nonprofit health organization, MCA's mission is to improve the maternity care system through family-centered maternity care and parenting education which supports and empowers women and their families, provides resource and referral services, technical assistance, training and consultation on early discharge, postpartum services, continuing professional education and access to reference library by professionals, students, and writers by appointment. Sponsors research; administers nurse-midwifery student assistance fund. Co-sponsors commu-

nity-based Nurse-Midwifery Education Program. **Founded:** 1918. **Membership:** 450. **Staff:** 7. **Budget:** $1,000,000.

MEDICAL CYBERNETICS FOUNDATION (MCF)
3804 Arrow Lake Dr.
Jacksonville, FL 32257
Bob Frost, CEO
PH: (904)268-2086
Description: Medical and medically affiliated professionals. Works to assist members in researching, developing, and marketing new medical machinery such as monitoring equipment and robotics systems; to improve life through medical cybernetics. (Medical cybernetics refers to the relationship between machinery and medical practices and procedures.) Sponsors charitable program. Compiles statistics. Publications: none. **Convention/Meeting:** none. **Founded:** 1985. **Membership:** 1000. **Staff:** 4. **Languages:** English.

MEDICAL EDUCATION FOR SOUTH AFRICAN BLACKS (MESAB)
e-mail: MESAB@CHARITIESUSA.com
2101 E. Jefferson St.
Box 6611
Rockville, MD 20849-6611
Frank C. Strasburger, Pres.
PH: (301)816-6320
FX: (301)816-7473
Description: Supports the training of South African black health professionals to bring better health care to all South Africans. Provides scholarships for black students in the health professions at South African universities. Develops health-related training programs, rural outreach programs, and offers scholarship support for nurses enrolled in university-level nursing programs. **Founded:** 1985. **Staff:** 3. Multinational. **Languages:** English. **Budget:** $1,000,000. **Publication:** *Annual Report* ▪ *MESAB News*, 1-2/year. Newsletter. Includes information about the organization and its programs. Price: free. Circulation: 3,000. Advertising: not accepted.

MEDICAL GROUP MANAGEMENT ASSOCIATION (MGMA)
url: http://www.mgma.com
104 Inverness Terr. E.
Englewood, CO 80112-5306
Thomas Adams, CAE, Contact
PH: (303)799-1111
TF: 888608-5601
FX: (303)643-4439
Description: Persons actively engaged in the business management of medical groups consisting of three or more physicians in medical practice with centralized business functions. Sponsors educational training programs. Provides placement and information services. Compiles statistics. **Founded:** 1926. **Membership:** 18000. **Staff:** 154. **Regional Groups:** 4. **Languages:** English. **Publication:** *Administrators' Bookshelf*, annual. Bibliography. Lists new books in the health administration field. Includes directory of publishers and list of recommended journals. Price: $12.00/copy for affiliates; $25.00/copy for nonmembers. Advertising: not accepted ▪ *Cost Survey Report*, annual. Provides revenue and expense data on the operation of medical group practices by size, geographic location, and type of practice. Price: $200.00/copy for members; $250.00/copy for affiliates; $300.00/copy for nonmembers ▪ *Health Exchange*, quarterly. Newsletter. Contains general articles related to health and wellness. Circulation: 160,000 ▪ *Medical Group Management Journal*, bimonthly. Covers group practice management topics including financial management and accounting, data processing, and purchasing and maintenance. Price: $50.00/year. ISSN: 0025-7257. Circulation: 18,000. Advertising: accepted ▪ *Medical Group Management – Management Update*, monthly. Reports on current legislative activities, practical management issues, and trends in the health care community. Includes association news. Price: available to members only. ISSN: 0196-9455. Circulation: 14,000. Advertising: accepted ▪ *Medical Group Management Washington Report*, monthly. Legislative and regulatory news service. Price: $31.50/year for members; $41.50/

year for nonmembers ■ *MGMA Directory*, annual. Membership Directory. Geographical and alphabetical listing of members; cross-referenced by services, personnel, facilities, and equipment. Price: free to members and affiliates; $310.00/year for nonmembers ■ *MGMA Management Compensation Survey Report*, annual. Shows compensation and fringe benefits for group practice administrators. Price: free to members; $115.00/year for nonmembers ■ Booklets ■ Brochures. **Formerly:** (1946) Association of Clinic Managers; (1963) National Association of Clinical Managers.

MEDICAL LETTER (ML)
url: http://www.medletter.com
1000 Main St.
New Rochelle, NY 10801
Mark Abramowicz, M.D., Editor
PH: (914)235-0500
FX: (914)576-3377
Description: Gathers and publishes information on the therapeutic and side effects of drugs for the benefit of physicians and other members of the health professions. Emphasis is on new drugs. **Founded:** 1959. **Staff:** 30. **Languages:** English. Formerly Drug and Therapeutic Information.

MEDICAL OUTREACH FOR ARMENIANS (MOA)
PO Box 1333
Paramus, NJ 07653-1333
Arthur Halvajian, Dir.
Description: Health care professionals and other individuals wishing to improve delivery of medical services to needy Armenians and to upgrade medical facilities in Armenia. Gathers monetary donations, medical supplies and medications, and technological equipment for distribution to hospitals in Armenia; sponsors transportation to America for Armenian children in need of complex surgical procedures. Plans to construct a children's heart center in Yerovan, Armenia. **Languages:** English. **Publication:** *Activities of Medical Outreach for Armenians*, periodic. Newsletter. Includes financial reports ■ *Pediatric Intensive Care Unit and Pediatric Cardiac Surgery Center for Yerevan, Armenia*.

MEDICAL RECORDS INSTITUTE (MRI)
e-mail: cust_service@medrecinst.com
url: http://www.medrecinst.com
567 Walnut St.
PO Box 600770
Newton, MA 02160
C. Peter Waegemann, Exec.Dir.
PH: (617)964-3923
FX: (617)964-3926
Description: Conducts research and education in the fields of medical documentation and computerization of patient information. Maintains committees and network groups. Compiles statistics. **Founded:** 1979. **Staff:** 5. Multinational. **Languages:** English. **For-Profit. Budget:** $1,500,000. **Publication:** *Handbook of Optical Memory Systems*. Monthly updates available. Price: $100.50. Advertising: not accepted ■ *Toward An Electronic Patient Record*, 10/year. Price: $145.00. ISSN: 1063-973X. Circulation: 600. Advertising: not accepted ■ Proceedings. **Formerly:** (1988) Institute for Medical Record Economics.

MEDICAL RESEARCH MODERNIZATION COMMITTEE (MRMC)
e-mail: mrmcmed@aol.com
url: http://www.mrmcmed.org
PO Box 2751, Grand Central Sta.
New York, NY 10163
Stephen R. Kaufman, M.D., Co-Chair
PH: (212)832-3904
FX: (216)283-6702
Description: Individuals, primarily scientists and clinicians, who evaluate the medical and/or scientific merit of research modalities in an effort to identify outdated research methods and to promote sensible, reliable, and efficient methods. Represents positions to the public, health care professionals, and government officials. Maintains speakers' bureau; distributes literature to the public. **Founded:** 1978. **Membership:** 1000. **Staff:** 1. **Languages:** English. **Budget:** $30,000. **Publication:** *A Critical Look at Animal Experimentation*, annual. Booklet. Price: free to members; $1.00/copy for nonmembers. Circulation: 20,000. Advertising: not accepted ■ *MRMC Report*, quarterly. Newsletter. Price: free to members; $2.00/copy for nonmembers. Circulation: 1,500 ■ *Perspectives on Medical Research*, annual. Monograph. Includes essays and commentary. Price: $10.00/paperback; $16.00/hardback. ISSN: 1053-8984. Circulation: 1,500.

MEDICAL OFFICERS OF SCHOOLS ASSOCIATION
21 St. Botorpa's Rd.
Sevenoaks, Kent TN13 3AQ, England
Dr. Neil D. Arnott, Hon.Sec.
PH: 44 1732 459255
FX: 44 1732 750586
Description: School doctors and doctors with an interest in the health of the school child. To represent school doctors and those doctors with an interest in the health of the school child; to provide an advisory service for members, and non-members, on any aspect of school medicine. **Founded:** 1884. **Membership:** 440. **Staff:** 2. **Publication:** *Handbook of School Health*, quarterly. Price: 22. ISSN: 8585-6081. Advertising: accepted. Alternate Formats: magnetic tape ■ Newsletter, quarterly ■ Report, annual.

MEDICAL SOCIETY OF THE UNITED STATES AND MEXICO (MSUSM)
219 W. MonteBello
Phoenix, AZ 85013-1844
PH: (602)279-9444
FX: (602)279-9444
Description: Doctors of medicine in the United States (200) and in Mexico (200). Promotes scientific and international goodwill; sponsors research and educational programs; fosters interchange of doctors. Conducts scientific program. **Founded:** 1954. **Membership:** 400. Multinational. **Languages:** English, Spanish. **Publication:** Directory, annual.

MEDICAL WOMEN'S FEDERATION
e-mail: lyn@m-w-f.demon.co.uk
Tavistock Sq.
London WC1H 9HX, England
Lyn Perry, Contact
PH: 44 171 3877765
FX: 44 171 3877765
Description: Women doctors and medical students. The professional association of women doctors in the UK. **Founded:** 1917. **Membership:** 2000. **Staff:** 3. **Local Groups:** 20. **Budget:** L100,000. **Publication:** *Medical Woman* (in English), 3/year. Newsletter. Price: L20.00; free to members. ISSN: 0951-2810. Advertising: accepted.

MEDICARE RIGHTS CENTER
1460 Broadway, 8th Fl.
New York, NY 10036-7393
Diane Archer, Exec.Dir.
PH: (212)869-3850
FX: (212)869-3532
Description: Seeks to ensure the rights of senior citizens and people with disabilities to quality, affordable health care. Provides counseling services to Medicare beneficiaries with health insurance problems and questions; compiles information on inquiries to detect issues and systemic problems in Medicare claims administration. Educates beneficiaries, advocates, providers, and social workers about developments in Medicare law and how to handle problems. Monitors trends and changes in Medicare laws, regulations, and guidelines. **Founded:** 1989. **Staff:** 5. **Languages:** English. **Budget:** $250,000. Formerly (1997) Medicare Beneficiaries Defense Fund.

MEDICINE IN THE PUBLIC INTEREST (MIPI)
192 South St., Ste. 500
Boston, MA 02111
Louis Lasagna, M.D., Pres.
PH: (617)728-7977
FX: (617)728-9135
Description: Professionals in medicine, law, and the social sciences. Promotes and funds research into medicine and related social, legal, and ethical issues; disseminates research findings and proposals. Encourages the development of long-range public health, welfare, and social planning at the federal, state, and local levels. Cooperates with governmental representatives in analyzing and developing legislation and programs designed to serve the public health and welfare. **Founded:** 1973. **Staff:** 1. **Languages:** English. **Publication:** Reports.

**MEDITERRANEAN ASSOCIATION OF LOCOMOTOR
PATHOLOGY CONNECTED TO SPORT**
(Association Mediterraneene de Pathologies de l'Appareil
Locomoteur Liees au Sport)
20 avenue Notre Dame
F-06000 Nice, France
Dr. Yves Bence, Contact
PH: 33 4 93854677
Description: Physicians specializing in locomotive sports medicine. Seeks to advance the diagnosis and treatment of locomotor sports injuries. Serves as a clearinghouse on locomotor sports medicine; sponsors research programs and continuing professional education courses. Multinational. **Languages:** English, French.

MENDED HEARTS (MH)
7272 Greenville Ave.
Dallas, TX 75231-4596
Darla Bonham, Exec.Dir.
PH: (214)706-1442
TF: 800242-1793
FX: (214)987-4334
Description: Persons who have heart disease; their families and friends. Works to: provide advice, encouragement, and services to heart disease patients and to their families; establish programs of assistance to surgeons, physicians, and hospitals. Conducts and assists in research programs designed to benefit heart patients. **Founded:** 1951. **Membership:** 24000. **Local Groups:** 200. **Languages:** English. Formerly (1955) Mended Hearts Club.

MENINGITIS ASSOCIATION SCOTLAND (MAS)
9 Edwin St.
Edinburgh G51 1ND, Scotland
PH: 44 0141 4276698
Description: Individuals with meningitis and their families; health care personnel and other individuals providing therapy and treatment to people with meningitis. Seeks to improve the quality of life of people with meningitis; works to increase public awareness of meningitis and related disorders; promotes advancement in the diagnosis and treatment of meningitis. Serves as a clearinghouse on meningitis and related disorders; provides financial support to research projects; makes available counseling services and support groups to people with meningitis and their families. Sponsors children's services. **Languages:** English. **Publication:** Brochures.

MENOPAUZE: CLINIC
University Hospital Gasthuisberg
Dept. of Obstetrics and Gynecology
Herestraat 49
B-3000 Louvain, Belgium
Prof. P.R. Koninckx, Contact
PH: 32 16 344202
FX: 32 16 344238
Description: Promotes the study of menopause. Supports theories of psychosomatic menopause. Conducts clinical training and teaching programs in psychosomatic gynecology. Offers marriage and family therapy sessions. Conducts sexological research.

Founded: 1968. **Membership:** 8. **Staff:** 6. **Languages:** Dutch, English.

MENTAL AFTER CARE ASSOCIATION (MACA)
25 Bedford Sq.
London WC1B 3HW, England
Gil Hitchon, Chief Exec.
PH: 44 171 4366194
FX: 44 171 6371980
Description: Provides residential care and other community-based services for people with mental health needs and their carers. Services include: supported accomodation; community support; day care; social clubs; employment training; court liaison for offenders with mental health needs, training and information services. **Founded:** 1879. **Membership:** 100. **Staff:** 650. **Languages:** English. **Budget:** I.8,291,463. **Publication:** *Annual Report.* Advertising: accepted ■ Pamphlets, periodic.

MENTAL HEALTH FOUNDATION
8 Hallam St.
London W1N 6DH, England
June McKerrow, Contact
PH: 44 171 5800145
FX: 44 171 6313868
Description: Plays a vital role in pioneering new approaches to prevention, treatment and care. Allocates grants for research and community projects, contributes to public debate and strives to reduce the stigma attached to mental illness and learning disabilities. **Founded:** 1949. **Staff:** 38.

MENTAL HEALTH MATERIALS CENTER (MHMC)
PO Box 304
Bronxville, NY 10708
Alex Sareyan, Pres.
PH: (914)337-6596
Description: Professional workers in the field of mental health and health education. Seeks to stimulate the development of wider and more effective channels of communication between health educators and the public. Provides consulting services to nonprofit organizations on the implementation of their publishing operations in areas related to mental health and health. Develops new publishing and audiovisual properties. **Founded:** 1953. **Membership:** 10. **Staff:** 1. **Languages:** English.

MENTAL HEALTH MEDIA
e-mail: headline@mhmedia.u-net.com
356 Holloway Rd.
London N7 6PA, England
Claudia Feldner, Admin.
PH: 44 171 7000100
FX: 44 171 7000099
Description: Works with the media, statutory and voluntary organizations and service users to do away with the stigma of mental distress. Uses the power of the media to increase public understanding of social issues, particularly mental distress and learning disabilities. Works in partnership with users and survivors in trying to improve the quality of press coverage of mental health issues. Provides training and multi media resources to people with learning disabilities. Trains service users and workers in media skills. **Founded:** 1965. **Staff:** 10. **Languages:** French, German. **Publication:** Directories. Contains audio-visual resources on mental health. Price: L4.00; L6.00. Circulation: 1,000. Advertising: accepted ■ Video. Contains information on mental health and other related issues. **Formerly:** Mental Health Film Council; (1996) Mental Health Media Council.

MENTAL ILLNESS FOUNDATION
722 W 168th St.
New York, NY 10032
PH: (212)682-4699
FX: (212)682-4896
Description: Supports community housing, treatment, research, outreach and public awareness eforts for people with mental illness. **Founded:** 1983. **Staff:** 3. Local. **Languages:** English.

MERES ET ENFANTS D'HAITI (MEH)
Chemin des Dalles No. 13
Port-au-Prince, Haiti
Dr. Jean Ronald Cornely, Pres.
PH: 509 456211
Description: Obstetricians, gynecologists, pediatricians, nurses, and medical and nursing students in Haiti. Strives to improve maternal and child health and safe motherhood. Encourages advancements in the fields of obstetrics, gynecology, and pediatrics. Promotes research on human reproduction and women's and child health. Organizes courses and programs aimed at improving maternal and child health; communicates with directors of educational institutions. Operates family planning program; offers consulting services. Sponsors seminars and training programs. **Founded:** 1987. **Membership:** 200. **Staff:** 8. **Languages:** English, French. **Budget:** $20,000. **Publication:** *Bulletin*, periodic ∎ *MCI Bulletin*, quarterly.

MEXICAN ACADEMY OF DERMATOLOGY (MAD)
(Academia Mexicana de Dermatologia)
Georgia 114-503
Colonia Napoles
03810 Mexico City, DF, Mexico
Dr. Rocio Orozco, Contact
PH: 52 5 2110173
FX: 52 5 2509161
Description: Provides continuing medical education programs to members. Offers support to dermatology residents. **Founded:** 1952. **Membership:** 150. **Staff:** 5. **Languages:** English, Spanish. **Budget:** $30,000. **Publication:** *Dermatologia-Revista Mexicana* (in Spanish), monthly. Advertising: accepted.

MICHAEL E. DEBAKEY INTERNATIONAL SURGICAL SOCIETY (MEDISS)
e-mail: mediss@aol.com
c/o Kenneth L. Mattox
1 Baylor Plz.
Department of Surgery
Houston, TX 77030
Kenneth L. Mattox, M.D., Sec.-Treas.
PH: (713)798-4557
FX: (713)796-9605
Description: Physicians organized to encourage, advance, and promote scientific research relating to the treatment of general vascular, cardiac and cardiovascular defects and diseases through general vascular and cardiovascular surgery. **Founded:** 1976. **Membership:** 640. Multinational. **Languages:** English. Formerly (1983) Michael E. DeBakey International Cardiovascular Society.

MIDDLE EAST NEUROSURGICAL SOCIETY
(Societe de Neurochirurgie du Moyen Orient)
American Univ. Medical Center
PO Box 113-6044
Beirut, Lebanon
Dr. Fuad Sami Haddad, Pres.
PH: 961 1 353486
FX: 961 1 373 1450231
Description: Individuals in 12 countries. Disseminates information to the medical profession and to the public on clinical advancements and scientific research in neurosurgery and similar disciplines. **Founded:** 1958. **Membership:** 545. Multinational. **Languages:** English.

MIDWEST PARENTCRAFT CENTER (MPC)
5525 W. Henderson
Chicago, IL 60641
Margaret Gamper, R.N., Exec.Dir.
PH: (773)725-7767
Description: Prenatal instructors, parents, and professionals involved in parenting and pregnancy. To instruct and educate expectant mothers and others in the Gamper Method of childbirth. (The Gamper Method, based on the teachings of several 19th century physicians and developed by Margaret Gamper in 1946, is designed to prepare the prospective mother for childbirth by instilling self-determination and confidence in her ability to work with the physiological changes of her body during pregnancy, labor, and delivery.) Conducts prenatal and grandparenting classes and workshops; operates in-service programs for hospitals and clinics; sponsors programs on topics such as grieving and history of birth procedures. Disseminates teaching aids including slides, films, records, and tapes. Grants childbirth educator certificates to qualified applicants who have taught Gamper Method classes under the supervision of an instructor. Operates charitable program and speakers' bureau; maintains library of 6000 volumes on childbirth, midwifery, marriage, sex, and childcare. The center's activities are currently concentrated in Ohio, Illinois, Indiana, Wisconsin, and Michigan. **Founded:** 1950. **Staff:** 2. **Languages:** English.

MIDWIVES ALLIANCE OF NORTH AMERICA (MANA)
e-mail: manainfo@aol.com
url: http://www.mana.org
PO Box 175
Newton, KS 67114
Ina May Gaskin, Pres.
FX: (316)832-3566
Description: Midwives, student/apprentice midwives, and persons supportive of midwifery. Seeks to expand communication and support among midwives. Works to promote basic competency in midwives; develops and encourages guidelines for their education. Offers legal, legislative, and political information and resource referrals; conducts networking on local, state, and regional bases; compiles statistics. **Founded:** 1982. **Membership:** 1000. Multinational. **Regional Groups:** 10. **Languages:** English. **Budget:** $55,000.

MIDWIVES INFORMATION AND RESOURCE SERVICE (MIDIRS)
e-mail: midirs@dial.pipex.com
url: http://www.midirs.org
9 Elmdale Rd.
Clifton
Bristol BS8 1SL, England
Joy Rodwell, Contact
PH: 44 117 9251791
FX: 44 117 9251792
Description: Provides information to health professionals on maternal health care. Acts as a clearinghouse, offering articles, books, and other information concerning midwifery. Conducts educational programs. **Founded:** 1983. **Staff:** 19. Multinational. **Languages:** English. **Publication:** *Directory of Maternity Organisations*, periodic ∎ *MIDIRS Midwifery Digest*, quarterly. ISSN: 0961-5555. Circulation: 15,000. Advertising: accepted.

MIND - MENTAL HEALTH CHARITY
Granta House
15-19 Broadway
London E1S 4BQ, England
Judi Clements, Dir.
PH: 44 181 5192122
FX: 44 181 5221725
Description: Promotes mental health and encourages a better understanding of mental health disorders. Assists in the treatment and rehabilitation of mental health patients and seeks to eliminate the stigma associated with mental illness. Conducts research; disseminates information. Offers legal referral services. Sponsors charitable program. Maintains information service. Conducts training and educational courses and seminars. **Founded:** 1948. **Membership:** 1700. **Staff:** 72. **Languages:** English. **Publication:** *Annual Report* (in English) ∎ *OpenMIND* (in English), bimonthly. Magazine. Price: L3.50/issue; L16.50/year - individuals; L20.00/year - organizations. Advertising: accepted ∎ *Publications from MIND* (in English), periodic. Catalog. **Also Known As:** National Association for Mental Health.

MINISTRY OF CONCERN FOR PUBLIC HEALTH (MCPH)
PO Box 1487
Williamsville, NY 14231
Mary K. Bertell, Exec.Sec.
Description: A task force of Global Education Associates which provides scientific and informational services to individuals and groups who seek to understand, control, and, if possible, eliminate disease epidemics brought on by environmental pollution. Seeks: to prevent genetic damage and chronic degenerative diseases; to discover ways to lessen global security tensions and the threat of nuclear war; to promote understanding of pollution-health-environment systems and epidemic management through environment, host, or agent modification. Initiates research projects and programs; provides professional consultation on biostatistical, epidemiological, and public health-related projects; testifies and provides affida vits in legal suits. Maintains Citizen Health Register recording human health effects of a variety of environmental pollutants and occupational hazards. Operates Cluster Program to provide assistance to scientists. Provides assistance to government agencies, scientific research groups, citizens' organizations, and labor unions on problems of radioactive chemical exposure at the workplace or environment or other radiation exposure problems; arranges for blood tests, chromosome and urine analyses, and other biomedical tests for exposure to hazardous chemicals and radiation. Researches legal avenues for social change and strategies for strengthening international law in the areas of air and water pollution control, exporting of unsafe commodities, and damage to human health by degradation of the biosphere and gene pool. **Convention/Meeting:** none. **Founded:** 1978. **Staff:** 3. Multinational. **Languages:** English. **Budget:** $20,000.

MISCARRIAGE ASSOCIATION
c/o Clayton Hospital
Northgate
Wakefield, W. Yorkshire WF1 3JS, England
Mrs. Ruth Bender Atik, Dir.
PH: 44 1924 200799
FX: 44 1924 298834
Description: Provides support and information for all on the subject of pregnancy loss. Gath ers information about causes and treatments and promote good practice in the wa y pregnancy loss is managed in hospitals and in the community. **Founded:** 1982. **Membership:** 1400. **Staff:** 5. **Languages:** English. **Budget:** L90,000. **Publication:** Booklet (in English). Information on miscarriages ■ Newsletter (in English), quarterly.

MISSION DOCTORS ASSOCIATION (MDA)
313424 Wilshire Blvd.
Los Angeles, CA 90015
Timothy Lefevre, M.D., Pres.
PH: (626)285-8868
FX: (626)309-1716
Description: Recruits, trains, and supports volunteer Catholic physicians and sends them to serve in Third World hospitals or clinics for a period of 2-3 years. Mission doctors accepted in the program must display a genuine spirit of sacrifice and must participate in a 9-month course on theology, missiology, scripture, and Third World culture. Provides for complete support of doctors and their families while overseas; also provides small monthly stipend. Screens and trains physicians' spouses to be part-time lay missionaries. **Founded:** 1957. **Staff:** 1. Multinational. **Languages:** English.

MOLDOVA FAMILY PLANNING ASSOCIATION (MFPA)
277001 Christinau St.
MD-32 Bulgara, Moldova
PH: 373 2 260031
FX: 373 2 260507
Description: Promotes population control through family planning. Gathers and disseminates information on family planning and reproductive health. **Founded:** 1992. **Languages:** English, Russian.

MOROCCAN MIDWIVES ASSOCIATION (MMA)
(Association Marocaine des Sages Femmes)
College de Sante
Route de Casa, Km. 4
Rabat, Morocco
PH: 212 7 691938
FX: 212 7 693058
Description: Midwives and other health care personnel. Promotes delivery of improved maternal and child health care services. Gathers and disseminates information on reproductive health and family planning issues. **Founded:** 1991. **Languages:** Arabic, English.

MOROCCAN PAEDIATRIC SOCIETY (MPS)
(Societe Marocaine de Pediatrie)
Hopital d'Enfants
CHU Ibnou-Sina
Rabat, Morocco
Dr. M.T. Lahrech, Dir.
PH: 212 7 670921
FX: 212 7 733186
Description: Pediatricians and other doctors specializing in child health. Encourages contact and information exchange among members. **Founded:** 1965. **Membership:** 300. **Staff:** 9. **Regional Groups:** 5. **Languages:** French. **Publication:** *Lettre du Pediatre* (in French), monthly. Price: free. Advertising: accepted.

MOSCOW ASSOCIATION OF CARDIOLOGISTS
(Moskovskaya Assotsiatsiya Kardiologov)
ulitsa 3-aya Cherepkovskaya 15A
121552 Moscow, Russia
A.P. Yurenev, Pres.
PH: 7 95 1492802
FX: 7 95 4146699
Description: Works to improve cardiology in the Commonwealth of Independent States and lower levels of illness and death from heart disease. Protects the social and legal rights of cardiologists. **Founded:** 1990. **Membership:** 220. **Staff:** 4. **Budget:** $50,000.

MOTOR NEURONE DISEASE ASSOCIATION
PO Box 246
Northampton NN1 2PR, England
George Levvy, Contact
PH: 44 1604 250505
FX: 44 1604 24726
Description: Promotes interest in motor neurone disease (MND) research among medical and scientific communities and the public in the United Kingdom. Offers support services to people with MND and their families. Disseminates information about the disease. **Founded:** 1979. **Membership:** 6000. **Staff:** 50. **Local Groups:** 95. **Budget:** L2,900,000. **Publication:** *Annual Review*. Booklets. Information leaflets ■ *Thumbprint* (in English), quarterly. Magazine. Advertising: accepted.

MOTOR NEURONE DISEASE ASSOCIATION OF AUSTRALIA
e-mail: mndvic@vicnet.net.au
PO Box 262
Caulfield South, VIC 3162, Australia
Mavis Gallienne
PH: 61 3 95964761
FX: 61 3 95968005
Description: Promotes interests in motor neurone disease (MND) research among medical and scientific communities and the public in Australia. Offers support services to MND sufferers and their families. Disseminates information about the disease.

MOTOR NEURONE DISEASE ASSOCIATION OF NEW ZEALAND
PO Box 2129
Wellington, New Zealand
Mary Newman, Contact
PH: 64 4 4735555
FX: 64 4 4994675

Description: Supports people living with Motor Neurone Disease by providing emotional, social and practical support, advocacy, information, and by raising awareness. **Founded:** 1985. **Publication:** *MND Newsletter* (in English), annual. Price: NZ$20.00 per annum. ISSN: 1172-2665.

MOTOR NEURONE DISEASE ASSOCIATION OF SOUTH AFRICA
e-mail: dianeh@iafrica.com
c/o PO Box 781880
Sandton
Transvaal 2146, Republic of South Africa
Diane Heron, Contact
PH: 27 11 7064883
FX: 27 11 4636855
Description: Promotes interests in motor neurone disease (MND) research among medical and scientific communities and the public in South Africa. Offers support services to MND sufferers and their families. Disseminates information about the disease. **Founded:** 1991. **Regional Groups:** 3.

MOTOR NEURONE DISEASE AND ESCLEROSIS LATERAL AMIOTROFICA IN URUGUAY (MONDELA)
Av. Italia 3318
Montevideo, Uruguay
Dr. O. Vincent, Contact
PH: 598 2 4871616
FX: 598 2 475461
Description: Promotes interest in motor neurone disease (MND) and amyotrophic lateral sclerosis (ALS) research among medical and scientific communities and the public in Uruguay. Offers support services to MND sufferers and their families. Disseminates information about the disease. **Founded:** 1991. **Membership:** 30. **Staff:** 3. **Local Groups:** 4. **Languages:** English, French. **Budget:** $4,500. **Publication:** *A Downstream Event in the Spinal Cord Slice: A Model of Early Excitotoxic Injury* (in English and Spanish). Report. Circulation: 500. Advertising: not accepted. Alternate Formats: online ■ *Fisioterapia para las Enfermedades Neuromusculares* (in Spanish). Report ■ *Mioterapia Oro Faringo Facial* (in Spanish). Report. **Formerly:** (1992) Asociacion de Enfermedades Motoneuronales y Esclerosis Lateral Amiotrofica del Uruguay (MON DELA).

MOTOR NEURONE DISEASE SUPPORT GROUP
e-mail: apuri@giasdl01.vsnl.net.in
40 Kologarh Rd.
St. No. 5
Rajendra Nagar 248 001, Delhi, India
Nicky Bhagat
PH: 91 135 754487
FX: 91 135 754487
Description: Promotes interest in motor neurone disease (MND) research among medical and scientific communities and the public in India. Works as a support group to further the interests of MND sufferers and their families throughout the country. Disseminates information about the disease. **Founded:** 1993. **Membership:** 260. **Staff:** 5. **National Groups:** 1. **Languages:** English, Hindi. **Budget:** Rs 250,000. **Publication:** *MND Newsletter* (in English), biennial. Circulation: 1,000. Advertising: accepted. **Formerly:** (1994) The MND Support Group of India.

MOUVEMENT FRANCAIS POUR LE PLANNING FAMILIAL (MFPF)
4, sq. St. Irenee
F-75011 Paris, France
Ms. Monique Bellanger, Contact
PH: 33 1 48072910
FX: 33 1 47007977
Description: Works to enhance the quality of life for individuals living in France by promoting responsible parenthood and family planning. Advocates family planning as a basic human right and defends women's rights to contraception and abortion. Attempts to stop the spread of AIDS and other sexually transmitted diseases. Sponsors programs in sex education, family planning, and

health. Provides contraceptive and health care services. Acts as an advocate for family planning on a national level. Conducts research. **Languages:** French.

MOZAMBIQUE ASSOCIATION FOR FAMILY DEVELOPMENT (MAFD)
(Asociacao Mocambicana para o Desenvolvimento da Familia)
PO Box 1535
Maputo, Mozambique
PH: 258 1 741003
FX: 258 1 491236
Description: Promotes an improved quality of life for families. Sponsors reproductive health and family planning programs and services. Conducts public education campaigns; advocates on behalf of more effective public health policies. **Founded:** 1989. **Languages:** English, Portuguese.

MOZAMBIQUE PUBLIC HEALTH ASSOCIATION (MPHA)
(Asociacao Mocambicana de Saude Publica)
PO Box 264
Maputo, Mozambique
PH: 258 1 32103
FX: 258 1 32103
Description: Public health professionals and health care personnel. Promotes formulation and implementation of effective public health programs. Participates in the formation of public health policies; conducts training courses for health care workers; gathers and disseminates information to raise awareness of public health issues. **Founded:** 1961. **Languages:** English, Portuguese.

MULTI-DISCIPLINARY HEALTH RESOURCES, EDUCATION AND ASSISTANCE TEAM (MHREAT)
PO Box 51067
Addis Ababa, Ethiopia
PH: 251 1 152913
Description: Promotes increased availability of primary health care services in developing regions of Ethiopia. Formulates and implements health care delivery programs; advocates for enhanced public support for health services. **Founded:** 1992. **Languages:** English.

MULTIDISCIPLINARY ASSOCIATION FOR PSYCHEDELIC STUDIES (MAPS)
e-mail: maps@vnet.net
url: http://www.maps.org
2121 Commonwealth Ave., Ste. 220
Charlotte, NC 28205
Rick Doblin, Pres.
PH: (704)334-1798
FX: (704)334-1799
Description: Promotes the development of beneficial, socially sanctioned uses of psychedelic drugs and marijuana. Helps researchers design, obtain government approval for, fund, conduct and report on psychedelic research in human volunteers; funds MDMA psychotherapy studies; facilitates research and FDA approval for marijuana to be prescribed for medical uses. **Founded:** 1986. **Membership:** 1500. **Staff:** 3. Multinational. **Languages:** English. **Budget:** $125,000.

MULTIPLE SCLEROSIS ASSOCIATION OF AMERICA (MSAA)
url: http://www.msaa.com
706 Haddonfield Rd.
Cherry Hill, NJ 08002-2652
John G. Hodson, Sr., Pres./Chm.
PH: (609)488-4500
TF: 800833-4672
FX: (609)661-9797
Description: Works to fulfill the daily needs of multiple sclerosis patients. Provides patient support, counseling, local transportation, therapeutic equipment, MRI scans for initial diagnosis and barrier-free housing. Conducts public education programs and and symptom relief therapy research. **Founded:** 1970. **Member-**

ship: 18000. **Staff:** 51. Multinational. **Regional Groups:** 5. **Budget:** $12,800,000.

MULTIPLE SCLEROSIS FOUNDATION (MFS)

e-mail: msfacts@juno.com
url: http://www.msfacts.org
6350 N. Andrews Ave.
Fort Lauderdale, FL 33309-2130
William Cody Garden, Exec.Dir.
PH: (954)776-6805
TF: 800441-7055
FX: (305)938-8708
Description: Provides funding toward research into the cause, prevention, treatment, and cure of multiple sclerosis. Disseminates information on research, referral, and support services, and health-care options. Works to improve the quality of life for individuals with MS. **Founded:** 1986. **Languages:** English. **Publication:** *MS Facts.* Brochures ∎ *MS FYI.* Brochures.

MULTIPLE SCLEROSIS SOCIETY OF GREAT BRITAIN AND NORTHERN IRELAND

e-mail: info@mssociety.org.uk
url: http://www.mssociety.org.uk
25 Effie Rd.
London SW6 1EE, England
Peter Cardy, Chief Exec.
PH: 44 171 6107171
FX: 44 171 7369861
Description: Persons with an interest in multiple sclerosis. Promoting and funding research to find the cause and cure of multiple sclerosis and the provision of a welfare and support service for anyone affected by MS. **Founded:** 1953. **Membership:** 60000. **Staff:** 28. Multinational. **Regional Groups:** 400. **Publication:** *MS Matters* (in English), bimonthly. Magazine. Price: included in membership dues. Advertising: accepted.

MULTIPLE SCLEROSIS SOCIETY OF ZIMBABWE

PO Box CY1177
Causeway
Harare, Zimbabwe
Saira Khan, Administrator
PH: 263 4 740472
FX: 263 4 740472
Description: Works to alleviate the suffering of persons with multiple sclerosis. Supports research to discover the cause of and cure for the disease. Offers financial assistance and counseling to individuals suffering from the disease. The society has just completed the constuction of a daycare/rehabilitation which will be geared to rehabilitate pwms, offer sympton management, carer & family training as well as support. **Founded:** 1972. **Membership:** 50. **Staff:** 4. **National Groups:** 1. **Budget:** Z$70,000. **Publication:** *Missive* (in English), monthly. Newsletter. Price: Free. Circulation: 250. Advertising: accepted.

MUSCULAR DYSTROPHY ASSOCIATION (MDA)

url: http://www.mdausa.org
3300 E. Sunrise Dr.
Tucson, AZ 85718
Robert Ross, Sr. VP & Exec.Dir.
PH: (520)529-2000
FX: (520)529-5300
Description: National voluntary health agency fostering research into the cause and cure of neuromuscular diseases in the following 8 categories. Muscular dystrophies: Becker; congenital; distal; Duchenne (pseudohypertrophic); Emery-Dreifuss; facioscapulohumeral (Landouzy-Dejerine); limb-girdle; myotonic (Steinert's disease); oculopharyngeal. Motor Neuron Diseases: adult spinal muscular atrophy (Aran-Duchenne type); amyotrophic lateral sclerosis (ALS); infantile progressive spinal muscular atrophy (type 1, Werdnig-Hoffmann disease); intermediate spinal muscular atrophy (type 2); juvenile spinal muscular atrophy (type 3, Kugelberg-Welander disease). Inflammatory Myopathies: dermatomyositis; polymyositis. Diseases of Neuromuscular Junction: Eaton-Lambert (myasthenic) syndrome; myasthenia gravis.

Diseases of the Peripheral Nerve: Dejerine-Sottas disease; Friedreich's ataxia; Charcot-Marie-Tooth disease (peroneal muscular atrophy). Metabolic Diseases of Muscle: acid maltase deficiency (Pompe's disease); carnitine deficiency; carnitine palmityl transferase deficiency; Debrancher enzyme deficiency (Cori'sor Forbes' disease); lactate dehydrogenase deficiency; mitochondrial myopathy; myoadenylate deaminase deficiency; phosphofructokinase deficiency (Tarui's disease); phosphoglycerate kinase deficiency; phosphoglycerate mutase deficiency; phosphorylase deficiency (McArdle's disease). Myopathies due to Endocrine Abnormalities: hyperthyroid myopathy; hypothyroid myopathy. Other myopathies: central core disease; myotonia congenita; myotubular myopathy; nemaline myopathy; paramyotonia congenita; periodic paralysis. Supports international programs of more than 400 research awards, major university-based neuromuscular disease research/clinical centers, and 230 outpatient clinics in hospitals in the U.S. and Puerto Rico. Awards grants for neuromuscular disease research to individual scientific investigators. Renders services to patients locally through its chapters, including: diagnostic examinations; follow-up medical evaluations; wheelchairs; leg braces; physical therapy; flu shots; summer camps. **Founded:** 1950. **Staff:** 1000. **Local Groups:** 153. **Languages:** English. **Publication:** *Quest,* bimonthly. Magazine. Advertising: accepted ∎ Annual Report, annual. Advertising: not accepted.

MUTUAL HELP HOME ASSOCIATION (MHHA)

(Association d'Entraide vive Chez Nous)
84 rue Principale
St.-Fidele, PQ, Canada G0T 1T0
J. Savard, Pres.
PH: (418)434-2561
Description: Individuals and organizations. Seeks to improve the quality of lives of elderly people living in nursing homes. Monitors conditions in nursing homes; provides support and services to the elderly. **Languages:** English, French.

MYASTHENIA GRAVIS FOUNDATION OF AMERICA

222 S. Riverside Plaza, Ste. 1540
Chicago, IL 60606
Edward S. Trainer, Exec.Dir.
PH: (312)258-0522
TF: 800541-5454
FX: (312)258-0461
Description: Persons suffering from myasthenia gravis; their families, doctors, and nurses; others dedicated to the detection, treatment, and cure of MG. Raises funds for research and for professional and public education programs. Provides literature. Sponsors low-cost prescription service. Lay and professional materials available upon request. **Founded:** 1952. **Membership:** 30000. **Staff:** 4. **Local Groups:** 1. **Languages:** English. **Budget:** $1,800,000. **Publication:** Brochures. Alternate Formats: online ∎ Handbooks. For patients ∎ Manuals. For physicians and nurses ∎ Pamphlets. **Formerly:** (1998) Myasthenia Gracis Foundation.

MYOCLONUS FAMILIES UNITED (MFU)

1553 E. 35th St.
Brooklyn, NY 11234
Sharon Dobkin, Pres.
PH: (718)252-2133
Description: Persons who have or are interested in myoclonus or other movement disorders. Seeks to educate the public and medical profession and to serve as a support group for the families of persons with myoclonus or other movement disorders. Maintains speakers' bureau; compiles statistics on the various types of myoclonus, their onsets, and duration of illness prior to correct diagnosis. **Founded:** 1982. **Membership:** 30. **Languages:** English.

MYOPIA INTERNATIONAL RESEARCH FOUNDATION (MIRF)

1265 Broadway, Rm. 608
New York, NY 10001
Joel Weintraub, M.D., Pres.

PH: (212)684-2777
FX: (212)684-2888
Description: Physicians and other professionals, and other interested persons. Promotes interdisciplinary research in the causes, prevention, and treatment of myopia (condition of nearsightedness that may be progressive and result in blindness). Sponsors Myopia International Research Network to promote worldwide cooperative research on myopia. **Founded:** 1963. Multinational. **Languages:** English. Formerly Myopia Research Foundation.

NADD - AN ASSOCIATION FOR PERSONS WITH DEVELOPMENTAL DISABILITIES AND MENTAL HEALTH NEEDS
132 Farr St.
Kingston, NY 12401-4802
Robert Fletcher, Dir.
PH: (714)331-4336
TF: 800331-5362
FX: (714)331-4569
Description: People with developmental disabilities and mental health care needs; mental health professionals; other interested individuals. Promotes public and professional interest in developmental disability; seeks to improve access to mental health care. Supports research programs; facilitates exchange of information among mental health professionals and consumers; conducts advocacy to insure implementation of effective public mental health policies and legislation. Holds educational programs; maintains speakers' bureau. **Founded:** 1983. **Staff:** 4. Multinational. **Languages:** English. **Budget:** $450,000.

NARCOLEPSY NETWORK
url: http://www.websciences.org/narnet
277 Fairfield Rd., Ste. 310 B
Fairfield, NJ 07004
Howard Wolfe, Exec. Dir.
PH: (973)276-0115
FX: (973)227-8224
Description: Individuals with narcolepsy, their friends and families, sleep professionals, and interested others. Seeks to improve the quality of life of individuals who have narcolepsy. Works to educate members and the general public about narcolepsy. Fosters communication among members. Offers referral service. Supports research; disseminates information. **Founded:** 1986. **Local Groups:** 60. **Languages:** English.

NATIONAL ABORTION FEDERATION (NAF)
1755 Mass Ave. NW Ste 600
Washington, DC 20036
Vicki Saporta, Exec.Dir.
PH: (202)667-5881
FX: (202)667-5890
Description: National professional forum for abortion service providers (physician offices, clinics, feminist health centers, Planned Parenthood affiliates) and others committed to making safe, legal abortions accessible to all women. Unites abortion service providers into a professional community dedicated to health care; upgrades abortion services by providing continuing medical education, standards, and guidelines; serves as clearinghouse of information on variety and quality of services offered; keeps abreast of educational, legislative, and public policy developments in reproductive health care. Provides referrals. **Founded:** 1977. **Membership:** 300. **Staff:** 13. Multinational. **Languages:** English. **Budget:** $1,300,000. **Publication:** *Clinical Training Curriculum in Abortion Practice*. Curriculum for residency training, medical reference. Price: $130.00 ■ *Consumer's Guide to Abortion Services* (in English and Spanish) ■ *Unsure About Your Pregnancy? A Guide to Making the Right Decision for You* ■ Books ■ Bulletins. **Absorbed:** (1977) Association for the Study of Abortion. **Formed by Merger of:** National Abortion Council; National Association of Abortion Facilities.

NATIONAL ACCREDITING AGENCY FOR CLINICAL LABORATORY SCIENCES (NAACLS)
8410 W. Bryn Mawr Ave., Ste. 670
Chicago, IL 60631
Olive M. Kimball, Exec.Dir.
PH: (773)714-8880
FX: (773)714-8886
Description: Independently accredits academic programs in hospitals, colleges, and universities in four allied health professions - medical technologist, medical laboratory technician, histotechnologist, and pathologists assistant. Establishes standards for quality educational programs; determines if hospitals and colleges are maintaining standards through self-study and on-site visits. Provides workshops for program officials on self-study and accreditation. **Founded:** 1973. **Membership:** 695. **Staff:** 9. **Languages:** English. **Budget:** $550,000. **Publication:** *Guide to Accreditation* ■ *NAACLS News*, quarterly. Newsletter. Includes news related to allied health professions and listing of position vacancies. Price: free to members and accredited program officials; $15.00/year for nonmembers. Circulation: 1,700 ■ *NAACLS Program Approval Guide* ■ *National Accrediting Agency for Clinical Laboratory Sciences – Annual Report* ■ *National Accrediting Agency for Clinical Laboratory Sciences – Essentials.* **Formerly:** (1973) Board of Schools of the ASCP. **Supersedes:** Board of Schools of Medical Technology.

NATIONAL ALLIANCE OF BREAST CANCER ORGANIZATIONS (NABCO)
e-mail: NABCOinfo@aol.com
url: http://www.nabco.org
9 E. 37th St., 10th Fl.
New York, NY 10016
Amy Langer, Exec.Dir.
PH: (212)719-0154
TF: 800719-9154
FX: (212)689-1213
Description: Breast centers; hospitals; government health offices; and support and research organizations providing information about breast cancer and breast diseases from early detection through continuing care. Serves as a resource for: organizations requiring information about breast cancer programs and organizations and medical advances; individuals seeking information about research, developments, and treatment options for breast cancer. Seeks to influence public and private health policy on issues pertaining to breast cancer, such as insurance reimbursement, health care legislation, and research funding priorities. Offers advice on how to propose and lobby for or against legislation regarding discrimination, informed consent, and third-party reimbursement. Disseminates educational materials and information on support groups, breast care centers, and hospital programs. **Founded:** 1986. **Membership:** 375. **Staff:** 10. **Languages:** English. **Budget:** $3,000,000. **Publication:** *NABCO News*, quarterly. Newsletter. Monitors developments relating to breast cancer. Price: included in membership dues. Advertising: not accepted ■ *NABCO's Resource List*, annual. Contains information on materials and organizations that provide information about breast cancer. Price: included in membership dues; $3.00/copy.

NATIONAL ALLIANCE FOR THE MENTALLY ILL (NAMI)
e-mail: kelly@nami.org
url: http://www.NAMI.ORG
200 N. Glebe Rd., No. 1015
Arlington, VA 22203-3728
Laurie M. Flynn, Exec.Dir.
PH: (703)524-7600
TF: 800950-NAMI
FX: (703)524-9094
Description: Alliance of selfhelp/advocacy groups concerned with severe and chronic mentally ill individuals. Objectives are to provide emotional support and practical guidance to families, and to educate and inform the public about mental illness. Conducts consumer advocacy activities at the local, state, and national levels to enact legislation and to promote funding for institutional and community-based settings for the seriously mentally

ill. Monitors and assures quality treatment, rehabilitation, and support services. Promotes research in the neurosciences and clinical sciences. Many affiliates maintain libraries. National office coordinates and disseminates information and resource materials and maintains liaison with legislative agencies and other mental health organizations. Offers referrals to local groups. Operates speakers' bureau. **Founded:** 1979. **Membership:** 130000. **Staff:** 55. **Local Groups:** 1,000. **Languages:** English, Spanish. **Budget:** $4,400,000.

NATIONAL ALLIANCE OF METHADONE ADVOCATES (NAMA)
e-mail: nama@interport.net
url: http://www.methadone.org/
435 2nd Ave.
New York, NY 10010
Joycelyn Woods, Exec.VP
PH: (212)595-6262
FX: (212)595-6262
Description: Methadone maintenance patients and supporters of methadone maintenance treatment. Promotes quality methadone maintenance treatment as the most effective modality for the treatment of heroin addiction. **Founded:** 1988. **Membership:** 15000. **Staff:** 1. Multinational. **National Groups:** 5. **Languages:** Danish, Italian. **Budget:** $53,000.

NATIONAL ALLIANCE OF NURSE PRACTITIONERS (NANP)
325 Pennsylvania Ave. SE
Washington, DC 20003-1100
Judith Dempster, DNSC, Chairperson
PH: (202)675-6350
Description: Nurse practitioners. Seeks to emphasize the role of Nurse Practitioners in efficient and cost-effective health care services. Promotes continuing education for all health care professionals. Promotes and supports legislation & health policy for NPs. **Founded:** 1985. **Membership:** 25000. **National Groups:** 6. **Languages:** English.

NATIONAL ALLIANCE FOR ORAL HEALTH (NAOH)
1625 Massachusetts Ave. NW, Ste. 610
Washington, DC 20036-2212
Dr. John Rutkauskas, Pres.
PH: (202)667-9433
FX: (202)667-0642
Description: Seeks to improve the oral health of special patient populations through access to early comprehensive diagnosis, prevention strategies, and therapies. Educates the public on oral health needs; works to remove reimbursement barriers to improve access; promotes a national research agenda; encourages the training of oral health professionals; develops educational materials. **Founded:** 1991. **Membership:** 30. **Staff:** 1. **Regional Groups:** 18. **Languages:** English.

NATIONAL ALLIANCE FOR RESEARCH ON SCHIZOPHRENIA AND DEPRESSION (NARSAD)
url: http://www.mhsource.com/narsad.html
60 Cutter Mill Rd., Ste. 404
Great Neck, NY 11021
Constance E. Lieber, Pres.
PH: (516)829-0091
FX: (516)487-6930
Description: Raises funds for research on schizophrenia, depression, and other mental illnesses. **Founded:** 1986. **Staff:** 5. **Languages:** English.

NATIONAL ARAB AMERICAN MEDICAL ASSOCIATION (NAAMA)
e-mail: naamusa@aol.com
url: http://www.naama.com/home.htm
1025 E. Maple, Ste. 210
Birmingham, MI 48009-6483
Ellen R. Potter, Exec.Dir.
PH: (248)646-3661
FX: (248)646-0617
Description: Medical professionals of Arab descent. Fosters exchange of scientific information. Encourages continuing education for members. Provides financial and technical support for medical students and institutions in the United States and in Arab countries. Offers medical assistance to needy individuals of Arab descent. **Founded:** 1974. **Membership:** 1800. **Staff:** 2. **State Groups:** 20. **Languages:** English. **For-Profit. Publication:** *Al Hakeem*, quarterly. Newsletter. Price: included in membership dues; $50.00/year. Circulation: 2,000. Advertising: accepted. **Formerly:** (1997) Arab Americam Medical Association.

NATIONAL ARTHRITIS AND MUSCULOSKELETAL AND SKIN DISEASES INFORMATION CLEARINGHOUSE (NAMSIC)
url: http://wwwnih.gov/niams
1 AMS Circle
Bethesda, MD 20892-2350
Ann Taubenheim, Dir.
PH: (301)495-4484
FX: (301)587-4352
Description: Collects, publishes, and disseminates professional and public educational materials for persons concerned with arthritis and musculoskeletal and skin diseases. **Languages:** English.

NATIONAL ASSOCIATION OF ADVISORS FOR THE HEALTH PROFESSIONS (NAAHP)
PO Box 1518
Champaign, IL 61824-1518
Julian M. Frankenberg, Exec.Dir.
PH: (217)355-0063
FX: (217)355-1287
Description: College and university faculty who advise and counsel students on health careers. Seeks to improve and preserve advisement at all educational levels of the health professions. Fosters and coordinates communication among the health professions and advisers. Marshalls resources; provides services concerning health professions advisement. Goals include: informed counseling for students seeking careers in the health professions; proper preparation of student evaluations for the professional schools; participation of advisers in curriculum development; improved communication between secondary and undergraduate institutions; coordination of record keeping and information exchange among undergraduate schools and local, state, and regional preprofessional programs. Makes available Advisor's Supplementary Student Evaluation Tool software program; conducts surveys. **Founded:** 1974. **Membership:** 1275. **Staff:** 5. **Regional Groups:** 4. **Languages:** English. **Budget:** $230,000. **Publication:** *Directory of the National Association of Advisors for the Health Professions*, annual. Includes health professional school announcements and order forms. Price: $25.00/issue. Circulation: 1,200. Advertising: accepted ■ *The Medical School Interview* ■ *National Association of Advisors for the Health Professions – The Advisor*, quarterly. Focuses on manpower statistics, financial aid, admission procedures, curriculum, advising, recruitment, counseling practice, and ethics. Price: $70.00/year. ISSN: 0736-0436. Circulation: 1,200 ■ *Plan for Success* ■ *Special Edition of the Advisor*, annual ■ *Strategy for Success: A Handbook for Prehealth Students* ■ *Write for Success* ■ Audiotapes. Advertising: accepted ■ Videos.

NATIONAL ASSOCIATION OF APNEA PROFESSIONALS (NAAP)
e-mail: msherida@hpu.edu
url: http://www-pediatrics.acsd.edu
2957 Kalakaua Ave., Apt. 403
Honolulu, HI 96815-4613
Connie Blaser, RN, Contact
TF: 800392-2514
Description: Physicians, nurses, respiratory therapists, social workers, polysomnographers (specialists in sleep studies), and manufacturers and suppliers of apnea monitoring equipment.

Seeks to improve communication among infnat apnea professionals and services provided for infant apnea patients and their families. (Apnea consists of interruptions in breathing of more than 15-20 seconds, usually during sleep.) Gathers scientific and clinical information about causes and treatments of apnea and related sleep disorders. **Founded:** 1987. **Membership:** 200. **Languages:** English.

NATIONAL ASSOCIATION OF BOARDS OF EXAMINERS OF LONG TERM CARE ADMINISTRATORS
808 17th St. NW, Ste. 200
Washington, DC 20006
Randy Lindrer, CAE, Exec.Dir.
PH: (202)712-9040
FX: (202)216-9646
Description: State boards responsible for licensing nursing homes. Produces exam to test the competence of nursing home adminstrators; operates continuing education review service; disseminates information and educational materials on nursing home administration. **Founded:** 1972. **Membership:** 51. **Languages:** English. **Budget:** $800,000. Formerly National Association of Boards of Examiners of Nursing Home Administrators.

NATIONAL ASSOCIATION OF BOARDS OF PHARMACY (NABP)
700 Busse Hwy.
Park Ridge, IL 60068
Carmen A. Catizone, Exec.Dir.
PH: (847)698-6227
FX: (847)698-0124
Description: Pharmacy boards of several states, District of Columbia, Puerto Rico, Virgin Islands, several Canadian provinces, and the states of Victoria, Australia, and New South Wales. Provides for inter-state reciprocity in pharmaceutic licensure based upon a uniform minimum standard of pharmaceutic education and uniform legislation; improves the standards of pharmaceutical education licensure and practice. Provides legislative information; sponsors uniform licensure examination; also provides information on accredited school and college requirements. Maintains pharmacy and drug law statistics. **Founded:** 1904. **Membership:** 67. **Staff:** 36. Multinational. **Languages:** English. **Budget:** $4,000,000.

NATIONAL ASSOCIATION OF CHILDBEARING CENTERS (NACC)
e-mail: reachnacc@birthcenters.org
url: http://www.birthcenters.org
3123 Gottschall Rd.
Perkiomenville, PA 18074
Kate Bauer, Exec.Dir.
PH: (215)234-8068
FX: (215)234-8829
Description: Working on public and policy levels in government, industry and the health professions, NACC is dedicated to developing quality, holistic services for childbearing families that promote self-reliance and confidence in birth and parenting. Collects and disseminates information on birth centers. Sets national standards for birth center operation, promotes state regulation for licensure, and national accreditation by the Commission for the Accreditation of Birth Centers. Provides a Parent Information Service for consumers looking for birth centers. Provides information on birth center. **Founded:** 1983. **Membership:** 825. **Staff:** 5. **State Groups:** 2. **Languages:** English. **Budget:** $400,000. Supersedes Cooperative Birth Center Network.

NATIONAL ASSOCIATION OF CLINICAL NURSE SPECIALISTS
e-mail: dburgher@amctec.com
4700 W. Lake Ave.
Glenview, IL 60025
Diane Burgher, Exec.Dir.
PH: (847)375-4740
Description: Clinical Nurse Specialists. **Founded:** 1995.

NATIONAL ASSOCIATION OF COMMUNITY HEALTH CENTERS (NACHC)
url: http://www.nachc.com
1330 New Hampshire Ave. NW, Ste. 122
Washington, DC 20036
Thomas Van Coverden, Pres. & CEO
PH: (202)659-8008
FX: (202)659-8519
Description: Advocacy organization of ambulatory healthcare centers, administrators, clinicians, and consumers. Works to assure the continued growth and development of community-based healthcare delivery programs for medically underserved populations by providing technical assistance and education and training opportunities for health center staff and board members. Disseminates information and research data and provides representation in legislative and professional arenas. Sponsors educational institutes, workshops, and seminars throughout the year. **Founded:** 1970. **Membership:** 950. **Staff:** 20. **Languages:** English. **Publication:** *NACHC Link.* Newsletter. Price: included in membership dues. Advertising: not accepted ▪ *The Vanguard*, quarterly. Newsletter ▪ *Washington Update*, monthly. Newsletter. **Formerly:** National Association of Directors and Administrators; (1977) National Association of Neighborhood Health Centers.

NATIONAL ASSOCIATION OF COUNTY AND CITY HEALTH OFFICIALS (NACCHO)
e-mail: info@naccho.org
url: http://www.naccho.org
440 1st St. NW, Ste. 450
Washington, DC 20001
Thomas Milne, Exec.Dir.
PH: (202)783-5550
FX: (202)783-1583
Description: County and city (local) health officials. Purposes are to stimulate and contribute to the improvement of local health programs and public health practices throughout the U.S.; disseminate information on local health programs and practices; participate in the formulation of the policies of the National Association of Counties. Is developing self-assessment instrument for use by local health officials. Operates Primary Care Project which helps to strengthen the link between local health departments and community health centers. Provides educational workshops for local health officials. **Founded:** 1965. **Membership:** 1000. **Staff:** 35. **Languages:** English. **Budget:** $600,000 Formerly National Association of County Health Officials; (1975) National Association of County Health Officers.

NATIONAL ASSOCIATION OF COUNTY HEALTH FACILITY ADMINISTRATORS (NACHFA)
c/o National Association of Counties
440 1st St. NW, 8th Fl.
Washington, DC 20001
Tom Joseph, Staff Liaison
PH: (202)393-6226
FX: (202)393-2630
Description: Administrators of freestanding and hospital-based long-term care facilities owned and operated by county governments or city-county consolidations; elected local officials. Promotes interests of county long-term care facilities; offers guidance in relevant legislative and regulatory areas. Provides technical assistance; conducts training workshops. Compiles statistics on public policy changes, such as changes in the Medicaid program, which affect long-term care facilities. **Founded:** 1977. **Membership:** 250. **Staff:** 1. **Languages:** English.

NATIONAL ASSOCIATION OF DENTAL ASSISTANTS (NADA)
900 S. Washington St., No. G-13
Falls Church, VA 22046
Joseph Salta, Pres.
PH: (703)237-8616
Description: Professional dental auxiliaries. Seeks to: bring added stature and purpose to the profession through continuing education; make available to dental assistants the special benefits

normally limited to members of specialized professional and fraternal groups. **Founded:** 1974. **Membership:** 4000. **Staff:** 4. **Languages:** English. **Budget:** $100,000. **Publication:** *Communication in the Workplace* ▪ *Dental Assistant Salary Survey*, biennial ▪ *The Explorer*, monthly. Newsletter. Includes job exchange. Price: included in membership dues; $15.00/year for nonmembers. ISSN: 0894-7929. Circulation: 4,000. Advertising: accepted ▪ *Infection Control* ▪ *Mercury Poisoning* ▪ *Radiology*.

NATIONAL ASSOCIATION OF DENTAL LABORATORIES (NADL)
e-mail: nadl@nadl.org
url: http://www.inf1.com/nadl
8201 Greensboro Dr., Ste. 300
Mc Lean, VA 22102
Robert W. Stanley, Exec.Dir.
PH: (703)610-9035
TF: 800950-1150
FX: (703)610-9005
Description: Develops criteria for ethical dental laboratories. Offers business and personal insurance programs, Hazardous Materials Training Program, and an infectious disease prevention training program, business management and technical education programs. Compiles statistics; maintains speakers' bureau and museum; conducts educational and charitable programs and sponsors annual DentalTech Expo. **Founded:** 1951. **Membership:** 2900. **Staff:** 14. **State Groups:** 48. **Languages:** German, Spanish. **Budget:** $2,000,000. **Publication:** *Directory of Speakers and Lecturers*, periodic. Price: free. Advertising: not accepted ▪ *Executive Information Series*, periodic. Booklets ▪ *Fabrication Procedures*, periodic ▪ *Hazard Communication Manual*, periodic. Video ▪ *The Journal of Dental Technology*, 10/year. Magazine. Price: $40.00 for members; $50.00 for members outside U.S. ISSN: 0746-8962. Circulation: 18,000. Advertising: accepted ▪ *Leadership Newsletter*, periodic ▪ *Managing for Profit*. Book ▪ *NADL*, quarterly. Newsletter. Price: for members ▪ *Who's Who in the Dental Laboratory Industry*, annual. Directory. Circulation: 18,000. Advertising: accepted. **Formed by Merger of:** American Dental Laboratory Association; Dental Laboratory Institute of American. **Formerly:** National Association of Certified Dental Laboratories.

NATIONAL ASSOCIATION OF DEPUTISING DOCTORS
651a Fulham Rd.
London SW6 5PX, England
C.I. Dellaporta, Hon.Treas.
PH: 44 171 7312511
FX: 44 171 3717857
Description: Medical Doctors working for deputising companies. Defends deputising doctors working conditions. **Founded:** 1983. **Membership:** 500.

NATIONAL ASSOCIATION OF DIRECTORS OF NURSING ADMINISTRATION IN LONG TERM CARE (NADONA/LTC)
e-mail: JCSchleue@aol.com
url: http://www.nadona.org
10999 Reed Hartman Hwy., Ste. 233
Cincinnati, OH 45242
Joan C. Warden, R.N., Exec.Dir.
PH: (513)791-3679
TF: 800222-0539
FX: (513)791-3699
Description: Directors, assistant directors, and former directors of nursing in long term care. Goals are: to create and establish an acceptable ethical standard for practices in long term care nursing administration; to promote and encourage research in the profession; to develop and provide a consistent program of education and certification for the positions of director, associate director, and assistant director; to promote a positive image of the long term health care industry. Encourages members to share concerns and experiences; sponsors research programs. Advocates legislation pertaining to the practice of professional nursing. Maintains speakers' bureau. **Founded:** 1986. **Membership:** 4600. **Staff:** 4. Multinational. **State Groups:** 29. **Languages:** English. **Budget:** $500,000.

NATIONAL ASSOCIATION OF DISABILITY EVALUATING PROFESSIONALS (NADEP)
e-mail: mayrehab@aol.com
url: http://www.nadgp.com
PO Box 35407
Richmond, VA 23235-0407
Virgil Robert May, III, Dir.
PH: (804)378-8809
Description: Lawyers, doctors, psychologists, employers, and others interested or involved in disability claims process, evaluation, and case management. Provides a forum for the exchange of information. Serves as a training center which prepares health professionals to qualify for the Certified Disability Examiner credential offered by the Commission on Disability Examiner Certification. **Founded:** 1984. **Membership:** 1000. **Languages:** English. **Publication:** *Disability Evaluation and Rehabilitation Review*, quarterly. Newsletter. Price: included in membership. Advertising: not accepted. **Formerly:** (1991) International Health Consultants.

NATIONAL ASSOCIATION OF FUNDHOLDING PRACTICES
11 Chandos St.
Cavendish Sq.
London W1M 9DE, England
Maggie Marum, Gen.Mgr.
PH: 44 171 6367228
FX: 44 171 6361601
Description: GP fundholding practices in England, Scotland, Wales & N Ireland. Aims to: promote good communication amongst fundholding practices; develop and extend the scope of services to patients offered by fundholding practices; encourage education research for and within fundholding practices; maintain and promote the highest ethical standards on the part of practitioners in fundholding practices; encourage the creation of new fundholding practices. **Founded:** 1991. **Membership:** 1000. **Staff:** 2.

NATIONAL ASSOCIATION OF HEALTH AUTHORITIES AND TRUSTS (NAHAT)
url: http://www.nahat.net
Birmingham Research Park
Vincent Dr.
Edgbaston
Birmingham, W. Midlands B15 2SQ, England
Philip Hunt, Dir.
PH: 44 121 4714444
FX: 44 121 4141120
Description: Represents the vast majority of NHS trusts and health authorities, acting as their voice on unique and general issues and concerns. **Founded:** 1990. **Membership:** 1000. **Staff:** 43. **Languages:** English. **Budget:** L412,000. **Publication:** *Briefing Papers/Updates* ▪ *Health Authority Newsletters* ▪ *Health Director*, monthly. Newsletter. Price: L30.00/year ▪ *Research Papers*, periodic ▪ *Trust Newsletters*. **Formed by Merger of:** National Association of Health Authorities; Society of Family Practitioner Committees.

NATIONAL ASSOCIATION OF HEALTH CARE SUPPLIES MANAGERS
218 Kennington Rd.
Kennington
Oxford OX1 5PG, England
Miss. A.M. Hales, Hon.Sec.
PH: 44 1865 735646
FX: 44 1865 735646
Description: Persons engaged in health care supplies management and associated functions on SMP grades or equivalent: those below SMP grades who are qualified by examination of the Diploma of The Chartered Institute of Purchasing and Supply. To promote maintain and seek continuously to improve professional standards and training relating to supplies and associated

services in health care. To establish and maintain a professional link with appropriate statutory bodies. To liaise with professional and other organizations. Activities include two annual training schools for junior grades in the supplies discipline and an annual conference. **Founded:** 1960. **Membership:** 490. **Publication:** *Members' Reference Book and Buyers' Guide* (in English), annual. Price: L15.00 postage and handling. Advertising: accepted.

NATIONAL ASSOCIATION OF HEALTH CAREER SCHOOLS (NAHCS)

750 1st St. NE, Ste. 940
Washington, DC 20002
Jeanne Russell, Contact
PH: (202)842-1592
FX: (202)842-1565
Description: Private, vocational, technical, and junior colleges training allied health personnel. Objectives are to: promote the interests and general welfare of health career training schools and their students accredited by the Accrediting Bureau of Health Education Schools; conduct and promote research for the advancement of the educational offerings of such schools; cooperate with local, state, and federal authorities and organizations engaged in the healing arts and the allied health sciences and with business, commerce, and industry in the maintenance of proper standards and sound policies in the field of health career training. Compiles statistics; develops curricula for allied health programs. **Founded:** 1980. **Membership:** 180. **Staff:** 1. **Languages:** English. **Publication:** *News Update* ▪ Newsletter, monthly. **Formed by Merger of:** National Association of Allied Health Schools; National Health Careers Council.

NATIONAL ASSOCIATION OF HEALTH DATA ORGANIZATIONS (NAHDO)

e-mail: nahdo@pipeline.com
url: http://www.nahdo.org
254-B N. Washington St.
Falls Church, VA 22046
Mark H. Epstein, Exec.Dir.
PH: (703)532-3282
FX: (703)532-3593
Description: Members include state and federal health data organizations, employee benefits consultants, professional review organizations, data analysis firms, software vendors, and health services consultants, health care researchers, third-party payers, hospital associations, managed care organizations. Seeks to improve health care through the collection, dissemination, and application of health care data. Promotes public availability of and access to health data; supports use of health care data to guide formulation of health policy, purchasing, and establishment of needed health services. Sponsors educational programs, workshops, & seminars. Conducts surveys and comparative studies; maintains speakers' bureau. **Founded:** 1986. **Membership:** 240. **Staff:** 4. **Languages:** English. **Publication:** *A Guide to State-Level Ambultory Care Data Collection Activities.* Manual. Price: $175.00 ▪ *Ambulatory Health Care Data Collection: A Survey of State Health Data.* Report. Price: $25.00. Advertising: not accepted ▪ *Conference Proceedings*, annual. Audiotapes. Price: price varies ▪ *Developing a Uniform Approach for Collecting Ambulatory Health Care Data.* Report ▪ *Fostering Uniformity for Health Care Data Gathering.* Report. Price: $25.00 ▪ *State Health Data Resource Manual: Hospital Discharge Data Systems.* Price: $225.00 ▪ Annual Report, annual. Price: free.

NATIONAL ASSOCIATION OF HEALTH SERVICE PERSONNEL OFFICERS

The Queen Building
Park Parade
Harrogate, N. Yorkshire HG1 5AH, England
Sue Harrison, Contact
PH: 44 1423 500066
FX: 44 1423 500199

NATIONAL ASSOCIATION OF HEALTH SERVICE SECURITY OFFICERS

Bassetlaw District General Hospital
Kilton F81 OBD, England
Tim Matthews, Chief Exec.
PH: 44 171 9289292
Description: Aims to serve the South London population and the rest of the UK. **Founded:** 1993. **Staff:** 6500. **Publication:** Annual Report, annual.

NATIONAL ASSOCIATION OF HEALTH SERVICES EXECUTIVES (NAHSE)

e-mail: nahse@compuserve.com
8630 Fenton Street, No. 126
Silver Spring, MD 20910
Ozzie Jenkins, Exec. Dir.
PH: (202)628-3953
FX: (301)588-0011
Description: Black health care executive managers, planners, educators, advocates, providers, organizers, researchers, and consumers participating in academic ventures, educational forums, seminars, workshops, systems design, legislation, and other activities. Conducts National Work-Study Program and sponsors educational programs. **Founded:** 1968. **Membership:** 500. **Staff:** 6. **Local Groups:** 7. **Languages:** English. **Budget:** $125,000. **Publication:** *NAHSE Notes*, quarterly. Newsletter. Price: free. Circulation: 1,000. Advertising: accepted.

NATIONAL ASSOCIATION OF HEALTH UNIT COORDINATORS (NAHUC)

e-mail: nahuc@nursecominc.com
1211 Locust St.
Philadelphia, PA 19107-5400
Rosemary Boisselle, Pres.&CEO
PH: (215)545-3310
TF: 88822-NAHUC
FX: (215)545-8107
Description: Coordinators of nonclinical nursing unit activities; educators, supervisors, students, and graduates in the field. Promotes the professional practice of unit coordinating. Has established standards of practice defining the role and responsibilities of health unit coordinators in the nonclinical area of health care and ensuring delivery of quality patient care. Works to establish certification guidelines for individual practitioners with a goal of national certification. Seeks recognition of the change in job title from clerk to that of coordinator, which the group believes better describes the nature of the position. Promotes continuing education and research; endeavors to develop accreditation of educational programs and standards of education for job entry. Provides vocational information to prospective students in the field; recruits students into the profession. Represents members' interests before allied health professionals, educational institutions, governmental bodies, and the community. Sponsors regional workshops, seminars, and other educational programs; compiles statistics. Maintains certification board and speakers' bureau; offers annual national certification exam and annual educational conference. **Founded:** 1980. **Membership:** 3500. **Staff:** 110. **Local Groups:** 78. **Languages:** English. **Budget:** $170,000. **Publication:** *Information Booklet*, annual. Price: free. Circulation: 2,500. Advertising: not accepted ▪ *National Association of Health Unit Coordinators – Coordinator*, quarterly. Newsletter. Price: included in membership dues; $10.00/year for nonmembers. Circulation: 4,000. Advertising: accepted ▪ *National Association of Health Unit Coordinators - Education Program Procural Guide.* Booklet. Provides information to assist in the development or evaluation of a formal educational program. Price: $27.00 for members; $45.00 for nonmembers ▪ *National Association of Health Unit Coordinators – Membership Directory*, annual. Price: included in membership dues. Advertising: not accepted ▪ *Question & Answer Brochures.* **Formerly:** (1990) National Association of Health Unit Clerks-Coordinators.

NATIONAL ASSOCIATION FOR HEALTHCARE RECRUITMENT (NAHCR)

PO Box 5769
Akron, OH 44372
Karen A. Hart, Exec.Dir.
PH: (216)867-3088
Description: Individuals employed directly by hospitals and other health care organizations which are involved in the practice of professional health care recruitment. Promotes sound principles of professional health care recruitment. Provides financial assistance to aid members in planning and implementing regional educational programs. Offers technical assistance and consultation services. Compiles statistics. **Founded:** 1975. **Membership:** 1400. **Local Groups:** 50. **Languages:** English. **Budget:** $400,000. **Publication:** *Annual Recruitment Survey.* Advertising: not accepted ▪ *Recruiter Handbook* ▪ *Recruitment Directions,* bimonthly. Price: $200.00/year. Circulation: 1,400. Advertising: accepted ▪ *Who's Who in Recruitment Resources,* annual. **Formerly:** National Association of Nurse Recruiters; (1987) National Association of Healthcare Recruiters.

NATIONAL ASSOCIATION OF HISPANIC NURSES (NAHN)

e-mail: nahn@juno.com
url: http://www.incacorp.com.nahn
1501 16st NW
Washington, DC 20036
Dr. Antonio Villerruel, Pres.
PH: (202)387-2477
FX: (202)483-7183
Description: Nurses on all educational levels, from all Hispanic subgroups; non-Hispanic nurses concerned about the health delivery needs of the Hispanic community; nursing students. Serves the nursing and health care delivery needs of the Hispanic community and the professional needs of Hispanic nurses. Provides a forum in which Hispanic nurses can analyze, research, and evaluate the health care needs of the Hispanic community. Disseminates findings of that research to local, state, and federal agencies so as to affect policy-making and resource allocation. Aims to ensure that Hispanic nurses have equal access to educational, professional, and economic opportunities. Identifies Hispanic nurses throughout the nation to determine the size of the work force available to provide culturally sensitive nursing care to Hispanics. **Founded:** 1976. **Membership:** 1000. **National Groups:** 1. **Languages:** Spanish. **For-Profit** **Formerly** (1979) National Association of Spanish Speaking-Spanish Surnamed Nurses.

NATIONAL ASSOCIATION OF LOCAL BOARDS OF HEALTH (NALBOH)

e-mail: nalboh@wcnet.org
1840 E. Gypsy Lane Rd.
Bowling Green, OH 43402
Ned Baker, MPH, Exec.Dir.
PH: (419)353-7714
FX: (419)353-9680
Description: Represents the interests of local boards of health throughout the United States and relates their concerns to individuals responsible for developing public health policy at the national level. Offers educational programs and speakers' bureau. **Founded:** 1992. **Membership:** 2600. **Staff:** 2. **State Groups:** 10. **Languages:** English. **Budget:** $200,000.

NATIONAL ASSOCIATION OF MANAGED CARE PHYSICIANS (NAMCP)

e-mail: sreed@namcp.com
url: http://www.namcp.com
4435 Waterfront Dr., Ste. 101
PO Box 4765
Glen Allen, VA 23058-4765
Richard Romeis, Pres.
PH: (804)527-1905
TF: 800722-0376
FX: (804)747-5316
Description: Licensed physicians and allied health professionals working in managed health care programs; medical residents and students interested in managed health care; corporations or agencies providing services or goods to the industry; interested others. Enhances the ability of practicing physicians to proactively participate within the managed health care arena through research, communication, and education. Provides a forum for members to communicate their concerns about the changing health care environment, integrate into managed health care delivery systems, and assure continuous improvement in the quality of health care services provided. Develops practice criteria, quality assurance measures, and appropriate utilization management criteria. Offers educational programs; maintains speakers' bureau and placement services; conducts research programs; developing informational clearinghouse. **Founded:** 1991. **Membership:** 12000. **Staff:** 12. **State Groups:** 5. **Languages:** English. **Budget:** $750,000. **Publication:** *Managed Care Medicine,* bimonthly. Journal. Price: $95.00. Circulation: 30,000. Advertising: accepted. Alternate Formats: online ▪ *NAMCP Guide to Managed Care.* Monograph.

NATIONAL ASSOCIATION OF MEDICAID DIRECTORS (NASMD)

url: http://medicaid.apwa.org
810 1st St. NE, Ste. 500
Washington, DC 20002-4267
Lee Partridge, Contact
PH: (202)682-0100
FX: (202)289-6555
Description: Directors and senior staff of state and territorial medical assistance programs. Promotes effective Medicaid policy and program administration; works with the federal government on issues through technical advisory groups. Conducts forums on policy and technical issues. **Membership:** 54. **Staff:** 1. **Languages:** English. **Publication:** *MMI Bulletin,* monthly. Newsletter. Summary of legal decisions, legislation, regulations, waivers relating to Medicaid program. Price: $90.00/year. Circulation: 300. Advertising: not accepted. **Formerly:** (1995) State Medicaid Directors Association.

NATIONAL ASSOCIATION OF MEDICAL DIRECTORS FOR RESPIRATORY CARE (NAMDRC)

url: http://www.namdrc.org
5454 Wisconsin Ave., Ste. 1270
Chevy Chase, MD 20815
Phillip Porte, Exec.Dir.
PH: (301)718-2975
FX: (301)718-2976
Description: Works to provide educational opportunities to fit the needs of medical directors of respiratory care and represents the interests of members to regulatory agencies to ensure that the needs of respiratory patients are not overlooked. Offers educational programs; maintains speakers' bureau. **Founded:** 1977. **Membership:** 650. **Staff:** 4. **Languages:** English. **Budget:** $200,000.

NATIONAL ASSOCIATION OF MEDICAL EXAMINERS (NAME)

url: http://www.thename.org
1402 S. Grand Blvd.
St. Louis, MO 63104
Denise Randazzo, Exec.Sec.
PH: (314)577-8298
FX: (314)268-5124
Description: Medical examiners, pathologists, and other licensed physicians who have responsibilities in connection with the official investigation of sudden, suspicious, and violent deaths. Attempts to establish greater understanding and support for the medical examiner system among the public, government officials, and the medical and legal professions. Has established standards for inspection and accreditation of a modern medico-legal investigative system. **Founded:** 1966. **Membership:** 774. **Staff:** 3. **Languages:** English. **Publication:** *American Journal of Forensic Medicine and Pathology,* quarterly.

NATIONAL ASSOCIATION OF MEDICAL MINORITY
   EDUCATORS (NAMME)
Marquette University
Office of Multicultural Concerns
Milwaukee, WI 53233
Dr. Charles J. Alexander, Pres.
PH: (414)288-5861
FX: (414)288-5788
Description: Educators, administrators, and practitioners of medicine, osteopathic medicine, dentistry, veterinary medicine, optometry, podiatry, public health, and allied health. Promotes the increase of medical minority personnel; admissions of minority students to health professionals schools; retention and graduation of minority students in health profession schools; recruitment and development of minority faculty administrators and managerial personnel in the health professions; delivery of quality health care for minority populations; and recruitment, retention, and development of minority students in pre-health profession programs. Sponsors workshops for high school counselors and junior high and high school science teachers; provides training for minority affairs workers and officers. Offers annual student development sessions and recruitment fairs. Conducts research programs and systematic studies. **Founded:** 1975. **Membership:** 200. **Regional Groups:** 4. **Languages:** English. **Publication:** *Financing Your Medical Education*, annual. Book ▪ *James Stills Quarterly - NAMME Edition*. Newsletter.

NATIONAL ASSOCIATION MEDICAL STAFF SERVICES
   (NAMSS)
e-mail: namss@namss.org
url: http://www.namss.org
631 E Butterfield, Ste. 311
Lombard, IL 60148
Robert Dengler, Exec.Dir.
PH: (630)271-9814
FX: (630)271-0295
Description: Individuals involved in the management and administration of healthcare provider services. Seeks to: enhance the knowledge and experience of medical staff services professionals; promote the certification of those involved in the profession. **Founded:** 1971. **Membership:** 3100. **Staff:** 6. **Local Groups:** 32. **Languages:** English. **Budget:** $1,500,000. **Publication:** *Guidebook: Developing a Policy and Procedure Manual* ▪ *Job Classifications: Delineation of Clinical Privileges, Criteria, and Forms* ▪ *Medical Staff Leadership Orientation Manual* ▪ *NAMSS Membership Roster*, annual. Membership Directory ▪ *Overview*, bimonthly. Magazine. Price: included in membership dues; $65.00/year for nonmembers. Advertising: accepted.

NATIONAL ASSOCIATION OF NEONATAL NURSES (NANN)
e-mail: nannmbrs@aol.com
url: http://www.nann.org
1304 Southpoint Blvd., Ste. 280
Petaluma, CA 94954
Patricia J. Johnson, Interim Exec.Dir.
PH: (707)762-5588
FX: (707)762-0401
Description: Nurses currently working in neonatal intensive care units. Promotes professional development of members. Provides educational and networking opportunities. Disseminates legislative information. **Founded:** 1984. **Membership:** 11500. **Staff:** 9. Multinational. **Regional Groups:** 60. **Languages:** English. **Budget:** $1,600,000.

NATIONAL ASSOCIATION OF NURSE MASSAGE
   THERAPISTS (NANMT)
e-mail: nanmt6@aol.com
PO Box 1268
Osprey, FL 34229
Barbara Harris, RN,LMT, Pres.
PH: (813)966-6288
FX: (813)918-0522
Description: Educates the medical community and the general

public about bodywork therapies. Monitors legislation. **Founded:** 1987. **Membership:** 650. Multinational. **Languages:** English.

NATIONAL ASSOCIATION OF NURSE PRACTITIONERS IN
   REPRODUCTIVE HEALTH (NANPRH)
e-mail: nanprh@aol.com
1090 Vermont Ave. NW, Ste. 800
Washington, DC 20005
Susan Wysocki, Pres.
PH: (202)408-7025
FX: (202)408-0902
Description: Nurse practitioners involved in reproductive healthcare. Advocates quality reproductive healthcare services and reproductive freedom. Supports the rights of nurse practitioners to administer reproductive healthcare services to patients. Encourages nurses to participate in continuing education programs. Disseminates information. **Founded:** 1980. **Membership:** 1700. **Staff:** 4. **Languages:** English.

NATIONAL ASSOCIATION OF ORTHOPAEDIC NURSES
   (NAON)
e-mail: naon@mail.ajj.com
url: http://www.inurse.com/~naon
E. Holly Ave.
Box 56
Pitman, NJ 08071-0056
Pat Reichart, Exec. Sec.
PH: (609)256-2310
FX: (609)589-7463
Description: Registered, licensed practical, or licensed vocational nurses involved or knowledgeable in orthopedic nursing. Enhances the personal and professional growth of orthopedic nurses through continuing education programs. Promotes research development and advances in orthopedic nursing; promotes an awareness of patients' rights. Stresses the concept of man's physical, psychological, social, emotional, and spiritual needs in the development of patient care plans. Maintains liaison with and serves as resource to hospitals, universities, industries, and government agencies. Operates special interest groups. Sponsors workshops; maintains speakers' bureau; offers research grants. Makes available audiovisual presentation. **Founded:** 1980. **Membership:** 8300. **Local Groups:** 154. **Languages:** English. **Budget:** $2,000,000.

NATIONAL ASSOCIATION OF ORTHOPAEDIC
   TECHNOLOGISTS (NAOT)
PO Box 14148
Research Triangle Park, NC 27709-4148
Bill Wick, Pres.
Description: Allied health assistants working with orthopedic patients. Promotes continued professional education of members and other orthopedic health care providers; administers certification examination. Seeks to enhance public understanding of orthopedics. Conducts seminars; compiles statistics. **Founded:** 1982. **Membership:** 1100. **Staff:** 3. **Local Groups:** 23. **Languages:** English. **Publication:** *OnLine: Advancements in Orthopaedic Technology*, bimonthly. Newsletter. Includes orthopaedic articles, meeting updates, and technology tips. Circulation: 1,500. Advertising: accepted.

NATIONAL ASSOCIATION OF PEDIATRIC NURSE
   ASSOCIATES AND PRACTITIONERS (NAPNAP)
e-mail: 74224.51@compuserve.com
url: http://www.napnap.org
1101 Kings Hwy. N., No. 206
Cherry Hill, NJ 08034-1912
Mavis McGuire, Exec.Dir.
PH: (609)667-1773
FX: (609)667-7187
Description: Pediatric, school, and family nurse practitioners and interested persons. Seeks to improve the quality of infant, child, and adolescent health care by making health care services accessible and providing a forum for continuing education of members. Facilitates and supports legislation designed to promote the

role of pediatric nurse practitioners and associates; promotes salary ranges commensurate with practitioners' and associates' responsibilities; facilitates exchange of information between prospective employers and job seekers in the field. Participates in the implementation of certification and certification maintenance of practitioners and associates, in cooperation with the National Certification Board of Pediatric Nurse Practitioners and Nurses. Supports research programs; compiles statistics. **Founded:** 1973. **Membership:** 5600. **Staff:** 8. **State Groups:** 46. **Languages:** English. **Budget:** $1,019,000.

NATIONAL ASSOCIATION OF PHARMACEUTICAL
   IMPORTERS
   (Bundesverband der Arzneimittel-Importeure)
Althofstr. 46
D-45468 Muhlheim, Germany
Andreas Mohringer, Contact
PH: 49 208 360810
FX: 49 208 35433
Description: Pharmaceutical importers headquartered in Germany. Promotes the economic and professional interests of members. **Founded:** 1982. **Membership:** 7.

NATIONAL ASSOCIATION OF PHARMACEUTICAL
   MANUFACTURERS (NAPM)
e-mail: napmgenrx@aol.com
320 Old Country Rd., Ste. 205
Garden City, NY 11530-1752
Robert S. Milanese, Pres.
PH: (516)741-3699
FX: (516)741-3696
Description: Pharmaceutical manufacturers and repackagers. Associate members are distributors of raw material, component, and service suppliers. Purpose is to consider problems arising from laws and regulations, and to establish rapport with federal and state agencies. Organized the Foundation for Pharmaceutical Research. Conducts technical and regulatory symposia and seminars. **Founded:** 1954. **Membership:** 65. **Staff:** 3. **National Groups:** 1. **Languages:** English. **Budget:** $500,000. **Publication:** *NAPM News Bulletin*, monthly. Focuses on the legislative, regulatory, legal, and technical aspects of the pharmaceutical industry. Includes new product information. Price: free. Circulation: 1,500. Advertising: not accepted. **Formerly:** Drug and Allied Products Guild.

NATIONAL ASSOCIATION OF PHARMACEUTICAL
   WHOLESALERS (PHAGRO)
   (Bundesverband des Pharmazeutischen Grosshandels)
Savignystr. 55
D-60325 Frankfurt, Germany
Dr. Hilko Meyer, Contact
PH: 49 69 9758760
FX: 49 69 97587630
Description: Promotes the pharmaceutical full-line wholesale industry in Germany. **Founded:** 1909. **Membership:** 10. **Staff:** 5. **Publication:** *Geschaftsbericht* (in German), annual. Annual Report. Price: free. Advertising: not accepted.

NATIONAL ASSOCIATION OF PHYSICIAN NURSES (NAPN)
900 S. Washington St., No. G-13
Falls Church, VA 22046
Susan Young, Dir.
PH: (703)237-8616
Description: Physicians' nurses united to bring added stature and purpose to their profession and to create for themselves the benefits normally limited to members of specialized professional and fraternal groups. **Founded:** 1973. **Membership:** 3000. **Staff:** 4. **Languages:** English. **Budget:** $60,000.

NATIONAL ASSOCIATION OF PHYSICIAN RECRUITERS
   (NAPR)
e-mail: KMG-ASSN@worldnet.att.net
url: http://www.napr.org
PO Box 150127
Altamonte Springs, FL 32715-0127
Willard S. Kautter, CAE, Exec.VP
PH: (407)774-7880
TF: 800726-5613
FX: (407)774-6440
Description: Physician search firms (companies that recruit resident physicians or practicing physicians to fill positions nationwide). Promotes a positive public image of physician recruiting services. Seeks to establish accreditation standards for the field. Provides marketing services to the physician recruiting industry. Maintains speakers' bureau. Sponsors educational programs and seminars. Compiles statistics. **Founded:** 1983. **Membership:** 300. **Staff:** 5. **Languages:** English. **Budget:** $280,000. **Publication:** *NAPA Business Report (Newsletter)*, annual, Client Brochure. Brochures. Price:. Advertising: accepted ∎ *NAPR Business Report*, quarterly. Newsletter. Advertising: accepted.

NATIONAL ASSOCIATION FOR PRACTICAL NURSE
   EDUCATION AND SERVICE (NAPNES)
e-mail: napnes@bellatlantic.net
1400 Spring St., Ste. 330
Silver Spring, MD 20910
John H. Word, Exec.Dir.
PH: (301)588-2491
FX: (301)588-2839
Description: Licensed practical/vocational nurses, registered nurses, physicians, hospital and nursing home administrators, and interested others. Provides consultation service to advise schools wishing to develop a practical/vocational nursing program on facilities, equipment, policies, curriculum, and staffing. Promotes recruitment of students through preparation and distribution of recruitment materials. Sponsors seminars for directors and instructors in schools of practical/vocational nursing and continuing education programs for LPNs/LVNs; approves continuing education programs and awards contact hours; holds national certification courses in post licensure specialities such as pharmacology, long term care and gerontics. **Founded:** 1941. **Membership:** 30000. **Staff:** 5. **State Groups:** 20. **Languages:** English. **Publication:** *Journal of Practical Nursing*, quarterly. Contains news of association activities, nursing law, and pending legislation affecting the nursing profession. Price: included in membership dues; $15.00/year for nonmembers; $30.00/year for nonmembers outside the U.S. ISSN: 0022-3867. Circulation: 10,000. Advertising: accepted ∎ *NAPNES Forum*, 8/year. Journal. Supplement to the *Journal of Practical Nusing*. **Absorbed:** (1985) National Association of Licensed Practical Nurses.

NATIONAL ASSOCIATION OF PROFESSIONAL GERIATRIC
   CARE MANAGERS (PGCM)
1604 N. Country Club Rd.
Tucson, AZ 85716-3102
Laury L. Adsit, Exec.Dir.
PH: (520)881-8008
FX: (520)325-7925
Description: Promotes quality services and care for elderly citizens. Provides referral service and distributes information to individuals interested in geriatric care management. Maintains referral network. **Founded:** 1985. **Membership:** 1100. **Staff:** 15. **Languages:** English. **Budget:** $250,000. Formerly National Association of Private Geriatric Care Managers.

NATIONAL ASSOCIATION FOR PSEUDOXANTHOMA
   ELASTICUM
e-mail: pxenape@estreet.com
url: http://www.ttuhsc.edu/pages/nape/
3500 E. 12 Ave.
Denver, CO 80206
Dr. Kenneth Neldner, Chm.

PH: (303)355-3866
FX: (303)355-3859
Description: People who have Pseudoxanthoma Elasticum (PXE), as well as interested others. (Pseudoxanthoma elasticum is a rare skin disease marked by muscles and papules and an exaggeration of the normal creases and folds of the skin.) Provides educational information about PXE. Compiles statistics. Serves to unite PXE patients with professionals who treat the disease. **Founded:** 1989. **Membership:** 600. **Staff:** 1. **National Groups:** 1. **Languages:** English. **Budget:** $20,000.

NATIONAL ASSOCIATION OF PSYCHIATRIC HEALTH SYSTEMS (NAPHS)

e-mail: napgs@naphs.org
url: http://www.napus.org
1317 F Street, NW, Suite 301
Washington, DC 20004
Mark Covall, Exec.Dir.
PH: (202)393-6700
FX: (202)783-6041
Description: Represents behavioral healthcare systems that are committed to the delivery of responsive, accountable, and clinically effective treatment and prevention programs for people with mental and substance abuse disorders. **Founded:** 1933. **Membership:** 292. **Staff:** 7. **Languages:** English. **Budget:** $2,000,000. Formerly (1993) National Association of Private Psychiatric Hospitals.

NATIONAL ASSOCIATION OF PSYCHIATRIC SURVIVORS (NAPS)

PO Box 618
Sioux Falls, SD 57101
Rae Unzicker, Coord.
PH: (605)334-4067
Description: Current and former recipients of mental health services; families of psychiatric patients; others with an interest in psychiatry and the rights of mental health patients. Seeks to promote the rights of psychiatric patients and end what the group feels is involuntary psychiatric intervention, including civil commitment and forced treatments such as electroshock, psychosurgery, involuntary detention, and mood-altering drug therapies. Encourages development of voluntary alternatives, including selfhelp and peer support groups, and other nonmedical procedures; promotes freedom of choice for individuals in selecting mental treatments and the right to refuse any unwanted treatments. Challenges negative social attitudes regarding mental illness and promotes public understanding and sensitivity to people who have received psychiatric treatment. Provides referral and advocacy services; maintains speakers' bureau. **Founded:** 1985. **Membership:** 2000. **Languages:** English. Formerly (1989) National Alliance of Mental Patients.

NATIONAL ASSOCIATION OF PSYCHIATRIC TREATMENT CENTERS FOR CHILDREN (NAPTCC)

e-mail: naptcc@aol.com
2000 L St. NW, Ste. 200
Washington, DC 20036
Joy Midman, Exec.Dir.
PH: (202)416-1669
FX: (202)362-5145
Description: Promotes exellence in the care, delivery, accountability, and cost effectiveness of psychiatric services for children. Works to improve the business conditions in the industry. Supports and promotes standards, advocacy, educational programs, marketing, and research designed to ensure quality psychiatric care for children. Conducts lobbying activities and educational programs. **Founded:** 1983. **Membership:** 80. **Staff:** 3. **Languages:** English. **Budget:** $350,000. Formerly (1982) CHAMPUS Coalition.

NATIONAL ASSOCIATION OF PUBLIC HEALTH SERVICE DENTISTS

(Bundesverband der Zahnarzte des Offentlichen Gesundheitsdienstes)
Bergstr. 11
D-37308 Heiligenstadt, Germany
Dr. Martina Kroplin, Contact
PH: 49 551 61140
FX: 49 551 61140
Description: Safeguards the interests of public health service dentists and promotes their continuing education. Also promotes the prevention of oral diseases, especially in children. **Founded:** 1954. **Publication:** *Zahnaerztlichen Gesundheitsdienst* (in German), quarterly, always last week of March, June, September, and December. Magazine. Price: DM 30.00/year plus shipping and handling. ISSN: 0340-5478. Circulation: 800. Advertising: accepted.

NATIONAL ASSOCIATION OF REGISTERED NURSES (NARN)

11512 Allecingie Pky., Ste. D
Richmond, VA 23235
Francis R. deBondt, Ph.D., Admin.
PH: (804)794-6513
FX: (804)379-7698
Description: Nurses' associations. Seeks to offer nurses the opportunity to plan and create a financially sound future through financial management programs. Provides financial products, consultation, and services including Individual Retirement Accounts, full investment services, and group life insurance. Conducts educational programs. **Founded:** 1979. **Membership:** 250. **Staff:** 6. **Languages:** English.

NATIONAL ASSOCIATION OF RESIDENTS AND INTERNS (NARI)

e-mail: ppsone@msn.com
url: http://www.nari-assn.com
292 Madison Ave., 4th Fl.
New York, NY 10017
Mrs. Patricia Arden, Exec.Dir./CEO
PH: (212)949-5900
TF: 800221-2168
FX: (212)949-5910
Description: Medical and dental students, interns, residents, and fellows. Contributes to the economic welfare of members through unsecured loan plans, low-cost group insurance, group purchase discounts, physician search service, and special financial planning services. **Founded:** 1959. **Membership:** 18000. **Staff:** 50. **Languages:** English. **Publication:** *NARI Stethoscope*, quarterly. Newsletter. Provides advice on business interests and benefits news. Price: included in membership dues. Circulation: 18,000. Advertising: not accepted.

NATIONAL ASSOCIATION FOR RURAL MENTAL HEALTH (NARMH)

e-mail: NARMH@facts.ksu.edu
3700 W. Division St., Ste. 105
St. Cloud, MN 56301
Damian Kirwan, ACSW, Pres.
PH: (320)202-1820
TF: 800809-5879
FX: (320)202-1833
Description: Mental health practitioners and administrators and others dedicated to improving mental health services in rural areas. Promotes effective rural mental health services. Promotes the use of services by rural community dwellers. **Founded:** 1977. **Membership:** 300. **Staff:** 1. **Languages:** English. **For-Profit.**

NATIONAL ASSOCIATION OF SCHOOL NURSES (NASN)

e-mail: nasn@aol.com
url: http://www.VRmedia.com/nurses/
PO Box 1300
Scarborough, ME 04070-1300
Beverly Farquhar, Exec. Dir.

PH: (207)883-2117
FX: (207)883-2683
Description: School nurses who conduct comprehensive school health programs in public and private schools. Objectives are: to provide national leadership in the promotion of health services for schoolchildren; to promote school health interests to the nursing and health community and the public; to monitor legislation pertaining to school nursing. Provides continuing education programs at the national level and assistance to states for program implementation. Has established workshops and grants for study of child and drug abuse, the female body, and skin care. **Founded:** 1969. **Membership:** 10000. **Staff:** 6. **State Groups:** 47. **Languages:** English. **Budget:** $1,000,000. Formerly (1977) Department of School Nurses/NEA.

NATIONAL ASSOCIATION OF SEVENTH-DAY ADVENTIST DENTISTS (NASDAD)
c/o Karen Sutton
PO Box 101
Loma Linda, CA 92354
Karen Sutton, Exec.Dir.
PH: (909)824-4633
FX: (909)824-4638
Publication: *News*, quarterly ▪ *SDA Dentist*, annual.

NATIONAL ASSOCIATION OF STATE MENTAL HEALTH PROGRAM DIRECTORS (NASMHPD)
e-mail: bob.glover@nasmhpd.org
url: http://www.nasmhpd.org
66 Canal Center Plz., Ste. 302
Alexandria, VA 22314
Dr. Robert W. Glover, Exec.Dir.
PH: (703)739-9333
FX: (703)548-9517
Description: State commissioners in charge of the state mental disability programs; associate members are assistant commissioners for children and youth, aged, legal services, forensic services, and adult services. Promotes cooperation of state government agencies in delivery of services to mentally disabled persons; fosters the exchange of scientific and programmatic information in the administration of public mental health programs including mental illness treatment programs, community and hospital care of mentally ill, mentally retarded, alcoholic, and drug addicted persons. Monitors state and federal and congressional activities; gathers and analyzes information on organization, structure, funding, and programming of state government mental health programs. A cooperating agency of the National Governors' Association and the Council of State Governments. **Founded:** 1963. **Membership:** 55. **Staff:** 18. **Languages:** English.

NATIONAL ASSOCIATION OF SUPERVISORS AND ADMINISTRATORS OF HEALTH OCCUPATIONS EDUCATION (NASAHOE)
e-mail: jwakelyn@pen.kiz.va.us
Virginia Department of Education
PO Box 2120
Richmond, VA 23216-2060
Jo Ann Wakelyn, Pres.
PH: (804)225-2842
FX: (804)371-2456
Description: State administrators and local supervisors of health occupations education. Acts as resource sharing group, particularly in the area of curriculum development. Seeks to develop shared resources for recruitment. **Membership:** 35. **Languages:** English. **Publication:** *NASAHOE News*, quarterly. Newsletter. **Formerly:** (1988) National Association for State Administrators of Health Occupations Education.

NATIONAL ASSOCIATION OF THEATRE NURSES
e-mail: hq@natn.org.uk
url: http://www.natn.org.uk
Daisy Aysir House
6 Grove Park Ct.
Harrogate HG1 4DP, England
Dot Chadwick
PH: 44 1423 508079
FX: 44 1423 531613
Description: Operating theatre nurses. Workshops and study days are organized locally and nationally throughout the year. Annual three day congress organised. **Founded:** 1964. **Membership:** 6500. **Staff:** 7. **Regional Groups:** 47. **Publication:** *British Journal of Theatre Nurses*, monthly. Circulation: 6,500. Advertising: accepted.

NATIONAL ASSOCIATION OF THE VETERINARY PHARMACEUTICAL INDUSTRY
(Bundesfachverband der Veterinar-Pharmazeutischen Industry)
Universitatsstr. 27
D-35037 Marburg, Germany
B. Aretz, Contact
PH: 49 6421 22073
FX: 49 6421 22074
Description: Manufacturers, importers, exporters, and wholesalers of veterinary pharmaceutical products. Represents the economic interests of members. Advises members and agencies on political issues. **Membership:** 30.

NATIONAL ASSOCIATION OF TRAVELING NURSES (NATN)
PO Box 35189
Chicago, IL 60707-0189
L. David Stoller, Chm.
PH: (708)453-0080
FX: (708)453-0083
Description: Members of the medical profession. Provides travel information. Offers substantial discounts for members at major hotels, resorts, and car rental agencies. Provides members with complete list of approved travel industry suppliers, including travel agents, vendors, airlines, cruise ship companies, and hotels. **Founded:** 1990. **Membership:** 78951. **Staff:** 10. Multinational. **Languages:** English.

NATIONAL ASSOCIATION OF VA PHYSICIANS AND DENTISTS (NAVAPD)
e-mail: navapd@navapd.dgs.com
1414 Prince St.
Alexandria, VA 22314
Samuel V. Spagnolo, M.D., Pres.
PH: (703)548-0280
FX: (703)548-8024
Description: Physicians and dentists at Veterans Administration Medical Centers. Purpose is to strengthen and improve the quality of care and conditions at VA health care facilities. Works to assure that veterans receive quality care. **Founded:** 1975. **Membership:** 2000. **Languages:** English. **Publication:** *NAVAPD News*, bimonthly. Newsletter. Price: included in membership. Circulation: 2,000. Advertising: accepted ▪ *NAVAPD Notes*, bimonthly.

NATIONAL ASSOCIATION OF VISION PROFESSIONALS (NAVP)
e-mail: prvblind@pop.erols.com
1775 Church St. NW
Washington, DC 20036
Arnold Simonse, Exec.Sec.
PH: (202)234-1010
FX: (202)234-1020
Description: Individuals responsible for or connected with vision conservation and eye health programs in public or private agencies and institutions. Serves as a forum for ideas and programs, cooperates with other agencies, and promotes professional standards. Certifies vision screening personnel. **Founded:** 1976. **Membership:** 200. **Staff:** 1. **Languages:** English. **Budget:** $25,000.

Formerly (1986) National Association of Vision Program Consultants.

NATIONAL ASSOCIATION OF VOLUNTARY SERVICE MANAGERS

Queen's Medical Centre
Nottingham NG7 2UH, England
Theresa Collen, Contact
PH: 44 115 9249924
Description: Voluntary services managers working in the field of health care. Offers support and training for voluntary services managers working in health care. **Founded:** 1968. **Membership:** 102. **Publication:** Report.

NATIONAL ATAXIA FOUNDATION (NAF)

e-mail: naf@mr.net
url: http://www.ataxia.org
2600 Fernbrook Ln. N.
Minneapolis, MN 55447
Donna Gruetzmacher, Exec.Dir.
Description: Objectives are: to make an early diagnosis of ataxia by locating all potential victims and encouraging them to have an examination; to educate the public and the helping professions about ataxia; to initiate basic research and coordinate efforts of worldwide research centers. Emphasis is on locating the genes responsible. Provides services and information to ataxia victims and their families. **Founded:** 1957. **Membership:** 2000. **Staff:** 6. **Local Groups:** 45. **Languages:** English. **For-Profit. Budget:** $250,000. **Publication:** *Generations* (in English), quarterly. Newsletter. Includes foundation news, calendar of events, and research updates. Price: free to members and those who suffer from ataxia. Circulation: 10,000. Advertising: not accepted ▪ *Together<el3>We Can*. Video ▪ Brochures.

NATIONAL ATTENTION-DEFICIT DISORDER ASSOCIATION (NATIONAL ADDA)

e-mail: natladda@aol.com
url: http://www.add.org
PO Box 972
Mentor, OH 44061-0972
Peter Jaksa, PhD, Pres.
PH: (216)350-9595
TF: 800487-2282
FX: (216)350-0223
Description: Seeks to: promote a greater public awareness of the multiple needs of individuals with ADD and their families; address their educational, psychological, and social needs; encourage more responsiveness with regard to ADD in the academic and health care communities. Maintains database of support groups throughout the country. **Founded:** 1989. **Languages:** English. **Publication:** *Addalog*. Catalog. Lists books, brochures, momographs, and other materials available for purchasing. Advertising: not accepted ▪ *Focus*. Newsletter. Advertising: not accepted ▪ Monographs ▪ Pamphlets. **Formerly:** (1992) Attention-Deficit Disorder Association.

NATIONAL BLACK NURSES ASSOCIATION (NBNA)

e-mail: nbna@erols.com
1511 K St. NW, Ste. 415
Washington, DC 20005
Millicent Gorham, Exec.Dir.
PH: (202)393-6870
FX: (202)347-3808
Description: Registered nurses, licensed practical nurses, licensed vocational nurses, and student nurses. Functions as a professional support group and as an advocacy group for the black community and their health care. Recruits and assists blacks interested in pursuing nursing as a career. Presents scholarships to student nurses, including the Dr. Lauranne Sams Scholarship. Compiles statistics; maintains biographical archives. **Founded:** 1971. **Membership:** 5000. **Staff:** 4. **Languages:** English.

NATIONAL BLOOD TRANSFUSION SERVICE

e-mail: lloyd@healthnet.zw
PO Box A101
Avondale
Harare, Zimbabwe
D.M. Connolly, Gen.Mgr.
PH: 263 4 707801
FX: 263 4 707820
Description: Promotes the availability of blood supplies for tranfusions in Zimbabwe. Disseminates information. **Founded:** 1986. **Staff:** 160. **Budget:** Z$51,000,000. **Publication:** *Annual Report* (in English). Price: Free. Advertising: not accepted ▪ Booklet. AIDS awareness and giving blood.

NATIONAL BOARD FOR CERTIFICATION OF DENTAL LABORATORIES (CDL)

e-mail: nadl@nadl.org
url: http://www.nadl.org
8201 Greensboro Dr., Ste. 300
Mc Lean, VA 22102
Robert W. Stanley, Exec.Dir.
PH: (703)610-9036
FX: (703)610-9005
Description: Certified dental laboratories, including commercial, private, and dental or dental technology schools. Purpose is the certification and recognition of dental laboratories that demonstrate and document compliance with standards set by the industry for laboratory facilities, technical resources, safety, prevention of cross-contamination, and competence of personnel. **Founded:** 1979. **Membership:** 600. **Staff:** 4. **Languages:** English. **Budget:** $300,000. **Publication:** *Certified Mail*, periodic. Newsletter. Circulation: 600. Advertising: not accepted ▪ Directory, semiannual.

NATIONAL BOARD FOR CERTIFICATION IN DENTAL TECHNOLOGY (NBC)

e-mail: cdts@erols.com
url: http://www.nadl.org
555 E. Braddock Rd.
Alexandria, VA 22314-2106
Sandra Stewart Ludes, Program Dir.
PH: (703)683-5310
TF: 800684-5310
FX: (703)549-4788
Description: Certifies dental technicians with formal education in dental technology and a minimum of three years' experience who have passed written and practical exams administered by the NBC. Provides continuing education to certificants and recognizes competent dental technicians. Also certifies dental laboratories that meet published standards for personnel, facility and infection control practice. **Founded:** 1958. **Membership:** 10000. **Staff:** 4. Multinational. **Languages:** English. **Budget:** $511,000. **Publication:** *Who's Who in the Dental Laboratory Industry*, annual. Directory. Published in conjunction with the National Association of Dental Laboratories. Price: $45.00. Circulation: 14,000. Advertising: accepted.

NATIONAL BOARD OF MEDICAL EXAMINERS (NBME)

3750 Market St.
Philadelphia, PA 19104
L. Thompson Bowles, M.D., Pres.
PH: (215)590-9500
FX: (215)590-9555
Description: Purposes are: to prepare and administer qualifying examinations either independently or in conjunction with other organizations, of such high quality that legal agencies governing the practice of medicine within each state may, in their discretion, grant a license without further examination for those who have successfully completed such examinations; to cooperate with and, where appropriate, to make its specialized services available to the examining boards of the states, specialty boards, and other organizations concerned with the education and qualification of personnel in the fields of health; to assist medical schools, hospitals and related organizations and institutions in

evaluation of the effectiveness of their educational programs; to initiate, develop, and participate in research designed to evaluate the effectiveness of educational programs and techniques, and to assess ever more precisely the knowledge, competence, and qualification of professionals in public health care; to provide educational opportunities for professional personnel in the methods, techniques, and values of testing methods related to knowledge and competence in the broad field of medicine. **Founded:** 1915. **Membership:** 75. **Staff:** 190. **Languages:** English. **Publication:** *National Board Examiner*, quarterly. Newsletter. Reports on new medical evaluation programs and new directions in the research and development of examinations. Price: free. Circulation: 65,000 ▪ Annual Report.

NATIONAL BOARD FOR NURSING, MIDWIFERY AND HEALTH VISITING FOR NORTHERN IRELAND

79 Chichester St.
Belfast, Antrim BT1 4JE, Northern Ireland
E.N. Thom, Contact
PH: 44 1232 238152
FX: 44 1232 333298
Description: Non-executive members appointed by the Head of Department of Health and Social Services for Northern Ireland, executive members ie the Chief Executive, Director of Education & Standards and Director of Finance & Administration of the National Board. The majority of members are registered nurses, midwives or health visitors. To approve institutions in relation to provision of training courses for nurses, midwives and health visitors which meet Central Council standards; to arrange examinations; to collaborate with Council in the promotion of improved training methods; and such other functions as the Head of the Department of Health may by order prescribe. **Founded:** 1979. **Membership:** 10. **Publication:** Annual Report (in English), annual. Price: L8.50. Advertising: not accepted ▪ Papers.

NATIONAL BOARD FOR NURSING, MIDWIFERY AND HEALTH VISITING FOR SCOTLAND

url: http://www.nbs.org.uk
22 Queen St.
Edinburgh EH2 1NT, Scotland
David Benton, Chief Exec.
PH: 44 131 2267371
FX: 44 131 2259970
Description: All 10 members appointed by the Secretary of State for Scotland. There are 7 non-executive members (including the Chairman) and 3 executive members. The non-executive members include at least one registered nurse, one registered midwife and one. registered health visitor. Statutory body responsible for the education and training of nurses, midwives and health visitors in Scotland. **Founded:** 1983. **Membership:** 10. **Staff:** 48. **Budget:** L3,500,000. **Publication:** *Corporate Plan* (in English), annual. Advertising: not accepted ▪ *NBS Annual Report*. Price: L6.00. Advertising: not accepted ▪ *NBS News*, quarterly. Newsletter.

NATIONAL BRAIN TUMOR FOUNDATION (NBTF)

e-mail: nbtf@braintumor.org
url: http://www.braintumor.org
785 Market St., Ste. 1600
San Francisco, CA 94103
Walter S. Newman, Chm.
PH: (415)284-0208
TF: 800934-CURE
FX: (415)284-0209
Description: Medical researchers, doctors, brain tumor patients, and relatives working together to improve the quality of life for brain tumor patients and their families and find a cure through research. Raises funds for brain tumor research; offers patient services such as educational materials, a toll-free brain tumor information line, a quarterly newsletter, information about support groups and patient networks, and national and regional conferences. **Founded:** 1981. **Staff:** 6. **Languages:** English. **Budget:** $783,000. Doing business as Brain Tumor Foundation of America. Formerly (1989) Friends of Brain Tumor Research.

NATIONAL CANCER INSTITUTE OF CANADA (NCIC)

(Institut National du Cancer du Canada)
e-mail: ncic@cancer.ca
url: http://www.cancer.ca
10 Alcorn Ave., Ste. 200
Toronto, ON, Canada M4V 3B1
Dr. Robert Phillips, Exec.Dir.
PH: (416)961-7223
FX: (416)961-4189
Description: Coordinates and correlates the efforts of individuals and organized bodies with the goal of reducing the morbidity and mortality of cancer. This role is fulfilled through the support of clinical and laboratory-based research activities and research personnel. **Founded:** 1947. **Membership:** 48. **Staff:** 16. **Languages:** English, French. **Budget:** C$50,000,000. **Publication:** *Breast Cance Bulletin*, semiannual. Newsletter ▪ *Canadian Cancer Statistics*, annual ▪ *Scientific Report* (in English and French), annual ▪ *UPDATE* (in English and French), quarterly. Newsletter ▪ Annual Report (in English and French), annual. Price: Free. Circulation: 6,000. Advertising: not accepted.

NATIONAL CARE HOMES ASSOCIATION

e-mail: ncha1@compuserve.com
45/49 Leather Ln.
4th Fl.
London EC1N 7TJ, England
Sheila Scott, Contact
PH: 44 171 8317090
FX: 44 171 8317040
Description: Members run residential care and nursing homes for the infirm and elderly. **Founded:** 1981. **Membership:** 3000. **Staff:** 5. **Publication:** *Newsletter*, monthly. Price: for members.

NATIONAL CENTER FOR THE ADVANCEMENT OF BLACKS IN THE HEALTH PROFESSIONS (NCABHP)

PO Box 21121
Detroit, MI 48221
Della McGraw Goodwin, Pres.
TF: 313345-4480
Description: Participants belong to organizations including the American Public Health Association, National Urban League, National Black Nurses Association, and the American Hospital Association. Promotes the advancement of blacks in the health professions. Publicizes the disparity between the health of black and white Americans and its relationship to the underrepresentation of blacks in the health professions. (According to the National Center for Health Statistics, blacks have a higher death rate from cancer, heart disease, stroke, and diabetes than whites; blacks also have a higher infant mortality rate.) Acts as clearinghouse. Conducts skills development seminars for college recruiters and employers and empowerment seminars for new graduates. Demonstrates recruitment projects. Bestows Pathfinder Award. **Founded:** 1988. **Languages:** English. **Publication:** *Improving the Health Status of Black Americans*, annual. Lists priorities and agenda for the coming year. Price: $8.00. Advertising: accepted ▪ *Pathways to Parity*, 8/year. Newsletter. Contains updates on programs of interest; announces recipient of Pathfinder of the Month award. Price: $15.00. Circulation: 5,000. Advertising: accepted ▪ Proceedings, periodic.

NATIONAL CENTER FOR AMERICAN INDIAN AND ALASKA NATIVE MENTAL HEALTH RESEARCH (NCAIANMHR)

e-mail: billie.greene@uchsc.edu
Psychiatry Department
Campus Box A011-13,
4455 E. 12th Ave.
Denver, CO 80220
Spero M. Manson, Ph.D., Dir.
PH: (303)315-9232
TF: 800444-6472
FX: (303)315-9579
Description: Faculty, staff, and research associates in the mental health field. Conducts and supports research on management,

prevention, and investigation of mental illness among Native Americans and Alaska Natives. Assists organizations in conducting and implementing mental health research. Disseminates information and statistics to public. **Founded:** 1987. **Languages:** English.

NATIONAL CENTER FOR EDUCATION IN MATERNAL AND CHILD HEALTH (NCEMCH)

e-mail: info@ncemch.org
url: http://www.ncemch.org
2000 15th St. N, Ste. 701
Arlington, VA 22201-2617
Dr. Rochelle Mayer, Dir.
PH: (703)524-7802
FX: (703)524-9335
Description: Provides information services to professionals and the public on maternal and child health. Collects and disseminates information on available materials, programs, and research. Offers internships for graduate students in public health schools. Participates in policy initiatives of the U.S. Maternal and Child Health Bureau. Conducts conferences and workshops. Convention/Meeting: none. **Founded:** 1982. **Staff:** 55. **Languages:** English Formerly (1982) National Clearinghouse for Human Genetic Diseases.

NATIONAL CENTER FOR FARM WORKERS HEALTH

url: http://www.ncfh.org
1515 Capital of Texas Hwy. S, Ste. 220
Austin, TX 78746
E. Roberta Ryder, Exec.Dir.
PH: (512)328-7682
FX: (512)328-8559
Description: Seeks to make quality primary health care accessible to migrant and seasonal farm workers. Supports the establishment of a national network of migrant health centers through the production, processing, and distribution of information, including information on health problems specific to or more prevalent in the migrant community. Works to provide technical assistance for health development and research. Develops collaborative working relationship between agencies serving migrant farmworkers. Disseminates portable health referral cards, which contain English/Spanish health records designed to assist migrants in the transfer of medical information. Maintains job/resume bank, biographical archives, library, and speakers' bureau. Bestows awards; operates placement service; compiles statistics. **Founded:** 1975. **Staff:** 16. **Languages:** English, Spanish. **Publication:** *Migrant Health Newsline*, bimonthly. Newsletter. Includes clinical supplement. Circulation: 4,000. Advertising: not accepted ■ *Migrant Health Referral Directory*, annual ■ *Migrant Health Resource Catalog*. Catalogs ■ Books ■ Directory ■ Videos. **Formerly:** (1989) National Migrant Referral Project.

NATIONAL CENTER FOR HEALTH EDUCATION (NCHE)

url: http://www.nche.org
72 Spring St., Ste. 208
New York, NY 10012-4019
Lynne Whitt, Exec. VP
PH: (212)334-9470
TF: 800551-3488
FX: (212)334-9845
Description: Professionals promoting health education in schools, communities, and family settings. Aims to "extend the reach and power of education for health." Advocates health education and health promotion; builds coalitions of private and public sector groups; documents, develops, and disseminates model programs. Developes and manages Growing Healthy, a comprehensive school health education curriculum for kindergarten through grade six and "Starting Healthy" pre-kindergarten curriculum. **Founded:** 1975. **Staff:** 10. **Languages:** English. **Budget:** $1,000,000. **Supersedes:** Health Education Research Council.

NATIONAL CERTIFICATION AGENCY FOR MEDICAL LAB PERSONNEL (NCA)

url: http://www.applmaapro.com/nca
PO Box 15945-289
Lenexa, KS 66285
Michelle Cheney, Assn.Mgr.
PH: (913)438-5110
FX: (913)541-0156
Description: Persons who direct, educate, supervise, or practice in clinical laboratory science. To assure the public and employers of the competence of clinical laboratory personnel; to provide a mechanism for individuals demonstrating competency in the field to achieve career mobility. Develops and administers competency-based examinations for certification of clinical laboratory personnel; provides for periodic recertification by examination or through documentation of continuing education. Compiles statistics. **Founded:** 1977. **Membership:** 65000. **Staff:** 4. **Languages:** English.

NATIONAL CERTIFICATION BOARD OF PEDIATRIC NURSE PRACTITIONERS AND NURSES (NCBPNP/N)

e-mail: ncbpnp@pnpcert.org
url: http://www.pnpcert.org
800 S. Frederick Ave., Ste. 104
Gaithersburg, MD 20877-4150
Jeane Cole, CPNP, Interim Exec.Dir.
PH: (301)330-2921
FX: (301)330-1504
Description: Participants include physician and nurse representatives from the American Academy of Pediatrics, National Association of Pediatric Nurse Associates and Practitioners, the Association of Faculties of Pediatric Nurse Associate/Practitioner Programs, the Society of Pediatric Nurses and a consumer representative. Seeks to ensure quality child health care. Administers certification, recertification, continuing education, and self-assessment programs for general and advanced practice pediatric nursing. **Founded:** 1976. **Staff:** 8. **Languages:** English Formerly (1989) National Board of Pediatric Nurse Practitioners and Associates.

NATIONAL CERTIFICATION CORPORATION FOR THE OBSTETRIC, GYNECOLOGIC AND NEONATAL NURSING SPECIALTIES (NCC)

645 N. Michigan Ave., Ste. 900
Chicago, IL 60611
Betty Burns, CAE, Exec.Dir.
PH: (312)951-0207
Description: Promotes quality nursing care by encouraging nurses to demonstrate special knowledge by participating in a voluntary national certification program for obstetric/ gynecologic nurse practitioners, inpatient obstetric nurses, neonatal intensive care nurses, neonatal nurse practitioners, low-risk neonatal nurses, reproductive endocrinology/infertility nurses, ambulatory women's health care nurses, high obstetric nurses, and maternal newborn nurses. **Founded:** 1975. **Membership:** 50000. **Staff:** 12. **Languages:** English. **Budget:** $2,000,000. Formerly (1991) NAACOG Certification Corporation.

NATIONAL CHILDREN'S EYE CARE FOUNDATION (NCECF)

PO Box 795069
Dallas, TX 75379-5069
Suzanne C. Beauchamp, Exec.Dir.
PH: (972)407-0404
FX: (972)407-0616
Description: Purposes are to promote and advance the medical care of children's eyes and to decrease the incidence, prevalence, and severity of children's visual disorders. Sponsors public information campaign targeted toward parents, teachers, and children, stressing early detection and treatment. Sponsors Vision 2020: The Amblyopia Program, aimed at climinating preventable blindness and vision loss from amblyopia. **Founded:** 1970. **Languages:** English. **Budget:** $125,000. Formerly (1982) Children's Eye Care Foundation.

NATIONAL CHRONIC FATIGUE SYNDROME AND FIBROMYALGIA ASSOCIATION (NCFSFA)

e-mail: keal55A@prodigy.com
PO Box 18426
Kansas City, MO 64133
Orvalene Prewitt, Pres.
PH: (816)313-2000
FX: (816)313-2001
Description: Individuals suffering from chronic fatigue syndrome and Fibromyalgia health care professionals. Chronic fatigue syndrome, also known as Chronic Epstein-Barr Virus syndrome, is characterized by persistent, recurring feelings of general weakness; other symptoms include sore throat, unexplained muscle pain, new headaches, devastating fatigue, impaired memory or concentration, tender lymph nodes, unrefreshing sleep and post-exertion malaise. Fibromyalgia is characterized as pain, generally felt all over, and can be compounded by fatique, sleep disturbances, changes in mood, headaches and gastro-intestinal problems. Sponsors educational programs. Maintains speakers' bureau. **Founded:** 1985. **Membership:** 2000. **Staff:** 5. **Local Groups:** 400. **Languages:** English. **Budget:** $50,000. **Publication:** *A Guide for Physicians When Considering a Diagnosis of Chronic Fatigue Syndrom in Children.* Brochure ▪ *A School's Guide for Students with CFS* ▪ *CFS: Addressing the Realities of a Chronic Illness.* Video. Includes educational information ▪ *CFS and School Success.* Brochure ▪ *CFS in the Workplace.* Brochure ▪ *CFS: Thief of Vitality.* Brochure ▪ *Chronic Fatigue Syndrome.* Bibliography ▪ *Coping Skills.* Brochure ▪ *Heart of America News*, quarterly. Newsletter. Price: $25.00/year; $35.00/year outside the U.S. Advertising: not accepted ▪ *How to be a Phone Contact Packet* ▪ *How to Start a Support Group Packet* ▪ *Neuro-Psychological Rehabilitation Techniques.* Brochure ▪ *Patient Information Packet* ▪ *Physician Information Packet* ▪ *Social Security Disability Benefits.* Brochure ▪ *Understanding the Emotions Surrounding CFS.* Brochure. **Formerly:** (1985) National Chronic Epstein-Barr Virus Association; (1993) National Chronic Fatigue Syndrome Association.

NATIONAL COALITION FOR ADULT IMMUNIZATION (NCAI)

e-mail: adultimm@aol.com
url: http://www.medscape.com/NCAI
4733 Bethesda Ave., Ste. 750
Bethesda, MD 20814-5228
Bettie W. Orr, Dir.
PH: (301)656-0003
FX: (301)907-0878
Description: Medical associations, advocacy groups, vaccine manufacturers and government health agencies. Dedicated to promoting adult immunization and to raise immunization levels in high-risk and other adult target groups. Promotes and supports National Adult Immunization Week. Educates physicians and public on vaccines for diptheria, hepatitis A and B, influenza, measles, mumps, pneumococcal pneumonia and rubella. Maintains speakers' bureau. **Founded:** 1988. **Membership:** 85. **Staff:** 2. **Languages:** English.

NATIONAL COALITION FOR CANCER RESEARCH (NCCR)

426 C St. NE
Washington, DC 20002
Marguerite Donoghue, Exec.Dir.
PH: (202)544-1880
FX: (202)543-2565
Description: Lay and professional organizations committed to the eradication of cancer. Dedicated to strengthening the National Cancer Program through public education and communication about the value of cancer research, treatment, and prevention. **Founded:** 1986. **Membership:** 19. **Languages:** English. **Budget:** $150,000.

NATIONAL COALITION FOR CANCER SURVIVORSHIP (NCCS)

e-mail: info@cansearch.org
url: http://www.cansearch.org
1010 Wayne Ave., Ste. 505
Silver Spring, MD 20910
Ellen Stovall, Exec.Dir.
PH: (301)650-8868
FX: (301)565-9670
Description: Institutions and organizations (400) and individuals (2100) concerned with survivorship and interested in supporting cancer survivors and their loved ones. (A survivor is anyone with a history of cancer.) Seeks to show that cancer survivors can continue leading productive and fulfilling lives. Facilitates communication among individuals involved with cancer survivorship and fosters peer support. Provides a forum for discussion of related issues and concerns. Promotes the interests of cancer survivors and advocates the reduction of cancer-based discrimination. Encourages study in survivorship. Collects and disseminates information and resources on supporting and helping survivors deal with life after cancer is diagnosed. Operates speakers' bureau. **Founded:** 1986. **Membership:** 2500. **Staff:** 8. **Regional Groups:** 7. **Languages:** English. **Budget:** $750,000. **Publication:** *Best Loved Books of Cancer Survivors* ▪ *Charting the Journey: An Almanac of Resources for Cancer Survivors.* Book ▪ *NCCS Networker*, quarterly. Newsletter. News and articles on cancer survivorship, interviews, and reviews. Price: included in membership dues. Circulation: 8,000 ▪ *Teamwork: The Cancer Patient's Guide to Talking With Your Doctor.* Booklet ▪ Bibliography.

NATIONAL COALITION FOR RESEARCH IN NEUROLOGICAL DISORDERS (NCR)

e-mail: brainnet@brainnet.org
url: http://www.brainnet.org
1250 24th St. NW, Ste. 300
Washington, DC 20037
Morgan Downey, Exec.Dir.
PH: (202)293-5453
FX: (202)466-0585
Description: Represents voluntary health agencies and professional societiesconcerned with obtaining funds for neurological research. Seeks to stimulate public information regarding the field of neurological disorders. Lobbies for increased funding for training and research in neurological disorders. **Founded:** 1952. **Membership:** 57. **Staff:** 3. **Languages:** English. **Budget:** $65,000. **Publication:** *NCR News*, quarterly. **Formerly:** National Committee for Research in Neurological Disorders; (1988) National Committee for Research in Neruological and Communicative Disorders; (1989) National Coalition for Research in Neurological and Communicative Disorders.

NATIONAL COMMISSION ON CERTIFICATION OF PHYSICIAN ASSISTANTS (NCCPA)

2845 Henderson Mill Rd, NE
Atlanta, GA 30341
Kate Hill, Exec.VP
Description: Certifies physician assistants at the entry level and for continued competence. Has certified 22,750 physician assistants. **Founded:** 1975. **Staff:** 9. **Languages:** English. Formerly (1987) National Commission on Certification of Physician's Assistants.

NATIONAL COMMISSION ON CORRECTIONAL HEALTH CARE (NCCHC)

e-mail: NCCHC@ncchc.org
url: http://www.corrections.com/ncchc
1300 W. Belmont Ave.
Chicago, IL 60657
Edward A. Harrison, Pres.
PH: (312)880-1460
FX: (312)880-2421
Description: Professional organizations in the fields of medical and health care. Works to improve the quality of and set standards for medical care in correctional institutions in the U.S. in-

cluding prisons, jails, and detention and juvenile facilities. Acts as an accrediting body for such facilities; develops training programs and conducts seminars; provides technical assistance; organizes special task forces on issues such as suicide and AIDS; annually bestows Award of Merit for achievement in the field of correctional health care. Compiles statistics; conducts research; disseminates information. **Founded:** 1983. **Membership:** 37. **Staff:** 9. **Languages:** English. **Budget:** $750,000. **Publication:** *CorrectCare*, quarterly. Newspaper. Advertising: accepted ▪ *Journal of Correctional Health Care*, semiannual. Contains articles on correctional health care topics including law, medicine, and ethics. Price: $30.00/year for individuals; $65.00/year for institutions. ISSN: 0731-8332. Circulation: 500. Advertising: not accepted ▪ *Prison Health Care: Guidelines for the Management of an Adequated Delivery System*. Manuals ▪ Films ▪ Monographs ▪ Proceedings.

NATIONAL COMMISSION ON HUMAN LIFE, REPRODUCTION AND RHYTHM (NCHLRR)
PO Box 101501
Pittsburgh, PA 15237
Herbert Ratner, M.D., Sec.-Treas.
PH: (412)369-4544
FX: (412)369-4550
Description: Physicians united to strengthen the family unit and support what the commission views as traditional concepts of marriage, sex, and life. Encourages physicians to place more emphasis on personal attention to patients and less emphasis on the prescribing of medication; promotes pro-life values. Conducts scientific meetings dealing with subjects including: the role of the mother, particularly during her child's first three years; sex education; natural family planning; obstetric delivery; breastfeeding; abortion. Sponsors public meetings. **Founded:** 1967. **Membership:** 25. **Staff:** 3. Multinational. **Languages:** English. **Budget:** $60,000. **Publication:** *Child and Family*, quarterly. Journal. Contains scientific and philosophical articles in support of the traditional family. Consists primarily of reprinted material. Price: $12.00/year; $16.00/year outside U.S. ISSN: 0009-3882. Circulation: 1,000. Advertising: not accepted.

NATIONAL COMMITTEE FOR MEDICAL RESEARCH ETHICS (NEM)
(Den Nasjonale Forskningsetiske Komite for Medisin)
Gaustadalleen 21
N-0371 Oslo, Norway
Dr. Knut W. Ruyter, Exec. Officer
PH: 47 22958780
FX: 47 22958492
Description: Health care professionals, attorneys, ethicists, and others with an interest in ethical aspects of medical research. Promotes increased awareness of ethical issues within the medical research industry; conducts continuing professional education and public education programs. **Founded:** 1990. **Membership:** 12. **Staff:** 3. **Regional Groups:** 5. **Languages:** English, Norwegian. **Budget:** 1,700,000 NKr. **Publication:** *NEM-Nytt* (in Norwegian), quarterly. Newsletter. ISSN: 0804-3175. Circulation: 300.

NATIONAL COMMITTEE FOR QUALITY HEALTH CARE (NCQHC)
1800 Massachusetts Ave. NW, Ste. 401
Washington, DC 20036
Pamela G. Bailey, Pres.
PH: (202)347-5731
FX: (202)347-5836
Description: Coalition of health care professionals and organizations principally involved in the health care industry; includes hospitals, physicians, health maintenance organizations, nursing homes, manufacturers of health care equipment, investment bankers, architects, contractors, and accountants. Works to maintain and strengthen quality health care in the U.S. **Founded:** 1978. **Membership:** 151. **Staff:** 4. **Languages:** English. **Budget:** $900,000. **Publication:** *An American Health Strategy: Ensuring the Availability of Quality Health Care* ▪ *Critical Condition: America's Health Care in Jeopardy* ▪ *Quality Bulletin*, bimonthly ▪ *Quality*

Outlook, bimonthly ▪ Pamphlets ▪ Papers. **Formerly:** National Committee on Hospital Capital Expenditures.

NATIONAL COMMUNITY MENTAL HEALTHCARE COUNCIL
12300 Twinbrook Pkwy., No. 320
Rockville, MD 20852
Charles Ray, Contact
PH: (301)984-6200
FX: (301)881-7159
Description: Conducts educational programs. Maintains speakers' bureau. **Founded:** 1969. **Membership:** 900. **Staff:** 20. **State Groups:** 38. **Languages:** English. **Budget:** $2,000,000. Formerly (1997) National Council on Community Mental Health Centers.

NATIONAL CONFERENCE OF LOCAL ENVIRONMENTAL HEALTH ADMINISTRATORS (NCLEHA)
1395 Blue Tent Ct.
Cool, CA 95614-2120
Richard Swenson, Exec. Officer
PH: (530)823-1736
Description: Professional environmental health personnel engaged in or officially concerned with municipal (city, county, or district) environmental health administration or teaching of environmental health. Promotes improvement and greater use of science and practice of environmental health in community life. **Founded:** 1939. **Membership:** 220. **Languages:** English. Formerly (1969) Conference of Municipal Public Health Engineers; (1981) Conference of Local Environmental Health Administrators.

NATIONAL CONSORTIUM OF CHEMICAL DEPENDENCY NURSES (NCCDN)
1720 Willow Creek Cir., Ste. 519
Eugene, OR 97402
Randy Bryson, Exec.Dir.
PH: (503)485-4421
TF: 80087-NCCDN
FX: (503)485-7372
Description: Professional nurses specializing in chemical dependency treatment. Goals are: to increase the effectiveness of nursing services for chemical dependency; to establish a professional standard in chemical dependency nursing through a system of competency-based testing and programs of professional development and certification. Aims to increase public awareness of the need for chemical dependency treatment and nurses specializing in this field. Encourages the growth of knowledge, skills, and competency in chemical dependency nursing. Offers certification exam for nurses with 4000 hours experience in the previous 5 years and 30 hours of chemical dependency coursework; conducts educational programs. Maintains speakers' bureau. **Founded:** 1987. **Membership:** 1500. **Regional Groups:** 12. **Languages:** English.

NATIONAL COUNCIL FOR HOSPICE AND SPECIALIST PALLIATIVE CARE SERVICES
Heron House
322 High Holborn
London WC1V 7PW, England
Mrs. Jean Gaffin, Exec.Dir.
PH: 44 171 2694550
FX: 44 171 2694548
Description: Members are nominated by national charities and professional organisations or elected by regional hospice and palliative care units. To represent the views and interests of hospice and palliative care services to ministers, civil servants, MPs, the media and statutory and other agencies. To provide advice to hospice and specialist palliative care services in their relations with health authorities, local authorities and other agencies. **Founded:** 1991. **Membership:** 35. **Staff:** 4. **Regional Groups:** 15. **Budget:** L180,000. **Publication:** *Information Exchange* (in English), quarterly. Newsletter. ISSN: 1359-2424. Circulation: 2,500 ▪ Papers.

NATIONAL COUNCIL ON PATIENT INFORMATION AND EDUCATION (NCPIE)
e-mail: wrbull@aol.com
666 11th St. NW, Ste. 810
Washington, DC 20001-4542
William Ray Bullman, Exec.Dir.
PH: (202)347-6711
FX: (202)638-0773
Description: Health care professional organizations, pharmaceutical manufacturing organizations, federal agencies, voluntary health agencies, and consumer groups. Increases the availability of information and improves the dialogue between consumers and health care providers about prescription medicines; increases professional awareness of the need to give adequate information on prescription therapy; expands consumers' participation with health professionals on matters of drug therapy. Communicates with health care providers on the importance of giving consumers oral and written information on prescription medicines and encourages consumers to ask questions about medicines and explain factors that may affect their ability to follow prescriptions. **Founded:** 1982. **Membership:** 389. **Staff:** 4. **Languages:** English. **Budget:** $500,000.

NATIONAL COUNCIL FOR PRESCRIPTION DRUG PROGRAMS (NCPDP)
e-mail: ncpdp@ncpdp.org
url: http://www.ncpdp.org
4201 N. 24th St., Ste. 365
Phoenix, AZ 85016
Lee Ann C. Stember, Pres.
PH: (602)957-9105
FX: (602)955-0749
Description: Works to create and promote data interchange and processing standards to the pharmacy services sector of the health care industry; and to provide a continuing source of accurate and reliable information that supports the diverse needs of its membership. **Founded:** 1977. **Membership:** 1300. **Staff:** 17. **Languages:** English. **Budget:** $1,500,000.

NATIONAL COUNCIL FOR RELIABLE HEALTH INFORMATION (NCRHI)
url: http://www.ncanf.org
PO Box 1276
Loma Linda, CA 92354
Dr. William Jarvis, Exec.Dir.
PH: (909)824-4690
FX: (909)824-4838
Description: Health professionals, researchers, legal professionals, and other interested individuals. Seeks to educate the public on fraud and quackery in health care; offers advice to consumers; provides witnesses for health fraud trials; assists law enforcement officials with health fraud cases. Administers the National Council Against Health Fraud Resource Center in Kansas City, MO. Maintains a collection of "quack medical devices." Sponsors speakers' bureau, museum, and research programs. Offers aid to victims in the form of legal screening free of charge. **Founded:** 1977. **Membership:** 1200. Multinational. **Local Groups:** 1. **Languages:** English. **Budget:** $50,000. **Publication:** *Available Resource Materials*. Pamphlet. Lists available materials by category. Circulation: 2,000. Advertising: not accepted ▪ *Join in Combatting Health Fraud, Misinformation, and Quackery*. Pamphlet ▪ *National Council Against Health Fraud Newsletter*, bimonthly. Price: included in membership dues; $15.00/year for nonmember subs; $18.00/year for library subs. ISSN: 0890-3417. Advertising: not accepted ▪ *NCAHF Bulletin Board*, bimonthly. Price: available to members only ▪ *Recommended Consumer Protection Publications*, bimonthly. Pamphlet ▪ Reports. **Formerly:** California Council Against Health Fraud. **Status Note:** (1998) Formerly national Council Against Health Fraud.

NATIONAL COUNCIL OF STATE BOARDS OF NURSING (NCSBN)
url: http://www.ncsbn.org
676 N. St. Clair St., Ste. 550
Chicago, IL 60611
PH: (312)787-6555
FX: (312)787-6898
Description: State boards of nursing. Assists member boards in administering the National Council Licensure Examinations for Registered Nurses and Practical Nurses and works to insure relevancy of the exams to current nursing practice. Aids boards in the collection and analysis of information pertaining to the licensure and discipline of nurses. Provides consultative services, conducts research, develops model nursing legislation and administrative regulations, and sponsors educational programs. **Founded:** 1978. **Membership:** 61. **Staff:** 48. **Languages:** English.

NATIONAL COUNCIL OF STATE PHARMACY ASSOCIATION EXECUTIVES (NCSPAE)
c/o Al Mebane
PO Box 151
Chapel Hill, NC 27514-0151
Al Mellbane, Sec.-Treas.
PH: (919)967-2237
TF: 800852-7343
FX: (919)968-9430
Description: Professional society of the executive officers of state pharmacy associations. **Founded:** 1927. **Membership:** 52. **Staff:** 1. **Languages:** English. **Budget:** $20,000. Formerly (1964) National Conference of State Pharmaceutical Association Secretaries; (1992) National Council of State Pharmaceutical Association.

NATIONAL DENTAL ASSISTANTS ASSOCIATION (NDAA)
c/o Robert Johns
5506 Connecticut Ave. NW, Ste. 24
Washington, DC 20015
Dr. Robert John, Exec.Dir.
PH: (202)244-7555
FX: (202)244-5992
Description: An auxiliary of the National Dental Association. Works to encourage education and certification among dental assistants. Conducts clinics and workshops to further the education of members. Bestows annual Humanitarian Award; offers scholarships. **Membership:** 500. **Languages:** English. **Publication:** *NDAA Journal*, annual.

NATIONAL DENTAL ASSOCIATION (NDA)
3517 16th St., NW
Washington, DC 20010
Robert S. Johns, Exec.Dir.
PH: (202)244-7555
FX: (202)588-1244
Description: Professional society for dentists. Aims to provide quality dental care to the unserved and underserved public and promote knowledge of the art and science of dentistry. Advocates the inclusion of dental care services in health care programs on local, state, and national levels. Fosters the integration of minority dental health care providers in the profession, and promotes dentistry as a viable career for minorities through support programs. Conducts research programs. Group is distinct from the former name of the American Dental Association. **Founded:** 1913. **Membership:** 5000. Multinational. **Local Groups:** 48. **Languages:** English. **Budget:** $294,050. **Publication:** *Flossline*, quarterly. Contains educational news. Price: included in membership dues. Circulation: 5,000. Advertising: accepted ▪ Journal, quarterly. **Absorbed:** Tri-State Dental Association. **Formerly:** (1932) Interstate Dental Association.

NATIONAL DENTAL HYGIENISTS' ASSOCIATION (NDHA)
1126 City County Building
Detroit, MI 48226
Darchelle Strickland, Pres.
PH: (313)224-4733
FX: (313)224-4433

Description: Minority dental hygienists. To cultivate and promote the art and science of dental hygiene and to enhance the professional image of dental hygienists. Attempts to meet the needs of society through educational, political, and social activities while giving the minority dental hygienist a voice in shaping the profession. Encourages cooperation and mutual support among minority professionals. Seeks to increase opportunities for continuing education and employment in the field of dental hygiene. Works to improve individual and community dental health. Sponsors annual seminar, fundraising events, and scholarship programs; participates in career orientation programs; counsels and assists students applying for or enrolled in dental hygiene programs. Maintains liaison with American Dental Hygienists' Association. **Founded:** 1932. **Membership:** 100. **State Groups:** 10. **Languages:** English. **Budget:** $50,000. **Publication:** *The Lore*, quarterly. Newsletter. Information relative to NDHA and Dental Hygiene Activities. Circulation: 500. Advertising: accepted.

NATIONAL DENTURIST ASSOCIATION (NDA)
PO Box 637
Poulsbo, WA 98370
Dr. James Davis, Exec.Dir.
Description: Denturists, dental laboratory technicians, and other dental professionals. Promotes recognition and authorization of the profession of denturism. Conducts research regarding law pertaining to the dental profession and to the profession and practice of denturism. Offers seminars to prepare denturists for certification. Compiles statistics. Provides political action counseling and organizing guidance. **Founded:** 1975. **Membership:** 350. **Staff:** 1. **State Groups:** 22. **Languages:** English. **Budget:** $40,000. **Publication:** *NDA Denturist News*, quarterly. Newsletter. Contains educational and business management articles and political reports. Includes new product information and legal news. Price: included in membership or free upon request. Circulation: 1,000. Advertising: accepted.

NATIONAL DEPRESSIVE AND MANIC DEPRESSIVE ASSOCIATION (NDMDA)
url: http://www.ndmda.org
730 N. Franklin, Ste. 501
Chicago, IL 60610-3526
Lydia Lewis, Exec. Dir.
PH: (312)642-0049
TF: 800826-3632
FX: (312)642-7243
Description: Seeks to educate patients, families, professionals, and the public concerning the nature of depressive and manic-depressive illnesses as treatable medical diseases; to foster self-help for patients and families; to eliminate discrimination and stigma; to improve access to care; and to advocate for research toward the elimination of these illnesses. **Founded:** 1986. **Membership:** 65000. **Staff:** 18. Multinational. **Local Groups:** 275. **Languages:** English. **Budget:** $2,000,000. Formerly (1978) Manic Depressive and Depressive Association.

NATIONAL ECZEMA ASSOCIATION FOR SCIENCE AND EDUCATION
1221 SW Yamhill, No. 303
Portland, OR 97205
PH: (503)228-4430
TF: 800818-7546
FX: (503)273-8778
Description: Works to raise awareness of the inflammatory condition of the skin called eczema. Provides patient education materials. Supports research. **Founded:** 1988. **Membership:** 4000. **Languages:** English. Formerly (1997) Eczema Association for Science and Education.

NATIONAL EYE CARE PROJECT (NECP)
url: http://www.eyenet.org
PO Box 429098
San Francisco, CA 94142-9098
B. Thomas Hutchinson, M.D., Chm.

PH: (415)561-8520
TF: 800222-3937
FX: (415)561-8567
Description: Ophthalmologists dedicated to ensuring eye care for the elderly, particularly those who are economically disadvantaged. Provides medical and surgical eye care to individuals 65 and over who normally would not have access or the means to consult an ophthalmologist. Disseminates information on participating physicians and eye diseases of the aging. Offers referral services. A project of the Foundation of the American Academy of Ophthalmology. **Founded:** 1986. **Staff:** 5. **Languages:** English.

NATIONAL FAMILY PLANNING AND REPRODUCTIVE HEALTH ASSOCIATION (NFPRHA)
e-mail: info@nfprha.org
url: http://www.nfprha.org
122 C St. NW, Ste. 380
Washington, DC 20001
Judith M. DeSarno, Pres.
PH: (202)628-3535
FX: (202)737-2690
Description: Hospitals, state and city departments of health, health care providers, private nonprofit clinics, and consumers concerned with the maintenance and improvement of family planning and reproductive health services. Serves as a national communications network and advocacy organization. Maintains contact with Congress and government agencies in order to monitor government policy and regulations. **Founded:** 1971. **Membership:** 1000. **Languages:** English. **Budget:** $1,000,000. **Publication:** *NFPRHA Alert*, periodic ■ *NFPRHA News*, bimonthly ■ *NFPRHA Report*, bimonthly. **Formerly:** (1979) National Family Planning Forum.

NATIONAL FEDERATION OF HOUSESTAFF ORGANIZATIONS (NFHO)
386 Park Ave. S, Rm. 1502
New York, NY 10016
Angela Moore, Contact
PH: (212)683-7475
FX: (212)779-2413
Description: Federation of housestaff physicians unions. (Housestaff physicians are employed by the hospitals in which they practice, and are currently in speciality training.) Assists members in collective bargaining, lobbying state and local governments, and promoting unionization among housestaff physicians. Maintains speakers' bureau. **Founded:** 1984. **Membership:** 11. **Languages:** English. **Publication:** *NFHO Newsletter*, quarterly.

NATIONAL FEDERATION INTERSCHOLASTIC SPEECH AND DEBATE ASSOCIATION (NFISDA)
url: http://www.nfhs.org
11724 NW Plaza Cir.
Kansas City, MO 64195-0626
Treva Dayton, Asst.Dir.
PH: (816)464-5400
FX: (816)464-5571
Description: High school and college speech, drama, and debate directors, coaches, and sponsors. Coordinates speech, drama, and debate programs at the state and national level. Provides a network of educators who prepare students for contests and festivals. Provides personal liability insurance for members. **Founded:** 1986. **Membership:** 1008. **Staff:** 2. **Languages:** English.

NATIONAL FEDERATION OF LICENSED PRACTICAL NURSES (NFLPN)
url: http://www.nflpn.com
1418 Aversboro Rd.
Garner, NC 27529-4547
Charlene Barbour, Admin.
PH: (919)779-0046
TF: 800948-2511
FX: (919)779-5642
Description: Federation of state associations of licensed practical and vocational nurses. Aims to: preserve and foster the ideal of

comprehensive nursing care for the ill and aged; improve standards of practice; secure recognition and effective utilization of LPNs; further continued improvement in the education of LPNs. Acts as clearinghouse for information on practical nursing and cooperates with other groups concerned with better patient care. Maintains loan program. **Founded:** 1949. **Membership:** 5000. **Staff:** 3. **State Groups:** 22. **Languages:** English. **Budget:** $200,000.

NATIONAL FEDERATION FOR SPECIALTY NURSING ORGANIZATIONS (NFSNO)
e-mail: nfsno@mail.ajj.com
E. Holly Ave., Box 56
Pitman, NJ 08071
Cynthia Nowicki, Exec.Dir.
PH: (609)256-2333
FX: (609)589-7463
Description: Nursing specialty organizations representing approximately 400,000 individuals. Provides a forum for the discussion of issues of mutual concern to members; attempts to gain more input in the establishment of nursing standards. Sponsors Nurse in Washington Internship. **Founded:** 1972. **Membership:** 43. **Languages:** English. **Budget:** $181,350. Formerly (1981) Federation of Specialty Nursing Organizations and the American Nurses Association.

NATIONAL FEDERATION OF SPIRITUAL HEALERS
Church St.
Sunbury-on-Thames TW16 6RG, England
P. Dowall, Contact
PH: 44 1932 783164
FX: 44 1932 779648

NATIONAL FLIGHT NURSES ASSOCIATION (NFNA)
url: http://www.nfna.org
216 Higgins Rd.
Park Ridge, IL 60068
H. Stephen Lieber, CAE, Exec.Dir.
PH: (847)698-1733
FX: (847)698-9407
Description: Flight nurses. Seeks to promote the quality of flight nursing by developing standards for the profession and exploring educational opportunities. Seeks optimum working conditions for members. Provides assistance to hospitals for developing air medical services programs. Maintains speakers' bureau. **Founded:** 1981. **Membership:** 1700. Multinational. **Regional Groups:** 10. **Languages:** English. **Budget:** $145.

NATIONAL FOUNDATION FOR BRAIN RESEARCH (NFBR)
e-mail: brainnet@brainnet.org
url: http://www.brainnet.org/nfbr.htm
1250 24th St. NW, Ste. 300
Washington, DC 20037
Lawrence S. Hoffheimer, J.D., Exec.Dir.
PH: (202)466-0577
FX: (202)466-3079
Description: Promotes the prevention and cure of disorders and diseases of the brain. Supports brain research. Collects, organizes, and disseminates information relating to the Decade of the Brain (the years 1990-2000, which were so designated by United States Congress and President George Bush to acknowledge the importance of neurological and mental research). Maintains the Decade of the Brain Coalition which strives to achieve by the end of the decade a large increase in federal funding for research on the brain. Seeks to increase public awareness of the importance of brain research through sponsoring educational symposia, the distribution of reports and pamphlets, and the organization of traveling museum exhibits. Provides educational programs for professionals. **Languages:** English. **Publication:** *Decade of the Brain News*, quarterly. Newsletter.

NATIONAL FOUNDATION OF DENTISTRY FOR THE HANDICAPPED (NFDH)
1800 Glenarm Pl., Ste. 500
Denver, CO 80202
Larry Coffee, D.D.S., Exec.Dir.
PH: (303)298-9650
FX: (303)573-0267
Description: Promotes preventive dentistry for handicapped individuals in order to reduce dental disease. Sponsors Campaign of Concern which enlists the cooperation of members of the dental profession, special education personnel, disabled individuals and their parents, counselors, and civic organizations in helping developmentally disabled people enjoy good dental health. The campaign currently serves 35,000 people in seven states. Conducts preventive health education through in-service training for members of participating special education schools, sheltered workshops, day centers, and group/nursing homes; teaches handicapped individuals how to maintain their own oral hygiene and provide them with dental supplies; evaluate the oral health status of each participant; suggests dentists who will accept handicapped patients if such a referral is desired. Sponsors Donated Dental Services Programs, which match indigent, elderly, and handicapped individuals with volunteer dentists. Operates a portable dental treatment system for the homebound, nursing home residents, and the developmentally disabled that is currently in use in Denver, CO, Newark, NJ, and Chicago, IL; has assisted in developing similar programs in Detroit, MI and Houston, TX. Convention/Meeting: none. **Founded:** 1974. **Staff:** 40. **State Groups:** 12. **Languages:** English. **Budget:** $2,200,000. **Publication:** *Guidelines for Dental Programs in Institutions for Developmentally Disabled Persons* ▪ *Guidelines for Using Fluorides Among Handicapped Persons* ▪ *Special Smiles*, periodic ▪ Annual Report.

NATIONAL FOUNDATION FOR DEPRESSIVE ILLNESS (NAFDI)
url: http://www.depression.org
PO Box 2257
New York, NY 10116
Peter Ross, Exec.Dir.
PH: (212)268-4260
TF: 800248-4344
FX: (212)268-4434
Description: Provides public and professional education and information on recent medical advances in affective mood disorders. Conducts seminars on affective disorders, pharmaceutical development, and disease-related loss of productivity. Maintains speakers' bureau. Provides support group and referral services to appropriate doctors. **Founded:** 1983. **Staff:** 3. **Languages:** English. **For-Profit.**

NATIONAL FOUNDATION FOR NON-INVASIVE DIAGNOSTICS (NFNID)
163 Loomis Ct.
Princeton, NJ 08540
Dr. Benedict Kingsley, Trustee
PH: (609)921-9493
Description: Provides continuing education program for physicians and technologists in the field of echocardiography (the use of ultrasound in examining the heart and diagnosing abnormalities). Bestows designation of Professional Ultrasound Technologist to seminar participants who meet certification standards. **Founded:** 1977. **Staff:** 10. **Languages:** English.

NATIONAL FOUNDATION FOR RESEARCH IN MEDICINE (NFRM)
c/o Jeanette Baptiste
2296-83 Caminito Pajarito
San Diego, CA 92107
Jeanette Baptiste, Pres.
Description: Supports medical research in areas where other support is not available; is particularly interested in the independent medical research investigator. **Founded:** 1959. Local.

Languages: English. **Formerly:** (1961) National Foundation for Independent Medical Research.

NATIONAL GUILD OF CATHOLIC PSYCHIATRISTS (NGCP)
Taylor Manor Hopital
4100 College Ave.
Ellicott City, MD 21041-0396
Dr. Taylor, Pres.
PH: (410)465-3322
FX: (410)461-7075
Description: Purposes are: to unite psychiatrists and other mental health professionals who share a belief in the spiritual dimension of human experience; to promote mutual respect for and to affirm the unique knowledge and skills of all members of the mental health professions; to establish a forum to further the integration of psychiatry and religion through the exchange of clinical experience and knowledge; to stimulate research on problems relating to psychiatry and religion. Conducts scientific program annually. **Founded:** 1949. **Membership:** 75. **Languages:** English. Formerly Guild of Catholic Psychiatrists.

NATIONAL HEALTH COUNCIL (NHC)
e-mail: info@nhcouncil.org
1730 M St. NW, Ste. 500
Washington, DC 20036
Myrl Weinberg, Pres.
PH: (202)785-3910
FX: (202)785-5923
Description: National membership association of voluntary and professional societies in the health field; national organizations and business groups with strong health interests. Seeks to improve the health of the nation through conferences, publications, policy briefings and special projects. Distributes printed material on health careers and related subjects. Promotes standardization of financial reporting for voluntary health groups. **Founded:** 1920. **Membership:** 130. **Staff:** 7. **Languages:** English. **Budget:** $977,000. **Publication:** *Congress and Health*. Book ■ *Council Currents*, bimonthly. Books. Price: free. Circulation: 700. Advertising: not accepted. Alternate Formats: diskette ■ *Directory of Health Groups in Washington* ■ *Guide to America's Voluntary Health Agencies*. Directory ■ *Long-Term Care*. Book ■ *Standards of Accounting and Reporting for Voluntary Health and Welfare Organizations (The Black Book)* ■ *200 Ways to Put Your Talent to Work in the Health Field*. Book.

NATIONAL HEALTH FEDERATION (NHF)
e-mail: nhf@HealthFreedom.org
url: http://www.healthfreedom.org
PO Box 688
Monrovia, CA 91016
Dr. Jonathan Wright, Pres.
PH: (818)357-2181
FX: (818)303-0642
Description: Persons interested in individual freedom of choice in matters relating to health. Represents belief "that organized medicine, the pharmaceutical industry, and other special interests have been responsible for many laws, rules, and regulations which very often better serve the interests of these groups than the interests of the American public...that through the activities of these groups monopolies in the field of health have been created and thus, that American free enterprise is threatened." Seeks to serve as a "watch dog" and to institute corrective measures through investigation, education, legislation, and coordination of organizations with similar purposes. Supports research in areas such as laetrile testing; supports numerous educational foundation programs. Conducts lobbying activities. **Founded:** 1955. **Membership:** 55000. **Staff:** 7. Multinational. **Local Groups:** 123. **Languages:** English. **Budget:** $425,000. **Publication:** *Health Freedom News*, periodic. Journal. Price: $3.95. Circulation: 70,000. Advertising: accepted. **Absorbed:** (1976) National Committee Against Fluoridation.

NATIONAL HEALTH LAW PROGRAM (NHELP)
e-mail: nhetp@healthlaw.org
url: http://www.healthlaw.org
2639 S. La Cienega Blvd.
Los Angeles, CA 90034
Laurence M. Lavin, Dir.
PH: (310)204-6010
FX: (310)204-0891
Description: Attorneys, health specialists, and other interested persons. Provides assistance to legal services program attorneys and their clients in matters involving health problems of the poor. Offers information, referral, and consultation on litigation strategy. Prepares materials for and conducts training sessions for and with field program attorneys and paralegals. Coordinates testimony for particular hearings. **Founded:** 1969. **Staff:** 10. **Languages:** English, Spanish. **For-Profit. Budget:** $900,000. **Publication:** *Health Advocate*, quarterly. Newsletter. Updates on issues affecting low-income/disabled health care consumers. Price: $75.00/years. Circulation: 1,000. Advertising: not accepted.

NATIONAL HEALTH LAWYERS ASSOCIATION (NHLA)
e-mail: healthlaw@nhla.org
url: http://www.nhla.org
1120 Connecticut Ave. NW, Ste. 950
Washington, DC 20036
Marilou King, Exec.Dir.
PH: (202)833-1100
FX: (202)833-1105
Description: Private, corporate, institutional, and governmental lawyers, and health professionals. Seeks to establish a forum for nonpartisan objective treatment of issues in the field of health law and to disseminate differing points of view. Conducts research; sponsors educational programs for lawyers, their clients, and other professional and technical personnel in the health field. Maintains small library of information pertaining to health and legal issues. **Founded:** 1971. **Membership:** 10000. **Staff:** 24. **Languages:** English. **Budget:** $6,500,000. **Publication:** *Health Law Digest*, monthly. Journal. Price: included in membership dues; $225.00/year. Advertising: not accepted. Alternate Formats: CD-ROM ■ *Health Lawyers News*, monthly. Magazine. Advertising: accepted.

NATIONAL HEALTH POLICY FORUM (NHPF)
2021 K St. NW, Ste. 800
Washington, DC 20052
Judith Miller Jones, Dir.
PH: (202)872-1390
FX: (202)862-9837
Description: Nonpartisan education program serving primarily senior federal legislative and regulatory health staff but also addressing the interests of state officials and their Washington representatives. Seeks to foster more informed government decision making. Helps decision makers forge the personal acquaintances and understanding necessary for cooperation among government agencies and between government and the private sector. Provides technical assistance to staff and grantees of its sponsoring foundations and corporate contributors. **Founded:** 1971. **Staff:** 13. **Languages:** English. **Budget:** $1,500,000. **Publication:** *Issue Briefs*, 25-30/year. Advertising: not accepted.

NATIONAL HEART COUNCIL (NHC)
306 W. Joppa Rd.
Baltimore, MD 21204
Howard H. Farrington, Pres.
PH: (410)494-0300
FX: (410)494-0725
Description: A project of the National Emergency Medicine Association. Seeks to further advances made in the field of emergency medicine, particularly as related to heart trauma. Awards grants to organizations and individuals for the purpose of conducting research, meetings, or other activities that gather and disseminate information on traumatic medicine, particularly cardiac disorders. Convention/Meeting: none. **Founded:** 1982.

Staff: 6. **Languages:** English Formerly (1994) National Heart Research.

NATIONAL HEART SAVERS ASSOCIATION (NHSA)

9140 W. Dodge Rd.
Omaha, NE 68114
Phil Sokolof, Pres.
PH: (402)398-1993
FX: (402)398-1994
Description: Promotes cardiac health care by informing the public of the dangers of a high-cholesterol diet. Conducts public cholesterol screening program; secured congressional designation of September as National Cholesterol Education Month. Has been successful in persuading major food processing and fast food restaurants companies to stop using palm and coconut oil, lard, and beef tallow, which are high in saturated fats, as ingredients in prepared foods. Promotes nutrition education in public schools and lobbies for more healthful school lunches. Convention/Meeting: none. **Founded:** 1985. **Languages:** English.

NATIONAL IMMUNOTHERAPY CANCER RESEARCH FOUNDATION

PO Box 1027
Flemington, NJ 08822
Dale A. Facchina, Pres.& CEO
PH: (908)806-4300
FX: (908)806-3548
Description: Promotes the use of immune system stimulation including vaccines, biological response modifiers, and other immuno-augmentative treatments as a cure for cancer. Raises funds for immunotherapy and immunology research in the prevention and treatment of cancer. Publications: none. **Founded:** 1990. **Languages:** English.

NATIONAL INSTITUTE OF HEALTH (NIH)

(Instituto Nacional de Salud)
Cesar Nicholas Penson 36
Edificio Miguelina II, Apto. 303
Gazcue
Santo Domingo, Dominican Republic
PH: (809)689-2027
FX: (809)689-2027
Description: Health care professionals, academics in the field of public health, and other individuals and organizations with an interest in public health programs in the Dominican Republic. Seeks to ensure availability of primary health care services. Conducts research on public health issues; makes recommendations to government agencies and health care institutions. **Founded:** 1991. **Languages:** English, Spanish.

NATIONAL INSTITUTE OF MEDICAL HERBALISTS

56 Longbrook St.
Exeter EX4 6AH, England
PH: 44 1392 426022
FX: 44 1392 498963
Description: Practitioners of herbal medicine. **Founded:** 1864. **Membership:** 410. **Staff:** 2. Multinational. **Publication:** *European Journal of Herbal Medicine* (in English), 3/year. Price: $25.50 individual; L31.50 institution. ISSN: 1352-4755. Advertising: accepted ■ *Register of Members.* Directory.

NATIONAL IRIDOLOGY RESEARCH ASSOCIATION

PO Box 31013
Seattle, WA 98103
William Caradonna, Pres.
PH: (206)282-6604
FX: (206)282-9631
Description: Researches iridology, the study of the iris of the eye for indications of bodily health and disease. Offers educational programs and certification. **Founded:** 1982. **Languages:** English.

NATIONAL LEAGUE FOR NURSING (NLN)

url: http://www.nln.org
61 Broadway, 33rd Fl.
New York, NY 10006-2701
Dr. Sheila Ryan, Pres.
PH: (212)989-9393
TF: 800669-9656
FX: (212)989-2272
Description: Individuals and leaders in nursing and other health professions, and community members interested in solving health care problems (9,000); agencies, nursing educational institutions, departments of nursing in hospitals and related facilities, and home and community health agencies (1800). Works to assess nursing needs, improve organized nursing services and nursing education, and foster collaboration between nursing and other health and community services. Provides tests used in selection of applicants to schools of nursing; also prepares tests for evaluating nursing student progress and nursing service tests. Nationally accredits nursing education programs and community health agencies. Collects and disseminates data on nursing services and nursing education. Conducts studies and demonstration projects on community planning for nursing and nursing service and education. **Founded:** 1952. **Membership:** 11000. **Staff:** 80. **State Groups:** 45. **Languages:** English, Spanish. Formed by Merger of Association of Collegiate Schools of Nursing; Joint Committee on Careers in Nursing; National Committee for the Improvement of Nursing Services; National League of Nursing Education.

NATIONAL MATERNAL AND CHILD HEALTH CLEARINGHOUSE (NMCHC)

e-mail: nmchc@circsol.com/nmchc
url: http://www.circsol.com/mch/
2070 Chain Bridge Rd., Ste. 450
Vienna, VA 22182-2536
Paul F. Seidman, Project Dir.
PH: (703)356-1964
FX: (703)821-2098
Description: Federal, state, and local agencies; voluntary organizations; health professionals; consumers. Collects, and disseminates information on maternal and child health, including perinatal health; prenatal care; infant, child, and adolescent health; immunization; newborn screening; oral health; emergency medical services for children; health and safety in child care; lead poisoning prevention; violence and injury prevention; children with special health needs; family support and family-centered care; maternal and child health programs and services; human genetics, nutrition, and pregnancy care, primarily from materials developed by the U.S. Department of Health and Human Services, Health Resources and Services Administration, and Maternal and Child Health Bureau. **Founded:** 1983. Multinational. **Languages:** Spanish, Ukrainian.

NATIONAL MEDIC-CARD SYSTEMS (NMCS)

e-mail: mikeb@bhprint.com
url: http://www.bhprint.com
1070 Commerce St., Ste. F
San Marcos, CA 92069
Michael C. Barksdale, Sales Mgr.
PH: (760)744-1560
FX: (760)744-1569
Description: Produces wallet-size medical cards that have five sections, fold into the size of a credit card, and describe individuals' medical conditions in detail. Convention/Meeting: none. **Founded:** 1978. **Languages:** English. **For-Profit. Formerly:** (1986) National Medic-Card Society.

NATIONAL MEDICAL ASSOCIATION (NMA)

1012 10th St. NW
Washington, DC 20001
Lorraine Cole, PhD, Exec.Dir.
PH: (202)347-1895
FX: (202)842-3293
Description: Professional society of black physicians. Maintains

24 scientific sections representing major specialties of medicine. Plans to establish library. Conducts symposia and workshops. **Founded:** 1895. **Membership:** 22000. **Staff:** 28. **Local Groups:** 93. **Languages:** English. **Publication:** *Journal of the National Medical Association*, monthly. Contains scientific articles. Price: $35.00. Circulation: 28,000. Advertising: accepted ▪ *National Medical Association Newsletter*, quarterly.

NATIONAL MEDICAL FELLOWSHIPS (NMF)
110 W. 32nd St., 8th Fl.
New York, NY 10001-3205
Leon Johnson, Jr., Pres.
PH: (212)714-0933
FX: (212)239-9718
Description: Promotes education of minority students in medicine. Conducts financial assistance program for first- and second-year minority medical students who are U.S. citizens. Conducts workshops in financial planning and management for medical and premedical students, administrators, and parents. **Founded:** 1946. **Staff:** 11. **Regional Groups:** 2. **Languages:** English. **Budget:** $1,630,000. **Publication:** *Informed Decison Making* ▪ *NMF Update*, biennial. Newsletter ▪ *Special Report*, annual ▪ Annual Report ▪ Brochure, annual. **Formerly:** (1952) Provident Medical Associates.

NATIONAL MENTAL HEALTH ASSOCIATION (NMHA)
e-mail: nmhainfo@aol.com
url: http://www.nmha.org
1021 Prince St.
Alexandria, VA 22314-2971
Michael Faenza, CEO/Pres.
PH: (703)684-7722
TF: 800969-NMHA
FX: (703)684-5968
Description: Addresses all aspects of mental health and mental illness and is dedicated to improving mental health, preventing mental disorders, and achieving victory over mental illnesses. NMHA, in partnership with more than 330 affiliates across the country, accomplishes its mission through advocacy, public education, research, and service. **Founded:** 1909. **Membership:** 416000. **Staff:** 45. **Local Groups:** 330. **Languages:** English. **Budget:** $2,414,554. Absorbed National Organization for Mentally Ill Children. Formed by Merger of National Committee for Mental Hygiene; National Mental Health Foundation; Psychiatric Foundation.

NATIONAL MENTAL HEALTH CONSUMER SELF-HELP CLEARINGHOUSE (NMHCSHC)
e-mail: THEKEY@delphi.com
url: http://www.libertynet.org/~mha/clhouse.html
1211 Chestnut St.
Philadelphia, PA 19107
Joseph Rogers, Exec.Dir.
PH: (215)751-1810
TF: 800553-4539
FX: (215)636-6310
Description: Serves mental health consumers/ex-patients and consumer/ex-patient self-help groups. Provides technical assistance in the development of self-help projects. Offers informational referrals, written material, and consulting services. **Founded:** 1985. **Staff:** 8. **Languages:** English, Spanish. **Budget:** $350,000.

NATIONAL MULTIPLE SCLEROSIS SOCIETY (NMSS)
e-mail: IRC@nmss.org
url: http://www.nmss.org
733 3rd Ave.
New York, NY 10017
Gen. Michael Dugan, Pres. & CEO
PH: (212)986-3240
TF: 800FIGHT-MS
FX: (212)986-7981
Description: Stimulates, supports, and coordinates research into the cause, treatment, and cure of multiple sclerosis; provides ser-

vices for persons with MS and related diseases and their families; aids in establishing MS clinics and therapy centers. Conducts Creative Will, biennial competition for artists with MS. Maintains numerous committees including international and research and medical programs, and services. Maintains speakers' bureau; compiles statistics. **Founded:** 1946. **Membership:** 470000. **Staff:** 900. **State Groups:** 93. **Languages:** English. **Budget:** $58,000,000. **Publication:** *Inside MS*, 4/year. Magazine. Contains book reviews, research updates, legislative updates, and annual report. Price: included in membership dues. ISSN: 0739-9774. Circulation: 400,000. Advertising: accepted. **Formerly:** (1947) Association for Advancementof Research on Multiple Sclerosis.

NATIONAL MYOSITIS ASSOCIATION
PO Box 890
Cooperstown, NY 13326
Karan Zopatti, Pres.
TF: 800821-7356
FX: (540)432-0206
Description: Seeks to educate members in ways to avoid future degeneration process of myositis, give emotional support, investigate the different causes of the disease, act as a clearinghouse to physicians and scientists, and disseminate information to patients to inform on some of the known causes, pursue additional funding for research, investigate the most effective medical treatments available that have the least side effects and, most important, research a cure into these debilitating diseases. **Founded:** 1986. **Membership:** 1000. **Regional Groups:** 22. **Languages:** English. **Publication:** *Newsletter for Myositis*, quarterly. Price: $4.00 for past Newsletters. Advertising: accepted. Also Known As (1995) National Support Group for Myositis.

NATIONAL NEUROFIBROMATOSIS FOUNDATION
e-mail: nnf@aol.com
url: http://www.nf.org/
95 Pine St.
New York, NY 10005
Peter Bellermann, Pres.
PH: (212)344-6633
TF: 800323-7938
FX: (212)529-6094
Description: Persons with neurofibromatosis and their families. (Neurofibromatosis is the most common neurological disorder caused by a single gene.) Sponsors scientific research to find treatments and a cure for neurofibromatosis. Promotes clinical activities for patients. Educates the public about neurofibromatosis. Provides support services to patients and their families. Conducts research programs. **Founded:** 1978. **Membership:** 33000. **Staff:** 17. **State Groups:** 27. **Languages:** English. **Budget:** $2,000,000. **Publication:** *Neurofibromatosis: A General Newsletter for Patients, Families, and the General Public*, quarterly ▪ *Neurofibromatosis: Research Newsletter*, semiannual.

NATIONAL NURSES ASSOCIATION OF KENYA (NNAK)
PO Box 49422
Nairobi, Kenya
Heme Noungu Geoffrey, Contact
PH: 254 2 229083
FX: 254 2 335438
Description: Nurses in Kenya. Goal is to ensure health for all by the year 2000. Promotes primary health care; facilitates exchange and cooperation between members; upholds ethics of the profession and encourages high standards. Represents members' interests before the government; provides help for members in times of difficulty; offers scholarships and operates trust fund. Operates foster child program. Works in conjunction with the National Council of Women in Kenya. Conducts workshops and seminars. **Founded:** 1958. **Local Groups:** 19. **Languages:** English. **Budget:** 500,000 KSh. **Publication:** *Kenya Nurses Newsletter*, quarterly ▪ *Kenya Nursing Journal*, semiannual.

NATIONAL NURSES SOCIETY ON ADDICTIONS (NNSA)
4101 Lake Boone Trl., Ste. 201
Raleigh, NC 27607

PH: (919)783-5181
FX: (919)787-4916
Description: Promotes quality nursing care for persons addicted to alcohol and other drugs, and their families. Fosters continuing education and development of skills among nurses involved in the field; works to enhance the professional image of addictions nurses. Participates in public policy and social issues related to alcohol or chemical abuse. Serves as liaison between members and professional groups with common goals. Represents members' interests before national organizations. Regional groups sponsor workshops. Provides certification program. **Founded:** 1975. **Membership:** 800. **Regional Groups:** 10. **Languages:** English. Formerly (1983) National Nurses Society on Alcoholism.

NATIONAL ORAL HEALTH INFORMATION CLEARINGHOUSE (NOHIC)
e-mail: nidr@aerie.com
url: http://www.nidr.nih.gov
1 NOHIC Way
Bethesda, MD 20892-3500
Anna-Marie Montague, Prj.Mgr.
PH: (301)402-7364
FX: (301)907-8830
Description: Serves as resource for patients, health professionals, and the public seeking information on the oral health of special care patients, including people with genetic or systemic disorders that compromise oral health, people whose medical treatment causes oral problems, and people with mental or physical disabilities that make good oral hygiene practices difficult. Collects and maintains an online database on oral health and special care issues. **Languages:** English.

NATIONAL ORGANIZATION OF ADOLESCENT PREGNANCY, PARENTING AND PREVENTION (NOAPP)
1319 F St. NW, Ste. 401
Washington, DC 20004-1106
Donna M. Butts, Exec.Dir.
PH: (301)913-0378
FX: (301)913-0380
Description: Professionals, policymakers, community and state leaders, and other concerned individuals and organizations. Promotes comprehensive and coordinated services designed for the prevention and resolution of problems associated with adolescent pregnancy, parenthood and prevention. Supports families in expanding their capability of nurturing children and setting standards that encourage their healthy development through loving, stable relationships. Programs include: providing advocacy services at local, state, and national levels for adolescent pregnancy issues; sharing information and promoting public awareness; conducting conferences, training institutes and workshops to encourage the establishment of effective programs; coalition building assistance. **Founded:** 1979. **Membership:** 2000. **Languages:** English. **Publication:** *NOAPP Network Newsletter*, quarterly. Contains resource and research reviews, state highlights, legislative focus, and successful program models. **Formerly:** (1993) National Organization of Adolescent Pregnancy and Parenting.

NATIONAL ORGANIZATION FOR ASSOCIATE DEGREE NURSING (NOADN)
e-mail: noadn@noadn.org
url: http://www.noadn.org/adnursing/
11250 Roger Bacon Dr., Ste. 8
Reston, VA 20190-5202
Randall C. Price, CAE, Exec.Dir.
PH: (703)437-4377
FX: (703)435-4390
Description: Individuals interested in retaining current competency level examinations and endorsement of RN licensure from state to state for associate degree nursing graduates. Represents and advances the status of associate degree nursing education and practice. Provides networking among members to facilitate the exchange of legislative information and support. Offers clearinghouse for interpretation of legal issues and liability insurance. **Founded:** 1986. **Membership:** 1600. **Staff:** 3. **State Groups:** 10.

Languages: English. **For-Profit. Budget:** $250,000. Formerly (1991) National Organization for Advancement of Associate Degree Nursing.

NATIONAL ORGANIZATION FOR COMPETENCY ASSURANCE (NOCA)
url: http://www.noca.org
1200 19th St. NW, Ste. 300
Washington, DC 20036-2401
Bonnie M. Aubin, Exec.Dir.
PH: (202)857-1165
FX: (202)223-4579
Description: Nonprofit organizations conducting certification programs for occupations and professionals and trade associations representing these professionals. Seeks to increase public awareness, understanding, and acceptance of private sector credentialing as an alternative to licensure; promotes nonlicensed but certified practitioners as a means to achieving high quality and cost containment. **Founded:** 1977. **Staff:** 2. Multinational. **Languages:** English. **Publication:** *Professional Regulation News*, monthly. Newsletter. Price: $95.00/year. Advertising: accepted. **Formerly:** (1989) National Commission for Health Certifying Agencies.

NATIONAL ORGANIZATION OF NURSE PRACTITIONERS FACULTIES
e-mail: nonpf@aacn.nche.edu
url: http://www.nonpf.com
1 Dupont Cir., NW, No. 530
Washington, DC 20036
Kathryn Werner, Admin.Dir.
PH: (202)452-1405
FX: (202)452-1406
Description: Works to promote public health by developing and implementing nurse practitioner education. Disseminates research related to nurse practitioner education; provides a forum for the exchange of information; works to influence policy affecting nurse practitioners; and develops national guidelins and criteria for nurse practitioner educational programs. **Founded:** 1981. **Membership:** 750. **Staff:** 2. **For-Profit. Budget:** $200,000. Formerly (1998) National Organization of Nursing Pratitioners.

NATIONAL ORGANIZATION FOR RARE DISORDERS (NORD)
e-mail: orphan@nord-rdb.com
url: http://www.NORD-RDB.com/~orphan
PO Box 8923
New Fairfield, CT 06812-8923
Abbey S. Meyers, Pres.
PH: (203)746-6518
TF: 800999-6673
FX: (203)746-6481
Description: Doctors, professionals, academics, voluntary health organizations, and individuals interested in rare disorders. Serves as a clearinghouse for information concerning rare disorders. Objectives are: to monitor the Orphan Drug Act; to link individuals with rare disorders together for mutual support; to stimulate research on rare diseases; to foster communication among voluntary agencies, health-related industries, and government bodies. (Orphan drugs are used in the treatment of rare disorders. Since their use is not widespread, most drug companies cannot expect to profit from the development and manufacture of these drugs. The Orphan Drug Act gives financial assistance and tax incentives to drug companies that develop these drugs.) Provides information on rare disorders and referrals to organizations. **Founded:** 1983. **Membership:** 65000. **Staff:** 32. **National Groups:** 130. **Languages:** English. **Budget:** $1,500,000. **Publication:** *NORD On-Line Bulletin*, monthly. Newsletter. Updating service for voluntary health agency members on legislation and other issues related to orphan drugs and diseases. Includes meeting schedule. Price: included in membership dues, for organizations. Circulation: 285. Advertising: not accepted ■ *NORD Resource Guide*. An alphabetical listing of national support groups and foundations that service the needs of people with rare dis-

orders and disabilities ∎ *Orphan Disease Update*, 3/year. Newsletter. For individual members updating information on orphan diseases and orphan drug research; discusses legislative issues related to health. Price: included in membership dues. Circulation: 65,000. Advertising: not accepted ∎ *Physician Guide to Rare Diseases*. Book.

NATIONAL PARKINSON FOUNDATION (NPF)
e-mail: mailbox@npf.med.miami.edu
url: http://www.parkinson.org
1501 NW 9th Ave./Bob Hope Rd.
Miami, FL 33136
Nathan Slewett, Chairperson
PH: (305)547-6666
TF: 800327-4545
FX: (305)548-4403
Description: Doctors, nurses, scientists, pharmacologists, and therapists who research, diagnose, and treat Parkinsonism. Supports basic and clinical research for Parkinsonism and related neurological disorders and provides physical, speech, and occupational therapy. NPF is associated with the University of Miami School of Medicine, and supports the National Parkinson Institute, which provides diagnosis, treatment, care, and rehabilitation. Conducts educational programs. Distributes literature to medical libraries, nurses training schools, health clinics, physicians, and patients. Sponsors regional patient self-support groups where problems are discussed and experiences are exchanged under guidance of physicians, social workers, and psychologists. Maintains offices at 122 E. 42nd St., New York, NY 10017 and 4929 Wilshire Blvd., Los Angeles, CA 90010. **Founded:** 1957. **Staff:** 50. Multinational. **Languages:** English. **Budget:** $3,650,000. **Publication:** *How to Start and Run a Support Group* ∎ *Membership List*, periodic ∎ *The Parkinson Handbook* ∎ *Parkinson Report*, quarterly. Newsletter. Contains research reports. Price: included in membership dues; available free of charge to others upon request. Circulation: 115,000. Advertising: not accepted.

NATIONAL PEDICULOSIS ASSOCIATION (NPA)
e-mail: webmaster@HeadLice.org
url: http://www.headlice.org
PO Box 610189
Newton, MA 02161
Deborah Z. Altschuler, Pres.
PH: (781)449-NITS
TF: 800446-4NPA
FX: (781)449-8129
Description: Parents, physicians, school nurses, and individuals representing hospitals and county health departments. Works to eliminate the incidence, particularly among children, of pediculosis (head lice). Conducts public education campaign to make pediculosis control a public health priority; acts as consumer advocate to ensure the quality and safety of products for treating pediculosis and scabies; encourages scientific research to discover methods of treatment that minimize the use of pesticides, which may harm pregnant and nursing women as well as infants and children. Disseminates information on identifying, treating, and preventing pediculosis, with emphasis on finding and removing nits (louse eggs) in the hair. Provides consultations to schools, camps, and other organizations. Maintains speakers' bureau and creates exhibits for professional meetings and conferences. Operates lending library of audiovisual aids; makes available other educational tools including posters and pamphlets. Sponsors National Pediculosis Prevention Month in September. Sponsors scientific advisory board of experts in such fields as entomology, dermatology, toxicology, pediatrics, parasitology, and pharmacology. Has testified before and works closely with the U.S. Food and Drug Administration. **Founded:** 1983. **Membership:** 1200. **Staff:** 5. **Languages:** Spanish.

NATIONAL PHARMACEUTICAL ASSOCIATION
Mallinson House
38-42 Saint Peter's St.
St. Albans, Herts. AL1 3NP, England
Colette McCreedy, Contact

PH: 44 1727 832161
FX: 44 1727 840858
Description: Represents 7000 pharmacy owners in UK, who collectively own 10,000 retail pharmacies. Provides members with legal and financial services; insurance; defence and indemnity; training; publications; public relations; business services and pharmacy planning. **Founded:** 1921. **Membership:** 9631. **Staff:** 81. **Publication:** *The Supplement*, monthly. Price: Available to members only. ∎ Pamphlets. Price: Available to members only.

NATIONAL PHARMACEUTICAL COUNCIL (NPC)
1894 Preston White Dr.
Reston, VA 20191
Karren Williams, Pres./CEO
PH: (703)620-6390
FX: (703)476-0904
Description: Pharmaceutical manufacturers producing high quality prescription medication and other pharmaceutical products. Generates research; compiles statistics; conducts specialized educational programs, and forums. **Founded:** 1953. **Membership:** 29. **Staff:** 14. **Languages:** English. **Budget:** $3,500,000. **Publication:** Directory, annual.

NATIONAL PSORIASIS FOUNDATION (NPF)
e-mail: 76135.2746@compuserve.com
url: http://www.psoriasis.org
6600 SW 92nd, Ste. 300
Portland, OR 97223-7195
Gail M. Zimmerman, Exec.Dir.
PH: (503)244-7404
TF: 800723-9166
FX: (503)245-0626
Description: Individuals suffering from psoriasis, or psoriatic arthritis, their families and friends; physicians, nurses, and representatives of pharmaceutical companies. Supports research at various university research centers. Facilitates communication through pen pal programs, group sessions, and other activities. Testifies annually to Congress for psoriasis research. Provides literature to schools and libraries; works with the media to disseminate information on psoriasis. Makes physician recommendations. Sponsors regional educational symposia. Established and maintains a public tissue bank for gene research in psoriasis and psoriatic arthritis. **Founded:** 1968. **Membership:** 37000. **Staff:** 11. **Local Groups:** 40. **Languages:** English. **Budget:** $2,400,000.

NATIONAL RARE BLOOD CLUB (NRBC)
Associated Health Foundation
99 Madison Ave.
New York, NY 10016
Edward Birnbaum, Pres.
PH: (212)889-8245
FX: (212)448-1811
Description: Persons ages 18-65 with rare blood types who are physically able to donate blood. Operates as a voluntary community service with no fees or dues involved. **Founded:** 1978. **Membership:** 16000. **Languages:** English. **Absorbed:** New York Blood Center.

NATIONAL RENAL ADMINISTRATORS ASSOCIATION (NRAA)
e-mail: nraa@NRAA.org
url: http://www.nraa.org/renal/
11250 Roger Bacon Dr., Ste 8
Reston, VA 20190
Keith Krueger, Exec.Dir.
PH: (703)437-4377
FX: (703)435-4390
Description: Administrative personnel involved with dialysis programs for patients suffering from kidney failure. Provides a vehicle for the development of educational and informational services for members. Maintains contact with health care facilities and government agencies. Operates placement service; compiles statistics; conducts political action committee. **Founded:** 1977. **Membership:** 475. **Staff:** 3. **Languages:** English. **Budget:**

$500,000. **Publication:** *NRAA Journal*, annual. Serves as an educational and informational resource for administrative personnel involved in the End Stage Renal Disease Program. Price: free; $50.00 for nonmembers. Circulation: 500 ∎ *Presidents Letter*, monthly. Price: free to members; $10.00 nonmembers.

NATIONAL RESIDENT MATCHING PROGRAM (NRMP)
url: http://www.aamc.org/nrmp
2501 M St. NW, Ste. 1
Washington, DC 20037-1307
Liz Lostumbo, Assoc.Dir.
PH: (202)828-0676
FX: (202)828-1121
Description: National clearinghouse for matching the preferences of applicants for medical residencies with the hospitals' choice of applicants, in order to assist, to the extent possible, their choices of residencies. **Founded:** 1951. **Languages:** English. **Publication:** *NRMP Data*, annual. **Formerly:** (1953) National InterAssociation Committee on Internships; (1968) National Intern Matching Program; (1978) National Intern and Resident Matching Program.

NATIONAL RURAL HEALTH ASSOCIATION (NRHA)
url: http://www.nrharural.org
One W. Armour Blvd., Ste. 203
Kansas City, MO 64111
Donna M. Williams, Exec.VP
PH: (816)756-3140
FX: (816)756-3144
Description: Administrators, physicians, nurses, physician assistants, health planners, academicians, and others interested or involved in rural health care. Creates a better understanding of health care problems unique to rural areas; utilizes a collective approach in finding positive solutions; articulates and represents the health care needs of rural America; supplies current information to rural health care providers; serves as a liaison between rural health care programs throughout the country. Offers continuing education credits for medical, dental, nursing, and management courses. **Founded:** 1989. **Membership:** 1800. **Staff:** 12. **Languages:** English. Absorbed American Small and Rural Hospital Association. Formed by Merger of American Rural Health Association; National Rural Health Care Association.

NATIONAL SCHIZOPHRENIA FELLOWSHIP (NSF)
url: http://www.nsf.org.uk
28 Castle St.
Kingston-upon-Thames, Surrey KT1 1SS, England
Bharat Mehta, Chief Exec.
PH: 44 181 5473937
FX: 44 181 5473862
Description: Majority are carers and the remainder is made up from users/people suffering from schizophrenia or other severe mental illness, interested professionals or people interested in mental health issues. Concerned with supporting people with a severe mental illness, their families and carers. Believes that all of these people have the right to equal opportunitites; to enjoy the challenges and the responsibilities of everyday life while receiving the support of the whole community. **Founded:** 1972. **Membership:** 7102. **Staff:** 900. **Local Groups:** 280. **Budget:** L16,000,000. **Publication:** *A Meeting Of Minds - A Positive Response To Mental Disorder*. Video. Features the perspectives of schizophrenia sufferers, their careers, CPNs, social workers, and police officers. Price: L20.00 ∎ *Cognitive Therapy*. Report. Covers a complimentary form of treatment ∎ *Does Severe Mental Illness Run In Families?* ∎ *Finding The Right Medication*. Handbook. A guide to drugs available to treat schizophrenia. Price: L2.00 ∎ *500 Million More - Where and Why it is Needed*. Report. Highlights the underfunding of community care for people with a severe mental illness. Price: L2.50 ∎ *Is Cost A Factor*. Survey. Price: L4.50 for members; L6.00 for non-members ∎ *One in Ten*. Report. Covers suicide and other unnatural deaths involving people with schizophrenia. Price: L4.50 for members; L6.00 for non-members ∎ *Schizophrenia*. Pamphlet. Covers the causes and symptoms of schizophrenia, including treatment. Price: free ∎

Schizophrenia And Research - UK. Report. Price: L50.00 ∎ *Schizophrenia - Notes for Relatives and Friends*. Pamphlet. Price: L50.00 ∎ *The Silent Partners - The Needs and Experiences of People Who Care For People With A Severe Mental Illness*. Reprint. Price: L4.50 for members; L8.00 for non-members ∎ *What is Schizophrenia?*. Price: free.

NATIONAL SJOGREN'S SYNDROME ASSOCIATION (NSSA)
e-mail: nssa@aol.com
url: http://www.sjogrens.org
5815 N Black Canyon Hwy., Ste. 103
Phoenix, AZ 85015-2200
Barbara Henry, Exec.Dir.
PH: (602)433-9844
TF: 800395-6772
FX: (602)433-9838
Description: Promotes public awareness of Sjogren's Syndrome; encourages research into the cause and cure of the disorder. (Sjogren's Syndrome is an autoimmune disorder characterized by dryness of all mucous membranes resulting from deficient secretion of the glands. Approximately 50% of Sjogren's Syndrome patients also have rheumatoid arthritis.) Sponsors chapters and offers information to the medical community. Conducts educational and research programs; maintains speakers' bureau. **Founded:** 1990. **Membership:** 4500. **Staff:** 6. **Languages:** English. **Budget:** $120,000.

NATIONAL SLEEP FOUNDATION
e-mail: natsleep@erols.com
url: http://www.sleepfoundation.org
729-15th St., Fourth Floor
Washington, DC 20005
Bill McLin, Exec. Dir.
PH: (202)347-3471
FX: (202)347-3472
Description: Works to improve the quality of life of people suffering from sleep disorders and to prevent accidents related to sleep disorders. (Sleep disorders include: insomnia, narcolepsy, sleep apnea syndrome, sudden infant death syndrome, stroke, e-pilepsy, and other disorders of sleep and daytime alertness.) Educates health care professionals and the public about the existance and treatment of sleep disorders. Promotes the development of patient services, community resources, and support groups for individuals affected by sleep disorders. Sponsors educational and research programs. **Founded:** 1990. **Staff:** 7. **Languages:** English. **Budget:** $1,000,000.

NATIONAL SOCIETY FOR EPILEPSY
url: http://www.erg.ion.ucl.ac.uk/nsehome
Chalfont St Peter
Gerrards Cross SL9 0RJ, England
PH: 44 1494 601300
FX: 44 1494 871927
Description: Anyone with an interest in epilepsy who wishes to support epilepsy education and research. Provides assessment, treatment, rehabilitation, long term and respite care for adults with epilepsy. The education department provides support and information, produces educational resources and runs conferences and seminars. There is a community network of groups around the UK offering support and advice... **Founded:** 1892. **Membership:** 1400. **Staff:** 216.

NATIONAL SOCIETY FOR HISTOTECHNOLOGY (NSH)
url: http://www.nsh.org
4201 Northview Dr., Ste. 502
Bowie, MD 20716-2604
Roberta Mosedale, Exec.Sec.
PH: (301)262-6221
FX: (301)262-9188
Description: Histology laboratory technicians, pathologists, laboratory equipment manufacturers' representatives, and interested individuals. Encourages the professional growth and advancement of histoprofessionals and promotes the exchange of ideas and knowledge significant to histotechnology. Assists in the es-

tablishment and mutual understanding of related societies. Provides continuing education training courses. Investigates health hazards in the laboratory; ensures the safety of the laboratory; and participates in formulating federal laboratory regulations. **Founded:** 1973. **Membership:** 4800. **Staff:** 5. **State Groups:** 42. **Languages:** English. **Publication:** *Journal of Histotechnology*, quarterly. Topics include anatomy, pathology, enzyme histochemistry, special stains, immunohistochemistry, cytology, and electron microscopy. Price: included in membership dues; $50.00/year for nonmembers; $60.00/year for nonmembers outside U.S. ISSN: 0147-8885. Circulation: 5,200. Advertising: accepted ■ *NSH In Action*, quarterly. Annual Report. Price: for members. Advertising: not accepted ■ *NSH in Action*, quarterly. Newsletter ■ Booklets. Pertains to careers ■ Films.

NATIONAL SPASMODIC DYSPHONIA ASSOCIATION (NSDA)
e-mail: NSDA@aol.com
1 E. Wacker Dr., Ste. 2430
Chicago, IL 60601-1905
Valerie F. Levitan, Ph.D.
TF: 800795-6732
Description: Individuals diagnosed with spasmodic dysphonia; doctors and scientists providing treatment and conducting research on the disease; interested others. Promotes public awareness of spasmodic dysphonia and the care, welfare, and rehabilitation of those with the disease. (Spasmodic dysphonia is a neurological movement disorder affecting muscular control of the vocal cords, often resulting in an abnormally raspy, breathy, or choppy speech pattern.) Makes information on the disease available to patients, their families, and the public. Encourages research to uncover the causes and treatments of spasmodic dysphonia; offers referral information on specialists administering the botulinum toxin (Botox) presently used in many cases to temporarily treat the disease. Assists in the formation of local support groups to assist patients. **Founded:** 1990. **Membership:** 5400. **National Groups:** 85. **Languages:** English. **Publication:** *NSDA Newsletter*, biennial. Circulation: 6,700. Advertising: not accepted.

NATIONAL SPASMODIC TORTICOLLIS ASSOCIATION (NSTA)
e-mail: nstassoc@aol.com
url: http://www.blueberonweb.com/nsta/nsta.htm
PO Box 424
Mukwonago, WI 53149
Patricia Murray, Exec.Dir.
PH: (714)516-1824
TF: 800HURTFUL
FX: (714)516-1824
Description: Persons afflicted with spasmodic torticollis (ST), a syndrome in which the muscles on one side of the neck contract and pull the head to the side, sometimes pushing the chin up or down. ST usually occurs in adults and can sometimes be treated successfully with medication and physical therapy. Educates the public on ST so that persons with early symptoms know to seek proper medical help from a neurologist or neurosurgeon. Provides forum for discussion among ST sufferers and their families in order to share information and experiences and diminish feelings of alienation and self-consciousness. **Founded:** 1980. **Membership:** 3400. **Staff:** 2. Multinational. **Local Groups:** 48. **Languages:** English. **Budget:** $150,000. **Publication:** *NSTA News Magazine*, quarterly. Includes medical advisor's column. Price: included in membership dues. Circulation: 3,500. Advertising: not accepted ■ *P.T. In-Home Videotape*. Price: $21.95 ■ *Physicians Referral Directory*, annual. Lists neurologists who treat spasmodic torticollis. Price: free. Advertising: not accepted ■ *Relaxation/Affirmation Audiotape*. Price: $5.95 ■ *Series of "Helpful Hints" Letters* ■ *What is NSTA?*. **Absorbed:** (1993) American Spasmodic Torticollis Association. **Formerly:** Project S.T.

NATIONAL STUDENT NURSES' ASSOCIATION (NSNA)
e-mail: nsna@nsna.org
url: http://www.nsna.org
555 W. 57th St., Ste. 1327
New York, NY 10019
Diane J. Mancino, Ed.D., RN CAE, Exec. Dir.
PH: (212)581-2211
FX: (212)581-2368
Description: Students enrolled in state-approved schools for the preparation of registered nurses. Seeks to aid in the development of the individual nursing student and to urge students of nursing, as future health professionals, to be aware of and to contribute to improving the health care of all people. Encourages programs and activities in state groups concerning nursing, health, and the community. Provides assistance for state board review, as well as materials for preparation for state RN licensing examination. Cooperates with nursing organizations in recruitment of nurses and in professional, community, and civic programs. Sponsors Foundation of the National Student Nurses' Association in memory of Frances Tompkins to award scholarships to student nurses. **Founded:** 1952. **Membership:** 40000. **Staff:** 12. **Local Groups:** 650. **Languages:** English. **Budget:** $2,000,000. **Publication:** *Convention News* ■ *Dean's Notes*, 5/year ■ *Imprint*, 5/year. Magazine. Price: included in membership dues. Advertising: accepted ■ *NSNA News*, 5/year ■ Manuals.

NATIONAL SUBACUTE CARE ASSOCIATION (NSCA)
7315 Wisconsin Ave., Ste. 424 E
Bethesda, MD 20814
Sanford. J. Hill, Exec.Dir.
PH: (301)961-8680
FX: (301)961-8681
Description: Hospitals, nursing facilities, professionals and suppliers. Works to serve and represent the subacute and transitional healthcare industry. Provides information on subacute healthcare; promotes high level of ethics; develops standards. **Founded:** 1995. **Membership:** 1500. **Staff:** 3. **Languages:** English.

NATIONAL SURGICAL ASSISTANT ASSOCIATION (NSAA)
1111 N. Dunlap St.
Savoy, IL 61874-9604
Lori Jones, Contact
PH: (217)356-3182
FX: (217)398-4119
Description: Professional surgical assistants throughout the United States. Provides standard guidelines and regulations. Establishes rules for those who practice and function as surgical assistants. Examines, reviews, and certifies the training, duration, experience, skills, and knowledge of its members. **Founded:** 1983. **Languages:** English.

NATIONAL TAY-SACHS AND ALLIED DISEASES ASSOCIATION (NTSAD)
e-mail: NTSAD-Boston@worldnet.att.net
url: http://mcrcr4.med.nyu.edu/~murphp01/taysachs.htm
2001 Beacon St.
Brookline, MA 02146
Debra Dunkless, Dir.
PH: (617)277-4463
TF: 800906-8723
FX: (617)277-0134
Description: Supports educational, prevention, family service, and research programs concerning Tay-Sachs and allied degenerative lysosomal and neurological diseases occurring in infants, children, and adults. Provides educational literature on Tay-Sachs and allied diseases; serves as a referral agency for the layperson and professional on all aspects of Tay-Sachs and related diseases; promotes mass screening programs and appropriate legislation locally and nationally. Sponsors International Laboratory Quality Control and Reference Sample Center for TSD laboratories. Offers support groups and services for parents of children with Tay-Sachs and related diseases. Compiles statistics; operates speakers' bureau. **Founded:** 1956. **Membership:** 5000.

D&B/Gale Industry Reference Handbooks

Staff: 2. Multinational. State Groups: 6. Languages: English, Russian. For-Profit. Budget: $230,000. Publication: *For My Sister, Elyssa*. Video. Price: $30.00 video includes postage & handling; $65.00 sound slide includes postage & handling ▪ *Home Care Manual*. Price: $3.00 includes shipping and handling ▪ *Jewish Genetic Diseases*. Video. Price: $30.00 includes postage & handling ▪ *Lay-Onset Tay-Sachs*. Booklet. Price: free ▪ *National Tay-Sachs and Allied Diseases Association – Breakthrough*, semiannual. Newsletter ▪ *One Day At A Time*. Booklet. Price: ▪ *Service To Families*. Brochure. Price: ▪ *Tay Sachs Is*. Pamphlet. Price: ▪ *Tay Sachs Is (Russian Translation)*. Price: ▪ *Tay-Sachs/The Dreaded Inheritance*. Booklet. Price: $5.00 over 25 copies ▪ *Understanding Lysosomal Storage Diseases*. Booklet. Price: $1.00 copy ▪ *What Every Family Should Know*. Booklet. Price:. Advertising: not accepted ▪ Pamphlets. Formerly: (1966) National Tay-Sachs Association.

NATIONAL TUBERCULOSIS CONTROLLERS ASSOCIATION
e-mail: ntca@bellsouth.net
Atlanta Koger Center
3355 NE Express Access Rd.
Cormell Bldg., Ste. 131
Atlanta, GA 30341-4000
Walter Q. Page, Exec.Dir.
PH: (770)455-0801
FX: (770)455-4221
Description: Seeks to provide a collective voice for TB controllers to advance and advocate for tuberculosis control and elimination activites in the U.S. Advocates for policies and laws to advance tuberculosis control and elimination at the sate, local, and territorial levels. Founded: 1995. Staff: 2.

NATIONAL TUBEROUS SCLEROSIS ASSOCIATION (NTSA)
e-mail: ntsa@capcon.net
8181 Professional Place, Ste. 110
Landover, MD 20785
Barbara K. Witten, Pres.
PH: (301)459-9888
TF: 800225-6872
FX: (301)459-0394
Description: Encourages and provides grants for research into the diagnosis, cause, management, and cure of tuberous sclerosis. (Tuberous sclerosis is a genetic disease characterized by one or more of the following: epileptic seizures, mental retardation, behavioral problems, tumors, or skin lesions.) Provides support to families affected by the disease through a nationwide network of volunteer area representatives and the distribution of informational packets. Conducts educational programs for medical and allied professionals. Founded: 1974. Membership: 4000. Staff: 9. Multinational. Languages: Chinese, Japanese. Budget: $100,050. Publication: *Perspective Newsletter*, quarterly. Contains research articles, current resources for patients and parents, legislative news, and patient /parent question and answer column. Price: available to members and professionals. Circulation: 8,000. Advertising: not accepted ▪ *Resource Newsletter*, semiannual.

NATIONAL UNION OF HOSPITAL AND HEALTH CARE EMPLOYEES/SEIU
310 W. 43rd St.
New York, NY 10036
Jerome Brown, Acting Pres.
PH: (212)582-1890
Description: An affiliate of the Service Employees International Union, Health Care Division. Works to organize hospital and health care employees into a labor union. Founded: 1973. Membership: 60000. Languages: English. Publication: *Health Care Update*, quarterly. Also Known As: 1199/SEIU. Formerly: (1973) National Union of Hospital and Nursing Home Employees; (1989) National Union of Hospital and Health Care Employees.

NATIONAL VASCULAR MALFORMATIONS FOUNDATION
8320 Nightingale
Dearborn Heights, MI 48127
Mary P. Burris, Pres./Founder
PH: (313)274-1243
FX: (313)274-1393
Description: Vascular malformation patients and their families. (Vascular malformations are tumors or flat lesions made up of abnormally sized blood vessels and include such conditions as port wine stains, hemangiomas, arteriovenous malformations (AVMs), and Sturge-Weber Syndrome.) Provides support and information to patients and medical professionals. Collects information on vascular malformations, specialist doctors, and reference sources. Conducts fundraising for research activities; maintains speakers' bureau. Founded: 1990. Membership: 500. Languages: English.

NATIONAL VITILIGO FOUNDATION (NVFI)
e-mail: 73071.33@compuserve.com
url: http://www.nvfi.org
PO Box 6337
Tyler, TX 75711
Jerri Bossley, Exec.Dir.
PH: (903)531-0074
FX: (903)531-9767
Description: Doctors and patients; contributors and supporters. Provides information and counseling to vitiligo patients and their families. (Vitiligo is a skin disease which destroys pigment cells causing smooth, white-colored patches of skin.) Seeks to increase awareness and concern for the vitiligo patient. Raises funds for scientific and clinical research on the cause, treatment, and cure of vitiligo. Convention/Meeting: none. Founded: 1985. Membership: 25000. Staff: 1. Multinational. Regional Groups: 11. Languages: Spanish.

NATIONAL WHOLESALE DRUGGISTS' ASSOCIATION (NWDA)
1821 Michael Faraday Dr., Ste. 400
Reston, VA 20190
Ronald J. Streck, Pres. and CEO
PH: (703)787-0000
FX: (703)787-6930
Description: Wholesalers and manufacturers of drug and health care products and industry service providers. Compiles statistics; sponsors research and specialized education programs. Has online e-mail bulletin service. Founded: 1876. Membership: 456. Staff: 41. Multinational. Languages: English. Budget: $9,350,000. Absorbed (1984) Drug Wholesalers Association. Formerly (1881) Western Wholesale Druggists.

NATIONAL YOUTH SPORTS SAFETY FOUNDATION (NYSSF)
e-mail: NYSSF@aol.com
url: http://www.nyssf.org
333 Longwood Ave., Ste. 202
Boston, MA 02115
Michelle Glassman, Exec.Dir.
PH: (617)277-1171
FX: (617)277-2278
Description: Works to promote the safety and well-being of children and adolescents participating in sports. Strives to reduce the number and severity of injuries youth sustain in sports activities. Sponsors educational programs. Maintains speakers' bureau. Founded: 1989. Languages: English. Formerly National Youth Sports Foundation for the Prevention of Athletic Inuries.

NATURAL-SOURCE VITAMIN E ASSOCIATION (NSVEA)
c/o William R. Pendergast
1050 Connecticut Ave. NW,
Washington, DC 20036-5339
William R. Pendergast, Exec.Dir.
PH: (202)857-6029
FX: (202)857-6395
Description: Corporations engaged in the manufacture of natural

source vitamin E. Purpose is to promote the sale of natural source vitamin E. **Founded:** 1984. **Membership:** 3. **Languages:** English.

NEED BANGLADESH
Tajmahal Rd., 20/3, Block C
Mohamed Pur
Dhaka 1207, Bangladesh
PH: 880 2 314995
Description: Individuals interested in public health and family planning issues. Seeks to insure availability of health services to all socioeconomic strata. Conducts family planning, health, education, and income generation programs. **Founded:** 1992. **Languages:** Bangla, English.

NETHERLANDS PHYSICAL SOCIETY
e-mail: A.Jelles@nnv.nl
url: http://www.nikhef.nl/pub/eps/europa/nederl.html
PO Box 302
NL 1170 AM Badhoevedorp, Netherlands
Dr. E.W.A. Lingeman, Sec.
Description: Physicists, physics teachers, and others with an interest in the physical sciences. Seeks to improve the quality of physics education, research, and knowledge. **Founded:** 1921. **Membership:** 3500. **Languages:** Dutch, English. **Budget:** 500,000 f. **Publication:** *Nederlands Tydschrift voor Natuurkunde* (in Dutch and English), monthly. Price: 150.00 f. Advertising: accepted. Alternate Formats: online ▪ *NNV-Gids*. Membership list.

NETWORK FOR CONTINUING MEDICAL EDUCATION (NCME)
1425 Broad St.
Clifton, NJ 07013
Paul Gersh, V.Chm.
PH: (973)473-9500
TF: 800223-0272
FX: (973)591-1224
Description: Hospitals that subscribe to receive NCME services. Produces and distributes monthly course package including videotape, posters, program brochure, and workbook to members. Course packages cover the full spectrum of medical topics and are designed to provide category 1 continuing medical education credit to physicians. Convention/Meeting: none. **Founded:** 1965. **Membership:** 800. **Staff:** 50. Multinational. **Languages:** English. **For-Profit. Publication:** *Video Journal Dermatology*, quarterly ▪ *Video Journal Oncology*, quarterly.

NEURO-DEVELOPMENTAL TREATMENT ASSOCIATION (NDTA)
e-mail: webmaster@ndta.org
url: http://www.nata.org
401 N. Michigan Ave.
Chicago, IL 60611-4267
Ruth Easterling, Exec.Dir.
PH: (312)321-5151
TF: 800869-9295
FX: (312)321-5194
Description: Physical and occupational therapists, speech pathologists, special educators, physicians, parents, and others interested in neurodevelopmental treatment. (NDT is a form of therapy for individuals who suffer from central nervous system disorders resulting in abnormal movement. Treatment attempts to initiate or refine normal stages and processes in the development of movement.) Informs members of new developments in the field and with ideas that will eventually improve fundamental independence. Locates articles related to NDT. Regional groups maintain libraries. **Founded:** 1967. **Membership:** 3800. **Staff:** 3. Multinational. **Regional Groups:** 14. **Languages:** English. **Budget:** $311,000. **Publication:** *NDTA Network* (in English), bimonthly. Newsletter. Price: for members. Advertising: accepted. **Formerly:** International Bobath Alumni Association.

NEUROPATHY ASSOCIATION
e-mail: info@neuropahty.org
url: http://www.neuropathy.org
Lincoln Bldg.
60 E 42nd St., Ste. 942
New York, NY 10165
PH: (212)692-0662
TF: 800247-6968
FX: (212)692-0668
Description: Provides resources and support for people who suffer from disorders that affect the peripheral nerves. Offers educational and research programs. **Founded:** 1995. **Membership:** 2500. **Staff:** 1. Multinational. **Local Groups:** 20.

NEUROSURGICAL SOCIETY OF AMERICA (NSA)
Division of Neurosurgery
7703 Floyd Curl Drive
San Antonio, TX 78284-7843
Dr. Willis E. Brown, Jr., Sec.
PH: (210)567-6725
Description: Young specialists in neurological surgery. **Founded:** 1948. **Membership:** 162. **Languages:** English.

NEW EYES FOR THE NEEDY (NEN)
PO Box 332
549 Millburn Ave.
Short Hills, NJ 07078
Susannah Likins, Dir.
PH: (973)376-4903
FX: (973)376-3807
Description: Provides new prescription eyeglasses for individuals in the United States to whom no other funds, public or private, are available. Tests, grades, and distributes reusable framed glasses to overseas missions and hospital clinics upon request. Funds are derived from the melt of precious metals found in jewelry and eyeglass frames donated to the organization and through contributions from individuals and grants. Funds are also derived from the sale of donated jewelry in our shop. **Founded:** 1932. **Membership:** 200. **Staff:** 2. Multinational. **Languages:** English. **Budget:** $292,000.

NEW PROFESSIONALS SECTION OF THE AMERICAN PUBLIC HEALTH ASSOCIATION (NPSAPHA)
Temple Family Planning
Hudson Bldg., Lower Level
3425 N. Carlisle St.
Philadelphia, PA 19140
Ruth Scarborough, Chairperson
PH: (215)707-3061
FX: (215)707-7918
Description: A section of the American Public Health Association. Professionals and paraprofessionals in the human service areas. Offers specialized education and forum for health advisors. **Founded:** 1969. **Membership:** 300. **Languages:** English **Formerly** (1982) National New Professional Health Workers.

NEW ZEALAND COLLEGE OF MIDWIVES
e-mail: nzcom@clear.net.nz
PO Box 21-106
906-908 Colombo St.
Christchurch, New Zealand
Karen Guilliland, Natl. Dir.
PH: 64 3 3772732
FX: 64 3 3775662
Description: Midwives, consumer groups, and interested individuals. Promotes midwifery services and education, and represents the interests of midwives to governmental bodies and the public. Prescribes and monitors standards for the practice and education of midwifery. Acts as a consultant for governmental agencies; engages in the negotiation of government funding for community and independent midwifery services. Offers courses jointly with colleges and universities. **Founded:** 1990. **Membership:** 1500. **Staff:** 6. **Regional Groups:** 10. **Languages:** English. **Budget:** NZ$100,000. **Publication:** *New Zealand College of Midwives* (in

English), semiannual. Journal. Contains articles on midwifery. Price: NZ$6.00. ISSN: 0114-7870. Circulation: 1,500. Advertising: accepted ▪ *New Zealand College of Midwives National Newsletter*, bimonthly.

NEW ZEALAND DENTAL ASSOCIATION (NZDA)
e-mail: nzda.info@nzda.org.nz
PO Box 28084
Remeura
Auckland 5, New Zealand
Dr. L.J. Croxson, Exec.Dir.
PH: 64 9 5242778
FX: 64 9 5205256
Description: Registered dental practitioners in New Zealand. Promotes improved dental health through the increased availability of dental and allied services. Collects and disseminates data on topics including AIDS, infection control, and oral health costs. **Founded:** 1905. **Membership:** 1500. **Staff:** 5. **Local Groups:** 16. **Languages:** English. **Publication:** *Membership Booklet of the New Zealand Dental Association* (in English), annual. Directory ▪ *New Zealand Dental Journal* (in English), quarterly ▪ *NZDA News* (in English), bimonthly. Newsletter.

NEW ZEALAND DENTAL THERAPISTS ASSOCIATION
115 Captain Scott Rd.
Titrangi
Auckland 7, New Zealand
Andrea Jarrold, Contact
PH: 64 9 8174140
Description: Women dental therapists of New Zealand. Promotes the professional interests of members. Works to ensure the provision of dental services to children and adults in New Zealand. Establishes industry standards. **Founded:** 1921. **Membership:** 400. **Languages:** English. **Budget:** NZ$12,000. **Publication:** *Dental Therapist Journal*, annual.

NEW ZEALAND FAMILY PLANNING ASSOCIATION (NZFPA)
PO Box 11515
Wellington, New Zealand
Sue Ineson, Exec.Dir.
PH: 64 4 3844349
FX: 64 4 3828356
Description: Promotes a positive view of sexuality to enable people to make informed choices about their sexual health. Works to reduce the number of unintended pregnancies and abortions. Attempts to stop the spread of AIDS and other sexually transmitted diseases through education and contraceptive services. **Founded:** 1936. **Membership:** 300. **Staff:** 400. **Local Groups:** 12. **Languages:** English. **Budget:** NZ$8,000,000. **Publication:** *Forum* (in English), quarterly. Newsletter. Price: NZ$25.00/year. Circulation: 1,200. Advertising: not accepted.

NEW ZEALAND NURSES ORGANIZATION (NZNO)
e-mail: nzno@xtra.co.nz
PO Box 2128
Wellington, New Zealand
Ms. Brenda Wilson, CEO
Description: Nurses, nurses' aids and medical radiation technologist. Represents and promotes nurses' interests and concerns on health issues through participation in health and social policy development. Conducts research on health issues. Offers health education programs. **Founded:** 1909. **Membership:** 26500. **Staff:** 60. **Regional Groups:** 11. **Budget:** NZ$5,600,000. **Publication:** *New Zealand Nursing Journal*, 11/year. **Formed by Merger of:** New Zealand Nurses Association (NZNA).

NICARAGUA MEDICAL AID (NMA)
2560 9th St., Ste. 213 B
Berkeley, CA 94709
Dr. Paul Kranz, Exec.Dir.
PH: (510)841-1644
FX: (510)644-2923
Description: Supports community-based health care organiza-

tions in Nicaragua. Provides medical supplies and equipment for primary and preventative care; promotes accessiblity of quality health care to the Nicaraguan poor. Convention/Meeting: none. **Founded:** 1986. **Membership:** 10000. **Staff:** 1. Multinational. **Languages:** English, Spanish. **Budget:** $250,000. **Publication:** Brochure.

NIGHTINGALE RESEARCH FOUNDATION (NRF)
383 Danforth Ave.
Ottawa, ON, Canada K2A 0E1
Byron M. Hyde, M.D., Chm.
Description: Individuals with Myalgic Encephalomyelitis (Chronic Fatigue Syndrome); health care providers and medical researchers with an interest in non-HIV acquired immune deficiency syndromes. Seeks to advance scientific knowledge of the causes of non-HIV immune deficiency syndromes, and to develop more effective treatments for these diseases. Conducts research and educational programs for the public, health care professionals, and medical researchers; sponsors fundraising activities. **Founded:** 1988. **Membership:** 8000. **Languages:** English, French. **Publication:** *Nightingale*, annual. Newsletter. Advertising: accepted ▪ Booklets ▪ Brochure.

NIGHTINGALE RESEARCH FOUNDATION - UNITED KINGDOM (NRFUK)
12 Copper Gate Close
Nafferton
Driffield, Northd. YO25 0LX, England
Description: Individuals with Myalgic Encephalomyelitis (Chronic Fatigue Syndrome); health care providers and medical researchers with an interest in non-HIV acquired immune deficiency syndromes. Seeks to advance scientific knowledge of the causes of non-HIV immune deficiency syndromes, and to develop more effective treatments for these diseases. Conducts research and educational programs for the public, health care professionals, and medical researchers; sponsors fundraising activities. **Languages:** English.

NONPRESCRIPTION DRUG MANUFACTURERS ASSOCIATION (NDMA)
1150 Connecticut Ave. NW
Washington, DC 20036
James D. Cope, Pres.
PH: (202)429-9260
Description: Marketers (70) of nonprescription drugs, which are packaged, over-the-counter medicines; associate members (150) include suppliers, advertising agencies, and advertising media. Obtains and disseminates business, legislative, regulatory, and scientific information; conducts voluntary labeling review service to assist members in complying with laws and regulations. **Founded:** 1881. **Membership:** 225. **Staff:** 40. **Languages:** English. **Budget:** $7,000,000. **Publication:** *Compilation of Laws Affecting Nonprescription Drug and Allied Industries*, annual. Booklets. 3 volume set ▪ *Compilation of OTC Drug Regulations*, quarterly. Advertising: not accepted ▪ *Executive Newsletter*, biweekly ▪ *State Legislative News Bulletin*, periodic ▪ *Who's Who in the Nonprescription Drug Industry*, annual. Directory ▪ Pamphlets. Subjects include self-medication and the safe use of over-the-counter medications. **Formerly:** (1989) The Proprietary Association.

NORDIC FEDERATION OF HEART AND LUNG ASSOCIATIONS (NHL)
Box 9090
S-102 72 Stockholm, Sweden
Bo Mansson, Sec.Gen.
PH: 46 8 6169300
FX: 46 8 6682385
Description: Lung and heart disease specialists in 5 countries. Addresses medical issues in the context of social welfare. Engages in political activities; operates vocational and training centers. **Founded:** 1948. **Membership:** 130000. Multinational. **Regional Groups:** 126. **Languages:** Danish, Finnish. **Publication:** *BM-Bladet* (in Danish), monthly ▪ *Silmu* (in Finnish), monthly ▪

Status (in Swedish), monthly ■ *Trygd og Arbeid* (in Norwegian), monthly.

NORDIC FEDERATION FOR MEDICAL EDUCATION (NFME)
(Nordisk Federation for Medicinsk Undervisning)
e-mail: nofenfme@inet.uni-c.dk
Rigshospitalet
Tagensvej 18
DK-2200 Copenhagen, Denmark
Jorgen Nystrup, M.D., Sec.Gen.
PH: 45 35375252
FX: 45 31357043
Description: Organizations in 5 countries involved in medical education. Promotes medical education in the Nordic countries; encourages Nordic cooperation. Sponsors teacher-training program and quarterly symposia. **Founded:** 1966. **Membership:** 92. **Staff:** 2. Multinational. **Languages:** Danish, English. **Budget:** 744,000 DKr. **Publication:** *NFMU NYTT* (in English and Swedish), 3-4/year. Newsletter. Advertising: not accepted ■ Articles ■ Reports.

NORDIC INSTITUTE FOR ADVANCED TRAINING IN OCCUPATIONAL HEALTH (NIATOH)
(Nordisk Arbetsmiljoutbildning)
e-mail: niva@occuphealth.fi
url: http://www.occuphealth.fi/eng/dept/niva
Topeliuksenkatu 41 A
FIN-00250 Helsinki, Finland
Guy Ahonen, Ph.D., Dir.
PH: 358 9 47471
FX: 358 9 4747497
Description: Occupational health service personnel, doctoral students, researchers, and other interested individuals. Provides refresher courses in occupational health. **Founded:** 1982. **Staff:** 3. Multinational. **Languages:** English, Finnish. **For-Profit. Budget:** FM 3,000,000. **Publication:** Catalog (in English), annual. Price: free. Advertising: not accepted. **Formerly:** (1989) Nordic Institute of Advanced Occupational Environment Studies.

NORDIC INSTITUTE FOR THEORETICAL PHYSICS (NITP)
(Nordisk Institut for Teoretisk Fysik)
e-mail: nordita@nordita.dk
url: http://www.nordita.dk/
Blegdamsvej 17
DK-2100 Copenhagen, Denmark
Prof. Paul Hoyer, Dir.
PH: 45 35325500
FX: 45 35389157
Description: Representatives of Denmark, Finland, Iceland, Norway, and Sweden. Promotes cooperation among research institutes in Nordic countries. Sponsors research in the areas of nuclear physics, high energy physics, astrophysics, and solid state physics. Conducts training of young physicists. Awards fellowships to physicists from member countries. **Founded:** 1957. Multinational. **Budget:** 16,000,000 DKr. **Publication:** *Annual Report* ■ *NORDITA Preprint* (in English), 80/year.

NORTH AMERICAN CLINICAL DERMATOLOGIC SOCIETY (NACDS)
Mayo Clinic
4500 San Pablo Rd.
Jacksonville, FL 32224
John W. White, Jr.,MD, Sec.Gen.
PH: (904)953-2219
FX: (904)953-2005
Description: Dermatologists practicing primarily in the U.S. and Canada and leaders of dermatology throughout the world. Promotes the interchange of information and research. **Founded:** 1959. **Membership:** 210. Multinational. **Languages:** English. **Budget:** $200,000.

NORTH AMERICAN MENOPAUSE SOCIETY (NAMS)
e-mail: nams@apk.net
url: http://www.menopause.org
Department of OB/GYN
11100 Euclid
Cleveland, OH 44106
Wulf H. Utian, M.D., Exec. Dir.
PH: (216)844-8748
FX: (216)844-8708
Description: Physicians, scientists, research and clinical personnel, and other health care professionals are active members; student or physicians serving residencies or fellowships are associate members. Promotes the study of the climacteric in men and women. Advances the exchange of research plans and experience between members. Offers educational programs. **Founded:** 1989. **Membership:** 1900. **Staff:** 3. Multinational. **Languages:** English.

NORTH AMERICAN NURSING DIAGNOSIS ASSOCIATION (NANDA)
e-mail: nanda@nyrsecominc.com
1211 Locust St.
Philadelphia, PA 19107
Dorothy Jones, RN, Pres.
PH: (215)545-8105
TF: 800647-9002
FX: (215)545-8107
Description: Registered nurses; individuals interested in nursing diagnosis. Purpose is to develop, refine, and promote a taxonomy of diagnostic terminology for use by professional nurses. **Founded:** 1972. **Membership:** 1000. Multinational. **Regional Groups:** 7. **Languages:** Chinese, French. **Budget:** $250,000.

NORTH AMERICAN SKULL BASE SOCIETY (NASBS)
4815 Rugby Ave., Ste. 203
Bethesda, MD 20814
Lawrence H. Leung, Exec.Dir.
PH: (301)654-6802
FX: (301)718-8692
Description: Neurosurgeons, otolaryngologists, and others with an interest in diseases associated with the skull base. Promotes advancement of medical practice relating to diseases of the skull base. Conducts continuing professional education programs. **Founded:** 1989. **Membership:** 500. **Staff:** 2. **Languages:** English. **Budget:** $250,000.

NORTH AMERICAN SOCIETY OF PACING AND ELECTROPHYSIOLOGY (NASPE)
e-mail: info@naspe.org
url: http://www.naspe.org
2 Vision Dr.
Natick, MA 01760-2059
Carol J. McGlinchey, Exec.Dir.
PH: (508)647-0100
FX: (508)647-0124
Description: Physicians, scientists, and allied professionals throughout the world dedicated to the study and management or cardiac arrhythmias; to improve the care of patients by promoting research, education and training, and providing leadership towards optimal health care policies and standards. **Founded:** 1979. **Membership:** 2600. **Staff:** 29. Multinational. **Languages:** English. **Budget:** $4,000,000.

NORTH AMERICAN SPINE SOCIETY (NASS)
url: http://www.spine.org
6300 N. River Rd., Ste. 500
Rosemont, IL 60018-4231
Eric J. Muehlbauer, Exec.Dir.
PH: (847)698-1630
FX: (847)823-8668
Description: Educational organization of physicians, osteopaths, orthopedists, neurosurgeons, physiatrists, radiologists, and other professionals interested in the human spine. Works to improve the quality of scientific practice in spinal disorders; exchange ideas and disseminate scientific information about clinical tech-

niques; investigate and propagate methods by which malfunction of the spine can be corrected. Makes inquiries into practice characteristics, language usage and terminology, and treatment methods. **Founded:** 1985. **Membership:** 1750. **Staff:** 9. Multinational. **Languages:** English. **Budget:** $1,900,000. **Publication:** *Contemporary Concepts in Spine Care* ▪ *NASS News*, quarterly. Newsletter. Contains news on association activities. Price: included in membership dues. Circulation: 4,000. Alternate Formats: online. **Formed by Merger of:** American College of Spine Surgeons; North American Lumbar Spine Association.

NORTHERN IRELAND ASSOCIATION FOR MENTAL HEALTH
80 University St.
Belfast, Antrim BT7 1HE, Northern Ireland
Pauline Rainey, Education Ofcr.
PH: 44 1232 328474
FX: 44 1232 234940
Description: Promotes dignity, choice, integration and participation for those with mental health needs living in the community. Aims to offer services of the highest standard to people with mental health needs; inform and educate the public about mental health; and press for high standards in the provision of mental health services. **Founded:** 1959. **Membership:** 280. **Staff:** 145. **Local Groups:** 32. **Publication:** *Mental Health Matters* (in English), quarterly. Price: free. ISSN: 0963-0201. Circulation: 1,500. Advertising: accepted.

NORWEGIAN ASSOCIATION FOR CHILDREN AND ADULTS WITH MINIMAL BRAIN DYSFUNCTION
(MBD-foreningen)
e-mail: mbd-for@online.no
Alexandragarden
Arnstein Arnebergsv 30
N-1324 Lysaker, Norway
Brita Drabitzius, Sec.
PH: 47 67583757
FX: 47 67583747
Description: Parents of children with Minimal Brain Dysfunction; health personnel. Acts as support group. **Founded:** 1979. **Membership:** 2500. **Staff:** 2. **Local Groups:** 18. **Languages:** English, Norwegian. **Budget:** 2,100,000 NKr. **Publication:** *Artikkelsamling om MBD.* Book ▪ *Ett Oyeblikk* ▪ *Sta Pa* (in Norwegian), quarterly, always March, June, July, and December. Magazine. Price: 100.00 NKr. Advertising: accepted.

NORWEGIAN ASSOCIATION FOR CLASSICAL ACUPUNCTURE (NFKA)
(Norsk Forening for Klassisk Akupunktur)
e-mail: nkfa@akupunktur.no
Munchsgate 7
N-0165 Oslo, Norway
Bernt Rognlien, Pres.
PH: 47 22361774
FX: 47 22361853
Description: Doctors, nurses, dentists, and physiotherapists; students. Encourages the practice of acupuncture in Norway. Operates training institute for members. Conducts educational programs. **Founded:** 1978. **Membership:** 210. **Staff:** 2. **Languages:** English, Norwegian. **Publication:** *DE Qi-Tidsskrift for Kinesisk Medisin* (in Norwegian), 3/year. Journal. Includes information on acupuncture and Chinese medicine. Price: 250.00 NKr. Advertising: accepted ▪ Brochure, periodic.

NORWEGIAN ASSOCIATION FOR HUNTINGTON'S DISEASE (NAHD)
(Landsforening for Huntingtons Sykdom)
Jerpeleina 30
N-1415 Oppegard, Norway
Sigrun Rosenlund, Exec. Officer
PH: 47 66991496
Description: Persons with Huntington's chorea and their families. Conducts seminars. **Founded:** 1980. **Membership:** 350. **Local Groups:** 7. **Languages:** English, Norwegian. **Publication:**

Tidsskrift for Huntingtons Sykdom (in Norwegian), 3/year. Magazine. Also Cited As: *THS.*

NORWEGIAN ASSOCIATION OF MIDWIVES
Tollbugt. 35
N-0157 Oslo, Norway
Description: Promotes the practice of midwifery, and works to maintain high standards in the field. Conducts research and educational programs. **Languages:** Dutch, English.

NORWEGIAN BIOCHEMICAL SOCIETY (NBS)
(Norsk Biokjemisk Selskap)
e-mail: knut-jan.andersen@meda.uib.no
url: http://www.no.embnnet.org/NBS/nbsnytt-tp.html
PO Box 7
Haukeland Sykehus Postkontor
N-5022 Bergen, Norway
Dr. Knut-Jan Andersen, Sec.Gen.
PH: 47 55973054
FX: 47 55972950
Description: Biochemistry students, scientists, and companies. Promotes research and education in biochemistry. Sponsors symposia and lecture series. **Founded:** 1968. **Membership:** 1500. **Local Groups:** 5. **Languages:** English, Norwegian. **Budget:** 250,000 NKr. **Publication:** *NBSnytt* (in Norwegian), quarterly. Magazine. ISSN: 0801-3535. Advertising: accepted ▪ *Newsletter*, periodic.

NORWEGIAN CANCER REGISTRY (NCR)
Montebello
N-0310 Oslo, Norway
PH: 47 22451300
FX: 47 22451370
Description: National cancer registries. Promotes availability of data on cancer patients; seeks to advance the prevention, diagnosis, and treatment of cancer. Serves as a clearinghouse on cancer and its treatment; sponsors health screenings and other services; conducts research. **Languages:** English, Norwegian.

NORWEGIAN DERMATOLOGICAL SOCIETY (NDS)
(Norsk Dermatologisk Selskap)
e-mail: jolangel@sn.no
Rikshospitalet, Hudavd.
N-0027 Oslo, Norway
Dr. Jon Langeland, Contact
PH: 47 2 868411
FX: 47 2 868433
Description: Dermatologists and residents in dermatology. Promotes the advancement of dermatology in Norway; represents members' interests. Offers courses for pre- and postgraduates in dermatology. **Founded:** 1914. **Membership:** 163. **Staff:** 1. **Languages:** English, Norwegian.

NORWEGIAN DIABETES ASSOCIATION (NDF)
(Norges Diabetesforbund)
e-mail: norges.diabetesforbund@online.no
url: http://home.sol.no/~naf/
Postboks 6442
Etterstad
N-0605 Oslo, Norway
Bjornar Allgot, Sec.Gen.
PH: 47 23 051800
FX: 47 23 051801
Description: Diabetics and their families; health personnel. Acts as support group. Disseminates information on availability of insulin, diabetes products, and health care. Lobbies the government to incorporate diabetes treatment into national health care plans and to provide free insulin, syringes, and urine and blood glucose strips. Provides research and medical services. Offers educational courses; conducts camps; maintains youth club. **Founded:** 1948. **Membership:** 25000. **Staff:** 17. **National Groups:** 5. **Languages:** English. **Budget:** 18,900,000 NKr. **Publication:** *Diabetikeren* (in Norwegian), bimonthly. Magazine. Features educational material. Includes Annual medical supplement. Price: included in membership dues; 290.00 NKr nonmembers. Circula-

tion: 26,000. Advertising: accepted. Also Cited As: Norwegian Diabetic Journal ∎ Booklets.

NORWEGIAN EPILEPSY ASSOCIATION (NEA)
(Norsk Epilepsiforbund)
Storgaten 39
N-0182 Oslo, Norway
Lise Soether, Consultant
PH: 47 22206021
FX: 47 22115976
Description: Disseminates information to individuals with epilepsy and their families, health care centers, hospitals, and schools. Collaborates with related groups. **Founded:** 1974. **Membership:** 4800. **Staff:** 5. **Local Groups:** 39. **Languages:** English, Norwegian. **Budget:** 2,500,000 NKr. **Publication:** *Epilepsy News* (in Norwegian), quarterly. Magazine. Price: included in membership dues. Advertising: accepted. Alternate Formats: magnetic tape.

NORWEGIAN FIBROMYALGIA PATIENTS' ASSOCIATION
(NFP)
(Norges Fibromyalgi Forbund)
Oksenoeystien 4
N-1324 Lysaker, Norway
Kari Toftoy-Andersen, Chm.
PH: 47 67583067
FX: 47 67583158
Description: Persons in Norway suffering from fibrositis or fibromyalgia (rheumatic disorders involving fibrous tissues). Funds research into the cause and cure of fibrositis or fibromyalgia. Promotes understanding of the disease; disseminates information. Conducts educational programs. **Founded:** 1985. **Membership:** 8000. **Staff:** 2. **Local Groups:** 67. **Languages:** English, Norwegian. **Budget:** 3,300,000 NKr. **Publication:** *Fibromyalgi* (in Norwegian), quarterly. Magazine. Price: 200.00 NKr/year. Advertising: accepted. **Formerly:** Norges Fibromyalgi Forbund.

NORWEGIAN IMMUNE DEFICIENCY FOUNDATION
(NIDF)
(Norsk Immunsviktforening)
e-mail: evabrox@online.no
Brunholmgt. 3A
N-6004 Alesund, Norway
Eva Brox, Pres.
PH: 47 71 28388
FX: 47 71 28388
Description: Persons with primary immunological disorders and their families; private companies. Acts as support group. Disseminates information. **Founded:** 1983. **Membership:** 120. **National Groups:** 1. **Languages:** Norwegian. **Budget:** 200,000 NKr. **Publication:** *Immunsvikt hos Voksne og Barn* (in Norwegian), periodic.

THE NORWEGIAN MULTIPLE SCLEROSIS SOCIETY
(NMSS)
(Multipel Sklerose Forbundet i Norge)
url: http://mcs.no/ms
Sorkedalsveien 3
N-0369 Oslo, Norway
Mrs. Gerd Hagen, Contact
PH: 47 22 604960
FX: 47 22 567695
Description: Promotes interest in multiple sclerosis research among medical and scientific communities and the public in Norway. Facilitates exchange of information among members. **Founded:** 1961. **Membership:** 4100. **Staff:** 4. **Regional Groups:** 45. **Languages:** English. **Publication:** *MS-bladet* (in Norwegian), 5/year. Magazine. Price: 100.00 NKr/year. Advertising: accepted ∎ Books ∎ Pamphlets.

NORWEGIAN PARKINSON ASSOCIATION (NPA)
(Norges Parkinsonforbund)
Schweigaardsgt 34, F.2
N-0191 Oslo, Norway
Frank Marring, Pres.
PH: 47 22 175861
FX: 47 22 175862
Description: Parkinson patients and their relatives. Teaches patients about their disease and how to deal with the related problems. Represents members' interests in matters of social and health politics. Supports research efforts; conducts educational seminars. Offers lectures. **Founded:** 1984. **Membership:** 4000. **Staff:** 1. **National Groups:** 1. **Languages:** English. **Budget:** 895,000 NKr. **Publication:** *Ergoterapy*. Booklet. Advertising: not accepted ∎ *Hjemmeovelser*. Booklet ∎ *Hva er NPF?*. Also Cited As: *What is NPF?* ∎ *Informasjon om Fylkesforeninger*. Also Cited As: *Information About Country Vacanches* ∎ *Parkinsonposten* (in Norwegian), quarterly. Newsletter. Advertising: accepted ∎ *Parkinsons Disease and the treatment*. ∎ *Parkinsons Sykdom*. Booklet. Also Cited As: Parkinsons Disease ∎ *Parkinsons Sykdom og Behandlingen au den*.

NORWEGIAN PHYSICAL SOCIETY
e-mail: tove.svendby@fys.uio.no
url: http://www.fys.vio.no/~tovesv/hfseng.htm
Dept. of Physics
University Of Oslo
PO Box 1048
N-0316 Oslo, Norway
Thormod Henriksen, Pres.
PH: 47 22 855641
FX: 47 22 855671
Description: Physicists, physics teachers, and others with an interest in the physical sciences. Seeks to improve the quality of physics education, research, and knowledge. **Founded:** 1953. **Membership:** 900. **Languages:** English, Norwegian. **Publication:** *FRA Fysikkens Verden* (in Norwegian), quarterly. Newsletter. Price: included in membership dues; 100.00 NKr.

NSF INTERNATIONAL
e-mail: info@nsf.org
url: http://www.nsf.org
3475 Plymouth Rd.
PO Box 130140
Ann Arbor, MI 48105
Dr. Dennis Mangino, Pres. & CEO
PH: (734)769-8010
TF: 800673-6275
FX: (734)769-0109
Description: Specializes in the areas of public health and environmental quality focusing on water quality, food safety, indoor air health and the environment. Develops standards, operates product certification and listings programs for products that meet or exceed public health safety standards. Maintains a worldwide network of auditors who conduct unannounced inspections of manufacturer facilities to ensure compliance and to protect the integrity of the NSF Certification Mark. Provides special research and testing services to industry, government, and foundations. **Founded:** 1944. **Membership:** 2000. **Staff:** 230. Multinational. **Languages:** English. **Formerly** (1993) National Sanitation Foundation.

NURSES ASSOCIATION OF JAMAICA (NAJ)
Mary Seacole Annex 4
Trevennion Park Rd.
Kingston 5, Jamaica
Description: Nurses, nursing students, and educators. Promotes professional recognition of members. Maintains standards of nursing education and practice. **Founded:** 1946. **Languages:** English. **Formerly:** (1951) Jamaica General Trained Nurses Association.

NURSES EDUCATIONAL FUNDS (NEF)
555 W. 57th St., 13th Fl., Ste. 1327
New York, NY 10019
Barbara Butler, Scholarship Coord.
PH: (212)399-1428
FX: (212)586-5462
Description: Seeks to establish, maintain, and administer funds to provide financial assistance to registered nurses studying for advanced degrees; masters/doctoral level only formulate policies for the administration of such funds; collect and manage all funds contributed to it. Masters study must be full-time only GRE/or MAT scores are required. **Founded:** 1954. **Membership:** 30. **Staff:** 1. **Languages:** English. **Budget:** $120,000. Formerly (1954) Isabel Hampton Robb Memorial Fund.

NURSES' HOUSE
2113 Western Ave., Ste. 2
Guilderland, NY 12084-9501
Patricia B. Barry, Exec.Dir.
Description: Registered nurses and interested individuals united to assist registered nurses in financial and other crises. Provides short-term financial aid for shelter, food, and utilities until nurses obtain entitlements or jobs. Offers counseling and referrals. Encourages homebound or retired nurses through a volunteer corps. Participates in the American Nurses Association and the National League for Nursing conventions. Convention/Meeting: none. **Founded:** 1925. **Membership:** 1100. **Staff:** 1. **Regional Groups:** 6. **Languages:** English. **Budget:** $163,500.

NURSES ORGANIZATION OF VETERANS AFFAIRS (NOVA)
e-mail: nova@nanurse.org
1726 M St. NW, Ste. 1101
Washington, DC 20036
Deborah Beck, Exec.Dir.
PH: (202)296-0888
FX: (202)833-1577
Description: Voluntary, nonprofit professional society of Department of Veterans Affairs registered nurses. Objective is to provide VA nurses with the opportunity to preserve and improve quality care and professionalism through legislative influence. Conducts competitions, seminars, and educational programs. **Founded:** 1980. **Membership:** 2782. **Staff:** 3. **Regional Groups:** 99. **Languages:** English, Spanish. **Budget:** $250. Formerly (1989) Nurses Organization of the Veterans Administration.

OBSESSIVE-COMPULSIVE ANONYMOUS (OCA)
PO Box 215
New Hyde Park, NY 11040
Roy C., Contact
PH: (516)741-4901
FX: (212)768-4679
Description: Individuals suffering from obsessive-compulsive disorders. (OCD is characterized by recurrent unpleasant thoughts and/or repetitive, irrational mannerisms the sufferer feels compelled to perform.) Follows the 12-step method originated by Alcoholics Anonymous World Services to assist members in their recovery. **Founded:** 1988. **Membership:** 1000. **Staff:** 7. **Regional Groups:** 45. **Languages:** English.

OBSESSIVE-COMPULSIVE FOUNDATION (OCF)
e-mail: info@ocfoundation.org
url: http://pages.prodigy.com/alwillen/ocf.html
PO Box 70
Milford, CT 06460-0070
James W. Broatch, Exec.Dir.
PH: (203)878-5669
FX: (203)874-2826
Description: Individuals with obsessive-compulsive disorders and their families and friends; professionals involved in the treatment of OCD. (OCD is often chronic and characterized by recurrent unpleasant thoughts and/or repetitive behaviors that the person feels driven to perform. Individuals with OCD realize their obsessions and compulsions are irrational or excessive, yet find they have no control over them. Individuals with OCD often be-

come demoralized, depressed, and anxious.) Seeks to control and find a cure for OCD while improving the welfare of its individuals with OCD. Disseminates information on OCD and possible new therapies. Offers educational programs for professionals and the public. Assists with fundraising and forming local support groups; fosters communication between members. Funds research into causes and treatments. Hosts annual membership meeting. **Founded:** 1986. **Membership:** 9400. **Staff:** 4. **State Groups:** 8. **Languages:** English. **Budget:** $900,000. Formerly (1988) Obsessive Compulsive Disorder Foundation.

OBSTETRIC ANAESTHETIST'S ASSOCIATION
Hucknall Rd.
Nottingham NG5 1PB, England
Dr. D. Bogod, Contact
PH: 44 115 9691169
FX: 44 115 9627713
Description: Anaesthetists and other medical practitioners with an interest in obstetric analgesia and anaesthesia. To promote the highest standards of care for mother and baby in every respect of anaesthetic practice. **Founded:** 1969. **Membership:** 1000. **Publication:** *International Journal of Obstetric Anaesthesia*, quarterly.

OBSTETRICAL AND GYNAECOLOGICAL SOCIETY OF HONG KONG
url: http://medicine.orghk/ogs/home.htm
Duke of Windsor Social Service Bldg., 4/F
15 Hennessy Rd.
Wanchai, Hong Kong
Dr. S.K. Lam, Sec.
PH: 852 25278898
FX: 852 28650345
Description: Obstetricians and gynecologists; medical students with an interest in the field. Seeks to advance the study and practice of obstetrics and gynecology. Conducts continuing professional development courses for members. **Founded:** 1961. **Membership:** 300. **Languages:** Chinese, English. **Publication:** Newsletter, periodic.

OBSTETRICIAN FAMILY CENTER
(Centro Obstetrico Familiar)
Pasaje Trevino 144 Y
AV. 12, De Octubre
Apartado 17-17438 CCNU
Quito, Ecuador
Dr. Orlando Batallas, Dir
PH: 593 2 226515
FX: 593 2 226515
Description: Works to increase public awareness of all aspects of sexuality and family life. Conducts educational and orientational programs for adolescents and parents on family planning, reproduction, sexuality, and family issues. Trains health care workers and family planning service providers. Investigates relevant topics and disseminates information. **Founded:** 1984. **Membership:** 56. **Staff:** 54. **Languages:** Spanish. **Budget:** $250,000. **Publication:** *Informe Anual* (in Spanish), annual. Price: free. Circulation: 500. Advertising: not accepted ■ *Manual Metodos Anticonceptivos* ■ *Revista Boletin Informativo Bi Mensual* (in Spanish). Price: free. Circulation: 500.

ODPHP NATIONAL HEALTH INFORMATION CENTER (NHIC)
e-mail: nhicinfo@health.org
url: http://www.nhic-nt.health.org
PO Box 1133
Washington, DC 20013-1133
Jill Herzog, Dir.
PH: (301)565-4167
TF: 800336-4797
FX: (301)984-4256
Description: A referral service to aid consumers and health professionals in locating health information. Funded by the Office of Disease Prevention and Health Promotion, Public Health Serv-

ice, U.S. Department of Health and Human Services. Convention/Meeting: none. **Founded:** 1979. **Staff:** 10. **Languages:** Spanish. **Publication:** *National Health Observances Planner*, annual ■ *Prevention Report*, quarterly. Newsletter. **Formerly:** (1986) National Health Information Clearinghouse; (1987) ODPHP Health Information Center.

OFFICE OF HEALTH ECONOMICS
12 Whitehall
London SW1A 2DY, England
Elizabeth Aulsford, Sec.
PH: 44 171 9309203
FX: 44 171 7471419
Description: Undertakes research on the economic aspects of medical care, with particular reference to the pharmaceutical industry. **Founded:** 1962. **Staff:** 7. **Publication:** Papers.

OMICRON KAPPA UPSILON
Coll. of Dentistry
University of Nebraska
40th & Hodrege
Lincoln, NE 68583-0740
Jan John, Sec.
PH: (402)472-1339
FX: (402)472-5290
Description: Honorary society of men and women in the field of dentistry. **Founded:** 1914. **Membership:** 17500. **Languages:** English. **Publication:** Bulletin, annual.

ONCOLOGY NURSING SOCIETY (ONS)
e-mail: member@ons.org
url: http://www.ons.org
501 Holiday Dr.
Pittsburgh, PA 15220
Pearl Moore, Exec.Dir.
PH: (412)921-7373
FX: (412)921-6565
Description: Registered nurses interested in oncology. Seeks to: promote high professional standards in oncology nursing; provide a network for the exchange of information, resources, and peer support; encourage nurses to specialize in oncology; promote and develop educational programs in oncology nursing extending through the graduate level; identify, encourage, and foster nursing research in improving the quality of patient care. Conducts instructional and abstract sessions. Compiles statistics. **Founded:** 1975. **Membership:** 25000. **Staff:** 75. **Local Groups:** 195. **Languages:** English. **Budget:** $6,600,000.

OPERATION SMILE INTERNATIONAL (OSI)
url: http://www.operationsmile.org
220 Boush St.
Norfolk, VA 23510
Thomas Fox, Ph.D, CEO
PH: (757)321-7645
TF: 888OPSMILE
FX: (757)321-3201
Description: Provides reconstructive surgery and quality health care to individuals from Third World countries and in the United States. Sponsors the World Care Program, which allows children and adults with severe deformities to reside with an American host family while awaiting reconstructive surgery in the U.S. Also sponsors the Operation Happy Clubs, an organization run by students across the nation, that raises funds and holds special activities for needy children in the U.S. and abroad. Conducts annual medical mission in 11 countries: the Philippines, China, Nicaragua, Venezuela, Kenya, Panama, Russia, Romania, Colombia, Vietnam, and the Middle East. Maintains speakers' bureau; conducts research programs. **Founded:** 1982. **Staff:** 5. Multinational. **Languages:** English. **Publication:** *Operation Smile Newsletter*, quarterly. **Formerly:** (1993) Operation Smile.

OPERATION SMILE INTERNATIONAL - VIETNAM (OSIV)
1 Tran Hung Dao
Hanoi, Vietnam

PH: 84 4 254627
Description: Reconstructive surgeons and other health care professionals. Seeks to increase the availability of cosmetic and reconstructive surgery among impoverished children. Performs free reconstructive surgery on needy children; conducts training programs for surgeons; distributes medical equipment and supplies to indigenous health care centers. **Languages:** English, French.

OPERATION U.S.A. (OPUSA)
e-mail: opusa@lafn.org
url: http://opusa.org
8320 Melrose Ave., No. 200
Los Angeles, CA 90069
Richard Walden, Pres. & Founder
PH: (213)658-8876
TF: 800678-7255
FX: (213)653-7846
Description: Provides relief aid to crisis areas in the U.S. and worldwide; makes available financial and material support and technical to clinics, hospitals, and orphanages. Maintains speakers' bureau. **Founded:** 1979. **Staff:** 10. Multinational. **Languages:** French, Spanish. **Budget:** $1,100,000. **Publication:** *OP USA Newsletter*, semiannual. Price: free. Circulation: 11,000. Advertising: not accepted. **Formerly:** (1988) Operation California.

OPHTHALMIC PHOTOGRAPHERS' SOCIETY (OPS)
e-mail: opsmember@aol.com
url: http://www.webeye.ophth.uiowa.edu/ops
213 Lorene St.
Nixa, MO 65714-9230
Lawrence M. Merin, RBP, Pres.
PH: (417)725-0181
TF: 800403-1677
FX: (417)724-8450
Description: Ophthalmologists, pathologists, medical and ophthalmic photographers, nurses, ophthalmic assistants, technicians, technologists, researchers, and engineers; organizations and individuals who are actively involved with ophthalmology or ophthalmic photography. Objective is to encourage the highest quality of ophthalmic photography and to promote development of new and improved techniques and equipment. (Ophthalmic photography involves photography of the eye for documentation and diagnostic purposes.) Provides continuing education and technical information. Serves as a forum for the discussion of ophthalmic photography. Provides testing, and subsequent certification as Certified Retinal Angiographer in performance of ophthalmic photography. **Founded:** 1969. **Membership:** 1200. **Staff:** 1. Multinational. **Regional Groups:** 9. **Languages:** English. **Budget:** $250,000.

OPTIONS SERVICE OF PROJECT CONCERN (OSPC)
3550 Afton Rd.
San Diego, CA 92123
Patricia Brown, Options Prog. Mgr.
PH: (619)279-6990
FX: (619)694-0294
Description: Nonsectarian, nonpolitical agency serving worldwide areas of health care shortage. Functions in volunteer matching health care and development personnel with domestic and overseas clinics, hospitals, and agencies where their services are needed. Assignments are volunteer as well as stipend by the participatingprograms. 95% of the voluntary assignments offer room, board. Long-term assignments sometimes offer subsistence allowance. Recruits health care personnel through medicine magazines and other sources. **Founded:** 1966. **Staff:** 2. **Languages:** English. **Publication:** *OPTIONS*, bimonthly. Newsletter. Lists volunteer opportunities in areas in need of health professionals, especially rural America and the developing countries. Advertising: accepted. **Also Known As:** Options. **Formerly:** (1972) American Doctors; (1973) AmDoc; (1976) Options/ AmDoc.

ORAL HEALTH AMERICA
410 N. Michigan Ave., Ste. 352
Chicago, IL 60611-4211
Robert J. Klaus, Pres. & CEO
PH: (312)836-9900
TF: 800523-3438
FX: (312)836-9986
Description: Funds dental education, research, and service programs. Operates speakers' bureau. **Founded:** 1955. **Staff:** 7. **Languages:** English. **Budget:** $3,500,000. **Publication:** *Oral Health 2000 News*, quarterly ▪ *Programs and Priorities*, periodic ▪ Annual Report. **Formerly:** (1963) Fund for Dental Education; (1973) American Fund for Dental Education; (1998) American Fund for Dental Health.

ORBIS INTERNATIONAL
url: http://www.orbis.org
330 W. 42nd St., Ste. 1900
New York, NY 10036
Pina Taormina, Pres. and Exec.Dir.
PH: (212)244-2525
TF: 800ORBIS-US
FX: (212)244-2744
Description: Dedicated to fighting blindness worldwide through medical education and hands-on training for ophthalmologists, nurses, anesthesiologists, biomedical technicians, and community health care workers. Conducts programs in local hospitals and in ORBIS, a DC-10 jet converted into a fully equipped eye surgery hospital and teaching facility. (Visiting faculty members join ORBIS's 25-member team of healthcare professionals to demonstrate their subspecialties and share their skills with their host-country colleagues.) Offers programs without the plane in surgery, nursing, technical services, and community health. **Founded:** 1973. **Staff:** 100. Multinational. **Languages:** English. **Budget:** $9,700,000. Formerly Project Orbis.

ORGANISATION GESTOSIS - SOCIETY FOR THE STUDY OF PATHOPHYSIOLOGY OF PREGNANCY (OG)
(Geburtshilfe und Gynakologie FMH)
Geburtshilfe und Gynakologie FMH
Gerbergasse 14
CH-4051 Basel, Switzerland
PD Ernest T. Rippmann, Sec.Gen.
PH: 41 61 2615555
FX: 41 61 2615934
Description: Obstetricians, gynecologists, neonatologists, nephrologists, epidemiologists, pathologists, geneticists, immunologists, physiologists, and health officials in 75 countries in the field of EPH-Gestosis. EPH-Gestosis is a term adopted by the society to describe a malady that may occur during pregnancy wherein a woman exhibits excessive accumulation of body water, protein in the urine, and/or abnormal elevation of blood pressure; EPH is derived from the terms for 3 conditions: edema, proteinuria, and hypertension; gestosis is derived from the word gestation and the suffix - osis which means disturbance. The condition is prevalent in socioeconomically depressed areas where poor hygiene and malnutrition aggravate the effects of inadeq uate prenatal care. The society reports that EPH-Gestosis occurs in 10% of world population births, is responsible for as much as 50% of perinatal/fetal death, and is the cause of up to 33% of maternal mortality. Objectives are to: disseminate information to medical and lay personnel and the public; foster research, preventive health care, and therapy; internationalize nomenclature, classification, and definitions in the field of EPH-Gestosis for diagnosis, therapy, and comparative techniques; standardize methods of investigation; serve as documentation center; foster exchange of scientists. Conducts discussion groups and study groups on topics such as edema, proteinuria, cytology, serumprotein, and hypertension. Suggests alterations of definitions of E-PH-Gestosis as offered by International Classification of Diseases of the World Health Organization. Makes recommendations for the most modern and successful measures of prevention and treatment of EPH-Gestosis. Collects and publishes papers submitted by researchers worldwide. Sponsors symposia and work-

shops; conducts surveys. Operates Organisation Gestosis Press, a publishing house. **Founded:** 1969. **Membership:** 4500. Multinational. **Regional Groups:** 11. **Languages:** English, German. **Publication:** *Congress Volume*, annual ▪ *Instruction Bulletin*, periodic ▪ *International Journal of Feto-Maternal Medicine*, periodic ▪ *La Malformazioni Uterine* (in Italian). Book. Price: 50,000.00 Lr; 50.00 SFr; $40.00 ▪ *OG News*, periodic ▪ Proceedings. **Also Known As:** Society for the Study of Pathophysiology of Pregnancy.

ORGANISATION MONDIALE DE LA SANTE - CONGO
BP 6
Brazzaville, Congo
Dr. Ebrahim Malick Samba
PH: 242 83 3860
FX: 242 83 9400
Description: Promotes health and nutrition in the Congo. Provides educational programs. Monitors healthcare programs. Conducts research. **Languages:** English, French.

ORGANISATION OF PHARMACEUTICAL PRODUCERS OF INDIA (OPPI)
Cook's Bldg., 1st Fl.
324 Dr. Dadabhoy Naoroji Rd.
Bombay 400 001, Maharashtra, India
R.D. Joshi, Sec.Gen.
PH: 91 22 2045509
FX: 91 22 2044705
Description: Manufacturers of pharmaceuticals and related products. Seeks to "ensure a healthy environment for profitable growth while making a contribution to the healthcare aims of the nation." Represents the collective interests of members; conducts educational and charitable programs; compiles industry statistics. **Founded:** 1965. **Membership:** 68. **Staff:** 18. **Languages:** English, Hindi. **Budget:** Rs 70. **Publication:** Directory, periodic.

ORGANIZATION FOR COORDINATION AND COOPERATION IN THE STRUGGLE AGAINST ENDEMIC DISEASES -BURKINA FASO (OCCSED)
(Organisation de Coordination et de Cooperation pour la Lutte Contre les Grandes Endemies)
01 Boite Postale 153
Bobo-Dioulasso 01, Burkina Faso
Abdoulaye Rhaly, Sec.Gen.
PH: 226 970101
FX: 226 970099
Description: Health care professionals, researchers, and services. Seeks to eradicate selected contagious diseases. Conducts medical research; delivers medical services to populations prone to endemic diseases. Multinational. **Languages:** English, French.

ORGANIZATION FOR INTEGRATION OF WOMEN IN DEVELOPMENT (WID)
e-mail: alwd@Padis.gn.apc.org
PO Box 31802
Addis Ababa, Ethiopia
Alemu Hailu, Dir.
PH: 251 1 118460
FX: 251 1 551499
Description: Promotes increased availability of nutrition and family planning services. Conducts primary health care and nutrition programs, HIV/AIDS prevention programs and counseling, community based urban/rural poverty alleviation programs, child welfare, education/vocational training for youth/school dropout girls. **Founded:** 1993. **Membership:** 100. **Staff:** 13. **Languages:** English, French. **Budget:** $70,000.

ORIENTATION CENTER FOR ADOLESCENTS (OCA)
(Centro de Orientacion para Adolescentes)
Tenayuca 29
Colonia Vertiz Navarte, 03400
Apartado Postal 21-205
04021 Mexico City, DF, Mexico
Anameli Monroy, Contact

PH: 52 5 6054370
FX: 52 5 6055372
Description: Health and education professionals and youth promoters. Promotes reproductive and sexual education within an integral health context for people between the ages of 10 and 24. Conducts youth-to-youth reproductive health and sex education programs; sponsors training courses for health and education professionals. Undertakes research on adolescent health; produces educational radio and television programs; develops and distributes teaching aids. Organizes social activities for youth. **Founded:** 1978. **Staff:** 15. **Languages:** English, Spanish. **Budget:** $220,000.

**ORTHODONTIC EDUCATION AND RESEARCH
  FOUNDATION (OERF)**
3320 Rutger
St. Louis, MO 63104-1008
Peter G. Sotiropoulos, Exec.Dir.
PH: (314)577-8189
FX: (314)268-5191
Description: Orthodontists. Promotes research; conducts continuing education programs, seminars, and clinical and professional training. **Founded:** 1957. **Membership:** 500. **Staff:** 1. **Languages:** English. **Publication:** *OERF Journal*, annual. Proceedings. Includes new members listing. Price: included in membership dues. Advertising: not accepted ▪ *OERF Newsletter*, annual.

**OSTEOPATHIC COLLEGES OF OPHTHALMOLOGY AND
  OTOLARYNGOLOGY-HEAD AND NECK SURGERY
  (OCOO)**
e-mail: practicesa@aol.com
url: http://www.aocoohns.org
3 Mac Koil Ave.
Dayton, OH 45403
Sharon D. Alexiades, Contact
PH: (937)252-0868
TF: 800782-5355
FX: (937)252-0968
Description: Osteopathic physicians who have completed formal specialty training or are acquiring such training in ophthalmology, otorhinolaryngology, and facial plastic surgery, and those who are certified specialists in one or more of the above named areas. Develops application of osteopathic concepts in this specialty; determines minimum standards of education at undergraduate and postgraduate levels. Sponsors research programs. **Founded:** 1916. **Membership:** 580. **Staff:** 2. **Languages:** English. **Budget:** $250,000. Formerly Osteopathic College of Ophthalmology and Otorhinolaryngology.

**OSTERREICHISCHE GESELLSCHAFT FUR
  FAMILIENPLANUNG (OGF)**
e-mail: epracht@fem.wien.clsub.de
Ignaz-Semmelweis-Frauenklinik
Bastiengasse 36-38
A-1180 Vienna, Austria
Elisabeth Pracht, Sec.
PH: 43 1 4785242
FX: 43 1 4785242
Description: Works to improve the quality of life for individuals living in Austria by promoting family planning and responsible parenthood. Works to reduce the number of unwanted pregnancies and abortions and stop the spread of sexually transmitted diseases, especially AIDS. Provides programs in family planning, sex education, and health. Provides contraceptive services. **Founded:** 1966. **Membership:** 107. **Staff:** 6. **Languages:** German. **Budget:** 2,230,000 AS.

OUTPATIENT OPHTHALMIC SURGERY SOCIETY (OOSS)
e-mail: ooss@amainc.com
url: http://www.amainc.com/
PO Box 23220
San Diego, CA 92193
Karen Morgan, Admin.

PH: (619)692-4426
FX: (619)692-3143
Description: Ophthalmic surgeons. Purpose is to gather and share information about outpatient eye surgery in order to promote high-quality, low-cost patient care. **Founded:** 1981. **Membership:** 700. **Languages:** English.

PACIFIC DERMATOLOGIC ASSOCIATION (PDA)
e-mail: straficano@aad.org
930 N. Meacham Rd.
Schaumburg, IL 60173-6016
Sandra N. Minor, M.D., Sec.-Treas.
PH: (847)330-9830
FX: (847)330-0050
Description: Dermatologists united to provide opportunities for exchange of information and advancement of knowledge of dermatology and syphilology among physicians within the Pacific Rim. Conducts specialized education programs; sponsors competitions. **Founded:** 1948. **Membership:** 1200. **Staff:** 1. Multinational. **Regional Groups:** 1. **Languages:** English.

PACIFIC WOMEN'S TRADITIONAL MEDICINE NETWORK
Private Mail Bag
Suva, Fiji
PH: 679 313900
FX: 679 301594
Description: Women practitioners of traditional medicine in Fiji, the Cook Islands, Naura, Kiribati, Tonga, Vanuatu, Papua New Guinea, the Solomon Islands, and Tahiti. Encourages: conservation of medicinal plants and their habitats; dissemination of information on traditional healing practices; communication among members; establishment of national traditional medicine associations. Local. **Languages:** English.

**PAN-AFRICAN ASSOCIATION OF NEUROLOGICAL
  SCIENCES (PAANS)**
(Association Pan-Africaine des Sciences Neurologiques)
PO Box 20413
Nairobi, Kenya
Prof. R.F. Ruberti, Exec. Officer
PH: 254 2 722487
FX: 254 2 725776
Description: African neurologists specializing in neurosurgery, neuroradiology, neuropathology, neurophysiology, neurobiochemistry, and other branches of neuroscience; non-African neurologists maintaining connections with Africa. Furthers neurological sciences and encourages the exchange of ideas and information among neurologists in Africa and worldwide. Strives to acquaint the public and interested laymen with current developments in neuroscience. Conducts epidemiological research. **Founded:** 1972. **Membership:** 250. Multinational. **Languages:** English, French. **Publication:** *African Journal of Neurological Sciences* (in English and French), semiannual. Contains information on neurology, neurosurgery, and neuroscience. Price: $75.00/ year. Advertising: accepted ▪ *Pan African Association of Neurological Sciences Rules*.

**PAN-AMERICAN ASSOCIATION OF BIOCHEMISTRY AND
  MOLECULAR BIOLOGY (PABMB)**
e-mail: preiss@pilot.msu.edu
url: http://www.ibt.unam.mx/virtual.cgi?pabmbpabmbhome
Michigan State University Dep. of Biochemistry
East Lansing, MI 48824-1319
Dr. Jack Preiss, V. Chm.
PH: (517)353-3137
FX: (517)353-9334
Description: Societies of professional biochemists in the Americas and culturally related European countries. Promotes the science of biochemistry by disseminating information and encouraging contacts between its members. Cooperates with other organizations having similar objectives. Conducts workshops and symposia. **Founded:** 1969. **Membership:** 12. Multinational. **National Groups:** 12. **Languages:** Portuguese, Spanish. **Publication:**

Symposium Proceedings, periodic. Advertising: accepted. **Formerly:** Pan American Association of Biochemical Societies.

PAN-AMERICAN ASSOCIATION OF OPHTHALMOLOGY (PAAO)

e-mail: paao@flash.net
url: http://www.flash.net/~paao
1301 S. Bowen Rd., Ste. 365
Arlington, TX 76013
Teresa J. Bradshaw, Admin.
PH: (817)265-2831
FX: (817)275-3961
Description: Ophthalmologists throughout the Western Hemisphere. Seeks to improve the treatment of eye diseases and prevention of blindness in the Americas through the exchange of ideas and treatments. **Founded:** 1939. **Membership:** 10000. Multinational. **Languages:** English, Portuguese. **Budget:** $200,000. **Publication:** *Noticiero* (in Spanish), quarterly. Circulation: 15,000. Advertising: not accepted ■ *Pan-American Association of Ophthalmology – OJO-EYE-OLHO*, semiannual. Newsletter. Includes obituaries and conference calendar. Price: free. Circulation: 15,000. Advertising: accepted. Also Cited As: *Insights.*

PAN AMERICAN FEDERATION FOR VOLUNTARY BLOODGIVING

(Federacion Panamericana pro Donacion Voluntaria de Sangre)
Apartado Postal 5830
Caracas, Venezuela
Jaime Gonzalez Angel, Exec.Pres.
Description: Promotes voluntary bloodgiving throughout the Americas. Collects and diffuses blood for hospitals and clinics throughout the region. Multinational.

PAN AMERICAN HEALTH AND EDUCATION FOUNDATION (PAHEF)

e-mail: marksric@paho.org
525 23rd St. NW
Washington, DC 20037
Richard Marks, Exec.Sec.
PH: (202)974-3416
FX: (202)974-3658
Description: Seeks to mobilize financial and human resources for the improvement of health and education, particularly in Latin America; to advance the objectives of the Pan American Health Organization and World Health Organization. Cosponsors Program for Textbooks and Instructional Materials, which makes needed items available for the training of health personnel at all levels, including professional, technical, and auxiliary. Works cooperatively with organizations and governmental bodies which share the same objectives. Convention/Meeting: none. **Founded:** 1968. **Staff:** 5. Multinational. **Languages:** English. **Budget:** $3,000,000. **Publication:** *Boletin de Medicamentos y Terapeutica* (in Spanish), quarterly. Bulletin. Price: free. ISSN: 0257-7836. Circulation: 30,000. Advertising: not accepted ■ Manuals. Provides information for primary health care workers.

PAN AMERICAN HEALTH ORGANIZATION (PAHO)

url: http://www.paho.org
525 23rd St. NW
Washington, DC 20037
Dr. George Alleyne, Dir.
PH: (202)974-3086
FX: (202)338-0869
Description: Governments of Western Hemisphere nations united to improve physical and mental health in the Americas. Coordinates regional activities combating disease including exchange of statistical and epidemiological information, development of local health services, and organization of disease control and eradication programs. Encourages development in health systems and technology; provides consulting services; conducts educational courses on public health topics including environmental health, food and nutrition, and tropical diseases. Has established Emergency Preparedness and Disaster Relief Coordination Pro

gram in order to increase the ability of health institutions to effectively handle emergencies. Operates the Natural Disaster Relief Voluntary Fund to support disaster relief activities. Maintains the Pan American Sanitary Bureau, the regional office for the Americas of the World Health Organization. Develops health documentaries and coordinates teleconferences. **Founded:** 1902. **Membership:** 41. **Staff:** 1100. Multinational. **Languages:** English, Spanish. **Publication:** *Disaster Preparedness in the Americas*, quarterly. Newsletter. PAHO Emergency Preparedness and Disaster Relief Coordination Program. Covers disaster preparedness, mitigation, and management. Price: free. ISSN: 0251-4494 ■ *EPI Newsletter*, bimonthly. Provides information on immunization programs in the Americas. Covers new technologies available for the execution of programs. Price: Distributed free to health workers. ISSN: 0251-4710 ■ *Epidemiological Bulletin* (in English and Spanish), bimonthly. Disseminates epidemiological information regarding communicable and noncommunicable diseases of public health importance. Price: free. ISSN: 0256-1859 ■ *Health Conditions in the Americas*, quadrennial. Each edition, different price ■ *Revista Panamericana de Salud Publica/Pan American Journal of Public Health* (in English, Portuguese, and Spanish), monthly. Serves as a reference source regarding health problems in the Americas and progress made toward solutions. Includes book reviews and results. Price: $68.00/year. ISSN: 1020-4989. Circulation: 15,000. Alternate Formats: online ■ Manuals ■ Monographs ■ Reports.

PAN AMERICAN HEALTH ORGANIZATION - COSTA RICA

(Organizacion Panamericana de la Salud - Costa Rica)
e-mail: opscor@netsalud.sa.cr
url: http://www.netsalud.sa.cr/ops
Apartado 3745
San Jose, Costa Rica
Dr. Merlin Fernandez, Rep.
PH: 503 2338878
FX: 503 2338061
Description: Works to improve the health and standard of living for individuals in Costa Rica. **Publication:** *Bulletin*, quarterly.

PAN AMERICAN HEALTH ORGANIZATION - ECUADOR

e-mail: postmast@opsecu.ecx.ec
Apartado Postal 8982
Sucursal 7
Quito, Ecuador
Dr. Patricio Hevia Rivas, Rep.
PH: 593 2 544642
FX: 593 2 502830
Description: Promotes quality health care for individuals in Ecuador. Sponsors public health educational programs. Works to improve the standard of living for those living in Ecuador. **Founded:** 1902. **Staff:** 18. **Languages:** English, Portuguese. **Publication:** *Boletin de la Oficina Sanitaria Panamericana* (in English and Spanish), monthly. Newsletter. Price: $30.00. ISSN: 0030-0632. Advertising: accepted. Alternate Formats: CD-ROM ■ *Bulletin*, quarterly.

PAN AMERICAN HEALTH ORGANIZATION - MEXICO

e-mail: cervante@servidor.dgsca.unam.mx
Apartado Postal 10-880
110000 Mexico City, DF, Mexico
Dr. Jose Luis Zeballos, PAHO Rep. in Mexico
PH: 52 1 2028200
FX: 52 1 5208868
Description: Promotes the well-being and health of individuals in Mexico. Sponsors health education programs. **Languages:** English, French.

PAN-AMERICAN IMPLANT ASSOCIATION (PAIA)

e-mail: uvision@generation.net
5591 Cote des Neiges Rd., Ste. 1
Montreal, PQ, Canada H3T 1Y8
Dr. Marvin L. Kwitko, Pres.
PH: (514)735-1133
FX: (514)731-0651

Description: Eye surgeons from North, Central, and South America dedicated to improving their skills and disseminating information to the medical communities in their homelands. **Membership:** 250. **Staff:** 2. Multinational.

PAN AMERICAN LEAGUE AGAINST RHEUMATISM (PANLAR)

Clinicas Hospital Herrera Llerandi
6a Avenida 7-55, Zona 10
Ala Norte 2o Pisa
Guatemala City, Guatemala
Dr. Duncan A. Gordon, Pres.
Description: Physicians and other professionals devoted to the prevention and treatment of rheumatic diseases. Seeks to educate health professionals. Conducts biomedical and epidemiological research. Offers assistance in the coordination of national, professional, and social agencies. Makes available professional publications. **Founded:** 1942. **Membership:** 5500. Multinational.

PAN AMERICAN MEDICAL ASSOCIATION (PAMA)

745 5th Ave., Ste. 403
New York, NY 10151
Frederic C. Fenig, M.D., Sec.
PH: (212)753-6033
FX: (212)308-6847
Description: Fosters the exchange of medical information and research results among physicians in Western Hemisphere countries. **Founded:** 1925. **Membership:** 6000. Multinational. **National Groups:** 58. **Languages:** English. **Publication:** *Journal of the Pan American Medical Association* (in English and Spanish), biennial. Price: free, for members only. Circulation: 5,000. Advertising: accepted. **Also Known As:** Associacion Medica Pan Americana.

PAN-PACIFIC SURGICAL ASSOCIATION (PPSA)

e-mail: congress@ppsa.org
1360 S Beretania St., Ste. 304
Honolulu, HI 96814-1520
Gayle Yoshida, Exec.Admin.
PH: (808)528-1180
FX: (808)528-1188
Description: Professional international association of surgeons. Coordinates exchange programs and educational projects. Conducts volunteer pogram in which surgeons go to Micronesia and the Pacific for two or more weeks. Sponsors educational programs; operates speakers' bureau. **Founded:** 1929. **Membership:** 2716. **Staff:** 1. Multinational. **Regional Groups:** 3. **Languages:** English. **Publication:** *Pan-Pacific Surgical Association Bulletin*, quarterly. Newsletter. Circulation: 1,700. Advertising: accepted.

PANAMANIAN ASSOCIATION FOR PLANNED PARENTHOOD

(Asociacion Panamena para el Planeamiento de la Familia)
Edificio Fundavico, Planta Baja
La Loceria Cl. Principal
Apartado Postal 4637
Panama City 5, Panama
Dr. Alfonso A. Lavergne, Exec.Dir.
PH: 507 2364428
FX: 507 2362979
Description: Fosters family values that include responsible parenting; educates the public about birth control options; conducts programs on health, children's concerns, and women in development. **Founded:** 1965. **Membership:** 100. **Staff:** 62. **Regional Groups:** 7. **Budget:** $1,000,000.

PAPUA NEW GUINEA PAEDIATRIC SOCIETY (PNGPS)

Medical Faculty
PO Box 5623
Boroko, Papua New Guinea
J. Vince, Sec.
PH: 675 3248461
FX: 675 3254935
Description: Formulates practices and procedures in pediatric

medicine in Papua New Guinea; advises the government on health policy; facilitates information exchange in the field; advises on undergraduate and postgraduate curricula in regards to child health. **Founded:** 1974. **Membership:** 30. **Languages:** English. **Budget:** 300 K. **Publication:** *Standard Treatment for Common Illnesses of Children in Papua New Guinea* (in English), periodic. Handbook. Contains information on the management of commonly present pediatric problems. Circulation: 10,000. Advertising: not accepted.

PARENTERAL DRUG ASSOCIATION (PDA)

e-mail: info@pda.org
url: http://www.pda.org
7500 Old Georgetown Rd., Ste. 620
Bethesda, MD 20814
Edmund M. Fry, Pres.
PH: (301)986-0293
FX: (301)986-0296
Description: Individuals working in the research, development, or manufacture of parenteral (injectable) drugs and sterile products. Promotes the advance of parenteral science and technology in the interest of public health. Encourages the exchange of information and technical expertise. Conducts open forums for manufacturers, suppliers, users, regulatory agencies, and academia; sponsors research and educational programs; operates placement service and speakers' bureau. **Founded:** 1946. **Membership:** 8500. **Staff:** 21. Multinational. **Regional Groups:** 16. **Languages:** English. **Budget:** $4,000,000. **Publication:** *PDA Journal of Pharmaceutical Science and Technology*, bimonthly. Covers pharmaceutical science research, production, and development. Price: $135.00/year; $90.00/year (outside U.S.). Circulation: 9,000. Advertising: accepted. Alternate Formats: CD-ROM ■ *PDA Letter*, monthly. Newsletter. Covers governmental and industrial developments relating to pharmaceutical manufacturing and quality control. Price: included in membership dues. Circulation: 8,500. Advertising: accepted ■ Membership Directory, annual.

PARKINSON FOUNDATION OF CANADA (PFC)

e-mail: sarah.hoddinott@parkinson.ca
url: http://www.parkinson.ca
710-390 Bay St.
Toronto, ON, Canada M5H 2Y2
Mr. Blair R. McRovie, Pres. Exec. Officer Chief
PH: (416)366-0099
TF: 800565-3000
FX: (416)366-9190
Description: Provides services to people with Parkinson's or related disorders, their families, and interested health care professionals. Seeks to publicize the nature and availability of treatment and assistance programs available to people with Parkinson's. Promotes research into the cause and cure of Parkinson's. Conducts fundraising activities; maintains support groups; makes available referral services. Sponsors research and educational programs. **Founded:** 1965. **Membership:** 16000. **Staff:** 20. **Local Groups:** 100. **Languages:** English, French. **Budget:** C$3,000,000. **Publication:** *Network* (in English and French), quarterly. Newsletter. Current information on Parkinson's and The Parkinson Foundation of Canada.

PARKINSON SUPPORT GROUPS OF AMERICA (PSGA)

11376 Cherry Hill Rd., No. 204
Beltsville, MD 20705
Ida M. Raitano, Pres.
PH: (301)937-1545
Description: Selfhelp groups whose members are Parkinson's disease patients and their relatives and friends. To provide encouragement, companionship, physical therapy, and counseling; to offer programs and activities to aid Parkinsonians in sustaining and improving the quality of their lives and the lives of their families and friends. Seeks to define needs of support groups and their members; makes recommendations and supplies resources necessary for satisfying such needs; encourages research into the causes and treatment of Parkinson's disease.

Works to educate Parkinsonians and the public on the importance of activity for Parkinsonians. Promotes state and national legislative and administrative efforts of benefit to Parkinsonians. Plans regional advisory groups, seminars, and symposia with health care professionals; sponsors speakers' bureau. Facilitates exchange of information among Parkinson's patients and health care professionals. Is in the process of establishing a library. Maintains ad hoc committees on Enactment of National Commission on Parkinson's Disease and Continuing and Expanding Training for Care Providers of Parkinson Patients. **Founded:** 1981. **Membership:** 150. **Languages:** English. **Publication:** *PSGA Update*, bimonthly. Newsletter.

PARKINSON'S DISEASE FOUNDATION (PDF)
710 West 168th St.
3rd Fl.
New York, NY 10032
Robin Elliott, Exec.Dir.
PH: (212)923-4700
TF: 800457-6676
FX: (212)923-4778
Description: Raises funds for support of scientific research into causes, prevention, and cure of Parkinson's disease. Supports its own laboratories for research in Parkinsonism. Prepares and distributes information on patient care and rehabilitation including list of clinics where treatment is available, and a list of patient selfhelp groups. Supports a brain bank to permit anatomical and chemical studies. Sponsors scientific symposia. Offers patient and family counseling and advocacy services. Maintains research advisory board. Sponsors summer fellowship program for medical students and undergraduate. **Founded:** 1957. **Membership:** 95000. **Staff:** 7. Multinational. **Local Groups:** 500. **Languages:** English. **Budget:** $2,088,000. **Publication:** *Exercises for the Parkinson Patient and Hints for Daily Living* ■ *Health Care Manual for the Professional Team*. Price: $10.00 ■ *Information Packet*. Booklets. Price: free ■ *PDF Newsletter*, 3-4/year. Covers developments in Parkinson's disease research, hints for daily living, and advice to health care professionals. Includes case studies. Price: free. Circulation: 98,000 ■ *Progress, Promise, and Hope: The Parkinson Patient at Home* ■ Brochures.

PAROPAKAR PRIMARY HEALTH CARE CENTER
PO Box 2919
Kathmandu, Nepal
Mr. Manik Lama, Chm.
PH: 977 1 417437
FX: 977 1 224431
Description: Promotes improved construction of housing as a means to better public health; seeks to minimize use of thatch as a building material. Introduces use of cement tile as a roofing material to replace thatch, which the group believes is more profitably utilized as fodder for livestock. **Languages:** English, Nepali.

PATHFINDER INTERNATIONAL (PI)
url: http://www.pathfind.org
9 Galen St., Ste. 217
Watertown, MA 02472
Daniel E. Pellegrom, Pres.
PH: (617)924-7200
FX: (617)924-3833
Description: Established to find, demonstrate, and promote new and more efficient family planning programs in developing countries. Objectives are to introduce and expand the availability of effective family planning services; improve the welfare of families in developing countries; assist developing countries in implementing population policies favorable to national development. Conducts activities with a concern for upholding human rights, enhancing the status and role of women, and respecting the views of family planning clients. Convention/Meeting: none. **Founded:** 1957. **Staff:** 170. Multinational. **Languages:** English. **Budget:** $50,000,000. **Publication:** *Pathways*, quarterly. Newsletter. Provides information on programs and updates on services. Circula-

tion: 6,000. Advertising: not accepted ■ Annual Report, annual. **Also Known As:** PF.

PATHFINDER INTERNATIONAL - BOLIVIA (PI)
Calle Goytia 141
La Paz, Bolivia
PH: 591 2 376331
FX: 591 2 391503
Description: Makes available low- and no-cost family planning services to the needy. Promotes population control through educational programs involving youth; trains indigenous people to sustain family planning services in their local areas. Multinational. **Languages:** Spanish.

PATHFINDER INTERNATIONAL - BRAZIL (PI)
Rua Itabuna 304
Rio Vermelho
41940-650 Salvador, Bahia, Brazil
PH: 55 71 2453255
FX: 55 71 2472070
Description: Makes available low- and no-cost family planning services to the needy. Promotes population control through educational programs involving youth; trains indigenous people to sustain family planning services in their local areas. Multinational. **Languages:** Portuguese, Spanish.

PATHFINDER INTERNATIONAL - MEXICO (PI)
Ximilpa 5 esp. Congreso
Tlalpan
14140 Mexico City, DF, Mexico
PH: 52 5 5736540
FX: 52 5 6550315
Description: Makes available low- and no-cost family planning services to the needy. Promotes population control through educational programs involving youth; trains indigenous people to sustain family planning services in their local areas. Multinational. **Languages:** English, Spanish.

PATHOLOGICAL SOCIETY OF GREAT BRITAIN AND IRELAND
2 Carlton House Terrace
London SW1Y 5AF, England
Mrs. J.E. Edwards, Contact
PH: 44 171 9761260
FX: 44 171 9761267
Description: Those engaged in research or teaching in connection with pathology or allied science. Holds two scientific meetings each year. **Founded:** 1906. **Membership:** 1700. **Staff:** 1. **Publication:** *Journal of Medical Microbiology*, monthly ■ *Journal of Pathology*, monthly ■ *Reviews in Medical Microbiology*, quarterly.

PATIENT ADVOCATES FOR ADVANCED CANCER TREATMENT (PAACT)
e-mail: paact@compuserve.com
url: http://www.osz.com/paact
1143 Parmelee NW
Grand Rapids, MI 49504-3844
Lloyd J. Ney, Sr., Exec. Officer
PH: (616)453-1477
FX: (616)453-1846
Description: Prostate cancer patients and physicians. Engages in advocacy activities. Provides educational materials to those with prostate cancer. Conducts protocol studies and research. **Founded:** 1984. **Membership:** 33000. **Staff:** 3. Multinational. **Languages:** English. **Publication:** *Cancer Communication*, quarterly. Newsletter. Circulation: 26,000. Advertising: not accepted ■ *Prostate Cancer Report*. Advertising: not accepted.

PEDIATRIC PROJECTS
e-mail: medpubl@kaiwan.com
PO Box 571555
Tarzana, CA 91357
Ms. Pat Azarnoff, Exec.Dir.

PH: 800-947-0947
FX: (818)705-3660
Description: Professionals in health & mental health and parents of ill, disabled, or hospitalized children. Strives to provide information to prepare children for surgery, and toll-free phone consultation. Offers educational and research programs and children's services. Distribute medical toys & books to help children & families understand healthcare. **Founded:** 1981. Multinational. **Languages:** English.

PEOPLE AGAINST CANCER (PAC)
e-mail: nocancer@ix.netcom.com
url: http://www.dodgenet.com/nocancer
604 East St.
PO Box 10
Otho, IA 50569-0010
Frank D. Wiewel, Contact
PH: (515)972-4444
TF: 800NO-CANCER
FX: (515)972-4415
Description: Promotes research into alternative cancer therapy and prevention. Conducts educational, charitable, and research programs. **Founded:** 1985. **Membership:** 2000. **Staff:** 5. Multinational. **Languages:** English. **Budget:** $300,000. **Publication:** *Options*, quarterly. Newsletter ■ Bulletin ■ Directory.

PEOPLE'S HEALTH CENTRE (PHC)
(Gonoshasthaya Kendra)
e-mail: gk.mail@drik.bgd.toolnet.org
Nayarhat
Dhaka 1350, Bangladesh
Mr. Tarun Chakrabarti Phiaoo, Finance Dir.
PH: 880 2 9332245
FX: 880 2 863567
Description: Health care professionals and other individuals with an interest in public health, nutrition, civil and human rights issues, and agricultural development. Seeks to insure a higher standard of living for people living in rural areas of southern Asia. Provides primary health care services; manufactures and distributes vaccines and other medications. Conducts leadership training courses for women; sponsors educational and vocational training programs. Facilitates the establishment of income generating microenterprises. **Founded:** 1971. **Membership:** 1500. **Staff:** 1753. Multinational. **Budget:** $10,000,000.

PEOPLE'S MEDICAL SOCIETY (PMS)
e-mail: media@peoplesmed.org
url: http://www.peoplesmed.org
462 Walnut St.
Allentown, PA 18102
Charles B. Inlander, Pres.
PH: (610)770-1670
TF: 800624-8773
FX: (610)770-0607
Description: Promotes citizen involvement in the cost, quality, and management of the American health care system. Seeks to: train and encourage individuals to study local health care systems, practitioners, and institutions and promote preventive health care and medical cost control by these groups; address major policy issues and control health costs; encourage more preventive practice and research; promote self-care and alternative health care procedures; launch an information campaign to assist individuals in maintaining personal health and to prepare them for appointments with medical professionals. Convention/Meeting: none. **Founded:** 1982. **Membership:** 80000. **Staff:** 11. **Languages:** English. **Publication:** *Allergies: Questions You Have...Answers You Need* ■ *Alzheimer's and Dementia: Questions You Have...Answers You Need* ■ *Arthritis: Questions You Have, Answers You Need* ■ *Asthma: Questions You Have, Answers You Need* ■ *Breathe Better, Feel Better* ■ *The Consumer's Medical Desk Reference* ■ *Depression: Questions You Have, Answers You Need* ■ *Good Operations – Bad Operations* ■ *Headaches: 47 Ways to Stop the Pain* ■ *Healthy Body Book* ■ *Hearing Loss: Questions, You Have, Answers You Need* ■ *Long-Term Care and Alternatives* ■

Medicare Made Easy ■ *Medicine on Trial* ■ *Misdiagnosis: Woman as a Disease* ■ *Natural Recipes for the Good Life* ■ *150 Ways to Be a Savvy Medical Consumer* ■ *People's Medical Society Newsletter*, bimonthly. Includes membership activities information. Price: included in membership dues. ISSN: 0736-4873. Circulation: 65,000 ■ *Prostate: Questions You Have...Answers You Need* ■ *77 Ways to Beat Colds and Flu* ■ *So You're Going to be a Mother* ■ *Tai Chi Made Easy* ■ *Take This Book to the Gynecologist With You* ■ *Take This Book to the Hospital With You* ■ *28 Days to a Better Body* ■ *Vitamins & Minerals: Questions You Have, Answers You Need* ■ *Your Complete Medical Record* ■ Bibliographies ■ Bulletins.

PERINATAL SOCIETY OF NEW ZEALAND (PSNZ)
Dept. of Obstetrics and Gynecology
Private Bag 4711
Christchurch
Aucules, New Zealand
Prof. Rita Teele, Pres.
PH: 3 364 4630
FX: 3 364 4634
Description: Pediatricians, obstetricians, neo-natal and obstetric nurses, scientists, other paediatric specialists and midwives in New Zealand. Aims to foster continued improvement in the standards of perinatal medicine and nursing. Works to increase public understanding of the activities in and the objectives of perinatology. Sponsors continuing education programs in perinatology. Promotes collaboration and open discussion among members. **Founded:** 1979. **Membership:** 240. **Local Groups:** 12. **Languages:** English. **Budget:** NZ$4,000. **Formerly:** (1990) New Zealand Perinatal Society.

PERUVIAN HEART ASSOCIATION (PHA)
100 S Greenleaf Ave.
Gurnee, IL 60031-3378
Luis Vasquez, M.D., Intl.Dir.
PH: (847)249-2111
TF: 800367-7378
FX: (847)249-2772
Description: Peruvian physicians, nurses, and other health care professionals specializing in cardiology who are devoted to research, training, teaching, and patient care. Offers continuing education courses for Peruvian physicians, enabling them to fulfill coursework required by Peruvian law for continuance of medical practice. Provides community health care information to residents of Lima, Peru concerning heart attacks, high blood pressure, cholesterol, diabetes, diet, and exercise. Conducts programs in conjunction with the American College of Cardiology and the American Heart Association, providing printed information and speakers on health care. Also provides information to U.S. doctors who wish to study and assist with Peruvian health care. **Founded:** 1967. **Membership:** 400. **Staff:** 10. Multinational. **Regional Groups:** 6. **Languages:** English, Spanish.

PHARMACEUTICAL CARE MANAGEMENT ASSOCIATION (PCMA)
2300 9th St. S., Ste. 210
Arlington, VA 22204-2320
Delbert D. Konnor, Pres. & CEO
PH: (703)920-8480
TF: 888SAY-PCMA
FX: (703)920-8491
Description: Represents managed care pharmacy and its healthcare partners in pharmaceutical care: managed healthcare organizations, PBMs, HMOs, PPOs, third party administrators, healthcare insurance companies, drug wholesalers, pharmaceutical manufacturers, and community pharmacy networks. Serves its members and America's healthcare system by promoting education, legislation, practice standards, and research that foster quality, afforable pharmaceutical care. PCMA members serve more than 150 million enrolled livcs. **Founded:** 1975. **Membership:** 100. **Staff:** 10. **Languages:** English. Formed by Merger of (1997) American Managed Care Pharmacy Association. Formerly (1989) National Association of Mail Service Pharmacies.

PHARMACEUTICAL RESEARCH AND MANUFACTURERS OF AMERICA (PMA)
url: http://www.phrma.org
1100 15th St. NW, Ste. 900
Washington, DC 20005
Gerald J. Mossinghoff, Pres.
PH: (202)835-3400
FX: (202)835-3429
Description: Research based manufacturers of ethical pharmaceutical and biological products that are distributed under their own labels. Encourages high standards for quality control and good manufacturing practices; research toward development of new and better medical products; enactment of uniform and reasonable drug legislation for the protection of public health. Disseminates information on governmental regulations and policies, but does not maintain or supply information on specific products, prices, distribution, promotion, or sales policies of its individual members. Has established the Pharmaceutical Manufacturers Association Foundation to promote public health through scientific and medical research. **Founded:** 1958. **Membership:** 63. **Staff:** 80. **Languages:** English. **Publication:** *Fact Book*, annual ▪ *Trademarks Listed with the Pharmaceutical Manufacturers Association*, periodic. Includes monthly supplements. Price: $25.00/year ▪ Annual Report ▪ Newsletter, weekly. **Formed by Merger of:** American Drug Manufacturers Association; American Pharmaceutical Manufacturers Association. **Formerly:** Pharmaceutical Manufacturers Association.

PHARMACEUTICAL SOCIETY OF NORTHERN IRELAND
73 University St.
Belfast, Antrim BT7 1HL, Northern Ireland
D.J. Lawson, Contact
PH: 44 1232 326927
FX: 44 1232 439919
Description: Registered pharmacists. Acts as a professional and registration body for pharmacists and pharmacies in Northern Ireland. **Founded:** 1925. **Membership:** 1350. **Staff:** 3.

PHARMACEUTICAL SOCIETY OF SINGAPORE (PSS)
e-mail: pss@pacific.net.sg
url: http://home1.pacific.net.sg/~pss/
Alumni Medical Centre
2 College Rd.
Singapore 169850, Singapore
Mr. Eng Tong Seng, Hon.Sec.
PH: 65 2211136
FX: 65 2230969
Description: Seeks to maximize the contribution of pharmacists to health care by enforcing a code of ethics, cooperating with other organizations, and providing educational programs. Sponsors competitions. **Founded:** 1967. **Membership:** 788. **Staff:** 3. **Languages:** English. **Publication:** *Singapore Pharmaceutical Bulletin* (in English), quarterly. Price: Available to members only. Advertising: accepted. **Formerly:** (1967) Malayan Pharmaceutical Association.

PHARMACEUTICAL SOCIETY OF SOUTH AFRICA (PSSA)
26 Juta St.
PO Box 31360
Braamfontein 2017, Republic of South Africa
Mr. I. Kotze, Exec.Dir.
PH: 27 11 3391752
FX: 27 11 4031309
Description: Registered pharmacists. Promotes high standards of ethics and practice in pharmacy. Conducts continuing professional education courses; facilitates communication among members; maintains museum. **Founded:** 1946. **Membership:** 5500. **Staff:** 16. **Languages:** Afrikaans, English. **Publication:** *South Africa Pharmaceutical Journal*, monthly. Circulation: 6,000. Advertising: accepted.

PHARMACISTS IN OPHTHALMIC PRACTICE (PIOP)
Wills Eye Hospital
900 Walnut Sts.
Philadelphia, PA 19107
Clement A. Weisbecker, Bd.Chm.
PH: (215)928-3002
FX: (215)928-3002
Description: Pharmacists who serve as directors or chief pharmacists of institutions that specialize in ophthalmology or otolaryngology. Exchanges information and determines standards relating to ophthalmological pharmacy, pharmacology, and formulations. Conducts research and compiles statistics on ophthalmic pharmacy, products, and medication. **Founded:** 1984. **Membership:** 26. **Languages:** English.

PHI ALPHA SIGMA
313 S. 10th St.
Philadelphia, PA 19107
Paul J. Antal, Pres.
Description: Professional fraternity - medicine. **Founded:** 1886. **Membership:** 120. **Languages:** English. **Publication:** *Bubbling Rales*, annual. Newsletter. Price: free to alumni. Circulation: 650. Advertising: not accepted.

PHI CHI MEDICAL FRATERNITY (PCMF)
1201 E. Spring St.
New Albany, IN 47150
Daniel H. Cannon, M.D., Chm., Exec. Trustees
PH: (812)948-0581
TF: 800800-7442
FX: (812)941-8850
Description: Professional fraternity - medicine. Maintains Phi Chi Welfare Association, which accepts voluntary contributions to a student loan fund and other services. **Founded:** 1889. **Membership:** 40818. **Staff:** 1. Multinational. **Local Groups:** 12. **Languages:** English. **Budget:** $50,000. **Publication:** *Constitution and Statutes* ▪ *Officers' Manual* ▪ *PC Chronicles*, semiannual. Magazine. Provides chapter news and information. Price: included in membership dues. Circulation: 4,300. Advertising: accepted ▪ *Phi Chi Directory* ▪ *Psi Chi History, 1889-1989* ▪ *Psi Chi Songs*. **Formerly:** (1989) Phi Chi.

PHI DELTA EPSILON MEDICAL FRATERNITY
2284 Diamond Point Rd.
Alpena, MI 49707-4608
S. M. Greenstone, Exec.Dir.
Description: Professional fraternity - medicine. **Founded:** 1904. **Membership:** 25000. **Staff:** 5. **Local Groups:** 41. **Languages:** English. **Publication:** *Phi Delta Epsilon News and Scientific Journal*, quarterly.

PHI LAMBDA KAPPA MEDICAL FRATERNITY
60 Fountain Rd.
Levittown, PA 19056-1915
Eleanor G. Halprin, Exec.Sec.
Description: Professional fraternity - medicine. **Founded:** 1907. **Membership:** 4800. **Local Groups:** 20. **Languages:** English. **Publication:** *Quarterly*.

PHI RHO SIGMA MEDICAL SOCIETY
e-mail: hrodenbe@wpo.iupui.edu
PO Box 90264
Indianapolis, IN 46290
Martin B. Wice, M.D., Sec.-Treas.
PH: (317)255-4379
FX: (317)253-5067
Description: Professional society - medicine. **Founded:** 1890. **Membership:** 31260. **Staff:** 1. **State Groups:** 12. **Languages:** English. **Publication:** *Journal of Phi Rho Sigma*, quarterly. Price: free, for members only.

PHYSICIANS ASSOCIATION FOR ANTHROPOSOPHICAL MEDICINE (PAAM)
1923 Geddes Ave.
Ann Arbor, MI 48104
Christian Wessling, MD, Sec.
PH: (734)930-9462
FX: (734)662-1727
Description: Physicians promoting the use of anthroposophical medicine. Sponsors educational programs. Studies the legal issues involving the use of anthroposophical medical treatment. **Membership:** 300. **Languages:** English. **Publication:** *Directory of Physicians* ▪ *Journal of Anthroposophical Medicine*, quarterly. Price: $50.00/year. ISSN: 1067-4640. Advertising: accepted.

PHYSICIANS COMMITTEE FOR RESPONSIBLE MEDICINE (PCRM)
e-mail: pcrm@pcrm.org
url: http://www.pcrm.org
PO Box 6322
Washington, DC 20015
Neal D. Barnard, M.D., Pres.
PH: (202)686-2210
FX: (202)686-2216
Description: Physicians, scientists, healthcare professionals, and interested others. Increases public awareness about the importance of preventive medicine and nutrition, and raises scientific and ethical questions pertaining to the use of humans and animals in medical research. Supports research into U.S. agricultural and public health policies. Promotes the New Four Food Groups, a no-cholesterol, low-fat alternative to U.S.D.A. dietary recommendations. Maintains the Gold Plan program which includes information on low-fat, cholesterol-free entrees and nutrition for institutional food services. Offers fact sheets on nutrition, preventive medicine, and non-animal research topics. Maintains speakers' bureau. **Founded:** 1985. **Membership:** 60000. **Staff:** 16. **Languages:** English. **For-Profit. Publication:** *Alternatives in Medical Education* ▪ *Eat Right, Live Longer* ▪ *Food for Life* ▪ *Good Medicine*, quarterly. Magazine. Provides information about preventive medicine, nutrition, public health policy, medical/nutrition research updates, and AIDS research. Price: included in membership dues ▪ *The Power of Your Plate* ▪ Brochures.

PHYSICIANS FORUM (PF)
1507 53rd St., Ste. 155
Chicago, IL 60615-4509
Raymond Demers, M.D., Pres.
PH: (312)922-1968
FX: (312)633-6442
Description: Professional organization of physicians, particularly those holding salaried positions, who work for health care as a human right. Promotes development of a national health service with a single class of medical care for all, financed by a progressive income tax surcharge for health. **Founded:** 1939. **Languages:** English. **Publication:** *Physicians Forum Bulletin*, quarterly.

PHYSICIANS WHO CARE (PWC)
e-mail: pwcorg@flash.net
url: http://www.pwc.org
10615 Perrin Beitel Rd., Ste. 201
San Antonio, TX 78217-3140
Stephen C. Cohen, M.D., Pres.
TF: 800545-9305
Description: A patient advocacy group devoted to protecting the traditional doctor-patient relationship and ensuring quality health care. Believes the responsibility for medical care belongs to physicians, as provider of care, and patients, who have the choice of determining the type of treatment received. Promotes communication between members and their patients on health care issues. **Founded:** 1985. **Membership:** 3500. **Languages:** English. **For-Profit. Publication:** *Are You Thinking of Joining a HMO?*. Brochure ▪ *Patients Who Care Newsletter*, periodic ▪ *Physicians Who Care Newsletter*, bimonthly. **Also Known As:** (1989) National Organization of Physicians Who Care.

PHYSIOLOGICAL SOCIETY - ENGLAND
e-mail: knewton@physoc.org
url: http://physiology.cup.cam.uk/
PO Box 11319
London WC1E 7JF, England
Keith Newton, Admin.
PH: 44 171 6311457
FX: 44 171 6311462
Description: Physiologists at senior levels in universities, research institutions, hospitals and relevant industries and government departments, about a third of whom are resident overseas. Affiliation is now available for younger physiologists such as. postgraduate students and postdoctoral workers. To promote the advancement of physiology. Covers all areas of physiology. Main activities are Scientific publishing; organising/funding scientific meetings, symposia, seminars, workshops, lectures for members, students, school-teachers, sixthformers; school and university liaison; 25 special interest groups, plus 13 subcommittees. **Founded:** 1876. **Membership:** 1775. **Staff:** 19. Multinational. **Publication:** *Experimental Physiology*, bimonthly ▪ *The Journal of Physiology*, bimonthly ▪ *Study Guides*, periodic ▪ Monographs.

PHYSIOLOGICAL SOCIETY - FRANCE
(Societe de Physiologie)
url: http://alize.ere.umontreal.ca/-molotchn/physio.html
Laboratoire de Physiologie
Rue Haute-de-Reculee
F-49045 Angers, France
Jean Louis Saumet, Gen.Sec.
PH: 33 2 41735845
FX: 33 2 41735895
Description: Physiologists from universities, hospitals, and research organizations. Purpose is to promote and facilitate scientific contacts among professionals in the field of physiology. **Founded:** 1926. **Membership:** 1046. Multinational. **National Groups:** 4. **Languages:** English, French. **Budget:** $37,000. **Publication:** *Directory*, triennial ▪ *Journal*, quarterly.

PI KAPPA DELTA
e-mail: rlittlef@badlands.nodak.edu
Box 5075, University Sta.
North Dakota State University
Fargo, ND 58105-5075
Dr. Robert Littlefield, Sec.Treas.
PH: (701)231-7783
FX: (701)231-7784
Description: Recognition fraternity - men and women, forensics. Maintains hall of fame; compiles statistics; sponsors competitions. **Founded:** 1913. **Membership:** 60000. **Local Groups:** 235. **Languages:** English.

PIERRE FAUCHARD ACADEMY (PFA)
url: http://www.fauchard.org
8021 W. 79th St.
Justice, IL 60458-1607
Dr. Richard Kozal, Sec.-Treas.
PH: (708)594-5884
TF: 800232-0099
FX: (708)496-1066
Description: Dentists "of high standards and leadership" who are nominated to the academy by state or section chairmen. Objectives are to educate dentists by providing literature on developments and opinions in dentistry; promote continuing education for all members of the dental profession; facilitate the exchange of knowledge among dentists; foster contact between dentistry leaders and those who seek advice on scientific, technical, or economic subjects; encourage advancement of professional and scientific standards; further the improvement of oral health of the public through prevention, therapy, and restoration; emphasize professional responsibility to the public. Sponsors annual Memorial Lecture honoring a past leader of dentistry. The academy is named for Pierre Fauchard (1678-1761), a French dentist who pioneered modern dental practice and dental education. **Founded:** 1936. **Membership:** 6000. **Staff:** 2. Multina-

tional. **State Groups:** 50. **Languages:** English. **Budget:** $250,000. **Publication:** *Dental Abstracts*, quarterly. Price: $22.00/year. Circulation: 6,000. Advertising: accepted ■ *Dental World*, bimonthly. Newsletter. Includes member news, meeting announcements, abstracts, book reviews, and editorials. Also Cited As: *PFA Newsletter* ■ *Leadership Manual of the PFA* ■ *Legacy, The Dental Profession*. Book ■ *The Life and Times of Pierre Fauchard*. Book ■ Membership Directory, periodic.

PLANNED PARENTHOOD ASSOCIATION OF SIERRA LEONE (PPASL)
2 Lightfoot-Boston St.
PO Box 1094
Freetown, Sierra Leone
Dr. W.E. Taylor, Exec.Dir.
PH: 232 22 22774
FX: 232 22 229139
Description: Works to enhance the standard of living for individuals living in Sierra Leone by promoting family planning. Advocates family planning as a basic human right. Attempts to stop the spread of sexually transmitted diseases, especially AIDS. Offers programs in sex education, family planning, and health. Provides contraceptive and health care services. **Founded:** 1959. **Membership:** 750. **Staff:** 98. **Languages:** English. **Budget:** $345,000. **Publication:** *PPASL News Letter* (in English), semiannual. Newsletter. Advertising: accepted ■ Annual Report. Advertising: not accepted ■ Reports. From baseline studies.

PLANNED PARENTHOOD ASSOCIATION OF SLOVENIA (PPA)
Kotnikova 5
SLO-61000 Ljubljana, Slovenia
PH: 386 61 1713404
FX: 386 61 1713411
Description: Works to improve accessibility of family planning and reproductive health services in Slovenia. Conducts educational programs to raise awareness of family planning programs. **Founded:** 1994. **Languages:** English, Slovene.

PLANNED PARENTHOOD ASSOCIATION OF THAILAND (PPAT)
8 Soi Vibhavadi-Rangsit 44
Vibhavadi-Rangsit Super Hwy.
Lard-Yao, Chatuchak
Bangkok 19000, Thailand
Mr. Sombhong Pattawichaiporn, Exec.Dir.
PH: 66 2 5790084
FX: 66 2 5799559
Description: Works to improve the quality of life for people living in Thailand by promoting responsible parenthood and family planning. Attempts to reduce the number of unwanted pregnancies and abortions. Offers programs in sex education, family planning, and health. Provides contraceptive and health care services. Conducts research. **Languages:** Thai. **Publication:** *PPAT News/Sarn Samphan Newsletter* (in English and Thai), bimonthly. Explains PPAT activities. Advertising: not accepted.

PLANNED PARENTHOOD FEDERATION OF AMERICA (PPFA)
url: http://www.plannedparenthood.org/
810 7th Ave.
New York, NY 10019
Gloria Feldt, Pres.
PH: (212)541-7800
FX: (212)245-1845
Description: Organizations providing leadership in making effective means of voluntary fertility regulation, including contraception, abortion, sterilization, and infertility services, available and fully accessible to all as a central element of reproductive health; stimulating and sponsoring relevant biomedical, socioeconomic, and demographic research; developing appropriate information, education, and training programs to increase knowledge about human reproduction and sexuality. Supports and assists efforts to achieve similar goals worldwide. Operates more than 900

centers that provide medically supervised reproductive health services and educational programs. **Founded:** 1916. **Staff:** 10961. **Regional Groups:** 169. **Languages:** English. **Budget:** $200,000. **Publication:** Annual Report ■ Books ■ Pamphlets. **Absorbed:** World Population Emergency Campaign. **Also Known As:** Planned Parenthood; Planned Parenthood/World Population. **Formerly:** (1939) American Birth Control League.

PLANNED PARENTHOOD FEDERATION OF CANADA (PPFC)
(Federation pour le Planning des Naissances du Canada)
1 Nicholas St., Ste. 430
Ottawa, ON, Canada K1N 7B7
Barbara Hestrin, Pres.
PH: (613)241-4474
FX: (613)241-7550
Description: Promotes family planning and responsible parenthood. Encourages public awareness of contraceptive methods and the need for family planning. Works to reduce the number of unwanted pregnancies and abortions. Sponsors programs in family planning, sex education, and sexually transmitted diseases, especially AIDS. Provides contraceptive services. Acts as an advocate for family planning issues on a national level. Conducts research. **Founded:** 1964. **Staff:** 5. **Local Groups:** 54. **Languages:** English. **Budget:** C$600,000. **Publication:** *PPFC Bulletin* (in English), 3/year. Newsletter. Circulation: 1,500. Advertising: not accepted.

PLANNED PARENTHOOD FEDERATION OF NIGERIA (PPFN)
e-mail: ppfn@rcl.dircon.co.uk
224 Ikorodu Rd.
Palmgrove
Somolu
Lagos, Lagos, Nigeria
Dr. A.B. Sulaiman, Exec.Dir.
PH: 234 1 820945
FX: 234 1 820526
Description: Works to improve the quality of life for individuals living in Nigeria by promoting responsible parenthood and family planning. Advocates family planning as a basic human right. Attempts to stop the spread of AIDS and other sexually transmitted diseases. Offers programs in sex education, family planning, and health. Provides contraceptive and health care services. **Founded:** 1964. **Membership:** 3000. **Staff:** 280. **National Groups:** 1. **Languages:** English. **Budget:** N 66,055,730. **Publication:** *Planned News* (in English), semiannual. Newsletter. Price: free. Advertising: accepted. **Formerly:** (1979) Family Planning Council of Nigeria.

POLIO SOCIETY (PS)
4200 Wisconsin Ave. NW, Ste. 106273
Washington, DC 20016
Becky Evans, Contact
PH: (301)897-8180
FX: (202)466-1911
Description: Polio survivors and health care professionals interested in the long-term health of patients who have had the disease. Gathers and disseminates information on post-polio syndrome. (PPS is a condition in which polio survivors suffer unaccustomed fatigue, joint and muscle pain, weakening or loss of muscle function, and respiratory problems.) Acts as liaison between members and medical facilities; maintains outreach program and referral service; sponsors support groups. Advocates on issues of disability and benefits. **Founded:** 1984. **Membership:** 3500. **Staff:** 1. **Local Groups:** 3. **Languages:** English. **Budget:** $10,000. **Publication:** *Options*, quarterly. Newsletter ■ Brochures. Informational brochures. **Formerly:** Post-Polio League for Information and Outreach.

POLISH ASSOCIATION OF PEOPLE SUFFERING FROM EPILEPSY (PAPSE)
Fabryczna Str. 57
PL-15-482 Bialystok, Poland
Tadeusz Zarebski, Pres.
PH: 48 85 754420
FX: 48 85 754420
Description: Nongovernmental organizations, foundations, funds, and individuals with an interest in people with epilepsy. Promotes an improved quality of life for people with epilepsy. Represents the rights and interests of people with epilepsy before government agencies; makes available international exchange program; identifies and seeks to acquire and distribute emerging technologies and equipment for the diagnosis and treatment of epilepsy. **Founded:** 1985. **Membership:** 400000. **Regional Groups:** 6. **Languages:** English, Polish. **Budget:** 400,000 Zl. **Publication:** *Padaezki - Pytania l Odpowicdzi* (in Polish). Book.

POLISH MEDICAL ASSOCIATION
(Polski Towarzystwo Lekarskie)
Al. Ujazdowskie St. 24
PL-00-478 Warsaw, Poland
Jerzy Woy-Wojciechowski, Pres.
PH: 48 26 288699
FX: 48 26 288699
Description: Aims to maintain high professional and ethical standards in the medical profession. **Founded:** 1820. **Membership:** 30000. **Local Groups:** 284. **Languages:** Polish. **Publication:** *Polski Tygodnik Lekavski also cited as: Polish Medical Weekly* (in Polish). Magazine. Advertising: accepted ■ *Przeylad Lekavski also cited as: Medical Review* ■ *Wiadomoici Leharshie also cited as: News for Physicians*.

POLISH PAEDIATRIC PATHOLOGY SOCIETY
(Polski Towarzystwo Patologii Dzieciecej)
e-mail: annals@usa.net
Aleja Dzieci Polskich 20
PL-04736 Warsaw, Poland
Piotr M. Dobosz, Sec.
PH: 48 22 151971
FX: 48 22 151971
Description: Pediatric pathologists. Seeks to advance the science and practice of pediatric pathology. Facilitates integration of scientific developments in the field; conducts continuing medical education programs. **Founded:** 1996. **Membership:** 50. **Staff:** 1. **Languages:** English, Polish. **Publication:** *Annals of Diagnostic Paediatric Pathology* (in English), quarterly. Journal. Price: 40.00 Zl/year for individuals; 290.00 Zl/year for institutions. ISSN: 1427-4426. Advertising: accepted.

POLISH PHYSICAL SOCIETY
e-mail: ptf@fuw.edu.pl
url: http://www.fuw.edu.pl
Main Board
Hoza 69
PL-00-681 Warsaw, Poland
Ireneusz Strzalkowski, Pres.
PH: 48 22 6212668
FX: 48 22 6212668
Description: Physicists, physics teachers, and others with an interest in the physical sciences. Seeks to improve the quality of physics education, research, and knowledge. Maintains wide internal collaboration. **Founded:** 1920. **Membership:** 1792. **Staff:** 4. **State Groups:** 2. **Languages:** English, Polish. **Publication:** *Poste Py Fizyki* (in English and Polish), bimonthly. Journal. Devoted to physics knowledge and diffusion. Price: 12.00 Zl. Advertising: accepted.

POLISH SOCIETY FOR IMMUNOLOGY (PSI)
(Polskie Towarzystwo Immunologii Doswiadczalnej i Klinicznej)
e-mail: igzelak@ib.amwaw.edu.pl
Department of Surgical Research and Transplantology
Medical Research Centre
Polish Academy of Sciences
PL-02-106 Warsaw, Poland
Dr. Irena Grzelak, Sec.Gen.
PH: 48 22 6685316
FX: 48 22 6685334
Description: Researchers. Encourages, coordinates, and supervises immunological research activities in Poland. Assists instruction at universities and medical centers. Disseminates scientific information. Conducts educational and research programs. **Founded:** 1969. **Membership:** 298. **Staff:** 1. **Local Groups:** 10. **Languages:** English, Polish. **Budget:** 20,000 Zl. **Publication:** *Bulletin* (in Polish), periodic. Price: Free. Circulation: 65. Advertising: accepted. Also Cited As: *INTEGRYNA* ■ *Central European Journal of Immunology* (in English and Polish), quarterly. Price: 500.00 Zl. ISSN: 0324-8534. Advertising: accepted. Alternate Formats: online. Also Cited As: Immunologia Polska, Polish Journal of Immunology.

POPULATION AND ENVIRONMENT SOCIETY OF CHINA (PESC)
PO Box A-1
No. 14 E Chang'An St.
Beijing 100741, People's Republic of China
PH: 86 1 5121005
FX: 86 1 5121005
Description: Promotes scientific research and increased public awareness of population control and environmental protection issues. Provides information and technical assistance to government bodies. **Founded:** 1992. **Languages:** Chinese, English.

POPULATION PROGRAMME UNIT
Anchorage House
84 Independence St.
Port of Spain, Trinidad and Tobago
Selwyn Ragoonanan, Contact
PH: (809)623-4373
Description: Seeks to heighten public awareness of overpopulation issues. Works to improve family planning and primary health care programs. Disseminates information. **Founded:** 1966. **Staff:** 14. **Languages:** English. **Budget:** TT$4,000,000.

PORTUGUESE SOCIETY OF STOMATOLOGY AND DENTAL MEDICINE (PSSDM)
(Sociedade Portugesa de Estomatolgia Emedicina Dentaria)
e-mail: mail.spend@medisis.pt
Rua Prof. Fernando de Fonseca, 10A
Esc. 7
P-1600 Lisbon, Portugal
Leite da Silva, Pres.
PH: 351 1 7593948
FX: 351 1 7593948
Description: Stomatologists, dentists, and oral and maxillofacial surgeons in Portugal. Promotes research in all disciplines of oral medicine. Sponsors community dental hygiene programs. Establishes standards and qualifications for oral medicine specialists. Represents' members interests; operates legal defense fund for members. Monitors the manufacture of dental materials in Portugal. Promotes continuing education programs for members. **Founded:** 1919. **Membership:** 2200. **Staff:** 6. **Local Groups:** 3. **Languages:** English, Portuguese. **Budget:** $300,000. **Publication:** *Revista Portugese de Estomatologia e Cirurgia Maxilofacial* (in English and Portuguese), quarterly. Journal. Journal of dentistry and maxillofacial surgery. Price: $30.00 annual. ISSN: 0035-0397. Circulation: 2,200. Advertising: accepted. Also Cited As: *Rev Port de Estometo Cir Maxilofac* ■ *Stoma* (in Portuguese), quarterly. ISSN: 0870-4287.

POSITIVE PREGNANCY AND PARENTING FITNESS (PPPF)
RR 1, Box 172 Glenview Rd.
Waitsfield, VT 05673
Robert L. Olkin, Contact
PH: (802)496-4944
TF: 800433-5523
FX: (802)496-5222
Description: Sells products for pregnant women, expectant parents and new parents. Products include books, videos, cassette tapes, etc. **Founded:** 1982. **Membership:** 350. **Staff:** 1. **Languages:** English. **For-Profit**Also Known As Be Healthy.

POSTPARTUM ADJUSTMENT SERVICES - CANADA (PASS-CAN)
url: http://www.passcan.c
PO Box 7282, Sta. Main
Oakville, ON, Canada L6J 6L6
Christine Long, Exec.Dir.
PH: (905)844-9009
FX: (905)844-5973
Description: Health care and mental health professionals; parents of preschool children. Seeks to "ease the transition to parenthood for families of infants or preschoolers" and to "reduce the stigma of postpartum depression or anxiety." Serves as the national clearinghouse on postpartum depression. Conducts advocacy, networking, and educational activities; maintains discussion and support groups for mothers experiencing postpartum anxiety or depression. Participates in charitable activities; maintains speakers' bureau. **Founded:** 1972. **Membership:** 500. **Staff:** 1. **Languages:** English, French. **Budget:** C$18,000. **Publication:** *Ups and Downs - A New Mother's Guide.* Booklet.

PREGNANCY COUNSELING SERVICES
PO Box 33-423
Takapuna
Auckland, New Zealand
Nina Barry-Martin, Dir.
PH: 64 9 4896505
FX: 64 9 4897271
Description: Provides counseling and support to pregnant women in New Zealand. Works to ensure maternal and child health; conducts educational programs. Offers post abortion counselling. **Founded:** 1980. **Local Groups:** 24. **Languages:** English. **Publication:** *Diary Notes*, semiannual. Provides information to supporters and pro life groups ▪ Annual Report.

PREMIER
400 N. Capitol St. NW, Ste. 590
Washington, DC 20001
James L. Scott, Pres.
PH: (202)393-0860
FX: (202)393-0864
Description: Nonprofit multi-hospital systems. Sponsors educational programs for corporate officers and trustees of multi-hospital systems. Monitors, investigates, and develops policy positions on developments in the health care field. **Founded:** 1984. **Membership:** 40. **Staff:** 6. **Languages:** English. **Formed by Merger of:** Associated Health Systems; United Healthcare Systems. **Formerly:** Association AMHS Institute; (1988) American Healthcare Institute.

PRO FAMILIA: DEUTSCHE GESELLSCHAFT FUR FAMILIENPLANUNG, SEXUALPADAGOGIK, UND SEXUALBERATUNG
url: http://www.profamilia.de
Stresemann Allee 3
D-60596 Frankfurt am Main, Germany
Ms. Elke Thoss, Exec.Dir.
PH: 49 69 639002
FX: 49 69 639852
Description: Promotes family planning as a basic human right. Works to reduce the number of unwanted pregnancies and abortions. Attempts to stop the spread of AIDS and other sexually transmitted diseases through education and contraceptive servi-

ces. Sponsors programs in family planning, sex education, and health. Conducts research. **Founded:** 1952. **Membership:** 5800. **Staff:** 10. **National Groups:** 1. **Languages:** German. **Budget:** DM 1,500,000. **Publication:** *Pro Familia Magazin* (in German), bimonthly. Magazine. Price: DM 6.50. ISSN: 0175-2960. Circulation: 7,000. Advertising: accepted. **Also Known As:** Pro Familia. **Formerly:** Pro Familia: Deutsche Gesellschaft fur Sexualberatung und Familienplanung.

PRO FAMILIA HUNGARIAN SCIENTIFIC SOCIETY (HSSFWW)
e-mail: klinger.office@office.ksh.hu
Keleti Karoly utca 5-7
H-1024 Budapest, Hungary
Dr. Arpad Meszaros, Sec.
PH: 36 1 3456666
FX: 36 1 3456678
Description: Advocates family planning as a basic human right. Encourages public awareness of family planning and responsible parenthood. Works to reduce the number of unwanted pregnancies and abortions. Offers programs in sex education, family planning, and health care. **Founded:** 1975. **Membership:** 531. **Staff:** 4. **Languages:** English, French. **Budget:** $50,000.

PROFESSIONAL ASSOCIATION OF GERMAN INTERNISTS
(Berufsverband Deutscher Internisten)
e-mail: info@bdi.de
url: http://www.bdi.de
Schone Aussicht 5
D-65193 Wiesbaden, Germany
Max Broglie, Contact
PH: 49 611 181330
FX: 49 611 1813350
Description: Protects and represents the interests of internal medicine specialists in Germany. Promotes continuing education. **Founded:** 1959. **Membership:** 28000. **Staff:** 15. **Local Groups:** 77. **Languages:** English, French. **Publication:** *BDI - Ruudschveiben*, monthly. Newsletter ▪ *Der Internist* (in German), monthly. Magazine. Price: included in membership. ISSN: 0020-9554. Circulation: 33,000. Advertising: accepted.

PROFESSIONAL ASSOCIATION OF HEALTH CARE OFFICE MANAGERS (PAHCOM)
e-mail: pahcom@pahcom.com
url: http://www.pahcom.com
461 E. Ten Mile Rd.
Pensacola, FL 32534
Richard Blanchette, Contact
PH: (850)474-9460
TF: 800451-9311
FX: (850)474-6352
Description: Office managers of small group and solo medical practices. Operates certification program for health care office managers. **Founded:** 1988. **Membership:** 3700. **Staff:** 8. **National Groups:** 1. **Languages:** English. **For-Profit. Budget:** $650,000. **Publication:** *Medical Office Management*, bimonthly. Newsletter. Provides current event information. Price: free, for members only. ISSN: 0896-6583. Circulation: 7,000. Advertising: accepted.

PROFESSIONAL ASSOCIATION OF NURSERY NURSES
e-mail: pann@pat.org.uk
url: http://www.pat.org.uk
2 St. James' Ct.
Friar Gate
Derby DE1 1BT, England
Tricia Pritchard, Professional Officer
PH: 44 1332 343029
FX: 44 1332 290310
Description: Qualified and experienced child care practitioners within education, social services, the health service, the private sector (including nannies). Represents the interests of qualified and student nursery nurses, nannies, and other cild care workers throughout the UK. Promotes professionalism at all times. **Founded:** 1982. **Membership:** 4000. **Staff:** 5. **Publication:** *All You Need*

to Know About Working as a Nanny. Book. Price: L5.00 ▪ *Professional Nursery Nurse* (in English), quarterly. Journal. Price: L1.50. ISSN: 1364-5641. Circulation: 4,000. Advertising: accepted.

PROFESSIONAL ASSOCIATION OF PHYSICIANS IN THE PHARMACEUTICAL INDUSTRY (PAPPI)

(Fachgesellschaft der Aerzte in der Pharmazeutischen
Industrie)
Gneisenaustrasse 23
D-30175 Hannover, Germany
Dr. Peter Kloepel, Contact
PH: 49 511 819138
FX: 49 511 819138
Description: Physicians working for pharmaceutical manufacturers and related research facilities. Works to insure the safety and effectiveness of pharmaceutical products; promotes high standards of professional ethics and practice among members. Conducts continuing education and training programs. **Founded:** 1973. **Membership:** 1200. **Regional Groups:** 6. **Languages:** English, German. **Publication:** *FAPI Intern,* bimonthly. Journal. Price: free for members. Advertising: accepted.

PROFESSIONAL BOARD FOR RADIOGRAPHY (PBR)

533 Vermenlen St.
Arcadia
PO Box 205
Pretoria 0083, Republic of South Africa
Mr. N.M. Prinsloo, Registrar
PH: 27 12 3286680
FX: 27 12 3285120
Description: Works to maintain professional standards of education and conduct of radiographers; strives to prevent the admission of unqualified individuals into the radiography profession. Cooperates with the Interim National Medical and Dental Council of South Africa in approving training courses in radiography. Investigates reports of unprofessional conduct. Represents members' interests before government authorities. Disseminates information; compiles statisics. **Founded:** 1974. **Membership:** 3500. **Languages:** Afrikaans, English. **Publication:** *SAMDC Bulletin* (in Afrikaans and English), quarterly. Price: free to members. Advertising: not accepted ▪ *Technical Journal,* periodic.

PROFESSIONAL MIDWIVES ASSOCIATION OF GERMANY

(Bund Freiberuflicher Hebammen Deutschlands eV)
Am Alten Nordkanal 9
D-41748 Viersen, Germany
Clea Nuss-Troles, Contact
PH: 49 2162 352149
FX: 49 2162 358542
Description: Midwives in Germany. Represents the interests of midwives. Informs and contributes to the health education of the population. Promotes continuing education for midwives in the interests of mother and child. **Founded:** 1984. **Membership:** 750. **Staff:** 6. **Regional Groups:** 12. **Languages:** English, Spanish. **Budget:** DM 140,000. **Publication:** *Hebammen Info* (in German), semimonthly. Newsletter. Contains articles about midwifery. Price: Included in membership fee. Advertising: accepted.

PROGRAM FOR APPROPRIATE TECHNOLOGY IN HEALTH (PATH)

e-mail: info@path.org
url: http://www.path.org
4 Nickerson St., Ste. 300
Seattle, WA 98109-1699
Gordon W. Perkin, M.D., Pres.
PH: (206)285-3500
FX: (206)285-6619
Description: Works to improve reproductive and child health, immunization programs, and diagnostic technologies in developing countries. Focuses on the effectiveness, availability, safety, and appropriateness of technologies for health and family planning. Conducts research and development, field assessment, communications, and technology transfer programs. Offers loans to assist developing countries in producing the essential health

products. **Founded:** 1977. **Staff:** 150. Multinational. **Languages:** English. **Budget:** $17,000,000. **Publication:** *Lending for Health,* semiannual ▪ *Outlook,* quarterly. **Absorbed:** Program for the Introduction and Adaptation of Contraceptive Technology. **Supersedes:** Health Division of Program for the Introduction and Adaptation of Contraceptive Technology.

PROJECT CONCERN HONG KONG

Pak Tin Estate, Block 11, Unit 1, G/F
Shamshuipo
Kowloon, Hong Kong
Mrs. Ng Chu Lai-Fong, Exec.Dir.
PH: 852 27769081
FX: 852 27769083
Description: Health care practitioners and other interested individuals. Seeks to reduce morbidity and mortality, particularly among women and children. Establishes and operates medical and dental clinics and provides social services in economically disadvantaged areas. Sponsors charitable activities. **Founded:** 1961. **Staff:** 70. **Languages:** Chinese, English. **Publication:** Annual Report, annual.

PROJECT CONCERN INTERNATIONAL (PCI)

e-mail: postmaster@projcon.cts.com
url: http://www.serve.com/pci
3550 Afton Rd.
San Diego, CA 92123
Daniel E. Shaughnessy, Exec.Dir.
PH: (619)279-9690
FX: (619)694-0294
Description: Works with communities worldwide to ensure low-cost, basic health care for those most in need, particularly mothers and children. Provides education, training, and medical assistance to safeguard the world's impoverished children. Works with volunteers to prepare local communities to care for their own children with long-term, self-sustaining projects. Maintains programs in Bolivia, Guatemala, El Salvador, Mexico, Nicaragua, India, Indonesia, Romania, and the United States. Operates OPTIONS recruitment and referral service. **Founded:** 1961. **Staff:** 160. Multinational. **Languages:** English. **Budget:** $8,400,000. **Publication:** *OPTIONS Newsletter,* bimonthly. Lists volunteer opportunities available to members. Price: $25.00/year. Circulation: 5,000. Advertising: accepted ▪ *Project Concern International–Annual Report.* Contains financial statements. Price: free. Advertising: not accepted ▪ *Project Concern International–Concern News,* quarterly. Provides information on Project Concern health and education programs and activities worldwide. Price: free. Circulation: 5,000. Advertising: not accepted. **Formerly:** (1978) Project Concern, Inc.

PROJECT CONCERN INTERNATIONAL - BOLIVIA (PCIB)

Calle J. Castro No. 1508, 3er piso
Casilla 4678
La Paz, Bolivia
Dudley Conneely, Dir.
PH: 591 1 351353
FX: 591 2 367625
Description: Works to reduce morbidity and mortality, particularly among women and children, through immunization and proper care of preventable and treatable diseases. Cooperates with local governmental agencies to provide public health services; conducts training programs for health service providers. Facilitates organization of local health care workers; sponsors publicity campaigns to raise public awareness of public health issues. Maintains Food for Work Program, which provides food for local laborers in exchange for their work on community public health projects. **Founded:** 1976. **Staff:** 15. **Languages:** English, Spanish. **Budget:** $963,514.

PROJECT CONCERN INTERNATIONAL - INDONESIA (PCII)
e-mail: pcijkt@rad.net.id
JR. PE Jompongan V/140
PO Box 99, JKPJ
10210 Jakarta, Indonesia
Barbie Rasmussen, Country Dir.
PH: 62 21 5707904
FX: 62 21 5707904
Description: National branch of the international organization. Works to reduce morbidity and mortality, particularly among children, through immunization and proper care of preventable and treatable diseases. Integrates local governing bodies into the provision of public health services; conducts training programs for local public health service providers. Prevent STD/HIV transmission in collaboration with local NGOs.

PROJECT CONCERN INTERNATIONAL - NICARAGUA (PCI)
e-mail: cepsnic@nicarao.apc.org
Edificio El Carmen
del Parque el Carmen 1c. Al Lago
Apartado Postal 4667
Managua, Nicaragua
Dr. Juan Alvaro Munguia, Contact
PH: 505 2 223073
FX: 505 2 224075
Description: Health care personnel and other individuals with an interest in public health. Promotes improved child health in urban areas. Conducts Nino-a-Nino Program, through which schoolchildren educate each other about public health topics. Trains community volunteers to disseminate health care and vaccination information. Sponsors child welfare education programs for new mothers. **Founded:** 1991. **Languages:** English, Spanish. **Budget:** $227,234.

PROJECT HOPE - JAMAICA
53 Old Hope Rd.
PO Box 6000
Kingston, Jamaica
Description: Health care professionals and other individuals. Promotes improved access to health care for people living in previously underserved areas. Conducts training programs for health care personnel in fields including anesthesia, family medicine, radiology, and health administration, with the aim of local autonomy in health care. Plans to offer services in areas including audiology, occupational therapy, and integrated urban development. **Founded:** 1971. **Languages:** English.

PROJECT HOPE - SWAZILAND
PO Box 2493
Manzini, Swaziland
PH: 268 52017
Description: Health care professionals and other individuals. Promotes improved access to health care for people living in previously underserved areas. Conducts training programs for health care personnel in fields including anesthesia, family medicine, radiology, and health administration, with the aim of local autonomy in health care. Plans to offer services in areas including audiology, occupational therapy, and integrated urban development. **Founded:** 1984. **Languages:** English.

PROJECT: HEARTS AND MINDS (PHAM)
Veterans for Peace
33 Portola Ave.
Monterey, CA 93940
Gordon Smith, Exec. Officer
PH: (408)649-5599
FX: (408)646-8376
Description: A project of Veterans for Peace. Collects surplus medical supplies and equipment for delivery to hospitals in Vietnam, Cambodia, and Cuba. **Languages:** English.

PROJECT OVERCOME (PO)
1821 University Ave., W.
St. Paul, MN 55104-2803
Margaret Correll, Exec.Dir.
Description: Recovered and recovering mental health patients. Works to eliminate the stigma attached to mental illness. Sponsors speakers' bureau of former mental health patients. Conducts advocacy services, seminars, support groups, lectures, and training events; offers professional consultation on the mental health system. **Founded:** 1977. **Membership:** 10. **Staff:** 1. Local. **Local Groups:** 1. **Languages:** English. **Budget:** $32,000.

PROPRIETARY ARTICLES TRADE ASSOCIATION
Watford Business Park
5 Caxton Way
Watford WD1 8UA, England
G. Harraway, Dir.
PH: 44 1923 211647
FX: 44 1923 211648
Description: Manufacturers, wholesalers and retailers operators in pharmaceutical industry. **Founded:** 1896. **Membership:** 10538. **Staff:** 2.

PROPRIETARY ASSOCIATION OF GREAT BRITAIN
e-mail: pagb@pagb.org.uk
Vernon House
Sicilian Ave.
London WC1A 2QH, England
Sheila Kelly, Exec.Dir.
PH: 44 171 2428331
FX: 44 171 4057719
Description: Trade association representing manufacturers of over-the-counter (OTC) medicines, health care and food supplements. Promotes responsible consumer and aims to increase the size of the OTC market. **Founded:** 1919. **Membership:** 70. **Staff:** 15. **Publication:** *OTC Update*, quarterly ▪ *PAGB Bulletin*, monthly. Price: Available to members only. ▪ *PAGB Monitor*, periodic ▪ Annual Report, annual.

PROTEIN SOCIETY OFFICE (FASEB)
e-mail: Newburgh@protein.faseb.org
url: http://www.faseb.org/protein
9650 Rockville Pike
Bethesda, MD 20814
Robert W. Newburgh, Ph.D., Exec. Officer
PH: (301)571-0662
FX: (301)571-0666
Description: Scientists, graduate students, and corporations interested in the study of the structure and function of proteins. Promotes discussion and interaction in the scientific community; provides a forum for exchange of ideas, findings, and research techniques on topics such as molecular biology, analytical chemistry, immunology, spectroscopy, and diffraction. Sponsors educational programs. **Founded:** 1986. **Membership:** 3200. **Staff:** 1. Multinational. **Languages:** English.

PSI OMEGA
e-mail: psio@ibm.net
1040 Savannah Hwy.
Charleston, SC 29407
Dr. B. Thomas Kays, Co-Exec.Dir.
PH: (803)556-0573
FX: (803)556-6311
Description: Professional fraternity - dentistry. **Founded:** 1892. **Membership:** 30000. **Staff:** 3. **State Groups:** 36. **Languages:** English. **Publication:** *Frater*, quarterly. Magazine. Circulation: 5,000. Advertising: accepted.

PSORIASIS RESEARCH ASSOCIATION (PRA)
107 Vista del Grande
San Carlos, CA 94070
Diane Bradley Mullins, Founder & Exec.Sec.
PH: (415)593-1394
Description: Supported by psoriasis patients, physicians, and oth-

ers interested in research to find the cause and cure of psoriasis, a chronic skin disease characterized by red patches covered with white scales. Provides patient-volunteers across the U.S. for studies at University of California Medical School, San Francisco, and at the Psoriasis Research Institute. Maintains library of 1500 volumes on psoriasis and related subspecialties. Supports individual researchers applying for small grants from PRA. Has received grants from several pharmaceutical companies to compile medical statistics on psoriasis patients, including detailed epidemiologic data and names of patient-volunteers. Maintains speakers' bureau. Convention/Meeting: none. **Founded:** 1952. **Languages:** English.

PSORIASIS RESEARCH INSTITUTE (PRI)
url: http://www.psoriasis-help.org
600 Town and Country Village
Palo Alto, CA 94301
Eugene M. Farber, M.D., Pres./CEO
PH: (415)326-1848
FX: (415)326-1262
Description: Creates projects for the study, diagnosis, treatment, and eventual cure of psoriasis. Collects and disseminates information about psoriasis in an effort to advance the science of dermatology. Maintains Psoriasis Medical Center, which offers advanced therapeutic programs and equipment to treat all aspects of the disease. Offers counseling and biofeedback stress control for patients. Compiles statistics; conducts epidemiological study of psoriasis patients. Sponsors monthly selfhelp workshop for psoriasis patients utilizing audiovisual presentations, written materials, and discussions. **Founded:** 1979. **Staff:** 13. Multinational. **Languages:** English. **Budget:** $1,400,000. Formerly (1983) International Psoriasis Research Foundation.

PSYCHIATRIC NURSES ASSOCIATION OF CANADA (PNAC)
e-mail: info@tnac.ca
url: http://www.pnac.ca
509 Pandora Ave. W
Winnipeg, MB, Canada R2C 1M8
Wendy Robillard, Pres.
PH: (204)222-6984
FX: (204)222-6984
Description: Psychiatric nursing associations. Seeks to advance the study and practice of psychiatric nursing; encourages professional advancement of psychiatric nurses. Makes available educational programs; compiles statistics. **Founded:** 1951. **Membership:** 3. **Staff:** 1. **Languages:** English, French. **Budget:** C$105,000. **Publication:** *Psychiatric Nursing: A Unique Profession.* Brochure.

PSYCHIATRIC SURVIVORS USING ALTERNATIVE METHODS
77 Main St., No. 914
Lockport, NY 14094
Joseph Hillegas, Contact
Description: Survivors of what the group believes is abuse at the hands of mental health professionals; other individuals with an interest in psychiatric malpractice. Seeks to improve the quality of life of psychiatric survivors. Promotes increased public awareness of what the group feels is the mental health system's treatment of patients as "second-class citizens." Encourages use of alternative mental health treatments including yoga, naturopathy, and aroma therapy. Conducts research and educational programs; maintains speakers' bureau. **Founded:** 1992. **Staff:** 1.

PUBLIC CITIZEN HEALTH RESEARCH GROUP (PCHRG)
e-mail: public_citizen@citizen.org
url: http://www.citizen.org/hrq/
1600 20th St. NW
Washington, DC 20009
Sidney M. Wolfe, M.D., Dir.
PH: (202)588-1000
FX: (202)588-7796
Description: Works on issues of health care delivery, workplace safety and health, drug regulation, food additives, medical device safety, and environmental influences on health. Petitions or sues

federal agencies on consumers' behalf, testifies before Congress on health matters, and monitors the enforcement of health and safety legislation. Publicizes important health findings; makes available to the public a broad spectrum of research and consumer action materials in the form of books and reports. **Founded:** 1971. **Staff:** 10. **Languages:** English.

PUBLIC HEALTH COMMITTEE OF THE COUNCIL OF EUROPE
Council of Europe
F-67075 Strasbourg, France
Dr. Peter Baum, Adm. Officer
PH: 33 388 412000
Description: A committee of the Council of Europe. Representatives of national ministries of health. Coordinates activities of the committees of experts assembled by CE under the Partial Agreement in the Social and Pubic Health Field. (The Goal of the Agreement is to assist in the development of uniform legislation in participating countries in the areas of public health and consumer protection. States party to the agreement are all CE member countries). Multinational.

QUALIFIED PRIVATE MEDICAL PRACTITIONERS ASSOCIATION (QMPA)
68 HB Panampilly Nagar
Kochi 682 036, Kerala, India
Dr. T. M. Paul, Pres.
PH: 91 484 312357
Description: Physicians. Promotes exchange of information among members; seeks to improve delivery of health care services. Informs members of legislation and research impacting on the practice of medicine. Conducts research and educational programs. **Founded:** 1973. **Membership:** 1015. **Languages:** English, Hindi. **Publication:** *QPMPA Journal of Medical Sciences,* monthly.

R. A. BLOCH CANCER FOUNDATION
url: http://www.blochcancer.org
4410 Main
Kansas City, MO 64111
Donna O'Connor, Contact
PH: (816)932-8453
FX: (816)931-7486
Description: Sponsors the Cancer Hot Line, a support group that matches cancer patients with volunteers who have been cured, are in remission, or are being treated for the same type of cancer. Volunteers describe treatments they have received and offer information referrals to newly diagnosed cancer victims. A second opinion may have physical and psychological benefits; it can reassure the patient that he is receiving the best available treatment or, in some cases, suggest that additional or alternative treatments be considered. Maintains speakers' bureau in Kansas City, MO. **Founded:** 1980. Multinational. **Languages:** English. **Publication:** *Cancer<el3>There's Hope.* Book ▪ *Cancer Hot Line News,* quarterly ▪ *Fighting Cancer.* Book ▪ *Guide for Cancer Supporters.* Book. Formerly: (1989) Cancer Connection.

RADIANCE TECHNIQUE AND RADIANT PEACE ASSOCIATION INTERNATIONAL
e-mail: trtpeace@aol.com
url: http://www.trt-rpai.org
PO Box 40570
St. Petersburg, FL 33743-0570
PH: (813)347-2106
TF: 888878-7724
FX: (813)347-2106
Description: Students of The Official Reiki Program - The Radiance Technique, a "science of universal energy which harmonizes and aligns the mind-body-spirit dynamic." Provides a network for those interested in The Radiance Technique. Maintains speakers' bureau. Compiles statistics and conducts research on the effectiveness of The Radiance Technique. **Founded:** 1980. Multinational. **Languages:** English. **Publication:** *News of TRT&RPAI Journal* (in English, German, Italian, and Spanish),

semiannual. Newsletter. Price: included in membership dues. ISSN: 1040-5836. Circulation: 2,000. Advertising: accepted. Alternate Formats: online. **Formerly:** American Reiki Association; Radiance Technique Association International; (1988) American-International Reiki Association; (1998) Radiance Technique and Peace Association International.

RADICAL CAUCUS IN PSYCHIATRY (RCP)
SUNY Downstate Med. Center
Box 1203
450 Clarkson Ave.
Brooklyn, NY 11203
Carl Cohen, M.D., Coord.
PH: (718)270-2907
FX: (718)287-0337
Description: Members of the American Psychiatric Association and individuals interested in mental health issues who take a politically progressive stand in psychiatry. Objective is to examine the socioeconomic and sociopolitical aspects of mental health issues from a left-oriented perspective. Areas of study have included a critical analysis of biological psychiatry, patient rights, and psychiatric treatment of mental patients in Latin America. Presents research findings to professionals and laypersons. Maintains speakers' bureau. **Founded:** 1969. **Membership:** 75. **Languages:** English.

RADIOLOGICAL SOCIETY OF NORTH AMERICA (RSNA)
url: http://www.rsna.org
2021 Spring Rd., Ste. 600
Oak Brook, IL 60521
Delmar J. Stauffer, Exec.Dir.
PH: (630)571-2670
FX: (630)571-7837
Description: Radiologists and scientists in fields closely related to radiology. Promotes study and practical application of radiology, radium, electricity, and other branches of physics related to medical science. **Founded:** 1915. **Membership:** 26000. **Staff:** 80. Multinational. **Languages:** English. **Budget:** $18,000,000. **Publication:** *Radiographics*, bimonthly. Features pictorial presentations of selected scientific exhibits from the society's annual meeting. Includes case studies. ISSN: 0271-5333. Circulation: 26,000. Advertising: accepted ■ *Radiology*, monthly. Journal. Covers diagnostic radiology, neuroradiology, nuclear medicine, pediatric radiology, therapeutic radiology, cardiovascular radiology, and ultrasound. ISSN: 0033-8419. Circulation: 36,000. Advertising: accepted ■ *RSNA Educational Materials*, annual. Catalog. Lists video/slide set series for CME credits ■ Membership Directory, annual. **Formerly:** (1918) Western Roentgen Society.

RADIOLOGY BUSINESS MANAGEMENT ASSOCIATION (RBMA)
url: http://www.rbma.org
1550 S. Coast Hwy., Ste. 201
Laguna Beach, CA 92651
Sharon Urch, Exec.Dir.
PH: (888)224-RBMA
FX: (714)376-2246
Description: Business managers for private radiology groups; corpoorate members include: vendors of equipment, services, or supplies. Purposes are to improve business administration of radiologists' practices to better serve patients and the medical profession; and to provide opportunities for professional development and recognition. Offers extensive educational and networking opportunities and informal placement service. Maintains information services emphasizing those aspects unique to the business of radiology. **Founded:** 1968. **Membership:** 1600. **Staff:** 4. Local Groups: 10. **Languages:** English. **Budget:** $700,000. **Publication:** *Radiology Business Management Association – Bulletin*, 10/year. Newsletter. Covers organizational topics, industry trends, and legislative developments affecting the private practice of radiology; includes annual index. Price: included in membership dues; $100.00/year for nonmembers. Circulation: 1,600. Advertising: accepted ■ *Radiology Business Management Association – Membership Directory*, annual. Includes list of industry ven-

dors and suppliers. Price: included in membership dues. Circulation: 1,600. Advertising: accepted. **Formerly:** (1990) Radiologists Business Managers Association.

REACH TO RECOVERY
url: http://www.cancer.org
c/o American Cancer Society
1599 Clifton Rd. NE
Atlanta, GA 30329
TF: 800ACS-2345
FX: (404)636-5567
Description: A short-term, one-on-one visitation program sponsored by the American Cancer Society that provides information and support to women with a personal concern about breast cancer by the Reach to Recovery visitor. Helps women meet the physical, emotional, and cosmetic needs related to their disease and its treatment. The Reach to Recovery volunteer visitor gives information and practical tips, but not medical advice. To request a visit, the patient or her doctor, nurse, family member, or friend can call the American Cancer Society office listed in the telephone book. Convention/Meeting: none. **Founded:** 1952. Multinational. **Languages:** English. **Publication:** Brochure.

READ NATURAL CHILDBIRTH FOUNDATION (RNCF)
PO Box 150956
San Rafael, CA 94915-0956
Margaret B. Farley, Pres.
PH: (415)456-8462
Description: Doctors, nurses, childbirth instructors, and parents. Promotes and teaches expectant parents the philosophies of natural childbirth pioneered by Grantly Dick-Read, a British doctor who began writing in 1932 about the then extremely controversial concept of natural childbirth and advocated relaxation as the key to comfortable labor. Techniques include abdominal and rib cage breathing and alleviation of fear, and thus pain, through knowledge. Acts as resource agency for the International Childbirth Education Association. Conducts charitable programs. Offers speakers' bureau. **Founded:** 1978. **Membership:** 30. **State Groups:** 3. **Languages:** English.

RECLAMATION (INC.)
2502 Waterford Dr.
San Antonio, TX 78217
Don H. Culwell, Dir.
PH: (210)822-3569
Description: Former mental patients; interested others. Seeks to eliminate the stigma of mental illness and reclaim members' "human dignity." Serves as a voice for mental health patients in consumer, social, and political affairs. Helps members to live outside a hospital setting by providing assistance in the areas of resocialization, employment, and housing. Monitors media coverage; encourages "positive" presentations of mental health patients and increased coverage of mental health community service projects and events. **Founded:** 1974. **Membership:** 200. **Staff:** 1. State. **Local Groups:** 1. **Languages:** English. **Budget:** $10,000.

REFLEX SYMPATHETIC DYSTROPHY ASSOCIATION OF AMERICA
url: http://www.cyboard.com/RSDS
PO Box 821
Haddonfield, NJ 08033
Francis J. Davis, Jr., Pres.
PH: (609)795-8845
FX: (609)795-8845
Description: People with Reflex Sympathetic Dystrophy Syndrome; health care professionals treating RSDS patients. (RSDS is a disorder of the autonomic nervous system whose onset is usually preceded by a minor trauma such as a muscle sprain; symptoms of RSDS include severe pain, loss of muscle motion and use, swelling, skin and nail changes, and softening of the bones in affected areas.) Promotes increased awareness of RSDS among health care professionals and the public; conducts media campaigns; maintains national network of physicians involved in RSDS treatment and research. Encourages and supports RSDS

research; has a national data bank for the coordination of RSDS research and treatment information. Aids in the formation of support groups for people with RSDS; develops in-service programs and seminars for use at hospitals and educational institutions. Makes available referral services. Conducts educational programs; maintains speakers' bureau; compiles statistics. **Founded:** 1984. **Membership:** 2300. **Local Groups:** 100. **Languages:** English. **Budget:** $140,000. **Publication:** *Help Us to Stop the Pain.* Brochure ▪ *RSDS Digest*, annual. Lists articles published in America and Canada and foreign articles from the previous year. Price: $6.00 for members; $12.00 for nonmembers ▪ *RSDSA Review*, quarterly. Newsletter. Price: included in membership dues. Circulation: 2,300. **Formerly:** (1998) Reflex Sympathetic Dystrophy Association.

REFUGEE RELIEF INTERNATIONAL (RRI)
PO Box 693
Boulder, CO 80306
Alexander M. S. McColl, Pres.
PH: (303)449-3750
FX: (303)444-5617
Description: Physicians, paramedics, and nurses with prior military experience. Provides medical and other help to refugees and other victims of war and oppression throughout the world. Major efforts have been in Central America, although significant contributions to multi-national, multi-agency relief efforts have been made in Afghanistan, Azerbaijan, and in support of the Karens in Burma. Transports and distributes medical supplies and equipment. Conducts classes on first aid, hygeine, public health and sanitation for indigenous paramedics, refugees and others. **Founded:** 1982. Multinational. **Languages:** English. **Absorbed:** (1994) Parachute Medical Rescue Service.

REGISTER OF TRADITIONAL CHINESE MEDICINE
19 Trinity Rd.
London N2 8JJ, England
Carol Daglish, Contact
PH: 44 181 8838431
Description: Professional acupuncture practitioners. Committed to maintaining proper standards of professional health care by its members for the protection and benefit of the public. **Founded:** 1984. **Membership:** 220. **Publication:** Newsletter.

REGISTERED NURSING HOME ASSOCIATION
e-mail: rnhaho@aol.com
url: http://www.intercarenet.co.uk/carenet/
Calthorpe House
Hagley Rd.
Birmingham, W. Midlands B16 8QY, England
F.E. Ursell, CEO
PH: 44 121 4542511
FX: 44 121 4540932
Description: Nursing Home Owners. **Founded:** 1968. **Membership:** 1600. **Staff:** 8. **Regional Groups:** 33. **Publication:** *RNHA Guide* (in English), annual. Book. A reference book on nursing homes in U.K. Price: Free to members and libraries; L50.00 for commercial companies. Circulation: 2,000. Advertising: accepted ▪ Newsletter, monthly.

REGISTRY OF COMPARATIVE PATHOLOGY (RCP)
c/o Armed Forces Institute of Pathology
Washington, DC 20306
Timothy P. O'Neill, D.V.M., Chief Pathologist
PH: (202)782-2440
FX: (202)782-9150
Description: Veterinary and medical pathologists; biomedical scientists in related fields; medical personnel. To collect, classify, and disseminate information on comparative pathology of animals to the biomedical community. Promotes communication in biomedical research by scientists interested in comparative pathology. Sponsors exhibits, lectures, and symposia; offers annual continuing education course in comparative pathology. **Founded:** 1966. **Membership:** 11. **Staff:** 3. Multinational. **Languages:** English. **Publication:** *Animal Models of Human Disease*, biennial.

Handbook. Price: $295.00/set 4% shipping & handling. Advertising: not accepted. Alternate Formats: CD-ROM ▪ *Comparative Pathology Bulletin*, quarterly. Price: $15.00/year; $25.00 for 2 years; $40.00 for 3 years ▪ *Educational Opportunities in Comparative Pathology*, periodic. Price: free ▪ *Resources of Biomedical and Zoological Specimens*, periodic. Directory. Price: free ▪ *Symposia Proceedings*, periodic ▪ *Training Programs in Pathology and Clinical Pathology in North American Colleges and Schools of Veterinary Medicine*, periodic. Price: free.

REGULATORY AFFAIRS PROFESSIONALS SOCIETY (RAPS)
e-mail: raps@raps.org
url: http://www.raps.org
12300 Twinbrook Pky., Ste. 350
Rockville, MD 20852
Sherry Keramidas, PhD, CAE
PH: (301)770-2920
FX: (301)770-2924
Description: Represents the regulatory affairs profession and the individuals who are part of this dynamic field. RAPS members are the health regulatory leaders of today and tomorrow in areas such as medical devices, pharmaceuticals, biologics, biotechnology and in vitro diagnostics. **Founded:** 1976. **Membership:** 6700. **Staff:** 13. Multinational. **Languages:** English. **Budget:** $4,000,000. **Publication:** *RA Focus*, monthly. Magazine. Advertising: accepted ▪ *RAPS*, annual. Membership Directory. Advertising: accepted.

REIKI ALLIANCE
e-mail: reikialliance@compuserve.com
PO Box 41
Cataldo, ID 83810
Susan Mitchell, Exec.Dir.
PH: (208)682-3535
FX: (208)682-4848
Description: Teachers of Reiki, the Usui System of Natural Healing. Supports teachers of the Usui System Of Natural Healing in 40 countries. Promotes exchange among teachers and students; provides member referrals; supports workshops for additional teacher training. **Founded:** 1983. **Membership:** 870. **Staff:** 8. Multinational. **Languages:** English, Finnish. **Budget:** $450,000. **Publication:** *Reiki Alliance Membership Newsletter* (in English and German), 3/year. Price: included in membership dues. Circulation: 870. Advertising: not accepted ▪ *Student Book*.

RENAL PATHOLOGY SOCIETY (RPS)
url: http://www.med.ualberta.ca/rps
Department of Pathology, CB7525
814 Brinkhous-Bullitt Bldg.
University of North Carolina
Chapel Hill, NC 27599-7525
Dr. Arthur Cohen, Pres.
Description: Works to spread and increase knowledge of pathology of the kidney and seeks to develop renal pathology as a subspecialty. Conducts research and educational programs. **Founded:** 1993. **Membership:** 170. Multinational.

REPHAEL SOCIETY (RS)
1123 Broadway
New York, NY 10010
Joel Schwartz, Exec.Dir.
PH: (212)229-2340
FX: (212)691-0573
Description: A section of the Association of Orthodox Jewish Scientists. Jewish Orthodox doctors, dentists, physical therapists, nurses, and others in the health care field. Objectives are to study medical issues and problems as they relate to Orthodox Jewish law and to promote the welfare of Orthodox Jews in the health care field. Sponsors lectures and seminars. Compiles listing of residency programs recommended for Orthodox Jewish medical students. **Founded:** 1966. **Membership:** 600. **Languages:** English. **Publication:** *Practical Medical Halacha*, periodic. Reports on studies and meetings.

REPRODUCTIVE HEALTH RESEARCH ASSOCIATION IN YUNNAN
Department of Public Health
Kunming University
Kunming 650031, People's Republic of China
PH: 86 10 8181911
FX: 86 10 8182571
Description: Health care professionals active in public health and reproductive medicine. Promotes availability of health care for women and children living in rural areas. Makes available family planning services. **Founded:** 1982. **Languages:** Chinese, English.

RESEARCH CENTER AGAINST MENINGITIS AND SCHISTOSOMIASIS
(Centre de Recherches sur les Meningites et les Schistosomiases)
e-mail: cermes@raimey.orstom.ne
url: http://www.orstom.ne/cermes
Boite Postale 10887
Niamey, Niger
J.-P. Chippaux, Dir.
PH: 227 752045
FX: 227 753180
Description: Health care professionals and researchers. Promotes development of improved diagnostic techniques and treatments for meningitis and schistosomiasis. Conducts research; gathers and disseminates information; makes available health services. **Founded:** 1978. **Staff:** 50. Multinational. **Languages:** English, French. **Budget:** $500,000.

RESEARCH! AMERICA
e-mail: researcham@aol.com
url: http://www.researchamerica.org
908 King St. No. 400E
Alexandria, VA 22314-3067
Mary Woolley, Pres. & CEO
TF: 800366-CURE
Description: Academia, voluntary health organizations, professional and scientific societies, colleges and universities, businesses and industries, and foundations and philanthropists. Works to increase public awareness of the benefits to humankind of medical research and to build a strong base of citizen support for research into the cure, treatment, and prevention of physical and mental disorders. Seeks to stimulate interest in medical research careers. Appeals to institutions and the government to provide essential funding for medical research. Engages in multimedia communications programs and serves as a clearinghouse and source of information to members, the media, the general public, and elected officials. **Founded:** 1989. **Membership:** 350. **Staff:** 7. **Languages:** English. **Budget:** $900,000. **Publication:** *Membership Matters* (in English), monthly. Newsletter. Price: included in membership dues. Circulation: 1,000. Advertising: not accepted.

RESPIRATORY NURSING SOCIETY (RNS)
e-mail: rnsatpns@aol.com
7794 Grow Dr.
Pensacola, FL 32514
Belinda E. Puetz, Exec.Dir.
PH: (850)474-8869
TF: 888330-4767
FX: (850)484-8762
Description: Nurses who care for clients with pulmonary dysfunction, and who are interested in the promotion of pulmonary health. Fosters the personal and professional development of respiratory nurses, and quality care of their clients. Provides educational opportunities and promotes research in the field. **Founded:** 1990. **Membership:** 400. **Local Groups:** 2. **Languages:** English.

RICHMOND FELLOWSHIP OF AUSTRIA (RFA)
e-mail: kuna.pmk@carinthia.com
url: http://www.happynet.at/pro-mente-kaernten
Society for Mental Health
Hoffmanngasse 12
A-9020 Klagenfurt, Austria
Prim. Dr. Thomas Platz, Contact
PH: 43 46355112
FX: 43 463501256
Description: Community mental health services. Seeks to insure ethical and efficient administration of community mental health care programs and institutions. Conducts training programs for community mental health personnel; participates in charitable activities. **Founded:** 1979. **Membership:** 400. **Staff:** 250. **Languages:** English, Slovene. **Budget:** 20,000,000 AS.

RICHMOND FELLOWSHIP INTERNATIONAL (RFI)
e-mail: RFI.UK@virgin.net
109 Strawberry Vale
Twickenham
Middlcscx, Greater London TW1 4SJ, England
Elly Jansen, OBE, CEO
PH: 44 181 7449585
FX: 44 181 8910500
Description: Promotes the establishment and operation of halfway houses and day centers for abused children, former psychiatric patients and recovering drug addicts. Organizes mental health training programs for social workers, psychologists, psychotherapists, and psychiatric nurses. Offers placement services. **Founded:** 1981. **Membership:** 18. **Staff:** 7. Multinational. **National Groups:** 26. **Languages:** English, French. **Budget:** L150,000. **Publication:** *Annual Report* (in English) ▪ Newsletter (in English), periodic. Price: free. Advertising: not accepted.

RIKSFORBUNDET FOR SEXUELL UPPLYSNING (RFSU)
e-mail: katarina.lindahl@rfsu.se
PO Box 121 28
S-102 24 Stockholm, Sweden
Ms. Katarina Lindahl, Head International Unit
PH: 46 8 6920700
FX: 46 8 6530823
Description: Promotes family planning as a basic human right. Works to reduce the number of unwanted pregnancies and abortions. Attempts to stop the spread of AIDS and other sexually transmitted diseases. Offers programs in sex education, youth sexuality, sexual and reproductive health. Provides contraceptive and health care services. Conducts research. **Founded:** 1933. **Languages:** Swedish.

RNA SOCIETY (RNAS)
e-mail: rna@faseb.org
url: http://www.cup.org/journals/rna/rnasoc.html
9650 Rockville Pike
Bethesda, MD 20814-3998
Chris Greer, CEO
PH: (301)530-7120
FX: (301)530-7049
Description: Professionals working in molecular, evolutionary, and structural biology, biochemistry, biomedical sciences, chemistry, genetics, virology, and related disciplines with an interest in the structure and functions of ribonucleic acid (RNA). Serves as a multidisciplinary forum for exchange of information and research results among members. Promotes and supports RNA research; gathers and disseminates information. **Founded:** 1993. **Membership:** 800. **Staff:** 3. **Languages:** English.

ROGER WYBURN-MASON AND JACK M. BLOUNT FOUNDATION FOR THE ERADICATION OF RHEUMATOID DISEASE (RDF)
e-mail: taf@telalink.net
url: http://www.telalink.net/~taf
5106 Old Harding Rd.
Franklin, TN 37064
Perry A. Chapdelaine, Exec.Dir. & Sec.

PH: (615)646-1030
FX: (615)646-1030
Description: Seeks to eradicate rheumatoid disease. Promotes professional university research and supplies free information to physicians and disease victims on Dr. Roger Wyburn-Mason's treatment protocol as modified by other physicians. (Such treatment includes oral medications, intraneural injections, and dietary control and, according to the foundation, has been successful in 80% of patients treated.) Conducts educational programs for the public and physicians; sponsors medical seminars; provides physician referrals and speakers' bureau. Emphasizes complementary, alternative, and holistic treatments especially for forms of arthritides. **Founded:** 1982. **Membership:** 14000. **Staff:** 1. Multinational. **National Groups:** 2. **Languages:** English. **Budget:** $1,000,000. Also Known As Rheumatoid Disease Foundation; The Arthritis Trust of America.

ROMANIAN PHYSICAL SOCIETY
e-mail: calbo@roifa.bitnet
Institute of Atomic Physics
PO Box MG 9
Bucharest, Romania
A. Calboreanu, Gen.Sec.
PH: 40 1 7807040
FX: 40 1 122247
Description: Physicists, physics students and educators, and others with an interest in the physical sciences. Promotes advancement in the study and teaching of physics in Romania. **Founded:** 1990. **Membership:** 450. **Staff:** 2. **National Groups:** 12. **Languages:** English, Romanian. **Publication:** *Curierul de Fizica* (in English and Romanian), quarterly. Journal. Advertising: accepted.

ROMANIAN SOCIETY OF CARDIOLOGY (SRC)
(Societatea de Cardiologie)
Sos. Fundeni 258, Sec. 2
R-72435 Bucharest, Romania
Prof. Eduard Apetrei, Pres.
PH: 40 1 2402827
FX: 40 1 2402827
Description: Cardiologists. Promotes investigation into cardiovascular diseases. Areas of research include: clinical physiopathology; epidemiology; physiopathology; prophylaxy; therapeutics. Maintains educational programs. **Founded:** 1947. **Membership:** 250. **National Groups:** 3. **Languages:** English, Romanian. **Budget:** 625,000 L. **Publication:** *Romanian Heart Journal* (in English and Romanian), quarterly. Price: $30.00. Advertising: accepted. **Formerly:** (1991) Society of Cardiology.

ROMANIAN SOCIETY OF CLINICAL NEUROPHYSIOLOGY (RSCN)
(Societatea Romana de Neurofiziologie Clinica)
e-mail: neurofiz@dsp.pub.ro
Neurological Clinic
Soseaua Berceni 10-12
Bucharest, Romania
Dr. Aurora Constantinovici, Pres.
PH: 40 1 3214924
FX: 40 1 3214924
Description: Scientists, physicians, and professors united to develop the electrophysiologic investigation of neurological diseases. Conducts basic and clinical research. Organizes symposia, lectures, and EEG, EMG, and Evoked Potentials demonstrations. **Founded:** 1952. **Membership:** 40. **Staff:** 1. **Local Groups:** 5. **Languages:** English, French. **Budget:** $400. **Publication:** *Romanian Journal of Neurology* (in English and Romanian), semiannual. Price: 3.00 L. Advertising: accepted ▪ *Romanian Journal of Neurology and Psychiatry* (in English), quarterly. Price: 2.00 L. Advertising: accepted ▪ *Romanian Neurosurgery* (in English). Advertising: accepted. **Formerly:** (1993) Romanian Society of Clinical Neurophysiology.

ROSE KUSHNER BREAST CANCER ADVISORY CENTER (RKBCAC)
PO Box 224
Kensington, MD 20895
Harvey D. Kushner, Exec.Dir.
PH: (301)897-3445
FX: (301)897-3444
Description: Information service for people, mostly women concerned about or with breast cancer. Provides information to public, patients and physicians concerning current knowledge about breast cancer detection, diagnosis, treatment and follow-up. **Founded:** 1975. **Staff:** 2. **Languages:** English. **Publication:** *If You've Thought About Breast Cancer by Rose Kushner*, biennial. Booklet. Price: free. Advertising: not accepted. **Formerly:** Breast Cancer Advisory Center; (1991) Women's Breast Cancer Advisory Center; (1991) Women's Breast Cancer Advisory Center.

ROYAL COLLEGE OF GENERAL PRACTITIONERS
e-mail: info@rcgp.org.uk
url: http://www.rcgp.org.uk
14 Princes Gate
London SW7 1PU, England
PH: 44 171 5813232
FX: 44 171 2253047
Description: General practitioners. Responsible for the promotion of high quality general practice through education, research and standard setting. **Founded:** 1952. **Membership:** 18400. **Staff:** 130. Multinational. **Publication:** *British Journal of General Practice* (in English), monthly. Price: L124.00 Pounds. Circulation: 19,500. Advertising: accepted.

ROYAL COLLEGE OF MIDWIVES
13-15 Mansfield St.
London W1M 0BE, England
Karlene Davis, Gen.Sec.
PH: 44 171 3123535
FX: 44 171 3123536
Description: Promotes the practice of midwifery, and works to maintain high standards in the field. Provides educational programs to midwives in the areas of maternity, child care, and personal development. Represents worker rights of midwives to national legal and political authorities. Encourages and supports research. **Founded:** 1881. **Membership:** 36000. **Staff:** 60. Multinational. **National Groups:** 4. **Languages:** English. **Publication:** *Delivery.* Newsletter ▪ *Midwives.* Magazine.

ROYAL COLLEGE OF NURSING OF THE UNITED KINGDOM
20 Cavendish Sq.
London W1M 0AB, England
Christine Hancock, Gen.Sec.
PH: 44 171 4093333
FX: 44 171 6473435
Description: Nurses, midwives and health visitors. Represents nurses working at all levels of responsibility and in a wide variety of settings, from the NHS to the independent sector and from local government to private industry. **Founded:** 1916. **Membership:** 310000. **Staff:** 480. **Publication:** *Nursing Standard*, weekly. Journal. Price: L1.10. ISSN: 0029-6570. Advertising: accepted.

ROYAL COLLEGE OF OBSTETRICIANS AND GYNAECOLOGISTS
e-mail: coll.sec@rcog.org.uk
url: http://www.rcog.org.uk
27 Sussex Pl.
London NW1 4RG, England
P. Barnett, Sec.
PH: 44 171 7726200
FX: 44 171 7230575
Description: Obstetricians and gynecologists, having completed a period of training recognised by the College and passed all components of the MRCOG examination. The encouragement of the study and the improvement of the practice of obstetrics and gynaecology. This is achieved by running examinations, postgra-

duate meetings, publications, committees and working parties. **Founded:** 1929. **Membership:** 9568. **Staff:** 85. **Publication:** *British Journal of Obstetrics and Gynaecology*, monthly. Advertising: accepted ■ *The Diplomate*, quarterly ■ *Journal of the Diplomates of the Royal College of Obstetricians and Gynaecologists*.

ROYAL COLLEGE OF OPHTHALMOLOGISTS

17 Cornwall Terr.
London NW1 4QW, England
Miss M. Hallendorff, Contact
PH: 44 171 9350702
FX: 44 171 9359838
Description: Medical Practitioners (ophthalmologists). **Founded:** 1988. **Membership:** 2876. **Staff:** 14. Multinational. **Publication:** *EYE* (in English), bimonthly. Circulation: 3,500. Advertising: accepted.

ROYAL COLLEGE OF PAEDIATRICS AND CHILD HEALTH

5 St. Andrews Pl.
Regents Park
London NW1 4LB, England
James Kempton, Contact
PH: 44 171 4866151
FX: 44 171 4866009
Description: Consultant paediatricians, community child health doctors, trainee paediatricians, research workers, general practitioners and other medical specialists who work with children. Aims to advance the understanding, treatment and prevention of disease in childhood, to further the study of child health and to promote excellence in paediatric practice. **Founded:** 1928. **Membership:** 3751. **Staff:** 25. **Formerly:** (1996) British Paediatric Association.

ROYAL COLLEGE OF PATHOLOGISTS

e-mail: secretary@repath.org
url: http://www.repath.org
2 Carlton House Terrace
London SW1Y 5AF, England
Keith Lockyer, College Sec.
PH: 44 171 9305861
FX: 44 171 3210523
Description: Postgraduate medical and scientific graduates who have successfully completed all or part of the college's examinations following a specified period of approved training, or elected under specified college ordinances. Advances the science and practice of pathology, furthers public education, promotes study and research work in pathology and related subjects and publishes the results of such study and research. **Founded:** 1962. **Membership:** 7300. **Staff:** 20. **Budget:** L1,500,000. **Publication:** *College Bulletin*, quarterly. Journal. Advertising: accepted ■ *Manpower and Management Policy Documents* ■ *Training and Examination Guidelines* ■ Reports.

ROYAL COLLEGE OF PHYSICIANS (RCP)

11 St. Andrew's Pl.
London NW1 4LE, England
Mr. D.B. Lloyd, Sec.
PH: 44 171 9351174
FX: 44 171 4875218
Description: Individuals in 64 countries. Establishes standards and quality controls for the medical practice. Advises the government, public, and members of the profession on health and medical issues. Conducts educational and training programs; organizes examinations; operates research unit. **Founded:** 1518. **Membership:** 7300. **Staff:** 102. Multinational. **Languages:** English. **Budget:** L6,500,000. **Publication:** *Annual Report* ■ *College List*, annual ■ *Working Party Reports* ■ Journal, bimonthly.

ROYAL COLLEGE OF PHYSICIANS AND SURGEONS OF CANADA (RCPSC)

e-mail: pierrette.leonard@rcpsc.edu
url: http://rcpsc.medical.org
774 Echo Dr.
Ottawa, ON, Canada K1S 5N8
Henry B. Dinsdale, M.D., Exec.Dir.
PH: (613)730-8177
TF: 800668-3740
FX: (613)730-8830
Description: Medical fellows (19,411); surgical fellows (9,742). Founded by the Canadian Medical Association. Prescribes requirements of specialty training in 53 medical, laboratory, and surgical specialties and subspecialties. Accredits specialty residency programs in 16 Canadian faculties, judges the acceptability of residency education medicine, and conducts the certifying examinations. Also assists its fellows to maintain their competence through the MOCOMP Program. Interested in health and public policy and biomedical ethics; it is not a licensing or disciplinary body. **Founded:** 1929. **Membership:** 30474. **Staff:** 96. **Languages:** English, French. **Budget:** C\$12,500,000. **Publication:** *Annals RCPSC* (in English and French), 8/year. Journal. Peer reviewed scientific articles. Price: C\$40.00/year. ISSN: 0035-8800. Circulation: 29,000. Advertising: accepted ■ *Annual Meeting Scientific Programme* ■ *Annual Report*. Bulletin ■ *Newsletter*, 8/year. Bulletin.

ROYAL COLLEGE OF PSYCHIATRISTS

e-mail: rcpsych@rcpsych.ac.uk
url: http://www.demon.co.uk/rcpsych/
17 Belgrave Sq.
London SW1X 8PG, England
PH: 44 171 2352351
FX: 44 171 2451231

ROYAL COLLEGE OF RADIOLOGISTS (RCR)

e-mail: enquiries@rcr.ac.uk
url: http://www.rcr.ac.uk/enquiries
38 Portland Pl.
London W1N 4JQ, England
Anthony J. Cowles, Gen.Sec.
PH: 44 171 6364432
FX: 44 171 3233100
Description: Diagnostic and interventional radiologists, nuclear medicine specialists, oncologists, radiotherapists, and ultrasound specialists. Works to advance the science and practice of radiological technology. Offers courses to further the education of practitioners. Establishes qualifications and examinations for fellowships and diplomas. **Founded:** 1939. **Membership:** 4900. **Staff:** 20. Multinational. **Languages:** English. **Publication:** *Clinical Oncology* (in English), bimonthly. Journal ■ *Clinical Radiology* (in English), monthly. Journal ■ *Members' Handbook* (in English), biennial ■ *Newsletter* (in English), quarterly. **Formed by Merger of:** British Association of Radiologists; Society of Radiotherapists. **Formerly:** (1975) Faculty of Radiologists.

ROYAL INSTITUTE OF HEALTH AND HYGIENE AND SOCIETY OF PUBLIC HEALTH

28 Portland Place
London W1N 4DE, England
Group Capt. R.A. Smith, Sec.
PH: 44 171 5802731
Description: Medical practitioners, dental practitioners, and environmental health officers from 19 countries. Seeks to advance public health and integrated health services. Provides a forum for information exchange among specialists. Reviews existing methodologies and proposes new practices. Serves as an advisory body to governmental and other organizations. Assists in developing continuing professional training for specialists in public health and preventive medicine. Conducts research. **Founded:** 1856. **Membership:** 1700. **Staff:** 18. Multinational. **National Groups:** 12. **Languages:** English. **Publication:** *Faculty Newsletter* (in English), quarterly. Price: free to members of the faculty ■ *Health and Hygiene*, quarterly. Journal. Features articles on

health hygiene. Advertising: accepted ▪ *Public Health* (in English), bimonthly. Journal. Contains articles submitted on public health matters worldwide. Price: L105.00/year for nonmembers. Circulation: 2,000. Advertising: accepted ▪ *Public Health Matters!* ▪ *Society Newsletter* (in English), quarterly. Price: free to members. Advertising: not accepted. **Formerly:** Society of Public Health; (1856) Society of Medical Officers of Health; (1973) Society of Community Medicine.

ROYAL INSTITUTE OF PUBLIC HEALTH AND HYGIENE (RIPHH)
e-mail: riphh@corpex.com
url: http://www.corpex
28 Portland Pl.
London W1N 4DE, England
R.A. Smith, Sec.
PH: 44 171 5802731
FX: 44 171 5806157
Description: Caterers, doctors, environmental health officers, food technologists, laboratory and mortuary technicians, microbiologists, nurses, and teachers promoting the advancement of domestic, industrial, and personal health and hygiene. Encourages the study of hygiene, preventive medicine, and public health. Offers courses; holds seminars. **Founded:** 1937. **Membership:** 3100. **Staff:** 22. Multinational. **Languages:** English. **Publication:** *Handbook of Mortuary Practice and Safety for Anatomical Pathology Technicians* (in English). ISBN: 0-9514655-1-1. Price: L6.00. Advertising: not accepted ▪ *Health and Hygiene*, quarterly. Journal ▪ *Public Health*, bimonthly. Journal ▪ *Supervisors Handbook of Food Safety* (in English). **Formed by Merger of:** Institute of Hygiene' Royal Institute of Public Health; Society of Public Health.

ROYAL IRISH ACADEMY - NATIONAL COMMITTEE FOR PHYSICS
19 Dawson St.
Dublin 2, Ireland
Prof. J.A. Slevin, MRIA, Chm.
PH: 353 1 6762570
FX: 353 1 6762346
Description: Physicists, physics teachers, and others with an interest in the physical sciences. Seeks to improve the quality of physics education, research, and knowledge. **Membership:** 17. **Languages:** English, Irish.

ROYAL MEDICAL SOCIETY
Student Centre
5/5 Bristol Sq.
Edinburgh EH8 9AL, Scotland
Mrs. P. Strong, Sec.
PH: 44 131 6502672
Description: Mainly medical students. Fellows and Life Members are medical graduates. An educational charity for medical students, run by medical students. **Founded:** 1737. **Membership:** 2500. **Staff:** 1. **Publication:** *Res Medica*, periodic.

ROYAL SOCIETY OF HEALTH
e-mail: rsh@cygnet.co.uk
RSH House
38a St. George's Dr.
London SW1V 4BH, England
Mrs. Heather Brandon, Sec.
PH: 44 171 6300121
FX: 44 171 9766847
Description: Members are drawn from a wide variety of professions and occupations with an interest in improving the health of the population. They range from architects and engineers, the health related profession, to food scientists and caterers. Aims to improve the quality and dignity of human life worldwide and to promote the continuous improvement of health and safety through education communication and the encouragement of scientific research. **Founded:** 1876. **Membership:** 10000. **Staff:** 22. Multinational. **Publication:** *RSH* (in English), bimonthly. Jour-

nal. Price: for members. ISSN: 0264-0325. Circulation: 10,000. Also Cited As: *J'Roy Soc Health.*

ROYAL SOCIETY OF MEDICINE
1 Wimpole St.
London W1M 8AE, England
Sir. Christopher Paine, Pres.
PH: 44 171 2902900
FX: 44 171 2902909
Description: Doctors, dentists, vets and lay members with interest in medicine. **Founded:** 1805. **Membership:** 18000. **Staff:** 150. **Publication:** *The AIDS Letter*, bimonthly ▪ *International Journal of STD and AIDS*, bimonthly ▪ *Journal of Medical Biography*, quarterly ▪ *Journal of Royal Society of Medicine*, monthly ▪ *Journal of Telemedicine and Telecare*, quarterly ▪ *Tropical Doctor*, quarterly.

ROYAL SOCIETY OF MEDICINE FOUNDATION (RSMF)
16 E 69th St.
New York, NY 10021-4906
William G. O'Reilly, Exec. Officer
PH: (212)371-1150
FX: (212)371-1151
Description: Serves as a forum for the discussion of topics relevant to the medical community in the U.S. and the United Kingdom. Sponsors conference series and exchange programs in conjunction with the Royal Society of Medicine. **Founded:** 1967. **Membership:** 3500. **Staff:** 2. **Languages:** English. **Publication:** *Digest*, quarterly.

RUSSIAN FAMILY PLANNING ASSOCIATION
e-mail: rfpa@dol.ru
18/20 Vadkovsky Per.
101479 Moscow, Russia
Inga Grebesheva, Dir.Gen.
PH: 7 95 9731559
FX: 7 95 9731917
Description: Advocates family planning and responsible parenthood as a basic human right and as a means to enhance the quality of life. Works to reduce the number of unwanted pregnancies and abortions. Attempts to stop the spread of AIDS and other sexually transmitted diseases. Offers programs in sex education, family planning, and health. Provides contraceptive and health care services. Conducts research. **Founded:** 1991. **Membership:** 4000. **Staff:** 22. **Languages:** Russian. **Budget:** 900,000 Rb. **Publication:** *Family Planning* (in Russian), quarterly. Magazine. Provides information on family planning, contraception, and sex education. Circulation: 4,000. Advertising: accepted.

RUTGERS STICHTING
e-mail: lcc@euronet.nl
Postbus 17430
Groot Hertoginnelaan 201
NL-2502 CK The Hague, Netherlands
Ms. Doortje Braeken, Contact
PH: 31 70 3631750
FX: 31 70 3561049
Description: Advocates family planning as a basic human right and a means to enhance the quality of life for individuals living in the Netherlands. Works to stop the spread of AIDS and other sexually transmitted diseases. Offers programs in sex education, family planning, and health. Acts as an advocate for family planning on a national level. Conducts research. **Founded:** 1965. **Staff:** 150. **Languages:** Dutch. **Budget:** 3,500,000 f. **Publication:** Books. Contains educational materials ▪ Pamphlets, periodic.

SAFE - SELF ABUSE FINALLY ENDS
c/o Karen Conterio
PO Box 267810
Chicago, IL 60626
Karen Conterio, Contact
PH: (312)722-3113
TF: 708783-0171
Description: Professional group assisting self-injurious individ-

uals in the treatment of their addictive behavior patterns. Maintains speakers' bureau; compiles statistics. **Founded:** 1984. **Local Groups:** 1. **Languages:** English. Formerly (1987) Self-Mutilators Support Group.

SAFE MOTHERHOOD INITIATIVE
Plot 196 Upper Mawanda Rd.
PO Box 1191
Kampala, Uganda
Dr. Josephine Kaselo, Contact
PH: 256 41 530500
FX: 256 41 230784
Description: Seeks to improve women's health and to reduce the number of women who die from complications of pregnancy and childbirth. Promotes family planning activities; conducts educational programs on teenage sexuality, sexually transmitted diseases, AIDS, and parenting. **Founded:** 1988. **Staff:** 372. **National Groups:** 1. **Languages:** English. **Budget:** $300,000. **Publication:** *Africa Women and Health* (in English), quarterly. Magazine. Price: $2.00. Circulation: 1,000. Advertising: accepted.

SALVATION ARMY MEDICAL FELLOWSHIP (SAMF)
101 Queen Victoria St.
London EC4P 4EP, England
Commissioner Kay F. Rader, World Pres.
PH: 44 171 2365222
Description: Purpose is to support members of the International Headquarters of the Salvation Army involved in the field of medicine, particularly those involved in nursing. **Founded:** 1943. **Membership:** 10895. **Staff:** 80. **Multinational. Languages:** English, French.

SARGENT CANCER CARE FOR CHILDREN (SCCC)
158 South St.
St. Andrews, Fife, Scotland
Dr. Chris Brittain, Coordinator
PH: 44 01334 470044
FX: 44 01334 470144
Description: Health care professionals and other individuals working with children with cancer. Seeks to improve the quality of life of children with cancer; promotes advancement of cancer diagnosis and treatment techniques. Provides support and assistance to families of children with cancer; makes available children's services; conducts educational programs; participates in charitable activities. **Founded:** 1969. **Languages:** English.

SCANDINAVIAN ASSOCIATION OF PAEDIATRIC SURGEONS (SCAPS)
(Nordisk Barnkirurgisk Forening)
Dept. of Pediatric Surgery
Regionsykehuset
N-7006 Trondheim, Norway
Torbjorn Kufaas, Contact
PH: 47 7 3998000
FX: 47 7 3997428
Description: Pediatric surgeons in 5 countries. Promotes the development of pediatric surgery and cooperation among members; represents members internationally. Encourages cooperative studies. **Founded:** 1964. **Membership:** 146. **Staff:** 2. **Multinational. National Groups:** 5. **Languages:** Danish, English.

SCANDINAVIAN ASSOCIATION OF ZONE-THERAPEUTISTS (SFFF)
(Skandinavisk Forening for (Fodreflexologer) Zoneterapeutes)
Krogholmgardsvej 50
DK-2950 Vedbek, Denmark
Birgitte Bendjellal, Contact
PH: 45 45890188
FX: 45 45890188
Description: Zone therapy practitioners and students. (Zone therapy involves the division of the body into parts or zones. Certain zones are then studied and/or manipulated in order to maintain health or treat particular health problems.) Examines the impact of vitamins, minerals, and diet on health. Studies related therapeutic procedures. **Founded:** 1975. **Membership:** 500. **Multinational. Languages:** Danish, English. **Budget:** 250,000 DKr. **Publication:** *Fodnoten.* Magazine. ISSN: 0905-1430 ■ *SFFF Medlemsblad* (in Danish), periodic.

SCANDINAVIAN NEUROLOGICAL ASSOCIATION (SNA)
(Nordisk Neurologisk Forening)
e-mail: jorma.palo@helsinki.fi
Department of Neurology
University of Helsinki
FIN-00290 Helsinki, Finland
Prof. J. Palo, Pres.
PH: 358 0 4712261
FX: 358 0 4714009
Description: Scandinavian national societies representing 900 neurologists and other specialists with an interest in neuroscience. Promotes neurological research and cooperation among Scandinavian neurologists. Provides educational counseling. **Founded:** 1922. **Membership:** 5. **Multinational. Languages:** Danish, English. **Publication:** *Congress Abstracts*, biennial. Proceedings.

SCANDINAVIAN NEUROSURGICAL SOCIETY (SNS)
(Nordisk Neurokirurgisk Forening)
e-mail: tiitm@neuro.ks.se
Institute of Clinical Neuroscience
Department of Neurosurgery
Karolinska Hospital
S-171 76 Stockholm, Sweden
Tiit Mathiesen, MD,PHD, Contact
PH: 46 8 51770000
FX: 46 31 416719
Description: Scandinavian neurosurgeons and neurosurgical residents; practicing neurosurgeons outside of Scandinavia. Works to facilitate collaboration among Scandinavian neurosurgeons. **Founded:** 1945. **Membership:** 160. **Multinational. Languages:** English.

SCANDINAVIAN SURGICAL SOCIETY (SSS)
Univ. of Turku
Lemminkaisenkatu 14-18 B
FIN-20520 Turku, Finland
Peter Roberts, Sec.Gen.
PH: 358 2 2612203
FX: 358 2 2612284
Description: Surgeons in Denmark, Finland, Iceland, Norway, and Sweden. Seeks to: promote clinical and research work and training in the field of surgery; encourage scientific and clinical communication between surgeons in the Scandinavian countries and elsewhere. Offers courses in surgical disciplines. **Founded:** 1893. **Membership:** 4352. **Multinational. National Groups:** 5. **Languages:** Danish, English. **Publication:** *European Journal of Surgery* (in English), semiannual. **Formerly:** (1994) Nordic Surgical Society.

SCHIZOPHRENICS ANONYMOUS (SA)
1209 California Rd.
Eastchester, NY 10709
Elizabeth A. Plante, Dir.
PH: (914)337-2252
Description: Self-help organization sponsored by American Schizophrenia Association. Groups are comprised of diagnosed schizophrenics who meet to share experiences, strengths, and hopes in an effort to help each other cope with common problems and recover from the disease; rehabilitation program follows the 12 principles of Alcoholics Anonymous World Services. Discussion topics include: symptoms and how to deal with them; the need to be responsible even though one is ill; overcoming guilt related to the illness. Each of the local groups attempts to recruit a volunteer mental health consultant from the area. The volunteer aids in program development and group discussion. **Founded:** 1967. **National Groups:** 5. **Languages:** English.

SCHOOL NURSE ACHIEVEMENT PROGRAM
c/o Ann Smith
University of Colorado School of Nursing
4200 E. 9th Ave.
Denver, CO 80262
Ann Smith, Project Dir.
PH: (303)270-8733
Description: Network of registered nurses in 26 states who conduct courses in the treatment of handicapped children in a school setting. Trains and certifies state course coordinators. Maintains library of materials pertaining to treatment of handicapped children in a school setting. Convention/Meeting: none. **Founded:** 1980. **Membership:** 34. **State Groups:** 26. **Languages:** English.

SCHOOL OF PHYTOTHERAPY
e-mail: medherb@pavilion.co.uk
url: http://www.blazeweb.com./phytotherapy/
Bucksteep Manor
Bodle St. Green
Hailsham BN27 4RJ, England
PH: 44 1323 834800
FX: 44 1323 834801
Description: Runs a training school for practitioners of phytotherapy (herbal medicine) incorporating a 4 year Bachelor of Science (Honours) degree course, a 5-year BSC Degree Distance Learning Course, specially structured course for practising general practitioners, plus a one-year basic home study course. **Founded:** 1982. **Membership:** 500. **Staff:** 6. **Publication:** *British Journal of Phytotherapy* (in English), semiannual. Price: L16.00/year for U.K. students; L38.00/year - overseas for an individual; L45.00/year - institution. ISSN: 0959-6879. Advertising: not accepted ∎ *Training for a Career in Herbal Medicine* (in English), annual.

SCIENTIFIC COMMITTEE ON SOLAR TERRESTRIAL PHYSICS (SCOSTEP)
e-mail: jallen@ngdc.noao.gov
url: http://www.ngdc.noaa.gov/STP/SCOSTEP
NOAA/NGDC
325 Broadway
Boulder, CO 80303
Prof. C. H. Liu, Pres.
PH: (303)497-7284
FX: (303)497-6513
Description: Countries interested in promoting and coordinating international scientific programs in solar terrestrial physics, the study of the relationship between the sun and earth. **Founded:** 1967. **Membership:** 55. **Staff:** 1. Multinational. **National Groups:** 40. **Languages:** English. **Budget:** $000,000. **Publication:** *International STEP NL* (in English), quarterly. Proceedings. Features scientific program activities. Circulation: 5,000. Advertising: not accepted. Alternate Formats: online. **Formerly:** Inter-Union Commission on Solar Terrestrial Physics.

SCIENTIFIC SOCIETY AGAINST EPILEPSY
Katedra po Nevrologia
Sv.G.Sofiiski 1
BG-1431 Sofia, Bulgaria
Dimitar Chavdarov, Pres.
PH: 359 2 542941
FX: 359 2 594094
Description: Fosters research in epilepsy. **Founded:** 1990.

SCIENTIFIC SOCIETY OF ANAESTHESIOLOGISTS IN BULGARIA
e-mail: tempus@ns.medfac.acad.bg
St. G. Sofiski 1
BG-1431 Sofia, Bulgaria
Prof. Ivan Smilov, Ph.D., Pres.
PH: 359 2 521046
FX: 359 2 548038
Description: Fosters research in anaesthesiology. **Founded:** 1970. **Membership:** 800. **Budget:** 1,000 Lv.

SCIENTIFIC SOCIETY OF ANGIOLOGY AND VASCULAR SURGERY
Miko Papo 65
National Centre for Cardio-Vascular Disease
BG-1309 Sofia, Bulgaria
Veselin Petrov, Sec.
PH: 359 2 223142
FX: 359 2 223128
Description: Fosters research in vessel surgery. **Founded:** 1993. **Membership:** 120. Multinational. **Languages:** English. **Publication:** *Journal of Angiology and Vascular Surgery* (in Bulgarian and English), 36/year. Price: 400.00 Lv. Advertising: accepted. **Formerly:** (1993) Scientific Society of Angiology and Vessel Surgery.

SCIENTIFIC SOCIETY OF BIOMEDICAL PHYSICS AND TECHNICS
Katedra po Fizika i Biofizika
Zdrave 2
BG-1431 Sofia, Bulgaria
Ventsilav Todorov, Pres.
PH: 359 2 51661
FX: 359 2 517266
Description: Fosters research in biomedical physics and technics. **Founded:** 1971.

SCIENTIFIC SOCIETY OF CARDIOLOGY
Tsentar po Sardechno-Sadovi Zaboliavania
Miko Papo 65
BG-1309 Sofia, Bulgaria
Ilia Tomov, Pres.
PH: 359 2 223134
Description: Fosters research in cardiology. **Founded:** 1973.

SCIENTIFIC SOCIETY OF CLINICAL NEUROPHYSIOLOGY
Klinika po Funktsionalna Diagnostika
Sv.G.Sofiiski 3
BG-1606 Sofia, Bulgaria
Slavcho Slavchev, Pres.
PH: 359 2 51542719
FX: 359 2 555006
Description: Fosters research in functional diagnostics. **Founded:** 1978.

SCIENTIFIC SOCIETY OF DERMATOLOGY AND VENEOROLOGY
Katedra po Dermatologia
Sv.G.Sofiiski 1
BG-1431 Sofia, Bulgaria
Nikolai Tsankov, Pres.
PH: 359 2 521261
FX: 359 2 594094
Description: Fosters research in dermatology and venerology. **Founded:** 1920.

SCIENTIFIC SOCIETY OF IMMUNOLOGY
Laboratoria po Imunologia
Madrid 26
BG-1504 Sofia, Bulgaria
Snezhina Marinova, Pres.
PH: 359 2 4347304
Description: Fosters research in immunology. **Founded:** 1991.

SCIENTIFIC SOCIETY OF MEDICAL EDUCATION
Katedra po Sotsialna Meditsina
Bialo more 8
BG-1504 Sofia, Bulgaria
Tsekomir Vodenicharov, Pres.
PH: 359 2 432275
FX: 359 2 443114
Description: Fosters research in medical education, social medicine and physicians' ethics. **Founded:** 1992.

SCIENTIFIC SOCIETY OF NEUROLOGY
Katedra po Nevrologia
Tsarigradsko Shose, 4 klm.
BG-1113 Sofia, Bulgaria
Dimitar Hadzhiev, Pres.
PH: 359 2 709390
Description: Fosters research in neuropathology and acupuncture. **Founded:** 1960.

SCIENTIFIC SOCIETY OF NEUROSURGERY
Katedra po Nevrohirurgia
Sv.G.Sofiiski 1
BG-1431 Sofia, Bulgaria
Andrush Karkeselian, Pres.
PH: 359 2 520233
FX: 359 2 594094
Description: Fosters research in neurosurgery. **Founded:** 1977.

SCIENTIFIC SOCIETY OF OBSTETRICS AND GYNECOLOGY
Institutska bolnitsa Maichin dom
Zdrave 2
BG-1431 Sofia, Bulgaria
Ilko Karagiozov, Pres.
PH: 359 2 521026
FX: 359 2 511650
Description: Fosters research in perinatal medicine. **Founded:** 1946.

SCIENTIFIC SOCIETY OF PATHOLOGY
e-mail: hristova@medfac.acad.bg
Dept. of Pathology
Central Labor. of Cytopathology
University Alexander's Hospital
BG-1431 Sofia, Bulgaria
Prof. Ivan Valkov, MD, Pres.
PH: 359 2 518651
FX: 359 2 517162
Description: Fosters research in pathomorphology and cytology. **Founded:** 1945. **Membership:** 120. **Languages:** English, French. **Publication:** *Savremenna Medicina* (in Bulgarian, English, and Russian), monthly. Journal. Alternate Formats: CD-ROM.

SCIENTIFIC SOCIETY OF PEDIATRICS
Katedra po Pediatria
D.Nestorov 11
BG-1431 Sofia, Bulgaria
Dragan Bobev, Pres.
PH: 359 2 541289
FX: 359 2 521650
Description: Fosters research in pediatrics. Immunological, diabetological, neonatological, oncochematology, cardiological. **Founded:** 1961. **Membership:** 829.

SCIENTIFIC SOCIETY OF PHARMACOLOGY
Institut po Fiziologia
Akad.G.Bonchev Blok 23
BG-1113 Sofia, Bulgaria
Hristofor Dishovski, Pres.
PH: 359 2 7132137
FX: 359 2 719108
Description: Fosters research in toxicology and clinical pharmacology. **Founded:** 1954.

SCIENTIFIC SOCIETY OF PHARMACY
Farmatsevtichen fakultet
Dunav 2
BG-1000 Sofia, Bulgaria
Evgenii Minkov, Pres.
PH: 359 2 879804
FX: 359 2 876265
Description: Fosters research in pharmacy. **Founded:** 1952.

SCIENTIFIC SOCIETY OF PSYCHIATRY
Psihiatrichna Klinika
Sv.G.Sofiiski 1
BG-1431 Sofia, Bulgaria
Kiril Kirov, Pres.
PH: 359 2 523503
FX: 359 2 594094
Description: Fosters research in psychiatry.

SCIENTIFIC SOCIETY OF RHEUMATOLOGY
Klinika po Revmatologia
Urvich 13
BG-1612 Sofia, Bulgaria
Kaniu Kanev, Pres.
PH: 359 2 585086
Description: Fosters research in rheumatology. **Founded:** 1983.

SCIENTIFIC SOCIETY OF ROENTGENOLOGY, RADIOLOGY AND RADIOBIOLOGY
Rentgenovo Otdelenie
Sv.G.Sofiiski 1
BG-1431 Sofia, Bulgaria
Licho Velichkov, Pres.
PH: 359 2 541123
FX: 359 2 594094
Description: Fosters research in roentgenology, radiology and radiobiology. **Founded:** 1959.

SCIENTIFIC SOCIETY OF SANITATION AND ORGANIZATION OF PUBLIC HEALTH SERVICES
Katedra po Sotsialna Meditsina
Bialo more 8
BG-1504 Sofia, Bulgaria
Zlatka Glutnikova, Pres.
PH: 359 2 442388
FX: 359 2 443114
Description: Fosters research in medical law, public health economics, informatics and automation of medicine and public health services. **Founded:** 1969.

SCIENTIFIC SOCIETY OF SPORT MEDICINE AND REMEDIAL GYM
Katedra po Fiziologia
V.Aprilov 15-A
BG-4000 Plovdiv, Bulgaria
Slavcho Savov, Pres.
PH: 359 32 44180
Description: Fosters research in remedial gym. **Founded:** 1953.

SCIENTIFIC SOCIETY OF STOMATOLOGY
Katedra po Protetichna Stomatologia
Dept. of Prosthetic Dentistry
Sv.G.Sofiiski 1
BG-1431 Sofia, Bulgaria
Todor Peev, Sec.Gen/Prof.
PH: 359 2 5169361
FX: 359 2 594094
Description: Fosters research in all diseases of the mouth. **Founded:** 1952. **Membership:** 85. **Languages:** English. **Publication:** *Stomatologia - Sofia BG* (in Bulgarian), semimonthly. Price: 1.00 Lv. ISSN: 0491-0982.

SCIENTIFIC SOCIETY OF SURGERY
Katedra po Obshta Hirurgia
Sv.G.Sofiiski 1
BG-1431 Sofia, Bulgaria
Stanislav Baev, Pres.
PH: 359 2 518663
FX: 359 2 594094
Description: Fosters research in infant surgery, plastic surgery, thoracic surgery, and artificial organs. **Founded:** 1944.

SCIENTIFIC SOCIETY OF VIROLOGY
Otdel po Virusologia
Stoletov 44-A
BG-1233 Sofia, Bulgaria
Stefan Dundarov, Pres.
PH: 359 2 329118
FX: 359 2 442260
Description: Fosters research in virology. **Founded:** 1991. **Membership:** 48. **Staff:** 3. **Languages:** English, German.

SCLERODERMA FOUNDATION (SF)
e-mail: sclerofed@aol.com
url: http://www.scleroderma.org
Peabody Office Bldg.
1 Newbury St.
Peabody, MA 01960
Karl Kastorf, Exec.Dir.
PH: (508)535-6600
TF: 800422-1113
FX: (508)535-6696
Description: Scleroderma organizations. Promotes medical research to find a cure for scleroderma, a chronic systemic disease affecting all organs resulting from uncontrolled growth of connective tissue. Seeks to foster an understanding of the disease through media and outreach programs; raises funds. Provides patients with educational materials and referrals to local organizations and medical specialists. Offers encouragement and consultation services towards the formation and development of local support groups. Acts as a clearinghouse for information about scleroderma research, drugs, and therapies. Conducts accredited programs for professionals. Maintains speakers' bureau; compiles statistics. **Founded:** 1983. **Membership:** 21000. **Staff:** 7. **Regional Groups:** 100. **Languages:** English. **Budget:** $1,300,000. Absorbed (1992) Scleroderma Association of New England. Formerly (1984) International Scleroderma Federation; (1998) Scleroderma Federation.

SCLERODERMA INTERNATIONAL FOUNDATION (SIF)
704 Gardner Center Rd.
New Castle, PA 16101
Mrs. Arkie Barlet, Pres.
PH: (412)652-3109
Description: Membership in 11 countries includes: individuals with scleroderma; family and friends of patients; doctors and nurses. (Scleroderma is a chronic condition resulting in the hardening of the skin, and in some cases, the connective tissue, arterial linings, and digestive tract.) Provides a supportive network for individuals with the disease. Supports research into the cause, cure, and control of scleroderma and strives to educate patients, physicians, and the public. **Founded:** 1971. **Membership:** 4500. Multinational. **Languages:** English. **Budget:** $35,000. **Publication:** *From Isolation to Communication <el3 >An Anthology of Scleroderma Patient's Experiences* ▪ *Scleroderma International Foundation – The Connector*, quarterly. Newsletter. Includes calendar of events. Circulation: 4,500 ▪ Pamphlet. **Formerly:** (1978) National Scleroderma Club.

SCLERODERMA RESEARCH FOUNDATION (SRF)
Box 200
Columbus, NJ 08022
Emanuel A. Coronis, Jr., Chm.
PH: (609)723-2600
TF: 800637-4005
FX: 800-723-6700
Description: Interested individuals and those who have had firsthand experience with scleroderma. Seeks to: supplement and implement medical research on the cause, treatment, and cure of scleroderma; develop a national network of support centers for patients and their families; inform the medical community and public about scleroderma symptoms to promote early diagnosis and treatment; encourage and gather donations, bequests, and memorials. Holds meetings featuring speakers on various aspects of the disease. Makes available a slide/sound program. **Founded:**

1978. **Membership:** 1500. Multinational. **Regional Groups:** 1. **Languages:** Greek.

SCLERODERMA SUPPORT GROUP (SSG)
e-mail: scleroderma@juno.com
8852 Enloe Ave.
Garden Grove, CA 92644
Clara K. Ihlbrock, Pres.
PH: (714)892-5297
FX: (714)893-2427
Description: Scleroderma patients and interested individuals. Serves as a support group for patients; provides information; raises funds for research; holds medical meetings and rap sessions. **Founded:** 1989. **Membership:** 1000. **National Groups:** 1. **Languages:** German, Spanish.

SCOTTISH ASSOCIATION OF HEALTH COUNCILS
18 Alva St.
Edinburgh EH2 4QG, Scotland
Patricia Dawson, Dir.
PH: 44 131 2204101
FX: 44 131 2204108
Description: Membership is open to all 18 health councils in Scotland. Provides information, training resources and development of public participation to all health related matters. The organisation is the focal point between Local Health Councils, the Scottish Office and Health Department and other national organisations, SAHC is voluntary and funded by LHC's subscriptions. **Founded:** 1977. **Membership:** 18. **Staff:** 2. **Budget:** L99,000. **Publication:** Papers.

SCOTTISH ASSOCIATION FOR MENTAL HEALTH
Atlantic House
38 Gardner's Crescent
Edinburgh EH3 8DQ, Scotland
Shona Barcus, Dir.
PH: 44 131 2299687
FX: 44 131 2293558
Description: Health Boards, Regional Councils, District Councils, Psychiatric Hospitals, local and regional voluntary organisations, Trade Unions, Professional Bodies Universities, individuals, local associations for mental health. Campaigns for better hospital and community services; seeks to increase understanding of mental distress; provides direct services to people who have suffered from mental health problems, namely supported accommodation and training for employment on projects all over Scotland. Information, training and a development consultancy are also offered to local groups, professionals and affiliated local mental health associations. **Founded:** 1923. **Membership:** 239. **Staff:** 381. **Local Groups:** 23. **Budget:** L9,178,000. **Publication:** *Mental Health Matters*, quarterly. Newsletter. Price: free to members. Circulation: 3,000. Advertising: not accepted.

SCOTTISH MOTOR NEURONE DISEASE ASSOCIATION (SMNDA)
76 Firhill Rd.
Glasgow G20 7BA, Scotland
Anne Jarvis, Contact
PH: 44 141 9451077
FX: 44 141 9451077
Description: Promotes interest in motor neurone disease (MND) research among medical and scientific communities and the public in Scotland. Offers support services to MND sufferers and their families. Disseminates information about the disease. **Founded:** 1981. **Membership:** 600. **Staff:** 7. **Regional Groups:** 14. **Budget:** L300,000. **Publication:** Newsletter (in English), 3/year. Advertising: not accepted.

SCOTTISH NATIONAL BLOOD TRANSFUSION ASSOCIATION (SNBTA)
2 Otterburn Park
Edinburgh EH14 1JX, Scotland
William Mack, Sec.-Treas.
PH: 44 0131 4437636

Description: Blood donors. Promotes donation of blood; seeks to insure a reliable and safe supply of blood and plasma for use in medical transfusions. Represents the interests of blood and bone marrow donors before medical organizations and government agencies; provides support and assistance to the Scottish National Blood Transfusion Service; consults with medical organizations to improve blood donation and transfusion techniques. Maintains speakers' bureau. **Founded:** 1940. **Membership:** 250000. **Languages:** English. **Publication:** *Annual Report and Statement of Accounts.* Advertising: not accepted.

SCOTTISH USERS NETWORK (SUN)
Firs Park
Firs St.
Falkirk FK2 7AY, Scotland
George H. Ronald, Contact
PH: 44 01324 632869
FX: 44 01324 632869
Description: Consumers of mental health services. Seeks to improve the quality of life of people with mental illness; promotes increased availability and effectiveness of mental health services. Represents members before mental health service provider organizations; sponsors self-advocacy groups for members; conducts educational and charitable programs; maintains speakers' bureau; compiles statistics. **Founded:** 1987. **Membership:** 550. **Staff:** 3. **Languages:** English. **Budget:** L75,000. **Publication:** *Shine,* bimonthly. Newsletter ▪ Directory, periodic ▪ Bulletin.

SEAMEO REGIONAL CENTRE FOR MEDICAL MICROBIOLOGY, PARASITOLOGY AND ENTOMOLOGY (SEAMEO TRO)
Jalan Pahang
Kuala Lumpur, Malaysia
Dr. M. Jegathesan, Centre Dir.
Description: A project of the Southeast Asian Ministers of Education Organization. Works to improve medical education and related programs in southeast Asia. Encourages study and research in the field. Conducts training programs and 2 graduate programs in medical microbiology and parasitology/entomology. **Founded:** 1970. Multinational.

SEAMEO REGIONAL CENTRE FOR PUBLIC HEALTH
e-mail: vchan@cph.upm.edu.ph
625 Pedro Gil St.
Ermita
Manila, Philippines
Dr. Veronica F. Chan, Dean
PH: 63 2 5242703
FX: 63 2 5211394
Description: A project of the Southeast Asian Ministers of Education Organization. Encourages excellence in public health education programs in southeast Asia. Conducts training programs. **Founded:** 1927. **Membership:** 59. **Staff:** 52. Multinational. **Budget:** $780,000.

SECTION FOR PSYCHIATRIC AND SUBSTANCE ABUSE SERVICES (SPSPAS)
url: http://www.aha.org
One N. Franklin
Chicago, IL 60606
PH: (312)422-3326
TF: 800242-4890
FX: (312)422-4590
Description: Institutional members, both general hospitals and freestanding specialty hospitals, of the American Hospital Association who provide psychiatric, substance abuse, clinical psychology, and other behavioral health services. Assists the AHA in development and implementation of policies and programs to promote improvement of and advocacy for the nation's behavioral health care providers. Active in formulating and commenting on federal legislation and regulations relating to psychiatric and substance abuse services. Develops and maintains liaison relationships with key organizations important to behavioral health providers. **Founded:** 1969. **Membership:** 3000. **Languages:** English. Formerly (1972) Psychiatric Hospital Section; (1984) Psychiatric Services Section; (1991) Special Constituency Section for Mental Health and Psychiatric Services; (1997) Special Constituency Section for Psychiatric and Substance Abuse Services.

SELECTIVE MUTISM FOUNDATION
url: http://personal.mia.bellsouth.net
PO Box 450632
Sunrise, FL 33345
Sue Newman, Co-Founder & Dir.
PH: (305)748-7714
FX: (305)748-7714
Description: Individuals and families affected by selective mutism, an inherited anxiety disorder in which children with normal language skills or deficient language skills are unable to speak in school or other social situations. SM is often mistaken for normal shyness, and may go undetected for as long as two years. Promotes awareness and understanding of this condition. Encourages research and treatment. Maintains speakers' bureau. **Founded:** 1991. **Membership:** 3000. **Staff:** 8. Multinational. **Languages:** Portuguese. Formerly (1993) Foundation for Elective Mutism, Inc.

SENEGAL FAMILY PLANNING ASSOCIATION (SFPB)
(Association Senegalaise pour le Bien-Etre Familial)
5, Route du Font de Terre
Boite Postale 6084
Dakar, Senegal
Belgasime Drame, Exec.Dir.
PH: 221 245261
Description: Promotes sustainable population growth through family planning. Seeks to increase participation by youth in family planning initiatives. Conducts educational programs to raise public awareness of population issues and family planning services. Makes available reproductive health, nutrition, and family planning services. Produces and distributes educational materials. **Languages:** French.

SEX INFORMATION AND EDUCATION COUNCIL OF CANADA (SIECC)
e-mail: sieccan@web.net
850 Coxwell Ave.
Toronto, ON, Canada M4C 5R1
Michael Barrett, Ph.D., Exec.Dir.
PH: (416)466-5304
FX: (416)778-0785
Description: Individuals and organizations in fields including sex education, counselling, reproductive health and medicine, and rehabilitation and therapy. Fosters public and professional education about human sexuality. Facilitates networking among members. Maintains information service and speakers' bureau; conducts research programs; sponsors educational programs. **Founded:** 1964. **Membership:** 800. **Staff:** 3. **Languages:** English, French. **Publication:** *Being Sexual: An Illustrated Series on Sexuality and Relationships.* Booklet ▪ *Canadian Journal of Human Sexuality,* quarterly. ISSN: 1188-4517. Circulation: 800. Advertising: accepted ▪ *SIECCAN Newsletter,* 2-3/year.

SIDELINES NATIONAL SUPPORT NETWORK
e-mail: sidelines@earthlink.net
url: http://www.sidelines.org
PO Box 1808
Laguna Beach, CA 92652
Candace Hurley, Exec.Dir.
PH: (949)497-2265
FX: (949)497-5598
Description: Former high-risk mothers dedicated to supporting women and their families experiencing a complicated or high-risk pregnancy. A pregnancy is termed "complicated" when the life or health of the mother and/or baby may be at risk. Committed to helping women overcome the risks of preterm birth, low birthweight, and other serious consequences of high risk pregnancies. Operates the One-On-One program where a mother

and her family are paired with a trained "Phone Friend" who has previously been through a complicated pregnancy. Offers prenatal care information and grief and loss counseling. Provides the families with resources and referrals to local businesses, agencies, and services that can assist them. Convention/Meeting: none. **Founded:** 1992. **Membership:** 20000. **Staff:** 35. **Regional Groups:** 32. **Languages:** Chinese, Japanese.

SIDRAN FOUNDATION AND PRESS
e-mail: sidran@access.digex.net
url: http://www.sidran.org
2328 W. Joppa Rd., Ste. 15
Lutherville, MD 21093
Esther Giller, Exec.Dir.
PH: (410)825-8888
FX: (410)337-0747
Description: Seeks to support people with trauma-generated psychological disorders and educate the public through the development of programs, projects and publications. Provides advocacy services; maintains speakers' bureau; information clearinghouse; professional training. **Founded:** 1986. **Staff:** 5. **Budget:** $200,000.

SIGMA PHI ALPHA
1919 7th Ave S, Rm. 311, Box 89
Birmingham, AL 35294-0007
Caren Barnes, Sec.-Treas.
PH: (205)934-7016
FX: (205)934-7013
Description: Honorary society, dental hygiene. **Founded:** 1958. **Membership:** 9000. **Staff:** 1. Multinational. **Local Groups:** 163. **Languages:** English. **Publication:** *Sigma Phi Alpha*, annual. Newsletter. **Also Known As:** National Dental Hygiene Honor Society.

SIGMA THETA TAU INTERNATIONAL (STTI)
e-mail: stti@stti.iupui.edu
url: http://www.iupui.edu
550 W. North St.
Indianapolis, IN 46202
Nancy Dickenson-Hazard, Exec. Officer
PH: (317)634-8171
TF: 888634-7575
FX: (317)634-8188
Description: Honor society - nursing. **Founded:** 1922. **Membership:** 262000. **Staff:** 65. Multinational. **Local Groups:** 383. **Languages:** English. **Budget:** $7,000,000. Formerly (1985) Sigma Theta Tau.

SINGAPORE MEDICAL ASSOCIATION (SMA)
e-mail: sma_org@pacific.net.sg
url: http://www.sma.org.sg
Alumni Medical Centre
2 College Rd.
Singapore 0316, Singapore
Gek Eng Chua, Exec.Sec.
PH: 65 2231264
FX: 65 2247827
Description: Promotes medicine and allied sciences in Singapore. Maintains the honour and interests of the medical profession. Represents the medical profession before government and other organizations. Maintains standards of medical ethics and conduct. Provides a forum for social, cultural, and professional contact among members. Organizes public health educational programs; offers CPR training; administers a training programme for health care assistants. **Founded:** 1959. **Membership:** 3200. **Staff:** 13. **Languages:** English. **Publication:** *Singapore Medical Association*, monthly. Newsletter. News article, classified ads. Price: Available to members only. Circulation: 4,000. Also Cited As: *merged with SMJ* ▪ *Singapore Medical Journal* (in English), monthly. Includes scientific papers. Price: S$10.00/issue. ISSN: 0037-5675. Circulation: 4,000. Advertising: accepted.

SINGAPORE PLANNED PARENTHOOD ASSOCIATION (SPPA)
e-mail: sppassn@signet.com.sg
03-04 Pek Chuan Bldg.
116 Lavender St.
Singapore 1233, Singapore
Mrs. Alice Tay, Admin.
PH: 65 2942691
FX: 65 2938719
Description: Promotes family planning as a basic human right and as a means to improve the quality of life for people living in Singapore. Works to reduce the number of unwanted pregnancies and abortions. Offers programs in sex education, family planning, and health. Provides contraceptive services. Acts as an advocate for family planning on a national level. **Founded:** 1949. **Membership:** 155. **Staff:** 6. **Languages:** English. **Publication:** *Monthly News Bulletin* (in English), bimonthly. Circulation: 200 ▪ Report, annual. Price: free ▪ Newsletter, biweekly. Price: free. **Formerly:** (1986) Family Planning Association of Singapore.

SJOGREN'S SYNDROME FOUNDATION (SSF)
e-mail: ssf@idt.net
url: http://www.sjogrens.com
333 N. Broadway, Ste. 2000
Jericho, NY 11753
Alexis Stegemann, Exec.Dir.
PH: (516)933-6365
TF: 800475-6473
FX: (516)933-6368
Description: Individuals who have Sjogren's Syndrome, xerostomia (dry mouth), or keratoconjunctivitis sicca (dry eyes); specialists, internists, immunologists, rheumatologists, otolaryngologists, opthalmologists, gynecologists, gastroenterologists, pulmonologists, dermatologists, neurologists, urologists, pharmaceutical companies, and dentists. (Sjogren's Syndrome is a disorder marked by dryness of all mucous membranes, resulting from deficient secretion of the glands, particularly the lacrimal and salivary glands, those of the upper respiratory tract, the sweat glands, and the vaginal area. Approximately 50% of Sjogren's Syndrome patients also have rheumatoid arthritis, lupus, or scleroderma.) Objectives are to increase public awareness and medical knowledge about Sjogren's Syndrome, educate patients and their families, and allow patients to share information on coping with the syndrome. Supports research. Sponsors support groups with meetings in which doctors speak on aspects of the syndrome. Compiles statistics. **Founded:** 1983. **Membership:** 6750. **Staff:** 3. **Regional Groups:** 7. **Languages:** English. **Budget:** $388,000. Formerly (1985) Moisture Seekers.

SKIN CANCER FOUNDATION (SCF)
e-mail: info@skincancer.org
url: http://www.skincancer.org
245 5th Ave., Ste. 1403
New York, NY 10016
Perry Robins, Pres.
PH: (212)725-5176
TF: 800SKIN-490
FX: (212)725-5751
Description: Sponsors medical symposia and public education programs on the prevention and early recognition of skin cancer. Grants its Seal of Recommendation to sunscreen products that meet the criteria and standards established by the SCF as effective aids in the prevention of sun-induced damage to the skin. **Founded:** 1977. **Staff:** 20. **Languages:** English. **Budget:** $2,000,000. **Publication:** *Flash!*. Newsletter. Price: $5.00 ▪ *Melanoma Letter*, quarterly. Newsletter. Contains articles and commentary on advances in the prevention and treatment of skin cancer. Price: $25.00/year (minimum donation). Advertising: not accepted ▪ *Play it Safe in the Sun*. Book. Price: $9.95 ▪ *Skin Cancer Foundation Journal*, annual. Contains short articles on the prevention, early detection, and treatment of skin cancer. Includes publications list. Price: $8.00/copy. Circulation: 30,000. Advertising: accepted ▪ *Sun and Skin News*, quarterly. Newsletter. Provides practical advice on the prevention, treatment, and

early detection of skin cancer. Includes research updates. Price: $25.00/year (minimum donation). Circulation: 60,000. Advertising: not accepted ■ *Sun Sense: A Complete Guide*. Book. Price: $14.95 ■ *Understanding Melanoma, What you need to know*. Book. Price: $14.95 ■ *Worldwide Melanoma Update*. Newsletter. Price: $6.00. **Formerly:** (1978) National Skin Cancer Foundation.

SLEEP DISORDERS DENTAL SOCIETY (SDDS)
e-mail: sdds@nb.net
url: http://www.nb.net/~sdds/
10592 Perry Hwy., No. 220
Wexford, PA 15090-9244
Mary Beth Rogers, Exec.Dir.
Description: Dentists, physicians, and Ph. D's active in sleep disorder medicine. Seeks to improve the treatment of patients with sleep disorders through the involvement of dental practicioners and use of oral appliances in overall therapy and to enhance the lives of people suffering form sleep disorders. Supports research in application of dental appliances in the treatment of sleep disorders, such as snoring and sleep apnea; conducts educational and certification programs; establishes dental treatment protocol; disseminates information on sleep disorder treatment; facilitates the exchange of information; operates the SDDS Resource Center. **Founded:** 1991. **Languages:** English.

SLEEP RESEARCH SOCIETY (SRS)
url: http://bisleep.medsch.ucla.edu/srs/
6301 Bandel Rd., Ste. 101
Rochester, MN 55901
Dr. Adrian Morrison, Pres.
PH: (216)444-8275
FX: (216)445-7471
Description: Physiologists, psychologists, and physicians with research interests in the study of sleep. Disseminates scientific papers on the physiological and psychological aspects of sleep. Facilitates communication among research workers in this field, but does not sponsor research investigations on its own. **Founded:** 1961. **Membership:** 600. Multinational. **Languages:** English. Formerly (1983) Association for the Psychophysiological Study of Sleep.

SLEEP/WAKE DISORDERS CANADA (SWDC)
e-mail: swdc@globalserve.net
url: http://www.geocities.com/~sleepwake/
3080 Yonge St., Ste. 5055
Toronto, ON, Canada M4N 3N1
Bev Devins, Exec.Dir.
PH: (416)483-9654
FX: (416)483-7081
Description: People with narcolepsy, insomnia, and other sleeping disorders and their families. Promotes self-help for people with sleep disorders; seeks to increase public awareness of sleep disorders and their causes and treatment. Encourages and facilitates establishment of local self-help and support groups for people with sleep disorders; conducts fundraising activities; sponsors National Sleep Awareness Week. Serves as a clearinghouse on sleep disorders; maintains register of sleep laboratories; functions as liaison between members and the Canadian Sleep Society, the national organization of doctors and sleep researchers. **Founded:** 1985. **Membership:** 1000. **Staff:** 3. **Languages:** English, French. **Publication:** *Good Night/Good Day*, periodic. Newsletter ■ *Sleep Solutions*. Booklet ■ Books ■ Brochures.

SLOVAK MEDICAL SOCIETY (SMS)
(Slovenska Learska Spolocnost)
Legionarska 4
SK-813 22 Bratislava, Slovakia
Zelmira Macova, Contact
PH: 421 7 211156
FX: 421 7 212363
Description: Chemical engineers, doctors, medical workers, and pharmacists. **Founded:** 1969. **Membership:** 31125. **Local Groups:** 67. **Languages:** English, French. **For-Profit. Publication:** *Avicennum*, periodic. Directory.

SLOVAK PHYSICAL SOCIETY
e-mail: sfs@savba.sk
url: http://www.savba.sk/~fyzists
Dubravska cesta 9
SK-842 28 Bratislava, Slovakia
Dr. Dalibor Krupa, Pres.
PH: 421 7 395676
FX: 421 7 376085
Description: Physicists, physics students and educators, mathematicians, and others with an interest in the physical sciences. Promotes advancement in physics research and training in the Slovak Republic. **Founded:** 1993. **Membership:** 260. **Languages:** English, Slovak. **Budget:** Kcs 150,000. **Publication:** *Gradient* (in Slovene). Bulletin. Advertising: not accepted. **Formerly:** (1993) Union of Slovak Mathematicians and Physicists.

SLOVAK SOCIETY OF ANESTHESIOLOGY AND INTENSIVE CARE MEDICINE
e-mail: aro@pos-tel.sk
Hodska cesta 373/38
SK-924 22 Galanta, Slovakia
Milan Ondercanin, M.D., Contact
PH: 42 1 7072441
FX: 42 1 7074572
Description: Health care professionals working in the fields of anesthesiology and intensive care medicine. Works to enhance members' professional development and to advance the quality of practice in the fields. Represents members' interests. **Founded:** 1991. **Membership:** 600. **Languages:** English, Slovak.

SLOVAK SOCIETY OF CLINICAL NEUROPHYSIOLOGY
Derer Hospital
Limbova 5
SK-833 05 Bratislava, Slovakia
Peter Kukumberg, M.D., Contact
PH: 421 7 371141
FX: 421 7 373708
Description: Neurologists, neurosurgeons, and other health care professionals with an interest in neurophysiology. Promotes continued professional advancement of members; represents members' interests. **Founded:** 1991. **Membership:** 190. **Staff:** 8. **National Groups:** 1. **Languages:** English, Slovak. **Formerly:** (1990) Czechoslovak Society of Clinical Neurophysiology.

SLOVAK SOCIETY FOR FAMILY PLANNING AND PARENTHOOD EDUCATION (SSPRVR)
e-mail: ssppr@netlab.sk
Ruzinovska 1
SK-82102 Bratislava, Slovakia
Cupanik Vladimir, MD, Pres.
PH: 42 17 5223880
FX: 42 17 5223880
Description: National branch of the International Planned Parenthood Federation. Promotes family planning and facilitates access to reproductive health services; works to ensure responsible parenthood. Conducts educational programs on population control, family planning, parenthood, and reproductive health. **Founded:** 1990. **Membership:** 172. **Staff:** 3. Multinational. **Languages:** English, Slovak. **Budget:** Kcs 35,000. **Publication:** *Empatia*, quarterly. Journal. Price: free.

SLOVAK SOCIETY OF NEUROLOGY
e-mail: lisy@ivzba.sk
Hospital Ruzinov
Ruzinovska 6
SK-826 06 Bratislava, Slovakia
Peter Spalek, M.D., Contact
PH: 42 7 233148
FX: 42 7 236433
Description: Neurologists. Works to improve the treatment of neuromuscular diseases, and to advance the professional standing of members. Represents members' interests. **Founded:** 1953. **Membership:** 652. **Staff:** 11. **Languages:** English, Slovak.

SLOVAK SOCIETY OF PEDIATRICS
1 Children's Clinic
Limbova 1
SK-833 40 Bratislava, Slovakia
Marta Benedekova, M.D., Contact
PH: 42 7 374511
FX: 42 7 376243
Description: Pediatricians and other health care professionals with an interest in child health. Promotes proper pediatric medical care; represents members' interests. **Membership:** 2000. **Languages:** English, Slovak.

SLOVENIAN BIOCHEMICAL SOCIETY (SBS)
(Slovensko Biokemijsko Drustvo)
e-mail: franc.gubensek@ijs.si
url: http://www.bio.ijs.si/sbd.htm
J. Stefan Institute
Department of Biochemistry
Jamova 39
SLO-1001 Ljubljana, Slovenia
Prof.Dr. Franc Gubensek, Pres.
PH: 386 61 1773900
FX: 386 61 273594
Description: Promotes scientific research in biochemistry. Acts as a forum for the exchange of information among biochemists. Disseminates research results. **Founded:** 1977. **Membership:** 140. **Staff:** 2. **Languages:** English, Slovene. **Budget:** $1,500. **Publication:** *Novice* (in Slovene), periodic. Newsletter. Price: free. Circulation: 150. Advertising: not accepted. **Formerly:** (1992) Union of the Biochemical Societies of Yugoslavia.

SLOVENIAN DENTAL ASSOCIATION (SDA)
Komenskega 4
SLO-61000 Ljubljana, Slovenia
Dr. M. Rode, Exec. Officer
PH: 386 61 317868
FX: 386 61 301955
Description: Dentists and others interested in promoting and maintaining good dental health. Conducts educational programs; makes available children's services. **Founded:** 1945. **Membership:** 350. **State Groups:** 1. **Languages:** English, German. **Publication:** *Informator* (in Slovene), periodic. Bulletin. Price: free. Advertising: accepted.

SLOVENIAN PHYSICAL SOCIETY
e-mail: normamankoc@iis.si
PO Box 64
SLO-1111 Ljubljana, Slovenia
Narma Susana, Pres.
PH: 386 61 1766525
FX: 386 61 217281
Description: Physicists and other scientists with an interest in physics. Promotes scholarship and continuing professional development of members; conducts research and educational programs. **Membership:** 200. **Languages:** Slovene. **Budget:** 6,200 Din.

SOCIAL PSYCHIATRY RESEARCH INSTITUTE (SPRI)
150 E. 69th St., Ste. 2H
New York, NY 10021
Ari Kiev, MD, JD, Pres.
PH: (212)628-4800
FX: (212)249-8546
Description: Promotes, supports, and conducts, in and outside the U.S., research in the fields of mental health and psychiatry; to assemble data and findings for mental health and psychiatry. Is presently conducting double-blind psychopharmacological studies of antidepressant and antianxiety medications with volunteers. Has supported several suicide prevention and drug abuse projects. Has developed a 15-week home-study program on panic and agoraphobia. **Founded:** 1970. **Languages:** English.

SOCIETATEA DE EDUCATIE CONTRACEPTIVA SI SEXUALA (SECS)
e-mail: secs@starnets.ro
Calea 13 Septembrie 85
BL 77C, ET8, AP 74, Sector 5
R-76100 Bucharest, Romania
Dr. Borbala Koo, Exec.Dir.
PH: 40 1 4101108
FX: 40 1 4101097
Description: Works to improve the quality of life for individuals living in Romania by promoting responsible parenthood and family planning. Attempts to reduce the number of unwanted pregnancies and abortions. Offers programs in family planning, sex education, and health. Acts as an advocate for family planning on a national level. **Founded:** 1990. **Membership:** 1027. **Staff:** 32. **Regional Groups:** 32. **Languages:** Romanian. **Budget:** $500,000. **Publication:** *Newsletter* (in Romanian), quarterly. Price: Free with membership. Circulation: 1,072. Advertising: accepted. Alternate Formats: magnetic tape.

SOCIETE FRANCAISE D'ANESTHESIE ET DE REANIMATION (SFAR)
e-mail: sfar@invivo.edu
74, rue Raynouard
F-75016 Paris, France
Prof. C. Conseiller, Pres.
PH: 33 1 45258225
FX: 33 1 40503522
Description: Anesthesiologists; interested others in France. Promotes scientific research and high standards of practice in the field. **Founded:** 1936. **Membership:** 4125. **Staff:** 7. **Languages:** French. **Publication:** *Annales Francaises d'Anesthesie et de Reanimation* (in French), bimonthly. Journal. Price: 1,075.00 Fr. Advertising: accepted ■ *Conferences d'Actuausation - Congrs 1997.*

SOCIETY OF APOTHECARIES OF LONDON
Apothecaries Hall
Black Friars Ln.
London EC4V 6EJ, England
R.J. Stringer, Clerk
PH: 44 171 2361189
FX: 44 171 3293177
Description: Members of the medical profession. Functions as City of London Livery Company and medical examining body. **Founded:** 1617. **Membership:** 1650.

SOCIETY OF BIOLOGICAL PSYCHIATRY (SBP)
e-mail: maggie@mayo.edu
url: http://www.sobp.org
Mayo Clinic of Jacksonville
4500 San Pablo Rd.
Jacksonville, FL 32224
Elliott Richelson, M.D., Contact
PH: (904)953-2842
FX: (904)953-7117
Description: International professional society of psychiatrists, neurologists, neurosurgeons, pharmacologists, neuropharmacologists, physiologists, psychologists, and physicians in related biological studies. Studies the neuronal basis of human behavior and the biological basis of psychiatry. Compiles statistics. **Founded:** 1945. **Membership:** 950. **Staff:** 1. Multinational. **Languages:** English. **Budget:** $275,000.

SOCIETY FOR BIOMATERIALS (SFB)
e-mail: member@biomaterials.org
url: http://www.biomaterials.org
6518 Walker St., Ste. 150
Minneapolis, MN 55426
Rosealee M. Lee, Exec.Dir.
PH: (612)927-8108
FX: (612)927-8127
Description: Bioengineers and materials scientists; dental, orthopedic, cardiac, and other surgeons and scientists interested

in developing biomaterials as tissue replacements in patients; corporations interested in the research manufacture of biomaterials. Provides an interdisciplinary forum for research in biomaterials. Promotes research, development, and education in the biomaterials sciences. **Founded:** 1974. **Membership:** 1900. **Staff:** 5. Multinational. **Languages:** English. **Publication:** *BioMaterials Forum*, periodic. Newsletter. Reports on developments in the science of biomaterials; includes society news. Price: free to members. Advertising: accepted. Also Cited As: *The Torch* ■ *Journal of Applied Biomaterials*, quarterly. Price: included in membership dues. Advertising: accepted ■ *Journal of Biomedical Materials Research*, monthly. Price: included in membership dues. Advertising: accepted.

SOCIETY FOR BIOMEDICAL EQUIPMENT TECHNICIANS (SBET)
3330 Washington Blvd., Ste. 400
Arlington, VA 22201
Patrick Thomas, Liaison
PH: (703)525-4890
TF: 800332-2264
FX: (703)276-0793
Description: Biomedical equipment technicians, hospital maintenance engineers, managers of hospital medical equipment departments, sales representatives, and others involved with the repair or installation of biomedical hospital machinery. Seeks to recognize biomedical equipment technicians and engineers as a specialty group. Supports certification programs including CBET (Certified Biomedical Equipment Technician), CRES (Certified Radiologic Equipment Specialist), and CLES (Certified Laboratory Equipment Specialist). Works with local biomedical organizations. Maintains speakers' bureau and placement service; compiles statistics. **Founded:** 1976. **Membership:** 1100. **Staff:** 1. **Languages:** English. **Budget:** $100,000. **Formerly:** (1987) Society of Biomedical Equipment Technicians; (1992) National Society of Biomedical Equipment Technicians.

SOCIETY FOR CARDIAC ANGIOGRAPHY AND INTERVENTIONS (SCA&I)
url: http://www.scai.org
4101 Lake Boone Tr., No. 201
Raleigh, NC 27607
Mary Alice Dilday, Exec.Dir.
PH: (919)787-5181
FX: (919)787-4916
Description: Angiographers united to foster excellence in the field of cardiac catheterization, especially coronary arteriography and interventional angiography. (Angiography involves injecting substances opaque to radiation into blood vessels so that diagnostic X-rays of those blood vessels may be made.) Conducts clinical research. **Founded:** 1978. **Membership:** 1100. **Staff:** 5. **Languages:** English. **Budget:** $550,000.

SOCIETY FOR CARDIOLOGICAL SCIENCE AND TECHNOLOGY
e-mail: egt@ulth.northy.nhs.uk
url: http://bcs.rbh.nthames.nhs.uk/scst.nsf
General Infirmary
Great George St.
Leeds LS1 3EX, England
Graham Tate, Contact
PH: 44 113 2926736
FX: 44 113 2926359
Description: Persons whom the Council of the Society consider to be qualified to practice cardiography, technical cardiology and allied subjects. Aims to advance for the public benefit the science and practice of cardiography, technical cardiology and allied subjects by the promotion of improved standards of education and training and of research work therein and by making the results of such study and research available to practitioners and the general public. **Founded:** 1948. **Membership:** 800. Multinational. **Regional Groups:** 3. **Publication:** *SCST Update*, monthly. Circulation: 800. Advertising: accepted.

SOCIETY OF CARDIOTHORACIC SURGEONS OF GREAT BRITAIN AND IRELAND
e-mail: 101611.3314@compuserve.com
10 Wendell Rd.
London W12 9RT, England
Miss Deirdre Watson, Surgeon
PH: 44 181 7433106
FX: 44 181 7431010
Description: Cardiac and thoracic surgeons. Concerned with the study of cardiothoracic disease. **Founded:** 1933. **Membership:** 520. **Publication:** Bulletin, semiannual. Price: free to members. Circulation: 650. Advertising: accepted.

SOCIETY AND COLLEGE OF RADIOGRAPHERS
14 Upper Wimpole St.
London W1M 8BN, England
Peter Smith, Contact
PH: 44 171 9355726
FX: 44 171 4873483
Description: Radiographers. Sets, maintains and, where appropriate, enhances training and professional standards for diagnostic imaging and therapeutic radiography and promotes radiography and allied sciences. It is also the trade union and professional association representing the interests of radiographers. **Founded:** 1920. **Membership:** 13000. **Staff:** 36. **Publication:** *Radiography*, quarterly ■ *Radiography Today*, monthly.

SOCIETY OF CARDIOVASCULAR ANESTHESIOLOGISTS (SCA)
e-mail: 75112.2053@compuserve.com
1910 Byrd Ave., No. 100
PO Box 11086
Richmond, VA 23230-1086
John A. Hinckley, Exec.Sec.
PH: (804)282-0084
FX: (804)282-0090
Description: Anesthesiologists who specialize in cardiovascular surgical conditions. Purpose is to further medical education of cardiovascular anesthesiologists. Establishes goals and objectives for education of trainees in cardiovascular anesthesia; promotes personnel exchange between the U.S. and other countries; reviews related literature; maintains workshops; conducts research competitions. Sponsors Anesthesia Grand Rounds: Case Presentations as a section of the annual meeting. **Founded:** 1977. **Membership:** 6000. **Staff:** 5. Multinational. **Languages:** English. **Budget:** $1,000,000.

SOCIETY OF CARDIOVASCULAR AND INTERVENTIONAL RADIOLOGY (SCVIR)
10201 Lee Hwy., Ste. 500
Fairfax, VA 22030
PH: (703)691-1805
TF: 800488-7284
FX: (703)691-1855
Description: Physicians who are leaders in the field of cardiovascular and interventional radiology. Facilitates exchange of new ideas and techniques and provides educational courses for all physicians working in the field. Conducts annual postgraduate course. Conducts Interventional Radiology Political Action. **Founded:** 1973. **Membership:** 2190. **Staff:** 4. **Languages:** English. **Publication:** *Directory of Angiography and Interventional Radiology Fellowship Programs* ■ *Journal of Vascular and Interventional Radiology*, bimonthly. Advertising: accepted ■ *SCVIR Membership Directory*, annual ■ *SCVIR Newsletter*, bimonthly. **Formerly:** (1983) Society of Cardiovascular Radiology.

SOCIETY FOR CARDIOVASCULAR MAGNETIC RESONANCE (SCMR)
19 Mantua Rd.
Mount Royal, NJ 08061
Dale Zeigler, Exec.Dir.
PH: (609)423-7222
FX: (609)423-3420
Description: Physicians and scientists with an interest in cardio-

vascular magnetic resonance imaging are members; physiciansin-training and doctoral candidates with an interest in the field are associates; medical technologists with at least two years of experience in cardiovascular magnetic resonance are technologist members; nonscientific professionals employed by companies engaged in magnetic resonance imaging are industrial members. Seeks to advance the practice of cardiovascular magnetic resonance; works to improve study and teaching in the field. Facilitates exchange of information among members and between members and physicians and scientists working in related fields. Conducts educational programs in the application of magnetic resonance imaging to cardiovascular conditions. Serves as a clearinghouse on cardiovascular magnetic resonance imaging; sets equipment standards; conducts multicenter trials to develop cardiovascular magnetic resonance imaging methods, clinical applications, and practice standards. **Founded:** 1994. **Membership:** 275. Multinational. **Languages:** English. **Budget:** $300,000.

SOCIETY FOR CLINICAL TRIALS (SCT)

url: http://members.aol.com/sctbalt/index.htm
600 Wyndhurst Ave.
Baltimore, MD 21210
Lawrence Friedman, Pres.
PH: (410)433-4722
FX: (410)435-8631
Description: Persons with training and expertise in behavioral science, bioethics, biostatistics, computer science, dentistry, epidemiology, law, management, medicine, nursing, and pharmacology. To promote the development and dissemination of knowledge about the design and conduct of clinical trials and other research employing similar methods. **Founded:** 1978. **Membership:** 1450. Multinational. **Languages:** English.

SOCIETY OF COMMUNITY HEALTH COUNCIL STAFF

23 Queens Rd.
Barnsley, N. Yorkshire S71 1AN, England
Tricia Hicks, Admin.Officer
PH: 44 1226 770441
FX: 44 1226 770441
Description: Permanent staff of Community Health Councils. Exists to promote the development of good practice, to exchange views and information among members and represents the concerns and interests of members to appropriate bodies. Organizes skills training for staff. **Founded:** 1978. **Membership:** 230. **Publication:** *Working for the CHC.* Handbook.

SOCIETY OF COMPUTED BODY TOMOGRAPHY AND MAGNETIC RESONANCE (SCBT/MR)

c/o Matrix Meetings
PO Box 1026
Rochester, MN 55903-1026
Barbara McLeod, Exec.Dir.
PH: (507)288-5620
FX: (507)288-0014
Description: Radiologists. Provides continuing medical educational courses on computed tomography and magnetic resonance imaging of the body. **Founded:** 1977. **Membership:** 80. **Staff:** 4. **Languages:** English. **Formerly:** (1991) Society of Computed Body Tomography.

SOCIETY FOR COMPUTER APPLICATIONS IN RADIOLOGY (SCAR)

e-mail: scar@acr.org
url: http://www.scar.rad.washington.edu/
10105 Cottesmore Ct.
Great Falls, VA 22066
Anna Marie Mason, Exec. Dir.
PH: (703)757-0054
Description: Individuals, corporations, and health facilities with an interest in medical imaging organized to promote and advance through study research, design and testing, the development and application of advanced technology information systems that will improve the delivery of medical imaging services. **Languages:** English.

SOCIETY FOR DEVELOPMENTAL AND BEHAVIORAL PEDIATRICS (SDBP)

e-mail: nmspota@aol.com
c/o Noreen M. Spota
19 Station Ln.
Philadelphia, PA 19118-2939
Noreen M. Spota, Admin.Dir.
PH: (215)248-9168
FX: (215)248-1981
Description: Pediatricians, child psychologists, and other related health care professionals. Seeks to improve the health care of infants, children, and adolescents by promoting research and scholarly instruction in the area of developmental-behavioral pediatrics. **Founded:** 1982. **Membership:** 615. **Staff:** 1. **State Groups:** 2. **Languages:** English. **Budget:** $175,000. Formerly Society for Behavioral Pediatrics.

SOCIETY OF EYE SURGEONS (SES)

7801 Norfolk Ave.
Bethesda, MD 20814
PH: (301)986-1830
Description: Ophthalmologists promoting the science of ophthalmic surgery worldwide. Supports the blindness prevention efforts of the International Eye Foundation. Provides educational, training, and eye care services by sponsoring teaching teams and professors to visit countries worldwide; fosters social exchange among physicians and scientists in the field of ophthalmology. Address unknown since 1993 edition. **Founded:** 1969. **Membership:** 1000. **Languages:** English.

SOCIETY OF GHANA MEDICAL AND DENTAL PRACTITIONERS

PO Box 18
Korlebu, Ghana
PH: 233 21 665481
Description: Physicians and dentists; students. Promotes availability of health care. Accredits physicians and dentists; maintains standards of practice and professional conduct. Sponsors social programs for women in health care. **Founded:** 1965.

SOCIETY FOR HEALTH EDUCATION (SHE)

M. Kothanmaage S
Maaveyo Magu
Male, Maldives
PH: 960 327117
FX: 960 315042
Description: Promotes family and community well-being. Conducts health education programs; makes available primary health care services. **Founded:** 1988. **Languages:** English.

SOCIETY OF HOMEOPATHS

2 Artizan Rd.
Northampton NN1 4HU, England
Mary Clarke, Contact
PH: 44 1604 621400
FX: 44 1604 622622
Description: Professional homeopaths on the Society's register. Aims to develop and maintain high standards for the practise of homeopathy and to promote public awareness of homeopathy. It also supports the establishment of education and training in homeopathy. **Founded:** 1978. **Membership:** 2200. **Staff:** 4. **Publication:** *The Homoeopath Journal,* quarterly. Advertising: accepted ▪ *Register of Professional Homoeopaths,* semiannual ▪ Newsletter, quarterly.

SOCIETY OF MEDICAL LABORATORY TECHNOLOGISTS OF SOUTH AFRICA (SMLTSA)

(Vereniging van Geneeskundige Laboratorium Tegnoloe van Suid-Afrika)
PO Box 6014
Roggebaai
Cape Town 8012, Republic of South Africa
Miss K.J. Lehmensich, Contact

PH: 27 21 4194857
FX: 27 21 212566
Description: Medical technologists, students, and interested persons organized to promote the medical technology profession. Works to: establish standards of practice; influence public policy; provide a forum for the exchange of ideas. Acts as an advisory and consulting body. Represents the profession before certifying, educational, employment, and registering authorities. Sponsors activities that advance scientific knowledge and encourage original work. **Founded:** 1951. **Membership:** 1700. **Staff:** 2. **Local Groups:** 15. **Languages:** Afrikaans, English. **Publication:** *Constitution of the Society of Medical Laboratory Technologists of South Africa*. Book ▪ *Medical Technology* (in Afrikaans and English), semiannual. Journal ▪ *Medical Technology News* (in Afrikaans and English), periodic. Newspaper ▪ Newsletter. **Formed by Merger of:** Society of Medical Laboratory Technologists of the Cape; Society of Medical Laboratory Technologists of Natal; Society of Medical Laboratory Technologists of Southern Transvaal.

SOCIETY FOR MEDICINAL PLANT RESEARCH

(Gesellschaft fur Arzneipflanzenforschung)
Steinbachtal 43
D-97082 Wurzburg, Germany
Dr. B. Frank, Sec.
PH: 49 931 8002271
FX: 49 931 8002275
Description: Scientists in 70 countries who promote medicinal plant research. Organized to serve as an international focal point for such interests as pharmacognosy, pharmacology, phytochemistry, plant biochemistry and physiology, chemistry of natural products; plant cell culture and application of medicinal plants in medicine. Acts as liaison with governments, pharmacopoeia commissions, and international health organizations on matters pertaining to the medicinal plant field. Serves as forum for international exchange of information on the different aspects of medicinal plant research. **Founded:** 1953. **Membership:** 850. Multinational. **Languages:** English, German. **Publication:** *Newsletter*, semiannual ▪ *Planta Medica*, bimonthly. Journal. **Formerly:** (1970) German Society for Medicinal Plant Research.

SOCIETY FOR MEDICINES RESEARCH (SMR)

e-mail: info@iob.primex.ac.uk
url: http://sgl.pcy.kcl.ac.uk/smr.html
Institute of Biology
20 Queensberry Pl.
London SW7 2DZ, England
Mrs. B.J. Cavilla, Sec.
PH: 44 171 5818333
FX: 44 171 8239409
Description: Researchers at academic institutions and in the pharmaceutical industry; other concerned individuals. Promotes advancement in the field of drug education and research in order to provide the public with proper information on drug usage for relief of sickness. **Founded:** 1966. **Membership:** 900. **Staff:** 1. **Languages:** English. **Publication:** *Proceedings*, periodic ▪ Newsletter, 3-4/year. **Formerly:** (1994) Society for Drug Research.

SOCIETY OF NURSERY NURSING ADMINISTRATORS

(SNNA)
40 Archdale Rd.
East Dulwich
London SE22 9HJ, England
Dr. R.A. Herbert-Blankson, Sec.
PH: 44 181 5161366
FX: 44 181 2745103
Description: Nursing administrators and nurses, nursery teachers, school nurses, nannies, and other workers and employers with an interest in the health and welfare of children from birth to five years of age. Seeks to establish professional standards and a uniform code of ethics within the field; works to enhance the professional standing of members. Gathers and disseminates information to inform legislative debate concerning child health issues. Conducts educational programs and maintains speakers'

bureau. **Founded:** 1991. **Membership:** 1500. **Staff:** 2. Multinational. **Local Groups:** 3. **Languages:** English. **Publication:** *Nursery Nursing Administrator* (in English), quarterly. Newsletter. Advertising: accepted.

SOCIETY OF PHARMACEUTICAL MEDICINE

20-22 Queensbury Pl.
London SW7 2DZ, England
Martin Perry, Hon.Sec.
PH: 44 171 5818333
FX: 44 171 8234909
Description: Open to all those involved within drug development - both in the pharmaceutical industry and also in academic/clinical medicine and the drug regulatory agencies. Aims to provide a focus for questions relating to the development of medicinal agents. This is promoted by the organisation of regular meetings and occasional workshops. Topics are wide ranging and collaboration with other societies is encouraged. **Founded:** 1987. **Membership:** 500. **Staff:** 2. **Publication:** *Journal of Pharmaceutical Medicine*, quarterly.

SOCIETY OF PHYSICIANS IN THE PHARMACEUTICAL INDUSTRY

(Fachgesellschaft der Artze in der Pharmazeutische Industrie)
Thalvischerstrasse 88
D-80337 Munich, Germany
Description: Physicians employed by pharmaceutical manufacturers. Promotes sound research and testing of pharmaceutical products. Represents members' interests; conducts educational and continuing professional training courses. **Languages:** German.

SOCIETY OF PHYSICISTS OF THE REPUBLIC OF MACEDONIA

Faculty of Natural Sciences and Mathematics
Cyril and Methodius University
PO Box 162
91000 Skopje, Macedonia
Vasil Micevski, Pres.
PH: 389 91 117055
FX: 389 91 228141
Description: Physicists, physics teachers, and others with an interest in the physical sciences. Seeks to improve the quality of physics education, research, and knowledge. **Founded:** 1949. **Membership:** 60. **Languages:** English, French. **Budget:** 6,000 Din. **Publication:** *Bulletin* (in Macedonian), annual. Journal. Contains educational material. Circulation: 250 ▪ *IMPULS*, semiannual. Discusses the popularization of physics among high school students. Price: $1.25. Circulation: 10,000.

SOCIETY OF RADIOGRAPHERS (SR)

14 Upper Wimpole St.
London W1M 8BN, England
Mr. S. Evans, Exec. Officer
PH: 44 171 9355726
FX: 44 171 4873483
Description: Represents the interests of radiographers in the United Kingdom. **Founded:** 1920. **Membership:** 12500. **Staff:** 25. **Regional Groups:** 14. **Languages:** English. **Publication:** *Radiography Today* (in English), monthly. Journal. Circulation: 17,000. Advertising: accepted.

SOCIETY OF RADIOGRAPHERS OF SOUTH AFRICA (SORSA)

(Vereniging van Radiograwe van Suid-Afrika)
PO Box 6014
Rogge Baai 8012, Republic of South Africa
Mrs. W. Bower, Natl.Sec.
PH: 27 21 4194857
FX: 27 21 212566
Description: Radiographers in South Africa. Strives for the establishment and maintenance of professional standards in the training and practice of radiography. Cooperates with governmental bodies in order to improve working conditions, salaries,

and benefits. Represents members' interests nationally and internationally. Communicates with relevant authorities on educational and employment matters. Maintains liaisons with similar national and international organizations. Sponsors seminars and workshops. **Founded:** 1951. **Membership:** 1500. **Languages:** English. **Publication:** *The South African Radiographer* (in Afrikaans and English), 3/year. Journal. Price: Free to members; R 62.40 for subscribers. ISSN: 0258-0241. Circulation: 1,800. Advertising: accepted ▪ Newsletter, quarterly.

SOCIETY OF RURAL PHYSICIANS OF CANADA (SRPC)
e-mail: bullhits@infonet.ca
url: http://www.gretmar.com/srp/home.html
PO Box 893
Shawville, PQ, Canada J0X 2Y0
Lee Teperman, Admin. Officer
PH: (819)647-3971
FX: (819)647-3971
Description: Physicians practicing in rural areas of Canada. Promotes delivery of health care services to individuals in remote areas nationwide. Seeks to ensure suitable working conditions for members. Sponsors annual continuing professional development course. Develops model policies for regulation and delivery of health care in rural areas; encourages medical research; provides support and services to members and to communities seeking to improve their health care resources; plans to establish a library. Offers free membership to students, residents, and honourary members. **Founded:** 1992. **Membership:** 450. **Staff:** 1. **Languages:** English, French. **Budget:** C$80,000. **Publication:** *Canadian Journal of Rural Medicine*, periodic. Newsletter.

SOCIETY FOR SURGERY OF THE ALIMENTARY TRACT (SSAT)
e-mail: ssat@slackinc.com
url: http://www.ssat.com
6900 Grove Rd.
Thorofare, NJ 08086
Clifford Brownstein, Exec.Dir.
PH: (609)251-0558
FX: (609)853-5991
Description: Physicians specializing in alimentary tract surgery. Purposes are: to stimulate and foster the study of and research in the function and diseases of the alimentary tract; to provide a forum for presentation of such information; to edit, encourage, or sponsor publications. **Founded:** 1960. **Membership:** 1200. Multinational. **Languages:** English. **For-Profit. Budget:** $500,000.

SOCIETY OF GENERAL PHYSIOLOGISTS (SGP)
PO Box 257
Woods Hole, MA 02543
Dr. Olaf Andersen, Pres.
PH: (508)540-6719
FX: (508)540-0155
Description: Biologists interested in fundamental physiological principles and phenomena. **Founded:** 1946. **Membership:** 1000. **Languages:** English.

SOCIETY OF GERIATRIC OPHTHALMOLOGY (SGO)
63 2nd St.
South Orange, NJ 07079
John Norris, Exec.Dir.
PH: (973)763-1381
FX: (973)762-9449
Description: Ophthalmologists interested in the vision problems of the elderly. Works to disseminate information regarding the problems of geriatric patients and to stimulate research. Provides speakers and programs dealing with the needs of the elderly. **Founded:** 1975. **Membership:** 80. **Languages:** English.

SOCIETY OF GRADUATE SURGEONS (SGS)
5820 Wilshire Blvd., Ste. 500
Los Angeles, CA 90036
C. James Dowden, Exec.Dir.

PH: (213)937-5514
FX: (213)937-0959
Description: Surgeons who've completed general surgery residencies. Conducts post-graduate educational programs for members and surgeons. **Founded:** 1950. **Membership:** 375. **Staff:** 9. Multinational.

SOCIETY FOR GYNECOLOGIC INVESTIGATION (SGI)
e-mail: sgiava@aol.com
url: http://www.socgyninv.org
409 12th St. SW
Washington, DC 20024-2188
Ava Tayman, Dir.
PH: (202)863-2544
FX: (202)863-0739
Description: Present and former faculty members of institutions interested or engaged in fundamental gynecologic research. Purpose is to stimulate, encourage, assist, and conduct gynecologic research. **Founded:** 1953. **Membership:** 850. **Staff:** 2. Multinational. **Languages:** English.

SOCIETY FOR HEMATOPATHOLOGY (SH)
471 Porpoise Circle
Fripp Island, SC 29920-9795
Peter M. Banks, M.D., Pres.
PH: (803)838-5564
Description: Physicians; doctors of science, osteopathy, veterinary medicine, and dental surgery. Promotes exchange of information and encourages clinical, morphologic, and functional investigation of the hematopoietic (pertaining to the formation of blood cells) and lymphoreticular (regarding reticuloendothelial cells of the lymph glands) systems. **Founded:** 1981. **Membership:** 500. Multinational. **Languages:** English. **Publication:** Newsletter. Advertising: not accepted.

SOCIETY OF INFECTIOUS DISEASES PHARMACISTS (SIDP)
e-mail: esmith@solar.cini.utk.edu
PO Box 891154
Houston, TX 77289-1154
PH: (713)795-8389
FX: (713)795-8383
Description: Pharmacists with a primary interest and practice in infectious diseases pharmacotherapy, and who have spent at least two years performing pharmacotherpeutic research are active members; pharmacists and other individuals not meeting the requirements for active membership, but who share an interest in infectious diseases pharmacotherapy, are associate members. Seeks to advance the study and practice of infectious diseases pharmacotherapy, and to enhance the professional status of members. Serves as a forum for discussion and exchange of information among members. Encourages pharmacotherapeutic research. **Languages:** English.

SOCIETY OF INVASIVE CARDIOVASCULAR PROFESSIONALS (SICP)
url: http://www.sicp.com
950 W. Valley Rd., Ste. 2800
Wayne, PA 19087
Jacquline Wells, Association Liason
TF: 800237-7285
FX: (610)688-8050
Description: Cardiac catheterization laboratory personnel. Supports the highest quality of patient care. Serves as a forum for exchange of information among members. Defines core curricula for cardiovascular professionals; makes available educational opportunities to members; establishes standards of ethics and practice for the field. Facilitates cardiovascular research. **Founded:** 1992. **Membership:** 1000. **Languages:** English.

SOCIETY FOR INVESTIGATIVE DERMATOLOGY (SID)
e-mail: sid@sidnet.org
url: http://www.sidnet.org
820 W. Superior Ave., Ste. 340
Cleveland, OH 44113-1800
Angela Welsh, Admin.Dir.
PH: (216)579-9300
FX: (216)579-9333
Description: Professional society promoting research in dermatology and allied subjects. Founded: 1937. Membership: 2300. Staff: 4. Multinational. Languages: English.

SOCIETY OF LAPAROENDOSCOPIC SURGEONS (SLS)
e-mail: info@sls.org
url: http://www.sls.org
7330 SW 62nd Pl., Ste. 410
South Miami, FL 33143-4825
Paul A. Wetter, M.D., Contact
PH: (305)665-9959
TF: 800446-2659
FX: (305)667-4123
Description: Laparoendoscopic surgeons and other health care professionals. Promotes improvement in laparoendoscopic surgical techniques; facilitates professional growth of members. Conducts educational programs. Membership: 5000. Staff: 9. Languages: English.

SOCIETY OF MEDICAL ADMINISTRATORS (SMA)
3500 E. Fletcher Ave., Ste. 530
University of South Florida
Tampa, FL 33613
Ronald Kaufman, Exec. VP
PH: (813)974-8420
FX: (813)974-8487
Description: Medical doctors in hospital or health care administration. Discusses issues concerning health care administration. Founded: 1920. Membership: 50. Languages: English. Publication: Directory, annual. Formerly: (1951) Medical Superintendents Club.

SOCIETY FOR MEDICAL DECISION MAKING (SMDM)
url: http://www.gwu.edu/~smdm
2300 K St. NW
Office of Continuing Medical Education in the Health
Professions
Washington, DC 20037
Thomas E. Piemme, MD, Admin. Dir.
PH: (202)994-8929
FX: (202)994-1791
Description: Individuals with an interest in "arational and systematic approaches" to medical decision making, including educators, clinicians, managers, and policy makers. Promotes improvement in all aspects of medical decision making. Evaluates decision making applications and disseminates conclusions. Facilitates multidisciplinary scholarship and research; conducts continuing professional education programs. Founded: 1979. Membership: 1000. Languages: English.

SOCIETY OF MEDICAL-DENTAL MANAGEMENT
CONSULTANTS (SMD)
e-mail: chuck@smdmc.org
url: http://www.smamc.org
3646 E. Ray Rd., B16-45
Phoenix, AZ 85044
Charles R. Wold, Exec.Sec.
TF: 800826-2264
FX: (602)759-3530
Description: Professional medical and/or dental management consultants associated for educational and information sharing purposes. Objectives are to: advance the profession; share management techniques; improve individual skills; provide clients with competent and capable business management. Provides information on insurance and income tax. Conducts surveys; compiles statistics. Founded: 1968. Membership: 80. Staff: 2. State

Groups: 43. Languages: English. Publication: *Membership Roster*, annual. Membership Directory ■ *SMD Statistics* ■ *Society of Medical-Dental Management Consultants – Newsletter*, monthly. Price: included in membership dues. Circulation: 80. Advertising: accepted ■ Bulletin.

SOCIETY FOR MENSTRUAL CYCLE RESEARCH (SMCR)
10559 N. 104th Pl.
Scottsdale, AZ 85258
Mary Anna Friederich, M.D., Sec.-Treas.
PH: (602)451-9731
Description: Physicians, nurses, endocrinologists, geneticists, physiologists, psychologists, sociologists, researchers, educators, students, and others interested in the health needs of women as related to the menstrual cycle. Goals are: to identify research priorities, recommend research strategies, and promote interdisciplinary research on the menstrual cycle; to establish a communication network for facilitating interdisciplinary dialogue on menstrual cycle events; to disseminate information and promote discussion of issues among public groups. Founded: 1979. Membership: 100. Languages: English.

SOCIETY FOR OCCLUSAL STUDIES (SOS)
c/o Dr. Bernard Williams
1010 Carondelet Dr., No. 410
Kansas City, MO 64114
Dr. Bernard Williams, Pres.
PH: (816)941-0509
FX: (816)941-4832
Description: Dentists and laboratory technicians who have completed the society's continuing education course in occlusion (bringing opposing surfaces of the teeth of the two jaws into contact). Promotes effective occlusal treatment. Conducts Principles of Occlusion Seminar, Advanced Restorative Seminar, laboratory technician program, and practice management program. Founded: 1964. Membership: 800. Staff: 3. Local Groups: 95. Languages: English. Publication: *Roster*, annual ■ *SOS Newsletter*, quarterly. Covers developments in the treatment and diagnosis of temporomandibular joint dysfunction and principles of occlusion instrumentation. Price: included in membership dues. Circulation: 1,000.

SOCIETY OF OTORHINOLARYNGOLOGY AND HEAD/
NECK NURSES (SOHN)
116 Canal St., Ste. A
New Smyrna Beach, FL 32168
Sandra Schwartz, R.N., Exec.Dir.
PH: (904)428-1695
FX: (904)423-7766
Description: Registered nurses specializing in otorhinolaryngology (the study of the ear, nose, and throat) and the head and neck. Seeks to: promote awareness of professional techniques and new developments in the field; enhance professional standards; create a channel for the exchange of ideas, concerns, and information; develop interaction with similar groups. Offers programs and seminars that have been approved for continuing education credits by the American Nurses' Association. Founded: 1976. Membership: 1200. Staff: 3. Local Groups: 15. Languages: English.

SOCIETY FOR PEDIATRIC DERMATOLOGY (SPD)
e-mail: patrici107@aol.com
5422 N. Bernard
Chicago, IL 60625
Amy S. Paller, M.D., Sec.-Treas.
PH: (773)583-9780
FX: (773)583-9765
Description: Pediatricians, dermatologists, pediatric or dermatologic house officers, manufacturers of children's skin products, and researchers in biomedicine with studies in pediatric dermatology. Conducts research programs. Founded: 1975. Membership: 450. Languages: English.

SOCIETY OF PEDIATRIC NURSES (SPN)
url: http://www.pednurse.org
2170 S Parker Rd., Ste. 350
Denver, CO 80231-5711
Gina Vargas, Contact
TF: 800723-2902
FX: (303)750-3212
Description: Registered pediatric nurses are ordinary members; nursing students and other professionals with an interest in pediatric nursing are associate members. Promotes quality health and nursing care of children. Conducts advocacy campaigns to improve access to affordable care for children; works to advance techniques of pediatric nursing and health care. Sponsors research and educational programs for members; formulates standards of practice and ethics; fosters collaboration between members and other health care professionals, child health care advocates, and related organizations. **Founded:** 1990. **Membership:** 2142. **Staff:** 1. **Local Groups:** 27. **Languages:** English.

SOCIETY FOR PEDIATRIC RADIOLOGY (SPR)
2021 Spring Rd., Ste. 600
Oak Brook, IL 60523-1860
Jennifer Boylan, Contact
PH: (630)571-2197
FX: (630)571-7837
Description: Physicians working in the field of pediatric radiology. Seeks to advance knowledge in pediatric imaging and improve medical care of infants and children. **Founded:** 1958. **Membership:** 800. **Languages:** English. **Budget:** $160,000. **Publication:** Membership Directory, annual.

SOCIETY FOR PEDIATRIC RESEARCH (SPR)
e-mail: info@aps-spr.org
url: http://www.aps-spr.org
3400 Research Forest Dr., Ste. B7
The Woodlands, TX 77381
Debbie Anagnostelis, Exec.Dir.
PH: (281)296-0244
FX: (281)296-0255
Description: Physicians and scientists under age 46 who are engaged in research in diseases of infancy and childhood; those over age 46 are senior members. **Founded:** 1929. **Membership:** 2000. **Staff:** 9. Multinational. **Languages:** English. **Budget:** $250,000. Formerly (1932) Eastern Society for Pediatric Research.

SOCIETY OF PELVIC SURGEONS (SPS)
e-mail: cohen@smtplink.mssm.edu
Indiana University School of Medicine
535 N. Barnhill Dr., Ste. 420
Indianapolis, IN 46202
Dr. John Donohue, Pres.
PH: (317)274-7338
FX: (317)274-0174
Description: Professional society of physicians specializing in surgery of the pelvis. Purpose is to hold meetings for the free and informal interchange of ideas pertaining to various phases of pelvic surgery and related fields and to exert influence for the betterment of the teaching and practice of pelvic surgery. Membership is by nomination. Maintains library and archives. Conducts educational programs. **Founded:** 1952. **Membership:** 125. **Languages:** English.

SOCIETY OF PROFESSORS OF CHILD AND ADOLESCENT PSYCHIATRY (SPCAP)
3615 Wisconsin Ave. NW
Washington, DC 20016-3007
Martin Drell, M.D., Pres.
PH: (202)966-7300
FX: (202)966-2891
Description: Selected representatives from university psychiatric departments who meet annually to discuss issues in child and adolescent psychiatry. **Founded:** 1969. **Membership:** 170. **Staff:** 1.

Languages: English. **Budget:** $20,000. Formerly (1987) Society of Professors of Child Psychiatry.

SOCIETY FOR PROGRESSIVE SUPRANUCLEAR PALSY (SPSP)
e-mail: epkatz@erols.com
url: http://www.psp.org
Johns Hopkins Outpatient Center
601 N. Caroline St., Ste. 5065
Baltimore, MD 21287
Ellen Katz, Dir.
PH: (410)955-2954
TF: 800457-4777
FX: (410)614-9260
Description: Works to provide help and support to persons with progressive supranuclear palsy (PSP), a degenerative brain disorder related to Parkinson's Disease. Sponsors medical research; educates physicians, persons with PSP and their families on the disease and care; provides advocacy and support; maintains speakers' bureau. **Founded:** 1990. **Membership:** 5000. **Staff:** 2. Multinational.

SOCIETY FOR PUBLIC HEALTH EDUCATION (SOPHE)
e-mail: sopheauld@aol.com
1015 Fifteenth St., NW, Ste., 410
Washington, DC 20005
Elaine Auld, Exec.Dir.
PH: (202)408-9804
FX: (202)408-9815
Description: Professional workers in health education concerned with personal and community health problems. Seeks to promote, encourage, and contribute to the advancement of health of all people by encouraging research, improving health practices, elevating standards of achievement in public health education, and advocating for public health policies. **Founded:** 1950. **Membership:** 2100. **Staff:** 2. **Local Groups:** 17. **Languages:** English. **Budget:** $350,000. Formerly Society of Public Health Educators.

SOCIETY FOR RADIATION ONCOLOGY ADMINISTRATORS (SROA)
e-mail: jendra@rsna.org
url: http://www.radonc.uchicago.edu/~SROA/
2021 Spring Rd., Ste. 600
Oak Brook, IL 60023-1860
Jeanne Jeandra, Exec. Sec.
PH: (630)571-9065
FX: (630)571-7837
Description: Individuals with managerial responsibilities in radiation oncology at the executive, divisional, or departmental level, and whose functions include personnel, budget, and development of operational procedures and guidelines for therapeutic radiology departments. Strives to improve the administration of the business and nonmedical management aspects of therapeutic radiology, to promote the field of therapeutic radiology administration, to provide a forum for communication among members, and to disseminate information among members. Maintains speakers' bureau; offers placement service. **Founded:** 1984. **Membership:** 500. **Staff:** 11. **Languages:** English. **For-Profit.** **Budget:** $125,000. **Publication:** *SROA Membership Directory*, annual. Price: included in membership dues. Circulation: 500. Advertising: accepted ■ *SROA Newsletter*, quarterly. Includes calendar of events and employment listings. Price: included in membership dues; $50.00 for non-members in U.S.; $60.00 for non-members outside U.S. Circulation: 520. Advertising: accepted. **Formerly:** (1985) Radiation Oncology Administrators.

SOCIETY OF TEACHERS OF FAMILY MEDICINE (STFM)
e-mail: admstaff@stfm.org
url: http://stfm.org
8880 Ward Pky.
Kansas City, MO 64114
Roger A. Sherwood, CAE, Exec.Dir.

PH: (816)333-9700
TF: 800274-2237
FX: (816)333-3884
Description: Physicians involved in teaching or promoting family medicine; individuals in related fields. Organized to promote public welfare by maintaining and improving standards and practices of medical service, especially in the field of family medicine. Promotes these objectives by: supporting and expressing the tenets of family medicine as an academic discipline; maintaining and continually improving the quality of instructional and scientific skills and knowledge in the field of family medicine; providing a forum for the interchange of experience and ideas among its members and other interested persons; and encouraging research and teaching in family medicine. **Founded:** 1967. **Membership:** 4500. **Staff:** 16. Multinational. **Languages:** English. **Budget:** $4,000,000. **Publication:** *Family Medicine*, monthly. Journal. Includes annual index, book reviews, and employment opportunities. Price: included in membership dues; $12.50/copy for nonmembers; $75.00/year for individual nonmembers; $100.00/year for institutions. ISSN: 0742-3225. Circulation: 4,500. Advertising: accepted. Also Cited As: *Family Medicine Teacher* ▪ *STFM Membership Directory*, biennial. Arranged alphabetically and geographically. Price: included in membership dues; $25.00 for nonmembers. Circulation: 4,300. Advertising: not accepted ▪ *STFM Messenger*, bimonthly. Newsletter. Covers geneal information related to family medicine issues. Includes research and education columns. Price: included in membership dues. Circulation: 4,300. Advertising: accepted ▪ Monographs.

SOCIETY FOR THE WELFARE OF MOTHERS AND BABIES
32 Ramses St.
Cairo, Egypt
PH: 20 2 750302
Description: Health and child care personnel. Seeks to improve the social and health condition of women and children. Provides primary health care and family planning services; makes available financial assistance; operates day and therapeutic care facilities for people with infantile paralysis. **Founded:** 1928. **Languages:** Arabic, English.

SOCIETY OF THORACIC RADIOLOGY (STR)
PO Box 1925
Roswell, GA 30077-1925
Mary Ryals, Pres.
PH: (770)641-9773
FX: (770)552-9859
Description: Radiologists. Provides for continuing medical education. **Founded:** 1983. **Membership:** 200. **Languages:** English.

SOCIETY OF TOXICOLOGIC PATHOLOGISTS (STP)
e-mail: srphq@stp.smarthub.com
url: http://www.toxpath.org
19 Mantua Road
Mount Royal, NJ 08061
Stephanie Dickinson, Dir.
PH: (609)423-3610
FX: (609)423-3420
Description: Promotes the advancement of the Individuals interested in toxicology and toxicologic pathology from industry, academic institutions, and government. **Founded:** 1971. **Membership:** 700. **Staff:** 3. Multinational. **Regional Groups:** 5. **Languages:** English. **Publication:** *STP Newsletter*, quarterly. Price: available to members only. Circulation: 700. Advertising: accepted ▪ *Toxicologic Pathology*, bimonthly. Journal. Price: $175.00/year for individuals in the U.S.; $195.00/year for individuals outside the U.S.; $195.00/year for institutions in the U.S.; $215.00/year for institutions outside the U.S. ISSN: 0192-6233. Circulation: 1,000. Advertising: accepted.

SOCIETY OF TOXICOLOGY (SOT)
e-mail: sothq@toxicology.org
url: http://www.toxicology.org
1767 Business Center Dr., Ste. 302
Reston, VA 20190-5332
Shawn Douglas Lamb, Exec.Dir.
PH: (703)438-3115
FX: (703)438-3113
Description: Persons who have conducted and published original investigations in some phase of toxicology and who have a continuing professional interest in this field. (Toxicology is the quantitative study of materials that may or may not adversely affect the health of humans, animals, and/or the environment.) Sponsors placement service at Annual Meeting. **Founded:** 1961. **Membership:** 4500. **Staff:** 5. Multinational. **Regional Groups:** 17. **Languages:** English. **For-Profit.** **Budget:** $3,000,000.

SOCIETY OF TRAUMA NURSES (STN)
224 N. DesPlaines St., Ste. 601
Chicago, IL 60661-1134
Eileen Whalen, Pres.
PH: (312)993-0559
TF: 888STN-5400
FX: (312)993-0362
Description: Nurses involved in all facets of trauma care. Seeks to communicate trauma nursing information and recognize excellence and innovation in trauma nursing. Addresses legislative issues; assists in the development of standards. Facilitates research. Convention/Meeting: none. **Founded:** 1989. **Membership:** 650. **Regional Groups:** 7. **Languages:** English.

SOCIETY FOR ULTRASTRUCTURAL PATHOLOGY
url: http://sup.ultrakohl.com/
Louisiana State University
1501 Kings Hwy.
PO Box 33932
Shreveport, LA 71130-3932
Bruce Mackay, MD, Pres.
PH: (318)675-5860
FX: (318)675-7662
Description: Promotes the art and science of diagnostic electron microscopy. Fosters the application of electron microscopy in the diagnosis and research of human diseases. Also provides an opportunity for the exchange of information, particularly ultrastructural and immunohistochemical, relevant to diagnostic pathology. **Founded:** 1986. **Membership:** 185. Multinational.

SOCIETY OF UNIVERSITY SURGEONS (SUS)
e-mail: samokar@1-2000.com
url: http://www.sus.org
PO Box 16549
West Haven, CT 06516
Mary E. Samokar, Admin. Dir.
PH: (203)932-0541
FX: (203)937-7716
Description: Professional society of surgeons connected with university teaching. Works to advance the art and science of surgery by encouraging original investigations both in the clinic and in the laboratory and by developing methods of graduate teaching of surgery with particular reference to the resident system. **Founded:** 1938. **Membership:** 1280. **Staff:** 1. Multinational. **Languages:** English. **Budget:** $50,000.

SOCIETY OF UROLOGIC NURSES AND ASSOCIATES (SUNA)
E Holly Ave.
PO Box 56
Pitman, NJ 08071-0056
Ronald Brady, Exec.Dir.
Description: Nurses and other health care providers working in the field of urology. Promotes excellence in urological education; establishes standards of care for urology patients. Conducts educational programs; holds examinations and bestows professional

certification; facilitates communication among members. **Membership:** 2000. **Staff:** 6. **Local Groups:** 36. **Languages:** English.

SOCIETY FOR VASCULAR NURSING (SVN)
e-mail: aspmn@aol.com
7794 Grow Dr.
Pensacola, FL 32514
Belinda Puetz, PhD, R.N., Exec.Dir.
PH: (904)484-8762
TF: 888536-4SVN
Description: Nurses and other health care professionals interested in providing comprehensive care for persons with vascular disease. Seeks to educate public about prevention of PVD. Provides educational programs; conducts research. Operates speakers' bureau. **Founded:** 1982. **Membership:** 780. **Staff:** 4. **Languages:** English. **Budget:** $200,000. Formerly (1992) Society for Peripheral Vascular Nursing.

SOLOMON ISLANDS PLANNED PARENTHOOD ASSOCIATION (SIPPA)
PO Box 554
Lombi Cress
Honiara, Solomon Islands
Charles Kelly, Exec.Dir.
PH: 677 22991
FX: 677 23653
Description: Advocates family planning as a basic human right and as a means to enhance the standard of living for individuals living in the Solomon Islands. Work to stop the spread of sexually transmitted diseases such as AIDS. Offers programs in sex education, family planning, and health. Provides contraceptive services. Conducts research. **Founded:** 1981. **Membership:** 9. **Staff:** 12. **Languages:** English. **Budget:** $125,000. **Publication:** Video.

SOUTH AFRICAN ASSOCIATION OF PAEDIATRIC SURGEONS (SAAPS)
(Suid-Afrikaanse Vereniging van Kinderchirurge)
e-mail: amillar@ich.uct.ac.za
Dept. of Paediatric Surgery
Red Cross War Memorial Children's Hospital
Rondebosch 7700, Republic of South Africa
Prof. A.J.W. Millar, Hon.Sec.-Treas.
PH: 27 21 6585339
FX: 27 21 6891287
Description: Pediatric surgeons in South Africa. Promotes research, training, and clinical services in pediatric surgery. Grants postgraduate fellowships. Conducts educational programs; compiles statistics. **Founded:** 1975. **Membership:** 50. **Staff:** 1. **Languages:** Afrikaans, English. **Budget:** R 5,000.

SOUTH AFRICAN DENTAL ASSOCIATION (SADA)
e-mail: info@sada.co.za
url: http://www.dentalhiway.co.za
Private Bag 1
Houghton 2041, Republic of South Africa
Dr. J.T. Barnard, Exec.Dir.
PH: 27 11 4845288
FX: 27 11 6425718
Description: Practicing and retired dentists. Represents the dental profession in South Africa. Promotes research and investigation into dentistry and allied sciences. Sponsors National Dental Health Week in South Africa. **Founded:** 1922. **Membership:** 2793. **Staff:** 12. **Languages:** Afrikaans, English. **Budget:** R 1,600,000. **Publication:** Dental Journal (in Afrikaans and English), monthly. Includes original scientific articles and general dental material. Price: included in membership dues. ISSN: 0011-8561. Circulation: 4,500. Advertising: accepted. **Formerly:** (1998) Dental Association of South Africa.

SOUTH AFRICAN DIABETES ASSOCIATION (SADA)
(Suid-Afrikaanse Diabetesberniging)
PO Box 1715
Saxonwold 2132, Republic of South Africa
R. Leoner, National Chmn.

PH: 21 11 788459516
FX: 21 11 4476265
Description: Individuals concerned with diabetes and associated diseases. Develops educational methods designed to give diabetics a better understanding and control of their disease. Promotes advancements in medical research and service to improve standards of treatment. Fosters exchange of information among members. Disseminates data on diabetes to increase public awareness of the disease; seeks to protect diabetics against discrimination due to their disease. Conducts research. Arranges social events and educational guidance for diabetics; organizes lectures. **Founded:** 1969. **Membership:** 6000. **Staff:** 7. **Local Groups:** 9. **Languages:** Afrikaans, English. **Budget:** R 200,000. **Publication:** Diabetes Focus (in Afrikaans and English), quarterly. Price: Free, for members only. Circulation: 10,000. Advertising: accepted ▪ Sada News, semiannual.

SOUTH PACIFIC ALLIANCE FOR FAMILY HEALTH (SPAFH)
PO Box 729
Nuku'alofa, Tonga
PH: 676 23133
FX: 676 24047
Description: Provides technical and financial support to family planning and family health programs throughout the South Pacific. Focuses efforts on enabling indigenous populations to sustain their own family planning and health services. **Founded:** 1987. **Languages:** English, Polynesian.

SPANISH ALS ASSOCIATION (ADELA)
(Association Espanola de ELA)
e-mail: adela@readysoft.es
Apartado Correos 40030
E-28080 Madrid, Spain
Nieves Rodriguez, Dir.
PH: 34 1 3142854
FX: 34 1 3144535
Description: Promotes interest in amyotrophic lateral sclerosis or ALS (also called Lou Gehrig's disease) research among medical and scientific communities and the public in Spain. Offers support services to ALS sufferers and their families. Disseminates information about the disease. **Founded:** 1990. **Membership:** 1500. **Staff:** 3. **National Groups:** 1. **Languages:** Spanish. **Budget:** 5,000 Ptas. **Publication:** Adela Informa (in Spanish), quarterly. Bulletin. Contains general information about ALS. Price: for members. Advertising: accepted ▪ Adela Informa, Suplemento Cientifico.

SPANISH ASSOCIATION OF PHYSICIANS IN THE PHARMACEUTICAL INDUSTRIES
(Asociacion de Medicos de la Industria Farmaceutica Espanola)
Villanueva 11, 3
E-28001 Madrid, Spain
Description: Physicians employed by pharmaceutical manufacturers. Promotes thorough testing of pharmaceutical products prior to their release on the market. Represents members' interests. Sponsors educational programs. **Founded:** 1975. **Membership:** 350. **Languages:** English, Spanish.

SPANISH ROYAL SOCIETY OF PHYSICS
(Real Sociedad Espanola de Fisica)
e-mail: fite207@is.ucm.es
url: http://www.ucm.es/info/rsef
Facultades de Fisica y Quimica
Pabellon de Quimica
E-28040 Madrid, Spain
J. M. Los Arcos Merino, Exec.Off.
PH: 34 1 3944359
FX: 34 1 5433879
Description: Physicists, physics students and educators, and others with an interest in the physical sciences. Promotes advancement in the study and teaching of physics in Spain. **Founded:** 1903. **Membership:** 700. **Staff:** 1. **National Groups:** 18. **Lang-**

uages: English, Spanish. **Publication:** *Anales de Fisica* (in English and Spanish), 3/year. Price: 12.00 Ptas. ISSN: 1133-0376. Circulation: 1,000. Advertising: accepted ■ *Anales De Fisica - Monografias*, annual ■ *Revista Espanola de Fisica* (in English and Spanish), quarterly. Price: 11.00 Ptas. ISSN: 0213-862X. Advertising: accepted. Alternate Formats: CD-ROM. **Formerly:** (1980) Real Sociedad Espanola de Fisica Y Quimica.

SPIRITUAL EMERGENCE NETWORK (SEN)
e-mail: sen@cruzio.com
url: http://www.elfi.com/sen
930 Mission St., No. 7
Santa Cruz, CA 95060
Craig Turek, Dir.
PH: (408)426-0902
FX: (408)429-1614
Description: Seeks to develop an expanded model of mental health care to help people in crisis by using scientific and spiritual assistance. Operates an information and referral service. Offers educational programs. Maintains speakers' bureau. **Founded:** 1980. **Membership:** 10000. **Staff:** 3. Multinational. **Languages:** English.

SPONDYLITIS ASSOCIATION OF AMERICA (SAA)
e-mail: info@spondylitis.org
url: http://www.spondylitis.org
PO Box 5872
Sherman Oaks, CA 91413
Jane Bruckel, Exec.Dir.
PH: (818)981-1616
TF: 800777-8189
Description: Individuals affected by Ankylosing Spondylitis, psoriatic arthritis, and Reiter's Syndrome; and their families and friends; health care professionals; scientific researchers. (Ankylosing Spondylitis is a condition most often affecting those between 17-40 years of age and characterized by pain or stiffness in the back. Although the cause and cure are not known, the condition may be contained through a program of anti-inflammatory drugs, posture awareness, and regular, therapeutic exercise; it is believed to be a hereditary condition.) Disseminates information; promotes public awareness and research; conducts educational programs. **Founded:** 1983. **Membership:** 4000. **Staff:** 3. **Languages:** English. Formerly (1993) Ankylosing Spondylitis Association.

STANDING REPRESENTATIVE COMMITTEE FOR MEDICAL LABORATORY TECHNOLOGY IN THE EEC (SRCMLT)
Swedish Association of Health Officers
Adolf Fredriks Kyrkogate 11
Box 3260
S-103 65 Stockholm, Sweden
Kristina Malm Janson, Contact
PH: 46 8 8147771
FX: 46 8 8204096
Description: Professional organizations representing medical laboratory technologists in the European Community. Offers advice to the European Commission in matters concerning the medical laboratory technological profession. **Founded:** 1973. **Membership:** 10. Multinational. **Languages:** English.

STICHTING ALS ONDERZOEKFONDS
e-mail: ETrietsch@ktu.ruu.nl
Joos van Clevelaan 8
NL-3723 PG Bilthoven, Netherlands
Eric Trietsch, Contact
PH: 31 30 2533591
FX: 31 30 2533665
Description: Individuals interested in amyotropic lateral sclerosis or ALS (also known as Lou Gehrig's Disease). Works to: heighten public awareness and understanding of the disease; encourage research among medical and scientific communities. Sponsors researchers. **Founded:** 1981. **For-Profit.**

STOMATOLOGICAL SOCIETY OF GREECE
17 Kallirroes St.
GR-117 43 Athens, Greece
R. Karapa-Damigos, Sec.Gen.
PH: 30 1 9214325
FX: 30 1 9214204
Description: Dentists. Promotes dentistry in Greece. Provides members with the latest technological information. **Founded:** 1937. **Membership:** 600. **Staff:** 1. **Languages:** English, Greek. **Budget:** 16,000,000 Dr. **Publication:** *Stomatologia* (in Greek), quarterly. Journal. Includes English summaries. Price: $80.00. ISSN: 0039-1700. Circulation: 3,000. Advertising: accepted.

STRATIS HEALTH
2901 Metro Dr., Ste. 400
Bloomington, MN 55425
David M. Ziegenhagen, CEO
PH: (612)854-3306
FX: (612)853-8503
Description: Physicians interested in ensuring the availabilty of quality health care at reasonable costs. Evaluates health care services at hospitals, retirement homes, and other facilities. Develops health care standards for hospitals and offers consultation services to operators of health care facilities to improve efficiency in services. Conducts research and development on latest treatments and medical technologies. Tests new medical technologies. **Founded:** 1971. **Membership:** 3500. **Staff:** 60. **Languages:** English. **Budget:** $7,000,000.

STUDENT NATIONAL MEDICAL ASSOCIATION (SNMA)
url: http://www.snma.org
1012 10th St. NW
Washington, DC 20001
Dr. Imo Aisiku, Chm.
PH: (202)371-1616
FX: (202)371-5676
Description: Medical students, residents, and undergraduates of color. Seeks to help students in recruitment, admission, and retention in medical school and publishes information on problems and achievement in this area. Conducts annual research forum and community service projects. **Founded:** 1964. **Membership:** 4000. **Staff:** 3. **Local Groups:** 155. **Languages:** English. **Budget:** $350,000. **Publication:** *Journal of the Student National Medical Association*, quarterly. Circulation: 5,000. Advertising: accepted ■ *SNMA News*, quarterly. Circulation: 5,000. Advertising: accepted.

STURGE-WEBER FOUNDATION (SWF)
e-mail: swf@sturge-weber.com
url: http://www.sturge-weber.com
PO Box 418
Mount Freedom, NJ 07970-0418
Karen L. Ball, CEO
PH: (973)895-4445
TF: 800627-5482
FX: (973)895-4846
Description: Persons with Sturge-Weber syndrome and their families; concerned professionals and supporters. Serves as an information clearinghouse on Sturge-Weber syndrome, port-wine stains, and Klippel-Trenaunay Weber syndrome. (Sturge-Weber syndrome is a congenital neurological disorder characterized by facial port-wine stains, seizures, glaucoma, and loss of motor control, accompanied in rare cases by internal organ irregularities.) Disseminates information; offers support to afflicted persons. Maintains speakers' bureau; compiles statistics. Funds research. **Founded:** 1986. **Membership:** 900. **Staff:** 2. Multinational. **Regional Groups:** 21. **Languages:** English. **Budget:** $155,000. **Publication:** *Branching Out Newsletter*, quarterly. Price: $30.00/year; $40.00/year outside U.S. Advertising: accepted ■ Brochures.

SURGICAL RESEARCH SOCIETY

Academic Surgical Unit
The University of Hull
Castle Hill Hospital
Cottingham HU6 SJQ, Wales
Prof. J.R.T. Monson, Hon.Sec.
PH: 44 1482 623225
FX: 44 1482 623274
Description: Surgeons. To provide for the interchange of information about research related to surgery and surgical disease..
Membership: 547. **Publication:** *British Journal of Surgery*.

SURGICAL RESEARCH SOCIETY OF SOUTHERN AFRICA (SRSSA)

(Chirurgiese Navorsingsvereniging van Suidelike Afrika)
Dept. of Surgery
Univ. of Natal Medical School
Pnvaiz Bag 7
Congella 4013, Republic of South Africa
Prof. P.C. Borwmaw, Pres.
Description: Surgeons and surgeons in training. Promotes research, particularly among younger members, in clinical and experimental surgery. Sets surgical research standards. Provides funding to surgery departments of South African universities; offers grants and scholarships; sponsors competitions. **Founded:** 1972. **Membership:** 270. **Local Groups:** 5. **Languages:** Afrikaans, English. **Publication:** *Abstracts of Society Meeting*, annual ■ *South Africa Journal of Surgery*, periodic.

SUSAN G. KOMEN BREAST CANCER FOUNDATION (SGKF)

url: http://www.breastcancerinfo.com
5005 LBJ, Ste. 370
PO Box 97100
Dallas, TX 75244
Susan Braun, CEO/Pres.
PH: (972)385-5000
TF: 800IM-AWARE
FX: (972)385-5005
Description: Breast cancer patients, health care professionals, and other interested individuals. Works to: increase the recovery and survival rates of breast cancer patients; heighten public awareness of the risks of breast cancer and the need for early detection. Establishes breast screening and training in self-examination procedures; provides funding through grants for research and screening programs. Operates the Komen Alliance for Breast Disease Research, Education and Treatment, which conducts research into the genesis, progression, and treatment of the disease; sponsors educational programs. Bestows awards; sponsors competitions; maintains speakers' bureau. **Founded:** 1982. **Membership:** 1000. **Staff:** 11. **Local Groups:** 77. **Languages:** English, Spanish. **Publication:** *Frontline*, quarterly. Newsletter. Highlights current breast cancer issues and Komen events. Price: free. **Formerly:** (1989) Susan G. Komen Foundation.

SWEDISH ASSOCIATION OF OCCUPATIONAL THERAPISTS (SAOT)

(Forbundet Sveriges Arbetsterapeuter)
e-mail: fsa@akademiderhuset.se
Planiavagen 13
Box 760
S-131 24 Nacka, Sweden
Mrs. Inga-Britt Lindstom, Pres.
PH: 46 8 4662440
FX: 46 8 4662424
Description: Union of occupational therapists in Sweden. Compiles statistics; conducts research and educational programs; negotiates working conditions and wages. **Founded:** 1979. **Membership:** 7800. **Staff:** 20. **Regional Groups:** 30. **Languages:** English, Swedish. **Budget:** 16,500,000 SKr. **Publication:** *Arbetsterapeuten* (in Swedish), 16/year. Journal. Price: 400.00 SKr. ISSN: 0345-0988. Circulation: 7,300. Advertising: accepted ■ *Arbetsterapeuten Publicerar Sig* (in Swedish) ■ *FOU-Rapporter* (in Swedish), bi-

monthly. **Formed by Merger of:** Foreningen Sveriges Arbetsterapeuter; Ergoterapeutsektionen.

SWEDISH ASSOCIATION OF REGISTERED PHYSICAL THERAPISTS

(Legitmerade Sjukgymnasters Riksforbund)
e-mail: kansli@lsr.se
url: http://www.lsr.se
Vasagatan 48
Box 3196
S-103 63 Stockholm, Sweden
Asa Holmstrand, Pres.
PH: 46 8 6969730
FX: 46 8 6969754
Description: Union of physical therapists in Sweden. Sponsors educational programs; compiles statistics. **Founded:** 1943. **Membership:** 11000. **Staff:** 20. **Languages:** English, Swedish. **Publication:** *Nordisk Fysioterapi* (in English), quarterly. Journal. ISSN: 1402-3024 ■ *Sjukgymnasten* (in Swedish), monthly. Magazine. ISSN: 0037-6019. Advertising: accepted.

SWEDISH DENTAL ASSOCIATION (SDA)

(Sveriges Tandlakarforbund)
e-mail: info@tandeakarforbunder.se
url: http://www.tandlakarforbunder.se
Nybrogatan 53
Box 5843
S-102 48 Stockholm, Sweden
Mr. Gunnar Luthman, Contact
PH: 46 8 6661500
FX: 46 8 6625842
Description: Union of dentists in Sweden. Offers over 200 continuing dental education courses annually. **Founded:** 1908. **Membership:** 11900. **Staff:** 25. **Languages:** English, Swedish. **Budget:** 21,000,000 SKr. **Publication:** *Swedish Dental Journal*, bimonthly ■ *Tandlakartidningen*, 18/year. Journal. Also Cited As: *The Journal of the SDA*.

SWEDISH DENTAL TRADE ASSOCIATION

(Foreningen Svensk Dentalhandel)
e-mail: fsd@branschkansliet.se
Box 1416
S-111 84 Stockholm, Sweden
Joakim Strignert, Dir.
PH: 46 8 240700
FX: 46 8 218496
Description: Companies manufacturing dental equipment and supplies. Establishes international standards and technical harmonization for dental equipment. Represents members' interests before government bodies, international agencies, and the public. Maintains liaison with organizations representing dentists, dental technicians, and dental supply dealers and distributors. Compiles statistics. **Founded:** 1989. **Membership:** 50. **Languages:** English, Swedish.

SWEDISH DIABETES ASSOCIATION (SDA)

(Svenska Diabetesforbundet)
Box 1545
S-171 29 Solna, Sweden
Marie Jeanette Bergvall, Contact
PH: 46 8 6298580
FX: 46 8 982555
Description: Provides support and information for diabetics in Sweden. Conducts educational and research programs. **Founded:** 1943. **Membership:** 34500. **Staff:** 16. **Local Groups:** 107. **Languages:** English, Swedish. **For-Profit. Budget:** 13,000,000 SKr. **Publication:** *Diabetes* (in Swedish), bimonthly. **Formerly:** (1997) Swedish Diabetic Association.

SWEDISH MEDICAL ASSOCIATION
(Sveriges Laekarfoerbund)
Villagatan 5
PO Box 5610
S-114 86 Stockholm, Sweden
Dr. Anders Milton, CEO
PH: 46 8 7903300
FX: 46 8 205718
Description: Union of physicians in Sweden. Advocates collective negotiations on physicians' employment conditions, health policy, and medical education issues. Maintains professional and specialist groups. **Founded:** 1903. **Membership:** 35000. **Staff:** 90. **Regional Groups:** 29. **Budget:** 000,000 SKr. **Publication:** *Laekartidningen* (in Swedish), weekly. Journal. Price: 813.00 SKr/members; 925.00 SKr/others. ISSN: 0023-7205. Circulation: 31,000. Advertising: accepted.

SWEDISH PHYSICAL SOCIETY
e-mail: barany@atom.msi.se
url: http://www2.tsl.uu.se:8001/
Atomfysik
Frescativagen 24
S-104 05 Stockholm, Sweden
A. Barany, Pres.
PH: 46 8 161022
FX: 46 8 158674
Description: Physicists, physics educators, and others with an interest in the physical sciences. Promotes increased public interest in physics, and more effective public education in the physical sciences. **Founded:** 1920. **Membership:** 915. **Languages:** English, Swedish. **Publication:** *Fysik-Aktuellt* (in Swedish), quarterly. Newsletter. Price: included in membership dues. ISSN: 0283-9148. Advertising: accepted ■ *Kosmos*, annual. Book.

SWEDISH PSYCHOLOGICAL ASSOCIATION (SPA)
(Sveriges Psykologforbund)
url: http://www.psykologtorbundej.se
Vasagatan 48
Box 3287
S-103 65 Stockholm, Sweden
Hans Persson, Contact
PH: 46 8 6969760
FX: 46 8 247855
Description: Union of psychologists in Sweden. **Founded:** 1955. **Membership:** 7000. **Staff:** 20.

SWEDISH SOCIETY FOR DERMATOLOGY AND VENEREOLOGY
Dept. of Dermatology
University Hospital
S-581 85 Linkoping, Sweden
Thomas Andersson, Sec.
PH: 46 13 222596
FX: 46 13 222562
Description: Dermatologists in Sweden. Represents members' interests. **Founded:** 1901. **Membership:** 450. **Languages:** English. **Publication:** *Forum for Nordic Dermatu-Venereology* (in English), quarterly. Newsletter. Advertising: accepted. **Formerly:** Swedish Dermatological Society.

SWISS PHYSICAL SOCIETY
Institut de Physique
Universite de Neuchatel
CH-2000 Neuchatel, Switzerland
PH: 41 38 256991
FX: 41 38 244973
Description: Physicists, physics teachers, and others with an interest in the physical sciences. Seeks to improve the quality of physics education, research, and knowledge. **Membership:** 1400. **Languages:** English, French.

SWISS TROPICAL INSTITUTE (STI)
(Bureau Appui Sante Environnement)
Boite Postale 972
N'Djamena, Chad
Jean Naissengar, Admin.
PH: 51 235 513060
FX: 51 235 512663
Description: Swiss organizations and government agencies concerned with international development and relief operations. Promotes improved health and quality of life in Chad. Seeks to develop local administrative capacities to ensure sustained economic and social development. Facilitates cooperation among development agencies; works to increase awareness of development issues among people in developing areas. Makes available health care services; conducts training courses to enable local communities to maintain autonomous primary health care facilities. Monitors environmental impact of development programs. **Founded:** 1987. **Staff:** 35. **Languages:** French. **Budget:** $2,000,000.

SYNDICAT DES INDUSTRIES FRANCAISES POUR L'ART DENTAIRE (SIFADENT)
8, rue Blanche
F-75009 Paris, France
Maurice Thermoz, Contact
PH: 33 1 48741108
FX: 33 1 42852032
Description: Companies manufacturing dental equipment and supplies. Establishes international standards and technical harmonization for dental equipment. Represents members' interests before government bodies, international agencies, and the public. Maintains liaison with organizations representing dentists, dental technicians, and dental supply dealers and distributors. Compiles statistics. **Founded:** 1924. **Membership:** 30. **Staff:** 3. **Languages:** French. **Budget:** 280,000 Fr. **Publication:** *Sifadent News* (in French), monthly. Newsletter. Price: free. Advertising: not accepted ■ Directory. **Formerly:** (1986) Chambre Esndicale des Fabricants de Materiel et Aroduits Pour Liart Dentaire.

TACHOGRAPH ANALYSIS ASSOCIATION
131 Mount Pleasant
Liverpool L3 5TF, England
Dr. N.E. Kirkwood, Contact
PH: 44 151 7080123
FX: 44 151 7070230
Description: Those associated with, or undertaking, the analysis of tachograph charts. Aims to encourage quality of analysis and the standardisation of interpretation of tachograph charts. A Code of Practice has been produced to provide a framework for those analysing charts. **Founded:** 1987. Multinational. **Publication:** *Tachnograph Review* (in English), semiannual. Newsletter. Price: free. Circulation: 75 ■ *Tachograph Analysis Code of Practice* (in English), annual.

TARDIVE DYSKINESIA/TARDIVE DYSTONIA NATIONAL ASSOCIATION (TD/TDNA)
4244 University Way NE
PO Box 45732
Seattle, WA 98145-0732
S.K. Kjaer, Exec.Dir.
Description: Tardive Dyskinesia and Tardive Dystonia patients and others disabled due to use of psychotropic and other prescription drugs; relatives of afflicted individuals and concerned citizens; legal and health care professionals. (Tardive Dyskinesia and Tardive Dystonia are neuromuscular disorders of the face, trunk, and extremities that occur primarily as a side effect of certain psychotropic and neuroleptic drugs.) Seeks to establish national legislation requiring that patients be warned of the potential side effects of prescription drug induced movement disorders, and that patients' informed consent be obtained before these drugs are administered. Works to increase public awareness of the disorders. Encourages research into alternative modalities and the prevention and cure of the dis orders. Provides guidance, support networks, referral services, and assistance for afflicted individuals and their families. Operates speak-

ers' bureau; compiles statistics. Maintains library and biographical archives. **Founded:** 1985. **Membership:** 510. **Staff:** 2. **Local Groups:** 5. **Languages:** English. **Publication:** *International Tardive Dyskinesia/Tardive Dystonia Newsletter*, semiannual ▪ *Living with TD/TD - Personal Perspectives* ▪ *Tardive Dyskinesia: Questions and Answers.*

TASK FORCE FOR CHILD SURVIVAL AND DEVELOPMENT (TFCSD)

The Carter Presidential Center
1 Copenhill Ave.
Atlanta, GA 30307
William H. Foege, M.D., Exec.Dir.
PH: (404)872-4122
FX: (404)873-7000
Description: Sponsored by United Nations Children's Fund, United Nations Development Programme, World Health Organization, Rockefeller Foundation, and The World Bank. Seeks to further efforts to immunize children worldwide against vaccine-preventable diseases (measles, polio, diphtheria, tuberculosis, neonatal tetanus, and whooping cough). Assists in the implementation of immunization programs; conducts research. Plans to implement programs dealing with dietary deficiency-related disorders. Coordinates activities between sponsoring organizations. **Founded:** 1984. **Membership:** 5. **Languages:** English. **Publication:** *Child Survival - World Development* (in English, French, and Spanish), bimonthly. Newsletter.

TEL-MED

e-mail: telmed@ix.netcom.com
url: http://www.tel-med.com
PO Box 1768
Colton, CA 92324
Michael Carpenter, Pres.
PH: (909)825-6034
FX: (909)825-6455
Description: Hospitals, medical societies, universities, medical centers, public libraries, and other organizations offering the Tel-Med program. Tel-Med is a library of three to five minute recorded health related messages created to be played over the telephone for public use, free of charge. Provides messages to communities; local libraries are established where individuals from the community can call to listen to messages. Operates as an information service intended to educate and assist in recognizing early signs of illness and is not designed to diagnose or treat medical problems. Scripts are written by medical professionals and examined by a team of physicians; messages are reviewed at least annually. Offers services and information on a wide range of medical subjects including alcoholism, arthritis, bee stings, cancer, diabetes, drug abuse, influenza, medical costs, mental health, nutrition, parenting, sex education, smoking, vasectomies, and vaginitis. **Founded:** 1971. **Membership:** 200. **Staff:** 3. **Languages:** English, Spanish. **For-Profit. Publication:** *Tel-Med Newsletter*, quarterly ▪ Annual Report, annual ▪ Brochures.

TENOVUS - SCOTLAND (TS)

234 St. Vincent St.
Glasgow G2 5RJ, Scotland
Christine Timm, Sec.-Treas.
PH: 44 0141 2216268
FX: 44 01292 311433
Description: Individuals and organizations. Promotes advancement of medical research projects undertaken by Scottish hospitals and university medical schools. Provides financial support and other assistance to medical research programs. Conducts fundraising activities. **Founded:** 1967. **Languages:** English. **Publication:** Newsletter, periodic. Advertising: not accepted ▪ Brochure.

TERRY FOX FOUNDATION (TFF)

e-mail: ontario@terryfoxrun.org
url: http://www.terryfoxrun.org
60 St. Clair Ave. E, Ste. 605
Toronto, ON, Canada M4T 1N5
Darrell Fox, National Dir.
PH: (416)924-8252
FX: (416)924-6597
Description: Individuals and organizations. Seeks to "maintain the vision and principles of Terry Fox;" promotes and supports research into the causes and treatment of cancer. Conducts fundraising activities benefitting cancer research. **Founded:** 1981. **Staff:** 18. **Languages:** English, French. **Budget:** C$10,000,000. **Publication:** Newsletter, periodic ▪ Brochure.

TETRAPYRROLE DISCUSSION GROUP (TG)

e-mail: d.i.vernon@leeds.ac.uk
University of Leeds
Dept. of Biochemistry and Molecular Biology
Leeds, W. Yorkshire LS2 9JT, England
Dr. D.I. Vernon
PH: 44 113 2333143
FX: 44 113 2333167
Description: Individuals interested in the tetrapyrrole group of chemicals, which includes components of hemoglobin, chlorophylls, vitamin B12, and bile pigments. Facilitates exchange of information among members. **Founded:** 1976. **Membership:** 95. **Languages:** English.

TONGA FAMILY PLANNING ASSOCIATION (TFPA)

PO Box 1142
Nuku'alofa, Tonga
PH: 676 21209
FX: 676 23766
Description: National affiliate of the International Family Planning Federation. Provides family planning information and counseling services; conducts family life education programs; sponsors training courses for family planning workers. **Founded:** 1975. **Languages:** English, Tongan.

TOUCH FOR HEALTH KINESIOLOGY ASSOCIATION

e-mail: admin@tfh.org
url: http://www.tfh.org
11262 Washington Blvd.
Culver City, CA 90230-4616
Larry Green, Pres.
PH: (310)313-5580
TF: 800466-8342
FX: (310)313-9319
Description: International network of independent instructors comprising laypersons, medical doctors, chiropractors, osteopaths, nurses, teachers, physical therapists, massage therapists, and other professionals. Promotes techniques for restoring natural energies and improving postural balance through muscle testing using applied kinesiology and acupressure points to improve muscle function and balance the body's energy. Stimulates trained professionals to utilize natural health care research techniques with laypeople and their associates, and disseminates information on research plans, methodology, and results of self-development programs in health care, both mental and physical. Increases the level of professional confidence and keeps interested instructors, trainers, laypeople, and those in the health care profession regularly and reliably informed on development in natural health care. Conducts research projects on Touch for Health methods and results. **Founded:** 1974. **Membership:** 1500. **Staff:** 3. **Languages:** English. **Budget:** $150,000. **Publication:** *Annual Meeting Journal.* Price: $30.00. Circulation: 1,000 ▪ *Keeping in Touch*, quarterly. Newsletter. Includes coverage of research developments, book reviews, calendar of events tips for professionals, anecdotal reports, news of upcoming events. Price: $250.00 full page; $150.00 1/2 page; $75.00 1/4 page; $35.00 business card ▪ *Touch for Health Association Directory*, annual. Membership Directory. Price: $125.00 full page; $75.00 1/2 page; $50.00 1/4 page; $35.00 business card. Circulation: 1,000 ▪ *Touch for Health*

Book (in English, French, German, Italian, Spanish, and Swedish). Reference manual. Price: $24.95. Circulation: 4,000. Advertising: not accepted ■ *Touch for Health Folios*. Price: $19.95 full size; $14.95 pocket size ■ *Touch for Health in Practice*, monthly. Newsletter. Price: included w/professional membership ■ *Touch for Health Reference Chart*. Price: $33.95. **Formerly:** (1990) Touch for Health Foundation; (1993) Touch for Health Association of America. **Status Note:** (1998) Formerly Touch for Health Association.

TOURETTE SYNDROME ASSOCIATION (TSA)
e-mail: tourette@ix.netcom.com
url: http://TSA.mgh.harvard.edu
42-40 Bell Blvd.
Bayside, NY 11361
Judit Ungar, Exec.Dir.
PH: (718)224-2999
TF: 800237-0717
FX: (718)279-9596
Description: People with Tourette Syndrome (TS) and their families and friends; physicians, nurses, teachers, psychologists, social workers, and other professionals; organizations such as mental health agencies. (TS is characterized by involuntary muscular movements and utterances of sounds or words, and is often undiagnosed or misdiagnosed.) Develops and disseminates educational materials to families, professionals, and agencies involved in health care, education, and governments. Schedules meetings and seminars for professionals and families to explore the latest information on TS. Stimulates support for research into the nature and causes of the disorder. Apprises members of rights, services, and benefits provided by the government and other organizations. Provides lists of doctors experienced in treating the disorder. Operates support groups and other services to help persons with TS and their families. Maintains sources for advocacy referral services in the areas of education, employment, and housing. **Founded:** 1972. **Membership:** 30000. **Staff:** 20. Multinational. **Local Groups:** 300. **Languages:** English. **Budget:** $1,800,000. **Publication:** *Leadership Bulletins*, 4/year. Price: free. Circulation: 50. Advertising: not accepted ■ *Medical Letter: Summary of the Recent Literature*, annual ■ *Tourette Syndrome Association Newsletter*, quarterly. Includes book reviews. Price: included in membership dues. **Formerly:** Gilles de la Tourette Syndrome Association.

TOXICOLOGICAL HISTORY SOCIETY (THIS)
5757 Hall St. SE
Grand Rapids, MI 49546-3845
John H. Trestrail, III, Sec.
PH: (616)774-5329
Description: Individuals interested in the researching and documentation of the history of poisons, antidotes, and the impact of toxicology on events in world history. Maintains speakers' bureau; has compiled bibliography. **Founded:** 1990. **Membership:** 70. **Staff:** 1. Multinational. **Languages:** English. Absorbed Venomological Artifact Society.

TRIGEMINAL NEURALGIA ASSOCIATION (TNA)
e-mail: tna@csuonline.net
url: http://neurosurgery/mgr.harvard.edu/tna
PO Box 340
Barnegat Light, NJ 08006
Claire W. Patterson, Pres.
PH: (609)361-1014
FX: (609)361-0982
Description: Individuals with trigeminal neuralgia, a neurological disorder characterized by sudden attacks of pain along the distribution of one or more branches of the trigeminal nerve in the face and head. Works to increase public and professional awareness and understanding of the disorder. Provides a forum for discussion among individuals with trigeminal neuralgia in order to share information and experiences and offer support to patients and their families. Offers physician referrals. Conducts educational programs. **Founded:** 1989. **Membership:** 6000. **Staff:** 2. **Languages:** English. **For-Profit. Budget:** $75,000. **Publication:**

TNAlert, quarterly. Newsletter. Price: free. Circulation: 7,000. Advertising: not accepted ■ *Trigeminal Neuralgia - An Overview for Patients and Their Parents*.

TRINIDAD AND TOBAGO REGISTERED NURSES' ASSOCIATION
4 Fitz Blackman Dr.
Wrighton Rd., Opposite Jean Pierre Sporting Complex
Port of Spain, Trinidad and Tobago
Yvonne Pilgrim, Exec.Sec.
PH: (809)632-1567
FX: (809)632-1567
Description: Registered nurses. Promotes and facilitates the professional advancement of members; works to insure that members receive the "recognition due to them." Represents members' interests before public and professional agencies. **Founded:** 1930. **Membership:** 700. **Staff:** 2. Multinational. **Regional Groups:** 3. **Languages:** English. **Publication:** *TTRNA News* (in English), monthly. Newsletter. Contains information aimed at keeping members updated on current changes in health care and nursing. Price: TT$5.00. Advertising: not accepted.

TROPICAL AFRICAN INSTITUTE OF OPHTHALMOLOGY
(Institut d'Ophtalmologie Tropicale Africaine)
e-mail: iota@malinet.ml
Boite Postale 248
Bamako, Mali
Dr. Pierre Huguet, Dir.
PH: 223 223421
FX: 223 225186
Description: Ophthalmologists practicing in tropical areas of Africa. Seeks to advance the study and practice of ophthalmology. Conducts continuing professional development courses for members. Serves as a clearinghouse on ophthalmology. **Founded:** 1953. **Staff:** 1. Multinational. **Languages:** English, French.

TROPICAL HEALTH AND EDUCATION TRUST (THET)
21 Edenhurst Ave.
London SW6 3PD, England
Elderyd Parry, Contact
PH: 44 0171 9272411
FX: 44 0171 6374314
Description: Medical training institutions specializing in tropical medicine. Seeks to advance the study, teaching, and practice of tropical medicine. Serves as a liaison linking medical education institutions in Europe and the developing world; sponsors research and educational programs. **Founded:** 1989. **Staff:** 2. Multinational. **Languages:** English. **Budget:** $225,000.

TURKISH AMERICAN PHYSICIANS ASSOCIATION (TAPA)
373 Smithtown Byp., No. 128
Hauppauge, NY 11788-2516
Dr. Cemil Bikmen, Exec. Officer
PH: (516)724-0777
Description: To develop closer relationships among physicians of Turkish origin, facilitate the exchange of information, and develop cultural and medical exchange with physicians in Turkey. **Founded:** 1969. **Membership:** 1260. **Regional Groups:** 4. **Languages:** English. **Publication:** *Membership Roster*, biennial.

TURKISH BIOCHEMICAL SOCIETY (TBS)
(Turk Biyokimya Dernegi)
PO Box 407
Yenisehir
TR-06444 Ankara, Turkey
Canan Bayar, Sec.Gen.
PH: 90 312 3110588
FX: 90 312 3116616
Description: Professionals and students concerned with biochemistry, clinical chemistry, and molecular biology. Promotes the development of educational techniques used in biochemistry; works to standardize terminology and laboratory procedures. Offers financial support to efforts aimed at alleviating the shortage of capable scientists. **Founded:** 1975. **Membership:** 1100. **Local**

Groups: 3. **Languages:** English, Turkish. **Budget:** TL 000,000. **Publication:** *Biyokimya Dergisi* (in English and Turkish), quarterly. Journal. Scientific research, articles, reviews, and case or methodology reports. Price: $45.00/year. ISSN: 0250-4685. Advertising: accepted. Also Cited As: Turkish Journal of Biochemistry ▪ *Klinik Laboratuvar Bulteni* (in English and Turkish), 3/year. Bulletin. Organization news and lab research. Advertising: accepted. **Formerly:** Biochemical Society.

TURKISH SOCIETY OF CARDIOLOGY (TSC)
(Turk Kardiyoloji Dernegi)
e-mail: tkd@turk.net
url: http://www.tkd.org.tr
Ortaklar Caddesi 4/7
Mecidiyekoy
TR-80240 Istanbul, Turkey
Dr. Altan Onat, Pres.
PH: 90 212 2884455
FX: 90 212 2884433
Description: Cardiologists and specialists in related fields. Promotes increased public and professional awareness of cardiovascular diseases. Encourages and funds cardiological research; gathers and disseminates information to members. Offers postgraduate course in cardiology. Has conducted survey on heart disease and risk factors. **Founded:** 1963. **Membership:** 430. **Staff:** 2. **National Groups:** 7. **Languages:** English, Turkish. **Budget:** $90,000. **Publication:** *Archives of the Turkish Society of Cardiology* (in Turkish), 9/year. Journal. Contains research work, reviews, and case reports. English summaries available. Price: $40.00 plus mailing charges. ISSN: 1016-5169. Circulation: 1,100. Advertising: accepted. Alternate Formats: magnetic tape. Also Cited As: *Turk Kardiyoloji Dernegi Arsivi* ▪ *Congress Supplement for Abstracts*, annual ▪ Directory, biennial.

UKRAINIAN MEDICAL ASSOCIATION OF NORTH AMERICA (UMANA)
url: http://www.umana.org
2247 W. Chicago Ave., 2nd Fl.
Chicago, IL 60622
Dr. Maria Hrycelak, Dir.
PH: (773)278-6262
TF: 888RXUMANA
FX: (773)278-6962
Description: Physicians, surgeons, dentists, and persons in related professions who are of Ukrainian descent. Provides assistance to members; sponsors lectures. Maintains placement service, museum, biographical and medical archives, and library of 1800 medical books and journals in Ukrainian. **Membership:** 1000. **Staff:** 14. **Local Groups:** 17. **Languages:** English. **Publication:** *Medical Journal*, quarterly. Contains medical research articles and news. Price: free to members; $10.00 otherwise. Circulation: 1,000. Advertising: not accepted ▪ *Newsletter to Membership*, quarterly ▪ *Umana News*. **Formerly:** American Ukrainian Medical Society.

ULSTER CANCER FOUNDATION (UCF)
e-mail: mwood_ucf@unite.net
40-42 Eglantine Ave.
Belfast, Antrim BT9 6DX, Northern Ireland
Michael A. Wood, M.B.E.
PH: 44 1232 663281
FX: 44 1232 660081
Description: Encourages and facilitates research on cancer prevention and early diagnosis. Seeks to help patients and their families cope with cancer. Works for new and better treatments for cancer, helps people reduce their risk of developing the disease. Conducts educational programs including clinics and training sessions for health care professionals; makes available children's services; sponsors competitions and bestows awards. Compiles statistics. **Founded:** 1970. **Staff:** 20. **Local Groups:** 59. **Languages:** English. **Budget:** L750,000. **Publication:** *Cancer Control in Practice*. Book. A training and resource park for practice nurses. Price: L7.00 ▪ *Cancer Education and Care in the Workplace* (in English). Book. Price: L15.00 ▪ *Environmental Health Perspec-*

tives on Cancer. Price: L15.00 ▪ *Focus on Cancer in Schools* ▪ *Smoking Matters for Young People*. Price: L8.50.

ULSTER PREGNANCY ADVISORY ASSOCIATION
719A Lisburn Rd.
Belfast, Antrim BT9 7GU, Northern Ireland
Joan Wilson, Dir.
PH: 44 1232 381345
Description: Offers counseling and support to women with unplanned pregnancies in Northern Ireland, where 1967 Abortion Law does not apply. Disseminates information on contraception methods and abortion alternatives. **Founded:** 1971. **Membership:** 10.

UNION OF AMERICAN PHYSICIANS AND DENTISTS (UAPD)
e-mail: uapd@uapd.com
1330 Broadway, Ste. 730
Oakland, CA 94612
Robert Weinmann, M.D., Pres.
PH: (510)839-0193
TF: 800622-0909
FX: (510)763-8756
Description: Independent national labor organization made up of self-employed medical doctors and dentists as well as those employed by hospitals, teaching institutions, counties, and municipalities. Seeks to: provide optimum medical care for the people; ensure quality facilities for the provision of medical care; enable physicians to give of themselves, unhindered by extraneous forces, for the welfare of their patients; ensure reasonable compensation for physicians commensurate with their training, skill, and the responsibility they bear for the life and health of their fellow human beings. **Founded:** 1972. **Membership:** 10000. **Staff:** 19. **National Groups:** 1. **Languages:** English. **Budget:** $1,600,000. **Publication:** *UAPD Report* (in English), monthly. Newsletter. Price: free with membership. Advertising: not accepted. **Formerly:** Union of American Physicians and Dentists.

UNION OF CZECH MATHEMATICIANS AND PHYSICISTS
e-mail: cieply@ujf.cas.cz
url: http://www.ujf.cas.cz/~fvs
Institute of Physics
Na Slovance 2
CZ-180 40 Prague, Czech Republic
A. Cieply, Sec.
PH: 420 2 66052910
FX: 420 2 8584569
Description: Physicists, and others with an interest in the physical sciences. Seeks to improve the quality of physics education, research, and knowledge. **Founded:** 1968. **Membership:** 640. **Staff:** 2. **Languages:** Czech, English. **Budget:** Kcs 40,000. **Publication:** *Zpravodaj FVS* (in Czech), bimonthly. Newsletter. Price: for members. Advertising: not accepted.

UNION OF DISPENCERS IN BULGARIA
G. Vashington 24
BG-1000 Sofia, Bulgaria
PH: 359 2 835280
FX: 359 2 833865
Description: Defends and represents the interests of pharmaceutists. **Founded:** 1992.

UNION OF ESTONIAN EMERGENCY MEDICAL SERVICES
(Eesti Kiirabi Liit)
e-mail: ekbiit@uninet.ee
Riia 18,
EE-2400 Tartu, Estonia
Ago Korgvee, MD, Pres.
PH: 372 2 525457
FX: 372 2 525457
Description: Organizations and individuals providing emergency medical services; members of other medical specialty associations. Assists members in clarifying their rights and responsibilities under the present Estonian healthcare system. Represents

the interests of EMS providers. Participates in training for EMS providers. Certifies emergency healthcare providers. Provides first aid training to the public. **Founded:** 1992. **Membership:** 1000. **Staff:** 10. **Regional Groups:** 50. **Languages:** Estonian. **Formerly:** Estonian First Medical Aid Association.

UNION OF MIDDLE EASTERN AND MEDITERRANEAN PEDIATRIC SOCIETIES (UMEMPS)
(Union des Societes de Pediatrie du Moyen-Orient et de la Mediterranee)
Milioni 6
GR-106 73 Athens, Greece
Prof. Thedore Thomaidis, Sec.Gen.
PH: 30 1 3615168
FX: 30 1 6444260
Description: National societies of pediatricians and pediatric surgeons. **Founded:** 1966. **Membership:** 23. **Multinational. Regional Groups:** 1. **Languages:** English, French. **Budget:** $2,200. **Publication:** *Newsletter* (in English and French), annual. Bulletin. Price: Free. Advertising: not accepted.

UNION NATIONALE DES ASSOCIATIONS DE SOINS ET SERVICE A DOMICILE (UNASSAD)
108-110 rue St. Maur
F-75011 Paris, France
C. Martel, Gen.Dir.
PH: 33 1 49238252
FX: 33 1 43385533
Description: Organizations providing home health care for the elderly or disabled and their families. Promotes high industry standards. **Founded:** 1970. **Membership:** 1700. **Staff:** 12. **Languages:** English, French. **Publication:** *Information Paper*, monthly. **Also Known As:** National Organisation for Home Care.

UNION OF PHYSICISTS IN BULGARIA
Administrative Council
Blvd. James Bourchier 5
BG-1126 Sofia, Bulgaria
Prof. I. Lalov, Pres.
PH: 359 2 627660
FX: 359 2 689085
Description: Physicists, physics teachers, and others with an interest in the physical sciences. Seeks to improve the quality of physics education, research, and knowledge. **Founded:** 1898. **Membership:** 100. **Staff:** 2. **State Groups:** 1. **Languages:** Bulgarian, English. **Budget:** 2,000 Lv. **Publication:** *Physics World* (in Bulgarian), quarterly. Contains information about popular publications, anniversaries, and reports. Price: $2.00. Advertising: not accepted.

UNION OF SCIENTIFIC MEDICAL SOCIETIES IN BULGARIA
Centre of Hygiene, Fl. XII, Rm. 19
15, D.Nestorov Str.
BG-1431 Sofia, Bulgaria
Nacho Nachev, Pres.
PH: 359 2 595032
FX: 359 2 595032
Description: Promotes development of medical science. **Founded:** 1968. **Membership:** 13000. **Publication:** *Modern Medicine* (in English).

UNIONE NAZIONALE INDUSTRIE DENTARIE ITALIANE
Via Tamburini 2
I-20123 Milan, Italy
Dr. Arturo Chiurazzi, Sec.
PH: 39 2 48008650
FX: 39 2 461330
Description: Companies manufacturing dental equipment and supplies. Establishes international standards and technical harmonization for dental equipment. Represents members' interests before government bodies, international agencies, and the public. Maintains liaison with organizations representing dentists, dental technicians, and dental supply dealers and distributors. Compiles

statistics. **Founded:** 1969. **Membership:** 135. **Staff:** 10. **Languages:** English, French. **Publication:** *Unidipress* (in Italian), bimonthly. Magazine. Circulation: 17,000. Advertising: accepted.

UNITED KINGDOM HOME CARE ASSOCIATION
42b Banstead Rd.
Carshalton Beeches
Carshalton SM5 3NW, England
Lesley Rimmer, Contact
PH: 44 181 2881551
FX: 44 181 2881550
Description: Represents independent home care organizations providing home care and nursing care to people in their own homes. Identifies and promotes the highest standards of home care. **Founded:** 1988. **Membership:** 1000. **Staff:** 8. **Publication:** *The Homecarer*, quarterly. Newsletter ∎ *VAT: The Effect on Care Agencies*.

UNITED LEUKODYSTROPHY FOUNDATION (ULF)
e-mail: ulf@ceet.niu.edu
url: http://www.ceet.niu.edu/ulf.html
2304 Highland Dr.
Sycamore, IL 60178
Ron Brazeal, Exec.Dir.
PH: (815)895-3211
TF: 800728-5483
FX: (815)895-2432
Description: Leukodystrophy patients, their families, and medical care professionals. (Leukodystrophy refers to a group of disorders which affect the brain, spinal cord, and peripheral nerves by damaging the insulating sheath around nerve strands, interfering with the flow of electrical impulses.) Provides information on leukodystrophy to patients, their families, and the general public; assists in identifying sources of medical care, social services, and counseling; coordinates a communication network among affected families. Promotes and supports research into the causes, treatment, and prevention of white matter disorders. Coordinates cooperation between donor and government agencies, scientific programs, and the private sector. Conducts educational and research programs. **Founded:** 1982. **Membership:** 3000. **Staff:** 3. **Multinational. Languages:** English. **Budget:** $250,000. **Publication:** *The Facts About Leukodystrophy*. Brochures ∎ *ULF News*, quarterly. Newsletter. Price: included in membership dues. Circulation: 3,000. Advertising: accepted ∎ *What to Expect When the Diagnosis is a Neurodegenerative Disease*. Booklet.

UNITED METHODIST ASSOCIATION OF HEALTH AND WELFARE MINISTRIES (UMA)
e-mail: uma@umassociation.org
url: http://www.umassociation.org
601 W. Riverview Ave.
Dayton, OH 45406-5543
Mr. Dean W. Pulliam, CEO
PH: (937)227-9494
TF: 800411-9901
FX: (937)222-7364
Description: Membership association for 400 United Methodist related hospitals, retirement homes, community based ministries, youth and family service organizations, children's homes, churches, and individuals. Offers communications and church relations guidance. Provides leadership development training for health and human service professionals in United Methodist related organizations and agencies. Develops ethical and theological statements on institutional care. Operates Educational Assessment Guidelines Leading Toward Excellence (EAGLE), a self-assessment and peer review accreditation program. Operates a Field Consultation Program; members may access skilled professionals to assist with governance questions. Offers audiovisual services to members. Administers the Order of Good Shepherds program designed to recognize ministry in the workplace by employees at member organizations. Maintains speakers' bureau; compiles statistics. **Founded:** 1940. **Membership:** 400. **Staff:** 5. **Languages:** English. **Budget:** $450,000. **Publication:** *Articles depicting innovative ministries by member organizations* (in Eng-

lish), quarterly. Magazine. Professional journal related to operation of United Methodist related institutional ministries. Price: $40.00/year member; $60.00/year nonmember. Circulation: 2,200. Advertising: accepted ■ *Children, Youth, & Family Services Section Salary & Benefit Study* ■ *National Directory of all United Methodist Related Health and Welfare Ministries*, annual. Price: $17.00/year for members; $27.00/year for nonmembers. Circulation: 400. Advertising: accepted ■ *Older Adult Ministries Section Salary & Benefit Study* ■ *The UMA Journal*, quarterly. Magazine. Depicts innovative ministries by member organizations. Circulation: 2,200. Advertising: accepted. **Formerly:** (1968) Board of Hospitals and Homes of The Methodist Church; (1972) Division of Health and Welfare Ministries of The United Methodist Church; (1983) National Association of Health and Welfare Ministries of The United Methodist Church.

UNITED PARKINSON FOUNDATION (UPF)
e-mail: upf_itf@msn.com
833 W. Washington Blvd.
Chicago, IL 60607
Judy Rosner, Exec.Dir.
PH: (312)733-1893
FX: (312)733-1896
Description: Patients, family members, medical personnel and other interested persons. Assembles and publishes reliable information about symptoms, medications and therapy helpful to sufferers of Parkinson's disease and related illnesses. Fosters and supports scientific research on the disease. Assists patients and their families with medical referrals, education and other means. **Founded:** 1963. **Membership:** 38000. **Staff:** 3. **Languages:** English. **Publication:** *One Step At a Time* ■ *Patient Experience* ■ *United Parkinson Foundation Newsletter*, quarterly. Includes research updates. Price: included in membership dues. Circulation: 40,000. Advertising: not accepted ■ *Your Questions Answered.*

UNITED SCLERODERMA FOUNDATION (USF)
e-mail: sclerofed@aol.com
url: http://www.scleroderma.com
89 Newbury St., Ste. 201
Danvers, MA 01923-1075
Karl Kastorf, Exec.Dir.
PH: (978)750-4499
TF: 800722-HOPE
FX: (978)750-9902
Description: Provides educational and emotional support to persons with scleroderma and their families. Stimulates and supports research designed to identify the cause and cure of scleroderma, as well as improve methods of treatment. Enhances the public's awareness of this disease. **Founded:** 1975. **Membership:** 20000. **Staff:** 5. Multinational. **Regional Groups:** 67. **Languages:** English. **Budget:** $540,000. Formerly (1977) Monterey Bay Scleroderma Foundation.

UNITED STATES AND CANADIAN ACADEMY OF PATHOLOGY
e-mail: iap@uscap.usa.com
3643 Walton Way Extension
Augusta, GA 30909
F. Stephen Vogel, Sec.-Treas.
PH: (706)733-7550
FX: (706)733-8033
Description: Works for the advancement of pathology teaching, practice, and research. Disseminates information to members. Sponsors educational programs to serve the needs of pathologists of various levels of experience. Presents Maude Abbott Lectureship to a recognized and respected person in contemporary pathology. **Founded:** 1906. **Membership:** 6700. **Staff:** 5. Multinational. **Languages:** English. **Budget:** $1,500,000. **Publication:** *Directory of Members*, annual. Membership Directory. Price: free to members ■ *Laboratory Investigation*, monthly. Journal. Focuses on significant advances in research dealing with human and experimental diseases. Price: free to members ■ *Modern Pathology*, bimonthly. Journal. Concentrates on the practice of diagnostic human pathology. Price: free to members.

UNITED STATES-MEXICO BORDER HEALTH ASSOCIATION (USMBHA)
e-mail: officer@usmbha.org
url: http://www.usmbha.org
6006 N. Mesa, Ste. 600
El Paso, TX 79912
Dr. Xavier Leus, Contact
PH: (915)581-6645
FX: (915)833-4768
Description: Physicians, public health administrators, nurses, sanitary engineers, veterinarians, scientists, laboratory workers, and other health officers from the 4 American and 6 Mexican states bordering the two countries. Seeks to make easier and more efficient the improvement of public health along both sides of the border; provides for exchange of experiences, discussion of mutual problems in human and animal diseases, and development of personal and professional contacts necessary for carrying out health projects. Sponsors seminars and workshops covering topics such as: food handling; rabies; tuberculosis; epidemiological principles; sexually transmitted diseases. Compiles statistics. **Founded:** 1943. **Membership:** 500. Multinational. **Languages:** Spanish. **Publication:** *Journal of Border Health* (in English and Spanish), quarterly. Contains articles on U.S.-Mexico border health issues. Price: $5.00/issue. Circulation: 800. Advertising: accepted ■ *Report of Activities*, annual ■ *U.S.-Mexico Border Health Association – News/Noticias*, quarterly. **Formerly:** (1975) United States-Mexico Border Health Association.

UNITED STATES PHARMACOPEIAL CONVENTION (USP)
e-mail: jac@usp.org
url: http://www.usp.org
12601 Twinbrook Pky.
Rockville, MD 20852
Jerome A. Halperin, Exec.VP & CEO
PH: (301)881-0666
TF: 800227-8772
FX: (301)816-8299
Description: Dedicated to promoting the public health by establishing and disseminating officially recognized standards of quality and authoritive information for the use of medicines and other health care technologies by health professionals, patients and consumers. **Founded:** 1820. **Membership:** 395. **Staff:** 230. **Languages:** English. **Budget:** $20,000,000.

UNIVERSITIES ASSOCIATED FOR RESEARCH AND EDUCATION IN PATHOLOGY (UAREP)
9650 Rockville Pike
Bethesda, MD 20814-3993
Frances A. Pitlick, Ph.D., Exec. Officer
PH: (301)571-1880
FX: (301)571-1879
Description: University pathology departments, including faculty members, residents, and research fellows. Provides core material in convenient form for updating and enriching teaching and researching of pathology, with special emphasis on toxicology and chemical carcinogens. Encourages biomedical projects; administers contracts. Has developed guidelines for the National Highway Safety Bureau for use in scientific investigations in accidents. Operates the Registry of Comparative Pathology which provides news of progress in the experimental study of disease from animal models. Convention/Meeting: none. **Founded:** 1964. **Membership:** 25. **Languages:** English. **Publication:** *Atlas of Tumor Pathology*. Book. Advertising: not accepted ■ Monographs.

VANUATU FAMILY HEALTH ASSOCIATION (VFHA)
Private Mail Bag 0065
Port Vila, Vanuatu
Mme. Blandine Boulekone
PH: 678 22140
FX: 678 24627
Description: Advocates family planning as a basic human right. Works to stop the spread of sexually transmitted diseases and reduce the number of unwanted pregnancies and abortions. Offers

educational programs in family planning and health. Provides contraceptive and health care services. Works with volunteers. **Languages:** English.

VERENIGING SPIERZIEKTEN NEDERLAND
e-mail: vsn@vsn.nl
url: http://www.vsn.nl
Lt. Gen. van Heutszlaan 6
NL-3743 JN Baarn, Netherlands
PH: 31 35 5180480
FX: 31 35 5480499
Description: Works as a support group for individuals suffering from neuromuscular diseases, among others amyotropic lateral sclerosis or ALS (also known as Lou Gehrig's Disease) in the Netherlands. Strives to: heighten public awareness and understanding of the diseases; encourage research among medical and scientific communities.

VIETNAM FAMILY PLANNING ASSOCIATION (VFPA)
138A Giang Vo
Hanoi, Vietnam
PH: 84 4 247231
FX: 84 4 247232
Description: National affiliate of the International Planned Parenthood Federation. Provides services and training programs to complement the activities of existing family planning and reproductive health services; facilitates local control of ongoing family planning initiatives. **Founded:** 1993. **Languages:** English, French.

VISITING NURSE ASSOCIATIONS OF AMERICA (VNAA)
3801 E. Florida, Ste. 900
Denver, CO 80210
Alexine Janiszewski, Interim CEO
PH: (303)753-0218
TF: 800426-2547
FX: (303)753-0258
Description: Voluntary, nonprofit home health care agencies. Develops competitive strength among community-based nonprofit visiting nurse organizations; works to strengthen business resources and economic programs through contracting, marketing, governmental affairs and publications. **Founded:** 1982. **Membership:** 210. **Staff:** 20. **Languages:** English. **Budget:** $1,300,000. Formerly (1985) American Affiliation of Visiting Nurses Associations and Services.

VOLUNTEER OPTOMETRIC SERVICES TO HUMANITY/ INTERNATIONAL (VOSH)
e-mail: vosher@aol.com
132 S. First Ave.
Iowa City, IA 52245
Phillip E. Hottel, O.D., Pres.
PH: (319)338-3267
FX: (319)338-2499
Description: Optometrists, optometric students, opticians, and other interested individuals. Conducts missions to disadvantaged countries, mostly in the Caribbean, Central and South America, Africa, Asia, and Eastern Europe to provide free visual care to the needy. Members pay their own travel, food, and lodging expenses, establish temporary clinics, and examine and distribute eyeglasses to an average of 2500 patients during each one-week mission. (Glasses are donated by civic clubs, churches, private citizens, and optical companies.). **Founded:** 1973. **Membership:** 900. Multinational. **State Groups:** 22. **Languages:** English. **For-Profit. Publication:** Brochure ■ Newsletter, quarterly. Circulation: 550. Advertising: not accepted.

VON HIPPEL-LINDAY SYNDROME FAMILY ALLIANCE (VHLSFA)
171 Clinton Rd.
Brookline, MA 02146
Joyce Graff, Chair
PH: (617)232-5946
TF: 800767-4VHL
FX: (617)734-8233

Description: People with von Hippel-Lindau Syndrome (a neurological disorder affecting the retinas, cerebellum and fourth ventrical of the brain, and, occasionally, the spinal cord and kidneys); health care professionals with an interest in the disease. Seeks to improve the diagnosis and treatment of von Hippel-Lindau Syndrome, and to improve the quality of life of people with the disease. Conducts research and educational programs; makes available children's services; compiles statistics; maintains speakers' bureau. **Founded:** 1993. **Membership:** 3000. Multinational. **State Groups:** 27. **Languages:** English. **Budget:** $80,000.

VULVAR PAIN FOUNDATION
url: http://www.vulvarpainfoundation.org
PO Drawer 177
Graham, NC 27253
Joanne J. Yount, Exec.Dir.
PH: (910)226-0704
FX: (910)226-8518
Description: Women with vulvar pain; medical doctors, scientists, physical therapists, clinical psychologists, nurse practitioners, and other healthcare professionals interested in the treatment of vulvar pain. Seeks to provide women with vulvar pain information about their conditions and appropriate treatments. Educates patients, physicians, and the public about vulvar pain, its causes, diagnostic techniques, treatments, and current research. Provides physician referral and physical therapy services. Promotes research into the causes and treatments of vulvar pain. Develops support networks for women with vulvar pain. Maintains speakers' bureau. **Founded:** 1992. **Membership:** 4900. **Staff:** 3. Multinational. **Local Groups:** 100. **Languages:** English. **Budget:** $120,000. The VP Foundation.

WEIGHT WATCHERS INTERNATIONAL (WWI)
url: http://www.weightwatchers.com
175 Crossways Park West
North Woodbury, NY 11797-2055
Kent Q. Kreh, Pres. & CEO
PH: (516)390-1400
FX: (516)390-1795
Description: The Weight Watchers Program includes a balanced diet, exercise and behavior modification. At weekly meetings, Weight Watchers members learn how to modify their current eating and exercise habits. Operates centers worldwide. **Founded:** 1963. Multinational. **Languages:** English. **For-Profit.**

WELLNESS CENTER (AWCI)
145 W. 28th St., Rm. 9R
New York, NY 10001
Howard Morse, Contact
PH: (212)465-8062
Description: Individuals concerned with wellness and preventive health care; firms, institutions, and organizations with wellness centers or employee assistance programs. Educates health practitioners and the public on methods of developing healthier lifestyles through the prevention and treatment of degenerative diseases and other health disorders. Provides professional training workshops in wellness counseling, an approach that integrates many scientific and medical disciplines, to assist members with problems related to weight control, stress, alcoholism, personal relationships, drug addiction, and other physical, mental, or social problems. Conducts individual and group counseling sessions and support groups for individuals suffering from arthritis, asthma, cancer, depression, diabetes, and hypertension. Provides speakers on topics such as wellness, lifestyle changes, longevity, diseases, and medical and alternative therapies. Convention/Meeting: none. **Founded:** 1979. **Membership:** 1500. **Staff:** 6. **Languages:** English. **Budget:** $50,000. **Publication:** *Bibliographical Essay*, periodic ■ *Directory of Members*, annual. Membership Directory ■ *Life-Style for Wellness*, quarterly. Journal. Includes research reports, book reviews, and listings of employment opportunities. Price: $50.00/year. Circulation: 1,500. Advertising: accepted. Alternate Formats: online. Also Cited As: *Lifestyle Changes for Wellness* ■ *Mailing List*, periodic.

WELLNESS INTERNATIONAL
4426 Avon Dr.
Harrisburg, PA 17112
Susan Shapiro, Contact
PH: (717)545-6373
Description: Promotes application of the precepts of health maintenance organizations to public health problems in developing areas. Provides technical assistance to health services operating in developing regions. Multinational. **Languages:** English.

WESTERN SAMOA FAMILY HEALTH ASSOCIATION (WSFHA)
PO Box 3029
Apia, Western Samoa
Miss Calmar Annandale, Exec.Dir.
PH: 685 26929
FX: 685 24560
Description: Advocates family planning and responsible parenthood as a means to improve the quality of life for individuals in Western Samoa. Works to reduce the number of unwanted pregnancies and abortion. Attempts to stop the spread of AIDS and other sexually transmitted diseases. Offers programs in family planning, health, and sex education. Acts as an advocate for family planning on a national level. **Founded:** 1974. **Membership:** 20. **Staff:** 11. **Languages:** English. **Budget:** $80,000. **Publication:** *Information Brochures* (in English and Samoan), periodic. Contains information on MCH/FP, sexual and reproductive health, and contraceptive technology. Advertising: not accepted.

WESTERN SURGICAL ASSOCIATION (WSA)
e-mail: jdrich01@ulkyum.louisville.edu
University of Louisville
Dept. of Surgery
530 S. Jackson St.
Louisville, KY 40292
Dr. J. David Richardson, Sec.
PH: (502)852-1704
FX: (502)852-8915
Description: Surgeons who have contributed to surgical education and advancement. Objectives are: to cultivate, promote, and diffuse knowledge of the art and science of surgery; to sponsor and maintain the highest standards of practice; to deliver the best possible care to all people. **Founded:** 1891. **Membership:** 600. **Languages:** English.

WILDERNESS MEDICAL SOCIETY (WMS)
e-mail: wms@indy.net
url: http://www.wms.org/wms
PO Box 2463
Indianapolis, IN 46206
David Van DerWege, Deputy Exec.-Exec.Dir.
PH: (317)631-1745
FX: (317)259-8150
Description: Persons with advanced degrees in the biomedical or life sciences with an interest in the medical, behavioral, and life sciences aspects of wilderness environments. Objectives are to promote research and educational activities that increase scientific knowledge about human activities in wilderness environments; stimulate interest and research in health consequences of wilderness activities; serve as central information source. Areas of interest include treatment of overpressure accident victims and victims of bites and stings, exotic infectious diseases and toxic plants, desert survival, avalanche control, and search and rescue. **Founded:** 1983. **Membership:** 3600. **Staff:** 3. Multinational. **Languages:** English. **Budget:** $600,000. **Publication:** *Wilderness and Environmental Medicine*, quarterly. Journal ■ *Wilderness Medicine Letter*, quarterly. Newsletter. Price: included in membership dues. Circulation: 3,600. Advertising: accepted.

WOMEN IN DENTISTRY
609 Nelson House
Dolphin Sq.
London SW1V 3NZ, England
Marion Press, Gen.Sec.

PH: 44 171 7885628
FX: 44 171 7985628
Description: Women dentists in the United Kingdom. Strives to assist women dentists in achieving professional goals through advice, practical support, and political representation. Cooperates with organizations in France, the United States, and Australia with similar aims. Disseminates information. **Founded:** 1985. **Membership:** 500. **Staff:** 2. **Regional Groups:** 17. **Languages:** English. **Publication:** *Women in Dentistry* (in English), quarterly. Newsletter. Advertising: accepted.

WOMEN IN MANAGED CARE (WMC)
4435 Waterfront Dr., Ste. 101
Glen Allen, VA 23060
Helen White, Pres.
PH: (804)527-1906
FX: (804)747-5316
Description: Women working for managed care health services providers. Promotes professional advancement of members. Conducts research and educational programs. **Founded:** 1996. **Membership:** 1000. **Languages:** English. **Publication:** *Women in Managed Care*, monthly. Newsletter.

WOMEN'S INTERNATIONAL PUBLIC HEALTH NETWORK (WIPHN)
7100 Oak Forest Ln.
Bethesda, MD 20817
Dr. Naomi Baumslag, Pres.
PH: (301)469-9210
FX: (301)469-8423
Description: Individuals and organizations with an interest in women's health issues. Promotes adoption of public health policies and programs providing greater access to health care for women. Conducts educational programs. **Founded:** 1987. **Membership:** 12500. **Staff:** 2. Multinational. **Languages:** English. **Budget:** $25,000.

WOMEN'S NATIONWIDE CANCER CONTROL CAMPAIGN (WNCCC)
e-mail: am40@dial.pipex.com
url: http://dspace.dial.pipex.com/town/square/gm40
Suna House
128-130 Curtain Rd.
London EC2A 3AR, England
Mary Button, Information Off.
PH: 44 171 7294688
FX: 44 171 6130771
Description: Women experienced in health care and counseling. Promotes education about cancer risks for women. Disseminates information on breast and cervical cancer. Operates confidential helpline. Sponsors mobile screening units. Maintains speakers' bureau; conducts research. **Founded:** 1965. **Membership:** 400. **Staff:** 8. **National Groups:** 2. **Budget:** L300,000. **Publication:** *A Ray of Hope - Mammography and Breast Examination*. Video. Price: L25.00/each VAT ■ *An Abnormal Smear - What Does It Mean? (WHRRIC)*. Brochure ■ *Being Breast Aware is for Life*. Video. Price: L25.00/each VAT ■ *Breast Awareness*. Pamphlet. Price: L3.00/per 100 ■ *Breast Awareness Poster* ■ *Calling All Women - Smears and Breast Self-Examination* (in Bengali, Cantonese, English, Gujarati, Hindi, Punjabi, Somali, Turkish, Urdu, and Vietnamese). Booklet. Price: L15.00/copy ■ *Cervical Cancer*. Pamphlet. Price: Free - limited to 100 per order. ■ *Cervical Smear Poster* ■ *Cervical Smear Test*. Pamphlet. Price: L2.50/per 100 ■ *Choice for Life*. Video. Covers the risk factors associated with cancer. Price: L25.00/each VAT ■ *Clinic Lists*. Lists of NHS and private clinics for almost every Health Authority and Board in the UK. Price: 3 pence per page photocopied ■ *Genital Warts Fact Sheet (WHRRIC)*. Brochure ■ *Have You Been Recalled for a Repeat Smear Test?*. Pamphlet. Price: L2.50/per 100 ■ *Have Your Mother and Grandmother Had a Smear Test?*. Pamphlet. Price: L2.50/per 100 ■ *Health Care for the Older Woman*. Pamphlet. Price: L10.00/copy ■ *Helpline Poster*. Price: Free. ■ *Mammography Poster* ■ *Positive Smear*. Book. Practical guide to the medical issues, i.e. what a positive smear can indicate and deals fully and

directly with the emotional issues. Price: L7.95 ■ *Screening Helpline*. Pamphlet. Price: Free. ■ *Test in Time*. Video. Price: L25.00/ each VAT ■ *What is the Wart Virus?*. Pamphlet. Price: L2.50/per 100 ■ *Why Won't You Have Your Cervical Smear Test?*. Pamphlet. Price: L2.50/per 100. **Formerly:** (1991) Women's National Cancer Control Campaign.

WORKING GROUP ON HEALTH AND DEVELOPMENT ISSUES (DEAG)
(Werkgroep Medische Ontwikkelingssamenwerking)
e-mail: Wemos@antenna.nl
Postbus 1693
NL-1000 BR Amsterdam, Netherlands
Jaap Kemkes, Contact
PH: 31 20 4202222
FX: 31 20 6205094
Description: Provides information on health problems in Third World countries: women's issues, pharmaceuticals, availability of basic health care, and nutrition. **Founded:** 1980. **Staff:** 10. **Languages:** Dutch, English. **Budget:** 800,000 f. **Publication:** *Exposed Deadly Exports: The Story of European Community Exports of Banned or Withdrawn Drugs to the Third World*. Book ■ *WEMOScoop* (in Dutch), bimonthly. Magazine. Price: 40.00 f/ year. ISSN: 0926-2059. Advertising: not accepted ■ Books (in German).

WORLD ASSOCIATION FOR DYNAMIC PSYCHIATRY (WADP)
Dynamic-Psychiatric Clinic
Geiselgasteigstrasse 203
Menterschwaige
D-81545 Munich, Germany
Maria Ammon, Contact
PH: 49 89 6427230
FX: 49 89 64272395
Description: Disseminates the theory and practice of dynamic psychiatry developed at Gunter Ammon's Berlin School of Dynamic Psychiatry. Fosters and creates opportunities for dynamic psychiatry study in universities and other institutions. Promotes continuous advanced training in dynamic psychiatry for better patient care and improvement of public health. Conducts research into disease prevention, therapeutic method efficiency, and education standards; disseminates results. **Founded:** 1980. **Membership:** 500. Multinational. **National Groups:** 22. **Languages:** English, German. **Publication:** *Dynamische Psychiatrie/ Dynamic Psychiatry* (in English and German), bimonthly ■ *WADP* (in English), semiannual. Newsletter.

WORLD ASSOCIATION FOR INFANT MENTAL HEALTH (WAIMH)
url: http://www.msu.edu/user/waimh
Kellogg Center/1 CYF, Ste. 1
East Lansing, MI 48824-1022
Hiram E. Fitzgerald, Exec.Dir.
PH: (517)432-3793
FX: (517)432-3694
Description: Child development specialists, child psychiatrists, child psychoanalysts, infant care workers, linguists, nurses, obstetricians, pediatricians, psychologists, and social workers. Works to further research and understanding of mental development and disorders in children from conception through age 3. Promotes studies on the conditions affecting the mental health of infants, their parents, and other caregivers; explores mental development during infancy and its subsequent effects on psychopathological development. Advocates international multidisciplinary discussions of research and intervention in infant psychiatry within the framework of the total life cycle. Facilitates communication and exchange of information and theories; fosters discussion of questions, problems, and issues in infant mental health. **Founded:** 1992. **Membership:** 1300. **Staff:** 1. Multinational. **Regional Groups:** 19. **Languages:** English, French. **Publication:** *Infant Mental Health Journal*, quarterly. Price: $37.50 for members; $50.00 for members outside the U.S.; $154.00 for nonmembers; $71.25 for nonmembers outside the U.S. ISSN: 0163-

9641. Circulation: 1,000 ■ *The Signal*, quarterly. Newsletter. **Formed by Merger of:** World Association for Allied Disciplines and Infant Psychiatry; International Association for Infant Mental Health.

WORLD ASSOCIATION FOR SOCIAL PSYCHIATRY (WASP)
656 Romero Cannon Rd.
Santa Barbara, CA 93108
John L. Carleton, M.D., Honorary Pres.
PH: (805)969-1376
FX: (805)969-1376
Description: Professionals, contributors, and interested individuals active in allied fields of social psychiatry including anthropology, social work, nursing, or occupational therapy. Objectives are to: study the nature of man and his surrounding culture; research methods to prevent and treat internal changes and behavioral disorders; advance the physical, social, and philosophic well-being of mankind. Fosters collaboration among members and distributes theoretical and practical information. Conducts workshops and demonstrations of rehabilitation centers. **Founded:** 1964. **Membership:** 3000. Multinational. **Regional Groups:** 26. **Languages:** English. **Publication:** *French Journal of Social Psychiatry* (in English and French), quarterly. Advertising: accepted ■ *International Journal of Social Psychiatry*, quarterly ■ *World Journal of Social Psychiatry* (in English and French), quarterly. Advertising: accepted. **Formerly:** (1978) International Association for Social Psychiatry.

WORLD ASSOCIATION OF SOCIETIES OF PATHOLOGY - ANATOMIC AND CLINICAL (WASP)
(Association Mondiale des Societes de Pathologie - Anatomique et Clinique)
e-mail: mickey@dokkyomed.ac.jp
url: http://www.dokkyomed.ac.jp/dep-k/cli-path/WASP.html
Mitsui-Sugamo Bldg. 7F
Sugamo 2-11-1, Toshima-ku
Tokyo 170, Japan
Mikio Mori, M.D.
PH: 81 3 39188161
FX: 81 3 39496168
Description: National societies of anatomic and clinical pathology in 40 countries united to foster cooperation between members and improve standards in anatomic and clinical pathology. Maintains a variety of committees and educational programs. **Founded:** 1947. **Membership:** 54. Multinational. **Languages:** English. **Publication:** *Directory* (in English), biennial ■ *News Bulletin of the World Association of Societies of Pathology/Commission on World Standards*, quarterly. **Formerly:** (1969) International Society of Clinical Pathology.

WORLD FEDERATION OF DOCTORS WHO RESPECT HUMAN LIFE (UNITED STATES SECTION) (WFDRHL)
PO Box 101501
Pittsburgh, PA 15237
Herbert Ratner, M.D., Sec.-Treas.
PH: (412)369-4544
FX: (412)369-4550
Description: Physicians united to restore the "traditional Hippocratic medical position" through firm opposition to abortion, suicide, and direct euthanasia. Sponsors educational programs and seminars. Presently inactive. **Founded:** 1976. **Membership:** 1400. **Languages:** English. **Publication:** *Primum Non Nocere*, quarterly. Newsletter.

WORLD FEDERATION FOR MEDICAL EDUCATION (WFME)
(Federation Mondiale pour l'Enseignement Medical)
Panum Institute
Blegdamsvej 3
DK-2200 Copenhagen, Denmark
Dr. Hans Karle, Pres.
PH: 45 35 32790009
FX: 45 35 327070
Description: Regional medical associations and associations of

medical schools. Promotes the integrated study of medical education worldwide. Evaluates the effectiveness of medical education in meeting the needs of contemporary society. Acts as international representative of medical education before the World Health Organization, UNICEF, UNESCO, United Nations Development Programme, and the World Bank. **Founded:** 1972. **Staff:** 4. Multinational. **Regional Groups:** 6. **Languages:** English. **Budget:** L6. **Publication:** *Report of the World Conference on Medical Education, Edinburgh, 1988/Proceedings of the World Summit on Medical Education, Edinburgh, 1994* ▪ *Report of the World Summit on Medical Education, Edinburgh, 1994.*

WORLD FEDERATION FOR MENTAL HEALTH (WFMH)
e-mail: wfmh@erols.com
url: http://www.wfmh.org
1021 Prince St.
Alexandria, VA 22314
Richard Hunter, Dep.Sec.Gen.
PH: (703)838-7543
FX: (703)519-7648
Description: Associations and individuals dedicated to achieving the highest level of public mental health. Objectives include charitable, scientific, literary, and educational activities in the field of mental health. Organizes training programs. Sponsors World Mental Health Day. **Founded:** 1948. **Membership:** 3500. **Staff:** 6. Multinational. **Languages:** English. **Budget:** $432,000. **Publication:** Newsletter, quarterly. Price: free to members. Advertising: not accepted. **Formerly:** (1948) International Committee for Mental Hygiene.

WORLD FEDERATION OF NEUROLOGY (WFN)
e-mail: 100675.761@compuserve.com
London Neurological Centre
110 Harley St.
London W1N 1AF, England
Dr. Clifford Rose, Sec.-Treas.
PH: 44 171 9353546
FX: 44 171 9354172
Description: Neurologists and neuroscientists dedicated to improving the care of neurological patients and to preventing diseases of the nervous system. Disseminates information in the field of neurology. Organizes research groups on disease topics; compiles statistics. Maintains speakers' bureau. Conducts educational and research programs. **Founded:** 1955. **Membership:** 23000. **Staff:** 1. Multinational. **National Groups:** 70. **Languages:** English. **Budget:** L50,000. **Publication:** *Journal of Neurological Sciences* (in English), bimonthly. Contains research papers. Circulation: 1,000. Advertising: accepted ▪ *World Neurology*, quarterly.

WORLD FEDERATION OF NEUROSURGICAL SOCIETIES (WFNS)
University of Virginia Health Services
Department of Neuro-Societies
Box 212
Charlottesville, VA 22908
Dr. Edward Laws, Sec.
PH: (804)924-2650
FX: (804)924-5894
Description: National neurosurgical societies representing approximately 17,400 neurosurgeons. Works for the advancement of neurological surgery. **Founded:** 1957. **Membership:** 64. **Staff:** 1. Multinational. **Regional Groups:** 5. **Languages:** English. **Budget:** $65,000. **Publication:** *Critical Reviews in Neurosurgery.* Journal ▪ *Federation News*, quarterly. Newsletter. Price: $75.00. Circulation: 19,000. Advertising: accepted ▪ *Proceedings of International Congress*, quadrennial ▪ *World Directory*, periodic.

WORLD FEDERATION OF PUBLIC HEALTH ASSOCIATIONS (WFPHA)
1015 15th St. NW
Ste. 300
Washington, DC 20005
Diane Kuntz, Exec.Sec.
PH: (202)789-5696
FX: (202)789-5661
Description: National public health associations united "to strengthen the public health profession and to improve community health throughout the world." Encourages formation of national public health associations. Organizes field projects; conducts special studies; offers lectures; compiles reports. **Founded:** 1967. **Membership:** 48. Multinational. **Languages:** English. **Publication:** *Reports of Triennial International Congresses* ▪ *WFPHA Report*, quarterly.

WORLD HEALTH ORGANIZATION (WHO)
(Organisation Mondiale de la Sante)
20, ave. Appia
CH-1211 Geneva, Switzerland
Hiroshi Nakajima, M.D., Dir.Gen.
PH: 41 22 7912111
FX: 41 22 7910746
Description: International health agency of the United Nations consisting of countries working toward the goal of "health for all," seeking to obtain the highest level of health care for all people. Believes health is a fundamental right of every human being without distinction of race, religion, political belief, economic situation, or social conditions and holds that all people deserve equal access to health services to enable them to lead socially and economically productive lives. Objectives are to: act as directing and coordinating authority on international health work; ensure valid and productive technical cooperation; promote research; prevent and combat diseases; generate and transfer information. Strives to eliminate poverty. Emphasizes the health needs of developing countries lacking resources and funds for modern medical technologies; works toward developing new techniques that will fulfill these needs by utilizing available resources, integrating educational, agricultural, town planning, and sanitation programs with health programs, combining peripheral health services and existing health systems, and applying appropriate technologies at reasonable costs. Establishes standards for food, biological, and pharmaceutical needs, develops standardized diagnostic procedures, and determines environmental health criteria. Promotes 8 elements of primary health care including: health education on prevention and cures; proper food supply and nutrition; adequate supply of safe water and sanitation; maternal and child health care; immunization; control of endemic diseases; and provisions of essential drugs. Acts as clearinghouse; coordinates activities with the United Nations on health and socioeconomic development; works with international nongovernmental organizations in the health sector. Supports International Agency for Research on Cancer. Maintains expert and scientific committees. Recognizes March 24 as World TB Day, April 7th as World Health Day, May 31 as World No-Tobacco Day, and December 1 as World AIDS Day. **Founded:** 1948. **Membership:** 192. **Staff:** 4500. Multinational. **Regional Groups:** 6. **Languages:** Arabic, Chinese. **Budget:** $654,000. **Publication:** *Bulletin of WHO* (in English and French), bimonthly ▪ *International Digest of Health Legislation* (in English and French), quarterly ▪ *Weekly Epidemiological Record* (in English and French) ▪ *WHO Drug Information* (in English, French, and Spanish), quarterly ▪ *World Health* (in English, French, German, Portuguese, Russian, and Spanish), 10/year. Magazine ▪ *World Health* (in Arabic and Farsi) ▪ *World Health Forum* (in Arabic, Chinese, English, French, Russian, and Spanish), quarterly ▪ *World Health Statistics Annual* (in English, French, and Russian) ▪ *World Health Statistics Quarterly* (in English and French). Includes summaries in Arabic, Chinese, Russian, and Spanish.

WORLD HEALTH ORGANIZATION - REGIONAL OFFICE FOR THE EASTERN MEDITERRANEAN (EMRO)
e-mail: emro@who.sci.eg
url: http://www.who.sci.eg
PO Box 1517
Alexandria 21511, Egypt
Dr. Hussein A. Gezairy, Reg. Dir.
PH: 20 3 4820223
FX: 20 3 4838916

Description: Regional office of the World Health Organization. Works to ensure that WHO programs effectively meet the particular public health needs of the Eastern Mediterranean; serves as a liaison between national and local public health agencies and the WHO. **Founded:** 1949. **Membership:** 22. **Staff:** 250. Multinational. **Languages:** Arabic, English. **Publication:** *Eastern Mediterranean Health Journal* (in English and French), 3/year. Price: LE 12.00. Circulation: 2,000. Advertising: not accepted. Alternate Formats: online.

WORLD HEALTH ORGANIZATION - REGIONAL OFFICE FOR EUROPE (EURO)
e-mail: postmaster@who.dk
8 Scherfigsvej
DK-2100 Copenhagen, Denmark
PH: 45 39171717
FX: 45 39171818
Description: Regional office of the World Health Organization. Works to ensure that WHO programs effectively meet the particular public health needs of Europe; serves as a liaison between national and local public health agencies and the WHO. Multinational. **Languages:** Danish, English.

WORLD HEALTH ORGANIZATION - REGIONAL OFFICE FOR SOUTH-EAST ASIA (SEARO)
e-mail: postmaster@who.ernet.in
World Health House
Indraprastha Estate
Mahatma Gandhi Rd.
New Delhi 110 002, Delhi, India
PH: 91 11 3317804
FX: 91 11 3318607
Description: Regional branch of the World Health Organization. Works to ensure that WHO programs effectively meet the particular public health needs of southeast Asia; serves as a liaison between national and local public health agencies and the WHO. Multinational.

WORLD HEALTH ORGANIZATION - ZIMBABWE (WHOZ)
PO Box 5160
Harare, Zimbabwe
Karamo M. L. Sanneh, Contact
PH: 263 4 728991
FX: 263 4 728998
Description: Public health services and programs. Seeks to ensure that programs of the World Health Organization (WHO) effectively meet the particular needs of people in Zimbabwe. Serves as a liaison between local public health programs and agencies and the WHO. **Languages:** English.

WORLD MEDICAL ASSOCIATION (WMA)
(Association Medicale Mondiale)
e-mail: wma@iprolink.fr
28, ave. des Alpes
BP 63
F-01212 Ferney-Voltaire, France
Dr. Ian Field, Sec.Gen.
PH: 33 450 407575
FX: 33 450 405937
Description: Federation of national medical associations throughout the world. Goal is to achieve the highest international standards in medical education, medical science, medical ethics, and health care for people worldwide. Promotes closer ties and better communication among medical organizations and doctors of the world; studies professional problems in different countries. Represents and protects the rights and interests of physicians and people internationally. Encourages proper nutrition in developing countries; urges the teaching of human values in the practice of medicine. Seeks to improve maternal and child health care. Issues declarations on ethical topics including: abortion; AIDS; abuse of children and the elderly; euthanasia; genetic engineering; organ transplantation; the use and misuse of psychotropic drugs; torture; biomedical research on human subjects; medical care in rural areas; an international code of medi-

cal ethics; and rights of the patient. **Founded:** 1947. **Membership:** 65. Multinational. **Regional Groups:** 6. **Languages:** English, French. **Budget:** $1,000,000. **Publication:** *World Medical Journal* (in English), bimonthly. Contains medical and medico-political articles. Advertising: not accepted.

WORLD MEDICAL MISSION (WMM)
e-mail: jcastle@samaritan.org
PO Box 3000
Boone, NC 28607
W. Franklin Graham, III, Pres.
PH: (828)262-1980
FX: (704)266-1055
Description: Coordinates medical activities of the evangelical group Samaritan's Purse. Places Christian physicians who serve voluntarily in evangelical mission hospitals overseas and conducts emergency medical relief. Provides assistance in refurbishing and equipping mission hospitals and conducts training sessions. **Founded:** 1977. **Languages:** English. **Publication:** *On Call*, quarterly. Advertising: not accepted ▪ *The PaceMaker*, quarterly. Advertising: not accepted ▪ *World Medical Mission Newsletter*, 6/year. Advertising: not accepted ▪ Brochures.

WORLD MEDICAL RELIEF (WMR)
11745 Rosa Parks Blvd.
Detroit, MI 48206
Carolyn E. George, President & CEO
PH: (313)866-5333
FX: (313)866-5588
Description: Nonsectarian, philanthropic organization contributing medical supplies and equipment for the care of the world's destitute sick. Instruments, equipment, and pharmaceuticals are donated to WMR, which in turn sends them to relief agencies and charitable medical clinics and hospitals worldwide. Provides prescriptions and medical supplies to needy senior citizens in the Detroit, MI, area. Convention/Meeting: none. **Founded:** 1953. **Staff:** 14. Multinational. **Languages:** English. **Budget:** $650,000. **Publication:** *Annual Report*. Brochure ▪ *World Medical Relief News*, quarterly. Advertising: not accepted.

WORLD ORGANIZATION OF NATIONAL COLLEGES, ACADEMIES, AND ACADEMIC ASSOCIATIONS OF GENERAL PRACTITIONERS/FAMILY PHYSICIANS (WONCA)
(Organisation Mondiale des Colleges Nationaux, Academies, et Associations Academiques des Generalistes et des Medecins de Famille)
e-mail: wonca@interserve.com.hk
url: http://www.ncl.ac.uk/~nphcare/WONCA/home.html
Hong Cong College of General Practitioners
15 Hennessy Rd., 8th Fl.
Wanchai, Hong Kong
Dr. Paul Lam, Hon.Sec.
PH: 852 25286618
FX: 852 28660616
Description: Colleges, academies, or organizations in 53 countries concerned with the academic aspects of general family practice. Objectives are to: promote and maintain high standards of general family practice through education and research; foster worldwide communication and understanding among general practitioners; represent the academic and research activities of general practitioners to other worldwide bodies concerned with health or medical care. **Founded:** 1972. **Membership:** 56. **Staff:** 1. Multinational. **Regional Groups:** 5. **Languages:** English, French. **Publication:** *The Family Doctor*, semiannual. Magazine. Price: free to members. Circulation: 130,000. Advertising: not accepted ▪ *International Classification of Health Problems in Primary Care*. Book ▪ *Membership Directory* (in English), annual. Circulation: 1,300 ▪ *WONCA News*, 6/year. **Also Known As:** (1992) World Organization of Family Doctors.

WORLD PSYCHIATRIC ASSOCIATION (WPA)
e-mail: wpa@dti.net
url: http://www.wpanet.org
University of NY
Fifth Ave. & 100th St.
Box 1093
New York, NY 10029-6574
Prof. Juan E. Mezzich, Jr., Sec.Gen.
PH: (212)241-6133
FX: (212)426-0437
Description: Psychiatric societies and individuals in 90 countries. Objectives are: to promote international cooperation in the field of psychiatry; to advance inquiry into the etiology, pathology, and treatment of mental illness; to strengthen relations among psychiatrists working in various fields. Encourages the exchange of information concerning the medical problems of mental diseases; sponsors educational and research programs. Comprises 40 sections representing different specialties in psychiatry. **Founded:** 1961. **Membership:** 465. **Staff:** 18. Multinational. **National Groups:** 93. **Languages:** English, French. **Publication:** *WPA Bulletin* (in English, French, German, and Spanish), quarterly. Circulation: 10,000. Advertising: accepted ▪ *WPA News*, quarterly. Newsletter. Price: free for members. Circulation: 800. Advertising: not accepted.

WORLD RESEARCH FOUNDATION (WRF)
41 Bell Rock Plz.
Sedona, AZ 86351-8804
Steven A. Ross, Pres.
PH: (818)999-5483
FX: (818)227-6484
Description: Informs the public of the latest developments in health and environmental issues. Provides health care professionals and the public with information on health tools and technologies currently available outside the U.S. but which have been overlooked or are unavailable in the U.S. Acts as a depository of public information. **Founded:** 1980. **Staff:** 25. Multinational. **Languages:** German, Spanish. **Publication:** *World Research News*, quarterly. Newsletter ▪ Journal, quarterly. Contains traditional and nontraditional international health news. Price: $20.00. Circulation: 40,000. Advertising: not accepted ▪ Proceedings, annual ▪ Reports.

WORLD SOCIETY FOR STEREOTACTIC AND FUNCTIONAL NEUROSURGERY (WSSFN)
6624 Fannin St., Ste. 1620
Houston, TX 77030
Philip L. Gildenberg, M.D., Past Pres.
PH: (713)790-0795
FX: (713)669-0388
Description: Neurosurgeons and professors dedicated to the advancement of stereotactic studies and procedures. Original manuscripts submitted at meetings are published and used as reference books throughout the world. **Founded:** 1963. **Membership:** 600. **Staff:** 2. Multinational. **Regional Groups:** 4. **Languages:** English. **Publication:** *Stereotactic and Functional Neurosurgery*, quarterly. Journal. Circulation: 2,000. Advertising: accepted ▪ *Studies in Stereoencephalotomy*, quadrennial. **Also Known As:** World Stereotactic Society; WSSFN. **Formerly:** (1973) International Society for Research in Stereoencephalotomy.

WORLD SPORTS MEDICINE ASSOCIATION OF REGISTERED THERAPISTS (WORLD SMAR)
206 Marine Ave.
PO Box 5642
Newport Beach, CA 92662
PH: (626)574-1999
FX: (626)574-1999
Description: Sports medicine therapist, trainer, technician, and individuals involved in sports medicine and certified by any nationally recognized athletic trainers association. Establishes standards of competency for trainers, therapists, and sports medicine care providers that are recognized worldwide. **Founded:**

1993. **Membership:** 4000. **Staff:** 3. Multinational. **Languages:** English. Also Known As World Smart.

XI PSI PHI
c/o Dr. Keith W. Dickey
1623 Washington Ave., No. 300
Alton, IL 62002
Dr. Keith W. Dickey, Sec.-Treas.
PH: (618)463-1889
Description: Professional dental fraternity - dentistry. Maintains Hall of Fame. Conducts educational programs. **Founded:** 1889. **Membership:** 19000. **Staff:** 2. **Local Groups:** 22. **Languages:** English. **Publication:** *Quarterly*. Price: $8.00. Advertising: accepted.

Y-ME NATIONAL BREAST CANCER ORGANIZATION (Y-ME)
e-mail: YMEONE@AOL.com
url: http://www.y-me.org
212 W. Van Buren
Chicago, IL 60607
Susan N. Nathanson, Ph.D, Exec. Dir.
PH: (312)986-8338
TF: 800221-2141
FX: (312)294-8597
Description: Purpose is to provide peer support and information to women who have or suspect they have breast cancer. Activities include presurgical counseling and referral service, inservice programs for health professionals, hot line volunteer training, and technical assistance. Administers the Deborah David Dewar Fund, the Billie Klein Memorial Fund, Shellie Broutman Memorial, Eve & Susan Feldman Memorial and Mimi Kaplan Memorial. **Founded:** 1978. **Membership:** 4600. **Staff:** 14. Multinational. **Local Groups:** 14. **Languages:** Spanish. **Budget:** $1,056,900. **Publication:** *For Single Women with Breast Cancer*. Price: one copy is free ▪ *Guidelines for Breast Cancer Support Groups* ▪ *When the Woman You Love Has Breast Cancer* ▪ *Y-ME Hotline*, bimonthly. Newsletter. **Formerly:** (1989) Y-Me Breast Cancer Support; (1994) Y-Me National Organization for Breast Cancer Information and Support.

YEMEN FAMILY CARE ASSOCIATION (YFCA)
e-mail: yfca@y.net.ye
PO Box 795
Al-Tahreer Sq.
Near Arab Bank
Sana'a, Yemen
Dr. Yahia Al-Babily
PH: 967 1 288145
FX: 967 1 270948
Description: Promotes family planning and responsible parenthood. Works to reduce the number of unwanted pregnancies and abortions and stop the spread of sexually transmitted diseases such as AIDS. Offers programs in sex education, family planning, and health. Provides contraceptive and health care services. Conducts research. **Founded:** 1978. **Membership:** 350. **Staff:** 46. **Languages:** Arabic, English. **Budget:** 500,000 YRl. **Publication:** *Al Osra* (in Arabic), bimonthly. Newsletter. Price: free. Circulation: 6,000. Advertising: accepted.

YUGOSLAV ASSOCIATION OF ANATOMISTS (YAA)
(Drustvo Anatoma Jugoslavije)
Medical Faculty
Hajduk Veljkova 3
YU-21000 Novi Sad, Serbia
Maria Mihalj, M.D., Sec.Gen.
PH: 381 21 615775
FX: 381 21 624153
Description: Exchanges scientific information. Organizes courses in methodology. **Founded:** 1956. **Membership:** 120. **Languages:** English, French. **Budget:** 15,000 Din. **Publication:** *Folia Anatomica* (in English), semiannual. Price: 80.00 Din. ISSN: 0354-5431. **Formerly:** (1994) Union of the Yugoslav Association of Anatomists.

ZERO TO THREE
734 15th St. NW, No. 10
Washington, DC 20005-1013
Matthew E. Melmed, Exec.Dir.
PH: (202)638-1144
TF: 800899-4301
FX: (202)638-0851
Description: Professionals and researchers in the health care industry, policymakers, and parents working to improve the healthy physical, cognitive and social development of infants, toddlers, and their families. Members share their expertise about infants, toddlers, and their families. Sponsors training and technical assistance activities. **Founded:** 1977. **Staff:** 27. **Languages:** English. **Budget:** $4,040,956. Formerly (1992) National Center for Clinical Infant Programs.

ZIMBABWE INSTITUTE OF MEDICAL LABORATORY
 SCIENTISTS
PO Box 8220
Causeway
Harare, Zimbabwe
Dr. Obadiah Moyo, Pres.
PH: 263 705639
FX: 263 792588
Description: Medical laboratory scientists. Seeks to maintain high standards in the practice of medical laboratory science, and to insure effective and economical laboratory services. Promotes continuing professional education of members. **Membership:** 250. **Staff:** 12. **National Groups:** 1. **Languages:** English. **Budget:** Z$100,000. **Publication:** *Journal of the Zimbabwe Institute of Med. Lab. Scientists* (in English), annual. Price: free. Circulation: 500. Advertising: not accepted. **Formerly:** (1990) Association of Medical Laboratory Technologists of Zimbabwe.

ZIMBABWE NATIONAL ASSOCIATION FOR MENTAL
 HEALTH
PO Box A 196
Avondale
Harare, Zimbabwe
I.H. Nyamatore, Dir.
PH: 263 4 792946
Description: Works to educate and rehabilitate the mentally ill. Informs the public about mental health issues. **Founded:** 1981. **Membership:** 150. **Staff:** 22. **Budget:** Z$750,000. **Publication:** Handbooks. Containing information about mental health ■ Newsletter, quarterly. Advertising: accepted ■ Pamphlets. Containing information about mental health ■ Video.

ZIMBABWE NATIONAL FAMILY PLANNING COUNCIL
 (ZNFPC)
PO Box ST220
Highfield Rd.
Southerton
Harare, Zimbabwe
Dr. Alex Zinanga, Contact
PH: 263 4 67656
FX: 263 4 68678
Description: Promotes family planning and responsible parenthood as a means to improve the quality of life for individuals living in Zimbabwe. Advocates family planning as a basic human right. Works to reduce the number of unwanted pregnancies and abortions. Offers programs in family planning, sex education, and health. Provides contraceptive and health care services. Conducts research. **Founded:** 1957. **Staff:** 1225. **Languages:** English. **Budget:** Z$36,000,000. **Publication:** Annual Report (in English). Advertising: not accepted.

ZIMBABWE NATIONAL TRADITIONAL HEALERS
 ASSOCIATION (ZINATHA)
PO Box 116
Reliance House
Corner of Takcawira and Speke Ave.
Harare, Zimbabwe
B. Makoni, Mgr

PH: 263 4 751902
Description: Promotes public awareness of alternative medicine. Coordinates actions of the Ministry of Health of Zimbabwe and traditional healers. Disseminates information. **Founded:** 1980. **Membership:** 45000. **Staff:** 10. **Budget:** Z$300,000. **Publication:** *ZINATHA* (in English and Shona). Booklet. Advertising: accepted.

CHAPTER 8

CONSULTANTS

Consultants and consulting organizations active in the Health and Medical Services sector are featured in this chapter. Entries are adapted from Gale's *Consultants and Consulting Organizations Directory* (*CCOD*). Each entry represents an expertise which may be of interest to business organizations, government agencies, nonprofit institutions, and individuals requiring technical and other support. The listees shown are located in the United States and Canada.

In Canada, the use of the term "consultant" is restricted. The use of the word, in this chapter, does not necessarily imply that the firm has been granted the "consultant" designation in Canada.

Entries are arranged in alphabetical order. Categories include contact information (address, phone, fax, web site, e-mail); names and titles of executive officers; description; special services offered; geographical areas served; and other information (e.g., seminars, workshops).

ABC CONSULTANTS
37442 Park Ave.
Willoughby, OH 44094
Kathleen Malec
PH: (216)951-7422
Founded: 1978. **Staff:** 4. Health consultants who identify, develop, educate, and initiate programs for staff development, patient education, performance evaluation (hospital), and patient and family education (outpatient areas). Also designs educational programs for nursing homes. Additional expertise on meeting requirements of state and federal guidelines on nursing homes and home health agencies. Industries served: health services (administration, management, healthcare programs), home healthcare, (LTC) nursing homes, and hospitals. Geographic areas served: U.S., especially Ohio.

ACI SERVICE GROUP
url: http://www.flash.net/~dws1
3111 Castro Valley Blvd., Ste. 210
Castro Valley, CA 94546
D.W. Smothers, President
PH: (510)728-9861
FX: (510)788-9874
Founded: 1978. **Staff:** 12. Provides investigative consulting regarding loss prevention in areas of personnel safety and physical security. Active in systems and procedures design as well as development of same. Serves private industries as well as government agencies. Geographic areas served: western U.S. **Conferences and Meetings:** *Offers seminars on drug/alcohol abuse in workplace.*

ADCARE HEALTH SYSTEMS, INC.
5057 Troy Rd.
Springfield, OH 45502-9032
Gary Wade
PH: (937)964-8974
FX: (937)964-8961
Founded: 1986. **Staff:** 17. Consulting firm offers expertise in the areas of healthcare systems management. Focus is on senior housing (retirement communities, asorted living and nursing homes), movement feasibility and Medicare/Medicaid reimbursement.

ADCARE HOSPITAL OF WORCESTER, INC., CHEMICAL DEPENDENCY PROGRAMS
107 Lincoln St.
Worcester, MA 01605
David W. Hills, President
FX: (508)799-9000
Health care consulting group with primary focus on alcohol and drug abuse programs. Industries served: small to large businesses, unions, and self-insured employers. Geographic areas served: northeast U.S. **Conferences and Meetings:** *Drug Free Workplace Issues; Workplace Intervention; Substance Abuse in the Workplace.* **Computer/Special Services:** Consultation is available for policy development regarding employee substance abuse, complying with the Drug Free Workplace Act, and implementing employee assistance services.

ADVANCE HEALTH SOCIAL & EDUCATIONAL ASSOCIATES, INC.
12405 PO Box
Chicago, IL 60612
Dr. Leon Dingle, Jr., President
PH: (312)666-0202
FX: (312)666-1943
Founded: 1977. **Staff:** 30. Management consulting firm specializing in health and social issues.

ADVANCED BIOSEARCH ASSOCIATES INC.
3880 Blackhawk Rd.
Danville, CA 94506-4617
Howard R. Asher

PH: (510)736-2500
FX: (510)736-2800
Provides management services for the health and medical fields.

ADVANCED HEALTH CARE CONCEPTS
3799 Turnwood Dr.
Richfield, WI 53076-9633
Nancy Doleysh, President
PH: (414)628-9007
FX: (414)628-3590
Founded: 1980. Consulting and continuing education for nurses/aides/emergency medical technicians. Consulting services to nursing service departments in hospitals, nursing homes, HMOS, and public health facilities. **Conferences and Meetings:** *Summer Trauma; Update of Cerebrovascular Disorders; Neurologic History and Physical Exam; Neurocritical Care; Compartment Syndrome; Nursing Care of Patient in Traction; Essentials of Orthopaedic Nursing; Motorcycle Trauma; Physical Assessment Skills.*

ADVANCED LASER SERVICES CORP.
819 Phillipi Rd.
Columbus, OH 43228
PH: (614)351-8321
FX: (614)351-8328
Founded: 1985. Offers expertise on the medical and surgical applications of lasers.

ADVANTAGE HEALTH SYSTEMS, INC.
e-mail: info@advantagehealth.com
url: http://www.advantagehealth.com
8704 Bourgade
Lenexa, KS 66219
Anne Tramposh
PH: (913)438-8400
TF: 800279-0491
FX: (913)438-8445
Founded: 1989. **Staff:** 30. Health care consulting firm; Ergonomics Consulting Firm. **Conferences and Meetings:** *Training Institute, 3-4 classes per month.* **Computer/Special Services:** Health and Productivity Software.

AFFILIATED HEALTHCARE MANAGEMENT
30 Summer St., Ste. 1
PO Box 811
Bangor, ME 04402-0811
Frank Hannon, President
PH: (207)945-5553
FX: (207)941-0873
Founded: 1977. **Staff:** 19. Management consulting firm specializes in serving the healthcare industry.

AIDS PARTNERSHIP MICHIGAN
url: http://www.aidspartnership.org
2751 E. Jefferson, Ste. 301
Detroit, MI 48207
Barbara Murray, Executive Director
PH: (313)446-9800
TF: 800872-AIDS
FX: (313)446-9039
Founded: 1983. **Staff:** 40. Offers customized advice to corporations on the effects of HIV & AIDS in the workplace. Covers strategies for dealing with HIV/AIDS in work situations. Focus is on infected employee rights, co-worker rights, and employer responsibilities. Serves all industries. Geographic areas served: southeastern Michigan.

C. KNIGHT ALDRICH M.D.
905 Cottage Ln.
Charlottesville, VA 22903
C. Knight Aldrich, M.D.
PH: (804)296-4816
FX: (804)982-4306
Founded: 1982. **Staff:** 2. Offers administrative consultations, on a single or continuing basis, with mental health centers and similar

organizations for planning, staff development, and trouble-shooting. Also provides editorial services for assistance in the preparation of psychiatric and medical articles, books, and other materials. Serves private industries as well as government agencies. Geographic areas served: U.S. **Conferences and Meetings:** *Workshops on executive mental health.*

ALEGENT HEALTH BERGAN MERCY MEDICAL CENTER RADIOLOGY CONSULTANTS, PC
e-mail: SamMehr@sprintmail.com
url: http://www.RadiologyConsultants.com
13918 Gold Cir.
Omaha, NE 68144
Samuel H. Mehr, MD, Director of Nuclear Medicine
PH: (402)398-6984
FX: (402)697-0116
Specializes in documentation of brain injury with positron emission tomography (PET scan). Experience in personal injury, including workers' compensation.

ALESSANDRO, INC.
e-mail: ewildgg@aol.com
2112 Spruce St.
Baldwin, NY 11510
Eileen J. Wild, President
PH: (516)867-7608
FX: (516)623-4537
Founded: 1971. Staff: 4. Health management consultant specializing in patient classification systems and staffing (new or modify old) nursing delivery system design; materials management analysis and control systems; and documentation systems - nursing care plans and charting. Also develops human capital blueprints to meet organizational goals, including workload/caseload distributions. Serves private industries as well as government agencies. Restructure and redesign strategies, budget analysis and budget control mechanism development. Geographic areas served: U.S., will travel to Europe.

A. ALLEN CONSULTING
4707 College Blvd., Ste. 213
Leawood, KS 66211
Ace Allen
PH: (913)338-1496
FX: (913)338-3631
Founded: 1993. Staff: 2. Dr. Allen provides strategic planning, workshops, and other expert services in telemedicine. He has been a principal with the U. of Kansas-affiliated Telemedicine Project since 1992. Has widely lectured in North America, Europe, and Latin America; organized and participated in dozens of telemedicine workshops and seminars. Serves university and private hospitals, governmental agencies, and private corporations worldwide.

ALLEN EVANS GROUP LTD.
13 Gatehouse Rd.
Bedminster, NJ 07921-1861
Michael E. Allen
Founded: 1990. Staff: 5. Offers medical supplies services to New Jersey businesses.

ALLIANCE SEARCH MANAGEMENT, INC.
e-mail: kflorip@flex.net
25307 I-45 N., 102
The Woodlands, TX 77380
Kathy Powell-Florip, President
PH: (281)367-8630
TF: 800444-0573
FX: (281)419-0335
Founded: 1988. Staff: 8. Offers healthcare executive recruitment in the U.S. Special emphasis on financial leadership, medically based fitness & wellness, integrated delivery systems, physician leadership and provider sponsored health plans. **Conferences and Meetings:** *Healthcare trends and career development work-*

shops. **Computer/Special Services:** Data base development and management services.

ALPHA CENTER FOR HEALTH PLANNING
1350 Connecticut Ave. NW, Ste. 1100
Washington, DC 20036
PH: (202)296-1818
FX: (202)296-1825
Founded: 1976. Medical consultants.

ALPHA CONSULTING ASSOCIATES
e-mail: alphafm@aol.com
url: http://www.knowledgetree.com/alpha
4741 Larkwood Ave.
Woodland Hills, CA 91364-3737
Francine Moskowitz, President
PH: (818)224-4224
TF: 800898-1354
FX: (818)224-4343
Founded: 1985. Staff: 16. Counsels on healthcare, specializing in managed care, strategic and market planning, business planning and development, feasibility studies, and new venture start-ups. Industries served: healthcare and government in the U.S. and Canada. **Conferences and Meetings:** *Managed Care Market Evolution.*

ALTURA & ALTURA CONSULTANTS
380 Rector Pl.
New York, NY 10280-1443
Burton M. Altura
PH: (718)270-2618
FX: (718)270-3103
Founded: 1984. Staff: 2. Cardiovascular and nutritionist consultants specializing in the etiology and treatment of cardiovascular disease processes. Investigates the role of magnesium in health and nutrition. Conducts research on the effects of alcohol, cocaine, and PCP on brain and cardiovascular system. Offers expertise in the mechanisms and treatment of shock-trauma, and the toxicological effects of substances of abuse. Also serve as editorial consultants in biomedical publishing. Industries served: pharmaceutical, biomedical research establishments, universities, colleges, medical centers, biomedical publishers, and government agencies. Geographic areas served: U.S., Canada, Europe, and Asia.

AM MEDICA COMMUNICATIONS LIMITED
e-mail: action@ammadelphi.com
305 E. 46th St., 7th Fl.
New York, NY 10017
PH: (212)751-1818
FX: (212)751-2005
Founded: 1986. Medical consulting.

MADALON O. AMENTA
5512 Northumberland
Pittsburgh, PA 15217
Madalon O. Amenta, President
PH: (412)687-3852
FX: (412)687-9095
Founded: 1982. Staff: 1. Offers healthcare consultation including hospice programs (all aspects), nursing policy, medical and nursing writing projects (editorial and writing), nursing research, and quality assurance in hospice care and nursing. Geographic areas served: U.S. **Conferences and Meetings:** *Communication with the Dying; Writing for Hospice Workers; Hospice Care and Nursing Expertise; Certification of Hospice Nurses: Determination of Need; Hospice Care in the Prison Environment.*

AMERICAN COLLEGE OF CHIROPRACTIC CONSULTANTS
e-mail: drwjahn@ix.netcom.com
url: http://www.ACCC-chiro.com
117 W. Harrison Bldg., 6th Fl., Ste. A-392
Chicago, IL 60605

PH: (770)740-1999
FX: (770)740-0567
Independent contractors who provide advisory consulting services to major insurance carriers. Experienced in independent medical examinations, educational training, medicologeal, risk management, and healthcare administration activities.

AMERICAN INSTITUTE FOR BIOSOCIAL RESEARCH, INC. -AIBR LIFE SCIENCES DIV.
e-mail: aibr@halcyon.com
PO Box 1174
Tacoma, WA 98401-1174
Alexander G. Schauss, PhD., President
PH: (253)922-0448
FX: (253)922-0479
Founded: 1980. **Staff:** 6. Prepares comprehensive databases on any area concerning public health issues. Examines products in the healthcare-giving marketplace. Conducts in-service training programs on public health topics for insurance companies, government agencies (federal, state, and local), and universities and colleges. Prepares scientific papers for publication to assist researchers desiring to submit manuscripts for publication. Industries served: insurance companies, hospitals, federal, state and local government agencies, colleges and universities, food processors, food distributors, food manufacturers, and informational database developers. Geographic areas served: worldwide. **Conferences and Meetings:** *The Institute has given over 800 seminars and workshops; the Institute's director offers courses on the role of diet, nutrition, and toxic environmental substances on brain function and behavior.* **Computer/Special Services:** Maintains a library of 10,000 plus volumes, in-house computer reference database, subscribes to Dialog and STN; also maintains over 14,000 individual research reports from over 4,000 journals on topics related to Institute's activities and research.

AMERICAN INSTITUTE FOR PREVENTIVE MEDICINE
url: http://www.aipm.healthy.net
30445 Northwestern Highway, Ste. 350
Farmington Hills, MI 48334
Don R. Powell, Ph.d., Founder, President
PH: (248)539-1800
FX: (248)539-1808
Founded: 1983. **Staff:** 37. Firm offers expertise in health promotion, wellness, and medical self care. Publishes 14 self care guides that address the needs of families, women, seniors, children, hispanics, and medicaid recipients. **Conferences and Meetings:** *Health at Home Workshop; Smokeless, Healthy Weigh, Systematic Stress Management, Self Esteem & Positive Performance.* **Computer/Special Services:** Provides self care information for websites and intranets.

AMERICAN SELECTCARE CORP.
820 Parish St.
Pittsburgh, PA 15220
PH: (412)922-2853
FX: (412)922-3071
Founded: 1990. Healthcare consulting services firm.

ANAHEIM ORTHOPEDIC SURGERY
1741-F W. Romneya Dr.
Anaheim, CA 92801
Arthur Bunzel, MD, Principal
PH: (714)776-7920
FX: (714)776-3786
Provides expert witness testimony in the areas of orthopedic surgery, arthroscopy spine surgery, and hand surgery.

DR. REBECCA COGWELL ANDERSON, PH.D.
e-mail: Rander5727@atsaol.com
1104 Riverway Ct.
Pewaukee, WI 53072
PH: (414)454-5464
A psychologist specializing in the areas of women's health issues, breast cancer adjustment, depression, wellness, stress manage-

ment, post traumatic stress disorder, silicone breast implants/issues and adjustments, chronic disease, adjustment to loss of function and disfigurement, and parenting issues.

APOLLO MANAGED CARE CONSULTANTS
e-mail: mbischel@rain.org
url: http://www.apollomanagedcare.com
860 Ladera Ln.
Santa Barbara, CA 93108
Margaret D. Bischel, M.D.
PH: (805)969-2606
FX: (805)969-3749
Founded: 1987. **Staff:** 3. Specializes in healthcare strategic planning, utilization, and quality management for managed healthcare, hospitals, and physicians' practices. Serves public and private sector in the U.S. **Conferences and Meetings:** *Managed Health Care; Capitation; Credentialing; and medical publishing.*

APPLIED HEALTH PHYSICS INC.
2986 Industrial Blvd.
Bethel Park, PA 15102-2536
Todd Y. Mobley, Technical Services Supervisor
PH: (412)835-9555
TF: 800332-6648
FX: (412)835-9559
Founded: 1962. **Staff:** 14. Provides radiation services for industry and nuclear users in the United States. **Conferences and Meetings:** *Radiation Safety Training.*

APPLIED MANAGEMENT SYSTEMS, INC.
e-mail: ams508@aol.com
3 New England Executive Park
Burlington, MA 01803
Alan J. Goldberg, President
PH: (617)272-8001
FX: (617)272-5666
Founded: 1967. **Staff:** 80. Health care consultants providing management engineering, reengineering, nursing management, operations improvement, product cost identification, information systems, health information management, materials management, accounts receivables management, and facilities design to the healthcare industry. **Conferences and Meetings:** *Critical Thinking; Bedside Computing and Patient Care Technology: Linking the Latest Advancements in Bedside Terminal Systems; Patient Classification Data in Costing Nursing Service; Opportunities in a Time of Change: Management Initiatives for Today; Quality First Conference; Hospital Departmental Profiles; Clinical Outreach: Beyond Traditional Markets.* **Computer/Special Services:** Management database reporting; production reporting.

APPLIED PSYCHOMETRICS
1450 Frazee Rd., Ste. 300
San Diego, CA 92108
Nancy Haller, Ph.D., President
PH: (619)260-8280
FX: (619)295-2597
Founded: 1989. Consulting firm that specializes in the application of psychology to problems in business and industry, including all phases of personnel selection, evaluation, training, executive development, conflict resolution, marketing research, and departmental communication. Industries served: transportation, automobile agencies, educational institutions, biotech and start-up, security, both government and private. Geographic areas served: California, West Coast, and the Southwest. **Conferences and Meetings:** *Communication Skills; Stress Management; Decision Making; Low Authority/High Power People Management; Performance Enhancement; Managing Conflict.* **Computer/Special Services:** Computerized personality testing.

JACK L. ARONOWITZ
6591 Skyline Dr.
Delray Beach, FL 33446-2201
Jack L. Aronowitz, President

PH: (561)498-3954
FX: (561)498-3954
Founded: 1971. An association of individual scientists, engineers, technicians, managers, and several specialty consulting companies. Offer clients access to the following areas of expertise and services: biomedical chemistry, pharmaceutical veterinary, analytical and diagnostic instrumentation, reagent development and production, management, quality control, regulatory affairs, toxicological studies, clinical trials and marketing. **Computer/Special Services:** Maintains extensive computer expertise utilizing both Borneuli equipped 486 and mainframe technology; senior consultants have extensive expertise in software design for both systems and equipment functionality; company has authored and published laboratory software systems for quality control, lab management and statistical analysis.

ARTERIAL & VENOUS DIAGNOSIS & TREATMENT CENTER
e-mail: bravura@pacbell.net
6357 Coyle Ave.
Carmichael, CA 95608
Dr. Sebastian Conti, Principal
PH: (916)965-5050
FX: (916)965-4040
An examiner and expert consultant for the Medical Board of California. Specializes in both venous and arterial pathology, including phlebitis, varicose veins, thrombotic disorders, chronic venous insufficiency, arterial occlusion, carotid stenosis, aortic aneurysm, doppler ultrasound and other vascular disorders.

ASPARTAME CONSUMER SAFETY NETWORK
url: http://web2.airmail.net/marystod
PO Box 780634
Dallas, TX 75378
Mary Nash Stoddard, Founder
PH: (214)352-4268
TF: 800969-6050
FX: (214)352-2480
Founded: 1987. **Staff:** 3. Maintains a network of consultants with expertise regarding the safety of aspartame. Provides in-house consulting services and speeches and will conduct seminars and workshops. Also offers referrals of expert witnesses for trial lawyers. Industries served: Fortune 500 companies and others. Geographic areas served: international. **Conferences and Meetings:** *Aspartame in the Workplace - The Economic Impact; The Aspartame Coverup; Aspartame - Symposium on Product Safety. Aspartame and Flying.* **Computer/Special Services:** Maintains a 24-hour hotline for pilots, healthcare professionals, and other consumers. E-mails welcomed.

ASSOCIATION MANAGEMENT RESOURCES
url: http://www.ihha.org
1151 E. Warrenville Rd.
PO Box 3015
Naperville, IL 60566
Ken Robbins, President
PH: (630)505-7777
FX: (630)505-0877
Founded: 1979. **Staff:** 12. Specialists in solving problems in the healthcare environment. Clients include hospitals, extented care facilities, and physicians' offices. Geographic areas served: statewide.

ASSOCIATION OF OPERATING ROOM NURSES, INC.
url: http://www.aorn.org
2170 S. Parker Rd. Ste. 300
Denver, CO 80231-5711
Lola M. Fehr, Executive Director
PH: (303)755-6300
FX: (303)755-5494
Founded: 1954. **Staff:** 88. AORN consultation services cover organizational efficiency of the surgical suite (operating room) in the areas of space and facility utilization, management, technical practices, staffing, scheduling, and interpersonal relationships of the surgical team members. Industries served: healthcare and government agencies. **Conferences and Meetings:** *Provides numerous seminars on operating room nursing throughout the year.* **Computer/Special Services:** Offers programs in healthcare field through computer assisted learning software including: Fundamentals of Aseptic Technique; Electrosurgery: Principles and Practices; and OR Credentialing software; also sponsors a tape-of-the-month club for continuing education purposes.

ATLANTIC REHABILITATION SERVICES, INC.
550 East Main St., Ste. 303
Norfolk, VA 23510
Barbara K. Byers, CEO
PH: (757)640-0500
TF: 800476-4394
FX: (757)627-8047
Founded: 1989. **Staff:** 8. A private vocational rehabilitation company that provides services to attorneys, insurance companies, and government agencies on the vocational impact of injuries and the need for vocational rehabilitation services. Firm routinely testifies as vocational experts. Geographic areas served: eastern U.S., Virginia, and northern North Carolina.

AUGUSTA NUTRITION CONSULTANTS
PO Box 799
Evans, GA 30809-0799
Tony Black, Secretary/Treasurer
PH: (706)860-8935
FX: (706)860-8932
Founded: 1985. **Staff:** 13. Provides nutrition consultation for individuals, groups, businesses, health departments, hospitals, private physicians, health maintenance organizations, and prepaid group plans. **Conferences and Meetings:** *Offers seminars and workshops on nutrition and lactation related services to professionals and the general public.*

KATHLEEN BABBITT
1590 Court St., No. 50
Port Allen, LA 70767
PH: (504)343-5539
Provides consultations on alternate healing processes to health problems and health issues using a natural healing approach instead of drugs and surgery. Serves all industries in all geographic locations.

BACK IN THE SADDLE: LONG-TERM RESIDENTIAL SERVICES FOR HEAD INJURED ADULTS
9775 Mockingbird Ave.
Apple Valley, CA 92308
Richard K. Smith, Ph.D., Clinical Director
PH: (760)240-3217
FX: (760)240-3274
A vocational and transitional program design for adult head injured. Specializes in head injury, CVA, spinal injury and other catastrophic rehabilitation pictures.

CONNIE BADILLO
5530 Wisconsin Ave., Ste. 1400
Chevy Chase, MD 20815
Connie Badillo
PH: (301)656-9170
FX: (301)654-5893
Consulting nutritionist in the Chesapeake Bay area and registered dietitian in private practice. **Conferences and Meetings:** *Vegetarian Cooking, Eating Out Healthfully, Supermarket Tours (Learning to Make Healthy Choices in the Grocery Store).*

JAMES BAHR ASSOCIATES, LTD.
44450 Pinetree Dr., Ste. 202
Plymouth, MI 48170
M. James Bahr, President
PH: (313)455-8260
FX: (313)455-0850
Founded: 1979. **Staff:** 6. Hospital management engineering con-

sultant with special expertise in patient classification and nursing management information system (ARIC). Also offers consultative services for hospital facilities planning. Industries served: hospitals and hospital corporations, government agencies, and healthcare industry. Geographic areas served: entire United States and Canada. **Conferences and Meetings:** *ARIC User Workshops; Patient Classification Seminars.*

BARBARA J. BARBU
6506 Deidre Terr.
McLean, VA 22101-1605
Barbara J. Barbu, R.D., L.D.
PH: (703)848-8110
FX: (703)848-8110
Registered dietitian in private practice. Consultant to companies, health care and medical facilities. Board Member of the Northern District, Virginia Dietetic Association Member of Consulting Nutritionist in the Chesapeake Bay Area Association. **Conferences and Meetings:** *Classes in low cholesterol cooking and weight control; work site presentations.* **Computer/Special Services:** Computerized nutrition analysis; body fat measurement.

ROBERT J. BARISH
211 E. 70th St.
New York, NY 10021
Robert J. Barish
PH: (212)288-7201
Founded: 1981. **Staff:** 1. Consultant in radiological physics and radiation safety. Specializes in radiation therapy calibrations, planning, architectural design, equipment selection, and medical-legal aspects of radiology including expert opinion in malpractice suits. Serves private industries as well as government agencies.

PHYLLIS M. BARRIER
e-mail: pbarrier@diabetes.org
226 N. Saint Asaph
Alexandria, VA 22314
Phyllis M. Barrier
PH: (703)549-3684
FX: (703)683-1839
Registered dietician in private practice, specializing in diabetes, weight management, and eating disorders. **Computer/Special Services:** Certified diabetes educator.

KENNETH BASHAM
e-mail: kendoc@compuserve.com
PO Box 22037
Ottawa, ON, Canada K1V 0C2
Kenneth Basham
PH: (613)738-0106
FX: (613)738-0106
Founded: 1985. **Staff:** 3. Consultant to the health field provides expertise in research, analysis and reports for the industry. Assists in the preparation of articles, pamphlets, and speeches. Also helps with the preparation of presentations and submissions to government bodies and committes. Conducts seminars and lectures. All the above services related to healthcare systems (especially alternatives to dominant, conventional system), healthcare delivery systems and the social and legislative factors associated therewith. Industries served: health food manufacturing and distribution, and alternative healthcare professionals. Geographic areas served: Canada, United States, United Kingdom and European Community; Australia, and New Zealand. **Conferences and Meetings:** *Practice Management to Development; The Cholesterol Controversy; Management of DJD; Effective Nutritional Practice; Media Training.*

TERRANCE E. BAULCH
103 E. Liberty, Ste. 207
Ann Arbor, MI 48104
Terrance E. Baulch
PH: (313)930-0800
FX: (313)930-0801
Founded: 1987. Healthcare management consultant specializing

in financial and economic analysis including changes in third party payment systems and other operating issues for the healthcare industry.

BEALE MEDICAL INC.
1601 Connecticut Ave. NW
Washington, DC 20009
PH: (202)328-1747
FX: (202)328-1766
Founded: 1977. Medical consultants.

JOE BEAN & ASSOCIATES, INC.
e-mail: beansafe@aol.com
171 Edison Rd.
Trumbull, CT 06611-4136
Joe E. Bean, President
PH: (203)459-0121
FX: (203)459-0121
Founded: 1989. Safety management consulting firm specializes in OSHA-type inspections, OSHA compliance training - all subjects, long or short-term safety management, OSHA defense, accident investigation and reconstruction, process safety management, expert witnessing, and total loss control. Industries served: all - special expertise in the automotive, pulp and paper industry and lockout/tagout.

K.O. BEATTY, PH.D., P.E.
e-mail: kobeatty@eos.ncsu.edu
323 Shepherd St.
Raleigh, NC 27607
K.O. Beatty, Jr.
PH: (919)833-7626
FX: (919)515-3465
Founded: 1950. **Staff:** 2. Legal expert in cases of fires and explosions (including arson), slips, trips and falls, and biomedical engineering. Works with attorneys for plaintiffs or defendants. Geographic areas served: North Carolina and surrounding states.

BEDFORD HEALTH ASSOCIATES, INC.
e-mail: tpweil@.aol.com
1400 Town Mountain Rd.
Asheville, NC 28804
Thomas P. Weil, President
PH: (828)252-1616
FX: (828)253-3820
Founded: 1975. **Staff:** 3. Offers health services and hospital consulting with emphasis on strategic and financial planning, cost containment, managed care, health alliances, and third party reimbursement problems. Geographic Areas Served: U.S. and Canada. **Conferences and Meetings:** *Contact firm for list.*

BEHAVIORAL HEALTH SYSTEMS, INCORPORATED
31 W. Carson Rd.
Phoenix, AZ 85041
Brent B. Geary, Ph.D., President
PH: (602)268-8404
FX: (602)268-5396
Founded: 1974. **Staff:** 13. Offers direct and consulting services to consumers and providers of behavioral health programming. Direct services include outpatient individual and group psychotherapy. Also offers social development and psychotherapeutic services to the physically handicapped. Other services include statewide behavioral health planning, training, program design and evaluation as well as executive assessment and career counseling assessment to management personnel in transitional positions.

RITA BEHLING
17 28th Ave., Apt. 306
Venice, CA 90291
PH: (310)822-0190
Medical-legal consultant, specializing in fetal heart rate monitoring analysis.

INA K. BENDIS, MD
851 Fremont Ave., Ste. 114
Los Altos, CA 94024
PH: (415)941-4100
FX: (415)948-2161
Specializes in internal medicine, pulmonary diseases, geriatrics, psychosomatics, HMO benefits denials, and claims fraud. Performs Record reviews, examinations, reports, detailed case analyses, and testimony.

BEVERLY ANN BENEDICT
2414 16th St.
Anacortes, WA 98221
Beverly Ann Benedict
PH: (360)293-9086
FX: (360)299-9151
Founded: 1993. Produces newsletter, including research and writing, which discusses rails-to-trails issues across the country. Serves as network for landowners adjacent to rails-to-trails corridors.

DAVID M. BENJAMIN, PH.D.
e-mail: medlaw@channel1.com
url: http://www.channel1.com/users/medlaw
2 Hammond Pond Pkwy., Ste. 605
Chestnut Hill, MA 02167
David M. Benjamin, Ph.D.
PH: (617)969-1393
TF: 800355-9915
FX: (617)969-4285
Founded: 1986. **Staff:** 1. Develops educational and risk management programs for physicians, hospitals, healthcare professionals and the pharmaceutical industry. Areas of expertise include drug information, root cause analysis, preparation of IND and New Drug Applications (NDAs), development of clinical research studies, medical-legal case review, and alternative dispute resolution. Industries served: healthcare professionals, pharmaceutical industry, insurance companies, and legal professionals. **Conferences and Meetings:** *Understanding Statistics in Science - 1/2 day course for lawyers and judges. Medical Risk Management- Risk Management seminars and syllabus for self-learning to improve prescribing skills and minimize the risk of medication prescribing, dispensing & administrate errors. For physicians, pharmacists, nurses, Rm/QA professionals and insurance claims managers.* **Computer/Special Services:** Full service.

IRENE C. BERMAN-LEVINE - NUTRITION PROGRAM PLANNING
650 N. 12th St.
Lemoyne, PA 17043
Irene Berman-Levine, Ph.D., R.D.
PH: (717)763-1798
FX: (717)238-5147
Founded: 1986. **Staff:** 1. Develops educational programs on the topics of nutrition and health. Frequently speaks on subjects such as diet and cancer and diet and oils in coronary heart disease. Expertise in consumer food purchasing patterns, nutrition labeling, and development/evaluation of nutrition education materials. Geographic areas served: Harrisburg, Central Pennsylvania, Philadelphia/Baltimore. **Conferences and Meetings:** *Nutrition Update; Nutrition and Cancer Update; Dietary Guidelines for Americans; Dietary Treatment of Diabetes Mellitus; Nutrition Claims in Food Advertising and Labeling.* **Computer/Special Services:** Nutrient analysis of diet, menu development for special diets.

ROY BERRY CONSULTANTS & DENTAL PRACTICE BROKERS
url: http://realty.mibor.net/rbc/
4936 Cavendish Rd.
Indianapolis, IN 46220
PH: (317)251-9169
TF: 800659-6117
FX: (317)251-3106

Sells and appraises dental practices. Provides consulting services to help dentists grow profitable dental practices, acquisition financing, valuations, etc.

JEAN M. BIGAOUETTE
460 Krumkill Rd.
Albany, NY 12203
Jean Bigaouette
PH: (518)482-8704
Founded: 1976. **Staff:** 1. Nutritionist and registered dietitian offering private counseling in nutrition. Services include nutritional assessment of dietary intake and body composition analysis. Provides dietary counseling for obesity, underweight, eating disorders, hypertension, high cholesterol, elevated triglycerides, vitamin and mineral deficiencies and excesses, pregnancy, lactation vegetariarism, adolescence, body builders, and professional athletes. Serves private industries as well as government agencies. Geographic areas served: tri-city area of New York (Albany, Schenetady, and Troy). **Computer/Special Services:** Nutritional analysis of dietary intake for protein, CHO, fat, 11 vitamins, and 7 minerals.

BILINGUAL HEALTH CARE CONSULTANTS INC.
137 S. San Fernando Blvd., Ste. 407
Burbank, CA 91502-1322
Virgilio C. Orozco, Pres.
PH: (818)557-6582
FX: (213)251-9512
Founded: 1989. **Staff:** 11. Offers medical administration expertise to businesses in southern California.

IRENE BILYEU
313 N. Adams St.
Owenton, KY 40359
Irene Bilyeu, President
PH: (502)484-2149
Founded: 1982. **Staff:** 1. Nursing service consultant who assists providers of healthcare in the effective use of their assets, helps them to visualize potential growth, and minimize or eliminate deficiencies. Serves hospitals, nursing homes, and home health agencies throughout the state of Kentucky. Serves private industries as well as government agencies. Geographic areas served: Polk County, Florida, and northern and Blue Grass area in Kentucky. **Conferences and Meetings:** *Why Communication Gaps; Burn-out Prevention; Realistic Staffing of Health Care Facility; Peer Review Development; Leadership-Authority; History of Nursing; A Hospice for AIDS Patients.*

BIO-RESEARCH CONSULTANTS, INC.
675 Massachusetts Ave.
Cambridge, MA 02139
F. Homburger, President
PH: (617)864-8735
FX: (617)661-9488
Founded: 1957. **Staff:** 1. Specializes in planning, monitoring, and interpreting safety evaluations of chemicals by means of in vivo bio-assay. Risk assessment and safety evaluation of drugs and chemicals in general. Expert witness on tobacco carcinogenesis. Geographic areas served: no limitations.

BIO-SENTRY ENGINEERING INC.
9205 Main St.
Whitmore Lake, MI 48189-9411
Orlin P. O'Brien, Pres.
PH: (313)449-4407
FX: (313)449-8408
Founded: 1971. **Staff:** 12. Offers medical equipment engineering design and repair services to healthcare and medical equipment manufacturing industries in the United States.

BIOBEHAVIORAL RESEARCH FOUNDATION, INC.
218 Beech View Ct.
Baltimore, MD 21286
Faith K. Jaffe, President

PH: (410)337-7319
FX: (410)337-0205
Founded: 1974. **Staff:** 3. Offers consultation to pharmaceutical corporations, law firms, government agencies, and not-for-profit organizations in areas of problems in pharmacology, substance abuse, toxicology, and forensic medicine.

BIOENERGETICS, INC.
PO Box 259141
Madison, WI 53725
Roy U. Schenk
PH: (608)255-4028
FX: (608)251-0658
Founded: 1973. **Staff:** 3. Offers technical counsel on chemical toxicology for forensic problems. Consultant has done numerous studies for insurance companies, legal firms, and others on a wide spectrum of problems, including paint identification, fuel and lubricant contaminants, identification of flammable solvents, Breathalyzer, Intoxilyzer and blood testing, and other chemical and biochemical problems. Also experienced with gender issues including sexual harassment defense. Geographic areas served: primarily midwestern U.S. **Conferences and Meetings:** *Seminars on Driving While Intoxicated Defenses, improving gender dialog.*

BIOPHARMACEUTICAL RESEARCH CONSULTANTS
e-mail: brci@compuserve.com
PO Box 2506
Ann Arbor, MI 48106
JP Hsu
PH: (313)426-2820
FX: (313)426-2849
Firm provides pharmaceutical research services including clinical trial monitoring, data management, statistical analysis and report writing. Geographical Areas Served: North America. **Conferences and Meetings:** *Biopharmaceutical Applied Statistics Symposium (BASS).* **Computer/Special Services:** Case report form scanning.

BIOTEK INC.
21 Olympia Ave., Ste. C
Woburn, MA 01801
PH: (617)938-0938
FX: (617)938-8939
Founded: 1980. Privately-owned medical research corporation.

BIRMAN & ASSOCIATES INC.
502 Gould Dr.
Cookeville, TN 38506
David Birman
PH: (615)432-6532
FX: (615)432-6536
Consulting firm offers expertise in the healthcare field.

JAMES BISSONETT & ASSOCIATES INC.
e-mail: bissonett@bissonett.com
7901 Flying Cloud Dr., Ste. 154
Eden Prairie, MN 55344-5342
James Bissonett, President
PH: (612)944-7117
FX: (612)944-7056
Founded: 1982. **Staff:** 16. Specializes in employee benefits, group insurance, and corporate retirement plans. **Conferences and Meetings:** *1996 Hol(k) Update; Benefits for Growing Companies.*

REBECCA BITZER
7218 D Hanover Pkwy.
Greenbelt, MD 20770
Rebecca Bitzer
PH: (301)474-2499
FX: (301)474-6709
Consulting nutritionist in the Chesapeake Bay area and registered dietitian in private practice. **Conferences and Meetings:** *Nutrition support groups.* **Computer/Special Services:** Nutrient analysis; Macintosh office/client management.

JOAN SALGE BLAKE
e-mail: salgeblake@aol.com
300 Old Lancaster Rd.
Sudbury, MA 01776
Joan Salge Blake
PH: (508)443-0172
FX: (508)443-0172
Founded: 1987. **Staff:** 1. Offers nutrition and weight loss counseling, blood pressure reduction, cholesterol lowering, pre and post pregnancy care, nutrition planning for athletes, and meal planning for busy families. **Computer/Special Services:** Computerized nutritional dietary analysis.

MARTIN BLINDER, MD
130 Melville Ave.
San Anselmo, CA 94960
Martin Blinder, MD, Principal
PH: (415)453-8920
FX: (415)346-1195
Founded: 1967. Offers expert testimony in claims of emotional distress and psychic trauma, sexual harassment and molestation, wrongful death, post traumatic stress disorder, closed head injury, and psychogenic pain syndromes. Offers detection of malingering and eyewitness fallibility. Distinguishes authentic from false psychological claims. Provides disability assessments. Geographic Areas Served: U.S.

BLOCK, MCGIBONY, BELLMORE AND ASSOCIATES
e-mail: bmb600@home.com
3609 Woodvalley Dr.
Baltimore, MD 21208
Mandell Bellmore
PH: (410)484-9880
TF: 800554-7200
FX: (410)484-9884
Founded: 1958. Hospital administration consultants focusing on four areas: (1) strategic planning, to strengthen the hospital's competitive and financial position; (2) market development, to identify market segments in which the client has distinct competencies, establishing specific market share objectives for each segment, and applying marketing techniques to achieve these objectives; (3) regulatory agency activities, to prepare and defend certificates of need or changes; and (4) litigation support, to prepare technical analyses and expert testimony at the request of the hospital's counsel.

WILLIAM H. BLOOM, MD
url: http://www.claims.com
270 E. Main St.
Bay Shore, NY 11706
William H. Bloom, MD, Principal
PH: (516)665-6685
FX: (516)665-6686
Provides expert testimony on neurological and medical matters.

BODY BASICS
e-mail: bodybasics@theriver.com
url: http://www.theriver.com/bodybasics
926 Plaza Topaz
PO Box 67
Sierra Vista, AZ 85636
Pam Germain
PH: (520)459-6145
TF: 800762-6232
FX: (520)452-1320
Founded: 1987. **Staff:** 2. Offers fitness and health education; programming for health clubs; and quality improvement for clubs. Also speaks professionally on the training of fitness instructors; and designs wellness programs for business employees. Certification Programs for Fitness Instructors and Personal Tarriners. Industries served: all in New Mexico, Texas, Colorado, Arizona, California, and Utah. **Conferences and Meetings:** *Healthy Image, weight loss workshops; CQI-IQ for Fitness, continuing quality improvement; The Mind/Body Journey, the connection between physi-*

cal fitness and mental processes; Specialty and Style, aerobic instructor training; and Aerobics: Basic and Creative, instructor training program. Also custom designs health and wellness workshops for the needs of the client.

JOHN D. BOGDEN, PH.D.
e-mail: bogden@umdnj.edu
UMDNJ - New Jersey Medical School
Department of Preventive Medicine
185 South Orange Ave.
Newark, NJ 07103-2714
John D. Bogden, Ph.D., Professor
PH: (973)972-5432
FX: (973)972-7625
An environmental toxicology and nutrition consultant, specializing in mineral and trace element nutrition and toxicology, including lead poisoning, chromium toxicity, overdoses of minerals and trace elements, air, soil and water pollutants, and environmental toxins. Analyzes body tissues and fluids. Provides expert reports, deposition and court testimony experience.

GEORGE E. BOLDUC, JR., MD
e-mail: gebolduc@atsconcentric.net
PO Box 5224
San Mateo, CA 94402-5224
George E. Bolduc, Jr., M, Principal
PH: (415)259-6500
FX: (415)388-3732
Provides expert witness testimony in forensic pathology for both: criminal and civil law cases.

BORON, LEPORE & ASSOCIATES INC.
17-17 State Rte. 208 N.
Fair Lawn, NJ 07410-2819
Patrick Le Pore, President
PH: (201)791-7272
FX: (201)791-1121

BOSTON BIOMEDICAL CONSULTANTS, INC.
e-mail: bostonbio@aol.com
1000 Winter St., Ste. 1600
Waltham, MA 02154
Henry M. Weinert, President
PH: (617)890-5060
FX: (617)890-6746
Founded: 1976. **Staff:** 18. Offers strategic management services to the biomedical industry, including business strategy formulation, strategic market planning, technology assessment, business development planning, design of new product portfolios, and due diligence searches. Conducts appraisals of potential acquisition, and licensing and divestiture candidates for investment organizations. Primarily serves manufacturers and distributors of human diagnostic and therapeutic products and life science instruments and reagents. Geographic areas served: worldwide.

**BOSTON MEDICAL CENTER, OCCUPATIONAL HEALTH
  PROGRAM**
e-mail: barbanel@bu.edu
88 E. Newton St., D203
Boston, MA 02118
PH: (617)638-8400
FX: (617)638-8406
Founded: 1989. **Staff:** 15. Provides occupational and environmental medicine services.

**BRADY & ASSOCIATES - CONSULTANTS TO HEALTH
  CARE MANAGEMENT**
e-mail: brady@bradyinc.com
url: http://www.bradyinc.com
7211 NW 83rd St., Ste. 230
Kansas City, MO 64152-6036
Frank J. Brady
PH: (816)587-2120
FX: (816)587-1698

Founded: 1983. **Staff:** 5. Provides consulting services to hospitals and other healthcare related organizations. Activities focus on the areas of continuous quality improvement, productivity improvement, cost effectiveness, cost reduction and management development. Geographic areas served: U.S. **Conferences and Meetings:** *Managing for Productivity, a one-day, in-house education program to introduce hospitals department heads to proven productivity improvement and cost-reduction techniques.*

NACHMAN BRAUTBAR, MD
6200 Wilshire Blvd., Ste. 1000
Los Angeles, CA 90048
Nachman Brautbar, MD, Principal
PH: (213)634-6500
FX: (213)634-6501
Medical doctor specializing in internal medicine, nephrology, pharmacology, occupational medicine, toxicology, internal medicine, and nephrology. Offers consultations, assessments, review records, and expert opinion testimony.

WILLIAM S. BREALL, MD
St. Francis Memorial Hospital
1150 Bush St., Ste. 4A
San Francisco, CA 94109
PH: (415)775-2277
Specializes in cardiology, cardiovascular disease, peripheral vascular disease, cerebrovascular disease, and hypertension.

BRENNAN COUNSELING, INC.
e-mail: ada@icanect.net
7955 Biscayne Point Cir.
Miami Beach, FL 33141
Michael Brennan, President/Treasurer
PH: (305)864-7070
FX: (305)864-4140
Founded: 1984. **Staff:** 2. Provides expert witness services for legal and insurance firms regarding personal injury, specifically disability versus ability to work. Also serves government agencies. Geographic areas served: Dade, Monroe, and Broward Counties, and Palm Beach.

MORLEY BRICKMAN & ASSOCIATES, LTD.
9221 Drake Ave., Unit 410
Evanston, IL 60203-1626
Morley Brickman, President
PH: (847)674-2664
FX: (847)674-0096
Founded: 1986. **Staff:** 1. Occupational safety and health consultants provide forensic services primarily to construction and manufacturing industry. Serves private industry as well as government agencies.

BRIM HEALTHCARE, INC.
e-mail: jonelle.totman@brimhealthcare.com
305 NE 102nd Ave.
Portland, OR 97220
James O. McKinney
PH: (503)256-2070
FX: (503)254-7619
Founded: 1973. **Staff:** 250. A diversified healthcare services company offering management and consulting services to the healthcare industry including direct management services, healthcare planning and full development. Services include full-service management, interim administrative management, fiscal services management, accounts receivable recovery, operational assessment, strategic planning, and quality assurance.

HELEN MERRILL BRINSON
313 Pinewood Rd.
Greenville, NC 27858
Helen Merrill Brinson
PH: (919)756-4104
Founded: 1982. Provides management consulting services to the healthcare field. **Conferences and Meetings:** *Offers workshops on*

the following topics: Preceptor Training for Nurses; Management-Performance Appraisal; Health Promotion/Disease Prevention.

BRISTOL GROUP INC.
10 Post Office Sq.
Boston, MA 02109
Peter F. Rettig
PH: (617)423-2464
FX: (617)423-2466
Founded: 1985. **Staff:** 10. Provides counsel to healthcare organizations, including hospitals and physician groups.

B.G. BROGDON, MD
e-mail: vbrown@usamail.usouthal.edu
University of South Alabama
2451 Fillingim St.
Mobile, AL 36617
B.G. Brogdon, MD, Univ.Disting.Prof.Emeritus of Radiology
PH: (334)471-7868
FX: (334)471-7882
Forensic radiology consultant specializing in individual and mass identification matters, child abuse, trauma and gunshot evaluation, missed diagnoses and malpractice, and personal injury cases. Prepares courtroom exhibits. Geographic areas served: U.S. **Conferences and Meetings:** *Forensic Radiology in many states and European countries.*

PAUL K. BRONSTON, MD
1 Jib St., Ste. 202
Marina del Rey, CA 90292
Paul K. Bronston, MD, Principal
PH: (310)301-9426
FX: (310)823-2433
Acts as plaintiff or defense expert consultant or witness in medical insurance bad faith evaluations; medical quality assurance evaluations; utilization review; liability evaluations; medical malpractice evaluations; emergency medicine and quality assurance and utilization review; hospital liability; and HMO/managed care liability evaluation. Geographic Areas Served: U.S.A.

ANNE D. BROWN
Albemarle Center for Family Medicine
535 Westfield Rd., Ste. 200
Charlottesville, VA 22901
Anne D. Brown
PH: (804)973-4040
FX: (804)974-1780
Founded: 1982. **Staff:** 1. Provides nutritional consultation for individuals referred by physician. All areas of nutrition addressed with primary emphasis on low cholesterol diets, weight reduction, gestational diabetes, as well as prudent diet restrictions.

WALLACE B. BROWN, DDS
e-mail: percha@earthlink.net
1955 S. 1300 E., Ste. 6
Salt Lake City, UT 84105
PH: (801)487-0758
FX: (801)487-0750
Founded: 1973. Endodontist providing diagnosis and treatment of pain of dental origin; as well as malpractice evaluation.

DAVID L. BROWN MANAGEMENT CO., INC.
21 Mt. Vernon St.
Boston, MA 02108-1801
David L. Brown, Pres., Treas.
PH: (617)720-1280
FX: (617)227-9091
Founded: 1979. **Staff:** 19. Advises doctors on professional practice management in the United States.

DAVID BUANNO
4560 S. Eastern Ave., Ste. 15
Las Vegas, NV 89119
David Buanno, DC, Principal

PH: (702)735-2311
FX: (702)731-1767
Offers chiropractic consulting.

ALAN BUCHWALD, MD INC.
PO Box 2009
Santa Cruz, CA 95063
Alan Buchwald, MD, Principal
PH: (408)761-0260
FX: (408)761-0260
Medical consultant specializing in medical toxicology, poisoning, overdose, envenomation, industrial/occupational injuries, environmental, hazardous materials, agricultural, food toxicology, and indoor air problems.

BUCKMAN CO. INC.
e-mail: nocaldave@msn.com
200 Gregory Ln., Ste. C-100
Pleasant Hill, CA 94523
Pamela M. Buckman, CEO
PH: (925)356-2640
TF: 800358-8785
FX: (925)356-2654
Founded: 1983. **Staff:** 12. Services include medical device regulatory planning/evaluation, study design, study monitoring, 510(K) submissions, I.D.E. design/development, PMAA preparation and filing, and FDA panel presentations. Industries served: medical device manufacturers, and in-vitro diagnostic manufacturers.

JOHN D. BULLOCK, MD
e-mail: jbullock@wright.edu
url: http://www.forop.com
Department of Ophthalmology
Wright State University
500 Lincoln Park Blvd., Ste. 104
Dayton, OH 45429-3487
John D. Bullock, MD, Principal
PH: (937)643-2301
FX: (937)297-7690
Opthamologist and forensic examiner experienced in medical-legal investigations, depositions and court appearances. Specializes in accident reconstruction and analysis, product liability (including contact lenses and pharmaceuticals), malingering, biophysics of ocular and orbital trauma, post-operative blindness, optometric liability, and forensic ocular and orbital microbiology. Geographic areas served: USA and Worldwide.

SARAH GREENE BURGER
3403 Woodley Rd. NW
Washington, DC 20016
Sarah Greene Burger
PH: (202)966-3025
Founded: 1976. Nursing consultant in management and supervision of long-term patient care facilities. Works with individuals and families making decisions about the combination of services needed for long-term care in the community or in institutions. **Conferences and Meetings:** *Chemical and Physical Restraint Reduction; Working with the Minimum Data Set.*

RICHARD G. BURNS
Box 276
Corte Madera, CA 94976-0276
Richard G. Burns
PH: (415)924-8902
Founded: 1990. **Staff:** 2. Specialist in alcoholism and drug abuse counseling. Serves the health, recovery, and religious community. Geographic areas served: U.S., Canada, and Great Britain.

HAROLD J. BURSZTAJN, MD
e-mail: burszt@atswarren.med.harvard.edu
url: http://www.forensic-psych.com
96 Larchwood Dr.
Cambridge, MA 02138
Harold J. Bursztajn, MD, Principal

PH: (617)492-8366
FX: (617)441-3195
An expert consultant and witness specializing in forensic psychiatry and medicine; medical and psychiatric malpractice; managed medical care, product liability and informed consent; emotional injury (PTSD, loss of consortium); true vs. false memories of trauma; sexual abuse in professional relationships; psychiatric and medical disability evaluation; workers' compensation; supervisory responsibility; premises liability; and competence assessment.

DONALD B. BUTLER, MD, MS, JD
PO Box 1165
La Porte, TX 77572-1165
PH: (281)471-8100
FX: (281)471-8116
Quality of care consultant, Physicians and Hospitals, medical-legal expert. Geographical Areas Served: U.S.

THE BYRD NETWORK
PO Box 6534
Raleigh, NC 27628
Annette Byrd, President
PH: (919)832-6777
FX: (919)832-6775
Founded: 1989. **Staff:** 6. Performs needs analysis in health hazard surveillance, medical monitoring and protection; safety, emergency response, injury care, accident control, and disability follow-up; alcohol and drug education, screening and referral; and wellness programming. Also provides quality assurance audits in the area of occupational health. Program support/management services include development of tailored systems and procedures to integrate or redirect existing health services, to fully install a new occupational health, health promotion or employee assistance program, or to manage workers' compensation. Also offers training for nurses, doctors, employee assistance programs, human resources personnel and wellness professionals. All training customized to increase staff's effectiveness in health program delivery. Industries served: advertising, utilities, manufacturing, research, financial and professional services, universities, consumer and professional products, healthcare, and government agencies. Geographic areas served: United States, Puerto Rico, Canada, and Europe. **Conferences and Meetings:** *What You Always Wanted to Know About a Drug Screening, Education, and Referral Program, But Could Not Find Anywhere Else; Providing Occupational Health Services to the Diverse Workforce of the Future; Planning and Implementation of an Employee Wellness Program.*

C-A-B CONSULTANTS, INC.
url: http://www.webspawner.com/users/cabinfo
4921 Butterfield Rd.
Hillside, IL 60162-1413
Carol A. Bacon
PH: (708)449-2221
FX: (708)449-2223
Founded: 1985. **Staff:** 10. Safety, OSHA related, Workers Compensation and Occupational Health. Geographic Areas Served: Chicago matropolitan area but will travel. **Conferences and Meetings:** *Drugs and the Employer; First Aid for the Industrial Setting; and Accident Investigation Dynamics of Occupational Health Nursing; Safe Driving Principles and Practices; Back Safety/Education; Developing In-House Safety Programs and Internet and Safety Computers.*

CAL/OSHA CONSULTATION SERVICES
7827 Convoy Ct., Ste. 406
San Diego, CA 92111-1218
William Obert
PH: (619)279-3771
FX: (619)279-2454
Founded: 1973. **Staff:** 6. The CAL/OSHA Consultation Service is a government funded, technical assistance program designed to help employers protect their workers from accidents and illness on the job through hazard identification and control, educa-

tion and training, and development of effective on-the-job safety and health programs.

CAMBRIDGE CONSULTING CORP.
e-mail: ccc@worldweb.net
1410 Spring Hill Rd., Ste. 450
McLean, VA 22102
Richard Alvarez, President
PH: (703)917-7909
FX: (703)917-7918
Founded: 1985. **Staff:** 81. An international health, management, and research organization. Serves private industries as well as government agencies. Geographic areas served: international.

YALE H. CAPLAN
3411 Philips Dr.
Baltimore, MD 21208
Yale H. Caplan
PH: (410)486-7486
FX: (410)653-4824
Founded: 1974. Consultant in toxicology, drug and chemical analysis, workplace drug testing, and interpretation of toxicologic information. Serves as expert witness in drunk driving and drug testing cases.

**CARDIOVASCULAR THORACIC SURGERY MEDICAL
   LEGAL CONSULTATIONS**
11828 Rancho Bernardo Rd., Ste. 123-173
San Diego, CA 92128
Michael J. O'Sullivan, MD, Principal
PH: (619)451-1270
FX: (619)451-1270
Provides medical-legal consultation and expert testimony in the area of cardio-vascular surgery.

CARE COMMUNICATIONS, INC.
e-mail: ccommun487@aol.com
205 W. Wacker Dr., Ste. 1900
Chicago, IL 60606-1214
S. Paul Musco, Chairman
PH: (312)551-3100
TF: 800458-3544
FX: (312)422-0106
Founded: 1976. **Staff:** 62. Care Communications, a temporary staffing services company, provides hands-on help for HIM functions including coding (on or off-site), abstracting, clerical functions, interim management, operations review/planning, reengineering, coding/DRG validation improvement, coding training, Chargemaster review, Master Patient Index clean-up, and other consulting services related to health and information management. Cancer/trauma registry services include outsourcing or temporary staffing for abstracting, staging, survey preparation, studies, and annual reports. Geographic Areas Served: national

CARING OPTIONS RESIDENTIAL EXPERTS
e-mail: chucklesn@aol.com
2306 American Dr.
Lago Vista, TX 78645
Sharyl Norman, Director
PH: (512)267-3439
FX: (512)267-2193
Staff: 1. Counsels in long-term care, Medicare, and Medicaid. Serves Geriatric in Texas.

CARLSON PRICE FASS & CO. INC.
520 Linen Ln.
Walnut Creek, CA 94598
Allen Carlson
PH: (510)746-3255
FX: (510)256-0222
Consulting firm provides management services to medical institutions.

M.L. CARTER ASSOCIATES INC.
3347 W. Hospital Ave.
Atlanta, GA 30341-3419
M.L. Carter, Pres.
PH: (770)455-6035
FX: (770)457-2560
Founded: 1971. **Staff:** 9. Offers employment recruiting, management, and healthcare services to hospitals worldwide.

DR. DARRELL B. CARTER
e-mail: dcarter@spectacle.berkeley.edu
School of Optometry
University of California
Berkeley, CA 94720
PH: (510)642-2153
FX: (510)653-8604
Acts as an expert witness in optometric standard of care, ocular disease, ocular pharmacology, vision loss, economic effects, and visibility in auto and other accidents.

CHARLES W. CASELLA
701 Welch Rd., Ste. 211
Palo Alto, CA 94304
Charles Casella
PH: (415)326-6638
FX: (415)326-8746
Founded: 1971. **Staff:** 1. Medical-legal consultant specializing in legal psychiatry, occupational psychiatry, and psychiatric disability evaluation. Industries served: insurance, legal, peace officers, government agencies, and all employees. Geographic areas served: West Coast.

VERONICA K. CASEY
8 Webster Valley Rd.
Darien, CT 06820
Veronica K. Casey
PH: (203)655-0196
FX: (203)655-0196
Founded: 1971. **Staff:** 1. Maternal-child healthcare nurse specialist. Geographic areas served: New England. Woman owned firm. **Conferences and Meetings:** *Topics related to parenting, pregnancy, and lactation.*

CDM GROUP INC.
5530 Wisconsin Ave., Ste. 1600
Chevy Chase, MD 20815-4301
Vincent Castro
PH: (301)654-6740
FX: (301)656-4012
Consulting firm provides management services and consults on healthcare issues.

CDP SERVICES INC.
e-mail: cdpatl@aol.com
1050 Crown Pointe Pkwy., Ste. 210
Atlanta, GA 30338
David G. Fulcher
PH: (770)391-9872
FX: (770)395-6544
Founded: 1973. Health care firm offers medical schools, hospital and physician consulting for cancer programs and facilities. Geographic Areas Served: International.

CELSIS LABORATORY GROUP LABORATORY DIVISION
e-mail: leberco@celsis.com
123 Hawthorne St.
Roselle Park, NJ 07204-0206
Edwin C. Rothstein, President
PH: (908)245-1933
TF: 800523-LABS
FX: (908)245-6253
Founded: 1939. **Staff:** 47. Offers consulting in animal toxicology, in-vitro toxicology, microbiology and chemical analysis to the pharmaceutical, cosmetic, toiletry, medical device, bacteriocide,

pesticide, coatings, graphic arts, and specialty chemical industries. Also serves government agencies. Geographic areas served: New Jersey, New York, Pennsylvania, and Connecticut.

MONICA A. CENGIA, R.D., L.D.
7707 Paragon Rd., Ste. 105
Centerville, OH 45459
Monica A. Cengia
PH: (937)436-1985
Founded: 1985. **Staff:** 1. Registered dietitian offers nutritional assessments and consultations. Also provides individualized nutrition counseling, wellness programs, nutrition education programs, long-term healthcare counseling, and media presentations. Industries served: long-term healthcare, hospitals, universities, private businesses, health clubs/spas, physicians' offices, food industry, radio, television, and newspaper. **Conferences and Meetings:** *Caring for the Tube-fed Resident; Rehabilitation: Team Approach in Long-Term Care; Long-Term Care Update: Ask the Experts; Wellness.*

THE CENTER FOR CORPORATE HEALTH, INC.
url: http://www.optiumcare.com
8201 Greenboro Dr., Ste. 500
Mclean, VA 22102
Terry Goplerud
PH: (703)394-7600
TF: 800745-1333
FX: (703)394-7585
Founded: 1984. **Staff:** 65. Consultants on integrated health promotion programs. Offers a variety of products and services to educate people on taking better care of themselves and using medical services wisely. Products include health-oriented newsletters, health counseling, medical self-care books, and health risk appraisals. Works with individual organizations to assess healthcare cost management and tailor a program for client company. Industries served: human resources/employee benefits executives, managed care organizations, and government agencies. Geographic areas served: national. **Computer/Special Services:** Offers Informed Care, a telephone-based healthcare decision counseling service. Also offers a health risk appraisal.

CENTER FOR COUNSELING & HEALTH RESOURCES, INC.
e-mail: thecenterinc@msn.com
url: http://www.3.imall.com/the_center/
611 Main
Edmonds, WA 98020
Gregory L. Jantz, Ph.D., Director, Authoer, Prof. Speaker
PH: (425)771-5166
TF: 888771-5166
FX: (425)670-2807
Founded: 1983. **Staff:** 23. Consulting services of the Center include education and training, as well as counseling and treatment programs concerning family relationships, eating disorders, weight loss, and addictions and compulsions. Emphasis is on health programs and nutrition. **Conferences and Meetings:** *Remarkable Relationships; Sexual Boundaries; Becoming Strong Again.*

THE CENTER FOR FORENSIC ECONOMIC STUDIES
e-mail: cfes@cfes.com
url: http://www.cfes.com
1608 Walnut St., Ste. 1200
Philadelphia, PA 19103
Jerome M. Staller, Ph.D., President
PH: (215)546-5600
TF: 800966-6099
FX: (215)732-8158
Founded: 1980. **Staff:** 25. Provides economic and statistical analysis in litigation, including personal injury, commercial, employment and civil rights matters: as well as business valuations. Geographic Areas Served: U.S. & other countries.

**CENTER FOR LIFESTYLE ENHANCEMENT - COLUMBIA
MEDICAL CENTER OF PLANO**
3901 W. 15th St.
Plano, TX 75075
Steven C. Kendall, Ph.D.
PH: (972)519-1208
FX: (972)519-1299
Founded: 1982. **Staff:** 10. Provides professional health counseling
in the areas of general nutrition for weight management, eating
disorders, diabetic education, cholesterol reduction, and adolescent weight management. Offers work site health promotion and
preventive services. Also coordinates speaker's bureau, cooking
classes, and physician referrals. Industries served: education, insurance, healthcare, retail/wholesale, data processing, and manufacturing in Dallas, Ft. Worth, and Collin County, Texas. **Conferences and Meetings:** *Rx Diet and Exercise; Smoking Cessation;
Stress Management; Health Fairs; Fitness Screenings; Body Composition; Nutrition Analysis; Exercise Classes; Prenatal Nutrition;
SHAPEDOWN; and Successfully Managing Diabetes.*

CESSNA CONSULTING
37966 S. Spoon Dr.
Tucson, AZ 85739
PH: (520)825-0030
TF: 800548-3141
FX: (520)825-0034
Founded: 1987. **Staff:** 4. Firm offers expertise in medical management.

CHI SYSTEMS, INC.
130 S. First St.
Ann Arbor, MI 48104
Karl G. Bartscht, Chairman/CEO
PH: (313)761-3912
TF: 800521-7210
FX: (313)761-9366
Founded: 1969. **Staff:** 70. Provides results-oriented health care
management consulting services in strategy development and
business planning, operations and quality improvement, facility
planning, information systems, physician services, and post-acute
services to health care organizations including hospitals, health
systems, and group practices. Clients include rural, inner-city,
and university hospitals; multi-institutional systems; hospital associations; shared service organizations; and state and federal
governments. **Conferences and Meetings:** *Gaining Competitive
Advantage in Ambulatory Care; Developing a Cancer Center of
Excellence; Integrating the Post-Acute Continuum; Retooling Your
Primary Care Network.* **Computer/Special Services:** Offers two
software packages: The Quality/Productivity Management Reporting System and The Nursing Productivity Management Reporting System. Also offers space planning workbook with computer templates in space modeling in a variety of healthcare organizations.

CHILDREN'S EYE CARE MEDICAL GROUP
e-mail: rls@bigfoot.com
3565 Torrance Blvd., Ste. A
Torrance, CA 90503
Robert L. Schwartz, MD, Medical Director
PH: (310)543-1310
FX: (310)316-8148
Specializes in pediatric ophthalmology and strabismus; children's
eye surgery and diseases; adult disorders of eye muscles, double
vision and cosmetic misalignments of the eye; retinopathy of
prematurity; visual difficulties in children; surgical and medical
problems of children's and infant's eyes; surgical and medical
complications in children and adult strabismus surgery; and ocular birth defects.

CHIROPRACTIC CONSULTANTS MANAGEMENT CO.
e-mail: info@cc-mc.com
url: http://www.cc-mc.com/
11444 Seminole Blvd.
Largo, FL 33778

PH: (813)319-6199
FX: (813)393-5461
Founded: 1993. **Staff:** 350. Assists independent chiropractic practitioner in obtaining provider status in various managed care
companies, in negotiating contracts for them, in case management, and claims submission and collection of their professional
fees.

THE CIOTOLAS
4 Bateau Landing
Grasonville, MD 21638
Linda A. Ciotola, President
PH: (410)827-7100
FX: (410)544-6168
Founded: 1982. **Staff:** 2. Designs and assists in implementation of
major lifestyle changes for optimum health and wellness, including nutrition, exercise, stress management, and communication
skills. Creates comprehensive programs for integrated mind-body wellness. Prevention of and lifestyle management of eating
disorders, weight management, smoking cessation, hypertension,
adult on-set diabetes, premenstrual syndrome, coronary artery
disease, osteoporosis and other lifestyle-related issues. Industries
served: individuals, groups, corporations, schools, colleges, and
community organizations. Geographic areas served: Howard
County/Baltimore; Washington, DC, area; and Anne Arundel
County. **Conferences and Meetings:** *Dieting Will Make You Fat
(Really!); Fitness Facts, Frauds, and Myths; Don't Die by the Fork
(nutrition); Know Bones About It (osteoporosis); Stress Distress
(stress management); Exercise as Medicine for Diabetics; Out of
the Danger Zone (exercise guidelines); Eating Disorders: Diagnosis
and Treatment; Food Addiction - Unrecognized Eating Disorder;
Up in Smoke (smoking cessation); Cancer Prevention - What You
Can Do; Body Image; Eating Disorders - An Overview.* **Computer/Special Services:** Dietary analysis software; "Think Light"
lowfat living plan (includes daily menus, recipes, and weekly
grocery lists, book, tape).

CLAIMSWARE, INC.
e-mail: lbarnett@claimsware.com
PO Box 6125
Greenville, SC 29606
PH: (803)234-8200
TF: 800992-8088
FX: (803)234-8202
Founded: 1986. **Staff:** 20. Offers health services administration,
specializing in benefit administration systems, including medical,
dental, disability, and flexible spending accounts.

MARY ANNE CLAIRMONT
e-mail: Fse452@erols.com
3127 Colony Ln.
Plymouth Meeting, PA 19462
Mary Anne Clairmont, R.D.
PH: (610)941-9429
Founded: 1985. **Staff:** 1. Consultant in nutrition and health to
hospitals and long-term care facilities, schools, colleges and private industry. Areas covered include: all topics of general nutrition, wellness, sports topics, weight loss programs, vegetarianism,
nutrition over fifty, drug and alcohol rehabilitation, and long-term care regulations for dietary departments. Consultant to
weight loss groups. Also offers presentations to groups, on limited or ongoing basis. Industries served: individuals, groups, hospitals, health centers, nursing homes, colleges, schools, and government agencies. **Conferences and Meetings:** *Healthy Eating;
Weight Loss Seminars; Basic Nutrition for Health Care Professionals; Medical Nutrition Therapy for Individuals; Healthy Dividends
Low-Fat Eating Program.*

DONALD P. CLIGGETT, PH.D.
e-mail: dpc@itsa.ucsf.edu
1255 Post St., Ste. 742
San Francisco, CA 94109-6710
PH: (415)346-3761
FX: (415)479-6539

Consultation services include use and limitations of psychological and neuropsychological testing and psychological testing/assessment. Provides expert testimony in cases such as mental competence, criminal responsibility, child custody, post-traumatic stress disorder, chronic pain, personal injury, psychological disability, job stress, sexual abuse or harassment, and fitness-for-duty/practice for firefighters, police, airline personnel and attorneys.

CLIN/REGS ASSOCIATES
12707 High Bluff Dr., Ste. 200
San Diego, CA 92130
Bruce Merchant, MD, Ph, President
PH: (619)350-4324
FX: (619)350-4325
Specializes in all aspects of biotech/biopharmaceuticals new product development, including research, pre-clinical, clinical, regulatory, quality control, manufacturing practices, FDA interactions, immunology, pathology, cancer, viral diseases, monoclonal antibodies, cytokines, recombinant proteins, and gene therapy.

CLINTRIALS RESEARCH INC.
20 Burton Hills Blvd., Ste. 500
Nashville, TN 37215
Jerry R. Mitchell, MD, Ph.D.
PH: (615)665-9665
TF: 800346-7931
FX: (615)665-0971
Founded: 1989. **Staff:** 1400. A contract research services company, designs and performs high quality preclinical and clinical trials. From IND/IDE preparation and Phase I trials, through Phases II, III, IIIB, IV, V, and specialized post-marketing surveillance. Maintains the resources and experiences to handle clinical trials of any size and complexity. Industries served: pharmaceutical, biotechnology, goverment, and medical devices. Geographic areas served: U.S., Canada, United Kingdom, and Europe, Australia, and South America. **Computer/Special Services:** Computer-assisted New Drug Applications (CANDAs) plus Medical Review Tools and Remote Site Software Management Systems; Client to ClinTrials on line project management systems.

JEROLD S. COHEN
e-mail: jcohen287@aol.com
PO Box 900
Cape May Court House, NJ 08210
Jerold S. Cohen
PH: (609)785-2199
FX: (609)785-2199
Founded: 1975. **Staff:** 2. Consultant in healthcare and nursing management. Active in the development of programs that provide information on AIDS. Geographic areas served: U.S.

RICHARD J. COHEN, MD
e-mail: rcohen3@aol.com
3838 California St., Ste. 707
San Francisco, CA 94118
PH: (415)668-0160
FX: (415)752-4635
A consultant in medical oncology and hematology. Special expertise in cancers of breast, colon, lung, lymphomas, and melanoma.

COLORADO ORTHOPEDIC CONSULTANTS, P.C.
e-mail: info@colo-ortho.com
url: http://www.colo-ortho.com/
1411 S. Potomac, Ste. 400
Aurora, CO 80012
Peter L. Weingarten, M.D.
PH: (303)695-6060
FX: (303)369-7776
Staff: 6. A group of accredited orthopedic surgeons in private practice. Scope of practice ranges throughout the spectrum of surgical and non-surgical care for disorders affecting the musculoskeletal system. Interests range from sports injuries, and reconstructive surgery of the shoulder, hip, knee, ankle, and foot to micro- vascular and reconstrucive nerve surgery of the hand.

COMPREHENSIVE RESOURCES INC.
1663 E. 17th St.
Brooklyn, NY 11229-1259
Joseph Geliebter, President
PH: (718)998-0200

CONCENTRA MEDICAL CENTERS
405 County Ave.
Secaucus, NJ 07094-2606
Ardith Grandbouche, CEO
PH: (201)319-0952
TF: 800851-0034
FX: (201)319-1611
Founded: 1991. **Staff:** 80. Advises businesses on environmental and occupational healthcare issues. Geographic areas served: New Jersey.

CONNECTICUT CARE REVIEW
100 Roscommon Dr.
Middletown, CT 06457-1591
Dr. Edward Kamans
PH: (860)632-2008
FX: (860)632-5865
Founded: 1987. **Staff:** 20. Offers healthcare management services to businesses in the United States.

PHYLLIS M. CONNOLLY
e-mail: connolly@sjsuvm1.sjsu.edu
6627 Bose Ln.
San Jose, CA 95120
Phyllis M. Connolly
PH: (408)924-3144
FX: (408)924-3135
Founded: 1981. **Staff:** 1. Offers counseling on individual, group, family, and organizational interpersonal relationships, conflict resolution, crisis intervention, assertiveness training, and collaboration partnership models. Also active in nursing research, TQI activities, and organizational development. Industries served: education, healthcare, and government. **Conferences and Meetings:** *List of seminars and workshops available from firm upon request.*

CONOMIKES ASSOCIATES INC.
6033 W. Century Blvd., Ste. 990
Los Angeles, CA 90045
George S. Conomikes, Chairman & CEO
PH: (310)645-5100
TF: 800421-6512
FX: (310)645-3224
Founded: 1970. **Staff:** 16. Offers medical management consulting services. Focus is on the following areas: improving medical practice management, mergers and acquisitions, valuations for practice sales or mergers, strategic planning, income and expense sharing arrangements, and coding and reimbursement review. Industries served: medical practices. **Conferences and Meetings:** *Medical Office Management (series); Office Staff Workshops; Physician and Manager Workshops; Coding and Reimbursement Workshops; Managed Care Workshops.*

CONSOLIDATED SAFETY SERVICES INC.
url: http://www.consolidatedsafety.com
4031 University Dr., Ste. 400
Fairfax, VA 22030
Dr. Jolanda N. Janczewski, President
PH: (703)691-4612
TF: 800888-4612
FX: (703)691-4615
Founded: 1988. **Staff:** 35. Provides services in occupational health and safety; industrial hygiene; transportation safety; information services; and testing and certification of bio-hazard safety cabinets, clean rooms, and fume hoods. Industries served: government agencies, transportation, manufacturing, construction, and institutions in the United States. **Conferences and Meetings:** *Provides OSHA, D.O.T., and compliance monitoring training.*

CONSULTANTS IN MEDICAL IMAGING
url: http://www.cmixray.com
718 Huntingdon Pike
Jenkintown, PA 19046
PH: (215)663-2450
FX: (215)663-2451
A radiology consultation service providing independent film reviews and second opinion radiology interpretations to the legal community and insurance companies.

CONSULTANTS IN OPTHALMIC PLASTIC SURGERY
url: http://www.facialworks.com
Comerica Southfield Twr.
29201 Telegraph Rd., Ste. 305
Southfield, MI 48034
Dr. Frank A. Nesi, President
PH: (248)357-5100
FX: (248)746-0683
Offers plastic surgery on the eyes and the latest advances in laser resurfacing. Specific problems seen by consultants in ophthalmic plastic surgery include ptosis-drooping of upper eyelid, entropion-eyelid rolling inward, ectropion-sagging of lower eyelid, tearing-due to injury or disease, skin cancers (basal cell, melanoma, squamous cell, etc.), tumors and cysts-growth of eyelids and surrounding tissues, orbital fractures, trauma, congenital problems (lids or tearing), cosmetic surgery, and laser resurfacing. Surgical counselors are available to answer questions regarding proposed procedures including pre-op and post-opcare, surgical facilities, and transportation.

CONSULTATION FOR NURSING EXCELLENCE
3410 Hillsborough St.
Raleigh, NC 27607
Carolyn V. Billings, MSN, RN, CS
PH: (919)834-2708
FX: (919)833-6430
Founded: 1982. Offers direct consultation services to nursing departments in healthcare delivery systems to create "nurse-friendly" environments for retention and recruitment of professional nurses. Provides particular expertise in organizational development, change management, problem-solving, and training for professional practice models. Serves private industries as well as government agencies. Geographic areas served: U.S. **Conferences and Meetings:** *Models for Professional Practice; Barriers to Professional Actualization; Nursing Diagnosis; Focus Charting; Participatory Management (Quality Circles).*

CONSULTING NUTRITIONISTS
1501 S. Essex
Springfield, MO 65809
Susan S. Wood
PH: (417)882-7575
Founded: 1984. **Staff:** 1. Nutrition consultant for nursing homes and small hospitals. Also covers offices on aging. Conducts private practice work with a major health clinic. Serves private industries as well as government agencies. Geographic areas served: southwestern Missouri.

CONSUMER HEALTH INFORMATION CORP.
8300 Greensboro Dr., Ste. 1220
McLean, VA 22102-3604
Dr. Dorothy Smith, President
PH: (703)734-0650
FX: (703)734-1459
Founded: 1983. Full-service patient education programs on medications and disease. Industries served: pharmaceutical companies, general public, and managed care industry. Geographic areas served: international.

CONTINUING EDUCATION CONSULTING
e-mail: ca1birdre@aol.com
PO Box 600
Bomoseen, VT 05732
Wenda Bird

PH: (802)468-3200
FX: (802)468-8989
Founded: 1979. **Staff:** 2. Consultant for healthcare systems. Services include analysis, planning and management services for health clinics, ambulance services, hospitals, and nursing homes. **Conferences and Meetings:** *ACLS and Emergency Nursing Courses; Stress Management.*

COOK INTERNATIONAL INC.
PO Box 2128
Columbia, MD 21045
Clarence Cook, President
PH: (301)596-0462
FX: (410)992-7318
Founded: 1983. **Staff:** 12. Offers both consultation and operational field services for both basic and complex security problems required by government and private industry. Services include security surveys and vulnerability studies, personnel background investigations, security guard training, preboard screening for airlines, internal/external investigations, building security planning and design, and drug abuse programs. Industries served: automobile dealers, retail stores, U.S. and local governments, and military installations. Geographic areas served: national. **Conferences and Meetings:** *Drug Abuse in Industry.*

CORESOURCE INC.
6100 Fairview Rd., Ste. 1000
Charlotte, NC 28210-3291
PH: (704)552-0900
FX: (704)552-8635
Third party consulting firm offers expertise in managed healthcare.

CORPORATE HEALTH ADVANTAGE
411 S Sangamon, Ste. 1A
Chicago, IL 60607
Michael Carney
PH: (312)455-2510
FX: (312)455-8170
Founded: 1994. **Staff:** 5.

CORPORATE PSYCHOLOGICAL SERVICES PC
e-mail: howardg@idt.net
2166 Broadway, No. 6D
New York, NY 10024
Howard I. Glazer, Ph.D., President
PH: (212)832-0477
FX: (212)371-6102
Specializes in discrimination, harassment, wrongful termination, and disability. Geographic areas served: USA.

COST REVIEW SERVICES INC.
3724 Executive Center Dr., Ste. 101
Austin, TX 78731
Leigh Goodwin, Pres.
PH: (512)338-9196
FX: (512)338-4972
Founded: 1991. **Staff:** 18. Offers business related health services, providing auditing expertise for workmen's compensation claims for Texas workers. Also offers cost containment services. Industries served: businesses and municipal governments in Texas.

ROY C. CRAFT
e-mail: rcraft@iamerica.net
1707 Pecan St.
Bay City, TX 77414
Roy C. Craft
PH: (409)245-9991
A consultant in health physics concerning control, protection, contamination, regulation, and environmental impact.

CREATIVE HEALTHCARE MANAGEMENT, INC.
url: http://www.chcm.com
614 E. Grant St.
Minneapolis, MN 55404
Marie Manthey, President
PH: (612)339-7766
TF: 800728-7766
FX: (612)339-2065
Founded: 1981. Staff: 5. Offers organization and management of professional services in all healthcare settings including work redesign, executive and management team building, leadership development, competency, care delivery, professional practice and case management. Conferences and Meetings: *Professional Nursing; Work Redesign; Successfully Implementing Change in Hospitals; Documentation; 2-day Primary Nursing Assessment; Leading and Empowered Organization; Case Management; Competency.*

CRITERION SYSTEMS INC.
e-mail: criterionsys@prodigy.com
100 Crother Rd.
Applegate, CA 95703
Anthon C. Freitas, President
PH: (916)878-6689
FX: (916)878-6585
Founded: 1978. Staff: 10. Health services consulting firm focusing on medical equipment. Industries served: hospitals and medical office buildings. Geographic areas served: international.

CRITICAL CARE CONSULTANTS
4429 Kingsway
Box 72052
Burnaby, BC, Canada V5H 4P9
Kristy Molnar
PH: (604)438-7080
FX: (604)438-4013
Founded: 1985. Staff: 20. Health care consultants providing support services in the following areas: educational programs, decentralized management, clinical practice, policy and procedure, management/leadership, legal issues, ethics, and nursing theory. Training can be custom designed and offered on an in-house basis. Industries served: hospitals, professional nursing organizations, and healthcare manufacturers. Geographic areas served: Canada. Conferences and Meetings: *Clinical specialties & management topics.*

BRIAN CROWLEY, MD
5225 Connecticut Ave., NW, Ste. 215
Washington, DC 20015
Brian Crowley, MD, Principal
PH: (202)537-3300
FX: (202)686-7443
Provides forensic psychiatry consultation and expert testimony for civil and criminal: malpractice cases, including personal injury, pain and suffering, sexual harassment and abuse, and sexual misconduct by professionals. Also specializes in post-traumatic stress disorder; professional ethics and peer review; hospital and outpatient treatment standards; recovered memories; workplace violence; sanity; trial competency; and diminished capacity.

CROZER-KEYSTONE HEALTH SYSTEM
url: http://www.crozer.org
1400 N. Providence Rd., Ste. 4010
Media, PA 19063
John C. McMeekin, President and CEO
PH: (610)892-8000
FX: (610)892-8030
Founded: 1990. Staff: 68. Health services specialists in hospital administration and integrated healthcare systems.

CSCA CONSULTING INC.
e-mail: shellyc1@earthlink.net
18954 Strathern St.
Reseda, CA 91335-1150
Sheila L. Conrad, President
PH: (818)727-7158
FX: (818)727-1949
Founded: 1986. Staff: 5. Full-service marketing, planning and management consulting firm with emphasis on services to the healthcare industry. Major activities are the production of implementation-ready strategic marketing and communications plans which produce bottom line results and market research which defines new opportunities for increasing market share. The firm serves hospitals, Health Maintenance Organizations (HMOs), Preferred Provider Organizations (PPOs), physician groups, ambulatory care centers, clinics, public health agencies, and advertising agencies.

CUNNINGHAM'S SAFETY
e-mail: waltzxtx@aol.com
url: http://www.waltzxtx.com
6410 Ira Ingram Dr.
Austin, TX 78749-1852
W.B. Cunningham, III, P.E., C.S.P.
PH: (512)288-3416
FX: (512)288-3416
Founded: 1970. Staff: 1. Provides services regarding OSHA and JCAHO requirements with special expertise in hospitals. Geographic areas served: Texas and Southwest. Conferences and Meetings: *Permit required confined space workshops and lockout/tag out workshops for small thru large hospitals.*

CYLL ENTERPRISES MEDICAL SERVICES - DIVISION OF CYLL ENTERPRISES
4814 E. Monte Cristo Ave.
Scottsdale, AZ 85254
Michael P. Cyll, CEO
PH: (602)241-3775
FX: (602)788-7236
Founded: 1983. Staff: 2. Provides medical and technical services, temporary staffing, and consulting to private clinics, physicians, and hospitals. Services include specialized non-invasive cardiology diagnostic testing in private physicians' offices. Also provides temporary relief staffing for hospitals/clinics for echocardiography, holter monitoring scanning services, stress testing, stress echocardiography, trans esophageal echocardiography, front office consulting practices and operations, back office staff training/consulting, diagnostic equipment evaluation/recommendations, and used equipment brokerage/disposal. Maintains a technical network for equipment service repair/replacement and offers sales brokerage referrals. Industries served: medical community, private practice physician groups, HMO's, PPO's, clincis, community and general hospitals. Geographic areas served: metropolitan Phoenix area, Page, Arizona, Wickenburg, Arizona, and Flagstaff, Arizona.

ROBERT H. DAILEY, MD
e-mail: yeliad@aol.com
29 Charles Hill Cir.
Orinda, CA 94563
PH: (925)253-8275
FX: (925)253-8373
Expert in emergency medicine and medicolegal experience, including court appearances.

DAMSEY & ASSOCIATES LTD.
e-mail: dawcllc@juno.com
420 North Center Dr., Ste. 119
Norfolk, VA 23502
Joan Damsey, FACMPE
PH: (757)455-5554
FX: (757)455-5558
Founded: 1982. Staff: 15. Offers medical management services, including operations audits, marketing plans, managed care

contracting, mergers, management recruitment, professional practice setup, cost controls, productivity enhancement, and coding issues. Serves more than 1,500 physicians and hospitals in fourteen states. Serves three medical schools. **Conferences and Meetings:** *Presents seminars and workshops on practice management (at medical schools), coding, reimbursement enhancement, customer service, TQM, and CQI.* **Computer/Special Services:** Provides medical office systems design, evaluation, selection, and conversion.

BEVERLY L. DANIEL - CONSULTING NUTRITIONIST
865 W. End Ave., Ste. 14B
New York, NY 10025
Beverly L. Daniel
PH: (212)663-4830
Founded: 1988. **Staff:** 1. Provides individualized nutrition consultation. Receives referrals from health professionals, physicians, and psychologists, as well as self-referrals. Expertise in special medical problems. Serves government agencies also. Geographic areas served: New York City and vicinity primarily; available elsewhere upon request. **Conferences and Meetings:** *Nutrition education seminars.*

DAVE M. DAVIS
1938 Peachtree Rd. NW, Ste. 505
Atlanta, GA 30309-1253
Dave M. Davis, M.D.
PH: (404)355-2914
FX: (404)355-2917
Founded: 1976. **Staff:** 1. Offers nationwide consultations for psychiatric/mental health facilities in program development, planning, troubleshooting, and conflict resolution. Also provides forensic psychiatric services for criminal, civil, and probate cases. **Conferences and Meetings:** *Administrative Psychiatry Review Courses.*

LARRY M. DAY & ASSOCIATES INC.
23731 Willow Herb Ln.
Golden, CO 80401-9180
Larry M. Day, Pres.
PH: (303)526-0168
FX: (303)526-9343
Founded: 1979. **Staff:** 25. Provides medical practice management services to physicians and hospitals in the United States.

R.G.M. DECKER, INTERNATIONAL CONSULTANT
103 Roswell Green Ln.
Roswell, GA 30075
R. Gundy M. Decker
PH: (770)587-5708
FX: (770)587-5708
Founded: 1978. International healthcare consultant who assists management teams at treatment facilities worldwide. Experienced, multi-lingual resource person with competency in technical/clinical areas and management, specializing in Eastern Europe. Expertise in all phases of hospital commissioning, needs analysis and problem solving, cost control, program development (including preventive health/fitness), budgeting, nursing research, technical training, quality assurance, infection control, talent search, and marketing new products. Industries served: governments, industry, hospitals, and individuals. Offers nursing escort services worldwide. **Conferences and Meetings:** *Export Promotion; International Trade-Technical Assistance; Entrepreneur Strategies and the Role of Government.*

SUSAN B. DECRISTOFARO
e-mail: susan_decristofaro@dfcl.harvard.edu
1466 Broadway
Hanover, MA 02339
Susan B. DeCristofaro, RN, MS, OCN
PH: (617)826-0327
FX: (617)632-3710
Founded: 1979. **Staff:** 3. Consultant in healthcare administration and oncology nursing serving hospitals and other healthcare or-

ganizations including such nonprofit organizations as the American Red Cross, Home Care Associations, and Hospice. Also consults on complementary therapies (ie homeopathy). **Conferences and Meetings:** *Time Management; Complementary Homeopathy TherapiesTeam; Oncology.*

DEE & SMITH ASSOCIATES
1509 Via Fernandez
Palos Verdes Estates, CA 90274
Vivien Dee
PH: (310)373-4466
FX: (310)373-4466
Founded: 1983. **Staff:** 3. Offers consultation and case analysis for litigation on unsafe health practices and wrongful termination; specializes in psychiatric settings. Clients include hospitals and law firms. Geographic areas served: Greater Los Angeles metropolitan area.

RUTH DEVOE
17708 Parkridge Dr.
Gaithersburg, MD 20878
Ruth Devoe
PH: (301)330-3944
Consulting nutritionist in the Chesapeake Bay area and registered Dietitian in private practice.

JOHN H. DEVOR, MD
e-mail: Jdevor@aol.com
970 Dewing Ave., Ste. 200
Lafayette, CA 94549
PH: (925)284-5100
FX: (925)284-5551
Specializes in general orthopedics; occupational and forensic orthopedics; neck and lower back problems; provides medical-legal evaluations for personal injury and workers' compensation. Offers medical record review/analysis; reviews myelograms, MRIS and CT scans; gives expert witness testimony.

DFW ENTERPRISES
e-mail: dwenterprises@msn.com
352 S. Denvr St.
Salt Lake City, UT 84111
Robert Mucci, President
PH: (801)328-4027
TF: 800561-4231
FX: (801)530-1550
Founded: 1995. **Staff:** 7. Firm provides consulting services to private businesses and public sector entities on the establishment of drug- and alcohol-free workplace policies and programs. Will write policy and procedures manuals, provide training and technical assistance, design and manage drug testing programs and provide expert witness testimony throughout the U.S. **Conferences and Meetings:** *Policy Development for Drug- and Alcohol-Free Workplaces; Drugand Alcohol-Testing in the Workplace; Recognizing the Drug- and Alcohol-Dependent Worker; The Legal Ramifications of a Drug-Free Workplace.* **Computer/Special Services:** Designs and manages random drug selection by computer.

DICKSON GABBAY CORPORATION
1205 Westlakes Dr., Ste. 150
Berwyn, PA 19312
Brian Dickson, Chairman
PH: (610)640-2035
FX: (610)640-2036
Founded: 1989. **Staff:** 26. Offers expertise in the design and conduct of clinical development programs for pharmaceuticals. Also provides strategic advice on pharmaceutical research and development management and drug compound portfolio management. Performs executive search function for pharmaceutical and healthcare industry. Industries served: pharmaceuticals, healthcare including hospitals and universities, and government agencies. Geographic areas served: worldwide. **Conferences and Meetings:** *Foundation Course on Pharmaceutical Drug Develop-*

ment; Advanced Course on Anti-Infective Drug Development; Economic Assessment of Drug Development (cost benefit analysis).

NATALIE R. DICKSTEIN, DIETICIAN, CERT., DIABETES EDUCATOR

56 Clover Hill
Poughkeepsie, NY 12603
Natalie R. Dickstein
PH: (914)462-3113
Founded: 1968. **Staff:** 1. Provides nutrition counseling for individuals and groups. Specializes in weight control, diabetes, sports, cardiovascular system, and wellness. Geographic areas served: Dutchess and Ulster County, New York. **Conferences and Meetings:** *Diabetes update seminars for Dutchess Community College for health professionals.*

DIETARY MANAGEMENT ADVISORY INC.

625 Ridge Pike, Ste. E405
Conshohocken, PA 19428
John S. Vaughan, President
PH: (610)941-9787
FX: (610)941-9790
Founded: 1975. **Staff:** 5. Provides specialized food service consulting to healthcare institutions. Provides evaluation studies and program improvement implementation. Provides diagnosis of people/systems/facilities and equipment deficiencies to lead client to practical, economic and effective solutions and visible quantifiable results. Also specializes in food facilities design. Hospital agent in food service management contract bids, negotiations, elimination et al. Industries served: hospitals, life care complexes, nursing homes, and government agencies. Geographic areas served: United States. **Conferences and Meetings:** *Increasing Food Service Productivity; Determining and Increasing Food Service Productivity; Financial Management of the Food Service Department; Effective Budgeting for Health Care Food Service; Computer Hardware/Software: Taking the First Steps; Improving Clinical and Diet Office Productivity.* **Computer/Special Services:** Provides consulting or food service computer applications (software, hardware, et al) to healthcare programs.

DIETARY MANAGEMENT SERVICES

e-mail: cag@eaglesol.com
50 Cherry St.
Milford, CT 06460
Constance A. Greene, RN, MS, CDE, RD, CHT
PH: (203)874-6019
FX: (203)877-5918
Founded: 1984. **Staff:** 3. Offers wholistic health options and nutritional consulting services to individuals, families, and industry. Emphasis is placed on assessment of health and wellness status and developing a lifestyle program suited to each client. Programs enforce dietary variation and modification reflecting the client's needs including weight management, diabetes, cholesterol, infectious disease, and hypertension counseling. Also offers preconceptual and material nutritional counseling. Consultant to: manufacturing, hospitals, and healthcare programs. Geographic areas served: Fairfield and New Haven counties, Connecticut. **Conferences and Meetings:** *List of seminars and workshops available from firm upon request.* **Computer/Special Services:** Seventy-eight dietary nutrient analysis as part of assessment.

DIETS LIMITED

e-mail: rxnutriton@aolcom
527 Sawyer St.
South Portland, ME 04106
Paula A. Allen
PH: (207)799-6394
FX: (207)799-7695
Founded: 1978. **Staff:** 1. Provides professional healthcare counseling, specializing in nutrition and diet modification for individuals of all ages, groups, healthcare professionals, business/industry, and the media. Also offers food service management to institutions. Geographic areas served: Southern Maine Cumberland and York counties. **Conferences and Meetings:** *Nutrition for*

the Elderly; Feeding the Young Child; Menu Planning to Reduce Stress; Nutri-Wise Tours - supermarket tour offered to small groups to enhance knowledge of food labeling and best choices at point of purchase.

DIGESTIVE DISEASES FOUNDATION

e-mail: pixiedoc@aol.com
465 N. Roxbury Dr., Ste. 711
Beverly Hills, CA 90210
Herbert Rubin, MD, Medical Director
PH: (310)271-5650
TF: 800900-5650
FX: (310)271-3847
Founded: 1975. Specializes in stomach, intestine, colon, and liver diseases. Consultant to Department of Corrections, State of California (HMO oversight). Consultant to Medical Board of California (Doctor oversight). Medico Legal Consulation.

DIGITAL VISION INC.

6805 SE Milwaukie Ave.
Portland, OR 97202-5619
Gordon H. Keane, Jr., Pres.
PH: (503)231-6606
Founded: 1983. **Staff:** 1. Offers optical laboratory research and services, and related computer support to government and private sector industries on the West Coast.

DIVERSIFIED HEALTH MANAGEMENT INC.

1210 8th Ave. S.
Nashville, TN 37203-5004
James W. Carell, President
PH: (615)256-3590
FX: (615)742-8842

DIVERSIFIED HEALTH RESOURCES, INC.

875 N. Michigan Ave.
Chicago, IL 60611
Marshall S. Yablon, Chairman
PH: (312)266-0466
FX: (312)266-0715
Founded: 1979. **Staff:** 8. Offers healthcare consulting for hospitals, nursing homes (including homes for the aged), and other health-related facilities and companies. Specializes in planning and marketing. Also conducts executive searches for top level healthcare administrative positions. Serves private industries as well as government agencies.

DIVERSIFIED MEDICAL GROUP INC.

1125 S. Beverly Dr., Ste. 720
Los Angeles, CA 90035-1148
Richard Cirami, President
PH: (310)282-7125
FX: (310)785-0348
Founded: 1986. **Staff:** 9. Healthcare consulting firm serving clients in the medical institutional sector.

DR. ISAACS NEUROLOGICAL CONSULTANT

9030 C Three Chopt Rd.
Richmond, VA 23229-4614
Dr. Edward R. Isaacs
PH: (804)282-7671
Founded: 1977. **Staff:** 10. Medical consultants offer expertise in the neurological field.

DOCTORS PROFESSIONAL CONSULTING

Box S-3061
Carmel, CA 93921
Dr. George Elmstrom
PH: (408)625-5210
FX: (408)625-9372
Founded: 1987. **Staff:** 6. Serves as advisor to optometrists and ophthalmologists, covering both the technical and administrative aspects. Primary interest is the evaluation of the value of practices. Serves as troubleshooter for doctors who have management

problems and concerns. Certified by the courts as an expert witness. Geographic areas served: U.S.

THE DOGWOOD INSTITUTE, INC.
e-mail: rgpeyton@aol.com
url: http://dogwoodinstitute.com
16600 Alpharetta Hwy., Ste. 330
Roswell, GA 30076
Ronald G. Peyton, President
PH: (770)751-9571
TF: 800533-2440
FX: (770)751-9572
Founded: 1970. **Staff:** 7. Provides training for healthcare professionals, particularly for physical therapists and orthopaedic specialists. Training covers both management and clinical physical therapy related topics. Industries served: physical therapists, rehabilitation managers and administrators, hospital physical therapy directors, private practice owners, and office managers.

ROBERT K. DOLGOFF, MD
1749 Martin Luther King Way
Berkeley, CA 94709
Robert K. Dolgoff, MD, Principal
PH: (510)841-8484
FX: (510)540-1707
General psychiatry assessment of injuries and disability, fitness for duty, mental competence, and testamentary capacity. Evaluates professionals whose hospital privileges or licenses are being challenged. Offer both plaintiff and defense testimonials.

MALIN DOLLINGER, MD
e-mail: malinml@aol.com
700 Via Somonte
Palos Verdes Estates, CA 90274
PH: (310)375-4349
FX: (310)791-0969
Specializes in oncology and cancer, including causation, diagnosis, treatment, standard of care, asbestos, chemical, and radiation-related cancers. Assists attorneys in likely causation/liability prior to client representation. Gives pretrial reviews, conferences, reports, and depositions.

DOLLINGER PATHOLOGY MEDICAL GROUP
9270 Las Lomas Ave.
Atascadero, CA 93422
A.L. Dollinger, MD, Principal
PH: (805)466-5313
FX: (805)466-5231
Specializes in forensic pathology. Offers expert witness testimony. Geographic Areas Served: Central Coast and Central Valley of California.

SHELDON I. DORENFEST & ASSOCIATES, LTD.
e-mail: info@dorenfest.com
url: http://www.dorenfest.com
515 N. State St., Ste. 1801
Chicago, IL 60610
Sheldon I. Dorenfest, President
PH: (312)464-3000
FX: (312)464-3030
Founded: 1976. **Staff:** 80. Helps integrated healthcare delivery systems, as well as individual acute care hospitals, ambulatory clinics, long-term care facilities, and physician offices develop and implement successful information systems strategies that maximize the benefits of automation. Consulting services include: competitive analysis studies, strategic planning, vendor evaluation and selection, contract negotiations, managing implementation of new systems, process reengineering, benefits realizations, networking strategies, and education. Also assists suppliers shape better products for the health care information systems industry. Geographic Areas Served: Worldwide. **Conferences and Meetings:** *Current Trends and Future Directions in Health Care Information Systems; The Multihospital Invitational Symposium on Information Systems; and The CEO Symposium.* **Computer/Special**

Services: THE DORENFEST INTEGRATED HEALTHCARE DELIVERY SYSTEM (IHDS) DATABASE(tm) is an annual survey of the automation efforts in all U.S. integrated healthcare delivery systems, including key contracts, enterprise-wide and facility-specific installed information technology and buying plans. THE DORENFEST IHDS DATABASE(tm) is the latest in a generation of databases that have included THE DORENFEST IHDS 3000 SURROUND DATABASE(tm) and THE DORENFEST 3000 DATABASE(tm).

THE DRB GROUP, INC.
1661 Commerce Ave., N
St. Petersburg, FL 33716
Don Brophy, Pres.
PH: (813)568-0088
FX: (813)568-9776
Founded: 1990. **Staff:** 9. Medical equipment consultants provide service and maintenance.

TOBY DREWS
PO Box 19910
Baltimore, MD 21211
Toby Rice Drews
PH: (410)243-8352
FX: (410)243-8558
Staff: 1. Acts as expert witness and offers consultation in the field of substance abuse and addiction. Industries served: legal, healthcare, and government. Geographic areas served: mid-Atlantic and northeastern United States. **Conferences and Meetings:** *One-day seminars: Attachments and Excited Miseries in the Workplace; Getting Past Stuck-Points in Recovery; Replacing the Excitement of Sickness; and Getting Your Children Sober and Clean.*

DRUG EDUCATION ASSOCIATES, INC.
4739 Utica St., Ste. 207
Metairie, LA 70006
Harold C. Patin, President
PH: (504)454-0412
TF: 800938-3782
FX: (504)454-6934
Founded: 1981. **Staff:** 12. Develops, designs, and implements corporate, government and educational institutions' response to drug abuse prevention, detection and suppression. Provides assistance in policy and procedure design, training, education and establishment of setting of employer-based drug prevention and detection programs, especially involving drug testing, searches, use of drug detector dogs, undercover approaches, honesty testing and traditional investigative means. Principals have expertise in areas of drug enforcement, law, pharmacology, toxicology, research and behavior; and have testified as expert witnesses in many courts. Geographic areas served: worldwide. **Conferences and Meetings:** *Offers Drug Abuse Awareness Seminars frequently throughout the United States.*

DRUG FREE INC.
100 S. University Ave., Ste. 401
Little Rock, AR 72205-5213
J. David Eades, President
PH: (501)664-4434
FX: (501)664-8886
Founded: 1989. **Staff:** 25. Consulting firm managing and administering drug treatment programs for business in the U.S.

DRUG RESEARCH AND ANALYSIS CORPORATION
e-mail: indtznda@aol.com
PO Box 240308
Montgomery, AL 36124-0308
Henry A. Frazer, President
PH: (334)265-2700
FX: (334)265-2704
Founded: 1978. **Staff:** 12. Offers pharmaceutical/device product development service which provides support to pharmaceutical and healthcare industries in areas of clinical research, new pro-

duct development, and regulatory affairs. Clinical safety/efficacy studies and clinical pharmacology studies can be conducted using in-house facilities or management/monitoring on a multi-center basis. Consultation services available on product research and development issues and on regulatory affairs.

DRUG TESTING CONSULTANTS INC.
PO Box 706
Fairfax, VA 22030-0706
Robert Schoening, Pres.
PH: (703)273-1757
FX: (703)352-7124
Founded: 1987. **Staff:** 3. Conducts workplace drug testing programs for government and private sector in the United States.

RALPH E. DUNCAN, MD
25 Monument Rd., Ste. 100
York, PA 17403
Ralph E. Duncan, MD, Principal
PH: (717)741-4785
FX: (717)741-4696
Specializes in urologic surgery, uroradiology, and adult and pediatric urology. Provides expert witness testimony in urology for plaintiff and defense in medical-legal cases. Gives medical-legal reviews, peer reviews, second opinion consultations, and quality assurance consultations.

JUDITH L. DVORAK
13949 Friendship Ln.
Odessa, FL 33556
Judith Dvorak
PH: (813)376-0078
FX: (813)376-0078
Founded: 1982. **Staff:** 1. Nursing care consultant whose activities include consultation, managed care services, education, workshops, support groups for staff, individual counseling, group counseling, and marital counseling. Serves healthcare industries, nursing services, insurance companies, and colleges. Geographic areas served: U.S. **Conferences and Meetings:** *Pre Menstrual Syndrome; All Stressed Out and What To Do About It; The Impaired Nurse; Pain Management; Psychological Aspects in Physical Illness; Understanding Managed Care Services.*

DYNAMIC HEALTHCARE CONSULTANT INC.
3359 W. Main St.
Skokie, IL 60076
Marshall Maver, President
PH: (847)679-8219
FX: (847)679-7377
Founded: 1984. Healthcare consulting firm specialing in bookkeeping and accounting services to the medical and healthcare industries in Illinois.

MARY J. DYRA, REGISTERED DIETITIAN
c/o Association of Internal Medicine
211 E. Chicago Ave., Ste. 930
Chicago, IL 60611
Mary J. Dyra
PH: (312)944-6677
FX: (312)944-3346
Founded: 1977. **Staff:** 3. Applied clinical nutritionist provides individual consultation on nutrition and conducts weight loss classes as well as cholesterol screening program for corporations. **Conferences and Meetings:** *Cholesterol Levels for Diabetic; Eating Disorders Among Older Adults; The New Cholesterol Guidelines; Hypertension; Obesity; Diabetes.*

THE EAR MEDICAL GROUP, APC
e-mail: salth@aol.com
5201 Norris Canyon Rd., Ste. 230
San Ramon, CA 94583
Sean R. Althaus, MD, President
PH: (510)830-9116
FX: (510)866-1699

Provides evaluation and treatment of hearing and balance disorders.

ECRI
e-mail: ecri@hslc.org
5200 Butler Pike
Plymouth Meeting, PA 19462-1298
Joel Nobel, President
PH: (610)825-6000
FX: (610)834-1275
Founded: 1965. **Staff:** 200. Offers counseling in healthcare technology including strategic planning, management consulting, assessment, evaluation, specification and acquisition of medical devices and systems, healthcare facilities and equipment planning, risk managers, accident investigation, and forensic engineering. Additional services in industrial hygiene and environmental sciences including hazardous materials management, and general industrial hygiene services. Also offers expertise in medical technology assessment, medical equipment acquisition, and medical equipment purchasing. Industries served: healthcare and insurance, as well as government worldwide. **Conferences and Meetings:** *Seminars on assessment and acquisition of healthcare technology.* **Computer/Special Services:** Electronic On-Line Bulletin Board Health Technology Information Service, Computer Models (Radiology, Telemetry, ECG, etc.); Hospital Equipment Capital System (HECS) software.

EDUCATION CONSULTANTS
255 Oakland Park Ave.
Columbus, OH 43214
Beth Ann Stevenson, President
PH: (614)267-6020
Founded: 1984. **Staff:** 8. Nursing consultants primarily serving the healthcare industry through product flow studies, organizational evaluations, staff education, management enhancement, and employee health programs. Also serves government and industry primarily through employee health enhancement programs such as cardiovascular health, positive communication skills, stress reduction, and exercise. Geographic areas served: East of Mississippi. **Conferences and Meetings:** *Frequently provides cardiovascular programming for healthcare employees in the central Ohio area.*

EDUCATION DESIGN, INC.
e-mail: edi@eddesign.com
2170 S. Parker Rd., Ste. 140
Denver, CO 80231
Carol J. Applegeet, President
PH: (303)745-5996
TF: 800832-5115
FX: (303)745-5856
Founded: 1980. **Staff:** 20. Offers education and consultation to hospitals and surgery centers specifically in surgical services. Firm works in conjunction with the Association of Operating Room Nurses. Works with medical industry in the area of education and marketing of products. Accredited as a sponsor of CME. **Conferences and Meetings:** *Stress Management; Productivity; Basic Management; Aseptic Practice; Less Invasive Surgery Workshops for Nurses and Physicians, Consensus Decision Making and Team Building.* **Computer/Special Services:** Interactive Tutorial Computer Learning; Anatomy and Physiology.

EDUCATIONAL SERVICES
e-mail: edsers@buffnet.net
6748 Boston State Rd.
Hamburg, NY 14075
Merrily A. Kuhn, President
PH: (716)649-1350
TF: 800724-9866
FX: (716)649-1959
Founded: 1981. **Staff:** 3. Consultants in critical care nursing, complemenetary therapies, herbs, pharmcology, and general management programs providing educational services for nurses seeking continuing education units and certification in nursing.

Conferences and Meetings: *Programs are available in the following areas: management, critical care, pharmacology, medical-surgical nursing certification review, 12-lead EKG interpretation, assessment, NCLEX review, and arrhythmias recognition.* **Computer/Special Services:** CCRN audio tapes, a 19-hour program; Critical Care Challenge Game.

THE EDUMED CORP.
e-mail: eddy@skypoint.com
url: http://www.edumed.com
5610 Rowland Rd., Ste. 165
Minnetonka, MN 55343
Dale B. Moser, President
PH: (612)932-9922
TF: 800338-6339
FX: (612)932-9939
Founded: 1988. **Staff:** 9. Offers consulting to medical startup companies, physicians, and healthcare organizations in medical diagnostics for the PC and software systems with a particular focus on nursing and radiology. Industries served: healthcare and biotechnology in the U.S.

EINSTEIN CONSULTING GROUP INC.
501 Washington Ln., Ste. 302
Jenkintown, PA 19046
Gary Moran, President
PH: (215)886-4622
TF: 800765-9975
FX: (215)886-4640
Founded: 1985. **Staff:** 20. Firm offers expertise in healthcare consulting.

ELAN SYSTEMS INC.
415 Detroit St., Ste. 200
Ann Arbor, MI 48104-1117
Leo W. DiGiulio, Pres.
PH: (313)668-6738
FX: (313)668-0182
Founded: 1976. **Staff:** 7. Advises U.S. hospitals in medical management and planning.

CHARLOTTE ELIOPOULOS AND ASSOCIATES
e-mail: charlotte@charm.net
11104 Glen Arm Rd.
Glen Arm, MD 21057
Charlotte Eliopoulos
PH: (410)668-7055
FX: (410)668-7718
Founded: 1978. Offers consultation and educational programs to long-term care facilities and geriatric care agencies. Services include workshop presentation, form development, determination of staffing needs, and planning and development of new programs. Industries served: long-term care facilities and hospitals. **Conferences and Meetings:** *Alternative therapies in LTC, Hotlistic Chronic Care Nurising, Gerontological Nursing Update; LTC Clinical and Managerial Updates; Geriatric Care.*

PAUL D. ELLNER ASSOCIATES, INC.
e-mail: pdel@columbia.edu
url: http://lawinfo.com/biz/ellner
28 Jean Dr.
Cortlandt Manor, NY 10566
Paul D. Ellner, Ph.D., Principal
PH: (914)736-2122
FX: (914)736-0223
Specializes in clinical microbiology and infectious disease. Acts as a testifying witness or litigation consultant in medical malpractice, product liability, or disputes.

ELM SERVICES, INC.
e-mail: elmconsulting@worldnet.att.net
11600 Nebel St., Ste. 201
Rockville, MD 20852
Lee E. Mortenson, President/CEO
PH: (301)984-1242
FX: (301)770-1949
Founded: 1976. **Staff:** 30. For the past 20 years, ELM Services, Inc., has been the leader in guiding, advising, and supporting the practice and delivery of oncology nationwide. ELM has influence the art, business, and science of this industry as it continues to undergo radical change and transformation. ELM, oncology's premier consulting firm, is assisting hospitals, physicians, health care systems, and academic/university programs in the development of whole new approaches to cancer program management.

EMERGENCY MEDICAL TRAINING ASSOCIATES
507 Hoboken Rd.
Carlstadt, NJ 07072-1119
Kevin M. Agard, Director
PH: (201)935-4983
FX: (201)935-4831
Founded: 1991. **Staff:** 5. Coordinates education for prehospital care provider agencies; develops continuing education scheduling and tracking methods; monitors OSHA compliance for public and private sectors; and implements Emergency Medical Service/First Response program. Firm serves the Northern New Jersey area. **Conferences and Meetings:** *Mass Casualty Incident Management & Operations; Principles of Prehospital Documentation.* **Computer/Special Services:** Customized Automated Ambulance Call Report and Continuing Education Systems.

EMERGENCY & SAFETY PROGRAMS
Main St., Ste. 911
Chester, PA 19015-2902
Frank Poliafico
PH: (610)872-7447
FX: (610)872-5727
Founded: 1979. **Staff:** 15. Healhcare consulting firm offering expertise in emergency and safety programs and training to business and government agencies worldwide.

EMERITUS CORP.
1919 University Ave., Ste. 160
St. Paul, MN 55104
PH: (612)645-5300
FX: (612)645-0976
Health care consulting firm offers mental health management services.

THOMAS L. ENGEL, MD
California Pacific Medical Center, California Campus
3838 California St., Ste. 505
San Francisco, CA 94118
PH: (415)751-4914
FX: (415)751-1414
Specializes in otolaryngology, head and neck surgery, and pediatric otolaryngology.

ENI LAB INC.
e-mail: enilab@aol.com
2394 Rte. 130
Dayton, NJ 08810-1519
Ralph Shapiro, President
PH: (732)329-2999
TF: 800841-1110
FX: (732)329-1031
Founded: 1969. **Staff:** 30. Designs and develops tests for evaluating efficacy and safety of products and provides guidance for claims substantiation. Also advises on subjects related to analytical chemistry, microbiology, quality control, toxicology, nutrition, and product labeling. Geographic areas served: U.S., Canada, Mexico, Europe, and Japan. **Conferences and Meetings:** *Methods for Evaluating Bio-Availability of Nutrients and Calories; Current Aspects of the New Nutrition Labeling Regulations; Concepts in Acute Toxicology.*

ENVIROMED CORPORATION
e-mail: EARSZU@Bellatlantic.net
555 Blackwood-Clementon Rd.
55 Blackwood-Clementon Rd.
Lindenwold, NJ 08021
Richard L. Stepkin, President
PH: (609)435-7200
TF: 800521-5051
FX: (609)435-4599
Founded: 1977. **Staff:** 7. Industrial audiologist consults on the development and implementation of effective hearing conservation programs for industry. Services include mobile audiometry, audiogram interpretation, educational training, noise surveys, hearing protection programs, computerization, custom audiometric software sales, and expert testimony. Geographic areas served: New England and Mid-Atlantic states. **Conferences and Meetings:** *Loss Prevention in Hearing Conservation; Audiometric Workshops for CAOHC Certification.*

ENVIRONMENTAL INNOVATIONS CORP.
e-mail: hanshid@ix.netcom.com
url: http://www.busair.com/enviroco/index.html
7901 Oakport St., Ste. 3100
Oakland, CA 94621
Farshid Salamati, President
PH: (510)632-0104
TF: 800554-0037
FX: (510)632-0474
Offers Environmental Protection Agency, Occupational Health and Safety Administration, National Institute for Occupational Health and Safety, and American Industrial Hygiene Association certified field and lab services; comprehensive I.H. services; asbestos inspection and design management planning; real estate environmental assessments; and indoor air quality assessment. Industries served: aerospace, city and state government, school districts, retail, and public works. **Conferences and Meetings:** *Quarterly seminar by expert and professional to develop the program; training center with Majore University in India for overseas program.* **Computer/Special Services:** Special program for real estate site assessment; special program for fibers and particle movement in the cubical high-rise building; ISO 1400 specialist.

ENVIRONMENTAL SERVICE CONSULTANTS, INC.
url: http://www.esct.com/esct
501 Metroplex Dr., Ste. 316
Nashville, TN 37211
Philip Lee, Principal
PH: (615)833-6602
TF: 800260-8665
FX: (615)833-5443
Founded: 1986. **Staff:** 16. Specialists in the design of housekeeping and maintenance systems and laundry facilities for healthcare institutions. Geographic Areas Served: U.S. & Canada. **Computer/Special Services:** Vertical software systems for environmental service department.

ROBERT A. EPSTEIN MD
2702 Dana St.
Berkeley, CA 94705
PH: (510)848-0900
FX: (510)540-5343
Provides forensic psychiatric consultation, independent medical evaluations, and psychiatric evaluation and testimony. Specializes in child, adolescent and adult psychiatric disorders, psychological trauma, child custody, and physical and sexual abuse.

EQUIPMENT PLANNERS, INC.
557 Morris Ave.
Summit, NJ 07901-1308
Jay S. Pulaski, President
PH: (908)273-1616
FX: (908)273-7411
Founded: 1981. **Staff:** 9. Specialists in the management and purchase of fixed and moveable medical equipment. Works with healthcare institutions to provide accurate and pertiennt information during the various phases of new construction and renovations.

EQUITY FUNDING INC.
url: http://www.equityfund@earthlink.net
7071 Orchard Lake Rd., Ste. 300
West Bloomfield, MI 48322
John Cini, Pres.
PH: (248)932-3040
TF: 800444-7763
FX: (248)932-0827
Founded: 1987. **Staff:** 18. Vocational rehabilitational consultants. Geographic Areas Served: Michigan.

ERNACO, INC.
PO Box 6522
Silver Spring, MD 20906
M.M. Lippman, President
PH: (301)598-5025
Founded: 1979. Provides expert services in the biomedical, health and environmental sciences. Also offers specialized programs in biological and biomedical topics for professionals. Industries served: pharmaceutical, health, environmental; nonprofit organizations; and federal, state, and local government. Geographic areas served: U.S., primarily mid-Atlantic states.

HOLISTIC CHIROPRACTIC, DR. KEITH ERWIN
24 Onassy Plain St.
Bethel, CT 06801
Brice E. Vickery, President
PH: (203)798-7930
Founded: 1985. **Staff:** 2. Teaches professionals in chiropractic, medicine, dentistry and osteopathy how to identify the basic cause of spinal pain - the intervertebral cartilage (disc) lesion. Also involved in advertising, marketing, and sports medicine. Industries served: health insurance firms. Geographic areas served: worldwide. **Conferences and Meetings:** *Offers seminars on request for medical, chiropractice, osteopathic and dental organizations.*

FRANCIS M. ESPOSITO, PH.D.
8613 Abbotsbury Ct.
Raleigh, NC 27615
PH: (919)676-8779
Specializes in forensic toxicology, including blood alcohol interpretation, and blood and urine drug interpretation; board certified forensic toxicologist. Estimates blood alcohol levels and/or amount of alcohol consumed based on laboratory result or drinking history. Predicts impairment based on blood alcohol or blood drug level. Gives expert witness testimony.

ESTRIN CONSULTING GROUP, INC.
e-mail: estrin@cpcug.org
9109 Copenhaver Dr.
Potomac, MD 20854
Norman F. Estrin,, Ph.D., President
PH: (301)279-2899
FX: (301)294-0126
Founded: 1990. **Staff:** 1. Current areas of consulting include: regulatory submissions (510(k), PDP, NDA, IDE), Food and Drug Administration (FDA) liaison, interpreting FDA requirements, preparing for and participating in FDA meetings, regulatory strategy development, labeling compliance, litigation support and special projects. Industries served: medical device, drug, and cosmetic. Geographic Areas Served: NS, Europe, Asia. **Conferences and Meetings:** *Making Effective FDA Medical Device Submissions.* **Computer/Special Services:** Technical committee management for trade associations.

EXCEL CONSULTANTS INC.
e-mail: 73512.1271@compuserve.com
12305 Hardwick Ct.
Glen Allen, VA 23060
Joe R. Cabaleiro, Principal

PH: (804)360-5667
FX: (804)360-5733
Consulting company specializing in home infusion therapy. Offers assistance to organizations involved in or considering involvement in the provision of home care services. Services include JCAHO survey preparation, policies and procedures for home infusion therapy, competency testing services, infusion therapy resources, survey preparation tips, home infusion therapy guidelines, and competency test-a sample home infusion therapy competency test relating to total parental nutrition.

EYE CENTER
url: http://www.pkleaser.com
6500 Fairmont Ave., Ste. 2
El Cerrito, CA 94530
William Ellis, MD, Principal
PH: (510)525-2600
FX: (510)524-1887
Specializes in eye disability evaluation and rehabilitation, vision loss and related emotional effects; toxicology, pharmacological and chemical injury, radial keratotomy, cataract surgery, retroactive surgery, and diseases and surgery of the eyes and eyelids. Offers expert testimony and records analysis in workers' compensation, ophthalmic product liability, and medical malpractice.

EYTEK CONSULTING COMPANY
e-mail: eytek@txdirect.net
210 Bluff Knoll, Ste. 1
San Antonio, TX 78216-1915
Theodore B. Eyrick
PH: (210)496-9663
FX: (210)496-3481
Founded: 1981. **Staff:** 1. Offers technical management and biomedical engineering expertise to attorneys, medical device manufacturers and importers, insurance companies, hospitals, and other healthcare facilities. Provides inspection, evaluation, and testing services related to the design, manufacture, labeling, maintenance, regulatory compliance, and pre-use readiness of medical devices. These services include incident and failure analysis, forensic engineering studies, and hazard and risk analyses. Geographic areas served: North America and Europe.

FAIR OAKS PSYCHIATRIC ASSOCIATES
2277 Fair Oaks, Ste. 150
Sacramento, CA 95825
Janak Mehtani, MD, Principal
PH: (916)567-6622
FX: (916)567-6620
Acts as an expert medical witness specializing in neuropsychiatry and psychopharmacology for civil and criminal cases, including medical malpractice, personal injury, workers' compensation, and employee assistance.

FALTER & ASSOCIATES, INC.
e-mail: falter@bestweb.net
6 Joseph Wallace Dr.
Croton on Hudson, NY 10520
Elizabeth J. Falter, President
PH: (914)271-2761
FX: (914)271-0722
Founded: 1990. **Staff:** 2. Healthcare specialist with nursing background, providing change management, retreat facilitation, and management seminars on managed care, leadership, change, process analysis, and problem solving. Industries served: full range of business environments, as well as service and educational institutions. Comprehensive financial planning and management consulting to individuals and small business. **Conferences and Meetings:** *"Managed Care Continuum: Where are You?"; "Emerging Presence of Wall Street in Healthcare; Creative Change; Merging Education and Service in Healthcare"*

THE FARRIS GROUP
12161 Lackland Rd.
St. Louis, MO 63146-4003
Michael R. Farris, CEO, President
PH: (314)576-1563
FX: (314)576-0059
Founded: 1994. **Staff:** 30. Offers healthcare management services to healthcare providers and managed care organizations in the United States. **Conferences and Meetings:** *Numerous presentations on integrated healthcare delivery systems (integrating hospitals and physicians).*

RICHARD FEINBERG, PH.D.
e-mail: feinberg@pobox.com
38950 Blacow Rd., Ste. D
Fremont, CA 94536
PH: (510)794-2800
FX: (510)791-8572
Specializes in clinical and forensic psychology. Offers expert witness testimony in both, civil and criminal cases, including workers' compensation. Provides psychological assessments and psychotherapy for adults and children.

MINDY B. FEIRMAN
2440 M. St.
Washington, DC 20037
Mindy Block Feirman, R.D., L.D., L.N.
PH: (202)296-0777
FX: (202)251-7050
Founded: 1984. **Staff:** 5. Presents nutrition counseling and education programs presented to business, industry, and government, including Culinary Hearts Kitchen program developed by American Heart Association. Nutrition and health-promotion services also provided to individuals and groups. Nutrition topics include cardiovascular disease, weight management, gastrointestinal disorders, sports nutrition, eating disorders, prenatal and postnatal nutrition, and infant and pediatric nutrition. Serves private industries as well as government agencies. Geographic areas served: Washington, DC, and Baltimore, Maryland, metropolitan areas. **Conferences and Meetings:** *American Heart Association Culinary Hearts Kitchen Course and Seminar; The Choose to Lose Diet Weight Loss Program.* **Computer/Special Services:** Computerized menu analysis.

AVNER I. FELDMAN, MD
323 N. Prairie Ave.
Inglewood, CA 90301
PH: (310)674-0873
FX: (310)412-7948
Specializes in neurosurgery, head and spine trauma, tumors, aneurysms, disc surgery, and peripheral nerve injury. Provides industrial, personal injury and malpractice evaluations, and reports and medical record reviews. Offers consultation and expert witness testimony.

GEORGE G. FEUSSNER, MD
6241 NW 23rd St., Ste. 101
Gainesville, FL 32653-1599
PH: (352)371-6330
FX: (352)371-2338
Specializes in neurology, chronic pain management, and disability analysis. Acts as a medical expert witness.

FINAL ANALYSIS
e-mail: finalanalysis@msn.com
PO Box 6888
Tacoma, WA 98407-0385
Jon J. Nordby, Ph.D., Forensic Sci. Investigative Consultant
PH: (253)627-2739
FX: (253)627-0350
Forensic science investigative consultant specializing in death & medical investigation, including cause, manner of death, investigation of scenes, histories; criminalistics, including trace evidence, organic/inorganic identifications, comparisons, ballistics;

scene investigation, including bloodstain pattern analysis, evidence collection, event/accident reconstruction; forensic analysis; and analysis of scientific evidence, including chain of custody, recognition/collection issues, assess limitations/scope of sciences applied, assessment of omissions, opinions, and investigation and evaluation of expert testimony. Geographic areas served: International. **Computer/Special Services:** Computerized Timeline & Case Data Basescase Management.

MARVIN FIRESTONE
e-mail: firestone@pol.net
225 South Cabillo Hwy., Ste. 105D
Half Moon Bay, CA 94019
PH: (415)712-0880
FX: (415)712-0882
A brain injury rehabilitation specialist. Serves as a consultant in cases involving head injuries, brain dysfunction, and mental distress. Also specializes in clinical psychiatry, psychopharmacology, forensic psychiatry, legal medicine, and neuropsychiatry.

FIRST FITNESS EQUIPMENT CO.
841 Southway Cir.
Fort Worth, TX 76115
Jim Steenbergen, President
PH: (817)921-9919
FX: (817)921-1780
Founded: 1983. **Staff:** 8. Serving the fitness industry. Firm aids health/exercise club owners (nonprofit organizations, corporations, hospitals, government agencies, and schools) in saving time and money through involvement with facility design, exercise equipment purchase and layout, membership marketing, and club management. Geographic areas served: international **Computer/Special Services:** Club Fitness Area layout and design

PETER FISHER, MD
e-mail: brianwilson@wcgi.com
2100 3rd Ave., Ste. 2302
Seattle, WA 98121
PH: (206)728-9997
FX: (206)728-1460
Evaluates the biodynamics and medical aspects of aviation, industrial, criminal, civil and slip and fall injuries, and highway injuries, including the relationship of vehicle damage and claimed passenger injuries, multiple impacts, motorcycle, bicycle and pedestrian injuries, child seats and the role of safety belts, helmets, airbags and vehicular design. Analyzes the role of alcohol and other drugs in driver performance and accident occurrence, roadside hazards, and product liability.

FITCH & ASSOCIATES, LLC
e-mail: fitchassoc@aol.com
303 Marshall Rd., Ste. 5
Platte City, MO 64079
Joseph J. Fitch, Ph.D., President
PH: (816)431-2600
FX: (816)431-2653
Founded: 1984. **Staff:** 10. Offers emergency medical services counsel to private and public ambulence services, medical institutions, and government agencies in the United States, Canada, Latin America, Europe and Middle East. **Conferences and Meetings:** *EMS Management Academy - focus is on management and administration of medical transportation and pre-hospital care providers.*

FITNESS BY FISHER, INC.
e-mail: sfisherfit@aol.com
535 E. 86th St.
New York, NY 10028
Sandra Lotz Fisher, M.S., M.A., President
PH: (212)744-5900
FX: (212)879-0032
Founded: 1985. **Staff:** 5. Offers expertise as exercise physiologist, speaker, seminar leader, and writer on stress management, fitness, wellness, women's issues, marketing yourself, personal/

professional development, and adventure travel. **Conferences and Meetings:** *You Can't Sell if You Feel Like Hell; Stress Reduction on the Job; Balancing Work and Family; Staying in Shape on the Road; Personal Wellness for Peak Performance; When the door to opportunity opens - Are You There?; Marketing Yourself for Success.*

ANNE M. FLETCHER
e-mail: amfrdc@aol.com
PO Box 1352
Mankato, MN 56002
Anne M. Fletcher
PH: (507)345-6015
FX: (507)345-5268
Founded: 1983. **Staff:** 1. Registered dietician who serves as spokesperson for health, food, and nutrition-related companies. Also available for public speaking engagements for both professional and lay audiences. Has written extensively on health, medical, food, and nutrition-related subjects. Active in development of healthful low-fat food products and brochures. Geographic areas served: international. **Conferences and Meetings:** *Fish for all Ages; Learning From Losers: Keys to Success From People Who Have Lost Weight & Kept It Off.*

FLORIDA INSTITUTE OF NUTRITION AND DIETETICS, INC.
2627 NE 203rd St., Ste. 116
North Miami Beach, FL 33180
Vicki Ellis, MS, RD/LD, Associate
PH: (305)932-9155
FX: (305)932-3989
Founded: 1978. **Staff:** 4. Offers consulting in nutrition for athletes, weight control, diabetes, failure to thrive, cholesterol reduction, eating disorders, heart disease, and pediatrics. Specializes in the development of wellness programs. Industries served: law enforcement, education, banking, private and public sector industry in southern Florida. **Conferences and Meetings:** *Nutrition and Stress; Wellness in the 90s; Fat and Fiber; Supermarket Sleuth; Sport Nutrition Workshops, Ergogenic Aids; Feeding Children and Infants.* **Computer/Special Services:** Analysis by nutritionist - computer software.

LEONARD FLYNN CONSULTING
e-mail: lynnflynn@compuserve.com
254 Tennent Rd.
Morganville, NJ 07751
Dr. Leonard T. Flynn
PH: (732)591-1328
Founded: 1985. **Staff:** 2. Provides scientific and regulatory consultation for the pharmaceutical, personal products, and other manufacturing industries. Services include document preparation of scientific reports and submissions to regulatory agencies and review of compliance with federal and state regulatory requirements. Industries served: manufacturers and importers of pharmaceutical, medical device and related health and personal/consumer products plus their raw material suppliers. Geographic areas served: worldwide.

FMAS CORP.
11300 Rockville Pike, Ste. 1001
Rockville, MD 20852
PH: (301)984-6180
FX: (301)770-1423
Founded: 1980. Provides clients with healthcare management information concerning quality and cost effectiveness of services they pay for, deliver, or receive. Offers services focusing on company's ability to manage data derived from clinical care process reliably and efficiently. Includes developing clinical practice profiles through measurement of medical care processes, outcomes, and costs; health information management services; professional liability consulting; and professional education. Evaluations can range from one to thousands of medical records.

FMC
PO Box 1604
Simpsonville, SC 29681
Robert K. Ferguson, RN, President
PH: (864)967-9887
Founded: 1990. **Staff:** 1. Provides "consumer-end" services to manufacturers of medical products in the U.S.; uses a multidisciplinary approach to product development/improvement. **Conferences and Meetings:** *Offers image and pride workshops to cardiovascular services at Greenville Hospital system.*

FOOD, DRUG, CHEMICAL SERVICES
3771 Center Wy.
Fairfax, VA 22033
Bob West, Ph.D., President
PH: (703)352-5913
FX: (703)255-6434
Founded: 1976. **Staff:** 10. Provides scientific, regulatory, and management consulting services for a wide variety of product lines and industries including pharmaceutical, industrial and agricultural chemicals, biotechnology, toiletries and cosmetics, food additives, diagnostics, and devices. Areas of expertise include product integrity, scientific affairs, management, medical communications, environmental science, pharmacology and toxicology, clinical studies, FDA liaison, and product licensing. Geographic areas served: worldwide. **Conferences and Meetings:** *Product Safety Testing; Regulatory Compliance.*

FORENSIC ADDICTION MEDICAL ASSOCIATES
e-mail: deutsch@slipnet.com
PO Box 719
Clovis, CA 93613
Raymond Deutsch, MD, Principal
PH: 800-974-3578
FX: (209)638-1769
Serves as an expert witness specializing in the correlation of behavior with laboratory and clinical evidence of toxicity; characterological and personality disorders involving drugs and the law; and fetal alcohol syndrome.

FOWLER HEALTHCARE AFFILIATES, INC.
e-mail: fha@cyberatl.net
900 Cir. 75 Pkwy. NW, Ste. 1360
Atlanta, GA 30339-3035
Frances J. Fowler, President
PH: (770)955-5957
TF: 800784-9829
FX: (770)916-1278
Founded: 1984. **Staff:** 10. With a nationwide client base representing virtually all provider entities, our clinical, financial, operational and regulatory staff are experienced in acute, post-acute, specialty and senior services emphasizing the total continuum of care, including: Managed care, network integration, restructuring, facilities design, product line analysis, Medicare/Medicaid, senior services and physicians/MSOs.

RAYMOND FOX & ASSOCIATES
5090 Shoreham Pl., Ste. 100
San Diego, CA 92122-5934
Raymond Fox, President
PH: (619)296-4595
FX: (619)296-1838
Founded: 1984. Architecture firm specializes in medical facilities.
Computer/Special Services: Computer Design (C.A.O.).

ROGER FREED, MD
3020 Fillmore St.
San Francisco, CA 94123
PH: (415)563-1811
FX: (415)435-0220
Specializes in forensic psychiatry and pain management. Provides medical-legal evaluations in workers' compensation and personal injury cases, child abuse, criminal behavior, and post-traumatic stress. Offers social security and disability evaluations. Offers ex-

pert witness testimony in industrial psychiatry and medical malpractice cases.

FREEDOM WORKSHOP
Box 5881
Berkeley, CA 94705
Nancy Freedom
PH: (510)428-1184
Founded: 1981. **Staff:** 1. Interpersonal communication consultant specializing in personal development, human relations, family relations, library services, indexing, planning for aging, religion (comparative), and women's concerns. Additional expertise in neurolinguistic programming, Yoga, eating habits, and food and sugar addictions. Industries served: companies wanting stress relief for their employees, adult schools, recreation departments, libraries, authors and publishing companies desiring indexes, counselors starting up practice. Geographic areas served: northern California, primarily Bay area. **Conferences and Meetings:** *Freedom Workshop (NLP); Neurolinguistic Apprenticeship; Self-hypnosis; Soft & Gentle Yoga for Stress Reduction; Good News About Weight Loss.*

CHRISTOPHER S. FRINGS, PH.D.
e-mail: sfrings@compuserve.com
633 Winwood Dr.
Birmingham, AL 35226-2837
Christopher S. Frings, Ph.D., President
PH: (205)823-5044
FX: (205)823-4283
Founded: 1978. **Staff:** 2. Provides expert testimony and consultation for court and arbitration regarding abused drug testing. Consultant to industry and labor relations attorneys with abused drug testing needs and problems. Also offers seminars and workshops and keynote speeches on management issues. **Conferences and Meetings:** *Workplace Drug Testing; Effective Time Management; Stress Management; Managing Change; Management and Leadership Strategies for Succeeding in the 21st Century.*

GA ENVIRONMENTAL SERVICES
23 S. Warren St.
Trenton, NJ 08608
Robert J. Gogats, President
PH: (609)393-5089
FX: (609)393-7304
Founded: 1987. **Staff:** 19. Specializes in environmental audits; remediation planning and coordination; asbestos inspection, abatement, and monitoring; and occupational health investigation and monitoring. The firm serves governments, school boards, commercial building owners, realtors, lending institutions, and attorneys. Geographic areas served: New Jersey/New York. **Conferences and Meetings:** *Offers seminars on: New Jersey technical requirements for site remediation; technical report writing; preliminary investigation and document review; site inspections; bloodborne pathogens; lead abatement; technical assessments; and septic system inspection.* **Computer/Special Services:** Environmental Health Institute, an environmental services training center.

PETER G. GAAL, MD
145 N. Brent St., Ste. 102
Ventura, CA 93003
PH: (805)643-2375
FX: (805)643-3511
Specializes in thoracic and cardiovascular surgery. Reviews medical-legal matters for lawsuits.

GARRETT ASSOCIATES INC.
e-mail: lgarr95868@aol.com
PO Box 53359
Atlanta, GA 30355
Don Garrett
PH: (404)364-0001
FX: (404)364-0726
Founded: 1982. **Staff:** 5. Garrett Associates Inc. is a retained ex-

ecutive search firm specializing in coast-to-coast healthcare recruiting since 1982. We recruit for all management levels from CEOs to director level for hospitals and healthcare related organizations.

GASTROENTEROLOGY ASSOCIATES OF MEMORIAL CITY
e-mail: klein@insync.net
url: http://www.driraklein.com
Memorial City Professional Bldg.
10565 Katy Fwy., Ste. 305
Houston, TX 77024
Ira Klein, MD
PH: (713)932-8651
FX: (713)465-1940
Founded: 1978. Staff: 1. Offers consulting services regarding medical malpractice in gastroenterology and internal medicine.

GASTROENTEROLOGY CONSULTANTS
url: http://www.gastro.com/
166 W. Broad St., Ste. 303
Stamford, CT 06902
Peter W. Gardner, MD, FACP
PH: (203)967-2100
FX: (203)967-4872
Founded: 1989. Medical practice in gastroenterology and liver disease, providing information on and treating symptoms and conditions in chest pain, heartburn, liver diseases, jaundice, gallstones, colitis, diarrhea, abdominal pain, ulcers, ulcerative colitis, Crohn's disease, nervous stomach, hemochromatosis, lactose intolerance, hepatitis, hemorrhoids, constipation, and bleeding.

GENESIS TECHNOLOGY
e-mail: genmed@abs.net
11403 Cronhill Dr., Ste. B
Owings Mills, MD 21117
Stuart L. Gallant, Pres.
PH: (410)654-0090
FX: (410)654-0138
Founded: 1994. Designs and develops medical products; and process controls and instrumentation. Computer/Special Services: Offers systems design/integration.

THE GENSER GROUP
e-mail: genser@lawecon.com
url: http://www.lawecon.com
2200 Powell St., Ste. 890
Emeryville, CA 94608
Joshua G. Genser, Principal
PH: (510)237-6916
FX: (510)236-9851
Provides services for lawyers to increase effectiveness of economic testimony in litigation, including identifying economic issues which might enhance or threaten a case; locating appropriate economists to act as consultants or expert witnesses; translating the legal standards so economist understands the constraints; interpreting economist's analysis and opinions; t defending expert's deposition and deposing opponent's economist; assisting in the presentation of economic issues to the trier of fact.

MICHELE L. GERARD, PH.D.
1750 30th St., Ste. 224
Boulder, CO 80301
PH: (303)939-9650
FX: (303)939-9677
Specializes in brain injury medical cases. Offers expert witness testimony in the areas of neuropsychology; neurology, and neurosurgery for personal injury cases; ADA cases; and return to work evaluation.

GERONTOLOGICAL PLANNING ASSOCIATES
3041 Queensbury Dr.
Los Angeles, CA 90064
Louis E. Gelwicks, President
PH: (310)838-9400
FX: (310)838-6069
Founded: 1974. Staff: 3. Offers consulting services including planning, programming, and design of homes for the elderly. Services include assessment of existing facilities and services, new program implementation, and marketing to the consumer. Expertise is based upon the knowledge and experience of the needs and desires of older persons, derived from surveys and interviews of 400,000 senior citizens. Geographic areas served: U.S., Europe, and Asia.

C.L. GERWICK & ASSOCIATES, INC.
9500 Nall Ave., Ste. 404
Overland Park, KS 66207
Carl L. Gerwick, President
PH: (913)383-3464
FX: (913)383-3729
Founded: 1965. Staff: 24. Consulting dietitians provide service to small hospitals and extended care facilities. Also conduct individual client counseling. Serves government agencies. Geographic areas served: Kansas - Missouri. Conferences and Meetings: *Seminars on various food production topics are presented two or more times per year.*

GLASS & INSERRA
309 Middle Country Rd.
Smithtown, NY 11787
Kenneth S. Glass, President
PH: (516)360-2200
FX: (516)360-1328
Founded: 1990. Staff: 2. Offers medical consulting for insurance companies, including second opinions for orthopaedic surgery. Industries served: health, medicine, and safety (particularly insurance and orthopaedics), including government agencies. Geographic areas served: Long Island, New York (especially Suffolk County).

GLOBAL SAFETY & SECURITY, INC.
4739 Utica St., Ste. 207
Metairie, LA 70006
Harold C. Patin, President
PH: (504)454-6933
TF: 800938-3782
FX: (504)454-6934
Founded: 1983. Staff: 16. Designs, develops and delivers drug abuse detection programs, including: drug investigators, drug detector dogs, drug screen urinalysis, and urine sample collection. Serves private industries as well as government agencies. Conferences and Meetings: *Principals speak at national and regional conferences, conventions and seminars throughout the United States on numerous drug related topics.*

HERBERT L. GOLDBERG, DDS
e-mail: hlgoldberg@aol.com
url: http://www.libertynet.org:80/~goldberg/
528 Delancey St.
Philadelphia, PA 19106-4106
PH: (215)925-9551
FX: (215)627-7417
A certified dental consultant. Provides orofacial pain, dental, temporomandibular consultant expert witness testimony.

ARTHUR S. GOLDENBERG, DDS
151 E. Post Rd.
White Plains, NY 10601
PH: (914)682-8883
Provides consultation concerning pain of dental and non-dental origin; also provides case reviews and assessments and expert opinion testimony.

PETER G. GOLDSCHMIDT
e-mail: pgg@has.com
5272 River Rd., Ste. 650
Bethesda, MD 20816-1405
Peter G. Goldschmidt
PH: (301)652-1818
FX: (301)652-1250
Founded: 1968. Health care consultant whose work intends to improve the quality and productivity of healthcare, including research and development. Services include policy formulation and analysis; strategic management, including market analysis and product evaluation; information management; quality management; medical technology assessment; and health services research. Serves private industries as well as government agencies. Geographic areas served: worldwide.

JAY P. GOLDSMITH, DMD
121 E. 60th St.
New York, NY 10022
PH: (212)838-5895
FX: (212)838-6007
Specializes in oral and maxillofacial surgery.

GRANCARE HOME HELATH CARE
38933 Ann Arbor Rd.
Livonia, MI 48150
Sherry Cummings, Regional Vice President
PH: (313)432-6565
TF: 800932-5202
FX: (313)432-6788
Founded: 1985. Health services consultants offer expertise in elderly care services, wound care, home health care, private duty services, hospice care, skilled nursing, physical, speech & occupational therapy in, home x-ray, medical social workers, diabetes management, spiritual care, grief counseling, pain management. Conferences and Meetings: *Seminars and workshops are available.*

NANCY GREEN, R.M., M.S.N., STRESS MANAGEMENT
  CONSULTANT
5861 Sacramento Ave.
Alta Loma, CA 91701
Nancy Green
PH: (909)987-5157
FX: (909)987-9347
Founded: 1982. Staff: 2. Offers stress management consultation and seminars to all businesses and industries, as well as government agencies. Conferences and Meetings: *Time Management; Interpersonal Communications and Conflict Resolution (includes role-playing); Teen Suicide Seminar; Stress Management; Substance Abuse.*

GREENBAUM EYE ASSOCIATES
40 Park Ave.
New York, NY 10016
Scott Greenbaum, MD, Ophthalmologist
PH: (212)686-6075
FX: (212)532-1192
Ophthalmology surgeon specializing in cataracts, the cornea, and glaucoma.

CAROL B. GREENBAUM, R.D., C.D.E.
490 Bleeker Ave.
Mamaroneck, NY 10543
Carol B. Greenbaum
PH: (914)698-4743
Founded: 1986. Staff: 1. Provides nutrition counseling for all therapeutic needs; weight reduction and maintenance; and guidance for normal nutrition for all ages, sports, etc., MD-referred or verified. Consultant is a Certified Diabetes Educator. Serves individuals or groups (lecture or round-table). Geographic areas served: Westchester County, New York.

CADVAN O. GRIFFITHS JR., MD
e-mail: cadvan@aol.com
url: http://www.plasticsurgery.org
11600 Wilshire Blvd., Ste. 120
Los Angeles, CA 90025
PH: (310)477-5558
FX: (310)274-7564
Offers medical-legal consultation and malpractice review related to cosmetic and reconstructive surgery involving the head, neck, hands, and extremities.

MURRAY GROSSAN, MD
e-mail: entconsult@aol.com
url: http://www.ent-consult.com
Cedars Sinai Medical Towers
8631 W. 3rd St., Ste. 440E
Los Angeles, CA 90048
PH: (310)659-1006
FX: (310)652-9906
Specializes in problems that involve hearing loss, tinnitus, and dizziness. Provides audiograms, tinnitus diagnosis and treatment, electronystagmography, brain stem auditory evoked response, otoacoustic emissions for objective hearing loss/damage recording, sinus and nasal evaluation for toxic exposure, objective measurements of mucocilliary impairment, and scar evaluation.

THOMAS C. HALL, M.D.
e-mail: all4halls@earthlink.net
1348 Sudden Valley
Bellingham, WA 98226-4836
Thomas C. Hall
PH: (360)734-8170
FX: (360)738-6711
Founded: 1970. Staff: 1. Offers medical consultation services related to medical malpractice, medical disability, and general medico-legal problems, with special emphasis on cancer cases. Serves private industries as well as government agencies.

RICHARD HAMER ASSOCIATES INC.
e-mail: bbkp18c@prodigy.com
Wedgwood Sta.
PO Box 16598
Fort Worth, TX 76162
Richard A. Hamer, President
PH: (817)294-3644
FX: (817)294-3761
Founded: 1983. Staff: 4. Active in the development of premarket approval strategies for new drug and medical device products; preparation, and submission and approval monitoring of investigational and/or premarketing approval applications (IND, IDE, NDA, ANDA, PMA, 510(k), etc.); monitoring of preclinical and clincial studies for compliance with GLP and GCP compliance; and review of labeling, advertising and promotional materials. Conducts comprehensive facility audits to evaluate GMP compliance, develops practical standard operation procedures and documentation systems to facilitate GMP compliance, and provides effective representation of clients' interests during FDA site inspections or meetings with regulatory agencies. Offers continuous monitoring of regulatory developments and provides recommendations for dealing with issues of specific interest. Industries served: pharmaceuticals, medical devices, cosmetics, and food. Geographic areas served: U.S., Canada, Western Europe, and Far East. Conferences and Meetings: *FDA Good Manufacturing Practices Regulations for Drug Products; FDA Good Manufacturing Practices Regulations for Medical Devices; GMP Training Seminars (specifically adapted to client's operations).*

HAMILTON/KSA
url: http://www.kurtsalmon.com
1355 Peachtree St. NE, Ste. 900
Atlanta, GA 30309-0900
W. Barry Moore, Exec VP
PH: (404)892-3436
FX: (404)898-9590

Founded: 1946. Staff: 65. Healthcare management consultants with experience in strategic planning, physician organization and relationships, facilities planning, technology process reengineering, quality improvement, and organization structure for the healthcare industry.

PETER F. HAMPL, DDS
e-mail: phampl@narrows.com
url: http://www.phampl.com
1901 S. Cedar, Ste. 106
Tacoma, WA 98405
PH: (253)383-5722
FX: (253)383-0696
Dentistry services include Human Identification; Bite Mark Analysis; Dental Liability in malpractice; mass disaster prepardness; human abuse

HANS TRONNES ASSOCIATES
e-mail: trornes@innocent.com
4311 Cedarwood Rd., Ste. 106
Minneapolis, MN 55416-3828
Hans F. Tronnes, CEO & President
PH: (612)546-3866
FX: (612)546-2417
Founded: 1986. Staff: 6. Works with healthcare leaders in strategic planning, physician/hospital integration, consolidation of hospitals, master planning, and programming. Geographic areas served: U.S. and Canada.

RONALD B. HARPER INC.
232 S. Beverly Dr., Ste. 222
Beverly Hills, CA 90212
Ronald B. Harper, Ed.D., President
PH: (310)550-8367
FX: (310)550-8483
Founded: 1978. Staff: 3. Performs vocational evaluations on disabled persons, and develops rehabilitation programs to return them to work. Consults with attorneys on impact of physical, mental, or social disabilities on earning capacity, including appearances as expert witness in personal injury, family law, wrongful death, and wrongful termination litigation. Conferences and Meetings: *Brain Injury Delegation; City Ambassador Program to China.*

HARVEY TROIANO & ASSOCIATES INC.
7750 N. MacArthur Blvd., Ste. 120-333
Irving, TX 75063
Nan M. Troiano, RN, MSN, President
PH: (972)257-0034
FX: (972)257-1104
Founded: 1986. Staff: 16. Healthcare consulting firm with expertise in adult, child, and baby health; risk factors; and human fertility. Serves hospitals and medical professionals in the U.S.

BARBARA HASS, P.D.
1321 Crestline Dr.
Santa Barbara, CA 93105
Barbara Hass
PH: (805)682-8907
FX: (805)682-0120
Founded: 1980. Staff: 1. Nutrition counseling for individuals or groups, recipe and menu planning for institutions (nursing home, retirement center, half-way house), and nutrition editing for newsletters, brochures, and articles. Conferences and Meetings: *Thinner Thru Choice, a ten-week weight management and nutrition course.*

HATCH AND ASSOCIATES, INC.
5 Revere Dr., Ste. 200
Northbrook, IL 60062
Stephen W. Hatch, President
PH: (847)498-7363
FX: (847)205-5330
Founded: 1990. Works with healthcare organizations to provide

strategic direction, consulting on medical staff development and physician relationships. Also assist clients with issues of organization and governance.

HAYES INC.
157 S. Broad St., Ste. 200
Lansdale, PA 19446
Winnie Hayes, Ph.D., Pres.
PH: (215)855-0615
FX: (215)855-5218
Founded: 1989. Staff: 16. Offers healthcare services, focusing on environment health. Industries served: healthcare, insurance, and businesses regionally.

HC ASSOCIATES INTERNATIONAL, INC.
e-mail: info@hcassoc.com
url: http://www.hcassoc.com
1455 Lincoln Pkwy., Ste. 180
Atlanta, GA 30346-2209
Nancy Sypniewski, President
PH: (770)673-0543
FX: (770)673-0648
Founded: 1988. Offers training, implementation consulting, software selection consulting and related computer development. Industries served: all. Geographic areas served: U.S., Canada, and Europe. Woman owned firm. Conferences and Meetings: *Transition Management - The People Issues Caused by Technology Change; Project Management; Using Your AS/400 - both tech and user programs.*

HCIA, INC.
e-mail: info@hcia.com
300 E. Lombard St.
Baltimore, MD 21202
George Pillari, Chairman/CEO
PH: (410)576-4600
TF: 800568-3282
FX: (410)930-7611
Founded: 1985. Staff: 500. Provides comparative/normative information concerning the cost and quality of healthcare. Specific areas of expertise include review of patterns of patient care, drug and clinical service utilization, and approaches for quality improvement and utilization management, primarily for acute care facilities. Industries served: education, government agencies, healthcare, nonprofit organizations, and pharmaceutical. Geographic areas served: U.S. and international. Conferences and Meetings: *Managed Care; JCAHO Preparation; Physician Education; Health Care Resource Consumption.*

H.C.L.S. INC.
45150 Polaris Ct.
Plymouth, MI 48170
Donna Konopka, President
TF: 800829-4257
FX: (313)414-3421
Founded: 1987. Staff: 22. Provides dental and medical healthcare counsel, including expertise in periodontal, quality assurance, training, and CLIA issues. Industries served: dental, medical, veterinary, and podiatry. Geographic areas served: U.S., Canada, and several other countries. Conferences and Meetings: *OSHA Compliance; Periodontal Patient Management; CLIA; Quality Assurance.*

HEALTH ACTION COUNCIL OF NORTHEAST OHIO
33610 Solon Rd., Ste. 4
Solon, OH 44139
PH: (440)248-2559
FX: (440)248-5830
Founded: 1983. Conducts management training sessions.

HEALTH ADVANCEMENT, INC.
PO Box 53444
Knoxville, TN 37950-3444
Judy B. Cox, CHES, President

PH: (423)691-4689
FX: (423)588-1319
Founded: 1990. **Staff:** 2. Health care consultants offer computerized health risk appraisals, pre-employment health screening, health education workshops, corporate health fairs, and health education consultation. Serves private industries as well as government agencies. **Conferences and Meetings:** *Blood Pressure; Cholesterol; Back Care; First Aid/CPR; Nutrition/Weight Management; Lifestyle Management; Smoke Cessation; Stress Management.*

HEALTH CARE CONSULTANTS OF AMERICA, INC.
e-mail: hccaol@aol.com
1054 Claussen Rd., Ste. 307
Augusta, GA 30907
PH: (706)738-2078
TF: 800253-4945
FX: (706)738-9839
Founded: 1988. Offers hospital and physician services regarding managed care and fees and coding issues.

HEALTH CARE EQUITY GROUP INC.
2025 E. Beltline Ave. SE
Grand Rapids, MI 49546-7630
Mark Nadel, Pres.
PH: (616)957-4478
FX: (616)285-5422
Founded: 1989. **Staff:** 10. Advises U.S. hospitals on healthcare management.

HEALTH CARE MANAGEMENT ASSOCIATES INC.
200 Broadway, Ste. 301
Lynnfield, MA 01940-2349
Michael O. Pulling, Pres., Treas.
PH: (781)596-0122
FX: (781)595-3540
Founded: 1979. **Staff:** 6. Advises nursing homes and hospitals on healthcare management practices. Geographic areas served: New York, New Jersey, and New England.

HEALTH CARE RESOURCES INC.
e-mail: hcrl@ntplx.net
url: http://www.mysticflame.com/hcr
936 Silas Deane Hwy.
Wethersfield, CT 06109-4202
George Moser, Pres.
PH: (860)563-4566
FX: (860)257-4004
Founded: 1973. **Staff:** 27. Advises state agencies, healthcare providers and corporations on healthcare management; medicare/medicaid regulations, billing, cost reporting, and appeal representation; recovering state and federal reimbursements feasibility studies and special studies. **Conferences and Meetings:** *To various healthcare associations.* **Computer/Special Services:** Medicare/Medicaid billing.

HEALTH CARE REVIEW CONSULTANTS, INC.
PO Box 36949
Shreveport, LA 71133-3941
Ellie M. Higginbotham, President/CEO
PH: (318)635-2077
FX: (318)636-9736
Founded: 1986. **Staff:** 8. Provides healthcare review consulting services to hospitals, physicians, and others. Specializes in utilization/quality assurance medical review, healthcare data analysis, and healthcare cost containment issues. Helps organizations in coping, dealing, and responding to Medicare's regulations and policies especially the Peer Review Organization (PRO) review activities and functions. Industries served: hospitals, outpatient surgery centers, ambulatory surgery centers (ASC), home health agencies, nursing homes, physicians, hospital associations, medical associations, and other consulting firms. Geographic areas served: national. **Conferences and Meetings:** *Advance and Basic Techniques for Coping with PRO Review; The New PRO Scope of*

Work - Plus More Information; Ways to Reduce PRO Liability and Cope with PRO Review; Understanding and Coping with PRO Review; Reducing your PRO Liability.

HEALTH CARE SERVICES, INC.
Prospective Medicine Center
6220 Lawrence Dr.
Indianapolis, IN 46226
Jack H. Hall, President
PH: (317)549-3600
FX: (317)549-3670
Founded: 1976. **Staff:** 5. Health care consulting group provides expertise in health wellness programs and health hazard appraisal and analysis. Geographic areas served: U.S. **Computer/Special Services:** Maintains Health Hazard Appraisal, a health risk appraisal computer program.

HEALTH COMMUNICATIONS, INC.
e-mail: info@hcomm.com
url: http://www.hcomm.com
20 Highland Ave., Ste. 6
Metuchen, NJ 08840-1949
Joel L. Shapiro
PH: (732)548-9130
FX: (732)548-8555
Founded: 1984. **Staff:** 20. The company's activities focuses on medical writing for pharmaceuticals, producing principally clinical manuscripts, scientific exhibits, regulatory support documents, product monographs, and related projects. The firm offers a complete range of pre-marketing and post-marketing services, including symposium development as well as audiovisual and other specialized programs. Industries served: healthcare, pharmaceutical, and medical device manufacturers. Geographic areas served: U.S. and Europe.

HEALTH CONSULTANTS INC.
420-D Madison St.
Clarksville, TN 37040
Ronald J. Lott
PH: (931)552-4655
FX: (931)552-7596
Founded: 1986. **Staff:** 11. Specialists in occupational safety and health. Industries served: manufacturing. Geographic areas served: U.S. **Conferences and Meetings:** *Safety Managers Update (OSHA Reform Act, Regulatory Trends); The Aging Workforce; Lockout/Tagout - A Practical Approach.*

HEALTH COST CONSULTANTS INC.
1850 Centennial Park Dr., Ste. 200
Reston, VA 20191
Debbie L. Scheff, Pres.
PH: (703)262-7800
FX: (703)262-7940
Founded: 1993. **Staff:** 35. Advises businesses and public healthcare organizations on health costs and economics. Geographic areas served: Washington, D.C. Metro area.

HEALTH ENHANCEMENT SYSTEMS, INC.
9 Mercer St.
Princeton, NJ 08540
Louis Young
PH: (609)924-7799
TF: 800437-6668
FX: (609)497-0739
Founded: 1981. **Staff:** 4. Offers consulting services in the evaluation, planning, implementation and assessment of medical care services to employees, including cost containment strategies and health and fitness programs.

HEALTH EQUIPMENT LOGISTICS & PLANNING INC.
850 Central Pkwy. E., Ste. 260
Plano, TX 75074
Larry Hampton, President/CEO

PH: (972)985-1313
FX: (972)423-2398
Founded: 1983. **Staff:** 23. Medical equipment consultants and planners. Industries served: healthcare. **Computer/Special Services:** Maintains third generation custom software integrating medical equipment budgeting, planning, specification development, purchasing and expediting.

HEALTH EVALUATION SYSTEMS
130 7th St., Ste. 1140
Pittsburgh, PA 15222-3409
Carol Swan, M.D., Owner
PH: (412)281-8727
FX: (412)281-8728
Founded: 1987. **Staff:** 7. Offers expertise in health evaluation. Industries served: insurance, transportation, certified medical/review offices (all safety sensitive areas for drug and alcohol testing, workers compensation issues). Geographic areas served: U.S. **Conferences and Meetings:** *Drug and Alcohol Testing: Countdown to Implementation; U.S. Department of Transportation Regulations and The Omnibus Transportation Act.*

HEALTH AND HYGIENE/ELB
url: http://www.health-hygiene.com
605 Eastowne Dr.
Chapel Hill, NC 27514
Hank Barnum, C.O.O.
PH: (919)967-2228
FX: (919)493-2263
Founded: 1969. **Staff:** 140. Offers occupational safety and health counseling services to a wide range of industries relative to workers compensation and OSHA activities. Also offers a full range of environmental monitoring services and a full line of health screening equipment. Geographic areas served: U.S., Canada, and Europe. **Conferences and Meetings:** *OSHA Update (annual program to update clients on OSHA activities); numerous training courses including pulmonary and audiometric technician and safety and industrial hygiene topics.* **Computer/Special Services:** The Industrial Workstation - computer program that lets you store audiometric and pulmonary test data. Sprintware software - to help companies manage employee health, safety, and personnel data.

HEALTH INFORMATION CENTER
RR1 Box 850
Woodstock, VT 05091
Susan N. Hastings
PH: (802)457-3455
Specializes in aspects of healthcare.

HEALTH MANAGEMENT ASSOCIATES INC.
e-mail: info@hlthmgt.com
url: http://www.hlthmgt.com
120 Washington Sq. N., Ste. 705
Lansing, MI 48933-1608
Jay Rosen, Principal
PH: (517)482-9236
FX: (517)482-0920
Founded: 1985. **Staff:** 30. Provides expertise in the areas of health and human services policy, finance and economics, evaluation, and health data analysis. Serves public and private sector health and human services clients in the U.S., primarily Michigan.

HEALTH MANAGEMENT INC.
e-mail: hmi123@aol.com
1828 L St. NW, Ste. 908
Washington, DC 20036
Robinson Abraham, President
PH: (202)887-8110
FX: (202)659-8983
Founded: 1983. **Staff:** 12. Healthcare consultants experienced with programs in management consultation; management of healthcare institutions; staff development and training; manage-

ment development and training; operations of hospitals, nursing homes, and clinics; institutional research and feasibility studies; corporate fitness program development; patient and public relations; and healthcare service organizational analysis and change management. Industries served: hospital referrals from Washington, DC, including government. Geographic areas served: Washington, DC, and Maryland. **Conferences and Meetings:** *Nursing Management; Criteria Based Performance Appraisal; Manager Development - Key to Improved Productivity.*

HEALTH MANAGEMENT RESOURCES INC.
e-mail: hmrrudy@aol.com
url: http://www.microtechgrp.com/hmr.html
8401 Corporate Dr., Ste. 400
Landover, MD 20785
Rudolph A. Coleman, CEO & President
PH: (301)429-2300
FX: (301)429-2314
Founded: 1983. **Staff:** 60. Health care consultants. Industries served: healthcare. Geographic areas served: U.S. and international. **Conferences and Meetings:** *Immunization; Women's Health; Managed Healthcare; Health Promotion Research and Evaluation; Business Process Reengineering; and Malcolm Baldrige Research; Facilities Management; Information systems.*

HEALTH MANAGEMENT STRATEGIES INTERNATIONAL, INC.
1725 Duke St., Ste. 300
Alexandria, VA 22314
William R. Vandervennet, Jr., President/CEO
TF: 800624-6472
FX: (703)706-4803
Founded: 1985. **Staff:** 250. Provides tailored, comprehensive, and mental health cost management services. Services include inpatient and outpatient utilization management, case management, retrospective record audits, data consulting, and network development. Mental Health Review Criteria are available for licensing and also provides on-site training in their application. As a leader in the managed mental healthcare field, firm has developed mental health provider networks throughout the country and offers them through its Mental Health Managed Care Program. Industries served: employer groups, insurance companies, TPAs, HMOs/PPOs, and government agencies. Geographic areas served: national. **Conferences and Meetings:** *Mental Health Strategies Forums.*

HEALTH METRICS, INC.
15312 Spencerville Ct., Ste. 201
Burtonsville, MD 20866
Thomas Armeli
PH: (301)384-0800
TF: 800878-3466
FX: (301)384-9854
Founded: 1976. **Staff:** 8. A consulting, research and occupational health service firm specializing in human factors applications with expertise and capabilities in human factors research, work physiology, biomechanics, occupational health, medical information management, and program development. The principal areas of service and research include: applied physiology, occupational health, preventive medicine, job/task analysis, human nutrition, health and fitness program development, biomechanics, physical fitness assessment, medical/physical standards, and sports medicine. Projects have included: design of job-related physical ability tests, studies on the effects of physical fitness programs on overall occupational health, development of physical performance standards for public safety workers, military physical performance task analysis, expert testimony in litigation and occupational health hearings, development of fitness testing and training centers, and design and instruction of exercise leadership classes. **Conferences and Meetings:** *Certified physical fitness coordinator workshops for public safety employees. Fitness professionals.* **Computer/Special Services:** FITSCAN software for physical fitness assessment and exercise prescription, Dine Healthy software for nutrittional analysis.

THE HEALTH AND NUTRITION EDUCATION RESOURCE GROUP INC.
1507 Druid Hill Ave.
Baltimore, MD 21217
Catherine Campbell, WIC Coordinator
PH: (410)383-3337
FX: (410)383-3338
Founded: 1991. **Staff:** 5. Registered dietitians who counsel patients referred by physicians regarding nutrition. Also plan menus for healthcare institutions and sometimes train staff. Conduct continuing education activities for dietitians also. Industries served: pregnant Medicaid recipients, diabetic Medicaid recipients, pediatric Medicaid recipients from birth through age 20, and subscribers to Travelers Managed Care Services are covered; other clients are expected to pay at the time of service. Geographic areas served: Baltimore, Maryland, and surrounding counties. **Conferences and Meetings:** *Make Dietetics Your Business (how to set-up, position, and expand a private group dietetic practice).* **Computer/Special Services:** Training regarding Nutrient Analysis, Food Service Software, and Newton/Software Products.

HEALTH OUTREACH PROJECT INC.
3030 Campbellton Rd. SW
Atlanta, GA 30311-5410
Sandea McDonald, Pres.
PH: (404.)346-3922
FX: (404)346-3036
Founded: 1986. **Staff:** 5. Educates HIV positive patients and alcohol and substance abusers in healthcare techniques regionally.

HEALTH QUEST AFFILIATES, INC.
600 Corporate Pt., Ste. 200
Culver City, CA 90230
Charles Klivans, MHA, Vice President
PH: (805)495-3100
FX: (310)388-0345
Founded: 1991. Offers healthcare services for integrated provider and payer systems. **Conferences and Meetings:** *Presents integrated healthcare symposia.*

HEALTH SCIENCE, INC.
418 Wall St.
Princeton, NJ 08540
David S. Goldberg, President
PH: (609)924-7616
TF: 800841-8923
Founded: 1984. **Staff:** 2. Specialists in rehabilitation technology for speech disorder and physically disabled persons. Offers demonstrations, evaluations and sales of the following types of equipment: augmentative speech communication systems, adaptive switches and specialty controls, and computer access devices. Industries served: hospitals and rehabilitation centers, schools, and special service organizations such as United Cerebral Palsy Association, Department of Human Services, etc. Geographic areas served: New Jersey, New York, Pennsylvania, Delaware, Connecticut, Vermont, and Massachusetts. **Conferences and Meetings:** *Augmentative Communication and Assistive Devices.*

HEALTH SERVICES CONSULTANTS INC.
8 Dunlap Ct.
Savoy, IL 61874-9501
Deana Wilson, Managing Director
PH: (217)398-0754
FX: (217)398-0944
Founded: 1988. **Staff:** 30. Offers healthcare management services to the general public in Illinois.

HEALTH SYSTEMS MANAGEMENT NETWORK, INC.
url: http://www.hsmn.com
PO Box 366
Chatham, NY 12037
Cathy M. Idema, President
PH: (518)392-6610
FX: (518)392-6606
Founded: 1977. Healthcare management consultants with extensive experience in hospital/clinical operations, utilization, finance, medical records and quality assurance.

HEALTH SYSTEMS RESEARCH INC.
e-mail: hsr@worldweb.net
2021 L St. NW, Ste. 400
Washington, DC 20036-4992
Larry Bartlett, President
PH: (202)828-5100
FX: (202)728-9469
Founded: 1981. **Staff:** 25. Advises government agencies worldwide on healthcare and financial management.

HEALTH SYSTEMS TECHNOLOGY CORP.
11701 Yates Ford Rd.
Fairfax Station, VA 22039-1507
Barry Cline, Pres.
PH: (703)978-2084
FX: (703)978-2197
Founded: 1990. **Staff:** 4. Provides healthcare and case management services to businesses in the United States.

HEALTH TECHNOLOGIES INC.
13801 Riverport Dr., Ste. 100
Maryland Heights, MO 63043
Carol Sapp, CEO/President
PH: (314)344-5060
TF: 800544-3059
FX: (314)344-0893
Founded: 1984. **Staff:** 12. Advises regional hospitals on nutrition and food service. **Computer/Special Services:** Capabilities include computer software and analysis services for menus.

HEALTH WATCH INTERNATIONAL
e-mail: rschmidt@sfsu.edu
California Pacific Medical Center/UCSF
2100 Webster St., Ste. 508
San Francisco, CA 94115-2381
Robert M. Schmidt, MD, Professor and Director
PH: (415)923-3993
FX: (415)923-0536
Provides health assessments in the areas of morbidity, mortality, prediction, longevity, quality of life, and function. Consultation on estimated survival, effective function, and job-related productivity. Assists in claims preparation, discovery, depositions. Reviews medical records. Gives patient interviews, physical examinations, and comparative productivity estimates.

HEALTHCARE ADMINISTRATIVE SERVICES INC.
6400 Prospect Ave., Ste. 216
Kansas City, MO 64132
Arthur Vogel, M.D., Pres.
PH: (816)822-8853
FX: (816)523-2355
Founded: 1988. **Staff:** 26. Advises physicians in private practice on administrative, accounting, and billing processes. Geographic areas served: Kansas City and St. Louis, Missouri.

HEALTHCARE AFFILIATES, INC.
121 County Rd.
Tenafly, NJ 07670
Dr. E. Charles Eckstein, President and CEO
PH: (201)568-4011
FX: (201)568-9031
Founded: 1985. **Staff:** 10. Medical and Dental consultants/expert witnesses to the legal profession. Medical and Dental malpractice case analysis and consultations, including examinations before trial for litigants. Scrves both plaintiffs and defendants. Industries served: legal profession and government agencies. Verification and evaluation of injuries, including temporo-mandibular joint (TMJ) dysfunction syndrome, and secondary to personal

injury insurance claims. All medical and dental specialties represented or accessible.

HEALTHCARE CONCEPTS, INC.

e-mail: hccinc@ix.netcom.com
url: http://www.hccinc.com
30 Creekview Ct.
Greenville, SC 29615
PH: (864)288-8386
FX: (864)458-9422

HEALTHCARE CONCEPTS INC.

url: http://www.healthconcepts.com
266 S. Font
Memphis, TN 38103-3213
Laurel Reisman
PH: (901)527-7701
FX: (901)529-9101
Founded: 1980. **Staff:** 16. Provides compliance assessments, compliance programming and monitoring, accreditation preparation and mock surveys, program development, temporary and permanent executive placement, operational assessments and training. Geographic Areas Served: International.**Founded:** 1977. **Staff:** 10. A healthcare consulting firm dedicated to rendering professional services in the areas of strategic planning, marketing plan development and implementation, facility planning, systems development and implementation, and management assistance in areas of strategic and operational plans for hospitals and related healthcare centers. Geographic areas served: U.S.

HEALTHCARE CONNECTIONS

25 Braintree Hill Pk., Ste. 308
Braintree, MA 02184
Pamela Buckley, Vice President
PH: (617)848-8080
TF: 800892-2880
FX: (617)848-3961
Staff: 6. Managed care consulting to insurance companies, HMO's, providers and other healthcare organizations. Areas of expertise include marketing, management, medical management, and communications consulting for the healthcare industry in the U.S.

HEALTHCARE FORECASTING INC.

110 National Dr.
Glastonbury, CT 06033
Janice Udesen Cohen, President
PH: (860)659-4077
FX: (860)633-6480
Founded: 1984. **Staff:** 12. Pharmaceutical industry consultants. Industries served: pharmaceuticals, medical supply, and biotechnology. **Conferences and Meetings:** *Forecasting New Products in an Era of Change; and Predicting the Future of the U.S. Pharmaceutical Industry.* **Computer/Special Services:** &Beyond(tm) forecasting software.

HEALTHCARE MANAGEMENT CONSULTANTS, INC.

5856 Sutters Ln.
Bloomfield Hills, MI 48301
Michael Hagan
PH: (810)851-4980
FX: (810)851-0943
Services include utilization review and quality assurance, pre-admission review, and audit preparation. Consultants assist hospitals with improving coding and documentation procedures in order to achieve accurate billing. Industries served: hospitals and third party payers.

HEALTHCARE MANAGEMENT CONSULTING SERVICES

e-mail: hotex1@aol.com
url: http://www.hmcpracticemgt.com
5723 Benning St.
Houston, TX 77096
Margaret A. Radzwill, RN, BSN, AAHC

PH: (713)723-0297
FX: (713)723-0297
Founded: 1991. Offers healthcare consulting services in such areas as utilization and quality management, credentializing program development physician/medical practice management, case management, clinical risk management, and PHO development (managed care Provider development and utilization management). Clients include hospitals, SPA;/medical groups, and MSO's managed care plans. Geographic Areas Served: U.S. **Conferences and Meetings:** *GHAA Annual Convention, Miami, FL; ASHRM Annual Convention, Seattle, WA.*

HEALTHCARE MANAGEMENT COUNSELORS, DIVISION OF RICHARD A. EISNER & COMPANY,

575 Madison Ave.
New York, NY 10022
Peter Weil, Practice Leader
PH: (212)891-8750
FX: (212)979-2429
Founded: 1982. Provides management expertise, specializing in healthcare information technology. Focus is on identifying the organization's need for automation, developing information technology strategic plans, generating Requests For Proposals, performing vendor selection activities, negotiating contracts with the vendor of choice, and providing implementation project management support. Industries served: Integrated Delivery Networks community hospitals, academic health centers, multihospital systems, medical centers, clinics, physician groups, faculty practice plans, nursing homes, and information technology vendors. Geographic areas served: U.S. **Conferences and Meetings:** *HIMMS - Two platform presentations: Internet/Intranet - facility management.*

HEALTHCARE SENTRY

e-mail: hcsentry@ix.netcom.com
24232 Mimosa Dr.
Laguna Niguel, CA 92677
Jeannette Cole
PH: (714)363-9448
FX: (714)362-9450
Founded: 1984. **Staff:** 2. Specializes in computer-enhanced facilitated meeting projects designed to help companies make smarter decisions in a significantly shorter time frame. The process provides a means of achieving consensus on issues ranging from strategic planning to move forward smoothly after major reorganizations, to improving an organization's creativity. The computer process generates a large amount of information in minutes. All input and ranking of ideas is anonymous, which encourages honest participation and ensures the same quality of feedback from outgoing and quiet members alike. The unbiased trained facilitator guides the group to reach the predetermined goals. **Computer/Special Services:** We provide consulting services that have computer enhanced decision making as their core. The process can be used when obtaining consensus is crucial or in situations where diverse goals and objectives hinder reaching a unified plan of action. The technique shortens the time to reach decisions, drives to consensus, generates solutions, creates an action plan, and guarantees buy-in from all participants to that plan. And, we take the process through full plan implementations.

HEALTHCHOICE, A CAREQUEST, INC., COMPANY

e-mail: rlpearson@carequestplrs.com
url: http://www.carequesyplrs.com
583 D'Onofrio Dr., Ste. 103
Madison, WI 53719
Robert L. Pearson, CEO
PH: (608)833-7988
TF: 800833-2524
FX: (608)833-7540
Founded: 1989. **Staff:** 40. Work and Family Life and Long-term care employee assistance program (EAP) offering Eldercare Plus and Information Line. It serves all industries, including unions and some associations, in the U.S. Maintains a branch office in

Minneapolis, Minnesota, Neenah Wisconsin and 7 regional branch sales offices. Geographic Areas Served: All 50 U.S. States. **Computer/Special Services:** Maintains databases of support services for long-term care and elder care needs in the U.S. Includeding a comprehensive work and family life employee assistance program.

HEALTHCHOICE INC.
1220 SW Morrison St.
Portland, OR 97205-2294
Colleen Cain, Exec. Dir.
PH: (503)228-2567
FX: (503)273-4211
Founded: 1982. **Staff:** 125. Offers third party health insurance administration to governmental and granting agencies, and private employers in the United States.

HEALTHSCOPE MANAGEMENT SERVICES CORP.
345 Hudson St., 16th Fl.
New York, NY 10014-4502
PH: (914)741-5044
FX: (914)741-5049
Founded: 1984. Health care management consultants serving hospitals. Offers expertise in the field of managed care.

HEALY & ASSOCIATES
121 Springfield Ave.
Joliet, IL 60435-6561
Carolyn B. Healy, President
PH: (815)741-0102
FX: (815)741-0163
Founded: 1982. **Staff:** 21. Personal development consultant with experience in alcoholism and family treatment; employee assistance program consultation and implementation; health promotion programming on stress, smoking cessation, weight control; alcohol and drug related prevention and educational programming; and individual, group and family counseling. Serves private industries as well as government agencies. Geographic areas served: Chicago metropolitan area. **Conferences and Meetings:** *Assertive Communication; Alcohol and Drug Problems in the Workplace; Chemical Dependency: Enabling vs. Intervention; Stress Management; Employee Assistance Programs; Smoking Cessation in the Workplace; Eating and Weight Issues; Cultural Diversity Training; Adapting to Change in the Workplace; Adapting to Shift Work.*

THE HEARING CENTER
29 Birch 2
Redwood City, CA 94062
Gustav F. Haas
PH: (650)369-4327
FX: (650)369-4327
Founded: 1979. **Staff:** 2. Consultancy specializing in audiology research and development, field testing and selection, and fitting procedures of hearing aids with new signal processing schemes; improvement of noisy communication channels; and hearing conservation and design of active hearing protection devices. Also offers expert witness services. Serves private industries as well as government agencies. Geographic areas served: no limitations.

HEINEMANN ASSOCIATES, INC.
e-mail: heine018@gold.tc.umn.edu
Crosstown Cir., Ste. 105
Eden Prairie, MN 55344
Charles A. Heinemann, President
PH: (612)941-9770
FX: (612)941-9771
Founded: 1988. **Staff:** 6. Specialists in planning medical facilities and equipment. Serves healthcare clients in the U.S. and overseas.

DOUGLAS E. HERITAGE, MD
2026A Opitz Blvd.
Woodbridge, VA 22191

PH: (703)491-7155
FX: (703)690-3958
Founded: 1978. Private practice of obstetrics and gynecology. Special qualifications in GYN laser surgery, laparoscopic surgery, pelvic microsurgery. Experience in treatment of endometriosis, abnormal PAP smears, and pelvic pain. Offers expert witness testimony.

THE HERMANN GROUP
e-mail: hermanngroup@compuserve.com
50 Barker St., Ste. 529
Mount Kisco, NY 10549
Mindy G. Hermann
PH: (914)241-8714
FX: (914)666-0919
Founded: 1988. Offers public relations, communications and marketing consultation in nutrition and healthcare. Industries served: public relations, pharmaceutical, food, publishing, and healthcare. Geographic areas served: metropolitan New York based; active nationwide. **Conferences and Meetings:** *Marketing for Health Care Professionals; Working with the Media to Get Your Message Across; Using Public Relations to Promote Your Service.*

HERMES MEDICAL SEARCH SERVICES
269 Reservation Rd.
PO Box 111
Marina, CA 93933
Terry C. Olesen, Lead Researcher
TF: 800486-9863
Founded: 1992. **Staff:** 3. Online researcher of medical and health information, using over 200 databases, 2 news services, and 10 medical/technical libraries. Also specializes in alternative and complementary therapies, customer attitudes and buying habits, and health information from overseas sources. Serves private companies interested in employee health, employee assistance, writers, editors, and researchers in medicine. Works in the U.S. and Canada. **Conferences and Meetings:** *Dates and locations of health related seminars may be obtained by contacting firm.* **Computer/Special Services:** Provides translations from Spanish, French, Russian, and Italian sources.

HEYER ENVIRONMENTAL SAFETY & HEALTH SERVICES INC.
30296 Stage Coach Ln.
Evergreen, CO 80439
PH: (303)670-3378
FX: (303)670-3378
Founded: 1991. Environmental safety and health consultants.

THE HILL TOP COMPANIES
PO Box 429501
Cincinnati, OH 45242
J. James Pearce, Jr., President/CEO
PH: (513)831-3114
TF: 800669-1947
FX: (513)831-1217
Founded: 1947. **Staff:** 235. Specialists in the design, evaluation, and conduct of testing programs for safety, efficacy, and registration of cosmetics, prescription and over-the-counter pharmaceuticals, personal care and household products, specialty chemicals, paper products, nonwovens, and medical devices. Recent activities include consumer and descriptive studies (sensory analysis), as well as research in dermal conditions and dermal products. Services include toxicology and microbiology. Toxicology offers acute testing and delayed contact hypersensitivity (the Buehler Method), as well as photobiology, sunscreen, and intratracheal procedures. The Microbiology Division tests for disinfectant efficacy, preservatives, and topical antimicrobials. Geographic areas served: international. **Conferences and Meetings:** *Hill Top Research sponsors the Dermatological Conference in conjunction with the Robert Wood Johnson Medical School.*

STEVEN HIRSCH & ASSOCIATES
950 South Coast Dr., Ste. 106
Costa Mesa, CA 92626
Steven Hirsch, President
PH: (714)557-5900
TF: 800624-3750
FX: (714)557-4420
Founded: 1987. **Staff:** 18. Offers healthcare administration expertise in these areas: hospital regulatory compliance, medicare certification, licensing, and joint commission, quality improvement, infection control, safety management, and staff support. Industries served: hospitals, ambulatory healthcare providers, and long-term care facilities in the United States.

MELANIE S. HITCH
4962 Walther Rd.
Kettering, OH 45429
Melanie S. Hitch
PH: (937)299-1721
Founded: 1969. **Staff:** 1. Nursing care consultant with particular expertise in homecare and orthopedics. Serves private industries as well as government agencies. Geographic areas served: U.S. and Canada. **Conferences and Meetings:** *Offers hands-on workshops, audiovisuals, and lectures for healthcare professional groups, nursing associations and the general public, as well as government agencies. Representative titles include: Home Care and the A.I.D.S. Patient; Basics of Orthopaedic Nursing (one day); Home Care of the Patient with Terminal Illness; Nutritional Support for the Orthopedic Patient; Sexuality and the Immobile Patient; Child Abuse; Home Care for Technology Dependent Children; Home Care for Chronically Ill Children.*

HLA SYSTEMS - HAROLD LAUFMAN ASSOCIATES, INC.
e-mail: hlasystems@aol.com; halaus@aol.com
31 E. 72 St.
New York, NY 10021
Harold Laufman, President
PH: (212)737-4343
TF: 800447-7899
FX: (212)737-4628
Founded: 1977. **Staff:** 12. Consultants in surgical and special care facilities and systems for hospitals. Industries served: healthcare - surgical and special care facilities and systems.

HMA BEHAVIORAL HEALTH INC.
PO Box 706
Worcester, MA 01613
PH: (508)757-2290
FX: (508)754-3616
Founded: 1982. **Staff:** 5. Offers services in psychiatric and substance abuse managed care network development.

LOWELL HOKIN
e-mail: hokin@macc.wisc.edu
University of Wisconsin Medical School
1300 University Ave.
Madison, WI 53706
PH: (608)262-9823
FX: (608)262-1257
Performs pharmacology research on psychoactive drugs. Skilled in forensic pharmacology and psychopharmacology.

HOLLINGSWORTH MED X-PRESS REHABILITATION & CONSULTING SERVICES, INC.
e-mail: hrcs@intrepid.net
442 Winchester Ave.
Martinsburg, WV 25401
Nancy B. Hollingsworth, CRC, Mgr., Sr. Disability Analyst
PH: (304)263-3400
TF: 800734-2238
FX: (304)263-3860
Founded: 1990. **Staff:** 15. Provides medical and vocational coordination services regarding the legal medical, and vocational issues inherent in the rehabilitation process of the industrially injured. Also Med X-Press provides transportation. **Computer/ Special Services:** Transportation services for injured workers.

RONALD D. HOOD & ASSOCIATES - CONSULTING TOXICOLOGISTS
e-mail: rhood@biology.as.ua.edu
University of Alabama
Box 870344
Tuscaloosa, AL 35487-0344
Dr. Ronald D. Hood
PH: (205)348-1817
FX: (205)348-1786
Founded: 1978. **Staff:** 4. Specializes in toxicology, especially developmental toxicology (teratology), reproductive toxicology, and environmental toxicology. Provides data interpretation, hazard assessment, literature review, and litigation support. Also conducts laboratory research on a wide range of chemicals, including industrial and agricultural chemicals, pesticides, pharmaceuticals, and environmental pollutants. Special expertise offered in the toxicology and pharmacology of arsenicals. Clients served include: state and federal agencies, especially the Environmental Protection Agency, law firms, and a wide variety of industrial clients. Geographic Areas Served: U.S. **Computer/Special Services:** On-line literature searches; Retrieval of chemical agent summaries from Reprotox and Teris databases.

PERRY HOOKMAN, MD
e-mail: hookman@hookman.com
url: http://www.hookman.com
9605 Halter Ct.
Potomac, MD 20854
Perry Hookman, M.D.
PH: (301)983-1890
FX: (301)983-8625
Specialist in evaluation and/or testimony and/or mediation in medical malpractice, alleged health care fraud and abuse, utilization review, and quality assurance. Geographic Area Served: National.

JOHN E. HOOVER - CONSULTANT
363 Riverview Rd.
Swarthmore, PA 19081
John E. Hoover
PH: (610)328-9786
Founded: 1978. **Staff:** 1. Consultant in bio-medical communications; offers editorial and writing services for wide variety of clients in pharmaceutical, medical, and other healthcare fields. Geographic areas served: U.S.

HOSPITAL MAINTENANCE CONSULTANTS INC.
PO Box 100
Lebanon, WI 53047
Michael Brinkman, President
PH: (414)925-3558
TF: 800953-6372
FX: (414)925-3321
Founded: 1972. Experts in the field of hospital maintenance. Industries served: hospitals, multi-hospital groups, medical and scientific manufacturers, leasing companies, shared clinical engineering services, and independent service companies. Geographic areas served: U.S. and Canada. **Conferences and Meetings:** *Seminars for hospital administration on the topics of Assessing Suitability of Plant and Equipment; Evaluating Hospital Engineering Departments; Technology Assessment; Maintenance Management.* **Computer/Special Services:** Maintains an extensive database on clinical equipment maintenance.

ERIC R. HUBBARD
2333 Pacific Ave.
Long Beach, CA 90806
Jan Wynne, Principal
PH: (562)427-7443
FX: (562)424-3395
Offers foot and ankle medical evaluations and consultations.

Provides personal injury evaluation; footprint identification, and medical record review. Offers expert testimony in workers comp and personal injury cases. Reviews insurance claims.

HUDSON VALLEY EYE SURGEONS, PC
e-mail: AndrewDahl@atspol.net
335 Rte. 52
Fishkill, NY 12524
Andrew A. Dahl, MD, President
PH: (914)896-9280
FX: (914)896-0246
Specializes in ophthalmology and ophthalmic surgery and forensic eye cases.

THE HUMAN FACTORS CONSULTANCY
4519 Arendale Sq.
Alexandria, VA 22309
Martin I. Kurke
PH: (703)780-2475
FX: (703)780-2475
Founded: 1978. Staff: 1. Offers human factors/safety consultation, forensic human factors (ergonomics) consultation, and expert witness testimony in litigation alleging defective equipment, systems, or delivery of services (e.g., malpractice). Assists with compliance with Americans With Disability Act. Industries served: attorneys, insurance companies and all industries nationwide. Geographic areas served: U.S. and Canada.

HUMANICS ERGOSYSTEMS, INC.
e-mail: humanics@aol.com
PO Box 17388
Encino, CA 91416-7388
Rani Lueder, CPE
PH: (818)345-3746
FX: (818)705-3903
Founded: 1982. Staff: 2. Specializes in occupational ergonomics; ergonomic workplace evaluations; ergonomics research; ergonomic seminars and training; psychological and biomechanics testing (EMG, dynamic lumbar motion, strength assessment, nerve conduction); product evaluations; compliance with ergonomic standards; and expert witnessing. Serves all industries in the U.S. and worldwide. Conferences and Meetings: *Presents a variety of seminars, including How to Conduct a Workplace Assessment; How to Reduce Cumulative Trauma in Your Workplace; and How to Evaluate Ergonomic Seats, Workstations, Keyboards, and Other Products.* Computer/Special Services: Accesses variety of online commercial, academic, and government databases. Skilled in the areas of technical ergonomics research and analysis.

HAL H. HUNT, M.D.
700 Crockett, Ste. 405
Seattle, WA 98109
Hal H. Hunt, M.D.
PH: (206)285-5596
Consults with healthcare providers on physician recruitment, practice merger/acquisition/sale and/or liquidations, practice valuation, strategic and life structure planning. Geographic areas served: Arizona, California, Idaho, Montana, Oregon, and Washington.

IN-FLIGHT RADIATION PROTECTION SERVICES, INC.
211 E. 70th St., Ste. 12G
New York, NY 10021
Robert J. Barish, President
PH: (212)288-7201
Founded: 1988. Staff: 1. Provides education and training regarding cosmic ray radiation exposure of airline crew members. Produces seminars and briefing sessions for airline executives. Provides monitoring instrument for radiation dose measurements on airplanes. Industries served: aviation and government agencies. Geographic areas served: national.

THERESA INCAGNOLI, PH.D., A.B.P.P.
240 Central Park, S., Ste. 24-C
New York, NY 10019
Theresa Incagnoli
PH: (212)757-0375
FX: (212)757-0376
Specialist in neuropsychology. Offers particular expertise in the evaluation of brain damage. Services include medical-legal work for plaintiff and defense and insurance companies. Specific focus is toward quantification of brain damage. Conferences and Meetings: *Neuropsychological Examination for Attorneys: The Quantification of Brain Damage; Trying the Head Injury Case; Medicine in the Courtroom.*

INDEPENDENT REHABILITATION CONSULTANTS, INC.
3475 Lenox Rd. NE, Ste. 400
Atlanta, GA 30326-1232
Marlene Cox, R.N., C.R.C., C.I.R.S.
PH: (404)238-0520
FX: (404)240-7201
Founded: 1982. Provides case management, life care planning, medical and vocational rehabilitation and medical-legal consulting services. Industries served: insurance, self-insured companies, and attorneys. Geographic areas served: Georgia and Alabama.

INFOTEQ
8484 Georgia Ave., Ste. 320
Silver Spring, MD 20910
Robert J. Waris, President
PH: (301)565-4020
FX: (301)565-5112
Founded: 1984. Staff: 80. Health care consultants offer consulting expertise in the following areas: technical assistance, information technology services, publications, conference management, logistics support, and clearinghouse operations. Industries served: information service. Geographic areas served: U.S.

INNOVATIVE HEALTHCARE SERVICES, INC. (IHS)
3765 Wetherburn Dr.
Clarkston, GA 30021
Avis D. Dickey, President
PH: (404)298-6490
Founded: 1996. Staff: 3. Provides executive search services and experience in the areas of integrated healthcare services and systems management.

INSECT CONTROL & RESEARCH, INC.
e-mail: icr@erols.com
1330 Dillon Heights Ave.
Baltimore, MD 21228
Robin G. Todd, Director
PH: (410)747-4500
FX: (410)747-4928
Founded: 1946. Staff: 10. Pesticide registration, testing, and screening specialists offer consulting on vector borne diseases and household and public health pests. Industries served: chemical, pest control, pharmaceutical, and government agencies. Geographic areas served: worldwide. Conferences and Meetings: *US AID Malaria Strategy Workshop.*

INSOURCE MANAGEMENT GROUP
1020 Holcombe Blvd., Ste. 1650
Houston, TX 77030
M. Ann Moser, CRN, BSN, MBA, CHC, Vice President
PH: (713)790-0800
FX: (713)852-2151
Founded: 1985. Nationally recognized in healthcare delivery reform, the firm provides services in the fields of strategic, facilities, organization, and financial planning. Also consults on all types of product-line evaluations (including five-year business plans), mergers/consolidations, and regulatory assistance. Facilities to retreat and conduct workshops on the changing delivery system. Speaks regularly at conventions and for other groups. Conferences and Meetings: *Dennis Moser speaks regularly at con-*

ventions and meetings across the U.S. Shares experience on the E-volving Integrated Healthcare Delivery System. **Computer/Special Services:** Has developed integrated planning software utilizing advanced spreadsheet and database technologies.

INSTITUTE FOR ALTERNATIVE FUTURES
e-mail: futurist@altfutures.com
url: http://www.altfutures.com
100 N. Pitt St., Ste. 235
Alexandria, VA 22314-3134
Clement Bezold, Ph.D., President
PH: (703)684-5880
FX: (703)684-0640
Founded: 1977. **Staff:** 13. Counsels in the areas of healthcare, information/communications technology, the environment, work, and the future in general.

INSTITUTIONAL PHARMACY CONSULTANTS OF GEORGIA INC.
816 Everee Inn Rd.
Griffin, GA 30224
Armon Neel
PH: (770)229-5050
TF: 800253-6962
FX: (770)229-8704
Founded: 1977. **Staff:** 20. Pharmacy consultants specialize in serving nursing homes.

INTEGRATED BEHAVIORAL SYSTEMS, INC.
656C N. Wellwood Ave., Ste. 303
Lindenhurst, NY 11757
Michael J. Chambers, CEO
PH: (516)951-1121
FX: (516)225-7076
Founded: 1995. A progressive behavioral healthcare consulting company specializing in innovative solutions to the problems encountered in today's challenging healthcare environment.

INTEGRATED HEALTHCARE AUDITING SERVICES (IHAS)
14435 Cherry Ln. Ct., Ste. 418
Laurel, MD 20707
PH: (301)206-2006
FX: (301)369-3454
Founded: 1987. Health care consultants.

INTER-GLOBE ASSOCIATES
e-mail: quantum@intergate.bc.ca
308-700 Chilco St.
Vancouver, BC, Canada V6G 2R1
Nuri Vellani, Ph.D., Consultant
PH: (604)687-3470
FX: (604)687-3470
Founded: 1994. **Staff:** 3. Evaluates health education and risk reduction projects. Industries served: health, medicine, and safety worldwide.

INTERACTIVE SOLUTIONS, INC.
e-mail: fapep@aol.comassee.net
PO Box 6325
Tallahassee, FL 32314-6325
Malcolm Kemp, President
PH: (850)942-0079
FX: (850)942-6630
Founded: 1984. **Staff:** 4. Provides marketing and technical support for all of the major medical software publishers, as well as IBM multimedia system hardware. Consults with healthcare training institutions to determine how computer-based training can be utilized as part of their educational programs. Industries served: healthcare in southeastern U.S.

INTERNATIONAL HEALTHCARE CONSULTANTS INC.
3657 Canton Rd.
Marietta, GA 30066
Don R. Wakefield
PH: (770)926-0062
FX: (770)926-0437
Founded: 1985. Offers healthcare consulting for insurance companies. **Conferences and Meetings:** *Fraud and Deception in Healthcare Billing and Utilization; Understanding Medical Records and Negotiating Techniques; and Recognition and Management of Abusive Claims.*

INTERNATIONAL MEDICAL PRODUCTS INC.
4503 Moorland Ave.
Edina, MN 55424
Dr. J.R. Shidema
PH: (612)835-4018
FX: (612)832-5806
Founded: 1981. Health services consulting firm specializes in medical products. Industries served: medical device. Geographic areas served: U.S., Europe, Canada, and Asia.

INTERNATIONAL NUTRITION CONSULTANTS, INC.
e-mail: feedback@inc-inc.com
url: http://www.inc-inc.com
101 Quail Hollow Dr.
San Jose, CA 95128
Robert E. Menkemeller, President and Founder
PH: (408)879-9141
TF: 800249-4554
FX: 800-311-7171
Founded: 1995. A nutritional education and analysis services company providing California state licensed home study nutrition courses. Offers in-depth health status reports and laboratory analyses for our graduates and individuals and on-line vitamin deficiency analysis software to health enthusiasts. Offers an Nutritional Counseling Course, which provides nutritional foundation, carries a diploma, and is licensed by the State of California. Analysis services complement educational programs. Available to graduates who become consultants are analysis services that include in-depth symptomology questionnaires as well as laboratory services, such as, tissue mineral analysis, blood testing and a DHEA saliva analysis.

INVERESK RESEARCH (NORTH AMERICA), INC.
e-mail: inveresk@aol.com
4470 Redwood Hwy., Ste. 101
San Rafael, CA 94903
Richard J. D'Agostino, President
PH: (415)491-6460
FX: (415)491-6464
Founded: 1974. **Staff:** 7. Project management, strategic development, clinical trial monitoring, regulatory affairs are tailored to the sponsors needs for manufacturers of medical devices, diagnostics, pharmaceuticals, and cosmetics.

IRVINE CONSULTING INC.
e-mail: irves224@msn.net
2207 Lakeside Dr.
Bannockburn, IL 60015-1265
Ronald Irvine, President
PH: (847)615-0040
FX: (847)615-0192
Founded: 1987. **Staff:** 7. Firm provides expertise in marketing to the healthcare industry nationwide.

IRVINE ORTHOPAEDIC ASSOCIATES
16300 Sand Canyon Ave., Ste. 511
Irvine, CA 92618
Robert A. Baird, MD, Principal
PH: (949)727-3636
FX: (949)727-9515
Offers consulting and expert witness testimony in civil and criminal litigation in the area of orthopedics. Provides case evaluations and independent medical evaluation.

ISENBERG & ASSOCIATES, INC.
1316 Rockbridge Rd., Ste. J
Stone Mountain, GA 30087
Walter G. Isenberg, President
PH: (770)381-0359
TF: 800533-0359
FX: (770)381-5226
Founded: 1981. **Staff:** 15. Staff of insurance/benefit specialists, registered professional nurses and medical/psychiatric professionals to assist in providing cost containment services, including claims administration audits, hospital audits, medical case management/home healthcare reviews, consulting services, disability programs and psychiatric peer reviews; and to assist in evaluation, development and administration of benefit programs. Industries served: corporations, insurance companies/brokers, third party administrators, and government agencies. Geographic areas served: national. **Conferences and Meetings:** *Claims Processing; Accident and Health Claims Auditing.*

JOSEPH M. JABBOUR, MD
e-mail: jabbourj@asprsdial.org
2 Fifth Ave.
New York, NY 10011
PH: (212)674-5200
FX: (212)674-5801
A plastic and reconstructive surgeon providing expert witness testimony.

KAREN JAMES, PH.D.
e-mail: karenjames@appstate.campus.mci.net
1584 Hattie Hill Rd.
Vilas, NC 28692
Karen James
PH: (704)297-4084
FX: (704)297-4084
Founded: 1986. **Staff:** 1. Offers consulting in clinical immunology including enzyme immunoassays, complement, and immunofluorescence. Provides additional consulting in laboratory management, particularly hospital laboratories for JCAHO preparedness, CAP preparedness, quality assurance, financial management and assessments. Also maintains expertise in physician office laboratories in areas of needs assessment, quality assurance, quality control, staff assessments and CLIA 88, as well as consulting in bedside laboratory test systems such as glucose monitoring, coagulation, and others. Industries served: hospitals, laboratory reagent/kit manufacturers, reference laboratories, physician groups, and government agencies. Geographic areas served: no limitations. **Conferences and Meetings:** *Immunoserology of Infectious and Autoimmune Diseases; Marketing Hospital Laboratory Services; Viral Serology: What Do the Results Mean; Managed Care and Hospital Laboratories; Hospital Laboratories in the 21st Century; The ABCs of Hospital Information Systems.*

HERMAN E. JASS
29 Platz Dr.
Skillman, NJ 08558
Herman E. Jass, Owner
PH: (908)874-4356
FX: (609)683-0079
Founded: 1976. **Staff:** 2. Active in the development, monitoring, and conduct of preclinical and clinical studies. Offers expertise with investigational new drug and new drug application development, label review, and regulatory services (FDA and FTC). Also provides expert witness testimony in area of skin treatment products, liability, new product development programs, and acquisition aid. Particularly accommodating to foreign firms attempting to market drugs and cosmetics in the U.S. Industries served: pharmaceutical and cosmetic. Geographic areas served: worldwide.

JEST FOR THE HEALTH OF IT
e-mail: pwooten@jesthealth.com
PO Box 4040
Davis, CA 95617
Patty Wooten
PH: (916)758-3826
FX: (916)753-7638
Founded: 1982. Develops and presents seminars, keynotes, and skill shops about the power of humor. Provides consulting services for development of humor rooms and comedy carts in hospitals. Conducts training for clowns to make visits in hospitals and nursing homes. Industries served: health professionals and businesses wishing to educate staff about healthy lifestyle choices. Geographic areas served: U.S., Canada, England, and Australia. Woman-owned firm. **Conferences and Meetings:** *Professional Survival - You Can Laugh or Cry: Stress Control; Choosing the Amusing - Humor Techniques for Work and Home; Laughter's the Best Medicine - Science and Research about Laughter and Healing; What's So Funny - What Humor Is, Isn't and Should Be; You've Got To Be Kidding - Learning to Laugh at Life's Upsets and Setbacks; and Tickle While You Teach - Learning with Laughter.*

JOHNSON, BASSIN & SHAW INC.
e-mail: jbsinc@netcom.com
url: http://www.jbsinc.com
8630 Fenton St., 12th Fl.
Silver Spring, MD 20910
Gail Bassin, Chairperson
PH: (301)495-1080
FX: (301)587-4352
Founded: 1985. **Staff:** 100. Health and social services issues-oriented consulting firm.

JOHNSON INSTITUTE
e-mail: info@johnsoninstitute.com
url: http://www.johnsoninstitute.com
7205 Ohms Ln.
Minneapolis, MN 55439-2159
Delano Remboldt, President
PH: (612)831-1630
TF: 800231-5165
FX: (612)831-1631
Founded: 1965. **Staff:** 20. Provides consultation services on Behavioral Health prevention, intervention, and treatment programming. These services are offered to corporations, civic groups, schools, judicial and law enforcement agencies, hospitals, mental health centers, professional groups such as lawyers, physicians and nurses, social workers, and a wide spectrum of others involved in providing social services. Has served as consultant in developing and implementing medical detoxification, primary inpatient treatment, primary outpatient treatment, aftercare, family programming, and adolescent treatment programs throughout the nation addressing clinical and management objectives. **Conferences and Meetings:** *Intervention: How to Help Those Who Don't Want Help; Alcohol, Drugs and the Family; Chemical Dependency and Family Violence. Adolescents, Alcohol, and Drugs; How to Prevent Violence at Work; Respect and Protect: Violence Prevention, Interventions for Schools, Parenting Techniques: Skills for Parents and other Concerned Adults.*

ROBERT T. JOHNSON, M.D.
e-mail: cpnbob@aol.com
672 Clay Shown Rd.
Hartford, KY 42347
Robert T. Johnson
PH: (502)298-9401
FX: (502)298-5252
Founded: 1982. **Staff:** 2. Physician and wellness expert who serves as free-lance writer for several publishing firms. Accepts speaking engagements for wellness forums, camps, and other programs. Also provides stress management and drug abuse seminars, as well as life style and behavioral modification consultation. Industries served: hospitals, schools, public service organi-

zations, parent-teacher organizations, self-help organizations, and support groups. Geographic areas served: U.S.

STEVEN JONAS, M.D., M.P.H.
Department of Preventive Medicine
School of Medicine
State University of New York
Stony Brook, NY 11794-8036
Steven Jonas
PH: (516)444-2147
FX: (516)444-7525
Founded: 1968. **Staff:** 1. Specialized expertise in health promotion, disease prevention, and health policy. Industries served: health services industry and government agencies. **Conferences and Meetings:** *Health Promotion in Clinical Practice; Taking Control of Your Weight; Putting Health into National Health Care Reform.*

JORDAN SERVICES INC.
e-mail: rehab@webspan.net
url: http://www.jordansrvs.com
900 Merchants Concourse, Ste. 112
Westbury, NY 11590-5114
Dr. Morris Ehrenreich
PH: (516)683-0100
FX: (516)683-0259
Founded: 1975. **Staff:** 95. Provides private rehabilitation management services. Serves private industries as well as government agencies.

J.P. CONSULTING, INC.
e-mail: jpeters1@d.umn.edu
url: http://members.aol.com/jpforesal/index.html
354 Kenilworth Ave.
PO Box 3053
Duluth, MN 55803
Jerrold M. Peterson, Ph.D., President and Director of Research
PH: (218)724-8920
FX: (218)724-8920
Specializes in valuation of lost earnings from death or injury, valuation of lost business profits and property, market and financial assessment, and business start up.

JULES STEIN EYE INSTITUTE
e-mail: leeda@jsei.ucla.edu
100 Stein Plaza, Rm. 2-235
Los Angeles, CA 90095-7004
David A. Lee, MD, Principal
PH: (213)206-0387
FX: (213)206-3652
Specializes in the diagnosis and medical and surgical treatment of eye diseases, including glaucoma. Performs clinical research in ophthalmology.

K & S ASSOCIATES INC.
1926 Elm Tree Dr.
Nashville, TN 37210-3718
Thomas W. Slowey
PH: (615)883-9760
TF: 800522-2325
FX: (615)871-0856
Founded: 1973. **Staff:** 12. Firm specializes in offering expertise on healthcare issues to medical institutions and hospitals. Serves individuals and commercial accounts in the U.S.

MEDHAT A. KADER, MD, INC.
988 Centerville Rd.
Warwick, RI 02886
PH: (401)828-4510
FX: (401)828-4370
Founded: 1972. Provides consultation, medical records review, and expert testimony in orthopedics.

KAM HEALTH CARE CONSULTING INC.
1847 Lincoln St.
Evanston, IL 60201
Kenneth A. March, President
PH: (847)869-6934
FX: (847)869-0838
Founded: 1990. **Staff:** 5. Health care research and consulting. Industries served: pharmaceuticals, diagnostics, OTC manufacturers, healthcare advertising agencies, and consumer advertising agencies. Geographic areas served: U.S.; international subcontractors.

KARCH & ASSOCIATES INC.
1701 K St. NW, Ste. 1000
Washington, DC 20006-1503
Nathan J. Karch, President
PH: (202)463-0400
FX: (202)463-0502
Founded: 1982. **Staff:** 20. Consultants on toxicology, epidemiology and risk assessment. Other services include regulatory/litigation support in relevant cases as well as hazards communications policies and procedures. Industries served: chemical, paper, plastics, and pharmaceutical industries; law firms; trade associations; and federal government.

KENNETH ASSOCIATES INC.
2014 Judah St.
San Francisco, CA 94122
PH: (415)665-6500
FX: (415)664-6400
Founded: 1971. Consultants for hospitals.

KING & ASSOCIATES, INC.
e-mail: marieking@writeme.com
2477 Valleydale Rd, Ste. B-1
Birmingham, AL 35244
Marie A. King, President
PH: (205)988-4222
FX: (205)988-4101
Founded: 1980. **Staff:** 10. Offers services in the area of healthcare, including reimbursement, documentation, and administration. **Conferences and Meetings:** *Medicare-Managing an Effective Medicare Program; Medicare Overview; Staff Development (Train-The-Trainer); Nursing Management in Long-Term Care; and Skilled Care Issues.*

KNOPF CO.
e-mail: knopf@oeonline.com
url: http://www.tmaxx.com/netmax/knopfcompany.html
1126 S. Main St.
Plymouth, MI 48170-2214
Jeanne Knopf DeRoche, Pres.
PH: (734)455-4343
TF: 800420-4343
FX: (734)455-0015
Founded: 1984. **Staff:** 6. Advises businesses and school districts, and general public locally on health issues in the areas of substance abuse, prevention programs, conflict resolution programs. Meeting and conference planning services. Geographic areas served: USA & Canada for training and consulting services. **Conferences and Meetings:** *Conflict Resolution Curriculum Training; Peer Mediation Train-the Trainer Program; Peer Mediation Student Training Program; Managing Conflicts on the Playground; Middle School Leadership Conference - Tobacco Prevention; Middle School Leadership Conference - Conflict Management; ParentPlus Facilitator Training Program; Using Risk & Protective factors in ATOD Prevention; Using the Internet in ATOD Prevention; Educational Support Group Facilitator Training Program; Drug-affected Children Training Program; Drug Matrix - Adolescent Drug Use; Paper People Facilitator Training Program; Children in Focus Facilitator Training Program.*

KOFFEL ASSOCIATES, INC.
3300 N. Ridge Rd., Ste. 120
Ellicott City, MD 21043
William E. Koffel, President
PH: (410)750-2246
FX: (410)750-2588
Founded: 1986. **Staff:** 9. Independent firm providing fire protection engineering and code consulting services. Offers a broad range of services including fire protection engineering surveys, fire protection system design and analysis, fire loss investigations, product testing and development, community fire defense planning, seminars, and building and fire code consulting. Although services are offered for a variety of occupancies, the firm has specialized experience in detention and healthcare facilities. Industries served: architectural, building owners, developers, engineering, fire service, legal, manufacturers, municipalities, and producers. Geographic areas served: worldwide. **Conferences and Meetings:** *But It Complies with the Code; A Systems Approach to Inspection, Testing, and Maintenance of Fire Protection and Life Safety Systems; Estimating the Effectiveness of State-of-the-Art Detectors and Automatic Sprinklers on Life Safety in Health Care Occupancies.* **Computer/Special Services:** Computer fire modeling, hydraulic analysis.

RICHARD M. KRIEG, MD
University of California, San Francisco
505 ParnaSSUS L-08, Box 0226
San Francisco, CA 94143
PH: (415)476-4815
FX: (415)476-8734
Specializes in radiation oncology brachytherapy, lymphoma, breast cancer, rectal and anal cancer.

RICHARD B. KRUEGER, MD
e-mail: rbk1721305@aol.com
210 E. 68th St., Ste. 1-H
New York, NY 10021-6024
PH: (212)517-6624
FX: (212)517-4073
Assesses and treats sex offenders and forensic populations, as well as neuropsychiatry and head injury. Oversees a program for treating sex offenders and for treating professionals accused of professional sexual misconduct. Specializes in psychopharmacology, malpractice, forensic psychiatry, competency, criminal responsibility, PTSD, and psychiatric disability.

KUAKINI PATHOLOGISTS, INC.
347 N. Kuakini St.
Box 5
Honolulu, HI 96817
Francis Fukunaga, President
PH: (808)547-9139
FX: (808)547-9497
Founded: 1983. **Staff:** 5. Professional medical consultants in the fields of medical pathology or diseases including occupational and environmental disease; anatomic pathology, clinical pathology, and forensic pathology; legal medicine; accidental and industrial fatalities for insurance, industry, and legal profession; and epidemiology of cancer in the Pacific. Serves private industries as well as government agencies. Geographic areas served: city and county of Honolulu, Hawaii. **Conferences and Meetings:** *Periodic cancer and oncology seminars.*

KUNITZ AND ASSOCIATES, INC.
e-mail: kai@dgs.dgsys.com
6001 Montrose Rd., Ste. 920
Rockville, MD 20852
Selma C. Kunitz, President
PH: (301)770-2730
TF: 800710-8053
FX: (301)770-4183
Founded: 1986. **Staff:** 50. Offers extensive expertise regarding clinical research, health research data management, clinical information systems and data management, and life quality assess-

ment tools and studies. Services include clinical studies, coordinating center services, surveys, focus groups, and evaluation studies. Industries served: pharmaceutical, healthcare, rehabilitation, and government agencies worldwide. **Conferences and Meetings:** *Clinical Information Systems; Clinical Research Methods; Quality Assurance.*

ANNA KURAMOTO
e-mail: Kuramoto@ix.netcom.com
1617 Koch Ln.
San Jose, CA 95125
Anna Kuramoto, President
PH: (408)723-9361
FX: (408)723-0623
Founded: 1985. **Staff:** 1. Health enhancement consultant offers services for corporate wellness, associations and groups, and individuals. Provides consultation in health risk assessment, stress management, back care and injury prevention, weight control and management, personalized exercise programs, workshops and presentations. Geographic areas served: northern California. **Conferences and Meetings:** *Presentations, workshops, and seminars related to exercise, health and wellness; topics include making wellness work for your company, exercise fundamentals, heart health and physical activity, exercise for seniors, and pregnancy and exercise; also educational in-service training for health/fitness professionals.*

L & M ELECTRONICS INC.
541 Taylor Way, No. 10
San Carlos, CA 94070-6254
PH: (650)631-3758
Founded: 1955. Electronics consulting firm serving the medical field in public and private sector as well as internationally.

THE LA PENNA GROUP
url: http://www.lapenna.com
2110 Enterprise SE, Ste. 300
Kentwood, MI 49508
A. Michael La Penna, Principal
PH: (616)281-2882
TF: 800527-3662
FX: (616)281-0573
Founded: 1987. Health care consulting firm.

LABORATORY SPECIALISTS INC.
PO Box 50577
New Orleans, LA 70150
Robert Gardebled, Controller
PH: (504)392-7961
TF: 800433-3823
FX: (504)394-5434
Founded: 1978. **Staff:** 65. Provides consulting services for industry and business requiring drug screens and confirmations of drug usage in employees. Offers four basic types of programs: for cause, preemployment, accident related, and random screens. Services include expert legal testimony. **Conferences and Meetings:** *Presents numerous seminars on drug use and abuse in the workplace.*

LACASSE INC.
6727 Quartzite Canyon Pl.
Tucson, AZ 85718
Lorne A. Campbell
PH: (520)299-6171
FX: (520)299-4362
Founded: 1983. **Staff:** 1. Involved in regulatory matters concerning the food and drug industry, both domestic and foreign, including food additive petitions, NADAs, NDAs, ANDAs, INDs, and pesticide and fungicide regulation. Consults in the development of drugs and their approval by the FDA. Develops protocols on all aspects of pre-clinical and clinical studies, both animal and human. Advises on establishing a pharmaceutical presence in the U.S. for foreign pharmaceutical companies. Expert in generic drug industry.

LACHMAN CONSULTANT SERVICES, INC.
1600 Stewart Ave., Ste. 604
Westbury, NY 11590
Robert W. Pollock
PH: (516)222-6222
FX: (516)683-1887
Founded: 1978. **Staff:** 13. Consultant to pharmaceutical, biological, biotechnology, device, and diagnostic industries in areas dealing with validation/qualification of equipment and systems, quality control/quality assurance, facilities design incorporating FDA and other governmental requirements, air and water systems design, research and development, and FDA related matters. Advisory to industry and law firms. **Conferences and Meetings:** *Qualification and Validation of Pharmaceutical Processes and Systems; Quality Control/Quality Assurance of Pharmaceuticals; Pharmaceutical Dosage Form Design.*

LAMMERS & ASSOCIATES, INC.
e-mail: llammersA@aol.com
1801 Alexander Bell Dr., Ste. 600
Reston, VA 20191
Lawrence P. Lammers, Chairman/CEO
PH: (703)476-8400
FX: (703)476-8541
Founded: 1979. **Staff:** 19. A healthcare consulting firm that specializes in planning and development services. The firm has a national practice and offers a comprehensive range of consultative assistance to healthcare providers, including: strategic and program planning, marketing, market research, facility evaluations, master planning, functional/space programming, and materials management. Geographic areas served: U.S.

CAROL LANGE, R.D.
1012 SW King
Portland, OR 97205
Carol Lange, R.D.
PH: (503)221-1793
Founded: 1976. **Staff:** 1. Provides full-spectrum nutrition counseling to bring about comfortable, permanent lifestyle changes. This includes classes, private clients and physican referrals for general compulsive eating, compulsive eating, all weight problems, diabetes, gestational diabetes, high cholesterol and triglycerides, vegetarian diets, maternal nutrition, government, and food allergies. Combines expertise in nutrition, psychology, counseling, and education.

LANGLEY & ASSOCIATES, P.C.
100 Glenborough Dr., Ste. 930
Houston, TX 77067
PH: (281)873-5320
FX: (281)873-5216
Founded: 1980. Medical management consulting firm.

LILLIAN LANGSETH
PO Box 700
Palisades, NY 10964
Lillian Langseth, President
PH: (914)359-8282
FX: (914)359-1229
Founded: 1980. **Staff:** 8. Consultants who produce technical documents in biomedical science, specializing in clinical nutrition, nutrition, food safety, and toxicology. Serves private industries as well as government agencies. Geographic areas served: United States and international.

LASCOLA QUALITATIVE RESEARCH
e-mail: lindalascdia@com
3900 Connecticut Ave., Ste. 101F
Washington, DC 20008
Linda J. LaScola, President
PH: (202)363-9367
FX: (202)244-1623
Founded: 1984. **Staff:** 1. Provides qualitative research, including focus groups, in-depth interviewing and analysis. Specializes in health and mental health, public affairs, human resources, and social issues. Has expertise with exploratory studies, sensitive topics and difficult respondents. Serves private industries as well as government agencies. Geographic areas served: Washington DC, and national. **Conferences and Meetings:** *Focus Group Demonstrations; Conducting Issues Research; Contributions of Social Science Disciplines to Qualitative Research; Reaching Minorities on Mental Health Issues.*

LATHAM ASSOCIATES
9702 Gayton Rd., Ste. 220
Richmond, VA 23233
David J. Latham
PH: (804)741-6507
FX: (804)750-2374
Founded: 1989. **Staff:** 1. Medicare consultant specializing in Medicare Part B physician reimbursement, coding and billing advice. Offers physician guidance regarding Medicare allowances, appeals process, electronic claim submission and cash flow enhancement techniques. Provides training for office staffs in procedure and diagnostic coding, Medicare eligibility and coverage, form completion, improved billing methods and how to increase Medicare payments. Industries served: physicians, dentists, podiatrists, chiropractors, optometrists, ambulance services, durable medical equipment suppliers, independent laboratories, and government agencies. Geographic areas served: Virginia. **Conferences and Meetings:** *Series on ICD-9-CM Diagnostic Coding.*

DEBRA F. LATIMER NUTRITION ASSOCIATES
7505 Fannin, Ste. 203
Houston, TX 77054
Debra Fermer Latimer, R.D., L.D., C.D.E.
PH: (713)795-0876
FX: (713)795-5126
Founded: 1981. **Staff:** 2. Provides nutrition education and counseling. Plans and conducts corporate wellness programs. Serves food service and food manufacturing industries, as well as government agencies. Geographic Areas Served: Greater Houston. **Conferences and Meetings:** *Preventive and Treatment Plans for Cardiac Care; Pre and Post-natal Nutrition; Pre-menstrual Syndrome; Eating for the Health of It; Weight Management and Wellness Program; Supermarket Nutrition Tours.* **Computer/Special Services:** Nutritional analysis, body composition analysis.

LEES-HALEY CORPORATION
21331 Costanso St.
Woodland Hills, CA 91364
Cheryl Lees-Haley, President
PH: (818)887-2874
FX: (818)887-9034
Founded: 1988. **Staff:** 5. Specialists in the evaluation of mass injury claims and fear of future illness claims, environmental and toxic claims, psychological and neuropsychological injury claims, sexual harassment claims, and numerous other types of personal injury claims. Provides training and consulting to risk managers, claims managers, and attorneys. Offers in-house lectures for selfinsured companies, insurers and reinsurers, and literature reviews in complex litigation. Industries served: chemical, oil, insurance, medical device manufacturers - almost any industry involved in litigation. Geographic areas served: U.S. **Conferences and Meetings:** *New Trends in Environmental Injury; Good Science Versus Junk Science in the Evaluation of Traumatic Injury; Vocational Neuropsychological Evaluations of Head Injury Patients.*

PAUL D. LEPORE
e-mail: glpuru@aol.com
url: http://glpguru.com
5724 Cedar Ln.
Columbia, MD 21044
Paul D. Lepore
PH: (410)720-0102
FX: (410)730-3095

Provides information on biomedical laboratory practices and quality assurance.

DR. STEVEN E. LERNER & ASSOCIATES
e-mail: mail@drlerner.com
url: http://www.drlerner.com
930 Irwin St., Ste. 209
San Rafael, CA 94901-3363
Steven E. Lerner, President/CEO
PH: (415)453-6900
TF: 800952-7563
FX: (415)454-0126
Founded: 1974. Multidisciplinary group of medical specialists (DPM, OD, OTR, PharmD, RN and RPT) who are available for case evaluations and expert testimony. All physicians are board-certified. Most are medical school faculty members.

MARILYN LEVASSEUR
2595 Hickory Grove
Bloomfield Hills, MI 48302
Marilyn LeVasseur
PH: (248)335-5924
FX: (248)335-5924
Founded: 1984. **Staff:** 3. Provides seminars, programs or individual consultation for home healthcare, either Medicare/Medicaid, private pay or other insurances. The emphasis ranges from agency start-up and encompasses any area of the home care agency: i.e., financial, management, nursing, marketing, and public relations. Serves government agencies also. Geographic areas served: U.S. and Canada.

MARK I. LEVY, MD, FAPA
e-mail: mark@levymd.com
url: http://www.levymd.com
655 Redwood Hwy., Ste. 271
Mill Valley, CA 94941
PH: (415)388-8040
FX: (415)388-1225
Specializes in post traumatic stress disorder, including witnessing or sustaining injury from disaster, violence, bereavement, torture, terrorization, auto/aircraft/industrial accidents, severe pain, rape, divorce, anxiety, work/school performance, sleep disturbance, depression, fearfulness, sexual dysfunction, psychotic states, molestation, sexual harassment, drug/alcohol abuse, job stress/violence/harassment, and psychiatric malpractice.

JOHN J. LICCARDO, MD
2239 S. Broad St.
Trenton, NJ 08610-5503
PH: (609)396-0964
FX: (609)396-1018
Evaluates and testifies in cases involving child abuse, termination of parental rights, medical malpractice, criminal cases (competency, diminished capacity, insanity defense), workers' compensation, personal injury, and sexual harassment.

CAROLE LIEBERMAN, MD
247 S. Beverly Dr., Ste. 202
Beverly Hills, CA 90212
PH: (310)278-5433
FX: (310)456-2458
A witness and legal consultant forensic psychiatry, specializing in high-profile cases, sexual harassment, entertainment law, divorce, custody, psychiatric malpractice, sports injuries, criminal behavior, violence, and work/personal injury law. Geographic areas served: U.S. **Conferences and Meetings:** *How to Use A Psychiatric Expert to Win Cases.*

RICHARD LIEBERMAN, MD
2112 Divisadero St.
San Francisco, CA 94115
PH: (415)346-9333
FX: (415)346-8170
Provides expert witness testimony and psychiatric-legal evalua-

tions, in matters that include criminal behavior, sexual harassment, workers' compensation, divorce, custody, psychiatric malpractice, post-traumatic stress disorders, false memory syndromes, and violence.

LIFE-LINE
e-mail: healthie1@aol.com
url: http://www.hlthmall.com/healthmall/life-line/
PO Box 482
Bronxville, NY 10708
Joan A. Friedrich, Ph.D., President
PH: (914)423-3531
FX: (914)423-3531
Founded: 1985. **Staff:** 2. Stress and lifestyle management consulting on nutrition, biofeedback, fitness, holistic health, and wellness. Services include research, writing, educational programs, and media presentations on various health and nutrition related areas. Seminars and workshops conducted on topics such as family health, wellness, stress management, osteoporosis, aging, immunity and others. Presentations given to hospitals, corporations, colleges, schools and special groups. Industries served: health, nutrition, public relations, education, and government agencies. Geographic areas served: United States and international. **Conferences and Meetings:** *Better Health Series; 8-week Weight Management; Stress Management, Nutrition, Wellness; general workshops on diet and nutrition, wellness, weight, disease prevention, consumer workshops, and professional trainings.*

LINDA MILES & ASSOCIATE
e-mail: llmile@ix.netcom.com
4356-2 Bonney Rd., Ste. 103
Virginia Beach, VA 23452
Linda Miles, Pres.
PH: (757)498-0014
FX: (757)498-0290
Founded: 1978. **Staff:** 15. Offers staff management development services to dentists in the United States and Canada.

ANN K. LOMBARD, R.D., NUTRITION COUNSELING SERVICES
48 Main St.
Bridgton, ME 04009
Ann K. Lombard
PH: (207)647-3889
Founded: 1987. **Staff:** 1. Provides individualized therapeutic and weight loss diet counseling. Conducts group weight loss programs. Acts as a resource and referral person for physicians. Geographic areas served: Oxford and Cumberland Counties, Maine. **Conferences and Meetings:** *Provides community lectures on various nutrition topics.*

DAVID A. LOMBARDI, MD
e-mail: David_Lombardi@msn.com
1125 E. 17th St., Ste. W-117
Santa Ana, CA 92701
PH: (714)558-7050
FX: (714)558-8942
A board certified neurologist and medical evaluator specializing workers' compensation.

LONGSHORE SIMMONS
625 Richpike, Ste. 410
Conshohocken, PA 19428
H.J. Simmons, III, Principal
PH: (610)941-3400
FX: (610)941-2424
Firm offers expertise on healthcare-related issues.

LYDA ASSOCIATES INC.
e-mail: l.langseth@worldnet.att.net
PO Box 700
Palisades, NY 10964
Lillian Langseth, President

PH: (914)359-8282
FX: (914)359-1229
Founded: 1980. **Staff:** 5. Offers consulting services in clinical nutrition, food safety, toxicology, and health sciences. Provides technical writing, editing, technical documents, and ghost writing services. Specializes in newsletters. Industries served: food, food supplements, vitamins and minerals, food-related trade organizations, as well as government agencies. Geographic areas served: U.S. and international.

M C P C GROUP INC.
9602 Montemar Dr.
Spring Valley, CA 91977-3425
Dave Cowan, Executive Director
PH: (619)462-8585
FX: (619)698-3348
Founded: 1989. **Staff:** 3. Nonprofit organization consults on drug education programs, including programs for families.

SISTER MARY CHRISTELLE MACALUSO -R.S.M., OFN. PH.D., THE FUN NUN
e-mail: funnun@csm.edu
url: http://www.speakers-podium.com/funnun
College of Saint Mary
1901 72nd St.
Omaha, NE 68124-2377
Sister Mary Christelle Macaluso, R.S.M., OFN, Ph.D.
PH: (402)399-2474
FX: (402)399-2686
Founded: 1980. **Staff:** 1. Personal skills development specialist focuses on being a seminar presenter, a convention speaker, and an after banquet speaker. Seminars and tapes include: Wellness and Your Funny Bone; Self-Image and Interpersonal Relationships; Stress: What's It All About, and others. Serves education, healthcare, nonprofit organizations and associations, business, government, and religious organizations in the U.S. and Canada. **Conferences and Meetings:** *Topic areas: Humor, Stress, Self-Image*

MACKEEN CONSULTANTS LIMITED
e-mail: d4903@msn.com
4903 Sangamore Rd.
Bethesda, MD 20816
PH: (301)229-7445
FX: (301)229-3541
Founded: 1980. Health services consulting firm focuses on medical product development.

M.A.F. EMERGENCY VACCINE DELIVERY
35 Pinelawn Rd., Ste. LL8
Melville, NY 11747
Nancy Seidman, R.N. and Medical Advisor
PH: (516)696-5932
FX: (516)420-1657
Founded: 1994. **Staff:** 3. Consults with public health officials, physicians, and families in need of emergency delivery of vaccines that are not readily available (or that are not being served by the WHO program) for infants and pre-natal mothers. Assists with overcoming logistical, transportation, cold-packaging, and syringe related problems; also assists with the relatively rapid delivery of vaccines to distant locations and with the orientation and training of vaccine providers. Offers these services and other special projects to the public health sector worldwide with special focus on developing nations.

MALLOY & ASSOCIATES, INC.
354 Whites Landing
Long Beach, CA 90803-6823
John J. Malloy, President
PH: (562)494-1632
FX: (562)494-2842
Founded: 1986. **Staff:** 3. Provides guidance to medical device and pharmaceutical manufacturers in the area of U.S. Food and Drug Administration and International Standards Organization requirements. Areas of expertise include good manufacturing practices (GMP), International Standards (ISO 9001), and operation audits: 510(k), IDE, PMA, and other submissions to the U.S. Food and Drug Administration. The firm also presents GMP, ISO, and software development seminars. Clients include start-ups, large corporations, international firms, and government agencies worldwide. **Conferences and Meetings:** *Good Manufacturing Practices for the Medical Device Industry; Good Laboratory Practices; Software, The FDA and Your Medical Device; Preproduction Quality Assurance; ISO-9000 and Medical Devices.*

E. DAVID MANACE, MD
e-mail: e.d.manace@aol.com
California Pacific Medical Center
2100 Webster St., Ste. 200
San Francisco, CA 94115
PH: (415)923-3133
FX: (415)931-5849
Specializes in otolaryngology (ear, nose and throat and facial plastic surgery).

MANAGED CARE SOLUTIONS, INC.
7600 N. 16th St., Ste. 150
Phoenix, AZ 85020
James Burns, President
PH: (602)331-5100
TF: 800377-2055
FX: (602)331-5199
Founded: 1989. **Staff:** 105. Offer managed care, HMO and Medicaid consulting services. Industries served: HMO's, Medicaid health plans, hospitals, and physicians. Geographic areas served: U.S. **Conferences and Meetings:** *Medicaid Managed Care Opportunities.* **Computer/Special Services:** Proprietary software used to manage the company's HMO, Medicaid, and long-term care service products.

MANAGED HEALTH CONSULTANTS INC.
100 Grandview Rd., Ste. 210
Braintree, MA 02184
PH: (781)356-4994
TF: 800526-8613
FX: (781)356-2998
Founded: 1988. **Staff:** 20. Health care consultants specializing in reimbursement management, indigent patient programs, patient compliance and case management.

MANAGEMENT 1-PRACTICE SYSTEMS
7302 E. Helm Dr., Ste. 2006
Scottsdale, AZ 85260
PH: (602)991-3319
FX: (602)368-8754
Founded: 1985. Offers medical/chiropractic practice management counsel.

MANAGEMENT SCIENCES FOR HEALTH INC.
e-mail: development@msh.org
url: http://www.msh.org
165 Allardale Rd.
Boston, MA 02130-3400
Ronald W. O'Connor, CEO and President
PH: (617)524-7799
FX: (617)965-2208
Founded: 1971. **Staff:** 300. Nonprofit public health management organization. Manages the Family Planning Management Development project, and the National Pharmaceutical Management and Rational Pharmaceutical Management Projects, both of which are funded by the U.S. Agency for International Development. **Conferences and Meetings:** *1998 Management Training Courses: Executive Course in Health Financing and Sustainability, Strategic Leadership for the 21st Century: Impact and Sustainability, Planning and Managing Information and Communications Systems, Leadership Strategique pour l'Efficacite' des Programmes au 21 Siecle, Managing Decentralized Health Systems, Managing Suc-*

cessful Training Programs, Gerencia de Programas: Gestion Administrativa para Asegurar la Calidad, Gestion Decentralisee des Systemes de Sante.

KARL MANDERS, MD
c/o Neurosurgical Associates of Indiana
7209 N. Shadeland Ave.
Indianapolis, IN 46250
Karl Manders, MD
PH: (317)577-3900
FX: (317)579-7459
Medico-legal consultancy offers expertise in neurological surgery, review, depositions, and trial testimony.

THE MARCANTELLI GROUP – NEW ORLEANS
PO Box 29744
New Orleans, LA 70129
Carlos J. Marcantelli, Ph.D., Managing Partner
PH: (504)522-5111
Specializes in investigations attorney services, asset searches, skip tracing, certified fraud investigations, security consulting, and travel security consulting for Mexico, Central and South America.

SHELDON MARGULIES, MD
e-mail: Ismarg@erols.com
2411 W. Belvedere Ave., Ste. 202
Baltimore, MD 21215
PH: (410)367-7600
FX: (410)578-6871
A neurologist and neurology consultant specializing in medical malpractice, mild and severe head injury, spinal cord injury, peripheral nerve injury, toxic torts, neuropsychologic testing, and issues of causation.

MARINER HEALTHCARE, INC.
44 Maritime Dr.
Mystic, CT 06355-2521
Dr. Arthur L. Stratton, Jr.
PH: (860)572-1700
FX: (860)572-7830
Founded: 1986. **Staff:** 1300. Health care consultants.

WILLIAM A. MARKEY
866 Princeton Dr.
PO Box F
Sonoma, CA 95476
William A. Markey
PH: (707)996-2212
FX: (707)935-6744
Founded: 1984. Health care consultant offering advice on hospital management improvement programs, middle management involvement in strategic planning, goal setting, professional practice enhancement, implementation, and IPA, PPO, and HMO networking. Geographic areas served: primarily northern California.

ROBERT J. MARSHALL & ASSOCIATES INC.
1010 Crenshaw Blvd., Ste. 170
Torrance, CA 90501-2055
Robert J. Marshall
PH: (310)787-8751
FX: (310)320-8930
Founded: 1975. **Staff:** 20. Provides nutrition information and consulting.

MARSHFIELD CLINIC VIDEO NETWORK
1000 N. Oak Ave.
Marshfield, WI 54449
Ed Korlesky
PH: (715)387-5127
FX: (715)387-5240
Founded: 1978. **Staff:** 8. Medical education specialists serving physicians, nurses, laboratories, and allied healthcare organiza-tions, as well as various government agencies. Produces audiovisual and other educational programs as well as numerous supplemental medical evaluation videotapes ranging in subject content from allergies to cost containment topics of urology and rheumatology; available in single or series format. Geographic areas served: United States and Canada. **Conferences and Meetings:** *Presents over 100 seminars yearly.*

MARYVIEW WELLSPRING HOME CARE
3636 High St.
Portsmouth, VA 23707
Marie Biggers-Gray
PH: (757)398-2338
FX: (757)393-4762
Founded: 1979. **Staff:** 55. Consulting services include hospital-based home care. Serves home health agencies and hospices. **Conferences and Meetings:** *Principal serves as facilitator of programs on managing quality and productivity in healthcare.*

JOSEPH B. MARZOUK MD
e-mail: jobm@aol.com
350 30th St., Ste. 511
Oakland, CA 94609
PH: (510)923-6225
FX: (510)923-1649
Specializes in infectious diseases, infection control; AIDS; food poisoning. Provides independent medical evaluations. Offers medical malpractice testimony.

MASSACHUSETTS HEALTH DATA CONSORTIUM INC.
url: http://www.mahealthdata.org
460 Totten Pond Rd., 3rd Fl.
Waltham, MA 02451
Elliot Stone, Exec. Director
PH: (781)890-6040
FX: (781)890-5460
Founded: 1978. **Staff:** 10. Offers healthcare management services to medical institutions in the eastern United States. **Conferences and Meetings:** *Health Mart Carnival in September, Strategic Issue in Ambulatory Care Carnival in June.* **Computer/Special Services:** Affiliated Health Information Networks of New England.

DR. MATHIS AND ASSOCIATES
3435 Valle Verde Dr., Ste. C
Napa, CA 94558
R. William Mathis, Principal
PH: (707)252-2151
FX: (707)252-1349
Specializes in clinical and industrial psychology. Offers expert witness testimony for personnel and wrongful termination, discrimination (sexual, age, etc.), and personal injury cases. Offers social security, disability, workers' compensation, stress management and post-traumatic stress, and medical malpractice evaluation and assessment, and abuse valuations.

CHARLES M. MATHIS ASSOCIATES INC.
45 S. Broadway, Ste. 206
Yonkers, NY 10701
Charles M. Mathis, Pres.
PH: (914)476-0454
FX: (914)476-1932
Founded: 1986. **Staff:** 7. Medical management consultants serving community healthcare centers.

MATTSON JACK GROUP INC.
e-mail: vickim@mattsonjack.com
url: http://www.mattsonjack.com
11960 Westline Industrial Dr., Ste. 180
St. Louis, MO 63146
William R. Mattson, Jr., Pres.
PH: (314)469-7600
FX: (314)469-6794
Founded: 1986. **Staff:** 45. Advises pharmaceutical companies on strategic issues or opportunities, and corporate development ac-

tivities. Geographic Areas Served: North America, Europe and Japan. **Conferences and Meetings:** *Offers model building workshops.* **Computer/Special Services:** Produces MEDSTRATEGY(tm)Management Reports.

MAXIMUS INC.
e-mail: info@maxinc.com
url: http://www.maximus-inc.com
1356 Beverly Rd.
McLean, VA 22101
David V. Mastran, CEO
PH: (703)734-4200
TF: 800368-2152
FX: (703)734-4277
Founded: 1975. **Staff:** 1000. Offers health and human services, information technolgy, surveys and evaluation, reverse maximization, and management support. **Computer/Special Services:** MAXSTAR (tn)- Human Services Application Builder.

MBC CONSULTANTS INC.
e-mail: mbc@wealthnet.com
url: http://www.planetmbc.com
1023 32nd Ave. East
Seattle, WA 98112-3703
Marc B. Cooper, DDS, MSD, CPC, President and CEO
PH: (206)323-2820
FX: (206)325-5180
Founded: 1985. Educates, trains and develops executives, care providers and board directors in organizational development, leadership, management and integration in the United States.

LINDA S. MCDONALD, MS, RD, LD
e-mail: linda@supermarketsavvy.com
url: http://www.supermarketsavvy.com
11102 Lakeside Forest Ln.
Houston, TX 77042-1032
Linda McDonald
PH: (713)978-6960
FX: (713)978-7044
Founded: 1984. **Staff:** 1. Specializes in providing nutrition support for the food industry - processors, producers and food service. Solutions start with the development or reformulation of products, continue through the labeling process, and provide expertise to position products in the health conscious marketplace. Expertise in the health and medical fields can help position products for the best results. Also experienced in media and material development for the consumer and health professional. Mrs. McDonald is also available as a speaker on related nutrition topics. Geographic Areas Served: National and International. **Conferences and Meetings:** *Healthy Trends in the Retail Food Industry.* **Computer/Special Services:** Computer nutrient analysis of food ingredients, new FDA food label camera ready design.

T.R. MCDOUGAL & ASSOCIATES INC.
1345 Carmichael Way
Montgomery, AL 36106-3692
T.R. McDougal, President
PH: (334)260-8600
TF: 800826-9410
FX: (334)260-0023
Founded: 1990. **Staff:** 9. Firm offers expertise in medicine and healthcare. Serves hospitals, physici ans, living facilities and commercial concerns in the southeastern U.S. **Conferences and Meetings:** *Strategic planning, CQI, managed care, managing change.*

R.S. MCQUATE & ASSOCIATES INC.
e-mail: mcquate@aol.com
3636 E. Columbine Dr.
Phoenix, AZ 85032
Robert S. McQuate, President
PH: (602)485-5495
FX: (602)485-5495
Founded: 1987. **Staff:** 4. Provides technical regulatory assistance

with emphasis on FDA approvals and compliance issues associated with foods and medical devices. Offers particular expertise with food and color additives, food labeling, and in vitro diagnostic products. Industries served: foods and food ingredients; medical device manufacturers and distributors. Geographic areas served: Pacific Rim countries and western states.

BARBARA H. MCSHEFFERY
2720 Tremont Rd.
Columbus, OH 43221
Barbara McSheffery
PH: (614)481-8465
FX: (614)481-8465
Founded: 1981. **Staff:** 1. Offers nutrition and diet consultation services for all age groups and health levels, well or with medical diagnosis. Serves private industries as well as government agencies. **Conferences and Meetings:** *Weight Management; Cholesterol Reduction; Whats New in Nutrition; Nutrition and Environmental Concerns; Cooking for Singles or Twosomes; Using the New (1994) Nutrition Facts Food Label.*

MD CONSULTANT
621 Pine Brook Blvd.
New Rochelle, NY 10804
Toni Gloria Novick, M.D.
PH: (914)235-1526
FX: (914)235-3797
Founded: 1992. **Staff:** 2. Firm is a medical information and research service that accesses the most current information and research from journals around the world. Clients are individual patients or medical or legal professionals.

MDI CONSULTING, INC.
e-mail: info@mdiconsultants.com
url: http://www.mdiconsultant.com
55 Northern Blvd., Ste. 410
Great Neck, NY 11021
Alan P. Schwartz, Senior Advisor
PH: (516)482-9001
TF: 800448-4407
FX: (516)482-0186
Founded: 1978. Management consulting company assisting companies to comply with FDA regulations, quality assurance programs, ISO certification, strategic partnering, strategic planning.

MEC HEALTH CARE, INC.
100 Park Ave.
Baltimore, MD 21201
Mark Gordon, CEO & President
PH: (410)752-1980
TF: 800766-4393
FX: (410)752-1990
Founded: 1986. Managed healthcare firm devotes itself to eliminating unnecessary medical costs in eye care while promoting superior quality care. Firm has formulated a successful model incorporating customized software, utilization review, credentialing, quality assurance, claims and billings, authorizations and triage.

THE MED GROUP, INC.
url: http://www.medgroup.com
3223 S. 289 Loop, Ste. 600
Lubbock, TX 79423
David Miller, President
PH: (806)793-8421
TF: 800825-5633
FX: (806)793-6480
Founded: 1986. **Staff:** 25. General medical supplies consultant. Provides education and training materials, accreditation system "maps", and independent medical equipment network provider.

MEDFALL, INC.
6150 Valley Way, Ste. 207
Niagara Falls, ON, Canada L2E 1Y3
Patrick Gibney, M.D., President
PH: (905)357-6644
FX: (905)357-2601
Staff: 5. Firm specializes in the recruitment of specialist physicians and medical executives. Serves hospitals, clinics, insurance companies, government, and other health-related services in Canada, as well as international clients.

MEDI-LEGAL SERVICES
url: http://www.autopsy-organretrieval.com
PO Box 1464
El Cajon, CA 92022
Steven H. Keyser, President
PH: (619)579-2135
TF: 800343-2135
FX: (619)444-6473
Founded: 1973. Offers evaluation of potential medical, dental and legal malpractice cases. Immediate autopsy services by Certified Pathologists also available in any type case, civil or criminal. Provides highly qualified medical and legal experts to testify in meritorious cases. Types of cases involve medical malpractice, personal injury, worker's compensation, medical product liability, drug related liability issues, legal malpractice and other professional liability litigation. Experts available include physicians, osteopaths, surgeons, dentists, attorneys, nurses, chiropractors, podiatrists, and accountants. Serves plaintiff and defense. Industries served: attorneys, hospitals, governmental agencies, medical societies, news media and insurance companies. Geographic Areas Served: All U.S. & Canada. **Conferences and Meetings:** *Medical Malpractice Defense Seminars; seminars on laparoscopy and nurse malpractice; seminars on radiology malpractice, and hospital/staff negligence avoidance.*

MEDI-SHARE INC.
24725 W. 12 Mile Rd.
Southfield, MI 48034-1801
James G. Moschini, Pres.
PH: (248)354-6225
FX: (248)354-5892
Founded: 1986. **Staff:** 8. Offers total healthcare management services, focusing primarily on managed care and shared services. Industries served: healthcare in the Midwest.

MEDICAL AUDIT CONSULTANTS
12915 Jones Maltsberger Rd.
San Antonio, TX 78247-4254
Elaine Munoz, Owner
PH: (210)494-1167
FX: (210)494-8332
Founded: 1982. **Staff:** 11. Provides accounting services, specializing in the auditing of healthcare facilities. Industries served: commercial concerns in the United States.

MEDICAL CARE MANAGEMENT CORPORATION
e-mail: mcman@mcman.com
url: http://www.mcman.com
5272 River Rd., Ste. 650
Bethesda, MD 20816-1405
Peter G. Goldschmidt
PH: (301)652-1818
FX: (301)652-1250
Founded: 1992. Provides expert reviews of high technology, high cost, high risk medical procedures, and of appeals and other centuries of high technology cases. Also offers a wide range of other programs pertaining to high technology, high risk, high cost medical procedures. Provides experts to help organizations learn how to do the following: create an identification program for high technology, high cost, high risk cases; establish a second opinion program; organize an outcomes research program; set up a "center of excellence" program to determine criteria for patients who may undergo high technology, high risk, high cost procedures;

and structure communication with providers and patients to inform them of program purposes and case review procedures. Industries served: employers, insurers, managed care organizations, lawyers, physicians and patients. Geographic areas served: international. **Conferences and Meetings:** *Provides seminars on the latest advances in and issues surrounding high technology, high risk, high cost medical procedures.*

MEDICAL CITIES INC.
7777 Forest Ln., Ste. C840
Dallas, TX 75230-2594
R.J. Wright, Pres.
PH: (972)566-6101
TF: 800633-7305
FX: (972)566-8882
Founded: 1972. **Staff:** 10. Offers medical facilities planning and real estate development. Industries served: healthcare regionally.

MEDICAL CONSULTANTS NORTHWEST INC.
url: http://www.ncn.com
901 Boren Ave., Ste. 1400
Seattle, WA 98104-3529
Brian Grant, Pres.
PH: (206)622-8128
FX: (206)343-2196
Founded: 1985. Offers independent medical advice to insurance companies, the state of Washington, and the general public.

MEDICAL EDUCATION CONSULTANTS LTD.
PO Box 315, Sta. A
Richmond Hill, ON, Canada L4C 4Y2
PH: (416)321-1056
FX: (905)737-0533
Founded: 1985. **Staff:** 6. Provides programs in hospital training and industrial health and accident prevention. The company produces programs from existing material suitable for implementing as professional healthcare training programs for healthcare workers and other professionals. **Conferences and Meetings:** *Back in Motion.*

MEDICAL INTEGRATED SERVICES, INC.
2000 Chestnut Blvd.
Cuyahoga Falls, OH 44223
Philip Wojcik, President/CEO
PH: (216)928-0706
TF: 800828-0706
FX: (216)928-0077
Founded: 1973. **Staff:** 32. Provides clinical/professional engineering consulting, preventive maintenance, and repair services to client hospitals. Also provides environmental testing, thermography, medical gas systems verification, anesthesia, laboratory, EtO waste gas, vapor testing, computer/data processing, codes and standards, and JCAHO consulting services to hospital clients. Industries served: healthcare and construction. Geographic areas served: Ohio, Michigan, Kentucky, West Virginia, and Pennsylvania. **Conferences and Meetings:** *Ethylene Oxide/OSHA Regulations; Thermography.*

MEDICAL-LEGAL CONSULTANTS, INC.
6361 Nancy Ridge Dr.
San Diego, CA 92121
Mark A. Gomez, Ph.D., Principal
PH: (619)457-9711
FX: (619)457-9775
Provides forensic, biomechanical, and medical analysis of causation and prevention of accidental injury, including vehicular, industrial, sport, construction and other accident environments. Evaluates protective devices and safety systems, including seat belts and helmets. Evaluates work place hazards. Offers computer reconstruction and animation.

MEDICAL LIABILITY CONSULTANTS
1500 Marina Bay Dr., Ste. 1600
Clear Lake Shores, TX 77565
M. Lee Gunter, Principal
PH: (281)334-5166
FX: (281)334-7712
Provides evaluations, fee assessments, and expert testimony in medical negligence and personal injury claims.

MEDICAL MANAGEMENT SERVICES INC.
1651 W. Front St.
Berwick, PA 18603-2305
Thomas J. Powell, Manager
PH: (717)759-7619
TF: 800982-0886
FX: (717)759-7613
Founded: 1981. **Staff:** 10. Business related health services firm provides expertise on billing services for doctors offices.

MEDICAL MANAGEMENT SYSTEMS OF MICHIGAN INC.
1701 Lake Lansing Rd., Ste. 100
Lansing, MI 48912-3708
Jeanne Rutledge, Pres.
PH: (517)485-0001
FX: (517)485-2622
Founded: 1983. **Staff:** 50. Advises physicians and hospitals in Michigan on healthcare management, billing, and audits. **Conferences and Meetings:** *Workers Compensation; I & D 9-CM, CPY and HCPCS coding; Exceptional Receptionist.* **Computer/Special Services:** On-line services.

MEDICAL MARKETING MANAGEMENT LTD.
e-mail: actonsell@aol.com
24333 Southfield Rd., Ste. 201
Southfield, MI 48075-2822
Stephen Sell, Pres.
PH: (248)569-5460
TF: 800473-5460
FX: (248)569-5469
Founded: 1982. **Staff:** 7. Advises on health services management, specializing in physician recruiting and general healthcare employment and interviewing. Industries served: businesses in the United States.

MEDICAL OPINIONS ASSOCIATES
31 Rich Valley Rd.
Wayland, MA 01778
Arthur S. Fine, Principal
PH: 800-874-7677
FX: (508)358-4716
Board-certified physicians evaluate medical records, write opinion letters, and are available for consultation, deposition, or trial.

MEDICAL PHYSICS CONSULTANTS INC.
2309 Shelby Ave.
Ann Arbor, MI 48103
James Carey, President
PH: (313)662-3197
TF: 800321-2207
FX: (313)662-9224
Founded: 1978. **Staff:** 20. Medical consulting group provides hospitals with nuclear medicine and physics support. Industries served: medical and industrial using radiation. Geographic areas served: Michigan, Ohio, Indiana, and Kentucky. **Conferences and Meetings:** *Regulatory compliance seminars.* **Computer/Special Services:** Specially developed software for testing nuclear medicine cameras and x-ray machines.

MEDICAL PLANNING & CONSULTANTS, INC.
1545 Whitstable Ct.
Heathrow, PA 32746
Joseph L. Beisler, President
PH: (407)444-5958
FX: (407)444-5658
Founded: 1979. **Staff:** 4. Specialists in the development of healthcare facilities including ambulatory surgical centers, cardiology, diagnostic imaging, home IV therapy, and radiation therapy centers. Consulting focuses on business development, financing/leasing, program planning, and facility design and construction.

MEDICAL RESEARCH CONSORTIUM INC.
6220 Lawrence Dr.
Indianapolis, IN 46226
Jack H. Hall, President
PH: (317)549-3131
FX: (317)549-3670
Founded: 1993. **Staff:** 4. Conduct and consult on research studies and clinical trials. Geographic areas served: U.S.

MEDICAL REVIEW FOUNDATION, INC.
e-mail: medexperts@aol.com
url: http://www.malpracticeexperts.com
120 Beulah Rd. NE., Ste. 200
Vienna, VA 22180
Renee Jacobs, President
TF: 800336-0332
FX: (703)255-6134
Founded: 1976. **Staff:** 5. A large medical-legal consulting firm made up of more than 5000 independent, board certified medical experts, in all specialities. Consultants review medical records, prepare written reports and testify. Offers free case evaluations. **Conferences and Meetings:** *Medical Malpractice and Personal Injury Weekend Teaching Seminars are held in the San Diego, CA. area.*

MEDICAL STRATEGIES INC.
1709 Westbelt Dr.
Columbus, OH 43228
Lisa M. Stein, General Manager
PH: (614)274-0200
TF: 800825-3742
FX: (614)529-1259
Founded: 1986. Advises U.S. drug manufacturers on healthcare issues, marketing, and advertising; and develops computer software.

MEDILEX, INC.
175 E. 96th St., Ste. 8H
New York, NY 10128-6204
PH: (212)860-8700
FX: (212)860-8263
Medical-legal case review, consultation and expert testimony. Provides high quality, cost-effective medical and scientific expertise. Specializes in malpractice, toxic tort, forensic pathology, products liability and behavioral science matters.

MEDISYS INC.
1170 Delsea Dr.
Westville, NJ 08093
Alex Makris
PH: (609)848-2954
FX: (609)848-3453
Founded: 1988. **Staff:** 8. Medical consultants specialize in infection control.

MEDRICON INC.
2702 Whitney Ave.
Hamden, CT 06518
Vince Manopoli, President
PH: (203)281-1899
FX: (203)288-7687
Founded: 1985. **Staff:** 7. Medical consultants specializing in ophthalmology. Industries served: healthcare reimbursement consulting. **Conferences and Meetings:** *Conducts seminars on physician practice management.* **Computer/Special Services:** Provides Medricon Information Clearinghouse Hotline, manned by policy analysts specializing in Medicare policy information.

MEDTRONIC INC.
7000 Central Ave. NE
Minneapolis, MN 55432
PH: (612)574-4000
FX: (612)574-4879
Founded: 1972. **Staff:** 34. Works with industrial and government agencies to develop procedures to test chemicals and drugs or medical device products to meet federal regulations for Food and Drug Administration, Environmental Protection Agency, Department of Transportation, and other regulatory agencies.

H.M. MEHENDALE
e-mail: pymehendale@alpha.nlu.edu
url: http://www.198.79.220.3/farmacy/mahendale/default.htm
Northeast Louisiana University
College of Pharmacy & Health Science
Div. of Toxicology
Monroe, LA 71209-0470
PH: (318)342-1691
FX: (318)342-1686
Toxicology specialist. Areas of expertise include chemical toxicology, pesticides, solvents, and other industrial chemicals; cancer; regulatory affairs,; occupational or accidental exposures and short- or long-term hazards; hazardous wastes; forensic toxicological analysis of extraneous evidence; body fluids and tissues, drugs, and intoxicants; and exposure to single or combinations of chemicals; and toxicological data interpretations.

MERCY MERCY HEALTH PLANS
34605 W. 12 Mile Rd.
Farmington Hills, MI 48331-3263
Robert J. Flanagan, CEO
PH: (248)489-6000
FX: (248)489-6932
Founded: 1986. **Staff:** 185. Offers organizational development and management services to NASA and U.S. Air Force healthcare providers.

MERRITT HAWKINS & ASSOCIATES
e-mail: info@practice-net.com
222 W. Las Colinas Blvd., Ste. 1920
Irving, TX 75039
James Merritt, President
PH: (972)868-2200
TF: 800876-0500
FX: (972)868-2222
Founded: 1988. **Staff:** 130. Physician recruitment firm. Industries served: healthcare. Geographic areas served: U.S.

C.W. METCALF & CO.
e-mail: gayemetco@aol.com
2801 S. Remington, Ste. 2
Fort Collins, CO 80525
Roma Felible, President
PH: (970)226-0610
TF: 800LIT-ENUP
FX: (970)226-6755
Founded: 1980. **Staff:** 3. Offers programs to corporate, healthcare, government and education industry clients focusing on humor, risk, and change adaptation; creativity; communication; and health and humor. Geographic areas served: international. **Conferences and Meetings:** *Practical Imagination; Humor and Creativity; Humor, Risk and Change(tm); Liten-Up(tm).*

METHODIST HEALTH SYSTEMS FOUNDATION INC.
5620 Read Blvd.
New Orleans, LA 70127-2647
Frederick C. Young, Jr., Pres.
PH: (504)244-5950
FX: (504)244-4585
Founded: 1981. **Staff:** 23. Advises regional hospitals on healthcare management and fund-raising.

METIS ASSOCIATES, LTD.
e-mail: metisltd@aol.com
10 S. Riverside Plaza, Ste. 1710
Chicago, IL 60606
Andrew S. Mazurek, President
PH: (312)648-0040
FX: (312)648-1067
Founded: 1984. **Staff:** 20. Specializes in healthcare facilities planning, including long-range master facility planning, functional and space programming, departmental space planning and design, equipment planning and code and compliance reviews. Serves healthcare facilities in the U.S. and worldwide.

DANIEL W. MEUB, INC.
1101 Welch Rd., Ste. C-9
Palo Alto, CA 94304
PH: (415)327-9373
FX: (415)327-1942
Active practicing neurologist providing arbitration appearances in personal injury and medical malpractice cases.

A.F. MEYER & ASSOCIATES INC.
e-mail: afma@afmeyer.com
url: http://www.afmeyer.com
1364 Beverly Rd., Ste. 201
McLean, VA 22101
Alvin F. Meyer, President
PH: (703)734-9093
FX: (703)734-9866
Founded: 1976. **Staff:** 25. Offers consulting services in hazardous material control and management, industrial hygiene and occupational safety including design of control measures, safety and occupational health program development and audits, indoor air pollution evaluation and control, noise evaluation and design of controls, and computer based safety and health, and cost estimation. Serves private industries as well as government agencies. Geographic areas served: national.

BASIL R. MEYEROWITZ, MD, INC.
101 South San Mateo Dr., Ste. 112
San Mateo, CA 94401
PH: (650)343-8042
FX: (650)348-5378
Specializes in bariatric surgery (for morbid obesity) and malpractice and quality assurance. Geographic areas served: California; Western States.

MARC S. MICOZZI
College of Physicians
19 S. 22nd St.
Philadelphia, PA 19103
Marc S. Micozzi
PH: (215)563-3737
FX: (215)567-1967
Founded: 1984. **Staff:** 1. General health services consultant offers expertise in the following areas: public health, medicine, medical technology, public health organization and policy, diet and nutrition, forensic science, and anthropology. Also provides preparation and presentation of seminars, lectures, articles, workshops, case review and preparation. Industries served: health industry manufacturers, pharmaceuticals, food, legal, print and broadcast media, museums, education and entertainment. Geographic areas served: national. **Conferences and Meetings:** *Continuing Medical Course with Dr. C. Everett Koop: Natural Medicine.*

MICRO MANAGEMENT TECHNOLOGIES, INC.
e-mail: fmays@aol.com
165 Winchester St.
Brookline, MA 02146
Reed Mays, President
PH: (617)731-3737
FX: (617)738-8601
Founded: 1979. **Staff:** 12. Health care consulting market. Accounting systems for the Healthcare, legal distribution, manufac-

turing, and service industries. Geographic areas served: New England. **Computer/Special Services:** On-site installers, operator training and support.

MICROTEST CONSULTING AND RESEARCH, INC.
779 Mill Rd.
Feeding Hills, MA 01030
Nancy Richter, President
PH: (413)786-5840
FX: (413)786-8751
Founded: 1991. **Staff:** 12. Offers consulting services relating to FDA regulations. These services include audits, regulatory consulting, sterilization validation, testing, FDA submissions, and EPA disinfection consulting regarding indoor air quality, microbiology, food testing and sanitation, product safety, and toxicology. Industries served: medical devices, foods, drugs (pharmaceuticals), cosmetics, environmental air quality, and government agencies. Geographic areas served: continental United States and Puerto Rico. **Conferences and Meetings:** *Fungal Identifications of Air Borne Contaminants; Sterilization of Medical Devices; LAL-Endotoxin Testing of Medical Devices.*

MIDWEST MEDICALK HOMECARE
12970 W. Bluemound Rd., Ste. 105
Elm Grove, WI 53122
John E. Conway, Pres.
PH: (414)789-2150
FX: (414)789-2155
Founded: 1961. **Staff:** 430. Advises Wisconsin healthcare industry on management issues.

MARGARET L. MIKKOLA
PO Box 659
Acton, MA 01720
Margaret L. Mikkola
PH: (978)264-9040
Founded: 1982. **Staff:** 1. Nutrition consultant provides expertise for individuals and groups regarding food/health related issues.

THOMAS H. MILBY, M.D.
e-mail: tmilby@aol.com
url: http://www.lawinfo.com/biz/milby/index.htm
1399 Yganacio Valley Rd., Ste. 25
Walnut Creek, CA 94598
PH: (510)284-4944
FX: (510)256-4617
A physician-toxicologist and medical-legal consultant specializing in the effects of toxic chemical exposures, spills, air and water pollution, hazardous dumps, molds and workplace exposures.

BILL MILLER & ASSOCIATES INC.
12696 Pacato Cir. N.
San Diego, CA 92128-2370
Bill Miller, President
PH: (619)487-2455
FX: (619)487-2611
Founded: 1975. **Staff:** 7. Recruits senior executives and management teams for healthcare industry, telecommunications, engineering and M.I.S., attorneys and finance, hotel and casino management. Geographic areas served: U.S. **Conferences and Meetings:** *Conducts seminars on executive wellness and executive self-defense; how to survive the mean streets; karate/judo/jiu-jitsu/ attache case as a weapon. Presents seminars in La Jolla, CA, or at corporate office.* **Computer/Special Services:** Highly effective at providing CEO's, CFO's and new management teams for venture capital firms in new start-ups and turnaround situations.

MINNESOTA MINING & MANUFACTURING CO. HEALTH INFORMATION SYSTEMS
12501 Prosperity Dr.
Silver Spring, MD 20904-1689
James C. Vertrees, President
PH: (301)680-0390
FX: (301)680-0393

Founded: 1987. **Staff:** 10. Provides healthcare and computer counsel to government and private sector in the United States.

THOMAS MINTZ, MD, INC.
1500 Montana Ave., Ste. 201
Santa Monica, CA 90403
PH: (310)394-3010
FX: (310)393-4939
Psychiatrist and psychoanalyst specializing in testimony and evaluation on all medical-psychiatric issues, including diagnosis, treatment, supervision, standards of care, medical malpractice, stress disorders, custody issues, boundary and ethical violations, competency, pre-trial case evaluation and analysis, sexual exploitation and harassment, wrongful death, wrongful termination, employment discrimination, witness and expert preparation, and jury-selection.

MIRFAK ASSOCIATES,INC.
e-mail: susan@mirfak.com
url: http://www.mirfak.com
201 Lafayette Cir., Ste. 100
Lafayette, CA 94549-4370
Susan Van de Bittner, Vice President
PH: (510)283-4100
FX: (510)283-9549
Pain resolution consultant handling physical and psychiatric injuries, head injuries, severe and complex medical cases, work injuries, personal injuries.

CHRISTINE I. MITCHELL
178 Oakland Ave.
Arlington, MA 02174
Christine I. Mitchell
PH: (617)643-6442
FX: (617)735-7429
Founded: 1979. **Staff:** 1. Offers consultation to nurses, physicians, social workers, administrators, and other healthcare professionals on ethical issues and methods for recognition and resolution. Informs healthcare consumers of the moral viewpoints and obligations of nurses. **Conferences and Meetings:** *Establishing Ethics Committees; Ethics in Long Term Care; Moral Imagination and Decision Making; Nursing Ethics and Economics; Federal Legislation and Ethics Committees; Ethical Dilemmas in Nursing; Ethical Issues and Decision Making in the Care of the Developmentally Disabled; The Nurse Patient Relationship-A Source of Some Moral Duties.*

MITCHELL & HEALTH COST ASSOCIATES
5138 Stage House Trail
Madison, WI 53714-2767
Paul J. Mitchell
PH: (608)249-0300
Founded: 1987. **Staff:** 1. Consultant will advise corporations on health cost management, including cost control, value enhancement, and design and development of health promotion programs. Also develops and writes marketing/promotional materials, professional reports, position papers, and policies/procedures. Additional duties include long-range health planning and conducting research/analytical studies of fiscal, budget, administrative and policy matters. Industries served: public, private, non-profit agencies, and businesses. Geographic areas served: primarily midwest, although will travel nationwide. **Conferences and Meetings:** *Health Cost Management; Worksite Wellness Programs.*

MOOREINFO INC.
url: http://www.mooreinfo.com
42 Westwood Cir.
Irvington, NY 10533-1843
Dianne S. Moore, CNM, MPA, Ph.D.
PH: (914)591-6748
FX: (914)591-6748
Founded: 1986. **Staff:** 2. Provides medical information service for professionals and consumers including scientific and medical-legal research. Services include manuscript consultation, grant

writing and fundraising, medical-legal research, training programs, and childbirth preparation, including Lamaze instruction. Industries served: medical, pharmaceutical, educational, and government agencies. **Conferences and Meetings:** *Conducts workshops on healthcare topics.*

MORRISY & CO., INC.
url: http://www.hwcsoft.com
3840 Park Ave., Ste. 208
Edison, NJ 08820
James J. Morrisy, Pres.
PH: (732)906-9313
FX: (732)906-9138
Founded: 1987. **Staff:** 14. Offers financial and data processing services to hospital and healthcare industries. **Conferences and Meetings:** *Information Resources - A Tool for Management and Care, Association des Hospitaux du Quebec; A Straightforward Look at Managed Care Requirements, Colegio de Administracion de Hospitales Servicios de Salud; History of Reimbursement and Various Reimbursement Systems, Rutgers University Center for Management, Development, and the Healthcare Financial Management Association; and Financial Management under New Jersey's DRG System, University Hospital.* **Computer/Special Services:** Developed application software for hospitals and healthcare providers for PC use: PHO Model, Managed Information System, and TRANSAM.

MOSBY
7250 Parkway Dr., Ste. 510
Hanover, MD 21076
Jay M. Katz, President
PH: (410)712-4110
TF: 800325-4177
FX: (410)712-4424
Founded: 1979. **Staff:** 150. Diversified communications company providing a wide range of educational services for healthcare professionals. These services include: seminars and workshops, in-house/in-service programs, national conferences, publications, management services, corporate health, and consultation services. **Conferences and Meetings:** *High Risk Labor and Delivery; Pediatric Emergencies; Setting Standards of Patient Care; First Line Nursing Management; and others.*

JUDITH MOYLAN
PO Box 5057
Daytona Beach, FL 32118
Judith Moylan, President
PH: (912)234-1732
FX: (904)257-5577
Founded: 1967. **Staff:** 3. Consultant dietitian and nutritionist in healthcare to hospitals, nursing homes, adult congregate living facilities, and government agencies. Also performs book reviews and provides expert legal witness services. Additional expertise in governmental compliance. Serves as a licensed consultant dietitian, adjunct professor, and specializes in kitchen design. Geographic areas served: U.S.

MSCH
2600 N. Loop W., Ste. 620
Houston, TX 77092
PH: (713)683-2900
FX: (713)683-2929
Founded: 1984. Health care-related consulting firm.

MURER CONSULTANTS
url: http://www.murer.com
62 W. Washington St.
Joliet, IL 60432
Cherilyn Murer, Owner
PH: (815)727-3331
FX: (815)727-3360
Founded: 1984. **Staff:** 25. Offers healthcare management services to healthcare networks, hospitals, and physicians' groups in all areas of post acute care, including rehabilitation, subacute care,

outpatient, and home health. Geographic areas served: worldwide.

MUSTA-DYDEK TOXICOLOGY CONSULTING SERVICES
e-mail: mde-tox@eden.com
url: http://www.eden.com/~mde-tox
5400 Brodie Ln., Ste. 1270
Austin, TX 78745
Dr. Thomas Musta-Dydek, PhD, D.A.B.T., P.E.
PH: (512)280-5477
FX: (512)280-8900
Founded: 1994. Environmental toxicologist and engineer specializing in toxicological/human health risk analyses for community/occupational exposures to metals, solvents, pesticides, and other chemicals; Superfund risk assessments; and air quality. Provides expert witness litigation support and trainings in toxicology and risk assesment. Geographic Areas Served: Nationwide. **Conferences and Meetings:** *Toxicology and Risk Assessment.* **Computer/Special Services:** Chemical Toxicity Reviews and Evaluations.

RALPH M. MYERSON
310 Maplewood Ave.
Merion Station, PA 19066
Ralph M. Myerson
PH: (215)664-0406
FX: (215)896-2750
Founded: 1985. **Staff:** 2. Provides consultation services to pharmaceutical industries and healthcare establishments by supplying data such as patient information and manuscripts for use in health journals for promotional and educational purposes. Industries served: publishing and pharmaceutical. Geographic areas served: greater Philadelphia area primarily, but also national.

NARAD AND ASSOCIATES
e-mail: rnarad@oavax.csuchico.edu
18 Carriage Ln.
Chico, CA 95926-5002
Richard A. Narad
PH: (916)893-5907
FX: (916)893-5907
Founded: 1985. **Staff:** 1. Offers emergency medical services and disaster medical services planning, implementation, and evaluation. Industries served: healthcare and local government. Geographic areas served: California.

NATIONAL BOARD OF FORENSIC CHIROPRACTORS (TM) (NBOFC)
e-mail: omyback@aol.com
601 S. Mill St.
PO Box 356
Manning, SC 29102
Preston B. Fitzgerald, Sr., D.C., Executive Director (SC)
PH: (803)435-5078
FX: (803)435-8096
Founded: 1996. **Staff:** 6. Administers exams and designates qualifying chiropractic physicians as having the credential of Certified Independent Forensic Chiropractic Medical Examiner (TM), or CIVCME (TM). After receiving this credentail, a doctor is qualified to assist insurance companies, workers' compensation commissions, social security boards, employres, police departments, and attorneys by providing independnet assessments of challenging bodily injury cases. The purpose of the NBOFC is to advance the profession of forensic examination and consultation throughout the chiropractic profession by elevating standards through education, and advanced training, and certification. The Board serves as a national center for this purpose and disseminates information and knowledge by coordinating lectures, seminars, conferences, workshops, Internet, continuing education courses and publications. Geographic Areas Served: U.S. **Conferences and Meetings:** *Dr. Fitzgerald developed the curriculum and is a faculty lecturer of the postdoctoral seminar series leading to Board Eligibility with the National Board of Forensic Chiropractors. The seminar series is co-sponsored by Logan College of Chiropractic. Topics covered in the NBOFC/Logan College seminar*

series include rules of evidence, application of forensic evidence, scientific reasoning, medical record review, case analysis, federal rules applicable to forensics, legal communications, risk management, evaluations for work functional capacity and forensic clincial examination. The locations for instruction for 1998 and 1999 are in Atlanta, GA; Miami, FL; Philadelphia, PA; Schaumburg, IL; and St. Louis, MO. **Computer/Special Services:** State of the art photographic report writing capabilities.

NATIONAL FARM MEDICINE CENTER
url: http://www.marshmed.org/nfmc/
1000 N. Oak Ave.
Marshfield, WI 54449-5790
Stephen A. Olenchock, PhD, Director
PH: (715)387-9298
FX: (715)389-4950
Staff: 30. Offers a variety of research, education, and service projects focusing on clinical health issues affecting farm workers and families. Special focus areas include: respiratory disease, noise-induced hearing loss, and degenerative joint disease. Industries served: rural Americans and healthcare workers and educators who provide services to the rural community.

NATIONAL FEDERATION OF MEDICAL/LEGAL NETWORKS, INC.
840 Spring Mill Ln.
Indianapolis, IN 46260
Gabriel J. Rosenberg, M.D.
PH: (317)253-9080
FX: (317)257-2375
Founded: 1987. **Staff:** 1. Provides consultative advice and renders expert medical opinions to attorneys, hospitals and insurance companies involving medical-legal problems, i.e., medical malpractice litigation and risk management problems. Primary expertise involves pediatric patients (age 0-21 years) with special interest in areas of infectious diseases, newborn, pulmonary and kidney problems. Also provides "networking" service for attorneys who desire non-pediatric medical experts and non-medical experts as the case merits it. Offers additional consultative advice on risk management for ambulatory medical settings. **Conferences and Meetings:** *How to Immunize Your Practice Against Legal Termites and Pests; Medical Review Panel Practice; Doctor in the Courtroom.*

NATIONAL HEALTH ADVISORS LTD.
1650 Tysons Blvd., Ste. 300
McLean, VA 22102-3810
Scott A. Mason
PH: (703)883-0400
FX: (703)883-0426
Founded: 1981. **Staff:** 6. A management consulting firm specializing in strategic management in today's healthcare industry. Emphasis on diversification and development, merger and acquisition planning, trustee education, and corporate reorganization. The firm has provided services to independent hospitals, multi-institutional arrangements and networks, and health-related companies in over 30 states throughout the United States. **Conferences and Meetings:** *Diversification Strategy and Organization in the 1990's; Rural Hospital Issues.*

NATIONAL HEALTH SYSTEMS INC.
1104 Fernwood Ave.
Camp Hill, PA 17011-6912
Wayne M. Pecht, Pres.
PH: (717)763-8578
TF: 800222-2607
FX: (717)763-9291
Founded: 1988. **Staff:** 27. Offers practice management counsel to hospitals and physicians in the United States.

NATIONAL LEAGUE FOR NURSING AND CHAP, COMMUNITY HEALTH ACCREDITATION
url: http://www.NLN.org
350 Hudson St., 4th Fl.
New York, NY 10014
Claire Fagin, President
PH: (212)989-9393
TF: 800669-1656
FX: (212)989-3710
Founded: 1952. **Staff:** 125. The National League for Nursing's consulting network is a comprehensive resource to develop, maintain, and refine nursing's standards of education and service in the most cost-effective way. NLN consultants use a variety of techniques that will help an education program or nursing service administration achieve maximum effectiveness. These include community or agency needs analysis, development of budgetary process and management strategies, aid in curriculum issues, statistical reporting systems, marketing and recruitment strategies, labor relations policies, and quality assurance programs. Active with nursing education programs and nursing service departments in hospitals, long-term care facilities, and community health agencies, as well as government agencies. Industries served: nursing, healthcare, education, universities, hospital, public health agencies, AIDS service organizations, healthcare political action agencies, medicine, pharmaceutical, and pharmaceutical research. Geographic areas served: international. **Conferences and Meetings:** *Continuing education programs*

NATIONAL MEDICAL ADVISORY SERVICE, INC.
6001 Montrose Rd., Ste. 400
Rockville, MD 20852
Ronald E. Gots, President
PH: (301)230-2999
TF: 800258-0014
FX: (301)230-2996
Founded: 1975. **Staff:** 30. National insurance claims and litigation support practice uniquely integrates medical, occupational health and technical environmental services. Primary expertise involves complex personal injury claims, multi-party toxic waste and environmental matters, workers' compensation and medical malpractice cases. Special interests consist of chemical exposure/ poisoning, clinical ecology, sick building syndrome and multiple chemical sensitivity claims. Most popular services include medical causation reviews, exposure assessment, risk communication, product stewardship programs (product risk analysis), industrial hygiene and environmental testing for insurers, law firms, government, associations and industry. Scientific specialties: medicine, toxicology, industrial hygiene, chemical engineering, environmental science and other related disciplines. Geographic areas served: U.S. **Conferences and Meetings:** *Seven Steps to Toxic Claims Analysis; Health & Safety Audits; principals lecture frequently on toxic tort litigation support, environmental and occupational health and safety compliance, and developing product stewardship programs.*

NATIONAL MEDICAL SERVICES, INC.
3701 Welsh Rd.
Willow Grove, PA 19090
Robert A. Middleberg, Director
PH: (215)657-4900
TF: 800522-6671
FX: (215)657-2631
Forensic-, clinical-, analytical toxicology and criminalistics. Specializes in toxic tort and occupational chemical product liability; worker's compensation and disability claims; referee drug testing; dram shop and social host liability; life insurance claims; pharmacological malpractice and therapeutic misadventure; driving under the influence of alcohol and/or drugs; forensic abuse substance testing; criminalistics; product tampering and product integrity; employee drug and alcohol testing; forensic toxicology; occupational toxicology; community and ecological toxicology; forensic hair testing for drugs and other toxicants.

NATIONAL PEDICULOSIS ASSOCIATION
e-mail: npa@headlice.org
url: http://www.headlice.org
PO Box 610189
Newton, MA 02161
Deborah Altschuler, President
PH: (617)449-6487
TF: 800446-4672
FX: (617)449-8129
Founded: 1982. **Staff:** 8. Consultants in head lice and scabies management, treatment, prevention, and education. Specializes in monitoring health policy administration in schools and trends in the treatment of head lice. Emphasis is on educational activities. Industries served: schools, health professionals, medical professionals, child care centers, health departments, hospitals, HMO's, clinics, libraries, parents, PTA's, camps, military bases, and churches.

NATIONAL SAFETY ALLIANCE CORP.
446 Metroplex Dr., Ste. 226
PO Box 159060
Nashville, TN 37211-3139
William R. Grainger, Pres.
PH: (615)832-0046
FX: (615)832-0054
Founded: 1988. **Staff:** 13. Offers health services counsel, specializing in substance abuse programs, administration, testing, research, legal support, and education. Industries served: U.S. businesses.

NATIONAL TECHNOMICS INC.
e-mail: jimccrea@bellatlantic.net
814 Sunset Hollow Rd.
West Chester, PA 19380
Joan I. McCrea, President
PH: (610)436-4551
FX: (610)436-0255
Founded: 1983. **Staff:** 3. Specializes in organizational development, education and training, and computer systems in health services industries. Industries served: hospitals, services, government agencies, and civilian employees of the U.S. Army, Navy, Marine Corps, and Veterans Administration in the United States. **Conferences and Meetings:** *Leadership Styles; Leadership for Women; Leadership in LongTerm Care; Effective Supervision; Nursing Management Revisited; Conflict Management; Situational Leadership; Empowerment; Effective Treatment Teams; When You Can't Be All Things to All Men; Holistic Communication; Trade-Offs; Risk-Taking.*

NCES, INC.
e-mail: info@nescatalog.com
url: http://www.ncescatalog.com
1904 E. 123rd
Olathe, KS 66061
Patricia G. Stein
PH: (913)782-4385
FX: (913)782-8230
Founded: 1980. **Staff:** 5. Nutrition consultants who offer mail order book services. Geographic areas served: U.S. Industries served: individuals, companies, organizations, and government.

NORMAN J. NEMOY, MD
e-mail: nnn635@village.ios.com
8631 W. 3rd St., Ste. 915E
Los Angeles, CA 90048
PH: (310)854-9898
FX: (310)854-0267
Specializes in pediatric and adult urology.

NETWORK INC.
8 S Morris St., Ste. 202
Dover, NJ 07801
James F. Hull, President

PH: (973)442-2990
TF: 800523-1394
FX: (973)442-2883
Founded: 1977. **Staff:** 14. Firm offers management expertise to medical institutions and hospitals. Serves boards of education in New York and New Jersey.

BETTY M. NEUMAN
Box 488
Beverly, OH 45715
Betty Neuman
PH: (614)749-3322
FX: (614)749-3322
Founded: 1974. **Staff:** 1. Nursing curriculum consultant for implementation of the Neuman Systems Model into both educational and nursing practice settings. Also offers organizational development assistance with emphasis on conflict resolution and leadership skill development. Geographic areas served: international. **Conferences and Meetings:** *The Neuman Systems Model for Nursing Practice; Group Leadership Skill Development.*

NEW HYPNOSIS INSTITUTE
e-mail: info@anodyne.org
url: http://www.anodyne.org
Box 150090
San Rafael, CA 94915
PH: (415)454-2500
TF: 800449-4422
Provides specialized training and consulting services to hospitals and other medial institutions through anodyne awareness.

NEW YORK LIFE HEALTH SYSTEMS
1 Liberty Plaza
New York, NY 10006
Joseph T. Lynaugh, Pres.
PH: (212)437-1000
FX: (212)437-1100
Founded: 1987. **Staff:** 2000. Offers expertise in the health insurance field to businesses and general public in New York, Washington, D.C., Dallas, Houston, and Chicago.

JOY NEWBY AND ASSOCIATES, INC.
e-mail: newbyassoc@aol.com
6828 Hawthorne Park Dr.
Indianapolis, IN 46220
Joy Newby, President
PH: (317)577-3066
FX: (317)577-3061
Founded: 1991. **Staff:** 10. Consults with physicians and their staffs on third-party pay or issues, accounts receivable management, personnel reviews, and new office setup. Geographic areas served: Midwest. **Conferences and Meetings:** *List of seminars and workshops available from firm upon request.* **Computer/Special Services:** Microsoft Word, WordPerfect, Quickbooks.

ANDREW NEWMAN, MD
301 City Line Ave., Ste. 210
Bala Cynwyd, PA 19004
PH: (610)660-0805
FX: (610)660-9270
Orthopedist, consultant, and expert witness specializing in workers' compensation and medical malpractice.

NORTHEAST PAIN CONSULTANTS
e-mail: info@painmd.com
url: http://www.painmd.com/
255 Route 108
Somersworth, NH 03878
PH: (603)692-3166
FX: (603)692-3168
Founded: 1992. Patient care services include spinal catheters and pump implants; medication management; home care pain supervision; diagnostic work-up to determine the exact cause of the pain; nerve blocks and trigger point injections; assistance in re-

storing functional status; pain coping strategies such as hypnosis, biofeedback, music; and emotional support. Professional consulting services covers the full spectrum of professional pain practice management, including all aspects of financial and medical practice, development.

NOTEWORTHY CREATIONS, INC.
e-mail: mayfield@dcwi.com
107 W. Franklin St.
PO Box 335
Delphi, IN 46923
Barbara J. Mayfield
PH: (765)564-4167
TF: 800305-4167
FX: (765)564-4280
Founded: 1982. **Staff:** 3. Offers nutritional assessment and dietary education consultation to individuals and groups. Makes presentations to all age groups on nutrition-related topics. Also sells nutrition education curricula, books, and tapes. **Conferences and Meetings:** *Nutrition Education for Children.*

NRH NUTRITION CONSULTANTS, INC.
100 Rosedale Rd.
Valley Stream, NY 11581
Annette Natow, President
PH: (718)229-0606
FX: (516)791-1289
Founded: 1975. **Staff:** 3. Registered dietitians and nutritionists providing services as translators of nutrition concepts and information. To this end, they prepare educational and audiovisual materials; prepare, implement and evaluate research; conduct seminars, conferences, and in-service education programs; represent and/or advise clients at conferences and meetings; interpret theoretical nutrition information into practical material to enhance promotion and sales of a product, concept or service; and serve as a resource to other medical specialties. Serves private industries as well as government agencies. Geographic areas served: United States, located in New York metropolitan area. **Computer/Special Services:** Maintains a nutrient database of 23,000 brand name and generic foods. Can provide product comparison and recipe analysis.

NUCRO-TECHNICS INCORPORATED
2000 Ellesmere Rd., Unit 16
Scarborough, ON, Canada M1H 2W4
John C. Fanaras, President
PH: (416)438-6727
FX: (416)438-3463
Founded: 1971. **Staff:** 60. Health and safety consultants to the food, cosmetic, chemical, and pharmaceutical industry, as well as to government agencies. Consulting staff are backed up with analytical laboratories in the areas of chemistry, microbiology, and animal toxicology.

NURSING CONSULTATION, INC.
Box 255
Winona, MN 55987
Lynn S. Theurer, RN, MSCS
PH: (507)454-1680
Founded: 1975. **Staff:** 1. Offers mental health consultations and workshop development. All services arranged by client request. Services related to human relations and interpersonal communication are provided to individuals, families, nonprofit associations and organizations, the healthcare field, and government as an industry. Geographic areas served: United States, **Conferences and Meetings:** *Seminars on family therapy, mental health and aging and adolescence.*

NURSING KNOWLEDGE, INC.
e-mail: nursknow@aol.com
2540 Severn Ave., Ste. 206
Metairie, LA 70002
Jackson Townsend, Treasurer

PH: (504)887-0401
TF: 800359-5114
Founded: 1979. **Staff:** 5. Consultants in continuing education programs for nurses principally in hospitals, other healthcare agencies, and colleges. Also serves government agencies. Additionally provides courses on instructional media production and use. Geographic areas served: national. **Conferences and Meetings:** *Critical Care Nursing; Medical-Surgical Acute Care Nursing; CCRN Review Course; CCRN: The Keys to the Care; Critical Care Course; CEN Review.*

NURSING TECHNOMICS
e-mail: jimccrea@bellatlantic.net
814 Sunset Hollow Rd.
West Chester, PA 19380
Joan I. McCrea, President
PH: (610)436-4551
FX: (610)436-0255
Founded: 1983. **Staff:** 17. Administrative nursing consultants offer expertise in the design and implementation of customized software applications for departments of nursing, organizational design and implementation, and executive nurse search. Also specializes in department staffing, scheduling and nurse recruitment. Serves private industries as well as government agencies. Geographic areas served: United States and Canada. **Conferences and Meetings:** *Basic Supervisory Skills for RNs; Advanced Management Skills for Nurse Executives; Achieving Agreement; Problem-Solving; Decision-making.* **Computer/Special Services:** Maintains Executive Nurse Management Information Systems (ENMIS), staffing, scheduling, personnel management; basic patient data management; and cost and budget reporting systems; also automated patient care plans, operating room management system. All software applications available to large hospitals for installation in minicomputers and mainframe. All applications available to smaller hospitals for PC's and LAN.

ELIEZER NUSSBAUM, MD
e-mail: enussbaum@compuserve.com
Memorial Miller Children's Hospital
University of Calif., Irvine
2801 Atlantic Ave.
Long Beach, CA 90801-1428
PH: (562)933-8740
FX: (562)933-8744
Specializes in pediatrics, pediatric pulmonary, pediatric critical care, and emergency medicine. Offers expert testimony.

NUTRITION ASSOCIATES, INC.
9428 Baymeadows Rd., Ste. 129
Jacksonville, FL 32256
Catherine Christie, Ph.D., RD., President
PH: (904)636-8640
FX: (904)636-0617
Founded: 1986. **Staff:** 3. Provides nutrition information and consultation to individuals and healthcare professionals through seminars and writing. **Conferences and Meetings:** *Women's Nutrition Issues; The Food-Mood Connection; Stress Eating Management; and Nutrition Update.*

NUTRITION CONSULTANTS, INC.
1643-B Owen Dr.
Fayetteville, NC 28304
Karen E. Gantt, President
PH: (910)483-4202
FX: (910)483-4202
Founded: 1985. **Staff:** 2. Nutrition consultants offering the following services: weight reduction and maintenance (individual and group sessions); wellness consultations and presentations for business and industry; nutrient analysis of individual diets and menus;supermarket sense tours; and adult and children's cooking classes. Additional expertise provided on sports nutrition, pediatric nutrition, and prenatal nutrition. Serves private industries as well as government agencies. Geographic areas served: Cumberland County, North Carolina. **Conferences and Meetings:** *Nutri-*

tion Issues for Women; Weight Loss the Healthy Way; Feeding But Not Fattening - How To's for Families; Private Practice: Creating, Building and Managing Successfully; Nutrition Intervention and Eating Disorders; Using the Food Guide Pyramid Effectively; Preventive Nutrition: Steps You Can Take Now.

NUTRITION COUNSELING SERVICE

311 S. Duck
Stillwater, OK 74074
Glee Kincannon, President
PH: (405)624-1343
FX: (405)377-5561
Founded: 1978. Provides nutrition counseling for both individuals and group in central Oklahoma.

THE NUTRITION COUNSELLING CENTER

The Gallery, Ste. 202
46 Newport Rd.
New London, NH 03257
Hope E. Damon
PH: (603)526-2078
Founded: 1987. **Staff:** 1. Offers individual nutrition counselling for weight control and therapeutic diets (low cholesterol, diabetic, prenatal, etc.); also provides group nutrition programs for business, industry and community groups (weight control, heart healthy eating). Geographic areas served: predominantly the Dartmouth-Lake Sunapee area of New Hampshire. **Conferences and Meetings:** *Shop Smart Eat Smart Supermarket Tours - seminars for hands-on education in label reading and shopping healthfully; Anorexia Recovery support group ongoing.* **Computer/ Special Services:** Computerized analysis of diets and recipes now available for individuals, restaurants, or institutions.

NUTRITION & DIET COUNSELING OF ROCKLAND

e-mail: rb.nutritn@aol.com
PO Box 299
New City, NY 10956
Roberta Becker, RD, CDN
PH: (914)354-8652
FX: (914)354-9221
Founded: 1979. **Staff:** 2. Registered Dietitian and NYS Certified Dietitian/Nutritionist who offers individual and group counseling for medical diets, weight control, nutrition and maintenance of good health, and corporate weight loss seminars and workshops for allied health professionals. Geographic areas served: Rockland County, New York. Geographic Areas Served: Rookland County, NY; N. Bergan City, NJ. **Conferences and Meetings:** *Counseling Skills; Permanent Weight Loss; Lunch Box Losing Weight Management Program; Healthy Heart.* **Computer/ Special Services:** Nutritional analysis by computer.

NUTRITION ENTREPRENEURS

e-mail: nedpg@aol.com
url: http://www.nutritionentrepreneurs.org
9212 Delphi Rd. SW
Olympia, WA 98502
PH: (360)956-1367
FX: (360)956-1367
Founded: 1977. Serves as the clearinghouse for nutrition entrepreneurs throughout the U.S. and Canada. Members provide consultation to a variety of clients which include consumers, medical clinics, physician's offices, outpatient departments of hospitals, restaurants, corporations, long-term care facilities, television, radio-television-print media, supermarkets, and food companies. In addition, many members produce and market nutrition related products. Industries served: acute and long term healthcare settings, all forms of media, consumer and professional education, corporate wellness, entrepreneurial production and marketing of products for consumers and/or professionals.

NUTRITION & FOOD ASSOCIATES

e-mail: patgodfrey@worldnet.att.net
url: http://www.nutriform.com
PO Box 47007
Minneapolis, MN 55447
Patricia Godfrey, President
PH: (612)550-9475
FX: (612)559-3675
Founded: 1984. **Staff:** 5. Nutritional consultants specializing in product regulations, nutrition labeling, nutritional recipe analysis and nutrition copy for product labels, national magazines and publishing companies. The purpose is to provide the nutrition information for recipes and products. Also offers food-styling and photography services, as well as nutritional and medical communication services. The purpose is to provide accurate nutrition and medical information copy for magazines and publishers. Industries served: food manufacturers, restaurants, bakeries, and grocers worldwide. **Conferences and Meetings:** *Ins and Outs of Nutritional Recipe Analysis and Product Labeling.* **Computer/ Special Services:** Maintain nutrition database and computer software for nutrition analysis, food product labeling for bakeries, grocers, restaurants, food manufacturers, and publications.

NUTRITION FOR YOU

e-mail: nfyopg@aol.com
Box 2521
Fair Oaks, CA 95628-9521
Judith D. Fields, President
PH: (916)965-4012
FX: (916)965-4012
Founded: 1985. **Staff:** 1. Nutrition counseling services designed for the individual including: personalized meal planning, recipes and informational brochures, behavior modification, exercise guidelines, body composition analysis, breath acetone levels, and image mirror with picture to illustrate weight goals. Serves private industries as well as government agencies. **Conferences and Meetings:** *Shape Up: Weight Reduction for Adults; Trim Down: Weight Reduction for Adolescents; Love Your Heart - Low Fat, Low Salt.* **Computer/Special Services:** Uses Food Processor 6.11 for nutrient analysis.

NUTRITIONAL CARE MANAGEMENT INSTITUTE

e-mail: psmith1@mindspring.com
1528 Harbour Oaks Rd.
Tucker, GA 30084
Alice Smith
PH: (770)414-9541
FX: (770)279-8818
Founded: 1987. **Staff:** 2. Works with hospitals and managed care firms to identify hospital patients who are at risk for protein calorie malnutrition, the 60 percent to 200 percent extra costs associated with their care, and to develop programs and strategies to reduce them with appropriate nutritional interventions systems. Geographic areas served: U.S. **Computer/Special Services:** The Malnutrition Cost Survey(tm) nutritional risk and care audit technique uses client data measures malnourished patient costs, savings associated with nutritional intervention and the opportunities to increase savings with expanded or improved clinical nutrition services.

NUTRITIONAL CONSULTANTS GROUP, INC.

e-mail: ncgroup@ix.netcom.com
6806 Vista del Mar Ln.
Playa del Rey, CA 90293
Jerzy W. Meduski, President
PH: (310)821-6456
FX: (310)821-0780
Founded: 1982. **Staff:** 5. Specialists in nutritional supplements, and food product and pharmaceutical formulation and development with emphasis on nutritional needs in different life periods, different occupations and different health status. Industries served: food processing, pharmaceutical, health food, and Orange County government agencies. Geographic areas served: United States, Europe and Asia.

NYH HEALTH CARE ASSOCIATES
e-mail: nyhcare@eznet.net
url: http://www.nyhwriter.com
16 San Rafael Dr.
Rochester, NY 14618
Nancy Yanes Hoffman, President
PH: (716)385-1515
FX: (716)385-3858
Founded: 1985. Staff: 1. Writes, and advises on the writing of, medical and scientific books and articles. Also engages in editing, speechwriting, and lecturing on all phases of healthcare. Conducts healthcare symposia and lectures. Focuses on prevention, diagnosis, treatment of disease, and strategies for coping with disease; improving doctor-patient relations; sex over 40; improving one's Type A personality; preventing heart disease; secondary prevention of, and dealing with, breast cancer; and coping with prostate cancer. Geographic areas served: worldwide. **Conferences and Meetings:** *List of seminars and workshops available from firm upon request.*

OCCU-HEALTH INC.
e-mail: occu@pop.erols.com
24 Frederick Rd.
Ellicott City, MD 21043-4710
Patricia McCullough, President
PH: (410)418-8205
FX: (410)381-9249
Founded: 1991. Staff: 74. Advises government and private sector organizations on occupational healthcare; industrial hygiene; quality assurance; wellness programs; and drug testing. Geographic areas served: Maryland, Virginia, and Washington D.C.

OCCUPATIONAL & ENVIRONMENTAL HEALTH CONSULTING SERVICES
e-mail: oehcs@flash.net
url: http://www.safety-epa.com
635 Harding Rd.
Hinsdale, IL 60521
Robert C. Brandys, President
PH: (630)325-2083
FX: (630)325-2098
Founded: 1984. Staff: 8. Provides consulting to industry on safety program development and implementation, industrial hygiene monitoring programs, occupational health nursing, wellness programs, medical monitoring, accident trending and statistics, emergency response planning, multilingual training, right-to-know compliance and training, hazardous waste management, radon monitoring and mitigation, asbestos school inspection, and project management. Also offers indoor air quality, expert witnessing service. Geographic Areas Served: US, Europe, Mexico, Canada, PR. **Conferences and Meetings:** *Right-To-Know Compliance; Setting Internal Exposure Standards; Hospital Right-to-Know and Contingency Response; Ethylene Oxide Control; Industrial Hygiene Training; Asbestos Worker Training; Asbestos Operations and Maintenance.* **Computer/Special Services:** Capabilities include software for both PC and Macintosh, such as OSHA 200 Log, Workers Compensation First Report of Injury, EPA Tier II report, EPA Form R, audioprogram analysis, annual hazardous waste report, material safety data sheets, and product label pictograms.

OCCUPATIONAL HEALTH & HYGIENE CORP. OF AMERICA
900 W. Main St.
Lebanon, IN 46052-2318
Jack Jeffries, Pres.
PH: (765)482-7652
FX: (765)482-7658
Founded: 1989. Staff: 27. Counsels in industrial health, offering mobile/industrial and environmental health testing. Industries served: manufacturing and utilites in the United States.

OCCUPATIONAL HEALTH REGISTRY & CONSULTING SERVICE INC.
1734 Stratfield Rd.
Fairfield, CT 06432
PH: (203)372-3768
FX: (203)371-7240
Founded: 1980. Offers consultation regarding medical services and agencies.

OCCUPATIONAL HEALTH RESEARCH
e-mail: webmaster@systoc.com
url: http://www.systoc.com
28 Research Dr.
PO Box 900
Skowhegan, ME 04976
Michael Keller, President
PH: (207)474-8432
TF: 800444-8432
FX: (207)474-6398
Founded: 1985. Staff: 50. OHR offers a cost effective approach to occupational health program development, product enhancement and operational improvement. Our consulting associates provide a broad range of services to help health care organiations establish high quality, competitive occupational health programs tailored to their market areas. Each project is unique and our consultants always create client-specif solutions. No assessment or report is ever produced using standardized forms, templates, or methods. Geographic areas served: Nationwide. **Conferences and Meetings:** *OHR presents annual national conferences where industry leaders provide insight into clinical issues, administrative challenges and managed workers' compensation care. Other one and two-day seminars provide strategies for occupational medicine providers to improve quality and control costs. OHR offers monthly computer training courses which teach our software program, SYSTOC.* **Computer/Special Services:** Occupational Health Research invented PC based case management systems for Workers' Compensation in 1981. Its information system, SYSTOC is the nation's most widely used software for managing healthcare and disability costs in worker's compensation. It is currently in use at over 300 hospitals and clinics to manage workplace injuries and employee health screening for over 100,000 employers in 42 states.

OCCUPATIONAL HEALTH STRATEGIES INC.
e-mail: kwp@cstone.net
901 Preston Ave., Ste. 400
Charlottesville, VA 22903-4491
Kent W. Peterson, M.D., Pres.
PH: (804)977-3784
FX: (804)977-8570
Founded: 1984. Staff: 15. Offers expertise in the areas of occupational medicine; regulatory compliance; planning and development; and safety programs to manufacturers worldwide, but primarily in the United States.

OFFICE WORKOUTS
e-mail: owinc@aol.com
29399 Agoura Rd., Ste. 113
Agoura, CA 91301
Denise Donlon, President
PH: (818)991-6256
TF: 800442-9255
FX: (818)991-9315
Staff: 4. Corporate wellness programs consulting firm offers the design and development of comprehensive, educational, and fun programs to client's employees. **Conferences and Meetings:** *The Energy Feat Fitness Walking Program - Safety Stretching.* **Computer/Special Services:** Newsletter based outrearch program designed for multi-location businesses.

JOSEPH J. OKON ASSOCIATES
e-mail: jjokonmd@jjpa.com
url: http://www.jjoa.com
1 Hermit Ln.
Westport, CT 06880
Dr. Joseph J. Okon
PH: (203)341-3394
TF: 800367-6566
FX: (203)341-3393
Founded: 1982. Provides a variety of services to hospitals and graduate medical education programs ranging from assistance with grant and accreditation applications to help with resident and faculty recruitment. Can also provide planning and management strategies for ambulatory care, long-term care, prepaid plans, faculty practice, marketing and facilities improvement. Industries served: hospitals, medical schools, foundations, ambulatory care facilities, professional organizations and law firms, and other healthcare institutions. Geographic areas served: national. **Conferences and Meetings:** *Grants for Graduate Training in Family Medicine; Grants for Residency Training in General Internal Medicine and/or General Pediatrics; Mastering Grantsmanship.*

MARY O'LEARY
1400 N. State Pkwy., Ste. 2B
Chicago, IL 60610
Mary O'Leary
PH: (312)337-7487
Founded: 1980. Serves medical and healthcare institutions and government agencies in the following areas: nursing administration, continuing education and patient/family education; psychiatric administration with focus on managed care contracting, Medicare, Medicaid, product/service development, research/development, marketing and patient/family mental health education.

OMEGA COMMUNICATIONS INC.
875 Greentree Rd., Ste. 275
Pittsburgh, PA 15220-3503
Jack Serra, Pres.
PH: (732)968-9181
Founded: 1976. **Staff:** 27. Provides health management, marketing, and sales training to pharmaceutical industry in the United States and Canada.

OMEGA EHS, INC.
One Pierce Place, Ste. 245C
Itasca, IL 60143
Mary Ann Latko, CSP - President
PH: (630)250-5877
TF: 800285-0194
FX: (630)250-5771
Founded: 1990. **Staff:** 25. Firm serves as a single resource for environmental, health, safety, and energy management services. Can integrate environmental, energy management, and health and safety considerations into an overall asset management program that efficiently minimizes liabilities and reduces long-term dependence on outside consultants. Offers a core staff of professionals certified in regulatory compliance; environmental, health, and safety issues; indoor air quality; and energy management. Serves businesses worldwide, with a concentration of personnel in the Midwest and Southeast. **Conferences and Meetings:** *List of seminars and workshops available from firm upon request.* **Computer/Special Services:** Regulatory compliance bulletins provided via e-mail or other electronic means, specifically tailored to clients operations and needs; Indoor Air Constituent Database developed for use by indoor air, industrial hygiene, and health and safety professionals; integration of existing client information systems and software to track and report environmental, health, and safety regulatory and corporate compliance status; and MSDS management and system automation.

OPTIONS & CHOICES
url: http://www.optis.com
2232 Dell Range Blvd., Ste. 300
Cheyenne, WY 82009-4005
Harold Gardner, M.D., Pres.
PH: (307)635-3777
FX: (307)634-0828
Founded: 1985. **Staff:** 52. Offers health education expertise to businesses on dealing with disabilities. Geographic areas served: Wyoming, Maryland, Tennessee, and Washington, D.C.

GERALD A. O'ROURKE
e-mail: orourke@isrv.com
244 Madison Ave.
New York, NY 10016
PH: (212)557-2422
Offers security and litigation support in matters that concern co-ops, condominiums, malls, parking lots, commercial and residential high rise, transportation, air-ground, hotels, casinos, public events, concerts, educational institutions, security training, court security.

DR. RODOFL OROZ
2229 Santa Clara Ave.
Alameda, CA 94501
PH: (510)523-0150
FX: (510)523-0152
Specializes in TMJ, temporomandibular disorders, jaw/face pain, orofacial pain, whiplash, implants, and restorative dentistry.

O'TOOLE-EWALD ART ASSOCIATES
e-mail: otoole_ewald@compuserve.com
1133 Broadway R 1107
New York, NY 10010
Elin Lake Ewald, ASA, Principal
PH: (212)989-5151
FX: (212)242-1629
Founded: 1932. **Staff:** 12. Appraisal experts and consultants specializing in damage/loss/fraud cases relating to fine/decorative art. Expertise in painting, sculpture, antiques, Asian art, ethnographic art, works on paper, ceramics and glassware, rugs and textiles, silver, etc., Provides forensic appraisals, fully documented and with photographs, adhering to USPAP standards. Geographic Areas Served: USA

OUTREACH NUTRITION SERVICE
CVPH Medical Center
75 Beekman St.
Plattsburgh, NY 12901
Mary M. Noone, M.A., R.D., C.D.E., CN
PH: (518)562-7562
FX: (518)562-7093
Founded: 1985. **Staff:** 2. Offers group and individual counseling in comprehensive nutrition assessment, and education with follow-up of nutrition management in disease prevention and treatment. Serves private industries as well as government agencies. Geographic areas served: Clinton County, New York. **Conferences and Meetings:** *Diabetic Education Program (twelve hours); Behavior Modification/Nutrition Management Program (eighteen months); Liquid Diet Program Nutrimed.*

LARRY J. OVERTON & ASSOCIATES INC.
101 E. College Ave., Ste. 302
Tallahassee, FL 32301-7703
Larry J. Overton, Pres.
PH: (850)224-2859
FX: (850)561-6311
Founded: 1988. **Staff:** 5. Provides healthcare services to U.S. businesses.

OXFORD RESEARCH INTERNATIONAL CORP.
e-mail: emalid@oric.com
url: http://www.oric.com
1425 Broad St.
Clifton, NJ 07013-4221
Richard A. Guarino, M.D., Pres.
PH: (201)777-2800
FX: (201)777-9847
Founded: 1979. **Staff:** 43. Provides medical, legal, and statistical services to pharmaceutical and healthcare industry worldwide.

P. M. MEDICAL CONSULTANTS INC.
e-mail: pmorl@aol.com
1752 Howell Branch Rd.
Winter Park, FL 32789-1120
Richard C. Davis
PH: (407)645-1150
FX: (407)645-2178
Founded: 1979. Advises general public on healthcare management in central Florida.

P R S INC. - PHARMACY SERVICES
PO Box 852
Latrobe, PA 15650
Harry A. Lattanzio, RPH, President
PH: (412)539-7820
TF: 800338-3688
FX: (412)539-1388
Founded: 1983. **Staff:** 70. Pharmacy consultants. Industries served: grocery and retail pharmacy. Geographic areas served: U.S. **Conferences and Meetings:** *How to Open an In-Store Supermarket Pharmacy.*

NORBERT P. PAGE
17601 Stoneridge Ct.
Gaithersburg, MD 20878
Norbert P. Page, President
PH: (301)948-9408
FX: (301)948-9408
Founded: 1984. **Staff:** 2. Provides consultation on toxicology; risk assessment of chemicals and radiation; literature compilation and evaluation; design of toxicology studies; compliance with TSCA, FIFRA, international law; new drug applications; toxicology data and experiment evaluation; and report preparation. **Conferences and Meetings:** *Participates in or organizes seminars/workshops on toxicology issues and right-to-know legislation.*

PAL-MED HEALTH SERVICES
7150 W. 20th Ave., Ste. 412
Hialeah, FL 33016-5533
Alvaro I. Martinez, MD, Chairman
PH: (305)362-1986
FX: (305)556-6028
Founded: 1985. **Staff:** 160. Advises local businesses on healthcare management.

PALMER ASSOCIATES INC.
PO Box 717
Homewood, CA 96141
Diane Palmer, Pres.
PH: (916)532-3213
Founded: 1978. **Staff:** 11. Offers management services to healthcare industry in United States.

PAN PACIFIC UROLOGY
2100 Webster St., Ste. 309
San Francisco, CA 94115
Ira D. Sharlip, MD, Principal
PH: (415)202-0250
FX: (415)202-0255
Specializes in prostate diseases, prostate cancer, male infertility, impotence, sexual dysfunction, penile prostheses, vasectomy, vasectomy reversal, incontinence, urinary stones, and general urology.

PAREXEL INTERNATIONAL CORPORATION
url: http://www.PARAEXEL.com
195 West St.
Waltham, MA 02154
Josef von Rickenbach, Chairman, CEO
PH: (617)487-9900
TF: 800PAR-EXEL
FX: (617)487-0525
Founded: 1982. **Staff:** 700. An independent pharmaceutical research organization offering clinical trials management, global regulatory affairs, data management, biostatistics, medical writing, strategy development consultation and performance improvement services to the pharmaceutical, biotechnology, medical device and diagnostics industries in North America, the United Kingdom, Asia, and Europe. **Conferences and Meetings:** *Benchmarks '95; Risk Management '95; MCO Customer Service '95; Information Technology '95; Global Bio/Pharmaceutical Manufacturing '95; and Capitalizing on Technology Transfer.*

PARKER MEDICAL INC.
137 New Milford Rd. E.
Bridgewater, CT 06752
PH: (203)350-4304
FX: (203)350-3432
Founded: 1984. Consultants on radiologic procedures and equipment; x-ray equipment components such as high voltage cables, x-ray tube cooling units, x-ray tube shields, and x-ray tubes. Expertise in equipment design and manufacture.

PATH NUTRITION SERVICE
3735 Woodhill Rd.
Montgomery, AL 36109
Patricia C. Harris
PH: (205)270-1308
FX: (205)270-1308
Founded: 1976. **Staff:** 1. Consulting dietitian offering nutrition services to healthcare and private organizations. Has served rural populations, handicapped children, children's homes, and chronic renal failure and dialysis, psychiatric patients, and private patients. Additional consultation services available in sports nutrition and wellness programs in Alabama. **Computer/Special Services:** Writes and produces menus and conducts analysis of menus and diets.

CHARLES PEARSON ASSOCIATES
2025 First Ave., Ste. 1020
Seattle, WA 98121
PH: (206)443-1664
Founded: 1979. Management consultant offers hospital and health system management services with major focus on restructuring hospital-physician contractual relationships. Geographic areas served: U.S.

MICHAEL PECK, PH.D. & ASSOCIATES
10642 Santa Monica Blvd., Ste. 300
Los Angeles, CA 90025
PH: (310)475-3018
FX: (310)475-3018
Specializes in clinical psychology assessment and consultation. Forensic psychology services in wrongful death, suicide and accident, alcohol and drug abuse, personal injury, and medical malpractice (psychology).

AGNEW PECKHAM & ASSOCIATES, LTD.
e-mail: agnew@interlog.com
1300 Yonge St., Ste. 500
Toronto, ON, Canada M4T 1X3
Lucy Brun
PH: (416)924-7451
FX: (416)924-2268
Founded: 1955. **Staff:** 13. Healthcare planning consultants providing the following services: strategic planning (role review); functional programming, master programming, and master plan development.

PENINSULA PSYCHIATRIC ASSOCIATES
285 Hamilton Ave, Ste. 470
4153234704
4153422350
Palo Alto, CA 94301
Ronnie Sue Leith, MD, Psychiatrist
FX: (650)342-2350
Provides assessment of emotional injury. An expert witness and consultant in civil litigation regarding sexual harassment, intentional infliction of emotional distress, wrongful termination, and psychiatric malpractice.

PAUL PERCHONOCK, MD
e-mail: prpmd@aol.com
425 28th St.
Oakland, CA 94609
PH: (510)452-1390
FX: (510)452-0834
Performs record review to establish pre-existing conditions/ apportionment of treatment, to establish prognosis and future medical costs, and to establish medical necessity and reasonableness of care.

PERFORMANCE MANAGEMENT SERVICES INC.
13522 Newport Ave., Ste. 200
Tustin, CA 92780-3707
Eliott H. Saulten, President
PH: (714)731-3414
FX: (714)731-4620

JON A. PERLMAN, MD
e-mail: jonap@ucla.edu
414 N. Camden Dr., Ste. 800
Beverly Hills, CA 90210
PH: (310)854-0031
FX: (310)275-5079
Specializes in plastic surgery, cosmetic surgery, nasal and facial injuries, hand surgery, and scars.

REED C. PERRON, MD
Neurology Group of Bergen County, PA
106 Prospect St.
Ridgewood, NJ 07450
PH: (201)444-0868
FX: (201)444-7363
Specializes in medical malpractice involving diagnosis and management of stroke, hemorrhage, injury, infection of brain, spine or peripheral nerves.

PERSONAL CARE RESOURCE CENTER, INC.
41 Londonvale Rd.
Gordonville, PA 17529
Margaret R. Eby
PH: (717)768-7271
TF: 800725-7395
FX: (717)768-8553
Residential healthcare consultants provide training programs. **Conferences and Meetings:** *Fire Prevention and Emergency Planning; First Aid, Medication, Medical Terminology and Personal Hygiene; Local, State and Federal Laws and Regulations; Nutrition, Food Handling and Sanitation; Recreation, Mental Illness and Gerontology.*

PETTSONS INC.
2804 Martin L. King Jr. Ave.
Washington, DC 20032
Bruce A. Petty, Pres., Treas.
PH: (202)561-4500
FX: (202)562-2011
Founded: 1984. **Staff:** 189. Advises government and private sector worldwide on home healthcare.

PHARMACEUTICAL CONSULTANTS INC.
url: http://www.pharmconsult.com
5033 W. 117th
Leawood, KS 66211
Dr. Beth Maggio, CEO
PH: (888)491-9825
TF: 888491-9825
FX: (888)491-9829
Founded: 1985. **Staff:** 10. Pharmaceutical consultants specializing in the F.D.A. drug approval process. Offers full-service research services in Rx to OTC switch, multicenter trials management, statistical analysis, protocol development, and toxicology studies. Industries served: pharmaceutical. Geographic areas served: national and international. Woman owned firm.

PHARMACEUTICAL RECRUITERS, INC.
271 Madison Ave., Ste. 1200
New York, NY 10016
Linda S. Weiss, President
PH: (212)557-5627
FX: (212)557-5866
Firm recruits medical professionals for clinical research positions.

PHARMACEUTICAL SYSTEMS INC.
url: http://www.pharmsystems.com
102 Terrace Dr.
Mundelein, IL 60060-3826
Robert Reich
PH: (847)566-9229
FX: (847)566-4960
Founded: 1988. **Staff:** 20. Offers legal, contract auditing, regulatory compliance, lab research, business planning, technology, sterility assurance and quality assurance services to U.S. health-care medical device and pharmaceutical industries. Geographic Areas Served: Worldwide. **Conferences and Meetings:** *Seminars include, but are not limited to the following topics: Ethylene Oxide Sterilization; Steam Sterilization; Emerging Sterilization Technologies; D-Value and Z-Value Calculations; Microbial Barrier Evaluation of Packaging; Bioburden Quantitation; Environmental Microbial Monitoring; LAL Pyrogen Testing; Biological Indicators; Quality Management; Handling FDA Inspections; GMP-The Real World.* **Computer/Special Services:** Software validations, computer control systems.

PHARMACY CONSULTANTS INC.
348 E. Blackstock Rd., Ste. A
Spartanburg, SC 29301
PH: (864)574-5220
FX: 800-842-2238
Founded: 1976. Medication consultation services to long-term care facilities, nursing homes, residential-care facilities, group homes for the mentally retarded, prison systems, and trauma recovery centers.

PHASE V TECHNOLOGIES INC.
20 Walnut St.
Wellesley, MA 02181-2104
Marcia Testa Simonson
PH: (781)237-7737
FX: (781)237-4407
Founded: 1987. **Staff:** 7. Medical research consultants.

PATRICK PHILBIN & ASSOCIATES
No. 2 Hidden Cove
Austin, TX 78746
Patrick W. Philbin, President
PH: (512)450-1788
FX: (512)450-1902
Founded: 1980. **Staff:** 8. Provides healthcare consulting with emphasis on ambulatory care and community network. Also offers expertise in marketing, strategic planning, management reorganization, system development, ambulatory care product lines, physician practice enhancement services, regional systems develop-

ment, ambulatory care assessment/development, long-term care, feasibility studies, seminars, retreats, and management information systems. Focus is on hospitals. Also serves government agencies. Geographic areas served: U.S.

RUSSELL PHILLIPS & ASSOCIATES INC.
e-mail: rusphill@aol.com
33 W. Outer Dr.
Rochester, NY 14615
Russell Phillips, President
PH: (716)621-3700
FX: (716)621-7300
Founded: 1976. Staff: 11. Team of professional fire protection experts offers facility inspections, evacuation system design and staff training, code review, and statements of condition and fire safety evaluation systems. Industries served: healthcare and government agencies. Geographic areas served: U.S. and international. Conferences and Meetings: *Health Care Fire Evacuation; Health Care Educational Seminars for many state associations. Environment of Care Seminars.*

PHILLIPS & FENWICK
5550 Scotts Valley Dr.
Scotts Valley, CA 95066-3460
Celeste Phillips, RN, EDD, Pres.
PH: (408)439-5150
FX: (408)439-5158
Founded: 1988. Staff: 11. Offers medical services, specializing in women's healthcare. Industries served: hospitals in United States and Canada.

PIVIROTTO & BOTHAMLEY CONSULTING
e-mail: h.pivirotto@alon.com
PO Box 787
Cheshire, CT 06410-0787
Dennis Bothamley, Partner
PH: (203)272-9204
FX: (203)271-2070
Founded: 1986. Staff: 8. Offers healthcare and financial management services to businesses in Connecticut.

PLACEMENT ASSOCIATES, LTD.
e-mail: placementa@ibm.net
url: http://expertpages.com/cv/mooney.htm
14222 Blarney Cir.
Cement City, MI 49233
Raymond P. Mooney, Physician Assistant
PH: (517)688-4637
FX: (517)688-4235
Physician's assistant experienced in family medicine, emergency medicine and urgent care medicine. Provides pre- and post-litigation analysis, written opinion, deposition and trial testimony concerning medical malpractice cases involving physician assistant practice. Experienced in recruitment of physician assistants. Knowledge of laws concerning the scope of practice and rules and regulations concerning physician assistant practice.

ROBERT S. POGRUND
11022 Windsor Dr.
Sun City, AZ 85351-3339
Robert S. Pogrund
PH: (602)977-2940
Founded: 1974. Specialist in occupational and environmental health and safety with consulting expertise in environmental physiology and toxicology, occupational or industrial hygiene, human factors (ergonomics, man-machine integration), nutrition, public health and preventive medicine, human health effects of air and water pollution, and pesticides. Legal expert testimony provided for toxic occupational exposures; specialty in carbon monoxide toxicity, low level ionizing radiation, and ELF (extremely low frequency) radiation. Serves private industries as well as government agencies. Geographic areas served: southwestern United States.

POLICE CONSULTANTS INC.
825 N. Cass Ave., Ste. 210
Westmont, IL 60559-1132
Avrum J. Mendelsohn
PH: (630)325-2336
FX: (630)325-3318
Founded: 1968. Consultants specialize in police and fire testing for entrace and promotion. Offers in-depth psychological exams. Geographic Areas Served: U.S.

DAVID G. POLIN, MD
230 Harrisburg Ave., Ste. 06
Lancaster, PA 17603
PH: (717)399-4364
FX: (717)392-8160
Specializes in brain injury, spinal cord injury, amputations, reflex sympathetic dystrophy, myopascial pain, and EMG testing.

JAY M. PORTNOW
167 Washington St., Ste. 14
Norwell, MA 02061
Jay M. Portnow
PH: (617)659-2521
FX: (617)871-4648
Founded: 1987. Staff: 7. Offers consultation on establishing rehabilitation services in hospital, ambulatory or home care setting, case management of high cost cases, and level of care decisions and alternative care options. Available for subacute programs. Additional expertise available on establishing home care programs, coordination and clinical concerns. Industries served: insurance companies, government agencies, and private organizations in the U.S. Conferences and Meetings: *Presents home care talks and numerous national and regional conferences.*

JO ANNE POWELL
228 Pinehurst Way
South San Francisco, CA 94080
Jo Anne Powell
PH: (650)875-1721
Founded: 1977. Independent nursing administration consultant in staff development and executive coaching primarily within the healthcare delivery system.

PRAGMA CORP.
e-mail: pragma1@ix.netcom.com
116 E. Broad St.
Falls Church, VA 22046-4501
Jacques Defay, Pres.
PH: (703)237-9303
FX: (703)237-9326
Founded: 1977. Staff: 65. Offers expertise in the fields of agricultural health and nutrition; research; feasibility studies; transportation; employment; and energy use. Also provides training services. Industries served: U.S. and foreign governments, and private businesses.

PREFERRED MEDICAL MARKETING CORP.
url: http://www.pmmconline.com
7400 Carmel Executive Pk., Ste. 240
Charlotte, NC 28226
Roger L. Shaul, Jr., President
PH: (704)543-8103
FX: (704)543-8106
Founded: 1987. Staff: 20. Health care consultants. Conferences and Meetings: *List of seminars and workshops available from firm upon request.* Computer/Special Services: Offers managed care software, insurance company managed care strategy database, inpatient and outpatient pricing database, and numerous statewide and national hospital databases.

PRESCRIPTION PLAN SERVICE CORP.
710 Penn Plaza, Ste. 910
New York, NY 10001
Alvin Konigsberg, Pres.

PH: (212)279-3232
TF: 800647-2677
FX: (212)629-0749
Founded: 1975. Provides national health plan administration, PPO, and cost containment services.

PRO-FIT
e-mail: alice.lockridge@cl.seattle.wa.us
url: http://www.quikpage.com/E/exercise
12012 156th Ave. SE
Renton, WA 98059-1613
Alice Lockridge, Owner
PH: (425)255-3817
FX: (425)255-0478
Founded: 1983. **Staff:** 5. Health fitness consultant offers expertise on simple steps to start doing what's good for you. Consultant stresses correct techniques of exercise and their importance. Topics include: aerobics for real people, back fitness, nutrition, stretching, food fats, office exercises, correct exercise form, physiology facts, principles of adult exercise and exercise abuse. Will also discuss client/requested topic at public presentations. Programs designed and operated in occupationally pertinent fitness programs for physically demanding careers. Geographic Areas Served: Focus on Pacific NW - travels nation-wide. **Conferences and Meetings:** *Fitness Instructor Training includes basic training, continuing education, master training course, and home-study courses as well as convention activity breaks: "Motivating Movement Moments".*

PROBE SCIENTIFIC-TOXICOLOGY
e-mail: 105133.3035@compuserve.com
2109 Pinehurst Ct.
El Cerrito, CA 94530-1879
Kenneth Dean Parker, Principal
PH: (510)233-2300
FX: (510)223-2290
Founded: 1973. **Staff:** 1. Serves attorneys, insurance companies, and individuals with forensic toxicology consulting and laboratory services. Emphasizes DUI-DUID cases; alcohol and drug use and abuse; human factors vs. driving skills; disorders and errors with breath, urine, and blood tests; correct diagnosis of intoxication, dose related to blood alcohol or drug concentration and action and effects on persons. Industries served: non-governmental companies' programs for employee drug use prevention, detection, forensic urine drug testing (FUDT), and consultation for certification of laboratory FUDT by College of American Pathologists. Also serves government agencies. Geographic areas served: primarily, the West Coast of United States, specifically, the Greater San Francisco Bay Area.

PROFESSIONAL COUNSELING CENTERS OF INDIANA
9595 N. Whitley Dr.
Indianapolis, IN 46240
PH: (317)846-7999
FX: (317)574-5063
Business counselors offer expertise in the following areas: employee assistance, managed care, alcohol and drug treatment, labor and union consultation, and industrial mental health.

PROFESSIONAL HEALTHCARE ASSOCIATES INC.
e-mail: sales@vistapubl.com
url: http://www.vistapubl.com
422 Morris Ave., Ste. 1
Long Branch, NJ 07740
Carolyn S. Zagury, President
PH: (732)229-4545
FX: (732)229-9647
Founded: 1989. **Staff:** 5. Offers healthcare consulting services in the areas of geriatric service development; grant funding research, development and application preparation; and system development and strategic planning for nursing. Additional work in education and training for healthcare professionals in management training, clinical areas, and writing skills. Other services include manuscript development, editing, publishing and marketing

of books, journals and articles related to healthcare, human services and women's issues. Industries served: healthcare, long term care, human services, and municipal government agencies. Geographic areas served: U.S. **Conferences and Meetings:** *Aging: Issues for Those Who Care (children of aging parents); The Sandwich Generation (women in the middle); Grant Writing Workshops; The Business of Nursing Management: Transformational Leadership in Nursing; Business Skills for Nursing Management; Beating Nursing Burn Out; Nurse Entrepreneur; The "In Basket" Crative Problem Solving.*

PROFILE MANAGEMENT INC.
7600 France Ave., Ste. 421
Minneapolis, MN 55435-5938
Jerry Nye
PH: (612)832-0511
FX: (612)832-0510
Founded: 1989. **Staff:** 10. Offers medical management and reimbursement counsel, including accounting, billing, and reporting services to physicians and hospitals regionally.

PROSPECT ASSOCIATES
e-mail: @prospectassoc.com
1801 Rockville Pike, Ste. 500
Rockville, MD 20852
Laura Henderson, President/CEO
PH: (301)468-6555
FX: (301)770-5164
Founded: 1979. **Staff:** 140. A health sciences research and communications firm which provides support to scientific, health and technical clients to help them combat and solve the nation's foremost health problems. Prospect offers particular expertise and experience on such issues as AIDS; cancer; heart, lung, and blood diseases; diabetes; digestive diseases; kidney and urologic diseases; arthritis; mental disorders; dental problems; and concerns of the aging population. Communications services include support in health education, mass media, minority health, and public affairs. Scientific support includes services in research and evaluation, information services, and biomedical and behavioral sciences. Information services are also offered which include integrated support in information services and management, computer applications, and library services. Prospect specializes in the dissemination of health and scientific information to consumers and professionals. Support services such as conference logistics, graphics support, word processing, data processing, publications management, editorial services, messenger service, warehousing and distribution, and clerical and administrative support are also available. Industries served: government agencies, universities and other nonprofit organizations, foundations and associations, and private industry. Small women-owned firm. **Conferences and Meetings:** *Firm has supported over 2,000 conferences and meetings for clients in the health, science and technology arenas.*

PROVIDENCE VENTURES INC.
6 E. Mountain Ave.
South Williamsport, PA 17701
PH: (717)321-7784
FX: (717)321-7780
Founded: 1986. Provides medical management services including shared mobile services.

PSA CONSULTING
e-mail: psacons@ix.netcom.com
6101 Imperata St., NE, No. 1625
Albuquerque, NM 87111
Patricia S. Albani, RN, MBA
PH: (505)823-1926
FX: (505)823-2670
Founded: 1983. **Staff:** 1. Acts as guide through maze of home health agency operations for new as well as experienced home health agencies. Specializes in variety of operational and clinical services designed to achieve and maintain regulatory compliance. Offers policy/manual development; program evaluation; licens-

ing, survey, and accreditation preparation; clinical record documentation development/review; and performance improvement activities. Skilled in agency management, fiscal intermediation, CHAP accreditation site visitation, and providing expert advice. Industries served: home health in the U.S., primarily HCFA Region VI (NM, TX, LA, AR, and OK).

PSYCHIATRIC CONSULTATION - LIAISON PROGRAM
e-mail: eisen@itsa.ucsf.edu
University of California, San Francisco
School of Medicine
401 Parnassus
San Francisco, CA 94143-0984
Stuart J. Eisendrath, MD, Director
PH: (415)476-7868
FX: (415)476-7371
Provides psychiatric consultation. Specializes in psychosomatic medicine, psychiatric aspects of medical illness, factitious disorders, hysterical conversion, post-traumatic stress disorder, and Munchausen syndrome. Provides claim analysis, depositions, and trial testimony.

THE PSYCHOLOGICAL TRAUMA CENTER
2024 Divisadero St.
San Francisco, CA 94115
Gilbert Kliman, MD, Medical Director
PH: (415)474-0955
FX: (415)474-7514
Treats those with psychological trauma claimed from stressors including institutional negligence, vehicular and aviation accidents, wrongful death in the family, rape, molestation, fire, explosion, flood, earthquake, loss of parents, terrorism, kidnapping, disfiguring events, emotional damage from social work, medical malpractice or defective products. Provides evaluation and reports to referring professionals. Experienced in forensic consultation and testimony.

PSYCHOTHERAPY ASSOCIATES
40 Old Pond Rd.
South Salem, NY 10590
Naomi F. Garrell
PH: (914)763-5916
FX: (914)763-6567
Founded: 1986. **Staff:** 4. Nutritional consultants with expertise in weight reduction or maintenance and stress-related modification. Offers a weight modifying program based on an eclectic approach consisting of medical, psychological and nutritional services. Also provide a stress reduction program utilizing this eclectic approach. Additional areas of expertise include: post traumatic stress disorders and electric burn trauma. Geographic areas served: north Westchester County, New York; and Ridgefield, New Cannan, and Greenwich, Connecticut.

ARNOLD D. PURISCH, PH.D.
e-mail: APurisch@aol.com
7700 Irvine Center Dr., Ste. 750
Irvine, CA 92618
PH: (714)753-7711
FX: (714)753-7708
Provides neuropsychological evaluation, psychometric testing, areas include forensic psychology and forensic neuropsychology for criminal behavior and workers' compensation cases. Provides neuropsych/psychological evaluation.

QUALITY MANAGEMENT ASSOCIATES INC.
PO Box 32516
Louisville, KY 40232
Evelyn Strange, Pres.
PH: (502)499-6760
Founded: 1991. **Staff:** 3. Advises businesses on quality healthcare management practices. Geographic areas served: United States.

QUALITY MANAGEMENT RESOURCES LIMITED
107 E. Main
Buford, GA 30518
Dr. Richard F. Kaine, President
PH: (770)614-4600
TF: 800762-1967
FX: (770)614-6885
Founded: 1988. **Staff:** 4. Firm offers expertise in medicine, healthcare, and quality assurance. Serves hospitals, insurance companies, doctors, and HMO's in the U.S.

QUALITY MEDI-CAL ADJUDICATION INC.
2897 Kilgore Rd.
Rancho Cordova, CA 95670
PH: (916)852-2500
FX: (916)852-2669
Founded: 1990. Offers expertise regarding medical billing.

QUINTILES BRI
1300 N. 17th St., Ste. 300
Arlington, VA 22209
PH: (703)276-0400
FX: (703)243-9746
Founded: 1971. Consults on pharmaceuticals and medical devices.

R. H. MEDICAL GROUP INC.
PO Box 820889
Houston, TX 77282-0889
Richard C. Holdren, Pres.
PH: (281)496-7777
FX: (281)496-9574
Founded: 1982. **Staff:** 6. Advises physicians on professional practice management in the United States. Geographic Areas Served: Nationwide.

RADIOLOGICAL SCIENCE ASSOCIATES INC.
e-mail: jbhatnagar@mercy.pmhs.org
PO Box 677
Ingomar, PA 15127
PH: (412)232-7805
FX: (412)232-5753
Founded: 1984. Radiological physicists offer consulting expertise.

RADIOLOGY ASSOCIATES OF WICHITA FALLS, PA
e-mail: sutton@wf.net
url: http://www.wf.net/~sutton
808 Brook Ave.
Wichita Falls, TX 76301
Richard N. Sutton, MD, President
PH: (940)766-0217
FX: (940)691-4305
Specializes in diagnostic radiology, angiography, mammography, myelography, computed tomography. Provides film and case reviews and expert witness services.

RADON ENVIRONMENTAL MONITORING, INC.
e-mail: REMRadon@compuserve.com
url: http://www.REMRadon.com
3334 Commercial Ave.
Northbrook, IL 60062-1909
Michael J. Myers
PH: (847)205-0110
TF: 800206-0110
FX: (847)205-0114
Founded: 1985. **Staff:** 9. Offers consultation for radon testing surveys and mitigation system planning and design, radon evaluation project design for wide geographic surveys, schoo ls, soil studies and public outreach. Mitigation system design for schools and large commercial and public buildings. Radon resistant construction tatnieves. Industries served: medical, industrial and government agencies. Geographic areas served: international. **Conferences and Meetings:** *Radon Measurement Operations Course, 2 1/2 days; Radon Mitigation Specialis t Course, 5 days*

with hands-on training. **Computer/Special Services:** Manufactures and analyzes Passive Alpha Track and Liquid Scintillation Detectors.

MARK M. RASENICK
e-mail: raz@uic.edu
Department of Physiology & Biophysics
Univ. of Illinois, College of Medicine
901 S. Wolcott
Chicago, IL 60612-7342
Mark M. Rasenick
PH: (312)996-6641
FX: (312)996-1414
Offers consultation on various aspects of neuropharmacology and psychopharmacology, especially those relating to GTP-binding proteins and neuronal signal transduction. Serves as expert witness for all drug effects upon the central nervous system, especially antidepressant drugs and treatments. Also provides consultation for the preparation of research grant applications. Industries served: biomedical, scientific, legal applications, and government agencies. Geographic areas served: worldwide.

RBH ASSOCIATES, INC.
e-mail: rbh@interramp.com
62-44 99th St.
Rego Park, NY 11374
Ruben Robert Ben-Harari, Ph.D.
TF: 800461-9227
FX: (718)592-6573
Founded: 1993. **Staff:** 2. Provides customized resources drawing together talents of independent specialists to address specific client needs. Services include strategic thinking and creative development; successful new products and product repositioning; client presentations; scientific review and analysis of medical communications ideas and materials; effective publication development for products; advisory and editorial board development from medical opinion leaders; writing expanded into new clinical areas; electronic, video, and slides applied to educational, promotional, and sales training programs; and cost effectiveness studies. **Conferences and Meetings:** *Has designed and presented exhibits and lectures.* **Computer/Special Services:** Produces CD-ROM, Internet, and video products.

RCFA HEALTHCARE MANAGEMENT SERVICES, LLC
url: http://www.rcfa.com
9648 Kingston Pike, Ste. 8
Knoxville, TN 37922
Paul L. King, Pres.
PH: (423)531-0176
TF: 800635-4040
FX: (423)531-0722
Founded: 1956. **Staff:** 24. Have served clients in 44 states since 1956. Full management services with specialty departments including human resources, coding, reimbursement, OSHA, CLIA and accounting, and marketing. Geographic Areas Served: National. **Conferences and Meetings:** *Coding, human resources, collection*

RD NETWORK INC.
e-mail: rd-network@msn.com
Shawmont Ave., Ste. 303-D
Philadelphia, PA 19128
Leslie Grant, President
PH: (215)482-4461
FX: (215)482-9947
Founded: 1983. **Staff:** 6. Dietitians, diet technicians, and certified dietary managers available nationwide and worldwide through an international registry (over 2000 members) for consulting positions to wellness/employee education programs, drug/alcohol rehabilitation, hospital, LTC, nutrition/labeling communications, nutrition consultation, weight control classes, healthcare staff supplementation, media and program development, and all nutrition and food-related needs. Expert witness and speakers bureau also available. Industries served: healthcare, food industry, food

service, restaurateurs, corrections, supermarkets, pharmaceutical companies, home health agencies, insurance companies, HMOs, and government agencies. **Conferences and Meetings:** *Healthy Dining Etiquette for Executives and Sales Staff Diet and Wellness; Cardiovasular Nutrition; Starting a Nutrition Consulting Practice; AIDS and Diet Therapy; Nutrition Care for Your Parents in Their Elder Years; Increase Your Energy - Increase Your Sales.* **Computer/Special Services:** Nutrient analysis, menu planning.

REED GROUP LTD.
3200 Cherry Creek Dr. S., Ste. 220
Denver, CO 80209
PH: (303)777-0515
TF: 800347-7443
FX: (303)871-0599
Founded: 1981. Offers medical disability case management and occupational health and medical services.

REHABILITATION CASE MANAGEMENT CONSULTANTS INC.
e-mail: rcmc-ssc@ix.netcom.com
PO Box 1006
Okemos, MI 48805-1006
Maggie Miez, RN, CRRN, CDMS, CCM
PH: (517)349-8221
TF: 800968-4087
FX: (517)349-1290
Founded: 1989. **Staff:** 10. Specializes in case management services for catastrophic accident and auto accident victims, group health, and short- and long-term disability and worker compensation claimants. **Computer/Special Services:** Email & Internet access available.

REHABINC EAST CORP.
175 Canal St.
Manchester, NH 03101
Lorraine F. Gerstin, Pres.
PH: (603)669-7833
FX: (603)669-1224
Founded: 1986. **Staff:** 7. Advises insurance companies on rehabilitation services, focusing on workers' compensation injuries. Geographic areas served: New Hampshire and Massachusetts.

REMINGTON ADVISORY GROUP INC.
30100 Town Center Dr., Ste. 421
Laguna Niguel, CA 92677-2064
Lisa Remington, Pres.
PH: (714)365-5533
FX: (714)365-5528
Founded: 1982. **Staff:** 7. Advises healthcare industry in the United States.

THE RESCUE COMPANY
514 Tobacco Quay
Alexandria, VA 22314
PH: (703)549-7783
FX: (703)683-1320
A healthcare consulting firm providing occupational health and safety programs, and management training to individuals and businesses, as well as government agencies. **Conferences and Meetings:** *Stress Management; Ergonomics; Regulatory Compliance; Corporate Wellness; Exercise; Weight Management; Disease Specific Topics; Nutrition.*

RESOURCE OPPORTUNITIES, INC.
2 Perimeter Park S, Ste. 410E
Birmingham, AL 35243
Myrtice Carr, District Manager
PH: (205)969-0084
TF: 800297-2926
FX: (205)969-0932
Founded: 1979. Rehabilitation services consultants with primary focus on medical case management.

RESOURCES FOR EXCELLENCE
112 Evans St.
Rockville, MD 20850
Anita W. Finkelman, R.N., M.S.N., Director
PH: (301)340-2077
FX: (301)340-2077
Founded: 1988. **Staff:** 1. Offers consultative services that focus on healthcare, particularly skilled in the areas of nursing and psychiatric-mental health. Specific areas include: leadership and management development; policy, procedure, and standards development; quality assessment and improvement; staff development; writing/healthcare issues; and medical-legal issues. Industries served: healthcare. Geographic areas served: U.S. **Conferences and Meetings:** *Management and Leadership for Nurse Managers; The Borderline Patient; The Seriously Disturbed Adolescent; Depression in the Medical Patient; Development of QA Programs; Home Care for the Psychiatric Patient.*

RETINA VITREOUS ASSOCIATES, INC.
2485 Hospital Dr., Ste. 200
Mountain View, CA 94040
Sterling J. Haidt, MD, President
PH: (415)988-7480
FX: (415)988-7482
Offers consulting on vision and automobile driving and medical malpractice.

REVELL'S DIET SERVICE
2407 E. Country Club Dr.
Fargo, ND 58103
Dorothy T. Revell, L.R.D.
PH: (701)235-9810
Founded: 1977. **Staff:** 1. Provides individual diet instruction according to the nutritional needs of the patient. Patients are either physician referrals or self-referrals. All types of diet are calculated, individually and personalized. Geographic areas served: Fargo and surrounding small cities or towns.

CAROL K. REVILOCK
1004 Tuxedo Ave.
Parma, OH 44134
Carol K. Revilock
PH: (216)749-2293
Founded: 1984. **Staff:** 1. Offers healthcare consulting services, specializing in the following areas: home healthcare, geriatrics, non-profit organizations, and staff development.

REYER & ASSOCIATES
24172 Jerome Ct.
Golden, CO 80401
Dianne K. Reyer
PH: (303)526-7371
FX: (303)526-7471
Founded: 1986. **Staff:** 1. Offers consultation to hospitals and medical care groups in developing new program strategies and alternative delivery systems for government agencies. Geographic areas served: continental United States. Woman owned firm.

RHA, INC.
4766 Sunset Blvd. Ste. B-1
Lexington, SC 29072
Jerry W. Sheffield, President
PH: (803)957-4646
FX: (803)957-3607
Founded: 1978. **Staff:** 8. Specializes in medical equipment planning and management for healthcare facilities. The scope of services includes space design guidance, budget development, long-range equipment replacement plans, inventory evaluation, and procurement assistance. The firm assists administrators, physicians, technologists and equipment users to establish need, analyze alternatives, and recommend practical, cost effective solutions. Industries served: medical facilities and government agencies in the U.S.

THE RINER GROUP, INC.
url: http://www.rinergroup.com
1034 S. Brentwood Blvd., Ste. 1640
St. Louis, MO 63117
Ronald N. Riner, President
PH: (314)727-7098
FX: (314)727-2735
Founded: 1981. **Staff:** 3. Provides health care advisory and management services, specializing in strategic planning, organizational development, professional medical practice/hospital mergers and acquisitions. Educational efforts are focused on hospital-medical staff organizational structure and board structures. Industries served: healthcare private medical practices, universities, pharmaceutical and medical device manufacturers, law firms, accounting firms, other consultancies, government in the U.S. and worldwide. **Conferences and Meetings:** *Courses on strategic development and new business development: clinical integration. Practice management and strategies for merging of clinical practices, heart institute development, cardiovascular diagnostic testing facilities, practice mergers, clinical and pharaco-economic studies, managed care strategies.*

EDWARD R. RITVO, MD
UCLA Medical School
Neuropsychiatric Institute
Los Angeles, CA 90024
PH: (310)825-0220
FX: (310)476-8345
Specializes in child and adult psychiatry, results of head trauma, mental retardation, psychiatric disability, developmental disabilities, learning disabilities, and autism.

RMC MEDICAL
url: http://www.mca1.com/rmc
3019 Darnell Rd.
Philadelphia, PA 19154-3201
Gil Cosnett, C.H.E.M. Program Manager
PH: (215)824-4100
TF: 800322-0672
FX: (215)824-1371
Founded: 1969. **Staff:** 15. Offers training in Chemical/Biological and Hazardous management and treatment to U.S. industries.

SUE ROBERTS HEALTH CONCEPTS
1515 Linden St., Ste. 220
Des Moines, IA 50309-3120
Susan L. Roberts
PH: (515)247-0014
FX: (515)247-0016
Founded: 1981. **Staff:** 8. Nutrition consultants providing individual patient consulting: group seminars and workshops; development and implementation of employee wellness programs for business and industry; and consultation to food producers, processors and marketers. Serves private industries as well as government agencies. **Conferences and Meetings:** *Nutrition for the Nineties; Healthy Employees; Preventing Heart Disease; Preventing Cancer; Losing Weight and Keeping It Off.*

RONALD H. ROBERTS, PH.D.
World Trade Center, Ste. 283
San Francisco, CA 94111
PH: (415)362-8202
FX: (415)362-3612
Clinical psychologist/neuropsychologist specializing in personal injury, automobile accidents, head injuries, chronic pain, toxic exposure, discrimination, post-traumatic stress, disability, back injuries, and forensic psychology.

ROBINSON HEALTH CARE COMPANIES INC.
4458 Cleveland Ave.
Fort Myers, FL 33901-9010
Kenneth D. Robinson, CEO, Pres.
PH: (941)275-2666
FX: (941)337-3180

Founded: 1975. **Staff:** 47. Advises healthcare industry worldwide on employment benefits.

ROBINSON INSTITUTE
1841 Broadway, Ste. 201
New York, NY 10023
Jeremy Robinson, President
PH: (212)459-8900
FX: (212)459-8959
Founded: 1990. **Staff:** 22. Offers intensive outpatient treatment program for drugs, alcohol and eating disorders. Provides dual-diagnosis psychiatric and addiction counseling. Conducts relapse prevention training. Many programs nationally are based on the philosophy and methodology of treatment utilized at the Institute for food addictions. Industries served: unlimited but have served automotive, transportation, educational, and government agencies. Geographic areas served: New York City metropolitan area.

ROCKY MOUNTAIN HEALTH CARE CORP.
url: http://www.bcbsco.com
700 Broadway
Denver, CO 80273
David Kikumoto, CEO, Pres.
PH: (303)831-2131
FX: (303)830-0887
Founded: 1987. **Staff:** 2128. Offers healthcare and benefits services, business administration, and education to businesses statewide.

ROCKY MOUNTAIN INSTRUMENTAL LABORATORIES, INC.
e-mail: rklantz@rockylab.com
url: http://www.rockylab.com
456 S. Link Ln.
Fort Collins, CO 80524
Robert K. Lantz, Ph.D.
PH: (970)221-3116
Founded: 1978. **Staff:** 7. Provides the following consulting services: pharmacologic and pharmacokinetic drug and toxin studies, forensic analysis in toxicology and serology, and product and method development in analytical chemistry and toxicology. Also provides expert witness testimony in state and federal courts. Serves pharmaceutical, forensic, chemical, as well as government agencies. Geographic areas served: U.S., Canada, and Europe. **Conferences and Meetings:** *Structure-Function Relationships in Psychoactive Drugs.*

THE GLORIA ROSE GOURMET LONG LIFE COOKING SCHOOL
48 Norwood Rd.
Springfield, NJ 07081
Gloria Rose
PH: (201)376-0942
FX: (908)352-2855
Founded: 1984. **Staff:** 12. Registered dieticians assist with the operation of nutritional schools teaching those with hypertension, high cholesterol, diabetes, and obesity (as well as a preventative healthy lifestyle) how to prepare delicious meals without the use of oils, fats, sugar, or salt. Provide individual attention upon request; with fine restaurants, hotels, and gourmet chefs. Serving physicians, hospitals, as well as large corporations in the New Jersey and New York. **Conferences and Meetings:** *Conducts seminars and classes on healthy eating habits and how to prepare delicious foods quickly and simply.*

ALDO M. ROSEMBLAT, MD
6316 Castle Pl., Ste. 200
Falls Church, VA 22044
PH: (703)241-8989
FX: (703)532-6247
Specializes in surgery of the brain, spine, spinal cord and peripheral nerves. Provides disability evaluations for workers' compensation, personal injury and social security pertaining to the neurological system and to the joint and muscular skeletal systems.

FRED ROSENTHAL
825 Van Ness Ave., Ste. 411
San Francisco, CA 94109
PH: (415)346-4608
FX: (415)885-5815
Provides expert witness testimony in legal cases and medical-legal evaluations. Areas include criminal behavior, sexual harassment, workers' compensation, divorce, custody, violence. Performs record review, psychiatric evaluations and psychological testing.

IVAR E. ROTH
e-mail: ifabs@earthlink.net
351 Hospital Rd., Ste. 407
Newport Beach, CA 92663
Ivar E. Roth
PH: (714)650-1147
FX: (714)650-6434
Founded: 1986. **Staff:** 4. Experienced expert witness concerning the foot and ankle. Areas of specialty are malpractice, accident reconstruction and forensic issues. Extensive experience in case management and strategic case planning issues. Consultation available concerning billing and insurance coverage issues. Personal evaluation and treatment available. Will handle urgent cases and complex, difficult cases. Industries served: insurance industry, malpractice, legal, and professional sports teams. Geographic areas served: U.S.

ROUNDTABLE OF TOXICOLOGY CONSULTANTS
url: http://lawinfo.com/biz/toxicology/index.html
31308 Via Colinas, Ste. 107
Westlake Village, CA 91362
Dr. Patricia Frank, President
PH: (818)706-2410
FX: (818)706-2413
Founded: 1980. **Staff:** 50. Provides general toxicology consulting by experienced doctoral-level scientists. Specialty areas include: legal support in product liability cases, new drug applications, FDA approvals, OSHA and EPA standards, pesticides, food additives, workplace safety, animal testing for regulatory approval, expert testimony, EPA compliance, and many related areas. Offers expert reviews in toxicology, medical, chemical, and other scientific databases. Industries served: attorneys, pharmaceutical, chemical, government, general manufacturing, as well as government agencies. Geographic areas served: Worldwide.

R.O.W. SCIENCES, INC.
url: http://www.rowsciences.com
1700 Research Blvd., Ste. 400
Rockville, MD 20850
PH: (301)294-5400
FX: (301)294-5401
Founded: 1983. **Staff:** 500. Performs biomedical and health services research and consulting. Also provides computer and telecommunications services.

RAPHAELA ROZANSKI, REGISTERED DIETITIAN
5 Virginia Rd.
Medway, MA 02053
Raphaela Rozanski
PH: (508)533-8560
Founded: 1966. **Staff:** 1. Consulting nutritionist offers dietetic expertise in areas of management, education, and for clinical settings to individuals, groups, long-term care institutions, and corporations. Particular counsel provided in products or healthcare benefits.

RPH CONSULTING INC.
1238 Stuivesant
Union, NJ 07083
Joseph P. Grosso, Jr.

PH: (973)284-1681
FX: (908)686-2473
Founded: 1986. **Staff:** 8. Pharmacy consultants for nursing homes.

RICHARD A. RUBENSTEIN, MD
2970 Hilltop Mall Rd., Ste. 203
Richmond, CA 94806
PH: (510)222-4479
FX: (510)222-4092
Neurologist providing worker's compensation disability evaluations and personal and bodily injury evaluations.

S. H. R. ASSOCIATES INC.
9690 Deereco Rd., Ste. 3270
Timonium, MD 21093-6902
Edwin Saionty, Pres.
PH: (410)561-0070
FX: (410)561-0781
Founded: 1981. **Staff:** 10. Advises on shared health resources, assisting physicians, hospitals, and nursing homes in Illinois, Michigan, New York, New Jersey, Maryland, and Washington D.C.

DENISE A. SADOWSKI
e-mail: 1035766.35@compuserve.com
7312 Plainfield Rd.
Cincinnati, OH 45236
Denise A. Sadowski
PH: (513)791-9439
Founded: 1988. Clinical nurse specialist provides educational classes, lectures and seminars to hospitals, schools of nursing and medical companies. Also offers consulting to medical companies for new product development as well as conducting research on their new products in the clinical area. Primary areas include burns, trauma, wounds, hemodynamic monitoring IV therapy. Industries served: hospitals and medical companies. Geographic areas served: continental United States. **Conferences and Meetings:** *Total Care of Thermally Injured Patient; Concepts of Hemodynamic Monitoring; IV Therapy; Pre-hospital and Emergency Care of Burn Victims; Total Concepts of Wound Care.*

SAFETY & LOSS CONTROL ASSOCIATES
PO Box 611
South Elgin, IL 60177-0611
Donald A. Neslund
PH: (847)622-1690
FX: (847)622-1695
Founded: 1984. **Staff:** 2. Assists contractors and industrial operators in reducing worker injuries and illnesses. Safety and training consulting includes employee training, supervisor and management seminars, OSHA compliance audits, pre-job inspections, expert witness work, accident investigation and reconstruction. Also provides expertise in ladders/scaffolds, fall protection, drugs/alcohol in work place, confined space entry, blasting and man produced vibration, driving, trench safety, Hazcom, and lockout/tagout. Serves the construction, insurance, legal profession, and manufacturing industries. Geographic Areas Served: USA **Conferences and Meetings:** *Hazard Communication-Construction, Trench Safety, OSHA 30-hour Hazard Recognition Course; Communication and Interpersonal Skills Workshops; also designs and conducts specialized safety seminars.*

SAFETY SCIENCES INC.
7586 Trade St.
San Diego, CA 92121
Kelly King, President
PH: (619)578-8400
FX: (619)578-1447
Founded: 1974. **Staff:** 25. Provides safety, health research, and consulting services for governmental agencies and large corporations, as well as forensic services for attorneys.

SAFETY SHORT PRODUCTION INC.
2960 N. 23rd St.
La Porte, TX 77571
PH: (281)470-9999
TF: 800458-2236
FX: (281)470-8653
Firm offers video and computer-based training programs designed to reduce accident rates, meet with OSHA training regulations, and reduce liability exposures through employee and management training.

SAN FRANCISCO SPORTS MEDICINE
Davies Medical Center
45 Castro, Ste. 117
San Francisco, CA 94114
Scott F. Dye, MD, Principal
PH: (415)861-9966
FX: (415)861-0174
Orthopedic surgeons and board certified medical-legal evaluators. Provide medical record reviews, expert witness testimony, and Spanish and German translation.

SAPONARO INC.
e-mail: psaponaro@en.com
url: http://www.allamart.com/saponaro
2168 Mentor Ave.
Painesville, OH 44077
James N. Saponaro, President
PH: (440)639-1413
TF: 800327-3026
FX: (440)639-1013
Founded: 1974. **Staff:** 6. A consulting firm that provides objective evaluations of medical care, medical literature research, and experts for plaintiff and defense, attorneys, and hospitals.

SAS MANAGEMENT CONSULTANTS
e-mail: sas1@nh.ultanet.com
92 Walden Pond Dr.
Nashua, NH 03060
Sally A. Stalker, President
PH: (603)880-7621
FX: (603)886-3302
Founded: 1991. Offers management consulting services in organizational development. Services include organizational assessments; work and role design; leadership coaching and development; team building; conflict resolution; and design and facilitation of retreats. Geographic Areas Served: National. **Conferences and Meetings:** *AAHU and IMU; Fundamentals of Consulting.*

RONALD E. SAUL, MD
550 N. Brand Blvd., Ste. 700
Glendale, CA 91203
PH: (818)546-5034
FX: (818)247-1414
Provides neurobehavioral disability evaluation limited to adult-adolescent cases of suspected brain injury, head trauma, epilepsy, dementia, anoxia, toxic exposure, and stroke. Provides expert witness testimony for personal injury cases.

SCAN - SPORTS, CARDIOVASCULAR AND WELLNESS NUTRITIONISTS
e-mail: scan@fleckcorporation.com
url: http://www.nutrifit.org
90 S. Cascade Ave., Ste. 1190
Colorado Springs, CO 80903
PH: (719)475-7751
FX: (719)475-8748
Founded: 1982. Nutrition consultants offering the following services: nutrition education for public via clinics, hospitals, health clubs, physicians' offices; clinical nutrition counseling via clinics, hospitals, cardiac rehab and eating disorders programs; and preventive and wellness program design and implementation. Geographic Areas Served: National. **Conferences and Meetings:** *1999*

Annual Meeting - Weight Control and Disordered Eating - March 26 - March 28, Cincinnati, OH.

SCHICK & AFFILIATES, INC.
3220 N St. NW, Ste. 161
Washington, DC 20007
Curt M. Huff, VP
PH: (202)338-1048
Founded: 1984. **Staff:** 13. Firm provides general management consulting services to the healthcare industry. Areas of specialized knowledge include systems for quantification of nursing care requirements in a variety of settings. Microcomputer based software supports results of projects. Geographic areas served: national. **Computer/Special Services:** Has developed and markets PACS, a complete stand-alone Patient Acuity System. Program includes its own ADT, classification, and cost reports and can be integrated with hospital mainframe systems.

SCHIRMER ENGINEERING CORPORATION
e-mail: schirmerhq@aol.com
707 Lake Cook Rd.
Deerfield, IL 60015-4997
Carl F. Baldassarra, P.E., President
PH: (847)272-8340
FX: (847)272-2639
Founded: 1939. **Staff:** 86. Fire protection engineering consultants providing fire protection master planning, building/fire code consultation, fire suppression system design, fire and security alarm system design, Americans With Disabilities Act (ADA) Accessibility Code consultation, loss control services, and litigation support services. Industries served: design and engineering, commercial, retail, health care, education, high tech, transportation, sports, office, industrial, attorneys, insurance brokers, insurance companies, risk managers, and government agencies. Geographic areas served: North and Central America. **Conferences and Meetings:** *Building Code Consultation Seminars and Fire Codes and Standards Seminars.*

TERRY L. SCHMIDT INC. - PHYSICIAN SERVICES GROUP
7770 Regents Rd., Ste. 113-611
San Diego, CA 92122
Terry L. Schmidt, President
PH: (619)597-8888
FX: (619)457-1960
Founded: 1974. **Staff:** 4. Physician practice management; assists clients in maximizing their reimbursement for health and medical services under various third-party reimbursement systems and marketing programs. The firm is heavily involved in healthcare reimbursement issues pending before the Health Care Financing Administration including Medicare and Medicaid, emergency physician practice management, hospital contract negotiations, medical group organization and reorganization. Clients include individual physician practices; physician group practices; hospitals; medical centers; individual providers and groups. **Conferences and Meetings:** *Maximizing Air Medical Transportation Reimbursement; Physician Medical Staff Leadership; Integrated Medical Group/Management Services Organization Development.*

MAX A. SCHNEIDER, MD, INC.
e-mail: alexron@aol.com
3311 E. Kirkwood Ave.
Orange, CA 92869-5211
PH: (714)639-0062
FX: (714)639-0987
A consultant on substance abuse issues. An expert witness in court cases involving alcohol and other mood altering drugs in criminal, civil, and malpractice issues. Lectures, seminars provided on all phases of substance use/abuse educatinal videos.

MARK S. SCHROEDER, MD
611 Windham Rd.
Willimantic, CT 06226
PH: (860)456-8444
FX: (860)456-0127

Specializes in mental harm and disability, medical and hospital malpractice, civil competence, and commitment.

MICHAEL SCHULDER, MD
e-mail: schulder@umdnj.edu
Section of Neurological Surgery
New Jersey Medical School
90 Bergen St., Ste. 7300
Newark, NJ 07103-2499
PH: (973)972-2323
FX: (973)972-2333
Specializes in neurosurgery, treatment of head and spinal injury, and treatment of brain tumors.

DR. DANIEL C. SCHUMAN
23 Summer St.
Weston, MA 02193
Daniel C. Schuman
PH: (617)891-0100
FX: (617)891-0100
Founded: 1970. Offers clinical psychiatric and forensic (legal) psychiatric evaluations. Special emphasis on: domestic relations (divorce, child custody, visitation, guardianship, testamentary competency); and forensic psychiatry (malpractice, emotional consequences of injuries, sexual abuse, review of questionable claims, etc.)

SCIENCE, TOXICOLOGY & TECHNOLOGY AND AIL LABORATORIES
e-mail: toxinfo@aol.com
url: http://www.toxinfo.com
PO Box 470116
San Francisco, CA 94147
Michael Scott, President
TF: 800869-4636
FX: (415)441-3204
Founded: 1983. Provides consultant and expert services in medical toxicology (adverse reactions to chemicals or drugs), veterinary toxicology (food chain contamination), and pharmacology (efficacy and safety). Areas covered include industrial, occupational and environmental toxicology (including "sick building" syndrome); drug/chemical risk assessment and management; veterinary, dietary and environmental chemical exposures; drug regulation and promotion; hospital and pharmacy risk management; terato and carcinogenesis research; and medicolegal evaluation. Industries served: insurance, corporate (industrial and manufacturing), pharmaceutical, pharmacies, legal, public utilities, and state governments. Geographic areas served: United States, Canada, Mexico, Europe, and Taiwan. **Conferences and Meetings:** *Risk and Liability Issues for Health Care Professionals and Organizations; Defining Indoor Air Quality and Risk Assessment Tools Used in Industry; Environmental, Legal and Regulatory Issues for the Food Industry.* **Computer/Special Services:** Document research - chemical and drug reactions; medical malpractice literature searches.

SCOTT GROUP
675 North Ct., Ste. 200
Palatine, IL 60067
Terrence J. Scott, CEO & President
PH: (708)394-9774
FX: (708)934-1290
Founded: 1989. Focuses on acute care hospitals and systems seeking to serve senior (elderly) needs; these systems include nursing home administration, in-home life care, housing with services for the elderly, and senior care networks.

SCOTT-LEVIN ASSOCIATES INC.
60 Blacksmith Rd.
Newtown, PA 18940
Joy Scott, President
PH: (215)860-0440
FX: (215)860-5477

Founded: 1982. **Staff:** 80. Firm offers expertise in healthcare and pharmaceutical consulting.

SECURITY AUDIT INC.
e-mail: secaudit@interramp.com
PO Box 1005
Notre Dame, IN 46556
Robert O. Murphy, CPP, President
PH: (219)277-2560
FX: (219)277-2560
Founded: 1977. **Staff:** 3. A management consulting firm specializing in security. Areas of expertise include security management and loss prevention security. Serves healthcare, financial and educational institutions, businesses and industrial firms. Geographic areas served: national. **Conferences and Meetings:** *Provides training programs for university and college security personnel and bank personnel.*

RONALD O. SEGALL, DMD
e-mail: sr1234@erols.com
196 Thomas Johnson Dr., Ste. 235
Frederick, MD 21702
PH: (301)663-5133
FX: (301)663-6943
A board certified endodontist (root canal specialist). Available for diagnosis and treatment evaluation for root canal therapy, consultation, malpractice case review, and expert testimony.

GABRIEL E. SELLA
e-mail: davicsv@ovnet.com
92 N. 4th St.
Martins Ferry, OH 43935
Gabriel E. Sella, President
PH: (614)633-4485
FX: (614)633-4141
Founded: 1987. **Staff:** 4. Consulting physician provides independent medical evaluations, examinee evaluation, file review, trial preparation for insurance or attorneys, and data research. Available for expert witness testimony. Industries served: insurance, industrial enterprises, attorneys, and judges. **Conferences and Meetings:** *Litigating TMJ, Back and Neck Injury Cases; S-EMG Analysis of Somatic Dysfunction: Case Reports; Soft Tissue Injury: Diagnosis and Treatment. Soft tissue injury evaluation seminars and S-EMG biofeedback and assessment training.*

S.E.M. INC.
c/o Marion E. Simon
1515 N. Astor St.
Chicago, IL 60610
Marion E. Simon, President
PH: (312)642-1515
FX: (312)642-7227
Founded: 1988. **Staff:** 1. Assists and educates healthcare providers in methods of providing humane and concerned care for patients. Experienced with large, urban medical center; consultant to many other medical centers to facilitate the development of this type of service for patients and families. Also offers consulting for fundraising for universities and assistance to groups who are beginning to raise funds for charitable purposes. Industries served: healthcare providers, charitable groups, and government agencies. Geographic areas served: United States, Britain, and Japan. **Conferences and Meetings:** *Consultant lectures frequently on the function of patient-representative departments in hospitals.*

SENSENBRENNER & ASSOCIATES
e-mail: wysiwyg51@aol.com
3431 S. Topanga Canyon Blvd.
Malibu, CA 90265
Lex Sensenbrenner, Principal
PH: (310)717-6206
FX: (310)456-6487
Specializes in medical device applications, safety and training, medical equipment, surgical instrumentation, physiologic monitoring, endoscopic technologies and instrumentation, anes-

thesia equipment, clinical equipment management and maintenance, repair and service, device testing and evaluation, clinical engineering, and intra-operative incident evaluation.

SEQUEST HEALTH CARE RESOURCES
e-mail: sales@sequestresources.com
url: http://www.sequestresources.com
2 Transam Plaza Dr., No. 280
Oakbrook Terrace, IL 60181
Leonard J. Brink, Pres.
PH: (630)953-0808
FX: (630)953-0896
Founded: 1983. **Staff:** 6. Offers management services to U.S. hospitals and other healthcare facilities. Geographic areas served: International. **Conferences and Meetings:** *Jcaho Mock Surveys.* **Computer/Special Services:** Information management consulting; automated patient record software-tier.

SERGEI CHIDLOWSKY DC
3637 Sacramento St., Ste. B
San Francisco, CA 94118
Sergei Chidlowsky, DC, Principal
PH: (415)753-2300
FX: (415)346-2449
Provides chiropractic consulting services. Acts as an expert witness in personal injury and workers' compensation testimony. Also serves as an industrial disability evaluator. Offers claims reviews. Proficient in med-legal report writing. A certified industrial consultant, as well as a certified "BAKSAFE" consultant in injury prevention at the work place and ergonomic/safety inspection of the workplace.

J.L. SHAPIRO ASSOCIATES INC.
e-mail: info@jlshapiro.com
url: http://www.jlshapiro.com
20 Highland Ave., Ste. 6
Metuchen, NJ 08840-1949
Joel L. Shapiro
PH: (732)548-7561
FX: (732)548-8555
Founded: 1974. **Staff:** 25. A healthcare communications and marketing firm servicing the pharmaceutical and allied health industry. Offers a wide range of services in medical communications, educational programs, electronic media, and medical publishing. Includes preparing preclinical and clinical manuscripts for publication, product monographs, formulary kits integrating print and video, retrospective studies, product backgrounders, IND/NDA submissions, scientific exhibits, and developing, coordinating, and conducting symposia and medical meetings. Also offers medical education videos and computer programs, audioconfering, Internet programs, laptop computer and CD-ROM training programs, patient education videos, and interactive multimedia display.

SHARED CARE RESEARCH & EDUCATION CONSULTING INC.
e-mail: sharedcare@aol.com
24254 Hawthorne Blvd., Ste. C
Torrance, CA 90505-6502
Carlene Minks Grim
PH: (310)375-2273
TF: 800962-7787
FX: (310)791-2733
Founded: 1985. **Staff:** 2. Develops and sells video tutored courses and services for healthcare professionals. Also supplies healthcare/medical equipment. Current specialties: training volunteers and professionals in proper blood pressure measurement technique. Maintains certification database for anti-hypertensive research. **Conferences and Meetings:** *Train-the-Trainer Workshops; Blood Pressure Management Standardization; Tracking Persons With Consistently Elevated Blood Pressure Readings to Improve Blood Pressure Control.* **Computer/Special Services:** Provides interactive video disc format, as well as self-instruction video taped

learning systems. Designs and tailors educational presentations on a variety of topics.

NEIL SHEEHAN
e-mail: neiljs@aol.com
2850 Middlefield Rd., Ste. 231
Palo Alto, CA 94306
PH: (415)324-3353
FX: (415)324-1143
A consulting engineer specializing in medical device design and development. Emphasis on disposables, intravenous systems and components, hemodialysis, catheters, electrodes, pipettors, including manufacturing processes (injection molding, compression molding, vacuum forming, die cutting). An expert witness in patent infringement, product liability and malpractice cases. Provides demonstrative evidence and litigation graphics.

ROY J. SHEPHARD
e-mail: rjshep@mountain-inter.net
PO Box 521
Brackendale, ON, Canada V0N 1HO
Roy J. Shephard
PH: (604)898-5527
FX: (604)898-5724
Founded: 1964. **Staff:** 20. Provides consulting services regarding exercise, environment, health and aging. Offers forensic services in the areas of air pollution, employment standards and physical work capacity. Serves private industries as well as government agencies. **Conferences and Meetings:** *Offers numerous lectures, seminars and workshops at various locations around the world.*

SHEPPARD PRATT HEALTH PLAN
6501 N. Charles St.
PO Box 6815
Baltimore, MD 21285-6815
Steven Sharfstein, President
PH: (410)938-3947
TF: 800765-0770
FX: (410)938-4099
Founded: 1891. **Staff:** 950. Firm specializes in employee assistance programs, behavioral managed care and Organizational Consulting Services which include: educational and wellness training, executive staff training, medication, ombuds and conflict resolution services, employee opinion surveys.

SHOTWELL & CARR, INC.
e-mail: shotcar@earthlink.com
url: http://www.shotcarr.com
3535 Fire Wheel Dr., Ste. A
Flower Mound, TX 75028
Thomas K. Shotwell, President
PH: (972)243-1634
TF: 800929-3003
FX: (972)243-3567
Founded: 1974. **Staff:** 7. Specializes in maximizing cost effectiveness in development, approval, production, and distribution of animal and human drugs, medical devices, and in vitro diagnostics worldwide. **Conferences and Meetings:** *New and Generic Animal Drug Applications Seminar; A Unique Seminar for Venture Capitalists and Investment Bankers: Development of Health Care Products; Getting the Product to Market; In Vitro Diagnostic Products. Sponsor of FDA/FDLI Satellite Downlinks on Medical Devices.* **Computer/Special Services:** Maintains computerized database of information on approved animal drugs in the U.S.

SIGMA ASSOCIATES, LTD.
105 Timber Ridge Blvd.
Pass Christian, MS 39571
A.J. Scardino, Jr., President
PH: (228)452-4866
TF: 800348-4866
FX: (228)452-7202
Founded: 1975. **Staff:** 7. Offers counsel on industrial accident reconstruction, risk management, risk management/loss control,

hazard identification and control, ergonomics (human factors engineering), systems analysis, forensics, and security. Also assists firms regarding compliance with Americans with Disabilities Act. Industries served: insurance, maritime, petroleum, construction, manufacturing, education, and government agencies worldwide. **Conferences and Meetings:** *Fire, Explosion, Arson Investigation Seminar; Risk Management The Loss Frontier; HazWoper (40 hours); Competent Person (45 hours).*

NORMA E. SIMBRA - DIET COUNSELING SERVICE
800 Briarwood Rd.
Morgantown, WV 26505
Norma E. Simbra
PH: (304)599-1555
Founded: 1983. Provides diet counseling on various areas such as weight control, pre-admission surgical diets, hypertension, diabetes education, allergies, sports nutrition, kidney disease, digestive disorders, general nutrition, and pre-natal care. Provides workshops and seminars on weight loss, eating disorders, and general nutrition, as well as cooking demonstrations. Geographic areas served: West Virginia. **Conferences and Meetings:** *Offers seminars on osteoporosis, general nutrition, cholesterol and other topics. Disorders; Cooking Demonstrations.*

SANDRA SIMMONS
90 Seeley Dr.
Midland, MI 48640
Sandra Simmons
PH: (517)631-0366
FX: (517)839-1796
Founded: 1966. **Staff:** 1. Offers management development and consultation for nursing administrators in service and educational settings. Services include organizational assessment and functioning, legal aspects of nursing, and management approaches to use during organizational decline. Industries served: hospitals, home health agencies, and government agencies. Geographic areas served: U.S., primarily Great Lakes and midwest. **Conferences and Meetings:** *Management Principles Applied to Nursing Service; Unit Management for New RN Employees; Practical Application of Management Principles; Employer Cost Savings Through Home Health Options; Hospital Revenue Generation Through Home Health Options; Motivation and Change.*

STEVEN M. SIMONS, MD
e-mail: simons@csmc.edu
Cedars - Sinai Medical Center
435 N. Roxbury, Ste. 311
Beverly Hills, CA 90210
PH: (310)274-7303
FX: (310)274-8572
Offers expert witness testimony in the medical matters, including pulmonary, internal medicine, critical care, asthma, pulmonary embolism, ventilator management, pneumonia, pleural effusion, and bronchoscopy.

ARTHUR SITELMAN, MD
e-mail: sitelman.path@worldnet.att.net
Phoenix Memorial Hospital
1201 South 7th Ave.
Phoenix, AZ 85007
PH: (602)824-3235
FX: (602)824-3139
Specializes in surgical pathology, cancer and tumor diagnosis, anatomic and clinical pathology, autopsy pathology, cytopathology, clinical pathology consultations, and hematopathology. Services include expert witness, depositions, independent review, case preparation consultant, literature review, court testimony, and private autopsies.

SITTING ON THE JOB
5540 South St., Ste. 200
Lincoln, NE 68506
Scott Donkin

PH: (402)488-1500
TF: 800552-6347
FX: (402)488-6651
Evaluates office ergonomics, and counsels on health and wellness, performance, and safety issues. Geographic Areas Served: United States and Canada.

ANNE SULLIVAN SMITH
24831 Ross Dr.
Redford, MI 48239
Anne Sullivan Smith
PH: (313)532-0464
Founded: 1982. Staff: 1. Offers healthcare expertise in the areas of development, refinement, and evaluation of services and programs of community health and social service agencies, hospitals, ambulatory care programs, and senior citizen facilities and services. Serves public and private sector in the U.S.

HERMAN SMITH ASSOCIATES, A DIVISION OF COOPERS AND LYBRAND, L.L.P.
203 N. LaSalle St.
Chicago, IL 60601
Jeffrey J. Frommelt
PH: (312)701-6239
FX: (312)701-6540
Founded: 1947. Staff: 30. Hospital and healthcare consulting division of Coopers & Lybrand L.L.P. offering services in strategic planning and marketing, facilities and equipment planning, management, clinical operations, physician/hospital integration, system planning studies,and organizational development. Industries served: hospitals, healthcare providers, long-term care providers, and government agencies. Geographic areas served: United States and international. **Conferences and Meetings:** *Staff of Herman Smith Associates lecture extensively throughout the United States on all aspects of hospital management, integrated delivery network development, managed care, and related topics.* **Computer/Special Services:** Comprehensive healthcare library; collection has more than 7,000 documents and 125 current periodicals.

SMITH DIABETES RESEARCH
PO Box 543
Topsham, ME 04086
Rowland E.M. Smith, Founder
PH: (207)725-4823
FX: (207)729-3219
Offers information to doctors, patients, and lawyers on a correlation between thorazine (chlorpomazine), a psychiatric drug, and insulin-dependent diabetes. Seeks to substantiate the working hypothesis that CPZ causes diabetes in general.

LILLIAN E. SMITH
19367 Whispering Trail
Traverse City, MI 49686
L.E. Smith
PH: (616)223-4817
FX: (616)922-8980
Founded: 1987. Staff: 1. Provides nutrition consulting for individuals, corporations, educational institutions, and private sector. Geographic areas served: U.S. Woman-owned firm. **Conferences and Meetings:** *Weight Management Support Groups; Meatless Meals; Label Reading; Cooking with Tofu; Behavior Modification; PMS and Women; Calcium Thru the Lifespan; Eating in the Fast Lane.* **Computer/Special Services:** Nutritional analysis of recipes, menus, and daily food intake records; "nutritional label" set-up available of recipes, food products.

CLARK SMITH, MD
e-mail: DoctrClark@aol.com
591 Camino de la Reina, Ste. 1020
San Diego, CA 92108
PH: (619)298-0518
FX: (619)298-1613
Founded: 1982. Specializes in substance abuse matters. Testimony in personal injury, malpractice, wrongful death, workers' com-

pensation, employment, alcohol and drug abuse, PTSD, impulse control, disability, diminished actuality, insanity, drug and alcohol abuse, intoxication, and death penalty. **Conferences and Meetings:** *A case of Diminished Actuality, University of San Diego School of Law.*

EDWARD A. SMITH, MD, INC.
426 E. Barcellus, Ste. 202
Santa Maria, CA 93454
Edward Smith, MD, Principal
PH: (805)922-8346
TF: 800638-7674
FX: (805)925-5151
Founded: 1975. Staff: 3. A neurologic surgeon specializing in acute and chronic head injury evaluation and treatment; brain injury; post-traumatic pain syndromes; and spinal injuries. Gives medical record reviews, written reports, and expert testimony. Provides impartial analysis for both plaintiff and defense.

SMITH-PIGG CONSULTING, INC.
1928 Fairhaven Dr.
Cedarburg, WI 53012
Janice Smith Pigg
PH: (414)377-8938
Founded: 1978. Staff: 2. Musculoskeletal (arthritis and orthopedics) product line development. **Conferences and Meetings:** *Arthritis: A Nursing Perspective.*

JOHN SMITHKEY, III, RN
1271 Overland Ave., NE
North Canton, OH 44720
John Smithkey, III
PH: (330)494-3729
Specializes in public and occupational health, HIV/AIDS education and prevention programs, grant and proposal writing, and programs for businesses and employees.

JOHN SNOW INC.
e-mail: jsinfo@jsi.com
url: http://www.jsi.com
44 Farnsworth St.
Boston, MA 02210-1211
Joel Lamstein, Pres., Treas.
PH: (617)482-9485
FX: (617)482-0617
Founded: 1978. Staff: 375. Advises hospitals and government agencies on public healthcare practices worldwide.

J.J. SNYDER AGRICULTURAL AVIATION CONSULTANT
e-mail: acesup@inreach.com
2350 19th Ave.
Kingsburg, CA 93631
PH: (209)897-3076
FX: (209)897-3076
Specializes in agricultural aircraft accidents and wire strikes. Provides aircraft maintenance and repair. Involved in handling pesticide drift claims.

BRUCE J. SOBOL
275 Ridgebury Rd.
Ridgefield, CT 06877
Bruce J. Sobol, M.D.
PH: (203)438-3650
Founded: 1983. Staff: 2. Offers medical writing expertise including clinical summaries for submission to the FDA, clinical trial reports for scientific journals, critiquing and writing research protocols, and medical articles for lay publications. Industries served: pharmaceutical and marketing.

SONOMA COAST ASSOCIATES
PO Box 1458
Santa Rosa, CA 95402
Alfredo Fornos, Ph.D., Principal
PH: (707)824-8141

Specializes in vocational rehabilitation and expert testimony, physical capacity assessments, labor market and job analysis, vocational feasibility and wage earning capacity determination, long term disability management, ADA consultation, job site analysis, medical management, and career counseling.

SORTOR OCCUPATIONAL SAFETY CONSULTING
e-mail: sortor@safestyle.com
url: http://www.safestyle.com
6327 S. Queensway Dr.
Tampa, FL 33617
Gary Sortor, President
PH: (813)988-7493
FX: (813)988-7493
Safety & health consulting, training and expert witness services. See web site for useful safety & health resources, including the Safestyle.com bookstore, compliance software, professional articles, job postings, a bulletin board, and valuable links. Geographic Areas Served: Nationwide. **Computer/Special Services:** Literature searches and expert witness serivces.

SOUTH SHORE NUTRITIONAL CONSULTANTS
2723 Aldred Ave.
Oceanside, NY 11572
Joyce Savoy
PH: (516)536-7885
FX: (516)536-4108
Founded: 1982. **Staff:** 2. Offers nutritional counseling.

SOUTHERN CALIFORNIA PSYCHIATRIC LEGAL
  CONSULTANTS
e-mail: peterson@hsc.usc.edu
65 N. Madison Ave., Ste. 302
Pasadena, CA 91101
Kaushal K. Sharma, MD, Principal
PH: (818)796-4052
FX: (818)796-3772
Forensic psychiatrists and independent contractors specializing in psychiatric evaluations, report preparation, and expert witness testimony in most areas of the law (civil, criminal, probate and conservatorship, insurance, personal injury, mental health law, wills and trusts, malpractice, professional liability, sexual harassment, and others).

SOUTHERN PAIN CONTROL CENTER
150 Medical Way, Ste. D-2
Riverdale, GA 30274
Tracy Frambro, Principal
PH: (770)997-7655
FX: (770)991-1843
Specializes in multi-disciplinary pain management, physical therapy, nerve blocks, epidural injections, and bio feedback therapy.

SOUTHWEST HEALTH CONSULTANTS
1030 Andrews Hwy., Ste. 210
Midland, TX 79701
John W. Stevenson
PH: (915)699-0923
FX: (915)699-5032
Founded: 1987. **Staff:** 1. Specializes in laboratory operational analysis and planning. Performs CPT-4 Code audits to enhance laboratory revenue. Writes strategic business plans, establishes and develops new laboratories. Develops marketing strategies and performs mock CAP, JCAHO and Medicare inspections. Designs client and patient satisfaction questionnaires serving medical laboratories in hospitals, physician's offices, and independent laboratories. **Conferences and Meetings:** *So You Want to Be a Supervisor.*

LAURA L. SOUTHWICK
1001 Lake Point Ln.
Columbia, MO 65203
Laura L. Southwick
PH: (573)443-6373

Founded: 1988. **Staff:** 1. Nutrition consultant for nursing homes, hospitals, physicians in private practice, wellness centers, etc. when the expertise of a registered dietitian is needed. Performs nutritional assessments; advises managers of dietary departments; and teaches weight loss seminars and other group classes. Geographic areas served: Midwestern United States. **Conferences and Meetings:** *Feeding Your Ego (wellness and weight loss); Be Trim (weight loss/maintenance program).*

SPA, INC.
e-mail: spa@concentric.net
203 W. 11th Ave.
Baltimore, MD 21225
Stanley D. Pulz, President
PH: (410)789-5888
FX: (410)636-7310
Founded: 1981. **Staff:** 2. Provides research analysis and consultative services in the areas of safety, health, human factors engineering, and risk management to private industry, insurance and legal communities, government, and trade organizations. These services include, but are not limited to analysis of facilities, products, operations, and equipment; programs to detect programmatic, physical or environmental hazards/failures, coupled with recommendations of needed solutions/methods to mitigate or eliminate hazardous and/or high risk conditions and/or lower insurance and worker compensation costs; and seminar development production. **Conferences and Meetings:** *Seminars on loss control and risk management for organizations in the construction and transportation industries.*

SPECIAL RESPONSE CORP. INC.
303 Allgheny Ave.
Towson, MD 21204
PH: (410)494-1900
FX: (410)494-1903
Firm provides special knowledge in health and safety issues.

SPECIALIZED HEALTHCARE CONSULTANTS
1141 Tamarack Ln.
Pittsburgh, PA 15237
Peter M. Vercilla, President
PH: (412)367-7291
FX: (412)367-7291
Founded: 1988. **Staff:** 3. Provides a wide range of services to the hospital, longterm care, home care/durable medical equipment companies, and governmental health agencies. These services include regulatory agency review and compliance, reorganization and financial analysis, continuing education, risk management, policy/procedure review, services utilization review, and rehabilitation program design. Geographic areas served: national and international. **Conferences and Meetings:** *Subacute ventilator unit development.* **Computer/Special Services:** Collaborates with programmers in the development of patient data and therapy protocols.

SPECTRUM CONSULTING
e-mail: iarons@usa1.com
4 Harvard St.
Peabody, MA 01960-1304
Irving J. Arons, Managing Director
PH: (508)531-0939
FX: (508)531-0939
Founded: 1989. **Staff:** 1. Provides technology assessments and market projections on technology and applications for medical lasers and ophthalmic devices and refractive surgery. Serves vision care and medical industries worldwide. **Conferences and Meetings:** *Ophthalmology Update; Medical Laser Market Update; Medical Laser Market Trends.*

SPIEHLER & ASSOCIATES
e-mail: spiehleraa@aol.com
422 Tustin Ave.
Newport Beach, CA 92663
Vina R. Spiehler, Ph.D., President

PH: (714)642-0574
FX: (714)642-2852
Specializes in pharmacology, pharmacokinetics and toxicology of cocaine, morphine and heroin, amphetamines, phencyclidine, alcohol, pharmaceuticals, poisons and drugs of abuse, immunoassay development and FDA submissions. Reviews employee drug testing, QA/QC, postmortem toxicology and drug testing in hair, saliva or sweat. Also specializes in drugs and DUI, memory, drug concentrations, combinations, time and cause of death.

SPINAL HEALTH CHIROPRACTIC
2340 Santa Rita Rd., Ste. 3
Pleasanton, CA 94566
Steven C. Hickey, Principal
PH: (510)484-2558
FX: (510)484-3951
Specializes in work, auto, sports, and recreational injuries. X-ray and physiotherapy services available.

SPIVEY CHIROPRACTIC CLINIC
667 Parker Ave.
Rodeo, CA 94572
Paula A. Spivey, Principal
PH: (510)799-3112
FX: (510)799-9013
Provides chiropractic, IDE, QME, services, chiropractic treatment, and permanent and stationary evaluation.

SPRINGDELL GROUP
e-mail: sg@cccbi.chester.pa.us
PO Box 877
Unionville, PA 19375
B.W. Langer, President
PH: (610)380-1874
FX: (610)380-9808
Founded: 1983. Offers wide variety of consulting services including occupational health and industrial hygiene consulting. Expertise encompasses testing and remediation of indoor air quality, hazard communications programs, medical surveillance programs, respiratory protection programs, and a program for the protection of employees from bloodborne pathogens.

RAY STAMMIR, D.C.
6325 Topanga Canyon Blvd., Ste. 111
Woodland Hills, CA 91367
PH: (818)716-6112
FX: (818)716-1810
Provides workers' compensation and private investigation. Evaluation and treatment. Offers case reviews and expert testimony.

K. DAVID STEIDLEY
50 Baltusrol Way
Short Hills, NJ 07078
K. David Steidley
PH: (973)533-5630
FX: (973)533-5648
Founded: 1965. Radiation health and safety consultant offering expert witness services and relevant safety surveys.

THE STEINER COMPANY
130 S. 1st St.
Ann Arbor, MI 48104
Mathew W. Steiner, President
PH: (313)663-3322
FX: (313)761-9366
Founded: 1980. **Staff:** 4. Consultants to healthcare organizations with specialization in systems analysis and the development of quality and productivity monitoring programs. Implements programs that are tailored to the specialized needs of each client hospital and assists management in the improvement of productivity, while maintaining a high quality of care. Conducts indepth studies for all hospital departments, including organization, systems, procedures, staffing levels, workloads, budgeting, delivery of care, and patient classification systems. TSC places a strong emphasis on education throughout all phases of consultation or program development, with the client's management personnel becoming integrally involved in each step of the process.

STEINMAN ASSOCIATES
1033 N. Fairfax St., Ste. 304
Alexandria, VA 22314
Steve Steinman, President
PH: (703)836-2686
FX: (703)836-4084
Founded: 1982. **Staff:** 17. Provides consulting services to pharmaceutical and biotechnology firms, regulated under the Federal Food, Drug and Cosmetic Act. Specific expertise in quality assurance, government affairs, drug and biologicals licensing, drug manufacturing, clinical trials management, data management and statistical analysis. Recent emphasis on investigations in cytokine therapy of cancer. Clinical applications of monoclonal antibodies, and investigations in drug therapy of hepatitis B. Specific and ongoing experience with clinical trials of AIDS drugs and biologicals. Geographic Areas Served: U.S., Europe, and Japan.

STENS CORP.
e-mail: stensco@aol.com
url: http://www.stens.biofeedback.com
6451 Oakwood Dr.
Oakland, CA 94611
Stephen Stern, President
PH: (510)339-9053
TF: 800257-8367
FX: (510)339-2222
Founded: 1979. **Staff:** 15. Offers consulting and training on the use of biofeedback equipment. Industries served: healthcare. **Conferences and Meetings:** *Pain Management and Biofeedback, EMC, EEC, ADWD* **Computer/Special Services:** System Sales, VAR, Instrumentation.

DANIEL STERN & ASSOCIATES INC.
url: http://www.danielstern.com/docjobs
211 N. Whitfield St.
Pittsburgh, PA 15206-3042
John Dempster, President/C.E.O.
PH: (412)363-9700
TF: 800438-2476
FX: (412)363-6032
Founded: 1970. **Staff:** 30. Firm offers expertise in medicine and healthcare issues, executive recruitment, staff employment, and planning. Serves commercial concerns in the U.S.

THOMAS STERN, MD
2636 Telegraph Ave.
Berkeley, CA 94704
PH: (510)841-1647
FX: (510)848-4924
Specializes in orthopedic surgery, joint replacement, sports medicine, hand surgery, neck and lower back problems, and pediatric orthopedics. Provides medical-legal evaluations and expert testimony for personal injury, workers' compensation, and medical malpractice.

FRANK D. STEVENS, PH.D.
12714 La Belle
Houston, TX 77015
PH: (713)455-2288
FX: (713)455-2288
Specializes in toxic chemical exposure, testimony, consultation, and investigations, as well as industrial hygiene, occupational health, and epidemiology air quality.

SUSAN Y. STEVENS
e-mail: sstevens@qben.edu
3573 Chelsea Crescent NE
Atlanta, GA 30319
Susan Y. Stevens

PH: (404)256-4350
FX: (404)265-6225
Founded: 1976. Nursing administration consultant and educator serving schools of nursing, hospital education services, and healthcare institutions. Services include improving nursing's image, curriculum development and planning for nursing schools, nursing education for nursing homes, and general consulting on creating better healthcare environments. Serves private industries as well as government agencies. Geographic areas served: no limitations. **Conferences and Meetings:** *Managing Violence in Health Care Settings; Creating Health; Promoting Healthy Environments in Children's Treatment Settings; Planning for Healthy Family Environments; Creativity in Nursing; Nursing Care of Patients With Pain; Creating Positive Nursing Images: Lessons from the Newsreels; Psychophysiologic Aspects of Mental Illness; Preventing and Addressing Delerium and Dementia in the Elderly; Preparation for Psychiatric Nursing C.N.S. Certifying Exam; History of Nurses in World War II, Images of Nursing in the Media.*

WYONNA STIFFLER - DOREEN WHITE
1496 Bowman Ave.
Kettering, OH 45409
Wyonna Stiffler, RN, BSN, CETN
PH: (937)294-8855
FX: (937)294-8855
Founded: 1984. **Staff:** 2. Offers community-based specialized nursing care for persons with an ostomy, draining wounds, fistulas, drains, and ulcers. Also provides patient care consults, product evaluation, continuing education courses, and program development. Industries served: healthcare. **Conferences and Meetings:** *Ostomy Prothesis; Skin Care Products; Wound Debridement.*

JONI STINSON ENTERPRISES
PO Box 21
Boys Town, NE 68010
Joni Kay Stinson, President
PH: (402)496-0167
Founded: 1982. **Staff:** 6. Primarily a consulting firm specializing in the field of long term care food service management and dietetics. Firm's kitchen design department provides expert consultation on the design, layout, and equipment for new construction and renovation projects. Offers systems design services including: food cost accounting systems, purchasing programs, cost effective menus and recipe services, policy and procedure development, nutritional assessment and quality assurance programs. The A La Carte Division is the Nutrition Education Division providing group and individual nutrition education and counseling programs. Geographic areas served: midwestern U.S. **Conferences and Meetings:** *The Dietary Treatment of Pressure Sores; Training the Dietary Manager; Malnutrition in the Chronically Ill.* **Computer/Special Services:** Nutritional assessment/menu services for individuals and groups.

LARRY H. STRASBURGER
527 Concord Ave.
Belmont, MA 02178
Larry H. Strasburger
PH: (617)484-8271
Founded: 1961. Consults with attorneys, governmental agencies, insurance companies, hospitals, physicians and individuals regarding legal-psychiatric issues. **Conferences and Meetings:** *Decision-making in Forensic Psychiatry; A Clinician Looks at the Assessment of Violence; Proving Psychiatric Damages.*

STS OF AMERICA CORPORATION
21548 Anthony Rd., Ste. 1910
Noblesville, IN 46060
W.C. Smith, CEO
PH: (317)758-9424
TF: 800435-8850
FX: (317)758-1439
Founded: 1990. **Staff:** 6. Consulting firm provides safety training/testing, safety audits/inspections reports, written program

development, and onsite task analysis. Occupational safety and health specialists (OSHA Standards 1910 and 1926). Industries served: all. Geographic areas served: Indiana.

JAMES STUBBLEBINE, MD
900 S. Eliseo Dr.
Greenbrae, CA 94904
PH: (415)485-0324
FX: (415)922-6075
Specializes in post traumatic stress disorder, witnessing or sustaining injury from disaster, violent loss/bereavement, and other major mental disorders from accidents.

MICHAEL S. STULBARG MD
e-mail: michae@itsa.ucsf.edu
University of California Medical Center, Box 0111
Rm. M-1093
San Francisco, CA 94143-0111
PH: (415)476-0631
FX: (415)381-4286
Serves as an expert witness. Specializes in pneumonia, asthma, asbestosis, pleural effusion, shortness of breath, pulmonary embolism, inhalation injury, respiratory failure, malignancy, malpractice, unusual pulmonary problems, and critical care.

THE STUPAK NETWORK, INC.
e-mail: tsni@netside.com
1115 Mt. Vernon Church Rd.
PO Box 785
White Rock, SC 29177
Jennifer M. Stupak, President
FX: (803)732-7937
Founded: 1988. Specialists in medical equipment management and planning services including equipment inventory/evaluation, budget development, and procurement assistance. Works with architects, engineers, and healthcare facility planners. Geographic areas served: U.S. and international.

STURZA ENTERPRISES, INC.
e-mail: sturza@localaccess.com
376 Avery Rd. W.
Winlock, WA 98596
Thomas A. Sturza, Safety Engineer
PH: (360)740-6390
FX: (360)740-6391
Specializes in product liability, compliance inspections, safety code development, accident investigation, forest road design and inspection, logging system analyses, code interpretation, forest products, and logging and sawmills.

SUCCESSFUL SOLUTIONS INC.
url: http://www.ssinc-usa.com
900 E. 1st St.
Vidalia, GA 30474-2337
Ronnie R. Smith, President
PH: (912)537-1665
TF: 800682-7153
FX: (912)537-6387
Founded: 1985. **Staff:** 10. Firm specializes in offering expertise in management and medical and health institutions to commercial concerns in the Southeast area.

D.J. SULLIVAN & ASSOCIATES INC.
775 Technology Dr., Ste. 100
Ann Arbor, MI 48108
D.J. Sullivan, Pres.
PH: (313)327-4000
FX: (313)662-0857
Founded: 1976. **Staff:** 24. Provides medical management, legal counsel, and contract services to physicians, hospitals, and healthcare operations in the United States.

SURGICAL RESOURCE MANAGEMENT INC.
e-mail: surgresmgt@aol.com
582 Revere Ave.
Westmont, IL 60559-1237
Judith L. Schanilec, President
PH: (630)323-0540
FX: (630)323-0576
Founded: 1983. **Staff:** 5. Specializes in surgical services in the following areas: operating rooms, post anesthesia care units, ambulatory surgery, and endoscopy.

SWEETLAND ASSOCIATES
1720 Elljobean Rd., Ste. 211
Port Charlotte, FL 33948
John Sweetland, Chairman of the Board
PH: (941)629-2630
FX: (941)629-3832
Founded: 1985. Firm offers healthcare management and facilities consultation.

ROBERT SWOTINSKY, MD
e-mail: swotinsky@aol.com
Boston University Medical Center
88 E. Newton St.
Boston, MA 02118-2393
PH: (617)638-8410
FX: (617)638-8406
A medical review officer specializing in workplace drug and alcohol testing, toxicology, occupational medicine, environmental medicine, biological monitoring, and medical surveillance.

CHARLES S. SYERS, DDS
PO Box 1879
San Mateo, CA 94401-9991
PH: (650)347-2614
FX: (650)347-2680
Specializes in temporomandibular joint injury, dento-facial nerve injury, dento-facial trauma, dental implants, dental pain, and orthognathic surgery. Also works with work compensation cases. Standard of care determination as it is applied to professional negligence.

SYSTEMS RESEARCH INC.
Box 925, Village Sta.
New York, NY 10014-0925
Carlton E. Wynter, President
PH: (212)473-5647
FX: (212)473-5647
Staff: 1. Offers management services in healthcare finance. Provides services in program planning, evaluation, receivables management, and information systems. Assists with third party payer systems and compliance, including Medicaid and Medicare. Industries served: healthcare providers, insurers, and government.

DONNA B. TAYLOR
e-mail: dbtaylor@seidata.com
213 West William St.
Lawrenceburg, IN 47025-1929
PH: (812)537-9840
FX: (812)537-9845
Provides employability evaluations, transferable skills analysis, job analysis, and labor market assessment and surveys. Concerned with wage loss, loss of earning capacity and work life expectancy, rehabilitation potential, ADA compliance, job modification, job development, placement, and case management.

TECHNOCLIN CONSULTING, INC.
830 Warwick Rd.
Deerfield, IL 60015
David T. Griffin, President
PH: (847)945-0030
FX: (847)945-0124
Founded: 1990. Consultants on laboratory management and radi-

ology, combining management skills with knowledge of laboratory technologies, procedures, and operations.

THA SOLUTIONS GROUP
e-mail: jwhitton@tha.com
url: http://www.tha.com
500 Interstate Blvd. S.
Nashville, TN 37210-4634
Jeffery H. Whitton, Fache, Senior Vice President
PH: (615)256-8240
FX: (615)248-4803
Specializes in strategic planning, operations analysis, re-engineering, management engineering, and managed care. Geographic Areas Served: Tennessee.

THERADEX SYSTEMS INC.
e-mail: 10200.1507@compuserve.com
url: http://www.theradex.com
14 Washington Rd.
Princeton Junction, NJ 08550-1028
Dr. Robert Royds
PH: (609)799-7580
FX: (609)799-4148
Founded: 1982. **Staff:** 65. Pharmaceutical consultants.

FRIDA THEROS
Sterling, VA 20164
Frida Theros
PH: (703)404-2547
Consulting nutritionist in the Chesapeake Bay area and registered dietitian in private practice.

PAULETTE THOMPSON
e-mail: paulettt@capaccess.org
3117 Belleview Ave.
Cheverly, MD 20785
Paulette Thomspon
PH: (301)772-5831
FX: (301)618-4968
Consulting nutritionist in the Chesapeake Bay area and registered dietitian in private practice. **Computer/Special Services:** Computer analysis of diet.

THOUGHT TECHNOLOGY LTD.
e-mail: mail@thoughttechnology.com
url: http://www.thought.technology.com
8396 Rte. 9
West Chazy, NY 12992
Hal K. Myers, President
PH: (518)489-8251
FX: (518)489-8255
Founded: 1974. **Staff:** 35. Personal development specialists train individuals in stress control, taking tests with confidence, weight control, sleeping well, smoking cessation, athletic peak performance, flying free of fear, evaluation of alcohol and drug abuse, public speaking with confidence, breathing for health, and pain control for medical, educational, athletic, corporate and military markets. **Computer/Special Services:** Has developed software programs for stress control through the computer, and physiological monitoring; EMG, EEG, EKG, heart rate, blood volume pulse, temperature, respiration on 16 channels.

TIDEWATER EMERGENCY MEDICAL SERVICES COUNCIL INC. (TEMS)
855 W. Brambleton Ave.
Norfolk, VA 23510
James M. Chandler, Director
PH: (757)446-5179
FX: (757)446-5906
Founded: 1974. Emergency medical training organization consults on appropriate training.

CAROL TILFORD
9910 Brink Rd.
Gaithersburg, MD 20879
Carol Tilford, Owner
PH: (301)926-6751
FX: (301)924-1844
Consulting nutritionist in the Chesapeake Bay area and registered dietitian in private practice.

JOHN F. TOMERA
354 South St.
Medfield, MA 02052-3127
John F. Tomera
PH: (508)359-4072
FX: (508)359-4072
Founded: 1986. **Staff:** 1. Consulting pharmacologist with experience in the following client markets: pharmaceutical, chemical, agricultural, cosmetic, medical diagnostic, and environmental toxicology. Significant expertise in medical applications in vivo and in vitro, with additional experience in cardiovascular, breast cancer, biochemical, and trauma research. Geographic areas served: worldwide. **Computer/Special Services:** Capabilities include multivariate testing, pharmacokinetics advanced statistical analysis and data interpretation, research proposal writing, research design, and reporting research findings.

TOXICOLOGY CONSULTANTS ROUNDTABLE
e-mail: jabudny@earthlink.net
url: http://lawinfo.com/biz/toxicology/index.html
31308 Via Colinas, Ste. 107
Westlake Village, CA 91362
John A. Budny, Ph.D., Director, Publicity
PH: (805)655-7604
FX: (805)655-7604
Toxicology consultants.

TOXICOLOGY PATHOLOGY SERVICES
e-mail: tps@toxpath.com
url: http://www.toxpath.com
10424 Middle Mt. Vernon Rd.
Mount Vernon, IN 47620
J.A. Botta, Jr., President
PH: (812)985-5900
TF: 800837-8771
FX: (812)985-3403
Founded: 1975. **Staff:** 34. Evaluates animal safety data including toxicology, body weight, clinical pathology, gross and microscopic pathology, organ weights, clinical signs and statistics for the pharmaceutical, chemical, petrochemical, and agricultural industries. Emphasis is on product safety through animal research. Geographic areas served: United States. **Computer/Special Services:** Developed TOPAX, a customized toxicology and pathology software system for evaluation of toxicological data.

TOXICON, INC.
6337 Highland Dr., Ste. 2054
Salt Lake City, UT 84121
Carol B. Done, President
PH: (801)277-2241
FX: (801)277-0867
Founded: 1988. **Staff:** 12. Safety consulting firm provides toxicologic advice, evaluation, research, publication, and litigation support. Offers additional services in toxic risk assessment, toxic incident investigation, toxicity diagnosis, employee drug abuse or safety programs, case evaluation and trial preparation, drug or toxin causation of disease or birth defects, toxicity or drug data presentation, employee education, and temporary or part-time project or management employment. In addition to its own staff, toxicologic consultants from various parts of the world can be supplied for whatever expertise or credentials are required. Industries served: health services, pharmaceutical/chemical industry, government, legal, and business. Geographic areas served: no limits. **Conferences and Meetings:** *Toxic Tort Case Presentation;*

Teratology Workshops; Toxic Catastrophe Lessons; Toxicology Highlights.

TRAINING SERVICES
24 Baylor Cres.
Georgetown, ON, Canada L7G 1A6
John Ford
PH: (905)873-3031
FX: (905)877-7147
Founded: 1989. **Staff:** 10. Offers occupational health and safety training for managers, supervisors, and safety committees. Also has training expertise in lift truck and crane operation, management and supervisor skills, and die setting (punch presses). Serves metal workers and manufacturers worldwide. **Conferences and Meetings:** *List of seminars and workshops available from firm upon request.*

HELEN TREDWAY
1638 Rd. W
Neosho Rapids, KS 66864-8700
Helen Tredway
PH: (316)343-3637
Founded: 1982. **Staff:** 1. Nursing consultant to nursing homes. Services include inservice education. **Conferences and Meetings:** *Meeting the Needs of the Nursing Home Nurse; Adult Day Care.*

TREIMIER
PO Box 668800
Charlotte, NC 28266-8800
Ben Latimer, President
PH: (704)529-3300
FX: (704)527-3654
Founded: 1969. **Staff:** 556. Provides management consulting services to healthcare providers. The purpose of these services is to assist healthcare providers to become high quality, cost effective providers of healthcare. Geographic areas served: 15 states, primarily southeastern region.

TRI FIT
e-mail: marsden@trifit.com
url: http://www.trifit.com
2914 Rainbow Crescent
Mississauga, ON, Canada L5L 2K6
Veronica Marsden, Partner
PH: (905)820-9641
FX: (905)569-8619
Founded: 1986. **Staff:** 35. A service oriented company specializing in the design, implementation and management of corporate wellness programs. Develops programs for small-to-medium sized businesses as well as major corporations. Programs are suitable for manufacturing companies, service-oriented groups, office personnel, and plant employees. Geographic areas served: Canada. **Conferences and Meetings:** *Stress Management Workshops and Guides.*

TRIBROOK/AM&G, LLC
e-mail: tbgamg@aol.com
999 Oakmont Plaza Dr., Ste. 600
Westmont, IL 60559-5504
Michael C. Carroll, Vice President
PH: (630)990-8070
FX: (630)325-0337
Founded: 1972. **Staff:** 30. National healthcare consulting practice active in strategic planning, integrated delivery system development, facilities and equipment planning, ambulatory care strategies, business and financial planning, and analysis of governance requirements.

TRIGON HEALTH VENTURES, INC.
5215 N. O'Connor Blvd., Ste. 1050
Irving, TX 75039
Dale L. Thomas
PH: (972)869-6565
FX: (972)869-6530

Founded: 1987. Offers healthcare services emphasizing provider-based managed care programs, including turnkey development and ongoing management. Industries served: physicians and hospitals worldwide. **Conferences and Meetings:** *Made presentations on PHOs at AAFP National Meeting and at Texas Medical Association regional meetings. Also offers utilization management workshops.* **Computer/Special Services:** Provides reimbursement and capitation analyses; and fee schedule development.

TSC STEINER CO.
130 S. 1st St.
Ann Arbor, MI 48104-1304
Matthew W. Steiner, Pres.
PH: (313)663-3322
FX: (313)761-9366
Founded: 1980. **Staff:** 2. Advises U.S. healthcare industry on quality control and productivity issues.

DR. M. UCAR, PE
31 Campanilla
San Clemente, CA 92673
Dr. M. Ucar
PH: (949)496-4330
FX: (949)240-8826
Founded: 1984. Services include: accident reconstruction, computer animations, failure analysis, product liability, computer animation, design analysis, safety, warnings, codes, standards, human factors, seat belt defense, litigation and defense strategies, computer reconstructions, automotive industrial and construction accidents. Serves clients in the U.S. and Canada. **Computer/Special Services:** Resources for computer reconstruction, simulation, and visualization of accidents; extensive expertise and experience in evidence photography and photogrammetry.

UCLA STATISTICAL/BIOMATHEMATICAL CONSULTING CLINIC
e-mail: gornbein@ucla.edu
url: http://www.biomath.medsch.ucla.edu
AV-516 CHS
10833 LeConte Ave.
Box 951766
Los Angeles, CA 90095-1766
PH: (310)825-3296
FX: (310)825-8685
Staff: 7. Offers biomathematical services, including clinical trial design, planning, and analysis; general statistical analysis, modeling, and report writing; statistical methods for laboratory data; data management design and implementation; data acquisition; assistance in preparation of grant proposals, publications, and reports; review of biomedical journal articles with regard to statistical methods and experimental or observational design; applied programming using commercial and specialized statistical and mathematical packages; data transfer between computing platforms; data extraction and processing from major databases, including UCLA hospital, California, and national data banks; statistical genetics; statistical graphics; and customized courses in statistics. Industries served: medicine, health sciences, social sciences, and education.

UCSF PSORIASIS CENTER
515 Spruce St.
San Francisco, CA 94118
John Koo, MD, Director
PH: (415)476-4701
FX: (415)502-4126
Specializes in dermatology, psychodermatology, phototherapy, psoriasis treatment, transcultural psychiatry, and stress-induced skin conditions.

UNITED REHABILITATION, INC.
7025 Tall Oak Dr., Ste. 200
Colorado Springs, CO 80919
John M. Bermudez, President

PH: (719)594-9987
FX: (719)594-4152
Founded: 1982. **Staff:** 25. Rehabilitation and disability management specialists offering the following services: income impairment, vocational rehabilitation evaluation/services, labor market analysis, transferrable skill analysis, and displaced homemaker evaluation. Conducts aptitude, interest, and abilities testing. Additional services are; adoption studies, family counseling, marriage counseling, and custody evaluations. Serves private industries as well as government agencies. Geographic areas served: southern Colorado.

U.S. COUNSELING SERVICES INC.
url: http://www.uscounselingcom
120 Bishops Way, Ste. 100
Brookfield, WI 53005-6241
Duane M. Bluemke, President
PH: (414)784-5600
FX: (414)784-8771
Founded: 1969. Advises U.S. healthcare industry, government agencies, and other businesses on medical equipment, maintenance cost reduction, and asset management.

U.S. INDUSTRIAL MEDICINE CORP.
763 Chestnut Ridge Rd.
Morgantown, WV 26505-2815
Thomas Clark, M.D., Pres.
PH: (304)599-6367
FX: (304)599-0400
Founded: 1980. **Staff:** 22. Specializes in occupational medicine, training, and development. Industries served: **manufacturing in the United States.**

U.S. OCCUPATIONAL HEALTH INC.
205 W. Randolph St., Ste. 720
Chicago, IL 60606
Dr. Barry L. Fischer, CEO & President
PH: (312)641-1449
TF: 800548-5909
FX: (312)641-1714
Founded: 1986. **Staff:** 20. Occupational health consultants and health testing. Particular expertise available in OSHA medical compliance exams including: asbestos or respirator wearer - certification at time of exam, benzene, coke oven, hearing conservation (audio), and HAZMAT and emergency response. Serves private industries as well as government agencies. Geographic areas served: Chicago metropolitan area.

URBAN HEALTH INSTITUTE INC.
101 Eisenhower Pkwy.
Roseland, NJ 07068-1028
Donald Malafronte, Pres.
PH: (973)228-9000
FX: (973)228-3128
Founded: 1973. **Staff:** 6. Assists hospitals, healthcare operations, and government agencies in healthcare management planning. Geographic areas served: New York, New Jersey, and Connecticut.

MAXINE UTTENREITHER, INC., HEALTHCARE RESOURCE MANAGEMENT GROUP
8348 Streamwood Dr.
Baltimore, MD 21208
TF: 800533-2834
FX: (410)521-7590
Staff: 3. Offers healthcare consulting services.

V-LABS, INC.
e-mail: v-labs@wild.net
url: http://www.v-labs.com
423 N. Theard St.
Covington, LA 70433
Sharon V. Vercellotti

PH: (504)893-0533
FX: (504)893-0517
Founded: 1979. Offers analytical service for carbohydrates and polysaccharides. Performs contract research and consulting for pharmaceutical, chemical, and food companies. Services include analysis of sugar processing products, dietary fiber determination, custom synthesis and polysaccharide modification, and computerized data acquisition and reporting.

JIMMIE L. VALENTINE, PH.D.
e-mail: valentinejimmiel@exchange.uams.edu
University of Arkansas for Medical Sciences
Department of Pediatrics
800 Marshall St.
Little Rock, AR 72202
Jimmie L. Valentine, Ph.D.
PH: (501)320-2802
FX: (501)320-3551
Specializes in drug abuse cases, accidents and medical malpractice, and forensic toxicology.

LUCAS S. VAN ORDEN MD, PH.D.
e-mail: 103465.766@compuserve.com
4 Moya Pl.
Santa Fe, NM 87505
PH: (505)466-8718
FX: (505)466-8718
Offers expert witness testimony in civil and criminal cases, including medical malpractice and wrongful death; capital crimes involving substance abuse or insanity plea; competency to stand trial; and civil commitment.

N.J. VAUGHAN & ASSOCIATES, INC.
11501 Chimney Rock Rd.
Houston, TX 77035-2948
Newal J. Vaughan
PH: (713)729-5310
Founded: 1977. **Staff:** 1. Offers consulting services in health administration.

VECTOR RESEARCH, INC.
PO Box 1506
Ann Arbor, MI 48106
Seth Bonder, President
PH: (313)973-9210
FX: (313)973-7845
Founded: 1969. **Staff:** 107. Broad-based operations research and data-processing effort with sharp focus on solving complex healthcare planning and delivery problems for private industry and government, including Department of Defense, Veterans Administration and Public Health Service. Consulting experience spans large-scale computer modeling of healthcare demand and demographics of physician supply, automated quality-of-care monitoring, medical database management and information quality engineering, site-specific economic analyses, software development for integrated hospital information systems, and graduate medical education.

VENCARE HEALTH SERVICES
1926 Harrison St.
Hollywood, FL 33020
Brent A. Spechler, President
PH: (954)921-2255
TF: 800842-9339
FX: (954)921-4496
Founded: 1979. **Staff:** 12. Consultants specializing in staffing requirements of rehabilitative hospitals, skilled nursing facilities, pediatric facilities, hospitals, home health and outpatient clinics in physical therapy, occupational therapy, and speech therapy on a short- or long-term basis. Firm's divisions include: Full Service/Management Contract Division, Long Term Staffing Division, Temporary Division, Traveling Therapist Division, and Physical Therapist/Occupational Therapist Placement Division. Serves government agencies. Geographic areas served: Florida.

Conferences and Meetings: *Resumes, Interviewing (and career planning for therapists PT/OT/ST) in the 1990's.*

VERK CONSULTANTS, INC.
e-mail: verk@rio.com
url: http://www.rio.com/~verk
PO Box 11277
Eugene, OR 97440
Larry H. Malmgren, M.S.
PH: (541)687-9170
FX: (541)687-9758
Founded: 1979. **Staff:** 6. Specializes in vocational rehabilitation, worksite evaluations for managing workers'compensation, and the Americans with Disabilities Act, Title I.

BRUCE S. VICTOR, MD
1819 Union St.
San Francisco, CA 94123
PH: (415)346-7025
FX: (415)346-0931
Specializes in mood and anxiety disorders and ethics violations. Offers expert testimony and consultation in malpractice litigation.

NAOMI VOLAIN, MS, RD
34 Virginia St.
Springfield, MA 01108-2623
Naomi Volain
PH: (413)785-1792
Founded: 1986. **Staff:** 1. Registered dietitian offering advertising copywriting, specializing in pharmaceuticals, medical instrumentation, and nutrition. Also writes advertising copy, promotional materials, feature articles, direct mail and public relations material. Serves the consumer and healthcare industries in addition to those mentioned above. Geographic areas served: northeastern United States.

W-F PROFESSIONAL ASSOCIATES INC.
400 Lake Cook Rd., Ste. 207
Deerfield, IL 60015
PH: (847)945-8050
Founded: 1977. Consulting firm conducts pharmacy continuing education programs.

JOHN M. WADSWORTH
313 Summer St.
Buffalo, NY 14222
PH: (716)883-5367
Psychiatric forensic work in areas that include competency, sanity, disability, stress and workers' compensation. Offers expert witness testimony.

KENDALL B. WALLACE
1925 Waverly Ave.
Duluth, MN 55803
PH: (218)348-8025
Provides human health risk assessments of environmental or occupational exposures. Provides forensic toxicology consultation and litigation support.

JOHN D. WARBRITTON III, MD
350 - 30th St., Ste. 530
Oakland, CA 94609
PH: (510)839-5564
FX: (510)839-1692
Specializes in orthopedic surgery. Provides medi-legal evaluations and consultations. A Spanish language translator.

WARREN & WARREN
e-mail: cjwarren@slipnet.com
url: http://www.slip.net/~cjwarren
2033 Powell St.
San Francisco, CA 94133
Charles B. Warren, Principal

PH: (415)433-0959
FX: (415)982-1441
Firm specializes in forensic appraisal, land economic/feasibility studies, economic geography, assessment/assessment appeals. Unusual properties a specialty-damaged, contaminated, wetlands; also small craft harbors and other maritime related property. Geographic Areas Served: Most consultation and valuation work in the Western U.S. Education and training in economic geography, appraisal and assessment available worldwide. **Conferences and Meetings:** *Uniform Standard of Professional Appraisal Practice (1998); Custom Training avialable-inquire.* **Computer/Special Services:** Automated Valuation Models, Computer Assisted Mass Assessment, Acquisition and interpretation of remote imagery.

WASHINGTON OCCUPATIONAL HEALTH ASSOCIATES, INC.
e-mail: kchase@woha.com
url: http://www.woha.com
1120 19th St. NW, Ste. 410
Washington, DC 20036
Kenneth H. Chase, President
PH: (202)463-6698
TF: 800777-9642
FX: (202)223-6525
Founded: 1980. **Staff:** 25. Occupational health consultants offering clinical, epidemiologic, industrial hygiene and toxicologic services in the areas of occupational and environmental health. Typical activities include toxic substance monitoring, audiometric testing and evaluation, respirator certification programs, epidemiologic surveys, expert opinion formulation and pre-placement and in-service physical examination programs throughout the U.S. Geographic Areas Served: North America. **Conferences and Meetings:** *Seminars and training courses are offered in hearing conservation and other occupational/environmental medicine issues.*

ROBERT L. WEINMANN, MD
2040 Forest Ave., Ste. 4
San Jose, CA 95128
PH: (408)292-0802
FX: (408)292-9574
Specializes in neurology, soft tissue, back and neck, head injury, alterations in consciousness (epilepsy, seizure disorders), cervical and lumbar radiculitis, post-concussion, headache, wrongful death from brain injury, post-traumatic head syndrome, brain death, carpal tunnel syndrome, Bell's palsy, Parkinson's disease, and Huntington's Chorea. Serves as an expert witness. Provides QME- AME Evaluations.

NORMAN WEISS, MD
231 E. 76th St., Ste. 7F
New York, NY 10021
PH: (212)861-8168
FX: (914)723-4343
Clinical and medico-legal psychiatry consultation and expert witness testimony.

WELLNESS GROUP INC.
e-mail: Wellnesgroup@compuserve.com
24800 Denso Dr., Ste. 255
Southfield, MI 48034
Delores C. Tripp, Pres.
PH: (248)351-7890
FX: (248)351-7896
Founded: 1982. **Staff:** 15. Human Resources consulting firm provides expertise in: employee assistance programs, counseling, seminars, stress management, and organizational development. **Conferences and Meetings:** *Prevention of Workplace Violence; Valuing Diversity; and Diversity Management; Leadership Development-Team Building.*

WELLPLAN INC.
617 E. Elm
Salina, KS 67401
Lori E. Henke, R.D.L.D.
PH: (913)825-8224
FX: (913)825-0644
Founded: 1981. **Staff:** 5. Offers consultation on health maintenance and improvement through positive lifestyles. Individual counseling on disease prevention and maintenance through medical nutrition and exercise therapy. Group programs are also offered. **Conferences and Meetings:** *Healthy Heart Workshop (cholesterol reduction); Slim Plan Workshop (body fat loss); Preventative Services for the Primary Care Physician (consultation on establishment and implementation of preventative, wellness services in the family practice office).* **Computer/Special Services:** Health Check Booklet (fat gram booklet and dietary recall and exercise sheets).

JOSHUA H. WERBLOWSKY
Presidential Apts. D-111, -112, Madison House
City Line/Presidential Blvd.
Philadelphia, PA 19131
Joshua H. Werblowsky
PH: (215)878-3954
FX: (610)667-1691
Founded: 1971. Forensic psychiatric consultant for civil, family, and criminal cases with particular expertise in workmen's compensation and personal injury.

HUGH H. WEST, MD
10 Morning Sun
Mill Valley, CA 94941
PH: (415)383-2301
FX: (415)383-2388
Emergency medicine consulting in pre-hospital care, emergency physician performance, and hospital staff performance.

WESTWOOD RESEARCH LABORATORY INC.
PO Box 3126
West Chester, PA 19381-3126
John Cornell, Executive Director/President
PH: (610)692-6933
Founded: 1957. **Staff:** 2. Offers consulting in the dental field in vitro testing and product development. Industries served: dental and medical organizations, and government agencies. Geographic areas served: worldwide.

THE WHITMAN GROUP
3501 Masons Mill Rd., Building 5
Huntingdon Valley, PA 19006
John Whitman, Chairman/CEO
PH: (215)657-9990
FX: (215)657-9547
Founded: 1985. **Staff:** 85. Nationally recognized consultation and management firm assisting hospitals, nursing facilities, and other healthcare organizations in identification, analysis, design, development, implementation, and management of programs and services for senior adults and chronic care populations. The organization's multidisciplinary expertise spans the areas of clinical gerontology, subacute facility contract management, financial analysis (including Medicare reimbursement of subacute units), expert witness testimony, long-term care continuum planning, and assisted living. Serves hospitals, nursing facilities, subacute care providers, rehabilitation hospitals, physicians, attorneys, government agencies, and professional healthcare organizations (as speakers) in the U.S. and worldwide. **Conferences and Meetings:** *Presents seminars on above topics throughout the country. Schedule available from firm.*

WHOLE PERSON ASSOCIATES, INC.
e-mail: wholeperson@aol.com
url: http://www.wholeperson.com
210 W. Michigan St.
Duluth, MN 55802-1908
Donald A. Tubesing, President
PH: (218)727-0500
TF: 800247-6789
FX: (218)727-0505
Founded: 1977. **Staff:** 13. Consulting firm specializing in the design and implementation of programs and products for stress management, wellness promotion, and reduction of employee burnout. Has assisted clients in healthcare, government, business, education, social service, and military settings. Geographic areas served: national and international. **Conferences and Meetings:** *Offers numerous seminars on stress management and other personal/personnel issues, specifically, Minimizing Stress Maximizing Vitality; Staying Evergreen; Charting Your Spiritual Path.*

THE WILKERSON GROUP
1748 Carovel Cir.
Vestavia Hills, AL 35216
Robert G. Wilkerson, President
PH: (205)823-4139
FX: (205)823-4139
Founded: 1990. **Staff:** 2. Offers consulting services to help hospitals benefit from the growing number of older people in their communities by developing housing and programs for the elderly that help them fulfill their mission, improve their image, increase their revenues, and create loyalty and gratitude among their elderly patients. Specific services include market-feasibility studies, program/facility design, development and management, strategic planning, seminars, and public speaking. Industries served: healthcare, universities, nursing homes, and retirement housing industry. Geographic areas served: U.S. **Conferences and Meetings:** *Long-term Care Insurance: What's Good and What's Not; The Future of the Retirement Housing Industry; The Graying of America: The Hospitals Role; Ethical Dilemmas in Long-term Care; The Aging in Place Phenomena: How to Cope; How to Select a Nursing Home; How to Select a Retirement Community; Community Resources for the Aging; Medicare: What it Covers and What It Don't; How to Select an Emergency Call System; How to Know Quality Senior Housing When You Manage It.*

PHILIP WILLEN ASSOCIATES
8 Church Ln.
Baltimore, MD 21208-3736
Philip Willen
PH: (410)486-2512
FX: (410)486-2797
Health care specialists providing public relations and advertising services. **Computer/Special Services:** Desktop Publishing and Graphic Design.

WILMA J. WINTER - MEDICAL COMMUNICATIONS
2111 Jefferson Davis Hwy., Apt. 513 N
Arlington, VA 22202
Wilma J. Winter
PH: (703)415-0610
Founded: 1984. **Staff:** 1. Provides research and writing expertise on medical affairs. Attends and summarizes science seminars. Writes and researches clinical papers, drug brochures, audiovisuals on drugs, and salesperson's mail pieces. Summarizes pharmacologic and clinical data for government application and review. Industries served: pharmaceutical firms, federal government, medical journals, and local TV (cable). Geographic areas served: national.

A.M. WOLVEN, INC.
175 W. Wieuca Rd., Ste. 118
Atlanta, GA 30342
Anne M. Wolven, President
PH: (404)252-6377
FX: (404)303-0052
Founded: 1978. **Staff:** 4. Involved in regulatory compliance: EPA, FDA, FHSA (CPSC), OSHA, product development, GLP's, GMP's, quality assurance audits, claim substantiation, planning and contract proposals, PRG-clinical and clinical studies, in vitro technology, and risk assessment. Industries served: chemical, cosmetic, toiletries, food, household products, medical device, and pharmaceuticals. Geographic areas served: U.S. and Europe. **Conferences and Meetings:** *In-house seminars presented to clients on in vitro testing and current regulatory requirements for medical devices, pesticides/disinfectants, and indirect food additives.* **Computer/Special Services:** Adjunct laboratory testing facilities (clinical, animal, microbiological, environmental).

WOMEN'S HEALTH CARE CONSULTANTS INC.
500 Davis St., Ste. 700
Evanston, IL 60201-4623
Sally J. Rynne, Pres.
PH: (847)869-1200
FX: (847)328-9056
Founded: 1984. **Staff:** 23. Provides women's healthcare services to hospitals and institutions in the United States.

WOMEN'S WELLNESS CENTER
1301 Seminole Blvd.
Plaza Center, Ste. 150
Largo, FL 33770
Dr. Carolyn Chambers Clark
PH: (813)581-6479
FX: (813)585-4089
Founded: 1977. **Staff:** 2. Involved in promotion of wellness and health promotion programs at the worksite and at the Women's Wellness Center to improve employee morale and productivity and reduce costs due to employee illness, absenteeism and turnover. Conducts stress management and support groups for executive women. Provides low cost wellness and health promotion resources including: company newsletters, self-help tapes, wellness selfassessments and healthy living booklets. Provides consultation for corporations to develop their own newsletters. Geographic areas served: northeast and southeast U.S. **Conferences and Meetings:** *Self-Care; Stress Management; Communication Skills/Interpersonal Relationships; Wellness Strategies. Will design workshops to suit client.*

DONNA LEE WONG
url: http://www.mosby.com/mosby/wong_on_web
7535 S. Urbana Ave.
Tulsa, OK 74136-6113
Donna Lee Wong
PH: (918)496-0544
FX: (918)496-8344
Founded: 1975. **Staff:** 3. Pediatric nurse consultant specializing in management of complex nursing care problems, family counseling related to childhood adjustment disorders and grief therapy, and in pain assessment and management. Consultant authors publications and conducts workshops and seminars on these topics; schedule available upon request. **Conferences and Meetings:** *Advancing the Practice of Pain Management; Assessment of Pain in Children; Pharmacologic Management of Pain in Children (includes infants); Transition from Hospital to Home: Caring for the Child with Complex Care; Family Assessment; Practice Makes Perfect, but Research Makes (it) Right; Communicating Effectively with Children: Using Creative Techniques; Beyond First Do No Harm: Principles of Atraumatic Care; Achieving Balance: Strategies for Success; Writing and Publishing: From Basics to Results.*

LINDA F. WOOD
e-mail: lfwood@worldnet.att.net
43 Village View Rd.
Westford, MA 01886-2359
Linda F. Wood, President
PH: (508)692-2369
FX: (508)692-0144
Founded: 1990. **Staff:** 1. Offers writing services for the pharmaceutical, device, and biotechnology industries. Experience in-

cludes expertise in regulatory submissions, clinical protocols, case report forms, investigator brochures, study manuals, clinical summaries, INDs, and NDAs. Clinical monitoring services and trial management offered as needed. Geographic areas served: no limitations.

WORK RETURN
e-mail: onabeth
155 Montgomery St., Ste. 606
San Francisco, CA 94104
Ona Schissel, Principal
PH: (415)391-8435
FX: (415)391-1543
A certified vocational rehabilitation counselor with experience in vocational rehabilitation and economic wage loss. Testifies in all types of civil litigation. Provides vocational evaluation, testing labor market regarding job availability, salaries, trends, employment, wage loss and economic ramifications, job site analysis, medical management, job placement, career counseling, and outplacement services. Geographic Areas Served: California, Nevada, Hawaii.

WORLDWIDE PROMEDICA INC.
577 Airport Blvd., Ste. 130
Burlingame, CA 94010
Joan R. Day, President
PH: (650)344-6242
FX: (650)344-3217
Founded: 1984. Consulting firm offers marketing research expertise for medical products and services. Industries served: healthcare (pharmaceuticals, diagnostics, biotech). Woman owned firm.

YEAST CONSULTING SERVICES
PO Box 11157
Torrance, CA 90510-1157
Marjorie Crandall, Ph.D., Founder and Owner
PH: (310)375-1073
Founded: 1988. **Staff:** 1. Provides confidential telephone counseling of Candida patients. Also offers public seminars, scientific lectures with slide presentations, consultations with physicians and review of medical records, referrals for testing and healthcare. Also offers expert witness testimony, research and development of antifungals and diagnostics. Industries served: patients, physicians, attorneys, health insurance companies, pharmaceutical firms, diagnostic companies, nonprofit health organizations, health book publishers, and manufacturers. Geographic areas served: U.S. **Conferences and Meetings:** *How to Prevent Yeast Infections; The Candidiasis Hypersensitivity Syndrome - Mucosal and Systemic Manifestations.*

HANK YUROW & ASSOCIATES, INC.
1905 Stonehaven Ct.
Marriottsville, MD 21104
Hank Yurow, President
PH: (410)795-5507
FX: (410)653-1296
Founded: 1990. **Staff:** 1. Offers a variety of healthcare management consulting services that include but are not limited to: physician networking, hospital/physician ventures, capitation/HMO agreements, mergers/practice acquisitions, practice reviews, accounts receivable management, facility planning, and cost containment strategies for purchasers of healthcare. Industries served: physicians, hospitals, and other sectors of the healthcare industry. Geographic areas served: mid-Atlantic. **Conferences and Meetings:** *Mergers and Networking, AHA, Phoenix, AR (October 1994); Physician Mergers and Other Collaborative Arrangements, MICPEL (November 1994).*

THOMAS J. ZAYDON, JR., MD
3661 S. Miami Ave., Ste. 509
Miami, FL 33133
PH: (305)856-3030
FX: (305)285-9423

Evaluates and manages scars and other deformities resulting from accidents.

ZELNER AND BADNER INC.
e-mail: hlasystems@aol.com
url: http://www.hlasystems.com
163 Engle St.
Englewood, NJ 07631
Barry Badner, President
PH: (201)569-5522
TF: 800447-7899
FX: (201)569-1793
Founded: 1969. **Staff:** 4. Provides materials handling, physical distribution, and cost reduction consulting services for healthcare and industrial organizations. Health care services include facilities programming and systems improvement studies for surgical, nursing, other special care and other support areas. Industrial services include: functional facility design and cost reduction studies for warehousing and manufacturing materials handling operations; automation and work simplification studies; significant activity in food processing layout and equipment studies. Industries served: healthcare, distribution, and food processing.

JEAN ZIMMERMANN
PO Box 934
Meadow Vista, CA 95722
Jean Zimmermann
PH: (530)878-8553
Founded: 1982. **Staff:** 3. Offers consulting services in psychiatric and mental health nursing, nursing leadership, and the nursing process. Serves hospitals, businesses, individuals, government agencies, institutions, and firms in stress management, interpersonal relationships, leadership, nursing process and evaluation, psychiatric and mental health crises, and drug and alcohol counseling. Also provides advertising evaluations from the consumer's view point. Geographic areas served: United States and Canada. **Conferences and Meetings:** *Stress Management; Nursing Process; Nursing Leadership; Mental Health Nursing; Working with Difficult Individuals; Psychiatric Principles; Choice and Changes for Women.*

ZOL CONSULTANTS INC.
340 W. 57th St.
New York, NY 10019
Saul Green, President
PH: (212)957-8029
Founded: 1982. **Staff:** 1. Specialist in the investigation of health frauds, offering scientific evaluation of unproved or questionable medical treatments particularly for cancer and AIDS. Also offers scientific evaluation of proposals to venture capitalists or individuals interested in setting up bioengineering companies and cancer research projects. Serves attorneys, insurance companies, and government agencies. Geographic areas served: United States.

LORAINE S. ZUCKERMAN
13006 Middlevale Ln.
Silver Spring, MD 20906
Loraine S. Zuckerman
PH: (301)933-5144
Founded: 1974. Provides nutrition consulting to government agencies, institutions, healthcare facilities, and individuals. **Conferences and Meetings:** *Weight Control Seminars; Diabetes Education, Cholesterol Education Seminars; Adolescent Nutrition Workshops.* **Computer/Special Services:** Computerized nutritional analysis, database of 7000 foods.

CHAPTER 9

TRADE INFORMATION SOURCES

Adapted from Gale's *Encyclopedia of Business Information Sources* (*EBIS*), the entries featured in this chapter show trade journals and other information sources, including web sites and databases.

Entries for publications and electronic databases list the title of the work, the name of the author (where available), name of the publisher, frequency or year of publication, prices or fees, and Internet address (in many cases).

Entries for trade associations and research centers provide the organization name, address, telephone numbers, e-mail address, and web site URL. Many of these entries include brief descriptions of the organization.

AAHSA RESOURCE CATALOG
e-mail: info@aahsa.org
url: http://www.aahsa.org
901 E St., N. W., Suite 500
Washington, DC 20004-2011
PH: 800-508-9442
FX: (202)783-2255
American Association of Homes and Services for the Aging. Annual. Free. Provides descriptions of material relating to managed care, senior housing, assisted living, continuing care retirement communities (CCRCs), nursing facilities, and home health care. Publishers are AAHSA and others.

ADVANCES IN HEALTH ECONOMICS AND HEALTH SERVICES RESEARCH
P.O. Box 1678
Greenwich, CT 06836-1678
PH: (203)661-7602
FX: (203)661-0792
JAI Press, Inc. Annual. $73.25.

ADVERTISING HANDBOOK FOR HEALTH CARE SERVICES
e-mail: getinfo@haworth.com
url: http://www.haworth.com
10 Alice St.
Binghamton, NY 13904-1580
PH: 800-429-6784
FX: 800-895-0582
William J. Winston. The Haworth Press, Inc. 1986. $49.95. (Health Marketing Quarterly Series.)

AHA GUIDE TO THE HEALTH CARE FIELD
url: http://www.aha.org
One North Franklin St.
Chicago, IL 60606
PH: (312)422-3537
FX: (312)422-4569
American Hospital Association Data and Information Business Group. Annual. $195.00. A directory of hospitals and health care systems.

AHA HOSPITAL STATISTICS
url: http://www.aha.org
One North Franklin St.
Chicago, IL 60606
PH: (312)422-3541
FX: (312)422-4651
American Hospital Association. Annual. Members, $59.00 per year; non-members $139.00 per year. Provides detailed statistical data on the nation's hospitals, including revenues, expenses, utilization, and personnel. Formerly *Hospital Statistics.*

AHA NEWS
737 North Michigan Ave., Suite 700
Chicago, IL 60611-2615
PH: 800-621-6902
FX: (312)951-8491
American Hospital Publishing, Inc. Weekly. Members, $45.00 per year; non-members, $100.00 per year. Newsletter edited for hospital and health care industry administrators. Covers health care news events and legislative activity. (An American Hospital Association publication.)

ALMANAC OF BUSINESS AND INDUSTRIAL FINANCIAL RATIOS
url: http://www.prenhall.com
One Lake St.
Upper Saddle River, NJ 07458
PH: 800-223-1360
FX: 800-445-6991
Leo Troy. Prentice Hall. Annual. $99.95. Contains financial ratios derived from federal tax returns. Ratios for each of about 200 industries are arranged according to company asset size.

AMERICAN ACADEMY OF DENTAL GROUP PRACTICE
5110 N. 40th St., Suite 250
Phoenix, AZ 85018
PH: (602)381-1185
FX: (602)381-1093

AMERICAN ACADEMY OF DENTAL PRACTICE ADMINISTRATION
c/o Kathleen Uebel
1063 Whippoorwill Lane
Palatine, IL 60067
PH: (847)934-4404

AMERICAN ACADEMY OF FAMILY PHYSICIANS
8880 Ward Parkway
Kansas City, MO 64114
PH: 800-274-2237
FX: (816)822-0580

AMERICAN ACADEMY OF MEDICAL ADMINISTRATORS
e-mail: aama@netquest.com
30555 Southfield Rd., Suite 150
Southfield, MI 48076-7747
PH: (810)540-4310
FX: (810)645-0590
Members are executives and middle managers in health care administration.

AMERICAN ASSOCIATION OF BIOANALYSTS
917 Locust St., Suite 1100
St. Louis, MO 63101-1413
PH: (314)241-1445
FX: (314)241-1449
Members are owners and managers of bioanalytical clinical laboratories.

AMERICAN ASSOCIATION FOR CONTINUITY OF CARE
638 Prospect Ave.
Hartford, CT 06105-4250
PH: (860)586-7525
FX: (860)586-7550
Members are professionals concerned with continuity of care, health care after hospital discharge, and home health care.

AMERICAN ASSOCIATION OF HEALTH PLANS
url: http://www.aahp.org
1129 20th St., N.W., Suite 600
Washington, DC 20036-3403
PH: (202)728-3200
FX: (202)331-7487
Members are alternate health care organizations, including HMOs.

AMERICAN ASSOCIATION OF HEALTHCARE CONSULTANTS
11208 Waples Mill Rd., Suite 109
Fairfax, VA 22030
PH: 800-362-4674
FX: (703)691-2247
Members are professional consultants who specialize in the health care industry.

AMERICAN ASSOCIATION OF HOMES AND SERVICES FOR THE AGING
e-mail: aahsa@aahsa.org
901 E. St., N.W., Suite 500
Washington, DC 20004-2037
PH: (202)783-2242
FX: (202)783-2255

AMERICAN BOARD OF MEDICAL SPECIALTIES
1007 Church St., Suite 404
Evanston, IL 60201-5913

PH: (847)491-9091
FX: (847)328-3596
Functions as the parent organization for U.S. medical specialty boards.

AMERICAN CLINICAL LABORATORY ASSOCIATION
1250 Eye St., N. W., Suite 880
Washington, DC 20005
PH: (202)637-9466
FX: (202)637-2050
Members are owners of clinical laboratories operating for a profit.

**AMERICAN COLLEGE OF HEALTH CARE
ADMINISTRATORS**
e-mail: achca@achca.usa.com
325 S. Patrick St.
Alexandria, VA 22314
PH: (703)739-7900
FX: (703)739-7901

AMERICAN COLLEGE OF HEALTHCARE EXECUTIVES
One N. Franklin, Suite 1700
Chicago, IL 60606-3491
PH: (312)424-2800
FX: (312)424-0023

**AMERICAN COLLEGE OF MEDICAL PRACTICE
EXECUTIVES**
104 Inverness Terrace East
Englewood, CO 80112-5306
PH: (303)397-7869
FX: (303)643-4427

**AMERICAN COLLEGE OF OCCUPATIONAL AND
ENVIRONMENTAL MEDICINE-MEMBERSHIP
DIRECTORY**
55 W. Seegers Rd.
Arlington Heights, IL 60005
PH: (847)228-6850
FX: (847)228-1856
Annual. $155.00. Lists 6,500 medical directories and plant physicians specializing in occupational medicine and surgery; coverage includes Canada and other foreign countries. Geographically arranged.

AMERICAN DENTAL ASSOCIATION
211 E. Chicago Ave.
Chicago, IL 60611
PH: (312)440-2500
FX: (312)440-7494

AMERICAN DENTAL ASSOCIATION JOURNAL
211 E. Chicago Ave.
Chicago, IL 60611
PH: 800-947-4746
FX: (312)440-3538
American Dental Association. Monthly. Members, $25.00 per year; non-members, $90.00 per year. Formerly *Journal of the American Dental Association.*

AMERICAN DENTAL DIRECTORY
211 E. Chicago Ave.
Chicago, IL 60611
PH: 800-947-4746
FX: (312)440-9970
American Dental Association. Annual. Members, $125.00; non-members, $187.50. Contains brief information for over 170,000 dentists.

AMERICAN DENTAL TRADE ASSOCIATION
4222 King St., W.
Alexandria, VA 22302-1597

PH: (703)379-7755
FX: (703)931-9429

AMERICAN HEALTH CARE ASSOCIATION
1201 L St., N. W.
Washington, DC 20005
PH: (202)842-4444
FX: (202)842-3860
Formerly American Nursing Home Association.

AMERICAN HEALTH CARE ASSOCIATION: PROVIDER
1201 L St., N.W.
Washington, DC 20005-4046
PH: (202)842-4444
FX: (202)842-3860
American Health Care Association. Monthly. $48.00 per year. Formerly *American Health Care Association Journal.*

AMERICAN HOSPITAL ASSOCIATION
One N. Franklin, Suite 27
Chicago, IL 60606
PH: (312)422-3000
FX: (312)422-4796

AMERICAN INDUSTRIAL HEALTH COUNCIL
e-mail: membershipservices@ainc.org
2001 Pennsylvania Ave., N.W., Suite 760
Washington, DC 20006
PH: (202)833-2131
FX: (202)833-2201

AMERICAN INDUSTRIAL HYGIENE ASSOCIATION
e-mail: infonet@aiha.org
2700 Prosperity Ave., Suite 250
Fairfax, VA 22031
PH: (703)849-8888
FX: (703)207-3561

**AMERICAN INDUSTRIAL HYGIENE ASSOCIATION
JOURNAL: A PUBLICATION FOR THE SCIENCE OF
OCCUPATIONAL AND ENVIRONMENTAL HEALTH**
e-mail: infonet@aiha.org
url: http://www.aiha.org
2700 Prosperity Ave., Suite 250
Fairfax, VA 22031-4307
PH: (703)849-8888
FX: (703)207-3561
American Industrial Hygiene Association. Monthly. $120.00 per year.

**AMERICAN INSTITUTE FOR MEDICAL AND BIOLOGICAL
ENGINEERING**
1901 Pennsylvania Ave., NW, Ste. 401
Washington, DC 200065
PH: (202)496-9660
FX: (202)466-8489

AMERICAN JOURNAL OF INDUSTRIAL MEDICINE
605 Third Ave.
New York, NY 10158-0012
PH: 800-225-5945
FX: (212)850-6088
John Wiley & Sons, Inc., Journals Div. Monthly. $999.00 per year.

AMERICAN JOURNAL OF NURSING
url: http://www.lrpub.com
227 E. Washington Sq.
Philadelphia, PA 19106
PH: 800-777-2295
FX: (215)238-4227
American Nurses' Association. Lippincott-Raven Publishers. Monthly. Individuals, $26.95 per year; institutions, $47.00 per

year. For registered nurses. Emphasis on the latest technological advances affecting nursing care.

AMERICAN MEDICAL ASSOCIATION
url: http://www.ama-assn.org
515 N. State St.
Chicago, IL 60610
PH: (312)464-5000
FX: (312)464-4184
Concerned with retirement planning and other financial planning for physicians 55 years of age or older.

AMERICAN MEDICAL GROUP ASSOCIATION
1422 Duke St.
Alexandria, VA 22314-3430
PH: (703)838-0033
FX: (703)548-1890

AMERICAN MEDICAL NEWS
e-mail: amnews-comments@ama.assn.org
url: http://www.ama-assn.org
515 N. State St.
Chicago, IL 60610
PH: 800-262-2350
FX: (312)464-5831
American Medical Association. 48 times a year. Individuals, $99.00 per year, institutions, $140.00 per year. Economic and legal news for the medical profession.

AMERICAN MEDICAL TECHNOLOGISTS
e-mail: amtmail@aol.com
710 Higgins Rd.
Park Ridge, IL 60068
PH: 800-275-1268
FX: (847)823-0458
National professional registry of medical laboratory technicians and medical assistants.

AMERICAN NURSES' ASSOCIATION
600 Maryland Ave., S.W., Suite 100 West
Washington, DC 20024-2571
PH: 800-637-0323
FX: (202)651-7001

AMERICAN PHARMACEUTICAL ASSOCIATION/ACADEMY OF PHARMACY PRACTICE AND MANAGEMENT
url: http://www.aphanet.org
2215 Constitution Ave., N.W.
Washington, DC 20037-2895
PH: 800-237-2742
FX: (202)783-2351

AMERICAN PROFESSIONAL PRACTICE ASSOCIATION
292 Madison Ave., 4th Fl.
New York, NY 10017
PH: 800-221-2168
FX: (212)949-5910
Concerned with financial planning for physicians and dentists.

AMERICAN SOCIETY FOR CLINICAL LABORATORY SCIENCE
7910 Woodmont Ave., Suite 530
Bethedsa, MD 20814
PH: (301)657-2768
FX: (301)657-2909
Seeks to promote high standards in clincal laboratory methods.

AMERICAN SOCIETY FOR HEALTH CARE MARKETING AND PUBLIC RELATIONS -MEMBERSHIP DIRECTORY
One N. Franklin
Chicago, IL 60606
PH: 800-621-6902
FX: (312)422-4579

American Society for Health Care Marketing and Public Relations. American Hospitals Publishing. Annual. Membership.

AMERICAN SOCIETY FOR HEALTHCARE MATERIALS MANAGEMENT
c/o American Hospital Association
One N. Franklin St., 30th Fl.
Chicago, IL 60606
PH: (312)422-3840
FX: (312)422-3573
Members are involved with the purchasing and distribution of supplies and equipment for hospitals and other healthcare establishments. Affiliated with the American Hospital Association.

AMERICAN SOCIETY FOR HEALTHCARE MATERIALS MANAGEMENT-ROSTER
One N. Franklin
Chicago, IL 60606
PH: 800-621-6902
FX: (312)422-4573
American Society for Healthcare Materials Management. Annual. Membership.

ANNUAL REVIEW OF MEDICINE: SELECTED TOPICS IN THE CLINICAL SCIENCES
e-mail: service@annurev.org
url: http://www.annurev.org
Post Office Box 10139
Palo Alto, CA 94303-0139
PH: 800-523-8635
FX: (650)424-0910
Annual Reviews, Inc. Annual. $40.00.

ANNUAL REVIEW OF PUBLIC HEALTH
e-mail: service@annurev.org
url: http://www.annurev.org
Post Office Box 10139
Palo Alto, CA 94303-0139
PH: 800-523-8635
FX: (650)855-9815
Annual Reviews, Inc. Annual. Individuals, $64.00; institutions, $128.00.

ANNUAL SURVEY OF MANUFACTURES
e-mail: gpoaccess@gpo.gov
url: http://www.access.gpo.gov
Washington, DC 20402
PH: (202)512-1800
FX: (202)512-2250
Available from U.S. Government Printing Office. Annual. Issued by the U.S. Census Bureau as an interim update to the *Census of Manufactures*. Includes data on number of manufacturing establishments in various industries, employment, labor costs, value of shipments, capital expenditures, inventories, energy costs, and assets. (See also Census Bureau home page, http://www.census.gov/.)

APPLIED SCIENCE AND TECHNOLOGY INDEX
e-mail: hwwmsg@info.hwwilson.com
url: http://www.hwwilson.com
950 University Ave.
Bronx, NY 10452
PH: 800-367-6770
FX: (718)590-1617
H. W. Wilson Co. 11 times a year. Quarterly and annual cumulations. Service basis. Indexes a wide variety of English language technical, industrial, and engineering periodicals.

ARCHIVES OF ENVIRONMENTAL HEALTH
url: http://www/helderf.org
1319 18th St., N.W.
Washington, DC 20036-1802
PH: (202)296-6267
FX: (202)296-5149

Helen Dwight Reid Educational Foundation. Heldref Publications. Bimonthly. $123.00 per year. Objective documentation of the effects of environmental agents on human health.

ASSOCIATION FOR THE ADVANCEMENT OF MEDICAL INSTRUMENTATION
3330 Washington Blvd., Suite 400
Arlington, VA 22201
PH: 800-332-2264
FX: (703)276-0793
Members are engineers, technicians, physicians, manufacturers, and others with an interest in medical instrumentation.

ASSOCIATION FOR THE ADVANCEMENT OF MEDICAL INSTRUMENTATION: MEMBERSHIP DIRECTORY
3330 Washington Blvd.
Suite 400
Arlington, VA 22201-4598
PH: 800-332-2264
FX: (703)276-0793
Association for the Advancement of Medical Instrumentation. Annual. $100.00. List 6,500 physicians, clinical engineers, biomedical engineersand technicians and nurses, researchers, and medical equipment manufacturers.

ASSOCIATION OF MANAGED HEALTHCARE ORGANIZATIONS
One Bridge Plaza, Suite 350
Fort Lee, NJ 07024
PH: (703)255-5340
FX: (201)947-8406

ATTORNEYS' DICTIONARY OF MEDICINE
Two Park Ave.
New York, NY 10016
PH: 800-223-1940
FX: (212)244-3188
J. E. Schmidt. Matthew Bender & Co., Inc. Five looseleaf volumes. Price on application. Periodic supplementation. Includes common lay words that lead to correct medical terms.

ATTORNEYS' TEXTBOOK OF MEDICINE
Two Park Ave.
New York, NY 10016
PH: 800-223-1940
FX: (212)244-3188
Matthew Bender & Co., Inc. 17 looseleaf volumes. Price on application. Periodic supplementation. Medico-legal material.

BASIC HOSPITAL FINANCIAL MANAGEMENT
e-mail: lynnantosz@aspenpubl.com
200 Orchard Ridge Dr., Suite 200
Gaithersburg, MD 20878
PH: 800-638-8437
FX: (301)417-7550
Donald F. Beck. Aspen Publishers, Inc. 1989. $62.00. Second edition.

THE BBI NEWSLETTER: A PERCEPTIVE ANALYSIS OF THE HEALTHCARE INDUSTRY AND MARKETPLACE FOCUSING ON NEW TECHNOLOGY, STRATEGIC PLANNING, AND MARKETSHARE P
16269 Laguna Canyon Rd, Suite 100
Invine, CA 92618-3603
PH: (714)755-5757
FX: (714)755-5724
Biomedical Business International, Inc. Monthly. $725.00 per year.

BESTLINK
Ambest Rd.
Oldwick, NJ 08858
PH: (908)439-2200
FX: (908)439-3296

A. M. Best Co. Financial data on about 4,400 insurance companies. Updated quarterly. Inquire as to online cost and availability.

BEST'S INSURANCE REPORTS
url: http://www.ambest.com
Ambest Rd.
Oldwick, NJ 08858
PH: (908)439-2200
FX: (908)439-3296
A. M. Best Co. Annual. $695.00 per edition. Two editions, Life-health insurance covering about 1,750 companies, and property-casualty insurance covering over 2,500 companies. Includes one year subscription to both *Best's Review* and *Best's Insurance Management Reports*.

BEST'S REVIEW. LIFE-HEALTH INSURANCE EDITION
url: http://www.ambest.com
Ambest Rd.
Oldwick, NJ 08858
PH: (908)439-2200
FX: (908)439-3296
A. M. Best Co. Monthly. $21.00 per year. Editorial coverage of significant trends and happenings.

BIOBUSINESS
2100 Arch St.
Philadelphia, PA 19103
PH: 800-523-4806
FX: (215)587-2016
BIOSIS. Provides abstracts of international periodical literature relating to business applications of biological and medical research, 1985 to date. Inquire as to online cost and availability.

BIOMEDICAL INSTRUMENTATION AND TECHNOLOGY
210 South 13th St.
Philadelphia, PA 19107
PH: (215)546-7293
FX: (215)790-9330
Association for the Advancement of Medical Instrumentation. Hanley and Belfus, Inc. Bimonthly. Individuals, $100.00 per year; institutions, $120.00 per year.

BIOMEDICAL PRODUCTS
url: http://www.bioprodmag
P.O. Box 650
Morris Plains, NJ 07950-0650
PH: (973)292-5100
FX: (973)605-1220
Gordon Publications, Inc. Monthly. $36.00 per year. Features new products and services.

BIOMEDICAL TECHNOLOGY INFORMATION SERVICE
url: http://www.lrpub.com
227 E. Washington Square
Philadelphia, PA 19106-3780
PH: 800-777-2295
FX: (215)238-4227
Lippincott-Raven Publishers. Semimonthly. Individuals, $320.00 per year; institutions, $370.00 per year. Newsletter on developments in medical devices and medical electronics.

BIOSCAN: THE WORLDWIDE BIOTECH INDUSTRY REPORTING SERVICE
e-mail: info@oryxpress.com
url: http://www.oryxpress.com
4041 North Central Ave.
Phoenix, AZ 85012-3397
PH: 800-279-6799
FX: 800-279-4663
Oryx Press. Bimonthly. $975.00 per year. Looseleaf. Provides detailed information on over 900 U.S. and foreign companies broadly classified as biotechnological. In addition to medical technology and advanced pharmaceutical firms, includes firms

doing research in food processing, waste management, agriculture, and veterinary science. Formerly *BioScan: The Biotechnology Corporate Directory Service.*

BLUE CROSS AND BLUE SHIELD ASSOCIATION
url: http://www.bluecares.com
225 N. Michigan Ave.
Chicago, IL 60611
PH: (312)297-6000
FX: (312)297-6609

THE BLUE SHEET: HEALTH POLICY AND BIOMEDICAL RESEARCH
e-mail: fdcr@fdcr.com
url: http://www.fdcr.com
5550 Friendship Blvd., Suite One
Chevy Chase, MD 20815-7278
PH: 800-332-2181
FX: (301)664-7248
F-D-C Reports, Inc. Weekly. $480.00 per year. Newsletter. Health policy topics include Medicare, the education and supply of health professionals, and public health. Biomedical topics are related to research, regulations, and the role of the National Science Foundation.

BNA'S SAFETY NET
url: http://www.bna.com
1250 23rd St., N.W.
Washington, DC 20037
PH: 800-372-1033
FX: (202)822-8092
Bureau of National Affairs, Inc. Biweekly. $680.00 per year. Looseleaf. Formerly *Job Safety and Health.*

BUREAU OF ECONOMIC AND BUSINESS RESEARCH
url: http://www.cba.uiuc.edu/research
University of Illinois at Urbana-Champaign
1206 South Sixth St.
428 Commerce W.
Champaign, IL 61820
PH: (217)333-2330
FX: (217)244-7410
Includes Office of Accounting Research, Office of Business Innovation and Entrepreneurship, Office of Real Estate Research, Center for Economic Education, Center for International Strategic Management, Program for Health Economics, Management, and Policy, and Center for Organizational Research. Publishes *Quarterly Review of Economics and Finance.*

BUREAU OF LABOR STATISTICS (BLS)
e-mail: labstat.helpdesk@bls.gov
url: http://www.bls.gov
PH: (202)523-1092
U.S. Department of Labor, Bureau of Labor Statistics. Web site provides a great variety of employment, wage, price, and economic data. Some links are "Data," "Economy at a Glance," "Keyword Search of BLS Web Pages," "Regional Information," and "Other Statistical Sites." Fees: Free.

BUSINESS AND HEALTH
e-mail: medec.com
url: http://www.medec.com
Five Paragon Drive
Montvale, NJ 07645-1742
PH: 800-232-7379
FX: (201)573-1045
Medical Economics Co., Inc. Monthly. $99.00 per year. Edited for business, government, and other buyers of employee health-care insurance or HMO coverage.

BUSINESS ORGANIZATIONS, AGENCIES, AND PUBLICATIONS DIRECTORY
e-mail: galeord@gale.com
url: http://www.gale.com
835 Penobscot Bldg.
Detroit, MI 48226-4094
PH: 800-877-GALE
FX: (313)961-6083
Gale Research Inc. 1996. $390.00. Eighth edition. Over 30,000 entries describing 39 types of business information sources. Classified by type of organization, publication, or service. Includes state, national, and international agencies and organizations. Master index to names and keywords.

BUSINESS PERIODICALS INDEX
e-mail: hwwmsg@info.hwwilson.com
url: http://www.hwwilson.com
950 University Ave.
Bronx, NY 10452
PH: 800-367-6770
FX: (718)590-1617
H. W. Wilson Co. Monthly, except August, with quarterly and annual cumulations. Price on application.

BUYERS' GUIDE FOR THE HEALTH CARE MARKET: A DIRECTORY OF PRODUCTS AND SERVICES FOR HEALTH CARE INSTITUTIONS
737 North Michigan Ave., Suite 700
Chicago, IL 60611-2615
PH: 800-621-6902
FX: (312)440-1158
American Hospital Publishing, Inc. Annual. $14.95. Lists 1.200 suppliers and manufacturers of health care products and services for hospitals, nursing homes, and related organizations. (An American Hospital Association publication.)

CARING FOR FRAIL ELDERLY PEOPLE: NEW DIRECTIONS IN CARE
e-mail: washcont@oecd.org
url: http://www.oecd.org
OECD Washington Center
2001 L St., N.W., Suite 650
Washington, DC 20036-4922
PH: 800-456-6323
FX: (202)785-0350
Organization for Economic Cooperation and Development. 1994. $27.00. Discusses the problem in OECD countries of providing good quality care to the elderly at manageable cost. Includes trends in family care, housing policies, and private financing.

CENTER FOR ADVANCED STUDY IN HEALTH CARE FISCAL MANAGEMENT, ORGANIZATION AND CONTROL
University of Wisconsin-Madison
1155 Observatory Dr.
Madison, WI 53706
PH: (608)262-4239
FX: (608)263-0477
Concerned with cost containment.

CENTER FOR HEALTH ADMINISTRATION STUDIES
e-mail: chas@uchichago.edu
University of Chicago
969 E. 60th St.
Chicago, IL 60637
PH: (773)702-7104
FX: (773)702-7222

CENTER FOR HEALTH ECONOMICS RESEARCH
e-mail: jan@her-cher.org
300 Fifth Ave., 6th Floor
Waltham, MA 02154
PH: (617)487-0200
FX: (617)487-0202

Studies the financing of Medicare.

CENTER FOR HEALTH POLICY RESEARCH AND EDUCATION
e-mail: match001@mc.duke.edu
Duke University
125 Old Chemistry Bldg.
Box 90253
Durham, NC 27708
PH: (919)684-3023
FX: (919)684-6246

CENTER FOR HEALTH RESEARCH
e-mail: ajacox@cms.cc.wayne.edu
url: http://www.comm.wayne.edu/nursing/nursing.html
Wayne State University
College of Nursing
5557 Cass Ave.
Detroit, MI 48202
PH: (313)577-4134
FX: (313)577-5777
Studies innovation in health care organization and financing.

CENTER FOR MEDICAL ECONOMICS STUDIES
360 Huntington Ave.
Boston, MA 02115
PH: (617)373-2884

CENTER FOR RESEARCH IN AMBULATORY HEALTH CARE ADMINISTRATION
url: http://www.mgma.com/
104 Inverness Terrace E
Englewood, CO 80112-5306
PH: (303)397-7879
FX: (303)397-1827
Fields of research include medical group practice management.

CHANGING MEDICAL MARKETS: THE MONTHLY NEWSLETTER FOR EXECUTIVES IN THE HEALTHCARE AND BIOTECHNOLOGY INDUSTRIES
url: http://www.thetareports.co.uk
2433 Main St., Suite One
Rocky Hill, CT 06067-2539
PH: 800-995-1550
FX: (860)257-0014
Theta Corp. Monthly. $295.00 per year. Newsletter on medical marketing, new products, new technology, company mergers, etc.

CHOOSING AND USING AN HMO
e-mail: info@bloomberg.com
url: http://www.bloomberg.com
Post Office Box 888
Princeton, NJ 08542-0888
PH: 800-388-2749
FX: (609)279-5967
Ellyn Spragins. Bloomberg Press. 1997. $19.95. Includes advice on finding a doctor, going outside the plan, and avoiding excess costs. (Bloomberg Personal Library.)

CLINICAL LAB LETTER
url: http://www.lrpub.com
227 E. Washington Square
Philadelphia, PA 19106-3780
PH: 800-777-2295
FX: (215)238-4227
Lippincott-Raven Publishers. Semimonthly. Individuals, $296.00 per year; institutions, $350.00 per year. Newsletter on clinical laboratory management, safety, and technology.

CLINICAL LABORATORY MANAGEMENT ASSOCIATION
989 Old Eagle School Rd., Suite 815
Wayne, PA 19087
PH: (610)995-9580
FX: (610)995-9568

Members are individuals who manage or supervise clinical laboratories.

CLINICAL LABORATORY MANAGEMENT REVIEW
url: http://www.wwilkins.com
351 W. Camden St.
Baltimore, MD 21201-2436
PH: 800-222-3790
FX: (410)528-4422
Clinical Laboratory Management Association. Williams and Wilkins. Bimonthly. Individuals, $86.00 per year; institutions, $119.00 per year.

CLR: CLINICAL LABORATORY REFERENCE
Five Paragon Drive
Montvale, NJ 07645-1742
PH: 800-232-7379
FX: (201)573-4956
Medical Economics Co., Inc. Annual. $32.00. Describes diagnostic reagents, test systems, instruments, equipment, and services for medical laboratories. Includes "Directory of Diagnostic Marketers" and "Index of Tests, Equipment, and Services."

THE COMPETITIVE EDGE
url: http://www.hmodata.com
Post Office Box 4366
St. Paul, MN 55104
PH: 800-844-3351
FX: (612)584-5698
InterStudy Publications. Semiannual. Price on application. Provides highly detailed statistical, directory, and market information on U.S. health maintenance organizations. Consists of three parts: *The HMO Directory, The HMO Industry Report,* and *The Regional Market Analysis.* Emphasis is on market research. (InterStudy Publications is a division of Decision Resources, Inc., http://www.dresources.com/)

THE COMPLETE BOOK OF INSURANCE: THE CONSUMER'S GUIDE TO INSURING YOUR LIFE, HEALTH, PROPERTY, AND INCOME
e-mail: customer.service@mcgraw-hill.com
url: http://www.mhhe.com
1333 Burr Ridge Parkway
Burr Ridge, IL 60521
PH: 800-634-3966
FX: 800-926-9495
Ben G. Baldwin. Irwin/McGraw-Hill. 1996. $24.95. Revised edition. Provides basic information and advice on various kinds of insurance: life, health, property (fire), disability, long-term care, automobile, liability, and annuities.

COMPULSORY HEALTH INSURANCE: THE CONTINUING AMERICAN DEBATE
88 Post Rd. W.
Westport, CT 06881
PH: 800-225-5800
FX: (203)222-1502
Ronald L. Numbers, editor. Greenwood Publishing Group Inc. 1982. $49.95.

THE CONSUMER HEALTH INFORMATION SOURCE BOOK
e-mail: info@oryxpress.com
url: http://www.oryxpress.com
4041 N. Central Ave.
Phoenix, AZ 85012-3397
PH: 800-279-6799
FX: 800-279-4663
Alan Rees, editor. Oryx Press. 1997. $59.50. Fifth edition. Bibliography of current literature and guide to organizations.

CONSUMER INSITE
e-mail: info@informationaccess.com
url: http://www.iac-insite.com

PH: 800-419-0313
FX: (415)378-5368
Information Access Co. A fee-based Web site based on IAC's online service, Magazine Database. Provides searching of about 350 popular periodicals on a wide variety of topics. Includes indexing of reviews and product evaluations. Time span is five years, with daily updates. Fees: Apply.

CONSUMERS' DIRECTORY OF CONTINUING CARE RETIREMENT COMMUNITIES
e-mail: info@aahsa.org
url: http://www.aahsa.org
901 E St., N. W., Suite 500
Washington, DC 20004-2011
PH: 800-508-9442
FX: (202)783-2255
American Association of Homes and Services for the Aging. 1997. $33.50. Contains information on fees, services, and accreditation of about 500 U. S. retirement facilities providing lifetime housing, meals, and health care. Introductory text discusses factors to be considered in selecting a continuing care community.

CONSUMERS' GUIDE TO HEALTH PLANS
733 15th St., N. W., Suite 820
Washington, DC 20005
PH: (202)347-7283
FX: (202)347-4000
Center for the Study of Services. 1996. $12.00. Revised edition. Presents the results of a consumer survey on satisfaction with specific managed care health insurance plans, and related information. Includes "Top-Rated Plans," "Health Plans That Chose Not to Have Their Members Surveyed," and other lists. General advice is provided on choosing a plan, finding a good doctor, getting good care, etc.

CONTEMPORARY LONG TERM CARE
e-mail: cltc1@aol.com
url: http://www.billcom.com
355 Park Ave. South, 3rd Fl.
New York, NY 10010-1789
PH: 800-266-4712
FX: (212)592-6339
Bill Communications, Inc. Monthly. $60.00 per year. Edited for the long term health care industry, including retirement centers with life care, continuing care communities, and nursing homes.

CONTEMPORARY LONG TERM CARE FAX DIRECTORY
e-mail: cltcl@aol.com
url: http://www.billcom.com
355 Park Ave. South, 3rd Fl.
New York, NY 10010-1789
PH: 800-266-4712
FX: (212)867-0019
Bill Communications, Inc. Annual. $27.50. Lists over 900 manufacturers and suppliers of equipment, products, and services for retirement communities and nursing homes. Formerly *Contemporary Administration for Long-Term Care Product Directory and Buyer's Guide.*

THE CONTINUING CARE RETIREMENT COMMUNITY, A GUIDEBOOK FOR CONSUMERS
e-mail: info@ahsa.org
url: http://www.aahsa.org
901 E St., N. W., Suite 500
Washington, DC 20004-2011
PH: 800-508-9442
FX: (202)783-2255
American Association of Homes and Services for the Aging. 1993. $10.45. Provides information for the evaluation of continuing care retirement communities and nursing facilities, including services and finances.

CREDIT CONSIDERATIONS: FINANCIAL AND CREDIT CHARACTERISTICS OF SELECTED INDUSTRIES, VOLUME ONE
url: http://www.rmahq.org
One Liberty Place, Suite 2300
1650 Market St.
Philadelphia, PA 19103
PH: 800-677-7621
FX: (215)446-4100
Robert Morris Associates. Looseleaf. $115.00. Provides financial characteristics, credit risk appraisal, and general description of 44 industries or businesses. An appendix outlines six forms of financing.

CREDIT CONSIDERATIONS: FINANCIAL AND CREDIT CHARACTERISTICS OF SELECTED INDUSTRIES, VOLUME TWO
url: http://www.rmahq.org
One Liberty Place, Suite 2300
1650 Market St.
Philadelphia, PA 19103
PH: 800-677-7621
FX: (215)446-4100
Robert Morris Associates. Looseleaf. $130.00. Provides financial characteristics, credit risk appraisal, and general description of 37 industries, businesses, professions, governments or institutions. An appendix outlines four methods of financing.

CUMULATIVE INDEX TO NURSING AND ALLIED HEALTH LITERATURE
e-mail: cinahl@cinahl.com
url: http://www.cinahl.com
P.O. Box 871
Glendale, CA 91209-0871
PH: 800-959-7167
FX: (818)546-5679
CINAHL Information Systems. Bimonthly. $315.00 per year. Annual cumulation.

CURRENT CONTENTS SEARCH
3501 Market St.
Philadelphia, PA 19104
PH: 800-386-4474
FX: (215)386-2911
Institute for Scientific Information. Provides online abstracts of articles listed in the tables of contents of about 7,000 journals. Coverage is very broad, including science, social science, life science, technology, engineering, industry, agriculture, the environment, economics, and arts and humanities. Time period is two years, with weekly updates. Inquire as to online cost and availability.

DENTAL DEALERS OF AMERICA
123 S. Broad St., Suite 2531
Philadelphia, PA 19109-1025
PH: (215)731-9975
FX: (215)731-9984

DENTAL ECONOMICS
url: http://w.pennwell.com
P.O. Box 3408
Tulsa, OK 74101
PH: 800-752-9764
FX: (918)831-9497
Pennwell Publishing Co., Dental Economics Div. Monthly. $75.00 per year.

DENTAL GROUP MANAGEMENT ASSOCIATION
c/o Ann Pakalski
North Point Dental Group
7040 N. Port Washington
Glendale, WI 53217
PH: (414)224-1020
FX: (414)251-6148

DENTAL LAB PRODUCTS
e-mail: medec.com
url: http://www.medec.com
Five Paragon Dr.
Montvale, NJ 07645-1742
PH: 800-232-7379
FX: (201)573-1045
Medical Economics Co., Inc. Bimonthly. $27.00 per year. Edited for dental laboratory managers. Covers new products and technical developments.

DENTAL MANUFACTURERS OF AMERICA
e-mail: staff@dmanews.org
Fidelity Bldg.
123 S. Broad St., Suite 2531
Philadelphia, PA 19109-1025
PH: (215)731-9975
FX: (215)731-9984

DENTAL PRACTICE AND FINANCE
Five Paragon Dr.
Montvale, NJ 07645-1742
PH: 800-232-7379
FX: (201)573-4956
Medical Economics Publishing Co., Inc. Bimonthly. Controlled circulation. Covers practice management and financial topics for dentists. Includes investment advice.

DENTAL PRODUCTS REPORT EUROPE
Five Paragon Dr.
Montvale, NJ 07645-1742
PH: (201)358-7200
FX: (201)573-4956
Medical Economics Co., Inc. Bimonthly. $30.00 per year. Covers new dental products for the European market.

DENTAL PRODUCTS REPORT: TRENDS IN INDUSTRY
Five Paragon Dr.
Montvale, NJ 07645-1742
PH: 800-232-7379
FX: (201)573-4956
Medical Economics Co., Inc. 11 times a year. $90.00 per year. Provides information on new dental products, technology, and trends in dentistry.

DENTAL TRADE NEWSLETTER
4222 King St.
Alexandria, VA 22302
PH: (703)379-7755
American Dental Trade Association. Bimonthly.

DENTISTRY TODAY: EQUIPMENT BUYERS' GUIDE
26 Park St.
Montclair, NJ 07042
PH: (201)783-3190
FX: (201)783-6835
Dentistry Today, Inc. Annual. Price on application. Provides purchasing information for more than 500 dental products.

DETWILER DIRECTORY OF HEALTH AND MEDICAL RESOURCES
Post Office Box 15308
Warsaw, IN 46581-1533
PH: (219)749-6534
FX: (219)493-6717
S. M. Detwiler & Associates, Inc. Annual. $200.00. Lists sources of information relating to the healthcare industry, including government agencies, medical experts, directories, newsletters, research groups, associations, and mailing list producers. Four indexes are provided: subject, publication, service, and acronym.

DICTIONARY OF AMERICAN MEDICAL BIOGRAPHY
88 Post Rd. W.
Westport, CT 06881

PH: 800-225-5800
FX: (203)222-1502
Martin Kaufman and others. Greenwood Publishing Group Inc. 1984. $195.00. Two volumes. Vol. one, $100.00; vol. two, $100.00.

DICTIONARY OF INSURANCE
4720 Boston Way
Lanham, MD 20706
PH: 800-462-6420
FX: (301)459-2118
Lewis E. Davids. Rowman and Littlefield Publishers, Inc. 1990. $17.95. Seventh revised edition.

DICTIONARY OF INSURANCE TERMS
250 Wireless Blvd.
Hauppauge, NY 11788
PH: 800-645-3476
FX: (516)434-3217
Harvey W. Rubin. Barron's Educational Series, Inc. 1995. $10.95. Third edition. Defines terms in a wide variety of insurance fields. Price on application.

DIRECTORY OF HOSPITAL PERSONNEL
Five Paragon Drive
Montvale, NJ 07645-1742
PH: 800-232-7379
FX: (201)573-4956
Medical Economics Co., Inc. Annual. $310.00. Lists over 200,000 healthcare professionals in 7,100 U.S. hospitals. Geographic arrangement, with indexes by personnel, hospital name, and bed size.

DIRECTORY OF INVESTOR-OWNED HOSPITALS, RESIDENTIAL TREATMENT FACILITIES AND CENTERS, HOSPITAL MANAGEMENT COMPANIES AND HEALTH SYSTEMS
1405 N. Pierce St., Suite 308
Little Rock, AR 72207
PH: (501)661-9555
FX: (501)663-4903
Federation of American Health Systems. Annual. $125.00. Supersedes *Directory of Investor-Owned Hospitals.*

DIRECTORY OF NURSING HOMES
300 East Lombard St., Suite 750
Baltimore, MD 21202
PH: (410)576-9600
FX: (410)539-5220
HCIA: Health Care Investment Analysts. Annual. $249.00. Provides information on over 16,000 licensed nursing homes in the U.S. Includes names of administrative personnel, admission requirements, number of beds, ownership, and certification information. (Formerly published by Oryx Press.)

DIRECTORY OF PHYSICIANS IN THE UNITED STATES
e-mail: amnews-comments@ama.assn.org
url: http://www.ama-assn.org
515 North State St.
Chicago, IL 60610-4377
PH: 800-621-8335
FX: (312)464-5600
American Medical Association. Biennial. $545.00. Four volumes. Brief information for more than 686,000 physicians. Formerly*American Medical Directory.*

DISPOSABLE MEDICAL SUPPLIES
625 Ave. of the Americas
New York, NY 10011
PH: 800-346-3787
FX: (212)645-7681
Available from FIND/SVP, Inc. 1996. $3,500.00. Published by the Freedonia Group. Market data with forecasts to 2000 and 2004. Includes disposable syringes, catheters, kits, trays, etc.

DISTRESSED HOSPITAL QUARTERLY
300 East Lombard St., Suite 750
Baltimore, MD 21202
PH: 800-568-3282
FX: (410)783-0575
HCIA: Health Care Investment Analysts. Quarterly. $500.00 per year. Names and provides information on specific distressed hospitals, which are defined as those "exhibiting substantial adverse changes" in such factors as capital structure, profitability, liquidity, payor mix, and utilization.

DIVISION OF HEALTH SERVICES RESEARCH AND POLICY
e-mail: krale001@maroon-tc.umn.edu
url: http://ihsr-hsr.umn.edu
University of Minnesota
P.O. Box 729 UMCH
Minneapolis, MN 55455
PH: (612)624-6151
FX: (612)624-2196
Fields of research include health insurance, consumer choice of health plans, quality of care, and long-term care.

DIVISION OF LABORATORY MEDICINE
University of Wisconsin-Madison
Clinical Science Center, Room B4-249
600 Highland Ave.
Madison, WI 53792
PH: (608)263-7507
FX: (608)263-1568
Conducts research relating to clinical laboratory instrument design and applications.

DRG HANDBOOK (DIAGNOSIS RELATED GROUP): COMPARATIVE CLINICAL AND FINANCIAL STANDARDS
300 East Lombard St., Suite 750
Baltimore, MD 21202
PH: 800-568-3282
FX: (410)539-5220
HCIA: Health Care Investment Analysts. Annual. $399.00. Presents summary data for all 477 DRGs (diagnosis-related groups) and the 23 MDCs (major diagnostic categories), based on information from more than 11 million Medicare patients. Ranks DRG information for 100 hospital groups according to number of beds, payor mix, case-mix, system affiliation, and profitability. Emphasis is financial. Formerly *Medicare DRG Handbook.*

EBRI DATABOOK ON EMPLOYEE BENEFITS
e-mail: publications@ebri.org
url: http://www.ebri.org
2121 K St., N. W., Suite 600
Washington, DC 20037-1986
PH: (202)659-0670
FX: (202)775-6312
Employee Benefit Research Institute. 1995. $35.95. Third edition. Contains more than 350 tables and charts presenting data on employee benefits in the U.S., including pensions, health insurance, social security, and medicare. Includes a glossary of employee benefit terms.

ECONOMIC TRENDS
url: http://www.aha.org
One North Franklin St.
Chicago, IL 60606
PH: (312)422-3527
FX: (312)422-4651
American Hospital Association. Quarterly. Members, $85.00 per year; non-members $135.00 per year. Provides statistics and analysis relating to hospital utilization, finances, and staffing.

ECRI: EMERGENCY CARE RESEARCH INSTITUTE
e-mail: ecri@hscl.org
5200 Butler Pike
Plymouth Meeting, PA 19462
PH: (610)825-6000
FX: (610)834-1275
Major research area is health care technology.

ELECTROMEDICAL EQUIPMENT AND IRRADIATION EQUIPMENT, INCLUDING X-RAY
url: http://www.census.gov
Washington, DC 20233-0800
PH: (301)457-4100
FX: (301)457-3842
U.S. Bureau of the Census. Annual. Contains shipment quantity, value of shipment, export, and import data. (Current Industrial Report No. MA-38R.)

EMBASE
655 Ave. of the Americas
New York, NY 10010
PH: (212)989-5800
FX: (212)633-3975
Elsevier Science, Inc. Worldwide medical literature, 1974 to present. Weekly updates. Inquire as to online cost and availability.

EMPLOYEE BENEFIT RESEARCH INSTITUTE
e-mail: dallassalisbury@ebri.org
url: http://www.ebri.org
2121 K St., N. W., Suite 600
Washington, DC 20037-1896
PH: (202)659-0670
FX: (202)775-6312
Conducts research on employee benefits, including various kinds of pensions, individual retirement accounts (IRAs), health insurance, social security, and long-term health care benefits.

EMPLOYEE BENEFITS IN MEDIUM AND LARGE PRIVATE ESTABLISHMENTS
Washington, DC 20402
PH: (202)512-1800
FX: (202)512-2250
Available from U.S. Government Printing Office. Biennial. Issued by Bureau of Labor Statistics, U.S. Department of Labor. Provides data on benefits provided by companies with 100 or more employees. Covers benefits for both full-time and part-time workers, including health insurance, pensions, a wide variety of paid time-off policies (holidays, vacations, personal leave, maternity leave, etc.), and other fringe benefits.

EMPLOYEE BENEFITS IN SMALL PRIVATE ESTABLISHMENTS
Washington, DC 20402
PH: (202)512-1800
FX: (202)512-2250
Available from U.S. Government Printing Office. Biennial. Issued by Bureau of Labor Statistics, U.S. Department of Labor. Supplies data on a wide variety of benefits provided by companies with fewer than 100 employees. Includes statistics for both full-time and part-time workers.

ENCYCLOPEDIA OF HEALTH INFORMATION SOURCES
835 Penobscot Bldg.
Detroit, MI 48226-4094
PH: 800-877-GALE
FX: (313)961-6083
Gale Research Inc. 1993. $175.00. Second edition. Both print and nonprint sources of information are listed for 450 health-related topics.

ENCYCLOPEDIA OF MEDICAL ORGANIZATIONS AND AGENCIES
835 Penobscot Bldg.
Detroit, MI 48226-4094
PH: 800-877-GALE
FX: 800-414-5043
Gale Research Inc. 1997. $239.00. Seventh edition. Information

on over 14,000 public and private organizations in medicine and related fields.

ENCYCLOPEDIA OF OCCUPATIONAL HEALTH AND SAFETY 1983
e-mail: webinfo@ilo.org
url: http://www.ilo.org
1828 L St., N.W., Suite 801
Washington, DC 20036
PH: (202)653-7652
FX: (202)653-7687
International Labor Office. 1991. $270.00. Third revised edition. Two volumes.

ENCYCLOPEDIA OF PHYSICAL SCIENCES AND ENGINEERING INFORMATION SOURCES
835 Penobscot Bldg.
Detroit, MI 48226-4094
PH: 800-877-GALE
FX: (313)961-6083
Gale Research Inc. Irregular. $155.00. Includes print, electronic, and other information sources for a wide range of scientific, technical, and engineering topics.

ENVIRONMENTAL TOXICOLOGY AND WATER QUALITY: AN INTERNATIONAL JOURNAL
605 Third Ave.
New York, NY 10158-0012
PH: 800-225-5945
FX: (212)850-6088
John Wiley and Sons, Inc. Journals Div. Quarterly. $395.00 per year. Formerly *Toxicity Assessment*.

ERISA: A COMPREHENSIVE GUIDE
605 Third Ave.
New York, NY 10158-0012
PH: 800-225-5945
FX: (212)850-6088
Martin Wald and David E. Kenty. John Wiley & Sons, Inc. 1991. $140.00. Provides a detailed analysis of the Employee Retirement Income Security Act of 1974 (ERISA). Covers pension plans, health and welfare plans, and other employee plans regulated by ERISA. Discusses the requirements of the Consolidated Omnibus Budget Reconciliation Act (COBRA) relative to providing health benefits for terminated or retired employees. Supplement available.

EXCERPTA MEDICA: BIOPHYSICS, BIOENGINEERING, AND MEDICAL INSTRUMENTATION
e-mail: usinfo-f@elsevier.com
url: http://www.elsevier.com
655 Ave. of the Americas
New York, NY 10010
PH: (888)437-4636
FX: (212)633-3680
Elsevier Science. 16 times a year. $1,876.00 per year. Section 27 of *Excerpta Medica*.

EXCERPTA MEDICA: HEALTH POLICY, ECONOMICS AND MANAGEMENT
e-mail: usinfo-f@elsevier.com
url: http://www.elsevier.com
655 Ave. of the Americas
New York, NY 10010
PH: (888)437-4636
FX: (212)633-3680
Elsevier Science. Bimonthly. $940.00 per year. Section 36 of *Excerpta Medica*.

EXCERPTA MEDICA: OCCUPATIONAL HEALTH AND INDUSTRIAL MEDICINE
e-mail: usinfo-f@elsevier.com
url: http://www.elsevier.com
655 Ave. of the Americas
New York, NY 10010
PH: (888)437-4636
FX: (212)633-3680
Elsevier Science. Monthly. $1,557.00 per year. Section 35 of *Excerpta Medica*.

F-D-C REPORTS
5550 Friendship Blvd., Suite One
Chevy Chase, MD 20815
PH: (301)657-9830
FX: (301)656-3094
FDC Reports, Inc. An online version of "The Gray Sheet" (medical devices), "The Pink Sheet" (pharmaceuticals), and "The Rose Sheet" (cosmetics). Contains full-text information on legal, technical, corporate, financial, and marketing developments from 1987 to date, with weekly updates. Inquire as to online cost and availability.

FACTS ON FILE DICTIONARY OF HEALTH CARE MANAGEMENT
11 Penn Plaza
New York, NY 10001
PH: 800-322-8755
FX: (212)967-9311
Joseph C. Rhea and others. Facts on File, Inc. 1988. $50.00.

FAULKNER AND GRAY'S MEDICINE AND HEALTH
url: http://www.faulknergray.com
Healthcare Information Center
1133 15th St., N.W., Suite 450
Washington, DC 20005
PH: 800-535-8403
FX: (202)828-2352
Faulkner & Gray. Weekly. $525.00 per year. Newsletter on socio-economic developments relating to the health care industry. Formerly *McGraw-Hill's Washington Report on Medicine and Health*.

FDC REPORTS, "THE BLUE SHEET": HEALTH POLICY AND BIOMEDICAL RESEARCH
5550 Friendship Blvd., Suite One
Chevy Chase, MD 20815-7278
PH: 800-332-2181
FX: (301)986-4495
FDC Reports, Inc. Weekly. $390.00 per year. Newsletter. Emphasis is on news of medical research agencies and institutions, especially the National Institutes of Health (NIH).

FDC REPORTS, "THE GRAY SHEET": MEDICAL DEVICES, DIAGNOSTICS, AND INSTRUMENTATION REPORTS
5550 Friendship Blvd., Suite One
Chevy Chase, MD 20815-7278
PH: 800-332-2181
FX: (301)986-4495
FDC Reports, Inc. Weekly. $630.00 per year. Newsletter. Provides industry and financial news, including a medical sector stock index. Monitors regulatory developments at the Center for Devices and Radiological Health of the U.S. Food and Drug Administration.

THE FINANCIAL MANAGEMENT OF HOSPITALS
Publications Service Center
One N. Franklin, Suite 1700
Chicago, IL 60106-3491
PH: (312)424-2800
FX: (312)424-0014
Howard J. Berman and others. Health Administration Press. 1992. $60.00. Eighth edition.

**FITCH HOSPITAL AND OTHER NON-PROFIT
   INSTITUTIONAL RATINGS**
One State Street Plaza
New York, NY 10004
PH: 800-753-4824
FX: (212)480-4435
Fitch Investors Service. Annual.

FUNDAMENTALS OF EMPLOYEE BENEFIT PROGRAMS
e-mail: publications@ebri.org
url: http://www.ebri.org
2121 K St., N. W., Suite 600
Washington, DC 20037-1986
PH: (202)659-0670
FX: (202)775-6312
Employee Benefit Research Institute. 1996. $29.95. Fifth edition.
Provides basic explanation of employee benefit programs in both
the private and public sectors, including health insurance, pension plans, retirement planning, social security, and long-term
care insurance.

**FUNDAMENTALS OF STRATEGIC PLANNING FOR
   HEALTHCARE ORGANIZATIONS**
e-mail: getinfo@haworth.com
url: http://www.haworth.com
10 Alice St.
Binghamton, NY 13904-1580
PH: 800-429-6784
FX: 800-895-0582
Stan Williamson and others. Haworth Press, Inc. 1996. $34.95.

GERIATRIC CARE NEWS
7435 S.E. 71st St.
Mercer Island, WA 98040
PH: (206)232-9689
Frances Greer, editor. DRS Geriatric Publishing Co. Monthly.
$89.00 per year. Latest information for health care professionals
in the geriatric field. Formerly *Geriatric and Residential Care
Newsmonthly.*

GLOBALBASE
e-mail: cemarketing@iacnet.com
url: http://www.iacnet.com
362 Lakeside Dr.
Foster City, CA 94404
PH: 800-321-6388
FX: (650)358-4759
Information Access Co. Provides more than one million online
summaries of business, industrial, and economic news reports
from more than 1,000 publications worldwide. Covers a wide
range of material appearing in international trade journals, professional magazines, and newspapers. Time period is 1984 to
date, with weekly updates. Inquire as to online cost and availability.

**THE GRAY SHEET: MEDICAL DEVICES, DIAGNOSTICS,
   AND INSTRUMENTATION REPORTS**
e-mail: fdcr@fdcr.com
url: http://www.fdcr.com
5550 Friendship Blvd., Suite One
Chevy Chase, MD 20815-7278
PH: 800-332-2181
FX: (301)664-7248
F-D-C Reports, Inc. Weekly. $775.00 per year. Newsletter on
new medical devices, Food and Drug Administration (FDA) regulations, industry trends, and financial matters. Includes medical
device stock price index (MDDI Index).

GROUP PRACTICE JOURNAL
e-mail: fredh@amga.org
1422 Duke St.
Alexandria, VA 22314-3430
PH: (703)838-0033
FX: (703)548-1890

American Group Practice Association. Bimonthly. $65.00 per
year.

**GUIDE TO HEALTH INSURANCE FOR PEOPLE WITH
   MEDICARE**
7500 Security Blvd.
C-3-11-07
Baltimore, MD 21244
U.S. Health Care Financing Administration. Annual. Free. Con-
tains detailed information on private health insurance as a sup-
plement to Medicare.

THE GUIDE TO THE NURSING HOME INDUSTRY
300 East Lombard St., Suite 750
Baltimore, MD 21202
PH: 800-568-3282
FX: (410)539-5220
HCIA: Health Care Investment Analysts. Annual. $249.00. Con-
tains aggregate financial and operating data and 18 key performance indicators, based on information from more than 15,000
nursing homes. A review of major industry trends is provided.

**GUIDEBOOK TO MANAGED CARE AND PRACTICE
   MANAGEMENT TERMINOLOGY**
e-mail: getinfo@haworth.com
url: http://www.haworth.com
10 Alice St.
Binghamton, NY 13904-1580
PH: 800-429-6784
FX: 800-895-0582
Norman Winegar. Haworth Press, Inc. 1998. $39.95. Provides
definitions of managed care "terminology, jargon, and concepts."

**HANDBOOK: A DIRECTORY OF HEALTH CARE
   MEETINGS AND CONVENTIONS**
5775 Peachtree-Dunwoody Rd., Suite 500-G
Atlanta, GA 30342
PH: (404)252-3663
FX: (404)252-0774
Healthcare Convention and Healthcare Exhibitors Association.
Semiannual. Free to members; non-members, $168.00 per year.
Lists more than 1,600 health care meetings, most of which have
an exhibit program.

HANDBOOK OF INDUSTRIAL TOXICOLOGY
192 Lexington Ave, Suite 603
New York, NY 10016
PH: 800-786-3659
FX: (212)889-1537
E. R. Plunkett, editor. Chemical Publishing Co., Inc. 1987.
$100.00.

**HANDBOOK OF TOXIC AND HAZARDOUS CHEMICALS
   AND CARCINOGENS**
369 Fairview Ave.
Westwood, NJ 07675
PH: (201)666-2121
FX: (201)666-5111
Marshall Sittig. Noyes Data Corp,. 1992. $197.00. Third edition.
Two volumes.

**HANDBOOK OF U.S. LABOR STATISTICS: EMPLOYMENT,
   EARNINGS, PRICES, PRODUCTIVITY, AND OTHER
   LABOR DATA**
e-mail: info@bernan.com
url: http://www.bernan.com
4611-F Assembly Drive
Lanham, MD 20706-4391
PH: 800-274-4447
FX: 800-865-3450
Eva E. Jacobs, editor. Bernan Associates. Annual. $65.00. Based
on *Handbook of Labor Statistics,* formerly issued by the Bureau
of Labor Statistics, U.S. Department of Labor. Includes the Bureau's projections of employment in the U.S. by industry and oc-

cupation. Provides a wide variety of data on the work force, prices, fringe benefits, and consumer expenditures.

HAYES DIRECTORY OF DENTAL SUPPLY HOUSES
4229 Birch St.
Newport Beach, CA 92660
PH: (714)756-9063
FX: (714)756-0921
Edward N. Hayes. Annual. $80.00. Lists about 700 dental supply houses.

HAYES DIRECTORY OF MEDICAL SUPPLY
4229 Birch St.
Newport Beach, CA 92660
PH: (714)756-9063
FX: (714)756-0921
Edward N. Hayes. Annual. $200.00 per year. Lists 5,100 medical supply houses. Formerly *Hayes Directory of Physician and Hospital Supply Houses.*

HAZARDOUS AND TOXIC MATERIALS: SAFE HANDLING AND DISPOSAL
605 Third Ave.
New York, NY 10158-0012
PH: 800-526-5368
FX: (212)850-6088
Howard H. Fawcett. John Wiley and Sons, Inc. 1988. $110.00. Second edition.

HEALTH AGAINST WEALTH: HMOS AND THE BREAKDOWN OF MEDICAL TRUST
url: http://www.hmco.com
222 Berkeley St.
Boston, MA 02116
PH: 800-225-3362
FX: (617)227-5409
George Anders. Houghton Mifflin Co. 1996. $24.95. The author, a *Wall Street Journal* reporter, presents the negative side of HMO cost cutting.

HEALTH ALLIANCE ALERT
url: http://www.faulknergray.com
Healthcare Information Center
1133 15th St., N.W., Suite 450
Washington, DC 20005
PH: 800-535-8403
FX: (202)828-2352
Faulkner & Gray. Biweekly. $450.00 per year. Newsletter. Formerly *Health Business.*

HEALTH CARE COST CONTAINMENT
2715 N. Charles St.
Baltimore, MD 21218-4319
PH: 800-537-5487
FX: (410)516-6998
Karen Davis and others. Johns Hopkins University Press. 1990. $48.00.

HEALTH CARE COSTS
24 Hartwell Ave.
Lexington, MA 02173
PH: (617)863-5100
FX: (617)860-6332
DRI/McGraw-Hill. Quarterly. $605.00 per year. Cost indexes for hospitals, nursing homes, and home healthcare agencies.

HEALTH CARE ECONOMICS
e-mail: cbutler@delmar.com
url: http://www.thomson.com/delmar/default.htm
Albany, NY 12212-5015
PH: 800-347-7707
FX: (518)459-3552
Paul J. Feldstein. Delmar Publishers, Inc. 1993. $47.50. Fourth edition.

HEALTH CARE FACILITY MANAGEMENT
4025 West Peterson Ave.
Chicago, IL 60646-6085
PH: 800-248-3248
FX: 800-224-8299
Commerce Clearing House, Inc. Two looseleaf volumes. $570.00 per year, including biweekly updates. Reports on federal and state laws and regulations affecting the day-to-day operation of hospitals, nursing homes, and other health care facilities.

HEALTH CARE FINANCING REVIEW
Washington, DC 20402
PH: (202)512-1800
FX: (202)512-2250
Available from U.S. Government Printing Office. Quarterly. $30.00 per year. Issued by the Health Care Financing Administration, U.S. Department of Health and Human Services. Presents articles by professionals in the areas of health care costs and financing.

HEALTH CARE PRODUCTS AND REMEDIES
e-mail: catalog@findsvp.com
url: http://www.findsvp.com
625 Ave. of the Americas
New York, NY 10011-2002
PH: 800-346-3787
FX: (212)807-2716
Available from FIND/SVP, Inc. 1997. $600.00 each. Consists of market reports published by Simmons Market Research Bureau on each of about 25 health care product categories. Examples are cold remedies, contraceptives, hearing aids, bandages, headache remedies, eyeglasses, contact lenses, and vitamins. Each report covers buying patterns and demographics.

HEALTH CARE RESOURCE MANAGEMENT SOCIETY
e-mail: 102546.3221@compuserve.com
PO Box 29253
Cincinnati, OH 45229-0253
PH: (513)520-1058
FX: (513)872-6158
Members are materials management (purchasing) personnel in hospitals and the healthcare industry. The Society is concerned with hospital costs, distribution, logistics, recycling, and inventory management.

HEALTH CARE STRATEGIC MANAGEMENT: THE NEWSLETTER FOR HOSPITAL STRATEGIES
e-mail: sandyc@businessword.com
5350 S. Roslyn St., Suite 400
Englewood, CO 80111-2145
PH: (303)290-8500
FX: (303)290-9025
Business Word, Inc. Monthly. $249.00 per year. Planning, marketing and resource allocation.

HEALTH CARE, TECHNOLOGY, AND THE COMPETITIVE ENVIRONMENT
88 Post Rd., W.
Westport, CT 06881-5007
PH: 800-225-5800
FX: (203)222-1502
Henry P. Brehm and Ross M. Mullner, editors. Greenwood Publishing Group, Inc. 1989. $65.00.

HEALTH DATA MANAGEMENT
11 Penn Plaza, 17th Fl.
New York, NY 10001
PH: 800-535-8403
FX: (212)564-8879
Faulkner & Gray, Inc. Monthly. $98.00 per year. Covers the management and automation of clinical data and health care insurance claims. Includes information on claims processors and third-party administrators.

HEALTH DEVICES ALERTS [ONLINE]
5200 Butler Pike
Plymouth Meeting, PA 19462
PH: (610)825-6000
FX: (610)834-1275
ECRI. Provides online reports of medical equipment defects, problems, failures, misuses, and recalls. Time period is 1977 to date, with weekly updates. Inquire as to online cost and availability.

HEALTH DEVICES ALERTS: A SUMMARY OF REPORTED PROBLEMS, HAZARDS, RECALLS, AND UPDATES
5200 Butler Pike
Plymouth Meeting, PA 19462
PH: (610)825-6000
FX: (610)834-1275
ECRI (Emergency Care Research Institute). Weekly. $595.00 per year. Newsletter containing reviews of health equipment problems. Includes *Health Devices Alerts Action Items, Health Devices Alerts Abstracts, Health Devices Alerts FDA Data, Health Devices Alerts Implants, Health Devices Alerts Hazards Bulletin.*

HEALTH DEVICES ALERTS [CD-ROM]
5200 Butler Pike
Plymouth Meeting, PA 19462
PH: (610)825-6000
FX: (610)834-1275
ECRI. Weekly. $2,450.00 per year. Provides CD-ROM reports of medical equipment defects, problems, failures, misuses, and recalls.

HEALTH DEVICES SOURCEBOOK
e-mail: ecri@hsic.org
ECRI
5200 Butler Pike
Plymouth Meeting, PA 19462
PH: (610)825-6000
FX: (610)834-1275
Emergency Care Research Institute. Annual. $365.00. Lists over 6,000 manufacturers of a wide variety of medical equipment and supplies, including clinical laboratory equipment, testing instruments, surgical instruments, patient care equipment, etc.

HEALTH AND ENVIRONMENT IN AMERICA'S TOP-RATED CITIES: A STATISTICAL PROFILE
e-mail: dg@atscitystats.com
url: http://www.citystats.com
1355 West Palmetto Park Rd., Suite 315
Boca Raton, FL 33486-9927
PH: 800-377-7551
FX: (561)997-6756
Andrew Garoogian, editor. Universal Reference Publications. Biennial. $75.00. Covers 75 U.S. cities. Includes statistical and other data on a wide variety of topics, such as air quality, water quality, recycling, hospitals, physicians, health care costs, death rates, infant mortality, accidents, and suicides.

HEALTH FACILITIES MANAGEMENT
737 N. Michigan Ave., Suite 700
Chicago, IL 60611-2615
PH: 800-621-6902
FX: (312)951-8491
American Hospital Publishing, Inc. Monthly. $30.00 per year. Covers building maintenance and engineering for hospitals and nursing homes. (An American Hospital Association publication.)

HEALTH GRANTS AND CONTRACTS WEEKLY: SELECTED FEDERAL PROJECT OPPORTUNITIES
1101 King St., Suite 444
Alexandria, VA 22314
PH: 800-655-5597
FX: 800-645-4104
Capitol Publications, Inc. Weekly. $379.00 per year. Lists new health-related federal contracts and grants.

HEALTH INDUSTRY BUYERS GUIDE
P.O. 908
Spring House, PA 19477-0903
PH: 800-621-4432
S N Publications. Annual. $95.00. About 4,000 manufacturers of hospital and physician's supplies and equipment. Formerly *Surgical Trade Buyers Guide.*

HEALTH INDUSTRY DISTRIBUTORS ASSOCIATION
66 Canal Center Plaza, Suite 250
Alexandria, VA 22314-1591
PH: (703)549-4432
FX: (703)549-6495

HEALTH INDUSTRY MANUFACTURERS ASSOCIATION
url: http://www.himanet.com
1200 G St., N.W., Suite 400
Washington, DC 20005
PH: (202)783-8700
FX: (202)783-8750

HEALTH INDUSTRY REPRESENTATIVES ASSOCIATION
6740 E. Hampden Ave., Suite 306
Denver, CO 80224
PH: (303)756-8115
FX: (303)756-5699
Members are manufacturers' representatives working within the health care industry.

HEALTH INDUSTRY TODAY: THE MARKET LETTER FOR HEALTH CARE INDUSTRY VENDORS
e-mail: curthit@buisnessword.com
5350 S. Roslyn St., Suite 400
Englewood, CO 80111-2145
PH: (303)290-8500
FX: (303)290-9025
Business Word, Inc. Monthly. $325.00 per year.

HEALTH INSURANCE ASSOCIATION OF AMERICA
url: http://www.hiaa.org
555 13th St., N.W. Suite 600E
Washington, DC 20004-1109
PH: (202)824-1600
FX: (02))24-1722
Members are commercial health insurers. Includes a Managed Care and Group Insurance Committee, a Disability Insurance Committee, a Medicare Administration Committee, and a Long-Term Care Task Force.

HEALTH INSURANCE COMPANY FINANCIAL DATA
url: http://www/naco.com
505 Gest St.
Cincinnati, OH 45203
PH: 800-543-0874
FX: (513)721-0126
The National Underwriter Co. Annual.

HEALTH INSURANCE TERMINOLOGY: A GLOSSARY OF HEALTH INSURANCE TERMS
555 13th St., NW, No. 600
Washington, DC 20004-1109
PH: (202)223-7853
FX: (202)223-7885
Margaret Lynch, editor. Health Insurance Association of America. 1992. Price on application.

HEALTH INSURANCE UNDERWRITER
1000 Connecticut Ave., N. W., Suite 1111
Washington, DC 20036
PH: (202)223-5533
FX: (202)785-2274
National Association of Health Underwriters. 11 times a year. Members, $18.00 per year; non-members, $40.00 per year. Includes special feature issues on long-term care insurance, disabi-

lity insurance, managed health care, and insurance office management.

HEALTH LAW HANDBOOK
url: http://www.westgroup.com
155 Pfingsten Rd.
Deerfield, IL 60015
PH: 800-328-4880
FX: (847)948-8955
Alice G. Gosfield, editor. Clark Boardman Callaghan. 1992. $75.00. Periodic supplementation.

HEALTH LEGISLATION
url: http://www.faulknergray.com
Healthcare Information Center
1133 15th St., N.W., Suite 450
Washington, DC 20005
PH: 800-535-8403
FX: (202)828-2352
Faulkner & Gray. 50 times a year. $595.00 per year. Newsletter. Formerly *Health Legislation and Regulation*.

HEALTH LETTER
1600 20th St., N. W.
Washington, DC 20009
PH: (202)588-1000
FX: (202)785-3584
Sidney M. Wolfe, editor. Public Citizen Health Research Group. Monthly. $18.00 per year. Newsletter for healthcare consumers. Also known as *Public Citizen Health Letter*.

HEALTH MANAGEMENT TECHNOLOGY
6151 Powers Ferry Rd., N.W.
Atlanta, GA 30339-2491
PH: 800-443-4969
FX: (770)955-2500
Argus, Inc. Monthly. $38.00 per year. Formerly *Computers in Healthcare*.

HEALTH MARKETING QUARTERLY
10 Alice St.
Binghamton, NY 13904-1580
PH: 800-429-6784
FX: (607)722-1424
The Haworth Press, Inc. Quarterly. Individuals, $45.00 per year; institutions, $80.00 per year; libraries, $375.00 per year.

HEALTH NEWS DAILY
5550 Friendship Blvd., Suite 1
Chevy Chase, MD 20815-7278
PH: 800-332-2181
FX: (301)664-7238
FDC Reports, Inc. Daily. $1,350.00 per year. Newsletter providing broad coverage of the healthcare business, including government policy, regulation, research, finance, and insurance. Contains news of pharmaceuticals, medical devices, biotechnology, and healthcare delivery in general.

HEALTH PLANNING AND ADMINISTRATION
National Library of Medicine
8600 Rockville Pike
Bethesda, MD 20209
PH: 800-638-8480
Medlars Management Section. Provides indexing and abstracting of non-clinical literature relating to health care delivery, 1975 to date. Monthly updates. Inquire as to online cost and availability.

HEALTH POLICY INSTITUTE
e-mail: dlow@admin4.hsc.uth.tmc.edu
url: http://utsph.sph.uth.tmc.edu/www/utsph/ts/hpi.htm
University of Texas-Houston Health Science Center
P.O. 20186
Houston, TX 77225

PH: (713)500-9485
FX: (713)500-9493

HEALTH REFERENCE CENTER
362 Lakeside Drive
Foster City, CA 94404
PH: 800-227-8431
FX: (650)378-5369
Information Access Co. Monthly. $5,000.00 per year. Provides CD-ROM citations, abstracts, and selected full-text articles on many health-related subjects. Includes references to medical journals, general periodicals, newsletters, newspapers, pamphlets, and medical reference books.

HEALTH RESEARCH INSTITUTE
3538 Torino Way
Concord, CA 94518
PH: (510)676-2320
FX: (510)676-2342
Conducts applied research in health care financing and delivery of health services, with emphasis on cost containment.

HEALTH SERVICES MANAGEMENT AND POLICY
url: http://www.smp.umich.edu/
University of Michigan
109 S. Observatory St.
Ann Arbor, MI 48109-2029
PH: (313)763-9903
FX: (313)764-4338
Research fields include health care economics, health insurance, and long-term care.

HEALTH SERVICES RESEARCH AND DEVELOPMENT CENTER
e-mail: hsrdc.center@phnet.sph.jhu.edu
Johns Hopkins University
624 N. Broadway
Baltimore, MD 21205
PH: (410)955-3625
FX: (410)955-0470

HEALTHCARE CAREER DIRECTORY: NURSES AND PHYSICIANS
835 Penobscot Bldg.
Detroit, MI 48226-4094
PH: 800-877-GALE
FX: (313)961-6083
Gale Research Inc. 1993. $34.00. Second edition. Includes information on careers in nursing, family medicine, surgery, and other medical areas. Provides advice from "insiders," resume suggestions, a directory of companies that may offer entry-level positions, and a directory of career information sources. (Career Advisor Series.)

HEALTHCARE CONVENTION AND EXHIBITORS ASSOCIATION
5775 Peachtree-Dunwoody Rd., Suite 500-G
Atlanta, GA 30342
PH: (404)252-3663
FX: (404)252-0774
Promotes more effective display of health care products at professional conventions.

HEALTHCARE EXECUTIVE
One N. Franklin St., Suite 1700
Chicago, IL 60606-3491
PH: (708)450-9952
FX: (312)424-0023
American College of Healthcare Executives. Bimonthly. $50.00 per year. Focuses on critical management issues.

HEALTHCARE FINANCE FOR THE NON-FINANCIAL MANAGER: BASIC GUIDE TO FINANCIAL ANALYSIS & CONTROL
e-mail: customer.service@mcgraw-hill.com
url: http://www.mhhe.com
1333 Burr Ridge Parkway
Burr Ridge, IL 60521
PH: 800-634-3966
FX: 800-926-9495
Louis Gapenski. Irwin/McGraw-Hill. 1994. $47.50.

HEALTHCARE FINANCIAL MANAGEMENT
Two Westbrook Corporate Center, Suite 700
Westchester, IL 60154
PH: 800-252-4362
FX: (708)531-0032
Healthcare Financial Management Association. Monthly. $82.00 per year.

HEALTHCARE FINANCIAL MANAGEMENT ASSOCIATION
Two Westbrook Corporate Center, Suite 700
Westchester, IL 60154
PH: (708)531-9600
FX: (708)531-0032

HEALTHCARE FINANCING STUDY GROUP
1919 Pennsylvania Ave., N.W., Suite 800
Washington, DC 20006
PH: (202)887-1400
FX: (202)466-3215
Concerned with the provision of capital financing for health care institutions.

HEALTHCARE FORUM JOURNAL: LEADERSHIP STRATEGIES FOR HEALTHCARE EXECUTIVES
url: http://www.healthonline
425 Market St.
San Francisco, CA 94105
PH: (415)436-4300
FX: (415)356-9300
Healthcare Forum. Bimonthly. $55.00 per year.

HEALTHCARE INFORMATION MANAGEMENT
url: http://www.josseybass.com
350 Sansome St.
San Francisco, CA 94104
PH: 800-956-7739
FX: 800-605-2665
Healthcare Information and Management Systems Society. Jossey-Bass Inc. Quarterly. Formerly *Health Care Systems.* Free to librarians; individuals, $60.00 per year; institutions, $85.00 per year.

HEALTHCARE INFORMATION AND MANAGEMENT SYSTEMS SOCIETY
e-mail: himss@himss.org
232 E. Ohio St., Suite 600
Chicago, IL 60611
PH: (312)664-4467
FX: (312)664-6143

HEALTHCARE MARKETING REPORT
P.O. Box 76002
Atlanta, GA 30358-1002
PH: (404)457-6105
FX: (404)457-0049
HMR Publication Group. Monthly. $135.00 per year.

HEALTHCARE PR AND MARKETING NEWS
1201 Seven Locks Rd., Suite 300
Potomac, MD 20854
PH: 800-777-5006
FX: (301)309-3847
Phillips Business Information, Inc. Biweekly. $397.00 per year.

Newsletter on public relations and client communications for the healthcare industry.

HEALTHCARE PURCHASING NEWS: A MAGAZINE FOR HOSPITAL MATERIALS MANAGEMENT CENTRAL SERVICE, INFECTION CONTROL PRACTITIONERS
e-mail: hpn@medec.com
url: http://www.medec.com
Two Northfield Plaza, Suite 300
Northfield, IL 60093-1217
PH: 800-451-7838
FX: (847)441-3701
McKnight Medical Communications. Monthly. $44.95 per year. Edited for personnel responsible for the purchase of medical, surgical, and hospital equipment and supplies. Features new purchasing techniques and new products. Includes news of the activities of two major purchasing associations, Health Care Material Management Society and International Association of Healthcare Central Service Materiel Management.

HMO MAGAZINE (HEALTH MAINTENANCE ORGANIZATION)
1129 20th St., N.W., Suite 600
Washington, DC 20036
PH: (202)778-3247
FX: (202)331-7487
Group Health Association of America. Six times a year. $75.00 per year.

HMO PRACTICE (HEALTH MAINTENANCE ORGANIZATION)
e-mail: hmop@moran.com
900 Guaranty Bldg.
Buffalo, NY 14202
PH: (716)857-6361
FX: (716)847-0047
HMO Group. Quarterly. $150.00 per year.

HMO REPORT AND DIRECTORY
url: http://www.smgusa.com
875 N. Michigan Ave., 31st Fl.
Chicago, IL 60611
PH: 800-678-3026
FX: (312)642-9729
SMG Marketing Group, Inc. Annual. $395.00. Contains information relating to over 700 HMOs. Relevant market data is also provided.

HOSPITAL COST MANAGEMENT
url: http://www.prenhall.com
One Lake St.
Upper Saddle River, NJ 07458
PH: 800-223-1360
FX: 800-445-6991
John G. Steinle. Prentice Hall. Looseleaf. Periodic supplementation. Price on application.

HOSPITAL FINANCE ALMANAC
Two Westbrook Corporate Center, Suite 700
Westchester, IL 60154
PH: 800-252-4362
FX: (708)531-0032
Healthcare Financial Management Association. Annual. $350.00. Provides five-year data relating to the financial and operating performance of the U.S. hospital industry. A consolidation of the former *Financial Report of the Hospital Industry* and *Performance Report of the Hospital Industry.*

HOSPITAL AND HEALTH ADMINISTRATION INDEX
url: http://www.aha.org
One North Franklin St.
Chicago, IL 60606
PH: (312)422-3541
FX: (312)422-4651

American Hospital Association. Quarterly, with annual cumulation. Members, $240.00 per year; non-members, $310.00 per year. Provides indexing of the literature of health care management, organization, finance, and insurance. Covers hospitals, nursing homes, health maintenance organizations, hospices, and other health care entities. Formerly *Hospital Literature Index*.

HOSPITAL AND HEALTH SERVICES ADMINISTRATION
url: http://www.ache.org
Publications Sevice Center
One North Franklin St., Suite 1700
Chicago, IL 60606
PH: (312)424-2800
FX: (312)424-0014
Foundation of the American College of Healthcare Executives. Health Administration Press. Quarterly. $55.00 per year. Information on the latest trends, developments and innovations in the industry.

HOSPITAL PHARMACIST REPORT
Five Paragon Drive
Montvale, NJ 07645-1742
PH: 800-232-7379
FX: (201)573-4956
Medical Economics Co., Inc. Monthly. $39.00 per year. Covers both business and clinical topics for hospital pharmacists.

HOSPITAL REVENUE REPORT
11300 Rockville Pike, Suite 1100
Rockville, MD 20852-3030
PH: (301)816-8950
FX: (301)816-8945
United Communications News. 25 times a year. $379.00 per year. Newsletter. Advises hospitals on how to cut costs, increase patient revenue, and maximize Medicare income. Incorporates the former *Part A News* and *Health Care Marketer*.

HOSPITALS AND HEALTH NETWORKS
737 North Michigan Ave., Suite 700
Chicago, IL 60611-2615
PH: 800-621-6902
FX: (312)951-8491
American Hospital Publishing, Inc. Biweekly. $65.00 per year. Covers the general management of hospitals, nursing homes, and managed care organizations. Formerly *Hospitals*. (An American Hospital Association publication.)

HOUSING THE ELDERLY REPORT
8204 Fenton St.
Silver Spring, MD 20910-2889
PH: 800-666-6380
FX: (301)588-6385
Community Development Services, Inc. CD Publications. Monthly. $175.00 per year. Newsletter. Edited for retirement communities, apartment projects, and nursing homes. Covers news relative to business and property management issues.

HOW TO COVER THE GAPS IN MEDICARE: HEALTH INSURANCE AND LONG-TERM CARE OPTIONS FOR THE RETIRED
e-mail: info@aier.org
url: http://www.aier.org
Division St.
Great Barrington, MA 01230
PH: (413)528-1216
FX: (413)528-0103
Robert A. Gilmour. American Institute for Economic Research. 1997. $5.00. 11th edition. Four parts: "The Medicare Quandry," "How to Protect Yourself Against the Medigap," "Long-Term Care Options", and "End-of-Life Decisions" (living wills). Includes discussions of long-term care insurance, retirement communities, and HMO Medicare insurance. (Economic Education Bulletin.)

IAC INDUSTRY EXPRESS
e-mail: cemarketing@iacnet.com
url: http://www.iacnet.com
362 Lakeside Dr.
Foster City, CA 94404
PH: 800-321-6388
FX: (650)358-4759
Information Access Co. Industry Express is an industry-focused database providing current, full-text material appearing in trade journals, newsletters, and other business publications. A wide range of business, industrial, and technical topics are covered. Time period is the most current 30 days, with comprehensive indexing. Inquire as to online cost and availability.

IEEE ENGINEERING IN MEDICINE AND BIOLOGY MAGAZINE
345 E. 47th St.
New York, NY 10017-2394
PH: 800-678-4333
FX: (212)752-4929
Institute of Electrical and Electronics Engineers, Inc. Quarterly. Free to members; non-members, $125.00 per year. Published for biomedical engineers.

INDEPENDENT MEDICAL DISTRIBUTORS ASSOCIATION
5818 Reeds Rd.
Shawnee Mission, KS 66202
PH: (913)262-4510
FX: (913)262-0174
Members are distributors of high technology health care products.

INDEX TO HEALTH INFORMATION
e-mail: info@cispubs.com
url: http://www.cispubs.com
4520 East-West Highway, Suite 800
Bethesda, MD 20814-3389
PH: 800-638-8380
FX: (301)654-4033
Congressional Information Service, Inc. Quarterly. $945.00 per year, including two-volume annual cumulation. Provides index and abstracts covering the medical and health field in general, with emphasis on statistical sources and government documents. Service with microfiche source documents, $4,995.00 per year.

INDEX MEDICUS
Washington, DC 20402
PH: (202)512-1800
FX: (202)512-2250
National Library of Medicine. Available from U.S. Government Printing Office. Monthly. $509.00 per year. Bibliographic listing of references to current articles from approximately 3,000 of the world's biomedical journals.

INDUSTRIAL HYGIENE NEWS
e-mail: rimbach@sgi.net
8650 Babcock Blvd.
Pittsburgh, PA 15237
PH: 800-245-3182
FX: (412)369-9720
Rimbach Publishing, Inc. Seven times a year. Free to qualified personnel; others, $25.00 per year.

INDUSTRIAL HYGIENE NEWS BUYER'S GUIDE
e-mail: rimbach@sgi.net
8650 Babcock Blvd.
Pittsburgh, PA 15237
PH: 800-245-3182
FX: (412)369-9720
Rimbach Publishing, Inc. Annual. $50.00. List of about 1,000 manufacturers and suppliers of products, equipment, and services to the occupational health, industrial hygiene, and high-tech safety industry.

INDUSTRIAL SAFETY AND HEALTH MANAGEMENT
url: http://www.prenhall.com
One Lake St.
Upper Saddle River, NJ 07458
PH: 800-223-1360
FX: 800-445-6991
C. Ray Asfahl. Prentice Hall. 1995. $82.00. Third edition.

INDUSTRY NORMS AND KEY BUSINESS RATIOS. DESK TOP EDITION
url: http://www.dnb.com
One Diamond Hill Rd.
Murray Hill, NJ 07974
PH: 800-223-0141
FX: (908)665-5418
Dun and Bradstreet Corp., Business Information Services. Annual. Five volumes. $475.00 per volume. $1890.00 per set. Covers over 800 kinds of businesses, arranged by Standard Industrial Classification number. More detailed editions covering longer periods of time are also available.

INQUIRY: THE JOURNAL OF HEALTH CARE ORGANIZATION, PROVISION, AND FINANCING
Post Office Box 25399
Rochester, NY 14625
PH: (716)264-9122
FX: (716)264-9122
Finger Lakes Blue Cross and Blue Shield Association. Quarterly. Individuals, $50.00 per year; institutions, $70.00 per year.

INSTITUTE OF CERTIFIED PROFESSIONAL BUSINESS CONSULTANTS
330 S. Wells St., Suite 1422
Chicago, IL 60606-7101
PH: 800-447-1684
FX: (312)360-0388
Members are advisors to physicians and dentists.

INSTITUTE OF ELECTRICAL AND ELECTRONICS ENGINEERS-ENGINEERING IN MEDICINE AND BIOLOGY SOCIETY
url: http://www.ieee.org
345 E. 47th St.
New York, NY 10017-2394
PH: (212)705-7900
FX: (212)752-4929
Members are engineers, technicians, physicians, manufacturers, and others with an interest in medical instrumentation.

INSTITUTE FOR ENVIRONMENTAL HEALTH SCIENCES
School of Public Health
University of Michigan
1420 Washington Heights
Ann Arbor, MI 48109-2029
PH: (313)764-3188
FX: (313)936-7283

INSTITUTE FOR HEALTH, HEALTH CARE POLICY, AND AGING RESEARCH
Rutgers University
30 College Ave.
New Brunswick, NJ 08903
PH: (908)932-8413
FX: (908)982-6872
Areas of study include HMO use by older adults.

INSTITUTE FOR HEALTH SERVICES AND POLICY STUDIES
e-mail: http://www.nwu.edu/ihsrps
Northwestern University
629 Noyes St.
Evanston, IL 60208-4170
PH: (847)491-5643
FX: (847)491-2202

INSURANCE ALMANAC: WHO, WHAT, WHEN AND WHERE IN INSURANCE
50 E. Palisade Ave.
Englewood, NJ 07631
PH: 800-526-4700
FX: (201)569-8817
Donald E. Wolff, editor. Underwriter Printing and Publishing Co. Annual. $115.00. Lists insurance agencies and brokerage firms; U.S. and Canadian insurance companies, adjusters, appraisers, auditors, investigators, insurance officials and insurance organizations.

THE INSURANCE FORUM: FOR THE UNFETTERED EXCHANGE OF IDEAS ABOUT INSURANCE
Post Office Box 245
Ellettsville, IN 47429
PH: (812)876-6502
Joseph M. Belth, editor. Insurance Forum, Inc. Monthly. $75.00 per year. Newsletter. Provides analysis of the insurance business, including occasional special issues showing the ratings of about 1,600 life-health insurance companies, as determined by four major rating services: Duff & Phelps Credit Rating Co., Moody's Investors Service, Standard & Poor's Corp., and Weiss Research, Inc.

AN INSURANCE GUIDE FOR SENIORS
Post Office Box 245
Ellettsville, IN 47429-0245
PH: (812)876-6502
Insurance Forum, Inc. 1997. $15.00. Provides concise advice and information on Medicare, Medicare supplement insurance, HMOs, long-term care insurance, automobile insurance, life insurance, annuities, and pensions. An appendix lists "Financially Strong Insurance Companies." (*The Insurance Forum*, vol. 24, no. 4.)

INSURANCE HANDBOOK FOR THE MEDICAL OFFICE
url: http://www.wbsaunders.com
Curtis Center, 3rd Fl.
Independence Square West
Philadelphia, PA 19106-3399
PH: 800-545-2522
FX: (215)238-7883
Marilyn T. Fordney. W. B. Saunders Co. 1997. Fifth edition. Price on application.

INSURANCE PERIODICALS INDEX [ONLINE]
21625 Prairie St.
Chatsworth, CA 91311
PH: 800-423-5910
FX: (818)718-8482
NILS Publishing Co. Compiled by the Insurance and Employee Benefits Div., Special Libraries Association. Corresponds to the printed *Insurance Periodicals Index*, but with abstracts and bi-weekly updates. Time period is 1984 to date. Inquire as to online cost and availability.

INSURANCE PERIODICALS INDEX
P.O. Box 2507
Chatsworth, CA 91313
PH: 800-423-5910
FX: (818)718-8482
NILS Publishing Co. Annual. $120.00. Two volumes. Compiled by the Insurance and Employee Benefits Div., Special Libraries Association. A yearly index of over 15,000 articles from about 35 insurance periodicals. Arrangement is by subject, with an index to authors.

INSURANCE PERIODICALS INDEX ON CD-ROM
url: http://www.nils.com
21625 Prairie St.
Chatsworth, CA 91311
PH: 800-423-5910
FX: (818)718-8482

NILS Publishing Co. Semiannual. $250.00 per year. Compiled by the Insurance and Employee Benefits Division, Special Libraries Association. A semiannual index on CD-ROM of more than 180,000 articles from about 40 insurance, risk management, and employee benefits journals. Full search capability is provided for indexes and abstracts over a time period of about 10 years.

INSURANCE STATISTICS YEARBOOK
e-mail: washcont@oecd.org
url: http://www.oecd.org
OECD Washington Center
2001 L St., N. W., Suite 650
Washington, DC 20036-4922
PH: 800-456-6323
FX: (202)785-0350
Organization for Economic Cooperation and Development. Annual. $72.00. Presents detailed statistics on insurance premiums collected in OECD countries, by type of insurance.

INSURANCE WORDS AND THEIR MEANINGS: A DICTIONARY OF INSURANCE TERMS
e-mail: rnc@in.net
url: http://www.roughnotes.com
11690 Techonology Dr.
Carmel, IN 46032-5600
PH: 800-428-4384
FX: (317)816-1003
Diana Kowatch. The Rough Notes Co., Inc. 1996. $30.25. 15th revised edition.

INSWEB
e-mail: info@insweb.com
url: http://www.insweb.com
PH: (650)372-2129
InsWeb Corp. Web site offers a wide variety of advice and information on automobile, life, health, and "other" insurance. Includes glossaries of insurance terms, Standard & Poor's ratings of individual insurance companies, and "Financial Needs Estimators." Searching is available. Fees: Free.

INTERNATIONAL ASSOCIATION OF HEALTHCARE CENTRAL SERVICE MATERIEL MANAGEMENT
e-mail: fvzz67@prodigy.com
213 West Institute Place, Suite 307
Chicago, IL 60610
PH: 800-962-8274
FX: (312)440-9474
Members are professional personnel responsible for management and distribution of supplies from a central service material management (purchasing) department of a hospital.

INTERNATIONAL JOURNAL OF HEALTH PLANNING AND MANAGEMENT
605 Third Ave.
New York, NY 10158-0012
PH: 800-526-5368
FX: (212)850-6088
Available from John Wiley & Sons, Inc., Journals Div. Quarterly. $715.00 per year. Published in England by John Wiley & Sons Ltd.

INTERNATIONAL JOURNAL OF OCCUPATIONAL MEDICINE, IMMUNOLOGY AND TOXICOLOGY
PO Box 2155
428 E. Preston St.
Princeton, NJ 08543
PH: (609)683-4750
FX: (609)683-0838
International Society of Occupational Medicine and Toxicology. Princeton Scientific Publishing Co., Inc. Quarterly. $160.00 per year. Formerly *Journal of Occupational Medicine and Toxicology.*

INTRODUCTION TO HOSPITAL ACCOUNTING
Two Westbrook Corporate Center, Suite 700
Westchester, IL 60154
PH: 800-252-4362
FX: 800-926-9495
L. Vann Seawell. Healthcare Financial Management Educational Foundation. 1992. $65.00. Third edition.

JAMA: THE JOURNAL OF THE AMERICAN MEDICAL ASSOCIATION
e-mail: amnews-comments@ama.assn.org
url: http://www.ama-assn.org
515 North State St.
Chicago, IL 60610
PH: 800-262-2350
FX: (312)464-4814
American Medical Association. 48 times a year. Individuals, $133.00 per year; institutions, $193.00 per year.

JOURNAL OF CLINICAL LABORATORY ANALYSIS
605 Third Ave.
New York, NY 10158-0012
PH: 800-526-5368
FX: (212)850-6088
John Wiley & Sons, Inc., Journals Div. Bimonthly. $725.00 per year. Original articles on newly developing assays.

JOURNAL OF HEALTH CARE MARKETING
e-mail: info@ama.org
url: http://www.ama.org
250 S. Wacker Dr., Suite 200
Chicago, IL 60606-5819
PH: 800-262-1150
FX: (312)993-7542
American Marketing Association. Quarterly. Members, $45.00 per year; non-members, $70.00 per year; institutions, $90.00 per year.

JOURNAL OF HOSPITAL MARKETING
e-mail: getinfo@haworth.com
url: http://www.haworth.com
10 Alice St.
Binghamton, NY 13904-1580
PH: 800-429-6784
FX: 800-895-0582
Haworth Press, Inc. Semiannual. Individuals, $60.00 per year; institutions, $85.00 per year; libraries, $225.00 per year.

JOURNAL OF LONG-TERM CARE ADMINISTRATION
e-mail: jan-1@spaceworks.com
325 South Patrick St.
Alexandria, VA 22314
PH: (703)739-7900
FX: (703)739-7901
American College of Health Care Administrators. Quarterly. Free to members; non-members, $70.00 per year. Includes research papers and articles on the administration of long term care facilities.

JOURNAL OF MEDICAL PRACTICE MANAGEMENT
e-mail: custserv@wilkins.com
url: http://www.wwilkins.com
351 W. Camden St.
Baltimore, MD 21201-2436
PH: 800-527-5597
FX: (410)528-4422
Williams and Wilkins. Bimonthly. Individuals, $139.00 per year; institutions, $160.00 per year.

JOURNAL OF PROFESSIONAL SERVICES MARKETING
10 Alice St.
Binghamton, NY 13904-1580
PH: 800-429-6784
FX: 800-895-0582

The Haworth Press, Inc. Semiannual. Individuals, $48.00 per year; institutions, $90.00 per year; libraries, $225.00 per year. Two volumes. Supplies "how to" marketing tools for specific sectors of the expanding service sector of the economy.

KEITHWOOD DIRECTORY OF MEDICAL /HOME HEALTH CARE SUPPLY DEALERS
P.O. Box 2963
Upper Darby, PA 19082
PH: (215)729-0320
FX: (215)727-1200
Keithwood Publishing Co. Annual. $125.00. Approximately 6,500 medical supply dealers. Updated continuously. Formerly *Keithwood Directory of Hospital and Surgical Dealers*

LABORATORIES MEDICAL DIRECTORY
e-mail: directory@abii.com
url: http://www.abii.com
American Business Information, Inc.
5711 S. 86th Circle
Omaha, NE 68127
PH: 800-555-6124
FX: (402)331-5481
American Business Directories, Inc. Annual. Price on application. Lists over 8,611 laboratories. Compiled from telephone company yellow pages.

LABORATORY OF ELECTRONICS
e-mail: ros@rockvax.rockefeller.edu
Rockefeller University
1230 York Ave.
New York, NY 10021
PH: (212)327-8613
FX: (212)327-7974
Studies the application of computer engineering and electronics to biomedicine.

LEONARD DAVIS INSTITUTE OF HEALTH ECONOMICS
e-mail: levy@wharton.upenn.edu
url: http://www.upenn.edu/ldi/
University of Pennsylvania
3641 Locust Walk
Philadelphia, PA 19104-6218
PH: (215)898-1655
FX: (215)898-0229
Research fields include health care management and cost-quality trade-offs.

LIFE ASSOCIATION NEWS
e-mail: jkosnett@nalu.org
url: http://www.agents-online.com
1922 F St., N. W.
Washington, DC 20006-4387
PH: 800-247-4074
FX: (202)835-9068
National Association of Life Underwriters. Monthly. Free to members; non-members, $7.00 per year. Edited for individual life and health insurance agents. Among the topics included are disability insurance and long-term care insurance.

LIFE, HEALTH, AND ACCIDENT INSURANCE LAW REPORTS
4025 W. Peterson Ave.
Chicago, IL 60646
PH: 800-248-3248
FX: 800-224-8299
Commerce Clearing House, Inc. $835.00 per year. Looseleaf service. Monthly updates.

LIFE AND HEALTH INSURANCE LAW
url: http://www.westgroup.com
155 Pfingsten Rd.
Deerfield, IL 60015

PH: 800-328-4880
FX: (847)948-8955
William F. Meyer. Clark Boardman Callaghan. $125.00. Second edition. Periodic supplementation. Covers the legal aspects of life, health, and accident insurance.

LIFE IN MEDICINE: BUSINESS AND LIFESTYLE ISSUES FOR NEW PHYSICIANS
6000 N. Forest Park Dr.
Peoria, IL 61614-3592
PH: 800-255-8800
FX: (309)698-8515
Dynamic Graphics, Inc. Bimonthly. $42.00 per year. Covers practice management and financial topics for new physicians.

THE LIFETIME BOOK OF MONEY MANAGEMENT
835 Penobscot Bldg.
Detroit, MI 48226-4094
PH: 800-877-GALE
FX: (313)961-6083
Gale Research Inc. 1993. $40.00. Third edition. Gives popularly-written advice on investments, life and health insurance, owning a home, credit, retirement, estate planning, and other personal finance topics.

LILLY HOSPITAL PHARMACY SURVEY
Lilly Corporate Center
Indianapolis, IN 46285
PH: (317)276-3641
FX: (317)276-5985
Eli Lilly and Co. Annual. $30.00. Includes financial data for drug stores located in hospitals.

LIST OF WORTHWHILE LIFE AND HEALTH INSURANCE BOOKS
1001 Pennsylvania Ave., N. W.
Washington, DC 20004-2599
PH: (202)624-2000
American Council of Life Insurance. Annual. Free. Books in print on life and health insurance and closely related subjects.

LONG TERM CARE ADMINISTRATION; THE MANAGEMENT OF INSTITUTIONAL AND NON-INSTITUTIONAL COMPONENTS OF THE CONTINUUM OF CARE
10 Alice St.
Binghamton, NY 13904-1580
PH: 800-429-6784
FX: 800-895-0582
Ben Abramovice. The Haworth Press, Inc. 1987. $39.95. Explores the multidisciplinary nature of long-term care.

LONG-TERM CARE: AN ANNOTATED BIBLIOGRAPHY
88 Post Rd. West
Westport, CT 06881
PH: 800-225-5800
FX: (203)222-1502
Theodore H. Koff. Greenwood Publishing Group, Inc. 1995. $59.95.

THE LONG-TERM CARE INDUSTRY
625 Ave. of the Americas
New York, NY 10011
PH: 800-346-3787
FX: (212)645-7681
FIND/SVP, Inc. 1995. $2,500.00. Market data with forecasts to the year 2005. Emphasis is on the over-85 age group. Covers health insurance, the nursing home industry, pharmaceuticals, healthcare supplies, etc.

LONG-TERM CARE AND ITS ALTERNATIVES
462 Walnut St.
Allentown, PA 18102

PH: 800-624-8773
FX: (610)770-0607
Charles B. Inlander. People's Medical Society. 1996. $16.95. Provides practical advice on the financing of long-term health care. The author is a consumer advocate and president of the People's Medical Society.

LONG-TERM HEALTH CARE: CURRENT RESEARCH ON FINANCING AND DELIVERY
e-mail: bibooks@brook.edu
url: http://www.brook.edu
1775 Massachusetts Ave., N. W.
Washington, DC 20036-2188
PH: 800-275-1447
FX: (202)797-6004
Joshua M. Wiener and others, editors. Brookings Institution. 1995. $12.95.

MAGAZINE INDEX PLUS
url: http://www.iacnet.com
362 Lakeside Drive
Foster City, CA 94404
PH: 800-227-8431
FX: (650)378-5369
Information Access Co. Monthly. $4,000.00 per year (includes InfoTrac workstation). Provides full text on CD-ROM for about 100 popular, general interest magazines and indexing for 300 others. Includes special indexing of reviews and product evaluations. Time period is 1980 to date.

MAJOR NON-HOSPITAL CLINICAL LABORATORIES
875 N. Michigan Ave., 31st Fl.
Chicago, IL 60611
PH: 800-678-3026
FX: (312)642-9729
SMG Marketing Group, Inc. Annual. $345.00.

MALCOLM WIENER CENTER FOR SOCIAL POLICY
e-mail: juliewilson@harvard.edu
url: http://www.ksg.harvard.edu/socpol
John F. Kennedy School of Government
79 JFK St.
Cambridge, MA 02138
PH: (617)495-1461
FX: (617)496-9053
Does multidisciplinary research on health care access and financing.

MANAGED CARE: A SURVIVAL GUIDE FOR LONG-TERM CARE PROVIDERS
e-mail: info@aahsa.org
url: http://www.aahsa.org
901 E St., N. W., Suite 500
Washington, DC 20004-2011
PH: 800-508-9442
FX: (202)783-2255
American Association of Homes and Services for the Aging. 1994. $90.00. Emphasis is on contracts, finances, taxes, and ethical issues. Published in association with Ernst and Young consultants.

THE MANAGED CARE CONTRACTING HANDBOOK: PLANNING AND NEGOTIATING THE MANAGED CARE RELATIONSHIP
e-mail: info@aahsa.org
url: http://www.aahsa.org
901 E St., N. W., Suite 500
Washington, DC 20004-2011
PH: 800-508-9442
FX: (202)783-2255
Maria K. Todd. Available from American Association of Homes and Services for the Aging. 1997. $78.00. Copublished by McGraw-Hill Healthcare Education Group and the Healthcare Financial Management Association. Covers managed care plan-

ning, proposals, strategy, negotiation, and contract law. Written for healthcare providers.

MANAGED CARE HANDBOOK: A COMPREHENSIVE GUIDE TO PREPARING YOUR PRACTICE FOR THE MANAGED CARE REVOLUTION
url: http://www.medicalbookstore.com
4727 Wilshire Blvd., Suite 300
Los Angeles, CA 90010
PH: 800-633-4215
FX: (213)954-0253
James Lyle and Hoyt Torras. Practice Management Information Corp. 1994. $49.95. A management guide for physicians in private practice.

MANAGED CARE LAW OUTLOOK: THE LEGAL BRIEFING ON HMOS, PPOS, AND BENEFITS OPTIONS
1101 King St., Suite 444
Alexandria, VA 22314
PH: 800-655-5597
FX: 800-645-4104
Capitol Publications, Inc. Monthly. $427.00 per year. Newsletter. Covers developments in laws and regulations affecting managed care groups, such as health maintenance organizations (HMOs) and preferred provider organizations (PPOs).

MANAGED CARE MARKETING
820 Bear Tavern Rd.
West Trenton, NJ 08628
PH: (609)530-0044
FX: (609)530-0207
Engel Publishing Partners. Quarterly. $24.00 per year. Edited for executives of managed health care companies and organizations.

MANAGED CARE OUTLOOK: THE INSIDER'S BUSINESS BRIEFING ON MANAGED HEALTH CARE
1101 King St., Suite 444
Alexandria, VA 22314
PH: 800-655-5597
FX: 800-645-4104
Capitol Publications, Inc. Biweekly. $449.00 per year. Newsletter relating to health maintenance organizations (HMOs), preferred provider organizations (PPOs), and other managed care systems.

MANAGED CARE: THE VISION AND THE STRATEGY
e-mail: info@aahsa.org
url: http://www.aahsa.org
901 E St., N. W., Suite 500
Washington, DC 20004-2011
PH: 800-508-9442
FX: (202)783-2255
American Association of Homes and Services for the Aging. 1996. $30.00. A report on an AAHSA national managed care summit. Topics include delivery models, regulatory conflicts, costs, finances, consumer choice, and related subjects.

MANAGED HEALTH CARE DIRECTORY
url: http://www.aahp.org
AAHP Foundation
1129 20th St., N.W., Suite 600
Washington, DC 20036
PH: (202)728-3247
FX: (202)331-7487
American Association of Health Plans. Annual. $280.00. Formerly *Directory of Preferred Provider Organizations*. Over 2,100 foundations for medical care, health maintenance organizations, preferred provider organizations, point of service plans and utilization review organizations.

MANAGED HEALTHCARE: THE NEWS MAGAZINE FOR MANAGERS OF HEALTHCARE COSTS AND QUALITY
url: http://www.advanstar.com
7500 Old Oak Blvd.
Cleveland, OH 44130

PH: 800-346-0085
FX: (216)891-2726
Advanstar Communications, Inc. Monthly. $64.00 per year. Edited for managers of HMOs and other managed care organizations. Covers outcomes, quality assurance, technology, long term care, and trends in the health care industry.

THE MANAGED MEDICARE AND MEDICAID MARKET
e-mail: catalog@findsvp.com
url: http://www.findsvp.com
625 Ave. of the Americas
New York, NY 10011-2002
PH: 800-346-3787
FX: (212)807-2716
FIND/SVP, Inc. 1997. $2,500.00. Market research report on medicare HMOs. Includes analysis of legal issues and the impact of managed care on older consumers. Providers such as Kaiser Permanente, Humana, and U.S. Healthcare are profiled.

MANAGEMENT ACCOUNTING FOR HEALTHCARE ORGANIZATIONS
e-mail: webmaster@bonus-books.com
url: http://www.bonus.books.com
160 E. Illinois St.
Chicago, IL 60611
PH: 800-225-3775
FX: (312)467-9271
James D. Suver and others. Precept Press. 1995. $59.95. Fourth edition. Published by Pluribus Press. Written for two distinct groups: healthcare managers who are not accountants and accountants who are not healthcare managers.

MANAGEMENT OF HEALTHCARE ORGANIZATIONS
5101 Madison Rd.
Cincinnati, OH 45227
PH: 800-543-0487
FX: (513)527-6956
Kerry D. Carson and others. South-Western Publishing Co. 1995. $69.95.

MANUFACTURING PROFILES
e-mail: gpoaccess@gpo.gov
url: http://www.access.gpo.gov
Washington, DC 20402
PH: (202)512-1800
FX: (202)512-2250
Available from U.S. Government Printing Office. Annual. $35.00. Issued by the U.S. Census Bureau. A printed consolidation of the entire *Current Industrial Report* series, presenting "all the data compiled." Contains statistics on production, shipments, inventories, consumption, exports, imports, and orders for a wide variety of manufactured products. (See also Census Bureau home page, http://www.census.gov/.)

MANUFACTURING USA: INDUSTRY ANALYSES, STATISTICS, AND LEADING COMPANIES
835 Penobscot Bldg.
Detroit, MI 48226-4094
PH: 800-877-GALE
FX: 800-414-5043
Gale Research Inc. Biennial. $205.00. Two volumes. A guide to economic activity in 458 manufacturing industries, providing analysis and synthesis of federal statistics. Up to 75 leading companies in each industry are ranked by sales, with addresses, number of employees, and other information. Selected business ratios are given for each industry.

MARKETING AND ADVERTISING REFERENCE SERVICE
362 Lakeside Dr.
Foster City, CA 94404
PH: 800-321-6388
FX: (650)358-4759
Information Access Co. Provides abstracts of literature relating to consumer marketing and advertising, including all forms of advertising media. Time period is 1984 to date. Daily updates. Inquire as to online cost and availability.

MARKETING HEALTH CARE INTO THE TWENTY-FIRST CENTURY: THE CHANGING DYNAMIC
e-mail: getinfo@haworth.com
url: http://www.haworth.com
10 Alice St.
Binghamton, NY 13904-1580
PH: 800-429-6784
FX: 800-895-0582
Alan K. Vitberg. Haworth Press, Inc. 1996. $29.95.

MCGILL'S LIFE INSURANCE
url: http://www.amercoll.edu
270 South Bryn Mawr Ave.
Bryn Mawr, PA 19010-2196
PH: 800-421-0654
FX: (610)526-1310
Edward E. Graves, editor. The American College. 1994. $61.00. Contains 44 chapters by various authors on diverse kinds of life insurance, as well as annuities, disability insurance, long-term care insurance, risk management, reinsurance, and other insurance topics. Originally by Dan M. McGill.

MCKNIGHT'S LONG TERM CARE NEWS
url: http://www.medec.com
Two Northfield Plaza
Northfield, IL 60093
PH: 800-451-7838
FX: (847)441-3701
McKnight Medical Communications, Inc. Monthly. $44.95 per year. Edited for retirement housing directors and nursing home administrators.

MCKNIGHT'S LONG-TERM CARE NEWS BUYER'S GUIDE
e-mail: Itcnewsatsmedec.com
url: http://www.medec.com
Two Northfield Plaza
Northfield, IL 60093
PH: 800-451-7838
FX: (847)441-3701
McKnight Medical Communications Co. Annual. $9.00. Lists suppliers of goods and services for retirement homes and nursing homes.

MEDICAL BENEFITS
1185 Avenue of the Americas
New York, NY 10036-8102
PH: (212)597-0200
FX: (212)597-0338
Panel Publishers, Inc. Semimonthly. $172.00 per year. Newsletter. Provides summaries of periodical articles.

MEDICAL CARE, MEDICAL COSTS: THE SEARCH FOR A HEALTH INSURANCE POLICY
79 Garden St.
Cambridge, MA 02138
PH: (617)495-2600
FX: (617)495-8924
Rashi Fein. Harvard University Press. 1986. $29.00.

MEDICAL CARE PRODUCTS
P.O. Box 650
Morris Plains, NJ 07950-0650
PH: (973)361-9060
FX: (973)898-9281
Gordon Publications, Inc. Eight times a year. $24.00 per year.

MEDICAL CLAIMS PROCESSING
2392 Morse Ave.
Irvine, CA 92714
PH: 800-421-2300
FX: (714)851-9088

Entrepreneur, Inc. Looseleaf. $59.50. A practical guide to starting a medical claims processing service. Covers profit potential, start-up costs, market size evaluation, owner's time required, site selection, pricing, accounting, advertising, promotion, etc. (Start-Up Business Guide No. E1345.)

MEDICAL CYBERNETICS FOUNDATION
Medical Design Center
3804 Arrow Lake Dr.
Jacksonville, FL 32257
PH: (904)268-2086
Members are medical professionals. Promotes research and development of new medical machinery, especially in the areas of monitoring equipment and robotics systems.

MEDICAL DEVICE AND DIAGNOSTIC INDUSTRY
e-mail: canon@cancom.com
url: http://www.cancom.com
3340 Ocean Park Blvd., Suite 1000
Santa Monica, CA 90405-3207
PH: (310)392-5509
FX: (310)392-4920
Canon Communications, Inc. Monthly. Free to qualified personnel; other, $125.00 per year.

MEDICAL DEVICE REGISTER
Five Paragon Drive
Montvale, NJ 07645-1742
PH: 800-222-3045
FX: (201)573-4956
Medical Economics. Annual. $325.00. Lists more than 12,000 suppliers of a wide variety of medical devices and clinical laboratory products.

MEDICAL DEVICE TECHNOLOGY
url: http://www.advanstar.com
7500 Old Oak Blvd.
Cleveland, OH 44130
PH: 800-346-0085
FX: (216)891-2726
Advanstar Communications, Inc. Ten times a year. Free to qualified personnel; others, $180.00 per year.

MEDICAL ECONOMICS
Five Paragon Drive
Montvale, NJ 07645-1742
PH: 800-232-7379
FX: (201)573-4956
Medical Economics Co., Inc. Semimonthly. $109.00 per year. Covers the financial, economic, insurance, administrative, and other non-clinical aspects of private medical practice. Provides investment and estate planning advice.

MEDICAL ECONOMICS FOR SURGEONS
Five Paragon Drive
Montvale, NJ 07645-1742
PH: 800-232-7379
FX: (201)573-4956
Medical Economics Co., Inc. Monthly. $64.00 per year. Provides information and advice on practice management (non-clinical) for surgeons.

MEDICAL ELECTRONICS
2994 West Liberty Ave.
Pittsburgh, PA 15216-2595
PH: (412)343-9666
FX: (412)343-9685
Measurements & Data Corp. Bimonthly. $22.00 per year. Includes information on new medical electronic products, technology, industry news, and medical safety.

MEDICAL ELECTRONICS AND EQUIPMENT NEWS
e-mail: rcgroup@flash.net
16 E. Schaumberg Rd.
Schaumberg, IL 60194-3536
PH: (847)882-3536
FX: (847)519-0166
Reilly Publishing Co. Bimonthly. Free to qualified personnel; others, $45.00 per year. Provides medical electronics industry news and new product information.

MEDICAL ELECTRONICS LABORATORY
University of Wisconsin
1300 University Ave.
Madison, WI 53706
PH: (608)262-1326
FX: (608)262-2327
Develops electronic instrumentation for medical and biological research.

MEDICAL GROUP MANAGEMENT ASSOCIATION
104 Inverness Terrace E.
Englewood, CA 80112
PH: (303)799-1111
FX: (303)643-4427
Members are medical group managers.

MEDICAL GROUP MANAGEMENT JOURNAL
104 Inverness Terrace East
Englewood, CO 80112-5306
PH: (303)759-1111
FX: (303)799-1683
Medical Group Management Association. Bimonthly. $48.00 per year.

MEDICAL AND HEALTH CARE BOOKS AND SERIALS IN PRINT: AN INDEX TO LITERATURE IN HEALTH SCIENCES
121 Chanlon Rd.
New Providence, NJ 07974
PH: 800-521-8110
FX: (908)665-6688
R. R. Bowker. Annual. $249.95. Two volumes.

MEDICAL AND HEALTH INFORMATION DIRECTORY
835 Penobscot Bldg.
Detroit, MI 48226-4094
PH: 800-877-GALE
FX: 800-414-5043
Gale Research Inc. 1997. $569.00. Three volumes. Ninth edition. Volume one covers medical organizations, agencies, and institutions ($235.00). Volume two includes bibliographic, library, and database information ($235.00). Volume three is a guide to services available for various medical and health problems ($235.00).

MEDICAL AND HEALTHCARE MARKETPLACE GUIDE
1617 JFK Blvd., Suite 960
Philadelphia, PA 19103
PH: (215)557-2300
FX: (215)557-2301
Legal Communications, Ltd. Annual. $670.00. Over 5,500 American firms, including over 300 subsidiaries of foreign firms operating in the U.S. which offer medical products and services; covers over 4,200 separate operating units.

MEDICAL INSTRUMENTATION LABORATORY
e-mail: webster@engr.wisc.edu
url: http://www.engr.wisc.edu/ece/faculty/websterjohn.html
University of Wisconsin-Madison
1415 Engineering Dr.
Madison, WI 53706
PH: (608)263-1574
FX: (608)265-4623
Research subjects include medical electrodes, medical amplifiers, bioimpedance techniques, and miniature tactile pressure sensors.

MEDICAL LASER REPORT
url: http://www.pennwell.com
10 Tara Blvd., 5th Fl.
Nashua, NH 03062-2801
PH: 800-331-4463
FX: (603)891-0574
PennWell Publishing Co. Monthly. $345.00 per year. Newsletter. Covers the business and financial side of the medical laser industry, along with news of technological developments and clinical applications. Supplement available *Buyers' Guide*. Formerly *Medical Laser Industry Report*.

MEDICAL PRODUCT MANUFACTURING NEWS
e-mail: canon@cancom.com
url: http://www.cancom.com
3340 Ocean Park Blvd., Suite 1000
Santa Monica, CA 90405-3207
PH: (310)392-5509
FX: (310)392-4920
Canon Communications, Inc. 10 times a year. Free to qualified personnel; others, $125.00 per year. Directed at manufacturers of medical devices and medical electronic equipment. Covers industry news, service news, and new products.

MEDICAL PRODUCT MANUFACTURING NEWS BUYER'S GUIDE AND DESIGNER'S SOURCEBOOK
e-mail: canon@cancom.com
url: http://www.cancom.com
3340 Ocean Park Blvd., Suite 1000
Santa Monica, CA 90405-3216
PH: (310)392-5509
FX: (310)392-4920
Canon Communications, Inc. Annual. Controlled circulation. A directory of over 2,800 medical device and medical electronic equipment. Formerly *Medical Product Manufacturing News-Buyer's Guide and Designer's Sourcebook*.

MEDICAL PRODUCT SALES
url: http://www.medec.com
Two Northfield Plaza
Northfield, IL 60093
PH: 800-451-7838
FX: (847)441-3701
Health Industry Distribution Association. McKnight Medical Communications, Inc. Monthly. $49.95 per year.

MEDICAL REFERENCE SERVICES QUARTERLY
10 Alice St.
Binghamton, NY 13904-1580
PH: 800-429-6784
FX: 800-895-0582
Haworth Press, Inc. Quarterly. Individuals, $35.00 per year; institutions and libraries, $140.00 per year. An academic and practical journal for medical reference librarians.

MEDICAL RESEARCH CENTRES: A WORLD DIRECTORY OF ORGANIZATIONS AND PROGRAMMES
e-mail: galeord@gale.com
url: http://www.gale.com
835 Penobscot Bldg.
Detroit, MI 48226
PH: 800-877-GALE
FX: 800-414-5043
Gale Research Inc. Irregular. $595.00. Two volumes. Published by The Longman Group. Contains profiles of about 9,000 medical research facilities around the world. Includes medical, dental, nursing, pharmaceutical, psychiatric, and surgical research centers.

MEDICAL SCIENCES INTERNATIONAL WHO'S WHO
345 Park Ave., S., 10th Fl.
New York, NY 10010
PH: 800-221-2123
FX: (212)689-9711

Groves Dictionaries. 1996. $595.00. Sixth edition. Volume seven. Provides biographical data for over 8,000 international figures active in medical research. Published in England by Longman.

MEDICAL TECHNOLOGISTS AND TECHNICIANS CAREER DIRECTORY
835 Penobscot Bldg.
Detroit, MI 48226-4094
PH: 800-877-GALE
FX: (313)961-6083
Gale Research Inc. 1993. $34.00. Includes career information relating to clinical laboratory technicians and other kinds of healthcare technical specialists. Provides advice from "insiders," resume suggestions, a directory of companies that may offer entry-level positions, and a directory of career information sources. (Career Advisor Series.)

MEDICAL TECHNOLOGY AND SOCIETY: AN INTERDISCIPLINARY PERSPECTIVE
e-mail: journals-orders@mit.edu
url: http://www.mit.edu
55 Hayward St.
Cambridge, MA 02142-1399
PH: 800-356-0343
FX: (617)253-1709
Joseph Bronzino and Vincent Smith. MIT Press. 1990. $42.00.

MEDICAL TECHNOLOGY STOCK LETTER
P.O. Box 40460
Berkeley, CA 94704
PH: (510)843-1857
FX: (510)843-0901
Piedmont Venture Group. Semimonthly. $320.00 per year. Newsletter. Provides health care industry investment recommendations, including information on initial public offerings.

MEDICAL TRIBUNE: WORLD NEWS OF MEDICINE AND ITS PRACTICE
url: http://www.medtrib.com
100 Ave. of the Americas, 9th Fl.
New York, NY 10013-1606
PH: (212)674-8500
FX: (212)529-8490
Medical Tribune, Inc. 26 times a year. Free to qualified personnel; others, $75.00 per year.

MEDICAL ULTRASOUND MARKETS
Theta Bldg.
Eight Old Indian Trail
Middlefield, CT 06455
PH: 800-995-1550
FX: (203)349-1227
Theta Corp. 1994. $795.00. Provides basic data and market forecasts to 1998 for ultrasound products used in the U.S. and foreign healthcare industries. Twenty corporate profiles are provided.

MEDICAL UTILIZATION MANAGEMENT
url: http://www.faulknergray.com
Healthcare Information Center
11 Penn Plaza, 17th Fl.
New York, NY 10001
PH: 800-535-5403
FX: (212)967-7155
Faulkner & Gray. Biweekly. $395.00 per year. Newsletter. Formerly *Medical Utilization Review*.

MEDICAL WASTE NEWS
e-mail: bpinews@bpinews.com
url: http://www.bpinews.com
951 Pershing Drive
Silver Spring, MD 20910-4464
PH: 800-274-0122
FX: (301)585-9075

Business Publishers, Inc. Biweekly. $377.00 per year. Newsletter on medical waste management and disposal.

MEDICARE COMPLIANCE ALERT
11300 Rockville Pike, Suite 1100
Rockville, MD 20852-3030
PH: (301)816-8950
FX: (301)816-8945
United Communications News. Biweekly. $370.00 per year. Supplement available, *Civil Money Penalties Reporter.* Newsletter. Provides news of changes in Medicare regulations and legislation. Advises physicians on Medicare rules relating to physician investments, joint ventures, limited partnerships, and patient referrals.

MEDICARE AND COORDINATED CARE PLANS
Department 59
Pueblo, CO 81009
Available from Consumer Information Center. Free. Published by the U.S. Department of Health and Human Services. Contains detailed information on services to Medicare beneficiaries from health maintenance organizations (HMOs). (Publication No. 509-X.)

MEDICARE: EMPLOYER HEALTH PLANS
Department 59
Pueblo, CO 81009
Available from Consumer Information Center. Free. Published by the U.S. Department of Health and Human Services. Explains the special rules that apply to Medicare beneficiaries who have employer group health plan coverage. (Publication No. 520-Y.)

MEDICARE EXPLAINED
4025 W. Peterson Ave.
Chicago, IL 60646
PH: 800-248-3248
FX: 800-224-8299
Commerce Clearing House, Inc. Annual. 19.00.

MEDICARE MADE EASY: EVERYTHING YOU NEED TO KNOW TO MAKE MEDICARE WORK FOR YOU
462 Walnut St.
Allentown, PA 18102
PH: 800-624-8773
FX: (610)770-0607
Charles B. Inlander. People's Medical Society. 1998. $18.95. Revised edition. Provides basic information on Medicare claims processing and the manner in which Medicare relates to other health insurance. The author is a consumer advocate and president of the People's Medical Society.

MEDICARE AND MEDICAID CLAIMS AND PROCEDURES
url: http://www.westpub.com
P.O. Box 64526
St. Paul, MN 55164-0526
PH: 800-328-9424
FX: (612)687-5388
Harvey L. McCormick. West Publishing Co. College and School Div. 1986. Two volumes. Periodic supplementation. Price on application. (West's Handbook Series).

MEDICARE SUPPLEMENT PRICE SURVEY
url: http://www.weissinc.com
Post Office Box 109665
Palm Beach Gardens, FL 33410
PH: 800-289-9222
FX: (561)625-6685
Weiss Ratings, Inc. Continuous revision. Price on application. Available for individual geographic areas to provide detailed price information for various types of Medicare supplement health insurance policies issued by specific insurance companies.

MEDLINE
National Library of Medicine
8600 Rockville Pike
Bethesda, MD 20894
PH: 800-638-8480
FX: (301)480-3537
Medlars Management Section. Provides indexing and abstracting of worldwide medical literature, 1966 to date. Inquire as to online cost and availability.

MENTAL HEALTH AND SOCIAL WORK CAREER DIRECTORY
835 Penobscot Bldg.
Detroit, MI 48226-4094
PH: 800-877-GALE
FX: (313)961-6083
Gale Research Inc. 1993. $34.00. Includes career information relating to family therapists, marriage counselors, behavioral psychologists, and others. Provides advice from "insiders," resume suggestions, a directory of companies that may offer entry-level positions, and a directory of career information sources. (Career Advisor Series.)

THE MILBANK QUARTERLY
e-mail: subscript@blackwellpub.com
url: http://www/blackwellpub.com
350 Main St.
Cambridge, MA 02148-5018
PH: 800-216-2522
FX: (617)388-8210
Milbank Memorial Fund. Blackwell Publishers. Quarterly. Individuals, $45.50 per year; institutions, $92.00 per year. Formerly*Health and Society.*

MLO (MEDICAL LABORATORY OBSERVER)
Five Paragon Drive
Montvale, NJ 07645-1742
PH: 800-232-7379
FX: (201)573-4956
Medical Economics Publishing Co., Inc. Monthly. $70.00 per year. Covers management, regulatory, and technical topics for clinical laboratory administrators.

MODERN HEALTHCARE: THE NEWSMAGAZINE FOR ADMINSTRATORS AND MANAGERS IN HOSPITALS AND OTHER HEALTHCARE INSTITUTIONS
e-mail: ckosek@crain.com
url: http://www.crain.com
740 N. Rush St.
Chicago, IL 60611-2590
PH: 800-678-9595
FX: (312)649-5443
Crain Communications, Inc. Weekly. $125.00 per year; students, $63.00 per year.

MODERN MEDICINE
url: http://www.advanstar.com
7500 Old Oak Blvd.
Cleveland, OH 44130
PH: 800-346-0085
FX: (216)891-2726
Advanstar Communications, Inc.,. Monthly. $55.00 per year.

NATIONAL ACCREDITING AGENCY FOR CLINICAL LABORATORY SCIENCES
8410 W. Bryn Mawr Ave., Suite 670
Chicago, IL 60631
PH: (773)714-8880
FX: (773)714-8886
Accredits hospital and college programs for the training of medical laboratory technicians.

NATIONAL ASSOCIATION FOR MEDICAL EQUIPMENT SERVICES
e-mail: info@names.org
625 Slaters Lane, Suite 200
Alexandria, VA 22314-1171
PH: (703)836-6263
FX: (703)836-6730
Members are durable medical equipment and oxygen suppliers, mainly for home health care. Has Legislative Affairs Committee that is concerned with Medicare/Medicaid benefits.

NATIONAL ASSOCIATION OF RESIDENTS AND INTERNS
292 Madison Ave.
New York, NY 10017
PH: 800-221-2168
FX: (212)949-5910
Seeks to improve economic welfare of members. Affiliated with American Professional Practice Association.

NATIONAL COMMITTEE FOR CLINICAL LABORATORY STUDYS
e-mail: exoffice@nccls.org
940 W. Valley Rd., Suite 1400
Wayne, PA 19087-1898
PH: (610)688-0100
FX: (610)688-0700
Promotes the development of national standards for clinical laboratory testing.

NATIONAL COMMITTEE FOR QUALITY HEALTH CARE
1800 Massachusetts Ave., N.W., Suite 401
Washington, DC 20036
PH: (202)347-5731
FX: (202)347-5836
Promotes efficient expenditures in the health care field. Members include hospitals, health maintenance organizations, and nursing homes.

NATIONAL CONTINUING CARE DIRECTORY
url: http://www.aarp.org
601 E St., N. W.
Washington, DC 20049
PH: (202)728-4700
American Association of Retired Persons. 1993. $20.00. Provides detailed descriptions of continuing care retirement communities located throughout the United States. Formerly published (1988) by Scott, Foresman & Co.

NATIONAL DIRECTORY OF HMOS
1129 20th St., N. W.
Suite 600
Washington, DC 20036
PH: (202)778-3247
FX: (202)331-7487
Group Health Association of America. Annual. $125.00. Includes names of key personnel and benefit options.

NATIONAL ECONOMIC, SOCIAL, AND ENVIRONMENTAL DATA BANK
Economics and Statistics Administration
Office of Business Analysis
Washington, DC 20230
PH: (202)482-4940
FX: (202)482-0325
U.S. Department of Commerce. Quarterly. $360.00 per year. Contains CD-ROM full text of *Economic Report of the President, U.S. Industrial Outlook, Digest of Education Statistics*, and many other government documents. Subjects include economics, education, health, crime, environmental issues, the federal budget, population, and energy.

NATIONAL HEALTH DIRECTORY
e-mail: lynnantosz@aspenpubl.com
200 Orchard Ridge Dr., Suite 200
Gaithersburg, MD 20878
PH: 800-638-8437
FX: (301)417-7550
Aspen Publishers, Inc. Annual. $95.00. Lists about 11,500 federal and state public health care officials.

NATIONAL LIBRARY OF MEDICINE (NLM)
e-mail: access@nlm.nih.gov
url: http://www.nlm.nih.gov
PH: (888)346-3656
FX: (301)480-3537
National Institutes of Health (NIH). NLM Web site offers free access through MEDLINE ("PubMed") to about nine million references to articles appearing in some 3,800 biomedical journals, with abstracts. Search interfaces range from "simple keywords to advanced Boolean expressions." The NLM site offers many links to other sources of biomedical and technical information (the National Center for Biotechnology Information, for example). Fees: Free.

NCHS: MONITORING THE NATION'S HEALTH
e-mail: nchsquery@cdc.gov
url: http://www.cdc.gov.nchswww
PH: (301)436-8500
National Center for Health Statistics, Centers for Disease Control and Prevention, U.S. Department of Health and Human Services. Web site provides detailed data on diseases, vital statistics, and health care in the U.S. Includes a search facility and links to many other health-related Web sites. Fees: Free. Frequent updates.

NEW ENGLAND JOURNAL OF MEDICINE
url: http://www.nejm.org
10 Shattuck St.
Boston, MA 02115
PH: 800-843-6356
FX: (617)893-8103
Massachusetts Medical Society, Publishing Div. Weekly. $109.00 per year. The offical journal of the Massachusetts Medical Society.

NEWSPAPER AND PERIODICAL ABSTRACTS
url: http://www.umi.com
300 North Zeeb Rd.
Ann Arbor, MI 48103
PH: 800-521-0600
FX: 800-864-0019
UMI. Provides online coverage (citations and abstracts) of 25 major newspapers, 1,600 perodicals, and 70 TV programs. Covers business, economics, current affairs, health, fitness, sports, education, technology, government, consumer affairs, psychology, the arts, and the social sciences. Time period is 1986 to date, with daily updates. Inquire as to online cost and availability.

NEXIS SERVICE
Post Office Box 933
Dayton, OH 45401-0933
PH: 800-543-6862
FX: (937)865-6909
LEXIS-NEXIS. Makes available the full text of a wide variety of periodicals and some major newspapers, including the *New York Times*.

NTIS ALERTS: BIOMEDICAL TECHNOLOGY & HUMAN FACTORS ENGINEERING
U.S. Department of Commerce
Technology Administration
5285 Port Royal Rd.
Springfield, VA 22161
PH: 800-553-6847
FX: (703)321-8547

National Technical Information Service. Semimonthly. 145.00 per year. Formerly *Abstract Newsletter*. Provides descriptions of government-sponsored research reports and software, with ordering information. Covers biotechnology, ergonomics, bionics, artificial intelligence, prosthetics, and related subjects.

NTIS ALERTS: HEALTH CARE
U.S. Department of Commerce
Technology Administration
5285 Port Royal Rd.
Springfield, VA 22161
PH: 800-553-6847
FX: (703)321-8547
National Technical Information Service. Semimonthly. $145.00 per year. Formerly *Abstract Newsletter*. Provides descriptions of government-sponsored research reports and software, with ordering information. Covers a wide variety of health care topics, including quality assurance, delivery organization, economics (costs), technology, and legislation.

NTIS BIBLIOGRAPHIC DATA BASE
5285 Port Royal Rd.
Springfield, VA 22161
PH: 800-553-6847
FX: (703)487-4134
National Technical Information Service. Contains citations and abstracts to unrestricted reports of government-sponsored research, 1964 to date. Covers a wide range of technical, engineering, business, and social science topics. Monthly updates. Inquire as to online cost and availability.

NTIS ON SILVERPLATTER
100 River Ridge Rd.
Norwood, MA 02062-5026
PH: 800-343-0064
FX: (781)769-8763
Available from SilverPlatter Information, Inc. Quarterly. $2,850.00 per year. Produced by the National Technical Information Service. Provides a CD-ROM guide to over 500,000 government reports on a wide variety of technical, industrial, and business topics.

NURSING ECONOMICS: BUSINESS PERSPECTIVES FOR
  NURSES
e-mail: nejrnl@mail.ajj.com
P.O. Box 56
Pitman, NJ 08071-0056
PH: (609)256-2300
FX: (609)589-7463
Jannetti Publications, Inc. Bimonthly. Individuals, $36.00 per year; institutions, $52.00 per year.

NURSING HOME CHAIN DIRECTORY
875 N. Michigan Ave., 31st Fl.
Chicago, IL 60611
PH: 800-678-3026
FX: (312)642-9729
SMG Marketing Group, Inc. Annual. $495.00. Contains information relating to almost 450 for profit and nonprofit U.S. nursing home chains.

NURSING HOME REPORT AND DIRECTORY
875 N. Michigan Ave., 31st Fl.
Chicago, IL 60611
PH: 800-678-3026
FX: (312)642-9729
SMG Marketing Group, Inc. Annual. $445.00. Lists 18,000 nursing homes with 50 beds or more.

NURSING MANAGEMENT
P.O. 908
Spring House, PA 19477-0903
PH: 800-950-0879

Springhouse Corp. Monthly. Individuals, $38.00 per year; institutions, $60.00 per year. Non-clinical subject matter.

OB/GYN REFERENCE GUIDE
e-mail: access@accesspub.com
url: http://www.accesspub.com
1301 West Park Ave.
Ocean, NJ 07712
PH: 800-458-0990
FX: (732)493-9713
Access Publishing Co. Annual. Price on application. Includes directory information for obstetrical/gynecological equipment, supplies, pharmaceuticals, services, organizations, and publications.

OCCUPATIONAL HEALTH AND SAFETY
3700 J.H. Kultgen Freeway
Waco, TX 76706
PH: (817)776-9000
FX: (817)776-9018
Stevens Publishing Corp. Monthly. $69.00 per year. Includes news, interviews, feature articles, legal developments, and reviews of literature. Contains *Buyer's Guide*.

OCCUPATIONAL HEALTH AND SAFETY
LETTER...TOWARDS PRODUCTIVITY AND PEACE OF
  MIND
e-mail: bpinews@bpinews.com
url: http://www.bpinews.com
951 Pershing Dr.
Silver Spring, MD 20910-4464
PH: 800-274-0122
FX: (301)585-9075
Business Publishers, Inc. Biweekly. $273.00 per year.

OCCUPATIONAL HEALTH AND SAFETY PURCHASING
  SOURCEBOOK
3700 J.H. Kultgen Freeway
Waco, TX 76706
PH: (817)776-9000
FX: (817)776-9018
Stevens Publishing Corp. Annual. $69.00. Over 1,500 manufacturers, distributors and consultants of poducts and services in the field of safety, health and environmental protection.

OFFICIAL ABMS DIRECTORY OF BOARD CERTIFIED
  MEDICAL SPECIALISTS
e-mail: info@reedref.com
url: http://www.reedref.com
121 Chanlon Rd.
New Providence, NJ 07974
PH: 800-521-8110
FX: (908)665-6688
Marquis Who's Who. Annual. $485.00. Four volumes. Published in conjunction with the American Board of Medical Specialties. Includes information on more than 496,000 specialists. Volumes are arranged by medical specialty and then geographically, with an overall index to physicians' names. Formerly *Directory of Medical Specialists*.

OLDER AMERICANS REPORT
e-mail: bpinews@bpinews.com
url: http://www.bpinews.com
951 Pershing Drive
Silver Spring, MD 20910-4464
PH: 800-274-0122
FX: (301)585-9075
Business Publishers, Inc. Weekly. $320.00 per year. Newsletter on health, economic, and social services for the aging, including social security, medicare, pensions, housing, nursing homes, and programs under the Older Americans Act. Edited for service providers.

OPTOMETRIC MANAGEMENT: THE BUSINESS AND MARKETING MAGAZINE FOR OPTOMETRY
1300 Virginia Drive, Suite 400
Fort Washington, PA 19034
PH: 800-306-6332
FX: (215)643-4827
Cardinal Business Media, Inc. Monthly. $37.00 per year. Provides information and advice for optometrists on practice management and marketing.

PAIS INTERNATIONAL
e-mail: inquiries@pais.org
url: http://www.pais.org
521 W. 43rd St.
New York, NY 10036
PH: 800-288-7247
FX: (212)643-2848
Public Affairs Information Service, Inc. Corresponds to the former printed publications, *PAIS Bulletin* (1976-90) and *PAIS Foreign Language Index* (1972-90), and to the current *PAIS International in Print* (1991 to date). Covers economic, political, and sociological material appearing in periodicals, books, government documents, and other publications. Updating is monthly. Inquire as to online cost and availability.

PART B NEWS
11300 Rockville Pike, Suite 1100
Rockville, MD 20852-3030
PH: (301)816-8950
FX: (301)816-8945
United Communications News. Biweekly. $426.00 per year. Newsletter. Explains Medicare Part B reimbursement program and rules for healthcare providers. Gives advice and strategies for physicians.

PATTY'S INDUSTRIAL HYGIENE AND TOXICOLOGY
605 Third Ave.
New York, NY 10158-0012
PH: 800-225-5945
FX: (212)850-6088
George D. Clayton and Florence E. Clayton, editors. John Wiley and Sons, Inc. 1996. $2,195.00. Three volumes in 10 parts. Provides broad coverage of environmental factors and stresses affecting the health of workers. Contains detailed information on the effects of specific substances.

PEOPLE'S MEDICAL SOCIETY
e-mail: peoplesmed@compuserve.com
462 Walnut St.
Allentown, PA 18102
PH: 800-624-8773
FX: (610)770-0607
A consumer affairs society concerned with the cost, quality, and management of the American health care system.

PHARMACEUTICAL LITIGATION REPORTER: THE NATIONAL JOURNAL OF RECORD OF PHARMACEUTICAL LITIGATION
175 Strafford Ave., Bldg. 4, Suite 140
Wayne, PA 19087
PH: 800-345-1101
FX: (610)622-0501
Andrews Publications. Monthly. $750.00 per year. Reports on a wide variety of legal cases involving the pharmaceutical and medical device industries. Includes product liability lawsuits.

PHARMACEUTICAL RESEARCH AND MANUFACTURERS ASSOCIATION
1100 15th St., N.W.
Washington, DC 20005
PH: (202)835-3400
FX: (202)835-3429

PHYSICIANS & COMPUTERS
810 S. Waukegan Rd., Suite 200
Lake Forest, IL 60045-2672
PH: (847)615-8333
FX: (847)615-8345
Moorhead Publications Inc. Monthly. $35.00 per year. Includes material on computer diagnostics, online research, medical and non-medical software, computer equipment, and practice management.

PHYSICIANS' DESK REFERENCE FOR OPHTHALMOLOGY
Five Paragon Drive
Montvale, NJ 07645-1742
PH: 800-232-7379
FX: (201)573-4956
Medical Economics Publishing Co., Inc. Irregular. $39.95. Provides detailed descriptions of ophthalmological instrumentation, equipment, supplies, lenses, and prescription drugs. Indexed by manufacturer, product name, product category, active drug ingredient, and instrumentation. Editorial discussion is included.

PHYSICIANS FINANCIAL NEWS
1221 Ave. of the Americas
New York, NY 10020
PH: 800-722-4726
FX: (212)512-2821
McGraw-Hill. Monthly. $75.00 per year.

PHYSICIAN'S MARKETING AND MANAGEMENT
3525 Piedmont Rd., N.W.
Bldg. 6, Suite 400
Atlanta, GA 30305
PH: 800-284-3291
FX: 800-688-2421
American Health Consultants, Inc. Monthly. $179.00 per year. Formerly *Physician's Marketing*.

PLUNKETT'S HEALTH CARE INDUSTRY ALMANAC: THE ONLY COMPLETE GUIDE TO THE FASTEST-CHANGING INDUSTRY IN AMERICA
e-mail: orders@hoovers.com
url: http://www.hoovers.com
1033 La Posada Drive, Suite 250
Austin, TX 78752
PH: 800-486-8666
FX: (512)374-4501
Available from Hoover's, Inc. Annual. $156.49. Published by Plunkett Research. Includes detailed profiles of 500 large companies providing health care products or services, with indexes by products, services, and location. Provides statistical and trend information for the health insurance industry, HMOs, hospital utilization, Medicare, medical technology, and national health expenditures.

PODIATRY MANAGEMENT MAGAZINE
7000 Terminal Square, Suite 210
Upper Darby, PA 19082
PH: (610)734-2420
FX: (610)734-2423
Kane Communications, Inc. Nine times a year. $30.00 per year. Non-clinical subject matter.

PREDICASTS F & S INDEX UNITED STATES
e-mail: cemarketing@iacnet.com
url: http://w.iacnet.com
362 Lakeside Dr.
Foster City, CA 94404
PH: 800-321-6388
FX: (650)358-4759
Information Access Co. Monthly, with quarterly and annual cumulations. $975.00 per year. Provides citations to U.S. business, marketing, and industrial material appearing in a large assortment of trade journals, newspapers, and other publications. Arranged by expanded Standard Industrial Classification (SIC)

number and by company name. Originally known as *Funk & Scott Index.*

PREDICTING SUCCESSFUL HOSPITAL MERGERS AND ACQUISITIONS: A FINANCIAL AND ANALYTICAL MARKETING TOOL
e-mail: getinfo@haworth.com
url: http://www.haworth.com
10 Alice St.
Binghamton, NY 13904-1580
PH: 800-429-6784
FX: 800-895-0582
David P. Angrisani and Robert L. Goldman. Haworth Press, Inc. 1996. $49.95.

PRIVATE PRACTICE
P.O. Box 1485
Shawnee, OK 74802-1485
Congress of County Medical Societies (CCMS) Publishing Co. Monthly. $18.00 per year.

PROMT: PREDICASTS OVERVIEW OF MARKETS AND TECHNOLOGY
e-mail: cemarketing@iacnet.com
url: http://www.iacnet.com
362 Lakeside Dr.
Foster City, CA 94404
PH: 800-321-6388
FX: (650)358-4759
Information Access Co. Companies, products, applied technologies and markets. U.S. and international literature coverage, 1972 to date. Daily updates. Inquire as to online cost and availability. Provides abstracts from more than 1,500 publications.

PROOFS: BUYERS' GUIDE AND MANUFACTURERS' DIRECTORY ISSUE
url: http://www.pennwell.com
P.O. Box 3408
Tulsa, OK 74101
PH: 800-235-6862
FX: (918)831-9497
Dental Economics Div. PennWell Publishing Co. Annual. $40.00. List of over 500 manufacturers of dental products and equipment; coverage includes foreign listings.

PROOFS: THE MAGAZINE OF DENTAL SALES
url: http://www.pennwell.com
P.O. Box 3408
Tulsa, OK 74101
PH: 800-752-9764
FX: (918)831-9497
PennWell Publishing Co., Dental Economics Div. 10 times a year. $29.95 per year.

PROVIDER: LTC BUYERS' GUIDE ISSUE
1201 L St., N. W.
Washington, DC 20005-4046
PH: (202)898-6319
FX: (202)842-3860
American Health Care Association. Annual. $10.00. Lists several hundred manufacturers and suppliers of products and services for long term care (LTC) facilities.

R M A ANNUAL STATEMENT STUDIES, INCLUDING COMPARATIVE HISTORICAL DATA AND OTHER SOURCES OF COMPOSITE FINANCIAL DATA
url: http://www.rmahq.org
One Liberty Place, Suite 2300
1650 Market St.
Philadelphia, PA 19103
PH: 800-677-7621
FX: (215)446-4100
Robert Morris Associates: The Association of Lending and Credit Risk Professionals. Annual. $125.00. Median and quartile financial ratios are given for over 400 kinds of manufacturing, wholesale, retail, construction, and consumer finance establishments. Data is sorted by both asset size and sales volume. Includes a clearly written "Definition of Ratios," a bibliography of financial ratio sources, and an alphabetical industry index.

RADIOLOGY REFERENCE GUIDE
e-mail: access@accesspub.com
url: http://www.accesspub.com
1301 West Park Ave.
Ocean, NJ 07712
PH: 800-458-0990
FX: (732)493-9713
Access Publishing Co. Annual. Price on application. Includes directory information for radiological equipment, supplies, services, organizations, and publications.

REFORM OF HEALTH CARE SYSTEMS: A REVIEW OF SEVENTEEN OECD COUNTRIES
e-mail: washcont@oecd.org
url: http://www.oecd.org
OECD Washington Center
2001 L St., N. W., Suite 650
Washington, DC 20036-4922
PH: 800-456-6323
FX: (202)785-0350
Organization for Economic Cooperation and Development. 1994. $86.00. An extensive review of attempts by major countries to control health care costs.

REPORT ON HEALTHCARE INFORMATION MANAGEMENT: A STRATEGIC GUIDE TO TECHNOLOGY AND DATA INTEGRATION
1101 King St., Suite 444
Alexandria, VA 22314
PH: 800-655-5597
FX: 800-645-4104
Capitol Publications, Inc. Monthly. $335.00 per year. Newsletter. Covers management information sytems for hospitals and physicicans' groups.

RESIDENT AND STAFF PHYSICIAN
80 Shore Rd.
Port Washington, NY 11050
PH: (516)883-6350
FX: (516)883-6609
Romaine Pierson Publishers, Inc. Monthly. $55.00 per year.

RETIREMENT SECURITY: UNDERSTANDING AND PLANNING YOUR FINANCIAL FUTURE
e-mail: business@jwiley.com
url: http://www.wiley.com
605 Third Ave.
New York, NY 10158-0012
PH: 800-225-5945
FX: (212)850-6088
David M. Walker. John Wiley and Sons, Inc. 1996. $29.95. Topics include investments, social security, Medicare, health insurance, and employer retirement plans.

SAFETY AND HEALTH AT WORK
e-mail: webinfo@ilo.org
url: http://www.ilo.org
1828 L St., N.W., Suite 801
Washington, DC 20036
PH: (202)653-7652
FX: (202)653-7687
International Labor Office. Bimonthly. $240.00 per year. Formerly *Occupational Safety and Health Abstracts.*

SCIENCE CITATION INDEX
3501 Market St.
Philadelphia, PA 19104

PH: 800-386-4474
FX: (215)386-2991
Institute for Scientific Information. Bimonthly. $15,020.00 per year. Annual cumulation.

SCISEARCH
url: http://www.isinet.com
3501 Market St.
Philadelphia, PA 19104
PH: 800-523-1850
FX: (215)386-2911
Institute for Scientific Information. Broad, multidisciplinary index to the literature of science and technology, 1974 to present. Inquire as to online cost and availability. Coverage of literature is worldwide, with weekly updates.

SEMINARS IN ULTRASOUND, CT, AND MR
(COMPUTERIZED TOMOGRAPHY AND MAGNETIC
RESONANCE)
e-mail: http://www.wbsaunders.com
Curtis Center, 3rd Fl.
Independence Square West
Philadelphia, PA 19106-3399
PH: 800-545-2522
FX: (215)238-6445
W. B. Saunders Co. Bimonthly. $169.00 per year.

SMARTER INSURANCE SOLUTIONS
e-mail: info@bloomberg.com
url: http://www.bloomberg.com
Post Office Box 888
Princeton, NJ 08542-0888
PH: 800-388-2749
FX: (609)279-5967
Janet Bamford. Bloomberg Press. 1996. $19.95. Provides practical advice to consumers, with separate chapters on the following kinds of insurance: automobile, homeowners, health, disability, and life. (Bloomberg Personal Library.)

SOCIAL SCIENCE SOURCE
e-mail: ep@epnet.com
url: http://www.epnet.com
10 Estes St.
Ipswitch, MA 01938
PH: 800-653-2726
FX: (978)356-6565
EBSCO Publishing. Monthly. $1,495.00 per year. Provides CD-ROM citations and abstracts to social science articles in more than 400 periodicals, with full text from 60 periodicals. Covers economics, political science, public policy, international relations, psychology, and other topics. Time period is most recent five years.

SOCIAL SCIENCES CITATION INDEX: COMPACT DISC
EDITION WITH ABSTRACTS
3501 Market St.
Philadelphia, PA 19104
PH: 800-523-1850
FX: (215)386-6362
Institute for Scientific Information. Quarterly. $6,540.00 per year. Provides CD-ROM indexing and abstracting of "significant articles" from 1,400 social science journals worldwide, with additional selections from 3,200 other journals, 1986 to date. Includes economics, business, finance, management, communications, demographics, information and library science, political science, sociology, and many other subjects.

SOCIAL SCIENCES INDEX
e-mail: hwwmsg@info.hwwilson.com
url: http://www.hwwilson.com
950 University Ave.
Bronx, NY 10452
PH: 800-367-6770
FX: (718)590-1617

H. W. Wilson Co. Quarterly, with annual cumulation. Service basis. Indexes more than 400 periodicals covering economics, environmental policy, government, insurance, labor, health care policy, plannning, public administration, public welfare, urban studies, women's issues, criminology, and related topics.

SOCIAL WELFARE RESEARCH INSTITUTE
e-mail: paul.schervish@bc.edu
515 McGuinn Hall
Chestnut Hill, MA 02167
PH: (617)552-4070

SOCIETY OF MEDICAL-DENTAL MANAGEMENT
CONSULTANTS
3646 E. Ray Rd. B16-45
Phoenix, AZ 85044
PH: 800-826-2264
FX: (602)759-3530

SOCIETY OF MEDICAL-DENTAL MANAGEMENT
CONSULTANTS: MEMBERSHIP DIRECTORY
4959 Olsen Memorial Highway
Minneapolis, MN 55422
PH: (612)544-9621
Society of Medical-Dental Management Consultants. Annual. Free. About 100 consultants in business and financial aspects of the management of medical and dental practices.

SOURCE BOOK OF HEALTH INSURANCE DATA
555 13th St., NW, No. 600
Washington, DC 20004-1109
PH: (202)223-7853
FX: (202)223-7885
Health Insurance Association of America. Annual. $25.00. Data on health insurance, medical care costs, morbidity and health manpower in the U.S.

SPECIAL INTEREST GROUP FOR BIOMEDICAL
COMPUTING
e-mail: rivikin@acm.org
url: http://:://www.org/sigart/
Association for Computing Machinery
1515 Broadway, 17th Fl.
New York, NY 10036
PH: (212)626-0607
FX: (212)302-5826
Subject area is the use of computer technology in the health and biological sciences.

STANDARD & POOR'S INDUSTRY SURVEYS
e-mail: speqwebmaster@mcgraw-hill.com
url: http://www.stockinfo.standardpoor.com
25 Broadway
New York, NY 10004-1010
PH: 800-221-5277
FX: (212)208-0040
Standard & Poor's. Semiannual. $2,250.00 per year. Two loose-leaf volumes. Provides detailed, individual surveys of 52 major industry groups. Each survey is revised on a semiannual basis. Also includes "Monthly Investment Review" (industry group investment analysis) and monthly "Trends & Projections" (economic analysis).

STATISTICAL FORECASTS OF THE UNITED STATES
835 Penobscot Bldg.
Detroit, MI 48226-4094
PH: 800-877-GALE
FX: 800-414-5043
Gale Research Inc. 1995. $99.00. Second edition. Provides both long-term and short-term statistical forecasts relating to basic items in the U.S.: population, employment, labor, crime, education, and health care. Data in the form of charts, graphs, and tables has been taken from a wide variety of government and pri-

vate sources. Includes a subject index and an "Index of Forecast by Year."

STRATEGIC HEALTH CARE MARKETING

625 Ave. of the Americas
New York, NY 10011
PH: 800-346-3787
Available from FIND/SVP, Inc. Monthly. $249.00 per year. Newsletter. Published by Health Care Communications.

STRATIS HEALTH

e-mail: reieroo3@maroon.tc.umn.edu
2901 Metro Dr., 400
Bloomington, MN 55425-1529
PH: (612)858-9188
FX: (612)858-9189
Formerly Health Outcomes Institute.

SURGEONS' DESK REFERENCE FOR MINIMALLY INVASIVE SURGERY PRODUCTS

Five Paragon Drive
Montvale, NJ 07645-1742
PH: 800-232-7379
FX: (201)573-4956
Medical Economics Co., Inc. Annual. $125.00. A directory of products for laparoscopic surgery. Includes commentary.

TOXLINE

8600 Rockville Pike
Bethesda, MD 20894
PH: 800-638-8480
FX: (301)480-3537
National Library of Medicine. Abstracting service covering human and animal toxicity studies, 1981 to present (older studies available in *Toxback* file). Monthly updates. Inquire as to online cost and availability.

TRUSTEE: THE MAGAZINE FOR HOSPITAL GOVERNING BOARDS

737 North Michigan Ave., Suite 700
Chicago, IL 60611-2615
PH: 800-621-6902
FX: (312)951-8491
American Hospital Publishing, Inc. Monthly. $25.00 per year. Emphasis is on community health care. (An American Hospital Association publication.)

U.S. INDUSTRY AND TRADE OUTLOOK

e-mail: customer.service@mcgraw-hill.com
url: http://www.mcgraw-hill.com
1221 Ave. of the Americas
New York, NY 10020
PH: 800-722-4726
FX: (212)512-2821
McGraw-Hill. Annual. $69.95. Produced by the International Trade Administration, U.S. Department of Commerce, in a "public-private" partnership with DRI/McGraw-Hill and Standard & Poor's. Provides basic data, outlook for the current year, and "Long-Term Prospects" (five-year projections) for a wide variety of products and services. Includes high technology industries. Formerly *U.S. Industrial Outlook.*

THE U.S. MARKET FOR ASSISTED-LIVING FACILITIES

e-mail: catalog@findsvp.com
url: http://www.findsvp.com
625 Ave. of the Americas
New York, NY 10011-2002
PH: 800-346-3787
FX: (212)807-2716
FIND/SVP, Inc. 1997. $2,250.00. Market research report. Includes market demographics and estimates of future revenues. Facility operators such as Emeritus, Manor Care, and Marriott Senior Living are profiled.

U.S. INSURANCE: LIFE, ACCIDENT, AND HEALTH

150 Cambridge Park Drive
Cambridge, MA 02140
PH: 800-554-5501
FX: (617)225-7058
OneSource Information Services. Monthly. Price on application. Provides detailed CD-ROM information on the financial characteristics of more than 2,300 life, accident, and health insurance companies.

UNIVERSAL HEALTHCARE ALMANAC: A COMPLETE GUIDE FOR THE HEALTHCARE PROFESSIONAL -FACTS, FIGURES, ANALYSIS

e-mail: uhaeditor@aol.com
10221 North 32nd St., Suite J-1
Phoenix, AZ 85028-3849
PH: (602)996-2220
Silver & Cherner. Looseleaf, with quarterly updates. $180.00 for first year, then $125.00 per year. Includes a wide variety of health care statistics: national expenditures, hospital data, health insurance, health professionals, vital statistics, demographics, etc. Years of coverage vary, with long range forecasts provided in some cases.

VITAL AND HEALTH STATISTICS

Washington, DC 20402
PH: (202)512-1800
FX: (202)512-2250
Available from U.S. Government Printing Office. Annual. Free. Lists government publications. (GPO Subject Bibliography Number 121).

WEFA INDUSTRIAL MONITOR

e-mail: business@jwiley.
url: http://www.wiley.com
605 Third Ave.
New York, NY 10158-0012
PH: 800-225-5945
FX: (212)850-6088
John Wiley and Sons, Inc. Annual. $59.95. Prepared by industry analysts at WEFA, an economic forecasting and consulting firm (originally Wharton Econometric Forecasting Associates). Contains discussions of the outlook for major U.S. industries, with many 10-year forecasts (WEFA Web site is http://www.wefa.com).

WHO WRITES WHAT IN LIFE AND HEALTH INSURANCE

url: http://www.naco.com
505 Gest St.
Cincinnati, OH 45203
PH: 800-543-0874
FX: (513)721-0126
National Underwriter Co. Annual. $22.95.

WHO'S WHO IN THE DENTAL LABORATORY INDUSTRY

555 E. Braddock Rd.
Alexandria, VA 22314-2601
PH: (703)683-5263
FX: (703)549-4788
National Association of Dental Laboratories. Annual. $55.00. About 3,300 dental laboratories; 12,000 certified dental technicians, manufacturers, and schools of dental technology.

WHO'S WHO IN TECHNOLOGY [ONLINE]

835 Penobscot Bldg.
Detroit, MI 48226-4094
PH: 800-877-GALE
FX: (313)961-6083
Gale Research Inc. Provides online biographical profiles of over 25,000 American scientists, engineers, and others in technology-related occupations. Inquire as to online cost and availability.

**WILSONDISC: APPLIED SCIENCE AND TECHNOLOGY
  ABSTRACTS**
950 University Ave.
Bronx, NY 10452
PH: 800-367-6770
FX: (718)590-1617
H. W. Wilson Co. Monthly. $1,495.00 per year, including un-
limited access to the online version of *Applied Science and Technology Abstracts* through WILSONLINE. Provides CD-ROM
indexing and abstracting of 400 prominent scientific, technical,
engineering, and industrial periodicals. Indexing coverage is provided from 1983 to date and abstracting from 1993 to date.

WILSONDISC: WILSON SOCIAL SCIENCES ABSTRACTS
e-mail: hwwmsg@info.hwwilson.com
url: http://www.hwwilson.com
950 University Ave.
Bronx, NY 10452
PH: 800-367-6770
FX: (718)590-1617
H. W. Wilson Co. Monthly. $2,295.00 per year, including un-
limited online access to *Social Sciences Index* through WILSON-
LINE. Provides CD-ROM indexing from 1983 and abstracting
from 1994 of more than 400 periodicals covering economics, area
studies, community health, public administration, public welfare,
urban studies, and many other topics related to the social sciences. (Also available without abstracts at $1,295.00 per year.)

**WILSONLINE: APPLIED SCIENCE AND TECHNOLOGY
  ABSTRACTS**
e-mail: hwwmsg@info.hwwilson.com
url: http://www.hwwilson.com
950 University Ave.
Bronx, NY 10452
PH: 800-367-6770
FX: (718)590-1617
H. W. Wilson Co. Provides online indexing and abstracting of
400 major scientific, technical, industrial, and engineering periodicals. Time period is 1983 to date for indexing and 1993 to date
for abstracting, with updating twice a week. Inquire as to online
cost and availability.

WILSONLINE: WILSON BUSINESS ABSTRACTS
e-mail: hwwmsg@info.hwwilson.com
url: http://ww.hwwilson.com
950 University Ave.
Bronx, NY 10452
PH: 800-367-6770
FX: (718)590-1617
H. W. Wilson Co. Indexes and abstracts 400 major business periodicals, plus the *Wall Street Journal* and the business section of
the *New York Times*. Indexing is from 1982, abstracting from
1990, with the two newspapers included from 1993. Updated
daily. Inquire as to online cost and availability. (*Business Periodicals Index* without abstracts is also available online.)

WILSONLINE: WILSON SOCIAL SCIENCES ABSTRACTS
e-mail: hwwmsg@info.hwwilson.com
url: http://www.hwwilson.com
950 University Ave.
Bronx, NY 10452
PH: 800-367-6770
FX: (718)590-1617
H. W. Wilson Co. Provides online abstracting and indexing of
more than 415 periodicals covering area studies, community
health, public administration, public welfare, urban studies, and
many other social science topics. Time period is 1994 to date for
abstracts and 1983 to date for indexing, with updates twice a
week. Inquire as to online cost and availability.

CHAPTER 10

TRADE SHOWS

Information presented in this chapter is adapted from Gale's *Trade Shows Worldwide* (*TSW*) or, where appropriate, from Gale's *Encyclopedia of Associations* (industry conferences). Entries present information needed for all those planning to visit or to participate in trade shows for the Health and Medical Services sector. *TSW* entries include U.S. and international shows and exhibitions as well as companies, organizations, and information sources relating to the trade industry. Events, such as conferences and conventions, are included only if they feature exhibitions.

Entries are arranged in alphabetical order by the name of the event and include the exhibition management company with full contact information, frequency of the event, audience, principal exhibits, dates and locations, and former name of the show (if applicable).

AAAAI ANNUAL CONFERENCE AND EXHIBITION
e-mail: info@aaaai.org
611 E. Wells St.
Milwaukee, WI 53202
PH: (414)272-6071
FX: (414)272-6070
Frequency: Annual. **Principal Exhibits:** Pharmaceuticals, medical supplies, and books. **Dates and Locations:** 1998 Mar 13-18; Washington, DC ▪ 1999 Feb 26 - Mar 03; Orlando, FL ▪ 2000 Mar 17-22; San Diego, CA.

AAOMS ANNUAL SCIENTIFIC SESSION
9700 W. Bryn Mawr Ave.
Rosemont, IL 60018-5701
PH: (708)678-6200
TF: 800822-6637
FX: (708)678-6286
Frequency: Annual. **Audience:** Oral and maxillofacial surgeons. **Principal Exhibits:** Products, services, and publications related to the practice of oral and maxillofacial surgery. **Dates and Locations:** 1998 Sep 16-20; New Orleans, LA ▪ 1999 Sep 29 - Oct 03; Boston, MA.

ACADEMY OF DENTISTRY WINTER CLINIC
e-mail: admin@tordent.com
170 Bloor St. W., Ste. 902
Toronto, ON, Canada M5S 1T9
PH: (416)967-5649
FX: (416)967-5081
Frequency: Annual. **Audience:** Dentists, assistants, hygienists, dental nurses, and other trade professionals. **Principal Exhibits:** Financial, dental equipment, supplies, and services. **Dates and Locations:** 1998 Nov; Toronto, ON.

ACADEMY OF GENERAL DENTISTRY ANNUAL MEETING
e-mail: agd.dented@aol.com
url: http://www.agd.org
211 E. Chicago Ave., Ste. 1200
Chicago, IL 60611
PH: (312)440-4300
TF: 888243-3368
FX: (312)440-0559
Frequency: Annual. **Audience:** General practitioners in dentistry. **Principal Exhibits:** Dental products and services. **Dates and Locations:** 1998 Jul 10-13; Boston, MA ▪ 1999 Jul 22-25; Salt Lake City, UT.

AEROSPACE MEDICAL ASSOCIATION EXHIBITION
url: http://www.asma.org
320 S. Henry St.
Alexandria, VA 22314
PH: (703)739-2240
FX: (703)739-9652
Frequency: Annual. **Audience:** Aviation medical examiners; scientists and bioengineers engaged in biomedical research; physicians and nurses of Aerospace Medical Association. **Principal Exhibits:** Products related to aerospace medicine; safety products; diagnostic and research instrumentation for the field of human factors. **Dates and Locations:** 1998 May 17-21; Seattle, WA ▪ 1999 May 16-20; Detroit, MI.

AIHE - ASHGABAT INTERNATIONAL HEALTHCARE EXHIBITION
e-mail: healthcare@ITE-Group.com
Byron House
112A Shirland Rd.
London W9 EQ, England
PH: 44 171 286 9720
FX: 44 171 266 1126
Frequency: Annual. **Principal Exhibits:** Healthcare equipment, supplies, and services.

ALABAMA DENTAL ASSOCIATION ANNUAL SESSION
836 Washington Ave.
Montgomery, AL 36104
PH: (205)265-1684
FX: (205)262-6218
Frequency: Annual. **Audience:** Dental assistants, dentists, family, and related professionals. **Principal Exhibits:** Dental equipment, sundry dental supplies, computer software, and pharmaceutical and dental instruments. **Dates and Locations:** 1998 Jun 14-21; Orange Beach, AL ▪ 1999 Jun 15-20; Orange Beach, AL.

ALABAMA HOSPITAL ASSOCIATION CONVENTION AND HOSPAC TRADE FAIR
PO Box 210759
Montgomery, AL 36121-0759
PH: (334)272-8781
TF: 800489-2542
FX: (334)270-9527
Frequency: Annual. **Audience:** Hospital administrators, nurses, purchasing managers, pharmacists, and other hospital-related professionals. **Principal Exhibits:** Hospital equipment, supplies, and services. **Dates and Locations:** 1998 Jun 09-12; Birmingham, AL ▪ 1999 Jun 08-11; Birmingham, AL.

ALBERTA ASSOCIATION OF REGISTERED NURSES ANNUAL CONVENTION
11620 168th St.
Edmonton, AB, Canada T5M 4A6
PH: (403)451-0043
FX: (403)452-3276
Frequency: Biennial. **Audience:** All registered nurses. **Principal Exhibits:** Medical supplies and nursing publications and supplies. **Dates and Locations:** 1999 Apr 20-23; Calgary, AB ▪ 2001 Apr 03-06; Edmonton, AB.

ALBERTA HEALTH CARE EXPO
11659-72 Ave.
Edmonton, AB, Canada T6G 0B9
PH: (403)436-0983
FX: (403)437-5984
Frequency: Annual. **Audience:** Chief executive officers, hospital trustees, purchasing agents, materials managers, O.R. nurses, directors of nursing, and hospital planners. **Principal Exhibits:** Hospital-related equipment, supplies, and services. **Dates and Locations:** 1998 Oct 27-28; Edmonton, AB ▪ 1999 Oct 26-27; Edmonton, AB. **Formerly:** Alberta Healthcare Association Convention; Alberta Hospital Association Convention.

AMERICAN ACADEMY OF ENVIRONMENTAL MEDICINE CONFERENCE
url: http://www.netplace.net/aaem/
PO Box CN 10018001
New Hope, PA 18938
Frequency: Annual. **Audience:** Physicians. **Principal Exhibits:** Environmental medicine equipment, supplies, and services. **Dates and Locations:** 1998.

AMERICAN ACADEMY OF FAMILY PHYSICIANS, WEST VIRGINIA CHAPTER, ANNUAL SCIENTIFIC ASSEMBLY
4760 Fire Creek Rd.
Charleston, WV 25313
PH: (304)776-1178
FX: (304)776-7784
Frequency: Annual. **Audience:** Physicians, students, interns, registered nurses, and physician assistants. **Principal Exhibits:** Pharmaceutical companies, hospitals, and home healthcare equipment, supplies, and services. **Dates and Locations:** 1998.

AMERICAN ACADEMY OF GNATHOLOGIC ORTHOPEDICS CONFERENCE
1585 N. Barrington Rd., Ste. 106
Hoffman Estates, IL 60194
PH: (847)884-1220
FX: (847)884-1638

Frequency: Annual. **Audience:** Dentists dealing with the prevention or correction of malocclusion and bony misformations. **Principal Exhibits:** Exhibits of interest to those in the fields of maxillofacial orthopedics/orthodontics and preventative and corrective orthodontics. **Dates and Locations:** 1998 Oct 21-24; Sacramento, CA ■ 1999 Oct 20-23; San Antonio, TX.

AMERICAN ACADEMY OF GOLD FOIL OPERATORS ANNUAL MEETING
17922 Tallgrass Ct.
Noblesville, IN 46060
PH: (317)867-3011
FX: (317)867-3011
Frequency: Annual. **Audience:** Dentists who perform restorative procedures utilizing gold foil, cast gold, and the rubber dam. **Principal Exhibits:** Exhibits relating to gold restorations and the rubber dam for dental procedures. **Dates and Locations:** 1998 Oct 07-11; Minneapolis, MN.

AMERICAN ACADEMY OF IMPLANT DENTISTRY ANNUAL MEETING
e-mail: aaid@aaid-implant.org
url: http://www.aaid-implant.org
211 E. Chicago Ave., Ste. 750
Chicago, IL 60611
PH: (312)335-1550
FX: (312)335-9090
Frequency: Annual. **Principal Exhibits:** Dental equipment, supplies, and services. **Dates and Locations:** 1998.

AMERICAN ACADEMY OF MEDICAL ADMINISTRATORS ANNUAL CONFERENCE AND CONVOCATION
30555 Southfield Rd., Ste. 150
Southfield, MI 48076
PH: (313)540-4310
FX: (313)645-0590
Frequency: Annual. **Audience:** Members and nonmembers. **Principal Exhibits:** Equipment, supplies, and services related to health care. **Dates and Locations:** 1998.

AMERICAN ACADEMY OF OPHTHALMOLOGY ANNUAL MEETING
e-mail: meetings@aao.org
655 Beach St.
PO Box 7424
San Francisco, CA 94120-7424
PH: (415)561-8500
FX: (415)561-8576
Frequency: Annual. **Audience:** Ophthalmologists and related trade professionals. **Principal Exhibits:** Ophthalmic equipment and instruments. **Dates and Locations:** 1998 Nov 08-12; New Orleans, LA ■ 1999 Oct 24-27; Orlando, FL ■ 2000 Oct 22-25; Dallas, TX.

AMERICAN ACADEMY OF OPTOMETRY
e-mail: aaoptom@aol.com
6110 Executive Blvd., Ste. 506
Rockville, MD 20910
PH: (301)984-1441
FX: (301)984-4737
Frequency: Annual. **Principal Exhibits:** Exhibits focusing on the latest research and patient treatments relating to clinical practice standards, optometric education, and experimental research in visual problems. **Dates and Locations:** 1998 Dec; San Francisco, CA.

AMERICAN ACADEMY OF OROFACIAL PAIN SCIENTIFIC CONFERENCE
19 Mantua Rd.
Mount Royal, NJ 08061
PH: (609)423-7222
FX: (609)423-3420
Frequency: Annual. **Audience:** Medical and dental doctors. **Principal Exhibits:** Exhibits relating to orofacial pain and temporomandibular disorders. **Dates and Locations:** 1998 May 01-03; Washington, DC.

AMERICAN ACADEMY OF ORTHODONTICS FOR THE GENERAL PRACTITIONER CONVENTION
920 Bascom Hill Dr.
Baraboo, WI 53913-1281
Frequency: Annual. **Audience:** Dentists. **Principal Exhibits:** Orthodontic equipment, supplies, and services. **Dates and Locations:** 1998 Jun.

AMERICAN ACADEMY OF ORTHOPEDIC SURGEONS ANNUAL MEETING
url: http://www.aaos.org
6300 N. River Rd.
Rosemont, IL 60018-4262
PH: (847)823-7186
FX: (847)823-8031
Frequency: Annual. **Audience:** Orthopedic surgeons and related professionals. **Principal Exhibits:** Surgical equipment, supplies, and services used by orthopaedic surgeons. **Dates and Locations:** 1998 Mar 19-23; New Orleans, LA ■ 1999 Feb 04-08; Anaheim, CA ■ 2000 Mar 15-19; Orlando, FL.

AMERICAN ACADEMY OF OSTEOPATHY WORKSHOP
3500 DePauw Blvd., Ste. 1080
Indianapolis, IN 46268-1136
PH: (317)879-1881
FX: (317)879-0563
Frequency: Annual. **Principal Exhibits:** Osteopathic manipulative treatment equipment, supplies, and services, including osteopathic structural diagnostic and therapeutic procedures. **Dates and Locations:** 1998 Mar 25-28; Colorado Springs, CO.

AMERICAN ACADEMY OF PHYSICAL MEDICINE AND REHABILITATION ANNUAL MEETING
url: http://www.aapmr.org
330 N. Wabash Ave., No. 2500
Chicago, IL 60611-3514
PH: (312)464-9700
FX: (312)464-0227
Frequency: Annual. **Audience:** Physicians specializing in physical medicine and rehabilitation. **Principal Exhibits:** Pharmaceuticals, electrodiagnostic equipment, wheelchairs, and related equipment, supplies, and services. **Dates and Locations:** 1998 Nov 05-08; Seattle, WA ■ 1999 Nov 11-14; Washington, DC ■ 2000 Nov 02-05; San Francisco, CA ■ 2001 Sep 13-16; New Orleans, LA ■ 2002 Nov 21-24; Orlando, FL.

AMERICAN ALLIANCE FOR HEALTH, PHYSICAL EDUCATION, RECREATION, AND DANCE -MIDWEST DISTRICT CONVENTION
e-mail: conv@aahperd.org
url: http://www.aahperd.org
1900 Association Dr.
Reston, VA 20191-1599
PH: (703)476-3400
TF: 800213-7193
FX: (703)476-9527
Frequency: Annual. **Audience:** Educators in the field of health, recreation, and dance. **Principal Exhibits:** Sporting goods, recreational equipment, clothing, publications, and health materials. **Dates and Locations:** 1998 Apr 05-09.

AMERICAN ALLIANCE FOR HEALTH, PHYSICAL EDUCATION, RECREATION, AND DANCE -NATIONAL CONFERENCE AND EXPOSITION
e-mail: conv@aahperd.org
url: http://www.aahperd.org
1900 Association Dr.
Reston, VA 20191-1599

PH: (703)476-3400
TF: 800213-7193
FX: (703)476-9527
Frequency: Annual. **Audience:** Health and physical education teachers, coaches, athletic directors, trainers, officials, dance teachers, and related professionals and students. **Principal Exhibits:** Physical educational sporting goods, supplies, equipment, publishers, and service organization representatives. **Dates and Locations:** 1998 Mar; St. Louis, MO.

AMERICAN ASSOCIATION FOR CLINICAL CHEMISTRY ANNUAL MEETING

url: http://www.aacc.org
2101 L St. NW, Ste. 202
Washington, DC 20037-1526
PH: (202)857-0717
TF: 800892-1400
FX: (202)887-5093
Frequency: Annual. **Audience:** Clinical laboratory scientists and others engaged in the practice of clinical chemistry in independent laboratories, hospitals, and allied institutions. **Principal Exhibits:** Clinical chemistry equipment, supplies, and services. **Dates and Locations:** 1998 Aug 02-06; Chicago, IL.

AMERICAN ASSOCIATION FOR CONTINUITY OF CARE ANNUAL CONFERENCE

e-mail: Ipiorek@csunet.ctstateu.edu
638 Prospect Ave.
Hartford, CT 06105-4250
PH: (203)586-7525
FX: (203)586-7550
Frequency: Annual. **Audience:** Discharge planners, nurses, social workers, hospital administrators, and related professionals. **Principal Exhibits:** Health care delivery resources, products, and services. **Dates and Locations:** 1998 Sep; Boston, MA.

AMERICAN ASSOCIATION OF DENTAL CONSULTANTS FALL MEETING

e-mail: JSALIS913@aol.com
PO Box 3345
Lawrence, KS 66046
PH: (913)749-2727
TF: 800896-0707
FX: (913)749-1140
Frequency: Annual. **Audience:** Dental insurance consultants and others concerned with dental insurance plans from administrative and design perspectives. **Principal Exhibits:** Exhibits relating to dental insurance plans, including the interrelationship between insurance carriers, the dental profession, and the insured. **Dates and Locations:** 1998.

AMERICAN ASSOCIATION OF DENTAL CONSULTANTS SPRING WORKSHOP

e-mail: JSALIS913@aol.com
PO Box 3345
Lawrence, KS 66046
PH: (913)749-2727
TF: 800896-0707
FX: (913)749-1140
Frequency: Annual. **Audience:** Dental insurance consultants and others concerned with dental insurance plans from administrative and design perspectives. **Principal Exhibits:** Exhibits relating to dental insurance plans, including the interrelationship between insurance carriers, the dental profession, and the insured. **Dates and Locations:** 1998 May 14-16; Scottsdale, AZ.

AMERICAN ASSOCIATION FOR DENTAL RESEARCH ANNUAL SESSION

e-mail: research@iadr.com
url: http://medhlp.netvsa.net/iadr/iadr.htm
1619 Duke St.
Alexandria, VA 22314
PH: (703)548-0066
FX: (703)548-1883

Frequency: Annual. **Audience:** Active dental researchers involved in buying. **Principal Exhibits:** Equipment, supplies, and services required by dental researchers for laboratory work and teaching with a focus on cell biology. **Dates and Locations:** 1998 Mar 04-08; Minneapolis, MN ▪ 1999 Mar 10-14; Vancouver, BC ▪ 2000 Apr 05-09; Washington, DC.

AMERICAN ASSOCIATION OF DENTAL SCHOOLS ANNUAL SESSION AND EXPOSITION

1625 Massachusetts Ave., NW
Washington, DC 20036
PH: (202)667-9433
FX: (202)667-0642
Frequency: Annual. **Audience:** Dental educators and dental auxiliary educators. **Principal Exhibits:** Dental equipment and supplies, publications, video equipment, and computers. **Dates and Locations:** 1998 Mar.

AMERICAN ASSOCIATION OF ENDODONTISTS ANNUAL CONVENTION AND TRADE SHOW

211 E. Chicago Ave., Ste. 1100
Chicago, IL 60611
PH: (312)266-7255
FX: (312)266-9867
Frequency: Annual. **Audience:** Endodontists and general practitioner dentists. **Principal Exhibits:** Industry related equipment, supplies, and services. **Dates and Locations:** 1998 May 06-10; New York, NY ▪ 1999 Apr 21-25; Atlanta, GA ▪ 2000 Mar 29 - Apr 02; Honolulu, HI.

AMERICAN ASSOCIATION FOR THE HISTORY OF MEDICINE MEETING

url: http://www.allegheny.edu/aahm/
Boston University School of Medicine
80 E. Concord St.
Boston, MA 02118-2394
PH: (617)638-4328
FX: (617)638-4329
Frequency: Annual. **Principal Exhibits:** Exhibits relating to the history of medicine. **Dates and Locations:** 1998 Apr; Williamsburg, VA ▪ 1998 May 07-10; Toronto, ON ▪ 1999 May 09-12; New Brunswick, NJ.

AMERICAN ASSOCIATION FOR LABORATORY ANIMAL SCIENCE CONFERENCE & EXHIBITS

70 Timber Creek Dr., Ste. 5
Cordova, TN 38018
PH: (901)754-8620
FX: (901)753-0046
Frequency: Annual. **Audience:** Research veterinarians, medical doctors, PhDs, laboratory animal technicians, and commercial animal breeders. **Principal Exhibits:** Pharmaceuticals and laboratory animal facility equipment and supplies. **Dates and Locations:** 1998 Oct 18-22; Cincinnati, OH ▪ 1999 Nov 07-11; Indianapolis, IN ▪ 2000 Nov 05-09; San Diego, CA.

AMERICAN ASSOCIATION FOR MEDICAL TRANSCRIPTION ANNUAL MEETING

PO Box 576187
Modesto, CA 95357-6187
PH: (209)551-0883
TF: 800982-2182
FX: (209)551-9317
Frequency: Annual. **Principal Exhibits:** Medical transcription equipment, supplies, and services. **Dates and Locations:** 1998.

AMERICAN ASSOCIATION OF NATUROPATHIC PHYSICIANS CONVENTION

e-mail: 74602,3715@compuserve.com
url: http://www.naturopathic.org
601 Valley St. 105
Seattle, WA 98109
PH: (206)298-0126
FX: (206)298-0129

Frequency: Annual. **Audience:** Naturopatric physicians and students. **Principal Exhibits:** Naturopathic medicine equipment, supplies, and services. **Dates and Locations:** 1998.

AMERICAN ASSOCIATION OF NEUROSCIENCE NURSES CONVENTION
url: http://www.aann.org
224 N. Des Planes No. 601
Chicago, IL 60661
PH: (312)993-0043
TF: 800477-2266
FX: (312)993-0362
Frequency: Annual. **Audience:** Neuroscience specialty nurses and general public. **Principal Exhibits:** Neurological and neurosurgical supplies and services, and industry-related recruiters. **Dates and Locations:** 1998 Apr 05-09; Chicago, IL.

AMERICAN ASSOCIATION OF ORTHODONTISTS TRADE SHOW AND SCIENTIFIC SESSION
e-mail: aao@worldnet.att.net
url: http://www.aaortho.org
401 N. Lindbergh Blvd.
St. Louis, MO 63141-7816
PH: (314)993-1700
FX: (314)997-1745
Frequency: Annual. **Audience:** Orthodontists and orthodontic assistants. **Principal Exhibits:** Orthodontic equipment and materials. **Dates and Locations:** 1998 May 16-20; Dallas, TX.

AMERICAN ASSOCIATION FOR PEDIATRIC OPHTHALMOLOGY AND STRABISMUS SCIENTIFIC SESSIONS
PO Box 193832
San Francisco, CA 94119
PH: (415)561-8505
FX: (415)561-8575
Frequency: Annual. **Principal Exhibits:** Pediatric ophthalmology equipment, supplies, and services. **Dates and Locations:** 1998 Apr 04-08; Palm Springs, CA.

AMERICAN ASSOCIATION OF PHYSICIAN SPECIALISTS CONVENTION
804 Main St., Ste. D
Forest Park, GA 30050
PH: (404)363-8263
FX: (404)361-2285
Frequency: Annual. **Audience:** Physicians, particularly those involved in specialty practice. **Principal Exhibits:** Pharmaceuticals, surgical and medical supplies, medical publications, and related equipment, supplies, and services. **Dates and Locations:** 1998 Jun; Philadelphia, PA. **Formerly:** American Association of Osteopathic Specialists Convention.

AMERICAN ASSOCIATION OF PUBLIC HEALTH DENTISTRY CONFERENCE
e-mail: natoff@aol.com
url: http://www.pitt.edu/~aaphd
3760 SW Lyle Ct.
Portland, OR 97221
PH: (503)242-0712
FX: (503)242-0721
Frequency: Annual. **Audience:** dentists, dental hygienists, and health educators. **Principal Exhibits:** Dental public health equipment, supplies, and services. **Dates and Locations:** 1998.

AMERICAN ASSOCIATION FOR THE STUDY OF HEADACHE MEETING
19 Mantua Rd.
Mount Royal, NJ 08061
PH: (609)845-0322
FX: (609)384-5811
Frequency: Annual. **Audience:** Physicians, dentists, and related scientists. **Principal Exhibits:** Headache research equipment,

supplies, and services. **Dates and Locations:** 1998 Jun 26-28; San Francisco, CA.

AMERICAN BOARD OF PODIATRIC ORTHOPEDICS AND PRIMARY MEDICINE CONFERENCE
22910 Crenshaw Blvd., No. B
Torrance, CA 90505
PH: (310)891-0100
FX: (310)891-0500
Frequency: Annual. **Principal Exhibits:** Podiatric equipment, supplies, and services. **Dates and Locations:** 1998.

THE AMERICAN BURN ASSOCIATION EXHIBITION
716 Lee St.
Des Plaines, IL 60016-4515
PH: (708)824-5700
FX: (708)824-0394
Frequency: Annual. **Audience:** Surgeons, nurses, physical and occupational therapists, technicians, researchers, emergency medical technicians, and firefighters. **Principal Exhibits:** Equipment, supplies and services related to burn-care treatment. **Dates and Locations:** 1998 Mar 18-21; Chicago, IL.

AMERICAN COLLEGE OF CHEST PHYSICIANS ANNUAL INTERNATIONAL SCIENTIFIC ASSEMBLY
3300 Dundee Rd.
Northbrook, IL 60062
PH: (847)498-1400
FX: (847)498-5460
Frequency: Annual. **Audience:** Cardiopulmonary physicians and surgeons. **Principal Exhibits:** Medical equipment, supplies, surgical instruments related to cardiopulmonary medicine. **Dates and Locations:** 1998 Nov 08-12; Toronto, ON ■ 1999 Oct 31 - Nov 04; Chicago, IL.

AMERICAN COLLEGE OF FOOT AND ANKLE SURGEONS ANNUAL MEETING AND SCIENTIFIC SEMINAR
e-mail: acfas@pop.mbsi.net
515 Busse Hwy.
Park Ridge, IL 60068
PH: (847)292-2237
TF: 800421-2237
FX: (847)292-2022
Frequency: Annual. **Audience:** Foot & Ankle surgeons. **Principal Exhibits:** Surgical and podiatric products. **Dates and Locations:** 1999 Feb 17-20; Beverly Hills, CA.

AMERICAN COLLEGE HEALTH ASSOCIATION TRADE SHOW
e-mail: acha@access.digex.net
url: http://www.acha.org
PO Box 28937
Baltimore, MD 21240-8937
PH: (410)859-1500
FX: (410)859-1510
Frequency: Annual. **Audience:** Physicians, nurses, nurse practitioners, psychologists, health educators, dentists adminstrators, all college healthcare professionals. **Principal Exhibits:** Pharmaceuticals, insurance plans, laboratory services, and medical equipment, medical textbooks and publications. **Dates and Locations:** 1998 Jun 03-06; San Diego, CA ■ 1999 Jun 02-05; Philadelphia, PA.

AMERICAN COLLEGE OF HEALTHCARE INFORMATION ADMINISTRATORS CONFERENCE
30555 Southfield Rd., Ste. 150
Southfield, MI 48076
PH: (810)540-4310
FX: (810)645-0590
Frequency: Annual. **Principal Exhibits:** Healthcare management equipment, supplies, and services. **Dates and Locations:** 1998 May 02-05; Atlanta, GA.

AMERICAN COLLEGE OF MEDICAL PHYSICS
e-mail: acmp@acr.org
1891 Preston White Dr.
Reston, VA 22091
PH: (703)648-8966
FX: (703)648-9176
Frequency: Annual. **Principal Exhibits:** Medical physics equipment, supplies, and services. **Dates and Locations:** 1998 Jun; Lake Tahoe, NV.

AMERICAN COLLEGE OF MEDICAL QUALITY
e-mail: acma@aol.com
url: http://www.acmq.org
PO Box 34493
Bethesda, MD 20827-0493
PH: (301)365-3570
TF: 800924-2149
FX: (301)365-3202
Frequency: Annual. **Audience:** Physicians, nurses, and other healthcare professionals interested in medical quality assurance and utilization review and risk management. **Principal Exhibits:** Computer hardware and software, pharmaceuticals, medical publications, and related equipment, supplies, and services. **Dates and Locations:** 1998. **Formerly:** Managed Care and Care Managers Focusing on Clinical Quality.

AMERICAN COLLEGE OF ORAL AND MAXILLOFACIAL
SURGEONS ANNUAL CONFERENCE
1100 NW Loop 410, Ste. 506
San Antonio, TX 78213-2266
PH: (210)344-5674
TF: 800522-6676
FX: (210)344-9754
Frequency: Annual. **Principal Exhibits:** Exhibits for oral and maxillofacial surgery. **Dates and Locations:** 1998 Apr 30 - May 03; Cleveland, OH.

AMERICAN COLLEGE OF PHYSICIANS ANNUAL SESSION
url: http://www.gesexpo.com
950 Crier Dr.
Las Vegas, NV 89119
Frequency: Annual. **Audience:** Members, trade professionals and general public. **Principal Exhibits:** Medical equipment, supplies, and services. **Dates and Locations:** 1998 Apr 02-05; San Diego, CA ▪ 1999 Apr 22-25; New Orleans, LA ▪ 2000 Apr 06-09; San Diego, CA.

AMERICAN COLLEGE OF SURGEONS ANNUAL CLINICAL
CONGRESS
e-mail: postmaster@facs.org
url: http://www.facs.org
55 E. Erie St.
Chicago, IL 60611
PH: (312)664-4050
FX: (312)440-7014
Frequency: Annual. **Audience:** Medical professionals. **Principal Exhibits:** Medical products, pritent care, practice management & educationa services and products. **Dates and Locations:** 1998 Oct 25-30; Orlando, FL ▪ 1999 Oct 10-15; San Francisco, CA ▪ 2000 Oct 22-27; Chicago, IL.

AMERICAN COLLEGE OF VETERINARY
OPHTHALMOLOGISTS CONFERENCE
c/o Dr. Mary B. Glaze
Louisiana State University
Veterinary Teaching Hospital
Baton Rouge, LA 70803
Baton Rouge, LA 70803
PH: (504)346-3333
FX: (504)346-3295
Frequency: Annual. **Principal Exhibits:** Veterinary ophthalmology equipment, supplies, and services. **Dates and Locations:** 1998.

AMERICAN DENTAL ASSOCIATION ANNUAL SESSION &
COMMERCIAL EXPOSITION
211 E. Chicago Ave.
Chicago, IL 60611-2678
PH: (312)440-2581
FX: (312)440-2707
Frequency: Annual. **Audience:** Dentists, dental hygienists, assistants, dealers, manufacturers, and lab technicians. **Principal Exhibits:** Dental equipment, instruments, materials, therapeutics, and services. **Dates and Locations:** 1998 Oct 24-28; San Francisco, CA ▪ 1999 Oct 16-21; Las Vegas, NV ▪ 2000 Oct 28 - Nov 02; Chicago, IL ▪ 2001 Oct 13-18; Honolulu, HI. **Formerly:** American Dental Association Annual Convention.

AMERICAN DENTAL HYGIENISTS' ASSOCIATION
CONVENTION
444 N. Michigan Ave., Ste. 3400
Chicago, IL 60611
PH: (312)440-8900
FX: (312)440-8929
Frequency: Annual. **Audience:** Dental hygienists and other dental professionals. **Principal Exhibits:** Dental hygiene products and services. **Dates and Locations:** 2000; Washington, DC.

AMERICAN DENTAL SOCIETY OF ANESTHESIOLOGY
SCIENTIFIC MEETING
211 E. Chicago Ave., Ste. 948
Chicago, IL 60611
PH: (312)664-8270
TF: 800722-7788
FX: (312)642-9713
Frequency: Annual. **Audience:** Dentists, oral surgeons, and dental anesthesiologists. **Principal Exhibits:** Anesthetics and anesthesia monitoring equipment. **Dates and Locations:** 1998 Apr; Chicago, IL.

AMERICAN ELECTROENCEPHALOGRAPHIC SOCIETY
CONVENTION
1 Regency Dr.
PO Box 30
Bloomfield, CT 06002
PH: (860)243-3977
FX: (860)286-0787
Frequency: Annual. **Audience:** Physicians, technologists. **Principal Exhibits:** Electroencephalographic and neurophysiology equipment, supplies, and services. **Dates and Locations:** 1998 Oct; New Orleans, LA.

AMERICAN GASTROENTEROLOGICAL ASSOCIATION
MEETING
7910 Woodmont Ave., Ste. 914
Bethesda, MD 20814
PH: (301)654-2055
FX: (301)654-5920
Principal Exhibits: Gastroenterology equipment, supplies, and services. **Dates and Locations:** 1998 May.

AMERICAN HEALTH CARE ASSOCIATION ANNUAL
CONVENTION AND EXPOSITION
1201 L St. NW
Washington, DC 20005
PH: (202)842-4444
FX: (202)842-3860
Frequency: Annual. **Audience:** Long-term care and nursing home owners and administrators. **Principal Exhibits:** Supplies for the long-term health care industry. **Dates and Locations:** 1998.

AMERICAN HEALTH INFORMATION MANAGEMENT
ASSOCIATION NATIONAL CONVENTION
919 North Michigan Avenue, Ste. 1400
Chicago, IL 60611
PH: (312)787-2672
FX: (312)787-9793
Frequency: Annual. **Principal Exhibits:** Health information man-

agement technologies and microfilm for health-related centers. **Dates and Locations:** 1998 Oct; New Orleans, LA ▪ 1999 Oct; Anaheim, CA.

AMERICAN HEART ASSOCIATION SCIENTIFIC SESSIONS
url: http://www.amhrt.org
7272 Greenville Ave.
Dallas, TX 75231-4596
PH: (214)706-1425
FX: (214)373-3406
Frequency: Annual. **Audience:** Cardiologists, cardiovascular surgeons and scientists, radiologists, cardiology nurses, and others involved in cardiology. **Principal Exhibits:** Equipment, books, pharmaceuticals, exercise equipment, heart healthy food, and services relevant to cardiological research or physician practice. **Dates and Locations:** 1998 Nov 08-11; Dallas, TX ▪ 1999 Nov 07-10; Atlanta, GA ▪ 2000 Nov 12-15; New Orleans, LA ▪ 2001 Nov 08-11; Anaheim, CA.

AMERICAN INSTITUTE OF BIOLOGICAL SCIENCES ANNUAL MEETING
1444 I St. NW, Ste. 200
Washington, DC 20005
PH: (202)628-1500
TF: 800992-2427
FX: (202)628-1509
Frequency: Annual. **Audience:** Biologists, botanists, ecologists, and mycologists. **Principal Exhibits:** Publishers, scientific equipment companies, and computer companies. **Dates and Locations:** 1998; Montreal, PQ.

AMERICAN LITHOTRIPSY SOCIETY CONVENTION
70 Walnut St.
Wellesley, MA 02181
PH: (617)239-8215
FX: (617)239-7553
Frequency: Annual. **Principal Exhibits:** Equipment, supplies, and services relating to lithotripsy (a non-invasive procedure to treat kidney stones and gall stones). **Dates and Locations:** 1998 Mar; La Jolla, CA ▪ 1999 Mar 16-19; San Antonio, TX.

AMERICAN MEDICAL STUDENT ASSOCIATION CONVENTION
e-mail: amsa@www.amsa.org
url: http://www.amsa.org
1902 Association Dr.
Reston, VA 22091
PH: (703)620-6600
TF: 800767-2266
FX: (703)620-5873
Frequency: Annual. **Audience:** Medical students and hospital housestaff. **Principal Exhibits:** Pharmaceuticals, medical instruments, medical publications, physician recruitment, residency programs, and professional associations. **Dates and Locations:** 1998 Mar.

AMERICAN MEDICAL WOMEN'S ASSOCIATION ANNUAL MEETING
801 N. Fairfax St., Ste. 400
Alexandria, VA 22314
PH: (703)838-0500
FX: (703)549-3864
Frequency: Annual. **Audience:** Women physicians and medical students. **Principal Exhibits:** Medical equipment, supplies, pharmaceuticals, and services. **Dates and Locations:** 1998 Nov 17-23; New Orleans, LA ▪ 1999 Nov 10-14; San Francisco, CA.

AMERICAN OCCUPATIONAL HEALTH CONFERENCE & EXHIBITS
6900 Grove Rd.
Thorofare, NJ 08086
PH: (609)848-1000
FX: (609)848-3522
Frequency: Annual. **Audience:** Occupational physicians, occupa-

tional health nurses, and industrial hygienists. **Principal Exhibits:** Pharmaceuticals, medical equipment, computer software packages for medical offices, lab services, diagnostic testing, and EAP's., ergonomics, environmental products and services. **Dates and Locations:** 1998 Apr 25 - May 01; Boston, MA ▪ 1999 Apr 24-30; Philadelphia, PA.

AMERICAN OPTOMETRIC ASSOCIATION CONGRESS
url: http://www.acanet.org/acanet
243 N. Lindbergh Blvd.
St. Louis, MO 63141
PH: (314)991-4100
FX: (314)991-4101
Frequency: Annual. **Principal Exhibits:** Optometry equipment, supplies, and services. **Dates and Locations:** 1998 Jun 24-28; Orlando, FL.

AMERICAN OPTOMETRIC STUDENT ASSOCIATION ANNUAL MEETING
243 N. Lindbergh
St. Louis, MO 63141
PH: (314)991-4100
FX: (314)991-4101
Frequency: Annual. **Audience:** Optometric students, state optometric associations, and family members of optometric students. **Principal Exhibits:** Optometry equipment, supplies, and services. **Dates and Locations:** 1999 Jan; Houston, TX.

AMERICAN ORGANIZATION OF NURSE EXECUTIVES MEETING AND EXPOSITION
Convention and Meetings Division
840 N. Lake Shore Dr.
Chicago, IL 60611
PH: (312)280-6000
FX: (312)280-6462
Frequency: Annual. **Audience:** Senior nursing administrators from U.S. and Canadian hospitals. **Principal Exhibits:** Patient-care equipment and supplies; computer hardware and software related to the administration of hospital nursing services; communications systems; intensive care units; medical supplies and equipment; recruiting and staffing services; and related equipment, supplies, and services. **Dates and Locations:** 1998 Apr.

AMERICAN ORTHOPAEDIC SOCIETY FOR SPORTS MEDICINE CONVENTION
e-mail: aossm@aossm.org
url: http://www.sportsmed.org
6300 N. River Rd., Ste. 200
Rosemont, IL 60018
PH: (847)292-4900
FX: (847)292-4905
Frequency: Annual. **Audience:** Orthopaedic surgeons. **Principal Exhibits:** Equipment, supplies, and services for orthopedic surgeons working in sports medicine or related fields. **Dates and Locations:** 1998 Jul 12-15; Vancouver, BC ▪ 1999 Jun 19-22; Traverse City, MI ▪ 2000 Jul 02-05; Washington, DC.

AMERICAN ORTHOPSYCHIATRIC ASSOCIATION ANNUAL MEETING
e-mail: amerortho@aol.com
330 7th Ave., 18th Fl.
New York, NY 10001
PH: (212)564-5930
FX: (212)564-6180
Frequency: Annual. **Audience:** Mental health professionals. **Principal Exhibits:** Social service agencies, publications, computer software, and pharmaceuticals. **Dates and Locations:** 1998 May.

AMERICAN ORTHOTIC AND PROSTHETIC ASSOCIATION NATIONAL ASSEMBLY
url: http://www.theaopa.org
1650 King St., Ste. 500
Alexandria, VA 22314

PH: (703)836-7116
FX: (703)836-0838
Frequency: Annual. **Audience:** Orthotic and prosthetic practitioners, business owners, and suppliers. **Principal Exhibits:** Orthotic and prosthetic devices, parts, supplies, and materials. **Dates and Locations:** 1998 Sep 15-19; Chicago, IL.

AMERICAN OSTEOPATHIC ASSOCIATION MEETING & EXHIBITS
142 E. Ontario St.
Chicago, IL 60611
PH: (312)280-5814
Frequency: Annual. **Audience:** Hospital chief executive officers and trustees, and directors of medical education institutions. **Principal Exhibits:** Products and services relating to the osteopathic healthcare industry, including: buildings, financing, marketing, and operations. **Dates and Locations:** 1998.

AMERICAN PAIN SOCIETY SCIENTIFIC MEETING
e-mail: info@ampainsoc.org
url: http://www.ampainsoc.org
4700 W. Lake Ave.
Glenview, IL 60025
PH: (847)375-4715
FX: (847)975-4777
Frequency: Annual. **Audience:** Medical doctors; registered nurses; and other professionals. **Principal Exhibits:** Pharmaceutical and medical instruments, medical equipment, products, supplies, services and alternative delivery systems (homecare, hospice). **Dates and Locations:** 1998.

AMERICAN PHYSICAL THERAPY ASSOCIATION ANNUAL CONFERENCE
1111 N. Fairfax St.
Alexandria, VA 22314
PH: (703)684-2782
TF: 800999-2782
Frequency: Annual. **Audience:** Physical therapists, physical therapists assistants, and allied health professionals. **Principal Exhibits:** Physical therapy products, equipment, and services. **Dates and Locations:** 1998 Jun 06-10; Orlando, FL ▪ 1999 Jun 05-09; Washington, DC ▪ 2000 Jun; Indianapolis, IN.

AMERICAN PHYSICAL THERAPY ASSOCIATION, CALIFORNIA CHAPTER ANNUAL CONFERENCE
2295 Gateway Oaks Dr., Ste. 200
Sacramento, CA 95833
PH: (916)929-2782
Frequency: Annual. **Audience:** Physical therapists; physical therapist assistants; students; and PTA students. **Principal Exhibits:** Physical therapy equipment, products, books, and supplies. **Dates and Locations:** 1998.

AMERICAN PHYSICAL THERAPY ASSOCIATION PRIVATE PRACTICE SESSION
1111 N. Fairfax St.
Alexandria, VA 22314
PH: (703)684-2782
TF: 800999-2782
Frequency: Annual. **Audience:** Trade professionals and students. **Principal Exhibits:** Physical therapy and rehabilitation equipment, supplies, and physical therapy software. **Dates and Locations:** 1998.

AMERICAN PODIATRIC MEDICAL ASSOCIATION ANNUAL MEETING
9312 Old Georgetown Rd.
Bethesda, MD 20814-1698
PH: (301)571-9200
FX: (301)530-2752
Frequency: Annual. **Audience:** Practicing podiatrists, hospital and college administrators, students, residents, association leaders, non-members, and affiliates. **Principal Exhibits:** Podiatric supplies and services. **Dates and Locations:** 1998 Aug 06-08;

Boston, MA ▪ 1999 Aug 12-14; Houston, TX ▪ 2000 Aug 10-12; Philadelphia, PA.

AMERICAN PSYCHIATRIC ASSOCIATION ANNUAL MEETING
url: http://www.psych.org
1400 K St., NW
Washington, DC 20005
PH: (202)682-6100
FX: (202)682-6132
Frequency: Annual. **Audience:** Psychiatrists, mental health professionals, and general public. **Principal Exhibits:** Pharmaceuticals, data processing hardware & software, biofeedback instrumentation; furnishings; information from private psychiatric hospitals and state mental health agencies; and related publications. **Dates and Locations:** 1998 May 31 - Jun 03; Toronto, ON.

AMERICAN PSYCHIATRIC ASSOCIATION INSTITUTE ON PSYCHIATRIC SERVICES
url: http://www.psych.org
1400 K St., NW
Washington, DC 20005
PH: (202)682-6100
FX: (202)682-6132
Frequency: Annual. **Audience:** Psychiatrists, social workers, psychiatric nurses, occupational therapists, and mental health administrators. **Principal Exhibits:** Psychiatric equipment, supplies, and services, including pharmaceuticals, computer software, and publications. **Dates and Locations:** 1998 May 31 - Jun 03; Toronto, ON ▪ 1998 Oct 02-06; Los Angeles, CA ▪ 1999 Oct 30 - Nov 02; New Orleans, LA. **Formerly:** American Psychiatric Association Institute on Hospital and Community Psychiatry.

AMERICAN PUBLIC HEALTH ASSOCIATION ANNUAL EXHIBITION
1015 15th St., NW
Washington, DC 20005
PH: (202)789-5672
FX: (202)789-5661
Frequency: Annual. **Audience:** Public health professionals, physicians, nurses, and social workers. **Principal Exhibits:** Industry-related equipment, supplies, and services. **Dates and Locations:** 1998 Nov 15-19; Washington, DC ▪ 1999 Nov 07-11; Chicago, IL ▪ 2000 Nov 12-16; Boston, MA.

AMERICAN SCHOOL HEALTH ASSOCIATION NATIONAL SCHOOL HEALTH CONFERENCE
e-mail: lhrobak@ashaweb.org
url: http://www.ashaweb.org
7263 State Rte. 43
PO Box 708
Kent, OH 44240
PH: (330)678-1601
TF: 800445-2742
FX: (330)678-4526
Frequency: Annual. **Audience:** School nurses, health educators, physicians, teachers, school administrators, dentists, school counselors, and physical educators. **Principal Exhibits:** Publications, pharmaceuticals, clinical and medical equipment and supplies, information on health organizations, and health education methods and materials. **Dates and Locations:** 1998 Oct 07-11; Colorado Springs, CO.

AMERICAN SOCIETY OF DIRECTORS OF VOLUNTEER SERVICES LEADERSHIP TRAINING CONFERENCE AND EXHIBITION
American Hospital Association
1 N. Franklin
Chicago, IL 60606
PH: (312)422-3939
FX: (312)442-4575
Frequency: Annual. **Audience:** Hospital directors of volunteer services; hospital gift shop managers; hospital auxilians. **Principal Exhibits:** Health care administration equipment, supplies,

and services. **Dates and Locations:** 1998 Sep 20-23; Chicago, IL ∎ 1999 Sep 12-15; Denver, CO ∎ 2000 Sep 07-10; Orlando, FL.

AMERICAN SOCIETY OF ECHOCARDIOGRAPHY SCIENTIFIC SESSION
e-mail: asc@mercury.interpath.net
4101 Lake Boone Trl., Ste. 201
Raleigh, NC 27607
PH: (919)787-5181
FX: (919)787-4916
Frequency: Annual. **Principal Exhibits:** Ultrasound heart imaging and diagnosis equipment, supplies, and services. **Dates and Locations:** 1998 Jun 10-12; San Francisco, CA.

AMERICAN SOCIETY FOR HEAD AND NECK SURGERY MEETING
e-mail: rlwa@med.pitt.edu
url: http://www.headandneckcancer.org
Dept. of Otolaryngology
203 Lothrop St., Ste. 519
Pittsburgh, PA 15213
PH: (412)647-2227
FX: (412)647-8944
Frequency: Annual. **Audience:** Professional MD's. **Principal Exhibits:** Head and neck surgical equipment, supplies, and services. **Dates and Locations:** 1998 May 14-16; Palm Beach, FL.

AMERICAN SOCIETY FOR HEALTH CARE MARKETING AND PUBLIC RELATIONS CONFERENCE
c/o American Hospital Association
1 N. Franklin
Chicago, IL 60606
PH: (312)422-3737
FX: (312)422-4579
Frequency: Annual. **Principal Exhibits:** Hospital and health care marketing and public relations equipment, supplies, and services. **Dates and Locations:** 1998.

AMERICAN SOCIETY FOR HEALTHCARE RISK MANAGEMENT CONVENTION
American Hospital Association
1 N. Franklin
Chicago, IL 60606
PH: (312)422-3980
FX: (312)422-4580
Frequency: Annual. **Principal Exhibits:** Healthcare industry risk management equipment, supplies, and services. **Dates and Locations:** 1998.

AMERICAN SOCIETY FOR HOSPITAL CENTRAL SERVICE PERSONNEL OF THE AMERICAN HOSPITAL ASSOCIATION EXHIBITION
1 N. Franklin
Chicago, IL 60302
PH: (312)422-3751
FX: (312)422-4572
Frequency: Annual. **Principal Exhibits:** Medical devices, packaging, sterilization, infection control, and medical supplies. **Dates and Locations:** 1998.

AMERICAN SOCIETY OF INTERNAL MEDICINE MEETING
2011 Pennsylvania Ave. NW, Ste. 800
Washington, DC 20006-1808
PH: (202)835-2746
FX: (202)835-0443
Frequency: Annual. **Principal Exhibits:** Internal medicine equipment, supplies, and services. **Dates and Locations:** 1998 Oct 08-11; Phoenix, AZ.

AMERICAN SOCIETY FOR LASER MEDICINE AND SURGERY CONFERENCE
2404 Stewart Sq.
Wausau, WI 54401
PH: (715)845-9283
FX: (715)848-2493
Frequency: Annual. **Audience:** Physicians, physicists, and other scientists; nurses, dentists, podiatrists, and veterinarians. **Principal Exhibits:** Laser medicine equipment, supplies, and services. **Dates and Locations:** 1998 Apr; Phoenix, AZ.

AMERICAN SOCIETY OF OPHTHALMIC ADMINISTRATORS EXHIBITION
e-mail: ascrs@ascrs.org
url: http://www.ascrs.org
4000 Legato Rd., No. 850
Fairfax, VA 22033-4003
PH: (703)591-2220
TF: 800451-1339
FX: (703)591-0614
Frequency: Annual. **Audience:** Ophthalmologists, administrators, nurses, technicians. **Principal Exhibits:** Opthalmolic related instruments, equipment, and publications. **Dates and Locations:** 1998 May 18-22; San Diego, CA.

AMERICAN SOCIETY OF PLASTIC AND RECONSTRUCTIVE SURGEONS SCIENTIFIC MEETING & EXHIBITS
url: http://www.plasticsurgery.org
444 E. Algonquin Rd.
Arlington Heights, IL 60005
PH: (847)228-9900
FX: (847)228-9131
Frequency: Annual. **Audience:** Plastic surgical nurses and trade professionals. **Principal Exhibits:** Instrument equipment company. **Dates and Locations:** 1998 Oct 03-07; Boston, MA.

AMERICAN SOCIETY OF POST ANESTHESIA NURSES
6900 Grove Rd.
Thorofare, NJ 08086
PH: (609)848-1000
FX: (609)848-3522
Frequency: Annual. **Audience:** Post anesthesia care nurses. **Principal Exhibits:** Pharmaceuticals and recovery room supplies. **Dates and Locations:** 1998 Apr 19-22; Philadelphia, PA.

AMERICAN SOCIETY OF TROPICAL MEDICINE AND HYGIENE ANNUAL SCIENTIFIC MEETING
e-mail: astmh@astmh.org
url: http://www.astmh.org
60 Revere Dr., Ste. 500
Northbrook, IL 60062
PH: (847)480-9592
FX: (847)480-9282
Frequency: Annual. **Audience:** MD's, PhD's, PPH's, researchers, scientists, educators, students. **Principal Exhibits:** Exhibits related to tropical medicine and hygiene, including the areas of arbovirology, entomology, medicine, nursing, and parasitology. **Dates and Locations:** 1998 Oct 18-22; San Juan, PR.

AMERICAN UROGYNECOLOGIC SOCIETY ANNUAL SCIENTIFIC MEETING
e-mail: augs@sba.com
401 N. Michigan Ave.
Chicago, IL 60611
PH: (312)644-6610
Frequency: Annual. **Principal Exhibits:** Equipment, supplies, and services for persons suffering from incontinence and other pelvic dysfunctions. **Dates and Locations:** 1998 Nov 12-15; Washington, DC ∎ 1999 Oct 14-17; San Diego, CA.

AMSECT INTERNATIONAL CONFERENCE
e-mail: webmaster@amsect.org
url: http://www.amsect.org
11480 Sunset Hills Rd., No. 210E
Reston, VA 20190-5208
PH: (703)435-8556
FX: (703)435-0056

Frequency: Annual. Audience: Perfusionists, technologists, doctors, nurses. Principal Exhibits: Exhibits relating to the practice of extracorporeal technology (involving heart-lung machines). Dates and Locations: 1998 Mar 12-15; Philadelphia, PA ■ 1999 Apr 08-11; New Orleans, LA.

ANALABASIA - ASIAN INTERNATIONAL LABORATORY AND ANALYTICAL TECHNOLOGY AND EQUIPMENT EXHIBITION

e-mail: info@sesmontnet.com
url: http://www.sesmontnet.com
2 Handy Rd.
15-09 Cathay Bldg.
Singapore 229233, Singapore
PH: 65 3384747
FX: 65 3395651
Frequency: Biennial. Audience: Trade professionals. Principal Exhibits: Laboratory equipment, including equipment for wet and dry chemical analyses; biological analyses equipment; microbiological analyses equipment; biochemical analyses equipment; pharmacological analyses equipment; and medical analyses equipment.

ANALIZA - ANALYTIC, DIAGNOSTIC, AND BIOTECHNOLOGICAL EQUIPMENT AND INSTRUMENTS

e-mail: expo@stier.co.il
url: http://www.stier.co.il
12 Tverski St.
67210 Tel Aviv, Israel
PH: 972 3 5626090
FX: 972 3 5615463
Frequency: Biennial. Audience: Scientists, engineers, technicians, lab workers in the biotechnology field; pharmaceutical chemists, biochemists, microbiologists, biologists. Principal Exhibits: Analytic, diagnostic, and biotechnological equipment, supplies, and services. Held in conjunction with: ISRACHEM.

ANNUAL ARIZONA STATE OSTEOPATHIC MEDICAL ASSOCIATION CONVENTION

5150 N. 16th St., Ste. A-122
Phoenix, AZ 85016-3934
PH: (602)266-6699
FX: (602)266-1393
Frequency: Annual. Audience: Doctors of Osteopathy (DOs) from Arizona and many other states. Principal Exhibits: Medical equipment, supplies, and services; pharmaceuticals; U.S. Army and Navy. Dates and Locations: 1998.

ANNUAL CONFERENCE AND ADMINISTRATORS WORKSHOP

11250 Roger Bacon Dr., Ste 8
Reston, VA 22090-5202
PH: (703)437-4377
FX: (703)435-4390
Frequency: Semiannual. Audience: Administrators of kidney dialysis facilities, nephrology nurses, and renal physicians. Principal Exhibits: Pharmaceuticals, medical equipment, and other healthcare equipment, supplies, and services related to nephrology and the treatment of renal disease. Dates and Locations: 1998.

ANNUAL CONFERENCE ON HEALTHCARE MARKETING

url: http://www.alliancehlth.org/hlthmktg/
11 S. LaSalle St., Ste. 2300
Chicago, IL 60603
PH: (312)704-9700
FX: (312)704-9709
Frequency: Annual. Audience: Directors, vice presidents, and others from health-care facilities. Principal Exhibits: Marketing communications, information systems, health information lines, strategic planning, productive development, and marketing research. Dates and Locations: 1998 Mar 29 - Apr 01; Orlando, FL ■ 2000 Mar; Orlando, FL.

ANNUAL CONFERENCE ON LEGAL MEDICINE

e-mail: info@aclm.org
url: http://execpc.com/~aclm
611 E. Wells St.
Milwaukee, WI 53202
PH: (414)276-1881
TF: 800433-9137
FX: (414)276-3349
Frequency: Annual. Principal Exhibits: Exhibits related to the field of legal medicine or medical jurisprudence. Dates and Locations: 1998 Mar 19-21; Las Vegas, NV.

ANNUAL CONTACT LENS SEMINAR

e-mail: mioptoassn@aol.com
530 W. Ionia St., Ste. A
Lansing, MI 48933-1062
PH: (517)482-0616
FX: (517)482-1611
Frequency: Annual. Audience: Professional optometrists, optometric technicians and assistants, and ophthalmic suppliers. Principal Exhibits: Ophthalmic supplies and services. Dates and Locations: 1998 Oct 07-08; Lansing, MI ■ 1999 Oct 06-07; Lansing, MI ■ 2000 Oct 04-05; Lansing, MI.

ANNUAL CONVENTION & SCIENCE SEMINAR OF THE AMERICAN OSTEOPATHIC ASSOCIATION

330 E. Algonquin Rd.
Arlington Heights, IL 60005
PH: (708)228-6090
Frequency: Annual. Audience: General practitioners in osteopathic medicine and surgery. Principal Exhibits: Medical/pharmaceutical equipment, supplies, and services. Dates and Locations: 1998 Mar 11-15.

ANNUAL CONVOCATION OF AMERICAN COLLEGE OF HEALTH CARE ADMINISTRATORS

e-mail: info@achca.org
url: http://www.achca.org
325 S. Patrick
Alexandria, VA 22314
PH: (703)739-7900
TF: 888882-2422
FX: (703)739-7901
Frequency: Annual. Audience: Long term care administrators, healthcare. Principal Exhibits: Healthcare equipment, supplies, and services. Dates and Locations: 1998 May 02-06; Atlanta, GA ■ 1999 Apr 10-14; Providence, RI ■ 2000 May 06-10; St. Louis, MO.

ANNUAL MEETING OF THE EUROPEAN ASSOCIATION FOR CARDIOTHORACIC SURGERY

e-mail: bc@bella.dk
url: http://www.bellacenter.dk
Center Blvd.
DK-2300 Copenhagen S, Denmark
PH: 45 32 52 88 11
FX: 45 32 51 96 36
Frequency: Annual. Principal Exhibits: Equipment, supplies, and services for cardiothoracic surgery. Dates and Locations: 1998.

ANNUAL MEETING OF THE MICROSCOPY SOCIETY OF AMERICA

e-mail: BusinessOffices@MSA.Microscopy.com
4 Barlows Landing Rd., Ste. 8
Pocasset, MA 02559
PH: (508)563-1155
TF: 800538-3672
FX: (508)563-1211
Frequency: Annual. Audience: Medical, biological, metallurgical, and polymer research scientists and technicians; physicists interested in instrument design and improvement. Principal Exhibits: Microscopes and related instruments, equipment, supplies, and services. Dates and Locations: 1998 Jul 12-16; Atlanta, GA.

ANNUAL MEETING OF THE MID-AMERICA ORTHOPAEDIC ASSOCIATION
20 2nd Ave. SW
Rochester, MN 55902-3013
PH: (507)281-3431
FX: (507)281-0291
Frequency: Annual. **Principal Exhibits:** Orthopaedic surgery and office supplies and products. **Dates and Locations:** 1998 Apr; Hilton Head Island, SC. **Formerly:** Mid-America Orthopedic Association Convention.

ANNUAL NATIONAL CONFERENCE ON CLINICAL HOSPICE CARE/PALLIATIVE
e-mail: drsnho@cais.com
url: http://www.nho.org
1901 N. Moore St., Ste. 901
Arlington, VA 22209
PH: (703)243-5900
TF: 800658-8898
FX: (703)525-5762
Frequency: Annual. **Principal Exhibits:** equipment, supplies, and services for hospice organizations. **Dates and Locations:** 1998 Aug.

ANNUAL NATIONAL MANAGED HEALTH CARE CONGRESS
e-mail: register@mnhcc.com
url: http://www.nmhcc.org
71 2nd Ave., 3rd Fl.
Waltham, MA 02154
TF: 888882-2500
FX: (941)365-0157
Frequency: Annual. **Principal Exhibits:** Services and products dedicated to improving the quality of health care. **Dates and Locations:** 1998.

AOSA/SCST ANNUAL MEETING
e-mail: assoc@navix.net
PO Box 81152
Lincoln, NE 68501-1152
PH: (402)476-3852
FX: (402)476-6547
Frequency: Annual. **Principal Exhibits:** Seed testing and research laboratory equipment, supplies, and services. **Dates and Locations:** 1998 Jun; Savannah, GA.

ARAB DENTISTRY - MIDDLE EAST DENTAL AND ORAL HEALTH EQUIPMENT AND MATERIALS EXHIBITION
Accurist House, Ste. 12
44 Baker St.
London W1M 1DH, England
PH: 44 171 935 8537
FX: 44 171 935 8161
Frequency: Biennial. **Audience:** Trade and professional personnel from the health care industries. **Principal Exhibits:** Medical and dental equipment, supplies, and services.

ARAB HEALTH CAIRO - THE INTERNATIONAL EXHIBITION FOR HOSPITAL & MEDICAL EQUIPMENT AND SERVICES
e-mail: iirx@emirates.net.ae
PO Box 28943
Dubai, United Arab Emirates
PH: 9714 365161
FX: 9714 360137
Frequency: Biennial. **Principal Exhibits:** Medical, dental, and pharmaceutical equipment, supplies, and services. **Incorporating:** Arab Dentistry; Arab Eyecare & Optical.

ARAB HEALTH - INTERNATIONAL HOSPITAL, MEDICAL EQUIPMENT AND SERVICES EXHIBITION
e-mail: iirx@emirates.net.ae
PO Box 28943
Dubai, United Arab Emirates

PH: 9714 365161
FX: 9714 360137
Frequency: Biennial. **Audience:** Health-care specialists and related professionals. **Principal Exhibits:** Equipment and services for healthcare, dentistry, eye care, hospital management, information technology, physiology, and fitness. **Held in conjunction with:** Arab Dentistry.

ARIZONA HEALTH CARE ASSOCIATION ANNUAL CONVENTION AND EXHIBITION
5020 N. 8th Pl., Ste. A
Phoenix, AZ 85014-3201
PH: (602)265-5331
FX: (602)265-4401
Frequency: Annual. **Audience:** Hospital administrators, directors, owners, nursing homes, social service and physical plant directors. **Principal Exhibits:** Furniture, bathing equipment, durable medical equipment, computers, pharmacy, therapies, waste co., nursing supplies, food vendors, time & attendance, respiratory care, ambulance, and related equipment, supplies, and services. **Dates and Locations:** 1999.

ARIZONA STATE DENTAL ASSOCIATION SCIENTIFIC SESSION
4131 N. 36th St.
Phoenix, AZ 85018
PH: (602)957-4777
FX: (602)957-1342
Frequency: Annual. **Audience:** Dental professionals, hygienists, and lab technicians. **Principal Exhibits:** Dental supplies and services. **Dates and Locations:** 1998 Mar; Phoenix, AZ.

ARKANSAS MEDICAL SOCIETY ANNUAL SESSION
10 Corporate Hill Drive
Little Rock, AR 72205
PH: (501)224-8967
FX: (501)224-6489
Frequency: Annual. **Audience:** Doctors and allied health professionals. **Principal Exhibits:** Pharmaceuticals, computers, insurance, investments, office supplies, and medical equipment. **Dates and Locations:** 1998 Apr.

ASHCSP ANNUAL CONFERENCE AND EXHIBIT
c/o American Hospital Association
1 N. Franklin
Chicago, IL 60606
PH: (312)422-3750
FX: (312)422-4572
Frequency: Annual. **Principal Exhibits:** Healthcare administration equipment, supplies, and services. **Dates and Locations:** 1998.

ASIAN AUSTRALIAN CONGRESS OF NEUROLOGICAL SURGERY
c/o Dr. Leigh Atkinson
201 Wickham Terr.
Brisbane, QLD 4000, Australia
PH: 61 7 38393393
FX: 61 7 38322005
Frequency: Quadrennial. **Audience:** Neuro surgeons. **Principal Exhibits:** Neurosurgical equipment, supplies, and services.

ASSOCIATION OF BRITISH DISPENSING OPTICIANS CONFERENCE
6 Hurlingham Business Park
Sulivan Rd.
London SW6 3DU, England
PH: 44 171 736 0088
FX: 44 171 731 5531
Frequency: Annual. **Principal Exhibits:** Equipment, supplies, and services for dispensing opticians.

ASSOCIATION OF CHILD AND ADOLESCENT PSYCHIATRIC NURSES CONFERENCE

e-mail: acapn@nursecominc.com
1211 Locust St.
Philadelphia, PA 19107
PH: (215)545-2843
TF: 800826-2950
FX: (215)545-8107
Frequency: Annual. Principal Exhibits: Child and adolescent psychiatric nursing equipment, supplies, and services. Dates and Locations: 1998.

ASSOCIATION FOR HEALTHCARE PHILANTHROPY ANNUAL INTERNATIONAL EDUCATIONAL CONFERENCE

e-mail: ahp@go-ahp.org
url: http://www.go-ahp.org
313 Park Ave., Ste. 400
Falls Church, VA 22046
PH: (703)532-6243
FX: (703)532-7170
Frequency: Annual. Audience: Development officers in healthcare. Principal Exhibits: Equipment, supplies, and services for the healthcare development and fundraising industry, including computer software, recognition gifts, direct mail companies, executive recruiters, special events, and consultants. Dates and Locations: 1998 Oct 21-25; Toronto, ON ▪ 1999 Oct 06-10; San Diego, CA ▪ 2000 Oct 11-15; Boston, MA. Formerly: National Association for Hospital Development Annual Educational Conference.

ASSOCIATION OF MILITARY SURGEONS OF THE U.S. CONVENTION AND EXHIBITION

e-mail: amsus@amsus.org
9320 Old Georgetown Rd.
Bethesda, MD 20814
PH: (301)897-8800
FX: (301)530-5446
Frequency: Annual. Audience: Federal health care professionals. Principal Exhibits: Pharmaceutical and medical equipment companies, medical book publishers. Dates and Locations: 1998 Nov 08-13; San Antonio, TX.

ASSOCIATION OF OPERATING ROOM NURSES ANNUAL CONGRESS

url: http://www.aorn.org
2170 S. Parker Rd., Ste. 300
Denver, CO 80231-5711
PH: (303)755-6300
TF: 800755-2676
FX: (303)752-0299
Frequency: Annual. Audience: Operating room nurses, purchasing agents, materials managers, central supply infection control personnel. Principal Exhibits: Surgical equipment, supplies, and services. Dates and Locations: 1998 Mar 29 - Apr 03; Orlando, FL.

ASSOCIATION FOR WORKSITE HEALTH PROMOTION ANNUAL INTERNATIONAL CONFERENCE

e-mail: awhp@awhp.org
url: http://www.awhp.org
60 Revere Dr., Ste. 500
Northbrook, IL 60062-1577
PH: (847)480-9574
FX: (847)480-9282
Frequency: Annual. Audience: Health and fitness professionals who conduct wellness fitness programs for employees; fitness centers. Principal Exhibits: Equipment, supplies, and services related to the development of quality programs of health and fitness in business and industry. Dates and Locations: 1998 Sep 24-27; Anaheim, CA ▪ 1999 Oct 06-10; Nashville, TN ▪ 2000 Sep 20-24; Orlando, FL.

BIO - BIOLOGICAL SCIENCES EXPO

2200 Berkley, No. 222
Berkley, MI 48072
Frequency: Annual. Audience: Scientists, researchers, professors, laboratory technicians. Principal Exhibits: Equipment, supplies, and services for biological research. Dates and Locations: 1998 May.

BIOTEK & LAB INDIA - INTERNATIONAL TRADE SHOW ON BIOTECHOLOGY AND LABORATORY TECHNOLOGY INDUSTRIES

e-mail: glahe@glahe.com
PO Box 2460
Germantown, MD 20875-2460
PH: (301)515-0012
FX: (301)515-0016
Frequency: Biennial. Audience: Trade professionals. Principal Exhibits: Biotechnology, and laboratory equipment, supplies, and services.

CALIFORNIA ASSOCIATION FOR HEALTH, PHYSICAL EDUCATION, RECREATION, AND DANCE STATE CONFERENCE

e-mail: cahperd@aol.com
1501 El Camino Ave., Ste. 3
Sacramento, CA 95815
PH: (916)922-3596
TF: 800499-3596
FX: (916)922-0133
Frequency: Annual. Audience: Member and non-member professionals, presenters, guests, and vendors. Principal Exhibits: Activity clothing, equipment, financial services, curriculum materials, computer software, and publications. Dates and Locations: 1998 Mar 06-08; San Diego, CA ▪ 1999 Mar; Fresno, CA ▪ 2000 Mar; San Francisco, CA.

CALIFORNIA COLLEGE OF PODIATRIC MEDICINE CONVENTION-SUPER SEMINAR

1210 Scott St.
San Francisco, CA 94115
PH: (415)292-0470
FX: (415)292-0439
Frequency: Annual. Audience: Podiatric physicians and staff. Principal Exhibits: Podiatric medicine supplies and services. Dates and Locations: 1998; Las Vegas, NV.

CALIFORNIA DENTAL ASSOCIATION SAN FRANCISCO CONVENTION

1201 K. St.
PO Box 13749
Sacramento, CA 95853
PH: (916)443-0505
FX: (916)443-2943
Frequency: Annual. Audience: Dentists, laboratory technicians, dental assistants, dental hygienists, and dental students. Principal Exhibits: Dental supplies, equipment, financial services, computers, and oral health care supplies. Dates and Locations: 1998 Sep 25-27; San Francisco, CA ▪ 1999 Aug 20-22; San Francisco, CA ▪ 2000 Oct 06-08; San Francisco, CA.

CALIFORNIA DENTAL ASSOCIATION SCIENTIFIC SESSION

1201 K. St.
PO Box 13749
Sacramento, CA 95853
PH: (916)443-0505
FX: (916)443-2943
Frequency: Annual. Principal Exhibits: Dental supplies, equipment, financial services, computers, and oral health care supplies. Dates and Locations: 1998; Anaheim, CA.

CALIFORNIA OPTOMETRIC ASSOCIATION CONGRESS

PO Box 2591
Sacramento, CA 95812

PH: (916)441-3990
FX: (916)448-1423
Frequency: Annual. **Principal Exhibits:** Optometric equipment, supplies, and services. **Dates and Locations:** 1998 Mar.

**CANADIAN DENTAL ASSOCIATION ANNUAL
CONVENTION**
url: http://www.cda-adc.ca
1815 Alta Vista Dr.
Ottawa, ON, Canada K1G 3Y6
PH: (613)523-1770
FX: (613)523-3062
Frequency: Annual. **Audience:** Dentists, hygienists, dental assistants, dental technicians, dental office personnel, and spouse and children. **Principal Exhibits:** Dental products and related supplies and services. **Dates and Locations:** 1998 May 07-09; Toronto, ON ▪ 1999 Aug 05-08; Halifax, NS.

**CANADIAN INTRAVENOUS NURSES ASSOCIATION
CONFERENCE**
e-mail: cinacsot@idirect.com
url: http://web.idirect.com/~csotcina
4433 Sheppard Ave. E, Ste. 200
Agincourt, ON, Canada M1S 1V3
PH: (416)292-0687
FX: (416)292-1038
Frequency: Annual. **Audience:** Registered nurses specializing in intravenous therapy. **Principal Exhibits:** Intravenous nursing equipment, supplies, and services. **Dates and Locations:** 1998 Oct 21-23; Scarborough, ON ▪ 1999 Oct 20-22; Scarborough, ON.

CANADIAN NURSES ASSOCIATION CONVENTION
e-mail: commdiv@cna-nurses.ca
url: http://www.cna-nurses.ca
50 The Driveway
Ottawa, ON, Canada K2P 1E2
PH: (613)237-2133
FX: (613)237-3520
Frequency: Biennial. **Audience:** Senior directors of nursing, nursing educators, nursing administrators and nursing students. **Principal Exhibits:** Pharmaceuticals, medical health equipment, and nursing publications. **Dates and Locations:** 1998 Jun 14-17; Ottawa, ON ▪ 2000 Jun 18-21; Vancouver, BC ▪ 2002 Jun 16-19; St. John's, NF ▪ 2004 Jun 20-23; Saskatoon, SK.

**CANADIAN OPHTHALMOLOGICAL SOCIETY ANNUAL
MEETING AND EXHIBITION**
e-mail: cos@eyesite.ca
url: http://www.eyesite.ca
1525 Carling Ave., Ste. 610
Ottawa, ON, Canada K1Z 8R9
PH: (613)729-6779
FX: (613)729-7209
Frequency: Annual. **Audience:** Ophthalmologists, ophthalmic assistants, orthoptists, and nurses. **Principal Exhibits:** Ophthalmic equipment, medical devices, and pharmaceutical products. **Dates and Locations:** 1998 Jun 26-29; Calgary, AB ▪ 1999 Jun 25-28; Halifax, NS.

**CANADIAN PSYCHIATRIC ASSOCIATION ANNUAL
CONVENTION**
url: http://www.medical.org
200-237 Argyle
Ottawa, ON, Canada K2P 1B8
PH: (613)234-2815
FX: (613)234-9857
Frequency: Annual. **Principal Exhibits:** Equipment, supplies, and services for Canadian psychiatrists. **Dates and Locations:** 1998.

**CANADIAN SOCIETY OF HOSPITAL PHARMACISTS
CONFERENCE**
e-mail: bleslie@cshp.cq
1145 Hunt Club Rd., Ste. 350
Ottawa, ON, Canada K1V 0Y3
PH: (613)736-9733
FX: (613)736-5660
Frequency: Annual. **Audience:** Hospital pharmacists, graduate pharmacists, and students. **Principal Exhibits:** Hospital pharmacy equipment, supplies, and services. **Dates and Locations:** 1999 Feb; Toronto, ON.

**CANADIAN SOCIETY OF ORTHOPAEDIC
TECHNOLOGISTS ANNUAL MEETING**
e-mail: cinacsot@idirect.com
url: http://web.idirect.com/~csotcina
4433 Sheppard Ave. E, Ste. 200
Agincourt, ON, Canada M1S 1V3
PH: (416)292-0687
FX: (416)292-1038
Frequency: Biennial. **Principal Exhibits:** Plaster casts, traction assemblies, and other orthopedic equipment and supplies. **Dates and Locations:** 1998 Apr 30 - May 03; Scarborough, ON ▪ 2000 Apr 28-30; Scarborough, ON.

**CARE PROVIDERS OF MINNESOTA CONVENTION AND
EXPOSITION**
2850 Metro Dr., Ste. 200
Bloomington, MN 55425
PH: (612)854-2844
FX: (612)854-6214
Frequency: Annual. **Audience:** Health care personnel, including long-term care professionals. **Principal Exhibits:** Products and services for long-term care facilities, including medical supplies, furniture, food vendors, accounting services, architects, pharmaceuticals, and energy management systems. **Dates and Locations:** 1998 Nov 02-05; Minneapolis, MN.

CHARLOTTE EMPLOYERS' HEALTH CARE EXPO
431 Ohio Pike, Ste. 104 S.
Cincinnati, OH 45255
PH: (704)331-9095
FX: (704)344-0504
Principal Exhibits: Hospitals, health maintenance organizations, corporate fitness plans, and dental and optical plans. **Dates and Locations:** 1998; Charlotte, NC.

**CHEM - INTERNATIONAL EXHIBITION OF CHEMISTRY,
ENVIRONMENT, AND WATER**
e-mail: kee-expo@otenet.gr
Halepa 1 and Aegealias 21
Marousi
GR-151 25 Athens, Greece
PH: 3 01 6844961
FX: 3 01 6841796
Frequency: Triennial. **Audience:** Chemists, chemical engineers, environmentalists, technical managers from food, plastic, chemical, cosmetic, pharmaceutical, and detergents industries. **Principal Exhibits:** Laboratory equipment, chemical processing systems and machines, raw chemicals, industrial chemicals, specialty chemicals, medicine, environmental protection equipment, and water treatment equipment.

CHICAGO DENTAL SOCIETY MIDWINTER MEETING
e-mail: mwm@chicagodentalsociety.org
401 N. Michigan Ave., Ste. 300
Chicago, IL 60611-4205
PH: (312)836-7300
FX: (312)836-7337
Frequency: Annual. **Audience:** Dentists and ancillary professional groups. **Principal Exhibits:** Dental equipment, services, and related business services. **Dates and Locations:** 1999 Feb 18-21; Chicago, IL ▪ 2000 Feb 24-27; Chicago, IL.

CHICAGO NATURAL HEALTH SHOW
e-mail: nhf@earthlink.net
url: http://www.healthfreedom.org
212 W. Foothill Blvd.
PO Box 688
Monrovia, CA 91017
PH: (626)357-2181
FX: (626)303-0642
Frequency: Annual. Audience: Health conscious consumers, chiropractors, medical doctors, acupuncturists, naturopaths, homeopaths, massage therapists, physical therapists, and trainers. Principal Exhibits: Vitamin, mineral, amino acids, food supplements, herb, food preparation, health books, and health aids. Dates and Locations: 1998; Chicago, IL.

CHICAGO OPHTHALMOLOGICAL SOCIETY CLINICAL CONFERENCE
c/o Conchita Valdes
515 N. Dearborn
Chicago, IL 60610
PH: (312)670-2583
Frequency: Annual. Audience: Ophthalmologists. Principal Exhibits: Ophthalmological equipment, supplies, and services. Dates and Locations: 1998 May; Chicago, IL.

CHILDREN & YOUNG PEOPLE
url: http://www.swefair.se
PO Box 5222
412 94 Goteborg, Sweden
PH: 46 31 708 80 00
FX: 46 31 16 03 30
Principal Exhibits: Health and well-being, life situation, development, and education.

CHINA INTERNATIONAL OPTICS FAIR
Frequency: Annual. Audience: Trade professionals. Principal Exhibits: Optical frames & glasses, contact lenses & lens care products, spectacle parts & accessories, quality control & laboratory testing equipment, spectacle manufacturing machinery, store & workshop fittings, instruments for optometry & ophthalmology.

CHINA OPTICS - INTERNATIONAL OPTICAL EXHIBITION FOR CHINA
Unit 1223, 12/F, Hong Kong International Trade & Exhibition
1 Trademart Dr.
Kowloon Bay, Hong Kong
PH: 852 2865 2633
FX: 852 2866 1770
Frequency: Annual. Audience: Trade professionals. Principal Exhibits: Optical supplies and equipment, including: glasses, lenses, processing machinery, parts and accessories, testing and cleaning equipment, and raw materials. Held in conjunction with: CHINA JEWELLERY; CHINA TIME.

CINCINNATI EMPLOYERS' HEALTH CARE EXPO
431 Ohio Pike, Ste. 104 S.
Cincinnati, OH 45255
PH: (704)331-9095
FX: (704)344-0504
Principal Exhibits: Hospitals, health maintenance organizations, corporate fitness plans, and dental and optical plans. Dates and Locations: 1998; Cincinnati, OH.

CITY MEDICARE
Level 21, 19A-21-2, UOA Centre
19 Jalan Pinang
50450 Kuala Lumpur, Malaysia
PH: 60 3 264 5663
FX: 60 2 264 5660
Frequency: Annual. Principal Exhibits: Equipment, supplies, and services for the medical and health industry.

CIVIL AVIATION MEDICAL ASSOCIATION CONFERENCE
PO Box 23864
Oklahoma City, OK 73123-3864
PH: (405)840-0199
FX: (405)848-1053
Frequency: Annual. Audience: Aviation medical examiners, physicians who are pilots, aviation medical educators. Principal Exhibits: Aviation medical equipment, supplies, and services. Dates and Locations: 1998.

CLEANROOMS, THE SHOW OF CONTAMINATION CONTROL TECHNOLOGY
PennWell Publishing Co.
Ten Tara Blvd., 5th Fl.
Nashua, NH 03062
PH: (603)891-9265
FX: (603)891-9490
Frequency: 3/yr. Audience: Engineers and managers from any industry using cleanrooms. Principal Exhibits: Products and services used in cleanroom facilities, including filtration systems, apparel, work stations, filters, monitors, and particle counters. Dates and Locations: 1998 Mar 02-04; Baltimore, MD.

CLINICAL ASSEMBLY OF OSTEOPATHIC SPECIALISTS
123 N. Henry St.
Alexandria, VA 22314-2903
PH: (703)684-0416
TF: 800888-1312
FX: (703)684-3280
Frequency: Annual. Audience: Surgeons. Principal Exhibits: Pharmaceuticals, medical equipment and supplies, and related equipment. Dates and Locations: 1998 Sep 26-29; Chicago, IL ∎ 1999 Oct 02-05; Seattle, WA.

CLINICAL LABORATORY MANAGEMENT ASSOCIATION ANNUAL CONFERENCE AND EXHIBITION
e-mail: 103033.1730@compuserve.com
url: http://www.clma.org
989 Old Eagle School Rd., Ste. 815
Wayne, PA 19087-1704
PH: (610)995-9580
FX: (610)995-9568
Frequency: Annual. Audience: Laboratory managers and administrators. Principal Exhibits: Laboratory equipment, supplies, and services. Dates and Locations: 1998; Philadelphia, PA.

CLINICAL LIGAND ASSAY SOCIETY NATIONAL MEETING
3139 S. Wayne Rd.
Wayne, MI 48184
PH: (313)722-6290
FX: (313)722-7006
Frequency: Annual. Principal Exhibits: Exhibits relating to ligand assay, a quantitative clinical laboratory technique for a specific area of diagnostic testing which measures proteins, peptides, or haptens. Dates and Locations: 1998 Apr; Chicago, IL.

CLINICAL AND RESEARCH BASICS FOR AIDS VIRUS
16126 E. Warren
PO Box 24224
Detroit, MI 48224
PH: (313)882-0641
FX: (313)882-5110
Frequency: Annual. Principal Exhibits: Medical and laboratory related exhibits. Dates and Locations: 1998 Jul 15-18; Santa Fe, NM.

COLLEGE OF OPTOMETRISTS IN VISION DEVELOPMENT ANNUAL MEETING
243 N. Lindbergh Blvd., No. 310
St. Louis, MO 63141
PH: (314)991-4007
FX: (314)991-1167
Frequency: Annual. Principal Exhibits: Exhibits relating to

orthoptics and optometric vision therapy with emphasis on visual information processing in visually related learning problems. **Dates and Locations:** 1998.

COLORADO HOSPITAL ASSOCIATION ANNUAL MEETING
2140 S. Holly St.
Denver, CO 80222-5607
PH: (303)758-1630
FX: (303)758-0047
Frequency: Annual. **Audience:** Hospital administrators and other healthcare professionals. **Principal Exhibits:** Equipment, supplies, and services for the health care industry. **Dates and Locations:** 1998.

COLORADO SOCIETY OF OSTEOPATHIC MEDICINE ANNUAL MEETING
e-mail: www.capcon.com/csom
50 S. Steele, Ste. 770
Denver, CO 80209
PH: (303)322-1752
FX: (303)322-1956
Frequency: Annual. **Audience:** Health care professionals and general public. **Principal Exhibits:** Pharmaceutical companies equipment, supplies, and services. **Dates and Locations:** 1998 Jun; Vail, CO.

COLORADO SOCIETY OF OSTEOPATHIC MEDICINE MIDWINTER SKI AND CONTINUING MEDICAL EDUCATION PROGRAM
e-mail: www.capcon.com/csom
50 S. Steele, Ste. 770
Denver, CO 80209
PH: (303)322-1752
FX: (303)322-1956
Frequency: Annual. **Audience:** Physicians and health care professionals. **Principal Exhibits:** Medical, pharmaceutical equipment, supplies, and services. **Dates and Locations:** 1999 Feb; Keystone, CO.

CONFERENCE ON CLASSIFICATION OF NURSING DIAGNOSIS
e-mail: nanda@nursecominc.com
1211 Locust St.
Philadelphia, PA 19107
PH: (215)545-8105
TF: 800647-9002
FX: (215)545-8107
Frequency: Biennial. **Principal Exhibits:** Exhibits relating to the development of a taxonomy of diagnostic terminology for use by professional nurses. **Dates and Locations:** 1998 Mar; St. Louis, MO.

CONFERENCE OF THE NATIONAL ASSOCIATION OF PEDIATRIC NURSE ASSOCIATES AND PRACTITIONERS
e-mail: 74224.51@compuserve.com
1101 Kings Hwy. N., No. 206
Cherry Hill, NJ 08034-1912
PH: (609)667-1773
FX: (609)667-7187
Frequency: Annual. **Principal Exhibits:** Equipment, supplies, and services for pediatric, school, and family nurse practitioners. **Dates and Locations:** 1998 Mar; Washington, DC.

CONGRESO ESTATAL DE PLANIFICACION FAMILIAR
Almagro 28
E-28010 Madrid, Spain
PH: 34 1 3199276
FX: 34 1 3081589
Frequency: Biennial. **Principal Exhibits:** Exhibits relating to family planning, responsible parenthood, contraception, and sexually transmitted disease.

CONGRESS ON BURN INJURIES
c/o Naoki Aikawa, MD
Keio University Hospital
35 Shinanomachi Shinjuku
Tokyo 160, Japan
PH: 81 333531368
FX: 81 332269877
Frequency: Quadrennial. **Principal Exhibits:** Exhibits related to burn prevention.

CONGRESS OF CONTINUING EDUCATION IN DENTISTRY
6, rue G. Tell
F-75017 Paris, France
PH: 33 1 44010270
FX: 33 1 47639028
Frequency: Annual. **Principal Exhibits:** Dental equipment, supplies, and services.

CONGRESS EUROPEAN COLLEGE OF NEUROPSYCHOPHARMACOLOGY
e-mail: ecnp@congrex.nl
A.J. Ernststraat 5g5
1082 LD Amsterdam, Netherlands
PH: 0 20 50 40 200
FX: 0 20 50 40 225
Frequency: Annual. **Principal Exhibits:** Neuropsychopharmacology.

CONGRESS OF THE INTERNATIONAL SOCIETY OF BLOOD TRANSFUSION
Box 7609 Skillebekk
0205 Oslo, Norway
PH: 66 99 66 00
FX: 66 99 67 99
Frequency: Biennial. **Audience:** Professionals involved in the blood transfusion field and the general public. **Principal Exhibits:** Products and services related to the blood transfusion field.

CONGRESS OF THE INTERNATIONAL SOCIETY FOR ELECTROPHYSIOLOGICAL KINESOLOGY (ISEK)
P.O. Box 560
7500 AN Enschede, Netherlands
PH: 053 335800
Principal Exhibits: Medicine.

CONGRESS ON OPHTHALMOLOGY
Institute of Ophthalmology
Philips van Leydenlaan 15
NL-6525 EX Nijmegen, Netherlands
PH: 31 80 613138
FX: 31 80 540522
Frequency: Quadrennial. **Principal Exhibits:** Ophthalmology equipment, supplies, and services.

DALLAS MID-WINTER DENTAL CLINIC
e-mail: renee@dcds.org
url: http://www.dcds.org
4100 McEwen, Ste. 141
Dallas, TX 75244
PH: (972)386-5741
FX: (972)233-8636
Frequency: Annual. **Audience:** Dentists, hygienists, assistants, and laboratory technicians. **Principal Exhibits:** Dental products and supplies, dental laboratory services, computer hardware and software, practice management consultancy services, financial planning services, pharmaceuticals, and related equipment, supplies, and services. **Dates and Locations:** 1999 Mar 11-13; Dallas, TX ■ 2000 Mar 02-04; Dallas, TX.

DENTAL ASSOCIATION OF SOUTH AFRICA ANNUAL CONVENTION
e-mail: dasa@pixie.co.za
Private Bag 1
Houghton 2041, Republic of South Africa

PH: 27 11 4845288
FX: 27 11 6425718
Frequency: Annual. **Principal Exhibits:** Dentistry equipment, supplies, and services.

DENTAL - DENTAL TRADE FAIR
e-mail: nv@messe.no
url: http://www.messe.no
Drammensveien 154
PO Box 130 Skoyen
N-0212 Oslo, Norway
PH: 47 22 439100
FX: 47 22 431914
Frequency: Annual. **Principal Exhibits:** Dental equipment, supplies, and services.

DENTAL INFORMA - EXHIBITION OF DENTAL SURGERY AND LABORATORY EQUIPMENT
url: http://www.heckmanngmbh.de
Hohenzollerstr.4
30161 Hannover, Germany
PH: 0511 99095 0
FX: 0511 99095 50
Frequency: Annual. **Audience:** Trade professionals. **Principal Exhibits:** Dental surgical and laboratory equipment, supplies, and services.

DENTAL VIETNAM
Postfach 120709
80033 Munich, Germany
PH: 89 500610
FX: 89 5028497
Frequency: Biennial. **Principal Exhibits:** Medical technology and supplies, electro-medicine, dental medicine, orthopedic and rehabilitation technology.

DENVER MIDWINTER DENTAL CONVENTION
3690 S. Yosemite St., Ste. 200
Denver, CO 80237
PH: (303)488-9700
TF: 800637-6337
FX: (303)488-0177
Frequency: Annual. **Audience:** Dentists, hygienists, dental assistants, office managers, laboratory technicians, physical therapists, and speech therapists. **Principal Exhibits:** Dental equipment, supplies, and services, including: dental instruments, office equipment, pharmaceuticals, dental laboratory services, and financial services. **Dates and Locations:** 1999 Jan 14-16; Denver, CO ■ 2000 Jan 13-15; Denver, CO ■ 2001 Jan 11-13; Denver, CO. **Formerly:** Denver Winteregional Dental Meeting.

DETROIT DENTAL REVIEW
460 Fisher Bldg.
Detroit, MI 48202
PH: (313)871-3500
Frequency: Annual. **Audience:** Dentists, hygienists, dental assistants, and other auxiliary personnel. **Principal Exhibits:** Dental equipment, supplies, and services, including office systems. **Dates and Locations:** 1998; Detroit, MI.

DIGESTIVE ENDOSCOPY LIVE
Academic Medical Center
G4-2uid, Meibergdreef 9
1105 AZ Amsterdam, Netherlands
PH: 31 20 566 39 26
FX: 31 20 691 48 58
Frequency: Annual. **Audience:** Gastroenlerologists. **Principal Exhibits:** Equipment, supplies, and services for digestive medicine.

DISTRICT OF COLUMBIA DENTAL SOCIETY SPRING MEETING
502 C St., NE
Washington, DC 20002-5810

PH: (202)547-7613
FX: (202)546-1482
Frequency: Annual. **Audience:** Dentists and dental auxiliaries. **Principal Exhibits:** Equipment, clothing, dental supplies, office management systems, and publications. **Dates and Locations:** 1998; Washington, DC.

EAST COAST DISTRICT DENTAL SOCIETY MIAMI WINTER MEETING AND DENTAL EXPO
e-mail: ecdds@ecdental.org
420 S. Dixie Hwy., Ste. 2-E
Coral Gables, FL 33146
PH: (305)667-3647
TF: 800344-5860
FX: (305)665-7059
Frequency: Annual. **Audience:** Hygienists, dental assistants, technicians and office staff. **Principal Exhibits:** Dental equipment, supplies, services. **Dates and Locations:** 1999 Jan 28-30; Miami, FL.

EASTERN ORTHOPAEDIC ASSOCIATION CONVENTION
Pier 5, N., Ste. 5D
7 N. Columbus Blvd.
Philadelphia, PA 19106-1486
PH: (215)351-4110
FX: (215)351-1825
Frequency: Annual. **Audience:** Orthopedic surgeons. **Principal Exhibits:** Orthopedic implants products. **Dates and Locations:** 1998 Oct 14-18; Dorado Beach, PR ■ 2000 Oct 11-15; Lake Buena Vista, FL.

ELMIA LAB - INTERNATIONAL TRADE FAIR FOR QUALITY ASSURANCE IN LABORATORIES
e-mail: international@elmia.se
Elmiavagen
PO Box 6066
S-550 06 Jonkoping, Sweden
PH: 46 36 152000
FX: 46 36 164692
Frequency: Biennial. **Audience:** Trade. **Principal Exhibits:** Laboratory services, analysis equipment, standards and chemicals, laboratory automation equipment, laboratory computer systems, scales, fittings, ergonomic services and supplies, and climate control.

EMERGENCY NURSES ASSOCIATION ANNUAL MEETING
e-mail: enainfo@iqnow.com
url: http://www.ena.org
216 Higgins Rd.
Park Ridge, IL 60068
PH: (847)698-9400
TF: 800243-8362
FX: (847)698-9406
Frequency: Annual. **Audience:** Registered nurses, licensed practical nurses, and licensed vocational nurses; emergency medical technicians or nurses. **Principal Exhibits:** Exhibits relating to emergency room care. **Dates and Locations:** 1998 Sep.

EMV DRESDEN - INTERNATIONAL EXHIBITION ON ELECTROMAGNETIC COMPATIBILITY IN INDUSTRY AND SKILLED TRADE
e-mail: buss@mesago.de
url: http://www.mesago.de
Rotebuhlstrasse 83-85
D-70178 Stuttgart, Germany
PH: 49 11 619460
FX: 49 11 6194698
Frequency: Biennial. **Principal Exhibits:** Testing and laboratory equipment.

EUROHOSPITAL AND REHAB
e-mail: bc@bella.dk
url: http://www.bellacenter.dk
Center Blvd.
DK-2300 Copenhagen S, Denmark
PH: 45 32 52 88 11
FX: 45 32 51 96 36
Frequency: Biennial. **Principal Exhibits:** Health care.

EUROPAISCHES SYMPOSIUM AUF RUGEN
Mallwitzstr. 16
53177 Bonn, Germany
PH: 49 228 85570
FX: 49 228 347967
Frequency: Annual. **Principal Exhibits:** Dentistry equipment, supplies, and services.

EUROPEAN CONGRESS ON INTENSIVE CARE MEDICINE
e-mail: staff@stofair.se
url: http://www.stofair.se
Massvagen 1, Alvsjo
S-125 80 Stockholm, Sweden
PH: 46 8 7494100
FX: 46 8 992044
Principal Exhibits: Equipment, supplies, and services for intensive care.

EUROPEAN DISPOSABLES AND NONWOVENS ASSOCIATION CONFERENCE
e-mail: edana@euronet.be
157 Avenue E. Plasky
B-1030 Brussels, Belgium
PH: 32 2 7349310
FX: 32 2 7333518
Frequency: Triennial. **Principal Exhibits:** Equipment, supplies, and services for the manufacture of hygiene products and nonwoven fabrics used in medicine and industry.

EXHIBITION OF THE INTERNATIONAL ASSOCIATION FOR DENTAL RESEARCH
c/o Faculty of Dentistry
National University of Singapore
5 Lower Kent Ridge Rd.
Singapore 0511, Singapore
PH: 7724944
FX: 7732602
Frequency: Annual. **Audience:** Dental research personnel involved in purchasing. **Principal Exhibits:** Equipment, supplies, and services for dental research, including laboratory supplies and educational materials. **Dates and Locations:** 1999 Mar 10-14; Vancouver, BC ▪ 2000 Mar 15-19; Washington, DC.

EXPO OPTICA - INTERNATIONAL OPTICS AND OPTOMETRY EXHIBITION
url: http://www.arco.sei.es.
PO Box 67067
Parque Ferial Juan Carlos I
28067 Madrid, Spain
PH: 34 1 722 5000
FX: 34 1 722 5788
Frequency: Annual. **Audience:** Professionals in optics, optometry, acoustics, audiometry, electro-optics wholesalers, and retailers of products in these fields. **Principal Exhibits:** Materials and services related to the optics, optometry, and acoustics industries.

EXPOANALITICA Y BIOCIENCIA - LABORATORY INSTRUMENTATION TRADE FAIR (MADRID)
Av. Reina Maria Cristina, s/n
E-08004 Barcelona, Spain
PH: 93 804 0102
FX: 93 805 4802
Frequency: Triennial. **Principal Exhibits:** Information on laboratory instrumentation.

EXPODENTAL - DENTAL EQUIPMENT, SUPPLIES, AND SERVICES SHOW
url: http://www.arco.sei.es.
PO Box 67067
Parque Ferial Juan Carlos I
28067 Madrid, Spain
PH: 34 1 722 5000
FX: 34 1 722 5788
Frequency: Biennial. **Audience:** Dentists, dental technicians and hygienists, and professional buyers. **Principal Exhibits:** Dental equipment, supplies, and services.

EXPOMED - EXHIBITION FOR HEALTHCARE PROFESSIONALS
url: http://www.bitf.be
Parc des Expositions
Place de Belgique
B-1020 Brussels, Belgium
PH: 32 2 474 8447
FX: 32 2 474 8540
Frequency: Biennial. **Principal Exhibits:** Hospital and medical equipment, supplies, and services.

EXPOMEDICA - INTERNATIONAL TRADE FAIR FOR MEDICINE, MEDICAL AND HOSPITAL ENGINEERING AND HOSPITAL SUPPLIES
url: http://www.arco.sei.es.
PO Box 67067
Parque Ferial Juan Carlos I
28067 Madrid, Spain
PH: 34 1 722 5000
FX: 34 1 722 5788

EXPOPHARM - INTERNATIONAL PHARMACEUTICAL TRADE FAIR
url: http://www.abda.de/wv/expoharm.html
Carl-Mannich Str. 26
Postfach 6144
D-65735 Eschborn, Germany
PH: 06196 928410
FX: 06196 928404
Frequency: Annual. **Principal Exhibits:** Pharmaceuticals, cosmetics, surgery equipment, shop fittings, laboratory apparatus, nursing equipment, nourishment, hygienics and plant protection.

EXPOSALUD
El Viento 14051
Lo Barnechea
Santiago, Chile
PH: 56 2 243 4678
Frequency: Every 18 mos. **Principal Exhibits:** Technogies, equipment, supplies, and services for the healthcare sector of Chile and Latin America.

EXPOSALUD - INTERNATIONAL EXHIBIT FOR HEALTH AND FITNESS
Av. Reina Maria Cristina, s/n
E-08004 Barcelona, Spain
PH: 93 804 0102
FX: 93 805 4802
Frequency: Biennial. **Audience:** General public. **Principal Exhibits:** Nutrition; infusions, herbs, beverages, and curative products; natural therapeutics; diagnostics and therapy; physical fitness, body culture, clothing, natural cosmetology, and dermopharmaceutics; vitamin products; structure biology; alternative and renewable energies; instruments and accessories; astronomy and astrology.

FACHDENTAL SUDWEST - TRADE FAIR FOR DENTAL SURGERIES AND LABORATORIES
url: http://www.mcssc-stuttgart.de
Am Kochenhof 16
Postfach 103252
D-70028 Stuttgart, Germany

PH: 711 2589 0
FX: 711 2589 440
Principal Exhibits: Dental surgeries and laboratories.

FALL EYECARE CONFERENCE
1266 SW Topeka Blvd.
Topeka, KS 66612
PH: (913)232-0225
Frequency: Annual. **Audience:** Optometrists and other eye care professionals. **Principal Exhibits:** Ophthalmic goods, services, and equipment. **Dates and Locations:** 1998 Oct 10-11; Wichita, KS.

FDI ANNUAL WORLD DENTAL CONGRESS
81-7, Songiong-dong
Songdong-gu
Seoul 133-160, Republic of Korea
PH: 02 498 6320
FX: 02 468 4655
Frequency: Annual. **Audience:** Dentists. **Principal Exhibits:** Dentistry.

FEDERATION OF AMERICAN HEALTH SYSTEMS ANNUAL CONVENTION & BUSINESS EXPOSITION
1405 N. Pierce, Ste. 311
Little Rock, AR 72217-8708
PH: (501)661-9555
TF: 800880-FAHS
FX: (501)663-4903
Frequency: Annual. **Audience:** Hospital and health care executives. **Principal Exhibits:** Hospital, health care, and educational equipment, supplies, and services. **Dates and Locations:** 1998 Apr; Las Vegas, NV.

FIT & GEZOND - THE COMPLETE FAIR FOR FITNESS, HEALTH AND BODY CARE
e-mail: com.expo@pophost.eunet.be
url: http://www.flexpo.be
Maaltekouter 1
B-9051 Gent, Belgium
PH: 9 2419211
FX: 9 2419325
Frequency: Annual. **Principal Exhibits:** Equipment, accessories, products for the fitness, health and body care sector.

FLORIDA NATIONAL DENTAL CONGRESS
e-mail: fndc@floridadental.org
1111 E. Tennessee St., Ste. 102
Tallahassee, FL 32301
PH: (904)681-3629
TF: 800877-9922
FX: (904)681-3629
Frequency: Annual. **Audience:** Dentists, dental hygienists, dental assistants, and laboratory technicians. **Principal Exhibits:** Dental products and services. **Dates and Locations:** 1998 Jun 11-13; Orlando, FL ▪ 1999 Jun 17-19; Orlando, FL.

FLORIDA NURSES ASSOCIATION ANNUAL CONVENTION
e-mail: theflnurse@aol.com
1235 E. Concord St.
PO Box 536985
Orlando, FL 32853-6985
PH: (407)896-3261
FX: (407)896-9042
Frequency: Annual. **Audience:** Nurses, nursing students, allied health care professionals, and nonmembers. **Principal Exhibits:** Hospital and health care agency information; hospital products and supplies; pharmaceuticals; insurance information; employment information; textbooks and related publications; nursing school information; and graduate program information for the health care industry. **Dates and Locations:** 1998; Panama City, FL.

FLORIDA OSTEOPATHIC MEDICAL ASSOCIATION ANNUAL CONVENTION
e-mail: admin@foma.org
2007 Apalachee Pkwy.
Tallahassee, FL 32301
PH: (904)878-7364
FX: (904)942-7538
Frequency: Annual. **Audience:** Osteopaths. **Principal Exhibits:** Pharmaceutical and health-related displays, computers, medical equipment, X-ray equipment, and exercise equipment. **Dates and Locations:** 1998 Mar; Miami Beach, FL.

FLYING PHYSICIANS ASSOCIATION ANNUAL MEETING
e-mail: 75114,1632@compuserve.com
url: http://www.fpadrs.org
PO Box 677427
Orlando, FL 32867-7427
PH: (407)359-1423
FX: (407)359-1167
Frequency: Annual. **Audience:** Physicians who are also pilots. **Principal Exhibits:** Aircraft and electronics. **Dates and Locations:** 1998 Jun 27 - Jul 03; Rockport, ME.

FORUM LABO
19 rue d'athenes
75009 Paris, France
PH: 33 1 44 53 72 20
FX: 33 1 44 53 72 22
Frequency: Annual. **Principal Exhibits:** Laboratory equipment, supplies, and services.

THE FOUNDATION FOR PODIATRIC MEDICINE ANNUAL CONFERENCE
1255 5th Ave.
New York, NY 10029
PH: (212)876-6719
FX: (212)996-4389
Frequency: Annual. **Audience:** Podiatrist and podiatric medical assistants and students. **Principal Exhibits:** Podiatric products and services. **Dates and Locations:** 1999 Jan; New York, NY.

GENERAL ASSEMBLY OF THE WORLD MEDICAL ASSOCIATION
28, ave. des Alpes
BP 63
F-01212 Ferney-Voltaire, France
PH: 33 450 407575
FX: 33 450 405937
Frequency: Annual. **Principal Exhibits:** Exhibits relating to the achievement of the highest international standards in medical education, medical science, medical ethics, and health care for people worldwide. **Dates and Locations:** 1998 Oct; Ottawa, ON.

GENERAL SESSION AND EXHIBITION OF THE IADR
e-mail: research@iadr.com
url: http://medhlp.netvsa.net/iadr/iadr.htm
1619 Duke St.
Alexandria, VA 22314
PH: (703)548-0066
FX: (703)548-1883
Frequency: Annual. **Principal Exhibits:** Dentistry equipment, supplies, and services.

GEORGIA HOSPITAL ASSOCIATION ANNUAL CONVENTION & EXPOSITION
1675 Terrell Mill Rd.
Marietta, GA 30067
PH: (404)955-0324
TF: 800233-2964
FX: (404)955-5801
Frequency: Annual. **Audience:** Hospital administrators and department heads. **Principal Exhibits:** Health care/hospital durable goods, information systems, physician services/recruit-

ment, and major medical equipment. **Dates and Locations:** 1999 Jan; Atlanta, GA.

GEORGIA NURSING HOME ASSOCIATION MIDYEAR CONVENTION AND EXPOSITION
3735 Memorial Dr.
Decatur, GA 30032
PH: (404)284-8700
FX: (404)286-0752
Frequency: Annual. **Audience:** Nursing home administrators and owners; directors of nursing; dietary, housekeeping, laundry, and maintenance supervisors; activity directors. **Principal Exhibits:** Health care equipment, supplies, and services for nursing homes. **Dates and Locations:** 1999 Jan; Atlanta, GA.

GERMAN DENTAL CONFERENCE
Universitatsstr. 71-73
50931 Cologne, Germany
PH: 49 221 40010
FX: 49 221 404035
Frequency: Quadrennial. **Principal Exhibits:** Dentistry equipment, supplies, and services.

GLOBAL HEALTH NETWORKING: A VISION FOR NEXT MILLENNIUM
e-mail: b.g.solheim@rh.uio.no
url: http://www.mi.med.uni-goettingen.de/imia
IMIA Secretary
TS, ITI
N-0027 Oslo, Norway
PH: 47 22 867479
FX: 47 22 203693
Frequency: Triennial. **Principal Exhibits:** Exhibits related to health care and biomedical research through medical informatics.

THE GLOBAL NETWORK OF WHO COLLABORATING CENTERS FOR NURSING DEVELOPMENT ON P.C.
Yonsei University
134, Shinch'on-dong, Sodaemun-gu
Seoul 120-752, Republic of Korea
PH: 02 361 5103
FX: 02 392 5440
Principal Exhibits: Nursing.

GREATER HOUSTON DENTAL MEETING
e-mail: ghds@flash.net
1 Greenway Plz., Ste. 110
Houston, TX 77046
PH: (713)961-4337
FX: (713)961-3617
Frequency: Annual. **Principal Exhibits:** Dental equipment, supplies, and dental office amenities. **Dates and Locations:** 1998 Mar; Houston, TX.

GREATER NEW YORK DENTAL MEETING
e-mail: gnydm@aol.com
New York Marriott Marquis
1535 Broadway
3rd Fl.
New York, NY 10036
PH: (212)398-6922
FX: (212)398-6934
Frequency: Annual. **Audience:** Dentists and allied health professionals. **Principal Exhibits:** Dental products and services. **Dates and Locations:** 1998 Nov 27 - Dec 02; New York, NY ▪ 1999 Nov 26 - Dec 01; New York, NY ▪ 2000 Nov 24-29; New York, NY.

GROUP HEALTH ASSOCIATION OF AMERICA INSTITUTE
1129 20th St., NW, Ste. 600
Washington, DC 20036
PH: (202)778-3225
FX: (202)955-4395
Frequency: Annual. **Audience:** Trade professionals. **Principal Ex-**

hibits: Suppliers to managed health care community. **Dates and Locations:** 1998 Jun 14-17; Boston, MA.

HEALTH CARE
url: http://www.mf-exhibitions.co.uk
630 Chiswick High Rd.
London W4 5BG, England
PH: 44 181 742 2828
FX: 44 181 747 3856
Frequency: Biennial. **Principal Exhibits:** Medical products, equipment, and supplies.

HEALTH CARE EXPO/CONNECTICUT
e-mail: rdpsteven@aol.com
30 Tower Ln.
Avon, CT 06001-4231
PH: (860)677-0094
TF: 800243-9774
FX: (860)677-6869
Frequency: Annual. **Audience:** Doctors, nurses, hospital and long-term care personnel, and other healthcare professionals. **Principal Exhibits:** Healthcare related products and services, including medical products and services, insurance, beds, laboratory equipment, pharmaceuticals, x-ray equipment, food services, waste management, and hospitals. **Dates and Locations:** 1998 Apr 29-30; Hartford, CT ▪ 1999 Apr 28-29; Hartford, CT. **Formerly:** Medical Expo.

HEALTH AND FITNESS EXPO
e-mail: jerryd@wtp.net
208 N. 29th St., Ste. 214
Billings, MT 59101
PH: (406)245-0404
FX: (406)245-3897
Frequency: Annual. **Audience:** Health professionals and general public. **Principal Exhibits:** Equipment, supplies, and services for health and medicine, recreation, sports, and education. **Dates and Locations:** 1999 Jan 15-17; Billings, MT ▪ 2000 Jan 21-23; Billings, MT.

HEALTH INDUSTRY DISTRIBUTORS ASSOCIATION ANNUAL EXHIBIT
225 Reinekers Lane, Ste. 650
Alexandria, VA 22314
PH: (703)549-4432
FX: (703)549-6495
Frequency: Annual. **Principal Exhibits:** Health equipment, supplies, and services. **Dates and Locations:** 1998 Aug 30 - Sep 01; New Orleans, LA.

HEALTH RESORT MEDICINE
e-mail: pratzel@imbk.med.uni-muenchen.de
c/o Dr. Helmut G. Pratzel
Institut fur Med. Baineologie und Klimatologie
Universitat Munich
81377 Munich, Germany
81377 Munich, Germany
PH: 49 89 70954287
FX: 49 89 70958829
Frequency: Quadrennial. **Principal Exhibits:** Medical hydrology and climatology equipment, supplies, and services.

HEALTH SERVICES RESEARCH: IMPLICATIONS FOR POLICY, MANAGEMENT AND CLINICAL PRACTICE
1130 Connecticut Ave. NW, Ste. 700
Washington, DC 20036
PH: (202)223-2477
FX: (202)835-8972
Frequency: Annual. **Audience:** Researchers, public and private funding agencies, health professionals, policy makers. **Principal Exhibits:** Exhibits relating to health services research in improving health care in the U.S. **Dates and Locations:** 1998 Jun; Chicago, IL.

HEALTHCARE ASSOCIATION OF HAWAII ANNUAL MEETING
932 Ward Ave., Ste. 430
Honolulu, HI 96814
PH: (808)521-8961
FX: (808)599-2879
Frequency: Annual. **Audience:** Nurses, health care administrators, purchasing agents, and related professionals. **Principal Exhibits:** Health care equipment, supplies, and services, including accounting systems, audiovisual equipment, communications systems, training services, furniture, home health care services, hospital equipment, paper products, pharmaceuticals, rehabilitation programs, safety aids, and word processing equipment. **Dates and Locations:** 1998 Oct; Honolulu, HI.

HEALTHCARE CONVENTION AND EXHIBITORS ASSOCIATION
e-mail: HCEA@assnhq.com
5775 Peachtree - Dunwoody Rd.
Suite 500 G
Atlanta, GA 30342
PH: (404)252-3663
FX: (404)252-0774
Frequency: Annual. **Audience:** Healthcare professionals. **Principal Exhibits:** Industry related supplies and services. **Dates and Locations:** 1998 Jun; Tampa, FL.

HEALTHCARE INFORMATION AND MANAGEMENT SYSTEMS SOCIETY CONFERENCE & EXHIBITION
Convention and Meetings Division
840 N. Lake Shore Dr.
Chicago, IL 60611
PH: (312)280-6000
FX: (312)280-6462
Frequency: Annual. **Audience:** Information systems trade professionals. **Principal Exhibits:** Health care information systems, telecommunications, consulting firms, hardware, software, and service providers. **Dates and Locations:** 1999 Jan.

HEALTHCARE ISTANBUL - INTERNATIONAL TRADE FAIR FOR HOSPITAL AND MEDICAL INSTRUMENTS, SYSTEMS, AND APPARATUS
Mim Kemal Oke Cad, No. 10 Nisantasi
TR-80200 Istanbul, Turkey
PH: 212 2250920
FX: 212 2250933
Frequency: Annual.

HONG KONG OPTICAL FAIR
e-mail: exhibitions@tdc.org.hk
Hong Kong Convention & Exhibition Centre
Exhibitions Dept.
Unit 13, Expo Galleria
Wanchai, Hong Kong
Wanchai, Hong Kong
PH: 852 2584 4333
FX: 852 2824 0249
Frequency: Annual. **Principal Exhibits:** Spectables, sunglasses, goggles, contact lenses, lenses, frames and mountings, parts and accessories, related chemicals and materials, manufacturing equipment and technology, optometry instruments, spectacle cases and holders, related packaging materials, and related services and publications.

HOPITEX - HEALTH CARE SHOW
3565 Edgar Leduc
Lachine, PQ, Canada H8T 3L5
PH: (514)639-6806
FX: (514)639-6629
Frequency: Annual. **Audience:** Hospital and health care center purchasing agents and management; nursing and medical professionals. **Principal Exhibits:** Material, equipment, and services related to hospitals and health care centers. **Dates and Locations:** 1998 May; Montreal, PQ.

HOSPITAL - INTERNATIONAL HEALTHCARE AND STOMATOLOGY EXHIBITION
url: http://www.gima.de
Heidenkampsweg 51
D-20097 Hamburg, Germany
PH: 040 235240
FX: 040 2352 4400
Frequency: Annual. **Principal Exhibits:** Hospital and medical equipment.

HOSPITALAR - INTERNATIONAL FAIR FOR PRODUCTS, EQUIPMENTS AND SERVICES FOR HOSPITALS AND HEALTH CLINICS
e-mail: couromod@mandic.com.br
379 Rua Oscar Freire, 19th Fl.
01426-001 Sao Paulo, Brazil
PH: 11 8811900
FX: 11 2803140
Frequency: Annual. **Audience:** Trade professionals. **Principal Exhibits:** Products, equipments, and services for hospitals and health clinics.

HOUSE OF DELEGATES MEETING
e-mail: exhibits@ana.org
url: http://www.nursingworld.org
600 Maryland Ave. SW, Ste. 100 W
Washingotn, DC 20024-2571
PH: (202)651-7203
FX: (202)651-7003
Frequency: Biennial. **Audience:** Registered nurses, hospital administrators, and school, operating room, public health, and nursing home nurses. **Principal Exhibits:** Equipment, supplies, and services for nurses, including publications, uniforms and shoes, computers, laboratory services, medical equipment, and nutritional products. **Dates and Locations:** 1998 Jun 25 - Jul 02; San Diego, CA ■ 2000 Jun 09-14; Indianapolis, IN ■ 2002 Jun 22-27; Philadelphia, PA.

ICN QUADRENNIAL CONGRESS: SHARING THE HEALTH CHALLENGE
3, place Jean-Marteau
CH-1201 Geneva, Switzerland
PH: 41 22 7312960
FX: 41 22 7381036
Frequency: Quadrennial. **Principal Exhibits:** Nursing equipment, supplies, and services. **Dates and Locations:** 2001 Jun; Vancouver, BC.

IDEA CONVENTION
url: http://www.ideafit.com
69190 Cornerstone Ct., E., Ste. 204
San Diego, CA 92121
PH: (619)535-8979
TF: 800999-4332
FX: (619)535-8234
Frequency: Annual. **Audience:** Professional aerobic/fitness instructors; studio owners; personal trainers. **Principal Exhibits:** Aerobic clothing and footwear; exercise products; equipment companies; related services. **Dates and Locations:** 1998; Ontario, ON. **Formerly:** International Dance Exercise Association Convention.

IDS - INTERNATIONAL DENTAL SHOW
url: http://www.koelnmesse.de
Messeplatz 1
D-50679 Cologne, Germany
PH: 221 821 0
FX: 221 821 2574
Frequency: Biennial. **Audience:** Trade professionals. **Principal Exhibits:** Dental equipment, supplies, and services.

**IKAL - INTERNATIONAL SPECIALIZED TRADE FAIR OF
EQUIPMENT FOR HOSPITALS, LABORATORIES, AND
MEDICAL OFFICES**
e-mail: info@messe.at
url: http://www.messe.at
Lagerhausstr. 7
PO Box 277
A-1021 Vienna, Austria
PH: 43 1 727 200
FX: 43 1 727 20443
Frequency: Biennial. **Audience:** General public. **Principal Exhibits:** Hospital, medical, and laboratory equipment, supplies, and services.

**ILLINOIS HEALTH CARE ASSOCIATION CONVENTION
AND TRADE SHOW**
url: http://www.ihca.com
1029 S. Fourth St.
Springfield, IL 62703
PH: (217)528-6455
TF: 800252-8988
FX: (217)528-0452
Frequency: Annual. **Audience:** Long-term care providers, nursing homes, and corporate officers. **Principal Exhibits:** Long-term (nursing homes) healthcare industry service providers. **Dates and Locations:** 1998; Rosemont, IL.

IMPERIAL COUNCIL SESSION
PO Box 31356
Tampa, FL 33631-3356
PH: (813)281-0300
FX: (813)281-8174
Frequency: Annual. **Principal Exhibits:** Exhibits relating to the Shriners' support of hospitals for crippled children. **Dates and Locations:** 1998 Jun 28 - Jul 02; Orlando, FL ■ 1999 Jul 04-08; Dallas, TX.

INCOF - OPTICS AND OPTOMETRY FAIR
url: http://www.bitf.be
Parc des Expositions
Place de Belgique
B-1020 Brussels, Belgium
PH: 32 2 474 8447
FX: 32 2 474 8540
Frequency: Annual. **Audience:** Trade professionals. **Principal Exhibits:** Frames, lenses, glasses and optical instruments and equipment.

**INDIANA ASSOCIATION OF OSTEOPATHIC PHYSICIANS
AND SURGEONS CONVENTION**
3520 Guion Rd., No. 202
Indianapolis, IN 46222
PH: (317)926-3009
FX: (317)926-3984
Frequency: Semiannual. **Audience:** Physicians and physicians assistants. **Principal Exhibits:** Pharmaceuticals; medical equipment and supplies, services for physicians. **Dates and Locations:** 1998 May 14-17; Indianapolis, IN.

INDIANA DENTAL ASSOCIATION CONVENTION
PO Box 2467
Indianapolis, IN 46206-2467
PH: (317)634-2610
TF: 800562-5646
FX: (317)634-2612
Frequency: Annual. **Audience:** Dentists, dental hygienists, dental assistants, and laboratory technicians. **Principal Exhibits:** Dental equipment, supplies, and services. **Dates and Locations:** 1998 Jun; Indianapolis, IN.

**INDIANA HOSPITAL ASSOCIATION MEETING AND
EXHIBITS**
e-mail: corcexpo@aol.com
33 N. Dearborn, Ste. 505
Chicago, IL 60602
PH: (312)541-0567
TF: 800541-0359
FX: (312)541-0573
Frequency: Annual. **Audience:** Association members, hospital CEO's, COO's, CFO's, dept. heads and middle managers. **Principal Exhibits:** Patient care equipment and supplies; financial and administrative service information; construction and maintenance service information; and hospital information systems. **Dates and Locations:** 1998; Indianapolis, IN.

**INDIANA STATE MEDICAL ASSOCIATION ANNUAL
CONVENTION**
322 Canal Walk
Indianapolis, IN 46202-3252
PH: (317)261-2060
TF: 800969-7545
FX: (317)264-0500
Frequency: Annual. **Audience:** Physicians and allied health professionals. **Principal Exhibits:** Health services, insurance companies, and health care givers. **Dates and Locations:** 1998; Indianapolis, IN.

**INDOMED - INDONESIA INTERNATIONAL MEDICAL,
PHARMACEUTICAL AND HEALTH CARE EXHIBITION**
21/F Tung Wai Commercial Bldg.
109-111 Gloucester Rd.
Wanchai, Hong Kong
PH: 5110511
FX: 5075014
Frequency: Biennial. **Audience:** Trade professionals. **Principal Exhibits:** Medical equipment, computer management systems, pharmaceuticals, supplies and materials, health products, tools, medical aids.

INSALABO - LABORATORY EQUIPMENT EXHIBITION
9, Ave. Louis Bleriot
69683 Lyon, France
PH: 72 223 212
FX: 72 223 182
Frequency: Biennial. **Principal Exhibits:** Biotechnology and chemical laboratory equipment, supplies, and services.

**INTERBAD - INTERNATIONAL TRADE FAIR FOR
SWIMMING POOLS, POOL AND BATH TECHNOL OGY,
SAUNAS, AND PHYSIOTHERAPY**
url: http://messe.dus.tradefair.de
Stockumer Kirchstrasse 61
PO Box 101006
D-40474 Dusseldorf, Germany
PH: 211 4560 01
FX: 211 4560 668
Frequency: Biennial. **Audience:** Trade professionals. **Principal Exhibits:** Physiotherapy; pools, bath and sauna equipment, supplies, and services.

INTERHOSPITAL MIT INTERFAB - HOSPITAL CONGRESS
Tersteegenstr. 9
D-40474 Dusseldorf, Germany
PH: 211 4541945
FX: 069 451834
Frequency: Annual. **Audience:** Administrators, distributors, representatives, and other medical professionals; general public. **Principal Exhibits:** Medical equipment, technical instruments, rehabilitation systems and related equipment, supplies, and services.

**INTERLINK - TEXAS HEALTHCARE FACILITIES AND
ENVIRONMENTAL MANAGEMENT**
url: http://www.thaonline.org
PO Box 15587
Austin, TX 78761
PH: (512)465-1000
TF: 800252-9403
FX: (512)465-1090
Frequency: Annual. Audience: Hospital engineers and related
professionals. Principal Exhibits: Hospital engineering/ house-
keeping equipment and services. Dates and Locations: 1998. For-
merly: Texas Hospital Engineer Exhibition.

**INTERNATIONAL ASSOCIATION OF ENVIRONMENTAL
TESTING LABORATORIES ANNUAL CONFERENCE**
700 13th St. NW, Ste. 950
Washington, DC 20005
PH: (202)434-4547
Frequency: Annual. Principal Exhibits: Equipment, supplies,
and services for environmental testing laboratories. Dates and
Locations: 1998.

**INTERNATIONAL ASSOCIATION OF HEALTHCARE
CENTRAL SERVICE MATERIALS MANAGEMENT
CONVENTION**
213 W. Institute Pl., Ste. 307
Chicago, IL 60610
PH: (312)440-0078
TF: 800962-8274
FX: (312)440-9474
Frequency: Annual. Audience: Hospital central service materil
management personnel. Principal Exhibits: Hospital central
service department equipment, supplies, and services. Dates and
Locations: 1998 May 03-06; Miami, FL ■ 1998 Nov 08-11;
Albuquerque, NM ■ 1999 May 02-05; Philadelphia, PA ■ 1999
Oct 31 - Nov 03; Chicago, IL ■ 2000 May 07-10; Reno, NV.

**INTERNATIONAL ASSOCIATION OF ORAL AND
MAXILLOFACIAL SURGEONS CONFERENCE**
Medical College of Virginia
Box 410, MCV
Richmond, VA 23298
PH: (804)828-8515
FX: (804)828-1753
Frequency: Biennial. Principal Exhibits: Oral and maxillofacial
surgery equipment, supplies, and services. Dates and Locations:
1999 Apr 25-29; Orlando, FL.

**INTERNATIONAL ASSOCIATION FOR ORTHODONTICS/
AMERICAN ORTHODONIC SOCIETY ANNUAL MEETING**
1100 Lake St., No. 240
Oak Park, IL 60301
PH: (708)445-0320
TF: 800447-8770
FX: (708)445-0321
Frequency: Annual. Audience: Dentists. Principal Exhibits: Or-
thodontic equipment and services. Dates and Locations: 1998;
Chicago, IL.

**INTERNATIONAL ASSOCIATION OF PAEDIATRIC
DENTISTRY CONGRESS**
7 Carlisle St.
London W1V 5RG, England
PH: 44 171 3777000
FX: 44 171 3777058
Frequency: Biennial. Audience: Dentists, dental and medical lib-
raries, bookshops, and research institutions. Principal Exhibits:
Paediatric dentistry equipment, supplies, and services.

**INTERNATIONAL COLLEGE OF SURGEONS WORLD
BIENNIAL CONGRESS**
e-mail: icsus@icsus.org
1516 N. Lake Shore Dr.
Chicago, IL 60610-1694

PH: (312)787-6274
TF: 800766-FICS
FX: (312)787-4289
Frequency: Annual. Audience: Surgeons. Principal Exhibits:
Medical equipment, including: pharmaceuticals, surgery books,
surgical equipment, new hospital devices, and anatomy models.

**INTERNATIONAL COMMISSION FOR UNIFORM
METHODS OF SUGAR ANALYSIS MEETING**
c/o CSR Ltd.
70 John St.
Pyrmont, NSW 2009, Australia
PH: 61 2 3257505
FX: 61 2 3257500
Frequency: Quadrennial. Principal Exhibits: Sugar analysis e-
quipment, supplies, and services.

**INTERNATIONAL CONFERENCE OF THE EUROPEAN
SOCIETY OF GASTRO-INTESTINAL & ABDOMINAL
RADIOLOGY**
Meibergdreef 9
1105 AZ Amsterdam, Netherlands
PH: 020 5662824
Principal Exhibits: Intestinal and abdominal medicine.

**INTERNATIONAL CONGRESS OF AGRICULTURAL
MEDICINE AND RURAL HEALTH**
Saku Central Hospital
197, Usuda
Minamisaku-gun
Nagano 384-03, Japan
PH: 81 267 823131
FX: 81 267 829602
Frequency: Triennial. Principal Exhibits: Exhibits relating to the
problems of agricultural medicine and rural health around the
world. Dates and Locations: 2000.

INTERNATIONAL CONGRESS FERTILITY AND PRACTICE
Stad en Landschap 53
2923 VL Krimpen a/d IJssel, Netherlands
PH: 01807 14991
Principal Exhibits: Fertility medicine.

**INTERNATIONAL CONGRESS FOR MATERNAL AND
NEONATAL HEALTH**
c/o Mrs. Gerda M. Santschi
16, chemin Grande Gorge
CH-1255 Veyrier, Switzerland
PH: 41 22 7840658
FX: 41 22 7840658
Frequency: Triennial. Audience: Medical professionals. Principal
Exhibits: Equipment, supplies, and services for improving mater-
nal and neonatal care throughout the world.

INTERNATIONAL CONGRESS OF NEUROPATHOLOGY
e-mail: jra20@cam.ac.uk
url: http://www.his.path.cam.ac.uk/npsoc/welcome.html
c/o Dr. Janice R. Anderson
Dept. of Histopathology
Addenbrooke's Hospital
Cambridge CB2 2QQ, England
PH: 44 1 223217170
FX: 44 1 223216980
Frequency: Triennial. Audience: Members of national societies
of neuropathology. Principal Exhibits: Exhibits concerning neu-
ropathology.

INTERNATIONAL CONGRESS OF OPHTHALMOLOGY
e-mail: bspivey@nmh.org
c/o Bruce E. Spivey
Northwestern Healthcare Network
980 N. Michigan Ave., Ste. 1500
Chicago, IL 60611

PH: (312)335-6035
FX: (312)335-6035
Frequency: Quadrennial. **Principal Exhibits:** Ophthalmology equipment, supplies, and services.

**INTERNATIONAL EDUCATION CONGRESS OF DENTAL
     TECHNOLOGY**
e-mail: dlany@aol.com
url: http://www.webmark/com/dlany/welcome.htm
Barstow Rd., Ste. P-20
Great Neck, NY 11021-3501
PH: (516)829-1144
FX: (516)829-1988
Frequency: Annual. **Audience:** Dental technicians, dentists, vendors, and other dental health care professionals. **Principal Exhibits:** Dental laboratory supplies and services. **Dates and Locations:** 1998 Sep 25-27; Tarrytown, NY.

**INTERNATIONAL EXPO DENTAL - EXHIBITION OF
     EQUIPMENT AND MATERIALS FOR DENTISTRY AND
     DENTAL TECHNICS**
e-mail: mce@planet.it
url: http://www.fmi.it
Largo Domodossola, 1
I-20145 Milan, Italy
PH: 39 2 48550 1
FX: 39 2 4800545 0
Frequency: Annual. **Principal Exhibits:** Dental equipment, supplies, and services.

**INTERNATIONAL GLAUCOMA CONGRESS AND
     EXHIBITION**
4711 W. Golf Rd., Ste. 408
Skokie, IL 60076
PH: (312)951-1400
FX: (312)951-1410
Frequency: Annual. **Audience:** Practicing ophthalmologists. **Principal Exhibits:** Pharmaceuticals and instrumentation related to the practice of ophthalmology. **Dates and Locations:** 1998.

INTERNATIONAL HEADACHE CONGRESS
P.O. Box 83005
1080 AA Amsterdam, Netherlands
PH: 020 6793218
Principal Exhibits: Headache medicine.

INTERNATIONAL HOSPITAL FEDERATION CONGRESS
e-mail: 101662.1262@compuserve.com
4 Abbots Pl.
London NW6 4NP, England
PH: 44 171 3727181
FX: 44 171 3287433
Frequency: Biennial. **Principal Exhibits:** Hospitals and health service management equipment, supplies, and services.

**INTERNATIONAL MEDICAL AND DENTAL
     HYPNOTHERAPY ASSOCIATION (IMDHA)**
e-mail: aspencer@infinityinst.com
url: http://www.infinityinst.com
4110 Edgeland, Ste. 800
Royal Oak, MI 48073-2285
PH: (248)549-5594
FX: (248)549-5421
Frequency: Annual. **Audience:** Hypnotherapists. **Principal Exhibits:** Hypnotherapy. **Dates and Locations:** 1998 Oct 24-25; Southfield, MI ▪ 1999 Oct 23-24; Southfield, MI ▪ 2000 Oct 28-29; Southfield, MI.

INTERNATIONAL MENOPAUSE SOCIETY CONGRESS
e-mail: staff@stofair.se
url: http://www.stofair.se
Massvagen 1, Alvsjo
S-125 80 Stockholm, Sweden

PH: 46 8 7494100
FX: 46 8 992044
Frequency: Triennial. **Principal Exhibits:** Exhibits relating to the treatment and study of the menopausal stages of life for men and women.

INTERNATIONAL ORTHOPTIC CONGRESS
Moorfields Eye Hospital
City Rd.
London EC1V 2PD, England
PH: 44 171 2533411
Frequency: Quadrennial. **Principal Exhibits:** Exhibits related to defects in binocular vision.

**INTERNATIONAL SOCIETY FOR THE STUDY OF LUMBAR
     SPINE**
c/o Communication Consultants
336 Smith St., No. 06-302
New Bridge Centre
Singapore 0105, Singapore
PH: 227 9811
FX: 227 0257
Frequency: Annual. **Principal Exhibits:** Orthopaedic products, spinal implants and instruments.

INTERNATIONAL SYMPOSIUM ON ATHEROSCLEROSIS
url: http://www.bcm.tmc.edu/ias/
c/o Barbara Gordin
6550 Fannin, No. 1423
Houston, TX 77030
PH: (713)790-4226
FX: (713)793-1080
Frequency: Triennial. **Audience:** Researchers, clinicians. **Principal Exhibits:** Exhibits on lipoproteins and apoliproteins, molecular genetics, cell biology, epidemiology and prevention, nutrition, drug treatment, diabetes, diagnostic and clinical aspects, and growth factors.

**INTERNATIONAL SYMPOSIUM ON COLOR VISION
     DEFICIENCIES**
e-mail: coa09@cc.keele.ac.uk
url: http://orlab.optom.unsw.edu.au./irgcvd/
c/o Prof. J.D. Moreland
Dept. of Communication and Neuroscience
Keele University
Stafford ST5 5BG, England
PH: 44 1782 583060
FX: 44 1782 583055
Frequency: Biennial. **Principal Exhibits:** Exhibits related to the study of congenital and acquired color vision deficiencies.

**INTERNATIONAL UNION AGAINST VENEREAL DISEASES
     AND TREPONEMATOSES GENERAL ASSEMBLY**
c/o Dr. M.A. Waugh
General Infirmary at Leeds
Great George St.
Leeds, W. Yorkshire LS1 3EX, England
PH: 44 113 2926762
FX: 44 113 2926387
Frequency: Biennial. **Principal Exhibits:** Exhibits relating to the study of sexually transmitted and HIV related disease.

INTERNATIONAL VISION EXPO AND CONFERENCE/EAST
e-mail: inquiry@nepcon.reedexpo.com
383 Main Ave.
PO Box 6059
Norwalk, CT 06851
PH: (203)840-5358
FX: (203)840-4804
Frequency: Annual. **Principal Exhibits:** Equipment, supplies and services for the vision industry. **Dates and Locations:** 1998 Mar; New York, NY.

INTERNATIONAL VISION EXPO AND CONFERENCE/ WEST
e-mail: inquiry@nepcon.reedexpo.com
383 Main Ave.
PO Box 6059
Norwalk, CT 06851
PH: (203)840-5358
FX: (203)840-4804
Frequency: Annual. **Audience:** Industry buyers, opticians, and optometrists. **Principal Exhibits:** Contact lenses, solutions, and care kits; frames; glass and plastic ophthalmic lenses; plano sunglasses; specialty lenses; business and record management systems; computer systems; dispensing, display, and examination equipment; laboratory systems; office furniture and design services; training programs; vision aids. **Dates and Locations:** 1998 Sep; Anaheim, CA.

INTERPHEX WEST
e-mail: inquiry@nepcon.reedexpo.com
383 Main Ave.
PO Box 6059
Norwalk, CT 06851
PH: (203)840-5358
FX: (203)840-4804
Frequency: Annual. **Audience:** Engineers. **Principal Exhibits:** Equipment, materials and supplies. **Dates and Locations:** 1998 Sep; Santa Clara, CA.

INTRAVENOUS NURSES SOCIETY ANNUAL MEETING
2 Brighton St.
Belmont, MA 02178
PH: (617)489-5205
FX: (617)489-0656
Frequency: Annual. **Audience:** Intravenous nurses and nursing supervisors; pharmacists. **Principal Exhibits:** IV medical devices such as pumps, controllers, catheters, IV solutions blood products, administration sets, dressings, and home-care services. **Dates and Locations:** 1998; Salt Lake City, UT.

IOFT - INTERNATIONAL OPTICAL FAIR TOKYO
2F Ginza-Eiwa Bldg.
8-18-7 Ginza Chuo-Ku
Tokyo 104, Japan
PH: 81 3 5565 0861
FX: 81 3 5565 0860
Frequency: Annual. **Audience:** Retailers, wholesalers, manufacturers, export/import traders. **Principal Exhibits:** Lens and lens processing equipment and tools; frames and frame processing equipment and tools; examination and measuring equipment; industrial glasses; computer systems; accessories; display equipment; and related equipment, supplies, and services.

ISPD - CONGRESS OF THE INTERNATIONAL SOCIETY FOR PERITONEAL DIALYSIS
e-mail: staff@stofair.se
url: http://www.stofair.se
Massvagen 1, Alvsjo
S-125 80 Stockholm, Sweden
PH: 46 8 7494100
FX: 46 8 992044
Frequency: Biennial. **Principal Exhibits:** Dialysis and related subjects. **Dates and Locations:** 1999.

ITALMEDICA - INTERNATIONAL EXHIBITION FOR MEDICAL AND HOSPITAL EQUIPMENT
e-mail: inquiry@nepcon.reedexpo.com
383 Main Ave.
PO Box 6059
Norwalk, CT 06851
PH: (203)840-5358
FX: (203)840-4804
Frequency: Annual. **Audience:** Trade professionals. **Principal Exhibits:** Healthcare equipment, supplies, and services.

IVAN - SEMINARS AND EXHIBITION ON ANAESTHESIA AND INTENSIVE CARE
e-mail: staff@stofair.se
url: http://www.stofair.se
Massvagen 1, Alvsjo
S-125 80 Stockholm, Sweden
PH: 46 8 7494100
FX: 46 8 992044
Frequency: Annual. **Audience:** Delegates at IVAN study days, and nurses belonging to the IVAN association. **Principal Exhibits:** Healthcare and medical products aimed specially at intensive care nurses and nurse anesthetists.

KANSAS ASSOCIATION OF OSTEOPATHIC MEDICINE ANNUAL CONVENTION
e-mail: kansasdo@aol.com
1260 SW Topeka Blvd.
Topeka, KS 66612
PH: (913)234-5563
FX: (913)234-5564
Frequency: Annual. **Audience:** Physicians. **Principal Exhibits:** Pharmaceutical companies, medical equipment, and finance management. **Dates and Locations:** 1998 Apr; Overland Park, KS.

KANSAS OPTOMETRIC ASSOCIATION CONVENTION AND EDUCATIONAL SEMINAR
1266 SW Topeka Blvd.
Topeka, KS 66612
PH: (913)232-0225
Frequency: Annual. **Audience:** Optometrists. **Principal Exhibits:** Ophthalmic goods, services, and equipment. **Dates and Locations:** 1998 Apr 22-25; Overland Park, KS.

KENTUCKY DENTAL ASSOCIATION MEETING AND EXHIBITS
1940 Princeton Dr.
Louisville, KY 40205-1873
PH: (502)459-5373
FX: (502)458-5915
Frequency: Annual. **Principal Exhibits:** Dental equipment, supplies, and services. **Dates and Locations:** 1998 Apr 03-05; Louisville, KY ▪ 1999 Apr 08-11; Louisville, KY.

KENTUCKY MEETING
1940 Princeton Dr.
Louisville, KY 40205-1873
PH: (502)459-5373
FX: (502)458-5915
Frequency: Annual. **Audience:** Dentists, dental hygienists, dental assistants, and laboratory technicians. **Principal Exhibits:** Dental, pharmaceutical, and health-care supplies and services. **Dates and Locations:** 1998 Apr 02-05; Louisville, KY ▪ 1999 Apr 08-11; Louisville, KY.

KENTUCKY NURSES ASSOCIATION ANNUAL CONVENTION
e-mail: kentucky.nurses@internet.mci.com
1400 S. 1st
PO Box 2616
Louisville, KY 40201
PH: (502)637-2546
FX: (502)637-8236
Frequency: Annual. **Audience:** Registered Nurses and students. **Principal Exhibits:** Health industry related services and equipment, including pharmaceuticals and recruitment services. **Dates and Locations:** 1998 Oct 22-23; Louisville, KY.

KIHE - INTERNATIONAL HEALTHCARE AND STOMATOLOGY EXHIBITION
url: http://www.gima.de
Heidenkampsweg 51
D-20097 Hamburg, Germany
PH: 040 235240
FX: 040 2352 4400

Frequency: Annual. **Principal Exhibits:** Equipment, supplies, and services for the healthcare industry.

LAB - LABORATORY EXHIBITION
e-mail: nv@messe.no
url: http://www.messe.no
Drammensveien 154
PO Box 130 Skoyen
N-0212 Oslo, Norway
PH: 47 22 439100
FX: 47 22 431914
Frequency: Biennial. **Principal Exhibits:** Industrial and medical laboratory equipment, supplies, and services.

LABORATORY LONDON - LABORATORY EXHIBITION AND CONFERENCE
Burlington House
Piccadilly
London W1V 0BN, England
PH: 71 4378656
FX: 71 4378883
Frequency: Annual. **Audience:** Trade. **Principal Exhibits:** Laboratory equipment, instruments and supplies. **Formerly:** British Laboratory Week.

LABORATORY MANCHESTER
e-mail: inquiry@nepcon.reedexpo.com
383 Main Ave.
PO Box 6059
Norwalk, CT 06851
PH: (203)840-5358
FX: (203)840-4804
Frequency: Annual. **Audience:** Trade professionals. **Principal Exhibits:** Scientific technology for industry and medicine.

LABORATORY SCOTLAND
e-mail: inquiry@nepcon.reedexpo.com
383 Main Ave.
PO Box 6059
Norwalk, CT 06851
PH: (203)840-5358
FX: (203)840-4804
Frequency: Biennial. **Audience:** Trade professionals. **Principal Exhibits:** Scientific technology for industry and medicine.

LAEGENDAGE - CONFERENCE AND EXHIBITION FOR GENERAL MEDICAL PRACTITIONERS
e-mail: bc@bella.dk
url: http://www.bellacenter.dk
Center Blvd.
DK-2300 Copenhagen S, Denmark
PH: 45 32 52 88 11
FX: 45 32 51 96 36
Frequency: Biennial. **Principal Exhibits:** Medical equipment, supplies, and services for general practitioners.

LESBIAN, GAY AND BISEXUAL PEOPLE IN MEDICINE CONFERENCE
c/o American Medical Student Association
1902 Association Dr.
Reston, VA 22091
PH: (703)620-6600
FX: (703)620-5873
Frequency: Annual. **Principal Exhibits:** Exhibits relating to the improvement of the treatment of homosexuals in the health care profession. **Dates and Locations:** 1998 Mar; New Orleans, LA.

LIBERTY DENTAL CONFERENCE
225 Washington E.
Philadelphia, PA 19106
PH: (215)925-6050
FX: (215)925-6998
Frequency: Annual. **Audience:** Dentists, dental assistants, dental hygienists, and dental technicians. **Principal Exhibits:** Dental e-

quipment, supplies, and products. **Dates and Locations:** 1998 Mar; Philadelphia, PA.

LOUISIANA-MISSISSIPPI OPHTHALMOLOGICAL AND OTOLARYNGOLOGICAL SOCIETY ANNUAL MEETING
Frequency: Annual. **Audience:** Ophthalmologists and otolaryngologists. **Principal Exhibits:** Surgical instruments, optical instruments, publications, pharmaceuticals, prosthetics, and hearing instruments. **Dates and Locations:** 1998 Apr.

MAINE DENTAL ASSOCIATION ANNUAL MEETING
PO Box 215
Manchester, ME 04351
PH: (207)622-7900
Frequency: Annual. **Audience:** Dentists, hygienists, lab technicians, and dental assistants. **Principal Exhibits:** Dental equipment, office equipment and supplies, and related products and supplies. **Dates and Locations:** 1998 Jun; Rockport, ME.

MANITOBA HEALTH ORGANIZATIONS ANNUAL HEALTH CONFERENCE AND EXHIBITION
PO Box 116
Winnipeg, MB, Canada R3C 2G1
PH: (204)958-7540
FX: (204)958-7547
Frequency: Annual. **Audience:** Health care administrators, board members, purchasing managers, nursing directors, dieticians, pharmacists, lawyers, and related professionals. **Principal Exhibits:** Pharmaceuticals, medical equipment, facility information, and related supplies and services. **Dates and Locations:** 1998 Nov 05-06; Winnipeg, MB ∎ 1999 Nov 03-04; Winnipeg, MB.

MASSACHUSETTS ACADEMY OF FAMILY PHYSICIANS CONVENTION
PO Box 1406
Manchester, MA 01944
PH: (508)526-9753
FX: (508)526-4417
Frequency: Annual. **Audience:** Family physicians. **Principal Exhibits:** Medical services, supplies, and equipment. **Dates and Locations:** 1998.

MEASUREX EXHIBITION
url: http://www.machinery.com.hk/machine.html
Room 15, 5/F Wah Shing Centre
11 Shing Yip Street
1 Kwun Tong
Kowloon, Hong Kong
PH: 27639011
FX: 23410379
Frequency: Annual. **Audience:** Trade. **Principal Exhibits:** Laboratory equipment, supplies, and services. **Formerly:** (970418) Labtech - Exhibition of Modern Laboratory Equipment Supplies & Services.

MEDAX - ISRAEL MEDICAL WEEK
e-mail: expo@stier.co.il
url: http://www.stier.co.il
12 Tverski St.
67210 Tel Aviv, Israel
PH: 972 3 5626090
FX: 972 3 5615463
Frequency: Biennial. **Principal Exhibits:** Medical technologies, hospital equipment, lab equipment, dental equipment, and supply for care centers.

MEDEC - MEDICAL CONGRESS AND EXHIBITION FOR PRACTICIONERS
e-mail: international@cepexposium.fr
74, av. Kleber
F-75116 Paris, France
PH: 01 45 53 36 24
FX: 01 45 53 68 04

Frequency: Annual. **Audience:** Health professionals. **Principal Exhibits:** Medical equipment, supplies, and services.

MEDIC VIETNAM
Postfach 120709
80033 Munich, Germany
PH: 89 500610
FX: 89 5028497
Frequency: Annual. **Principal Exhibits:** Medical technology and supplies, electro-medicine, dental medicine, orthopedic and rehabilitation technology.

MEDICA - INTERNATIONAL HEALTH CARE EXHIBITION AND PAVILION FOR INFORMATION SUPPLY AND COMMUNICATION
e-mail: info@jaarbeursutrecht.nl
url: http://www.jaarbeursutrecht.nl
Jaarbeursplein-Utrecht
PO Box 8500
NL-3503 RM Utrecht, Netherlands
PH: 30 295 5911
FX: 30 294 0379
Frequency: Biennial. **Audience:** Hospital administrators, physicians, pharmacists, biologists, chemists, processing engineers and technicians, medical assistants, nurses. **Principal Exhibits:** Medical, nursing and technical equipment, supplies, and services.

MEDICAL/HOSPITECH - INTERNATIONAL MEDICAL, HOSPITAL, AND DENTAL FACILITIES AND EQUIPMENT EXHIBITION
Waldhöheweg 21
Postfach 288
CH-3000 Bern, Switzerland
PH: 31 331 3724
FX: 31 333 1861
Frequency: Biennial. **Audience:** Manufacturers, traders, suppliers, medical practitioners, Thai Ministry of Public Health, trade professionals, and general public. **Principal Exhibits:** Acupuncture; accident and emergency equipment; anaesthetic baby care products; diagnostics; catheters; cardiology equipment; dental equipment, supplies, and dialysis; nose instruments and apparatus; electromedical apparatus; hospital beds; furniture and incubators; operation theater respirators; ultrasound, and ward equipment.

MEDICAL WOMEN'S INTERNATIONAL ASSOCIATION CONGRESS
e-mail: mwia@aol.com
Herbert-Lewin-Strasse 1
50931 Cologne, Germany
PH: 49 221 4004558
FX: 49 221 4004557
Frequency: Triennial. **Principal Exhibits:** Exhibits of interest to women in medical professions.

MEDICINA/TEHNIKA - INTERNATIONAL EXHIBITION OF MEDICAL EQUIPMENT, PHARMACEUTICALS, AND LABORATORY EQUIPMENT
url: http://www.zv.hr
Avenija Dubrovnik 15
10020 Zagreb, Croatia
PH: 385 1 6503 111
FX: 385 1 6520 643
Frequency: Annual. **Principal Exhibits:** Medical, pharmaceutical, and laboratory equipment, supplies, and services.

MEDICINE - EXHIBITION OF MEDICINE, NURSING AND HEALTH CARE
e-mail: info@finnexpo.fi
url: http://www.finnexpo.fi
Helsinki Fair Centre
Messuaukio 1
PO Box 21
FIN-00521 Helsinki, Finland

PH: 358 9 150 91
FX: 358 9 142 358
Frequency: Annual. **Audience:** Trade professionals. **Principal Exhibits:** Medicine and other pharmaceuticals, diagnostics, surgical instruments and equipment, physiotherapy equipment, protheses and aids, related instruments, materials, accessories, hospital equipment, computer applications, first aid and rescue equipment, publications and information services, and allied services and organizations.

MEDICINE GOES ELECTRONIC - INNOVATIVE MEDICAL CONGRESS WITH EXHIBITION
Frequency: Biennial. **Audience:** Trade professionals; doctors, hospital managers, nurses, pharmaceutical companies, medical software companies, health insurance funds, policy makers. **Principal Exhibits:** Innovative endoscopic methods, virtual reality in medicine, robotics in surgery, modern imaging methods.

MEDIKAL DENTAL BUDAPEST - INTERNATIONAL FAIR FOR HOSPITALS, DOCTORS AND LABORATORIES, PHARMACIES, REHABILITATION, DENTISTS AND DENTAL LABORATORI
e-mail: hungexpo@hungexpo.hu
url: http://www.hungexpo.hu
PO Box 44
H-1441 Budapest, Hungary
PH: 36 1 263 6000
FX: 36 1 263 6098
Frequency: Biennial. **Principal Exhibits:** Equipment, supplies, and services for hospitals, nursing homes, sanatorium, private practices, dental laboratories and facilities, rehabilitation, and home care: diagnostic aids, drugs, data processing, technical installations, and medical consumer goods. **Held in conjunction with:** Budatranspack; Printexpo.

MEDIVITAL - MEDICINE AND HEALTH TRADE FAIR
e-mail: marketing@messe-berlin.de
url: http://www.messe-berlin.de
Messedamm 22
D-14055 Berlin, Germany
PH: 49 30 3038 0
FX: 49 30 3038 2325
Frequency: Annual. **Principal Exhibits:** Equipment, supplies, and services for the fields of medicine, health, and the promotion of well-being. Exhibits include pharmaceuticals, life-saving and laboratory equipment, hospital logistics and computer applications, holistic and alternative medicine, and spa resorts.

MEDNAT - INTERNATIONAL FAIR OF NATURAL MEDICINES, BETTER LIVING, HEALTH, AND PREVENTION
e-mail: beaulieu@comptoir.ch
url: http://www.beaulieu.comptoir.ch
CP 89
CH-1000 Lausanne, Switzerland
PH: 6432111
FX: 6433711
Frequency: Annual. **Audience:** Health professionals and general public. **Principal Exhibits:** Natural medicine, thermalism, thalasso and balneotherapy, nutrition, personal hygiene, sports and health, geobiology, therapeutical equipments, natural cosmetics, literature and healthy living.

MEDTEKHNIKA - INTERNATIONAL EXHIBITION ON MEDICAL ENGINEERING
Krasnopresnenskaya nab. 14
123100 Moscow, Russia
PH: 095 268 1340
FX: 095 205 60 55
Frequency: Biennial. **Audience:** Trade professionals and general public. **Principal Exhibits:** Medical equipment, supplies, and services.

**MENTAL HEALTH WORKERS AND EDUCATORS
  NATIONAL CONFERENCE**
1789 N. Neltor Blvd., Ste. 260
West Chicago, IL 60185-2997
TF: 800391-7589
Frequency: Biennial. **Audience:** Psychiatric technicians, behavioral health technicians, mental health workers, and counselors. **Principal Exhibits:** Exhibits for the mental health industry. **Dates and Locations:** 1998 May; Chicago, IL.

MICHIGAN DENTAL ASSOCIATION ANNUAL SESSION
230 N. Washington Sq., Ste. 208
Lansing, MI 48933
PH: (517)372-9070
FX: (517)372-0008
Frequency: Annual. **Audience:** Dentists, dental hygienists, dental assistants, lab technicians, business staff and students. **Principal Exhibits:** Dental equipment, materials, and instruments; computers; software; uniforms; and estate planners. **Dates and Locations:** 1998 Apr 22-25; Detroit, MI ▪ 1999; Detroit, MI ▪ 2000; Grand Rapids, MI.

**MICHIGAN NURSES ASSOCIATION ANNUAL
  CONVENTION**
e-mail: mna@voyager.net
2310 Jolly Oak Rd.
Okemos, MI 48864-3546
PH: (517)349-5640
FX: (517)349-5818
Frequency: Annual. **Audience:** Trade professionals. **Principal Exhibits:** Recruiters, pharmaceutical companies, medical supplies, uniforms, insurance companies and financial planners. **Dates and Locations:** 1998 Oct 01-02; Lansing, MI ▪ 1999 Oct 07-08; Kalamazoo, MI.

**MICHIGAN OPTOMETRIC ASSOCIATION ANNUAL
  CONVENTION**
e-mail: mioptoassn@aol.com
530 W. Ionia St., Ste. A
Lansing, MI 48933-1062
PH: (517)482-0616
FX: (517)482-1611
Frequency: Annual. **Audience:** Optometrists, optometric technicians, and assistants. **Principal Exhibits:** Ophthalmic supplies, equipment, and services. **Dates and Locations:** 1998 Jul 23-26; Harbor Springs, MI ▪ 1999 Aug 06-09; Acme, MI.

**MICRO - EXHIBITION OF THE LATEST INSTRUMENTS
  AND ANCILLARY EQUIPMENT OF THE MODERN
  MICROSCOPE INDUSTRY**
e-mail: rms@uak.ox.ac.uk
37-38 St. Clements
Oxford OX4 1AJ, England
PH: 865 248768
FX: 865 791237
Frequency: Biennial. **Audience:** Trade professionals. **Principal Exhibits:** Microscopes (LM, EM etc), image analysis equipment, and other ancillary equipment.

MID-CONTINENT DENTAL CONGRESS CONVENTION
13667 Manchester Rd.
St. Louis, MO 63131
PH: (314)965-5960
FX: (314)965-4746
Frequency: Annual. **Audience:** Dentists and related professionals. **Principal Exhibits:** Dental equipment, supplies, and services. **Dates and Locations:** 1998 Sep 17-19; St. Louis, MO ▪ 1999 Sep 16-18; St. Louis, MO ▪ 2000 Sep 21-23; St. Louis, MO ▪ 2001 Sep 13-15; St. Louis, MO ▪ 2002 Sep 19-21; St. Louis, MO.

**MIDDLE ATLANTIC SOCIETY OF ORTHODONTISTS
  ANNUAL SESSION**
1039 Louise Ln.
Allentown, PA 18103

PH: (610)820-4062
TF: 610820-0330
Frequency: Annual. **Principal Exhibits:** Orthodontics equipment, supplies, and services. **Dates and Locations:** 1998.

MIDWEST DENTAL CONFERENCE
650 E. 25th St.
Kansas City, MO 64108
PH: (816)235-2060
TF: 800887-4477
FX: (816)235-2157
Frequency: Annual. **Principal Exhibits:** Dental equipment, supplies, and services. **Dates and Locations:** 1998 Mar 19-22; Kansas City, MO.

MISSISSIPPI ACADEMY OF FAMILY PHYSICIANS
5903 Ridgewood Rd., Ste. 200
Jackson, MS 39211-3707
PH: (601)981-0774
FX: (601)981-4583
Frequency: Annual. **Audience:** Trade professionals, members only. **Principal Exhibits:** Medical equipment, supplies, and services. **Dates and Locations:** 1998; Orange Beach, AL.

MISSISSIPPI DENTAL ASSOCIATION ANNUAL SESSION
2630 Ridgewood Rd.
Jackson, MS 39216
PH: (601)982-0442
FX: (601)366-3050
Frequency: Annual. **Audience:** Dentists. **Principal Exhibits:** Pharmaceuticals and dental laboratory services. **Dates and Locations:** 1998 Jun 12-16.

**MISSISSIPPI NURSES ASSOCIATION ANNUAL
  CONVENTION**
e-mail: mna@netdoor.com
31 Woodgreen Place
Madison, MS 39110-9531
PH: (601)898-0670
FX: (601)898-0190
Frequency: Annual. **Audience:** Trade professionals. **Principal Exhibits:** Nursing industry equipment, supplies, and services. **Dates and Locations:** 1998 Oct 21-23; Biloxi, MS.

MISSOURI STATE MEDICAL ASSOCIATION CONVENTION
url: http://www.msma.org
113 Madison St.
PO Box 1028
Jefferson City, MO 65101
PH: (573)636-5151
FX: (573)636-8552
Frequency: Annual. **Audience:** Physicians. **Principal Exhibits:** Pharmaceuticals, insurance information, and computers. **Dates and Locations:** 1998 Apr 16-19; St. Louis, MO ▪ 1999 Apr 08-11; Osage Beach, MO ▪ 2000 Apr 06-09; Kansas City, MO.

**MOUNTAIN STATES CONGRESS OF OPTOMETRY
  COLORADO OPTOMETRIC ASSOCIATION TRADE SHOW**
419 W. Main
PO Box 204
Sterling, CO 80751
PH: (970)522-4396
FX: (970)522-8476
Frequency: Annual. **Audience:** Optometrists. **Principal Exhibits:** Optometric supplies and laboratory equipment, including contact lenses and frames. **Dates and Locations:** 1998; Snowmass, CO.

MULTIDISCIPLINARY TRAINING CONFERENCE
e-mail: achsa@achsa.meinet.com
PO Box 2307
Dayton, OH 45401-2307
PH: (937)586-3708
FX: (937)586-3699
Frequency: Annual. **Audience:** Multidisciplinary health care pro-

fessionals. **Principal Exhibits:** Medical equipment, supplies, and services, including laboratory services, pharmacy services, automated equipment, and nursing and psychiatric educational materials. **Dates and Locations:** 1998 Apr; Atlanta, GA. **Formerly:** American Correctional Health Services Association Convention.

MUSIC MEDICINE CONFERENCE
Paulmannshoher Str. 17
58515 Ludenscheid, Germany
PH: 49 2351 9452260
FX: 49 2351 94517
Frequency: Biennial. **Audience:** Medical doctors, scientists, and music therapists. **Principal Exhibits:** Equipment, supplies, and services for interdisciplinary research into the psychological basis for and applications of music in medicine.

NAIDEX CARE MANAGEMENT
e-mail: info@reedexpo.co.uk
url: http://www.reedexpo.com
Oriel House
26 The Quadrant
Richmond, Surrey TW9 1DL, England
PH: 181 910 7825
FX: 181 910 7926
Frequency: Annual. **Principal Exhibits:** Equipment and services for disabled and elderly people, nursing and rest homes.

NASN ANNUAL CONFERENCE
Lamplighter Ln.
PO Box 1300
Scarborough, ME 04070
PH: (207)883-2117
FX: (207)883-2683
Frequency: Annual. **Principal Exhibits:** School nursing equipment, supplies, and services. **Dates and Locations:** 1998 Jun; Dallas, TX.

NATIONAL ADRN CONGRESS
PO Box 880244
San Diego, CA 92168-0244
PH: (619)292-1864
Frequency: Annual. **Principal Exhibits:** Operating room equipment, supplies, and services. **Dates and Locations:** 1998 Mar 29 - Apr 03; Orlando, FL ▪ 1999; San Francisco, CA.

NATIONAL ASSOCIATION OF BIOLOGY TEACHERS NATIONAL CONVENTION
e-mail: nabter@aol.com
11250 Roger Bacon Dr., Ste. 19
Reston, VA 22090
PH: (703)471-1134
TF: 800406-0775
FX: (703)435-5582
Frequency: Annual. **Audience:** Biology teachers and administrators. **Principal Exhibits:** Publications, biological supplies, laboratory equipment, and computer software. **Dates and Locations:** 1998 Nov 18-21; Reno, NV ▪ 1999 Oct 27-30; Fort Worth, TX ▪ 2000 Oct 25-28; Orlando, FL.

NATIONAL ASSOCIATION OF DENTAL LABORATORIES
url: http://www.inf1.com/nadl
555 E. Braddock Rd.
Alexandria, VA 22314-2106
PH: (703)683-5263
TF: 800950-1150
FX: (703)549-4788
Frequency: Annual. **Audience:** Owners, managers, technicians, students, and dentists. **Principal Exhibits:** Supplies for the commercial dental industry. **Dates and Locations:** 1998 Sep 09-12; Las Vegas, NV ▪ 1999 Sep; Las Vegas, NV.

NATIONAL ASSOCIATION OF HOSPITAL HOSPITALITY HOUSES CONFERENCE
e-mail: nahhhcom@aol.com
4915 Auburn Ave., Ste. 303
Bethesda, MD 20814
PH: (301)961-5264
TF: 800542-9730
FX: (301)961-3094
Frequency: Annual. **Principal Exhibits:** Equipment, supplies, and services for hospital hospitality houses, which are temporary residential facilities for patients and their families. **Dates and Locations:** 1998 Jun; Rochester, MN.

NATIONAL ASSOCIATION OF ORTHOPEDIC NURSES ANNUAL CONGRESS
E. Holly Ave. Box 56
Pitman, NJ 08071
PH: (609)256-2300
FX: (609)589-7463
Frequency: Annual. **Audience:** Orthopedic nurses, operating room nurses, rehabilitation nurses, and related professionals. **Principal Exhibits:** Pharmaceuticals, medical equipment, medical instruments, and publications. **Dates and Locations:** 1998 May 12-21; San Francisco, CA ▪ 1999 May 23-27; Atlanta, GA.

NATIONAL ASSOCIATION OF SCIENTIFIC MATERIALS MANAGERS CONVENTION
e-mail: cmwcm@uno.edu
University of New Orleans
Chemistry Dept.
New Orleans, LA 70148
PH: (504)280-6324
FX: (504)280-7039
Frequency: Annual. **Audience:** Stockroom managers of educational, industrial, hospital, dental and pharmaceutical warehouses. **Principal Exhibits:** Scientific material and equipment, including research material, chemicals, packaging, and glassware. **Dates and Locations:** 1998 Jul; Portland, ME.

NATIONAL DENTAL ASSOCIATION ANNUAL CONVENTION
3517 16th St., NW
Washington, DC 20010
PH: (202)588-1697
FX: (202)588-1244
Frequency: Annual. **Audience:** Dentists, dental assistants, dental hygienists, and dental students. **Principal Exhibits:** Dental and Pharmaceutical equipment, supplies, and services. **Dates and Locations:** 1998; Scottsdale, AZ.

NATIONAL HOSPICE ORGANIZATION ANNUAL SYMPOSIUM AND EXPOSITION
e-mail: drsnho@cais.com
url: http://www.nho.org
1901 N. Moore St., Ste. 901
Arlington, VA 22209
PH: (703)243-5900
TF: 800658-8898
FX: (703)525-5762
Frequency: Annual. **Principal Exhibits:** equipment, supplies, and services for hospice organizations. **Dates and Locations:** 1998; Atlanta, GA.

NATIONAL LEAGUE FOR NURSING CONVENTION
6900 Grove Rd.
Thorofare, NJ 08086
PH: (609)848-1000
FX: (609)848-3522
Frequency: Biennial. **Audience:** Nurses, and related health care professionals. **Principal Exhibits:** Equipment, supplies, and services for nurses and related healthcare professionals. **Dates and Locations:** 1999 Jun; San Diego, CA.

NATIONAL MEDICAL ASSOCIATION ANNUAL CONVENTION AND SCIENTIFIC ASSEMBLY
1012 10th St. NW
Washington, DC 20001
PH: (202)347-1895
FX: (202)842-3293
Frequency: Annual. **Audience:** Physicians. **Principal Exhibits:** Medical equipment, supplies, and services. **Dates and Locations:** 1998 Aug 01-05; New Orleans, LA ▪ 1999 Aug; Las Vegas, NV.

NATIONAL OSTEOPATHIC HEALTH CONFERENCE
1423 Randy Lane
PO Box 748
Jefferson City, MO 65102
PH: (314)634-3415
FX: (314)634-5635
Frequency: Annual. **Audience:** Osteopathic physicians, medical assistants, students, interns, and residents; hospital administrators. **Principal Exhibits:** Pharmaceuticals and medical/surgical services, professional liability insurance, office/computer equipment. **Dates and Locations:** 1998 May 27-31; Lake Ozark, MO ▪ 1999 May; Lake Ozark, MO ▪ 2000 May; Lake Ozark, MO.

NATIONAL PERINATAL ASSOCIATION ANNUAL CLINICAL CONFERENCE
e-mail: npaonline@aol.com
3500 E. Fletcher Ave., Ste. 209
Tampa, FL 33613
PH: (813)971-1008
FX: (813)971-9306
Frequency: Annual. **Principal Exhibits:** Perinatal health care equipment, supplies, and services. **Dates and Locations:** 1998 Nov 12-15; Providence, RI.

NATIONAL RURAL HEALTH ASSOCIATION ANNUAL CONFERENCE ON RURAL HEALTH
1 W. Armour Blvd., Ste. 301
Kansas City, MO 64111
PH: (816)756-3140
FX: (816)756-3144
Frequency: Annual. **Audience:** Rural physicians, administrators, health educators, nurses, physicians assistants, federal and state officials, and other trade professionals. **Principal Exhibits:** Equipment, supplies, services, and programs for persons interested or involved in rural health issues and rural health care delivery. **Dates and Locations:** 1998 May.

NATIONAL SOCIETY FOR HISTOTECHNOLOGY SYMPOSIUM AND CONVENTION
e-mail: histo@nsh.org
url: http://www.nsh.org
4201 Northview Dr., Ste. 502
Bowie, MD 20716-1073
PH: (301)262-6221
FX: (301)262-9188
Frequency: Annual. **Audience:** Laboratory technicians and pathologists. **Principal Exhibits:** Equipment for the histology and pathology laboratories. **Dates and Locations:** 1998 Sep 12-16; Salt Lake City, UT ▪ 1999 Oct 16-20; Providence, RI ▪ 2000 Sep 16-20; Milwaukee, WI.

NATIONAL STUDENT NURSES' ASSOCIATION CONVENTION
e-mail: nsna.net@internetmci.com
url: http://www.nsna.org
555 W. 57th St., Ste. 1327
New York, NY 10019
PH: (212)581-2211
FX: (212)581-2368
Frequency: Annual. **Principal Exhibits:** Equipment, supplies, and services for the student nurse. **Dates and Locations:** 1998 Apr 15-19; Cincinnati, OH ▪ 1999 Apr 21-25; Pittsburgh, PA.

NATURVITA - EXHIBITION FOR NATURE AND ENVIRONMENT, HEALTH AND NUTRITION
Rheinlanddamm 200
Postfach 104444
D-44139 Dortmund, Germany
PH: 231 1204521
FX: 231 1204678
Frequency: Biennial. **Audience:** General public. **Principal Exhibits:** Nutritional foods, dietary aides, and related equipment, supplies, and services.

NEBRASKA DENTAL ASSOCIATION ANNUAL SESSION
e-mail: nda@binary.net
3120 O St.
Lincoln, NE 68510
PH: (402)476-1704
FX: (402)476-2641
Frequency: Annual. **Audience:** Dentists, hygienists, dental assistants, dental students, lab technicians, spouses, and office staff. **Principal Exhibits:** Dental supplies, office equipment, insurance companies, and laboratory services, software companies. **Dates and Locations:** 1998 Apr 19-21; Lincoln, NE ▪ 1999 Apr 18-20; Omaha, NE ▪ 2000; Omaha, NE.

NEBRASKA NURSES' ASSOCIATION CONVENTION
e-mail: ne.nurses@internetmci.com
715 S. 14th St.
Lincoln, NE 68508
PH: (402)475-3859
FX: (402)475-3961
Frequency: Annual. **Audience:** Registered nurses. **Principal Exhibits:** Nursing-related equipment, supplies, and services. **Dates and Locations:** 1998 Oct.

NEW ENGLAND HEALTHCARE ASSEMBLY ANNUAL MEETING
500 Spaulding Tpke., Ste. W-310
PO Box 7100
Portsmouth, NH 03802
Frequency: Annual. **Audience:** Healthcare personnel. **Principal Exhibits:** Healthcare manufactured products and services. **Dates and Locations:** 1998 Mar 30 - Apr 02; Boston, MA ▪ 1999 Mar 30 - Apr 01; Boston, MA ▪ 2000 Apr 04-06; Boston, MA.

NEW HAMPSHIRE DENTAL SOCIETY ANNUAL MEETING
PO Box 2229
Concord, NH 03302
PH: (603)225-5961
FX: (603)226-4880
Frequency: Annual. **Audience:** Dental professionals. **Principal Exhibits:** Dental supplies and equipment, office equipment, and insurance publications. **Dates and Locations:** 1998 Jun.

NEW JERSEY DENTAL ASSOCIATION ANNUAL SESSION
Dept. of Communications
1 Dental Plaza
North Brunswick, NJ 08902
PH: (908)821-9400
FX: (908)821-1082
Frequency: Annual. **Audience:** Dentists, dental hygienists, dental assistants, students, and guests. **Principal Exhibits:** Dental supplies, including laboratory supplies, computers, insurance information, manufacturers, dealers, and related professionals. **Dates and Locations:** 1998 Jun; Atlantic City, NJ.

NEW JERSEY HEALTHCARE CONGRESS
760 Alexander Rd.
PO Box 1
Princeton, NJ 08543-0001
PH: (609)924-0049
FX: (609)275-4114
Frequency: Annual. **Audience:** Hospital, nursing home, and health-care personnel. **Principal Exhibits:** Products and services used by hospitals, nursing homes, and health-care organizations.

Dates and Locations: 1998; Atlantic City, NJ. **Formerly:** Middle Atlantic Health Congress.

NEW JERSEY STATE NURSES ASSOCIATION CONVENTION
e-mail: njsna@njsna.org
1479 Pennington Rd.
Trenton, NJ 08618
PH: (609)883-5335
FX: (609)883-5343
Frequency: Annual. **Audience:** Registered nurses. **Principal Exhibits:** Nursing publications, medical supplies, and nurse recruiters. **Dates and Locations:** 1998 Apr; Atlantic City, NJ.

NEW MEXICO OSTEOPATHIC MEDICAL ASSOCIATION ANNUAL BALLOON FIESTA MEDICAL SYMPOSIUM
PO Box 90396
Albuquerque, NM 87199-0396
PH: (505)828-1905
FX: (505)821-1050
Frequency: Annual. **Audience:** Family practice physicians. **Principal Exhibits:** Pharmaceuticals and medical products; financial information; real estate industry information; jewelry; insurance information. **Dates and Locations:** 1998 Oct 06-10; Albuquerque, NM ▪ 1999 Oct 05-09; Albuquerque, NM.

NEW ORLEANS DENTAL CONFERENCE
e-mail: nodc@acadiacom.net
2121 N. Causeway Blvd., No. 153
Metairie, LA 70001
PH: (504)834-6449
FX: (504)838-6909
Frequency: Annual. **Audience:** Dentists. **Principal Exhibits:** Dental laboratory representatives; dental supplies and equipment; computers; office management services. **Dates and Locations:** 1998 Aug; New Orleans, LA.

NEW YORK STATE NURSES ASSOCIATION ANNUAL CONVENTION & EXHIBITS
46 Cornell Rd.
Latham, NY 12110-1403
Frequency: Annual. **Audience:** Registered professional nurses representing all areas of administrative and clinical nursing. **Principal Exhibits:** Nursing equipment, supplies, and services. **Dates and Locations:** 1998 Oct 29 - Nov 01; Saratoga Springs, NY ▪ 1999 Oct 14-17; Lake Placid, NY.

NORTH AMERICAN SPINE SOCIETY ANNUAL MEETING
url: http://www.spine.org
6300 N. River Rd., Ste. 500
Rosemont, IL 60018-4231
PH: (847)698-1630
FX: (847)823-8668
Frequency: Annual. **Audience:** Physicians, osteopaths, orthopedists, neurosurgeons, radiologists. **Principal Exhibits:** Exhibits relating to research and treatment methods in the human spine. **Dates and Locations:** 1998 Oct 20-27; San Francisco, CA ▪ 1999 Oct 20-27; Chicago, IL.

NORTH AMERICAN STROKE MEETING
url: http://www.stroke.org
96 Inverness Dr. E, Ste. I
Englewood, CO 80112-5112
PH: (303)649-9299
TF: 800STROKES
FX: (303)649-1328
Frequency: Annual. **Audience:** Stroke survivors and their families; health care professionals. **Principal Exhibits:** Exhibits related to stroke prevention, treatment, rehabilitation, resocialization, and research. **Dates and Locations:** 1998 Oct.

NORTH CAROLINA NURSES ASSOCIATION CONVENTION
e-mail: ncnurses@aol.com
103 Enterprise St.
PO Box 12025
Raleigh, NC 27605
PH: (919)821-4250
TF: 800626-2153
FX: (919)829-5807
Frequency: Annual. **Audience:** Registered nurses. **Principal Exhibits:** Nursing equipment, supplies, and services. **Dates and Locations:** 1998 Oct 14-16; Raleigh, NC.

NORTH CENTRAL STATES OPTOMETRIC CONFERENCE
e-mail: assoc@navix.net
201 N. 8th, Ste. 400
PO Box 80896
Lincoln, NE 68501-0896
PH: (402)476-8016
FX: (402)476-6547
Frequency: Annual. **Audience:** Optometrists, optometric assistants, and ophthalmic suppliers. **Principal Exhibits:** Ophthalmic equipment and supplies, including computer systems and clothing. **Dates and Locations:** 1999 Jan 29-31; Minneapolis, MN ▪ 2000 Jan 28-30; Minneapolis, MN.

NORTH DAKOTA MEDICAL ASSOCIATION CONVENTION
PO Box 1198
Bismarck, ND 58502
PH: (701)223-9475
FX: (701)223-9476
Frequency: Annual. **Audience:** Physicians. **Principal Exhibits:** Medical equipment, supplies, and services. **Dates and Locations:** 1998 May 07-09; Grand Forks, ND.

NORTHEASTERN SOCIETY OF ORTHODONTISTS MEETING & EXHIBIT
427 Kenwood Ave.
Delmar, NY 12054
PH: (518)439-0981
FX: (518)439-0980
Frequency: Annual. **Audience:** Orthodontists and related personnel. **Principal Exhibits:** Orthodontic equipment, supplies, and services, including computer hardware and software. **Dates and Locations:** 1998; New York, NY.

NORWAY HEALTH EXHIBITION
e-mail: nv@messe.no
url: http://www.messe.no
Drammensveien 154
PO Box 130 Skoyen
N-0212 Oslo, Norway
PH: 47 22 439100
FX: 47 22 431914
Frequency: Biennial. **Audience:** Trade professionals and general public. **Principal Exhibits:** Equipment, supplies, and services for health and social services professionals, including medical equipment, economic furniture, non-prescription medicines and training equipment.

NTRS INSTITUTE
e-mail: ntrsnrpa@aol.com
url: http://www.NRPA.org/NRPA
22377 Belmont Ridge Rd.
Ashburn, VA 20148-4501
PH: (703)578-5548
TF: 800626-6772
FX: (703)671-6772
Frequency: Annual. **Principal Exhibits:** Therapeutic recreation equipment, supplies, and services. **Dates and Locations:** 1998 Sep 23-27; Miami, FL.

NURSES CARE FAIR
7600 Burnet Rd., Ste. 440
Austin, TX 78757-1292

PH: (512)452-0645
FX: (512)452-0648
Frequency: Biennial. **Audience:** Student nurses and trade professionals. **Principal Exhibits:** Medical supplies, pharmaceuticals, employers, schools of nursing, book, and educational companies. **Dates and Locations:** 1998 Apr; Corpus Christi, TX ▪ 2000; Dallas, TX ▪ 2002; San Antonio, TX ▪ 2004; Fort Worth, TX.

NURSING MANAGEMENT CONGRESS AND EXPOSITION
40 Richards Ave.
Norwalk, CT 06856-4990
PH: (203)852-0500
FX: (203)838-3710
Frequency: Annual. **Audience:** Nursing managers responsible for recommending and purchasing patient care equipment, products, and services. **Principal Exhibits:** Medical and hospital equipment, products, and services, including computers and bedding. **Dates and Locations:** 1998; Springhouse, PA.

NURSING PRAKTIJK DAGEN
e-mail: info@jaarbeursutrecht.nl
url: http://www.jaarbeursutrecht.nl
Jaarbeursplein-Utrecht
PO Box 8500
NL-3503 RM Utrecht, Netherlands
PH: 30 295 5911
FX: 30 294 0379
Frequency: Annual. **Audience:** Trade professionals. **Principal Exhibits:** Medical and health care.

ODMAFAIR
e-mail: melb@eff.com.au
311 Montague St.
Albert Park, VIC 3206, Australia
PH: 6139696 0666
FX: 6139696 0808
Frequency: Biennial. **Principal Exhibits:** Optical.

OHA JOINT EDUCATIONAL SUMMIT
155 E. Broad St.
Columbus, OH 43215-3620
PH: (614)221-7614
FX: (614)241-2933
Frequency: Annual. **Audience:** Management, administration, and purchasing professionals; general support and paient services personnel; related professionals, nursing home adminstration. **Principal Exhibits:** Health care products, equipment, supplies, and services. **Dates and Locations:** 1998 Apr 06-08; Columbus, OH ▪ 1999 Apr 19-21; Columbus, OH ▪ 2000 Apr 17-19; Columbus, OH ▪ 2001 Apr 14-19; Columbus, OH.

OHIO DENTAL ASSOCIATION ANNUAL SESSION
e-mail: 103244.3447@compuserve.com
1370 Dublin Rd.
Columbus, OH 43215
PH: (614)486-2700
FX: (614)486-0381
Frequency: Annual. **Audience:** Dentists, dental hygienists & assistants, office staff. **Principal Exhibits:** Dental equipment, supplies, and services, computers, and insurance. **Dates and Locations:** 1998 Sep 17-20; Columbus, OH.

OHIO OSTEOPATHIC ASSOCIATION ANNUAL MEETING AND SCIENTIFIC SEMINAR
53 W. 3rd Ave.
Box 8130
Columbus, OH 43201
PH: (614)299-2107
FX: (614)294-0457
Frequency: Annual. **Audience:** Physicians and allied health professions. **Principal Exhibits:** Pharmaceutical products, clinical laboratory services, health equipment, computer-based practice management systems, medical books, automobile leasing, insur-

ance, and financial planning. **Dates and Locations:** 1998 Jun; Cleveland, OH.

OHIO PODIATRIC MEDICAL ASSOCIATION ANNUAL MEETING AND SCIENTIFIC SEMINAR
e-mail: opma@ee.net
url: http://www.opma.org
5310 McKitrick Blvd.
Columbus, OH 43235-7366
PH: (614)457-6269
FX: (614)457-3375
Frequency: Annual. **Audience:** Podiatrists and podiatry assistants. **Principal Exhibits:** Medical supplies, publications, office equipment, computer firms, personal and professional services, investment firms, insurance companies and pharmaceutical companies. **Dates and Locations:** 1998 May; Columbus, OH.

OKLAHOMA DENTAL MEETING
e-mail: okdental@aol.com
629 W. I-44 Service Rd.
Oklahoma City, OK 73118
PH: (405)848-8873
TF: 800876-8890
FX: (405)848-8875
Frequency: Annual. **Audience:** Dental practitioners. **Principal Exhibits:** Dental equipment, supplies, and services. **Dates and Locations:** 1998 May; Oklahoma City, OK. **Formerly:** Oklahoma Dental Association Convention.

ONCOLOGY NURSING SOCIETY MEETING
501 Holiday Dr.
Pittsburgh, PA 15220
PH: (412)921-7373
FX: (412)921-6565
Frequency: Annual. **Principal Exhibits:** Oncology nursing equipment, supplies, and services. **Dates and Locations:** 1998 May 07-10; San Francisco, CA.

ONTARIO DENTAL ASSOCIATION ANNUAL SPRING MEETING
e-mail: pdasm@oda.nn.ca
4 New St.
Toronto, ON, Canada M5R 1P6
PH: (416)922-4162
FX: (416)922-9005
Frequency: Annual. **Audience:** Dentists, dental students, dental assistants, dental hygienists, dental technicians, exhibitors, and other trade professionals. **Principal Exhibits:** Dental equipment, supplies, and services, investment opportunities and recreational items. **Dates and Locations:** 1998 May 07-09; Toronto, ON ▪ 1999 Apr 29 - May 01; Toronto, ON ▪ 2000 May 04-06; Toronto, ON.

ONTARIO HOSPITAL ASSOCIATION CONVENTION & EXHIBITION
150 Ferrand Dr.
Don Mills, ON, Canada M3C 1H6
PH: (416)429-2661
FX: (416)429-5651
Frequency: Annual. **Principal Exhibits:** Healthcare products, equipment and services. **Dates and Locations:** 1998 Oct 26-28; Toronto, ON ▪ 1999 Nov 01-03; Toronto, ON ▪ 2000 Nov 20-22; Toronto, ON ▪ 2001 Nov 19-21; Toronto, ON.

OPTATEC - INTERNATIONAL TRADE FAIR FOR OPTICS AND OPTOELECTRONICS
e-mail: info@schall-messen.de
url: http://www.schall-messen.de
Gustav-Werner-Strasse 6
D-72636 Frickenhausen-Linsenhofen, Germany
PH: 70 25 92 06 0
FX: 70 25 92 06 20
Frequency: Biennial. **Audience:** Optronics users. **Principal Exhibits:** Optics and Optoelectronics application and technology.

OPTEX - INTERNATIONAL TRADE FAIR FOR THE OPTICIAN
e-mail: info@reedexpo.at
url: http://www.reedexpo.at
Postfach 285
Am Messezentrum
A-5021 Salzburg, Austria
PH: 43 662 4477 0
FX: 662 4477 161
Frequency: Annual. **Audience:** Opticians, eye specialists, lenses. **Principal Exhibits:** Spectacle lenses and frames, contact lenses, sunglasses, trade goods and accessories, optical instruments, workshop supplies and equipment, shop fittings and computer equipment, microscopes, thermometers, barometers, and hearing aids.

OPTICA FASHION - INTERNATIONAL TREND EVENT FOR EYEWEAR FASHION
url: http://www.koelnmesse.de
Messeplatz 1
D-50679 Cologne, Germany
PH: 221 821 0
FX: 221 821 2574
Frequency: Biennial. **Principal Exhibits:** Eyewear.

OPTICA - INTERNATIONAL TRADE FAIR FOR OPHTHALMIC OPTICS AND ANNUAL CONGRESS OF THE WVAO
url: http://www.koelnmesse.de
Messeplatz 1
D-50679 Cologne, Germany
PH: 221 821 0
FX: 221 821 2574
Frequency: Annual. **Audience:** Trade professionals. **Principal Exhibits:** Ophthalmic optic equipment, supplies, and services, including contact lenses and accessories, workshop and shop equipment, and eyeglass frames, lenses, and cases.

OPTICA/SAO PAULO - OPTICAL PRODUCTS AND EQUIPMENT SHOW
Av. Paulista, 726 17th A
01310-910 Sao Paulo, Brazil
PH: 11 289 0833
FX: 11 251 5549
Frequency: Annual. **Audience:** Trade professionals and general public. **Principal Exhibits:** Glasses, frames, machines, equipment and components for the optical industry; accessories, sunglasses, ophthlamic lenses, raw materials.

OPTICAL LABORATORIES ASSOCIATION CONVENTION
PO Box 2000
Merrifield, VA 22116-2000
PH: (703)359-2830
FX: (703)359-2834
Frequency: Annual. **Principal Exhibits:** Ophthalmic laboratory equipment, supplies, and services. **Dates and Locations:** 1998 Nov; San Antonio, TX ■ 1999 Nov; Nashville, TN.

OPTICIANS ASSOCIATION OF AMERICA CONVENTION
10341 Democracy Lane
Fairfax, VA 22030
PH: (703)691-8355
FX: (703)691-3929
Frequency: Annual. **Principal Exhibits:** Optical lenses, frames, accessories. **Dates and Locations:** 1998 Jun; Philadelphia, PA.

OPTICS IN STOCKHOLM - NATIONAL OPTICS FAIR
e-mail: staff@stofair.se
url: http://www.stofair.se
Massvagen 1, Alvsjo
S-125 80 Stockholm, Sweden
PH: 46 8 7494100
FX: 46 8 992044

Frequency: Annual. **Audience:** Opticians and retailers. **Principal Exhibits:** Frames, lenses, contacts, and vision testing equipment.

OPTIKA - OPTICS AT MAN'S SERVICE INTERNATIONAL
Krasnopresnenskaya nab. 14
123100 Moscow, Russia
PH: 095 268 1340
FX: 095 205 60 55
Frequency: Biennial. **Audience:** Trade professionals and general public. **Principal Exhibits:** Optical equipment, supplies, and services.

OPTITECNICA - OPTICIANS AND OPTICAL EQUIPMENT EXHIBITION
e-mail: fildg@mail.telepac.pt
url: http://www.aip.pt
Praca das Industrias, Apt. 3200
1301 Lisbon Codex, Portugal
PH: 351 1 360 1502
FX: 351 1 363 90 48
Frequency: Biennial. **Audience:** Trade professionals, including suppliers and importers. **Principal Exhibits:** Optical articles and equipment.

OPTRAFAIR - OPHTHALMIC TRADE FAIR
37-41 Bedford Row
London WC1R 4JH, England
PH: 71 4058101
FX: 71 8312797
Frequency: Biennial. **Audience:** Optical professionals. **Principal Exhibits:** Optical equipment, supplies, and services.

ORPROTEC - TECHNICAL ORTHOPEDICS AND REHABILITATION SHOW
e-mail: feriavalencia@feriavalencia.com
url: http://www.feriavalencia.com
Avda. de las Ferias s/n
PO Box 476
E-46080 Valencia, Spain
PH: 34 9 6 386 11 00
FX: 34 9 6 363 61 11
Frequency: Biennial. **Audience:** Trade professionals. **Principal Exhibits:** Technical orthopedics, diagnosis, analysis, and orthopedic machinery. **Formerly:** ORTOE.

ORS ANNUAL MEETING
6300 N. River Rd., Ste. 727
Rosemont, IL 60018-4238
PH: (847)698-1625
FX: (847)823-0536
Frequency: Annual. **Principal Exhibits:** Orthopedic surgery equipment, supplies, and services. **Dates and Locations:** 1998 Mar 16-19; New Orleans, LA.

ORTHOPADIE & REHA-TECHNIK - INTERNATIONAL TRADE FAIR AND CONGRESS FOR ORTHOPEDICS AND REHABILITATION TECHNOLOGY
Reinoldistr. 7-9
44135 Dortmund, Germany
PH: 0231 557050 0
FX: 0231 557050 40
Frequency: Triennial. **Audience:** Trade professionals; scientists, physicians, engineers, technicians, supply trade. **Principal Exhibits:** Orthopedics, rehabilitation equipment, technical medical equipment, supplies, and services.

OSTEOPATHIC PHYSICIANS AND SURGEONS OF CALIFORNIA ANNUAL CONVENTION
455 Capitol Mall, Ste. 230
Sacramento, CA 95814-4405
PH: (916)447-2004
FX: (916)447-4828
Frequency: Annual. **Audience:** Osteopathic physicians and related professionals. **Principal Exhibits:** Pharmaceutical, scientific,

educational, hospital, and medical services and equipment; insurance information; and computers. **Dates and Locations:** 1998 Mar 01-05; Las Vegas, NV ▪ 1999 Feb 17-22; Palm Springs, CA.

PACIFIC NORTHWEST DENTAL CONFERENCE
e-mail: wsda@sprynet.com
url: http://www.wsda.org
2033 6th Ave., Ste. 333
Seattle, WA 98121
PH: (206)448-1914
FX: (206)728-4470
Frequency: Annual. **Audience:** Dentists, hygienists, assistants, and lab technicians. **Principal Exhibits:** Dental supplies, instruments, and equipment. **Dates and Locations:** 1998 Jul 15-17; Seattle, WA ▪ 1999 Jul 14-16; Seattle, WA. **Formerly:** Washington State Dental Association Scientific Session.

PAN-AMERICAN ALLERGY SOCIETY CONFERENCE
e-mail: paas@worldnett.att.net
PO Box 947
Fredericksburg, TX 78624
PH: (830)997-9853
FX: (830)997-8625
Frequency: Annual. **Principal Exhibits:** Exhibits related to the diagnosis and treatment of allergic disorders. **Dates and Locations:** 1998 Mar; San Antonio, TX.

PAN-AMERICAN ASSOCIATION OF OPHTHALMOLOGY MEETING
1301 S. Bowen Rd., Ste. 365
Arlington, TX 76013
PH: (817)265-2831
FX: (817)275-3961
Frequency: Biennial. **Principal Exhibits:** Ophthalmology equipment, supplies, and services.

PARACELSUS-MESSE
e-mail: info@messe.at
url: http://www.messe.at
Lagerhausstr. 7
PO Box 277
A-1021 Vienna, Austria
PH: 43 1 727 200
FX: 43 1 727 20443
Principal Exhibits: Health and welfare products.

PEDORTHIC FOOTWEAR ASSOCIATION SYMPOSIUM & EXPOSITION
9861 Broken Land Pky., Ste. 255
Columbia, MD 21046-1151
PH: (410)381-7278
TF: 800673-8447
FX: (410)381-1167
Frequency: Annual. **Audience:** Allied health professionals. **Principal Exhibits:** Exhibits relating to pedorthics, the design, manufacture, fit and modification of shoes and foot orthoses to alleviate foot problems caused by disease, overuse or injury. **Dates and Locations:** 1998 Nov 20-22; Scottsdale, AZ.

PHYSICIAN INSURERS ASSOCIATION OF AMERICA ANNUAL MEETING
2275 Research Blvd., Ste. 250
Rockville, MD 20850
PH: (301)947-9000
FX: (301)947-9090
Frequency: Annual. **Audience:** Physician liability insurance companies, including domestic physician and dental liability insurers, international affiliates, and reinsurers. **Principal Exhibits:** Exhibits related to physician liability insurance. **Dates and Locations:** 1998 May 27-30; Orlando, FL.

PREMIERE VISION - LE SALON
e-mail: info@premierevision.fr
url: http://www.premierevision.fr
le britannia a 20 bd. eugene deruelle
69432 Lyon, France
PH: 33 72 60 65 00
FX: 33 72 60 65 09
Frequency: Semiannual. **Principal Exhibits:** Eye care.

PREVENTION
e-mail: info@acpm.org
url: http://www.acpm.org
1660 L St., Ste. 206
Washington, DC 20036-5603
PH: (202)466-2044
FX: (202)466-2662
Frequency: Annual. **Principal Exhibits:** Exhibits for medical doctors specializing in preventive medicine, public health, aerospace medicine, and occupational medicine. **Dates and Locations:** 1998 Apr 02-05; San Francisco, CA.

RADTECH
Queensway House
2 Queensway
Redhill, Surrey RH1 1QS, England
PH: 44 1737 768611
FX: 44 1737 761685
Frequency: Biennial. **Principal Exhibits:** Raw materials, additives, photo initiators, ultra violet equipment, electron beam equipment, process equipment, formulation, and laboratory equipment.

REHA - INTERNATIONAL TRADE FAIR FOR REHABILITATION, EQUIPMENT AND CARE FOR THE DISABLED
url: http://messe.dus.tradefair.de
Stockumer Kirchstrasse 61
PO Box 101006
D-40474 Dusseldorf, Germany
PH: 211 4560 01
FX: 211 4560 668
Frequency: Biennial. **Audience:** Trade professionals and general public; hospitals, rehabilitation centers, self-help groups, orthopedic professionals, care providers, cost carriers, insurers. **Principal Exhibits:** Auxiliary appliances for the medical, educational, and social fields; technical literature related to medical, educational, professional, and social rehabilitation of the disabled; clothing, personal care and hygiene products; communication devices; walking and mobility aids, including wheelchairs; and transportation equipment. **Held in conjunction with:** International Conference of the European Association for Advance in Support Technology.

REHAB AND HOSPITAL
Bredballe Byvej 63
DK-7120 Vejle, Denmark
PH: 45 75814088
FX: 45 75814605
Frequency: Annual. **Audience:** Administrators, doctors, nurses, therapists, caterers, managers, and other trade professionals. **Principal Exhibits:** Furniture, clothing, sanitary appliances, cleaning articles and systems, laboratory, EDP, electromedical, rehabilitation, communication, and office equipment, transportation, surgical instruments, central kitchen machines, and therapy materials. **Formerly:** Cure and Care, Forsorg and Hospital Exhibition.

RESUSCITATION
e-mail: bc@bella.dk
url: http://www.bellacenter.dk
Center Blvd.
DK-2300 Copenhagen S, Denmark
PH: 45 32 52 88 11
FX: 45 32 51 96 36

Principal Exhibits: Resuscitation items.

ROSPA - INTERNATIONAL HEALTH & SAFETY EXHIBITION & CONGRESS
NEC House
National Exhibition Centre
Birmingham B40 1NT, England
PH: 44 121 767 2651
FX: 44 121 767 2880
Frequency: Annual. **Principal Exhibits:** Safety and health products, consultancy, prevention of accidents.

ROYAL COLLEGE OF PHYSICIANS AND SURGEONS OF CANADA SCIENTIFIC MEETING
e-mail: meetings@rcpsc.medical.org
url: http://www.rcpsc.medical.org
774 Echo Dr.
Ottawa, ON, Canada K1S 5N8
PH: (613)730-8177
TF: 800668-3740
FX: (613)730-8830
Frequency: Annual. **Audience:** Specialist physicians & surgeons. **Principal Exhibits:** Medical and surgical equipment, supplies, and services. **Dates and Locations:** 1998 Sep 24-27; Toronto, ON ■ 1999 Sep 23-26; Montreal, PQ ■ 2000 Sep 21-24; Edmonton, AB.

SAIGON MEDICAL, DENTAL AND PHARMACEUTICAL EXPO
e-mail: cpexhbit@hk.super.net
url: http://www.hk.super.net/~cpexhbit
Tung Wai Commercial Bldg., Rm. 1703
109 Gloucester Rd.
Wanchai, Hong Kong
PH: 852 2 511 7427
FX: 852 2 511 9692
Frequency: Annual. **Principal Exhibits:** Hospital facilities, dental apparatus and equipment, and pharmaceutical products.

SAIGON OPTICS EXPO
e-mail: cpexhbit@hk.super.net
url: http://www.hk.super.net/~cpexhbit
Tung Wai Commercial Bldg., Rm. 1703
109 Gloucester Rd.
Wanchai, Hong Kong
PH: 852 2 511 7427
FX: 852 2 511 9692
Principal Exhibits: Equipment, supplies, and services for the optical industry.

SALON DU LABORATOIRE/BIOEXPO - LABORATORY TRADE EXHIBITION AND CONFERENCE
39-41 Nue Lours Blanc
CEDEX 72
92038 Paris La Defense, France
PH: 1 47235 940
Frequency: Biennial. **Audience:** Trade professionals. **Principal Exhibits:** Laboratory equipment, supplies, and services. **Held in conjunction with:** INTERCHIMIE.

SASKATCHEWAN ASSOCIATION OF HEALTH ORGANIZATIONS ANNUAL CONVENTION AND EXHIBITION
PO Box 116
Winnipeg, MB, Canada R3C 2G1
PH: (204)958-7540
FX: (204)958-7547
Frequency: Annual. **Audience:** Conference delegates and trade professionals. **Principal Exhibits:** Pharmaceuticals, medical equipment, related supplies, and facility information. **Dates and Locations:** 1999 Mar; Regina, SK.

SAUDI DENTISTRY
e-mail: oes@montnet.com
url: http://www.montnet.com
11 Manchester Sq.
London W1M 5AB, England
PH: 44 0 171 862 2000
FX: 44 0 171 862 2098
Frequency: Biennial. **Principal Exhibits:** Dental health.

SAUDIMEDICARE - TOTAL HEALTHCARE, HOSPITAL SUPPLIES, AND MEDICAL EQUIPMENT SHOW
e-mail: recsa@midleast.net
PO Box 56010
Riyadh 11554, Saudi Arabia
PH: 966 1 454 1448
FX: 966 1 454 4846
Frequency: Biennial. **Audience:** Health care, hospital supplies, and medical equipment trades. **Principal Exhibits:** Medical and surgical instruments and equipment; hospital systems, equipment, and supplies; health care products, equipment, and services; pharmaceuticals; dental equipment and supplies; hospital management services and consulting services; special training services.

SCANDEFA - SCANDINAVIAN DENTAL FAIR
e-mail: bc@bella.dk
url: http://www.bellacenter.dk
Center Blvd.
DK-2300 Copenhagen S, Denmark
PH: 45 32 52 88 11
FX: 45 32 51 96 36
Frequency: Annual. **Audience:** Trade professionals. **Principal Exhibits:** Dental equipment, supplies, and services.

SCANDINAVIAN ASSOCIATION FOR THORACIC SURGERY ANNUAL MEETING
e-mail: CHROLTHX@HOLIO.LIU.SE
c/o Mr. Christian Olin
Department of Cardio-Thoracic Surgery
University Hospital
S-581 85 Linkoping, Sweden
PH: 46 13 224800
FX: 46 13 100246
Frequency: Annual. **Principal Exhibits:** Thoracic and cardiovascular surgery equipment, supplies, and services.

SCHIZOPHRENIA - INTERNATIONAL CONGRESS
e-mail: congress@venuewest.com
375 Water St., Ste. 645
Vancouver, BC, Canada V6B 5C6
PH: (604)681-5226
FX: (604)681-2503
Frequency: Biennial. **Principal Exhibits:** Pharmaceutical equipment, supplies, and services. **Dates and Locations:** 1998 Oct.

SCIENCE AND TECHNOLOGY WEEK
e-mail: owpshk@netvigator.com
6/F China Harbour Blvd.
370 King's Rd.
Hong Kong, Hong Kong
PH: 28077633
FX: 25705903
Frequency: Biennial. **Audience:** Scientist, researchers, engineers, factory managers, quality control, doctors, lab technicians, and factory owners. **Principal Exhibits:** Scientific instrument, test and measurement equipment, and labware. **Formerly:** Thai Instrumex/Thai Labtech.

SCIENTIFIC AND STANDARDIZATION COMMITTEE MEETING
url: http://www.med.unc.edu/isth/welcome
University of North Carolina Medical School
CB 7035
Chapel Hill, NC 27599-7035

PH: (919)929-3807
FX: (919)929-3935
Frequency: Annual. **Principal Exhibits:** Exhibits related to thrombosis (the presence of a clot in a blood vessel), hemostasis (the arrest of bleeding), blood clotting, and vascular biology. **Dates and Locations:** 1999 Aug 14-21; Washington, DC.

SHSTF - HEALTH AND MEDICAL CARE
e-mail: staff@stofair.se
url: http://www.stofair.se
Massvagen 1, Alvsjo
S-125 80 Stockholm, Sweden
PH: 46 8 7494100
FX: 46 8 992044
Frequency: Biennial. **Audience:** Nurses, politicians, doctors, administrators, midwives, and others involved in the health and medical care fields. **Principal Exhibits:** Health and medical care fields equipment, supplies, and services, including laboratory and computer equipment, literature, pharmaceuticals, handicap aids, and operation equipment.

SIBDENT - INTERNATIONAL STOMATOLOGICAL EXHIBITION
e-mail: siberian.fair@sovcust.sprint.com
16 Gorky St.
6300099 Novosibirsk, Russia
PH: 7 3832 102674
FX: 7 3832 236335
Frequency: Annual. **Audience:** Buyers and general public. **Principal Exhibits:** Stomatological industry.

SIBMEDICA - INTERNATIONAL HEALTHCARE, MEDICAL EQUIPMENT, AND SOCIAL WELFARE EXHIBITION
e-mail: siberian.fair@sovcust.sprint.com
16 Gorky St.
6300099 Novosibirsk, Russia
PH: 7 3832 102674
FX: 7 3832 236335
Frequency: Annual. **Audience:** Medical and biological personnel. **Principal Exhibits:** Diagnostic instruments, tomographs, analytic and laboratory equipment, hospital equipment, pharmaceuticals.

SIBOPTICA - INTERNATIONAL OPTICAL TECHNOLOGY EQUIPMENT AND PRODUCTS EXHIBITION
e-mail: siberian.fair@sovcust.sprint.com
16 Gorky St.
6300099 Novosibirsk, Russia
PH: 7 3832 102674
FX: 7 3832 236335
Frequency: Annual. **Principal Exhibits:** Optical technology equipment and products.

SILMO - INTERNATIONAL OPTICS AND EYEWEAR EXHIBITION
e-mail: info@comite-expo-paris.asso.fr
url: http://www.comite-expo-paris.asso.fr
55, quai Alphonse Le Gallo
BP 317
92107 Boulogne, France
PH: 33 1 49 09 60 00
FX: 33 1 49 09 60 03
Frequency: Annual. **Audience:** Trade professionals. **Principal Exhibits:** Sunglasses, prescription glasses, contact lenses equipment, eyeglass frames, and accessories.

SLOVAKIADENT - INTERNATIONAL EXHIBITION OF STOMATOLOGIC AND DENTALTECHNICAL APPARATUS, INSTRUMENTS AND AMBULANCE EQUIPMENT
e-mail: inchmar@mbox.bts.sk
url: http://www.incheba.sk
28, Rijna 13
PO Box 555
CR-111 21 Prague, Czech Republic

PH: 420 2 24 19 51 11
FX: 420 2 24 19 52 86
Frequency: Annual. **Audience:** Trade professionals and the general public. **Principal Exhibits:** Dental apparatus, appliances, ambulance equipment, dental devices and equipment, complete equipment of work sets for dentist technicians, and dental materials.

SOCIETY OF CRITICAL CARE MEDICINE ANNUAL EDUCATIONAL AND SCIENTIFIC SYMPOSIUM
e-mail: info@sccm.org
url: http://www.sccm.org
8101 E. Kaiser Blvd. Ste. 300
Anaheim, CA 92808-2259
PH: (714)282-6000
FX: (714)282-6050
Frequency: Annual. **Audience:** Physicians, nurses, and allied health professionals; critical care equipment trade. **Principal Exhibits:** Equipment, supplies, and services pertaining to the practice of critical care medicine.

SOCIETY OF GENERAL INTERNAL MEDICINE CONFERENCE
url: http://www.sgim.html
700 13th St. NW, Ste. 250
Washington, DC 20005
PH: (202)393-1662
TF: 800822-3060
FX: (202)783-1347
Frequency: Annual. **Principal Exhibits:** Equipment, supplies, and services for general internal medicine. **Dates and Locations:** 1998 Apr 23-25; Chicago, IL.

SOCIETY FOR HEALTHCARE PLANNING AND MARKETING CONVENTION
Convention and Meetings Division
840 N. Lake Shore Dr.
Chicago, IL 60611
PH: (312)280-6000
FX: (312)280-6462
Frequency: Annual. **Audience:** Health care executives, including administrators, physicians, planning executives, marketing vice presidents, directors, and CEOs. **Principal Exhibits:** Equipment, supplies, and services for marketing planning, strategic planning, physician development, market research, advertising, management training, financial planning, resources management, facilities planning, and regulatory consulting. **Dates and Locations:** 1998 May.

SOCIETY FOR MEDICAL DECISION MAKING ANNUAL MEETING
url: http://www.nemc.org/smdm
c/o Elizabeth Paine
2300 K St. NW
Office of Continuing Medical Education
Washington, DC 20037
Washington, DC 20037
PH: (202)994-8929
FX: (202)994-1791
Frequency: Annual. **Audience:** Educators, clinicians, managers, and policy makers. **Principal Exhibits:** Exhibits related to medical decision making. **Dates and Locations:** 1998 Oct 24-28; Cambridge, MA ■ 1999 Oct; Reno, NV.

SOCIETY OF TEACHERS OF FAMILY MEDICINE ANNUAL SPRING CONFERENCE
e-mail: admstaff@stfm.org
url: http://www.stfm.org
8880 Ward Pkwy.
PO Box 8729
Kansas City, MO 64114
PH: (816)333-9700
TF: 800274-2237
FX: (816)333-3884

Frequency: Annual. **Audience:** Family medicine educators, physicians, social workers, and behavioral scientists. **Principal Exhibits:** Physician recruitment firms, medical-related videotapes and software, and medical books. **Dates and Locations:** 1998 Apr 22-26; Chicago, IL ▪ 1999 Apr 28 - May 02; Seattle, WA.

SOUTH AFRICAN ASSOCIATION OF PEDIATRIC SURGEONS CONGRESS
e-mail: amillar@ich.uct.ac.za
c/o Prof. A.J.W. Millar
Dept. of Paediatric Surgery
Red Cross War Memorial Children's Hospital
Rondebosch 7700, Republic of South Africa
PH: 27 21 6585339
FX: 27 21 6891287
Frequency: Biennial. **Audience:** Pediatric surgeons in South Africa. **Principal Exhibits:** Exhibits relating to research, training, and clinical services in pediatric surgery.

SOUTH CAROLINA DENTAL ASSOCIATION ANNUAL SESSION
e-mail: communications@scda.org
120 Stonemark Ln.
Columbia, SC 29210-3841
PH: (803)750-2277
FX: (803)750-1644
Frequency: Annual. **Principal Exhibits:** Oral Health Care equipment, supplies, and services. **Dates and Locations:** 1998 Apr 30 - May 03; Myrtle Beach, SC ▪ 1999 Apr 29 - May 02; Myrtle Beach, SC ▪ 2000; Myrtle Beach, SC ▪ 2001; Myrtle Beach, SC.

SOUTH CAROLINA LABORATORY MANAGEMENT SOCIETY ANNUAL CONFERENCE AND EXHIBITION
PO Box 1814
Irmo, SC 29731
PH: (803)329-8704
FX: (803)329-0095
Frequency: Annual. **Audience:** Scientific, environmental, technical professionals. **Principal Exhibits:** Scientific instrument manufacturers, equipment, apparatus, and professional services. **Dates and Locations:** 1998.

SOUTH CAROLINA MEDICAL ASSOCIATION ANNUAL MEETING
3210 Fernandina Rd.
PO Box 11188
Columbia, SC 29211-1188
PH: (803)798-6207
TF: 800327-1021
FX: (803)772-6783
Frequency: Annual. **Audience:** Physicians. **Principal Exhibits:** Pharmaceuticals, surgical supplies, investment services, military representatives, computers, books, treatment centers, and electronic paging equipment. **Dates and Locations:** 1998 May; Charleston, SC.

SOUTH CAROLINA NURSES ASSOCIATION CONVENTION
1821 Gadsden St.
Columbia, SC 29201
PH: (803)252-4781
FX: (803)779-3870
Frequency: Annual. **Audience:** Registered nurses. **Principal Exhibits:** Medical supplies and services, including schools, hospital recruiters, pharmaceuticals, and textbooks. **Dates and Locations:** 1998 Sep; Columbia, SC.

SOUTH DAKOTA DENTAL ASSOCIATION ANNUAL SESSION
e-mail: sddentex@dtgnet.com
330 S. Poplar Ave.
Box 1194
Pierre, SD 57501
PH: (605)224-9133
FX: (605)224-9168

Frequency: Annual. **Audience:** Dentists, hygienists, and assistants. **Principal Exhibits:** Dental equipment and supplies. **Dates and Locations:** 1998 May 14-17; Rapid City, SD ▪ 1999 May 13-16; Sioux Falls, SD ▪ 2000 May 18-21; Sioux Falls, SD.

SOUTH DAKOTA STATE MEDICAL ASSOCIATION ANNUAL MEETING
e-mail: jjanders@sunflowr.usd.edu
1323 S. Minnesota Ave.
Sioux Falls, SD 57105
PH: (605)336-1965
FX: (605)336-0270
Frequency: Annual. **Principal Exhibits:** Medical equipment, supplies, and services. **Dates and Locations:** 1998 Jun 04-06; Rapid City, SD.

SOUTHEASTERN CHAPTER-SOCIETY OF NUCLEAR MEDICINE EXHIBITION
5987 Turpin Hills Dr.
Cincinnati, OH 45244
PH: (513)231-6955
Frequency: Annual. **Audience:** Physicians, radiologists, cardiologists, nuclear medicine, technologists, and scientists. **Principal Exhibits:** Nuclear medical equipment and related medical supplies. **Dates and Locations:** 1998.

SOUTHEASTERN SURGICAL CONGRESS ANNUAL SCIENTIFIC MEETING
1581 Cahaba Valley Rd.
PO Box 330
Pelham, AL 35124
PH: (205)403-2791
TF: 800622-0901
FX: (205)403-2793
Frequency: Annual. **Audience:** Surgeons and surgical nurses. **Principal Exhibits:** Surgical equipment, supplies, and services including pharmaceuticals, instruments, recruiting information, and hospital information. **Dates and Locations:** 1999 Jan.

SOUTHERN ASSOCIATION OF ORTHODONTISTS CONVENTION
32 Lenox Pointe NE
Atlanta, GA 30324-3169
PH: (404)261-5528
TF: 800261-5528
FX: (404)261-6856
Frequency: Annual. **Principal Exhibits:** Orthodontic equipment, supplies, and services. **Dates and Locations:** 1998 Oct 15-20; Asheville, NC.

SOUTHERN EDUCATIONAL CONGRESS OF OPTOMETRY
4661 N. Shallowford Rd.
Atlanta, GA 30338
PH: (404)451-8206
FX: (404)451-3156
Frequency: Annual. **Audience:** Optometrists, paraoptometrics, assistants, and opticians. **Principal Exhibits:** Ophthalmic supplies, diagnostic equipment, reference books, frames for glasses, office equipment, computers, contact lenses, and ophthalmic pharmaceuticals. **Dates and Locations:** 1999 Feb; Atlanta, GA.

SOUTHWESTERN CHAPTER, SOCIETY OF NUCLEAR MEDICINE EXHIBITION
e-mail: society@hooked.net
PO Box 411106
San Francisco, CA 94141-1106
PH: (415)487-9802
FX: (415)487-9803
Frequency: Annual. **Audience:** Nuclear medicine physicians, scientists, and technologists also nuclear medicine pharmacists. **Principal Exhibits:** Industry related technology and pharmaceuticals. **Dates and Locations:** 1998 Mar 20-22; Houston, TX.

STAR OF THE NORTH DENTAL MEETING
e-mail: mndental@mn.uswest.net
2236 Marshall Ave.
St. Paul, MN 55104
PH: (612)646-7454
FX: (612)646-8246
Frequency: Annual. Audience: Dentists, dental assistants, dental hygienists, receptionists and office managers, and dental students; general public. Principal Exhibits: Dental equipment and supplies, dental laboratory equipment, office equipment, and service organizations. Dates and Locations: 1998 Apr 25-27; St. Paul, MN ▪ 1999 Apr 24-26; St. Paul, MN ▪ 2000 Apr 29 - May 01; St. Paul, MN.

STATE MEDICAL SOCIETY OF WISCONSIN ANNUAL
CONVENTION
330 E. Lakeside St.
Box 1109
Madison, WI 53701
PH: (608)257-6781
FX: (608)283-5401
Frequency: Annual. Audience: Medical professionals. Principal Exhibits: Pharmaceuticals, computers, and surgical supplies. Dates and Locations: 1998 Apr 02-05; Lake Geneva, WI ▪ 1999 Apr; Madison, WI.

STOMATOLOGY - INTERNATIONAL TRADE FAIR FOR
DENTAL MEDICINE
e-mail: healthcare@ITE-Group.com
Byron House
112A Shirland Rd.
London W9 EQ, England
PH: 44 171 286 9720
FX: 44 171 266 1126
Frequency: Annual. Audience: Dentists, dental hygienists, and related professionals. Principal Exhibits: Dental equipment, supplies, services, and related products.

SWEDENTAL - FAIR AND ODONTOLOGICAL CONGRESS
OF THE SWEDISH DENTAL SOCIETY
e-mail: staff@stofair.se
url: http://www.stofair.se
Massvagen 1, Alvsjo
S-125 80 Stockholm, Sweden
PH: 46 8 7494100
FX: 46 8 992044
Frequency: Annual. Audience: Dental care professionals. Principal Exhibits: Dental hygiene articles; pharmaceutical products; expendable articles; implants/systems; fixtures and fittings for clinics, laboratories, waiting rooms; clinical and laboratory equipment; office furnishings and equipment; computer equipment; protective clothing; dental technology; technical information; specialized literature; consulting services.

SWISS OPTIC - TRADE FAIR FOR OPTICS
Postfach
CH-8022 Zurich, Switzerland
PH: 1 221 35 05
FX: 1 221 36 71
Frequency: Annual. Principal Exhibits: Lenses, contacts, spectacle frames, sunglasses, instruments, workshop equipment and supplies, and shop fittings.

SYMPOSIUM ON CATARACT 10L & REFRACTIVE
SURGERY
e-mail: ascrs@ascrs.org
url: http://www.ascrs.org
4000 Legato Rd., No. 850
Fairfax, VA 22033-4003
PH: (703)591-2220
TF: 800451-1339
FX: (703)591-0614
Frequency: Annual. Audience: Ophthalmologists, administrators, nurses, and technicians. Principal Exhibits: Ophthalmic surgical equipment, pharmaceuticals, management programs, diagnostic supplies, and related equipment, supplies, and services. Dates and Locations: 1998 Apr 18-22; San Diego, CA ▪ 1999 Apr 10-14; Seattle, WA. Formerly: American Society of Cataract and Refractive Surgery Convention.

SYMPOSIUM ON COMPUTER APPLICATIONS IN
MEDICAL CARE
4915 St. Elmo, Ste. 302
Bethesda, MD 20814
PH: (301)657-1291
FX: (301)657-1296
Frequency: Annual. Principal Exhibits: Commercial and scientific medical informatics hardware and software, supplies, and services. Dates and Locations: 1998 Nov 07-11; Orlando, FL.

SYMPOSIUM OF NEW ORLEANS ACADEMY OF
OPTHALMOLOGY
E.E.N.T. Hospital
2626 Napoleon Ave., Rm. 2076
New Orleans, LA 70115
PH: (504)899-9955
FX: (504)899-4948
Frequency: Annual. Audience: Ophthalmologists and related medical professionals. Principal Exhibits: Medical instruments, drug companies, and computers. Dates and Locations: 1998 Apr 03-05; New Orleans, LA. Formerly: New Orleans Academy of Ophthalmology Convention.

SYMPOSIUM AND TRADE EXHIBITION ON HEALTHCARE,
SAFETY, AND THE ENVIRONMENT
Convention and Meetings Division
840 N. Lake Shore Dr.
Chicago, IL 60611
PH: (312)280-6000
FX: (312)280-6462
Frequency: Biennial. Audience: Administrators, support service directors, safety officials, regulatory officials, directors of environmental services. Principal Exhibits: Waste management/disposal systems, recycling products and services, storage products, air and waste purification products. Dates and Locations: 1999.

TENNESSEE DENTAL ASSOCIATION ANNUAL SESSION
P.O. Box 120188
2104 Sunset Place
Nashville, TN 37212
PH: (615)383-8962
FX: (615)383-0214
Frequency: Annual. Audience: Dentists, hygienists, and assistants. Principal Exhibits: Dental equipment, supplies, and services; laboratory supplies. Dates and Locations: 1998 May 14-17; Chattanooga, TN ▪ 1999 May 13-16; Nashville, TN.

TENNESSEE HOSPITAL ASSOCIATION TECHNICAL AND
EDUCATIONAL EXPOSITION
500 Interstate Blvd. S.
Nashville, TN 37210-4634
PH: (615)256-8240
FX: (615)242-4803
Frequency: Annual. Audience: Hospital executives and staff. Principal Exhibits: Health care products and services. Dates and Locations: 1998 Nov; Nashville, TN.

TENNESSEE MEDICAL ASSOCIATION ANNUAL MEETING
2301 21st Ave., S.
PO Box 120909
Nashville, TN 37212
PH: (615)385-2100
FX: (615)383-5918
Frequency: Annual. Audience: Physicians. Principal Exhibits: Medical equipment, supplies, and services, including pharmaceuticals, insurance, research services, and computers. Dates and Locations: 1998 Apr; Nashville, TN.

**TENNESSEE SOCIETY OF HOSPITAL PHARMACISTS
ANNUAL MEETING**
226 Capitol Blvd., Ste. 810
Nashville, TN 37219
PH: (615)256-3023
FX: (615)255-3528
Frequency: Annual. **Audience:** Licensed hospital pharmacists.
Principal Exhibits: Pharmaceuticals and sundries. **Dates and
Locations:** 1998 Apr; Nashville, TN.

**TEXAS ASSOCIATION FOR HEALTH, PHYSICAL
EDUCATION, RECREATION, AND DANCE ANNUAL STATE
CONVENTION**
url: http://www.tahperd.org
6300 La Calma Dr., Ste. 100
Austin, TX 78752-3890
PH: (512)459-1299
TF: 800880-7300
FX: (512)459-1290
Frequency: Annual. **Audience:** Teachers and administrators of
health, physical education, recreation, and dance; park and recre-
ational professionals; and health educators. **Principal Exhibits:**
Publications, equipment, and supplies for health, physical educa-
tion, recreation, and dance. **Dates and Locations:** 1998 Dec; Fort
Worth, TX.

TEXAS DENTAL ASSOCIATION ANNUAL SESSION
e-mail: tda@tda.org
1946 S. International Hwy.
Austin, TX 78704
PH: (512)443-3675
FX: (512)443-3031
Frequency: Annual. **Audience:** Dentists, hygienists, dental assis-
tants, and dental students, lab technicians. **Principal Exhibits:**
Pharmaceutical, laser, computer software/hardware, equipment
and instruments, tooth brushes & pastes, and gloves. **Dates and
Locations:** 1998 May 07-09; San Antonio, TX ▪ 1999 May 06-08;
San Antonio, TX ▪ 2000 May 04-06; San Antonio, TX.

**TEXAS HEALTH CARE ASSOCIATION CONVENTION AND
TRADESHOW**
PO Box 4554
Austin, TX 78765
PH: (512)458-1257
FX: (512)467-9575
Frequency: Annual. **Audience:** Trade professionals. **Principal Ex-
hibits:** Food DME, furniture, drugs, computers, insurance, and
construction. **Dates and Locations:** 1998 Sep.

**TEXAS HEALTH INFORMATION MANAGEMENT
CONVENTION**
PO Box 14423
Austin, TX 78761
PH: (512)465-1077
FX: (512)465-1090
Frequency: Annual. **Principal Exhibits:** Equipment, supplies,
and services for health information management professionals.
Dates and Locations: 1998 Jun; Austin, TX.

**TEXAS HOSPITAL ASSOCIATION ANNUAL CONVENTION
AND EXHIBITS SHOW**
url: http://www.thaonline.org
PO Box 15587
Austin, TX 78761
PH: (512)465-1000
TF: 800252-9403
FX: (512)465-1090
Frequency: Annual. **Audience:** Hospital administrators, trustees,
nurses, and allied personnel. **Principal Exhibits:** Health-care and
administrative equipment, supplies, and services. **Dates and
Locations:** 1998 May 31 - Jun 02; Dallas, TX.

TEXAS MEDICAL ASSOCIATION ANNUAL CONVENTION
url: http://www.texmed.org
401 W. 15th St.
Austin, TX 78701
PH: (512)370-1455
FX: (512)370-1635
Frequency: Annual. **Audience:** Physicians, medical students, registered nurses, and related medical personnel. **Principal Exhibits:** Medical equipment, supplies, and services, including pharmaceuticals and computer hardware and software. **Dates and
Locations:** 1998 Apr 23-25; Austin, TX.

**TEXAS PHYSICAL THERAPY ASSOCIATION ANNUAL
CONFERENCE**
400 W. 15th St., Ste. 805
Austin, TX 78701-1647
PH: (512)477-1818
FX: (512)477-1434
Frequency: Annual. **Audience:** Physical therapists and assistants.
Principal Exhibits: Physical therapy recruiters, equipment, sup-
plies, books, and services. **Dates and Locations:** 1998 Oct; Ar-
lington, TX.

THEMES IN TROPICAL MEDICINE AND DISEASES
16126 E. Warren
PO Box 24224
Detroit, MI 48224
PH: (313)882-0641
FX: (313)882-5110
Frequency: Annual. **Principal Exhibits:** Tropical medicine equip-
ment, supplies, and services. **Dates and Locations:** 1998 Jul 15-
18; Santa Fe, NM.

**THERMALIES - HYDROTHERAPY, THALASSOTHERAPY
AND HEALTH EXHIBITION**
e-mail: international@cepexposium.fr
74, av. Kleber
F-75116 Paris, France
PH: 01 45 53 36 24
FX: 01 45 53 68 04
Frequency: Annual. **Principal Exhibits:** Equipment, supplies,
and services for hydrotherapy, thalassotherapy and health.

THOMAS P. HINMAN DENTAL MEETING & EXHIBITS
60 Lenox Pte.
Atlanta, GA 30324
PH: (404)231-1476
FX: (404)231-9638
Frequency: Annual. **Audience:** Dentists, auxiliary personnel,
office managers, and dental educators. **Principal Exhibits:** Den-
tal equipment, supplies, and services. **Dates and Locations:** 1998
Mar; Atlanta, GA.

THREE RIVERS DENTAL CONFERENCE
900 Cedar Ave.
Pittsburgh, PA 15212
PH: (412)321-5810
FX: (412)321-7719
Frequency: Annual. **Audience:** Dentists and dental auxiliaries.
Principal Exhibits: Dental products and equipment, computers,
office equipment, and insurance. **Dates and Locations:** 1998 Oct.

TIHE - INTERNATIONAL HEALTHCARE EXHIBITION
url: http://www.gima.de
Heidenkampsweg 51
D-20097 Hamburg, Germany
PH: 040 235240
FX: 040 2352 4400
Frequency: Annual. **Principal Exhibits:** Equipment, supplies,
and services for the healthcare industry.

TRADE FAIR FOR SHOE MANUFACTURERS AND REPAIRERS, ORTHOPEDISTS, AND CHIROPODISTS
Ieperstraat 7
B-8800 Roeselare, Belgium
PH: 51 226932
FX: 51 225584
Frequency: Biennial. **Audience:** Trade. **Principal Exhibits:** Equipment, supplies, and services for the shoe industry.

TRIOLOGICAL SOCIETY EASTERN SECTION MEETING
555 N 30th St.
Omaha, NE 68131-2136
Frequency: Annual. **Principal Exhibits:** Medical equipment, supplies, and services as related to Otolaryngology. **Dates and Locations:** 1999 Jan.

TRIOLOGICAL SOCIETY SOUTHERN SECTION MEETING
555 N 30th St.
Omaha, NE 68131-2136
Frequency: Annual. **Principal Exhibits:** Medical equipment, supplies, and services as related to Otolaryngology. **Dates and Locations:** 1999 Jan.

UNDERSEA AND HYPERBARIC MEDICAL SOCIETY ANNUAL SCIENTIFIC MEETING
e-mail: uhms@radix.net
10531 Metropolitan Ave.
Kensington, MD 20895
PH: (301)942-2980
FX: (301)942-7804
Frequency: Annual. **Audience:** Diving physiologists, physicians, biologists, and bioengineers with subsea or hyperbaric interests. **Principal Exhibits:** Equipment, supplies, and services for undersea and hyperbaric medicine, and the safe penetration of oceans by humans. **Dates and Locations:** 1998 May 20-24; Seattle, WA.

UNIFORMED SERVICES ACADEMY OF FAMILY PHYSICIANS ANNUAL MEETING
1301 North Hamilton Street, Ste. 312
Richmond, VA 23230-3959
PH: (804)358-4002
Frequency: Annual. **Audience:** Uniformed family physicians from U.S. services. **Principal Exhibits:** Pharmaceutical companies, recruiters, and medical equipment companies. **Dates and Locations:** 1998 Mar; Norfolk, VA.

U.S. PSYCHIATRIC & MENTAL HEALTH CONGRESS
e-mail: customer.service@mhsource.com
2801 McGaw Ave.
Irvine, CA 92714-5835
PH: (714)250-1008
TF: 800447-4474
FX: (714)250-0445
Frequency: Annual. **Audience:** Psychiatrists, psychoanalysts, psychologists, counselors, social workers, and other mental health professionals. **Principal Exhibits:** Pharmaceuticals, books, and recruitment opportunities. **Dates and Locations:** 1998 Nov 19-22; San Francisco, CA ■ 2000 Nov 16-19; San Diego, CA.

UNIVERSITY OF DELAWARE AND JEFFERSON MEDICAL COLLEGE/EASTERN SHORE MEDICAL SYMPOSIUM
e-mail: Jerri.Heater@mus.udel.edu
Division of Continuing Education
Newark, DE 19716-7410
PH: (302)831-3475
FX: (302)831-1077
Frequency: Annual. **Audience:** Family practice professionals and internists. **Principal Exhibits:** Equipment, supplies, and services for family practitioners and internists. **Dates and Locations:** 1998 Jun.

UPPER MIDWEST OSTEOPATHIC HEALTH CONFERENCE
1113 Locust St., Ste. 2B
Des Moines, IA 50309
PH: (515)283-0002
FX: (515)283-0355
Frequency: Annual. **Audience:** Physicians (primarily general practice). **Principal Exhibits:** Pharmaceutical companies, medical equipment, and hospitals. **Dates and Locations:** 1998 May; Des Moines, IA. **Formerly:** Iowa Osteopathic Medical Association Convention.

URBAN TRANSPORT, SUBWAY & RAILWAY EXPO/CHINA
Frequency: Biennial. **Audience:** Manufacturers, suppliers, distributors. **Principal Exhibits:** Railway, subway, light rail facilities & equipment, urban transport, road & highway construction.

VIRGINIA HEALTH CARE ASSOCIATION ANNUAL CONVENTION AND TRADE SHOW
2112 W. Laburnum Ave., Ste. 206
Richmond, VA 23227
PH: (804)353-9101
FX: (804)353-3098
Frequency: Annual. **Audience:** Nursing home owners, administrators, purchasing agents, and nurses; dietary, housekeeping, social services, and activities departments heads. **Principal Exhibits:** Equipment, supplies, and services for nursing home operations, including food, medical supplies, furniture, computer systems, linen, medical equipment, insurance, and pharmaceuticals. **Dates and Locations:** 1998 Sep; Richmond, VA ■ 1999 Sep; Richmond, VA ■ 2000 Sep; Richmond, VA.

WASHINGTON ACADEMY OF EYE PHYSICIANS AND SURGEONS TRADE SHOW
2033 6th Ave., Ste. 1100
Seattle, WA 98121
PH: (206)441-9762
TF: 800552-0612
FX: (206)441-5863
Frequency: Annual. **Audience:** Ophthalmologists, registered nurses, physician assistants, and other medical professionals. **Principal Exhibits:** Ophthalmic, technical, and scientific equipment, supplies, and services. **Dates and Locations:** 1998 Mar 13-14; Seattle, WA. **Formerly:** Washington State Academy of Ophthalmology Annual President's Meeting.

WEST VIRGINIA ACADEMY OF OPHTHALMOLOGY CONVENTION
PO Box 5008
Charleston, WV 25361
PH: (304)343-5842
FX: (304)344-3130
Frequency: Annual. **Audience:** Ophthalmologists. **Principal Exhibits:** Pharmaceuticals, surgical instruments, books, and capital equipment. **Dates and Locations:** 1998 Apr 23-26; White Sulphur Springs, WV ■ 1999 Apr 22-25; White Sulphur Springs, WV ■ 2000 Apr 20-23; White Sulphur Springs, WV.

WEST VIRGINIA SOCIETY OF OSTEOPATHIC MEDICINE GENERAL PRACTICE UPDATE
PO Box 5266
Charleston, WV 25361
PH: (304)345-9836
FX: (304)345-9836
Frequency: Annual. **Audience:** General practitioners; osteopathic physicians; interns and students; residents. **Principal Exhibits:** Pharmaceuticals, computers, medical supplies and equipment, management firm information, and insurance information. **Dates and Locations:** 1998 Sep 17-20; White Sulphur Springs, WV ■ 1999 Sep 16-19; White Sulphur Springs, WV ■ 2000 Sep 21-24; White Sulphur Springs, WV.

WESTERN PODIATRIC MEDICAL CONGRESS
2430 K St., Ste. 200
Sacramento, CA 95816

PH: (916)448-0248
FX: (916)448-0258
Frequency: Annual. Audience: Doctors' assistants and other trade professionals. Principal Exhibits: Surgical supplies, X-ray equipment, computers, pharmaceuticals and general medical supplies and equipment. Dates and Locations: 1998 May.

WESTERN SAFETY CONGRESS & EXHIBIT
3450 Wilshire Blvd., Ste. 700
Los Angeles, CA 90010
PH: (213)385-6461
FX: (213)385-8405
Frequency: Annual. Audience: Safety and Health professionals, supervisors, managers, risk managers, purchasing agents, business owners. Principal Exhibits: Safety and health products and services. Dates and Locations: 1998 May; Anaheim, CA.

WESTERN STATES OSTEOPATHIC CONVENTION
6730 E. McDowell Rd., Ste. 114
Scottsdale, AZ 85257-3142
PH: (602)941-8981
TF: 800528-9906
Frequency: Annual. Audience: Osteopathic physicians, nurses, and physicians assistants. Principal Exhibits: Medical equipment, supplies, and services, including pharmaceuticals. Dates and Locations: 1998 Apr; Las Vegas, NV.

WILLS EYE HOSPITAL ANNUAL CONFERENCE
1621 Norristown Rd.
Maple Glen, PA 19002
PH: (215)641-9569
Frequency: Annual. Audience: Ophthalmologists and related health professionals. Principal Exhibits: Ophthalmic equipment, supplies, and services. Dates and Locations: 1998 Mar 12-14; Philadelphia, PA.

WISCONSIN DENTAL ASSOCIATION ANNUAL SESSION
111 E. Wisconsin Ave., Ste. 1300
Milwaukee, WI 53202-4811
PH: (414)276-4520
FX: (414)276-8431
Frequency: Annual. Audience: Dentists, dental hygienists, dental assistants, students, and lab technicians. Principal Exhibits: Dental equipment and supplies, office supplies, publications, and data processing. Dates and Locations: 1998 Nov; Milwaukee, WI.

WISCONSIN NURSES ASSOCIATION CONVENTION
6117 Monona Dr.
Madison, WI 53716
PH: (608)221-0383
FX: (608)221-2788
Frequency: Annual. Audience: Registered nurses. Principal Exhibits: Nursing equipment, supplies, and services. Dates and Locations: 1998 Oct 23-24; Eau Claire, WI.

WORLD CONFERENCE
e-mail: wonca@interserve.com.hk
url: http://www.ncl.ac.uk/~nphcare/WONCA/home.html
Hong Cong College of General Practitioners
15 Hennessy Rd., 8th Fl.
Wanchai, Hong Kong
PH: 852 25286618
FX: 852 28660616
Frequency: Triennial. Principal Exhibits: Exhibits concerned with the academic aspects of general family practice and maintaining high standards in the field.

WORLD CONFERENCE ON HEALTH PROMOTION AND HEALTH EDUCATION
e-mail: iuhpemcl@worldnet.fr
2, rue Auguste Comte
F-92170 Vanves, France
PH: 33 1 46450059
FX: 33 1 46450045
Frequency: Triennial. Principal Exhibits: Services for the promotion of worldwide health. Dates and Locations: 1998 Jun 21-26; San Juan, PR. Formerly: (970414) World Conference of the IUIIPE.

WORLD CONFERENCE OF OPERATING ROOM NURSES
url: http://www.aorn.org
2170 S. Parker Rd., Ste. 300
Denver, CO 80231-5711
PH: (303)755-6300
TF: 800755-2676
FX: (303)752-0299
Frequency: Biennial. Audience: Operating room nurses, health care professionals, registered nurses, doctors, and hospital administrators, material managers. Principal Exhibits: Equipment, supplies, and services used in operating room suites and pre-surgical areas.

WORLD CONGRESS OF THE IHPBA
Gastrointestinal Surgical Unit
Dept. of Surgery
Flinders Medical Center
Adelaide, SA 5042, Australia
Adelaide, SA 5042, Australia
Frequency: Biennial. Audience: Endoscopists, hepatologists, radiologists, and surgeons. Principal Exhibits: Exhibits related to diagnostic and treatment modalities of lymphatic, pancreatic, and biliary disorders.

WORLD CONGRESS OF INTENSIVE AND CRITICAL CARE
University Hospital
Intensive Care
CH-1211 Geneva, Switzerland
PH: 41 22 3827452
FX: 41 22 3827455
Frequency: Quadrennial. Principal Exhibits: Equipment, supplies, and services for intensive and critical care medicine, the branch of medicine dealing with patients in life-threatening pathophysiological conditions. Dates and Locations: 2001 Jun; Ottawa, ON.

WORLD CONGRESS OF ISOST
40, rue Washington, bte. 9
B-1050 Brussels, Belgium
PH: 32 2 6486823
FX: 32 2 6498601
Frequency: Triennial. Principal Exhibits: Exhibits related to orthopedic surgery and traumatology.

WORLD CONGRESS OF NEUROLOGICAL SURGERY
c/o Dr. Edward Laws
University of Virginia Health Services
Box 212
Charlottesville, VA 22904
FX: (804)924-5894
Frequency: Quadrennial. Principal Exhibits: Neurosurgical equipment, supplies, and services.

WORLD CONGRESS OF SURGERY - INTERNATIONAL SURGICAL WEEK (ISW)
e-mail: 101762,1434@compuserve.com
url: http://www.surgery.nbs.ch
Netzibodenstr. 34
PO Box 1527
CH-4133 Pratteln, Switzerland
PH: 41 61 8114770
FX: 41 61 8114775
Frequency: Biennial. Audience: Surgeons. Principal Exhibits: Surgical equipment, supplies, and services, including that for various types of surgery such as digestive tract visceral, endocrine, hepato-bilary, trauma, military, burn, pediatric, infection, and esophagus; also for surgical education, research, and nutrition. Dates and Locations: 2003 Aug ▪ 2005 Aug; Seattle, WA.

WORLD DENTAL CONGRESS
e-mail: congress@fdi.uk.org
url: http://www.fdi.org.uk/worldental
7 Carlisle St.
London W1V 5RG, England
PH: 44 171 9357852
FX: 44 171 4860183
Frequency: Annual. **Principal Exhibits:** Dental equipment, supplies, and services.

WORLD ROUND TABLE CONFERENCE ON SINTERING
e-mail: maria@mi.sanv.oc.yu
Serbian Academy of Sciences and Arts
Postanski Fah 745
YU-11001 Belgrade, Yugoslavia
PH: 381 11 637239
FX: 381 11 182825
Frequency: Quadrennial. **Principal Exhibits:** Equipment, supplies, and services for the theory, science, and technology of sintering (the scientific process involving the creation of a coherent mass through heating without melting).

WOUND, OSTOMY AND CONTINENCE NURSES SOCIETY
   (WOCN)
1550 S. Coast Hwy., Ste. 201
Laguna Beach, CA 92651
PH: (949)497-9007
TF: 888224-9626
FX: (949)376-3456
Frequency: Annual. **Audience:** Speciality nurses. **Principal Exhibits:** Products and equipment relating to wound, ostomy, and incontinence care. **Dates and Locations:** 1998 Jun 08-13; Salt Lake City, UT ■ 1999 Jun 20-24; Minneapolis, MN. **Formerly:** International Association for Enterostomal Therapy Annual Convention.

YANKEE DENTAL CONGRESS
e-mail: massdental@massdental.org
url: http://www.massdental.org
83 Speen St.
Natick, MA 01760-4125
PH: (508)651-7511
TF: 800342-8747
FX: (508)653-7115
Frequency: Annual. **Audience:** Dentists, dental students, dental hygienists, dental assistants, and dental technicians. **Principal Exhibits:** Dental products, equipment, and services. **Dates and Locations:** 1999 Jan 21-24; Boston, MA.

ZDRAVOOKHRANENIYE - INTERNATIONAL EXHIBITION
   ON HEALTHCARE, MEDICAL ENGINEERING, AND
   PHARMACEUTICALS
Krasnopresnenskaya nab. 14
123100 Moscow, Russia
PH: 095 268 1340
FX: 095 205 60 55
Frequency: Biennial. **Principal Exhibits:** Diagnostic instrument, including: bomographs, centrifuges, analytical and laboratory equipment; hospital equipment; drugs; and medical tools.

MASTER INDEX

The Master Index presents company and organization names, names of individuals, SIC industry names, and terms. Each entry in the index is followed by one or more page numbers.

American Academy of Anesthesiologist Assistants,
p. 576

American Academy of Child and Adolescent
Psychiatry, p. 576

American Academy of Clinical Neurophysiology, p.
576

American Academy of Clinical Psychiatrists, p. 576

American Academy of Clinical Toxicology, p. 577

American Academy of Dental Electrosurgery, p. 577

American Academy of Dental Group Practice, pp.
577, 926

American Academy of Dental Practice
Administration, pp. 577, 926

American Academy of Dermatology, p. 577

American Academy of Environmental Medicine
Conference, p. 958

American Academy of Esthetic Dentistry, p. 577

American Academy of Family Physicians, pp. 577,
926

American Academy of Family Physicians, West
Virginia Chapter, Annual Scientific Assembly, p.
958

American Academy of Fixed Prosthodontics, p. 578

American Academy of Gnathologic Orthopedics, p.
578

American Academy of Gnathologic Orthopedics
Conference, pp. 958-959

American Academy of Gold Foil Operators, p. 578

American Academy of Gold Foil Operators Annual
Meeting, p. 959

American Academy of Husband-Coached
Childbirth, p. 578

American Academy of Implant Dentistry, p. 578

American Academy of Implant Dentistry Annual
Meeting, p. 959

American Academy of Implant Prosthodontics, p.
578

American Academy of Insurance Medicine, p. 578

American Academy of Medical Administrators, pp.
579, 926

American Academy of Medical Administrators
Annual Conference and Convocation, p. 959

American Academy of Medical Administrators
Research and Educational Foundation, p. 579

American Academy of Neurological and
Orthopaedic Surgeons, p. 579

American Academy of Neurological Surgery, p. 579

American Academy of Neurology, p. 579

American Academy of Nurse Practitioners, p. 579

American Academy of Nursing, p. 579

American Academy of Ophthalmology, p. 579-580

American Academy of Ophthalmology Annual
Meeting, p. 959

American Academy of Optometry, p. 959

American Academy of Oral and Maxillofacial
Pathology, p. 580

American Academy of Oral and Maxillofacial
Radiology, p. 580

American Academy of Oral Medicine, p. 580

American Academy of Orofacial Pain, p. 580

American Academy of Orofacial Pain Scientific
Conference, p. 959

American Academy of Orthodontics for the General
Practitioner, p. 580

American Academy of Orthodontics for the General
Practitioner Convention, p. 959

American Academy of Orthopedic Surgeons Annual
Meeting, p. 959

American Academy of Osteopathy Workshop, p. 959

American Academy of Pediatric Dentistry, p. 580

American Academy of Pediatrics, p. 580-581

American Academy of Periodontology, p. 581

American Academy of Physical Medicine and
Rehabilitation Annual Meeting, p. 959

American Academy of Physician Assistants, p. 581

American Academy of Physiologic Dentistry, p. 581

American Academy of Podiatric Sports Medicine, p.
581

American Academy of Procedural Coders, p. 581

American Academy of Psychiatry and the Law, p.
581

American Academy of Restorative Dentistry, p. 581

American Academy of Somnology, p. 581-582

American Academy of Sports Physicians, p. 582

American Academy of the History of Dentistry, p.
578

American Alliance for Health, Physical Education,
Recreation, and Dance, p. 959

American Apitherapy Society, p. 582

American Assembly for Men in Nursing, p. 582

American Association for Accreditation of
Ambulatory Surgery Facilities, p. 582

American Association for Cancer Education, p. 583

American Association for Clinical Chemistry Annual
Meeting, p. 960

American Association for Community Dental
Programs, p. 583

American Association for Continuity of Care, p. 926

American Association for Continuity of Care Annual
Conference, p. 960

American Association for Dental Research, p. 584

American Association for Dental Research Annual
Session, p. 960

American Association for Functional Orthodontics,
p. 585

American Association for Geriatric Psychiatry, p.
585

American Association for Health Education, p. 585

American Association for Laboratory Animal
Science Conference & Exhibits, p. 960

American Association for Medical Transcription, p.
586-587

American Association for Medical Transcription
Annual Meeting, p. 960

American Association for Pediatric Ophthalmology
and Strabismus, p. 588

American Association for Pediatric Ophthalmology
and Strabismus Scientific Sessions, p. 961

American Association for the History of Medicine
Meeting, p. 960

American Association for the Study of Headache
Meeting, p. 961

American Association for Women Radiologists, p.
590

American Association of Ambulatory Surgery
Centers, p. 582

American Association of Anatomists, p. 582

American Association of Bioanalysts, p. 926

American Association of Blood Banks, p. 582-583

American Health Assistance Foundation, p. 602
American Health Care Advisory Association, p. 602
American Health Care Association, pp. 8, 602, 927
American Health Care Association Annual
  Convention and Exposition, p. 962
American Health Care Association: Provider, p. 927
American Health Care Centers, pp. 82, 475, 513
American Health Centers Inc, pp. 82, 447, 504
American Health Decisions, p. 602-603
American Health Foundation, p. 603
American Health Information Management
  Association, p. 603
American Health Information Management
  Association National Convention, p. 962-963
American Health Lawyers Association, p. 603
American Health Planning Association, p. 603
American Healthcare Radiology Administrators, p.
  603
American Healthcorp Inc, pp. 82, 479, 531
American Heart Association, p. 603
American Heart Association Scientific Sessions, p.
  963
American Home Patient Inc, pp. 82, 430, 502, 556-
  558
American Home Products Corp, pp. 82, 487
American Hospital Association, pp. 8, 927
American Hospital Mgt Corp, pp. 82, 469, 536
American Industrial Health Council, p. 927
American Industrial Hygiene Association, p. 927
American Industrial Hygiene Association Journal, p.
  927
American Institute for Biosocial Research, Inc., p.
  850
American Institute for Medical and Biological
  Engineering, p. 927
American Institute for Preventive Medicine, p. 850
American Institute of Biological Sciences Annual
  Meeting, p. 963
American Institute of Oral Biology, p. 604
American International Health Alliance, p. 601
American-Israeli Ophthalmological Society, p. 604
American Journal of Industrial Medicine, p. 927
American Journal of Nursing, p. 927-928
American Juvenile Arthritis Organization, p. 604
American Lebanese Medical Association, p. 604
American Legion Hospital, pp. 82-83, 487, 544
American Licensed Practical Nurses Association, p.
  604
American Lithotripsy Society Convention, p. 963
American Lyme Disease Foundation, p. 604
American Managed Behavioral Healthcare
  Association, p. 604
American Medical Association, pp. 12, 604-605, 928
American Medical Association Alliance, p. 605
American Medical Association (AMA), pp. 8, 14
American Medical Association Education and
  Research Foundation, p. 605
American Medical Directors Association, p. 605
American Medical Group Association, pp. 605-606,
  928
American Medical Holdings Inc, pp. 83, 428
American Medical Laboratories, pp. 83, 464, 521
American Medical Network, p. 606
American Medical News, p. 928
American Medical Student Association, p. 606

American Medical Student Association Convention,
  p. 963
American Medical Technologists, pp. 606, 928
American Medical Women's Association, p. 606
American Medical Women's Association Annual
  Meeting, p. 963
American Mental Health Counselors Association, p.
  606
American Mental Health Foundation, p. 606
American Neurological Association, p. 606
American Neuropsychiatric Association, p. 607
American Nurses Association, pp. 12, 607
American Nurses in Business Association, p. 607
American Nurses' Association, p. 928
American Nurses' Foundation, p. 607
American Nursing Association, p. 8
American Occupational Health Conference &
  Exhibits, p. 963
American Oncologic Hospital, pp. 83, 456, 529
American Ophthalmological Society, p. 607
American Optometric Association Congress, p. 963
American Optometric Student Association Annual
  Meeting, p. 963
American Organization of Nurse Executives, p. 607
American Organization of Nurse Executives
  Meeting and Exposition, p. 963
American Orthodontic Society, p. 607
American Orthopaedic Society for Sports Medicine,
  p. 607
American Orthopaedic Society for Sports Medicine
  Convention, p. 963
American Orthopsychiatric Association, p. 607
American Orthopsychiatric Association Annual
  Meeting, p. 963
American Orthoptic Council, p. 607-608
American Orthotic and Prosthetic Association
  National Assembly, p. 963
American Osler Society, p. 608
American Osteopathic Academy of Sports Medicine,
  p. 608
American Osteopathic Association Meeting &
  Exhibits, p. 964
American Osteopathic College of Anesthesiologists,
  p. 608
American Osteopathic College of Dermatology, p.
  608
American Osteopathic College of Radiology, p. 608
American Pain Society Scientific Meeting, p. 964
American Parkinson's Disease Association, p. 608
American Pathology Foundation, p. 608
American Pediatric Society, p. 608
American Pharmaceutical Association, p. 608-609
American Pharmaceutical Association/Academy of
  Pharmacy Practice and Management, p. 928
American Phrm Svcs Del, pp. 83, 433, 513
American Physical Society, p. 609
American Physical Therapy Association Annual
  Conference, p. 964
American Physical Therapy Association, California
  Chapter Annual Conference, p. 964
American Physical Therapy Association Private
  Practice Session, p. 964
American Physiological Society, p. 609
American Podiatric Medical Association Annual
  Meeting, p. 964

Associacao Brasileira de Distrofia Muscular, p. 628

Associacao Portuguesa de Miastenia Gravis e Doencas Neuromusculares, p. 628

Associated Health Foundation, p. 628

Associated Medical Services, p. 628

Associated Professional Sleep Societies, p. 628

Associated Therapists Corp, pp. 87, 457, 472, 515

Associates of Clinical Pharmacology, p. 628-629

Association Centrafricaine pour le Bien-Etre Familial, p. 639

Association Congolaise pour le Bien-Etre Familial, p. 639

Association Dentaire Francaise, p. 640

Association des Medecins de Langue Francaise du Canada, p. 642

Association des Neurologues Liberaux de Langue Francaise, p. 643

Association for Academic Surgery, p. 629

Association for Ambulatory Behavioral Healthcare, p. 630

Association for Child Psychology and Psychiatry, p. 639

Association for Childbirth at Home, International, p. 632

Association for Common European Nursing Diagnoses, Interventions and Outcomes, p. 639

Association for Continuing Education, p. 632

Association for Dental Education in Europe, p. 640

Association for Eye Research, p. 640

Association for Faculty in the Medical Humanities, p. 632

Association for Health-Care Institutions, p. 641

Association for Health Services Research, p. 633

Association for Health Without Vaccination, p. 641

Association for Healthcare Philanthropy Annual International Educational Conference, p. 968

Association for Macular Diseases, p. 633

Association for Medical Education in Europe, p. 642

Association for Medical Education in the Eastern Mediterranean, p. 642

Association for Medical Education in the Western Pacific Region, p. 642

Association for Molecular Pathology, p. 634

Association for Protection of the Moroccan Family, p. 644

Association for Public Health, p. 644

Association for Quality in Healthcare, p. 644-645

Association for Research in Nervous and Mental Disease, p. 637

Association for Research in Vision and Ophthalmology, p. 637

Association for Research of Childhood Cancer, p. 636

Association for Responsible Medicine, p. 637

Association for Surgical Education, p. 638

Association for the Advancement of Applied Sport Psychology, p. 630

Association for the Advancement of Medical Instrumentation, pp. 630, 929

Association for the Advancement of Wound Care, p. 630

Association for the Development of Tropical Atmospheric Physics, p. 640

Association for Voluntary Surgical Contraception, p. 646

Association for Worksite Health Promotion Annual International Conference, p. 968

Association Ivoirienne de Bien-Etre Familial, p. 642

Association Management Resources, p. 851

Association of Academic Health Centers, p. 629

Association of African Optometric Educators, p. 629

Association of American Cancer Institutes, p. 630

Association of American Indian Physicians, p. 630

Association of American Medical Colleges, p. 630-631

Association of American Physicians, p. 631

Association of American Physicians and Surgeons, p. 631

Association of Anaesthetists of Great Britain and Ireland, p. 629

Association of Asia Pacific Physical Societies, p. 629

Association of Asian/Pacific Community Health Organizations, p. 631

Association of Behavioral Healthcare Management, p. 631

Association of Biological Manufacturers of Japan, p. 629

Association of Black Cardiologists, p. 631

Association of Black Nursing Faculty, p. 631

Association of British Dental Surgery Assistants, p. 629

Association of British Dispensing Opticians Conference, p. 967

Association of British Neurologists, p. 629

Association of Camp Nurses, p. 631

Association of Canadian Faculties of Dentistry, p. 638

Association of Canadian Medical Colleges, p. 638

Association of Canadian Pharmaceutical Physicians, p. 638

Association of Cardiothoracic Anaesthetists, p. 638-639

Association of Chartered Physiotherapists in Sports Medicine, p. 639

Association of Child and Adolescent Psychiatric Nurses, p. 632

Association of Child and Adolescent Psychiatric Nurses Conference, p. 968

Association of Clinical Biochemists, p. 639

Association of Clinical Research for the Pharmaceutical Industry, p. 639

Association of Clinical Scientists, p. 632

Association of Community Cancer Centers, p. 632

Association of Community Health Councils for England and Wales, p. 639

Association of County Public Health Officers, p. 639-640

Association of Democratic Pharmacists, p. 640

Association of Dental Dealers in Europe, p. 640

Association of European Cancer Leagues, p. 640

Association of European Paediatric Cardiologists, p. 640

Association of European Psychiatrists, p. 640

Association of Faculties of Pharmacy of Canada, p. 640-641

Association of Family Practice Administrators, p. 632

Association of Family Practice Residency Directors, p. 632-633

Canadian Medic Alert Foundation, p. 665
Canadian Medical and Biological Engineering
   Society, p. 665-666
Canadian Medical Association, p. 665
Canadian Medical Foundation, p. 666
Canadian Medical Malpractice Prevention
   Association, p. 666
Canadian Medical Protective Association, p. 666
Canadian Mental Health Association, p. 666
Canadian Natural Health Association, p. 666
Canadian Network of Toxicology Centres, p. 666
Canadian Neurological Society, p. 666
Canadian Neurosurgery Society, p. 666
Canadian Nurses Association, p. 666-667
Canadian Nurses Association Convention, p. 969
Canadian Nurses Foundation, p. 667
Canadian Nurses Respiratory Society, p. 667
Canadian Nursing Research Group, p. 667
Canadian Obstetric Gynecologic and Neonatal
   Nurses, p. 667
Canadian Occupational Health Nurses Association,
   p. 667
Canadian Ophthalmological Society, p. 667
Canadian Ophthalmological Society Annual Meeting
   and Exhibition, p. 969
Canadian Orthopaedic Nurses Association, p. 667
Canadian Orthoptic Council, p. 667
Canadian Paediatric Society, p. 667
Canadian Physiological Society, p. 667
Canadian Psoriasis Foundation, p. 668
Canadian Psychiatric Association, p. 668
Canadian Psychiatric Association Annual
   Convention, p. 969
Canadian Public Health Association, p. 668
Canadian Reference Centre for Cancer Pathology,
   p. 668
Canadian Rheumatology Association, p. 668
Canadian Schizophrenia Foundation, p. 668
Canadian Sleep Society, p. 668
Canadian Society for Clinical Pharmacology, p. 669
Canadian Society for Exercise Physiology, p. 669
Canadian Society for Immunology, p. 669
Canadian Society for International Health, p. 669
Canadian Society for Medical Laboratory Science, p.
   669
Canadian Society for Psychomotor Learning and
   Sport Psychology, p. 670
Canadian Society of Allergy and Clinical
   Immunology, p. 668
Canadian Society of Cardiology Technologists, p.
   669
Canadian Society of Clinical Neurophysiologists, p.
   669
Canadian Society of Gastroenterology Nurses and
   Associates, p. 669
Canadian Society of Hospital Pharmacists
   Conference, p. 969
Canadian Society of Orthopaedic Technologists
   Annual Meeting, p. 969
Canadian Society of Plant Physiologists, p. 669
Canadian Thoracic Society, p. 670
Canadian Wholesale Drug Association, p. 670
Canadians for Health Research, p. 670
Cancer Biotherapy Research Group, p. 670
Cancer Care, p. 670

Cancer Control Society, p. 670
Cancer Federation, p. 670-671
Cancer Information Service, p. 671
Cancer Information Service (Canada), p. 671
Cancer Research Fund of the Damon Runyon, p.
   671
Cancer Research Society, p. 671
Cancer Therapy, pp. 110, 453, 547
Cancer Treatment Ctrs of America, pp. 110, 492, 533
Candlelighters Childhood Cancer Foundation, p. 671
Candlelighters Childhood Cancer Foundation
   Canada, p. 671
Candler Health System Inc, pp. 110, 433, 509
Candler Hospital Inc, pp. 110, 434, 511
Cannon, Walter Bradford, p. 12-13
Canonsburg General Hospital, pp. 110, 482, 542
Cantex Health Care Centers, pp. 110, 483, 517
Canton-Potsdam Hospital, pp. 110, 480, 539
Cape Canaveral Hospital, pp. 110, 458, 526
Cape Cod Hospital, pp. 110, 439, 517
Cape Medical Inc, pp. 110-111, 493, 554
Capital Dst Physicians Health Plan, pp. 111, 431, 546
Capital Health Services Inc, pp. 111, 482, 529
Capital Health Systems Inc, pp. 111, 437, 488, 503
Capital Region Medical Center, pp. 111, 450, 517
Capital Senior Living Inc, pp. 111, 478, 512
Caplan, Yale H., p. 857
Carbon Schuylkill Comm Htlh, pp. 111, 490, 544
Carbondale Clinic S C, pp. 111, 489, 549
Cardiac Solutions, Inc, pp. 111, 488, 552
Cardiovascular Consultants Inc, pp. 111, 484, 551
Cardiovascular Credentialing International, p. 671
Cardiovascular Thoracic Surgery Medical Legal
   Consultations, p. 857
Care America Integrated Health Care Services Inc.,
   p. 562
Care Communications, Inc., p. 857
Care Enterprises Inc, pp. 111, 440, 500
Care Enterprises West, pp. 111, 450, 503
Care Group Inc, pp. 111-112, 474, 495, 525, 547
Care Initiatives, pp. 112, 449, 504
Care Providers of Minnesota Convention and
   Exposition, p. 969
Carefirst of Maryland, Inc, pp. 112, 428, 502
Caregivers Inc, pp. 112, 495, 514
Caremark Inc, pp. 112, 494
Caremark International Inc, pp. 112, 486
Careselect Group Inc, pp. 112, 495, 544
Caretenders Health Corp, pp. 112, 447, 503, 560
Carilion Medical Centers Inc, pp. 112, 431, 453, 502
Carilion Services Inc, pp. 112, 429, 523
Carillon House Nursing Fcilty, pp. 112, 493, 546
Caring for Frail Elderly People: New Directions in
   Care, p. 930
Caring Options Residential Experts, p. 857
Caritas Norwood Hospital Inc, pp. 112, 474, 528
Caritas Southwood Hospital, pp. 112, 477, 529
Carle Clinic Association Pc, pp. 112-113, 431, 505
Carle Foundation, The, pp. 378, 435, 508
Carlisle Hospital, pp. 113, 460, 531
Carlson Price Fass & Co. Inc., p. 857
Carmel Richmond Nursing Home, pp. 113, 487, 535
Carnegie Partners Inc, pp. 113, 473, 537
Carney Hospital Inc, pp. 113, 447, 516
Carolina Home Oxygen Medical Supply, p. 556-558

Columbia Bay Area Healthcare, pp. 128, 493
Columbia/Cape Fear Healthcare, pp. 131, 487, 537
Columbia Chicago Ostpthc Hospt, pp. 128, 436, 528
Columbia Chppnhm Mdcl Ctr, pp. 128, 443, 474, 506
Columbia Csa/Hs Greater Clvlnd, pp. 128, 452, 486, 512
Columbia Dunwoody Medical Ctr, pp. 128, 493, 539
Columbia East Houston Med Ctr, pp. 128, 493, 539
Columbia El Drado Hospital Med Ctr, pp. 128, 474, 536
Columbia Four Rivers Med Ctr, pp. 128, 466, 532
Columbia/HCA, p. 558
Columbia/HCA Healthcare Corporation, pp. 20, 131-132, 428, 450, 461-462, 468, 475, 478-479, 487, 490, 495-499, 556, 560, 562-563
Columbia/HCA John Randolph Med Ctr, pp. 128, 467, 523
Columbia Healthcare of Centl VA, pp. 128-129, 439, 454, 457, 463, 508
Columbia-Healthone L L C, pp. 130-131, 429, 459, 473, 486, 494, 499
Columbia Hospital Corp Bay Area, pp. 129, 483, 533
Columbia Hospital Corp KY, pp. 129, 477, 529
Columbia Hospital Corp of S Broward, pp. 129, 470, 525
Columbia Hospital for Women Med Ctr, pp. 129, 447, 529
Columbia Hospital Frankfort, pp. 129, 491, 537
Columbia Hospital, Inc., pp. 129, 441, 514
Columbia Hospital L P, pp. 129, 481, 532
Columbia Huntington Beach Med Ctr, pp. 129, 471, 537
Columbia La Grange Mem Hosp, pp. 129, 450, 511
Columbia Med Ctr of San Angelo, pp. 129, 481, 531
Columbia Medical Plan Inc, pp. 129-130, 439, 521
Columbia Memorial Hospital, pp. 130, 463, 521
Columbia Metrowest Medical Ctr, pp. 130, 442, 506
Columbia North Bay Hospital, pp. 130, 470, 549
Columbia Outpatient Surgical Svcs, pp. 130, 486, 553
Columbia Palmyra Park Hospital, pp. 130, 484, 534
Columbia Pine Lk Regional Hosp, pp. 130, 485
Columbia Pk Healthcare Systems, pp. 130, 448, 509
Columbia Putnam Hospital Inc, pp. 130, 483, 536
Columbia Regional Medical Ctr, pp. 130, 456, 530
Columbia Tops Surgical Hosp, pp. 130, 482, 551
Columbus Community Hospital, pp. 132, 493, 547
Columbus Doctors Hospital Inc, pp. 132, 489, 536
Columbus Hospital Inc, pp. 132, 449, 524
Columbus Reg Healthcr Sys Inc, pp. 132, 435, 505
Columbus Regional Hospital, pp. 132, 444, 516
Comanche County Hospital Auth Tr, pp. 132, 442, 514
Commission on Accreditation of Allied Health Education Programs, p. 680
Commission on Graduates of Foreign Nursing Schools, p. 680
Commissioned Officers Association of the United States Public Health Service, p. 680-681
Committee for Freedom of Choice in Medicine, p. 681
Committee for National Health Insurance, p. 681
Committee for the Promotion of Medical Research, p. 681
Committee for Truth in Psychiatry, p. 681
Committee of Interns and Residents, p. 681

Committee on Accreditation for Opthalmic Medical Personnel, p. 681
Commonwealth Dental Association, p. 681
Commonwealth Health Corp, pp. 132, 441, 545
Commonwealth Medical Association, p. 681
Commonwealth Nurses Federation, p. 682
Commonwealth Pharmaceutical Association, p. 682
Commonwealth Regional Health Secretariat, p. 682
Commun Mem Hospital of Menomonee Falls, pp. 132, 456, 519
Community Behavioral Health Sys, pp. 132-133, 469, 525
Community Bio Resources, pp. 133, 451, 537
Community Care of America Inc, pp. 133, 447, 502
Community Care Systems Inc, pp. 133, 488, 505
Community Gen Hospital of Thomasville, pp. 133, 485, 540
Community Gen Osteopathic Hosp, pp. 133, 462, 531
Community General Hospital, pp. 133, 456, 526
Community Health Association, pp. 133, 492, 547
Community Health Care Sys, pp. 452, 512
Community Health Care Sys of San Bernardino, p. 134
Community Health Counseling Svcs, pp. 134, 469, 520
Community Health Ctr of Branch Cnty, pp. 134, 473, 544
Community Health Group, pp. 133, 461, 552
Community Health Inv Corp, pp. 133, 442, 506
Community Health Network, Inc, pp. 133, 472, 540
Community Health Nurses Association of Canada, p. 682
Community Health Plan Inc, pp. 133, 429, 503
Community Health Plan of Ohio, pp. 133, 494, 553
Community Health Systems Inc, pp. 133, 429, 499
Community Healthlink Inc, pp. 133-134, 482, 549
Community Hospital, p. 512
Community Hospital - SB, p. 437
Community Hospital Assn Inc, pp. 134, 444, 514
Community Hospital Chanl Inc, pp. 134-135, 451, 521
Community Hospital Group Inc, pp. 135, 434, 504
Community Hospital Inc, pp. 135, 482, 537
Community Hospital of Andalusia, pp. 134, 463, 547
Community Hospital of Anderson, pp. 134, 459, 521
Community Hospital of Brzsport Inc, pp. 134, 457, 537
Community Hospital of Lancaster, pp. 134, 470, 526
Community Hospital of Monterey, pp. 134, 438, 514
Community Hospital of Ottawa, pp. 134, 474, 535
Community Hospital of San Bernardino, p. 134
Community Hospital of Springfield, pp. 134, 484, 517
Community Hospital Williams County, pp. 134, 491, 537
Community Hospitals of Galen, pp. 135, 489, 536
Community Hospitals of Indiana, pp. 135, 430, 473, 498, 501
Community Living Options Inc, pp. 135, 494, 539
Community Medical Center Inc, pp. 135, 434, 445, 461, 506, 519, 524
Community Memorial Hospital, pp. 135, 471, 490, 529, 543
Community Memorial Hospital/Sa, pp. 135, 449, 517

European Association of Centres of Medical Ethics, p. 694

European Association of Dental Graphology, p. 694-695

European Association of Multidisciplinary Practice in Child, Adolescent and Family Mental Health, p. 695

European Association of Neurosurgical Societies, p. 695

European Association of New Medical Techniques, p. 695

European Association of Poisons Centres and Clinical Toxicologists, p. 695

European Bank of Frozen Blood of Rare Groups, p. 695

European Brain and Behaviour Society, p. 695

European Chemoreception Research Organization, p. 695

European Congress on Intensive Care Medicine, p. 973

European Department for the Quality of Medicines, p. 696

European Diabetes Pregnancy Study Group, p. 696

European Disposables and Nonwovens Association Conference, p. 973

European Federation of Pharmaceutical Industries' Associations, p. 696

European Health Policy Forum, p. 696

European Healthcare Management Association, p. 696

European League Against Rheumatism, p. 696

European Medical Research Councils, p. 696

European Midwives Liaison Committee, p. 697

European Organization for Caries Research, p. 697

European Organization for Research and Treatment of Cancer, p. 697

European Orthodontic Society, p. 697

European Physical Society, p. 697

European Proprietary Medicines Manufacturers' Association, p. 697

European Public Health Alliance, p. 697-698

European Regional Organization of the International Dental Federation, p. 698

European Society for Cardiovascular Surgery, p. 698

European Society for Noninvasive Cardiovascular Dynamics, p. 698-699

European Society of Biomechanics, p. 698

European Society of Child and Adolescent Psychiatry, p. 698

European Society of Comparative Physiology and Biochemistry, p. 698

European Society of Neuroradiology, p. 698

European Society of Ophthalmic Plastic and Reconstructive Surgery, p. 699

European Society of Paediatric Radiology, p. 699

European Society of Pathology, p. 699

European Society of Regional Anaesthesia, p. 699

European Union of Medical Specialists, p. 699

Eurotox, p. 699

Evangelical Community Hosp, pp. 159, 468, 528

Evangelical Homes of Michigan, pp. 159, 482, 531

Evangelical Lutheran, pp. 429, 499

Evangelical Lutheran Good Samaritan, p. 159

Evans Syndrome Research and Support Group, p. 699

Evanston Northwestern, pp. 159, 430, 449, 501

Everest Healthcare Svcs Corp, pp. 159-160, 439, 513

Everett Clinic, The, pp. 379, 452, 457, 521

Everett House, pp. 160, 494

Evergreen Healthcare, Inc, pp. 160, 445, 500

Evergreen Healthcare Mgt Llc, pp. 160, 468, 553

Examination Management Svcs, pp. 160, 445, 502

Examination Mgt Svcs Inc Amer, pp. 160, 430, 500

Excel Consultants Inc., p. 868

Excelcare System Inc, pp. 160, 470, 554

Excerpta Medica, p. 935

Excerpta Medica: Health Policy, Economics and Management, p. 935

Executive Health Group, MD PC, pp. 160, 483, 543

Executive Office of The Government, pp. 160, 478

Exeter Hospital Inc, pp. 160, 458, 530

Exhibition of the International Association for Dental Research, p. 973

EXPO OPTICA - International Optics and Optometry Exhibition, p. 973

EXPOANALITICA Y BIOCIENCIA, p. 973

Expodental - Dental Equipment, Supplies, and Services Show, p. 973

EXPOMED - Exhibition for Healthcare Professionals, p. 973

EXPOMEDICA, p. 973

Expopharm - International Pharmaceutical Trade Fair, p. 973

EXPOSALUD, p. 973

EXPOSALUD - International Exhibit for Health and Fitness, p. 973

Express Scripts Inc., p. 560

Extendicare Facilities Inc, pp. 160, 433, 501

Extendicare Health Services, pp. 160, 428, 499

Extendicare Homes, Inc, pp. 160, 430, 499

Extendicare Inc., pp. 557, 560

Eye Center, p. 869

Eyexam 2000 of California, Inc, pp. 160, 491, 540

Eytek Consulting Company, p. 869

F-D-C Reports, p. 935

Facey Medical Foundation Inc, pp. 161, 458, 538

Facey Medical Group, Pc, pp. 161, 473, 536

Fachdental Sudwest, p. 973

Facts on File Dictionary of Health Care Management, p. 935

Faculty of Dental Surgery, p. 699

Faculty of Homeopathy, p. 700

Faculty of Public Health Medicine, p. 700

Fair Acres Center, pp. 161, 466, 519

Fair Acres Geriatric Center, pp. 161, 464, 521

Fair Oaks Psychiatric Associates, p. 869

Fairfield Medical Center, pp. 161, 447, 516

Fairmont General Hospital Inc, pp. 161, 460, 525

Fairview Clinics, pp. 161, 485, 544

Fairview Extended Care Svcs, pp. 161, 466, 524

Fairview Hm Care & Hospice Inc, pp. 161, 485, 530

Fairview Hospital, pp. 161-162, 437, 506

Fairview Hospital Healthcare Svcs, pp. 161, 447, 476, 485, 499

Fairview Redwing Health Svcs, pp. 162, 491, 543

Faith Regional Health Services, pp. 162, 466, 521

Fall Eyecare Conference, p. 974

Fallon Clinic Inc, pp. 162, 443

Fallston General Hospital Inc, pp. 162, 464, 527

Falmouth Hospital Association, pp. 162, 464, 529

Health Outreach Project Inc., p. 877
Health Partners of Philadelphia, pp. 189, 434, 548
Health Physics Society, p. 714
Health Plan of Nevada Inc, pp. 189, 430, 549
Health Plan of Upper Ohio, pp. 189, 443, 552
Health Planning and Administration, p. 939
Health Plus of Louisiana Inc, pp. 189, 492, 553
Health Policy Institute, p. 939
Health Professions Council Zimbabwe, p. 714
Health Quest Affiliates, Inc., p. 877
Health Reference Center, p. 939
Health Research Council of New Zealand, p. 714
Health Research Institute, p. 939
Health Resort Medicine, p. 975
Health Resources Corporation, pp. 189-190, 473, 477, 543, 548
Health Science Center, p. 714
Health Science, Inc., p. 877
Health Security Action Council, p. 714
Health Services Consultants Inc., p. 877
Health Services Management and Policy, p. 939
Health Services Medical Corp, pp. 190, 438, 520
Health Services Research, p. 975
Health Services Research and Development Center, p. 939
Health Services Union of Australia, p. 714
Health Span Hm Care & Hospice, pp. 190, 482, 527
Health Svcs Assn of Central NY, pp. 190, 457, 529
Health Systems International, Inc., pp. 556, 561
Health Systems Management Network, Inc., p. 877
Health Systems Research Inc., p. 877
Health Systems Technology Corp., p. 877
Health Tech Affiliates Inc, pp. 190, 480, 543
Health Technologies Inc., p. 877
Health Volunteers Overseas, p. 714
Health Volunteers Overseas - Vietnam, p. 714
Health Watch International, p. 877
Health Workers Union of the Russian Federation, p. 715
Healthaccess Inc, pp. 190, 478, 553
Healthalliance Hospitals Inc, pp. 190, 464, 470, 515
Healthcare Administrative Services Inc., p. 877
Healthcare Affiliates, Inc., p. 877-878
Healthcare Association of Hawaii Annual Meeting, p. 976
Healthcare Career Directory: Nurses and Physicians, p. 939
HealthCare Compliance Packaging Council, p. 715
HealthCare Concepts, Inc., p. 878
HealthCare Connections, p. 878
Healthcare Convention and Exhibitors Association, pp. 939, 976
Healthcare Executive, p. 939
Healthcare Finance for the Non-Financial Manager, p. 940
Healthcare Financial Management, p. 940
Healthcare Financial Management Association, pp. 715, 940
Healthcare Financing Study Group, pp. 715, 940
Healthcare Forecasting Inc., p. 878
Healthcare Forum Journal, p. 940
Healthcare Forum, The, p. 715
Healthcare Information and Management Systems Society, p. 940

Healthcare Information and Management Systems Society Conference & Exhibition, p. 976
Healthcare Information Management, p. 940
Healthcare Istanbul, p. 976
Healthcare Management Consultants, Inc., p. 878
Healthcare Management Consulting Services, p. 878
Healthcare Management Counselors, Division of Richard A. Eisner & Company,, p. 878
Healthcare Marketing Report, p. 940
Healthcare Mgt Alternatives, pp. 190, 435, 551
Healthcare Partners Med Group, pp. 190, 444, 512
Healthcare PR and Marketing News, p. 940
Healthcare Properties Inc, pp. 190, 492, 538
Healthcare Purchasing News, p. 940
Healthcare San Antonio Inc, pp. 190, 495, 548
Healthcare Sentry, p. 878
HealthChoice, a Carequest, Inc., Company, p. 878-879
Healthchoice Inc., p. 879
Healthcor Holdings Inc, pp. 190, 439, 503
Healthcor, Inc, pp. 190-191, 443, 451, 518, 550
Healtheast Companies, Inc, pp. 191, 470, 506
Healtheast St John's Hospital, pp. 191, 446, 529
Healtheast St Joseph's Hosp, pp. 191, 443, 520
Healthfirst Inc, pp. 191, 449, 547
Healthlink Inc, pp. 191, 490, 546
Healthmark of Walton Inc, pp. 191, 497, 551
HealthMax Inc., p. 561
HealthNet Botswana, p. 715
HealthNet South Africa, p. 715-716
HealthNet Zimbabwe, p. 716
HealthOhio, Inc, pp. 191, 458, 553
Healthpartners, Inc, pp. 191, 428, 500
HealthPartners of Arizona, Inc., p. 565
Healthplex Inc, pp. 191, 496, 553
Healthplus Corporation, pp. 191, 463, 543
Healthright Inc, pp. 191, 461, 553
Healthscope Management Services Corp., p. 879
Healthsource Health Plans Inc, pp. 191, 431, 542
Healthsource Inc., pp. 556, 560
Healthsource Maine Inc, pp. 191, 441, 550
Healthsource South Carolina, pp. 191-192, 435, 549
Healthsouth Corporation, pp. 192-193, 428, 499, 557-558, 561-562
Healthsouth Doctors' Hospital, pp. 193, 451, 529
Healthsouth Medical Center Inc, pp. 193, 451, 531
Healthsouth of Austin, Inc, pp. 192, 483, 545
Healthsouth of Ft. Lauderdale, pp. 192, 482, 543
Healthsouth of Midland, Inc, pp. 192, 494, 551
Healthsouth of Montgomery, pp. 192, 496, 549
Healthsouth of New Mexico, pp. 192, 497, 549
Healthsouth of Pittsburgh,, pp. 192, 471, 538
Healthsouth of San Antonio,, pp. 192, 486, 544
Healthsouth of South Carolina,, pp. 192, 474, 549
Healthsouth of Texarkana Inc, pp. 192, 486, 551
Healthsouth of Treasure Coast, pp. 192, 470, 550
Healthsouth of Virginia, Inc, pp. 192, 467, 535
Healthsouth of York, Inc, pp. 192, 471, 547
Healthsouth Orthopedic Svcs, pp. 193, 451, 519
Healthsouth Rehabilitation Hosp, pp. 193, 492, 549
Healthsouth Rehabiltiation, pp. 193, 490, 540
Healthsouth Sub-Acute Ctr, pp. 193, 498, 531
Healthsphere of America Inc, pp. 193, 493, 533
Healthtexas Provider Network, pp. 193, 455, 548

St Mary's Hospital, pp. 360, 454, 466, 523, 535
St Mary's Hospital, pp. 360, 465, 524
St Mary's Hospital & Med Ctr, pp. 360-361, 441, 447, 509, 521
St Mary's Hospital At Amsterdam, pp. 360, 466, 526
St Mary's Hospital Corporation, pp. 360, 440, 512
St Mary's Hospital for Children, pp. 361, 492, 541
St Mary's Hospital Inc, pp. 360, 437, 497, 509, 545
St. Mary's Hospital of Blue Sprng, pp. 363, 464, 536
St Mary's Hospital of Brooklyn, pp. 360, 454, 513
Saint Mary's Hospital of Huntington, pp. 326, 438, 513
St Mary's Hospital of Milwaukee, pp. 360, 442, 508
St Mary's Hospital of Richmond, pp. 361, 431, 509
St Mary's Hospital of St Mrys Cnty, pp. 360, 471, 532
St Mary's Hospital Ozaukee, pp. 360, 465, 531
St Mary's Med Ctr of Evansville, pp. 361, 439, 505
St Mary's Med Ctr of Saginaw, pp. 361, 439, 510
St. Mary's Medical Center, p. 564
St Mary's Medical Center, pp. 360, 436, 511
St Mary's Medical Center Inc, pp. 360, 461, 519
St Mary's Regional Health Sys, pp. 361, 478, 539
St Mary's Regional Medical Ctr, pp. 361, 440, 457, 475, 478, 515, 525, 528, 531
St Michael Hospital, pp. 361, 449, 521
St Michael's Hospital, pp. 361, 466, 537
St Nicholas Hospital, pp. 361, 465, 534
St Olaf Hospital Association, pp. 361-362, 471, 530
St Patrick Hospital Corp, pp. 362, 446, 519
St Patrick Hospital Inc, pp. 362, 455, 514
Saint Patrick's Home, pp. 326, 492, 546
St Peter's Hospital, pp. 362, 435, 506
St Peter's Medical Center, pp. 362, 435, 505
St. Peters Community Hospital, pp. 363, 460, 530
St Petrsburg Sncoast Med Group, pp. 362, 475, 539
St Rita's Medical Center, pp. 362, 440, 509
St. Rose Dominican Hospital, pp. 363, 457, 528
St Tammany Parish Hospital, pp. 362, 441, 525
St Tammany Parish Hospital Dst 2, pp. 362, 465, 522
St Vincent Hospital, pp. 362, 440, 507
Saint Vincent Hospital & Health Ctr, pp. 326, 459, 517
St Vincent Hospital Health Care Ctr, pp. 362, 430, 501
St Vincent Hospital Inc, pp. 362, 444, 521
Saint Vincent Hospital, Llc, pp. 326-327, 445, 507
St Vincent Infirmary Med Ctr, pp. 362, 433, 504
St Vincent Mercy Medical Ctr, pp. 362, 430, 501
St Vincent's Ambulatory Care, pp. 362-363, 497, 553
St Vincent's Hospital, pp. 363, 442, 514
St Vincent's Medical Center, pp. 363, 433, 506
St Vincnts Hospital Med Ctr of Ny, pp. 363, 430, 502
Saints Memorial Medical Center, pp. 327, 451, 518
Salem Community Hospital, pp. 327, 460, 531
Salem Hospital, pp. 327, 437, 463, 506
Salem Hospital Inc, pp. 381, 449, 510
Salick Health Care Inc, pp. 327, 464, 512
Salina Regional Health Center, pp. 327, 458, 516
Salinas Valley Memorial Health, pp. 327, 436, 513
Salo Inc, pp. 327, 469, 503
Salon du Laboratoire/Bioexpo, p. 990
Salvation Army Medical Fellowship, p. 816
Samaritan Health Partners Shp, pp. 327, 434, 507
Samaritan Health System, pp. 327-328, 428, 437, 450, 455, 464, 495, 499, 523

Samaritan Hospital, pp. 328, 456, 514
Samaritan Medical Center, pp. 328, 441, 516
Sampson Regional Medical Ctr, pp. 328, 474, 534
San Antonio Community Hosp, pp. 328, 441, 510
San Benito Health Care Dst, pp. 328, 487, 542
San Diego Hospital Assn, pp. 328, 438
San Francisco City & County, pp. 328, 438, 448
San Francisco Sports Medicine, p. 910
San Gabriel Valley Med Ctr, pp. 328, 456, 525
San Jacinto Methodist Hosp, pp. 328, 452, 520
San Joaquin Community Hosp, pp. 328, 451, 524
San Joaquin, County of, pp. 328, 454
San Juan Regional Medical Ctr, pp. 328-329, 451, 524
San Leandro Hospital, pp. 329, 461, 553
San Luis Obispo, County of, pp. 329, 487
San Mateo Health Commission, pp. 329, 450, 552
San Mateo Individual Practice, pp. 329, 475, 553
San Pedro Peninsula Hospital, pp. 329, 453, 525
Sansum Medical Clinic Inc, pp. 329, 473, 541
Santa Ana Tustin Radiology, pp. 329, 451, 554
Santa Barbara Cottage Hosp, pp. 329, 450, 510
Santa Barbara Mdcl Fndn Clc, pp. 329, 461, 535
Santa Cruz Medical Clinic, pp. 329, 479, 554
Santa Marta Hospital Inc, pp. 329, 480, 542
Santa Paula Memorial Hospital, pp. 329, 493, 550
Santa Rosa Health Care Corp, pp. 329, 449
Santa Rosa Memorial Hospital, pp. 329-330, 444, 521
Santa Teresita Hospital, pp. 330, 492, 542
Saponaro Inc., p. 910
Sarah Bush Lincoln Health Ctr, pp. 330, 452, 515
Sarasota County Pub Hospital Bd, pp. 330, 432, 505
Sarasota Doctor's Hospital, pp. 330, 453, 528
Saratoga Community Hospital, pp. 330, 466, 524
Saratoga Hospital (Inc), pp. 330, 460, 522
Sargent Cancer Care for Children, p. 816
Sartori Memorial Hospital, pp. 330, 494, 546
SAS Management Consultants, p. 910
Saskatchewan Association of Health Organizations Annual Convention and Exhibition, p. 990
Satellite Dialysis Centers, pp. 330, 468, 544
Satilla Health Services Inc, pp. 330, 452, 522
Saudi Dentistry, p. 990
Saudi Medicare, p. 990
Sauk Prairie Memorial Hospital, pp. 330, 487, 540
Saul, Ronald E., MD, p. 910
SCAN - Sports, Cardiovascular and Wellness Nutritionists, p. 910-911
Scan Health Plan, pp. 330, 445, 549
Scandefa - Scandinavian Dental Fair, p. 990
Scandinavian Association for Thoracic Surgery Annual Meeting, p. 990
Scandinavian Association of Paediatric Surgeons, p. 816
Scandinavian Association of Zone-Therapeutists, p. 816
Scandinavian Neurological Association, p. 816
Scandinavian Neurosurgical Society, p. 816
Scandinavian Surgical Society, p. 816
Sch Health Care System, pp. 330-331, 447, 458, 484, 496
Schick & Affiliates, Inc., p. 911
Schirmer Engineering Corporation, p. 911
Schizophrenia - International Congress, p. 990

South African Association of Paediatric Surgeons, p. 831

South African Association of Pediatric Surgeons Congress, p. 992

South African Dental Association, p. 831

South African Diabetes Association, p. 831

South Austin Medical Center, pp. 342, 482, 532

South Baldwin County Healthcar, pp. 342, 488, 542

South Bay Community Hospital, pp. 342, 489, 550

South Bend Medical Foundation, pp. 342, 467, 538

South Broward Hospital Dst, pp. 342, 430, 481, 502

South Carolina Dental Association Annual Session, p. 992

South Carolina Dept Mental Health, pp. 342-343, 475, 483

South Carolina Laboratory Management Society Annual Conference and Exhibition, p. 992

South Carolina Medical Association Annual Meeting, p. 992

South Carolina Nurses Association Convention, p. 992

South Central Regional Med Ctr, pp. 342, 454, 519

South County Hospital Inc, pp. 342, 465, 539

South Dade Healthcare Group, pp. 343, 483, 533

South Dakota Dental Association Annual Session, p. 992

South Dakota Dept HumanSvcs, pp. 343, 497

South Dakota State Medical Association Annual Meeting, p. 992

South Florida Baptist Hospital, pp. 343, 470, 533

South Fulton Medical Center, pp. 343, 449, 515

South Hills Health System, pp. 343, 438, 447, 505

South Miami Hospital Inc, pp. 343, 438, 507

South Mississippi Home Health, pp. 343, 482, 528

South Nassau Communities Hosp, pp. 343, 463, 520

South Pacific Alliance for Family Health, p. 831

South Shore Hospital Corp, pp. 343, 479, 537

South Shore Hospital Inc, pp. 343, 436, 506

South Shore Mntal Health Ctr Inc, pp. 343, 493, 551

South Shore Nutritional Consultants, p. 915

Southampton Hospital Assn, pp. 343, 457, 528

Southampton Memorial Hospital, pp. 343-344, 478, 541

Southboro Medical Group Inc, pp. 344, 482, 542

Southcoast Hospital Group Inc, pp. 344, 431, 447-448, 502

Southeast Alaska Reg Health, pp. 344, 460, 535

Southeast Missouri Hospital Assn, pp. 344, 444, 515

Southeastern Chapter-Society of Nuclear Medicine Exhibition, p. 992

Southeastern Regional Med Ctr, pp. 344, 443, 512

Southeastern Surgical Congress Annual Scientific Meeting, p. 992

Southern Association of Orthodontists Convention, p. 992

Southern Baptist Hospital of Fla, pp. 344, 433, 505

Southern Cal Permanente Med Group, pp. 344, 436, 441

Southern California Psychiatric Legal Consultants, p. 915

Southern Chester County Med Ctr, pp. 344, 485, 544

Southern Educational Congress of Optometry, p. 992

Southern Health Care of Ala, pp. 344, 490, 546

Southern Health Management, pp. 344, 454, 522

Southern Health Services, Inc, pp. 344-345, 449, 554

Southern Healthcare Systems, pp. 345, 478, 532

Southern Illinois Hospital Svcs, pp. 345, 474

Southern Management Services, pp. 345, 462, 544

Southern Maryland Hospital, pp. 345, 446, 516

Southern Medical Group, Inc, pp. 345, 487, 553

Southern NH Regional Med Ctr, pp. 345, 454, 521

Southern Ocean County Hosp, pp. 345, 465, 534

Southern Ohio Medical Center, pp. 345, 442, 456, 509

Southern Pain Control Center, p. 915

Southern Regional Medical Ctr, pp. 345, 453, 512

Southside Community Hospital Assn, pp. 345, 482, 540

Southside Hospital Inc, pp. 345, 448, 509

Southside Virginia Training Ctr, pp. 345, 461, 512

Southstern Ohio Regional Med Ctr, pp. 345-346, 471, 531

Southwest Catholic Health Network, pp. 346, 440, 551

Southwest Community Health Systems, pp. 346, 445, 509

Southwest Fla Regional Med Ctr, pp. 346, 436, 512

Southwest General Health Ctr, pp. 346, 442, 509

Southwest Health Consultants, p. 915

Southwest Hospital, p. 561

Southwest Jefferson Community Hosp, pp. 346, 475, 546

Southwest LA Health Care Sys, pp. 346, 446, 514

Southwest Louisiana Hospital Assn, pp. 346, 445, 513

Southwest Medical Associates, pp. 346, 447, 537

Southwest Medical Center, pp. 346, 476, 539

Southwest Miss Regional Med Ctr, pp. 346, 457, 522

Southwest Washington Med Ctr, pp. 346, 437, 506

Southwestern Chapter, Society of Nuclear Medicine Exhibition, p. 992

Southwestern Ill Health Fcilities, pp. 346-347, 464, 534

Southwestern Ohio Seniors Svcs, pp. 346, 490, 545

Southwestern VT Medical Center, pp. 346, 468, 532

Southwick, Laura L., p. 915

SP Acquisition Corp, pp. 324, 464, 551

SPA, Inc., p. 915

Spanish ALS Association, p. 831

Spanish Association of Physicians in the Pharmaceutical Industries, p. 831

Spanish Royal Society of Physics, p. 831-832

Sparks Regional Medical Ctr, pp. 347, 442, 510

Spartanburg Cnty Health Svcs Dst, pp. 347, 432, 504

Spaulding Rhbltation Hospital Corp, pp. 347, 451, 519

Special Interest Group for Biomedical Computing, p. 954

Special Response Corp. Inc., p. 915

Specialized Healthcare Consultants, p. 915

Specialty Hospitals exc. Psychiatric (SIC 8069), pp. 3-4, 17-18, 44, 64

Specialty Outpatient Clinics, nec (SIC 8093), pp. 4, 19-20, 49, 69

Spectera Inc, pp. 347, 459, 545

Spectrum Consulting, p. 915

Spectrum Health - Dwntwn Campus, pp. 347, 431, 503

Spencer Municipal Hospital, pp. 347, 490, 541

SIC TO NAICS AND NAICS TO SIC CONVERSION GUIDE

This appendix presents complete conversion tables from SIC codes to NAICS codes. SIC stands for *Standard Industrial Classification*, the "old" system of classifying economic activities. NAICS stands for *North American Industry Classification System*, the new classification for classifying economic activities in the United States, Canada, and Mexico.

The first part of the appendix presents the SIC to NAICS Conversion Guide. Four-digit SIC codes and names are shown in bold type. NAICS codes and names are shown beneath, indented, each item labelled "NAICS". An SIC industry may convert to one or more NAICS industries.

The second part, starting on page 1107, shows the same information but in the reverse format: the NAICS to SIC Conversion Guide. NAICS codes and names are shown in bold type; the equivalent SIC codes, beneath, are shown indented. A NAICS-coded industry may have one, more than one, or no SIC equivalent (two instances).

SIC TO NAICS CONVERSION GUIDE

AGRICULTURE, FORESTRY, & FISHING

0111 Wheat
NAICS 11114 Wheat Farming
0112 Rice
NAICS 11116 Rice Farming
0115 Corn
NAICS 11115 Corn Farming
0116 Soybeans
NAICS 11111 Soybean Farming
0119 Cash Grains, nec
NAICS 11113 Dry Pea & Bean Farming
NAICS 11112 Oilseed Farming
NAICS 11115 Corn Farming
NAICS 111191 Oilseed & Grain Combination Farming
NAICS 111199 All Other Grain Farming
0131 Cotton
NAICS 11192 Cotton Farming
0132 Tobacco
NAICS 11191 Tobacco Farming
0133 Sugarcane & Sugar Beets
NAICS 111991 Sugar Beet Farming
NAICS 11193 Sugarcane Farming
0134 Irish Potatoes
NAICS 111211 Potato Farming
0139 Field Crops, Except Cash Grains, nec
NAICS 11194 Hay Farming
NAICS 111992 Peanut Farming
NAICS 111219 Other Vegetable & Melon Farming
NAICS 111998 All Other Miscellaneous Crop Farming
0161 Vegetables & Melons
NAICS 111219 Other Vegetable & Melon Farming
0171 Berry Crops
NAICS 111333 Strawberry Farming
NAICS 111334 Berry Farming
0172 Grapes
NAICS 111332 Grape Vineyards
0173 Tree Nuts
NAICS 111335 Tree Nut Farming
0174 Citrus Fruits
NAICS 11131 Orange Groves
NAICS 11132 Citrus Groves
0175 Deciduous Tree Fruits
NAICS 111331 Apple Orchards
NAICS 111339 Other Noncitrus Fruit Farming
0179 Fruits & Tree Nuts, nec
NAICS 111336 Fruit & Tree Nut Combination Farming
NAICS 111339 Other Noncitrus Fruit Farming
0181 Ornamental Floriculture & Nursery Products
NAICS 111422 Floriculture Production
NAICS 111421 Nursery & Tree Production
0182 Food Crops Grown under Cover
NAICS 111411 Mushroom Production
NAICS 111419 Other Food Crops Grown under Cover
0191 General Farms, Primarily Crop
NAICS 111998 All Other Miscellaneous Crop Farming
0211 Beef Cattle Feedlots
NAICS 112112 Cattle Feedlots
0212 Beef Cattle, Except Feedlots
NAICS 112111 Beef Cattle Ranching & Farming

0213 Hogs
NAICS 11221 Hog & Pig Farming
0214 Sheep & Goats
NAICS 11241 Sheep Farming
NAICS 11242 Goat Farming
0219 General Livestock, Except Dairy & Poultry
NAICS 11299 All Other Animal Production
0241 Dairy Farms
NAICS 112111 Beef Cattle Ranching & Farming
NAICS 11212 Dairy Cattle & Milk Production
0251 Broiler, Fryers, & Roaster Chickens
NAICS 11232 Broilers & Other Meat-type Chicken
                     Production
0252 Chicken Eggs
NAICS 11231 Chicken Egg Production
0253 Turkey & Turkey Eggs
NAICS 11233 Turkey Production
0254 Poultry Hatcheries
NAICS 11234 Poultry Hatcheries
0259 Poultry & Eggs, nec
NAICS 11239 Other Poultry Production
0271 Fur-bearing Animals & Rabbits
NAICS 11293 Fur-bearing Animal & Rabbit Production
0272 Horses & Other Equines
NAICS 11292 Horse & Other Equine Production
0273 Animal Aquaculture
NAICS 112511 Finfish Farming & Fish Hatcheries
NAICS 112512 Shellfish Farming
NAICS 112519 Other Animal Aquaculture
0279 Animal Specialities, nec
NAICS 11291 Apiculture
NAICS 11299 All Other Animal Production
0291 General Farms, Primarily Livestock & Animal Specialties
NAICS 11299 All Other Animal Production
0711 Soil Preparation Services
NAICS 115112 Soil Preparation, Planting & Cultivating
0721 Crop Planting, Cultivating & Protecting
NAICS 48122 Nonscheduled Speciality Air Transportation
NAICS 115112 Soil Preparation, Planting & Cultivating
0722 Crop Harvesting, Primarily by Machine
NAICS 115113 Crop Harvesting, Primarily by Machine
0723 Crop Preparation Services for Market, Except Cotton Ginning
NAICS 115114 Postharvest Crop Activities
0724 Cotton Ginning
NAICS 115111 Cotton Ginning
0741 Veterinary Service for Livestock
NAICS 54194 Veterinary Services
0742 Veterinary Services for Animal Specialties
NAICS 54194 Veterinary Services
0751 Livestock Services, Except Veterinary
NAICS 311611 Animal Slaughtering
NAICS 11521 Support Activities for Animal Production
0752 Animal Specialty Services, Except Veterinary
NAICS 11521 Support Activities for Animal Production
NAICS 81291 Pet Care Services
0761 Farm Labor Contractors & Crew Leaders
NAICS 115115 Farm Labor Contractors & Crew Leaders
0762 Farm Management Services
NAICS 115116 Farm Management Services
0781 Landscape Counseling & Planning
NAICS 54169 Other Scientific & Technical Consulting
                     Services
NAICS 54132 Landscape Architectural Services

0782 Lawn & Garden Services
NAICS 56173 Landscaping Services
0783 Ornamental Shrub & Tree Services
NAICS 56173 Landscaping Services
0811 Timber Tracts
NAICS 111421 Nursery & Tree Production
NAICS 11311 Timber Tract Operations
0831 Forest Nurseries & Gathering of Forest Products
NAICS 111998 All Other Miscellaneous Crop
NAICS 11321 Forest Nurseries & Gathering of Forest
Products
0851 Forestry Services
NAICS 11531 Support Activities for Forestry
0912 Finfish
NAICS 114111 Finfish Fishing
0913 Shellfish
NAICS 114112 Shellfish Fishing
0919 Miscellaneous Marine Products
NAICS 114119 Other Marine Fishing
NAICS 111998 All Other Miscellaneous Crop Farming
0921 Fish Hatcheries & Preserves
NAICS 112511 Finfish Farming & Fish Hatcheries
NAICS 112512 Shellfish Farming
0971 Hunting, Trapping, & Game Propagation
NAICS 11421 Hunting & Trapping

MINING INDUSTRIES

1011 Iron Ores
NAICS 21221 Iron Ore Mining
1021 Copper Ores
NAICS 212234 Copper Ore & Nickel Ore Mining
1031 Lead & Zinc Ores
NAICS 212231 Lead Ore & Zinc Ore Mining
1041 Gold Ores
NAICS 212221 Gold Ore Mining
1044 Silver Ores
NAICS 212222 Silver Ore Mining
1061 Ferroalloy Ores, Except Vanadium
NAICS 212234 Copper Ore & Nickel Ore Mining
NAICS 212299 Other Metal Ore Mining
1081 Metal Mining Services
NAICS 213115 Support Activities for Metal Mining
NAICS 54136 Geophysical Surveying & Mapping Services
1094 Uranium-radium-vanadium Ores
NAICS 212291 Uranium-radium-vanadium Ore Mining
1099 Miscellaneous Metal Ores, nec
NAICS 212299 Other Metal Ore Mining
1221 Bituminous Coal & Lignite Surface Mining
NAICS 212111 Bituminous Coal & Lignite Surface Mining
1222 Bituminous Coal Underground Mining
NAICS 212112 Bituminous Coal Underground Mining
1231 Anthracite Mining
NAICS 212113 Anthracite Mining
1241 Coal Mining Services
NAICS 213114 Support Activities for Coal Mining
1311 Crude Petroleum & Natural Gas
NAICS 211111 Crude Petroleum & Natural Gas Extraction
1321 Natural Gas Liquids
NAICS 211112 Natural Gas Liquid Extraction
1381 Drilling Oil & Gas Wells
NAICS 213111 Drilling Oil & Gas Wells

1382 Oil & Gas Field Exploration Services
NAICS 48122 Nonscheduled Speciality Air Transportation
NAICS 54136 Geophysical Surveying & Mapping Services
NAICS 213112 Support Activities for Oil & Gas Field
Operations
1389 Oil & Gas Field Services, nec
NAICS 213113 Other Oil & Gas Field Support Activities
1411 Dimension Stone
NAICS 212311 Dimension Stone Mining & Quarry
1422 Crushed & Broken Limestone
NAICS 212312 Crushed & Broken Limestone Mining &
Quarrying
1423 Crushed & Broken Granite
NAICS 212313 Crushed & Broken Granite Mining &
Quarrying
1429 Crushed & Broken Stone, nec
NAICS 212319 Other Crushed & Broken Stone Mining &
Quarrying
1442 Construction Sand & Gravel
NAICS 212321 Construction Sand & Gravel Mining
1446 Industrial Sand
NAICS 212322 Industrial Sand Mining
1455 Kaolin & Ball Clay
NAICS 212324 Kaolin & Ball Clay Mining
1459 Clay, Ceramic, & Refractory Minerals, nec
NAICS 212325 Clay & Ceramic & Refractory Minerals Mining
1474 Potash, Soda, & Borate Minerals
NAICS 212391 Potash, Soda, & Borate Mineral Mining
1475 Phosphate Rock
NAICS 212392 Phosphate Rock Mining
1479 Chemical & Fertilizer Mineral Mining, nec
NAICS 212393 Other Chemical & Fertilizer Mineral Mining
1481 Nonmetallic Minerals Services Except Fuels
NAICS 213116 Support Activities for Non-metallic Minerals
NAICS 54136 Geophysical Surveying & Mapping Services
1499 Miscellaneous Nonmetallic Minerals, Except Fuels
NAICS 212319 Other Crushed & Broken Stone Mining or
Quarrying
NAICS 212399 All Other Non-metallic Mineral Mining

CONSTRUCTION INDUSTRIES

1521 General Contractors-single-family Houses
NAICS 23321 Single Family Housing Construction
**1522 General Contractors-residential Buildings, Other than
Single-family**
NAICS 23332 Commercial & Institutional Building
Construction
NAICS 23322 Multifamily Housing Construction
1531 Operative Builders
NAICS 23321 Single Family Housing Construction
NAICS 23322 Multifamily Housing Construction
NAICS 23331 Manufacturing & Industrial Building
Construction
NAICS 23332 Commercial & Institutional Building
Construction
1541 General Contractors-industrial Buildings & Warehouses
NAICS 23332 Commercial & Institutional Building
Construction
NAICS 23331 Manufacturing & Industrial Building
Construction

1542 General Contractors-nonresidential Buildings, Other than Industrial Buildings & Warehouses
NAICS 23332 Commercial & Institutional Building Construction
1611 Highway & Street Construction, Except Elevated Highways
NAICS 23411 Highway & Street Construction
1622 Bridge, Tunnel, & Elevated Highway Construction
NAICS 23412 Bridge & Tunnel Construction
1623 Water, Sewer, Pipeline, & Communications & Power Line Construction
NAICS 23491 Water, Sewer & Pipeline Construction
NAICS 23492 Power & Communication Transmission Line Construction
1629 Heavy Construction, nec
NAICS 23493 Industrial Nonbuilding Structure Construction
NAICS 23499 All Other Heavy Construction
1711 Plumbing, Heating, & Air-conditioning
NAICS 23511 Plumbing, Heating & Air-conditioning Contractors
1721 Painting & Paper Hanging
NAICS 23521 Painting & Wall Covering Contractors
1731 Electrical Work
NAICS 561621 Security Systems Services
NAICS 23531 Electrical Contractors
1741 Masonry, Stone Setting & Other Stone Work
NAICS 23541 Masonry & Stone Contractors
1742 Plastering, Drywall, Acoustical & Insulation Work
NAICS 23542 Drywall, Plastering, Acoustical & Insulation Contractors
1743 Terrazzo, Tile, Marble, & Mosaic Work
NAICS 23542 Drywall, Plastering, Acoustical & Insulation Contractors
NAICS 23543 Tile, Marble, Terrazzo & Mosaic Contractors
1751 Carpentry Work
NAICS 23551 Carpentry Contractors
1752 Floor Laying & Other Floor Work, nec
NAICS 23552 Floor Laying & Other Floor Contractors
1761 Roofing, Siding, & Sheet Metal Work
NAICS 23561 Roofing, Siding, & Sheet Metal Contractors
1771 Concrete Work
NAICS 23542 Drywall, Plastering, Acoustical & Insulation Contractors
NAICS 23571 Concrete Contractors
1781 Water Well Drilling
NAICS 23581 Water Well Drilling Contractors
1791 Structural Steel Erection
NAICS 23591 Structural Steel Erection Contractors
1793 Glass & Glazing Work
NAICS 23592 Glass & Glazing Contractors
1794 Excavation Work
NAICS 23593 Excavation Contractors
1795 Wrecking & Demolition Work
NAICS 23594 Wrecking & Demolition Contractors
1796 Installation or Erection of Building Equipment, nec
NAICS 23595 Building Equipment & Other Machinery Installation Contractors
1799 Special Trade Contractors, nec
NAICS 23521 Painting & Wall Covering Contractors
NAICS 23592 Glass & Glazing Contractors
NAICS 56291 Remediation Services
NAICS 23599 All Other Special Trade Contractors

FOOD & KINDRED PRODUCTS

2011 Meat Packing Plants
NAICS 311611 Animal Slaughtering
2013 Sausages & Other Prepared Meats
NAICS 311612 Meat Processed from Carcasses
2015 Poultry Slaughtering & Processing
NAICS 311615 Poultry Processing
NAICS 311999 All Other Miscellaneous Food Manufacturing
2021 Creamery Butter
NAICS 311512 Creamery Butter Manufacturing
2022 Natural, Processed, & Imitation Cheese
NAICS 311513 Cheese Manufacturing
2023 Dry, Condensed, & Evaporated Dairy Products
NAICS 311514 Dry, Condensed, & Evaporated Milk Manufacturing
2024 Ice Cream & Frozen Desserts
NAICS 31152 Ice Cream & Frozen Dessert Manufacturing
2026 Fluid Milk
NAICS 311511 Fluid Milk Manufacturing
2032 Canned Specialties
NAICS 311422 Specialty Canning
NAICS 311999 All Other Miscellaneous Food Manufacturing
2033 Canned Fruits, Vegetables, Preserves, Jams, & Jellies
NAICS 311421 Fruit & Vegetable Canning
2034 Dried & Dehydrated Fruits, Vegetables, & Soup Mixes
NAICS 311423 Dried & Dehydrated Food Manufacturing
NAICS 311211 Flour Milling
2035 Pickled Fruits & Vegetables, Vegetables Sauces & Seasonings, & Salad Dressings
NAICS 311421 Fruit & Vegetable Canning
NAICS 311941 Mayonnaise, Dressing, & Other Prepared Sauce Manufacturing
2037 Frozen Fruits, Fruit Juices, & Vegetables
NAICS 311411 Frozen Fruit, Juice, & Vegetable Processing
2038 Frozen Specialties, nec
NAICS 311412 Frozen Specialty Food Manufacturing
2041 Flour & Other Grain Mill Products
NAICS 311211 Flour Milling
2043 Cereal Breakfast Foods
NAICS 31192 Coffee & Tea Manufacturing
NAICS 31123 Breakfast Cereal Manufacturing
2044 Rice Milling
NAICS 311212 Rice Milling
2045 Prepared Flour Mixes & Doughs
NAICS 311822 Flour Mixes & Dough Manufacturing from Purchased Flour
2046 Wet Corn Milling
NAICS 311221 Wet Corn Milling
2047 Dog & Cat Food
NAICS 311111 Dog & Cat Food Manufacturing
2048 Prepared Feed & Feed Ingredients for Animals & Fowls, Except Dogs & Cats
NAICS 311611 Animal Slaughtering
NAICS 311119 Other Animal Food Manufacturing
2051 Bread & Other Bakery Products, Except Cookies & Crackers
NAICS 311812 Commercial Bakeries
2052 Cookies & Crackers
NAICS 311821 Cookie & Cracker Manufacturing
NAICS 311919 Other Snack Food Manufacturing
NAICS 311812 Commercial Bakeries

2053 Frozen Bakery Products, Except Bread
NAICS 311813 Frozen Bakery Product Manufacturing
2061 Cane Sugar, Except Refining
NAICS 311311 Sugarcane Mills
2062 Cane Sugar Refining
NAICS 311312 Cane Sugar Refining
2063 Beet Sugar
NAICS 311313 Beet Sugar Manufacturing
2064 Candy & Other Confectionery Products
NAICS 31133   Confectionery Manufacturing from Purchased
            Chocolate
NAICS 31134   Non-chocolate Confectionery Manufacturing
2066 Chocolate & Cocoa Products
NAICS 31132   Chocolate & Confectionery Manufacturing from
            Cacao Beans
2067 Chewing Gum
NAICS 31134   Non-chocolate Confectionery Manufacturing
2068 Salted & Roasted Nuts & Seeds
NAICS 311911 Roasted Nuts & Peanut Butter Manufacturing
2074 Cottonseed Oil Mills
NAICS 311223 Other Oilseed Processing
NAICS 311225 Fats & Oils Refining & Blending
2075 Soybean Oil Mills
NAICS 311222 Soybean Processing
NAICS 311225 Fats & Oils Refining & Blending
2076 Vegetable Oil Mills, Except Corn, Cottonseed, & Soybeans
NAICS 311223 Other Oilseed Processing
NAICS 311225 Fats & Oils Refining & Blending
2077 Animal & Marine Fats & Oils
NAICS 311613 Rendering & Meat By-product Processing
NAICS 311711 Seafood Canning
NAICS 311712 Fresh & Frozen Seafood Processing
NAICS 311225 Edible Fats & Oils Manufacturing
2079 Shortening, Table Oils, Margarine, & Other Edible Fats &
    Oils, nec
NAICS 311225 Edible Fats & Oils Manufacturing
NAICS 311222 Soybean Processing
NAICS 311223 Other Oilseed Processing
2082 Malt Beverages
NAICS 31212   Breweries
2083 Malt
NAICS 311213 Malt Manufacturing
2084 Wines, Brandy, & Brandy Spirits
NAICS 31213   Wineries
2085 Distilled & Blended Liquors
NAICS 31214   Distilleries
2086 Bottled & Canned Soft Drinks & Carbonated Waters
NAICS 312111 Soft Drink Manufacturing
NAICS 312112 Bottled Water Manufacturing
2087 Flavoring Extracts & Flavoring Syrups nec
NAICS 31193   Flavoring Syrup & Concentrate Manufacturing
NAICS 311942 Spice & Extract Manufacturing
NAICS 311999 All Other Miscellaneous Food Manufacturing
2091 Canned & Cured Fish & Seafood
NAICS 311711 Seafood Canning
2092 Prepared Fresh or Frozen Fish & Seafoods
NAICS 311712 Fresh & Frozen Seafood Processing
2095 Roasted Coffee
NAICS 31192   Coffee & Tea Manufacturing
NAICS 311942 Spice & Extract Manufacturing
2096 Potato Chips, Corn Chips, & Similar Snacks
NAICS 311919 Other Snack Food Manufacturing

2097 Manufactured Ice
NAICS 312113 Ice Manufacturing
2098 Macaroni, Spaghetti, Vermicelli, & Noodles
NAICS 311823 Pasta Manufacturing
2099 Food Preparations, nec
NAICS 311423 Dried & Dehydrated Food Manufacturing
NAICS 111998 All Other Miscellaneous Crop Farming
NAICS 31134   Non-chocolate Confectionery Manufacturing
NAICS 311911 Roasted Nuts & Peanut Butter Manufacturing
NAICS 311991 Perishable Prepared Food Manufacturing
NAICS 31183   Tortilla Manufacturing
NAICS 31192   Coffee & Tea Manufacturing
NAICS 311941 Mayonnaise, Dressing, & Other Prepared Sauce
            Manufacturing
NAICS 311942 Spice & Extract Manufacturing
NAICS 311999 All Other Miscellaneous Food Manufacturing

TOBACCO PRODUCTS

2111 Cigarettes
NAICS 312221 Cigarette Manufacturing
2121 Cigars
NAICS 312229 Other Tobacco Product Manufacturing
2131 Chewing & Smoking Tobacco & Snuff
NAICS 312229 Other Tobacco Product Manufacturing
2141 Tobacco Stemming & Redrying
NAICS 312229 Other Tobacco Product Manufacturing
NAICS 31221   Tobacco Stemming & Redrying

TEXTILE MILL PRODUCTS

2211 Broadwoven Fabric Mills, Cotton
NAICS 31321   Broadwoven Fabric Mills
2221 Broadwoven Fabric Mills, Manmade Fiber & Silk
NAICS 31321   Broadwoven Fabric Mills
2231 Broadwoven Fabric Mills, Wool
NAICS 31321   Broadwoven Fabric Mills
NAICS 313311 Broadwoven Fabric Finishing Mills
NAICS 313312 Textile & Fabric Finishing Mills
2241 Narrow Fabric & Other Smallware Mills: Cotton, Wool,
    Silk, & Manmade Fiber
NAICS 313221 Narrow Fabric Mills
2251 Women's Full-length & Knee-length Hosiery, Except Socks
NAICS 315111 Sheer Hosiery Mills
2252 Hosiery, nec
NAICS 315111 Sheer Hosiery Mills
NAICS 315119 Other Hosiery & Sock Mills
2253 Knit Outerwear Mills
NAICS 315191 Outerwear Knitting Mills
2254 Knit Underwear & Nightwear Mills
NAICS 315192 Underwear & Nightwear Knitting Mills
2257 Weft Knit Fabric Mills
NAICS 313241 Weft Knit Fabric Mills
NAICS 313312 Textile & Fabric Finishing Mills
2258 Lace & Warp Knit Fabric Mills
NAICS 313249 Other Knit Fabric & Lace Mills
NAICS 313312 Textile & Fabric Finishing Mills
2259 Knitting Mills, nec
NAICS 315191 Outerwear Knitting Mills
NAICS 315192 Underwear & Nightwear Knitting Mills
NAICS 313241 Weft Knit Fabric Mills
NAICS 313249 Other Knit Fabric & Lace Mills

2261 Finishers of Broadwoven Fabrics of Cotton
NAICS 313311 Broadwoven Fabric Finishing Mills
2262 Finishers of Broadwoven Fabrics of Manmade Fiber & Silk
NAICS 313311 Broadwoven Fabric Finishing Mills
2269 Finishers of Textiles, nec
NAICS 313311 Broadwoven Fabric Finishing Mills
NAICS 313312 Textile & Fabric Finishing Mills
2273 Carpets & Rugs
NAICS 31411 Carpet & Rug Mills
2281 Yarn Spinning Mills
NAICS 313111 Yarn Spinning Mills
2282 Yarn Texturizing, Throwing, Twisting, & Winding Mills
NAICS 313112 Yarn Texturing, Throwing & Twisting Mills
NAICS 313312 Textile & Fabric Finishing Mills
2284 Thread Mills
NAICS 313113 Thread Mills
NAICS 313312 Textile & Fabric Finishing Mills
2295 Coated Fabrics, Not Rubberized
NAICS 31332 Fabric Coating Mills
2296 Tire Cord & Fabrics
NAICS 314992 Tire Cord & Tire Fabric Mills
2297 Nonwoven Fabrics
NAICS 31323 Nonwoven Fabric Mills
2298 Cordage & Twine
NAICS 314991 Rope, Cordage & Twine Mills
2299 Textile Goods, nec
NAICS 31321 Broadwoven Fabric Mills
NAICS 31323 Nonwoven Fabric Mills
NAICS 313312 Textile & Fabric Finishing Mills
NAICS 313221 Narrow Fabric Mills
NAICS 313113 Thread Mills
NAICS 313111 Yarn Spinning Mills
NAICS 314999 All Other Miscellaneous Textile Product Mills

APPAREL & OTHER FINISHED PRODUCTS MADE FROM FABRICS & SIMILAR MATERIALS

2311 Men's & Boys' Suits, Coats & Overcoats
NAICS 315211 Men's & Boys' Cut & Sew Apparel Contractors
NAICS 315222 Men's & Boys' Cut & Sew Suit, Coat, & Overcoat Manufacturing
2321 Men's & Boys' Shirts, Except Work Shirts
NAICS 315211 Men's & Boys' Cut & Sew Apparel Contractors
NAICS 315223 Men's & Boys' Cut & Sew Shirt, Manufacturing
2322 Men's & Boys' Underwear & Nightwear
NAICS 315211 Men's & Boys' Cut & Sew Apparel Contractors
NAICS 315221 Men's & Boys' Cut & Sew Underwear & Nightwear Manufacturing
2323 Men's & Boys' Neckwear
NAICS 315993 Men's & Boys' Neckwear Manufacturing
2325 Men's & Boys' Trousers & Slacks
NAICS 315211 Men's & Boys' Cut & Sew Apparel Contractors
NAICS 315224 Men's & Boys' Cut & Sew Trouser, Slack, & Jean Manufacturing
2326 Men's & Boys' Work Clothing
NAICS 315211 Men's & Boys' Cut & Sew Apparel Contractors
NAICS 315225 Men's & Boys' Cut & Sew Work Clothing Manufacturing
2329 Men's & Boys' Clothing, nec
NAICS 315211 Men's & Boys' Cut & Sew Apparel Contractors

NAICS 315228 Men's & Boys' Cut & Sew Other Outerwear Manufacturing
NAICS 315299 All Other Cut & Sew Apparel Manufacturing
2331 Women's, Misses', & Juniors' Blouses & Shirts
NAICS 315212 Women's & Girls' Cut & Sew Apparel Contractors
NAICS 315232 Women's & Girls' Cut & Sew Blouse & Shirt Manufacturing
2335 Women's, Misses' & Junior's Dresses
NAICS 315212 Women's & Girls' Cut & Sew Apparel Contractors
NAICS 315233 Women's & Girls' Cut & Sew Dress Manufacturing
2337 Women's, Misses' & Juniors' Suits, Skirts & Coats
NAICS 315212 Women's & Girls' Cut & Sew Apparel Contractors
NAICS 315234 Women's & Girls' Cut & Sew Suit, Coat, Tailored Jacket, & Skirt Manufacturing
2339 Women's, Misses' & Juniors' Outerwear, nec
NAICS 315999 Other Apparel Accessories & Other Apparel Manufacturing
NAICS 315212 Women's & Girls' Cut & Sew Apparel Contractors
NAICS 315299 All Other Cut & Sew Apparel Manufacturing
NAICS 315238 Women's & Girls' Cut & Sew Other Outerwear Manufacturing
2341 Women's, Misses, Children's, & Infants' Underwear & Nightwear
NAICS 315212 Women's & Girls' Cut & Sew Apparel Contractors
NAICS 315211 Men's & Boys' Cut & Sew Apparel Contractors
NAICS 315231 Women's & Girls' Cut & Sew Lingerie, Loungewear, & Nightwear Manufacturing
NAICS 315221 Men's & Boys' Cut & Sew Underwear & Nightwear Manufacturing
NAICS 315291 Infants' Cut & Sew Apparel Manufacturing
2342 Brassieres, Girdles, & Allied Garments
NAICS 315212 Women's & Girls' Cut & Sew Apparel Contractors
NAICS 315231 Women's & Girls' Cut & Sew Lingerie, Loungewear, & Nightwear Manufacturing
2353 Hats, Caps, & Millinery
NAICS 315991 Hat, Cap, & Millinery Manufacturing
2361 Girls', Children's & Infants' Dresses, Blouses & Shirts
NAICS 315291 Infants' Cut & Sew Apparel Manufacturing
NAICS 315223 Men's & Boys' Cut & Sew Shirt, Manufacturing
NAICS 315211 Men's & Boys' Cut & Sew Apparel Contractors
NAICS 315232 Women's & Girls' Cut & Sew Blouse & Shirt Manufacturing
NAICS 315233 Women's & Girls' Cut & Sew Dress Manufacturing
NAICS 315212 Women's & Girls' Cut & Sew Apparel Contractors
2369 Girls', Children's & Infants' Outerwear, nec
NAICS 315291 Infants' Cut & Sew Apparel Manufacturing
NAICS 315222 Men's & Boys' Cut & Sew Suit, Coat, & Overcoat Manufacturing
NAICS 315224 Men's & Boys' Cut & Sew Trouser, Slack, & Jean Manufacturing
NAICS 315228 Men's & Boys' Cut & Sew Other Outerwear Manufacturing
NAICS 315221 Men's & Boys' Cut & Sew Underwear & Nightwear Manufacturing
NAICS 315211 Men's & Boys' Cut & Sew Apparel Contractors

NAICS 315234 Women's & Girls' Cut & Sew Suit, Coat, Tailored Jacket, & Skirt Manufacturing

NAICS 315238 Women's & Girls' Cut & Sew Other Outerwear Manufacturing

NAICS 315231 Women's & Girls' Cut & Sew Lingerie, Loungewear, & Nightwear Manufacturing

NAICS 315212 Women's & Girls' Cut & Sew Apparel Contractors

2371 Fur Goods
NAICS 315292 Fur & Leather Apparel Manufacturing

2381 Dress & Work Gloves, Except Knit & All-leather
NAICS 315992 Glove & Mitten Manufacturing

2384 Robes & Dressing Gowns
NAICS 315231 Women's & Girls' Cut & Sew Lingerie, Loungewear, & Nightwear Manufacturing

NAICS 315221 Men's & Boys' Cut & Sew Underwear & Nightwear Manufacturing

NAICS 315211 Men's & Boys' Cut & Sew Apparel Contractors

NAICS 315212 Women's & Girls' Cut & Sew Apparel Contractors

2385 Waterproof Outerwear
NAICS 315222 Men's & Boys' Cut & Sew Suit, Coat, & Overcoat Manufacturing

NAICS 315234 Women's & Girls' Cut & Sew Suit, Coat, Tailored Jacket, & Skirt Manufacturing

NAICS 315228 Men's & Boys' Cut & Sew Other Outerwear Manufacturing

NAICS 315238 Women's & Girls' Cut & Sew Other Outerwear Manufacturing

NAICS 315291 Infants' Cut & Sew Apparel Manufacturing

NAICS 315999 Other Apparel Accessories & Other Apparel Manufacturing

NAICS 315211 Men's & Boys' Cut & Sew Apparel Contractors

NAICS 315212 Women's & Girls' Cut & Sew Apparel Contractors

2386 Leather & Sheep-lined Clothing
NAICS 315292 Fur & Leather Apparel Manufacturing

2387 Apparel Belts
NAICS 315999 Other Apparel Accessories & Other Apparel Manufacturing

2389 Apparel & Accessories, nec
NAICS 315999 Other Apparel Accessories & Other Apparel Manufacturing

NAICS 315299 All Other Cut & Sew Apparel Manufacturing

NAICS 315231 Women's & Girls' Cut & Sew Lingerie, Loungewear, & Nightwear Manufacturing

NAICS 315212 Women's & Girls' Cut & Sew Apparel Contractors

NAICS 315211 Mens' & Boys' Cut & Sew Apparel Contractors

2391 Curtains & Draperies
NAICS 314121 Curtain & Drapery Mills

2392 Housefurnishings, Except Curtains & Draperies
NAICS 314911 Textile Bag Mills

NAICS 339994 Broom, Brush & Mop Manufacturing

NAICS 314129 Other Household Textile Product Mills

2393 Textile Bags
NAICS 314911 Textile Bag Mills

2394 Canvas & Related Products
NAICS 314912 Canvas & Related Product Mills

2395 Pleating, Decorative & Novelty Stitching, & Tucking for the Trade
NAICS 314999 All Other Miscellaneous Textile Product Mills

NAICS 315211 Mens' & Boys' Cut & Sew Apparel Contractors

NAICS 315212 Women's & Girls' Cut & Sew Apparel Contractors

2396 Automotive Trimmings, Apparel Findings, & Related Products
NAICS 33636 Motor Vehicle Fabric Accessories & Seat Manufacturing

NAICS 315999 Other Apparel Accessories, & Other Apparel Manufacturing

NAICS 323113 Commercial Screen Printing

NAICS 314999 All Other Miscellaneous Textile Product Mills

2397 Schiffli Machine Embroideries
NAICS 313222 Schiffli Machine Embroidery

2399 Fabricated Textile Products, nec
NAICS 33636 Motor Vehicle Fabric Accessories & Seat Manufacturing

NAICS 315999 Other Apparel Accessories & Other Apparel Manufacturing

NAICS 314999 All Other Miscellaneous Textile Product Mills

LUMBER & WOOD PRODUCTS, EXCEPT FURNITURE

2411 Logging
NAICS 11331 Logging

2421 Sawmills & Planing Mills, General
NAICS 321913 Softwood Cut Stock, Resawing Lumber, & Planing

NAICS 321113 Sawmills

NAICS 321914 Other Millwork

NAICS 321999 All Other Miscellaneous Wood Product Manufacturing

2426 Hardwood Dimension & Flooring Mills
NAICS 321914 Other Millwork

NAICS 321999 All Other Miscellaneous Wood Product Manufacturing

NAICS 337139 Other Wood Furniture Manufacturing

NAICS 321912 Hardwood Dimension Mills

2429 Special Product Sawmills, nec
NAICS 321113 Sawmills

NAICS 321913 Softwood Cut Stock, Resawing Lumber, & Planing

NAICS 321999 All Other Miscellaneous Wood Product Manufacturing

2431 Millwork
NAICS 321911 Wood Window & Door Manufacturing

NAICS 321914 Other Millwork

2434 Wood Kitchen Cabinets
NAICS 337131 Wood Kitchen Cabinet & Counter Top Manufacturing

2435 Hardwood Veneer & Plywood
NAICS 321211 Hardwood Veneer & Plywood Manufacturing

2436 Softwood Veneer & Plywood
NAICS 321212 Softwood Veneer & Plywood Manufacturing

2439 Structural Wood Members, nec
NAICS 321913 Softwood Cut Stock, Resawing Lumber, & Planing

NAICS 321214 Truss Manufacturing

NAICS 321213 Engineered Wood Member Manufacturing

2441 Nailed & Lock Corner Wood Boxes & Shook
NAICS 32192 Wood Container & Pallet Manufacturing

2448 Wood Pallets & Skids
NAICS 32192 Wood Container & Pallet Manufacturing

2449 Wood Containers, nec
NAICS 32192 Wood Container & Pallet Manufacturing
2451 Mobile Homes
NAICS 321991 Manufactured Home Manufacturing
2452 Prefabricated Wood Buildings & Components
NAICS 321992 Prefabricated Wood Building Manufacturing
2491 Wood Preserving
NAICS 321114 Wood Preservation
2493 Reconstituted Wood Products
NAICS 321219 Reconstituted Wood Product Manufacturing
2499 Wood Products, nec
NAICS 339999 All Other Miscellaneous Manufacturing
NAICS 337139 Other Wood Furniture Manufacturing
NAICS 337148 Other Nonwood Furniture Manufacturing
NAICS 32192 Wood Container & Pallet Manufacturing
NAICS 321999 All Other Miscellaneous Wood Product
   Manufacturing

FURNITURE & FIXTURES

2511 Wood Household Furniture, Except Upholstered
NAICS 337122 Wood Household Furniture Manufacturing
2512 Wood Household Furniture, Upholstered
NAICS 337121 Upholstered Household Furniture
   Manufacturing
2514 Metal Household Furniture
NAICS 337124 Metal Household Furniture Manufacturing
2515 Mattresses, Foundations, & Convertible Beds
NAICS 33791 Mattress Manufacturing
NAICS 337132 Upholstered Wood Household Furniture
   Manufacturing
**2517 Wood Television, Radio, Phonograph & Sewing Machine
   Cabinets**
NAICS 337139 Other Wood Furniture Manufacturing
2519 Household Furniture, nec
NAICS 337143 Household Furniture (except Wood & Metal)
   Manufacturing
2521 Wood Office Furniture
NAICS 337134 Wood Office Furniture Manufacturing
2522 Office Furniture, Except Wood
NAICS 337141 Nonwood Office Furniture Manufacturing
2531 Public Building & Related Furniture
NAICS 33636 Motor Vehicle Fabric Accessories & Seat
   Manufacturing
NAICS 337139 Other Wood Furniture Manufacturing
NAICS 337148 Other Nonwood Furniture Manufacturing
NAICS 339942 Lead Pencil & Art Good Manufacturing
**2541 Wood Office & Store Fixtures, Partitions, Shelving, &
   Lockers**
NAICS 337131 Wood Kitchen Cabinet & Counter Top
   Manufacturing
NAICS 337135 Custom Architectural Woodwork, Millwork, &
   Fixtures
NAICS 337139 Other Wood Furniture Manufacturing
**2542 Office & Store Fixtures, Partitions Shelving, & Lockers,
   Except Wood**
NAICS 337145 Nonwood Showcase, Partition, Shelving, &
   Locker Manufacturing
2591 Drapery Hardware & Window Blinds & Shades
NAICS 33792 Blind & Shade Manufacturing
2599 Furniture & Fixtures, nec
NAICS 339113 Surgical Appliance & Supplies Manufacturing
NAICS 337139 Other Wood Furniture Manufacturing

NAICS 337148 Other Nonwood Furniture Manufacturing

PAPER & ALLIED PRODUCTS

2611 Pulp Mills
NAICS 32211 Pulp Mills
NAICS 322121 Paper Mills
NAICS 32213 Paperboard Mills
2621 Paper Mills
NAICS 322121 Paper Mills
NAICS 322122 Newsprint Mills
2631 Paperboard Mills
NAICS 32213 Paperboard Mills
2652 Setup Paperboard Boxes
NAICS 322213 Setup Paperboard Box Manufacturing
2653 Corrugated & Solid Fiber Boxes
NAICS 322211 Corrugated & Solid Fiber Box Manufacturing
2655 Fiber Cans, Tubes, Drums, & Similar Products
NAICS 322214 Fiber Can, Tube, Drum, & Similar Products
   Manufacturing
2656 Sanitary Food Containers, Except Folding
NAICS 322215 Non-folding Sanitary Food Container
   Manufacturing
2657 Folding Paperboard Boxes, Including Sanitary
NAICS 322212 Folding Paperboard Box Manufacturing
2671 Packaging Paper & Plastics Film, Coated & Laminated
NAICS 322221 Coated & Laminated Packaging Paper &
   Plastics Film Manufacturing
NAICS 326112 Unsupported Plastics Packaging Film & Sheet
   Manufacturing
2672 Coated & Laminated Paper, nec
NAICS 322222 Coated & Laminated Paper Manufacturing
2673 Plastics, Foil, & Coated Paper Bags
NAICS 322223 Plastics, Foil, & Coated Paper Bag
   Manufacturing
NAICS 326111 Unsupported Plastics Bag Manufacturing
2674 Uncoated Paper & Multiwall Bags
NAICS 322224 Uncoated Paper & Multiwall Bag
   Manufacturing
2675 Die-cut Paper & Paperboard & Cardboard
NAICS 322231 Die-cut Paper & Paperboard Office Supplies
   Manufacturing
NAICS 322292 Surface-coated Paperboard Manufacturing
NAICS 322298 All Other Converted Paper Product
   Manufacturing
2676 Sanitary Paper Products
NAICS 322291 Sanitary Paper Product Manufacturing
2677 Envelopes
NAICS 322232 Envelope Manufacturing
2678 Stationery, Tablets, & Related Products
NAICS 322233 Stationery, Tablet, & Related Product
   Manufacturing
2679 Converted Paper & Paperboard Products, nec
NAICS 322215 Non-folding Sanitary Food Container
   Manufacturing
NAICS 322222 Coated & Laminated Paper Manufacturing
NAICS 322231 Die-cut Paper & Paperboard Office Supplies
   Manufacturing
NAICS 322298 All Other Converted Paper Product
   Manufacturing

PRINTING, PUBLISHING, & ALLIED INDUSTRIES

2711 Newspapers: Publishing, or Publishing & Printing
NAICS 51111 Newspaper Publishers
2721 Periodicals: Publishing, or Publishing & Printing
NAICS 51112 Periodical Publishers
2731 Books: Publishing, or Publishing & Printing
NAICS 51223 Music Publishers
NAICS 51113 Book Publishers
2732 Book Printing
NAICS 323117 Book Printing
2741 Miscellaneous Publishing
NAICS 51114 Database & Directory Publishers
NAICS 51223 Music Publishers
NAICS 511199 All Other Publishers
2752 Commercial Printing, Lithographic
NAICS 323114 Quick Printing
NAICS 323110 Commercial Lithographic Printing
2754 Commercial Printing, Gravure
NAICS 323111 Commercial Gravure Printing
2759 Commercial Printing, nec
NAICS 323113 Commercial Screen Printing
NAICS 323112 Commercial Flexographic Printing
NAICS 323114 Quick Printing
NAICS 323115 Digital Printing
NAICS 323119 Other Commercial Printing
2761 Manifold Business Forms
NAICS 323116 Manifold Business Form Printing
2771 Greeting Cards
NAICS 323110 Commercial Lithographic Printing
NAICS 323111 Commercial Gravure Printing
NAICS 323112 Commercial Flexographic Printing
NAICS 323113 Commercial Screen Printing
NAICS 323119 Other Commercial Printing
NAICS 511191 Greeting Card Publishers
2782 Blankbooks, Loose-leaf Binders & Devices
NAICS 323110 Commercial Lithographic Printing
NAICS 323111 Commercial Gravure Printing
NAICS 323112 Commercial Flexographic Printing
NAICS 323113 Commercial Screen Printing
NAICS 323119 Other Commercial Printing
NAICS 323118 Blankbook, Loose-leaf Binder & Device
        Manufacturing
2789 Bookbinding & Related Work
NAICS 323121 Tradebinding & Related Work
2791 Typesetting
NAICS 323122 Prepress Services
2796 Platemaking & Related Services
NAICS 323122 Prepress Services

CHEMICALS & ALLIED PRODUCTS

2812 Alkalies & Chlorine
NAICS 325181 Alkalies & Chlorine Manufacturing
2813 Industrial Gases
NAICS 32512 Industrial Gas Manufacturing
2816 Inorganic Pigments
NAICS 325131 Inorganic Dye & Pigment Manufacturing
NAICS 325182 Carbon Black Manufacturing
2819 Industrial Inorganic Chemicals, nec
NAICS 325998 All Other Miscellaneous Chemical Product
        Manufacturing

NAICS 331311 Alumina Refining
NAICS 325131 Inorganic Dye & Pigment Manufacturing
NAICS 325188 All Other Basic Inorganic Chemical
        Manufacturing
2821 Plastics Material Synthetic Resins, & Nonvulcanizable Elastomers
NAICS 325211 Plastics Material & Resin Manufacturing
2822 Synthetic Rubber
NAICS 325212 Synthetic Rubber Manufacturing
2823 Cellulosic Manmade Fibers
NAICS 325221 Cellulosic Manmade Fiber Manufacturing
2824 Manmade Organic Fibers, Except Cellulosic
NAICS 325222 Noncellulosic Organic Fiber Manufacturing
2833 Medicinal Chemicals & Botanical Products
NAICS 325411 Medicinal & Botanical Manufacturing
2834 Pharmaceutical Preparations
NAICS 325412 Pharmaceutical Preparation Manufacturing
2835 In Vitro & in Vivo Diagnostic Substances
NAICS 325412 Pharmaceutical Preparation Manufacturing
NAICS 325413 In-vitro Diagnostic Substance Manufacturing
2836 Biological Products, Except Diagnostic Substances
NAICS 325414 Biological Product Manufacturing
2841 Soaps & Other Detergents, Except Speciality Cleaners
NAICS 325611 Soap & Other Detergent Manufacturing
2842 Speciality Cleaning, Polishing, & Sanitary Preparations
NAICS 325612 Polish & Other Sanitation Good Manufacturing
2843 Surface Active Agents, Finishing Agents, Sulfonated Oils, & Assistants
NAICS 325613 Surface Active Agent Manufacturing
2844 Perfumes, Cosmetics, & Other Toilet Preparations
NAICS 32562 Toilet Preparation Manufacturing
NAICS 325611 Soap & Other Detergent Manufacturing
2851 Paints, Varnishes, Lacquers, Enamels, & Allied Products
NAICS 32551 Paint & Coating Manufacturing
2861 Gum & Wood Chemicals
NAICS 325191 Gum & Wood Chemical Manufacturing
2865 Cyclic Organic Crudes & Intermediates, & Organic Dyes & Pigments
NAICS 32511 Petrochemical Manufacturing
NAICS 325132 Organic Dye & Pigment Manufacturing
NAICS 325192 Cyclic Crude & Intermediate Manufacturing
2869 Industrial Organic Chemicals, nec
NAICS 32511 Petrochemical Manufacturing
NAICS 325188 All Other Inorganic Chemical Manufacturing
NAICS 325193 Ethyl Alcohol Manufacturing
NAICS 32512 Industrial Gas Manufacturing
NAICS 325199 All Other Basic Organic Chemical
        Manufacturing
2873 Nitrogenous Fertilizers
NAICS 325311 Nitrogenous Fertilizer Manufacturing
2874 Phosphatic Fertilizers
NAICS 325312 Phosphatic Fertilizer Manufacturing
2875 Fertilizers, Mixing Only
NAICS 325314 Fertilizer Manufacturing
2879 Pesticides & Agricultural Chemicals, nec
NAICS 32532 Pesticide & Other Agricultural Chemical
        Manufacturing
2891 Adhesives & Sealants
NAICS 32552 Adhesive & Sealant Manufacturing
2892 Explosives
NAICS 32592 Explosives Manufacturing
2893 Printing Ink
NAICS 32591 Printing Ink Manufacturing

2895 Carbon Black
NAICS 325182 Carbon Black Manufacturing
2899 Chemicals & Chemical Preparations, nec
NAICS 32551   Paint & Coating Manufacturing
NAICS 311942 Spice & Extract Manufacturing
NAICS 325199 All Other Basic Organic Chemical
   Manufacturing
NAICS 325998 All Other Miscellaneous Chemical Product
   Manufacturing

PETROLEUM REFINING & RELATED INDUSTRIES

2911 Petroleum Refining
NAICS 32411   Petroleum Refineries
2951 Asphalt Paving Mixtures & Blocks
NAICS 324121 Asphalt Paving Mixture & Block Manufacturing
2952 Asphalt Felts & Coatings
NAICS 324122 Asphalt Shingle & Coating Materials
   Manufacturing
2992 Lubricating Oils & Greases
NAICS 324191 Petroleum Lubricating Oil & Grease
   Manufacturing 2999

RUBBER & MISCELLANEOUS PLASTICS PRODUCTS

3011 Tires & Inner Tubes
NAICS 326211 Tire Manufacturing
3021 Rubber & Plastics Footwear
NAICS 316211 Rubber & Plastics Footwear Manufacturing
3052 Rubber & Plastics Hose & Belting
NAICS 32622   Rubber & Plastics Hoses & Belting
   Manufacturing
3053 Gaskets, Packing, & Sealing Devices
NAICS 339991 Gasket, Packing, & Sealing Device
   Manufacturing
3061 Molded, Extruded, & Lathe-cut Mechanical Rubber Products
NAICS 326291 Rubber Product Manufacturing for Mechanical
   Use
3069 Fabricated Rubber Products, nec
NAICS 31332   Fabric Coating Mills
NAICS 326192 Resilient Floor Covering Manufacturing
NAICS 326299 All Other Rubber Product Manufacturing
3081 Unsupported Plastics Film & Sheet
NAICS 326113 Unsupported Plastics Film & Sheet
   Manufacturing
3082 Unsupported Plastics Profile Shapes
NAICS 326121 Unsupported Plastics Profile Shape
   Manufacturing
3083 Laminated Plastics Plate, Sheet, & Profile Shapes
NAICS 32613   Laminated Plastics Plate, Sheet, & Shape
   Manufacturing
3084 Plastic Pipe
NAICS 326122 Plastic Pipe & Pipe Fitting Manufacturing
3085 Plastics Bottles
NAICS 32616   Plastics Bottle Manufacturing
3086 Plastics Foam Products
NAICS 32615   Urethane & Other Foam Product
   Manufacturing
NAICS 32614   Polystyrene Foam Product Manufacturing

3087 Custom Compounding of Purchased Plastics Resins
NAICS 325991 Custom Compounding of Purchased Resin
3088 Plastics Plumbing Fixtures
NAICS 326191 Plastics Plumbing Fixtures Manufacturing
3089 Plastics Products, nec
NAICS 326122 Plastics Pipe & Pipe Fitting Manufacturing
NAICS 326121 Unsupported Plastics Profile Shape
   Manufacturing
NAICS 326199 All Other Plastics Product Manufacturing

LEATHER & LEATHER PRODUCTS

3111 Leather Tanning & Finishing
NAICS 31611   Leather & Hide Tanning & Finishing
3131 Boot & Shoe Cut Stock & Findings
NAICS 321999 All Other Miscellaneous Wood Product
   Manufacturing
NAICS 339993 Fastener, Button, Needle, & Pin Manufacturing
NAICS 316999 All Other Leather Good Manufacturing
3142 House Slippers
NAICS 316212 House Slipper Manufacturing
3143 Men's Footwear, Except Athletic
NAICS 316213 Men's Footwear Manufacturing
3144 Women's Footwear, Except Athletic
NAICS 316214 Women's Footwear Manufacturing
3149 Footwear, Except Rubber, nec
NAICS 316219 Other Footwear Manufacturing
3151 Leather Gloves & Mittens
NAICS 315992 Glove & Mitten Manufacturing
3161 Luggage
NAICS 316991 Luggage Manufacturing
3171 Women's Handbags & Purses
NAICS 316992 Women's Handbag & Purse Manufacturing
3172 Personal Leather Goods, Except Women's Handbags & Purses
NAICS 316993 Personal Leather Good Manufacturing
3199 Leather Goods, nec
NAICS 316999 All Other Leather Good Manufacturing

STONE, CLAY, GLASS, & CONCRETE PRODUCTS

3211 Flat Glass
NAICS 327211 Flat Glass Manufacturing
3221 Glass Containers
NAICS 327213 Glass Container Manufacturing
3229 Pressed & Blown Glass & Glassware, nec
NAICS 327212 Other Pressed & Blown Glass & Glassware
   Manufacturing
3231 Glass Products, Made of Purchased Glass
NAICS 327215 Glass Product Manufacturing Made of
   Purchased Glass
3241 Cement, Hydraulic
NAICS 32731   Hydraulic Cement Manufacturing
3251 Brick & Structural Clay Tile
NAICS 327121 Brick & Structural Clay Tile Manufacturing
3253 Ceramic Wall & Floor Tile
NAICS 327122 Ceramic Wall & Floor Tile Manufacturing
3255 Clay Refractories
NAICS 327124 Clay Refractory Manufacturing

3259 Structural Clay Products, nec
NAICS 327123 Other Structural Clay Product Manufacturing
3261 Vitreous China Plumbing Fixtures & China & Earthenware Fittings & Bathroom Accessories
NAICS 327111 Vitreous China Plumbing Fixture & China & Earthenware Fittings & Bathroom Accessories Manufacturing
3262 Vitreous China Table & Kitchen Articles
NAICS 327112 Vitreous China, Fine Earthenware & Other Pottery Product Manufacturing
3263 Fine Earthenware Table & Kitchen Articles
NAICS 327112 Vitreous China, Fine Earthenware & Other Pottery Product Manufacturing
3264 Porcelain Electrical Supplies
NAICS 327113 Porcelain Electrical Supply Manufacturing
3269 Pottery Products, nec
NAICS 327112 Vitreous China, Fine Earthenware, & Other Pottery Product Manufacturing
3271 Concrete Block & Brick
NAICS 327331 Concrete Block & Brick Manufacturing
3272 Concrete Products, Except Block & Brick
NAICS 327999 All Other Miscellaneous Nonmetallic Mineral Product Manufacturing
NAICS 327332 Concrete Pipe Manufacturing
NAICS 32739 Other Concrete Product Manufacturing
3273 Ready-mixed Concrete
NAICS 32732 Ready-mix Concrete Manufacturing
3274 Lime
NAICS 32741 Lime Manufacturing
3275 Gypsum Products
NAICS 32742 Gypsum & Gypsum Product Manufacturing
3281 Cut Stone & Stone Products
NAICS 327991 Cut Stone & Stone Product Manufacturing
3291 Abrasive Products
NAICS 332999 All Other Miscellaneous Fabricated Metal Product Manufacturing
NAICS 32791 Abrasive Product Manufacturing
3292 Asbestos Products
NAICS 33634 Motor Vehicle Brake System Manufacturing
NAICS 327999 All Other Miscellaneous Nonmetallic Mineral Product Manufacturing
3295 Minerals & Earths, Ground or Otherwise Treated
NAICS 327992 Ground or Treated Mineral & Earth Manufacturing
3296 Mineral Wool
NAICS 327993 Mineral Wool Manufacturing
3297 Nonclay Refractories
NAICS 327125 Nonclay Refractory Manufacturing
3299 Nonmetallic Mineral Products, nec
NAICS 32742 Gypsum & Gypsum Product Manufacturing
NAICS 327999 All Other Miscellaneous Nonmetallic Mineral Product Manufacturing

PRIMARY METALS INDUSTRIES

3312 Steel Works, Blast Furnaces , & Rolling Mills
NAICS 324199 All Other Petroleum & Coal Products Manufacturing
NAICS 331111 Iron & Steel Mills
3313 Electrometallurgical Products, Except Steel
NAICS 331112 Electrometallurgical Ferroalloy Product Manufacturing

NAICS 331492 Secondary Smelting, Refining, & Alloying of Nonferrous Metals
3315 Steel Wiredrawing & Steel Nails & Spikes
NAICS 331222 Steel Wire Drawing
NAICS 332618 Other Fabricated Wire Product Manufacturing
3316 Cold-rolled Steel Sheet, Strip, & Bars
NAICS 331221 Cold-rolled Steel Shape Manufacturing
3317 Steel Pipe & Tubes
NAICS 33121 Iron & Steel Pipes & Tubes Manufacturing from Purchased Steel
3321 Gray & Ductile Iron Foundries
NAICS 331511 Iron Foundries
3322 Malleable Iron Foundries
NAICS 331511 Iron Foundries
3324 Steel Investment Foundries
NAICS 331512 Steel Investment Foundries
3325 Steel Foundries, nec
NAICS 331513 Steel Foundries
3331 Primary Smelting & Refining of Copper
NAICS 331411 Primary Smelting & Refining of Copper
3334 Primary Production of Aluminum
NAICS 331312 Primary Aluminum Production
3339 Primary Smelting & Refining of Nonferrous Metals, Except Copper & Aluminum
NAICS 331419 Primary Smelting & Refining of Nonferrous Metals
3341 Secondary Smelting & Refining of Nonferrous Metals
NAICS 331314 Secondary Smelting & Alloying of Aluminum
NAICS 331423 Secondary Smelting, Refining, & Alloying of Copper
NAICS 331492 Secondary Smelting, Refining, & Alloying of Nonferrous Metals
3351 Rolling, Drawing, & Extruding of Copper
NAICS 331421 Copper Rolling, Drawing, & Extruding
3353 Aluminum Sheet, Plate, & Foil
NAICS 331315 Aluminum Sheet, Plate, & Foil Manufacturing
3354 Aluminum Extruded Products
NAICS 331316 Aluminum Extruded Product Manufacturing
3355 Aluminum Rolling & Drawing, nec
NAICS 331319 Other Aluminum Rolling & Drawing,
3356 Rolling, Drawing, & Extruding of Nonferrous Metals, Except Copper & Aluminum
NAICS 331491 Nonferrous Metal Rolling. Drawing, & Extruding
3357 Drawing & Insulating of Nonferrous Wire
NAICS 331319 Other Aluminum Rolling & Drawing
NAICS 331422 Copper Wire Drawing
NAICS 331491 Nonferrous Metal Rolling, Drawing, & Extruding
NAICS 335921 Fiber Optic Cable Manufacturing
NAICS 335929 Other Communication & Energy Wire Manufacturing
3363 Aluminum Die-castings
NAICS 331521 Aluminum Die-castings
3364 Nonferrous Die-castings, Except Aluminum
NAICS 331522 Nonferrous Die-castings
3365 Aluminum Foundries
NAICS 331524 Aluminum Foundries
3366 Copper Foundries
NAICS 331525 Copper Foundries
3369 Nonferrous Foundries, Except Aluminum & Copper
NAICS 331528 Other Nonferrous Foundries

3398 Metal Heat Treating
NAICS 332811 Metal Heat Treating
3399 Primary Metal Products, nec
NAICS 331111 Iron & Steel Mills
NAICS 331314 Secondary Smelting & Alloying of Aluminum
NAICS 331423 Secondary Smelting, Refining & Alloying of Copper
NAICS 331492 Secondary Smelting, Refining, & Alloying of Nonferrous Metals
NAICS 332618 Other Fabricated Wire Product Manufacturing
NAICS 332813 Electroplating, Plating, Polishing, Anodizing, & Coloring

FABRICATED METAL PRODUCTS, EXCEPT MACHINERY & TRANSPORTATION EQUIPMENT

3411 Metal Cans
NAICS 332431 Metal Can Manufacturing
3412 Metal Shipping Barrels, Drums, Kegs & Pails
NAICS 332439 Other Metal Container Manufacturing
3421 Cutlery
NAICS 332211 Cutlery & Flatware Manufacturing
3423 Hand & Edge Tools, Except Machine Tools & Handsaws
NAICS 332212 Hand & Edge Tool Manufacturing
3425 Saw Blades & Handsaws
NAICS 332213 Saw Blade & Handsaw Manufacturing
3429 Hardware, nec
NAICS 332439 Other Metal Container Manufacturing
NAICS 332919 Other Metal Valve & Pipe Fitting Manufacturing
NAICS 33251 Hardware Manufacturing
3431 Enameled Iron & Metal Sanitary Ware
NAICS 332998 Enameled Iron & Metal Sanitary Ware Manufacturing
3432 Plumbing Fixture Fittings & Trim
NAICS 332913 Plumbing Fixture Fitting & Trim Manufacturing
NAICS 332999 All Other Miscellaneous Fabricated Metal Product Manufacturing
3433 Heating Equipment, Except Electric & Warm Air Furnaces
NAICS 333414 Heating Equipment Manufacturing
3441 Fabricated Structural Metal
NAICS 332312 Fabricated Structural Metal Manufacturing
3442 Metal Doors, Sash, Frames, Molding, & Trim Manufacturing
NAICS 332321 Metal Window & Door Manufacturing
3443 Fabricated Plate Work
NAICS 332313 Plate Work Manufacturing
NAICS 33241 Power Boiler & Heat Exchanger Manufacturing
NAICS 33242 Metal Tank Manufacturing
NAICS 333415 Air-conditioning & Warm Air Heating Equipment & Commercial & Industrial Refrigeration Equipment Manufacturing
3444 Sheet Metal Work
NAICS 332322 Sheet Metal Work Manufacturing
NAICS 332439 Other Metal Container Manufacturing
3446 Architectural & Ornamental Metal Work
NAICS 332323 Ornamental & Architectural Metal Work Manufacturing
3448 Prefabricated Metal Buildings & Components
NAICS 332311 Prefabricated Metal Building & Component Manufacturing

3449 Miscellaneous Structural Metal Work
NAICS 332114 Custom Roll Forming
NAICS 332312 Fabricated Structural Metal Manufacturing
NAICS 332321 Metal Window & Door Manufacturing
NAICS 332323 Ornamental & Architectural Metal Work Manufacturing
3451 Screw Machine Products
NAICS 332721 Precision Turned Product Manufacturing
3452 Bolts, Nuts, Screws, Rivets, & Washers
NAICS 332722 Bolt, Nut, Screw, Rivet, & Washer Manufacturing
3462 Iron & Steel Forgings
NAICS 332111 Iron & Steel Forging
3463 Nonferrous Forgings
NAICS 332112 Nonferrous Forging
3465 Automotive Stamping
NAICS 33637 Motor Vehicle Metal Stamping
3466 Crowns & Closures
NAICS 332115 Crown & Closure Manufacturing
3469 Metal Stamping, nec
NAICS 339911 Jewelry Manufacturing
NAICS 332116 Metal Stamping
NAICS 332214 Kitchen Utensil, Pot & Pan Manufacturing
3471 Electroplating, Plating, Polishing, Anodizing, & Coloring
NAICS 332813 Electroplating, Plating, Polishing, Anodizing, & Coloring
3479 Coating, Engraving, & Allied Services, nec
NAICS 339914 Costume Jewelry & Novelty Manufacturing
NAICS 339911 Jewelry Manufacturing
NAICS 339912 Silverware & Plated Ware Manufacturing
NAICS 332812 Metal Coating, Engraving , & Allied Services to Manufacturers
3482 Small Arms Ammunition
NAICS 332992 Small Arms Ammunition Manufacturing
3483 Ammunition, Except for Small Arms
NAICS 332993 Ammunition Manufacturing
3484 Small Arms
NAICS 332994 Small Arms Manufacturing
3489 Ordnance & Accessories, nec
NAICS 332995 Other Ordnance & Accessories Manufacturing
3491
3492 Fluid Power Valves & Hose Fittings
NAICS 332912 Fluid Power Valve & Hose Fitting Manufacturing
3493 Steel Springs, Except Wire
NAICS 332611 Steel Spring Manufacturing
3494 Valves & Pipe Fittings, nec
NAICS 332919 Other Metal Valve & Pipe Fitting Manufacturing
NAICS 332999 All Other Miscellaneous Fabricated Metal Product Manufacturing
3495 Wire Springs
NAICS 332612 Wire Spring Manufacturing
NAICS 334518 Watch, Clock, & Part Manufacturing
3496 Miscellaneous Fabricated Wire Products
NAICS 332618 Other Fabricated Wire Product Manufacturing
3497 Metal Foil & Leaf
NAICS 322225 Laminated Aluminum Foil Manufacturing for Flexible Packaging Uses
NAICS 332999 All Other Miscellaneous Fabricated Metal Product Manufacturing
3498 Fabricated Pipe & Pipe Fittings
NAICS 332996 Fabricated Pipe & Pipe Fitting Manufacturing

3499 Fabricated Metal Products, nec
NAICS 337148 Other Nonwood Furniture Manufacturing
NAICS 332117 Powder Metallurgy Part Manufacturing
NAICS 332439 Other Metal Container Manufacturing
NAICS 33251 Hardware Manufacturing
NAICS 332919 Other Metal Valve & Pipe Fitting
Manufacturing
NAICS 339914 Costume Jewelry & Novelty Manufacturing
NAICS 332999 All Other Miscellaneous Fabricated Metal
Product Manufacturing

INDUSTRIAL & COMMERCIAL MACHINERY & COMPUTER EQUIPMENT

3511 Steam, Gas, & Hydraulic Turbines, & Turbine Generator Set Units
NAICS 333611 Turbine & Turbine Generator Set Unit
Manufacturing
3519 Internal Combustion Engines, nec
NAICS 336399 All Other Motor Vehicle Parts Manufacturing
NAICS 333618 Other Engine Equipment Manufacturing
3523 Farm Machinery & Equipment
NAICS 333111 Farm Machinery & Equipment Manufacturing
NAICS 332323 Ornamental & Architectural Metal Work
Manufacturing
NAICS 332212 Hand & Edge Tool Manufacturing
NAICS 333922 Conveyor & Conveying Equipment
Manufacturing
3524 Lawn & Garden Tractors & Home Lawn & Garden Equipment
NAICS 333112 Lawn & Garden Tractor & Home Lawn &
Garden Equipment Manufacturing
NAICS 332212 Hand & Edge Tool Manufacturing
3531 Construction Machinery & Equipment
NAICS 33651 Railroad Rolling Stock Manufacturing
NAICS 333923 Overhead Traveling Crane, Hoist, & Monorail
System Manufacturing
NAICS 33312 Construction Machinery Manufacturing
3532 Mining Machinery & Equipment, Except Oil & Gas Field Machinery & Equipment
NAICS 333131 Mining Machinery & Equipment Manufacturing
3533 Oil & Gas Field Machinery & Equipment
NAICS 333132 Oil & Gas Field Machinery & Equipment
Manufacturing
3534 Elevators & Moving Stairways
NAICS 333921 Elevator & Moving Stairway Manufacturing
3535 Conveyors & Conveying Equipment
NAICS 333922 Conveyor & Conveying Equipment
Manufacturing
3536 Overhead Traveling Cranes, Hoists & Monorail Systems
NAICS 333923 Overhead Traveling Crane, Hoist & Monorail
System Manufacturing
3537 Industrial Trucks, Tractors, Trailers, & Stackers
NAICS 333924 Industrial Truck, Tractor, Trailer, & Stacker
Machinery Manufacturing
NAICS 332999 All Other Miscellaneous Fabricated Metal
Product Manufacturing
NAICS 332439 Other Metal Container Manufacturing
3541 Machine Tools, Metal Cutting Type
NAICS 333512 Machine Tool Manufacturing
3542 Machine Tools, Metal Forming Type
NAICS 333513 Machine Tool Manufacturing

3543 Industrial Patterns
NAICS 332997 Industrial Pattern Manufacturing
3544 Special Dies & Tools, Die Sets, Jigs & Fixtures, & Industrial Molds
NAICS 333514 Special Die & Tool, Die Set, Jig, & Fixture
Manufacturing
NAICS 333511 Industrial Mold Manufacturing
3545 Cutting Tools, Machine Tool Accessories, & Machinists' Precision Measuring Devices
NAICS 333515 Cutting Tool & Machine Tool Accessory
Manufacturing
NAICS 332212 Hand & Edge Tool Manufacturing
3546 Power-driven Handtools
NAICS 333991 Power-driven Hand Tool Manufacturing
3547 Rolling Mill Machinery & Equipment
NAICS 333516 Rolling Mill Machinery & Equipment
Manufacturing
3548 Electric & Gas Welding & Soldering Equipment
NAICS 333992 Welding & Soldering Equipment Manufacturing
NAICS 335311 Power, Distribution, & Specialty Transformer
Manufacturing
3549 Metalworking Machinery, nec
NAICS 333518 Other Metalworking Machinery Manufacturing
3552
3553 Woodworking Machinery
NAICS 33321 Sawmill & Woodworking Machinery
Manufacturing
3554 Paper Industries Machinery
NAICS 333291 Paper Industry Machinery Manufacturing
3555 Printing Trades Machinery & Equipment
NAICS 333293 Printing Machinery & Equipment
Manufacturing
3556 Food Products Machinery
NAICS 333294 Food Product Machinery Manufacturing
3559 Special Industry Machinery, nec
NAICS 33322 Rubber & Plastics Industry Machinery
Manufacturing
NAICS 333319 Other Commercial & Service Industry
Machinery Manufacturing
NAICS 333295 Semiconductor Manufacturing Machinery
NAICS 333298 All Other Industrial Machinery Manufacturing
3561 Pumps & Pumping Equipment
NAICS 333911 Pump & Pumping Equipment Manufacturing
3562 Ball & Roller Bearings
NAICS 332991 Ball & Roller Bearing Manufacturing
3563 Air & Gas Compressors
NAICS 333912 Air & Gas Compressor Manufacturing
3564 Industrial & Commercial Fans & Blowers & Air Purification Equipment
NAICS 333411 Air Purification Equipment Manufacturing
NAICS 333412 Industrial & Commercial Fan & Blower
Manufacturing
3565 Packaging Machinery
NAICS 333993 Packaging Machinery Manufacturing
3566 Speed Changers, Industrial High-speed Drives, & Gears
NAICS 333612 Speed Changer, Industrial High-speed Drive, &
Gear Manufacturing
3567 Industrial Process Furnaces & Ovens
NAICS 333994 Industrial Process Furnace & Oven
Manufacturing
3568 Mechanical Power Transmission Equipment, nec
NAICS 333613 Mechanical Power Transmission Equipment
Manufacturing

3569 General Industrial Machinery & Equipment, nec
NAICS 333999 All Other General Purpose Machinery
           Manufacturing

3571 Electronic Computers
NAICS 334111 Electronic Computer Manufacturing

3572 Computer Storage Devices
NAICS 334112 Computer Storage Device Manufacturing

3575 Computer Terminals
NAICS 334113 Computer Terminal Manufacturing

3577 Computer Peripheral Equipment, nec
NAICS 334119 Other Computer Peripheral Equipment
           Manufacturing

3578 Calculating & Accounting Machines, Except Electronic Computers
NAICS 334119 Other Computer Peripheral Equipment
           Manufacturing
NAICS 333313 Office Machinery Manufacturing

3579 Office Machines, nec
NAICS 339942 Lead Pencil & Art Good Manufacturing
NAICS 334518 Watch, Clock, & Part Manufacturing
NAICS 333313 Office Machinery Manufacturing

3581 Automatic Vending Machines
NAICS 333311 Automatic Vending Machine Manufacturing

3582 Commercial Laundry, Drycleaning, & Pressing Machines
NAICS 333312 Commercial Laundry, Drycleaning, & Pressing
           Machine Manufacturing

3585 Air-conditioning & Warm Air Heating Equipment & Commercial & Industrial Refrigeration Equipment
NAICS 336391 Motor Vehicle Air Conditioning Manufacturing
NAICS 333415 Air Conditioning & Warm Air Heating
           Equipment & Commercial & Industrial
           Refrigeration Equipment Manufacturing

3586 Measuring & Dispensing Pumps
NAICS 333913 Measuring & Dispensing Pump Manufacturing

3589 Service Industry Machinery, nec
NAICS 333319 Other Commercial and Service Industry
           Machinery Manufacturing

3592 Carburetors, Pistons, Piston Rings & Valves
NAICS 336311 Carburetor, Piston, Piston Ring & Valve
           Manufacturing

3593 Fluid Power Cylinders & Actuators
NAICS 333995 Fluid Power Cylinder & Actuator
           Manufacturing

3594 Fluid Power Pumps & Motors
NAICS 333996 Fluid Power Pump & Motor Manufacturing

3596 Scales & Balances, Except Laboratory
NAICS 333997 Scale & Balance Manufacturing

3599 Industrial & Commercial Machinery & Equipment, nec
NAICS 336399 All Other Motor Vehicle Part Manufacturing
NAICS 332999 All Other Miscellaneous Fabricated Metal
           Product Manufacturing
NAICS 333319 Other Commercial & Service Industry
           Machinery Manufacturing
NAICS 33271 Machine Shops
NAICS 333999 All Other General Purpose Machinery
           Manufacturing

ELECTRONIC & OTHER ELECTRICAL EQUIPMENT & COMPONENTS, EXCEPT COMPUTER EQUIPMENT

3612 Power, Distribution, & Specialty Transformers
NAICS 335311 Power, Distribution, & Specialty Transformer
           Manufacturing

3613 Switchgear & Switchboard Apparatus
NAICS 335313 Switchgear & Switchboard Apparatus
           Manufacturing

3621 Motors & Generators
NAICS 335312 Motor & Generator Manufacturing

3624 Carbon & Graphite Products
NAICS 335991 Carbon & Graphite Product Manufacturing

3625 Relays & Industrial Controls
NAICS 335314 Relay & Industrial Control Manufacturing

3629 Electrical Industrial Apparatus, nec
NAICS 335999 All Other Miscellaneous Electrical Equipment
           & Component Manufacturing

3631 Household Cooking Equipment
NAICS 335221 Household Cooking Appliance Manufacturing

3632 Household Refrigerators & Home & Farm Freezers
NAICS 335222 Household Refrigerator & Home Freezer
           Manufacturing

3633 Household Laundry Equipment
NAICS 335224 Household Laundry Equipment Manufacturing

3634 Electric Housewares & Fans
NAICS 335211 Electric Housewares & Fan Manufacturing

3635 Household Vacuum Cleaners
NAICS 335212 Household Vacuum Cleaner Manufacturing

3639 Household Appliances, nec
NAICS 335212 Household Vacuum Cleaner Manufacturing
NAICS 333298 All Other Industrial Machinery Manufacturing
NAICS 335228 Other Household Appliance Manufacturing

3641 Electric Lamp Bulbs & Tubes
NAICS 33511 Electric Lamp Bulb & Part Manufacturing

3643 Current-carrying Wiring Devices
NAICS 335931 Current-carrying Wiring Device Manufacturing

3644 Noncurrent-carrying Wiring Devices
NAICS 335932 Noncurrent-carrying Wiring Device
           Manufacturing

3645 Residential Electric Lighting Fixtures
NAICS 335121 Residential Electric Lighting Fixture
           Manufacturing

3646 Commercial, Industrial, & Institutional Electric Lighting Fixtures
NAICS 335122 Commercial, Industrial, & Institutional Electric
           Lighting Fixture Manufacturing

3647 Vehicular Lighting Equipment
NAICS 336321 Vehicular Lighting Equipment Manufacturing

3648 Lighting Equipment, nec
NAICS 335129 Other Lighting Equipment Manufacturing

3651 Household Audio & Video Equipment
NAICS 33431 Audio & Video Equipment Manufacturing 3652
NAICS 51222 Integrated Record Production/distribution

3661 Telephone & Telegraph Apparatus
NAICS 33421 Telephone Apparatus Manufacturing
NAICS 334416 Electronic Coil, Transformer, & Other Inductor
           Manufacturing
NAICS 334418 Printed Circuit/electronics Assembly
           Manufacturing

3663 Radio & Television Broadcasting & Communication Equipment
NAICS 33422   Radio & Television Broadcasting & Wireless Communications Equipment Manufacturing
3669 Communications Equipment, nec
NAICS 33429   Other Communication Equipment Manufacturing
3671 Electron Tubes
NAICS 334411 Electron Tube Manufacturing
3672 Printed Circuit Boards
NAICS 334412 Printed Circuit Board Manufacturing
3674 Semiconductors & Related Devices
NAICS 334413 Semiconductor & Related Device Manufacturing
3675 Electronic Capacitors
NAICS 334414 Electronic Capacitor Manufacturing
3676 Electronic Resistors
NAICS 334415 Electronic Resistor Manufacturing
3677 Electronic Coils, Transformers, & Other Inductors
NAICS 334416 Electronic Coil, Transformer, & Other Inductor Manufacturing
3678 Electronic ConNECtors
NAICS 334417 Electronic ConNECtor Manufacturing
3679 Electronic Components, nec
NAICS 33422   Radio & Television Broadcasting & Wireless Communications Equipment Manufacturing
NAICS 334418 Printed Circuit/electronics Assembly Manufacturing
NAICS 336322 Other Motor Vehicle Electrical & Electronic Equipment Manufacturing
NAICS 334419 Other Electronic Component Manufacturing
3691 Storage Batteries
NAICS 335911 Storage Battery Manufacturing
3692 Primary Batteries, Dry & Wet
NAICS 335912 Dry & Wet Primary Battery Manufacturing
3694 Electrical Equipment for Internal Combustion Engines
NAICS 336322 Other Motor Vehicle Electrical & Electronic Equipment Manufacturing
3695 Magnetic & Optical Recording Media
NAICS 334613 Magnetic & Optical Recording Media Manufacturing
3699 Electrical Machinery, Equipment, & Supplies, nec
NAICS 333319 Other Commercial & Service Industry Machinery Manufacturing
NAICS 333618 Other Engine Equipment Manufacturing
NAICS 334119 Other Computer Peripheral Equipment Manufacturing Classify According to Function
NAICS 335129 Other Lighting Equipment Manufacturing
NAICS 335999 All Other Miscellaneous Electrical Equipment & Component Manufacturing

TRANSPORTATION EQUIPMENT

3711 Motor Vehicles & Passenger Car Bodies
NAICS 336111 Automobile Manufacturing
NAICS 336112 Light Truck & Utility Vehicle Manufacturing
NAICS 33612   Heavy Duty Truck Manufacturing
NAICS 336211 Motor Vehicle Body Manufacturing
NAICS 336992 Military Armored Vehicle, Tank, & Tank Component Manufacturing
3713 Truck & Bus Bodies
NAICS 336211 Motor Vehicle Body Manufacturing

3714 Motor Vehicle Parts & Accessories
NAICS 336211 Motor Vehicle Body Manufacturing
NAICS 336312 Gasoline Engine & Engine Parts Manufacturing
NAICS 336322 Other Motor Vehicle Electrical & Electronic Equipment Manufacturing
NAICS 33633   Motor Vehicle Steering & Suspension Components Manufacturing
NAICS 33634   Motor Vehicle Brake System Manufacturing
NAICS 33635   Motor Vehicle Transmission & Power Train Parts Manufacturing
NAICS 336399 All Other Motor Vehicle Parts Manufacturing
3715 Truck Trailers
NAICS 336212 Truck Trailer Manufacturing
3716 Motor Homes
NAICS 336213 Motor Home Manufacturing
3721 Aircraft
NAICS 336411 Aircraft Manufacturing
3724 Aircraft Engines & Engine Parts
NAICS 336412 Aircraft Engine & Engine Parts Manufacturing
3728
NAICS 336413 Other Aircraft Part & Auxiliary Equipment Manufacturing
3731 Ship Building & Repairing
NAICS 336611 Ship Building & Repairing
3732 Boat Building & Repairing
NAICS 81149   Other Personal & Household Goods Repair & Maintenance
NAICS 336612 Boat Building
3743 Railroad Equipment
NAICS 333911 Pump & Pumping Equipment Manufacturing
NAICS 33651   Railroad Rolling Stock Manufacturing
3751 Motorcycles, Bicycles, & Parts
NAICS 336991 Motorcycle, Bicycle, & Parts Manufacturing
3761 Guided Missiles & Space Vehicles
NAICS 336414 Guided Missile & Space Vehicle Manufacturing
3764
3769 Guided Missile Space Vehicle Parts & Auxiliary Equipment, nec
NAICS 336419 Other Guided Missile & Space Vehicle Parts & Auxiliary Equipment Manufacturing
3792 Travel Trailers & Campers
NAICS 336214 Travel Trailer & Camper Manufacturing
3795 Tanks & Tank Components
NAICS 336992 Military Armored Vehicle, Tank, & Tank Component Manufacturing
3799 Transportation Equipment, nec
NAICS 336214 Travel Trailer & Camper Manufacturing
NAICS 332212 Hand & Edge Tool Manufacturing
NAICS 336999 All Other Transportation Equipment Manufacturing

MEASURING, ANALYZING, & CONTROLLING INSTRUMENTS

3812 Search, Detection, Navigation, Guidance, Aeronautical, & Nautical Systems & Instruments
NAICS 334511 Search, Detection, Navigation, Guidance, Aeronautical, & Nautical System & Instrument Manufacturing
3821 Laboratory Apparatus & Furniture
NAICS 339111 Laboratory Apparatus & Furniture Manufacturing

**3822 Automatic Controls for Regulating Residential &
Commercial Environments & Appliances**
NAICS 334512 Automatic Environmental Control
Manufacturing for Regulating Residential,
Commercial, & Appliance Use
**3823 Industrial Instruments for Measurement, Display, &
Control of Process Variables & Related Products**
NAICS 334513 Instruments & Related Product Manufacturing
for Measuring Displaying, & Controlling
Industrial Process Variables
3824 Totalizing Fluid Meters & Counting Devices
NAICS 334514 Totalizing Fluid Meter & Counting Device
Manufacturing
**3825 Instruments for Measuring & Testing of Electricity &
Electrical Signals**
NAICS 334416 Electronic Coil, Transformer, & Other Inductor
Manufacturing
NAICS 334515 Instrument Manufacturing for Measuring &
Testing Electricity & Electrical Signals
3826 Laboratory Analytical Instruments
NAICS 334516 Analytical Laboratory Instrument
Manufacturing
3827 Optical Instruments & Lenses
NAICS 333314 Optical Instrument & Lens Manufacturing
3829 Measuring & Controlling Devices, nec
NAICS 339112 Surgical & Medical Instrument Manufacturing
NAICS 334519 Other Measuring & Controlling Device
Manufacturing
3841 Surgical & Medical Instruments & Apparatus
NAICS 339112 Surgical & Medical Instrument Manufacturing
3842 Orthopedic, Prosthetic, & Surgical Appliances & Supplies
NAICS 339113 Surgical Appliance & Supplies Manufacturing
NAICS 334510 Electromedical & Electrotherapeutic Apparatus
Manufacturing
3843 Dental Equipment & Supplies
NAICS 339114 Dental Equipment & Supplies Manufacturing
3844 X-ray Apparatus & Tubes & Related Irradiation Apparatus
NAICS 334517 Irradiation Apparatus Manufacturing
3845 Electromedical & Electrotherapeutic Apparatus
NAICS 334517 Irradiation Apparatus Manufacturing
NAICS 334510 Electromedical & Electrotherapeutic Apparatus
Manufacturing
3851 Ophthalmic Goods
NAICS 339115 Ophthalmic Goods Manufacturing
3861 Photographic Equipment & Supplies
NAICS 333315 Photographic & Photocopying Equipment
Manufacturing
NAICS 325992 Photographic Film, Paper, Plate & Chemical
Manufacturing
3873 Watches, Clocks, Clockwork Operated Devices & Parts
NAICS 334518 Watch, Clock, & Part Manufacturing

MISCELLANEOUS MANUFACTURING INDUSTRIES

3911 Jewelry, Precious Metal
NAICS 339911 Jewelry Manufacturing
3914 Silverware, Plated Ware, & Stainless Steel Ware
NAICS 332211 Cutlery & Flatware Manufacturing
NAICS 339912 Silverware & Plated Ware Manufacturing
3915 Jewelers' Findings & Materials, & Lapidary Work
NAICS 339913 Jewelers' Material & Lapidary Work
Manufacturing

3931 Musical Instruments
NAICS 339992 Musical Instrument Manufacturing
3942 Dolls & Stuffed Toys
NAICS 339931 Doll & Stuffed Toy Manufacturing
**3944 Games, Toys, & Children's Vehicles, Except Dolls &
Bicycles**
NAICS 336991 Motorcycle, Bicycle & Parts Manufacturing
NAICS 339932 Game, Toy, & Children's Vehicle
Manufacturing
3949 Sporting & Athletic Goods, nec
NAICS 33992 Sporting & Athletic Good Manufacturing
3951 Pens, Mechanical Pencils & Parts
NAICS 339941 Pen & Mechanical Pencil Manufacturing
3952 Lead Pencils, Crayons, & Artist's Materials
NAICS 337139 Other Wood Furniture Manufacturing
NAICS 337139 Other Wood Furniture Manufacturing
NAICS 325998 All Other Miscellaneous Chemical
Manufacturing
NAICS 339942 Lead Pencil & Art Good Manufacturing
3953 Marking Devices
NAICS 339943 Marking Device Manufacturing
3955 Carbon Paper & Inked Ribbons
NAICS 339944 Carbon Paper & Inked Ribbon Manufacturing
**3961 Costume Jewelry & Costume Novelties, Except Precious
Metals**
NAICS 339914 Costume Jewelry & Novelty Manufacturing
3965 Fasteners, Buttons, Needles, & Pins
NAICS 339993 Fastener, Button, Needle & Pin Manufacturing
3991 Brooms & Brushes
NAICS 339994 Broom, Brush & Mop Manufacturing
3993 Signs & Advertising Specialties
NAICS 33995 Sign Manufacturing
3995 Burial Caskets
NAICS 339995 Burial Casket Manufacturing
**3996 Linoleum, Asphalted-felt-base, & Other Hard Surface
Floor Coverings, nec**
NAICS 326192 Resilient Floor Covering Manufacturing
3999 Manufacturing Industries, nec
NAICS 337148 Other Nonwood Furniture Manufacturing
NAICS 321999 All Other Miscellaneous Wood Product
Manufacturing
NAICS 31611 Leather & Hide Tanning & Finishing
NAICS 335121 Residential Electric Lighting Fixture
Manufacturing
NAICS 325998 All Other Miscellaneous Chemical Product
Manufacturing
NAICS 332999 All Other Miscellaneous Fabricated Metal
Product Manufacturing
NAICS 326199 All Other Plastics Product Manufacturing
NAICS 323112 Commercial Flexographic Printing
NAICS 323111 Commercial Gravure Printing
NAICS 323110 Commercial Lithographic Printing
NAICS 323113 Commercial Screen Printing
NAICS 323119 Other Commercial Printing
NAICS 332212 Hand & Edge Tool Manufacturing
NAICS 339999 All Other Miscellaneous Manufacturing

TRANSPORTATION, COMMUNICATIONS, ELECTRIC, GAS, & SANITARY SERVICES

4011 Railroads, Line-haul Operating
NAICS 482111 Line-haul Railroads
4013 Railroad Switching & Terminal Establishments
NAICS 482112 Short Line Railroads
NAICS 48821 Support Activities for Rail Transportation
4111 Local & Suburban Transit
NAICS 485111 Mixed Mode Transit Systems
NAICS 485112 Commuter Rail Systems
NAICS 485113 Bus & Motor Vehicle Transit Systems
NAICS 485119 Other Urban Transit Systems
NAICS 485999 All Other Transit & Ground Passenger Transportation
4119 Local Passenger Transportation, nec
NAICS 62191 Ambulance Service
NAICS 48541 School & Employee Bus Transportation
NAICS 48711 Scenic & Sightseeing Transportation , Land
NAICS 485991 Special Needs Transportation
NAICS 485999 All Other Transit & Ground Passenger Transportation
NAICS 48532 Limousine Service
4121 Taxicabs
NAICS 48531 Taxi Service
4131 Intercity & Rural Bus Transportation
NAICS 48521 Interurban & Rural Bus Transportation
4141 Local Bus Charter Service
NAICS 48551 Charter Bus Industry
4142 Bus Charter Service, Except Local
NAICS 48551 Charter Bus Industry
4151 School Buses
NAICS 48541 School & Employee Bus Transportation
4173 Terminal & Service Facilities for Motor Vehicle Passenger Transportation
NAICS 48849 Other Support Activities for Road Transportation
4212 Local Trucking Without Storage
NAICS 562111 Solid Waste Collection
NAICS 562112 Hazardous Waste Collection
NAICS 562119 Other Waste Collection
NAICS 48411 General Freight Trucking, Local
NAICS 48421 Used Household & Office Goods Moving
NAICS 48422 Specialized Freight Trucking, Local
4213 Trucking, Except Local
NAICS 484121 General Freight Trucking, Long-distance, Truckload
NAICS 484122 General Freight Trucking, Long-distance, less than Truckload
NAICS 48421 Used Household & Office Goods Moving
NAICS 48423 Specialized Freight Trucking, Long-distance
4214 Local Trucking with Storage
NAICS 48411 General Freight Trucking, Local
NAICS 48421 Used Household & Office Goods Moving
NAICS 48422 Specialized Freight Trucking, Local
4215 Couriers Services Except by Air
NAICS 49211 Couriers
NAICS 49221 Local Messengers & Local Delivery
4221 Farm Product Warehousing & Storage
NAICS 49313 Farm Product Storage Facilities
4222 Refrigerated Warehousing & Storage
NAICS 49312 Refrigerated Storage Facilities

4225 General Warehousing & Storage
NAICS 49311 General Warehousing & Storage Facilities
NAICS 53113 Lessors of Miniwarehouses & Self Storage Units
4226 Special Warehousing & Storage, nec
NAICS 49312 Refrigerated Warehousing & Storage Facilities
NAICS 49311 General Warehousing & Storage Facilities
NAICS 49319 Other Warehousing & Storage Facilities
4231 Terminal & Joint Terminal Maintenance Facilities for Motor Freight Transportation
NAICS 48849 Other Support Activities for Road Transportation
4311 United States Postal Service
NAICS 49111 Postal Service
4412 Deep Sea Foreign Transportation of Freight
NAICS 483111 Deep Sea Freight Transportation
4424 Deep Sea Domestic Transportation of Freight
NAICS 483113 Coastal & Great Lakes Freight Transportation
4432 Freight Transportation on the Great Lakes - St. Lawrence Seaway
NAICS 483113 Coastal & Great Lakes Freight Transportation
4449 Water Transportation of Freight, nec
NAICS 483211 Inland Water Freight Transportation
4481 Deep Sea Transportation of Passengers, Except by Ferry
NAICS 483112 Deep Sea Passenger Transportation
NAICS 483114 Coastal & Great Lakes Passenger Transportation
4482 Ferries
NAICS 483114 Coastal & Great Lakes Passenger Transportation
NAICS 483212 Inland Water Passenger Transportation
4489 Water Transportation of Passengers, nec
NAICS 483212 Inland Water Passenger Transportation
NAICS 48721 Scenic & Sightseeing Transportation, Water
4491 Marine Cargo Handling
NAICS 48831 Port & Harbor Operations
NAICS 48832 Marine Cargo Handling
4492 Towing & Tugboat Services
NAICS 483113 Coastal & Great Lakes Freight Transportation
NAICS 483211 Inland Water Freight Transportation
NAICS 48833 Navigational Services to Shipping
4493 Marinas
NAICS 71393 Marinas
4499 Water Transportation Services, nec
NAICS 532411 Commercial Air, Rail, & Water Transportation Equipment Rental & Leasing
NAICS 48831 Port & Harbor Operations
NAICS 48833 Navigational Services to Shipping
NAICS 48839 Other Support Activities for Water Transportation
4512 Air Transportation, Scheduled
NAICS 481111 Scheduled Passenger Air Transportation
NAICS 481112 Scheduled Freight Air Transportation
4513 Air Courier Services
NAICS 49211 Couriers
4522 Air Transportation, Nonscheduled
NAICS 62191 Ambulance Services
NAICS 481212 Nonscheduled Chartered Freight Air Transportation
NAICS 481211 Nonscheduled Chartered Passenger Air Transportation
NAICS 48122 Nonscheduled Speciality Air Transportation
NAICS 48799 Scenic & Sightseeing Transportation , Other

4581 Airports, Flying Fields, & Airport Terminal Services
NAICS 488111 Air Traffic Control
NAICS 488112 Airport Operations, Except Air Traffic Control
NAICS 56172 Janitorial Services
NAICS 48819 Other Support Activities for Air Transportation
4612 Crude Petroleum Pipelines
NAICS 48611 Pipeline Transportation of Crude Oil
4613 Refined Petroleum Pipelines
NAICS 48691 Pipeline Transportation of Refined Petroleum
Products
4619 Pipelines, nec
NAICS 48699 All Other Pipeline Transportation
4724 Travel Agencies
NAICS 56151 Travel Agencies
4725 Tour Operators
NAICS 56152 Tour Operators
4729 Arrangement of Passenger Transportation, nec
NAICS 488999 All Other Support Activities for Transportation
NAICS 561599 All Other Travel Arrangement & Reservation
Services
4731 Arrangement of Transportation of Freight & Cargo
NAICS 541618 Other Management Consulting Services
NAICS 48851 Freight Transportation Arrangement
4741 Rental of Railroad Cars
NAICS 532411 Commercial Air, Rail, & Water Transportation
Equipment Rental & Leasing
NAICS 48821 Support Activities for Rail Transportation
4783 Packing & Crating
NAICS 488991 Packing & Crating
**4785 Fixed Facilities & Inspection & Weighing Services for
Motor Vehicle Transportation**
NAICS 48839 Other Support Activities for Water
Transportation
NAICS 48849 Other Support Activities for Road
Transportation
4789 Transportation Services, nec
NAICS 488999 All Other Support Activities for Transportation
NAICS 48711 Scenic & Sightseeing Transportation, Land
NAICS 48821 Support Activities for Rail Transportation
4812 Radiotelephone Communications
NAICS 513321 Paging
NAICS 513322 Cellular & Other Wireless Telecommunications
NAICS 51333 Telecommunications Resellers
4813 Telephone Communications, Except Radiotelephone
NAICS 51331 Wired Telecommunications Carriers
NAICS 51333 Telecommunications Resellers
4822 Telegraph & Other Message Communications
NAICS 51331 Wired Telecommunications Carriers
4832 Radio Broadcasting Stations
NAICS 513111 Radio Networks
NAICS 513112 Radio Stations
4833 Television Broadcasting Stations
NAICS 51312 Television Broadcasting
4841 Cable & Other Pay Television Services
NAICS 51321 Cable Networks
NAICS 51322 Cable & Other Program Distribution
4899 Communications Services, nec
NAICS 513322 Cellular & Other Wireless Telecommunications
NAICS 51334 Satellite Telecommunications
NAICS 51339 Other Telecommunications
4911 Electric Services
NAICS 221111 Hydroelectric Power Generation
NAICS 221112 Fossil Fuel Electric Power Generation
NAICS 221113 Nuclear Electric Power Generation

NAICS 221119 Other Electric Power Generation
NAICS 221121 Electric Bulk Power Transmission & Control
NAICS 221122 Electric Power Distribution
4922 Natural Gas Transmission
NAICS 48621 Pipeline Transportation of Natural Gas
4923 Natural Gas Transmission & Distribution
NAICS 22121 Natural Gas Distribution
NAICS 48621 Pipeline Transportation of Natural Gas
4924 Natural Gas Distribution
NAICS 22121 Natural Gas Distribution
**4925 Mixed, Manufactured, or Liquefied Petroleum Gas
Production And/or Distribution**
NAICS 22121 Natural Gas Distribution
4931 Electric & Other Services Combined
NAICS 221111 Hydroelectric Power Generation
NAICS 221112 Fossil Fuel Electric Power Generation
NAICS 221113 Nuclear Electric Power Generation
NAICS 221119 Other Electric Power Generation
NAICS 221121 Electric Bulk Power Transmission & Control
NAICS 221122 Electric Power Distribution
NAICS 22121 Natural Gas Distribution
4932 Gas & Other Services Combined
NAICS 22121 Natural Gas Distribution
4939 Combination Utilities, nec
NAICS 221111 Hydroelectric Power Generation
NAICS 221112 Fossil Fuel Electric Power Generation
NAICS 221113 Nuclear Electric Power Generation
NAICS 221119 Other Electric Power Generation
NAICS 221121 Electric Bulk Power Transmission & Control
NAICS 221122 Electric Power Distribution
NAICS 22121 Natural Gas Distribution
4941 Water Supply
NAICS 22131 Water Supply & Irrigation Systems
4952 Sewerage Systems
NAICS 22132 Sewage Treatment Facilities
4953 Refuse Systems
NAICS 562111 Solid Waste Collection
NAICS 562112 Hazardous Waste Collection
NAICS 56292 Materials Recovery Facilities
NAICS 562119 Other Waste Collection
NAICS 562211 Hazardous Waste Treatment & Disposal
NAICS 562212 Solid Waste Landfills
NAICS 562213 Solid Waste Combustors & Incinerators
NAICS 562219 Other Nonhazardous Waste Treatment &
Disposal
4959 Sanitary Services, nec
NAICS 488112 Airport Operations, Except Air Traffic Control
NAICS 56291 Remediation Services
NAICS 56171 Exterminating & Pest Control Services
NAICS 562998 All Other Miscellaneous Waste Management
Services
4961 Steam & Air-conditioning Supply
NAICS 22133 Steam & Air-conditioning Supply
4971 Irrigation Systems
NAICS 22131 Water Supply & Irrigation Systems

WHOLESALE TRADE

5012 Automobiles & Other Motor Vehicles
NAICS 42111 Automobile & Other Motor Vehicle
Wholesalers

5013 Motor Vehicle Supplies & New Parts
NAICS 44131 Automotive Parts & Accessories Stores - Retail
NAICS 42112 Motor Vehicle Supplies & New Part
          Wholesalers
5014 Tires & Tubes
NAICS 44132 Tire Dealers - Retail
NAICS 42113 Tire & Tube Wholesalers
5015 Motor Vehicle Parts, Used
NAICS 42114 Motor Vehicle Part Wholesalers
5021 Furniture
NAICS 44211 Furniture Stores
NAICS 42121 Furniture Wholesalers
5023 Home Furnishings
NAICS 44221 Floor Covering Stores
NAICS 42122 Home Furnishing Wholesalers
5031 Lumber, Plywood, Millwork, & Wood Panels
NAICS 44419 Other Building Material Dealers
NAICS 42131 Lumber, Plywood, Millwork, & Wood Panel
          Wholesalers
5032 Brick, Stone & Related Construction Materials
NAICS 44419 Other Building Material Dealers
NAICS 42132 Brick, Stone & Related Construction Material
          Wholesalers
5033 Roofing, Siding, & Insulation Materials
NAICS 42133 Roofing, Siding, & Insulation Material
          Wholesalers
5039 Construction Materials, nec
NAICS 44419 Other Building Material Dealers
NAICS 42139 Other Construction Material Wholesalers
5043 Photographic Equipment & Supplies
NAICS 42141 Photographic Equipment & Supplies
          Wholesalers
5044 Office Equipment
NAICS 42142 Office Equipment Wholesalers
5045 Computers & Computer Peripheral Equipment & Software
NAICS 42143 Computer & Computer Peripheral Equipment
          & Software Wholesalers
NAICS 44312 Computer & Software Stores - Retail
5046 Commercial Equipment, nec
NAICS 42144 Other Commercial Equipment Wholesalers
5047 Medical, Dental, & Hospital Equipment & Supplies
NAICS 42145 Medical, Dental & Hospital Equipment &
          Supplies Wholesalers
NAICS 446199 All Other Health & Personal Care Stores -
          Retail
5048 Ophthalmic Goods
NAICS 42146 Ophthalmic Goods Wholesalers
5049 Professional Equipment & Supplies, nec
NAICS 42149 Other Professional Equipment & Supplies
          Wholesalers
NAICS 45321 Office Supplies & Stationery Stores - Retail
5051 Metals Service Centers & Offices
NAICS 42151 Metals Service Centers & Offices
5052 Coal & Other Minerals & Ores
NAICS 42152 Coal & Other Mineral & Ore Wholesalers
5063 Electrical Apparatus & Equipment Wiring Supplies, & Construction Materials
NAICS 44419 Other Building Material Dealers
NAICS 42161 Electrical Apparatus & Equipment, Wiring
          Supplies & Construction Material Wholesalers
5064 Electrical Appliances, Television & Radio Sets
NAICS 42162 Electrical Appliance, Television & Radio Set
          Wholesalers

5065 Electronic Parts & Equipment, Not Elsewhere Classified
NAICS 42169 Other Electronic Parts & Equipment
          Wholesalers
5072 Hardware
NAICS 42171 Hardware Wholesalers
5074 Plumbing & Heating Equipment & Supplies
NAICS 44419 Other Building Material Dealers
NAICS 42172 Plumbing & Heating Equipment & Supplies
          Wholesalers
5075 Warm Air Heating & Air-conditioning Equipment & Supplies
NAICS 42173 Warm Air Heating & Air-conditioning
          Equipment & Supplies Wholesalers
5078 Refrigeration Equipment & Supplies
NAICS 42174 Refrigeration Equipment & Supplies
          Wholesalers
5082 Construction & Mining Machinery & Equipment
NAICS 42181 Construction & Mining Machinery &
          Equipment Wholesalers
5083 Farm & Garden Machinery & Equipment
NAICS 42182 Farm & Garden Machinery & Equipment
          Wholesalers
NAICS 44421 Outdoor Power Equipment Stores - Retail
5084 Industrial Machinery & Equipment
NAICS 42183 Industrial Machinery & Equipment Wholesalers
5085 Industrial Supplies
NAICS 42183 Industrial Machinery & Equipment Wholesalers
NAICS 42184 Industrial Supplies Wholesalers
NAICS 81131 Commercial & Industrial Machinery &
          Equipment Repair & Maintenence
5087 Service Establishment Equipment & Supplies
NAICS 42185 Service Establishment Equipment & Supplies
          Wholesalers
NAICS 44612 Cosmetics, Beauty Supplies, & Perfume Stores
5088 Transportation Equipment & Supplies, Except Motor Vehicles
NAICS 42186 Transportation Equipment & Supplies
          Wholesalers
5091 Sporting & Recreational Goods & Supplies
NAICS 42191 Sporting & Recreational Goods & Supplies
          Wholesalers
5092 Toys & Hobby Goods & Supplies
NAICS 42192 Toy & Hobby Goods & Supplies Wholesalers
5093 Scrap & Waste Materials
NAICS 42193 Recyclable Material Wholesalers
5094 Jewelry, Watches, Precious Stones, & Precious Metals
NAICS 42194 Jewelry, Watch , Precious Stone, & Precious
          Metal Wholesalers
5099 Durable Goods, nec
NAICS 42199 Other Miscellaneous Durable Goods
          Wholesalers
5111 Printing & Writing Paper
NAICS 42211 Printing & Writing Paper Wholesalers
5112 Stationery & Office Supplies
NAICS 45321 Office Supplies & Stationery Stores
NAICS 42212 Stationery & Office Supplies Wholesalers
5113 Industrial & Personal Service Paper
NAICS 42213 Industrial & Personal Service Paper
          Wholesalers
5122 Drugs, Drug Proprietaries, & Druggists' Sundries
NAICS 42221 Drugs, Drug Proprietaries, & Druggists'
          Sundries Wholesalers

5131 Piece Goods, Notions, & Other Dry Goods
NAICS 313311 Broadwoven Fabric Finishing Mills
NAICS 313312 Textile & Fabric Finishing Mills
NAICS 42231 Piece Goods, Notions, & Other Dry Goods
    Wholesalers
5136 Men's & Boys' Clothing & Furnishings
NAICS 42232 Men's & Boys' Clothing & Furnishings
    Wholesalers
5137 Women's Children's & Infants' Clothing & Accessories
NAICS 42233 Women's, Children's, & Infants' Clothing &
    Accessories Wholesalers
5139 Footwear
NAICS 42234 Footwear Wholesalers
5141 Groceries, General Line
NAICS 42241 General Line Grocery Wholesalers
5142 Packaged Frozen Foods
NAICS 42242 Packaged Frozen Food Wholesalers
5143 Dairy Products, Except Dried or Canned
NAICS 42243 Dairy Products Wholesalers
5144 Poultry & Poultry Products
NAICS 42244 Poultry & Poultry Product Wholesalers
5145 Confectionery
NAICS 42245 Confectionery Wholesalers
5146 Fish & Seafoods
NAICS 42246 Fish & Seafood Wholesalers
5147 Meats & Meat Products
NAICS 311612 Meat Processed from Carcasses
NAICS 42247 Meat & Meat Product Wholesalers
5148 Fresh Fruits & Vegetables
NAICS 42248 Fresh Fruit & Vegetable Wholesalers
5149 Groceries & Related Products, nec
NAICS 42249 Other Grocery & Related Product Wholesalers
5153 Grain & Field Beans
NAICS 42251 Grain & Field Bean Wholesalers
5154 Livestock
NAICS 42252 Livestock Wholesalers
5159 Farm-product Raw Materials, nec
NAICS 42259 Other Farm Product Raw Material Wholesalers
5162 Plastics Materials & Basic Forms & Shapes
NAICS 42261 Plastics Materials & Basic Forms & Shapes
    Wholesalers
5169 Chemicals & Allied Products, nec
NAICS 42269 Other Chemical & Allied Products Wholesalers
5171 Petroleum Bulk Stations & Terminals
NAICS 454311 Heating Oil Dealers
NAICS 454312 Liquefied Petroleum Gas Dealers
NAICS 42271 Petroleum Bulk Stations & Terminals
5172 Petroleum & Petroleum Products Wholesalers, Except Bulk Stations & Terminals
NAICS 42272 Petroleum & Petroleum Products Wholesalers
5181 Beer & Ale
NAICS 42281 Beer & Ale Wholesalers
5182 Wine & Distilled Alcoholic Beverages
NAICS 42282 Wine & Distilled Alcoholic Beverage
    Wholesalers
5191 Farm Supplies
NAICS 44422 Nursery & Garden Centers - Retail
NAICS 42291 Farm Supplies Wholesalers
5192 Books, Periodicals, & Newspapers
NAICS 42292 Book, Periodical & Newspaper Wholesalers
5193 Flowers, Nursery Stock, & Florists' Supplies
NAICS 42293 Flower, Nursery Stock & Florists' Supplies
    Wholesalers
NAICS 44422 Nursery & Garden Centers - Retail

5194 Tobacco & Tobacco Products
NAICS 42294 Tobacco & Tobacco Product Wholesalers
5198 Paint, Varnishes, & Supplies
NAICS 42295 Paint, Varnish & Supplies Wholesalers
NAICS 44412 Paint & Wallpaper Stores
5199 Nondurable Goods, nec
NAICS 54189 Other Services Related to Advertising
NAICS 42299 Other Miscellaneous Nondurable Goods
    Wholesalers

RETAIL TRADE

5211 Lumber & Other Building Materials Dealers
NAICS 44411 Home Centers
NAICS 42131 Lumber, Plywood, Millwork & Wood Panel
    Wholesalers
NAICS 44419 Other Building Material Dealers
5231 Paint, Glass, & Wallpaper Stores
NAICS 42295 Paint, Varnish & Supplies Wholesalers
NAICS 44419 Other Building Material Dealers
NAICS 44412 Paint & Wallpaper Stores
5251 Hardware Stores
NAICS 44413 Hardware Stores
5261 Retail Nurseries, Lawn & Garden Supply Stores
NAICS 44422 Nursery & Garden Centers
NAICS 453998 All Other Miscellaneous Store Retailers
NAICS 44421 Outdoor Power Equipment Stores
5271 Mobile Home Dealers
NAICS 45393 Manufactured Home Dealers
5311 Department Stores
NAICS 45211 Department Stores
5331 Variety Stores
NAICS 45299 All Other General Merchandise Stores
5399 Miscellaneous General Merchandise Stores
NAICS 45291 Warehouse Clubs & Superstores
NAICS 45299 All Other General Merchandise Stores
5411 Grocery Stores
NAICS 44711 Gasoline Stations with Convenience Stores
NAICS 44511 Supermarkets & Other Grocery Stores
NAICS 45291 Warehouse Clubs & Superstores
NAICS 44512 Convenience Stores
5421 Meat & Fish Markets, Including Freezer Provisioners
NAICS 45439 Other Direct Selling Establishments
NAICS 44521 Meat Markets
NAICS 44522 Fish & Seafood Markets
5431 Fruit & Vegetable Markets
NAICS 44523 Fruit & Vegetable Markets
5441 Candy, Nut, & Confectionery Stores
NAICS 445292 Confectionary & Nut Stores
5451 Dairy Products Stores
NAICS 445299 All Other Specialty Food Stores
5461 Retail Bakeries
NAICS 722213 Snack & Nonalcoholic Beverage Bars
NAICS 311811 Retail Bakeries
NAICS 445291 Baked Goods Stores
5499 Miscellaneous Food Stores
NAICS 44521 Meat Markets
NAICS 722211 Limited-service Restaurants
NAICS 446191 Food Supplement Stores
NAICS 445299 All Other Specialty Food Stores
5511 Motor Vehicle Dealers
NAICS 44111 New Car Dealers

5521 Motor Vehicle Dealers
NAICS 44112 Used Car Dealers
5531 Auto & Home Supply Stores
NAICS 44132 Tire Dealers
NAICS 44131 Automotive Parts & Accessories Stores
5541 Gasoline Service Stations
NAICS 44711 Gasoline Stations with Convenience Store
NAICS 44719 Other Gasoline Stations
5551 Boat Dealers
NAICS 441222 Boat Dealers
5561 Recreational Vehicle Dealers
NAICS 44121 Recreational Vehicle Dealers
5571 Motorcycle Dealers
NAICS 441221 Motorcycle Dealers
5599 Automotive Dealers, nec
NAICS 441229 All Other Motor Vehicle Dealers
5611 Men's & Boys' Clothing & Accessory Stores
NAICS 44811 Men's Clothing Stores
NAICS 44815 Clothing Accessories Stores
5621 Women's Clothing Stores
NAICS 44812 Women's Clothing Stores
5632 Women's Accessory & Specialty Stores
NAICS 44819 Other Clothing Stores
NAICS 44815 Clothing Accessories Stores
5641 Children's & Infants' Wear Stores
NAICS 44813 Children's & Infants' Clothing Stores
5651 Family Clothing Stores
NAICS 44814 Family Clothing Stores
5661 Shoe Stores
NAICS 44821 Shoe Stores
5699 Miscellaneous Apparel & Accessory Stores
NAICS 315   Included in Apparel Manufacturing Subsector
             Based on Type of Garment Produced
NAICS 44819 Other Clothing Stores
NAICS 44815 Clothing Accessories Stores
5712 Furniture Stores
NAICS 337133 Wood Household Furniture, Except
             Upholstered, Manufacturing
NAICS 337131 Wood Kitchen Cabinet & Counter Top
             Manufacturing
NAICS 337132 Upholstered Household Furniture
             Manufacturing
NAICS 44211 Furniture Stores
5713 Floor Covering Stores
NAICS 44221 Floor Covering Stores
5714 Drapery, Curtain, & Upholstery Stores
NAICS 442291 Window Treatment Stores
NAICS 45113 Sewing, Needlework & Piece Goods Stores
NAICS 314121 Curtain & Drapery Mills
5719 Miscellaneous Homefurnishings Stores
NAICS 442291 Window Treatment Stores
NAICS 442299 All Other Home Furnishings Stores
5722 Household Appliance Stores
NAICS 443111 Household Appliance Stores
5731 Radio, Television, & Consumer Electronics Stores
NAICS 443112 Radio, Television, & Other Electronics Stores
NAICS 44131 Automotive Parts & Accessories Stores
5734 Computer & Computer Software Stores
NAICS 44312 Computer & Software Stores
5735 Record & Prerecorded Tape Stores
NAICS 45122 Prerecorded Tape, Compact Disc & Record
             Stores

5736 Musical Instrument Stores
NAICS 45114 Musical Instrument & Supplies Stores
5812 Eating & Drinking Places
NAICS 72211 Full-service Restaurants
NAICS 722211 Limited-service Restaurants
NAICS 722212 Cafeterias
NAICS 722213 Snack & Nonalcoholic Beverage Bars
NAICS 72231 Foodservice Contractors
NAICS 72232 Caterers
NAICS 71111 Theater Companies & Dinner Theaters
5813 Drinking Places
NAICS 72241 Drinking Places
5912 Drug Stores & Proprietary Stores
NAICS 44611 Pharmacies & Drug Stores
5921 Liquor Stores
NAICS 44531 Beer, Wine & Liquor Stores
5932 Used Merchandise Stores
NAICS 522298 All Other Non-depository Credit
             Intermediation
NAICS 45331 Used Merchandise Stores
5941 Sporting Goods Stores & Bicycle Shops
NAICS 45111 Sporting Goods Stores
5942 Book Stores
NAICS 451211 Book Stores
5943 Stationery Stores
NAICS 45321 Office Supplies & Stationery Stores
5944 Jewelry Stores
NAICS 44831 Jewelry Stores
5945 Hobby, Toy, & Game Shops
NAICS 45112 Hobby, Toy & Game Stores
5946 Camera & Photographic Supply Stores
NAICS 44313 Camera & Photographic Supplies Stores
5947 Gift, Novelty, & Souvenir Shops
NAICS 45322 Gift, Novelty & Souvenir Stores
5948 Luggage & Leather Goods Stores
NAICS 44832 Luggage & Leather Goods Stores
5949 Sewing, Needlework, & Piece Goods Stores
NAICS 45113 Sewing, Needlework & Piece Goods Stores
5961 Catalog & Mail-order Houses
NAICS 45411 Electronic Shopping & Mail-order Houses
5962 Automatic Merchandising Machine Operator
NAICS 45421 Vending Machine Operators
5963 Direct Selling Establishments
NAICS 72233 Mobile Caterers
NAICS 45439 Other Direct Selling Establishments
5983 Fuel Oil Dealers
NAICS 454311 Heating Oil Dealers
5984 Liquefied Petroleum Gas Dealers
NAICS 454312 Liquefied Petroleum Gas Dealers
5989 Fuel Dealers, nec
NAICS 454319 Other Fuel Dealers
5992 Florists
NAICS 45311 Florists
5993 Tobacco Stores & Stands
NAICS 453991 Tobacco Stores
5994 News Dealers & Newsstands
NAICS 451212 News Dealers & Newsstands
5995 Optical Goods Stores
NAICS 339117 Eyeglass & Contact Lens Manufacturing
NAICS 44613 Optical Goods Stores
5999 Miscellaneous Retail Stores, nec
NAICS 44612 Cosmetics, Beauty Supplies & Perfume Stores
NAICS 446199 All Other Health & Personal Care Stores
NAICS 45391 Pet & Pet Supplies Stores

NAICS 45392 Art Dealers
NAICS 443111 Household Appliance Stores
NAICS 443112 Radio, Television & Other Electronics Stores
NAICS 44831 Jewelry Stores
NAICS 453999 All Other Miscellaneous Store Retailers

FINANCE, INSURANCE, & REAL ESTATE

6011 Federal Reserve Banks
NAICS 52111 Monetary Authorities-central Banks
6019 Central Reserve Depository Institutions, nec
NAICS 52232 Financial Transactions Processing, Reserve, & Clearing House Activities
6021 National Commercial Banks
NAICS 52211 Commercial Banking
NAICS 52221 Credit Card Issuing
NAICS 523991 Trust, Fiduciary & Custody Activities
6022 State Commercial Banks
NAICS 52211 Commercial Banking
NAICS 52221 Credit Card Issuing
NAICS 52219 Other Depository Intermediation
NAICS 523991 Trust, Fiduciary & Custody Activities
6029 Commercial Banks, nec
NAICS 52211 Commercial Banking
6035 Savings Institutions, Federally Chartered
NAICS 52212 Savings Institutions
6036 Savings Institutions, Not Federally Chartered
NAICS 52212 Savings Institutions
6061 Credit Unions, Federally Chartered
NAICS 52213 Credit Unions
6062 Credit Unions, Not Federally Chartered
NAICS 52213 Credit Unions
6081 Branches & Agencies of Foreign Banks
NAICS 522293 International Trade Financing
NAICS 52211 Commercial Banking
NAICS 522298 All Other Non-depository Credit Intermediation
6082 Foreign Trade & International Banking Institutions
NAICS 522293 International Trade Financing
6091 Nondeposit Trust Facilities
NAICS 523991 Trust, Fiduciary, & Custody Activities
6099 Functions Related to Deposit Banking, nec
NAICS 52232 Financial Transactions Processing, Reserve, & Clearing House Activities
NAICS 52313 Commodity Contracts Dealing
NAICS 523991 Trust, Fiduciary, & Custody Activities
NAICS 523999 Miscellaneous Financial Investment Activities
NAICS 52239 Other Activities Related to Credit Intermediation
6111 Federal & Federally Sponsored Credit Agencies
NAICS 522293 International Trade Financing
NAICS 522294 Secondary Market Financing
NAICS 522298 All Other Non-depository Credit Intermediation
6141 Personal Credit Institutions
NAICS 52221 Credit Card Issuing
NAICS 52222 Sales Financing
NAICS 522291 Consumer Lending
6153 Short-term Business Credit Institutions, Except Agricultural
NAICS 52222 Sales Financing
NAICS 52232 Financial Transactions Processing, Reserve, & Clearing House Activities

NAICS 522298 All Other Non-depository Credit Intermediation
6159 Miscellaneous Business Credit Institutions
NAICS 52222 Sales Financing
NAICS 532 Included in Rental & Leasing Services Subsector by Type of Equipment & Method of Operation
NAICS 522293 International Trade Financing
NAICS 522298 All Other Non-depository Credit Intermediation
6162 Mortgage Bankers & Loan Correspondents
NAICS 522292 Real Estate Credit
NAICS 52239 Other Activities Related to Credit Intermediation
6163 Loan Brokers
NAICS 52231 Mortgage & Other Loan Brokers
6211 Security Brokers, Dealers, & Flotation Companies
NAICS 52311 Investment Banking & Securities Dealing
NAICS 52312 Securities Brokerage
NAICS 52391 Miscellaneous Intermediation
NAICS 523999 Miscellaneous Financial Investment Activities
6221 Commodity Contracts Brokers & Dealers
NAICS 52313 Commodity Contracts Dealing
NAICS 52314 Commodity Brokerage
6231 Security & Commodity Exchanges
NAICS 52321 Securities & Commodity Exchanges
6282 Investment Advice
NAICS 52392 Portfolio Management
NAICS 52393 Investment Advice
6289 Services Allied with the Exchange of Securities or Commodities, nec
NAICS 523991 Trust, Fiduciary, & Custody Activities
NAICS 523999 Miscellaneous Financial Investment Activities
6311 Life Insurance
NAICS 524113 Direct Life Insurance Carriers
NAICS 52413 Reinsurance Carriers
6321 Accident & Health Insurance
NAICS 524114 Direct Health & Medical Insurance Carriers
NAICS 52519 Other Insurance Funds
NAICS 52413 Reinsurance Carriers
6324 Hospital & Medical Service Plans
NAICS 524114 Direct Health & Medical Insurance Carriers
NAICS 52519 Other Insurance Funds
NAICS 52413 Reinsurance Carriers
6331 Fire, Marine, & Casualty Insurance
NAICS 524126 Direct Property & Casualty Insurance Carriers
NAICS 52519 Other Insurance Funds
NAICS 52413 Reinsurance Carriers
6351 Surety Insurance
NAICS 524126 Direct Property & Casualty Insurance Carriers
NAICS 52413 Reinsurance Carriers
6361 Title Insurance
NAICS 524127 Direct Title Insurance Carriers
NAICS 52413 Reinsurance Carriers
6371 Pension, Health, & Welfare Funds
NAICS 52392 Portfolio Management
NAICS 524292 Third Party Administration for Insurance & Pension Funds
NAICS 52511 Pension Funds
NAICS 52512 Health & Welfare Funds
6399 Insurance Carriers, nec
NAICS 524128 Other Direct Insurance Carriers

6411 Insurance Agents, Brokers, & Service
NAICS 52421 Insurance Agencies & Brokerages
NAICS 524291 Claims Adjusters
NAICS 524292 Third Party Administrators for Insurance &
Pension Funds
NAICS 524298 All Other Insurance Related Activities
6512 Operators of Nonresidential Buildings
NAICS 71131 Promoters of Performing Arts, Sports & Similar
Events with Facilities
NAICS 53112 Lessors of Nonresidential Buildings
6513 Operators of Apartment Buildings
NAICS 53111 Lessors of Residential Buildings & Dwellings
6514 Operators of Dwellings Other than Apartment Buildings
NAICS 53111 Lessors of Residential Buildings & Dwellings
6515 Operators of Residential Mobile Home Sites
NAICS 53119 Lessors of Other Real Estate Property
6517 Lessors of Railroad Property
NAICS 53119 Lessors of Other Real Estate Property
6519 Lessors of Real Property, nec
NAICS 53119 Lessors of Other Real Estate Property
6531 Real Estate Agents & Managers
NAICS 53121 Offices of Real Estate Agents & Brokers
NAICS 81399 Other Similar Organizations
NAICS 531311 Residential Property Managers
NAICS 531312 Nonresidential Property Managers
NAICS 53132 Offices of Real Estate Appraisers
NAICS 81222 Cemeteries & Crematories
NAICS 531399 All Other Activities Related to Real Estate
6541 Title Abstract Offices
NAICS 541191 Title Abstract & Settlement Offices
6552 Land Subdividers & Developers, Except Cemeteries
NAICS 23311 Land Subdivision & Land Development
6553 Cemetery Subdividers & Developers
NAICS 81222 Cemeteries & Crematories
6712 Offices of Bank Holding Companies
NAICS 551111 Offices of Bank Holding Companies
6719 Offices of Holding Companies, nec
NAICS 551112 Offices of Other Holding Companies
6722 Management Investment Offices, Open-end
NAICS 52591 Open-end Investment Funds
**6726 Unit Investment Trusts, Face-amount Certificate Offices, &
Closed-end Management Investment Offices**
NAICS 52599 Other Financial Vehicles
6732 Education, Religious, & Charitable Trusts
NAICS 813211 Grantmaking Foundations
6733 Trusts, Except Educational, Religious, & Charitable
NAICS 52392 Portfolio Management
NAICS 523991 Trust, Fiduciary, & Custody Services
NAICS 52519 Other Insurance Funds
NAICS 52592 Trusts, Estates, & Agency Accounts
6792 Oil Royalty Traders
NAICS 523999 Miscellaneous Financial Investment Activities
NAICS 53311 Owners & Lessors of Other Non-financial
Assets
6794 Patent Owners & Lessors
NAICS 53311 Owners & Lessors of Other Non-financial
Assets
6798 Real Estate Investment Trusts
NAICS 52593 Real Estate Investment Trusts
6799 Investors, nec
NAICS 52391 Miscellaneous Intermediation
NAICS 52392 Portfolio Management
NAICS 52313 Commodity Contracts Dealing
NAICS 523999 Miscellaneous Financial Investment Activities

SERVICE INDUSTRIES

7011 Hotels & Motels
NAICS 72111   Hotels & Motels
NAICS 72112   Casino Hotels
NAICS 721191 Bed & Breakfast Inns
NAICS 721199 All Other Traveler Accommodation
7021 Rooming & Boarding Houses
NAICS 72131   Rooming & Boarding Houses
7032 Sporting & Recreational Camps
NAICS 721214 Recreational & Vacation Camps
7033 Recreational Vehicle Parks & Campsites
NAICS 721211 Rv & Campgrounds
**7041 Organization Hotels & Lodging Houses, on Membership
Basis**
NAICS 72111   Hotels & Motels
NAICS 72131   Rooming & Boarding Houses
7211 Power Laundries, Family & Commercial
NAICS 812321 Laundries, Family & Commercial
7212 Garment Pressing, & Agents for Laundries
NAICS 812391 Garment Pressing & Agents for Laundries
7213 Linen Supply
NAICS 812331 Linen Supply
7215 Coin-operated Laundry & Drycleaning
NAICS 81231   Coin-operated Laundries & Drycleaners
7216 Drycleaning Plants, Except Rug Cleaning
NAICS 812322 Drycleaning Plants
7217 Carpet & Upholstery Cleaning
NAICS 56174   Carpet & Upholstery Cleaning Services
7218 Industrial Launderers
NAICS 812332 Industrial Launderers
7219 Laundry & Garment Services, nec
NAICS 812331 Linen Supply
NAICS 81149   Other Personal & Household Goods Repair &
Maintenance
NAICS 812399 All Other Laundry Services
7221 Photographic Studios, Portrait
NAICS 541921 Photographic Studios, Portrait
7231 Beauty Shops
NAICS 812112 Beauty Salons
NAICS 812113 Nail Salons
NAICS 611511 Cosmetology & Barber Schools
7241 Barber Shops
NAICS 812111 Barber Shops
NAICS 611511 Cosmetology & Barber Schools
7251 Shoe Repair Shops & Shoeshine Parlors
NAICS 81143   Footwear & Leather Goods Repair
7261 Funeral Services & Crematories
NAICS 81221   Funeral Homes
NAICS 81222   Cemeteries & Crematories
7291 Tax Return Preparation Services
NAICS 541213 Tax Preparation Services
7299 Miscellaneous Personal Services, nec
NAICS 62441   Child Day Care Services
NAICS 812191 Diet & Weight Reducing Centers
NAICS 53222   Formal Wear & Costume Rental
NAICS 812199 Other Personal Care Services
NAICS 81299   All Other Personal Services
7311 Advertising Agencies
NAICS 54181   Advertising Agencies
7312 Outdoor Advertising Services
NAICS 54185   Display Advertising

7313 Radio, Television, & Publishers' Advertising Representatives
NAICS 54184 Media Representatives
7319 Advertising, nec
NAICS 481219 Other Nonscheduled Air Transportation
NAICS 54183 Media Buying Agencies
NAICS 54185 Display Advertising
NAICS 54187 Advertising Material Distribution Services
NAICS 54189 Other Services Related to Advertising
7322 Adjustment & Collection Services
NAICS 56144 Collection Agencies
NAICS 561491 Repossession Services
7323 Credit Reporting Services
NAICS 56145 Credit Bureaus
7331 Direct Mail Advertising Services
NAICS 54186 Direct Mail Advertising
7334 Photocopying & Duplicating Services
NAICS 561431 Photocopying & Duplicating Services
7335 Commercial Photography
NAICS 48122 Nonscheduled Speciality Air Transportation
NAICS 541922 Commercial Photography
7336 Commercial Art & Graphic Design
NAICS 54143 Commercial Art & Graphic Design Services
7338 Secretarial & Court Reporting Services
NAICS 56141 Document Preparation Services
NAICS 561492 Court Reporting & Stenotype Services
7342 Disinfecting & Pest Control Services
NAICS 56172 Janitorial Services
NAICS 56171 Exterminating & Pest Control Services
7349 Building Cleaning & Maintenance Services, nec
NAICS 56172 Janitorial Services
7352 Medical Equipment Rental & Leasing
NAICS 532291 Home Health Equipment Rental
NAICS 53249 Other Commercial & Industrial Machinery & Equipment Rental & Leasing
7353 Heavy Construction Equipment Rental & Leasing
NAICS 23499 All Other Heavy Construction
NAICS 532412 Construction, Mining & Forestry Machinery & Equipment Rental & Leasing
7359 Equipment Rental & Leasing, nec
NAICS 53221 Consumer Electronics & Appliances Rental
NAICS 53231 General Rental Centers
NAICS 532299 All Other Consumer Goods Rental
NAICS 532412 Construction, Mining & Forestry Machinery & Equipment Rental & Leasing
NAICS 532411 Commercial Air, Rail, & Water Transportation Equipment Rental & Leasing
NAICS 562991 Septic Tank & Related Services
NAICS 53242 Office Machinery & Equipment Rental & Leasing
NAICS 53249 Other Commercial & Industrial Machinery & Equipment Rental & Leasing
7361 Employment Agencies
NAICS 541612 Human Resources & Executive Search Consulting Services
NAICS 56131 Employment Placement Agencies
7363 Help Supply Services
NAICS 56132 Temporary Help Services
NAICS 56133 Employee Leasing Services
7371 Computer Programming Services
NAICS 541511 Custom Computer Programming Services
7372 Prepackaged Software
NAICS 51121 Software Publishers
NAICS 334611 Software Reproducing

7373 Computer Integrated Systems Design
NAICS 541512 Computer Systems Design Services
7374 Computer Processing & Data Preparation & Processing Services
NAICS 51421 Data Processing Services
7375 Information Retrieval Services
NAICS 514191 On-line Information Services
7376 Computer Facilities Management Services
NAICS 541513 Computer Facilities Management Services
7377 Computer Rental & Leasing
NAICS 53242 Office Machinery & Equipment Rental & Leasing
7378 Computer Maintenance & Repair
NAICS 44312 Computer & Software Stores
NAICS 811212 Computer & Office Machine Repair & Maintenance
7379 Computer Related Services, nec
NAICS 541512 Computer Systems Design Services
NAICS 541519 Other Computer Related Services
7381 Detective, Guard, & Armored Car Services
NAICS 561611 Investigation Services
NAICS 561612 Security Guards & Patrol Services
NAICS 561613 Armored Car Services
7382 Security Systems Services
NAICS 561621 Security Systems Services
7383 News Syndicates
NAICS 51411 New Syndicates
7384 Photofinishing Laboratories
NAICS 812921 Photo Finishing Laboratories
NAICS 812922 One-hour Photo Finishing
7389 Business Services, nec
NAICS 51224 Sound Recording Studios
NAICS 51229 Other Sound Recording Industries
NAICS 541199 All Other Legal Services
NAICS 81299 All Other Personal Services
NAICS 54137 Surveying & Mapping Services
NAICS 54141 Interior Design Services
NAICS 54142 Industrial Design Services
NAICS 54134 Drafting Services
NAICS 54149 Other Specialized Design Services
NAICS 54189 Other Services Related to Advertising
NAICS 54193 Translation & Interpretation Services
NAICS 54135 Building Inspection Services
NAICS 54199 All Other Professional, Scientific & Technical Services
NAICS 71141 Agents & Managers for Artists, Athletes, Entertainers & Other Public Figures
NAICS 561422 Telemarketing Bureaus
NAICS 561432 Private Mail Centers
NAICS 561439 Other Business Service Centers
NAICS 561491 Repossession Services
NAICS 56191 Packaging & Labeling Services
NAICS 56179 Other Services to Buildings & Dwellings
NAICS 561599 All Other Travel Arrangement & Reservation Services
NAICS 56192 Convention & Trade Show Organizers
NAICS 561591 Convention & Visitors Bureaus
NAICS 52232 Financial Transactions, Processing, Reserve & Clearing House Activities
NAICS 561499 All Other Business Support Services
NAICS 56199 All Other Support Services
7513 Truck Rental & Leasing, Without Drivers
NAICS 53212 Truck, Utility Trailer & Rv Rental & Leasing

7514 Passenger Car Rental
NAICS 532111 Passenger Cars Rental
7515 Passenger Car Leasing
NAICS 532112 Passenger Cars Leasing
7519 Utility Trailer & Recreational Vehicle Rental
NAICS 53212 Truck, Utility Trailer & Rv Rental & Leasing
7521 Automobile Parking
NAICS 81293 Parking Lots & Garages
7532 Top, Body, & Upholstery Repair Shops & Paint Shops
NAICS 811121 Automotive Body, Paint, & Upholstery Repair
& Maintenance
7533 Automotive Exhaust System Repair Shops
NAICS 811112 Automotive Exhaust System Repair
7534 Tire Retreading & Repair Shops
NAICS 326212 Tire Retreading
NAICS 811198 All Other Automotive Repair & Maintenance
7536 Automotive Glass Replacement Shops
NAICS 811122 Automotive Glass Replacement Shops
7537 Automotive Transmission Repair Shops
NAICS 811113 Automotive Transmission Repair
7538 General Automotive Repair Shops
NAICS 811111 General Automotive Repair
7539 Automotive Repair Shops, nec
NAICS 811118 Other Automotive Mechanical & Electrical
Repair & Maintenance
7542 Carwashes
NAICS 811192 Car Washes
7549 Automotive Services, Except Repair & Carwashes
NAICS 811191 Automotive Oil Change & Lubrication Shops
NAICS 48841 Motor Vehicle Towing
NAICS 811198 All Other Automotive Repair & Maintenance
7622 Radio & Television Repair Shops
NAICS 811211 Consumer Electronics Repair & Maintenance
NAICS 443112 Radio, Television & Other Electronics Stores
7623 Refrigeration & Air-conditioning Services & Repair Shops
NAICS 443111 Household Appliance Stores
NAICS 81131 Commercial & Industrial Machinery &
Equipment Repair & Maintenance
NAICS 811412 Appliance Repair & Maintenance
7629 Electrical & Electronic Repair Shops, nec
NAICS 443111 Household Appliance Stores
NAICS 811212 Computer & Office Machine Repair &
Maintenance
NAICS 811213 Communication Equipment Repair &
Maintenance
NAICS 811219 Other Electronic & Precision Equipment
Repair & Maintenance
NAICS 811412 Appliance Repair & Maintenance
NAICS 811211 Consumer Electronics Repair & Maintenance
7631 Watch, Clock, & Jewelry Repair
NAICS 81149 Other Personal & Household Goods Repair &
Maintenance
7641 Reupholster & Furniture Repair
NAICS 81142 Reupholstery & Furniture Repair
7692 Welding Repair
NAICS 81149 Other Personal & Household Goods Repair &
Maintenance
7694 Armature Rewinding Shops
NAICS 81131 Commercial & Industrial Machinery &
Equipment Repair & Maintenance
NAICS 335312 Motor & Generator Manufacturing
7699 Repair Shops & Related Services, nec
NAICS 561622 Locksmiths
NAICS 562991 Septic Tank & Related Services

NAICS 56179 Other Services to Buildings & Dwellings
NAICS 48839 Other Supporting Activities for Water
Transportation
NAICS 45111 Sporting Goods Stores
NAICS 81131 Commercial & Industrial Machinery &
Equipment Repair & Maintenance
NAICS 11521 Support Activities for Animal Production
NAICS 811212 Computer & Office Machine Repair &
Maintenance
NAICS 811219 Other Electronic & Precision Equipment
Repair & Maintenance
NAICS 811411 Home & Garden Equipment Repair &
Maintenance
NAICS 811412 Appliance Repair & Maintenance
NAICS 81143 Footwear & Leather Goods Repair
NAICS 81149 Other Personal & Household Goods Repair &
Maintenance
7812 Motion Picture & Video Tape Production
NAICS 51211 Motion Picture & Video Production
7819 Services Allied to Motion Picture Production
NAICS 512191 Teleproduction & Other Post-production
Services
NAICS 56131 Employment Placement Agencies
NAICS 53222 Formal Wear & Costumes Rental
NAICS 53249 Other Commercial & Industrial Machinery &
Equipment Rental & Leasing
NAICS 541214 Payroll Services
NAICS 71151 Independent Artists, Writers, & Performers
NAICS 334612 Prerecorded Compact Disc , Tape, & Record
Manufacturing
NAICS 512199 Other Motion Picture & Video Industries
7822 Motion Picture & Video Tape Distribution
NAICS 42199 Other Miscellaneous Durable Goods
Wholesalers
NAICS 51212 Motion Picture & Video Distribution
7829 Services Allied to Motion Picture Distribution
NAICS 512199 Other Motion Picture & Video Industries
NAICS 51212 Motion Picture & Video Distribution
7832 Motion Picture Theaters, Except Drive-ins.
NAICS 512131 Motion Picture Theaters, Except Drive-in
7833 Drive-in Motion Picture Theaters
NAICS 512132 Drive-in Motion Picture Theaters
7841 Video Tape Rental
NAICS 53223 Video Tapes & Disc Rental
7911 Dance Studios, Schools, & Halls
NAICS 71399 All Other Amusement & Recreation Industries
NAICS 61161 Fine Arts Schools
7922 Theatrical Producers & Miscellaneous Theatrical Services
NAICS 56131 Employment Placement Agencies
NAICS 71111 Theater Companies & Dinner Theaters
NAICS 71141 Agents & Managers for Artists, Athletes,
Entertainers & Other Public Figures
NAICS 71112 Dance Companies
NAICS 71131 Promoters of Performing Arts, Sports, &
Similar Events with Facilities
NAICS 71132 Promoters of Performing Arts, Sports, &
Similar Events Without Facilities
NAICS 51229 Other Sound Recording Industries
NAICS 53249 Other Commercial & Industrial Machinery &
Equipment Rental & Leasing
**7929 Bands, Orchestras, Actors, & Other Entertainers &
Entertainment Groups**
NAICS 71113 Musical Groups & Artists
NAICS 71151 Independent Artists, Writers, & Performers

NAICS 71119 Other Performing Arts Companies
7933 Bowling Centers
NAICS 71395 Bowling Centers
7941 Professional Sports Clubs & Promoters
NAICS 711211 Sports Teams & Clubs
NAICS 71141 Agents & Managers for Artists, Athletes,
           Entertainers , & Other Public Figures
NAICS 71132 Promoters of Arts, Sports & Similar Events
           Without Facilities
NAICS 71131 Promoters of Arts, Sports, & Similar Events
           with Facilities
NAICS 711219 Other Spectator Sports
7948 Racing, Including Track Operations
NAICS 711212 Race Tracks
NAICS 711219 Other Spectator Sports
7991 Physical Fitness Facilities
NAICS 71394 Fitness & Recreational Sports Centers
7992 Public Golf Courses
NAICS 71391 Golf Courses & Country Clubs
7993 Coin Operated Amusement Devices
NAICS 71312 Amusement Arcades
NAICS 71329 Other Gambling Industries
NAICS 71399 All Other Amusement & Recreation Industries
7996 Amusement Parks
NAICS 71311 Amusement & Theme Parks
7997 Membership Sports & Recreation Clubs
NAICS 48122 Nonscheduled Speciality Air Transportation
NAICS 71391 Golf Courses & Country Clubs
NAICS 71394 Fitness & Recreational Sports Centers
NAICS 71399 All Other Amusement & Recreation Industries
7999 Amusement & Recreation Services, nec
NAICS 561599 All Other Travel Arrangement & Reservation
           Services
NAICS 48799 Scenic & Sightseeing Transportation, Other
NAICS 71119 Other Performing Arts Companies
NAICS 711219 Other Spectator Sports
NAICS 71392 Skiing Facilities
NAICS 71394 Fitness & Recreational Sports Centers
NAICS 71321 Casinos
NAICS 71329 Other Gambling Industries
NAICS 71219 Nature Parks & Other Similar Institutions
NAICS 61162 Sports & Recreation Instruction
NAICS 532292 Recreational Goods Rental
NAICS 48711 Scenic & Sightseeing Transportation, Land
NAICS 48721 Scenic & Sightseeing Transportation, Water
NAICS 71399 All Other Amusement & Recreation Industries
8011 Offices & Clinics of Doctors of Medicine
NAICS 621493 Freestanding Ambulatory Surgical &
           Emergency Centers
NAICS 621491 Hmo Medical Centers
NAICS 621112 Offices of Physicians, Mental Health Specialists
NAICS 621111 Offices of Physicians
8021 Offices & Clinics of Dentists
NAICS 62121 Offices of Dentists
8031 Offices & Clinics of Doctors of Osteopathy
NAICS 621111 Offices of Physicians
NAICS 621112 Offices of Physicians, Mental Health Specialists
8041 Offices & Clinics of Chiropractors
NAICS 62131 Offices of Chiropractors
8042 Offices & Clinics of Optometrists
NAICS 62132 Offices of Optometrists
8043 Offices & Clinics of Podiatrists
NAICS 621391 Offices of Podiatrists

8049 Offices & Clinics of Health Practitioners, nec
NAICS 62133 Offices of Mental Health Practitioners
NAICS 62134 Offices of Physical, Occupational, & Speech
           Therapists & Audiologists
NAICS 621399 Offices of All Other Miscellaneous Health
           Practitioners
8051 Skilled Nursing Care Facilities
NAICS 623311 Continuing Care Retirement Communities
NAICS 62311 Nursing Care Facilities
8052 Intermediate Care Facilities
NAICS 623311 Continuing Care Retirement Communities
NAICS 62321 Residential Mental Retardation Facilities
NAICS 62311 Nursing Care Facilities
8059 Nursing & Personal Care Facilities, nec
NAICS 623311 Continuing Care Retirement Communities
NAICS 62311 Nursing Care Facilities
8062 General Medical & Surgical Hospitals
NAICS 62211 General Medical & Surgical Hospitals
8063 Psychiatric Hospitals
NAICS 62221 Psychiatric & Substance Abuse Hospitals
8069 Specialty Hospitals, Except Psychiatric
NAICS 62211 General Medical & Surgical Hospitals
NAICS 62221 Psychiatric & Substance Abuse Hospitals
NAICS 62231 Specialty Hospitals
8071 Medical Laboratories
NAICS 621512 Diagnostic Imaging Centers
NAICS 621511 Medical Laboratories
8072 Dental Laboratories
NAICS 339116 Dental Laboratories
8082 Home Health Care Services
NAICS 62161 Home Health Care Services
8092 Kidney Dialysis Centers
NAICS 621492 Kidney Dialysis Centers
8093 Specialty Outpatient Facilities, nec
NAICS 62141 Family Planning Centers
NAICS 62142 Outpatient Mental Health & Substance Abuse
           Centers
NAICS 621498 All Other Outpatient Care Facilities
8099 Health & Allied Services, nec
NAICS 621991 Blood & Organ Banks
NAICS 54143 Graphic Design Services
NAICS 541922 Commercial Photography
NAICS 62141 Family Planning Centers
NAICS 621999 All Other Miscellaneous Ambulatory Health
           Care Services
8111 Legal Services
NAICS 54111 Offices of Lawyers
8211 Elementary & Secondary Schools
NAICS 61111 Elementary & Secondary Schools
8221 Colleges, Universities, & Professional Schools
NAICS 61131 Colleges, Universities & Professional Schools
8222 Junior Colleges & Technical Institutes
NAICS 61121 Junior Colleges
8231 Libraries
NAICS 51412 Libraries & Archives
8243 Data Processing Schools
NAICS 611519 Other Technical & Trade Schools
NAICS 61142 Computer Training
8244 Business & Secretarial Schools
NAICS 61141 Business & Secretarial Schools
8249 Vocational Schools, nec
NAICS 611513 Apprenticeship Training
NAICS 611512 Flight Training
NAICS 611519 Other Technical & Trade Schools

8299 Schools & Educational Services, nec
NAICS 48122 Nonscheduled speciality Air Transportation
NAICS 611512 Flight Training
NAICS 611692 Automobile Driving Schools
NAICS 61171 Educational Support Services
NAICS 611691 Exam Preparation & Tutoring
NAICS 61161 Fine Arts Schools
NAICS 61163 Language Schools
NAICS 61143 Professional & Management Development
           Training Schools
NAICS 611699 All Other Miscellaneous Schools & Instruction
8322 Individual & Family Social Services
NAICS 62411 Child & Youth Services
NAICS 62421 Community Food Services
NAICS 624229 Other Community Housing Services
NAICS 62423 Emergency & Other Relief Services
NAICS 62412 Services for the Elderly & Persons with
           Disabilities
NAICS 624221 Temporary Shelters
NAICS 92215 Parole Offices & Probation Offices
NAICS 62419 Other Individual & Family Services
8331 Job Training & Vocational Rehabilitation Services
NAICS 62431 Vocational Rehabilitation Services
8351 Child Day Care Services
NAICS 62441 Child Day Care Services
8361 Residential Care
NAICS 623312 Homes for the Elderly
NAICS 62322 Residential Mental Health & Substance Abuse
           Facilities
NAICS 62399 Other Residential Care Facilities
8399 Social Services, nec
NAICS 813212 Voluntary Health Organizations
NAICS 813219 Other Grantmaking & Giving Services
NAICS 813311 Human Rights Organizations
NAICS 813312 Environment, Conservation & Wildlife
           Organizations
NAICS 813319 Other Social Advocacy Organizations
8412 Museums & Art Galleries
NAICS 71211 Museums
NAICS 71212 Historical Sites
8422 Arboreta & Botanical or Zoological Gardens
NAICS 71213 Zoos & Botanical Gardens
NAICS 71219 Nature Parks & Other Similar Institutions
8611 Business Associations
NAICS 81391 Business Associations
8621 Professional Membership Organizations
NAICS 81392 Professional Organizations
8631 Labor Unions & Similar Labor Organizations
NAICS 81393 Labor Unions & Similar Labor Organizations
8641 Civic, Social, & Fraternal Associations
NAICS 81341 Civic & Social Organizations
NAICS 81399 Other Similar Organizations
NAICS 92115 American Indian & Alaska Native Tribal
           Governments
NAICS 62411 Child & Youth Services
8651 Political Organizations
NAICS 81394 Political Organizations
8661 Religious Organizations
NAICS 81311 Religious Organizations
8699 Membership Organizations, nec
NAICS 81341 Civic & Social Organizations
NAICS 81391 Business Associations
NAICS 813312 Environment, Conservation, & Wildlife
           Organizations

NAICS 561599 All Other Travel Arrangement & Reservation
           Services
NAICS 81399 Other Similar Organizations
8711 Engineering Services
NAICS 54133 Engineering Services
8712 Architectural Services
NAICS 54131 Architectural Services
8713 Surveying Services
NAICS 48122 Nonscheduled Air Speciality Transportation
NAICS 54136 Geophysical Surveying & Mapping Services
NAICS 54137 Surveying & Mapping Services
8721 Accounting, Auditing, & Bookkeeping Services
NAICS 541211 Offices of Certified Public Accountants
NAICS 541214 Payroll Services
NAICS 541219 Other Accounting Services
8731 Commercial Physical & Biological Research
NAICS 54171 Research & Development in the Physical
           Sciences & Engineering Sciences
NAICS 54172 Research & Development in the Life Sciences
**8732 Commercial Economic, Sociological, & Educational
     Research**
NAICS 54173 Research & Development in the Social Sciences
           & Humanities
NAICS 54191 Marketing Research & Public Opinion Polling
8733 Noncommercial Research Organizations
NAICS 54171 Research & Development in the Physical
           Sciences & Engineering Sciences
NAICS 54172 Research & Development in the Life Sciences
NAICS 54173 Research & Development in the Social Sciences
           & Humanities
8734 Testing Laboratories
NAICS 54194 Veterinary Services
NAICS 54138 Testing Laboratories
8741 Management Services
NAICS 56111 Office Administrative Services
NAICS 23   Included in Construction Sector by Type of
           Construction
8742 Management Consulting Services
NAICS 541611 Administrative Management & General
           Management Consulting Services
NAICS 541612 Human Resources & Executive Search Services
NAICS 541613 Marketing Consulting Services
NAICS 541614 Process, Physical, Distribution & Logistics
           Consulting Services
8743 Public Relations Services
NAICS 54182 Public Relations Agencies
8744 Facilities Support Management Services
NAICS 56121 Facilities Support Services
8748 Business Consulting Services, nec
NAICS 61171 Educational Support Services
NAICS 541618 Other Management Consulting Services
NAICS 54169 Other Scientific & Technical Consulting
           Services
8811 Private Households
NAICS 81411 Private Households
8999 Services, nec
NAICS 71151 Independent Artists, Writers, & Performers
NAICS 51221 Record Production
NAICS 54169 Other Scientific & Technical Consulting
           Services
NAICS 51223 Music Publishers
NAICS 541612 Human Resources & Executive Search
           Consulting Services
NAICS 514199 All Other Information Services

NAICS 54162 Environmental Consulting Services

PUBLIC ADMINISTRATION

9111 Executive Offices
NAICS 92111 Executive Offices
9121 Legislative Bodies
NAICS 92112 Legislative Bodies
9131 Executive & Legislative Offices, Combined
NAICS 92114 Executive & Legislative Offices, Combined
9199 General Government, nec
NAICS 92119 All Other General Government
9211 Courts
NAICS 92211 Courts
9221 Police Protection
NAICS 92212 Police Protection
9222 Legal Counsel & Prosecution
NAICS 92213 Legal Counsel & Prosecution
9223 Correctional Institutions
NAICS 92214 Correctional Institutions
9224 Fire Protection
NAICS 92216 Fire Protection
9229 Public Order & Safety, nec
NAICS 92219 All Other Justice, Public Order, & Safety
9311 Public Finance, Taxation, & Monetary Policy
NAICS 92113 Public Finance
9411 Administration of Educational Programs
NAICS 92311 Administration of Education Programs
9431 Administration of Public Health Programs
NAICS 92312 Administration of Public Health Programs
9441 Administration of Social, Human Resource & Income Maintenance Programs
NAICS 92313 Administration of Social, Human Resource & Income Maintenance Programs
9451 Administration of Veteran's Affairs, Except Health Insurance
NAICS 92314 Administration of Veteran's Affairs
9511 Air & Water Resource & Solid Waste Management
NAICS 92411 Air & Water Resource & Solid Waste Management
9512 Land, Mineral, Wildlife, & Forest Conservation
NAICS 92412 Land, Mineral, Wildlife, & Forest Conservation
9531 Administration of Housing Programs
NAICS 92511 Administration of Housing Programs
9532 Administration of Urban Planning & Community & Rural Development
NAICS 92512 Administration of Urban Planning & Community & Rural Development
9611 Administration of General Economic Programs
NAICS 92611 Administration of General Economic Programs
9621 Regulations & Administration of Transportation Programs
NAICS 488111 Air Traffic Control
NAICS 92612 Regulation & Administration of Transportation Programs
9631 Regulation & Administration of Communications, Electric, Gas, & Other Utilities
NAICS 92613 Regulation & Administration of Communications, Electric, Gas, & Other Utilities
9641 Regulation of Agricultural Marketing & Commodity
NAICS 92614 Regulation of Agricultural Marketing & Commodity

9651 Regulation, Licensing, & Inspection of Miscellaneous Commercial Sectors
NAICS 92615 Regulation, Licensing, & Inspection of Miscellaneous Commercial Sectors
9661 Space Research & Technology
NAICS 92711 Space Research & Technology
9711 National Security
NAICS 92811 National Security
9721 International Affairs
NAICS 92812 International Affairs
9999 Nonclassifiable Establishments
NAICS 99999 Unclassified Establishments

NAICS TO SIC CONVERSION GUIDE

AGRICULTURE, FORESTRY, FISHING, & HUNTING

11111   Soybean Farming
SIC 0116 Soybeans
11112   Oilseed Farming
SIC 0119 Cash Grains, nec
11113   Dry Pea & Bean Farming
SIC 0119 Cash Grains, nec
11114   Wheat Farming
SIC 0111 Wheat
11115   Corn Farming
SIC 0115 Corn
SIC 0119 Cash Grains, nec
11116   Rice Farming
SIC 0112 Rice
111191 Oilseed & Grain Combination Farming
SIC 0119 Cash Grains, nec
111199 All Other Grain Farming
SIC 0119 Cash Grains, nec
111211 Potato Farming
SIC 0134 Irish Potatoes
111219 Other Vegetable & Melon Farming
SIC 0161 Vegetables & Melons
SIC 0139 Field Crops Except Cash Grains
11131   Orange Groves
SIC 0174 Citrus Fruits
11132   Citrus Groves
SIC 0174 Citrus Fruits
111331 Apple Orchards
SIC 0175 Deciduous Tree Fruits
111332 Grape Vineyards
SIC 0172 Grapes
111333 Strawberry Farming
SIC 0171 Berry Crops
111334 Berry Farming
SIC 0171 Berry Crops
111335 Tree Nut Farming
SIC 0173 Tree Nuts
111336 Fruit & Tree Nut Combination Farming
SIC 0179 Fruits & Tree Nuts, nec
111339 Other Noncitrus Fruit Farming
SIC 0175 Deciduous Tree Fruits
SIC 0179 Fruit & Tree Nuts, nec
111411 Mushroom Production
SIC 0182 Food Crops Grown Under Cover
111419 Other Food Crops Grown Under Cover
SIC 0182 Food Crops Grown Under Cover
111421 Nursery & Tree Production
SIC 0181 Ornamental Floriculture & Nursery Products
SIC 0811 Timber Tracts
111422 Floriculture Production
SIC 0181 Ornamental Floriculture & Nursery Products
11191   Tobacco Farming
SIC 0132 Tobacco
11192   Cotton Farming
SIC 0131 Cotton
11193   Sugarcane Farming
SIC 0133 Sugarcane & Sugar Beets

11194   Hay Farming
SIC 0139 Field Crops, Except Cash Grains, nec
111991 Sugar Beet Farming
SIC 0133 Sugarcane & Sugar Beets
111992 Peanut Farming
SIC 0139 Field Crops, Except Cash Grains, nec
111998 All Other Miscellaneous Crop Farming
SIC 0139 Field Crops, Except Cash Grains, nec
SIC 0191 General Farms, Primarily Crop
SIC 0831 Forest Products
SIC 0919 Miscellaneous Marine Products
SIC 2099 Food Preparations, nec
112111 Beef Cattle Ranching & Farming
SIC 0212 Beef Cattle, Except Feedlots
SIC 0241 Dairy Farms
112112 Cattle Feedlots
SIC 0211 Beef Cattle Feedlots
11212   Dairy Cattle & Milk Production
SIC 0241 Dairy Farms
11213   Dual Purpose Cattle Ranching & Farming
No SIC equivalent
11221   Hog & Pig Farming
SIC 0213 Hogs
11231   Chicken Egg Production
SIC 0252 Chicken Eggs
11232   Broilers & Other Meat Type Chicken Production
SIC 0251 Broiler, Fryers, & Roaster Chickens
11233   Turkey Production
SIC 0253 Turkey & Turkey Eggs
11234   Poultry Hatcheries
SIC 0254 Poultry Hatcheries
11239   Other Poultry Production
SIC 0259 Poultry & Eggs, nec
11241   Sheep Farming
SIC 0214 Sheep & Goats
11242   Goat Farming
SIC 0214 Sheep & Goats
112511 Finfish Farming & Fish Hatcheries
SIC 0273 Animal Aquaculture
SIC 0921 Fish Hatcheries & Preserves
112512 Shellfish Farming
SIC 0273 Animal Aquaculture
SIC 0921 Fish Hatcheries & Preserves
112519 Other Animal Aquaculture
SIC 0273 Animal Aquaculture
11291   Apiculture
SIC 0279 Animal Specialties, nec
11292   Horse & Other Equine Production
SIC 0272 Horses & Other Equines
11293   Fur-Bearing Animal & Rabbit Production
SIC 0271 Fur-Bearing Animals & Rabbits
11299   All Other Animal Production
SIC 0219 General Livestock, Except Dairy & Poultry
SIC 0279 Animal Specialties, nec
SIC 0291 General Farms, Primarily Livestock & Animal
      Specialties;
11311   Timber Tract Operations
SIC 0811 Timber Tracts
11321   Forest Nurseries & Gathering of Forest Products
SIC 0831 Forest Nurseries & Gathering of Forest Products
11331   Logging
SIC 2411 Logging

114111 Finfish Fishing
SIC 0912 Finfish
114112 Shellfish Fishing
SIC 0913 Shellfish
114119 Other Marine Fishing
SIC 0919 Miscellaneous Marine Products
11421 Hunting & Trapping
SIC 0971 Hunting & Trapping, & Game Propagation;
115111 Cotton Ginning
SIC 0724 Cotton Ginning
115112 Soil Preparation, Planting, & Cultivating
SIC 0711 Soil Preparation Services
SIC 0721 Crop Planting, Cultivating, & Protecting
115113 Crop Harvesting, Primarily by Machine
SIC 0722 Crop Harvesting, Primarily by Machine
115114 Other Postharvest Crop Activities
SIC 0723 Crop Preparation Services For Market, Except Cotton
Ginning
115115 Farm Labor Contractors & Crew Leaders
SIC 0761 Farm Labor Contractors & Crew Leaders
115116 Farm Management Services
SIC 0762 Farm Management Services
11521 Support Activities for Animal Production
SIC 0751 Livestock Services, Except Veterinary
SIC 0752 Animal Specialty Services, Except Veterinary
SIC 7699 Repair Services, nec
11531 Support Activities for Forestry
SIC 0851 Forestry Services

MINING

211111 Crude Petroleum & Natural Gas Extraction
SIC 1311 Crude Petroleum & Natural Gas
211112 Natural Gas Liquid Extraction
SIC 1321 Natural Gas Liquids
212111 Bituminous Coal & Lignite Surface Mining
SIC 1221 Bituminous Coal & Lignite Surface Mining
212112 Bituminous Coal Underground Mining
SIC 1222 Bituminous Coal Underground Mining
212113 Anthracite Mining
SIC 1231 Anthracite Mining
21221 Iron Ore Mining
SIC 1011 Iron Ores
212221 Gold Ore Mining
SIC 1041 Gold Ores
212222 Silver Ore Mining
SIC 1044 Silver Ores
212231 Lead Ore & Zinc Ore Mining
SIC 1031 Lead & Zinc Ores
212234 Copper Ore & Nickel Ore Mining
SIC 1021 Copper Ores
212291 Uranium-Radium-Vanadium Ore Mining
SIC 1094 Uranium-Radium-Vanadium Ores
212299 All Other Metal Ore Mining
SIC 1061 Ferroalloy Ores, Except Vanadium
SIC 1099 Miscellaneous Metal Ores, nec
212311 Dimension Stone Mining & Quarrying
SIC 1411 Dimension Stone
212312 Crushed & Broken Limestone Mining & Quarrying
SIC 1422 Crushed & Broken Limestone
212313 Crushed & Broken Granite Mining & Quarrying
SIC 1423 Crushed & Broken Granite

212319 Other Crushed & Broken Stone Mining & Quarrying
SIC 1429 Crushed & Broken Stone, nec
SIC 1499 Miscellaneous Nonmetallic Minerals, Except Fuels
212321 Construction Sand & Gravel Mining
SIC 1442 Construction Sand & Gravel
212322 Industrial Sand Mining
SIC 1446 Industrial Sand
212324 Kaolin & Ball Clay Mining
SIC 1455 Kaolin & Ball Clay
212325 Clay & Ceramic & Refractory Minerals Mining
SIC 1459 Clay, Ceramic, & Refractory Minerals, nec
212391 Potash, Soda, & Borate Mineral Mining
SIC 1474 Potash, Soda, & Borate Minerals
212392 Phosphate Rock Mining
SIC 1475 Phosphate Rock
212393 Other Chemical & Fertilizer Mineral Mining
SIC 1479 Chemical & Fertilizer Mineral Mining, nec
212399 All Other Nonmetallic Mineral Mining
SIC 1499 Miscellaneous Nonmetallic Minerals, Except Fuels
213111 Drilling Oil & Gas Wells
SIC 1381 Drilling Oil & Gas Wells
213112 Support Activities for Oil & Gas Operations
SIC 1382 Oil & Gas Field Exploration Services
SIC 1389 Oil & Gas Field Services, nec
213113 Other Gas & Field Support Activities
SIC 1389 Oil & Gas Field Services, nec
213114 Support Activities for Coal Mining
SIC 1241 Coal Mining Services
213115 Support Activities for Metal Mining
SIC 1081 Metal Mining Services
**213116 Support Activities for Nonmetallic Minerals, Except
Fuels**
SIC 1481 Nonmetallic Minerals Services, Except Fuels

UTILITIES

221111 Hydroelectric Power Generation
SIC 4911 Electric Services
SIC 4931 Electric & Other Services Combined
SIC 4939 Combination Utilities, nec
221112 Fossil Fuel Electric Power Generation
SIC 4911 Electric Services
SIC 4931 Electric & Other Services Combined
SIC 4939 Combination Utilities, nec
221113 Nuclear Electric Power Generation
SIC 4911 Electric Services
SIC 4931 Electric & Other Services Combined
SIC 4939 Combination Utilities, nec
221119 Other Electric Power Generation
SIC 4911 Electric Services
SIC 4931 Electric & Other Services Combined
SIC 4939 Combination Utilities, nec
221121 Electric Bulk Power Transmission & Control
SIC 4911 Electric Services
SIC 4931 Electric & Other Services Combined
SIC 4939 Combination Utilities, NEC
221122 Electric Power Distribution
SIC 4911 Electric Services
SIC 4931 Electric & Other Services Combined
SIC 4939 Combination Utilities, nec
22121 Natural Gas Distribution
SIC 4923 Natural Gas Transmission & Distribution
SIC 4924 Natural Gas Distribution

SIC 4925 Mixed, Manufactured, or Liquefied Petroleum Gas
  Production and/or Distribution
SIC 4931 Electronic & Other Services Combined
SIC 4932 Gas & Other Services Combined
SIC 4939 Combination Utilities, nec
22131 Water Supply & Irrigation Systems
SIC 4941 Water Supply
SIC 4971 Irrigation Systems
22132 Sewage Treatment Facilities
SIC 4952 Sewerage Systems
22133 Steam & Air-Conditioning Supply
SIC 4961 Steam & Air-Conditioning Supply

CONSTRUCTION

23311 Land Subdivision & Land Development
SIC 6552 Land Subdividers & Developers, Except Cemeteries
23321 Single Family Housing Construction
SIC 1521 General contractors-Single-Family Houses
SIC 1531 Operative Builders
23322 Multifamily Housing Construction
SIC 1522 General Contractors-Residential Building, Other
  Than Single-Family
SIC 1531 Operative Builders
23331 Manufacturing & Industrial Building Construction
SIC 1531 Operative Builders
SIC 1541 General Contractors-Industrial Buildings &
  Warehouses
23332 Commercial & Institutional Building Construction
SIC 1522 General Contractors-Residential Building Other than
  Single-Family
SIC 1531 Operative Builders
SIC 1541 General Contractors-Industrial Buildings &
  Warehouses
SIC 1542 General Contractor-Nonresidential Buildings, Other
  than Industrial Buildings & Warehouses
23411 Highway & Street Construction
SIC 1611 Highway & Street Construction, Except Elevated
  Highways
23412 Bridge & Tunnel Construction
SIC 1622 Bridge, Tunnel, & Elevated Highway Construction
2349 Other Heavy Construction
23491 Water, Sewer, & Pipeline Construction
SIC 1623 Water, Sewer, Pipeline, & Communications & Power
  Line Construction
**23492 Power & Communication Transmission Line
  Construction**
SIC 1623 Water, Sewer, Pipelines, & Communications & Power
  Line Construction
23493 Industrial Nonbuilding Structure Construction
SIC 1629 Heavy Construction, nec
23499 All Other Heavy Construction
SIC 1629 Heavy Construction, nec
SIC 7353 Construction Equipment Rental & Leasing
23511 Plumbing, Heating & Air-Conditioning Contractors
SIC 1711 Plumbing, Heating & Air-Conditioning
23521 Painting & Wall Covering Contractors
SIC 1721 Painting & Paper Hanging
SIC 1799 Special Trade Contractors, nec
23531 Electrical Contractors
SIC 1731 Electrical Work

23541 Masonry & Stone Contractors
SIC 1741 Masonry, Stone Setting & Other Stone Work
23542 Drywall, Plastering, Acoustical & Insulation Contractors
SIC 1742 Plastering, Drywall, Acoustical, & Insulation Work
SIC 1743 Terrazzo, Tile, Marble & Mosaic work
SIC 1771 Concrete Work
23543 Tile, Marble, Terrazzo & Mosaic Contractors
SIC 1743 Terrazzo, Tile, Marble, & Mosaic Work
23551 Carpentry Contractors
SIC 1751 Carpentry Work
23552 Floor Laying & Other Floor Contractors
SIC 1752 Floor Laying & Other Floor Work, nec
23561 Roofing, Siding & Sheet Metal Contractors
SIC 1761 Roofing, Siding, & Sheet Metal Work
23571 Concrete Contractors
SIC 1771 Concrete Work
23581 Water Well Drilling Contractors
SIC 1781 Water Well Drilling
23591 Structural Steel Erection Contractors
SIC 1791 Structural Steel Erection
23592 Glass & Glazing Contractors
SIC 1793 Glass & Glazing Work
SIC 1799 Specialty Trade Contractors, nec
23593 Excavation Contractors
SIC 1794 Excavation Work
23594 Wrecking & Demolition Contractors
SIC 1795 Wrecking & Demolition Work
**23595 Building Equipment & Other Machinery Installation
  Contractors**
SIC 1796 Installation of Erection of Building Equipment, nec
23599 All Other Special Trade Contractors
SIC 1799 Special Trade Contractors, nec

FOOD MANUFACTURING

311111 Dog & Cat Food Manufacturing
SIC 2047 Dog & Cat Food
311119 Other Animal Food Manufacturing
SIC 2048 Prepared Feeds & Feed Ingredients for Animals &
  Fowls, Except Dogs & Cats
311211 Flour Milling
SIC 2034 Dehydrated Fruits, Vegetables & Soup Mixes
SIC 2041 Flour & Other Grain Mill Products
311212 Rice Milling
SIC 2044 Rice Milling
311213 Malt Manufacturing
SIC 2083 Malt
311221 Wet Corn Milling
SIC 2046 Wet Corn Milling
311222 Soybean Processing
SIC 2075 Soybean Oil Mills
SIC 2079 Shortening, Table Oils, Margarine, & Other Edible
  Fats & Oils, nec
311223 Other Oilseed Processing
SIC 2074 Cottonseed Oil Mills
SIC 2079 Shortening, Table Oils, Margarine & Other Edible
  Fats & Oils, nec
SIC 2076 Vegetable Oil Mills, Except Corn, Cottonseed, &
  Soybean
311225 Edible Fats & Oils Manufacturing
SIC 2077 Animal & Marine Fats & Oil, nec
SIC 2074 Cottonseed Oil Mills
SIC 2075 Soybean Oil Mills

SIC 2076 Vegetable Oil Mills, Except Corn, Cottonseed, &
  Soybean
SIC 2079 Shortening, Table Oils, Margarine, & Other Edible
  Fats & Oils, nec
31123 Breakfast Cereal Manufacturing
SIC 2043 Cereal Breakfast Foods
311311 Sugarcane Mills
SIC 2061 Cane Sugar, Except Refining
311312 Cane Sugar Refining
SIC 2062 Cane Sugar Refining
311313 Beet Sugar Manufacturing
SIC 2063 Beet Sugar
**31132 Chocolate & Confectionery Manufacturing from Cacao
  Beans**
SIC 2066 Chocolate & Cocoa Products
31133 Confectionery Manufacturing from Purchased Chocolate
SIC 2064 Candy & Other Confectionery Products
31134 Non-Chocolate Confectionery Manufacturing
SIC 2064 Candy & Other Confectionery Products
SIC 2067 Chewing Gum
SIC 2099 Food Preparations, nec
311411 Frozen Fruit, Juice & Vegetable Processing
SIC 2037 Frozen Fruits, Fruit Juices, & Vegetables
311412 Frozen Specialty Food Manufacturing
SIC 2038 Frozen Specialties, NEC
311421 Fruit & Vegetable Canning
SIC 2033 Canned Fruits, Vegetables, Preserves, Jams, & Jellies
SIC 2035 Pickled Fruits & Vegetables, Vegetable Sauces, &
  Seasonings & Salad Dressings
311422 Specialty Canning
SIC 2032 Canned Specialties
311423 Dried & Dehydrated Food Manufacturing
SIC 2034 Dried & Dehydrated Fruits, Vegetables & Soup
  Mixes
SIC 2099 Food Preparation, nec
311511 Fluid Milk Manufacturing
SIC 2026 Fluid Milk
311512 Creamery Butter Manufacturing
SIC 2021 Creamery Butter
311513 Cheese Manufacturing
SIC 2022 Natural, Processed, & Imitation Cheese
311514 Dry, Condensed, & Evaporated Milk Manufacturing
SIC 2023 Dry, Condensed & Evaporated Dairy Products
31152 Ice Cream & Frozen Dessert Manufacturing
SIC 2024 Ice Cream & Frozen Desserts
311611 Animal Slaughtering
SIC 0751 Livestock Services, Except Veterinary
SIC 2011 Meat Packing Plants
SIC 2048 Prepared Feeds & Feed Ingredients for Animals &
  Fowls, Except Dogs & Cats
311612 Meat Processed from Carcasses
SIC 2013 Sausages & Other Prepared Meats
SIC 5147 Meat & Meat Products
311613 Rendering & Meat By-product Processing
SIC 2077 Animal & Marine Fats & Oils
311615 Poultry Processing
SIC 2015 Poultry Slaughtering & Processing
311711 Seafood Canning
SIC 2077 Animal & Marine Fats & Oils
SIC 2091 Canned & Cured Fish & Seafood
311712 Fresh & Frozen Seafood Processing
SIC 2077 Animal & Marine Fats & Oils
SIC 2092 Prepared Fresh or Frozen Fish & Seafood

311811 Retail Bakeries
SIC 5461 Retail Bakeries
311812 Commercial Bakeries
SIC 2051 Bread & Other Bakery Products, Except Cookies &
  Crackers
SIC 2052 Cookies & Crackers
311813 Frozen Bakery Product Manufacturing
SIC 2053 Frozen Bakery Products, Except Bread
311821 Cookie & Cracker Manufacturing
SIC 2052 Cookies & Crackers
**311822 Flour Mixes & Dough Manufacturing from Purchased
  Flour**
SIC 2045 Prepared Flour Mixes & Doughs
311823 Pasta Manufacturing
SIC 2098 Macaroni, Spaghetti, Vermicelli & Noodles
31183 Tortilla Manufacturing
SIC 2099 Food Preparations, nec
311911 Roasted Nuts & Peanut Butter Manufacturing
SIC 2068 Salted & Roasted Nuts & Seeds
SIC 2099 Food Preparations, nec
311919 Other Snack Food Manufacturing
SIC 2052 Cookies & Crackers
SIC 2096 Potato Chips, Corn Chips, & Similar Snacks
31192 Coffee & Tea Manufacturing
SIC 2043 Cereal Breakfast Foods
SIC 2095 Roasted Coffee
SIC 2099 Food Preparations, nec
31193 Flavoring Syrup & Concentrate Manufacturing
SIC 2087 Flavoring Extracts & Flavoring Syrups
**311941 Mayonnaise, Dressing & Other Prepared Sauce
  Manufacturing**
SIC 2035 Pickled Fruits & Vegetables, Vegetable Seasonings, &
  Sauces & Salad Dressings
SIC 2099 Food Preparations, nec
311942 Spice & Extract Manufacturing
SIC 2087 Flavoring Extracts & Flavoring Syrups
SIC 2095 Roasted Coffee
SIC 2099 Food Preparations, nec
SIC 2899 Chemical Preparations, nec
311991 Perishable Prepared Food Manufacturing
SIC 2099 Food Preparations, nec
311999 All Other Miscellaneous Food Manufacturing
SIC 2015 Poultry Slaughtering & Processing
SIC 2032 Canned Specialties
SIC 2087 Flavoring Extracts & Flavoring Syrups
SIC 2099 Food Preparations, nec

BEVERAGE & TOBACCO PRODUCT MANUFACTURING

312111 Soft Drink Manufacturing
SIC 2086 Bottled & Canned Soft Drinks & Carbonated Water
312112 Bottled Water Manufacturing
SIC 2086 Bottled & Canned Soft Drinks & Carbonated Water
312113 Ice Manufacturing
SIC 2097 Manufactured Ice
31212 Breweries
SIC 2082 Malt Beverages
31213 Wineries
SIC 2084 Wines, Brandy, & Brandy Spirits
31214 Distilleries
SIC 2085 Distilled & Blended Liquors

31221 Tobacco Stemming & Redrying
SIC 2141 Tobacco Stemming & Redrying
312221 Cigarette Manufacturing
SIC 2111 Cigarettes
312229 Other Tobacco Product Manufacturing
SIC 2121 Cigars
SIC 2131 Chewing & Smoking Tobacco & Snuff
SIC 2141 Tobacco Stemming & Redrying

TEXTILE MILLS

313111 Yarn Spinning Mills
SIC 2281 Yarn Spinning Mills
SIC 2299 Textile Goods, nec
313112 Yarn Texturing, Throwing & Twisting Mills
SIC 2282 Yarn Texturing, Throwing, Winding Mills
313113 Thread Mills
SIC 2284 Thread Mills
SIC 2299 Textile Goods, NEC
31321 Broadwoven Fabric Mills
SIC 2211 Broadwoven Fabric Mills, Cotton
SIC 2221 Broadwoven Fabric Mills, Manmade Fiber & Silk
SIC 2231 Broadwoven Fabric Mills, Wool
SIC 2299 Textile Goods, nec
313221 Narrow Fabric Mills
SIC 2241 Narrow Fabric & Other Smallware Mills: Cotton, Wool, Silk & Manmade Fiber
SIC 2299 Textile Goods, nec
313222 Schiffli Machine Embroidery
SIC 2397 Schiffli Machine Embroideries
31323 Nonwoven Fabric Mills
SIC 2297 Nonwoven Fabrics
SIC 2299 Textile Goods, nec
313241 Weft Knit Fabric Mills
SIC 2257 Weft Knit Fabric Mills
SIC 2259 Knitting Mills nec
313249 Other Knit Fabric & Lace Mills
SIC 2258 Lace & Warp Knit Fabric Mills
SIC 2259 Knitting Mills nec
313311 Broadwoven Fabric Finishing Mills
SIC 2231 Broadwoven Fabric Mills, Wool
SIC 2261 Finishers of Broadwoven Fabrics of Cotton
SIC 2262 Finishers of Broadwoven Fabrics of Manmade Fiber & Silk
SIC 2269 Finishers of Textiles, nec
SIC 5131 Piece Goods & Notions
313312 Textile & Fabric Finishing Mills
SIC 2231 Broadwoven Fabric Mills, Wool
SIC 2257 Weft Knit Fabric Mills
SIC 2258 Lace & Warp Knit Fabric Mills
SIC 2269 Finishers of Textiles, nec
SIC 2282 Yarn Texturizing, Throwing, Twisting, & Winding Mills
SIC 2284 Thread Mills
SIC 2299 Textile Goods, nec
SIC 5131 Piece Goods & Notions
31332 Fabric Coating Mills
SIC 2295 Coated Fabrics, Not Rubberized
SIC 3069 Fabricated Rubber Products, nec

TEXTILE PRODUCT MILLS

31411 Carpet & Rug Mills
SIC 2273 Carpets & Rugs
314121 Curtain & Drapery Mills
SIC 2391 Curtains & Draperies
SIC 5714 Drapery, Curtain, & Upholstery Stores
314129 Other Household Textile Product Mills
SIC 2392 Housefurnishings, Except Curtains & Draperies
314911 Textile Bag Mills
SIC 2392 Housefurnishings, Except Curtains & Draperies
SIC 2393 Textile Bags
314912 Canvas & Related Product Mills
SIC 2394 Canvas & Related Products
314991 Rope, Cordage & Twine Mills
SIC 2298 Cordage & Twine
314992 Tire Cord & Tire Fabric Mills
SIC 2296 Tire Cord & Fabrics
314999 All Other Miscellaneous Textile Product Mills
SIC 2299 Textile Goods, nec
SIC 2395 Pleating, Decorative & Novelty Stitching, & Tucking for the Trade
SIC 2396 Automotive Trimmings, Apparel Findings, & Related Products
SIC 2399 Fabricated Textile Products, nec

APPAREL MANUFACTURING

315111 Sheer Hosiery Mills
SIC 2251 Women's Full-Length & Knee-Length Hosiery, Except socks
SIC 2252 Hosiery, nec
315119 Other Hosiery & Sock Mills
SIC 2252 Hosiery, nec
315191 Outerwear Knitting Mills
SIC 2253 Knit Outerwear Mills
SIC 2259 Knitting Mills, nec
315192 Underwear & Nightwear Knitting Mills
SIC 2254 Knit Underwear & Nightwear Mills
SIC 2259 Knitting Mills, nec
315211 Men's & Boys' Cut & Sew Apparel Contractors
SIC 2311 Men's & Boys' Suits, Coats, & Overcoats
SIC 2321 Men's & Boys' Shirts, Except Work Shirts
SIC 2322 Men's & Boys' Underwear & Nightwear
SIC 2325 Men's & Boys' Trousers & Slacks
SIC 2326 Men's & Boys' Work Clothing
SIC 2329 Men's & Boys' Clothing, nec
SIC 2341 Women's, Misses', Children's, & Infants' Underwear & Nightwear
SIC 2361 Girls', Children's, & Infants' Dresses, Blouses & Shirts
SIC 2369 Girls', Children's, & Infants' Outerwear, nec
SIC 2384 Robes & Dressing Gowns
SIC 2385 Waterproof Outerwear
SIC 2389 Apparel & Accessories, nec
SIC 2395 Pleating, Decorative & Novelty Stitching, & Tucking for the Trade
315212 Women's & Girls' Cut & Sew Apparel Contractors
SIC 2331 Women's, Misses', & Juniors' Blouses & Shirts
SIC 2335 Women's, Misses' & Juniors' Dresses
SIC 2337 Women's, Misses', & Juniors' Suits, Skirts, & Coats
SIC 2339 Women's, Misses', & Juniors' Outerwear, nec

SIC 2341 Women's, Misses', Children's, & Infants' Underwear & Nightwear

SIC 2342 Brassieres, Girdles, & Allied Garments

SIC 2361 Girls', Children's, & Infants' Dresses, Blouses, & Shirts

SIC 2369 Girls', Children's, & Infants' Outerwear, nec

SIC 2384 Robes & Dressing Gowns

SIC 2385 Waterproof Outerwear

SIC 2389 Apparel & Accessories, nec

SIC 2395 Pleating, Decorative & Novelty Stitching, & Tucking for the Trade

315221 Men's & Boys' Cut & Sew Underwear & Nightwear Manufacturing

SIC 2322 Men's & Boys' Underwear & Nightwear

SIC 2341 Women's, Misses', Children's, & Infants' Underwear & Nightwear

SIC 2369 Girls', Children's, & Infants' Outerwear, nec

SIC 2384 Robes & Dressing Gowns

315222 Men's & Boys' Cut & Sew Suit, Coat & Overcoat Manufacturing

SIC 2311 Men's & Boys' Suits, Coats, & Overcoats

SIC 2369 Girls', Children's, & Infants' Outerwear, nec

SIC 2385 Waterproof Outerwear

315223 Men's & Boys' Cut & Sew Shirt Manufacturing

SIC 2321 Men's & Boys' Shirts, Except Work Shirts

SIC 2361 Girls', Children's, & Infants' Dresses, Blouses, & Shirts

315224 Men's & Boys' Cut & Sew Trouser, Slack & Jean Manufacturing

SIC 2325 Men's & Boys' Trousers & Slacks

SIC 2369 Girls', Children's, & Infants' Outerwear, NEC

315225 Men's & Boys' Cut & Sew Work Clothing Manufacturing

SIC 2326 Men's & Boys' Work Clothing

315228 Men's & Boys' Cut & Sew Other Outerwear Manufacturing

SIC 2329 Men's & Boys' Clothing, nec

SIC 2369 Girls', Children's, & Infants' Outerwear, nec

SIC 2385 Waterproof Outerwear

315231 Women's & Girls' Cut & Sew Lingerie, Loungewear & Nightwear Manufacturing

SIC 2341 Women's, Misses', Children's, & Infants' Underwear & Nightwear

SIC 2342 Brassieres, Girdles, & Allied Garments

SIC 2369 Girls', Children's, & Infants' Outerwear, nec

SIC 2384 Robes & Dressing Gowns

SIC 2389 Apparel & Accessories, NEC

315232 Women's & Girls' Cut & Sew Blouse & Shirt Manufacturing

SIC 2331 Women's, Misses', & Juniors' Blouses & Shirts

SIC 2361 Girls', Children's, & Infants' Dresses, Blouses & Shirts

315233 Women's & Girls' Cut & Sew Dress Manufacturing

SIC 2335 Women's, Misses', & Juniors' Dresses

SIC 2361 Girls', Children's, & Infants' Dresses, Blouses & Shirts

315234 Women's & Girls' Cut & Sew Suit, Coat, Tailored Jacket & Skirt Manufacturing

SIC 2337 Women's, Misses', & Juniors' Suits, Skirts, & Coats

SIC 2369 Girls', Children's, & Infants' Outerwear, nec

SIC 2385 Waterproof Outerwear

315238 Women's & Girls' Cut & Sew Other Outerwear Manufacturing

SIC 2339 Women's, Misses', & Juniors' Outerwear, nec

SIC 2369 Girls', Children's, & Infants' Outerwear, nec

SIC 2385 Waterproof Outerwear

315291 Infants' Cut & Sew Apparel Manufacturing

SIC 2341 Women's, Misses', Children's, & Infants' Underwear & Nightwear

SIC 2361 Girls', Children's, & Infants' Dresses, Blouses, & Shirts

SIC 2369 Girls', Children's, & Infants' Outerwear, nec

SIC 2385 Waterproof Outerwear

315292 Fur & Leather Apparel Manufacturing

SIC 2371 Fur Goods

SIC 2386 Leather & Sheep-lined Clothing

315299 All Other Cut & Sew Apparel Manufacturing

SIC 2329 Men's & Boys' Outerwear, nec

SIC 2339 Women's, Misses', & Juniors' Outerwear, nec

SIC 2389 Apparel & Accessories, nec

315991 Hat, Cap & Millinery Manufacturing

SIC 2353 Hats, Caps, & Millinery

315992 Glove & Mitten Manufacturing

SIC 2381 Dress & Work Gloves, Except Knit & All-Leather

SIC 3151 Leather Gloves & Mittens

315993 Men's & Boys' Neckwear Manufacturing

SIC 2323 Men's & Boys' Neckwear

315999 Other Apparel Accessories & Other Apparel Manufacturing

SIC 2339 Women's, Misses', & Juniors' Outerwear, nec

SIC 2385 Waterproof Outerwear

SIC 2387 Apparel Belts

SIC 2389 Apparel & Accessories, nec

SIC 2396 Automotive Trimmings, Apparel Findings, & Related Products

SIC 2399 Fabricated Textile Products, nec

LEATHER & ALLIED PRODUCT MANUFACTURING

31611 Leather & Hide Tanning & Finishing

SIC 3111 Leather Tanning & Finishing

SIC 3999 Manufacturing Industries, nec

316211 Rubber & Plastics Footwear Manufacturing

SIC 3021 Rubber & Plastics Footwear

316212 House Slipper Manufacturing

SIC 3142 House Slippers

316213 Men's Footwear Manufacturing

SIC 3143 Men's Footwear, Except Athletic

316214 Women's Footwear Manufacturing

SIC 3144 Women's Footwear, Except Athletic

316219 Other Footwear Manufacturing

SIC 3149 Footwear Except Rubber, NEC

316991 Luggage Manufacturing

SIC 3161 Luggage

316992 Women's Handbag & Purse Manufacturing

SIC 3171 Women's Handbags & Purses

316993 Personal Leather Good Manufacturing

SIC 3172 Personal Leather Goods, Except Women's Handbags & Purses

316999 All Other Leather Good Manufacturing

SIC 3131 Boot & Shoe Cut Stock & Findings

SIC 3199 Leather Goods, nec

WOOD PRODUCT MANUFACTURING

321113 Sawmills
SIC 2421 Sawmills & Planing Mills, General
SIC 2429 Special Product Sawmills, nec
321114 Wood Preservation
SIC 2491 Wood Preserving
321211 Hardwood Veneer & Plywood Manufacturing
SIC 2435 Hardwood Veneer & Plywood
321212 Softwood Veneer & Plywood Manufacturing
SIC 2436 Softwood Veneer & Plywood
321213 Engineered Wood Member Manufacturing
SIC 2439 Structural Wood Members, nec
321214 Truss Manufacturing
SIC 2439 Structural Wood Members, nec
321219 Reconstituted Wood Product Manufacturing
SIC 2493 Reconstituted Wood Products
321911 Wood Window & Door Manufacturing
SIC 2431 Millwork
321912 Hardwood Dimension Mills
SIC 2426 Hardwood Dimension & Flooring Mills
321913 Softwood Cut Stock, Resawing Lumber, & Planing
SIC 2421 Sawmills & Planing Mills, General
SIC 2429 Special Product Sawmills, nec
SIC 2439 Structural Wood Members, nec
321914 Other Millwork
SIC 2421 Sawmills & Planing Mills, General
SIC 2426 Hardwood Dimension & Flooring Mills
SIC 2431 Millwork
32192 Wood Container & Pallet Manufacturing
SIC 2441 Nailed & Lock Corner Wood Boxes & Shook
SIC 2448 Wood Pallets & Skids
SIC 2449 Wood Containers, NEC
SIC 2499 Wood Products, nec
321991 Manufactured Home Manufacturing
SIC 2451 Mobile Homes
321992 Prefabricated Wood Building Manufacturing
SIC 2452 Prefabricated Wood Buildings & Components
321999 All Other Miscellaneous Wood Product Manufacturing
SIC 2426 Hardwood Dimension & Flooring Mills
SIC 2499 Wood Products, nec
SIC 3131 Boot & Shoe Cut Stock & Findings
SIC 3999 Manufacturing Industries, nec
SIC 2421 Sawmills & Planing Mills, General
SIC 2429 Special Product Sawmills, nec

PAPER MANUFACTURING

32211 Pulp Mills
SIC 2611 Pulp Mills
322121 Paper Mills
SIC 2611 Pulp Mills
SIC 2621 Paper Mills
322122 Newsprint Mills
SIC 2621 Paper Mills
32213 Paperboard Mills
SIC 2611 Pulp Mills
SIC 2631 Paperboard Mills
322211 Corrugated & Solid Fiber Box Manufacturing
SIC 2653 Corrugated & Solid Fiber Boxes
322212 Folding Paperboard Box Manufacturing
SIC 2657 Folding Paperboard Boxes, Including Sanitary

322213 Setup Paperboard Box Manufacturing
SIC 2652 Setup Paperboard Boxes
322214 Fiber Can, Tube, Drum, & Similar Products Manufacturing
SIC 2655 Fiber Cans, Tubes, Drums, & Similar Products
322215 Non-Folding Sanitary Food Container Manufacturing
SIC 2656 Sanitary Food Containers, Except Folding
SIC 2679 Converted Paper & Paperboard Products, NEC
322221 Coated & Laminated Packaging Paper & Plastics Film Manufacturing
SIC 2671 Packaging Paper & Plastics Film, Coated & Laminated
322222 Coated & Laminated Paper Manufacturing
SIC 2672 Coated & Laminated Paper, nec
SIC 2679 Converted Paper & Paperboard Products, nec
322223 Plastics, Foil, & Coated Paper Bag Manufacturing
SIC 2673 Plastics, Foil, & Coated Paper Bags
322224 Uncoated Paper & Multiwall Bag Manufacturing
SIC 2674 Uncoated Paper & Multiwall Bags
322225 Laminated Aluminum Foil Manufacturing for Flexible Packaging Uses
SIC 3497 Metal Foil & Leaf
322231 Die-Cut Paper & Paperboard Office Supplies Manufacturing
SIC 2675 Die-Cut Paper & Paperboard & Cardboard
SIC 2679 Converted Paper & Paperboard Products, nec
322232 Envelope Manufacturing
SIC 2677 Envelopes
322233 Stationery, Tablet, & Related Product Manufacturing
SIC 2678 Stationery, Tablets, & Related Products
322291 Sanitary Paper Product Manufacturing
SIC 2676 Sanitary Paper Products
322292 Surface-Coated Paperboard Manufacturing
SIC 2675 Die-Cut Paper & Paperboard & Cardboard
322298 All Other Converted Paper Product Manufacturing
SIC 2675 Die-Cut Paper & Paperboard & Cardboard
SIC 2679 Converted Paper & Paperboard Products, NEC

PRINTING & RELATED SUPPORT ACTIVITIES

323110 Commercial Lithographic Printing
SIC 2752 Commercial Printing, Lithographic
SIC 2771 Greeting Cards
SIC 2782 Blankbooks, Loose-leaf Binders & Devices
SIC 3999 Manufacturing Industries, nec
323111 Commercial Gravure Printing
SIC 2754 Commercial Printing, Gravure
SIC 2771 Greeting Cards
SIC 2782 Blankbooks, Loose-leaf Binders & Devices
SIC 3999 Manufacturing Industries, nec
323112 Commercial Flexographic Printing
SIC 2759 Commercial Printing, NEC
SIC 2771 Greeting Cards
SIC 2782 Blankbooks, Loose-leaf Binders & Devices
SIC 3999 Manufacturing Industries, nec
323113 Commercial Screen Printing
SIC 2396 Automotive Trimmings, Apparel Findings, & Related Products
SIC 2759 Commercial Printing, nec
SIC 2771 Greeting Cards
SIC 2782 Blankbooks, Loose-leaf Binders & Devices
SIC 3999 Manufacturing Industries, nec

323114 Quick Printing
SIC 2752 Commercial Printing, Lithographic
SIC 2759 Commercial Printing, nec
323115 Digital Printing
SIC 2759 Commercial Printing, nec
323116 Manifold Business Form Printing
SIC 2761 Manifold Business Forms
323117 Book Printing
SIC 2732 Book Printing
323118 Blankbook, Loose-leaf Binder & Device Manufacturing
SIC 2782 Blankbooks, Loose-leaf Binders & Devices
323119 Other Commercial Printing
SIC 2759 Commercial Printing, nec
SIC 2771 Greeting Cards
SIC 2782 Blankbooks, Loose-leaf Binders & Devices
SIC 3999 Manufacturing Industries, nec
323121 Tradebinding & Related Work
SIC 2789 Bookbinding & Related Work
323122 Prepress Services
SIC 2791 Typesetting
SIC 2796 Platemaking & Related Services

PETROLEUM & COAL PRODUCTS MANUFACTURING

32411 Petroleum Refineries
SIC 2911 Petroleum Refining
324121 Asphalt Paving Mixture & Block Manufacturing
SIC 2951 Asphalt Paving Mixtures & Blocks
324122 Asphalt Shingle & Coating Materials Manufacturing
SIC 2952 Asphalt Felts & Coatings
324191 Petroleum Lubricating Oil & Grease Manufacturing
SIC 2992 Lubricating Oils & Greases
324199 All Other Petroleum & Coal Products Manufacturing
SIC 2999 Products of Petroleum & Coal, nec
SIC 3312 Blast Furnaces & Steel Mills

CHEMICAL MANUFACTURING

32511 Petrochemical Manufacturing
SIC 2865 Cyclic Organic Crudes & Intermediates, & Organic Dyes & Pigments
SIC 2869 Industrial Organic Chemicals, nec
32512 Industrial Gas Manufacturing
SIC 2813 Industrial Gases
SIC 2869 Industrial Organic Chemicals, nec
325131 Inorganic Dye & Pigment Manufacturing
SIC 2816 Inorganic Pigments
SIC 2819 Industrial Inorganic Chemicals, nec
325132 Organic Dye & Pigment Manufacturing
SIC 2865 Cyclic Organic Crudes & Intermediates, & Organic Dyes & Pigments
325181 Alkalies & Chlorine Manufacturing
SIC 2812 Alkalies & Chlorine
325182 Carbon Black Manufacturing
SIC 2816 Inorganic pigments
SIC 2895 Carbon Black
325188 All Other Basic Inorganic Chemical Manufacturing
SIC 2819 Industrial Inorganic Chemicals, nec
SIC 2869 Industrial Organic Chemicals, nec

325191 Gum & Wood Chemical Manufacturing
SIC 2861 Gum & Wood Chemicals
325192 Cyclic Crude & Intermediate Manufacturing
SIC 2865 Cyclic Organic Crudes & Intermediates & Organic Dyes & Pigments
325193 Ethyl Alcohol Manufacturing
SIC 2869 Industrial Organic Chemicals
325199 All Other Basic Organic Chemical Manufacturing
SIC 2869 Industrial Organic Chemicals, nec
SIC 2899 Chemical & Chemical Preparations, nec
325211 Plastics Material & Resin Manufacturing
SIC 2821 Plastics Materials, Synthetic & Resins, & Nonvulcanizable Elastomers
325212 Synthetic Rubber Manufacturing
SIC 2822 Synthetic Rubber
325221 Cellulosic Manmade Fiber Manufacturing
SIC 2823 Cellulosic Manmade Fibers
325222 Noncellulosic Organic Fiber Manufacturing
SIC 2824 Manmade Organic Fibers, Except Cellulosic
325311 Nitrogenous Fertilizer Manufacturing
SIC 2873 Nitrogenous Fertilizers
325312 Phosphatic Fertilizer Manufacturing
SIC 2874 Phosphatic Fertilizers
325314 Fertilizer Manufacturing
SIC 2875 Fertilizers, Mixing Only
32532 Pesticide & Other Agricultural Chemical Manufacturing
SIC 2879 Pesticides & Agricultural Chemicals, nec
325411 Medicinal & Botanical Manufacturing
SIC 2833 Medicinal Chemicals & Botanical Products
325412 Pharmaceutical Preparation Manufacturing
SIC 2834 Pharmaceutical Preparations
SIC 2835 In-Vitro & In-Vivo Diagnostic Substances
325413 In-Vitro Diagnostic Substance Manufacturing
SIC 2835 In-Vitro & In-Vivo Diagnostic Substances
325414 Biological Product Manufacturing
SIC 2836 Biological Products, Except Diagnostic Substance
32551 Paint & Coating Manufacturing
SIC 2851 Paints, Varnishes, Lacquers, Enamels & Allied Products
SIC 2899 Chemicals & Chemical Preparations, nec
32552 Adhesive & Sealant Manufacturing
SIC 2891 Adhesives & Sealants
325611 Soap & Other Detergent Manufacturing
SIC 2841 Soaps & Other Detergents, Except Specialty Cleaners
SIC 2844 Toilet Preparations
325612 Polish & Other Sanitation Good Manufacturing
SIC 2842 Specialty Cleaning, Polishing, & Sanitary Preparations
325613 Surface Active Agent Manufacturing
SIC 2843 Surface Active Agents, Finishing Agents, Sulfonated Oils, & Assistants
32562 Toilet Preparation Manufacturing
SIC 2844 Perfumes, Cosmetics, & Other Toilet Preparations
32591 Printing Ink Manufacturing
SIC 2893 Printing Ink
32592 Explosives Manufacturing
SIC 2892 Explosives
325991 Custom Compounding of Purchased Resin
SIC 3087 Custom Compounding of Purchased Plastics Resin
325992 Photographic Film, Paper, Plate & Chemical Manufacturing
SIC 3861 Photographic Equipment & Supplies

**325998 All Other Miscellaneous Chemical Product
    Manufacturing**
SIC 2819 Industrial Inorganic Chemicals, nec
SIC 2899 Chemicals & Chemical Preparations, nec
SIC 3952 Lead Pencils & Art Goods
SIC 3999 Manufacturing Industries, nec

PLASTICS & RUBBER PRODUCTS MANUFACTURING

326111 Unsupported Plastics Bag Manufacturing
SIC 2673 Plastics, Foil, & Coated Paper Bags
**326112 Unsupported Plastics Packaging Film & Sheet
    Manufacturing**
SIC 2671 Packaging Paper & Plastics Film, Coated, &
    Laminated
326113 Unsupported Plastics Film & Sheet Manufacturing
SIC 3081 Unsupported Plastics Film & Sheets
326121 Unsupported Plastics Profile Shape Manufacturing
SIC 3082 Unsupported Plastics Profile Shapes
SIC 3089 Plastics Product, nec
326122 Plastics Pipe & Pipe Fitting Manufacturing
SIC 3084 Plastics Pipe
SIC 3089 Plastics Products, nec
32613 Laminated Plastics Plate, Sheet & Shape Manufacturing
SIC 3083 Laminated Plastics Plate, Sheet & Profile Shapes
32614 Polystyrene Foam Product Manufacturing
SIC 3086 Plastics Foam Products
32615 Urethane & Other Foam Product Manufacturing
SIC 3086 Plastics Foam Products
32616 Plastics Bottle Manufacturing
SIC 3085 Plastics Bottles
326191 Plastics Plumbing Fixture Manufacturing
SIC 3088 Plastics Plumbing Fixtures
326192 Resilient Floor Covering Manufacturing
SIC 3069 Fabricated Rubber Products, nec
SIC 3996 Linoleum, Asphalted-Felt-Base, & Other Hard
    Surface Floor Coverings, nec
326199 All Other Plastics Product Manufacturing
SIC 3089 Plastics Products, nec
SIC 3999 Manufacturing Industries, nec
326211 Tire Manufacturing
SIC 3011 Tires & Inner Tubes
326212 Tire Retreading
SIC 7534 Tire Retreading & Repair Shops
32622 Rubber & Plastics Hoses & Belting Manufacturing
SIC 3052 Rubber & Plastics Hose & Belting
326291 Rubber Product Manufacturing for Mechanical Use
SIC 3061 Molded, Extruded, & Lathe-Cut Mechanical Rubber
    Goods
326299 All Other Rubber Product Manufacturing
SIC 3069 Fabricated Rubber Products, nec

NONMETALLIC MINERAL PRODUCT MANUFACTURING

**327111 Vitreous China Plumbing Fixture & China &
    Earthenware Fittings & Bathroom Accessories
    Manufacturing**
SIC 3261 Vitreous China Plumbing Fixtures & China &
    Earthenware Fittings & Bathroom Accessories

**327112 Vitreous China, Fine Earthenware & Other Pottery
    Product Manufacturing**
SIC 3262 Vitreous China Table & Kitchen Articles
SIC 3263 Fine Earthenware Table & Kitchen Articles
SIC 3269 Pottery Products, nec
327113 Porcelain Electrical Supply Manufacturing
SIC 3264 Porcelain Electrical Supplies
327121 Brick & Structural Clay Tile Manufacturing
SIC 3251 Brick & Structural Clay Tile
327122 Ceramic Wall & Floor Tile Manufacturing
SIC 3253 Ceramic Wall & Floor Tile
327123 Other Structural Clay Product Manufacturing
SIC 3259 Structural Clay Products, nec
327124 Clay Refractory Manufacturing
SIC 3255 Clay Refractories
327125 Nonclay Refractory Manufacturing
SIC 3297 Nonclay Refractories
327211 Flat Glass Manufacturing
SIC 3211 Flat Glass
**327212 Other Pressed & Blown Glass & Glassware
    Manufacturing**
SIC 3229 Pressed & Blown Glass & Glassware, nec
327213 Glass Container Manufacturing
SIC 3221 Glass Containers
327215 Glass Product Manufacturing Made of Purchased Glass
SIC 3231 Glass Products Made of Purchased Glass
32731 Hydraulic Cement Manufacturing
SIC 3241 Cement, Hydraulic
32732 Ready-Mix Concrete Manufacturing
SIC 3273 Ready-Mixed Concrete
327331 Concrete Block & Brick Manufacturing
SIC 3271 Concrete Block & Brick
327332 Concrete Pipe Manufacturing
SIC 3272 Concrete Products, Except Block & Brick
32739 Other Concrete Product Manufacturing
SIC 3272 Concrete Products, Except Block & Brick
32741 Lime Manufacturing
SIC 3274 Lime
32742 Gypsum & Gypsum Product Manufacturing
SIC 3275 Gypsum Products
SIC 3299 Nonmetallic Mineral Products, nec
32791 Abrasive Product Manufacturing
SIC 3291 Abrasive Products
327991 Cut Stone & Stone Product Manufacturing
SIC 3281 Cut Stone & Stone Products
327992 Ground or Treated Mineral & Earth Manufacturing
SIC 3295 Minerals & Earths, Ground or Otherwise Treated
327993 Mineral Wool Manufacturing
SIC 3296 Mineral Wool
**327999 All Other Miscellaneous Nonmetallic Mineral Product
    Manufacturing**
SIC 3272 Concrete Products, Except Block & Brick
SIC 3292 Asbestos Products
SIC 3299 Nonmetallic Mineral Products, nec

PRIMARY METAL MANUFACTURING

331111 Iron & Steel Mills
SIC 3312 Steel Works, Blast Furnaces , & Rolling Mills
SIC 3399 Primary Metal Products, nec
331112 Electrometallurgical Ferroalloy Product Manufacturing
SIC 3313 Electrometallurgical Products, Except Steel

33121 Iron & Steel Pipes & Tubes Manufacturing from Purchased Steel
SIC 3317 Steel Pipe & Tubes
331221 Cold-Rolled Steel Shape Manufacturing
SIC 3316 Cold-Rolled Steel Sheet, Strip & Bars
331222 Steel Wire Drawing
SIC 3315 Steel Wiredrawing & Steel Nails & Spikes
331311 Alumina Refining
SIC 2819 Industrial Inorganic Chemicals, nec
331312 Primary Aluminum Production
SIC 3334 Primary Production of Aluminum
331314 Secondary Smelting & Alloying of Aluminum
SIC 3341 Secondary Smelting & Refining of Nonferrous Metals
SIC 3399 Primary Metal Products, nec
331315 Aluminum Sheet, Plate & Foil Manufacturing
SIC 3353 Aluminum Sheet, Plate, & Foil
331316 Aluminum Extruded Product Manufacturing
SIC 3354 Aluminum Extruded Products
331319 Other Aluminum Rolling & Drawing
SIC 3355 Aluminum Rolling & Drawing, nec
SIC 3357 Drawing & Insulating of Nonferrous Wire
331411 Primary Smelting & Refining of Copper
SIC 3331 Primary Smelting & Refining of Copper
331419 Primary Smelting & Refining of Nonferrous Metal
SIC 3339 Primary Smelting & Refining of Nonferrous Metals, Except Copper & Aluminum
331421 Copper Rolling, Drawing & Extruding
SIC 3351 Rolling, Drawing, & Extruding of Copper
331422 Copper Wire Drawing
SIC 3357 Drawing & Insulating of Nonferrous Wire
331423 Secondary Smelting, Refining, & Alloying of Copper
SIC 3341 Secondary Smelting & Refining of Nonferrous Metals
SIC 3399 Primary Metal Products, nec
331491 Nonferrous Metal Rolling, Drawing & Extruding
SIC 3356 Rolling, Drawing & Extruding of Nonferrous Metals, Except Copper & Aluminum
SIC 3357 Drawing & Insulating of Nonferrous Wire
331492 Secondary Smelting, Refining, & Alloying of Nonferrous Metal
SIC 3313 Electrometallurgical Products, Except Steel
SIC 3341 Secondary Smelting & Reining of Nonferrous Metals
SIC 3399 Primary Metal Products, nec
331511 Iron Foundries
SIC 3321 Gray & Ductile Iron Foundries
SIC 3322 Malleable Iron Foundries
331512 Steel Investment Foundries
SIC 3324 Steel Investment Foundries
331513 Steel Foundries,
SIC 3325 Steel Foundries, nec
331521 Aluminum Die-Castings
SIC 3363 Aluminum Die-Castings
331522 Nonferrous Die-Castings
SIC 3364 Nonferrous Die-Castings, Except Aluminum
331524 Aluminum Foundries
SIC 3365 Aluminum Foundries
331525 Copper Foundries
SIC 3366 Copper Foundries
331528 Other Nonferrous Foundries
SIC 3369 Nonferrous Foundries, Except Aluminum & Copper

FABRICATED METAL PRODUCT MANUFACTURING

332111 Iron & Steel Forging
SIC 3462 Iron & Steel Forgings
332112 Nonferrous Forging
SIC 3463 Nonferrous Forgings
332114 Custom Roll Forming
SIC 3449 Miscellaneous Structural Metal Work
332115 Crown & Closure Manufacturing
SIC 3466 Crowns & Closures
332116 Metal Stamping
SIC 3469 Metal Stampings, nec
332117 Powder Metallurgy Part Manufacturing
SIC 3499 Fabricated Metal Products, nec
332211 Cutlery & Flatware Manufacturing
SIC 3421 Cutlery
SIC 3914 Silverware, Plated Ware, & Stainless Steel Ware
332212 Hand & Edge Tool Manufacturing
SIC 3423 Hand & Edge Tools, Except Machine Tools & Handsaws
SIC 3523 Farm Machinery & Equipment
SIC 3524 Lawn & Garden Tractors & Home Lawn & Garden Equipment
SIC 3545 Cutting Tools, Machine Tools Accessories, & Machinist Precision Measuring Devices
SIC 3799 Transportation Equipment, nec
SIC 3999 Manufacturing Industries, nec
332213 Saw Blade & Handsaw Manufacturing
SIC 3425 Saw Blades & Handsaws
332214 Kitchen Utensil, Pot & Pan Manufacturing
SIC 3469 Metal Stampings, nec
332311 Prefabricated Metal Building & Component Manufacturing
SIC 3448 Prefabricated Metal Buildings & Components
332312 Fabricated Structural Metal Manufacturing
SIC 3441 Fabricated Structural Metal
SIC 3449 Miscellaneous Structural Metal Work
332313 Plate Work Manufacturing
SIC 3443 Fabricated Plate Work
332321 Metal Window & Door Manufacturing
SIC 3442 Metal Doors, Sash, Frames, Molding & Trim
SIC 3449 Miscellaneous Structural Metal Work
332322 Sheet Metal Work Manufacturing
SIC 3444 Sheet Metal Work
332323 Ornamental & Architectural Metal Work Manufacturing
SIC 3446 Architectural & Ornamental Metal Work
SIC 3449 Miscellaneous Structural Metal Work
SIC 3523 Farm Machinery & Equipment
33241 Power Boiler & Heat Exchanger Manufacturing
SIC 3443 Fabricated Plate Work
33242 Metal Tank Manufacturing
SIC 3443 Fabricated Plate Work
332431 Metal Can Manufacturing
SIC 3411 Metal Cans
332439 Other Metal Container Manufacturing
SIC 3412 Metal Shipping Barrels, Drums, Kegs, & Pails
SIC 3429 Hardware, nec
SIC 3444 Sheet Metal Work
SIC 3499 Fabricated Metal Products, nec
SIC 3537 Industrial Trucks, Tractors, Trailers, & Stackers
33251 Hardware Manufacturing
SIC 3429 Hardware, nec
SIC 3499 Fabricated Metal Products, nec

332611 Steel Spring Manufacturing
SIC 3493 Steel Springs, Except Wire
332612 Wire Spring Manufacturing
SIC 3495 Wire Springs
332618 Other Fabricated Wire Product Manufacturing
SIC 3315 Steel Wiredrawing & Steel Nails & Spikes
SIC 3399 Primary Metal Products, nec
SIC 3496 Miscellaneous Fabricated Wire Products
33271 Machine Shops
SIC 3599 Industrial & Commercial Machinery & Equipment, nec
332721 Precision Turned Product Manufacturing
SIC 3451 Screw Machine Products
332722 Bolt, Nut, Screw, Rivet & Washer Manufacturing
SIC 3452 Bolts, Nuts, Screws, Rivets, & Washers
332811 Metal Heat Treating
SIC 3398 Metal Heat Treating
332812 Metal Coating, Engraving , & Allied Services to Manufacturers
SIC 3479 Coating, Engraving, & Allied Services, nec
332813 Electroplating, Plating, Polishing, Anodizing & Coloring
SIC 3399 Primary Metal Products, nec
SIC 3471 Electroplating, Plating, Polishing, Anodizing, & Coloring
332911 Industrial Valve Manufacturing
SIC 3491 Industrial Valves
332912 Fluid Power Valve & Hose Fitting Manufacturing
SIC 3492 Fluid Power Valves & Hose Fittings
SIC 3728 Aircraft Parts & Auxiliary Equipment, nec
332913 Plumbing Fixture Fitting & Trim Manufacturing
SIC 3432 Plumbing Fixture Fittings & Trim
332919 Other Metal Valve & Pipe Fitting Manufacturing
SIC 3429 Hardware, nec
SIC 3494 Valves & Pipe Fittings, nec
SIC 3499 Fabricated Metal Products, nec
332991 Ball & Roller Bearing Manufacturing
SIC 3562 Ball & Roller Bearings
332992 Small Arms Ammunition Manufacturing
SIC 3482 Small Arms Ammunition
332993 Ammunition Manufacturing
SIC 3483 Ammunition, Except for Small Arms
332994 Small Arms Manufacturing
SIC 3484 Small Arms
332995 Other Ordnance & Accessories Manufacturing
SIC 3489 Ordnance & Accessories, nec
332996 Fabricated Pipe & Pipe Fitting Manufacturing
SIC 3498 Fabricated Pipe & Pipe Fittings
332997 Industrial Pattern Manufacturing
SIC 3543 Industrial Patterns
332998 Enameled Iron & Metal Sanitary Ware Manufacturing
SIC 3431 Enameled Iron & Metal Sanitary Ware
332999 All Other Miscellaneous Fabricated Metal Product Manufacturing
SIC 3291 Abrasive Products
SIC 3432 Plumbing Fixture Fittings & Trim
SIC 3494 Valves & Pipe Fittings, nec
SIC 3497 Metal Foil & Leaf
SIC 3499 Fabricated Metal Products, NEC
SIC 3537 Industrial Trucks, Tractors, Trailers, & Stackers
SIC 3599 Industrial & Commercial Machinery & Equipment, nec
SIC 3999 Manufacturing Industries, nec

MACHINERY MANUFACTURING

333111 Farm Machinery & Equipment Manufacturing
SIC 3523 Farm Machinery & Equipment
333112 Lawn & Garden Tractor & Home Lawn & Garden Equipment Manufacturing
SIC 3524 Lawn & Garden Tractors & Home Lawn & Garden Equipment
33312 Construction Machinery Manufacturing
SIC 3531 Construction Machinery & Equipment
333131 Mining Machinery & Equipment Manufacturing
SIC 3532 Mining Machinery & Equipment, Except Oil & Gas Field Machinery & Equipment
333132 Oil & Gas Field Machinery & Equipment Manufacturing
SIC 3533 Oil & Gas Field Machinery & Equipment
33321 Sawmill & Woodworking Machinery Manufacturing
SIC 3553 Woodworking Machinery
33322 Rubber & Plastics Industry Machinery Manufacturing
SIC 3559 Special Industry Machinery, nec
333291 Paper Industry Machinery Manufacturing
SIC 3554 Paper Industries Machinery
333292 Textile Machinery Manufacturing
SIC 3552 Textile Machinery
333293 Printing Machinery & Equipment Manufacturing
SIC 3555 Printing Trades Machinery & Equipment
333294 Food Product Machinery Manufacturing
SIC 3556 Food Products Machinery
333295 Semiconductor Machinery Manufacturing
SIC 3559 Special Industry Machinery, nec
333298 All Other Industrial Machinery Manufacturing
SIC 3559 Special Industry Machinery, nec
SIC 3639 Household Appliances, nec
333311 Automatic Vending Machine Manufacturing
SIC 3581 Automatic Vending Machines
333312 Commercial Laundry, Drycleaning & Pressing Machine Manufacturing
SIC 3582 Commercial Laundry, Drycleaning & Pressing Machines
333313 Office Machinery Manufacturing
SIC 3578 Calculating & Accounting Machinery, Except Electronic Computers
SIC 3579 Office Machines, nec
333314 Optical Instrument & Lens Manufacturing
SIC 3827 Optical Instruments & Lenses
333315 Photographic & Photocopying Equipment Manufacturing
SIC 3861 Photographic Equipment & Supplies
333319 Other Commercial & Service Industry Machinery Manufacturing
SIC 3559 Special Industry Machinery, nec
SIC 3589 Service Industry Machinery, nec
SIC 3599 Industrial & Commercial Machinery & Equipment, nec
SIC 3699 Electrical Machinery, Equipment & Supplies, nec
333411 Air Purification Equipment Manufacturing
SIC 3564 Industrial & Commercial Fans & Blowers & Air Purification Equipment
333412 Industrial & Commercial Fan & Blower Manufacturing
SIC 3564 Industrial & Commercial Fans & Blowers & Air Purification Equipment
333414 Heating Equipment Manufacturing
SIC 3433 Heating Equipment, Except Electric & Warm Air Furnaces

SIC 3634 Electric Housewares & Fans
333415 Air-Conditioning & Warm Air Heating Equipment & Commercial & Industrial Refrigeration Equipment Manufacturing
SIC 3443 Fabricated Plate Work
SIC 3585 Air-Conditioning & Warm Air Heating Equipment & Commercial & Industrial Refrigeration Equipment
333511 Industrial Mold Manufacturing
SIC 3544 Special Dies & Tools, Die Sets, Jigs & Fixtures, & Industrial Molds
333512 Machine Tool Manufacturing
SIC 3541 Machine Tools, Metal Cutting Type
333513 Machine Tool Manufacturing
SIC 3542 Machine Tools, Metal Forming Type
333514 Special Die & Tool, Die Set, Jig & Fixture Manufacturing
SIC 3544 Special Dies & Tools, Die Sets, Jigs & Fixtures, & Industrial Molds
333515 Cutting Tool & Machine Tool Accessory Manufacturing
SIC 3545 Cutting Tools, Machine Tool Accessories, & Machinists' Precision Measuring Devices
333516 Rolling Mill Machinery & Equipment Manufacturing
SIC 3547 Rolling Mill Machinery & Equipment
333518 Other Metalworking Machinery Manufacturing
SIC 3549 Metalworking Machinery, nec
333611 Turbine & Turbine Generator Set Unit Manufacturing
SIC 3511 Steam, Gas, & Hydraulic Turbines, & Turbine Generator Set Units
333612 Speed Changer, Industrial High-Speed Drive & Gear Manufacturing
SIC 3566 Speed Changers, Industrial High-Speed Drives, & Gears
333613 Mechanical Power Transmission Equipment Manufacturing
SIC 3568 Mechanical Power Transmission Equipment, nec
333618 Other Engine Equipment Manufacturing
SIC 3519 Internal Combustion Engines, nec
SIC 3699 Electrical Machinery, Equipment & Supplies, nec
333911 Pump & Pumping Equipment Manufacturing
SIC 3561 Pumps & Pumping Equipment
SIC 3743 Railroad Equipment
333912 Air & Gas Compressor Manufacturing
SIC 3563 Air & Gas Compressors
333913 Measuring & Dispensing Pump Manufacturing
SIC 3586 Measuring & Dispensing Pumps
333921 Elevator & Moving Stairway Manufacturing
SIC 3534 Elevators & Moving Stairways
333922 Conveyor & Conveying Equipment Manufacturing
SIC 3523 Farm Machinery & Equipment
SIC 3535 Conveyors & Conveying Equipment
333923 Overhead Traveling Crane, Hoist & Monorail System Manufacturing
SIC 3536 Overhead Traveling Cranes, Hoists, & Monorail Systems
SIC 3531 Construction Machinery & Equipment
333924 Industrial Truck, Tractor, Trailer & Stacker Machinery Manufacturing
SIC 3537 Industrial Trucks, Tractors, Trailers, & Stackers
333991 Power-Driven Hand Tool Manufacturing
SIC 3546 Power-Driven Handtools
333992 Welding & Soldering Equipment Manufacturing
SIC 3548 Electric & Gas Welding & Soldering Equipment

333993 Packaging Machinery Manufacturing
SIC 3565 Packaging Machinery
333994 Industrial Process Furnace & Oven Manufacturing
SIC 3567 Industrial Process Furnaces & Ovens
333995 Fluid Power Cylinder & Actuator Manufacturing
SIC 3593 Fluid Power Cylinders & Actuators
333996 Fluid Power Pump & Motor Manufacturing
SIC 3594 Fluid Power Pumps & Motors
333997 Scale & Balance Manufacturing
SIC 3596 Scales & Balances, Except Laboratory
333999 All Other General Purpose Machinery Manufacturing
SIC 3599 Industrial & Commercial Machinery & Equipment, nec
SIC 3569 General Industrial Machinery & Equipment, nec

COMPUTER & ELECTRONIC PRODUCT MANUFACTURING

334111 Electronic Computer Manufacturing
SIC 3571 Electronic Computers
334112 Computer Storage Device Manufacturing
SIC 3572 Computer Storage Devices
334113 Computer Terminal Manufacturing
SIC 3575 Computer Terminals
334119 Other Computer Peripheral Equipment Manufacturing
SIC 3577 Computer Peripheral Equipment, nec
SIC 3578 Calculating & Accounting Machines, Except Electronic Computers
SIC 3699 Electrical Machinery, Equipment & Supplies, nec
33421 Telephone Apparatus Manufacturing
SIC 3661 Telephone & Telegraph Apparatus
33422 Radio & Television Broadcasting & Wireless Communications Equipment Manufacturing
SIC 3663 Radio & Television Broadcasting & Communication Equipment
SIC 3679 Electronic Components, nec
33429 Other Communications Equipment Manufacturing
SIC 3669 Communications Equipment, nec
33431 Audio & Video Equipment Manufacturing
SIC 3651 Household Audio & Video Equipment
334411 Electron Tube Manufacturing
SIC 3671 Electron Tubes
334412 Printed Circuit Board Manufacturing
SIC 3672 Printed Circuit Boards
334413 Semiconductor & Related Device Manufacturing
SIC 3674 Semiconductors & Related Devices
334414 Electronic Capacitor Manufacturing
SIC 3675 Electronic Capacitors
334415 Electronic Resistor Manufacturing
SIC 3676 Electronic Resistors
334416 Electronic Coil, Transformer, & Other Inductor Manufacturing
SIC 3661 Telephone & Telegraph Apparatus
SIC 3677 Electronic Coils, Transformers, & Other Inductors
SIC 3825 Instruments for Measuring & Testing of Electricity & Electrical Signals
334417 Electronic Connector Manufacturing
SIC 3678 Electronic Connectors
334418 Printed Circuit/Electronics Assembly Manufacturing
SIC 3679 Electronic Components, nec
SIC 3661 Telephone & Telegraph Apparatus

334419 Other Electronic Component Manufacturing
SIC 3679 Electronic Components, nec
334510 Electromedical & Electrotherapeutic Apparatus Manufacturing
SIC 3842 Orthopedic, Prosthetic & Surgical Appliances & Supplies
SIC 3845 Electromedical & Electrotherapeutic Apparatus
334511 Search, Detection, Navigation, Guidance, Aeronautical, & Nautical System & Instrument Manufacturing
SIC 3812 Search, Detection, Navigation, Guidance, Aeronautical, & Nautical Systems & Instruments
334512 Automatic Environmental Control Manufacturing for Residential, Commercial & Appliance Use
SIC 3822 Automatic Controls for Regulating Residential & Commercial Environments & Appliances
334513 Instruments & Related Products Manufacturing for Measuring, Displaying, & Controlling Industrial Process Variables
SIC 3823 Industrial Instruments for Measurement, Display, & Control of Process Variables; & Related Products
334514 Totalizing Fluid Meter & Counting Device Manufacturing
SIC 3824 Totalizing Fluid Meters & Counting Devices
334515 Instrument Manufacturing for Measuring & Testing Electricity & Electrical Signals
SIC 3825 Instruments for Measuring & Testing of Electricity & Electrical Signals
334516 Analytical Laboratory Instrument Manufacturing
SIC 3826 Laboratory Analytical Instruments
334517 Irradiation Apparatus Manufacturing
SIC 3844 X-Ray Apparatus & Tubes & Related Irradiation Apparatus
SIC 3845 Electromedical & Electrotherapeutic Apparatus
334518 Watch, Clock, & Part Manufacturing
SIC 3495 Wire Springs
SIC 3579 Office Machines, nec
SIC 3873 Watches, Clocks, Clockwork Operated Devices, & Parts
334519 Other Measuring & Controlling Device Manufacturing
SIC 3829 Measuring & Controlling Devices, nec
334611 Software Reproducing
SIC 7372 Prepackaged Software
334612 Prerecorded Compact Disc , Tape, & Record Reproducing
SIC 3652 Phonograph Records & Prerecorded Audio Tapes & Disks
SIC 7819 Services Allied to Motion Picture Production
334613 Magnetic & Optical Recording Media Manufacturing
SIC 3695 Magnetic & Optical Recording Media

ELECTRICAL EQUIPMENT, APPLIANCE, & COMPONENT MANUFACTURING

33511 Electric Lamp Bulb & Part Manufacturing
SIC 3641 Electric Lamp Bulbs & Tubes
335121 Residential Electric Lighting Fixture Manufacturing
SIC 3645 Residential Electric Lighting Fixtures
SIC 3999 Manufacturing Industries, nec
335122 Commercial, Industrial & Institutional Electric Lighting Fixture Manufacturing
SIC 3646 Commercial, Industrial, & Institutional Electric Lighting Fixtures

335129 Other Lighting Equipment Manufacturing
SIC 3648 Lighting Equipment, nec
SIC 3699 Electrical Machinery, Equipment, & Supplies, nec
335211 Electric Housewares & Fan Manufacturing
SIC 3634 Electric Housewares & Fans
335212 Household Vacuum Cleaner Manufacturing
SIC 3635 Household Vacuum Cleaners
SIC 3639 Household Appliances, nec
335221 Household Cooking Appliance Manufacturing
SIC 3631 Household Cooking Equipment
335222 Household Refrigerator & Home Freezer Manufacturing
SIC 3632 Household Refrigerators & Home & Farm Freezers
335224 Household Laundry Equipment Manufacturing
SIC 3633 Household Laundry Equipment
335228 Other Household Appliance Manufacturing
SIC 3639 Household Appliances, nec
335311 Power, Distribution & Specialty Transformer Manufacturing
SIC 3548 Electric & Gas Welding & Soldering Equipment
SIC 3612 Power, Distribution, & Speciality Transformers
335312 Motor & Generator Manufacturing
SIC 3621 Motors & Generators
SIC 7694 Armature Rewinding Shops
335313 Switchgear & Switchboard Apparatus Manufacturing
SIC 3613 Switchgear & Switchboard Apparatus
335314 Relay & Industrial Control Manufacturing
SIC 3625 Relays & Industrial Controls
335911 Storage Battery Manufacturing
SIC 3691 Storage Batteries
335912 Dry & Wet Primary Battery Manufacturing
SIC 3692 Primary Batteries, Dry & Wet
335921 Fiber-Optic Cable Manufacturing
SIC 3357 Drawing & Insulating of Nonferrous Wire
335929 Other Communication & Energy Wire Manufacturing
SIC 3357 Drawing & Insulating of Nonferrous Wire
335931 Current-Carrying Wiring Device Manufacturing
SIC 3643 Current-Carrying Wiring Devices
335932 Noncurrent-Carrying Wiring Device Manufacturing
SIC 3644 Noncurrent-Carrying Wiring Devices
335991 Carbon & Graphite Product Manufacturing
SIC 3624 Carbon & Graphite Products
335999 All Other Miscellaneous Electrical Equipment & Component Manufacturing
SIC 3629 Electrical Industrial Apparatus, nec
SIC 3699 Electrical Machinery, Equipment, & Supplies, nec

TRANSPORTATION EQUIPMENT MANUFACTURING

336111 Automobile Manufacturing
SIC 3711 Motor Vehicles & Passenger Car Bodies
336112 Light Truck & Utility Vehicle Manufacturing
SIC 3711 Motor Vehicles & Passenger Car Bodies
33612 Heavy Duty Truck Manufacturing
SIC 3711 Motor Vehicles & Passenger Car Bodies
336211 Motor Vehicle Body Manufacturing
SIC 3711 Motor Vehicles & Passenger Car Bodies
SIC 3713 Truck & Bus Bodies
SIC 3714 Motor Vehicle Parts & Accessories
336212 Truck Trailer Manufacturing
SIC 3715 Truck Trailers

336213 Motor Home Manufacturing
SIC 3716 Motor Homes
336214 Travel Trailer & Camper Manufacturing
SIC 3792 Travel Trailers & Campers
SIC 3799 Transportation Equipment, nec
336311 Carburetor, Piston, Piston Ring & Valve Manufacturing
SIC 3592 Carburetors, Pistons, Piston Rings, & Valves
336312 Gasoline Engine & Engine Parts Manufacturing
SIC 3714 Motor Vehicle Parts & Accessories
336321 Vehicular Lighting Equipment Manufacturing
SIC 3647 Vehicular Lighting Equipment
336322 Other Motor Vehicle Electrical & Electronic Equipment Manufacturing
SIC 3679 Electronic Components, nec
SIC 3694 Electrical Equipment for Internal Combustion Engines
SIC 3714 Motor Vehicle Parts & Accessories
33633 Motor Vehicle Steering & Suspension Components Manufacturing
SIC 3714 Motor Vehicle Parts & Accessories
33634 Motor Vehicle Brake System Manufacturing
SIC 3292 Asbestos Products
SIC 3714 Motor Vehicle Parts & Accessories
33635 Motor Vehicle Transmission & Power Train Parts Manufacturing
SIC 3714 Motor Vehicle Parts & Accessories
33636 Motor Vehicle Fabric Accessories & Seat Manufacturing
SIC 2396 Automotive Trimmings, Apparel Findings, & Related Products
SIC 2399 Fabricated Textile Products, nec
SIC 2531 Public Building & Related Furniture
33637 Motor Vehicle Metal Stamping
SIC 3465 Automotive Stampings
336391 Motor Vehicle Air-Conditioning Manufacturing
SIC 3585 Air-Conditioning & Warm Air Heating Equipment & Commercial & Industrial Refrigeration Equipment
336399 All Other Motor Vehicle Parts Manufacturing
SIC 3519 Internal Combustion Engines, nec
SIC 3599 Industrial & Commercial Machinery & Equipment, NEC
SIC 3714 Motor Vehicle Parts & Accessories
336411 Aircraft Manufacturing
SIC 3721 Aircraft
336412 Aircraft Engine & Engine Parts Manufacturing
SIC 3724 Aircraft Engines & Engine Parts
336413 Other Aircraft Part & Auxiliary Equipment Manufacturing
SIC 3728 Aircraft Parts & Auxiliary Equipment, nec
336414 Guided Missile & Space Vehicle Manufacturing
SIC 3761 Guided Missiles & Space Vehicles
336415 Guided Missile & Space Vehicle Propulsion Unit & Propulsion Unit Parts Manufacturing
SIC 3764 Guided Missile & Space Vehicle Propulsion Units & Propulsion Unit Parts
336419 Other Guided Missile & Space Vehicle Parts & Auxiliary Equipment Manufacturing
SIC 3769 Guided Missile & Space Vehicle Parts & Auxiliary Equipment
33651 Railroad Rolling Stock Manufacturing
SIC 3531 Construction Machinery & Equipment
SIC 3743 Railroad Equipment
336611 Ship Building & Repairing
SIC 3731 Ship Building & Repairing

336612 Boat Building
SIC 3732 Boat Building & Repairing
336991 Motorcycle, Bicycle, & Parts Manufacturing
SIC 3944 Games, Toys, & Children's Vehicles, Except Dolls & Bicycles
SIC 3751 Motorcycles, Bicycles & Parts
336992 Military Armored Vehicle, Tank & Tank Component Manufacturing
SIC 3711 Motor Vehicles & Passenger Car Bodies
SIC 3795 Tanks & Tank Components
336999 All Other Transportation Equipment Manufacturing
SIC 3799 Transportation Equipment, nec

FURNITURE & RELATED PRODUCT MANUFACTURING

337121 Upholstered Household Furniture Manufacturing
SIC 2512 Wood Household Furniture, Upholstered
SIC 2515 Mattress, Foundations, & Convertible Beds
SIC 5712 Furniture
337122 Nonupholstered Wood Household Furniture Manufacturing
SIC 2511 Wood Household Furniture, Except Upholstered
SIC 5712 Furniture Stores
337124 Metal Household Furniture Manufacturing
SIC 2514 Metal Household Furniture
337125 Household Furniture Manufacturing
SIC 2519 Household Furniture, NEC
337127 Institutional Furniture Manufacturing
SIC 2531 Public Building & Related Furniture
SIC 2599 Furniture & Fixtures, nec
SIC 3952 Lead Pencils, Crayons, & Artist's Materials
SIC 3999 Manufacturing Industries, nec
337129 Wood Television, Radio, & Sewing Machine Cabinet Manufacturing
SIC 2517 Wood Television, Radio, Phonograph, & Sewing Machine Cabinets
337131 Wood Kitchen & Counter Top Manufacturing
SIC 2434 Wood Kitchen Cabinets
SIC 2541 Wood Office & Store Fixtures, Partitions, Shelving, & Lockers
SIC 5712 Furniture Stores
337132 Upholstered Wood Household Furniture Manufacturing
SIC 2515 Mattresses, Foundations, & Convertible Beds
SIC 5712 Furniture Stores
337133 Wood Household Furniture
SIC 5712 Furniture Stores
337134 Wood Office Furniture Manufacturing
SIC 2521 Wood Office Furniture
337135 Custom Architectural Woodwork, Millwork, & Fixtures
SIC 2541 Wood Office & Store Fixtures, Partitions, Shelving, and Lockers
337139 Other Wood Furniture Manufacturing
SIC 2426 Hardwood Dimension & Flooring Mills
SIC 2499 Wood Products, nec
SIC 2517 Wood Television, Radio, Phonograph, & Sewing Machine Cabinets
SIC 2531 Public Building & Related Furniture
SIC 2541 Wood Office & Store Fixtures, Partitions., Shelving, & Lockers
SIC 2599 Furniture & Fixtures, nec
SIC 3952 Lead Pencils, Crayons, & Artist's Materials

337141 Nonwood Office Furniture Manufacturing
SIC 2522 Office Furniture, Except Wood
337143 Household Furniture Manufacturing
SIC 2519 Household Furniture, NEC
337145 Nonwood Showcase, Partition, Shelving, & Locker Manufacturing
SIC 2542 Office & Store Fixtures, Partitions, Shelving, & Lockers, Except Wood
337148 Other Nonwood Furniture Manufacturing
SIC 2499 Wood Products, NEC
SIC 2531 Public Building & Related Furniture
SIC 2599 Furniture & Fixtures, nec
SIC 3499 Fabricated Metal Products, nec
SIC 3952 Lead Pencils, Crayons, & Artist's Materials
SIC 3999 Manufacturing Industries, nec
337212 Custom Architectural Woodwork & Millwork Manufacturing
SIC 2541 Wood Office & Store Fixtures, Partitions, Shelving, & Lockers
337214 Nonwood Office Furniture Manufacturing
SIC 2522 Office Furniture, Except Wood
337215 Showcase, Partition, Shelving, & Locker Manufacturing
SIC 2542 Office & Store Fixtures, Partitions, Shelving & Lockers, Except Wood
SIC 2541 Wood Office & Store Fixtures, Partitions, Shelving, & Lockers
SIC 2426 Hardwood Dimension & Flooring Mills
SIC 3499 Fabricated Metal Products, nec
33791 Mattress Manufacturing
SIC 2515 Mattresses, Foundations & Convertible Beds
33792 Blind & Shade Manufacturing
SIC 2591 Drapery Hardware & Window Blinds & Shades

MISCELLANEOUS MANUFACTURING

339111 Laboratory Apparatus & Furniture Manufacturing
SIC 3829 Measuring & Controlling Devices, nec
339112 Surgical & Medical Instrument Manufacturing
SIC 3841 Surgical & Medical Instruments & Apparatus
SIC 3829 Measuring & Controlling Devices, nec
339113 Surgical Appliance & Supplies Manufacturing
SIC 2599 Furniture & Fixtures, nec
SIC 3842 Orthopedic, Prosthetic, & Surgical Appliances & Supplies
339114 Dental Equipment & Supplies Manufacturing
SIC 3843 Dental Equipment & Supplies
339115 Ophthalmic Goods Manufacturing
SIC 3851 Opthalmic Goods
SIC 5995 Optical Goods Stores
339116 Dental Laboratories
SIC 8072 Dental Laboratories 339117 Eyeglass & Contact Lens Manufacturing
SIC 5995 Optical Goods Stores
339911 Jewelry Manufacturing
SIC 3469 Metal Stamping, nec
SIC 3479 Coating, Engraving, & Allied Services, nec
SIC 3911 Jewelry, Precious Metal
339912 Silverware & Plated Ware Manufacturing
SIC 3479 Coating, Engraving, & Allied Services, nec
SIC 3914 Silverware, Plated Ware, & Stainless Steel Ware
339913 Jewelers' Material & Lapidary Work Manufacturing
SIC 3915 Jewelers' Findings & Materials, & Lapidary Work

339914 Costume Jewelry & Novelty Manufacturing
SIC 3479 Coating, Engraving, & Allied Services, nec
SIC 3499 Fabricated Metal Products, nec
SIC 3961 Costume Jewelry & Costume Novelties, Except Precious Metal
33992 Sporting & Athletic Goods Manufacturing
SIC 3949 Sporting & Athletic Goods, nec
339931 Doll & Stuffed Toy Manufacturing
SIC 3942 Dolls & Stuffed Toys
339932 Game, Toy, & Children's Vehicle Manufacturing
SIC 3944 Games, Toys, & Children's Vehicles, Except Dolls & Bicycles
339941 Pen & Mechanical Pencil Manufacturing
SIC 3951 Pens, Mechanical Pencils, & Parts
339942 Lead Pencil & Art Good Manufacturing
SIC 2531 Public Buildings & Related Furniture
SIC 3579 Office Machines, nec
SIC 3952 Lead Pencils, Crayons, & Artists' Materials
339943 Marking Device Manufacturing
SIC 3953 Marking Devices
339944 Carbon Paper & Inked Ribbon Manufacturing
SIC 3955 Carbon Paper & Inked Ribbons
33995 Sign Manufacturing
SIC 3993 Signs & Advertising Specialties
339991 Gasket, Packing, & Sealing Device Manufacturing
SIC 3053 Gaskets, Packing, & Sealing Devices
339992 Musical Instrument Manufacturing
SIC 3931 Musical Instruments
339993 Fastener, Button, Needle & Pin Manufacturing
SIC 3965 Fasteners, Buttons, Needles, & Pins
SIC 3131 Boat & Shoe Cut Stock & Findings
339994 Broom, Brush & Mop Manufacturing
SIC 3991 Brooms & Brushes
SIC 2392 Housefurnishings, Except Curtains & Draperies
339995 Burial Casket Manufacturing
SIC 3995 Burial Caskets
339999 All Other Miscellaneous Manufacturing
SIC 2499 Wood Products, NEC
SIC 3999 Manufacturing Industries, nec

WHOLESALE TRADE

42111 Automobile & Other Motor Vehicle Wholesalers
SIC 5012 Automobiles & Other Motor Vehicles
42112 Motor Vehicle Supplies & New Part Wholesalers
SIC 5013 Motor Vehicle Supplies & New Parts
42113 Tire & Tube Wholesalers
SIC 5014 Tires & Tubes
42114 Motor Vehicle Part Wholesalers
SIC 5015 Motor Vehicle Parts, Used
42121 Furniture Wholesalers
SIC 5021 Furniture
42122 Home Furnishing Wholesalers
SIC 5023 Homefurnishings
42131 Lumber, Plywood, Millwork & Wood Panel Wholesalers
SIC 5031 Lumber, Plywood, Millwork, & Wood Panels
SIC 5211 Lumber & Other Building Materials Dealers - Retail
42132 Brick, Stone & Related Construction Material Wholesalers
SIC 5032 Brick, Stone, & Related Construction Materials
42133 Roofing, Siding & Insulation Material Wholesalers
SIC 5033 Roofing, Siding, & Insulation Materials

42139 Other Construction Material Wholesalers
SIC 5039 Construction Materials, nec

42141 Photographic Equipment & Supplies Wholesalers
SIC 5043 Photographic Equipment & Supplies

42142 Office Equipment Wholesalers
SIC 5044 Office Equipment

42143 Computer & Computer Peripheral Equipment & Software Wholesalers
SIC 5045 Computers & Computer Peripherals Equipment & Software

42144 Other Commercial Equipment Wholesalers
SIC 5046 Commercial Equipment, nec

42145 Medical, Dental & Hospital Equipment & Supplies Wholesalers
SIC 5047 Medical, Dental & Hospital Equipment & Supplies

42146 Ophthalmic Goods Wholesalers
SIC 5048 Ophthalmic Goods

42149 Other Professional Equipment & Supplies Wholesalers
SIC 5049 Professional Equipment & Supplies, nec

42151 Metal Service Centers & Offices
SIC 5051 Metals Service Centers & Offices

42152 Coal & Other Mineral & Ore Wholesalers
SIC 5052 Coal & Other Mineral & Ores

42161 Electrical Apparatus & Equipment, Wiring Supplies & Construction Material Wholesalers
SIC 5063 Electrical Apparatus & Equipment, Wiring Supplies & Construction Materials

42162 Electrical Appliance, Television & Radio Set Wholesalers
SIC 5064 Electrical Appliances, Television & Radio Sets

42169 Other Electronic Parts & Equipment Wholesalers
SIC 5065 Electronic Parts & Equipment, nec

42171 Hardware Wholesalers
SIC 5072 Hardware

42172 Plumbing & Heating Equipment & Supplies Wholesalers
SIC 5074 Plumbing & Heating Equipment & Supplies

42173 Warm Air Heating & Air-Conditioning Equipment & Supplies Wholesalers
SIC 5075 Warm Air Heating & Air-Conditioning Equipment & Supplies

42174 Refrigeration Equipment & Supplies Wholesalers
SIC 5078 Refrigeration Equipment & Supplies

42181 Construction & Mining Machinery & Equipment Wholesalers
SIC 5082 Construction & Mining Machinery & Equipment

42182 Farm & Garden Machinery & Equipment Wholesalers
SIC 5083 Farm & Garden Machinery & Equipment

42183 Industrial Machinery & Equipment Wholesalers
SIC 5084 Industrial Machinery & Equipment
SIC 5085 Industrial Supplies

42184 Industrial Supplies Wholesalers
SIC 5085 Industrial Supplies

42185 Service Establishment Equipment & Supplies Wholesalers
SIC 5087 Service Establishment Equipment & Supplies Wholesalers

42186 Transportation Equipment & Supplies Wholesalers
SIC 5088 Transportation Equipment and Supplies, Except Motor Vehicles

42191 Sporting & Recreational Goods & Supplies Wholesalers
SIC 5091 Sporting & Recreational Goods & Supplies

42192 Toy & Hobby Goods & Supplies Wholesalers
SIC 5092 Toys & Hobby Goods & Supplies

42193 Recyclable Material Wholesalers
SIC 5093 Scrap & Waste Materials

42194 Jewelry, Watch, Precious Stone & Precious Metal Wholesalers
SIC 5094 Jewelry, Watches, Precious Stones, & Precious Metals

42199 Other Miscellaneous Durable Goods Wholesalers
SIC 5099 Durable Goods, nec
SIC 7822 Motion Picture & Video Tape Distribution

42211 Printing & Writing Paper Wholesalers
SIC 5111 Printing & Writing Paper

42212 Stationary & Office Supplies Wholesalers
SIC 5112 Stationery & Office Supplies

42213 Industrial & Personal Service Paper Wholesalers
SIC 5113 Industrial & Personal Service Paper

42221 Drug, Drug Proprietaries & Druggists' Sundries Wholesalers
SIC 5122 Drugs, Drug Proprietaries, & Druggists' Sundries

42231 Piece Goods, Notions & Other Dry Goods Wholesalers
SIC 5131 Piece Goods, Notions, & Other Dry Goods

42232 Men's & Boys' Clothing & Furnishings Wholesalers
SIC 5136 Men's & Boys' Clothing & Furnishings

42233 Women's, Children's, & Infants' & Accessories Wholesalers
SIC 5137 Women's, Children's, & Infants' Clothing & Accessories

42234 Footwear Wholesalers
SIC 5139 Footwear

42241 General Line Grocery Wholesalers
SIC 5141 Groceries, General Line

42242 Packaged Frozen Food Wholesalers
SIC 5142 Packaged Frozen Foods

42243 Dairy Product Wholesalers
SIC 5143 Dairy Products, Except Dried or Canned

42244 Poultry & Poultry Product Wholesalers
SIC 5144 Poultry & Poultry Products

42245 Confectionery Wholesalers
SIC 5145 Confectionery

42246 Fish & Seafood Wholesalers
SIC 5146 Fish & Seafoods

42247 Meat & Meat Product Wholesalers
SIC 5147 Meats & Meat Products

42248 Fresh Fruit & Vegetable Wholesalers
SIC 5148 Fresh Fruits & Vegetables

42249 Other Grocery & Related Products Wholesalers
SIC 5149 Groceries & Related Products, nec

42251 Grain & Field Bean Wholesalers
SIC 5153 Grain & Field Beans

42252 Livestock Wholesalers
SIC 5154 Livestock

42259 Other Farm Product Raw Material Wholesalers
SIC 5159 Farm-Product Raw Materials, nec

42261 Plastics Materials & Basic Forms & Shapes Wholesalers
SIC 5162 Plastics Materials & Basic Forms & Shapes

42269 Other Chemical & Allied Products Wholesalers
SIC 5169 Chemicals & Allied Products, nec

42271 Petroleum Bulk Stations & Terminals
SIC 5171 Petroleum Bulk Stations & Terminals

42272 Petroleum & Petroleum Products Wholesalers
SIC 5172 Petroleum & Petroleum Products Wholesalers, Except Bulk Stations & Terminals

42281 Beer & Ale Wholesalers
SIC 5181 Beer & Ale

42282 Wine & Distilled Alcoholic Beverage Wholesalers
SIC 5182 Wine & Distilled Alcoholic Beverages
42291 Farm Supplies Wholesalers
SIC 5191 Farm Supplies
42292 Book, Periodical & Newspaper Wholesalers
SIC 5192 Books, Periodicals, & Newspapers
42293 Flower, Nursery Stock & Florists' Supplies Wholesalers
SIC 5193 Flowers, Nursery Stock, & Florists' Supplies
42294 Tobacco & Tobacco Product Wholesalers
SIC 5194 Tobacco & Tobacco Products
42295 Paint, Varnish & Supplies Wholesalers
SIC 5198 Paints, Varnishes, & Supplies
SIC 5231 Paint, Glass & Wallpaper Stores
42299 Other Miscellaneous Nondurable Goods Wholesalers
SIC 5199 Nondurable Goods, nec

RETAIL TRADE

44111 New Car Dealers
SIC 5511 Motor Vehicle Dealers, New and Used
44112 Used Car Dealers
SIC 5521 Motor Vehicle Dealers, Used Only
44121 Recreational Vehicle Dealers
SIC 5561 Recreational Vehicle Dealers
441221 Motorcycle Dealers
SIC 5571 Motorcycle Dealers
441222 Boat Dealers
SIC 5551 Boat Dealers
441229 All Other Motor Vehicle Dealers
SIC 5599 Automotive Dealers, NEC
44131 Automotive Parts & Accessories Stores
SIC 5013 Motor Vehicle Supplies & New Parts
SIC 5731 Radio, Television, & Consumer Electronics Stores
SIC 5531 Auto & Home Supply Stores
44132 Tire Dealers
SIC 5014 Tires & Tubes
SIC 5531 Auto & Home Supply Stores
44211 Furniture Stores
SIC 5021 Furniture
SIC 5712 Furniture Stores
44221 Floor Covering Stores
SIC 5023 Homefurnishings
SIC 5713 Floor Coverings Stores
442291 Window Treatment Stores
SIC 5714 Drapery, Curtain, & Upholstery Stores
SIC 5719 Miscellaneous Homefurnishings Stores
442299 All Other Home Furnishings Stores
SIC 5719 Miscellaneous Homefurnishings Stores
443111 Household Appliance Stores
SIC 5722 Household Appliance Stores
SIC 5999 Miscellaneous Retail Stores, nec
SIC 7623 Refrigeration & Air-Conditioning Service & Repair Shops
SIC 7629 Electrical & Electronic Repair Shops, nec
443112 Radio, Television & Other Electronics Stores
SIC 5731 Radio, Television, & Consumer Electronics Stores
SIC 5999 Miscellaneous Retail Stores, nec
SIC 7622 Radio & Television Repair Shops
44312 Computer & Software Stores
SIC 5045 Computers & Computer Peripheral Equipment & Software
SIC 7378 Computer Maintenance & Repair
SIC 5734 Computer & Computer Software Stores

44313 Camera & Photographic Supplies Stores
SIC 5946 Camera & Photographic Supply Stores
44411 Home Centers
SIC 5211 Lumber & Other Building Materials Dealers
44412 Paint & Wallpaper Stores
SIC 5198 Paints, Varnishes, & Supplies
SIC 5231 Paint, Glass, & Wallpaper Stores
44413 Hardware Stores
SIC 5251 Hardware Stores
44419 Other Building Material Dealers
SIC 5031 Lumber, Plywood, Millwork, & Wood Panels
SIC 5032 Brick, Stone, & Related Construction Materials
SIC 5039 Construction Materials, nec
SIC 5063 Electrical Apparatus & Equipment, Wiring Supplies, & Construction Materials
SIC 5074 Plumbing & Heating Equipment & Supplies
SIC 5211 Lumber & Other Building Materials Dealers
SIC 5231 Paint, Glass, & Wallpaper Stores
44421 Outdoor Power Equipment Stores
SIC 5083 Farm & Garden Machinery & Equipment
SIC 5261 Retail Nurseries, Lawn & Garden Supply Stores
44422 Nursery & Garden Centers
SIC 5191 Farm Supplies
SIC 5193 Flowers, Nursery Stock, & Florists' Supplies
SIC 5261 Retail Nurseries, Lawn & Garden Supply Stores
44511 Supermarkets & Other Grocery Stores
SIC 5411 Grocery Stores
44512 Convenience Stores
SIC 5411 Grocery Stores
44521 Meat Markets
SIC 5421 Meat & Fish Markets, Including Freezer Provisioners
SIC 5499 Miscellaneous Food Stores
44522 Fish & Seafood Markets
SIC 5421 Meat & Fish Markets, Including Freezer Provisioners
44523 Fruit & Vegetable Markets
SIC 5431 Fruit & Vegetable Markets
445291 Baked Goods Stores
SIC 5461 Retail Bakeries
445292 Confectionery & Nut Stores
SIC 5441 Candy, Nut & Confectionery Stores
445299 All Other Specialty Food Stores
SIC 5499 Miscellaneous Food Stores
SIC 5451 Dairy Products Stores
44531 Beer, Wine & Liquor Stores
SIC 5921 Liquor Stores
44611 Pharmacies & Drug Stores
SIC 5912 Drug Stores & Proprietary Stores
44612 Cosmetics, Beauty Supplies & Perfume Stores
SIC 5087 Service Establishment Equipment & Supplies
SIC 5999 Miscellaneous Retail Stores, nec
44613 Optical Goods Stores
SIC 5995 Optical Goods Stores
446191 Food Supplement Stores
SIC 5499 Miscellaneous Food Stores
446199 All Other Health & Personal Care Stores
SIC 5047 Medical, Dental, & Hospital Equipment & Supplies
SIC 5999 Miscellaneous Retail Stores, nec
44711 Gasoline Stations with Convenience Stores
SIC 5541 Gasoline Service Station
SIC 5411 Grocery Stores
44719 Other Gasoline Stations
SIC 5541 Gasoline Service Station

44811 Men's Clothing Stores
SIC 5611 Men's & Boys' Clothing & Accessory Stores
44812 Women's Clothing Stores
SIC 5621 Women's Clothing Stores
44813 Children's & Infants' Clothing Stores
SIC 5641 Children's & Infants' Wear Stores
44814 Family Clothing Stores
SIC 5651 Family Clothing Stores
44815 Clothing Accessories Stores
SIC 5611 Men's & Boys' Clothing & Accessory Stores
SIC 5632 Women's Accessory & Specialty Stores
SIC 5699 Miscellaneous Apparel & Accessory Stores
44819 Other Clothing Stores
SIC 5699 Miscellaneous Apparel & Accessory Stores
SIC 5632 Women's Accessory & Specialty Stores
44821 Shoe Stores
SIC 5661 Shoe Stores
44831 Jewelry Stores
SIC 5999 Miscellaneous Retailer, nec
SIC 5944 Jewelry Stores
44832 Luggage & Leather Goods Stores
SIC 5948 Luggage & Leather Goods Stores
45111 Sporting Goods Stores
SIC 7699 Repair Shops & Related Services, NEC
SIC 5941 Sporting Goods Stores & Bicycle Shops
45112 Hobby, Toy & Game Stores
SIC 5945 Hobby, Toy, & Game Stores
45113 Sewing, Needlework & Piece Goods Stores
SIC 5714 Drapery, Curtain, & Upholstery Stores
SIC 5949 Sewing, Needlework, & Piece Goods Stores
45114 Musical Instrument & Supplies Stores
SIC 5736 Musical Instruments Stores
451211 Book Stores
SIC 5942 Book Stores
451212 News Dealers & Newsstands
SIC 5994 News Dealers & Newsstands
45122 Prerecorded Tape, Compact Disc & Record Stores
SIC 5735 Record & Prerecorded Tape Stores
45211 Department Stores
SIC 5311 Department Stores
45291 Warehouse Clubs & Superstores
SIC 5399 Miscellaneous General Merchandise Stores
SIC 5411 Grocery Stores
45299 All Other General Merchandise Stores
SIC 5399 Miscellaneous General Merchandise Stores
SIC 5331 Variety Stores
45311 Florists
SIC 5992 Florists
45321 Office Supplies & Stationery Stores
SIC 5049 Professional Equipment & Supplies, nec
SIC 5112 Stationery & Office Supplies
SIC 5943 Stationery Stores
45322 Gift, Novelty & Souvenir Stores
SIC 5947 Gift, Novelty, & Souvenir Shops
45331 Used Merchandise Stores
SIC 5932 Used Merchandise Stores
45391 Pet & Pet Supplies Stores
SIC 5999 Miscellaneous Retail Stores, NEC
45392 Art Dealers
SIC 5999 Miscellaneous Retail Stores, nec
45393 Manufactured Home Dealers
SIC 5271 Mobile Home Dealers

453991 Tobacco Stores
SIC 5993 Tobacco Stores & Stands
453999 All Other Miscellaneous Store Retailers
SIC 5999 Miscellaneous Retail Stores, nec
SIC 5261 Retail Nurseries, Lawn & Garden Supply Stores
45411 Electronic Shopping & Mail-Order Houses
SIC 5961 Catalog & Mail-Order Houses
45421 Vending Machine Operators
SIC 5962 Automatic Merchandise Machine Operators
454311 Heating Oil Dealers
SIC 5171 Petroleum Bulk Stations & Terminals
SIC 5983 Fuel Oil Dealers
454312 Liquefied Petroleum Gas Dealers
SIC 5171 Petroleum Bulk Stations & Terminals
SIC 5984 Liquefied Petroleum Gas Dealers
454319 Other Fuel Dealers
SIC 5989 Fuel Dealers, nec
45439 Other Direct Selling Establishments
SIC 5421 Meat & Fish Markets, Including Freezer Provisioners
SIC 5963 Direct Selling Establishments

TRANSPORTATION & WAREHOUSING

481111 Scheduled Passenger Air Transportation
SIC 4512 Air Transportation, Scheduled
481112 Scheduled Freight Air Transportation
SIC 4512 Air Transportation, Scheduled
481211 Nonscheduled Chartered Passenger Air Transportation
SIC 4522 Air Transportation, Nonscheduled
481212 Nonscheduled Chartered Freight Air Transportation
SIC 4522 Air Transportation, Nonscheduled
481219 Other Nonscheduled Air Transportation
SIC 7319 Advertising, nec
48122 Nonscheduled Speciality Air Transportation
SIC 0721 Crop Planting, Cultivating, & Protecting
SIC 1382 Oil & Gas Field Exploration Services
SIC 4522 Air Transportation, Nonscheduled
SIC 7335 Commercial Photography
SIC 7997 Membership Sports & Recreation Clubs
SIC 8299 Schools & Educational Services, nec
SIC 8713 Surveying Services
482111 Line-Haul Railroads
SIC 4011 Railroads, Line-Haul Operating
482112 Short Line Railroads
SIC 4013 Railroad Switching & Terminal Establishments
483111 Deep Sea Freight Transportation
SIC 4412 Deep Sea Foreign Transportation of Freight
483112 Deep Sea Passenger Transportation
SIC 4481 Deep Sea Transportation of Passengers, Except by Ferry
483113 Coastal & Great Lakes Freight Transportation
SIC 4424 Deep Sea Domestic Transportation of Freight
SIC 4432 Freight Transportation on the Great Lakes - St. Lawrence Seaway
SIC 4492 Towing & Tugboat Services
483114 Coastal & Great Lakes Passenger Transportation
SIC 4481 Deep Sea Transportation of Passengers, Except by Ferry
SIC 4482 Ferries
483211 Inland Water Freight Transportation
SIC 4449 Water Transportation of Freight, nec
SIC 4492 Towing & Tugboat Services

483212 Inland Water Passenger Transportation
SIC 4482 Ferries
SIC 4489 Water Transportation of Passengers, nec
48411 General Freight Trucking, Local
SIC 4212 Local Trucking without Storage
SIC 4214 Local Trucking with Storage
484121 General Freight Trucking, Long-Distance, Truckload
SIC 4213 Trucking, Except Local
484122 General Freight Trucking, Long-Distance, Less Than Truckload
SIC 4213 Trucking, Except Local
48421 Used Household & Office Goods Moving
SIC 4212 Local Trucking Without Storage
SIC 4213 Trucking, Except Local
SIC 4214 Local Trucking With Storage
48422 Specialized Freight Trucking, Local
SIC 4212 Local Trucking without Storage
SIC 4214 Local Trucking with Storage
48423 Specialized Freight Trucking, Long-Distance
SIC 4213 Trucking, Except Local
485111 Mixed Mode Transit Systems
SIC 4111 Local & Suburban Transit
485112 Commuter Rail Systems
SIC 4111 Local & Suburban Transit
485113 Bus & Motor Vehicle Transit Systems
SIC 4111 Local & Suburban Transit
485119 Other Urban Transit Systems
SIC 4111 Local & Suburban Transit
48521 Interurban & Rural Bus Transportation
SIC 4131 Intercity & Rural Bus Transportation
48531 Taxi Service
SIC 4121 Taxicabs
48532 Limousine Service
SIC 4119 Local Passenger Transportation, nec
48541 School & Employee Bus Transportation
SIC 4151 School Buses
SIC 4119 Local Passenger Transportation, nec
48551 Charter Bus Industry
SIC 4141 Local Charter Bus Service
SIC 4142 Bus Charter Services, Except Local
485991 Special Needs Transportation
SIC 4119 Local Passenger Transportation, nec
485999 All Other Transit & Ground Passenger Transportation
SIC 4111 Local & Suburban Transit
SIC 4119 Local Passenger Transportation, nec
48611 Pipeline Transportation of Crude Oil
SIC 4612 Crude Petroleum Pipelines
48621 Pipeline Transportation of Natural Gas
SIC 4922 Natural Gas Transmission
SIC 4923 Natural Gas Transmission & Distribution
48691 Pipeline Transportation of Refined Petroleum Products
SIC 4613 Refined Petroleum Pipelines
48699 All Other Pipeline Transportation
SIC 4619 Pipelines, nec
48711 Scenic & Sightseeing Transportation, Land
SIC 4119 Local Passenger Transportation, nec
SIC 4789 Transportation Services, nec
SIC 7999 Amusement & Recreation Services, nec
48721 Scenic & Sightseeing Transportation, Water
SIC 4489 Water Transportation of Passengers, nec
SIC 7999 Amusement & Recreation Services, nec
48799 Scenic & Sightseeing Transportation, Other
SIC 4522 Air Transportation, Nonscheduled
SIC 7999 Amusement & Recreation Services, nec

488111 Air Traffic Control
SIC 4581 Airports, Flying Fields, & Airport Terminal Services
SIC 9621 Regulation & Administration of Transportation Programs
488112 Airport Operations, except Air Traffic Control
SIC 4581 Airports, Flying Fields, & Airport Terminal Services
SIC 4959 Sanitary Services, nec
488119 Other Airport Operations
SIC 4581 Airports, Flying Fields, & Airport Terminal Services
SIC 4959 Sanitary Services, nec
48819 Other Support Activities for Air Transportation
SIC 4581 Airports, Flying Fields, & Airport Terminal Services
48821 Support Activities for Rail Transportation
SIC 4013 Railroad Switching & Terminal Establishments
SIC 4741 Rental of Railroad Cars
SIC 4789 Transportation Services, nec
48831 Port & Harbor Operations
SIC 4491 Marine Cargo Handling
SIC 4499 Water Transportation Services, nec
48832 Marine Cargo Handling
SIC 4491 Marine Cargo Handling
48833 Navigational Services to Shipping
SIC 4492 Towing & Tugboat Services
SIC 4499 Water Transportation Services, nec
48839 Other Support Activities for Water Transportation
SIC 4499 Water Transportation Services, nec
SIC 4785 Fixed Facilities & Inspection & Weighing Services for Motor Vehicle Transportation
SIC 7699 Repair Shops & Related Services, nec
48841 Motor Vehicle Towing
SIC 7549 Automotive Services, Except Repair & Carwashes
48849 Other Support Activities for Road Transportation
SIC 4173 Terminal & Service Facilities for Motor Vehicle Passenger Transportation
SIC 4231 Terminal & Joint Terminal Maintenance Facilities for Motor Freight Transportation
SIC 4785 Fixed Facilities & Inspection & Weighing Services for Motor Vehicle Transportation
48851 Freight Transportation Arrangement
SIC 4731 Arrangement of Transportation of Freight & Cargo
488991 Packing & Crating
SIC 4783 Packing & Crating
488999 All Other Support Activities for Transportation
SIC 4729 Arrangement of Passenger Transportation, nec
SIC 4789 Transportation Services, nec
49111 Postal Service
SIC 4311 United States Postal Service
49211 Couriers
SIC 4215 Courier Services, Except by Air
SIC 4513 Air Courier Services
49221 Local Messengers & Local Delivery
SIC 4215 Courier Services, Except by Air
49311 General Warehousing & Storage Facilities
SIC 4225 General Warehousing & Storage
SIC 4226 Special Warehousing & Storage, nec
49312 Refrigerated Storage Facilities
SIC 4222 Refrigerated Warehousing & Storage
SIC 4226 Special Warehousing & Storage, nec
49313 Farm Product Storage Facilities
SIC 4221 Farm Product Warehousing & Storage
49319 Other Warehousing & Storage Facilities
SIC 4226 Special Warehousing & Storage, nec

INFORMATION

51111 Newspaper Publishers
SIC 2711 Newspapers: Publishing or Publishing & Printing
51112 Periodical Publishers
SIC 2721 Periodicals: Publishing or Publishing & Printing
51113 Book Publishers
SIC 2731 Books: Publishing or Publishing & Printing
51114 Database & Directory Publishers
SIC 2741 Miscellaneous Publishing
511191 Greeting Card Publishers
SIC 2771 Greeting Cards
511199 All Other Publishers
SIC 2741 Miscellaneous Publishing
51121 Software Publishers
SIC 7372 Prepackaged Software
51211 Motion Picture & Video Production
SIC 7812 Motion Picture & Video Tape Production
51212 Motion Picture & Video Distribution
SIC 7822 Motion Picture & Video Tape Distribution
SIC 7829 Services Allied to Motion Picture Distribution
512131 Motion Picture Theaters, Except Drive-Ins.
SIC 7832 Motion Picture Theaters, Except Drive-In
512132 Drive-In Motion Picture Theaters
SIC 7833 Drive-In Motion Picture Theaters
512191 Teleproduction & Other Post-Production Services
SIC 7819 Services Allied to Motion Picture Production
512199 Other Motion Picture & Video Industries
SIC 7819 Services Allied to Motion Picture Production
SIC 7829 Services Allied to Motion Picture Distribution
51221 Record Production
SIC 8999 Services, nec
51222 Integrated Record Production/Distribution
SIC 3652 Phonograph Records & Prerecorded Audio Tapes & Disks
51223 Music Publishers
SIC 2731 Books: Publishing or Publishing & Printing
SIC 2741 Miscellaneous Publishing
SIC 8999 Services, nec
51224 Sound Recording Studios
SIC 7389 Business Services, nec
51229 Other Sound Recording Industries
SIC 7389 Business Services, nec
SIC 7922 Theatrical Producers & Miscellaneous Theatrical Services
513111 Radio Networks
SIC 4832 Radio Broadcasting Stations
513112 Radio Stations
SIC 4832 Radio Broadcasting Stations
51312 Television Broadcasting
SIC 4833 Television Broadcasting Stations
51321 Cable Networks
SIC 4841 Cable & Other Pay Television Services
51322 Cable & Other Program Distribution
SIC 4841 Cable & Other Pay Television Services
51331 Wired Telecommunications Carriers
SIC 4813 Telephone Communications, Except Radiotelephone
SIC 4822 Telegraph & Other Message Communications
513321 Paging
SIC 4812 Radiotelephone Communications
513322 Cellular & Other Wireless Telecommunications
SIC 4812 Radiotelephone Communications
SIC 4899 Communications Services, nec

51333 Telecommunications Resellers
SIC 4812 Radio Communications
SIC 4813 Telephone Communications, Except Radiotelephone
51334 Satellite Telecommunications
SIC 4899 Communications Services, NEC
51339 Other Telecommunications
SIC 4899 Communications Services, NEC
51411 News Syndicates
SIC 7383 News Syndicates
51412 Libraries & Archives
SIC 8231 Libraries
514191 On-Line Information Services
SIC 7375 Information Retrieval Services
514199 All Other Information Services
SIC 8999 Services, nec
51421 Data Processing Services
SIC 7374 Computer Processing & Data Preparation & Processing Services

FINANCE & INSURANCE

52111 Monetary Authorities - Central Bank
SIC 6011 Federal Reserve Banks
52211 Commercial Banking
SIC 6021 National Commercial Banks
SIC 6022 State Commercial Banks
SIC 6029 Commercial Banks, nec
SIC 6081 Branches & Agencies of Foreign Banks
52212 Savings Institutions
SIC 6035 Savings Institutions, Federally Chartered
SIC 6036 Savings Institutions, Not Federally Chartered
52213 Credit Unions
SIC 6061 Credit Unions, Federally Chartered
SIC 6062 Credit Unions, Not Federally Chartered
52219 Other Depository Credit Intermediation
SIC 6022 State Commercial Banks
52221 Credit Card Issuing
SIC 6021 National Commercial Banks
SIC 6022 State Commercial Banks
SIC 6141 Personal Credit Institutions
52222 Sales Financing
SIC 6141 Personal Credit Institutions
SIC 6153 Short-Term Business Credit Institutions, Except Agricultural .
SIC 6159 Miscellaneous Business Credit Institutions
522291 Consumer Lending
SIC 6141 Personal Credit Institutions
522292 Real Estate Credit
SIC 6162 Mortgage Bankers & Loan Correspondents
522293 International Trade Financing
SIC 6081 Branches & Agencies of Foreign Banks
SIC 6082 Foreign Trade & International Banking Institutions
SIC 6111 Federal & Federally-Sponsored Credit Agencies
SIC 6159 Miscellaneous Business Credit Institutions
522294 Secondary Market Financing
SIC 6111 Federal & Federally Sponsored Credit Agencies
522298 All Other Nondepository Credit Intermediation
SIC 5932 Used Merchandise Stores
SIC 6081 Branches & Agencies of Foreign Banks
SIC 6111 Federal & Federally-Sponsored Credit Agencies
SIC 6153 Short-Term Business Credit Institutions, Except Agricultural
SIC 6159 Miscellaneous Business Credit Institutions

52231 Mortgage & Other Loan Brokers
SIC 6163 Loan Brokers
52232 Financial Transactions Processing, Reserve, & Clearing House Activities
SIC 6019 Central Reserve Depository Institutions, nec
SIC 6099 Functions Related to Depository Banking, nec
SIC 6153 Short-Term Business Credit Institutions, Except Agricultural
SIC 7389 Business Services, nec
52239 Other Activities Related to Credit Intermediation
SIC 6099 Functions Related to Depository Banking, nec
SIC 6162 Mortgage Bankers & Loan Correspondents
52311 Investment Banking & Securities Dealing
SIC 6211 Security Brokers, Dealers, & Flotation Companies
52312 Securities Brokerage
SIC 6211 Security Brokers, Dealers, & Flotation Companies
52313 Commodity Contracts Dealing
SIC 6099 Functions Related to depository Banking, nec
SIC 6799 Investors, nec
SIC 6221 Commodity Contracts Brokers & Dealers
52314 Commodity Brokerage
SIC 6221 Commodity Contracts Brokers & Dealers
52321 Securities & Commodity Exchanges
SIC 6231 Security & Commodity Exchanges
52391 Miscellaneous Intermediation
SIC 6211 Securities Brokers, Dealers & Flotation Companies
SIC 6799 Investors, nec
52392 Portfolio Management
SIC 6282 Investment Advice
SIC 6371 Pension, Health, & Welfare Funds
SIC 6733 Trust, Except Educational, Religious, & Charitable
SIC 6799 Investors, nec
52393 Investment Advice
SIC 6282 Investment Advice
523991 Trust, Fiduciary & Custody Activities
SIC 6021 National Commercial Banks
SIC 6022 State Commercial Banks
SIC 6091 Nondepository Trust Facilities
SIC 6099 Functions Related to Depository Banking, nec
SIC 6289 Services Allied With the Exchange of Securities or Commodities, nec
SIC 6733 Trusts, Except Educational, Religious, & Charitable
523999 Miscellaneous Financial Investment Activities
SIC 6099 Functions Related to Depository Banking, nec
SIC 6211 Security Brokers, Dealers, & Flotation Companies
SIC 6289 Services Allied With the Exchange of Securities or Commodities, nec
SIC 6799 Investors, nec
SIC 6792 Oil Royalty Traders
524113 Direct Life Insurance Carriers
SIC 6311 Life Insurance
524114 Direct Health & Medical Insurance Carriers
SIC 6324 Hospital & Medical Service Plans
SIC 6321 Accident & Health Insurance
524126 Direct Property & Casualty Insurance Carriers
SIC 6331 Fire, Marine, & Casualty Insurance
SIC 6351 Surety Insurance
524127 Direct Title Insurance Carriers
SIC 6361 Title Insurance
524128 Other Direct Insurance Carriers
SIC 6399 Insurance Carriers, nec
52413 Reinsurance Carriers
SIC 6311 Life Insurance
SIC 6321 Accident & Health Insurance

SIC 6324 Hospital & Medical Service Plans
SIC 6331 Fire, Marine, & Casualty Insurance
SIC 6351 Surety Insurance
SIC 6361 Title Insurance
52421 Insurance Agencies & Brokerages
SIC 6411 Insurance Agents, Brokers & Service
524291 Claims Adjusters
SIC 6411 Insurance Agents, Brokers & Service
524292 Third Party Administration for Insurance & Pension Funds
SIC 6371 Pension, Health, & Welfare Funds
SIC 6411 Insurance Agents, Brokers & Service
524298 All Other Insurance Related Activities
SIC 6411 Insurance Agents, Brokers & Service
52511 Pension Funds
SIC 6371 Pension, Health, & Welfare Funds
52512 Health & Welfare Funds
SIC 6371 Pension, Health, & Welfare Funds
52519 Other Insurance Funds
SIC 6321 Accident & Health Insurance
SIC 6324 Hospital & Medical Service Plans
SIC 6331 Fire, Marine, & Casualty Insurance
SIC 6733 Trusts, Except Educational, Religious, & Charitable
52591 Open-End Investment Funds
SIC 6722 Management Investment Offices, Open-End
52592 Trusts, Estates, & Agency Accounts
SIC 6733 Trusts, Except Educational, Religious, & Charitable
52593 Real Estate Investment Trusts
SIC 6798 Real Estate Investment Trusts
52599 Other Financial Vehicles
SIC 6726 Unit Investment Trusts, Face-Amount Certificate Offices, & Closed-End Management Investment Offices

REAL ESTATE & RENTAL & LEASING

53111 Lessors of Residential Buildings & Dwellings
SIC 6513 Operators of Apartment Buildings
SIC 6514 Operators of Dwellings Other Than Apartment Buildings
53112 Lessors of Nonresidential Buildings
SIC 6512 Operators of Nonresidential Buildings
53113 Lessors of Miniwarehouses & Self Storage Units
SIC 4225 General Warehousing & Storage
53119 Lessors of Other Real Estate Property
SIC 6515 Operators of Residential Mobile Home Sites
SIC 6517 Lessors of Railroad Property
SIC 6519 Lessors of Real Property, nec
53121 Offices of Real Estate Agents & Brokers
SIC 6531 Real Estate Agents Managers
531311 Residential Property Managers
SIC 6531 Real Estate Agents & Managers
531312 Nonresidential Property Managers
SIC 6531 Real Estate Agents & Managers
53132 Offices of Real Estate Appraisers
SIC 6531 Real Estate Agents & Managers
531399 All Other Activities Related to Real Estate
SIC 6531 Real Estate Agents & Managers
532111 Passenger Car Rental
SIC 7514 Passenger Car Rental
532112 Passenger Car Leasing
SIC 7515 Passenger Car Leasing

53212 Truck, Utility Trailer, & RV Rental & Leasing
SIC 7513 Truck Rental & Leasing Without Drivers
SIC 7519 Utility Trailers & Recreational Vehicle Rental
53221 Consumer Electronics & Appliances Rental
SIC 7359 Equipment Rental & Leasing, nec
53222 Formal Wear & Costume Rental
SIC 7299 Miscellaneous Personal Services, nec
SIC 7819 Services Allied to Motion Picture Production
53223 Video Tape & Disc Rental
SIC 7841 Video Tape Rental
532291 Home Health Equipment Rental
SIC 7352 Medical Equipment Rental & Leasing
532292 Recreational Goods Rental
SIC 7999 Amusement & Recreation Services, nec
532299 All Other Consumer Goods Rental
SIC 7359 Equipment Rental & Leasing, nec
53231 General Rental Centers
SIC 7359 Equipment Rental & Leasing, nec
532411 Commercial Air, Rail, & Water Transportation Equipment Rental & Leasing
SIC 4499 Water Transportation Services, nec
SIC 4741 Rental of Railroad Cars
SIC 7359 Equipment Rental & Leasing, nec
532412 Construction, Mining & Forestry Machinery & Equipment Rental & Leasing
SIC 7353 Heavy Construction Equipment Rental & Leasing
SIC 7359 Equipment Rental & Leasing, nec
53242 Office Machinery & Equipment Rental & Leasing
SIC 7359 Equipment Rental & Leasing
SIC 7377 Computer Rental & Leasing
53249 Other Commercial & Industrial Machinery & Equipment Rental & Leasing
SIC 7352 Medical Equipment Rental & Leasing
SIC 7359 Equipment Rental & Leasing, nec
SIC 7819 Services Allied to Motion Picture Production
SIC 7922 Theatrical Producers & Miscellaneous Theatrical Services
53311 Owners & Lessors of Other Nonfinancial Assets
SIC 6792 Oil Royalty Traders
SIC 6794 Patent Owners & Lessors

PROFESSIONAL, SCIENTIFIC, & TECHNICAL SERVICES

54111 Offices of Lawyers
SIC 8111 Legal Services
541191 Title Abstract & Settlement Offices
SIC 6541 Title Abstract Offices
541199 All Other Legal Services
SIC 7389 Business Services, nec
541211 Offices of Certified Public Accountants
SIC 8721 Accounting, Auditing, & Bookkeeping Services
541213 Tax Preparation Services
SIC 7291 Tax Return Preparation Services
541214 Payroll Services
SIC 7819 Services Allied to Motion Picture Production
SIC 8721 Accounting, Auditing, & Bookkeeping Services
541219 Other Accounting Services
SIC 8721 Accounting, Auditing, & Bookkeeping Services
54131 Architectural Services
SIC 8712 Architectural Services

54132 Landscape Architectural Services
SIC 0781 Landscape Counseling & Planning
54133 Engineering Services
SIC 8711 Engineering Services
54134 Drafting Services
SIC 7389 Business Services, nec
54135 Building Inspection Services
SIC 7389 Business Services, nec
54136 Geophysical Surveying & Mapping Services
SIC 8713 Surveying Services
SIC 1081 Metal Mining Services
SIC 1382 Oil & Gas Field Exploration Services
SIC 1481 Nonmetallic Minerals Services, Except Fuels
54137 Surveying & Mapping Services
SIC 7389 Business Services, nec
SIC 8713 Surveying Services
54138 Testing Laboratories
SIC 8734 Testing Laboratories
54141 Interior Design Services
SIC 7389 Business Services, nec
54142 Industrial Design Services
SIC 7389 Business Services, nec
54143 Commercial Art & Graphic Design Services
SIC 7336 Commercial Art & Graphic Design
SIC 8099 Health & Allied Services, nec
54149 Other Specialized Design Services
SIC 7389 Business Services, nec
541511 Custom Computer Programming Services
SIC 7371 Computer Programming Services
541512 Computer Systems Design Services
SIC 7373 Computer Integrated Systems Design
SIC 7379 Computer Related Services, nec
541513 Computer Facilities Management Services
SIC 7376 Computer Facilities Management Services
541519 Other Computer Related Services
SIC 7379 Computer Related Services, nec
541611 Administrative Management & General Management Consulting Services
SIC 8742 Management Consulting Services
541612 Human Resources & Executive Search Consulting Services
SIC 8742 Management Consulting Services
SIC 7361 Employment Agencies
SIC 8999 Services, nec
541613 Marketing Consulting Services
SIC 8742 Management Consulting Services
541614 Process, Physical, Distribution & Logistics Consulting Services
SIC 8742 Management Consulting Services
541618 Other Management Consulting Services
SIC 4731 Arrangement of Transportation of Freight & Cargo
SIC 8748 Business Consulting Services, nec
54162 Environmental Consulting Services
SIC 8999 Services, nec
54169 Other Scientific & Technical Consulting Services
SIC 0781 Landscape Counseling & Planning
SIC 8748 Business Consulting Services, nec
SIC 8999 Services, nec
54171 Research & Development in the Physical Sciences & Engineering Sciences
SIC 8731 Commercial Physical & Biological Research
SIC 8733 Noncommercial Research Organizations

54172 Research & Development in the Life Sciences
SIC 8731 Commercial Physical & Biological Research
SIC 8733 Noncommercial Research Organizations
54173 Research & Development in the Social Sciences & Humanities
SIC 8732 Commercial Economic, Sociological, & Educational Research
SIC 8733 Noncommercial Research Organizations
54181 Advertising Agencies
SIC 7311 Advertising Agencies
54182 Public Relations Agencies
SIC 8743 Public Relations Services
54183 Media Buying Agencies
SIC 7319 Advertising, nec
54184 Media Representatives
SIC 7313 Radio, Television, & Publishers' Advertising Representatives
54185 Display Advertising
SIC 7312 Outdoor Advertising Services
SIC 7319 Advertising, nec
54186 Direct Mail Advertising
SIC 7331 Direct Mail Advertising Services
54187 Advertising Material Distribution Services
SIC 7319 Advertising, NEC
54189 Other Services Related to Advertising
SIC 7319 Advertising, nec
SIC 5199 Nondurable Goods, nec
SIC 7389 Business Services, nec
54191 Marketing Research & Public Opinion Polling
SIC 8732 Commercial Economic, Sociological, & Educational Research
541921 Photography Studios, Portrait
SIC 7221 Photographic Studios, Portrait
541922 Commercial Photography
SIC 7335 Commercial Photography
SIC 8099 Health & Allied Services, nec
54193 Translation & Interpretation Services
SIC 7389 Business Services, NEC
54194 Veterinary Services
SIC 0741 Veterinary Services for Livestock
SIC 0742 Veterinary Services for Animal Specialties
SIC 8734 Testing Laboratories
54199 All Other Professional, Scientific & Technical Services
SIC 7389 Business Services

MANAGEMENT OF COMPANIES & ENTERPRISES

551111 Offices of Bank Holding Companies
SIC 6712 Offices of Bank Holding Companies
551112 Offices of Other Holding Companies
SIC 6719 Offices of Holding Companies, nec
551114 Corporate, Subsidiary, & Regional Managing Offices
No SIC equivalent

ADMINISTRATIVE & SUPPORT, WASTE MANAGEMENT & REMEDIATION SERVICES

56111 Office Administrative Services
SIC 8741 Management Services

56121 Facilities Support Services
SIC 8744 Facilities Support Management Services
56131 Employment Placement Agencies
SIC 7361 Employment Agencies
SIC 7819 Services Allied to Motion Pictures Production
SIC 7922 Theatrical Producers & Miscellaneous Theatrical Services
56132 Temporary Help Services
SIC 7363 Help Supply Services
56133 Employee Leasing Services
SIC 7363 Help Supply Services
56141 Document Preparation Services
SIC 7338 Secretarial & Court Reporting
561421 Telephone Answering Services
SIC 7389 Business Services, nec
561422 Telemarketing Bureaus
SIC 7389 Business Services, nec
561431 Photocopying & Duplicating Services
SIC 7334 Photocopying & Duplicating Services
561432 Private Mail Centers
SIC 7389 Business Services, nec
561439 Other Business Service Centers
SIC 7334 Photocopying & Duplicating Services
SIC 7389 Business Services, nec
56144 Collection Agencies
SIC 7322 Adjustment & Collection Services
56145 Credit Bureaus
SIC 7323 Credit Reporting Services
561491 Repossession Services
SIC 7322 Adjustment & Collection
SIC 7389 Business Services, nec
561492 Court Reporting & Stenotype Services
SIC 7338 Secretarial & Court Reporting
561499 All Other Business Support Services
SIC 7389 Business Services, NEC
56151 Travel Agencies
SIC 4724 Travel Agencies
56152 Tour Operators
SIC 4725 Tour Operators
561591 Convention & Visitors Bureaus
SIC 7389 Business Services, nec
561599 All Other Travel Arrangement & Reservation Services
SIC 4729 Arrangement of Passenger Transportation, nec
SIC 7389 Business Services, nec
SIC 7999 Amusement & Recreation Services, nec
SIC 8699 Membership Organizations, nec
561611 Investigation Services
SIC 7381 Detective, Guard, & Armored Car Services
561612 Security Guards & Patrol Services
SIC 7381 Detective, Guard, & Armored Car Services
561613 Armored Car Services
SIC 7381 Detective, Guard, & Armored Car Services
561621 Security Systems Services
SIC 7382 Security Systems Services
SIC 1731 Electrical Work
561622 Locksmiths
SIC 7699 Repair Shops & Related Services, nec
56171 Exterminating & Pest Control Services
SIC 4959 Sanitary Services, NEC
SIC 7342 Disinfecting & Pest Control Services
56172 Janitorial Services
SIC 7342 Disinfecting & Pest Control Services
SIC 7349 Building Cleaning & Maintenance Services, nec
SIC 4581 Airports, Flying Fields, & Airport Terminal Services

56173 Landscaping Services
SIC 0782 Lawn & Garden Services
SIC 0783 Ornamental Shrub & Tree Services
56174 Carpet & Upholstery Cleaning Services
SIC 7217 Carpet & Upholstery Cleaning
56179 Other Services to Buildings & Dwellings
SIC 7389 Business Services, nec
SIC 7699 Repair Shops & Related Services, nec
56191 Packaging & Labeling Services
SIC 7389 Business Services, nec
56192 Convention & Trade Show Organizers
SIC 7389 Business Services, NEC
56199 All Other Support Services
SIC 7389 Business Services, nec
562111 Solid Waste Collection
SIC 4212 Local Trucking Without Storage
SIC 4953 Refuse Systems
562112 Hazardous Waste Collection
SIC 4212 Local Trucking Without Storage
SIC 4953 Refuse Systems
562119 Other Waste Collection
SIC 4212 Local Trucking Without Storage
SIC 4953 Refuse Systems
562211 Hazardous Waste Treatment & Disposal
SIC 4953 Refuse Systems
562212 Solid Waste Landfill
SIC 4953 Refuse Systems
562213 Solid Waste Combustors & Incinerators
SIC 4953 Refuse Systems
562219 Other Nonhazardous Waste Treatment & Disposal
SIC 4953 Refuse Systems
56291 Remediation Services
SIC 1799 Special Trade Contractors, nec
SIC 4959 Sanitary Services, nec
56292 Materials Recovery Facilities
SIC 4953 Refuse Systems
562991 Septic Tank & Related Services
SIC 7359 Equipment Rental & Leasing, nec
SIC 7699 Repair Shops & Related Services, nec
562998 All Other Miscellaneous Waste Management Services
SIC 4959 Sanitary Services, nec

EDUCATIONAL SERVICES

61111 Elementary & Secondary Schools
SIC 8211 Elementary & Secondary Schools
61121 Junior Colleges
SIC 8222 Junior Colleges & Technical Institutes
61131 Colleges, Universities & Professional Schools
SIC 8221 Colleges, Universities, & Professional Schools
61141 Business & Secretarial Schools
SIC 8244 Business & Secretarial Schools
61142 Computer Training
SIC 8243 Data Processing Schools
61143 Professional & Management Development Training Schools
SIC 8299 Schools & Educational Services, nec
611511 Cosmetology & Barber Schools
SIC 7231 Beauty Shops
SIC 7241 Barber Shops
611512 Flight Training
SIC 8249 Vocational Schools, nec
SIC 8299 Schools & Educational Services, nec

611513 Apprenticeship Training
SIC 8249 Vocational Schools, nec
611519 Other Technical & Trade Schools
SIC 8249 Vocational Schools, NEC
SIC 8243 Data Processing Schools
61161 Fine Arts Schools
SIC 8299 Schools & Educational Services, nec
SIC 7911 Dance Studios, Schools, & Halls
61162 Sports & Recreation Instruction
SIC 7999 Amusement & Recreation Services, nec
61163 Language Schools
SIC 8299 Schools & Educational Services, nec
611691 Exam Preparation & Tutoring
SIC 8299 Schools & Educational Services, nec
611692 Automobile Driving Schools
SIC 8299 Schools & Educational Services, nec
611699 All Other Miscellaneous Schools & Instruction
SIC 8299 Schools & Educational Services, nec
61171 Educational Support Services
SIC 8299 Schools & Educational Services nec
SIC 8748 Business Consulting Services, nec

HEALTH CARE & SOCIAL ASSISTANCE

621111 Offices of Physicians
SIC 8011 Offices & Clinics of Doctors of Medicine
SIC 8031 Offices & Clinics of Doctors of Osteopathy
621112 Offices of Physicians, Mental Health Specialists
SIC 8011 Offices & Clinics of Doctors of Medicine
SIC 8031 Offices & Clinics of Doctors of Osteopathy
62121 Offices of Dentists
SIC 8021 Offices & Clinics of Dentists
62131 Offices of Chiropractors
SIC 8041 Offices & Clinics of Chiropractors
62132 Offices of Optometrists
SIC 8042 Offices & Clinics of Optometrists
62133 Offices of Mental Health Practitioners
SIC 8049 Offices & Clinics of Health Practitioners, nec
62134 Offices of Physical, Occupational & Speech Therapists & Audiologists
SIC 8049 Offices & Clinics of Health Practitioners, nec
621391 Offices of Podiatrists
SIC 8043 Offices & Clinics of Podiatrists
621399 Offices of All Other Miscellaneous Health Practitioners
SIC 8049 Offices & Clinics of Health Practitioners, nec
62141 Family Planning Centers
SIC 8093 Speciality Outpatient Facilities, NEC
SIC 8099 Health & Allied Services, nec
62142 Outpatient Mental Health & Substance Abuse Centers
SIC 8093 Specialty Outpatient Facilities, nec
621491 HMO Medical Centers
SIC 8011 Offices & Clinics of Doctors of Medicine
621492 Kidney Dialysis Centers
SIC 8092 Kidney Dialysis Centers
621493 Freestanding Ambulatory Surgical & Emergency Centers
SIC 8011 Offices & Clinics of Doctors of Medicine
621498 All Other Outpatient Care Centers
SIC 8093 Specialty Outpatient Facilities, nec
621511 Medical Laboratories
SIC 8071 Medical Laboratories
621512 Diagnostic Imaging Centers
SIC 8071 Medical Laboratories

62161 Home Health Care Services
SIC 8082 Home Health Care Services
62191 Ambulance Services
SIC 4119 Local Passenger Transportation, nec
SIC 4522 Air Transportation, Nonscheduled
621991 Blood & Organ Banks
SIC 8099 Health & Allied Services, nec
621999 All Other Miscellaneous Ambulatory Health Care Services
SIC 8099 Health & Allied Services, nec
62211 General Medical & Surgical Hospitals
SIC 8062 General Medical & Surgical Hospitals
SIC 8069 Specialty Hospitals, Except Psychiatric
62221 Psychiatric & Substance Abuse Hospitals
SIC 8063 Psychiatric Hospitals
SIC 8069 Specialty Hospitals, Except Psychiatric
62231 Specialty Hospitals
SIC 8069 Specialty Hospitals, Except Psychiatric
62311 Nursing Care Facilities
SIC 8051 Skilled Nursing Care Facilities
SIC 8052 Intermediate Care Facilities
SIC 8059 Nursing & Personal Care Facilities, nec
62321 Residential Mental Retardation Facilities
SIC 8052 Intermediate Care Facilities
62322 Residential Mental Health & Substance Abuse Facilities
SIC 8361 Residential Care
623311 Continuing Care Retirement Communities
SIC 8051 Skilled Nursing Care Facilities
SIC 8052 Intermediate Care Facilities
SIC 8059 Nursing & Personal Care Facilities, nec
623312 Homes for the Elderly
SIC 8361 Residential Care
62399 Other Residential Care Facilities
SIC 8361 Residential Care
62411 Child & Youth Services
SIC 8322 Individual & Family Social Services
SIC 8641 Civic, Social, & Fraternal Organizations
62412 Services for the Elderly & Persons with Disabilities
SIC 8322 Individual & Family Social Services
62419 Other Individual & Family Services
SIC 8322 Individual & Family Social Services
62421 Community Food Services
SIC 8322 Individual & Family Social Services
624221 Temporary Shelters
SIC 8322 Individual & Family Social Services
624229 Other Community Housing Services
SIC 8322 Individual & Family Social Services
62423 Emergency & Other Relief Services
SIC 8322 Individual & Family Social Services
62431 Vocational Rehabilitation Services
SIC 8331 Job Training & Vocational Rehabilitation Services
62441 Child Day Care Services
SIC 8351 Child Day Care Services
SIC 7299 Miscellaneous Personal Services, nec

ARTS, ENTERTAINMENT, & RECREATION

71111 Theater Companies & Dinner Theaters
SIC 5812 Eating Places
SIC 7922 Theatrical Producers & Miscellaneous Theatrical Services

71112 Dance Companies
SIC 7922 Theatrical Producers & Miscellaneous Theatrical Services
71113 Musical Groups & Artists
SIC 7929 Bands, Orchestras, Actors, & Entertainment Groups
71119 Other Performing Arts Companies
SIC 7929 Bands, Orchestras, Actors, & Entertainment Groups
SIC 7999 Amusement & Recreation Services, nec
711211 Sports Teams & Clubs
SIC 7941 Professional Sports Clubs & Promoters
711212 Race Tracks
SIC 7948 Racing, Including Track Operations
711219 Other Spectator Sports
SIC 7941 Professional Sports Clubs & Promoters
SIC 7948 Racing, Including Track Operations
SIC 7999 Amusement & Recreation Services, nec
71131 Promoters of Performing Arts, Sports & Similar Events with Facilities
SIC 6512 Operators of Nonresidential Buildings
SIC 7922 Theatrical Procedures & Miscellaneous Theatrical Services
SIC 7941 Professional Sports Clubs & Promoters
71132 Promoters of Performing Arts, Sports & Similar Events without Facilities
SIC 7922 Theatrical Producers & Miscellaneous Theatrical Services
SIC 7941 Professional Sports Clubs & Promoters
71141 Agents & Managers for Artists, Athletes, Entertainers & Other Public Figures
SIC 7389 Business Services, nec
SIC 7922 Theatrical Producers & Miscellaneous Theatrical Services
SIC 7941 Professional Sports Clubs & Promoters
71151 Independent Artists, Writers, & Performers
SIC 7819 Services Allied to Motion Picture Production
SIC 7929 Bands, Orchestras, Actors, & Other Entertainers & Entertainment Services
SIC 8999 Services, nec
71211 Museums
SIC 8412 Museums & Art Galleries
71212 Historical Sites
SIC 8412 Museums & Art Galleries
71213 Zoos & Botanical Gardens
SIC 8422 Arboreta & Botanical & Zoological Gardens
71219 Nature Parks & Other Similar Institutions
SIC 7999 Amusement & Recreation Services, nec
SIC 8422 Arboreta & Botanical & Zoological Gardens
71311 Amusement & Theme Parks
SIC 7996 Amusement Parks
71312 Amusement Arcades
SIC 7993 Coin-Operated Amusement Devices
71321 Casinos
SIC 7999 Amusement & Recreation Services, nec
71329 Other Gambling Industries
SIC 7993 Coin-Operated Amusement Devices
SIC 7999 Amusement & Recreation Services, nec
71391 Golf Courses & Country Clubs
SIC 7992 Public Golf Courses
SIC 7997 Membership Sports & Recreation Clubs
71392 Skiing Facilities
SIC 7999 Amusement & Recreation Services, nec
71393 Marinas
SIC 4493 Marinas

71394 Fitness & Recreational Sports Centers
SIC 7991 Physical Fitness Facilities
SIC 7997 Membership Sports & Recreation Clubs
SIC 7999 Amusement & Recreation Services, nec
71395 Bowling Centers
SIC 7933 Bowling Centers
71399 All Other Amusement & Recreation Industries
SIC 7911 Dance Studios, Schools, & Halls
SIC 7993 Amusement & Recreation Services, nec
SIC 7997 Membership Sports & Recreation Clubs
SIC 7999 Amusement & Recreation Services, nec

ACCOMMODATION & FOODSERVICES

72111 Hotels & Motels
SIC 7011 Hotels & Motels
SIC 7041 Organization Hotels & Lodging Houses, on
        Membership Basis
72112 Casino Hotels
SIC 7011 Hotels & Motels
721191 Bed & Breakfast Inns
SIC 7011 Hotels & Motels
721199 All Other Traveler Accommodation
SIC 7011 Hotels & Motels
721211 RV Parks & Campgrounds
SIC 7033 Recreational Vehicle Parks & Campgrounds
721214 Recreational & Vacation Camps
SIC 7032 Sporting & Recreational Camps
72131 Rooming & Boarding Houses
SIC 7021 Rooming & Boarding Houses
SIC 7041 Organization Hotels & Lodging Houses, on
        Membership Basis
72211 Full-Service Restaurants
SIC 5812 Eating Places
722211 Limited-Service Restaurants
SIC 5812 Eating Places
SIC 5499 Miscellaneous Food Stores
722212 Cafeterias
SIC 5812 Eating Places
722213 Snack & Nonalcoholic Beverage Bars
SIC 5812 Eating Places
SIC 5461 Retail Bakeries
72231 Foodservice Contractors
SIC 5812 Eating Places
72232 Caterers
SIC 5812 Eating Places
72233 Mobile Caterers
SIC 5963 Direct Selling Establishments
72241 Drinking Places
SIC 5813 Drinking Places

OTHER SERVICES

811111 General Automotive Repair
SIC 7538 General Automotive Repair Shops
811112 Automotive Exhaust System Repair
SIC 7533 Automotive Exhaust System Repair Shops
811113 Automotive Transmission Repair
SIC 7537 Automotive Transmission Repair Shops

**811118 Other Automotive Mechanical & Electrical Repair &
        Maintenance**
SIC 7539 Automotive Repair Shops, nec
**811121 Automotive Body, Paint & Upholstery Repair &
        Maintenance**
SIC 7532 Top, Body, & Upholstery Repair Shops & Paint
        Shops
811122 Automotive Glass Replacement Shops
SIC 7536 Automotive Glass Replacement Shops
811191 Automotive Oil Change & Lubrication Shops
SIC 7549 Automotive Services, Except Repair & Carwashes
811192 Car Washes
SIC 7542 Carwashes
811198 All Other Automotive Repair & Maintenance
SIC 7534 Tire Retreading & Repair Shops
SIC 7549 Automotive Services, Except Repair & Carwashes
811211 Consumer Electronics Repair & Maintenance
SIC 7622 Radio & Television Repair Shops
SIC 7629 Electrical & Electronic Repair Shops, nec
811212 Computer & Office Machine Repair & Maintenance
SIC 7378 Computer Maintenance & Repair
SIC 7629 Electrical & Electronic Repair Shops, nec
SIC 7699 Repair Shops & Related Services, nec
811213 Communication Equipment Repair & Maintenance
SIC 7622 Radio & Television Repair Shops
SIC 7629 Electrical & Electronic Repair Shops, nec
**811219 Other Electronic & Precision Equipment Repair &
        Maintenance**
SIC 7629 Electrical & Electronic Repair Shops, nec
SIC 7699 Repair Shops & Related Services, NEC
**81131 Commercial & Industrial Machinery & Equipment
        Repair & Maintenance**
SIC 7699 Repair Shops & Related Services, nec
SIC 7623 Refrigerator & Air-Conditioning Service & Repair
        Shops
SIC 7694 Armature Rewinding Shops
811411 Home & Garden Equipment Repair & Maintenance
SIC 7699 Repair Shops & Related Services, nec
811412 Appliance Repair & Maintenance
SIC 7623 Refrigeration & Air-Conditioning Service & Repair
        Shops
SIC 7629 Electrical & Electronic Repair Shops, NEC
SIC 7699 Repairs Shops & Related Services, nec
81142 Reupholstery & Furniture Repair
SIC 7641 Reupholstery & Furniture Repair
81143 Footwear & Leather Goods Repair
SIC 7251 Shoe Repair & Shoeshine Parlors
SIC 7699 Repair Shops & Related Services
**81149 Other Personal & Household Goods Repair &
        Maintenance**
SIC 3732 Boat Building & Repairing
SIC 7219 Laundry & Garment Services, nec
SIC 7631 Watch, Clock, & Jewelry Repair
SIC 7692 Welding Repair
SIC 7699 Repair Shops & Related Services, nec
812111 Barber Shops
SIC 7241 Barber Shops
812112 Beauty Salons
SIC 7231 Beauty Shops
812113 Nail Salons
SIC 7231 Beauty Shops
812191 Diet & Weight Reducing Centers
SIC 7299 Miscellaneous Personal Services, nec

812199 Other Personal Care Services
SIC 7299 Miscellaneous Personal Services, nec,
81221 Funeral Homes
SIC 7261 Funeral Services & Crematories
81222 Cemeteries & Crematories
SIC 6531 Real Estate Agents & Managers
SIC 6553 Cemetery Subdividers & Developers
SIC 7261 Funeral Services & Crematories
81231 Coin-Operated Laundries & Drycleaners
SIC 7215 Coin-Operated Laundry & Drycleaning
812321 Laundries, Family & Commercial
SIC 7211 Power Laundries, Family & Commercial
812322 Drycleaning Plants
SIC 7216 Drycleaning Plants, Except Rug Cleaning
812331 Linen Supply
SIC 7213 Linen Supply
SIC 7219 Laundry & Garment Services, nec,
812332 Industrial Launderers
SIC 7218 Industrial Launderers
812391 Garment Pressing, & Agents for Laundries
SIC 7212 Garment Pressing & Agents for Laundries
812399 All Other Laundry Services
SIC 7219 Laundry & Garment Services, NEC
81291 Pet Care Services
SIC 0752 Animal Speciality Services, Except Veterinary
812921 Photo Finishing Laboratories
SIC 7384 Photofinishing Laboratories
812922 One-Hour Photo Finishing
SIC 7384 Photofinishing Laboratories
81293 Parking Lots & Garages
SIC 7521 Automobile Parking
81299 All Other Personal Services
SIC 7299 Miscellaneous Personal Services, nec
SIC 7389 Miscellaneous Business Services
81311 Religious Organizations
SIC 8661 Religious Organizations
813211 Grantmaking Foundations
SIC 6732 Educational, Religious, & Charitable Trust
813212 Voluntary Health Organizations
SIC 8399 Social Services, nec
813219 Other Grantmaking & Giving Services
SIC 8399 Social Services, NEC
813311 Human Rights Organizations
SIC 8399 Social Services, nec
813312 Environment, Conservation & Wildlife Organizations
SIC 8399 Social Services, nec
SIC 8699 Membership Organizations, nec
813319 Other Social Advocacy Organizations
SIC 8399 Social Services, NEC
81341 Civic & Social Organizations
SIC 8641 Civic, Social, & Fraternal Organizations
SIC 8699 Membership Organizations, ncc
81391 Business Associations
SIC 8611 Business Associations
SIC 8699 Membership Organizations, nec
81392 Professional Organizations
SIC 8621 Professional Membership Organizations
81393 Labor Unions & Similar Labor Organizations
SIC 8631 Labor Unions & Similar Labor Organizations
81394 Political Organizations
SIC 8651 Political Organizations
81399 Other Similar Organizations
SIC 6531 Real Estate Agents & Managers
SIC 8641 Civic, Social, & Fraternal Organizations

SIC 8699 Membership Organizations, nec
81411 Private Households
SIC 8811 Private Households

PUBLIC ADMINISTRATION

92111 Executive Offices
SIC 9111 Executive Offices
92112 Legislative Bodies
SIC 9121 Legislative Bodies
92113 Public Finance
SIC 9311 Public Finance, Taxation, & Monetary Policy
92114 Executive & Legislative Offices, Combined
SIC 9131 Executive & Legislative Offices, Combined
92115 American Indian & Alaska Native Tribal Governments
SIC 8641 Civic, Social, & Fraternal Organizations
92119 All Other General Government
SIC 9199 General Government, nec
92211 Courts
SIC 9211 Courts
92212 Police Protection
SIC 9221 Police Protection
92213 Legal Counsel & Prosecution
SIC 9222 Legal Counsel & Prosecution
92214 Correctional Institutions
SIC 9223 Correctional Institutions
92215 Parole Offices & Probation Offices
SIC 8322 Individual & Family Social Services
92216 Fire Protection
SIC 9224 Fire Protection
92219 All Other Justice, Public Order, & Safety
SIC 9229 Public Order & Safety, nec
92311 Administration of Education Programs
SIC 9411 Administration of Educational Programs
92312 Administration of Public Health Programs
SIC 9431 Administration of Public Health Programs
92313 Administration of Social, Human Resource & Income Maintenance Programs
SIC 9441 Administration of Social, Human Resource & Income Maintenance Programs
92314 Administration of Veteran's Affairs
SIC 9451 Administration of Veteran's Affairs, Except Health Insurance
92411 Air & Water Resource & Solid Waste Management
SIC 9511 Air & Water Resource & Solid Waste Management
92412 Land, Mineral, Wildlife, & Forest Conservation
SIC 9512 Land, Mineral, Wildlife, & Forest Conservation
92511 Administration of Housing Programs
SIC 9531 Administration of Housing Programs
92512 Administration of Urban Planning & Community & Rural Development
SIC 9532 Administration of Urban Planning & Community & Rural Development
92611 Administration of General Economic Programs
SIC 9611 Administration of General Economic Programs
92612 Regulation & Administration of Transportation Programs
SIC 9621 Regulations & Administration of Transportation Programs
92613 Regulation & Administration of Communications, Electric, Gas, & Other Utilities
SIC 9631 Regulation & Administration of Communications, Electric, Gas, & Other Utilities

92614 Regulation of Agricultural Marketing & Commodities
  SIC 9641 Regulation of Agricultural Marketing & Commodities
92615 Regulation, Licensing, & Inspection of Miscellaneous Commercial Sectors
  SIC 9651 Regulation, Licensing, & Inspection of Miscellaneous Commercial Sectors
92711 Space Research & Technology
  SIC 9661 Space Research & Technology
92811 National Security
  SIC 9711 National Security
92812 International Affairs
  SIC 9721 International Affairs
99999 Unclassified Establishments
  SIC 9999 Nonclassifiable Establishments